Financial Accounting
Standards Board

ACCOUNTING STANDARDS

Original Pronouncements

July 1973 – June 1, 1984

1984/85 Edition

Distributed by McGRAW-HILL BOOK COMPANY
New York St. Louis San Francisco Auckland Bogotá Hamburg
Johannesburg London Madrid Mexico Montreal New Delhi
Panama Paris São Paulo Singapore Sydney Tokyo Toronto

Published by the
Financial Accounting Standards Board

High Ridge Park, P.O. Box 3821, Stamford, Connecticut 06905-0821

Printed in the United States of America
Library of Congress Catalog Card Number: 84-80965

FOREWORD

This volume contains:

- FASB Statements of Financial Accounting Standards
- Statements of Financial Accounting Concepts
- Interpretations
- Technical Bulletins

These pronouncements were issued by the FASB from its inception in July 1973 to June 1, 1984.

A companion volume contains the following materials issued by the FASB's predecessor standard-setting bodies—the American Institute of Certified Public Accountants and its committees:

- Accounting Research Bulletins
- Accounting Principles Board Opinions
- Accounting Principles Board Statements
- Accounting Terminology Bulletins

Superseded, amended, or changed material is highlighted to alert the reader. A status page at the beginning of each pronouncement identifies the pronouncement that is the source of the change. The status page also identifies pronouncements affected by that pronouncement and the principal effective date.

The Financial Accounting Standards Board has neither reviewed, approved, nor otherwise acted with respect to the aforementioned AICPA pronouncements, except as may be stated in FASB pronouncements.

In this regard, Section III(K) of the FASB's *Rules of Procedure* (as amended January 1, 1978 by the Standards Board) states that Accounting Research Bulletins and Opinions of the Accounting Principles Board should be considered as continuing in force except to the extent altered, amended, supplemented, revoked, or superseded by one or more Statements of Financial Accounting Standards or Statements of Financial Accounting Concepts issued by the Financial Accounting Standards Board.

June 1, 1984

ORIGINAL PRONOUNCEMENTS
JULY 1973–JUNE 1, 1984

TABLE OF CONTENTS

Statements of

Financial Accounting Standards

TABLE OF CONTENTS

Table of Contents

Table of Contents

Table of Contents

Table of Contents

(The next page is 1001.)

Statement of Financial Accounting Standards No. 1 Disclosure of Foreign Currency Translation Information

STATUS

Issued: December 1973

Effective Date: For fiscal periods ending after November 30, 1973

Affects: No other pronouncements

Affected by: Superseded by FAS 8
Superseded by FAS 52

Statement of Financial Accounting Standards No. 1
Disclosure of Foreign Currency Translation Information

CONTENTS

Introduction

1. The Financial Accounting Standards Board (FASB) currently has the subject of accounting for foreign currency translation on its technical agenda. As part of that project, the FASB will examine the alternative methods of accounting for foreign currency translation. At the completion of that project, the FASB expects to issue a comprehensive Statement specifying the financial accounting and reporting standards to be applied. The disclosures required by this Statement should not be interpreted to imply that any accounting method is more or less acceptable than any other method.

2. Under existing pronouncements of the Accounting Principles Board (APB) and its predecessor, several significantly different alternatives are acceptable in accounting for foreign currency translation (see Appendix A). These pronouncements, however, are lacking in specific disclosure requirements. A recent survey[1] of foreign currency translation practices indicates that various accounting methods are used. The survey also indicates that a significant proportion of the companies surveyed presented incomplete disclosures of translation methods and the disposition of translation adjustments. Research conducted by the FASB staff supports those findings of the survey. (See paragraph 18.)

3. Because of (a) continuing realignments of exchange rates, (b) the number of accounting alternatives available, (c) the diversity of practice, (d) the lack of specific disclosure requirements in existing accounting pronouncements, and (e) the limited amount of information concerning translation practices presently being disclosed by some companies with important foreign operations, the FASB has concluded that more specific disclosure of current practices in foreign currency translation is now needed.

4. The disclosures required by this Statement are designed to provide information concerning a company's translation practices to facilitate assessment of possible implications with respect to its financial position and results of operations. This Statement does not supersede, alter, or amend any APB Opinion or Accounting Research Bulletin (ARB).

EXPLANATION OF TERMS

5. The following are explanations of certain terms used in this Statement:

a. *Exchange rate* is the ratio between a unit of one currency and the amount of another currency for which that unit can be exchanged at a particular time. A given currency may, in fact, have several categories of exchange rates, such as the financial rate or the commercial rate. Where such categories exist, this Statement does not attempt to specify a particular category as being more appropriate than another.
b. *Current rate* is the exchange rate in effect at the balance sheet date.[2]
c. *Historical rate* is the exchange rate that was in effect when a specific transaction or event occurred.
d. *Exchange adjustment* is the effect of an exchange rate change on the carrying amount of assets and liabilities denominated in terms of foreign currency. This term includes adjustments arising from (1) expression, in terms of one currency, of financial statements maintained in another currency, (2) expression, in terms of its own currency, of an entity's unsettled receivables and payables denominated in terms of another cur-

[1]Financial Executives Institute, *Survey of U.S. Company Foreign Translation Practices,* July 31, 1973.

[2]See paragraph 14 of Chapter 12 of ARB 43 regarding forward exchange contracts.

rency, (3) settlement of receivables and payables denominated in terms of another currency at an exchange rate different from that at which the receivable or payable was recorded, and (4) for purposes of this Statement, gains or losses on forward exchange contracts.

STANDARDS OF DISCLOSURE

6. The FASB has concluded that certain disclosures shall be made in financial statements that include amounts denominated in a foreign currency which have been translated into the currency of the reporting entity. The amounts may result from transactions, the consolidation of subsidiaries, and the equity method of accounting for investees. The following information[3] shall be disclosed (see Appendix B for examples):

a. A statement of translation policies including identification of: (1) the balance sheet accounts that are translated at the current rate and those translated at the historical rate, (2) the rates used to translate income statement accounts (e.g., historical rates for specified accounts and a weighted average rate for all other accounts), (3) the time of recognition of gain or loss on forward exchange contracts, and (4) the method of accounting for exchange adjustments (and if any portion of the exchange adjustment is deferred, the method of disposition of the deferred amount in future years).
b. The aggregate amount of exchange adjustments originating in the period, the amount thereof included in the determination of income and the amount thereof deferred.
c. The aggregate amount of exchange adjustments included in the determination of income for the period, regardless of when the adjustments originated.
d. The aggregate amount of deferred exchange adjustments, regardless of when the adjustments originated, included in the balance sheet (e.g., such as in a deferral or in a "reserve" account) and how this amount is classified.
e. The amount by which total long-term receivables and total long-term payables translated at historical rates would each increase or decrease at the balance sheet date if translated at current rates.
f. The amount of gain or loss which has not been recognized on unperformed forward exchange contracts at the balance sheet date.

EFFECTIVE DATE

7. The disclosures required by this Statement shall be made in financial statements reporting results of operations for fiscal periods ending after November 30, 1973 and in financial statements reporting financial position dated after November 30, 1973.

The provisions of this Statement need not be applied to immaterial items.

This Statement was adopted by the unanimous vote of the seven members of the Financial Standards Accounting Board.

Marshall S. Armstrong, *Chairman*
Donald J. Kirk
Arthur L. Litke
Robert E. Mays
John W. Queenan
Walter Schuetze
Robert T. Sprouse

Appendix A

BACKGROUND INFORMATION

Summary of Pronouncements[4] and Practices

8. Chapter 12 of ARB 43, as modified by paragraph 18 of APB Opinion No. 6, is the authoritative pronouncement with respect to accounting for foreign currency translation. Chapter 12 calls for translation by the "current-noncurrent method," that is, translation of current assets and liabilities at the current rate and translation of noncurrent assets and liabilities at historical rates. Under Chapter 12, all exchange losses are charged to income, realized gains are credited to income, and unrealized gains are preferably deferred, except that such gains may be credited to income to the extent that they offset previously recognized losses.

9. Chapter 12 of ARB 43 provides exceptions to these general rules. Under special circumstances (see

[3]This Statement does not require companies to change accounting methods. On occasion, the accounting methods employed may be such that it is not reasonably possible to provide all amounts required in paragraphs 6(b), (c) or (d). For example, an importer may have recorded as a part of the cost of merchandise an amount defined in the Statement as an exchange adjustment, and, therefore, may be unable to determine all or part of an amount required. Where this is so, an estimate shall be furnished if feasible. If an estimate cannot be furnished, an explanation shall be provided.

[4]The purpose of paragraphs 8-17 of this Appendix is to provide references to relevant pronouncements. These paragraphs should not be considered as interpretations by the FASB of any pronouncement cited.

paragraph 16 of Chapter 12), inventory may be stated at the historical rate. Long-term debt incurred or capital stock issued in connection with the acquisition of long-term assets shortly before a substantial and presumably permanent change in the exchange rate may be restated at the new rate. If the debt or stock is restated, an equivalent adjustment is to be made to the long-term assets. (See paragraphs 12 and 18 of Chapter 12.)

10. A research report[5] published in 1960 describes the current-noncurrent distinction as one which "seems to reflect the use of an established balance sheet classification for a purpose to which it is not relevant." In addition, the report describes the monetary-nonmonetary distinction. Based on this distinction, inventory, being nonmonetary, should be translated at historical rates of exchange, and noncurrent receivables and payables, being monetary items, should be translated at current rates.

11. The development in practice of translating all payables and receivables at current rates was given official recognition with the issuance in 1965 of APB Opinion No. 6. Paragraph 18 of Opinion No. 6 states, without specifying the circumstances, that "translation of long-term receivables and long-term liabilities at current exchange rates is appropriate in many circumstances." This modification of Chapter 12 of ARB 43, in effect, permits use of the monetary-nonmonetary method of translation.

12. Because of extensive currency realignments in 1971, the APB considered the problem of foreign currency translation and issued an exposure draft proposing that companies using the monetary-nonmonetary method defer exchange adjustments to the extent they did not exceed those attributable to long-term debt. Amounts deferred were to be accounted for in a manner similar to debt discount.[6] This draft, in effect, gave rise to another method of accounting for exchange adjustments. An Accounting Research Study[7] was in process at the time and the U.S. dollar was devalued during the exposure period. The APB deferred action on the exposure draft and announced that companies should disclose how they accounted for exchange adjustments. The APB also noted that some companies had adopted the recommendations of the exposure draft, thus achieving somewhat the same effect as translating long-term receivables and payables at historical rates.[8]

13. Paragraph 13 of APB Opinion No. 22 specifies that disclosure should be made of accounting policies with respect to translation of foreign currencies. This disclosure should "describe the accounting principles followed . . . and the methods of applying those principles that materially affect the determination of financial position, changes in financial position, or results of operations." (Paragraph 12 of APB Opinion No. 22.)

14. While there is no specific reference to foreign currency translation in APB Opinion No. 19, the APB did conclude that "the statement summarizing changes in financial position should be based on a broad concept embracing all changes in financial position" and that the statement of changes in financial position "should disclose all important aspects of its financing and investing activities regardless of whether cash or other elements of working capital are directly affected." (Paragraph 8 of APB Opinion No. 19.)

15. Chapter 12 of ARB 43 states, ". . . it is important that especial care be taken to make full disclosure in the financial statements of United States companies of the extent to which they include significant foreign items" (paragraph 6) and ". . . adequate disclosure of foreign operations should be made" (paragraph 8).

16. Chapter 12 of ARB 43 was amended as of 1967 by APB Opinion No. 9. Paragraph 21 of APB Opinion No. 9 states the conditions under which an exchange adjustment should be reported as an extraordinary item, and paragraph 22 states when it should not be reported as an extraordinary item. These paragraphs have been superseded by APB Opinion No. 30 for events and transactions occurring after September 30, 1973. Paragraph 23 of Opinion No. 30 states that "certain gains or losses should not be reported as extraordinary items" and names "gains or losses from exchange or translation of foreign currencies, including those relating to major devaluations and revaluations" as not qualifying as extraordinary items. Paragraph 27 of Opinion No. 30 states that "differences in classification . . . of the current and any prior periods presented should be disclosed in notes to the financial statements."

17. A company that changes its methods of accounting for foreign currency translation is required to make certain disclosures by APB Opinion No. 20. Those disclosures are not discussed here.

[5] National Association of Accountants, *Management Accounting Problems in Foreign Operations*, Research Report No. 36 (New York: NAA, 1960), p. 17.

[6] Proposed APB Opinion, *Translating Foreign Operations*, Exposure Draft, December 20, 1971.

[7] Leonard Lorensen, *Reporting Foreign Operations of U.S. Companies in U.S. Dollars*, Accounting Research Study No. 12 (New York: AICPA, 1972).

[8] *Accounting Research Association Newsletter*, January 28, 1972, p. 1.

Summary of Research Findings

18. The FASB research staff reviewed recent annual financial statements of seventy-seven companies engaged in foreign operations with regard to the disclosure of translation practices. The population used in this study consisted of the companies appearing on the following lists:

a. The Financial Executives Institute, *Survey of U.S. Company Foreign Translation Practices* (July 31, 1973).
b. The major multinational companies as reported by *Business Week,* August 18, 1973.
c. The U.S. companies that derived the most sales from their overseas operations in 1970 as reported by *Dun's,* April, 1973.

A variety of methods of determining and accounting for foreign currency exchange adjustments was found. Further, it was found that a significant proportion of the companies made incomplete disclosures of translation methods and the disposition of exchange adjustments.

Summary of Considerations of Comments on Exposure Draft

19. In response to the request for comments on the Exposure Draft dated October 19, 1973, seventy-four letters were received and considered by the FASB in its deliberations on this Statement. Certain of the comments and the FASB's consideration of them are summarized in paragraphs 20-25.

20. Suggestions were made that the definition in paragraph 5(d) explicitly include realized exchange gains and losses as well as gains and losses on forward exchange contracts. The FASB adopted these suggestions and, for emphasis, the term "translation adjustment" used in the Exposure Draft has been changed to "exchange adjustment" in this Statement.

21. The importance of the use of forward exchange contracts in the financial management of foreign operations was emphasized. In recognition of this and because of the apparent variety of methods of recognizing gain or loss on forward exchange contracts,[9] the FASB added specific requirements with respect thereto in paragraphs 6(a)(3) and 6(f).

22. A need was indicated for disclosure of tax effects of exchange adjustments and for a statement of policy with regard to interperiod tax allocation on exchange adjustments. Because of the complexity in determining the taxability of exchange adjustments and the interrelationship of such with the provisions of APB Opinions No. 23 and No. 24, the FASB concluded that it would prefer to consider the matter further before requiring such disclosures. This Statement requires before tax amounts as opposed to after tax amounts. Where appropriate, the FASB encourages the separate disclosure of tax effects.

23. The Exposure Draft contained the following proposed disclosure requirement which is not included in this Statement:

> *The amounts of changes in long-term receivables or long-term payables reflected in the statement of changes in financial position that are attributable to translation and the effect of translation on the net change in working capital.*

The belief was expressed that APB Opinion No. 19 was not intended to cover such changes in financial position or that compliance was impracticable because of the number of transactions and balances affected by numerous exchange rate changes. Research by the FASB disclosed that some companies are furnishing in the statement of changes in financial position the type of information contemplated in the proposed requirement. However, because it was indicated that many companies would have difficulty in furnishing the desired information, the FASB decided not to require such information at the present time. This subject will be considered further as part of the comprehensive project on accounting for foreign currency translation. The FASB encourages those companies which have been furnishing the information to continue to do so and others to do so where practicable.

24. The Exposure Draft contained the following proposed disclosure requirement:

> *If historical rates have been used in translating long-term receivables or long-term payables, the amount each of these classifications would increase or decrease in the balance sheet if translated at the current rate.*

a. The assertion was made that, by proposing this disclosure, the FASB appeared to be indicating a preference for translation at the current rate. Translation of long-term receivables and payables at historical rates is an acceptable accounting method, and in proposing this requirement, the FASB did not, in fact, intend to imply any preference for translation at current rates.
b. Objections were expressed because companies using an acceptable method of accounting were being asked to disclose the effect of using a different method. The use of historical rates to translate long-term receivables and payables in

[9]Financial Executives Institute, *Survey of U.S. Company Foreign Translation Practices,* July 31, 1973.

effect defers the recording of an exchange adjustment until the asset or liability is reclassified as current. Companies using the current rate to translate long-term receivables and payables record an exchange adjustment related thereto when an exchange rate changes, but may defer exchange adjustments. The FASB believes that information as to all deferrals of exchange adjustments should be furnished. Therefore the requirement is retained in slightly different form as paragraph 6(e).

25. It was suggested that the required disclosures be considered only after public hearings as a portion of the FASB's previously announced comprehensive study on accounting for foreign currency translation or that the effective date of applicability be deferred. After considering these suggestions, however, the FASB judged that, on the basis of existing data, it could make an informed decision on this Statement without a public hearing. Also, on consideration of the circumstances mentioned in paragraph 3 of this Statement, the FASB judged that the effective date specified in paragraph 7 would be advisable.

Appendix B

EXAMPLES OF DISCLOSURE

26. The disclosures specified by paragraph 6 of this Statement may be accomplished in various ways; for example, by a clearly captioned amount separately identified in the body of the financial statements, by a description in the summary of significant accounting policies, by explanation in the notes to the financial statements, or by combinations thereof. The following are to be considered only as examples of the disclosures which might be made to comply with the disclosure requirements specified by this Statement.

27. Paragraph 6(a) calls for a statement of translation policies including identification of: (1) the balance sheet accounts that are translated at the current rate and those translated at the historical rate, (2) the rates used to translate income statement accounts, (3) the time of recognition of gain or loss on forward exchange contracts, and (4) the method of accounting for exchange adjustments. For example, a company which uses the current-noncurrent method of translation might state the following concerning its policy for translating assets and liabilities, for time of recognition of gain or loss on forward exchange contracts, and for disposition of the exchange adjustment:

> Current assets and current liabilities are translated at the rate of exchange in effect at the close of the period. Long-term assets are translated at the rates in effect at the dates these assets were acquired, and long-term liabilities are translated at the rates in effect at the dates these obligations were incurred. Exchange adjustments, including gain or loss on settled forward exchange contracts, are charged or credited to income.
>
> Or, the following might replace the last sentence:
>
> Net unrealized losses from foreign currency translation are charged to income currently. Net unrealized gains from foreign currency translation are credited to Deferred Foreign Currency Exchange Gains, except that these gains are credited to income currently to the extent of losses previously charged to income. Gain or loss on forward exchange contracts is recognized in income upon settlement.

A company which uses the monetary-nonmonetary method of translation might state:

> Inventory, property, plant, equipment, deferred charges, . . . are translated at the rates of exchange in effect when acquired. All other assets and liabilities are translated at the rate of exchange in effect at the close of the period. Exchange adjustments are deferred to the extent that they do not exceed those that are attributable to long-term debt and are amortized by the interest method over the remaining term of the debt. Otherwise, they are charged or credited to income currently. Gain or loss on forward exchange contracts is recognized in income upon settlement.

As to rates used to translate income statement accounts, the accounting policy might be stated as follows:

> Revenue and expense accounts for each month are translated at the average rate of exchange in effect during the month, except for depreciation and amortization which are translated at the rates of exchange which were in effect when the respective assets were acquired.
>
> Or, as follows:
>
> Revenue and expense accounts are translated at a weighted average of exchange rates which were in effect during the year, except for depreciation . . . etc.

28. Paragraph 6(b) calls for disclosure of the aggregate amount of exchange adjustments originating in the period, the amount thereof included in the determination of income and the amount thereof deferred. A company which includes all exchange

adjustments in the determination of income for the year and so states in a description of its accounting policies might identify the amount by reporting it separately in its income statement as follows:

> Foreign Currency Exchange
> Losses . . . .$XX,XXX

A company that follows the recommendations of paragraph 11 of Chapter 12 of ARB 43 might state in a note:

> In 1973, the Company charged unrealized foreign currency exchange losses of $12,345 for the year to income. In 1974, the Company credited $12,345 of its $54,321 unrealized foreign currency exchange gain for the year to income and credited the remaining $41,976 to Deferred Foreign Currency Exchange Gains.

29. Paragraph 6(c) calls for disclosure of the aggregate amount of exchange adjustments included in the determination of income for the period, regardless of when the adjustments originated. This disclosure will generally be fulfilled by the disclosure called for under paragraph 6(b) unless amortization of exchange adjustments originating in prior periods has been included in income for the current year. For example, a company that defers the exchange adjustment (wholly or partially) and amortizes it would disclose the amount amortized in the current year from past years plus or minus any portion of the current year's exchange adjustment included in income.

A company might state the following:

> Foreign currency exchange adjustments of $100,000 originating during the year and amortization of $10,000 of previously deferred exchange adjustments have both been charged to income.

30. Paragraph 6(d) calls for disclosure of the aggregate amount of deferred exchange adjustments included in the balance sheet and how this amount is classified. The disclosures called for here may be accomplished by a separate caption in the balance sheet or by disclosure in a note.

For example, a company might have a separate caption in its balance sheet as follows:

> Deferred Foreign Currency
> Exchange Gains . . . .$XXX,XXX

Another company might state in a note:

> Deferred Charges at December 31, 1973, includes foreign currency exchange adjustments amounting to $XXX,XXX.

31. Paragraph 6(e) calls for disclosure of the amount by which long-term receivables and payables translated at historical rates would each increase or decrease at the balance sheet date if translated at current rates.

A company might state the following:

> The Company translates foreign currency long-term receivables at the rates of exchange in effect when the sales were made and translates foreign currency long-term debt at the rates of exchange in effect when these obligations were incurred. Translated at the rates of exchange in effect on December 31, 1973, long-term receivables would increase by $3,210,000 and long-term debt would increase by $5,432,000.

As an alternative, that same company (assuming the company disclosed in its balance sheet at December 31, 1973, total U.S. dollar and foreign currency long-term receivables in the amount of $65,432,000 and total U.S. dollar and foreign currency long-term debt in the amount of $76,543,000) might substitute for the last sentence above the following:

> . . . Translated at the rates of exchange in effect on December 31, 1973, total long-term receivables would be $68,642,000 and total long-term debt would be $81,975,000.

32. Paragraph 6(f) calls for disclosure of the amount of gain or loss which has not been recognized on unperformed forward exchange contracts at the balance sheet date. A company which accrues losses on such contracts might state the following:

> The Company accrues losses on all unperformed forward exchange contracts and records gains at maturity. At December 31, 1973, unrecorded gains based on exchange rates then in effect amounted to $XX,XXX.

Statement of Financial Accounting Standards No. 2
Accounting for Research and Development Costs

STATUS

Issued: October 1974

Effective Date: For fiscal years beginning on or after January 1, 1975

Affects: Amends APB 17, paragraph 6
Amends APB 22, paragraph 13

Affected by: Paragraph 14 superseded by FAS 71

Statement of Financial Accounting Standards No. 2
Accounting for Research and Development Costs

CONTENTS

INTRODUCTION

1. This Statement establishes standards of financial accounting and reporting for research and development costs with the objectives of reducing the number of alternative accounting and reporting practices presently followed and providing useful financial information about research and development costs. This Statement specifies:

a. Those activities that shall be identified as research and development for financial accounting and reporting purposes.
b. The elements of costs that shall be identified with research and development activities.
c. The accounting for research and development costs.
d. The financial statement disclosures related to research and development costs.

2. Accounting for the costs of research and development activities conducted for others under a contractual arrangement is a part of accounting for contracts in general and is beyond the scope of this Statement. Indirect costs that are specifically reimbursable under the terms of a contract are also excluded from this Statement.

3. This Statement does not apply to activities that are unique to enterprises in the extractive industries, such as prospecting, acquisition of mineral rights, exploration, drilling, mining, and related mineral development. It does apply, however, to research and development activities of enterprises in the extractive industries that are comparable in nature to research and development activities of other enterprises, such as development or improvement of processes and techniques including those employed in exploration, drilling, and extraction.

4. *APB Opinion No. 17,* "Intangible Assets," is hereby amended to exclude from its scope those research and development costs encompassed by this Statement.

5. Paragraph 13 of *APB Opinion No. 22,* "Disclosure of Accounting Policies," is amended to delete "research and development costs (including basis for amortization)" as an example of disclosure "commonly required" with respect to accounting policies.

6. Standards of financial accounting and reporting for research and development costs are set forth in paragraphs 7-16. The basis for the Board's conclusions, as well as alternatives considered by the Board and reasons for their rejection, are discussed in Appendix B to this Statement. Background information is presented in Appendix A.

STANDARDS OF FINANCIAL ACCOUNTING AND REPORTING

Activities Constituting Research and Development

7. Paragraphs 8-10 set forth broad guidelines as to the activities that shall be classified as research and development.

8. For purposes of this Statement, research and development is defined as follows:

a. *Research* is planned search or critical investigation aimed at discovery of new knowledge with the hope that such knowledge will be useful in developing a new product or service (hereinafter "product") or a new process or technique (hereinafter "process") or in bringing about a significant improvement to an existing product or process.
b. *Development* is the translation of research find-

ings or other knowledge into a plan or design for a new product or process or for a significant improvement to an existing product or process whether intended for sale or use. It includes the conceptual formulation, design, and testing of product alternatives, construction of prototypes, and operation of pilot plants. It does not include routine or periodic alterations to existing products, production lines, manufacturing processes, and other on-going operations even though those alterations may represent improvements and it does not include market research or market testing activities.

9. The following are examples of activities that typically would be included in research and development in accordance with paragraph 8 (unless conducted for others under a contractual arrangement—see paragraph 2):

a. Laboratory research aimed at discovery of new knowledge.
b. Searching for applications of new research findings or other knowledge.
c. Conceptual formulation and design of possible product or process alternatives.
d. Testing in search for or evaluation of product or process alternatives.
e. Modification of the formulation or design of a product or process.
f. Design, construction, and testing of pre-production prototypes and models.
g. Design of tools, jigs, molds, and dies involving new technology.
h. Design, construction, and operation of a pilot plant that is not of a scale economically feasible to the enterprise for commercial production.
i. Engineering activity required to advance the design of a product to the point that it meets specific functional and economic requirements and is ready for manufacture.

10. The following are examples of activities that typically would be excluded from research and development in accordance with paragraph 8:

a. Engineering follow-through in an early phase of commercial production.
b. Quality control during commercial production including routine testing of products.
c. Trouble-shooting in connection with breakdowns during commercial production.
d. Routine, on-going efforts to refine, enrich, or otherwise improve upon the qualities of an existing product.
e. Adaptation of an existing capability to a particular requirement or customer's need as part of a continuing commercial activity.
f. Seasonal or other periodic design changes to existing products.
g. Routine design of tools, jigs, molds, and dies.
h. Activity, including design and construction engineering, related to the construction, relocation, rearrangement, or start-up of facilities or equipment other than (1) pilot plants (see paragraph 9(h)) and (2) facilities or equipment whose sole use is for a particular research and development project (see paragraph 11(a)).
i. Legal work in connection with patent applications or litigation, and the sale or licensing of patents.

Elements of Costs to Be Identified with Research and Development Activities

11. Elements of costs shall be identified with research and development activities as follows:

a. *Materials, equipment, and facilities.* The costs of materials (whether from the enterprise's normal inventory or acquired specially for research and development activities) and equipment or facilities that are acquired or constructed for research and development activities and that have alternative future uses (in research and development projects or otherwise) shall be capitalized as tangible assets when acquired or constructed. The cost of such materials consumed in research and development activities and the depreciation of such equipment or facilities used in those activities are research and development costs. However, the costs of materials, equipment, or facilities that are acquired or constructed for a particular research and development project and that have no alternative future uses (in other research and development projects or otherwise) and therefore no separate economic values are research and development costs at the time the costs are incurred.
b. *Personnel.* Salaries, wages, and other related costs of of personnel engaged in research and development activities shall be included in research and development costs.
c. *Intangibles purchased from others.* The costs of intangibles that are purchased from others for use in research and development activities and that have alternative future uses (in research and development projects or otherwise) shall be capitalized and amortized as intangible assets in accordance with *APB Opinion No. 17*. The amortization of those intangible assets used in research and development activities is a research and development cost. However, the costs of intangibles that are purchased from others for a particular research and development project and that have no alternative future uses (in other research and development projects or otherwise) and therefore no separate economic values are research and development costs at the time the costs are incurred.

d. *Contract services.* The costs of services performed by others in connection with the research and development activities of an enterprise, including research and development conducted by others in behalf of the enterprise, shall be included in research and development costs.

e. *Indirect costs.* Research and development costs shall include a reasonable allocation of indirect costs. However, general and administrative costs that are not clearly related to research and development activities shall not be included as research and development costs.

Accounting for Research and Development Costs

12. All research and development costs encompassed by this Statement shall be charged to expense when incurred.

Disclosure

13. Disclosure shall be made in the financial statements of the total research and development costs charged to expense in each period for which an income statement is presented.

14. A government-regulated enterprise that defers research and development costs for financial accounting purposes in accordance with the Addendum to *APB Opinion No. 2,* "Accounting for the 'Investment Credit,'" shall disclose the following additional information about its research and development costs:

a. Accounting policy, including basis for amortization.

b. Total research and development costs incurred in each period for which an income statement is presented and the amount of those costs that has been capitalized or deferred in each period.

Effective Date and Transition

15. This Statement shall be effective for fiscal years beginning on or after January 1, 1975, although earlier application is encouraged. The requirement of paragraph 12 that research and development costs be charged to expense when incurred shall be applied retroactively by prior period adjustment (described in paragraphs 18 and 26 of *APB Opinion No. 9,* "Reporting the Results of Operations"). When financial statements for periods before the effective date or financial summaries or other data derived therefrom are presented, they shall be restated to reflect the prior period adjustment. The prior period adjustment shall recognize any related income tax effect. The nature of a restatement and its effect on income before extraordinary items, net income, and related per share amounts for each period presented shall be disclosed in the period of change.

16. The disclosures specified in paragraphs 13-14 are encouraged but not required for fiscal periods prior to the effective date of this Statement. If disclosures for those earlier periods are made, amounts shall be based to the extent practicable on the guidelines in paragraphs 8-11 of this Statement for identifying research and development activities and costs.

The provisions of this Statement need not be applied to immaterial items.

This Statement was adopted by the unanimous vote of the seven members of the Financial Accounting Standards Board:

Marshall S. Armstrong, *Chairman*
Donald J. Kirk
Arthur L. Litke
Robert E. Mays
John W. Queenan
Walter Schuetze
Robert T. Sprouse

Appendix A

BACKGROUND INFORMATION

17. Expenditures for research and development constitute a significant element of the United States economy and are vital for its growth. Based on statistics for research and development as defined by the National Science Foundation (see paragraph 25), total expenditures were over $30 billion in 1973, approximately two-thirds of which was spent for research and development conducted by business enterprises and the balance for research and development conducted by the government, universities and colleges, and other organizations.

18. In recognition of the significance of research and development and the alternative accounting and reporting practices presently followed for research and development costs, in April 1973 the FASB placed on its technical agenda a project on "Accounting for Research and Development and Similar Costs." The scope of the project encompassed accounting and reporting by companies in the development stage.

19. A task force of 16 persons from industry, government, public accounting, the financial community, and academe was appointed in July 1973 to provide counsel to the Board in preparing a Discussion Memorandum analyzing issues related to the project.

20. In February 1973 the AICPA published *Accounting Research Study No. 14,* "Accounting for Research and Development Expenditures." In view of the availability of that study and other published research studies and articles, which are cited in Appendix B and in the Discussion Memorandum, the FASB did not undertake a major research effort for the project. The FASB staff interviewed a limited number of selected financial analysts and commercial bankers and reviewed a substantial number of published financial statements.

21. The Board issued the Discussion Memorandum on December 28, 1973, and held a public hearing on the subject on March 15, 1974. The Board received 74 position papers, letters of comment, and outlines of oral presentations in connection with the public hearing and heard 14 oral presentations at the hearing.

22. In its deliberations following the hearing, the Board concluded that the initial Statement of Financial Accounting Standards resulting from the project should address solely accounting for research and development costs. An Exposure Draft of a proposed Statement on "Accounting for Research and Development Costs" was issued on June 5, 1974. The Board received 168 letters of comment on the Exposure Draft.

Appendix B

BASIS FOR CONCLUSIONS

23. This Appendix discusses factors deemed significant by members of the Board in reaching the conclusions in this Statement, including the various alternatives considered and reasons for accepting some and rejecting others.

ACTIVITIES CONSTITUTING RESEARCH AND DEVELOPMENT

24. The guidelines in paragraphs 8-10 for activities that should be identified as research and development are designed to accommodate a wide variety of research and development activities. Adherence to those guidelines should result in a reasonable degree of comparability. Differences among enterprises and among industries are so great that a detailed prescription of the activities and related costs includable in research and development, either for all companies or on an industry-by-industry basis, is not a realistic undertaking for the FASB.

25. The Board began its consideration of a definition of research and development with the following definition by the National Science Foundation (NSF):[1]

> *Research and development*—Basic and applied research in the sciences and engineering and the design and development of prototypes and processes. This definition excludes quality control, routine product testing, market research, sales promotion, sales service, research in the social sciences or psychology, and other nontechnological activities or technical services.

26. The NSF further classifies research and development activities by type, as follows:[2]

> *Basic research*—Original investigations for the advancement of scientific knowledge not having specific commercial objectives, although such investigations may be in fields of present or potential interest to the reporting company.
>
> *Applied research*—Investigations directed to the discovery of new scientific knowledge having specific commercial objectives with respect to products or processes. This definition differs from that of basic research chiefly in terms of the objectives of the reporting company.
>
> *Development*—Technical activities of a nonroutine nature concerned with translating research findings or other scientific knowledge into products or processes. [Development] does not include routine technical services to customers or other activities excluded from . . . research and development.

27. The NSF definition has the advantage of being relatively widely used and understood. However, it is oriented primarily to research in the physical and biological sciences and excludes research in the social sciences.

28. Respondents to the Discussion Memorandum recommended modifications of the NSF definition as well as various other definitions which were gen-

[1] National Science Foundation, *Research and Development in Industry 1971* (Washington, D.C.: U.S. Government Printing Office, May 1973), p. 19.

[2] *Ibid.*

erally similar to or broader than the NSF definition. The Board agreed that a broad definition including research and development activities in the social sciences such as those conducted by service-type business enterprises is appropriate for financial accounting and reporting purposes. Accordingly, the definition in paragraph 8 has been adopted.

29. The Exposure Draft had included research and development activities conducted for others under a contractual arrangement within the definition of research and development and had proposed that all research and development costs not directly reimbursable by others be charged to expense when incurred. Some respondents to the Exposure Draft contended that costs incurred in research and development activities conducted for others under a contractual arrangement should continue to be accounted for in accordance with financial accounting standards for contracts in general rather than as research and development costs. The Board agrees with this view and the change is reflected in paragraph 2.

30. The examples in paragraphs 9-10 incorporate certain changes, many of which were recommended by respondents to the Exposure Draft. The Board believes that those paragraphs as changed more clearly reflect its intent regarding the inclusion or exclusion of particular types of activities within the definition of research and development.

31. Several respondents to the Exposure Draft raised questions about the inclusion or exclusion of the development of various types of computer software within the definition of research and development. Computer software is developed for many and diverse uses. Accordingly, in each case the nature of the activity for which the software is being developed should be considered in relation to the guidelines in paragraphs 8-10 to determine whether software costs should be included or excluded. For example, efforts to develop a new or higher level of computer software capability intended for sale (but not under a contractual arrangement) would be a research and development activity encompassed by this Statement.

ELEMENTS OF COSTS TO BE IDENTIFIED WITH RESEARCH AND DEVELOPMENT ACTIVITIES

32. To achieve a reasonable degree of comparability among enterprises, the Board concluded that broad guidelines are appropriate to identify the elements of costs that should be included as research and development. Those guidelines are in paragraph 11.

33. Consideration was given to the alternative that the costs of materials, equipment, or facilities that are acquired or constructed for a particular research and development project and that have no alternative future uses (in other research and development projects or otherwise) be apportioned over the life of the project rather than treated as research and development costs when incurred. The Board reasoned, however, that if materials, equipment, or facilities are of such a specialized nature that they have no alternative future uses, even in another research and development project, those materials, equipment, or facilities have no separate economic values to distinguish them from other types of costs such as salaries and wages incurred in a particular project. Accordingly, all costs of those materials, equipment, and facilities should be treated as research and development costs when incurred.

34. Paragraph 11(c) reflects certain changes from the Exposure Draft to treat the costs of intangibles purchased from others in a manner similar to that in paragraph 11(a) for the costs of materials, equipment, or facilities. Paragraph 11(c) is not intended to alter the conclusions in paragraphs 87-88 of *APB Opinion No. 16,* "Business Combinations," regarding allocation of cost to assets acquired in a business combination accounted for by the purchase method.

35. The conclusion that general and administrative costs not be allocated to research and development activities (unless clearly related) conforms to present accounting practice, which generally treats such costs as expenses when incurred.

36. One question in the Discussion Memorandum was whether interest or other cost of capital should be allocated to research and development activities. At present, interest or other cost of capital generally is not allocated to the cost of assets or specific activities for financial accounting purposes. The Board believes that allocation of interest or other cost of capital to research and development activities is part of a broader question beyond the scope of this Statement.

ACCOUNTING FOR RESEARCH AND DEVELOPMENT COSTS

37. The Board considered four alternative methods of accounting at the time research and development costs are incurred:

a. Charge all costs to expense when incurred.
b. Capitalize all costs when incurred.
c. Capitalize costs when incurred if specified conditions are fulfilled and charge all other costs to expense.
d. Accumulate all costs in a special category until

the existence of future benefits can be determined.

38. In concluding that all research and development costs be charged to expense when incurred (see paragraph 12), Board members considered the factors discussed in paragraphs 39-59. Individual Board members gave greater weight to some factors than to others.

Uncertainty of Future Benefits

39. There is normally a high degree of uncertainty about the future benefits of individual research and development projects, although the element of uncertainty may diminish as a project progresses. Estimates of the rate of success of research and development projects vary markedly—depending in part on how narrowly one defines a "project" and how one defines "success"—but all such estimates indicate a high failure rate. For example, one study of a number of industries found that an average of less than 2 percent of new product ideas and less than 15 percent of product development projects were commercially successful.[3]

40. Even after a project has passed beyond the research and development stage, and a new or improved product or process is being marketed or used, the failure rate is high. Estimates of new product failures range from 30 percent to 90 percent, depending on the definition of failure used.[4] One study concludes that "for about every three products emerging from research and development departments as technical successes, there is an average of only one commercial success."[5] That study goes on to say that "of all the dollars of new product expense, almost three-fourths go to unsuccessful products; about two-thirds of these . . . dollars are in the 'development stage.'"[6]

Lack of Causal Relationship between Expenditures and Benefits

41. A direct relationship between research and development costs and specific future revenue generally has not been demonstrated, even with the benefit of hindsight. For example, three empirical research studies, which focus on companies in industries intensively involved in research and development activities, generally failed to find a significant correlation between research and development expenditures and increased future benefits as measured by subsequent sales,[7] earnings,[8] or share of industry sales.[9]

Accounting Recognition of Economic Resources

42. In paragraph 57 of *APB Statement No. 4,* "Basic Concepts and Accounting Principles Underlying Financial Statements of Business Enterprises," economic resources are defined as the scarce means for carrying on economic activities. The economic resources of a particular enterprise are generally regarded as those *scarce* resources for which there is an *expectation of future benefits to the enterprise* either through use or sale.

43. Not all of the economic resources of an enterprise are recognized as assets for financial accounting purposes. However, criteria for identifying those economic resources that should be recognized as the assets of an enterprise for accounting purposes have not been specified in the official accounting literature. One criterion that has been suggested in published research studies and articles and in position papers, letters of comment, and oral presentations the Board received in connection with the public hearing is that of *measurability.*

44. The criterion of measurability would require that a resource not be recognized as an asset for accounting purposes unless at the time it is acquired or developed its future economic benefits can be identified and objectively measured.

45. Paragraphs 39-40 indicate that at the time most research and development costs are incurred the future benefits are at best uncertain. In other words, there is no indication that an economic resource has been created. Moreover, even if at some point in the progress of an individual research and development project the expectation of future benefits becomes sufficiently high to indicate that an economic resource has been created, the question remains whether that resource should be recognized as an asset for financial accounting purposes. Although future benefits from a particular research and devel-

[3]Booz-Allen & Hamilton, Inc., *Management of New Products* (Chicago: Booz-Allen & Hamilton, Inc., 1968), p. 12.

[4]John T. Gerlach and Charles Anthony Wainwright, *Successful Management of New Products* (New York: Hastings House, Publishers, Inc., 1968), p. 126.

[5]Booz-Allen & Hamilton, Inc., *Management of New Products,* p. 2.

[6]*Ibid.,* p. 11.

[7]Maurice S. Newman, "Equating Return from R & D Expenditures," *Financial Executive,* April 1968, pp. 26-33.

[8]Orace Johnson, "A Consequential Approach to Accounting for R & D," *Journal of Accounting Research,* Autumn 1967, pp. 164-172.

[9]Alex J. Milburn, "An Empirical Study of the Relationship of Research and Development Expenditures to Subsequent Benefits" (Unpublished Research Study, Department of Accountancy of the University of Illinois, 1971).

opment project may be foreseen, they generally cannot be measured with a reasonable degree of certainty. According to the research data cited in paragraph 41, there is normally little, if any, direct relationship between the amount of current research and development expenditures and the amount of resultant future benefits to the enterprise. Research and development costs therefore fail to satisfy the suggested measurability test for accounting recognition as an asset.

46. The criterion of exchangeability, which was discussed in the Exposure Draft, was not considered a significant factor by the Board in reaching its final conclusion on accounting for research and development costs. The Board believes that exchangeability needs further study and at this time the Board neither accepts nor rejects exchangeability as a criterion for accounting recognition of an economic resource.

Expense Recognition and Matching

47. *APB Statement No. 4* explicitly avoids using the term "matching" because it has a variety of meanings in the accounting literature. In its broadest sense, matching refers to the entire process of income determination—described in paragraph 147 of *APB Statement No. 4* as "identifying, measuring, and relating revenues and expenses of an enterprise for an accounting period." Matching may also be used in a more limited sense to refer only to the process of expense recognition or in an even more limited sense to refer to the recognition of expenses by associating costs with revenue on a cause and effect basis. In the following discussion, matching is used in its most limited sense to refer to the process of recognizing costs as expenses on a cause and effect basis.

48. Three pervasive principles for recognizing costs as expenses are set forth in paragraphs 156-160 of *APB Statement No. 4* as follows:

> *Associating Cause and Effect.* Some costs are recognized as expenses on the basis of a presumed direct association with specific revenue. . . . recognizing them as expenses accompanies recognition of the revenue.
>
> *Systematic and Rational Allocation.* . . . If an asset provides benefits for several periods its cost is allocated to the periods in a systematic and rational manner in the absence of a more direct basis for associating cause and effect.
>
> *Immediate Recognition.* Some costs are associated with the current accounting period as expenses because (1) costs incurred during the period provide no discernible future benefits, (2) costs recorded as assets in prior periods no longer provide discernible benefits, or (3) allocating costs either on the basis of association with revenue or among several accounting periods is considered to serve no useful purpose. . . . The principle of immediate recognition also requires that items carried as assets in prior periods that are discovered to have no discernible future benefit be charged to expense, for example, a patent that is determined to be worthless.

49. As noted in paragraph 41, evidence of a direct causal relationship between current research and development expenditures and subsequent future benefits generally has not been found. Also, there is often a high degree of uncertainty about whether research and development expenditures will provide any future benefits. Thus, even an indirect cause and effect relationship can seldom be demonstrated. Because there is generally no direct or even indirect basis for relating costs to revenues, the Board believes that the principles of "associating cause and effect" and "systematic and rational allocation" cannot be applied to recognize research and development costs as expenses. That is, the notion of "matching"—when used to refer to the process of recognizing costs as expenses on any sort of cause and effect basis—cannot be applied to research and development costs. Indeed, the general lack of discernible future benefits at the time the costs are incurred indicates that the "immediate recognition" principle of expense recognition should apply.

Usefulness of Resulting Information

50. *APB Statement No. 4* indicates that certain costs are immediately recognized as expenses because allocating them to several accounting periods "is considered to serve no useful purpose." There is general agreement that two of the basic elements in the decision models of many financial statement users are (a) expected return—the predicted amount and timing of the return on an investment—and (b) risk—the variability of that expected return. The data cited in paragraphs 39-41, the views of security analysts and other professional investors submitted to the Board in connection with the public hearing, and FASB interviews with selected analysts and bankers suggest that the relationship between current research and development costs and the amount of resultant future benefits to an enterprise is so uncertain that capitalization of any research and development costs is not useful in assessing the earnings potential of the enterprise. Therefore, it is unlikely that one's ability to predict the return on an investment and the variability of that return would be enhanced by capitalization.

Capitalization of All Costs When Incurred

51. Enterprises undertake research and development activities with the hope of future benefits. If there were no such hope, the activities would not be conducted. Some persons take the position that the accounting treatment for research and development costs should be determined by considering in the aggregate all of the research and development activities of an enterprise. In their view, if there is a high probability of future benefits from an enterprise's total research and development program, the entire cost of those activities should be capitalized without regard to the certainty of future benefits from individual projects.

52. The Board believes, however, that it is not appropriate to consider accounting for research and development activities on an aggregate or total-enterprise basis for several reasons. For accounting purposes the expectation of future benefits generally is not evaluated in relation to broad categories of expenditures on an enterprise-wide basis but rather in relation to individual or related transactions or projects. Also, an enterprise's total research and development program may consist of a number of projects at varying stages of completion and with varying degrees of uncertainty as to their ultimate success. If research and development costs were capitalized on an enterprise-wide basis, a meaningful method of amortization could not be developed because the period of benefit could not be determined. Moreover, over 90 percent of the respondents to a survey reported in AICPA *Accounting Research Study No. 14* indicated that their company's philosophy is that research and development expenditures are intended to be recovered by current revenues rather than by revenue from new products.[10]

Selective Capitalization

53. Selective capitalization—capitalizing research and development costs when incurred if specified conditions are fulfilled and charging to expense all other research and development costs—requires establishment of conditions that must be fulfilled before research and development costs are capitalized. The Board considered a number of factors on which prerequisite conditions might be based, including the following:

a. *Definition of product or process.* The new or improved product or process must be defined.
b. *Technological feasibility.* The new or improved product or process must be determined to be technologically feasible.
c. *Marketability/Usefulness.* The marketability of the product or process or, if it is to be used internally rather than sold, its usefulness to the enterprise must be substantially assured.
d. *Economic feasibility.* Probability of future economic benefits sufficient to recover all capitalized costs must be high. Encompassed by the notion of economic feasibility is measurability of future benefits. Also implicit is the ability to associate particular future benefits with particular costs.
e. *Management action.* Management must have definitely decided to produce and market or use the new product or process or to incorporate the significant improvement into an existing product or process.
f. *Distortion of net income comparisons.* Capitalization or immediate charging to expense of research and development costs must be determined on the basis of whether interperiod comparisons of net income would be materially distorted.

54. None of those factors, however, lends itself to establishing a condition that could be objectively and comparably applied by all enterprises. Considerable judgment is required to identify the point in the progress of a research and development project at which a new or improved product or process is "defined" or is determined to be "technologically feasible," "marketable," or "useful." Nor can the "probability of future benefits" be readily assessed. A "management decision" to proceed with production does not necessarily assure future benefits. The Board does not believe that "distortion of net income comparisons," which a few respondents to the Discussion Memorandum suggested, is an operable criterion by which to decide whether research and development costs should be capitalized because the point at which net income comparisons might be "distorted" cannot be defined. Moreover, in assessing risk, financial statement users have indicated that they seek information about the variability of earnings.

55. The Board has concluded that no set of conditions that might be established for capitalization of costs could achieve the comparability among enterprises that proponents of "selective capitalization" cite as a primary objective of that approach.

56. If selective capitalization were applied only to costs incurred after fulfillment of the specified conditions, only a portion of the total costs of a particular research and development project would be capitalized and amortized. Thus, the capitalized amount would not indicate the total costs incurred

[10]Oscar S. Gellein and Maurice A. Newman, *Accounting Research Study No. 14,* "Accounting for Research and Development Expenditures" (New York: AICPA, 1973), p. 100.

to produce future benefits; nor would the amount of periodic amortization of capitalized costs represent a "matching" of costs and benefits.

57. Selective capitalization might involve retroactive capitalization of previously incurred costs in addition to capitalization of costs incurred after fulfillment of the specified conditions. However, many research and development costs incurred before fulfillment of the conditions are not likely to be directly identifiable with the particular new or improved product or process for which costs would be capitalized. Moreover, retroactive capitalization of costs previously charged to expense is contrary to present accounting practice for other transactions whose initial accounting is not altered as a result of hindsight. The preparation of periodic financial statements requires many estimates and judgments for which restatements are not made in retrospect.

Accumulation of Costs in a Special Category

58. The Board considered the proposal that all research and development costs be accumulated in a special category distinct from assets and expenses until a determination can be made about whether future benefits exist. That special category might be reported either below the asset section of the balance sheet (with segregation of a corresponding amount of stockholders' equity) or as a negative (contra) element of stockholders' equity. Ultimately, the accumulated costs would be transferred to assets (if future benefits become reasonably established) or written off (if it were reasonably established that no significant future benefits would ensue).

59. A feature cited by proponents of this approach is that it draws attention to the uncertainty surrounding most research and development costs and it enables postponement of the capitalize vs. expense decision. This alternative was rejected, however, for the following reasons. First, financial analysts and others have indicated that costs accumulated in that special category would not be useful in assessing the earning power of an enterprise because of the uncertainties involved, and the research data cited earlier tend to support that view. Second, use of a special category would alter the nature of the basic financial statements and would complicate the computation of ratios and other financial data.

DISCLOSURE

60. Regardless of their position on the accounting treatment for research and development costs, respondents to the Discussion Memorandum generally pointed out that current disclosure practices for research and development costs vary and that requirements for informative disclosure need to be established. The disclosures specified in paragraphs 13-14 reflect the Board's general agreement with that view.

61. The Exposure Draft had proposed that disclosure also be required of (a) the accounting policy for research and development costs, (b) the amount of directly reimbursable research and development costs incurred, (c) the costs of research and development conducted in behalf of the enterprise by others, and (d) the amounts and classifications in the income statement of research and development costs charged to expense during the period. The Board has accepted the recommendation of some respondents to the Exposure Draft that disclosure of accounting policy not be required[11] because this Statement permits only one method of accounting for research and development costs. Some letters of comment on the Exposure Draft indicated that data related to items (b), (c), and (d) above are frequently difficult to obtain and that those disclosures generally would not be meaningful. The Board agrees with this view; this Statement does not require those disclosures.

62. The Board recognizes that disclosure of additional information about an enterprise's research and development activities might be useful to some financial statement users. However, many respondents to the Discussion Memorandum contended that certain kinds of information should not be required to be included in financial statements because the information is not sufficiently objective, is confidential in nature, or is beyond the scope of financial accounting information. For that reason, the Board concluded that disclosure of (a) the nature, status, and costs of individual research and development projects, (b) the nature and status of patents, (c) projections about new or improved products or processes, and (d) an enterprise's philosophy regarding research and development, all of which were included in the Discussion Memorandum as disclosure possibilities, should not be required. In addition, most respondents said that forecasts of research and development expenditures should not be considered in this project, and the Board agrees with that view. Disclosure of research and development costs by line of business is a matter included in "Financial Reporting for Segments of a Business Enterprise," another project presently on the Board's agenda.

EFFECTIVE DATE AND TRANSITION

63. The Board considered three alternative approaches to reporting a change in the method of accounting for research and development costs: (1)

[11] That disclosure is required by this Statement for certain government-regulated enterprises (see paragraph 14).

prior period adjustment, (2) the "cumulative effect" method described in *APB Opinion No. 20,* "Accounting Changes," and (3) continued amortization of previously capitalized costs. The Board concluded that the prior period adjustment method will provide the most useful information about research and development costs for comparing financial data for periods after the effective date of this Statement with data presented for earlier periods.

64. Upon consideration of all circumstances, the Board judged that the effective date specified in paragraph 15, which had been proposed in the Exposure Draft, is advisable.

Statement of Financial Accounting Standards No. 3
Reporting Accounting Changes in Interim Financial Statements

an amendment of APB Opinion No. 28

STATUS

Issued: December 1974

Effective Date: For interim periods ending on or after December 31, 1974

Affects: Amends APB 28, paragraph 31
Supersedes APB 28, paragraph 27 and footnote 5

Affected by: No other pronouncements

Statement of Financial Accounting Standards No. 3
Reporting Accounting Changes in Interim Financial Statements

an amendment of APB Opinion No. 28

CONTENTS

INTRODUCTION AND BACKGROUND INFORMATION

1. As a result of numerous inquiries concerning the appropriate procedures for reporting a change to the LIFO method of inventory pricing in interim financial reports, the FASB has examined certain conclusions of *APB Opinion No. 28,* "Interim Financial Reporting," with respect to two aspects of reporting accounting changes in interim financial reports:

a. Reporting a cumulative effect type accounting change (as described in *APB Opinion No. 20,* "Accounting Changes") including a change to the LIFO method of inventory pricing for which a cumulative effect cannot be determined.
b. Reporting an accounting change made during the fourth quarter of a fiscal year by a company whose securities are publicly traded.

2. *APB Opinion No. 28* became effective for interim periods relating to fiscal years beginning on or after January 1, 1974, and paragraphs 23-29 of that Opinion set forth standards for reporting accounting changes in interim financial reports. Those paragraphs provide that, in general, an accounting change made in an interim period should be reported in accordance with the provisions of *APB Opinion No. 20.*

3. Paragraphs 9-14 of this Statement establish standards of financial accounting and reporting that address the matters identified in paragraph 1. The Appendices to this Statement contain examples of application of *APB Opinion No. 28* (as amended by this Statement) and the requirements of *APB Opinion No. 20* as they are incorporated by reference in *APB Opinion No. 28.*

4. An Exposure Draft of a proposed Statement on "Reporting Accounting Changes in Interim Financial Statements" was issued on November 11, 1974. Fifty-five letters were received in response to the request for comments. This Statement incorporates a number of changes suggested by those respondents. The principal change is to require that, if an accounting change is made in other than the first interim period of an enterprise's fiscal year, the cumulative effect of the change on retained earnings at the beginning of that year shall be included in the determination of net income of the first interim period of the year of change (by restatement of that period's financial information).

5. The Board has concluded that it can make an informed decision on the matters identified in paragraph 1 of this Statement without a public hearing. It has also concluded that the effective date in paragraph 16 of this Statement is advisable to permit application of the provisions of this Statement before divergent interpretations of *APB Opinion No. 28* develop in practice.

Cumulative Effect Type Accounting Changes

6. Paragraph 27 of *APB Opinion No. 28* provides that "a change in accounting principle or practice adopted in an interim period that requires an adjustment for the cumulative effect of the change to the beginning of the current fiscal year should be reported in the interim period in a manner similar to that to be followed in the annual report. . . . The effect of the change from the beginning of the annual period to the period of change should be reported as a determinant of net income in the interim period in which the change is made." That paragraph goes on to require, however, that when information is subsequently presented for the period in which the change is made or for pre-change interim periods of that year, that information should be restated to give effect to the accounting change.

7. As a result of those requirements, if a cumulative effect type accounting change is made, the cumulative effect of the change on retained earnings at the beginning of that fiscal year is a component of net income of the interim period in which the change is adopted. If a change is made in other than the first interim period, since the cumulative effect remains a component of that interim period's income when financial information for that period is subsequently reported, reissued pre-change interim period balance sheets would not reflect the cumulative effect of the change on retained earnings at the beginning of the fiscal year on a retroactive basis, whereas reissued pre-change interim period income statements would be restated. In addition, an enterprise may issue interim financial information knowing that the information will subsequently have to be revised. For example, during the second quarter of its fiscal year an enterprise may make an accounting change as of the beginning of that quarter. If, subsequently during that second quarter, the enterprise issues first quarter financial information (perhaps in a report to its securityholders, in a report to a bank, or in a filing with the SEC), that first quarter information would be prepared on the basis of the old accounting principle—not the newly adopted one. When that enterprise later issues second quarter information, both the cumulative effect of the change up to the beginning of the fiscal year and the effect from the beginning of the second quarter would be included in the determination of second quarter net income. However, in any subsequent report that separately presents information either for that first quarter or that second quarter, the first quarter information would be retroactively restated on the basis of the newly adopted accounting principle, and the effect of the change from the beginning of the year to the beginning of the second quarter would no longer be included in second quarter net income. Thus the enterprise issued both first and second quarter information that had to be restated in subsequent periods. A similar situation arises if the accounting change were made during the third or fourth quarters.

Fourth Quarter Accounting Changes Made by Publicly Traded Companies

8. Paragraphs 30-33 of *APB Opinion No. 28* set forth special requirements for disclosure of summarized financial data by publicly traded companies (as defined in footnote 1 to that Opinion). Some publicly traded companies are required by paragraph 31 of the Opinion to disclose certain fourth quarter information in a note to the annual financial statements. Information about the effects of an accounting change made during the fourth quarter is not explicitly identified as one of the items for which disclosure is required.

STANDARDS OF FINANCIAL ACCOUNTING AND REPORTING

Cumulative Effect Type Accounting Changes Other Than Changes to LIFO

9. If a cumulative effect type accounting change is made during the *first* interim period of an enterprise's fiscal year, the cumulative effect of the change on retained earnings at the *beginning of that fiscal year* shall be included in net income of the first interim period (and in last-twelve-months-to-date financial reports that include that first interim period).

10. If a cumulative effect type accounting change is made in *other than the first* interim period of an enterprise's fiscal year, *no* cumulative effect of the change shall be included in net income of the period of change. Instead, financial information for the pre-change interim periods of the fiscal year in which the change is made shall be restated by applying the newly adopted accounting principle to those pre-change interim periods. The cumulative effect of the change on retained earnings at the *beginning of that fiscal year* shall be included in restated net income of the first interim period of the fiscal year in which the change is made (and in any year-to-date or last-twelve-months-to-date financial reports that include the first interim period). Whenever financial information that includes those pre-change interim periods is presented, it shall be presented on the restated basis.

11. The following disclosures about a cumulative effect type accounting change shall be made in interim financial reports:

a. In financial reports for the interim period in which the new accounting principle is adopted, disclosure shall be made of the nature of and justification for the change.
b. In financial reports for the interim period in which the new accounting principle is adopted, disclosure shall be made of the effect of the change on income from continuing operations, net income, and related per share amounts for the interim period in which the change is made. In addition, when the change is made in other than the first interim period of a fiscal year, financial reports for the period of change shall also disclose (i) the effect of the change on income from continuing operations, net income, and related per share amounts for each pre-change interim period of that fiscal year and (ii) income from continuing operations, net income, and related per share amounts for each pre-change interim period restated in accordance with paragraph 10 of this Statement.
c. In financial reports for the interim period in

which the new accounting principle is adopted, disclosure shall be made of income from continuing operations, net income, and related per share amounts computed on a pro forma basis for (i) the interim period in which the change is made and (ii) any interim periods of prior fiscal years for which financial information is being presented. If no financial information for interim periods of prior fiscal years is being presented, disclosure shall be made, in the period of change, of the actual and pro forma amounts of income from continuing operations, net income, and related per share amounts for the interim period of the immediately preceding fiscal year that corresponds to the interim period in which the change is made. In all cases, the pro forma amounts shall be computed and presented in conformity with paragraphs 19, 21, 22, and 25 of *APB Opinion No. 20*.

d. In year-to-date and last-twelve-months-to-date financial reports that include the interim period in which the new accounting principle is adopted, the disclosures specified in the first sentence of subparagraph (b) above and in subparagraph (c) above shall be made.
e. In financial reports for a subsequent (post-change) interim period of the fiscal year in which the new accounting principle is adopted, disclosure shall be made of the effect of the change on income from continuing operations, net income, and related per share amounts for that post-change interim period.

Changes to the LIFO Method of Inventory Pricing and Similar Situations

12. Paragraph 26 of *APB Opinion No. 20* indicates that in rare situations—principally a change to the LIFO method of inventory pricing[1]—neither the cumulative effect of the change on retained earnings at the beginning of the fiscal year in which the change is made nor the pro forma amounts can be computed. In those situations, that paragraph requires an explanation of the reasons for omitting (a) accounting for a cumulative effect and (b) disclosure of pro forma amounts for prior years. If a change of that type is made in the *first* interim period of an enterprise's fiscal year, the disclosures specified in paragraph 11 of this Statement shall be made (except the pro forma amounts for interim periods of prior fiscal years called for by paragraph 11(c) will not be disclosed).

13. If the change is made in *other than* the first interim period of an enterprise's fiscal year, the disclosure specified in paragraph 11 of this Statement shall be made (except the pro forma amounts for interim periods of prior fiscal years called for by paragraph 11(c) will not be disclosed) and in addition, financial information for the pre-change interim periods of that fiscal year shall be restated by applying the newly adopted accounting principle to those pre-change interim periods. Whenever financial information that includes those pre-change interim periods is presented, it shall be presented on the restated basis.

Fourth Quarter Accounting Changes Made by Publicly Traded Companies

14. When a publicly traded company that regularly reports interim information to its securityholders makes an accounting change during the fourth quarter of its fiscal year and does not report the data specified by paragraph 30 of *APB Opinion No. 28* in a separate fourth quarter report or in its annual report[2] to its securityholders, the disclosures about the effect of the accounting change on interim periods that are required by paragraphs 23-26 of *APB Opinion No. 28* or by paragraphs 9-13 of this Statement, as appropriate, shall be made in a note to the annual financial statements for the fiscal year in which the change is made.

Amendments to Existing Pronouncement

15. Paragraph 27 of *APB Opinion No. 28* is superseded by paragraphs 9-13 of this Statement. Paragraph 31 of that Opinion is amended by this Statement to require the additional disclosures set forth in paragraph 14.

Effective Date

16. The provisions of this Statement shall apply to accounting changes made in interim periods ending on or after December 31, 1974.

The provisions of this Statement need not be applied to immaterial items.

---

[1] In making disclosures about changes to the LIFO method, enterprises should be aware of the limitations the Internal Revenue Service has placed on such disclosures.

[2] See footnote 1.

This Statement was adopted by the unanimous vote of the seven members of the Financial Accounting Standards Board:

Marshall S. Armstrong, *Chairman*
Donald J. Kirk
Arthur L. Litke
Robert E. Mays
John W. Queenan
Walter Schuetze
Robert T. Sprouse

Appendix A

REPORTING A CUMULATIVE EFFECT TYPE ACCOUNTING CHANGE (OTHER THAN A CHANGE TO LIFO)

The following are examples of application of *APB Opinion No. 28* (as amended by this Statement) and the requirements of *APB Opinion No. 20* as they are incorporated by reference in *APB Opinion No. 28*. The examples do not encompass all possible circumstances and are not intended to indicate the Board's preference for a particular format.

FACTS

In the year 19x5, ABC Company decides to adopt the straight-line method of depreciation for plant equipment. The straight-line method will be used for new acquisitions as well as for previously acquired plant equipment for which depreciation had been provided on an accelerated method.

These examples assume that the effects of the change are limited to the effect on depreciation, incentive compensation, and related income tax provisions and that the effect on inventories is not material. The pro forma amounts have been adjusted for an assumed 10% pre-tax effect of the change on the provisions for incentive compensation and an assumed 50% income tax rate. The per share amounts are computed assuming that throughout the two years 19x4 and 19x5, 1,000,000 shares of common stock were issued and outstanding with no potential dilution. Other data assumed for these examples are:

Period	Net Income on the Basis of Old Accounting Principle (Accelerated Depreciation)	Gross Effect of Change to Straight-Line Depreciation	Gross Effect Less Income Taxes	Net Effect After Incentive Compensation and Related Income Taxes
Prior to first quarter 19x4		$20,000	$10,000	$9,000
First quarter 19x4	$1,000,000	30,000	15,000	13,500
Second quarter 19x4	1,200,000	70,000	35,000	31,500
Third quarter 19x4	1,100,000	50,000	25,000	22,500
Fourth quarter 19x4	$1,100,000	80,000	40,000	36,000
Total at beginning of 19x5	$4,400,000	$250,000	$125,000	$112,500
First quarter 19x5	$1,059,500	$90,000	$45,000	$40,500
Second quarter 19x5	1,255,000	100,000	50,000	45,000
Third quarter 19x5	1,150,500	110,000	55,000	49,500
Fourth quarter 19x5	1,146,000	120,000	60,000	54,000
	$4,611,000	$420,000	$210,000	$189,000

EXAMPLE 1

The change in depreciation method is made in the first quarter of 19x5. The manner of reporting the change in the first quarter of 19x5, with comparative information for the first quarter of 19x4, is as follows:

	Three Months Ended March 31,	
	19x5	19x4
Income before cumulative effect of a change in accounting principle	$1,100,000	$1,000,000
Cumulative effect on prior years (to December 31, 19x4) of changing to a different depreciation method (Note A)	125,000	
Net income	$1,225,000	$1,000,000
Amounts per common share:		
Income before cumulative effect of a change in accounting principle	$1.10	$1.00
Cumulative effect on prior years (to December 31, 19x4) of changing to a different depreciation method (Note A)	.13	
Net income	$1.23	$1.00
Pro forma amounts assuming the new depreciation method is applied retroactively (Note A):		
Net income	$1,100,000	$1,013,500
Net income per common share	$1.10	$1.01

NOTE A: Change in Depreciation Method for Plant Equipment

In the first quarter of 19x5, the method of computing depreciation of plant equipment was changed from the . . . (state previous method) . . . used in prior years, to the straight-line method . . . (state justification for the change in method) . . . and the new method has been applied to equipment acquisitions of prior years. The $125,000 cumulative effect of the change on prior years (after reduction for income taxes of $125,000) is included in income of the first quarter of 19x5. The effect of the change on the first quarter of 19x5 was to increase income before cumulative effect of a change in accounting principle $40,500 ($.04 per share) and net income $165,500 ($.17 per share). The pro forma amounts reflect the effect of retroactive application on depreciation, the change in provisions for incentive compensation that would have been made in 19x4 had the new method been in effect, and related income taxes.

EXAMPLE 2

Assume the same facts as in Example 1, except that the change is made in the third quarter of 19x5.

The manner of reporting the change in the third quarter of 19x5, with year-to-date information and comparative information for similar periods of 19x4, is as follows:

	Three Months Ended September 30,		Nine Months Ended September 30,	
	19x5	19x4	19x5	19x4
Income before cumulative effect of a change in accounting principle	$1,200,000	$1,100,000	$3,600,000	$3,300,000
Cumulative effect on prior years (to December 31, 19x4) of changing to a different depreciation method (Note A)			125,000	
Net income	$1,200,000	$1,100,000	$3,725,000	$3,300,000
Amounts per common share:				
Income before cumulative effect of a change in accounting principle	$1.20	$1.10	$3.60	$3.30
Cumulative effect on prior years (to December 31, 19x4) of changing to a different depreciation method (Note A)			.13	
Net income	$1.20	$1.10	$3.73	$3.30
Pro forma amounts assuming the new depreciation method is applied retroactively (Note A):				
Net income	$1,200,000	$1,122,500	$3,600,000	$3,367,500
Net income per common share	$1.20	$1.12	$3.60	$3.37

NOTE A: Change in Depreciation Method for Plant Equipment

In the third quarter of 19x5, the method of computing depreciation of plant equipment was changed from the . . . (state previous method) . . . used in prior years, to the straight-line method . . . (state justification for the change in method) . . . and the new method has been applied to equipment acquisitions of prior years. The $125,000 cumulative effect of the change on prior years (after reduction for income taxes of $125,000) is included in income of the nine months ended September 30, 19x5. The effect of the change on the three months ended September 30, 19x5 was to increase net income $49,500 ($.05 per share); the effect of the change on the nine months ended September 30, 19x5 was to increase income before cumulative effect of a change in accounting principle $135,000 ($.14 per share) and net income $260,000 ($.26 per share). The pro forma amounts reflect the effect of retroactive application on depreciation, the change in provisions for incentive compensation that would have been made in 19x4 had the new method been in effect, and related income taxes. The effect of the change on the first quarter of 19x5 was to increase income before cumulative effect of a change in accounting principle $40,500 ($.04 per share) to $1,100,000 ($1.10 per share) and net income $165,500 ($.17 per share) to $1,225,000 ($1.23 per share); the effect of the change on the second quarter was to increase net income $45,000 ($.04 per share) to $1,300,000 ($1.30 per share).

Alternatively, the last sentence of Note A could be replaced with the following tabular disclosure:

The effect of the change on the first and second quarters of 19x5 is as follows:

	Three Months Ended	
	March 31, 19x5	**June 30, 19x5**
Net income as originally reported*	$1,059,500	$1,255,000
Effect of change in depreciation method	40,500	45,000
Income before cumulative effect of a change in accounting principle	1,100,000	1,300,000
Cumulative effect on prior years (to December 31, 19x4) of changing to a different depreciation method	125,000	
Net income as restated	$1,225,000	$1,300,000
Per share amounts:		
Net income as originally reported*	$1.06	$1.26
Effect of change in depreciation method	.04	.04
Income before cumulative effect of a change in accounting principle	1.10	1.30
Cumulative effect on prior years (to December 31, 19x4) of changing to a different depreciation method	.13	
Net income as restated	$1.23	$1.30

*Disclosure of net income as originally reported is not required.

Appendix B

REPORTING A CHANGE TO THE LIFO METHOD OF INVENTORY PRICING

The following are examples of application of *APB Opinion No. 28* (as amended by this Statement) and the requirements of *APB Opinion No. 20* as they are incorporated by reference in *APB Opinion No. 28*. The examples do not encompass all possible circumstances and are not intended to indicate the Board's preference for a particular format.

FACTS

In the year 19x5, XYZ Company decides to change to the LIFO method of inventory pricing. These examples assume that the effects of the change are limited to the effect on inventory, incentive compensation, and related income tax provisions. A 10% pre-tax effect of the change on incentive compensation and a 50% income tax rate are assumed.The per share amounts are computed assuming that throughout 19x4 and 19x5, 1,000,000 shares of common stock were issued and outstanding with no potential dilution. Other data assumed for these examples are:

Period	Net Income on the Basis of Old Accounting Principle	Gross Effect of Change to LIFO	Net Effect After Incentive Comprehensive and Income Taxes
First quarter 19x5	$1,095,500	$(90,000)	$(40,500)
Second quarter 19x5	1,295,000	(100,000)	(45,000)
Third quarter 19x5	1,194,500	(110,000)	(49,500)
Fourth quarter 19x5	1,194,000	(120,000)	(54,000)
	$4,779,000	$(420,000)	$(189,000)

EXAMPLE 3

The change to LIFO is made in the first quarter of 19x5. The manner of reporting the change in the first quarter of 19x5, with comparative information for the first quarter of 19x4, is as follows:

	Three Months Ended March 31,	
	19x5	19x4
Net income (Note A)	$1,055,000	$1,000,000
Net income per common share (Note A)	$1.06	$1.00

NOTE A: Change to LIFO Method of Inventory Pricing

In the first quarter of 19x5, the Company changed its method of inventory pricing from . . . (state previous method) . . . used previously to the LIFO method because . . . (state justification for change and reasons for not disclosing a cumulative effect on, and pro forma amounts for, prior periods). The effect of the change on the first quarter of 19x5 was to decrease net income $40,500 ($.04 per share).

EXAMPLE 4

Assume the same facts as in Example 3, except that the change is made in the third quarter of 19x5. The manner of reporting the change in the third quarter of 19x5, with year-to-date information and comparative information for similar periods of 19x4, is as follows:

	Three Months Ended September 30,		Nine Months Ended September 30,	
	19x5	19x4	19x5	19x4
Net income (Note A)	$1,145,000	$1,200,000	$3,450,000	$3,400,000
Net income per common share (Note A)	$1.15	$1.20	$3.45	$3.40

NOTE A: Change to LIFO Method of Inventory Pricing

In the third quarter of 19x5, the Company changed its method of inventory pricing from . . . (state previous method) . . . used previously to the LIFO method because . . . (state justification for change and reasons for not disclosing a cumulative effect on, and pro forma amounts for, prior periods). The effect of the change on the three months and nine months ended September 30, 19x5 was to decrease net income $49,500 ($.05 per share) and $135,000 ($.14 per share), respectively. The effect of the change on the first and second quarters of 19x5 was to decrease net income $40,500 ($.04 per share) to $1,055,000 ($1.06 per share) and $45,000 ($.05 per share) to $1,250,000 ($1.25 per share), respectively.

Alternatively, the last sentence of Note A could be replaced with the following tabular disclosure:

The effect of the change on the first and second quarters of 19x5 is as follows:

	Three Months Ended	
	March 31, 19x5	June 30, 19x5
Net income as originally reported*	$1,095,500	$1,295,000
Effect of change to LIFO method of inventory pricing	(40,500)	(45,000)
Net income as restated	$1,055,000	$1,250,000
Per share amounts:		
Net income as originally reported*	$1.10	$1.30
Effect of change to LIFO method of inventory pricing	(.04)	(.05)
Net income as restated	$1.06	$1.25

*Disclosure of net income as originally reported is not required.

Statement of Financial Accounting Standards No. 4 Reporting Gains and Losses from Extinguishment of Debt

an amendment of APB Opinion No. 30

STATUS

Issued: March 1975

Effective Date: For extinguishments after March 31, 1975

Affects: Amends APB 26, paragraph 20
Supersedes APB 26, footnote 1
Amends APB 30, paragraph 20

Affected by: Paragraph 7 superseded by FAS 71
Paragraph 8 and footnote 2 amended by FAS 64

Statement of Financial Accounting Standards No. 4 Reporting Gains and Losses from Extinguishment of Debt

an amendment of APB Opinion No. 30

CONTENTS

INTRODUCTION AND BACKGROUND INFORMATION

1. *APB Opinion No. 26,* "Early Extinguishment of Debt," became effective for extinguishment of debt occurring on or after January 1, 1973. Paragraph 19 of that Opinion states "that all extinguishments of debt before scheduled maturities are fundamentally alike. The accounting for such transactions should be the same regardless of the means used to achieve the extinguishment." Paragraph 20 of the same Opinion states that "a difference between the reacquisition price and the net carrying amount of the extinguished debt should be recognized currently in income of the period of extinguishment as losses or gains and identified as a separate item.... The criteria in *APB Opinion No. 9* ['Reporting the Results of Operations'] should be used to determine whether the losses or gains are ordinary or extraordinary items. Gains and losses should not be amortized to future periods."

2. *APB Opinion No. 30,* "Reporting the Results of Operations," became effective for events and transactions occurring after September 30, 1973 and superseded *APB Opinion No. 9* with respect to the determination of extraordinary items. *APB Opinion No. 30* and the related Accounting Interpretation issued by the AICPA staff (see *The Journal of Accountancy,* November 1973, pages 82-84) can be read literally to preclude classifying most if not all gains or losses from early extinguishment of debt as an extraordinary item in the income statement. The Board has observed that in those cases coming to its attention where a gain or loss from early extinguishment of debt has been reported in an income statement to which *APB Opinion No. 30* was applicable, the gain or loss was included in income before extraordinary items.

3. Since the effective date of *APB Opinion No. 30,* the Board has had inquiries regarding that Opinion because application of the criteria, especially as illustrated in the related AICPA Accounting Interpretation, appears to preclude classifying gains or losses from most transactions or events as extraordinary items in the income statement. Many respondents to the Board's July 12, 1973 request for views concerning APB Opinions and Accounting Research Bulletins suggested that the conclusions of *APB Opinion No. 26* relating to *early* extinguishment of debt be reconsidered. Since that time, concern also has been expressed to the Board with respect to the accounting for extinguishment of debt at its *scheduled maturity date or later* because the authoritative accounting pronouncements do not address that issue. In addition, the Securities and Exchange Commission and others have expressed concern to the Board about including gains and losses from extinguishment of debt in the determination of income before extraordinary items in the income statement.

4. The Board considered carefully the suggestions that *APB Opinion No. 26* be reconsidered and concluded that the issues extend beyond *APB Opinion No. 26* and could involve *APB Opinion No. 14,* "Accounting for Convertible Debt and Debt Issued with Stock Purchase Warrants," and *APB Opinion No. 21,* "Interest on Receivables and Payables,"

and could extend to exchanges or sales and related purchases of similar monetary assets. The Board concluded that the pervasiveness of those issues makes broad reconsideration of all these Opinions and the other related issues a more comprehensive undertaking than can be accomplished in the near future. The Board also considered carefully the questions raised with respect to *APB Opinion No. 30* and concluded that there is insufficient experience under that Opinion to warrant a general reconsideration of the criteria set forth therein at this time.

5. Prior to the issuance of the Exposure Draft of this Statement, the Board had been considering an Interpretation of *APB Opinion No. 26* that would have specified disclosure requirements regarding gains and losses from extinguishment of debt, but that course of action was changed when it became clear to the Board that the income statement classification of gains or losses on extinguishment of debt also required attention. The Board believes that an immediate response is needed to the concern expressed regarding income statement classification of gains and losses from certain extinguishments of debt. Further, the Board continues to believe that guidelines are needed regarding disclosures related to certain debt extinguishments because a review of a number of financial statements by the FASB staff indicates that disclosures often have been unclear, particularly with regard to the income tax effects.

6. The Board has concluded that on the basis of existing data it can make an informed decision on the narrow issues identified in paragraph 5 without a public hearing and that the effective date and transition requirements set forth in paragraphs 11 and 12 are advisable.

7. This Statement applies to regulated enterprises in accordance with the provisions of the Addendum to *APB Opinion No. 2,* "Accounting for the 'Investment Credit.'"

STANDARDS OF FINANCIAL ACCOUNTING AND REPORTING

Income Statement Classification

8. Gains and losses from extinguishment of debt that are included in the determination of net income shall be aggregated and, if material,[1] classified as an extraordinary item, net of related income tax effect. That conclusion shall apply whether an extinguishment is early or at scheduled maturity date or later. The conclusion does not apply, however, to gains or losses from cash purchases of debt made to satisfy current or future sinking-fund requirements.[2] Those gains and losses shall be aggregated and the amount shall be identified as a separate item.

Disclosure

9. Gains or losses from extinguishment of debt that are classified as extraordinary items should be described sufficiently to enable users of financial statements to evaluate their significance. Accordingly, the following information, to the extent not shown separately on the face of the income statement, shall be disclosed in a single note to the financial statements or adequately cross-referenced if in more than one note:

a. A description of the extinguishment transactions, including the sources of any funds used to extinguish debt if it is practicable to identify the sources.
b. The income tax effect in the period of extinguishment.
c. The per share amount of the aggregate gain or loss net of related income tax effect.

Amendment to Existing Pronouncement

10. This Statement amends *APB Opinion No. 30* only to the extent that classification of gains or losses from extinguishment of debt as an extraordinary item pursuant to the first two sentences of paragraph 8 of this Statement shall be made without regard to the criteria in paragraph 20 of that Opinion.

Effective Date and Transition

11. This Statement shall be effective for extinguishments occurring after March 31, 1975, except that it need not be applied to extinguishments occurring on or after April 1, 1975 pursuant to the terms of an offer or other commitment made prior to that date. Application to *all* extinguishments occurring during a fiscal year in which April 1, 1975 falls is encouraged. Retroactive application to extinguishments occurring in prior fiscal years is encouraged but not required.

12. Although the requirements of this Statement may be applied retroactively, such application is not

[1]See the first sentence of paragraph 24 of *APB Opinion No. 30.*

[2]Some obligations to acquire debt have the essential characteristics of sinking-fund requirements, and resulting gains or losses are not required to be classified as extraordinary items. For example, if an enterprise is required each year to purchase a certain percentage of its outstanding bonds before their scheduled maturity, the gain or loss from such purchase is not required to be classified as an extraordinary item. Debt maturing serially, however, does not have the characteristics of sinking-fund requirements, and gain or loss from extinguishment of serial debt shall be classified as an extraordinary item.

intended to change the accounting for amounts deferred on refundings of debt that occurred prior to the effective date of *APB Opinion No. 26* or the income statement classification of the amortization of those amounts.

The provisions of this Statement need not be applied to immaterial items.

This Statement was adopted by the affirmative votes of six members of the Financial Accounting Standards Board. Mr. Kirk dissented.

Mr. Kirk dissents because he believes that extinguishments of debt are reportable transactions that seldom, if ever, warrant extraordinary item treatment. In many cases, extinguishments are neither unusual nor infrequent. In most cases, they are certainly no more extraordinary than other infrequent gains or losses for which *APB Opinion No. 30* prohibits extraordinary item classification. That Opinion sharply restricted—for good reasons—the types of gains and losses that may be identified as extraordinary items and reported on a net-of-tax basis, and Mr. Kirk can see no inherent characteristic of debt extinguishments that justifies overriding the criteria in *APB Opinion No. 30.* He believes that disclosures, like those required by paragraph 20 of *APB Opinion No. 26* and paragraph 26 of *APB Opinion No. 30,* are sufficient to prevent a financial statement user from being misled. In his view, accounting standards cannot satisfy everyone's perception of economic reality, but they should at least be logically consistent in their result. Mr. Kirk believes that this Statement fails in that regard and may well encourage piecemeal erosion of *APB Opinion No. 30.*

Members of the Financial Accounting Standards Board:

Marshall S. Armstrong, *Chairman*
Oscar S. Gellein
Donald J. Kirk
Arthur L. Litke
Robert E. Mays
Walter Schuetze
Robert T. Sprouse

Appendix A

SUMMARY OF CONSIDERATION OF COMMENTS ON EXPOSURE DRAFT

13. In response to the request for comments on the Exposure Draft issued January 31, 1975, the FASB received and considered 120 letters in its deliberations on this Statement. Certain of the comments and the FASB's consideration of them are summarized in paragraphs 14-17.

14. For a variety of reasons, many respondents recommended that the FASB not adopt the Exposure Draft as a final Statement. Some respondents recommended that *APB Opinion No. 26* and related issues be reconsidered. Others recommended that the criteria for determining extraordinary items as set forth in *APB Opinion No. 30* be reconsidered. The Board concluded not to address these issues for the reasons stated in paragraph 4.

15. Some respondents suggested that the proposals in the Exposure Draft, if adopted, would result in erosion of the criteria in *APB Opinion No. 30* for determining extraordinary items. However, this Statement is neither an amendment nor an interpretation of the criteria for classifying and reporting an event or transaction as an extraordinary item as set forth in paragraph 20 of that Opinion. Rather, the Board is proscribing the application of those criteria to certain extinguishments of debt in the same way that the application of those criteria has been proscribed with respect to the realization of tax benefits from an operating loss carryforward and to certain profits or losses resulting from the disposal of a significant part of the assets or a separable segment acquired in a business combination accounted for as a pooling of interests.[3] The Board recognizes that the application of the criteria in *APB Opinion No. 30* to extinguishments of debt would seldom, if ever, require that resulting gains and losses be classified as extraordinary items. In issuing this Statement requiring that a gain or loss from certain debt extinguishments be classified as an extraordinary item in the income statement, the Board is neither modifying the criteria set forth in that Opinion nor intending to start a piecemeal revision of those criteria. Although as a result of this Statement questions may be raised regarding the application of the criteria for determining extraordinary items pursuant to *APB Opinion No. 30,* the Board has concluded that, on balance, this Statement represents a practical and reasonable solution to the question regarding income statement classification of gains or losses

[3]See paragraph 7 of *APB Opinion No. 30.*

from extinguishment of debt until such time as the broader issues involved can be addressed.

16. Many respondents argued that gains and losses from extinguishment of debt pursuant to sinking-fund requirements should not be required to be classified as extraordinary items. The Board agrees primarily because acquisitions for sinking-fund purposes are made to meet continuing contractual requirements assumed in connection with the incurrence of the debt.

17. In addition to the fact that many respondents recommended that the Exposure Draft not be issued as a final Statement, some respondents objected to the proposal that the Statement be applied retroactively. On further consideration of all the circumstances, the Board concluded that application of the Statement should be required only on a prospective basis although retroactive application is encouraged.

Statement of Financial Accounting Standards No. 5
Accounting for Contingencies

STATUS

Issued: March 1975

Effective Date: For fiscal years beginning on or after July 1, 1975

Affects: Supersedes ARB 43, Chapter 6
Supersedes ARB 50

Affected by: Paragraph 13 superseded by FAS 71
Paragraph 20 amended by FAS 11
Paragraphs 41 and 102 amended by FAS 60
Footnote 3 superseded by FAS 16

Statement of Financial Accounting Standards No. 5
Accounting for Contingencies

CONTENTS

INTRODUCTION

1. For the purpose of this Statement, a contingency is defined as an existing condition, situation, or set of circumstances involving uncertainty as to possible gain (hereinafter a "gain contingency") or loss[1] (hereinafter a "loss contingency") to an enterprise that will ultimately be resolved when one or more future events occur or fail to occur. Resolution of the uncertainty may confirm the acquisition of an asset or the reduction of a liability or the loss or impairment of an asset or the incurrence of a liability.

2. Not all uncertainties inherent in the accounting process give rise to contingencies as that term is used in this Statement. Estimates are required in financial statements for many on-going and recurring activities of an enterprise. The mere fact that an estimate is involved does not of itself constitute the type of uncertainty referred to in the definition in paragraph 1. For example, the fact that estimates are used to allocate the known cost of a depreciable asset over the period of use by an enterprise does not make depreciation a contingency; the eventual expiration of the utility of the asset is not uncertain. Thus, depreciation of assets is not a contingency as defined in paragraph 1, nor are such matters as recurring repairs, maintenance, and overhauls, which interrelate with depreciation. Also, amounts owed for services received, such as advertising and utilities, are not contingencies even though the accrued amounts may have been estimated; there is nothing uncertain about the fact that those obligations have been incurred.

3. When a loss contingency exists, the likelihood that the future event or events will confirm the loss or impairment of an asset or the incurrence of a liability can range from probable to remote. This Statement uses the terms *probable, reasonably possible,* and *remote* to identify three areas within that range, as follows:

a. *Probable.* The future event or events are likely to occur.
b. *Reasonably possible.* The chance of the future event or events occurring is more than remote but less than likely.
c. *Remote.* The chance of the future event or events occurring is slight.

4. Examples of loss contingencies include:

a. Collectibility of receivables.
b. Obligations related to product warranties and product defects.
c. Risk of loss or damage of enterprise property by fire, explosion, or other hazards.
d. Threat of expropriation of assets.
e. Pending or threatened litigation.
f. Actual or possible claims and assessments.
g. Risk of loss from catastrophes assumed by property and casualty insurance companies including reinsurance companies.
h. Guarantees of indebtedness of others.

[1]The term *loss* is used for convenience to include many charges against income that are commonly referred to as *expenses* and others that are commonly referred to as *losses*.

i. Obligations of commercial banks under "standby letters of credit."[2]
j. Agreements to repurchase receivables (or to repurchase the related property that have been sold.

5. Some enterprises now accrue estimated losses from some types of contingencies by a charge to income prior to the occurrence of the event or events that are expected to resolve the uncertainties while, under similar circumstances, other enterprises account for those losses only when the confirming event or events have occurred.

6. This Statement establishes standards of financial accounting and reporting for loss contingencies (see paragraphs 8-16) and carries forward without reconsideration the conclusions of *Accounting Research Bulletin (ARB) No. 50,* "Contingencies," with respect to gain contingencies (see paragraph 17) and other disclosures (see paragraphs 18-19). The basis for the Board's conclusions, as well as alternatives considered and reasons for their rejection, are discussed in Appendix C. Examples of application of this Statement are presented in Appendix A, and background information is presented in Appendix B.

7. This Statement supersedes both *ARB No. 50* and Chapter 6, "Contingency Reserves," of *ARB No. 43*. The conditions for accrual of loss contingencies in paragraph 8 of this Statement do not amend any other present requirement in an Accounting Research Bulletin or Opinion of the Accounting Principles Board to accrue a particular type of loss or expense. Thus, for example, accounting for pension cost, deferred compensation contracts, and stock issued to employees are excluded from the scope of this Statement. Those matters are covered, respectively, in *APB Opinion No. 8,* "Accounting for the Cost of Pension Plans," *APB Opinion No. 12,* "Omnibus Opinion—1967," paragraphs 6-8, and *APB Opinion No. 25,* "Accounting for Stock Issued to Employees." Accounting for other employment-related costs, such as group insurance, vacation pay, workmen's compensation, and disability benefits, is also excluded from the scope of this Statement. Accounting practices for those types of costs and pension accounting practices tend to involve similar considerations.

STANDARDS OF FINANCIAL ACCOUNTING AND REPORTING

Accrual of Loss Contingencies

8. An estimated loss from a loss contingency (as defined in paragraph 1) shall be accrued by a charge to income[3] if *both* of the following conditions are met:

a. Information available prior to issuance of the financial statements indicates that it is probable that an asset had been impaired or a liability had been incurred at the date of the financial statements.[4] It is implicit in this condition that it must be probable that one or more future events will occur confirming the fact of the loss.
b. The amount of loss can be reasonably estimated.

Disclosure of Loss Contingencies

9. Disclosure of the nature of an accrual[5] made pursuant to the provisions of paragraph 8, and in some circumstances the amount accrued, may be necessary for the financial statements not to be misleading.

10. If no accrual is made for a loss contingency because one or both of the conditions in paragraph 8 are not met, or if an exposure to loss exists in excess of the amount accrued pursuant to the provisions of paragraph 8, disclosure of the contingency shall be made when there is at least a reasonable possibility that a loss or an additional loss may have

[2]As defined by the Federal Reserve Board, "standby letters of credit" include "every letter of credit (or similar arrangement however named or designated) which represents an obligation to the beneficiary on the part of the issuer (1) to repay money borrowed by or advanced to or for the account of the account party or (2) to make payment on account of any evidence of indebtedness undertaken by the account party or (3) to make payment on account of any default by the account party in the performance of an obligation." A note to that definition states that "as defined, 'standby letter of credit' would not include (1) commercial letters of credit and similar instruments where the issuing bank expects the beneficiary to draw upon the issuer and which do not 'guaranty' payment of a money obligation or (2) a guaranty or similar obligation issued by a foreign branch in accordance with and subject to the limitations of Regulation M [of the Federal Reserve Board]." Regulations of the Comptroller of the Currency and the Federal Deposit Insurance Corporation contain similar definitions.

[3]Paragraphs 23-24 of *APB Opinion No. 9,* "Reporting the Results of Operations," describe the "rare" circumstances in which a prior period adjustment is appropriate. Those paragraphs are not amended by this Statement.

[4]*Date of the financial statements* means the end of the most recent accounting period for which financial statements are being presented.

[5]Terminology used shall be descriptive of the nature of the accrual (see paragraphs 57-64 of *Accounting Terminology Bulletin No. 1,* "Review and Resume").

been incurred.[6] The disclosure shall indicate the nature of the contingency and shall give an estimate of the possible loss or range of loss or state that such an estimate cannot be made. Disclosure is not required of a loss contingency involving an unasserted claim or assessment when there has been no manifestation by a potential claimant of an awareness of a possible claim or assessment unless it is considered probable that a claim will be asserted and there is a reasonable possibility that the outcome will be unfavorable.

11. After the date of an enterprise's financial statements but before those financial statements are issued, information may become available indicating that an asset was impaired or a liability was incurred after the date of the financial statements or that there is at least a reasonable possibility that an asset was impaired or a liability was incurred after that date. The information may relate to a loss contingency that existed at the date of the financial statements, e.g., an asset that was not insured at the date of the financial statements. On the other hand, the information may relate to a loss contingency that did not exist at the date of the financial statements, e.g., threat of expropriation of assets after the date of the financial statements or the filing for bankruptcy by an enterprise whose debt was guaranteed after the date of the financial statements. In none of the cases cited in this paragraph was an asset impaired or a liability incurred at the date of the financial statements, and the condition for accrual in paragraph 8(a) is, therefore, not met. Disclosure of those kinds of losses or loss contingencies may be necessary, however, to keep the financial statements from being misleading. If disclosure is deemed necessary, the financial statements shall indicate the nature of the loss or loss contingency and give an estimate of the amount or range of loss or possible loss or state that such an estimate cannot be made. Occasionally, in the case of a loss arising after the date of the financial statements where the amount of asset impairment or liability incurrence can be reasonably estimated, disclosure may best be made by supplementing the historical financial statements with pro forma financial data giving effect to the loss as if it had occurred at the date of the financial statements. It may be desirable to present pro forma statements, usually a balance sheet only, in columnar form on the face of the historical financial statements.

12. Certain loss contingencies are presently being disclosed in financial statements even though the possibility of loss may be remote. The common characteristic of those contingencies is a guarantee, normally with a right to proceed against an outside party in the event that the guarantor is called upon to satisfy the guarantee. Examples include (a) guarantees of indebtedness of others, (b) obligations of commercial banks under "standby letters of credit," and (c) guarantees to repurchase receivables (or, in some cases, to repurchase the related property) that have been sold or otherwise assigned. The Board concludes that disclosure of those loss contingencies, and others that in substance have the same characteristic, shall be continued. The disclosure shall include the nature and amount of the guarantee. Consideration should be given to disclosing, if estimable, the value of any recovery that could be expected to result, such as from the guarantor's right to proceed against an outside party.

13. This Statement applies to regulated enterprises in accordance with provisions of the Addendum to *APB Opinion No. 2,* "Accounting for the 'Investment Credit.'" If, in conformity with the Addendum, a regulated enterprise accrues for financial accounting and reporting purposes an estimated loss without regard to the conditions in paragraph 8, the following information shall be disclosed in its financial statements:

a. The accounting policy including the nature of the accrual and the basis for estimation.
b. The amount of any related "liability" or "asset valuation" account included in each balance sheet presented.

General or Unspecified Business Risks

14. Some enterprises have in the past accrued so-called "reserves for general contingencies." General or unspecified business risks do not meet the conditions for accrual in paragraph 8, and no accrual for loss shall be made. No disclosure about them is required by this Statement.

Appropriation of Retained Earnings

15. Some enterprises have classified a portion of retained earnings as "appropriated" for loss contingencies. In some cases, the appropriation has been shown outside the stockholders' equity section of the balance sheet. Appropriation of retained earnings is not prohibited by this Statement provided that it is shown within the stockholders' equity section of the balance sheet and is clearly identified as an appropriation of retained earnings. Costs or

---

[6] For example, disclosure shall be made of any loss contingency that meets the condition in paragraph 8(a) but that is not accrued because the amount of loss cannot be reasonably estimated (paragraph 8(b)). Disclosure is also required of some loss contingencies that do not meet the condition in paragraph 8(a)—namely, those contingencies for which there is a *reasonable possibility* that a loss may have been incurred even though information may not indicate that it is *probable* that an asset had been impaired or a liability had been incurred at the date of the financial statements.

losses shall not be charged to an appropriation of retained earnings, and no part of the appropriation shall be transferred to income.

Examples of Application of This Statement

16. Examples of application of the conditions for accrual of loss contingencies in paragraph 8 and the disclosure requirements in paragraphs 9-11 are presented in Appendix A.

Gain Contingencies

17. The Board has not reconsidered *ARB No. 50* with respect to gain contingencies. Accordingly, the following provisions of paragraphs 3 and 5 of that Bulletin shall continue in effect:

a. Contingencies that might result in gains usually are not reflected in the accounts since to do so might be to recognize revenue prior to its realization.
b. Adequate disclosure shall be made of contingencies that might result in gains, but care shall be exercised to avoid misleading implications as to the likelihood of realization.

Other Disclosures

18. Paragraph 6 of *ARB No. 50* required disclosure of a number of situations including "unused letters of credit, long-term leases, assets pledged as security for loans, pension plans, the existence of cumulative preferred stock dividends in arrears, and commitments such as those for plant acquisition or an obligation to reduce debts, maintain working capital, or restrict dividends." Subsequent Opinions issued by the Accounting Principles Board established more explicit disclosure requirements for a number of those items, i.e., leases (see *APB Opinions No. 5* and *31*), pension plans (see *APB Opinion No. 8*), and preferred stock dividend arrearages (see *APB Opinion No. 10,* paragraph 11(b)).

19. Situations of the type described in the preceding paragraph shall continue to be disclosed in financial statements, and this Statement does not alter the present disclosure requirements with respect to those items.

Effective Date and Transition

20. This Statement shall be effective for fiscal years beginning on or after July 1, 1975, although earlier application is encouraged. A change in accounting principle resulting from compliance with paragraph 8 or 14 of this Statement shall be reported in accordance with *APB Opinion No. 20,* "Accounting Changes." Accordingly, except in the special circumstances referred to in paragraphs 29-30 of *APB Opinion No. 20,* the cumulative effect of the change on retained earnings at the beginning of the year in which the change is made shall be included in net income of the year of the change, and the disclosures specified in *APB Opinion No. 20* shall be made. Reclassification of an appropriation of retained earnings to comply with paragraph 15 of this Statement shall be made in any financial statements for periods before the effective date of this Statement, or financial summaries or other data derived therefrom, that are presented after the effective date of this Statement.

The provisions of this Statement need not be applied to immaterial items.

This Statement was adopted by the unanimous vote of the seven members of the Financial Accounting Standards Board:

Marshall S. Armstrong, *Chairman*
Oscar S. Gellein
Donald J. Kirk
Arthur L. Litke
Robert E. Mays
Walter Schuetze
Robert T. Sprouse

Appendix A

EXAMPLES OF APPLICATION OF THIS STATEMENT

21. This Appendix contains examples of application of the conditions for accrual of loss contingencies in paragraph 8 and of the disclosure requirements in paragraphs 9-11. Some examples have been included in response to questions raised in letters of comment on the Exposure Draft. It should be recognized that no set of examples can encompass all possible contingencies or circumstances. Accordingly, accrual and disclosure of loss contingencies should be based on an evaluation of the facts in each particular case.

Collectibility of Receivables

22. The assets of an enterprise may include receivables that arose from credit sales, loans, or other transactions. The conditions under which receivables exist usually involve some degree of uncertainty about their collectibility, in which case a

contingency exists as defined in paragraph 1. Losses from uncollectible receivables shall be accrued when both conditions in paragraph 8 are met. Those conditions may be considered in relation to individual receivables or in relation to groups of similar types of receivables. If the conditions are met, accrual shall be made even though the particular receivables that are uncollectible may not be identifiable.

23. If, based on available information, it is probable that the enterprise will be unable to collect all amounts due and, therefore, that at the date of its financial statements the net realizable value of the receivables through collection in the ordinary course of business is less than the total amount receivable, the condition in paragraph 8(a) is met because it is probable that an asset has been impaired. Whether the amount of loss can be reasonably estimated (the condition in paragraph 8(b)) will normally depend on, among other things, the experience of the enterprise, information about the ability of individual debtors to pay, and appraisal of the receivables in light of the current economic environment. In the case of an enterprise that has no experience of its own, reference to the experience of other enterprises in the same business may be appropriate. Inability to make a reasonable estimate of the amount of loss from uncollectible receivables (i.e., failure to satisfy the condition in paragraph 8(b)) precludes accrual and may, if there is significant uncertainty as to collection, suggest that the installment method, the cost recovery method, or some other method of revenue recognition be used (see paragraph 12 of *APB Opinion No. 10,* "Omnibus Opinion—1966"); in addition, the disclosures called for by paragraph 10 of this Statement should be made.

Obligations Related to Product Warranties and Product Defects

24. A warranty is an obligation incurred in connection with the sale of goods or services that may require further performance by the seller after the sale has taken place. Because of the uncertainty surrounding claims that may be made under warranties, warranty obligations fall within the definition of a contingency in paragraph 1. Losses from warranty obligations shall be accrued when the conditions in paragraph 8 are met. Those conditions may be considered in relation to individual sales made with warranties or in relation to groups of similar types of sales made with warranties. If the conditions are met, accrual shall be made even though the particular parties that will make claims under warranties may not be identifiable.

25. If, based on available information, it is probable that customers will make claims under warranties relating to goods or services that have been sold, the condition in paragraph 8(a) is met at the date of an enterprise's financial statements because it is probable that a liability has been incurred. Satisfaction of the condition in paragraph 8(b) will normally depend on the experience of an enterprise or other information. In the case of an enterprise that has no experience of its own, reference to the experience of other enterprises in the same business may be appropriate. Inability to make a reasonable estimate of the amount of a warranty obligation at the time of sale because of significant uncertainty about possible claims (i.e., failure to satisfy the condition in paragraph 8(b)) precludes accrual and, if the range of possible loss is wide, may raise a question about whether a sale should be recorded prior to expiration of the warranty period or until sufficient experience has been gained to permit a reasonable estimate of the obligation; in addition, the disclosures called for by paragraph 10 of this Statement should be made.

26. Obligations other than warranties may arise with respect to products or services that have been sold, for example, claims resulting from injury or damage caused by product defects. If it is probable that claims will arise with respect to products or services that have been sold, accrual for losses may be appropriate. The condition in paragraph 8(a) would be met, for instance, with respect to a drug product or toys that have been sold if a health or safety hazard related to those products is discovered and as a result it is considered probable that liabilities have been incurred. The condition in paragraph 8(b) would be met if experience or other information enables the enterprise to make a reasonable estimate of the loss with respect to the drug product or the toys.

Risk of Loss or Damage of Enterprise Property

27. At the date of an enterprise's financial statements, it may not be insured against risk of future loss or damage to its property by fire, explosion, or other hazards. The absence of insurance against losses from risks of those types constitutes an existing condition involving uncertainty about the amount and timing of any losses that may occur, in which case a contingency exists as defined in paragraph 1. Uninsured risks may arise in a number of ways, including (a) noninsurance of certain risks or co-insurance or deductible clauses in an insurance contract or (b) insurance through a subsidiary or investee[7] to the extent not reinsured with an inde-

[7]The effects of transactions between a parent or other investor and a subsidiary or investee insurance company shall be eliminated from an enterprise's financial statements (see paragraph 6 of *ARB No. 51,* "Consolidated Financial Statements," and paragraph 19(a) of *APB Opinion No. 18,* "The Equity Method of Accounting for Investments in Common Stock").

pendent insurer. Some risks, for all practical purposes, may be noninsurable, and the self-assumption of those risks is mandatory.

28. The absence of insurance does not mean that an asset has been impaired or a liability has been incurred at the date of an enterprise's financial statements. Fires, explosions, and other similar events that may cause loss or damage of an enterprise's property are random in their occurrence.[8] With respect to events of that type, the condition for accrual in paragraph 8(a) is not satisfied prior to the occurrence of the event because until that time there is no diminution in the value of the property. There is no relationship of those events to the activities of the enterprise prior to their occurrence, and no asset is impaired prior to their occurrence. Further, unlike an insurance company, which has a contractual obligation under policies in force to reimburse insureds for losses, an enterprise can have no such obligation to itself and, hence, no liability.

Risk of Loss from Future Injury to Others, Damage to the Property of Others, and Business Interruption

29. An enterprise may choose not to purchase insurance against risk of loss that may result from injury to others, damage to the property of others, or interruption of its business operations.[9] Exposure to risks of those types constitutes an existing condition involving uncertainty about the amount and timing of any losses that may occur, in which case a contingency exists as defined in paragraph 1.

30. Mere exposure to risks of those types, however, does not mean that an asset has been impaired or a liability has been incurred. The condition for accrual in paragraph 8(a) is not met with respect to loss that may result from injury to others, damage to the property of others, or business interruption that may occur after the date of an enterprise's financial statements. Losses of those types do not relate to the current or a prior period but rather to the *future* period in which they occur. Thus, for example, an enterprise with a fleet of vehicles should not accrue for injury to others or damage to the property of others that may be caused by those vehicles in the future even if the amount of those losses may be reasonably estimable. On the other hand, the conditions in paragraph 8 would be met with respect to uninsured losses resulting from injury to others or damage to the property of others that took place prior to the date of the financial statements, even though the enterprise may not become aware of those matters until after that date, if the experience of the enterprise or other information enables it to make a reasonable estimate of the loss that was incurred prior to the date of its financial statements.

Write-Down of Operating Assets

31. In some cases, the carrying amount of an operating asset not intended for disposal may exceed the amount expected to be recoverable through future use of that asset even though there has been no physical loss or damage of the asset or threat of such loss or damage. For example, changed economic conditions may have made recovery of the carrying amount of a productive facility doubtful. The question of whether, in those cases, it is appropriate to write down the carrying amount of the asset to an amount expected to be recoverable through future operations is not covered by this Statement.

Threat of Expropriation

32. The threat of expropriation of assets is a contingency within the definition of paragraph 1 because of the uncertainty about its outcome and effect. If information indicates that expropriation is imminent and compensation will be less than the carrying amount of the assets, the condition for accrual in paragraph 8(a) is met. Imminence may be indicated, for example, by public or private declarations of intent by a government to expropriate assets of the enterprise or actual expropriation of assets of other enterprises. Paragraph 8(b) requires that accrual be made only if the amount of loss can be reasonably estimated. If the conditions for accrual are not met, the disclosures specified in paragraph 10 would be made when there is at least a reasonable possibility that an asset has been impaired.

Litigation, Claims, and Assessments

33. The following factors, among others, must be considered in determining whether accrual and/or disclosure is required with respect to pending or threatened litigation and actual or possible claims and assessments:

a. The period in which the underlying cause (i.e., the cause for action) of the pending or threatened litigation or of the actual or possible claim or assessment occurred.
b. The degree of probability of an unfavorable outcome.

---

[8]The Board recognizes that, in practice, experience regarding loss or damage to depreciable assets is in some cases one of the factors considered in estimating the depreciable lives of a group of depreciable assets, along with such other factors as wear and tear, obsolescence, and maintenance and replacement policies. This Statement is not intended to alter present depreciation practices (see paragraph 2)

[9]As to injury or damage resulting from products that have been sold, see paragraph 26.

c. The ability to make a reasonable estimate of the amount of loss.

34. As a condition for accrual of a loss contingency, paragraph 8(a) requires that information available prior to the issuance of financial statements indicate that it is probable that an asset had been impaired or a liability had been incurred at the date of the financial statements. Accordingly, accrual would clearly be inappropriate for litigation, claims, or assessments whose underlying cause is an event or condition occurring after the date of financial statements but before those financial statements are issued, for example, a suit for damages alleged to have been suffered as a result of an accident that occurred after the date of the financial statements. Disclosure may be required, however, by paragraph 11.

35. On the other hand, accrual may be appropriate for litigation, claims, or assessments whose underlying cause is an event occurring on or before the date of an enterprise's financial statements even if the enterprise does not become aware of the existence or possibility of the lawsuit, claim, or assessment until after the date of the financial statements. If those financial statements have not been issued, accrual of a loss related to the litigation, claim, or assessment would be required if the probability of loss is such that the condition in paragraph 8(a) is met and the amount of loss can be reasonably estimated.

36. If the underlying cause of the litigation, claim, or assessment is an event occurring before the date of an enterprise's financial statements, the probability of an outcome unfavorable to the enterprise must be assessed to determine whether the condition in paragraph 8(a) is met. Among the factors that should be considered are the nature of the litigation, claim, or assessment, the progress of the case (including progress after the date of the financial statements but before those statements are issued), the opinions or views of legal counsel and other advisers, the experience of the enterprise in similar cases, the experience of other enterprises, and any decision of the enterprise's management as to how the enterprise intends to respond to the lawsuit, claim, or assessment (for example, a decision to contest the case vigorously or a decision to seek an out-of-court settlement). The fact that legal counsel is unable to express an opinion that the outcome will be favorable to the enterprise should not necessarily be interpreted to mean that the condition for accrual of a loss in paragraph 8(a) is met.

37. The filing of a suit or formal assertion of a claim or assessment does not automatically indicate that accrual of a loss may be appropriate. The degree of probability of an unfavorable outcome must be assessed. The condition for accrual in paragraph 8(a) would be met if an unfavorable outcome is determined to be probable. If an unfavorable outcome is determined to be reasonably possible but not probable, or if the amount of loss cannot be reasonably estimated, accrual would be inappropriate, but disclosure would be required by paragraph 10 of this Statement.

38. With respect to unasserted claims and assessments, an enterprise must determine the degree of probability that a suit may be filed or a claim or assessment may be asserted and the possibility of an unfavorable outcome. For example, a catastrophe, accident, or other similar physical occurrence predictably engenders claims for redress, and in such circumstances their assertion may be probable; similarly, an investigation of an enterprise by a governmental agency, if enforcement proceedings have been or are likely to be instituted, is often followed by private claims for redress, and the probability of their assertion and the possibility of loss should be considered in each case. By way of further example, an enterprise may believe there is a possibility that it has infringed on another enterprise's patent rights, but the enterprise owning the patent rights has not indicated an intention to take any action and has not even indicated an awareness of the possible infringement. In that case, a judgment must first be made as to whether the assertion of a claim is probable. If the judgment is that assertion is not probable, no accrual or disclosure would be required. On the other hand, if the judgment is that assertion is probable, then a second judgment must be made as to the degree of probability of an unfavorable outcome. If an unfavorable outcome is probable and the amount of loss can be reasonably estimated, accrual of a loss is required by paragraph 8. If an unfavorable outcome is probable but the amount of loss cannot be reasonably estimated, accrual would not be appropriate, but disclosure would be required by paragraph 10. If an unfavorable outcome is reasonably possible but not probable, disclosure would be required by paragraph 10.

39. As a condition for accrual of a loss contingency, paragraph 8(b) requires that the amount of loss can be reasonably estimated. In some cases, it may be determined that a loss was incurred because an unfavorable outcome of the litigation, claim, or assessment is probable (thus satisfying the condition in paragraph 8(a)), but the range of possible loss is wide. For example, an enterprise may be litigating an income tax matter. In preparation for the trial, it may determine that, based on recent decisions involving one aspect of the litigation, it is probable that it will have to pay additional taxes of $2 million. Another aspect of the litigation may, however, be open to considerable interpretation, and depending on the interpretation by the court the enterprise may have to pay taxes of $8 million over and above the $2 million. In that case, paragraph 8 requires

accrual of the $2 million if that is considered a reasonable estimate of the loss. Paragraph 10 requires disclosure of the additional exposure to loss if there is a reasonable possibility that additional taxes will be paid. Depending on the circumstances, paragraph 9 may require disclosure of the $2 million that was accrued.

Catastrophe Losses of Property and Casualty Insurance Companies

40. At the time that a property and casualty insurance company or reinsurance company issues an insurance policy covering risk of loss from catastrophes, a contingency arises. The contingency is the risk of loss *assumed* by the insurance company, that is, the risk of loss from catastrophes that may occur *during the term of the policy.* The insurance company has not assumed risk of loss for catastrophes that may occur *beyond* the term of the policy. Clearly, therefore, no asset has been impaired or liability incurred with respect to catastrophes that may occur beyond the terms of policies in force.

41. The conditions in paragraph 8 should be considered with respect to the risk of loss assumed by an insurance company for catastrophes that may occur during the terms of policies in force to determine whether accrual of a loss is appropriate. To satisfy the condition in paragraph 8(a) that it be probable that a liability has been incurred to existing policyholders, the occurrence of catastrophes (i.e., the confirming future events) would have to be reasonably predictable within the terms of policies in force. Further, to satisfy the condition in paragraph 8(b), the amounts of losses therefrom would have to be reasonably estimable. Actuarial techniques are employed by insurance companies to predict the rate of occurrence of and amounts of losses from catastrophes over long periods of time for insurance rate-setting purposes. Predictions over relatively short periods of time, such as an individual accounting period or the terms of a large number of existing insurance policies in force, are subject to substantial deviations. Consequently, assumption of risk of loss from catastrophes by property and casualty insurance companies and reinsurance companies fails to satisfy the conditions for accrual in paragraphs 8(a) and 8(b). Moreover, deferral of unearned premiums *within* the terms of policies in force represents the "unknown liability" for loss (including catastrophe losses) on unexpired policies, making an accrual inappropriate—see paragraphs 94-96 in Appendix C. Recognition of premium income as earned revenue within the terms of policies in force is discussed in the AICPA Industry Audit Guide, "Audits of Fire and Casualty Insurance Companies."

42. Although some property and casualty insurance companies have accrued an estimated amount for catastrophe losses, other insurance companies have accomplished the same objective by deferring a portion of the premium income. Deferral of any portion of premium income *beyond the terms of policies in force* is, in substance, similar to premature accrual of catastrophe losses and, therefore, also does not meet the conditions of paragraph 8.

43. The conditions for accrual in paragraph 8 do not prohibit a property and casualty insurance company from accruing probable catastrophe losses that have been incurred on or before the date of its financial statements but that have not been reported by its policyholders as of that date. If the amount of loss can be reasonably estimated, paragraph 8 requires accrual of those incurred-but-not-reported losses.

Payments to Insurance Companies That May Not Involve Transfer of Risk

44. To the extent that an insurance contract or reinsurance contract does not, despite its form, provide for indemnification of the insured or the ceding company by the insurer or reinsurer against loss or liability, the premium paid less the amount of the premium to be retained by the insurer or reinsurer shall be accounted for as a deposit by the insured or the ceding company. Those contracts may be structured in various ways, but if, regardless of form, their substance is that all or part of the premium paid by the insured or the ceding company is a deposit, it shall be accounted for as such.

45. Operations in certain industries may be subject to such high risks that insurance is unavailable or is available only at what is considered to be a prohibitively high cost. Some enterprises in those industries have "pooled" their risks by forming a mutual insurance company in which they retain an equity interest and to which they pay insurance premiums. For example, some electric utility companies have formed such a mutual insurance company to insure risks related to nuclear power plants, and some oil companies have formed a company to insure against risks associated with petroleum exploration and production. Whether the premium paid represents a payment for the transfer of risk or whether it represents merely a deposit will depend on the circumstances surrounding each enterprise's interest in and insurance arrangement with the mutual insurance company. An analysis of the contract is required to determine whether risk has been transferred and to what extent.

Appendix B

BACKGROUND INFORMATION

46. In April 1973, the FASB placed on its technical

agenda a project then entitled "Accounting for Future Losses." The project addressed accrual and disclosure of loss contingencies. The Board believes that "Accounting for Contingencies" is a more descriptive title for this Statement than "Accounting for Future Losses."

47. A task force of 16 persons from industry, public accounting, the financial community, and academe was appointed in the summer of 1973 to provide counsel to the Board in preparing a Discussion Memorandum analyzing issues related to the project.

48. The Discussion Memorandum gave examples of various types of contingencies and considered several of those at length to assist in the development of standards of financial accounting and reporting. These included (a) uninsured risks ("self-insurance"), (b) risk of losses from catastrophes assumed by property and casualty insurance companies, and (c) risk of losses from expropriations by foreign governments.

49. Research undertaken in connection with this project included (a) a search of relevant literature, (b) an examination of published financial statements in annual reports to shareholders and in filings with the SEC on Form 10-K, (c) a questionnaire survey conducted by the Financial Executives Institute to which 64 companies responded, and (d) a study of catastrophe reserve accounting methods employed by property and casualty insurance companies. Summaries of research findings are included in appendices to the Discussion Memorandum.

50. On January 3, 1973 (prior to the date the Board placed this subject on its agenda), the Securities and Exchange Commission issued its *Accounting Series Release No. 134,* which pointed out that a number of property and casualty insurance companies had adopted the accounting policy of making a provision from each period's income to cover a portion of major losses expected to occur in future periods. The SEC Release indicated that the Committee on Insurance Accounting and Auditing of the AICPA was working actively on the subject in cooperation with industry groups. The Release set forth certain disclosure requirements pending resolution of the question of accrual.

51. The AICPA committee's report (dated July 17, 1973) was in the form of a memorandum setting forth the views of those committee members favoring and those opposing accrual of losses from future catastrophes. In the course of its study, the AICPA committee had gathered considerable data on the subject, in part from a survey of member companies of the American Insurance Association, and this information was made available to the Board.

52. On August 2, 1973, the SEC announced in *Accounting Series Release No. 145* that property and casualty insurance companies should not change their method of accounting for catastrophe losses "until a single method has been adopted by the Financial Accounting Standards Board."

53. The Board issued the Discussion Memorandum on March 13, 1974, and held a public hearing on the subject on May 13, 1974. The Board received 87 position papers, letters of comment, and outlines of oral presentations in response to the Discussion Memorandum. Eighteen presentations were made at the public hearing.

54. An Exposure Draft of a proposed Statement on "Accounting for Contingencies" was issued on October 21, 1974. The Board received 212 letters of comment on the Exposure Draft.

Appendix C

BASIS FOR CONCLUSIONS

55. This Appendix discusses factors deemed significant by members of the Board in reaching the conclusions in this Statement, including various alternatives considered and reasons for accepting some and rejecting others.

SCOPE OF THIS STATEMENT

56. Some respondents to the Exposure Draft proposed that the Statement not deal with accrual and disclosure of loss contingencies in general but, rather, only with the following three specific matters: "self-insurance," risks of losses from catastrophes assumed by property and casualty insurance companies including reinsurance companies, and threat of expropriation. As the basis for that position, they noted that the Discussion Memorandum considered those three matters at length. Other respondents suggested that catastrophe losses be dealt with in a separate Statement.

57. The Board has concluded, however, that the broad issue of accrual and disclosure of loss contingencies should be dealt with in a single Statement, just as the Discussion Memorandum encompassed "the broad issue of accounting for future losses."[10] As the Discussion Memorandum stated, "future losses of all types presently known to affect enterprises and new types of future losses that may arise are conceptually included in the scope of this project." The three matters dealt with at length in

[10]The Board believes that *contingencies* is a more descriptive term than *future losses,* and the Discussion Memorandum indicated that the project would necessarily involve reconsideration of both *ARB No. 50* and Chapter 6 of *ARB No. 43*.

the Discussion Memorandum were used "as examples to assist in the evaluation and development of criteria for accounting for future losses," and other examples were discussed. The Board has concluded that loss contingencies such as those given as examples in paragraph 4 of this Statement have common characteristics and that questions about accounting for and reporting of those contingencies should be resolved comprehensively. It is for that reason, also, that the Board believes it inappropriate to deal with catastrophe losses in a separate Statement.

58. A question has been raised whether uncollectibility of receivables and product warranties constitute contingencies within the scope of this Statement. The Board recognizes that uncertainties associated with uncollectibility of some receivables and some product warranties are likely to be, in part, inherent in making accounting estimates (described in paragraph 2) as well as, in part, the type of uncertainties that give rise to a contingency (described in paragraph 1). The Board believes that no useful purpose would be served by attempting to distinguish between those two types of uncertainties for purposes of establishing conditions for accrual of uncollectible receivables and product warranties. Consequently, those matters are deemed to be contingencies within the definition of paragraph 1 and should be accounted for pursuant to the provisions of this Statement.

ACCRUAL OF LOSS CONTINGENCIES

59. Paragraph 8 requires that a loss contingency be accrued if the two specified conditions are met. The purpose of those conditions is to require accrual of losses when they are reasonably estimable and relate to the current or a prior period. The requirement that the loss be reasonably estimable is intended to prevent accrual in the financial statements of amounts so uncertain as to impair the integrity of those statements. The Board has concluded that disclosure is preferable to accrual when a reasonable estimate of loss cannot be made. Further, even losses that are reasonably estimable should not be accrued if it is not probable that an asset has been impaired or a liability has been incurred at the date of an enterprise's financial statements because those losses relate to a future period rather than the current or a prior period. Attribution of a loss to events or activities of the current or prior periods is an element of asset impairment or liability incurrence.

60. In establishing the conditions in paragraph 8, Board members considered the factors discussed in paragraphs 61-101. Individual Board members gave greater weight to some factors than to others.

Accounting Accruals Do Not Provide Protection against Losses

61. Accrual of a loss related to a contingency does not create or set aside funds to lessen the possible financial impact of a loss, although some respondents to the Discussion Memorandum and the Exposure Draft argued to the contrary. The Board believes that confusion exists between accounting accruals (sometimes referred to as "accounting reserves") and the reserving or setting aside of specific assets to be used for a particular purpose or contingency. Accounting accruals are simply a method of allocating costs among accounting periods and have no effect on an enterprise's cash flow. An enterprise may choose to maintain or have access to sufficient liquid assets to replace or repair lost or damaged property or to pay claims in case a loss occurs. Alternatively, it may transfer the risk to others by purchasing insurance. Those are financial decisions, and if enterprise management decides to do neither, the presence or absence of an accrued credit balance on the balance sheet will have no effect on the consequences of that decision. The accounting standards set forth in this Statement do not affect the fundamental business economics of that decision.

62. In that regard, some respondents to the Discussion Memorandum and the Exposure Draft contended that an accounting standard that does not permit periodic accrual of so-called "self-insurance reserves" and, in the case of insurance companies, so-called "catastrophe reserves" will force enterprises to purchase insurance or reinsurance because the "protection" afforded by the accrual would no longer exist. Those accruals, however, in no way protect the assets available to replace or repair uninsured property that may be lost or damaged, or to satisfy claims that are not covered by insurance, or, in the case of insurance companies, to satisfy the claims of insured parties. Accrual, in and of itself, provides no financial protection that is not available in the absence of accrual.

63. The sole result of accrual, for financial accounting and reporting purposes, is allocation of costs among accounting periods. Some respondents to the Discussion Memorandum and the Exposure Draft took the position that estimated losses from loss contingencies should be accrued even before available information indicates that it is probable that an asset has been impaired or a liability has been incurred to avoid reporting net income that fluctuates widely from period to period. In their view, financial statement users may be misled by those fluctuations. They believe that estimated losses should be accrued without regard to whether the loss relates to the current period if, based on experience, it is reasonable to expect losses sometime in the future.

64. Financial statement users have indicated, however, that information about earnings variability is important to them. Two elements often cited as basic to the decision models of many financial statement users are (a) expected return—the predicted amount and timing of the return on an investment—and (b) risk—the variability of that expected return. If the nature of an enterprise's operations is such that irregularities in the incurrence of losses cause variations in periodic net income, that fact should not be obscured by accruing for anticipated losses that do not relate to the current period.

65. The Board recognizes that some investors may have a preference for investments in enterprises having a stable pattern of earnings, because that indicates lesser uncertainty or risk than fluctuating earnings. That preference, in turn, is perceived by many as having a favorable effect on the market prices of those enterprises' securities. If accruals for such matters as future uninsured losses and catastrophes were prohibited, some respondents contended, enterprises would be forced to purchase insurance or reinsurance to achieve the more stable pattern of reported earnings that tends to accompany the use of an "accounting reserve." Insurance or reinsurance reduces or eliminates risks and the inherent earnings fluctuations that accompany risks. Unlike insurance and reinsurance, however, the use of "accounting reserves" does not reduce or eliminate risk. The Board rejects the contention, therefore, that the use of "accounting reserves" is an alternative to insurance and reinsurance in protecting against risk. Earnings fluctuations are inherent in risk retention, and they should be reported as they occur. The Board cannot sanction the use of an accounting procedure to create the illusion of protection from risk when, in fact, protection does not exist.

66. The Board has also considered the argument that periodic accrual of losses without regard to whether an asset has been impaired or liability incurred is justified on grounds of comparability of financial statements among enterprises. Some respondents contended, for example, that accrual is necessary to make the financial statements of enterprises that do not purchase insurance comparable to those of enterprises that do purchase insurance (and report the premiums as expenses) and to make the financial statements of property and casualty insurance companies comparable regardless of the extent to which reinsurance has been purchased. In the Board's view, however, to report activity when there has been none would obscure a fundamental difference in circumstance between enterprises that transfer risks to others and those that do not.

Financial Accounting and Reporting Reflects Primarily the Effects of Past Transactions and Existing Conditions

67. Financial accounting and reporting reflects primarily the effects of past transactions and existing conditions, not future transactions or conditions. For example, paragraph 35 of *APB Statement No. 4,* "Basic Concepts and Accounting Principles Underlying Financial Statements of Business Enterprises," states:

> Financial accounting and financial statements are primarily historical in that information about events that have taken place provides the basic data of financial accounting and financial statements.

68. The first condition in paragraph 8—that a loss contingency not be accrued until it is probable that an asset has been impaired or a liability has been incurred—is consistent with this concept of financial accounting and financial statements. That condition is not so past-oriented that accrual of a loss must await the occurrence of the confirming future event, for example, final adjudication or settlement of a lawsuit. The condition requires only that it be probable that the confirming future event will occur. The condition is intended to prohibit the recognition of a liability when it is not probable that one has been incurred and to prohibit the accrual of an asset impairment when it is not probable that an asset of an enterprise has been impaired.

The Concept of a Liability

69. In many cases, the accrual of a loss contingency results in the recording of a liability, for example, accruals for a probable tax assessment, a warranty obligation, or a probable loss resulting from the guarantee of indebtedness of others. In the course of its deliberations, therefore, the Board found it relevant to consider the concept of a liability as expressed in accounting literature.

70. The economic obligations of an enterprise are defined in paragraph 58 of *APB Statement No. 4* as "its present responsibilities to transfer economic resources or provide services to other entities in the future." Two aspects of that definition are especially relevant to accounting for contingencies: first, that liabilities are *present* responsibilities and, second, that they are obligations to *other entities.* Those notions are supported by other definitions of liabilities in published accounting literature, for example:

> Liabilities are claims of creditors against the enterprise, arising out of past activities, that are to be satisfied by the disbursement or utilization of corporate resources.[11]

> A liability is the result of a transaction of the past, not of the future.[12]

71. The condition in paragraph 8(a)—that a loss contingency shall be accrued if it is probable that a liability has been incurred—is intended to proscribe recognition of losses that relate to future periods but to require accrual of losses that relate to the current or a prior period (assuming the amount of loss can be reasonably estimated—see paragraph 8(b)).

72. Liability definitions also generally require that the amount of an economic obligation be known or susceptible of reasonable estimation before it is recorded as a liability. For example:

> [Liabilities] are measured by cash received, by the established price of noncash assets or services received, or by estimates of a definitive character when the amount owing cannot be measured more precisely.[13]

> The amount of the liability must be the subject of calculation or of close estimation.[14]

73. The condition in paragraph 8(b)—that an estimated loss from a loss contingency not be accrued until the amount of loss can be reasonably estimated—is consistent with this feature of the liability concept.

Accounting for Impairment of Value of Assets

74. The accrual of some loss contingencies may result in recording the impairment of the value of an asset rather than in recording a liability, for example, accruals for expropriation of assets or uncollectible receivables. Accounting presently recognizes impairments of the value of assets such as the following:

a. Paragraph 9 of Chapter 3A, "Current Assets and Current Liabilities," of *ARB No. 43* provides that "in the case of marketable securities where market value is less than cost by a substantial amount and it is evident that the decline in market value is not due to a mere temporary condition, the amount to be included as a current asset should not exceed the market value."
b. Statement 5 of Chapter 4, "Inventory Pricing," of *ARB No. 43* states that "a departure from the cost basis of pricing the inventory is required when the utility of the goods is no longer as great as its cost. . . . A loss of utility is to be reflected as a charge against the revenues of the period in which it occurs."
c. Paragraph 19(h) of *APB Opinion No. 18,* "The Equity Method of Accounting for Investments in Common Stock," states that "a loss in value of an investment which is other than a temporary decline should be recognized the same as a loss in value of other long-term assets."
d. Paragraph 15 of *APB Opinion No. 30,* "Reporting the Results of Operations," states that "if a loss is expected from the proposed sale or abandonment of a segment, the estimated loss should be provided for at the measurement date. . . ." Paragraph 14 states that the measurement date is the date on which management "commits itself to a formal plan to dispose of a segment of the business, whether by sale or abandonment."
e. Paragraph 183 of *APB Statement No. 4* states that "when enterprise assets are damaged by others, asset amounts are written down to recoverable costs and a loss is recorded."

75. A recurring principle underlying all of these references to asset impairments in the accounting literature is that a loss should not be accrued until it is probable that an asset *has been* impaired and the amount of the loss can be reasonably estimated. As indicated by those references, impairment is recognized, for instance, when a non-temporary decline in the market price of marketable securities below cost *has taken place,* when the utility of inventory *is no longer* as great as its cost, when a commitment, in terms of a formal plan, *has been made* to abandon a segment of a business or to sell a segment at less than its carrying amount, when enterprise assets *are damaged,* and so forth. The condition in paragraph 8(a) is intended to proscribe accrual of losses that relate to future periods, and the condition in paragraph 8(b) further requires that the amount of loss be reasonably estimable before it is accrued.

The Matching Concept

76. A number of respondents to the Discussion Memorandum and the Exposure Draft noted that losses from certain types of contingencies are likely to occur irregularly over an extended period of time encompassing a number of accounting periods. In their view, the matching process in accounting

[11]American Accounting Association, *Accounting and Reporting Standards for Corporate Financial Statements and Preceding Statements and Supplements* (Sarasota, Fla.: AAA, 1957), p. 16.

[12] Maurice Moonitz, "The Changing Concept of Liabilities," *The Journal of Accountancy,* May 1960, p. 44.

[13]American Accounting Association, *Accounting and Reporting Standards for Corporate Financial Statements,* p. 16.

[14] Maurice Moonitz, "The Changing Concept of Liabilities," p. 44.

requires that estimated losses from those types of contingencies be accrued in each accounting period even if not directly related to events or activities of the period.

77. *APB Statement No. 4* explicitly avoids using the term "matching" because it has a variety of meanings in the accounting literature. In its broadest sense, matching refers to the entire process of income determination—described in paragraph 147 of *APB Statement No. 4* as "identifying, measuring, and relating revenue and expenses of an enterprise for an accounting period." Matching may also be used in a more limited sense to refer only to the process of expense recognition or in an even more limited sense to refer to the recognition of expenses by associating costs with revenue on a cause and effect basis.

78. Three pervasive principles for recognizing costs as expenses are set forth in paragraphs 156-160 of *APB Statement No. 4* as follows:

> *Associating Cause and Effect.* . . . Some costs are recognized as expenses on the basis of a presumed direct association with specific revenue . . . recognizing them as expenses accompanies recognition of the revenue.
>
> *Systematic and Rational Allocation.* . . . If an asset provides benefits for several periods its cost is allocated to the periods in a systematic and rational manner in the absence of a more direct basis for associating cause and effect.
>
> *Immediate Recognition.* Some costs are associated with the current accounting period as expenses because (1) costs incurred during the period provide no discernible future benefits, (2) costs recorded as assets in prior periods no longer provide discernible benefits or (3) allocating costs either on the basis of association with revenue or among several accounting periods is considered to serve no useful purpose.

79. Some who believe that matching requires accrual of losses that are likely to occur irregularly over an extended period of time encompassing a number of accounting periods cite the systematic and rational allocation principle of expense recognition as justification for their position. That principle, however, involves the systematic and rational allocation of the cost of an asset (an asset that *has been* acquired) throughout the estimated periods that the asset provides benefits or the systematic and rational accrual of the amount of some obligations (obligations that *have been* incurred) throughout the estimated periods that the obligations are incurred. The customary depreciation of plant and equipment is an example of the former; when reasonably estimable, the accrual of vacation pay is an example of the latter. The systematic and rational allocation principle has no application to assets that are expected to be acquired in the future or to obligations that are expected to be incurred in the future.

80. Matching, in the sense of recognizing expenses by associating costs with specific revenue on a cause and effect basis, is a consideration in relation to accrual for such matters as uncollectible receivables and warranty obligations. For example, most enterprises that make credit sales or warrant their products or services regularly incur losses from uncollectible receivables and warranty obligations. Frequently, those losses can be associated with revenue on a cause and effect basis. If the amount of those losses can be reasonably estimated, paragraph 8 of this Statement requires accrual if it is probable that an asset has been impaired (estimated uncollectible receivables) or that a liability has been incurred (estimated warranty claims).

Spreading the Burden of Irregularly Occurring Costs to Successive Generations of Customers and Shareholders

81. Some respondents to the Discussion Memorandum and the Exposure Draft contended that all costs of doing business should be accrued in each accounting period so that successive generations of customers and shareholders would bear their share of all costs including those that occur irregularly. It would seem, however, that those irregularly occurring costs are usually borne by customers through pricing policy and that pricing is not necessarily dependent upon financial accounting and reporting practices. With regard to accrual on grounds that it enables successive generations of shareholders to bear their share of irregularly occurring costs, see paragraphs 63-65.

Conservatism

82. On the grounds of conservatism, some respondents supported accrual of estimated losses from loss contingencies before available information indicates that it is probable that an asset has been impaired or a liability has been incurred. Conservatism is indicated as one of the "characteristics and limitations" of financial accounting in paragraph 35 of *APB Statement No. 4* as follows:

> *Conservatism.* The uncertainties that surround the preparation of financial statements are reflected in a general tendency toward early recognition of unfavorable events and minimization of the amount of net assets and net income.

83. Conservatism is further discussed in paragraph 171 of *APB Statement No. 4:*

Conservatism. Frequently, assets and liabilities are measured in a context of significant uncertainties. Historically, managers, investors, and accountants have generally preferred that possible errors in measurement be in the direction of understatement rather than overstatement of net income and net assets. This has led to the convention of conservatism. . . .

84. The conditions for accrual in paragraph 8 are not inconsistent with the accounting concept of conservatism. Those conditions are not intended to be so rigid that they require virtual certainty before a loss is accrued. They require only that it be *probable* that an asset has been impaired or a liability has been incurred and that the amount of loss be *reasonably* estimable. In the absence of that probability or estimability, however, the Board has concluded that disclosure is preferable to accruing in the financial statements amounts so uncertain as to impair the integrity of the financial statements.

Risk of Future Loss or Damage of Enterprise Property, Injury to Others, Damage to the Property of Others, and Business Interruption

85. Some persons contend that the decision not to purchase insurance against losses that can be reasonably expected some time in the future (such as risk of loss or damage of enterprise property, injury to others, damage to the property of others, and business interruption) justifies periodic accrual for those losses without regard to whether it is probable that an asset has been impaired or a liability incurred at the date of the financial statements. As a basis for their position, they frequently cite the following factors: matching of revenue and expense, spreading the burden of irregularly occurring costs to successive generations of customers, and conservatism. They also believe that accrual of estimated losses from those types of risks improves the comparability of the financial statements of enterprises that do not insure with those of enterprises that purchase insurance. Some contend that a prohibition against periodic accrual for uninsured losses will force enterprises to purchase insurance coverage that would not otherwise be purchased.

86. In the Board's judgment, however, the mere existence of risk, at the date of an enterprise's financial statements, does not mean that a loss should be accrued. Anticipation of asset impairments or liabilities or losses from business interruption that do not relate to the current or a prior period is not justified by the matching concept.

87. The Board's views regarding the contention that periodic accrual for uninsured losses is a way of providing protection against loss and improving comparability among enterprises that do and do not purchase insurance, and the contention that prohibition of accrual will force enterprises to purchase insurance, are discussed in paragraphs 61-66. The Board's position regarding periodic accrual for uninsured risks and other loss contingencies on the grounds of spreading the burden of irregularly occurring costs to successive generations of customers or on the grounds of conservatism is discussed in paragraphs 81-84.

88. Some respondents to the Exposure Draft said that prohibition against periodic accrual for uninsured losses would be detrimental to government contractors because requirements of Federal government agencies in auditing costs subject to procurement regulations currently allow reimbursement for periodic accruals for uninsured losses only if they are included in the contractor's financial statements. Contract reimbursement and financial accounting and reporting may well have different objectives. Accordingly, the provisions of this Statement may not be appropriate for contract reimbursement purposes.

Catastrophe Losses of Property and Casualty Insurance Companies

89. At the time that a property and casualty insurance company or reinsurance company issues an insurance policy covering risk of loss from catastrophes, a contingency arises. The contingency is the risk of loss *assumed* by the insurance company, that is, the risk of loss from catastrophes that may occur *during the term of the policy.*

90. Some respondents to the Discussion Memorandum and the Exposure Draft proposed that insurance companies accrue estimated losses from catastrophes including both those that may occur during the terms of insurance policies in force and those that may occur beyond the terms of policies in force. Other respondents proposed that some portion of the premium revenue of a property and casualty insurance company be deferred beyond the terms of insurance policies in force to provide what, in substance, is an estimated liability for future catastrophe losses. Some respondents proposed that accrual of estimated losses or deferral of premiums be permitted but not required. On the other hand, some respondents to the Discussion Memorandum and the Exposure Draft were opposed to any accrual for future catastrophe losses by means of an estimated liability or deferral of premium revenue. Because those estimated liabilities and revenue deferrals have come to be referred to as "catastrophe reserves," that term will be used in paragraphs 91-101 for convenience.

91. In response to the Exposure Draft, it was recommended that the FASB appoint a special commit-

tee to study further the matter of catastrophe reserve accounting and to make recommendations thereon. The Board has concluded, however, that its own research and that of others (mentioned in Appendix B to this Statement and summarized in the Discussion Memorandum), the written responses received to the Discussion Memorandum, the presentations made at the public hearing, and the letters of comment on the Exposure Draft provide the Board with sufficient information with which to reach a conclusion.

92. Proponents of catastrophe reserve accounting generally cite the following reasons for their position:

a. *Catastrophes certain to occur.* Over the long term, catastrophes are certain to occur; therefore, they are not contingencies.
b. *Predictability of catastrophe losses.* On the basis of experience and by application of appropriate statistical techniques, catastrophe losses can be predicted over the long term with reasonable accuracy.
c. *Matching.* Some portion of property and casualty insurance premiums is intended to cover losses that usually occur infrequently and at intervals longer than both the terms of the policies in force and the financial accounting and reporting period. Catastrophe losses should, therefore, be accrued when the revenue is recognized (or premiums should be deferred beyond the terms of policies in force to periods in which the catastrophes occur) to match catastrophe losses with the related revenue.
d. *Stabilization of reported income.* Catastrophe reserve accounting stabilizes reported income and avoids erratic variations caused by irregularly occurring catastrophes.
e. *Comparability.* Reinsurance premiums paid by a prime insurer are said to be similar to accrual of catastrophe losses prior to their occurrence because the reinsurance premiums paid reduce income before a catastrophe loss occurs. Accrual of catastrophe losses as an expense prior to occurrence of a catastrophe makes the financial statements of property and casualty insurance companies comparable regardless of the extent to which reinsurance has been purchased.
f. *Non-accrual would force purchase of reinsurance.* Non-accrual of catastrophe losses will force property and casualty insurance companies to purchase reinsurance.
g. *Generations of policyholders.* Periodic accrual of estimated catastrophe losses charges each generation of policyholders with its share of the loss through the premium structure.

93. The Board does not find those arguments persuasive. The fact that over the long term catastrophes are certain to occur does not justify accrual before the catastrophes occur. As stated in paragraph 59, the purpose of the conditions for accrual in paragraph 8 is to require accrual of losses if they are reasonably estimable *and relate to the current or a prior period.* An enterprise may know with certainty, for example, next year's administrative salaries, but that does not justify accrual in the current accounting period because those salaries do not relate to that period. As indicated in paragraphs 67-68, financial accounting and reporting reflects primarily the effects of past transactions and existing conditions, not future transactions or conditions; accrual for losses from catastrophes that are expected to occur *beyond the terms of insurance policies in force* would amount to accrual of a liability before one has been incurred. Existing policyholders are insured only during the period covered by their insurance contracts; an insurance company is not presently obligated to policyholders for catastrophes that may occur after expiration of their policies. Accrual for those catastrophe losses would record a liability that is inconsistent with the concept of a liability discussed in paragraphs 69-73.

94. The Board recognizes that the costs of catastrophes to insurance companies are large and are incurred irregularly and that insurance companies recoup those costs in the long run through periodic adjustments in the premiums charged to policyholders. It is the view of the Board, however, that the long-run nature of pricing of premiums should not be a determinant of the time when a liability is recorded.

95. The AICPA Industry Audit Guide, "Audits of Fire and Casualty Insurance Companies," describes accounting for premiums as follows (pp. 24-25):

> As soon as a policy is issued promising to indemnify for loss, the insurance company incurs a potential liability. The company may be called upon to pay the full amount of the policy, a portion of the policy, or nothing. It would be impossible to try to measure the liability under a single policy. However, since insurance is based on the law of averages, one may estimate from experience the loss on a large number of policies.
>
> As state supervision of insurance developed, the insurance departments set about providing a legal basis for determining the potential liability under outstanding policies in order to establish an ample reserve for the protection of policyholders and provide a uniform method of calculation. It was recognized that, since the premium is expected to pay losses and expenses, and provide a margin of profit over the term of the policy, the portion measured by the unexpired term should be adequate to pay policy liabilities (prin-

cipally losses and loss expenses) and return premiums during the unexpired term on a uniform basis for all companies. Therefore the unearned premium was adopted as the basis for computing the unknown liability on unexpired policies.

96. Because unearned premiums represents the "unknown liability," the Board is of the view that it is inappropriate to accrue an additional amount as an estimate for that same unknown liability. Further, in the Board's view, deferral of premiums beyond the terms of policies in force is inconsistent with the concept of revenue recognition set forth in the Audit Guide and is without any conceptual basis. Moreover, the Board believes that its conclusion regarding the time at which accruals shall be made for catastrophic losses is consistent with the Audit Guide. It should be noted that this Statement does not prohibit (and, in fact, requires) accrual of a *net* loss (that is, a loss in excess of deferred premiums) that probably will be incurred on insurance policies that are in force, provided that the loss can be reasonably estimated, just as accrual of net losses on long-term construction-type contracts is required (see *ARB No. 45,* "Long-Term Construction-Type Contracts").

97. With respect to catastrophes that may occur within the terms of policies in force, to satisfy the conditions for accrual in paragraph 8, the occurrence of catastrophes would have to be probable during the terms of those policies, and the amounts of losses therefrom would have to be reasonably estimable. The letters of comment and position papers received in response to the Discussion Memorandum and the Exposure Draft and presentations at the public hearing lead the Board to conclude that neither the timing of catastrophes nor the amounts of losses therefrom are reasonably predictable within the terms of policies in force.

98. The Board is of the view that accrual of losses from catastrophes is not justified by the accounting concept of matching. Systematic and rational allocation does not apply to costs that have not been incurred. The Board recognizes that large and irregularly occurring costs must of necessity be considered in systematically and rationally determining premiums to be charged to customers but does not believe that pricing considerations should dictate the accrual of losses for financial accounting purposes. The Board also does not believe that matching in the sense of recognizing expenses by associating losses with specific revenue on a cause and effect basis is, in and of itself, a basis for accrual of catastrophe losses prior to the event causing the loss. The Board believes that, for the reasons stated in paragraphs 94-96, there can be no presumed direct association with specific revenue prior to the event causing the catastrophe loss.

99. The Board's views regarding justification of periodic accrual of catastrophe reserves on grounds of (a) stabilizing reported income, (b) improving comparability among financial statements of insurance companies, and (c) preventing the "forced" purchase of reinsurance are discussed in paragraphs 61-66.

100. The argument that accrual of catastrophe reserves enables each generation of policyholders to bear its share of the losses through the premiums that it is charged is also questionable because amounts established for premiums are not necessarily dependent on financial accounting and reporting practices.

101. The Board considered the proposal that catastrophe reserve accounting be permitted but not made mandatory. Whether it is probable that an asset has been impaired or a liability incurred is determined by the circumstances, not by choice. Accordingly, the conditions for accrual in paragraph 8 apply to all loss contingencies, including risk of loss from catastrophes assumed by property and casualty insurance companies and reinsurance companies. In the Board's view, the use of different methods to report catastrophe losses in similar circumstances cannot be justified.

APPLICABILITY TO LIFE INSURANCE COMPANIES

102. Some respondents to the Exposure Draft inquired as to whether the conditions for accrual in paragraph 8 are intended to change accounting practices of life insurance companies. This Statement does not amend the AICPA Industry Audit Guide, "Audits of Stock Life Insurance Companies."

DISCLOSURE OF NONINSURANCE

103. A number of respondents to the Exposure Draft inquired as to whether it is the Board's intent to require disclosure of noninsurance or underinsurance. Some recommended that the Board require disclosures with respect to uninsured risks that enterprises ordinarily insure against. Others said that they were unable to define risks that would ordinarily be insured against because the insurance practices of enterprises are so varied. Because of the problems involved in developing operational criteria for disclosure of noninsured or underinsured risks, this Statement does not require disclosure of uninsured risks. However, the Board does not discourage those disclosures in appropriate circumstances.

EFFECTIVE DATE AND TRANSITION

104. The Board considered three alternative approaches to a change in the method of accounting for contingencies: (1) prior period adjustment, (2) the "cumulative effect" method described in *APB Opinion No. 20,* "Accounting Changes," and (3) retention of amounts accrued for contingencies that do not meet the conditions for accrual in paragraph 8 until those amounts are exhausted by actual losses charged thereto. The Exposure Draft had proposed the change be effected by the prior period adjustment method. A large number of respondents to the Exposure Draft, however, opposed the prior period adjustment method for a number of reasons, including significant difficulties involved in determining the degree of probability and estimability that had existed in prior periods as would have been required if the conditions in paragraph 8 were applied retroactively. On further consideration of all the circumstances, the Board has concluded that use of the "cumulative effect" method described in *APB Opinion No. 20* represents a satisfactory solution and has concluded that the effective date in paragraph 20 is advisable.

Statement of Financial Accounting Standards No. 6 Classification of Short-Term Obligations Expected to Be Refinanced

an amendment of ARB No. 43, Chapter 3A

STATUS

Issued: May 1975

Effective Date: For fiscal periods ending on or after December 31, 1975

Affects: Amends ARB 43, Chapter 3A, paragraph 6(a) and footnote 1
Amends ARB 43, Chapter 3A, paragraph 8
Supersedes ARB 43, Chapter 3A, footnote 4

Affected by: No other pronouncements

Statement of Financial Accounting Standards No. 6
Classification of Short-Term Obligations Expected to Be Refinanced

an amendment of ARB No. 43, Chapter 3A

CONTENTS

INTRODUCTION AND BACKGROUND INFORMATION

1. Some short-term obligations are expected to be refinanced on a long-term basis and, therefore, are not expected to require the use of enterprise working capital during the ensuing fiscal year. Examples include commercial paper, construction loans, and the currently maturing portion of long-term debt. Those obligations have been presented in balance sheets in a number of ways, including the following: (a) classification as current liabilities, (b) classification as long-term liabilities, and (c) presentation as a class of liabilities distinct from both current liabilities and long-term liabilities.

2. For purposes of this Statement, *short-term obligations* are those that are scheduled to mature within one year after the date of an enterprise's balance sheet or, for those enterprises that use the operating cycle concept of working capital described in paragraphs 5 and 7 of Chapter 3A, "Current Assets and Current Liabilities," of *Accounting Research Bulletin (ARB) No. 43,* within an enterprise's operating cycle that is longer than one year. *Long-term obligations* are those scheduled to mature beyond one year (or the operating cycle, if applicable) from the date of an enterprise's balance sheet. *Refinancing a short-term obligation on a long-term basis* means either replacing it with a long-term obligation or with equity securities or renewing, extending, or replacing it with short-term obligations for an uninterrupted period extending beyond one year (or the operating cycle, if applicable) from the date of an enterprise's balance sheet. Accordingly, despite the fact that the short-term obligation is scheduled to mature during the ensuing fiscal year (or the operating cycle, if applicable), it will not require the use of working capital during that period.

3. Exclusion of some short-term obligations from the current liability classification has been supported by paragraph 8 of Chapter 3A of *ARB No. 43,* which states that the current liability classification "is not intended to include a contractual obligation falling due at an early date which is expected to be refunded." In assessing whether a short-term obligation is "expected to be refunded," enterprise *intent* to refinance on a long-term basis and its *prior ability* to refinance its short-term obligations have sometimes been considered sufficient for exclusion of the short-term obligation from current liabilities. In other cases, *future ability* to refinance as demonstrated by the existence of an agreement for long-term financing has been viewed as necessary.

4. SEC *Accounting Series Release (ASR) No. 148,* issued November 13, 1973, requires that commercial paper and other short-term debt be classified as a current liability unless (a) the borrower has a non-cancelable binding agreement from a creditor to refinance the paper or other short-term debt and (b) the refinancing would extend the maturity date beyond one year (or operating cycle, if longer) and (c) the borrower's intention is to exercise this right.

5. Because of the diverse practices referred to in paragraphs 1 and 3 of this Statement and questions brought to the Board's attention concerning the differences between the criteria in paragraph 8 of Chapter 3A of *ARB No. 43* and those in *ASR No. 148,* the Board concluded that it should examine the criteria for classification of short-term obligations that are expected to be refinanced on a long-term basis.

6. The Board concluded that on the basis of existing data it could make an informed decision on the classification of short-term obligations expected to be refinanced without a public hearing. An Exposure

Draft of a proposed Statement on "Classification of Short-Term Obligations Expected to Be Refinanced" was issued on November 11, 1974. Ninety-two letters were received in response to the request for comments. On January 9, 1975, the Board announced that it would not issue a final statement effective for fiscal periods ending December 31, 1974, as had been proposed in the Exposure Draft, to allow additional time for consideration of points raised in the comment letters. Appendix A describes the principal changes from the Exposure Draft and also sets forth the basis for the Board's conclusions, including alternatives considered and reasons for accepting some and rejecting others. Examples of application of this Statement are presented in Appendix B.

APPLICABILITY

7. The balance sheets of most enterprises show separate classifications of current assets and current liabilities (commonly referred to as classified balance sheets) permitting ready determination of working capital. Enterprises in several specialized industries (including broker-dealers and finance, real estate, and stock life insurance companies) for which the current/noncurrent distinction is deemed in practice to have little or no relevance prepare unclassified balance sheets. The standards established by this Statement apply only when an enterprise is preparing a classified balance sheet for financial accounting and reporting purposes.

STANDARDS OF FINANCIAL ACCOUNTING AND REPORTING

Classification

8. Short-term obligations arising from transactions in the normal course of business that are due in customary terms shall be classified as current liabilities. Those obligations (as described in the second sentence of paragraph 7 of Chapter 3A of *ARB No. 43*) are "obligations for items which have entered into the operating cycle, such as payables incurred in the acquisition of materials and supplies to be used in the production of goods or in providing services to be offered for sale; collections received in advance of the delivery of goods or performance of services; . . . and debts which arise from operations directly related to the operating cycle, such as accruals for wages, salaries, commissions, rentals, royalties, and income and other taxes."

9. A short-term obligation other than one classified as a current liability in accordance with paragraph 8 shall be excluded from current liabilities only if the conditions in paragraphs 10 and 11 are met.[1]

Intent to Refinance

10. The enterprise intends to *refinance the obligation on a long-term basis* (see paragraph 2).

Ability to Consummate the Refinancing

11. The enterprise's intent to refinance the short-term obligation on a long-term basis is supported by an ability to consummate the refinancing demonstrated in either of the following ways:

a. *Post-balance-sheet-date issuance of a long-term obligation or equity securities.* After the date of an enterprise's balance sheet but before that balance sheet is issued, a long-term obligation or equity securities[2] have been issued for the purpose of refinancing the short-term obligation on a long-term basis; or
b. *Financing agreement.* Before the balance sheet is issued, the enterprise has entered into a financing agreement that clearly permits the enterprise to refinance the short-term obligation on a long-term basis on terms that are readily determinable, and all of the following conditions are met:

   (i) The agreement does not expire within one year (or operating cycle—see paragraph 2) from the date of the enterprise's balance sheet and during that period the agreement is not cancelable by the lender or the prospective lender or investor (and obligations incurred under the agreement are not callable during that period) except for violation

[1]Paragraph 8 of Chapter 3A, *ARB No. 43,* describes a circumstance, unaffected by this Statement, in which obligations maturing within one year would be excluded from current liabilities as follows: "The current liability classification, however, is not intended to include . . . debts to be liquidated by funds which have been accumulated in accounts of a type not properly classified as current assets. . . ." Footnote 1 to paragraph 6(a) of Chapter 3A, *ARB No. 43,* describes another circumstance, also unaffected by this Statement. Under that paragraph, "funds that are clearly to be used in the near future for liquidation of long-term debts, payments to sinking funds, or for similar purposes should . . . be excluded from current assets. However, where such funds are considered to offset maturing debt which has properly been set up as a current liability, they may be included within the current asset classification." Accordingly, funds obtained on a long-term basis prior to the balance sheet date would be excluded from current assets if the obligation to be liquidated is excluded from current liabilities.

[2]If equity securities have been issued, the short-term obligation, although excluded from current liabilities, shall not be included in owners' equity.

of a provision[3] with which compliance is objectively determinable or measurable.[4]

(ii) No violation of any provision in the financing agreement exists at the balance-sheet date and no available information indicates that a violation has occurred thereafter but prior to the issuance of the balance sheet, or, if one exists at the balance-sheet date or has occurred thereafter, a waiver has been obtained.

(iii) The lender or the prospective lender or investor with which the enterprise has entered into the financing agreement is expected to be financially capable of honoring the agreement.

12. If an enterprise's ability to consummate an intended refinancing of a short-term obligation on a long-term basis is demonstrated by post-balance-sheet-date issuance of a long-term obligation or equity securities (paragraph 11(a)), the amount of the short-term obligation to be excluded from current liabilities shall not exceed the proceeds of the new long-term obligation or the equity securities issued. If ability to refinance is demonstrated by the existence of a financing agreement (paragraph 11(b)), the amount of the short-term obligation to be excluded from current liabilities shall be reduced to the amount available for refinancing under the agreement when the amount available is less than the amount of the short-term obligation. The amount to be excluded shall be reduced further if information (such as restrictions in other agreements or restrictions as to transferability of funds) indicates that funds obtainable under the agreement will not be available to liquidate the short-term obligation. Further, if amounts that could be obtained under the financing agreement fluctuate (for example, in relation to the enterprise's needs, in proportion to the value of collateral, or in accordance with other terms of the agreement), the amount to be excluded from current liabilities shall be limited to a reasonable estimate of the minimum amount expected to be available at any date from the scheduled maturity of the short-term obligation to the end of the fiscal year (or operating cycle—see paragraph 2). If no reasonable estimate can be made, the entire outstanding short-term obligation shall be included in current liabilities.

13. The enterprise may intend to seek an alternative source of financing rather than to exercise its rights under the existing agreement when the short-term obligation becomes due. The enterprise must intend to exercise its rights under the existing agreement, however, if that other source does not become available.[5]

14. Replacement of a short-term obligation with another short-term obligation after the date of the balance sheet but before the balance sheet is issued is not, by itself, sufficient to demonstrate an enterprise's ability to refinance the short-term obligation on a long-term basis. If, for example, the replacement is made under the terms of a revolving credit agreement that provides for renewal or extension of the short-term obligation for an uninterrupted period extending beyond one year (or operating cycle—see paragraph 2) from the date of the balance sheet, the revolving credit agreement must meet the conditions in paragraph 11(b) to justify excluding the short-term obligation from current liabilities. Similarly, if the replacement is a roll-over of commercial paper accompanied by a "stand-by" credit agreement, the stand-by agreement must meet the conditions in paragraph 11(b) to justify excluding the short-term obligation from current liabilities.

Disclosure

15. A total of current liabilities shall be presented in classified balance sheets. If a short-term obligation is excluded from current liabilities pursuant to the provisions of this Statement, the notes to the financial statements shall include a general description of the financing agreement and the terms of any new obligation incurred or expected to be incurred or equity securities issued or expected to be issued as a result of a refinancing.

Amendments to Existing Pronouncement

16. The Board's conclusions require deletion of the following words from the second sentence of paragraph 8 of Chapter 3A, *ARB No. 43: a contractual obligation falling due at an early date which is expected to be refunded, or.* Footnote 4 and the reference to it in paragraph 8 of Chapter 3A are also deleted.

Effective Date and Transition

17. The provisions of this Statement shall be effective December 31, 1975 and shall apply to balance

[3]For purposes of this Statement, *violation of a provision* means failure to meet a condition set forth in the agreement or breach or violation of a provision such as a restrictive covenant, representation, or warranty, whether or not a grace period is allowed or the lender is required to give notice.

[4]Financing agreements cancelable for violation of a provision that can be evaluated differently by the parties to the agreement (such as "a material adverse change" or "failure to maintain satisfactory operations") do not comply with this condition.

[5]The intent to exercise may not be present if the terms of the agreement contain conditions or permit the prospective lender or investor to establish conditions, such as interest rates or collateral requirements, that are unreasonable to the enterprise.

sheets dated on or after that date and to related statements of changes in financial position. Reclassification in financial statements for periods ending prior to December 31, 1975 is permitted but not required.

The provisions of this Statement need not be applied to immaterial items.

This Statement was adopted by the affirmative votes of six members of the Financial Accounting Standards Board. Mr. Mays dissented.

Mr. Mays dissents because this Statement permits the exclusion of short-term obligations from current liabilities under circumstances in which, in his view, such exclusion is unwarranted. He beleives that the criteria for exclusion set forth in the Statement tend to blur rather than to sharpen the accounting concept of working capital.

He is of the opinion that more restrictive criteria would result in a more meaningful portrayal of current and long-term cash requirements. He believes that information concerning management's ability and intent to refinance certain of its obligations can be communicated in financial statements by footnote disclosure or by disclosures within the current liabilities section of the balance sheet. However, those considerations, while important, should not be permitted to obscure the nature of the obligations themselves.

In Mr. Mays' opinion, classification of an obligation as a current liability or as a long-term liability should be based on the maturity date of the obligation, and only in exceptional circumstances should the existence of a financing agreement affect that classification. Those circumstances would be (1) the agreement is noncancelable by the lender (whereas the Statement provides for reclassification even though the lender may cancel if a provision of the agreement is violated); and (2) the agreement is entered into for the stated purpose of refinancing the particular short-term obligation (whereas the Statement requires merely that the agreement not prohibit such refinancing); and (3) the enterprise fully intends to refinance the obligation on a long-term basis under the agreement (whereas the Statement provides for reclassification even if the enterprise intends to seek other sources of financing).

In Mr. Mays' view, since the Statement permits general lines of bank credit to be used to justify the exclusion of unrelated short-term debt from current liabilities, logic would suggest that any solvent corporation with sufficient unused borrowing capacity should be permitted to exclude from current liabilities any kind of short-term obligation that it intends to refinance on a long-term basis. While not in agreement with the criteria that the Statement establishes, given those criteria, he sees no logical basis for denying their application to any short-term obligation, including those payables for which reclassification is ruled out by paragraph 8 of the Statement.

Members of the Financial Accounting Standards Board:

Marshall S. Armstrong, *Chairman*
Oscar S. Gellein
Donald J. Kirk
Arthur L. Litke
Robert E. Mays
Walter Scheutze
Robert T. Sprouse

Appendix A

BASIS FOR CONCLUSIONS

18. This Appendix discusses factors deemed significant by members of the Board in reaching the conclusions in this Statement. Individual Board members gave greater weight to some factors than to others. The Appendix also sets forth suggestions made by those responding to the Exposure Draft and reasons for accepting some and rejecting others.

SCOPE OF THIS STATEMENT

19. Some respondents indicated that the Exposure Draft appeared to require all enterprises to prepare a classified balance sheet regardless of normal industry practice or other justification for adopting a balance sheet format that does not identify current assets and current liabilities. The question of whether it is appropriate for an enterprise to present an unclassified balance sheet is beyond the scope of this Statement. Accordingly, paragraph 7 indicates that the standards established by this Statement

apply only if an enterprise is preparing a classified balance sheet.

20. The Board also concluded that it should not, as part of this project, re-examine the accounting concept of working capital described in detail in Chapter 3A of *ARB No. 43*. Paragraph 7 of Chapter 3A defines current liabilities as those whose liquidation "is reasonably expected to require the use of existing resources properly classified as current assets, or the creation of other current liabilities." That paragraph goes on to say that the current liabilities classification "is intended to include obligations for items which have entered into the operating cycle. . . . and debts which arise from operations directly related to the operating cycle. . . ." Accordingly, paragraph 8 of this Statement requires that short-term obligations arising from transactions in the normal course of business that are to be paid in customary terms shall be included in current liabilities. On the other hand, short-term obligations arising from the acquisition or construction of noncurrent assets would be excluded from current liabilities if the conditions in paragraphs 10 and 11 are met. Similarly, short-term obligations not directly related to the operating cycle—for example, a note given to a supplier to replace an account payable that originally arose in the normal course of business and had been due in customary terms—would be excluded if the conditions in paragraphs 10 and 11 are met. This Statement does not specify disclosures relating to short-term obligations that are *included* in current liabilities, although the Statement does make explicit that a total of current liabilities shall be presented in classified balance sheets (see paragraph 15).

BALANCE SHEET CLASSIFICATION

21. The alternative solutions considered by the Board with regard to the question of how to classify a short-term obligation that is expected to be refinanced on a long-term basis (see paragraph 2) ranged between:

a. A *strict maturity-date* approach under which all obligations scheduled to mature within one year (or, in certain cases, within an enterprise's operating cycle) would be classified as current liabilities regardless of any intention to refinance on a long-term basis.
b. An approach based *solely* on management's intention to seek refinancing on a long-term basis without requiring evidence of the enterprise's ability to do so.

22. The Board also considered alternatives within that range. Those alternatives all require that the *intent* of the enterprise to refinance a short-term obligation on a long-term basis be demonstrated by an *ability* to consummate the refinancing, but they differ in terms of the conditions required to demonstrate that ability.

23. The Board rejected a strict maturity-date approach because the scheduled maturity date of an obligation is not necessarily indicative of the point in time at which that obligation will require the use of the enterprise's funds. Inclusion of all short-term obligations within the current liability classification ignores the fact that enterprises, for sound economic reasons, often use commercial paper and other short-term debt instruments as means of long-term financing or that they often replace the currently maturing portion of long-term debt with other long-term debt. Borrowings under long-term revolving credit agreements and borrowings backed by long-term stand-by credit agreements are commonplace. A strict maturity-date approach would deny that these borrowings are sometimes, in substance, long-term financing. That approach would also result in a major change in the concept of current liabilities described in paragraph 7 of Chapter 3A of *ARB No. 43* as "obligations whose liquidation is reasonably expected to require the use of existing resources properly classifiable as current assets, or the creation of other current liabilities."

24. The Board also rejected classification based solely on an enterprise's intention to seek refinancing on a long-term basis. The Board concluded that intent, while essential, is insufficient to justify excluding a short-term obligation from current liabilities. The intent of an enterprise is an essential condition because without intent to refinance there is a presumption that liquidation of the short-term obligation would require the use of current assets or the creation of other current liabilities. The existence of a financing agreement, even one that requires that funds obtained thereunder be used to liquidate the short-term obligation, is irrelevant if the enterprise does not intend to refinance on a long-term basis. In the Board's judgment, however, intent alone does not provide sufficiently objective evidence to overcome the presumption that a short-term obligation will require the use of funds at its scheduled maturity date. The intent must be supported by a demonstrated ability to carry out that intent.

25. The two conditions set forth in this Statement for exclusion of a short-term obligation from current liabilities—intent and ability—are essentially the same as the requirements proposed in the Exposure Draft. That draft had proposed that a short-term obligation be classified as a current liability unless all of the following conditions were met:

a. The borrower has a noncancelable binding agreement to refinance the obligation from a source reasonably expected to be financially capable of honoring the agreement.

b. The maturity date of the new obligation expected to be incurred by the borrower as a result of the refinancing under the agreement will be more than one year from the date of the financial statements.
c. The borrower intends to exercise its rights under the agreement.

26. Many respondents to the Exposure Draft indicated that the requirement of a "noncancelable binding agreement" was unrealistic because lenders generally do not make unqualified commitments. Financing agreements often include provisions that could restrict borrowing under the agreement. As indicated by the conditions in paragraphs 11(b)(i) and 11(b)(ii) of this Statement, the inclusion of a restrictive covenant, representation, warranty, or other provision in a financing agreement does not prevent a short-term obligation from being excluded from current liabilities provided that compliance with the provision can be objectively determined or measured and provided that there is no evidence of a violation for which a waiver has not been obtained. In the Board's view, inability to objectively determine or measure compliance, or the existence of a violation of a provision for which a waiver has not been obtained, raises a serious doubt about the enterprise's ability to consummate an intended refinancing to avoid the use of working capital and, consequently, requires classification of the short-term obligation as a current liability. The existence of a situation that permits the lender to cancel the agreement or otherwise to prevent the enterprise from exercising its rights thereunder after expiration of a grace period or after notice to the enterprise or both is also considered a violation of a provision that will, in the absence of a waiver, require classification of the short-term obligation as a current liability.

27. The Board has concluded that exclusion of a short-term obligation from current liabilities should not be precluded as long as the financing agreement *clearly permits* the enterprise to replace the short-term obligation with a long-term obligation or with equity securities or to renew, extend, or replace the short-term obligation with another short-term obligation for an uninterrupted period extending beyond one year (or operating cycle). The Board considered and rejected the proposal that a short-term obligation should be excluded from current liabilities only if a financing agreement is *specifically linked* to the short-term obligation, either by specifically permitting or requiring that funds obtained thereunder be used to liquidate the short-term obligation. In the Board's judgment, that proposal places undue emphasis on the form of an agreement rather than on its substance. It is neither practicable nor realistic to trace specific funds to their ultimate use. The financial position of an enterprise that has refinanced under a linked agreement will be indistinguishable from the financial position of an enterprise that has entered into the same transactions under an agreement that is not linked but clearly permits refinancing the short-term obligation. Moreover, whether or not a financing agreement is specifically linked to a particular short-term obligation, the enterprise is not precluded from issuing another short-term obligation at approximately the same time as the old obligation is refinanced under the agreement. The potential effect of such a transaction can be avoided only if a strict maturity-date approach is adopted, but the Board rejected that alternative for the reasons stated in paragraph 23. The Board believes that the requirement in paragraph 10 that the enterprise intend to refinance on a long-term basis and thus not to use working capital to repay the maturing short-term obligation more closely comports with the spirit of this Statement and Chapter 3A of *ARB No. 43* than would a requirement for specific linkage.

28. Respondents to the Exposure Draft indicated that many enterprises enter into agreements that assure their ability to refinance short-term obligations although they might not intend to exercise their rights under the agreement if an alternative source of financing becomes available. One of the conditions in the Exposure Draft was that the enterprise intend to exercise its rights under the agreement (see paragraph 25(c)). A footnote in the Exposure Draft indicated that this condition would be met if the enterprise intended to exercise its rights under the agreement when the short-term obligations could not continue to be refinanced on a short-term basis. Respondents asked the Board to clarify the intent of the condition in the Exposure Draft and the related footnote. The Board believes that the justification for excluding a short-term obligation from current liabilities is not negated simply because an enterprise may intend to seek a more advantageous source of financing (including, perhaps, short-term financing) than that provided under the financing agreement in existence when the balance sheet is issued.However, the condition in paragraph 11(b)(i) requires that the agreement extend beyond one year (or operating cycle) from the date of the enterprise's balance sheet to demonstrate clearly the enterprise's ability to avoid using working capital to repay the short-term obligation. Moreover, paragraph 13 requires that the enterprise intend to exercise its rights under the agreement if another source of financing does not become available.

29. A number of respondents to the Exposure Draft asked whether events occurring after the date

of the balance sheet but before the balance sheet is issued should be considered in assessing an enterprise's ability to consummate the refinancing of a short-term obligation on a long-term basis. In particular, the two types of post-balance-sheet-date events cited were (a) actual issuance of a long-term obligation or equity securities for the purpose of refinancing the short-term obligation on a long-term basis and (b) entering into a financing agreement after the balance-sheet date but before the balance sheet is issued. In the Board's judgment, both of those types of post-balance-sheet-date events should be considered in determining liability classification and in assessing an enterprise's ability to consummate an intended refinancing, and they are explicitly provided for in paragraphs 11(a) and 11(b).

30. Several respondents to the Exposure Draft asked whether a short-term obligation could be excluded from current liabilities if it is intended to be replaced (or, in fact, has been replaced after the balance sheet date) by issuing equity securities. A short-term obligation will not require the use of working capital regardless of whether refinancing on a long-term basis is accomplished by issuing debt securities or equity securities. Accordingly, *refinancing on a long-term basis* is defined in paragraph 2 to include issuance of equity securities, and a short-term obligation intended to be refinanced in that manner would be excluded from current liabilities if the conditions in paragraphs 10 and 11 are met. Although it is appropriate to exclude the short-term obligation from current liabilities when those conditions are met, the Board concluded that it is not appropriate to include the short-term obligation in owners' equity (see footnote 2 to paragraph 11(a)). The intent of an enterprise to refinance a short-term obligation on a long-term basis and its ability to do so relate to the question of whether the obligation is expected to require the use of working capital, not whether it is a liability. The obligation is a liability and not owners' equity at the date of the balance sheet.

EFFECTIVE DATE AND TRANSITION

31. Many respondents opposed the proposal in the Exposure Draft that balance sheets for dates prior to the effective date of the Statement be restated to conform to the provisions of the Statement. They indicated that restatement would not achieve comparability of balance sheets for dates prior to the effective date of the Statement with balance sheets for subsequent dates because of the new conditions established by paragraph 11. After considering all of the circumstances, the Board concluded that prospective application of this Statement is appropriate, with restatement permitted but not required, and that the effective date in paragraph 17 is advisable.

Appendix B

EXAMPLES OF APPLICATION OF THIS STATEMENT

32. The following examples provide guidance for applying this Statement. It should be recognized that these examples do not comprehend all possible circumstances and do not include all the disclosures that would typically be made regarding long-term debt or current liabilities.

GENERAL ASSUMPTIONS

33. The assumptions on which the examples are based are:

a. ABC Company's fiscal year end is December 31, 19x5.
b. The date of issuance of the December 31, 19x5 financial statements is March 31, 19x6; the Company's practice is to issue a classified balance sheet.
c. At December 31, 19x5, short-term obligations include $5,000,000 representing the portion of 6% long-term debt maturing in February 19x6 and $3,000,000 of 9% notes payable issued in November 19x5 and maturing in July 19x6.
d. The Company intends to refinance on a long-term basis both the current maturity of long-term debt and the 9% notes payable.
e. Accounts other than the long-term debt maturing in February 19x6 and the notes payable maturing in July 19x6 are:

Current assets	$30,000,000
Other assets	$50,000,000
Accounts payable and accruals	$10,000,000
Other long-term debt	$25,000,000
Shareholders' equity	$37,000,000

f. Unless otherwise indicated, the examples also assume that the lender or prospective lender is expected to be capable of honoring the agreement, that there is no evidence of a violation of any provision, and that the terms of borrowings available under the agreement are readily determinable.

EXAMPLE 1

34. The Company negotiates a financing agreement with a commercial bank in December 19x5 for a maximum borrowing of $8,000,000 at any time through 19x7 with the following terms:

a. Borrowings are available at ABC Company's request for such purposes as it deems appropriate and will mature three years from the date of borrowing.
b. Amounts borrowed will bear interest at the bank's prime rate.
c. An annual commitment fee of 1/2 of 1% is payable on the difference between the amount borrowed and $8,000,000.
d. The agreement is cancelable by the lender only if:
   (i) The Company's working capital, excluding borrowings under the agreement, falls below $10,000,000.
   (ii) The Company becomes obligated under lease agreements to pay an annual rental in excess of $1,000,000.
   (iii) Treasury stock is acquired without the prior approval of the prospective lender.
   (iv) The Company guarantees indebtedness of unaffiliated persons in excess of $500,000.

35. The enterprise's intention to refinance meets the condition specified by paragraph 10. Compliance with the provisions listed in paragraph 34(d) is objectively determinable or measurable; therefore, the condition specified by paragraph 11(b)(i) is met. The proceeds of borrowings under the agreement are clearly available for the liquidation of the 9% notes payable and the long-term debt maturing in February 19x6. Both obligations, therefore, would be classified as other than current liabilities.

36. Following are the liability section of ABC Company's balance sheet at December 31, 19x5 and the related footnote disclosures required by this Statement, based on the information in paragraphs 33 and 34. Because the balance sheet is issued subsequent to the February 19x6 maturity of the long-term debt, the footnote describes the refinancing of that obligation.

	December 31, 19x5
Current Liabilities:	
Accounts payable and accruals	$10,000,000
Total Current Liabilities	10,000,000
Long-Term Debt:	
9% notes payable (Note A)	3,000,000*
6% debt due February 19x6 (Note A)	5,000,000*
Other long-term debt	25,000,000
Total Long-Term Debt	33,000,000
Total Liabilities	$43,000,000

Note A

The Company has entered into a financing agreement with a commercial bank that permits the Company to borrow at any time through 19x7 up to $8,000,000 at the bank's prime rate of interest. The Company must pay an annual commitment fee of 1/2 of 1% of the unused portion of the commitment. Borrowings under the financing agreement mature three years after the date of the loan. Among other things, the agreement prohibits the acquisition of treasury stock without prior approval by the bank, requires maintenance of working capital of $10,000,000 exclusive of borrowings under the agreement, and limits the annual rental under lease agreements to $1,000,000. In February 19x6, the Company borrowed $5,000,000 at 8% and liquidated the 6% long-term debt, and it intends to borrow additional funds available under the agreement to refinance the 9% notes payable maturing in July 19x6.

EXAMPLE 2

37. A foreign subsidiary of the enterprise negotiates a financing agreement with its local bank in December 19x5. Funds are available to the subsidiary for its unrestricted use, including loans to affiliated companies; other terms are identical to those cited in paragraph 34. Local laws prohibit the transfer of funds outside the country.

38. The requirement of paragraph 11(b)(i) is met because compliance with the provisions of the agreement is objectively determinable or measurable. Because of the laws prohibiting the transfer of funds, however, the proceeds from borrowings under the agreement are not available for liquidation of the debt maturing in February and July 19x6. Accordingly, both the 6% debt maturing in February 19x6 and the 9% notes payable maturing in July 19x6 would be classified as current liabilities.

*These obligations may also be shown in captions distinct from both current liabilities and long-term debt, such as "Interim Debt," "Short-Term Debt Expected to Be Refinanced," and "Intermediate Debt."

EXAMPLE 3

39. Assume that instead of utilizing the agreement cited in paragraph 34, the Company issues $8,000,000 of ten-year debentures to the public in January 19x6. The Company intends to use the proceeds to liquidate the $5,000,000 debt maturing February 19x6 and the $3,000,000 of 9% notes payable maturing July 19x6. In addition, assume the debt maturing February 19x6 is paid prior to the issuance of the balance sheet, and the remaining proceeds from the sale of debentures are invested in a U.S. Treasury note maturing the same day as the 9% notes payable.

40. Since the Company refinanced the long-term debt maturing in February 19x6 in a manner that meets the conditions set forth in paragraph 11 of this Statement, that obligation would be excluded from current liabilities. In addition, the 9% notes payable maturing in July 19x6 would also be excluded because the Company has obtained funds expressly intended to be used to liquidate those notes and not intended to be used in current operations. In balance sheets after the date of sale of the debentures and before the maturity date of the notes payable, the Company would exclude the notes payable from current liabilities if the U.S. Treasury note is excluded from current assets (see paragraph 6 of Chapter 3A of *ARB No. 43,* which is not altered by this Statement).

41. If the debentures had been sold prior to January 1, 19x6, the $8,000,000 of obligations to be paid would be excluded from current liabilities in the balance sheet at that date if the $8,000,000 in funds were excluded from current assets.

42. If, instead of issuing the ten-year debentures, the Company had issued $8,000,000 of equity securities and all other facts in this example remained unchanged, both the 6% debt due February 19x6 and the 9% notes payable due July 19x6 would be classified as liabilities other than current liabilities, such as "Indebtedness Due in 19x6 Refinanced in January 19x6."

EXAMPLE 4

43. In December 19x5 the Company negotiates a revolving credit agreement providing for unrestricted borrowings up to $10,000,000. Borrowings will bear interest at 1% over the prevailing prime rate of the bank with which the agreement is arranged but in any event not less than 8%, will have stated maturities of ninety days, and will be continuously renewable for ninety-day periods at the Company's option for three years provided there is compliance with the terms of the agreement. Provisions of the agreement are similar to those cited in paragraph 34(d). Further, the enterprise intends to renew obligations incurred under the agreement for a period extending beyond one year from the balance-sheet date. There are no outstanding borrowings under the agreement at December 31, 19x5.

44. In this instance, the long-term debt maturing in February 19x6 and the 9% notes payable maturing in July 19x6 would be excluded from current liabilities because the Company consummated a financing agreement meeting the conditions set forth in paragraph 11(b) prior to the issuance of the balance sheet.

EXAMPLE 5

45. Assume that the agreement cited in Example 4 included an additional provision limiting the amount to be borrowed by the Company to the amount of its inventory, which is pledged as collateral and is expected to range between a high of $8,000,000 during the second quarter of 19x6 and a low of $4,000,000 during the fourth quarter of 19x6.

46. The terms of the agreement comply with the conditions required by this Statement; however, because the minimum amount expected to be available from February to December 19x6 is $4,000,000, only that amount of short-term obligations can be excluded from current liabilities (see paragraph 12). Whether the obligation to be excluded is a portion of the currently maturing long-term debt or some portions of both it and the 9% notes payable depends on the intended timing of the borrowing.

47. If the Company intended to refinance only the 9% notes payable due July 19x6 and the amount of its inventory is expected to reach a low of approximately $2,000,000 during the second quarter of 19x6 but be at least $3,000,000 in July 19x6 and thereafter during 19x6, the $3,000,000 9% notes payable would be excluded from current liabilities at December 31, 19x5 (see paragraph 12).

EXAMPLE 6

48. In lieu of the facts given in paragraphs 33(c) and 33(d), assume that during 19x5 the Company entered into a contract to have a warehouse built. The warehouse is expected to be financed by issuance of the Company's commercial paper. In addition, the Company negotiated a stand-by agreement with a commercial bank that provides for maximum borrowings equal to the expected cost of the warehouse, which will be pledged as collateral.

The agreement also requires that the proceeds from the sale of commercial paper be used to pay construction costs. Borrowings may be made under the agreement only if the Company is unable to issue new commercial paper. The proceeds of borrowings must be used to retire outstanding commercial paper and to liquidate additional liabilities incurred in the construction of the warehouse. At December 31, 19x5 the Company has $7,000,000 of commercial paper outstanding and $1,000,000 of unpaid construction costs resulting from a progress billing through December 31.

49. Because the commercial paper will be refinanced on a long-term basis, either by uninterrupted renewal or, failing that, by a borrowing under the agreement, the commercial paper would be excluded from current liabilities. The $1,000,000 liability for the unpaid progress billing results from the construction of a noncurrent asset and will be refinanced on the same basis as the commercial paper and, therefore, it would also be excluded from current liabilities (see paragraphs 8 and 20).

EXAMPLE 7

50. Following are two methods of presenting liabilities in ABC Company's balance sheet at December 31, 19x5 assuming the Company intends to refinance the 6% debt maturing in February 19x6 and the 9% notes payable maturing in July 19x6 but has not met the conditions required by this Statement to exclude those obligations from current liabilities.

Alternative 1

	December 31, 19x5
Current Liabilities:	
Accounts payable and accruals	$10,000,000
Notes payable, due July 19x6	3,000,000
6% debt due February 19x6	5,000,000
Total Current Liabilities	18,000,000
Long-Term Debt	25,000,000
Total Liabilities	$43,000,000

Alternative 2

		December 31, 19x5
Current Liabilities:		
Accounts payable and accruals		$10,000,000
Short-term debt expected to be refinanced:		
Notes payable, due July 19x6	$3,000,000	
6% debt due February 19x6	5,000,000	8,000,000
Total Current Liabilities		18,000,000
Long-Term Debt		25,000,000
Total Liabilities		$43,000,000

Statement of Financial Accounting Standards No. 7 Accounting and Reporting by Development Stage Enterprises

STATUS

Issued: June 1975

Effective Date: For fiscal periods beginning on or after January 1, 1976

Affects: Supersedes FIN 5

Affected by: Paragraph 5 amended by FAS 71

Statement of Financial Accounting Standards No. 7
Accounting and Reporting by Development Stage Enterprises

CONTENTS

INTRODUCTION

1. This Statement specifies the guidelines for identifying an enterprise in the development stage and the standards of financial accounting and reporting applicable to such an enterprise. The transition requirements of this Statement are also applicable to certain established operating enterprises.[1]

2. Some development stage enterprises have adopted special financial accounting and reporting practices, including special forms of financial statement presentation or types of disclosure, that are different from those used by established operating enterprises. Some of the special practices have resulted from applying regulations of the Securities and Exchange Commission; other practices appear simply to have evolved. Special accounting practices have included (a) deferral of all types of costs without regard to their recoverability, (b) nonassignment of dollar amounts to shares of stock issued for consideration other than cash, and (c) offset of revenue against deferred costs. Special reporting formats have included statements of (a) assets and unrecovered preoperating costs, (b) liabilities, (c) capital shares, and (d) cash receipts and disbursements. Sometimes, a balance sheet or a statement of operations is presented in conjunction with one or more special formats. Other development stage enterprises issue financial statements like those of established operating enterprises that present financial position, changes in financial position, and results of operations in conformity with generally accepted accounting principles.

3. No special standards of financial accounting and reporting were established for development stage enterprises by the AICPA Accounting Principles Board or its predecessor, the Committee on Accounting Procedure. In 1973, the AICPA Committee on Companies in the Development Stage issued an exposure draft of a proposed Audit Guide recommending special financial statements and accounting methods, but no action was taken on the exposure draft and the matter was referred to the FASB. *FASB Statement No. 2,* "Accounting for Research and Development Costs," issued in October 1974, has been interpreted by the FASB to apply to "the accounting for research and development costs of development stage enterprises whose financial statements present financial position, changes in financial position, or results of operations in conformity with generally accepted accounting principles."[2] However, pending the issuance of a Statement on the subject of accounting and reporting by development stage enterprises, the FASB Interpretation stated that "a development stage enterprise that issues financial statements that do not purport to present financial position, changes in financial position, or results of operations in conformity with generally accepted accounting principles need not apply *Statement No. 2* in accounting for its research and development costs."[3]

4. The standards of financial accounting and reporting set forth in this Statement apply to any separate financial statements of a development stage subsidiary or other investee[4] of an established operating enterprise, as well as to the financial statements of a separate development stage enterprise (or of a group of companies that, as a whole, is considered to be in the development stage). Hereinafter, the term "development stage enterprise" is used to include a development stage subsidiary or other investee that is issuing separate financial statements.

5. This Statement applies to development stage enterprises in all industries. This Statement applies

[1]See paragraphs 14-16.

[2]*FASB Interpretation No. 5,* "Applicability of FASB Statement No. 2 to Development Stage Enterprises," para. 6.

[3]Ibid., para. 7.

[4]The terms *subsidiary* and *investee* are defined in paragraph 3 of *APB Opinion No. 18,* "The Equity Method of Accounting for Investments in Common Stock."

to development stage enterprises in regulated industries in accordance with the provisions of the Addendum to *APB Opinion No. 2,* "Accounting for the 'Investment Credit.'" However, paragraphs 11-12 of this Statement, which require disclosure of additional information, apply to development stage enterprises in regulated industries in all cases.

6. This Statement supersedes *FASB Interpretation No. 5,* "Applicability of FASB Statement No. 2 to Development Stage Enterprises." It does not supersede, alter, or amend any other present requirement in an Accounting Research Bulletin (ARB), Accounting Principles Board (APB) Opinion, or FASB Statement or Interpretation. Neither does this Statement change generally accepted accounting principles that are currently applicable to established operating enterprises but that are not explicitly stated in an ARB, APB Opinion, or FASB Statement or Interpretation. For example, this Statement does not change generally accepted accounting principles applicable to (a) established operating enterprises generally in expanding their existing businesses, (b) established operating enterprises in the extractive industries in their exploration and development activities, and (c) established operating enterprises in the real estate industry in developing their properties.

7. Standards of financial accounting and reporting for development stage enterprises are set forth in paragraphs 8-16. Appendix B sets forth the basis for the Board's conclusions, including alternatives considered and reasons for accepting some and rejecting others. Appendix A provides background information.

STANDARDS OF FINANCIAL ACCOUNTING AND REPORTING

Guidelines for Identifying a Development Stage Enterprise

8. For purposes of this Statement, an enterprise shall be considered to be in the development stage if it is devoting substantially all of its efforts to establishing a new business and either of the following conditions exists:

a. Planned principal operations have not commenced.
b. Planned principal operations have commenced, but there has been no siginficant revenue therefrom.

9. A development stage enterprise will typically be devoting most of its efforts to activities such as financial planning; raising capital; exploring for natural resources; developing natural resources; research and development;[5] establishing sources of supply; acquiring property, plant, equipment, or other operating assets, such as mineral rights; recruiting and training personnel; developing markets; and starting up production.

Financial Accounting and Reporting

10. Financial statements issued by a development stage enterprise shall present financial position, changes in financial position, and results of operations in conformity with the generally accepted accounting principles that apply to established operating enterprises and shall include the additional information required by paragraphs 11-12. Special accounting practices and reporting formats, such as those described in paragraph 2 of this Statement, that are based on a distinctive accounting for development stage enterprises are no longer acceptable. Generally accepted accounting principles that apply to established operating enterprises shall govern the recognition of revenue by a development stage enterprise and shall determine whether a cost incurred by a development stage enterprise is to be charged to expense when incurred or is to be capitalized or deferred. Accordingly, capitalization or deferral of costs shall be subject to the same assessment of recoverability that would be applicable in an established operating enterprise. For a development stage subsidiary or other investee, the recoverability of costs shall be assessed within the entity for which separate financial statements are being presented.

11. In issuing the same basic financial statements as an established operating enterprise, a development stage enterprise shall disclose therein certain additional information. The basic financial statements to be presented[6] and the additional information shall include the following:

a. A balance sheet, including any cumulative net losses reported with a descriptive caption such as "deficit accumulated during the development stage" in the stockholders' equity section.
b. An income statement, showing amounts of revenue and expenses for each period covered by the income statement and, in addition, cumulative amounts from the enterprise's inception.[7]
c. A statement of changes in financial position,

---

[5]*Research and development* is defined in paragraph 8 of *FASB Statement No. 2,* "Accounting for Research and Development Costs."

[6]Under some circumstances, an established operating enterprise may issue less than a full set of financial statements, for example, only a balance sheet. This Statement does not preclude that possibility for development stage enterprises. Also, different titles or formats used by some established operating enterprises may be used provided that the prescribed information is included.

[7]For a dormant enterprise that is reactivated to undertake development stage activities, the disclosure of cumulative amounts required by this paragraph shall be from inception of the development stage.

showing the sources and uses of financial resources for each period for which an income statement is presented[8] and, in addition, cumulative amounts from the enterprise's inception.

d. A statement of stockholders' equity, showing from the enterprise's inception:[9]
   1. For each issuance, the date and number of shares of stock, warrants, rights, or other equity securities issued for cash and for other consideration.
   2. For each issuance, the dollar amounts (per share or other equity unit and in total) assigned to the consideration received for shares of stock, warrants, rights, or other equity securities. Dollar amounts shall be assigned to any noncash consideration received.
   3. For each issuance involving noncash consideration, the nature of the noncash consideration and the basis for assigning amounts.

12. The financial statements shall be identified as those of a development stage enterprise and shall include a description of the nature of the development stage activities in which the enterprise is engaged.

13. The financial statements for the first fiscal year in which an enterprise is no longer considered to be in the development stage shall disclose that in prior years it had been in the development stage. If financial statements for prior years are presented for comparative purposes, the cumulative amounts and other additional disclosures required by paragraphs 11-12 need not be shown.

Effective Date and Transition

14. This Statement shall be effective for fiscal periods beginning on or after January 1, 1976, although earlier application is encouraged. Thereafter, when financial statements, or financial summaries or other data derived therefrom, are presented for periods prior to the effective date of this Statement, they shall be restated, where necessary, to conform to the provisions of this Statement. Accordingly, any items that would have been accounted for differently by a development stage enterprise if the provisions of paragraph 10 had then been applicable shall be accounted for by prior period adjustment (described in paragraphs 18 and 26 of *APB Opinion No. 9,* "Reporting the Results of Operations").

15. An established operating enterprise that during its development stage would have accounted for any items differently if the provisions of paragraph 10 had then been applicable shall account for those items by prior period adjustment. In some cases, those items will have been amortized or otherwise included in an income statement in periods prior to the effective date of this Statement. Financial statements, or financial summaries or other data derived therefrom, for those periods shall be restated when they are included for comparative purposes with financial data for periods after the effective date of this Statement.

16. The nature of any adjustment or restatement resulting from application of paragraphs 14-15 and, where appropriate, its effect on income before extraordinary items, net income, and related per share amounts shall be disclosed in the period of change for all periods presented. Any related income tax effects shall be recognized and disclosed.

The provisions of this Statement need not be applied to immaterial items.

This Statement was adopted by the affirmative votes of six members of the Financial Accounting Standards Board. Mr. Schuetze dissented.

Although he agrees with the basic conclusions in this Statement that development stage enterprises should use the same accounting principles and prepare the same basic financial statements as established operating enterprises, Mr. Schuetze dissents because he believes that the Board should have addressed the question of accounting for start-up costs before issuing this Statement. Paragraph 10 states that "capitalization or deferral of costs [in a development stage enterprise] shall be subject to the same assessment of recoverability that would be applicable in an established operating enterprise." A substantial portion of the costs incurred by many development stage enterprises falls into the broad category that most persons would regard as start-up costs. In Mr. Schuetze's view, neither this Statement

[8]Subject to the exceptions described in paragraphs 7 and 16 of *APB Opinion No. 19,* "Reporting Changes in Financial Position."

[9]Separate issuances of equity securities within the same fiscal year for the same type of consideration and for the same amount per equity unit may be combined in the statement of stockholders' equity. Appropriate modification of the statement of stockholders' equity may be required for (a) a combined group of companies that, as a whole, is considered to be in the development stage and (b) in unincorporated development stage enterprise.

nor any other authoritative pronouncement furnishes adequate guidance as to how the recoverability of start-up costs should be assessed or as to how those start-up costs that are capitalized or deferred should be accounted for thereafter. Mr. Schuetze believes that until such a pronouncement is issued the accounting practices of development stage enterprises will vary significantly. In this regard, Mr. Schuetze is particularly concerned as to how the recoverability test in paragraph 10 would be applied by development stage enterprises in the extractive industries.

Members of the Financial Accounting Standards Board:

Marshall S. Armstrong, *Chairman*
Oscar S. Gellein
Donald J. Kirk
Arthur L. Litke
Robert E. Mays
Walter Schuetze
Robert T. Sprouse

Appendix A

BACKGROUND INFORMATION

17. In April 1973, the FASB placed on its technical agenda a project on "Accounting for Research and Development and Similar Costs." The scope of the project also encompassed accounting and reporting by development stage enterprises, the subject of this Statement.

18. A task force of sixteen persons from industry, government, public accounting, the financial community, and academe was appointed in July 1973 to provide counsel to the Board in preparing a Discussion Memorandum analyzing issues related to the project.

19. The FASB did not undertake a major research effort in connection with the project but rather relied primarily on published research studies and articles that are cited in the Discussion Memorandum. Especially important in this regard was *Accounting for Companies in the Development Stage,* an exposure draft of an Audit Guide originally issued for comment in 1973 by the Committee on Companies in the Development Stage of the American Institute of Certified Public Accountants.

20. The Discussion Memorandum was issued by the Board on December 28, 1973, and a public hearing on the subject was held on March 15, 1974. Seventy-four position papers, letters of comment, and outlines of oral presentations were received by the Board in response to the Discussion Memorandum. Thirty-nine of those responses included recommendations about development stage enterprises. Fourteen oral presentations were made at the public hearing.

21. In the course of its deliberations following the hearing, the Board concluded that accounting and reporting by development stage enterprises should be addressed in a separate Statement of Financial Accounting Standards. An Exposure Draft of a proposed Statement on "Accounting and Reporting by Development Stage Companies, Subsidiaries, Divisions and Other Components" was issued on July 19, 1974. The Board received 138 letters of comment on the Exposure Draft. In November 1974, the Board announced that "because of questions raised in many of the comment letters received during exposure of the proposed Statement on development stage companies, the Standards Board is continuing its consideration of that subject and a final Statement is not expected to be issued before April or May of 1975."[10]

Appendix B

BASIS FOR CONCLUSIONS

22. This Appendix discusses factors deemed significant by members of the Board in reaching the conclusions in this Statement, including various alternatives considered and reasons for accepting some and rejecting others.

SCOPE OF THIS STATEMENT

23. As indicated by the title, the Exposure Draft, "Accounting and Reporting by Development Stage Companies, Subsidiaries, Divisions and Other Components," explicitly encompassed a development stage subsidiary, division, or other component of an established operating enterprise as well as a separate development stage enterprise. A number of respondents to the Exposure Draft interpreted the inclusion of subsidiaries, divisions, or other components of an established operating enterprise to mean that new financial accounting standards were being proposed for the costs incurred by established operating enterprises in expanding their existing businesses. Those respondents suggested that any changes called for by the proposed new standards in

[10] *FASB Status Report,* No. 19, November 16, 1974.

that regard were unclear. They further suggested that the proposed new standards for financial statement presentation and disclosure were inapplicable to components of established operating enterprises except as they might apply to separate financial statements occasionally issued by subsidiaries in the development stage.

24. In addition to accounting for research and development costs and accounting for development stage enterprises, the Discussion Memorandum comprehended accounting for start-up costs and other costs that are similar to research and development costs in the sense that they share certain distinguishing characteristics.[11] In issuing the Exposure Draft, however, the Board did not intend to propose new financial accounting standards for start-up costs and those other "similar costs" incurred by established operating enterprises. To eliminate that possible source of confusion and to deal more directly with the financial accounting and reporting matters affecting development stage enterprises, the scope of this Statement is restricted to the financial statements of a development stage enterprise (or of a group of companies that, as a whole, is considered to be in the development stage) and to any separate financial statements of a development stage subsidiary or other investee of an established operating enterprise (see paragraph 4).

Development Stage Enterprises in the Extractive Industries

25. A number of respondents to the Exposure Draft questioned the application of this Statement to development stage enterprises in certain industries (see paragraph 5 of this Statement), especially to development stage enterprises in the extractive industries. The Discussion Memorandum made a distinction for the extractive industries between (1) costs that are indistinguishable in nature from those costs incurred in other industries and (2) costs that are incurred uniquely in the extractive industries. It stated that "research and development and similar costs that are indistinguishable in nature from the research and development and similar costs incurred in other industries are embraced by this project." The Discussion Memorandum also stated that costs that are incurred uniquely in the extractive industries are generally believed to warrant separate consideration and "are specifically outside the scope of this project."[12] *FASB Statement No. 2,* "Accounting for Research and Development Costs," in paragraph 3, recognized that distinction by indicating that it "does not apply to activities that are unique to enterprises in the extractive industries."

26. Chapter four, "Companies in the Development Stage," of the Discussion Memorandum states that "this Discussion Memorandum excludes from this project only those 'costs that are incurred uniquely in the extractive industries.' Therefore, whether extractive industry companies in the development stage have sufficiently different characteristics to warrant exclusion from or special handling in a definition of a company in the development stage requires consideration."[13]

27. The AICPA Committee on Companies in the Development Stage indicated in its 1973 exposure draft that the proposed provisions should be applicable to any development stage enterprise in any industry. Similarly, the APB Committee on Extractive Industries states, "new companies still in the exploratory and development stage in the oil and gas industry are no different than companies in a similar stage in other industries and probably should not be afforded any special treatment."[14]

28. The Board has concluded that consideration of the accounting for costs incurred in activities that are unique to enterprises in the extractive industries is outside the scope of this Statement. Paragraph 6 explains that this Statement does not change generally accepted accounting principles that are applicable to established operating enterprises but that are not explicitly stated in an ARB, APB Opinion, or FASB Statement or Interpretation, and cites as an example generally accepted accounting principles that are applicable to established operating enterprises in the extractive industries in their exploration and development activities. The effect of this Statement being applicable to development stage enterprises in all industries, therefore, is not to change the generally accepted accounting principles applicable to costs incurred in activities that are unique to enterprises in the extractive industries, but to require those generally accepted accounting principles applicable to established operating enterprises in the extractive industries to be applied to development stage enterprises in the extractive industries as well. This includes presentation of the same basic financial statements.

GUIDELINES FOR IDENTIFYING A DEVELOPMENT STAGE ENTERPRISE

29. The broad guidelines set forth in paragraphs 8-9

[11] *FASB Discussion Memorandum,* "Accounting for Research and Development and Similar Costs," pp. 2-5.

[12] Ibid., pp. 8-9.

[13] Ibid., p. 55.

[14] American Institute of Certified Public Accountants, Accounting Principles Board Committee on Extractive Industries, *Accounting and Reporting Practices in the Oil and Gas Industry* (New York: AICPA, May 31, 1973), p. 24.

for identifying a development stage enterprise are designed to include enterprises engaged in diverse areas of economic activity. The point at which an enterprise ceases to be in the development stage, and, therefore, need not present the cumulative amounts since its inception and other additional disclosures required by paragraphs 11-12, must be evaluated in each case.

ACCOUNTING

30. The Board has concluded that the generally accepted accounting principles that apply to established operating enterprises shall govern the recognition of revenue by a development stage enterprise and shall determine whether a cost incurred by a development stage enterprise is to be charged to expense when incurred or is to be capitalized or deferred. The primary reasons for this conclusion are:

a. The kinds of transactions engaged in by development stage enterprises are also common to established operating enterprises in expanding their existing businesses. Accounting treatment should be governed by the nature of the transaction rather than by the degree of maturity of the enterprise. Thus, the determination of whether a particular cost should be charged to expense when incurred or should be capitalized or deferred should be based on the same accounting standards regardless of whether the enterprise incurring the cost is already operating or is in the development stage.
b. Any different standards for a development stage enterprise that would result in deferral of costs that would not be deferred if the generally accepted accounting principles applicable to established operating enterprises had been applied may cause financial statement users to reach unjustified conclusions about the nature of the costs incurred by a development stage enterprise. The Board believes that adequate financial statement disclosures concerning the costs incurred by a development stage enterprise, both for the current period and cumulatively since its inception, will mitigate that possibility and provide useful financial information for decisions about that kind of enterprise.

31. Established operating enterprises incur costs under various circumstances and with varying degrees of uncertainty about future benefits, especially in expanding their existing businesses. Authoritative accounting literature does not contain general criteria or guidelines for determining when costs should be charged to expense as incurred and when costs should be capitalized or deferred,[15] and this Statement does not attempt to specify such criteria or guidelines.

32. The absence of explicit criteria or guidelines, however, does not provide a free choice to defer costs or to charge them to expense when incurred. The scope of generally accepted accounting principles is broader than the authoritative literature and encompass practices that have evolved and gained acceptance with time and experience. Many of those practices are described in *APB Statement No. 4,* "Basic Concepts and Accounting Principles Underlying Financial Statements of Business Enterprises." For example, paragraph 160 of *APB Statement No. 4* describes generally accepted accounting principles as calling for immediate recognition as expense when "(1) costs incurred during the period provide no discernible future benefits, (2) costs recorded as assets in prior periods no longer provide discernible benefits or (3) allocating costs either on the basis of association with revenue or among several accounting periods is considered to serve no useful purpose."[16]

33. In concluding that the generally accepted accounting principles applicable to established operating enterprises shall determine whether a cost incurred by a development stage enterprise is to be charged to expense when incurred or is to be capitalized or deferred, the Board is relying primarily on the assessment of recoverability of incurred costs that those principles require. Heretofore, some have felt that generally accepted accounting principles did not apply to the special accounting practices and special financial reporting formats that have been used by some development stage enterprises. The Board's conclusion that the generally accepted accounting principles applicable to established operating enterprises also apply to development stage enterprises, including presentation of the same basic financial statements, eliminates the special practices and formats and the question about the

---

[15]Guidance is provided for some specific situations. For example, *FASB Statement No. 2* prescribes that the research and development costs encompassed by that Statement shall be charged to expense when incurred and describes the considerations that led to that conclusion. Also, AICPA Industry Audit Guides provide guidance about accounting for costs incurred by enterprises in particular industries. Although Audit Guides do not constitute authoritative accounting literature, those issued in recent years state that members of the AICPA may be called upon to justify departures from the recommendations contained therein.

[16]*APB Statement No. 4,* in paragraph 4, describes its status as follows: "The accounting principles described are those that the [Accounting Principles Board] believes are generally accepted today. The Board has not evaluated or approved present generally accepted accounting principles except to the extent that principles have been adopted in Board Opinions. Publication of this Statement does not constitute approval by the Board of accounting principles that are not covered in its Opinions."

applicability of generally accepted accounting principles to them.

SEC Regulations and AICPA Committee Proposal

34. Both the regulations of the Securities and Exchange Commission (SEC) and the proposed Audit Guide issued by the AICPA Committee on Companies in the Development Stage provide for the use by development stage enterprises of certain accounting practices that differ from those appropriate for established operating enterprises.

35. Article 5A of SEC *Regulation S-X* prescribes the form and content of financial statements filed with the SEC by development stage enterprises. It provides for separate statements of (a) assets and unrecovered promotional, exploratory, and development costs; (b) liabilities; (c) capital shares; (d) other securities; and (e) cash receipts and disbursements. Among the types of costs indicated as includible in *unrecovered promotional, exploratory, and development costs* are:

> (a) development expenses, (b) plant and equipment maintenance expenses, (c) rehabilitation expenses, (d) general administrative expenses incurred in a period when there was little or no actual mining and (e) other expenses.... General administrative expenses incurred in connection with subcaptions (a), (b) and (c) should be included therein. Any other general administrative expenses not chargeable to those subcaptions nor written off as costs or other operating charges (including taxes, protection and conservation of property when inactive) shall be included under subcaption (d).[17]

Rule 12-06a of *Regulation S-X* allows for the offset of certain proceeds and other income against promotional, exploratory, and development costs.

36. The AICPA Committee proposed the presentation of cumulative cost outlays, together with assets, liabilities, and investment by stockholders, in a special statement referred to as a "preoperating accountability statement." Cumulative cost outlays would have been deferred and amortized by charges against income when operations commenced. Incidental revenue received during the development stage would have been deducted from the cumulative cost outlays.

37. The AICPA Committee stated the basis for its conclusion as follows:

> A company in the development stage is engaged in building an enterprise, and the expenditures it makes are in the nature of investments for the future. Costs incurred during the development stage are accumulated because they have been incurred in the expectation that they will generate future revenues or otherwise benefit periods after the company reaches the operating stage. Accumulating costs is consistent with the business fact that for many companies a development stage must precede the attainment of ordinary business operations. . . . The only outlays that should not be carried as accumulated costs during the preoperating period are those relating to known losses. . . .
>
> For a company in the development stage there is from inception a presumption that uncertainty as to cost recovery will both exist and persist. (By contrast, the presumption for an operating company is that cost recoverability can be reasonably evaluated.) It would be unrealistic and arbitrary to write off immediately the costs incurred during the development stage simply because of this predictable uncertainty.[18]

38. Both the SEC and AICPA Committee approaches draw attention to the uncertainty about cost recovery surrounding most development stage costs by segregating them in a special category and a special financial statement (or group of statements) similar to the conventional balance sheet. Those costs are not reported as "assets," and they need not be subjected to the assessment of recoverability that is applied to costs incurred by established operating enterprises. The Board believes, however, that the distinction between costs that would be reported as "assets" and costs that would be reported as "unrecovered costs" or "cumulative cost outlays" under the SEC and AICPA Committee approaches is one that is likely to be overlooked by many financial statement users. In addition, as indicated in paragraphs 30-33, the Board believes that all costs of a development stage enterprise should be subjected to the same assessment of recoverability applicable to costs incurred by established operating enterprises. In the Board's view, the nature of development stage activities and their related costs can best be indicated by the additional financial statement disclosures required by paragraphs 11-12, rather than by accumulation or deferral of costs that would be charged to expense when incurred if generally accepted accounting principles applicable to established operating enterprises were applied.

---

[17] U.S. Securities and Exchange Commission, *Regulation S-X,* Rule 5a-02, "Statement of Assets and Unrecovered Promotional, Exploratory, and Development Costs," item 14.

[18] American Institute of Certified Public Accountants, Committee on Companies in the Development Stage, *Accounting for Companies in the Development Stage,* an exposure draft of an Audit Guide (New York: AICPA, March 1973), pp. 25-26, 28.

39. Accumulation or deferral of development stage costs requires amortization after operations commence. Article 5A does not address the question of amortization, and the AICPA Committee noted that "while the current practices are anything but uniform, the most prevalent policy noted is to amortize such costs over a short period of time, usually not more than five years."[19] The Board believes that the difficulty in reasonably relating subsequent revenue to accumulated or deferred costs that would not be deferred under generally accepted accounting principles applicable to established operating enterprises limits the usefulness of the data that would result from such accumulation or deferral by a development stage enterprise. Moreover, the initial operating periods of such an enterprise would include both the amortization of those costs incurred during the development stage and the charging to expense of certain costs incurred currently.

40. Some respondents to the Discussion Memorandum and to the Exposure Draft supported the SEC approach, the proposed approach of the AICPA Committee, or similar approaches. The reasons offered were generally similar to those stated by the AICPA Committee (see paragraph 37). A number of respondents to the Discussion Memorandum and to the Exposure Draft recommended that development stage enterprises follow the same accounting standards as established operating enterprises. The reasons given by the respondents were generally similar to those specified in paragraph 30.

Relationship to "Similar Costs"

41. The Exposure Draft stated that the Board was considering an additional pronouncement on the "similar costs" identified in the Discussion Memorandum. A number of respondents to the Exposure Draft indicated that because, in their view, many costs incurred by development stage enterprises are within a broader category of costs that include start-up costs generally, the Board should address accounting for those "similar costs" before issuing a final Statement on development stage enterprises. The Board considered those suggestions, but concluded that it could reach an informed decision on the issues covered in this Statement without first addressing the more pervasive issues associated with accounting for "similar costs." In the Board's view, this Statement will significantly improve financial accounting and reporting for development stage enterprises.

FINANCIAL STATEMENT PRESENTATION AND ADDITIONAL DISCLOSURES

42. The Board believes that a development stage enterprise should present the same basic financial statements as any other enterprise. The conventional balance sheet, income statement, statement of changes in financial position, and statement of stockholders' equity are sufficiently adaptable to provide the distinctive information that might be considered useful for development stage enterprises. Unique financial statements for development stage enterprises might imply that the nature and results of the transactions entered into by those enterprises are unique, but many established operating enterprises have similar transactions. Further, unique financial statements would not be readily comparable with financial statements issued after an enterprise has emerged from the development stage. Also, the conclusion that the same accounting principles are appropriate for the transactions of development stage enterprises suggests that conventional basic financial statements should be presented.

43. A development stage enterprise typically will be incurring substantial costs in connection with development stage activities and will not have significant revenue. Development stage activities are likely to extend into two or more financial reporting periods. To reflect the significance of development stage activities, the Board believes that the basic financial statements presented by a development stage enterprise should be expanded to provide cumulative financial information since its inception, as well as current information. The Board concluded that disclosure of cumulative revenue and expenses and cumulative amounts of funds obtained from various sources to finance the development effort and initial operations will provide useful information about the activities of development stage enterprises without sacrificing the advantages of retaining the familiar format and content of the basic financial statements of established operating enterprises. Those additional disclosures are specified in paragraphs 11-12.

44. Some respondents to the Discussion Memorandum and Exposure Draft suggested that the differences between established operating enterprises and development stage enterprises are so fundamental as to require unique financial statements for development stage enterprises. The AICPA Committee concluded that, because of the absence of revenue, a conventional income statement would be

[19]Ibid., p. 11

inappropriate for a development stage enterprise; unique financial statements were deemed necessary to emphasize accountability for financial resources received and expended and to direct attention to accumulated costs rather than to measurement of performance. To accomplish those objectives, the Committee recommended the following special statements:

Preoperating accountability statement—to show the assets and cumulative cost outlays, the liabilities, and the investment by stockholders.

Statement of preoperating financial activities—to show the sources and uses of financial resources, preferably cumulative since an enterprise's inception along with data for the current period.

Statement of investment by stockholders—to show the classes and numbers of shares authorized, issued, and outstanding and the types of amounts of consideration received for the shares issued.

45. The AICPA Committee proposed extensive disclosures emphasizing that the enterprise is in the development stage, calling attention to the uncertainties that surround the enterprise and making clear that the financial statements do not purport to present financial position and results of operations.

46. Other respondents to the Discussion Memorandum and to the Exposure Draft took the position that different basic financial statements or additional disclosures are not necessary for a development stage enterprise. Still others asserted that the same basic financial statements are appropriate but should be supplemented by additional disclosures relevant to the distinctive features of a development stage enterprise.

Other Suggestions

47. The Board considered other presentation and disclosure possibilities for a development stage enterprise (including forecasts, disclosure of liquidation priorities and values, and a description of the business environment) and concluded that they should not be required solely for development stage enterprises. The Board also considered the possibility of a statement of cash receipts and disbursements and concluded that the statement of changes in financial position including amounts on a cumulative basis required by paragraph 11(c) would fulfill that need.

POTENTIAL ECONOMIC IMPACT

48. Some respondents to the Exposure Draft expressed concern that requiring development stage enterprises to present the same basic financial statements and to apply the same generally accepted accounting principles as established operating enterprises might make it difficult, if not impossible, for development stage enterprises to obtain capital. They suggested that those requirements would likely cause many development stage enterprises to report periodic losses in an income statement and a cumulative deficit in a balance sheet. Because those results would not be fully understood, suppliers of capital would be disinclined to invest in those enterprises.

49. During the course of developing the Discussion Memorandum and preparing the Exposure Draft, the FASB solicited information about the potential economic impact of applying to development stage enterprises the same generally accepted accounting principles that apply to established operating enterprises. Responses of financial statement users to the Discussion Memorandum and to the Exposure Draft provided only limited information about the potential economic impact. To obtain additional information, the FASB arranged for discussions with officers of fifteen venture capital enterprises. The consensus of those officers was that whether a development stage enterprise defers or expenses preoperating costs has little effect on (a) the amount of any venture capital to be provided to that enterprise and (b) the terms under which any venture capital is provided. According to those officers, the venture capital investor typically relies on an investigation of the technological, marketing, management, and financial aspects of an enterprise. That investigation provides a basis for estimating potential cash flows and the probabilities of achieving them. Whether a development stage enterprise defers or expenses its preoperating costs does not affect those estimates. Based on their experience, those officers also expressed the opinion that the accounting treatment of preoperating costs would have minimal impact on the availability of short-term credit from commercial banks, but might have impact on the investment and credit decisions of unsophisticated investors.

50. In January 1975, the U.S. Department of Commerce issued a report of a study entitled "Impact of FASB's Rule Two Accounting for Research and Development Costs on Small/Developing Stage Firms." The study involved interviews with forty lenders and investors, eleven small, high-technology firms, eleven accountants, and selected government agencies. It focused primarily on the impact on investment and credit decisions concerning development stage enterprises if they were required to charge research and development costs to expense when incurred. That issue is related to the issue at hand—that is, the potential economic impact on development stage enterprises of requiring certain

costs to be expensed when incurred rather than deferred. The conclusions of the Department of Commerce study were generally consistent with the FASB findings described in paragraph 49 of this Statement. Specifically, the study concluded that "FASB's Statement Two should not have a significant impact on those firms who have heretofore capitalized R&D."[20]

51. In summary, the Board has concluded that the cumulative income statement information and the cumulative information about changes in financial position required in paragraph 11 of this Statement will provide the cumulative information about preoperating costs that is typically provided by development stage enterprises currently when using special reporting formats and special accounting practices, such as those cited in paragraph 2. In addition, this Statement requires such information to be presented in financial statements whose formats are familiar and, therefore, less likely to be misinterpreted. As for the concerns of some respondents, the results of FASB discussions and the Department of Commerce study suggest that this Statement will have no significant adverse effect on the ability of development stage enterprises to obtain capital.

ISSUANCE OF SHARES OF STOCK OTHER THAN FOR CASH

52. Under the provisions of Article 5A of SEC *Regulation S-X,* dollar amounts are not assigned to shares of stock issued by a development stage enterprise for noncash consideration, or to the consideration received, unless the noncash consideration has a "fixed or objectively determinable value."

53. The proposed AICPA Audit Guide would have required assignment of dollar amounts to shares of stock issued for noncash consideration, and to the consideration received, at the time of issuance.

54. The Board agrees with the conclusion of the AICPA Committee, and of a number of respondents to the Discussion Memorandum and Exposure Draft who addressed this question, that those transactions should be accounted for when the shares are issued in accordance with the guidelines applicable to acquisition of assets or issuance of shares in general. The transactions are not unique to development stage enterprises and should not be accounted for differently by those enterprises, even if estimates and judgments are required to determine their values.

EFFECTIVE DATE AND TRANSITION

55. The Board adopted the restatement provisions set forth in paragraphs 14-16 because, in its view, this approach provides the most useful information about development stage enterprises and about those previously in the development stage in comparing financial data for periods after the effective date of this Statement with data presented for earlier periods.

[20]U.S. Department of Commerce, "Impact of FASB's Rule Two Accounting for Research and Development Costs on Small/Developing Stage Firms" (Washington, D.C.: U.S. Department of Commerce, January 20, 1975), p. 3.

Statement of Financial Accounting Standards No. 8 Accounting for the Translation of Foreign Currency Transactions and Foreign Currency Financial Statements

STATUS

Issued: October 1975

Effective Date: For fiscal years beginning on or after January 1, 1976

Affects: Amends ARB 43, Chapter 12, paragraph 5
Supersedes ARB 43, Chapter 12, paragraphs 7 and 10 through 22
Supersedes APB 6, paragraph 18
Amends APB 22, paragraph 13
Supersedes FAS 1

Affected by: Paragraphs 27 and 35 amended by FAS 20
Superseded by FAS 52

Note: This Statement has been superseded by FAS 52, "Foreign Currency Translation" effective for fiscal years beginning on, or after, December 15, 1982. Even though earlier application of FAS 52 is encouraged, this Statement may be applied prior to the effective date of FAS 52.

Statement of Financial Accounting Standards No. 8
Accounting for the Translation of Foreign Currency Transactions and Foreign Currency Financial Statements

CONTENTS

INTRODUCTION

1. The expansion of international business activities, extensive currency realignments—including two U.S. dollar devaluations—that followed the recent major revision of the international monetary system, and the acceptance in practice of significantly different methods of accounting have highlighted problems concerning **foreign currency translation.** (Terms defined in the glossary in Appendix E are in boldface type the first time they appear in this Statement.) Appendix B presents background information for this Statement.

2. This Statement establishes standards of financial accounting and reporting for **foreign currency transactions** in financial statements of a **reporting enterprise** (hereinafter *enterprise*). It also establishes standards of financial accounting and reporting for translating **foreign currency financial statements** incorporated in the financial statements of an enterprise by consolidation, combination, or the equity method of accounting. Translation of financial statements from one currency to another for purposes other than consolidation, combination, or the equity method is beyond the scope of this Statement. For example, this Statement does not cover translation of the financial statements of an enterprise from its **reporting currency** into another currency for the convenience of readers accustomed to that other currency.

3. To incorporate foreign currency transactions and foreign currency financial statements in its financial statements, an enterprise must translate—that is, express in its reporting currency[1]—all assets, liabilities, revenue, or expenses that are *measured in foreign currency* or *denominated in foreign currency*[2] and that arise in either of two ways:

---

[1]For convenience, this Statement assumes that the enterprise uses the U.S. dollar (dollar) as its reporting currency and unit of measure. A currency other than the dollar may be the reporting currency in financial statements that are prepared in conformity with U.S. generally accepted accounting principles. For example, a foreign enterprise may report in its local currency in conformity with U.S. generally accepted accounting principles. If so, the requirements of this Statement apply.

[2]To *measure in foreign currency* is to quantify an attribute of an item in a unit of currency other than the reporting currency. Assets and liabilities are *denominated in foreign currency* if their amounts are fixed in terms of a foreign currency regardless of exchange rate changes. An asset or liability may be both measured and denominated in one currency, or it may be measured in one currency and denominated in another. To illustrate: two foreign branches of a U.S. company, one Swiss and one German, purchase on credit identical assets from a Swiss vendor at identical prices stated in Swiss francs. The German branch measures the cost (an attribute) of that asset in German marks. Although the corresponding liability is also *measured* in marks, it remains *denominated* in Swiss francs since the liability must be settled in a specified number of Swiss francs. The Swiss branch measures the asset and liability in Swiss francs. Its liability is both measured and denominated in Swiss francs. Assets and liabilities can be measured in various currencies. However, currency and rights to receive or obligations to pay fixed amounts of a currency are denominated only in that currency.

Foreign currency transactions—an enterprise (a) buys or sells on credit goods or services whose prices are stated in **foreign currency,** (b) borrows or lends funds and the amounts payable or receivable are denominated in foreign currency, (c) is a party to an unperformed forward exchange contract, or (d) for other reasons, acquires assets or incurs liabilities denominated in foreign currency.

Foreign operations—an enterprise conducts activities through a **foreign operation** whose assets, liabilities, revenue, and expenses are measured in foreign currency.

The need for translation is discussed further in Appendix C.

4. This Statement supersedes paragraphs 7 and 10-22 of Chapter 12, "Foreign Operations and Foreign Exchange," of *ARB No. 43;* paragraph 18 of *APB Opinion No. 6,* "Status of Accounting Research Bulletins"; and *FASB Statement No. 1,* "Disclosure of Foreign Currency Translation Information." It also amends the last sentence of paragraph 5 of *ARB No. 43,* Chapter 12, to delete "and they should be reserved against to the extent that their realization in dollars appears to be doubtful," and paragraph 13 of *APB Opinion No. 22,* "Disclosure of Accounting Policies," to delete "translation of foreign currencies" as an example of disclosure "commonly required with respect to accounting policies."

5. Standards of financial accounting and reporting for the translation of foreign currency transactions and foreign currency financial statements (*foreign statements*) are presented in paragraphs 6-37. Those paragraphs deal in sequence with the following: objective of translation, foreign currency transactions, foreign statements, exchange gains and losses, income tax consequences of rate changes, forward exchange contracts, use of averages or reasonable approximations, exchange rates, disclosure, and effective date and transition. The basis for the Board's conclusions, as well as alternatives considered and reasons for their rejection, are discussed in Appendix D.

STANDARDS OF FINANCIAL ACCOUNTING AND REPORTING

Objective of Translation

6. For the purpose of preparing an enterprise's financial statements, the objective of translation is to measure and express (a) in dollars and (b) in conformity with U.S. generally accepted accounting principles the assets, liabilities, revenue, or expenses that are measured or denominated in foreign currency. Remeasuring in dollars the assets, liabilities, revenue, or expenses measured or denominated in foreign currency should not affect either the measurement bases for assets and liabilities or the timing of revenue and expense recognition otherwise required by generally accepted accounting principles. That is, translation should change the **unit of measure** without changing accounting principles.

Foreign Currency Transactions

7. The objective of translation requires that the following shall apply to all foreign currency transactions of an enterprise other than forward exchange contracts (paragraphs 22-28):

a. At the **transaction date,** each asset, liability, revenue, or expense arising from the transaction shall be translated into (that is, measured in) dollars by use of the exchange rate (*rate*) in effect at that date, and shall be recorded at that dollar amount.
b. At each balance sheet date, recorded dollar balances representing cash and amounts owed by or to the enterprise that are denominated in foreign currency shall be adjusted to reflect the current rate.[3]
c. At each balance sheet date, assets carried at market whose current market price is stated in a foreign currency shall be adjusted to the equivalent dollar market price at the balance sheet date (that is, the foreign currency market price at the balance sheet date multiplied by the current rate).

8. Although paragraph 7 refers to foreign currency transactions of an enterprise whose reporting currency is the dollar, the conclusions expressed therein also apply to a foreign operation that has transactions whose terms are stated in a currency other than its **local currency.**

Foreign Statements

9. The objective of translation requires that the assets, liabilities, revenue, and expenses in foreign statements be translated and accounted for in the same manner as assets, liabilities, revenue, and expenses that result from foreign currency transactions of the enterprise. Foreign currency transactions of an enterprise involve amounts denominated or measured in foreign currency, but the assets, liabilities, revenue, and expenses from foreign currency transactions are initially measured and recorded in dollars, and in conformity with U.S. generally accepted accounting principles, following the procedures in paragraph 7(a). In contrast,

[3]Debt securities held that are essentially equivalent to notes receivable shall be adjusted to reflect the current rate (paragraph 39).

assets, liabilities, revenue, and expenses in foreign statements are initially measured and recorded in foreign currency and may not be in conformity with U.S. generally accepted accounting principles. Since translation cannot transform the results obtained under dissimilar foreign accounting principles into acceptable measurements under U.S. accounting principles, special procedures are necessary to ensure that the translated statements are prepared in conformity with U.S. generally accepted accounting principles.

10. Accordingly, before translation, foreign statements that are to be included by consolidation, combination, or the equity method in an enterprise's financial statements shall be prepared in conformity with U.S. generally accepted accounting principles. Those financial statements shall then be translated into dollars following the standards in this Statement.[4]

11. In preparing foreign statements, balances representing cash and amounts receivable or payable that are denominated in other than the local currency shall be adjusted to reflect the current rate between the local and the foreign currency.[5] Those adjusted balances and other balances representing cash and amounts receivable or payable that are denominated in the local currency shall be translated into dollars at the current rate.

12. For assets and liabilities other than those described in paragraph 11, the particular measurement basis used shall determine the translation rate. Several measurement bases are used in financial accounting under present generally accepted accounting principles.[6] A measurement may be based on a price in a past exchange (for example, historical cost), a price in a current purchase exchange (for example, replacement cost), or a price in a current sale exchange (for example, market price). Foreign statements may employ various measurement bases. Accordingly, amounts in foreign statements that are carried at exchange prices shall be translated in a manner that retains their measurement bases as follows:

a. Accounts carried at prices in past exchanges (past prices) shall be translated at historical rates.
b. Accounts carried at prices in current purchase or sale exchanges (current prices) or future exchanges (future prices) shall be translated at the current rate.

13. Revenue and expense transactions shall be translated in a manner that produces approximately the same dollar amounts that would have resulted had the underlying transactions been translated into dollars on the dates they occurred. Since separate translation of each transaction is usually impractical, the specified result can be achieved by using an average rate for the period. However, revenue and expenses that relate to assets and liabilities translated at historical rates shall be translated at the historical rates used to translate the related assets or liabilities.

14. The procedures specified in paragraphs 10-13 generally result in translated statements in which the assets, liabilities, revenue, and expenses are measured in dollars in the same manner as those resulting from foreign currency transactions of the enterprise. Occasionally, however, translation of foreign statements in strict conformity with those paragraphs does not result in dollar measurements required by U.S. generally accepted accounting principles. For example, the test of *cost or market, whichever is lower,* must be applied *in dollars* to ensure that inventory in the translated statements conforms to that rule—a procedure that can result in dollar measurements that are sometimes different from translating inventory in foreign statements in the manner described in paragraph 12. Similarly, timing differences that affect deferred tax accounting sometimes increase or decrease *in dollars* even though their amounts measured in foreign currency remained unchanged.

15. Appendix A, "Translation of Certain Accounts," (paragraphs 38-52) explains and illustrates certain applications of the procedures set forth in paragraphs 11-13. It also describes and illustrates ways to ensure that amounts in translated statements conform to U.S. generally accepted accounting principles in those situations indicated in paragraph 14.

Exchange Gains and Losses

16. A change in the rate between the dollar and the foreign currency in which assets and liabilities are measured or denominated can result in an exchange gain or loss if the translation method uses the dollar as the unit of measure. Exchange gains or losses are a consequence of translation, that is, of remeasuring in dollars. They result from the procedures specified in paragraphs 7(b) and 11-13 (see paragraphs 167-

[4]In multilevel consolidation, foreign statements may be translated into another foreign currency and consolidated with other foreign statements before being consolidated with the enterprise's financial statements. Translation at each step of a multilevel consolidation shall be in conformity with the standards in this Statement.

[5]Since foreign statements are expressed in local currency, the term *foreign currency* in this context includes the dollar.

[6]Various measurement bases are described in paragraphs 70 and 179 of *APB Statement No. 4,* "Basic Concepts of Accounting Principles Underlying Financial Statements of Business Enterprises."

169). Exchange gains or losses also result from the **conversion** of foreign currency or the settlement of a receivable or payable denominated in foreign currency at a rate different from that at which the item is recorded.

17. Exchange gains and losses shall be included in determining net income for the period in which the rate changes. Exchange gains and losses are *gains* and *losses* as those terms are used in paragraph 15(d) of *APB Opinion No. 28,* "Interim Financial Reporting," which states: "Gains and losses that arise in any interim period similar to those that would not be deferred at year end should not be deferred to later interim periods within the same fiscal year."

Income Tax Consequences of Rate Changes

18. Interperiod tax allocation is required in accordance with *APB Opinion No. 11,* "Accounting for Income Taxes," if taxable exchange gains or tax-deductible exchange losses resulting from an enterprise's foreign currency transactions are included in income in a different period for financial statement purposes than for tax purposes. Partial or complete elimination of a foreign operation's exchange gains or losses through translation of its statements into dollars shall not alter current inclusion in the dollar income statement of the effects, if any, of the exchange gains or losses on foreign taxes (see paragraph 200).

19. The use of historical rates to translate certain revenue or expense items may result in an unusual relationship between the translated amounts of foreign pretax income and foreign income taxes. However, that effect of a rate change is not a timing difference as defined in *APB Opinion No. 11,* and interperiod tax allocation is not appropriate.

20. To the extent that exhange gains or losses arising from translating subsidiaries' and investees' foreign statements into dollars are not included currently in U.S. taxable income, the need for deferred taxes shall be determined in accordance with the provisions of *APB Opinion No. 23,* "Accounting for Income Taxes—Special Areas," and *APB Opinion No. 24,* "Accounting for Income Taxes—Investments in Common Stock Accounted for by the Equity Method (Other than Subsidiaries and Corporate Joint Ventures)."

21. Deferred taxes shall be recorded in accordance with *APB Opinion No. 11* for exchange gains or losses that are timing differences arising from including the operations of foreign branches of U.S. companies and certain foreign subsidiaries and investees in determining U.S. taxable income. Since various methods are allowed to measure exchange gains or losses for tax purposes, the determination of whether exchange gains or losses are timing differences or permanent differences must depend on the circumstances in each situation.

Forward Exchange Contracts

22. A forward exchange contract (*forward contract*) is an agreement to exchange at a specified future date currencies of different countries at a specified rate (the *forward rate*). The purpose of a forward contract may be to hedge either a foreign currency commitment or a foreign currency **exposed net asset position** or **exposed net liability position** or to speculate in anticipation of a gain.

23. A gain or loss shall be included in determining net income for the period in which the rate changes if the gain or loss pertains to a forward contract that is intended to be a (a) hedge of a foreign currency exposed net asset or net liability position, (b) hedge of a foreign currency commitment that does not meet the conditions described in paragraph 27, or (c) speculation.

24. A gain or loss shall be deferred and included in the measurement of the dollar basis of the related foreign currency transaction if the gain or loss pertains to a forward contract that is intended to be a hedge of an identifiable foreign currency commitment that meets the conditions described in paragraph 27. Losses on a forward contract shall not be deferred, however, if deferral could lead to recognizing losses in later periods.[7]

25. A gain or loss on a forward contract that is intended to be a hedge (paragraphs 23(a), 23(b), and 24) shall be determined by multiplying the foreign currency amount of the forward contract by the difference between the **spot rate** at the balance sheet date[8] and the spot rate at the date of inception of the contract (or the spot rate last used to measure a gain or loss on that contract for an earlier period). The discount or premium on the forward contract (that is, the foreign currency amount of the contract multiplied by the difference between the contracted forward rate and the spot rate at the date of inception of the contract) shall be accounted for separately from the gain or loss on the contract and shall be included in determining net income over the life

[7]For example, a loss on a forward contract shall not be deferred if future revenue from sale or other disposition of an asset is estimated to be less than the sum of (a) the asset's dollar cost including the deferred loss on the related forward contract and (b) reasonably predictable costs of sale or disposal.

[8]If the transaction date for a commitment that is hedged by a forward contract (paragraph 24) occurs during the period before the balance sheet date, the spot rate at the transaction date shall be used instead of the spot rate at the subsequent balance sheet date.

of the forward contract. If a gain or loss is deferred under paragraph 24, however, the forward contract's discount or premium that relates to the commitment period may be included in the measure of the dollar basis of the related foreign currency transaction when recorded.

26. A gain or loss on a forward contract that is a speculation shall be determined by multiplying the foreign currency amount of the forward contract by the difference between the forward rate available for the remaining maturity of the contract and the contracted forward rate (or the forward rate last used to measure a gain or loss on that contract for an earlier period). No separate accounting recognition is given to the discount or premium on a forward contract that is a speculation.

27. There shall be the presumption that the intent of entering into a forward contract is described in paragraph 23. However, a forward contract shall be considered a hedge of an identifiable foreign currency commitment (paragraph 24), provided *all* of the following conditions are met:

a. The life of the forward contract extends from the foreign currency commitment date to the anticipated transaction date[9] or a later date.[10]
b. The forward contract is denominated in the same currency as the foreign currency commitment and for an amount that is the same or less than the amount of the foreign currency commitment.
c. The foreign currency commitment is firm and uncancelable.

A forward contract is not a hedge of an identifiable commitment to the extent that its amount exceeds the amount of the commitment or its life extends beyond the transaction date of the commitment. Consequently, a gain or loss pertaining to an amount of a forward contract in excess of the related commitment or pertaining to a period after the transaction date of the related commitment shall not be deferred.

28. If a forward contract previously considered a hedge of a foreign currency commitment is sold or otherwise terminated before the transaction date, the deferred gain or loss, if any, shall continue to be deferred and accounted for in accordance with the requirements of paragraph 24.

Use of Averages or Reasonable Approximations

29. Since literal application of several of the standards in this Statement would require a degree of detail in record-keeping and computations that might be burdensome as well as unnecessary to produce reasonable approximations of the results desired, the use of averages or other methods of approximation is appropriate, provided the results obtained do not differ materially from the results prescribed by the standards. For example, the propriety of average rates in translating certain revenue and expense amounts is noted in paragraph 13. Likewise, the use of averages and other time- and effort-saving methods to approximate the results of detailed calculations will often prove useful in translating certain inventory, deferred income tax, and other accounts that involve translation of numerous individual elements at historical rates.

Exchange Rates

30. The exchange rate is the ratio between a unit of one currency and the amount of another currency for which that unit can be exchanged at a particular time. For purposes of applying this Statement, the *current rate* is the rate in effect at the balance sheet date (see paragraph 34), and the *historical rate* is the rate in effect at the date a specific transaction or event occurred.[11] The following shall apply if multiple rates exist:

a. *Foreign Currency Transactions.* The applicable rate at which a particular transaction could be settled at the transaction date shall be used to translate and record the transaction. At a subsequent balance sheet date, the current rate is that rate at which the related receivable or payable could be settled at that date.
b. *Foreign Statements.* In the absence of unusual circumstances, the rate applicable to conversion of a currency for purposes of dividend remit-

---

[9]A long-term commitment may have more than one transaction date. For example, the due date of each progress payment under a construction contract is an anticipated transaction date. For purposes of this Statement, each future progress payment due is a commitment, and the period between the commitment date for the entire contract and the due date of each progress payment is the minimum life for a forward contract that hedges that payment.

[10]The intended use of successive forward contracts satisfies the condition in paragraph 27(a) if the nature of the forward exchange market precludes a single forward contract's covering the entire period, provided the first contract commences at the commitment date.

[11]If exchangeability between the dollar and the foreign currency is temporarily lacking at the transaction date or balance sheet date, the first subsequent rate at which exchanges could be made shall be used for purposes of this Statement. If the lack of exchangeability is other than temporary, the propriety of consolidating, combining, or accounting for the foreign operation by the equity method in the financial statements of the enterprise shall be carefully considered (*ARB No. 43,* Chapter 12, paragraph 8).

tances shall be used to translate foreign statements.[12]

31. If a foreign operation whose balance sheet date differs from that of the enterprise is consolidated or combined with or accounted for by the equity method in the financial statements of the enterprise, the current rate is the rate in effect at the foreign operation's balance sheet date for purposes of applying the requirements of this Statement to that foreign operation.

Disclosure

32. The aggregate exchange gain or loss included in determining net income for the period shall be disclosed in the financial statements or in a note thereto.[13] For the purpose of that disclosure, gains and losses on forward contracts determined in conformity with the requirements of paragraphs 25 and 26 shall be considered exchange gains or losses.

33. Effects of rate changes on reported results of operations, other than the effects included in the disclosure required by paragraph 32, shall, if practicable, be described and quantified. If quantified, the methods and the underlying assumptions used to determine the estimated effects shall be explained (paragraphs 223-225).

34. An enterprise's financial statements shall not be adjusted for a rate change that occurs after the date of the financial statements or after the date of the foreign statements of a foreign operation that are consolidated or combined with or accounted for by the equity method in the financial statements of the enterprise. However, disclosure of the rate change and its effects, if significant, may be necessary.

Effective Date and Transition

35. This Statement shall be effective for fiscal years beginning on or after January 1, 1976,[14] although earlier application is encouraged. Thereafter, if financial statements for periods before the effective date, and financial summaries or other data derived therefrom, are presented, they shall be restated, if practicable, to conform to the provisions of paragraphs 7-31 of this Statement. In the year that this Statement is first applied, the financial statements shall disclose the nature of any restatement and its effect on income before extraordinary items, net income, and related per share amounts for each period restated.

36. If restatement of financial statements or summaries for all prior periods presented is not practicable, information presented shall be restated for as many consecutive periods immediately preceding the effective date of this Statement as is practicable, and the cumulative effect of applying paragraphs 7-31 on the retained earnings at the beginning of the earliest period restated (or at the beginning of the period in which the Statement is first applied if it is not practicable to restate any prior periods) shall be included in determining net income of that period (see paragraph 20 of *APB Opinion No. 20,* "Accounting Changes").[15] The effect on income before extraordinary items, net income, and related per share amounts of applying this Statement in a period in which the cumulative effect is included in determining net income shall be disclosed for that period, and the reason for not restating all of the prior periods presented shall be explained.

37. Financial statements for periods beginning on or after the effective date of this Statement shall include the disclosures specified by paragraphs 32 and 33 of this Statement. To the extent practicable, those disclosures shall also be included in financial statements for earlier periods that have been restated pursuant to paragraph 35 or paragraph 36.

The provisions of this Statement need not be applied to immaterial items.

This Statement was adopted by the affirmative votes of six members of the Financial Accounting Standards Board. Mr. Mays dissented.

---

[12]If unsettled intercompany transactions are subject to preference or penalty rates, translation at the rate applicable to dividend remittances may cause a difference between intercompany receivables and payables measured in dollars. Until that difference is eliminated by settlement of the intercompany transaction, it shall be treated as a receivable or payable in the enterprise's financial statements.

[13]Certain enterprises, primarily banks, are dealers in foreign exchange. Although certain gains or losses from dealer transactions may fit the definition of exchange gains or losses in this Statement, they need not be included in the aggregate exchange gain or loss required to be disclosed if dealer gains or losses are disclosed.

[14]For enterprises having fiscal years of 52 or 53 weeks instead of the calendar year, this Statement shall be effective for fiscal years beginning in late December 1975.

[15]Pro forma disclosures required by paragraphs 19(d) and 21 of *APB Opinion No. 20* are not applicable.

Mr. Mays dissents for two principal reasons: (1) he believes that the method adopted by the Board (which he views as essentially the temporal method) is generally inappropriate for translating financial statements of foreign operating entities; and (2) he believes that exchange differences arising from translation should not, in all cases, be treated as current gains or losses.

Mr. Mays would apply the current rate method in translating financial statements of foreign subsidiaries whose operations are largely conducted in foreign currency and whose assets and liabilities are exposed to foreign currency exchange risk. He believes that only that method meets two requirements which he deems essential: (1) that the translation process should preserve the essence of the foreign currency statements in terms of financial position and results of operations and (2) that it should produce results that are generally consistent with the economic effects of exchange rate changes. Mr. Mays disagrees with the objective of translation as stated in paragraphs 6 and 9 because it does not recognize the two requirements mentioned above, and because, in his opinion, it mistakenly views the assets of a foreign subsidiary as if they had been purchased individually by the domestic parent and recorded in dollars. Typically, however, the parent's dollar investment cannot be identified with individual assets acquired by the subsidiary and, from the parent's standpoint, all assets of the subsidiary are equally at risk in the same foreign exchange environment. In Mr. Mays' view, the temporal method, the selection of which automatically flows from the objective as stated, meets neither of the two requirements referred to above which he believes constitute important elements of the objective of translation. Translating inventories and fixed assets at historical rates, while translating the short- and long-term debt incurred to finance them at the current rate, causes the translated results and relationships, under the temporal method, to differ significantly from those reflected by the foreign currency statements. In addition, under that method, an exchange loss will be recognized when the economic effect of a rate change is considered beneficial and, conversely, an exchange gain will be recognized when the economic effect of a rate change is considered adverse. Mr. Mays believes that the use of the temporal method with the immediate recognition of the resulting exchange differences as gains and losses will, in the present environment of fluctuating exchange rates, cause erratic changes in the reported results of companies with significant foreign operations, especially for interim periods. In his opinion, these variations will depart markedly from economic results and, accordingly, will be misinterpreted by investors. He also has concern that current recognition in income of translation differences produced under the temporal method may induce uneconomic actions by companies to protect against what may be viewed as an accounting exchange exposure, as contrasted with the actual exchange exposure.

Mr. Mays contests the arguments that the temporal method is conceptually superior because it is compatible with generally accepted accounting practice, including the concept of historical cost, whereas the current rate method is not. He believes that assets acquired for local currency by a foreign subsidiary have no historical dollar costs; their historical cost exists only in local currency, and translation at the current rate does not change that basis. Translation of foreign statements is an accounting convention necessary for the preparation of consolidated financial statements. If use of the current rate with respect to nonmonetary assets introduces valuation into the translation process, as some contend, it may be equally contended that use of the current rate for debt and other monetary items as embraced by the temporal method also introduces valuation. Further, recognition of exchange differences from translation as current gains and losses is, per se, an acknowledgement of valuation. Thus, Mr. Mays concludes that the conceptual superiority claimed for the temporal method is illusory, but its practical deficiencies, as he sees them, are real.

Mr. Mays regards exchange differences arising from translation as unrealized gains and losses. He believes that generally accepted accounting principles, including the principle of conservatism, require the deferral of unrealized exchange gains to the extent they exceed unrealized exchange losses. An excess of unrealized exchange losses should, in his view, normally be recognized in the period in which the excess occurs.

In Mr. Mays' opinion, the nature of foreign operations of U.S. companies is sufficiently diverse and complex that no single accounting treatment for foreign currency translation, whatever its conceptual merits, can be universally applied without producing irrational results in many instances. The practical problems cited in Appendix D in identifying those situations in which the use of the current rate method would be appropriate, would require for their solution some latitude in the Statement for the use of judgment on the part of managements and auditors. Mr. Mays believes that these problems, while real, are of lesser magnitude than those inherent in the mandatory application of a single method to widely divergent situations.

Members of the Financial Accounting Standards Board:

Marshall S. Armstrong, *Chairman*
Oscar S. Gellein
Donald J. Kirk
Arthur L. Litke
Robert E. Mays
Walter Schuetze
Robert T. Sprouse

Appendix A

TRANSLATION OF CERTAIN ACCOUNTS

38. Paragraphs 11 and 12 distinguish those balance sheet accounts in foreign statements that shall be translated at either current or historical rates. The table on the following page indicates the rates at which certain common balance sheet accounts in foreign statements shall be translated. In addition, the following paragraphs discuss certain additional aspects of translating foreign statements. Two topics included in the discussion—applying the rule of cost or market, whichever is lower, to inventory and applying *APB Opinion No. 11* to deferred income taxes—require procedures not described in paragraphs 11 and 12 (see paragraph 14).

Holdings of Debt Securities

39. Debt securities held that are essentially equivalent to notes receivable shall be translated at the current rate. An example is a bond that is intended to be held to maturity and is carried at an amount that is the present value of future interest and principal payments based on the effective rate of interest at the date of purchase (that is, at maturity amount plus or minus an unamortized premium or discount). A debt security held that is not essentially equivalent to a note receivable shall be translated (a) at the current rate if carried at current market price or (b) at the historical rate if carried at cost.

Translation After a Business Combination[16]

40. The method an enterprise uses to account for the acquisition of a foreign operation affects certain aspects of translation. If a business combination with a foreign operation is accounted for by the *pooling-of-interests method,* the assets and liabilities of the foreign operation shall be translated as if the foreign operation had always been a subsidiary of the enterprise. Therefore, assets and liabilities that are translated at historical rates shall be translated at the rates in effect at the date the foreign operation recognized the specific transactions or events.

41. If a business combination with a foreign operation is accounted for by the *purchase method,* assets and liabilities that are translated at historical rates shall be translated at the rates in effect when the enterprise acquired its interest in the assets or liabilities. Thus, assets and liabilities of a foreign operation at the date of its acquisition shall be adjusted to their fair values in local currency and then translated at the rate in effect at the date of acquisition. A difference between the translated net assets and the dollar cost of acquisition by the enterprise is *goodwill* or *an excess of acquired net assets over cost* as those terms are used in *APB Opinion No. 16.* Translation at the date of acquisition, as described, establishes the dollar measures of the assets acquired and liabilities assumed as of the date of acquisition that are translated at historical rates in subsequent balance sheets.

[16] *APB Opinion No. 16,* "Business Combinations," prescribes generally accepted accounting principles for business combinations. Paragraphs 87-92 are particularly pertinent.

Rates Used to Translate Assets and Liabilities

	Translation Rates	
	Current	Historical
ASSETS		
Cash on hand and demand and time deposits	X	
Marketable equity securities:		
Carried at cost		X
Carried at current market price	X	
Accounts and notes receivable and related unearned discount	X	
Allowance for doubtful accounts and notes receivable	X	
Inventories:		
Carried at cost		X
Carried at current replacement price or current selling price	X	
Carried at net realizable value	X	
Carried at contract price (produced under fixed price contracts)	X	
Prepaid insurance, advertising, and rent		X
Refundable deposits	X	
Advances to unconsolidated subsidiaries	X	
Property, plant, and equipment		X
Accumulated depreciation of property, plant, and equipment		X
Cash surrender value of life insurance	X	
Patents, trademarks, licenses, and formulas		X
Goodwill		X
Other intangible assets		X
LIABILITIES		
Accounts and notes payable and overdrafts	X	
Accrued expenses payable	X	
Accrued losses on firm purchase commitments	X	
Refundable deposits	X	
Deferred income		X
Bonds payable or other long-term debt	X	
Unamortized premium or discount on bonds or notes payable	X	
Convertible bonds payable	X	
Accrued pension obligations	X	
Obligations under warranties	X	

Translation of an Investment Accounted for by the Equity Method[17]

42. The foreign statements of an investee that are accounted for by the equity method first shall be translated into dollars in conformity with the requirements of this Statement; then the equity method shall be applied.

Minority Interests

43. The minority interest reported in an enterprise's consolidated financial statements shall be based on the financial statements of the subsidiary in which there is a minority interest after they have been translated according to the requirements of this Statement.

Preferred Stock

44. Preferred stock that is essentially a permanent stockholder investment shall be translated in the same manner as common stock, that is, at historical rates. However, if preferred stock not owned by the enterprise is carried in the foreign operation's balance sheet at its liquidation or redemption price, and liquidation or redemption is either required or imminent, that preferred stock shall be translated at the current rate. If translation at the historical rate would result in stating a preferred stock above its stated liquidation or redemption price in foreign currency translated at the current rate, the preferred stock shall be carried at the lesser dollar amount.

[17] *APB Opinion No. 18*, "The Equity Method of Accounting for Investments in Common Stock," prescribes generally accepted accounting principles for the equity method.

Revenue and Expense Transactions

45. Paragraph 13 permits the use of average rates to translate revenue and expense transactions that do not relate to balance sheet accounts translated at historical rates. Average rates used shall be appropriately weighted by the foreign currency volume of transactions occurring during the accounting period. For example, to translate revenue and expense accounts for an annual period, individual revenue and expense accounts for each quarter or month may be translated at that quarter's or month's average rate. The translated amounts for each quarter or month should then be combined for the annual totals.

Applying the Rule of Cost or Market, Whichever Is Lower

46. To apply the rule of *cost or market, whichever is lower* (as described in Statement 6 of Chapter 4, "Inventory Pricing," of *ARB No. 43*), *translated historical cost* shall be compared with *translated market*. Application of the rule *in dollars* may require write-downs to market in the translated statements even though no write-down in the foreign statements is required by the rule. It may also require a write-down in the foreign statements to be reversed before translation if the translated market amount exceeds translated historical cost; the foreign currency cost shall then be translated at the historical rate.[18] Once inventory has been written down to market in the translated statements, that dollar amount shall continue to be the carrying amount in the dollar financial statements until the inventory is sold or a further write-down is necessary.[19]

47. Paragraphs 48 and 49 illustrate two different situations.

48. A foreign subsidiary of a U.S. company purchases a unit of inventory at a cost of FC500 when the rate is FC1 = $2.40. At the balance sheet date the *market* (as the term is used in Chapter 4 of *ARB No. 43*) of the item is FC450 and the rate is FC1 = $3.00. Thus, the item's historical cost is $1,200 (FC500 × $2.40) and its market is $1,350 (FC450 × $3.00). If inventory is written down to FC450 in the foreign accounting records, translation of that amount at the current rate would not result in the lower of cost or market measured in dollars. Therefore, the write-down should be reversed in the foreign statements before translation. After translating the foreign currency cost at the historical rate, the inventory will be properly stated in the dollar financial statements at its historical cost of $1,200.

49. A situation different from the one in the preceding paragraph could also exist. For example, a foreign operation purchases a unit of inventory at a cost of FC500 when the rate is FC1 = $2.40. At the balance sheet date the *market* of the item is FC600 and the rate is FC1 = $1.80. Thus, the item's historical cost is $1,200 (FC500 × $2.40), its market is $1,080 (FC600 × $1.80), and a write-down of the inventory to market in the translated financial statements is necessary.

Deferred Income Taxes

50. Present accounting for income taxes is governed by *APB Opinion No. 11,* which requires the *deferred method* of interperiod tax allocation. Consistent with the requirements of *APB Opinion No. 11* and paragraph 9 of this Statement, deferred taxes in the translated balance sheet of a foreign operation shall be stated the same as would the deferred tax effects of timing differences from foreign currency transactions of the enterprise that are subject to foreign taxes but measured and recorded in dollars. Accordingly, the following procedures shall apply:

a. Deferred taxes that (1) are determined by the *gross change* method (*APB Opinion No. 11,* paragraph 37(a)) and (2) do not relate to assets or liabilities translated at the current rate shall be translated at historical rates.
b. Deferred taxes that (1) are determined by the *net change* method (*APB Opinion No. 11,* paragraph 37(b)) and (2) do not relate to assets or liabilities translated at the current rate shall be measured in dollars by adding to or subtracting from the dollar balance at the beginning of the period the amount determined by translating (in accordance with paragraph 13 of this Statement) the foreign currency deferred tax expense or credit included in the foreign operation's income statement for the period. (Paragraph 51 illustrates that procedure.)
c. Deferred taxes that relate to assets or liabilities translated at the current rate shall be translated at the current rate. (Paragraph 52 illustrates that procedure.)

---

[18]An asset other than inventory may sometimes be written down from historical cost. Although that write-down is not under the rule of cost of market, whichever is lower, the standards prescribed in this paragraph shall be applied. That is, a write-down may be required in the translated statements even though not required in the foreign statements, and a write-down in the foreign statements may need to be reversed before translation to prevent the translated amount from exceeding translated historical cost.

[19]This paragraph is not intended to preclude recognition of gains in a later interim period to the extent of inventory losses recognized from market declines in earlier interim periods if losses on the same inventory are recovered in the same year, as provided by paragraph 14(c) of *APB Opinion No. 28,* "Interim Financial Reporting."

Applying the current rate to the balance of deferred taxes in (c) above complies with the objective of translation. Translating at the current rate the item in the foreign statements that gave rise to a timing difference remeasures the timing difference in dollars, and, therefore, the tax effect *in dollars* of the change in the timing difference should be recognized.

Illustrations of Applying Paragraph 50

51. A foreign subsidiary of a U.S. company uses the net change method of deferred tax allocation for timing differences from using an accelerated depreciation method on plant and equipment for tax purposes and the straight-line method of depreciation for financial statement purposes. The dollar measure of the deferred tax credit at the beginning of the year is $100,000 (determined in conformity with the requirements of paragraph 50(b)). The current year's deferred tax expense is FC50,000, and the average exchange rate for translating income tax expense is FC1 = $.50. Accordingly, the dollar amount of deferred taxes in the translated balance sheet is $125,000 [$100,000 + .50(50,000)].

52. A foreign subsidiary of a U.S. company accrues warranty obligations for financial statement purposes but is on the cash basis for tax purposes. The accrued warranty obligation at the beginning and end of the year is FC900. No warranty claims are paid during the year. The deferred tax charge using the net change method is FC450 (determined at the 50% local tax rate) at the beginning and end of the year. The exchange rate at the beginning and end of the year is FC1 = $1 and FC3 = $1, respectively. The dollar measure of the deferred tax charge at the beginning of the year is $450. Accordingly, the dollar amount of the deferred tax charge in the translated balance sheet at year end is $150 (FC450 ÷ 3). The warranty obligation measured in dollars has decreased $600 during the year; therefore, the deferred tax charge should be decreased by $300.

Appendix B

BACKGROUND INFORMATION

53. Before this Statement was issued, existing accounting pronouncements on foreign currency translation (summarized in paragraphs 60-64) dealt only with translating foreign statements and not with foreign currency transactions. Since publication of the basic existing pronouncement, the international business activities of U.S. companies have expanded rapidly. In addition, the international business environment has been affected by recent, significant changes in the world monetary system, exemplified by the U.S. dollar devaluations of 1971 and 1973 and the current prevalence of *floating* rather than *fixed* rates in most foreign exchange markets.

54. Because of those factors and the acceptance in practice of several different methods of accounting for foreign currency translation, the FASB in April 1973 placed on its technical agenda a project on "Accounting for Foreign Currency Translation."

55. A task force of 14 persons from industry, public accounting, the financial community, and academe was appointed in May 1973 to counsel the Board in preparing a Discussion Memorandum analyzing issues related to the project.

56. In the meantime, because a variety of methods of determining and accounting for exchange gains and losses existed in practice and not all companies completely disclosed their translation methods or their accounting for exchange gains and losses, the Board issued in October 1973 an Exposure Draft of a proposed FASB Statement on "Disclosure of Foreign Currency Translation Information." After considering the comments received on that Exposure Draft, the Board issued *FASB Statement No. 1* on that topic in December 1973.

57. The Board issued the Discussion Memorandum, "Accounting for Foreign Currency Translation," on February 21, 1974, and held a public hearing on the subject on June 10 and 11, 1974. The Board received 90 position papers, letters of comment, and outlines of oral presentations in response to the Discussion Memorandum. Fifteen presentations were made at the public hearing.

58. In 1972, the AICPA and the Canadian Institute of Chartered Accountants both published research studies on this subject.[20] While the Discussion Memorandum was being prepared, the Financial Executives Institute completed a survey of the translation practices of 45 major U.S. companies.[21] In addition to the availability of those studies, pronouncements of other professional accounting bodies, and other published research studies and articles that are cited in the Discussion Memorandum, the FASB staff prepared a *Financial Statement Model on Accounting for Foreign Currency Translation*.[22] Its purpose was to aid in identifying

[20]Leonard Lorensen, *Accounting Research Study No. 12,* "Reporting Foreign Operations of U.S. Companies in U.S. Dollars" (New York: AICPA, 1972); R. MacDonald Parkinson, *Translation of Foreign Currencies* (Toronto: Canadian Institute of Chartered Accountants, 1972).

[21]Financial Executives Institute, *Survey of U.S. Company Foreign Translation Practices,* 31 July 1973.

[22]Financial Accounting Standards Board, *Financial Statement Model on Accounting for Foreign Currency Translation* (Stamford, Connecticut: FASB, March 1974).

possible implementation problems related to adopting a particular method or combination of methods from among those that had been proposed or that were currently used in practice. The FASB staff also reviewed the disclosure of translation practices in recent annual financial statements of 77 companies engaged in foreign activities.

59. The Board received 190 letters of comment on its Exposure Draft of a proposed Statement on "Accounting for the Translation of Foreign Currency Transactions and Foreign Currency Financial Statements," dated December 31, 1974.

SUMMARY OF PAST PRONOUNCEMENTS AND PRACTICES

60. Chapter 12 of *ARB No. 43,* as modified by paragraph 18 of *APB Opinion No. 6,* was the basic authoritative pronouncement on accounting for foreign currency translation before this Statement. Chapter 12 called for translation of current assets and liabilities at the current rate and translation of noncurrent assets and liabilities at historical rates, that is, the *current-noncurrent* method. Under Chapter 12, exchange losses and realized exchange gains were included in net income, and unrealized exchange gains were preferably deferred, except that unrealized exchange gains might be included in net income to the extent that they offset exchange losses previously included in net income.

61. Chapter 12 of *ARB No. 43* provided certain exceptions to those general rules. Under special circumstances, inventory could be stated at historical rates. Long-term debt incurred or capital stock issued in connection with the acquisition of long-term assets shortly before a substantial and presumably permanent change in the rate could be restated at the new rate. If the debt or stock was restated, the difference was an adjustment of the cost of the assets acquired.

62. A research report[23] published in 1960 described the current-noncurrent distinction as one that "seems to reflect the use of an established balance sheet classification for a purpose to which it is not relevant." In addition, the report described the *monetary-nonmonetary* method, which had been proposed earlier.[24] Under that method, inventory is translated at historical rates because it is a nonmonetary asset, and both current and noncurrent receivables and payables are translated at the current rate because they are monetary items.

63. Translating all payables and receivables at the current rate received official recognition with the issuance in 1965 of *APB Opinion No. 6.* Paragraph 18 of *APB Opinion No. 6* stated, without specifying the circumstances, that "translation of long-term receivables and long-term liabilities at current exchange rates is appropriate in many circumstances." That modification of Chapter 12 of *ARB No. 43* in effect permitted use of the monetary-nonmonetary method of translation.

64. Because of extensive currency realignments in 1971, the APB considered the problem of foreign currency translation and issued an exposure draft proposing that companies using the monetary-nonmonetary method defer exchange gains and losses to the extent they did not exceed those attributable to long-term debt. Amounts deferred were to be accounted for in a manner similar to debt discount.[25] That draft in effect created another method of accounting for exchange gains and losses. *ARS No. 12* was in process at the time, and the U.S. dollar was devalued during the exposure period. The APB deferred action on the exposure draft and announced that companies should disclose how they accounted for exchange gains and losses. The APB also noted that some companies had adopted the recommendations of the exposure draft, thus achieving somewhat the same effect as translating long-term receivables and payables at historical rates.[26]

Appendix C

NEED FOR TRANSLATION

FOREIGN CURRENCY TRANSACTIONS

65. If an enterprise engages in a transaction that requires later settlement in a currency other than the one in which its accounts are maintained, translation is required to record the transaction.

66. An enterprise may be involved in various types of transactions that require settlement in foreign currency, including:

a. Operating transactions (importing, exporting, licensing, etc.);

[23]National Association of Accountants, *Research Report No. 36,* "Management Accounting Problems in Foreign Operations" (New York: NAA, 1960), p. 17.

[24]Samuel R. Hepworth, *Reporting Foreign Operations* (Ann Arbor, Michigan: University of Michigan, 1956).

[25]Proposed APB Opinion, "Translating Foreign Operations," Exposure Draft, 20 December 1971.

[26]*Accounting Research Association Newsletter,* 20 January 1972, p. 1.

b. Financing transactions (borrowing and lending);
c. Forward exchange contracts.

67. Foreign currency transactions may involve three stages:

a. Translation to record the transaction at the transaction date;
b. Subsequent adjustments of the unsettled portion of the transaction (the amount owed by or to the enterprise), if any, to reflect the current rate at balance sheet dates between the transaction date and the **settlement date;**
c. Conversion of one currency into the other at settlement date.[27]

Unit of Measure

68. At the transaction date it is necessary to measure and record in a particular currency (a unit of measure) the amount of the goods or services purchased or sold or the amount of the loan received or granted and the corresponding amount owed by or to the enterprise. Once the amount of the goods or services purchased or sold is measured and recorded in dollars,[28] it is not subject to further *translation.*

69. Because the dollar amount of any unsettled portion of the transaction (the amount to be paid in an import or borrowing transaction and the amount to be collected in an export or lending transaction) will be affected by a change in the rate between the dollar and the foreign currency (paragraphs 71 and 72), a potential for gain or loss exists.

70. If a foreign currency transaction is not settled when the transaction occurs, the question arises whether the amount receivable or payable should be presented in the financial statements of the enterprise until the settlement date at the dollar equivalent established at the transaction date or whether it should be adjusted at each intervening balance sheet date for the rate changes that may have occurred in the meantime. Paragraph 7(b) of this Statement states the Board's conclusion regarding that question, and paragraphs 112-115 and 161-166 give the Board's reasoning.

Effect of a Rate Change

71. An exchange rate is the ratio between a unit of one currency and the amount of another currency for which that unit can be exchanged (converted) at a particular time. For exemple, a spot rate of $1 = FC2 means that one dollar presently can be exchanged for two foreign currency units of money. A change in rate means that more or fewer units of one currency can be subsequently exchanged for a unit of another currency. For example, if the spot rate changed from $1 = FC2 to $1 = FC1, it would take $2 to obtain the same FC2 that $1 could have obtained at the old rate. Therefore, rate changes have a direct economic effect on transactions that require exchanges between a particular unit of money (for example, the dollar) and another unit of money.

Unsettled Foreign Currency Transactions

72. The effect of a rate change on foreign currency held is measurable in dollars. A rate change has a similar effect on an unsettled foreign currency transaction that was entered into before the rate change and involves the future payment or receipt of a fixed number of foreign currency units.

Future Foreign Currency Transactions

73. Once a rate changes, all subsequent exchanges between the two currencies are effected at the new rate until another rate change occurs. Therefore, a rate change may also affect the future earnings of an enterprise that has foreign currency transactions. For example, the future revenue in dollars of a U.S. company that exports its domestically manufactured product for sale to customers in a foreign country at a price stated in foreign currency may be affected by a rate change. Whether or not the translation process should consider the future effect of a rate change is discussed in paragraphs 96-111.

FOREIGN STATEMENTS

Unit of Measure

74. Foreign statements are derived from accounting records that are not kept in dollars. The unit of measure in foreign statements is usually the local currency of the foreign country, but another foreign currency may be chosen as the unit of measure in particular circumstances. Either way, transactions of a foreign operation are not measured in dollars

[27]Although conversion may be at a rate other than the one at which cash, a receivable, or a payable is recorded, *translation* is not involved. However, an exchange gain or loss results from conversion at a different rate.

[28]*APB Statement No. 4* (paragraph 165) states the following regarding the unit of measure:

> "In the United States, the U.S. dollar fulfills the functions of medium of exchange, unit of account, and store of value. It provides the unit of measure for financial accounting. Stating assets and liabilities and changes in them in terms of a common financial denominator is prerequisite to performing the operations—for example, addition and subtraction—necessary to measure financial position and periodic net income."

but in another currency. The foreign currency transactions of a foreign operation require the same translation process as foreign currency transactions of a U.S. company.

75. The need to translate foreign statements arises because an enterprise's financial statements cannot be prepared in dollars directly from accounting records kept in a different currency. The major issue raised in translating foreign statements is whether or not the statements should be translated, either for some or all foreign operations, in a manner that changes the unit of measure from the local currency to the dollar. Paragraph 6 states the Board's conclusion on that issue, and paragraphs 83-95 give the Board's reasoning.

Effect of a Rate Change

76. Paragraphs 72 and 73 mention the possible effects of a rate change on an enterprise's unsettled foreign currency transactions and future foreign currency transactions. That discussion applies equally to foreign currency transactions of U.S. and foreign operations. A rate change between the local currency of a foreign operation and the dollar may also affect the accounting results measured in dollars of future local currency transactions of that operation. For example, the measurement in dollars of future revenue and expenses of a French company whose transactions are solely in French francs may be affected by a rate change. Paragraphs 96-111 consider that possible consequence.

Appendix D

BASIS FOR CONCLUSIONS

CONTENTS

Appendix D

BASIS FOR CONCLUSIONS

77. This Appendix discusses factors deemed significant by members of the Board in reaching the conclusions in this Statement, including various alternatives considered and reasons for accepting some and rejecting others. Some Board members gave greater weight to some factors than to others.

OBJECTIVES OF TRANSLATION

78. The Board determined that the first step toward conclusions regarding the unique problems of translating foreign currency transactions and foreign statements should be to identify the objective of the translation process.

79. Letters of comment received, personal views of Board and task force members, and thoughts expressed in various writings on the subject sug-

gested the following objectives which were considered by the Board.

A. To present the financial statements of the enterprise in conformity with the U.S. generally accepted accounting principles that would apply had all assets, liabilities, revenue, and expenses been measured and recorded in dollars.
B. To retain in the enterprise's financial statements the accounting principles that are accepted in the foreign country for assets, liabilities, revenue, and expenses measured and recorded in foreign currency.
C. To have a single unit of measure for financial statements that include translated foreign amounts; that is, not only to express in dollars the assets, liabilities, revenue, or expenses that are measured or denominated in foreign currency, but also to measure them in dollars.
D. To retain as a unit of measure each currency in which assets, liabilities, revenue, and expenses are measured; that is, to express in dollars the assets, liabilities, revenue, and expenses that are measured in foreign currencies but to retain the foreign currencies as units of measure.
E. To produce an exchange gain or loss that is compatible with the expected economic effect of a rate change on business activities conducted in a currency other than dollars.

U.S. or Foreign Accounting Principles (Objective A v. Objective B)

80. Unless the same accounting principles are generally accepted in both the U.S. and the countries in which foreign operations are located, Objectives A and B are mutually exclusive. The translation process cannot retain both if the principles are different. One view is that the only meaningful foreign statements for translation purpospes are those based on accounting principles generally accepted in the foreign country. Thus, if an **attribute** of an asset is measured on a basis not in conformity with U.S. generally accepted accounting principles, that measurement basis should, nonetheless, be retained in the translation process.

81. The opposing view is that U.S. generally accepted accounting principles have been developed and are well known. Accordingly, readers of dollar financial statements, although perhaps not cognizant of all the principles used to prepare the statements, generally understand what the statements represent. Therefore, it is inappropriate to combine in an enterprise's financial statements assets and liabilities that are measured by different accounting principles.

82. After considering the alternatives, the Board concluded that it should require the concept that has been implicitly understood and applied in practice, namely, that all financial statements included in consolidated financial statements should be prepared in conformity with U.S. generally accepted accounting principles. The Board concluded that consistency of accounting procedures and measurement processes between foreign and domestic operations is desirable in the consolidation of foreign and domestic financial statements. Therefore, foreign statements prepared for purposes of combination, consolidation, or equity accounting should be prepared in conformity with U.S. generally accepted accounting principles, and translation should not change the measurement bases used in those foreign statements. The Board, therefore, accepted Objective A and rejected Objective B.

Single or Multiple Units of Measure (Objective C v. Objective D)

83. Objectives C and D are also mutually exclusive because after a rate change the translation process can either retain two or more currencies as units of measure or have a single unit of measure, but it cannot do both. For example, if an asset is acquired either by a foreign operation or a domestic operation for FC100 when the rate is FC1 = $1, its historical cost measured in either foreign currency or dollars can be expressed as $100 in the dollar financial statements. However, if the rate changes to FC1 = $2, the historical cost of the asset would be expressed as $200 (translated at the current rate) in the dollar financial statements to retain the foreign currency as the unit of measure. Expressing the cost as $100 after the rate change measures the historical cost of the asset in dollars, not in foreign currency.

84. The desire to retain the foreign currency as the unit of measure stems from the belief that the foreign statements represent the most meaningful presentation of a foreign operation and that translation should preserve the relationships in those statements. That view also supports retaining the foreign accounting principles (paragraphs 80-82) and is related to the view that the historical cost of a foreign asset can be measured only in foreign currency (paragraphs 133-138).

85. The unit-of-measure issue focuses principally on the assets and liabilities of foreign operations that are measured at past prices in foreign currency. There is general agreement that cash, receivables, and payables measured or denominated in foreign currency, and assets and liabilities measured at current or future prices in foreign currency are trans-

lated at the current rate regardless of which currency is considered the unit of measure.[29]

86. An important conceptual distinction between the two opposing views involves the way in which the effect of the translation process is recognized. If the dollar is the unit of measure, a change in the dollar carrying amounts of assets and liabilities resulting from a rate change affects net income. If, however, the foreign currency is the unit of measure in dollar statements of foreign operations, prior dollar translated statements need to be restated to current equivalent dollars to make them comparable with current translated statements. Restatement does not change the prior periods' statements in any way except to update the amounts to current equivalent dollars and, therefore, does not result in an exchange gain or loss.

87. The Board considered the purpose of consolidated financial statements under present generally accepted accounting principles in assessing whether the dollar or the foreign currency should be the appropriate unit of measure for foreign statements included in an enterprise's financial statements. *ARB No. 51,* "Consolidated Financial Statements," paragraph 1, states:

> The purpose of consolidated statements is to present, primarily for the benefit of the shareholders and creditors of the parent company, the results of operations and the financial position of a parent company and its subsidiaries essentially as if the group were a single company with one or more branches or divisions.

88. The Board believes that to be consistent with that purpose the translation process should reflect the transactions of the entire group, including foreign operations, as though the transactions were of a single enterprise. For example, when an enterprise purchases an entity, the cost of the investment to the enterprise establishes the cost for the assets acquired for consolidated financial statements regardless of the carrying amounts recorded by the acquired entity. Therefore, even though the acquired entity may have its own recorded cost for an asset, the acquiring enterprise's cost governs in the consolidation process (paragraph 41).

89. The dollar is usually the unit of measure for financial statements of a U.S. enterprise, and there is no controversy regarding the cost of an asset acquired by a U.S. company in a foreign currency transaction that is settled at the rate in effect at the transaction date. *Cost* is measured in dollars at the transaction date, and that cost does not subsequently change as a result of rate changes. Although advocates of a one-transaction perspective (paragraph 113) have a different view of what constitutes cost if settlement is at a rate different from the one in effect at the transaction date, they nevertheless recognize the dollar as the unit of measure.

90. Since translated cost in dollars may be affected by the foreign currency chosen, attempting to use a particular foreign currency as the unit of measure for foreign statements included in dollar financial statements creates a practical problem—that of selecting the particular currency to measure the cost of an asset. For example, if an oil tanker is acquired at a price negotiated in Japanese yen and its cost is recorded in financial statements that use the U.S. dollar as the unit of measure, the dollar cost of that asset remains constant regardless of rate changes (paragraph 89). If, however, the cost is measured and recorded in the financial statements of a foreign operation and translation retains the foreign currency as the unit of measure, the cost of the tanker reported in the dollar statements changes with changes in the dollar rate for that foreign currency. That is true regardless of the currency used to acquire the asset or the currency in which revenue from use of the asset will be generated. The tanker could be used to transport oil from the Middle East to France (and other European countries) and the revenue generated thereby might be stated in French francs (or other European currencies). But the historical cost of the asset in the translated dollar financial statements would fluctuate with changes in the dollar rate for, say, the pound sterling if that were the local currency in which the cost of the tanker was originally measured and recorded.

91. Another example that also illustrates the potential consequences of selecting the local currency of a foreign operation as the unit of measure involves goodwill. If a U.S. enterprise acquires for cash a foreign operation located in Germany at a price in excess of the fair value of the net assets acquired, the difference is recognized as goodwill. If the enterprise acquires the interest directly, the goodwill is measured in dollars and it does not change solely because of a rate change. If, however, the enterprise's Swiss subsidiary acquires the interest with the proceeds of a Eurodollar borrowing or financing from the enterprise and records the investment in the Swiss accounts, the basis for the same goodwill reported in the dollar statements will change with changes in the dollar rate for the Swiss

[29]Proposals to defer recognition of exchange gains and losses on long-term receivables and payables—either by deferring exchange gains and losses resulting from translating the assets and liabilities at the current rate or by translating the items at historical rates until collection or settlement (as, for example, by the current-noncurrent method)—raise issues separate from the unit-of-measure issue and are discussed in paragraphs 172-194 and 129-132.

franc even though it does not change in the Swiss accounts. Moreover, the dollar basis of the goodwill will begin a new pattern of changes based on the relation of the new currency to the dollar if the enterprise's investment in the foreign operation in Germany is shifted from the Swiss subsidiary to, say, a subsidiary in the United Kingdom, even if the shift is for good business or tax reasons. In other words, adopting a foreign currency rather than the dollar as the unit of measure allows the translated dollar cost of an asset to be affected by discretionary selection of the accounting records in which the asset is recorded.

92. To use more than one unit of measure in a single set of financial statements raises questions about describing the results. If various foreign currencies are used as the units of measure in translated financial statements of foreign operations of an enterprise, aggregating the resulting dollar amounts with each other and with the dollar amounts from domestic operations would produce totals that are neither dollar measures nor measures in any other currency. In the Board's judgment, the notion of a single enterprise that underlies consolidated financial statements requires a single unit of measure.

93. Since attempting to use a foreign currency as the unit of measure both produces results not in conformity with generally accepted accounting principles and creates conceptual and practical problems, the Board concluded that the dollar, not the local currency of the foreign operation, should be the unit of measure. Thus, the Board rejected Objective D and adopted Objective C.

94. Objectives A and C, adopted by the Board, are combined in paragraph 6 of this Statement as a single objective of translation. Some respondents to the Exposure Draft criticized that objective as an attempt to account for local and foreign currency transactions of foreign operations as if they were dollar transactions or, to a few respondents, as if they were dollar transactions in the United States. In the Board's judgment, those criticisms are not valid. Neither the objective nor the procedures to accomplish it change the denomination of a transaction or the environment in which it occurs. The procedures adopted by the Board are consistent with the purpose of consolidated financial statements. The foreign currency transactions of an enterprise and the local and foreign currency transactions of its foreign operations are translated and accounted for as transactions of a single enterprise. The denomination of transactions and the location of assets are not changed; however, the separate corporate identities within the consolidated group are ignored. Translation procedures are merely a means of remeasuring in dollars amounts that are denominated or originally measured in foreign currency. That is, the procedures do *not* attempt to simulate what the cost of a foreign plant would have been had it been located in the United States; instead, they recognize the factors that determined the plant's cost in the foreign location and express that cost in dollars.

95. If translation procedures were capable of changing the denomination of an asset or liability from foreign currency to dollars, no exchange risk would be present. Translation procedures obviously cannot accomplish that, and the procedures adopted in this Statement affirm the existence of an exchange risk in foreign currency transactions and foreign operations and specify accounting for the resulting exchange gains or losses.[30]

Compatibility with Expected Economic Effects of Rate Change (Objective E)

96. In its deliberations on each of several translation methods, the Board considered the views of respondents to the Discussion Memorandum and Exposure Draft and others who suggested, directly or indirectly, that the translation method should produce an exchange gain or loss that is compatible with the expected economic effects of a rate change. That is, the translation method should produce an exchange gain (or at least avoid producing an exchange loss) if the economic effect of a rate change appears to be beneficial and an exchange loss (or at least not an exchange gain) if the economic effect appears to be detrimental.

97. In the Board's opinion, that objective cannot be fulfilled without major changes in the present accounting model. The economic compatibility issue is usually raised in the context of a foreign operation with significant assets carried at cost in the foreign statements and significant long-term debt denominated in foreign currency. Methods used or proposed to achieve the compatibility objective fall into one or a combination of three categories: (a) exchange gains and losses are recognized by translating both assets carried at cost and long-term liabilities at the current rate, (b) no exchange gains or losses are recognized when exchange rates change on either assets or liabilities by translating both at historical rates,[31] and (c) no exchange gain or loss is recognized on assets translated at historical rates, and the gain or loss computed on the liabilities translated at the current rate is deferred and recognized over later periods by accounting for it (i) as an

[30]Some arguments supporting translation of all accounts at the current rate raise questions about whether translation can or should result in exchange gains and losses (paragraphs 80-82, 84-86, and 133-138).

[31]The argument that a rate change can be ignored because it will probably reverse before a debt is paid or a receivable is collected is a different issue which is considered in paragraphs 166 and 192.

adjustment of the translated cost of the assets, (ii) as an adjustment of the effective rate of interest on the liability (that is, as a premium or discount), or (iii) as a deferred credit or deferred charge.[32]

98. All of the proposed methods meet the compatibility objective in the sense that they at least avoid producing an exchange loss if a rate change is one that the proponents deem beneficial and avoid producing an exchange gain if a rate change is one that the proponents deem detrimental. In addition, if assets exceed liabilities, methods that translate both assets and liabilities at the current rate (paragraph 97(a)) produce a gain or loss that is in the right direction according to the proponents of the proposed objective. In the Board's view, however, the result cannot be described as an accurate measure of the beneficial or detrimental effect of a rate change because its computation involves multiplying the unamortized historical cost of assets in foreign currency by the current rate (paragraphs 106, 107, and 147-149). Further, in the Board's judgment, the proposed methods either conflict with present generally accepted accounting principles or are unacceptable for other reasons. The Board's views that are summarized in this and the preceding paragraph are expanded and illustrated in the following paragraphs.

99. Under present generally accepted accounting principles, the time for recognizing gains or losses on assets and liabilities depends on their carrying bases. Thus, recognition of gains and losses on assets accounted for at cost is usually deferred until the assets are sold or their costs are otherwise deducted from operating revenue. The translation method adopted by the Board retains that timing for recognition of gains and losses and by so doing amplifies or highlights one effect of carrying assets at cost. A simple example illustrates the type of translated result that proponents of the compatibility objective describe as not compatible with the expected economic effect of a rate change.

100. The balance sheet of a hypothetical foreign operation consists of FC125 in cash, FC100 owed to a local bank, and FC25 of stockholders' equity. The exchange rate is FC1 = $1. Under the translation procedures adopted by the Board, the asset and liability are translated into $125 and $100, respectively. If the rate changes to FC.50 = $1, translation at the new rate gives $250 for the asset and $200 for the liability. The net exchange gain of $25 ($125 gain on the asset less $100 loss on the liability) is almost universally accepted as the result of a valid translation procedure and few, if any, question whether it is a reasonable representation of the economic effect of the rate change.

101. However, a different pattern of gains and losses results and a difference of opinion arises if, instead of cash or a receivable, the asset held when the rate changes is one that is normally accounted for at its costs or amortized cost. If the foreign operation in the foregoing example spends its cash balance before the rate changes to buy an asset such as inventory, land, or equipment, the cost of the asset acquired is FC125 = $125. Under the procedures adopted by the Board, the translated dollar cost remains at $125 after the rate change. The liability is translated at $200, however, resulting in an exchange loss of $100 for the period of the rate change. Proponents of the compatibility objective hold that it is erroneous to report the $100 exchange loss on the liability when the rate changes because the expected economic effect of the rate change is beneficial by reason of an equal or greater expected eventual gain on the asset.

102. The eventual gain or loss on the asset is usually recognized when the asset is sold or its translated cost is otherwise deducted from operating revenue (translated at the new rate). Assuming the rate remains stable and the revenue in foreign currency equals cost in foreign currency, the reported gain on the sale is $125 (sales price FC125 × 1/.50 = $250 less cost $125 = $125 gain), the same as the exchange gain in paragraph 100.

103. Two criticisms of the translation procedures adopted by the Board may confuse discussions of the economic compatibility issue. The first is that the Board's procedures result in recognizing only the loss on the liability, thereby ignoring the gain on the asset and misstating the profitability of a net foreign investment. However, the example shows that the gain on the asset is often recognized in a later period than the loss on the liability and is often included in gain or loss on sale of the asset (as in the example), reflected in operating income as the difference between operating revenue translated at the new rate and depreciation or amortization translated at the old rate, or otherwise included in income as other than exchange gain or loss.

104. The second criticism is that the exchange loss on the liability, which is recognized by the Board's procedures, is not really a loss in dollars because the whole series of transactions from borrowing to repayment is in the same foreign currency. However, the difference between the original borrowing (initially translated as $100) and its repayment (equivalent to $200) must be accounted for. To satisfy the debt requires the equivalent of $200 whether dollars or foreign currency are paid. No question arises if a U.S. parent transfers $200 to settle the debt. The substance is the same if the debt is paid with foreign

[32] The three categories are discussed individually in paragraphs 140-152, 129-132, and 172-194.

currency received from operations in the foreign country. The cash (FC100) used to pay the debt is translated as $200 at all times between the rate change or the receipt of the cash and immediately before its use to pay the debt. Repayment of the debt requires cash with an equivalent dollar value of $200, and the loss of $100 is undeniable because cash held or received after the rate change cannot reasonably be translated at other than the new rate (FC.50 = $1). The only way to avoid recognizing a loss of $100 is to translate the original borrowing as $200 by restating the earlier financial statements as if the rate had always been FC.50 = $1. However, that is appropriate only if the foreign currency is the unit of measure in the translated statements (paragraphs 83-86), not if the dollar is the unit of measure.

105. Since the *incompatible* loss result described in paragraph 101 can be avoided only by anticipating the gain on the asset or by deferring recognition of the loss on the liability, the proposed objective directly conflicts with present generally accepted accounting principles. Under present generally accepted accounting principles, recognition of gains on assets carried at cost must normally await sale (or depreciation or amortization), and those gains may not be anticipated indirectly by deferring otherwise recognizable losses. In contrast, under present principles, identified losses should be recognized when they occur and should not be deferred as assets or deferred charges, offset against gains on unsold assets, or treated as valuation accounts to unsold assets.[33]

106. A major obstacle to implementing the compatibility objective is that to determine whether a translation method produces a compatible exchange gain or loss, one must first be able to ascertain the expected future economic effects of a rate change. The proposal seems to rest significantly on a general assumption that a local currency's strengthening is beneficial and its weakening is detrimental. That assumption rests on a further assumption that the relation between rate changes and economic effects is reasonably straightforward—that only the rate changes, while other variables—such as output, sales volume, production costs, and sales prices—remain essentially unaffected. However, determining the expected economic effect of a rate change is more complex than that.

107. For example, to assess the expected economic effect of a rate change on a foreign operation's investment in plant and equipment, and possibly other long-lived assets, requires a long-term economic forecast in which many interrelated and interacting forces involved in a rate change should be considered. The Board believes it may be difficult or impossible under most circumstances to predict with reasonable certainty the general effects over an extended future period of a rate change. A foreign operation in a country that experiences a major rate change may be affected both directly and indirectly by the adaptations and shifts that occur in that country's economy as a result of the currency adjustment. The nature and effect of those adaptations and modifications depend on a complex relation among factors, such as the relative degree to which general demand for imports and exports responds to changes in the foreign exchange price, the level of income and employment, the rate of economic expansion, monetary and fiscal policies instituted by the country whose currency has either weakened or strengthened, and conditions and forces existing in countries that are major trading partners. Accordingly, a foreign operation may experience complex changes in the local market demand and market price for its goods, changes in its local cost of goods and services procured, and in the local availability and cost of financing. Moreover, not all operations in the same environment will be affected in the same way because of differences in activities and realignments of price and cost structures within the local economy. In addition, a foreign operation's exposure to the effect of a rate change may go beyond its recorded assets and liabilities. A foreign operation's unrecorded exposure to rate changes might include, for example, sales and purchase backlog commitments at fixed foreign currency prices or fixed foreign currency streams of revenue or expense, such as rent payments. The proposed objective could be impractical in many circumstances because of the foresight required to identify the future economic effects of a rate change at the time it occurs.

108. Finally, the proposed compatibility objective seems to be based on an assumption that it is needed only in translating foreign statements that are to be incorporated in the financial statements of a U.S. enterprise. However, it appears to be a response to the fact that U.S. generally accepted accounting principles require certain assets to be accounted for at cost. The argument for economic compatibility of reported results with expected effects of rate changes could be directed with equal force to reporting foreign currency transactions of a U.S. enterprise or, with minor modification, even to reporting its domestic operations.

109. For example, a U.S. enterprise serves the needs of important foreign customers by selling them the entire output of a plant located in the United States. The enterprise also owes long-term debt denominated in the foreign currency, and as a result of the dol-

[33]Matters relating to recognizing gains on assets carried at cost or deferring losses on liabilities are discussed further in paragraphs 147-149 and 172-194.

lar's weakening against the foreign currency it incurs an exchange loss. However, the rate change appears to be beneficial to the enterprise because, other things remaining constant, the dollar value of its foreign revenue (and therefore also its dollar net income) should increase. To report a result compatible with that assessment requires recognition of a gain from an upward adjustment of the related plant assets. Further, a rate change involving a weakening dollar has the same effects on expected dollar revenue and expected dollar gross profit as an increased selling price in a U.S. market. Consistent with the compatibility objective, therefore, an increase in the selling price of the output of a U.S. plant that produces for the U.S. market should, other things being equal, result in a reported gain from revaluation of the plant compatible with the expectation of its improved future revenue and profits. That those kinds of gains are not now recognized reflects a characteristic of present generally accepted accounting principles, not a defect in the Board's translation procedures.

110. Present financial accounting and reporting reflects primarily the effects of past transactions and existing conditions, not future transactions or conditions. Accordingly, assets are generally carried at cost, and related gains are recognized only when assets are sold or the cost is otherwise deducted from revenue. Many have commented on the strengths and weaknesses of the present accounting model, and some have proposed major changes in it.This Statement pertains to translation of foreign currency transactions and foreign currency financial statements, and the Board believes that consideration of fundamental changes in generally accepted accounting principles relating to measurement bases of assets and liabilities is beyond this Statement's scope. The Board does not intend to use translation procedures to effect major changes in the accounting model presently in use.

111. Since, for the reasons given, the Board chose an objective of translation and a translation procedure that preserve the present accounting model, it rejected proposed Objective E. The Board rejected the view that the objective of compatibility can be implemented by changing translation procedures without considering the implications for underlying concepts and measurements.

Appendix D

FOREIGN CURRENCY TRANSACTIONS

Import or Export of Goods or Services

112. The Board's conclusions on accounting for foreign currency transactions reflect the view that collection of a receivable or payment of a liability is a transaction separate from the sale or purchase from which the receivable or liability arose. Thus, if an enterprise has foreign currency exchange exposure (*exchange exposure*) on a receivable from a sale or a liability from a purchase requiring settlement in foreign currency, the results, if any, of that exchange exposure should be accounted for separately from sales, cost of sales, or inventory. A rate change does not affect previously recorded revenue from exports or the cost of imported goods or services.

113. An alternate view, sometimes referred to as a one-transaction perspective, is that a transaction involving purchase or sale of goods or services with the price stated in foreign currency is incomplete until the amount in dollars necessary to liquidate the related payable or receivable is determined. The initial amount recorded in dollars as cost or revenue is considered to be an estimate until final settlement. According to that view, an exchange gain or loss related to the transaction should be treated as an adjustment of the cost of imports or revenue from exports.

114. The Board considered and rejected the one-transaction view. Specifically, the Board rejected the idea that the cost of an imported asset or the reported revenue from an export sale is affected by later changes in the related liability or receivable. The exchange exposure in a purchase or sale transaction whose price is denominated in foreign currency stems not from the purchase or sale itself but from a delay in payment or receipt of the equivalent dollars. No exchange gain or loss can occur if, as soon as the price is fixed in foreign currency, the U.S. purchaser immediately buys foreign currency with dollars and pays the foreign seller, or the U.S. seller receives foreign currency from the foreign buyer and immediately converts it into dollars. In other words, exchange gains and losses on import or export transactions result from a combination of a rate change and one of the following: the U.S. buyer owes an amount denominated in foreign currency, or the U.S. seller holds a receivable denominated in foreign currency or holds foreign currency received from a foreign buyer.

115. The exchange gain or loss that may result from an exchange exposure is the result of an event (a rate change) that is separate from the original purchase or sale transaction. Since an exchange exposure can usually be eliminated, a determination not to avoid exchange exposure should be accounted for by recognizing the gain or loss that results from that decision.

116. Paragraph 7(a) specifies that the purchase or sale price in foreign currency be translated into dollars at the rate in effect at the transaction date. Since

transactions are often preceded by commitments, and exchange exposure may be viewed as beginning at the commitment date if the price is fixed in foreign currency at that time, the dollar basis of the transaction might be established at the commitment date rather than the transaction date. However, a major obstacle to choosing the commitment date is the fact that, although certain commitments are often disclosed, rarely are commitments recorded under present generally accepted accounting principles. Losses on *firm* commitments are recorded[34] but not the commitments themselves. The Board believes that recognizing exchange gains and losses on a commitment date basis would be both impracticable and inconsistent with the timing of recognizing the underlying transaction in the financial statements.

117. A commitment date basis could present implementation problems because various degrees of commitment are possible before consummation of a business transaction. For example, a noncancelable sales contract negotiated in a foreign currency might be considered by some as a reasonable basis on which to recognize an exchange gain or loss. However, a firm commitment to provide goods or services might require a commitment by the seller to purchase goods or services in foreign currency to fulfill his obligation. Both commitments would need to be considered to reflect exchange gains and losses properly on a commitment date basis, but the purchase obligations might not necessarily be in the form of fixed contractual commitments. Moreover, since commitments are not now recorded, measuring exchange gains and losses from a commitment date would require ascertaining the commitment date on each individual transaction. An importer or exporter with relatively few individual transactions might manage that, but it would be burdensome, if not impossible, for one with numerous foreign currency transactions or for a foreign operation to separate transactions with commitments from those without commitments and maintain a record of commitment dates, prices, and applicable exchange rates.

118. The problem of inconsistency in using the commitment date under present generally accepted accounting principles is illustrated by a long-term supply contract for raw materials under which both the purchaser and the seller now recognize cost and revenue, respectively, in their financial statements on a performance basis. Since that kind of agreement might be considered a commitment, an enterprise that is party to a five-year supply contract requiring payments in a foreign currency may conceivably have a significant exchange gain or loss if the total future payments are considered on a commitment basis. Since the supplier recognizes revenue and operating profit over the life of the contract, for him to recognize as current gain or loss the expected effect of a rate change on future income would be inconsistent with the timing of recognition of the operating income from the contract. Likewise, an enterprise that must pay foreign currency for its raw materials could also have a significant exchange gain or loss, but its immediate recognition (except to the extent of "accrued net losses on firm purchase commitments"[35]) would be inappropriate for similar reasons.

Foreign Borrowing or Lending

119. The Board's conclusions on accounting for foreign currency transactions involving the borrowing or lending of foreign currency reflect the view that the effect of a rate change on the repayment or collection of a loan should be accounted for separately from the original borrowing or lending transaction. An alternate treatment considered by the Board is based on a one-transaction perspective similar to that described in paragraph 113: that an exchange gain or loss related to a loan payable denominated in foreign currency is an adjustment of the cost of assets purchased with the borrowed funds. The Board's reasoning in rejecting a one-transaction perspective for borrowing foreign currency is similar to that stated in paragraphs 114 and 115.

120. Another possibility in accounting for borrowing or lending of foreign currency is to treat a related exchange gain or loss as an adjustment of the cost of borrowing or the return from lending. Following that concept, an enterprise ideally would adjust the cost or return from funds borrowed or loaned by using the interest method to amortize expected exchange gains or losses on principal and interest over the life of the debt or receivable. Since at the date of lending or borrowing it is impossible to predict the rates that will prevail during the life of the loan, prospective (and partially retroactive) methods have been suggested to amortize the exchange gain or loss. The Board rejected those methods for the reasons stated in paragraphs 164, 181, and 182.

FOREIGN STATEMENTS

121. Paragraphs 123-139 compare four normative methods for translating assets and liabilities measured in foreign currency against the objective of translation adopted by the Board (a situational

[34] *ARB No. 43,* Chapter 4, Statement 10 reads: "Accrued net losses on firm purchase commitments for goods for inventory, measured in the same way as are inventory losses, should, if material, be recognized in the accounts."

[35] *ARB No. 43,* Chapter 4, Statement 10.

approach to the application of those methods is discussed in paragraphs 140-152). The principal distinction among various normative methods of translation is the requirement to translate particular classifications of assets and liabilities at either the current or historical rate.

a. The temporal method translates cash, receivables and payables, and assets and liabilities carried at present or future prices at the current rate and assets and liabilities carried at past prices at applicable historical rates.
b. The monetary-nonmonetary method generally translates monetary assets and liabilities at the current rate and nonmonetary assets and liabilities at applicable historical rates. For translation purposes, assets and liabilities are monetary if they are expressed in terms of a fixed number of foreign currency units. All other balance sheet items are classified as nonmonetary.
c. The current-noncurrent method generally translates current assets and liabilities at the current rate and noncurrent assets and liabilities at applicable historical rates.
d. The current rate method translates all assets and liabilities at the current rate.

122. The objective of translation requires that the assets, liabilities, revenue, and expenses in foreign statements be translated and accounted for in the same manner as assets, liabilities, revenue, and expenses that result from foreign currency transactions of the enterprise (paragraph 9). Since foreign statements are prepared in conformity with U.S. generally accepted accounting principles before translation, the objective is generally achieved by (a) translating cash, receivables, and payables at the current rate and (b) translating other assets and liabilities in a way that retains the accounting principles used to measure them in the foreign statements. The Board adopted intact none of the four normative methods considered but found the temporal method, proposed by *ARS No. 12* (see footnote 20), the most useful in meeting the objective.

Temporal Method

123. The temporal method generally translates assets and liabilities carried at past, current, or future prices expressed in foreign currency in a manner that retains the accounting principles used to measure them in the foreign statements. That is, the measurement bases of the assets and liabilities measured are the same after translation as before. Thus, the temporal method changes a measurement in foreign currency into a measurement in dollars without changing the basis of the measurement and thereby achieves one of the objectives of translation, which is to retain the measurement bases of foreign statement items (paragraph 82). The temporal method can also accommodate any basis of measurement—for example, historical cost, current replacement price, or current selling price—that is based on exchange prices.

124. The translation procedures to apply the temporal method are generally the same as those now used by many U.S. enterprises under the monetary-nonmonetary method.The results of the temporal method and the monetary-nonmonetary method now coincide because under present generally accepted accounting principles monetary assets and liabilities are usually measured at amounts that pertain to the balance sheet date and nonmonetary assets and liabilities are usually measured at prices in effect when the assets or liabilities were acquired or incurred. The monetary-nonmonetary classification itself contains nothing to preserve the measurement bases and timing of revenue and expenses recognition that are in the foreign statements (paragraphs 126 and 127). Rather, the coincidence of results between the monetary-nonmonetary method and the temporal method is due solely to the nature of present generally accepted accounting principles—assets and liabilities are measured on bases that happen to coincide with their classifications as monetary and nonmonetary. The results of the temporal method and the monetary-nonmonetary method would differ significantly under other accounting principles that, for example, required nonmonetary assets and liabilities to be measured at prices in effect at dates other than those at which they were acquired or incurred. Since the temporal method retains the measurement bases of the foreign statements equally as well under all accounting methods based on exchange prices as it does under historical cost accounting, the Board believes that it is the more generally valid method for achieving the objective of translation. It provides a conceptual basis for the procedures that are now used to apply the monetary-nonmonetary method.

125. The same point as in the preceding paragraph also applies to the current-noncurrent method. Some of the translation procedures under that method are the same as under the temporal method, but the major exceptions include translation of current assets carried at cost (inventory and prepaid expenses) and noncurrent liabilities and receivables. The current-noncurrent classification itself contains nothing to preserve accounting principles after translation (paragraph 129), but under present generally accepted accounting principles the measurement bases of many assets and liabilities happen to coincide with their classification as current or noncurrent. The major exceptions—inventory and long-term debt—show the deficiencies of the method when the measurement bases and the classifications do not coincide. As long as most foreign currencies weakened against the dollar, as they

usually did from the time of the original writing of Chapter 12 of *ARB No. 43* until about 1969, translating inventory at the current rate and long-term debt at historical rates under the current-noncurrent method probably produced conservative results. Inventory was stated lower in dollars than if translated at historical rates (though not necessarily at the lower of cost or market as described in paragraphs 46-49), and exchange gains (not losses) on long-term debt were deferred until the time of settlement or classification as a current liability. Once the dollar began to weaken against foreign currencies, however, that translation method lost its conservative appeal because it produced the opposite results.

Monetary-Nonmonetary Method

126. The monetary-nonmonetary method produces acceptable results under present generally accepted accounting principles (paragraph 124), but no comprehensive principle of translation can be derived solely from the monetary-nonmonetary distinction. Nonmonetary assets and liabilities are measured on different bases (for example, past prices or current prices) under different circumstances, and translation at a past rate does not always fit. Translating nonmonetary items at a past rate produces reasonable results if the items are stated at historical cost but not if they are stated at current market price in foreign currency.

127. For example, if a foreign operation purchases as an investment 100 shares of another company's common stock (a nonmonetary item) for FC1,000 when the rate is FC1 = $1, the cost of that investment is equivalent to $1,000. If the investment is carried at cost by the foreign operation, treating the investment as a nonmonetary item and translating it at the historical rate is appropriate. However, if the investment is carried at market price, translating that basis by the historical rate usually produces questionable results. For example, if the current market value of the investment is FC1,500 and the current rate is FC1 = $1.25, translating FC1,500 into $1,500 using the historical rate does not result in the current market value measured in dollars (FC1,500 × 1.25 = $1,875) or the historical cost in dollars. The monetary-nonmonetary method can produce the $1,875 current market value only if it is recognized that, under the method, the current rate is the applicable historical rate for nonmonetary assets carried at current prices. The point has been confusing enough to cause some proponents of the monetary-nonmonetary method to argue that nonmonetary assets, such as investments and inventories, become monetary assets if they are carried at market price.

128. Although the deficiencies of the monetary-nonmonetary method have been recognized and dealt with in practice, the Board found the monetary-nonmonetary method concept inadequate as a comprehensive method of translation.

Current-Noncurrent Method

129. Existing definitions of current and noncurrent assets and liabilities contain nothing to explain why that classification scheme should determine the rate used to translate. The attributes of assets and liabilities that are measured in financial statements differ from their characteristics that determine their classification as current or noncurrent. Consequently, different kinds of assets or liabilities may be measured the same way but classified differently or classified the same way but measured differently. For example, under present generally accepted accounting principles both inventory and plant and equipment are measured at historical cost, but inventory is classified as a current asset and plant and equipment as noncurrent assets. Since translation is concerned with measurement and not with classification, the characteristics of assets and liabilities that determine their classification for purposes of disclosure are not relevant for selecting the rate for translation. The weaknesses of the method are most pronounced in translating inventory and long-term debt.

130. Under the current-noncurrent method, inventory carried at historical cost in foreign statements is generally translated at the current rate. As indicated in paragraph 134, that translation results in a measure in dollars that departs from historical-cost-based accounting. Later changes in market prices or rates cannot change the historical cost of an asset already owned. Once recorded, the historical cost of an asset can be amortized or otherwise included in expense in accounting records but cannot be changed because of varying prices without changing the basis of accounting from historical cost to something else. (Paragraphs 153-158 give additional reasons for the Board's rejection of the current rate to translate inventory carried at cost.)

131. Measured in local currency, long-term debt denominated in local currency and a related unamortized discount or premium (determined by the interest method) together represent the present value of future interest and principal payments based on the effective rate of interest at the date the debt was incurred. Translating long-term debt and a related discount or premium at the historical rate after a rate change, as required by the current-noncurrent method, does not retain that measurement basis. Translation at the historical rate produces a result that is unrelated to the current dollar equivalent of the present value of the remaining interest and principal payments based on the effective rate of interest at the date the debt was incurred. Furthermore, unless the rate change reverses before

the debt is settled, translation at the historical rate merely delays recognition of the exchange gain or loss—it does not avoid the gain or loss. (Paragraph 164 gives additional reasons for translating long-term debt at the current rate.)

132. For the reasons set forth in paragraphs 129-131, the Board rejected the current-noncurrent method.

Current Rate Method

133. The current rate method is, of the four normative methods discussed, the most significant departure from present practice. The arguments for the current rate method discussed in this section are related to those for using the foreign currency as the unit of measure (paragraphs 83-93). The current rate is used under the situational approach, discussed in the next section, but the underlying concept there is different.

134. The Board believes that a foreign operation's assets and liabilities should be measured in the foreign statements in conformity with U.S. generally accepted accounting principles applicable to the reporting enterprise and that those principles should be retained in the translation process (paragraphs 82 and 122). If assets and liabilities that are measured at past prices in foreign statements are translated at the current rate and included in dollar financial statements, the dollar financial statements depart from historical-cost-based accounting because inventory, property, plant, equipment, and other assets normally carried at cost are reflected at varying dollar amounts resulting from changes in rates. The dollar amounts do not, except by coincidence, represent reasonable measure of replacement cost or selling price and would be unacceptable under present U.S. generally accepted accounting principles even if they did.

135. A contrary view expressed is that the historical cost of an asset acquired by a foreign operation can be measured only in the foreign currency and that the asset has no historical cost in dollars. According to that view, translating the foreign currency historical cost of an asset into a fewer or greater number of dollars following a rate change is simply the result of an *absolute, mathematical revision in the rate* and thus does not represent a departure from the historical-cost principle of accounting; the foreign currency cost is the only historical cost, and that cost has not changed.

136. Some advocates of the view described in paragraph 135 believe that the results of the *absolute, mathematical revision* is an exchange gain or loss and others do not. Those who support the foreign currency as the unit of measure would restate prior financial statements because of the rate change and, therefore, would report no exchange gain or loss. Those who support the dollar as the unit of measure would report an exchange gain or loss as a result of a rate change. The Board believes that latter approach is inconsistent with the view that there can be no dollar measure of the historical cost.

137. The Board believes that although an asset's acquisition price may have been stated in a particular currency, its equivalent cost in another currency can be approximated by multiplying the stated currency price by the rate in effect at the date of acquisition. Just as the length of an object can be measured in inches and then remeasured in centimeters by applying the appropriate conversion rate, the *cost* of an asset can likewise be measured in various units of measure (different currencies) by applying the appropriate translation rates.

138. Assets in foreign countries can be purchased indirectly for dollars by acquiring the necessary foreign currency in a foreign exchange market. The situation is not fundamentally different if the foreign currency is acquired before the purchase; the dollar cost of the purchase is known through the measurement conversion process (paragraph 137). Or, viewed another way, spending foreign currency to buy an asset means that the currency cannot be converted into dollars for remission to a U.S. parent. The dollars not received in conversion because the foreign currency was used to buy an asset—the dollars foregone—are the cost of the asset acquired in the most literal sense of the word *cost*.

139. Accordingly, the Board rejected the view that historical cost can be measured only in the foreign currency. It also rejected use of the current rate method based on that premise for the reason stated in paragraph 134 as well.

A Situational Approach to Translation

140. Paragraphs 123-139 compared the four basic normative methods for translating balance sheet accounts against the objectives of translation adopted by the Board. Another, somewhat different, approach to translation has also been suggested, which is not a normative method but looks instead at the nature of each foreign operation. It distinguishes between foreign operations that are extensions of affiliated domestic operations (*dependent* operations[36]) and those whose operations are essentially self-contained and, therefore, not dependent on affiliated domestic operations (*independent* operations[36]). The situational argument is that since many factors influence the creation of a foreign operation, translation must look further than the

[36]The terms *dependent* and *independent* were used by Parkinson (see footnote 20) and are used in the same context here.

location of a business operation; it should also look at its nature.

141. According to that view, if a foreign operation depends on domestic operations, the foreign operation should be accounted for as an extension of those domestic operations (that is, as part of a single domestic operation) and its foreign statements should be translated by one of the normative methods other than the current rate method. If a foreign operation is independent, its foreign statements should be translated by the current rate method.

142. A principal reason given to support using the current rate method to translate independent foreign operations is that the assets and liabilities of those operations are not individually at risk to rate changes; rather, the entire business is at risk. Since the foreign activities are conducted entirely in a foreign environment and future cash flows will be in a foreign currency, future operating results can be expressed in a meaningful way in dollars only if all revenue and costs (including those carried forward from a period before the rate change) are translated at the current rate. From the enterprise's viewpoint, its net investment in the foreign operation represents its total exposure to a rate change. Only by translating the net assets of the foreign operation at the current rate can the effect of rate changes be properly measured.

143. The situational approach involves both practical and conceptual problems, including the difficulty of finding or developing criteria or conditions to distinguish *independent* and *dependent* foreign operations. Proponents of the situational approach have explained the distinctions only broadly and have not given specific criteria. A few circumstances have been suggested or implied as indicating independence, such as regulation of the foreign operation by local authorities or a minimum of intercompany sale and borrowing transactions between the foreign operation and its parent or other domestic affiliates.

144. The Board considered criteria for independence of foreign operations but was unable to develop criteria that it believed to be satisfactory to identify an independent foreign operation. At least part of the difficulty lies in the inherently contradictory concept of an independent subsidiary, which seems to deny the single enterprise concept that underlies consolidated financial statements (*ARB No. 51,* paragraph 1). If foreign operations are as independent of their U.S. parent companies as some proponents of the situational approach seem to argue, the validity of consolidating them is questionable. Further, since many domestic subsidiaries may also have the characteristics of independent operations, however *independence* is defined, the distinction has implications that reach beyond the translation of foreign statements.

145. Certain respondents to the Discussion Memorandum and Exposure Draft, recognizing the purpose of consolidated financial statements as set forth in paragraph 87, recommended that if the current rate method were deemed appropriate for certain foreign operations for the reasons set forth in paragraph 142, those operations should be accounted for under the equity method rather than line-by-line consolidation. The Board believes that the situational approach raises broad questions about concepts of consolidation and the equity method applicable to domestic as well as foreign operations that are beyond the scope of this Statement.

146. Even if criteria could be developed, there are apt to be problems in applying any set of criteria to determine independence, including whether foreign operations should be viewed on the basis of country-by-country, foreign-operation-by-foreign-operation, or segment-by-segment of each foreign operation. In addition, changes in classification (from dependent to independent or vice versa) between reporting periods, presumably necessitating the use of different translation methods for each period, could produce results that would not be comparable with those of prior periods. It is also unclear how to translate the financial statements of a foreign operation that is independent of its parent but dependent on another foreign economy (for example, a foreign operation that manufactures its product in various European countries and sells its product to an unaffiliated or affiliated South American operation).

147. The situational approach is a way of looking at the exchange exposure of foreign operations that are considered independent, and the effect of a rate change on the net investment is a gain or loss to be included in income of some accounting period. Proponents of the approach believe that the results are erroneous if exchange gains and losses on liabilities are recognized earlier than exchange gains and losses on assets, especially since the latter are not identified in operating results as exchange gains and losses (paragraphs 100-102 contain an example). They argue that a foreign operation involves risk of rate changes in addition to the other risks involved in every business operation, and translation procedures should measure the effects of exchange risk. They argue further that since gains and losses can only be measured through valuations, translation must involve valuation at the current exchange rate—the effect of exchange risk is measured by valuing *all* assets and liabilities before and after movements in the rate. Or stated in another way, a net

investment is an integrated whole on which the effect of a rate change can best be determined by multiplying the investment by the change in rate. According to that view, all independent foreign operations in a country whose currency weakens should be worth less (the net investment multiplied by the decline in rate gives an exchange loss) and, conversely, independent foreign operations in a country whose currency strengthens should be worth more.

148. However, translation is a poor valuation process for assets carried in financial statements at cost because it relies on prices in a single market. It reflects only the exchange price between dollars and a single foreign currency and does not adequately reflect prices in other markets in which a foreign operation could buy or sell those assets. Thus, multiplying the historical foreign currency cost of an asset by the current rate cannot, except by coincidence, measure the value of the asset. For example, an enterprise in England acquired land in 1964 at a cost of 1,000,000 pounds sterling when the rate was £1 = $2.80; the dollar equivalent historical cost was, therefore, $2,800,000. If the land being carried at cost in the foreign statements at December 31, 1974 is multiplied by the current rate £1 = $2.35, the product will be $2,350,000. However, the current dollar equivalent of the value of that land may be more or less than $2,350,000 and depends on prices not included in either historical-cost-based financial statements or exchange rates. In other words, translation procedures cannot measure the dollar value of a foreign investment that is subject to exchange risk unless the current value of the investment is included in the foreign statements.

149. Some respondents to the Exposure Draft interpreted the Board's emphasis on a translation method that preserves the measurement bases of assets and liabilities in foreign statements as a denial that translation at the current rate involves valuation. On the contrary, the Board recognizes that accounting for certain assets and liabilities (for example, inventory or investments carried at market price, obligations for pensions and warranties) involves estimates and valuation in the foreign statements and that translating those items at the current rate after a rate change introduces an additional value change in dollars. Foreign currency and receivables and payables denominated in foreign currency are stated in a fixed number of foreign currency units regardless of rate changes, and their foreign currency measures do not change when the rate changes. However, their dollar measurements change solely as a result of a rate change; that value change, which does not exist in the foreign statements, is the exchange gain or loss. The Board believes that all of the value changes in dollars described in this paragraph are the valid result of remeasuring foreign statements in dollars. What the Board did reject, for reasons given in the preceding paragraph, was translation at the current rate of items carried at cost in the foreign statements. In the Board's view, that procedure is not a valid valuation process and, further, it is unacceptable under the historical-cost-basis of accounting required by current generally accepted accounting principles.

150. The key distinction in the situational approach to translation is between independent and dependent foreign operations, and the difference can result in significantly different accounting. Thus, if the purchase of land in the example in paragraph 148 was financed by locally incurred long-term debt due on December 31, 1974, the $2,350,000 equivalent of the payment to liquidate the debt is $450,000 less than the $2,800,000 equivalent proceeds of borrowing. If the foreign operation is considered to be independent by the advocates of the situational approach, both the land and the debt are translated at the current rate, and no exchange gain or loss is recognized when the rate changes because the amount of the debt equals the carrying basis (cost) of the asset, leaving no net investment subject to exchange risk. If, however, the foreign operation is assumed to be dependent on its parent, advocates of the situational approach agree that the $450,000 should be recognized as gain on the debt in determining net income over the 10-year period (although they may disagree on the timing of recognition) and that no exchange loss because of the weakening of the pound sterling should be recognized on the land, which is translated at the historical rate.

151. The Board can see no reason to base the calculation and recognition of exchange gains and losses solely on the dependence or independence of foreign operations. If the argument is sound that the net investment, rather than individual assets and liabilities, is subject to exchange exposure, it is as sound for dependent as for independent foreign operations. To hold that an independent foreign operation is fundamentally different from a dependent operation raises questions about the propriety of consolidation for independent operations that, as already noted, are beyond the scope of this Statement (paragraph 144). In summary, the Board recognized that foreign operations may be structured differently but could find no persuasive reasons to translate their financial statements differently for purposes of consolidation or combination with financial statements of a U.S. reporting enterprise.

152. A modification of the situational approach to translation is the suggestion that to apply the current rate method to foreign operations located in highly inflationary economies (for example, some South American countries), the foreign statements first should be restated in terms of units of the general

purchasing power of the local currency and then translated at the current rate because to do otherwise could produce unreasonable results in dollars. The Board believes that, even without the problem of identifying *highly inflationary* economies, restating part but not all of an enterprise's financial statements in units of general purchasing power mixes the units of measure used in the financial statements and results in an aggregation of numbers that cannot be meaningfully described except in terms of the procedures followed to obtain them. That is, adding units of general purchasing power (the unit of measure used in the restated foreign statements) translated at the current rate and units of money (the unit of measure used in conventional statements) produces a total that represents neither aggregate units of money nor aggregate units of general purchasing power. Moreover, to restate in units of general purchasing power only foreign statements in currencies that weaken against the dollar is to introduce a bias into the translated statements. According to its advocates, translation under the situational approach of all assets and liabilities at the current rate results in exchange losses on investments in countries with weakening currencies and exchange gains on investments in countries with strengthening currencies (paragraph 147). The proposed linking of translation at current rate and restatement in units of general purchasing power of foreign statements has the effect of reducing the exchange losses that normally result from translating net investments in countries with weakening currencies at the current rate while at the same time leaving undiminished the exchange gains that normally result from translating net investments in countries with strengthening currencies at the current rate.

Translation of Inventory

153. Numerous respondents to the Discussion Memorandum and Exposure Draft recommended that inventory carried at cost be translated at the current rate. Many of those recommendations were from supporters of the current rate or current-noncurrent methods. The Board rejected those methods for reasons given in paragraphs 129-139. Others argued or implied that inventory should be considered a monetary asset because it is but one step removed from accounts receivable and will soon bring cash into the enterprise. That view is rejected not only because inventory is a nonmonetary asset (paragraph 127) but also because the monetary-nonmonetary distinction is not an appropriate criterion in this Statement for choosing the applicable rate.

154. Several respondents who generally supported the monetary-nonmonetary or temporal methods recommended that inventory carried at cost—other than on a last in, first out (LIFO) basis—should be translated at the current rate. (Some respondents would apply the current rate to LIFO inventory.) The reasons they gave for that major exception to methods they otherwise supported was the need to reflect economic reality or the impracticality of applying historical rates to inventories.

155. Certain advocates of the exception described in the preceding paragraph argued that translating inventory at historical rates distorts the dollar gross profit during an inventory turnover period after a rate change. Related arguments given for reflecting economic reality by using the current rate were that inventory is exposed to exchange risk the same as a receivable and that deducting cost of goods sold translated at historical rates from operating revenue translated at the current rate produces *inventory profits* or *paper profits* if the foreign currency strengthens.

156. Translating inventory carried at cost at the current rate departs from historical-cost-based accounting (paragraph 134). A desire to approximate replacement cost of inventory may underlie some arguments for using the current rate, which are similar to those used to support replacement cost methods. However, even if the use of replacement cost were presently acceptable in principle, translating inventory cost in foreign currency at the current rate does not, except by coincidence, give a reasonable approximation of replacement cost for reasons given in paragraph 148. Nor does that translation method measure the exposure of inventory to rate changes because the basis of the exposure risk is unrecorded. The exchange exposure of inventory depends on its future selling price, not on its cost.

157. Applying historical rates to inventory may result in a dollar gross profit on sales immediately after a rate change that differs from the dollar gross profit both on sales before the rate change and on sales after the inventory turnover period following the rate change. The Board believes that is the expected result of using the dollar as the unit of measure in concert with generally accepted accounting principles. That is, when selling prices change, matching historical costs of inventory with sales affects gross profit both in dollar statements of the parent company and in translated statements of foreign operations. For example, gross profit increases in the parent's statements if cost of inventory is deducted from sales after a selling price increase, resulting in so-called *inventory profits* from inflation. In other words, the phenomenon criticized is a feature of historical cost accounting; translation of inventory at historical rates does not introduce that feature.

158. The Board rejected in principle the proposal to

translate inventory at the current rate for the reasons given in the preceding paragraphs. However, the Board recognized the practical aspects of applying historical rates to detailed inventory records and provided for the use of averages and other reasonable approximations as long as the result is not materially different from the result of following the standards of this Statement (paragraph 29). Translating all or part of an inventory at the current rate may under certain circumstances give a reasonable approximation of translation at historical rates.

Translation of Revenue and Expense Accounts

159. The Board believes that the transaction method, rather than the closing rate method, should be used to translate revenue and expense accounts because it satisfies an objective of translation adopted by the Board, namely, to measure all transactions in a single unit of measure (dollars).

160. The closing rate method, in contrast, is linked to the view that the foreign currency should be retained as the unit of measure, requiring at least two units of measure in an enterprise's financial statements. Translating revenue and expenses at the closing rate retains the foreign currency as the unit of measure for transactions occurring during the year (including those previously reported for interim periods). If the rate changes, dollar translations of prior local currency transactions during the current year are restated (updated) to reflect the new dollar equivalents of the transactions, and no exchange gain or loss on the current year's transactions is separately recognized. Since the Board believes that the dollar, rather than the foreign currency, should be the unit of measure in translated statements, it rejected the closing rate method.

EXCHANGE GAINS AND LOSSES

Foreign Currency Transactions

161. The Board concluded that an exchange gain or loss shall be recorded when a rate change occurs because (a) when the rate changes, certain assets and liabilities should be adjusted to reflect the new rate (paragraph 7(b)), (b) the resulting gain or loss is not an adjustment of the cost of an asset acquired in a foreign purchase or of the revenue recorded in a foreign sale (that is, the Board rejected the so-called *one-transaction* view), and (c) other methods of deferring recognition of the gain or loss are also unacceptable (paragraphs 163-166).

162. The Board also concluded that the accounting treatment specified in paragraph 17 offers more practical implementation than does a one-transaction view. Current recognition of an exchange gain or loss does not require, as does the one-transaction view, the tracing of exchange gains or losses on foreign currency payables or receivables to related assets, revenue, or expenses. Another implementation problem under the one-transaction view is that a purchase or sale of goods or services may take place in one accounting period and an exchange gain or loss on the related payable or receivable may occur in a subsequent period.

163. Other alternative answers considered and rejected were (1) to record an exchange gain or loss when payables or receivables are settled, (2) to record an exchange gain or loss when the rate changes more than a specified percentage from the rate previously used, and (3) to record no gain or loss if the rate change is likely to reverse.

164. The Board views an enterprise that holds foreign currency or has a receivable or a payable denominated in foreign currency as being in a special situation, namely, the enterprise is subject to a gain or loss solely as a result of a rate change. Accordingly, when the rate changes, an exchange gain or loss resulting from the adjustment of accounts denominated in foreign currency should be immediately included in the determination of net income to report properly the results of that situation at the time it occurs. Financial statement users are thus informed of the results of a rate change in the period of change rather than at conversion or settlement in a later period, which may be several years after the rate change for certain receivables and payables. Methods that involve amortizing exchange gains or losses also fail to recognize the effect of a rate change in the period of occurrence and are, therefore, also rejected (paragraphs 173-182).

165. The Board considered and rejected the possibility of recording exchange gains and losses only if the rate changes more than a specified percentage. The allowable percentage range chosen, within which rates might fluctuate without affecting the financial statements, would of necessity be arbitrary. A more serious weakness in the proposal is that, since even a relatively minor change in rate can sometimes have a material impact on the financial statements, depending on the size of an enterprise's exposed position in the foreign currency, the method may ignore material effects of rate changes. Therefore, the Board concluded that the rate at the balance sheet date should be used.

166. The Board also considered and rejected the view that an exchange gain or loss should be deferred if the rate change that caused it is likely to reverse. The argument is that to recognize gains and losses from all rate changes in determining net income creates needless fluctuations in reported

income by reporting exchange gains and losses that are cancelled by reversals of rate changes. The Board rejected the underlying argument and its implication for accounting (paragraphs 196-199). The proposal is also incapable of practical application. First, it requires distinguishing rate changes that will reverse from those that will not. Second, it requires predicting the changes in an enterprise's exposure to rate changes between the time of a rate change and the time of its reversal. And third, it requires an arbitrary time limit to prevent rate changes from being ignored indefinitely. The proposal contains no objective basis for accounting measurement.

Foreign Statements

167. In concept, exchange gains or losses from translating foreign statements are the direct effects, measured in dollars on existing assets and liabilities at the dates rates change, that are attributable solely to rate changes between the foreign currency and the dollar.

168. In practice, however, the exchange gain or loss is usually determined at the close of a period by translating both the ending balance sheet and income statement accounts at the rates required by the translation method (that is, current or historical rates for assets and liabilities and weighted average rate for most revenue and expenses). When the translation is completed and the net income less dividends in dollars is added to the beginning dollar balance of retained earnings, the sum of those amounts will usually not equal the ending dollar retained earnings shown in the translated balance sheet. The difference is the exchange gain or loss from translating foreign statements.

169. Applying the translation procedures for foreign statements (paragraphs 11-14) results in an appropriate measure in dollars of the net income of a foreign operation consistent with the objective of translation. However, the method in practice of calculating the exchange gain or loss from translating foreign statements, as described in paragraph 168, may sometimes include in exchange gains or losses other gains or losses from market price changes. For example, an enterprise that uses the dollar as its unit of measure acquires securities that it accounts for at current market price, and those securities' prices are stated in foreign currency. Since the cost of the securities acquired and subsequent changes in market price are recorded in dollars (not in foreign currency), following the procedures required by paragraphs 7(a) and 7(c), the accounting does not produce *exchange gains and losses* as described in paragraph 16. In the Board's view, it is unnecessary in measuring and recording transactions and events in dollars to distinguish between the effect of changes in the foreign market price of a security and changes in the market price of the foreign currency itself, even if that distinction can be made. To meet the objective of translation (paragraph 9), the same result should be obtained in translating similar securities presented in foreign statements. However, the averaging and approximations permitted by this Statement can result in exchange gains and losses that include gains and losses properly attributable to other revenue and expense accounts. The procedures that would be required to segregate those *other* gains and losses from exchange gains and losses for purposes of this Statement's disclosure requirements (paragraph 32) may not be practical. The Board accepted as reasonable the results determined by applying the requirements of paragraphs 11-14 by the procedures described in paragraph 168.

170. Some respondents to the Exposure Draft suggested that certain enterprises that carry investments in securities at current market price but do not include unrealized gains or losses on those investments *in the determination of net income* should be exempt from the requirement of paragraph 17 to include in the determination of net income *exchange* gains and losses relating to those investments.

171. The Board concluded that if unrealized appreciation or depreciation on investments is measured in dollars, the translation procedures required by this Statement do not produce exchange gains or losses that pertain thereto. Accordingly, the Board concluded the *exemption* for those enterprises was not necessary.

172. The Board considered the following possible methods to account for exchange gains or losses in arriving at its conclusion stated in paragraph 17:

a. Adjust cost of, or amortize over life of, assets carried at cost in dollars (assets translated at historical rates);
b. Amortize over remaining term of long-term liabilities;
c. Adjust stockholders' equity;
d. Defer based on certain criteria;
e. Include immediately in the determination of net income.

Adjustment Related to Assets Carried at Cost

173. One view to support accounting for exchange gains and losses as adjustments of the cost basis of assets is that the cost of an asset equals the total sacrifice required to discharge all related liabilities. Accordingly, if a foreign operation has an exposed net liability position at the time of a rate change, the exchange gain or loss is an element of the cost of the related assets. That view is similar to a one-

transaction perspective and is rejected for reasons similar to those in paragraphs 114 and 115.

174. Another view is that an exchange loss that results from the combination of the strengthening of a foreign currency and an exposed net liability position is considered *covered,* in whole or in part, by assets carried at cost in foreign currency. *Cover* is the amount by which the foreign currency cost of those assets translated at the current rate exceeds their cost translated at historical rates (their cost in dollars). According to the argument, the *covered* loss should be deferred rather than included in determining net income when the rate changes. The reduction in income over the lives of the assets from amortizing the deferred loss on the net exposed liability position is considered to be at least offset by the effect of depreciation based on lower historical translation rates (*lighter costs*) that will be deducted over the assets' lives from revenue (received in cash or receivables from sales) translated at the higher current rate.

175. Likewise, an exchange gain that results from the combination of the weakening of a foreign currency and an exposed net liability position should be deferred under the *cover* approach to the extent required to offset the unrecognized potential loss on the assets translated at the historical rate. The potential loss represents the difference between translating the foreign currency costs of the assets at the higher historical rates and translating them at the lower current rate. The cover approach views translating the assets at historical rates as speculation about the assets' ability to produce a product that will sell for an increased foreign currency selling price which, when translated at the lower current rate, will sufficiently cover the historical dollar cost of the assets. Amortization of the deferred gain over the life of the assets is, therefore, considered appropriate to offset the effect of depreciation based on higher historical rates (*heavier cost*) to be included in determining net income of later periods.

176. The Board rejected the cover approach because it is essentially a procedure whereby a change that has occurred in the dollar measure of liabilities is deferred to be offset against a *potential* change in the future dollar value of assets carried at cost. That potential dollar value of the assets depends on foreign currency proceeds from sale or other disposition of the assets. Since changes in the values of assets carried at cost (for example, property, plant, and equipment) are not normally recognized under generally accepted accounting principles until the assets are sold, offsetting is accomplished under the cover approach by *not* including immediately in the determination of net income gains or losses on changes in the dollar measure of liabilities denominated in foreign currency. The argument for deferral is in effect that changes in the dollar measure of one item should not be recognized because changes in the dollar value of another item are not recognized. However, the Board believes that offsetting of that type is not proper under present generally accepted accounting principles that recognize certain gains and losses only at time of sale or other disposition. If offsetting is desirable at all, it should be accomplished by changing generally accepted accounting principles to recognize changes in the dollar value of items now carried at cost. However, to do so would require reconsideration of historical cost as a fundamental concept of accounting—a process that is beyond the scope of this Statement.

177. The questionable result of offsetting recognizable gains and losses from changes in the dollar measurements of liabilities denominated in foreign currency against unrecognizable increases in the values of assets carried at cost in foreign currency is highlighted if the liability is paid but the asset remains unsold. For example, a rate change from FC1 = $1 to FC.80 = $1 occurs while a foreign operation has an exposed net liability position of FC80 and a depreciable asset with an undepreciated cost of FC100 and a remaining life of five years. The $20 loss on the exposed net liability position (FC80 ÷ .80 = $100; $100 − $80 = $20) is *covered* because the foreign currency cost of the asset translated at the current rate ($125) exceeds the cost translated at the historical rate ($100) by $25, which is $5 more than the loss on the liabilities. Thus, under the *cover* approach, the full $20 loss can be deferred and amortized over the remaining five-year life of the asset. Using straight-line depreciation and amortization, the expense for each of the succeeding five years is $24 ($20 depreciation based on cost translated at the historical rate plus $4 amortization of the deferred loss). The added expense ($4 amortization of the deferred loss) is said to be necessary to offset the effect of matching *light* depreciation expense translated at historical rates against foreign currency revenue translated at the higher rate after the rate change.

178. If, however, all liabilities outstanding at the time of the rate change are settled by the end of the second year, the loss has occurred, even to the satisfaction of those who believe that exchange gains and losses are *unrealized* until payment of liabilities and collection of receivables (paragraph 188). However, the result that is said to justify the *cover* approach—matching of the increased expense from adding the annual amortization of the deferred loss against the increased revenue from translating current sales at the new higher rate—cannot be achieved unless the loss is deferred and amortized after it has been *realized.*

179. The *cover* approach appears to be based on the presumption that a rate change may be expected to affect future earnings in a way that offsets an exchange gain or loss related to an exposed net liability position. The Board believes that future impacts of rate changes should be reflected in the future and not anticipated by deferring an exchange gain or loss.

180. Another apparent assumption of the cover approach is that future revenue generated by the assets carried at cost will be in the same currency as the exposed net liability position. That may not be valid for many foreign operations.

Adjustment Related to Life of Long-Term Liabilities

181. Another method that has been suggested would limit deferral of exchange gains or losses from an exposed net liability position to amounts associated with long-term liabilities denominated in foreign currency. The amount deferred would be amortized over the remaining term of the long-term liabilities, in effect accounting for the deferred exchange gain or loss as an adjustment of financing costs (interest expense). The Board rejected the method because of the Board's basic view (stated in paragraph 164) that the gain or loss results solely from the rate change and to recognize it in other periods obscures what has occurred. Furthermore, the method masks the economic difference in the source (denomination) of financing. That is, foreign currency denominated debt has an exchange exposure that dollar denominated debt or equity financing does not. Spreading the result of the exposure over the future rather than recognizing it in full when a rate changes fails to contrast an economic difference between financing denominated in foreign currency and dollar borrowings or equity financing.

182. The Board considered the argument that management assesses the likelihood of rate changes and differences in interest rates between countries in deciding to borrow foreign currency rather than dollars or one foreign currency rather than another and that all or part of the effect on long-term debt of a rate change is, therefore, an added or reduced cost of borrowing a particular foreign currency. The Board does not deny that management may assess borrowing alternatives in that manner. To be consistent with that view, though, would require interest accruals over the life of the borrowing at the anticipated effective interest rate. However, the Board concluded that it is inappropriate to attempt to account currently for the expected effect of future rate changes on interest and principal payments. The Board also concluded that adjusting translated long-term debt by the amount of the related exchange gain or loss at the time of a rate change and spreading that gain or loss as an adjustment of interest expense subsequent to the rate change does not produce a result consistent with the expected effective interest rate at the date of the borrowing even if the expectations about rate changes at the time of borrowing are realized. Therefore, the Board rejected the proposal.

Adjustment to Stockholders' Equity

183. Certain respondents to the Discussion Memorandum and Exposure Draft suggested that exchange gains or losses be accounted for as adjustments of stockholders' equity. The Board rejected that method because it believes that a gain or loss resulting from an exposure to rate changes should be included in the determination of net income in accordance with the all-inclusive income statement presently required of most enterprises by generally accepted accounting principles. A foreign investment exposes a U.S. company to the effects of rate changes which can be economically beneficial or detrimental. The Board believes that those benefits or detriments should be reflected in the determination of net income at a time and in a manner that is consistent with generally accepted accounting principles.

Deferral Based on Certain Criteria

184. The following criteria were suggested for deferring exchange gains or losses:

a. Realization;
b. Conservatism;
c. Likelihood of reversal of rate change;
d. The effect on future income of rate change.

185. It was suggested that exchange gains or losses be deferred based on the criterion of realization. Realized gains and losses should be recognized immediately while unrealized gains and (possibly) losses should be deferred until realized. Chapter 12 of *ARB No. 43* permitted different accounting treatment for *realized* and *unrealized* exchange gains and losses but gave no guidance on how to distinguish them. In the Board's view, the distinction between *realized* and *unrealized* exchange gains and losses is a questionable concept for the purpose of translation as well as a difficult concept to implement.

186. The concept of realization usually applied in accounting pertains to conversions of other assets into cash or receivables. It usually applies to conversion of inventory but is also applied to assets such as marketable securites, property, plant, equipment, and certain intangible assets. A sale of an asset is the most common basis of realization in accounting.

187. That meaning of realization is preserved if transmission of funds (for example, dividends) from a foreign operation to a domestic operation is the event that determines *realization* of exchange gains and losses from translating foreign statements, but that narrow view of realization is not particularly useful. First, it is questionable how transmission of funds causes an exchange gain or loss to be realized. For example, an exchange gain that results from translating a foreign operation's exposed net liability position cannot be reasonably associated with a dividend remittance. Likewise, an exchange gain that results from translating a foreign operation's exposed net asset position that primarily reflects accounts receivable cannot be reasonably associated with a dividend remittance if the foreign currency collected on settlement of the receivables is used to purchase other assets. Second, if remittance of dividends is the criterion for realization in translation of foreign statements, all of a foreign operation's unremitted earnings must be considered *unrealized*. That interpretation requires investments in foreign operations to be carried at cost and largely invalidates consolidation of foreign operations. It therefore is rejected.

188. The suggestion by some respondents to the Discussion Memorandum and Exposure Draft that realization of exchange gains and losses should be based on spending cash, collecting receivables, and paying liabilities is the opposite of the usual concept of realization, namely, converting assets into cash or receivables. Converting cash into other assets is usually called a *purchase* and does not constitute realization in any accepted sense of the word. Moreover, it is generally impracticable to determine whether or not a given transaction converts a previously unrealized gain or loss into a realized gain or loss. Under the proposed realization test, not all collections of receivables or payments of liabilities are bases of realization but only collections or payments of receivables and payables that were in existence at the date of a rate change. Similarly, not all cash spent realizes previously unrealized exchange gains or losses but only the spending of cash held at the time of a rate change. The problem was complicated when rate changes were official devaluations or revaluations. Floating rates increase the complexity. The Board believes that attempting to base realization of exchange gains and losses on cash disbursements and collections and settlements of receivables and payables would involve unreasonable effort to make a distinction between realized and unrealized gains or losses for which the Board sees no theoretical justification.

189. Another suggestion is that unrealized exchange gains should be deferred based on the criterion of conservatism. The Board believes that although the concept of conservatism may be appropriate in other areas of accounting, its application to exchange gains and losses is inappropriate.

190. Conservatism is a way of dealing with uncertainty and is intended to avoid recognizing income on the basis of inadequate evidence that a gain has occurred. The Board believes that a rate change in a foreign exchange market provides sufficient objective evidence of the occurrence of a gain or loss to warrant changes in the dollar carrying amounts of cash, receivables, payables, and other assets and liabilities measured in foreign currency at current or future prices. To defer an exchange gain *solely because it is a gain* in effect denies that a rate change has occurred. Thus, the Board believes that even if it were feasible to identify unrealized gains, to defer recognition of unrealized exchange gains while recognizing unrealized exchange losses is an unwarranted inconsistency in translation.

191. The inconsistency of deferring an exchange gain while recognizing an exchange loss is further illustrated by translation of two accounts receivable from the same customer, one from a sale just before a rate change and the other from a sale just afterwards. Both receivables are translated at the new rate after the rate change and are, therefore, treated as comparable. If the foreign currency weakens against the dollar, the *unrealized* exchange loss on the earlier receivable is recognized to be conservative. Otherwise, the deferral of the loss would have the effect of increasing the dollar measure of the receivable to the same amount as before the rate change. If, however, the foreign currency strengthens against the dollar, the *unrealized* exchange gain on the same receivable is deferred, again to be conservative. But the effect of deferring the gain is to reduce the dollar measure of the receivable to the same amount as before the rate change. Therefore, the earlier receivable is no longer treated as comparable to the later one. Moreover, the inconsistency is unwarranted because the dollar measure of the earlier receivable is as objectively determinable as that of the later receivable.

192. The Board rejected the recommendation that exchange gains or losses be deferred if rates are likely to reverse. That proposal is often a part of both the realization and conservatism proposals because those proposals are often based on arguments that gains should not be recognized because the related rate change might reverse *before the gain is realized*. But the proposal to defer if rates are likely to reverse raises separate issues because it depends on predicting rate changes in the future (paragraph 166). Given the high degree of unpredictability of exchange rates, the proposed method creates a situation in which operating results are misstated simply through errors in forecasting. A procedure of that type invariably causes divergent

decisions about the movements of rates. In addition, to determine how much of an exchange gain or loss will be reversed when the rate change reverses necessitates a forecast of the financial position at the time of the later rate change, which may be another extremely uncertain variable. In the Board's judgment, the proposal is not practical.

193. Another recommendation proposed is that accounting for exchange gains or losses vary depending on the likely effect of rate changes on future income. As pointed out in paragraph 107, the future effects of rate changes may vary widely, and the effects are uncertain. The Board believes it inappropriate to inject forecasting of future effects into the accounting for exchange gains or losses.

Additional Factors Considered

194. An additional factor in the Board's decision to include exchange gains or losses in the determination of net income at the time of a rate change is that deferral approaches generally raise significant questions of implementation. For example, should amounts deferred be determined on a global basis, currency-by-currency, country-by-country, foreign-operation-by-foreign operation, or some other basis? If exchange gains or losses are aggregated on a global basis, most suggested amortization approaches become exceedingly complex, if not impractical, for a company with numerous foreign operations to apply. Not aggregating on a global basis can result in exchange gains being included in the determination of net income at the time of a rate change and exchange losses being deferred, or vice versa, depending on the deferral method employed.

195. Another factor that supports including exchange gains or losses in the determination of net income at the time of a rate change is that after a rate change operating revenue (other than amortization of deferred income) as well as other cash receipts and disbursements are translated at the current rate. To recognize the effect of a rate change on current transactions (by reporting in the translated statements an increased or decreased dollar equivalent for the transactions) when they occur and yet defer the effect of a rate change on past unsettled transactions (for example, receivables from previously reported sales) places the enterprise in the anomalous position of having recognized the entire effect of the rate change on a recent transaction while holding in suspense its effect on a previous transaction.

Rate Changes and Earnings Fluctuations

196. Many respondents to the Discussion Memorandum and Exposure Draft commented that to include exchange gains and losses in determining net income when rates change would distort reported net income or otherwise confuse readers of the financial statements. Some of those arguments were based on the assumption that rate changes would reverse. Some respondents to the Exposure Draft presented examples showing how application of the proposed standard would have caused reported income to fluctuate in recent years. Since many of the rate changes did reverse, those comments, based on hindsight, argued that the proposed standard would have caused unnecessary fluctuations in their reported net income.

197. The Board's view has previously been indicated regarding the assumption that rate changes will reverse (paragraphs 166 and 192).

198. In addition, the Board rejected the implication that a function of accounting is to minimize the reporting of fluctuations. Past rate changes are historical facts, and the Board believes that users of financial statements are best served by accounting for the changes as they occur. It is the deferring or spreading of those effects, not their recognition and disclosure, that is the artificial process (see *FASB Statement No. 2,* "Accounting for Research and Development Costs," paragraph 54, and *FASB Statement No. 5,* "Accounting for Contingencies," paragraphs 64 and 65).

199. In the Board's opinion, readers of financial statements will not be confused by fluctuations in reported earnings caused by rate changes. That view was supported by comments of financial analysts who said they preferred to have exchange gains and losses accounted for when rates change. Exchange rates fluctuate; accounting should not give the impression that rates are stable.

INCOME TAX CONSEQUENCES OF RATE CHANGES

200. The Board concluded that if an exchange gain or loss related to a foreign currency transaction of a foreign operation is taxable in the foreign country, the related tax effect shall be included in the translated income statement when the rate change occurs. Inclusion is appropriate regardless of the fact that the foreign operation's exchange gain or loss may be partially or completely (for a dollar denominated asset or liability) eliminated upon translation, because the rate change is the event that causes the tax effect in the foreign operation's financial statements. The fact that the exchange gain or loss does not exist (or exists only partially) in dollars should in no way affect the accounting for the tax effect, which does exist in dollars.

201. A method has been proposed for measuring exchange gains or losses resulting from translating

foreign statements that in effect would correct what some might consider an erroneous relationship of translated tax expense to translated pretax income. Following the proposal, the exchange gain or loss would include the future tax effect in the translated financial statements of using the historical rate for translating inventory, plant, and equipment. The resulting deferred tax accounts would be amortized as an adjustment of tax expense as inventory and fixed assets are charged against operations.

202. In the Board's opinion, the use of historical rates to translate certain income or expense items (for example, cost of goods sold and depreciation) does not require interperiod tax allocation. Timing differences, defined as "differences between the periods in which transactions affect taxable income and the periods in which they enter into the determination of pretax accounting income" (paragraph 13(e) of *APB Opinion No. 11*), do not arise from translating assets or liabilities at historical rates. Accordingly, the effective tax rate in the translated dollar statements may differ from the effective tax rate in the foreign statements. Applying historical rates may also change various other relationships in the translated dollar statements from those in the foreign statements (for example, gross profit percentages). However, the Board believes that is the expected result of using the dollar as the unit of measure in concert with generally accepted accounting principles.

203. The Board concluded that the existing authoritative literature (*APB Opinions No. 11, 23,* and *24*) provides sufficient guidance about whether deferred taxes should be recognized for exchange gains or losses that result from applying the requirements of this Statement. *APB Opinions No. 23* and *24* apply because exchange gains and losses from translation of foreign statements are an integral part of measuring in dollars the undistributed earnings of foreign subsidiaries and investees.

FORWARD EXCHANGE CONTRACTS

204. A forward contract is an agreement to exchange at a specified future date currencies of different countries at a specified rate (the *forward rate*). The purpose of a forward contract may be to hedge either a foreign currency commitment or a foreign currency exposed net asset or net liability position or to speculate in anticipation of a gain.

Hedge of Foreign Currency Exposed Net Asset or Net Liability Position

205. The Board concluded that if a forward contract is intended to hedge an exposed foreign currency position, the gain or loss on the forward contract (determined by the method specified in paragraph 25) shall be included in determining net income currently. To recognize the gain or loss only at maturity of the contract could result in benefiting (penalizing) one period's income by recognizing an exchange gain (loss) resulting from the translation process currently to the detriment (benefit) of a later period's income when a loss (gain) on the forward contract is recorded.

Speculative Contract

206. An enterprise that uses a forward contract to speculate exposes itself to risks from movements in forward rates. Therefore, for reasons similar to those expressed in paragraphs 164-166, the Board concluded that the gain or loss on the forward contract (determined by the method stated in paragraph 26) shall be included in determining net income currently as the value of the contract changes.

Hedge of Identifiable Foreign Currency Commitment

207. Although the Board rejected the one-transaction approach as a general basis for translation of foreign currency transactions (paragraphs 114 and 115), it decided (for the reasons given in paragraphs 116-118) that the dollar basis of a foreign currency transaction shall be established at the transaction date. By rejecting the commitment date as the date for making that determination, the Board implicitly accepted a one-transaction view for an unrecorded future foreign currency transaction (that is, a commitment in foreign currency) for the period from the commitment date to the transaction date. In other words, the effects of rate changes between commitment date and transaction date are not separately identified and accounted for as exchange gains or losses; rather, they are included in the dollar basis of the transaction.

208. A number of respondents to the Exposure Draft opposed current recognition in income of the gain or loss on a forward contract intended to hedge a future foreign currency transaction. In their view, the exposure to rate changes during the commitment period could (or should) be hedged by a forward contract, even though the accounting does not separately recognize the exposure on the commitment. They believe that to include a gain or loss on a forward contract that hedges a commitment in determining net income when rates change rather than to include the gain or loss in the dollar basis of the related transaction could benefit (penalize) one period's income to the detriment (benefit) of a later period's income. For example, a U.S. enterprise contracts with a U.S. customer to sell for $1,000,000 certain equipment to be delivered in 18 months. At the same time the enterprise enters into a firm,

uncancelable commitment with a foreign company to manufacture the specified equipment for FC900,000 (equal to $900,000 at the existing current rate). Simultaneously, the enterprise enters into a forward contract to receive FC900,000 in 18 months. By so doing, the enterprise is viewed as having fixed its gross profit on the transaction at $100,000 (ignoring premium or discount on the forward contract). If at a balance sheet date between the commitment date and the anticipated transaction date for receipt of the equipment, the spot rate has changed from FC1 = $1 to FC1 = $1.07, a gain of $63,000 exists on the forward contract. However, the dollar price of the equipment has also increased $63,000. If the gain on the forward contract is not deferred, the gross profit of the sale when recorded will be $37,000 rather than $100,000. Since the enterprise's intent on entering into the forward contract was not to speculate in the forward market but to fix the equipment's dollar cost at $900,000 and thus fix the gross profit at $100,000, those respondents argued that the gain on the contract should be deferred until the transaction date. On further consideration, the Board concluded that gains or losses on forward contracts that meet the conditions stated in paragraph 27 shall be deferred until the date the commitment is recorded (that is, the transaction date). The deferred gain or loss shall then be included in the dollar basis of the transaction.

209. The requirements in this Statement for measuring gains or losses on forward contracts represent a modification of the requirements proposed in the Exposure Draft. That draft proposed accrual of the difference between the original market value of an unperformed forward contract (zero) and its current market value. Stated another way, the difference between the contracted forward rate (or the forward rate last used to measure a gain or loss on the contract) and the forward rate available for the remaining maturity of that forward contract multiplied by the amount of the forward contract is a gain or loss to be included in determining net income.

210. Certain respondents to the Exposure Draft questioned valuing a forward contract at current market value if the intent is to hold the contract to maturity to hedge a foreign currency receivable or payable. In their view, it is inconsistent to value, for example, a two-year contract at a forward rate because it is a forward contract and translate at the current rate the two-year foreign currency payable that is hedged.

211. The Board concluded that a gain or loss on a forward contract shall be determined on a basis consistent with management's intent for entering into the contract. That is, the results of a speculative forward contract should be determined by changes in its market value; the results of a forward contract intended to hedge an identifiable foreign currency commitment or exposed net asset or net liability position should be accounted for in a manner consistent with the accounting for the related exposure. Therefore, the Board specified the procedures in paragraphs 23-26.

212. An alternative approach for a forward contract intended to hedge a specific foreign currency transaction for the period between transaction date and settlement date is to use the rate in the forward contract rather than the spot rate at the transaction date to establish the related amounts payable or receivable. Although a forward contract may limit or eliminate exposure on a payable or receivable denominated in foreign currency, the Board views such a forward contract as an independent transaction that should be accounted for separately. It also believes that the original discount or premium on a forward contract normally reflects an interest rate differential between two countries which should be recognized over the life of the contract if the contract hedges a foreign currency exposed net asset or net liability position. Further, since specific identification of individual forward contracts with related unsettled foreign currency transactions may not be readily ascertainable, the procedures specified by paragraph 23 are a more practical approach.

DISCLOSURE

213. In reaching its conclusion regarding disclosures, the Board considered disclosures required by *FASB Statement No. 1* as well as additional possible disclosures presented in the Discussion Memorandum.

214. Since this Statement specifies a single accounting method for foreign currency translation, the Board concluded that the disclosure requirements as stated in *FASB Statement No. 1* are no longer appropriate.

215. Paragraph 32 herein requires disclosure of the aggregate exchange gain or loss included in the determination of net income for the period. An exchange gain or loss does not measure, nor is it necessarily an indicator of, the full economic effect of a rate change on an enterprise. The disclosure required by paragraph 32 provides information to users of financial statements about the effects of rate changes on certain assets and liabilities which may be useful in evaluating and comparing reported result of operations.

216. A few respondents to the Exposure Draft suggested that some components of the aggregate exchange gain or loss (for example, gains and losses on unperformed forward exchange contracts) be

separately disclosed. The Board concluded that since enterprises often manage and hedge their exchange exposure on an overall basis, separate disclosure of any of the components, particularly gains or losses on forward exchange contracts, should not be required.

217. Disclosure of gains or losses on forward exchange contracts that are deferred in accordance with paragraph 27 is not required by paragraph 32. The Board reasoned that those gains or losses are, in effect, offset by unrecorded exchange losses or gains on the related foreign currency commitments; therefore, separate disclosure would be inappropriate.

218. The Exposure Draft (paragraph 20) contained a proposed requirement that the aggregate amount of tax effects related to exchange gains or losses be disclosed. Some respondents to the Exposure Draft explained certain difficulties in determining the tax effects and pointed out that disclosure of tax effects might imply that the gain or loss was *extraordinary*—an implication contrary to the requirement of paragraph 23 of *APB Opinion No. 30* that exchange gains or losses not be reported as extraordinary items. Other respondents suggested that other accounting pronouncements already required explanations of unusual tax effects (for example, *APB Opinion No. 11,* paragraph 63). The Board concluded that those comments had merit, and, therefore, this Statement does not require disclosure of the tax effects of exchange gains or losses.

219. Certain respondents to the Exposure Draft proposed an exemption from the disclosure requirements of paragraph 32 for certain enterprises whose principal business purpose is investing in foreign securities and that present those investments at current market price (determined by applying the current rate to the market price of securities traded and quoted in foreign currency). They argued that it is impracticable and of questionable usefulness for those enterprises to attempt to isolate the portion of the change in market price measured in dollars that arises from rate changes from the portion that arises from changes in foreign currency market prices.

220. The Board concluded that *exemption* for those enterprises was not appropriate because the segregation described in paragraph 219 is not intended by paragraph 32 of this Statement (and was not intended in paragraph 20 of the Exposure Draft). Exchange gains and losses as described in paragraph 16 do not include the effects of rate changes on assets (other than those denominated in foreign currency) carried at current prices measured in dollars. However, those effects should be considered, if practicable, in providing the disclosures required by paragraph 33 (see paragraph 223).

221. Some respondents to the Exposure Draft stated that disclosing the exchange gain or loss from an exposed net liability position when the foreign currency strengthens would give the wrong signal (a loss) because the rate change is expected to have future beneficial effects. In the Board's opinion, an exchange gain or loss neither is nor should be a signal of the direction of future operating results. An exchange gain or loss merely reflects the effect of a rate change on a given financial position at a specific time. Other respondents indicated that other effects of rate changes on reported results of operations should be disclosed in addition to the disclosure of exchange gains or losses.

222. The Board acknowledges that more information than disclosure of exchange gains or losses is needed for an understanding of the effects of rate changes on the operating results of an enterprise. Therefore, it modified paragraph 21 of the Exposure Draft in paragraph 33 of this Statement.

223. Paragraph 33 of this Statement requires that, if practicable, the effects of rate changes on reported revenue and earnings be described and quantified. The Board concluded that a practicability qualification was necessary. As indicated in paragraph 107, it may be difficult or impossible to quantify the economic effects of rate changes (for example, on selling prices, sales volume, and cost structures). In the Board's opinion, disclosing only the mathematical effects of translating revenue and expenses at rates different from those used in a preceding period could be misinterpreted if other significant direct and indirect economic effects of rate changes on operations are not considered and disclosed. Thus, the Board concluded that since the effect of rate changes on revenue and earnings cannot always be measured with sufficient precision, it could not require disclosures of that type in all financial statements. The Board noted, however, that some companies have disclosed certain information (not necessarily in financial statements) that might be interpreted as showing the effect of rate changes on revenue and earnings. The Board's intention is to encourage disclosures of that kind if, in the opinion of management, they provide useful information. The Board believes that if that information is disclosed in financial statements, a clear explanation of the methods and underlying assumptions used to determine the amounts is also essential, as required by paragraph 33 of this Statement.

224. The Board believes that management can best decide how information about the effects of rate changes on revenue and earnings should be described or quantified. The nature and extent of foreign currency transactions or foreign operations of enterprises vary, and that which is possible or appropriate for one enterprise may not be possible

or appropriate for others. The purpose of disclosure of the effect of rate changes in addition to exchange gains and losses is to assist financial statement users in understanding the financial effects of rate changes on the reported results of operations. Disclosing only exchange gains and losses if rate changes significantly affect reported revenue and earnings in a way or to an extent that can be determined would not, in the view of the Board, comply with the intent of paragraph 33 of this Statement. The disclosures urged by that paragraph are not forecasts, but rather descriptions and estimates of the effect on reported results of operations of rate changes that the Board believes will assist users in comparing recent results with those of prior periods.

225. Some respondents requested clarification of the circumstances requiring an enterprise's financial statements to be *adjusted* for a change in rate subsequent to the date of the financial statements. The Board concluded that financial statements should not be adjusted for rate changes after their date; however, disclosure may be necessary (paragraph 34). If the estimated effect of a rate change is disclosed, the disclosure should include consideration of changes in financial position from the date of the financial statements to the date the rate changed. The Board recognizes that in some cases it may not be practicable to determine the changes in financial position; if so, that fact should be stated.

226. The disclosure of geographical, or otherwise segmented, information on foreign operations is being considered in the FASB project, "Financial Reporting for Segments of a Business Enterprise."

EXCHANGE RATES

Multiple Rates

227. The Board concluded that if multiple rates exist, the rate to be used to translate foreign statements should, in the absence of unusual circumstances, be the rate applicable to dividend remittances. Use of that rate expresses results of operations in dollars in a more meaningful way than any other rate because the earnings can be converted into dollars only at that rate. Further, in translating an asset carried at a current price, the dividend rate measures the dollar amount that might be realized from sale of the asset and remittance of the proceeds and thereby establishes the asset's value in dollars. In translating an asset carried at cost, the dividend rate at the time the asset was acquired measures the sacrifice made by the parent in foregoing a remission of the local-currency cost of the asset and thus establishes the asset's dollar cost.

228. The dividend rate measures the dollar sacrifice in all situations, including those involving multiple rates in which the foreign operation purchased an imported asset at a preferential or penalty rate. Before being used to pay for the imported asset, the local currency cash with which payment is made is translated at the dividend rate. That rate thus measures the translated cost of the asset. If the preferential or penalty rate, whichever applies, were used to translate the local currency cost of the asset, its translated cost would not represent the dollar sacrifice made.

Differing Balance Sheet Dates

229. If foreign statements of an operation are as of a date different from that of the enterprise and are combined or consolidated with or accounted for by the equity method in the financial statements of the enterprise, the Board concluded that for purposes of applying the requirements of this Statement, the current rate is the rate in effect at the foreign operation's balance sheet date. The use of that rate is necessary to present dollar measurements as of that date.

230. Some respondents to the Exposure Draft questioned that conclusion. In their view, use of a foreign operation's financial statements as of a date that differs from that of the enterprise's financial statements is justified only on the basis that those financial statements approximate financial statements as of the enterprise's year-end. Accordingly, they argue, the current rate should be the rate in effect at the date of the enterprise's financial statements, not the rate at the date of the foreign operation's financial statements.

231. Paragraph 4 of *ARB No. 51,* "Consolidated Financial Statements," states:

> A difference in fiscal periods of a parent and a subsidiary does not of itself justify the exclusion of the subsidiary from consolidation. It ordinarily is feasible for the subsidiary to prepare, for consolidation purposes, statements for a period which corresponds with or closely approaches the fiscal period of the parent. However, where the difference is not more than about three months, it usually is acceptable to use, for consolidation purposes, the subsidiary's statements for its fiscal period; when this is done, recognition should be given by disclosure or otherwise to the effect of intervening events which materially affect the financial position or results of operations.

Similarly, paragraph 19(g) of *APB Opinion No. 18* states:

> If financial statements of an investee are not

sufficiently timely for an investor to apply the equity method currently, the investor ordinarily should record its share of the earnings or losses of an investee from the most recent available financial statements. A lag in reporting should be consistent from period to period.

232. Reconsideration of *ARB No. 51* and *APB Opinion No. 18* was not within the scope of the project that led to the issuance of this Statement. Accordingly, the Board neither accepted nor rejected the view expressed in paragraph 230. However, the Board believes that if that view is appropriate, the determination that the operation's financial statements at other than the enterprise's year-end are reasonable approximations of its financial statements as of the enterprise's year-end should be based on dollar measurements (translated statements) and not local currency measurements (foreign statements). Using as the current rate a rate at a date other than the foreign operation's balance sheet date could produce translated financial statements that are not in accordance with the requirements of this Statement. For example, if between the date of the foreign operation's financial statements and the date of the enterprise's financial statements there have been changes in the foreign currency measure of the foreign operation's financial position (that is, total assets and total liabilities) or the components thereof (for example, cash and inventory), including changes that may have occurred in anticipation of a significant rate change, using the rate as of the enterprise's financial statements will not result in financial statements for the foreign operation that reflect dollar measures of financial position and results of operations as of either date.

233. Certain respondents to the Exposure Draft expressed another view opposing the Board's conclusion. In their view, using as the current rate a rate at other than the enterprise's balance sheet date raises implemental issues in eliminating intercompany transactions if the rate has changed during the intervening period. The Board believes that those implemental problems are similar to other implemental problems caused by intercompany transactions within the intervening period and, therefore, apparently can be accommodated in the consolidation, combination, or equity accounting process.

234. Another opposing view expressed in response to the Exposure Draft was that using as the current rate the rate in effect at the foreign operation's balance sheet date rather than the rate in effect on the date of the enterprise's balance sheet would be contrary to the principle underlying *FASB Statement No. 5*, "Accounting for Contingencies," if an intervening rate change resulted in an exchange loss. According to that view, the rate change causes an asset to be impaired or liability incurred, and the amount of the loss is known as of the date of the enterprise's balance sheet. The Board believes that if foreign statements are as of a date other than the balance sheet date of the enterprise, the terminology "date of the financial statement" as used in paragraph 8(a) of *FASB Statement No. 5* refers to the end of the most recent accounting period for which foreign statements are being combined, consolidated, or accounted for by the equity method.

235. The Board believes that rate changes subsequent to the date of a foreign operation's balance sheet are similar to those subsequent to the date of an enterprise's balance sheet. Disclosure may be necessary, but the financial statements should not be adjusted (paragraph 34).

DEFERRED INCOME TAXES

236. The procedures set forth in this Statement (paragraph 50) for determining the amount of deferred taxes in a translated balance sheet represent a modification of the procedures proposed in the Exposure Draft. That draft proposed that all deferred tax charges or credits be translated at historical rates.

237. Certain respondents to the Exposure Draft questioned translation at historical rates if the *net change* method of deferred tax allocation is followed. In their view, use of historical rates requires that originating and reversing timing difference be distinguished for translation purposes—a requirement that is inconsistent with the *net change* method. Under the *net change* method, a single computation is made at the *current* tax rate for the net effect of both originating and reversing differences occurring during a period relating to a particular group of similar timing differences. The method results in a balance of deferred taxes that is a residual, that is, the difference between the deferred taxes originally recorded and subsequent reduction of deferred taxes at different tax rates as timing differences reverse.

238. Other respondents to the Exposure Draft questioned translation at historical rates of deferred income tax charges or credits applicable to timing difference on items translated at the current rate. In their view, that approach does not result in proper dollar measures of deferred tax charges and credits relating to timing differences.

239. The Board considered those views and the objective of translation (paragraph 6) and concluded that the procedures set forth in paragraph 50 should be followed. The Board believes that those procedures result in deferred tax charges and credits in a translated balance sheet that are consistent with

the requirements of *APB Opinion No. 11* and the objective of translation.

EFFECTIVE DATE AND TRANSITION

240. The Board concluded that because of the various methods of translation or of recognition of exchange gains and losses now followed in practice and because of the complex nature of the translation process, a prospective method of transition is not feasible. The Board considered whether the transition should be by prior period restatement or by cumulative effect adjustment (the method specified in the Exposure Draft). The Board concluded that prior period restatement is the preferable method to provide useful information about foreign currency transactions and foreign operations for purposes of comparing financial data for periods after the effective date of this Statement with data presented for earlier periods.

241. The Board recognizes, however, that the procedures called for by this Statement may sometimes differ significantly from procedures followed in previous periods. In addition, restatement requires the availability of records or information that an enterprise may no longer have or that its past procedures did not require. Therefore, if the effect of the restatement on all individual periods presented cannot be computed or reasonably estimated, the cumulative effect adjustment method shall be used in accordance with paragraph 36.

242. On considering all circumstances, the Board judged the effective date specified in paragraph 35 to be advisable.

Appendix E

GLOSSARY

243. This Appendix defines certain terms used and not defined elsewhere in this Statement.

Attribute: The quantifiable characteristic of an item that is measured for accounting purposes. For example, historical cost and replacement cost are attributes of an asset.

Conversion: The exchange of one currency for another.

Enterprise: See Reporting Enterprise.

Exposed Net Asset Position: The excess of assets that are measured or denominated in foreign currency and translated at the current rate over liabilities that are measured or denominated in foreign currency and translated at the current rate.

Exposed Net Liability Position: The excess of liabilities that are measured or denominated in foreign currency and translated at the current rate over assets that are measured or denominated in foreign currency and translated at the current rate.

Foreign Currency: A currency other than the currency of the country being referred to; a currency other than the reporting currency of the enterprise being referred to; composites of currencies, such as the Special Drawing Rights on the International Monetary Fund (SDRs), used to set prices or denominate amounts of loans, etc., have the characteristics of foreign currency for purposes of applying this Statement.

Foreign Currency Financial Statements: Financial statements of a foreign operation that employ as the unit of measure a currency other than the reporting currency of the enterprise being referred to.

Foreign Currency Transactions: Transactions (for example, sales or purchases of goods or services or loans payable or receivable) whose terms are stated in a currency other than the local currency.

Foreign Currency Translation: The process of expressing amounts denominated or measured in one currency in terms of another currency by use of the exchange rate between the two currencies.

Foreign Operation: An operation whose financial statements are (a) combined or consolidated with or accounted for on an equity basis in the financial statements of the reporting enterprise and (b) prepared in a currency other than the reporting currency of the reporting enterprise.

Foreign Statements: See Foreign Currency Financial Statements.

Local Currency: Currency of a particular country being referred to; the reporting currency of a domestic or foreign operation being referred to.

Reporting Currency: The currency in which an enterprise prepares its financial statements.

Reporting Enterprise: An entity whose financial statements are being referred to; in this Statement, those financial statements reflect (a) the financial statements of one or more foreign operations by combination, consolidation, or equity accounting and/or (b) foreign currency transactions.

Settlement Date: The date at which a receivable is collected or a payable is paid.

Spot Rate: The exchange rate for immediate delivery of currencies exchanged.

Transaction Date: The date at which a transaction (for example, a sale or purchase of merchandise or services) is recorded in accounting records in conformity with generally accepted accounting principles.

Translation: See Foreign Currency Translation.

Unit of Measure: The currency in which assets, liabilities, revenue, and expenses are measured.

Statement of Financial Accounting Standards No. 9
Accounting for Income Taxes—Oil and Gas Producing Companies

an amendment of APB Opinions No. 11 and 23

STATUS

Issued: October 1975

Effective Date: For financial statements issued on or after December 1, 1975

Affects: Supersedes APB 11, paragraph 40
Amends APB 23, paragraph 2

Affected by: Superseded by FAS 19

Statement of Financial Accounting Standards No. 9
Accounting for Income Taxes—Oil and Gas Producing Companies

an amendment of APB Opinions No. 11 and 23

CONTENTS

INTRODUCTION AND BACKGROUND INFORMATION

1. *APB Opinion No. 11,* "Accounting for Income Taxes," issued in 1967, has not required interperiod income tax allocation with respect to "intangible development costs" incurred by oil and gas producing companies. Paragraph 40 of the Opinion states:

> Intangible development costs in the oil and gas industry are commonly deducted in the determination of taxable income in the period in which the costs are incurred. Usually the costs are capitalized for financial accounting purposes and are amortized over the productive periods of the related wells. A question exists as to whether the tax effects of the current deduction of these costs for tax purposes should be deferred and amortized over the productive periods of the wells to which the costs relate. Other items have a similar, or opposite, effect because of the interaction with "percentage" depletion for income tax purposes. The Board [APB] has decided to defer any conclusion on these questions until the accounting research study on extractive industries is completed and an Opinion is issued on that subject.

2. Paragraph 33 of *APB Opinion No. 11* cites as an example of a permanent difference (defined in paragraph 13(f) of that Opinion) "the excess of statutory depletion over cost depletion."

3. *APB Opinion No. 23,* "Accounting for Income Taxes—Special Areas," issued in 1972, amended *APB Opinion No. 11* in certain respects but did not modify paragraph 40 of *APB Opinion No. 11.* Paragraph 2 of *APB Opinion No. 23* states: "The Board [APB] continues to defer conclusions on intangible development costs in the oil and gas industry pending the issuance of an Opinion on extractive industries."

4. Prior to the effective date of *APB Opinion No. 11,* some oil and gas producing companies had allocated income taxes with respect to intangible drilling and development costs and some other costs associated with the exploration for and development of oil and gas reserves that entered into the determination of taxable income and pretax accounting income in different periods. Those companies generally have continued that practice since the issuance of *APB Opinion No. 11.*

5. On the other hand, both before and after the effective date of *APB Opinion No. 11,* many oil and gas producing companies have not allocated income taxes with respect to those costs. The fact that percentage depletion over the life of oil and gas properties was expected to exceed costs of that type that are capitalized and amortized in the determination of pretax accounting income (i.e., the interaction with percentage depletion described in the citation in paragraph 1 of this Statement) has generally been cited as the conceptual basis for not allocating income taxes.

6. The Tax Reduction Act of 1975 (hereinafter sometimes referred to as the *Act*) substantially reduced or eliminated percentage depletion as a Federal income tax deduction for many oil and gas producing companies as of January 1, 1975.

7. The Board has, among other things, (a) examined the provisions of the Act relating to percentage depletion for oil and gas production, (b) reviewed a report dated April 11, 1975 of an American Petroleum Institute survey of 25 oil and gas producing companies on interperiod tax allocation relating to the elimination of percentage depletion, and (c) reviewed the financial statements of a number of oil and gas producing companies.

8. The Board originally concluded not to hold a public hearing on the specific issue of interperiod

tax allocation related to intangible drilling and development costs and other costs associated with the exploration for and development of oil and gas reserves. An Exposure Draft of a proposed Statement on "Accounting for Income Taxes—Oil and Gas Producing Companies" was issued on April 25, 1975. Ninety-eight letters were received in response to the request for comments. Most of the respondents objected to the method of transition set forth in paragraph 15 of the Exposure Draft, but they held widely divergent views about other methods of transition. On June 26, 1975 the Board announced that it would hold a public hearing. A Notice of Public Hearing was issued on July 10, 1975 stating that the purpose of the public hearing was to provide an opportunity for the Board to receive additional information from, and to hear the views of, interested persons and groups with repect to the accounting problems and issues associated with this matter, in particular those issues discussed in paragraphs 11-17 and Appendix A of the Exposure Draft and those issues and questions set forth in Appendix 1 of the Notice of Public Hearing. The Board received 54 position papers, letters of comment, and outlines of oral presentations in response to the Notice of Public Hearing. Twenty-seven presentations were made at the public hearing.

9. The basis for the Board's conclusions, as well as alternatives considered and reasons for their rejection, are discussed in Appendix A to this Statement.

10. This Statement applies to regulated enterprises in accordance with the provisions of the Addendum to *APB Opinion No. 2,* "Accounting for the 'Investment Credit.'"

STANDARDS OF FINANCIAL ACCOUNTING AND REPORTING

Interperiod Tax Allocation

11. Commencing January 1, 1975, interperiod tax allocation is required[1] for intangible drilling and development costs[2] and other costs[3] associated with the exploration for and development of oil and gas reserves that enter into the determination of taxable income and pretax accounting income in different periods (hereinafter referred to as *IDC financial accounting/tax differences*) pursuant to the provisions of *APB Opinion No. 11.*

12. An oil or gas producing company that heretofore has not allocated income taxes related to IDC financial accounting/tax differences shall, as of January 1, 1975, begin allocating income taxes on the difference (hereinafter referred to as the *net change*) between (i) IDC financial accounting/tax differences originating in the period and (ii) the reversal of similar differences during the period. *APB Opinion No. 11,* particularly paragraphs 36-37 thereof, specifies the method for computing the income tax effect[4] relating to the net change. In any period during which reversals exceed originating timing differences, the resulting income tax effect shall reduce previously deferred income taxes attributable only to the costs described in paragraph 11 and footnotes 2 and 3. If deferred income taxes have not been provided or if previously deferred income taxes are eliminated, deferred tax credits attributable to other items shall not be reduced, and the excess income tax effect shall be charged to income tax expense in the period in which the excess arises.

13. In making the computation of deferred income tax expense as set forth in the first sentence of paragraph 12, an oil or gas producing company with excess statutory depletion[5] may elect, but is not required, to recognize interaction with percentage depletion. If this election is made, income taxes shall be deferred on the amount by which originating timing differences exceed reversals during the period, except that the amount on which income taxes are deferred in that period shall be limited to the excess of cumulative IDC financial accounting/tax differences at the end of the period over the sum of (a) excess statutory depletion and (b) cumulative IDC financial accounting/tax differences with respect to which income taxes have been allocated. In periods in which reversals exceed originating timing differences, previously deferred income taxes attributable only to the costs described in paragraph 11 and footnotes 2 and 3 shall be reduced.[6] If at the end of the period the sum of (a) excess statutory depletion

[1]See the exception provided by paragraph 13, however.

[2]Intangible drilling and development costs include costs incurred with respect to both producing and nonproducing wells or properties.

[3]These other costs include costs such as geological and geophysical costs, leasehold costs, delay rentals, advance or shut-in royalties, and ad valorem taxes, some of which may be charged to expense for financial accounting purposes before they are deducted for income tax purposes.

[4]The income tax effect referred to in this Statement is determined in the same manner as if income taxes had been allocated on IDC financial accounting/tax differences in the periods of their origination using the net change method as set forth in *APB Opinion No. 11.*

[5]*Excess statutory depletion* is the excess of estimated statutory depletion allowable as an income tax deduction in future years over the amount of cost depletion otherwise allowable as a tax deduction, determined on a total enterprise basis.

[6]If deferred income taxes have not been provided or if previously deferred income taxes are eliminated, deferred tax credits attributable to other items shall not be reduced, and any excess income tax effect shall be charged to income tax expense in the period in which the excess arises.

and (b) cumulative IDC financial accounting/tax differences with respect to which income taxes have been allocated is equal to or greater than cumulative IDC financial accounting/tax differences, income taxes shall not be allocated on the amount by which originating timing differences exceed reversals during the period. Previously deferred income taxes attributable to the costs described in paragraph 11 and footnotes 2 and 3 shall not be reduced unless reversals exceed originating timing differences during the period.[7] See Appendix B for examples of the application of this paragraph.

14. Prior to January 1, 1975, certain oil and gas producing companies allocated income taxes in accordance with the provisions of *APB Opinion No. 11* with respect to IDC financial accounting/tax differences without recognizing interaction with percentage depletion. This method of income tax allocation shall continue as an accepted method. Accordingly, an oil or gas producing company may change to that method of accounting and, if it does, shall apply the method retroactively by restating financial statements and financial summaries or other data derived therefrom presented for prior periods (see paragraphs 18, 26, and 27 of *APB Opinion No. 9,* "Reporting the Results of Operations"). If records are not available to make the detailed year-by-year "with and without" computations under this method (see paragraph 36 of *APB Opinion No. 11*), reasonable approximations shall be made. Considering the unique circumstance of the question at hand, the requirement of paragraphs 15-17 of *APB Opinion No. 20,* "Accounting Changes," for justification of a change in accounting principle need not be met in connection with a change made in accordance with this paragraph.

Disclosure

15. Because different methods of accounting are permitted in paragraphs 12-14 of this Statement and because of the uncertainties involved in estimating future statutory depletion, a company that allocates income taxes in accordance with paragraph 12 or 13 shall disclose in its financial statements the amount of cumulative IDC financial accounting/tax differences at the end of the period with respect to which income taxes have not been allocated. In addition, when it becomes probable that future reversals of IDC financial accounting/tax differences will exceed future originating differences of a similar nature and that the excess income tax effect (referred to in paragraphs 12 and 13) will be charged to income tax expense, the company shall disclose that probability.

Amendments to Existing Pronouncements

16. *APB Opinion No. 11* exempted "intangible development costs" from the requirement for interperiod tax allocation pending further study of the question of interaction with percentage depletion, and that exemption was continued in *APB Opinion No. 23.* The Board has not considered, and therefore does not in this Statement address, the question of whether interperiod tax allocation should or should not be affected by that interaction. In light of the substantial reduction in or elimination of percentage depletion for many companies resulting from the Tax Reduction Act of 1975, however, the exemption in *APB Opinions No. 11* and *23* of intangible development costs from the requirement for interperiod tax allocation is removed by this Statement. Accordingly, this Statement supersedes paragraph 40 of *APB Opinion No. 11* and the second sentence of paragraph 2 of *APB Opinion No. 23.*

Effective Date

17. This Statement shall be effective with respect to financial statements issued on or after December 1, 1975, although earlier application is encouraged.

18. If financial statements for the fiscal year that includes January 1, 1975 have been issued prior to December 1, 1975, when those financial statements or financial summaries or other data derived therefrom are subsequently presented, they shall be restated to reflect the requirements of this Statement. Interim financial reports issued prior to December 1, 1975 that include results of operations subsequent to December 31, 1974 also shall be restated to reflect the requirements of this Statement.

The provisions of this Statement need not be applied to immaterial items.

This Statement was adopted by the affirmative votes of five members of the Financial Accounting Standards Board. Mr. Kirk and Mr. Sprouse dissented.

Mr. Kirk and Mr. Sprouse dissent for two reasons:

First, they dissent because this Statement provides free choice to companies in similar circumstances to

[7]See footnote 6.

adopt either of two significantly different methods of implementation. Allowing companies to choose either the retroactive restatement method or the prospective net method insures that in similar circumstances significant differences in accounting for income taxes will exist indefinitely in the financial statements of oil and gas producing companies. Mr. Kirk and Mr. Sprouse hold that accounting for similar circumstances similarly and for different circumstances differently is a desirable objective that could have been achieved in this Statement. They consider the result of the Statement to be unacceptable.

Second, they dissent because in their opinion the prospective net method is based on a fiction and is not in conformity with the intention of *APB Opinion No. 11.* Under the prospective net method, income tax expense will be determined as if provisions for deferred income taxes had been made prior to 1975 when in fact the provisions had not been made. As a result, over a period of years enterprises electing the prospective net method will reflect in determining net income two tax benefits for one pre-1975 tax deduction. (Of the implementation methods considered by the Board, only the direct charge to retained earnings without restatement has similar results.) The first tax benefit was reflected in net income prior to 1975 when certain costs were deducted for income tax purposes and capitalized for financial statement purposes but no provision was made in the financial statements for related deferred income taxes. The second tax benefit will be reflected in net income when costs capitalized prior to 1975 are amortized, because under the prospective net method as those costs are amortized the provision for income taxes will be reduced as if the amortization caused a reversal of pre-1975 deferred income taxes even though no provision for those deferred income taxes was made. The Statement seems to recognize the impropriety of this result by precluding recognition of the second benefit to the extent that recognition would result in a "debit balance" to be reported among the assets (paragraph 12) and by requiring disclosure when it is probable that situation will occur in the future (paragraph 15). However, the Statement condones recognition of the second benefit as long as the debit is accounted for as a reduction in an existing deferred credit. Messrs. Kirk and Sprouse consider the prospective net method to be without merit. They do, however, support retroactive restatement, an alternative provided for in paragraph 14.

Mr. Kirk dissents for two additional reasons:

First, this Statement claims in paragraph 16 that "the Board has not considered, and therefore does not in this Statement address, the question of whether interperiod tax allocation should or should not be affected by . . . interaction." Mr. Kirk believes that for this Statement to conclude that it is permissible to recognize interaction, the conceptual basis for interaction had to be considered and accepted. He finds acceptance of the concept irreconcilable with the requirement of this Statement that the provisions of *APB Opinion No. 11* now apply to intangible drilling and development costs.

In particular, Mr. Kirk believes that paragraph 13 conflicts with *APB Opinion No. 11.* That Opinion cites the excess of statutory depletion over cost depletion as an example of a permanent difference and states that "since permanent differences do not affect other periods, interperiod tax allocation is not appropriate to account for such differences." In Mr. Kirk's view, *APB Opinion No. 11* therefore requires that the tax benefits of excess statutory depletion be accounted for in the year in which that excess is deducted for income tax purposes. Under paragraph 13 of this Statement, however, estimates of those benefits can be anticipated and included in net income for accounting purposes many years before the benefit is realized by income tax deduction of that excess.

Second, Mr. Kirk believes that the *anticipation* of the estimated tax benefits relating to a future permanent difference and the *offsetting* of that questionable *asset,* allowed by paragraph 13 of this Statement, against a deferred credit, required by *APB Opinion No. 11,* conflicts with the bases for conclusions in *FASB Statements No. 2, 5,* and *8* regarding asset recognition, matching and offsetting (i.e., the *cover* approach), respectively.

Members of the Financial Accounting Standards Board:

Marshall S. Armstrong, *Chairman*
Oscar S. Gellein
Donald J. Kirk
Arthur L. Litke
Robert E. Mays
Walter Schuetze
Robert T. Sprouse

Appendix A

BASIS FOR CONCLUSIONS

19. This Appendix discusses factors deemed significant by members of the Board in reaching the conclusions in this Statement, including various alternatives considered and reasons for accepting some and rejecting others.

20. The scope of this Statement is limited to the question of whether, in light of the Tax Reduction Act of 1975, interperiod tax allocation is now required for IDC financial accounting/tax differences. Although the Board has not considered the

question of whether interperiod tax allocation should or should not be affected by interaction with percentage depletion, it has set forth in paragraph 13 the method of computing deferred income taxes when interaction with percentage depletion is recognized.

21. Allocation of income taxes on timing differences is the basic concept of *APB Opinion No. 11*. That Opinion had allowed an exemption for "intangible development costs," however, pending further study of the question of interaction with percentage depletion. Because the Tax Reduction Act of 1975 substantially reduced or eliminated percentage depletion for many companies as of January 1, 1975, the Board concluded that the exemption of intangible drilling and development costs and other costs from the provisions of *APB Opinion No. 11* is no longer appropriate. Accordingly, paragraph 11 of this Statement requires that beginning January 1, 1975 income taxes be deferred on IDC financial accounting/tax differences. Because the Board has not considered whether interperiod tax allocation should or should not be affected by interaction with percentage depletion, paragraph 13 permits, but does not require, companies to recognize interaction with percentage depletion.

22. In the Exposure Draft, the Board set forth five methods of transition that had been considered:

a. *Retroactive restatement.* Record the cumulative income tax effect that had not been deferred prior to January 1, 1975 by restating the financial statements for prior periods. Thereafter, allocate income taxes in accordance with *APB Opinion No. 11*.
b. *Direct charge to retain earnings without restatement.* Record the cumulative income tax effect that had not been deferred prior to January 1, 1975 by a direct charge to retained earnings as of that date, with no restatement of financial statements for prior periods. Thereafter, allocate income taxes in accordance with *APB Opinion No. 11*.
c. *Allocate taxes prospectively—gross method.* Allocate income taxes only with respect to IDC financial accounting/tax differences arising after December 31, 1974.
d. *Allocate taxes prospectively—net method.* Allocate income taxes on the net change in (i) IDC financial accounting/tax differences originating in the period and (ii) the reversal of similar differences during the period.
e. *Charge in the income statement.* Record the cumulative income tax effect that had not been deferred prior to January 1, 1975 by a charge in the income statement, with no restatement of financial statements for prior periods. Thereafter, allocate income taxes in accordance with *APB Opinion No. 11*.

Charge in the Income Statement

23. The method proposed in the Exposure Draft would have required an income statement charge as of January 1, 1975 for the cumulative income tax effect that had not been deferred prior to that date; the charge in the income statement would have been reported between the captions "extraordinary items" and "net income." The Board reasoned that reporting the charge separately between the captions "extraordinary items" and "net income" would have highlighted the fact that passage of the Act was a unique event of considerable impact on oil and gas producing companies and would have segregated the charge in the presentation of results of current operations. Respondents to the Exposure Draft and the Notice of Public Hearing argued that users of financial statements in general would not understand the charge in the income statement. They reasoned that, as a result of the emphasis users place on net income, comparability of financial statements would be weakened since net income for none of the years 1974, 1975, and 1976 would be comparable. They also reasoned that to require a charge now based on a 1975 event, viz., passage of the Act, would be inconsistent with the fact that the effect of the Act is prospective in nature and that the accounting should reflect that fact. The Board took these arguments into consideration in concluding that this method of transition should not be adopted.

Allocate Taxes Prospectively—Net Method

24. The Board originally rejected the prospective net method because it appeared inconsistent with the rationale underlying paragraph 37 of *APB Opinion No. 11*. That paragraph states that the net change method is permitted only "if the applicable deferred taxes have been provided in accordance with this Opinion on the cumulative timing differences as of the beginning of the period." Certain respondents to the Exposure Draft and the Notice of Public Hearing argued that they had provided *applicable* deferred income taxes in prior years with respect to IDC financial accounting/tax differences in accordance with *APB Opinion No. 11*, either on the basis of interaction with percentage depletion or because of the exemption referred to in paragraph 40 of that Opinion, and that, therefore, use of the net change method on a prospective basis is appropriate and consistent with prior accounting. In addition, certain of those respondents suggested that the prospective net method would result in income statement presentations after 1974 that would facilitate comparisons of results of operations of oil and gas producing companies. Other respondents pointed out that considering the unique circumstance of the question at hand existing accounting pronouncements are ambiguous with respect to the

proper method of transition and that conceptual support is not limited to any one method of transition. They concluded that the prospective net method represents a practical solution to a unique and complex problem. The Board took these arguments into consideration in concluding that the prospective net method together with the disclosures required by paragraph 15 represent a practical and reasonable solution to the problem.

Retroactive Restatement

25. One question that arises in connection with retroactive restatement of prior year financial statements concerns the feasibility of making the computations for individual prior years, because of the detailed information that might be required in making the year-by-year "with and without" computations under paragraph 36 of APB Opinion No. 11. Some respondents indicated that the computations would be impossible or extremely difficult because, in certain cases, records are not available or were not kept on a basis suitable for that purpose. Other respondents indicated, however, that the retroactive restatement could be computed on a reasonable basis. The Board notes that some oil and gas producing companies have been allocating income taxes on IDC financial accounting/tax differences, and have been doing so without recognizing interaction with percentage depletion. Some respondents reasoned that this method would result in greater comparability of financial statements of an individual company among years, as well as among oil and gas producing companies in general, than would any of the other methods considered. After considering all of the circumstances, the Board decided that retroactive restatement should not be required but should be permitted. The Board concluded, therefore, that it would be appropriate for a company to change its method of accounting to that of allocating income taxes without recognizing interaction with percentage depletion and, if it does, financial statements presented for prior periods should be restated.

Direct Charge to Retained Earnings without Restatement

26. Direct charges or credits to retained earnings without restatement of prior period financial statements are prohibited by *APB Opinion No. 9*. Consequently, the Board concluded that it would be inappropriate to record the cumulative income tax effect at January 1, 1975 by a direct charge to retained earnings as of that date. To do so would be in conflict with the basic concepts underlying *APB Opinion No. 9*.

Allocate Taxes Prospectively—Gross Method

27. Allocation of income taxes only with respect to IDC financial accounting/tax differences arising after December 31, 1974 would result in substantial variations in the ratio of income tax expense to pretax accounting income reported in financial statements for periods ending after that date. Costs unamortized for financial accounting purposes as of January 1, 1975 but previously deducted for income tax purposes would be amortized in determination of pretax accounting income after December 31, 1974 with no corresponding reversal of deferred income taxes because none would have been recorded. As a result, a company's effective income tax rate might appear to be abnormally high. Moreover, the degree of "abnormality" could vary significantly among companies depending on the extent of IDC financial accounting/tax differences at January 1, 1975. Further, practical difficulties exist in applying this method because of the need to identify separately certain pre-1975 and post-1974 information. Accordingly, the Board rejected this method.

Other Matters

28. The Exposure Draft proposed disclosure of the amount of additional income taxes paid or payable for the first full fiscal year beginning on or after January 1, 1975 as a result of the reduction or elimination of percentage depletion. Certain respondents argued that this would be a burdensome, hypothetical calculation and that the disclosures required by paragraph 63(c) of *APB Opinion No. 11* will reflect the results of the reduction or elimination of percentage depletion caused by the Act. The Board found merit in these arguments and as a result concluded that this additional disclosure should not be required.

29. The Notice of Public Hearing included a question concerning what difficulties, if any, exist with respect to net operating loss carryforwards, investment tax credit carryforwards, and foreign tax credit carryforwards in the application of the transition method(s) preferred. Those respondents who addressed this point indicated that accounting for those carryforwards could be accommodated by the provisions of *APB Opinion No. 11*.

30. Several respondents commented that the recognition of interaction with percentage depletion should not be permitted. The Board concluded that interaction with percentage depletion should continue to be permitted as set forth by paragraph 13 of this Statement because to do otherwise would require examination of the conceptual basis of interaction. As stated in paragraph 16 of this Statement, the Board has not considered the question of whether interperiod tax allocation should or should not be affected by that interaction.

31. The Board has concluded it advisable that this Statement be effective as set forth in paragraph 17.

Appendix B

EXAMPLES OF APPLICATION OF PARAGRAPH 13

32. The following examples illustrate the computation of deferred income taxes under the election permitted by paragraph 13 of this Statement. It should be recognized that these examples do not comprehend all possible circumstances and do not include the disclosures required by paragraph 15.

General Assumptions

33. The assumptions on which the examples are based are as follows:

a. The company's fiscal year-end is December 31.
b. The rate for deferring income taxes resulting from applying the computation required by paragraph 12 is 48 percent.
c. Excess statutory depletion:

January 1, 1975	$ 505,000
December 31, 1975	400,000
December 31, 1976	650,000
December 31, 1977	860,000
December 31, 1978	1,020,000
December 31, 1979	1,000,000
December 31, 1980	800,000

d. Cumulative IDC financial accounting/tax differences:

January 1, 1975	$ 500,000
December 31, 1975	600,000
December 31, 1976	760,000
December 31, 1977	930,000
December 31, 1978	1,010,000
December 31, 1979	990,000
December 31, 1980	960,000

December 31, 1975

34. At December 31, 1975 cumulative IDC financial accounting/tax differences ($600,000) exceeds by $200,000 the sum of (a) excess statutory depletion ($400,000) and (b) cumulative IDC financial accounting/tax differences with respect to which taxes had been allocated (zero). Therefore, income taxes of $48,000 would be deferred with respect to the $100,000 increase in IDC financial accounting/tax differences during the year.

December 31, 1976

35. At December 31, 1976 cumulative IDC financial accounting/tax differences ($760,000) exceeds by $10,000 the sum of (a) excess statutory depletion ($650,000) and (b) cumulative IDC financial accounting/tax differences with respect to which income taxes had been allocated ($100,000). Although IDC financial accounting/tax differences increased $160,000 during the year, the amount on which income taxes would be deferred is limited to $10,000. Therefore, income taxes of $4,800 would be deferred in the current year.

December 31, 1977

36. At December 31, 1977 the sum of (a) excess statutory depletion ($860,000) and (b) cumulative IDC financial accounting/tax differences with respect to which income taxes had been allocated ($110,000) exceeds cumulative IDC financial accounting/tax differences ($930,000). Therefore, no income taxes would be deferred in the current year. Previously deferred income taxes would not be reduced.

December 31, 1978

37. At December 31, 1978 the sum of (a) excess statutory depletion ($1,020,000) and (b) cumulative IDC financial accounting/tax differences with respect to which income taxes had been allocated ($110,000) exceeds cumulative IDC financial accounting/tax differences ($1,010,000). Therefore, no income taxes would be deferred in the current year. Previously deferred income taxes would not be reduced.

December 31, 1979

38. Reversals exceed originating IDC financial accounting/tax differences during the year by $20,000. Therefore, previously deferred income taxes would be reduced by $9,600 in the current year.

December 31, 1980

39. Reversals exceed originating IDC financial accounting/tax differences during the year by $30,000. Therefore, previously deferred income taxes would be reduced by $14,400 in the current year.

40. The following summarizes the examples in paragraphs 33-39:

	1	2	3	4	5	6	7
		IDC Financial Accounting/Tax Differences					
	Excess Statutory Depletion	Cumulative	Net Change	Memo Amounts*	Portion of Net Change on Which Deferred Tax Is Computed	Deferred Tax Expense Dr. (Cr.)	Cumulative Deferred Tax
1/01/75	$ 505,000	$ 500,000	$ N/A	$ 505,000	$ -0-	$ -0-	$ -0-
12/31/75	400,000	600,000	100,000	400,000	100,000	48,000	48,000
12/31/76	650,000	760,000	160,000	750,000	10,000	4,800	52,800
12/31/77	860,000	930,000	170,000	970,000	-0-	-0-	52,800
12/31/78	1,020,000	1,010,000	80,000	1,130,000	-0-	-0-	52,800
12/31/79	1,000,000	990,000	(20,000)	1,110,000	(20,000)	(9,600)	43,200
12/31/80	800,000	960,000	(30,000)	890,000	(30,000)	(14,400)	28,800

*Memo amounts represent the sum of (a) excess statutory depletion and (b) cumulative IDC financial accounting/tax differences with respect to which income taxes have been allocated (column 1 plus the cumulative amount in column 5 at the beginning of the period).

Statement of Financial Accounting Standards No. 10 Extension of "Grandfather" Provisions for Business Combinations

an amendment of APB Opinion No. 16

STATUS

Issued: October 1975

Effective Date: November 1, 1975

Affects: Amends APB 16, paragraph 99
Amends AIN-APB 16, Interpretations No. 15 through 17, 24, and 26

Affected by: No other pronouncements

Statement of Financial Accounting Standards No. 10
Extension of "Grandfather" Provisions for Business Combinations

an amendment of APB Opinion No. 16

CONTENTS

INTRODUCTION AND BACKGROUND INFORMATION

1. *APB Opinion No. 16,* "Business Combinations," which became effective for business combinations initiated after October 31, 1970, establishes conditions that must be met for a business combination to be accounted for by the pooling of interests method. Paragraph 99 of that Opinion, however, provides an exemption from certain of those conditions for a business combination between two companies with certain intercorporate investments at October 31, 1970 if "the combination is completed within five years after October 31, 1970." That exemption has been referred to as a "grandfather clause." AICPA Accounting Interpretations No. 15, 16, 17, and 26 of *APB Opinion No. 16* relate to that grandfather clause.

2. In addition, AICPA Accounting Interpretation No. 24 of *APB Opinion No. 16* contains a grandfather provision related to paragraph 46(a) of that Opinion and permits certain subsidiaries to account for business combinations by the pooling of interests method. In part, the Interpretation states:

> Subsidiaries which had a *significant* outstanding minority interest at October 31, 1970 may take part in a pooling combination completed within five years after that date providing the significant minority also exists at the initiation of the combination. In addition, the combination must meet all of the other pooling conditions specified in paragraphs 46 through 48. . . .
>
> For purposes of this Interpretation, a significant minority means that at least 20 percent of the voting common stock of the subsidiary is owned by persons not affiliated with the parent company.
>
> This "grandfathering" is consistent with paragraph 99 of the Opinion and applies both to combinations where the subsidiary with a significant minority interest is the issuing corporation and those where it is the other combining company. However, it does not permit a pooling between a subsidiary and its parent.

3. The FASB presently has on its technical agenda a project entitled "Accounting for Business Combinations and Purchased Intangibles," which involves a reconsideration of *APB Opinion No. 16.* Consequently, accounting practices that would change if the grandfather provisions of that Opinion expire on October 31, 1975 might, once again, be changed as a result of the FASB's reconsideration of the Opinion. The Board believes that because it is reconsidering *APB Opinion No. 16* the grandfather provisions of the Opinion and related AICPA Accounting Interpretations should continue in effect so as to maintain the status quo during the Board's reconsideration of that Opinion.

4. An Exposure Draft of a proposed Statement on "Extension of 'Grandfather' Provisions for Business Combinations" was issued on September 8, 1975. Twenty-two letters were received in response to that Exposure Draft. No substantive changes were suggested by respondents, and this Statement contains no substantive changes from the Exposure Draft.

5. The Board concluded that on the basis of existing data it could make an informed decision on the matter addressed in this Statement without a public hearing and that the effective date set forth in paragraph 8 is advisable.

STANDARDS OF FINANCIAL ACCOUNTING AND REPORTING

6. The five-year limitation in the grandfather provisions contained in paragraph 99 of *APB Opinion No. 16* and in the AICPA Accounting Interpretations cited in paragraphs 1-2 of this Statement is eliminated.

Amendment to Existing Pronouncement

7. The wording "the combination is completed within five years after October 31, 1970 and" in paragraph 99 of *APB Opinion No. 16* and similar wording in the AICPA Accounting Interpretations cited in paragraphs 1-2 of this Statement, imposing an October 31, 1975 expiration date for the grandfather provisions, are deleted.

Effective Date

8. This Statement shall be effective on November 1, 1975.

The provisions of this Statement need not be applied to immaterial items.

This Statement was adopted by the unanimous vote of the seven members of the Financial Accounting Standards Board:

Marshall S. Armstrong, *Chairman*
Oscar S. Gellein
Donald J. Kirk
Arthur L. Litke
Robert E. Mays
Walter Schuetze
Robert T. Sprouse

Statement of Financial Accounting Standards No. 11
Accounting for Contingencies—Transition Method

an amendment of FASB Statement No. 5

STATUS

Issued: December 1975

Effective Date: For fiscal years beginning on or after July 1, 1975

Affects: Amends FAS 5, paragraph 20

Affected by: No other pronouncements

Statement of Financial Accounting Standards No. 11
Accounting for Contingencies—Transition Method

an amendment of FASB Statement No. 5

CONTENTS

INTRODUCTION AND BACKGROUND INFORMATION

1. *FASB Statement No. 5,* "Accounting for Contingencies," was issued by the Board in March 1975. With respect to that Statement's effective date and transition, paragraph 20 of that Statement reads as follows:

> This Statement shall be effective for fiscal years beginning on or after July 1, 1975, although earlier application is encouraged. A change in accounting principle resulting from compliance with paragraph 8 or 14 of this Statement shall be reported in accordance with *APB Opinion No. 20,* "Accounting Changes." Accordingly, except in the special circumstances referred to in paragraphs 29-30 of *APB Opinion No. 20,* the cumulative effect of the change on retained earnings at the beginning of the year in which the change is made shall be included in net income of the year of the change, and the disclosures specified in *APB Opinion No. 20* shall be made. Reclassification of an appropriation of retained earnings to comply with paragraph 15 of this Statement shall be made in any financial statements for periods before the effective date of this Statement, or financial summaries or other data derived therefrom, that are presented after the effective date of this Statement.

2. In Appendix C, "Basis for Conclusions," of that Statement, paragraph 104 reads as follows:

> The Board considered three alternative approaches to a change in the method of accounting for contingencies: (1) prior period adjustment, (2) the "cumulative effect" method described in *APB Opinion No. 20,* "Accounting Changes," and (3) retention of amounts accrued for contingencies that do not meet the conditions for accrual in paragraph 8 until those amounts are exhausted by actual losses charged thereto. The Exposure Draft had proposed the change be effected by the prior period adjustment method. A large number of respondents to the Exposure Draft, however, opposed the prior period adjustment method for a number of reasons, including significant difficulties involved in determining the degree of probability and estimability that had existed in prior periods as would have been required if the conditions in paragraph 8 were applied retroactively. On further consideration of all the circumstances, the Board has concluded that use of the "cumulative effect" method described in *APB Opinion No. 20* represents a satisfactory solution and has concluded that the effective date in paragraph 20 is advisable.

3. The Exposure Draft of *FASB Statement No. 5* proposed a transition requiring retroactive restatement by prior period adjustment. In Appendix B, "Basis for Conclusions," of the Exposure Draft, the Board stated a preference for the prior period adjustment method because, in its judgment at the time, it would provide the most useful information for comparing financial data for periods after the adoption of the Statement with prior periods.

4. The Board recently issued *FASB Statement No. 8,* "Accounting for the Translation of Foreign Currency Transactions and Foreign Currency Financial Statements." With respect to that Statement's effective date and transition, paragraphs 35 and 36 of that Statement read as follows:

> This Statement shall be effective for fiscal years beginning on or after January 1, 1976,[14] although earlier application is encouraged. Thereafter, if financial statements for periods before the effective date, and financial summaries or other data derived therefrom, are presented, they shall be restated, if practicable, to conform to the provisions of paragraphs 7-31 of this Statement. In the year that this Statement is first applied, the financial statements shall disclose the nature of any restatement and its effect on income before extraordinary items, net income, and related per share amounts for each period restated.
>
> If restatement of financial statements or summaries for all prior periods presented is not practicable, information presented shall be

restated for as many consecutive periods immediately preceding the effective date of this Statement as is practicable, and the cumulative effect of applying paragraphs 7-31 on the retained earnings at the beginning of the earliest period restated (or at the beginning of the period in which the Statement is first applied if it is not practicable to restate any prior periods) shall be included in determining net income of that period (see paragraph 20 of *APB Opinion No. 20,* "Accounting Changes").[15] The effect on income before extraordinary items, net income, and related per share amounts of applying this Statement in a period in which the cumulative effect is included in determining net income shall be disclosed for that period, and the reason for not restating all of the prior periods presented shall be explained.

---

[14]For enterprises having fiscal years of 52 or 53 weeks instead of the calendar year, this Statement shall be effective for fiscal years beginning in late December 1975.

[15]Pro forma disclosures required by paragraphs 19(d) and 21 of *APB Opinion No. 20* are not applicable.

5. Although the Exposure Draft of *FASB Statement No. 8* indicated that transition under that Statement would be required in accordance with paragraphs 19-21, 25, and 39 of *APB Opinion No. 20* (viz., to include in the determination of net income in the year of change the effect of the accounting change), in the final Statement, the Board concluded that prior period restatement is the preferable method to provide useful information about foreign currency transactions and foreign operations for comparing financial data for a number of periods. In Appendix D, "Basis for Conclusions," of that Statement, paragraphs 240 and 241 read as follows:

> The Board concluded that because of the various methods of translation or of recognition of exchange gains and losses now followed in practice and because of the complex nature of the translation process, a prospective method of transition is not feasible. The Board considered whether the transition should be by prior period restatement or by cumulative effect adjustment (the method specified in the Exposure Draft). The Board concluded that prior period restatement is the preferable method to provide useful information about foreign currency transactions and foreign operations for purposes of comparing financial data for periods after the effective date of this Statement with data presented for earlier periods.
>
> The Board recognizes, however, that the procedures called for by this Statement may sometimes differ significantly from procedures followed in previous periods. In addition, restatement requires the availability of records or information that an enterprise may no longer have or that its past procedures did not require. Therefore, if the effect of the restatement on all individual periods presented cannot be computed or reasonably estimated, the cumulative effect adjustment method shall be used in accordance with paragraph 36.

Reconsideration of the Transition Method of FASB Statement No. 5

6. In considering and resolving the issue of transition in *FASB Statement No. 8,* the Board was mindful that there were similarities in characteristics of certain accounts affected by *FASB Statement No. 8* and *FASB Statement No. 5.* As indicated in paragraph 104 of *FASB Statement No. 5,* one of the factors that led the Board to conclude that use of the cumulative effect method would be preferable to restatement of financial statements for prior periods was its concern about the cases in which there might be significant difficulties in determining the degree of probability and estimability that existed in the prior periods. After reconsideration of the differences in the transition methods required by *FASB Statements No. 5* and *8* and the factors that led the Board to reach different conclusions on transition in those two Statements, the Board has concluded that the cumulative effect method should not be required as it now is by *FASB Statement No. 5* in those cases in which the difficulties of determining probability and estimability retroactively are not present. On reconsideration of all the circumstances, the Board has concluded that in order to provide the most useful information, it is preferable for an enterprise adopting *FASB Statement No. 5* to restate its financial statements for as many immediately preceding periods as is practicable in accordance with the revised transition method set forth in paragraph 10 of this Statement.

7. Some enterprises elected to apply *FASB Statement No. 5* prior to its effective date (as encouraged in paragraph 20 of the Statement) and issued annual or interim financial statements or financial summaries or other data derived therefrom using the cumulative effect method of transition. The Board considered whether those enterprises should now be required to conform to the method of transition to *FASB Statement No. 5* specified by this Statement. Although the Board strongly encourages those enterprises to restate their financial statements in a manner similar to that required of enterprises that did not elect early application, it has concluded that it should not require them to do so.

8. An Exposure Draft of a proposed Statement on "Accounting for Contingencies—Transition Method" was issued on October 31, 1975. Forty-five letters were received in response to that Exposure Draft.

9. The Board concluded that on the basis of existing data it could make an informed decision on the matter addressed in this Statement without a public hearing and that the effective date in paragraph 11 is advisable.

STANDARDS OF FINANCIAL ACCOUNTING AND REPORTING

Amendment to FASB Statement No. 5

10. Paragraph 20 of *FASB Statement No. 5* is amended to read as follows:

> *FASB Statement No. 5* shall be effective for fiscal years beginning on or after July 1, 1975, although earlier application is encouraged. Thereafter, if financial statements for periods before the effective date, and financial summaries or other data derived therefrom, are presented, they shall be restated, if practicable, to conform to the provisions of paragraph 8 or 14 of *FASB Statement No. 5.** In the year that the Statement is first applied, the financial statements shall disclose the nature of any restatement and its effect on income before extraordinary items, net income, and related per share amounts for each period restated. If restatement of financial statements or summaries for all prior periods presented is not practicable, information presented shall be restated for as many consecutive periods immediately preceding the effective date of *FASB Statement No. 5* as is practicable, and the cumulative effect of applying paragraph 8 or 14 on the retained earnings at the beginning of the earliest period restated (or at the beginning of the period in which the Statement is first applied if it is not practicable to restate any prior periods) shall be included in determining net income of that period (see paragraph 20 of *APB Opinion No. 20*).** The effect on income before extraordinary items, net income, and related per share amounts of applying *FASB Statement No. 5* in a period in which the cumulative effect is included in determining net income shall be disclosed for that period, and the reason for not restating all of the prior periods presented shall be explained. Reclassification of an appropriation of retained earnings to comply with paragraph 15 of *FASB Statement No. 5* shall be made in any financial statements for periods before the effective date of the Statement, or financial summaries or other data derived therefrom, that are presented after the effective date of the Statement.
>
> *This does not alter the accounting for changes in estimates—see paragraph 31 of *APB Opinion No. 20.*
>
> **Pro forma disclosures required by paragraphs 19(d) and 21 of *APB Opinion No. 20* are not applicable.

Effective Date and Transition

11. This amendment to *FASB Statement No. 5* shall be effective retroactively to the effective date of *FASB Statement No. 5* except that enterprises that have issued financial statements for annual or interim periods, or financial summaries or other data derived therefrom, prior to January 1, 1976 based on the original transition requirement in paragraph 20 of *FASB Statement No. 5* are strongly encouraged but not required to comply with this Statement when those financial statements or financial summaries or other data derived therefrom are subsequently presented for the first time on or after January 1, 1976.

The provisions of this Statement need not be applied to immaterial items.

This Statement was adopted by the affirmative votes of six members of the Financial Accounting Standards Board. Mr. Litke dissented.

Mr. Litke dissents because paragraph 11 of this Statement permits companies that have issued financial statements using the cumulative effect method of transition to *FASB Statement No. 5* to elect not to change to the method specified by this Statement. He believes that the Board, once having determined that restatement is the appropriate method of transition to *FASB Statement No. 5,* should have required all companies to follow that method. In Mr. Litke's judgment, an important objective of the Board should be to eliminate, rather than create, accounting differences among enterprises that are not justified by differences in underlying circumstances.

Members of the Financial Accounting Standards Board:

Marshall S. Armstrong, *Chairman*
Oscar S. Gellein
Donald J. Kirk
Arthur L. Litke
Robert E. Mays
Walter Schuetze
Robert T. Sprouse

Statement of Financial Accounting Standards No. 12
Accounting for Certain Marketable Securities

STATUS

Issued: December 1975

Effective Date: For fiscal periods ending on or after December 31, 1975

Affects: No other pronouncements

Affected by: No other pronouncements

Statement of Financial Accounting Standards No. 12
Accounting for Certain Marketable Securities

CONTENTS

INTRODUCTION AND BACKGROUND INFORMATION

1. There has long been diversity in accounting for marketable securities. Paragraph 9, Chapter 3A, "Current Assets and Current Liabilities," of *Accounting Research Bulletin (ARB) No. 43* (originally adopted as *ARB No. 30* in 1947) narrowed practice somewhat by stating:

> . . . practice varies with respect to the carrying basis for current assets such as marketable securities and inventories. In the case of marketable securities where market value is less than cost by a substantial amount and it is evident that the decline in market value is not due to a mere temporary condition, the amount to be included as a current asset should not exceed the market value.

Chapter 3A of *ARB No. 43* did not, however, deal with the question of whether a write-up of a previous write-down might be permissible to reflect a recovery in the market. *Accounting Principles Board (APB) Opinion No. 18,* "The Equity Method of Accounting for Investments in Common Stock," dealt with accounting for investments by the equity method when the investor has "significant influence" over the investee, thus establishing accounting principles for those investments. In addition, a number of Industry Audit Guides, issued by the AICPA for certain industries, describe specialized accounting practices applied in those industries. At present, some enterprises are carrying marketable securities at cost, some at market (or variations of market), some at the lower of cost or market, and some are applying more than one of those methods to different classes of securities. During 1973 and 1974, there were substantial declines in market values of many securities. As a result, in many enterprises where securities are carried at cost, the carrying amount is in excess of current market value. In other enterprises where carrying amounts were written down to reflect the market decline, the partial recovery in the market in 1975 has given rise to a situation in which securities are being carried at amounts which are below both original cost and current market value.

2. Concern over the lack of definitive guidance in the authoritative literature with respect to certain accounting problems accentuated by these conditions led to requests for the FASB to consider those problems on an urgent basis. The issues raised were submitted to the members of the Board's Screening Committee on Emerging Problems, and their recommendations were weighed by the Board in arriving at its decision to proceed with a project of limited scope, based on the three questions stated in paragraph 3.

3. The Board has concluded that the following questions concerning financial accounting and reporting for marketable securities require resolution as soon as possible:

a. Under what circumstances should marketable equity securities that are carried on a cost basis be written down below cost?
b. Should marketable equity securities that have been written down be written back up based on market recoveries or other criteria?
c. If a parent company and one or more subsidiaries or investees follow different methods of accounting for marketable securities, should any adjustments be made to conform the subsidi-

aries' or investees' methods of accounting to that of the parent company in consolidated or parent company financial statements?[1]

4. An Exposure Draft of a proposed Statement on "Accounting for Certain Marketable Securities" was issued November 6, 1975, and a public hearing based on the Exposure Draft was held on December 8, 1975. The Board received 272 position papers and letters of comment in response to the Exposure Draft. Twenty presentations were made at the public hearing.

5. This Statement does not apply to not-for-profit organizations[2] or mutual life insurance companies; it does, however, apply to mutual savings banks (see paragraphs 39 and 40) as well as to other for-profit mutual enterprises. This Statement also does not apply to employee benefit plans because that subject is a separate item on the FASB's current agenda.

6. Investments accounted for by the equity method, as described in *APB Opinion No. 18,* are beyond the scope of this Statement except for the provisions of paragraph 18.

STANDARDS OF FINANCIAL ACCOUNTING AND REPORTING

Enterprises in Industries Not Having Specialized Accounting Practices with Respect to Marketable Securities

7. For purposes of applying paragraphs 8-13 of this Statement, certain terms are defined as follows:

a. *Equity security* encompasses any instrument representing ownership shares (e.g., common, preferred, and other capital stock), or the right to acquire (e.g., warrants, rights, and call options) or dispose of (e.g., put options) ownership shares in an enterprise at fixed or determinable prices. The term does not encompass preferred stock that by its terms either must be redeemed by the issuing enterprise or is redeemable at the option of the investor, nor does it include treasury stock or convertible bonds.
b. *Marketable,* as applied to an equity security, means an equity security as to which sales prices or bid and ask prices are currently available on a national securities exchange (i.e., those registered with the Securities and Exchange Commission) or in the over-the-counter market. In the over-the-counter market, an equity security shall be considered marketable when a quotation is publicly reported by the National Association of Securities Dealers Automatic Quotations System or by the National Quotations Bureau Inc. (provided, in the latter case, that quotations are available from at least three dealers). Equity securities traded in foreign markets shall be considered marketable when such markets are of a breadth and scope comparable to those referred to above. Restricted stock[3] does not meet this definition.
c. *Market price* refers to the price (see paragraph 7(b)) of a single share or unit of a marketable equity security.
d. *Market value* refers to the aggregate of the market price times the number of shares or units of each marketable equity security in the portfolio. When an entity has taken positions involving short sales, sales of calls, and purchases of puts for marketable equity securities and the same securities are included in the portfolio, those contracts shall be taken into consideration in the determination of market value of the marketable equity securities.
e. *Cost* refers to the original cost of a marketable equity security unless a new cost basis has been assigned based on recognition of an impairment of value that was deemed other than temporary or as the result of a transfer between current and noncurrent classifications as described in paragraph 10. In such cases, the new cost basis shall be the cost for the purposes of this Statement.
f. The *valuation allowance* for a marketable equity securities portfolio represents the net unrealized loss (the amount by which aggregate cost exceeds market value) in that portfolio.
g. The *carrying amount* of a marketable equity securities portfolio is the amount at which that portfolio of marketable equity securities is reflected in the financial statements of an enterprise.
h. A *realized gain or loss* represents the difference between the net proceeds from the sale of a marketable equity security and its cost.
i. *Net unrealized gain or loss* on a marketable equity securities portfolio represents the difference between the market value of its securities and their aggregate cost at any given date.

---

[1]The term *parent company financial statements* as used in this Statement is limited to those parent company financial statements prepared for issuance as the financial statements of the primary reporting entity.

[2]For this purpose, not-for-profit organizations are those described in the third sentence of paragraph 5 of the Introduction to *ARB No. 43*.

[3]Restricted stock for purposes of this Statement shall mean securities for which sale is restricted by a governmental or contractual requirement except where such requirement terminates within one year or where the holder has the power by contract or otherwise to cause the requirement to be met within one year. Any portion of the stock which can reasonably be expected to qualify for sale within one year, such as may be the case under Rule 144 or similar rules of the Securities and Exchange Commission, is not considered restricted.

8. The carrying amount of a marketable equity securities portfolio shall be the lower of its aggregate cost or market value, determined at the balance sheet date. The amount by which aggregate cost of the portfolio exceeds market value shall be accounted for as the valuation allowance.

9. Marketable equity securities owned by an entity[4] shall, in the case of a classified balance sheet, be grouped into separate portfolios according to the current or noncurrent classification of the securities for the purpose of comparing aggregate cost and market value to determine carrying amount. In the case of an unclassified balance sheet, marketable equity securities shall for the purposes of this Statement be considered as noncurrent assets. The current portfolios of entities that are consolidated in financial statements and that do not follow specialized industry accounting practices with respect to marketable securities shall be treated as a single consolidated portfolio for the comparison of aggregate cost and market value; similarly, the noncurrent portfolios of entities that are consolidated in financial statements and that do not follow specialized industry accounting practices with respect to marketable securities shall be treated as a single consolidated portfolio for the comparison of aggregate cost and market value. The portfolios of marketable equity securities owned by an entity (subsidiary or investee) that is accounted for by the equity method shall not be combined with the portfolios of marketable equity securities owned by any other entity included in the financial statements.[5] However, such an entity is, itself, subject to the requirements of this Statement.

10. If there is a change in the classification of a marketable equity security between current and noncurrent, the security shall be transferred between the corresponding portfolios at the lower of its cost or market value at date of transfer. If market value is less than cost, the market value shall become the new cost basis, and the difference shall be accounted for as if it were a realized loss and included in the determination of net income.

11. Realized gains and losses shall be included in the determination of net income of the period in which they occur. Changes in the valuation allowance for a marketable equity securities portfolio included in current assets shall be included in the determination of net income of the period in which they occur. Accumulated changes in the valuation allowance for a marketable equity securities portfolio included in noncurrent assets or in an unclassified balance sheet shall be included in the equity section of the balance sheet and shown separately.

12. The following information with respect to marketable equity securities owned shall be disclosed either in the body of the financial statements or in the accompanying notes:

a. As of the date of each balance sheet presented, aggregate cost and market value (each segregated between current and noncurrent portfolios when a classified balance sheet is presented) with identification as to which is the carrying amount.
b. As of the date of the latest balance sheet presented, the following, segregated between current and noncurrent portfolios when a classified balance sheet is presented:
   (i) Gross unrealized gains representing the excess of market value over cost for all marketable equity securities in the portfolio having such an excess.
   (ii) Gross unrealized losses representing the excess of cost over market value for all marketable equity securities in the portfolio having such an excess.
c. For each period for which an income statement is presented:
   (i) Net realized gain or loss included in the determination of net income.
   (ii) The basis on which cost was determined in computing realized gain or loss (i.e., average cost or other method used).
   (iii) The change in the valuation allowance(s) that has been included in the equity section of the balance sheet during the period and, when a classified balance sheet is presented, the amount of such change included in the determination of net income.

13. An enterprise's financial statements shall not be adjusted for realized gains or losses or for changes in market prices with respect to marketable equity securities when such gains or losses or changes occur after the date of the financial statements but prior to their issuance, except for situations covered by paragraph 21. However, significant net realized and net unrealized gains and losses arising after the date of the financial statements, but prior to their issuance, applicable to marketable equity securities owned at the date of the most recent balance sheet shall be disclosed.

---

[4]For this purpose, marketable equity securities owned by an investee accounted for by the equity method shall not be considered owned by the entity (investor).

[5]This constitutes an exception to paragraph 19 of *APB Opinion No. 18* in those cases in which a subsidiary accounted for under the equity method has a net unrealized gain or loss on a portfolio of marketable equity securities that would serve to offset, in whole or in part, the net unrealized gain or loss on a comparable portfolio of marketable equity securities of the parent or consolidated entity. If the subsidiary were consolidated and its portfolios were combined with comparable portfolios of other entities in the consolidation in accordance with this paragraph, a different effect on consolidated net income would be produced, as compared with the equity method.

Enterprises in Industries Having Specialized Accounting Practices with Respect to Marketable Securities

14. Certain industries apply specialized industry accounting practices with respect to marketable securities. Such industries include investment companies, brokers and dealers in securities, stock life insurance companies, and fire and casualty insurance companies. Except for the requirements in paragraphs 15, 21, and 22, this Statement does not alter any industry's specialized accounting practices. Paragraphs 15, 17, and 19 deal with marketable equity securities as that term is defined in paragraph 7. Paragraphs 16, 18, and 20-22 deal with marketable securities as that term is used in the particular industries concerned, including, but not limited to, marketable equity securities.

15. Entities that carry marketable equity securities at cost shall hereafter carry them at the lower of their aggregate cost or market value.[6] In making this determination, the provisions of paragraphs 7-9 shall be applied with the exception of the third sentence of paragraph 9. The portfolios of entities that are consolidated in financial statements and that follow the same specialized industry accounting practices with respect to marketable equity securities shall be treated as a single portfolio for the comparison of aggregate cost and market value. This Statement does not alter any entity's specialized industry practice for reporting gains and losses, whether realized or unrealized, for marketable equity securities.

16. Entities that do not include unrealized gains and losses[7] on marketable securities in the determination of net income but that do include them in the equity section of the balance sheet shall disclose the following information, either in the body of the financial statements or in the accompanying notes:

a. Gross unrealized gains and gross unrealized losses as of the date of the latest balance sheet presented.
b. Change in net unrealized gain or loss (the amount by which equity has been increased or decreased as a result of unrealized gains and losses) for each period for which an income statement is presented.

17. An enterprise's financial statements shall not be adjusted for realized gains or losses or for changes in market prices with respect to marketable equity securities when such gains or losses or changes occur after the date of the financial statements, but prior to their issuance, except for situations covered by paragraph 21. However, significant net realized and net unrealized gains and losses arising after the date of the financial statements, but prior to their issuance, applicable to marketable equity securities in the portfolio at the date of the most recent balance sheet shall be disclosed.

Enterprises That Include Entities Whose Accepted Accounting Practices Differ with Respect to Marketable Securities

18. If an investee accounted for by the equity method or a subsidiary follows accepted accounting practices that are different from those of the parent or investor with respect to marketable securities, those practices shall be retained in the consolidated or parent company financial statements in which those entities are included. As an exception to this requirement, if it is the practice of the parent or investor to include realized gains and losses in the determination of net income, or would so include them if present, the accounting treatment of a subsidiary or an investee that does not follow such practice shall be conformed to that of the parent or investor in that particular respect in consolidated or parent company financial statements.

19. If the parent company in a consolidation follows specialized industry accounting practices with respect to marketable securities but two or more consolidated subsidiaries do not (and hence are subject to the provisions of paragraphs 8-13 of this Statement), the current and noncurrent portfolios of marketable equity securities of such subsidiaries shall be consolidated as separate current and noncurrent portfolios in the manner provided in paragraph 9, exclusive of the portfolios of the parent company, for the purpose of determining carrying amounts in accordance with paragraph 9. The information required by paragraph 12 shall be disclosed in the consolidated financial statements with respect to such subsidiaries.

20. If the consolidated financial statements reflect more than one accepted practice of accounting for marketable securities, the disclosures required by this Statement and those encompassed by specialized industry practice, as applicable, shall be disclosed either in the body of the financial statements or in the accompanying notes for the marketable securities accounted for under each such practice.

---

[6]This does not preclude entities in industries in which either the cost basis or the market basis is an accepted specialized practice from electing the market basis where such election is permissible in that industry. In such an election, the provisions of paragraphs 15-17 of *APB Opinion No. 20,* "Accounting Changes," shall not apply.

[7]For the purposes of paragraph 16, unrealized gains and losses shall have the same meaning as is presently accepted in the particular industry's specialized accounting practice.

Decline in Market Value Is Assessed to Be Other Than Temporary

21. For those marketable securities for which the effect of a change in carrying amount is included in stockholders' equity rather than in net income (including marketable securities in unclassified balance sheets), a determination must be made as to whether a decline in market value below cost as of the balance sheet date of an individual security is other than temporary.[8] If the decline is judged to be other than temporary, the cost basis of the individual security shall be written down to a new cost basis and the amount of the write-down shall be accounted for as a realized loss. The new cost basis shall not be changed for subsequent recoveries in market value.

Income Taxes

22. Unrealized gains and losses on marketable securities, whether recognized in net income or included in the equity section of the balance sheet, shall be considered as timing differences, and the provisions of *APB Opinion No. 11,* "Accounting for Income Taxes," shall be applied in determining whether such net unrealized gain or loss shall be reduced by the applicable income tax effect. A tax effect shall be recognized on an unrealized capital loss only when there exists assurance beyond a reasonable doubt that the benefit will be realized by an offset of the loss against capital gains.

Effective Date and Transition

23. The provisions of this Statement, other than those of paragraph 18, shall be effective for financial statements for annual and interim periods ending on or after December 31, 1975.[9] If initial application of this Statement necessitates establishment of a valuation allowance for a marketable equity securities portfolio included in current assets, the amount thereof shall be included in the determination of net income for the period in which this Statement is initially applied. If initial application of this Statement necessitates establishment of a valuation allowance for a marketable equity securities portfolio included in noncurrent assets or in an unclassified balance sheet, the amount thereof shall be reflected separately in stockholder's equity as of the end of the period in which this Statement is initially applied. For initial application of this Statement, the provisions of paragraph 10 shall not apply to transfers between current and noncurrent classifications made as of or before December 31, 1975.[10] Financial statements for annual and interim periods ending before December 31, 1975[11] shall not be restated except as stated below. The provisions of paragraph 18 of this Statement shall be effective for financial statements for annual and interim periods ending on or after December 31, 1975.[12] Those provisions shall be applied retroactively by prior period adjustment (described in paragraphs 18 and 26 of *APB Opinion No. 9,* "Reporting the Results of Operations"). When prior period financial statements or financial summaries or other data derived therefrom are presented, they shall be restated to conform to those provisions.

The provisions of this Statement need not be applied to immaterial items.

This Statement was adopted by the affirmative votes of five members of the Financial Accounting Standards Board. Messrs. Litke and Sprouse dissented.

Mr. Litke and Mr. Sprouse dissent primarily because this Statement requires some enterprises in industries not having specialized accounting practices to recognize unrealized gains in the determination of net income of the period in which they occur and prohibits other similar enterprises from recognizing unrealized gains in circumstances that are in substance identical. In their view, recognition of a gain should depend on underlying economic circumstance—in this case whether or not a security's market value has increased. Under this Statement, however, recognition of an unrealized gain in the determination of net income depends on accounting irrelevancies such as (1) whether the security is classified in the balance sheet as a current asset or a noncurrent asset, (2) whether unrealized losses on marketable securities had previously been recognized in net income of prior periods, and (3)

[8]For a recent discussion of this subject, see the Auditing Interpretation published by the staff of the Auditing Standards Division, AICPA, "Evidential Matter for the Carrying Amount of Marketable Securities," in *The Journal of Accountancy,* April 1975.

[9]For enterprises having fiscal years of 52 and 53 weeks instead of the calendar year, this Statement shall be effective for financial statements for periods ending in late December 1975.

[10]See footnote 9.

[11]See footnote 9.

[12]See footnote 9.

whether in a given accounting period an enterprise has unrealized losses in some securities that offset unrealized gains in others. Mr. Litke and Mr. Sprouse hold that accounting for similar circumstances similarly and for different circumstances differently is an important objective in establishing financial accounting standards. This Statement, in their judgment, ignores that objective.

Mr. Litke and Mr. Sprouse believe that accounting for marketable securities held as current assets on a portfolio basis has significant defects. In comparing the aggregate cost and market value of a portfolio, the Statement calls for unrealized gains to be recognized to the extent of any unrealized losses. In this way, unrealized gains may be recognized implicitly by some enterprises while the implicit or explicit recognition of similar unrealized gains by other enterprises is precluded. Also, reporting the carrying amount of a portfolio at the lower of the aggregate cost or market value may be deceptive because it may suggest that all unrealized losses have been recognized in the period in which market values have declined. Unrealized losses that are not recognized at the end of a period because they are offset by unrealized gains on other securities in the portfolio may have to be recognized in a future period when a component of the portfolio is sold. That could be the effect even in the absence of any further changes in market value. As a result, like the cost method it is intended to supplant, the lower of cost or market rule applied on a portfolio basis may cause losses from declines in market value to be recognized in the period of sale rather than in the period in which the loss in market value occurs.

Mr. Sprouse agrees that the scope of this Statement is properly confined to resolution of the three questions stated in paragraph 3. He also agrees that current assets should not be carried at amounts in excess of their net realizable value, that in the case of marketable equity securities the best measure of net realizable value is their current market value, and that unrealized losses on marketable securities classified as current assets should be included in the determination of net income of the period in which they occur. However, since the Board concluded that it is not feasible at this time to consider comprehensively the recognition of unrealized gains on marketable equity securities, in the interest of equity and comparability among enterprises Mr. Sprouse believes that no recognition of unrealized gains is preferable to the partial and arbitrary recognition required by this Statement.

Mr. Litke believes that marketable securities should not be carried in amounts in excess of their net realizable value and that the best measure of net realizable value is their current market value. He believes that this Statement should require that all marketable equity securities be carried at market value in the balance sheet. While his inclination at this time would be to recognize unrealized market value changes in the determination of net income, he believes that the Board should not take that step in this Statement given the limited scope of the project. In Mr. Litke's opinion, the solution to the emerging problem of accounting for marketable equity securities would be for the financial statements to include in income only: (1) realized gains and losses resulting from exchange transactions, and (2) provisions to recognize the effect of permanent impairment of the security's value. Under this solution, he believes all unrealized gains and losses on both current and noncurrent marketable equity securities should be added to or deducted from stockholders' equity, except that the effect of permanent impairment would be deducted from income.

Members of the Financial Accounting Standards Board:

Marshall S. Armstrong, *Chairman*
Oscar S. Gellein
Donald J. Kirk
Arthur L. Litke
Robert E. Mays
Walter Schuetze
Robert T. Sprouse

Appendix A

BASIS FOR CONCLUSIONS

24. This Appendix discusses factors deemed significant by members of the Board in reaching the conclusions in this Statement, including alternatives considered and the reasons for accepting some and rejecting others.

Scope

25. The three questions which the Board addressed as constituting financial reporting problems requiring early resolution are those listed in paragraph 3. Questions (a) and (b) relate to the determination of carrying amount for marketable equity securities, whereas question (c) relates to the issue of conformity in consolidated or parent company financial statements of different methods of accounting with respect to all marketable securities, whether or not they are equity securities.

26. Because of the urgency of resolving these questions within a limited time frame, the Board concluded that the scope of the project should be limited essentially to the questions as presented.

Although a number of respondents objected to the short exposure period and the proximity of the proposed effective date, the Board determined that the problems should be resolved for application in 1975. As stated in paragraph 2, the requests that the Board deal with the problems had indicated that such a timely answer was needed. On the basis of available information, including that obtained at the public hearing and in position papers and letters of comment, the Board concluded that it could make an informed decision on the questions as presented and that the effective date and method of transition specified herein are advisable.

27. The Board is mindful of the fact that enterprises in certain industries apply specialized accounting practices presently accepted in those industries. The Board concluded that consideration of questions (a) and (b) with respect to those particular industries should be limited to the enterprises within those industries that carry marketable equity securities on the basis of cost. The alternative bases for carrying marketable equity securities (e.g., market value, appraised value, fair value) which are permitted in certain specialized industry accounting practices with respect to marketable securities have not been considered by the Board and are not altered by this Statement. The Board further concluded that it would not, as a part of this project, examine or change specialized industry practice for reporting gains and losses, whether realized or unrealized, for marketable securities. To do so would expand the scope of the project in that consideration of the fundamental issues that led to the adoption of those specialized practices would be required. This, the Board decided, could not be done in the limited time available for the completion of this project.

28. For the reasons discussed in paragraph 27, the "Standards of Financial Accounting and Reporting" of this Statement contain separate provisions for two categories of enterprises: those in industries not having specialized accounting practices with respect to marketable securities, and those in industries having such specialized accounting practices.

Enterprises in Industries Not Having Specialized Accounting Practices with Respect to Marketable Securities

29. In considering questions (a) and (b) of paragraph 3 the Board noted that the questions pertain to marketable equity securities carried on a cost basis. The Board's conclusion that the lower of cost or market should apply in the determination of carrying amount for such securities was based on the following factors:

a. The Board excluded from its consideration market value alone as the determinant of carrying value. Consideration of that alternative would raise pervasive issues concerning the valuation of other types of assets, including the concept of historic cost versus current or realizable value. The Board concluded that it could not examine these conceptual issues in a project of such limited scope.
b. The Board noted that continuance of original cost as the carrying amount of a portfolio of marketable equity securities when its market value is lower has the effect of deferring recognition of the decline in the realizable value of such securities based on the expectation of a future recovery in market value which may or may not occur. Because of the uncertainty of such future recovery, the Board concluded that original cost is not a proper determinant of carrying amount for marketable equity securities when market value is below cost. A number of respondents advanced the argument that, in the case of securities held as long-term investments, a decline in market value viewed as temporary should not be reflected in net income. While not necessarily accepting this argument, the Board took into account the fact that this argument has considerable support in current practice, and that the Auditing Interpretation referred to in footnote 8 is consistent with it. The Board concluded that the conceptual question of whether such differences should or should not be included in income could not be dealt with in this project, and hence no such requirement should be made at this time. However, the Board concluded that a decline in market value below cost should in all cases be reflected in the balance sheet and when such securities are classified as current assets, the decline in market value below cost should enter into the determination of net income. In the case of current assets, it is the Board's view that the realization of the loss in value of the securities should be regarded as imminent and therefore should be recognized in the determination of net income.
c. In adopting the lower of cost or market as the determinant for carrying amount, the Board required that when write-downs have been made because the market value of the portfolio has dropped below cost, if market value subsequently rises, the write-down be reversed to the extent that the resulting carrying amount does not exceed cost. The Board does not regard the reversal of the write-down as representing recognition of an unrealized gain. Rather, the Board views the write-down as establishing a valuation allowance representing the estimated reduction in the realizable value of the portfolio, and it views a subsequent market increase as having reduced or eliminated the requirement for such an allowance. In the Board's view, the reversal of the write-down represents a change in an

accounting estimate of an unrealized loss (see paragraph 2 of *FASB Statement No. 5,* "Accounting for Contingencies," and paragraph 10 of *APB Opinion No. 20*).

30. The Exposure Draft required that all changes in the carrying amounts of the marketable equity securities portfolio be reflected in income currently and made no distinction in that regard between the current or noncurrent classifications of such securities. Some respondents favored the separation of the single portfolio called for by the Exposure Draft into current and noncurrent portfolios with the change in carrying amount for the noncurrent portfolio to be reflected in equity rather than in income. They argued that fluctuations in the market value of long-term investments should not be reflected in income and to do so would cause distortions which would not be understood by investors. While not necessarily agreeing with these arguments, for the reasons discussed in paragraph 29(b), the Board decided not to require in this Statement that declines in the market value below cost of noncurrent marketable equity securities be reflected in net income. In reaching this decision, the Board recognized that the present concepts of income require authoritative clarification with respect to the recognition of unrealized gains and losses on long-term assets. Such clarification, the Board noted, is beyond the scope of this Statement. For these reasons, the Board concluded that marketable equity securities classified as noncurrent assets should constitute a separate portfolio from those securities classified as current assets for the determination of carrying amount, and that changes in the carrying amount of the noncurrent portfolio should be reflected in the equity section of the balance sheet rather than included in income, provided that the decline in market value is assessed as temporary.

31. An issue inherent in the determination of carrying amount for marketable equity securities was whether the lower of cost or market method adopted by the Board should be applied on the basis of individual security holdings or on a portfolio basis. In deciding to require application on a portfolio basis (with the exceptions noted in paragraph 9), the Board considered the following factors: Many enterprises regard their portfolios of marketable equity securities (excluding long-term investments accounted for under the equity method) as collective assets. A requirement that the application of lower of cost or market be made on an individual security basis would, in the Board's view, be unduly conservative and at variance with the manner in which enterprises generally view their investment in marketable equity securities. The Board recognized that the application of the criterion on a portfolio basis may be regarded as having the effect of offsetting the unrealized losses on one security with unrealized gains on another. However, the Board agrees with those respondents who regard the current and noncurrent portfolios of marketable equity securities each as collective assets, hence the determination of the carrying amount on a collective (portfolio) basis is in the Board's view appropriate despite the offsets referred to. The disclosures required by paragraph 12(b) are intended to inform as to the extent to which such offsets exist in the portfolio.

32. Paragraph 30 discussed the reasons for the Board's decision to change from a single portfolio basis as provided by the Exposure Draft to separate portfolios for current and noncurrent assets. The Exposure Draft noted that such a separation of portfolios would provide opportunities for transfers between portfolios simply by changing classifications and that such transfers could result in significant changes in net income. The Board had this feature in mind in requiring that transfers between the current and noncurrent portfolios be accounted for in the manner prescribed by paragraph 10. This has the effect of accounting for an unrealized loss at the date of transfer in the same manner as if it had been realized, thus reducing the incentive to cause significant changes in income by transferring securities between portfolios. The Board recognized, however, that the above requirement would not be effective in the case of a transfer from noncurrent to current classifications of a security having an excess of market value over cost which would serve to offset a reverse situation in the current portfolio, thus affecting the determination of net income. However, as mentioned in paragraph 31, the disclosures required by paragraph 12(b) should assist users of financial statements in assessing the effects of such transfers.

33. The definition of "equity security" in the Exposure Draft included convertible bonds. Many respondents believed that such inclusion was in conflict with *APB Opinion No. 14,* "Accounting for Convertible Debt and Debt Issued with Stock Purchase Warrants." It was pointed out further that the market sometimes values a convertible bond primarily on its equity characteristics and at other times primarily on its debt characteristics. The Board concluded that it was impractical to apply criteria under which a convertible bond might in some time intervals come under the definition and at other times be excluded. Accordingly, the Board decided that convertible bonds, and, for consistency, convertible preferred stock with redemption requirements, would be excluded from the definition of equity securities.

34. A number of respondents asked for clarification of what was encompassed by the term "restricted stock" with respect to the statement in the Exposure Draft that restricted stock did not

meet the definition of "marketable." Footnote 3 of this Statement is intended to provide the requested clarification. The Board's decision to consider restricted stock as meeting the definition of marketable where the restriction terminates or can be terminated by the holder within one year is based on the view that current market value is relevant in applying the lower of cost or market determination to such securities, whereas in the case of longer term restrictions, the application of current market value is of lesser relevance.

35. Paragraph 9 provides, as did the Exposure Draft, that "The portfolios of marketable equity securities owned by an entity (subsidiary or investee) that is accounted for by the equity method shall not be combined with the portfolios of marketable equity securities owned by any other entity included in the financial statements.[5]" Some respondents were of the opinion that the portfolio(s) of unconsolidated subsidiaries accounted for by the equity method should be so combined, especially in the case of 100 percent owned subsidiaries, and that failure to do so would be contrary to paragraph 19 of *APB Opinion No. 18*. Some of the respondents expressing this view acknowledged that there were both conceptual and mechanical problems involved in implementing this recommendation, but none offered specific suggestions for resolving them. The Board noted in the Exposure Draft and in footnote 5 of this Statement that the procedure called for constitutes an exception to paragraph 19 of *APB Opinion No. 18*. The Board rejected the recommendation that the portfolios of equity method subsidiaries be combined with others, because to do so could produce illogical results either with respect to the carrying amount of marketable securities as reflected in the consolidated balance sheet, or the carrying amount of the equity method subsidiary as reflected in the same balance sheet.

Enterprises in Industries Having Specialized Accounting Practices with Respect to Marketable Securities

36. Paragraph 14 states that, with the exception of paragraphs 15, 21, and 22, this Statement does not alter any industry's specialized accounting practices with respect to marketable securities.

37. Paragraph 15 requires that entities that carry marketable equity securities at cost shall hereafter carry them at the lower of their aggregate cost or market value with the following exception: entities in industries whose specialized accounting practices permit market value as an acceptable alternate carrying basis may elect that basis. The cost basis is no longer acceptable for determining carrying amount for marketable equity securities and is replaced by the lower of aggregate cost or market value.

38. The Board's decision to replace the cost basis with the lower of cost or market basis in industries having specialized accounting practices took into account the following factors:

a. Having concluded that the cost basis should be replaced in all enterprises in industries with nonspecialized accounting practices, the Board could find no justification for maintaining cost as a basis for marketable equity securities in the other industries.
b. As stated in paragraph 27, this Statement does not alter specialized industry practice for reporting gains and losses on marketable securities because to do so would involve a reconsideration of fundamental issues in those industries. However, a change in the carrying basis for marketable equity securities does not, in the Board's view, necessitate such a reconsideration.
c. Elimination of cost as a carrying basis for marketable equity securities in the industries having specialized accounting practices serves to reduce some of the disparity in practice among those industries as well as with industries not having specialized accounting practices.

Applicability

39. Numerous responses from the mutual savings bank industry urged that mutual savings banks be excluded from the scope of this Statement. The principal arguments advanced were: mutual savings banks are regulated and, in some states, are required to carry marketable securities at cost; the exclusion of not-for-profit organizations should apply to mutual savings banks; the element of mutuality (absence of shareholders) applies equally to these organizations as it does to mutual life insurance companies. The Board did not find these arguments persuasive. When mutual savings banks, which are in an industry not having specialized accounting practices, present financial statements purporting to be in conformity with generally accepted accounting principles, the fact that they are regulated or that they do not have shareholders does not, in the Board's view, justify different accounting for marketable equity securities from that required to be followed by other entities not having specialized accounting practices. Accordingly, the provisions of this Statement apply to mutual savings banks, as well as to other for-profit mutual enterprises, except mutual life insurance companies.

40. Mutual life insurance companies were excluded from the scope of this Statement because, unlike stock life insurance companies (see paragraph 14), there is disagreement as to whether generally accepted accounting principles exist for mutual life

insurance companies.[13] This coupled with the complexity of some of the issues involved in life insurance accounting caused the Board to conclude that it could not resolve these questions within this project. On the other hand, mutual savings banks, which are not excluded from the scope of this Statement, do present financial statements prepared in conformity with generally accepted accounting principles and there are no complex related accounting issues involved as is the case with mutual life insurance companies.

41. The Exposure Draft proposed that the Statement be applied retroactively by prior period restatement. That method of transition was proposed on the premise that it would afford maximum comparability among financial statements. The Board has obtained information, subsequent to the issuance of the Exposure Draft, that a number of companies have in past years made substantial reclassifications of marketable equity securities as between current and noncurrent assets. With the Board's decision to provide for separate portfolios of current and noncurrent marketable equity securities with different accounting for changes in carrying value of the two portfolios, the number of and seemingly divergent bases for reclassifications that have occurred in recent years would, in the case of retroactive restatement, result in less rather than more comparability. The new requirement that transfers between current and noncurrent portfolios be accounted for in a manner to treat reductions in market value below cost as realized losses at the date of transfer would, if applied retroactively, accentuate this effect. For these reasons, the Board concluded that the interests of users of financial statements would best be served by making the Statement effective December 31, 1975[14] (except for paragraph 18 for which retroactive application is still required).

Appendix B

ILLUSTRATION OF DISCLOSURES REQUIRED BY PARAGRAPH 12 OF THIS STATEMENT

42. The following example illustrates the disclosure requirements of paragraph 12 for an enterprise having a classified balance sheet. For purposes of this illustration it is presumed that the only marketable securities that the enterprise owns are marketable equity securities as defined in paragraph 7. The illustration does not encompass all possible circumstances that may arise in connection with the disclosure requirements, nor does it indicate the Board's preference for a particular format.

Computational Information

The details on the following pages pertain to marketable equity securities owned at December 31:

[13]See the Preface to *AICPA Industry Audit Guide*, "Audits of Stock Life Insurance Companies."

[14]See footnote 9.

	1975			1974		
	Cost	Market	Unrealized Gain (Loss)	Cost	Market	Unrealized Gain (Loss)
In Current Assets:						
Security A	$100,000	$100,000	$ —	$200,000	$250,000	$ 50,000
B	200,000	150,000	(50,000)	300,000	250,000	(50,000)
C	200,000	175,000	(25,000)	200,000	150,000	(50,000)
D	150,000	100,000	(50,000)	150,000	200,000	50,000
E	50,000	100,000	50,000	50,000	75,000	25,000
F	200,000	225,000	25,000	—	—	—
Total of Portfolio	$900,000	$850,000	$(50,000)	$900,000	$925,000	$ 25,000
Valuation Allowance—Current			$(50,000)			Not Applicable
In Noncurrent Assets:						
Security G	$300,000	$200,000	$(100,000)	$300,000	$100,000	$(200,000)
H	100,000	190,000	90,000	100,000	250,000	150,000
I	250,000	150,000	(100,000)	250,000	150,000	(100,000)
Total of Portfolio	$650,000	$540,000	$(110,000)	$650,000	$500,000	$(150,000)
Valuation Allowance—Noncurrent			$(110,000)			Not Applicable

During 1975 the following sales of securities took place. (There were no sales of securities in 1974.):

	Net Proceeds of Sale	Cost	Realized Gain (Loss)
Security A	$125,000	$100,000	$ 25,000
Security B	65,000	100,000	(35,000)
	$190,000	$200,000	$(10,000)

The valuation allowances required at December 31, 1975 are as follows:

	Charged Against Income	Charged Against Equity
In Current Assets:		
Cost $900,000 less market $850,000	$50,000*	
In Noncurrent Assets:		
Cost $650,000 less market $540,000		$110,000*

*No tax effect was recognized because there is no assurance beyond a reasonable doubt that the benefit will be realized by an offset of the loss against capital gains.

Disclosure Requirements

BALANCE SHEET

	December 31, 1975	December 31, 1974
Current Assets		
Marketable equity securities, carried at market in 1975 and at cost in 1974 (Note 1)	$850,000	$900,000
Noncurrent Assets		
Marketable equity securities, carried at market in 1975 and at cost in 1974 (Note 1)	540,000	650,000
Stockholders' Equity		
Net unrealized loss on noncurrent marketable equity securities (Note 1)	(110,000)	—

NOTES TO FINANCIAL STATEMENTS

Note 1—Marketable Equity Securities

At December 31, 1975, the current and noncurrent portfolios of marketable equity securities are each carried at their lower of cost or market at the balance sheet date. Marketable equity securities included in current and noncurrent assets had a cost of $900,000 and $650,000, respectively, at December 31, 1975.

To reduce the carrying amount of the current marketable equity securities portfolio to market, which was lower than cost at December 31, 1975, a valuation allowance in the amount of $50,000 was established with a corresponding charge to net income at that date. To reduce the carrying amount of the noncurrent marketable equity securities portfolio to market, which was lower than cost at December 31, 1975, a valuation allowance in the amount of $110,000 was established by a charge to stockholders' equity representing the net unrealized loss.

At December 31, 1974, the current and noncurrent portfolios of marketable equity securities were not required to be carried at their lower of cost or market at the balance sheet date and were carried at cost. Marketable equity securities included in current and noncurrent assets had a market value of $925,000 and $500,000, respectively, at December 31, 1974.

At December 31, 1975, gross unrealized gains and gross unrealized losses pertaining to the marketable equity securities in the portfolios were as follows:

	Gains	Losses
Current	$75,000	$125,000
Noncurrent	$90,000	$200,000

A net realized loss of $10,000 on the sale of marketable equity securiites was included in the determination of net income for 1975. The cost of the securities sold was based on the average cost of all the shares of each such security held at the time of sale. There were no sales of marketable equity securities during 1974.

Statement of Financial Accounting Standards No. 13 Accounting for Leases

STATUS

Issued: November 1976

Effective Date: For leasing transactions and revisions entered into on or after January 1, 1977

Affects: Supersedes APB 5
Supersedes APB 7
Supersedes APB 18, paragraph 15 and footnote 5
Supersedes APB 27
Supersedes APB 31
Supersedes AIN-APB 7, Interpretation No. 1
Supersedes AIN-APB 22, Interpretation No. 1

Affected by: Paragraph 3 superseded by FAS 71
Paragraph 5(b) superseded by FAS 23
Paragraphs 5(j)(i), 5(n), 12, 16(a)(iv), 17(b), and 18(b) amended by FAS 29
Paragraph 5(m) superseded by FAS 17
Paragraphs 6(b)(i) and (ii) superseded by FAS 27
Paragraphs 8(b), 10, 17(a), 18(a), 26(a)(i), and 43(c) amended by FAS 23
Paragraph 8 amended by FAS 26
Paragraph 12 amended by FAS 34
Paragraphs 14 and 17(f) amended by FAS 22
Paragraph 17(f)(ii) amended by FAS 27
Paragraph 20 amended by FAS 77
Paragraphs 32 and 33 superseded by FAS 28
Footnote 13 superseded by FAS 29

Statement of Financial Accounting Standards No. 13
Accounting for Leases

CONTENTS

INTRODUCTION

1. This Statement establishes standards of financial accounting and reporting for leases by lessees and lessors. For purposes of this Statement, a lease is defined as an agreement conveying the right to use property, plant, or equipment (land and/or depreciable assets) usually for a stated period of time. It includes agreements that, although not nominally identified as leases, meet the above definition, such as a "heat supply contract" for nuclear fuel.[1] This definition does not include agreements that are contracts for services that do not transfer the right to use property, plant, or equipment from one contracting party to the other. On the other hand, agreements that do transfer the right to use property, plant, or equipment meet the definition of a lease for purposes of this Statement even though substantial services by the contractor (lessor) may be called for in connection with the operation or maintenance of such assets. This Statement does not apply to lease agreements concerning the rights to explore for or to exploit natural resources such as oil, gas, minerals, and timber. Nor does it apply to licensing agreements for items such as motion picture films, plays, manuscripts, patents, and copyrights.

2. This Statement supersedes *APB Opinion No. 5,* "Reporting of Leases in Financial Statements of Lessee"; *APB Opinion No. 7,* "Accounting for Leases in Financial Statements of Lessors"; paragraph 15 of *APB Opinion No. 18,* "The Equity Method of Accounting for Investments in Common Stock"; *APB Opinion No. 27,* "Accounting for Lease Transactions by Manufacturer or Dealer Lessors"; and *APB Opinion No. 31,* "Disclosure of Lease Commitments by Lessees."

3. This Statement applies to regulated enterprises in accordance with the provisions of the Addendum to *APB Opinion No. 2,* "Accounting for the 'Investment Credit'."

4. Appendix A provides background information. Appendix B sets forth the basis for the Board's conclusions, including alternatives considered and reasons for accepting some and rejecting others. Illustrations of the accounting and disclosure requirements for lessees and lessors called for by this Statement are contained in Appendixes C and D. An example of the application of the accounting and disclosure provisions for leveraged leases is provided in Appendix E.

[1] Heat supply (also called "burn-up") contracts usually provide for payments by the user-lessee based upon nuclear fuel utilization in the period plus a charge for the unrecovered cost base. The residual value usually accrues to the lessee, and the lessor furnishes no service other than the financing.

STANDARDS OF FINANCIAL ACCOUNTING AND REPORTING

Definitions of Terms

5. For purposes of this Statement, certain terms are defined as follows:

a. *Related parties in leasing transactions.* A parent company and its subsidiaries, an owner company and its joint ventures (corporate or otherwise) and partnerships, and an investor (including a natural person) and its investees, provided that the parent company, owner company, or investor has the ability to exercise significant influence over operating and financial policies of the related party, as significant influence is defined in *APB Opinion No. 18,* paragraph 17. In addition to the examples of significant influence set forth in that paragraph, significant influence may be exercised through guarantees of indebtedness, extensions of credit, or through ownership of warrants, debt obligations, or other securities. If two or more entities are subject to the significant influence of a parent, owner company, investor (including a natural person), or common officers or directors, those entities shall be considered related parties with respect to each other.
b. *Inception of the lease.* With the exception noted below, the date of the lease agreement or commitment, if earlier. For purposes of this definition, a commitment shall be in writing, signed by the parties in interest to the transaction, and shall specifically set forth the principal terms of the transaction. However, if the property covered by the lease has yet to be constructed or has not been acquired by the lessor at the date of the lease agreement or commitment, the inception of the lease shall be the date that construction of the property is completed or the property is acquired by the lessor.
c. *Fair value of the leased property.* The price for which the property could be sold in an arm's-length transaction between unrelated parties. (See definition of related parties in leasing transactions in paragraph 5(a).) The following are examples of the determination of fair value:
   i. When the lessor is a manufacturer or dealer, the fair value of the property at the inception of the lease (as defined in paragraph 5(b)) will ordinarily be its normal selling price, reflecting any volume or trade discounts that may be applicable. However, the determination of fair value shall be made in light of market conditions prevailing at the time, which may indicate that the fair value of the property is less than the normal selling price and, in some instances, less than the cost of the property.
   ii. When the lessor is not a manufacturer or dealer, the fair value of the property at the inception of the lease will ordinarily be its cost, reflecting any volume or trade discounts that may be applicable. However, when there has been a significant lapse of time between the acquisition of the property by the lessor and the inception of the lease, the determination of fair value shall be made in light of market conditions prevailing at the inception of the lease, which may indicate that the fair value of the property is greater or less than its cost or carrying amount, if different. (See paragraph 6(b).)
d. *Bargain purchase option.* A provision allowing the lessee, at his option, to purchase the leased property for a price which is sufficiently lower than the expected fair value of the property at the date the option becomes exercisable that exercise of the option appears, at the inception of the lease, to be reasonably assured.
e. *Bargain renewal option.* A provision allowing the lessee, at his option, to renew the lease for a rental sufficiently lower than the fair rental[2] of the property at the date the option becomes exercisable that exercise of the option appears, at the inception of the lease, to be reasonably assured.
f. *Lease term.* The fixed noncancelable term of the lease plus (i) all periods, if any, covered by bargain renewal options (as defined in paragraph 5(e)), (ii) all periods, if any, for which failure to renew the lease imposes a penalty on the lessee in an amount such that renewal appears, at the inception of the lease, to be reasonably assured, (iii) all periods, if any, covered by ordinary renewal options during which a guarantee by the lessee of the lessor's debt related to the leased property is expected to be in effect, (iv) all periods, if any, covered by ordinary renewal options preceding the date as of which a bargain purchase option (as defined in paragraph 5(d)) is exercisable, and (v) all periods, if any, representing renewals or extensions of the lease at the lessor's option; however, in no case shall the lease term extend beyond the date a bargain purchase option becomes exercisable. A lease which is cancelable (i) only upon the occurrence of some remote contingency, (ii) only with the permission of the lessor, (iii) only if the lessee enters into a new lease with the same lessor, or (iv) only upon payment by the lessee of a penalty in an amount such that continuation of the lease appears, at inception, reasonably assured shall be considered "noncancelable" for purposes of this definition.

[2] "Fair rental" in this context shall mean the expected rental for equivalent property under similar terms and conditions.

g. *Estimated economic life of leased property*. The estimated remaining period during which the property is expected to be economically usable by one or more users, with normal repairs and maintenance, for the purpose for which it was intended at the inception of the lease, without limitation by the lease term.

h. *Estimated residual value of leased property*. The estimated fair value of the leased property at the end of the lease term (as defined in paragraph 5(f)).

i. *Unguaranteed residual value*. The estimated residual value of the leased property (as defined in paragraph 5(h)) exclusive of any portion guaranteed by the lessee[3] or by a third party unrelated to the lessor.[4]

j. *Minimum lease payments*.

  i. From the standpoint of the lessee: The payments that the lessee is obligated to make or can be required to make in connection with the leased property. However, a guarantee by the lessee of the lessor's debt and the lessee's obligation to pay (apart from the rental payments) executory costs such as insurance, maintenance, and taxes in connection with the leased property shall be excluded. If the lease contains a bargain purchase option, only the minimum rental payments over the lease term (as defined in paragraph 5(f)) and the payment called for by the bargain purchase option shall be included in the minimum lease payments. Otherwise, minimum lease payments include the following:

  (a) The minimum rental payments called for by the lease over the lease term.

  (b) Any guarantee by the lessee[5] of the residual value at the expiration of the lease term, whether or not payment of the guarantee constitutes a purchase of the leased property. When the lessor has the right to require the lessee to purchase the property at termination of the lease for a certain or determinable amount, that amount shall be considered a lessee guarantee. When the lessee agrees to make up any deficiency below a stated amount in the lessor's realization of the residual value, the guarantee to be included in the minimum lease payments shall be the stated amount, rather than an estimate of the deficiency to be made up.

  (c) Any payment that the lessee must make or can be required to make upon failure to renew or extend the lease at the expiration of the lease term, whether or not the payment would constitute a purchase of the leased property. In this connection, it should be noted that the definition of lease term in paragraph 5(f) includes "all periods, if any, for which failure to renew the lease imposes a penalty on the lessee in an amount such that renewal appears, at the inception of the lease, to be reasonably assured." If the lease term has been extended because of that provision, the related penalty shall not be included in minimum lease payments.

  ii. From the standpoint of the lessor: The payments described in (i) above plus any guarantee of the residual value or of rental payments beyond the lease term by a third party unrelated to either the lessee[6] or the lessor,[7] provided the third party is financially capable of discharging the obligations that may arise from the guarantee.

k. *Interest rate implicit in the lease*. The discount rate that, when applied to (i) the minimum lease payments (as defined in paragraph 5(j)), excluding that portion of the payments representing executory costs to be paid by the lessor, together with any profit thereon, and (ii) the unguaranteed residual value (as defined in paragraph 5(j)) accruing to the benefit of the lessor,[8] causes the aggregate present value at the beginning of the lease term to be equal to the fair value of the leased property (as defined in paragraph 5(c)) to the lessor at the inception of the lease, minus any investment tax credit retained by the lessor and expected to be realized by him. (This definition does not necessarily purport to include all factors that a lessor might recognize in determining his rate of return, e.g., see paragraph 44.)

l. *Lessee's incremental borrowing rate*. The rate that, at the inception of the lease, the lessee would have incurred to borrow over a similar term the funds necessary to purchase the leased asset.

m. *Initial direct costs*. Those incremental direct costs incurred by the lessor in negotiating and consummating leasing transactions (e.g., commissions and legal fees).

---

[3]A guarantee by a third party related to the lessee shall be considered a lessee guarantee.

[4]If the guarantor is related to the lessor, the residual value shall be considered as unguaranteed.

[5]See footnote 3.

[6]See footnote 3.

[7]See footnote 4.

[8]If the lessor is not entitled to any excess of the amount realized on disposition of the property over a guaranteed amount, no unguaranteed residual value would accrue to his benefit.

Classification of Leases for Purposes of This Statement

6. For purposes of applying the accounting and reporting standards of this Statement, leases are classified as follows:

a. Classifications from the standpoint of the lessee:
   i. *Capital leases*. Leases that meet one or more of the criteria in paragraph 7.
   ii. *Operating leases*. All other leases.
b. Classifications from the standpoint of the lessor:
   i. *Sales-type leases*. Leases that give rise to manufacturer's or dealer's profit (or loss) to the lessor (i.e., the fair value of the leased property at the inception of the lease is greater or less than its cost or carrying amount, if different) and that meet one or more of the criteria in paragraph 7 and both of the criteria in paragraph 8. Normally, sales-type leases will arise when manufacturers or dealers use leasing as a means of marketing their products. Leases involving lessors that are primarily engaged in financing operations normally will not be sales-type leases if they qualify under paragraphs 7 and 8, but will most often be direct financing leases, described in paragraph 6(b)(ii) below. However, a lessor need not be a dealer to realize dealer's profit (or loss) on a transaction, e.g., if a lessor, not a dealer, leases an asset that at the inception of the lease has a fair value that is greater or less than its cost or carrying amount, if different, such a transaction is a sales-type lease, assuming the criteria referred to are met. A renewal or an extension[9] of an existing sales-type or direct financing lease shall not be classified as a sales-type lease; however, if it qualifies under paragraphs 7 and 8, it shall be classified as a direct financing lease. (See paragraph 17(f).)
   ii. *Direct financing leases*. Leases other than leveraged leases that do not give rise to manufacturer's or dealer's profit (or loss) to the lessor but that meet one or more of the criteria in paragraph 7 and both of the criteria in paragraph 8. In such leases, the cost or carrying amount, if different, and fair value of the leased property are the same at the inception of the lease. An exception arises when an existing lease is renewed or extended.[10] In such cases, the fact that the carrying amount of the property at the end of the original lease term is different from its fair value at that date shall not preclude the classification of the renewal or extension as a direct financing lease. (See paragraph 17(f).)
   iii. *Leveraged leases*. Leases that meet the criteria of paragraph 42.
   iv. *Operating leases*. All other leases.

Criteria for Classifying Leases (Other Than Leveraged Leases)

7. The criteria for classifying leases set forth in this paragraph and in paragraph 8 derive from the concept set forth in paragraph 60. If at its inception (as defined in paragraph 5(b)) a lease meets one or more of the following four criteria, the lease shall be classified as a capital lease by the lessee. Otherwise, it shall be classified as an operating lease. (See Appendix C for an illustration of the application of these criteria.)

a. The lease transfers ownership of the property to the lessee by the end of the lease term (as defined in paragraph 5(f)).
b. The lease contains a bargain purchase option (as defined in paragraph 5(d)).
c. The lease term (as defined in paragraph 5(f)) is equal to 75 percent or more of the estimated economic life of the leased property (as defined in paragraph 5(g)). However, if the beginning of the lease term falls within the last 25 percent of the total estimated economic life of the leased property, including earlier years of use, this criterion shall not be used for purposes of classifying the lease.
d. The present value at the beginning of the lease term of the minimum lease payments (as defined in paragraph 5(j)), excluding that portion of the payments representing executory costs such as insurance, maintenance, and taxes to be paid by the lessor, including any profit thereon, equals or exceeds 90 percent of the excess of the fair value of the leased property (as defined in paragraph 5(c)) to the lessor at the inception of the lease over any related investment tax credit retained by the lessor and expected to be realized by him. However, if the beginning of the lease term falls within the last 25 percent of the total estimated economic life of the leased property, including earlier years of use, this criterion shall not be used for purposes of classifying the lease. A lessor shall compute the present value of the minimum lease payments using the interest rate implicit in the lease (as defined in paragraph 5(k)). A lessee shall compute the present value of the minimum lease payments using his incremental borrowing rate (as defined in paragraph 5(l)), unless (i) it is practicable for him to learn the implicit rate computed by the lessor and (ii) the implicit rate computed by the lessor is less than the lessee's incremental borrowing rate. If both

[9]As used here, renewal or extension includes a new lease under which the lessee continues to use the same property.

[10]See footnote 9.

of those conditions are met, the lessee shall use the implicit rate.

8. From the standpoint of the lessor, if at inception a lease meets any one of the preceding four criteria and in addition meets both of the following criteria, it shall be classified as a sales-type lease or a direct financing lease, whichever is appropriate (see paragraphs 6(b)(i) and 6(b)(ii)). Otherwise, it shall be classified as an operating lease.

a. Collectibility of the minimum lease payments is reasonably predictable. A lessor shall not be precluded from classifying a lease as a sales-type lease or as a direct financing lease simply because the receivable is subject to an estimate of uncollectibility based on experience with groups of similar receivables.
b. No important uncertainties surround the amount of unreimbursable costs yet to be incurred by the lessor under the lease. Important uncertainties might include commitments by the lessor to guarantee performance of the leased property in a manner more extensive than the typical product warranty or to effectively protect the lessee from obsolescence of the leased property. However, the necessity of estimating executory costs such as insurance, maintenance, and taxes to be paid by the lessor (see paragraphs 17(a) and 18(a)) shall not by itself constitute an important uncertainty as referred to herein.

9. If at any time the lessee and lessor agree to change the provisions of the lease, other than by renewing the lease or extending its term, in a manner that would have resulted in a different classification of the lease under the criteria in paragraphs 7 and 8 had the changed terms been in effect at the inception of the lease, the revised agreement shall be considered as a new agreement over its term, and the criteria in paragraphs 7 and 8 shall be applied for purposes of classifying the new lease. Likewise, except when a guarantee or penalty is rendered inoperative as described in paragraphs 12 and 17(e), any action that extends the lease beyond the expiration of the existing lease term (see paragraph 5(f)), such as the exercise of a lease renewal option other than those already included in the lease term, shall be considered as a new agreement, which shall be classified according to the provisions of paragraphs 6-8. Changes in estimates (for example, changes in estimates of the economic life or of the residual value of the leased property) or changes in circumstances (for example, default by the lessee), however, shall not give rise to a new classification of a lease for accounting purposes.

Accounting and Reporting by Lessees

Capital Leases

10. The lessee shall record a capital lease as an asset and an obligation at an amount equal to the present value at the beginning of the lease term of minimum lease payments during the lease term, excluding that portion of the payments representing executory costs such as insurance, maintenance, and taxes to be paid by the lessor, together with any profit thereon. However, if the amount so determined exceeds the fair value of the leased property at the inception of the lease, the amount recorded as the asset and obligation shall be the fair value. If the portion of the minimum lease payments representing executory costs, including profit thereon, is not determinable from the provisions of the lease, an estimate of the amount shall be made. The discount rate to be used in determining present value of the minimum lease payments shall be that prescribed for the lessee in paragraph 7(d). (See Appendix C for illustrations.)

11. Except as provided in paragraphs 25 and 26 with respect to leases involving land, the asset recorded under a capital lease shall be amortized as follows:

a. If the lease meets the criterion of either paragraph 7(a) or 7(b), the asset shall be amortized in a manner consistent with the lessee's normal depreciation policy for owned assets.
b. If the lease does not meet either criterion 7(a) or 7(b), the asset shall be amortized in a manner consistent with the lessee's normal depreciation policy except that the period of amortization shall be the lease term. The asset shall be amortized to its expected value, if any, to the lessee at the end of the lease term. As an example, if the lessee guarantees a residual value at the end of the lease term and has no interest in any excess which might be realized, the expected value of the leased property to him is the amount that can be realized from it up to the amount of the guarantee.

12. During the lease term, each minimum lease payment shall be allocated between a reduction of the obligation and interest expense so as to produce a constant periodic rate of interest on the remaining balance of the obligation.[11] (See Appendix C for illustrations.) In leases containing a residual guarantee by the lessee or a penalty for failure to renew the lease at the end of the lease term,[12] following the above method of amortization will result in a bal-

[11]This is the "interest" method described in the first sentence of paragraph 15 of *APB Opinion No. 21*, "Interest on Receivables and Payables," and in paragraphs 16 and 17 of *APB Opinion No. 12*, "Omnibus Opinion—1967."

[12]Residual guarantees and termination penalties that serve to extend the lease term (as defined in paragraph 5(f)) are excluded from minimum lease payments and are thus distinguished from those guarantees and penalties referred to in this paragraph.

ance of the obligation at the end of the lease term that will equal the amount of the guarantee or penalty at that date. In the event that a renewal or other extension of the lease term or a new lease under which the lessee continues to lease the same property renders the guarantee or penalty inoperative, the asset and the obligation under the lease shall be adjusted by an amount equal to the difference between the present value of the future minimum lease payments under the revised agreement and the present balance of the obligation. The present value of the future minimum lease payments under the revised agreement shall be computed using the rate of interest used to record the lease initially. In accordance with paragraph 9, other renewals and extensions of the lease term shall be considered new agreements, which shall be accounted for in accordance with the provisions of paragraph 14. Contingent rentals,[13] including rentals based on variables such as the prime interest rate, shall be charged to expense when actually incurred.

13. Assets recorded under capital leases and the accumulated amortization thereon shall be separately identified in the lessee's balance sheet or in footnotes thereto. Likewise, the related obligations shall be separately identified in the balance sheet as obligations under capital leases and shall be subject to the same considerations as other obligations in classifying them with current and noncurrent liabilities in classified balance sheets. Unless the charge to income resulting from amortization of assets recorded under capital leases is included with depreciation expense and the fact that it is so included is disclosed, the amortization charge shall be separately disclosed in the financial statements or footnotes thereto.

14. Prior to the expiration of the lease term, a change in the provisions of a lease, a renewal or extension[14] of an existing lease, and a termination of a lease shall be accounted for as follows:

a. If the provisions of the lease are changed in a way that changes the amount of the remaining minimum lease payments and the change either (i) does not give rise to a new agreement under the provisions of paragraph 9 or (ii) does give rise to a new agreement but such agreement is also classified as a capital lease, the present balances of the asset and the obligation shall be adjusted by an amount equal to the difference between the present value of the future minimum lease payments under the revised or new agreement and the present balance of the obligation. The present value of the future minimum lease payments under the revised or new agreement shall be computed using the rate of interest used to record the lease initially. If the change in the lease provisions gives rise to a new agreement classified as an operating lease, the asset and obligation under the lease shall be removed, gain or loss shall be recognized for the difference, and the new lease agreement shall thereafter be accounted for as any other operating lease.
b. Except when a guarantee or penalty is rendered inoperative as described in paragraph 12, a renewal or an extension[15] of an existing lease shall be accounted for as follows:
   i. If the renewal or extension is classified as a capital lease, it shall be accounted for as described in subparagraph (a) above.
   ii. If the renewal or extension is classified as an operating lease, the existing lease shall continue to be accounted for as a capital lease to the end of its original term, and the renewal or extension shall be accounted for as any other operating lease.
c. A termination of a capital lease shall be accounted for by removing the asset and obligation, with gain or loss recognized for the difference.

Operating Leases

15. Normally, rental on an operating lease shall be charged to expense over the lease term as it becomes payable. If rental payments are not made on a straight-line basis, rental expense nevertheless shall be recognized on a straight-line basis unless another systematic and rational basis is more representative of the time pattern in which use benefit is derived from the leased property, in which case that basis shall be used.

Disclosures

16. The following information with respect to leases shall be disclosed in the lessee's financial statements or the footnotes thereto (see Appendix D for illustrations).

a. For capital leases:
   i. The gross amount of assets recorded under capital leases as of the date of each balance sheet presented by major classes according to nature or function. This information may be combined with the comparable information for owned assets.
   ii. Future minimum lease payments as of the date of the latest balance sheet presented, in

[13]The term "contingent rentals" includes all or any portion of the stipulated rental that is contingent.

[14]See footnote 9.

[15]See footnote 9.

the aggregate and for each of the five succeeding fiscal years, with separate deductions from the total for the amount representing executory costs, including any profit thereon, included in the minimum lease payments and for the amount of the imputed interest necessary to reduce the net minimum lease payments to present value (see paragraph 10).

iii. The total of minimum sublease rentals to be received in the future under noncancelable subleases as of the date of the latest balance sheet presented.

iv. Total contingent rentals (rentals on which the amounts are dependent on some factor other than the passage of time) actually incurred for each period for which an income statement is presented.

b. For operating leases having initial or remaining noncancelable lease terms in excess of one year:

i. Future minimum rental payments required as of the date of the latest balance sheet presented, in the aggregate and for each of the five succeeding fiscal years.

ii. The total of minimum rentals to be received in the future under noncancelable subleases as of the date of the latest balance sheet presented.

c. For all operating leases, rental expense for each period for which an income statement is presented, with separate amounts for minimum rentals, contingent rentals, and sublease rentals. Rental payments under leases with terms of a month or less that were not renewed need not be included.

d. A general description of the lessee's leasing arrangements including, but not limited to, the following:

i. The basis on which contingent rental payments are determined.

ii. The existence and terms of renewal or purchase options and escalation clauses.

iii. Restrictions imposed by lease agreements, such as those concerning dividends, additional debt, and further leasing.

Accounting and Reporting by Lessors

Sales-Type Leases

17. Sales-type leases shall be accounted for by the lessor as follows:

a. The minimum lease payments (net of amounts, if any, included therein with respect to executory costs such as maintenance, taxes, and insurance to be paid by the lessor, together with any profit thereon) plus the unguaranteed residual value (as defined in paragraph 5(i)) accruing to the benefit of the lessor shall be recorded as the gross investment in the lease.

b. The difference between the gross investment in the lease in (a) above and the sum of the present values of the two components of the gross investment shall be recorded as unearned income. The discount rate to be used in determining the present values shall be the interest rate implicit in the lease. The net investment in the lease shall consist of the gross investment less the unearned income. The unearned income shall be amortized to income over the lease term so as to produce a constant periodic rate of return on the net investment in the lease.[16] However, other methods of income recognition may be used if the results obtained are not materially different from those which would result from the prescribed method. The net investment in the lease shall be subject to the same considerations as other assets in classification as current or noncurrent assets in a classified balance sheet. Contingent rentals, including rentals based on variables such as the prime interest rate, shall be credited to income when they become receivable.

c. The present value of the minimum lease payments (net of executory costs, including any profit thereon), computed at the interest rate implicit in the lease, shall be recorded as the sales price. The cost or carrying amount, if different, of the leased property, plus any initial direct costs (as defined in paragraph 5(m)), less the present value of the unguaranteed residual value accruing to the benefit of the lessor, computed at the interest rate implicit in the lease, shall be charged against income in the same period.

d. The estimated residual value shall be reviewed at least annually. If the review results in a lower estimate than had been previously established, a determination must be made as to whether the decline in estimated residual value is other than temporary. If the decline in estimated residual value is judged to be other than temporary, the accounting for the transaction shall be revised using the changed estimate. The resulting reduction in the net investment shall be recognized as a loss in the period in which the estimate is changed. An upward adjustment of the estimated residual value shall not be made.

e. In leases containing a residual guarantee or a penalty for failure to renew the lease at the end of the lease term,[17] following the method of amortization described in (b) above will result in a balance of minimum lease payments receivable at the end of the lease term that will equal the amount of the guarantee or penalty at that date.

[16]See footnote 11.

[17]See footnote 12.

In the event that a renewal or other extension[18] of the lease term renders the guarantee or penalty inoperative, the existing balances of the minimum lease payments receivable and the estimated residual value shall be adjusted for the changes resulting from the revised agreement (subject to the limitation on the residual value imposed by subparagraph (d) above) and the net adjustment shall be charged or credited to unearned income.

f. Prior to the expiration of the lease term, a change in the provisions of a lease, a renewal or extension[19] of an existing lease, and a termination of a lease shall be accounted for as follows:
   i. If the provisions of a lease are changed in a way that changes the amount of the remaining minimum lease payments and the change either (a) does not give rise to a new agreement under the provisions of paragraph 9 or (b) does give rise to a new agreement but such agreement is classified as a direct financing lease, the balance of the minimum lease payments receivable and the estimated residual value, if affected, shall be adjusted to reflect the change (subject to the limitation on the residual value imposed by subparagraph (d) above), and the net adjustment shall be charged or credited to unearned income. If the change in the lease provisions gives rise to a new agreement classified as an operating lease, the remaining net investment shall be removed from the accounts, the leased asset shall be recorded as an asset at the lower of its original cost, present fair value, or present carrying amount, and the net adjustment shall be charged to income of the period. The new lease shall thereafter be accounted for as any other operating lease.
   ii. Except when a guarantee or penalty is rendered inoperative as described in subparagraph (e) above, a renewal or an extension[20] of an existing lease shall be accounted for as follows:
      (a) If the renewal or extension is classified as a direct financing lease, it shall be accounted for as described in subparagraph (f)(i) above.
      (b) If the renewal or extension is classified as an operating lease, the existing lease shall continue to be accounted for as a sales-type lease to the end of its original term, and the renewal or extension shall be accounted for as any other operating lease.
   iii. A termination of the lease shall be accounted for by removing the net investment from the accounts, recording the leased asset at the lower of its original cost, present fair value, or present carrying amount, and the net adjustment shall be charged to income of the period.

Direct Financing Leases

18. Direct financing leases shall be accounted for by the lessor as follows (see Appendix C for illustrations):

a. The minimum lease payments (net of amounts, if any, included therein with respect to executory costs such as maintenance, taxes, and insurance to be paid by the lessor, together with any profit thereon) plus the unguaranteed residual value accruing to the benefit of the lessor shall be recorded as the gross investment in the lease.
b. The difference between the gross investment in the lease in (a) above and the cost or carrying amount, if different, of the leased property shall be recorded as unearned income. The net investment in the lease shall consist of the gross investment less the unearned income. Initial direct costs (as defined in paragraph 5(m)) shall be charged against income as incurred, and a portion of the unearned income equal to the initial direct costs shall be recognized as income in the same period. The remaining unearned income shall be amortized to income over the lease term so as to produce a constant periodic rate of return on the net investment in the lease.[21] However, other methods of income recognition may be used if the results obtained are not materially different from those which would result from the prescribed method in the preceding sentence. The net investment in the lease shall be subject to the same considerations as other assets in classification as current or noncurrent assets in a classified balance sheet. Contingent rentals, including rentals based on variables such as the prime interest rate, shall be credited to income when they become receivable.
c. In leases containing a residual guarantee or a penalty for failure to renew the lease at the end of the lease term,[22] the lessor shall follow the accounting procedure described in paragraph 17 (e). The accounting provisions of paragraph 17(f) with respect to renewals and extensions not dealt with in paragraph 17(e), terminations, and other changes in lease provisions shall also be fol-

[18]See footnote 9.

[19]See footnote 9.

[20]See footnote 9.

[21]See footnote 11.

[22]See footnote 12.

lowed with respect to direct financing leases.

d. The estimated residual value shall be reviewed at least annually and, if necessary, adjusted in the manner prescribed in paragraph 17(d).

Operating Leases

19. Operating leases shall be accounted for by the lessor as follows:

a. The leased property shall be included with or near property, plant, and equipment in the balance sheet. The property shall be depreciated following the lessor's normal depreciation policy, and in the balance sheet the accumulated depreciation shall be deducted from the investment in the leased property.
b. Rent shall be reported as income over the lease term as it becomes receivable according to the provisions of the lease. However, if the rentals vary from a straight-line basis, the income shall be recognized on a straight-line basis unless another systematic and rational basis is more representative of the time pattern in which use benefit from the leased property is diminished, in which case that basis shall be used.
c. Initial direct costs shall be deferred and allocated over the lease term in proportion to the recognition of rental income. However, initial direct costs may be charged to expense as incurred if the effect is not materially different from that which would have resulted from the use of the method prescribed in the preceding sentence.

Participation by Third Parties

20. The sale or assignment of a lease or of property subject to a lease that was accounted for as a sales-type lease or direct financing lease shall not negate the original accounting treatment accorded the lease. Any profit or loss on the sale or assignment shall be recognized at the time of the transaction except that (a) when the sale or assignment is between related parties, the provisions of paragraphs 29 and 30 shall be applied, or (b) when the sale or assignment is with recourse, the profit or loss shall be deferred and recognized over the lease term in a systematic manner (e.g., in proportion to the minimum lease payments).

21. The sale of property subject to an operating lease, or of property that is leased by or intended to be leased by the third-party purchaser to another party, shall not be treated as a sale if the seller or any party related to the seller retains substantial risks of ownership in the leased property. A seller may by various arrangements assure recovery of the investment by the third-party purchaser in some operating lease transactions and thus retain substantial risks in connection with the property. For example, in the case of default by the lessee or termination of the lease, the arrangements may involve a formal or informal commitment by the seller to (a) acquire the lease or the property, (b) substitute an existing lease, or (c) secure a replacement lessee or a buyer for the property under a remarketing agreement. However, a remarketing agreement by itself shall not disqualify accounting for the transaction as a sale if the seller (a) will receive a reasonable fee commensurate with the effort involved at the time of securing a replacement lessee or buyer for the property and (b) is not required to give priority to the re-leasing or disposition of the property owned by the third-party purchaser over similar property owned or produced by the seller. (For example, a first-in, first-out remarketing arrangement is considered to be a priority.)

22. If a sale to a third party of property subject to an operating lease or of property that is leased by or intended to be leased by the third-party purchaser to another party is not to be recorded as a sale because of the provisions of paragraph 21 above, the transaction shall be accounted for as a borrowing. (Transactions of these types are in effect collateralized borrowings.) The proceeds from the "sale" shall be recorded as an obligation on the books of the "seller." Until that obligation has been amortized under the procedure described herein, rental payments made by the lessee(s) under the operating lease or leases shall be recorded as revenue by the "seller," even if such rentals are paid directly to the third-party purchaser. A portion of each rental shall be recorded by the "seller" as interest expense, with the remainder to be recorded as a reduction of the obligation. The interest expense shall be calculated by application of a rate determined in accordance with the provisions of *APB Opinion No. 21*, "Interest on Receivables and Payables," paragraphs 13 and 14. The leased property shall be accounted for as prescribed in paragraph 19(a) for an operating lease, except that the term over which the asset is depreciated shall be limited to the estimated amortization period of the obligation. The sale or assignment by the lessor of lease payments due under an operating lease shall be accounted for as a borrowing as described above.

Disclosures

23. When leasing, exclusive of leveraged leasing, is a significant part of the lessor's business activities in terms of revenue, net income, or assets, the following information with respect to leases shall be disclosed in the financial statements or footnotes thereto (see Appendix D for illustrations):

a. For sales-type and direct financing leases:
   i. The components of the net investment in sales-type and direct financing leases as of

the date of each balance sheet presented:

(a) Future minimum lease payments to be received, with separate deductions for (i) amounts representing executory costs, including any profit thereon, included in the minimum lease payments and (ii) the accumulated allowance for uncollectible minimum lease payments receivable.

(b) The unguaranteed residual values accruing to the benefit of the lessor.

(c) Unearned income (see paragraphs 17(b) and 18(b)).

ii. Future minimum lease payments to be received for each of the five succeeding fiscal years as of the date of the latest balance sheet presented.

iii. The amount of unearned income included in income to offset initial direct costs charged against income for each period for which an income statements is presented. (For direct financing leases only.)

iv. Total contingent rentals included in income for each period for which an income statement is presented.

b. For operating leases:

i. The cost and carrying amount, if different, of property on lease or held for leasing by major classes of property according to nature or function, and the amount of accumulated depreciation in total as of the date of the latest balance sheet presented.

ii. Minimum future rentals on noncancelable leases as of the date of the latest balance sheet presented, in the aggregate and for each of the five succeeding fiscal years.

iii. Total contingent rentals included in income for each period for which an income statement is presented.

c. A general description of the lessor's leasing arrangements.

Leases Involving Real Estate

24. For purposes of this Statement, leases involving real estate can be divided into four categories: (a) leases involving land only, (b) leases involving land and building(s), (c) leases involving equipment as well as real estate, and (d) leases involving only part of a building.

Leases Involving Land Only

25. If land is the sole item of property leased and the criterion in either paragraph 7(a) or 7(b) is met, the lessee shall account for the lease as a capital lease; otherwise, as an operating lease. If the criteria set forth in paragraph 8 are also met, the lessor shall account for the lease as a sales-type or direct financing lease, whichever is appropriate (see paragraphs 6(b)(i) and 6(b)(ii)); otherwise, as an operating lease. Criteria 7(c) and 7(d) are not applicable to land leases. Because ownership of the land is expected to pass to the lessee if either criterion 7(a) or 7(b) is met, the asset recorded under the capital lease would not normally be amortized.

Leases Involving Land and Building(s)

26. Leases involving both land and building(s) shall be accounted for as follows:

a. Lease meets either criterion 7(a) or 7(b):

i. Lessee's accounting: If either criterion (a) or (b) of paragraph 7 is met, the land and building shall be separately capitalized by the lessee. For this purpose, the present value of the minimum lease payments after deducting executory costs, including any profit thereon, shall be allocated between the two elements in proportion to their fair values at the inception of the lease. The building shall be amortized in accordance with the provisions of paragraph 11(a). As stated in paragraph 25, land capitalized under a lease that meets criterion (a) or (b) of paragraph 7 would not normally be amortized.

ii. Lessor's accounting: If either criterion (a) or (b) of paragraph 7 is met and the criteria of paragraph 8 are also met, the lessor shall account for the lease as a single unit, either as a sales-type lease or as a direct financing lease as appropriate under paragraphs 6(b)(i) and 6(b)(ii). If the criteria of paragraph 8 are not met, the lessor shall account for the lease as an operating lease.

b. Lease meets neither criterion 7(a) nor 7(b):

i. If the fair value of the land is less than 25 percent of the total fair value of the leased property at the inception of the lease: Both the lessee and the lessor shall consider the land and the building as a single unit for purposes of applying the criteria of paragraphs 7(c) and 7(d). For purposes of applying the criterion of paragraph 7(c), the estimated economic life of the building shall be considered as the estimated economic life of the unit.

(a) Lessee's accounting: If either criterion (c) or (d) of paragraph 7 is met, the lessee shall capitalize the land and building as a single unit and amortize it in accordance with the provisions of paragraph 11(b); otherwise, the lease shall be accounted for as an operating lease.

(b) Lessor's accounting: If either criterion (c) or (d) of paragraph 7 and the criteria of paragraph 8 are met, the lessor shall account for the lease as a single unit, either as a sales-type lease or as a direct financing lease as appropriate under paragraphs 6(b)(i) and 6(b)(ii); otherwise, the lease shall be accounted for as an operating lease.

ii. If the fair value of the land is 25 percent or more of the total fair value of the leased property at the inception of the lease: Both the lessee and lessor shall consider the land and the building separately for purposes of applying the criteria of paragraphs 7(c) and 7(d). The minimum lease payments after deducting executory costs, including any profit thereon, applicable to the land and the building shall be separated both by the lessee and the lessor by determining the fair value of the land and applying the lessee's incremental borrowing rate to it to determine the annual minimum lease payments applicable to the land element; the remaining minimum lease payments shall be attributed to the building element.

(a) Lessee's accounting: If the building element of the lease meets criterion (c) or (d) of paragraph 7, the building element shall be accounted for as a capital lease and amortized in accordance with the provisions of paragraph 11(b). The land element of the lease shall be accounted for separately as an operating lease. If the building element of the lease meets neither criterion (c) nor (d) of paragraph 7, both the building element and the land element shall be accounted for as a single operating lease.

(b) Lessor's accounting: If the building element of the lease meets criterion (c) or (d) of paragraph 7 and the criteria of paragraph 8, the building element shall be accounted for as a sales-type lease or a direct financing lease as appropriate under paragraphs 6(b)(i) and 6(b)(ii). The land element of the lease shall be accounted for separately as an operating lease. If the building element of the lease meets neither criterion (c) nor (d) of paragraph 7 or does not meet the criteria of paragraph 8, both the building element and the land element shall be accounted for as a single operating lease.

Leases Involving Equipment as Well as Real Estate

27. If a lease involving real estate also includes equipment, the portion of the minimum lease payments applicable to the equipment element of the lease shall be estimated by whatever means are appropriate in the circumstances. The equipment shall be considered separately for purposes of applying the criteria in paragraphs 7 and 8 and shall be accounted for separately according to its classification by both lessees and lessors.

Leases Involving Only Part of a Building

28. When the leased property is part of a larger whole, its cost (or carrying amount) and fair value may not be objectively determinable, as for example, when an office or floor of a building is leased. If the cost and fair value of the leased property are objectively determinable, both the lessee and the lessor shall classify and account for the lease according to the provisions of paragraph 26. Unless both the cost and the fair value are objectively determinable, the lease shall be classified and accounted for as follows:

a. Lessee:
   i. If the fair value of the leased property is objectively determinable, the lessee shall classify and account for the lease according to the provisions of paragraph 26.
   ii. If the fair value of the leased property is not objectively determinable, the lessee shall classify the lease according to the criterion of paragraph 7(c) only, using the estimated economic life of the building in which the leased premises are located. If that criterion is met, the leased property shall be capitalized as a unit and amortized in accordance with the provisions of paragraph 11(b).
b. Lessor: If either the cost or the fair value of the property is not objectively determinable, the lessor shall account for the lease as an operating lease.

Because of special provisions normally present in leases involving terminal space and other airport facilities owned by a governmental unit or authority, the economic life of such facilities for purposes of classifying the lease is essentially indeterminate. Likewise, the concept of fair value is not applicable to such leases. Since such leases also do not provide for a transfer of ownership or a bargain purchase option, they shall be classified as operating leases. Leases of other facilities owned by a governmental unit or authority wherein the rights of the parties are essentially the same as in a lease of airport facilities described above shall also be classified as operating leases. Examples of such leases may be those involving facilities at ports and bus terminals.

Leases between Related Parties

29. Except as noted below, leases between related parties (as defined in paragraph 5(a)) shall be classified in accordance with the criteria in paragraphs 7 and 8. Insofar as the separate financial statements of the related parties are concerned, the classification and accounting shall be the same as for similar leases between unrelated parties, except in cases where it is clear that the terms of the transaction have been significantly affected by the fact that the

lessee and lessor are related. In such cases the classification and/or accounting shall be modified as necessary to recognize economic substance rather than legal form. The nature and extent of leasing transactions with related parties shall be disclosed.

30. In consolidated financial statements or in financial statements for which an interest in an investee is accounted for on the equity basis, any profit or loss on a leasing transaction with the related party shall be accounted for in accordance with the principles set forth in *ARB No. 51*, "Consolidated Financial Statements," or *APB Opinion No. 18*, whichever is applicable.

31. The accounts of subsidiaries (regardless of when organized or acquired) whose principal business activity is leasing property or facilities to the parent or other affiliated companies shall be consolidated. The equity method is not adequate for fair presentation of those subsidiaries because their assets and liabilities are significant to the consolidated financial position of the enterprise.

Sale-Leaseback Transactions

32. Sale-leaseback transactions involve the sale of property by the owner and a lease of the property back to the seller.

33. If the lease meets one of the criteria for treatment as a capital lease (see paragraph 7), the seller-lessee shall account for the lease as a capital lease; otherwise, as an operating lease. Except as noted below, any profit or loss on the sale shall be deferred and amortized in proportion to the amortization of the leased asset,[23] if a capital lease, or in proportion to rental payments over the period of time the asset is expected to be used, if an operating lease. However, when the fair value of the property at the time of the transaction is less than its undepreciated cost, a loss shall be recognized immediately up to the amount of the difference between undepreciated cost and fair value.

34. If the lease meets the criteria in paragraphs 7 and 8, the purchaser-lessor shall record the transaction as a purchase and a direct financing lease; otherwise, he shall record the transaction as a purchase and an operating lease.

Accounting and Reporting for Subleases and Similar Transactions

35. This section deals with the following types of leasing transactions:

a. The leased property is re-leased by the original lessee to a third party, and the lease agreement between the two original parties remains in effect (a sublease).
b. A new lessee is substituted under the original lease agreement. The new lessee becomes the primary obligor under the agreement, and the original lessee may or may not be secondarily liable.
c. A new lessee is substituted through a new agreement, with cancellation of the original lease agreement.

Accounting by the Original Lessor

36. If the original lessee enters into a sublease or the original lease agreement is sold or transferred by the original lessee to a third party, the original lessor shall continue to account for the lease as before.

37. If the original lease agreement is replaced by a new agreement with a new lessee, the lessor shall account for the termination of the original lease as provided in paragraph 17(f) and shall classify and account for the new lease as a separate transaction.

Accounting by the Original Lessee

38. If the nature of the transaction is such that the original lessee is relieved of the primary obligation under the original lease, as would be the case in transactions of the type described in paragraphs 35(b) and 35(c), the termination of the original lease agreement shall be account for as follows:

a. If the original lease was a capital lease, the asset and obligation representing the original lease shall be removed from the accounts, gain or loss shall be recognized for the difference, and, if the original lessee is secondarily liable, the loss contingency shall be treated as provided by *FASB Statement No. 5*, "Accounting for Contingencies." Any consideration paid or received upon termination shall be included in the determination of gain or loss to be recognized.
b. If the original lease was an operating lease and the original lessee is secondarily liable, the loss contingency shall be treated as provided by *FASB Statement No. 5*.

39. If the nature of the transaction is such that the original lessee is not relieved of the primary obligation under the original lease, as would be the case in transactions of the type described in paragraph 35(a), the original lessee, as sublessor, shall account for the transaction as follows:

a. If the original lease met either criterion (a) or (b) of paragraph 7, the original lessee shall classify the new lease in accordance with the criteria of

[23]If the leased asset is land only, the amortization shall be on a straight-line basis over the lease term.

paragraphs 7 and 8. If the new lease meets one of the criteria of paragraph 7 and both of the criteria of paragraph 8, it shall be accounted for as a sales-type or direct financing lease, as appropriate, and the unamortized balance of the asset under the original lease shall be treated as the cost of the leased property. If the new lease does not qualify as a sales-type or direct financing lease, it shall be accounted for as an operating lease. In either case, the original lessee shall continue to account for the obligation related to the original lease as before.

b. If the original lease met either criterion (c) or (d) but not criterion (a) or (b) of paragraph 7, the original lessee shall, with one exception, classify the new lease in accordance with the criteria of paragraphs 7(c) and 8 only. If it meets those criteria, it shall be accounted for as a direct financing lease, with the unamortized balance of the asset under the original lease treated as the cost of the leased property; otherwise, as an operating lease. In either case, the original lessee shall continue to account for the obligation related to the original lease as before. The one exception arises when the timing and other circumstances surrounding the sublease are such as to suggest that the sublease was intended as an integral part of an overall transaction in which the original lessee serves only as an intermediary. In that case, the sublease shall be classified according to the criteria of paragraphs 7(c) and 7(d), as well as the criteria of paragraph 8. In applying the criterion of paragraph 7(d), the fair value of the leased property shall be the fair value to the original lessor at the inception of the original lease.

c. If the original lease is an operating lease, the original lessee shall account for both it and the new lease as operating leases.

Accounting by the New Lessee

40. The new lessee shall classify the lease in accordance with the criteria of paragraph 7 and account for it accordingly.

Accounting and Reporting for Leveraged Leases

41. From the standpoint of the lessee, leveraged leases shall be classified and accounted for in the same manner as non-leveraged leases. The balance of this section deals with leveraged leases from the standpoint of the lessor.

42. For purposes of this Statement, a leveraged lease is defined as one having all of the following characteristics:

a. Except for the exclusion of leveraged leases from the definition of a direct financing lease as set forth in paragraph 6(b)(ii), it otherwise meets that definition. Leases that meet the definition of sales-type leases set forth in paragraph 6(b)(i) shall not be accounted for as leveraged leases but shall be accounted for as prescribed in paragraph 17.
b. It involves at least three parties: a lessee, a long-term creditor, and a lessor (commonly called the equity participant).
c. The financing provided by the long-term creditor is nonrecourse as to the general credit of the lessor (although the creditor may have recourse to the specific property leased and the unremitted rentals relating to it). The amount of the financing is sufficient to provide the lessor with substantial "leverage" in the transaction.
d. The lessor's net investment, as defined in paragraph 43, declines during the early years once the investment has been completed and rises during the later years of the lease before its final elimination. Such decreases and increases in the net investment balance may occur more than once.

A lease meeting the preceding definition shall be accounted for by the lessor using the method described in paragraphs 43-47; an exception arises if the investment tax credit is accounted for other than as stated in paragraphs 43 and 44,[24] in which case the lease shall be classified as a direct financing lease and accounted for in accordance with paragraph 18. A lease not meeting the definition of a leveraged lease shall be accounted for in accordance with its classification under paragraph 6(b).

43. The lessor shall record his investment in a leveraged lease net of the nonrecourse debt. The net of the balances of the following accounts shall represent the initial and continuing investment in leveraged leases:

a. Rentals receivable, net of that portion of the rental applicable to principal and interest on the nonrecourse debt.
b. A receivable for the amount of the investment tax credit to be realized on the transaction.
c. The estimated residual value of the leased asset.
d. Unearned and deferred income consisting of (i) the estimated pretax lease income (or loss), after deducting initial direct costs, remaining to be allocated to income over the lease term and (ii) the investment tax credit remaining to be allocated to income over the lease term.

[24] It is recognized that the investment tax credit may be accounted for other than as prescribed in this Statement, as provided by Congress in the Revenue Act of 1971.

The investment in leveraged leases less deferred taxes arising from differences between pretax accounting income and taxable income shall represent the lessor's net investment in leveraged leases for purposes of computing periodic net income from the lease, as described in paragraph 44.

44. Given the original investment and using the projected cash receipts and disbursements over the term of the lease, the rate of return on the net investment in the years[25] in which it is positive shall be computed. The rate is that rate which when applied to the net investment in the years in which the net investment is positive will distribute the net income to those years (see Appendix E, Schedule 3) and is distinct from the interest rate implicit in the lease as defined in paragraph 5(k). In each year, whether positive or not, the difference between the net cash flow and the amount of income recognized, if any, shall serve to increase or reduce the net investment balance. The net income recognized shall be composed of three elements: two, pretax lease income (or loss) and investment tax credit, shall be allocated in proportionate amounts from the unearned and deferred income included in net investment, as described in paragraph 43; the third element is the tax effect of the pretax lease income (or loss) recognized, which shall be reflected in tax expense for the year. The tax effect of the difference between pretax accounting income (or loss) and taxable income (or loss) for the year shall be charged or credited to deferred taxes. The accounting prescribed in paragraph 43 and in this paragraph is illustrated in Appendix E.

45. If the projected net cash receipts[26] over the term of the lease are less than the lessor's initial investment, the deficiency shall be recognized as a loss at the inception of the lease. Likewise, if at any time during the lease term the application of the method prescribed in paragraphs 43 and 44 would result in a loss being allocated to future years, that loss shall be recognized immediately. This situation might arise in cases where one of the important assumptions affecting net income is revised (see paragraph 46).

46. Any estimated residual value and all other important assumptions affecting estimated total net income from the lease shall be reviewed at least annually. If during the lease term the estimate of the residual value is determined to be excessive and the decline in the residual value is judged to be other than temporary or if the revision of another important assumption changes the estimated total net income from the lease, the rate of return and the allocation of income to positive investment years shall be recalculated from the inception of the lease following the method described in paragraph 44 and using the revised assumption. The accounts constituting the net investment balance shall be adjusted to conform to the recalculated balances, and the change in the net investment shall be recognized as a gain or loss in the year in which the assumption is changed. An upward adjustment of the estimated residual value shall not be made. The accounting prescribed in this paragraph is illustrated in Appendix E.

47. For purposes of presenting the investment in a leveraged lease in the lessor's balance sheet, the amount of related deferred taxes shall be presented separately (from the remainder of the net investment), as prescribed in *APB Opinion No. 11*, "Accounting for Income Taxes," paragraphs 57, 59, and 64. In the income statement or the notes thereto, separate presentation (from each other) shall be made of pretax income from the leveraged lease, the tax effect of pretax income, and the amount of investment tax credit recognized as income during the period. When leveraged leasing is a significant part of the lessor's business activities in terms of revenue, net income, or assets, the components of the net investment balance in leveraged leases as set forth in paragraph 43 shall be disclosed in the footnotes to the financial statements. Appendix E contains an illustration of the balance sheet, income statement, and footnote presentation for a leveraged lease.

Effective Date and Transition

48. The preceding paragraphs of this Statement shall be effective for leasing transactions and lease agreement revisions (see paragraph 9) entered into on or after January 1, 1977. However, leasing transactions or revisions of agreements consummated on or after January 1, 1977 pursuant to the terms of a commitment made prior to that date and renewal options exercised under agreements existing or committed prior to that date shall not be considered as leasing transactions or lease agreement revisions entered into after January 1, 1977 if such commitment is in writing, signed by the parties in interest to the transaction, including the financing party,[27] if any, when specific financing is essential to the transaction, and specifically sets forth the principal terms

[25]The use of the term "years" is not intended to preclude application of the accounting prescribed in this paragraph to shorter accounting periods.

[26]For purposes of this paragraph, net cash receipts shall be gross cash receipts less gross cash disbursements exclusive of the lessor's initial investment.

[27]For purposes of this paragraph, the term "financing party" shall include an interim lender pending long-term financing.

of the transaction. The disclosures called for in the preceding paragraphs of this Statement shall be included in financial statements for calendar or fiscal years ending after December 31, 1976.[28] Earlier application of the preceding paragraphs of this Statement, including retroactive application to all leases regardless of when they were entered into or committed is encouraged but, until the effective date specified in paragraph 49, is not required. If applied retroactively, financial statements presented for prior periods shall be restated according to the provisions of paragraph 51.

49. For purposes of financial statements for calendar or fiscal years beginning after December 31, 1980, paragraphs 1-47 of this Statement shall be applied retroactively, and any accompanying financial statements presented for prior periods shall be restated as may be required by the provisions of paragraph 51.

50. If paragraphs 1-47 are not applied initially on a retroactive basis, as permitted by paragraph 48, those leases existing or committed at December 31, 1976 shall be subject to the following provisions until such time as paragraphs 1-47 are applied retroactively to all leases.

a. For purposes of applying the presentation and disclosure requirements of this Statement applicable to lessees, those leases existing or committed at December 31, 1976 that are capitalized in accordance with the provisions of superseded *APB Opinion No. 5* shall be considered as capital leases, and those leases existing or committed at December 31, 1976 that are classified and accounted for as operating leases shall be considered as operating leases. For those leases that are classified and accounted for as operating leases but that meet the criteria of paragraph 7 for classification as capital leases, separate disclosure of the following information shall be made for purposes of financial statements for the year ending December 31, 1977 and for years ending thereafter:
   i. The amounts of the asset and the liability that would have been included in the balance sheet had those leases been classified and accounted for in accordance with the provisions of paragraphs 1-47. This information shall also be disclosed for balance sheets as of December 31, 1976 and thereafter when such balance sheets are included in the financial statements referred to in paragraph 50(a) above.
   ii. The effect on net income that would have resulted if those leases had been classified and accounted for in accordance with the provisions of paragraphs 1-47. This information shall also be disclosed for income statements for periods beginning after December 31, 1976 when such income statements are included in the aforementioned financial statements.

b. For purposes of applying the presentation and disclosure requirements of this Statement applicable to lessors, those leases existing or committed at December 31, 1976 that are accounted for as sales, financing leases, and as operating leases in accordance with superseded *APB Opinions No. 7* and *27* shall be considered as sales-type leases, as direct financing leases, and as operating leases, respectively. (Refer to (c) below for provisions applicable to leveraged leases.) For those leases existing or committed at December 31, 1976 that are classified and accounted for as operating leases but that meet the criteria of paragraphs 7 and 8 for classification as direct financing leases or sales-type leases, separate disclosure of the following information shall be made for purposes of financial statements for the year ending December 31, 1977 and for years ending thereafter:
   i. The amount of the change in net worth that would have resulted had the leases been classified and accounted for in accordance with the provisions of paragraphs 1-47. This information shall also be disclosed for balance sheets as of December 31, 1976 and thereafter when such balance sheets are included in the foregoing financial statements referred to in paragraph 50(b) above.
   ii. The effect on net income that would have resulted if the leases had been classified and accounted for in accordance with the provisions of paragraphs 1-47. This information shall also be disclosed for income statements for periods beginning after December 31, 1976 when such income statements are included in the aforementioned financial statements.

c. For those leases that meet the criteria of paragraph 42 (leveraged leases) but that are accounted for other than as prescribed in paragraphs 1-47, separate disclosure of the following information shall be made for purposes of lessors' financial statements for the year ending December 31, 1977 and for years ending thereafter:
   i. The amounts of the net changes in total assets and in total liabilities that would have resulted had the leases been classified and accounted for in accordance with the provisions of paragraphs 1-47. This information shall also be

[28]For an enterprise having a fiscal year of 52 or 53 weeks ending in the last seven days in December or the first seven days in January, references to December 31 in paragraphs 48-51 shall mean the date in December or January on which the fiscal year ends.

disclosed for balance sheets as of December 31, 1976 and thereafter when such balance sheets are included in the financial statements referred to in paragraph 50(c) above.

ii. The effect on net income that would have resulted if the leases had been classified and accounted for in accordance with the provisions of paragraphs 1-47. This information shall also be disclosed for income statements for periods beginning after December 31, 1976 when such income statements are included in the aforementioned financial statements.

51. Paragraph 49 requires retroactive application of paragraphs 1-47 for purposes of financial statements for calendar or fiscal years beginning after December 31, 1980, and paragraph 48 encourages earlier retroactive application. If after retroactive application is adopted, financial statements for earlier periods and financial summaries or other data derived from them are presented, they shall be restated in accordance with the following requirements to conform to the provisions of paragraphs 1-47:

a. Such restatements shall include the effects of leases that were in existence during the periods covered by the financial statements even if those leases are no longer in existence.
b. Balance sheets presented as of December 31, 1976 and thereafter and income statements presented for periods beginning after December 31, 1976 and financial summaries and other data derived from those financial statements shall be restated to conform to the provisions of paragraphs 1-47.
c. Balance sheets as of dates before December 31, 1976 and income statements for periods beginning before December 31, 1976 shall, when presented, be restated to conform to the provisions of paragraphs 1-47 for as many consecutive periods immediately preceding December 31, 1976 as is practicable. Summaries or other data presented based on such balance sheets and income statements shall be treated in like manner.
d. The cumulative effect of applying paragraphs 1-47 on the retained earnings at the beginning of the earliest period restated shall be included in determining net income of that period (see paragraph 20 of *APB Opinion No. 20*, "Accounting Changes").[29]

The effect on net income of applying paragraphs 1-47 in the period in which the cumulative effect is included in determining net income shall be disclosed for that period, and the reason for not restating the prior periods presented shall be explained.

The provisions of this Statement need not be applied to immaterial items.

This Statement was adopted by the affirmative votes of five members of the Financial Accounting Standards Board. Mr. Kirk dissented.

Mr. Kirk dissents primarily because he does not believe that the front-ending of lease income required by paragraph 44 for leveraged leases versus the method of lease income recognition required by paragraph 18(b) for direct financing leases is justified by any significant economic (i.e., cash flow) differences between the two types of leases. The front-ending of leveraged lease income results from treating the related debt and deferred tax benefits (principally the latter) as valuation accounts, and Mr. Kirk believes that the treatment as valuation accounts is unwarranted.

The leasing business is a leveraged business. Many leases are partially financed by recourse debt; some leases are partially financed by nonrecourse debt. Mr. Kirk believes the cash inflows from the lessee and the outflows to the creditor can be similar whether the debt is recourse or nonrecourse, and he does not believe that a difference in the method of financing a lease should be a factor in determining the pattern of recognizing lease income (and interest expense) as is required by this Statement. Mr. Kirk also objects to the inconsistent classification of nonrecourse debt required by this Statement (i.e., if the lease meets the criteria of paragraph 42, the nonrecourse debt financing the lease is a valuation account and *not* a liability; if the lessor is the manufacturer of the leased asset or if the lease does not meet all the criteria of paragraph 42, the nonrecourse debt *is* a liability).

The amount and timing of the cash flow benefits resulting from the tax attributes of a leased asset are the same to the lessor whether he finances the asset with recourse debt, with nonrecourse debt, or with equity. A difference in the method of financing the lease should not, in the opinion of Mr. Kirk, result in a difference in accounting for deferred taxes. This Statement, however, requires that deferred income tax balances arising from tax timing differences be accounted for as a valuation account (for purposes of computing periodic lease income) only if (a) the lease is financed with *substantial* nonrecourse debt

[29]Pro forma disclosures required by paragraphs 19(d) and 21 of *APB Opinion No. 20* are not applicable.

and (b) the lessor accounts for the benefit from the investment tax credit as a valuation account. The special treatment of these deferred tax benefits as valuation accounts results in a net investment that declines in the early years and rises during the later years; that result then requires the front-ending of lease income. Also, Mr. Kirk can see no reason why the method of accounting for the investment tax credit should determine the accounting for deferred income taxes and, therefore, the pattern of lease income recognition.

Mr. Kirk also believes the treatment of deferred taxes and the required method of accounting for changes in assumptions (paragraph 46) result in the deferred taxes related to leveraged leases being accounted for by the *liability method*, which is not in conformity with the requirements of *APB Opinion No. 11*, "Accounting for Income Taxes," and the accounting for deferred taxes related to other leases.

In order to avoid having (a) the method of financing, (b) the debt repayment schedule, and (c) the method of accounting for deferred tax benefits influence the pattern of recognition of lease income, interest expense, and initial direct costs (as is the case for those leases meeting the criteria of paragraph 42), Mr. Kirk believes it is necessary to use the ordinary financing lease method (paragraph 109(a)) for all financing leases, including those financed with nonrecourse debt. However, in view of the present inconsistencies in accounting for nonrecourse debt, Mr. Kirk would not have dissented to a requirement that the three-party financing lease method (paragraph 109(b)) be used for financing leases financed with nonrecourse debt. Both methods avoid the inconsistent treatment of nonrecourse debt and the front-ending of lease income.

Mr. Kirk also dissents because he objects to the exemption in paragraph 28 that applies to certain facilities leased from governmental units because of special provisions *normally* present in those leases. Mr. Kirk believes the classification of all leases, regardless of the nature of the asset or lessor, should be determined by application of the criteria in paragraphs 7 and 8.

Members of the Financial Accounting Standards Board:

Marshall S. Armstrong, *Chairman*
Oscar S. Gellein
Donald J. Kirk
Arthur L. Litke
Robert E. Mays
Robert T. Sprouse

Appendix A

BACKGROUND INFORMATION

52. The growing importance of leasing as a financing device was recognized by the accounting profession as early as 1949, when the AI[CPA] issued *Accounting Research Bulletin No. 38*, "Disclosure of Long-Term Leases in Financial Statements of Lessees." In early 1960, the newly formed APB recognized the importance of the matter by including lease accounting as one of the first five topics to be studied by the AICPA's Accounting Research Division. That project culminated in 1962 with the publication of *Accounting Research Study No. 4*, "Reporting of Leases in Financial Statements," and shortly thereafter the APB took up the subject. In all, during the ten years ending June 30, 1973, the APB issued four Opinions (No. 5, 7, 27, and 31) dealing with leases. They were supplemented by three AICPA Accounting Interpretations. The last of the APB Opinions, *APB Opinion No. 31*, "Disclosure of Lease Commitments by Lessees," as its name implies, dealt only with disclosure. The APB had previously acknowledged that certain questions remained in connection with Opinions 5 and 7 and had publicly announced its intention to give those questions further consideration. The APB decided, however, to deal only with additional disclosure requirements. In paragraph 5 of *APB Opinion No. 31*, which was approved in June 1973, the APB noted that:

> . . . disclosure of lease commitments is part of the broad subject of accounting for leases by lessees, a subject which has now been placed on the agenda of the Financial Accounting Standards Board. The Board [APB] also recognizes that the forthcoming report of the Study Group on the Objectives of Financial Statements may contain recommendations which will bear on this subject and which the FASB may consider in its deliberations. Accordingly, the Board is refraining from establishing any disclosure requirements which may prejudge or imply any bias with respect to the outcome of the FASB's undertaking, particularly in relation to the questions of which leases, if any, should be capitalized and how such capitalization may influence the income statement. Nevertheless, in the meantime the Board recognizes the need to improve the disclosure of lease commitments in order that users of financial statements may be better informed.

53. The SEC, too, has issued a number of pronouncements on accounting for leases, including three Accounting Series Releases: No. 132, 141, and 147, adopted on October 5, 1973. The latter Release

imposes essentially the same disclosure requirements with respect to total rental expense and minimum rental commitments as *APB Opinion No. 31*. However, it makes mandatory the disclosure of the present value of certain lease commitments (defined differently from the optional present value disclosure included in *APB Opinion No. 31*). In addition, it requires disclosure of the impact on net income had "financing" leases been capitalized, a disclosure not called for by *APB Opinion No. 31*.

54. Despite the attention that the accounting profession has given to the matter of accounting for leases, inconsistencies remain in lease accounting practices, and differences of opinion as to what should be done about them remain. In recognition of that fact, the FASB placed on its initial agenda a project on Accounting for Leases. In October 1973, a task force of 11 persons from industry, government, public accounting, the financial community, and academe was appointed to provide counsel to the Board in preparing a Discussion Memorandum analyzing issues related to the project.

55. As indicated above, accounting for leases is a subject which has been thoroughly studied over a long period of time and on which numerous pronouncements have been made. Extensive research has been carried out; several public hearings have been held for which position papers were filed by many interested parties and groups; especially appointed committees, not only of the Accounting Principles Board, but of a number of other organizations, have analyzed and debated the issues. A considerable number of the studies and articles on lease accounting were available to the Board, many of which are summarized or identified in the Discussion Memorandum. In addition, the FASB staff surveyed the accounting and reporting practices of a number of lessee and lessor companies, the results of which are set forth in Appendix C to the Discussion Memorandum. The staff also met on a number of occasions with representatives of various organizations interested in leasing for the purpose of obtaining specialized information helpful to the Board's consideration of the various issues involved in accounting for leases.

56. The Board issued its Discussion Memorandum on July 2, 1974, and on November 18-21, 1974 held a public hearing on the subject. The Board received 306 position papers, letters of comment, and outlines of oral presentations in response to the Discussion Memorandum, and 32 presentations were made at the public hearing.

57. On August 26, 1975, the Financial Accounting Standards Board issued an Exposure Draft of a Proposed Statement of Financial Accounting Standards on Accounting for Leases that, if adopted, would have been effective for leasing transactions entered into on or after January 1, 1976. Two hundred and fifty letters of comment were received in response to that Exposure Draft. The Board announced on November 25, 1975 that, because of the need to analyze the large number of responses and the complexity of the issues involved, it would be unable to issue a final Statement in 1975 but expected to do so early in 1976. A further announcement made by the Board on June 2, 1976 stated that a number of modifications were being made to the Exposure Draft and that a second Exposure Draft would be issued for public comment preparatory to the expected issuance of a final Statement in 1976.

58. The Board issued the second Exposure Draft of a Proposed Statement of Financial Accounting Standards on Accounting for Leases on July 22, 1976. Two hundred and eighty-two letters of comment were received in response to that Exposure Draft.

Appendix B

BASIS FOR CONCLUSIONS

59. This Appendix discusses factors deemed significant by the Board in reaching the conclusions in this Statement, including various alternatives considered and reasons for accepting some and rejecting others.

60. The provisions of this Statement derive from the view that a lease that transfers substantially all of the benefits and risks incident to the ownership of property should be accounted for as the acquisition of an asset and the incurrence of an obligation by the lessee and as a sale or financing by the lessor. All other leases should be accounted for as operating leases. In a lease that transfers substantially all of the benefits and risks of ownership, the economic effect on the parties is similar, in many respects, to that of an installment purchase. This is not to say, however, that such transactions are necessarily "in substance purchases" as that term is used in previous authoritative literature.

61. The transfer of substantially all the benefits and risks of ownership is the concept embodied in previous practice in lessors' accounting, having been articulated in both *APB Opinion No. 7*, "Accounting for Leases in Financial Statements of Lessors," and *APB Opinion No. 27*, "Accounting for Lease Transactions by Manufacturer or Dealer Lessors," as a basis for determining whether a lease should be accounted for as a financing or sale or as an operating lease. However, a different concept has existed in the authoritative literature for lessees' accounting, as evidenced by *APB Opinion No. 5*, "Reporting of Leases in Financial Statements of Lessee."

That Opinion required capitalization of those leases that are "clearly in substance installment purchases of property," which it essentially defined as those leases whose terms "result in the creation of a material equity in the property." Because of this divergence in both concept and criteria, a particular leasing transaction might be recorded as a sale or as a financing by the lessor and as an operating lease by the lessee. This difference in treatment has been the subject of criticism as being inconsistent conceptually, and some of the identifying criteria for classifying leases, particularly those applying to lessees' accounting, have been termed vague and subject to varied interpretation in practice.

62. The Board believes that this Statement removes most, if not all, of the conceptual differences in lease classification as between lessors and lessees and that it provides criteria for such classification that are more explicit and less susceptible to varied interpretation than those in previous literature.

63. Some members of the Board who support this Statement hold the view that, regardless of whether substantially all the benefits and risks of ownership are transferred, a lease, in transferring for its term the right to use property, gives rise to the acquisition of an asset and the incurrence of an obligation by the lessee which should be reflected in his financial statements. Those members nonetheless support this Statement because, to them, (i) it clarifies and improves the guidelines for implementing the conceptual basis previously underlying accounting for leases and (ii) it represents an advance in extending the recognition of the essential nature of leases.

Definition of a Lease

64. Some respondents took the position that nuclear fuel leases, sometimes called "heat supply" or "burn up" contracts, should be excluded from the definition of a lease on the grounds that such agreements are of the same nature as take-or-pay contracts to supply other types of fuel such as coal or oil which are excluded. The Board's conclusion that nuclear fuel leases meet the definition of a lease as expressed in paragraph 1 is based on the fact that under present generally accepted accounting principles a nuclear fuel installation constitutes a depreciable asset. Thus, a nuclear fuel lease conveys the right to use a depreciable asset whereas contracts to supply coal or oil do not. The fact that the latter contracts may be take-or-pay, in the Board's view, is irrelevant to this central point.

Classification of Leases

65. The Board believes that the characteristics of a leasing transaction should determine its classification in terms of the appropriate accounting treatment by both the lessee and lessor; this is to say that the characteristics that identify a lease as a capital lease, as distinct from an operating lease, from the standpoint of the lessee should, with certain exceptions identified in this Statement, be the same attributes that identify a direct financing or sales-type lease, as distinct from an operating lease, from the standpoint of the lessor. The principal exceptions referred to are those stated in paragraph 8.

66. The Board considered and rejected, for the reason set forth in paragraph 65, the argument that the difference in the nature of the lessor's and lessee's businesses is often sufficient to warrant different classification of a lease by the two parties.

67. Some respondents to the Discussion Memorandum and Exposure Drafts, while agreeing generally with the premise that the nature of the transaction should govern its classification by both the lessee and lessor, pointed out that there is no assurance that the transaction will be discerned identically by both parties. However, the Board believes that by adopting essentially the same criteria for classification of leases by both parties (see paragraph 65), as contrasted with the difference in criteria previously existing between *APB Opinion No. 5*, concerning lessee accounting, and *APB Opinions No. 7* and *27*, concerning lessor accounting, and, by virtue of the fact that the criteria adopted are in some respects more explicit than those referred to in those Opinions, that a significant improvement in consistency of classification can be achieved.

68. A large number of respondents favored capitalization by lessees of only those leases that they would classify as "in substance installment purchases." A wide range of preferences was expressed as to the criteria to be used to identify such leases. Most prominent among these was the "material equity" criterion that is the basic criterion of *APB Opinion No. 5* and that is discussed in paragraph 73. Most of those favoring this concept would apply it only to the lessee rather than to both parties.

69. The Board considered the concept for capitalization by the lessee of those leases that are "in substance installment purchases." Such leases, if identifiable, would be encompassed within the concept described in paragraph 60, but, by itself, the installment purchase concept, in the Board's view, is too limiting as a basis for lease capitalization. Taken literally, the concept would apply only to those leases that automatically transfer ownership. All other leases contain characteristics not found in installment purchases, such as the reversion of the property to the lessor at the termination of the lease.

70. Some respondents advocated capitalization of leases that give rise to what they term "debt in a

strict legal sense." A number of the respondents in this group were also represented in the group referred to in paragraph 68, indicating that they view the two concepts as not being mutually exclusive. The argument advanced is essentially that some leases contain clauses that make the lessee's obligation absolute and unconditional, and because the obligation is absolute, such clauses should be made the determinant for capitalization of leases containing them. Those advancing this view generally appeared to be focusing on the liability aspect of the transaction rather than on the nature of the corresponding asset to be recorded. Few had any comment to offer concerning cases in which the "legal debt" assumed by the lessee represents only a portion of the asset's cost; nor was it clear from the comments how, if at all, the concept of "legal debt" standing alone should affect accounting for the lease by the lessor.

71. The Board noted that the determination of whether a lease obligation represents debt in the strict legal sense would of necessity rest primarily on court decisions, and that such decisions have arisen almost entirely from litigation involving bankruptcy, reorganization, or taxation. The Board concluded that legal distinctions of this nature were apt to be neither relevant nor practical in application to the accounting issue of lease capitalization. The Board believes further that, in most instances where the lessee has assumed an unconditional obligation that the courts might hold to be legal debt, it is reasonable to assume that he will have protected his interest through other features in the agreement that are likely to meet one or more of the criteria for capitalization stated in paragraph 7. The Board accordingly rejected the concept of "legal debt" as a determinant for lease capitalization.

Criteria for Classification

72. The Discussion Memorandum listed 14 criteria as having some support for use in classifying leases by lessees. A number of criteria, including some of the 14, were also listed for possible use in classifying leases by lessors. Among the respondents, opinion was divided as to the criteria that identify leases that should be capitalized by the lessee as well as to those criteria that identify leases that should be recorded as sales or financing leases by lessors. The Board concluded that many of the listed criteria were overlapping, i.e., that the basic idea contained in one also was embodied in others designed to identify the same attribute. The Board believes that the criteria stated in paragraphs 7 and 8 contain the essence of the listed criteria except those that the Board did not consider relevant or suitable. The basis for the Board's adoption or rejection of individual criteria is the concept discussed in paragraph 60, namely, the transfer of substantially all of the benefits and risks incident to the ownership of property. The following discusses the Board's conclusions with respect to each of the 14 criteria listed in the lessee section of the Discussion Memorandum together with 5 other criteria that were dealt with in the lessor section. These last 5 are discussed in paragraphs 87-90.

73. *Lessee builds up a material equity in the leased property*. Many of the respondents favored the material equity criterion as contained in *APB Opinion No. 5* as the principal basis for lease capitalization by the lessee. Of the criteria selected by the Board, the criterion stated in paragraph 7(b) wherein the lease contains a bargain purchase option is evidential that a material equity is being established. The criterion stated in paragraph 7(a) wherein ownership is transferred by the end of the lease term may in some circumstances be evidential that a material equity is being established. However, in relating material equity to the concept discussed in paragraph 60, the Board concluded that leases in which no material equity is established by the lessee may effectively transfer substantially all of the benefits and risks of ownership. For example, a lease whose term extends over the entire economic life of the asset and thus transfers all of the benefits and risks of ownership need not give rise to a material equity. Accordingly, the Board rejected material equity as a separate criterion and considered it too limiting to represent the central basis for lease capitalization by lessees.

74. *Leased property is special purpose to the lessee.* The Board rejected this criterion for two reasons. First, "special purpose property" is a relative concept that is hard to define objectively. Second, the fact that the leased property is special purpose does not, of itself, evidence a transfer of substantially all of the benefits and risks of asset ownership. Although it is expected that most lessors would lease special purpose property only under terms that transfer substantially all of those benefits and risks to the lessee, nothing in the nature of special purpose property necessarily entails such lease terms. The Board concluded that, if the lease, in fact, contains such terms, it is likely that one or more of the adopted criteria in paragraph 7 would be met.

75. *Lease term is substantially equal to the estimated useful life of the property*. This criterion was modified as adopted in criterion (c) of paragraph 7 as follows:

> The lease term (as defined in paragraph 5(f)) is equal to 75 percent or more of the estimated economic life of the leased property (as defined in paragraph 5(g)).

In the Board's view, the fact that the lease term need be for only 75 percent of the economic life of the property is not inconsistent with the concept discussed in paragraph 60 for the following reasons:

> Although the lease term may represent only 75 percent of the economic life of the property in terms of years, the lessee can normally expect to receive significantly more than 75 percent of the total economic benefit to be derived from the use of the property over its life span. This is due to the fact that new equipment, reflecting later technology and in prime condition, can be assumed to be more efficient, and hence yield proportionately more use benefit, than old equipment which has been subject to obsolescence and the wearing-out process. Moreover, that portion of use benefit remaining in the equipment after the lease term, in terms of the dollar value that may be estimated for it, when discounted to present worth, would represent a still smaller percentage of the value of the property at inception.

As a result of comments received in response to the second Exposure Draft, the following qualification has been added to paragraph 7(c):

> However, if the beginning of the lease term falls within the last 25 percent of the total estimated economic life of the leased property, including earlier years of use, this criterion shall not be used for purposes of classifying the lease.

The Board found persuasive the argument that it would be inconsistent to require that a lease covering the last few years of an asset's life be recorded as a capital lease by the lessee and as a sales-type or direct financing lease by the lessor when a lease of the asset for a similar period earlier in its life would have been classified as an operating lease. Without the above qualification, in the case of a tank car having an estimated economic life of 25 years and placed under five successive 5-year leases, the first four leases would be classified as operating leases under this criterion and the last lease would be classified as a capital lease. The Board considered such a result illogical.

76. *Lessee pays costs normally incident to ownership.* This criterion was rejected by the Board since it can be presumed that, one way or another, the lessee bears the costs of ownership in virtually all lease agreements.

77. *Lessee guarantees the lessor's debt with respect to the leased property.* The Board concluded that this criterion does not necessarily evidence a lease that transfers substantially all of the benefits and risks of property ownership; the amount guaranteed may represent only a portion of the fair value of the property. When there is a guarantee, the Board believes it likely that the lessee will have protected his interest through other features in the agreement that may meet one or more of the adopted criteria stated in paragraph 7. In this regard, any periods covered by renewal options in which a lessee guarantee is expected to be outstanding are to be included in the lease term, as provided by paragraph 5(f), and the corresponding renewal rentals are to be included in minimum lease payments, as provided by paragraph 5(j). Thus, such periods would be recognized in applying criterion 7(c) to the property's economic life, and both the periods and the corresponding rentals would be recognized in applying the 90 percent recovery criterion (paragraph 7(d)).

78. *Lessee treats the lease as a purchase for tax purposes.* The Board rejected this criterion. There are many instances in which tax and financial accounting treatments diverge, and the question of a possible need for conformity between them is beyond the scope of this Statement.

79. *Lease is between related parties.* The Board did not consider this criterion as suitable, in itself, for determining lease classification. Leases between related parties are discussed in paragraphs 29-31.

80. *Lease passes usual risks and rewards to lessee.* The Board considered this to be a concept rather than a criterion. It is closely related to the basic concept underlying the conclusions of this Statement, described in paragraph 60.

81. *Lessee assumes an unconditional liability for lease rentals.* This criterion was rejected by the Board for the reasons given in paragraph 71.

82. *Lessor lacks independent economic substance.* The Board considered the argument advanced by some that, if the lessor has no economic substance, the lessor serves merely as a conduit in that the lender looks to the lessee for payment and thus, it is asserted, the lessee is, in fact, the real debtor and purchaser. Whether the lessee is judged to be a debtor does not, in the Board's view, constitute a suitable criterion for determining lease classification for the reasons expressed in paragraph 71. The Board finds unpersuasive the argument that the lessee's accounting for a leasing transaction should be determined by the economic condition of an unrelated[30] lessor. If a lease qualifies as an operating lease because it does not meet the criteria in paragraph 7, the Board finds no justification for requiring that it be accounted for as a capital lease by the lessee simply because an unrelated lessor lacks independent economic substance. In such a case, it probably means that someone else, presumably the lender, is in substance the lessor, but this circumstance, per se, should not alter the lessee's accounting. Accordingly, the Board rejected this criterion.

[30]If the lessee and the lessor are related parties, the provisions of paragraphs 29-31 apply.

83. *Residual value at end of lease is expected to be nominal.* Some respondents recommended that such a criterion, if adopted, should be based on the present value of the residual, which, because of the long-term nature of many leases, would represent a much smaller percentage of asset value at inception than the undiscounted residual value. However, other respondents who favored the addition of a recovery criterion based on the relationship of the present value of the lease payments to the fair value of the leased property argued that a criterion based on residual value would be redundant in that it would essentially measure the complement of that relationship. Since, for the reasons set forth in paragraph 84 below, the Board favored the recovery criterion, it was adopted in lieu of a criterion based on residual values.

84. *Lease agreement provides that the lessor will recover his investment plus a fair return (a) guaranteed by the lessee or (b) not so guaranteed.* A variation of this criterion was adopted as criterion (d) of paragraph 7. In the form adopted, the criterion is met when the present value of the minimum lease payments, defined in paragraph 5(j), excluding executory costs, equals or exceeds 90 percent of the excess of the fair value of the leased property, defined in paragraph 5(c), to the lessor at the inception of the lease over any related investment tax credit retained by the lessor and expected to be realized by him. The Board concluded that if the present value of the contractual receipts of the lessor provide for recovery of substantially all (defined as 90 percent or more) of his net investment in the fair value of the leased asset, the lessor has transferred substantially all of the benefits and risks of asset ownership. Likewise, if the present value of the lessee's lease obligations provide for that degree of recovery by the lessor, the conclusion was that the lessee has acquired those benefits and risks. Some respondents pointed out that a recovery criterion more clearly evidences the transfer of risks than of benefits since a substantial residual value may revert to the lessor at the end of the lease term. However, the Board concluded that, in leases meeting the recovery criterion, the residual amount, when discounted to its present value at the inception of the lease, is likely to represent only a small percentage of the fair value of the property. For the reasons cited above, the Board adopted a criterion based on recovery of substantially all (defined as 90 percent or more) of the fair value of the leased property. A lessee guarantee of recovery to the lessor is recognized through inclusion in the definition of minimum lease payments. Thus, such guarantees are taken into account in the application of the 90 percent recovery criterion. As a result of comments received in response to the second Exposure Draft, the following qualification has been added to paragraph 7(d):

> However, if the beginning of the lease term falls within the last 25 percent of the total estimated economic life of the leased property, including earlier years of use, this criterion shall not be used for purposes of classifying the lease.

The above qualification is the same as that added to criterion 7(c) and the reasons are the same as those discussed in paragraph 75.

85. *Lessee has the option at any time to purchase the asset for the lessor's unrecovered investment.* The Board concluded that the existence of a purchase option is significant only if it is a bargain purchase option as defined in paragraph 5(d) and as adopted in paragraph 7(b); otherwise, there is no presumption that the lessee will exercise the option. Accordingly, the Board rejected this criterion.

86. *Lease agreement is noncancelable for a "long term."* This criterion was rejected by the Board in favor of criterion (c) of paragraph 7.

87. *Lease transfers title (ownership) to the lessee by the end of the lease term.* This criterion was adopted by the Board as criterion (a) of paragraph 7. Such a provision effectively transfers all of the benefits and risks of ownership and, thus, the criterion is consistent with the concept discussed in paragraph 60.

88. *Lease provides for a bargain purchase or a renewal option at bargain rates.* The existence of a bargain purchase option was adopted by the Board as criterion (b) of paragraph 7. Such a provision effectively transfers all of the benefits and risks of ownership and, thus, the criterion is consistent with the concept discussed in paragraph 60. The period covered by a bargain renewal option is included in the lease term, as defined in paragraph 5(f), and the option rentals are included in minimum lease payments, as defined in paragraph 5(j). Thus, a bargain renewal option enters into the determination of whether the lease meets either criterion (c) or criterion (d) of paragraph 7. Accordingly, the Board rejected the existence of a bargain renewal option as a separate criterion.

89. *Collection of the rentals called for by the lease is reasonably assured.* This criterion relates only to lessors. It has been restated as follows and adopted by the Board as a necessary criterion (paragraph 8(a)): "Collectibility of the minimum lease payments is reasonably predictable." The wording change reflects the Board's view that lessors should not be precluded from classifying leases as direct financing or sales-type leases, when they meet one of the criteria for such classification in paragraph 7, if losses are reasonably predictable based on experience with groups of similar receivables. When other than normal credit risks are involved in a leasing transaction,

it was the Board's conclusion that collectibility is not reasonably predictable and classification as a sales-type or direct financing lease, in such cases, is therefore not appropriate.

90. *No important uncertainties surround costs yet to be incurred by lessor*. The matter of uncertainties surrounding future costs was dealt with in the Discussion Memorandum as one of the risks of ownership relevant to the classification of leases by lessors. This criterion is essentially equivalent to one of the criteria set forth in *APB Opinion No. 27*, paragraph 4, as a requirement for treating a lease by a manufacturer or dealer lessor as a sale. In adopting this as a necessary criterion, the Board believes that if future unreimbursable costs to be incurred by the lessor under the lease are not reasonably predictable, the risks under the lease transaction may be so great that it should be accounted for as an operating lease instead of as a sales-type or direct financing lease.

Accounting by Lessees

91. *APB Opinion No. 5*, paragraph 15, prescribed accounting for leases that were to be capitalized as "in substance installment purchases" as follows:

> Leases which are clearly in substance installment purchases of property . . . should be recorded as purchases. The property and the obligation should be stated in the balance sheet at an appropriate discounted amount of future payments under the lease agreement. . . . The method of amortizing the amount of the asset to income should be appropriate to the nature and use of the asset and should be chosen without reference to the period over which the related obligation is discharged.

As stated in paragraph 60, the concept underlying this Statement is that a lease that transfers substantially all of the benefits and risks incident to the ownership of property should be accounted for as the acquisition of an asset and the incurrence of an obligation by the lessee, and as a sale or financing by the lessor. The concept for capitalization by the lessee of only those leases that are "in substance installment purchases" was rejected by the Board as too limiting a basis for lease capitalization (see paragraph 69).

92. Despite this difference in the concept for capitalization, the Board viewed the accounting prescribed by *APB Opinion No. 5* for capitalized leases as generally appropriate. While respondents expressed varying opinions as to the characteristics of leases that should be capitalized, there was little opposition to the method of accounting for such leases prescribed by *APB Opinion No. 5*. The accounting provisions of this Statement applicable to lessees, with the exceptions noted below, generally follow that Opinion; however, these provisions are more specific with respect to implementation.

93. With respect to the rate of interest to be used in determining the present value of the minimum lease payments for recording the asset and obligation under a capital lease, the Board concluded the rate should generally be that which the lessee would have incurred to borrow for a similar term the funds necessary to purchase the leased asset (the lessee's incremental borrowing rate). An exception to that general rule occurs when (a) it is practicable for the lessee to ascertain the implicit rate computed by the lessor and (b) that rate is less than the lessee's incremental borrowing rate; if both of those conditions are met, the lessee shall use the implicit rate. However, if the present value of the minimum lease payments, using the appropriate rate, exceeds the fair value of the leased property at the inception of the lease, the amount recorded as the asset and obligation shall be the fair value. A number of respondents pointed out that in many instances, the lessee does not know the implicit rate as computed by the lessor. Also, since the implicit rate is affected by the lessor's estimate of the residual value of the leased property in which the lessee will usually have no interest, and may also be affected by other factors extraneous to the lessee, it may, if higher than the lessee's incremental borrowing rate, produce a result that is less representative of the transfer of use benefit to the lessee than would be obtained from use of the lessee's incremental borrowing rate. For those reasons, the Board concluded that the lessee's use of the implicit rate for discounting purposes should be limited to circumstances in which he is able to ascertain that rate, as computed by the lessor, and it is less than his incremental borrowing rate. In the revised Exposure Draft, the Board had defined this rate as that which "the lessee would have incurred to borrow the funds necessary to buy the leased asset on a secured loan with repayment terms similar to the payment schedule called for in the lease." A number of respondents objected to this definition pointing out that they would not have financed the asset on a secured loan basis and, hence, would be unable to determine such a theoretical rate. Those respondents suggested that the definition be revised to allow the lessee to use a rate consistent with the type of financing that would have been used in the particular circumstances. The Board found merit in those suggestions because it intended that the rate should be both determinable and reasonable. The definition of the lessee's incremental borrowing rate has been revised accordingly. Some respondents pointed out that the use of the lessee's incremental rate, however determined, would in some cases produce an amount to be capitalized that would be greater than the known fair value of the leased asset.

It was suggested that in such cases the amount to be capitalized be limited to the fair value. The Board agreed with that recommendation.

94. The method of amortization of the capitalized asset prescribed in this Statement (see paragraph 11) differs from that called for in *APB Opinion No. 5* in that, except for those leases that meet criterion 7(a) or 7(b), the period of amortization is limited to the lease term. *APB Opinion No. 5* did not so limit the period of amortization since the leases to be capitalized were those that were considered "in substance installment purchases." The Board concluded that, for leases which are capitalized under criterion 7(c) or 7(d) of this Statement, the amortization period should be the lease term. It is presumed for accounting purposes that, in such leases, the lessee's period of use of the asset will end at the expiration of the lease term.

95. Some respondents asked for clarification and more specific treatment in the Statement with respect to the accounting to be followed in connection with the situations referred to in paragraph 9 having to do with changes in lease provisions that would have resulted in a different classification of the lease at its inception and renewals and extensions of existing leases. The clarification requested has been incorporated in paragraph 14. Additionally, respondents asked for clarification with respect to the accounting to be followed when a guarantee or penalty provision in a lease is rendered inoperative by a renewal or extension. That clarification has been provided in paragraph 12.

Disclosure by Lessees

96. Users of financial statements have indicated a strong desire for disclosure by lessees of information concerning leasing transactions whether leases are capitalized or not. In some cases, the information desired was similar to that now provided in accordance with *APB Opinion No. 31* or SEC *Accounting Series Release No. 147*. However, some respondents objected to the requirement to disclose future minimum rental payments by periods beyond the next succeeding five years. It was contended that any such projections are apt to be misleading since the accumulating effect of new leases and lease renewals on future payments in those periods is not reflected. In addition, some users and many other respondents opposed requiring disclosure of the estimated effect on net income had certain leases been capitalized. The Board agreed with both of those views except that during the transition period until full retroactive application of this Statement is required, the Board decided that the disclosure called for in paragraph 50 is needed by users of financial statements pending retroactive application. The Board concluded that the disclosures called for in paragraph 16(a) with respect to capital leases would provide information helpful to users of financial statements in assessing the financial condition and results of operations of lessees. In the Board's view, such disclosures are consistent with the information presently required to be disclosed with respect to owned property and to long-term obligations in general. The Board further concluded that users' assessments would be facilitated by the disclosures called for in paragraphs 16(b) and 16(c) with respect to operating leases. The requirement to disclose information concerning commitments for rental payments under operating leases during the succeeding five years is consistent with the similar requirement for capital leases.

Accounting by Lessors

97. As stated in paragraph 61, the concept underlying the accounting for leases by lessors in this Statement is essentially the same as the concept embodied in *APB Opinions No. 7* and *27*; that is, a lease that transfers substantially all of the benefits and risks incident to the ownership of property should be accounted for as a sale or financing by the lessor. Accordingly, the accounting provisions of this Statement applicable to lessors, with the principal exceptions noted below, generally follow those of the two APB Opinions.

98. In computing the manufacturer's or dealer's profit on a sales-type lease, the cost of the property leased will be reduced by the present value of the estimated residual value. This represents a liberalization of the provisions of *APB Opinion No. 27*, which did not permit recognition of any residual value in determining manufacturer's or dealer's profit. Some respondents favored continuing the provisions of Opinion 27 in this regard. Others believed that the present value of the residual should be recognized in profit determination and that the accounting for the financing element of a leasing transaction should be essentially the same in a sales-type lease as in a direct financing lease. The Board agreed with this latter view and concluded that the difference between the estimated residual and its present value should be included in unearned income and recognized in income over the lease term.

99. This Statement calls for the estimated residual value, along with rentals and other minimum lease payments receivable, to be included in the balance sheet presentation of the investment in sales-type and in direct financing leases. Under *APB Opinion No. 7*, the estimated residual value was to be included with property, plant, and equipment. Several respondents contended that inclusion of the residual with depreciable assets of the lessor would blur the distinction between property on lease and

property used in the lessor's internal operations. Others pointed out that, in the vast majority of leases, the estimated residual value is realized by a sale or re-lease of the property and, for that reason, the residual should be looked upon as a last payment similar to the minimum lease payments. In addition, it was contended, presentation of the estimated residual value as part of the lease investment rather than as part of property, plant, and equipment is necessary to portray the proper relationship between the gross investment in leases and the related unearned income, since a portion of the unearned income relates to the residual value. The Board agreed with those views.

100. This Statement requires that the selling price in a sales-type lease be determined by computing the present value of payments required under the lease. In this respect, it follows Opinion 27. However, this Statement is more specific than Opinion 27 in identifying the payments that are to be included in the computation, and it requires use of the rate of interest implicit in the lease for discounting instead of an interest rate determined in accordance with the provisions of *APB Opinion No. 21*, as called for by Opinion 27. Use of the latter rate was rejected by the Board on the grounds that it would yield an amount to be recorded as the sales price that would be at variance with the known fair value of the leased asset (after adjusting that price for the present value of any investment tax credit or residual retained).

101. This Statement requires different treatment of initial direct costs (see paragraph 5(m)) as between sales-type leases and direct financing and leveraged leases. In the case of sales-type leases, initial direct costs are to be charged against income of the period in which the sale is recorded, which is consistent with the general practice of accounting for similar costs incurred in connection with installment sales on the basis that such costs are incurred primarily to produce sales revenue. In this respect, the Statement follows *APB Opinion No. 27*, which, although not mentioning initial direct costs specifically, in paragraph 6 called for estimated "future costs" related to leases accounted for as sales to be charged to income of the period in which the sale is recorded. The second Exposure Draft called for initial direct costs incurred in connection with direct financing leases to be accounted for in the manner that *APB Opinion No. 7*, paragraph 11, described as preferred, that is, to be deferred and allocated to future periods in which the related financing income is reported. This requirement recognized that, unlike the initial direct costs in sales-type leases, such costs in direct financing leases are not primarily related to income of the period in which the costs are incurred. A number of respondents objected to the deferral of initial direct costs incurred in connection with direct financing leases because it is at variance with predominant industry practice and would, it was reported, necessitate a major revision of existing record systems and computer programs with no appreciable effect on net income over the lease term. The predominant industry practice as cited by those respondents consists of expensing such costs as incurred and recognizing as income in the same period a portion of unearned income equal to the amount of the costs expensed. It was pointed out that this method produces essentially the same income effect as if the initial direct costs were deferred and amortized separately, as was called for by the revised Exposure Draft, or as if these costs were charged to unearned income, as is called for in the case of leveraged leases. The Board accepted this recommendation for practical considerations and has revised the accounting prescribed for initial direct costs incurred in connection with direct financing leases accordingly. In the case of leveraged leases, the accounting for initial direct costs is consistent with the central concept underlying the accounting for leveraged leases by the investment with separate phases method, that concept being that the net income should be recognized at a level rate of return on the investment in the lease in the years in which the investment is positive.

102. As was the case with lessee accounting, respondents requested clarification and more specific guidance as to the accounting to be followed by lessors with respect to the situations referred to in paragraph 95. The requested guidance for lessor accounting for those situations has been provided in paragraphs 17(e) and 17(f). In addition, respondents objected to the provisions of the revised Exposure Draft allowing, in some instances, gain to be recognized immediately on renewals or extensions of sales-type or direct financing leases. Those who objected contended that gain recognition in those circumstances was equivalent to allowing upward revisions of residual value estimates, a practice specifically prohibited in the Statement. The Board found those objections persuasive and, accordingly, revised the accounting for renewals or extensions of sales-type or direct financing leases to prohibit immediate recognition of gain.

Disclosure by Lessors

103. A number of those respondents who addressed the question of what information should be disclosed by lessors thought that the disclosures called for by *APB Opinion No. 7* were adequate. Some, however, thought there should be consistency, where relevant, between the disclosure requirements for lessors and those for lessees and noted that disclosure requirements for lessees had been recently made more extensive by *APB Opinion No. 31* and SEC *Accounting Series Release No. 147*. The Board agreed with this latter view. As in the case of lessees,

the Board believes that the information required to be disclosed by paragraph 23 will be helpful to users of financial statements in assessing the financial condition and results of operations of lessors. Several respondents to the second Exposure Draft objected to the limitation of lessor disclosure requirements to those lessors for which leasing is the predominant activity. It was contended that the disclosures should be required whenever leasing is a significant part of the lessor's business activities rather than only when leasing is predominant. Other respondents thought that a single test of predominance based on revenues was inappropriate and pointed to the difference in the nature of lease rentals as compared to sales revenue of a manufacturing concern. It was recommended that significance be determined in terms of revenue, net income, or assets as separate indicators. The Board found merit in these recommendations and revised the disclosure limitation accordingly.

104. Some respondents recommended the elimination of the requirement in the Exposure Drafts that the cost or carrying amount of property on operating leases and that of property held for lease be separately disclosed. They contended that in companies having thousands of operating leases it would be difficult, if not impossible, to make such a split. Since the information would be based on one particular point in time, it may well be unrepresentative. The Board found those arguments persuasive and believes, moreover, that a better indication of the productivity of property on or held for lease is its relationship to the minimum future rentals by years and in the aggregate from noncancelable operating leases, which latter information is required by the Statement.

Leases Involving Real Estate

105. The second Exposure Draft provided that criteria 7(c) and 7(d) were not applicable to leases of land and that, unless criterion 7(a) or 7(b) was met, leases of land should be accounted for as operating leases. In a lease involving both land and building, if the land element represented 15 percent or more of the total fair value of the leased property, the land and building elements of the lease were required to be separated and each classified and accounted for as if it were a separate lease. Some respondents objected to this, contending that the recovery criterion, 7(d), should be applicable to land leases the same as to other leases. Others objected to the required separate treatment of the land and building elements in a lease involving both, contending that the property should be classified and accounted for as a unit and that to require separation would be inconsistent with the economic substance of the transaction. Some, particularly in the case of retail leases, cited the difficulties and cost involved in separating the land and building elements for companies with large numbers of such leases. They recommended that separation not be required and that all such leases be classified as operating leases. However, if separation were to continue to be required, some suggested that the 15 percent limitation be raised to permit treating as a unit a greater number of leases in which land would still not represent a major element. The Board's conclusion that, unless criterion 7(a) or 7(b) was met, leases of land should be classified as operating leases is based on the concept that such leases do not transfer substantially all the benefits and risks of ownership. Land normally does not depreciate in value over time, and rental payments for the use of land are not predicated on compensation for depreciation plus interest, as is the case with leases of depreciable assets, but are in the nature of interest only or, as some may prefer to say, interest plus whatever additional profit element may be included. The requirement for separation of the land and building elements in a lease involving both is based on this distinction. The Board found merit, however, in the recommendation that the 15 percent limitation be raised in order to reduce the practical problems involved in separating the land and building elements for large numbers of leases. The Board concluded that the 15 percent limitation established in the second Exposure Draft should accordingly be raised to 25 percent.

106. A number of respondents pointed out that leases of facilities such as airport and bus terminals and port facilities from governmental units or authorities contain features that render the criteria of paragraph 7 inappropriate for classifying such leases. Leases of such facilities do not transfer ownership or contain bargain purchase options. By virtue of its power to abandon a facility during the term of a lease, the governmental body can effectively control the lessee's continued use of the property for its intended purpose, thus making its economic life essentially indeterminate. Finally, since neither the leased property nor equivalent property is available for sale, a meaningful fair value cannot be determined, thereby invalidating the 90 percent recovery criterion. For those reasons, the Board concluded that such leases shall be classified as operating leases by both the lessee and lessor.

Sale-Leaseback Transactions

107. Of those respondents who addressed the issues of accounting for sale-leaseback transactions, opinions were divided between those who favored (a) treatment as a single transaction with deferral of profit on the sale and (b) treatment as two independent transactions unless the lease meets criteria for capitalization by the lessee. Generally, those favoring treatment as a single transaction would make

certain exceptions, such as "leasebacks to accommodate a short-term property requirement of the seller" and "leasebacks of only a relatively small part of the property sold." The Board noted that most sale-leasebacks are entered into as a means of financing, for tax reasons, or both and that the terms of the sale and the terms of the leaseback are usually negotiated as a package. Because of this interdependence of terms, no means could be identified for separating the sale and the leaseback that would be both practicable and objective. For that reason, the Board concluded that the present general requirement that gains and losses on sale-leaseback transactions be deferred and amortized should be retained. An exception to that requirement arises when the fair value of the property at the time of the transaction is less than its undepreciated cost. In that case, the Board decided that the loss should be recognized up to the amount of the difference between the undepreciated cost and fair value.

Accounting for Leveraged Leases by Lessors

108. The first issue concerning leveraged leases in the Discussion Memorandum asked whether leveraged leases are unique in the sense that special standards are required to recognize their economic nature. The affirmative responses to this issue generally gave as reasons the arguments stated in the Discussion Memorandum. The essence of those arguments is that the combination of nonrecourse financing and a cash flow pattern that typically enables the lessor to recover his investment in the early years of the lease and thereafter affords him the temporary use of funds from which additional income can be derived produces a unique economic effect. Those respondents who did not agree that leveraged leases are unique generally cited the contra argument in the Discussion Memorandum, namely, that each of the attributes of leveraged leases that serve to support the uniqueness claim has its counterpart in other types of business transactions. Information communicated by respondents, as well as that obtained through staff investigation, indicates that the use of a variety of accounting methods for leveraged leases has grown rapidly. The methods in use generally correspond, although frequently with variations, to those illustrated in the Discussion Memorandum. The Board noted with concern the increasing disparity in practice in accounting for leveraged leases. Despite the fact that each of the attributes of a leveraged lease is found in other types of transactions, the Board believes that in a leveraged lease those attributes are combined in a manner that produces an overall economic effect that is distinct from that of other transactions. Accordingly, the Board concluded that a leveraged lease, as defined in paragraph 42, should be accounted for in a manner that recognizes this overall economic effect. However, the Board emphasizes that the qualification "as defined in paragraph 42" is an important one since the term "leveraged lease" is used by some respondents to refer to any lease involving nonrecourse debt. There is further discussion of this distinction in paragraph 110.

109. The Discussion Memorandum described and illustrated four different methods of accounting for leveraged leases. Three of those methods are designed to recognize what their adherents see as the economic effect of a leveraged lease, while the other method, the ordinary financing lease method, is that presently prescribed for financing leases by *APB Opinion No. 7*. The Board's conclusions and the reasons therefor concerning the four methods are as follows:

a. *The ordinary financing lease method.* This accounting method makes no distinction between a leveraged lease and an ordinary two-party financing lease. Even though the debt is nonrecourse to the lessor and the lessor has no claim on the debt service payments, the transaction is recorded "gross" with the lessor's investment based on the present value of the gross rentals plus the residual value as prescribed by *APB Opinion No. 7*. In fact, however, the lessor's real investment is not a function of the amount of the future rental payments, which amount represents neither the funds he has at risk nor the asset from which he derives earnings. Further, no recognition is given to the separate investment phases of a leveraged lease as defined in paragraph 42. This method was rejected by the Board because it is incompatible with the essential features of the transaction.
b. *The three-party financing lease method.* This method does reflect the three-party nature of the transaction in that the lessor's investment is recorded net of the nonrecourse debt, and rental receipts are reduced by the debt service payments. However, it gives no recognition to the fact that a leveraged lease has separate investment phases, which is one of the characteristics included in the definition (see paragraph 42(d)). The lessor's unrecovered investment balance declines during the early years of a leveraged lease from the strong cash inflow in that period. Typically, the cumulative cash inflow during the early years exceeds the investment, producing a negative investment balance during the middle years. The investment returns to a positive balance again in the later years as funds are reinvested and then goes to zero with realization of the residual value at the termination of the lease. This pattern of cash flow results from the fact that income tax reductions from the investment tax credit, accelerated depreciation, and greater interest deductions in earlier years are replaced

by additional income taxes in the later years after the investment tax credit has been utilized and as tax benefits from depreciation and interest diminish. By ignoring these separate investment phases, the three-party financing method shows a gradually declining investment balance throughout the years of the lease, with income recognized at a level rate of return on the declining balance. The Board believes that the accounting treatment for a leveraged lease should reflect these separate investment phases, which have different economic effects, and should provide for the recognition of income in appropriate relation to them. To do otherwise, in the Board's view, is to negate the reason for having a separate standard for leveraged leases, that reason being that leveraged leases have a distinct combination of economic features that sets them apart from ordinary financing leases. While the three-party financing lease method reflects the three-party nature of the transaction, it fails to recognize the other economic features referred to above; as a consequence, it produces results that are inconsistent with the manner in which the lessor-investor views the transaction. For those reasons, the Board rejected the three-party financing lease method.

c. *The investment with separate phases method.* This method recognizes the separate investment phases and the reversing cash flow pattern of a leveraged lease. By recognizing income at a level rate of return on net investment in the years in which the net investment is positive, it associates the income with the unrecovered balance of the earning asset in a manner consistent with the investor's view of the transaction. In the middle years of the lease term, the investment balance is generally negative, indicating that the lessor has not only recovered his initial investment but has the temporary use of funds that will be reinvested in the later years. The earnings on these temporary funds are reflected in income as and if they occur in the years in which the investment is negative. The income that is recognized at a level rate of return in the years in which the net investment balance is positive consists only of the so-called "primary" earnings from the lease, as distinct from the earnings on temporary funds to be reinvested, sometimes referred to as "secondary" earnings. The lessor-investor looks upon these secondary earnings from the temporarily held funds as one of the economic benefits inherent in the transaction. The integral investment method discussed in (d) below allocates both the primary and secondary earnings to annual income on a level rate of return basis. It is asserted by some that because of this feature, the integral investment method is more consistent with the manner in which the lessor-investor views the transaction. However, this feature involves estimation of the secondary earnings and recognition of a substantial portion of them in advance of their occurrence, which the Board did not favor for reasons stated below in the discussion of the integral investment method. The Board believes that secondary earnings should be recognized in income only as they occur (in the negative investment years), and that this treatment, coupled with the recognition of primary earnings in the positive investment years, appropriately portrays the economic effects of the separate investment phases. Accordingly, the Board concluded that the investment with separate phases method as prescribed in paragraphs 43-47 is the appropriate method for accounting for leveraged leases.

d. *The integral investment method.* Several variations of the method illustrated in Schedule 7, page 126, of the Discussion Memorandum were suggested by respondents who supported its concept. That concept looks upon the earnings from the use of temporarily held funds (discussed in (c) above) as constituting an integral part of the lease income, rather than as secondary earnings to be accounted for as they occur (the treatment called for in the separate phases method). Advocates of the integral method point out that the equity participant (lessor) in a leveraged lease is actually buying a series of cash flows consisting not only of the equity portion of the rental payments, the investment tax credit and other tax benefits, and the amount to be realized from the sale of the residual, but also including the earnings to be obtained from the use of temporarily held funds. Failure to include the latter in the calculation and recognition of lease income, in their view, understates lease income and is inconsistent with the manner in which the lessor-investor views the transaction. In considering these arguments, the Board noted (1) that the earnings in question, in effect, represent an estimate of interest expected to be earned (or interest cost to be saved) in future years through the application of the temporarily held funds; (2) although these earnings will not be realized until future years, their inclusion in lease income under the integral investment method would result in their recognition in substantial amounts beginning with the first year of the lease; and (3) the actual occurrence and amount of those earnings cannot be verified because this would involve tracing the source of specific investment dollars, generally acknowledged to be impractical. The Board noted further that the other cash flows that constitute the source of the primary earnings, with the exception of the residual value, are either contractual or based on existing tax law and thus provide a firmer basis for income recognition than the secondary earnings. Admittedly, there is uncertainty involved in the estimate of residual value to be realized; however, the Board noted that recognition of residual value is consistent with the accounting prescribed for ordinary financing leases, whereas the anticipation of future interest on funds expected to be held temporarily has no support in present generally accepted accounting principles. For the foregoing reasons, the Board rejected the integral investment method.

110. Some respondents who objected to the inclusion of paragraph 42(d) in the definition of a leveraged lease argued that leveraged leases can have a variety of rental payment arrangements, some of which would not produce the separate investment phases specified as part of the definition, but that, nevertheless, such leases should be accorded the accounting method prescribed in the Statement. The Board did not agree with this view, since the method prescribed is designed to recognize the unique economic aspects of the separate investment phases. It concluded that leases not having this characteristic should not be accounted for as leveraged leases and that the presence of nonrecourse debt in a leasing transaction is not by itself justification for special accounting treatment. Nonrecourse debt occurs in many types of transactions other than leases and, as discussed in paragraph 108, it is only the combination of attributes, not the presence of nonrecourse debt alone, that produces an overall economic effect that is distinct from that of other transactions.

111. Some have contended that the inclusion of deferred taxes in the determination of the lessor's unrecovered investment is what gives rise to the separate investment phases, which is then used to justify the Board's adoption of the separate phases method and its rejection of the three-party financing method. The Board believes that the essential difference between the three-party financing method and the separate phases method is that the latter method closely follows the cash flow of the transaction, whereas the former does not. The three-party financing method portrays a gradually declining investment balance over the entire lease term, thus failing to recognize the short-term nature of the lessor's initial investment, which is typically recovered through the cash flow in the early years of the lease. That this early cash flow comes in large part from tax benefits does not alter the fact that the lessor has recovered his investment and is then provided with the temporary use of funds by which additional income can be generated. It is this feature which provides much of the incentive for the lessor to enter into the transaction in the first place and, in fact, without those tax benefits some leveraged leases would yield negative results. The Board concluded that leveraged leases should be accounted for in a manner that recognizes this cash flow pattern, both in determining the lessor's unrecovered investment balance and in the allocation of income relating to it. The assertion by some that the separate phases method results in an unwarranted "front ending" of income, in the Board's view, fails to take into account that the economic benefits of the transaction are themselves "front-ended," as has been described above. It is precisely this feature and the lack of recognition given it by the three-party financing method that caused the Board to reject that method.

112. A number of respondents to the second Exposure Draft objected to the exclusion of the 90 percent recovery criterion, 7(d), in determining whether or not a lease meets the requirement of paragraph 42(a) as part of the definition of a leveraged lease. These respondents pointed out that the majority of leveraged leases would not meet any of the other criteria of paragraph 7 and that, if criterion 7(d) was not to be applicable, few leases would meet the definition of a leveraged lease. They took exception to the Board's reasons for having excluded criterion 7(d) as expressed in the second Exposure Draft. In their view, the determination of whether the lease would qualify as a direct financing lease, as required by paragraph 42(a), should be made in the same manner as with any other lease and that the presence of nonrecourse debt should thus not enter into such determination. The Board agreed with this reasoning and has changed the requirement of paragraph 42(a) accordingly.

113. Some respondents asked that the Board reconsider its decision reflected in the second Exposure Draft that leases meeting the definition of sales-type leases should not be accounted for as leveraged leases. The argument was advanced that manufacturers and dealers often engaged in leasing transactions that, except for the exclusion of sales-type leases, would otherwise meet the definition of a leveraged lease as set forth in paragraph 42. Specifically, it was asked why should not a manufacturer record manufacturing profit for a sales-type lease and then also account for it as a leveraged lease, if it otherwise meets the definition? In the Board's view, the recognition of manufacturing profit by the lessor at the beginning of the lease is incompatible with the concept underlying the accounting method prescribed by this Statement for leveraged leases. As stated in paragraph 109(c), that method recognizes income at a level rate of return on the lessor's net investment in the years in which the net investment is positive. The annual cash flow is thus allocated between that portion recognized as income and that applied as a reduction of net investment. Net investment at any point is considered to represent the lessor's unrecovered investment. If manufacturing profit is recognized at the beginning of the lease, an element of the overall profit in the transaction has been abstracted at the outset, thus changing the pat-

tern of income recognition contemplated. The lessor's investment as recorded after recognition of manufacturing profit would not represent his unrecovered investment. That fact plus the deferral of income taxes related to the manufacturing profit recognized would alter both the investment base and the income to be allocated, thus departing from the cash flow concept on which the prescribed method is based. For these reasons, the Board did not accept the recommendation.

114. For much the same reason, the Board concluded that if the investment tax credit is accounted for other than as described in paragraphs 43 and 44, the leveraged lease should not be accounted for by the investment with separate phases method but, instead, by the method prescribed for a direct financing lease. Accounting for the credit other than as prescribed by the investment with separate phases method would abstract an important element of the overall profit in the transaction, thereby changing the lessor's net investment and the pattern of income recognition contemplated by the investment with separate phases method and thus, in the Board's view, rendering the use of that method inappropriate.

Effective Date and Transition

115. The Board considered three methods of transition in the application of the Statement:

a. Retroactive application with restatement of prior period financial statements
b. Retroactive application without restatement
c. Prospective application

The first alternative maximizes comparability of a company's financial statements with those of other companies and with its own statements for prior periods. However, respondents expressed concern that it would require the accumulation of a considerable amount of information about existing and expired leases and that some companies might have problems relating to restrictive covenants in loan indentures and other contracts. In addition, it requires estimates that in some cases would be made with after-the-fact knowledge. The second alternative reduces the problem of data accumulation but at the cost of impairing interperiod comparability of a company's financial statements before and after the date of retroactive application. Depending on the particular circumstances, it may or may not mitigate the possible problems relating to loan indenture covenants. The third alternative avoids most of the problems of the other two but would result in noncomparability of financial statements, both as among different companies and those of the same company for different periods, for years in the future.

116. While the majority of respondents favored prospective application, others strongly urged that the Statement be applied retroactively with restatement. The long period of time that would ensue before comparability would be achieved was given as the prime reason by those advocating retroactivity. Some preparers, on the other hand, cited problems involving loan indenture restrictions should the Statement require retroactive application. Some companies with large numbers of leases stated in their responses that the task of gathering the necessary data for retroactive application would be onerous as well as time consuming for existing leases, and that it would be more difficult, if not impossible, to obtain the information on expired leases necessary for restatement.

117. Included in the responses was the suggestion that a transition period be established during which companies would be given time both for the purpose of accumulating the necessary data for retroactive application and for taking steps toward resolving problems that might arise in connection with restrictive clauses in loan indentures or other agreements.

118. In considering these conflicting recommendations, the Board was sympathetic to the problems of data accumulation for companies with large numbers of leases and to the problems that some companies believe might be associated with indenture restrictions. On the other hand, the objections raised, particularly by users of financial statements, to the long period of noncomparability of financial statements that would be entailed by prospective application concerned the Board. The Board concluded that the use of a transition period at the end of which full retroactive application would be required would best meet the needs of users while at the same time giving significant recognition to the problems referred to by preparers.

119. The procedure adopted by the Board calls for immediate prospective application of the Statement (see paragraph 48), with retroactive restatement required after a four-year transition period (see paragraph 49). Thus, companies that might have problems arising from loan indenture restrictions are given at least four full years in which, depending on the nature of the restrictions, resolution of such problems may be possible. Further, restatement is required for periods beginning before December 31, 1976 only to the extent that it is practicable (see paragraph 51), in recognition of the fact that some companies may be unable to obtain or reconstruct the necessary information about leases expiring in prior years. Finally, interim disclosures (see paragraph 50) are called for to facilitate comparability before retroactive application of the Statement is required; however, since the Board recognizes that the accumulation of information to make such dis-

closures may require time, companies are given at least one full year before such disclosure is called for. Although the Board recognizes that the period of time provided for transition will not completely eliminate the problems of retroactive restatement, it believes that those problems will be alleviated under the method outlined above and that the benefit to be gained through comparability of financial statements is substantial.

120. Upon consideration of the relevant circumstances, the Board concluded that the interests of users of financial statements would be best served by making the statement effective for leasing transactions and lease agreement revisions entered into on or after January 1, 1977, as provided by paragraph 48.

Appendix C

ILLUSTRATIONS OF ACCOUNTING BY LESSEES AND LESSORS

121. This Appendix contains the following schedules illustrating the accounting requirements of this Statement as applied to a particular example (an automobile lease):

1. Lease example—terms and assumptions, Schedule 1
2. Computation of minimum lease payments (lessee and lessor) and lessor's computation of rate of interest implicit in the lease, Schedule 2
3. Classification of the lease, Schedule 3
4. Journal entries for the first month of the lease as well as for the disposition of the leased property at the end of the lease term, Schedule 4

SCHEDULE 1 — Lease Example Terms and Assumptions

Lessor's cost of the leased property (automobile)	$5,000
Fair value of the leased property at inception of the lease (1/1/77)	$5,000
Estimated economic life of the leased property	5 years

Lease terms and assumptions: The lease has a fixed noncancelable term of 30 months, with a rental of $135 payable at the beginning of each month. The lessee guarantees the residual value at the end of the 30-month lease term in the amount of $2,000. The lessee is to receive any excess of sales price of property over the guaranteed amount at the end of the lease term. The lessee pays executory costs. The lease is renewable periodically based on a schedule of rentals and guarantees of the residual values decreasing over time. The rentals specified are deemed to be fair rentals (as distinct from bargain rentals), and the guarantees of the residual are expected to approximate realizable values. No investment tax credit is available.

The residental value at the end of the lease term is estimated to be $2,000. The lessee depreciates his owned automobiles on a straight-line basis. The lessee's incremental borrowing rate is 10 1/2% per year. There were no initial direct costs of negotiating and closing the transaction. At the end of the lease term the asset is sold for $2,100.

SCHEDULE 2 — Computation of Minimum Lease Payments (Lessee and Lessor)

In accordance with paragraph 5(j), minimum lease payments for both the lessee and lessor are computed as follows:

Minimum rental payments over the lease term ($135 × 30 months)	$4,050
Lessee guarantee of the residual value at the end of the lease term	2,000
Total minimum lease payments	$6,050

Lessor's Computation of Rate of Interest Implicit in the Lease

In accordance with paragraph 5(k), the interest rate implicit in the lease is that rate implicit in the recovery of the fair value of the property at the inception of the lease ($5,000) through the minimum lease payments (30 monthly payments of $135 and the lessee's guarantee of the residual value in the amount of $2,000 at the end of the lease term). That rate is 12.036% (1.003% per month).

SCHEDULE 3

Classification of the Lease

Criteria set forth in paragraph	
7(a)	*Not met*. The lease does not transfer ownership of the property to the lessee by the end of the lease term.
7(b)	*Not met*. The lease does not contain a bargain purchase option.
7(c)	*Not met*. The lease term is not equal to 75% or more of the estimated economic life of the property. (In this case, it represents only 50% of the estimated economic life of the property.)
7(d)	*Met*. In the lessee's case, the present value ($5,120) of the minimum lease payments using his incremental borrowing rate (10 1/2%) exceeds 90% of the fair value of the property at the inception of the lease. (See computation below.) Even if the lessee knows the implicit rate, he uses his incremental rate because it is lower. The lessee classifies the lease as a capital lease. In the lessor's case, the present value ($5,000) of the minimum lease payments using the implicit rate also exceeds 90% of the fair value of the property. (See computation below.) Having met this criterion and assuming that the criteria of paragraph 8 are also met, the lessor will classify the lease as a direct financing lease (as opposed to a sales-type lease) because the cost and fair value of the asset are the same at the inception of the lease. (See paragraph 6(b)(ii).)

	Present Values	
	Lessee's computation using his incremental borrowing rate of 10 1/2% (.875% per month)*	**Lessor's computation using the implicit interest rate of 12.036% (1.003% per month)**
Minimum lease payments:		
Rental payments	$3,580	$3,517
Residual guarantee by lessee	1,540	1,483
Total	$5,120	$5,000
Fair value of the property at inception of the lease	$5,000	$5,000
Minimum lease payments as a percentage of fair value	102%	100%

*In this case, the lessee's incremental borrowing rate is used because it is lower than the implicit rate. (See paragraph 7(d).)

SCHEDULE 4

Journal Entries for the First Month of the Lease as Well as for the Disposition of the Leased Property at the End of the Lease Term

First Month of the Lease

LESSEE

Date	Entry	Debit	Credit
1/1/77	Leased property under capital leases	5,000	
	Obligations under capital leases		5,000
	To record capital lease at the fair value of the property. (Since the present value of the minimum lease payments using the lessee's incremental borrowing rate as the discount rate (see paragraph 7(d) for selection of rate to be used) is greater than the fair value of the property, the lessee capitalizes only the fair value of the property. (See paragraph 10.))		
1/1/77	Obligations under capital leases	135	
	Cash		135
	To record first month's rental payment.		
1/31/77	Interest expense	49	
	Accrued interest on obligations under capital leases		49*
	To recognize interest expense for the first month of the lease. Obligation balance outstanding during month \$4,865 (\$5,000 − \$135) × 1.003% (rate implicit in the liquidation of the \$5,000 obligation through (a) 30 monthly payments of \$135 made at the beginning of each month and (b) a \$2,000 guarantee of the residual value at the end of 30 months) = \$49. (See paragraph 12.)		
1/31/77	Depreciation expense	100	
	Leased property under capital leases		100
	To record first month's depreciation on a straight-line basis over 30 months to a salvage value of \$2,000, which is the estimated residual value to the lessee. (See paragraph 11(b).)		

LESSOR

Date	Entry	Debit	Credit
1/1/77	Minimum lease payments receivable	6,050	
	Automobile		5,000
	Unearned income		1,050
	To record lessor's investment in the direct financing lease. (See paragraphs 18(a) and (b).)		
1/1/77	Cash	135	
	Minimum lease payments receivable		135
	To record receipt of first month's rental payment under the lease.		
1/31/77	Unearned income	49	
	Earned income		49
	To recognize the portion of unearned income that is earned during the first month of the lease. Net investment outstanding for month \$4,865 (gross investment \$5,915 (\$6,050 − \$135) less unearned income (\$1,050) × 1.003% (monthly implicit rate in the lease) = \$49. (See paragraph 18(b).)		

*In accordance with paragraph 12, the February 1, 1977 rental payment of \$135 will be allocated as follows: \$86 (principal reduction) against obligations under capital leases and \$49 against accrued interest on obligations under capital leases.

Disposition of Asset for $2,100

		Debit	Credit
LESSEE			
7/1/79	Cash	100	
	Obligations under capital leases	1,980	
	Accrued interest on obligations under capital leases	20	
	Leased property under capital leases		2,000
	Gain on disposition of leased property		100
	To record the liquidation of the obligations under capital leases and receipt of cash in excess of the residual guarantee through the sale of the leased property.		
LESSOR			
7/1/79	Cash	2,000	
	Minimum lease payments receivable		2,000
	To record the receipt of the amount of the lessee's guarantee.		

Note to Disposition of Asset

Had the lessee elected at July 1, 1979 to renew the lease, it would render inoperative the guarantee as of that date. For that reason, the renewal would not be treated as a new agreement, as would otherwise be the case under paragraph 9, but would instead be accounted for as provided in paragraph 12. The lessee would accordingly adjust the remaining balances of the asset and obligation from the original lease, which at June 30, 1979 were equal, by an amount equal to the difference between the present value of the future minimum lease payments under the revised agreement and the remaining balance of the obligation. The present value of the future minimum lease payments would be computed using the rate of interest used to record the lease initially.

From the lessor's standpoint, the revised agreement would be accounted for in accordance with paragraph 17(e). Accordingly, the remaining balance of minimum lease payments receivable would be adjusted to the amount of the payments called for by the revised agreement, and the adjustment would be credited to unearned income.

Appendix D

ILLUSTRATIONS OF DISCLOSURE BY LESSEES AND LESSORS

122. This Appendix illustrates one way of meeting the disclosure requirements of this Statement, except for those relating to leveraged leases which are illustrated in Appendix E. The illustrations do not encompass all types of leasing arrangements for which disclosures are required. For convenience, the illustrations have been constructed as if the Statement had been in effect in prior years.

LESSEE'S DISCLOSURE

Company X
BALANCE SHEET

ASSETS	December 31, 1976	December 31, 1975
Leased property under capital leases, less accumulated amortization (Note 2)	XXX	XXX

LIABILITIES	December 31, 1976	December 31, 1975
Current:		
Obligations under capital leases (Note 2)	XXX	XXX
Noncurrent:		
Obligations under capital leases (Note 2)	XXX	XXX

Footnotes appear on the following pages.

FOOTNOTES

Note 1—Description of Leasing Arrangements

The Company conducts a major part of its operations from leased facilities which include a manufacturing plant, 4 warehouses, and 26 stores. The plant lease, which is for 40 years expiring in 1999, is classified as a capital lease. The warehouses are under operating leases that expire over the next 7 years. Most of the leases of store facilities are classified as capital leases. All of the leases of store facilities expire over the next 15 years.

Most of the operating leases for warehouses and store facilities contain one of the following options: (a) the Company can, after the initial lease term, purchase the property at the then fair value of the property or (b) the Company can, at the end of the initial lease term, renew its lease at the then fair rental value for periods of 5 to 10 years. These options enable the Company to retain use of facilities in desirable operating areas. The rental payments under a store facility lease are based on a minimum rental plus a percentage of the store's sales in excess of stipulated amounts. Portions of store space and warehouse space are sublet under leases expiring during the next 5 years.

In addition, the Company leases transportation equipment (principally trucks) and data processing equipment under operating leases expiring during the next 3 years.

In most cases, management expects that in the normal course of business, leases will be renewed or replaced by other leases.

The plant lease prohibits the Company from entering into future lease agreements if, as a result of new lease agreements, aggregate annual rentals under all leases will exceed $XXX.

Note 2—Capital Leases

The following is an analysis of the leased property under capital leases by major classes:

Classes of Property	Asset Balances at December 31, 1976	1975
Manufacturing plant	$ XXX	$ XXX
Store facilities	XXX	XXX
Other	XXX	XXX
Less: Accumulated amortization	(XXX)	(XXX)
	$ XXX	$ XXX

The following is a schedule by years of future minimum lease payments under capital leases together with the present value of the net minimum lease payments as of December 31, 1976:

Year ending December 31:	
1977	$ XXX
1978	XXX
1979	XXX
1980	XXX
1981	XXX
Later years	XXX
Total minimum lease payments[1]	XXX
Less: Amount representing estimated executory costs (such as taxes, maintenance, and insurance), including profit thereon, included in total minimum lease payments	(XXX)
Net minimum lease payments	XXX
Less: Amount representing interest[2]	(XXX)
Present value of net minimum lease payments[3]	$ XXX

Note 3—Operating Leases

The following is a schedule by years of future minimum rental payments required under operating leases that have initial or remaining noncancelable lease terms in excess of one year as of December 31, 1976:

Year ending December 31:	
1977	$ XXX
1978	XXX
1979	XXX
1980	XXX
1981	XXX
Later years	XXX
Total minimum payments required*	$ XXX

The following schedule shows the composition of total rental expense for all operating leases except those with terms of a month or less that were not renewed:

	Year ending December 31,	
	1976	1975
Minimum rentals	$ XXX	$ XXX
Contingent rentals	XXX	XXX
Less: Sublease rentals	(XXX)	(XXX)
	$ XXX	$ XXX

[1]Minimum payments have not been reduced by minimum sublease rentals of $XXX due in the future under noncancelable subleases. They also do not include contingent rentals which may be paid under certain store leases on the basis of a percentage of sales in excess of stipulated amounts. Contingent rentals amounted to $XXX in 1976 and $XXX in 1975.

[2]Amount necessary to reduce net minimum lease payments to present value calculated at the Company's incremental borrowing rate at the inception of the leases.

[3]Reflected in the balance sheet as current and noncurrent obligations under capital leases of $XXX and $XXX, respectively.

*Minimum payments have not been reduced by minimum sublease rentals of $XXX due in the future under noncancelable subleases.

LESSOR'S DISCLOSURE (Other Than for Leveraged Leases)

Company X
BALANCE SHEET

ASSETS	December 31, 1976	1975
Current assets:		
Net investment in direct financing and sales-type leases (Note 2)	XXX	XXX
Noncurrent assets:		
Net investment in direct financing and sales-type leases (Note 2)	XXX	XXX
Property on operating leases and property held for leases (net of accumulated depreciation of $ XXX and $ XXX for 1976 and 1975, respectively) (Note 3)	XXX	XXX

Footnotes appear [below and] on the following pages.

FOOTNOTES

Note 1—Description of Leasing Arrangements

The Company's leasing operations consist principally of the leasing of various types of heavy construction and mining equipment, data processing equipment, and transportation equipment. With the exception of the leases of transportation equipment, the bulk of the Company's leases are classified as direct financing leases. The construction equipment and mining equipment leases expire over the next ten years and the data processing equipment leases expire over the next eight years. Transportation equipment (principally trucks) is leased under operating leases that expire during the next three years.

Note 2—Net Investment in Direct Financing and Sales-Type Leases

The following lists the components of the net investment in direct financing and sales-type leases as of December 31:

	1976	1975
Total minimum lease payments to be received*	$ XXX	$ XXX
Less: Amounts representing estimated executory costs (such as taxes, maintenance, and insurance), including profit thereon, included in total minimum lease payments	(XXX)	(XXX)
Minimum lease payments receivable	XXX	XXX
Less: Allowance for uncollectibles	(XXX)	(XXX)
Net minimum lease payments receivable	XXX	XXX
Estimated residual values of leased property (unguaranteed)	XXX	XXX
Less: Unearned income	(XXX)	(XXX)
Net investment in direct financing and sales-type leases	$ XXX	$ XXX

*Minimum lease payments to do include contingent rentals which may be received under certain leases of data processing equipment on the basis of hours of use in excess of stipulated minimums. Contingent rentals amounted to $XXX in 1976 and $XXX in 1975. At December 31, 1976, minimum lease payments for each of the five succeeding fiscal years are as follows: $XXX in 1977, $XXX in 1978, $XXX in 1979, $XXX in 1980, and $XXX in 1981.

Note 3—Property on Operating Leases and Property Held for Lease

The following schedule provides an analysis of the Company's investment in property on operating leases and property held for lease by major classes as of December 31, 1976:

Construction equipment	$ XXX
Mining equipment	XXX
Data processing equipment	XXX
Transportation equipment	XXX
Other	XXX
	XXX
Less: Accumulated depreciation	(XXX)
	$ XXX

Note 4—Rentals under Operating Leases

The following is a schedule by years of minimum future rentals on noncancelable operating leases as of December 31, 1976:

Year ending December 31:	
1977	$ XXX
1978	XXX
1979	XXX
1980	XXX
1981	XXX
Later years	XXX
Total minimum future rentals*	$ XXX

Appendix E

ILLUSTRATIONS OF ACCOUNTING AND FINANCIAL STATEMENT PRESENTATION FOR LEVERAGED LEASES

123. This Appendix illustrates the accounting requirements of this Statement and one way of meeting its disclosure requirements as applied to a leveraged lease. The illustrations do not encompass all circumstances that may arise in connection with leveraged leases; rather, the illustrations are based on a single example of a leveraged lease, the terms and assumptions for which are stated in Schedule 1. The elements of accounting and reporting illustrated for this example of a leveraged lease are as follows:

a. Leveraged lease example—terms and assumptions, Schedule 1
b. Cash flow analysis by years, Schedule 2
c. Allocation of annual cash flow to investment and income, Schedule 3
d. Journal entries for lessor's initial investment and first year of operation, Schedule 4
e. Financial statements including footnotes at end of second year
f. Accounting for a revision in the estimated residual value of the leased asset assumed to occur in the eleventh year of the lease (from $200,000 to $120,000):
   i. Revised allocation of annual cash flow to investment and income, Schedule 5
   ii. Balances in investment accounts at beginning of the eleventh year before revised estimate, Schedule 6
   iii. Journal entries, Schedule 7
   iv. Adjustment of investment accounts, Schedule 8

*This amount does not include contingent rentals which may be received under certain leases of data processing equipment on the basis of hours of use in excess of stipulated minimums. Contingent rentals amounted to $XXX in 1976 and $XXX in 1975.

SCHEDULE 1

Leveraged Lease Example
Terms and Assumptions

Cost of leased asset (equipment)	$1,000,000
Lease term	15 years, dating from January 1, 1975
Lease rental payments	$90,000 per year (payable last day of each year)
Residual value	$200,000 estimated to be realized one year after lease termination. In the eleventh year of the lease the estimate is reduced to $120,000.
Financing:	
Equity investment by lessor	$400,000
Long-term nonrecourse debt	$600,000, bearing interest at 9% and repayable in annual installments (on last day of each year) of $74,435.30
Depreciation allowable to lessor for income tax purposes	Seven-year ADR life using double-declining-balance method for the first two years (with the half-year convention election applied in the first year) and sum-of-years digits method for remaining life, depreciated to $100,000 salvage value
Lessor's income tax rate (federal and state)	50.4% (assumed to continue in existence throughout the term of the lease)
Investment tax credit	10% of equipment cost or $100,000 (realized by the lessor on last day of first year of lease)
Initial direct costs	For simplicity, initial direct costs have not been included in the illustration.

SCHEDULE 2

Cash Flow Analysis by Years

Year	1 Gross lease rentals and residual value	2 Depreciation (for income tax purposes)	3 Loan interest payments	4 Taxable income (loss) (col. 1 − 2 − 3)	5 Income tax credits (charges) (col. 4 × 50.4%)	6 Loan principal payments	7 Investment tax credit realized	8 Annual cash flow (col. 1 − 3 + 5 − 6 + 7)	9 Cumulative cash flow
Initial investment	—	—	—	—	—	—	—	$(400,000)	(400,000)
1	$ 90,000	$ 142,857	$ 54,000	$(106,857)	$ 53,856	$ 20,435	$100,000	169,421	(230,579)
2	90,000	244,898	52,161	(207,059)	104,358	22,274	—	119,923	(110,656)
3	90,000	187,075	50,156	(147,231)	74,204	24,279	—	89,769	(20,887)
4	90,000	153,061	47,971	(111,032)	55,960	26,464	—	71,525	50,638
5	90,000	119,048	45,589	(74,637)	37,617	28,846	—	53,182	103,820
6	90,000	53,061	42,993	(6,054)	3,051	31,442	—	18,616	122,436
7	90,000	—	40,163	49,837	(25,118)	34,272	—	(9,553)	112,883
8	90,000	—	37,079	52,921	(26,672)	37,357	—	(11,108)	101,775
9	90,000	—	33,717	56,283	(28,367)	40,719	—	(12,803)	88,972
10	90,000	—	30,052	59,948	(30,214)	44,383	—	(14,649)	74,323
11	90,000	—	26,058	63,942	(32,227)	48,378	—	(16,663)	57,660
12	90,000	—	21,704	68,296	(34,421)	52,732	—	(18,857)	38,803
13	90,000	—	16,957	73,043	(36,813)	57,478	—	(21,248)	17,555
14	90,000	—	11,785	78,215	(39,420)	62,651	—	(23,856)	(6,301)
15	90,000	—	6,145	83,855	(42,263)	68,290	—	(26,698)	(32,999)
16	200,000	100,000	—	100,000	(50,400)	—	—	149,600	116,601
Totals	$1,550,000	$1,000,000	$516,530	$ 33,470	$(16,869)	$600,000	$100,000	$116,601	

SCHEDULE 3

Allocation of Annual Cash Flow to Investment and Income

	1	2	3	4	5	6	7
		Annual Cash Flow			Components of Income[2]		
Year	Lessor's net investment at beginning of year	Total (from Schedule 2, col. 8)	Allocated to investment	Allocated to income[1]	Pretax income	Tax effect of pretax income	Investment tax credit
1	$400,000	$169,421	$134,833	$34,588	$9,929	$(5,004)	$29,663
2	265,167	119,923	96,994	22,929	6,582	(3,317)	19,664
3	168,173	89,769	75,227	14,542	4,174	(2,104)	12,472
4	92,946	71,525	63,488	8,037	2,307	(1,163)	6,893
5	29,458	53,182	50,635	2,547	731	(368)	2,184
6	(21,177)	18,616	18,616	—	—	—	—
7	(39,793)	(9,553)	(9,553)	—	—	—	—
8	(30,240)	(11,108)	(11,108)	—	—	—	—
9	(19,132)	(12,803)	(12,803)	—	—	—	—
10	(6,329)	(14,649)	(14,649)	—	—	—	—
11	8,320	(16,663)	(17,382)	719	206	(104)	617
12	25,702	(18,857)	(21,079)	2,222	637	(321)	1,906
13	46,781	(21,248)	(25,293)	4,045	1,161	(585)	3,469
14	72,074	(23,856)	(30,088)	6,232	1,789	(902)	5,345
15	102,162	(26,698)	(35,532)	8,834	2,536	(1,278)	7,576
16	137,694	149,600	137,694	11,906	3,418	(1,723)	10,211
Totals		$516,601	$400,000	$116,601	$33,470	$(16,869)	$100,000

[1]Lease income is recognized as 8.647% of the unrecovered investment at the beginning of each year in which the net investment is positive. The rate is that rate which when applied to the net investment in the years in which the net investment is positive will distribute the net income (net cash flow) to those years. The rate for allocation used in this Schedule is calculated by a trial and error process. The allocation is calculated based upon an initial estimate of the rate as a starting point. If the total thus allocated to income (column 4) differs under the estimated rate from the net cash flow (Schedule 2, column 8) the estimated rate is increased or decreased, as appropriate, to derive a revised allocation. This process is repeated until a rate is selected which develops a total amount allocated to income that is precisely equal to the net cash flow. As a practical matter, a computer program is used to calculate Schedule 3 under successive iterations until the correct rate is determined.

[2]Each component is allocated among the years of positive net investment in proportion to the allocation of net income in column 4.

SCHEDULE 4

Illustrative Journal Entries for Year Ending December 31, 1975

Lessor's Initial Investment

Rentals receivable (Schedule 2, total of column 1 less residual value, less totals of columns 3 and 6)	233,470	
Investment tax credit receivable (Schedule 2, column 7)	100,000	
Estimated residual value (Schedule 1)	200,000	
Unearned and deferred income (Schedule 3, totals of columns 5 and 7)		133,470
Cash		400,000
Record lessor's initial investment		

First Year of Operation

Journal Entry 1

Cash	15,565	
Rentals receivable (Schedule 2, column 1 less columns 3 and 6)		15,565
Collection of first year's net rental		

Journal Entry 2

Cash *	100,000	
Investment tax credit receivable (Schedule 2, column 7)		100,000
Receipt of investment tax credit		

Journal Entry 3

Unearned and deferred income	9,929	
Income from leveraged leases (Schedule 3, column 5)		9,929

Recognition of first year's portion of pretax income allocated in the same proportion as the allocation of total income

$$\left(\frac{34,588}{116,601}\right) \times 33,470 = 9,929$$

Journal Entry 4

Unearned and deferred income	29,663	
Investment tax credit recognized (Schedule 3, column 7)		29,663

Recognition of first year's portion of investment tax credit allocated in the same proportion as the allocation of total income

$$\left(\frac{34,588}{116,601}\right) \times 100,000 = 29,663$$

Journal Entry 5

Cash (Schedule 2, column 5) *	53,856	
Income tax expense (Schedule 3, column 6)	5,004	
Deferred taxes		58,860

To record receipt of first year's tax credit from lease operation, to charge income tax expense for tax effect of pretax accounting income, and to recognize as deferred taxes the tax effect of the difference between pretax accounting income and the tax loss for the year, calculated as follows:

Tax loss (Schedule 2, column 4)	\$(106,857)
Pretax accounting income	9,929
Difference	\$(116,786)
Deferred taxes (\$116,786 × 50.4%)	\$ 58,860

*Receipts of the investment tax credit and other tax benefits are shown as cash receipts for simplicity only. Those receipts probably would not be in the form of immediate cash inflow. Instead, they likely would be in the form of reduced payments of taxes on other income of the lessor or on the combined income of the lessor and other entities whose operations are joined with the lessor's operations in a consolidated tax return.

ILLUSTRATIVE PARTIAL FINANCIAL STATEMENTS INCLUDING FOOTNOTES

BALANCE SHEET

ASSETS	December 31, 1976	December 31, 1975	LIABILITIES	December 31, 1976	December 31, 1975
Investment in leveraged leases	$334,708	$324,027	Deferred taxes arising from leveraged leases	$166,535	$58,860

INCOME STATEMENT

(Ignoring all income and expense items other than those relating to leveraged leasing)

	1976	1975
Income from leveraged leases	$ 6,582	$ 9,929
Income before taxes and investment tax credit	6,582	9,929
Less: Income tax expense*	(3,317)	(5,004)
	3,265	4,925
Investment tax credit recognized*	19,664	29,663
Net income	$22,929	$34,588

FOOTNOTES

Investment in Leveraged Leases

The Company is the lessor in a leveraged lease agreement entered into in 1975 under which mining equipment having an estimated economic life of 18 years was leased for a term of 15 years. The Company's equity investment represented 40 percent of the purchase price; the remaining 60 percent was furnished by third-party financing in the form of long-term debt that provides for no recourse against the Company and is secured by a first lien on the property. At the end of the lease term, the equipment is turned back to the Company. The residual value at that time is estimated to be 20 percent of cost. For federal income tax purposes, the Company receives the investment tax credit and has the benefit of tax deductions for depreciation on the entire leased asset and for interest on the long-term debt. Since during the early years of the lease those deductions exceed the lease rental income, substantial excess deductions are available to be applied against the Company's other income. In the later years of the lease, rental income will exceed the deductions and taxes will be payable. Deferred taxes are provided to reflect this reversal.

The Company's net investment in leveraged leases is composed of the following elements:

	December 31, 1976	December 31, 1975
Rentals receivable (net of principal and interest on the nonrecourse debt)	$202,340	$217,905
Estimated residual value of leased assets	200,000	200,000
Less: Unearned and deferred income	(67,632)	(93,878)
Investment in leveraged leases	334,708	324,027
Less: Deferred taxes arising from leveraged leases	(166,535)	(58,860)
Net investment in leveraged leases	$168,173	$265,167

*These two items may be netted for purposes of presentation in the income statement, provided that the separate amounts are disclosed in a note to the financial statements.

SCHEDULE 5

Allocation of Annual Cash Flow to Investment and Income Revised to Include New Residual Value Estimate

	1	2	3	4	5	6	7
		Annual Cash Flow			Components of Income		
Year	Lessor's net investment at beginning of year	Total	Allocated to investment	Allocated to income[1]	Pretax loss	Tax effect of pretax loss	Investment tax credit
1	$400,000	$169,421	$142,458	$26,963	$(16,309)	$ 8,220	$ 35,052
2	257,542	119,923	102,563	17,360	(10,501)	5,293	22,568
3	154,979	89,769	79,323	10,446	(6,319)	3,184	13,581
4	75,656	71,525	66,425	5,100	(3,085)	1,555	6,630
5	9,231	53,182	52,560	622	(377)	190	809
6	(43,329)	18,616	18,616	—	—	—	—
7	(61,945)	(9,553)	(9,553)	—	—	—	—
8	(52,392)	(11,108)	(11,108)	—	—	—	—
9	(41,284)	(12,803)	(12,803)	—	—	—	—
10	(28,481)	(14,649)	(14,649)	—	—	—	—
11	(13,832)	(16,663)	(16,663)	—	—	—	—
12	2,831	(18,857)	(19,048)	191	(115)	58	248
13	21,879	(21,248)	(22,723)	1,475	(892)	450	1,917
14	44,602	(23,856)	(26,862)	3,006	(1,819)	916	3,909
15	71,464	(26,698)	(31,515)	4,817	(2,914)	1,469	6,262
16	102,979	109,920	102,979	6,941	(4,199)	2,116	9,024
Totals		$476,921	$400,000	$76,921	$(46,530)	$23,451	$100,000

[1] The revised allocation rate is 6.741%.

SCHEDULE 6

Balances in Investment Accounts before Revised Estimate of Residual Value

	1	2	3	4	5	6	7
				Unearned & Deferred Income			
	Rentals receivable[1]	Estimated residual value	Investment tax credit receivable	Pretax income (loss)[2]	Investment tax credit[3]	Deferred taxes[4]	Net investment (col. 1+2+3) less (col. 4+5+6)
Initial investment	$233,470	$200,000	$100,000	$33,470	$100,000	$ —	$400,000
Changes in year of operation							
1	(15,565)	—	(100,000)	(9,929)	(29,663)	58,860	(134,833)
2	(15,565)	—	—	(6,582)	(19,664)	107,675	(96,994)
3	(15,565)	—	—	(4,174)	(12,472)	76,308	(75,227)
4	(15,565)	—	—	(2,307)	(6,893)	57,123	(63,488)
5	(15,565)	—	—	(731)	(2,184)	37,985	(50,635)
6	(15,565)	—	—	—	—	3,051	(18,616)
7	(15,565)	—	—	—	—	(25,118)	9,553
8	(15,564)	—	—	—	—	(26,672)	11,108
9	(15,564)	—	—	—	—	(28,367)	12,803
10	(15,565)	—	—	—	—	(30,214)	14,649
Balances, beginning of eleventh year	$ 77,822	$200,000	$ —	$ 9,747	$ 29,124	$230,631	$ 8,320

[1] Schedule 2, column 1, excluding residual value, less columns 3 and 6.

[2] Schedule 3, column 5.

[3] Schedule 3, column 7.

[4] 50.4% of difference between taxable income (loss), Schedule 2, column 4, and pretax accounting income (loss), Schedule 3, column 5.

SCHEDULE 7

Illustrative Journal Entries
Reduction in Residual Value in Eleventh Year

Journal Entry 1			
Pretax income (or loss)		60,314	
Unearned and deferred income		27,450	
Pretax income (loss):			
Balance at end of 10th year	9,747[1]		
Revised balance	(9,939)[2]		
Adjustment	(19,686)		
Deferred investment tax credit:			
Balance at end of 10th year	29,124[3]		
Revised balance	21,360[4]		
Adjustment	(7,764)		
Investment tax credit recognized			7,764
Estimated residual value			80,000

To record:

i. The cumulative effect on pretax income and the effect on future income resulting from the decrease in estimated residual value:

Reduction in estimated residual value	$80,000
Less portion attributable to future years (unearned and deferred income)	(19,686)
Cumulative effect (charged against current income)	$60,314

ii. The cumulative and future effect of the change in allocation of the investment tax credit resulting from the reduction in estimated residual value

Journal Entry 2		
Deferred taxes	30,398	
Income tax expense		30,398

To recognize deferred taxes for the difference between pretax accounting income (or loss) and taxable income (or loss) for the effect of the reduction in estimated residual value.

Pre-tax accounting loss per journal entry 1	$(60,314)
Tax income (or loss)	—
Difference	$(60,314)
Deferred taxes ($60,314 × 50.4%)	$(30,398)

[1]Schedule 6, column 4.

[2]Schedule 5, total of column 5 less amounts applicable to the first 10 years.

[3]Schedule 6, column 5.

[4]Schedule 5, total of column 7 less amounts applicable to the first 10 years.

SCHEDULE 8

Adjustment of Investment Accounts for Revised Estimate of Residual Value in Eleventh Year

	1	2	3	4	5	6
			Unearned & Deferred Income			Net investment
	Rentals receivable	Estimated residual value	Pretax income (loss)	Investment tax credit	Deferred taxes	(col. 1 + 2) less (col. 3 + 4 + 5)
Balances, beginning of eleventh year (Schedule 6)	$77,822	$200,000	$ 9,747	$29,124	$230,631	$ 8,320
Adjustment of estimated residual value and unearned and deferred income (Schedule 7 – journal entry 1)	—	(80,000)	(19,686)	(7,764)	—	(52,550)
Adjustment of deferred taxes for the cumulative effect on pretax accounting income (Schedule 7 – journal entry 2)	—	—	—	—	(30,398)	30,398
Adjusted balances, beginning of eleventh year	$77,822	$120,000	$ (9,939)	$21,360	$200,233	$(13,832)[1]

[1]Schedule 5, column 1.

Statement of Financial Accounting Standards No. 14 Financial Reporting for Segments of a Business Enterprise

STATUS

Issued: December 1976

Effective Date: For fiscal years beginning after December 15, 1976 and interim periods within those years (but amended by FAS 18, FAS 21, and FAS 24)

Affects: No other pronouncements

Affected by: Paragraphs 4 and 73 and footnote 15 superseded by FAS 18
Paragraph 7 amended by FAS 24
Paragraph 39 superseded by FAS 30
Paragraph 41 amended by FAS 18
Paragraph 41 amended by FAS 21

Statement of Financial Accounting Standards No. 14
Financial Reporting for Segments of a Business Enterprise

CONTENTS

INTRODUCTION

1. In recent years, many business enterprises have broadened the scope of their activities into different industries, foreign countries, and markets. This Statement requires that the financial statements of a business enterprise (hereinafter enterprise) include information about the enterprise's operations in different industries, its foreign operations and export sales, and its major customers. This Statement also requires that an enterprise operating predominantly or exclusively in a single industry identify that industry.

2. Appendix A contains background information. Appendix B sets forth the basis for the Board's conclusions, including alternatives considered and reasons for accepting some and rejecting others. Appendix C describes two systems that have been developed for classifying business activities, and Appendix D describes a number of factors to be considered in grouping products and services by industry lines. An illustration of applying paragraph 15(b) is presented in Appendix E, and illustrations of the disclosures required by this Statement are presented in Appendix F.

STANDARDS OF FINANCIAL ACCOUNTING AND REPORTING

Inclusion in Financial Statements

3. When an enterprise issues a complete set of financial statements that present financial position at the end of the enterprise's fiscal year and results of operations and changes in financial position for that fiscal year in conformity with generally accepted accounting principles, those financial statements shall include certain information relating to:

a. The enterprise's operations in different industries—paragraphs 9-30.
b. Its foreign operations and export sales—paragraphs 31-38.
c. Its major customers—paragraph 39.

If such statements are presented for more than one fiscal year, the information required by this Statement shall be presented for each such year, except as provided in paragraph 41.

4. If an enterprise issues for an interim period a complete set of financial statements that are expressly described as presenting financial position, results of operations, and changes in financial position in conformity with generally accepted accounting principles, this Statement requires that the information referred to in paragraph 3 be included in those interim financial statements. If an enterprise issues for an interim period financial statements that are not a complete set or are otherwise complete but not expressly described as presenting financial position, results of operations, and changes in financial position in conformity with generally accepted accounting principles, this Statement does not require that the information referred

to in paragraph 3 be included in those interim financial statements.

Purpose of Segment Information

5. The purpose of the information required to be reported by this Statement is to assist financial statement users in analyzing and understanding the enterprise's financial statements by permitting better assessment of the enterprise's past performance and future prospects. As noted in paragraph 76, information prepared in conformity with this Statement may be of limited usefulness for comparing a segment of one enterprise with a similar segment of another enterprise.

Accounting Principles Used in Preparing Segment Information

6. The information required to be reported by this Statement is a disaggregation of the consolidated financial information[1] included in the enterprise's financial statements. The accounting principles underlying the disaggregated information should be the same accounting principles as those underlying the consolidated information, except that most intersegment transactions that are eliminated from consolidated financial information are included in segment information (see paragraph 8). For example, a segment for which information is required to be reported by this Statement may include a consolidated subsidiary that prepares separate financial statements. Amounts reported in the subsidiary's financial statements sometimes differ from amounts included in consolidation for reasons other than intersegment transactions, for instance, because the subsidiary was acquired in a business combination accounted for by the purchase method. In that event, the segment information required to be reported by this Statement with respect to the consolidated financial statements shall be based on the amounts included in consolidation, not on the amounts reported in the subsidiary's financial statements.

7. Enterprises are not required by this Statement to disaggregate financial information pertaining to unconsolidated subsidiaries or other unconsolidated investees. Unconsolidated subsidiaries and investments in corporate joint ventures and 50 percent or less owned companies are normally accounted for by the equity method, and financial information about equity method investees is required to be disclosed in the investor's financial statements in accordance with paragraph 20 of *APB Opinion No. 18,* "The Equity Method of Accounting for Investments in Common Stock." In addition, *ARB No. 43,* Chapter 12, "Foreign Operations and Foreign Exchange," requires the disclosure of certain financial information about foreign subsidiaries of an enterprise. This Statement does not amend those disclosure requirements. However, in addition to those disclosures, identification shall be made of both the industries and the geographic areas in which the equity method investees operate. Also, paragraph 27(c) of this Statement requires special disclosures with respect to an equity method investee whose operations are vertically integrated with those of a reportable segment of the enterprise. Disaggregation of financial information pertaining to unconsolidated subsidiaries and other unconsolidated equity method investees is encouraged when that is considered to be desirable for an understanding of the enterprise's operations. When a complete set of financial statements that present financial position, results of operations, and changes in financial position in conformity with generally accepted accounting principles is presented for a subsidiary, corporate joint venture, or 50 percent or less owned investee, each such entity is considered to be an enterprise as that term is used in this Statement and thus is subject to its requirements whether those financial statements are issued separately or included in another enterprise's financial report.

8. Transactions between a parent and its subsidiaries or between two subsidiaries are eliminated in preparing consolidated financial statements (see paragraph 6 of *ARB No. 51,* "Consolidated Financial Statements"). In preparing the information required to be reported by this Statement, however, transactions between the segments of an enterprise shall be included in the segment information. Thus, for example, revenue reported for a segment includes both sales to unaffiliated customers (i.e., customers outside the enterprise) and intersegment sales or transfers. Similarly, expenses relating both to sales to unaffiliated customers and to intersegment sales or transfers are deducted in measuring a segment's profitability. Exceptions to the general rule that intersegment transactions are not eliminated from segment information are provided in paragraphs 10(c)-10(e) for certain intersegment advances and loans and related interest revenue and expense. Paragraphs 30 and 38 require reconciliation of segment information with amounts reported in consolidated financial statements.

Information about an Enterprise's Operations in Different Industries

9. The financial statements of an enterprise shall include certain information about the industry seg-

[1]The term "consolidated financial information" is used herein to refer to aggregate information relating to an enterprise as a whole whether or not the enterprise has consolidated subsidiaries.

ments of the enterprise. Criteria for determining industry segments for which information shall be reported are in paragraphs 11-21. The type of information to be presented for each reportable industry segment is specified in paragraphs 22-27. Requirements for presenting that information in financial statements are in paragraphs 28-30.

Definitions

10. Certain terms are defined for purposes of this Statement as follows:

a. *Industry segment.*[2] A component of an enterprise engaged in providing a product or service or a group of related products and services primarily to unaffiliated customers (i.e., customers outside the enterprise) for a profit.[3] By defining an industry segment in terms of products and services that are sold primarily to unaffiliated customers, this Statement does not require the disaggregation of the vertically integrated operations of an enterprise.
b. *Reportable segment.* An industry segment (or, in certain cases, a group of two or more closely related industry segments—see paragraph 19) for which information is required to be reported by this Statement.
c. *Revenue.* The revenue of an industry segment includes revenue both from sales[4] to unaffiliated customers (i.e., revenue from customers outside the enterprise as reported in the enterprise's income statement) and from intersegment sales or transfers, if any, of products and services similar to those sold to unaffiliated customers.[5] Interest from sources outside the enterprise and interest earned on intersegment trade receivables is included in revenue if the asset on which the interest is earned is included among the industry segment's identifiable assets (see paragraph 10(e)), but interest earned on advances or loans to other industry segments is not included.[6] For purposes of this Statement, revenue from intersegment sales or transfers shall be accounted for on the basis used by the enterprise to price the intersegment sales or transfers.
d. *Operating profit or loss.* The operating profit or loss of an industry segment is its revenue as defined in paragraph 10(c) minus all operating expenses. As used herein, operating expenses include expenses that relate to both revenue from sales to unaffiliated customers and revenue from intersegment sales or transfers; those operating expenses incurred by an enterprise that are not directly traceable to an industry segment shall be allocated on a reasonable basis among those industry segments for whose benefit the expenses were incurred (see paragraph 24). For purposes of this Statement, intersegment purchases shall be accounted for on the same basis as intersegment sales or transfers (i.e., on the basis used by the enterprise to price the intersegment sales or transfers—see the last sentence of paragraph 10(c)). None of the following shall be added or deducted, as the case may be, in computing the operating profit or loss of an industry segment: revenue earned at the corporate level and not derived from the operations of any industry segment; general corporate expenses;[7] interest expense;[8] domestic and foreign income taxes; equity in income or loss from unconsolidated subsidiaries and other unconsolidated investees; gain or loss on discontinued operations (as defined in *APB Opinion No. 30,* "Reporting the Results of Operations"); extraordinary items; minority interest; and the cumulative effect of a change in accounting principles (see *APB Opinion No. 20,* "Accounting Changes").
e. *Identifiable assets.* The identifiable assets of an industry segment are those tangible and intangible enterprise assets that are used by the industry segment, including (i) assets that are used exclu-

---

[2]The meaning of the term "industry segment" as it is used in this Statement is different from the use of the term "segment" in pronouncements of the Cost Accounting Standards Board.

[3]In some industries, it is normal practice for an enterprise to purchase and sell substantially identical commodities to minimize transportation or other costs. In those situations, sales and purchases of substantially identical commodities shall be netted for the purpose of determining whether a product or service or a group of related products and services is sold primarily to unaffiliated customers. Although those sales and purchases are netted for the purpose of identifying an industry segment, it is not intended that this rule change an enterprise's accounting practice with respect to determining the revenue of the enterprise or any of its industry segments.

[4]For convenience, the term "sales" is used in this Statement to include the sale of a product, the rendering of a service, and other types of transactions by which revenue is earned.

[5]Intersegment billings for the cost of shared facilities or other jointly incurred costs do not represent intersegment sales or transfers as that term is used in this Statement.

[6]Interest earned on advances or loans to other industry segments is included in computing the operating profit or loss of an industry segment whose operations are principally of a financial nature (e.g., banking, insurance, leasing, or financing).

[7]Some of the expenses incurred at an enterprise's central administrative office may not be general corporate expenses, but rather may be operating expenses of industry segments that should therefore be allocated to those industry segments. The nature of an expense rather than the location of its incurrence shall determine whether it is an operating expense. Only those expenses identified by their nature as operating expenses shall be allocated as operating expenses in computing an industry segment's operating profit or loss.

[8]Interest expense is deducted in computing the operating profit or loss of an industry segment whose operations are principally of a financial nature (e.g., banking, insurance, leasing, or financing).

sively by that industry segment and (ii) an allocated portion of assets used jointly by two or more industry segments. Assets used jointly by two or more industry segments shall be allocated among the industry segments on a reasonable basis. Because the assets of an industry segment that transfers products or services to another industry segment are not used in the operations of the receiving segment, no amount of those assets shall be allocated to the receiving segment. Assets that represent part of an enterprise's investment in an industry segment, such as goodwill, shall be included in the industry segment's identifiable assets.[9] Assets maintained for general corporate purposes (i.e., those not used in the operations of any industry segment) shall not be allocated to industry segments. The identifiable assets of an industry segment shall not include advances or loans to or investments in another industry segment, except that advances or loans to other industry segments shall be included in the identifiable assets of a financial segment because the income therefrom is included in computing the financial segment's operating profit or loss (see footnote 6). Asset valuation allowances such as the following shall be taken into account in computing the amount of an industry segment's identifiable assets: allowance for doubtful accounts, accumulated depreciation, and marketable securities valuation allowance.

Determining Reportable Segments

11. The reportable segments of an enterprise shall be determined by (a) identifying the individual products and services from which the enterprise derives its revenue, (b) grouping those products and services by industry lines into industry segments (see paragraphs 12-14), and (c) selecting those industry segments that are significant with respect to the enterprise as a whole (see paragraphs 15-21).

Grouping Products and Services by Industry Lines

12. Several systems have been developed for classifying business activities, such as the Standard Industrial Classification (SIC) and the Enterprise Standard Industrial Classification (ESIC). (The SIC and ESIC systems are described in Appendix C to this Statement.) The Board has examined those systems and has judged that none is, by itself, suitable to determine industry segments for purposes of this Statement. Moreover, although certain characteristics can be identified that assist in differentiating among industries (such as those discussed in Appendix D to this Statement), no single set of characteristics is universally applicable in determining the industry segments of all enterprises, nor is any single characteristic determinative in all cases. Consequently, determination of an enterprise's industry segments must depend to a considerable extent on the judgment of the management of the enterprise.

13. Many enterprises presently accumulate information about revenue and profitability on a less-than-total-enterprise basis for internal planning and control purposes. Frequently, that type of information is maintained by profit centers for individual products and services or for groups of related products and services, particularly with respect to an enterprise's domestic operations. The term "profit center" is used in this Statement to refer only to those components of an enterprise *that sell primarily to outside markets* and *for which information about revenue and profitability is accumulated.* An enterprise's existing profit centers—the smallest units of activity for which revenue and expense information is accumulated for internal planning and control purposes—represent a logical starting point for determining the enterprise's industry segments. If an enterprise's existing profit centers cross industry lines, it will be necessary to disaggregate its existing profit centers into smaller groups of related products and services (except as provided in paragraph 14). If an enterprise operates in more than one industry but does not presently accumulate any information on a less-than-total-enterprise basis (i.e., its only profit center is the enterprise as a whole), it shall disaggregate its operations along industry lines (except as provided in paragraph 14).

14. Industry segmentation on a worldwide basis is a desirable objective but it may be impracticable for some enterprises. To the extent that revenue and profitability information is accumulated along industry lines for an enterprise's foreign operations, as defined in paragraph 31, or that it would be practicable to do so, industry segments shall be determined on a worldwide basis. To the extent that it is impracticable to disaggregate part or all of its foreign operations along industry lines, the enterprise shall disaggregate along industry lines its domestic operations and its foreign operations for which disaggregation is practicable and shall treat the aggregate of its foreign operations for which disaggregation is not practicable as a single industry segment. When that segment qualifies as a reportable industry segment (see paragraphs 15-21), disclosure shall be made of the types of industry operations included in the foreign operations that have not been disaggregated.

Selecting Reportable Segments

15. Each industry segment that is significant to an

[9]Any related depreciation or amortization expense is deducted in determining the operating profit of the industry segment.

enterprise as a whole shall be identified as a reportable segment. For purposes of this Statement, an industry segment shall be regarded as significant—and therefore identified as a reportable segment (see paragraph 16)—if it satisfies one or more of the following tests. The tests shall be applied separately for each fiscal year for which financial statements are presented, except as provided in paragraph 41.

a. Its revenue (including both sales to unaffiliated customers and intersegment sales or transfers) is 10 percent or more of the combined revenue (sales to unaffiliated customers and intersegment sales or transfers) of all of the enterprise's industry segments.
b. The absolute amount of its operating profit or operating loss is 10 percent or more of the greater, in absolute amount, of:
   (i) The combined operating profit of all industry segments that did not incur an operating loss, or
   (ii) The combined operating loss of all industry segments that did incur an operating loss. (Appendix E illustrates the application of paragraph 15(b).)
c. Its identifiable assets are 10 percent or more of the combined identifiable assets of all industry segments.

Revenue, operating profit or loss, and identifiable assets relating to those foreign operations that have not been disaggregated along industry lines on grounds of impracticability (see paragraph 14) shall be included in computing the combined revenue, combined operating profit or operating loss, and combined identifiable assets of the enterprise's industry segments.

16. The results of applying the percentage tests in paragraph 15 shall be evaluated from the standpoint of interperiod comparability before final determination of an enterprise's reportable segments is made. For instance, interperiod comparability would most likely require that an industry segment that has been significant in the past and is expected to be significant in the future be regarded as a reportable segment even though it fails to satisfy the tests in paragraph 15 in the current year. Conversely, a relatively insignificant industry segment may happen to satisfy the tests in paragraph 15 in the current fiscal year because its revenue or operating profit or loss is abnormally high or the combined revenue or operating profit or loss of all industry segments is abnormally low. In that case, it may be inappropriate to regard it as a reportable segment. Appropriate explanation of such circumstances shall be included as a part of the enterprise's segment information.

17. The reportable segments of an enterprise shall represent a substantial portion of the enterprise's total operations. The following test shall be applied to determine whether a substantial portion of an enterprise's operations is explained by its segment information: The combined revenue from sales to unaffiliated customers of all reportable segments (that is, revenue not including intersegment sales or transfers) shall constitute at least 75 percent of the combined revenue from sales to unaffiliated customers of all industry segments. The test shall be applied separately for each fiscal year for which financial statements are presented, except as provided in paragraph 41. Revenue relating to those foreign operations that have not been disaggregated along industry lines on grounds of impracticability shall be included in the denominator of the computation required by this paragraph and will be included in the numerator if those operations have been identified (in accordance with paragraphs 14 and 15) as a reportable segment.

18. If the industry segments identified as reportable in accordance with paragraphs 15 and 16 do not satisfy the 75-percent test in paragraph 17, additional industry segments shall be identified as reportable segments (subject to the provisions of paragraph 19) until the 75-percent test is met.

19. The Board recognizes the need for a practical limit to the number of industry segments for which an enterprise reports information; beyond that limit, segment information may become overly detailed. Without attempting to define that limit precisely, the Board suggests that as the number of industry segments that would be identified as reportable segments in accordance with paragraphs 15-18 increases above 10, the question of whether a practical limit has been reached comes increasingly into consideration, and combining the most closely related industry segments into broader reportable segments may be appropriate. Combinations shall be made, however, only to the extent necessary to contain the number of reportable segments within practical limits while still meeting the 75-percent test.

20. An enterprise may operate exclusively in a single industry or a dominant portion of an enterprise's operations may be in a single industry segment with the remaining portion in one or more other industry segments. The Board has concluded that the disclosures required by paragraphs 22-30 of this Statement need not be applied to a dominant industry segment, except that the financial statements of an enterprise that operates predominantly or exclusively in a single industry shall identify that industry. An industry segment may be regarded as dominant if its revenue, operating profit or loss, and identifiable assets (as defined in paragraphs 10(c)-(e)) each constitute more than 90 percent of related combined totals for all industry segments,

and no other industry segment meets any of the 10-percent tests in paragraph 15.

21. Paragraphs 11-20 and the guidelines for grouping products and services into industry segments set forth in Appendix D are not intended to prohibit a more detailed disaggregation if that is considered to be desirable for an understanding of the enterprise's operations.

Information to Be Presented

22. The following shall be presented for each of an enterprise's reportable segments determined in accordance with paragraphs 11-21 (including those foreign operations that have not been disaggregated along industry lines on grounds of impracticability—see paragraph 14) and in the aggregate for the remainder of the enterprise's industry segments not deemed reportable segments:

a. Revenue information as set forth in paragraph 23.
b. Profitability information as set forth in paragraphs 24 and 25.
c. Identifiable assets information as set forth in paragraph 26.
d. Other related disclosures as set forth in paragraph 27.

In addition, the types of products and services from which the revenue of each reportable segment is derived shall be identified, and the accounting policies relevant to the information reported for industry segments shall be described to the extent not adequately explained by the disclosures of the enterprise's accounting policies required by *APB Opinion No. 22,* "Disclosure of Accounting Policies." Presentation of additional information for some or all of an enterprise's reportable segments beyond that specified in paragraphs 23-27 may be considered to be desirable, and this Statement does not preclude those additional disclosures.

23. *Revenue.* Sales to unaffiliated customers and sales or transfers to other industry segments of the enterprise shall be separately disclosed in presenting revenue of a reportable segment. As indicated in paragraph 10(c), for purposes of this Statement sales or transfers to other industry segments shall be accounted for on the basis used by the enterprise to price the intersegment sales or transfers. The basis of accounting for intersegment sales or transfers shall be disclosed. If the basis is changed, disclosure shall be made of the nature of the change and its effect on the reportable segments' operating profit or loss in the period of change.

24. *Profitability.* Operating profit or loss as defined in paragraph 10(d) shall be presented for each reportable segment. As part of its segment information, an enterprise shall explain the nature and amount of any unusual or infrequently occurring items (see paragraph 26 of *APB Opinion No. 30)* reported in its consolidated income statement that have been added or deducted in computing the operating profit or loss of a reportable segment in accordance with paragraph 10(d). Methods used to allocate operating expenses along industry segments in computing operating profit or loss should be consistently applied from period to period (but, if changed, disclosure shall be made of the nature of the change and its effect on the reportable segments' operating profit or loss in the period of change).

25. *Other profitability information.* In addition to presenting operating profit or loss as required by paragraph 24, an enterprise may choose to present some other measure of profitability for some or all of its segments. If the enterprise elects to present a measure of contribution to operating profit or loss, the enterprise shall describe the differences between contribution and operating profit or loss. If the enterprise elects to present net income or a measure of profitability between operating profit or loss and net income, the nature and amount of each category of revenue or expense that was added or deducted and the methods of allocation, if any, shall be disclosed. Those methods should be consistently applied from period to period (but, if changed, disclosure shall be made of the nature and effect of the change in the period of change).

26. *Identifiable assets.* The aggregate carrying amount of identifiable assets as defined in paragraph 10(e) shall be presented for each reportable segment.

27. *Other related disclosures.* Disclosures relating to the information for reportable segments shall be made as follows:

a. Disclosure shall be made of the aggregate amount of depreciation, depletion, and amortization expense for each reportable segment.
b. Disclosure shall be made of the amount of each reportable segment's capital expenditures, i.e., additions to its property, plant, and equipment.
c. For each reportable segment disclosure shall be made of the enterprise's equity in the net income from and investment in the net assets of unconsolidated subsidiaries and other equity method investees whose operations are vertically integrated with the operations of that segment. Disclosure shall also be made of the geographic areas in which those vertically integrated equity method investees operate.
d. Paragraph 17 of *APB Opinion No. 20* requires that the effect on income of a change in accounting principle be disclosed in the financial state-

ments of an enterprise in the period in which the change is made. Disclosure shall also be made of the effect of the change on the operating profit of reportable segments in the period in which the change is made.[10]

Methods of Presentation

28. Information about the reportable segments of a business enterprise shall be included in the enterprise's financial statements in any of the following ways:

a. Within the body of the financial statements, with appropriate explanatory disclosures in the footnotes to the financial statements.
b. Entirely in the footnotes to the financial statements.
c. In a separate schedule that is included as an integral part of the financial statements. If, in a report to securityholders, that schedule is located on a page that is not clearly a part of the financial statements, the schedule shall be referenced in the financial statements as an integral part thereof.

29. Financial information such as revenue, operating profit or loss, and identifiable assets of reportable segments shall be presented as dollar amounts. Corresponding percentages may be shown in addition to dollar amounts.

30. The information required to be presented by paragraphs 22-27 for individual reportable segments and in the aggregate for industry segments not deemed reportable shall be reconciled to related amounts in the financial statements of the enterprise as a whole, as follows: Revenue shall be reconciled to revenue reported in the consolidated income statement, and operating profit or loss shall be reconciled to pretax income from continuing operations (before gain or loss on discontinued operations, extraordinary items, and cumulative effect of a change in accounting principle) in the consolidated income statement. Also, identifiable assets shall be reconciled to consolidated total assets, with assets maintained for general corporate purposes separately identified in the reconciliation. An illustration is presented in Appendix F to this Statement.

Information about Foreign Operations and Export Sales

31. The financial statements of an enterprise shall include information about its foreign operations. The features that identify an operation as foreign vary among enterprises. Thus, the identification of foreign operations will depend on the facts and circumstances of the particular enterprise. For purposes of this Statement, an enterprise's foreign operations include those revenue-producing operations (except for unconsolidated subsidiaries and other unconsolidated investees (see paragraph 7)) that (a) are located outside of the enterprise's home country (the United States for U.S. enterprises)[11] and (b) are generating revenue either from sales to unaffiliated customers or from intraenterprise sales or transfers between geographic areas.[12] Similarly, an enterprise's domestic operations include those revenue-producing operations of the enterprise located in the enterprise's home country that generate revenue either from sales to unaffiliated customers or from intraenterprise sales or transfers between geographic areas. Operations, either domestic or foreign, (and regardless of whether part of a branch or division of the enterprise or part of a consolidated subsidiary) should have identified with them the revenues generated by those operations, the assets employed in or associated with generating those revenues, and the costs and expenses incurred in generating those revenues or employing those assets.

32. The information specified in paragraph 35 shall be presented for (1) an enterprise's foreign operations, either in the aggregate or, if appropriate under paragraph 33, by geographic area, and (2) its domestic operations,[13] if either of the following conditions is met:

[10]The pro forma effects of retroactive application, which are required to be disclosed on a consolidated basis by paragraph 21 of *APB Opinion No. 20,* need not be disclosed for individual reportable segments. Also, the pro forma supplemental information relating to a business combination accounted for by the purchase method required to be presented by paragraph 96 of *APB Opinion No. 16,* "Business Combinations," need not be presented for individual reportable segments.

[11]An enterprise whose home country is other than the United States but that prepares financial statements in conformity with U.S. generally accepted accounting principles shall classify operations outside of its home country as foreign operations.

[12]Difficulties may arise in classifying the activities of certain types of enterprises. The following examples may provide useful guidelines: (1) Determination of whether the employment of an enterprise's mobile assets, such as off-shore drilling rigs or ocean-going vessels, constitutes foreign operations should depend on whether such assets are normally identified with operations located and generating revenue from outside the home country. If they are normally identified with the enterprise's foreign operations, revenue generated from abroad would be considered foreign revenue. If they are normally identified with the enterprise's domestic operations, revenue generated from abroad would be considered export sales; (2) Services rendered by the foreign offices of a service enterprise, such as a consulting firm, having offices or facilities located both in the home country and in foreign countries would be considered foreign operations, and the revenue should be considered foreign revenue. Revenue generated abroad from services provided by domestic offices should be considered export sales.

[13]Separate information about domestic operations need not be presented if domestic operations' revenue from sales to unaffiliated customers and domestic operations' identifiable assets are less than 10 percent of related consolidated amounts.

a. Revenue generated by the enterprise's foreign operations from sales to unaffiliated customers is 10 percent or more of consolidated revenue as reported in the enterprise's income statement.
b. Identifiable assets of the enterprise's foreign operations are 10 percent or more of consolidated total assets as reported in the enterprise's balance sheet.

33. If an enterprise's foreign operations are conducted in two or more geographic areas as defined in paragraph 34, the information specified in paragraph 35 shall be presented separately for each significant foreign geographic area, and in the aggregate for all other foreign geographic areas not deemed significant. A geographic area shall be regarded as *significant,* for the purpose of applying this paragraph, if its revenue from sales to unaffiliated customers or its identifiable assets are 10 percent or more of related consolidated amounts.

34. For purposes of this Statement, foreign *geographic areas* are individual countries or groups of countries as may be determined to be appropriate in an enterprise's particular circumstances. No single method of grouping the countries in which an enterprise operates into the geographic areas can reflect all of the differences among international business environments. Each enterprise shall group its foreign operations on the basis of the differences that are most important in its particular circumstances. Factors to be considered include proximity, economic affinity, similarities in business environments, and the nature, scale, and degree of interrelationship of the enterprise's operations in the various countries.

35. The following information shall be presented for an enterprise's foreign operations and for its domestic operations as appropriate in accordance with paragraphs 32-34:

a. Revenue as defined in paragraph 10(c), with sales to unaffiliated customers and sales or transfers between geographic areas shown separately. For purposes of this Statement, intraenterprise sales or transfers between geographic areas shall be accounted for on the basis used by the enterprise to price the intraenterprise sales or transfers. The basis of accounting for intraenterprise sales or transfers shall be disclosed. If the basis is changed, disclosure shall be made of the nature of the change and its effect in the period of change.
b. Operating profit or loss as defined in paragraph 10(d) *or* net income *or* some other measure of profitability between operating profit or loss and net income. A common level of profitability shall be reported for all geographic areas, although an enterprise may choose to report additional profitability information for some or all of its geographic areas of operations.
c. Identifiable assets as defined in paragraph 10(e).

36. With respect to an enterprise's *domestic* operations, sales to unaffiliated customers include both (a) sales to customers within the enterprise's home country and (b) sales to customers in foreign countries, i.e., export sales. If the amount of export sales from an enterprise's home country to unaffiliated customers in foreign countries is 10 percent or more of total revenue from sales to unaffiliated customers as reported in the enterprise's consolidated income statement, that amount shall be separately reported, in the aggregate and by such geographic areas as are considered appropriate in the circumstances. The disclosure required by this paragraph shall be made even if the enterprise is not required by this Statement to report information about its operations in different industries or foreign operations.

37. Information about the foreign operations and export sales of a business enterprise may be included in the enterprise's financial statements in any of the ways identified in paragraph 28 of this Statement. Financial information shall be presented as U.S. dollar amounts; corresponding percentages may be shown in addition to dollar amounts. The geographic areas into which an enterprise's foreign operations have been disaggregated shall be identified.

38. The information about revenue, profitability, and identifiable assets required to be presented for foreign operations shall be reconciled to related amounts in the financial statements of the enterprise as a whole, in a manner similar to that described in paragraph 30. An illustration is presented in Appendix F to this Statement.

Information about Major Customers

39. If 10 percent or more of the revenue of an enterprise is derived from sales to any single customer, that fact and the amount of revenue from each such customer shall be disclosed. (For this purpose, a group of customers under common control shall be regarded as a single customer.) Similarly, if 10 percent or more of the revenue of an enterprise is derived from sales to domestic government agencies in the aggregate or to foreign governments in the aggregate, that fact and the amount of revenue shall be disclosed. The identity of the industry segment or segments making the sales shall be disclosed. The disclosures required by this paragraph shall be made even if the enterprise is not required by this Statement to report information about operations in different industries or foreign operations.

Restatement of Previously Reported Segment Information

40. When prior period information about an enterprise's reportable industry segments, its foreign operations and export sales, and its major customers is being presented with corresponding information for the current period, the prior period information shall be retroactively restated (at least as far back as the effective date of this Statement—see paragraph 41) in the following circumstances, with appropriate disclosure of the nature and effect of the restatement:

a. When the financial statements of the enterprise as a whole have been retroactively restated, for example, for a change in accounting principle of the type described in paragraphs 27 and 29 of *APB Opinion No. 20* or for a business combination accounted for by the pooling-of-interests method.
b. When there has been a change in the way the enterprise's products and services are grouped into industry segments or a change in the way the enterprise's foreign operations are grouped[14] into geographic areas and such changes affect the segment or geographic area information being reported.

Effective Date and Transition

41. The provisions of this Statement shall be effective for financial statements for fiscal years beginning after December 15, 1976 and for interim periods[15] within those fiscal years. Earlier application is encouraged in financial statements for periods beginning before December 16, 1976 that have not previously been issued. Information of the type required by this Statement need not be included in financial statements for periods beginning before the effective date of this Statement that are being presented for comparative purposes with financial statements for periods after the effective date, but if included, that information shall be prepared and presented in conformity with the provisions of this Statement to the extent practicable with appropriate explanation if the information for periods before the effective date is not comparable to that for periods after the effective date.

The provisions of this Statement need not be applied to immaterial items.

This Statement was adopted by the unanimous vote of the six members of the Financial Accounting Standards Board:

Marshall S. Armstrong, *Chairman*
Oscar S. Gellein
Donald J. Kirk
Arthur L. Litke
Robert E. Mays
Robert T. Sprouse

Appendix A

BACKGROUND INFORMATION

42. Although the authoritative accounting literature has heretofore dealt principally with financial statements prepared on a consolidated or total-enterprise basis, several pronouncements of the Accounting Principles Board and its predecessor, the Committee on Accounting Procedure, have required business enterprises to report information on a less-than-total-enterprise basis in a limited number of areas. For example, Chapter 12 of *ARB No. 43* requires certain disclosures related to an enterprise's foreign operations; *APB Opinion No. 18* requires disclosure of information about companies accounted for by the equity method; and *APB Opinion No. 30* requires information about the discontinued operations of a segment of a business.

43. Starting in the mid-1960s, a number of professional organizations, including the Financial Analysts Federation, the Financial Executives Research Foundation, and the National Association of Accountants, sponsored research studies to assess the desirability and feasibility of disclosing information for line-of-business segments in external financial reports. Several professional organizations have issued pronouncements that generally support segment reporting, including the APB (its Statement No. 2, "Disclosure of Supplemental Financial Information by Diversified Companies," issued in 1967, urged companies to report segment information voluntarily), the Financial Accounting Policy Com-

[14]Restatement is not required when an enterprise's reportable segments change as a result of a change in the nature of an enterprise's operations or as a result of applying the tests in paragraphs 15-20.

[15]See paragraph 4

mittee of the Financial Analysts Federation, the Financial Executives Institute, the Committee on Management Accounting Practices of the National Association of Accountants, and the Accountants International Study Group.

44. In 1969, the Securities and Exchange Commission issued requirements for reporting line-of-business information in registration statements. In 1970, those requirements were extended to annual reports filed with the SEC on Form 10-K, and in October 1974 they were extended to the annual reports to securityholders of companies filing with the SEC.

45. In 1973, the New York Stock Exchange issued a "white paper" urging that line-of-business information at least as extensive as that required in SEC Form 10-K be included in annual reports to securityholders.

46. In 1974, the Federal Trade Commission initiated an annual line-of-business reporting program to enable it to publish aggregate data on corporations engaged in commerce in the United States. Under the FTC program, large manufacturing companies are required to report detailed financial information for each line of business as defined by the FTC.[16]

47. In recognition of the broadened scope of operations of many business enterprises, the need for disaggregation of enterprise-wide information expressed by many financial statement users, and the variety of present reporting practices in reports to securityholders, in April 1973 the FASB placed on its technical agenda a project on Financial Reporting for Segments of a Business Enterprise.

48. A task force of 16 persons from industry, government, public accounting, the financial community, and academe was appointed in May 1973 to counsel the Board in preparing a Discussion Memorandum analyzing issues related to the project.

49. A considerable number of research studies and articles on the subject were available to the Board, many of which were summarized or identified in the Discussion Memorandum. In addition, two research reports were prepared by the FASB staff. One was a survey of the existing reporting practices of 100 companies disclosing segment information in annual reports to shareholders. The other, involving field interviews of corporate executives of 30 companies, was directed primarily at identifying the decision criteria used by management for purposes of internal and external segmentation. Those research reports were included as appendixes to the Discussion Memorandum.

50. The Board issued the Discussion Memorandum on May 22, 1974 and held a public hearing on the subject on August 1 and 2, 1974. The Board received 144 position papers, letters of comment, and outlines of oral presentations in response to the Discussion Memorandum. Twenty-one presentations were made at the public hearing.

51. An Exposure Draft of a proposed Statement on "Financial Reporting for Segments of a Business Enterprise" was issued on September 30, 1975. The Board received 233 letters of comment on the Exposure Draft.

52. In June 1976, the Organization for Economic Cooperation and Development (OECD) adopted a "Declaration on International Investment and Multinational Enterprises," recommending certain guidelines for a code of conduct for multinational corporations. Those guidelines include, but are not limited to, the following disclosures:

a. The geographical areas where operations are carried out and the principal activities carried on therein by the parent company and the main affiliates.
b. The operating results and sales by geographical area and the sales in the major lines of business for the enterprise as a whole.
c. Significant new capital investment by geographical area and, as far as practicable, by major lines of business for the enterprise as a whole.
d. The policies followed in respect of intergroup pricing.
e. The accounting policies, including those on consolidation, observed in compiling the published information.

The OECD is made up of representatives of the governments of 24 economically developed nations of Western Europe, North America, Asia, and the South Pacific.

Appendix B

BASIS FOR CONCLUSIONS

53. This Appendix discusses factors deemed significant by members of the Board in reaching the conclusions in this Statement, including alternatives considered and reasons for accepting some and rejecting others.

Inclusion in Financial Statements

54. The Board concluded that information relating to an enterprise's industry segments, foreign operations, export sales, and major customers is useful to

[16]A number of companies are challenging the FTC's line-of-business reporting program through legal proceedings.

analyze and understand the financial statements of the enterprise. Reasons for that conclusion are discussed in paragraphs 55-74.

55. The financial statements of an enterprise are usually prepared on a consolidated or total-enterprise basis, aggregating the financial data of the various activities of the enterprise. The principal exception to the rule of consolidation is that financial subsidiaries (such as banks, insurance companies, and finance companies) of a manufacturing company usually are not consolidated (see *ARB No. 51,* "Consolidated Financial Statements," especially paragraphs 1-5). Another exception to the rule of consolidation is that foreign subsidiaries sometimes are not consolidated (see *ARB No. 43,* Chapter 12, "Foreign Operations and Foreign Exchange," especially paragraphs 8 and 9).

56. Investors and lenders who acquire equity interests in or extend credit to an enterprise as a whole recognize the importance of consolidated financial statements for reporting the overall performance of the enterprise. At the same time, however, investors, credit grantors, and other financial statement users have indicated that disaggregation of total-enterprise financial data to provide information about the various segments of an enterprise, in addition to aggregate data for the enterprise, is useful to them.

57. Those financial statement users point out that the evaluation of risk and return is the central element of investment and lending decisions—the greater the perceived degree of risk associated with an investment or lending alternative, the greater is the required rate of return to the investor or lender. If return is defined as expected cash flows to the investor or creditor, the evaluation of risk involves assessment of the uncertainty surrounding both the timing and the amount of the expected cash flows to the enterprise, which in turn are indicative of potential cash flows to the investor or creditor. Users of financial statements indicate that uncertainty results, in part, from factors unique to the particular enterprise in which an investment may be made or to which credit may be extended. Uncertainty also results, in part, from factors related to the industries and geographic areas in which the enterprise operates and, in part, from national and international economic and political factors. Investors and lenders analyze factors at all of those levels to evaluate the risk and return associated with an investment or lending alternative.

58. Information contained in an enterprise's financial statements constitutes an important input to that analysis. Financial statements provide information about conditions, trends, and ratios that assist in predicting cash flows. In analyzing an enterprise, a financial statement user often compares information about the enterprise with information about other enterprises, with industry-wide information, and with national or international economic information in general. Those comparisons are helpful in determining whether a given enterprise's operations may be expected to move with, against, or independently of developments in its industry and in the economy within which it operates.

59. The broadening of an enterprise's activities into different industries or geographic areas complicates the analysis of conditions, trends, and ratios and, therefore, the ability to predict. The various industry segments or geographic areas of operations of an enterprise may have different rates of profitability, degrees and types of risk, and opportunities for growth. There may be differences in the rates of return on the investment commitment in the various industry segments or geographic areas and in their future capital demands.

60. Consequently, many financial statement users have said that consolidated financial information, while important, would be more useful if supplemented with disaggregated information to assist them in analyzing the uncertainties surrounding the timing and amount of expected cash flows—and, therefore, the risks—related to an investment in or a loan to an enterprise that operates in different industries or areas of the world. Since the progress and prospects of a diversified enterprise are composits of the progress and prospects of its several parts, financial statement users regard financial information on a less-than-total-enterprise basis as also important.

61. Although many business enterprises presently include disaggregated financial information in reports to securityholders, in filings with the Securities and Exchange Commission and in other types of reports, the nature and extent of the information disclosed and the methods of presentation vary, and that information generally is not included in the financial statements.

62. A few respondents to the Discussion Memorandum and the Exposure Draft contended that information on a less-than-total-enterprise basis is not useful to investors and creditors. They generally argued that investors and lenders who acquire equity interests in or extend credit to an enterprise as a whole should be concerned only with overall enterprise results as reported in its consolidated financial statements. For the reasons expressed in paragraphs 55-61, however, the Board concluded that investors and creditors find segment information to be useful in analyzing and understanding consolidated statements and therefore in analyzing overall enterprise results.

63. Although most respondents agreed that information on a less-than-total-enterprise basis is useful for investment and credit decisions, some said that the information should not be included in the financial statements of an enterprise, principally on two grounds:

a. Some said that while segment information may indeed be useful to investors and credit grantors, it is too analytical or interpretive to be classified as accounting information and, thus, does not belong in financial statements.
b. Others said that disaggregated information is not susceptible to the same degree of verifiability as consolidated information.

64. The Board has given careful consideration to those points of view because inclusion of segment information in financial statements is an important question to be resolved in this project. The Board does not agree that segment information of the type required to be reported by this Statement is too analytical or interpretive to be properly classified as accounting information. The information called for by this Statement is a rearrangement (that is, a disaggregation) of information included in an enterprise's consolidated financial statements, as is the information required in the statement of changes in financial position a rearrangement of information reported in or underlying the balance sheet and income statement. Thus, in the Board's judgment, this Statement does not go beyond or enlarge the boundaries of accounting, as some have contended.

65. As to the question of verifiability, the Board recognizes that disaggregated information is subject to certain limitations and that some of it may not be susceptible to the *same degree* of verifiability as some of the consolidated information. The Board believes, however, that the more critical question to be addressed is whether the disaggregated information is *sufficiently* verifiable to warrant its inclusion in an enterprise's financial statements.

66. Verifiability is identified in *APB Statement No. 4,* "Basic Concepts and Accounting Principles Underlying Financial Statements of Business Enterprises," as one of the qualitative objectives of financial accounting. Paragraph 90 of that Statement says:

> Verifiable financial accounting information provides results that would be substantially duplicated by independent measures using the same measurement methods.

That paragraph further states:

> Measurements cannot be completely free from subjective opinions and judgments. The process of measuring and presenting information must use human agents and human reasoning and therefore is not founded solely on an "objective reality." Nevertheless, the usefulness of information is enhanced if it is verifiable, that is, if the attribute or attributes selected for measurement and the measurement methods used provide results that can be corroborated by independent measures.

67. Other qualitative objectives set forth in paragraphs 87-93 of *APB Statement No. 4* are relevance (described as "the primary qualitative objective"), understandability, neutrality, timeliness, and comparability. Paragraph 94 sets forth a final qualitative objective, completeness: "Complete financial accounting information includes all financial accounting data that reasonably fulfill the requirements of the other qualitative objectives." Paragraph 94 goes on to say that the qualitative objectives are not absolute but, rather, must be met "in reasonable degree." That is, an appropriate balance must be maintained among the objectives. For example, some degree of verifiability might have to be sacrificed to improve the relevance of information included in financial statements. In the Board's judgment, the information required to be reported by this Statement meets the objective of verifiability in reasonable degree and is useful for analyzing and understanding an enterprise's financial statements. Moreover, consistency from period to period in the methods by which an enterprise's segment information is prepared and presented is as important as consistency in the application of the accounting principles used in preparing the enterprise's consolidated financial statements. Consistency is a quality that is comprehended by the objective of comparability and is an important aspect of segment reporting that does lend itself to objective verification. For those reasons, the Board concluded that the information required to be reported by this Statement shall be included as an integral part of an enterprise's financial statements.

68. Some respondents contended that the costs of compiling and processing the type of information called for by this Statement would be overly burdensome to many enterprises, particularly those that are relatively small or whose securities are not publicly traded. Many enterprises, however, already accumulate information similar to the type required to be reported by this Statement for various purposes, such as inclusion in filings with the SEC or internal planning and control. Those enterprises will be able to provide the information required to be reported by this Statement by using existing records.

69. To lessen the information processing costs to enterprises, the Board has modified the proposal in

the Exposure Draft that an enterprise's industry segments be determined by grouping its products and services by industry lines on a *worldwide* basis. Some respondents to the Exposure Draft felt that disaggregation of *foreign* operations was an especially burdensome requirement. Accordingly, this Statement does not require an enterprise to disaggregate its foreign operations to the extent that it is impracticable to do so (see paragraph 14).

70. In the Exposure Draft, the Board proposed that any requirement to include segment information in financial statements be applicable to all enterprises regardless of their size or whether their securities are publicly traded. The Board continues to believe that there are no fundamental differences in the types of decisions and the decision-making processes of those who use the financial statements of smaller or privately held enterprises. Many small or privately held enterprises operate in more than one industry or country or rely significantly on a single or a few major customers or export sales. Information of the type required to be disclosed by this Statement is as important to users of the financial statements of those enterprises as it is to users of the financial statements of larger or publicly held enterprises. Accordingly, this Statement applies to all enterprises, regardless of their size or whether their securities are publicly traded. In reaching that conclusion, the Board neither rejects nor accepts the recommendations of the AICPA Committee on Generally Accepted Accounting Principles for Smaller and/or Closely Held Businesses, in its August 1976 report.

71. Several respondents cited harm to an enterprise's competitive position as a basis for opposing disclosures about industry segments such as this Statement requires. However, the required disclosures about an industry segment are no more detailed or specific than the disclosures typically provided by an enterprise that operates in a single industry. The information required to be reported is intended primarily to permit users to make a better assessment of the past performance and future prospects of an enterprise operating in more than one industry. In the Board's judgment, the information specified by this Statement is useful in making that assessment and, therefore, the information should be required.

72. Some respondents recommended that the disclosure requirement of this Statement should apply only to annual financial statements and not to any interim financial statements. They said that an interim reporting requirement would be unnecessarily burdensome for many enterprises, particularly those enterprises not heretofore reporting any information of the type required by this Statement. Also, some said that for many enterprises, seasonal fluctuations could cause significant changes from quarter to quarter in the composition of an enterprise's significant industry segments, diminishing the interperiod comparability of segment information. On the other hand, some respondents took the position that segment information should be included in all interim reports, including those that present only condensed financial statements or selected financial data and that do not purport to present financial position, results of operations, and changes in financial position in conformity with generally accepted accounting principles. Those respondents contended that segment information is needed on a more timely basis than annually and that the difficulties of preparing it on an interim basis can be overcome.

73. After considering both views, the Board has concluded that segment information should not be required in interim financial statements or interim financial reports unless they are *expressly described* as presenting financial position, results of operations, and changes in financial position in conformity with generally accepted accounting principles. When an enterprise issues for an interim period a complete set of financial statements that are *expressly described* as presenting financial position, results of operations, and changes in financial position in conformity with generally accepted accounting principles, those financial statements should include all of the disclosures required by this Statement in similar financial statements for an entire fiscal year. Users have the right to expect that financial statements so described, even though for an interim period, would contain all of the disclosures required in similarly described financial statements for an entire fiscal year.

74. A number of respondents to both the Discussion Memorandum and the Exposure Draft said that differences among enterprises in the nature of their operations and in the extent to which components of the enterprise share common facilities, equipment, materials and supplies, or labor force make unworkable the prescription of highly detailed rules and procedures that must be followed by all enterprises. Moreover, they pointed out that differences in the accounting systems of business enterprises are a practical constraint on the degree of specificity with which standards of financial accounting and reporting for disaggregated information can be established. The Board agrees, in general, with those views. In the Board's judgment, the standards set forth in this Statement are sufficiently broad that when they are applied in the context of the objective stated in paragraph 5 they will result in reporting information that is useful in analyzing and understanding the financial statements of an enterprise that operates in different industries or geographic areas or that derives significant revenue

from export sales or from a single or a few major customers.

Purpose of Segment Information

75. As stated in paragraph 5, the purpose of the information required to be disclosed by this Statement about an enterprise's operations in different industries and different areas of the world and about the extent of its reliance on export sales or major customers is to assist financial statement users in analyzing and understanding the enterprise's financial statements by permitting better assessment of the enterprise's past performance and future prospects. The standards of financial accounting and reporting set forth in paragraphs 3-40 derive from that purpose.

76. Information prepared in conformity with those standards may be of limited usefulness for comparing an industry segment of one enterprise with a similar industry segment of another enterprise (i.e., for interenterprise comparison). Interenterprise comparison of industry segments would require a fairly detailed prescription of the basis or bases of disaggregation to be followed by all enterprises, as well as specification of the basis of accounting for intersegment transfers and methods of allocating costs common to two or more segments. As explained in paragraph 74, the Board concluded that it is not appropriate to specify rules and procedures in that degree of detail. Moreover, differences in the bases of accounting for intersegment sales or transfers may also militate against comparison of a segment of an enterprise with extensive intersegment transactions with a similar but autonomous segment of another enterprise or with a unitary enterprise in the same industry.

Information Required to Be Presented

77. This Statement requires that sales to outsiders be reported separately from sales or transfers to other segments because different types of uncertainties and measurement bases affect those two sources of a reportable segment's revenue. The Exposure Draft proposed that intersegment sales or transfers be accounted for at amounts that are consistent with the objective of determining segment profitability "as realistically as practicable." A number of respondents to the Exposure Draft asked the Board whether, under the draft, intersegment sales or transfers could be accounted for at other than market price, for example, at cost. The Board has concluded that for purposes of this Statement revenue from intersegment sales or transfers shall be accounted for on whatever basis is used by the enterprise to price the intersegment sales or transfers. No single basis is prescribed or proscribed, but disclosure of the basis of accounting for intersegment sales or transfers is required.

78. The Exposure Draft proposed that two specified levels of profitability—profit or loss contribution and operating profit or loss—be presented for each reportable segment. The former was defined as revenue less only those operating expenses that were directly traceable to the segment, and the latter was defined (as it is in paragraph 10(d) of this Statement) as revenue less all operating expenses including those allocated to segments on a reasonable basis as well as those that are directly traceable. This Statement, however, requires presentation of only operating profit or loss for reportable segments. In the Exposure Draft, the Board stated that "presenting profitability both before and after allocation of common costs and expenses highlights the extent to which the computation of operating profit or loss is affected by allocations." Although most respondents to the Exposure Draft did not disagree with the requirement that operating profit or loss be disclosed for individual reportable segments, many made the point that it is not practicable to distinguish between those operating expenses that may be said to be *directly traceable* to a segment and those that may be said only to be *allocable*. Some respondents pointed out that traceability often depends on the sophistication of an enterprise's internal recordkeeping system. They noted that traceability depends on the degree to which management of an enterprise's operations is decentralized. Some said that location of incurrence should not govern the attribution of a cost to a particular segment. In view of the problems cited by those who responded to the Exposure Draft, the Board has judged that disclosure of profit or loss contribution should not be required, although this Statement does not proscribe that disclosure if an enterprise wishes to include it.

79. The Board continues to believe that certain items of revenue and expense either do not relate to segments or cannot *always* be allocated to segments on the basis of objective evidence, and for that reason this Statement does not require that net income be disclosed for reportable segments. Those items are revenue earned at the corporate level and not derived from operations of any industry segment, general corporate expenses, interest expense, domestic and foreign income taxes, and equity in income or loss from unconsolidated subsidiaries and other unconsolidated investees. The Board also has not required that the following (which are normally reported net of income taxes) be allocated: extraordinary items, gain or loss on discontinued operations, minority interest, and the cumulative effect of a change in accounting principle. However, paragraph 25 permits additional disclosure of some other measure of profitability for some or all of an enterprise's reportable segments in addition to operating profit or loss, with appropriate disclosure of the nature and amount of each type of item allocated to segments and the method of allocation.

80. Disclosure of identifiable assets is required, as proposed in the Exposure Draft, to allow financial statement users to assess the relative investment commitment in an enterprise's various segments and to assess the results obtained by the various segments in relation to the investment committed. Some respondents to the Exposure Draft stated that the definition of a segment's identifiable assets as proposed in the Exposure Draft was inconsistent with the proposed definition of a segment's operating profit or loss. They indicated that although allocation of all operating expenses common to two or more segments was required to compute operating profit or loss, allocation of all assets used jointly by two or more segments was not required. In response to that view, the definition of identifiable assets in paragraph 10(e) of this Statement requires that a portion of assets used jointly by two or more industry segments be allocated among the industry segments on a reasonable basis.

81. To provide information useful in understanding the operating profit or loss and the identifiable assets of an industry segment, paragraph 27 requires disclosure of the aggregate amount of each reportable segment's depreciation, depletion, and amortization and of each reportable segment's capital expenditures. The Exposure Draft had identified certain additional disclosures that "may be important" in certain circumstances, including property, plant, and equipment and related accumulated depreciation, receivables and inventories, loans, deposits, or other monetary amounts, and research and development costs. A number of respondents to the Exposure Draft recommended that the final Statement not identify those disclosures as possibly "important" unless the circumstances were clearly specified. Some said the disclosures were overly detailed and would be of questionable benefit in many cases. The Board found those arguments persuasive and decided to delete them in the final Statement. As stated in paragraph 22, presentation of additional information beyond that required to be reported by this Statement may be considered to be desirable, and this Statement does not preclude those additional disclosures.

82. The Exposure Draft proposed that operating profit or loss and identifiable assets of an industry segment or geographic area of consolidated operations include, respectively, the income from and the investment in unconsolidated investees operating in the same industry or the same geographic area. Some respondents stated that, due to the complexity of many enterprises' unconsolidated operations, information called for by the Exposure Draft (i.e., operating profit or loss and identifiable assets) may not be available for some of those investees, especially for those investees in which the enterprise has less than a 50 percent ownership. Other respondents considered it inappropriate to combine the after-tax net income from the unconsolidated investees with operating profit of the consolidated operations. They also considered it inappropriate to combine the investment in the net assets of unconsolidated investees with identifiable assets of the consolidated operations. Such combinations, in their view, would distort the operating results and financial ratios for the industry segments and geographic areas and thereby make the reported information less useful in some cases and misleading in others. The Board found merit in those arguments and accordingly eliminated the requirement. The Board continues to believe, however, that if the operations of an unconsolidated investee are closely related with those of a reportable segment, information about the segment would be incomplete and therefore subject to possible misinterpretation without information about the relationship. For that reason, the Board concluded that disclosure should be made for each reportable segment of the enterprise's equity in the net income from and investment in the net assets of unconsolidated subsidiaries and other equity method investees whose operations are vertically integrated with the operations of that segment.[17] The Board further concluded that disclosure should also be made of the geographic areas in which those vertically integrated equity method investees operate.

Information about Foreign Operations and Export Sales

83. Several respondents to the Exposure Draft indicated that for their particular industries the distinction between domestic and foreign operations was very difficult to make and requested that the Board develop guidelines and allow judgment in determining the distinction between the two. The Board's intention had been to allow judgment and that intention is made explicit and guidelines are furnished in paragraph 31 and footnote 12 of this Statement.

84. With respect to reporting information about an enterprise's operations in different geographic areas, some respondents to the Exposure Draft requested that the Board clarify or elaborate on a number of matters, including (a) whether the Statement would require disclosure of information on an individual country-by-country basis and (b) how should significance be determined for an enterprise's foreign operations in the aggregate or in any geographic area. The Board's conclusion on each of those matters is clarified or elaborated on in paragraphs 32 and 33 of this Statement.

[17]If the operations of two or more equity method investees are vertically integrated with a reportable segment, the amounts required to be disclosed may be combined respectively.

85. The Board recognized in the Exposure Draft and in this Statement that the variety of ways in which foreign operations are conducted made it impossible to define appropriate geographic areas for all enterprises. Therefore, only general guidelines for that determination are set forth in paragraph 34 of this Statement. For those enterprises conducting foreign operations in two or more geographic areas, the Board considered several methods of associating foreign revenue, a measure of profitability, and identifiable assets with a particular geographic area. Those methods include associating this information with geographic areas in terms of the location of the accounting records, the location of the assets, the location of the risks associated with the assets and liabilities, and the location of the customers. However, the Board concluded that none of those methods would necessarily correlate the profitability and identifiable assets of a geographic area in a manner consistent with the objective expressed in paragraph 31. The Board believes that the description of geographic areas of foreign operations in paragraph 34 is sufficiently broad to permit management to accomplish that objective by determining the scope of its operations in each area and then identifying (i) the revenue generated from those operations, (ii) the assets employed in or associated with generating those revenues, and (iii) the costs and expenses related to those revenues and assets. The Board believes that disclosing a measure of assets or assets and liabilities that can be related to a measure of profitability for each significant geographic area will provide users of financial statements with useful financial information about an enterprise's foreign operations consistent with the purpose set forth in paragraph 5.

86. Some respondents to the Exposure Draft recommended that the Statement not require disclosure of operating profit or loss for each geographic area of an enterprise's operations if it is determined instead to present a level of profitability below operating profit or loss. They said that in many cases an after-tax profitability measure is more informative than a pretax measure and that because of significant differences in income tax rates among different geographic areas a pretax measure could at times be misinterpreted. They also said that many enterprises can more easily determine net income or another measure of profitability below operating profit or loss by geographic area than by industry segment. The Board found those arguments convincing, and paragraph 35(b) requires presentation of operating profit or loss, or net income, or some other measure of profitability between operating profit or loss and net income.

87. The Board considered whether this Statement should supersede any part of *ARB No. 43,* Chapter 12, "Foreign Operations and Foreign Exchange," especially paragraph 9 thereof. Since paragraph 9 of Chapter 12 deals with consolidation of foreign subsidiaries which is a subject beyond the scope of this Statement, the Board concluded that it should not be superseded. However, this Statement provides definitions and guidelines that may also be useful in applying that Bulletin.

88. The Board has determined that disclosure of working capital and property, plant, and equipment and related accumulated depreciation should not be required by geographic area. Those disclosures had been proposed in the Exposure Draft, but a number of respondents said, and the Board agreed, that the volume of detail that would be required would be excessive. However, as noted in paragraph 87, this Statement does not supersede the requirements of paragraph 9, Chapter 12, *ARB No. 43,* for certain disclosures with respect to the assets and liabilities of foreign subsidiaries.

89. A number of respondents to the Exposure Draft requested that the Board provide guidance as to when export sales should be considered significant, and paragraph 36 of this Statement provides a test of significance. The Board also was asked to clarify certain matters with respect to the disclosures about major customers, including a guideline as to significance and an elaboration on the type of information required to be presented. Paragraph 39 of this Statement reflects the appropriate revisions. Because many respondents argued that identification of the major customer could be competitively harmful to either the enterprise or the customer, the proposal for disclosure of the name of the customer has been dropped.

Effective Date and Transition

90. On considering all circumstances, the Board determined that prospective application of the standards set forth in this Statement effective for periods beginning after December 15, 1976 as stated in paragraph 41, is appropriate because enterprises may not have accumulated in prior years all of the information required to be disclosed by this Statement; the Board also determined that the effective date is advisable in the circumstances.

Appendix C

STANDARD INDUSTRIAL CLASSIFICATIONS

91. As indicated in paragraph 12, the Board has examined several systems that have been developed for classifying business activities, such as the Standard Industrial Classification and the Enterprise Standard Industrial Classification systems and has

judged that none is, by itself, suitable to determine industry segments as that term is used in this Statement. Nonetheless, those systems may provide guidance for the exercise of the judgment required to group an enterprise's products and services by industry lines.

92. As set forth in the *Standard Industrial Classification Manual* prepared by the Statistical Policy Division of the U.S. Office of Management and Budget, SIC is a system for classifying business establishments (generally, individual plants, stores, banks, etc.) by the type of economic activity in which they are engaged. An establishment is not necessarily identical with a business enterprise, which may consist of one or more establishments.

93. The 649-page manual contains one-digit, two-digit, three-digit, and four-digit SIC industry codes, each of which is described in detail. At the one-digit level, the SIC classifies business activities into 11 divisions:

A Agriculture, forestry, and fishing.
B Mining.
C Construction.
D Manufacturing.
E Transportation, communications, electric, gas, and sanitary services.
F Wholesale trade.
G Retail trade.
H Finance, insurance, and real estate.
I Services.
J Public administration.
K Nonclassifiable establishments.

94. Each of those divisions is subdivided into two-digit major groups. There is a total of 84 two-digit groups. For example, the 20 major groups in manufacturing are:

1. Food and kindred products.
2. Tobacco manufacturers.
3. Textile mill products.
4. Apparel and other finished products made from fabrics and similar materials.
5. Lumber and wood products, except furniture.
6. Furniture and fixtures.
7. Paper and allied products.
8. Printing, publishing, and allied products.
9. Chemicals and allied products.
10. Petroleum refining and related industries.
11. Rubber and miscellaneous plastics products.
12. Leather and leather products.
13. Stone, clay, glass, and concrete products.
14. Primary metal industries.
15. Fabricated metal products, except machinery and transportation equipment.
16. Machinery, except electrical.
17. Electrical and electronic machinery, equipment, and supplies.
18. Transportation equipment.
19. Measuring, analyzing, and controlling instruments; photographic, medical, and optical goods; watches and clocks.
20. Miscellaneous manufacturing industries.

95. Each of the two-digit SIC major groups, in turn, is further subdivided into three-digit industry groups. There are 421 three-digit industry groups. For example, the "machinery, except electrical" group includes the following industry groups:

1. Engines and turbines.
2. Farm and garden machinery and equipment.
3. Construction, mining, and materials handling machinery and equipment.
4. Metalworking machinery and equipment.
5. Special industry machinery, except metalworking machinery.
6. General industry machinery and equipment.
7. Office, computing, and accounting machines.
8. Refrigeration and service industry machinery.
9. Miscellaneous machinery, except electrical.

96. The three-digit SIC industry groups are still further subdivided by product lines into over 1,000 narrower four-digit industry groups. Metalworking machinery and equipment (a three-digit industry group), for example, is divided into metal cutting machine tools, metal forming machine tools, power driven hand tools, rolling mill machinery and equipment, and so on.

97. The *Standard Industrial Classification Manual* is revised periodically, most recently in 1972. It is available for sale by the Superintendent of Documents, U.S. Government Printing Office.

98. The *Enterprise Standard Industrial Classification Manual,* like the *SIC Manual,* is prepared by the Statistical Policy Division of the U.S. Office of Management and Budget. It classifies enterprises (companies, firms, partnerships, etc.) rather than establishments (plants, stores, banks, etc.). The structure of ESIC follows closely the structure of the SIC codes. It includes eight classes of enterprises at the one-digit level, 67 at the two-digit level, 216 at the three-digit level, and 252 at the four-digit level.

Appendix D

FACTORS TO BE CONSIDERED IN DETERMINING INDUSTRY SEGMENTS

99. This Appendix identifies a number of factors to be considered in grouping products and services by

industry lines into industry segments. As indicated in paragraph 12, although certain characteristics can be identified that assist in differentiating among industries, no single set of characteristics is universally applicable to determine the industry segments of all business enterprises. Nor is any single characteristic determinative in all cases.

100. Among the factors that should be considered in determining whether products and services are related (and, therefore, should be grouped into a single industry segment) or unrelated (and, therefore, should be separated into two or more industry segments) are the following:

a. *The nature of the product.* Related products or services have similar purposes or end uses. Thus, they may be expected to have similar rates of profitability, similar degrees of risk, and similar opportunities for growth.
b. *The nature of the production process.* Sharing of common or interchangeable production or sales facilities, equipment, labor force, or service group or use of the same or similar basic raw materials may suggest that products or services are related. Likewise, similar degrees of labor intensiveness or similar degrees of capital intensiveness may indicate a relationship among products or services.
c. *Markets and marketing methods.* Similarity of geographic marketing areas, types of customers, or marketing methods may indicate a relationship among products or services. For instance, the use of a common or interchangeable sales force may suggest a relationship among products or services. The sensitivity of the market to price changes and to changes in general economic conditions may also indicate whether products or services are related or unrelated.

101. Broad categories such as *manufacturing, wholesaling, retailing,* and *consumer products* are not per se indicative of the industries in which an enterprise operates, and those terms should not be used without identification of a product or service to describe an enterprise's industry segments.

Appendix E

ILLUSTRATION OF APPLYING PARAGRAPH 15(b)

102. Under paragraph 15(b), an industry segment is to be regarded as significant if the absolute amount of its operating profit or operating loss is 10 percent or more of the greater, in absolute amount, of:

(i) The combined operating profit of all industry segments that did not incur an operating loss, or

(ii) The combined operating loss of all industry segments that did incur an operating loss.

103. To illustrate how that paragraph is applied, assume that an enterprise has seven industry segments some of which incurred operating losses, as follows:

Industry Segment	Operating Profit or (Operating Loss)	
A	$ 100	
B	500	$1,000
C	400	
D	(295)	
E	(600)	(1,100)
F	(100)	
G	(105)	
	$(100)	

104. The combined operating profit of all industry segments that did not incur a loss (A, B, and C) is $1,000. The absolute amount of the combined operating loss of those segments that did incur a loss (D, E, F, and G) is $1,100. Under paragraph 15(b), therefore, Industry Segments B, C, D, and E are significant because the absolute amount of their individual operating profit or operating loss equals or exceeds $110 (10 percent of $1,100). Additional industry segments might, of course, also be deemed significant under the revenue and identifiable assets tests in paragraphs 15(a) and 15(c).

Appendix F

ILLUSTRATIONS OF FINANCIAL STATEMENT DISCLOSURES

105. This Appendix contains examples of disclosures of the type that this Statement requires to be included in the financial statements of an enterprise. The illustrations do not encompass all possible circumstances, nor do the formats used indicate a particular preference of the Board.

106. Exhibit A presents the consolidated income statement of a hypothetical company for the year ended December 31, 1977. Exhibit B illustrates how the company might present information about its operations in different industries and its reliance on major customers. Exhibit C illustrates how the company might present information about its foreign operations in different geographic areas and its export sales.

EXHIBIT A

X Company
Consolidated Income Statement
Year ended December 31, 1977

Sales		$4,700
Cost of sales	$3,000	
Selling, general, and administrative expense	700	
Interest expense	200	3,900
		800
Equity in net income of Z Co. (25% owned)		100
Income from continuing operations before income taxes		900
Income taxes		400
Income from continuing operations		500
Discontinued operations:		
Loss from operations of discontinued West Coast division (net of income tax effect of $50)	70	
Loss on disposal of West Coast division (net of income tax effect of $100)	130	200
Income before extraordinary gain and before cumulative effect of change in accounting principle		300
Extraordinary gain (net of income tax effect of $80)		90
Cumulative effect on prior years of change from straight-line to accelerated depreciation (net of income tax effect of $60)		(60)
Net income		$ 330

EXHIBIT B

X Company
Information about the Company's Operations in Different Industries
Year ended December 31, 1977

	Industry A	Industry B	Industry C	Other Industries	Adjustments and Eliminations	Consolidated
Sales to unaffiliated customers	$1,000	$2,000	$1,500	$ 200		$ 4,700
Intersegment sales	200		500		$(700)	
Total revenue	$1,200	$2,000	$2,000	$ 200	$(700)	$ 4,700
Operating profit	$ 200	$ 290	$ 600	$ 50	$ (40)	$ 1,100
Equity in net income of Z Co.						100
General corporate expenses						(100)
Interest expense						(200)
Income from continuing operations before income taxes						$ 900
Identifiable assets at December 31, 1977	$2,000	$4,050	$6,000	$1,000	$ (50)	$13,000
Investment in net assets of Z Co.						400
Corporate assets						1,600
Total assets at December 31, 1977						$15,000

See accompanying note.

Note

The Company operates principally in three industries, A, B, and C. Operations in Industry A involve production and sale of (describe types of products and services). Operations in Industry B involve production and sale of (describe types of products and services). Operations in Industry C involve production and sale of (describe types of products and services). Total revenue by industry includes both sales to unaffiliated customers, as reported in the Company's consolidated income statement, and intersegment sales, which are accounted for by (describe the basis of accounting for intersegment sales).

Operating profit is total revenue less operating expenses. In computing operating profit, none of the following items has been added or deducted: general corporate expenses, interest expense, income taxes, equity in income from unconsolidated investee, loss from discontinued operations of the West Coast division (which was a part of the Company's operations in Industry B), extraordinary gain (which relates to the Company's operations in Industry A), and the cumulative effect of the change from straight-line to accelerated depreciation (of which $30 relates to the Company's operations in Industry A, $10 to Industry B, and $20 to Industry C). Depreciation for Industries A, B, and C, respectively, was $80, $100, and $150. Capital expenditures for the three industries were $100, $200, and $400, respectively.

The effect of the change from straight-line to accelerated depreciation was to reduce the 1977 operating profit of Industries A, B, and C, respectively, by $40, $30, and $20.

Identifiable assets by industry are those assets that are used in the Company's operations in each industry. Corporate assets are principally cash and marketable securities.

The Company has a 25 percent interest in Z Co., whose operations are in the United States and are vertically integrated with the Company's operations in Industry A. Equity in net income of Z Co. was $100; investment in net assets of Z Co. was $400.

To reconcile industry information with consolidated amounts, the following eliminations have been made; $700 of intersegment sales; $40 relating to the net change in intersegment operating profit in beginning and ending inventories; and $50 intersegment operating profit in inventory at December 31, 1977.

Contracts with a U.S. government agency account for $1,100 of the sales to unaffiliated customers of Industry B.

EXHIBIT C

X Company
Information about the Company's Operations in Different Geographic Areas
Year ended December 31, 1977

	United States	Geographic Area A	Geographic Area B	Adjustments and Eliminations	Consolidated
Sales to unaffiliated customers	$3,000	$1,000	$ 700		$ 4,700
Transfers between geographic areas	1,000			$(1,000)	
Total revenue	$4,000	$1,000	$ 700	$(1,000)	$ 4,700
Operating profit	$ 800	$ 400	$ 100	$ (200)	$ 1,100
Equity in net income of Z Co.					100
General corporate expenses					(100)
Interest expense					(200)
Income from continuing operations before income taxes					$ 900
Identifiable assets at December 31, 1977	$7,300	$3,400	$2,450	$ (150)	$13,000
Investment in net assets of Z Co.					400
Corporate assets					1,600
Total assets at December 31, 1977					$15,000

See accompanying note.

Note

Transfers between geographic areas are accounted for by (describe the basis of accounting for such transfers). Operating profit is total revenue less operating expenses. In computing operating profit, none of the following items has been added or deducted: general corporate expenses, interest expense, income taxes, equity in income from unconsolidated investee, loss from discontinued operations of West Coast division (which was part of the Company's U.S. operations), extraordinary gain (which relates to the Company's operations in Geographic Area B), and the cumulative effect of the change from straight-line to accelerated depreciation (which relates entirely to the Company's operations in the United States).

Identifiable assets are those assets of the Company that are identified with the operations in each geographic area. Corporate assets are principally cash and marketable securities.

Of the $3,000 U.S. sales to unaffiliated customers, $1,200 were export sales, principally to Geographic Area C.

Statement of Financial Accounting Standards No. 15 Accounting by Debtors and Creditors for Troubled Debt Restructurings

STATUS

Issued: June 1977

Effective Date: For troubled debt restructurings consummated after December 31, 1977

Affects: Amends APB 26, paragraphs 2 and 3(a)
Supersedes FIN 2

Affected by: Paragraph 9 superseded by FAS 71

Statement of Financial Accounting Standards No. 15
Accounting by Debtors and Creditors for Troubled Debt Restructurings

CONTENTS

INTRODUCTION

1. This Statement establishes standards of financial accounting and reporting by the debtor and by the creditor for a troubled debt restructuring. The Statement does not cover accounting for allowances for estimated uncollectible amounts and does not prescribe or proscribe particular methods for estimating amounts of uncollectible receivables.

2. A restructuring of a debt constitutes a *troubled debt restructuring* for purposes of this Statement if the creditor for economic or legal reasons related to the debtor's financial difficulties grants a concession to the debtor that it would not otherwise consider. That concession either stems from an agreement between the creditor and the debtor or is imposed by law or a court. For example, a creditor may restructure the terms of a debt to alleviate the burden of the debtor's near-term cash requirements, and many troubled debt restructurings involve modifying terms to reduce or defer cash payments required of the debtor in the near future to help the debtor attempt to improve its financial condition and eventually be able to pay the creditor. Or, for example, the creditor may accept cash, other assets, or an equity interest in the debtor in satisfaction of the debt though the value received is less than the amount of the debt because the creditor concludes that step will maximize recovery of its investment.[1]

3. Whatever the form of concession granted by the creditor to the debtor in a troubled debt restructuring, the creditor's objective is to make the best of a difficult situation. That is, the creditor expects to obtain more cash or other value from the debtor, or to increase the probability of receipt, by granting the concession than by not granting it.

4. In this Statement, a *receivable* or *payable* (collectively referred to as *debt*) represents a contractual right to receive money or a contractual obligation to pay money on demand or on fixed or determinable dates that is already included as an asset or liability in the creditor's or debtor's balance sheet at the time of the restructuring. Receivables or payables that may be involved in troubled debt restructurings commonly result from lending or borrowing of cash, investing in debt securities that were previously issued, or selling or purchasing goods or services on credit. Examples are accounts receivable or payable, notes, debentures and bonds (whether those receivables or payables are secured or unsecured and whether they are convertible or nonconvertible), and related accrued interest, if any. Typically, each receivable or payable is negotiated separately, but

[1]Although troubled debt that is fully satisfied by foreclosure, repossession, or other transfer of assets or by grant of equity securities by the debtor is, in a technical sense, not restructured, that kind of event is included in the term *troubled debt restructuring* in this Statement.

sometimes two or more receivables or payables are negotiated together. For example, a debtor may negotiate with a group of creditors but sign separate debt instruments with each creditor. For purposes of this Statement, restructuring of each receivable or payable, including those negotiated and restructured jointly, shall be accounted for individually. The substance rather than the form of the receivable or payable shall govern. For example, to a debtor, a bond constitutes one payable even though there are many bondholders.

5. A troubled debt restructuring may include, but is not necessarily limited to, one or a combination of the following:

a. Transfer from the debtor to the creditor of receivables from third parties, real estate, or other assets to satisfy fully or partially a debt (including a transfer resulting from foreclosure or repossession).
b. Issuance or other granting of an equity interest to the creditor by the debtor to satisfy fully or partially a debt unless the equity interest is granted pursuant to existing terms for converting the debt into an equity interest.
c. Modification of terms of a debt, such as one or a combination of:
    1. Reduction (absolute or contingent) of the stated interest rate for the remaining original life of the debt.
    2. Extension of the maturity date or dates at a stated interest rate lower than the current market rate for new debt with similar risk.
    3. Reduction (absolute or contingent) of the face amount or maturity amount of the debt as stated in the instrument or other agreement.
    4. Reduction (absolute or contingent) of accrued interest.

6. Troubled debt restructurings may occur before, at, or after the stated maturity of debt, and time may elapse between the agreement, court order, etc. and the transfer of assets or equity interest, the effective date of new terms, or the occurrence of another event that constitutes consummation of the restructuring. The date of consummation is the *time of the restructuring* in this Statement.

7. A debt restructuring is not necessarily a troubled debt restructuring for purposes of this Statement even if the debtor is experiencing some financial difficulties. For example, a troubled debt restructuring is not involved if (a) the fair value[2] of cash, other assets, or an equity interest accepted by a creditor from a debtor in full satisfaction of its receivable at least equals the creditor's recorded investment in the receivable;[3] (b) the fair value of cash, other assets, or an equity interest transferred by a debtor to a creditor in full settlement of its payable at least equals the debtor's carrying amount of the payable; (c) the creditor reduces the effective interest rate on the debt primarily to reflect a decrease in market interest rates in general or a decrease in the risk so as to maintain a relationship with a debtor that can readily obtain funds from other sources at the current market interest rate; or (d) the debtor issues in exchange for its debt new marketable debt having an effective interest rate based on its market price that is at or near the current market interest rates of debt with similar maturity dates and stated interest rates issued by nontroubled debtors. In general, a debtor that can obtain funds from sources other than the existing creditor at market interest rates at or near those for nontroubled debt is not involved in a troubled debt restructuring. A debtor in a troubled debt restructuring can obtain funds from sources other than the existing creditor in the troubled debt restructuring, if at all, only at effective interest rates (based on market prices) so high that it cannot afford to pay them. Thus, in an attempt to protect as much of its investment as possible, the creditor in a troubled debt restructuring grants a concession to the debtor that it would not otherwise consider.

8. For purposes of this Statement, troubled debt restructurings do not include changes in lease agreements (the accounting is prescribed by *FASB Statement No. 13,* "Accounting for Leases") or employment-related agreements (for example, pension plans and deferred compensation contracts). Nor do troubled debt restructurings include debtors' failures to pay trade accounts according to their terms or creditors' delays in taking legal action to collect overdue amounts of interest and principal, unless thay involve an agreement between debtor and creditor to restructure.

9. The Addendum to *APB Opinion No. 2,* "Accounting for the 'Investment Credit'," states that "differences may arise in the application of generally accepted accounting principles as between regulated and nonregulated businesses, because of the effect in regulated businesses of the rate-making process" and discusses the application of generally accepted accounting principles to regulated industries. FASB Statements and Interpretations should therefore be applied to regulated companies that are subject to the rate-making process in accordance with the provisions of the Addendum.

10. This Statement supersedes *FASB Interpretation No. 2,* "Imputing Interest on Debt Arrangements Made under the Federal Bankruptcy Act," and shall

[2]Defined in paragraph 13.

[3]Defined in footnote 17.

be applied to the types of situations that were covered by that Interpretation. Thus, it shall be applied to troubled debt restructurings consummated under reorganization, arrangement, or other provisions of the Federal Bankruptcy Act or other Federal statutes related thereto.[4] It also amends *APB Opinion No. 26,* "Early Extinguishment of Debt," to the extent needed to exclude from that Opinion's scope early extinguishments of debt through troubled debt restructurings.

11. Appendix A provides background information. Appendix B sets forth the basis for the Board's conclusions, including alternatives considered and reasons for accepting some and rejecting others.

STANDARDS OF FINANCIAL ACCOUNTING AND REPORTING

Accounting by Debtors

12. A debtor shall account for a troubled debt restructuring according to the type of the restructuring as prescribed in the following paragraphs.

Transfer of Assets in Full Settlement

13. A debtor that transfers its receivables from third parties, real estate, or other assets to a creditor to settle fully a payable shall recognize a gain on restructuring of payables (see paragraph 21). The gain shall be measured by the excess of (i) the carrying amount of the payable settled (the face amount increased or decreased by applicable accrued interest and applicable unamortized premium, discount, finance charges, or issue costs) over (ii) the fair value of the assets transferred to the creditor.[5] The fair value of the assets transferred is the amount that the debtor could reasonably expect to receive for them in a current sale between a willing buyer and a willing seller, that is, other than in a forced or liquidation sale. Fair value of assets shall be measured by their market value if an active market for them exists. If no active market exists for the assets transferred but exists for similar assets, the selling prices in that market may be helpful in estimating the fair value of the assets transferred. If no market price is available, a forecast of expected cash flows may aid in estimating the fair value of assets transferred, provided the expected cash flows are discounted at a rate commensurate with the risk involved.[6]

14. A difference between the fair value and the carrying amount of assets transferred to a creditor to settle a payable is a gain or loss on transfer of assets.[7] The debtor shall include that gain or loss in measuring net income for the period of transfer, reported as provided in *APB Opinion No. 30,* "Reporting the Results of Operations."

Grant of Equity Interest in Full Settlement

15. A debtor that issues or otherwise grants an equity interest to a creditor to settle fully a payable shall account for the equity interest at its fair value.[8] The difference between the fair value of the equity interest granted and the carrying amount of the payable settled shall be recognized as a gain on restructuring of payables (see paragraph 21).

Modification of Terms

16. A debtor in a troubled debt restructuring involving only modification of terms of a payable—that is, not involving a transfer of assets or grant of an equity interest—shall account for the effects of the restructuring prospectively from the time of restructuring, and shall not change the carrying amount of the payable at the time of the restructuring unless the carrying amount exceeds the total

---

[4]This Statement does not apply, however, if under provisions of those Federal statutes or in a quasi-reorganization or corporate readjustment (*ARB No. 43,* Chapter 7, Section A, "Quasi-Reorganization or Corporate Readjustment . . .") with which a troubled debt restructuring coincides, the debtor restates its liabilities generally.

[5]Paragraphs 13, 15, and 19 indicate that the fair value of assets transferred or the fair value of an equity interest granted shall be used in accounting for a settlement of a payable in a troubled debt restructuring. That guidance is not intended to preclude using the fair value of the payable settled if more clearly evident than the fair value of the assets transferred or of the equity interest granted in a full settlement of a payable (paragraphs 13 and 15). (See paragraph 67 of *APB Opinion No. 16,* "Business Combinations.") However, in a partial settlement of a payable (paragraph 19), the fair value of the assets transferred or of the equity interest granted shall be used in all cases to avoid the need to allocate the fair value of the payable between the part settled and the part still outstanding.

[6]Some factors that may be relevant in estimating the fair value of various kinds of assets are described in paragraphs 88 and 89 of *APB Opinion No. 16,* paragraphs 12-14 of *APB Opinion No. 21,* "Interest on Receivables and Payables," and paragraph 25 of *APB Opinion No. 29,* "Accounting for Nonmonetary Transactions."

[7]The carrying amount of a receivable encompasses not only unamortized premium, discount, acquisition costs, and the like but also an allowance for uncollectible amounts and other "valuation" accounts, if any. A loss on transferring receivables to creditors may therefore have been wholly or partially recognized in measuring net income before the transfer and be wholly or partly a reduction of a valuation account rather than a gain or loss in measuring net income for the period of the transfer.

[8]See footnote 5.

future cash payments specified by the new terms.[9] That is, the effects of changes in the amounts or timing (or both) of future cash payments designated as either interest or face amount shall be reflected in future periods.[10] Interest expense shall be computed in a way that a constant effective interest rate is applied to the carrying amount of the payable at the beginning of each period between restructuring and maturity (in substance the "interest" method prescribed by paragraph 15 of *APB Opinion No. 21*). The new effective interest rate shall be the discount rate that equates the present value of the future cash payments specified by the new terms (excluding amounts contingently payable) with the carrying amount of the payable.

17. If, however, the total future cash payments specified by the new terms of a payable, including both payments designated as interest and those designated as face amount, are less than the carrying amount of the payable, the debtor shall reduce the carrying amount to an amount equal to the total future cash payments specified by the new terms and shall recognize a gain on restructuring of payables equal to the amount of the reduction (see paragraph 21).[11] Thereafter, all cash payments under the terms of the payable shall be accounted for as reductions of the carrying amount of the payable, and no interest expense shall be recognized on the payable for any period between the restructuring and maturity of the payable.[12]

18. A debtor shall not recognize a gain on a restructured payable involving indeterminate future cash payments as long as the maximum total future cash payments may exceed the carrying amount of the payable. Amounts designated either as interest or as face amount by the new terms may be payable contingent on a specified event or circumstance (for example, the debtor may be required to pay specified amounts if its financial condition improves to a specified degree within a specified period). To determine whether the debtor shall recognize a gain according to the provisions of paragraphs 16 and 17, those contingent amounts shall be included in the "total future cash payments specified by the new terms" to the extent necessary to prevent recognizing a gain at the time of restructuring that may be offset by future interest expense. Thus, the debtor shall apply paragraph 17 of *FASB Statement No. 5,* "Accounting for Contingencies," in which probability of occurrence of a gain contingency is not a factor, and shall assume that contingent future payments will have to be paid. The same principle applies to amounts of future cash payments that must sometimes be estimated to apply the provisions of paragraphs 16 and 17. For example, if the number of future interest payments is flexible because the face amount and accrued interest is payable on demand or becomes payable on demand, estimates of total future cash payments shall be based on the maximum number of periods possible under the restructured terms.

Combination of Types

19. A troubled debt restructuring may involve partial settlement of a payable by the debtor's transferring assets or granting an equity interest (or both) to the creditor and modification of terms of the remaining payable.[13] A debtor shall account for a troubled debt restructuring involving a partial settlement and a modification of terms as prescribed in paragraphs 16-18 except that, first, assets transferred or an equity interest granted in that partial settlement shall be measured as prescribed in paragraphs 13 and 15, respectively, and the carrying amount of the payable shall be reduced by the total fair value of those assets or equity interest.[14] A difference between the fair value and the carrying amount of assets transferred to the creditor shall be recognized as a gain or loss on transfer of assets. No gain on restructuring of payables shall be recognized unless the remaining carrying amount of the payable exceeds the total future cash payments (including amounts contingently payable) specified by the

---

[9]In this Statement, *total future cash payments* includes related accrued interest, if any, at the time of the restructuring that continues to be payable under the new terms.

[10]All or a portion of the carrying amount of the payable at the time of the restructuring may need to be reclassified in the balance sheet because of changes in the terms, for example, a change in the amount of the payable due within one year after the date of the debtor's balance sheet. A troubled debt restructuring of a short-term obligation after the date of a debtor's balance sheet but before that balance sheet is issued may affect the classification of that obligation in accordance with *FASB Statement No. 6,* "Classification of Short-Term Obligations Expected to Be Refinanced."

[11]If the carrying amount of the payable comprises several accounts (for example, face amount, accrued interest, and unamortized premium, discount, finance charges, and issue costs) that are to be continued after the restructuring, some possibly being combined, the reduction in carrying amount may need to be allocated among the remaining accounts in proportion to the previous balances. However, the debtor may choose to carry the amount designated as face amount by the new terms in a separate account and adjust another account accordingly.

[12]The only exception is to recognize interest expense according to paragraph 22.

[13]Even if the stated terms of the remaining payable, for example, the stated interest rate and the maturity date or dates, are not changed in connection with the transfer of assets or grant of an equity interest, the restructuring shall be accounted for as prescribed by paragraph 19.

[14]If cash is paid in a partial settlement of a payable in a troubled debt restructuring, the carrying amount of the payable shall be reduced by the amount of cash paid.

terms of the debt remaining unsettled after the restructuring. Future interest expense, if any, shall be determined according to the provisions of paragraphs 16-18.

Related Matters

20. A troubled debt restructuring that is in substance a repossession or foreclosure by the creditor or other transfer of assets to the creditor shall be accounted for according to the provisions of paragraphs 13, 14, and 19.

21. Gains on restructuring of payables determined by applying the provisions of paragraphs 13-20 of this Statement shall be aggregated, included in measuring net income for the period of restructuring, and, if material, classified as an extraordinary item, net of related income tax effect, in accordance with paragraph 8 of *FASB Statement No. 4,* "Reporting Gains and Losses from Extinguishment of Debt."

22. If a troubled debt restructuring involves amounts contingently payable, those contingent amounts shall be recognized as a payable and as interest expense in future periods in accordance with paragraph 8 of *FASB Statement No. 5.* Thus, in general, interest expense for contingent payments shall be recognized in each period in which (a) it is probable that a liability has been incurred and (b) the amount of that liability can be reasonably estimated. Before recognizing a payable and interest expense for amounts contingently payable, however, accrual or payment of those amounts shall be deducted from the carrying amount of the restructured payable to the extent that contingent payments included in "total future cash payments specified by the new terms" prevented recognition of a gain at the time of restructuring (paragraph 18).

23. If amounts of future cash payments must be estimated to apply the provisions of paragraphs 16-18 because future interest payments are expected to fluctuate—for example, the restructured terms may specify the stated interest rate to be the prime interest rate increased by a specified amount or proportion—estimates of maximum total future payments shall be based on the interest rate in effect at the time of the restructuring. Fluctuations in the effective interest rate after the restructuring from changes in the prime rate or other causes shall be accounted for as changes in estimates in the periods the changes occur. However, the accounting for those fluctuations shall not result in recognizing a gain on restructuring that may be offset by future cash payments (paragraphs 18 and 22). Rather, the carrying amount of the restructured payable shall remain unchanged, and future cash payments shall reduce the carrying amount until the time that any gain recognized cannot be offset by future cash payments.

24. Legal fees and other direct costs that a debtor incurs in granting an equity interest to a creditor in a troubled debt restructuring shall reduce the amount otherwise recorded for that equity interest according to paragraphs 15 and 19. All other direct costs that a debtor incurs to effect a troubled debt restructuring shall be deducted in measuring gain on restructuring of payables or shall be included in expense for the period if no gain on restructuring is recognized.

Disclosure by Debtors

25. A debtor shall disclose, either in the body of the financial statements or in the accompanying notes, the following information about troubled debt restructurings that have occurred during a period for which financial statements are presented:

a. For each restructuring:[15] a description of the principal changes in terms, the major features of settlement, or both.
b. Aggregate gain on restructuring of payables and the related income tax effect (paragraph 21).
c. Aggregate net gain or loss on transfers of assets recognized during the period (paragraphs 14 and 19).
d. Per share amount of the aggregate gain on restructuring of payables, net of related income tax effect.

26. A debtor shall disclose in financial statements for periods after a troubled debt restructuring the extent to which amounts contingently payable are included in the carrying amount of restructured payables pursuant to the provisions of paragraph 18. If required by paragraphs 9-13 of *FASB Statement No. 5,* a debtor shall also disclose in those financial statements total amounts that are contingently payable on restructured payables and the conditions under which those amounts would become payable or would be forgiven.

Accounting by Creditors

27. A creditor shall account for a troubled debt restructuring according to the type of the restructuring as prescribed in the following paragraphs. Paragraphs 28-42 do not apply to a receivable that the creditor is accounting for at market value in accordance with the specialized industry practice (for example, a marketable debt security accounted

[15]Separate restructurings within a fiscal period for the same category of payables (for example, accounts payable or subordinated debentures) may be grouped for disclosure purposes.

for at market value by a mutual fund). Estimated cash expected to be received less estimated costs expected to be incurred is not market value in accordance with specialized industry practice as that term is used in this paragraph.

Receipt of Assets in Full Satisfaction

28. A creditor that receives from a debtor in full satisfaction of a receivable either (i) receivables from third parties, real estate, or other assets or (ii) shares of stock or other evidence of an equity interest in the debtor, or both, shall account for those assets (including an equity interest) at their fair value at the time of the restructuring (see paragraph 13 for how to measure fair value).[16] The excess of (i) the recorded investment in the receivable[17] satisfied over (ii) the fair value of assets received is a loss to be recognized according to paragraph 35.

29. After a troubled debt restructuring, a creditor shall account for assets received in satisfaction of a receivable the same as if the assets had been acquired for cash.

Modification of Terms

30. A creditor in a troubled debt restructuring involving only modification of terms of a receivable—that is, not involving receipt of assets (including an equity interest in the debtor)—shall account for the effects of the restructuring prospectively and shall not change the recorded investment in the receivable at the time of the restructuring unless that amount exceeds the total future cash receipts specified by the new terms.[18] That is, the effects of changes in the amounts or timing (or both) of future cash receipts designated either as interest or as face amount shall be reflected in future periods.[19] Interest income shall be computed in a way that a constant effective interest rate is applied to the recorded investment in the receivable at the beginning of each period between restructuring and maturity (in substance the "interest" method prescribed by paragraph 15 of *APB Opinion No. 21*).[20] The new effective interest rate shall be the discount rate that equates the present value of the future cash receipts specified by the new terms (excluding amounts contingently receivable) with the recorded investment in the receivable.

31. If, however, the total future cash receipts specified by the new terms of the receivable, including both receipts designated as interest and those designated as face amount, are less than the recorded investment in the receivable before restructuring, the creditor shall reduce the recorded investment in the receivable to an amount equal to the total future cash receipts specified by the new terms. The amount of the reduction is a loss to be recognized according to paragraph 35. Thereafter, all cash receipts by the creditor under the terms of the restructured receivable, whether designated as interest or as face amount, shall be accounted for as recovery of the recorded investment in the receivable, and no interest income shall be recognized on the receivable for any period between the restructuring and maturity of the receivable.[21]

32. A creditor shall recognize a loss on a restructured receivable involving indeterminate future cash receipts unless the minimum future cash receipts specified by the new terms at least equals the recorded investment in the receivable. Amounts designated either as interest or as face amount that are receivable from the debtor may be contingent on a specified event or circumstance (for example, specified amounts may be receivable from the debtor if the debtor's financial condition improves to a specified degree within a specified period). To determine whether the creditor shall recognize a loss according to the provisions of paragraphs 30 and 31, those

[16]Paragraphs 28 and 33 indicate that the fair value of assets received shall be used in accounting for satisfaction of a receivable in a troubled debt restructuring. That guidance is not intended to preclude using the fair value of the receivable satisfied if more clearly evident than the fair value of the assets received in full satisfaction of a receivable (paragraph 28). (See paragraph 67 of *APB Opinion No. 16*.) However, in a partial satisfaction of a receivable (paragraph 33), the fair value of the assets received shall be used in all cases to avoid the need to allocate the fair value of the receivable between the part satisfied and the part still outstanding.

[17]*Recorded investment in the receivable* is used in paragraphs 28-41 instead of *carrying amount of the receivable* because the latter is net of an allowance for estimated uncollectible amounts or other "valuation" account, if any, while the former is not. The recorded investment in the receivable is the face amount increased or decreased by applicable accrued interest and unamortized premium, discount, finance charges, or acquisition costs and may also reflect a previous direct write-down of the investment.

[18]In this Statement, total future cash receipts includes related accrued interest, if any, at the time of the restructuring that continues to be receivable under the new terms. Uncertainty of collection of noncontingent amounts specified by the new terms (see paragraph 32 for inclusion of contingent amounts) is not a factor in applying paragraphs 30-32 but should, of course, be considered in accounting for allowances for uncollectible amounts.

[19]All or a portion of the recorded investment in the receivable at the time of restructuring may need to be reclassified in the balance sheet because of changes in the terms.

[20]Some creditors—for example, finance companies (*AICPA Industry Audit Guide,* "Audits of Finance Companies," Chapter 2)—use methods that recognize less revenue in early periods of a receivable than does the "interest" method. The accounting for restructured receivables described in this Statement is not intended to change creditors' methods of recognizing revenue to require a different method for restructured receivables from that for other receivables.

[21]The only exception is to recognize interest income according to paragraph 36.

contingent amounts shall be included in the "total future cash receipts specified by the new terms" only if at the time of restructuring those amounts meet the conditions that would be applied under the provisions of paragraph 8 of *FASB Statement No. 5* in accruing a loss. That is, a creditor shall recognize a loss unless contingent future cash receipts needed to make total future cash receipts specified by the new terms at least equal to the recorded investment in the receivable both are probable and can be reasonably estimated. The same principle applies to amounts of future cash receipts that must sometimes be estimated to apply the provisions of paragraphs 30 and 31. For example, if the number of interest receipts is flexible because the face amount and accrued interest is collectible on demand or becomes collectible on demand after a specified period, estimates of total future cash receipts should be based on the minimum number of periods possible under the restructured terms.

Combination of Types

33. A troubled debt restructuring may involve receipt of assets (including an equity interest in the debtor) in partial satisfaction of a receivable and a modification of terms of the remaining receivable.[22] A creditor shall account for a troubled debt restructuring involving a partial satisfaction and modification of terms as prescribed in paragraphs 30-32 except that, first, the assets received shall be accounted for at their fair values as prescribed in paragraph 28 and the recorded investment in the receivable shall be reduced by the fair value of the assets received.[23] No loss on the restructuring shall be recognized unless the remaining recorded investment in the receivable exceeds the total future cash receipts specified by the terms of the receivable remaining unsatisfied after the restructuring. Future interest income, if any, shall be determined according to the provisions of paragraphs 30-32.

Related Matters

34. A troubled debt restructuring that is in substance a repossession or foreclosure by the creditor, or in which the creditor otherwise obtains one or more of the debtor's assets in place of all or part of the receivable, shall be accounted for according to the provisions of paragraphs 28 and 33 and, if appropriate, 39.

35. Losses determined by applying the provisions of paragraphs 28-34 of this Statement shall, to the extent that they are not offset against allowances for uncollectible amounts or other valuation accounts, be included in measuring net income for the period of restructuring and reported according to *APB Opinion No. 30*. Although this Statement does not address questions concerning estimating uncollectible amounts or accounting for the related valuation allowance (paragraph 1), it recognizes that creditors use allowances for uncollectible amounts. Thus, a loss from reducing the recorded investment in a receivable may have been recognized before the restructuring by deducting an estimate of uncollectible amounts in measuring net income and increasing an appropriate valuation allowance. If so, a reduction in the recorded investment in the receivable in a troubled debt restructuring is a deduction from the valuation allowance rather than a loss in measuring net income for the period of restructuring. A valuation allowance can also be used to recognize a loss determined by applying paragraphs 28-34 that has not been previously recognized in measuring net income. For example, a creditor with an allowance for uncollectible amounts pertaining to a group of receivables that includes the restructured receivable may deduct from the allowance the reduction of recorded investment in the restructured receivable and recognize the loss in measuring net income for the period of restructuring by estimating the appropriate allowance for remaining receivables, including the restructured receivable.

36. If a troubled debt restructuring involves amounts contingently receivable, those contingent amounts shall not be recognized as interest income in future periods before they become receivable—that is, they shall not be recognized as interest income before both the contingency has been removed and the interest has been earned.[24] Before recognizing those amounts as interest income, however, they shall be deducted from the recorded investment in the restructured receivable to the extent that contingent receipts included in "total future cash receipts specified by the new terms" avoided recognition of a loss at the time of restructuring (paragraph 32).

37. If amounts of future cash receipts must be estimated to apply the provisions of paragraphs 30-32 because future interest receipts are expected to

[22]Even if the stated terms of the remaining receivable, for example, the stated interest rate and the maturity date or dates, are not changed in connection with the receipt of assets (including an equity interest in the debtor), the restructuring shall be accounted for as prescribed by paragraph 33.

[23]If cash is received in a partial satisfaction of a receivable, the recorded investment in the receivable shall be reduced by the amount of cash received.

[24]*FASB Statement No. 5*, paragraph 17 (which continued without reconsideration certain provisions of *ARB No. 50*, "Contingencies"), states, in part: "Contingencies that might result in gains usually are not reflected in the accounts since to do so might be to recognize revenue prior to its realization."

fluctuate—for example, the restructured terms may specify the stated interest rate to be the prime interest rate increased by a specified amount or proportion—estimates of the minimum total future receipts shall be based on the interest rate in effect at the time of restructuring. Fluctuations in the effective interest rate after the restructuring from changes in the prime rate or other causes shall be accounted for as changes in estimates in the periods the changes occur except that a creditor shall recognize a loss and reduce the recorded investment in a restructured receivable if the interest rate decreases to an extent that the minimum total future cash receipts determined using that interest rate fall below the recorded investment in the receivable at that time.

38. Legal fees and other direct costs incurred by a creditor to effect a troubled debt restructuring shall be included in expense when incurred.

39. A receivable from the sale of assets previously obtained in a troubled debt restructuring shall be accounted for according to *APB Opinion No. 21* regardless of whether the assets were obtained in satisfaction (full or partial) of a receivable to which that Opinion was not intended to apply. A difference, if any, between the amount of the new receivable and the carrying amount of the assets sold is a gain or loss on sale of assets.

Disclosure by Creditors

40. A creditor shall disclose, either in the body of the financial statements or in the accompanying notes, the following information about troubled debt restructurings as of the date of each balance sheet presented:

a. For outstanding receivables whose terms have been modified in troubled debt restructurings, by major category:[25] (i) the aggregate recorded investment; (ii) the gross interest income that would have been recorded in the period then ended if those receivables had been current in accordance with their original terms and had been outstanding throughout the period or since origination, if held for part of the period; and (iii) the amount of interest income on those receivables that was included in net income for the period. A receivable whose terms have been modified need not be included in that disclosure if, subsequent to restructuring, its effective interest rate (paragraph 30) has been equal to or greater than the rate that the creditor was willing to accept for a new receivable with comparable risk.
b. The amount of commitments, if any, to lend additional funds to debtors owing receivables whose terms have been modified in troubled debt restructurings.

41. A financial institution, or other creditor, may appropriately disclose the information prescribed by paragraph 40, by major category, for the aggregate of outstanding reduced-earning and nonearning receivables rather than separately for outstanding receivables whose terms have been modified in troubled debt restructurings.

Substitution or Addition of Debtors

42. A troubled debt restructuring may involve substituting debt of another business enterprise, individual, or government unit[26] for that of the troubled debtor or adding another debtor (for example, as a joint debtor). That kind of restructuring should be accounted for according to its substance. For example, a restructuring in which, after the restructuring, the substitute or additional debtor controls, is controlled by, or is under common control[27] with the original debtor is an example of one that shall be accounted for by the creditor according to the provisions of paragraphs 30-32. Those paragraphs shall also apply to a restructuring in which the substitute or additional debtor and original debtor are related after the restructuring by an agency, trust, or other relationship that in substance earmarks certain of the original debtor's funds or funds flows for the creditor although payments to the creditor may be made by the substitute or additional debtor. In contrast, a restructuring in which the substitute or additional debtor and the original debtor do not have any of the relationships described above after the restructuring shall be accounted for by the creditor according to the provisions of paragraphs 28 and 33.

---

[25]The appropriate major categories depend on various factors, including the industry or industries in which the creditor is involved. For example, for a commercial banking enterprise, at a minimum, the appropriate categories are investments in debt securities and loans. Information need not be disclosed, however, for non-interest-bearing trade receivables; loans to individuals for household, family, and other personal expenditures; and real estate loans secured by one-to-four family residential properties.

[26]Government units include, but are not limited to, states, counties, townships, municipalities, school districts, authorities, and commissions. See page 4 of *AICPA Industry Audit Guide,* "Audits of State and Local Governmental Units."

[27]"Control" in this paragraph has the meaning described in paragraph 3(c) of *APB Opinion No. 18,* "The Equity Method of Accounting for Investments in Common Stock": "The usual condition for control is ownership of a majority (over 50%) of the outstanding voting stock. The power to control may also exist with a lesser percentage of ownership, for example, by contract, lease, agreement with other stockholders or by court decree."

Effective Date and Transition

43. The preceding paragraphs of this Statement, other than paragraphs 39-41, shall be effective for troubled debt restructurings consummated after December 31, 1977.[28] Earlier application is encouraged for those consummated on or before December 31, 1977 but during fiscal years for which annual financial statements have not previously been issued. The paragraphs shall not be applied to those consummated during fiscal years for which annual financial statements have previously been issued.

44. Paragraph 39 shall be effective for receivables resulting from sales of assets after December 31, 1977 regardless of whether the provisions of this Statement were applied to the related troubled debt restructuring. Earlier application is encouraged for receivables from sales of assets on or before December 31, 1977 but during fiscal years for which annual financial statements have not previously been issued. It shall not be applied to those from sales of assets during fiscal years for which annual financial statements have previously been issued.

45. The information prescribed by paragraphs 40 and 41 shall be disclosed in financial statements for fiscal years ending after December 15, 1977. Earlier application is encouraged in financial statements for fiscal years ending before December 16, 1977. For the purpose of applying paragraph 40, "receivables whose terms have been modified in troubled debt restructurings" shall encompass not only (a) receivables whose terms have been modified in troubled debt restructurings to which the other provisions of this Statement have been applied in accordance with paragraph 43 but also (b) those whose terms have been modified in earlier restructurings that constitute troubled debt restructurings (paragraphs 2-8) but have been excluded from its other provisions because of the timing of the restructurings.

The provisions of this Statement need not be applied to immaterial items.

This Statement was adopted by the affirmative votes of five members of the Financial Accounting Standards Board. Messrs. Gellein and Kirk dissented.

Messrs. Kirk and Gellein dissent because they disagree with the conclusions in paragraphs 16 and 30 (which are also in paragraphs 19 and 33) about prospective treatment of the effect of a reduction of the face amount or maturity amount of debt. They would apply the fair value accounting required in paragraphs 13, 15, and 28 to reductions in the face amount of restructured debt. They point to the incontrovertible fact that a modification of terms that reduces the face amount or interest rate or extends the maturity date, without equivalent consideration, is a relinquishment of rights by the creditor and a corresponding benefit to the debtor, and note that debtors and creditors currently record a reduction in face amount when it occurs. They believe that this Statement takes a backward step in reversing, for the sake of consistency, the practice of current recognition, though not based on fair value. They do not accept the argument implicit in paragraphs 140-144, especially paragraph 144, that consistency in accounting for various modifications of terms should govern. They find no virtue in theoretical consistency if it means now ignoring a substantive consequence of an event—in this case relinquishment of rights—that prior to the issuance of this Statement was being recognized. Messrs. Kirk and Gellein accept prospective recognition of the relinquishment by the creditor and the contra benefit to the debtor associated with interest rate reductions and extensions of maturity dates pending further consideration of other aspects of accounting for interest.

Messrs. Kirk and Gellein believe that their proposal to apply fair value accounting (required in paragraphs 13, 15, and 28 of this Statement) to reduction in the face amount would eliminate a significant difference between the accounting required by this Statement and that required by *APB Opinion No. 26* for debt exchanges that involve changes in the face amount. They also believe that their proposal would result in a more conventional and understandable measure of gain or loss than that which results from the application of paragraphs 17, 19, 31, and 33. They believe that in situations considered to be recordable events, any gain or loss should be determined by comparing fair value, not an undiscounted amount of future cash flows, with previously recorded amounts.

Messrs. Kirk and Gellein also dissent because of disagreement with the guidelines in paragraph 42 for determining when a restructuring that involves a substitution of debtors is a recordable event. First, they believe that from the viewpoint of the creditor, there is no significant difference between a change from the original debtor to one under or to one not under the same control as the original debtor. To the

[28]For an enterprise having a fiscal year of 52 or 53 weeks ending in the last seven days in December or the first seven days in January, references to December 31, 1977 in paragraphs 43 and 44 shall mean the date in December 1977 or January 1978 on which the fiscal year ends.

creditor both are changes to a new and different credit risk that should be accounted for in the same way. Second, they believe the guideline in that paragraph concerning a substitute debtor and original debtor who are "related after the restructuring by an agency, trust, or other relationship that in substance earmarks certain of the original debtor's funds or funds flows for the creditor although payments to the creditor may be made by the substitute . . . debtor," is an unworkable criterion and is irrelevant if the right, or asset that gives rise to those funds flows, is irrevocably transferred. In the latter event, from the creditor's viewpoint, the transfer changes the risk and, in effect, results in a different asset—similar in substance to that described in paragraph 28. Further, they find insufficient guidance about the kind of relationship between the parties intended to govern. As an example, they disagree with the interpretation of that guideline in paragraph 161 where recent exchanges of bonds of the Municipal Assistance Corporation (the Corporation) for notes of the City of New York (the City) are noted as examples of debt substititions whose substance to creditors is modification of terms of an existing receivable rather than an acquisition of a new asset. They believe the relationship in that case goes beyond that of an agency, trust, or other relationship that earmarks funds. They note that the Corporation is a corporate governmental agency and an instrumentality of the State of New York (the State), not the City; that bonds of the Corporation do not constitute an enforceable obligation, or a debt, of either the State or the City and neither the State nor the City shall be liable thereon; and that neither the faith and credit nor the taxing power of the State or City is pledged to the payment of principal of or interest on the bonds. They note, too, that the Corporation is empowered to issue and sell bonds and notes and to pay or lend funds received from such sale to the City and to exchange the Corporation's obligations for obligations of the City. Those characteristics in their minds establish sufficient independence of the Corporation from the City to take the exchanges out from under the guidelines of paragraph 42.

Members of the Financial Accounting Standards Board:

Marshall S. Armstrong, *Chairman*
Oscar S. Gellein
Donald J. Kirk
Arthur L. Litke
Robert E. Mays
Robert T. Sprouse
Ralph E. Walters

Appendix A

BACKGROUND INFORMATION

46. There has been a substantial increase in recent years in the number of debtors that are unable to meet their obligations on outstanding debt because of financial difficulties. Sometimes the debtor and the creditor have restructured the debt to enable the debtor to avoid bankruptcy proceedings or other consequences of default, and the number of troubled debt restructurings receiving publicity has also increased. Although many of the most publicized troubled debt restructurings have involved debtors that are real estate companies or real estate investment trusts, debtors in other industries have also been involved in troubled debt restructurings.

47. *APB Opinion No. 26,* "Early Extinguishment of Debt," established the accounting by a debtor for debt extinguished before its scheduled maturity. A number of commentators have observed, however, that not all troubled debt restructurings are "extinguishments" as that term is used in *APB Opinion No. 26.* Also, since many troubled debt restructurings have occurred on or after the scheduled maturity of the debt, questions have arisen about accounting for debt restructurings that are not early extinguishments. It has been suggested that troubled debt restructurings should be considered separately from restructurings, including early extinguishments, that do not involve the economic or legal pressure to restructure on the creditor that characterizes troubled debt restructurings.

48. Concern over the lack of guidance in the authoritative literature on accounting for troubled debt restructurings, accentuated by their increasing number, led to requests that the Financial Accounting Standards Board consider the matter. The Board submitted the question to the Screening Committee on Emerging Problems and weighed its recommendations in deciding to proceed with a project limited in scope to accounting and reporting by a debtor whose debt is restructured in a troubled loan situation. The Board issued an Exposure Draft of a Proposed Statement, "Restructuring of Debt in a Troubled Loan Situation," dated November 7, 1975, and held a public hearing on December 12, 1975. The Board received 63 written responses to the Exposure Draft and heard five oral presentations at the public hearing. A number of respondents objected to the accounting prescribed by the Exposure Draft, but they held divergent views about the appropriate accounting. Major issues of concern centered on (a) whether certain kinds of troubled debt restructurings require reductions of carrying amounts of debt, (b) if they do, whether the effect of the reduction should be included in measuring

current net income, be deferred, or be considered a contribution to capital, and (c) whether interest that is contingently payable on restructured debt should be recognized before it becomes payable.

49. During the same period, uncertainties arose about the abilities of some state and local government units to pay their obligations when due. Some of those obligations have also been restructured, for example, by continuing the existing obligation for a designated period at a reduced interest rate or by substituting obligations with later maturities of the same or a related issuer. Questions about accounting and reporting by creditors for those restructured securities led various individuals and organizations to urge the Board to consider that matter.

50. The Board considered (a) the lack of authoritative guidance and divergent views about accounting and reporting by debtors for troubled debt restructurings and by creditors for restructured securities of state and local government units and (b) the similarities of the issues for debtors and creditors and concluded that the accounting and reporting issues affecting both debtors and creditors should be considered in a single project. The Board therefore announced on January 7, 1976, that it had added to its agenda a project to determine accounting and reporting by both debtors and creditors. At the same time the Board announced that since the new project concerned accounting by both debtors and creditors, the Board would not issue a Statement covering the limited topic of the November 7, 1975 Exposure Draft.

51. The Securities and Exchange Commission issued, also on January 7, 1976, *Accounting Series Release No. 188,* "Interpretive Statement by the Commission on Disclosure by Registrants of Holdings of Securities of New York City and Accounting for Securities Subject to Exchange Offer and Moratorium." The Commission did not require a particular accounting method because of the divergent views on accounting for the securities held and "the fact that the Financial Accounting Standards Board has agreed to undertake a study of the accounting problems . . . with the intention of developing standards which can be applied to year-end statements in 1976."

52. The Board appointed a task force in January 1976 to provide counsel in preparing a Discussion Memorandum. Its sixteen members included individuals from academe, the financial community, industry, law, and public accounting. The Board issued a Discussion Memorandum, "Accounting by Debtors and Creditors When Debt Is Restructured," dated May 11, 1976, comprehending accounting and reporting by debtors and creditors for "any change in the amount or timing of cash payments otherwise required under the terms of the debt at the date of restructuring." It received 894 written responses to the Discussion Memorandum and heard 37 oral presentations at a public hearing on July 27-30, 1976.

53. In addition, the FASB staff reviewed the accounting and reporting practices of a number of debtors and creditors involved in troubled debt restructurings and interviewed a limited number of individuals who were directly associated with some of those restructurings.

54. The Board issued an Exposure Draft of a proposed Statement on "Accounting by Debtors and Creditors for Troubled Debt Restructurings," dated December 30, 1976. It received 96 letters of comment on the Exposure Draft.

Appendix B

BASIS FOR CONCLUSIONS

CONTENTS

BASIS FOR CONCLUSIONS

55. This Appendix discusses factors deemed significant by members of the Board in reaching the conclusions in this Statement, including various alternatives considered and reasons for accepting some and rejecting others.

SCOPE OF THIS STATEMENT

56. Paragraph 1 states that this Statement establishes standards of financial accounting and reporting by the debtor and by the creditor for a troubled debt restructuring. In contrast, the Discussion Memorandum comprehended all restructurings that changed "the amount or timing of cash payments otherwise required under the terms of the debt at the date of the restructuring." The broader scope of the Discussion Memorandum, which encompassed nontroubled as well as troubled debt restructurings, was due to several factors. The Board considered it necessary to obtain additional information about accounting practices and problems for both troubled and nontroubled debt restructurings. Some respondents to the November 7, 1975 Exposure Draft of a Proposed Statement, "Restructuring of Debt in a Troubled Loan Situation," expressed concern that to apply its guidelines for identifying troubled loan situations would require considerable judgment. Some Task Force members and other commentators advised the Board to comprehend all restructurings accomplished by exchanges of debt for debt or of equity securities for debt that may not be covered by *APB Opinion No. 26.*[29]

[29]See paragraph 47 of this Statement.

57. Most respondents to the Discussion Memorandum that commented on the matter, however, recommended that a Statement at this time should be limited to accounting for troubled debt restructurings. Numerous respondents indicated that restructurings of debt in nontroubled situations present no significant or unusual accounting problems that merit consideration or require new accounting and reporting standards. Many respondents contended that the kinds of major changes that might result from new standards on accounting for all restructurings should be deferred pending progress on the FASB's existing projects on accounting for interest costs and the conceptual framework for financial accounting and reporting. Some respondents argued that a useful distinction between troubled and nontroubled restructurings of debt can be made and that the need to use judgment in some circumstances should not be a deterrent to making that distinction in a Statement. A number of respondents to the Exposure Draft[30] made similar comments.

58. The Board found persuasive the views described in the preceding paragraph and decided to limit the scope of this Statement to troubled debt restructurings. The Board also decided that conclusions in this Statement should not attempt to anticipate results of considering the issues in its Discussion Memorandum, "Conceptual Framework for Financial Accounting and Reporting: Elements of Financial Statements and Their Measurement," dated December 2, 1976. Rather, the Board believes that, to the extent possible, the accounting for troubled debt restructurings prescribed in this Statement should be consistent and compatible with the existing accounting framework.

59. Paragraph 1 also states that the Statement does not establish standards of financial accounting and reporting for allowances for uncollectible amounts and does not prescribe or proscribe particular methods for estimating amounts of uncollectible receivables. Several respondents to the Exposure Draft urged the Board to adopt the method of accounting for uncollectible amounts based on the net realizable value of collateral property set forth in *Statement of Position 75-2,* "Accounting Practices of Real Estate Investment Trusts," issued June 27, 1975 by the Accounting Standards Division of the American Institute of Certified Public Accountants. Others noted potential conflicts between the Exposure Draft and the AICPA publication and requested clarification. Still others urged the Board to reject the method for estimating amounts of uncollectible receivables in *Statement of Position 75-2.*

60. Since this Statement neither prescribes nor proscribes particular methods for estimating uncollectible amounts of receivables, it takes no position on whether the net realizable value of collateral is a proper basis for estimating allowances for uncollectible amounts of receivables. However, the accounting prescribed in this Statement for assets received in troubled debt restructurings differs from that in *Statement of Position 75-2,* for reasons given in paragraphs 65-105, and the accounting prescribed in this Statement governs.

61. Paragraphs 2-8 identify debt restructurings that fall within the scope of this Statement. This paragraph and the next are intended to clarify further the meaning of *troubled debt restructuring* for purposes of this Statement. The description of a troubled debt restructuring is based generally on that in the November 7, 1975 Exposure Draft, which many respondents to that Exposure Draft and the Discussion Memorandum found satisfactory. It focuses on the economic and legal considerations related to the debtor's financial difficulties that in effect compel the creditor to restructure a receivable in ways more favorable to the debtor than the creditor would otherwise consider. The creditor participates in a troubled debt restructuring because it no longer expects its investment in the receivable to earn the rate of return expected at the time of investment and may view loss of all or part of the investment to be likely unless the receivable is restructured. Thus, a troubled debt restructuring involves a receivable whose risk to the creditor has greatly increased since its acquisition, and if the creditor were not faced with the need to restructure to protect itself, it would require a much higher effective interest rate to invest in the same receivable currently. If the receivable has a market price, the effective interest rate based on that market price will have increased because of that increased risk to the creditor—that is, it will have increased more than market interest rates generally (or fallen less than market rates or increased while interest rates generally have fallen).

62. Although the broad description of a troubled debt restructuring in paragraphs 2-8 includes settlements of debt by transfers of assets and grants of equity interests in debtors, *troubled debt restructuring* refers in particular to modifications of terms intended to continue an existing debt by making the terms more favorable to the debtor to protect the creditor's investment. For purposes of this Statement, troubled debt restructurings do not include changes in terms resulting in an effective interest rate based on market price of the debt that is comparable to effective interest rates applicable to debt

[30]References to "Exposure Draft" in this Appendix are to "Accounting by Debtors and Creditors for Troubled Debt Restructurings," dated December 30, 1976, unless the reference specifically identifies the earlier Exposure Draft, "Restructurings of Debt in a Troubled Loan Situation," dated November 7, 1975.

issued by nontroubled debtors, for example, a situation in which a debtor is able to exchange for its outstanding debt new marketable debt with an effective interest rate at or near the market interest rates for debt issued by nontroubled debtors generally. The fact that the debtor can obtain that interest rate only by including a "sweetener," such as a conversion privilege, does not make that transaction a troubled debt restructuring because (a) the debtor is sufficiently strong financially that the kind of economic compulsion on the creditor described earlier is not present, (b) the "sweetener" represents so drastic a change in the terms of the debt that the transaction is in substance the exchange of new debt for outstanding debt rather than merely a modification of terms to continue an existing debt, or (c) some combination of both factors.

63. Some respondents to the Discussion Memorandum advocated that the scope of this Statement specifically exclude restructurings of receivables related to consumer finance activities or to all or certain residential properties. Their reasons focused primarily on the individual insignificance of those receivables in a creditor's financial position and on the cost involved to account for reductions in recorded investments in large numbers of receivables that may be restructured. The Board concluded that accounting for restructurings of those receivables in troubled situations should in general be the same as for other troubled debt restructurings. However, grouping like items or using statistical measures may be appropriate for receivables that are not individually material.

64. Some respondents to the Exposure Draft suggested that the *time of a troubled debt restructuring* be clarified because several dates or events may be involved. The time may be significant in matters relating to recognizing gains or losses from restructuring or to the effective date of the Statement. Paragraph 6 specifies the time of a restructuring to be the date of consummation, that is, the time that assets are transferred, new terms become effective, and the like. A debtor should not recognize a gain on restructuring before consummation of the restructuring; a creditor should record receipt of an asset or equity interest at that date or should formally write down a restructured receivable, but may already have recognized a loss on restructuring through estimated uncollectible amounts.

DIVERGENT VIEWS OF TROUBLED DEBT RESTRUCTURINGS

65. Respondents to the Discussion Memorandum expressed divergent views about the substance of various types of troubled debt restructurings and appropriate accounting for them within the existing accounting framework. Those views fall generally into three categories:

a. All troubled debt restructurings constitute events that are part of continuing efforts by creditors to recover amounts invested and obtain a return on investment despite debtors' financial difficulties; therefore, troubled debt restructurings may require certain disclosures, but usually do not require changes in carrying amounts of payables or recorded investments in receivables or recognition of gains or losses.
b. All debt restructurings, troubled and nontroubled, constitute transactions whose financial effect on assets or liabilities (receivables or payables) should be recognized, including recognition of gains or losses.
c. Accounting for a troubled debt restructuring depends on the characteristics of the restructuring. Some troubled debt restructurings constitute transactions requiring recognition of changes in receivables or payables and related gains or losses; other troubled debt restructurings do not.

Recognition of Changes Not Appropriate

66. Respondents who contended that troubled debt restructurings constitute events for which recognition of changes in assets or liabilities is usually not appropriate within the existing accounting framework generally focused on accounting by creditors. They reasoned that a troubled debt restructuring commonly involves a concession granted unilaterally by the creditor to increase its prospects of recovering the amount invested. The debtor is usually a passive beneficiary of the effects of the restructuring. Troubled debt restructurings typically result from the debtor's financial difficulties that existed before restructuring, and in the existing accounting framework the creditor should have considered the debtor's financial difficulties in estimating an allowance for uncollectible amounts regardless of whether those difficulties were likely to culminate in a restructuring. According to those respondents, the restructuring event in itself has no accounting significance except to sometimes provide more definitive evidence of the effect of the debtor's financial difficulties on the creditor's ability to recover the recorded investment in the receivable.

67. According to that view, the creditor should record no change in a receivable restructured in a troubled debt restructuring and no gain or loss whether the restructuring involves (i) transfer of receivables, real estate, or other noncash assets from the debtor to the creditor to satisfy the receivable, (ii) grant to the creditor of an equity interest in the debtor to satisfy the receivable, (iii) modification of the terms of the receivable, or (iv) some combina-

tion of transfer of assets or grant of equity interests (or both) and modification of terms. The normal, expected course of events in a creditor's activities is to invest cash, earn interest on the cash invested, and eventually recover the cash. Although a creditor initiates or agrees to a restructuring to protect the amount invested, not to acquire noncash assets, the creditor may accept noncash assets (including an equity interest) as a necessary intermediate step. The creditor previously held a claim on the debtor's assets, either through a receivable secured by specific collateral or through an unsecured general claim against the debtor's assets. Accepting noncash assets in a restructuring represents the exercise of that claim; the assets stand in the place of the receivable. According to that view, the creditor's recorded investment in the receivable should become the recorded investment in the surrogate assets obtained. Then, since whether the creditor recovers that investment depends on the cash received for the assets that replaced the receivable, recoverability of that recorded investment as a result of obtaining the surrogate assets should be assessed. An expected failure, if any, to recover all of the recorded investment should be recognized as a loss by the creditor to the extent not previously recognized. However, transfer of the assets to the creditor should not precipitate recognition of a loss that was not inherent in the receivable before the restructuring; at most, the transfer provides evidence of the existence and amount of a loss.

Recognition of Changes Appropriate for All Debt Restructurings

68. Some respondents advocated for virtually all debt restructurings, troubled and nontroubled, the accounting normally required in the existing accounting framework for initial recognition of assets and liabilities. They reasoned that each restructuring is an exchange resulting in a new asset for the creditor or liability for the debtor in place of the old one. According to that view, the presence or absence of financial difficulties does not affect the appropriate accounting for a restructuring; at most, a debtor's financial difficulties may affect the terms of the exchange. Those respondents contended that all assets and liabilities exchanged in debt restructurings should be measured at their fair values at the time of the restructuring by both debtors and creditors. They considered continued use of recorded amounts derived from previous exchange transactions to be inappropriate for restructured receivables and payables because it ignores a current exchange transaction and may ignore gains or losses that have occurred and should be recognized.

Accounting Depends on Circumstances

69. Some respondents contended that the controlling criterion in determining appropriate accounting for a debt restructuring within the existing accounting framework is whether the restructuring involves transfer of resources, obligations, or both between debtor and creditor. According to that view, a troubled debt restructuring involving transfer of resources, obligations, or both should be accounted for the same as other transfers of resources and obligations in the existing accounting framework and may involve recognizing a gain or loss. A troubled debt restructuring involving no transfer of resources or obligations requires no accounting for changes in assets or liabilities, except to recognize losses in accordance with *FASB Statement No. 5*.

70. Some respondents distinguished debt restructurings involving transfers of resources, obligations, or both from those involving no transfers on the basis of whether the debtor transferred assets or granted an equity interest to the creditor to satisfy the debt or the restructuring involved modification of terms only. Other respondents classified modifications of terms involving reduction of face amount of the debt with transfers of assets or grants of equity interests (discussed further in paragraphs 106-155).

Board Conclusions about Recognizing Changes in Assets or Liabilities

71. *APB Statement No. 4,* "Basic Concepts and Accounting Principles Underlying Financial Statements of Business Enterprises," describes relevant parts of the existing accounting framework. That Statement defines "economic resources" as "the scarce means (limited in supply relative to desired uses) available for carrying on economic activities" and identifies "claims to receive money" as an economic resource. It defines "economic obligations" as "present responsibilities to transfer economic resources or provide services to other entities in the future" and identifies "obligations to pay money" as an economic obligation. It also states that "events that change resources, obligations, and residual interest are the basis for the basic elements of results of operations . . . and other changes in financial position with which financial accounting is concerned." (See *APB Statement No. 4,* paragraphs 57, 58, and 61.)

72. According to *APB Statement No. 4,* almost all of the events that in the existing accounting framework normally change assets and liabilities and also affect net income for the period of change are either "exchanges" or "nonreciprocal transfers," the two classes that comprise "transfers of resources or obligations to or from other entities." The other classes of events—"external events other than transfers of resources or obligations to or from other entities" (price changes, interest rate changes, technological

changes, vandalism, etc.) and "internal events" (production and casualties)—result in revenues or gains only through "exceptions" and result in expenses or losses only because some produce losses by definition or by applying the "modifying convention" of conservatism. (See *APB Statement No. 4,* paragraphs 62 and 180-187.)

73. An exchange is a reciprocal transfer between the enterprise and another entity in which "the enterprise either sacrifices resources or incurs obligations in order to obtain other resources or satisfy other obligations." "Exchanges between the enterprise and other entities (enterprises or individuals) are generally recorded in financial accounting when the transfer of resources or obligations takes place or services are provided." Nonreciprocal transfers are "transfers in one direction of resources or obligations, either from the enterprise to other entities or from other entities to the enterprise." In nonreciprocal transfers between the enterprise and entities other than owners, "one of the two entities is often passive, a mere beneficiary or victim of the other's actions." Nonreciprocal transfers between the enterprise and entities other than owners "are recorded when assets are acquired (except that some noncash assets received as gifts are not recorded), when assets are disposed of or their loss is discovered, or when liabilities come into existence or are discovered." (See *APB Statement No. 4,* paragraphs 62, 181, and 182.)

74. The Board rejected the view that virtually all troubled debt restructurings have the same substance in the existing accounting framework. It therefore rejected both the view that accounting for all troubled debt restructurings should involve recognition of changes in assets or liabilities and perhaps gains and losses and the view that no troubled debt restructurings should require recognition of changes in assets or liabilities or gains or losses.

75. The Board concluded that a troubled debt restructuring that involves transfer of resources or obligations requires accounting for the resources or obligations transferred whether that restructuring involves an exchange transaction or a nonreciprocal transfer. Both kinds of transfers are accounted for in the existing accounting framework on essentially the same basis (exchange price received or paid or fair value received or given). In this Statement, therefore, the Board found it unnecessary to decide whether the transfer of resources and obligations in various types of troubled debt restructurings is reciprocal (an exchange) or nonreciprocal as those terms are used in paragraph 62 of *APB Statement No. 4*.

76. The Board also concluded that a troubled debt restructuring that does not involve a transfer of resources or obligations is a continuation of an existing debt. It is neither an event that results in a new asset or liability for accounting purposes nor an event that requires a new measurement of an existing asset or liability.

77. The Board noted that guidance regarding the types of troubled debt restructurings that involve transfers of resources, obligations, or both is sparse in existing accounting pronouncements, and various views exist. The Board concluded that to the extent a troubled debt restructuring involves (i) transfer of receivables, real estate, or other assets from debtor to creditor to satisfy debt or (ii) grant to the creditor of an equity interest in the debtor to satisfy debt (or a combination of both), a transfer of resources or obligations has occurred that in the existing accounting framework should be accounted for at fair value. The debtor has given up assets or granted an equity interest to settle a payable, and the creditor has received the assets or equity interest in satisfaction of a receivable. In contrast, to the extent a troubled debt restructuring involves only modification of terms of continuing debt, no transfer of resources or obligations has occurred. The substance of troubled debt restructurings involving modifications of continuing debt is discussed in paragraphs 106-155.

78. Several respondents to the Exposure Draft disagreed with the Board's distinction between troubled debt restructurings involving transfers of assets or grants of equity interests in debtors and those involving only modifications of terms. Some respondents wished to have fewer kinds of troubled debt restructurings accounted for as transactions between debtors and creditors and thus disagreed with the Exposure Draft's conclusions on accounting for transfers of assets; their views are noted in the next section. Others wished to account for more kinds of troubled debt restructurings as transactions between debtors and creditors and thus disagreed with the Exposure Draft's conclusions on accounting for modifications of terms; their views are noted in paragraphs 150-153.

ACCOUNTING FOR RESTRUCTURINGS INVOLVING TRANSFERS

Accounting by Debtors and Creditors for Transfer of Assets

Concept of Fair Value

79. Some respondents to the Exposure Draft continued to argue that all troubled debt restructurings should be accounted for as modifications of terms of debt and that none should be accounted for as

transfers of assets (paragraphs 66 and 67). Others accepted the need to account for some troubled debt restructurings as asset transfers but held that obtaining assets through foreclosure or repossession under terms included in lending agreements should be distinguished from obtaining assets in exchange for cash or in other "asset swaps." They contended that (a) only the form of the asset is changed by foreclosure or repossession, (b) the substance of a secured loan is that the lender may choose either to postpone receipt of cash or take the asset to optimize cash receipts and recovery of its investment, and (c) foreclosure or repossession is not the completion of a lending transaction but merely a step in the transaction that begins with lending cash and ends with collecting cash.

80. The Board rejected those arguments for the reasons given in paragraphs 71-77, emphasizing that an event in which (a) an asset is transferred between debtor and creditor, (b) the creditor relinquishes all or part of its claim against the debtor, and (c) the debtor is absolved of all or part of its obligation to the creditor is the kind of event that is the basis of accounting under the existing transaction-based accounting framework. To fail to recognize an event that fits the usual description of a transaction and to recognize only the lending and collection of cash as transactions would significantly change the existing accounting framework.

81. Use of the fair value of an asset transferred to measure the debtor's gain on restructuring and gain or loss on the asset's disposal or the creditor's cost of acquisition is not adopting some kind of "current value accounting." On the contrary, that use of fair value is common practice within the existing accounting framework. Paragraph 13 of this Statement explains briefly the meaning of *fair value* and refers to *APB Opinions No. 16, No. 21,* and *No. 29,* which use *fair value* in the same way and provide guidance about determining fair values within the existing accounting framework. The term *fair value* is used in essentially the same way as *market value* was used in the Discussion Memorandum to denote a possible attribute to be measured at the time a debt is restructured. *Fair value* is defined in paragraph 181 of *APB Statement No. 4* as "the approximation of exchange price in transfers in which money or money claims are not involved." Although a "money claim" is necessarily involved in transferring assets to settle a payable in a troubled debt restructuring, the troubled circumstances in which the transfer occurs make it obvious that the amount of the "money claim" does not establish an exchange price. Determining the fair value of the assets transferred in a troubled debt restructuring is usually necessary to approximate an exchange price for the same reasons that determining fair value is necessary to account for transfers of assets in nonmonetary transactions (*APB Opinion No. 29*).

82. That point is emphasized in this Appendix because some respondents to the Exposure Draft apparently misunderstood the concept of fair value (paragraph 11 of the Exposure Draft and paragraph 13 of this Statement) and the discounting of expected cash flows specified in those paragraphs. Paragraph 13 permits discounting of expected cash flows from an asset transferred or received in a troubled debt restructuring to be used to estimate fair value only if no market prices are available either for the asset or for similar assets. The sole purpose of discounting cash flows in that paragraph is to estimate a current market price as if the asset were being sold by the debtor to the creditor for cash. That estimated market price provides the equivalent of a sale price on which the debtor can base measurement of a gain on restructuring and a gain or loss on disposal of the asset and the equivalent of a purchase price on which the creditor can measure the acquisition cost of the asset. To approximate a market price, the estimate of fair value should use cash flows and discounting in the same way the marketplace does to set prices—in essence, the marketplace discounts expected future cash flows from a particular asset "at a rate commensurate with the risk involved" in holding the asset. An individual assessment of expected cash flows and risk may differ from what the marketplace's assessment would be, but the procedure is the same.

83. In contrast to the purpose of paragraph 13, *AICPA Statement of Position No. 75-2*[31] is concerned with different measures—net realizable value to a creditor of a receivable secured by real property and net realizable value of repossessed or foreclosed property. Its method of accounting for assets obtained by foreclosure or repossession thus differs from the method specified in this Statement. It proposes discounting expected cash flows at a rate based on the creditor's "cost of money" to measure the "holding cost" of the asset until its realizable value is collected in cash. The concept of fair value in paragraph 13 does not involve questions of whether interest is a "holding cost" or "period cost" because it is concerned with estimating market price, not net realizable value, however defined. Accounting for transfers of assets in troubled debt restructurings and for the assets after transfer is, of course, governed by this Statement.

84. Several respondents to the Exposure Draft suggested that the Statement should explicitly state that troubled debt restructurings that are in substance transfers of assets should be accounted for accord-

[31]See paragraphs 59 and 60 of this Statement.

ing to that substance. The Board agreed that a restructuring may be in substance a foreclosure, repossession, or other transfer of assets even though formal foreclosure or repossession proceedings are not involved. Thus, the Statement requires accounting for a transfer of assets if, for example, the creditor obtains control or ownership (or substantially all of the benefits and risks incident to ownership) of one or more assets of the debtor and the debtor is wholly or partially relieved of the obligations under the debt, or if both the debt and one or more assets of the debtor are transferred to another debtor that is controlled by the creditor.

Debtor's Recognition of Gain or Loss

85. Responses to the November 7, 1975 Exposure Draft, the May 11, 1976 Discussion Memorandum, and the Exposure Draft included two general procedures for a debtor to account for a gain or loss from a troubled debt restructuring involving a transfer of assets to settle a payable:

a. The debtor recognizes a difference, if any, between the carrying amount of assets transferred and the carrying amoung of the payable settled as a gain on restructuring of a payable.
b. The debtor (1) recognizes a difference, if any, between the fair value and carrying amount of assets transferred as a gain or loss on transfer of assets and (2) recognizes a difference, if any, between the fair value of assets transferred and the carrying amount of the payable settled, as a gain on restructuring of a payable.

86. Some respondents contended that debtors should not recognize the difference between the carrying amount and fair value of assets transferred to settle a payable as a gain or loss on assets. Instead, the net difference, if any, between the carrying amount of assets transferred and the carrying amount of a payable settled should be recognized as a gain or loss on restructuring of a payable. They argued that to measure the fair value of assets transferred would be costly and subjective in certain circumstances and that distinctions in the debtor's income statement between a gain or loss on disposition of assets and a gain on settlement of payables in the same troubled debt restructuring would probably not be helpful and might be arbitrary.

87. Other respondents who addressed the question emphasized the desirability of being able to assess separately the debtor's performance with respect to the transferred assets. They suggested that measuring the fair values of the transferred assets is essential to that assessment and conveys significant information that is obscured if fair values are not measured. For example, the fair values of some assets transferred (such as real estate) may often exceed their carrying amounts, while the fair values of other assets transferred (such as receivables) may sometimes be less than their face amounts. In the existing accounting framework, the first kind of difference is not recognized before disposal of the asset, but the second kind of difference is likely to have been recognized before restructuring by some debtors but not recognized by others for various reasons. Failure to include a gain or loss for the difference between the fair values and carrying amounts of assets transferred in troubled debt restructurings is likely to obscure differences and similarities between restructurings, according to that view, and respondents who advocated separate recognition of a debtor's gains or losses on assets transferred and gains on restructuring argued that separate recognition is required to provide consistent information about a single debtor for different periods and comparable information about different debtors for the same periods. The need for separate recognition is accentuated if gains and losses on transfer of assets are classed differently from gains on restructuring in the debtor's income statement (that is, if the latter are classified as extraordinary items).

88. The Board concluded that the fair value of the assets transferred in a troubled debt restructuring constitutes the best measure of the debtor's sacrifice to settle the payable and therefore that the fair value of assets transferred should be used to measure the gain on restructuring of the payable. In the existing accounting framework, gains, and losses on certain kinds of noncurrent assets, are usually recognized on assets only when the assets are sold or otherwise disposed of. For many assets, that gain or loss on sale or disposal is the only indication of whether the enterprise did well or poorly by having the asset. That indication is lost if the gain or loss on disposition is buried in a gain on restructuring of troubled debt, and the effect of the restructuring itself is also obscured. Further, unless fair value of the asset transferred is used to account for the transaction, the proportion of a payable settled by the transfer can usually be determined only by arbitrary and complicated allocations if the transfer settles only part of the payable and the terms are modified on the remainder (paragraph 19).

89. Since a gain or loss recognized by a debtor on the assets transferred to settle a payable in a troubled debt restructuring is closely related to a gain recognized by a debtor on restructuring of a payable, the Board concluded that the aggregate amount of each should be disclosed for restructurings that have occurred during a period for which financial statements are presented (paragraph 25).

Creditor's Subsequent Accounting

90. The Board considered two proposals for a creditor's accounting for assets received in full satisfaction of a receivable in a troubled debt restructuring: (a) the creditor accounts for the assets received at their fair value and recognizes as a loss a difference, if any, between the total fair value of assets received and the recorded investment in the receivable satisfied or (b) the creditor accounts for the assets received at the recorded investment in the receivable satisfied and recognizes no loss. Those alternatives are described in paragraphs 65-70, and the Board's reasons for adopting the first proposal are given in paragraphs 71-78.

91. Several respondents to the Exposure Draft requested guidance on a creditor's accounting after a troubled debt restructuring for assets received in the restructuring. Some asked the Board to require or permit creditors to accrue interest on all assets acquired through repossession or foreclosure. In response, paragraph 29 states that "after a troubled debt restructuring, a creditor shall account for assets received in satisfaction of a receivable the same as if the assets had been acquired for cash." The fair value at the time of transfer of an asset transferred to a creditor in a troubled debt restructuring is a measure of its cost to the creditor and generally remains its carrying amount (except for depreciation or amortization) until sale or other disposition if the asset is inventory, land, building, equipment, or other nonmonetary asset. That is, under the present accounting framework, interest is accrued only on some receivables and other monetary assets. Except for the effects of a few specialized rules that permit interest cost to be added to the cost of some assets under construction, etc., interest is not accrued on nonmonetary assets. That framework governs accounting for assets acquired in a troubled debt restructuring. The method of accounting for assets received through foreclosure, repossession, or other asset transfer to satisfy a receivable proposed by *Statement of Position 75-2* is not compatible with the accounting specified in this Statement.

Debtor's Accounting for Grant of Equity Interest

92. The Board considered three proposals for a debtor's accounting for an equity interest granted to a creditor to settle a payable in a troubled debt restructuring:

a. The debtor directly increases its owners' equity by the fair value of the equity interest granted[32] and recognizes the difference between that fair value and the carrying amount of the payable settled as a gain included in measuring net income.
b. Same as (a) except that the resulting gain is included directly in the owners' equity of the debtor.
c. The debtor directly increases its owners' equity by the carrying amount of the payable settled, recognizing no gain.

93. Respondents favoring use of fair value to record a grant of an equity interest contended that the increase in the owners' equity of the debtor as a result of a troubled debt restructuring should be measured by the consideration received for the equity interest granted, not by the carrying amount of the payable settled because that carrying amount has no current economic significance. They also contended that a separate measure of a gain on restructuring of payables provides useful information.

94. Among those who advocated use of fair value to record an equity interest granted to settle debt in a troubled debt restructuring and recognition of a resulting gain on restructuring, some advocated including that gain in measuring net income and others advocated including it directly in the debtor's equity accounts. Those favoring inclusion in net income argued that all gains from troubled debt restructurings are components of net income whether they arise from transfer of assets or grant of equity interests. Those favoring direct inclusion in owners' equity argued that, to the extent an equity interest is involved, the restructuring is a capital transaction and gains resulting from capital transactions should be recognized as direct increases in paid-in or contributed owners' equity rather than as components of net income.

95. Those who advocated that the debtor's increase in equity for an equity interest granted should be the carrying amount of the debt settled also argued that granting an equity interest is essentially a capital transaction to which the notion of a gain does not apply. That solution was proposed in the November 7, 1975 Exposure Draft. Advocates of that view noted that paragraph 187 of *APB Statement No. 4* states that, among other sources, increases in owners' equity arise from investments in an enterprise by its owners. According to that view, a creditor that accepts an equity interest in the debtor in satisfaction of a receivable becomes an owner; the debtor's measure of the owners' investment is the carrying amount of the payable settled.

96. After considering the comments received in response to the November 7, 1975 Exposure Draft,

[32]"Fair value" in this context normally means the fair value of the liability satisfied or the fair value of the equity interest granted, whichever is the more clearly evident (*APB Opinion No. 16,* paragraph 67 and *APB Statement No. 4,* paragraph 182).

the May 11, 1976 Discussion Memorandum, and the Exposure Draft, the Board concluded that a debtor should record an equity interest in the debtor granted to a creditor to settle a payable in a troubled debt restructuring at its fair value, and the difference between that fair value and the carrying amount of the payable settled should be recognized as a gain in measuring net income. The Board recognizes that, for some debtors involved in troubled debt restructurings, estimating either fair value of the equity interest granted or the fair value of the payable settled may be difficult. That estimate is necessary, however, to measure separately the consideration received for the equity interest and the gain on restructuring. To include the gain on restructuring in contributed equity would violate a clear principle for accounting for issues of stock—capital stock issued is recorded at the fair value of the consideration received (*APB Statement No. 4,* paragraph 182). The consideration received for the stock issued in that kind of troubled debt restructuring is cancellation of the payable (or part of it), but the fair value of the consideration received is not measured by the carrying amount of the payable. Whether the consideration received is measured by the fair value of the stock issued or the fair value of the payable cancelled, the consideration is less than the carrying amount of the payable. To record the stock issued at the carrying amount of the payable thus results in recording the stock at an amount in excess of the consideration received; to include the gain in restructuring in contributed equity instead of net income gives the same result.

97. To recognize a gain on restructuring acknowledges that the creditor accepted something less than the carrying amount of the payable to settle it. Since that is the essential result whether the restructuring is in the form of a transfer of assets from debtor to creditor or the form of a grant to the creditor of an equity interest in the debtor, the Board believes that essentially the same accounting applies in the existing accounting framework to both kinds of restructurings. Although the creditor becomes an owner of the debtor to the extent that the creditor accepts an equity interest in the debtor, that is a consequence of the kind of consideration used to settle a payable in a restructuring. The restructuring itself is an agreement between a debtor and a creditor, and the gain to the debtor results because the creditor accepted less consideration than the carrying amount of the debt.

Classification of Debtor's Gain on Restructuring

98. Alternatives considered by the Board for classifying gain on a troubled debt restructuring in the debtor's financial statements were that the gain is: (a) always included in measuring net income in accordance with *APB Opinion No. 30,* (b) always included in measuring net income as an extraordinary item, and (c) always included as a direct addition to paid-in capital. Most respondents addressing the question recommended classifying a gain on restructuring debt as an extraordinary item, primarily because they perceived it to be similar to gains or losses on extinguishment of debt that, according to *FASB Statement No. 4,* shall be aggregated and, if material, classified as an extraordinary item, net of related income tax effect. Some respondents recommended classifying the gain as a direct increase in paid-in capital, contending that since the gain results from a unilateral action by the creditor, the debtor has in effect received a contribution to equity from the creditor.

99. The Board concluded that a gain on restructuring (net of related income tax effect), if material, should always be classified as an extraordinary item in measuring the debtor's net income. The Board recognized that to apply the criteria in *APB Opinion No. 30* to a particular debtor's gain on restructuring would not necessarily result in its classification as an extraordinary item. The Board concluded, however, that a gain on restructuring of a payable in a troubled debt restructuring is indistinguishable from a gain or loss on other extinguishments of debt, and the same classification in financial statements is appropriate. Since *FASB Statement No. 4* classifies a gain or loss on extinguishment of debt as an extraordinary item, the classification is appropriate for a gain on restructuring of a payable.

100. Some respondents suggested that "legal fees and other direct costs that a debtor incurs in granting an equity interest to a creditor in a troubled debt restructuring" (paragraph 24) always be included as extraordinary items whether or not the debtor recognizes a gain on restructuring. Issuing equity interests is not an extraordinary event for a business enterprise, however, and related costs are not extraordinary items under any existing authoritative literature. Deducting those costs from the proceeds of issue has been customary practice, and this Statement does not change that custom. But only costs of issuing the equity interest may be accounted for that way. All other direct costs of a troubled debt restructuring are expenses of the period of restructuring but shall be deducted from a gain, if any, on restructuring.

Creditor's Accounting for Loss on Restructuring

101. Some respondents to the Discussion Memorandum, especially financial institutions, indicated that they hold and manage broad groups of earning assets (primarily loans and investments) as portfolios rather than as individual assets. According to them, their primary consideration in making a new loan or investment is to recover the amount

invested, and the rate of return on the amount invested is a secondary consideration. Although one objective is to obtain an appropriate rate of return for the particular credit risk, changes in market conditions and general economic conditions as well as changes affecting the individual asset or debtor may cause the actual return from a loan or investment to vary from that originally anticipated. Therefore, the objective is to maintain a portfolio with an average yield that provides an adequate margin over the cost of funds and that has risk, maturity, marketability, and liquidity characteristics that are appropriate for the particular institution. To achieve that objective, the contractual rate of return required on individual loans and investments must include a factor to offset the probability that some of them will become nonearning assets, some will ultimately recover amounts invested only with difficulty, and some will involve loss of at least a portion of the amounts invested.

102. The financial difficulties of a debtor that lead to a troubled debt restructuring usually require the creditor to consider those difficulties carefully in determining whether to recognize a loss on the existing receivable. Typically, before restructuring occurs, the creditor has determined the need for a related allowance for uncollectible amounts in light of those difficulties. An allowance for uncollectible amounts may have been based on individual receivables, on groups of similar receivables without necessarily attempting to identify particular receivables that may prove uncollectible, or both. The creditor typically has numerous lending transactions and expects loan losses to recur as a consequence of customary and continuing business activities. Almost all respondents who commented on the classification of a creditor's loss on restructuring recommended that the loss be accounted for in a manner consistent with the enterprise's method of accounting for other losses related to its receivables. Usually that involves recognizing specific losses as they are identified and periodically adjusting the allowance for uncollectible amounts based on an assessment of its adequacy for losses not yet specifically identified. Respondents recommended that the net effect of recognizing specific losses and adjusting the valuation allowance be included in measuring net income in accordance with the provisions of *APB Opinion No. 30.*

103. The Board considered the varied frequency and significance for creditors of troubled debt restructurings in the light of the discussion in *APB Opinion No. 30,* and agreed that (a) a creditor should account for a loss from a troubled debt restructuring in the same manner as a creditor's other losses on receivables (that is, as deductions in measuring net income or as reductions of an allowance for uncollectible amounts), and (b) *APB Opinion No. 30* should apply to losses on restructuring that are included in measuring net income.

Creditor's Sale of Assets Received in Restructuring

104. A creditor whose customary business activities include lending may sell an asset that was previously acquired in a troubled debt restructuring. The consideration received in that sale may be represented, in whole or in part, by a receivable. The Board considered whether a receivable received in that way is exempt from the provisions of *APB Opinion No. 21* because paragraph 3(d) of that Opinion states that, except for one paragraph, the Opinion does not apply to several kinds of receivables or payables or activities, including "the customary cash lending activities and demand or savings deposit activities of financial institutions whose primary business is lending money." Some respondents to the Exposure Draft held that acquiring and disposing of those assets is part of "the customary cash lending activities" of certain financial institutions.

105. The "lending activities" referred to in paragraph 3(d) of *APB Opinion No. 21* are modified by the words "customary" and "cash," and the Board concluded that the sale of an asset, such as real estate, by a financial institution is distinguishable from its customary cash lending activities. The view that the customary cash lending activities of a financial institution include repossession or foreclosure and resale of assets is part of the argument that repossessions and foreclosures are not transactions to be accounted for but merely changes in the form of the asset (paragraphs 66, 67, and 79-84). The Board rejected that contention and also rejected this part of it. *APB Opinion No. 21* focuses primarily on the possible misstatement of the exchange price (sale price or purchase price) in an exchange of a noncash asset for a receivable or payable, with consequent misstatement in the period of the transaction of gain or loss on sale or acquisition cost and misstatement in later periods of interest income or interest expense. The resale of repossessed or foreclosed assets is that kind of transaction and involves the same questions. Accordingly, the Board concluded that a receivable resulting from sale of an asset received in a troubled debt restructuring is covered by that Opinion, including paragraph 12, which prescribes the measurement of a note (receivable) exchanged "for property, goods, or service in a bargained transaction entered into at arm's length."

ACCOUNTING FOR RESTRUCTURINGS INVOLVING MODIFICATION OF TERMS

Background Information

106. A creditor holds a receivable with the expecta-

tion that the future cash receipts, both those designated as interest and those designated as face amount, specified by the terms of the agreement will provide a return of the creditor's investment in that receivable and a return on the investment (interest income).[33] That essential nature of a creditor's investment in a receivable is the same whether the creditor invested cash (for example, a cash loan to a debtor or a cash purchase of debt securities) or exchanged assets or services (for example, a sale of the creditor's services, product, or other assets) for the receivable.

107. Similarly, a debtor expects the future cash payments specified by the terms of a payable to include a cost (interest expense) for the privilege of deferring repayment of funds borrowed or deferring payment for goods or services acquired. The essential nature of a debtor's payable is the same whether the debtor received cash in exchange for the payable (for example, a cash loan or the issue of debt securities for cash) or received other assets or services (for example, a purchase of services, materials, or other assets from the creditor).

108. The difference between the amount a creditor invests in a receivable and the amount it receives from the debtor's payments of interest and face amount is the return on the investment (interest income) for the entire period the receivable is held. Similarly, the difference between the amount a debtor receives and the amount it pays for interest and face amount is the cost of deferring payment (interest expense) for the entire period the payable is outstanding. The question that must be answered to account for a debt (a receivable or payable) and related interest is how that total interest income or expense is to be allocated to the accounting periods comprising the entire period that the receivable is held or the payable is outstanding.

109. That allocation of interest income or expense to periods is normally accomplished in present accounting practices by the interest method, which measures the interest income or expense of each period by applying the effective interest rate implicit in the debt to the amount of the debt at the beginning of the period, assuming that all cash receipts or payments will occur as specified in the agreement. The effective interest rate implicit in the debt may be the same as or different from the interest rate stated in the agreement (the stated interest rate). The effective and stated rates are the same if the amount invested or borrowed equals the face amount; the rates differ if the amount invested or borrowed is greater or less than the face amount.

110. Thus, the recorded investment in a receivable or the carrying amount of a payable, both at the time of the originating transaction and at the beginning of each period comprising the entire period a receivable is held or a payable is outstanding, is the sum of the present values of (a) the amounts of periodic future cash receipts or payments that are designated as interest and (b) the face amount of cash due at maturity, both discounted at the effective interest rate implicit in the debt. If the effective interest rate differs from the stated interest rate, the recorded investment in the receivable or carrying amount of the payable in financial statements is the face amount plus unamortized premium or less unamortized discount, and that amount is used to measure the interest income or expense, as described in the preceding paragraph.

111. Numerous references to and descriptions of the concepts and procedures referred to in paragraphs 108-110 are found in the pronouncements of the Accounting Principles Board and the Financial Accounting Standards Board, for example, on accounting for leases *(FASB Statement No. 13);* accounting for the cost of pension plans *(APB Opinion No. 8);* accounting for interest on receivables and payables *(APB Opinions No. 12* and *No. 21);* accounting for early extinguishment of debt *(APB Opinion No. 26);* recording receivables and payables of a company acquired in a business combination (*APB Opinion No. 16,* paragraphs 87-89); and translating receivables and payables denominated in a foreign currency (*FASB Statement No. 8,* paragraph 39).

112. Pronouncements of the Accounting Principles Board also include several specific statements of broad principle. They include: "The general principles to apply the historical-cost basis of accounting to an acquisition of an asset depend on the nature of the transaction: . . . b. An asset acquired by incurring liabilities is recorded at cost—that is, at the present value of the amounts to be paid" (*APB Opinion No. 16,* paragraph 67); "Conceptually, a liability is measured at the amount of cash to be paid discounted to the time the liability is incurred" (*APB Statement No. 4,* paragraph 181 [M-1C]; and ". . . upon issuance, a bond is valued at (1) the present value of the future coupon interest payments plus (2) the present value of the future principal payments (face amount) . . . discounted at the prevailing market rate of interest . . . at the date of issuance of the debt" and ". . . the difference between the present value and the face amount should be treated as discount or premium and amortized as interest expense or income over the life of

[33]The terms of some short-term receivables and payables (for example, trade accounts receivable or payable) may not be expected to result in interest income or interest expense to the creditor or debtor except as it may be implicit in the transaction (for example, implicit in the price of a product sold or purchased on account).

the note in such a way as to result in a constant rate of interest when applied to the amount outstanding at the beginning of any given period. This is the 'interest' method described in and supported by paragraphs 16 and 17 of *APB Opinion No. 12"* (*APB Opinion No. 21,* paragraphs 18 [Appendix] and 15).

Kinds of Modifications and Accounting Issues

113. Agreements between a creditor and a debtor that modify the terms of an existing debt may affect (i) only the *timing* of future cash receipts or payments specified by the agreement—the timing of periodic interest, the maturity date, or both, (ii) only the *amounts* of cash to be received or paid—the amounts of interest, face amount, or both, or (iii) *both* timing and amounts of cash to be received or paid.

114. Two major issues arise in accounting for an existing debt whose terms are modified in a troubled debt restructuring. One issue involves whether to: (a) continue the same recorded investment for the receivable or carrying amount for the payable and recognize the effects of the new terms prospectively as reduced interest income or expense or (b) recognize a loss or gain by changing the recorded amount. The interest method (paragraph 109) is used in both (a) and (b) to allocate interest income or expense to periods between restructuring and maturity, but in general, the implicit annual interest rate will be higher, and the resulting interest income or expense will be larger in each of the remaining periods, if a loss (creditor) or gain (debtor) is recognized at the time of a troubled debt restructuring, as in (b), than if the effects of the new terms are recognized prospectively, as in (a).

115. The other issue involves two related questions: Should the same accounting (either (a) or (b) in paragraph 114) apply both to modifications of *timing* and to modifications of *amounts* to be received or paid under the agreement? And should the same accounting apply both to modifications of *interest* and to modifications of *face amount?* The following paragraphs explain and illustrate those issues and summarize the arguments advanced for various proposed solutions.

116. Modifications of terms that affect only the *timing* of amounts to be received or paid do not change the total amount to be received or paid. However, changes in timing of the amounts to be received or paid on a debt change its present value determined by discounting at the prerestructuring effective interest rate or a current market interest rate or change the effective interest rate needed to discount the amounts to the prerestructuring present value (recorded investment in receivable or carrying amount of payable) or market value. Modifications that affect only the *amount* of interest or face amount (or both unless they are exactly offsetting) to be received or paid change total amounts as well as present values, effective interest rates, or both. Modifications of *both timing and amount* to be received or paid combine those effects. A hypothetical case illustrates those kinds of modifications and their effects.

117. A creditor holds a receivable calling for receipt of $100 at the end of each year for five more years and receipt of the $1,000 face amount at the end of those five years. The stated interest rate is 10 percent, compounded annually. The recorded investment in the receivable is $1,000, and the effective annual interest rate implicit in the investment is also 10 percent. If all amounts are received as agreed, the creditor will receive total interest income of $500—the difference between the total amount to be received ($1,500) and the recorded investment in the receivable ($1,000)—and the effective interest rate on the $1,000 investment will be 10 percent. However, the terms of the receivable are to be modified in a troubled debt restructuring. The four modifications that follow are examples of the three kinds of modifications described in paragraphs 113 and 116 (change in amount of interest and change in face amount are both illustrated; change in timing of face amount raises no issues different from change in timing of interest and is not illustrated):

1. *Timing of interest only*—Terms modified to defer collection of interest until the receivable matures (a single collection of $500 at the end of five years is substituted for five annual collections at $100).
2. *Amount of interest only*—Terms modified to leave unchanged the timing of interest and the timing and amount of the face amount but reduce the annual interest from $100 to $60.
3. *Amount of face amount only*—Terms modified to leave unchanged the amounts and timing of interest but reduce the face amount to $800 due at the end of five years.
4. *Both timing of interest and amount of face amount*—Terms modified to defer collection of interest until the receivable matures and reduce the face amount to $800 (modifications 1 and 3 combined).

118. The following chart lists several factual observations that can be made about the effects on the creditor's receivable of each of those restructurings. In general, the same observations apply to the debtor's payable.

	Before Modification	Modification 1 (Timing Only)	Modification 2 (Amount of Interest Only)	Modification 3 (Amount of Face Amount Only)	Modification 4 (Timing and Amount)
Observation:					
a. Amount by which total cash receipts specified by the terms exceed recorded investment in the receivable:					
Interest	$ 500	$ 500	$ 300	$ 500	$ 500
Face amount	1,000	1,000	1,000	800	800
Total cash receipts	$1,500	$1,500	$1,300	$1,300	$1,300
Recorded investment	1,000	1,000	1,000	1,000	1,000
Excess of specified cash receipts over recorded investment	$ 500	$ 500	$ 300	$ 300	$ 300
b. Effective interest rate on the recorded investment ($1,000)	10.0%	8.5%	6.0%	6.5%	5.4%
c. Present value of the total cash receipts discounted at the pre-restructuring effective interest rate (10%)	$1,000	$ 931	$ 848	$ 876	$ 807
d. Present value of the total cash receipts discounted at the current market interest rate (assumed to be 12%)	$ 928	$ 851	$ 784	$ 814	$ 738
e. Face amount specified by the terms	$1,000	$1,000	$1,000	$ 800	$ 800

Alternatives Considered

119. Proposals for accounting for troubled debt restructurings tend to focus on the various observations (paragraph 118) about the effects of modifying the terms of a debt.

a. Some respondents focused on the effect of a troubled debt restructuring on the effective interest rate (observation (b)). They would not reduce the recorded investment in a receivable or carrying amount of a payable and recognize a loss (creditor) or gain (debtor) as long as the new terms did not result in a negative effective interest rate on the recorded investment or carrying amount—that is, as long as the total future cash receipts or payments specified by the new terms (including both amounts designated as interest and the amount designated as face amount) at least equaled the recorded investment or carrying amount (observation (a)). Thus, they would recognize no loss or gain for any of the four modifications in the illustration in paragraphs 117 and 118.
b. Some respondents focused on the effect of a troubled debt restructuring on the face amount of the debt (observation (e)). They would not reduce the recorded investment in a receivable or carrying amount of a payable as long as the restructuring modified only the timing or amount of designated interest or the timing of the designated face amount, but would recognize a loss (creditor) or gain (debtor) if restructuring reduced the face amount of the debt. Thus, they would recognize a loss or gain for modifications 3 and 4 in the illustration.
c. Some respondents focused on the effect of a troubled debt restructuring on the present value of the debt discounted at the effective interest rate before restructuring (observation (c)). They would reduce the recorded investment in a receivable or carrying amount of a payable to the present value of the total future cash receipts or payments under the new terms discounted at the prerestructuring effective interest rate and recognize a loss (creditor) or gain (debtor) equal to the reduction. Thus, they would recognize a loss or gain for each of the modifications in the illustration.
d. Some respondents focused on the fair or market value of the debt after a troubled debt restructuring. They would account for each restructuring as an exchange of debt, recording a new receivable or payable at its fair or market value and recognizing a loss (creditor) or gain (debtor) for the difference between that fair or market

value and the recorded investment or carrying amount of the receivable or payable replaced. Thus, they would recognize a loss or gain for each of the modifications in the illustration.

The following paragraphs summarize those four views and their variations.

Change in Effective Rate View

120. Some respondents emphasized that, in the absence of a transfer of resources or obligations, the existing accounting framework does not require losses to be recognized or permit gains to be recognized because of events that affect only future profitability of an investment but do not affect the recoverability of the investment itself. They contended that applying that principle to troubled debt restructurings means that no loss or gain should be recognized on a debt because of modification of terms of debt unless part of the recorded investment in a receivable is not recoverable or part of the carrying amount of a payable will not be paid under the new terms. In their view, a creditor should recognize a loss to the extent that the total future cash receipts specified by the new terms is less than the recorded investment in the receivable, and a debtor should recognize a gain to the extent that the total future cash payments specified by the new terms is less than the carrying amount of the payable.

121. According to that view, if the recorded investment in a receivable is recoverable or the carrying amount of a payable is to be paid under the new terms,[34] interest income or expense is allocated to the periods between restructuring and maturity of the debt by using the reduced effective interest rate that is implicit in the difference between the recorded investment or carrying amount before (and after) restructuring and the future cash receipts or payments specified by the new terms. If a loss or gain is recognized at the time of restructuring, the recorded investment or carrying amount equals the total future cash receipts or payments, and no interest income or expense is allocated to the remaining periods between restructuring and maturity.

122. Some of those respondents contended that the amount invested by a creditor in a receivable has some of the characteristics of, and is analogous to, an investment in plant, property, intangibles, and similar assets sometimes called "capital assets." According to that analogy, modifying the terms of receivables in troubled debt restructurings is similar to modifying selling prices of products produced by those capital assets; the modifications affect the profitability of those assets but are not recorded in the existing accounting framework unless they result in an inability to recover the investment in the assets. That capital asset analogy leads its proponents to accounting for troubled debt restructurings that is essentially the same as that described in paragraphs 120 and 121.

123. Certain respondents who supported the views described in paragraphs 120-122 argued that the resulting accounting not only is required by the existing accounting framework but also accurately describes a troubled debt restructuring involving only modification of terms. They held that, unless the effective interest rate on a debt becomes negative in a troubled debt restructuring, the essential effect of modifying terms is to reduce the effective interest rate on the debt—that is, to decrease the effective rate of return to the creditor and to decrease the effective cost to the debtor of deferring payment. For example, some responding financial analysts argued that to disclose the creditor's new effective interest rate on restructured receivables would be more useful for their purposes than for the creditor to report a loss on restructuring and then show those receivables to be earning the prerestructuring interest rate, the current market interest rate, or some other rate higher than the effective rate on the recorded investment in a receivable before restructuring.

124. According to respondents who emphasized the effect of a troubled debt restructuring on the effective interest rate, there is no economic basis for distinguishing modifications of future cash receipts or payments designated as interest from modifications of future cash receipts or payments designated as face amount. They argued that a creditor in a troubled debt restructuring attempts first to assure recovery of its investment (which is represented in its financial statements by the recorded investment in the receivable) and then to obtain the highest interest income commensurate with the situation. Whether the amounts to be received under the new terms are designated as receipts of interest or receipt of face amount is a minor consideration; the significant question is whether the new terms allow the creditor to recover its investment.

125. According to that view, since numerous combinations of receipts or payments designated as interest and face amount can be structured to produce a particular present value or effective interest rate, to base accounting on that distinction is likely to result in questionable, if not indefensible, financial reporting. The creditor in a troubled debt restructuring may have considerable flexibility in

[34]The likelihood of collection of the amounts specified by the new terms of a receivable should, of course, be assessed in determining allowances for estimated uncollectible amounts.

designating a proportion of the future receipts or payments under the new terms as interest and designating another proportion as face amount. If those designations were to dictate the accounting, a creditor desiring to recognize a loss on restructuring and to recognize higher interest income for later periods could restructure terms in one way, while a creditor desiring to avoid recognizing a loss on restructuring and to recognize lower interest income for later periods could restructure the terms in another way, even though the underlying cash receipts specified by the new terms were the same, both in timing and amount, for both creditors. A creditor desiring to recognize a gain on restructuring could conceivably increase the amount designated as face amount to an amount higher than the present recorded investment and reduce the amounts designated as receipt of interest; a debtor might agree to that arrangement if it were financially troubled at the time of restructuring but expected to be able to pay the higher face amount later.

Change in Face Amount View

126. Some respondents distinguished modifications of face amounts from modifications affecting only amounts or timing of receipts or payments designated as interest or timing of the maturity date. They would neither reduce recorded investment in a receivable or carrying amount of a payable nor recognize loss or gain in a troubled debt restructuring if a modification of terms of a debt changed only the *amounts or timing* of receipts or payments designated as interest or changed the *timing* of receipts or payments designated as face amount. They held, however, that if a troubled debt restructuring *reduces the face amount* of a debt, the creditor should recognize a loss, and the debtor should recognize a gain.[35]

127. To record a modification of terms involving reduction of face amount of a debt, proponents of that view would reduce the recorded investment in the receivable or carrying amount of the payable by the same proportion as the reduction of the face amount and recognize a loss (creditor) or gain (debtor) for that amount. If the restructuring changed the effective interest rate on the remaining recorded investment or carrying amount, they would allocate interest income or expense to the remaining periods between restructuring and maturity using that new effective interest rate. That rate would be implicit in the difference between the new recorded investment in the receivable or carrying amount of the payable and the future cash receipts or payments specified by the new terms. That rate would be higher for a debt whose face amount had been reduced, and would therefore result in more interest income or expense for those periods, than the rate described in paragraph 121.

128. Respondents who distinguished between modifications of terms that change the face amount of a debt and other kinds of modifications generally agreed with the view expressed in paragraphs 120 and 122 that the existing accounting framework does not recognize losses or gains from events that change the profitability of existing assets but requires a loss to be recognized if the event causes part or all of an investment in an asset to become unrecoverable. Those respondents gave several reasons for concluding that reduction of face amount of a debt in a troubled debt restructuring requires proportionate reduction of the recorded investment in the receivable or carrying amount of the payable and recognition of a resulting loss or gain.

129. Some respondents who favored accounting based on a distinction between modifications of face amount and other modifications argued that to the extent that the face amount of a debt is reduced, the debtor-creditor relationship has been terminated, and the accounting should recognize that termination. In other words, the face amount adjusted by a premium or discount, if any, measured in the market at the time a receivable or payable was created is recognized in the existing accounting framework as an asset for the creditor or liability for the debtor; reducing that face amount therefore reduces an asset or liability proportionately, and the reduction must be recognized. In their view, to the extent the face amount is reduced, a transfer of resources or obligations occurs.

130. Some respondents described the analogy between a creditor's investment in a receivable and an investment in "capital assets" that is noted in paragraph 122 and contended that reductions of face amounts of receivables in troubled debt restructurings are analogous to events that reduce the amount, rather than the future profitability, of capital assets. Both they and the respondents whose view is described in the preceding paragraph held that the act of reducing the face amount showed that the creditor and debtor agreed that the receivable and payable had been decreased.

131. Some respondents contended in effect that accounting for receivables and payables in the existing accounting framework is based on the face amount of a receivable or payable, or perhaps on the face amount plus a premium or minus a discount at the date of acquisition or issue, and a change in the face amount is a change in an asset

[35]Some proponents of this view opposed recognizing gains from troubled debt restructurings not involving transfers of assets or grants of equity interests.

(receivable) or liability (payable). They implicitly assumed or concluded that the present value concepts described in the pronouncements noted in paragraphs 111 and 112 did not apply to receivables or payables involved in troubled debt restructurings. Thus, they contended that the distinction between the face amount due at maturity and the amounts designated as interest to be received or paid periodically until maturity is vital in determining proper accounting for a troubled debt restructuring. According to that view, the face amount due at maturity (sometimes referred to as the "principal") is the basis of the recorded investment in a receivable or carrying amount of a payable; that investment or carrying amount does not include the present value of future receipts or payments designated as interest. That is, a creditor or debtor records the face amount (perhaps increased by premium or decreased by discount) when a receivable is obtained or a payable is incurred, and no value is ascribed in the accounts to rights to receive or obligations to pay amounts designated as interest; rather, cash receipts or payments designated as interest are recognized in the accounts only as they become receivable or payable in future periods. Some respondents holding that view added that to record a loss (creditor) or gain (debtor) because future cash receipts or payments designated as interest are modified in a troubled debt restructuring would represent abandonment of the existing historical cost framework and constitute piecemeal implementation of current value accounting.

132. Several respondents who supported the views described in paragraphs 126-131 held that the accounting required by those views is presently used, at least by some financial institutions. Some banker respondents indicated that troubled debt restructurings involving reductions in face amount or "principal" are exceedingly rare, but that most bankers would probably recognize a loss of "principal" in recording one in which their institution was the creditor.

133. Differences between the view that focuses on the effect of a troubled debt restructuring on face amount (paragraphs 126-132) and the view that focuses on its effect on the effective interest rate (paragraphs 120-125) pertain wholly to troubled debt restructurings that reduce the amount designated as face amount. Both views lead to the same accounting for troubled debt restructurings involving other kinds of modification of terms.

Present Value at Prerestructuring Rate View

134. Some respondents contended that accounting for troubled debt restructurings should recognize the revised pattern of cash receipts or payments under the new terms of the restructured debt. That is, they would continue to use the effective interest rate established when the receivable was acquired or payable was incurred and would reduce the recorded investment or carrying amount to the present value of the future cash receipts or payments specified by the new terms.

135. Those respondents in effect supported the accounting proposed in the FASB Exposure Draft, "Restructuring of Debt in a Troubled Loan Situation" (November 7, 1975): a debtor should account for a troubled debt restructuring that involves modification of terms of debt by adjusting the carrying amount of the payable to the present value of the cash payments (both those designated as interest and those designated as face amount) required of the debtor after restructuring, discounted at the prerestructuring effective interest rate, and recognizing a gain on restructuring of the payable equal to the difference, if any, between that present value and the carrying amount of the payable before restructuring (paragraph 6 of that Exposure Draft). Since a troubled debt restructuring almost invariably involves stretching out or deferring the debtor's payments, and may involve reducing amounts due as well, the present value of a restructured payable is almost invariably less than its carrying amount (both are determined by discounting at the same interest rate); a debtor would thus normally recognize a gain on the restructuring. The November 7, 1975 Exposure Draft dealt only with accounting by debtors, but if the counterpart accounting were adopted by creditors, the creditor would normally recognize a loss equal to the difference between its recorded investment in the receivable before restructuring and the present value at the prerestructuring effective interest rate. Interest expense or income in future periods would continue to be based on the prerestructuring interest rate.

136. Some respondents who held the view described in paragraphs 134 and 135 agreed with the view in paragraphs 124 and 125 that no economic basis exists for distinguishing between modifications of face amounts and other kinds of modifications. The major difference between the two views is that the accounting for one view (paragraphs 134 and 135) retains the same effective interest rate as before restructuring and changes the present value of the future cash receipts or payments specified by the new terms, while the other view (paragraphs 124 and 125) retains the same present value as before restructuring (the recorded investment in a receivable or carrying amount of a payable)[36] and changes the effective interest rate for the periods remaining between restructuring and maturity.

[36]Unless the restructuring causes the effective interest rate to fall below zero.

Fair Value View

137. Some respondents contended that modifying terms in a troubled debt restructuring results in an exchange of new debt for the previous debt. The new debt should be recorded at its fair value—usually the present value of the future cash receipts or payments specified by the new terms (whether designated as interest or face amount) discounted at the current market rate of interest for receivables or payables with similar terms and risk characteristics. Those respondents contended that every debt restructuring is an exchange transaction (paragraph 68), and they would recognize a loss (creditor) and gain (debtor) to the extent of the difference between the recorded investment in the receivable or carrying amount of the payable before restructuring and the fair value of the receivable or payable after restructuring. Interest income and expense in future periods would be based on the market rate of interest at the time of restructuring.

138. Respondents who supported the view just described agreed that designations of amounts as face amount or interest should not determine whether a loss or gain should be recognized (paragraphs 124 and 125) because only the amounts and timing of cash receipts or payments, and not their names, affect the present value of a receivable or payable. They disagreed with other respondents by contending that the current market interest rate—which gives the fair value of a receivable or payable—should be used because an exchange transaction had occurred.[37]

139. Some of the responding financial analysts indicated a preference for accounting that does not use a current interest rate to determine whether a creditor should recognize a loss in a troubled debt restructuring involving modification of terms. According to them, to use a current interest rate to discount future cash receipts only for receivables that have been restructured would not result in meaningful information about the earning potential of a creditor's entire loan or investment portfolio and might be confusing because receivables that were not restructured would continue to reflect the various historical interest rates at the time of each investment.

Conclusions on Modification of Terms

140. After considering the information received in connection with (i) the Exposure Draft, "Restructuring of Debt in a Troubled Loan Situation" (November 7, 1975), and the public hearing based on it (paragraph 48), (ii) the Discussion Memorandum, "Accounting By Debtors and Creditors When Debt Is Restructured" (May 11, 1976), and the public hearing based on it (paragraph 52), and (iii) the Exposure Draft, the Board concluded that the substance of all modifications of a debt in a troubled debt restructuring is essentially the same whether they are modifications of timing, modifications of amounts designated as interest, or modifications of amounts designated as face amounts. All of those kinds of modifications affect future cash receipts or payments and therefore affect (a) the creditor's total return on the receivable, its effective interest rate, or both and (b) the debtor's total cost on the payable, its effective interest rate, or both. The Board believes that accounting for restructured debt should be based on the substance of the modifications—the effect on cash flows—not on the labels chosen to describe those cash flows.

141. The Board thus rejected views that modifications involving changes in face amounts should be distinguished from and accounted for differently from modifications involving amounts of future cash receipts or payments designated as interest and modifications involving timing of future cash receipts or payments. The major reason for that rejection is given in the preceding paragraph: the substance of a troubled debt restructuring lies in its effect on the *timing and amounts* of cash receipts or payments due in the future. Whether an amount due at a particular time is described as face amount or interest is of no consequence to either the present value of the receivable or payable or its effective interest rate.

142. The Board considered the views described in paragraphs 129-132 and rejected them to the extent they conflict with the Board's conclusions. In the Board's view, a debtor-creditor relationship is described by the entire agreement between the debtor and creditor and not merely by the face amount of the debt. Changes in that relationship therefore encompass changes in timing and changes in amounts designated as interest as well as changes in an amount designated as face amount. The same reasoning applies to the analogy between debt and investment in "capital assets." A reduction in a troubled debt restructuring of an amount designated as face amount is not, in the Board's view, analogous to the loss or destruction of a portion of a capital asset. Indeed, the economic impact of reducing an amount designated as face amount is essentially the same as that of reducing by the same amount an amount designated as interest that is due at the same time. Thus, although an analogy between investment in a receivable and investment in a capital asset may have merit, an analogy between an amount des-

[37]Some respondents contended that the fair value of the receivable or payable after restructuring should be measured by discounting the future cash flows specified by the new terms at the cost of capital to the creditor or debtor, as appropriate.

ignated as the face amount of a receivable and the physical entirety of a capital asset does not.

143. The Board also rejected the view that accounting is based on the face amount or "principal" in the existing accounting framework. That view is not consistent with the weight of the pronouncements noted in paragraphs 111 and 112 to the effect that the recorded investment in a receivable or carrying amount of a payable is the present value of the future cash receipts or payments specified by the terms of the debt discounted at the effective interest rate that is implicit in the debt at its inception. That accounting explicitly excludes from the recorded investment in a receivable or carrying amount of a payable the interest income or expense to be recognized in future periods. The interest method recognizes that interest income or expense as a constant percent (the effective interest rate) of the recorded investment or carrying amount at the beginning of each future period as the interest income or expense becomes receivable or payable. The method is not a "current value method" as that term is generally used in the accounting literature, unless the effective interest rate used to determine present value and interest income or expense each period is the current market interest rate for the period.

144. The Board noted the argument that current practice in some financial institutions is to record losses based on reductions in troubled debt restructurings of amounts designated as face amount. The Board also noted that several respondents indicated that modifications of terms of that kind almost never occur. Presumably, a creditor would generally prefer to alleviate the debtor's cash difficulties by deferring payment of the amount designated as face amount rather than by reducing it because deferring payment preserves a creditor's maximum claim in the event of the debtor's bankruptcy. The Board decided that accounting for reductions in troubled debt restructurings of amounts designated as face amounts, although occurring only rarely, should be made consistent with accounting for other modifications of future cash receipts or payments in troubled debt restructurings and with the accounting pronouncements referred to in paragraphs 111 and 112.

145. The Board also considered the views described in paragraphs 134-139 and rejected them to the extent they conflict with the Board's conclusions. The Board concluded that since a troubled debt restructuring involving modifications of terms of debt does not involve transfers of resources or obligations (paragraph 77), restructured debt should continue to be accounted for in the existing accounting framework, on the basis of the recorded investment in the receivable or carrying amount of the payable before the restructuring. The effective interest rate on that debt should be determined by the relation of the recorded investment in the receivable or carrying amount of the payable and the future cash receipts or payments specified by the new terms of the debt.

146. To introduce the current market interest rate to provide a new measure of the recorded investment in a restructured receivable or carrying amount of a restructured payable is inappropriate in the existing accounting framework in the absence of a transfer of resources or obligations, that is, if only the terms of a debt are modified in a troubled debt restructuring. Moreover, since the new terms are not negotiated on the basis of the current market rates of interest, there is little or no reason to believe that a current market rate of interest applied to the restructured debt reflects the effective return to the creditor or the effective cost to the debtor. On the contrary, the circumstances of a troubled debt restructuring give every reason to believe that, except by coincidence, it does not. Similarly, there is little or no reason to believe that a restructured debt continues to earn or cost the same effective interest rate as before the restructuring. The restructuring reflected the creditor's recognition that its investment in the receivable no longer could earn that rate and that a lower effective rate was inevitable. In other words, the effect of the restructuring was to decrease the effective interest rate on a continuing debt, and the accounting should show that result.

147. The Board found persuasive the arguments that a creditor in a troubled debt restructuring is interested in protecting its unrecovered investment (represented in the accounts by the recorded investment in the receivable) and, if possible, obtaining a return. To the creditor, therefore, the effect of a restructuring that provides for recovery of the investment is to reduce the rate of return (the effective interest rate) between the restructuring and maturity. Similarly, the effect of that kind of restructuring to the debtor is to reduce the cost of credit (the effective interest rate) between the restructuring and maturity.

148. Thus, the Board concluded that no loss (creditor) or gain (debtor) should be recognized in a troubled debt restructuring if the total future cash receipts or payments (whether designated as interest or face amount) specified by the new terms at least equals the recorded investment or carrying amount of the debt before the restructuring. The creditor should reduce the recorded investment in the receivable and recognize a loss and the debtor should reduce the carrying amount of the payable and recognize a gain to the extent that the recorded investment or carrying amount exceeds the total cash receipts or payments specified by the new terms. Some respondents to the Exposure Draft apparently

misunderstood the reason for using *total* future cash receipts or payments to compare with the recorded investment in a receivable or the carrying amount of a payable to determine whether to recognize a loss or gain on restructuring. Some wondered if the failure to discount the future cash flows implied changes in pronouncements that require discounting or de-emphasis or abandonment by the Board of discounting methods. On the contrary, the Statement is based solidly on the need to consider the effect of interest. Indeed, the Board's conclusion is that a troubled debt restructuring affects primarily the effective interest rate and results in no loss or gain as long as the effective rate does not fall below zero. It requires recognition of a loss to prevent the effective rate from falling below zero. The effective interest rate inherent in the unrecovered receivable or unpaid payable and the cash flows specified by the modified terms is then used to recognize interest income or interest expense between restructuring and maturity.

149. The Board also concluded that the fair values of assets transferred or equity interest granted in partial settlement of debt in a troubled debt restructuring should be accounted for the same as a partial cash payment. The recorded investment in the receivable or carrying amount of the payable should be reduced by the amount of cash or fair value transferred, and the remaining receivable or payable should be accounted for the same as a modification of terms. That accounting avoids basing losses or gains on restructuring on arbitrary allocations otherwise required to determine the amount of a receivable satisfied or payable settled by transfer of assets or grant of an equity interest.

150. Several respondents to the Exposure Draft disagreed with its proposed conclusions on accounting for modifications of terms in troubled debt restructurings. One group, which favored accounting for all troubled debt restructurings at fair value as exchanges of debt, criticized the Exposure Draft for failing to recognize losses and gains from decreases in present values of receivables and payables, for being inconsistent with *APB Opinions No. 21* and *No. 26,* and for elevating form over substance. Another group, which agreed with the Exposure Draft except for restructurings in which face amounts of receivables are reduced, criticized it for failing to recognize losses and gains from decreases in face amounts, for changing existing practice, and for elevating form over substance. Both views are discussed individually in earlier paragraphs (126-139) and are there shown to be virtually opposite views to each other, but they have some similarities when compared to the accounting in the Exposure Draft and this Statement.

151. For example, both criticisms of the Exposure Draft noted in the preceding paragraph result from rejection of fundamental conclusions in the Exposure Draft. Thus, respondents who favor accounting for all troubled debt restructurings as exchanges of debt disagreed with the conclusions that "a troubled debt restructuring that does not involve a transfer of resources or obligations is a continuation of an existing debt" and "to the extent that a troubled debt restructuring involves only a modification of terms of continuing debt, no transfer of resources or obligations has occurred" (paragraphs 76 and 77). Respondents with that view presumably saw troubled debt restructurings as of the same essence as exchanges covered by *APB Opinions No. 21* and *No. 26* and found the Exposure Draft inconsistent with those Opinions. If, however, the conclusions quoted earlier in this paragraph are accepted, modifications of terms of continuing debt are different in substance from exchanges of resources or obligations, and the Exposure Draft is consistent with the Opinions.

152. Similarly, some respondents who favor recognizing losses and gains from reducing face amounts in troubled debt restructurings disagreed with the conclusion that "the substance of all modifications of a debt in a troubled debt restructuring is essentially the same whether they are modifications of timing, modifications of amounts designated as interest, or modifications of amounts designated as face amounts" (paragraph 140). That is, they think that financial institutions' customary distinctions between principal and interest have more substance than the effects of modifications on future cash flows, although they admit that changes in practice would be minimal because few troubled debt restructurings involve changes in face amounts (paragraph 144).

153. The fact that elevating form over substance is a criticism common to the arguments of respondents who fundamentally disagreed with the Exposure Draft emphasizes that various views on proper accounting depend on varying perceptions of the substance of modification of terms in a troubled debt restructuring. The preceding paragraphs note three different views of that substance: the view on which the Exposure Draft and this Statement are based and two other views that differ significantly not only from the view adopted but from each other. The Board carefully analyzed all three views before issuing the Exposure Draft and decided on one of them for the reasons stated in paragraphs 106-152.

154. Some respondents who agreed generally with the accounting for modifications of terms specified in the Exposure Draft and some who preferred to recognize debtors' gains and creditors' losses from decreases in face amounts expressed concern that a debtor's prepayment may result in recognizing a

creditor's loss in the wrong period (they are silent about a debtor's gain). That is, if a debtor may prepay a reduced face amount without penalty, total future cash receipts may actually be less than the recorded investment in the receivable even though the total future amounts specified by the restructured terms are at least equal to the recorded investment, and no loss is recognized by the creditor at the time of restructuring under paragraph 16. The loss would be recorded in the period of prepayment rather than the period of restructuring. They propose that a creditor be required to recognize a loss on restructuring in the period of restructuring to the extent that a reduction of face amount is not protected by a prepayment penalty.

155. This Statement does not include that kind of test based on prepayment penalties. The proposed test rests on the assumption that a loss resulting from prepayment necessarily is a loss on restructuring, and that presumption is questionable. At the time of restructuring, the most probable estimate of future cash receipts is usually that the debtor will not prepay, even if there is no prepayment penalty, because (a) prepayment of a debt with a relatively low effective interest rate is to the creditor's advantage, not the debtor's, (b) initiative for prepayment lies wholly with the debtor, and (c) the debtor is clearly unable to prepay at the time of a troubled debt restructuring and may never be able to prepay. If that most probable estimate later proves incorrect, and the debtor does prepay, a change of estimate should be recorded in the period of prepayment.

CREDITOR'S ACCOUNTING FOR SUBSTITUTION OR ADDITION OF DEBTORS

156. A change between the Exposure Draft and this Statement is that the Exposure Draft dealt with substitutions of debtors only if the debtors were government units. Several respondents to the Exposure Draft suggested that the principles developed there applied to substitutions or additions of nongovernment debtors as well.

157. The general principle developed in earlier paragraphs is that the accounting for a troubled debt restructuring depends on its substance. The issues raised if a creditor in a troubled debt restructuring accepts, or is required to accept, a new receivable from a different debtor to replace an existing receivable from a debtor experiencing financial difficulties pertains to the circumstances, if any, in which the substitution or addition is in substance similar to a transfer of assets to satisfy a receivable and the circumstances, if any, in which that kind of restructuring is in substance similar to a modification of terms only.

158. One view expressed by respondents was that the substitution of a receivable from a different debtor for an existing receivable or the addition of another debtor is always a transaction requiring accounting by the creditor for a new asset at its fair value, recognizing gain or loss to the extent that the fair value of the new asset differs from the recorded investment in the receivable it replaces. To some proponents, that view holds regardless of the relationship between the original debtor and the new debtor.

159. Another view expressed was that the kind of substitution involved in each restructuring must be considered, and the accounting depends on the relationship between the original and new debtors and between the original and new terms.

160. The Board rejected the view that the substitution or addition of a new debtor is always a transaction requiring recognition of a new asset by the creditor. In some troubled debt restructurings, the substitution or addition may be primarily a matter of form while the underlying debtor-creditor relationship, though modified, essentially continues. For example, to enhance the likelihood that the modified terms of a troubled debt restructuring will be fulfilled, a new legal entity may be created to serve as a custodian or trustee to collect designated revenues and disburse the cash received in accordance with the new debt agreement. The role of that new unit may be similar to that of a sinking fund trustee in an untroubled debt situation. The source of the funds required to fulfill the agreement may be the same, but some or all of those funds may be earmarked to meet specific obligations under the agreement. Similarly, if the new debtor controls, is controlled by, or is under common control with the original debtor, the substance of the relationship is not changed. Each troubled debt restructuring involving a substitution or addition of a debtor should be carefully examined to determine whether the substitution or addition is primarily a matter of form to facilitate compliance with modified terms or primarily a matter of substance.

161. The Board considers the exchanges of bonds of the Municipal Assistance Corporation (Corporation) for notes of the City of New York (City) described in recent exchange offers[38] to be examples of troubled debt restructurings whose substance to creditors for accounting purposes is a modification of the terms of an existing receivable rather than an

[38]Municipal Assistance Corporation for the City of New York, "Exchange Offer[s] to Holders of Certain Short-Term Notes of the City of New York," November 26, 1975, May 21, 1976, and March 22, 1977.

acquisition of a new asset (receivable). According to those exchange offers:

> The Corporation . . . was created in June 1975 . . . for the purposes of assisting the City in providing essential services to its inhabitants without interruption and in creating investor confidence in the soundness of the obligations of the City. To carry out such purposes, the Corporation is empowered, among other things, to issue and sell bonds and notes and to pay or lend funds received from such sale to the City and to exchange the Corporation's obligations for obligations of the City.[39]

The Board's understanding is that: (a) the Corporation receives its funds to meet debt service requirements and operating expenses from tax allocations from New York State's collections of Sales Taxes imposed by the State within the City, Stock Transfer Taxes, and Per Capita Aid (revenue sources previously available to the City); (b) Tax and Per Capita Aid amounts not allocated to the Corporation for its requirements are available to the City under the terms of the applicable statutes; and (c) the primary purpose in creating the Corporation was to enhance the likelihood that the City's debt will be paid, not to introduce new economic resources and activities.

RELATED MATTERS

162. Several respondents commenting on accounting for contingent future cash payments or receipts indicated a need for some clarification of the accounting described in the Exposure Draft. Accounting for contingent payments or receipts is complicated because it involves four separate situations—(1) accounting by the debtor at the time of restructuring, (2) accounting by the debtor after the time of restructuring, (3) accounting by the creditor at the time of restructuring, and (4) accounting by the creditor after the time of restructuring. It is further complicated because the view of both debtor and creditor shifts between "gain" contingencies and "loss" contingencies as the accounting shifts from the time of restructuring to after the time of restructuring. The accounting in the Exposure Draft and this Statement is governed by the following general principles:

a. Paragraph 17 (gain contingencies) of *FASB Statement No. 5* governs a debtor's accounting for contingent cash payments at the time of restructuring (paragraph 18) and a creditor's accounting for contingent cash receipts after the time of restructuring (paragraph 36). Since gain contingencies are not recognized until a gain is realized, (1) a *debtor* should not recognize a gain at the time of restructuring that may be offset by future contingent payments, which is equivalent to assuming that contingent future payments will be paid, and (2) a *creditor* should not recognize contingent cash receipts as interest income until they become unconditionally receivable, that is, until both the contingency has been removed and the interest has been earned.
b. Paragraph 8 (loss contingencies) of *FASB Statement No. 5* governs a debtor's accounting for contingent cash payments after the time of restructuring (paragraph 22) and a creditor's accounting for contingent cash receipts at the time of restructuring (paragraph 32). Since two conditions must be met to recognize an estimated loss, (1) a *debtor* should recognize an interest expense and payable for contingent payments when it is probable that a liability has been incurred and the amount can be reasonably estimated, and (2) a *creditor* should recognize a loss unless offsetting contingent cash receipts are probable and the amount can be reasonably estimated. Contingent cash receipts are unlikely to be probable at the time of restructuring.

163. The principles described in the preceding paragraph also apply to other situations in which future cash payments or receipts must be estimated to apply the provisions of the Statement, for example, future interest payments or receipts that are expected to fluctuate because they are based on the prime interest rate or indeterminate total interest payments or receipts because the debt is payable or collectible on demand or becomes payable or collectible on demand after a specified period (paragraphs 18 and 32).

DISCLOSURE

Disclosure by Debtors

164. Most respondents to the Discussion Memorandum commenting on disclosure by debtors for restructurings advocated essentially the disclosure prescribed for gains or losses from extinguishment of debt in *FASB Statement No. 4*. Paragraph 99 gives the Board's reasons for adopting for gains on troubled debt restructurings the guidelines for income statement classification prescribed in that Statement for gains from extinguishment of debt. Since troubled debt restructurings for which gains are recognized and extinguishments of debts thus use the same guidelines for income statement classification and are similar for disclosure purposes, the

[39]Municipal Assistance Corporation for the City of New York, "Exchange Offer to Holders of Certain Short-Term Notes of the City of New York," November 26, 1975, p. 15.

Board concluded that the kind of information prescribed in paragraph 9 of *FASB Statement No. 4* is generally appropriate for disclosing troubled debt restructurings involving recognition of gains. Since some of those restructurings involve transfers of assets to creditors to settle payables, the Board believes that it is appropriate also to disclose the aggregate net gain or loss recognized on transfers of assets. However, since several respondents to the Exposure Draft indicated that problems would arise in attempting to determine when a debtor's current difficulties began and perhaps in obtaining amounts of earlier losses, this Statement omits a requirement in the Exposure Draft to disclose also "the aggregate loss, if any, recognized on those assets in earlier periods in connection with the debtor's current financial difficulties."

165. Restructurings not involving recognition of gain or loss at the time of restructuring usually modify the timing, amounts, or both, of interest or face amount the debtor is to pay under the debt's terms (paragraphs 16-18). In the Board's view, the principal changes in terms should be disclosed to permit an understanding of the financial effects of those modifications.

166. Paragraph 26, specifying disclosure of the extent to which inclusion of contingent future cash receipts prevented recognizing a gain on restructuring was added in response to suggestions by respondents to the Exposure Draft. The Board agreed that information would be useful in assessing the relation between future cash payments and future interest expenses of the debtor.

Disclosure by Creditors

167. Most banking and other financial institutions responding to the Discussion Memorandum that commented on disclosure by creditors argued against separate disclosures about restructured receivables. They emphasized that to be the most meaningful to financial statement users information about receivables should disclose the interest rate characteristics of each broad group of earning assets (primarily loan or investment portfolios), by major category. They argued that information limited to receivables that have been restructured would not only be less meaningful than information about entire portfolios of receivables but also could be confusing because the same information is also needed about other receivables, particularly those that are earning no return but have not been restructured (nonearning receivables). Several of those institutions referred to the requirements of the Securities and Exchange Commission and of the banking regulatory agencies, which recently became effective, both concerning disclosure about categories of loan and investment portfolios—including their maturities, interest rates, and nonearning loans and investments—and the allowance for uncollectible amounts. They indicated that those requirements provide adequate information about the financial effects of restructurings, troubled or nontroubled. Financial analysts responding also recommended disclosure focusing on the characteristics of each broad group of earning assets. They expressed a desire for information about past and expected yields of entire portfolios, by major category, to enable them to make informed judgments about recent and prospective earnings performance.

168. Some respondents to the Discussion Memorandum that are not financial institutions recommended that the Board require information to be disclosed about each significant troubled debt restructuring in the period that it occurs, primarily the terms of the restructuring, gain or loss recognized, if any, and the related income tax effect. Most of those respondents focused on individual receivables rather than on groups of receivables and proposed that debtors and creditors disclose similar information.

169. The Board concluded that the information prescribed by paragraph 40 should be disclosed, by major category, for outstanding receivables whose terms have been modified in troubled debt restructurings. The information may be disclosed either separately for those receivables or as part of the disclosure about reduced-earning and nonearning receivables. The Board believes that the appropriate format for that disclosure depends primarily on the characteristics and number of receivables, including the proportion of those receivables that have reduced earning potential. It believes the argument has merit that the most meaningful disclosure about earnings potential for a financial institution typically should focus on entire portfolios of receivables, by major category, rather than only on receivables that have been restructured in troubled situations, but the Board acknowledges that determining appropriate disclosure for receivables in general is beyond the scope of this Statement. Accordingly, paragraphs 40 and 41 specify types of information that shall be disclosed and permit that information to be provided by major category for the aggregate of outstanding reduced-earning and nonearning receivables, by major category for outstanding receivables whose terms have been modified in troubled debt restructurings, or for each significant outstanding receivable that has been so restructured, depending on the circumstances.

170. This Statement contains three changes from the Exposure Draft concerning disclosure by creditors, all made in response to comments or suggestions from respondents to the Exposure Draft and all in paragraph 40, which was paragraph 34 of the

Exposure Draft: (1) disclosure of information more in conformity with SEC Guides 61 and 3[40] replaces disclosure of the weighted average effective interest rate and the range of maturities, (2) disclosure of the allowance for uncollectible amounts or other valuation allowance applicable to restructured receivables is deleted, and (3) disclosure of a commitment to lend additional funds to debtors owing restructured receivables is added.

171. Disclosure of commitments to lend additional funds was chosen instead of a penalty suggested by some respondents to the Exposure Draft. They expressed concern that a creditor might avoid recognizing a loss under paragraphs 30-32 by restructuring a troubled receivable in a way that the specified future cash receipts exceed the recorded investment in the receivable and then agree to lend funds to the debtor to meet those terms. They proposed that irrevocable commitments to lend to the debtor be included in the creditor's recorded investment to determine whether the creditor should recognize a loss at the time of restructuring. Since that test is equivalent to saying that a creditor must recognize a loss unless the restructured terms provide not only for recovery of the outstanding receivable but also for recovery of future loans to the same debtor (because future cash receipts from future loans are ignored), the test is excessively punitive. The Board decided that disclosure of those commitments is adequate. That disclosure may already be required by paragraphs 18 and 19 of *FASB Statement No. 5,* but paragraph 40(b) makes the disclosure explicit.

172. Some respondents who advocated that the scope of this Statement exclude restructurings of receivables related to consumer financing activities or to all or certain residential properties (paragraph 63) also argued that, if those restructurings were embraced by this Statement, applicable requirements for disclosure would likely be burdensome and not very meaningful to financial statement users. They point out that the accounting, including information normally disclosed in financial statements or in other reports, for those types of receivables has been tailored to fit special characteristics of the receivables, such as large numbers of relatively small balances, interest rates fixed by state law rather than in a fluctuating market, and numerous accounts on which collections are past due. The Board noted the special characteristics of those types of receivables and, since the scope of this Statement does not encompass appropriate disclosure for receivables generally, concluded that paragraphs 40 and 41 should not necessarily apply to those types of receivables that have been restructured.

ACCOUNTING SYMMETRY BETWEEN DEBTORS AND CREDITORS

173. The Discussion Memorandum contained several questions on whether particular accounting by debtors and creditors should be symmetrical. Most respondents considered a criterion of symmetry between debtors and creditors an insignificant factor in accounting for troubled debt restructurings. Many noted that existing accounting principles for accounting by creditors for receivables after their initial recording and for recognizing losses already differ from those for accounting by debtors for payables and for recognizing gains. Some respondents also noted that differences usually exist between the debtor and creditor in a particular restructuring (for example, differences in the industry or industries in which they are involved, in their financial viability, and in the significance and frequency of that kind of event for them). The accounting for troubled debt restructurings prescribed in this Statement is symmetrical between debtors and creditors in most matters. However, the Board considered the types of differences described above, among other factors, in concluding that different accounting is appropriate for debtors and creditors in matters such as classifying gains or losses recognized at the time of troubled debt restructurings, accounting for contingent interest, and disclosing information about troubled debt restructurings.

EFFECTIVE DATE AND TRANSITION

174. The Board concluded that prospective application of this Statement is appropriate and that the effective dates in paragraphs 43-45 are advisable. In the Board's view, comparability of financial statements would not be greatly enhanced by restating past, nonrecurring troubled debt restructurings. Further, difficulties in retroactive application of the provisions of this Statement include identifying restructurings for which fair values would need to be determined and determining those fair values. A number of enterprises that in recent years have had several restructurings of those types would be unlikely to have information available to restate retroactively.

[40]SEC, *Securities Exchange Act of 1934 Release No. 12748,* "Guides for Statistical Disclosure by Bank Holding Companies," August 31, 1976.

Statement of Financial Accounting Standards No. 16
Prior Period Adjustments

STATUS

Issued: June 1977

Effective Date: For fiscal years beginning after October 15, 1977

Affects: Amends ARB 43, Chapter 10A, paragraph 19
Amends ARB 43, Chapter 11B, paragraph 9 and footnote 4
Amends APB 9, paragraphs 3 and 18
Supersedes APB 9, paragraphs 23 and 24
Supersedes APB 20, footnote 9
Amends APB 30, paragraph 25
Supersedes AIN-APB 4, Interpretation No. 5
Supersedes FAS 5, footnote 3

Affected by: Paragraph 9 superseded by FAS 71

Statement of Financial Accounting Standards No. 16
Prior Period Adjustments

CONTENTS

INTRODUCTION AND BACKGROUND INFORMATION

1. The AICPA Committee on SEC Regulations and others have requested that the FASB consider the criteria for prior period adjustments stated in paragraph 23 of *APB Opinion No. 9,* "Reporting the Results of Operations," and provide further guidelines for the application of those criteria. Paragraph 23 of *APB Opinion No. 9* states:

> Adjustments related to prior periods—and thus excluded in the determination of net income for the current period—are limited to those material adjustments which (a) can be specifically identified with and directly related to the business activities of particular prior periods, and (b) are not attributable to economic events occurring subsequent to the date of the financial statements for the prior period, and (c) depend primarily on determinations by persons other than management and (d) were not susceptible of reasonable estimation prior to such determination. Such adjustments are rare in modern financial accounting. They relate to events or transactions which occurred in a prior period, the accounting effects of which could not be determined with reasonable assurance at that time, usually because of some major uncertainty then existing. Evidence of such an uncertainty would be disclosure thereof in the financial statements of the applicable period, or of an intervening period in those cases in which the uncertainty became apparent during a subsequent period. Further, it would be expected that, in most cases, the opinion of the reporting independent auditor on such prior period would have contained a qualification because of the uncertainty. Examples are material, nonrecurring adjustments or settlements of income taxes, of renegotiation proceedings or of utility revenue under rate processes. Settlements of significant amounts resulting from litigation or similar claims may also constitute prior period adjustments.

2. The requests referred to in paragraph 1 were prompted by Securities and Exchange Commission staff administrative interpretations of *APB Opinion No. 9* during 1975 limiting prior period adjustments for out-of-court settlements of litigation. The view of the SEC staff was later explained in *Staff Accounting Bulletin No. 8* (see Appendix C). In addition, differing interpretations of the criteria of paragraph 23 and of the provisions of paragraph 24 of *APB Opinion No. 9* have been cited as a basis for requesting a reconsideration of the concept of prior period adjustments.

3. Paragraph 24 of *APB Opinion No. 9* elaborates on paragraph 23 by giving examples of items that do not qualify as prior period adjustments. Paragraph 24 states:

> Treatment as prior period adjustments should not be applied to the normal, recurring corrections and adjustments which are the natural result of the use of estimates inherent in the accounting process. For example, changes in the estimated remaining lives of fixed assets affect the computed amounts of depreciation, but these changes should be considered prospective in nature and not prior period adjustments. Similarly, relatively immaterial adjustments of provisions for liabilities (including income taxes) made in prior periods should be considered recurring items to be reflected in operations of the current period. Some uncertainties, for example those relating to the realization of assets (collectibility of accounts receivable, ultimate recovery of deferred costs or realizability of inventories or other assets), would not qualify for prior period adjustment treatment, since economic events subsequent to the date of the financial statements must of necessity enter into the elimination of any previously-existing uncer-

tainty. Therefore, the effects of such matters are considered to be elements in the determination of net income for the period in which the uncertainty is eliminated. Thus, the Board [APB] believes that prior period adjustments will be rare.

4. *APB Opinion No. 20,* "Accounting Changes," affirmed the conclusions of paragraph 24 of *APB Opinion No. 9* by requiring that "a change in an estimate should not be accounted for by restating amounts reported in financial statements of prior periods . . . unless the change meets all the conditions for a prior period adjustment (paragraph 23 of *APB Opinion No. 9*)."

5. *FASB Statement No. 5,* "Accounting for Contingencies," (effective for fiscal years beginning on or after July 1, 1975) establishes the conditions for accrual of an estimated loss from a loss contingency and prohibits accrual before those conditions are met. The two conditions for accrual of an estimated loss from a loss contingency set forth in paragraph 8 of Statement No. 5 are that "(a) information available prior to issuance of the financial statements indicates that it is probable that an asset had been impaired or a liability had been incurred at the date of the financial statements . . ." and "(b) the amount of loss can be reasonably estimated." Paragraph 8 of the Statement requires that "an estimated loss from a loss contingency . . . shall be accrued by a charge to income. . . ." A footnote to that paragraph states that "paragraphs 23-24 of *APB Opinion No. 9* . . . describe the 'rare' circumstances in which a prior period adjustment is appropriate" and indicates that "those paragraphs are not amended" by Statement No. 5.

6. The Board has, among other things, (a) reviewed an FASB staff survey of prior period adjustments made in recent years pursuant to the criteria of *APB Opinion No. 9,* (b) considered the relationship of the criteria of *APB Opinion No. 9* for prior period adjustments to the rationale of subsequent APB Opinions (see paragraphs 29-36), and (c) examined the relationship of the criteria of *APB Opinion No. 9* for prior period adjustments to the conditions of *FASB Statement No. 5* for accrual of estimated losses from loss contingencies (see paragraph 37).

7. An Exposure Draft of a proposed Statement on "Prior Period Adjustments" was issued July 29, 1976, and a public hearing based on the Exposure Draft was held on October 15, 1976. The Board received 162 position papers and letters of comment in response to the Exposure Draft. Ten presentations were made at the public hearing. On April 12, 1977 the FASB announced that it was unable to attain the necessary five assenting votes for issuance of a final Statement on Prior Period Adjustments. That announcement stated that four FASB members agreed to support the position in the Exposure Draft, modified in certain respects for interim reporting, and that the other three Board members dissented for varied reasons. On June 21, 1977 the Trustees of the Financial Accounting Foundation announced that they had approved the implementation of a number of the recommendations made by the Trustees' Structure Committee in its April 1977 report, "The Structure of Establishing Financial Accounting Standards." The recommendations approved included amending the Foundation's bylaws to change the voting requirement for adoption of pronouncements by the FASB from five affirmative votes among the seven members to a simple majority. Subsequent to the action by the Trustees, the Board reconsidered the subject and voted to issue this Statement.

8. The Board concluded that, with limited exceptions, items of profit and loss recognized during a period shall be included in the determination of net income of that period. Paragraphs 11 and 13-15 describe the exceptions that shall be accounted for and reported as prior period adjustments. The basis for the Board's conclusions, as well as alternatives considered and reasons for their rejection, are discussed in Appendix A to this Statement. The results of the FASB staff survey of prior period adjustments made pursuant to the criteria of *APB Opinion No. 9* in annual financial statements for fiscal years ending from July 1973 through June 1975 are summarized in Appendix B to this Statement.

9. The Addendum to *APB Opinion No. 2,* "Accounting for the 'Investment Credit'," states that "differences may arise in the application of generally accepted accounting principles as between regulated and nonregulated businesses, because of the effect in regulated businesses of the rate-making process," and discusses the application of generally accepted accounting principles to regulated industries. FASB Statements and Interpretations should therefore be applied to regulated companies that are subject to the rate-making process in accordance with the provisions of the Addendum.

STANDARDS OF FINANCIAL ACCOUNTING AND REPORTING

10. Except as specified in paragraph 11 and in paragraphs 13 and 14 with respect to prior interim periods of the current year, all items of profit and loss recognized during a period,[1] including accruals of estimated losses from loss contingencies, shall be

[1] As used in this Statement, the term "period" refers to both annual and interim reporting periods.

included in the determination of net income for that period.[2]

11. Items of profit and loss related to the following shall be accounted for and reported as prior period adjustments[3] and excluded from the determination of net income for the current period:

a. Correction of an error in the financial statements of a prior period[4] and
b. Adjustments that result from realization of income tax benefits of pre-acquisition operating loss carryforwards of purchased subsidiaries.[5]

12. This Statement does not affect the manner of reporting accounting changes required or permitted by an FASB Statement, an FASB Interpretation, or an APB Opinion.[6]

Adjustments Related to Prior Interim Periods of the Current Fiscal Year

13. For purposes of this Statement, an "adjustment related to prior *interim* periods of the current fiscal year" is an adjustment or settlement of litigation or similar claims, of income taxes, of renegotiation proceedings, or of utility revenue under rate-making processes provided that the adjustment or settlement meets each of the following criteria:

a. The effect of the adjustment or settlement is material in relation to income from continuing operations of the current fiscal year or in relation to the trend of income from continuing operations or is material by other appropriate criteria, and
b. All or part of the adjustment or settlement can be specifically identified with and is directly related to business activities of specific prior interim periods of the current fiscal year, and
c. The amount of the adjustment or settlement could not be reasonably estimated prior to the current interim period but becomes reasonably estimable in the current interim period.

Criterion (b) above is not met solely because of incidental effects such as interest on a settlement. Criterion (c) would be met by the occurrence of an event with currently measurable effects such as new retroactive tax legislation or a final decision on a rate order. Treatment as adjustments related to prior interim periods of the current fiscal year shall not be applied to the normal recurring corrections and adjustments that are the result of the use of estimates inherent in the accounting process. Changes in provisions for doubtful accounts shall not be considered to be adjustments related to prior interim periods of the current fiscal year even though the changes result from litigation or similar claims.

14. If an item of profit or loss occurs in *other than the first* interim period of the enterprise's fiscal year and all or a part of the item of profit or loss is an adjustment related to prior interim periods of the current fiscal year, as defined in paragraph 13 above, the item shall be reported as follows:

a. The portion of the item that is directly related to business activities of the enterprise during the current interim period, if any, shall be included in the determination of net income for that period.
b. Prior interim periods of the current fiscal year shall be restated to include the portion of the item that is directly related to business activities of the enterprise during each prior interim period in the determination of net income for that period.
c. The portion of the item that is directly related to business activities of the enterprise during prior fiscal years, if any, shall be included in the determination of net income of the first interim period of the current fiscal year.

15. The following disclosures shall be made in interim financial reports about an adjustment related to prior interim periods of the current fiscal year. In financial reports for the interim period in which the adjustment occurs, disclosure shall be made of (a) the effect on income from continuing operations, net income, and related per share amounts for each prior interim period of the current fiscal year, and (b) income from continuing opera-

[2]Many items that would previously have been reported as prior period adjustments will be subject to existing disclosure requirements when that type of item is included in the determination of current net income. For example, *APB Opinion No. 28,* "Interim Financial Reporting," specifies certain disclosures for interim reporting periods and *APB Opinion No. 30,* "Reporting the Results of Operations," specifies disclosures for certain types of items discussed by that Opinion.

[3]The reporting of prior period adjustments is described in paragraph 18 of *APB Opinion No. 9,* as modified by paragraph 16 of this Statement, and in paragraph 26 of *APB Opinion No. 9.*

[4]As defined in paragraph 13 of *APB Opinion No. 20.* That paragraph also describes the distinction between a correction of an error and a change in accounting estimate.

[5]See paragraph 49 of *APB Opinion No. 11,* "Accounting for Income Taxes," and paragraph 88 of *APB Opinion No. 16,* "Business Combinations."

[6]In addition to transition requirements of these pronouncements, accounting changes resulting in restatement of previously issued financial statements of prior periods include a change in accounting method permitted by paragraph 52 of *APB Opinion No. 16,* a change in the reporting entity described in paragraph 34 of *APB Opinion No. 20,* and special changes in accounting principle described in paragraphs 27 and 29 of *APB Opinion No. 20.* See also footnote 5 to *APB Opinion No. 20.*

tions, net income, and related per share amounts for each prior interim period restated in accordance with paragraph 14 of this Statement.

Amendments to Existing Pronouncements

16. The conclusions of this Statement require the following amendments to existing pronouncements:

a. *APB Opinion No. 9.* Delete paragraphs 23 and 24. The first sentence of paragraph 18 is modified to read as follows:

   Those items that are reported as prior period adjustments shall, in single period statements, be reflected as adjustments of the opening balance of retained earnings.

b. *APB Opinion No. 20.* Delete footnote 9 to paragraph 31.
c. *APB Opinion No. 30.* Delete the following words from the second and third sentences of paragraph 25: "should not be reported as a prior period adjustment unless it meets the criteria for a prior period adjustment as defined in paragraph 23 of APB Opinion No. 9. An adjustment that does not meet such criteria," and combine the remainder of the two sentences into one sentence as follows:

   Each adjustment in the current period of a loss on disposal of a business segment or of an element of an extraordinary item that was reported in a prior period should be separately disclosed as to year of origin, nature, and amount and classified separately in the current period in the same manner as the original item.

d. *FASB Statement No. 5.* Delete footnote 3 to paragraph 8.

Effective Date and Transition

17. This Statement shall be effective for financial statements for fiscal years beginning after October 15, 1977. Application in financial statements for fiscal years beginning before October 16, 1977 that have not been previously issued, and in interim periods within those fiscal years, is encouraged but not required. This Statement shall not be applied retroactively to previously issued annual financial statements.

The provisions of this Statement need not be applied to immaterial items.

This Statement was adopted by the affirmative votes of four members of the Financial Accounting Standards Board. Messrs. Sprouse, Litke, and Walters dissented.

Mr. Sprouse and Mr. Litke dissent primarily because the effect of this Statement is to include in the current year's *income from continuing operations* adjustments related to prior years that previously would have been excluded in the determination of the current year's *net income.* In their opinion this is a quantum leap that detracts from the usefulness of the measure of income from continuing operations and that should not be undertaken without comprehensive consideration of the presentation of information about earnings activities. Mr. Sprouse and Mr. Litke believe that application of this Statement produces anomalous results including (i) reporting tax benefits of loss carryforwards as extraordinary items when realized (a practice with which they concur) but including other adjustments or settlements of income taxes related to prior periods in income from continuing operations, (ii) reporting gains and losses from extinguishing debt during the current period as extraordinary items (a practice with which they concur) but including adjudications and out-of-court settlements of litigation, results of renegotiation proceedings, and other financial results related to prior periods in income from continuing operations, and (iii) excluding adjustments related to prior interim periods from the net income of the current interim period (except that such adjustments made during the first interim period are included in that period's income from continuing operations) because the Board is reconsidering interim reporting and some respondents to the Exposure Draft argued that the inclusion of those adjustments would detract from the usefulness of interim reporting (paragraph 46) but rejecting similar considerations related to annual reporting (paragraphs 23 and 52). If, without comprehensive consideration of the presentation of information about earnings activities, certain adjustments related to prior periods that previously were excluded in the determination of net income for the current period are now to be included in that determination, Mr. Sprouse and Mr. Litke believe that, as a minimum, those adjustments should be specifically designated (as they are in paragraph 13) and be reported as extraordinary items.

Further, Mr. Litke would provide an additional specific exception in paragraph 11 (as is now provided by paragraph 23 of *APB Opinion No. 9*) for cost-of-service regulated utility companies in those instances where revenues collected subject to refund are required to be refunded. He believes that the circumstances applicable to regulated utility companies in those instances are sufficiently different from circumstances applicable to other industries to warrant such special treatment.

With respect to current practice for such companies, the amount of the refund generally is attributed to the year of collection and not to the year of the refund. Mr. Litke agrees with this practice. He notes that when management believes a reasonable estimate can be made of the amount of revenues currently being collected which are likely to be refunded, they generally record a reserve against revenue for that amount in accordance with *FASB Statement No. 5*. However, management is often unable to make a reasonable estimate as to what, if any, refunds may be required. In that case, all revenues resulting from such rate increases collected but subject to refund are frequently recorded as current revenue in the determination of the current period's income (even though the revenue and the income are subject to final adjudication), and the auditor's report is normally qualified. When the amount of the refund is determined, it generally is attributed to the year(s) of collection by prior period adjustment.

Mr. Litke believes that, if prior period adjustments were not permitted for a regulated company required to refund amounts previously collected subject to refund, the revenue, operating profit, and net income for prior periods could be materially misstated based on what the rate regulatory body finally allowed.

In addition, Mr. Litke believes that a specific exception is necessary because this Statement does not specifically respond to the questions raised by many as to the applicability of the Addendum to *APB Opinion No. 2* to refunds of utility revenues for which a reasonable estimate cannot be made.

Mr. Walters dissents because he does not believe the elimination of prior period adjustments improves financial reporting. To the contrary, he believes that there are clearly valid items, admittedly somewhat rare, whose inclusion in prior periods with which they are specifically identified, enhances the relevance, comparability, and understandability of financial statements and therefore their usefulness. He also does not believe the Board should tinker with this narrow, but basic, issue outside the conceptual framework project. As a minimum, it should be part of a broader project dealing with the meaning and presentation of results of operations.

Members of the Financial Accounting Standards Board:

Marshall S. Armstrong, *Chairman*
Oscar S. Gellein
Donald J. Kirk
Arthur L. Litke
Robert E. Mays
Robert T. Sprouse
Ralph E. Walters

Appendix A

BASIS FOR CONCLUSIONS

18. This Appendix contains a discussion of the factors deemed significant by members of the Board in reaching the conclusions in this Statement, including various alternatives considered and reasons for accepting some and rejecting others. Individual Board members gave greater weight to some factors than to others.

Scope

19. The initial request referred to in paragraph 1 was for clarification of the application of criterion (b)[7] and criterion (c)[8] of paragraph 23 of *APB Opinion No. 9* to negotiated settlements of litigation. Paragraph 23 of *APB Opinion No. 9* included "settlements of significant amounts resulting from litigation or similar claims" as an example of items that may qualify as prior period adjustments. SEC *Staff Accounting Bulletin No. 8* states the SEC staff's conclusion that "litigation is inevitably an 'economic event' and that settlements would constitute 'economic events' of the period in which they occur. Accordingly, it would seem that charges or credits relating to settlements would also not meet" criterion (b).[9] *Staff Accounting Bulletin No. 8* also states the view that when litigation is settled, management must make a number of significant judgments, and, hence, criterion (c)[10] has not been met.

20. As described in Appendix B, the FASB staff searched approximately 6,000 annual reports for fiscal years ended from July 1973 through June 1975 and identified 191 annual reports that showed prior period adjustments that appeared to have been made pursuant to the criteria of paragraph 23 of *APB Opinion No. 9*. The purpose of the research

[7]Criterion (b) of paragraph 23 of *APB Opinion No. 9* requires that the adjustments "are not attributable to economic events occurring subsequent to the date of the financial statements for the prior period."

[8]Criterion (c) of paragraph 23 of *APB Opinion No. 9* requires that the adjustment "depend primarily on determinations by persons other than management."

[9]See footnote 7.

[10]See footnote 8.

was to determine the extent and nature of those prior period adjustments and the possible interpretative problems the Board would face if it decided to clarify the criteria in paragraph 23 of *APB Opinion No. 9.* Over one-third of the identified adjustments resulted from litigation and similar claims, and most of these were negotiated. Income tax settlements also represented over one-third of the identified adjustments. Because of the similarity of the process involved in settling litigation and income taxes, and because they constitute most of the identified prior period adjustments made pursuant to the criteria of paragraph 23 of *APB Opinion No. 9,* the Board concluded that this Statement should not be limited to the area of negotiated settlements of litigation, but rather, should address all items reported as prior period adjustments pursuant to the criteria of paragraph 23 of *APB Opinion No. 9.*

21. Some respondents to the Exposure Draft questioned whether this Statement was intended to change the reporting of adjustments that are required by *APB Opinions No. 9, 11,* and *16* to be reported as adjustments to paid-in capital, goodwill, or other assets. This Statement is not intended to require those adjustments to be included in the determination of net income of the current period. This Statement is also not intended to proscribe restatements of earnings per share that are required by *APB Opinions No. 15,* "Earnings Per Share," and *16* or by other APB Opinions and FASB Statements.

Summary

22. In considering possible clarification of the criteria in paragraph 23 of *APB Opinion No. 9* (see paragraph 24), the purpose of the criteria (see paragraph 25), and the effect on prior period adjustments of subsequent pronouncements (see paragraphs 29-37), the Board determined that an amendment of *APB Opinion No. 9* was needed. The Board concluded for the reasons indicated in paragraphs 24-39 that all items of profit and loss recognized during a period, with the limited exceptions indicated in paragraphs 11 and 13-15 and explained in paragraphs 41-46, shall be included in the determination of net income for that reporting period. The Board also concluded, for the reasons indicated in paragraphs 47-51, that the manner of reporting accounting changes should not be modified at this time (see paragraph 12).

23. Some respondents recommended that this project be included in or deferred pending completion of the Board's agenda project entitled "Conceptual Framework for Financial Accounting and Reporting." The Board determined that this problem required resolution at this time and could be resolved in the existing accounting framework. As outlined in paragraphs 29-37, the all-inclusive income statement is predominant in the existing accounting framework.

Possible Clarification of Criteria

24. Relating the criteria of paragraph 23 of *APB Opinion No. 9* and the examples given in that paragraph to prior period adjustments identified in the FASB staff survey (see Appendix B) led to the conclusion that any attempted clarification could result in an amendment of *APB Opinion No. 9* and that the problem could not be satisfactorily resolved by an Interpretation as indicated by the following examples:

a. Settlements of income taxes and litigation constitute the majority of identified prior period adjustments. The former is included in paragraph 23 as an example of a prior period adjustment when material and nonrecurring and the latter is included as an example of an item that *may* qualify as a prior period adjustment. Such settlements are usually negotiated and often do not depend *primarily* on determinations by *any* single party. Accordingly, for out-of-court settlements of both income taxes and litigation to qualify as prior period adjustments, the phrase "depend primarily on determinations by persons other than management" (criterion (c)) would have to be amended to read "*not* depending primarily on management."
b. The term "economic events" in criterion (b)[11] has been interpreted in significantly different ways (see paragraph 19 and Appendix C). Refining the definition of this term could result in an effective amendment.
c. Refining the requirement that prior period adjustments be "material" or of the word "nonrecurring" in the examples in paragraph 23 would likely be an effective amendment.

Purpose of the Criteria of Paragraph 23 of APB Opinion No. 9

25. Paragraph 17 of *APB Opinion No. 9* states that "net income should reflect all items of profit and loss recognized during the period with the sole exception of . . . prior period adjustments. . . ." *APB Opinion No. 9* requires restatement of affected prior periods only if the statements of the affected prior periods are presented; otherwise, only the effect on beginning retained earnings of the earliest period presented is required. The Board believes that a decision to exclude certain items of profit and loss recognized during a period from the determina-

[11]See footnote 7.

tion of net income for that period should be based on a determination that some expected user or class of users would be benefited. Items of profit and loss clearly related to prior period operations and unrelated to the current period operations, for example, might be excluded from the determination of net income for the current period because existing and potential investors might be misled by their inclusion. The criteria of paragraph 23 of *APB Opinion No. 9* do not serve this purpose because they do not comprehend many other items of profit and loss related to prior periods and unrelated to the current period operations. The Board concluded that users will not be benefited by special treatment for some items of profit and loss recognized during a period but not for other similar items. The reasons for the limited exceptions indicated in paragraphs 11 and 13-15 are explained in paragraphs 41-46.

The Matching Concept

26. A number of respondents to the Exposure Draft noted that adjustments that are reported as prior period adjustments are unrelated to operations of the current period. In their view, inclusion in net income of the current period of costs or revenues that are directly related to business activities of prior periods distorts net income in the current period by matching revenue of one period with costs of another period.

27. *APB Statement No. 4,* "Basic Concepts and Accounting Principles Underlying Financial Statements of Business Enterprises," explicitly avoids using the term "matching" because it has a variety of meanings in the accounting literature. In its broadest sense, matching refers to the entire process of income determination—described in paragraph 147 of *APB Statement No. 4* as "identifying, measuring, and relating revenue and expenses of an enterprise for an accounting period." Matching may also be used in a more limited sense to refer only to the process of expense recognition or in an even more limited sense to refer to the recognition of expenses by associating costs with revenue on a cause and effect basis.

28. The Board reviewed items that were reported as prior period adjustments in recent years. The results of that review are summarized in Appendix B. Based on that review, the Board concluded that the items that were reported as prior period adjustments were not sufficiently different from other items that were included in the determination of net income in the current period to justify their exclusion.

Relationship to Subsequent Pronouncements

29. *APB Opinion No. 9* was issued in December 1966. Since then, other APB Opinions and FASB Statements have changed the standards of accounting for some items related to prior periods. The following paragraphs refer to certain of those changes and their relationship to prior period adjustments.

30. Paragraph 23 of *APB Opinion No. 9* includes "material, nonrecurring adjustments or settlements of income taxes" as an example of items that would meet the criteria for prior period adjustments. Paragraph 24 of Opinion No. 9 states that "relatively immaterial adjustments of provisions for liabilities (including income taxes) made in prior periods should be considered recurring items to be reflected in operations of the current period." *APB Opinion No. 11,* issued in December 1967, requires the use of comprehensive allocation in accounting for income taxes. Prior to the issuance of that Opinion, some enterprises applied partial allocation, a method that did not require taxes to be allocated for certain timing differences. Many settlements of income taxes involve timing differences. With the use of comprehensive allocation, tax settlements relating to timing differences normally do not affect income; thus, *APB Opinion No. 11* probably has reduced the income effect of some settlements of income tax and accordingly the number of settlements that would be accounted for as prior period adjustments.

31. Paragraph 45 of *APB Opinion No. 11* requires that the benefits of prior year tax loss carryforwards not recognized in the year of the loss be recognized as an extraordinary item in the year in which the benefits are realized. Previously, Chapter 10B, "Income Taxes," of *ARB No. 43* provided that ". . . where it is believed that misleading inferences would be drawn from such inclusion, the tax reduction should be credited to surplus." Thus, *APB Opinion No. 11* requires that an item that is related to specific prior periods be included in the determination of current income.

32. Paragraph 50 of *APB Opinion No. 11* requires that realized tax benefits of loss carryforwards arising prior to a "quasi-reorganization" be added to contributed capital if not recognized prior to the "quasi-reorganization." Thus, *APB Opinion No. 11* requires inclusion of an item that relates to specific prior periods as an addition to contributed capital in the current period. (See paragraph 34.)

33. Paragraphs 79-83 of *APB Opinion No. 16* require that adjustments resulting from resolution of certain contingencies be accounted for as adjustments of the cost of the acquired enterprise. The required accounting is prospective rather than retroactive. Thus, *APB Opinion No. 16* requires that resolution of certain contingencies relating to specific prior periods be reported as an adjustment of the purchase price of assets in the current period. (See paragraph 34.)

34. *APB Opinion No. 19,* "Reporting Changes in Financial Position," established the statement of changes in financial position as a new basic financial statement. This statement purports to present all changes in financial position that occur during the period. The interaction of Opinion No. 19, *APB Opinion No. 9,* and other APB Opinions results in the following anomalies:

a. Realized tax benefits of loss carryforwards arising prior to a "quasi-reorganization" are considered related to prior operations and are added to contributed capital, but are reported as changes in financial position in the current period (see paragraph 32); whereas settlements of income taxes, when they meet the criteria of paragraph 23 of *APB Opinion No. 9,* are reported as changes in financial position in the prior period.
b. Adjustments arising from resolution of certain pre-acquisition contingencies of acquired subsidiaries, considered unrelated to current operations and thus reported as adjustments to the cost of the acquired enterprise, are reported as changes in financial position in the current period (see paragraph 33); whereas adjustments of contingencies that meet the criteria of paragraph 23 of *APB Opinion No. 9* are reported as changes in financial position in the prior period.

The Board concluded that all items of profit and loss recognized in a period, with the limited exceptions indicated in paragraphs 11 and 13-15 and explained in paragraphs 41-46, shall be included in the determination of net income and accordingly shall be reported as changes in financial position in that reporting period.

35. Paragraph 31 of *APB Opinion No. 20* requires that the effect of changes in accounting estimates be accounted for in the current period, or the current and future periods if the change affects both. Restatement of amounts reported in prior periods and reporting of pro forma amounts for prior periods are prohibited. However, the Opinion includes a footnote that states:

> Financial statements of a prior period should not be restated for a change in estimate resulting from later resolution of an uncertainty which may have caused the auditor to qualify his opinion on previous financial statements unless the change meets all the conditions for a prior period adjustment (paragraph 23 of *APB Opinion No. 9*).

Thus, Opinion No. 20 requires that most items related to prior periods be included in the determination of current net income without disclosure of the pro forma effect of those items on prior periods but continues the requirements of paragraph 23 of *APB Opinion No. 9* that a few similar items be reported as prior period adjustments.

36. In addition to establishing criteria for prior period adjustments, which were expected to be rare, *APB Opinion No. 9* also established criteria for "extraordinary items," which were to be reported separately in net income of the current period. *APB Opinion No. 30,* "Reporting the Results of Operations," issued in June 1973, established new criteria for extraordinary items, including a change of "would not be expected to recur frequently" in *APB Opinion No. 9* to "not reasonably expected to recur in the foreseeable future" in *APB Opinion No. 30.* Although *APB Opinion No. 30* did not address prior period adjustments, it significantly restricted the eligibility for classification as an extraodinary item. Under Opinion No. 9 the statement that prior period adjustments would be *nonrecurring* adjustments was often interpreted in practice to mean adjustments that would not be expected to recur frequently, but in the current accounting environment, including *APB Opinion No. 30, nonrecurring* would be defined as "not reasonably expected to recur in the foreseeable future."

37. Paragraph 8 of *FASB Statement No. 5,* issued in March 1975, establishes two conditions for accrual of an estimated loss from a loss contingency and prohibits accrual before those conditions are met. The Board did not reexamine the concept of prior period adjustments at that time. Consideration in this Statement of the kinds of items, if any, to be accounted for as prior period adjustments led to the following questions: If pursuant to *FASB Statement No. 5* a loss cannot be accrued in the period when it is probable that an asset had been impaired or a liability had been incurred because the amount of loss cannot be reasonably estimated, should the loss be charged retroactively to that period when it can be reasonably estimated in a subsequent period? Does the loss accrue to the earlier period, when it was probable that an asset had been impaired or a liability had been incurred, or to the later period, when the amount of loss can be reasonably estimated? The Board believes that the requirement under *APB Opinion No. 9* that certain losses, when they can be reasonably estimated in a later period, be charged retroactively to an earlier period is inconsistent with the intent of *FASB Statement No. 5* in prohibiting accrual of an estimated loss when the amount of loss cannot be reasonably estimated, even though it is probable that an asset has been impaired or a liability has been incurred. The Board concluded that all estimated losses for loss contingencies should be charged to income rather than charging some to income and others to retained earnings as prior period adjustments.

Consideration of Specific Types of Adjustments

38. A number of respondents questioned the appropriateness of a rate-regulated utility's reporting refunds in the period in which the refunds are ordered if the refunded amounts were originally collected subject to refund. Upon request, several of those respondents furnished additional data that further explained the effect of those refunds. The Board is aware that there are differing views about the reporting of both the contingently refundable revenue when it is billed and the subsequent refunds. Determining the reporting that would be appropriate for the contingently refundable revenue when it is billed is outside the scope of this Statement. Except for the possible effect of the rate-making process, the Board does not believe that the reporting of any adjustment at the time that a subsequent refund is determined is sufficiently different from the reporting of other adjustments that result from previous uncertainties to justify special treatment in this Statement. However, the Board did not consider whether the effect of the rate-making process might permit or require special treatment for those refunds. (See also paragraphs 46, concerning adjustments related to prior interim periods of the current fiscal year, and 55, concerning the Addendum to *APB Opinion No. 2*.)

39. A number of respondents recommended that this Statement be modified to provide that specific types of adjustments, such as renegotiation, continue to be reported as prior period adjustments. The Board rejected this recommendation because none of the items cited is sufficiently different from other adjustments that are included in the determination of net income of the current period to justify special treatment. (However, see paragraph 46 concerning adjustments related to prior interim periods of the current fiscal year.)

Prior Period Adjustments That Are Not Affected by This Statement

40. The Board reviewed other kinds of items reported as prior period adjustments, described in paragraphs 41-45. In each case, the Board concluded that the accounting for these items should not be modified at this time.

Correction of an Error

41. Paragraph 13 of *APB Opinion No. 20* states:

> Errors in financial statements result from mathematical mistakes, mistakes in the application of accounting principles, or oversight or misuse of facts that existed at the time the financial statements were prepared. In contrast, a change in accounting estimate results from new information or subsequent developments and accordingly from better insight or improved judgment. Thus, an error is distinguishable from a change in estimate. A change from an accounting principle that is not generally accepted to one that is generally accepted is a correction of an error for purposes of applying this Opinion.

A major distinguishing feature of a correction of an error is that the financial statements of the affected prior period, when originally issued, should have reflected the adjustment. In contrast, a prior period adjustment that meets the criteria of paragraph 23 of *APB Opinion No. 9* could not have been determined when the financial statements were originally issued. The Board concluded that a correction of an error, as defined above, should continue to be reflected by restating the financial statements of the affected prior period.

42. Some respondents contended that the distinction between a correction of an error and a change in estimate is too vague to be a basis for different accounting. The Board noted that *APB Opinion No. 20* used that same distinction as the basis for different accounting for corrections of errors and changes in estimates that did not meet the criteria of Opinion No. 9 for prior period adjustments. No problems of application resulting from that requirement of Opinion No. 20 have been brought to the Board's attention.

43. Several respondents stated that an exception to permit the reporting of corrections of errors as prior period adjustments is not justified. The Board concluded that the normal procedures of revising and reissuing financial statements promptly when an error is discovered or otherwise advising users that the financial statements contain erroneous data appear to satisfy the interest of financial statement users. Those procedures also permit enterprises to disclose the inaccuracies on as timely a basis as is practicable in the circumstances.

Income Tax Benefits of Pre-Acquisition Operating Loss Carryforwards of Purchased Subsidiaries

44. Paragraph 88 of *APB Opinion No. 16* states that "an acquiring corporation should reduce the acquired goodwill retroactively for the realized tax benefits of loss carry-forwards of an acquired company not previously recorded by the acquiring corporation." The corresponding reduction in the amount of goodwill amortization in prior years is reported as a prior period adjustment as described in paragraph 49 of *APB Opinion No. 11*. The FASB presently has on its technical agenda a project entitled "Accounting for Business Combinations and Purchased Intangibles" that includes a re-

consideration of *APB Opinion No. 16*. The Board believes that because it is reconsidering *APB Opinion No. 16* the requirements of that Opinion should continue in effect so as to maintain the status quo during the Board's reconsideration.

45. Some respondents recommended that the acquired goodwill be reduced *in the current year* for the realized tax benefits of loss carryforwards of an acquired company not previously recorded by the acquiring corporation. The adjustment would thus in effect be amortized only prospectively rather than both retroactively, as a prior period adjustment, and prospectively. Accounting for realized tax benefits of loss carryforwards of an acquired company is addressed as Problem 2 of Technical Issue Two at paragraphs 512-520 of the August 19, 1976 FASB Discussion Memorandum, "Accounting for Business Combinations and Purchased Intangibles." As indicated in paragraph 44 above, the Board believes that the status quo should be maintained on that project during the Board's deliberations.

Adjustments Related to Prior Interim Periods of the Current Fiscal Year

46. A number of respondents to the Exposure Draft and to the October 7, 1976 Exposure Draft on "Accounting for Income Taxes in Interim Periods" recommended that this Statement be applied to annual financial statements only, rather than to annual and interim financial statements. Several of those respondents noted that the APB concluded in paragraph 9 of *APB Opinion No. 28* that "the usefulness of such [interim financial] information rests on the relationship that it has to the annual results of operations." In those respondents' view, restatement of interim periods is necessary to make interim data relate in a meaningful way to anticipated annual results. Several other of those respondents observed that the Board has on its technical agenda a project entitled "Interim Financial Reporting" that includes a reconsideration of *APB Opinion No. 28* and contended that, because Opinion No. 28 was issued when the criteria of Opinion No. 9 for prior period adjustments were in effect, the Board should not change interim reporting during its reconsideration of Opinion No. 28 by proscribing adjustments to prior interim periods. While not necessarily agreeing with these arguments, the Board decided to continue the practice of interim period restatements in the current fiscal year on a limited basis for the present. To avoid the interpretation problems that have resulted from the criteria of paragraph 23 of Opinion No. 9, the Board (a) limited such restatements to the specific examples cited in paragraph 23 of Opinion No. 9, (b) required that the adjustments meet the definition of materiality for extraordinary items (paragraph 24 of *APB Opinion No. 30*), and (c) required that the adjustments meet the two criteria of paragraph 23 of Opinion No. 9 that have not created interpretation problems in the past. The Board believes that application of the criteria in paragraph 13 will substantially continue existing practice for interim periods of the current fiscal year. Some Board members believe that this exception is inconsistent with some of the other conclusions of this Statement; however, they are willing to accept the provisions of paragraphs 13-15 during the Board's consideration of its project on interim financial reporting.

Accounting Changes

47. Paragraph 25 of *APB Opinion No. 9* addressed the subject of accounting changes as follows:

> A change in the application of accounting principles may create a situation in which retroactive application is appropriate. In such situations *these changes should receive the same treatment as that for prior period adjustments.* [Emphasis added]

While distinguishing a retroactive accounting change from the prior period adjustments covered by paragraph 23 of that Opinion, the APB did prescribe the same accounting treatment for both.

48. Accounting changes (but not prior period adjustments covered by paragraph 23 of *APB Opinion No. 9*) were subsequently dealt with in *APB Opinion No. 20*. Paragraph 5 of Opinion No. 20 states:

> Paragraph 25 of *APB Opinion No. 9* is superseded. Although the conclusion of that paragraph is not modified, this Opinion deals more completely with accounting changes.

49. The Board believes that retroactive accounting changes, whether specified in transition requirements of FASB Statements and Interpretations and APB Opinions or in the requirements of *APB Opinion No. 20,* differ significantly in nature from the prior period adjustments covered by paragraph 23 of *APB Opinion No. 9,* as described in the following paragraph. For that reason, the Board concluded that it should not, in this standard, reexamine existing requirements for retroactive accounting changes or proscribe the use of retroactive accounting changes in future Statements or Interpretations.

50. Requirements for restatements of prior periods to reflect changes in accounting principles address categories of transactions that are usually recurring and pervasive. Those restatements provide useful information for purposes of comparing financial data for periods after initial application of the

accounting principles with data presented for earlier periods. In contrast, the criteria of paragraph 23 of *APB Opinion No. 9* address isolated adjustments that are stated to be "rare in modern financial accounting." The purpose of restatement of prior periods for nonrecurring items cannot be to make the affected prior period comparable to subsequent periods because comparability cannot be accomplished by shifting nonrecurring items among periods. Instead, the purpose is to exclude material items directly related to prior periods from the determination of net income in the current period to avoid impairing the significance of net income of the current period (see paragraphs 10-12 of *APB Opinion No. 9*). As previously stated, the Board concluded that purpose is not accomplished by paragraph 23 of *APB Opinion No. 9* (see paragraph 25 above).

51. Paragraph 52 of *APB Opinion No. 16* states that a change in accounting method of one of the combining enterprises in a pooling of interests that is made to conform the accounting methods of the combining enterprises shall be applied retroactively. Like the item discussed in paragraph 44, this provision will be reconsidered as a part of the current FASB technical agenda project entitled "Accounting for Business Combinations and Purchased Intangibles," and the Board believes the status quo should be maintained in the meantime.

Income Statement Classification

52. Some respondents noted that most adjustments that would have been reported as prior period adjustments prior to the issuance of this Statement will not meet the criteria of *APB Opinion No. 30* for classification as extraordinary items. Some of those respondents recommended that this Statement require adjustments to be classified in the future as extraordinary items if they meet the present criteria of paragraph 23 of *APB Opinion No. 9*. Others contended that inclusion of such adjustments in income from continuing operations would obscure current income from ongoing operations. Considerations of income statement classification under Opinion No. 30 are not different for items previously classified as prior period adjustments and for other changes in estimates. The Board concluded that income statement classification is too pervasive to be dealt with in this project and that it probably should be considered in some phase of the FASB agenda project entitled "Conceptual Framework for Financial Accounting and Reporting."

53. A number of respondents observed that the "average" investor relies primarily on earnings per share data or earnings summaries in the financial press and thus might be misled by the inclusion of adjustments that are related to prior periods in income from continuing operations in the current period. The effect of random, irregular, or unpredictable events may make periodic earnings per share data unrepresentative of an enterprise's earning activities during that period. For example, completed contract accounting for long-term contracts may result in an enterprise's reporting activities of one period in a subsequent period. However, the Board does not believe that investors are served by excluding the effects of such events from reported earnings. Disclosure of the effects of such events is required by certain APB Opinions and FASB Statements. Thus, reliance on a single earnings per share amount or a summary in the financial press may not be a sound basis for investment decisions.

54. Some respondents to the Exposure Draft contended that this Statement substitutes a narrow rule for managements' and auditors' judgments. The Board agrees that judgment is necessary in financial reporting but does not believe that judgment should result in special treatment for some items of profit and loss recognized during a period but not for other similar items unless special treatment is justified by different circumstances. On the other hand, management's judgment may indicate that disclosure should be furnished to allow a user to properly evaluate the enterprise's earnings. For example, *APB Opinion No. 30* requires disclosure of the effect of "unusual" or "infrequently occurring" items. Similar disclosure for items that are not "unusual" or "infrequently occurring," as defined in that Opinion, may also be appropriate if management feels that such disclosure is needed.

Addendum to APB Opinion No. 2

55. A number of respondents requested that the FASB clarify how the Addendum to *APB Opinion No. 2* applies to prior period adjustments. The Board is aware that differing applications of the Addendum exist in practice and has not addressed that issue.

Effective Date and Transition

56. Some respondents recommended that the Statement not apply to certain categories of preexisting contingencies. Those respondents suggested a variety of criteria for determining the preexisting contingencies to be exempted, including prior disclosure of the contingency, prior partial settlements of the same or of a related matter that were reported as prior period adjustments, and qualifications of auditors' earlier reports with respect to the contingency. The Board concluded that there was no equitable basis for exempting certain preexisting contingencies and not others.

57. The Exposure Draft proposed that the State-

ment be applied to fiscal years beginning on or after December 15, 1976. Several respondents recommended earlier application to avoid an interim period of confusion. Several others recommended a delay in the effective date because management may have disclosed in good faith that an anticipated adjustment would be reported as a prior period adjustment and might as a result be charged with having misled investors if the adjustment is reported in income of the current period. Following further consideration the Board concluded that it was appropriate to modify the effective date of this Statement to fiscal years beginning after October 15, 1977.

Applicability to Interim Periods

58. Some respondents questioned whether this Statement was intended to apply to interim as well as annual financial statements. As a result the Board added footnote 1 to paragraph 10. In addition, as explained in paragraph 46, paragraphs 13-15 were added.

Disclosure

59. Some respondents recommended that this Statement specify the disclosures that should be made for an adjustment that would previously have been reported as a prior period adjustment under the criteria of *APB Opinion No. 9.* The Board concluded that existing disclosure requirements that have been applied to other similar items included in the determination of current net income also apply to items that would previously have been reported as prior period adjustments. For example, *APB Opinion No. 30* specifies the disclosure requirements for "unusual items," "infrequently occurring items," and "extraordinary items"; *APB Opinion No. 28* specifies the disclosure requirements for various categories of adjustments in interim financial reports; and other pronouncements specify disclosures that apply to certain types of items.

Appendix B

SUMMARY OF FASB STAFF RESEARCH

Other Studies Available

60. A recent survey of the annual reports of 600 industrial and commercial corporations contained the following summary of adjustments to the opening balances of retained earnings during the four fiscal years of those enterprises ended not later than February 2, 1975:[12]

Reasons for adjustment	1974	1973	1972	1971
Poolings of interests	30	56	67	69
Research and development expenditures charged to operations	23	—	—	—
Litigation or income tax settlements	12	29	26	15
Other	18	36	89	87
Total adjustments	83	121	182	171

Investigation revealed that the "other" category consisted principally of accounting changes (adopting tax allocation, adopting recommendations of AICPA Industry Audit Guides that required retroactive application, etc.) and changes in the reporting entity. The items categorized as "litigation or income tax settlements" were prior period adjustments made pursuant to the criteria of paragraph 23 of *APB Opinion No. 9.* Since the adjustments represented by this caption were few in number, the broader study described in the following paragraphs was undertaken. The adjustments in the above table that were determined to have been made pursuant to paragraph 23 of *APB Opinion No. 9* were used as a control to ensure that the selection procedures were adequate to locate substantially all of such adjustments made by enterprises included in the study.

[12]American Institute of Certified Public Accountants, *Accounting Trends & Techniques—1975,* 29th ed. (New York: AICPA, 1975), p. 363.

Methodology

61. The research by the FASB staff utilized the National Automated Accounting Research System (NAARS).[13] NAARS includes a file of annual reports of publicly held enterprises. Enterprises reporting or referring to prior period adjustments in either the footnotes or the retained earnings statement were identified. The control group referred to in paragraph 60 was used to provide assurance that no substantial number of items was omitted. Complete reliability of the results of such a search could not be assured because of the variety of ways that enterprises disclose such adjustments. Adjustments were located in approximately 1,200 reports and those adjustments were reviewed in detail, and the adjustments made pursuant to paragraph 23 of *APB Opinion No. 9* were identified. If it was unclear whether the adjustment belonged in this category, it was included, except that in a few instances where there was virtually no disclosure of the nature or circumstances of the adjustment, the adjustment was excluded from the study because no meaningful conclusions could be derived. Subsidiary companies that reported the same prior period adjustment reported in consolidated statements were excluded to avoid duplication. At the time the research was conducted, the NAARS system included:

Year*	Total reports including subsidiaries	Approximate total enterprises
1973	3,617	3,350
1974	3,150	2,800
1975	650	600
Total	7,417	6,750

The detail summaries following are limited to 1974 and 1973; 1975 was reviewed to determine whether significant trends were apparent (none were noted) but the file was considered not sufficiently complete to justify any further conclusions. In addition, later 1975 results, if available, would probably have reflected the effect of the recent SEC staff interpretations.

Overall Results

62. The following table compares 1974 and 1973 identified prior period adjustments:

	1974		1973	
Category	Number of enterprises reporting adjustments	Percentage of enterprises	Number of enterprises reporting adjustments	Percentage of enterprises
Income taxes	30	1.1%	53	1.6%
Litigation and similar claims	37	1.3%	37	1.1%
Utility rate and similar matters	13	0.5%	13	0.4%
Renegotiation	—	0.0%	6	0.2%
Economic Stabilization	1	0.0%	2	0.1%
Other	—	0.0%	5	0.1%
Total†	81		116	
Total enterprises†	79	2.8%	112	3.3%

[13]NAARS is a computer-assisted accounting retrieval system developed by the American Institute of Certified Public Accountants in conjunction with Mead Data Central, Inc.

*The NAARS system classifies fiscal year-ends from July through June as a "year" (e.g., 1974 includes fiscal years ended July 1974 through June 1975).

†Individual categories add to more than the total enterprises shown because some enterprises reported prior period adjustments in more than one category.

63. The following table compares the relative size of the identified adjustments reported for 1974 and 1973:

Range of prior period adjustment as a percentage of net income or loss in the year reported		Number of enterprises reporting adjustments in the range			
Over	But not over	Income taxes	Litigation and similar claims	Utility rate and similar matters	All other
0%	5%	13	18	7	4
5%	10%	29	7	6	3
10%	20%	17	17	6	3
20%	50%	16	19	4	1
50%	100%	5	8	—	—
100%		2	5	2	3
Not determinable		1	—	1	—
Total		83	74	26	14

64. Investigation of the adjustments relating to income taxes and litigation disclosed the following circumstances:

Apparent circumstances of the adjustment, based on financial statement disclosures	Adjustments relating to: Income taxes	Adjustments relating to: Litigation and similar claims
Negotiated settlements	56	45*
Adjudicated settlements	5	14
Combination of negotiated and adjudicated settlements	—	5
Not settled at the date the financial statements were issued	8	7
Negotiated by outside parties without participation by the enterprise	—	1
Change in estimate, with no other party involved	5	—
Not determinable	9	2
Total	83	74

Other Findings

65. Paragraphs 66-70 describe other findings of the survey.

Changes in Accounting Estimates

66. *APB Opinion No. 20* prohibits restatement of amounts reported in prior periods as a result of changes in accounting estimates except for adjustments that meet all of the criteria of paragraph 23 of *APB Opinion No. 9* (see paragraph 35). Twenty of the 197 identified 1974 and 1973 prior period adjustments were changes in previously recorded accounting estimates. These consisted of seven reversals of income tax accruals, six adjustments of prior year provisions for loss on disposal of discontinued operations, and seven adjustments of prior year provisions for other litigation and similar claims.

Frequency of Occurrence

67. Paragraph 23 of *APB Opinion No. 9* stated that prior period adjustments would be "nonrecurring." Paragraph 24 of Opinion No. 9 stated that "treatment as prior period adjustments should not be applied to the normal, recurring corrections. . . ." The term "nonrecurring" is discussed in paragraph 36 above. Many of the identified prior period adjustments appeared to be of a nature that would be reasonably expected to recur in the foreseeable future in the enterprise's operating environment. Nine enterprises reported similar or related prior period adjustments in both 1974 and 1973.

*17 required court approval.

Application of Criterion (a)

68. Criterion (a) of paragraph 23 of *APB Opinion No. 9* requires that an item "can be specifically identified with and directly related to the business activities of particular prior periods." Most of the identified prior period adjustments for settlements of litigation were charged to the period in which the underlying event that gave rise to the litigation occurred. Some, however, were charged or credited to a prior period subsequent to the underlying event, including (a) the period the litigation was initiated, (b) the period of a prior criminal conviction for the alleged acts, or (c) the period that an amount was accrued in excess of the eventual cost of the settlement.

Utility Rate and Similar Matters

69. Utility rate making processes sometimes allow rates to customers to be increased on a provisional basis prior to the regulatory commission's final action on a requested rate increase. If a portion of the requested increase is subsequently disallowed, the utility is required to refund the disallowed portion. Of the 26 identified adjustments relating to utility rate and similar matters, 14 relate to this process.

Income Taxes

70. Identified adjustments for income tax matters included 12 settlements for which the underlying basis of the settlement was recorded (e.g., retroactive adjustment of depreciation to reflect longer useful lives). These may have been corrections of errors. As explained in paragraph 61, these adjustments were included because it was unclear whether the adjustments were made pursuant to paragraph 23 of *APB Opinion No. 9*.

Appendix C

EXCERPTS FROM SEC STAFF ACCOUNTING BULLETIN NO. 8

71. On June 4, 1976 the SEC published *Staff Accounting Bulletin No. 8*. This Bulletin included a statement of the SEC staff's interpretation and application of the criteria of *APB Opinion No. 9* for prior period adjustments.

72. Staff Accounting Bulletins contain the following statement concerning their authoritative status:

> The statements in the Bulletin are not rules or interpretations of the Commission nor are they published as bearing the Commission's official approval; they represent interpretations and practices followed by the Division [of Corporation Finance] and the Chief Accountant in administering the disclosure requirements of the federal securities laws.

73. *Staff Accounting Bulletin No. 8* included the following:

> H. Prior Period Adjustments
>
> Facts:
>
> Accounting Principles Board Opinion No. 9, paragraph 23, limits treatment as a prior period adjustment "to those material adjustments which (a) can be specifically identified with and directly related to the business activities of particular prior periods, and (b) are not attributable to economic events occurring subsequent to the date of the financial statements for the prior period, and (c) depend primarily on determinations by persons other than management and (d) were not susceptible of reasonable estimation prior to such determination."
>
> It is not uncommon for parties to litigation to reach settlement of the matter at issue in an out-of-court settlement.
>
> Question:
>
> Do out-of-court settlements meet the criteria for prior period adjustments?
>
> Interpretative Response:
>
> The staff has been extremely reluctant to permit registrants to charge items to retained earnings as prior period adjustments in the light of the clear intent expressed in APB 9 to limit such charges severely. That opinion effectively adopted an all-inclusive approach to the measurement of periodic income. While such an approach may not result in the best matching of costs and revenues, it does provide assurance that all items will at some time be accounted for as elements of income and it prevents the abuses which were noted prior to the adoption of APB 9 whereby adverse circumstances could be at least partially obscured through the vehicle of a direct charge to retained earnings. If unusual items and items related to matters arising in prior years are properly isolated and described in the income statement, we believe that investors will be able to interpret results in an intelligent fashion. Were the Financial Accounting Standards Board to revise the basic accounting philosophy of the all-inclusive income statement, the staff would, of course, review its position in the light of that revision.
>
> In the meantime, however, the staff intends to

continue to apply the four restrictive tests set forth in paragraph 23 of Accounting Principles Board Opinion No. 9 strictly. In this connection, the issue which has arisen most frequently is the treatment of litigation settlements. It is the staff's view that when litigation is settled, the management must make a number of significant judgments and, hence, the test that the amounts must "depend primarily on determinations by persons other than management" (criterion (c) above) has not been met. In addition, in a business world increasingly characterized by litigation to an extent far in excess of that when Accounting Principles Board Opinion No. 9 was adopted (1966), it seems that litigation is inevitably an "economic event" and that settlements would constitute "economic events" of the period in which they occur. Accordingly, it would seem that charges or credits relating to settlements would also not meet the second test (criterion (b) above) set forth in paragraph 23 of Opinion 9 that they not be "attributable to economic events occurring subsequent to the date of the financial statements for the prior period."

Statement of Financial Accounting Standards No. 17 Accounting for Leases—Initial Direct Costs

an amendment of FASB Statement No. 13

STATUS

Issued: November 1977

Effective Date: For leasing transactions and revisions entered into on or after January 1, 1978

Affects: Supersedes FAS 13, paragraph 5(m)

Affected by: No other pronouncements

Statement of Financial Accounting Standards No. 17
Accounting for Leases—Initial Direct Costs

an amendment of FASB Statement No. 13

CONTENTS

INTRODUCTION AND BACKGROUND INFORMATION

1. *FASB Statement No. 13*, "Accounting for Leases," issued by the Board in November 1976, defined *initial direct costs* in paragraph 5(m) as follows:

> Those incremental direct costs incurred by the lessor in negotiating and consummating leasing transactions (e.g., commissions and legal fees).

2. Since issuance of *FASB Statement No. 13* the Board has received a number of requests to interpret the definition of *initial direct costs*, specifically to clarify the meaning of "incremental direct costs." On April 7, 1977, the Board submitted a proposed Interpretation of the definition to the members of the Financial Accounting Standards Advisory Council for comment. The proposed Interpretation stated that *direct* referred to those costs that are incurred in connection with specific leasing transactions and *incremental* limited such costs to those that vary directly with the number or dollar amount of leasing transactions, as distinct from ongoing, recurring expenses that ordinarily do not vary with the number or dollar amount of leasing transactions. Twenty-five letters of comment were received from Council members and from others representing businesses that would be affected by the Interpretation. Many respondents to the proposed Interpretation urged the Board to include in the definition of initial direct costs sales salaries and other costs that do not vary directly with specific leasing transactions but that do vary with the general level of leasing business acquired. The Board concluded that it should amend the definition of initial direct costs to encompass costs that are directly related to consummated leasing transactions and that vary either with specific leasing transactions or with the general level of leasing business acquired.

3. An Exposure Draft of a proposed Statement on "Accounting for Leases—Initial Direct Costs" was issued on August 8, 1977. The Board received 42 letters of comment in response to the Exposure Draft. Certain of those comments and the Board's consideration of them are discussed in paragraphs 4-6 below.

4. Some respondents recommended that the Board conform the accounting for initial direct costs of leases to the existing practices for other financing activities of finance companies; other respondents recommended that the Board conform the accounting for initial direct costs of leases to the existing practices for other financing activities of banks. The *AICPA Industry Audit Guide*, "Audits of Finance Companies," permits the use of any of three overall methods of recognizing finance income. All of the methods require that direct and indirect acquisition costs applicable to loans be charged to operations when incurred. Two of the methods require that an amount of deferred finance income equal to estimated acquisition costs be transferred to operations in the same period; such a transfer is prohibited under the other permitted method. Banks often charge all loan origination costs to expense without offsetting revenue recognition. Conforming the accounting for initial direct costs of leases to the accounting for initial direct costs of other financing activities of various types of enterprises would require alternative methods of accounting for similar leasing transactions. Still other respondents recommended that the Board permit the option of charging initial direct costs to expense without offsetting revenue recognition. The Board concluded that it should not prescribe alternative methods of accounting for similar leasing transactions.

5. Some respondents to the Exposure Draft stated that the cost of identifying the portion of salespersons' salaries that relates to specific completed leasing transactions would be excessive. The Board believes that salespersons can estimate the portion of their time that results in completed leases and the portion spent in negotiations for leases that were not

consummated and in other activities and that reasonable allocations of other costs can be made based on similar estimates. In some enterprises, the determinations can be made by periodic statistical samples. The Board believes that enterprises can perform the required allocations without excessive cost.

6. Some respondents to the Exposure Draft asked if the Board intended that a provision for bad debts be included in initial direct costs. The Board does not intend that initial direct costs, as defined, include a provision for bad debts. Accounting for bad debts that are expected to result from leases and other financing activities is a pervasive issue that the Board did not address in *FASB Statement No. 13*. The Board has not studied that question and did not intend that Statement No. 13 would change existing practices in accounting for bad debts.

7. The Board concluded that on the basis of existing data it could make an informed decision on the matter addressed in this Statement without a public hearing and that the effective date and transition prescribed in paragraph 9 are advisable.

STANDARDS OF FINANCIAL ACCOUNTING AND REPORTING

Amendment to FASB Statement No. 13

8. Paragraph 5(m) of *FASB Statement No. 13* is superseded by the following:

> *Initial direct costs.* Those costs incurred by the lessor that are directly associated with negotiating and consummating completed leasing transactions. Those costs include, but are not necessarily limited to, commissions, legal fees, costs of credit investigations, and costs of preparing and processing documents for new leases acquired. In addition, that portion of salespersons' compensation, other than commissions, and the compensation of other employees that is applicable to the time spent in the activities described above with respect to completed leasing transactions shall also be included in initial direct costs. That portion of salespersons' compensation and the compensation of other employees that is applicable to the time spent in negotiating leases that are not consummated shall not be included in initial direct costs. No portion of supervisory and administrative expenses or other indirect expenses, such as rent and facilities costs, shall be included in initial direct costs.

Effective Date and Transition

9. The provisions of this amendment to *FASB Statement No. 13* shall be effective for leasing transactions and lease agreement revisions (see paragraph 9 of Statement No. 13) entered into on or after January 1, 1978. Earlier application is encouraged. In addition, the provisions of this Statement shall be applied retroactively at the same time and in the same manner as the provisions of Statement No. 13 are applied retroactively (see paragraphs 49 and 51 of Statement No. 13). Enterprises that have already applied the provisions of Statement No. 13 retroactively and have published financial statements based on the retroactively adjusted accounts before the effective date of this Statement may, but are not required to, apply the provisions of this Statement retroactively.

The provisions of this Statement need not be applied to immaterial items.

This Statement was adopted by the affirmative votes of five members of the Financial Accounting Standards Board. Messrs. Gellein and Kirk dissented.

Messrs. Gellein and Kirk dissent because the Statement proliferates further, and therefore adds confusion to, the accounting for costs of acquiring business. As indicated in paragraph 4 of the Statement, financial-type enterprises, including banks, finance companies, leasing companies, and insurance companies, follow various methods of accounting for acquisition costs. Messrs. Gellein and Kirk object to piecemeal consideration of the accounting for such acquisition costs, particularly if the result is to establish a method followed by few, if any, companies, without offering the rationale for the method. Understanding of financial statements of companies in industries with similar operating circumstances is not enhanced by specifying a new accounting method based on a new meaning of terms for certain transactions of an enterprise while similar transactions are accounted for under different methods.

Messrs. Gellein and Kirk believe that the revenue of a period is not determined by the expenses of the period and therefore they can accept a transfer to revenue of an amount equivalent to certain expenses of the period only as an expedient, pending further consideration of the accounting for business acquisition costs. In the meantime they would limit the extent of that kind of transfer to additional costs incurred to obtain the business, as was the intention in *FASB Statement No. 13* and the proposed Interpretation referred to in paragraph 2 of this Statement.

Members of the Financial Accounting Standards Board:

Marshall S. Armstrong, *Chairman*	Donald J. Kirk	Robert T. Sprouse
Oscar S. Gellein	Arthur L. Litke	Ralph E. Walters
	Robert E. Mays	

Statement of Financial Accounting Standards No. 18
Financial Reporting for Segments of a Business Enterprise—Interim Financial Statements

an amendment of FASB Statement No. 14

STATUS

Issued: November 1977

Effective Date: December 1, 1977 retroactive to effective date of FAS14

Affects: Amends FAS 14, paragraph 41
Supersedes FAS 14, paragraphs 4 and 73 and footnote 15

Affected by: No other pronouncements

Statement of Financial Accounting Standards No. 18
Financial Reporting for Segments of a Business Enterprise—Interim Financial Statements

an amendment of FASB Statement No. 14

CONTENTS

INTRODUCTION AND BACKGROUND INFORMATION

1. Paragraph 4 of *FASB Statement No. 14,* "Financial Reporting for Segments of a Business Enterprise," issued by the Board in December 1976, provides for the inclusion of segment information in interim financial statements as follows:

> If an enterprise issues for an interim period a complete set of financial statements that are expressly described as presenting financial position, results of operations, and changes in financial position in conformity with generally accepted accounting principles, this Statement requires that the information referred to in paragraph 3 be included in those interim financial statements. If an enterprise issues for an interim period financial statements that are not a complete set or are otherwise complete but not expressly described as presenting financial position, results of operations, and changes in financial position in conformity with generally accepted accounting principles, this Statement does not require that the information referred to in paragraph 3 be included in those interim financial statements.

The alternatives considered by the Board and the basis for its conclusions are set forth in paragraphs 72 and 73 of the Statement.

2. Since the issuance of *FASB Statement No. 14,* the Board has received a number of questions about when the information specified in the Statement is required in financial statements for interim periods. On March 2, 1977, the Board submitted a proposed Interpretation of paragraph 4 of the Statement to the members of the Financial Accounting Standards Advisory Council for comment. That proposed Interpretation included examples of situations in which the "expressly described" test of paragraph 4 was met and segment information was required and other situations in which the "expressly described" test was not met and segment information was not required. A number of the comment letters received from Council members indicated that the proposed Interpretation did not provide adequate clarification and that an amendment of Statement No. 14 was necessary.

3. The Board has the subject of interim financial reporting on its technical agenda. The issues addressed in that project include consideration of the type of financial information that should be reported for interim periods.

4. The Board has reconsidered the question of whether segment information shall be included in interim financial statements and has decided to eliminate any requirement to report the information specified by *FASB Statement No. 14* in interim period financial statements pending completion of the interim financial reporting project.

5. An Exposure Draft of a proposed Statement on "Financial Reporting for Segments of a Business Enterprise—Interim Financial Statements" was issued on September 20, 1977. Sixty-five letters were received in response to that Exposure Draft, virtually all of which expressed agreement.

6. The Board concluded that on the basis of existing data it can reach an informed decision without a public hearing and that the effective date and transition specified in paragraph 9 are advisable in the circumstances.

STANDARDS OF FINANCIAL ACCOUNTING AND REPORTING

Amendment to FASB Statement No. 14

7. The information specified in paragraph 3 of *FASB Statement No. 14* is not required in financial statements for interim periods. Accordingly, Statement No. 14 is amended as follows:

a. Paragraphs 4 and 73 and footnote 15 to paragraph 41 are deleted.
b. The words "and for interim periods[15] within those fiscal years" are deleted from the first sentence of paragraph 41 and that sentence is modified to read as follows:

> The provisions of this Statement shall be effective for financial statements for fiscal years beginning after December 15, 1976.

8. Although segment information is not required in financial statements for interim periods, any segment information that is presented in interim period financial statements shall be consistent with the requirements of *FASB Statement No. 14.*

Effective Date and Transition

9. This amendment to *FASB Statement No. 14* shall be effective December 1, 1977, retroactive to the effective date of that Statement. Segment information presented in interim period financial statements issued prior to December 1, 1977 need not be included if those interim period financial statements are subsequently presented for comparative purposes after the effective date of this Statement.

The provisions of this Statement need not be applied to immaterial items.

This Statement was adopted by the affirmative votes of the seven members of the Financial Accounting Standards Board.

Marshall S. Armstrong, *Chairman*
Oscar S. Gellein
Donald J. Kirk
Arthur L. Litke
Robert E. Mays
Robert T. Sprouse
Ralph E. Walters

Statement of Financial Accounting Standards No. 19
Financial Accounting and Reporting by Oil and Gas Producing Companies

STATUS

Issued: December 1977

Effective Date: For fiscal years beginning after December 15, 1978 and interim periods within those years (but amended by FAS 25)

Affects: Supersedes FAS 9

Affected by: Paragraph 9 superseded by FAS 71
Paragraphs 48 through 59 superseded by FAS 69
Paragraphs 48 and 63 amended by FAS 25
Paragraph 271 and footnotes 11 and 12 superseded by FAS 25

Statement of Financial Accounting Standards No. 19
Financial Accounting and Reporting by Oil and Gas Producing Companies

CONTENTS

INTRODUCTION

1. This Statement establishes standards of financial accounting and reporting for the oil and gas producing activities of a business enterprise. Those activities involve the acquisition of mineral interests in properties, exploration (including prospecting), development, and production of crude oil, including condensate and natural gas liquids, and natural gas (hereinafter collectively referred to as oil and gas producing activities).

2. Existing authoritative accounting pronouncements do not explicitly or comprehensively establish standards of financial accounting and reporting for those activities. Numerous alternative accounting practices are presently followed by oil and gas producing companies, and the nature and extent of the information they disclose in their financial statements about their oil and gas producing activities vary considerably from company to company. The Board is issuing this Statement to address the financial accounting and reporting issues that led to the alternative practices.

3. Appendix A contains background information. Appendix B sets forth the basis for the Board's conclusions, including alternatives considered and reasons for accepting some and rejecting others. Appendix C is a glossary of terms.

4. The accounting standards in this Statement adhere to the traditional historical cost basis. Although the Board considered both *discovery value* and *current value* as alternative bases of accounting for oil and gas reserves, it determined for the reasons discussed in paragraphs 133-141 that any decision on applying value accounting to oil and gas companies should await resolution of the broader issue of the general applicability of value accounting in the Board's project, "Conceptual Framework for Financial Accounting and Reporting."

5. This Statement supersedes *FASB Statement No. 9,* "Accounting for Income Taxes—Oil and Gas Producing Companies."

SCOPE

6. This Statement applies only to *oil and gas producing* activities; it does not address financial accounting and reporting issues relating to the transporting, refining, and marketing of oil and gas. Also, this Statement does not apply to activities relating to the production of other wasting (nonregenerative) natural resources; nor does it apply to the production of geothermal steam or to the extraction of hydrocarbons as a by-product of the production of geothermal steam and associated geothermal resources as defined in the *Geothermal Steam Act of 1970;* nor does it apply to the extraction of hydrocarbons from shale, tar sands, or coal.

7. Accounting for interest on funds borrowed to finance an enterprise's oil and gas producing activities is excluded from consideration in this Statement because the broader subject of accounting for interest costs in general is a project presently on the Board's technical agenda.

8. This Statement prescribes disclosures related to an enterprise's oil and gas producing activities that are considered necessary for fair presentation of the enterprise's financial position, results of operations, and changes in financial position in conformity with generally accepted accounting principles. Those disclosures are only part of the information that may be needed for investment, regulatory, or national economic planning and energy policy decisions.

9. The Addendum to *APB Opinion No. 2,* "Accounting for the 'Investment Credit'," states that "differences may arise in the application of generally accepted accounting principles as between regulated and nonregulated businesses, because of the effect in regulated businesses of the rate-making process" and discusses the application of generally accepted accounting principles to regulated industries. Accordingly, the provisions of the Addendum shall govern the application of this Statement to those oil and gas producing operations of a company that are regulated for rate-making purposes on an individual-company-cost-of-service basis.

STANDARDS OF FINANCIAL ACCOUNTING AND REPORTING

Definitions

10. The glossary in Appendix C defines the following terms as they are used in this Statement:

a. Proved reserves.
b. Proved developed reserves.
c. Proved undeveloped reserves.
d. Field.
e. Reservoir.
f. Exploratory well.
g. Development well.
h. Service well.
i. Stratigraphic test well.
   i. Exploratory-type.
   ii. Development-type.
j. Proved area.

Basic Concepts

11. An enterprise's oil and gas producing activities involve certain special types of assets. Costs of those assets shall be capitalized when incurred. Those types of assets broadly defined are:

a. *Mineral interests in properties* (hereinafter referred to as *properties*), which include fee ownership or a lease, concession, or other interest representing the right to extract oil or gas subject to such terms as may be imposed by the conveyance of that interest. Properties also include royalty interests, production payments payable in oil or gas, and other nonoperating interests in properties operated by others. Properties include those agreements with foreign governments or authorities under which an enterprise participates in the operation of the related properties or otherwise serves as "producer" of the underlying reserves (see paragraph 53); but properties do not include other supply agreements or contracts that represent the right to *purchase* (as opposed to *extract*) oil and gas. Properties shall be classified as proved or unproved as follows:
   i. *Unproved properties*—properties with no proved reserves.
   ii. *Proved properties*—properties with proved reserves.

b. *Wells and related equipment and facilities,*[1] the costs of which include those incurred to:
   i. Drill and equip those exploratory wells and exploratory-type stratigraphic test wells that have found proved reserves.
   ii. Obtain access to proved reserves and provide facilities for extracting, treating, gathering, and storing the oil and gas, including the drilling and equipping of development wells and development-type stratigraphic test wells (whether those wells are successful or unsuccessful) and service wells.
c. *Support equipment and facilities used in oil and gas producing activities,* such as seismic equipment, drilling equipment, construction and grading equipment, vehicles, repair shops, warehouses, supply points, camps, and division, district, or field offices.
d. *Uncompleted wells, equipment, and facilities,* the costs of which include those incurred to:
   i. Drill and equip wells that are not yet completed.
   ii. Acquire or construct equipment and facilities that are not yet completed and installed.

12. The costs of an enterprise's wells and related equipment and facilities and the costs of the related proved properties shall be amortized as the related oil and gas reserves are produced. That amortization plus production (lifting) costs become part of the cost of oil and gas produced. Unproved properties shall be assessed periodically, and a loss recognized if those properties are impaired.

13. Some costs incurred in an enterprise's oil and gas producing activities do not result in acquisition of an asset and, therefore, shall be charged to expense. Examples include geological and geophysical costs, the costs of carrying and retaining undeveloped properties, and the costs of drilling those exploratory wells and exploratory-type stratigraphic test wells that do not find proved reserves.

14. The basic concepts in paragraphs 11-13 are elaborated on in paragraphs 15-41.

Accounting at the Time Costs Are Incurred

Acquisition of Properties

15. Costs incurred to purchase, lease, or otherwise acquire a property (whether unproved or proved) shall be capitalized when incurred. They include the costs of lease bonuses and options to purchase or lease properties, the portion of costs applicable to minerals when land including mineral rights is purchased in fee, brokers' fees, recording fees, legal costs, and other costs incurred in acquiring properties.

Exploration

16. Exploration involves (a) identifying areas that may warrant examination and (b) examining specific areas that are considered to have prospects of containing oil and gas reserves, including drilling exploratory wells and exploratory-type stratigraphic test wells. Exploration costs may be incurred both before acquiring the related property (sometimes referred to in part as prospecting costs) and after acquiring the property.

17. Principal types of exploration costs, which include depreciation and applicable operating costs of support equipment and facilities (paragraph 26) and other costs of exploration activities, are:

a. Costs of topographical, geological, and geophysical studies, rights of access to properties to conduct those studies, and salaries and other expenses of geologists, geophysical crews, and others conducting those studies. Collectively, those are sometimes referred to as geological and geophysical or "G&G" costs.
b. Costs of carrying and retaining undeveloped properties, such as delay rentals, *ad valorem* taxes on the properties, legal costs for title defense, and the maintenance of land and lease records.
c. Dry hole contributions and bottom hole contributions.
d. Costs of drilling and equipping exploratory wells.
e. Costs of drilling exploratory-type stratigraphic test wells.[2]

18. Geological and geophysical costs, costs of carrying and retaining undeveloped properties, and dry hole and bottom hole contributions shall be charged to expense when incurred.

19. The costs of drilling exploratory wells and the costs of drilling exploratory-type stratigraphic test wells shall be capitalized as part of the enterprise's uncompleted wells, equipment, and facilities pending determination of whether the well has found proved reserves. If the well has found proved reserves (paragraphs 31-34), the capitalized costs of drilling the well shall become part of the enterprise's wells and related equipment and facilities (even

[1] Often referred to in the oil and gas industry as "lease and well equipment" even though, technically, the property may have been acquired other than by a lease.

[2] While the costs of drilling stratigraphic test wells are sometimes considered to be geological and geophysical costs, they are accounted for separately under this Statement for reasons explained in paragraphs 200-202.

though the well may not be completed as a producing well); if, however, the well has not found proved reserves, the capitalized costs of drilling the well, net of any salvage value, shall be charged to expense.

20. An enterprise sometimes conducts G&G studies and other exploration activities on a property owned by another party, in exchange for which the enterprise is contractually entitled to receive an interest in the property if proved reserves are found or to be reimbursed by the owner for the G&G and other costs incurred if proved reserves are not found. In that case, the enterprise conducting the G&G studies and other exploration activities shall account for those costs as a receivable when incurred and, if proved reserves are found, they shall become the cost of the proved property acquired.

Development

21. Development costs are incurred to obtain access to proved reserves and to provide facilities for extracting, treating, gathering, and storing the oil and gas. More specifically, development costs, including depreciation and applicable operating costs of support equipment and facilities (paragraph 26) and other costs of development activities, are costs incurred to:

a. Gain access to and prepare well locations for drilling, including surveying well locations for the purpose of determining specific development drilling sites, clearing ground, draining, road building, and relocating public roads, gas lines, and power lines, to the extent necessary in developing the proved reserves.
b. Drill and equip development wells, development-type stratigraphic test wells, and service wells, including the costs of platforms and of well equipment such as casing, tubing, pumping equipment, and the wellhead assembly.
c. Acquire, construct, and install production facilities such as lease flow lines, separators, treaters, heaters, manifolds, measuring devices, and production storage tanks, natural gas cycling and processing plants, and utility and waste disposal systems.
d. Provide improved recovery systems.

22. Development costs shall be capitalized as part of the cost of an enterprise's wells and related equipment and facilities. Thus, all costs incurred to drill and equip development wells, development-type stratigraphic test wells, and service wells are development costs and shall be capitalized, whether the well is successful or unsuccessful. Costs of drilling those wells and costs of constructing equipment and facilities shall be included in the enterprise's uncompleted wells, equipment, and facilities until drilling or construction is completed.

Production

23. Production involves lifting the oil and gas to the surface and gathering, treating, field processing (as in the case of processing gas to extract liquid hydrocarbons), and field storage. For purposes of this Statement, the production function shall normally be regarded as terminating at the outlet valve on the lease or field production storage tank; if unusual physical or operational circumstances exist, it may be more appropriate to regard the production function as terminating at the first point at which oil, gas, or gas liquids are delivered to a main pipeline, a common carrier, a refinery, or a marine terminal.

24. Production costs are those costs incurred to operate and maintain an enterprise's wells and related equipment and facilities, including depreciation and applicable operating costs of support equipment and facilities (paragraph 26) and other costs of operating and maintaining those wells and related equipment and facilities. They become part of the cost of oil and gas produced. Examples of production costs (sometimes called lifting costs) are:

a. Costs of labor to operate the wells and related equipment and facilities.
b. Repairs and maintenance.
c. Materials, supplies, and fuel consumed and services utilized in operating the wells and related equipment and facilities.
d. Property taxes and insurance applicable to proved properties and wells and related equipment and facilities.
e. Severance taxes.

25. Depreciation, depletion, and amortization of capitalized acquisition, exploration, and development costs also become part of the cost of oil and gas produced along with production (lifting) costs identified in paragraph 24.

Support Equipment and Facilities

26. The cost of acquiring or constructing support equipment and facilities used in oil and gas producing activities shall be capitalized. Examples of support equipment and facilities include seismic equipment, drilling equipment, construction and grading equipment, vehicles, repair shops, warehouses, supply points, camps, and division, district, or field offices. Some support equipment or facilities are acquired or constructed for use exclusively in a single activity—exploration, development, or production. Other support equipment or facilities may serve two or more of those activities and may also serve the enterprise's transportation, refining, and marketing activities. To the extent that the support

equipment and facilities are used in oil and gas producing activities, their depreciation and applicable operating costs become an exploration, development, or production cost, as appropriate.

Disposition of Capitalized Costs

27. The effect of paragraphs 15-26, which deal with accounting at the time costs are incurred, is to recognize as assets: (a) unproved properties; (b) proved properties; (c) wells and related equipment and facilities (which consist of all development costs plus the costs of drilling those exploratory wells and exploratory-type stratigraphic test wells that find proved reserves); (d) support equipment and facilities used in oil and gas producing activities; and (e) uncompleted wells, equipment, and facilities. Paragraphs 28-41 which follow deal with disposition of the costs of those assets after capitalization. Among other things, those paragraphs provide that the acquisition costs of proved properties and the costs of wells and related equipment and facilities be amortized to become part of the cost of oil and gas produced; that impairment of unproved properties be recognized; and that the costs of an exploratory well or exploratory-type stratigraphic test well be charged to expense if the well is determined not to have found proved reserves.

Assessment of Unproved Properties

28. Unproved properties shall be assessed periodically to determine whether they have been impaired. A property would likely be impaired, for example, if a dry hole has been drilled on it and the enterprise has no firm plans to continue drilling. Also, the likelihood of partial or total impairment of a property increases as the expiration of the lease term approaches if drilling activity has not commenced on the property or on nearby properties. If the results of the assessment indicate impairment, a loss shall be recognized by providing a valuation allowance. Impairment of individual unproved properties whose acquisition costs are relatively significant shall be assessed on a property-by-property basis, and an indicated loss shall be recognized by providing a valuation allowance. When an enterprise has a relatively large number of unproved properties whose acquisition costs are not individually significant, it may not be practical to assess impairment on a property-by-property basis, in which case the amount of loss to be recognized and the amount of the valuation allowance needed to provide for impairment of those properties shall be determined by amortizing those properties, either in the aggregate or by groups, on the basis of the experience of the enterprise in similar situations and other information about such factors as the primary lease terms of those properties, the average holding period of unproved properties, and the relative proportion of such properties on which proved reserves have been found in the past.

Reclassification of an Unproved Property

29. A property shall be reclassified from unproved properties to proved properties when proved reserves are discovered on or otherwise attributed to the property; occasionally, a single property, such as a foreign lease or concession covers so vast an area that only the portion of the property to which the proved reserves relate—determined on the basis of geological structural features or stratigraphic conditions—should be reclassified from unproved to proved. For a property whose impairment has been assessed individually in accordance with paragraph 28, the *net* carrying amount (acquisition cost minus valuation allowance) shall be reclassified to proved properties; for properties amortized by providing a valuation allowance on a group basis, the gross acquisition cost shall be reclassified.

Amortization (Depletion) of Acquisition Costs of Proved Properties

30. Capitalized acquisition costs of proved properties shall be amortized (depleted) by the unit-of-production method so that each unit produced is assigned a pro rata portion of the unamortized acquisition costs. Under the unit-of-production method, amortization (depletion) may be computed either on a property-by-property basis or on the basis of some reasonable aggregation of properties with a common geological structural feature or stratigraphic condition, such as a reservoir or field. When an enterprise has a relatively large number of royalty interests whose acquisition costs are not individually significant, they may be aggregated, for the purpose of computing amortization, without regard to commonality of geological structural features or stratigraphic conditions; if information is not available to estimate reserve quantities applicable to royalty interests owned (paragraph 50), a method other than the unit-of-production method may be used to amortize their acquisition costs. The unit cost shall be computed on the basis of the total estimated units of proved oil and gas reserves. (Joint production of both oil and gas is discussed in paragraph 38.) Unit-of-production amortization rates shall be revised whenever there is an indication of the need for revision but at least once a year; those revisions shall be accounted for prospectively as changes in accounting estimates—see paragraphs 31-33 of *APB Opinion No. 20,* "Accounting Changes."

Accounting When Drilling of an Exploratory Well Is Completed

31. As specified in paragraph 19, the costs of drilling an exploratory well are capitalized as part of the

enterprise's uncompleted wells, equipment, and facilities pending determination of whether the well has found proved reserves. That determination is usually made on or shortly after completion of drilling the well, and the capitalized costs shall either be charged to expense or be reclassified as part of the costs of the enterprise's wells and related equipment and facilities at that time. Occasionally, however, an exploratory well may be determined to have found oil and gas reserves, but classification of those reserves as proved cannot be made when drilling is completed. In those cases, one or the other of the following subparagraphs shall apply depending on whether the well is drilled in an area requiring a major capital expenditure, such as a trunk pipeline, before production from that well could begin:

a. *Exploratory wells that find oil and gas reserves in an area requiring a major capital expenditure, such as a trunk pipeline, before production could begin.* On completion of drilling, an exploratory well may be determined to have found oil and gas reserves, but classification of those reserves as proved depends on whether a major capital expenditure can be justified which, in turn, depends on whether additional exploratory wells find a sufficient quantity of additional reserves. That situation arises principally with exploratory wells drilled in a remote area for which production would require constructing a trunk pipeline. In that case, the cost of drilling the exploratory well shall continue to be carried as an asset pending determination of whether proved reserves have been found only as long as both of the following conditions are met:
   i. The well has found a sufficient quantity of reserves to justify its completion as a producing well if the required capital expenditure is made.
   ii. Drilling of the additional exploratory wells is under way or firmly planned for the near future.

   Thus if drilling in the area is not under way or firmly planned, or if the well has not found a commercially producible quantity of reserves, the exploratory well shall be assumed to be impaired, and its costs shall be charged to expense.
b. *All other exploratory wells that find oil and gas reserves.* In the absence of a determination as to whether the reserves that have been found can be classified as proved, the costs of drilling such an exploratory well shall not be carried as an asset for more than one year following completion of drilling. If, after that year has passed, a determination that proved reserves have been found cannot be made, the well shall be assumed to be impaired, and its costs shall be charged to expense.

32. Paragraph 31 is intended to prohibit, in all cases, the deferral of the costs of exploratory wells that find some oil and gas reserves merely on the chance that some event totally beyond the control of the enterprise will occur, for example, on the chance that the selling prices of oil and gas will increase sufficiently to result in classification of reserves as proved that are not commercially recoverable at current prices.

Accounting When Drilling of an Exploratory-Type Stratigraphic Test Well Is Completed

33. As specified in paragraph 19, the costs of drilling an exploratory-type stratigraphic test well are capitalized as part of the enterprise's uncompleted wells, equipment, and facilities pending determination of whether the well has found proved reserves. When that determination is made, the capitalized costs shall be charged to expense if proved reserves are not found or shall be reclassified as part of the costs of the enterprise's wells and related equipment and facilities if proved reserves are found.

34. Exploratory-type stratigraphic test wells are normally drilled on unproved offshore properties. Frequently, on completion of drilling, such a well may be determined to have found oil and gas reserves, but classification of those reserves as proved depends on whether a major capital expenditure—usually a production platform—can be justified which, in turn, depends on whether additional exploratory-type stratigraphic test wells find a sufficient quantity of additional reserves. In that case, the cost of drilling the exploratory-type stratigraphic test well shall continue to be carried as an asset pending determination of whether proved reserves have been found only as long as both of the following conditions are met:

a. The well has found a quantity of reserves that would justify its completion for production had it not been simply a stratigraphic test well.
b. Drilling of the additional exploratory-type stratigraphic test wells is under way or firmly planned for the near future.

Thus if associated stratigraphic test drilling is not under way or firmly planned, or if the well has not found a commercially producible quantity of reserves, the exploratory-type stratigraphic test well shall be assumed to be impaired, and its costs shall be charged to expense.

Amortization and Depreciation of Capitalized Exploratory Drilling and Development Costs

35. Capitalized costs of exploratory wells and exploratory-type stratigraphic test wells that have

found proved reserves and capitalized development costs shall be amortized (depreciated) by the unit-of-production method so that each unit produced is assigned a pro rata portion of the unamortized costs. It may be more appropriate, in some cases, to depreciate natural gas cycling and processing plants by a method other than the unit-of-production method. Under the unit-of-production method, amortization (depreciation) may be computed either on a property-by-property basis or on the basis of some reasonable aggregation of properties with a common geological structural feature or stratigraphic condition, such as a reservoir or field. The unit cost shall be computed on the basis of the total estimated units of proved *developed* reserves, rather than on the basis of all proved reserves, which is the basis for amortizing acquisition costs of proved properties. If significant development costs (such as the cost of an off-shore production platform) are incurred in connection with a planned group of development wells before all of the planned wells have been drilled, it will be necessary to exclude a portion of those development costs in determining the unit-of-production amortization rate until the additional development wells are drilled. Similarly it will be necessary to exclude, in computing the amortization rate, those proved developed reserves that will be produced only after significant additional development costs are incurred, such as for improved recovery systems. However, in no case should future development costs be anticipated in computing the amortization rate. (Joint production of both oil and gas is discussed in paragraph 38.) Unit-of-production amortization rates shall be revised whenever there is an indication of the need for revision but at least once a year; those revisions shall be accounted for prospectively as changes in accounting estimates—see paragraphs 31-33 of *APB Opinion No. 20.*

Depreciation of Support Equipment and Facilities

36. Depreciation of support equipment and facilities used in oil and gas producing activities shall be accounted for as exploration cost, development cost, or production cost, as appropriate (paragraph 26).

Dismantlement Costs and Salvage Values

37. Estimated dismantlement, restoration, and abandonment costs and estimated residual salvage values shall be taken into account in determining amortization and depreciation rates.

Amortization of Costs Relating to Oil and Gas Reserves Produced Jointly

38. The unit-of-production method of amortization requires that the total number of units of oil or gas reserves in a property or group of properties be estimated and that the number of units produced in the current period be determined. Many properties contain both oil and gas reserves. In those cases, the oil and gas reserves and the oil and gas produced shall be converted to a common unit of measure on the basis of their approximate relative energy content (without considering their relative sales values). However, if the relative proportion of gas and oil extracted in the current period is expected to continue throughout the remaining productive life of the property, unit-of-production amortization may be computed on the basis of one of the two minerals only; similarly, if either oil or gas clearly dominates both the reserves and the current production (with dominance determined on the basis of relative energy content), unit-of-production amortization may be computed on the basis of the dominant mineral only.

Information Available after the Balance Sheet Date

39. Information that becomes available after the end of the period covered by the financial statements but before those financial statements are issued shall be taken into account in evaluating conditions that existed at the balance sheet date, for example, in assessing unproved properties (paragraph 28) and in determining whether an exploratory well or exploratory-type stratigraphic test well had found proved reserves (paragraphs 31-34).

Surrender or Abandonment of Properties

40. When an unproved property is surrendered, abandoned, or otherwise deemed worthless, capitalized acquisition costs relating thereto shall be charged against the related allowance for impairment to the extent an allowance has been provided; if the allowance previously provided is inadequate, a loss shall be recognized.

41. Normally, no gain or loss shall be recognized if only an individual well or individual item of equipment is abandoned or retired or if only a single lease or other part of a group of proved properties constituting the amortization base is abandoned or retired as long as the remainder of the property or group of properties continues to produce oil or gas. Instead, the asset being abandoned or retired shall be deemed to be fully amortized, and its cost shall be charged to accumulated depreciation, depletion, or amortization. When the *last* well on an individual property (if that is the amortization base) or group of properties (if amortization is determined on the basis of an aggregation of properties with a common geological structure) ceases to produce and the entire property or property group is abandoned, gain or loss shall be recognized. Occasionally, the partial abandonment or retirement of a proved property or group of

proved properties or the abandonment or retirement of wells or related equipment or facilities may result from a catastrophic event or other major abnormality. In those cases, a loss shall be recognized at the time of abandonment or retirement.

Mineral Property Conveyances and Related Transactions

42. Mineral interests in properties are frequently conveyed to others for a variety of reasons, including the desire to spread risks, to obtain financing, to improve operating efficiency, and to achieve tax benefits. Conveyances of those interests may involve the transfer of all or a part of the rights and responsibilities of operating a property (operating interest). The transferor may or may not retain an interest in the oil and gas produced that is free of the responsibilities and costs of operating the property (a non-operating interest). A transaction may, on the other hand, involve the transfer of a nonoperating interest to another party and retention of the operating interest.

43. Certain transactions, sometimes referred to as conveyances, are in substance borrowings repayable in cash or its equivalent and shall be accounted for as borrowings. The following are examples of such transactions:

a. Enterprises seeking supplies of oil or gas sometimes make cash advances to operators to finance exploration in return for the right to purchase oil or gas discovered. Funds advanced for exploration that are repayable by offset against purchases of oil or gas discovered, or in cash if insufficient oil or gas is produced by a specified date, shall be accounted for as a receivable by the lender and as a payable by the operator.
b. Funds advanced to an operator that are repayable in cash out of the proceeds from a specified share of future production of a producing property, until the amount advanced plus interest at a specified or determinable rate is paid in full, shall be accounted for as a borrowing. The advance is a payable for the recipient of the cash and a receivable for the party making the advance. Such transactions, as well as those described in paragraph 47(a) below, are commonly referred to as production payments. The two types differ in substance, however, as explained in paragraph 47(a).

44. In the following types of conveyances, gain or loss shall not be recognized at the time of the conveyance:

a. A transfer of assets used in oil and gas producing activities (including both proved and unproved properties) in exchange for other assets also used in oil and gas producing activities.
b. A pooling of assets in a joint undertaking intended to find, develop, or produce oil or gas from a particular property or group of properties.

45. In the following types of conveyances, gain shall not be recognized at the time of the conveyance:

a. A part of an interest owned is sold and substantial uncertainty exists about recovery of the costs applicable to the retained interest.
b. A part of an interest owned is sold and the seller has a substantial obligation for future performance, such as an obligation to drill a well or to operate the property without proportional reimbursement for that portion of the drilling or operating costs applicable to the interest sold.

46. If a conveyance is not one of the types described in paragraphs 44 and 45, gain or loss shall be recognized unless there are other aspects of the transaction that would prohibit such recognition under accounting principles applicable to enterprises in general.

47. In accordance with paragraphs 44-46, the following types of transactions shall be accounted for as indicated in each example.[3] No attempt has been made to include the many variations of those arrangements that occur, but paragraphs 44-46 shall, where applicable, determine the accounting for those other arrangements as well.

a. Some production payments differ from those described in paragraph 43(b) in that the seller's obligation is not expressed in monetary terms but as an obligation to deliver, free and clear of all expenses associated with operation of the property, a specified quantity of oil or gas to the purchaser out of a specified share of future production. Such a transaction is a sale of a mineral interest for which gain shall not be recognized because the seller has a substantial obligation for future performance. The seller shall account for the funds received as unearned revenue to be recognized as the oil or gas is delivered. The purchaser of such a production payment has acquired an interest in a mineral property that shall be recorded at cost and amortized by the unit-of-production method as delivery takes place. The related reserve estimates and production data shall be reported as those of the purchaser of the production payment and not of the seller (paragraphs 50-56).

[3] Costs of unproved properties are always subject to an assessment for impairment as required by paragraph 28.

b. An assignment of the operating interest in an unproved property with retention of a nonoperating interest in return for drilling, development, and operation by the assignee is a pooling of assets in a joint undertaking for which the assignor shall not recognize gain or loss. The assignor's cost of the original interest shall become the cost of the interest retained. The assignee shall account for all costs incurred as specified by paragraphs 15-41 and shall allocate none of those costs to the mineral interest acquired. If oil or gas is discovered, each party shall report its share of reserves and production (paragraphs 50-56).
c. An assignment of a part of an operating interest in an unproved property in exchange for a "free well" with provision for joint ownership and operation is a pooling of assets in a joint undertaking by the parties. The assignor shall record no cost for the obligatory well; the assignee shall record no cost for the mineral interest acquired. All drilling, development, and operating costs incurred by either party shall be accounted for as provided in paragraphs 15-41 of this Statement. If the conveyance agreement requires the assignee to incur geological or geophysical expenditures instead of, or in addition to, a drilling obligation, those costs shall likewise be accounted for by the assignee as provided in paragraphs 15-41 of this Statement. If reserves are discovered, each party shall report its share of reserves and production (paragraphs 50-56).
d. A part of an operating interest in an unproved property may be assigned to effect an arrangement called a "carried interest" whereby the assignee (the carrying party) agrees to defray all costs of drilling, developing, and operating the property and is entitled to all of the revenue from production from the property, excluding any third party interest, until all of the assignee's costs have been recovered, after which the assignor will share in both costs and production. Such an arrangement represents a pooling of assets in a joint undertaking by the assignor and assignee. The carried party shall make no accounting for any costs and revenue until after recoupment (payout) of the carried costs by the carrying party. Subsequent to payout the carried party shall account for its share of revenue, operating expenses, and (if the agreement provides for subsequent sharing of costs rather than a carried interest) subsequent development costs. During the payout period the carrying party shall record all costs, including those carried, as provided in paragraphs 15-41 and shall record all revenue from the property including that applicable to the recovery of costs carried. The carried party shall report as oil or gas reserves only its share of proved reserves estimated to remain after payout, and unit-of-production amortization of the carried party's property cost shall not commence prior to payout. Prior to payout the carrying party's reserve estimates and production data shall include the quantities applicable to recoupment of the carried costs (paragraphs 50-56).
e. A part of an operating interest owned may be exchanged for a part of an operating interest owned by another party. The purpose of such an arrangement, commonly called a joint venture in the oil and gas industry, often is to avoid duplication of facilities, diversify risks, and achieve operating efficiencies. Such reciprocal conveyances represent exchanges of similar productive assets, and no gain or loss shall be recognized by either party at the time of the transaction. In some joint ventures which may or may not involve an exchange of interests, the parties may share different elements of costs in different proportions. In such an arrangement a party may acquire an interest in a property or in wells and related equipment that is disproportionate to the share of costs borne by it. As in the case of a carried interest or a free well, each party shall account for its own cost under the provisions of this Statement. No gain shall be recognized for the acquisition of an interest in joint assets, the cost of which may have been paid in whole or in part by another party.
f. In a unitization all the operating and nonoperating participants pool their assets in a producing area (normally a field) to form a single unit and in return receive an undivided interest (of the same type as previously held) in that unit. Unitizations generally are undertaken to obtain operating efficiencies and to enhance recovery of reserves, often through improved recovery operations. Participation in the unit is generally proportionate to the oil and gas reserves contributed by each. Because the properties may be in different stages of development at the time of unitization, some participants may pay cash and others may receive cash to equalize contributions of wells and related equipment and facilities with the ownership interests in reserves. In those circumstances, cash paid by a participant shall be recorded as an additional investment in wells and related equipment and facilities, and cash received by a participant shall be recorded as a recovery of cost. The cost of the assets contributed plus or minus cash paid or received is the cost of the participant's undivided interest in the assets of the unit. Each participant shall include its interest in reporting reserve estimates and production data (paragraphs 50-56).
g. If the entire interest in an unproved property is sold for cash or cash equivalent, recognition of gain or loss depends on whether, in applying paragraph 28 of this Statement, impairment had been assessed for that property individually or

by amortizing that property as part of a group. If impairment was assessed individually, gain or loss shall be recognized. For a property amortized by providing a valuation allowance on a group basis, neither gain nor loss shall be recognized when an unproved property is sold unless the sales price exceeds the original cost of the property, in which case gain shall be recognized in the amount of such excess.

h. If a part of the interest in an unproved property is sold, even though for cash or cash equivalent, substantial uncertainty usually exists as to recovery of the cost applicable to the interest retained. Consequently, the amount received shall be treated as a recovery of cost.[4] However, if the sales price exceeds the carrying amount of a property whose impairment has been assessed individually in accordance with paragraph 28 of this Statement, or exceeds the original cost of a property amortized by providing a valuation allowance on a group basis, gain shall be recognized in the amount of such excess.

i. The sale of an entire interest in a proved property that constitutes a separate amortization base is not one of the types of conveyances described in paragraph 44 or 45. The difference between the amount of sales proceeds and the unamortized cost shall be recognized as a gain or loss.

j. The sale of a part of a proved property, or of an entire proved property constituting a part of an amortization base, shall be accounted for as the sale of an asset, and a gain or loss shall be recognized, since it is not one of the conveyances described in paragraph 44 or 45. The unamortized cost of the property or group of properties a part of which was sold shall be apportioned to the interest sold and the interest retained on the basis of the fair values of those interests. However, the sale may be accounted for as a normal retirement under the provisions of paragraph 41 with no gain or loss recognized if doing so does not significantly affect the unit-of-production amortization rate.

k. The sale of the operating interest in a proved property for cash with retention of a nonoperating interest is not one of the types of conveyances described in paragraph 44 or 45. Accordingly, it shall be accounted for as the sale of an asset, and any gain or loss shall be recognized. The seller shall allocate the cost of the proved property to the operating interest sold and the nonoperating interest retained on the basis of the fair values of those interests.[5]

l. The sale of a proved property subject to a retained production payment that is expressed as a fixed sum of money payable only from a specified share of production from that property, with the purchaser of the property obligated to incur the future costs of operating the property, shall be accounted for as follows:

   i. *If satisfaction of the retained production payment is reasonably assured.* The seller of the property, who retained the production payment, shall record the transaction as a sale, with recognition of any resulting gain or loss. The retained production payment shall be recorded as a receivable, with interest accounted for in accordance with the provisions of *APB Opinion No. 21,* "Interest on Receivables and Payables." The purchaser shall record as the cost of the assets acquired the cash consideration paid plus the present value (determined in accordance with *APB Opinion No. 21*) of the retained production payment, which shall be recorded as a payable. The oil and gas reserve estimates and production data, including those applicable to liquidation of the retained production payment, shall be reported by the purchaser of the property (paragraphs 50-56).

   ii. *If satisfaction of the retained production payment is not reasonably assured.* The transaction is in substance a sale with retention of an overriding royalty that shall be accounted for in accordance with paragraph 47(k).

m. The sale of a proved property subject to a retained production payment that is expressed as a right to a specified quantity of oil or gas out of a specified share of future production shall be accounted for in accordance with paragraph 47(k).

Disclosure

48. An enterprise engaged in oil and gas producing activities shall include in a complete set of annual financial statements the disclosures specified in paragraphs 50-59. Those disclosures may be made within the body of the financial statements, in the notes thereto, or in a separate schedule that is an integral part of the financial statements.

49. Disclosure of capitalized costs (paragraph 57) shall also be included in a complete set of interim financial statements that present financial position, results of operations, and changes in financial position in conformity with generally accepted accounting principles. Disclosures of reserve quantities and of costs incurred as set forth in paragraphs 50-56 and 58 and 59 are not required in such interim financial statements, though the Board encourages disclosure in those financial statements of information

[4]The carrying amount of the interest retained shall continue to be subject to the assessment for impairment as required by paragraph 28.

[5]A retained production payment denominated in money is not a mineral interest (see paragraphs 11(a) and 43).

about a major discovery or other favorable or adverse event that causes a significant change from the reserve data reported in the most recent annual financial statements.

Disclosure of Reserve Quantities

50. Net quantities of an enterprise's interests in proved reserves and proved developed reserves of (a) crude oil (including condensate and natural gas liquids) and (b) natural gas shall be reported as of the beginning and the end of each year for which a complete set of financial statements is presented. "Net" quantities of reserves include those relating to the enterprise's operating and nonoperating interests in properties as defined in paragraph 11(a). Quantities of reserves relating to royalty interests owned shall be included in "net" quantities if the necessary information is available to the enterprise; if reserves relating to royalty interests owned are not included because the information is unavailable, that fact and the enterprise's share of oil and gas produced for those royalty interests shall be reported for each year for which a complete set of financial statements is presented. "Net" quantities shall not include reserves relating to interests of others in properties owned by the enterprise.

51. Changes in the net quantities of an enterprise's proved reserves of oil and of gas during each year for which a complete set of financial statements is presented shall be reported. Changes resulting from each of the following shall be separately shown with appropriate explanation of significant changes:

a. *Revisions of previous estimates.* Revisions represent changes in previous estimates of proved reserves, either upward or downward, resulting from new information (except for an increase in proved acreage) normally obtained from development drilling and production history or resulting from a change in economic factors.
b. *Improved recovery.* Changes in reserve estimates resulting from application of improved recovery techniques shall be separately shown if significant. If not significant, such changes shall be included in revisions of previous estimates.
c. *Purchases of minerals-in-place.*
d. *Extensions, discoveries, and other additions.* Additions to an enterprise's proved reserves that result from (i) extension of the proved acreage of previously discovered (old) reservoirs through additional drilling in periods subsequent to discovery and (ii) discovery of new fields with proved reserves or of new reservoirs of proved reserves in old fields.
e. *Production.*
f. *Sales of minerals-in-place.*

52. If an enterprise's proved reserves of oil and gas are located entirely within its home country, that fact shall be disclosed. If some or all of its reserves are located in foreign countries, the disclosures of net quantities of reserves of oil and of gas and changes in them required by paragraphs 50 and 51 shall be separately reported for (a) the enterprise's home country (if significant reserves are located there) and (b) each foreign geographic area in which significant reserves are located. Foreign geographic areas are individual countries or groups of countries as appropriate for meaningful disclosure in the circumstances.

53. Net quantities disclosed in conformity with paragraphs 50-52 shall not include oil or gas subject to purchase under long-term supply, purchase, or similar agreements and contracts, including such agreements with foreign governments or authorities. However, quantities of oil or gas subject to such agreements with foreign governments or authorities as of the end of each year for which a complete set of financial statements is presented, and the net quantity of oil or gas received under the agreements during each such year, shall be separately disclosed if the enterprise participates in the operation of the properties in which the oil or gas is located or otherwise serves as the "producer" of those reserves, as opposed, for example, to being an independent purchaser, broker, dealer, or importer.

54. In determining the reserve quantities to be reported in conformity with paragraphs 50-53:

a. If the enterprise issues consolidated financial statements, 100 percent of the *net* reserve quantities attributable to the parent company and 100 percent of the *net* reserve quantities attributable to its consolidated subsidiaries (whether or not wholly owned) shall be included.
b. If the enterprise's financial statements include investments that are proportionately consolidated, the enterprise's reserve quantities shall include its proportionate share of the investee's net oil and gas reserves.
c. If the enterprise's financial statements include investments that are accounted for by the equity method, the investee's net oil and gas reserves shall *not* be included in the disclosures of the enterprise's reserves. However, the enterprise's (investor's) share of the investee's net oil and gas reserves shall be separately reported as of the end of each year for which a complete set of financial statements is presented.

55. In reporting reserve quantities and changes in them, oil reserves (which include condensate and natural gas liquids) shall be stated in barrels, and gas reserves in cubic feet. Disclosures of the type called for by paragraphs 50-54 are diagrammed on page 1288.

	Total Worldwide		*United States*		*Foreign Geographic Area A*		*Foreign Geographic Area B*		*Other Foreign Geographic Areas*	
	Oil	*Gas*	*Oil*	*Gas*	*Oil*	*Gas*	*Oil*	*Gas*	*Oil*	*Gas*
Proved developed and undeveloped reserves:										
Beginning of year	X	X	X	X	X	X	X	X	X	X
Revisions of previous estimates	X	X	X	X	X	X	X	X	X	X
Improved recovery	X	X	X	X	X	X	X	X	X	X
Purchases of minerals-in-place	X	X	X	X	X	X	X	X	X	X
Extensions, discoveries, and other additions	X	X	X	X	X	X	X	X	X	X
Production	(X)	(X)	(X)	(X)	(X)	(X)	(X)	(X)	(X)	(X)
Sales of minerals-in-place	(X)	(X)	(X)	(X)	(X)	(X)	(X)	(X)	(X)	(X)
End of year	X	X	X	X	X	X	X	X	X	X
Proved developed reserves:										
Beginning of year	X	X	X	X	X	X	X	X	X	X
End of year	X	X	X	X	X	X	X	X	X	X
Oil and gas applicable to long-term supply agreements with foreign governments or authorities in which the company acts as producer:										
Proved reserves at end of year	X	X			X	X	X	X	X	X
Received during the year	X	X			X	X	X	X	X	X
Company's proportional interest in reserves of investees accounted for by the equity method, end of year	X	X	X	X	X	X	X	X	X	X

56. If important economic factors or significant uncertainties affect particular components of an enterprise's proved reserves, explanation shall be provided. Examples include unusually high expected development or lifting costs; the necessity to build a major pipeline or other major facilities before production of the reserves can begin; or contractual obligations to produce and sell a significant portion of reserves at prices that are substantially below those at which the oil or gas could otherwise be sold in the absence of the contractual obligation.

Disclosure of Capitalized Costs

57. The aggregate amount of capitalized costs relating to an enterprise's oil and gas producing activities (paragraph 11) and the aggregate amount of the related accumulated depreciation, depletion, amortization, and valuation allowances shall be reported as of the end of each period for which financial statements are presented. Paragraph 5 of *APB Opinion No. 12,* "Omnibus Opinion—1967," requires disclosure of "balances of major classes of depreciable assets, by nature or function." Thus, separate disclosure of the amount of capitalized costs for one or more of asset categories (a) to (d) in paragraph 11 or for a combination of two or more of those categories often may be appropriate.

Disclosure of Costs Incurred in Oil and Gas Producing Activities

58. The financial statements of an oil and gas producing company shall disclose the amounts of each of the following types of costs for each year for which a complete set of financial statements is presented (whether those costs are capitalized or charged to expense at the time they are incurred under the provisions of paragraphs 15-26). As defined in the paragraphs cited, exploration, development, and production costs *include* depreciation of support equipment and facilities used in those activities and *do not include* the expenditures to acquire support equipment and facilities. Also, as stated in paragraph 25, production (lifting) costs do not include depreciation, depletion, and amortization of capitalized acquisition, exploration, and development costs.

a. Property acquisition costs (paragraph 15).
b. Exploration costs (paragraph 17).
c. Development costs (paragraph 21).
d. Production (lifting) costs (paragraph 24).

59. If some or all of those costs are incurred in foreign countries, the amounts shall be disclosed separately for each of the geographic areas for which reserve quantities are disclosed (paragraph 52).

Accounting for Income Taxes

60. Some costs incurred in an enterprise's oil and gas producing activities enter into the determination of taxable income and pretax accounting income in different periods. A principal example is intangible drilling and development costs, which are deductible in determining taxable income when incurred but which, for successful exploratory wells and for all development wells, are capitalized and amortized for financial accounting purposes under the provisions of this Statement. As another example, some geological and geophysical costs, which are charged to expense when incurred under the provisions of this Statement, are deferred and deducted in subsequent periods for income tax purposes.

61. Comprehensive interperiod income tax allocation by the deferred method, as described in *APB Opinion No. 11,* "Accounting for Income Taxes," shall be followed by oil and gas producing companies for intangible drilling and development costs and other costs incurred that enter into the determination of taxable income and pretax accounting income in different periods.

62. In applying the comprehensive interperiod income tax allocation provision of the preceding paragraph, the possibility that statutory depletion in future periods will reduce or eliminate the amount of income taxes otherwise payable shall not be taken into account. That is, the so-called *interaction* of book/tax timing differences with any anticipated future excess of statutory depletion allowed as a tax deduction over the amount of cost depletion otherwise allowable as a tax deduction shall not be recognized in determining the appropriate periodic provision for income taxes. Accordingly, the excess of statutory depletion over cost depletion for tax purposes shall be accounted for as a permanent difference in the period in which the excess is deducted for income tax purposes; it shall not be anticipated by recognizing interaction.

Effective Date and Transition

63. This Statement shall be effective for financial statements for fiscal years beginning after December 15, 1978 and for interim periods within those fiscal years. Accounting changes adopted to conform to the provisions of this Statement, including changes to apply comprehensive interperiod income tax allocation (paragraph 61) and to eliminate the recognition of the interaction of book/tax timing differences with the excess of statutory depletion over cost depletion for tax purposes (paragraph 62), shall be made retroactively by restating the financial statements of prior periods. Financial statements for

the fiscal year in which this Statement is first applied, and for interim periods of that year, shall disclose the nature of those accounting changes and their effect on income before extraordinary items, net income, and related per share amounts for each period restated. The disclosures specified by paragraphs 50-59 shall be included in complete sets of financial statements that have been restated pursuant to the provisions of this paragraph.

64. Retroactive application of the provisions of this Statement requires the use of estimates and approximations; a provision that would not have a significant effect on prior years' financial statements need not be retroactively applied. Further, retroactive application of some provisions of this Statement may require the use of estimates of a type that the enterprise had not previously made; information that may have become available some time after the year being restated may be taken into account in making those estimates, except that estimates of quantities of oil and gas reserves that had been made in prior years shall not currently be revised in retrospect.

The provisions of this Statement need not be applied to immaterial items.

This Statement was adopted by the affirmative votes of four members of the Financial Accounting Standards Board. Messrs. Litke, Mays, and Walters dissented.

Messrs. Litke and Walters dissent because this Statement endorses accounting measurements that in their opinion do not portray the unique economic characteristics of oil and gas exploration and discovery. As a result, it does not measure up to the fundamental objective of financial statements, as enunciated by the Trueblood Committee, that they be "useful for making economic decisions."

Conceptually, they believe it is necessary to account for mineral reserves at fair value for the financial statements to appropriately emphasize certain economic characteristics of the industry, which include:

1. The principal assets are the mineral reserves.
2. The most significant economic event is discovery of reserves.
3. There is no necessary correlation between finding costs and values of reserves found.

No historical cost method adequately emphasizes these facts; both full cost and successful efforts accounting in their traditional forms have significant defects.

In their view, the conceptual case for accounting for mineral reserves at fair value is so strong that it should be rejected only if it is infeasible to derive amounts meeting an acceptable standard of reliability. They are not satisfied that it is infeasible. The public record on this project indicates that many creditors and investors find value information relevant and useful and either obtain it from the enterprise or approximate it themselves. Nonetheless, the record further indicates most respondents may not be ready to accept the perceived sacrifice in reliability necessary to achieve relevance.

Under any approach that is not based on fair value accounting, Messrs. Litke and Walters believe that the estimated quantities and values of the mineral reserves should be disclosed as supplemental information. While recognizing that the Board has taken a positive step in requiring disclosure of the quantities of, and changes in, mineral reserves, they believe the Board failed to go far enough. Research included in the public record indicates that investment and lending decisions in the oil and gas industry are heavily dependent on information about the quantity and value of mineral reserves, as well as about expected cash flows. For reserve information to be useful to investors and creditors, they must assign values to the quantities of estimated reserves. The values of reserves can vary greatly, even within the same overall market price structure, because of differences in quality and in costs of developing, lifting, and transporting to market.

Messrs. Litke and Walters believe that the enterprise is in a better position to evaluate its own reserves than the users of its financial statements. Accordingly, they believe the company should disclose a measure of fair value attributable to its proven mineral reserves, together with the methods and principal assumptions used to develop that information. They believe that discounted cash flow procedures can be developed based on methodologies that are already widely used and understood. Though this information may not be perceived by some as reliable enough to be used as the basis for accounting for mineral reserves in the balance sheet or for recognizing income, they believe a lesser degree of reliability can be accepted for informative supplemental disclosures which have such a high degree of relevance.

If the Board will not adopt the conceptually superior value approach at this time, whether because that approach may be impracticable or ahead of its time, Messrs. Litke and Walters would have accepted an area-of-interest approach, supplemented by disclosure of mineral reserve values. The approach acceptable to them would be a modified full cost approach in which costs of prospecting, acquisition, exploration, and development in an area-of-interest where proven reserves are discovered would be capitalized as the cost of discovering and developing the reserves found in that area-of-interest, subject to a discounted cash flow ceiling. Similar costs in an area-of-interest where no reserves were found would be written off. This method:

1. Measures the costs incurred in each area-of-interest, and reflects "success or failure" with a decision model that would most commonly be used by management.
2. Avoids the worst fault of "pure" full costing—that of charging reserves with costs which are unrelated either temporally or geographically.
3. Avoids the worst faults of "pure" successful efforts accounting—the failures to recognize the principal asset and to capitalize costs that are logically and integrally related to the discovery and development of that asset.

Some say that it is not possible to define an area-of-interest with enough precision that it would be interpreted the same in each case by every company. While Messrs. Litke and Walters believe this concern is overstated, it has some validity if uniformity is the primary objective. While they agree that uniformity is an appropriate consideration and that "free choice" accounting alternatives should be narrowed or eliminated, Messrs. Litke and Walters believe some room for judgment, guided by relevant criteria, is both appropriate and necessary. They do not believe that uniformity for its own sake can be used to justify accounting standards. They observe that unless the uniform accounting and reporting provides *more meaningful economic* information to users of financial statements, the fact that the financial accounting and reporting is on a uniform basis is largely irrelevant.

Mr. Litke further dissents because he believes the Board should not impose successful efforts accounting upon the industry without having provided conceptual support for the superiority of that method in the Basis for Conclusions. Based on the public record (including FASB research) which strongly indicates that *neither* successful efforts *nor* full costing is sufficient to portray the economic substance of an enterprise's financial position or results of operations, he believes merely summarizing the faults of *either* method is not a sufficient basis for imposing the other method. He observes that because neither traditional method of accounting communicates the necessary and relevant investment and return-on-investment information to investors, creditors, regulators or other users of financial statements, an accounting method that adopts the strengths and minimizes the weaknesses of each method must be considered. He believes an area-of-interest method, with certain supplemental disclosures, would satisfy these criteria.

In addition to being unconvincing, Mr. Litke believes the arguments that are presented in the Basis for Conclusions are internally inconsistent. They represent, in his view, a series of inconsistent and unsupported assertions. Mr. Litke believes the need for such inconsistencies has not been supported. Some of those inconsistencies are discussed in the following paragraphs.

- The Statement emphasizes that full cost accounting obscures failures and risks in the search for oil and gas reserves and that successful efforts accounting highlights such failures and risks. This assertion evades the real issues. Mr. Litke observes that neither success nor failure, however defined, is satisfactorily measured based solely on the costs incurred. Success is most appropriately measured by the discovery and development of mineral reserves in sufficient quantity and of sufficient value to result in a return of the amounts invested, as well as a return on the amounts invested. Failure is a result of not discovering and developing sufficient reserves. Further, in Mr. Litke's view the purpose of accounting is neither to obscure nor to highlight "risks" or "failures" or "success." The purpose is to reflect the facts in the most meaningful and useful manner. Under the historical cost basis of accounting, the most meaningful and useful manner would be based on an area-of-interest approach, with certain supplemental disclosures.
- Mr. Litke finds substantial evidence in the accounting literature that an enterprise's assets include its natural resource deposits, including oil and gas reserves. The Statement does not define "assets" in a manner fully consistent with the accounting literature. Nor does the Statement choose to account for or determine the cost of all the enterprise's assets. By identifying only the individual properties, wells, equipment, and facilities as assets to be accounted for, it excludes oil and gas reserves-in-place from the assets to be accounted for and for which costs must be determined. Mr. Litke believes such an exclusion results in an inappropriate and unnecessary distinction between the economic substance of the enterprise's oil and gas operations and the method of accounting for them. Furthermore, some costs that meet the Statement's capitalization criteria are expensed because the criteria are not uniformly applied to all exploration and development costs, including G&G costs. Because of this inconsistent application of criteria, the Statement fails to recognize the benefits derived from the costs of geological and geophysical testing performed on the enterprise's own properties but requires capitalization of such costs, when contractually reimbursable, on G&G testing performed on property owned by another party. G&G costs are often a meaningful element of cost

in the acquisition and development of productive properties. They are an integral part of the costs of acquiring and developing an oil and gas property. It is therefore theoretically correct and both practicable and appropriate to capitalize G&G costs applicable to oil and gas properties, especially to the extent that expenditures are specifically identifiable with retained acreage in specific areas-of-interest. Such costs should be capitalized and amortized in the same manner as other acquisition, drilling, and development costs.

- The Statement requires that the costs of exploratory dry holes be expensed as incurred while the costs of development dry holes be capitalized and amortized. In other words, the accounting for these exploratory and development costs in an area may be different even though the costs of drilling the exploratory dry holes in the area are just as much a part of the costs invested as are the costs of drilling the development dry holes in that area. Further, the fact that a well may be classified as a development well, based on the definitions provided in this Statement, may depend on whether it is the first well drilled or whether it is drilled after a successful well. Mr. Litke observes that the cost of drilling both exploratory and development wells is an integral part of the cost of exploring and developing oil and gas properties. Mr. Litke believes such conflicting accounting requirements are not conceptually sound and will not necessarily result in uniform accounting and reporting. Such requirements will, however, result in such illogical results as having the amounts capitalized depend on the sequence in which the wells were drilled.
- Mr. Litke believes the costs of drilling exploration and development dry holes are integrally related to the other reasonable and necessary costs that are incurred in discovering and developing mineral reserves. He believes therefore that all such reasonable and necessary costs incurred in or related to the acquisition or enhancement of an asset in an area-of-interest in which commercially recoverable reserves are discovered and developed, or that result in increased discernible future benefits, should be deferred (temporarily capitalized) pending evaluation of the results of the exploration and development activities in that area-of-interest.

This Statement, however, prescribes that the costs of exploratory dry holes and certain stratigraphic wells be expensed as incurred. It also requires that the costs of development dry holes and certain other stratigraphic wells be capitalized. Mr. Litke observes that each of those types of wells has the same expected future benefits, but they are accounted for differently. The Statement also permits deferral of the costs of drilling in progress even though those wells on which those costs were incurred may prove to provide no discernible future benefits either. While Mr. Litke agrees that those costs should be capitalized, he believes the logical conceptual basis under which such costs should be capitalized also results in the capitalization of other costs under an area-of-interest approach—an approach which he believes is appropriate but which the Statement specifically rejects. He further observes that the reasons supporting these capitalization policies are inconsistent with the reasoning behind *FASB Statement No. 2,* "Accounting for Research and Development Costs."

Mr. Mays dissents because he considers some of the conclusions reached conceptually inconsistent with others. Mr. Mays believes that in adopting successful efforts accounting a choice must be made between two basic and distinct concepts. In the first concept, each well drilled is an individual "effort," the success or failure of which determines the capital/expense treatment. Thus, a well that is not capable of commercial production, whether it be exploratory, development, or stratigraphic, is expensed. In the second concept, a group of wells with a common geological objective is a collective "effort," and the capital/expense decision is based on the success or failure of the group as a whole. Although he prefers the first, Mr. Mays would accept either of these concepts but not a mixing of the two. In his view, the Statement contains elements of both concepts resulting in inconsistencies such as the following:

While affirming that the nature of a cost rather than a cost center should govern the capital/expense decision, the Statement uses the producing system as a collective asset, in effect a cost center, to justify the capitalization of development dry holes and certain nonproducible stratigraphic test wells. At the same time, the Statement excludes an exploratory dry hole having the same geological objective from capitalization even though that well also was intended to form part of the producing system and represents just as much a part of its cost as the development dry hole. The fact that the development location was not drilled first in the drilling program, and would thus have been an exploratory dry hole, may well be pure chance; in Mr. Mays's view, capital/expense decisions should not depend on sequential happenstance. Similar inconsistencies result from the distinction for capital/expense purposes that the Statement draws with respect to "successful" and "unsuccessful" stratigraphic wells, and the further distinction drawn between "unsuccessful development type" and "unsuccessful exploratory type" stratigraphic wells. Mr. Mays believes that, since none of such wells are to be produced, they should either all be expensed under the first concept or all be capitalized, assuming collective success, under the second concept.

Mr. Mays also dissents with respect to the changes

in accounting for income taxes promulgated by this Statement. The changes, which he views as major, represent a reversal of the Board's position taken only two years ago with the issuance of *FASB Statement No. 9,* and he points to the fact that nothing has happened in the interim to justify such a reversal. Mr. Mays considers these changes especially untimely in view of the Board's current consideration of the definition of the elements of financial statements, including the definition of a liability, in the conceptual framework project.

Members of the Financial Accounting Standards Board:

Marshall S. Armstrong, *Chairman*
Oscar S. Gellein
Donald J. Kirk
Arthur L. Litke
Robert E. Mays
Robert T. Sprouse
Ralph E. Walters

Appendix A

BACKGROUND INFORMATION

65. Financial accounting and reporting for oil and gas producing companies has been debated for many years in the United States by the accounting profession, regulatory agencies, industry groups, and the companies themselves. The principal focus in recent years has been on the two widely different methods of accounting followed by those companies—the full cost method and the successful efforts method.

66. In 1964, the American Institute of Certified Public Accountants commissioned Robert E. Field, a partner of Price Waterhouse & Co., to study the various accounting methods used by companies in the extractive industries and to make recommendations for consideration by the AICPA Accounting Principles Board in formulating a pronouncement. The study was published by the AICPA in 1969 as *Accounting Research Study No. 11,* "Financial Reporting in the Extractive Industries." The recommendations in *ARS No. 11* essentially supported the successful efforts method of accounting.

67. In 1970, the APB asked its Committee on Extractive Industries to (a) study the recommendations in *ARS No. 11* and (b) "determine the appropriate accounting practices with the intent of narrowing the different accounting practices in the extractive industries." In mid-1971, the Committee drafted a proposed APB Opinion dealing only with determination of the appropriate *cost center,* on the belief that issues associated with the cost center question were at the heart of the full cost/successful efforts controversy. The full APB decided, however, that limiting an Opinion to the cost center question was inappropriate. The APB directed its Committee to prepare a paper containing recommendations on (a) determination of the cost center, (b) accounting for prediscovery and postdiscovery costs, (c) disposition of capitalized costs, and (d) disclosure of supplementary information in financial reports.

68. The APB Committee paper was published in the fall of 1971 under the title "Accounting and Reporting Practices in the Petroleum Industry." The paper recommended using the *field* as the cost center and capitalizing all prediscovery and postdiscovery costs that could be directly associated with oil and gas reserves, including reinstatement of the costs of exploratory dry holes initially written off but later determined to be in a field. The APB scheduled a public hearing for November 1971, with the Committee paper to serve as the basis for the hearing.

69. While the APB Committee was deliberating and preparing its paper, the Federal Power Commission was studying the accounting practices of natural gas producing companies subject to its jurisdiction. In October 1970, the FPC issued a proposal to require application of the full cost concept in FPC filings by natural gas companies. During the following thirteen months, the FPC weighed arguments for and against its proposal, including a request from the APB that the FPC delay final action until an APB Opinion could be issued. On November 5, 1971, the FPC issued Order No. 440 adopting the full cost method for mineral leases acquired after October 6, 1969 with each country as a cost center. Petitions for rehearing, which were filed on December 5, 1971, were denied by the FPC in Order No. 440-A issued January 5, 1972.

70. The APB's public hearing was held on November 22 and 23, 1971. At the hearing, the recommendations in the APB Committee paper were opposed not only by advocates of the full cost method, who viewed the proposal to use the field as the cost center as effectively banning the full cost concept, but also by many advocates of successful efforts accounting, who disagreed with various aspects of the recommendations including, among other things, the capitalization of the costs of development dry holes and those exploratory dry holes determined to be in a field. After the hearing, the APB Committee on Extractive Industries continued to work on a proposed Opinion. The testimony given at that public hearing and the written submissions to the APB have been studied by the FASB.

71. On July 1, 1973, the FASB succeeded the APB as the private sector accounting standards-setting body. The APB Committee prepared for the FASB a detailed report on its activities entitled "Accounting and Reporting Practices in the Oil and Gas Industry." That report is reprinted as an appendix to the FASB Discussion Memorandum on the project.

72. In January 1973, a group of oil and gas producing companies that use the full cost method formed the Ad Hoc Committee (Petroleum Companies) on Full Cost Accounting. That Committee commissioned a research study by John H. Myers, Professor of Accounting at Indiana University. The study, entitled *Full Cost vs. Successful Efforts in Petroleum Accounting: An Empirical Approach,* was published in 1974. Dr. Myers simulated the results of accounting for various types of transactions under each of the two methods and concluded that full cost accounting together with disclosure of data on oil and gas reserves better serves the needs of users of financial statements.

73. In 1975, Congress substantially reduced or eliminated the percentage depletion deduction for many oil and gas producing companies, which led to the issuance in October 1975 of *FASB Statement No. 9.*

74. The FASB did not place accounting and reporting in the extractive industries on its initial technical agenda in 1973, but the foreign oil embargo of that year and the resulting substantial increases in world oil prices aroused great interest in the oil and gas industry on the part of both the American public and the federal government. With other energy legislation enacted or under active consideration by Congress, the FASB decided that accounting by oil and gas producing companies should receive high priority. In October 1975, it added to its technical agenda a project entitled "Financial Accounting and Reporting in the Extractive Industries."

75. In December 1975, President Gerald R. Ford signed Public Law 94-163, the *Energy Policy and Conservation Act* [42 U.S. Code, Sec. 6383]. Title V, Section 503 of the Act empowers the Securities and Exchange Commission either:

> to prescribe rules applicable to persons engaged in the production of crude oil or natural gas, or make effective by recognition, or by other appropriate means indicating a determination to rely on, accounting practices developed by the Financial Accounting Standards Board, if the Securities and Exchange Commission is assured that such practice will be observed by persons engaged in the production of crude oil or natural gas to the same extent as would result if the Securities and Exchange Commission had prescribed such practices by rule.

76. The effect of Section 503 is to require that the contemplated accounting practices be developed by December 22, 1977 (24 months after the Act was signed into law) for all persons engaged either exclusively or partially in the production of crude oil or natural gas in the United States. The Act requires the SEC to provide an opportunity for interested persons to submit written comments on whether the Commission should recognize or otherwise rely on the standards developed by the FASB. That comment period can be after December 22, 1977.

77. The Act further provides that the SEC shall assure that the accounting practices developed pursuant to Section 503 will, to the greatest extent practicable, permit the compilation of a national energy data base consisting of the following data with domestic and foreign operations treated separately:

> (1) The separate calculation of capital, revenue, and operating cost information pertaining to—
> (A) prospecting,
> (B) acquisition,
> (C) exploration,
> (D) development, and
> (E) production,
> including geological and geophysical costs, carrying costs, unsuccessful exploratory drilling costs, intangible drilling and development costs on productive wells, the cost of unsuccessful development wells, and the cost of acquiring oil and gas reserves by means other than development. Any such calculation shall take into account disposition of capitalized costs, contractual arrangements involving special conveyance of rights and joint operations, differences between book and tax income, and prices used in the transfer of products or other assets from one person to any other person, including a person controlled by, controlling, or under common control with such person.
> (2) The full presentation of the financial information of persons engaged in the production of crude oil or natural gas, including—
> (A) disclosure of reserves and operating activities, both domestic and foreign, to facilitate evaluation of financial effort and result; and
> (B) classification of financial information by function to facilitate correlation with reserve and operating statistics, both domestic and foreign.
> (3) Such other information, projections, and relationships of collected data as shall be necessary to facilitate the compilation of such data base.

78. The Board is issuing this Statement under its authority, which exists entirely apart from the Act, and also to assist the SEC in carrying out its obliga-

tions as contemplated by Congress under the Act as well as under the federal securities laws.

79. The FASB appointed a task force of 18 persons in December 1975 to counsel the Board in preparing a Discussion Memorandum analyzing issues related to the project. Members of the task force came from the oil and gas industry, petroleum geology and engineering, other extractive industries, public accounting, banking, securities underwriting, and academe. Professor Horace R. Brock of North Texas State University was engaged by the Board to serve as chairman of the task force and consultant to the Board during the preparation of the Discussion Memorandum. Meetings of the task force were attended by observers from the following federal agencies and Congressional committee:

a. Cost Accounting Standards Board.
b. Federal Energy Administration.
c. Federal Power Commission.
d. Securities and Exchange Commission.
e. Oversight and Investigations Subcommittee of the Committee on Interstate and Foreign Commerce, United States House of Representatives.
f. United States General Accounting Office.

80. The task force held its initial meeting in January 1976. Three additional meetings were held during that year. Much of the work of the task force was accomplished by correspondence, with task force members providing the Board with a significant amount of input concerning the accounting and reporting issues that they believed should be addressed in this project. Drafts of all sections of the Discussion Memorandum were sent to task force members and observers for written comment. Although the chairman of the task force and members of the staff of the FASB assumed primary responsibility for drafting the Discussion Memorandum, some sections were initially drafted by task force members expert on the particular matter being discussed.

81. In February 1976, the FASB concluded, on the basis of a task force recommendation, that the Discussion Memorandum should not be restricted to only the oil and gas industry, but should cover accounting and reporting issues relevant to companies engaged in the search for and production of all wasting (nonregenerative) natural resources. That recommendation was not unanimously supported by the task force. Some members believed that it would be preferable to focus initially on the oil and gas industry, as the APB Committee on Extractive Industries had done. Those members were also concerned that broadening the study could blur important distinctions between oil and gas companies and other extractive industries. The FASB, in accepting the recommendation of a majority of the task force members, concluded that apparent similarities of operations among extractive industries warranted the inclusion of all such industries in the scope of the Discussion Memorandum. The Board noted in the Discussion Memorandum, however, that inclusion of all extractive industries within the scope of the project at that stage did not mean that the Board intended to issue a single Statement covering all of those industries.

82. On March 23, 1976, the SEC issued *Accounting Series Release No. 190* amending Regulation S-X to require companies that meet specified size tests to disclose certain replacement cost data relating to "inventories" and "productive capacity" in financial statements filed with the Commission for fiscal years ending on or after December 25, 1976. In that Release, the SEC delayed for one year the effective date of the required replacement cost disclosures for "mineral resource assets." SEC *Staff Accounting Bulletin No. 10* defines mineral resource assets as "those costs shown on the balance sheet representing assets which are directly associated with and which derive value from mineral reserves." In June 1977, the American Petroleum Institute published and submitted to the SEC a study by Professors Glenn A. Welsch and Edward B. Deakin, of the University of Texas at Austin, entitled *Measuring and Reporting the "Replacement" Cost of Oil and Gas Reserves.* In transmitting the study to the SEC, the API stated its view that "the concept of replacement cost as envisioned in ASR 190 is not applicable to oil and gas reserves" and urged the SEC to "permanently exempt oil and gas reserves from replacement cost disclosure."

83. On May 12, 1976, the SEC issued *Securities Act Release No. 5706,* which requires that information relating to oil and gas properties, reserves, and production be disclosed in registration statements, proxy statements, and reports filed with the Commission.

84. In preparing the Discussion Memorandum, the task force and the Board considered many research studies and other publications in addition to *ARS No. 11* and the study by Dr. Myers, including the proceedings of the APB's public hearing and studies of accounting and reporting practices in the extractive industries by public accounting firms and industry associations. Approximately 100 recent (generally post-1968) publications on accounting and reporting in the extractive industries were reviewed by the FASB staff; a bibliography is included as an appendix to the Discussion Memorandum. Copies of those publications are in the FASB library.

85. The Board issued the Discussion Memorandum on December 23, 1976 with written comments due

by March 7, 1977. In response to the Discussion Memorandum, the Board received 140 position papers, letters of comment, and outlines (totalling approximately 2,600 pages), copies of which have been available for inspection at the Board's offices since March 14, 1977 and are available for purchase. Copies were made available to each of the observer groups identified in paragraph 79.

86. On January 31, 1977, in *Securities Act Release No. 5801,* the SEC called attention to publication of the FASB Discussion Memorandum and encouraged interested parties to obtain and comment on the Memorandum and to participate in the FASB public hearing. The Release states that "the Commission, consistent with its policy most recently expressed in Accounting Series Release No. 150, contemplates that the Financial Accounting Standards Board (FASB) will be providing the leadership in establishing financial accounting principles and standards for producers of oil and gas." A part of one of the chapters in the Discussion Memorandum was prepared by the staff of the SEC. It considers matters relating to the SEC's responsibilities regarding the national energy data base.

87. The Board held a public hearing on the subject on March 30 and 31 and April 1 and 4, 1977. Thirty-nine presentations were made at the hearing. A transcript of the hearing (nearly 1,000 pages in length) is available for inspection or purchase. Copies were made available to each of the observer groups identified in paragraph 79.

88. Seven days of concentrated preparatory sessions were held by the Board prior to deliberations on the issues. Those sessions were devoted to detailed examination of (a) the nature of acquisition, exploration, development, and production activities in the oil and gas industry; (b) the features and variations of the full cost method, the successful efforts method, discovery value accounting, and current value accounting; (c) reserve definitions and measurement; (d) reserve valuation; and (e) mineral property conveyances and contracts. Outside experts were invited to make presentations or otherwise assist the Board's staff in conducting the sessions. Those experts, eight of whom were task force members, included petroleum engineers and geologists, public accountants, corporate executives from the oil and gas industry, and academicians.

89. Subsequent to issuance of the Discussion Memorandum, the Board and its staff have maintained close contact with representatives of the SEC who, in turn, have been in contact with the other government agencies concerned with implementing the *Energy Policy and Conservation Act* and other federal energy legislation, with the mutual objective of keeping all parties informed of the others' activities regarding accounting and reporting by oil and gas producing companies. That close contact has continued after issuance of the FASB's Exposure Draft.

90. In addition to the Discussion Memorandum and the research studies and other publications mentioned earlier in paragraph 84, two other research efforts were undertaken at the Board's request during its deliberations on the Exposure Draft:

a. Academic consultants conducted interviews to ascertain how investment and credit decisions regarding oil and gas producing companies are reached. The 24 interviewees included loan officers of large and small banks that make loans to large and small oil and gas companies, bank trust department officers, institutional securities underwriters for both large and small companies, securities analysts, and an officer of a bond rating agency. The selection of interviewees from both the Northeast and the Southwest was designed to include organizations that invest or recommend investments in small as well as large companies. While the limited number of interviews did not provide conclusive evidence, the majority of interviewees indicated that the method of accounting would not affect their investment and credit decisions regarding oil and gas producing companies. The key factor in the decisions of a number of interviewees was their own valuations of oil and gas reserves and other assets; others relied heavily on cash flow data rather than earnings; still others took into consideration the method of accounting when evaluating earnings. Several interviewees believed that reduced earnings from accounting changes probably affected some investors and thus could adversely affect some stock prices.
b. A study was made of how *FASB Statement No. 9* was applied in practice. The study found no relationship between the way that Statement was applied and the method of accounting employed or company size.

91. On June 20, 1977, the SEC issued *Securities Act Release No. 5837* soliciting comments in connection with the Commission's responsibilities under the *Energy Policy and Conservation Act* to assure the development and observance of accounting practices to be followed by U.S. producers of crude oil and natural gas. That Release not only raised questions relating to the reporting of financial and operating data to the Federal Energy Administrator but also solicited comments about the extent to which that data should be "included in filings with the Commission in a manner which would require independent public accountants reporting on registrants' financial statements to be associated with the data." The Release indicated that "the Commission recognizes that the FASB is considering for inclusion

in its proposed standard the disclosure of functional financial data and information on oil and gas reserves. The Commission will be cognizant of the FASB's conclusions in this area and will attempt to coordinate the reporting requirements pursuant to the Act and any revisions proposed to the disclosure requirements under the Securities Acts with the disclosures required in financial statements by the FASB. Reporting pursuant to the Act and any changes to the Commission's disclosure rules may encompass matters . . . in addition to or in greater detail than those required by the FASB."

92. The Board issued an Exposure Draft of a proposed Statement on "Financial Accounting and Reporting by Oil and Gas Producing Companies" on July 15, 1977. It received letters of comment on the Exposure Draft from 195 respondents (totalling approximately 1,300 pages). Copies of the letters were made available to each of the observer groups identified in paragraph 79.

93. After the Exposure Draft was issued, two additional research studies were conducted at the Board's request:

a. A research consultant, with assistance from the FASB staff, studied the effect of the Exposure Draft on the market prices of common stock issued by both full cost and successful efforts oil and gas producing companies. The research was conducted by Professor Thomas R. Dyckman of Cornell University, using data part of which was supplied by the FASB staff. Two research methodologies were employed. The first required two samples of equal size and was applied to companies that derive more than 50 percent of their revenue from exploration and production activities. The market prices of common shares issued by 22 full cost companies and 22 successful efforts companies were studied for the 11 weeks before and the 11 weeks after the Exposure Draft was issued. The study did not find statistically significant evidence that issuance of the Exposure Draft affected the market prices of securities issued by the full cost companies as compared to those of the successful efforts companies—except for some possible effect on the full cost companies during the week preceding and the week of issuance of the Exposure Draft, but the market soon adjusted, and evidence of a permanent or lingering effect was not found. The second methodology employed different underlying statistical procedures and was applied to broader samples. Those samples were not limited to companies engaged primarily in exploration and production but were limited to oil and gas companies with annual revenues less than $1 billion each. The samples included 65 full cost companies and 40 successful efforts companies. Again, the evidence did not support the hypothesis that the prices of shares issued by full cost companies were adversely affected, other than for a very brief period, by issuance of the Exposure Draft. Both Professor Dyckman and the Board recognize that statistical testing may not necessarily be conclusive. Following issuance of this Statement, the Board will undertake a similar study with respect to whether this Statement adversely affects the market prices of securities of oil and gas producing companies that heretofore had been using the full cost method as compared to those that had been using the successful efforts method.
b. The Board commissioned a telephone interview survey of senior executive officers of 27 relatively small and medium sized, publicly traded, successful efforts oil and gas producing companies (with annual revenues ranging from $1 million to $441 million, average $68 million). No large integrated oil and gas companies were included. The study was conducted under the direction of Professor Horace R. Brock of North Texas State University. The purpose of the survey was to ascertain whether, in the judgment of those corporate officers, the use of the successful efforts method of accounting has had any negative effect on the ability of their companies to raise the capital necessary to finance their exploration and production activities. Most of the surveyed companies have raised capital externally during the past 10 years from one or more of the following sources: public issue of debt securities, public issue of equity securities, private placement of securities, special conveyances, borrowing from a local bank, international bank, or insurance company, and sale of participations in individual projects. None of the executive officers surveyed indicated that the company's use of successful efforts accounting had hindered its ability to raise capital. Four of the officers did indicate an uncertainty as to whether their continued use of the successful efforts method would affect their ability to raise capital in the future.

94. On August 31, 1977, the SEC issued *Securities Act Release No. 5861* proposing to amend the Commission's regulations to incorporate therein the accounting standards set forth in the FASB Exposure Draft. The Commission stated that the reason for the proposal is to place the Commission in a position to adopt by December 22, 1977 financial accounting and reporting standards for oil and gas producing activities in the unlikely event that the FASB has not adopted final standards by that date. The Release states that the proposed standards would be applicable to both (1) persons filing reports with the Department of Energy and (2) filings with the Commission under federal securities

laws. The Commission stated that it proposed the rules pursuant to its authority under the *Energy Policy and Conservation Act* and the federal securities laws. The Release deals only with accounting standards and does not address disclosure matters.

95. On October 26, 1977, the SEC issued two Releases dealing with disclosures by oil and gas producing companies. The first Release, *Securities Act Release No. 5877,* proposes to amend the Commission's regulations to provide for disclosure in financial statements of certain operating and financial data relating to oil and gas producing activities. Like the proposal mentioned in the preceding paragraph, the disclosure standards proposed in this Release would apply both to (1) filings with the Commission pursuant to federal securities laws and (2) reports filed with the Department of Energy pursuant to the *Energy Policy and Conservation Act.* The SEC's proposed disclosures are generally the same as those proposed in the FASB Exposure Draft.

96. The second SEC Release of October 26, 1977, *Securities Act Release No. 5878,* deals with replacement cost disclosures for mineral resource assets. The Release proposes (1) to rescind the requirement adopted in *ASR No. 190* for certain registrants to disclose replacement cost information about their mineral resource assets employed in oil and gas producing activities (see paragraph 82 of this Statement) and (2) to require, instead, that registrants with mineral resource assets employed in oil and gas producing activities disclose information based on the present value of future net revenues from estimated production of proved oil and gas reserves. The Release points out that "the proposed disclosures cannot be described as replacement cost information; however, they would provide information on the differences between the historical costs associated with proved oil and gas reserves shown in the financial statements and the future net revenues to be derived from these reserves." That proposal would be effective in filings covering fiscal years ending on or after December 25, 1978. Comments on the proposal are to be submitted to the Commission by March 31, 1978.

Appendix B

BASIS FOR CONCLUSIONS

CONTENTS

Appendix B

BASIS FOR CONCLUSIONS

97. This Appendix discusses factors deemed significant by members of the Board in reaching the conclusions in this Statement, including alternatives considered and reasons for accepting some and rejecting others.

Scope

98. Although the Discussion Memorandum for this project analyzed issues and solicited comments on accounting and reporting by companies in all extractive industries, this Statement applies only to the oil and gas producing industry as had been proposed in the Exposure Draft. Some respondents to the Discussion Memorandum and the Exposure Draft said that the mining industries are sufficiently different from the oil and gas industry to warrant separate pronouncements. For instance, some said that in the mining industries the principal emphasis is on the development and operation of existing mines and known deposits whereas in the oil and gas industry the principal emphasis is on the search for new mineral deposits. Also, some respondents said that mining operations involve substantially lower exploration and acquisition costs and substantially higher development and production costs relative to the oil and gas industry, which, they claimed, is characterized by high finding costs and a high proportion of unsuccessful search activities. In the view of those respondents, *discovery* is the critical event leading to the production of oil and gas whereas *development* and *extraction* are the critical events for most other minerals. Many who favored separating the oil and gas industry from other extractive industries pointed out also that the full cost versus successful efforts controversy has little significance in the mining industry while it is the primary issue for the oil and gas industry. Still others noted that there is greater uniformity in current accounting practices within the mining industries than within the oil and gas industry. Thus, they took the position that current generally accepted accounting principles are adequate for the mining industries and do not require the attention of the FASB at this time. The Board has not yet examined in depth those and other claimed dissimilarities between the oil and gas industry and other extractive industries; nor has it decided whether there is a need to address the other extractive industries in a separate pronouncement.

99. In response to questions raised in letters of comment on the Exposure Draft, paragraph 7 indicates that this Statement does not deal with accounting for interest costs because that matter is being addressed in another Board agenda project.

The Four Basic Accounting Alternatives

100. Four basic methods of accounting for a company's oil and gas producing activities were considered by the Board:

a. Full costing.
b. Successful efforts costing.
c. Discovery value accounting.
d. Current value accounting.

The principal features of each of those four methods, and variations within each method, are described in paragraphs 104-127.

101. Both full costing and successful efforts costing have been considered as conforming to generally accepted accounting principles, and both, in various forms, are widely used today. Discovery value accounting and current value accounting are both proposals that are not presently followed by oil and gas producing companies or by other companies (except in a few specialized industries and then only for certain assets with readily determinable market prices) in preparing their financial statements. The full costing method came into use around 1960 and only since the late 1960s has become widely used. A 1973 survey of nearly 300 oil and gas companies found that roughly half used full cost accounting and half used successful efforts costing.[6] A 1972 survey showed that companies employing the successful efforts method account for approximately 87 percent of U.S. oil and gas production, indicating that full costing has been adopted by relatively more small and medium sized companies than large companies.[7] Testimony given at the Board's public hearing by a spokesperson for an association of independent petroleum producers indicated that many independent oil and gas companies follow federal income tax accounting practices in preparing their financial statements; income tax accounting is a variation of successful efforts accounting.

Basic Differences between Full Costing and Successful Efforts Costing

102. The principal difference between full costing and successful efforts costing concerns costs that cannot be directly related to the discovery of specific oil and gas reserves. Under full costing those costs are carried forward to future periods as costs of oil and gas reserves generally; under successful efforts costing those costs are charged to expense. Full costing regards the costs of unsuccessful acquisition and exploration activities as necessary for the discovery of reserves. All of those costs are incurred with the knowledge that many of a company's prospects will not result directly in the discovery of reserves. However, the company expects that the benefits obtained from those prospects that do prove successful together with the benefits from past discoveries will be adequate to recover the costs of all activities, both successful and unsuccessful, and will result in an ultimate profit. Thus, all costs incurred in oil and gas producing activities are regarded as integral to the acquisition, discovery, and development of whatever reserves ultimately result from the efforts as a whole, and are thus associated with the company's reserves. Establishing a direct cause-and-effect relationship between costs incurred and specific reserves discovered is not relevant to full costing. Under successful efforts costing, however, except for acquisition costs of properties, a direct relationship between costs incurred and specific reserves discovered is required before costs are identified with assets; costs of acquisition and exploration activities that are known not to have resulted in the discovery of reserves are charged to expense.

103. Although many variations exist within the successful efforts method, two principal approaches can be identified. One approach relies on an "area-of-interest" (or "project" or "prospect") as a cost center because the oil and gas reserves in that area-of-interest are deemed to represent the asset for which cost is determined. Under that approach, all costs incurred within that cost center are capitalized; if the area-of-interest is abandoned, the costs are charged to expense; if the area-of-interest proves successful, the capitalized costs are amortized as the reserves are produced. The second approach does not rely on a cost center for capitalization purposes; the accounting treatment is determined by the nature of the costs at the time they are incurred. This approach does not assign costs to oil and gas reserves until they are extracted; prior to then, this approach regards properties, wells, equipment, and facilities as the assets to which costs relate. Under one variation of this approach, all exploratory costs are charged to expense when incurred, but the cost of an exploratory well is later capitalized by reinstatement if the well is successful. Under the other variation, all exploration costs except the costs of exploratory wells are charged to expense when incurred; the costs of exploratory wells are capitalized as "construction-in-progress" when incurred, to be expensed later if the well is determined to be unsuccessful.

Principal Features of Full Costing

104. Under the full cost concept, all costs incurred in acquiring, exploring, and developing properties within a relatively large geopolitical (as opposed to geological) cost center (such as a country) are capitalized when incurred and are amortized as mineral reserves in the cost center are produced, subject to a limitation that the capitalized costs not exceed the value of those reserves.

105. Many variations of the full cost method exist,

[6] Ginsburg, Feldman and Bress, Attorneys for Ad Hoc Committee (Petroleum Companies), *Comments of the Ad Hoc Committee (Petroleum Companies) on Full Cost Accounting,* File No. S7-464, presented to the Securities and Exchange Commission, 14 March 1973, p. 31.

[7] Porter, Stanley P., *"Full Cost" Accounting: The Problem It Poses for the Extractive Industries* (New York: Arthur Young & Company, 1972), p. 6.

one of which is in the selection of the cost center. Under the broadest concept of full costing, all acquisition, exploration, and development costs wherever and whenever incurred are capitalized and amortized on a pro rata basis over the production of all of the company's oil and gas reserves wherever and whenever discovered, subject to the aforementioned limitation. This approach is referred to as using a company-wide cost center. Most companies that use full costing, however, adopt a country or a continent as the cost center.

106. If full costing is applied on a less-than-company-wide basis, the limitation (sometimes called a ceiling) on capitalized costs generally is applied separately to each cost center, though sometimes the comparison of unamortized capitalized costs and reserve values is made on the basis of groups of cost centers or on a company-wide basis. Variations also exist in the categories of reserves used in computing the limitation and in the methods of valuing those reserves.

107. Under the full cost concept, acquisition, exploration, and development costs are sometimes included in the pool of capitalized costs associated with a cost center when incurred, so that if the cost center is producing, those costs are subject to amortization at once. In some cases, however, certain significant costs, such as those associated with offshore U.S. operations, are deferred separately without amortization until the specific property to which they relate is found to be either productive or nonproductive, at which time those deferred costs and any reserves attributable to the property are included in the computation of amortization in the cost center.

108. Although most proponents of full costing indicate that the reserve value limitation is an essential condition for use of that method, preproduction costs incurred in a nonproducing cost center (for example, a country or continent in which the company has only recently begun its first exploration activity) are sometimes capitalized without regard to a limitation or ceiling test, based on the expectation that reserves will be discovered in the future sufficient to assure recovery of the capitalized costs.

109. Under full costing and in many cases under successful efforts costing (if the amortization base comprises a number of properties), the unamortized costs relating to a property that is surrendered, abandoned, or otherwise disposed of are accounted for as an adjustment of accumulated amortization, rather than as a gain or loss that enters into the determination of net income, until *all* of the properties constituting the amortization base are disposed of, at which point gain or loss is recognized. Under full costing, the amortization base is normally a very large cost center—country or continent—whereas under successful efforts costing it is usually either individual properties or groups of properties with a common geological structural feature or stratigraphic condition. Therefore, recognition of gain or loss on abandonment of properties is more likely to be delayed under full costing than under successful efforts costing, although some proponents of full costing would recognize certain unusual or significant losses even before activities in an entire country or continent are discontinued.

110. Variations within both the full cost method and the successful efforts method exist in (a) the categories of reserves used in computing amortization, (b) whether future development costs are anticipated if capitalized acquisition, exploration, or development costs are amortized on the basis of all proved reserves, (c) the extent to which properties are aggregated for amortization purposes, (d) the bases for determining amortization rates if oil and gas are jointly produced, (e) the categories of reserves and methods of valuation used in computing a limitation on capitalized costs, and (f) allocation of overhead.

Principal Features of Successful Efforts Costing

111. Under successful efforts costing, except for acquisition costs of properties, a direct relationship between costs incurred and specific reserves discovered is required before costs are identified with assets. An acquired property is regarded as an asset until either a determination is made that it does not contain oil and gas reserves or the property is surrendered. Capitalized costs relating to producing properties are amortized as the reserves underlying those properties are produced.

112. Many variations of successful efforts accounting exist. As noted in paragraph 103, a conceptual difference centers around the role of the cost center—whether a cost center is needed for cost capitalization purposes or only to compute amortization. For example, some proponents of successful efforts accounting would capitalize all geological and geophysical costs and, possibly, all carrying costs relating to a cost center, such as an area-of-interest, on grounds that any mineral reserves in the cost center represent the asset with which the costs are associated. If mineral reserves are found in that area-of-interest, those capitalized costs are carried forward as the costs of those reserves; otherwise, they are charged to expense. Those proponents of successful efforts thus rely in part on the concept of a cost center for the capitalize/expense decision. Others who favor successful efforts accounting would use a cost center, such as a field or a lease, only for purposes of amortizing costs. They would let the nature of the cost govern the capitalize/

expense decision. For example, they might charge all G&G costs and all carrying costs to expense, based on the belief that such costs result in no identifiable future benefits, but they would capitalize all lease bonus expenditures on the basis that an asset (the right to explore for and extract oil and gas) has been acquired.

113. With respect to property acquisition costs, relatively minor variations exist within the successful efforts method concerning the extent to which such items as brokers' fees, recording fees, legal costs, other direct costs, and allocations of indirect costs are considered acquisition costs. Those minor variations aside, virtually all advocates of successful efforts accounting capitalize all property acquisition costs when incurred, though different accounting methods are used to dispose of those costs subsequent to capitalization.

114. Under successful efforts accounting, different methods are sometimes used to account for *pre*acquisition and *post*acquisition geological and geophysical costs. With respect to preacquisition G&G, some expense all such costs when incurred; others capitalize preacquisition G&G to the extent that those costs can be related to acquired properties and expense all other such costs. Some follow a practice of reinstating costs charged to expense in a prior period based on events and experience in subsequent periods. Others do not. With respect to postacquisition G&G, alternatives include (a) capitalize all postacquisition G&G as part of the cost of the acquired properties to which the G&G costs relate; (b) charge it all to expense when incurred; and (c) charge it all to expense when incurred but reinstate those costs that relate to reserves that are found. Some persons would capitalize only post*discovery* G&G while expensing when incurred all other postacquisition G&G as well as the preacquisition G&G.

115. At least two variations can be identified in accounting for the costs of carrying undeveloped properties (delay rentals, *ad valorem* taxes, etc.) under successful efforts accounting: (a) charge all to expense as incurred and (b) charge to expense as incurred but reinstate if subsequently associable with an area-of-interest in which reserves are found.

116. Some proponents of the successful efforts method defer all exploratory drilling costs as "construction-in-progress" for a period of time until a determination has been made whether reserves have been found, at which time the costs of dry holes are charged to expense. Others expense all exploratory drilling costs as incurred but reinstate costs relating to any reserves that are discovered. The costs of drilling a stratigraphic test well, which is drilled solely to obtain geological information and is not customarily intended to be completed as a producing well, are sometimes charged to expense when incurred; alternatively, those costs are sometimes capitalized to the extent that reserves are found (even though the well is not intended to be used to produce those reserves), with the costs of such wells that did not find reserves charged to expense when that determination is made.

117. The principal alternative with respect to accounting for development costs within a successful efforts framework concerns the treatment of development dry holes. Some proponents of successful efforts accounting capitalize the costs of drilling unsuccessful development wells on grounds that those costs were incurred as part of the capital investment required to extract reserves that were previously discovered. On the other hand, many successful efforts proponents take the position that those costs should be charged to expense on the basis that any dry hole, whether exploratory or development, has no future benefit. With respect to other development costs, some companies capitalize all while other companies—principally the smaller and closely held companies—follow the income tax accounting treatment under which intangible development costs are charged to expense as incurred.

118. Whether capitalized preproduction costs are amortized or otherwise written off before production begins is another area of difference within the successful efforts method. Some companies do not amortize any capitalized costs until production of the related reserves begins. If reserves are not found, the entire cost is written off when the property is surrendered. A variety of methods is used by those companies that do amortize costs before production begins. A distinction normally is made between (a) acquisition costs of unproved properties and (b) preproduction costs relating to properties that become proved. Some companies amortize the acquisition costs of unproved properties or provide an allowance for impairment; other companies carry unproved properties at their cost without regard to diminution of value until either reserves are found or the property is surrendered. With respect to the capitalized preproduction costs relating to proved properties, amortization generally does not begin until production commences. Reinstatement of costs is another accounting alternative, and whether to establish a limitation on capitalized costs of proved properties is yet another area of difference.

119. A number of other variations within the successful efforts method (which are also variations within full costing) were noted in paragraph 110.

Principal Features of Discovery Value Accounting

120. Under discovery value accounting as it has

generally been proposed, mineral reserves would be recorded at their estimated *value* when the reserves are discovered or, alternatively, when the reserves are developed. Property acquisition costs and other prediscovery costs generally would be deferred and written off when the areas to which the costs apply have been explored and the underlying reserves, if any, evaluated. Subsequent to discovery, the carrying amount of the reserves would not be adjusted for changes in prices; however, the carrying amount would be adjusted for revisions of estimated reserve quantities. The discovery value would be treated as revenue from the oil and gas exploration activities of the enterprise and would become the recorded value ("cost") of reserves for future accounting purposes. Those discovery value amounts would then be amortized against the revenues resulting from the production and sale of the minerals.

121. Several variations of discovery value accounting have been proposed. If only proved developed reserves are included in the value computation, generally all development costs associated with the reserves will have been incurred; if additional development costs are incurred, the value of any incremental quantity of reserves discovered is recorded and, simultaneously, the related costs are written off. If undeveloped reserves are included in the value computation, an adjustment must be made for the expected future development costs (generally by reducing the value otherwise attributable to the reserves in the ground). When the development costs are eventually incurred, it is generally proposed that they be added to the carrying value of the reserves.

122. Determination of the value of oil and gas reserves is critical to both discovery value accounting and current value accounting. Four principal valuation methods that might be used to measure the value of reserves (and other assets) were discussed at length in paragraphs 436-466 of the Discussion Memorandum. Briefly summarized, they are:

a. *Current cost.* Current cost is the amount of cash or its equivalent that would have to be paid if the same asset were acquired currently. The "same asset" may be an identical asset (current reproduction cost or current cost of replacement in kind) or an asset with equivalent productive capacity (current replacement cost).
b. *Current exit value in orderly liquidation.* Current exit value in orderly liquidation is the net amount of cash that could be obtained currently by selling the asset in orderly liquidation (current market value, if a market exists). The value of mineral reserves on a current exit value basis would equal the price at which the reserves could be sold in place by a willing seller to a willing buyer, neither being under any compulsion to sell or buy, both being competent and having reasonable knowledge of the facts.
c. *Expected exit value in due course of business.* Expected exit value in due course of business is the nondiscounted amount of cash or its equivalent into which an asset is expected to be converted in the due course of business less the direct costs necessary to make that conversion (sometimes referred to as net realizable value). The value of mineral reserves on this basis would be an amount equal to the estimated net cash flows attributable to the reserves.
d. *Present value of expected cash flows.* The present value of expected cash flows is the present value of future cash inflows into which an asset is expected to be converted in the due course of business, less the present value of cash outflows necessary to obtain those inflows. Present value measurements require information about estimated amounts of future cash inflows and outflows, the timing of those expected cash flows, and the appropriate discount rate. Various discount rates that have been proposed include the (i) rate applicable to long-term government bonds issued by the government of the country in which the reserves are located, (ii) prime rate, (iii) company's weighted average or incremental long-term borrowing rate, (iv) company's weighted average cost of capital, and (v) discount rate used by company management internally to make individual investment decisions.

123. Considerable disagreement exists as to which of those methods, if any, are suitable for valuation of oil and gas reserves, either at the time of discovery or subsequently. Also, under discovery value accounting, a decision must be made as to which categories of reserves enter into the value computation.

124. Some discovery value accounting proponents would report the value of periodic discoveries of reserves as operating income. Others would segregate the discovery value from realized revenues and gains reported in the income statement. Still others would report the discovery values in a special unrealized income section of stockholders' equity in the balance sheet until realized through the actual production and sale of oil and gas.

Principal Features of Current Value Accounting

125. Current value accounting involves the continuous use in the financial statements of one of the four methods of valuation identified in paragraph 122, or some other method. (Current value accounting could, of course, be applied to all of an enterprise's assets and liabilities, not just oil and gas reserves, but applying current value accounting beyond oil

and gas reserves was not included in the scope of this project. Alternative methods of measurement are to be considered in the Board's project to develop a conceptual framework for financial accounting and reporting.)

126. Most proponents of current value accounting for oil and gas reserves believe that the reserves should be valued at each financial statement date using the most current information available. Some proponents suggest that periodic changes in reserve values should be reflected directly in the income statement; others would report value changes directly in the stockholders' equity section of the balance sheet, perhaps by segregating or otherwise separately identifying the realized and unrealized amounts. Under current value accounting, separate data might be presented for (a) value increases resulting from new discoveries, (b) value changes resulting from adjustment of reserve quantities, and (c) holding gains and losses resulting from revaluing end-of-period reserve quantities to reflect the change in unit value during the period.

127. As with discovery value accounting, decisions must be made as to which method of valuation should be used and which reserve categories should be included in the current value computations.

A Single Accounting Method

128. The proposal that the two presently accepted accounting methods, full costing and successful efforts costing, be allowed to continue as optional alternatives received little support in the letters of comment submitted to the Board in response to the Discussion Memorandum or in the oral presentations made at the public hearing conducted by the Board before the Exposure Draft was issued. It was principally after the Exposure Draft was issued proposing to proscribe the full costing method that support for retaining both methods was expressed to the Board.

129. The Board has considered the question of accounting alternatives at length, not only in connection with its oil and gas project but also for other projects on its agenda, and has concluded that differences in accounting may be appropriate when significant differences in facts and circumstances exist, but different accounting among companies for the same types of facts and circumstances impedes comparability of financial statements and significantly detracts from their usefulness to financial statement users.

130. In the Board's judgment, the facts and circumstances surrounding the search for and development and production of oil and gas do not differ because of the size of the company or whether its securities are publicly traded. Similar types of risks of failure and potential rewards of success prevail among all companies engaged in oil and gas producing activities; only the magnitude and number of projects vary. Although the scale or location of operations may differ among companies, that should not affect the principles underlying recognition of assets, measurement of the cost of those assets, and measurement of earnings. The costs of exploratory dry holes or abandonded properties, for example, should not be included in the costs of assets for some companies and reported as losses by other companies. Yet if full costing and successful efforts costing were both retained as optional accounting alternatives, different principles of asset recognition and measurement and earnings measurement would be regarded as appropriate for companies whose circumstances are substantially similar.

131. Some respondents to the Exposure Draft cited the existence of other accounting alternatives—for instance, the use of both the last-in, first-out and the first-in, first-out methods in accounting for inventories—as justification for retaining full costing and successful efforts costing as optional alternatives. The Board does not believe that the availability of alternatives in unrelated areas of accounting should bear on a decision that the Board must make for a project on its agenda. In the Board's judgment, accounting for similar circumstances similarly and for different circumstances differently is a desirable objective in establishing standards of financial accounting and reporting. For that reason, the Board rejected the proposal, made by some respondents to the Exposure Draft, that intercompany comparability be achieved by footnote disclosure with retention of both full costing and successful efforts costing. Also, for that reason, the Board rejected the proposal that it simply "clean up" the many variations in full costing and the many variations in successful efforts costing presently used in practice by mandating only one acceptable approach to full costing and one acceptable approach to successful efforts costing and allowing companies to choose one of those two approaches.

132. One of the principal criticisms of the work of the FASB's predecessors that led to creation of the FASB was that they did not sufficiently narrow or eliminate free choice accounting alternatives. A report entitled *Federal Regulation and Regulatory Reform* (the "Moss Report") issued in 1976 by the Subcommittee on Oversight and Investigations of the U.S. House of Representatives and a report entitled *The Accounting Establishment* (the "Metcalf Report") prepared in 1976 by the staff of the Subcommittee on Reports, Accounting and Management of the U.S. Senate were both strongly critical of the availability of alternative accounting

principles. In its November 1977 report, "Improving the Accountability of Publicly Owned Corporations and Their Auditors," Senator Metcalf's Subcommittee concluded that "uniformity in the development and application of accounting standards must be a major goal of the standard-setting system." Moreover, two major financial statement user groups—the Financial Accounting Policy Committee of the Financial Analysts Federation (the national professional association of security analysts) and the Robert Morris Associates (the national professional association of bank lending officers)—have endorsed elimination of optional accounting alternatives not only for oil and gas producing companies but for other industries as well. The Securities and Exchange Commission, in *Securities Act Release No. 5877* (October 26, 1977), took a similar position, stating that the Board's oil and gas project "is expected to result in significant improvement in financial reporting through the establishment of uniform accounting standards so that investors are provided with a valid basis for comparing the financial statements of different companies." In the Board's judgment, when the same or similar facts and circumstances exist, as they do in the search for and development of oil and gas reserves, intercompany comparability requires a single method of accounting. Comparable reporting by companies competing for capital is, in the Board's judgment, in the public interest (see paragraphs 157-174).

Reasons for Rejecting Discovery Value Accounting

133. The Board concluded that financial statements of an oil and gas producing company should not be prepared on a discovery value basis for a number of reasons. One group of reasons relates to problems in measuring the value of reserves with reasonable accuracy at the point of discovery. Measurements of discovery value require estimates of (a) the quantity of reserves, (b) the amount and timing of costs to develop the reserves, (c) the timing of production of the reserves, (d) the production costs and income taxes, (e) selling prices, and (f) (for some valuation methods) appropriate discount rates that reflect both an interest element and a risk factor. Those estimates, in turn, might be based on predictions of changes in government regulations and restrictions (both domestic and foreign), technological changes (including not only the technology involved in oil and gas producing activities but also the technology of transportation, refining, and marketing of oil and gas products), and domestic and international economic conditions; or current regulations, technology, and conditions might be assumed to continue indefinitely. The uncertainties inherent in those estimates and predictions tend to make estimates of reserve values highly subjective and relatively unreliable for the purpose of providing the basis on which to prepare financial statements of an oil and gas producing company.

134. Under generally accepted accounting principles followed by companies in nearly all industries, revenue is normally recognized only when the earning process is complete or virtually complete and, then, only after an exchange transaction has taken place. The earning process is the continuum of profit-directed activities by which revenue is earned—purchasing, manufacturing, selling a product or rendering a service, delivery, cash collection, etc. The exchange transaction is the specific point at which the earning process is normally regarded as sufficiently complete to justify accounting recognition of revenue.

135. Discovery value accounting recognizes revenue from exploration activities at the point of discovery even though it may be many years until the property is developed and the oil and gas are produced and sold. That is, the earning process is far from complete, at least as completion of that process is generally determined for other industries. Discovery is certainly a critical event in the search for and extraction of oil and gas, but there are many uncertainties standing between discovery of reserves and the ultimate realization of related revenues. Often many years pass, very substantial amounts of money are spent, and significant revisions are made to estimated quantities of reserves discovered.

136. Exceptions to the general rule for revenue recognition are found in practice today. *APB Statement No. 4,* "Basic Concepts and Accounting Principles Underlying Financial Statements of Business Enterprises," paragraph 152, states:

> Sometimes revenue is recognized at the completion of production and before a sale is made. Examples include certain precious metals and farm products with assured sales prices. The assured price, the difficulty in some situations of determining costs of products on hand, and the characteristic of unit interchangeability are reasons given to support this exception.

137. As noted earlier, reserves often are discovered many years before they are produced, and many dollars often are spent for development and production costs before the oil and gas reserves are extracted. Moreover, while oil and gas may to some extent be regarded as fungible, sales prices, particularly in the present domestic and international economic and regulatory environments, are anything but assured. Thus, the reasons given in support of the special revenue recognition principles for precious metals and farm products that have been produced and have assured sales prices do not apply to oil and gas producing activities.

138. Proponents of discovery value accounting argue that it provides better information about the success or failure of exploration activities, which activities are the most important ones in oil and gas production. However, discovery value accounting represents a fundamental change from the traditional, historical cost basis of preparing financial statements. Various alternatives to the historical cost measurement basis are under examination as part of the Board's conceptual framework project. Although covered in the Discussion Memorandum for the extractive industries project, valuation methods were addressed by relatively few respondents, and discovery value accounting received only very limited support among respondents. On balance, the Board concluded that estimated discovery values do not provide a satisfactory basis of accounting for oil and gas producing activities for the reasons that (a) values that were current when initially recorded quickly become out-of-date and (b) the mixture of values of minerals measured at different dates of discovery lacks both the verifiability of historical costs and the relevance of current values. The Board believes that issues relating to the accounting measurement basis should await resolution in the conceptual framework project.

Reasons for Rejecting Current Value Accounting

139. Like discovery value accounting, current value accounting for oil and gas reserves requires estimation of reserve values.The uncertainties inherent in those estimates (discussed in paragraph 133) tend to make them subjective and relatively unreliable for the purpose of providing the underlying basis on which the financial statements of an oil and gas producing company are prepared.

140. As noted in paragraph 138, the historical cost basis of accounting and certain alternative measurement bases are currently under examination as part of the Board's project on a conceptual framework for financial accounting and reporting. The Board has concluded that it should not attempt to resolve those issues in the narrow context of the extractive industries project.

141. Moreover, as with discovery value accounting, adoption of current value accounting for oil and gas reserves would require reconsideration of the accounting concept of earnings (discussed in paragraphs 134-137). Decisions would have to be made as to whether the periodic value changes should be reflected in determining earnings or only in the stockholders' equity section of the balance sheet, and whether realized value changes should be treated differently from unrealized. Those issues, too, are part of the Board's conceptual framework project.

Reasons for Accepting Successful Efforts Accounting and for Rejecting Full Costing

142. None of the assenting or dissenting members of the Board consider it appropriate to capitalize costs of exploration efforts in a geological area in which no reserves are found simply because the company previously discovered valuable reserves in an unrelated geological area.

Successful Efforts Accounting Is Consistent with the Present Accounting Framework

143. In the presently accepted financial accounting framework, an asset is an economic resource that is expected to provide future benefits, and nonmonetary assets generally are accounted for at the cost to acquire or construct them. Costs that do not relate directly to specific assets having identifiable future benefits normally are not capitalized—no matter how vital those costs may be to the ongoing operations of the enterprise. If costs do not give rise to an asset with identifiable future benefits, they are charged to expense or recognized as a loss.

144. In the Board's judgment, successful efforts costing is consistent with that accounting framework, and full costing is not. Under full costing, even costs that are known *not* to have resulted in identifiable future benefits are nonetheless capitalized as part of the cost of assets to which they have no direct relationship.

145. In the oil and gas industry, ultimately the expected future benefits that an enterprise is attempting to obtain through its acquisition, exploration, and development activities are represented by oil and gas reserves. But, other than by purchasing minerals-in-place, an enterprise does not acquire reserves directly. Rather, it acquires properties (rights to extract any reserves that may be discovered in the future) and it acquires (develops) systems capable of producing the oil and gas reserves that are discovered. Costs that are known *not* to relate directly to the discovery of oil and gas reserves or in the development of a system for the extraction of previously discovered reserves should not be capitalized. To capitalize them is inconsistent with the presently accepted accounting framework based on measuring the historical cost of an asset.

146. Present accounting concepts place boundaries on the assets to be accounted for—boundaries determined by the transaction in which the asset was acquired, by physical attributes of the asset, by legal attributes of the asset, or by the way in which the asset is used. Full costing aggregates all oil and gas reserves within very broad cost centers (countries or continents), wherever those reserves may be located

in the cost center and whenever discovered, and accounts for that aggregation as a single asset. All acquisition, exploration, and development costs incurred in that cost center are deemed to be the cost of the aggregate asset, even if those costs relate to activities that are known *not* to have been successful in acquiring, discovering, or developing reserves.

147. The successful efforts method, on the other hand, circumscribes the boundaries of, and accounts separately for, individual assets. Under the "area-of-interest" approach to successful efforts costing, oil and gas reserves located in an individual area-of-interest are the assets accounted for. Under the approach to successful efforts in which no cost center is used for the capitalize/expense decision, individual properties or groups of geologically related properties and wells, equipment, and facilities are the assets accounted for. Either way, boundaries are placed on the assets being accounted for. Only those exploration and development costs that relate directly to specific oil and gas reserves are capitalized; costs that do not relate directly to specific reserves are charged to expense. The successful efforts method of accounting conforms to the traditional concept of the historical cost of an asset.

148. Under the successful efforts method, certain types of costs may be capitalized as "construction-in-progress" pending further information about the existence of future benefits, but as soon as the additional information becomes available, and it is known whether future benefits exist, those costs are either reclassified as an amortizable asset or charged to expense.

Financial Statements Should Reflect Risk and Unsuccessful Results

149. The function of the nation's capital markets is to direct capital to companies and institutions through decisions to invest and lend. Financial accounting and reporting provides one important source of information on which investment, lending, and related decisions are made.

150. Enterprises seeking capital operate in varying circumstances of possible success or failure. That is, they offer varying degrees of risk and opportunity to those supplying capital. Although investors and lenders differ among themselves with regard to the risks they are willing to accept, they have one thing in common: They seek a higher expected return for accepting higher risk. Business enterprises seeking capital offer different risks. Capital is equitably allocated if the prices paid are commensurate with the risk.

151. In the production of oil and gas, significant risks and returns arise in the search for reserves. In other words, discovery of oil and gas reserves is a critical event in determining failure or success, for assessing risks and returns. Because it capitalizes the costs of unsuccessful property acquisitions and unsuccessful exploratory activities as part of the costs of successful acquisitions and activities, full costing tends to obscure failure and risk. Successful efforts accounting, on the other hand, highlights failures and the risks involved in the search for oil and gas reserves by charging to expense costs that are known not to have resulted in identifiable future benefits.

152. Neither full costing nor successful efforts costing reflects success at the time of discovery. Under both methods, success is reported at the time of sale. It might be said, therefore, that both methods tend to obscure, or at least delay, the reporting of success, but that is the consequence of the historical cost basis of accounting, and its adherence to the realization concept. The obscuring of failure, however, results only from the full cost method. Under successful efforts accounting, unsuccessful costs are charged to expense and not carried forward as assets. In the Board's judgment, financial statements prepared on the successful efforts basis, including disclosures (as required by this Statement) of capitalized costs and costs incurred in oil and gas producing activities (to provide an indication of effort) and of reserve quantities and changes therein (to provide an indication of accomplishment) will provide investors with important information about success as well as failure.

153. Investors and creditors look to financial statements as an important source of information about companies' risks and returns. Investors and creditors focus on earnings—and in particular on earnings variability—as an indicator of risks and returns. As the Board noted in summarizing its *Tentative Conclusions on Objectives of Financial Statements of Business Enterprises:*[8]

> Earnings (or profits or net income) of a business enterprise are the focal point of the information communicated in financial statements. Earnings are a major motivating force in the economic activities of business enterprises and a major motivating force in the economic activities of those who lend to business enterprises, those who invest in them, and those who manage them. In general, earnings reduce the risk of those who lend funds to an enterprise or acquire its debt securities.
>
> Earnings also enable an enterprise to pay cash

[8]FASB Discussion Memorandum, "Conceptual Framework for Financial Accounting and Reporting: Elements of Financial Statements and Their Measurement," December 2, 1976, paragraph 4.

dividends to those who invest in its equity securities and enhance the prospects for increases in the market price of its stock. Thus, investors and creditors are generally more willing to commit funds to profitable enterprises than to unprofitable ones. Expectations of earnings, often based on a history of earnings, enable an enterprise to obtain both equity and debt financing.

154. Some persons criticize successful efforts accounting on grounds that a company's earnings tend to fluctuate more under that method than under full cost accounting, depending on the level and degree of success or failure of the company's acquisition and exploration activities in a given accounting period. While fluctuating earnings may, indeed, be a *characteristic* of successful efforts accounting, it is not a *fault*. The successful efforts method enables investors and lenders to observe the impact of the risks inherent in oil and gas producing activities on a company's results of operations from period to period.

155. A similar issue arose in connection with the Board's project on accounting by enterprises in the development stage. The Board concluded in *FASB Statement No. 7,* "Accounting and Reporting by Development Stage Enterprises," that a development stage enterprise should not be permitted to capitalize costs that would be charged to expense when incurred by an established operating enterprise because to do so would tend to obscure, in financial statements, the impact of risks inherent in starting up a new company.

156. The same issue has arisen in a number of other Board projects, for example, the projects on self-insurance, catastrophe losses, expropriations, and other contingencies and on foreign currency translation. A basic issue in each of those projects, as it is in the oil and gas project, was whether financial accounting standards should be adopted to normalize or average the effects of events that are inevitable over extended periods but occur at infrequent and relatively unpredictable intervals. Consistent with its conclusion in this Statement, the Board concluded in those projects that financial statements should report the effects of risk and not attempt to normalize them.

Ability to Raise Capital

157. Many proponents of full costing have said, in written submissions in response to the Discussion Memorandum, at the public hearing, and in comment letters on the Exposure Draft, that adoption of the successful efforts method of accounting will inhibit the ability of oil and gas producing companies to raise capital to finance their exploration activities. In particular, they contend, small exploration companies will have special difficulties in obtaining capital because, under a successful efforts approach, their income statements will be more likely to report earnings fluctuations and in some cases net losses, and their balance sheets could even show cumulative deficits. Potential suppliers of capital will not understand those fluctuations, losses, and deficits, it is argued, and sources of capital will diminish or be more costly. Those results, they say, are at variance with national economic goals. A particular national economic goal they cite is to encourage additional oil and gas exploration.

158. In the Board's judgment, the arguments put forth by those who say that adoption of successful efforts accounting and proscription of full costing will prevent them from raising the capital needed to finance their exploration and production activities are not persuasive. In a free enterprise economy in which capital is allocated among enterprises largely on the basis of individual investors' decisions, if a company is an economically successful enterprise, it will continue to attract capital. Its financial statements should provide those who supply capital with information that assists them in determining whether the expected returns on that capital are commensurate with the risks involved. In the Board's judgment, financial statements that are prepared in conformity with the provisions of this Statement will provide investors and creditors with that type of information. Many small oil and gas producing companies use the successful efforts method, not full costing; have done so for many years; and have generally been able to obtain capital to finance their exploration activities. Indeed, full costing is a relatively recent development in accounting for oil and gas producing activities. The 1973 survey (cited in paragraph 101 of this Statement), which was sponsored by a group of full costing petroleum companies, identified only *one* instance of its use prior to 1960, and it was not until the late 1960s that the use of full costing became relatively widespread.

159. In examining the ability-to-raise-capital issue, the Board focused in particular on three distinct types of small exploration companies:

a. Privately owned exploration companies. (A representative of the Independent Petroleum Association of America at the Board's public hearing estimated that there are 10,000 such companies in the United States.)
b. Publicly owned exploration companies. (A 1977 list of companies whose securities are registered with the SEC identifies 214 companies in "petroleum and natural gas extraction" Standard Industrial Classification.)
c. Oil and gas exploration subsidiaries and divisions of companies that are mainly in other lines of business.

160. As noted in paragraphs 101 and 117, a great many *privately* owned exploration companies follow federal income tax accounting practices in preparing their financial statements. Income tax accounting is a variation of successful efforts accounting. Those companies have for many years been able to obtain capital from external sources, including loans from local and international banks and insurance companies, from knowledgeable individual investors, and from private placements of securities.

161. Many publicly owned oil and gas exploration companies follow the successful efforts method. In connection with the research study described in paragraph 93(a) of this Statement, the staff of the FASB identified 79 oil and gas companies that (a) have securities currently traded on a securities exchange or in the over-the-counter market and (b) derive more than 50 percent of their revenue from exploration and production. (The latter criterion eliminates virtually all of the major integrated companies from the group.) Of the publicly owned companies so identified, 41 percent use successful efforts accounting.

162. Some responses to the Exposure Draft were from companies that are mainly in lines of business other than oil and gas but that have oil and gas exploration subsidiaries and divisions that use the full cost method. A number of the responses came from electric and gas public utility companies with oil and gas exploration subsidiaries recently formed or under active consideration. Those respondents urged retention of full costing for their subsidiaries and divisions on grounds that investors and lenders who supply capital to the enterprise do not regard the enterprise as an oil and gas producing company and thus would not understand the fluctuations of reported earnings or losses that, in their view, would more likely result from using successful efforts accounting, especially by a newly formed exploration subsidiary. In the Board's judgment, however, that is not an appropriate reason for allowing those subsidiaries and divisions to adopt or continue to use full costing. By choosing to seek the rewards of engaging in oil and gas exploration activities, those enterprises have assumed the risks associated with the search for oil and gas reserves, and their financial statements should provide information about those risks and not obscure them. Investors and creditors seek a return on their capital commensurate with the risks involved, and financial statements should assist them in assessing those risks. One would expect that those who supply capital for a high-risk activity such as oil and gas exploration would demand a higher return than for capital invested in less risky activity.

163. The telephone interview survey described in paragraph 93(b) provides additional evidence about the ability of small, publicly owned, successful efforts companies to raise capital. Professor Horace R. Brock of North Texas State University, or a person working under his direction, asked a senior executive officer of each of 27 small, publicly owned, successful efforts companies whether, in the officer's opinion, use of the successful efforts method has affected the company's ability to obtain the capital necessary to finance its exploration and production activities. None of the executive officers surveyed felt that the company's use of successful efforts accounting had hindered its ability to raise capital. Most of the surveyed companies raised capital externally during the past 10 years from public sales of equity and debt securities, loans from banks and insurance companies, private placements, investments by individual investors, or other outside sources. Those corporate officers were also asked whether they felt that their companies were denied access to any particular source of capital and, if so, whether the company's accounting method was a significant factor in any such situation. Again, they said that successful efforts accounting did not adversely affect their companies' ability to obtain capital from a desired source.

164. Interviews with suppliers of capital to oil and gas producing companies resulted in a similar finding. As described in paragraph 90(a), 24 bank loan officers, bank trust department officers, and securities underwriters, all of whom work directly with oil and gas companies, were interviewed to ascertain how investment and credit decisions regarding such companies are reached. The majority of interviewees indicated that the method of accounting would not affect their investment and credit decisions regarding oil and gas producing companies.

165. Some who favor retention of full costing argue that use of that method by newly formed exploration companies is essential to their viability, because investors will be disinclined to provide capital to those companies if their financial statements report net losses from operations and cumulative deficits. The Board found, however, in the course of its deliberations on *FASB Statement No. 7,* that those who supply capital to companies in the development stage understand the special circumstances of those companies and the possibility that their financial statements will report losses and deficits. In connection with that project, the Board surveyed officers of 15 venture capital companies that provide capital to development stage enterprises (though not necessarily to oil and gas ventures). Those officers said that whether a development stage enterprise defers preoperating costs or charges them to expense has little effect on (a) the amount of venture capital to be provided to that enterprise and (b) the terms under which any venture capital is provided. That

survey and related economic impact considerations were supported by a study conducted by the U.S. Department of Commerce, which is described in paragraph 50 of Statement No. 7.

166. Most proponents of full costing indicate that the reserve value ceiling on capitalized costs is an essential condition for use of that method. Except for those new companies that find relatively large quantities of proved reserves in their initial exploration efforts or that purchase interests in proved properties, it seems likely that many new exploration companies would be reporting operating losses and cumulative deficits under full costing as well as under successful efforts costing.

167. A few respondents to the Exposure Draft have said that their own companies' property acquisition and exploratory drilling programs would be sharply curtailed if they were forced to change from the full cost method of accounting to the successful efforts method. However, since the prospects of finding commercially recoverable reserves, the prices at which those reserves would be sold, the costs that would be incurred, and the income taxes that would be paid are totally unaffected by the method of accounting for the costs incurred, a decision not to go ahead with an otherwise commercially attractive project simply because successful efforts reporting is required would seem to be unlikely for the vast majority of companies. Conversely, a venture that is not otherwise commercially attractive does not become so simply because a particular method will be used to account for that venture in the company's financial statements. While a few respondents representing full cost companies did say that their companies would expect to reduce their exploration efforts because successful efforts accounting would reduce reported earnings, other companies that use full costing have said that an FASB Statement mandating successful efforts accounting will not affect their exploration plans. For example, one such company has publicly stated that while a mandated change to successful efforts accounting would have a substantial effect on previously reported earnings, it would not change the value of the company's assets, its reserves, or its cash flow, and that the company had decided not to change its exploration program if successful efforts accounting is required.

168. In support of their claim that adopting the successful efforts method will impair their companies' ability to raise capital and thereby reduce exploration activity, some persons have said that in November 1971 the Federal Power Commission adopted its Order No. 440 (which supports the full cost concept) to stimulate the search for and development of new natural gas supplies. (Order No. 440 is described in paragraph 69 of this Statement.) The petitions for rehearing of that Order that were filed with the FPC in December 1971 alleged, among other things, that the Commission had failed to reach any conclusion on what was stated to be the primary factor resulting in issuance of Order No. 440—namely, how full cost accounting would provide a stimulus for companies under the FPC's jurisdiction to conduct a search for and develop new gas supplies. In its Order No. 440-A denying the request for rehearing, the FPC stated: "Since we concluded that full-cost accounting on its merits should be adopted, it is not necessary for us to proceed further and reach a finding as to whether the accounting, as such, would provide a stimulus to discover and develop new gas supplies." (The Federal Power Commission is now the Federal Energy Regulatory Commission, a part of the Department of Energy.)

169. Some advocates of full costing apparently feel that the securities markets, which bring together those who provide capital and those who seek it, will not understand financial results reported by the successful efforts method. They imply that investors' willingness to provide capital to a given company or industry is affected by that company's or industry's use of a particular method of accounting. However, a number of research studies indicate that the securities markets generally recognize and compensate for intercompany differences in accounting practices for the same or similar events and transactions. In a 1973 summary of the findings of the then-extant research, Stanford University Professor William H. Beaver noted:[9]

> The prevailing opinion in the accounting profession is that the market reacts naively to financial statement information. This view is reinforced by the anecdotal data of the sort described earlier, and by the obvious fact that the market is populated with several million uninformed, naive investors, whose knowledge or concern for the subtleties of accounting matters is nil. However, in spite of this obvious fact, the formal research in this area is remarkably consistent in finding that the market, at least as manifested in the way in which security prices react, is quite sophisticated in dealing with financial statement data.

170. The research undertaken at the Board's request to examine the effect of the oil and gas Exposure Draft on the market prices of common stock issued by both full cost and successful efforts companies (described in paragraph 93(a) of this Statement) corroborates that the securities markets are generally able to assimilate financial information and to understand the underlying economics of

[9]Beaver, William H., "What Should Be the FASB's Objectives?," *The Journal of Accountancy*, August 1973, pp. 49-56.

the oil and gas exploration and production industry. That study did not find statistically significant evidence that issuance of the Exposure Draft affected the market prices of common shares issued by full cost companies as compared to successful efforts companies—except for some possible effect on the full cost companies during the week preceding and the week of issuance of the Exposure Draft, but the market soon adjusted, and evidence of a permanent or lingering effect was not found. (As noted in paragraph 93(a), the Board will undertake a similar study of the impact of this Statement following its issuance.)

171. The Board acknowledges that not all empirical evidence supports the view that the securities markets are entirely able to take into account the differences in accounting methods used by different companies. The studies referred to in paragraph 169 provide evidence only with respect to the securities markets as a whole; those researchers readily admit (and other research substantiates) the likelihood that decisions of individual investors in individual securities can be affected by accounting differences. As noted in paragraph 170, a Board-sponsored study found that the oil and gas Exposure Draft may have affected the prices of full cost companies' securities during the two weeks surrounding its issuance, though the effect was of brief duration. That finding supports the conclusions of other researchers that investors are sometimes unable to properly evaluate the impact of alternative accounting methods. Further, in situations in which accounting changes may have had a long-term effect on securities prices (as opposed to a temporary disruption), that result might well be viewed as an equitable adjustment of the cost of capital.[10]

172. Some respondents to the Exposure Draft said that adopting the successful efforts method and proscribing the full costing method would likely have anticompetitive effects and would be contrary to national economic or policy goals. Any national economic or policy goal that involves the use of data reported in or derived from financial statements can, in the Board's judgment, be best pursued if the relevant financial statements are prepared on a common basis, so that lenders, investors, government regulators, and others involved directly or indirectly in allocating capital can analyze and reach informed decisions on the basis of consistent and comparable financial data. To the extent that furtherance of competition in oil and gas exploration and production and the availability of increased capital resources to finance those efforts are perceived as national economic or policy goals and in the interest of the general public, those goals can best be fostered—and the likelihood of their attainment substantially increased—if all competitors disclose financial data in a marketplace free from the burdens of inconsistency, noncomparability, and misunderstanding, a marketplace in which risks and rewards are reported as objectively and as evenhandedly as possible.

173. Financial accounting should attempt to report the results of business decisions as nearly as those results can be determined in accordance with the accepted framework of accounting for all enterprises. If an enterprise's operations are subject to economic influences that are manifested in fluctuating earnings, financial statements should report those fluctuations and not obscure them. If the economic influences that affect an enterprise's operations are manifested in only minor fluctuations, that too should be portrayed. Otherwise, accounting is not evenhanded, for it fails to distinguish different characteristics of enterprises that investors may perceive as involving different risks. That evenhandedness becomes especially important for equitable allocation of capital. If financial reporting obscures differences that may be perceived as representing differences in risk or creates differences where none exist, it may contribute to channeling some capital into enterprises with expected returns and risks that are disparate—in effect, subsidizing the cost of capital to some companies at the expense of other companies.

174. As explained in paragraphs 157-173, the Board has not been presented with or able to obtain persuasive information indicating that adoption of successful efforts accounting and proscription of full costing will inhibit competition in exploration for and production of oil and gas reserves or in financing those activities. Indeed, the Board is of the view that, far from inhibiting competition, the removal of one or two significantly different optional alternative methods of accounting in similar situations will facilitate competition. The weight of the evidence before the Board is that independent oil and gas producing companies using successful efforts accounting do compete successfully and conduct effective exploration and production programs

[10]The contradictory conclusions of the various studies on accounting and securities prices and the implications of those conclusions are discussed in considerable depth in *Tentative Conclusions on Objectives of Financial Statements of Business Enterprises,* which was issued by the Board in December 1976. A number of specific studies are cited in Chapter 2, "Investors and Creditors," of *Tentative Conclusions;* additional studies are identified in the bibliography of the extractive industries Discussion Memorandum. Chapter 2 of *Tentative Conclusions* discusses both the traditional view of investors' and creditors' information needs (which concentrates on analysis of individual securities and enterprises that issue them) and the more recent capital market theory (which concentrates on portfolios and the extent to which individual securities increase or decrease the level of risk of a portfolio). An appendix to *Tentative Conclusions* provides an even more technical discussion of recent capital market theory.

that they are able to finance through a variety of capital sources.

The "Cover" Concept Is Inconsistent with the Present Accounting Framework

175. Under the full cost method, all costs incurred in acquiring, exploring, and developing properties within a relatively large geopolitical cost center (usually a country or a continent) are capitalized when incurred as costs of obtaining whatever reserves have been found in that cost center as long as the aggregate capitalized costs do not exceed the aggregate value of those reserves. If the value of previously discovered reserves exceeds the aggregate unamortized capitalized costs, unsuccessful acquisition and exploration costs are said to be adequately "covered" by the value of the previously discovered reserves, and a loss need not be recognized. In other words, current failures are "covered" and are not reported to the extent of past successes. Further, an increase in the market prices of previously discovered reserves in a cost center can enhance the amount of "cover" and further delay recognition of failures (losses) in that cost center.

176. In the Board's judgment, the "cover" concept is inconsistent with the present accounting framework, and it also obscures risk (see paragraphs 149-156). Reserves that may have been discovered ten, twenty, thirty, forty, or more years ago by a company under completely different management, with very different technology, and in very different domestic and international economic and political circumstances, should not be used, as they are under the full cost method, to justify nonrecognition of current failures. Similarly, reserves located in, say, West Texas should not be used to "cover" unsuccessful acquisition and exploration efforts in Louisiana, Alaska, or Canada, or in the offshore U.S. waters.

Successful Efforts Is Comparable to Accounting in Other Extractive Industries

177. Although not usually labeled as such, successful efforts accounting generally is followed in extractive industries other than the oil and gas industry. Because of its wide acceptance in those industries, requiring it for all oil and gas producing companies is likely to bring about greater comparability of financial statements among companies in the various extractive industries.

The Matching Concept Does Not Justify Full Costing

178. Some persons contend that full costing is justified because a "better matching" of revenues and expenses is achieved if all costs incurred in acquisition, exploration, and development activities are amortized on a pro rata basis as total reserves are produced. Proponents of full costing argue that it is impossible to discover oil and gas reserves without incurring the costs of some unsuccessful acquisition, exploration, and development activities, and they sometimes compare those activities with manufacturing operations in which spoilage or breakage is unavoidable. They argue that "proper matching" requires that the costs incurred in unavoidable unsuccessful efforts be accounted for as reasonable and necessary costs of successful efforts in the same way that the costs of unavoidable spoilage or breakage are accounted for as costs of good products.

179. Three pervasive principles by which revenues and expenses are matched are described in paragraphs 156-160 of *APB Statement No. 4,* as follows:

> *Associating Cause and Effect.* Some costs are recognized as expenses on the basis of a presumed direct association with specific revenue . . . recognizing them as expenses accompanies recognition of the revenue.
>
> *Systematic and Rational Allocation. . . .* If an asset provides benefits for several periods its cost is allocated to the periods in a systematic and rational manner in the absence of a more direct basis for associating cause and effect.
>
> *Immediate Recognition.* Some costs are associated with the current accounting period as expenses because (1) costs incurred during the period provide no discernible future benefits, (2) costs recorded as assets in prior periods no longer provide discernible benefits, or (3) allocating costs either on the basis of association with revenue or among several accounting periods is considered to serve no useful purpose.

180. A direct cause and effect justification for associating unsuccessful acquisition and exploration costs with revenues derived from successful activities has not been demonstrated. A direct cause and effect association can be said to exist between the costs of nonproductive fields and the revenues from reserves in productive fields, or between costs applicable to unsuccessful ventures and costs applicable to successful ventures, if there is a *reliable* association between total costs and reserves discovered as a direct result of incurring those costs. Only then could it be said that a cost gives rise to revenues, that is, causes revenues. Although some persons claim that *industry-wide* statistics indicate a general predictable relationship between total number of wells or total footage drilled and total reserves added, those relationships have not been constant, particularly over a relatively short period of time such as a year, and there can be no assurance that they will apply to the future. More importantly, to the best of the Board's knowledge no such relationship has

been demonstrated to be predictable for an *individual company.* Accounting is done for individual companies, not for an industry as a whole, and for companies a direct association between finding costs and mineral reserves emerges only at the level of an individual property unit or within a given field or other localized geological structure. Even that association often is not evident at the time the costs are incurred, and that is when accounting decisions must be made.

181. Systematic and rational allocation likewise does not justify attributing unsuccessful acquisition and exploration costs to the results of successful activities. As *APB Statement No. 4* states, allocation of an asset's cost is justified "if an asset provides benefits for several periods." In the full costing versus successful efforts costing controversy, the question is not whether or how to allocate capitalized costs but which costs to capitalize.

182. The "immediate recognition" principle referred to in *APB Statement No. 4* is appropriate for unsuccessful acquisition and exploration costs. According to that principle, costs are associated with the current period as expenses if they provide no discernible future benefits (for example, geological and geophysical costs) or, if previously capitalized, they no longer provide discernible benefits (for example, acquisition costs of abandoned properties). The application of the immediate recognition principle in this Statement is consistent with its application by the Board in other pronouncements. In paragraph 49 of *FASB Statement No. 2,* "Accounting for Research and Development Costs," for example, the Board stated that "the general lack of discernible future benefits at the time the costs are incurred indicates that the 'immediate recognition' principle of expense recognition should apply."

183. In *FASB Statement No. 2,* moreover, the Board considered and rejected the argument that research and development costs be capitalized when incurred and amortized on a company-wide basis. Paragraphs 51 and 52 state:

> 51. Enterprises undertake research and development activities with the hope of future benefits. If there were no such hope, the activities would not be conducted. Some persons take the position that the accounting treatment for research and development costs should be determined by considering in the aggregate all of the research and development activities of an enterprise. In their view, if there is a high probability of future benefits from an enterprise's total research and development program, the entire cost of those activities should be capitalized without regard to the certainty of future benefits from individual projects.
>
> 52. The Board believes, however, that it is not appropriate to consider accounting for research and development activities on an aggregate or total-enterprise basis for several reasons. For accounting purposes the expectation of future benefits generally is not evaluated in relation to broad categories of expenditures or an enterprise-wide basis but rather in relation to individual or related transactions or projects. . . .

Value Ceiling Is Subjective

184. Limiting capitalized costs to the estimated value of reserves, which is an integral part of the full cost method of accounting, requires estimation of reserve quantities, development costs, production costs, the timing of development and production, selling prices, and appropriate discount rates. The uncertainties inherent in those estimates and projections tend to make estimates of reserve values highly subjective, and estimates of value made by trained experts can differ markedly. Under the successful efforts method, the need to limit capitalized costs is much less crucial because the costs of unsuccessful efforts, which may represent a large part of the total capitalized costs under the full cost method, will have been charged to expense as incurred or recognized as a loss when the effort was determined to be unsuccessful.

Full Costing Does Not Represent Current Value on the Balance Sheet

185. Some persons contend that by using full costing, asset carrying amounts reported in the balance sheet will be closer to the current values of most companies' oil and gas reserves than they would under successful efforts costing. In the Board's judgment, however, under neither method do the *costs* to acquire, explore, and develop mineral properties indicate the *values* of reserves discovered. Those values change continually, depending on revisions of estimates of reserve quantities, development costs, production costs, income taxes, the timing of future development and production, selling prices, and appropriate discount rates. The capitalized costs, however, do not change. Neither full costing nor successful efforts costing is intended to portray current values; both of those methods are based on historical costs.

The Ability to Manage Earnings Is Not Unique to Successful Efforts Accounting

186. Some proponents of full costing contend that the ability of management to subjectively influence reported earnings is reduced under full costing. In their view, under successful efforts accounting,

management may be inclined to smooth or average periodic reported earnings by (a) deciding to delay final determination of the outcome of a project or to delay the write-off of an unsuccessful venture, thus postponing loss recognition, (b) incurring larger or smaller amounts of costs that are charged to expense as incurred, such as in exploration, and (c) postponing or moving forward the times at which such costs are to be incurred.

187. While a transaction-oriented accounting framework—which is the presently accepted framework—allows opportunities to postpone or accelerate earnings effects, those opportunities are not unique to the oil and gas industry. Nor are they unique to successful efforts accounting since full costing itself may be viewed as a method for averaging reported earnings over long periods of time. Most importantly, the Board does not believe that the potential actions described in the preceding paragraph should bear importantly on the accounting decisions confronting the Board in this project. Even if accounting results were to influence some managers' decisions, it does not follow that accounting standards should be designed to accomplish or prevent an action by management. That type of accounting standard would require a judgment by the Board as to which potential actions are desirable and which are undesirable. Accounting should evenhandedly report economic actions taken, regardless of motivation. Accounting should not obscure the effect of actions and events in order to prevent what some believe to be "uneconomic" actions.

Simplicity Is Not the Overriding Criterion for Selection of Accounting Method

188. Some persons advocate full costing on grounds that it reduces the amount of procedural and mechanical accounting work, thus saving time, effort, and cost in maintaining accounting records. They claim that since all costs incurred in acquisition, exploration, and development are capitalized, there is less need to make arbitrary cost allocations or to prepare separate computations of amortization on individual properties. The Board disagrees. Firstly, individual property records must be maintained for purposes of determining royalties, computing taxable income, and making management decisions to commit funds, abandon properties, and so forth, so the amount of additional effort that may be required under successful efforts accounting is not expected to be burdensome. More importantly, in the Board's judgment, accounting simplicity should not justify nonrecognition of losses at the time they are incurred.

Reasons for Specific Conclusions within the Successful Efforts Method

189. Paragraphs 142-188 set forth the Board's reasons for rejecting full cost accounting and accepting successful efforts accounting. As explained in paragraphs 111-119, however, there are many variations within the successful efforts method. Paragraphs 190-214 which follow explain the Board's conclusions regarding the principal variations considered.

Rejection of Area-of-Interest Approach

190. Some proponents of successful efforts accounting believe that a cost center (such as an area-of-interest) has a central role in accumulating certain types of prediscovery costs prior to the time that a reasonable determination can be made as to whether future benefits will result from having incurred those costs. They would capitalize some or all prediscovery costs relating to an area-of-interest until it is determined whether that area contains proved reserves. If it is determined that the area-of-interest does not contain reserves, the costs are written off and a loss is recognized. Even among proponents of the area-of-interest approach there are differences as to which prediscovery costs relating to an area-of-interest should be capitalized. Some proponents would capitalize prediscovery drilling costs but not G&G; others would capitalize the G&G as well. Other successful efforts proponents use a cost center only for computing amortization rates. They believe that the nature of a cost, and not the nature of a cost center, should be the primary consideration in the capitalize/expense decision (discussed further in paragraph 103).

191. The Board has adopted the latter view. Until discovery, delineation of the boundaries of a cost center such as an area-of-interest is arbitrary, and intercompany differences in defining cost centers are likely to be significant and unavoidable. Many years often elapse before reserves are discovered in an area-of-interest, if they are discovered at all. Thus, depending on the extent to which an area-of-interest proponent would capitalize prediscovery costs, exploration costs that have no identifiable future benefits may be carried forward as assets potentially for many years. The Board concluded that exploration expenditures that do not directly result in the acquisition of an asset having identifiable future benefits should not be capitalized simply because they fall within lines drawn on a map by individual companies, that is, lines drawn to circumscribe an area-of-interest or, as some would say, a project.

192. Some persons who advocate capitalization of all costs associated with an area-of-interest say that doing so is essential for financial statements to reflect the total "historical cost" of a project that ultimately proves successful. Many projects, however, do not ultimately prove successful, and determination of success or failure of an area-of-interest often takes a number of years. In the Board's judgment, periodic reporting of financial position and results of operations to investors and creditors is an overriding consideration that precludes the indefinite accumulation of costs of unknown future benefit. The Board reached a similar conclusion in *FASB Statement No. 2,* "Accounting for Research and Development Costs," in which the Board rejected the indefinite deferral of R&D costs on a project basis pending determination of success or failure of the project.

Charging G&G to Expense

193. This Statement requires that geological and geophysical costs, whether incurred before or after acquisition of the related property, be charged to expense when incurred. Those costs are information costs very much like research costs. To a considerable extent, G&G costs are incurred before any properties are acquired, and in the majority of cases the acreage surveyed is either never acquired or, if acquired, is ultimately abandoned or surrendered. It is difficult, and in many cases impossible, to correlate geological and geophysical expenditures with a specific discovery made many months or years later, even with the benefit of hindsight; such correlation clearly cannot be done at the time the G&G expenditures are incurred, which is when accounting decisions are made. For those reasons, the Board has concluded that G&G costs shall be charged to expense when incurred. While the costs of drilling stratigraphic test wells are sometimes considered to be geological and geophysical costs, they are accounted for separately under this Statement for reasons explained in paragraphs 200-202.

194. In response to recommendations made by commentators on the Exposure Draft, this Statement makes clear that dry hole contributions and bottom hole contributions are included in exploration costs (paragraph 17(c)). Also, in response to comments on the Exposure Draft, paragraph 20 has been added to provide for capitalization of contractually reimbursable G&G and other exploration costs.

Charging Carrying Costs to Expense

195. Costs of carrying and retaining undeveloped properties do not increase the potential of those properties to contain oil and gas reserves. Carrying costs are incurred to *maintain* an enterprise's rights, not to *acquire* those rights. In a sense, they are penalties for having delayed drilling and development activities and, thereby, having delayed potential production of oil and gas. Because carrying costs do not enhance the future benefits from the enterprise's properties and other assets, they are charged to expense when incurred under the provisions of this Statement.

Charging the Costs of Drilling Unsuccessful Exploratory Wells to Expense

196. Charging the costs of drilling unsuccessful exploratory wells to expense is generally regarded as an inherent part of the successful efforts method of accounting. Not all successful efforts proponents agree, however, on what constitutes unsuccessful exploratory wells, and there is also disagreement over the timing of expense recognition. Under this Statement, success is defined in terms of whether proved oil and gas reserves have been found. As to timing, under this Statement the costs of drilling exploratory wells are initially capitalized when incurred and are subsequently either charged to expense or reclassified as part of the enterprise's wells and related equipment and facilities when the determination is made as to whether proved reserves have been found. Further, this Statement establishes guidelines for determining whether the costs of drilling exploratory wells may continue to be carried as an asset pending determination of whether proved reserves have been found.

197. Several alternatives regarding the timing of expense recognition are proposed by successful efforts advocates. Some persons, on grounds that the majority of all exploratory wells (73 percent for the U.S. as a whole in 1976) are unsuccessful, would charge all costs of drilling exploratory wells to expense when incurred, rather than regard them as "construction-in-progress" pending determination of success or failure. Some would subsequently "reinstate" the costs of drilling an exploratory well that is determined to have been successful. In the Board's judgment, however, reinstatement of costs previously charged to expense is inconsistent with generally accepted accounting principles for other industries. For example, the Board has previously rejected the notion of cost reinstatement with respect to research and development costs (paragraph 57 of *FASB Statement No. 2*). Consequently, the Board concluded that a method of accounting for oil and gas producing activities based on cost reinstatement is inappropriate.

198. The best accounting, in the Board's judgment, is to capitalize as "construction-in-progress" the costs of drilling all exploratory wells pending determination of success or failure, that is, pending determination of whether proved reserves are found. The

length of time it takes to drill an exploratory well is relatively short—generally a matter of weeks or months, although a few occasionally take a year or longer—so the period during which costs of undetermined future benefit are capitalized usually is relatively brief, and this Statement requires that the costs be charged to expense as soon as a determination is made that proved reserves have not been found. In the Board's judgment, it is appropriate that the costs of drilling exploratory wells be treated differently from G&G and similar exploration costs because, first, determination of success or failure is much more clear-cut for exploratory drilling than it is for G&G and similar exploration costs, and, second, because successful exploratory wells result directly in the discovery of proved reserves whereas G&G does not.

199. The quantity of oil and gas reserves found by an exploratory well is normally estimated on or shortly after completion of drilling; occasionally that assessment takes a matter of weeks or months, rarely longer. If, however, a major capital expenditure is required before production could begin—such as for construction of a trunk pipeline—the reserves found may not be classifiable as proved unless sufficient quantities of additional reserves are found as a result of additional exploratory drilling. The additional exploratory drilling might take several years to complete. Paragraph 31 of this Statement therefore divides exploratory wells that find oil and gas reserves into two types: Those that are not drilled in an area requiring a major capital expenditure such as a trunk pipeline before production could begin and those that are drilled in such an area. For the former type, when classification of the reserves that are found cannot be made at the time drilling is completed, a one-year capitalization period is provided if that is necessary to allow a reasonable period of time for determining whether to classify those reserves as proved. Recognizing, however, that the decision to make a major capital expenditure, such as for a trunk pipeline, must sometimes await the results of additional exploratory wells, the Board concluded not to impose the one-year presumption of impairment on exploratory wells drilled in areas requiring a major capital expenditure before production could begin. Instead, paragraph 31(a) establishes two conditions for continued capitalization that take into account the realities and economics of exploratory drilling in remote areas and, at the same time, prohibit the indefinite deferral of the costs of exploratory wells merely on the hope that the selling prices of oil and gas will increase or on the possibility that unplanned exploratory drilling activity in the indefinite future might find additional quantities of reserves.

Stratigraphic Test Wells Treated Similarly to Exploratory Wells and Development Wells

200. Stratigraphic test wells are drilled to obtain information. They are not normally intended to be completed for hydrocarbon production and are customarily abandoned after drilling is completed and the information is obtained. Normally, stratigraphic test wells are drilled offshore to determine whether an offshore property contains sufficient reserves to justify the cost of constructing and installing a production platform and to determine where to locate such a platform.

201. Under this Statement, stratigraphic test wells are divided into two types—exploratory-type and development-type—and the standards of accounting for the two types parallel the accounting for exploratory wells and development wells, respectively. Thus, an exploratory-type stratigraphic test well is accounted for in a manner similar to an exploratory well drilled in an area requiring a major capital expenditure before production could begin: The costs of drilling the exploratory-type stratigraphic test well are capitalized pending determination of whether proved reserves are found, subject to the condition that those costs not continue to be carried as assets indefinitely if stratigraphic test drilling activity in the area has ceased or if the quantity of reserves found would not justify completion of the well for production had it not been simply a stratigraphic test well. The capitalized costs either are reclassified as part of the cost of the enterprise's wells and related equipment and facilities if proved reserves are found or are charged to expense if proved reserves are not found. Thus if an exploratory-type stratigraphic test well discovers reserves that are classified as proved and facilities are to be installed to produce those reserves, the cost of the exploratory-type stratigraphic test well is accounted for as part of the cost of the facilities even though the particular well itself may be abandoned. Accounting for the other type of stratigraphic test well—development-type—is identical to accounting for development wells and other development costs generally: capitalize as part of the cost of an enterprise's wells and related equipment and facilities (reasons therefor discussed in paragraph 207).

202. The method of accounting for exploratory-type stratigraphic test wells described in the preceding paragraph represents a change from the Exposure Draft, which had proposed that the costs of all stratigraphic test wells be charged to expense when incurred on grounds that they are similar to G&G costs. A number of respondents to the Expo-

sure Draft pointed out that an important difference exists between the costs of stratigraphic test wells and G&G costs: G&G information, no matter how persuasive, does not provide sufficient evidence to classify reserves as proved; reserves are classified as proved only after an exploratory well or a stratigraphic test well has been drilled. Thus a stratigraphic test well can result directly in the discovery of proved reserves whereas information obtained from geological and geophysical studies cannot. Discovery of proved reserves establishes the existence of future benefits and justifies the continued capitalization of the costs of those stratigraphic test wells that find proved reserves. Because of the foregoing differences, the costs of exploratory-type stratigraphic test wells are more like the costs of drilling exploratory wells than they are like G&G costs. The Board agrees with that view, and this Statement reflects the appropriate modification from the Exposure Draft. Further, paragraph 34 provides for deferral of the costs of exploratory-type stratigraphic test wells that find commercially producible quantities of reserves, even though those wells cannot be used to produce the reserves. That provision reflects the realities and economics of offshore drilling. Producible exploratory wells often are prohibitively expensive in offshore waters, and offshore exploratory drilling generally involves nonproducible, expendable wells.

All Development Costs Capitalized

203. Under this Statement, discovery of oil and gas reserves is viewed as the single most critical event in the search for and extraction of oil and gas. Discovery of proved reserves establishes the existence of future benefits and justifies the capitalization of the costs of successful exploratory wells and exploratory-type stratigraphic test wells as amortizable assets. After discovery, development costs are incurred to obtain additional access to those proved reserves and to provide facilities for extracting, treating, gathering, and storing the oil and gas. Those development costs result in the creation of a producing system of wells and related equipment and facilities—a system much like the production system of a manufacturing company.

204. After discovery, all costs incurred to build that producing system, including the costs of drilling unsuccessful development wells and development-type stratigraphic test wells, are capitalized as part of the cost of that system under the provisions of this Statement. With respect to development dry holes, some persons take the position that no costs incurred in drilling a dry hole—exploratory or development—can provide future benefits, and therefore the costs of all dry holes, including development dry holes, should be charged to expense.

205. In the Board's judgment, however, there is an important difference between exploratory dry holes and development dry holes. The purpose of an exploratory well is to search for oil and gas. The existence of future benefits is not known until the well is drilled. Future benefits depend on whether reserves are found. A development well, on the other hand, is drilled as part of the effort to build a producing system of wells and related equipment and facilities. Its purpose is to extract previously discovered proved oil and gas reserves. By definition (Appendix C, paragraph 274), a development well is a well drilled *within the proved area* of a reservoir to a *depth known to be productive.* The existence of future benefits is discernible from reserves already proved at the time the well is drilled. An exploratory well, because it is drilled outside a proved area, or within a proved area but to a previously untested horizon, is not directly associable with specific proved reserves until completion of drilling. An exploratory well must be assessed on its own, and the direct discovery of oil and gas reserves can be the sole determinant of whether future benefits exist and, therefore, whether an asset should be recognized. Unlike an exploratory well, a development well by definition is associable with known future benefits before drilling begins. The cost of a development well is a part of the cost of a bigger asset—a producing system of wells and related equipment and facilities intended to extract, treat, gather, and store known reserves.

206. Moreover, because they are drilled only in proved areas to proved depths, the great majority of development wells are successful; a much smaller percentage (22 percent in the United States in 1976), as compared to exploratory wells (73 percent in the United States in 1976) are dry holes. Development dry holes occur principally because of a structural fault or other unexpected stratigraphic condition or because of a problem that arose during drilling, such as tools or equipment accidentally dropped down the hole, or simply the inability to know precisely the limits and nature of a proven reservoir. Development dry holes are similar to normal, relatively minor "spoilage" or "waste" in manufacturing or construction. The Board believes that there is a significant difference between the *exploration for* and the *development of* proved reserves. Therefore, in the Board's judgment, it is appropriate to account for the costs of development dry holes different from exploratory dry holes.

207. For similar reasons, the Board believes that the costs of development-type stratigraphic test wells should be accounted for as other development costs. Development-type stratigraphic test wells are drilled *after* proved reserves have been discovered, and they are drilled *within* the proved area, generally either to

assess more accurately the quantity of reserves that has been found or to provide information as to where best to locate the production platform. The existence of future benefits is discernible from reserves already proved at the time the development-type stratigraphic test well is drilled. The costs of drilling the well are part of the costs of developing a system that will produce those reserves. In the Board's judgment, it is inappropriate to account for the costs of development-type stratigraphic test wells different from other development costs. As explained in paragraph 202, the method of accounting for stratigraphic test wells in this Statement represents a change from the proposal in the Exposure Draft as a result of comments made by respondents to the Exposure Draft.

Impairment Test for Unproved Properties

208. When unproved properties are acquired, their acquisition costs are capitalized when incurred. Whether the unproved property will ultimately provide future benefits—that is, whether it contains proved oil and gas reserves—is unknown at the time of acquisition. However, a *property right* is acquired. That property right, and the underlying *right to search for and extract* oil and gas reserves, in themselves are in the Board's judgment a sufficient future benefit to justify capitalizing the acquisition cost of an unproved property at the time it is incurred. Because a purchase price has been paid, there is a presumption that the property right has an independent market value at the time equivalent to the purchase price. Thereafter, either as a result of unsuccessful exploration activities including those of other parties on nearby or adjacent properties or as the expiration of the property right approaches, the future benefits inherent in the right to search for and extract oil and gas in an unproved property may diminish or disappear entirely, with no offsetting benefits in terms of oil and gas discovered. Consequently, this Statement requires that unproved properties be assessed periodically and a loss recognized if those properties have been impaired. Many respondents to the Exposure Draft recommended that for practical reasons the Board should permit recognition of impairment of individually insignificant properties by amortizing their costs, either in the aggregate or by groups, on the basis of the experience of the enterprise and other information. This Statement reflects the appropriate modification of the Exposure Draft to permit amortization of individually insignificant properties.

Question of a Limitation Test for Proved Properties and Capitalized Exploration and Development Costs

209. As explained in paragraphs 190 and 191, a cost center is not the primary consideration in the capitalize/expense decision under the approach to successful efforts accounting adopted by the Board in this Statement. Under that approach, the assets to which the capitalized acquisition, exploratory drilling, and development costs relate are *properties, wells, equipment, and facilities*. The question of whether to write down the carrying amount of productive assets to an amount expected to be recoverable through future use of those assets is unsettled under present generally accepted accounting principles. This is a pervasive issue that the Board has not addressed. Consequently, this Statement is not intended to change practice by either requiring or prohibiting an impairment test for proved properties or for wells, equipment, and facilities that constitute part of an enterprise's oil and gas producing systems.

Unit-of-Production Amortization

210. Nearly all respondents to the Discussion Memorandum and the Exposure Draft favored unit-of-production amortization for capitalized acquisition, exploratory drilling, and development costs. There was some disagreement, however, as to the appropriate reserve categories on which to base amortization. Some persons favor using the same reserve categories for all amortizations. Within that group, some would use only *proved developed* reserves while others would use *all proved* reserves. Some who would use all proved reserves would include estimated future development costs in the amortization computation; others would use only actual costs incurred. Some persons would use different reserve categories for different types of capitalized costs.

211. The Board believes that using estimated future development costs to compute amortization rates introduces an unnecessary and subjective element into the financial accounting and reporting process. Only development costs incurred to date should be amortized. Further, in the Board's judgment, costs should be amortized on the basis of estimates of quantities of proved reserves to which those costs relate. Proved developed reserves, by definition, relate to the costs of wells and related equipment and facilities. Acquisition costs relating to proved properties, on the other hand, were incurred to obtain not only the proved reserves that are already developed but also those proved reserves remaining to be developed. Accordingly, this Statement requires that acquisition costs of proved properties be amortized on the basis of all proved reserves, developed and undeveloped, and that capitalized exploratory drilling and development costs (wells and related equipment and facilities) be amortized on the basis of proved developed reserves.

212. Respondents to the Exposure Draft cited three

important aspects of its provisions regarding unit-of-production amortization that, in their view, required clarification or modification. The Board agrees that clarification or modification is needed for each of those matters, and the following changes have been made in this Statement:

a. Paragraph 29 has been modified to permit reclassification from unproved to proved of only a portion of an unusually large property to which proved reserves have been attributed. The acquisition cost of the portion remaining as unproved will therefore not be subject to unit-of-production amortization, though it will continue to be subject to assessment for impairment.
b. Paragraph 35 has been modified to permit amortization of natural gas cycling and processing plants by other than the unit-of-production method if another method is deemed more appropriate in the circumstances.
c. Paragraph 35 has been modified to provide for exclusion of certain large front-end development costs that relate to an entire planned group of wells as a whole from immediate early amortization pending completion of drilling the additional wells; similarly, that paragraph now provides for exclusion from the amortization rate determination those proved developed reserves that will be produced only after significant expenditures are made.

213. Two principal approaches were considered by the Board for equating, in computing amortization rates, oil and gas that are jointly produced from a property or group of properties. One is to equate the oil and gas on the basis of their relative energy content—their heat content based on the British Thermal Unit (BTU). The other approach is to equate oil and gas on the basis of their relative sales values.

214. The relative energy content approach stresses the physical relationship of oil and gas. The relative sales value method is intended to emphasize their economic relationship. The Board rejected the relative sales value method principally because of problems in determining and using relative sales values. For example, because market prices of much of the oil and gas sold are regulated, sometimes with widely disparate prices prevailing for the same commodity and with relatively significant year-to-year fluctuations, the economic relationship as of a given date could be quite artificial and quite different from a similar determination made for the same reserves as of some prior or future date. Consequently, the Board rejected the relative sales value method.

Importance of the Definition of Proved Reserves

215. Under the provisions of this Statement, capitalization and asset classification decisions hinge on whether *proved* reserves have been found. For that reason, the definition of proved reserves in Appendix C of this Statement assumes great importance. That definition is the one set forth in the rules and regulations of the Securities and Exchange Commission. The Board chose that definition, rather than definitions proposed by others and rather than creating a definition of its own, because the SEC definition is already required to be used in practice by oil and gas producing companies whose securities are publicly traded. The Board believes that conformity of the reserve definitions used in filings with the SEC, in information reported to the Department of Energy for the national energy data base, and in financial statements prepared in conformity with generally accepted accounting principles is desirable.

216. Under paragraph 11 of this Statement, properties are classified as either unproved or proved depending on whether those properties have proved reserves. Although some oil and gas producing companies currently make a developed/undeveloped or producing/nonproducing distinction among properties, in the Board's judgment *discovery,* rather than development or production, is the single most critical event in an enterprise's oil and gas producing activities. The Board recognizes that some companies presently refer to properties with no proved reserves as *undeveloped* or *nonproducing,* for disclosure purposes; conversely, some companies heretofore have referred to properties with proved reserves as *developed* or *producing* properties even though some or all of a property's proved reserves may not be developed or producing.

Information Available after the Balance Sheet Date

217. In response to questions raised in letters of comment on the Exposure Draft, paragraph 39 has been added to this Statement to clarify that information that becomes available after the balance sheet date but before the financial statements are issued shall be taken into account in evaluating conditions that existed at the balance sheet date, for example, in assessing unproved properties and in determining whether a well has found proved reserves. The Board believes that this position is consistent with the concepts in *FASB Statement No. 5,* "Accounting for Contingencies."

Mineral Property Conveyances and Related Transactions

218. Mineral property conveyances and related transactions may be classified according to their nature as a sale, a borrowing, an exchange of nonmonetary assets, a pooling of assets in a joint undertaking, or some combination thereof. In the Board's

judgment, the accounting principles set forth in the authoritative accounting literature and otherwise generally accepted in current practice for similar transactions in other industries should apply to the oil and gas industry. Paragraphs 43 and 47 apply accepted accounting practices to some of the more common types of conveyances.

219. The transactions described in paragraph 43(a) are classified as borrowings because the funds advanced are repayable in cash or its equivalent. Although the purpose of advancing funds for exploration is to obtain future supplies, successful exploration is not assured, and to the extent production is inadequate to satisfy the obligation, the balance is payable in cash. Accordingly, the transaction is in substance a borrowing.

220. A production payment repayable in cash out of the proceeds from a specified share of production until the amount advanced has been recovered with interest (paragraph 43(b)), is in substance a borrowing. Some hold the view that the recipient of the advance has no liability except to the extent that oil or gas is produced and that, accordingly, the recipient should account for the advance as deferred revenue. The Board did not find that reasoning persuasive. Normally, the advances are made by banks (often through an intermediary) or by other lenders under conditions that leave little doubt that the proved reserves are more than adequate to recover the funds advanced plus interest. The intent of the transaction is to obtain funds and not to sell oil or gas for future delivery. The recipient of the advance is at risk for any change in the price of oil or gas and for the cost of operating the property. The transaction is in substance a loan secured by reserves and is without recourse to other assets of the party receiving the advance. The reserves and production involved are reported by the recipient, not by the lender.

221. The Exposure Draft had proposed that neither gain nor loss be recognized at the time of conveyance if a part of an interest owned is sold and either (a) substantial uncertainty exists about recovery of the costs applicable to the retained interest or (b) the seller has a substantial obligation for future performance. While agreeing that because of those uncertainties recognition of a *gain* is not appropriate in those situations, some respondents to the Exposure Draft said that recognition of a *loss* should not be prohibited. The Board agrees, and paragraph 45 of this Statement prohibits only the recognition of a gain in those situations. In addition, the phrase "substantial obligation for future performance" in paragraph 45(b) has been expanded to include examples, as suggested by some respondents to the Exposure Draft.

222. A production payment to be satisfied by delivery of a specified quantity of oil or gas out of a specified share of production (paragraph 47(a)) is a sale for which income is not recognized because the earning process is not complete. The seller still has to perform the production and delivery function. Unlike the production payment payable in cash, the amount payable is not fixed, there is no specified or determinable rate of interest, and the risks of price changes rest with the purchaser rather than the seller. The purchaser, not the seller, reports the reserves and production because the substance of the transaction is the purchase of a mineral interest rather than the lending of cash.

223. In some transactions, the owner of an operating interest in an unproved property arranges for another party to assume some or all of the exploration, drilling, development, and operating obligations in return for a share of the rewards if those efforts are successful. This Statement addresses three types of such arrangements: (a) assignment of the operating interest with retention of a nonoperating interest in return for which the assignee assumes the drilling, development, and operating obligations (paragraph 47(b)); (b) assignment of a part of an operating interest in return for assumption by the assignee of the obligation to drill one or more exploratory wells at assignee's cost, after which the property is to be jointly owned and operated if the drilling is successful (paragraph 47(c)); and (c) a carried interest arrangement by which the assignee assumes all the exploration drilling and development risk in return for a fractional operating interest but recovers the cost incurred, if the venture is successful, before the assignor shares in the production from the property (paragraph 47(d)).

224. While the three types of conveyances described in the preceding paragraph have different features, in each instance one party has provided the property and the other party has agreed to incur certain high risk costs, and the benefits, if any, are to be shared in agreed proportions. The Board concluded that all those transactions represent a pooling of assets in a joint undertaking. The investment of each party in the joint operations consists of the carrying amount of the assets contributed by it. Each party will share in the resulting benefits, if any, according to the terms of the agreement. The cost of those benefits to the recipient is the amount of its investment. At the time of the transaction the earning process is incomplete and no gain or loss has been realized by either party. Each party records only its own costs and revenues and does not make a reassignment of costs to reflect the interest that it obtains, or may obtain, in assets contributed by the other party. Each party looks upon its earning assets as those contributed by it.

225. Some support the view that when part of an

interest in an unproved property is relinquished to obtain another type of interest in the same property or an interest in wells and equipment, both parties to the transaction should reassign the cost each has incurred so that their accounts will reflect some cost for each type of asset. The Board rejected that view because there is no true exchange of assets in this type of transaction. As stated above each party's earning assets are those contributed by it, and the carrying amounts of those assets should be retained at their historical cost.

226. In applying the above conclusions to carried interests, the Board recognizes that before payout a carried party will reflect no income and that at payout the carried party will own an interest in wells and related equipment and facilities, but its accounts will reflect only the original investment in the property. The Board believes, however, that the pooling concept best reflects the substance of the agreement between the parties. At the time expenditures are made it is not known whether payout will occur, and many carried interests, even in properties where production is obtained, do not pay out. The Board's conclusions in respect to accounting for this type of transaction are that a carried party has no revenue until payout and no cost of assets beyond the original leasehold cost; a carrying party's accounts reflect the investment, operating costs, and revenue that are at its risk or for its benefit; and the disclosures of reserves and production should be consonant with that basis of accounting.

227. Because an exchange of fractional operating interests in undeveloped mineral properties upon formation of a joint venture (paragraph 47(e)) is a nonmonetary exchange of similar productive assets, accounting as prescribed in *APB Opinion No. 29,* "Accounting for Nonmonetary Transactions," paragraph 21(b) is appropriate. In response to requests for clarification of gain or loss recognition in disproportional cost sharing arrangements paragraph 47(e) was expanded to provide that each party to a joint venture shall record its cost and that gain shall not be recognized if an interest in a property or other assets is acquired without cost or at a cost disproportionate to the interest acquired. This accounting is compatible with that prescribed for a free well or a carried interest.

228. The Board considered the transactions carried out to effect the unitization of oil and gas properties (paragraph 47(f)) to be a pooling of assets for which the earning process is incomplete. Unitizations result in a group of separate properties being combined and operated as a single property. Each participant normally has essentially the same quantity of oil and gas reserves immediately following the unitization as before. A payment of money to equalize the contributions of wells, equipment, and facilities does not in the Board's judgment change the substance of the transaction.

229. Paragraph 47(g) has been added to this Statement to clarify the appropriate accounting for the sale of an entire interest in an unproved property. Recognition of gain or loss on the sale of a property whose impairment has been assessed individually is consistent with accounting for the sales of assets generally. Nonrecognition of gain or loss on the sale of a property whose impairment has been assessed by amortizing its cost as part of a group is compatible with the normal accounting for a partial retirement of assets subject to group depreciation; paragraph 47(g) also provides for recognizing gain when the sales price exceeds the original cost of the property sold, a circumstance that does not normally arise in the usual group depreciation situation for other types of assets.

230. The sale of a part of an interest in an unproved property for cash (paragraph 47(h)) is viewed by some as the sale of an asset that results in a gain or loss. The Board does not agree with that view. The objective of the parties in this type of transaction is generally to diversify risks and jointly participate in any future costs and benefits. Since this Statement requires continuing evaluation of unproved properties for impairment, no loss need be recognized as stemming directly from the sale of a fractional interest. The Board concluded that because of the uncertainty of the recovery of costs applicable to the interest retained in an unproved property, the transaction should be accounted for as a recovery of cost and that a gain should be recognized only to the extent that proceeds from the fractional interest sold exceed the carrying amount of the property. The proposal in the Exposure Draft has been revised to clarify the question of gain recognition if the unproved property in which part or all of an interest is sold is part of a group for which an impairment allowance is provided in the aggregate.

231. The risk of nonrecovery of the remaining cost is usually not significant if proved properties or parts of interests in proved properties are sold (paragraph 47(i)-(m)). Accordingly, the Board concluded that gain or loss should normally be recognized in those transactions consistent with other sales of capital assets.

232. Paragraphs 47(l) and 47(m) have been added to clarify that accounting for the sale of a property with retention of a production payment shall be compatible with the accounting for the sale of production payments with retention of the operating interest. A retained production payment expressed in money may sometimes be so large that it is highly improbable that the production payment will be satisfied before the reserves are fully depleted. In

those situations, therefore, paragraph 47(l) provides that the retained production payment shall be treated as an overriding royalty interest rather than as a receivable or payable.

Disclosure

233. In establishing the disclosure standards in paragraphs 48-59 of this Statement, the Board relied on the following general guidelines:

a. The disclosures in financial statements do not and cannot include all information that may be needed for investment, credit, regulatory, or national economic planning and energy policy decisions, although the accounting standards established by this Statement should contribute importantly to the reliability and uniformity of financial data used in those types of decisions. Financial statements are intended to present fairly an enterprise's financial position, results of operations, and changes in financial position in conformity with generally accepted accounting principles. Thus, financial statement disclosures are those disclosures that are considered necessary for such a fair presentation. Criteria such as relevance, reliability, verifiability, freedom from bias, and comparability provide guidance in considering which disclosures are necessary for fair financial statement presentation.
b. Oil and gas producing companies currently disclose a considerable amount of information about their oil and gas producing activities in annual reports to shareholders, in published statistical summaries, in filings with the SEC, Department of Energy, and other regulatory agencies, and in other publicly available documents. Most of that information is currently presented outside the scope of the companies' financial statements. This Statement will result in some of that information being included in financial statements and, for many companies, will result in changes in the bases of preparing the information.
c. The disclosures required by this Statement relate only to those activities (acquisition, exploration, development, and production) for which this Statement establishes accounting standards; therefore, this Statement does not prescribe disclosures related to transporting, refining, and marketing of oil and gas or other activities of an oil and gas producing company.
d. As a general proposition, disclosures required for companies engaged in oil and gas producing activities should be similar to those required for companies in other industries.
e. As elaborated on in paragraphs 149-152, financial statements by themselves do not adequately portray the success of a company in finding and developing oil and gas reserves under either of the two historical cost methods of accounting for oil and gas producing activities—full costing or successful efforts costing. Under both methods, earnings are recognized at the time of sale, not at the time of discovery or production. Therefore, an important objective of the disclosures included in financial statements prepared by either of those historical cost methods should be to help the user of those statements relate a company's *efforts* (in terms of costs incurred in searching for and developing oil and gas reserves) and *accomplishments* (in terms of reserves discovered and developed).
f. The disclosure requirements must be consistent with and derived from the accounting standards established by this Statement. That is, a principal purpose of the disclosures should be to aid in understanding of the information *shown* in the financial statements of an oil and gas producing company. The disclosures should not be designed to present information that *might have been shown* in the financial statements had different accounting standards been established by this Statement.

Disclosures in Interim Financial Statements

234. This Statement does not require that the disclosures of reserve quantities and of acquisition, exploration, development, and production costs be included in interim financial statements, though they are required in annual financial statements. The Board reached that conclusion principally because problems in gathering data of that type on a timely basis become especially acute at interim reporting dates and, for some companies, the costs of that effort may be unduly burdensome. The Board presently has on its agenda a project on interim financial reporting in which the nature and extent of disclosures in interim financial statements are issues.

Disclosure of Information about Reserves

235. Most of the respondents to the Discussion Memorandum and most of the interviewees in the research effort described in paragraph 90(a) of Appendix A said that information about quantities of oil and gas reserves is essential to understand and interpret the financial statements of an oil and gas producing company. Many felt that reserve information is the single most important type of disclosure that could be required of an oil and gas producing company. They said that discovery of reserves is the critical event in the oil and gas production cycle and that reserves and changes in reserves are key indicators of the success of a company. In general, the Board agrees with those views. None of the methods of accounting considered by the Board in this project, not even discovery value

or current value accounting, would, in the Board's judgment, result in financial statements that would not need to be accompanied by disclosures of reserves and reserve changes. This Statement requires disclosure of information with respect to a company's oil and gas reserves.

236. The Board does not agree with the view, expressed by some, that mineral reserve information is not accounting information and, if disclosed at all, should not be included in financial statements. Those who take that position argue that while reserve information may indeed be important, it is too subjective, too frequently revised, too unreliable, too "soft" to be reported in financial statements. In the Board's judgment, however, certain reserve information has the qualities of verifiability, reliability, freedom from bias, comparability, and the like to a sufficiently reasonable degree to warrant its inclusion in financial statements. Accordingly, the Board concluded that reserve information is so helpful and essential to an understanding of the financial position, results of operations, and changes in financial position of an oil and gas producing company that the added relevance of the financial statements from including the information more than compensates for the lack of precision of estimates of reserves.

237. The Board considered the following broad areas of disclosure of information regarding oil and gas reserves:

a. Disclosure of reserve quantities:
   i. Estimated reserve quantities, by categories and types of reserves.
   ii. Changes in estimated reserve quantities, by categories and types of reserves.
   iii. Other disclosures relating to estimated reserve quantities, such as geographic locations, ownership characteristics, quality of reserves, and unusual risks and uncertainties.
b. Disclosure of reserve values:
   i. Estimated value of reserves.
   ii. Changes in estimated reserve values.
c. Description of assumptions and difficulties in estimating quantities or values of oil and gas reserves.

Disclosure of Reserve Quantities

238. This Statement relies on estimates of proved reserves and proved developed reserves for a number of capitalization and amortization determinations, and for the reasons discussed in paragraphs 235 and 236 disclosure of quantities of those categories of reserves, and of changes in those quantities, is required. In the Board's judgment, the constraints imposed on the estimator by the definitions of proved reserves and proved developed reserves in paragraph 271 of Appendix C will keep the subjectivity of the estimates to an acceptably low level for financial reporting purposes.

239. Reserve increases that result from successful exploration and development efforts and from purchases of minerals-in-place, net of decreases from production and sales of minerals-in-place, represent the *physical* expansion or contraction of the quantity of the company's reserves from the beginning to the end of the period. Revisions of previous estimates, on the other hand, represent a change to the quantity that was *perceived* to have existed at the beginning of the period. The categories of changes in reserve quantities required to be separately reported by paragraph 51 are intended to reflect those differences. Some respondents to the Exposure Draft disagreed with the inclusion of changes in reserves resulting from application of improved recovery techniques among other additions; they pointed out that such changes are normally classified by industry practice as revisions of previous estimates. This Statement reflects a change from the Exposure Draft in response to the foregoing concerns. Paragraph 51 provides for separate disclosure of changes resulting from improved recovery techniques if significant and for inclusion of those changes as revisions of previous estimates if not significant. Also, in response to comments on the Exposure Draft, paragraph 50 provides for exclusion of reserves relating to royalty interests owned if the reserve information is not available to the royalty owner. Also, paragraph 54(c) reflects a modification of the Exposure Draft to provide for separate disclosure of the investor's share of oil and gas reserves owned by an investee accounted for by the equity method.

240. Because enterprises' interests in foreign oil and gas reserves are affected by political, economic, and environmental risks and considerations that are often significantly different from the risks associated with domestic reserves, this Statement requires that reserve quantities and changes in them be reported separately for each geographic area in which significant reserves are located. That requirement comports with the conclusions of the Board in *FASB Statement No. 14,* "Financial Reporting for Segments of a Business Enterprise," which requires that the financial statements of a company that operates in different geographic areas report certain key information by geographic area.

241. Some persons propose that disclosure be required of estimated future development costs relating to proved undeveloped reserves. In the Board's view, disclosure of cost projections of that nature and tentativeness should not be required in financial statements of oil and gas producing companies. The question is not unique to the oil and gas

industry—indeed, the whole area of disclosure of forecasts is unsettled. To provide some indication of the extent to which development of proved reserves has been accomplished, paragraph 50 requires the separate reporting of year-end quantities of proved developed reserves. Further, the Board believes that estimates of reserves that are not classified as proved but that are regarded as probable reserves or possible reserves are too subjective to be required for inclusion in financial statements. Some persons have suggested that disclosure of those quantities be required.

242. Some foreign governments have nationalized or otherwise taken over, in whole or in part, certain properties in which oil and gas producing companies previously had mineral interests. Some of those interests have been converted into long-term supply, purchase, or similar agreements with the foreign government or a government authority. In some countries, oil and gas producing companies can obtain access to oil and gas reserves only through such agreements, and not through direct acquisition of a traditional type of mineral interest in a property. If an oil and gas producing company participates in the operation of a property subject to such an agreement or otherwise serves as "producer" of the reserves from the property, it is the Board's judgment that the reserve quantities identified with, and quantities of oil or gas received under, agreements with foreign governments or authorities should be disclosed in the company's financial statements. In view of the different nature of those agreements, however, paragraph 53 requires that those reserve quantities be separately reported from the company's regular proved reserves. The fact that the reserves are available to the company under agreements that differ from domestic agreements does not justify excluding those reserves from the accounting and disclosure provisions of this Statement as long as the foreign agreements, in substance, represent the right to *extract* oil and gas.

243. Although the Exposure Draft had proposed to include in an investor's reserve quantities, for purposes of the disclosures required by paragraphs 50-56 of this Statement, the investor's share of reserves owned by an investee accounted for by the equity method, some respondents to the Exposure Draft pointed out that the investor's financial statements do not include the investee's individual assets, liabilities, revenues, or expenses. They questioned therefore the propriety of including the investee's reserves in the investor's. The Board is persuaded that the better approach is not to commingle the investee's and investor's reserves in the investor's disclosures but, rather, to require separate disclosure of the investee's reserves at year-end. Paragraph 54(c) reflects the revised requirement.

244. Some persons believe that information about ownership characteristics (for example, whether reserves are owned in fee, by domestic lease agreement, or by concession from a foreign government) and about quality of reserves (for example, sulphur or paraffin content or specific gravity) should accompany disclosure of reserve quantities. Because of differences from property to property in those types of characteristics, for many companies the disclosures either would be so broad and general that they would be of little or no value to financial statement users or they would be so detailed and voluminous that they could overwhelm or confuse financial statement users rather than inform them. Consequently, the Board believes that explanations of that type should not be required in general purpose financial statements. For similar reasons, this Statement does not require a description of the assumptions used and difficulties involved in estimating quantities of oil and gas reserves.

Disclosure of Reserve Values

245. The fact that the Board rejected both discovery value and current value as bases of accounting for oil and gas reserves did not, of itself, mean that the Board automatically had rejected estimated reserve values as additional financial statement disclosures. The Board viewed the use of estimated reserve values as the basis of accounting for oil and gas producing companies and the disclosure of estimated reserve values as part of the financial statements of those companies as separable decisions, although, of course, many common considerations are involved.

246. The measurement problems discussed in paragraph 133 were important reasons for not requiring disclosure of estimated reserve values, as they were for not accepting discovery value or current value accounting. They were not, however, the only reasons.

247. As noted in paragraphs 138 and 140, various bases of accounting measurement, including both historical cost and current value measurements, are under consideration as part of the Board's conceptual framework project. The Discussion Memorandum on "Financial Accounting and Reporting in the Extractive Industries" did raise issues relating to methods of valuing mineral reserves. Relatively few respondents supported the use of discovery value or current value accounting or the disclosure of estimated reserve values, and the Board received only limited response to the valuation issues. The Board has decided not to resolve those issues for the limited purpose of this Statement.

248. The SEC's consideration of whether replacement cost disclosures or other reserve value disclo-

sures can be applied to mineral resource assets (discussed in paragraphs 82 and 96 of Appendix A to this Statement) is another reason that led the Board to reject disclosure of estimated reserve values at this time. The Welsch and Deakin study (paragraph 82) has two fundamental conclusions: that the replacement cost concept of SEC *Accounting Series Release No. 190* is not relevant to oil and gas reserves and that the preferred surrogate for replacement cost is a present value method that the study calls "Equivalent Purchase Cost." In its June 15, 1977 letter transmitting that study to the SEC, though, the American Petroleum Institute, sponsor of the study, stated:

> We see in the Equivalent Purchase Cost method many of the deficiencies which caused the research team to conclude that replacement cost is not relevant with respect to oil and gas reserves. The theoretical cost of a stream of future income fails to recognize that revenue sources cannot be replaced in kind and that they will originate in different environments with characteristics substantially different from the current revenue stream.
>
> The large majority of our Accounting Committee members cannot support this method on the grounds that the data provided would make little, if any, contribution to an investor's understanding of the economics of the business and, indeed, could be misleading.

249. In *Securities Act Release No. 5837,* dated June 20, 1977, the Commission stated:

> The Commission's staff has recently received, and is currently reviewing, the results of the research study together with recommendations of the American Petroleum Institute. No comments are being solicited on the disclosure of current value and current cost data until the evaluation of the American Petroleum Institute project is completed.

250. On October 26, 1977, in *Securities Act Release No. 5878,* the Commission proposed to rescind the requirement in *ASR No. 190* that certain registrants disclose replacement cost information about their mineral resource assets employed in oil and gas producing activities and, instead, to require registrants with mineral resource assets employed in oil and gas producing activities to disclose, in filings covering fiscal years ending on or after December 25, 1978, information based on the present value of future net revenues from estimated production of proved oil and gas reserves. The Commission has asked that comments on the proposal be submitted by March 31, 1978.

251. The FASB will be holding a public hearing beginning January 16, 1978 on the broad subject of accounting measurement, including the question of whether one or more of the various types of "current value" measurements should be reported in financial statements of companies generally.

252. The Board believes, therefore, that a decision as to whether reserve value information should be required to be included in financial statements should await consideration of the comments on the SEC proposal referred to in paragraph 250 and the written submissions and oral presentations in connection with the public hearing referred to in paragraph 251.

Disclosure of Capitalized Costs and of Costs Incurred

253. The disclosures of capitalized costs (paragraph 57) and of costs incurred (paragraphs 58 and 59) are intended to complement the disclosures of reserve quantities and changes therein. The reserve quantity disclosures are an indicator of *accomplishment.* Capitalized costs and costs incurred provide an indication of *effort.*

254. Reserves are considered the focal point for assessing *accomplishment* because of the importance of discovery as the most critical event in the oil and gas production cycle and of development as the next most important event. Similarly, *effort* is much more a function of incurring costs than it is a function of disbursing cash. As a consequence, the disclosures required by paragraphs 58 and 59 include not only expenditures for acquisition, exploration, development, and production but also the *depreciation* of support equipment and facilities that are *used* in those activities. It is not the *purchase* of seismic equipment or a drilling rig, for example, but rather the *use* of that seismic equipment and the drilling rig in exploration and development activities that is an indication of effort. Thus, as paragraph 58 points out, exploration, development, and production costs include the *depreciation* of the seismic equipment and drilling rig but exclude the *expenditures* to acquire that equipment. Likewise, it is the incurrence of acquisition, exploration, and development costs that best indicates effort in terms of *finding and developing reserves.*

255. The Exposure Draft had proposed to require certain special disclosures for a rate-regulated company that, under the Addendum to *APB Opinion No. 2,* follows an accounting policy that involves capitalizing or amortizing costs on a basis different from that otherwise required by this FASB Statement. Since the Exposure Draft, the Board has begun work on a project that involves reconsideration of the Addendum to *APB Opinion No. 2.* Because the question of special disclosures such as

those proposed in the Exposure Draft will be considered as part of that project, the Board has determined not to require the special disclosures that had been proposed.

Disclosure of Other Functional and Operating Data

256. Some persons propose that aggregate revenues and expenses for oil and gas producing activities be disclosed in financial statements. In the Board's view, a serious doubt exists as to whether those aggregate revenue and expense disclosures will contribute to an understanding of an enterprise's profitability as reflected in its financial statements. Many oil and gas producing companies do not derive revenue from oil and gas producing activities but rather from the sale of refined oil and gas products. For those companies, even if practicable, information about the results of operations of oil and gas producing activities standing alone, without similar information for the company's transportation, refining, and marketing activities and for its other operations, would represent only a fragment of the overall picture of the company.

257. Moreover, under the provisions of *FASB Statement No. 14,* the combined activities of acquisition, exploration, development, and production are not considered to be an industry segment of an integrated oil and gas company. Paragraph 10(a) of that Statement defines an industry segment as a "component of an enterprise engaged in providing a product or service or a group of related products and services *primarily to unaffiliated customers* (i.e., customers outside the enterprise) for a profit." (Emphasis added.) That paragraph goes on to say that "by defining an industry segment in terms of products and services that are sold primarily to unaffiliated customers, this Statement does not require the disaggregation of the vertically integrated operations of an enterprise." The Board reconsidered that decision as part of its project on the extractive industries and concluded that *FASB Statement No. 14* should not be amended to apply to oil and gas producing companies a disclosure requirement not required of companies in other industries.

258. For the reasons in paragraphs 256 and 257 this Statement does not require disclosure of functional data for oil and gas producing activities beyond the disclosures of capitalized costs and of costs incurred.

259. The Board considered various types of operating data as possible financial statement disclosures, in addition to the required disclosures relating to reserve quantities, including gross and net undeveloped acreage, gross and net productive acreage, and gross and net producing wells and well completions, and has concluded that those disclosures need not be included for a fair presentation of financial position, results of operations, and changes in financial position in conformity with generally accepted accounting principles.

Accounting for Income Taxes

260. This Statement reaffirms the conclusion of *FASB Statement No. 9* that oil and gas producing companies should apply interperiod income tax allocation, as described in *APB Opinion No. 11,* for all timing differences, including those relating to intangible drilling and development costs. *FASB Statement No. 9,* which this Statement supersedes, had permitted companies to recognize the interaction of book/tax timing differences with an anticipated future excess of statutory depletion over cost depletion in applying interperiod income tax allocation. As indicated in paragraph 16 of *FASB Statement No. 9,* the question of whether interaction should be recognized was left unresolved by the Accounting Principles Board in *APB Opinion No. 11* and was not addressed by the Financial Accounting Standards Board in *FASB Statement No. 9.* Although recognition of interaction was permitted by *FASB Statement No. 9,* it was not required. This Statement prohibits the recognition of interaction.

261. The Board has rejected the concept of interaction for several reasons. First, an excess of statutory depletion over the amount of cost depletion otherwise allowable as a tax deduction becomes a benefit only when it is actually realized via income tax deduction. The interaction concept anticipates the possible future benefit by recognizing it as a reduction of book income tax expense in advance of realization. In the Board's judgment, the uncertainties described in the next paragraph make it inappropriate to anticipate the possible future tax benefit in advance of realization.

262. Statutory depletion was eliminated or virtually eliminated for many companies by the *Tax Reduction Act of 1975* and was substantially reduced for many other companies by that Act. Further reductions are scheduled under that Act and subsequent legislation. Also, the law imposes certain limitations to statutory depletion that depend on future production, future sales prices, and future costs, all of which are difficult to estimate but which must be estimated if interaction is to be recognized. The uncertainties identified in this paragraph cause serious concern about anticipating tax benefits from future statutory depletion.

263. Moreover, the interaction concept is inconsistent with the deferred method of income tax allocation described in paragraphs 19 and 34-37 of *APB*

Opinion No. 11. Although the recognition of interaction is consistent, in some respects, to the "partial allocation" theory discussed in paragraphs 26-28 of that Opinion, the APB rejected the partial allocation theory in favor of comprehensive income tax allocation by the deferred method (paragraphs 29-32 of that Opinion).

264. The concept of interaction is, essentially, a "cover" concept: Deferred income taxes that otherwise relate to *current* period pretax accounting income need not be recognized to the extent of offsetting possible *future* income tax benefits from excess statutory depletion. The Board has expressly rejected the "cover" concept in reaching certain decisions in this Statement (see paragraphs 175 and 176) and in *FASB Statement No. 8,* "Accounting for the Translation of Foreign Currency Transactions and Foreign Currency Financial Statements" (see paragraphs 174-180 of that Statement).

Effective Date and Transition

265. This Statement was made effective for fiscal years beginning after December 15, 1978 to allow an oil and gas producing company sufficient time to gather the necessary data, modify its accounting systems, and otherwise prepare for transition to the accounting standards established by this Statement. The Exposure Draft had proposed a June 15, 1978 effective date; the change to December 15, 1978 is intended to give all companies at least one year to prepare for the change and to explain any impact it may have to investors and creditors. Voluntary adoption of the provisions of this Statement prior to its effective date is not prohibited by this Statement.

266. For several reasons, the Board has concluded that the provisions of this Statement should be applied retroactively by restating the financial statements of prior periods. First, unlike FASB pronouncements that deal with a comparatively narrow accounting question, the standards established by this Statement prescribe the fundamental basis by which the financial statements of an oil and gas producing company shall be prepared. Moreover, because many variations of successful efforts accounting have heretofore been applied in practice, this Statement is likely to have an impact on the financial statements of a great many oil and gas producing companies, not just those companies presently using the full cost method. In the Board's judgment, because of the magnitude and pervasiveness of the impact of this Statement, restatement will result in the most meaningful and comparable financial statements of all oil and gas producing companies.

267. Further, in paragraph 27 of *APB Opinion No. 20,* the Accounting Principles Board cited a change to or from the full cost method of accounting in the extractive industries as one of three special types of changes in accounting principle that should be reported by applying retroactively the new method in restatements of prior periods.

268. The Board recognizes that some companies may encounter some difficulties in accumulating the necessary data or in making after-the-fact estimates or judgments to apply the provisions of this Statement retroactively. The Board believes, however, that the added interperiod and intercompany comparability thus obtained outweighs any cost-saving advantages of prospective application or the cumulative effect method. Further, because of (a) the diversity of cost capitalization and amortization practices heretofore followed by both full cost and successful efforts companies and (b) the fact that amortization of some previously capitalized costs could continue for ten, twenty, thirty, forty, or more years, the Board concluded that prospective application of the standards established by this Statement is inappropriate.

269. With regard to some of the restatement problems cited by some respondents to the Exposure Draft, paragraph 64 points out that a provision of this Statement that would not have a significant effect on prior years' financial statements need not be retroactively applied. Also, in response to questions raised in letters of comment on the Exposure Draft, paragraph 64 allows the use of "hindsight" information in making the retroactive restatements except that reserve estimates should not now be revised in retrospect.

Appendix C

GLOSSARY

270. This glossary defines certain terms as they are used in this Statement.

271. The definitions of categories of *reserves* used in this Statement are those set forth in the regulations of the Securities and Exchange Commission:[11]

> *Proved reserves.* Those quantities of crude oil, natural gas, and natural gas liquids which, upon analysis of geologic and engineering data, appear with reasonable certainty to be recoverable in the future from known oil and gas reservoirs under existing economic and operating conditions. Proved reserves are limited to those

[11] Adopted May 12, 1976, in Securities Act Release No. 5706, which deals with disclosure of estimates of oil and gas reserves in registration statements, proxy statements, and reports filed with the Commission.

quantities of oil and gas which can be expected, with little doubt, to be recoverable commercially at current prices[12] and costs, under existing regulatory practices and with existing conventional equipment and operating methods. Depending upon their status of development, such proved reserves are subdivided into "proved developed reserves" and "proved undeveloped reserves."

Proved developed reserves. Reserves which can be expected to be recovered through existing wells with existing equipment and operating methods. Proved developed reserves include both (a) proved developed *producing* reserves (those that are expected to be produced from existing completion intervals now open for production in existing wells) and (b) proved developed *nonproducing* reserves (those that exist behind the casing of existing wells, or at minor depths below the present bottom of such wells, which are expected to be produced through these wells in the predictable future, where the cost of making such oil and gas available for production should be relatively small compared to the cost of a new well). Additional oil and gas expected to be obtained through the application of fluid injection or other improved recovery techniques for supplementing the natural forces and mechanisms of primary recovery should be included as "proved developed reserves" only after testing by a pilot project or after the operation of an installed program has confirmed through production response that increased recovery will be achieved.

Proved undeveloped reserves. Reserves which are expected to be recovered from new wells on undrilled acreage, or from existing wells where a relatively major expenditure is required for recompletion. Reserves on undrilled acreage shall be limited to those drilling units offsetting productive units, which are reasonably certain of production when drilled. Proved reserves for other undrilled units can be claimed only where it can be demonstrated with certainty that there is continuity of production from the existing productive formation. Under no circumstances should estimates for proved undeveloped reserves be attributable to any acreage for which an application of fluid injection or other improved recovery technique is contemplated, unless such techniques have been proved effective by actual tests in the area and in the same reservoir.

272. The following is the definition of a *field* used in this Statement:

Field. An area consisting of a single reservoir or multiple reservoirs all grouped on or related to the same individual geological structural feature and/or stratigraphic condition. There may be two or more reservoirs in a field which are separated vertically by intervening impervious strata, or laterally by local geologic barriers, or by both. Reservoirs that are associated by being in overlapping or adjacent fields may be treated as a single or common operational field. The geological terms "structural feature" and "stratigraphic condition" are intended to identify localized geological features as opposed to the broader terms of basins, trends, provinces, plays, areas-of-interest, etc.

273. The foregoing definition of a field relies, in turn, on the definition of a reservoir. The following definition shall be used for purposes of this Statement:

Reservoir. A porous and permeable underground formation containing a natural accumulation of producible oil or gas that is confined by impermeable rock or water barriers and is individual and separate from other reservoirs.

274. For purposes of this Statement, the following definitions of wells shall be used:

Exploratory well. An exploratory well is a well that is not a development well, a service well, or a stratigraphic test well as those terms are defined below.

Development well. A development well is a well drilled within the proved area of an oil or gas reservoir to the depth of a stratigraphic horizon known to be productive.

Service well. A service well is a well drilled or completed for the purpose of supporting production in an existing field. Wells in this class are drilled for the following specific purposes: gas injection (natural gas, propane, butane, or flue gas), water injection, steam injection, air injection, salt-water disposal, water supply for injection, observation, or injection for in-situ combustion.

Stratigraphic test well. A stratigraphic test is a

[12]The term *current prices* is elaborated on by the SEC in *Securities Act Release No. 5837* as follows: "Current prices include consideration of changes in existing prices provided by contractual arrangements, by law, or by regulatory agencies, where applicable; and for changes in prices for gas to be produced subsequent to termination or expiration of existing contracts, which latter prices should be based on current prices plus escalation for similar production subject to the entity's or other entities' recent contracts." The term "escalation" is further elaborated on in *SEC Release No. 5877* as follows: "The 'escalation' referred to in these releases is limited to specific escalation provisions in recent contracts. Escalations to reflect future price expectations are not permitted."

drilling effort, geologically directed, to obtain information pertaining to a specific geologic condition. Such wells customarily are drilled without the intention of being completed for hydrocarbon production. This classification also includes tests identified as core tests and all types of expendable holes related to hydrocarbon exploration. For purposes of this Statement, stratigraphic test wells (sometimes called "expendable wells") are classified as follows:

1. *Exploratory-type stratigraphic test well.* A stratigraphic test well not drilled in a proved area.
2. *Development-type stratigraphic test well.* A stratigraphic test well drilled in a proved area.

275. The term *proved area* is used in the foregoing definitions of development well, exploratory-type stratigraphic test well and development-type stratigraphic test well. As used therein, a *proved area* is the part of a property to which proved reserves have been specifically attributed.

Statement of Financial Accounting Standards No. 20
Accounting for Forward Exchange Contracts

an amendment of FASB Statement No. 8

STATUS

Issued: December 1977

Effective Date: January 1, 1978

Affects: Amends FAS 8, paragraphs 27 and 35

Affected by: Superseded by FAS 52

Statement of Financial Accounting Standards No. 20
Accounting for Forward Exchange Contracts

an amendment of FASB Statement No. 8

CONTENTS

INTRODUCTION AND BACKGROUND INFORMATION

1. Paragraph 27 of *FASB Statement No. 8,* "Accounting for the Translation of Foreign Currency Transactions and Foreign Currency Financial Statements," specifies conditions that must be met to defer a gain or loss on a forward exchange contract (*forward contract*). Paragraph 27 states that:

> . . . a forward contract shall be considered a hedge of an identifiable foreign currency commitment . . . , provided *all* of the following conditions are met:
> a. The life of the forward contract extends from the foreign currency commitment date to the anticipated transaction date . . . or a later date. . . .
> b. The forward contract is denominated in the same currency as the foreign currency commitment and for an amount that is the same or less than the amount of the foreign currency commitment.
> c. The foreign currency commitment is firm and uncancelable.

With respect to the application of those conditions, the FASB has been asked:

a. Whether an enterprise may defer a gain or loss on a forward contract that is intended to hedge a commitment that was entered into before the effective date of *FASB Statement No. 8*[1] even though the life of the forward contract does not extend from the commitment date.
b. Whether an enterprise may defer a gain or loss on a portion of a forward contract in excess of the related commitment to the extent that the forward contract is intended to provide a hedge of the commitment on an after-tax basis, i.e., to assure that the gain or loss on the forward contract offsets the effects of an exchange rate change on the foreign currency exposure related to the commitment, after considering the net related tax effects.

Hedging a Commitment Entered into before FASB Statement No. 8 Became Effective

2. By specifying that the life of a forward contract must extend from the foreign currency commitment date, paragraph 27(a) of *FASB Statement No. 8* would appear to preclude the deferral of a gain or loss on any forward contract entered into after the commitment date. However, that was not the intent of the Board if a forward contract is intended to hedge a commitment entered into before the effective date of Statement No. 8. Accordingly, the Board is specifying a transition period during which an enterprise may enter into a forward contract to hedge an existing commitment that was entered into before the effective date of Statement No. 8. For purposes of determining compliance with the conditions for deferral of a gain or loss, such a forward contract will be considered to have met the condition of paragraph 27(a) even though its life does not extend from the foreign currency commitment date.

Hedging on an After-Tax Basis

3. Paragraph 24 of *FASB Statement No. 8* states, "a gain or loss shall be deferred and included in the measurement of the dollar basis of the related foreign currency transaction if the gain or loss pertains to a forward contract that is intended to be a hedge of an identifiable foreign currency commitment that meets the conditions described in paragraph 27." The reason for that requirement is explained in paragraphs 207 and 208 of Statement No. 8.

4. Paragraph 27 of *FASB Statement No. 8* limits the deferral of a gain or loss on a forward contract to the gain or loss pertaining to the portion of the forward contract that is not in excess of the related

[1]For purposes of this Statement, the effective date of Statement No. 8 means the date that an enterprise first applied the provisions of Statement No. 8.

commitment. Thus, any gain or loss pertaining to a portion of a forward contract in excess of the related commitment is included in the determination of net income currently. After consideration of the question of hedging on an after-tax basis, the Board has decided that paragraph 27 of Statement No. 8 should be amended to require the deferral of a gain or loss on a portion of a forward contract *in excess of the related commitment* if certain conditions have been met. Those conditions are specified in paragraph 10 of this Statement.

5. An Exposure Draft of a proposed Statement on "Accounting for Forward Exchange Contracts" was issued on November 7, 1977. The Board received 30 letters of comment in response to the Exposure Draft, virtually all of which expressed agreement.

6. Some respondents recommended that the final Statement should include other amendments of *FASB Statement No. 8* in addition to the provisions in the Exposure Draft, including an amendment to permit the gain or loss pertaining to a hedge of a net monetary position on an after-tax basis to be determined by the method specified in paragraph 25 of Statement No. 8. The Board concluded that consideration of other possible amendments of Statement No. 8 should not delay the issuance of this Statement and noted that the determination of the gain or loss pertaining to a hedge of a net monetary position on an after-tax basis by the method specified in paragraph 25 is not now precluded by Statement No. 8.

7. Some respondents questioned whether the requirement of the Exposure Draft to include the gain or loss pertaining to the portion of a forward contract that is intended to provide a hedge on an after-tax basis as an offset to the related tax effects is contrary to *APB Opinion No. 11,* "Accounting for Income Taxes." The Board concluded that such a requirement is not contrary to Opinion No. 11 and does not modify the disclosure requirements of paragraph 60 of that Opinion. However, the Board concluded that tax effects related to a hedge of a net monetary position should not be offset. The Board believes that with respect to a hedge of a commitment the requirement to offset a gain or loss against the related tax effects is consistent with paragraph 24 of *FASB Statement No. 8,* which requires a deferred gain or loss pertaining to a forward contract that is intended to hedge an identifiable commitment to be included as an adjustment of the dollar basis of the foreign currency transaction. Further, the Board believes that with respect to a hedge of a net monetary position the requirement not to offset the related tax effects is consistent with the conclusion in paragraph 212 of Statement No. 8, which views such forward contracts as independent transactions.

8. The Board has concluded that on the basis of existing data it can reach an informed decision without a public hearing and that the effective date and transition specified in paragraphs 14 and 15 are advisable in the circumstances.

STANDARDS OF FINANCIAL ACCOUNTING AND REPORTING

9. For purposes of applying paragraph 27 of *FASB Statement No. 8,* a forward contract that is intended to hedge an identifiable foreign currency commitment entered into before the effective date of Statement No. 8 shall be deemed to have met the conditions specified in paragraph 27(a) of Statement No. 8 if the life of the forward contract extends from a date prior to March 31, 1978 to the anticipated transaction date[2] or a later date.[3]

10. If the conditions of paragraph 27 of *FASB Statement No. 8* as amended are met, a gain or loss pertaining to a portion of a forward contract *in excess of the related commitment* shall be deferred to the extent that the forward contract is intended to provide a hedge on an after-tax basis. A gain or loss so deferred shall be included as an offset to the related tax effects in the period in which such tax effects are recognized.[4] A gain or loss that has been offset against related tax effects shall not be included in the aggregate exchange gain or loss disclosure required by paragraph 32 of Statement No. 8.

11. A gain or loss pertaining to the portion of a forward contract in excess of the amount that provides a hedge on an after-tax basis shall not be deferred. Likewise, a gain or loss pertaining to a period after the transaction date of the related commitment shall not be deferred.

Amendments to FASB Statement No. 8

12. Paragraph 35 of *FASB Statement No. 8* is amended to add the following as the last sentence:

> For purposes of applying the provisions of paragraph 27(a) of this Statement, *FASB Statement No. 20* provides a limited exception for forward contracts that are intended to hedge commit-

[2]See footnote 9 of Statement No. 8.

[3]See footnote 10 of Statement No. 8.

[4]The requirement to offset such gains or losses against the related tax effects does not modify the disclosure requirements of paragraph 60 of *APB Opinion No. 11.*

ments entered into before the provisions of this Statement are initially applied.

13. The words "and for an amount that is the same or less than the amount of the foreign currency commitment" in paragraph 27(b) of *FASB Statement No. 8* are deleted. The last two sentences of paragraph 27 of Statement No. 8 are superseded by the following:

> The portion of a forward contract that shall be accounted for pursuant to paragraph 24 is limited to the amount of the related commitment. If a forward contract that meets conditions (a) through (c) above exceeds the amount of the related commitment, the gain or loss pertaining to a portion of the forward contract in excess of the commitment shall be deferred to the extent that the forward contract is intended to provide a hedge on an after-tax basis. A gain or loss so deferred shall be included as an offset to the related tax effects in the period in which such tax effects are recognized. A gain or loss that has been offset against related tax effects shall not be included in the aggregate exchange gain or loss disclosure required by paragraph 32. A gain or loss pertaining to the portion of a forward contract in excess of the amount that provides a hedge on an after-tax basis shall not be deferred. Likewise, a gain or loss pertaining to a period after the transaction date of the related commitment shall not be deferred.

Effective Date and Transition

14. This Statement shall be effective prospectively beginning January 1, 1978. Earlier application is encouraged in financial statements for annual and interim periods ending before January 1, 1978 that have not been previously issued. Previously issued annual or interim financial statements shall not be restated to comply with the provisions of this Statement.

15. An enterprise that has hedged a foreign currency commitment with a forward contract that meets the conditions of paragraph 27 of *FASB Statement No. 8* as amended, and, prior to March 31, 1978, has entered into a forward contract for an amount in excess of the related commitment shall defer the gain or loss on the amount of the excess that is intended to provide a hedge on an after-tax basis. Any gain or loss with respect to such excess that has been previously recognized in the determination of net income shall not be restated.

The provisions of this Statement need not be applied to immaterial items.

This Statement was adopted by the unanimous vote of the seven members of the Financial Accounting Standards Board.

Marshall S. Armstrong, *Chairman*
Oscar S. Gellein
Donald J. Kirk
Arthur L. Litke
Robert E. Mays
Robert T. Sprouse
Ralph E. Walters

Appendix A

EXAMPLE OF APPLICATION OF THIS STATEMENT

16. The following example provides guidance for applying paragraphs 10 and 11 of this Statement.

General Assumptions

17. Assume the following:

a. ABC Company and XYZ Company, a wholly owned foreign subsidiary of ABC Company, both have fiscal years ending December 31.
b. On November 1, 1978, when the exchange rate is FC1 = $1, XYZ Company enters into a commitment to sell for FC2,120,000 on March 1, 1979 certain previously acquired and paid for assets having a cost of FC1,720,000 ($1,720,000).
c. Foreign income is subject to foreign taxes at the rate of 10 percent.
d. U.S. income is subject to U.S. taxes at the rate of 48 percent.
e. XYZ Company will invest its undistributed earnings indefinitely. Accordingly, under the provisions of *APB Opinion No. 23,* "Accounting for Income Taxes—Special Areas," no U.S. income taxes are provided on XYZ Company's undistributed earnings in ABC Company's consolidated financial statements.
f. The forward rate is FC1 = $1. (This example assumes that there is no premium or discount.)

18. Given the above assumptions, if the exchange rate does not change, ABC Company's reportable pre-tax profit in dollars from the transaction is

$400,000 [$2,120,000 (FC2,120,000 × $1) selling price less $1,720,000 cost] and reportable after-tax profit in dollars is $360,000 [$400,000 pre-tax profit less $40,000 (FC40,000 × $1) foreign taxes].

19. Assume the same information as given in paragraph 17 and that the exchange rate changes on December 31, 1978 to FC1 = $.90 and that it remains unchanged through March 1, 1979. In this case, ABC Company's reportable pre-tax profit in dollars from the transaction is $188,000 [$1,908,000 (FC2,120,000 × $.90) selling price less $1,720,000 cost] and reportable after-tax profit is $152,000 [$188,000 pre-tax profit less $36,000 (FC40,000 × $.90) foreign taxes].

20. Assume further that on November 1, 1978 ABC Company entered into a forward contract to sell forward FC5,000,000 for delivery on March 1, 1979 to hedge XYZ Company's commitment on an after-tax basis and to hedge a specific exposed monetary item of FC1,000,000 of ABC Company. The amount of a forward contract necessary to hedge the sales commitment in full on an after-tax basis is FC4,000,000, computed by dividing the net foreign currency exposure of FC2,080,000 by 52 percent (the complement of the U.S. income tax rate of 48 percent). In other words, a forward contract of FC4,000,000 assures that the effects of any exchange rate change on the foreign currency exposure related to the commitment will be offset by the gain or loss on the forward contract, after considering the net related tax effects. Accordingly, pursuant to paragraph 11 of this Statement, ABC Company cannot defer any gain or loss pertaining to the portion of the forward contract in excess of FC4,000,000. Given the above assumptions, an exchange rate change to FC1 = $.90 on December 31, 1978 results in the following:

Gain on forward contract (determined by the method specified in paragraph 25 of Statement No. 8):

Total forward contract	FC	5,000,000
Exchange rate change	×	($1–$.90)
Gain on forward contract	$	500,000
Portion of gain deferrable as a hedge of foreign currency sales commitment:		
Forward contract	FC	2,120,000
Exchange rate change	×	($1–$.90)
Gain deferrable as a hedge of foreign currency sales commitment	$	212,000
Portion of gain deferrable as a hedge of the net related tax effects (pursuant to paragraph 10 of this Statement):		
Forward contract	FC	1,880,000
Exchange rate change	×	($1–$.90)
Gain deferrable as hedge of net related tax effects	$	188,000
Portion of gain to be recognized in period in which exchange rate changes (pursuant to paragraph 11 of this Statement):		
Forward contract	FC	1,000,000
Exchange rate change	×	($1–$.90)
Gain to be recognized in period in which exchange rate changes	$	100,000
Calculation of net related tax effects:		
Amount of forward contract intended to hedge the sales commitment on an after-tax basis	FC	4,000,000
Exchange rate change	×	($1–$.90)
Gain on forward contract	$	400,000
U.S. income tax rate		48%
U.S. income taxes attributable to the gain on the forward contract		192,000
Reduction of foreign taxes in dollars resulting from exchange rate change (see below)		4,000
Net related tax effects	$	188,000
Calculation of reduction of foreign taxes in dollars resulting from exchange rate change:		
Selling price	FC	2,120,000
Cost		1,720,000
Pre-tax profit	FC	400,000
Foreign tax rate		10%
Foreign taxes	FC	40,000
Exchange rate change	×	($1–$.90)
Reduction of foreign taxes in dollars resulting from exchange rate change	$	4,000

If the exchange rate remains at FC1 = $.90 through March 1, 1979, pursuant to paragraph 24 of *FASB Statement No. 8,* the deferred gain of $212,000 would be included in the measurement of the dollar basis of the selling price of the assets on March 1, 1979. Also, pursuant to paragraph 10 of this Statement, the deferred gain of $188,000 would be included as an offset to the related tax effects in the period in which such tax effects are recognized.

Statement of Financial Accounting Standards No. 21 Suspension of the Reporting of Earnings per Share and Segment Information by Nonpublic Enterprises

an amendment of APB Opinion No. 15 and FASB Statement No. 14

STATUS

Issued: April 1978

Effective Date: April 30, 1978 retroactive to fiscal years beginning after December 15, 1976

Affects: Amends APB 15, paragraphs 5 and 45
Amends FAS 14, paragraph 41

Affected by: No other pronouncements

Statement of Financial Accounting Standards No. 21
Suspension of the Reporting of Earnings per Share and Segment Information by Nonpublic Enterprises

an amendment of APB Opinion No. 15 and FASB Statement No. 14

CONTENTS

INTRODUCTION AND BACKGROUND INFORMATION

1. The Accounting Standards Division of the AICPA began a study of the application of generally accepted accounting principles (GAAP) to smaller or closely held enterprises in 1974 and issued its report on that study in August 1976. One of the major recommendations in that report states:

> The Financial Accounting Standards Board should develop criteria to distinguish disclosures that should be required by GAAP, which is applicable to the financial statements of all entities, from disclosures that merely provide additional or analytical data. (Some of these latter disclosures may, however, still be required in certain circumstances for certain types of entities.) The criteria should then be used in a formal review of disclosures presently considered to be required by GAAP and should also be considered by the Board in any new pronouncements.

The report also recommends that the FASB amend *APB Opinion No. 15,* "Earnings per Share," to require disclosure of earnings per share information only by enterprises whose securities are publicly traded. In addition to the recommendation contained in the AICPA report, a number of respondents to the FASB agenda project, "Conceptual Framework for Financial Accounting and Reporting: Objectives of Financial Reporting and Elements of Financial Statements of Business Enterprises," have expressed the view that the Board should distinguish between the information that should be included in financial statements and the so-called predictive, interpretive, or "soft" data that should be provided by financial reporting other than financial statements. Further, since the issuance in December 1976 of *FASB Statement No. 14,* "Financial Reporting for Segments of a Business Enterprise," the Board has received a number of suggestions that nonpublic enterprises be exempted from the requirements of that Statement. Others have suggested that segment information is an example of the type of interpretive or analytical information that should be presented outside the financial statements.

2. *APB Opinion No. 15* requires that earnings per share data be presented on the face of an enterprise's income statement and requires certain other disclosures in specified situations. *FASB Statement No. 14* requires disclosure of certain information relating to (a) the operations of an enterprise in different industries, (b) its foreign operations and export sales, and (c) its major customers. In its deliberations leading to the issuance of Statement No. 14, the Board considered whether certain enterprises should be exempted from disclosing segment information based on the size of the enterprise or whether its securities are publicly traded and concluded, for the reasons set forth in paragraph 70 of the Statement, that segment information should be included in the financial statements of all business enterprises.

3. The members of the Financial Accounting Standards Advisory Council and the FASB Screening Committee on Emerging Problems were consulted in January 1978 about the possibility of different applications of generally accepted accounting principles to small or closely held enterprises and large or public enterprises. Many of the members of the Advisory Council and the Screening Committee who advised the Board on this matter indicated that there should be a differentiation between disclosures required of small or closely held enterprises and disclosures required of large publicly traded enterprises and recommended that the Board add a project to its agenda to develop criteria for such a differentiation. Further, many of the members of the Advisory Council and the Screening Committee who advised the Board on this matter cited earnings per share and segment information as examples of disclosures that they believe should be optional for certain enterprises.

4. On February 23, 1978, the Board added to its agenda a major project to consider whether guidelines should be established for (a) distinguishing between information that should be disclosed in financial statements and information that should be disclosed in financial reporting otherwise and (b) distinguishing between information that all enterprises should be required to disclose and information that only designated types of enterprises should be required to disclose. Special attention will be given in that project to the financial statements and financial reporting of small or closely held enterprises.

5. In recognition of (a) the apparent pervasive public concern about the burden on small or closely held enterprises of compliance with certain financial statement disclosure requirements, (b) the recommendations of the AICPA report on "Generally Accepted Accounting Principles for Smaller and/or Closely Held Businesses," and (c) the recommendations of the members of the Board's Screening Committee on Emerging Problems and the Board's Advisory Council, the Board has concluded that application of *APB Opinion No. 15* and *FASB Statement No. 14* to nonpublic enterprises should be suspended, pending completion of the project referred to in paragraph 4. The Board will consider whether the disclosure requirements in pronouncements issued while that project is underway should be applicable to all enterprises.

6. An Exposure Draft of a proposed Statement of Financial Accounting Standards, "Suspension of the Reporting of Earnings per Share and Segment Information by Nonpublic Enterprises," was issued on February 27, 1978. The Board received 126 letters of comment in response to the Exposure Draft, most of which expressed agreement.

7. Some respondents recommended that the Board clarify whether the definition of "nonpublic" applies to a subsidiary, corporate joint venture, or other investee. The Board has a project on its agenda addressing the question of whether a complete set of financial statements of a parent company, a subsidiary, a corporate joint venture, or other investee accounted for by the equity method should include segment information when those financial statements are presented with consolidated financial statements. That project involves a reconsideration of the requirements of the last sentence of paragraph 7 of *FASB Statement No. 14.*[1] The Board concluded that it should not delay issuance of this Statement pending completion of its deliberations on that project. This Statement applies to a complete set of separately issued financial statements of a subsidiary, corporate joint venture, or other investee that is nonpublic as that term is used in this Statement. This Statement does not extend to those financial statements when presented in the financial report of another enterprise, as that matter is included in the scope of the project involving reconsideration of the last sentence of paragraph 7 of Statement No. 14 referred to above. An Exposure Draft of a proposed Statement of Financial Accounting Standards addressing that matter will be issued in the near future.

8. Some respondents noted that defining a nonpublic enterprise as an enterprise other than one whose debt or equity securities trade in a public market would exempt other kinds of enterprises with public participation from the requirements of *FASB Statement No. 14.* Those exempted enterprises include certain mutual associations, cooperatives, nonbusiness organizations, and partnerships that often make their financial statements available to a broad class, such as, insurance policyholders, depositors, members, contributors, or partners. The Board concluded that it should not delay the issuance of this Statement to refine the meaning of the term "nonpublic" at this time. Accordingly, the suspensions in paragraph 12 apply for the present to enterprises with a broad class of public participants that meet the "nonpublic" definition in paragraph 13. Those suspensions, however, should not be construed as an indication that the Board has decided that the information requirements for those enterprises are significantly different from those for an enterprise whose debt or equity securities are publicly traded.

9. Some respondents stated that the requirement of paragraph 39 of *FASB Statement No. 14* to disclose information about major customers should not be suspended. Those respondents believe that disclosure is necessary if an enterprise sells much of its output to one or relatively few other enterprises. Although this Statement suspends the application of Statement No. 14 to the financial statements of nonpublic enterprises, the Board notes that it does not

---

[1] The last sentence of paragraph 7 of *FASB Statement No. 14* states:

> When a complete set of financial statements that present financial position, results of operations, and changes in financial position in conformity with generally accepted accounting principles is presented for a subsidiary, corporate joint venture, or 50 percent or less owned investee, each such entity is considered to be an enterprise as that term is used in this Statement and thus is subject to its requirements whether those financial statements are issued separately or included in another enterprise's financial report.

affect the disclosure of information about economic dependency when such disclosure may be necessary for a fair presentation.[2]

10. Some respondents stated that the effective date and transition set forth in the Exposure Draft of the proposed Statement were too restrictive. They noted that financial statements issued prior to the effective date of this Statement may be reissued subsequent to its effective date for other than comparative purposes and recommended that disclosure of earnings per share and segment information for fiscal years ended prior to the effective date of this Statement should not be required in financial statements of nonpublic enterprises that are reissued for any reason subsequent to the effective date of this Statement. The Board accepted those views, and the provisions of this Statement are retroactive to fiscal years beginning after December 15, 1976, the effective date of *FASB Statement No. 14.*

11. The Board has concluded that on the basis of existing information it can reach an informed decision without a public hearing and the effective date and transition specified in paragraph 16 are advisable in the circumstances.

STANDARDS OF FINANCIAL ACCOUNTING AND REPORTING

12. This Statement suspends the requirements of *APB Opinion No. 15*[3] and *FASB Statement No. 14* in the financial statements of nonpublic enterprises as defined in paragraph 13. Therefore, this Statement suspends any requirement to disclose the information specified by Opinion No. 15 and Statement No. 14 in a complete set of separately issued financial statements of a subsidiary, corporate joint venture, or other investee that is a nonpublic enterprise.[4]

13. For purposes of this Statement, a nonpublic enterprise is an enterprise other than one (a) whose debt or equity securities trade in a public market on a foreign or domestic stock exchange or in the over-the-counter market (including securities quoted only locally or regionally) or (b) that is required to file financial statements with the Securities and Exchange Commission. An enterprise is no longer considered a nonpublic enterprise when its financial statements are issued in preparation for the sale of any class of securities in a public market.

14. Although the presentation of earnings per share and segment information is not required in the financial statements of nonpublic enterprises, any such information that is presented in the financial statements shall be consistent with the requirements of *APB Opinion No. 15* and *FASB Statement No. 14.*

Amendments to Existing Pronouncements

15. The following footnote is added to the end of the first sentence of paragraph 45 of *APB Opinion No. 15* and to the end of the first sentence of paragraph 41 of *FASB Statement No. 14* (as amended by *FASB Statement No. 18,* "Financial Reporting for Segments of a Business Enterprise—Interim Financial Statements: an amendment of FASB Statement No. 14"):

> The provisions of this [Opinion/Statement] were suspended by *FASB Statement No. 21* and need not be applied by a nonpublic enterprise as defined in that Statement pending further action by the FASB.

Effective Date and Transition

16. This Statement shall be effective April 30, 1978 retroactive to fiscal years beginning after December 15, 1976.

---

[2]Paragraph .05 of section 335, "Related Party Transactions," of *Statements on Auditing Standards* states:

> An entity may be economically dependent on one or more parties with which it transacts a significant volume of business, such as a sole or major customer, supplier, franchisor, franchisee, distributor, general agent, borrower, or lender. Such parties should not be considered related parties solely by virtue of economic dependency unless one of them clearly exercises significant management or ownership influence over the other. Disclosure of economic dependency may, however, be necessary for a fair presentation of financial position, results of operations, or changes in financial position in conformity with generally accepted accounting principles.

[3]This Statement does not suspend or modify other generally accepted accounting principles or practices (such as those specified in paragraph 15 of Chapter 13B, "Compensation Involved in Stock Option and Stock Purchase Plans," of *ARB No. 43* and paragraphs 10 and 11, "Liquidation Preference of Preferred Stock," of *APB Opinion No. 10*) that require disclosure of information concerning the capital structure of an enterprise.

[4]As mentioned in paragraph 7, the Board has a project on its agenda addressing the question of whether a complete set of financial statements of a parent company, a subsidiary, a corporate joint venture, or other investee accounted for by the equity method should include segment information when those financial statements are presented with consolidated financial statements.

The provisions of this Statement need not be applied to immaterial items.

This Statement was adopted by the affirmative votes of five members of the Financial Accounting Standards Board. Messrs. Mosso and Walters dissented.

Although Messrs. Mosso and Walters agree with the suspension of the application of *APB Opinion No. 15* and *FASB Statement No. 14* to the financial statements of small, closely held enterprises, they dissent because this amendment suspends the standards for many enterprises that do not meet reasonable tests of "small" or "closely held." Some are large complex enterprises whose financial reports are widely distributed. They may be in direct competition with enterprises whose securities are traded in public markets. The dissenters believe that suspension of Statement No. 14 for some of the large enterprises in an industry but not for others is not sustainable on the basis solely of differences in the form of ownership.

Members of the Financial Accounting Standards Board:

Donald J. Kirk, *Chairman*
Oscar S. Gellein
John W. March
Robert A. Morgan
David Mosso
Robert T. Sprouse
Ralph E. Walters

Statement of Financial Accounting Standards No. 22
Changes in the Provisions of Lease Agreements Resulting from Refundings of Tax-Exempt Debt

an amendment of FASB Statement No. 13

STATUS

Issued: June 1978

Effective Date: For lease agreement revisions entered into on or after July 1, 1978

Affects: Amends FAS 13, paragraphs 14 and 17(f)

Affected by: Footnote 1 superseded by FAS 76
Paragraph 11 superseded by FAS 71

Statement of Financial Accounting Standards No. 22 Changes in the Provisions of Lease Agreements Resulting from Refundings of Tax-Exempt Debt

an amendment of FASB Statement No. 13

CONTENTS

INTRODUCTION AND BACKGROUND INFORMATION

1. The FASB has been asked to reconcile an apparent inconsistency between *FASB Statement No. 13,* "Accounting for Leases," and *APB Opinion No. 26,* "Early Extinguishment of Debt," arising from refundings of tax-exempt debt, including advance refundings[1] that are accounted for as early extinguishments of debt. In some situations tax-exempt debt is issued to finance construction of a facility, such as a plant or hospital, that is transferred to a user of the facility by either lease or sale. A lease or, in the case of sale, a mortgage note generally serves as collateral for the guarantee of payments equivalent to those required to service the tax-exempt debt. Payments required by the terms of the lease or mortgage note are essentially the same, as to both amount and timing, as those required by the tax-exempt debt. In practice, a liability equivalent to the amount of the tax-exempt debt often has been included in the accounts of the lessee or the mortgagor. Some issuers of tax-exempt debt recently have entered into refundings and, concurrently, the terms of the related lease or mortgage note have been changed to conform with the terms of the refunding issue. If a refunding of tax-exempt debt results in a change in the provisions of a lease and the revised lease is classified as a capital lease by a lessee or a direct financing lease by a lessor, gain or loss is not recognized under Statement No. 13 (see paragraphs 14(a) and 17(f)(i) of the Statement). If a refunding of tax-exempt debt results in a change in the terms of a mortgage note, any gain or loss arising from the transaction because of the change in the carrying amount of the debt would be recognized currently in accordance with the provisions of Opinion No. 26.

Lessee Accounting

2. Paragraph 14(a) of *FASB Statement No. 13* sets forth the accounting by a lessee for a change in the provisions, a renewal, or an extension of an existing lease if the revised lease agreement is classified as a capital lease as follows:

> If the provisions of the lease are changed in a way that changes the amount of the remaining minimum lease payments and the change either (i) does not give rise to a new agreement . . . or (ii) does give rise to a new agreement but such agreement is also classified as a capital lease, the present balances of the asset and the obligation shall be adjusted by an amount equal to the difference between the present value of the future minimum lease payments under the revised or new agreement and the present balance of the obligation. The present value of the future minimum lease payments under the revised or new agreement shall be computed using the rate of interest used to record the lease initially.

3. In accounting for an early extinguishment of debt, paragraph 20 of *APB Opinion No. 26* requires that "a difference between the reacquisition price

[1]An advance refunding involves the issuance of new debt to replace existing debt with the proceeds from the new debt placed in trust or otherwise restricted to retire the existing debt at a determinable future date or dates. Descriptions of advance refundings that are and are not accounted for as early extinguishments of debt are presented in the AICPA Statement of Position on "Accounting for Advance Refundings of Tax-Exempt Debt."

and the net carrying amount of the extinguished debt should be recognized currently in income of the period of extinguishment as losses or gains. . . ." In this regard, paragraph 8 of *FASB Statement No. 4*, "Reporting Gains and Losses from Extinguishment of Debt," requires that "gains and losses from extinguishment of debt that are included in the determination of net income shall be aggregated and, if material, . . . classified as an extraordinary item, net of related income tax effect."

4. If a refunding of tax-exempt debt results in a change in the provisions of a capital lease that passes the perceived economic advantages of the refunding through to the lessee, paragraph 14(a) of *FASB Statement No. 13* requires the lessee to adjust both the asset and related obligation for any difference caused by a change in the provisions of a lease. If the perceived economic advantages of the same refunding had been passed through by a change in the terms of a mortgage note, the accounting specified by *APB Opinion No. 26* would result in the recognition of a gain or loss.

5. The Board considered the possibility of amending *APB Opinion No. 26* to defer recognition of gain or loss. That would not completely eliminate the inconsistency unless the gain or loss were included as an adjustment to the cost of the related property, because *FASB Statement No. 13* specifies that any difference resulting from a change in the provisions of a capital lease should be accounted for as an adjustment of the leased asset. In the interest of a timely resolution of the conflict, the Board decided that paragraph 14 of Statement No. 13 should be amended so that the accounting will be compatible with that specified by Opinion No. 26.

Lessor Accounting

6. Paragraph 17(f)(i) of *FASB Statement No. 13* specifies the accounting by a lessor for a change in the provisions, a renewal, or an extension of an existing lease if the revised lease agreement is classified as a direct financing lease as follows:

> If the provisions of a lease are changed in a way that changes the amount of the remaining minimum lease payments and the change either (a) does not give rise to a new agreement . . . or (b) does give rise to a new agreement but such agreement is classified as a direct financing lease, the balance of the minimum lease payments receivable and the estimated residual value, if affected, shall be adjusted to reflect the change . . . and the net adjustment shall be charged or credited to unearned income.

7. If a refunding of tax-exempt debt results in a change in the provisions of a lease that passes the perceived economic advantages of the refunding through to the lessee and the revised agreement is classified as a direct financing lease, paragraphs 18 (c) and 17(f)(i) of *FASB Statement No. 13* require the lessor to adjust the balance of the minimum lease payments receivable and unearned income. The lessor, on the other hand, would look to *APB Opinion No. 26* for guidance in accounting for a refunding. That Opinion requires recognition of a gain or loss concurrent with early extinguishments of debt. The Board has concluded that the accounting for changes in the provisions of a lease in connection with a refunding of tax-exempt debt should be compatible with the accounting for the refunding of the debt itself. The Board has, therefore, decided to amend paragraph 17 (f) of Statement No. 13 so that any gain or loss resulting from a change in the provisions of a lease agreement in connection with a refunding of tax-exempt debt is recognized when the tax-exempt debt is considered to have been extinguished.

Other Matters

8. An Exposure Draft of a proposed Statement on "Accounting for Leases: Changes in the Provisions of Lease Agreements Resulting from Refundings of Tax-Exempt Debt" was issued on December 19, 1977. The Board received 26 letters of comment in response to the Exposure Draft, most of which expressed general agreement.

9. Several respondents recommended that the final Statement should apply to all types of refundings and not be limited to refundings involving only tax-exempt debt. The Board noted that, typically, lessors in tax-exempt debt refundings are governmental or quasi-governmental agencies that are not affected by state or federal income tax regulations. For the most part, the governmental lessor's borrowing serves only to obtain necessary financing for the construction of the leased facilities. Refundings that do not involve tax-exempt debt may involve considerations beyond those normally present in the lessor/lessee relationship discussed above. The Board considered these recommendations and concluded that further consideration of the subject of refundings should not delay the issuance of this Statement.

10. The Board has concluded that on the basis of existing information it can reach an informed decision without a public hearing, and the effective date and transition specified in paragraph 16 are advisable in the circumstances.

11. The Addendum to *APB Opinion No. 2*, "Accounting for the 'Investment Credit'," states that "differences may arise in the application of generally accepted accounting principles as between reg-

ulated and nonregulated businesses, because of the effect in regulated businesses of the rate-making process" and discusses the application of generally accepted accounting principles to regulated industries. Accordingly, the provisions of the Addendum shall govern the application of this Statement to those operations of a company that are regulated for rate-making purposes on an individual-company-cost-of-service basis.

STANDARDS OF FINANCIAL ACCOUNTING AND REPORTING

12. If prior to the expiration of the lease term a change in the provisions of a lease results from a refunding by the lessor of tax-exempt debt, including an advance refunding,[2] in which the perceived economic advantages of the refunding are passed through to the lessee and the revised agreement is classified as a capital lease by the lessee or a direct financing lease by the lessor, the change shall be accounted for as follows:

a. Lessee accounting:

   i. If a change in the provisions of a lease results from a refunding by the lessor of tax-exempt debt, including an advance refunding that is accounted for as an early extinguishment of debt, the lessee shall adjust the lease obligation to the present value of the future minimum lease payments under the revised lease using the effective interest rate applicable to the revised agreement and shall recognize any resulting gain or loss currently as a gain or loss on early extinguishment of debt. Any gain or loss so determined shall be classified in accordance with *FASB Statement No. 4*.

   ii. If the provisions of a lease are changed in connection with an advance refunding by the lessor of tax-exempt debt that is not accounted for as an early extinguishment of debt at the date of the advance refunding and the lessee is obligated to reimburse the lessor for any costs related to the debt to be refunded that have been or will be incurred, such as unamortized discount or issue costs or a call premium, the lessee shall accrue those costs by the "interest" method[3] over the period from the date of the advance refunding to the call date of the debt to be refunded.

b. Lessor accounting:[4]

   i. If a change in the provisions of a lease results from a refunding of tax-exempt debt, including an advance refunding that is accounted for as an early extinguishment of debt, the lessor shall adjust the balance of the minimum lease payments receivable and the estimated residual value, if affected (i.e., the gross investment in the lease) in accordance with the requirements of paragraphs 18(c) and 17(f)(i) of *FASB Statement No. 13*. The adjustment of unearned income shall be the amount required to adjust the net investment in the lease to the sum of the present values of the two components of the gross investment based on the interest rate applicable to the revised lease agreement. The combined adjustment resulting from applying the two preceding sentences shall be recognized as a gain or loss in the current period.

   ii. If a change in the provisions of a lease results from an advance refunding that is not accounted for as an early extinguishment of debt at the date of the advance refunding, the lessor shall systematically recognize, as revenue, any reimbursements to be received from the lessee for costs related to the debt to be refunded, such as unamortized discount or issue costs or a call premium, over the period from the date of the advance refunding to the call date of the debt to be refunded.

13. The accounting prescribed in subparagraphs 12(a)(i) and 12(b)(i) for a refunding of tax-exempt debt is illustrated in Appendix A.

Amendments to FASB Statement No. 13

14. The introduction to paragraph 14 of *FASB Statement No. 13* is amended to read as follows:

> Except for a change in the provisions of a lease that results from a refunding by the lessor of tax-exempt debt, including an advance refunding, in which the perceived economic advantages of the refunding are passed through to the lessee by a change in the provisions of the lease agreement and the revised agreement is classified as a capital lease (see *FASB Statement No. 22*), a change in the provisions of a lease, a renewal or extension[14] of an existing lease, and a termina-

[2]See footnote 1.

[3]See paragraph 12 of *FASB Statement No. 13* and footnote 11 thereto.

[4]This paragraph prescribes the accounting for a direct financing lease by governmental units that classify and account for leases of that kind.

tion of a lease prior to the expiration of the lease term shall be accounted for as follows:

15. The introduction to paragraph 17(f) of *FASB Statement No. 13* is amended to read as follows:

> Except for a change in the provisions of a lease that results from a refunding by the lessor of tax-exempt debt, including an advance refunding, in which the perceived economic advantages of the refunding are passed through to the lessee by a change in the provisions of the lease agreement and the revised agreement is classified as a direct financing lease (see *FASB Statement No. 22*), a change in the provisions of a lease, a renewal or extension[19] of an existing lease, and a termination of a lease prior to the expiration of the lease term shall be accounted for as follows:

Effective Date and Transition

16. This Statement shall be effective for lease agreement revisions entered into on or after July 1, 1978. Earlier application is encouraged. In addition, the provisions of this Statement shall be applied retroactively at the same time and in the same manner as the provisions of *FASB Statement No. 13* are applied retroactively (see paragraphs 49 and 51 of Statement No. 13). Enterprises that have already applied the provisions of Statement No. 13 retroactively and have published annual financial statements based on the retroactively adjusted accounts before the effective date of this Statement may, but are not required to, apply the provisions of this Statement retroactively.

The provisions of this Statement need not be applied to immaterial items.

This Statement was adopted by the affirmative votes of five members of the Financial Accounting Standards Board. Messrs. March and Sprouse dissented.

Mr. March dissents because he believes the Statement will encourage differing treatment of similar transactions based merely on legal form rather than real substance. As stated in paragraph 1 of this Statement, tax-exempt debt refundings arise in situations where the user of a facility acquires that use by either a lease or sale. In either case, the governmental unit or authority often, if not usually, has no real liability to the holder of the debt who must look entirely to the resources of the lessee or mortgagor-purchaser. It is not logical to conclude that *FASB Statement No. 13* is even applicable under these circumstances. The logic of the provisions of paragraphs 7, 9, and 12(a) of this Statement rests on the substance of the lessee's obligations being the equivalent of debt.

The AICPA Statement of Position on "Accounting for Advance Refundings of Tax-Exempt Debt," referred to in footnote 1 of this Statement, requires users of such a facility that are mortgagors to record their obligations for both the refunding issue and the debt to be refunded in the future when the latter issue is not accounted for as an early extinguishment of debt. This Statement fails to state specific acceptance or rejection of the existing practice, referred to in paragraph 1, which recognizes the reality of the transaction by accounting for a lessee's obligations as debt in the same manner as a mortgagor. The Statement also fails to require presentation of the lessee's obligations under both the original and refunding debt issues still outstanding, in a manner parallel to the mortgagor; by such silence inviting the development of alternative practices.

Mr. Sprouse dissents because he believes that a loss related to an advance refunding is the result of past events (see paragraphs 8 and 9 of *APB Opinion No. 26*) and should be recognized at the time the refunding commitment is made and the loss becomes measurable (see paragraph 8 of *FASB Statement No. 5*). Despite identical changes in the cash flows required by a lease agreement, subparagraph 12(a)(i) of this Statement requires the lessee to immediately recognize a gain or loss while subparagraph 12(a)(ii) requires the lessee to spread the amount of that gain or loss over the period between the advance refunding and call date, depending on the way in which the lessor accounts for the related advance refunding of tax-exempt debt. Subparagraph 12(b)(i) and subparagraph 12(b)(ii) call for counterpart immediate recognition or systematic accrual by the lessor, respectively. Mr. Sprouse believes that a loss related to an advance refunding is not a function of future passage of time and therefore it should be recognized when it becomes known and measurable rather than spread over a future period of time.

Members of the Financial Accounting Standards Board:

Donald J. Kirk, *Chairman*
Oscar S. Gellein
John W. March
Robert A. Morgan
David Mosso
Robert T. Sprouse
Ralph E. Walters

Appendix A

ILLUSTRATION OF LESSOR AND LESSEE ACCOUNTING REQUIRED BY PARAGRAPH 12 OF THIS STATEMENT

17. The following example illustrates the application of the requirements of subparagraphs 12(a)(i) and 12(b)(i) of this Statement when a refunding of tax-exempt debt results in a change in the provisions of a lease agreement and the revised lease is classified as a direct financing lease by the lessor and as a capital lease by the lessee.

Computation Information

The following table summarizes the total debt service requirements of the serial obligation to be refunded and of the refunding obligation. It is presumed that the perceived economic advantages of the refunding results from the lower interest rate applicable to the refunding obligation. The resulting reduction in total debt service requirements will be passed through to the lessee by changing the terms of the related lease to conform with the debt service requirements of the refunding obligation. All costs that have been or that will be incurred by the lessor in connection with the refunding transaction will be passed through to the lessee.

Fifteen Year Serial Debt Service Requirements ($000 omitted):

Obligation to Be Refunded			Refunding Obligation*			
Face Amount	Interest 7%	Total	Face Amount	Interest 5%	Total	Difference
$50,000	$32,300	$82,300	$52,000	$23,150	$75,150	$7,150

LESSOR ACCOUNTING

Computation of Required Adjustments to Reflect Changes in the Terms of a Lease Resulting from a Refunding of Tax-Exempt Debt

Adjustment to Balance of Minimum Lease Payments Receivable:

Present balance of minimum lease payments receivable (equal to debt service requirements of obligation to be refunded)	$82,300,000
Minimum lease payments receivable under revised agreement (equal to debt service requirements of refunding obligation)	75,150,000
Adjustment to reflect reduction in minimum lease payments receivable	$ 7,150,000

Adjustment to Unearned Income:

Change in the sum of the present value of the two components of the gross investment using the interest rate applicable to each agreement	$ 2,000,000
Change in the balance of minimum lease payments receivable	7,150,000
Adjustment to reflect reduction in balance of unearned income	$ 9,150,000

Summary of Adjustments ($000 omitted):

	Minimum Lease Payments Receivable	Unearned Income	Net Investment
Balance before Refunding	$82,300	$32,300	$50,000
Adjustment	(7,150)	(9,150)	2,000
Balance after Refunding	$75,150	$23,150	$52,000

*The face amount of the refunding obligation ($52,000,000) is equal to the face amount of the obligation to be refunded ($50,000,000) plus the redemption premium applicable to the obligation to be refunded ($1,500,000) and the costs of issuance ($500,000).

Journal Entries to Record the Refunding and the Changes in the Terms of the Lease Resulting from the Refunding of Tax-Exempt Debt

Recoverable deferred issue costs	500,000	
Loss resulting from refunding of tax-exempt debt	1,500,000	
7% Outstanding obligation	50,000,000	
5% Refunding obligation		52,000,000

To record loss from refunding $50,000,000 – 7% obligation with $52,000,000 – 5% refunding obligation in accordance with the provisions of *APB Opinion No. 26*

Unearned income	9,150,000	
Minimum lease payments receivable		7,150,000
Gain resulting from adjustment of lease terms		1,500,000
Recoverable deferred issue costs		500,000

To adjust unearned income by the amount required to adjust the net investment in the lease to the sum of the present values of the two components of the gross investment based on the interest rate applicable to the revised lease agreement in accordance with *FASB Statement No. 22*.

LESSEE ACCOUNTING

Computation of Required Adjustment to Lease Obligation to Reflect Changes in the Terms of the Lease Resulting from a Refunding of Tax-Exempt Debt

Adjustment to Balance of Lease Obligation:

Present balance of lease obligation under original agreement	$50,000,000
Present value of future minimum lease payments under revised agreement	51,500,000
Adjustment to Lease Obligation	$ 1,500,000

Journal Entry to Record Adjustment to Lease Obligation Resulting from a Refunding of Tax-Exempt Debt

Loss resulting from revision to lease agreement	1,500,000	
Obligation under capital lease		1,500,000

To record the loss resulting from changes in the lease terms resulting from a refunding of tax-exempt debt. For purposes of calculating the present value of the future minimum lease payments, deferred issue costs were considered as additional interest in determining the effective interest rate applicable to the revised agreement. (The loss shall be classified in accordance with *FASB Statement No. 4*.)

Statement of Financial Accounting Standards No. 23
Inception of the Lease

an amendment of FASB Statement No. 13

STATUS

Issued: August 1978

Effective Date: For leasing transactions and revisions recorded as of December 1, 1978

Affects: Amends FAS 13, paragraphs 8(b), 10, 17(a), 18(a), 26(a)(i), and 43(c)
Supersedes FAS 13, paragraph 5(b)

Affected by: No other pronouncements

SUMMARY

Under *FASB Statement No. 13*, "Accounting for Leases," the *inception of the lease* is the date on which the classification of a lease is determined. The lease is recorded at the beginning of the lease term using the classification that was determined at the date of the inception of the lease. If property covered by a lease is yet to be constructed or has not yet been acquired by the lessor at the date of the lease agreement or any earlier commitment, this Statement:

- Changes the "inception of the lease" from the date that construction is completed or the property is acquired by the lessor to the date of the lease agreement or any earlier commitment. This change is intended to result in a lease classification that more closely reflects the substance of the transaction.
- Changes the lessee's determination of "fair value of the leased property" for a lease with a cost-based or similar escalator provision from the amount estimated on the inception date to an amount that is escalated to give effect to increases under the escalator clause, when:

  a. Fair value is used as a limitation on the amount of the asset to be recorded, or
  b. Fair value is used as a basis for allocation of recorded amounts between land and buildings.

  This change is intended to base the lessee's accounting on amounts that relate to the finally determined lease payments.

If the redefined "inception of the lease" is a date before the beginning of the lease term, with limited exceptions this Statement prohibits the recording of increases in estimated residual value that may occur between those two dates.

Statement of Financial Accounting Standards No. 23
Inception of the Lease

an amendment of FASB Statement No. 13

CONTENTS

INTRODUCTION AND BACKGROUND INFORMATION

1. The FASB has been asked to reconsider the application of *FASB Statement No. 13*, "Accounting for Leases," for a leasing transaction in which the lessor and lessee agree on lease terms prior to the construction of the asset to be leased. Paragraph 2 describes circumstances in which a literal application of Statement No. 13 can result in a lease classification that does not reflect the economic considerations that entered into the agreement.

2. A lease that is, in effect, a financing transaction might be classified as an operating lease by both parties rather than as a capital lease to the lessee and a direct financing lease to the lessor. That classification would result from application of the 90 percent recovery criterion in *FASB Statement No. 13* at the date of completion of construction instead of the earlier date of the agreement or commitment. If the fair value of the leased asset increases during the construction period, it is possible that the present value of the minimum lease payments at the beginning of the lease term could be more than 90 percent of the estimated fair value of the leased asset at the earlier agreement date but less than 90 percent of the fair value of the leased asset at the later date that construction is completed. On the other hand, if the fair value of the leased asset decreases during the construction period, a lease that would otherwise have been classified as a direct financing lease by the lessor might meet the criteria for classification as a sales-type lease, requiring recognition of a loss even though the terms of the lease were designed to provide full recovery of cost and a reasonable rate of return on net investment to the lessor.

3. In view of the matters discussed above, the Board concluded that it should amend the definition of "inception of the lease" in *FASB Statement No. 13* to make it the date of the lease agreement or any earlier commitment in all cases. Previously, if a lease were for property to be constructed or to be acquired by the lessor, the "inception of the lease" would have been the date that construction was completed or the property was acquired by the lessor. The purpose of the change is to make the classification of a lease, which is determined at its inception date, better reflect the economic considerations that entered into the agreement. This Statement also amends two paragraphs of Statement No. 13 to provide that, if a lease has a cost-based or similar construction period escalator clause, "fair value at the inception of the lease," for purposes of the lessee's recording of the lease, is escalated to reflect any increases under that clause.

4. An Exposure Draft of a proposed Statement on "Accounting for Leases—Inception of the Lease" was issued on December 19, 1977. The Board received 30 letters of comment in response to the Exposure Draft. Certain of the comments received and the Board's consideration of them are discussed in Appendix A, "Summary of Consideration of Comments on Exposure Draft."

5. The Board concluded that on the basis of existing information it can make an informed decision on the matters addressed by this Statement without a public hearing and that the effective date and transition specified in paragraph 11 are advisable in the circumstances.

STANDARDS OF FINANCIAL ACCOUNTING AND REPORTING

Amendments to FASB Statement No. 13

6. Paragraph 5(b) of *FASB Statement No. 13* is superseded by the following:

> *Inception of the lease.* The date of the lease agreement or commitment, if earlier. For purposes of this definition, a commitment shall be

in writing, signed by the parties in interest to the transaction, and shall specifically set forth the principal provisions of the transaction. If any of the principal provisions are yet to be negotiated, such a preliminary agreement or commitment does not qualify for purposes of this definition.

7. The following footnote is added to the end of the first sentence of paragraph 8(b) of *FASB Statement No. 13*:

> If the property covered by the lease is yet to be constructed or has not been acquired by the lessor at the inception of the lease, the classification criterion of paragraph 8(b) shall be applied at the date that construction of the property is completed or the property is acquired by the lessor.

8. The following footnote is added to the end of the second sentence of paragraph 10 of *FASB Statement No. 13* and to the end of the second sentence of paragraph 26(a)(i) of Statement No. 13:

> If the lease agreement or commitment, if earlier, includes a provision to escalate minimum lease payments for increases in construction or acquisition cost of the leased property or for increases in some other measure of cost or value, such as general price levels, during the construction or pre-acquisition period, the effect of any increases that have occurred shall be considered in the determination of "fair value of the leased property at the inception of the lease" for purposes of this paragraph.

9. Paragraphs 17(a) and 18(a) of *FASB Statement No. 13* are amended by adding the following final sentence and related footnote to each paragraph:

> The estimated residual value used to compute the unguaranteed residual value accruing to the benefit of the lessor shall not exceed the amount estimated at the inception of the lease except as provided in footnote*.
>
> ---
>
> *If the lease agreement or commitment, if earlier, includes a provision to escalate minimum lease payments for increases in construction or acquisition cost of the leased property or for increases in some other measure of cost or value, such as general price levels, during the construction or pre-acquisition period, the effect of any increases that have occurred shall be considered in the determination of "the estimated residual value of the leased property at the inception of the lease" for purposes of this paragraph.

10. Paragraph 43(c) of *FASB Statement No. 13* is amended by adding the following final sentence and related footnote:

> The estimated residual value shall not exceed the amount estimated at the inception of the lease except as provided in footnote†.
>
> ---
>
> †If the lease agreement or commitment, if earlier, includes a provision to escalate minimum lease payments for increases in construction or acquisition cost of the leased property or for increases in some other measure of cost or value, such as general price levels, during the construction or pre-acquisition period, the effect of any increases that have occurred shall be considered in the determination of "the estimated residual value of the leased property at the inception of the lease" for purposes of this paragraph.

Effective Date and Transition

11. The provisions of this amendment to *FASB Statement No. 13* shall be effective for leasing transactions recorded and lease agreement revisions (see paragraph 9 of Statement No. 13) recorded as of December 1, 1978 or thereafter. Earlier application is encouraged. In addition, except as provided in the next sentence, the provisions of this Statement shall be applied retroactively at the same time and in the same manner as the provisions of Statement No. 13 are applied retroactively (see paragraphs 49 and 51 of Statement No. 13). Enterprises that have already applied the provisions of Statement No. 13 retroactively and have published annual financial statements based on the retroactively adjusted accounts before the effective date of this Statement may, but are not required to, apply the provisions of this Statement retroactively.

The provisions of this Statement need not be applied to immaterial items.

This Statement was adopted by the unanimous vote of the seven members of the Financial Accounting Standards Board:

Donald J. Kirk, *Chairman*
Oscar S. Gellein
John W. March
Robert A. Morgan
David Mosso
Robert T. Sprouse
Ralph E. Walters

Appendix A

SUMMARY OF CONSIDERATION OF COMMENTS ON EXPOSURE DRAFT

12. The December 19, 1977 Exposure Draft proposed a complex amendment of the definition of *inception of the lease* in paragraph 5(b) of *FASB Statement No. 13*. The amended definition would have modified various determinations used for both classification of and accounting for a lease. The Exposure Draft also would have, in most cases, limited the amount recorded by the lessor for the residual value of the leased property to an amount not greater than the lessor's estimate as of inception of the lease.

13. Many respondents indicated that the proposed amendment was too complicated and requested clarification or simplification. Some respondents suggested that the Board separate lease classification from lease recording. Based on those comments, the Board made this final Statement a series of individual amendments that, in total, have approximately the same result as the Exposure Draft. The individual amendments are:

a. The definition of *inception of the lease* in paragraph 5(b) of *FASB Statement No. 13* is amended to make it the date of the lease agreement or any earlier commitment. This modification should result in a lessee's classification of a lease that reflects the economic considerations that entered into the agreement.
b. A footnote was added to paragraph 8(b) of Statement No. 13 to permit a lease of property that is to be constructed or acquired by the lessor to be classified as a sales-type lease or direct financing lease (providing it otherwise meets the criteria for those classifications) if there are no important uncertainties about unreimbursable costs yet to be incurred by the lessor at the date that the property is completed or acquired by the lessor, although there may have been such uncertainties at the inception of the lease. This modification and the modification described in paragraph 13(a) above, in combination, should result in a lessor's classification of a lease that reflects the economic considerations that entered into the agreement.
c. Footnotes were added to paragraphs 10 and 26(a)(i) of Statement No. 13 to require a lessee to escalate the "fair value at the inception of the lease," used as a limitation for amounts to be recorded and as a basis for allocation between land and buildings in a real estate lease, for the effects of an escalator provision. The footnotes apply only to leases that include cost-based or similar construction period or pre-acquisition period escalator provisions.
d. Paragraphs 9 and 10 of this Statement modify paragraphs 17(a), 18(a), and 43 of Statement No. 13 to limit the amount recorded by the lessor for the residual value of the leased property to an amount not greater than the estimate as of the inception of the lease. Footnotes were added to provide a limited exception to this requirement in the event that a lease includes a cost-based or similar construction period or pre-acquisition period escalator provision.
e. If a lease calls for adjustment of a lease provision because of specified changes occurring during a construction or pre-acquisition period, a new determination related to that occurrence may be appropriate if Statement No. 13 requires a determination at the inception of the lease for recording purposes. The Exposure Draft specified formula adjustments that would have applied to any lease provisions that call for adjustments. For simplicity, this Statement addresses only the usual cost-based or similar construction or pre-acquisition period escalator provisions (see paragraph 13(c) above). The parties to the lease should make the appropriate adjustments to record a lease if other types of construction period or pre-acquisition period contingency provisions are present. However, no adjustments should be made to reflect the effect of contingency provisions that continue during the lease term.

14. Some respondents questioned the application of the amended definition of inception of the lease to multiple "takedowns" of equipment under a master lease agreement. If a master lease agreement specifies that the lessee must take a minimum number of units or dollar value of equipment and if all other principal provisions are stated, the inception of the lease is the date of the master lease agreement with respect to the specified minimum. The inception of the lease for equipment "takedowns" in excess of the specified minimum is the date that the lessee orders the equipment because the lessee does not agree to lease the equipment until that date. To the extent that lease payments for required "takedowns" are based on value at the date of the "takedown," the lease, in effect, has a pre-acquisition period escalator provision based on value. Paragraphs 8-10 of this Statement address that situation. If a master lease agreement does not require the lessee to "takedown" any minimum quantity or dollar value of equipment, the agreement is merely an offer by the lessor to rent equipment at an agreed price and the inception of the lease is the date that the lessee orders the equipment.

15. Some respondents stated that retroactive application of the proposed Statement would require extensive recomputations to classify and account for

existing leases and questioned whether the cost would be justified. Many respondents, on the other hand, stated that retroactive application of the amended definition in the proposed Statement was necesary to reflect the economic considerations that entered into existing leases. The Board considered the problems of data accumulation and reconsidered whether to require retroactive application or to permit prospective application of this Statement. Paragraphs 115-119 of *FASB Statement No. 13* discuss the considerations that resulted in the requirement for retroactive application of that Statement. The same considerations influenced the Board in its decision to adopt the transition requirements in this Statement. This Statement permits, but does not require, retroactive application for enterprises that have already applied Statement No. 13 retroactively *and* have published *annual* financial statements based on the retroactively adjusted accounts. All other enterprises are required to apply the provisions of this Statement retroactively at the same time as they apply the provisions of Statement No. 13 retroactively. Companies with a large number of leases that are affected may be able to use aggregate computations or statistical sampling techniques to compute the required adjustments.

Statement of Financial Accounting Standards No. 24 Reporting Segment Information in Financial Statements That Are Presented in Another Enterprise's Financial Report

an amendment of FASB Statement No. 14

STATUS

Issued: December 1978

Effective Date: January 1, 1979 retroactive to fiscal years beginning after December 15, 1976

Affects: Amends FAS 14, paragraph 7

Affected by: No other pronouncements

SUMMARY

If consolidated or combined financial statements are accompanied by a complete set of separate parent company or investee company (or group of investee companies) financial statements, this Statement eliminates the requirement to disclose segment information in the separate financial statements of:

- The parent company or affiliated companies that have been consolidated or combined in that financial report.
- Certain foreign investee companies.
- Investee companies accounted for by the cost or equity method if that segment information is not significant in relation to the consolidated or combined financial statements.

Statement of Financial Accounting Standards No. 24
Reporting Segment Information in Financial Statements That Are Presented in Another Enterprise's Financial Report

an amendment of FASB Statement No. 14

CONTENTS

INTRODUCTION AND BACKGROUND INFORMATION

1. The FASB has been asked whether *FASB Statement No. 14,* "Financial Reporting for Segments of a Business Enterprise," requires segment information[1] to be disclosed in a complete set of parent company financial statements that are presented with the consolidated financial statements of that company. That question was raised apparently because of uncertainty about the intention of the last sentence of paragraph 7 of Statement No. 14, which states:

> When a complete set of financial statements that present financial position, results of operations, and changes in financial position in conformity with generally accepted accounting principles is presented for a subsidiary, corporate joint venture, or 50 percent or less owned investee, each such entity is considered to be an enterprise as that term is used in this Statement and thus is subject to its requirements whether those financial statements are issued separately or included in another enterprise's financial report.

The Board expanded this question and also considered the need for segment information in a complete set of financial statements[2] of a subsidiary, corporate joint venture, or other investee when those financial statements are presented in the parent's or investor's financial report.[3]

2. *FASB Statement No. 21,* "Suspension of the Reporting of Earnings per Share and Segment Information by Nonpublic Enterprises," suspended the requirement to disclose segment information in a complete set of separately issued financial statements of a subsidiary, corporate joint venture, or other investee that is a nonpublic enterprise (as that term is defined in Statement No. 21).

3. An Exposure Draft of a proposed Statement on "Reporting Segment Information in Financial Statements That Are Presented with Another Enterprise's Financial Report" was issued on July 19, 1978. Thirty-five letters of comment were received in response to the Exposure Draft. Virtually all respondents expressed or implied agreement with the proposal to eliminate the requirement to disclose segment information in the financial statements of a parent company or affiliated companies if those financial statements also are consolidated or combined in other financial statements that are presented in the same financial report. Many respondents also recommended that the Board reduce or eliminate the requirement to disclose segment information in the financial statements of other investees that are presented in the same finan-

[1]The term "segment information" as used in this Statement, is the information required to be disclosed by *FASB Statement No. 14* concerning:

a. The enterprise's operations in different industries.
b. Its foreign operations and export sales.
c. Its major customers.

[2]The term "complete set of financial statements," as used in this Statement, refers to a set of financial statements (including necessary footnotes) that present financial position, results of operations, and changes in financial position in conformity with generally accepted accounting principles.

[3]The term "financial report" as used in this Statement, includes any compilation of information that includes one or more complete sets of financial statements, such as in an annual report to stockholders or in a filing with the Securities and Exchange Commission.

cial report. The Board considered those recommendations and concluded that the exemption proposed in the Exposure Draft should be expanded in certain respects.

4. The Board has concluded that it can reach an informed decision on the basis of existing information without a public hearing and that the effective date and transition specified in paragraph 6 are advisable in the circumstances.

STANDARDS OF FINANCIAL ACCOUNTING AND REPORTING

Amendment to FASB Statement No. 14

5. The last sentence of paragraph 7 of *FASB Statement No. 14* is deleted and the following sentences and footnotes are added to the end of that paragraph:

> If a complete set of financial statements that present financial position, results of operations, and changes in financial position in conformity with generally accepted accounting principles is presented for a parent company, subsidiary, corporate joint venture, or 50 percent or less owned investee, each such entity or a combined group of such entities is considered to be an enterprise as that term is used in this Statement [Statement No. 14] and thus is subject to its requirements if those financial statements are *issued separately.** However, disclosure of the information that would otherwise be required by this Statement [Statement No. 14] need not be made in a complete set of financial statements that is presented in another enterprise's financial report (i.e., the primary reporting enterprise):
>
> a. If those financial statements are also consolidated or combined in a complete set of financial statements and both sets of financial statements are presented in the same financial report, or
>
> b. If those financial statements are presented for a foreign investee that is not a subsidiary of the primary reporting enterprise† unless that foreign investee's *separately issued* financial statements disclose the information required by this Statement [Statement No. 14], for example, because the investee prepares its *separately issued* financial statements in accordance with United States generally accepted accounting principles, or
>
> c. If those financial statements are presented in the financial report of an enterprise that is not subject to the requirements of *FASB Statement No. 14* because of the suspension provided by *FASB Statement No. 21*.
>
> Unless exempted above, if a complete set of financial statements for an investee (i.e., subsidiary, corporate joint venture, or 50 percent or less owned investee) accounted for by the cost or equity method is presented in another enterprise's financial report, the information required by this Statement [Statement No. 14] shall be presented for the investee if that information is significant in relation to the financial statements of the primary reporting entity in that financial report (e.g., the consolidated or combined financial statements). To determine the information required by this Statement [Statement No. 14] to be disclosed for an investee in such situations, the percentage tests specified in paragraphs 15, 32, and 39 of this Statement [Statement No. 14] shall be applied as specified in those paragraphs in relation to the financial statements of the primary reporting entity without adjustment for the revenues, operating profit or loss, or identifiable assets of the investee.

Effective Date and Transition

6. This Statement shall be effective January 1, 1979 retroactive to fiscal years beginning after December 15, 1976. Earlier application is encouraged.

The provisions of this Statement need not be applied to immaterial items.

This Statement was adopted by the affirmative votes of five members of the Financial Accounting Standards Board. Messrs. Kirk and Gellein dissented.

**FASB Statement No. 21* suspends the requirements of this Statement [Statement No. 14] for the *separately issued* financial statements of a nonpublic enterprise as defined by that Statement.

†The term "foreign investee that is not a subsidiary of the primary reporting enterprise," as used in this Statement [Statement No. 14] refers to an enterprise incorporated or otherwise organized and domiciled in a foreign country if fifty percent or more of that enterprise's voting stock is owned by residents of a foreign country.

Messrs. Kirk and Gellein dissent from the Statement because the exemption in paragraph 5b fails tests of usefulness and evenhandedness. Pursuant to that paragraph, the furnishing of segment information for an enterprise whose financial statements conform with generally accepted accounting principles depends on factors such as the extent to which the enterprise is owned by others, where it is incorporated, where it is domiciled, and where its shareholders reside. Those factors, in the view of Messrs. Kirk and Gellein, are not relevant to the usefulness of financial statements. Further, in their view, it is not evenhanded to single out for exemption a specified class of investees.

Mr. Gellein also disagrees with that aspect of the Statement that applies the tests for segment significance by comparing amounts in the separate financial statements with amounts in the consolidated statements, as reported. He believes it illogical to omit from the denominator of the ratios amounts for the segment being tested. The results may be irrational depending on the mix of industry segments among the enterprises and the extent of interenterprise transfers.

Members of the Financial Accounting Standards Board:

Donald J. Kirk, *Chairman*
Oscar S. Gellein
John W. March
Robert A. Morgan
David Mosso
Robert T. Sprouse
Ralph E. Walters

Statement of Financial Accounting Standards No. 25 Suspension of Certain Accounting Requirements for Oil and Gas Producing Companies

an amendment of FASB Statement No. 19

STATUS

Issued: February 1979

Effective Date: For fiscal years beginning after December 15, 1978

Affects: Amends FAS 19, paragraphs 48 and 63
Supersedes FAS 19, paragraph 271 and footnotes 11 and 12

Affected by: Paragraphs 6 and 8 superseded by FAS 69

SUMMARY

FASB Statement No. 19, "Financial Accounting and Reporting by Oil and Gas Producing Companies," requires the use of a form of the successful efforts method of accounting and disclosure of reserve quantities, costs incurred, and capitalized costs. The Securities and Exchange Commission (SEC) has incorporated into its rules all the substantive provisions of Statement No. 19 except that the Commission's rules permit, as an acceptable alternative for its reporting purposes, the use of a prescribed form of the full cost method of accounting. In light of this conflict between Statement No. 19 and the SEC's regulations, this Statement:

- Suspends the effective date for applying the requirements of Statement No. 19 related to the successful efforts method of accounting. Oil and gas producing companies not subject to SEC reporting requirements thus are permitted to continue their present methods of accounting.
- Retains, with revision of the effective date, the income tax allocation requirements of Statement No. 19. Those requirements supersede *FASB Statement No. 9,* "Accounting for Income Taxes—Oil and Gas Producing Companies."
- Retains, with revision of the effective date, the requirement of Statement No. 19 to classify production payments payable in cash as debt.
- Retains, with revision of the effective date, the requirements of Statement No. 19 related to disclosure of reserve quantities, costs incurred, and capitalized costs, but permits the required disclosure of reserve quantities to be made outside the financial statements.
- Requires disclosure of the method of accounting for costs incurred in oil and gas producing activities.
- Rescinds the reserve definitions as contained in Statement No. 19 and requires, for financial reporting purposes, the use of the reserve definitions developed by the Department of Energy for its Financial Reporting System and adopted by the SEC for its reporting purposes.

Statement of Financial Accounting Standards No. 25 Suspension of Certain Accounting Requirements for Oil and Gas Producing Companies

an amendment of FASB Statement No. 19

CONTENTS

INTRODUCTION AND BACKGROUND INFORMATION

1. *FASB Statement No. 19,* "Financial Accounting and Reporting by Oil and Gas Producing Companies," was issued in December 1977. That Statement was to have become effective for financial statements for fiscal years beginning after December 15, 1978 and for interim periods within those years.

2. By its issuance of *Accounting Series Release (ASR) No. 253,* "Adoption of Requirements for Financial Accounting and Reporting Practices for Oil and Gas Producing Activities," on August 31, 1978, the Securities and Exchange Commission (SEC): (a) adopted the form of successful efforts accounting and the disclosures prescribed by *FASB Statement No. 19;* (b) indicated its intention to develop a form of the full cost accounting method as an alternative acceptable for SEC reporting purposes; (c) concluded that both the full cost and successful efforts methods of accounting, based essentially on historical costs, fail to provide sufficient information on the financial position and operating results of oil and gas producing companies and, accordingly, that steps should be taken to develop an accounting method based on a valuation of proved oil and gas reserves; (d) adopted rules that require financial statement disclosure of certain financial and operating data regardless of the method of accounting followed; and (e) adopted definitions of proved reserves different from those in effect at the time Statement No. 19 was issued. On December 19, 1978, the SEC issued *ASR No. 257,* "Requirements for Financial Accounting and Reporting Practices for Oil and Gas Producing Activities," and *ASR No. 258,* "Oil and Gas Producers—Full Cost Accounting Practices," in which the SEC reaffirmed its conclusions reflected in *ASR No. 253,* adopted definitions of proved reserves developed by the Department of Energy (DOE) for its Financial Reporting System, and prescribed the form of full cost accounting acceptable as an alternative to successful efforts accounting for the SEC's reporting purposes. Those requirements are effective initially for fiscal years ending after December 25, 1978 that are contained in filings that include fiscal years ending after December 25, 1979.

3. After considering the foregoing, the Board has decided to suspend the effective date of *FASB Statement No. 19* for certain provisions related to the basic method of accounting while retaining certain requirements of that Statement related to tax allocation, production payments, and disclosure. Appendix A to this Statement sets forth the basis for the Board's conclusions.

STANDARDS OF FINANCIAL ACCOUNTING AND REPORTING

Amendment of FASB Statement No. 19

4. The effective date for application of paragraphs 11-41, 44-47, and 60 of *FASB Statement No. 19* is suspended insofar as those paragraphs pertain to a *required* form of successful efforts accounting. Those paragraphs are not suspended insofar as they provide definitions of terms in paragraph 11 or pro-

vide direction and guidance for financial statement disclosures required by paragraphs 57-59. Statement No. 19, including paragraphs 11-47, continues in effect as a Statement issued by the FASB for the purpose of applying paragraph 16 of *APB Opinion No. 20,* "Accounting Changes."[1]

5. If accounting changes are made to adopt the provisions of paragraphs 11-47 of *FASB Statement No. 19,* they shall be made by retroactive restatement as provided in paragraphs 63 and 64 of that Statement. Enterprises that presently follow a form of the full cost accounting method and that subsequently adopt accounting changes to conform to the form of the full cost accounting method specified by the SEC also shall make those changes retroactively by restating the financial statements of prior periods.

6. The disclosure requirements of *FASB Statement No. 19* are amended to permit the disclosures of reserve quantities to be made as supplementary information accompanying but outside the financial statements. The last sentence of paragraph 48 of Statement No. 19 is revised to read as follows: "Those disclosures shall be made within the body of the financial statements, in the notes thereto, or in a separate schedule that is an integral part of the financial statements, except that the disclosures of reserve quantities required by paragraphs 50-56 may be made as supplementary information accompanying but outside the financial statements." The last sentence of paragraph 63 is revised to read as follows: "The disclosures specified by paragraphs 50-59 shall be made when presenting complete sets of financial statements that have been restated pursuant to the provisions of this paragraph."

7. Paragraph 271 of *FASB Statement No. 19,* in which various categories of *reserves* are defined, is rescinded. For the purpose of applying this Statement and Statement No. 19, the definitions of proved reserves, proved developed reserves, and proved undeveloped reserves shall be the definitions adopted by the SEC for its reporting purposes that are in effect on the date(s) as of which reserve disclosures are to be made.[2] Previously reported quantities shall not be revised retroactively if the SEC definitions are changed.

8. An enterprise engaged in oil and gas producing activities shall disclose in its financial statements the method of accounting for costs incurred in those activities and the manner of disposing of capitalized costs related to those activities.

9. Paragraph 63 of *FASB Statement No. 19* is amended to change the effective date from "fiscal years beginning after December 15, 1978 and for interim periods within those fiscal years" to "fiscal years ending after December 25, 1979, although earlier application is encouraged." The provision of paragraph 4 of this Statement suspending application of a certain form of the successful efforts method of accounting is an indefinite suspension of that method as a mandatory requirement.

Effective Date

10. This Statement shall be effective for fiscal years beginning after December 15, 1978.

The provisions of this Statement need not be applied to immaterial items.

This Statement was adopted by the affirmative votes of four members of the Financial Accounting Standards Board. Messrs. March and Mosso dissented.

Mr. Mosso and Mr. March dissent because they think that this action at least partially abdicates the Board's standard-setting responsibility. By suspending *FASB Statement No. 19,* the Board passes an opportunity to significantly narrow the range of accounting alternatives in the oil and gas industry and steps aside while the federal government attempts to resolve the issues. They think the Board should have retained Statement No. 19 as the duly adopted private-sector accounting standard, with an exemption for those companies (registered or nonregistered) electing to use the alternative full cost method permitted under SEC-prescribed rules. Although they disagree with the SEC decision that fails to adopt a standard for uniform use, in their view the Board's failure to narrow the numerous alternatives available to nonregistered companies to at least the two methods that registered companies must follow is not in the public interest. The absence of effective FASB-adopted standards may limit the

[1]Paragraph 16 of *APB Opinion No. 20* states in part: "The presumption that an entity should not change an accounting principle may be overcome only if the enterprise justifies the use of an alternative acceptable accounting principle on the basis that it is preferable. . . . The issuance of [a Statement of Financial Accounting Standards] that creates a new accounting principle, that expresses a preference for an accounting principle, or that rejects a specific accounting principle is sufficient support for a change in accounting principle. The burden of justifying other changes rests with the entity proposing the change."

[2]The definitions of proved reserves, proved developed reserves, and proved undeveloped reserves adopted by the SEC on December 19, 1978 in *Accounting Series Release No. 257* are presented in Appendix B to this Statement.

Board from any significant role in the maintenance of these standards, including the successful efforts method of Statement No. 19. Mr. March and Mr. Mosso also believe more affirmative action would have placed the Board in a better position to maintain an active presence in this critical area of national concern and to reassert leadership in setting accounting standards for the oil and gas industry.

Mr. March also dissents because he believes the last sentence of paragraph 4, which asserts that *FASB Statement No. 19* continues in effect for the purpose of controlling accounting changes under *APB Opinion No. 20,* is not warranted in view of the Board's decision to suspend the effectiveness of that Statement. Since the Securities and Exchange Commission decided to permit two alternative accounting methods for companies subject to its jurisdiction and the Board declined to adopt the approach supported by the dissenting members for all companies, the matter of the justification for accounting changes for both registered and nonregistered companies cannot be guided by the Board.

Members of the Financial Accounting Standards Board:

Donald J. Kirk, *Chairman*
John W. March
Robert A. Morgan
David Mosso
Robert T. Sprouse
Ralph E. Walters

Appendix A

BASIS FOR CONCLUSIONS

Scope

11. For many years oil and gas producing companies generally have followed various forms of each of two accounting methods, commonly called successful efforts and full cost. In December 1977 the Board issued *FASB Statement No. 19,* "Financial Accounting and Reporting by Oil and Gas Producing Companies," which specified one form of the successful efforts method to be used by all oil and gas producing companies. That Statement was to have become effective for fiscal years beginning after December 15, 1978. The SEC reviewed the Board's decision and decided that, for the present, oil and gas producing companies subject to its reporting requirements should follow either the successful efforts method as provided by Statement No. 19 or a form of the full cost method specified by the SEC in *ASR No. 258*. Reporting to the SEC based on one of those two methods is effective initially for fiscal years ending after December 25, 1978 that are contained in filings that include fiscal years ending after December 25, 1979 as provided by *ASR No. 257*. This Statement addresses conflicts arising because of the differences between Statement No. 19 and the SEC's regulations.

12. The SEC also has concluded that, because it believes neither the full cost nor the successful efforts method provides sufficient information on the financial position and operating results of oil and gas producing companies, an accounting method based on valuations of proved oil and gas reserves should be developed. The proposed method is referred to by the SEC as Reserve Recognition Accounting (RRA). This Statement does not address RRA.

13. The Board issued an Exposure Draft of an amendment of *FASB Statement No. 19* on November 7, 1978 with a 60-day comment period. Letters of comment were received from 27 respondents.

Alternatives Considered

14. The Board considered the following four approaches for resolving conflicts between *FASB Statement No. 19*'s requirements and the SEC's decision to accept the continued use of alternative accounting methods while it considers the development of RRA:

a. Amend Statement No. 19 to suspend its effective date with respect to either the entire Statement or only portions of it.
b. Amend Statement No. 19 so as to permit all oil and gas producing companies (including those not subject to SEC reporting requirements) an election to follow the full cost method prescribed by the SEC for as long as the SEC permits that method to be an acceptable alternative for its reporting purposes.
c. Rescind Statement No. 19.
d. Take no action and let the American Institute of Certified Public Accountants (AICPA) amend or interpret its standards of reporting on financial statements or its rules of professional conduct to resolve the conflicts created by the different standards established by the FASB and the SEC.

15. For the reasons set forth in this Appendix, the Board decided to suspend the effective date for certain provisions of *FASB Statement No. 19*.

Reasons for Suspending the Effective Date for Certain Paragraphs of FASB Statement No. 19

16. The Board considered, during the deliberations that preceded the issuance of *FASB Statement No.*

19, the issue of whether oil and gas producing companies should be permitted to continue to choose between the full cost method and the successful efforts method. The Board rejected the continued use of alternative accounting methods by oil and gas producing companies for the reasons set forth in paragraphs 128-132 of that Statement. Paragraph 129 states:

> The Board has considered the question of accounting alternatives at length, not only in connection with its oil and gas project but also for other projects on its agenda, and has concluded that differences in accounting may be appropriate when significant differences in facts and circumstances exist, but different accounting among companies for the same types of facts and circumstances impedes comparability of financial statements and significantly detracts from their usefulness to financial statement users.

17. In the Board's view, the reasons cited in those paragraphs for not embracing alternatives continue to be valid. While the Board acknowledges the SEC's statutory authority to differ with the Board on substantive matters, such as in connection with the continued use of alternative methods of accounting for oil and gas producing companies subject to SEC reporting requirements while it considers the development of RRA, the Board sees no basis for reversing its earlier decision reached on the basis of extensive due process procedures.

18. The Board's recognition of the form of the full cost method as adopted by the SEC as an acceptable alternative would provide companies not subject to SEC reporting requirements with the same alternatives granted to companies that are subject to those requirements. Companies not subject to SEC reporting requirements are usually small, and the burden of implementing an accounting change can be particularly heavy for them. The Board was willing to impose that burden when it adopted *FASB Statement No. 19* because of the advantage of comparable reporting by all oil and gas producing companies. Now that two alternative methods are to be permitted for companies subject to SEC reporting requirements and the Commission is considering eventually replacing both of those methods with a completely different method based on RRA, the Board concluded that, at this time, it should not require companies not subject to SEC reporting requirements to adopt either alternative.

19. In addition, the Board's recognition of the form of the full cost method adopted by the SEC as an acceptable alternative would impose on companies not otherwise subject to SEC reporting requirements the regulations, rules, and interpretations of the SEC. The Board believes it is inappropriate for a private sector standard-setting body to impose requirements determined by a governmental agency.

20. Paragraph 4 of this Statement explains that *FASB Statement No. 19,* including paragraphs 11-47, continues in effect as an FASB Statement for the purpose of applying paragraph 16 of *APB Opinion No. 20,* "Accounting Changes." Statement No. 19 "expresses a preference for" the successful efforts method of accounting provided in paragraphs 11-47 and "rejects" other methods of accounting for oil and gas producing activities; accordingly, the Board considers it appropriate to indicate that paragraph 16 of Opinion No. 20 requires that entities proposing to change to an accounting method other than that provided in paragraphs 11-47 of Statement No. 19 bear the burden of justifying that change.

21. The SEC has indicated that, even though its judgment differs from that of the Board in certain respects in this instance, it reaffirms its basic policy of looking to the FASB for the initiative in establishing and improving accounting standards. The SEC has incorporated into its rules the provisions of *FASB Statement No. 19* related to the successful efforts method of accounting, conveyances, income tax allocation, and disclosure. The Board believes that rescinding Statement No. 19 would invalidate its intention to monitor the Statement and provide interpretations of it as they may be needed.

22. The Board considers it essential that it accept responsibility to resolve any problems that arise in implementing its standards. The conflicts between *FASB Statement No. 19* and the SEC's regulations do result in an implementation problem. Therefore, taking no action and letting the AICPA amend or interpret its standards of reporting on financial statements or its rules of professional conduct was not considered to be an acceptable alternative.

23. The Exposure Draft proposed to suspend the applicability of all of the conveyance requirements of paragraphs 42-47 of *FASB Statement No. 19.* It also discussed the possible retention of those conveyance requirements that did not appear to conflict with the form of full cost accounting then proposed by the SEC, but the limited provisions that might have been retained did not appear to have broad applicability, and it was possible that new conflicts could arise if the SEC's final requirements for full cost accounting differed from the proposed requirements. After considering the requirements for full cost accounting adopted by the SEC in *ASR No. 258,* the Board concluded that it should not suspend the applicability of paragraphs 42 and 43 of Statement No. 19, which address accounting for production payments payable in cash and funds advanced for exploration. The Board believes the conclusion

stated in Statement No. 19 that production payments payable in cash and funds advanced for exploration are, in substance, borrowings is consistent with the SEC's final regulations on accounting for those transactions under either the full cost or the successful efforts method of accounting. In other respects, the Board has decided to suspend the applicability of the conveyance requirements in paragraphs 44-47 of Statement No. 19 as proposed in the Exposure Draft because some of those requirements conflict with the full cost method of accounting.

Reasons for Retaining or Revising Certain Provisions of FASB Statement No. 19

24. The SEC has incorporated into its rules the requirements of *FASB Statement No. 19* that pertain to income tax allocation and to disclosures of costs incurred and capitalized costs. The retention of these requirements of Statement No. 19 does not conflict with the SEC's rules.

25. The income tax allocation provisions of *FASB Statement No. 19* superseded *FASB Statement No. 9,* "Accounting for Income Taxes—Oil and Gas Producing Companies," which had permitted different methods of accounting for income tax allocations. The Board believes the income tax allocation provisions of Statement No. 19 to be as appropriate for companies using the full cost method as they are for companies using the successful efforts method.

26. Many observers have advised the Board that information about quantities of oil and gas reserves is essential to understand and interpret the financial statements of oil and gas producing companies and that reserve information is the single most important type of disclosure that could be required. In general, the Board concurs with those views. In the Board's judgment, disclosure of reserve quantities and changes in reserve quantities should be required under any method of accounting.

27. The Board considered suspending the effective date for applicability of the disclosure requirements because they are effectively incremental disclosures only to companies not subject to SEC reporting requirements. However, information about reserves is essential, in the Board's judgment, for assessing the financial position and results of operations of an oil and gas producing company. Some, but not all, users of financial statements of companies not subject to SEC reporting requirements are in a position to obtain reserve information. The Board understood from responses to its Discussion Memorandum, "Financial Accounting and Reporting in the Extractive Industries," and testimony at its public hearing that the principal burden on companies not subject to SEC reporting requirements concerns accounting requirements rather than disclosure requirements. The suspension provision of paragraph 4 permits companies not subject to SEC reporting requirements to continue their present methods of accounting if they so desire.

28. The Exposure Draft proposed the retention of *FASB Statement No. 19*'s requirement to disclose information about reserve quantities in the financial statements. Some respondents suggested, however, that those disclosures be made outside the financial statements. Their concerns generally related to the cost, time, or difficulty of obtaining an independent verification of reserve quantity information that may be necessary if disclosure were made in the financial statements. Many companies have *staff* engineers who prepare estimates of proved reserves quantities, but questions have been raised as to whether there are enough *independent* professional engineers to verify those estimates on a timely basis or whether generally accepted engineering standards exist whereby an engineer can verify the work of another. The Board considered those comments in light of several recent developments. The issuance of *FASB Statement of Financial Accounting Concepts No. 1,* "Objectives of Financial Reporting by Business Enterprises," indicates that the Board intends to establish standards for reporting information outside financial statements, and the Board has issued a proposed Statement that would require disclosure *outside* financial statements of information about the effects of changing prices. In addition, as part of the Board's conceptual framework project, progress is being made in the development of distinctions between financial reporting and financial statements. The Board also understands that the petroleum engineering profession is initiating studies to develop uniform guidelines for estimating quantities of proved reserves and to develop standards whereby an independent professional engineer can verify the work of another engineer. Finally, the Board understands that the auditing profession is in the process of developing standards that establish an independent accountant's responsibility to review and verify compliance with a required disclosure permitted to be made outside the financial statements. In view of the evolutionary and experimental nature of deciding where information should be disclosed and the degree of independent verification, the Board believes that, for the present, permitting the required disclosure of reserve quantities to be made outside the financial statements will ensure the provision of this essential information without excessive burden.

29. The Board also reviewed the reasons given in Appendix B of *FASB Statement No. 19* for the requirements to disclose costs incurred and capitalized costs and found them equally valid for a full cost company as for a successful efforts company.

30. Because of the SEC action and the suspension of the effective date for the accounting requirements of *FASB Statement No. 19,* there will not be a single, uniform method of accounting used by all oil and gas producing companies. Therefore, the Board concluded that it is desirable to add a requirement to disclose in the financial statements the method of accounting for costs incurred in oil and gas producing activities and the manner of disposition of capitalized costs relating to those activities. Since the provision of this Statement suspending portions of Statement No. 19 allows companies not reporting to the SEC to apply various forms of successful efforts and full cost accounting, reference to those terms alone may not provide an adequate description of the method followed.

31. Paragraph 7 of this Statement rescinds the definitions of proved reserves, proved developed reserves, and proved undeveloped reserves contained in paragraph 271 of *FASB Statement No. 19* and requires the use of definitions adopted by the SEC for its reporting purposes. As stated in Statement No. 19, the Board believes that conformity of the reserve definitions used in filings with the SEC, in information reported to the DOE for its Financial Reporting System, and in financial statements prepared in conformity with generally accepted accounting principles is desirable. On December 19, 1978, the SEC adopted in *ASR No. 257* the definitions developed by the DOE for its Financial Reporting System. For convenience purposes, the definitions adopted by the SEC and DOE are reprinted in Appendix B to this Statement.

32. *ASR No. 257* provides an exemption from its disclosure requirements if a company's oil and gas operations represent 10 percent or less of total revenue, total earnings, and total assets, as defined. The Board considered whether more specific guidance for applying its general materiality provision should be presented in this Statement. The Board concluded that it would be inappropriate to resolve pervasive materiality issues in the context of this project and that more specific guidance should be provided only after having considered those issues on a comprehensive basis. The provisions of this Statement, as with all the Board's standards, need not be applied to immaterial items.

33. Paragraph 9 of this Statement amends paragraph 63 of *FASB Statement No. 19* to change its effective date to "fiscal years ending after December 25, 1979, although earlier application is encouraged." The SEC's accounting requirements are "effective initially for fiscal years ending after December 25, 1978 that are contained in filings that include fiscal years ending after December 25, 1979, although earlier application is encouraged." The Board believes that it would be unreasonable to impose on companies subject to SEC reporting requirements certain standards related to accounting for oil and gas producing activities, such as Statement No. 19's tax allocation provisions, prior to the time those companies are required to make accounting changes in accordance with the SEC's regulations.

Appendix B

DEFINITIONS OF PROVED RESERVES

34. The following definitions of proved reserves are those developed by the Department of Energy for its Financial Reporting System and adopted by the Securities and Exchange Commission on December 19, 1978 in *ASR No. 257.* Reference should be made to the SEC's reporting requirements for revisions that may have been made since the issuance of *ASR No. 257.*

Proved oil and gas reserves. Proved oil and gas reserves are the estimated quantities of crude oil, natural gas, and natural gas liquids which geological and engineering data demonstrate with reasonable certainty to be recoverable in future years from known reservoirs under existing economic and operating conditions, i.e., prices and costs as of the date the estimate is made. Prices include consideration of changes in existing prices provided only by contractual arrangements, but not on escalations based upon future conditions.

1. Reservoirs are considered proved if economic producibility is supported by either actual production or conclusive formation test. The area of a reservoir considered proved includes (a) that portion delineated by drilling and defined by gas-oil and/or oil-water contacts, if any, and (b) the immediately adjoining portions not yet drilled, but which can be reasonably judged as economically productive on the basis of available geological and engineering data. In the absence of information on fluid contacts, the lowest known structural occurrence of hydrocarbons controls the lower proved limit of the reservoir.
2. Reserves which can be produced economically through application of improved recovery techniques (such as fluid injection) are included in the "proved" classification when successful testing by a pilot project, or the operation of an installed program in the reservoir, provides support for the engineering analysis on which the project or program was based.
3. Estimates of proved reserves do not include the following: (a) oil that may become avail-

able from known reservoirs but is classified separately as "indicated additional reserves"; (b) crude oil, natural gas, and natural gas liquids, the recovery of which is subject to reasonable doubt because of uncertainty as to geology, reservoir characteristics, or economic factors; (c) crude oil, natural gas, and natural gas liquids, that may occur in undrilled prospects; and (d) crude oil, natural gas, and natural gas liquids, that may be recovered from oil shales, coal, gilsonite and other such sources.

Proved developed oil and gas reserves. Proved developed oil and gas reserves are reserves that can be expected to be recovered through existing wells with existing equipment and operating methods. Additional oil and gas expected to be obtained through the application of fluid injection or other improved recovery techniques for supplementing the natural forces and mechanisms of primary recovery should be included as "proved developed reserves" only after testing by a pilot project or after the operation of an installed program has confirmed through production response that increased recovery will be achieved.

Proved undeveloped reserves. Proved undeveloped oil and gas reserves are reserves that are expected to be recovered from new wells on undrilled acreage, or from existing wells where a relatively major expenditure is required for recompletion. Reserves on undrilled acreage shall be limited to those drilling units offsetting productive units that are reasonably certain of production when drilled. Proved reserves for other undrilled units can be claimed only where it can be demonstrated with certainty that there is continuity of production from the existing productive formation. Under no circumstances should estimates for proved undeveloped reserves be attributable to any acreage for which an application of fluid injection or other improved recovery technique is contemplated, unless such techniques have been proved effective by actual tests in the area and in the same reservoir.

Statement of Financial Accounting Standards No. 26 Profit Recognition on Sales-Type Leases of Real Estate

an amendment of FASB Statement No. 13

STATUS

Issued: April 1979

Effective Date: For leasing transactions and revisions recorded as of August 1, 1979

Affects: Amends FAS 13, paragraph 8

Affected by: Paragraph 7 amended by FAS 66

SUMMARY

This Statement specifies that a lease of real estate that would otherwise be classified as a sales-type lease under *FASB Statement No. 13* , "Accounting for Leases," and that results in a "sales-type" profit shall be classified as an operating lease by the lessor unless at the beginning of the lease term it also meets the conditions for full and immediate profit recognition as described in the *AICPA Industry Accounting Guide* , "Accounting for Profit Recognition on Sales of Real Estate." This means that a lessor would be precluded from classifying a lease as a sales-type lease and recognizing a "sales-type" profit unless, for example, the lessor receives lease payments as of the beginning of the lease term in an amount at least equal to the minimum down payment requirement specified by the *AICPA Industry Accounting Guide* . The down payment requirements of the Guide range from 5 to 25 percent depending on the type of property.

The Statement does not affect the classification of a sales-type lease of real estate that results in a "sales-type" loss, nor does it affect the classification of a lease of real estate that would be classified as a direct financing lease.

Statement of Financial Accounting Standards No. 26
Profit Recognition on Sales-Type Leases of Real Estate

an amendment of FASB Statement No. 13

CONTENTS

INTRODUCTION AND BACKGROUND INFORMATION

1. The FASB has been asked by as a committee of the American Institute of Certified Public Accountants to resolve a problem in the application of *FASB Statement No. 13*, "Accounting for Leases," to leases involving real estate. The problem arises because the classification criteria of paragraph 8 of Statement No. 13 are different from and not as specific as those that relate to the recognition of profits on sales of real estate under the *AICPA Industry Accounting Guide*, "Accounting for Profit Recognition on Sales of Real Estate" (the AICPA Accounting Guide). The AICPA Accounting Guide addresses the timing of profit recognition on real estate sales and concludes that the buyer's investment in the property acquired and the seller's continuing involvement in the property sold are matters of significance in determining the recognition of profits from real estate sales.

2. Paragraph 6(b)(i) of *FASB Statement No. 13* describes sales-type leases as:

> Leases that give rise to manufacturer's or dealer's profit (or loss) to the lessor (i.e., the fair value of the leased property at the inception of the lease is greater or less than its cost or carrying amount, if different) and that meet one or more of the criteria in paragraph 7 and both of the criteria in paragraph 8. Normally, sales-type leases will arise when manufacturers or dealers use leasing as a means of marketing their products. Leases involving lessors that are primarily engaged in financing operations normally will not be sales-type leases if they qualify under paragraphs 7 and 8, but will most often be direct financing leases, described in paragraph 6(b)(ii) below. However, a lessor need not be a dealer to realize dealer's profit (or loss) on a transaction, e.g., if a lessor, not a dealer, leases an asset that at the inception of the lease has a fair value that is greater or less than its cost or carrying amount, if different, such a transaction is a sales-type lease, assuming the criteria referred to are met.

The criteria for lessors to classify leases are set forth in paragraphs 7 and 8 of Statement No. 13. A lease that meets any one of the criteria of paragraph 7 and both of the criteria of paragraph 8 is classified as a sales-type lease if at inception the fair value of the leased property is greater or less than its cost or carrying amount, if different.

3. Those making the request described in paragraph 1 indicated that sales transactions of real estate that would not meet the requirements of the AICPA Accounting Guide for full and immediate profit recognition might qualify for profit recognition if they were consummated, instead, as sales-type leases under *FASB Statement No. 13*. They believe that the collectibility criterion of paragraph 8(a) of Statement No. 13 for sales-type leases of real estate should be equivalent to the tests relating to the adequacy of the buyer's initial and continuing investment in the property acquired as described in paragraphs 15-37 of the AICPA Accounting Guide. Further, they believe that the cost uncertainty criterion of paragraph 8(b) of Statement No. 13 would not be met if the lessor continues to be involved with the leased property in any of the ways described in paragraphs 38-60 of the AICPA Accounting Guide because of uncertainties about the amount of unreimbursable costs yet to be incurred by the lessor.

4. An Exposure Draft of a proposed Statement on "Profit Recognition on Sales-Type Leases of Real Estate" was issued for public comment on December 22, 1978. The Board received 33 letters of comment in response to the Exposure Draft, a majority of which expressed general agreement.

5. Several respondents stated that the accounting requirements of the AICPA Accounting Guide should govern profit recognition on sales-type leases of real estate and not the classification of a lease.

The Board considered the possibility of amending *FASB Statement No. 13* to adopt the accounting requirements prescribed in the AICPA Accounting Guide. However, the Board concluded that that approach would involve significant implementation problems and require significant modifications to Statement No. 13. Accordingly, in the interest of resolving this problem, the Board decided to amend paragraph 8 of Statement No. 13 to adopt the requirements of the AICPA Accounting Guide for full and immediate profit recognition as a condition for classifying a lease of real estate as a sales-type lease if a "sales-type" profit would result from the transaction (i.e., the fair value of the leased property at inception is greater than its cost or carrying amount, if different). In concluding that those requirements should be adopted as a condition for classifying a lease of real estate as a sales-type lease, the Board determined that those requirements should be met as of the beginning of the lease term rather than as of the inception date. Those requirements concern the adequacy of the buyer's initial and continuing investment in the property acquired and the conditions relating to the seller's continued involvement with the property sold.

6. The Board has concluded that it can reach an informed decision on the basis of existing data without a public hearing and that the effective date and transition specified in paragraph 8 are advisable in the circumstances.

STANDARDS OF FINANCIAL ACCOUNTING AND REPORTING

Amendment to FASB Statement No. 13

7. Paragraph 8 of *FASB Statement No. 13* is amended by adding the following at the end of that paragraph:

> However, a lease involving real estate that would otherwise be classified as of the inception date as a sales-type lease giving rise to a manufacturer's or dealer's profit as described in paragraph 6(b)(i) shall be classified as an operating lease unless at the beginning of the lease term it also meets the requirements that a *sale* of the same property would have to meet for full and immediate profit recognition under the *AICPA Industry Accounting Guide*, "Accounting for Profit Recognition on Sales of Real Estate." Those requirements relate to the adequacy of the buyer's initial and continuing investment in the property acquired and the conditions relating to the seller's continued involvement with the property sold.

Effective Date and Transition

8. The provisions of this amendment to *FASB Statement No. 13* shall be effective for leasing transactions recorded and lease agreement revisions (see paragraph 9 of Statement No. 13) recorded as of August 1, 1979 or thereafter. Earlier application is encouraged. In addition, except as provided in the next sentence, the provisions of this Statement shall be applied retroactively at the same time and in the same manner as the provisions of Statement No. 13 are applied retroactively (see paragraphs 49 and 51 of Statement No. 13). Enterprises that have already applied the provisions of Statement No. 13 retroactively and have published annual financial statements based on the retroactively adjusted accounts before the effective date of this Statement may, but are not required to, apply the provisions of this Statement retroactively.

The provisions of this Statement need not be applied to immaterial items.

This Statement was adopted by the unanimous vote of the seven members of the Financial Accounting Standards Board:

Donald J. Kirk, *Chairman*
Frank E. Block
John W. March
Robert A. Morgan
David Mosso
Robert T. Sprouse
Ralph E. Walters

Statement of Financial Accounting Standards No. 27 Classification of Renewals or Extensions of Existing Sales-Type or Direct Financing Leases

an amendment of FASB Statement No. 13

STATUS

Issued: May 1979

Effective Date: For lease agreement renewals and extensions recorded as of September 1, 1979

Affects: Amends FAS 13, paragraph 17(f)(ii)
Supersedes FAS 13, paragraphs 6(b)(i) and (ii)

Affected by: No other pronouncements

SUMMARY

This Statement modifies *FASB Statement No. 13*, "Accounting for Leases," to require a lessor to classify a renewal or an extension of a sales-type or direct financing lease as a sales-type lease if the lease would otherwise qualify as a sales-type lease and the renewal or extension occurs at or near the end of the lease term. If the renewal or extension occurs at other times during the lease term, the prohibition in Statement No. 13 against classifying the renewal or extension as a sales-type lease continues in effect. Furthermore, this Statement does not affect the classification of a lease that results from a change in the provisions of an existing lease or the accounting for changes in the provisions of a lease if those changes occur during the lease term.

Statement of Financial Accounting Standards No. 27 Classification of Renewals or Extensions of Existing Sales-Type or Direct Financing Leases

an amendment of FASB Statement No. 13

CONTENTS

INTRODUCTION AND BACKGROUND INFORMATION

1. The FASB has been asked to reconsider the provision of paragraph 6(b)(i) of *FASB Statement No. 13*, "Accounting for Leases," that states "a renewal or an extension[9] of an existing sales-type or direct financing lease shall not be classified as a sales-type lease; however, if it qualifies under paragraphs 7 and 8, it shall be classified as a direct financing lease." According to footnote 9 to paragraph 6(b)(i), a renewal or extension includes a new lease under which the lessee continues to use the same property. If the provisions of a sales-type or direct financing lease are changed, the revised agreement might be considered a new agreement under the provisions of paragraph 9 of Statement No. 13.

2. Those making the request described above stated that leases that have the same characteristics are classified and accounted for differently because of the prohibition in paragraph 6(b)(i) of *FASB Statement No. 13*. They noted that the prohibition against classifying a renewal or extension of an existing sales-type or direct financing lease is only applicable if the original lease was classified as a sales-type or direct financing lease and the same lessee continues to use the leased property. On the other hand, the prohibition is not applicable if the original lease was classified as an operating lease or if the property is leased to a different lessee. In their opinion, different lease classification and accounting should not be based on the identity of the lessee or the classification of an original or existing lease.

3. An Exposure Draft of a proposed Statement on "Classification of Renewals or Extensions of Existing Sales-Type or Direct Financing Leases" was issued for public comment on February 13, 1979. The Board received 25 letters of comment in response to the Exposure Draft.

4. The Exposure Draft made a distinction between renewals or extensions of existing sales-type or direct financing leases that occur during the lease term and those that occur at or near the end of the lease term. Several respondents stated that the timing of a renewal or an extension of an existing sales-type or direct financing lease should not affect the classification or the accounting for a revised or extended lease. They suggested completely eliminating the prohibition against recording a "second sale" for renewals or extensions of existing sales-type or direct financing leases. The Board considered that alternative but concluded that the prohibition against recording a "second sale" should continue if a renewal or extension occurs *during the term* of a lease. In limited circumstances, *FASB Statement No. 13* recognizes "partial sales" of leased property. In accounting for a sales-type lease, a "partial sale" is recognized by including only the present value of the minimum lease payments in "sales" revenue and excluding the present value of the unguaranteed residual value from the cost of the leased property charged against that revenue. Recognition of "partial sales" under Statement No. 13 is a liberalization of prior practice in accounting for leases, which did not permit recognition of "partial sales." This Statement extends those limited circumstances to certain renewals or extensions of existing sales-type or direct financing leases that occur at or near the end of the lease term. A further extension of those circumstances to permit recognition of a "partial sale" for a renewal or extension that occurs during the term of an existing lease would require significant modifications to many of the accounting and reporting provisions of Statement No. 13, and the Board does not believe that problem warrants the additional effort that would be required.

5. The Board has concluded that it can reach an informed decision on the basis of existing data without a public hearing and that the effective date

and transition specified in paragraph 9 are advisable in the circumstances.

STANDARDS OF FINANCIAL ACCOUNTING AND REPORTING

Amendments to FASB Statement No. 13

6. The last sentence of paragraph 6(b)(i) of *FASB Statement No. 13* is superseded by the following:

> A renewal or extension[9] of an existing sales-type or direct financing lease that otherwise qualifies as a sales-type lease shall be classified as a direct financing lease unless the renewal or extension occurs at or near the end of the original term* specified in the existing lease, in which case it shall be classified as a sales-type lease. (See paragraph 17(f).)

7. The third sentence of paragraph 6(b)(ii) of *FASB Statement No. 13* is superseded by the following sentence:

> An exception arises when an existing sales-type or direct financing lease is renewed or extended[10] during the term of the existing lease.

8. The following subparagraph is added to paragraph 17(f)(ii) of *FASB Statement No. 13*:

> c. If a renewal or extension that occurs at or near the end of the term† of the existing lease is classified as a sales-type lease, the renewal or extension shall be accounted for as a sales-type lease.

Effective Date and Transition

9. The provisions of this amendment to *FASB Statement No. 13* shall be effective for lease agreement renewals and extensions (see paragraph 9 of Statement No. 13) recorded as of September 1, 1979 or thereafter. Earlier application is encouraged. In addition, except as provided in the next sentence, the provisions of this Statement shall be applied retroactively at the same time and in the same manner as the provisions of Statement No. 13 are applied retroactively (see paragraphs 49 and 51 of Statement No. 13). Enterprises that have already applied the provisions of Statement No. 13 retroactively and have published annual financial statements based on the retroactively adjusted accounts before the effective date of this Statement may, but are not required to, apply the provisions of this Statement retroactively.

The provisions of this Statement need not be applied to immaterial items.

This Statement was adopted by the affirmative votes of six members of the Financial Accounting Standards Board. Mr. Walters dissented.

Mr. Walters dissents to this amendment because, while it properly removes one inconsistency in accounting for similar transactions, it substitutes another inconsistency based solely on timing. If one accepts that a transaction styled as a lease that does not transfer title is substantively a sale, one necessarily accepts the notion of a partial sale; that is, a sale of something less than all the rights to a property for all of its economic life. If one can sell a portion of the whole, one can also sell a portion or all of the remainder, and the accounting for a transaction that meets the criteria of a sale should not differ based solely on its proximity to the end of the original lease term.

Members of the Financial Accounting Standards Board:

Donald J. Kirk, *Chairman*
Frank E. Block
John W. March
Robert A. Morgan
David Mosso
Robert T. Sprouse
Ralph E. Walters

*A renewal or extension that occurs in the last few months of an existing lease is considered to have occurred at or near the end of the existing lease term.

†See footnote*.

Statement of Financial Accounting Standards No. 28
Accounting for Sales with Leasebacks

an amendment of FASB Statement No. 13

STATUS

Issued: May 1979

Effective Date: For leasing transactions and revisions recorded as of September 1, 1979

Affects: Supersedes FAS 13, paragraphs 32 and 33

Affected by: Paragraphs 3 and 23 through 25 and footnote * amended by FAS 66

SUMMARY

Paragraph 33 of *FASB Statement No. 13*, "Accounting for Leases," generally treats a sale-leaseback as a single financing transaction in which any profit or loss on the sale is deferred and amortized by the seller, who becomes the lessee. This Statement requires the seller to recognize some profit or loss in either of the following limited circumstances:

- If the seller retains the use of only a minor part of the property or a minor part of its remaining useful life through the leaseback, the sale and the lease would be accounted for based on their separate terms. However, if the rentals called for by the lease are unreasonable in relation to current market conditions, an appropriate amount would be deferred or accrued by adjusting the profit or loss on the sale. The amount deferred or accrued would be amortized as an adjustment of those rentals.
- If the seller retains more than a minor part but less than substantially all of the use of the property through the leaseback and the profit on the sale exceeds the present value of the minimum lease payments called for by the leaseback for an operating lease or the recorded amount of the leased asset for a capital lease, that excess would be recognized as profit at the date of the sale.

Statement of Financial Accounting Standards No. 28
Accounting for Sales with Leasebacks

an amendment of FASB Statement No. 13

CONTENTS

INTRODUCTION

1. The FASB has been asked whether the description of sale-leaseback transactions in paragraph 32 of *FASB Statement No. 13*, "Accounting for Leases," is intended to mean that any sale with a leaseback of all or any part of the property for all or part of its remaining life is subject to the sale-leaseback provisions of Statement No. 13. Paragraph 32 of Statement No. 13 states that "sale-leaseback transactions involve the sale of property by the owner and a lease of the property back to the seller." Those making the inquiry noted that deferral of the profit on a sale and amortization of that profit over the term of the leaseback would appear to be inappropriate in some cases in which the leaseback covers only a relatively small part of the property sold or the leaseback is for only a relatively short period of time. They noted that in some cases the profit on the sale might exceed the total rentals under the leaseback, resulting in a negative rental if the accounting provisions of Statement No. 13 were followed. Appendix A provides additional background information about this matter. Appendix B provides illustrations of accounting for sales with leasebacks.

STANDARDS OF FINANCIAL ACCOUNTING AND REPORTING

Amendments to FASB Statement No. 13

2. Paragraph 32 of *FASB Statement No. 13* is superseded by the following:

> Sale-leaseback transactions involve the sale of property by the owner and a lease of the property back to the seller. A sale of property that is accompanied by a leaseback of all or any part of the property for all or part of its remaining economic life shall be accounted for by the seller-lessee in accordance with the provisions of paragraph 33 [of Statement No. 13] and shall be accounted for by the purchaser-lessor in accordance with the provisions of paragraph 34 [of Statement No. 13].

3. Paragraph 33 of *FASB Statement No. 13* is superseded by the following:

> If the lease meets one of the criteria for treatment as a capital lease (see paragraph 7 [of Statement No. 13]), the seller-lessee shall account for the lease as a capital lease; otherwise as an operating lease. Any profit or loss on the sale* shall be deferred and amortized in proportion to the amortization of the leased asset,[23] if a capital lease, or in proportion to the related gross rental charged to expense over the lease term, if an operating lease, unless:
>
> a. The seller-lessee relinquishes the right to *substantially all* of the remaining use of the property sold (retaining only a *minor* portion of such use),† in which case the sale and the leaseback shall be accounted for as separate transactions based on their respective terms.

*"Profit or loss on the sale" is used in this paragraph to refer to the profit or loss that would be recognized on the sale if there were no leaseback. For example, on a sale of real estate subject to the *AICPA Industry Accounting Guide*, "Accounting for Profit Recognition on Sales of Real Estate," the profit on the sale to be deferred and amortized in proportion to the leaseback would be the profit that could otherwise be recognized in accordance with the Guide.

†"Substantially all" and "minor" are used here in the context of the concepts underlying the classification criteria of *FASB Statement No. 13*. In that context, a test based on the 90 percent recovery criterion of Statement No. 13 could be used as a guideline; that is, if the present value of a reasonable amount of rental for the leaseback represents 10 percent or less of the fair value of the asset sold, the seller-lessee could be presumed to have transferred to the purchaser-lessor the right to substantially all of the remaining use of the property sold, and the seller-lessee could be presumed to have retained only a minor portion of such use.

However, if the amount of rentals called for by the lease is unreasonable under market conditions at the inception of the lease, an appropriate amount shall be deferred or accrued, by adjusting the profit or loss on the sale, and amortized as specified in the introduction of this paragraph to adjust those rentals to a reasonable amount.

b. The seller-lessee retains more than a minor part but less than substantially all‡ of the use of the property through the leaseback and realizes a profit on the sale** in excess of (i) the present value of the minimum lease payments over the lease term, if the leaseback is classified as an operating lease, or (ii) the recorded amount of the leased asset, if the leaseback is classified as a capital lease. In that case, the profit on the sale in excess of either the present value of the minimum lease payments or the recorded amount of the leased asset, whichever is appropriate, shall be recognized at the date of the sale. For purposes of applying this provision, the present value of the minimum lease payments for an operating lease shall be computed using the interest rate that would be used to apply the 90 percent recovery criterion of paragraph 7(d) [of Statement No. 13].

c. The fair value of the property at the time of the transaction is less than its undepreciated cost, in which case a loss shall be recognized immediately up to the amount of the difference between undepreciated cost and fair value.

Effective Date and Transition

4. The provisions of this amendment to *FASB Statement No. 13* shall be effective for leasing transactions recorded and lease agreement revisions (see paragraph 9 of Statement No. 13) recorded as of September 1, 1979 or thereafter. Earlier application is encouraged. In addition, except as provided in the next sentence, the provisions of this Statement shall be applied retroactively at the same time and in the same manner as the provisions of Statement No. 13 are applied retroactively (see paragraphs 49 and 51 of Statement No. 13). Enterprises that have already applied the provisions of Statement No. 13 retroactively and have published annual financial statements based on the retroactively adjusted accounts before the effective date of this Statement may, but are not required to, apply the provisions of this Statement retroactively.

The provisions of this Statement need not be applied to immaterial items.

This Statement was adopted by the unanimous vote of the seven members of the Financial Accounting Standards Board:

Donald J. Kirk, *Chairman*
Frank E. Block
John W. March
Robert A. Morgan
David Moșso
Robert T. Sprouse
Ralph E. Walters

Appendix A

BACKGROUND INFORMATION

5. Paragraph 33 of *FASB Statement No. 13* requires that with one stated exception any profit or loss on the sale in a sale-leaseback transaction be deferred by the seller-lessee and amortized. Paragraph 33 states:

> Except as noted below, any profit or loss on the sale shall be deferred and amortized in proportion to the amortization of the leased asset, . . . if a capital lease, or in proportion to rental payments over the period of time the asset is expected to be used, if an operating lease. However, when the fair value of the property at the time of the transaction is less than its undepreciated cost, a loss shall be recognized immediately up to the amount of the difference between undepreciated cost and fair value.

6. Paragraph 107 of *FASB Statement No. 13* explains that the seller-lessee's accounting for a sale-leaseback transaction, described in paragraph 5 above, was prescribed because no means could be identified for separating the sale and the leaseback that would be both practicable and objective, with one exception. The one exception was that if an asset had a fair value less than its undepreciated cost at the time of the transaction, a loss should be recog-

‡"Substantially all" is used here in the context of the concepts underlying the classification criteria of *FASB Statement No. 13*. In that context, if a leaseback of *the entire property sold* meets the criteria of Statement No. 13 for classification as a capital lease, the seller-lessee would be presumed to have retained substantially all of the remaining use of the property sold.

**See footnote *.

nized up to the amount of the difference between undepreciated cost and fair value. Upon further consideration, the Board has concluded that it should provide two additional exceptions.

7. Paragraph 34 of *FASB Statement No. 13* requires the purchaser-lessor in a sale-leaseback transaction to classify the lease as a direct financing lease or an operating lease, based on the criteria of Statement No. 13 for those classifications. The principal effect of that paragraph is to prohibit the purchaser-lessor from classifying the lease to the seller-lessee as a sales-type lease. Paragraph 34 states:

> If the lease meets the criteria in paragraphs 7 and 8, the purchaser-lessor shall record the transaction as a purchase and a direct financing lease; otherwise, he shall record the transaction as a purchase and an operating lease.

8. The Board concluded that the provisions of paragraph 34 of *FASB Statement No. 13* should not be modified to permit a purchaser-lessor in a sale and leaseback transaction to classify the lease as a sales-type lease.

9. An Exposure Draft of a proposed Statement on "Accounting for Sales with Leasebacks" was issued on December 21, 1978. The Board received 37 letters of comment in response to the Exposure Draft. Certain of the comments received and the Board's consideration of them are discussed in paragraphs 10-21 below.

Sales with "Minor" Leasebacks

10. This Statement requires that sales with minor leasebacks be accounted for based on the separate terms of the sale and of the leaseback except when the rentals called for by the leaseback are unreasonable in relation to current market conditions. If the rentals called for by the leaseback are unreasonable, the rentals would be adjusted to a reasonable amount by adjusting the profit or loss on the sale. Some respondents asked why the Statement requires sales with minor leasebacks to be accounted for based on the separate terms of the sale and of the leaseback but prohibits that same accounting for sales with more significant leasebacks.

11. To the extent that the seller-lessee's use of the asset sold continues after the sale, the sale-leaseback transaction is in substance a method of financing that continuing use, and no profit or loss should result from that transaction. To the extent that the seller-lessee gives up the right to the use of the asset sold, the transaction is in substance a sale, and profit or loss recognition might be appropriate; however, the extent of the seller-lessee's continuing use of the asset would have to be evaluated to determine whether that continuing involvement is so major that no profit should be recognized. Paragraph 107 of *FASB Statement No. 13* states the Board's conclusion that no means could be identified for separating the sale and the leaseback that would be both practical and objective. That conclusion was arrived at after considering comments received in response to an Exposure Draft on "Accounting for Leases." The Board has not modified that general conclusion. However, if the leaseback is minor, the overall sale-leaseback transaction clearly is in substance a sale of the property. The Board concluded that accounting for the sale and the leaseback based on their respective terms, using the reasonableness of the rentals as a control, is appropriate for a sale with a minor leaseback because it reflects the overall nature of the transaction. However, if the leaseback is more than a minor one, accounting for the sale and the leaseback based on their terms would permit the seller-lessee to recognize a profit on the portion of the transaction that is in substance a financing. Recognition of a sales-type profit on a financing would be equivalent to profit recognition on a company's sale to itself. Therefore, the Board concluded that the terms of the sale and of the leaseback, using the reasonableness of the leaseback rentals as a control, should not be used as a basis for accounting for other sale-leaseback transactions.

Definition of a "Minor" Leaseback

12. Footnote† indicates that a test based on the 90 percent criterion of *FASB Statement No. 13* could be used as a guideline to distinguish a "minor" leaseback. In that context, if the present value of the leaseback based on reasonable rentals is 10 percent or less of the fair value of the asset sold, the leaseback could be presumed to be minor. Some respondents suggested that "minor" be defined using a test based on the 75 percent of economic life criterion of Statement No. 13. In that context, if the leaseback encompassed less than 25 percent of the remaining economic life of the asset sold, the leaseback could be presumed to be minor.

13. Paragraph 75 of *FASB Statement No. 13* explains that 75 percent of economic life was considered to be substantially all of the benefits and risks incident to the ownership of the property because (a) new equipment, reflecting later technology and in prime condition, can be assumed to be more efficient, and hence yield proportionately more use benefit, than old equipment which has been subject to obsolescence and the wearing-out process, and (b) the present worth, at inception of the lease, of the last 25 percent of the remaining economic life of the property would represent less than 25 percent of the fair value of the asset at the inception of the

lease. Both of those arguments indicate that the first 25 percent of an asset's economic life is more than a minor part of the asset's value. The Board decided to severely limit the minor leaseback exception from the usual sale-leaseback accounting, and accordingly, it used the 90 percent recovery criterion as a guideline to indicate the Board's intent for determination of a "minor" leaseback.

Sales with Other Than "Minor" Leasebacks

14. If a seller-lessee retains more than a minor part but less than substantially all of the use of an asset through a leaseback, this Statement requires the seller-lessee to recognize an amount of profit on the sale equal to the excess, if any, of the realized profit on the sale over the present value of the minimum lease payments (or the recorded amount of the leased asset if the leaseback is classified as a capital lease). Some respondents to the Exposure Draft suggested that the Board permit recognition of a pro rata portion of the realized profit on the sale for those sale-leaseback transactions, i.e., if the present value of the leaseback were equal to 60 percent of the fair value of the asset sold, 40 percent of the profit realized on the sale would be recognized, and the remaining 60 percent would be deferred and amortized over the leaseback term.

15. Paragraph 107 of *FASB Statement No. 13* states that the Board concluded that the present general requirement that gains and losses on sale-leaseback transactions be deferred and amortized should be retained. As discussed in paragraph 13 above, this Statement provides an exception for a minor leaseback because in that case the substance of the overall transaction is apparent. For sales with leasebacks that are not minor, the Board decided to limit profit recognition to amounts that could not represent borrowings to be repaid. Thus, any profits up to the amount of the present value of the leaseback rentals (the maximum amount of borrowing that could be repaid) must be deferred and amortized. The recorded amount of the leased asset is usually the present value of the minimum lease payments. Accordingly, if the leaseback of part of the asset sold is classified as a capital lease, any profit on the sale up to the recorded amount of the leased asset must be deferred and amortized.

16. In the Exposure Draft, the Board proposed to limit recognition of profits on sales with other than minor leasebacks to the excess of the realized profit over the aggregate rental payments for an operating leaseback. Some respondents noted that the purchaser-lessor would expect to receive interest on any amount of sales proceeds that was in substance a borrowing; thus, the present value of those payments would be a more appropriate measure of the borrowing that could be repaid through leaseback rentals. The Board agreed with those respondents and modified this Statement to reflect their suggestion.

17. If the seller-lessee retains, through a leaseback, substantially all of the benefits and risks incident to the ownership of the property sold, the sale-leaseback transaction is merely a financing. The Board concluded that the seller-lessee should not recognize any profit on the sale of an asset if the substance of the sale-leaseback transaction is merely a financing. Accordingly, the Statement does not permit any profit to be recognized on a sale if a related leaseback *of the entire property sold* meets one of the criteria of *FASB Statement No. 13* for classification as a capital lease.

Indicated Losses

18. This Statement continues the requirement of *FASB Statement No. 13* that an indicated loss on the sale in a sale-leaseback be recognized up to the amount of the excess of the carrying amount of the asset sold over its fair value and does not permit an indicated loss on the sale in a sale-leaseback to be deferred and amortized as prepaid rent without some evidence that the indicated loss is in substance a prepayment of rent. If the fair value of the asset sold is more than its carrying amount, any indicated loss on the sale is probably in substance a prepayment of rent, and thus, deferral of that indicated loss to be amortized as prepaid rent would be appropriate.

Amortization of Deferred Amounts

19. Some respondents asked why the profit or loss that is deferred on the sale should be amortized over the period of expected use of the leased asset for an operating leaseback. They noted that any borrowing to be repaid through leaseback rentals would be repaid during the lease term, as defined in *FASB Statement No. 13,* to ensure recovery to the purchaser-lessor. Any reduction of sales proceeds that was in substance a prepayment of rent would result in bargain rentals during the affected period, and the lease term includes any option periods with bargain rentals. The Board agreed and modified paragraph 3 of this Statement to require that the amount deferred or accrued be amortized over the lease term.

Classification of Leasebacks

20. A few respondents asked whether special classification criteria should be provided for leasebacks. They suggested a criterion based on 90 percent recovery of the sales price called for by the related sale rather than 90 percent recovery of fair value of the leased asset. They also suggested that any

deferred profit or loss be considered an adjustment of minimum lease payments for application of that criterion. This Statement addresses a narrow issue that was identified as a problem requiring urgent resolution. The Board concluded that it should not expand the scope of this Statement to provide special criteria for classification of a leaseback.

21. The Board concluded that on the basis of existing information it can make an informed decision on the matters addressed by this Statement without a public hearing and that the effective date and transition specified in paragraph 4 are advisable in the circumstances.

Appendix B

ILLUSTRATIONS OF ACCOUNTING FOR SALES WITH LEASEBACKS

22. The examples in this Appendix illustrate the accounting for certain sales with leasebacks but do not encompass all possible circumstances. Accordingly, each situation should be resolved based on an evaluation of the facts, using the examples in this Appendix as guidance to the extent that they are applicable to the facts of the individual sale and leaseback.

Minor Leaseback

23. An enterprise constructs a regional shopping center and sells it to a real estate management firm. The sale meets the cirteria of the *AICPA Industry Accounting Guide,* "Accounting for Profit Recognition on Sales of Real Estate," for full and immediate profit recognition. At the same time, the seller leases back for 40 years a part of the facility, estimated to be approximately 8 percent of the total rental value of the center. Pertinent data are:

Sales price	$11,200,000
Cost of shopping center	$10,000,000

The rental called for by the lease appears to be reasonable in view of current market conditions. The seller-lessee would record the sale and recognize $1,200,000 profit. The seller-lessee would account for the leaseback as though it were unrelated to the sale because the leaseback is minor as indicated in paragraph 3(a).

24. An enterprise sells real estate, consisting of land and a factory. The factory has an estimated remaining life of approximately 40 years. The sale meets the criteria of the *AICPA Industry Accounting Guide,* "Accounting for Profit Recognition on Sales of Real Estate," for full and immediate profit recognition. The seller negotiates a leaseback of the factory for one year because its new facilities are under construction and approximately one year will be required to complete the new facilities and relocate. Pertinent data are:

Sales price	$20,000,000
Carrying value of real estate	$ 6,000,000
Annual rental under leaseback	$ 900,000
Estimated annual market rental	$ 1,800,000

The leaseback is minor as indicated in paragraph 3(a) because the present value of the leaseback ($1,800,000) is less than 10 percent of the fair value of the asset sold (approximately $20,900,000, based on the sales price and the prepaid rental that apparently has reduced the sales price). Accordingly, the seller-lessee would record the sale and would recognize profit. An amount of $900,000 would be deferred and amortized as additional rent expense over the term of the leaseback to adjust the leaseback rentals to a reasonable amount.†† Accordingly, the seller-lessee would recognize $14,900,000 as profit on the sale ($14,000,000 of profit based on the terms of the sale increased by $900,000 to adjust the leaseback rentals to a reasonable amount).

Leasebacks That Are Not Minor but Do Not Cover Substantially All of the Use of the Property Sold

25. An enterprise sells an existing shopping center to a real estate management firm. The sale meets the criteria of the *AICPA Industry Accounting Guide,* "Accounting for Profit Recognition on Sales of Real Estate," for full and immediate profit recognition. At the same time, the seller leases back the "anchor" store (with corresponding use of the related land), estimated to be approximately 30 percent of the total rental value of the shopping center, for 20 years, which is substantially all of the remaining economic life of the building. Pertinent data are:

††If the term of a prepayment of rent were significant, the amount deferred would be the amount required to adjust the rental to the market rental for an equivalent property if that rental were also prepaid.

Sales price of shopping center	$3,500,000
Estimated to consist of:	
Land	$1,000,000
Buildings and improvements	2,500,000
	$3,500,000
Carrying value of shopping center	$1,000,000
Monthly rentals called for by leaseback	$ 12,600
*Seller-lessee's incremental borrowing rate	10%

*Believed to be approximately the same as the implicit rate calculated by the lessor.

The seller-lessee estimates the ratio of land to building for the leaseback to be the same as for the property as a whole. The seller-lessee would apply paragraph 26(b)(ii)(a) of *FASB Statement No. 13* because the land value exceeds 25 percent of the total fair value of the leased property and would account for the leaseback of the land as a separate operating lease. The seller-lessee would account for $2,500 as monthly land rental (10 percent annual rate applied to the $300,000 value of the land leased back—30 percent of the land value of the shopping center). The balance of the monthly rental ($10,100) would be allocated to the building and improvements and would be accounted for as a capital lease pursuant to the 75 percent of economic life criterion of Statement No. 13. The leased building and improvements would be recorded at the present value of the $10,100 monthly rentals for 20 years at the seller-lessee's 10 percent incremental borrowing rate, or $1,046,608. The seller-lessee would compute the profit to be recognized on the sale as follows:

Profit on the sale		$2,500,000
Recorded amount of leased asset (capital lease)	$1,046,608	
Present value of operating lease rentals at 10% rate	259,061	
Profit to be deferred and amortized		1,305,669
Profit to be recognized		$1,194,331

The deferred profit would be amortized in relation to the separate segments of the lease. The amount attributable to the capital lease ($1,046,608) would be amortized in proportion to the amortization of the leased asset over the term of the lease. The amount attributable to the operating lease ($259,061) would be amortized on a straight line basis over the term of the lease.

26. An enterprise sells an airplane with an estimated remaining economic life of 10 years. At the same time, the seller leases back the airplane for three years. Pertinent data are:

Sales price	$600,000
Carrying value of airplane	$100,000
Monthly rental under leaseback	$ 6,330
*Interest rate implicit in the lease as computed by the lessor	12%

*Used because it is lower than the lessee's incremental borrowing rate.

The leaseback does not meet any of the criteria for classification as a capital lease; hence, it would be classified as an operating lease. The seller-lessee would compute the profit to be recognized on the sale as follows:

Profit on the sale	$500,000
Present value of operating lease rentals ($6,330 for 36 months at 12%)	190,581
Profit to be recognized	$309,419

The $190,581 deferred profit would be amortized in equal monthly amounts over the lease term because the leaseback is classified as an operating lease.

Leaseback That Covers Substantially All of the Use of the Property Sold

27. An enterprise sells equipment with an estimated remaining economic life of 15 years. At the same time, the seller leases back the equipment for 12 years. All profit on the sale would be deferred and amortized in relation to the amortization of the leased asset because the leaseback of *all* of the property sold covers a period in excess of 75 percent of the remaining economic life of the property, and thus, meets one of the criteria of *FASB Statement No. 13* for classification as a capital lease.

Statement of Financial Accounting Standards No. 29
Determining Contingent Rentals

an amendment of FASB Statement No. 13

STATUS

Issued: June 1979

Effective Date: For leasing transactions and revisions recorded as of October 1, 1979

Affects: Amends FAS 13, paragraphs 5(j)(i), 5(n), 12, 16(a)(iv), 17(b), and 18(b)
Supersedes FAS 13, footnote 13

Affected by: No other pronouncements

SUMMARY

The Board has been asked to reconsider the definition of contingent rentals in *FASB Statement No. 13*, "Accounting for Leases," because differing views about the meaning of that definition result in similar leases being accounted for differently, for example, as a capital lease by one lessee and as an operating lease by another lessee. This Statement defines contingent rentals as the increases or decreases in lease payments that result from changes occurring subsequent to the inception of the lease in the factors on which lease payments are based. Lease payments that depend on a factor that exists and is measurable at the inception of the lease, such as the prime interest rate, would be included in minimum lease payments based on the factor at the inception of the lease. Lease payments that depend on a factor that does not exist or is not measurable at the inception of the lease, such as future sales volume, would be contingent rentals in their entirety and, accordingly, would be excluded from minimum lease payments and included in the determination of income as they accrue.

Statement of Financial Accounting Standards No. 29
Determining Contingent Rentals

an amendment of FASB Statement No. 13

CONTENTS

INTRODUCTION AND BACKGROUND INFORMATION

1. The FASB has been asked whether lease payments that depend on changes in a factor that is measurable at the inception of the lease should be included in minimum lease payments for purposes of lease classification, accounting, and reporting under *FASB Statement No. 13,* "Accounting for Leases." Examples of factors upon which lease payments can be based include sales volume in a leased facility, an interest rate such as the prime rate, or an index such as a construction cost index or consumer price index.

2. Paragraph 16(a)(iv) of *FASB Statement No. 13* refers to contingent rentals as "rentals on which the amounts are dependent on some factor other than the passage of time." Footnote 13 of Statement No. 13 further states that "the term 'contingent rentals' includes all or any portion of the stipulated rental that is contingent."

3. In specifying the accounting for capital leases by lessees, paragraph 12 of *FASB Statement No. 13* states that "contingent rentals, . . . including rentals based on variables such as the prime interest rate, shall be charged to expense when actually incurred." Paragraphs 17(b) and 18(b) of Statement No. 13 include similar reference to contingent rentals in specifying the accounting by lessors for sales-type leases and direct financing leases.

4. The Board has been advised that diverse accounting practices have developed with respect to determining contingent rentals. The following three practices have been identified: (a) all lease payments that depend on factors that can change are considered contingent rentals and are excluded from minimum lease payments in their entirety, (b) lease payments that depend on such factors are included in minimum lease payments to the extent that payment by the lessee is assessed as probable, and (c) only the amounts based on a measurable factor existing at the inception of the lease are included in minimum lease payments. Under the last approach, lease payments that depend on a factor like future sales volume of a leased facility are contingent rentals in their entirety and are excluded from minimum lease payments because future sales do not exist at the inception of the lease. Supporters of this approach point out that lease payments based on future sales should be excluded from minimum lease payments because those payments would terminate if the lessee discontinues use of the leased facility.

5. The diverse accounting practices described in the preceding paragraph cause different amounts to be included in minimum lease payments for similar leases. Because the amount of minimum lease payments affects the classification and accounting for leases, such diverse practices result in similar leases being classified and accounted for differently. For example, a lease may be classified as a capital lease by one lessee and a similar lease classified as an operating lease by another lessee because of differing views about the definition of contingent rentals.

6. An Exposure Draft of a proposed Statement on "Determining Contingent Rentals" was issued for public comment on December 21, 1978. The Board received 37 letters of comment in response to the Exposure Draft.

7. Several respondents stated that contingent rentals should be included in minimum lease payments to the extent that payment by the lessee is probable. The Board rejected that approach primarily because of the subjectivity inherent in estimating probable contingent rentals. However, the Board noted that, if certain rental payments to the lessor were required rather than probable under the terms of the lease or other agreement, *FASB Statement*

No. 13 requires that such payments be included in minimum lease payments.

8. The Board has considered various accounting practices with respect to determining contingent rentals and has concluded that lease payments that depend on factors that exist and are measurable at the inception of the lease should be included in minimum lease payments. The Board believes that the term *contingent rentals* contemplates an uncertainty about **future changes** in the factors on which lease payments are based. Accordingly, the Board has concluded that *FASB Statement No. 13* should be amended to identify the contingency in that way.

9. The Board has concluded that it can reach an informed decision on the basis of existing data without a public hearing and that the effective date and transition specified in paragraph 14 are advisable in the circumstances.

STANDARDS OF FINANCIAL ACCOUNTING AND REPORTING

Amendments to FASB Statement No. 13

10. The following footnote is added to the end of the first sentence of paragraph 5(j)(i) of *FASB Statement No. 13:*

> Contingent rentals as defined by paragraph 5(n) of *FASB Statement No. 13* shall be excluded from minimum lease payments.

11. Paragraph 5 of *FASB Statement No. 13* is amended by adding the following subparagraph:

> n. *Contingent rentals.* The increases or decreases in lease payments that result from changes occurring subsequent to the inception of the lease in the factors (other than the passage of time) on which lease payments are based, except as provided in the following sentence. Any escalation of minimum lease payments relating to increases in construction or acquisition cost of the leased property or for increases in some measure of cost or value during the construction or preconstruction period, as discussed in *FASB Statement No. 23,* "Inception of the Lease," shall be excluded from contingent rentals. Lease payments that depend on a factor directly related to the future use of the leased property, such as machine hours of use or sales volume during the lease term, are contingent rentals and, accordingly, are excluded from minimum lease payments in their entirety. However, lease payments that depend on an existing index or rate, such as the consumer price index or the prime interest rate, shall be included in minimum lease payments based on the index or rate existing at the inception of the lease; any increases or decreases in lease payments that result from subsequent changes in the index or rate are contingent rentals and thus affect the determination of income as accruable.

12. Footnote 13 and the parenthetical phrase following *contingent rentals* in paragraph 16(a)(iv) of *FASB Statement No. 13* are deleted.

13. The last sentence of paragraphs 12, 17(b), and 18(b) of *FASB Statement No. 13* is superseded by the following:

> Contingent rentals shall be included in the determination of income as accruable.

Effective Date and Transition

14. The provisions of this amendment to *FASB Statement No. 13* shall be effective for leasing transactions recorded and lease agreement revisions (see paragraph 9 of Statement No. 13) recorded as of October 1, 1979 or thereafter. Earlier application is encouraged. In addition, except as provided in the next sentence, the provisions of this Statement shall be applied retroactively at the same time and in the same manner as the provisions of Statement No. 13 are applied retroactively (see paragraphs 49 and 51 of Statement No. 13). Enterprises that have already applied the provisions of Statement No. 13 retroactively and have published annual financial statements based on the retroactively adjusted accounts before the effective date of this Statement may, but are not required to, apply the provisions of this Statement retroactively.

The provisions of this Statement need not be applied to immaterial items.

This Statement was adopted by the unanimous vote of the seven members of the Financial Accounting Standards Board:

Donald J. Kirk, *Chairman*	John W. March	Robert T. Sprouse
Frank E. Block	Robert A. Morgan	Ralph E. Walters
	David Mosso	

Appendix A

ILLUSTRATIONS OF THE APPLICATION OF THE PROVISIONS OF THIS STATEMENT

15. This Appendix illustrates the application of the provisions of paragraphs 10-13 of this Statement in determining contingent rentals. The examples do not comprehend all possible combinations of circumstances.

16. Paragraph 11 of this Statement indicates that lease payments that depend on an existing index or rate, such as the prime interest rate, shall be included in minimum lease payments based on the index or rate existing at the inception of the lease. As an example, an equipment lease could stipulate a monthly base rental of $2,000 and a monthly supplemental rental of $15 for each percentage point in the prime interest rate in effect at the beginning of each month. If the prime interest rate at the inception of the lease is 10 percent, minimum lease payments would be based on a monthly rental of $2,150 [$2,000 + ($15 × 10) = $2,150]. If the lease term is 48 months and no executory costs are included in the rentals, minimum lease payments would be $103,200 [$2,150 × 48]. If the lease is classified as a capital lease and the prime interest rate subsequently increases to 11 percent, the $15 increase in the monthly rentals would be a contingent rental included in the determination of income as it accrues. If the prime interest rate subsequently decreases to 9 percent, the $15 reduction in the monthly rentals would affect income as accruable. In the case of either the increase or decrease, minimum lease payments would continue to be $103,200.

17. Paragraph 11 of this Statement also indicates that lease payments that depend on a factor directly related to the future use of the leased property, such as machine hours of use or sales volume during the lease term, are contingent rentals and, accordingly, are excluded from minimum lease payments in their entirety. For example, a lease agreement for retail store space could stipulate a monthly base rental of $200 and a monthly supplemental rental of one-fourth of one percent of monthly sales volume during the lease term. Even if the lease agreement is a renewal for store space that had averaged monthly sales of $25,000 for the past 2 years, minimum lease payments would include only the $200 monthly base rental; the supplemental rental is a contingent rental that is excluded from minimum lease payments. The future sales for the lease term do not exist at the inception of the lease, and future rentals would be limited to $200 per month if the store were subsequently closed and no sales were made thereafter.

Statement of Financial Accounting Standards No. 30
Disclosure of Information about Major Customers

an amendment of FASB Statement No. 14

STATUS

Issued: August 1979

Effective Date: For fiscal years beginning after December 15, 1979

Affects: Supersedes FAS 14, paragraph 39

Affected by: No other pronouncements

SUMMARY

Paragraph 39 of *FASB Statement No. 14,* "Financial Reporting for Segments of a Business Enterprise," requires disclosure of the amount of revenue derived from sales to domestic governmental agencies in the *aggregate* or to foreign governments in the *aggregate* when those revenues are 10 percent or more of the enterprise's revenues. The Board was requested to consider the usefulness of disclosing aggregate amounts and concluded that such disclosure has limited general usefulness and should not be required. Therefore, this Statement amends that paragraph to require disclosure of the amount of sales to an individual domestic government or foreign government when those revenues are 10 percent or more of the enterprise's revenues. Consequently, disclosure of sales to a governmental customer is now the same as disclosure of sales to any other customer.

Statement of Financial Accounting Standards No. 30 Disclosure of Information about Major Customers

an amendment of FASB Statement No. 14

CONTENTS

INTRODUCTION AND BACKGROUND INFORMATION

1. Paragraph 39 of *FASB Statement No. 14,* "Financial Reporting for Segments of a Business Enterprise," requires disclosure of information about major customers as follows:

> If 10 percent or more of the revenue of an enterprise is derived from sales to any single customer, that fact and the amount of revenue from each such customer shall be disclosed. (For this purpose, a group of customers under common control shall be regarded as a single customer.) Similarly, if 10 percent or more of the revenue of an enterprise is derived from sales to domestic government agencies in the aggregate or to foreign governments in the aggregate, that fact and the amount of revenue shall be disclosed. The identity of the industry segment or segments making the sales shall be disclosed. The disclosures required by this paragraph shall be made even if the enterprise is not required by this Statement to report information about operations in different industries or foreign operations.

2. The Board has received a number of questions concerning the disclosure of revenue derived from sales to domestic governmental agencies in the aggregate or to foreign governments in the aggregate. The questions pertain to the usefulness of disclosing aggregate amounts, such as aggregate revenue derived from sales to federal, state, and county agencies when there is no apparent relationship, such as common control. Similar questions have been asked about aggregating sales to foreign governments.

3. The purpose of the major customer disclosure requirement of *FASB Statement No. 14* is to inform financial statement users of the extent of an enterprise's reliance on a customer. Accordingly, the Board has concluded that disclosure of revenue derived from sales to domestic governmental agencies in the *aggregate* or to foreign governments in the *aggregate* has limited general usefulness and should not be required. Instead, the major customer disclosure requirements of Statement No. 14 should apply for sales to domestic governmental agencies and foreign governments. Therefore, if 10 percent or more of the revenue of an enterprise is derived from sales to a domestic government or a foreign government, that fact and the amount of revenue from each such source should be disclosed.

4. An Exposure Draft of a proposed Statement on "Disclosure of Information about Major Customers" was issued on March 29, 1979. The Board received 36 letters of comment in response to that Exposure Draft, virtually all of which expressed agreement with the proposed Statement.

5. The Board has concluded that it can reach an informed decision on the basis of existing information without a public hearing and that the effective date and transition specified in paragraph 7 are advisable in the circumstances.

STANDARDS OF FINANCIAL ACCOUNTING AND REPORTING

Amendment to FASB Statement No. 14

6. Paragraph 39 of *FASB Statement No. 14* is superseded by the following:

> An enterprise shall disclose information about the extent of the enterprise's reliance on its major customers. If 10 percent or more of the revenue of an enterprise is derived from sales to any single customer, that fact and the amount of revenue from each such customer shall be disclosed. For this purpose, a group of entities under common control shall be regarded as a single customer, and the federal government, a state government, a local government (for

example, a county or municipality), or a foreign government shall each be considered as a single customer.* The identity of the customer need not be disclosed, but the identity of the industry segment or segments making the sales shall be disclosed. The disclosures required by this paragraph shall be made by an enterprise subject to this Statement [Statement No. 14] even if the enterprise operates only in one industry or has no foreign operations.

*If sales are concentrated in a particular department or agency of government, disclosure of that fact and the amount of revenue derived from each such source is encouraged.

Effective Date and Transition

7. This Statement shall be effective for fiscal years beginning after December 15, 1979. Earlier application is encouraged in financial statements for fiscal years beginning before December 16, 1979. This Statement may be, but is not required to be, applied retroactively to previously issued financial statements.

The provisions of this Statement need not be applied to immaterial items.

This Statement was adopted by the unanimous vote of the seven members of the Financial Accounting Standards Board:

Donald J. Kirk, *Chairman*
Frank E. Block
John W. March
Robert A. Morgan
David Mosso
Robert T. Sprouse
Ralph E. Walters

Statement of Financial Accounting Standards No. 31
Accounting for Tax Benefits Related to U.K. Tax Legislation concerning Stock Relief

STATUS

Issued: September 1979

Effective Date: For annual or interim financial statements issued after September 30, 1979 for periods ending on or after July 26, 1979

Affects: No other pronouncements

Affected by: No other pronouncements

SUMMARY

This Statement specifies how an enterprise subject to United States generally accepted accounting principles should account for income taxes relating to recent changes in the United Kingdom tax law concerning "stock relief," which permits an income tax deduction for increases in inventory. The changes have modified the provisions for recapture of the tax benefit of that deduction. The Statement requires that certain previously deferred tax benefits related to "stock relief" be recognized as of July 26, 1979 when the legislation was enacted. Other tax benefits related to "stock relief" should be deferred unless it is probable that those tax benefits will not be recaptured.

Statement of Financial Accounting Standards No. 31
Accounting for Tax Benefits Related to U.K. Tax Legislation concerning Stock Relief

CONTENTS

INTRODUCTION AND BACKGROUND INFORMATION

1. The FASB has been asked to clarify the accounting for income taxes relating to recent changes in the United Kingdom tax law with respect to "stock[1] relief" for enterprises reporting in conformity with United States generally accepted accounting principles. The U.K. "stock relief" legislation permits enterprises to deduct, for the purpose of determining taxable income, increases in the carrying amount of inventories. The FASB has been informed that tax benefits from "stock relief" have been deferred as if this deduction were a timing difference,[2] which reverses if inventories decrease in future years. The reversal increases taxable income, thereby resulting in the recapture of previously granted tax benefits. This recapture is known in the United Kingdom as the "clawback provision." In July 1979, the United Kingdom adopted legislation to limit the timing and the amount of tax that could be recaptured. Under the new legislation, the potential for recapture of tax benefits in 1973-1974 and 1974-1975 fiscal[3] years has been eliminated, effective from the beginning of an enterprise's 1979-1980 fiscal year. The legislation also provides that the potential for recapture of the "stock relief" tax benefit received in a year will terminate if it has not been recaptured during a six-year period.[4] Thus, for an enterprise with a December year-end, any "stock relief" for the year ended December 31, 1975 (1975-1976) not recaptured by December 31, 1981 (1981-1982) will not be subject to recapture after January 1, 1982.

2. The Board believes that the change in the U.K. tax law changes the character of the "stock relief" deduction for purposes of accounting for income taxes as of the date the legislation was enacted. Because the potential for recapture exists for six years, the Board concluded that the tax benefit resulting from "stock relief" should be deferred unless it is probable that the benefit will not be recaptured. The Board also concluded that the deferred benefit should be adjusted if circumstances change, indicating that the probability of recapture has changed; any accrual or reversal should be included in the determination of income tax expense of the period in which circumstances change. The Board believes that the change in the U.K. tax law with regard to "stock relief" creates a unique situation in accounting for income taxes and that the accounting specified by the Statement should not extend to other situations.

3. An Exposure Draft of a proposed Statement on "Accounting for Income Taxes Related to U.K. Tax Legislation concerning Stock Relief" was issued for public comment on July 30, 1979. The Board received 49 letters of comment in response to the Exposure Draft. Certain of the comments received and the Board's consideration of them are discussed in Appendix A, "Summary of Consideration of Comments on Exposure Draft."

4. The Board has concluded that it can reach an informed decision on the basis of existing data without a public hearing and that the effective date and transition specified in paragraphs 8 and 9 are advisable in the circumstances.

STANDARDS OF FINANCIAL ACCOUNTING AND REPORTING

5. Because of the potential recapture of "stock relief," the tax benefit related thereto shall be deferred unless it is probable that the tax benefit will not be recaptured prior to the end of the relevant

[1] In the United Kingdom, inventory is known as "stock."

[2] Timing differences are defined in paragraph 13(e) of APB Opinion No. 11, *Accounting for Income Taxes.*

[3] Fiscal is used in this Statement to indicate an enterprise's financial year ended after March 31 of one year and before April 1 of the following year, as that term is used in the United Kingdom.

[4] The legislation stipulates that any recapture will be on a LIFO basis; for example, a decrease in inventory in 1978-1979 would first be offset against any "stock relief" claimed in 1977-1978.

six-year recapture period. If the tax benefit related to "stock relief" has been deferred and circumstances subsequently change indicating that it is probable that the tax benefit will not be recaptured prior to the end of the relevant six-year recapture period, the tax benefit previously deferred shall be recognized by a reduction of income tax expense in the period in which circumstances change.[5] If the tax benefit related to "stock relief" has not been deferred and circumstances subsequently change, the tax benefit attributable to that "stock relief" shall be deferred to the extent appropriate by a charge to income tax expense of the period in which circumstances change.

6. For interim reporting purposes, except as provided in paragraph 9, any change in circumstances requiring an adjustment of the tax benefit related to "stock relief" shall be included as an adjustment of the estimated annual effective tax rate in the interim reporting period in which circumstances change.

7. If accounting for "stock relief" in accordance with this Statement creates a significant variation in the customary relationship between income tax expense and pretax accounting income, that fact shall be disclosed.

Effective Date and Transition

8. The provisions of this Statement shall be applied in the first annual or interim financial statements issued after September 30, 1979 for periods ending on or after July 26, 1979. Application in such statements issued by September 30, 1979 is encouraged but not required.

9. In the initial application of this Statement in an interim reporting period ending after July 26, 1979, any recognition of previously deferred tax benefits related to "stock relief" shall be reported as an item of income tax expense of that interim period only rather than as an adjustment of the estimated annual effective tax rate and shall not be reported as an extraordinary item.

The provisions of this Statement need not be applied to immaterial items.

This Statement was adopted by the unanimous vote of the seven members of the Financial Accounting Standards Board:

Donald J. Kirk,
Chairman
Frank E. Block

John W. March
Robert A. Morgan
David Mosso

Robert T. Sprouse
Ralph E. Walters

Appendix A

SUMMARY OF CONSIDERATION OF COMMENTS ON EXPOSURE DRAFT

10. Some respondents indicated that they believed the "stock relief" deduction is a timing difference that will reverse on recapture or become a permanent difference when the potential for recapture is eliminated, i.e., after the six-year time period. They therefore recommended that tax benefits deferred from 1975-1976 to date should not be recognized until the relevant six-year period has passed, when in their view the timing difference would become a permanent difference. Further, some respondents commented on the wording used in the Exposure Draft to describe the previous treatment of "stock relief": "the FASB has been informed that deferred taxes have been provided *as if* this deduction were a timing difference." (Emphasis added.) The Board believes that "stock relief" does not have the characteristics of a timing difference for the following reasons. Inventory and merchandise purchases are accounted for the same way each year for both income tax and financial reporting; an additional deduction for any increase in inventory is allowed for income tax purposes in the year the increase occurs. Because any increase in inventory is accounted for the same way each year for both income tax and financial reporting, the increase does not have the characteristics of a timing difference.[6] Likewise, the additional deduction does not have the characteristics of a permanent difference because the tax benefit is subject to recapture during the six-year period.[7] In some respects, "stock relief" is like the investment tax credit in that a tax benefit is realized because of an increase in particular assets and is recaptured if those assets or their equivalent are not held for the required period.

[5]An increase in net income of a U.K. subsidiary from recognition of the tax benefit related to "stock relief" may require income tax allocation under APB Opinion No. 23, *Accounting for Income Taxes—Special Areas,* when that increase is recognized by the U.S. parent company.

[6]See par. 13(e) of Opinion 11.

[7]See par. 13(f) of Opinion 11.

APB Opinion No. 11, *Accounting for Income Taxes,* defines differences as either timing differences or permanent differences and does not contemplate a timing difference that later changes into a permanent difference. The Board has therefore concluded that accounting for "stock relief" as a timing difference that becomes a permanent difference is inappropriate under the existing principles of income tax allocation.

11. Some respondents questioned the use of the probability approach and suggested that recapture was not simply probable or improbable. Other comments on this approach suggested that it was too subjective and would be difficult to implement in practice. The Board has modified the approach proposed in the Exposure Draft so that the tax benefit related to "stock relief" is deferred unless it is probable that the tax benefit will not be recaptured.

12. Some respondents recommended that for interim reporting purposes the reversal of previously deferred tax benefits should be treated as a discrete item and not as an adjustment of the estimated annual effective tax rate as proposed in the Exposure Draft because treatment as a discrete item would minimize any distortion of earnings and would not include a nonoperating item in the results of operations. The Board accepted this recommendation for initial application of this Statement because of the unusual nature of this unique situation. However, for ongoing accounting, paragraph 6 is consistent with FASB Interpretation No. 18, *Accounting for Income Taxes in Interim Periods,* which requires the tax effect of changes in estimates to be reflected in the computation of the estimated annual effective tax rate. The Board does not believe this existing principle should be modified for such future changes.

Statement of Financial Accounting Standards No. 32 Specialized Accounting and Reporting Principles and Practices in AICPA Statements of Position and Guides on Accounting and Auditing Matters

an amendment of APB Opinion No. 20

STATUS

Issued: September 1979

Effective Date: October 31, 1979

Affects: Amends APB 20, footnote 5

Affected by: Appendix A, Franchise Fee Revenue, amended by FAS 45
Appendix A, SOP 74-6 amended by FAS 77
Appendix A, SOPs 74-12 and 76-2 amended by FAS 65
Appendix A, SOP 75-1 amended by FAS 48
Appendix A, SOP 75-5 amended by FAS 63
Appendix A, SOPs 75-6 and 78-4 and Real Estate amended by FAS 66
Appendix A, SOP 78-3 and Appendix B, SOP 80-3 amended by FAS 67
Appendix A, SOP 78-5 amended by FAS 76
Appendix A, SOPs 78-6 and 79-3 and Insurance amended by FAS 60
Appendix A, SOP 78-8 amended by FAS 49
Appendix A, SOP 76-1 amended by FAS 50
Appendix A, SOP 79-2 amended by FAS 51
Appendix A, SOP 79-4 and Motion Picture Films amended by FAS 53
Appendix A, Construction Contractors and Appendix B, SOPs 81-1 and 81-2 amended by FAS 56
Appendix B, SOP 80-1 superseded by FAS 60

SUMMARY

The Board has agreed to exercise responsibility for the specialized accounting and reporting principles and practices in the AICPA Statements of Position and Guides on accounting and auditing matters by extracting those specialized principles and practices from those documents and issuing them as FASB Statements, after appropriate due process. This has created uncertainty regarding the ongoing status of those specialized principles and practices. This Statement specifies that the specialized accounting and reporting principles and practices contained in the AICPA Statements of Position and Guides on accounting and auditing matters designated herein are preferable accounting principles for purposes of justifying a change in accounting principles as required by APB Opinion No. 20, *Accounting Changes.*

Statement of Financial Accounting Standards No. 32
Specialized Accounting and Reporting Principles and Practices in AICPA Statements of Position and Guides on Accounting and Auditing Matters

an amendment of APB Opinion No. 20

CONTENTS

INTRODUCTION AND BACKGROUND INFORMATION

1. On November 7, 1978, the FASB issued a *Request for Written Comments on an FASB Proposal for Dealing with Industry Accounting Matters and Accounting Questions of Limited Application* (Proposal) that outlined proposed procedures for the Board to adopt the AICPA Statements of Position (SOPs) and Guides on accounting and auditing matters as FASB Statements and thereafter to exercise responsibility for amending and interpreting them. One hundred fifty-seven letters of comment were received on the Proposal. Some respondents expressed concern that the status and authority of the SOPs and Guides would be weakened by the Board's decision to begin due process proceedings toward issuing final FASB Statements concerning the accounting and reporting principles and practices in those SOPs and Guides. Their concern centered on the possibility that the accounting principles in those documents would not be followed pending release of final FASB Statements.

2. At its meetings on March 22 and April 26, 1979, the Board agreed to exercise responsibility for all the specialized[1] accounting and reporting principles and practices in the existing AICPA SOPs and Guides by extracting those specialized principles and practices from the SOPs and Guides and issuing them as FASB Statements, after appropriate due process. As explained in paragraph 8, the Board deferred similar action with regard to those specialized accounting and reporting principles and practices contained in the Industry Audit Guide, *Audits of State and Local Governmental Units,* and the two SOPs (75-3 and 77-2) that supplement that Guide.

3. The Board has considered respondents' concerns about the uncertainty regarding the status of the specialized accounting and reporting principles and practices in the SOPs and Guides and decided to clarify the ongoing status of those specialized principles and practices. The Board considers those specialized principles and practices in the SOPs and Guides listed in Appendix A to be preferable accounting principles for purposes of applying APB Opinion No. 20, *Accounting Changes.*

4. The Board also noted that four Guides and one SOP do not contain any specialized accounting and reporting principles and practices. The Guides, *The Auditor's Study and Evaluation of Internal Control in EDP Systems* (1977), *Audits of Service-Center-Produced Records* (1974), *Computer Assisted Audit Techniques* (1979), and *Medicare Audit Guide* (1969), relate solely to auditing procedures. SOP 75-4, *Presentation and Disclosure of Financial Forecasts,* relates to supplemental financial information that is not now required to be disclosed and is not part of basic historical financial statements prepared in conformity with generally accepted accounting principles. Accordingly, this Statement does not apply to those Guides and the SOP. In addition, the Board noted that the AICPA Auditing Standards Division has published four auditing SOPs that do not contain any specialized accounting and reporting principles and practices and, accordingly, are excluded from Appendix A.

[1]The term *specialized* is used to refer to those current accounting and reporting principles and practices in the existing AICPA Guides and SOPs that are neither superseded by nor contained in the ARBs, APB Opinions, FASB Statements, and FASB Interpretations.

5. An Exposure Draft of a proposed Statement on *Specialized Accounting and Reporting Principles and Practices in AICPA Industry Accounting Guides, Industry Audit Guides, and Statements of Position* was issued on June 1, 1979. The Board received 53 letters of comment in response to the Exposure Draft.

6. Several respondents expressed concern that without proper due process the Board was designating the specialized accounting and reporting principles and practices in those Guides and SOPs as standards covered by Rule 203 of the AICPA's Rules of Conduct, which explains the authority of FASB pronouncements. Such designation would have required enterprises to conform with those specialized principles and practices, a requirement that respondents noted was in conflict with paragraph 3 of the Exposure Draft, which stated that "this Statement does not require any enterprise to change the accounting principles it currently uses to those specified in the Guides and SOPs." The Board was not implying that the specialized accounting and reporting principles and practices in the Guides and SOPs are now standards covered by Rule 203; rather, the Board was acknowledging that those specialized principles and practices were encompassed in the conventions, rules, and procedures referred to as "generally accepted accounting principles." This Statement has been modified to clarify that point.

7. Several respondents noted that the Exposure Draft did not address the preferability of the specialized accounting and reporting principles and practices in the SOPs and Guides with respect to the initial adoption of an accounting principle. They recommended that the Board require enterprises to follow those specialized principles and practices upon initial adoption. The Board believes it should not take any position with respect to initial adoption prior to completion of appropriate due process on the specialized principles and practices.

8. The Board defers action with respect to exercising responsibility for the specialized accounting and reporting principles and practices in the Guide on state and local government accounting and the two related SOPs. In so doing, the Board notes that at the present time the accounting and reporting by such governmental units is addressed by the National Council on Governmental Accounting (NCGA) and the AICPA. The Board also notes that discussions are being held with interested parties, including the NCGA and AICPA, as to what the appropriate structure for accounting standard setting for such governmental units should be. Until the matter is resolved, the FASB is proposing no changes with respect to its involvement with pronouncements in that area and, accordingly, is omitting that Guide and related SOPs from Appendix A. However, some respondents have objected to this omission because they were concerned that it may create the impression that the specialized principles and practices in those documents would not be considered as generally accepted accounting principles. In deferring action with respect to state and local government accounting, the Board emphasizes that it does not intend to change the status or discourage the use of the Guide and SOPs on those matters.

9. The Accounting Standards Executive Committee (AcSEC) of the AICPA has a limited number of projects in process that it expects will result in the issuance of SOPs or Guide revisions within approximately a year. Those projects are listed in Appendix B. In addition, the Board may request AcSEC to undertake issuance of an SOP or Guide during the period prior to the extraction of the specialized accounting and reporting principles and practices from the SOPs and Guides and the issuance of them in FASB Statements. The Board plans to review any specialized principles and practices contained in any such SOPs and Guides before issuance and, if the Board finds them acceptable, it will, after appropriate due process, issue Interpretations of this Statement announcing that they are preferable accounting principles for purposes of applying Opinion 20.

STANDARDS OF FINANCIAL ACCOUNTING AND REPORTING

10. The specialized accounting and reporting principles and practices contained in the AICPA SOPs and Guides on accounting and auditing matters listed in Appendix A are preferable accounting principles for purposes of applying Opinion 20.[2]

Amendment to APB Opinion No. 20

11. Footnote 5 to paragraph 16 of Opinion 20 is superseded by the following:

> The specialized accounting and reporting principles and practices contained in the AICPA Statements of Position and Guides on accounting and auditing matters listed in Appendix A of FASB Statement No. 32 are preferable accounting principles for purposes of justifying a change in accounting principle (paragraph 4).

[2]By Interpretations of this Statement, the Board may also designate as preferable for purposes of applying Opinion 20 the specialized accounting and reporting principles and practices in future AICPA SOPs and Guides either related to AcSEC projects listed in Appendix B or undertaken by AcSEC at the Board's request.

Effective Date

12. This Statement shall be effective October 31, 1979. Earlier application is encouraged.

The provisions of this Statement need not be applied to immaterial items.

This Statement was adopted by the unanimous vote of the seven members of the Financial Accounting Standards Board:

Donald J. Kirk, *Chairman*	John W. March	Robert T. Sprouse
Frank E. Block	Robert A. Morgan	Ralph E. Walters
	David Mosso	

Appendix A

CERTAIN AICPA STATEMENTS OF POSITION AND GUIDES ON ACCOUNTING AND AUDITING MATTERS THAT CONTAIN SPECIALIZED ACCOUNTING AND REPORTING PRINCIPLES AND PRACTICES

Statements of Position

SOP 74-6	Recognition of Profit on Sales of Receivables with Recourse
SOP 74-8	Financial Accounting and Reporting by Colleges and Universities
SOP 74-11	Financial Accounting and Reporting by Face-Amount Certificate Companies
SOP 74-12	Accounting Practices in the Mortgage Banking Industry
SOP 75-1	Revenue Recognition When Right of Return Exists
SOP 75-2	Accounting Practices of Real Estate Investment Trusts
SOP 75-5	Accounting Practices in the Broadcasting Industry
SOP 75-6	Questions Concerning Profit Recognition on Sales of Real Estate
SOP 76-1	Accounting Practices in the Record and Music Industry
SOP 76-2	Accounting for Origination Costs and Loan and Commitment Fees in the Mortgage Banking Industry
SOP 76-3	Accounting Practices for Certain Employee Stock Ownership Plans
SOP 77-1	Financial Accounting and Reporting by Investment Companies
SOP 78-1	Accounting by Hospitals for Certain Marketable Equity Securities
SOP 78-2	Accounting Practices of Real Estate Investment Trusts
SOP 78-3	Accounting for Costs to Sell and Rent, and Initial Rental Operations of, Real Estate Projects
SOP 78-4	Application of the Deposit, Installment, and Cost Recovery Methods in Accounting for Sales of Real Estate
SOP 78-5	Accounting for Advance Refundings of Tax-Exempt Debt
SOP 78-6	Accounting for Property and Liability Insurance Companies
SOP 78-7	Financial Accounting and Reporting by Hospitals Operated by a Government Unit
SOP 78-8	Accounting for Product Financing Arrangements
SOP 78-9	Accounting for Investments in Real Estate Ventures
SOP 78-10	Accounting Principles and Reporting Practices for Certain Nonprofit Organizations
SOP 79-1	Accounting for Municipal Bond Funds
SOP 79-2	Accounting by Cable Television Companies
SOP 79-3	Accounting for Investments of Stock Life Insurance Companies
SOP 79-4	Accounting for Motion Picture Films

Industry Accounting Guides

Accounting for Franchise Fee Revenue, 1973
Accounting for Motion Picture Films, 1973 (see also SOP 79-4)
Accounting for Profit Recognition on Sales of Real Estate, 1973 (see also SOPs 75-6 and 78-4)

Accounting for Retail Land Sales, 1973

Industry Audit Guides

Audits of Banks, Including Supplement, 1969
Audits of Brokers and Dealers in Securities, 1973
Audits of Colleges and Universities, 1973 (see also SOP 74-8)
Audits of Construction Contractors, 1965
Audits of Employee Health and Welfare Benefit Funds, 1972
Audits of Finance Companies, 1973
Audits of Fire and Casualty Insurance Companies, 1966 (see also SOP 78-6)
Audits of Government Contractors, 1975
Audits of Investment Companies, 1973 (see also SOPs 74-11, 77-1, and 79-1)
Audits of Personal Financial Statements, 1968
Audits of Stock Life Insurance Companies, 1972 (see also SOP 79-3)
Audits of Voluntary Health and Welfare Organizations, 1974
Hospital Audit Guide, 1972 (see also SOPs 78-1 and 78-7)

Audit and Accounting Guide

Savings and Loan Associations, 1979

Appendix B

AICPA PROJECTS THAT ARE SCHEDULED TO RESULT IN 1980 IN REVISIONS TO AICPA GUIDES OR STATEMENTS OF POSITION THAT ARE ADDRESSED BY THIS STATEMENT AND EXPECTED TO CONTAIN SPECIALIZED ACCOUNTING AND REPORTING PRINCIPLES AND PRACTICES

Projects Expected to Result in Revisions to Guides

Guide for Banks
Guide for Personal Financial Statements
Guide for Construction Contractors
Guide for Brokers and Dealers in Securities

Projects Expected to Result in a Statement of Position

Accounting by Title Insurance Companies
Reporting Practices Concerning Hospital Related Organizations
Accounting for Real Estate Acquisition, Development, and Construction Costs
Accounting for Performance of Construction-Type and Certain Production-Type Contracts

Statement of Financial Accounting Standards No. 33
Financial Reporting and Changing Prices

STATUS

Issued: September 1979

Effective Date: For fiscal years ending on or after December 25, 1979

Affects: No other pronouncements

Affected by: Paragraphs 22, 29(a), 30, 31, 34, 35, 35(c), 36, 39, 41, 50, 53, 56, 59, and 66 amended by FAS 70
Paragraph 22(c) superseded by FAS 70
Paragraph 23 amended by FAS 54
Paragraphs 30(a) through (c), 35(c)(1) through (4), and 52 amended by FAS 39
Paragraphs 51(b), 52(b), and 53 superseded by FAS 39
Paragraphs 51(b) and 52(b) superseded by FAS 69
Paragraph 53 superseded by FAS 40
Paragraph 53 superseded by FAS 41
Paragraph 53 amended by FAS 46
Paragraph 53(a) superseded by FAS 69

SUMMARY

This Statement applies to public enterprises that have either (1) inventories and property, plant, and equipment (before deducting accumulated depreciation) amounting to more than $125 million or (2) total assets amounting to more than $1 billion (after deducting accumulated depreciation).

No changes are to be made in the primary financial statements; the information required by the Statement is to be presented as supplementary information in published annual reports.

For fiscal years ended on or after December 25, 1979, enterprises are required to report:

a. Income from continuing operations adjusted for the effects of general inflation
b. The purchasing power gain or loss on net monetary items.

For fiscal years ended on or after December 25, 1979, enterprises are also required to report:

a. Income from continuing operations on a current cost basis
b. The current cost amounts of inventory and property, plant, and equipment at the end of the fiscal year
c. Increases or decreases in current cost amounts of inventory and property, plant, and equipment, net of inflation.

However, information on a current cost basis for fiscal years ended before December 25, 1980 may be presented in the first annual report for a fiscal year ended on or after December 25, 1980.

Enterprises are required to present a five-year summary of selected financial data, including information on income, sales and other operating revenues, net assets, dividends per common share, and market price per share. In the computation of net assets, only inventory and property, plant, and equipment need be adjusted for the effects of changing prices.

Illustrative formats for disclosure of the required information are included in this Summary as Schedules A, B, and C (pages 1408-1410 of the Statement).

To present the supplementary information required by this Statement, an enterprise needs to measure the effects of changing prices on inventory, property, plant, and equipment, cost of goods sold, and depreciation, depletion, and amortization expense. No adjustments are required to other revenues, expenses, gains, and losses.

In computations of current cost income, expenses are to be measured at current cost or lower recoverable amount. Current cost measures relate to the assets owned and used by the enterprise and not to other assets that might be acquired to replace the assets owned. This Statement allows considerable flexibility in choice of sources of information about current costs: An enterprise may use specific price indexes or other evidence of a more direct nature. This Statement also encourages simplifications in computations and other aspects of implementation: In particular "recoverable amounts" need be measured only if they are judged to be significantly and permanently lower than current cost; that situation is unlikely to occur very often.

The Board believes that this Statement meets an urgent need for information about the effects of changing prices. If that information is not provided: Resources may be allocated inefficiently; investors' and creditors' understanding of the past performance of an enterprise and their ability to assess future cash flows may be severely limited; and people in government who participate in decisions on economic policy may lack important information about the implications of their decisions. The requirements of the Statement are expected to promote a better understanding by the general public of the problems caused by inflation: Statements by business managers about those problems are unlikely to have sufficient credibility until financial reports provide quantitative information about the effects of inflation.

Special problems arise in the application of the current cost requirements of this Statement to certain types of assets, notably natural resources and income-producing real estate property. The Board will consider those problems further and address them in an Exposure Draft with a view to publishing a Statement in 1980. This Statement gives guidance on the treatment of those assets and related expenses for enterprises that present current cost information for fiscal years ending before December 25, 1980.

This Statement calls for two supplementary income computations, one dealing with the effects of general inflation, the other dealing with the effects of changes in the prices of resources used by the enterprise. The Board believes that both types of information are likely to be useful. Comment letters on the Exposure Draft revealed differences of opinion on the relative usefulness of the two approaches. Many preparers and public accounting firms emphasized the need to deal with the effects of general inflation; users generally preferred information dealing with the effects of specific price changes. The Board believes that further experimentation is required on the usefulness of the two types of information and that experimentation is possible only if both are provided by large public enterprises. The Board intends to assess the usefulness of the information called for by this Statement. That assessment will provide a basis for ongoing decisions on whether or not provision of both types of information should be continued and on whether other requirements in this Statement should be reviewed. The Board will undertake a comprehensive review of this Statement no later than five years after its publication.

The measurement and use of information on changing prices will require a substantial learning process on the part of all concerned. In view of the importance of clear explanations to users of financial reports of the significance of the information, the Board is organizing an advisory group to develop and publish illustrative disclosures that might be appropriate as a guide to preparers in particular industries.

Statement of Financial Accounting Standards No. 33
Financial Reporting and Changing Prices

CONTENTS

INTRODUCTION

1. This Statement establishes standards for reporting certain effects of price changes on business enterprises. It deals with both general inflation and changes in the prices of certain specific types of assets. It requires no changes in the basic financial statements; the required information is to be presented in supplementary statements, schedules, or supplementary notes in financial reports. This Statement applies only to certain large, publicly held enterprises.

The Objectives of This Statement

2. This Statement is based on the objectives set out in FASB Concepts Statement No. 1, *Objectives of Financial Reporting by Business Enterprises*. That Statement concludes that financial reporting should provide information to help investors, creditors, and others assess the amounts, timing, and uncertainty of prospective net cash inflows to the enterprise (paragraph 37). It also calls for the provision of information about the economic resources of an enterprise in a manner that provides direct and indirect evidence of cash flow potential (paragraphs 40 and 41) and it concludes that management is accountable to the owners for "protecting them to the extent possible from unfavorable economic impacts of factors in the economy such as inflation or deflation" (paragraph 50).

3. The users of financial reports need to have an understanding of the effects of changing prices on a business enterprise to help their decisions on investment, lending, and other matters. This Statement is intended to help users in the following specific ways:

a. Assessment of future cash flows. Present financial statements include measurements of expenses and assets at historical prices. When prices are changing, measurements that reflect current prices are likely to provide useful information for the assessment of future cash flows.
b. Assessment of enterprise performance. The worth of an enterprise can be increased as a result of prudent timing of asset purchases when prices are changing. That increase is one aspect of performance even though it may be distinguished from operating performance. Measurements that reflect current prices can provide a basis for assessing the extent to which past decisions on the acquisition of assets have created opportunities for earning future cash flows.
c. Assessment of the erosion of operating capability. An enterprise typically must hold minimum quantities of inventory, property, plant, and equipment and other assets to maintain its ability to provide goods and services. When the prices of those assets are increasing, larger amounts of money investment are needed to maintain the previous levels of output. Information on the current prices of resources that are used to gener-

ate revenues can help users to assess the extent to which and the manner in which operating capability has been maintained.

d. Assessment of the erosion of general purchasing power. When general price levels are increasing, larger amounts of money are required to maintain a fixed amount of purchasing power. Investors typically are concerned with assessing whether an enterprise has maintained the purchasing power of its capital. Financial information that reflects changes in general purchasing power can help with that assessment.

4. The needs described in paragraph 3 are important to investors, creditors, and also to other users. If information about the effects of changing prices is not available, the cost of capital may be excessive for enterprises that can use capital most effectively. Resources may be allocated inefficiently and all members of society may suffer. Furthermore, people in government who participate in decisions on economic policy may not obtain the most relevant information on which to base their decisions.

5. Many people recognize that the effects of changing prices should be taken into account in the interpretation of information in the financial reports of business enterprises. However, there are several reasons for believing that those effects cannot be understood adequately until they are measured and disclosed in financial reports:

a. The effects depend on the transactions and circumstances of an enterprise and users do not have detailed information about those factors;
b. Effective financial decisions can take place only in an environment in which there is an understanding by the general public of the problems caused by changing prices; that understanding is unlikely to develop until business performance is discussed in terms of measures that allow for the impact of changing prices;
c. Statements by business managers about the problems caused by changing prices will not have credibility until specific quantitative information is published about those problems.

The Usefulness of Present Financial Statements

6. Most people believe that the primary financial statements should continue to incorporate measurements based mainly on historical prices. Those financial statements rely to a great extent on prices in transactions to which the enterprise was a party. Among the most common and important transactions are sales in which the historical selling prices are used to measure receivables and purchases in which the historical buying prices are used to measure the inventories and property, plant, and equipment acquired. In present financial statements, those historical prices are measured in terms of the number of units of money agreed upon by the buyer and seller at the time of the transaction.

7. There are at least four important reasons for supporting the dominant focus of present financial statements on historical prices. First, it is fitting that the financial statements depend on actual transactions of the enterprise because those transactions determine the changes in owners' equity in the long run. Business enterprises invest cash in assets in order to earn more cash. Historical prices provide the elementary measures of both the amounts invested and the amounts received in return. Second, because historical prices generally are the result of arms-length bargaining, they provide a basis for reliable measures of the results of transactions. Accordingly, financial statements prepared on the basis of historical prices tend to be capable of independent verification and can be prepared and used with confidence that the information presented is reliable. Third, users' understanding of the effect of changing prices may be enhanced if they are able to compare the measurements in the primary financial statements with measurements that reflect changing prices. Fourth, users are accustomed to the present financial statements.

The Need for Supplementary Information

8. The term "general inflation" means a rise in the general level of prices or a decline in the general purchasing power of the monetary unit. It is widely perceived to be an unfortunate but persistent current feature of the economies of most countries, including the United States. However, measurements in conventional statements are made in nominal dollars, with no direct allowance for the variability of their purchasing power. Many people believe that the users of financial reports need information about measurements that are made in units having the same (i.e., constant) general purchasing power. This Statement requires disclosure of certain supplementary information measured in units having the same general purchasing power. The method used to compute that information is known as constant dollar accounting.

9. Changes in the relative prices of specific goods and services are an integral feature of all modern economies. Many people believe that financial statements based on historical cost fail to provide sufficient information for users because those statements normally do not identify separately changes in prices of assets while they are held by an enterprise. This Statement requires disclosure of certain supplementary information based on measurement of the current cost of inventories and property, plant, and equipment. The method used to compute that information is known as current cost accounting.

10. The Board has concluded that there is an urgent need for enterprises to provide information about the effects on their activities of general inflation and other price changes. It believes that users' understanding of the past performance of an enterprise and their ability to assess future cash flows will be severely limited until such information is included in financial reports.

The Need for Experimentation

11. Both constant dollar accounting and current cost accounting have been subjects of intensive study for many years. Various methodologies similar to constant dollar accounting have been employed to some extent in several countries. In the United States, 101 enterprises participated in the Financial Accounting Standards Board field test experiment with constant dollar accounting by preparing experimental financial statements for one or more of the years 1972-1974. A few U.S. companies have published constant dollar financial statements for several years; others say that they have prepared similar statements for internal use.

12. Preparers and users of financial reports have had wide experience with measurements similar to current cost. The last-in, first-out inventory method typically produces cost of goods sold (but not inventory) measurements that are similar to those obtained from the use of current cost. Starting with 1976, reports filed by certain companies with the Securities and Exchange Commission (SEC) have included measurements of cost of goods sold, depreciation, inventory and property, plant, and equipment on the basis of replacement cost, an attribute that frequently is similar to current cost. Income statements and supplementary schedules based on current cost accounting recently have been presented by several enterprises in the United Kingdom, Canada, and Australia.

13. Preparers and users of financial reports have not yet reached a consensus on the general, practical usefulness of constant dollar information and current cost information. It seems unlikely that a consensus can be reached until further experience has been gained with the use of both types of information in systematic practical applications. This Statement therefore requires certain enterprises to present information both on a constant dollar basis and on a current cost basis.

14. The measurement and use of information on changing prices will require a substantial learning process on the part of all concerned. The Board makes no pretense of having solved all of the implementation problems. Rather, it encourages experimentation within the guidelines of this Statement and the development of new techniques that fit the particular circumstances of the enterprise. This Statement has been written to provide more flexibility than is customary in Board Statements in the belief that those involved will help to develop techniques that further the understanding of the effects of price changes on the enterprise. In view of the importance of clear explanations of the significance of information on the effects of changing prices, to assist users' understanding of the information, the Board is organizing an advisory group to develop illustrative disclosures that might be appropriate for particular industries.

15. The requirement to present information on both a constant dollar basis and a current cost basis provides a basis for studying the usefulness of the two types of information. The Board intends to study the extent to which the information is used, the types of people to whom it is useful, and the purpose for which it is used. The requirements of this Statement will be reviewed on an ongoing basis and the Board will amend or withdraw requirements whenever that course is justified by the evidence. This Statement will be reviewed comprehensively after a period of not more than five years.

Accounting Series Release No. 190

16. As noted in paragraph 12, the Securities and Exchange Commission has required the filing of information having some similarities to the current cost accounting information called for in this Statement. That requirement is included in Accounting Series Release No. 190, *Notice of Adoption of Amendments to Regulation S-X Requiring Disclosure of Certain Replacement Cost Data*. However, it is important that the differences between the two sets of information be recognized. This Statement requires presentation of a computation of income from continuing operations using current cost information. ASR 190, however, calls for information that is not suitable for integration into a computation of income. It requires the disclosure of cost of goods sold at current replacement cost and of depreciation on the basis of the current cost of replacing productive capacity; and the current cost of replacing productive capacity may not be commensurate with labor costs and other operating costs reflected in the income statement. Consequently, ASR 190 emphasizes information that would assist in understanding the "current economics of the business" and it specifically states that the SEC "determined not to require the disclosure of the effect on net income" and that it "did not believe that users should be encouraged to convert the data into a single revised net income figure" (page 7). Some users have nevertheless made that conversion.

17. This Statement emphasizes measurement of the assets owned by the enterprise, whereas ASR 190

focuses attention on the assets that would replace those owned if replacement were to occur currently. Furthermore, this Statement provides for use of current cost or lower recoverable amount as the measure of the asset and of its consumption, rather than requiring use of only one measure—replacement cost—with separate disclosure of net realizable value when it is lower. This Statement calls for disclosure of increases or decreases in the current cost amounts of inventory and property, plant, and equipment as well as calling for measurement of expenses and assets at current cost; and unlike ASR 190, it also requires specific disclosures of the effects of changes in the general price level.

18. The Board is aware of and agrees with the belief that the continuation of requirements to measure both replacement cost data as required by ASR 190 and current cost data as required by this Statement will involve excessive costs for business enterprises. If the Securities and Exchange Commission does not rescind ASR 190 when this Statement becomes effective, the Board will take that factor into account in its decisions about the timing of its review of this Statement and the nature of any revisions to this Statement.

Special Industry Problems

19. Special problems arise in the application of the provisions of this Statement to several particular industries. Special industry task groups have assisted the Board in its study of those problems. In the case of financial institutions such as commercial banks, thrift institutions, and insurance companies, the Board has concluded that the general provisions of this Statement are useful and applicable. In other cases, such as forest products, mining, oil and gas, and real estate, the Board has concluded that further studies are required to provide a basis for decisions on the applicability to certain types of assets and expenses, of the requirement to present information on a current cost basis. The Board intends to undertake those studies with the help of its advisory task groups, and it aims to publish one or more Exposure Drafts followed in 1980 by Statements dealing with the assets concerned. In the meantime, enterprises are not required to disclose information about the current costs of unprocessed natural resources and income-producing real estate properties. There are no special exemptions from requirements to disclose information on a historical cost/constant dollar basis.

Organization of This Statement

20. Paragraph 22 defines certain terms used in this Statement. Paragraphs 23-28 specify the applicability and scope of this Statement; and paragraphs 29-38 summarize the requirements for the disclosure of supplementary information. Paragraphs 39-50 contain provisions for the measurement of historical cost/constant dollar information in annual reports for fiscal years ended on or after December 25, 1979. Paragraphs 51-60 contain provisions for the measurement of current cost information by those enterprises. The current cost information is required for fiscal years ended on or after December 25, 1979 but first disclosure of the information may be postponed to annual reports for fiscal years ended on or after December 25, 1980. Paragraphs 61-64 contain provisions applicable to both historical cost/constant dollar measurements and current cost measurements. Paragraphs 65 and 66 contain provisions for the presentation of a five-year summary of selected data; and paragraphs 67-69 state the transitional provisions and effective dates of this Statement.

21. Illustrations of schedules that display the information required by this Statement are presented in Appendix A. Appendix B provides background information. The bases for the Board's conclusions are set out in Appendix C. Illustrative materials are presented in Appendix D and Appendix E. Appendix F provides information about the Consumer Price Index for All Urban Consumers.

STANDARDS OF FINANCIAL ACCOUNTING AND REPORTING

Definitions

22. For purposes of this Statement, certain terms are defined as follows:

a. *Constant dollar accounting*. A method of reporting financial statement elements in dollars each of which has the same (i.e., constant) general purchasing power. This method of accounting is often described as accounting in units of general purchasing power or as accounting in units of current purchasing power.
b. *Current cost accounting*. A method of measuring and reporting assets and expenses associated with the use or sale of assets, at their current cost or lower recoverable amount at the balance sheet date or at the date of use or sale.
c. *Current cost/constant dollar accounting*. A method of accounting based on measures of current cost or lower recoverable amount in terms of dollars, each of which has the same general purchasing power.
d. *Current cost/nominal dollar accounting*. A method of accounting based on measures of current cost or lower recoverable amount without restatement into units, each of which has the same general purchasing power.
e. *Historical cost/constant dollar accounting*. A

method of accounting based on measures of historical prices in dollars, each of which has the same general purchasing power.

f. *Historical cost/nominal dollar accounting*. The generally accepted method of accounting, used in the primary financial statements, based on measures of historical prices in dollars without restatement into units, each of which has the same general purchasing power.

g. *Income from continuing operations*. Income after applicable income taxes but excluding the results of discontinued operations, extraordinary items, and the cumulative effect of accounting changes.

h. *Public enterprise*. A business enterprise (a) whose debt or equity securities are traded in a public market on a domestic stock exchange or in the domestic over-the-counter market (including securities quoted only locally or regionally) or (b) that is required to file financial statements with the Securities and Exchange Commission. An enterprise is considered to be a public enterprise as soon as its financial statements are issued in preparation for the sale of any class of securities in a domestic market.

Applicability and Scope

23. The requirements of this Statement apply to public enterprises that prepare their primary financial statements in U.S. dollars and in accordance with U.S. generally accepted accounting principles and that have, at the beginning of the fiscal year for which financial statements are being presented either:

a. Inventories and property, plant, and equipment[1] (before deducting accumulated depreciation, depletion, and amortization) amounting in aggregate to more than $125 million; or
b. Total assets amounting to more than $1 billion (after deducting accumulated depreciation).

Both amounts shall be measured in accordance with generally accepted accounting principles as reported in the primary financial statements (consolidated if applicable) of the enterprise.

24. The requirements of this Statement do not apply, during the year of a business combination accounted for as a pooling of interests, to an enterprise created by the pooling of two or more enterprises, none of which individually satisfies the size test described in paragraph 23.

25. The Board encourages nonpublic enterprises and enterprises that do not meet the size test in paragraph 23 to present the information called for by this Statement.

26. This Statement does not change the standards of financial accounting and reporting used for the preparation of the primary financial statements of the enterprise.

27. The information required by this Statement shall be presented as supplementary information in any published annual report that contains the primary financial statements of the enterprise except that the information need not be presented in an interim financial report. The information required by this Statement need not be presented for segments of a business enterprise although such presentations are encouraged.

28. An enterprise that presents consolidated financial statements shall present the information required by this Statement on the same consolidated basis. The information required by this Statement need not be presented separately for a parent company, an investee company, or other enterprise in any financial report that includes the results for that enterprise in consolidated financial statements.

Requirement for Supplementary Information

29. An enterprise is required to disclose:

a. Information on income from continuing operations for the current fiscal year on a historical cost/constant dollar basis (paragraphs 39-46)
b. The purchasing power gain or loss on net monetary items for the current fiscal year (paragraphs 47-50).

The purchasing power gain or loss on net monetary items shall *not* be included in income from continuing operations.

30. An enterprise is required to disclose:

a. Information on income from continuing operations for the current fiscal year on a current cost basis (paragraphs 51-64)
b. The current cost amounts of inventory and property, plant, and equipment at the end of the current fiscal year (paragraph 51)
c. Increases or decreases for the current fiscal year in the current cost amounts of inventory and property, plant, and equipment, net of inflation (paragraphs 55 and 56).

The increases or decreases in current cost amounts shall *not* be included in income from continuing operations.

[1] For the purposes of this Statement, except where otherwise provided, inventory and property, plant, and equipment shall include land and other natural resources and capitalized leasehold interests but *not* goodwill or other intangible assets.

31. In some circumstances, there may be no material difference between the amount of income from continuing operations on a historical cost/constant dollar basis and the amount of income from continuing operations on a current cost basis. In those circumstances, the current cost information listed in paragraph 30 need not be disclosed for the fiscal year concerned, but the enterprise is required to state, in a note to the supplementary disclosures, the reason for the omission of the information.

32. Information on income from continuing operations (on a historical cost/constant dollar basis or on a current cost basis) may be presented either in a "statement format" (disclosing revenues, expenses, gains, and losses) or in a "reconciliation format" (disclosing adjustments to the income from continuing operations that is shown in the primary income statement). Whichever format is used, such information should disclose, unless they are immaterial, the amounts of or adjustments to cost of goods sold, depreciation, depletion, and amortization expense and (in the case of historical cost/constant dollar income from continuing operations) reductions of the historical cost amounts of inventory, property, plant, and equipment to lower recoverable amounts as required by paragraph 44. Formats for the presentation of the supplementary information are illustrated in Appendix A.

33. If depreciation expense has been allocated among various expense categories in the supplementary computations of income from continuing operations (for example, among cost of goods sold and other functional expenses), the aggregate amount of depreciation expense, on both a historical cost/constant dollar basis and a current cost basis, shall be disclosed in a note to the supplementary information.

34. An enterprise shall disclose, in notes to the supplementary information:

a. The principal types of information used to calculate the current cost of inventory, property, plant, and equipment, cost of goods sold, and depreciation, depletion, and amortization expense (paragraph 60)
b. Any differences between (1) the depreciation methods, estimates of useful lives, and salvage values of assets used for calculations of historical cost/constant dollar depreciation and current cost depreciation and (2) the methods and estimates used for calculations of depreciation in the primary financial statements (paragraph 61)
c. The exclusion from the computations of supplementary information of any adjustments to or allocations of the amount of income tax expense in the primary financial statements (paragraph 54).

35. An enterprise is required to disclose the following information for each of its five most recent fiscal years (paragraphs 65 and 66):

a. *Net Sales and Other Operating Revenues*
b. *Historical Cost/Constant Dollar Information*
   (1) Income from continuing operations
   (2) Income per common share from continuing operations
   (3) Net assets at fiscal year-end
c. *Current Cost Information* (except for individual years in which the information was excluded from the current year disclosures in accordance with paragraph 31)
   (1) Income from continuing operations
   (2) Income per common share from continuing operations
   (3) Net assets at fiscal year-end
   (4) Increases or decreases in the current cost amounts of inventory and property, plant, and equipment, net of inflation
d. *Other Information*
   (1) Purchasing power gain or loss on net monetary items
   (2) Cash dividends declared per common share
   (3) Market price per common share at fiscal year-end.

All enterprises shall report, in a note to the five-year summary, the average level or the end-of-year level (whichever is used for the measurement of income from continuing operations) of the Consumer Price Index for each year included in the summary (paragraphs 40 and 41).

36. If an enterprise chooses to state net assets, in the five-year summary, at amounts computed from comprehensive financial statements prepared on a historical cost/constant dollar basis or on a current cost/constant dollar basis, that fact shall be disclosed in a note to the five-year summary (paragraph 66).

37. Enterprises shall provide, in their financial reports, explanations of the information disclosed in accordance with this Statement and discussions of its significance in the circumstances of the enterprise.

38. The disclosures summarized in paragraphs 29-37 are required by this Statement. Enterprises are encouraged to provide additional information to help users of financial reports understand the effects of changing prices on the activities of the enterprise.

Historical Cost/Constant Dollar Measurements

39. The index used to compute information on a constant dollar basis shall be the Consumer Price Index for All Urban Consumers, published by the

Bureau of Labor Statistics of the U.S. Department of Labor.[2]

40. An enterprise that presents the minimum historical cost/constant dollar information required by this Statement shall restate inventory, property, plant, and equipment, cost of goods sold, depreciation, depletion, and amortization expense and any reductions of the historical cost amounts of inventory, property, plant, and equipment to lower recoverable amounts (paragraph 44) in constant dollars represented by the average level over the fiscal year of the Consumer Price Index for All Urban Consumers. Other financial statement elements need not be restated. An enterprise that chooses to present comprehensive financial statements on a historical cost/constant dollar basis may measure the components of those statements either in average-for-the-year constant dollars or in end-of-year constant dollars.

41. If the level of the Consumer Price Index at the end of the year and the data required to compute the average level of the index over the year have not been published in time for preparation of the annual report, they may be estimated by referring to published forecasts based on economic statistics or by extrapolation based on recently reported changes in the index.

42. Inventory and property, plant, and equipment (for computation of the amount of net assets at the end of the current fiscal year for inclusion in the five-year summary of selected financial data paragraph 35(b)(3)), cost of goods sold and depreciation, depletion, and amortization expense shall be measured at their historical cost/constant dollar amounts or lower recoverable amounts. Inventories may need to be reclassified as monetary assets at the date of the use on or commitment to a contract (Appendix D).

43. Measurements of historical cost/constant dollar amounts shall be computed by multiplying the components of the historical cost/nominal dollar measurements by the average level of the Consumer Price Index for the current fiscal year (or the level of the index at the end of the year if comprehensive financial statements are presented) and dividing by the level of the index at the date on which the measurement of the associated asset was established (i.e., the date of acquisition or the date of any measurement not based on historical cost). Those measurements may be restated in base-year dollars for inclusion in the five-year summary (paragraph 65).

44. If it is necessary to reduce the measurements of inventory and property, plant, and equipment, during the current fiscal year from historical cost/constant dollar amounts to lower recoverable amounts, the reduction shall be deducted in the computation of income from continuing operations.

45. Except as provided in paragraphs 42-44 and paragraph 61, the accounting principles used in computing historical cost/constant dollar income shall be the same as those used in computing historical cost/nominal dollar income. Only the measuring unit is changed.

46. Inventory, property, plant, and equipment, and related cost of goods sold and depreciation, depletion, and amortization expense that are originally measured in units of a foreign currency shall first be translated into U.S. dollars in accordance with generally accepted accounting principles and then restated in constant dollars in accordance with the provisions of paragraph 43.

Purchasing Power Gain or Loss on Net Monetary Items

47. A monetary asset is money or a claim to receive a sum of money the amount of which is fixed or determinable without reference to future prices of specific goods or services. A monetary liability is an obligation to pay a sum of money the amount of which is fixed or determinable without reference to future prices of specific goods or services. The economic significance of monetary assets and liabilities (monetary items) depends heavily on the general purchasing power of money, although other factors, such as the credit worthiness of debtors, may affect their significance.

48. All assets and liabilities that are not monetary are nonmonetary. The economic significance of nonmonetary items depends heavily on the value of specific goods and services. Nonmonetary assets include (a) goods held primarily for resale or assets held primarily for direct use in providing services for the business of the enterprise, (b) claims to cash in amounts dependent on future prices of specific goods or services, and (c) residual rights such as goodwill or equity interests. Nonmonetary liabilities include (a) obligations to furnish goods or services in quantities that are fixed or determinable without reference to changes in prices or (b) obligations to pay cash in amounts dependent on future prices of specific goods or services.

[2]The index is published in *Monthly Labor Review*. Those desiring prompt and direct information may subscribed to the Consumer Price Index (CPI) press release mailing list of the Department of Labor.

49. Guidance on the classification of balance sheet items as monetary or nonmonetary is set forth in Appendix D to this Statement.

50. The purchasing power gain or loss on net monetary items shall be equal to the net gain or loss found by restating in constant dollars the opening and closing balances of, and transactions in, monetary assets and liabilities. An enterprise that presents comprehensive supplementary financial statements on a historical cost/constant dollar basis may measure the purchasing power gain or loss in average-for-the-year constant dollars or in end-of-year constant dollars; other enterprises shall measure the purchasing power gain or loss in average-for-the-year dollars. An acceptable approximate method of calculating the purchasing power gain or loss on net monetary items is illustrated in Appendix E.

Current Cost Measurements

51. The current cost amounts of inventory and property, plant, and equipment shall be measured as follows:

a. Inventories at current cost or lower recoverable amount (paragraphs 57-64) at the measurement date. (This provision is qualified by paragraph 53 in respect of any depletion expense included in the measurement of inventories.)
b. Property, plant, and equipment (excluding income-producing real estate properties and unprocessed natural resources) at the current cost or lower recoverable amount (paragraphs 57-64) of the assets' remaining service potential at the measurement date.
c. Resources used on partly completed contracts shall be measured at current cost or lower recoverable amount at the date of use on or commitment to the contracts.

52. An enterprise that presents the minimum information required by this Statement on current cost income from continuing operations shall measure the amounts of cost of goods sold and depreciation and amortization expense as follows:

a. Cost of goods sold shall be measured at current cost or lower recoverable amount (paragraphs 57-64) at the date of sale or at the date on which resources are used on or committed to a specific contract. (This provision is qualified by paragraph 53 in respect of any depletion expense included in cost of goods sold.)
b. Depreciation and amortization expense of property, plant, and equipment (excluding income-producing real estate properties and unprocessed natural resources) shall be measured on the basis of the average current cost or lower recoverable amount (paragraphs 57-64) of the assets' service potential during the period of use.

Other revenues, expenses, gains, and losses may be measured by such an enterprise at the amounts included in the primary income statement. An enterprise that chooses to present comprehensive financial statements on a current cost/constant dollar basis may measure the components of those statements either in average-for-the-year constant dollars or in end-of-year constant dollars. (This paragraph is qualified by paragraph 64 for enterprises that are subject to rate regulation or other form of price control.)

53. This Statement does not contain provisions for the measurement, on a current cost basis, of income-producing real estate properties, unprocessed natural resources, and related depreciation, depletion, and amortization expense (paragraph 19). If an enterprise presents information on a current cost basis in an annual report for a fiscal year ended before December 25, 1980, it may measure the assets and the related expenses, described in this paragraph, at their historical cost/constant dollar amounts or by reference to an appropriate index of specific price changes.

54. The amount of income tax expense in computations of current cost income from continuing operations shall be the same as the amount of income tax expense charged against income from continuing operations in the primary financial statements. No adjustments shall be made to income tax expense for any timing differences that might be deemed to arise as a result of the use of current cost accounting methods. Income tax expense shall not be allocated between income from continuing operations and the increases or decreases in current cost amounts of inventory and property, plant, and equipment.

Increases or Decreases in the Current Cost Amounts of Inventory and Property, Plant, and Equipment

55. The increases or decreases in the current cost amounts of inventory and property, plant, and equipment represent the differences between the measures of the assets at their "entry dates" for the year and the measures of the assets at their "exit dates" for the year. "Entry dates" means the beginning of the year or the dates of acquisition, whichever is applicable; "exit dates" means the end of the year or the dates of use, sale, or commitment to a specific contract whichever is applicable. For the purposes of this paragraph, assets are measured in accordance with the provisions of paragraph 51.

56. The increases or decreases in current cost amounts of inventory and property, plant, and

equipment shall be reported both before and after eliminating the effects of general inflation. An enterprise that presents comprehensive supplementary statements on a current cost/constant dollar basis may measure increases or decreases in current cost amounts in average-for-the-year constant dollars or in end-of-year constant dollars; other enterprises shall measure those increases or decreases in average-for-the-year constant dollars. An acceptable approximate method of calculating the increases or decreases in current cost amounts and the inflation adjustment is illustrated in Appendix E.

Information about Current Costs

57. The current cost of inventory owned by an enterprise is the current cost of purchasing the goods concerned or the current cost of the resources required to produce the goods concerned (including an allowance for the current overhead costs according to the allocation bases used under generally accepted accounting principles), whichever would be applicable in the circumstances of the enterprise.

58. The current cost of property, plant, and equipment owned by an enterprise is the current cost of acquiring the same service potential (indicated by operating costs and physical output capacity) as embodied by the asset owned; the sources of information used to measure current cost should reflect whatever method of acquisition would currently be appropriate in the circumstances of the enterprise. The current cost of a used asset may be measured:

a. By measuring the current cost of a new asset that has the same service potential as the used asset had when it was new (the current cost of the asset as if it were new) and deducting an allowance for depreciation;
b. By measuring the current cost of a used asset of the same age and in the same condition as the asset owned;
c. By measuring the current cost of a new asset with a different service potential and adjusting that cost for the value of the differences in service potential due to differences in life, output capacity, nature of service, and operating costs.

Current cost may be measured by direct reference to current prices of comparable assets or methods such as functional pricing or unit pricing under which the current cost of a unit of service embodied in the asset owned is measured and the current cost per unit is multiplied by the appropriate number of service units.

59. If current cost is measured in a foreign currency, the amount shall be translated into dollars at the current exchange rate, that is, the rate at the date of use, sale, or commitment to a specific contract (in the cases of depreciation expense and cost of goods sold) or the rate at the balance sheet date (in the cases of inventory and property, plant, and equipment).

60. Enterprises may use various types of information to determine the current cost of inventory, property, plant, and equipment, cost of goods sold, and depreciation, depletion, and amortization expense.[3] The information may be gathered and applied internally or externally and may be applied to single items or broad categories, as appropriate in the circumstances. The following types of information are listed as examples of the information that may be used, but they are *not* listed in any order of preferability. Enterprises are expected to select types of information appropriate to their particular circumstances, giving due consideration to their availability, reliability, and cost:

a. Indexation
   (1) Externally generated price indexes for the class of goods or services being measured
   (2) Internally generated price indexes for the class of goods or services being measured
b. Direct pricing
   (1) Current invoice prices
   (2) Vendors' price lists or other quotations or estimates
   (3) Standard manufacturing costs that reflect current costs.

Depreciation Expense

61. There is a presumption that depreciation methods, estimates of useful lives, and salvage values of assets should be the same for purposes of current cost, historical cost/constant dollar, and historical cost/nominal dollar depreciation calculations. However, if the methods and estimates used for calculations in the primary financial statements have been chosen partly to allow for expected price changes, different methods and estimates may be used for purposes of current cost and historical cost/constant dollar calculations.

Recoverable Amounts

62. The term "recoverable amount" means the current worth of the net amount of cash expected to be recoverable from the use or sale of an asset. If the recoverable amount for a group of assets is judged

[3]Cost of goods sold measured on a LIFO basis may provide an acceptable approximation of cost of goods sold, measured at current cost, provided that the effect of any decreases in inventory layers is excluded.

to be materially and permanently lower than historical cost in constant dollars or current cost, the recoverable amount shall be used as a measure of the assets and of the expense associated with the use or sale of the assets. Decisions on the measurement of assets at their recoverable amounts need not be made by considering assets individually unless they are used independently of other assets.

63. Recoverable amounts may be measured by considering the net realizable values or the values in use of the assets concerned:

a. Net realizable value is the amount of cash, or its equivalent, expected to be derived from sale of an asset net of costs required to be incurred as a result of the sale. It shall be considered as a measurement of an asset only when the asset concerned is about to be sold.
b. Value in use is the net present value of future cash flows (including the ultimate proceeds of disposal) expected to be derived from the use of an asset by the enterprise. It shall be considered as a measurement of an asset only when immediate sale of the asset concerned is not intended. Value in use shall be estimated by discounting expected future cash flows at an appropriate discount rate that allows for the risk of the activities concerned.

64. An enterprise that is subject to rate regulation or other form of price control may be limited to a maximum recovery through its selling prices, based on the nominal dollar amount of the historical cost of its assets. In that situation, nominal dollar/historical costs may represent an appropriate basis for the measurement of the recoverable amounts associated with the assets at the end of the fiscal year. Recoverable amounts may also be lower than historical costs. However, cost of goods sold and depreciation, depletion, and amortization expense shall be measured at historical cost/constant dollar amounts (in measurements of historical cost/constant dollar income from continuing operations) or at current cost (in measurements of current cost income from continuing operations) provided that replacement of the service potential provided by the related assets would be undertaken, if necessary, in current economic conditions; if replacement would not be undertaken, expenses shall be measured at recoverable amounts.

Five-Year Summary of Selected Financial Data

65. The information presented in the five-year summary shall be stated either:

a. In average-for-the-year constant dollars or end-of-year constant dollars (whichever is used for the measurement of income from continuing operations) as measured by the Consumer Price Index for All Urban Consumers for the current fiscal year; or
b. In dollars having a purchasing power equal to that of dollars of the base period used by the Bureau of Labor Statistics in calculating the Consumer Price Index (currently 1967).

66. If an enterprise presents the minimum information required by this Statement, it shall measure net assets (i.e., shareholders' equity) for the purposes of the five-year summary:

a. On a historical cost/constant dollar basis at the amount reported in its primary financial statements adjusted for the difference between the historical cost/nominal dollar amounts and the historical cost/constant dollar amounts or lower recoverable amounts of inventory and property, plant, and equipment
b. On a current cost basis at the amount reported in its primary financial statements, adjusted for the difference between the historical cost/nominal dollar amounts and the current cost or lower recoverable amounts of inventory and property, plant, and equipment and restated in constant dollars in accordance with paragraph 65.

If an enterprise elects to present comprehensive supplementary financial statements on a current cost/constant dollar basis, or on a historical cost/constant dollar basis, it may report the amount of net assets in the five-year summary in accordance with the comprehensive statements.

Effective Date and Transition

67. The provisions of this Statement shall be effective for fiscal years ended on or after December 25, 1979. However, information on a current cost basis for fiscal years ended before December 25, 1980 may be presented in the first annual report for a fiscal year ended on or after December 25, 1980.

68. An enterprise is required to state, in the five-year summary of selected financial data, only the following amounts for fiscal years ended before December 25, 1979: net sales and other operating revenues, cash dividends declared per common share, and market price per common share at fiscal year-end (paragraph 35(a), (d)(2), and (d)(3)). Disclosure of the other items listed in paragraph 35, for fiscal years ended before December 25, 1979 is encouraged. Disclosure of current cost information in the five-year summary (paragraph 35(c)) for fiscal years ending before December 25, 1980 may be postponed to the first annual report for a fiscal year ending on or after December 25, 1980.

69. An enterprise that first applies the requirements

of this Statement for a fiscal year ended on or after December 25, 1980 is required to state for earlier years, in its five-year summary, only the following items listed in paragraph 35: net sales and other operating revenues (item (a)), cash dividends declared per common share (item (d)(2)), and market price per common share at fiscal year-end (item (d)(3)). Disclosure of the other items listed in paragraph 35 for earlier years is encouraged.

The provisions of this Statement need not be applied to immaterial items.

This Statement was adopted by the affirmative votes of five members of the Financial Accounting Standards Board. Messrs. Mosso and Walters dissented.

Mr. Mosso dissents because he believes that the Statement does not bring the basic problem it addresses—measuring the effect of inflation on business operations—into focus. Because of that he doubts that it will effectively communicate the erosive impact of inflation on profits and capital and the significance of that erosion on all who have an investment stake in business enterprises. The Statement seems to him to fail the cost-benefit test because potential benefits are diminished by diffusion and some costs are unnecessary regardless of benefits.

The lack of focus stems from the dual reporting requirements imposed by this Statement, reporting on both historical cost/constant dollar and current cost bases, and is compounded by the ambivalence of the income concepts in both approaches. The Statement offers at least four income numbers—historical cost/constant dollar or current cost, each with or without adjustments for purchasing power gains or losses on monetary items. Other income combinations are invited in the current cost approach because of the juxtaposition of the increase or decrease in current cost amounts of assets. This array of income numbers is a good reflection of the range of views existing among the Board's respondents; but a good mirror does not make a good standard.

Mr. Mosso does not share the widely-held view that the historical cost/constant dollar and current cost models have different objectives. The objective is the same: To measure the effect of inflation on a business enterprise. But there are two types of inflation effect. The Board's historical cost/constant dollar model captures one type, the effect of inflation on the purchasing power of money invested in a particular business. The Board's current cost model captures both types. It incorporates some features of the constant dollar model and also the effect on the prices of goods and services that a particular business deals in. Inflation affects different specific prices in different ways. Consequently, information about changes in an index of general inflation does not provide sufficient information about the effect of inflation on a specific business enterprise. The current cost model is a more comprehensive inflation measurement approach and it makes a free standing historical cost/constant dollar model superfluous.

The constant dollar approach has two uses that he would support: One, as a method of computing simple one-line adjustments of net income and owners' equity in the primary historical cost financial statements, in conjunction with current cost supplemental statements (a proposal that deserves more support than it has received so far); or two, as an integral part of a supplemental current cost model, essentially as in the current cost approach required by this Statement. As a complete model, however, the historical cost/constant dollar approach has little to recommend it except seniority.

A major criterion that the Board has established for choosing among alternative disclosure is usefulness of the information for predicting earnings and cash flows. The evidence presented to the Board on usefulness in this sense was sketchy, but virtually all of it favored the current cost approach. In fact, usefulness for predicting earnings and cash flows was rarely associated with the historical cost/constant dollar approach, even by its supporters.

Beyond the investor-oriented usefulness criterion, the current cost model bears directly on an urgent national economic policy issue, that of capital formation and its corollary, productivity. The current cost model is built around the notion of maintaining operating capacity, and the distributable income concept that goes with it is designed to trigger attention at the point where reduction of capacity sets in. The whole system pivots on the point where capital investment begins to rise or fall. In the historical cost/constant dollar model, reduction of operating capacity can occur without showing up in the financial statements. This is not to suggest that it is a function of the Board to design accounting standards to promote economic policy objectives. But it is a function of the Board to design standards that measure business income and investment and to be aware, in doing so, of the broader economic consequences of standards. The current cost model has the potential for measuring and communicating many effects of inflation in ways that will be useful both to investors, to policy makers, and to the business community.

Much of the resistance to current cost accounting derives from two interrelated misconceptions: First that it is a major step toward current value accounting and second that its measurements are subjective and open to income manipulation. These are valid concerns. They should not be dismissed or lulled. But neither is an inherent concomitant of current cost accounting.

The essence of current value accounting is revenue recognition on some prerealization basis. The increases in current cost amounts of assets (so-called "holding gains") arising in a current cost model can be viewed as income equivalents, but that view is not necessary. The model can classify those items as capital maintenance adjustments—necessary to keep the business on a level output trendline.

Subjectivity of measurement is also associated with the current cost model because in theory it breaks the link to historical transaction prices. In practice, this need not be a problem. Indexing can maintain a linkage to historical prices and preserve objectivity and reliability. Many other current costing techniques compare favorably, in terms of objectivity, with historical cost allocation techniques.

In Mr. Mosso's view, conventional accounting measurements fail to capture the erosion of business profits and invested capital caused by inflation. The urgent need is to focus attention on that basic problem. To do that effectively, it is essential to settle on a single inflation-adjusted bottom line within a framework that captures the price experience of individual firms. The door should be closed quickly and firmly on the dual approach with multiple income numbers.

Mr. Walters dissents because he believes that the dual approach in this Statement unfortunately attempts to deal with two very important but fundamentally different issues in combination. The result is most confusing.

The first issue is the need to measure and report the impact on the enterprise of the change in the exchange value of money. This need is urgent. Paton said: "A summation of unlike monetary units, even of the same name, is a misrepresentation." The integrity of the historical cost/nominal dollar system relies on a stable monetary system. We have experienced several decades of continuing debasement of the currency. It is essential to the credibility of financial reporting to recognize that the recovery of the real cost of investment is not earnings—that there can be no earnings unless and until the purchasing power of capital is maintained. The constant dollar information required by this Statement, provided one takes the monetary adjustment into consideration, will generally accomplish this within a reasonable order of magnitude. It is not experimental. It is ready to go.

The second issue is the need to introduce current costs or values into the financial reporting model. The record built in the Board's due process indicates that the Securities and Exchange Commission, some educators, and some financial analysts perceive such a need. Issuers of financial statements and auditors, in the main, either do not perceive a need at this time, or believe the proposed model needs further development and testing or that the costs exceed the benefits.

The current cost information introduced in this Statement has significant limitations. It is neither a comprehensive current cost nor a value system. It identifies as income from continuing operations an amount that is sometimes referred to as "distributable income." This amount may have use in funds flow analysis, but it is neither distributable nor income. In most cases, it is a result of subtracting the estimated cost of the next purchase from the revenue from the last sale. It is neither transaction-based income nor real economic income. It has no "bottom line." It is best an intermediate step, easily misinterpreted.

To reduce complexity, the Board elected to defer action or deal inconclusively with such significant matters as backlog depreciation, holding gains, tax allocation, gearing adjustments, and liability measurement. The sacrifice of completeness for understandability leaves us with a model that falls short of the mark on both counts.

This Statement reflects diverse views on the best way to report the effects of changing prices. The resulting product has something for everybody, but by requiring a number of supplemental income amounts which can be used in various combinations, it does not focus on a concept of real income. It offers a smorgasbord of data that fail to meet the tests of simplicity, understandability, and therefore cost-effectiveness.

The weight of evidence suggests that the Board is promulgating a current cost model that is not ready, for a constituency that is not ready for it. Experimentation with current cost and value information is sorely needed to establish their feasibility, reliability, cost, and usefulness. Mr. Walters believes that this experimentation should be conducted with volunteer companies working through professional organizations of business executives, accountants, and financial analysts. Regulators mandate experiments in financial reports; standard setters should not.

Members of the Financial Accounting Standards Board:

Donald J. Kirk, *Chairman*
Frank E. Block
John W. March
Robert A. Morgan
David Mosso
Robert T. Sprouse
Ralph E. Walters

Appendix A

ILLUSTRATIONS OF DISCLOSURES

70. This appendix gives illustrations of formats that may be used to disclose the information required by this Statement. The illustrations relate to a manufacturing enterprise. The Board has formed an advisory group to develop additional illustrations of formats for presenting the information required by this Statement. It intends to publish those illustrations as soon as possible. The illustrations will cover various types of manufacturing and other enterprises. The Board recognizes that clear presentations and explanations are important if information on the effects of changing prices is to be as useful as possible. It encourages enterprises to experiment with the use of different forms of presentation.

Schedule A

STATEMENT OF INCOME FROM CONTINUING OPERATIONS ADJUSTED FOR CHANGING PRICES

For the Year Ended December 31, 1980
(In (000s) of Average 1980 Dollars)

Income from continuing operations, as reported in the income statement		$ 9,000
Adjustments to restate costs for the effect of general inflation		
Cost of goods sold	(7,384)	
Depreciation and amortization expense	(4,130)	(11,514)
Loss from continuing operations adjusted for general inflation		(2,514)
Adjustments to reflect the difference between general inflation and changes in specific prices (current costs)		
Cost of goods sold	(1,024)	
Depreciation and amortization expense	(5,370)	(6,394)
Loss from continuing operations adjusted for changes in specific prices		$(8,908)
Gain from decline in purchasing power of net amounts owed		$ 7,729
Increase in specific prices (current cost) of inventories and property, plant, and equipment held during the year*		$24,608
Effect of increase in general price level		18,959
Excess of increase in specific prices over increase in the general price level		$ 5,649

*At December 31, 1980 current cost of inventory was $65,700 and current cost of property, plant, and equipment, net of accumulated depreciation was $85,100.

Schedule B

STATEMENT OF INCOME FROM CONTINUING OPERATIONS ADJUSTED FOR CHANGING PRICES

For the Year Ended December 31, 1980
(In (000s) of Dollars)

	As Reported in the Primary Statements	Adjusted for General Inflation	Adjusted for Changes in Specific Prices (Current Costs)
Net sales and other operating revenues	$253,000	$253,000	$253,000
Cost of goods sold	197,000	204,384	205,408
Depreciation and amortization expense	10,000	14,130	19,500
Other operating expense	20,835	20,835	20,835
Interest expense	7,165	7,165	7,165
Provision for income taxes	9,000	9,000	9,000
	244,000	255,514	261,908
Income (loss) from continuing operations	$ 9,000	$(2,514)	$(8,908)
Gain from decline in purchasing power of net amounts owed		$ 7,729	$ 7,729
Increase in specific prices (current cost) of inventories and property, plant, and equipment held during the year*			$ 24,608
Effect of increase in general price level			18,959
Excess of increase in specific prices over increase in the general price level			$ 5,649

*At December 31, 1980 current cost of inventory was $65,700 and current cost of property, plant, and equipment, net of accumulated depreciation was $85,100.

Schedule C

FIVE-YEAR COMPARISON OF SELECTED SUPPLEMENTARY FINANCIAL DATA ADJUSTED FOR EFFECTS OF CHANGING PRICES
(In (000s) of Average 1980 Dollars)

	Years Ended December 31,				
	1976	1977	1978	1979	1980
Net sales and other operating revenues	265,000	235,000	240,000	237,063	253,000
Historical cost information adjusted for general inflation					
Income (loss) from continuing operations				(2,761)	(2,514)
Income (loss) from continuing operations per common share				$ (1.91)	$ (1.68)
Net assets at year-end				55,518	57,733
Current cost information					
Income (loss) from continuing operations				(4,125)	(8,908)
Income (loss) from continuing operations per common share				$ (2.75)	$ (5.94)
Excess of increase in specific prices over increase in the general price level				2,292	5,649
Net assets at year-end				79,996	81,466
Gain from decline in purchasing power of net amounts owed				7,027	7,729
Cash dividends declared per common share	$ 2.59	$ 2.43	$ 2.26	$ 2.16	$ 2.00
Market price per common share at year-end	$ 32	$ 31	$ 43	$ 39	$ 35
Average consumer price index	170.5	181.5	195.4	205.0	220.9

Appendix B

BACKGROUND

71. Accounting literature has long recognized that price changes cause difficulties in measuring and comparing financial statement elements. As Professor William Paton noted in 1922, "the value of the dollar—its general purchasing power—is subject to serious change over a period of years. . . . Accountants . . . deal with an unstable, variable unit; and comparisons of unadjusted accounting statements prepared at intervals are accordingly always more or less unsatisfactory and are often positively misleading."[4] The subject of changes in general prices has been discussed widely in accounting literature and was extensively studied by the Accounting Principles Board (APB) of the American Institute of Certified Public Accountants (AICPA) and its predecessor, the Committee on Accounting Procedure. In 1947,[5] 1948,[6] and 1953[7] the Committee, and in 1965 the APB (in APB Opinion No. 6, *Status of Accounting Research Bulletins*), considered accounting problems related to sharp increases in the general level of prices. Several of these pronouncements were particularly concerned with the amount of depreciation to be charged against current income for facilities acquired at lower prices. The Committee concluded that depreciation charges should be based on historical cost, but gave full support to the use of supplementary financial schedules, explanations, or footnotes by which company management might explain the need for retention of earnings because of the effects of inflation.

72. The AICPA published ARS No. 6, *Reporting the Financial Effects of Price-Level Changes,* in 1963; and in June 1969, the APB issued APB Statement No. 3, *Financial Statements Restated for General Price-Level Changes*. The Statement recommended that "historical-dollar" financial statements be supplemented by general price-level information. But the APB stopped short of requiring general price-level information for fair presentation of financial position and results of operations in conformity with generally accepted accounting principles. Very few companies have followed the APB's recommendation.

73. The FASB added the subject of reporting the effects of general price-level changes in financial statements to its agenda in January 1974, issued an FASB Discussion Memorandum, *Reporting the Effects of General Price-Level Changes in Financial Statements,* on February 15, 1974, held a public hearing in April 1974, and on December 31, 1974 issued an FASB Exposure Draft, *Financial Reporting in Units of General Purchasing Power*. That Exposure Draft proposed to require supplementary disclosure of specified financial information, stated in units of general purchasing power, in addition to financial statements presented in units of money. The Board received 476 letters of comment on the Exposure Draft. In November 1975, the Board announced that a final Statement on general purchasing power accounting would not be issued that year, pending additional analysis of the results of a field test of the Exposure Draft provisions conducted by a large number of companies.

74. In March 1976, the Securities and Exchange Commission issued ASR 190 requiring certain publicly held companies to disclose replacement cost information about inventories, cost of sales, productive capacity, and depreciation. The Commission announced at that time that its requirements were not competitive with the Board's proposal for general price-level accounting information, and did not prejudge the Board's conceptual framework studies.

75. In June 1976, the Board deferred action on its Exposure Draft on general purchasing power accounting pending further progress on its project on a conceptual framework for accounting and reporting. The Board concluded that general purchasing power information was not sufficiently understood by preparers and users, and the need for it was not sufficiently demonstrated to justify imposing the cost of implementation upon all preparers of financial statements at that time. Another consideration was the effort required at that time of many of the largest corporations in providing the current replacement cost data required by the SEC.

76. On December 2, 1976, the Board published, as part of its conceptual framework project, an FASB Discussion Memorandum, *Conceptual Framework for Financial Accounting and Reporting: Elements of Financial Statements and Their Measurement*. Public hearings were conducted on the measurement issues in that Discussion Memorandum in January 1978. The Board received 270 letters of comment on measurement issues in response to the Discussion Memorandum and 27 presentations were made at the public hearing.

---

[4]William A. Paton, *Accounting Theory* (Houston, TX.: Reprinted by Scholars Book Co., 1973), p. 427.

[5]American Institute of Certified Public Accountants, Committee on Accounting Procedure, ARB No. 33, *Depreciation and High Costs* (New York: AICPA, December 1947).

[6]——,Committee on Accounting Procedure, letter to AICPA members reaffirming the recommendations of *ARB No. 33,* October 1948.

[7]——,Committee on Accounting Procedure, ARB No. 43, *Restatement and Revision of Accounting Research Bulletins* , Chap. 9, Section A, "Depreciation and High Costs" (New York: AICPA, June 1953).

77. In May 1977, the Board published an FASB Research Report, *Field Tests of Financial Reporting in Units of General Purchasing Power*. The Report summarized the results of field tests by 101 companies of the restatement techniques proposed in the December 1974 Exposure Draft.

78. On December 28, 1978, the Board issued an FASB Exposure Draft, *Financial Reporting and Changing Prices*, and on March 2, 1979, published an Exposure Draft, Supplement to the 1974 proposed Statement on general purchasing power adjustments. That Exposure Draft was entitled *Constant Dollar Accounting*.

79. Those Exposure Drafts were general in nature and did not address possible problems of measurement or disclosure that might be faced by different industries or for specialized assets. The Board recognized that those problems needed further attention and therefore appointed six special industry task groups for banking and thrift institutions, forest products, insurance, mining, oil and gas, and real estate. Those task groups were composed of industry executives, public accountants, financial analysts, and academicians. Their objectives were to identify the problems of measurement related to specialized assets and industries and to propose solutions that were consistent with the objectives and conceptual conclusions in the Exposure Drafts on changing prices and constant dollar accounting. An additional objective of the Oil and Gas Task Group was to maintain a close, direct liaison with the SEC and its staff as the Commission considered its proposed Reserve Recognition Accounting (RRA). To help assure this close contact, three of the members of the SEC's Advisory Committee on RRA also served on the Board's Oil and Gas Task Group.

80. The six industry task groups each held open meetings in January through May 1979, issued Preliminary Reports in April 1979, and held public hearings in May 1979 at which 30 organizations and individuals commented on the Preliminary Reports.

81. The Board received letters of comment on the Exposure Drafts and on the task groups' Preliminary Reports from 450 respondents. Copies of the letters commenting on the Preliminary Reports were sent to all members of the related task groups.

82. The Board sponsored a Conference on Financial Reporting and Changing Prices in New York City on May 31, 1979 to call attention to the urgent need for better disclosure of the effects of inflation on business operations. More than 400 financial executives, analysts, accountants, professors, and public sector policymakers heard the comments of 14 speakers representing all segments of the Board's constituency. At the Conference, and subsequently in written Interim Reports issued after considering comments on their Preliminary Reports, the six industry task groups presented their recommendations to the Board. The Board received comments from 50 individuals and organizations in response to the task groups' Interim Reports.

83. In June 1979, the Board conducted a public hearing on the Exposure Drafts. Thirty-one organizations and individuals presented their views at the three-day hearing.

84. After issuance of the Exposure Drafts, the Board and its staff maintained close contact with representatives of the SEC to keep them fully informed of the Board's and task groups' activities, particularly as they affected the SEC's reconsideration of its ASR 190 replacement cost disclosure requirements and its development of RRA for oil and gas producing activities. Members of the SEC's staff attended the meeting of the Board's Oil and Gas Task Group, and representatives of the Board attended all of the meetings of the SEC's RRA Advisory Committee.

85. In March 1978, the Board reorganized its Conceptual Framework Task Force and appointed 23 members to advise the Board and its staff on certain issues related to preparing the Exposure Drafts and this Statement. Members of the task force came from various industries, public accounting, the securities industry, and academe. The task force met four times in 1978 and 1979 and were consulted on several specific measurement and disclosure issues that are addressed in this Statement. Drafts of various sections of this Statement were sent to the task force members for comment.

86. The worldwide nature of the problem of disclosing effects of changing prices has led to active development of general price level and "current value accounting" proposals in other countries. Some of these proposals have been tested and have been withdrawn temporarily for further development before being implemented. Some of the countries in which proposals have been developed are Argentina, Australia, Brazil, Canada, France, Ireland, Japan, Mexico, Netherlands, New Zealand, South Africa, the United Kingdom, and West Germany. The European Economic Community (EEC) has issued a directive allowing member states to permit valuation methods that reflect inflation, and the International Accounting Standards Committee (IASC) is expected to issue an Exposure Draft of a proposed standard on changing prices in 1980.

Appendix C

BASIS FOR CONCLUSIONS

CONTENTS

Appendix C

BASIS FOR CONCLUSIONS

Introduction

87. This appendix reviews considerations that were deemed significant by members of the Board in reaching the conclusions in this Statement; it includes reasons for accepting certain views and rejecting others. Each consideration that was important to an individual Board member is discussed in this appendix. However the Board members who assented to this Statement did so on the basis of overall considerations and they do not attach equal weight to each consideration discussed.

88. This appendix first reviews the objectives of this Statement (paragraphs 92-96). In broad terms, the objectives are to provide information on the most significant effects on business enterprises of changing prices. This Statement calls for supplementary information about those effects in financial reports of large public enterprises. Alternative bases for the preparation of supplementary information are described in paragraphs 97-101. Paragraphs 102-115 explain two fundamental conclusions, on which all the other conclusions depend: (a) historical cost/nominal dollar accounting should continue to be

used in the primary financial statements and (b) all enterprises affected by this Statement should present two types of supplementary information—historical cost/constant dollar information and current cost information. During the next several years, the Board intends to examine additional evidence on the usefulness of the supplementary information. There are strong reasons for expecting that the information will be useful; however, the evidence will provide a basis for future decisions on the continuation or modification of the requirements of this Statement and possibly on extending them to a larger group of enterprises.

89. Paragraphs 116-155 explain the reasons for believing that each of the requirements of this Statement will be useful in providing information that is relevant to the objectives of this Statement.

90. The preparation of information on the effects of changing prices may present special difficulty in certain industries because of the nature of the resources that they use or because of other aspects of their operations. Some of those special difficulties are discussed in paragraphs 156-178.

91. The remainder of this appendix gives the bases for the Board's conclusions at a more detailed level. Issues that arise in current cost accounting are discussed in paragraphs 179-186; issues that arise in constant dollar accounting are discussed in paragraphs 187-192; issues that arise under both methods are discussed in paragraphs 193-198. Decisions on the applicability of this Statement and on the display of information are explained in paragraphs 199-207.

Objectives of This Statement

92. Changing prices have significant effects on business enterprises. If those effects are not recognized, poor decisions may be made in all sectors of society. Investors may lack important information for decisions on how much to invest, in which enterprises to invest, and on what terms; creditors may have a weak basis for decisions on the granting and pricing of credit. Consequently, the cost of capital may be too high or too low for individual enterprises: resources may be allocated inefficiently. Furthermore, people in government who participate in decisions on economic policy may not obtain the most relevant information on which to base their decisions.

93. Many people have a general understanding of the need to take account of changing prices in the interpretation of financial statements. However, there are several reasons for believing that the effects of changing prices cannot be understood adequately until they are directly reflected in financial reports:

a. The effects of changing prices depend partially on the transactions and circumstances of an enterprise and users do not have detailed information about those factors.
b. Alleviation of the problems caused by changing prices depends on a widespread understanding of those problems; a widespread understanding is unlikely to develop until business performance is discussed in terms of measures that explicitly allow for the effects of changing prices.
c. Statements by managers about the problems caused by changing prices will have greater credibility when enterprises publish financial information that addresses those problems.

94. This Statement calls for information that will be useful for users' assessments of the effects of changing prices in the following ways:

a. *Assessment of future cash flows*. In present financial statements, assets and expenses are generally measured on the basis of historical costs; changes in the prices of assets during the period between their acquisition and use or sale often are not reported. Supplementary information about those price changes will provide an up-to-date basis for users' assessments of future cash flows.
b. *Assessment of erosion of operating capability*. In assessing the future prospects of an enterprise, the users of financial reports are typically interested in whether or not an enterprise has maintained its operating capability. The maintenance of operating capability (the ability to supply a fixed quantity of goods and services) requires the holding of minimum quantities of inventory and property, plant, and equipment (and perhaps other assets). When the prices of those assets are increasing, larger amounts of money investment are needed to maintain the previous levels of output. For example, an enterprise may buy an item of inventory for $100 and sell it for $140. The transactions would contribute $40 to income determined on a historical cost/nominal dollar basis (i.e., under generally accepted accounting principles). However, the enterprise may need to replace the inventory at a cost of $115. The sale produces only $25 ($140 less $115), available for distribution without impairment of operating capability. A larger distribution, in payment of taxes or dividends, could result in an erosion of the capital required to maintain operating capability. Information on the current prices of resources that are used to generate revenues can help users to assess the extent to which and the manner in which operating capability has been maintained.
c. *Assessment of financial performance*. An enterprise may become better off as a result of holding assets while their prices increase. For example, an enterprise may decide to increase its

inventory beyond the minimum required level in order to avoid expected future increases in prices. If the price increases do take place, the decision will have increased the worth of resources. Moreover, if contribution margins (selling prices less buying prices) increase with buying prices, an enterprise may be able to sustain a given level of net cash inflows with a smaller physical investment: increases in buying prices may leave the enterprise better off in the sense of being able to earn higher nominal cash inflows. Disclosure of the effects of price changes may provide an improved basis for assessing the worth of the resources of an enterprise and hence for assessing its financial performance.

d. *Assessment of the erosion of general purchasing power.* Cash distributions by an enterprise to investors are used partly for consumption, that is for expenditures that will determine investors' standard of living. For most people, the ultimate objective of investing is to maintain or improve their standard of living or to increase their estate. When prices in general are increasing, larger sums of money are needed to maintain a fixed standard of living. If rates of return are (approximately) fixed, larger cash distributions may be obtained only as a result of increases in the amount of money invested: The amount of additional investment required depends on the rate of inflation and the extent to which it is compensated by changes in rates of return. For example, the investment of $1,000 at 10 percent will yield $100 per year. If the general price level increases by 15 percent, $115 will be needed to maintain the purchasing power of the yield. If the rate of return remains equal to 10 percent, the investment would need to be increased to $1,150 to maintain purchasing power. Financial information that reflects changes in general purchasing power can provide an improved basis for assessing whether an enterprise has maintained the purchasing power of its capital.

95. The objectives described in paragraph 94 are derived from the objectives of financial reporting set out in Concepts Statement 1. In particular that Statement calls for:

a. Information to help present and potential investors, creditors, and other users in assessing the amounts, timing, and uncertainty of prospective cash receipts from dividends or interest and the proceeds from the sale, redemption, or maturity of securities or loans. Since investors' and creditors' cash flows are related to enterprise cash flows, financial reporting should provide information to help investors, creditors, and others assess the amounts, timing, and uncertainty of prospective net cash inflows to the related enterprise (paragraph 37).
b. Information about the economic resources of an enterprise, claims to those resources, and transactions, events, and circumstances that change its resources and claims to those resources (paragraph 40).
c. Information about an enterprise's performance provided by measures of earnings and its components. Investors, creditors, and others who are concerned with assessing the prospects for enterprise net cash inflows are especially interested in that information (paragraph 43).

96. In fulfilling the objectives summarized in paragraph 94, this Statement requires information only about the effects of changes in the specific prices of resources used by an enterprise and the effects of changes in the general purchasing power of money. It is beyond the scope of this Statement to consider other matters that are relevant to the assessment of future cash flows. The Board believes that problems associated with changing prices are urgent and require immediate attention.

Alternative Accounting Systems

97. The alternatives considered by the Board may be grouped under three headings:

a. Measurements of inventory and property, plant, and equipment
    (1) Historical cost
    (2) Current reproduction cost
    (3) Current replacement cost
    (4) Net realizable value
    (5) Net present value of expected future cash flows (value in use)
    (6) Recoverable amount
    (7) Current cost
    (8) Value to the business (current cost or lower recoverable amount)
b. Concepts of capital maintenance
    (1) Financial capital maintenance
    (2) Physical capital maintenance (the maintenance of operating capability)
c. Measuring units
    (1) Measurements in nominal dollars
    (2) Measurements in constant dollars.

It is possible to combine any method of asset measurement with either concept of capital maintenance and with either measuring unit even though some combinations have greater coherence than others.

98. Paragraph 97 identifies alternatives for the measurement of certain nonmonetary assets but makes no reference to alternatives for the measurement of nonmonetary liabilities. Various alternatives are available for the measurement of liabilities. However, the Board decided to focus on alternatives available for asset measurement because it believes

that those alternatives have the greatest immediate importance for the urgent needs described in paragraph 94.

99. The asset measurements listed in paragraph 97 may be described as follows:

a. *Historical cost*. Assets are measured initially at the amount of cash (or its equivalent) paid to acquire them. Subsequently, the historical cost may be adjusted for depreciation or amortization.
b. *Current reproduction cost*. The amount of cash (or its equivalent) that would have to be paid to acquire an identical asset currently. If the reproduction cost of a used asset is measured by referring to the cost of a new asset it may need to be adjusted for depreciation or amortization.
c. *Current replacement cost*. The amount of cash (or its equivalent) that would have to be paid to acquire currently the best asset available to undertake the function of the asset owned (less depreciation or amortization if appropriate). This concept of replacement cost should be distinguished from the cost of replacing the service potential of the asset owned, called "current cost" in this Statement.
d. *Net realizable value*. Assets are measured at the amount of cash (or its equivalent) expected to be derived from sale of an asset, net of costs required to be incurred as a result of the sale.
e. *Net present value of expected future cash flows*. Assets are measured at the present value of expected future cash inflows into which the asset is expected to be converted in due course of business less the present value of expected future cash outflows necessary to obtain those inflows. This measurement of an asset is often described as value in use.
f. *Current cost*. Current cost is equal to the current replacement cost of the asset owned, adjusted for the value of any operating advantages or disadvantages of the asset owned. Current cost differs from current replacement cost in that current cost measurement focuses on the cost of the service potential embodied in the asset owned by the enterprise whereas current replacement cost may be a measurement of a different asset, available for use in place of the asset owned. Current cost will be less than current replacement cost if the service potential of the asset owned is less than the service potential of the asset that would replace it. That may be the case, for example, when the asset owned has a higher operating cost or produces an output of lower quality. Similarly, current cost may be less than current reproduction cost if identical used assets are not available for purchase and if acquisition of a new, but otherwise identical, asset would not be worthwhile because that asset is obsolete for the purposes of the enterprise concerned.
g. *Recoverable amount*. The net realizable value of an asset that is about to be sold or the net present value of expected cash flows (value in use) of an asset that is not about to be sold.
h. *Value to the business*. Value to the business may be defined as the lower of (1) current cost and (2) recoverable amount, where recoverable amount is measured at the higher of net realizable value and net present value of future cash flows. The rationale for measurement at value to the business is that the measurement of an asset should depend on the circumstances of the enterprise. Current cost is the appropriate measure if purchase of the asset would be worthwhile in current circumstances, i.e., if the value of the earning power of the asset is at least equal to current cost. In some cases, however, current purchase of the asset would not be worthwhile and current cost would then overstate the worth of the asset. If the asset is about to be sold, its worth to the business is limited to net realizable value. If the asset is not about to be sold (but would not be replaced), value in use would be an appropriate measure of the asset. Value to the business is often called "deprival value" because it can be assessed by assuming that the enterprise has been deprived of the use of an asset and asking how much the enterprise would need to be paid to compensate it for the loss. Current cost sets the upper limit for measurement of the asset. The maximum loss incurred by the enterprise, following deprival, would be limited to the current cost of the asset as long as replacement was possible. The assumption of deprival should not be interpreted literally; it is no more than a helpful analytical device. (As the above discussion indicates, the terms "value to the business," "deprival value," and "current cost or lower recoverable amount" all have the same meaning.)

100. Capital is maintained when revenues are at least equal to all costs and expenses. The appropriate measurement of costs and expenses depends on the concept of capital maintenance adopted. The capital maintenance concepts listed in paragraph 97 may be described as follows:

a. Financial capital maintenance. If capital is regarded as a quantity of financial resources, costs and expenses should be measured in terms of the financial resources (usually historical costs) used up in earning the revenues. Suppose, for example, that an enterprise is established with a capital of $1,000 in cash; that sum is used immediately to purchase inventory; the inventory is sold a year later for $1,500. Cost of goods sold would be measured at $1,000, the amount required to maintain the original money amount of capital invested in the inventory, and income would be measured at $500. Suppose, as an alternative, that the inventory is held and measured at its current cost ($1,200) at the end of the year. Those who believe in financial capital maintenance would recognize the increase in current cost ($200) as part of income: $1,000 is deducted from the current cost of $1,200 at the end of the year to maintain the amount of financial capital invested.

b. Physical capital maintenance (the maintenance of physical operating capability). According to this view, costs and expenses are measured at an amount sufficient to preserve the capacity of the enterprise to maintain previous levels of output of goods and services. Consider again the numerical example given in subparagraph (a) above. If the inventory is sold for $1,500, and if the current cost of the inventory is $1,200 at the date of sale, income would be measured at $300 ($1,500 less $1,200); $1,200 must be retained to maintain the physical operating capability of the enterprise. Similarly, if the inventory is held and measured at $1,200 at the end of the year, no income would be recognized.

101. The units of measurement listed in paragraph 97 may be described as follows:

a. Nominal dollars. All events, transactions, and other circumstances affecting the financial statements are measured and reported in actual money amounts without adjustment for the fact that one dollar represents a different amount of purchasing power at different times. Measurements are expressed in nominal dollars in the primary financial statements under generally accepted accounting principles.

b. Constant dollars (units of general purchasing power). All events, transactions, and other circumstances affecting the enterprise are measured in units of constant general purchasing power represented by the dollar at some specified base date. Advocates of this method of measurement often regard its main advantage as the use of homogeneous units whereas the nominal dollar method involves units having a variable worth. Consider again the simplified numerical example given in paragraph 100 and suppose that the general price level increases by 10 percent during the year under consideration. Suppose, also, that the purchasing power of the dollar at the end of the year is used as the unit of measure. The amount of capital to be maintained under the financial capital maintenance concept will be $1,100 because that amount in end-of-period dollars has the same purchasing power as $1,000 at the start of the period. If the inventory was sold at the end of the period for $1,500, income would be measured at $400 ($1,500 less $1,100). If the inventory was held and measured at a current cost of $1,200 at the end of the period, and the financial capital maintenance concept was again used, income would be measured at only $100 ($1,200 less $1,100). Constant dollars may be used as a measuring unit regardless of which attribute of assets is measured and regardless of whether the financial capital maintenance concept or the physical capital maintenance concept is used.

Selection of Supplementary Disclosures

102. In choosing among the alternatives described in paragraphs 97-101, the Board considered the benefits of each system in terms of usefulness in meeting the needs listed in paragraph 94 and it weighed those benefits against the costs of implementing the systems. Usefulness was assessed in terms of the relevance of the measurements to the objectives and in terms of the reliability of the measurements as indicated by representational faithfulness and verifiability. The Board recognized the desirability of limiting the costs of preparing information about the effects of changing prices by allowing an enterprise the flexibility to choose any one of several alternative sources of information to obtain the required measurements and by encouraging approximate methods of computation.

103. No accounting computation can represent perfectly all the complex considerations that are relevant to the assessment of future cash flows to an enterprise or to the evaluation of enterprise performance. It will always be necessary for users of financial reports to exercise independent judgment, taking account of their knowledge of the general economic environment and the structure of the industry in which an enterprise operates. Decisions on the desirability of new accounting requirements should be based on answers to questions such as: Would the new information provide an improved basis for users' judgment? Does the new information represent an improvement over existing information, an improvement that is sufficient to justify the extra costs?

104. The Board concluded that information in the primary financial statements should continue to be measured on a historical cost/nominal dollar basis and that enterprises should present certain supplementary information according to two main bases:

a. Historical cost/constant dollar accounting. Inventory and property, plant, and equipment, cost of goods sold, and depreciation expense would be measured at historical cost/constant dollar amounts or lower recoverable amounts. Constant dollar adjustments need not be applied comprehensively to the remaining nonmonetary items in the financial statements but would be applied to computation of the purchasing power gain or loss on net monetary items.

b. Current cost accounting. Inventory and property, plant, and equipment, cost of goods sold, and depreciation expense would be measured at current cost or lower recoverable amounts. Current cost adjustments would not be applied to other items in the financial statements. Constant dollar adjustments would not be applied comprehensively to the current cost information but would be applied to computations of the increase or decrease in current cost amounts of inventory, property, plant, and equipment and to the purchasing power gain or loss on net monetary items.

In the Exposure Draft, the Board expressed its conclusion that the financial capital maintenance concept is more useful than the physical capital maintenance concept. It has subsequently concluded that it should express no preference for either concept at this time and that enterprises should present information that would enable users to assess the amount of income under both concepts.

105. The Board believes that further experimentation is required on the usefulness of the two types of supplementary information described in paragraph 104. The basis for that belief is set out in paragraphs 109-115. However, the Board has concluded that there are strong reasons to expect that both types of supplementary information will be useful. Those reasons are reviewed in paragraphs 116-155 in terms of the objectives described in paragraph 94. Special considerations are applicable to certain types of enterprises and those considerations are discussed in paragraphs 156-178.

Continued Reliance on Historical Cost/ Nominal Dollar Accounting

106. Most financial statements prepared in the United States measure nonmonetary assets at historical costs. For example, under present practice, inventory and property, plant, and equipment are normally measured at historical cost or depreciated historical cost in the balance sheet; when an asset is wholly or partly used in revenue-producing activities, the related expense is also measured at historical cost. The measuring unit in financial statements is the nominal dollar; changes in the purchasing power of the dollar are ignored.

107. Historical cost/nominal dollar accounting is widely believed to provide useful information. Historical cost is accepted as a satisfactory measure of asset value at the date of acquisition. It can be measured with acceptable reliability in the vast majority of cases. The tradition of measuring profit on the sale of an asset as the excess of selling price over historical cost is simple to understand, as is the meaning of acquisition cost as the measure of an asset.

The Advantages of Requirements of Supplementary Information

108. Many observers concerned with financial reports have had little experience with the preparation and use of financial reports based on systems other than historical cost/nominal dollar accounting. A change in the measures of assets and expenses in the primary financial statements would be confusing to some. An approach based on supplementary information has several advantages over requirements for changes in the primary financial statements: Familiar types of information would continue to be available to users and would provide a basis for evaluation of the supplementary information; experience with supplementary information on the effects of changing prices would permit better assessment of the usefulness of alternative methods; possible disruption of the procedures involved in accounting, auditing, and financial analysis would be minimized; and the exemption of small and closely held enterprises from the requirements of a Statement on supplementary disclosure would be preferable to exemptions from requirements related to the primary financial statements. Moreover, the retention of historical cost as the basic measure for most enterprises makes it possible to justify the allowance of more flexibility in the preparation of information on the impact of changing prices. Experience with supplementary information based on different measurement concepts may or may not eventually lead to changes in measurements in the primary financial statements. The Board concluded that no change should be made to the primary financial statements at this time. That decision was widely supported by those who commented on the Exposure Draft.

The Need for Experimentation

109. The Exposure Draft proposed that enterprises should be permitted to choose between the provision of supplementary information on a historical cost/constant dollar basis and on a current cost basis. Guidelines were provided for the choice. The Board had tentatively concluded that a choice should be permitted because it believed that both methods would provide useful information but it had insufficient evidence to select one and reject the other. Moreover, the Board concluded that both methods could be implemented with acceptable reliability. Extensive field tests of historical cost/ constant dollar accounting had been carried out by the Board in 1975 and enterprises had obtained extensive experience, in complying with the SEC's replacement cost requirements in ASR 190, with the

measurement of data having many similarities to current cost data.

110. Constant dollar accounting and current cost accounting may be regarded as methods for dealing with two different problems. In times of general inflation, the nominal dollar has a variable purchasing power. Nominal dollar accounting therefore involves the aggregation of measures expressed in a variable unit. Constant dollar accounting overcomes that problem. However, historical cost/constant dollar accounting simply restates the primary financial statements in units of constant purchasing power. Current cost accounting deals with changes in the specific prices of resources used by the enterprise. Many comment letters on the Exposure Draft argued that the differences of purpose made it inappropriate to allow a choice between the two methods.

111. Many people have also argued that the provision of choice would make it difficult to gather valid evidence on the usefulness of the two methods. If similar enterprises chose different methods, the information in their reports would not be comparable. Moreover, choices might be biased in favor of one method with the result that insufficient evidence would be available for a comparative evaluation of the two methods. The Board accepted the arguments against the provision of choice between current cost information and historical cost/constant dollar information.

112. The comment letters and public hearings indicated sharp divisions of opinion on the relative usefulness of historical cost/constant dollar accounting and current cost accounting. Comments from the users of financial reports strongly supported a system that measured assets at current cost. Those comments appear to reflect the belief that current cost measures are more relevant than historical cost measures for the assessment of future cash flows. Many preparers of financial reports and public accounting firms favored historical cost/constant dollar accounting. Their comments typically emphasized the lower cost and the higher verifiability and representational faithfulness of historical cost/constant dollar accounting.

113. The arguments against permitting choice and the absence of a clear preference for one method suggest the need to call for supplementary information according to both methods. The Board considered whether such a requirement could be met within acceptable cost limits. It concluded that the incremental costs of implementation would not be excessive if it provided for simplifications in the methods of measurement and computation. Moreover, the incremental cost would be further limited if, as expected, the SEC rescinds its requirement for the disclosure of replacement cost data under ASR 190. The Board further noted that some of the preparatory work would be common to both methods. For example, if an enterprise determined current cost by using indexes of specific prices, the same "aging" of assets would be required for both historical cost/constant dollar measurements and current cost measurements. Moreover, most of the enterprises covered by this Statement would already have undertaken that "aging" in preparing data on replacement costs to comply with ASR 190.

114. Some people believe that the presentation of supplementary information about two different measures of income will be confusing to some users. The Board believes that confusion can be substantially avoided if enterprises include sufficient explanatory material in the financial reports to help users understand the supplementary information; this Statement requires presentation of that explanatory material. The Board also believes that the presentation of alternative measurements may be desirable in itself. A single measure may be insufficient to convey all the effects of changing prices on a business enterprise.

115. The Board intends to assess the usefulness of the information called for by this Statement. It proposes to carry out research to answer questions such as the following: Which supplementary information is used? By whom is it used? How is it used? The Board will review the requirements of the Statement comprehensively when it has obtained sufficient evidence on usefulness. It anticipates that a period of up to five years may be required to gather satisfactory evidence. However, the Board will also reassess the costs and benefits of providing the information required by this Statement on an ongoing basis and will amend or withdraw requirements whenever that course is justified by the evidence.

The Usefulness of Supplementary Information on Changing Prices

The Assessment of Future Cash Flows

116. Concepts Statement 1 expresses the Board's conclusion that financial reports should provide information to help users assess the amounts, timing, and uncertainty of future cash flows. That conclusion provides the primary basis for believing that the information required by this Statement will be useful.

117. Current cost income reflects current cost margins—sales revenues less the current cost of inputs. Information on current cost margins may be useful for assessing future cash flows particularly if the selling price of a product is closely related to its current cost at the date of sale. However, the Board

recognizes that selling prices are not determined by costs alone and that assessments of future cash flows must take account of changes in economic conditions as they affect the industry in which the enterprise operates.

118. The increase or decrease in current cost amounts of assets held by the enterprise may also provide a useful basis for the assessment of future cash flows. The results of holding activities and continuing operations will be affected differently by economic forces and the two measures may therefore be useful in different ways for the assessment of future cash flows. It is easier to take account of the various forces shaping the time patterns of operating income and changes in current cost amounts if the two items are separated as they are in the current cost information provided for by this Statement.

119. Some people have pointed out that the holding of assets is normally necessary to the continuation of business activities. They have argued that the results of holding and the income from continuing operations are joint effects, and they take the view that separation is therefore invalid. However, the Board believes that this argument is outweighed by the counterarguments: separation may well improve the basis for assessments of future cash flows. Moreover, the holding period is not absolutely fixed. It may be varied to take advantage of favorable buying opportunities that may not recur, and it is useful to disclose separately the results of such opportunities.

120. The measurement of the current costs or lower recoverable amounts of assets may be regarded as partial recognition of the net present values of future cash flows from the use of the assets. Current cost represents a conservative measure of the net present value of future cash flows because net present value represents the maximum price at which purchase of an asset would be worthwhile. Competitive market forces normally cause current costs to have a closer and more stable relationship than historical costs to net present values. Moreover, recoverable amounts will be approximately equal to the net present values of future cash flow. Consequently, current costs or lower recoverable amounts may be regarded as providing a useful supplement to historical cost information for the purposes of assessing future cash flows.

121. The measurement of income from continuing operations on a current cost basis may be regarded as a guide to assessments of whether an enterprise has maintained its operating capability, i.e., its capacity to supply a fixed quantity of goods and services. Current cost income from continuing operations does not measure the maintenance of operating capability exactly because it rests on certain simplifying assumptions. For example, an enterprise may need to increase its net monetary working capital to maintain operating capability and that factor is ignored in the measurement of current cost income. Moreover, an enterprise may be able to obtain some of the capital required to maintain operating capability by borrowing or by raising new equity capital from external sources: That possibility also is ignored in the measurement of current cost income. Subject to those factors, however, the difference between dividends paid by an enterprise and current cost income from continuing operations provides an indication of changes in operating capability: An excess of dividends over current cost income indicates that operating capability has decreased; an excess of current cost income over dividends indicates that operating capability has increased. An enterprise will not normally wish to maintain its operating capability at a constant level over time. Decisions on the desired level of operating capability depend on rates of increase in the costs of resources used by the enterprise, the strength of demand for its products, the opportunities for commencing new lines of business and other factors. However, users who wish to assess future cash flows may find it helpful to have information from which they can assess whether operating capability has changed during a fiscal year. The relationship between current cost income and operating capability is discussed more fully in paragraphs 124-130.

122. In paragraphs 118 and 119, it was noted that separation of current cost income and increases or decreases in current cost amounts of assets held may be useful for assessments of future cash flows because the two measures have different patterns over time. The usefulness of information of changes in current cost amounts may be explained in a different way. An increase in current costs of assets held by an enterprise represents an increase in its financial investment. Presumably, an enterprise can expect to earn a rate of return on that additional investment. Hence, information on changes in current cost amounts represents a basis for assessing changes in future cash flows and related returns on investment. That use of current cost information is discussed further in paragraphs 131-136.

123. The measurement of current cost amounts may be useful for the assessment of future cash flows in another, more general, manner. When users wish to assess future cash flows, they will often examine the components of financial statements in detail rather than focusing on summary measures such as income from continuing operations. Cost of goods sold at current cost, depreciation expense at current cost, and the current cost amounts of inventory and property, plant, and equipment will incorporate more up-to-date information about the

prices of resources used by an enterprise than the corresponding historical cost amounts. Information based on current prices may provide a more useful basis than historical cost amounts for assessing future prices of the resources concerned and hence for assessing future cash flows.

Information on the Erosion of Physical Capital

124. Some members of the Board attach particular importance to the use of information on current cost income from continuing operations for assessments of whether an enterprise has maintained its operating capability. Erosion of physical capital (or erosion of operating capability) may be regarded as the failure to retain sufficient financial resources to acquire the assets needed to maintain the capacity of the enterprise to provide a constant supply of goods and services. The concept of physical capital erosion may be linked to a concept of distributable income where distributable income is defined as the amount of cash that may be distributed without reducing the operating capability of an enterprise. The information on current cost income from continuing operations required by this Statement provides a basis for users' assessments of distributable income.

125. In computations of current cost income from continuing operations, cost of goods sold, and depreciation expense are measured at current cost or lower recoverable amounts. The relevance of those measures to the assessment of the operating capability of an enterprise may be demonstrated by considering various circumstances in which the measurements may need to be made. First, suppose that current cost is equal to replacement cost (there have been no changes in technology or fashion since the asset owned was purchased) and that recoverable amounts exceed current cost: replacement of the asset is worthwhile. In that situation, costs must be measured at current cost in order to provide for the maintenance of operating capability. Assume, for example, that inventory is purchased for $1,000 and sold for $1,500 at a time when current cost is $1,200. Although historical cost/nominal dollar income is $500 ($1,500 less $1,000), distributions may be limited to $300 ($1,500 less $1,200) to maintain operating capability. Costs are measured at $1,200 in order to provide for the replacement of the inventory out of revenues. An increase of $200 ($1,200 less $1,000) in current costs would be recognized but would not be regarded as part of income under concepts that address the maintenance of physical operating capability.

126. In other circumstances, current cost may be less than replacement cost for various reasons. The service potential of the asset owned may be less than the service potential of new assets that are available. That situation would be important if purchase of a new asset would be worthwhile. Alternatively, the replacement of the asset owned may not be worthwhile because the type of inventory or output of the asset is no longer marketable at a satisfactory price; in other words, the recoverable amounts are lower than current cost. In those circumstances, measurement of costs may reflect (1) replacement costs or (2) current costs or lower recoverable amounts. The nature of the alternatives may be illustrated by a simplified example. Suppose that inventory was purchased for $1,000 but that the item goes out of fashion and is sold for $900 when replacement cost is $1,200. The results of the transaction may be measured in the following two ways:

	Measurement at	
	Replacement Cost	Current Cost or Lower Recoverable Amount
Sales revenues	$ 900	$ 900
Cost of goods sold	1,200	900
Loss from continuing operations	$ (300)	$ 0
Cost at date of sale	$1,200	$ 900
Cost at date of acquisition	1,000	1,000
Increase (decrease) in current cost amounts	$ 200	$ (100)

Measurement at current cost or lower recoverable amount produces an income from continuing operations of zero. That concept may be justified by the argument that $100 has been lost while the asset was held and should be reported as a "decrease in current cost amounts"; operating capability can be maintained at the date of sale if revenues are at least equal to costs measured at $900. The alternative approach is to measure cost of goods sold at replacement cost, so that income would be measured at negative $300 and an increase in current cost amounts of $200 would be reported. That approach reflects the view that in order to continue with similar operations, an enterprise should maintain net assets at $1,200. The enterprise may not wish to replace the inventory but it would be assumed to wish to have capital of $1,200 available for purchase of other assets. The Board concluded that expenses should be measured at current cost or lower recoverable amount in the measurement of income on a current cost basis. It believes that replacement cost is not relevant to the measurement of income from continuing operations when replacement would not be worthwhile.

127. The discussion in paragraphs 125 and 126, illustrated by reference to the holding of inventory and the measurement of cost of goods sold, is applicable also to the measurement of depreciation expense. However, the concept is more complicated in the case of depreciation expense because the replacement of property, plant, and equipment may take place several years after the measurement date. Suppose, for example, that an enterprise buys a fixed asset for $1,000 and that the asset has a life of only two years. If the current cost of the asset increases by 10 percent per year, depreciation expense measured at the midpoint of each year would be $525 in year 1 and $577 in year 2, a total of $1,102 and less than the current cost of $1,210 at the replacement date. The gap between the total depreciation expense during the life of the asset and its current cost at the end of its life is often referred to as "backlog depreciation." However, the omission of backlog depreciation from expense does not prevent the maintenance of operating capability when assets are acquired at regular intervals. Suppose, for example, that an enterprise has 10 similar assets, each having a maximum life of 10 years, and present ages range evenly from 1 to 10 years. The aggregate depreciation expense on the 10 assets, at current cost, would represent the current cost of the one asset that needs to be purchased currently. If the pattern of asset acquisition is uneven to a significant extent, backlog depreciation may need to be considered in users' assessment of the maintenance of physical capital.

128. The discussion in paragraphs 125-127 has ignored two other influences on distributable income: The effect of changing prices on monetary working capital and the opportunity to increase the amount of debt in times of rising prices. The adjustments to cost of goods sold and depreciation expense, discussed above, recognize increases in costs that need to be recovered to provide for increases in capital invested in inventory and property, plant, and equipment. However, they do not provide for the increase in monetary working capital (for example, cash plus receivables less payables) that is commonly required as a result of increasing prices. It is also possible that the borrowing capacity of an enterprise may be related to the current costs of its assets so that part of the increase in assets required to maintain operating capability may be provided by increasing the amount of debt rather than by retention of earnings. Some people have argued that it would be desirable to include approximate adjustments for these factors in a supplementary measure of income.

129. The Board has concluded that no adjustments should be required at this time for the factors described in paragraph 128 because: (a) the adjustments would significantly increase the complexity of the requirements and (b) the amount of debt that is actually raised will depend on discretionary decisions of the enterprise. Moreover, the Board has a separate project on funds flows and liquidity and it believes that special aspects of the effects of changing prices on funds flows should be studied as part of that project. The Board believes that, pending completion of the project on funds flows and liquidity, assessments of changes in monetary working capital and of changes in borrowing capacity should be based on other information in the financial reports. It encourages enterprises to comment on these factors in explanations of the supplementary financial information. Some Board members regard the purchasing power gain or loss on net monetary items (paragraphs 150-155) as mitigating the need for adjustments of monetary working capital and for changes in borrowing capacity. That view is based on the observation that increases in the general price level produce a purchasing power loss on monetary assets, such as receivables (the loss may be seen as a provision for extra monetary working capital requirements) and a purchasing power gain on debt and payables (the gain may be regarded as a recognition of an increase in distributable income resulting from the use of additional debt or payables to provide financial resources for some of the additional investment required to maintain operating capability). However, those Board members recognize the deficiency of the purchasing power gain or loss for these purposes, resulting from the fact that it reflects changes in general price levels rather than changes in specific prices that affect the enterprise.

130. On the basis of the arguments set forth in paragraphs 125-129, some Board members believe that distributable income can represent a useful basis for certain aspects of users' assessments of future cash flows. The actual distribution made by an enterprise will normally differ from current cost income from continuing operations for various reasons. However, investors who wish to assess future cash flows are likely to find it useful to have some basis for assessing whether increases or reductions in operating capacity have taken place; and creditors and other users of financial reports may wish to assess whether an enterprise has been able to maintain operating capability without raising additional capital from external sources. Other Board members believe that consideration of the concept of distributable income and the related concerns with the needs for additional monetary working capital and changes in borrowing capacity is not appropriate in this Statement dealing as it does with measurements of earnings. In their view, those matters relate to

dividend policy and other aspects of financing policies and are more properly considered in the Board's project on funds flows and liquidity. Those Board members agree, however, that for the additional reasons discussed in paragraphs 131-136, information about income from continuing operations measured on a current cost basis is likely to be helpful to users in their assessments of future cash flows.

The Comprehensive Measurement of Enterprise Performance

131. Some Board members believe that an important use of current cost accounting is in providing an improved basis for the comprehensive assessment of enterprise performance; that basis is represented by the sum of current cost income from continuing operations and the increase or decrease in the current cost amounts of assets (referred to in the Exposure Draft as holding gains and losses). Those Board members believe that investors and creditors are primarily concerned with the performance of an enterprise in terms of its ability to generate cash flows and returns on financial investment rather than with its physical operating capability. Although potential cash flows are not independent of operating capability, an enterprise may be able to increase its cash flows and returns on investment without increasing its operating capability. According to this view, an enterprise invests financial resources with the expectation that the investment will generate acceptable levels of cash inflow. Recovery of the amount of financial resources invested is a return *of* capital; cash flows in excess of the amount invested are returns *on* invested capital. From that point of view, increased investments of financial resources to maintain physical operating capability are indistinguishable from increased investments of financial resources to expand physical operating capability. Both kinds of investments will be made only if expected cash flows provide an acceptable return on the investment.

132. The ideal measure of the worth of the resources of an enterprise might be obtained by measuring assets at the net present value of future cash flows. An asset is valuable to the extent that it can generate future cash flows and only to that extent. Moreover, if net present values would be ideal measures of worth, changes in net present value over a period would be ideal measures of enterprise performance. However, the Board has concluded that the general use of net present values is not practicable and it does not expect their use to become practicable. The use of net present value calculations required by this Statement is limited to some special situations in which they may be needed for measurements of recoverable amounts. There are at least two overriding objections to the general use of net present values. The measurements cannot be made with acceptable reliability. Furthermore, the jointness of cash flows to the enterprise means that net present values for individual assets cannot be obtained without using arbitrary allocations that lack economic significance. In general, net present values are better suited to measurement of the value of the whole enterprise than to measurements of individual assets. However, assessment of the value of the whole enterprise is the essence of the process of financial analysis; it is not properly a part of the information that should be provided directly in financial reports.

133. Having rejected the general use of net present values, the Board considered whether another system of measurement would provide a useful basis for users' assessment of the worth of the enterprise. Historical cost (less depreciation, if appropriate) may provide a useful basis for such assessments when prices are stable. However, when prices are increasing, historical cost measures tend to lose their significance as bases for assessment of the worth of an asset. Some Board members concluded that the measurement of assets at current cost or lower recoverable amount could provide a useful basis for assessing future cash flows to the enterprise because those measurements can be regarded as surrogates for the net present value of cash flows expected to be earned from the use of assets. Current costs may presumably be expected to have some relationship to net present values (and hence future cash flows) because estimated net present value will represent the maximum sum that an enterprise would be willing to pay for an asset. The exact nature of the relationship will depend on conditions in the markets in which the assets are bought and sold. Measurements of assets at their recoverable amounts represent direct estimates of the net present values of future cash flows (in the case of values in use) or approximations to net present values (in the case of net realizable values).

134. If measurements of assets at current cost or lower recoverable amounts are regarded as surrogates for measurements of the net present value of future cash flows, it follows that a basis for assessments of enterprise performance during a period may be provided by an income measure that reflects changes in current costs or lower recoverable amounts. Income from continuing operations on a current cost basis does not fully reflect those changes. It omits the difference between the measure of the asset at its acquisition date (i.e., acquisition cost) and the measure of the asset at the date of use or sale.

135. The increases or decreases in current cost or lower recoverable amounts are often known as holding gains or losses and they were so described in the Exposure Draft. However, several comment let-

ters argued that the terms "gain" and "loss" should not be applied to these items because they are not part of the income that is available for distribution without impairing the operating capability of the enterprise. That view reflects the physical capital maintenance concept described in paragraphs 124-130. However, those who favor the financial capital maintenance concept believe that capital is maintained when revenues are sufficient to recover the financial reserves invested; under that concept, holding gains or losses are regarded as part of income. After considering those alternative points of view, the Board concluded that it is preferable to use the neutral description "increase or decrease in current cost amounts" to describe differences between acquisition cost and current costs or lower recoverable amounts at the date of use or sale.

136. The Board concluded that enterprises should be required to report the increase or decrease in current cost amounts separately from income from continuing operations. Users may find it useful to add the two numbers together to obtain a basis for assessing the overall performance of an enterprise during the fiscal year. However, separate reporting of the two amounts may be helpful for the assessment of future cash flows for the reasons discussed in paragraph 118. It is easier to take account of the various forces shaping the time patterns of operating income and changes in current cost amounts if the two items are separated as they are in the current cost information provided for by this Statement. In assessing overall performance, users should take into account changes in market conditions governing the prices of assets held by the enterprise since those changes may affect the extent to which changes in current cost are associated with changes in expected future cash flows. Current cost measurements do not reflect all the factors that influence the value of an enterprise.

Maintenance of Purchasing Power

137. Paragraphs 138-144 explain the reasons for believing that current cost/constant dollar accounting can provide a useful basis for users' assessments of whether an enterprise has maintained the purchasing power of their investments. The focus is on two measures derived from current cost accounting: (a) income from continuing operations on a current cost basis and (b) the increase or decrease in current cost amounts, net of inflation.

138. The main purpose of investment by shareholders and others is to earn a return that is available, sooner or later, in cash to meet personal expenditures. Investors will hope to receive cash (in the form of dividends, interest payments and so on) in amounts that have a convenient pattern over time, particularly if they rely on the cash to meet fixed commitments. Investors are also concerned with the purchasing power of the cash that they receive. If they receive a fixed amount of money each year, in times of inflation, their purchasing power will decline year by year. In that situation, investors may wish to save money in order to provide a fund that can be used as needed to compensate for the decline in purchasing power. They may be interested in an estimate of the maximum amount they can spend in a given year without expecting a decline in future purchasing power, even if they decide, for personal reasons, to spend a different amount.

139. Investors' need for information about the purchasing power associated with their investments can be met by the use of a "constant dollar" measuring unit. The potential usefulness of such a system can be illustrated by a simplified numerical example. Suppose that an investor holds a fixed interest security having a very long life. Suppose also, to simplify the calculations, that effective interest rates for such securities have been 14 percent per year for several years; and that the rate of general inflation has been 10 percent per year for several years. In those circumstances, it may be reasonable to assume that the market value of the security will be constant over time. It is assumed that the market value of the security is $1,000, interest receipts are $140 per year and that all economic conditions are expected to remain constant for several years. If the investor spends $140 each year, purchasing power will steadily decline. In the second year, the interest receipt will provide enough to purchase only $140/1.1, i.e., $127 worth of goods and services measured in terms of the purchasing power of the dollar in year one. If the investor wishes to enjoy a constant amount of purchasing power in each year, the purchasing power of his investment must be maintained. That means that expenditures must be restricted in each year to produce savings equal to the rate of inflation multiplied by the value of the investments at the start of the year; the saving would have to be invested in securities that were similar to the original holding. The transactions would then run as follows:

	Value of Investments at Start of Year	Interest Receipts	Saving Reinvested	Personal Expenditure	Value of Investments at End of Year
Year 1	$1,000	$140	$100	$40	$1,100
Year 2	$1,100	$154	$110	$44	$1,210
Year 3	$1,210	$169	$121	$48	$1,331

Personal expenditures increase by 10 percent each year, in step with inflation.

140. If the methods of constant dollar accounting are applied to the illustration in paragraph 139, and the unit of measurement is the purchasing power of the dollar at the end of the year concerned, income will be measured at the amounts shown above as personal expenditure. Thus, constant dollar accounting may help to answer the question: How much can be spent this year if the investor wishes to maintain the purchasing power of expenditures from year to year? The computations would run as follows in year one:

Interest Income		$140
Change in value of security:		
Value at end of year	$1,000	
Value at beginning of year, restated in end-of-year dollars ($1,000 × 110/100)	1,100	(100)
Net income		$ 40

The computations involve, in effect, deducting a capital maintenance adjustment equal to the rate of inflation multiplied by the amount of net assets at the beginning of the year. Furthermore, if the computations for each year are restated in constant dollars of a fixed base year, each row in the table in paragraph 139 would contain the same numbers. For example, if all measurements were made in constant dollars as of the end of year one, income would be measured at $40 in each year, thus providing another way of illustrating that the investor can enjoy a fixed amount of purchasing power from year to year. The above illustration has been highly simplified particularly in its assumption that interest rates and rates of inflation are constant. In practice, an assessment of the future purchasing power available as a result of past activities would have to take account of possible changes in rates of return and in rates of inflation. However, constant dollar accounting may provide a useful basis for users' assessments of such factors.

141. The illustration in paragraph 140 of the usefulness of constant dollar accounting dealt with transactions undertaken by an investor. Some people believe that computations of performance in constant dollars should be regarded as useful for investors but that they should not be applied directly to information in the financial reports of an enterprise. Others believe that it can be useful to have information about the performance of an enterprise, measured in constant dollars. The reasons for that belief are examined next.

142. In paragraphs 131-136, it was argued that a useful indication of overall enterprise performance could be obtained by considering income from continuing operations on a current cost basis together with a computation of the increase or decrease in the current cost amounts of assets held by the enterprise. Users' assessments based on that information will need to take account of various external factors, including the extent to which assets held by the enterprise are traded in competitive markets and the implications for the extent to which current cost measures indicate potential future cash flows. The application of constant dollar accounting to information prepared on a current cost basis can be regarded as an adjustment for changes in the general purchasing power represented by the worth of the enterprise insofar as that worth is recognized under current cost accounting.

143. Income from continuing operations on a current cost basis may be regarded as a number measured, approximately, in constant dollars having the average purchasing power of dollars during the year concerned. Revenues are measured in average dollars if they are spread evenly over the year and expenses are measured at current costs at the dates of use or sale. The increase or decrease in current cost amounts over the year reflects the differences between measures of assets in end-of-year dollars and in beginning-of-year dollars. Those differences must be adjusted for the general inflation component to obtain a measure of changes in current costs in constant dollars (the adjustment is analogous to the adjustment of the changes in the value of the security, illustrated in paragraph 140).

144. On the basis of the discussion in paragraphs 138-143, the Board concluded that information disclosed by an enterprise on the increase or decrease in current cost amounts of assets should be reported net of inflation.

The Usefulness of Historical Cost/ Constant Dollar Accounting

145. One way of expressing the arguments for using a system of constant dollar accounting is to say that the measuring unit should serve as a common denominator for the adding, subtracting, and comparing of revenues and expenses, assets and liabilities, owners' equity, and earnings. Some observers question whether a nominal monetary unit such as the nominal dollar can serve that function. Conversion of nominal dollars to constant dollars is recommended by them as a means of obtaining the benefits of a common denominator. That process is considered analogous to the process under which measurements made in one currency are translated into another currency for comparative purposes. Constant dollar measurements may be added, subtracted, compared, and used without the need to make subjective allowances for inflation in a manner that would otherwise be necessary for valid comparisons. That, according to its advocates, is a pervasive advantage of using constant dollar information as a supplement to nominal dollar information.

146. The rate of return on investment is commonly used as a measure of investment performance. Investors who are concerned with purchasing power may want to compute their rate of return by dividing constant dollar income by constant dollar investment. A computation of a constant dollar return on investment may be useful for an individual who invests in securities, one who invests in his own business, or one who joins with others in a partnership or corporation. A shareholder cannot expect to obtain a net increase in purchasing power in the long run if the corporation does not increase the purchasing power equivalent of its net assets. If shareholders take an interest in the corporation's constant dollar return on investment, it follows that managers may be evaluated partly on that basis and may concern themselves with that measure of performance. Top managers may also appraise and compare divisional management and divisional activities on the same basis. Regulatory authorities and other governmental agencies may also be concerned with the preservation of the equity interest in the enterprise. Finally, the widely recognized desire of investors to compare the performance of different enterprises suggests the need for uniform computations of constant dollar returns on investment.

147. Constant dollar accounting and current cost accounting have been developed as solutions to fundamentally different problems: Constant dollar accounting deals with general inflation by adopting an appropriate measuring unit; current cost accounting deals with specific price changes by measuring an appropriate attribute of resources held and used by an enterprise.

148. However, some people believe that it is useful to regard measurements of assets and expenses at their historical cost/constant dollar amounts as rough approximations to the measurements obtained under current cost accounting. If the constant dollar selected as the measuring unit is the average purchasing power of the dollar over the fiscal year, certain revenues and expenses that are spread evenly over the year will be measured at approximately the same amount in the primary financial statements and under historical cost/ constant dollar accounting and current cost accounting. This Statement provides that those items may be reported at the same amounts in the supplementary information and in the primary financial statements. The principal differences between income in the primary financial statements and income under current cost accounting and historical cost/constant dollar accounting will be in the measurements of cost of goods sold and depreciation expense. In both cases, the numbers represent original cost of the related asset adjusted for changes in price levels between the date of acquisition and the date of use or sale. In the case of historical cost/constant dollar accounting, the adjustment is based on an index of general prices; in the case of current cost accounting, the adjustment reflects specific price changes. Similar differences characterize the balance sheet measurements of inventory and property, plant, and equipment under the two systems. It follows that historical cost/ constant dollar measurements will approximate current cost measurements only to the extent that general price changes are approximately the same as changes in the specific prices of resources used by the enterprise.

149. The view that historical cost/constant dollar measurements represent an approximation to current cost measurements may be helpful because it focuses attention on differences in the relevance and reliability of information produced under the two systems. The measurement of current cost may be a matter of practical difficulty. If the measurement is based on a specific price index, it will be necessary to choose an appropriate index and accept that the index may fail to reflect the effect of changing technology and the mix of assets used by the enterprise. If the measurement is based on a direct pricing method, it may be difficult to obtain evidence that is unambiguously relevant to the circumstances of the enterprise. Those problems of judgment are avoided in historical cost/constant dollar accounting. Even opponents of historical cost/constant dollar accounting agree that it is verifiable and represents accurately what it purports to represent. Many believe that current cost measurements have greater relevance to the assessment of future cash flows but historical cost/constant dollar measurements have greater reliability. The Board concluded that it should call for the disclosure of income from con-

tinuing operations under both historical cost/constant dollar accounting and current cost accounting partly in order to obtain evidence of users' trade-off between relevance and reliability.

The Purchasing Power Gain or Loss on Net Monetary Items

150. An enterprise often needs to hold cash and the effect of doing so may be analyzed according to the concepts of constant dollar accounting. The value of cash is fixed in nominal dollars. If an enterprise holds $100 in cash, it will still have $100 at any later time. Holding cash does not in itself produce a nominal dollar profit or loss; however, during a period of inflation there is a loss of purchasing power. For example, the holding of $100 for one year, when the inflation rate is 8 percent, involves a loss of $8 of purchasing power (measured in end-of-year dollars): one would need 108 end-of-year dollars to have the purchasing power equivalent of 100 beginning-of-year dollars.

151. The loss of purchasing power from holding cash is one component of the purchasing power gain or loss on net monetary items. Furthermore, if cash loses value, so does a claim to cash (a receivable)—and a payable is associated with a gain of purchasing power: Losses on monetary assets such as receivables, and gains on monetary liabilities such as payables, must be counted in the same way as the loss on holding cash. The reporting of purchasing power gains or losses on net monetary items may provide an improved understanding of some of the implications, in periods of inflation, of the monetary components of working capital and of the amount of debt included in the capital structure of the enterprise.

152. The foregoing discussion has explained the reasons for believing that constant dollar accounting provides a useful basis for assessment of the performance of an enterprise in maintaining the purchasing power of investors. The purchasing power gain or loss on net monetary items is another part of the information that may be useful for that assessment. Suppose, for example, that an enterprise is established with capital of $2,000. It invests $1,500 in inventory and holds $500 in cash. Inventory is sold for $1,950 at the end of the year; general inflation is 10 percent during the year. Cash (and total assets) at the end of the year amount to $2,450 ($1,950 plus $500) and the nominal dollar increase in owners' equity is $450 ($2,450 less $2,000). The adjustment for changes in the purchasing power of owners' equity is $200 ($2,000 times 0.1) and the increase in the purchasing power of the investment in the enterprise is $250 ($450 less $200), measured in "end-of-year dollars." The enterprise will report income from continuing operations, on a historical cost/constant dollar basis, of $300 (sales $1,950 less cost of sales measured at $1,500 times 110/100). However, income overstates the increase in purchasing power because it excludes the loss of purchasing power resulting from the holding of cash. The purchasing power loss on net monetary items will be $50 (cash at the end of the year, $500, less cash at the beginning of the year, in end-of-year dollars, $500 times 110/100). Total increase in purchasing power ($250) is equal to income from continuing operations ($300) less the loss of purchasing power on net monetary assets ($50). Similar results would be obtained under current cost accounting except that historical cost/constant dollar income from continuing operations would be divided between current cost income from continuing operations and the increase or decrease in current cost amounts, net of inflation. Generalization of this kind of reasoning indicates that the total increase or decrease in purchasing power resulting from the activities of an enterprise may be assessed on the basis of the sum of current cost income from continuing operations, the change in current cost amounts of assets net of inflation and the purchasing power gain or loss on net monetary items.

153. Several commentators on the Exposure Draft argued that it was inappropriate to describe the purchasing power adjustment as a gain or loss. They were particularly critical of the implicit suggestion that an enterprise could gain by borrowing. The Board believes that a gain in purchasing power associated with a prudent amount of debt may be a sign of successful management when the funds have been invested in assets that maintain their purchasing power or lose purchasing power less rapidly than monetary items. The full significance of gains or losses of purchasing power on monetary items can be understood only in the context of a study of all components of income.

154. Suppose that Enterprise A has $1,000 of equity capital; Enterprise B borrows $1,000 at 15 percent per year. Both enterprises buy inventory at a cost of $1,000 and sell it a year later for $1,500; general inflation is 10 percent per year. Computations of income from continuing operations on a historical cost/constant dollar basis and of the purchasing power gain on debt, in end-of-year dollars, would run as follows:

	Enterprise A	Enterprise B
Sales	$ 1,500	$ 1,500
Cost of goods sold ($1,000 times 110/100)	(1,100)	(1,100)
Gross margin	400	400
Interest expense	—	(150)
Income from continuing operations	$ 400	$ 250
Purchasing power gain on debt	$ 0	$ 100

A comparison of the performance of the two enterprises should take into account the purchasing power gain on debt. Both enterprises need to measure cost of goods sold at $1,100 in order to reflect the amount of general purchasing power invested in the inventory. Both enterprises obtain a gross margin of $400, measured in end-of-year dollars. Enterprise B must pay $150 in interest. However, Enterprise B's income from continuing operations, $250, understates the increase in purchasing power earned for equity investors. Enterprise B has earned a real cash surplus of $350 because it has received $1,500 and needs only $1,150 to repay the borrowing with interest. Another way of looking at the effect of the purchasing power gain on debt would be to regard it as a reduction in the interest expense incorporated in the computation of income. Similar arguments would be applicable when current cost accounting methods are used.

155. The arguments in paragraphs 150-154 suggest that there is a case for including the purchasing power gain or loss on net monetary items in the computation of income from continuing operations. That treatment would have the advantage that the purchasing power gain on debt could be set against the associated interest expense to produce a measure of interest expense, net of inflation, consistently with the general principles of constant dollar accounting. However, in view of some comments on the Exposure Draft, expressing doubt about the usefulness of the item, the Board concluded that it would be preferable for it to be displayed separately, pending further experience with its use in practice.

Special Industry Problems

156. Special considerations arise in the choice of a system for measuring the effects of changing prices on enterprises that own particular categories of assets. Discussions about which attribute of an asset should be measured involve weighing the relevance and reliability of various alternatives, taking account of the costs of preparing the information. Consideration of those factors may suggest the desirability of measuring different attributes of different assets. The Board has concluded that current cost is a useful measurement for inventory and property, plant, and equipment. However, measurements of the current costs of some assets may have relatively low relevance and reliability while other measures, for example net present value of future cash flows, may have more relevance and an acceptable level of reliability. In such cases, it may be desirable to call for measurement of a different attribute from the one that is required for other assets, provided that information about the measurements can be presented in a format that enables users to understand its significance.

157. Many different categories of assets could be regarded as suitable subjects for special study and the identification of categories that merit special treatment involves subjective judgment. Various types of natural resources, assets committed to long-term contracts, works of art (books, paintings, film libraries, and so on), and other assets all may merit special consideration. The Board selected six industries, in which special types of assets were judged to be particularly important and formed task groups to advise it on the applicability of the proposals in the Exposure Draft to the industries concerned. Those task groups dealt with banking and thrift institutions, forest products, insurance, mining, oil and gas, and real estate. The Board's conclusions for assets held in those industries and for certain other special classes of assets are summarized in paragraphs 158-178. The Board will monitor the experience of all enterprises in preparing the information required by this Statement and attempt to identify any other categories of assets that require special consideration.

Natural Resources

158. Natural resources, given special consideration by the Board, comprise mainly oil and gas reserves and resources held by mining enterprises (nonrenewable resources) and timberlands, including growing timber (renewable over a long time period). Those resources have a number of special characteristics that are relevant for this Statement. The primary special characteristic of natural resources may be described as a limitation on replacement. The supply of oil and gas reserves and mineral ore bodies, for example, is limited. An individual enterprise may expand its holdings of nonrenewable resources by exploration to discover previously unknown sup-

plies. However, the process will be subject to a high level of uncertainty and is likely to involve operations needing progressively higher levels of expenditure. The worthwhileness of further exploration at increasing levels of expenditure will depend on economic conditions in the industry concerned. The time may come, or may have come already in some cases, when increasing expenditures cause an enterprise to abandon the attempt to obtain additional supplies of existing types of resources.

159. The "replacement problem" described in paragraph 158 is important because it indicates unusual difficulties in measuring the current costs of nonrenewable resources. The measurement of current costs could be undertaken in at least three ways:

a. A restatement, in terms of current prices, of the actual historical costs incurred to obtain the resources; the result would be a measurement of the cost that would be incurred today to carry out the past process of exploration and development.
b. An estimate of the current cost of finding and developing an equivalent source of supply; the result would normally be a higher cost than that obtained under (a) because new sources of supply would normally be less accessible than previous sources and because costs may be affected by changes in other factors such as environmental and safety requirements.
c. An estimate of the current buying price of resources already found by another enterprise; the result would presumably reflect the net present value of future cash flows.

Method (b) would be most relevant in providing a basis for users' assessment of whether or not an enterprise had maintained its operating capability. Enterprises normally intend to seek new supplies by exploration and development; and current finding cost would represent an estimate of the cost of that process. However, any estimate of current finding cost would be subject to considerable uncertainty and, in some cases, might even be inapplicable because new supplies do not exist. Consequently, it may be necessary to consider methods (a) and (c) as surrogates for the measurement of current finding cost.

160. There are some special difficulties in measuring the actual historical cost of acquiring natural resource assets. In general, the balance sheet value of natural resources will reflect only some of the actual costs of acquisition. Many of the costs are commonly treated as expenses when they are incurred. The difficulty is noteworthy in the case of growing timber but it also applies to the assets of enterprises in the oil and gas industry and the mining industry. This factor may limit the relevance of the measurements obtained from method (a) in paragraph 159.

161. It may be desirable to consider the possibility of measuring certain natural resources on a net present value basis. The measurement of net present value depends on estimates of levels of demand, future selling prices, future operating costs, and discount rates. For most assets, such measurements cannot be made with a high standard of reliability at the present time (paragraph 132). Consequently, their use must be limited to special situations, where current cost measures are likely to be lacking in relevance and reliability.

162. Several problems of implementation remain to be considered before requirements can be introduced for the measurement and reporting of net present values for most natural resources. However, the quantity of some natural resources owned by an enterprise can be measured with sufficient reliability to provide useful information. For example, acceptable measurements can be made of the quantity of proved oil and gas reserves, of the quantity of mineral ore bodies, and the quantity of growing timber. A degree of objectivity can also be obtained by assuming the continuance of price levels prevailing at the date of the measurement. Such measurements of net present values may not be free from bias: They may tend to underestimate net present values if procedures for estimating quantities count only resources that are reasonably certain. Moreover, price fluctuations may cause difficulties in certain industries. However, the measurements can be regarded as partial recognition of the worth created by the enterprises in acquiring natural resources; and the information content of the measurements may be high because the worth of the enterprises depends heavily on their holdings of natural resources. Such measurements may be useful as a basis for the assessment of future cash flows and of enterprise performance during a period.

163. The Board concluded that it should consider further the usefulness of alternative measurements of natural resource assets and the problems of implementing those measurements before finalizing requirements for their treatment under current cost accounting. It plans to publish an Exposure Draft dealing with natural resource assets and to publish a final Statement in 1980. Enterprises are not required to disclose information on a current cost basis in annual reports for fiscal years ending before December 25, 1980. The Statement on the measurement of natural resources is expected to be published in time to provide a basis for the preparation of annual reports for fiscal years ending on or after December 25, 1980. If an enterprise publishes consolidated information on income from continuing operations on a current cost basis, in annual

reports for years ended before December 25, 1980, it may use historical cost/constant dollar measures or current cost measures based on appropriate special indexes of natural resources used and held.

164. The problems of implementation of current cost measures of natural resources do not apply to the measurement of historical cost/constant dollar income. Therefore the Board concluded that it should not exempt natural resources from the requirements to disclose information on income on a historical cost/constant dollar basis (or from the related requirement to report purchasing power gains and losses on net monetary items); the information would be important in the context of the Board's wish to obtain experimental evidence of usefulness and would provide a basis for the comparison of enterprises in all industries.

The Real Estate Industry

165. Income-producing property is an important asset of many real estate enterprises. It would be possible to measure such assets and the related depreciation expense on a current cost basis. However, the Real Estate Task Group recommended that income-producing properties should be measured either at net present value of future cash flows or at net realizable value in due course of business. The Task Group argued that those measurements would be most relevant in helping users to assess the worth of an enterprise and that they could be measured with acceptable reliability because the properties were typically leased under long-term contracts. The Task Group further argued that changes in the worth of income-producing property should be reflected directly in the income of real estate enterprises, thus obviating the need for a separate measurement of depreciation expense.

166. Many real estate enterprises have other important business activities, in particular, the development of real estate. The Board considered the desirability of establishing separate requirements for those activities. However, it concluded that it should deal with all the main activities of real estate enterprises at one time because of the interdependencies between the different activities. Such interdependencies arise, for example, when an enterprise develops a property that it subsequently holds to produce income.

167. The Board concluded that the arguments of the Real Estate Task Group established the need for further consideration of the special features of real estate enterprises. The Board believes that there may be net benefits in the disclosure of measurements of net present value of income-producing properties but that further study is required of the implementation problems before a decision is made on that issue. The Board plans to publish in 1980 a Statement dealing with the special characteristics of the real estate industry. It concluded that real estate enterprises should disclose information on a historical cost/constant dollar basis in the meantime.

The Banking Industry

168. A task group was established to advise the Board on the application of this Statement to commercial banks and thrift institutions. The Banking Task Group pointed out that the effects of inflation on banks are, in some respects, highly specialized. A critical factor is the impact of inflation on interest income and interest expense; information on a bank's asset-liability posture provides a basis for assessing the extent to which a bank is exposed to risk with respect to changing interest rates. This Statement does not call for any information that directly addresses those factors. However, many banks do provide supplementary information on rates of interest income and expense in relation to an analysis of assets and liabilities. The Board believes that such information is useful.

169. The Banking Task Group believes that property, plant, and equipment, and the associated depreciation expense are generally immaterial in the banking industry. Accordingly, it suggested that information on the current costs and on historical costs in constant dollars of those items would not be useful. It recommended that the requirements to present information on a current cost basis should not apply to banks and that banks should be permitted to treat all assets as monetary assets for the purposes of historical cost/constant dollar computations.

170. The Board accepted the assertion that current cost adjustments and constant dollar adjustments to depreciation expense might be immaterial for many banks. However, it concluded that no special exemptions or provisions were needed to deal with that situation. This Statement provides that current cost information need be presented only if current cost income from continuing operations is materially different from historical cost/constant dollar income from continuing operations; and the requirements of this Statement are qualified by the more general provision that they need not be applied to immaterial items. Those provisions appear to be adequate to meet the points raised by the task group. However, the Board believes that the adjustments discussed in paragraph 169 may be material for some banks and that there are no arguments of principle to justify exemptions in those cases.

The Insurance Industry

171. A task group was established to advise the Board on the application of this Statement to the insurance industry. In some respects, the special

characteristics of insurance enterprises are similar to those of banking enterprises. In particular, inventories and property, plant, and equipment are often small in relation to other balance sheet items. The Insurance Task Group recommended that insurance enterprises should be exempt from the requirement to present information on a current cost basis and that they should be permitted to treat all assets and liabilities as monetary for the purposes of constant dollar measurements. The Board agreed that current cost adjustments would often be immaterial for insurance enterprises. However, it concluded that no special provisions or exemptions were needed to deal with that situation. This Statement provides that current cost information need be presented only if current cost income from continuing operations is materially different from historical cost/constant dollar income from continuing operations.

172. The Insurance Task Group pointed out difficulties in classifying certain assets and liabilities as monetary or nonmonetary—for example, loss reserves for claims, deferred policy acquisition costs and unearned premium reserves. The task group was particularly concerned that this Statement should not call for a costly analysis of particular balance sheet categories (for example, an analysis of loss reserves between monetary and nonmonetary items) and that related assets and liabilities should be treated consistently (for example, deferred policy acquisition costs should be treated in the same manner as unearned premium reserves). The Board concluded that the general definitions of monetary and nonmonetary items should be applicable to insurance enterprises. It believes that those definitions meet the main concerns of the task group (Appendix D).

Regulated Businesses

173. The Board did not establish a task group to advise on the application of this Statement to utilities and other regulated businesses. However, meetings were arranged with representatives of the industry and several comment letters were received from utilities. The main problem arising in the application of this Statement to utilities concerns the measurement of assets and related expenses. Some people argue that inventory, property, plant, and equipment, and the associated expenses of a rate regulated enterprise should not be measured at an amount in excess of the historical cost/nominal dollar amount in the computations of income from continuing operations and related disclosures. That argument is based on the observation that utilities may not be permitted to recover more than historical cost/nominal dollar amounts in their selling prices; the provision that assets should be measured at cost or lower recoverable amount leads to measurement on a historical cost/nominal dollar basis. Other arguments point to a different conclusion. Utilities have the same problem as other enterprises in maintaining their operating capability and in avoiding erosion of general purchasing power. Historical cost/constant dollar measures and current cost measures may provide a useful basis for assessments of those factors. Furthermore, the presentation of information on a historical cost/constant dollar basis and on a current cost basis may be important to a general public understanding of the operations of utilities.

174. The Board believes that it is important to distinguish the measurement of expenses in the computation of income from continuing operations from the measurement of assets held at the end of the fiscal year. Choice of a measurement for assets (inventory and property, plant, and equipment) requires consideration of the worth to the business of the service potential provided by the assets. The Board concluded that assets should be measured at cost (historical cost in constant dollars or current cost) or lower recoverable amount. It believes that the special characteristics of utilities provide no justification for departure from the general requirement: Failure to consider recoverable amounts (which may be measured by historical cost in nominal dollars or by lower amounts) could give a misleading impression of the worth of resources owned by the enterprise.

175. Choice of a measurement for expenses involves different considerations. The Board focused on two main alternatives:

a. Measure expenses at cost (historical cost in constant dollars or current cost) or lower recoverable amount in all situations.
b. Measure expenses at cost or lower recoverable amount unless replacement of the related asset would be undertaken under current economic conditions, in which case measure expenses at cost and ignore lower recoverable amount.

The effect of the choice can be illustrated by a simplified numerical example. An enterprise has property, plant, and equipment measured at $10,000 at historical cost in nominal dollars at the beginning of the year (and no other assets and no liabilities). It is permitted to set its prices at a level that will result in income, on a historical cost/nominal dollar basis, equal to 15 percent of net assets, i.e. $1,500. Assets were purchased at various past dates and have varying lives. Depreciation for the year and asset values at the beginning and end of the year are as follows:

	Depreciation	Assets at Beginning of Year	Assets at End of Year
Historical cost in nominal dollars	$2,000	$10,000	$ 8,000
Historical cost in constant dollars	2,800	13,000	11,500
Current cost	4,000	18,000	16,700
Recoverable amount	3,500	10,000	8,000

It is assumed that recoverable amounts of assets are equal to historical costs in nominal dollars although that equality does not always hold because, for example, the allowed rate of return may be higher or lower than the appropriate discount rate. It is also assumed for simplicity that all sales are made and expenses incurred at the end of the year. The rate of inflation is 10 percent per year. Computations of income from continuing operations based on the alternative measures of expenses and of related changes in current cost amounts of assets would run as follows, in end-of-year dollars:

		Alternative (a) (cost or lower recoverable amount)		Alternative (b) (cost)	
	Historical Cost in Nominal Dollars	Historical Cost in Constant Dollars	Current Cost	Historical Cost in Constant Dollars	Current Cost
Sales revenues less expenses	$ 3,500	$ 3,500	$ 3,500	$ 3,500	$ 3,500
Depreciation expense	(2,000)	(2,800)	(3,500)	(2,800)	(4,000)
Reduction of historical cost to lower recoverable amount		(200)		(200)	
Income from continuing operations	$ 1,500	$ 500	$ 0	$ 500	$ (500)
Increase in current cost amounts, net of inflation			$ 500		$ 1,000

The increase in shareholders' equity, measured in constant dollars, is $500 (assets at the end of the year $11,500 = cash $3,500 plus plant $8,000—less assets at the beginning of the year $10,000 × 110/100). The current cost computations divide this amount between income from continuing operations and the increase in current cost amounts of assets. Current cost income is lower under method (b) (a loss of $500) than under method (a) because of the restriction of depreciation expense under method (a) to the recoverable amount. That restriction does not apply to the historical cost/constant dollar depreciation expense in this illustration.

176. Alternative (b) has the advantage that it provides a basis for the assessment of the extent to which income from continuing operations provides for maintenance of operating capability; current cost measures are relevant for that assessment. It can also be argued that the sacrifice involved in using up the service potential of assets is represented by current cost when that service potential would be replaced. An enterprise that is affected by rate regulation differs from other enterprises in that it is likely to wish to replace its assets even when the recoverable amount is lower than current cost. Recoverable amounts will normally be lower than current cost only because of the effect of rate regulation; replacement will be worthwhile provided that the enterprise expects to be able to recover an appropriate return on the expenditure involved in replacement when it is incurred. Similar arguments apply to historical cost/constant dollar computations. Consequently, the Board concluded that method (b) was preferable for rate regulated enterprises.

Sale under Contracts

177. The Board considered whether special procedures were required for measuring the costs (either historical costs in constant dollars or current costs) of goods and services used to carry out contracts. Two bases for measurement were considered:

a. Measure expenses at the date of use on or commitment to the contract and measure assets (partly completed contracts) at the dates when the resources were used on or committed to the contract

b. Measure expenses at the date of use on or commitment to the contract and measure assets (partly completed contracts) at the balance sheet date.

178. The choice between option (a) and option (b) rests essentially on a decision as to whether changes in current cost amounts should be recognized after resources have been used on or committed to a contract. (In many cases, the date of use on a contract will be the same as the date of commitment; however, reference is made to the date of commitment to allow for the possibility that materials are ordered specially or earmarked for a contract and held for some time before they are used.) The Board believes that there would be little significance in measures of changes in the cost of resources after their use on or commitment to a contract; their worth then cannot be measured independently of the revenues earned from the contract as a whole. Use of a resource on a contract may be regarded as similar to conversion to a receivable. Having regard also to the desirability of simplification, the Board concluded that option (a) was preferable.

Current Cost Measurement Issues

The Measurement of Current Cost

179. Paragraph 60 lists various sources of information to which reference may be made for the measurement of current costs. Those sources of information may be divided into two categories: direct pricing methods and methods based on the use of indexes. The Exposure Draft expressed a preference for direct pricing methods while recognizing the need to give due consideration to availability, reliability, and cost. Several comment letters on the Exposure Draft argued that the expression of preference for direct pricing methods would increase considerably the cost and complexity of the requirements. They stated that the use of indexes would be the only practicable method for measuring current cost in many cases. The Board recognizes that the choice of the best source of information about current cost, taking account of relevance, reliability, and cost, will vary according to the circumstances of the enterprise. It also recognizes the desirability of simplifications in the computations required by this Statement. Consequently, the Board concluded that it should *not* express a preference as between the use of direct pricing methods and methods based on the use of indexes.

Used Assets

180. In measurements of the current cost of property, plant, and equipment, the focus normally will be on used assets rather than new assets. The current cost of used assets may be estimated by three alternative methods:

a. A direct estimate of the buying price of an asset of the same age and in the same condition as the asset owned.
b. An estimate of the buying price of a similar new asset less an allowance for depreciation calculated according to an acceptable accounting method.
c. An estimate of the buying price of a new improved asset less an allowance for the operating disadvantages of the asset owned (higher operating costs or lower output potential) and an allowance for depreciation calculated according to an acceptable accounting method. This approach yields what may be described as a measurement of the current cost of the service potential of the asset owned.

Alternative (a) provides the more direct measurement of the current cost of a used asset than alternatives (b) and (c); however, alternative (a) will produce reliable results only if there is an active market in used assets.The choice between alternatives (b) and (c) should reflect the method of acquisition that would be appropriate in the circumstances of the case. If the enterprise would purchase a similar new asset, because the asset owned is not functionally obsolescent, alternative (b) would be appropriate. If the enterprise would purchase an improved asset, alternative (c) would be appropriate. The Board concluded that the choice of method should be made according to the circumstances of the case, taking account of the availability and reliability of the evidence.

Assets outside the United States

181. Many enterprises will need to measure the current cost of inventory and property, plant, and equipment located outside of the United States. The Board recognizes that such cases may present particular difficulty depending upon the availability of economic information in the country concerned. Experimentation in methods of measurement will be particularly necessary in such cases and approximate methods are acceptable in cases of difficulty. The concepts underlying current cost indicate that measurements should be based on production or purchase of the asset in whatever location or market would minimize total cost including transportation cost. In some cases, the purchase would be made in the United States and current cost would be estimated directly in dollars. In other cases, current cost would have to be estimated first in an external market, and that cost would have to be translated into dollars at the current exchange rate in order to obtain the current cost of the asset in dollars.

Income Tax Expense

182. A number of questions arise in relation to the calculation of income tax expense in measuring current cost income from continuing operations. Over the lifetime of an item of property, plant, and equipment, current cost depreciation expense will be higher than historical cost depreciation expense (provided that current costs are increasing). The difference will be exactly equal in the aggregate to changes in current cost amounts (before elimination of the inflation component). However, the equality between "excess depreciation expense" and changes in current cost amounts applies only to aggregates over the lifetime of an asset; it does not normally hold for a single year in isolation. Consequently, current cost methods may be seen as causing timing differences that should be recognized in the provision for deferred taxes.

183. An additional argument for adjusting the provision for deferred taxes would apply to supplementary information on income from continuing operations both on a historical cost/constant dollar basis and a current cost basis. It would be relevant if depreciation in the supplementary disclosures and depreciation in the primary financial statements were based on different estimates of length of asset life, amount of salvage value, or on the use of a different depreciation method: Such circumstances would indicate additional timing differences not recognized in the primary financial statements. The Board recognizes that all these circumstances give rise to arguments in favor of adjustments to deferred taxes. However, the Board believes that there are strong arguments for restricting the complexity of the requirements of this Statement at a time when users are inexperienced in the analysis of supplementary disclosures, and in order to limit the costs of preparing supplementary information. The Board has concluded therefore that no adjustments to the amount of the provision for income taxes in the primary financial statements should be made for the purposes of calculating supplementary information on income from continuing operations.

184. This Statement requires that changes in current cost amounts of assets should be disclosed separately from current cost income from continuing operations. Income tax expense will include tax attributable to those changes in current cost amounts that are realized during the year, and the question arises as to whether income tax expense should be divided into two parts: one to be deducted in computing income from continuing operations, the other to be deducted from changes in current cost amounts. The Exposure Draft called for such a division of income tax expense.

185. The Board has reviewed the treatment of income taxes proposed in the Exposure Draft, partly as a result of comments that the requirement obscured the effective burden of taxation. Those comments seem to be based partly on the view that current cost income from continuing operations should represent a basis for assessment of the extent to which provision has been made to maintain operating capability. Users who wish to assess the overall performance of the enterprise may wish to consider both current cost income from continuing operations and changes in the current cost amounts of assets. In that context, it may be preferable to assess income tax expense as a separate item rather than focusing on summary indicators obtained by allocating the expense. Allocations of income taxes between current cost income and changes in current cost amounts may also obscure the relationship between specific price changes and general inflation, reflected in changes in current cost amounts, net of inflation—an important factor in assessments of the effect of changing prices on the enterprise.

186. Some people believe that strong arguments exist in favor of the allocation of income tax expense between current cost income from continuing operations and changes in current cost amounts. In their view, taxes should be attributed to the gain to which they relate. They point out that income taxes would be less if changes in current cost had not occurred (and current cost income from continuing operations was as reported). They also point out that the principle of tax allocation is described in APB Opinion No. 11, *Accounting for Income Taxes* (paragraph 52) and is generally applied, for example, to the reporting of extraordinary items in the basic financial statements. After considering the alternative points of view, and having regard to the desirability of restricting the complexity of the requirements of this Statement, the Board concluded that no such allocations of income tax expense should be made for the purposes of the supplementary disclosures required by this Statement.

Constant Dollar Measurements

187. The Board considered various bases for the measuring unit used in the computation of information required to be presented in constant dollars:

a. Dollars having a purchasing power equal to that of dollars of the base period used by the Bureau of Labor Statistics in calculating the Consumer Price Index for All Urban Consumers
b. Dollars having a purchasing power equal to that represented by the average level over the current fiscal year of the Consumer Price Index
c. Dollars having a purchasing power equal to that represented by the level of the Consumer Price Index at the end of the current fiscal year.

188. Computations in "average-for-the-year dollars" may be made either directly or by using computations in "end-of-year dollars" as an intermediate step. Suppose, for example, that an enterprise holds a cash balance of $1,100 throughout its fiscal year. The Consumer Price Index stands at 100 at the start of the year and at 110 at the end of the year; the average level over the year is 106. The purchasing power loss on holding cash may be computed directly in average-for-the-year dollars by expressing beginning and ending balances in average dollars: $1,100 × 106/100 less $1,100 × 106/110 = $106. The computation in end-of-year dollars would run: $1,100 × 110/100 less $1,100 = $110 and that sum may be converted to average dollars: $110 × 106/110 = $106.

189. The Board concluded that option (b)—use of average-for-the-year dollars—should normally be used for computations relating to the current year. It has significant computational advantages in that context: Several revenues and expenses that are spread evenly throughout the period may be assumed to be the same in historical cost/nominal dollars and historical cost/constant dollars. Current cost measures of cost of goods sold and depreciation expense also approximate measures in average-for-the-year constant dollars without further adjustment. Comparisons of amounts in the primary financial statements with components of historical cost/constant dollar income and current cost income may be less confusing to users if many of the components are measured similarly. However, enterprises are encouraged to present comprehensive supplementary financial statements on a constant dollar basis. Use of the average-for-the-year dollar in comprehensive statements may be confusing to users because it results in balance sheet amounts that differ from the historical cost/nominal dollar equivalents for monetary assets and liabilities. Consequently, the Board concluded that enterprises that present comprehensive constant dollar statements should be permitted to use the end-of-year dollar as a measuring unit.

190. Somewhat different considerations apply to the presentation of the five-year summary. If information is presented in current dollars (options (b) or (c)), the information relating to previous years must be restated. If information is presented in "base-period" dollars (option (a)), information on income for the current year will be measured in different units in the supplementary income statement and in the five-year summary. Either possibility may be confusing to some users. The importance of the five-year summary is in presenting information about trends over time and each option seems equally useful for that purpose. The Board consequently concluded that enterprises should be permitted to present the five-year summary either in current dollars (average-for-the-year or end-of-year dollars whichever is used in the measurement of income for the current year) or in base period dollars.

191. The Board considered whether it would be appropriate to permit the use of different accounting principles in the computation of historical cost/constant dollar income from those used in the computation of historical cost/nominal dollar income. It concluded that the same accounting principles should be used under both measurement systems (except as provided in the special circumstances described in paragraphs 193-198). Thus, for example, the same principles should be used to determine the costs attributed to assets in the supplementary information as in the primary statements. The main advantage of historical cost/constant dollar accounting is that it provides a basis for comparing the measurements and estimates in the basic financial statements with measurements that reflect changes in general prices. That comparability would be lost if different accounting principles were generally to be used.

192. The Board considered whether transactions in foreign currency should be:

a. First translated into U.S. currency and then restated for U.S. inflation; or
b. First restated for local inflation and then translated into U.S. currency.

It concluded that option (a) was preferable because the usefulness of constant dollar measurements is partly to provide information about the erosion of investors' purchasing power and the relevant measure of purchasing power for most investors in U.S. enterprises is the purchasing power of the U.S. dollar. That conclusion is consistent with the requirements of FASB Statement No. 8, *Accounting for the Translation of Foreign Currency Transactions and Foreign Currency Financial Statements.* However, further consideration may need to be given to this issue as a result of the current review of that Statement.

Methods for Current Cost Measurements and Constant Dollar Measurements

Recoverable Amount

193. The value to the business of an asset cannot exceed the maximum sum that an enterprise would be willing to pay to acquire the asset. In some circumstances, the amount of cash recoverable from the use of an asset may be so small that the enterprise would not wish to buy the asset at its current cost if the asset were not already owned. The maximum sum that an enterprise would be willing

to pay for an asset is given by net realizable value or by the net present value of cash flows expected to be derived from its use, i.e., value in use. Accordingly, the Exposure Draft provided that an asset should be measured at its value in use if that amount is lower than current cost and immediate sale is not intended.

194. Several comment letters expressed concern about the need to measure value in use. They argued that the Exposure Draft implied the need to measure value in use for all assets to determine whether value in use is lower than current cost—a very expensive procedure. They emphasized the low reliability of measurements of value in use. They indicated that it is often difficult to determine value in use for individual assets because cash flows may be jointly attributable to several assets. They also suggested that the results of applying measurements of value in use might be confusing in cases of volatile prices, because the appropriate measurement might change from value in use to current cost and vice versa from year to year.

195. The Board concluded that the concept of limiting asset measurements to recoverable amounts should be retained. It also concluded that the limitation should be applied to historical cost/constant dollar measurements of assets as well as to current cost measurements. It believes that such a limitation is needed to avoid significant overstatements of the worth of assets. However, the Board also believes that it is desirable to avoid excessive complexity in applications of the provisions of this Statement and that the need to measure value in use should arise relatively rarely. Consequently, it concluded that value in use need be considered as a measurement of an asset only when it is judged to be materially and permanently lower than historical cost in constant dollars or current cost.

Depreciation Expense

196. Calculations of depreciation must be based on various estimates and assumptions, and if enterprises with similar circumstances make different estimates or select different assumptions, the comparability of their calculations of income from continuing operations will be impaired. Moreover, the usefulness of the supplementary disclosures might be impaired if an enterprise were to adopt different assumptions and estimates for calculations of depreciation in the primary financial statements on the one hand, and for calculations of depreciation in the supplementary information on the other hand. The estimates and assumptions in question are length of asset life, salvage value of the asset, and depreciation method (straight-line, declining-balance, sum-of-the-years-digits, and so on).

197. The Board considered the following possible requirements in relation to the measurement of depreciation:

a. A requirement that all enterprises should use the same assumptions and estimates in calculations of depreciation in both supplementary information and in the primary financial statements,
b. A requirement that all enterprises should use a particular specified depreciation method in calculations of depreciation for presentations of supplementary information, and
c. Recognition that an enterprise should be permitted to select different assumptions and estimates for calculations of depreciation in supplementary information from those used in the primary financial statements.

A disadvantage of alternative (a) is that some enterprises may have selected an accelerated method of depreciation for use in the primary financial statements in order to make some allowance for the impact of inflation: Accelerated methods of depreciation have the effect of increasing aggregate depreciation charges during periods in which the amount of property, plant, and equipment in use is growing. Similarly, an enterprise may have made conservative estimates of asset lives and salvage values for financial statement purposes in order to accelerate depreciation charges and thereby make some allowance for inflation. If the same methods and estimates were to be used for calculations of supplementary information, the effect might be to build in a double allowance for inflation and make an excessive depreciation charge. Alternative (b) has the disadvantage that it ignores the possible existence of valid reasons for differences in depreciation methods associated with the existence of various patterns of maintenance costs, usage, or output capacity over the asset life.

198. The Board concluded that, in the calculation of depreciation for presentations of supplementary information, an enterprise should be permitted to use different estimates and methods from those used in the primary financial statements, provided that allowance for inflation was a factor in choices made for the financial statements. However, it would be undesirable for an enterprise to adopt different estimates and methods in order to avoid disclosure of the full impact of changing prices, and there normally should be a presumption that estimated asset lives and salvage values will be the same for purposes of the primary financial statements and the supplementary disclosures. The Board believes that it will be a sufficient safeguard to require footnote disclosure of any differences in depreciation methods and estimates. The Exposure Draft provided that changes in estimates and methods used in

calculations of depreciation should be permitted only in the case of measurements of current cost information. However, the Board has subsequently concluded that the arguments are equally applicable to measurements on a historical cost/constant dollar basis.

The Foreign Exchange Gain or Loss

199. The Exposure Draft called for separate disclosure of the foreign exchange gain or loss. Several comment letters argued against that requirement, partly because of uncertainties regarding the outcome of the Board's review of Statement 8. Having regard to the desirability of simplifying the requirements of this Statement, the Board concluded that separate disclosure of the foreign exchange gain or loss should not be required as part of the supplementary information.

Scope of Supplementary Disclosure

200. In considering which enterprises should be required to comply with this Statement, the Board put considerable weight on the need to avoid the imposition of excessive costs on the preparers of financial reports. It believes that there are potential net benefits to users to be derived from the disclosure of current cost information and historical cost/constant dollar information by all enterprises. The Board concluded that all enterprises should be encouraged to comply with this Statement, but that compliance should be required initially only for large, publicly held corporations. Financial reporting by such corporations may be presumed to be of importance to a relatively large group of users and those corporations may benefit from economies of scale in preparing the information, partly because they have established sophisticated accounting systems. Moreover, many of them are already providing information similar to that required by this Statement in complying with ASR 190 of the Securities and Exchange Commission. The size test in paragraph 23 has been expressed partly in terms of amounts of inventories and property, plant, and equipment, rather than some alternative such as sales and other operating revenues, or stockholders' equity, because the differences between historical cost/nominal dollar income from continuing operations on the one hand and historical cost/constant dollar or current cost income from continuing operations on the other hand, are likely to be most affected by the amounts of those assets.

201. The Board considered the implications of the scope of this Statement in relation to enterprises that have merged during the year and are using the pooling of interests method for preparing basic financial statements. Two situations are particularly important:

a. Two or more enterprises merge during the year; none of them meets the size test individually at the start of the year although the combined assets of the enterprises would meet the size test. The Board concluded that this Statement should *not* apply to the enterprises during the year of the merger. Hence, no special provision is required for this situation.
b. Two or more enterprises merge during the year and one of them does meet the size test at the start of the year. The Board concluded that this Statement should apply during the year of the merger to the whole of the new enterprise created by the merger. It recognized that there might be some difficulties in developing the required data for the enterprises to which this Statement had not previously applied. However, the Board believes that it will be feasible for such enterprises to meet the requirements, given the permitted level of flexibility in the measurements; and it believes that the application of the requirements to the enterprise as a whole is preferable to the alternative of exempting part of the enterprise.

Partial Reporting

202. This Statement does not require an enterprise to present a statement of financial position and a complete statement of earnings on a historical cost/constant dollar basis or on a current cost basis. Required supplementary disclosures are limited to a five-year summary of important data, supplementary information on income from continuing operations, and certain other supplementary data. The Board considered and rejected a requirement that the amount of net assets presented in the five-year summary of selected financial data should be calculated by a comprehensive application of historical cost/constant dollar methods or of current cost methods. The Board hopes that enterprises will experiment with the preparation of more than the minimum required amount of supplementary information. However, it believes that experience should be gained in the preparation and use of partial information before consideration is given to the requirement of more comprehensive information. The disclosures required under this Statement have been chosen on the grounds that they are believed to be particularly important to users—they include items for which differences between historical cost/nominal dollar amounts and historical cost/constant dollar or current cost amounts are likely to be particularly great.

Choice of Format

203. The Board considered whether it should call for supplementary disclosures to be presented in a fixed format. It has decided that it is appropriate to

allow flexibility in the choice of format so that enterprises may experiment to find methods of presentation which they believe to be most effective in their particular circumstances. Some illustrations of possible formats are given in Appendix A. Similarly, some flexibility is thought to be desirable in the choice of line items to be disclosed in the supplementary statement of income from continuing operations. It is presumed that it will normally be appropriate to disclose the same line items in the supplementary statement as are disclosed in the basic financial statements. However, only cost of goods sold, depreciation, depletion, and amortization expense, and any reductions from historical cost/constant dollar amounts to lower recoverable amounts are specifically required to be disclosed separately because only those items would normally be material to an understanding of the supplementary information on income from continuing operations.

The Five-Year Summary of Selected Data

204. The use of constant dollar accounting may be particularly helpful in the comparison of a series of measurements relating to sequential periods. It has long been thought that such a comparison may be facilitiated by restating the measurements in terms of a common price level. For example, many policymakers emphasize the importance of "real growth" in the economy as measured by gross national product data restated in dollars of a specified base year. That same practice is viewed by some as helpful in comparing data relating to several periods in the life of one enterprise. Sales revenues, net assets, stockholders' equity, earnings, and dividends are obvious candidates for that treatment. Some observers think that "unsophisticated investors" may be misled if a company whose sales and earnings in nominal dollars have doubled in the last 10 years is described as a growth company. During that period, the general price level in the United States has roughly doubled. Restatement of the nominal dollar measurements of such a company would show that current sales and earnings represent approximately the same purchasing power as those of 10 years earlier.

205. The Board has selected certain data to be displayed in a five-year tabulation. The data required to be included in the tabulation were selected because of their importance to users; users may be directly interested in the trend of the series or they may be interested in using the data for the calculation of ratios.

206. Users are likely to be interested in the constant dollar trend of sales as a basis for assessing the success of the sales effort of the enterprise in the face of changing economic conditions and competitive pressures. The constant dollar series of income from continuing operations, purchasing power gain or loss on net monetary items, and increase or decrease in the current cost amounts of assets are all important in providing bases for the assessment of various aspects of future cash flows. Income from continuing operations in conjunction with net assets may be used to estimate rates of return earned by the enterprise. Earnings per common share, dividends per common share, and market price per common share are all directly important to investors. Their inclusion also permits users to compute "constant dollar price-earnings ratios" and "constant dollar market rates of return" (taking account of dividends and changes in stock prices). However, calculation of income from continuing operations, purchasing power gain or loss on net monetary items, increases or decreases in current cost amounts of assets, net assets, and earnings per common share all require a significant computational effort. Consequently, an enterprise is not required to report these data for years prior to the effective date of this Statement or prior to the year in which this Statement first applies to the enterprise, if later, although such reporting is encouraged.

Effective Date

207. The Exposure Draft provided that this Statement should apply to fiscal years ending on or after December 25, 1979. The feasibility of that provision has been generally acceptable to preparers in so far as the historical cost/constant dollar requirements are concerned. However, several comment letters as well as the special industry task groups have emphasized the difficulty in preparing information on a current cost basis for publication in 1979 annual reports. The Board recognizes that difficulty although it believes that there is an urgent need for information on a current cost basis and that the difficulty will be limited by experience gained in meeting the requirements of ASR 190. The Board considered the possibility of permitting late publication of the data for 1979, possibly in an interim report in 1980. However, that possibility would have the disadvantage of disrupting the normal pattern of reporting. The Board concluded that the requirements of this Statement should apply for fiscal years ended on or after December 25, 1979, but that enterprises should be permitted to delay first disclosure of information on a current cost basis to the annual report for the first year ending on or after December 25, 1980.

Appendix D

MONETARY AND NONMONETARY ITEMS

208. This appendix provides guidance on the interpretation of paragraphs 47 and 48 for the classification of certain asset and liability items as monetary or nonmonetary. The following table is not intended to provide answers that should be followed regardless of the circumstances of the case. Rather, the intent is to illustrate the application of the definitions to common cases under typical circumstances. In other circumstances the classification should be resolved by reference to the definitions.

ASSETS	Monetary	Nonmonetary
Cash on hand and demand bank deposits (U.S. dollars)	X	
Time deposits (U.S. dollars)	X	
Foreign currency on hand and claims to foreign currency†	X	
Securities:		
Common stocks (not accounted for on the equity method)		X
Common stocks represent residual interests in the underlying net assets and earnings of the issuer.		
Preferred stock (convertible or participating)		
Circumstances may indicate that such stock is either monetary or nonmonetary. See convertible bonds.	(see discussion)	
Preferred stock (nonconvertible, non-participating)		
Future cash receipts are likely to be substantially unaffected by changes in specific prices.	X	
Convertible bonds.		
If the market values the security primarily as a bond, it is monetary; if it values the security primarily as a stock, it is nonmonetary.	(see discussion)	
Bonds (other than convertibles)	X	
Accounts and notes receivable	X	
Allowance for doubtful accounts and notes receivable	X	
Variable rate mortgage loans	X	
The terms of such loans do not link them directly to the rate of inflation. Also, there are practical reasons for classifying all loans as monetary.		
Inventories used on contracts		
They are, in substance, rights to receive sums of money if the future cash receipts on the contracts will not vary due to future changes in specific prices. (Goods used on contracts to be priced at market upon delivery are nonmonetary.)	(see discussion)	
Inventories (other than inventories used on contracts)		X
Loans to employees	X	
Prepaid insurance, advertising, rent, and other prepayments.		
Claims to future services are nonmonetary. Prepayments that are deposits, advance payments or receivables are monetary because the prepayment does not obtain a given quantity of future services, but rather is a fixed money offset.	(see discussion)	
Long-term receivables	X	
Refundable deposits	X	
Advances to unconsolidated subsidiaries	X	
Equity investment in unconsolidated subsidiaries or other investees*		X
Pension, sinking, and other funds under an enterprise's control		
The specific assets in the fund should be classified as monetary or nonmonetary. (See listings under securities above.)	(see discussion)	
Property, plant, and equipment		X
Accumulated depreciaton of property, plant, and equipment		X
Cash surrender value of life insurance	X	
Purchase commitments—portion paid on fixed price contracts		X
An advance on a fixed price contract is the portion of the purchaser's claim to nonmonetary goods or services that is recognized in the accounts; it is not a right to receive money.		

	Monetary	Nonmonetary
Advances to supplier—not on a fixed price contract	X	
A right to receive credit for a sum of money; not a claim to a specified quantity of goods or services.		
Deferred income tax charges†	X	
Offsets to prospective monetary liabilities.		
Patents, trademarks, licenses and formulas		X
Goodwill		X
Deferred life insurance policy acquisition costs†	X	
The portion of future cash receipts for premiums that is recognized in the accounts. Alternatively, viewed as an offset to the policy reserve.		
Deferred property and casualty insurance policy acquisition costs		X
Related to unearned premiums.		
Other intangible assets and deferred charges		X
LIABILITIES		
Accounts and notes payable	X	
Accrued expenses payable (wages, etc.)	X	
Accrued vacation pay.		
Nonmonetary if it is paid at the wage rates as of the vacation dates and if those rates may vary.	(see discussion)	
Cash dividends payable	X	
Obligations payable in foreign currency	X	
Sales commitments—portion collected on fixed price contracts		X
An advance received on a fixed price contract is the portion of the seller's obligation to deliver goods or services that is recognized in the accounts; it is not an obligation to pay money.		
Advance from customers—not on a fixed price contract.	X	
Equivalent of a loan from the customer; not an obligation to furnish a specified quantity of goods or services.		
Accrued losses on firm purchase commitments.	X	
In essence, these are accounts payable.		
Deferred revenue		
Nonmonetary if an obligation to furnish goods or services is involved. Certain "deferred income" items of savings and loan associations are monetary.	(see discussion)	
Refundable deposits	X	
Bonds payable and other long-term debt	X	
Unamortized premium or discount and prepaid interest on bonds or notes payable	X	
Inseparable from the debt to which it relates—a monetary item.		
Convertible bonds payable	X	
Until converted these are obligations to pay sums of money.		
Accrued pension obligations		
Fixed amounts payable to a fund are monetary; all other amounts are nonmonetary.	(see discussion)	
Obligations under warranties		X
These are nonmonetary because they oblige the enterprise to furnish goods or services or their future price.		
Deferred income tax credits†	X	
Cash requirements will not vary materially due to changes in specific prices.		
Deferred investment tax credits		X
Not to be settled by payment of cash; associated with nonmonetary assets.		
Life insurance policy reserves	X	
Portions of policies face values that are now deemed liabilities		
Property and casualty insurance loss reserves	X	
Unearned property and casualty insurance premiums		X

	Monetary	Nonmonetary
These are nonmonetary because they are principally obligations to furnish insurance coverage. The dollar amount of payments to be made under that coverage might vary materially due to changes in specific prices.		
Deposit liabilities of financial institutions	X	

*If an investment is accounted for on the equity method, and if the investor is preparing comprehensive constant dollar financial statements, the financial statements of the investee theoretically should be restated in constant dollars and the equity method should then be applied. However, if restated financial statements cannot be obtained from the investee, the investor may be able to prepare such statements using nominal dollar information that is available, such as nominal dollar financial statements for a series of years. As a simpler alternative, an investor that prepares comprehensive constant dollar statements merely could restate the entries in the investment account as recorded in accordance with the equity method.

†Although classification of this item as nonmonetary may be technically preferable, the monetary classification provides a more practical solution for the purposes of constant dollar accounting.

Appendix E

ILLUSTRATIVE CALCULATIONS TO COMPUTE HISTORICAL COST/CONSTANT DOLLAR INFORMATION AND CURRENT COST INFORMATION

INTRODUCTION

209. This appendix gives an example of the methodology that might be used in calculating the disclosures illustrated in Appendix A (Schedules A and B).

210. Computation of historical cost/constant dollar information and of current cost information could be based on a detailed analysis of all transactions and an updating of all revenues, expenses, gains and losses to reflect changes in purchasing power. However, the Board believes that the costs of preparing the information can be reduced with little loss of usefulness by simplifying the methods of calculation. The Board has therefore concluded that revenues, expenses, gains and losses except cost of sales and depreciation expense need not be adjusted from the amounts shown in the primary income statement and that approximate methods of computation are acceptable for adjusting cost of sales and depreciation expense (and the related asset measurements). The *measurement* of current cost is not illustrated in this appendix. However, enterprises may find it convenient to follow the methods of measurement illustrated for historical cost/constant dollar measurements, using specific price indexes in place of general price indexes.

211. The objective in making these calculations is to obtain a *reasonable degree* of accuracy—complete precision is not required. Preparers are encouraged to devise short-cut methods of calculation, appropriate to their individual circumstances. Some useful simplifications are described in the FASB Research Report, *Field Tests of Financial Reporting in Units of General Purchasing Power,* published in May 1977.

212. Where inventories and cost of sales are accounted for under the LIFO method in the primary financial statements the only adjustment normally required in computing income from continuing operations would be to eliminate the effect of changing prices on any prior period LIFO layer liquidation.

213. The following sample calculations illustrate the minimum required calculations (in paragraphs 223-237). A method of checking the arithmetic accuracy of the calculations is included in paragraphs 238 and 239.

214. Throughout this illustration $ indicates nominal dollars and C$ indicates average 1980 constant dollars.

215. The results of these calculations, summarized in paragraph 240, are reflected in the illustrative disclosures in Appendix A.

STEPS TO RESTATE FINANCIAL INFORMATION

216. Seven basic steps to restate nominal dollar information (either on a historical cost basis or a current cost basis) into constant dollars are illustrated in this appendix:

1. Analyze inventory (at the beginning and end of the year) and cost of goods sold to determine when the costs were incurred.
2. Restate inventory and cost of goods sold into constant dollars and current cost.
3. Analyze property, plant, and equipment, and related depreciation, depletion, and amortization expense to determine when the related assets were acquired.
4. Restate property, plant, and equipment and depreciation, depletion, and amortization expense into constant dollars and current cost.
5. Identify amount of net monetary items at the beginning and end of the period and changes during the period (Appendix D).
6. Compute the purchasing power gain or loss on net monetary items.
7. Compute change in current cost of inventory and property, plant, and equipment and the related effect of the increase in the general price level.

217.

Historical Cost/Nominal Dollar Financial Statements and Other Background Information

Balance Sheets as at December 31, 1980 and 1979
(000s)

	1980	1979		1980	1979
Current assets:			Current liabilities:		
Cash	$ 1,000	$ 2,000	Bank indebtedness	$ 35,000	$ 22,000
Accounts receivable	36,000	30,000	Accounts payable and accrued expenses	12,000	10,000
Inventories, at FIFO cost	63,000	56,000	Income taxes payable	6,000	6,000
			Current portion of long-term debt	5,000	5,000
Total current assets	100,000	88,000	Total current liabilities	58,000	43,000
Property, plant, and equipment, at cost	100,000	85,000	Deferred income taxes	6,000	5,000
Less accumulated depreciation	56,000	46,000	Long-term debt	34,000	39,000
	44,000	39,000	Total liabilities	98,000	87,000
			Shareholders' equity	46,000	40,000
	$144,000	$127,000		$144,000	$127,000

217. (cont.)

Statement of Earnings and Shareholders' Equity

For The Years Ended December 31, 1980 and 1979
(000s)

	1980	1979
Sales	$253,000	$220,000
Cost of goods sold, exclusive of depreciation	197,000	170,600
Selling, general, and administrative expenses	20,835	25,500
Depreciation	10,000	8,500
Interest	7,165	3,400
	235,000	208,000
Earnings before taxes	18,000	12,000
Income taxes	9,000	6,000
Net income	9,000	6,000
Shareholders' equity at beginning of the year	40,000	37,000
	49,000	43,000
Dividends	3,000	3,000
Shareholders' equity at end of the year	$ 46,000	$ 40,000
Net income per share	$ 6.00	$ 4.00

218. Inventory and Production

a. Inventory is accounted for on a FIFO basis and turns over four times per year. There is no significant amount of work in progress or raw material.

b. At December 31, 1980 and 1979 inventory consisted of 900,000 units and 1,000,000 units respectively—representing production of the immediately preceding quarter. Management has measured the current cost of inventory at $73 per unit at December 31, 1980 ($65,700,000) and $58 per unit at December 31, 1979 ($58,000,000).

c. Costs were incurred and goods produced as follows:

	1979	1980				
	4th	1st	2nd	3rd	4th	Total
Historical Costs (000s)	$56,000	$39,560	$59,400	$42,040	$63,000	$204,000
Units produced (000s)	1,000	618	900	618	900	3,036
Units sold (000s)		1,000	618	900	618	3,136

d. At December 31, 1980 the selling price per unit was $85.

219. Property, Plant, and Equipment

a. Details of fixed assets at December 31, 1980 are as follows:

Date Acquired	Percent Depreciated	Historical Cost (000s)	Accumulated Depreciation (000s)
1973	80	$ 50,000	$40,000
1974	70	5,000	3,500
1975	60	5,000	3,000
1976	50	5,000	2,500
1977	40	5,000	2,000
1978	30	5,000	1,500
1979	20	10,000	2,000
1980	10	15,000	1,500
		$100,000	$56,000

b. Depreciation is calculated at 10% per annum, straight line. A full year's depreciation is charged in the year of acquisition.

c. There were no disposals.

d. Management has measured the current cost of property, plant, and equipment at December 31, 1980 and 1979 as follows:

(000s)

Date Acquired	December 31, 1980 Current Cost	December 31, 1980 Accumulated Depreciation	December 31, 1979 Current Cost	December 31, 1979 Accumulated Depreciation
1973	$120,000	$ 96,000	$110,000	$77,000
1974	10,000	7,000	6,000	3,600
1975	15,000	9,000	7,000	3,500
1976	18,000	9,000	12,000	4,800
1977	12,000	4,800	10,000	3,000
1978	17,000	5,100	15,000	3,000
1979	12,000	2,400	10,000	1,000
1980	16,000	1,600	—	—
	220,000	$134,900	170,000	$95,900
Accumulated depreciation	134,900		95,900	
Net current cost	$ 85,100		$ 74,100	

e. The "net recoverable amount" has been determined by management to be in excess of net current cost.

220. Dividends

Dividends were paid at the rate of $750,000 per quarter.

221. Consumer Price Index (All Urban Consumers)

Average	1973	133.1	Average 4th Qtr.	1979†	210.0
"	1974	147.7	Average 4th Qtr.	1980†	237.8
"	1975	161.2	December	1979	212.9*
"	1976	170.5	December	1980	243.5*
"	1977	181.5			
"	1978	195.4			
"	1979	205.0*			
"	1980	220.9‡			

*Estimated for illustrative purposes.
†Calculated by averaging the estimated monthly indexes for each quarter.
‡Calculated by averaging the estimated monthly indexes for 1980. The index for the last month of the year may not be available at the time of preparing the supplemental disclosures and may be estimated by extrapolating the rate of change for the previous month.

OBJECTIVE

222. The objective is to express the supplementary information in average 1980 dollars. As indicated in paragraph 210, nominal dollar measurements are to be used for all elements other than inventory, property, plant, and equipment, cost of sales, depreciation, and increases in current cost amounts of inventory and property, plant, and equipment.

Inventory and Cost of Goods Sold

Step 1: Analyze inventory and cost of goods sold.

223. Inventory is assumed to turn over four times per year (paragraph 218). Therefore inventory with an historical cost of $63,000 at December 31, 1980 is assumed to have been acquired during the fourth quarter of 1980 and inventory with an historical cost of $56,000 at December 31, 1979 is assumed to have been acquired in the fourth quarter of 1979.

Step 2: Restate historical cost of inventory and cost of goods sold into average 1980 dollars and at current cost.

224. Inventory:

	(000s) Historical Cost Constant Dollars	Current Cost
$63,000† × 220.9 (average 1980) / 237.8 (4th qtr. 1980)	C$58,523	$65,700‡

†From paragraph 218c.
‡From paragraph 218b.

225. Cost of goods sold, historical cost/constant dollar:

	Nominal Dollars		(000s) Conversion Factor	Average 1980 Dollars
Balance, January 1, 1980	$ 56,000	×	220.9 (avg. 1980) / 210.0 (4th qtr. 1979)	C$ 58,907
Production during 1980 (paragraph 218c)	204,000		*	204,000
Balance, December 31, 1980	(63,000)	×	220.9 (avg. 1980) / 237.8 (4th qtr. 1980)	(58,523)
Cost of goods sold	$197,000			C$204,384

*Assumed to be in average 1980 dollars.

226. Cost of goods sold, current cost:

Current cost at the beginning of the year	$ 58/unit
Current cost at the end of the year	73/unit
	$ 131/unit
Average current cost ($131 × 1/2)	$ 65.5/unit
Units sold during the year (000s)	3,136
Average current cost of goods sold (000s)	$205,408

227. In applying the standard the historical cost/constant dollar and current cost amounts should be compared to the "recoverable amount." This is illustrated below:

Market price/unit at year end (from paragraph 218d):	$85
Restated to average 1980 dollars:	
$85 × 220.9 (average 1980) / 243.5 (Dec. 1980)	C$ 77.11
Historical cost/constant dollar:	(000s)
Market value of inventory on hand at end of the year (77.11 × 900,000)	C$ 69,399
Restated historical cost (paragraph 225)	58,523
Excess—no write down required.	C$ 10,876
Current cost:	
Market value per unit at end of year	$85
Current cost per unit of inventory on hand at end of year (paragraph 218b)	73
Excess—no write down required	$12

Property, Plant, and Equipment and Depreciation, Depletion, and Amortization Expense

Step 3: Analyze property, plant, and equipment and depreciation, depletion, and amortization.

228. An analysis of property, plant, and equipment was given in paragraph 219. It normally will not be necessary to restate the cost and accumulated depreciation for each asset individually in order to obtain an acceptable level of accuracy. Satisfactory results can normally be obtained by using annual totals of acquisitions and dispositions and the average index for the year of acquisition and disposal. Moreover, assets acquired many years before the balance sheet date might be combined into convenient groups where there is some doubt about the specific years of acquisition or where changes in the index for several years can be considered on an average basis. For example, the cost of all assets acquired between 1945 and 1950 could be measured by reference to an index representing an average of those years.

Step 4: Restate property, plant, and equipment and depreciation, depletion, and amortization expense into constant dollars and current cost.

229. Historical cost of property, plant, and equipment in average 1980 dollars:

Date of Acquisition	(1) Historical Cost/ Nominal Dollars (000s)		(2) Conversion Factor		(3) (1) × (2) Historical Cost/ Constant Dollars (000s)	(4) Percent Depreciated	(5) (3) × (4) Accumulated Depreciation (000s)	(6) (3) – (5) Net
1973	$ 50,000	×	220.9 (Avg. 1980) / 133.1 (" 1973)	=	C$ 82,983	80	C$66,386	
1974	5,000	×	220.9 (" 1980) / 147.7 (" 1974)	=	7,478	70	5,235	
1975	5,000	×	220.9 (" 1980) / 161.2 (" 1975)	=	6,852	60	4,111	
1976	5,000	×	220.9 (" 1980) / 170.5 (" 1976)	=	6,478	50	3,239	
1977	5,000	×	220.9 (" 1980) / 181.5 (" 1977)	=	6,085	40	2,434	
1978	5,000	×	220.9 (" 1980) / 195.4 (" 1978)	=	5,652	30	1,696	
1979	10,000	×	220.9 (" 1980) / 205.0 (" 1979)	=	10,776	20	2,155	
1980	15,000	×	220.9 (" 1980) / 220.9 (" 1980)	=	15,000	10	1,500	
	$100,000				C$141,304		C$86,756	C$54,548

Historical cost/constant dollar depreciation expense for 1980 is calculated as follows:

C$141,304 (col. 3) × 10% straight line = C$14,130

Property, Plant, and Equipment at Current Cost

230. It will usually be appropriate to calculate current cost depreciation, depletion, and amortization expense by reference to average current cost of the related assets (current cost of assets at beginning of year and current cost of assets at end of year ÷ 2).

	Current Cost (000s)
Current cost, Dec. 31, 1979 (par. 219d)	$170,000
Current cost, Dec. 31, 1980 (par. 219d)	220,000
	$390,000
	÷2
Average current cost	$195,000
Current cost depreciation: 10% straight line	$ 19,500

In this example, management has determined that the "recoverable amount" is greater than net current cost of property, plant, and equipment and there is no write down required.

Purchasing Power Gain on Net Monetary Items

Step 5: ***Identify monetary items at the beginning and end of the period and change during the period.***

	(000s) Balance*	
	Dec. 1980	**Dec. 1979**
231. Monetary items:		
Cash	$ 1,000	$ 2,000
Accounts receivable	36,000	30,000
Bank indebtedness	(35,000)	(22,000)
Accounts payable and accrued expenses	(12,000)	(10,000)
Income taxes payable	(6,000)	(6,000)
Current portion of long-term debt	(5,000)	(5,000)
Deferred income taxes	(6,000)	(5,000)
Long-term debt	(34,000)	(39,000)
Net monetary liabilities	($61,000)	($55,000)

*Paragraph 217

Step 6: Compute the purchasing power gain or loss on net monetary items.

232. The amount of net monetary items at the beginning of the year, changes in the net monetary items and the amount at the end of the year are restated into average 1980 dollars. The purchasing power gain or loss on net monetary items is then the balancing item as illustrated below:

	Nominal Dollars		(000s) Conversion Factor	Average 1980 Dollars
Balance, January 1, 1980	$55,000	×	220.9 (avg. 1980) / 212.9 (Dec. 1979)	C$57,067
Increase in net monetary liabilities during the year	6,000		*	6,000
				63,067
Balance, December 31, 1980	61,000	×	220.9 (avg. 1980) / 243.5 (Dec. 1980)	55,338
Purchasing power gain on net monetary items				C$ 7,729

*Assumed to be in average 1980 dollars.

Increase in current cost of inventories and property, plant, and equipment

Step 7: Compute change in current cost of inventory and property, plant, and equipment and effect of the increase in the general price level.

233. Increase in current cost of inventories

	Current Cost/ Nominal Dollars		(000s) Conversion Factor	Current Cost/ Average 1980 Dollars
Balance, January 1, 1980 (paragraph 218b)	$ 58,000	×	220.9 (avg. 1980) / 212.9 (Dec. 1979)	C$ 60,179
Production (paragraph 218c)	204,000		*	204,000
Cost of goods sold (paragraph 226)	(205,408)		*	(205,408)
Balance, December 31, 1980 (paragraph 218b)	(65,700)	×	220.9 (avg. 1980) / 243.5 (Dec. 1980)	(59,602)
Increase/(decrease) current cost of inventories	$ 9,108			C$ 831

*Assumed to be in average 1980 dollars.

234. The "inflation component" of the increase in current cost amount is the difference between the nominal dollar and constant dollar measures. Using the numbers from paragraph 233:

	(000s)
Increase in current cost (nominal dollars)	$9,108
Increase in current cost (constant dollars)	C$ 831
Inflation component	8,277

235. Increase in current cost of property, plant, and equipment

	Current cost/ Nominal Dollars		(000s) Conversion Factor	Current cost/ Average 1980 Dollars
Balance, January 1, 1980 (paragraph 219d)	$ 74,100	×	220.9 (avg. 1980) / 212.9 (Dec. 1979)	C$ 76,884
Additions (paragraph 219a)	15,000		*	15,000
Depreciation expense (paragraph 230)	(19,500)		*	(19,500)
Balance, December 31, 1980 (paragraph 219d)	(85,100)	×	220.9 (avg. 1980) / 243.5 (Dec. 1980)	(77,202)
Increase in current cost of property, plant, and equipment	$ 15,500			C$ 4,818

*Assumed to be in average 1980 dollars.

236. The "inflation component" of the increase in current cost amount is the difference between the nominal dollar and constant dollars measures. Using the numbers from paragraph 235:

	(000s)
Increase in current cost (nominal dollars)	$15,500
Increase in current cost (constant dollars)	C$ 4,818
Inflation component	10,682

Summary of increase in current cost amounts

237. Summarizing paragraphs 234 and 236 above:

	Increase in Current Cost	(000s) Inflation Component	Increase Net of Inflation
Inventory	$ 9,108	8,277	C$ 831
Property, plant, and equipment	15,500	10,682	4,818
Totals	$24,608	18,959	C$5,649

Check of Calculations

238. A reconciliation of shareholders' equity, with changes in the amounts of net assets on a historical cost/constant dollar basis, and current cost/constant dollar basis although not required by this Statement, acts as a check on the arithmetical accuracy of the calculations.

Changes in shareholders' equity during 1980 in average 1980 dollars.

	Source Paragraph	(000s) Historical Cost/ Average 1980 Dollars	Source Paragraph	Current Cost/ Average 1980 Dollars
Equity at Jan. 1, 1980				
Inventory	(225)	C$ 58,907	(233)	C$ 60,179
Property, plant, and equipment—net	(239)	53,678	(235)	76,884
Net monetary items	(232)	(57,067)	(232)	(57,067)
		55,518		79,996
Loss from continuing operations	(App. A)	(2,514)	(App. A)	(8,908)
Dividends	(220)	(3,000)	(220)	(3,000)
Gain from decline in purchasing power of net monetary liabilities	(232)	7,729	(232)	7,729
Excess of increase in specific prices over increase in the general price level			(237)	5,649
		C$ 57,733		C$ 81,466
Equity at December 31, 1980				
Inventory	(224)	C$ 58,523	(233)	C$ 59,602
Property, plant, and equipment—net	(229)	54,548	(235)	77,202
Net monetary items	(232)	(55,338)	(232)	(55,338)
		C$ 57,733		C$ 81,466

239. Historical cost/constant dollar property, plant, and equipment at December 31, 1979 in average 1980 dollars.

Date of Acquisition	(000s) Historical Cost/ Constant Dollars*	Percent Depreciated	Accumulated Depreciation
1973	C$82,983	70	C$58,088
1974	7,478	60	4,487
1975	6,852	50	3,426
1976	6,478	40	2,591
1977	6,085	30	1,826
1978	5,652	20	1,130
1979	10,776	10	1,078
Totals	C$126,304		C$72,626
Accumulated depreciation	72,626		
Net property, plant, and equipment at Dec. 31, 1979, carried to paragraph 238	C$ 53,678		

*Paragraph 229

240. Restated amounts

Summary of Amounts Restated in Average 1980 Dollars
(000s)

	Source Paragraph	Historical Cost/ Constant Dollars	Source Paragraph	Current Cost/ Information
Cost of goods sold	(225)	C$204,384	(226)	C$205,408
Depreciation expense	(229)	C$ 14,130	(230)	C$ 19,500
Purchasing power gain on net monetary items	(232)	C$ 7,729	(232)	C$ 7,729
Increase in current cost of inventories			(234)	C$ 831
Increase in current cost amount of property, plant, and equipment			(236)	C$ 4,818
Inventory	(224)	C$ 58,523	(233)	C$ 59,602
Property, plant, and equipment—net	(229)	C$ 54,548	(235)	C$ 77,202

Appendix F

THE CONSUMER PRICE INDEX

241. The table included in this appendix is the official Department of Labor Consumer Price Index—CPI (U), U.S. City Average, All Items (1967 = 100). This table includes monthly indexes and the average index for the year from 1913.

Monthly updates to the table are published in the United States Department of Labor, Bureau of Labor Statistics, "News."

U.S. Department of Labor
Room 1539
Bureau of Labor Statistics
Washington, D.C. 20212
Consumer Price Index
All Urban Consumers—(CPI-U) U.S. City Average All items (1967 = 100)

YEAR	JAN.	FEB.	MAR.	APR.	MAY	JUNE	JULY	AUG.	SEP.	OCT.	NOV.	DEC.	AVG.
1913	29.4	29.3	29.3	29.4	29.2	29.3	29.6	29.8	29.9	30.1	30.2	30.1	29.7
1914	30.1	29.8	29.7	29.4	29.6	29.8	30.1	30.5	30.6	30.4	30.5	30.4	30.1
1915	30.3	30.1	29.8	30.1	30.2	30.3	30.3	30.3	30.4	30.7	30.9	31.0	30.4
1916	31.3	31.3	31.6	31.9	32.0	32.4	32.4	32.8	33.4	33.8	34.4	34.6	32.7
1917	35.0	35.8	36.0	37.6	38.4	38.8	38.4	39.0	39.7	40.4	40.5	41.0	38.4
1918	41.8	42.2	42.0	42.5	43.3	44.1	45.2	46.0	47.1	47.9	48.7	49.4	45.1
1919	49.5	48.4	49.0	49.9	50.6	50.7	52.1	53.0	53.3	54.2	55.5	56.7	51.8
1920	57.8	58.5	59.1	60.8	61.8	62.7	62.3	60.7	60.0	59.7	59.3	58.0	60.0
1921	57.0	55.2	54.8	54.1	53.1	52.8	52.9	53.1	52.5	52.4	52.1	51.8	53.6
1922	50.7	50.6	50.0	50.0	50.0	50.1	50.2	49.7	49.8	50.1	50.3	50.5	50.2
1923	50.3	50.2	50.4	50.6	50.7	51.0	51.5	51.3	51.6	51.7	51.8	51.8	51.1
1924	51.7	51.5	51.2	51.0	51.0	51.0	51.1	51.0	51.2	51.4	51.6	51.7	51.2
1925	51.8	51.6	51.7	51.6	51.8	52.4	53.1	53.1	52.9	53.1	54.0	53.7	52.5
1926	53.7	53.5	53.2	53.7	53.4	53.0	52.5	52.2	52.5	52.7	52.9	52.9	53.0
1927	52.5	52.1	51.8	51.8	52.2	52.7	51.7	51.4	51.7	52.0	51.9	51.8	52.0
1928	51.7	51.2	51.2	51.3	51.6	51.2	51.2	51.3	51.7	51.6	51.5	51.3	51.3
1929	51.2	51.1	50.9	50.7	51.0	51.2	51.7	51.9	51.8	51.8	51.7	51.4	51.3
1930	51.2	51.0	50.7	51.0	50.7	50.4	49.7	49.4	49.7	49.4	49.0	48.3	50.0
1931	47.6	46.9	46.6	46.3	45.8	45.3	45.2	45.1	44.9	44.6	44.1	43.7	45.6
1932	42.8	42.2	42.0	41.7	41.1	40.8	40.8	40.3	40.1	39.8	39.6	39.2	40.9
1933	38.6	38.0	37.7	37.6	37.7	38.1	39.2	39.6	39.6	39.6	39.6	39.4	38.8
1934	39.6	39.9	39.9	39.8	39.9	40.0	40.0	40.1	40.7	40.4	40.3	40.2	40.1
1935	40.8	41.1	41.0	41.4	41.2	41.1	40.9	40.9	41.1	41.1	41.3	41.4	41.1
1936	41.4	41.2	41.0	41.0	41.0	41.4	41.6	41.9	42.0	41.9	41.9	41.9	41.5
1937	42.2	42.3	42.6	42.8	43.0	43.1	43.3	43.4	43.8	43.6	43.3	43.2	43.0
1938	42.6	42.2	42.2	42.4	42.2	42.2	42.3	42.2	42.2	42.0	41.9	42.0	42.2
1939	41.8	41.6	41.5	41.4	41.4	41.4	41.4	41.4	42.2	42.0	42.0	41.8	41.6
1940	41.7	42.0	41.9	41.9	42.0	42.1	42.0	41.9	42.0	42.0	42.0	42.2	42.0
1941	42.2	42.2	42.4	42.8	43.1	43.9	44.1	44.5	45.3	45.8	46.2	46.3	44.1
1942	46.9	47.3	47.9	48.2	48.7	48.8	49.0	49.3	49.4	49.9	50.2	50.6	48.8
1943	50.6	50.7	51.5	52.1	52.5	52.4	52.0	51.8	52.0	52.2	52.1	52.2	51.8
1944	52.1	52.0	52.0	52.3	52.5	52.6	52.9	53.1	53.1	53.1	53.1	53.3	52.7

YEAR	JAN.	FEB.	MAR.	APR.	MAY	JUNE	JULY	AUG.	SEP.	OCT.	NOV.	DEC.	AVG.
1945	53.3	53.2	53.2	53.3	53.7	54.2	54.3	54.3	54.1	54.1	54.3	54.5	53.9
1946	54.5	54.3	54.7	55.0	55.3	55.9	59.2	60.5	61.2	62.4	63.9	64.4	58.5
1947	64.4	64.3	65.7	65.7	65.5	66.0	66.6	67.3	68.9	68.9	69.3	70.2	66.9
1948	71.0	70.4	70.2	71.2	71.7	72.2	73.1	73.4	73.4	73.1	72.6	72.1	72.1
1949	72.0	71.2	71.4	71.5	71.4	71.5	71.0	71.2	71.5	71.1	71.2	70.8	71.4
1950	70.5	70.3	70.6	70.7	71.0	71.4	72.1	72.7	73.2	73.6	73.9	74.9	72.1
1951	76.1	77.0	77.3	77.4	77.7	77.6	77.7	77.7	78.2	78.6	79.0	79.3	77.8
1952	79.3	78.8	78.8	79.1	79.2	79.4	80.0	80.1	80.0	80.1	80.1	80.0	79.5
1953	79.8	79.4	79.6	79.7	79.9	80.2	80.4	80.6	80.7	80.9	80.6	80.5	80.1
1954	80.7	80.6	80.5	80.3	80.6	80.7	80.7	80.6	80.4	80.2	80.3	80.1	80.5
1955	80.1	80.1	80.1	80.1	80.1	80.1	80.4	80.2	80.5	80.5	80.6	80.4	80.2
1956	80.3	80.3	80.4	80.5	80.9	81.4	82.0	81.9	82.0	82.5	82.5	82.7	81.4
1957	82.8	83.1	83.3	83.6	83.8	84.3	84.7	84.8	84.9	84.9	85.2	85.2	84.3
1958	85.7	85.8	86.4	86.6	86.6	86.7	86.8	86.7	86.7	86.7	86.8	86.7	86.6
1959	86.8	86.7	86.7	86.8	86.9	87.3	87.5	87.4	87.7	88.0	88.0	88.0	87.3
1960	87.9	88.0	88.0	88.5	88.5	88.7	88.7	88.7	88.8	89.2	89.3	89.3	88.7
1961	89.3	89.3	89.3	89.3	89.3	89.4	89.8	89.7	89.9	89.9	89.9	89.9	89.6
1962	89.9	90.1	90.3	90.5	90.5	90.5	90.7	90.7	91.2	91.1	91.1	91.0	90.6
1963	91.1	91.2	91.3	91.3	91.3	91.7	92.1	92.1	92.1	92.2	92.3	92.5	91.7
1964	92.6	92.5	92.6	92.7	92.7	92.9	93.1	93.0	93.2	93.3	93.5	93.6	92.9
1965	93.6	93.6	93.7	94.0	94.2	94.7	94.8	94.6	94.8	94.9	95.1	95.4	94.5
1966	95.4	96.0	96.3	96.7	96.8	97.1	97.4	97.9	98.1	98.5	98.5	98.6	97.2
1967	98.6	98.7	98.9	99.1	99.4	99.7	100.2	100.5	100.7	101.0	101.3	101.6	100.0
1968	102.0	102.3	102.8	103.1	103.4	104.0	104.5	104.8	105.1	105.7	106.1	106.4	104.2
1969	106.7	107.1	108.0	108.7	109.0	109.7	110.2	110.7	111.2	111.6	112.2	112.9	109.8
1970	113.3	113.9	114.5	115.2	115.7	116.3	116.7	116.9	117.5	118.1	118.5	119.1	116.3
1971	119.2	119.4	119.8	120.2	120.8	121.5	121.8	122.1	122.2	122.4	122.6	123.1	121.3
1972	123.2	123.8	124.0	124.3	124.7	125.0	125.5	125.7	126.2	126.6	126.9	127.3	125.3
1973	127.7	128.6	129.8	130.7	131.5	132.4	132.7	135.1	135.5	136.6	137.6	138.5	133.1
1974	139.7	141.5	143.1	143.9	145.5	146.9	148.0	149.9	151.7	153.0	154.3	155.4	147.7
1975	156.1	157.2	157.8	158.6	159.3	160.6	162.3	162.8	163.6	164.6	165.6	166.3	161.2
1976	166.7	167.1	167.5	168.2	169.2	170.1	171.1	171.9	172.6	173.3	173.8	174.3	170.5
1977	175.3	177.1	178.2	179.6	180.6	181.8	182.6	183.3	184.0	184.5	185.4	186.1	181.5
1978	187.2	188.4	189.8	191.5	193.3	195.3	196.7	197.8	199.3	200.9	202.0	202.9	195.4
1979	204.7	207.1	209.1	211.5	214.1	216.6	218.9	221.1					

Statement of Financial Accounting Standards No. 34
Capitalization of Interest Cost

STATUS

Issued: October 1979

Effective Date: For fiscal years beginning after December 15, 1979

Affects: Amends APB 21, paragraphs 15 and 16
Amends FAS 13, paragraph 12

Affected by: Paragraph 5 superseded by FAS 71
Paragraphs 8 and 9 amended by FAS 42
Paragraphs 9, 10, and 20 amended by FAS 58
Paragraphs 10, 13, and 17 amended by FAS 62

SUMMARY

This Statement establishes standards for capitalizing interest cost as part of the historical cost of acquiring certain assets. To qualify for interest capitalization, assets must require a period of time to get them ready for their intended use. Examples are assets that an enterprise constructs for its own use (such as facilities) and assets intended for sale or lease that are constructed as discrete projects (such as ships or real estate projects). Interest capitalization is required for those assets if its effect, compared with the effect of expensing interest, is material. If the net effect is not material, interest capitalization is not required. However, interest cannot be capitalized for inventories that are routinely manufactured or otherwise produced in large quantities on a repetitive basis.

The interest cost eligible for capitalization shall be the interest cost recognized on borrowings and other obligations. The amount capitalized is to be an allocation of the interest cost incurred during the period required to complete the asset. The interest rate for capitalization purposes is to be based on the rates on the enterprise's outstanding borrowings. If the enterprise associates a specific new borrowing with the asset, it may apply the rate on that borrowing to the appropriate portion of the expenditures for the asset. A weighted average of the rates on other borrowings is to be applied to expenditures not covered by specific new borrowings. Judgment is required in identifying the borrowings on which the average rate is based.

Statement of Financial Accounting Standards No. 34
Capitalization of Interest Cost

CONTENTS

INTRODUCTION

1. This Statement establishes standards of financial accounting and reporting for capitalizing interest cost as a part of the historical cost of acquiring certain assets. For the purposes of this Statement, *interest cost* includes interest recognized on obligations having explicit interest rates,[1] interest imputed on certain types of payables in accordance with APB Opinion No. 21, *Interest on Receivables and Payables,* and interest related to a capital lease determined in accordance with FASB Statement No. 13, *Accounting for Leases.*

2. Paragraphs 15 and 16 of Opinion 21 provide that the discount or premium that results from imputing interest for certain types of payables should be amortized as interest expense over the life of the payable and reported as such in the statement of income. Paragraph 12 of Statement 13 provides that, during the term of a capital lease, a portion of each minimum lease payment shall be recorded as interest expense. This Statement modifies Opinion 21 and Statement 13 in that the amount chargeable to interest expense under the provisions of those paragraphs is eligible for inclusion in the amount of interest cost capitalizable in accordance with this Statement.

3. Some enterprises now charge all interest cost to expense when incurred; some enterprises capitalize interest cost in some circumstances; and some enterprises, primarily public utilities, also capitalize a cost for equity funds in some circumstances. This diversity of practice and an observation that an increasing number of nonutility registrants were adopting a policy of capitalizing interest led the Securities and Exchange Commission to impose, in November 1974, a moratorium on adoption or extension of such a policy by most nonutility registrants until such time as the FASB established standards in this area.[2]

4. Appendix A provides additional background information. Appendix B sets forth the basis for the Board's conclusions, including alternatives considered and reasons for accepting some and rejecting others.

5. The Addendum to APB Opinion No. 2, *Accounting for the 'Investment Credit',* states that "differences may arise in the application of generally accepted accounting principles as between regulated and nonregulated businesses, because of the effect in regulated businesses of the rate-making process," and discusses the application of generally accepted accounting principles to regulated industries. Accordingly, the provisions of the Addendum shall govern the application of this Statement to those operations of an enterprise that are regulated for rate-making purposes on an individual-company-cost-of-service basis.

---

[1] Interest cost on these obligations includes amounts resulting from periodic amortization of discount or premium and issue costs on debt.

[2] Securities and Exchange Commission, ASR No. 163, *Capitalization of Interest by Companies Other Than Public Utilities* (Washington: November 14, 1974).

STANDARDS OF FINANCIAL ACCOUNTING AND REPORTING

6. The historical cost of acquiring an asset includes the costs necessarily incurred to bring it to the condition and location necessary for its intended use.[3] If an asset requires a period of time in which to carry out the activities[4] necessary to bring it to that condition and location, the interest cost incurred during that period as a result of expenditures for the asset is a part of the historical cost of acquiring the asset.

7. The objectives of capitalizing interest are (a) to obtain a measure of acquisition cost that more closely reflects the enterprise's total investment in the asset and (b) to charge a cost that relates to the acquisition of a resource that will benefit future periods against the revenues of the periods benefited.

8. In concept, interest cost is capitalizable for all assets that require a period of time to get them ready for their intended use (an "acquisition period"). However, in many cases, the benefit in terms of information about enterprise resources and earnings may not justify the additional accounting and administrative cost involved in providing the information. The benefit may be less than the cost because the effect of interest capitalization and its subsequent amortization or other disposition, compared with the effect of charging it to expense when incurred, would not be material. In that circumstance, interest capitalization is not *required* by this Statement.

Assets Qualifying for Interest Capitalization

9. Subject to the provisions of paragraph 8, interest shall be capitalized for the following types of assets ("qualifying assets"):

a. Assets that are constructed or otherwise produced for an enterprise's own use (including assets constructed or produced for the enterprise by others for which deposits or progress payments have been made)
b. Assets intended for sale or lease that are constructed or otherwise produced as discrete projects (e.g., ships or real estate developments).

10. However, interest cost shall not be capitalized for inventories that are routinely manufactured or otherwise produced in large quantities on a repetitive basis because, in the Board's judgment, the informational benefit does not justify the cost of so doing. In addition, interest shall not be capitalized for the following types of assets:

a. Assets that are in use or ready for their intended use in the earning activities of the enterprise
b. Assets that are not being used in the earning activities of the enterprise and that are not undergoing the activities necessary to get them ready for use.

11. Land that is not undergoing activities necessary to get it ready for its intended use is not a qualifying asset. If activities are undertaken for the purpose of developing land for a particular use, the expenditures to acquire the land qualify for interest capitalization while those activities are in progress. The interest cost capitalized on those expenditures is a cost of acquiring the asset that results from those activities. If the resulting asset is a structure, such as a plant or a shopping center, interest capitalized on the land expenditures is part of the acquisition cost of the structure. If the resulting asset is developed land, such as land that is to be sold as developed lots, interest capitalized on the land expenditures is part of the acquisition cost of the developed land.

The Amount of Interest Cost to Be Capitalized

12. The amount of interest cost to be capitalized for qualifying assets is intended to be that portion of the interest cost incurred during the assets' acquisition periods that theoretically could have been avoided (for example, by avoiding additional borrowings or by using the funds expended for the assets to repay existing borrowings) if expenditures for the assets had not been made.

13. The amount capitalized in an accounting period shall be determined by applying an interest rate(s) ("the capitalization rate") to the average amount of accumulated expenditures for the asset during the period. The capitalization rates used in an accounting period shall be based on the rates applicable to borrowings outstanding during the period. If an enterprise's financing plans associate a specific new borrowing with a qualifying asset, the enterprise may use the rate on that borrowing as the capitalization rate to be applied to that portion of the average accumulated expenditures for the asset that does not exceed the amount of that borrowing. If average accumulated expenditures for the asset exceed the amounts of specific new borrowings associated with the asset, the capitalization rate to be applied to such excess shall be a weighted average of the rates applicable to other borrowings of the enterprise.

---

[3]The term *intended use* embraces both readiness for use and readiness for sale, depending on the purpose of acquisition.

[4]See paragraph 17 for a definition of those activities for purposes of this Statement.

14. In identifying the borrowings to be included in the weighted average rate, the objective is a reasonable measure of the cost of financing acquisition of the asset in terms of the interest cost incurred that otherwise could have been avoided. Accordingly, judgment will be required to make a selection of borrowings that best accomplishes that objective in the circumstances. For example, in some circumstances, it will be appropriate to include all borrowings of the parent company and its consolidated subsidiaries; for some multinational enterprises, it may be appropriate for each foreign subsidiary to use an average of the rates applicable to its own borrowings. However, the use of judgment in determining capitalization rates shall not circumvent the requirement that a capitalization rate be applied to all capitalized expenditures for a qualifying asset to the extent that interest cost has been incurred during an accounting period.

15. The total amount of interest cost capitalized in an accounting period shall not exceed the total amount of interest cost incurred by the enterprise in that period. In consolidated financial statements, that limitation shall be applied by reference to the total amount of interest cost incurred by the parent company and consolidated subsidiaries on a consolidated basis. In any separately issued financial statements of a parent company or a consolidated subsidiary and in the financial statements (whether separately issued or not) of unconsolidated subsidiaries and other investees accounted for by the equity method, the limitation shall be applied by reference to the total amount of interest cost (including interest on intercompany borrowings) incurred by the separate entity.

16. For the purposes of this Statement, *expenditures* to which capitalization rates are to be applied are capitalized expenditures (net of progress payment collections) for the qualifying asset that have required the payment of cash, the transfer of other assets, or the incurring of a liability on which interest is recognized (in contrast to liabilities, such as trade payables, accruals, and retainages on which interest is not recognized). However, reasonable approximations of net capitalized expenditures may be used. For example, capitalized costs for an asset may be used as a reasonable approximation of capitalized expenditures unless the difference is material.

The Capitalization Period

17. The capitalization period shall begin when three conditions are present:

a. Expenditures (as defined in paragraph 16) for the asset have been made.
b. Activities that are necessary to get the asset ready for its intended use are in progress.
c. Interest cost is being incurred.

Interest capitalization shall continue as long as those three conditions are present. The term *activities* is to be construed broadly. It encompasses more than physical construction; it includes all the steps required to prepare the asset for its intended use. For example, it includes administrative and technical activities during the preconstruction stage, such as the development of plans or the process of obtaining permits from governmental authorities; it includes activities undertaken after construction has begun in order to overcome unforeseen obstacles, such as technical problems, labor disputes, or litigation. If the enterprise suspends substantially all activities related to acquisition of the asset, interest capitalization shall cease until activities are resumed. However, brief interruptions in activities, interruptions that are externally imposed, and delays that are inherent in the asset acquisition process shall not require cessation of interest capitalization.

18. The capitalization period shall end when the asset is substantially complete and ready for its intended use. Some assets are completed in parts, and each part is capable of being used independently while work is continuing on other parts. An example is a condominium. For such assets, interest capitalization shall stop on each part when it is substantially complete and ready for use. Some assets must be completed in their entirety before any part of the asset can be used. An example is a facility designed to manufacture products by sequential processes. For such assets, interest capitalization shall continue until the entire asset is substantially complete and ready for use. Some assets cannot be used effectively until a separate facility has been completed. Examples are the oil wells drilled in Alaska before completion of the pipeline. For such assets, interest capitalization shall continue until the separate facility is substantially complete and ready for use.

19. Interest capitalization shall not cease when present accounting principles require recognition of a lower value for the asset than acquisition cost; the provision required to reduce acquisition cost to such lower value shall be increased appropriately.

Disposition of the Amount Capitalized

20. Because interest cost is an integral part of the total cost of acquiring a qualifying asset, its disposition shall be the same as that of other components of asset cost.

Disclosures

21. The following information with respect to interest cost shall be disclosed in the financial statements or related notes:

a. For an accounting period in which no interest cost is capitalized, the amount of interest cost incurred and charged to expense during the period
b. For an accounting period in which some interest cost is capitalized, the total amount of interest cost incurred during the period and the amount thereof that has been capitalized.

Effective Date and Transition

22. This Statement shall be applied prospectively in fiscal years beginning after December 15, 1979. Earlier application is permitted, but not required, in financial statements for fiscal years begining before December 16, 1979 that have not been previously issued. With respect to qualifying assets in existence at the beginning of the fiscal year in which this Statement is first applied for which interest cost has not been previously capitalized, interest capitalization shall begin at that time. With respect to qualifying assets for which interest cost has been capitalized according to a method that differs from the provisions of this Statement, no adjustment shall be made to the amounts of interest cost previously capitalized, but interest cost capitalized after this Statement is first applied shall be determined according to the provisions of this Statement. With respect to assets in existence when this Statement is first applied for which interest cost has been capitalized but which do not qualify for interest capitalization according to the provisions of this Statement, no adjustments shall be made, but no additional amounts of interest cost shall be capitalized.

23. If early application is adopted in financial reports for interim periods of a fiscal year beginning before December 16, 1979, previously issued financial information for any interim periods of that fiscal year that precede the period of adoption shall be restated to give effect to the provisions of this Statement, and any subsequent presentation of that information shall be on the restated basis. This Statement shall not be applied retroactively for previously issued annual financial statements.

The provisions of this Statement need not be applied to immaterial items.

This Statement was adopted by the affirmative votes of four members of the Financial Accounting Standards Board. Messrs. Block, Kirk, and Morgan dissented.

Messrs. Block, Kirk, and Morgan dissent to this Statement because, in their opinion, it is founded on a view of interest cost that does not meet the needs of users of financial statements, because it makes the requirement to capitalize interest dependent on meeting an undefined test of materiality, and because it is not evenhanded in the application of its requirements.

Messrs. Block, Kirk, and Morgan consider interest to be a cost of a different order from the costs of materials, labor, and other services in two respects. First, cash—the resource obtained by the payment of interest on debt—has unique characteristics. It is fungible. It is obtained from a variety of sources (principally, earning activities, borrowings, issuance of equity securities, and sales of economic resources), only one of which (borrowings) gives rise to a cost that is recognized in the present accounting framework. The amount of cash (or cash equivalent) given in exchange for a noncash resource provides the basis for measuring the cost of a noncash resource. Because of those characteristics of cash, interest on debt cannot be assigned or allocated to noncash resources in the same way as material, labor, and overhead costs, and association of interest on debt with a particular category of noncash resources, such as assets undergoing a construction or production process, is inherently arbitrary. Second, interest cost is the return to lenders on capital provided by them to an enterprise for a certain period. In the view of Messrs. Block, Kirk, and Morgan, interest cost, like dividends, is more directly associable with the period during which the capital giving rise to it is outstanding than with the material, labor, and other resources into which capital is converted. They acknowledge that the conversion of cash into a nonearning asset entails the sacrifice of the return that the cash could otherwise have earned, but they do not believe that a measure of that sacrifice is a proper addition to the cost of acquiring the asset. In addition, they note that, by attaching an interest cost to all expenditures for a qualifying asset, the prescribed method in this Statement in effect imputes an interest cost to any equity funds that may have been used for it.

Information about the return earned by an enterprise during an accounting period on the capital existing during that period is important to investors and creditors in assessing the enterprise's periodic performance, in assessing the risks of financial leverage, and in assessing their prospects of receiving both return on and return of their investment. Users of financial statements often compute the return earned on the total of debt and equity capital by adding interest expense to reported earnings. Interest capitalization, however, merges interest cost into the costs of assets, with the result that, when the costs of those assets are charged to income in subsequent periods, the interest cost component cannot be distinguished. Thus, the return on total capital in those periods yielded by that computation is misstated. The disclosure requirements of this Statement do not provide the information needed to correct that misstatement.

Messrs. Block, Kirk, and Morgan conclude that charging interest on debt to expense when incurred results in information in the financial statements of all companies that allows the return earned on capital during a period to be readily related on a comparable basis to the capital existing during that period. They believe that information to be more useful in making rational investment, credit, and similar decisions than that provided by including interest cost in the cost of assets.

Messrs. Block, Kirk, and Morgan also believe the discussion of materiality in this Statement will cause confusion. All FASB Statements have contained the sentence, "the provisions of this Statement need not be applied to immaterial items." Heretofore, they believe, FASB standards generally have been followed whenever there was a possibility that noncompliance would have a material effect. In their opinion, paragraph 8 and the amplification of that paragraph in paragraphs 46 and 47 could be viewed as an invitation to search for a new but undefined test of materiality. They believe that search, with the attendant arguments between preparers and auditors and explanations to users as to why interest was not capitalized, will result in more cost, in terms of credibility as well as in a monetary sense, than would compliance with the concept of interest capitalization. They also believe that it is untimely for the Board to elaborate on materiality in a Statement on interest capitalization when an Exposure Draft, *Qualitative Characteristics: Criteria for Selecting and Evaluating Financial Accounting and Reporting Policies,* covering the subject of materiality is out for public comment.

Messrs. Block, Kirk, and Morgan believe a goal of standards is similar accounting for similar situations. In their opinion, because this Statement proscribes interest capitalization for certain inventories, even when the effect is material, and does not define those inventories clearly, this Statement will fail to achieve that goal.

Mr. Morgan also dissents because he believes that the application of this Statement may result in unfavorable economic consequences of significance, such as (a) restructuring of analysis models by financial analysts and other users of financial statements, and (b) possible changes in laws and regulations as a result of reaction to the more liberal profitability concept embodied in this Statement.

Members of the Financial Accounting Standards Board:

Donald J. Kirk, *Chairman*
Frank E. Block
John W. March
Robert A. Morgan
David Mosso
Robert T. Sprouse
Ralph E. Walters

Appendix A

BACKGROUND INFORMATION

24. Accounting for interest cost was the subject of considerable discussion in accounting literature during the first quarter of this century, but, apart from discussion in accounting textbooks and some articles in regulatory periodicals, relatively little was written on the subject during the next 40 years. The sharp rise in interest rates and increased use of borrowed funds in the last 10 years, however, resulted in renewed attention to the subject.

25. The question of capitalizing interest cost has never been resolved by an authoritative pronouncement of a standard-setting body.[5] In 1971, the Accounting Principles Board (APB) appointed a committee to study the subject. The committee prepared a comprehensive working paper setting forth the principal issues to be considered, but the APB terminated its activities before a pronouncement could be issued. Accounting for interest cost was also among the many topics originally suggested to the FASB by its Advisory Council and others; however, it was not included on the Board's initial technical agenda.

26. In 1974, the Securities and Exchange Commission became concerned with accounting for interest cost when it noted an increase in the number of nonutility registrants that were adopting a policy of capitalizing interest as part of the cost of certain assets. On June 21, 1974, the SEC issued a release that proposed a moratorium on adoption or exten-

[5]In 1917, the American Institute of Accountants (as it was then known) set up a Special Committee on Interest in Relation to Cost. The Committee concluded that interest on investment should not be included in production cost. At the Institute's 1918 annual meeting, the members in attendance voted their acceptance and approval of the Committee's report. Although the vote of the Institute's membership is of historical interest, it has not been incorporated into the body of authoritative pronouncements currently in force.

sion of a policy of capitalizing interest by registrants other than public utilities that had not, as of June 21, 1974, publicly disclosed such a policy. On November 14, 1974, the moratorium was imposed by ASR No. 163, *Capitalization of Interest by Companies Other Than Public Utilities.* "Public utilities" was defined to include electric, gas, water, and telephone utilities; registrants covered by AICPA Guides *Accounting for Retail Lands Sales* and *Audits of Savings and Loan Associations* were also excluded from the moratorium. In explaining its action, the SEC noted that:

> . . . it does not seem desirable to have an alternative practice grow up through selective adoption by individual companies without careful consideration of such a change by the Financial Accounting Standards Board, including the development of systematic criteria as to when, if ever, capitalization of interest is desirable.
>
> Accordingly, the Commission concludes that companies other than electric, gas, water and telephone utilities and those companies covered by the two exceptions in the authoritative literature described above which had not, as of June 21, 1974, publicly disclosed an accounting policy of capitalizing interest costs shall not follow such a policy in financial statements filed with the Commission covering fiscal periods ending after June 21, 1974. At such time as the Financial Accounting Standards Board develops standards for accounting for interest cost, the Commission expects to reconsider this conclusion. Until such time, companies which have publicly disclosed such a policy may continue to apply it on a consistent basis but not extend it to new types of assets. Return on equity invested shall not be capitalized by companies other than electric, gas, water and telephone utilities.

The Release amended *Regulation S-X* to require the disclosure of certain information by registrants continuing to capitalize interest.

27. At its meeting on September 18, 1974, the FASB's Advisory Council agreed that this matter should be considered by the FASB, and on November 25, 1974, the Board added the project to its technical agenda. In September 1975, a task force of 16 persons from academe, the financial community, industry, and public accounting was appointed to provide counsel to the Board in preparing a Discussion Memorandum.

28. The project began with a broad scope. It was to deal not only with accounting for interest on debt, but also to explore the proposal to give comprehensive accounting recognition to an imputed interest cost for equity capital. According to proponents of that proposal, accounting should recognize such imputed interest whether it is to be capitalized or not. The total of debt interest and imputed equity interest, they believe, should be allocated to enterprise assets and operations, just as material, labor, and overhead costs are presently allocated. However, as the project proceeded, the Board came to the conclusion that, because it could involve fundamental changes in the measurement of earnings and asset values—a subject that properly belongs in the Board's conceptual framework project—the Statement resulting from the interest cost project should not deal with that proposal. Accordingly, the scope of the project was narrowed to focus on accounting alternatives that are found in practice under the present accounting model.

29. Presently, some companies account for interest on debt as an expense of the period in which it is incurred. Some companies, on the other hand, capitalize interest on debt as part of the cost of certain kinds of assets, such as construction work in progress, land held for future development, and real estate in process of development; and some companies, notably public utility companies, capitalize a cost of equity funds as well as interest on debt as part of the cost of certain assets. Thus, the basic issue to be resolved by this project was stated in the Discussion Memorandum, *Accounting for Interest Costs,* to be a determination as to which of those accounting alternatives should be applied.

30. In addition to presenting arguments for and against each of the accounting alternatives, the Discussion Memorandum identified 10 implemental issues relating to interest capitalization and three implemental issues relating to information disclosures and application of this Statement. A chapter was devoted to the proposal for comprehensive accounting recognition of imputed equity interest to assist the reader to relate the basic issue being considered to the broader aspects of the subject but, because of the Board's decision not to deal with the proposal at the present time, the related issues were described as "advisory" issues.

31. The Board issued the Discussion Memorandum on December 16, 1977 and held a public hearing in New York on April 4 and 5, 1978. The Board received 145 position papers, letters of comment, and outlines of oral presentations in response to the Discussion Memorandum, and 18 presentations were made at the public hearing.

32. An Exposure Draft of a proposed Statement on *Capitalization of Interest Cost* was issued on December 15, 1978. The Board received 269 letters of comment in response to the Exposure Draft.

Appendix B

BASIS FOR CONCLUSIONS

33. This appendix discusses factors deemed significant by members of the Board in reaching the conclusions in this Statement, including various alternatives considered and reasons for accepting some and rejecting others. Individual assenting Board members gave greater weight to some factors than to others.

Scope

34. Some respondents to the Discussion Memorandum recommended that regulated enterprises be exempt from the provisions of this Statement because the rate-making process creates a special set of circumstances and because most regulatory agencies prescribe when and how interest shall be capitalized by companies subject to their jurisdiction. The Board concluded that the applicability of this Statement should not differ from that of other FASB Statements. Moreover, the effect of the rate-making process on accounting and reporting by regulated enterprises is the subject of another project on the Board's technical agenda, and the Board concluded that this Statement should not prejudge the outcome of that project.

35. Some respondents to the Exposure Draft urged that the scope of this Statement be expanded to include other costs, such as insurance and property taxes, that are sometimes capitalized in the same circumstances as interest cost. The Board did not adopt that suggestion because special considerations apply to interest cost and expansion of the scope of this Statement at that stage would have significantly delayed its issuance. The scope of the project was considered at length during the Discussion Memorandum stage, as indicated in Appendix A.

The Accounting Alternatives

36. As indicated in Appendix A, the Board considered three basic methods of accounting for interest cost:

a. Account for interest on debt as an expense of the period in which it is incurred.
b. Capitalize interest on debt as part of the cost of an asset when prescribed conditions are met.
c. Capitalize interest on debt and imputed interest on stockholders' equity as part of the cost of an asset when prescribed conditions are met.

The Board concluded that the second of those methods should be adopted. The reasons for that conclusion are presented in paragraphs 37-57.

Interest as a Cost of Acquiring an Asset

37. The Board determined that the primary question to be addressed was whether there are any circumstances in which interest cost should be considered to be part of the historical cost of *acquiring* an asset. The focus on the historical cost of acquiring an asset followed from the Board's decision, in developing the scope of this project, that the accounting alternatives that would be considered for this Statement should be limited to those found in practice based on the present accounting model, as stated in Appendix A. In the present accounting model, nonmonetary assets are generally carried at acquisition cost or some unexpired or unamortized portion of it.[6] The cost "at which assets are carried and expenses are measured in financial accounting today usually means historical or acquisition cost because of the conventions of initially recording assets at acquisition cost and of ignoring increases in assets until they are exchanged (the realization convention)."[7]

38. Some believe that interest should be capitalized as a cost of holding assets, but, in general, in the present accounting model, costs are not added to assets subsequent to their readiness for use. Consideration of that proposal would require a comprehensive reexamination of a fundamental principle underlying present practice. One of the consequences of restricting the focus to acquisition cost was that capitalization of interest as a holding cost was rejected. Thus, earning assets and nonearning assets not undergoing the activities necessary to get them ready for use do not qualify for interest capitalization under this Statement.

39. The Board concluded that interest cost is a part of the cost of acquiring an asset if a period of time is required in which to carry out the activities necessary to get it ready for its intended use. In reaching this conclusion, the Board considered that the point in time at which an asset is ready for its intended use is critical in determining its acquisition cost. Assets are expected to provide future economic benefits, and the notion of expected future economic benefits implies fitness for a particular purpose. Although assets may be capable of being applied to a variety of possible uses, the use intended by the enterprise in deciding to acquire an asset has an important bearing on the nature and value of the economic benefits that it will yield.

---

[6]APB Statement No. 4, *Basic Concepts and Accounting Principles Underlying Financial Statements of Business Enterprises*, par. 163.
[7]Ibid., par. 164.

40. Some assets are ready for their intended use when purchased. Others are constructed or otherwise developed for a particular use by a series of activities whereby diverse resources are combined to form a new asset or a less valuable resource is transformed into a more valuable resource. Activities take time for their accomplishment. During the period of time required, the expenditures for the materials, labor, and other resources used in creating the asset must be financed. Financing has a cost. The cost may take the form of explicit interest on borrowed funds, or it may take the form of a return foregone on an alternative use of funds, but regardless of the form it takes, a financing cost is necessarily incurred. On the premise that the historical cost of acquiring an asset should include all costs necessarily incurred to bring it to the condition and location necessary for its intended use, the Board concluded that, in principle, the cost incurred in financing expenditures for an asset during a required construction or development period is itself a part of the asset's historical acquisition cost.

41. Some assenting Board members believe that the informational value of historical cost as an indicator of an asset's cash flow potential is also a reason for capitalizing interest cost. At the time of the decision to acquire an asset, they point out, the enterprise believes that the present value of its cash flow service potential is at least as great as the sum of the costs that will have to be incurred to acquire it. Otherwise, the enterprise presumably would not acquire the asset. Accordingly, the enterprise's commitment of cash or other resources to acquire the asset provides the best available objective evidence of an asset's cash flow service potential at the time of acquisition.

42. Those Board members believe acquisition cost provides the most reliable measure of cash flow potential when assets are self-constructed or produced as well as when they are purchased in arms-length transactions. Measuring the acquisition cost of a self-constructed or produced asset is not as simple as measuring the acquisition cost of a purchased asset, but, those Board members believe, the objective should be the same—to obtain a measure of cash flow service potential that is supported by objective evidence. For such assets, therefore, acquisition cost should include all the cost components envisioned by the enterprise as being necessary to acquire the asset. The cost of financing the asset during the period of its construction or production is one of those cost components. Since the cash flow potential of an enterprise's assets is significant information in assessing the future net cash flows of the enterprise and hence the prospective cash receipts of investors and creditors,[8] a measure of acquisition cost that includes interest cost is likely to be more useful to investors and creditors than one that does not.

43. Some assenting Board members believe that a case could be made for allocating interest cost to all nonmonetary assets, whether being developed for use or in use. It could be argued that, since assets are *future* economic benefits, the historical cost of an asset at any point in time should be the unexpired portion of *all* costs incurred in relation to the asset prior to that time. All assets require financing, and therefore the cost of financing (interest) should be included in the historical cost of all nonmonetary assets. Those Board members, however, concluded that allocation of interest cost to assets in use or ready for use is not appropriate at present. The broad issue of dividing the long-term service potential of an asset into the services associated with periods of use would have to be reexamined before such an extension of the historical cost concept could be made. Further, allocation of interest cost to all nonmonetary assets often would have a relatively small effect on periodic earnings because the amount of interest capitalized in a period would tend to be offset by amortization of interest capitalized in prior periods. The incremental informational benefit would not be commensurate with the additional accounting and administrative costs. They concluded that interest cost should be capitalized only when it is part of the original acquisition cost of an asset.

44. The reasoning in the foregoing paragraphs would lead to the conclusion that interest should be included in the acquisition cost of all assets that are derived from a production, construction, or other time-consuming development process. However, in considering the circumstances in which interest capitalization should be required, the Board weighed the expected benefit in terms of information about enterprise resources and earnings against the expected cost of providing that information. With that consideration in mind when developing the Exposure Draft, the Board had concluded that interest should not be included in the cost of manufactured inventories that turn over relatively quickly and that interest capitalization should be confined to assets whose required development period is significant. But respondents to the Exposure Draft identified a number of problems with the proposal to delineate qualifying assets by the length of the development period. In particular, it was pointed out that a judgment about the benefit of interest capitalization in a given set of circumstances should focus on the significance of the amount of interest

[8]FASB Concepts Statement No. 1, *Objectives of Financial Reporting by Business Enterprises*, especially par. 37.

cost associable with an asset, and that the length of the development period is only one of the factors to be considered. Other factors include the amount of expenditures, the timing of expenditures, the capitalization rate, and the criterion by which significance is judged (e.g., periodic earnings). In addition, some respondents said that a review of their operations showed that, in any given year, a very large number of assets would meet the "significant period" test. They said that considerable costs would be involved in continually identifying assets that meet the test and the borrowings to be associated with each asset, and in additional recordkeeping.

45. Other respondents expressed concern that inventory items that require an extended maturation period (such as aging whiskeys and tobacco) would qualify for interest capitalization according to the Exposure Draft. They said that aging is not part of the production process. Moreover, such inventories are often accounted for on the last-in, first-out basis (LIFO), which would present special difficulties in concept, in implementation, and in application of "LIFO conformity" requirements for income tax purposes. Finally, it was observed that, although an individual batch of whiskey or tobacco may be held in inventory for a significant period, there is a constant flow of product into and out of inventory. Hence, the effect on earnings of capitalizing interest on maturing inventories usually would not be significant in the long run.

46. In the light of respondents' comments, the Board decided that cost/benefit considerations indicated that the circumstances in which interest capitalization is required should be more restricted than those set forth in the Exposure Draft and that those circumstances should be delineated by criteria other than the length of the required development period. The significance of the effect of interest capitalization in relation to enterprise resources and earnings is the most important consideration in assessing its benefit. The ease with which qualifying assets and related expenditures can be separately identified and the number of assets subject to interest capitalization are important factors in assessing the cost of implementation. Interest capitalization should be required only when the balance of the informational benefit and the cost of implementation is favorable. The Board judged that a favorable balance is most likely to be achieved where an asset is constructed or produced as a discrete project for which costs are separately accumulated and where construction of the asset takes considerable time, entails substantial expenditures, and hence is likely to involve a significant amount of interest cost. A favorable balance is unlikely in the case of inventory items that are routinely manufactured or otherwise produced in large quantities on a repetitive basis. Accordingly, this Statement proscribes interest capitalization on those types of inventories and provides for interest capitalization on assets that are constructed or produced as discrete projects. (Some Board members believe that another reason for not capitalizing interest on inventories generally is that, because variations presently exist in the methods of costing inventories, inclusion of interest cost would do little to improve comparability of inventory costs among enterprises.)

47. The Board recognized that, in many cases, the effect of interest capitalization and its subsequent amortization or other disposition, compared with the effect of charging it to expense when incurred, would not be material. Some assenting Board members noted that the primary factor in making materiality judgments in current practice usually is the relation to the level or trend of earnings. Accordingly, they anticipate that such a factor will be primary in making materiality judgments about the requirement for interest capitalization in accordance with this Statement.

48. Some respondents to the Discussion Memorandum and the Exposure Draft expressed the view that interest is a unique cost that cannot be allocated to cost objectives in the same way as material, labor, and overhead costs. The Board rejected that view. As explained in paragraph 51, the Board concluded that the cause-and-effect relationship between acquiring an asset and the incurrence of interest cost makes interest cost analogous to a direct cost that is readily and objectively assignable to the acquired asset. The Board believes that failure to capitalize the interest cost associated with the acquisition of qualifying assets improperly reduces reported earnings during the period of acquisition and increases reported earnings in later periods.

The Amount of Interest Cost to Be Capitalized

49. Some Board members believe that there is a valid conceptual argument for measuring the cost of financing acquisition of qualifying assets on the basis of the enterprise's cost of capital, which would include imputed interest on equity capital as well as interest on borrowed capital. Such a measure would recognize that both borrowed capital and equity capital provide funds to the enterprise and that, due to the fungible nature of cash, it is usually impossible to determine objectively the proportion of the funds expended for a particular purpose that was derived from each source. It would also recognize the interrelationship between an enterprise's cost of borrowing and its cost of equity. Some assenting Board members believe that it may be appropriate at some time in the future to consider whether the cost

of equity capital should be recognized within a framework for financial reporting that continues to be based primarily on historical cost. Accordingly, they think that the standards prescribed in this Statement should not be incompatible with that possible development. Other assenting Board members do not share that view. Nevertheless, all Board members agreed that recognition of the cost of equity capital does not conform to the present accounting framework. In the present accounting framework, the cost of a resource is generally measured by the historical exchange price paid to acquire it. However, funds are an unusual kind of resource in that, although an enterprise obtains funds from various sources, only borrowed funds give rise to a cost that can be described as a historical exchange price. Although a historical exchange transaction may occur when equity securities are issued, that transaction is not the basis generally advocated for measuring the cost of equity capital. It is generally agreed that use of equity capital entails an economic cost, but in the absence of a historical exchange price, the cost of equity capital is not reliably determinable. The Board concluded, therefore, that the cost of financing expenditures for a qualifying asset should be measured by assigning to the asset an appropriate portion of the interest cost incurred on borrowings during the period of its acquisition. (As a result of that conclusion, the issue presented in the Discussion Memorandum regarding the appropriate method of accounting for the credit corresponding to imputed interest on equity capital did not have to be addressed.)

50. The Board considered several methods of determining the amount of interest cost to be capitalized. Some suggested that the amount capitalized be limited to the interest incurred on specific borrowings associated with the qualifying asset by the enterprise. However, in the Board's view, association of sources and uses of funds is primarily subjective. If that suggestion had been adopted, the enterprise's identification of the source of the funds used for the asset would determine not only the amount of interest capitalized but also whether *any* interest is capitalized. Some suggested that interest cost be allocated to qualifying assets on a basis such as total assets or the total of debt and owner's equity. That method would be based on an assumption that funds used for all assets are obtained from borrowings and other sources proportionately. However, in many cases, it would result in an amount of capitalized interest that was unrealistically low as a measure of the economic cost of financing acquisition of the qualifying asset.

51. The Board concluded that the amount of interest cost to be capitalized should be the amount that theoretically could have been avoided during the acquisition period if expenditures for the asset had not been made. Clearly, interest cost can be avoided by repaying existing borrowings as well as by not borrowing additional funds. When an enterprise is contemplating investment in an asset, both those alternatives are available. When the decision to invest in the asset is made, those alternatives are rejected and the incurrence of interest cost during the acquisition period is a consequence of that decision. That cause-and-effect relationship between the investment in the asset and the incurrence of interest cost makes interest cost analogous to a direct cost in those circumstances. Also, the amount of interest cost that could have been avoided is one measure of the opportunity cost incurred. Admittedly, investment of funds in the asset also entails rejection of a wide range of other possible uses of funds, and therefore interest cost avoided is only one of several possible measures of opportunity cost. But it is the measure that can be recognized in the present accounting framework. (In adopting the notion of interest on borrowings as an avoidable cost, the Board does not intend that the practicability of repaying individual borrowings has to be considered.)

52. In the Exposure Draft, the Board proposed a method of associating interest on borrowings with qualifying assets that gave priority to recent borrowings. Respondents criticized that method on a number of grounds, most of which related to its complexity in practice and hence the cost of implementation. The Board concluded that the method should be simplified in order to reduce that cost. Two methods considered were (a) a general measure of the current cost of money, such as the prime rate and (b) the enterprise's incremental borrowing rate. However, the Board rejected those methods on the grounds that the historical exchange price convention requires that the interest rate used for capitalization purposes be based on rates actually being paid by the enterprise. The Board also considered a weighted average of the rates being paid on all borrowings. But it concluded that, despite the element of subjectivity, if an enterprise borrows additional funds with the intention of using them to finance a qualifying asset, the enterprise should not be prevented from using the rate on that borrowing as a capitalization rate. That rate would provide a readily determined measure of a major part of the interest cost that could have been avoided if funds had not been invested in the asset. This Statement therefore permits use of the rate(s) on specific new borrowing(s) associated with a qualifying asset and provides that an average rate shall be applied to expenditures not covered by specific new borrowings. Judgment is to be used in determining the borrowings on which the average rate is based. Thus, for example, depending on the facts and circumstances, it might be appropriate to include all borrowings of the parent company and consolidated

subsidiaries or to include only the borrowings of the corporate entity constructing the qualifying asset. It should be noted, however, that the provisions regarding capitalization rates are intended to allow an enterprise to determine a relevant measure of the cost of financing acquisition of the asset while minimizing the cost of implementing this Statement. Exclusion of borrowings from the computation of the average rate is not to circumvent the requirement to capitalize interest cost to the extent that interest cost has been incurred during a qualifying asset's acquisition period.

53. Some respondents to the Exposure Draft observed that, by attaching an interest cost to all of the expenditures for a qualifying asset, the prescribed method of determining the amount of interest capitalized in effect imputes an interest cost to any equity funds that may have been used. Board members' responses to that observation differ. Some would agree, arguing that the prescribed method uses the cost of borrowings as a surrogate measure of enterprise cost of capital. In their view, the prescribed method is an appropriate compromise between the conceptually desirable and the constraints of the present accounting framework. Other Board members do not share that view. They believe that the essence of this Statement is that interest on borrowings is a cost, which, like any other cost, is capitalizable in certain circumstances. In their view, the notion of interest on borrowings as an avoidable cost incurred as a consequence of the decision to acquire the qualifying asset supports the position that the capitalization method does not impute a cost to equity funds.

54. Some respondents to the Discussion Memorandum and to the Exposure Draft observed that limiting capitalized interest to interest on borrowings would preclude the "all-equity" enterprise from capitalizing interest, even though it incurs an economic cost of the same order as an enterprise that has borrowed funds. The Board concluded that, despite that consequence, capitalization of interest on borrowings in the circumstances specified in this Statement is preferable to the alternatives of (a) excluding interest from asset acquisition cost in all circumstances or (b) imputing interest on equity capital. In the Board's view, the fact that the present accounting framework does not recognize all economic costs should not control accounting for the costs that are recognized. Moreover, an "all-equity" enterprise is not the same as an enterprise that has borrowed funds. (Similarly, an enterprise that is making substantial expenditures for asset construction differs from one that is not.) Those who assert that comparability among enterprises would be greater if all interest cost were expensed would create an illusion of comparability that may disguise the differences in facts.

55. Some respondents disagreed with the conclusion in the Exposure Draft that the total amount of interest cost available for capitalization should be the amount recognized in the present accounting framework and hence include interest cost imputed on certain types of payables in accordance with Opinion 21 and interest cost related to a capital lease determined in accordance with Statement 13. In their view, interest cost determined in accordance with Opinion 21 and Statement 13 clearly relates to transactions other than the acquisition of qualifying assets. However, as previously indicated, the Board's conclusions in this Statement rest on an assumption that association of sources and uses of funds is primarily subjective. The Board believes that, just as association of a particular borrowing with a qualifying asset is an insufficiently objective basis for determining whether any interest cost should be capitalized, the form of financing transactions covered by Opinion 21 and Statement 13 is an inadequate basis for excluding interest cost recognized on those transactions from the pool of interest cost available for capitalization.

56. The Board concluded that, in determining the expenditures with which interest cost is associated, amounts corresponding to liabilities on which interest cost is not recognized (such as trade payables, accruals, and retainages) should be excluded. The Board does not intend that enterprises try to determine precisely when those liabilities are liquidated. Capitalized costs may be used as a reasonable approximation of expenditures unless the difference is material.

57. One of the issues raised in the Discussion Memorandum was whether capitalized interest should be compounded. The Board concluded that compounding is conceptually consistent with its conclusion that interest on expenditures for the asset is a cost of acquiring the asset. Admittedly, some portion of the interest incurred during an accounting period may be unpaid at the end of the period, but that complication usually may be ignored to simplify practical application.

The Capitalization Period

58. The capitalization period is determined by the definition of the circumstances in which interest is capitalizable. Essentially, the capitalization period covers the duration of the activities required to get the asset ready for its intended use, provided that expenditures for the asset have been made and interest cost is being incurred. Interest capitalization continues as long as those activities and the incurrence of interest cost continue. The capitalization period ends when the asset is substantially complete and ready for its intended use. The words "substantially complete" are used to prohibit continuation of

interest capitalization in situations in which completion of the asset is intentionally delayed. For example, it is customary for a condominium developer to defer installation of certain fixtures and fittings until units are sold, so that buyers may choose the types and colors they want. An intentional delay of that kind is related more to marketing of the asset than to the exigencies of the asset acquisition process. Similarly, interest is not to be capitalized during periods when the enterprise intentionally defers or suspends activities related to the asset. Interest cost incurred during such periods is a holding cost, not an acquisition cost. However, delays that are inherent in the asset acquisition process and interruptions in activities that are imposed by external forces are unavoidable in acquiring the asset and as such do not call for a cessation of interest capitalization. Brief interruptions may be disregarded on immateriality grounds.

59. Some respondents to the Exposure Draft asked for confirmation that interest capitalization is not restricted to times when physical change is taking place. Most cited the example of land development. Many activities, they pointed out, must be undertaken before work on the land itself can begin. In response to those requests, an explanation that the term *activities* is to be construed broadly in this context has been included in paragraph 17.

60. Some respondents to the Exposure Draft asked for clarification concerning the end of interest capitalization when an asset is completed in parts and the individual parts are capable of being used while work continues on other parts. Paragraph 18 now explains that interest capitalization stops on each part as it is completed.

61. Some respondents took issue with the conclusion in Appendix C to the Exposure Draft that interest capitalization on mineral interests should stop when the first well capable of producing oil or gas is completed. They argued that the oil or gas producing system is not ready for its intended use until the means of transporting the oil or gas from the well (e.g., a pipeline) is in place. The Board agreed, and that conclusion has been added to paragraph 18.

62. Some respondents to the Discussion Memorandum expressed the view that capitalization of interest for an asset intended for sale should end when the accumulated costs of the asset equal its net realizable value. The Board concluded that that view is inconsistent with the conclusion that interest is a cost of acquiring the asset. Capitalization of material, labor, and overhead costs does not end when a net realizable value limit is reached; interest cost should not be treated differently. The present accounting requirements for recognizing a lower asset value than acquisition cost should apply when total asset cost includes capitalized interest and when it does not.

Disposition of Capitalized Interest

63. Some companies that presently capitalize interest amortize it over a shorter period than the life of the related asset. The Board believes that the conclusion that interest is part of the cost of acquiring a qualifying asset requires that capitalized interest should not be accounted for differently from other components of asset cost.

Disclosures

64. Disclosure of the total amount of interest cost incurred in an accounting period is required because lenders, security analysts, and others may wish to know that amount in order to compute certain fixed-charge coverage ratios, etc. The amount of interest cost incurred and capitalized during a period is required because that amount is not included in the determination of earnings.

65. The Board concluded that the other possible disclosures listed in the Discussion Memorandum were not required. Descriptions of the method of accounting for interest, the circumstances in which interest is capitalized, and the method of determining the amount of interest capitalized are unnecessary because those matters are dealt with in this Statement. Information about amortization of capitalized interest is unnecessary; such disclosure is not required for other components of asset cost.

66. Some respondents to the Discussion Memorandum suggested that the net effect on periodic earnings of capitalizing interest as opposed to charging it to expense should be disclosed. The Board decided that such disclosure was unnecessary once accounting alternatives had been eliminated.

Effective Date and Transition

67. The Board concluded that this Statement should be applied prospectively. Inevitably, prospective application of a Statement entails some impairment of comparability among enterprises' financial statements during the periods immediately following its adoption. Retroactive application in this instance, however, would require greater accounting effort than would be justified by the resulting informational benefits.

Statement of Financial Accounting Standards No. 35
Accounting and Reporting by Defined Benefit Pension Plans

STATUS

Issued: March 1980

Effective Date: For plan years beginning after December 15, 1980 (but deferred indefinitely by FAS 75 for plans sponsored by state or local governments)

Affects: No other pronouncements

Affected by: Paragraph 30 amended by FAS 59
Paragraph 30 amended by FAS 75

SUMMARY

Standards

This Statement establishes standards of financial accounting and reporting for the annual financial statements of a defined benefit pension plan (*plan*). It applies both to plans in the private sector and to plans of state and local governmental units. It does not require the preparation, distribution, or attestation of financial statements for any plan.

The primary objective of a plan's financial statements is to provide financial information that is useful in assessing the plan's present and future ability to pay benefits when due. To accomplish that objective, the financial statements will include information regarding (a) the net assets available for benefits as of the end of the plan year, (b) the changes in net assets during the plan year, (c) the actuarial present value of accumulated plan benefits as of either the beginning or end of the plan year, and (d) the effects, if significant, of certain factors affecting the year-to-year change in the actuarial present value of accumulated plan benefits. If the date as of which the benefit information ((c) above) is presented (the *benefit information date*) is the beginning of the year, additional information is required regarding both the net assets available for benefits as of that date and the changes in net assets during the preceding year. Flexibility in the manner of presenting benefit information and changes therein (items (c) and (d) above) is permitted. Either or both of those categories of information may be presented on the face of one or more financial statements or in accompanying notes.

Information regarding net assets is to be prepared on the accrual basis of accounting. Plan investments (excluding contracts with insurance companies) are to be presented at fair value. Contracts with insurance companies are to be presented the same way as in the plan's annual report to certain governmental agencies pursuant to the Employee Retirement Income Security Act of 1974 (*ERISA*). Plans not subject to ERISA are to account for their contracts with insurance companies as though they also filed that annual report.

The primary information regarding participants' accumulated plan benefits reported in plan financial statements will be their actuarial present value. This Statement defines participants' accumulated plan benefits as those future benefit payments that are attributable under the plan's provisions to employees' service rendered to the benefit information date. Their measurement is primarily based on employees' history of pay and service and other appropriate factors as of that date. Future salary changes are not considered. Future years of service are considered only in determining employees' expected eligibility for particular types of benefits, for example, early retirement, death, and disability benefits. To measure their actuarial present value, assumptions are used to adjust those accumulated plan benefits to reflect the time value of money (through discounts for interest) and the probability of payment (by means of decrements such as for death, disability, withdrawal, or retirement) between the benefit information date and the expected date of payment. An assumption of an ongoing plan underlies those assumptions.

The use of averages and other methods of approximation consistent with recommended actuarial practice is permitted, provided the results are substantially the same as those contemplated by this Statement. Such simplified techniques may be particularly useful for plans sponsored by small employers.

Plan financial statements are required to include certain information about (a) the plan, (b) the results of transactions and other events that affect the information presented regarding net assets and participants' benefits, and (c) other factors necessary for users to understand the information provided.

This Statement is effective for plan years beginning after December 15, 1980.

Basis for Conclusions

In developing the foregoing standards, the Board first identified both the users of plan financial statements and the objectives of those statements. The Board believes that the content of plan financial statements should focus on the needs of participants because pension plans exist primarily for their benefit. However, plan financial statements should also be useful to others who either advise or represent participants, are present or potential investors or creditors of the employer(s), are responsible for funding the plan, or for other reasons have a derived or indirect interest in the plan's financial status.

Because employees render service long before they receive the benefits to which they are entitled as a result of that service, they are concerned with whether the plan will be able to pay their future benefits. Therefore, the Board concluded that the primary objective of plan financial statements should be to provide financial information that is useful in assessing the plan's present and future ability to pay benefits when due. However, plan financial statements do not provide all the information necessary for that assessment. They should be used in combination with other pertinent information, including information about the financial condition of the employer(s) and, for plans subject to ERISA, the guaranty of the Pension Benefit Guaranty Corporation. Also, financial statements for several plan years can provide information more useful in assessing the plan's future ability to pay benefits than can the financial statements for a single plan year.

Because a plan's net assets are the existing means by which it may provide benefits, information about them (the *net asset information*) is considered essential in assessing a plan's ability to pay benefits when due. The Board believes that measuring a plan's investments (other than contracts with insurance companies) at fair value will provide the most relevant information about those assets consistent with the primary objective of plan financial statements.

Insurance companies offer plans a wide variety of contracts. Because of their complexity, several difficult issues arise in recognizing and measuring the elements of such contracts that constitute plan assets. The Board decided that sufficient information was not available at this time to enable it to reach definitive conclusions about certain conceptual and implementation issues. It therefore chose the practical solution of requiring contracts with insurance companies to be reported in plan financial statements in the same way they are reported (for ERISA plans) or would have been reported (for non-ERISA plans) in the annual report required by ERISA to be filed with certain governmental agencies. That approach may result in such contracts being presented at other than fair value.

To be useful in assessing a plan's present and future ability to pay benefits when due, plan financial statements must also present information about the benefits to be paid. The Board believes that information (the *benefit information*) should relate to the benefits reasonably expected to be paid in exchange for employees' service to the benefit information date. Because the Board did not deem it essential at this time to resolve the issue of the accounting nature of the benefit information, this Statement does not prescribe its location in the financial statements.

The initial Exposure Draft required that both the benefit and net asset information be determined as of the same date. Thus, if the plan's annual financial statements were as of the end of the plan year, end-of-year benefit information was required. A number of respondents expressed the view that determination of end-of-year benefit information on a timely basis was not practical and would cause increased actuarial fees. They indicated that most actuarial valuations are performed during the year using data as of the beginning of the year. Changing that practice at this time might create significant timing problems in terms of scheduling the actuaries' workload and, in some cases, obtaining necessary end-of-year data.

The Board concluded that the perceived costs of requiring end-of-year benefit information at this time may exceed the potential benefits of such information. Therefore, this Statement provides for the presentation of benefit information as of either the beginning or end of the year. However, the Board continues to believe that presenting both net asset and benefit information as of the same date is necessary to present the financial status of the plan. Therefore, if benefit information is presented as of the beginning of the year, this Statement requires that net asset information also be presented as of that date.

The information about a plan's ability to pay benefits when due that is provided by its financial statements is affected whenever transactions and other events affect the net asset or benefit information presented in those statements. Normally, a plan's ability to pay participants' benefits does not remain constant. Therefore, users of the financial statements are concerned with assessing the plan's ability to pay participants' benefits not only as of a point in time but also on a continuing basis. To facilitate that latter assessment, users need to know the reasons for changes in the net asset and benefit information reported in successive financial statements. Therefore, the Board concluded that plan financial statements should include (a) information regarding the year-to-year change in the net assets available for benefits and (b) disclosure of the effects, if significant, of certain factors affecting the year-to-year change in the benefit information.

If the benefit information date is the beginning of the year, the required disclosure regarding the year-to-year change in the benefit information will relate to the preceding year. Presenting information regarding changes in both the net asset and benefit information for the same period is necessary to present the changes in the plan's financial status for that period. Therefore, if the benefit information date is the beginning of the year, information regarding the changes in net assets during the preceding year is also required.

Determination of the net asset and benefit information may be affected by estimates and judgment. The Board believes users can better evaluate that information if the underlying assumptions and methods are disclosed. In addition, certain explanations may be needed for users to understand the information provided by a plan's financial statements. Therefore, this Statement requires certain disclosures regarding the plan, the effects of certain transactions and events, and other factors necessary for users to understand the information provided.

Statement of Financial Accounting Standards No. 35
Accounting and Reporting by Defined Benefit Pension Plans

CONTENTS

INTRODUCTION

1. This Statement establishes standards of financial accounting and reporting for the annual financial statements of a **defined benefit pension plan (pension plan** or **plan**).* Plans covered are those that principally provide **pension benefits** but may also provide **benefits** on death, disability, or termination of employment.

2. This Statement applies to an ongoing plan that provides pension benefits for the **employees** of one or more employers, including state and local governments, or for the members of a trade or other employee association. Such a plan may have no intermediary **funding agency** or it may be financed through one or more trust funds, one or more contracts with insurance companies, or a combination thereof. This Statement applies to plans that are subject to the provisions of the Employee Retirement Income Security Act of 1974 (**ERISA** or the **Act**) as well as to those that are not. It is not intended to apply to a plan that is expected to be terminated, nor to a government-sponsored social security plan. This Statement does not require the preparation, distribution, or attestation of any plan's financial statements (paragraph 51).

3. Standards of financial accounting and reporting for defined benefit pension plans are presented in paragraphs 4-30. Background information for this Statement is presented in Appendix A. The basis for the Board's conclusions, as well as alternatives considered and reasons for their rejection, are discussed in Appendix B. Illustrations of certain applications of the requirements of this Statement appear in Appendixes D and E.

STANDARDS OF FINANCIAL ACCOUNTING AND REPORTING

Existing Generally Accepted Accounting Principles

4. Existing generally accepted accounting principles other than those discussed in this Statement may apply to the financial statements of defined benefit pension plans. The financial accounting standards discussed in this Statement are those of particular importance to pension plans or that differ from existing generally accepted accounting principles for other types of entities.

Primary Objective of Plan Financial Statements

5. The primary objective of a pension plan's financial statements is to provide financial information that is useful in assessing the plan's present and future ability to pay benefits when due.[1] To accomplish that objective, a plan's financial statements

*Terms defined in the Glossary (Appendix C) are in boldface type the first time they appear in this Statement.

[1]The Board recognizes that (a) information in addition to that contained in a plan's financial statements is needed in assessing the plan's present and future ability to pay benefits when due and (b) financial statements for several plan years can provide information more useful in assessing the plan's future ability to pay benefits than can the financial statements for a single plan year (paragraphs 58-63).

should provide information about (a) plan resources and how the stewardship responsibility for those resources has been discharged, (b) the **accumulated plan benefits** of **participants**, (c) the results of transactions and events that affect the information regarding those resources and benefits, and (d) other factors necessary for users to understand the information provided.

Financial Statements

6. The annual financial statements of a plan shall include:

a. A statement that includes information regarding the **net assets available for benefits** as of the end of the plan year
b. A statement that includes information regarding the changes during the year in the net assets available for benefits
c. Information regarding the **actuarial present value of accumulated plan benefits** as of either the beginning[2] or end of the plan year
d. Information regarding the effects, if significant, of certain factors affecting the year-to-year change in the actuarial present value of accumulated plan benefits.

7. The primary objective set forth in paragraph 5 is satisfied only if (a) information regarding both the net assets available for benefits and the actuarial present value of accumulated plan benefits is presented as of the same date and (b) information regarding both the changes in net assets available for benefits and the changes in the actuarial present value of accumulated plan benefits is presented for the same period. Therefore, if the **benefit information date** pursuant to paragraph 6(c) is the beginning of the year, a statement that includes information regarding the net assets available for benefits as of that date and a statement that includes information regarding the changes during the preceding year in the net assets available for benefits shall also be presented. Use of an end-of-year benefit information date is considered preferable. Plans are encouraged to develop procedures to enable them to use that date (paragraph 29).

8. The Board believes it is desirable to allow certain flexibility in presenting the information regarding the actuarial present value of accumulated plan benefits and the year-to-year changes therein. Therefore, either or both of those categories of information may be presented on the face of one or more financial statements or in notes thereto. Regardless of the format selected, each category of information shall be presented in its entirety in the same location. If a statement format is selected for either category, a separate statement may be used to present that information or, provided the information is as of the same date or for the same period, that information may be presented together with information regarding the net assets available for benefits and the year-to-year changes therein.

Net Assets Available for Benefits

9. The accrual basis of accounting[3] shall be used in preparing information regarding the net assets available for benefits. The information shall be presented in such reasonable detail as is necessary to identify the plan's resources that are available for benefits.

Contributions Receivable

10. Contributions receivable are the amounts due as of the **reporting date** to the plan from the employer(s), participants, and other sources of funding (for example, state subsidies or federal grants—which shall be separately identified). Amounts due include those pursuant to formal commitments as well as legal or contractual requirements. With respect to an employer's contributions, evidence of a formal commitment may include (a) a resolution by the employer's governing body approving a specified contribution, (b) a consistent pattern of making payments after the plan's year-end pursuant to an established **funding policy** that attributes such subsequent payments to the preceding plan year, (c) a deduction of a contribution for federal tax purposes for periods ending on or before the reporting date, or (d) the employer's recognition as of the reporting date of a contribution payable to the plan.[4]

Investments

11. Plan investments, whether equity or debt securities, real estate, or other (excluding contracts with insurance companies) shall be presented at their fair value at the reporting date. The fair value of an investment is the amount that the plan could reasonably expect to receive for it in a current sale between a willing buyer and a willing seller, that is, other than

[2]Financial information presented as of the beginning of the year shall be the amounts as of the end of the preceding year.

[3]The accrual basis requires that purchases and sales of securities be recorded on a trade-date basis. However, if the settlement date is after the reporting date and (a) the fair value of securities purchased or sold just before the reporting date does not change significantly from the trade date to the reporting date, and (b) the purchases or sales do not significantly affect the composition of the plan's assets available for benefits, accounting on a settlement-date basis for such sales and purchases is acceptable.

[4]The existence of accrued pension costs does not, by itself, provide sufficient support for recognition of a contribution receivable (paragraph 92).

a forced or liquidation sale. Fair value shall be measured by the market price if there is an active market for the investment. If there is not an active market for an investment but there is such a market for similar investments, selling prices in that market may be helpful in estimating fair value. If a market price is not available, a forecast of expected cash flows may aid in estimating fair value, provided the expected cash flows are discounted at a rate commensurate with the risk involved.[5]

12. Contracts with insurance companies shall be presented in the same manner as that contained in the annual report filed by the plan with certain governmental agencies pursuant to ERISA.[6] A plan not subject to ERISA shall similarly present its contracts with insurance companies, that is, as if the plan were subject to the reporting requirements of ERISA.

13. Information regarding a plan's investments shall be presented in enough detail to identify the types of investments and shall indicate whether reported fair values have been measured by quoted prices in an active market or are fair values otherwise determined. (Paragraphs 28(g) and 28(h) require certain additional disclosures related to investments.)

Operating Assets

14. Plan assets used in plan operations (for example, buildings, equipment, furniture and fixtures, and leasehold improvements) shall be presented at cost less accumulated depreciation or amortization.

Changes in Net Assets Available for Benefits

15. Information regarding changes in net assets available for benefits shall be presented in enough detail to identify the significant changes during the year. Minimum disclosure shall include:

a. The net appreciation (depreciation)[7] in fair value for each significant class of investments, segregated between investments whose fair values have been measured by quoted prices in an active market and those whose fair values have been otherwise determined
b. Investment income (exclusive of (a) above)
c. Contributions from the employer(s), segregated between cash and noncash contributions[8]
d. Contributions from participants, including those transmitted by the **sponsor**
e. Contributions from other identified sources (for example, state subsidies or federal grants)
f. Benefits paid to participants
g. Payments to insurance companies to purchase contracts that are excluded from plan assets[9]
h. Administrative expenses.

Actuarial Present Value of Accumulated Plan Benefits

16. Accumulated plan benefits are those future benefit payments that are attributable under the plan's provisions to employees' **service** rendered to the benefit information date. Accumulated plan benefits comprise benefits expected to be paid to (a) retired or terminated employees or their beneficiaries, (b) beneficiaries of deceased employees, and (c) present employees or their beneficiaries.

17. To the extent possible, plan provisions shall apply in measuring accumulated plan benefits. In some plans, benefits are a specified amount for each year of service. Even if a plan does not specify a benefit for each year of service, another of its provisions (for example, a provision applicable to terminated employees or to termination of the plan—if independent of funding patterns) may indicate how to measure accumulated plan benefits. If the benefit for each year of service is not stated by or clearly determinable from the provisions of the plan, the benefit shall be considered to accumulate in proportion to (a) the ratio of the number of years of service completed to the benefit information date to the number that will have been completed when the benefit will first be fully vested, if the type of benefit is includable in **vested benefits** (for example, a supplemental early retirement benefit that is a vested benefit after a stated number of years of service), or (b) the ratio of completed years of service to projected years of service upon anticipated separation from covered employment, if the type of benefit is not includable in vested benefits (for example, a death or disability benefit that is payable only if death or disability occurs during active service).

18. In measuring accumulated plan benefits, the following shall apply:

a. Except as indicated in (b) and (c) below, accumu-

[5]For an indication of factors to be considered in determining the discount rate, see paragraphs 13 and 14 of APB Opinion No. 21, *Interest on Receivables and Payables*. If significant, the fair value of an investment shall reflect the brokerage commissions and other costs normally incurred in a sale.

[6]For 1979 plan years, the pertinent governmental reporting requirements relate to item 13 of either Form 5500 or Form 5500-C.

[7]Realized gains and losses on investments that were both bought and sold during the year shall be included.

[8]A noncash contribution shall be recorded at fair value. The nature of noncash contributions shall be described, either parenthetically or in a note.

[9]Paragraph 28(e) requires disclosure of the plan's dividend income related to excluded contracts and permits that income to be netted against item (g).

lated plan benefits shall be based on employees' history of pay and service and other appropriate factors as of the benefit information date.[10]

b. Projected years of service shall be a factor only in determining employees' expected eligibility for particular benefits, such as:
   i. Increased benefits that are granted provided a specified number of years of service are rendered (for example, a pension benefit that is increased from $9 per month to $10 per month for each year of service if 20 or more years of service are rendered)
   ii. Early retirement benefits
   iii. Death benefits
   iv. Disability benefits.
c. Automatic benefit increases specified by the plan (for example, automatic cost-of-living increases) that are expected to occur after the benefit information date shall be recognized.
d. Benefits to be provided by means of contracts excluded from plan assets for which payments to the insurance company have been made shall be excluded.
e. Plan amendments adopted after the benefit information date shall not be recognized.
f. If it is necessary to take future compensation into account in the determination of Social Security benefits, employees' compensation as of the benefit information date shall be assumed to remain unchanged during their assumed future service. Increases in the wage base or benefit level pursuant to either the existing Social Security law or possible future amendments of the law shall not be recognized.

19. The actuarial present value of accumulated plan benefits is that amount as of the benefit information date that results from applying actuarial assumptions to the benefit amounts determined pursuant to paragraphs 16-18, with the actuarial assumptions being used to adjust those amounts to reflect the time value of money (through discounts for interest) and the probability of payment (by means of decrements such as for death, disability, withdrawal, or retirement) between the benefit information date and the expected date of payment.

20. An assumption of an ongoing plan shall underlie the other assumptions used in determining the actuarial present value of accumulated plan benefits. Every other significant assumption used in that determination and disclosed pursuant to paragraph 27(b) shall reflect the best estimate of the plan's future experience solely with respect to that individual assumption. As to certain assumptions, the following shall apply:

a. Assumed rates of return shall reflect the expected rates of return during the periods for which payment of benefits is deferred and shall be consistent with returns realistically achievable on the types of assets held by the plan and the plan's investment policy. To the extent that assumed rates of return are based on values of existing plan assets, the values used in determining assumed rates of return shall be the values presented in the plan's financial statements pursuant to the requirements of this Statement.
b. Expected rates of inflation assumed in estimating automatic cost-of-living adjustments shall be consistent with the assumed rates of return.
c. Administrative expenses expected to be paid by the plan (not those paid by the sponsor) that are associated with providing accumulated plan benefits shall be reflected either by appropriately adjusting the assumed rates of return or by assigning those expenses to future periods and discounting them to the benefit information date. If the former method is used, the adjustment of the assumed rates of return shall be separately disclosed (paragraph 27(b)).

21. In selecting certain assumptions to be used in determining the actuarial present value of accumulated plan benefits, an acceptable alternative to that discussed in paragraph 20 is to use those assumptions that are inherent in the estimated cost at the benefit information date to obtain a contract with an insurance company to provide participants with their accumulated plan benefits. Those other assumptions that are necessary but are not inherent in that estimated cost shall be selected pursuant to the requirements in paragraph 20.

Presentation of the Actuarial Present Value of Accumulated Plan Benefits

22. The total actuarial present value of accumulated plan benefits as of the benefit information date shall be segmented into at least the following categories:

a. Vested benefits of participants currently receiving payments
b. Other vested benefits
c. Nonvested benefits.

Category (a) shall include those benefits due and payable as of the benefit information date. Present employees' accumulated contributions as of the benefit information date (including interest, if any) shall be disclosed. If interest has been credited on employees' contributions, the rate(s) shall be disclosed.

[10]An example of the application of paragraphs 18(a) and 18(b) appears in Appendix E.

Changes in the Actuarial Present Value of Accumulated Plan Benefits

23. Changes in actuarial assumptions made to reflect changes in the plan's expected experience shall be viewed as changes in estimates. That is, the effects of those changes shall be accounted for in the year of change (or in the year of change and future years if the change affects both) and shall not be accounted for by restating amounts reported in financial statements for prior years or by reporting pro forma amounts for prior years.

24. Assumed rates of return used to determine the actuarial present value of accumulated plan benefits may change periodically due to changes in expected rates of return or as changes occur in the factors affecting estimates. A change in assumed rates of return need not necessarily result when a decision is made to replace fixed-income securities currently held with lower-rated fixed-income securities because the higher yield associated with the lower-rated securities reflects increased risk. Accordingly, a higher ultimate return on the aggregate investment portfolio may not result.

Presentation of Changes in the Actuarial Present Value of Accumulated Plan Benefits

25. If significant, either individually or in the aggregate, the effects of certain factors affecting the change in the actuarial present value of accumulated plan benefits from the preceding to the current benefit information date shall be identified. Effects that are individually significant shall be separately identified. Minimum disclosure shall include the significant effects of factors such as the following:

a. Plan amendments
b. Changes in the nature of the plan (for example, a plan spinoff or a merger with another plan)
c. Changes in actuarial assumptions.[11]

The significant effects of other factors may also be identified, including, for example, benefits accumulated,[12] the increase (for interest) as a result of the decrease in the discount period, and benefits paid. If presented, *benefits paid* shall not include benefit payments made by an insurance company in accordance with a contract that is excluded from plan assets. However, amounts paid by the plan to an insurance company pursuant to such a contract (including purchasing annuities with amounts allocated from existing investments with the insurance company) shall be included in *benefits paid*.[13] If the minimum required disclosure is presented in other than a statement format, the actuarial present value of accumulated plan benefits as of the preceding benefit information date shall also be presented.

26. Information regarding changes in the actuarial present value of accumulated plan benefits may be presented either (a) in a statement that accounts for the change between two benefit information dates or (b) elsewhere in the financial statements. If only the minimum required disclosure is presented, presentation in a statement format will necessitate an additional unidentified "other" category to reconcile the beginning and ending amounts.

Additional Financial Statement Disclosures

27. Disclosure of the plan's accounting policies[14] shall include the following:

a. A description of the method(s) and significant assumptions used to determine the fair value of investments and the reported value of contracts with insurance companies.
b. A description of the method and significant assumptions (for example, assumed rates of return, inflation rates, and retirement ages) used to determine the actuarial present value of accumulated plan benefits. Any significant changes of method or assumptions between benefit information dates shall be described.

28. The financial statements shall include the following additional disclosures, if applicable:

a. A brief, general description of the plan agreement, including—but not limited to—vesting and benefit provisions.[15]
b. A description of significant plan amendments adopted during the year ending on the latest benefit information date. If significant amend-

[11] Plans that measure the actuarial present value of accumulated plan benefits by insurance company rates pursuant to the alternative approach described in paragraph 21 shall, if practicable, disclose the effects of changes in actuarial assumptions reflected in changes in those insurance rates.

[12] Actuarial experience gains or losses may be included with the effects of additional benefits accumulated rather than being separately disclosed. If the effects of changes in actuarial assumptions discussed in footnote 11 cannot be separately disclosed, those effects shall be included in benefits accumulated.

[13] Due to the use of different actuarial assumptions, the amount paid by the plan to an insurance company may be different from the previous measure of the actuarial present value of the related accumulated plan benefits. That difference is an actuarial experience gain or loss (footnote 12).

[14] See APB Opinion No. 22, *Disclosure of Accounting Policies*.

[15] If a plan agreement or a description thereof providing this information is otherwise published and made available, the description required by paragraph 28(a) may be omitted provided that reference to such other source is made.

ments were adopted between the latest benefit information date and the plan's year-end, it shall be indicated that the actuarial present value of accumulated plan benefits does not reflect those amendments.

c. A brief, general description of (i) the priority order of participants' claims to the assets of the plan upon plan termination and (ii) benefits guaranteed by the Pension Benefit Guaranty Corporation (**PBGC**), including a discussion of the application of the PBGC guaranty to any recent plan amendment.[16]
d. The funding policy and any changes in such policy during the plan year.[17] For a **contributory plan**, the disclosure shall state the method of determining participants' contributions. Plans subject to ERISA shall disclose whether the minimum funding requirements of ERISA have been met. If a minimum funding waiver has been granted by the Internal Revenue Service (*IRS*) or if a request for a waiver is pending before the IRS, that fact shall be disclosed.
e. The policy regarding the purchase of contracts with insurance companies that are excluded from plan assets. The plan's dividend income for the year that is related to excluded contracts shall be disclosed, and for purposes of paragraph 15 may be netted against item (g).
f. The federal income tax status of the plan, if a favorable letter of determination has not been obtained or maintained.
g. Identification of investments that represent five percent or more of the net assets available for benefits.
h. Significant real estate or other transactions in which the plan and any of the following parties are jointly involved: (i) the sponsor, (ii) the employer(s), or (iii) the employee organization(s).
i. Unusual or infrequent events or transactions occurring after the latest benefit information date but before issuance of the financial statements that might significantly affect the usefulness of the financial statements in an assessment of the plan's present and future ability to pay benefits. For example, a plan amendment adopted after the latest benefit information date that significantly increases future benefits that are attributable to employees' service rendered before that date shall be disclosed. If reasonably determinable, the effects of such events or transactions shall be disclosed. If such effects are not quantified, the reasons why they are not reasonably determinable shall be disclosed.

Use of Averages or Reasonable Approximations

29. The Board recognizes that literal application of certain of the requirements of this Statement could require a degree of detail in recordkeeping and computation that might be unduly burdensome. Accordingly, the use of averages or other methods of approximation is appropriate, provided the results obtained are substantially the same as the results contemplated by this Statement. Thus, rolling back to the beginning of the year or projecting to the end of the year detailed employee service-related data as of a date within the year may be acceptable in approximating beginning- or end-of-year **benefit information**. The use of averages and other methods of approximation consistent with recommended actuarial practice may be useful in conjunction with other provisions of this Statement, particularly when applied to plans sponsored by small employers. If participants' individual historical salary data for plan years before the effective date of this Statement are not available, reasonable approximations thereof are acceptable.

Effective Date and Transition

30. This Statement shall be effective for plan years beginning after December 15, 1980. Earlier application is encouraged. Accounting changes adopted to conform to the provisions of this Statement shall be made retroactively. Financial statements of prior plan years are required to be restated to comply with the provisions of this Statement *only* if presented together with financial statements for plan years beginning after December 15, 1980. If accounting changes were necessary to conform to the provisions of this Statement, that fact shall be disclosed when financial statements for the year in which this Statement is first applied are presented either alone or only with financial statements of prior years.

[16]If material providing this information is otherwise published and made available to participants, the descriptions required by paragraph 28(c) may be omitted provided that (a) reference to such other source is made and (b) disclosure similar to the following is made in the financial statements: "Should the plan terminate at some future time, its net assets generally will not be available on a pro rata basis to provide participants' benefits. Whether a particular participant's accumulated plan benefits will be paid depends on both the priority of those benefits and the level of benefits guaranteed by the PBGC at that time. Some benefits may be fully or partially provided for by the then existing assets and the PBGC guaranty while other benefits may not be provided for at all."

[17]If significant costs of plan administration are being absorbed by the employer(s), that fact shall be disclosed.

Accounting and Reporting by Defined Benefit Pension Plans

The provisions of this Statement need not be applied to immaterial items.

This Statement was adopted by the affirmative votes of four members of the Financial Accounting Standards Board. Messrs. March, Morgan, and Walters dissented.

Messrs. March, Morgan, and Walters dissent to this Statement because, in their opinion, it establishes an unattainable objective for a plan's financial statements, it improperly includes what they consider to be actuarial statements within the financial statements rather than as supplementary information outside the financial statements, and it prescribes detailed reporting beyond reasonable usefulness to plan participants. They share an overriding concern that, taken as a whole, these provisions invite comparison of items that do not possess enough common properties to be directly comparable and lend an unjustified aura of reliability to estimates of the future.

They believe that the stated primary objective of a pension plan's financial statements, ". . . to provide financial information that is useful in assessing the plan's *present* and *future* ability to pay benefits when due," promises more than can be achieved and will foster unreasonable expectations. In most cases, the plan's ability to pay benefits will depend primarily on the continuing support and financial health of the plan sponsor far into the future. In their view, users are not well served by an objective and a presentation that suggest that a *spot comparison* of the estimated present value of benefits to the current market valuation of assets held is a relevant or reliable indicator of a plan's ability to pay benefits when due. The benefit information is a product of estimates of events and conditions and payments over decades; the asset information necessarily relates to specific assets existing and values prevailing at a specific moment, often emphasizing temporary or short-run conditions. The trend *over time* of accumulated assets and benefits payable may indicate funding progress and the historical record of the investment policy and actuarial assumptions, but even that has limited value in assessing ability to make remote benefit payments.

They believe the primary objective of a pension plan's financial reporting should be to provide financial information about resources and financial activities of the plan that is useful in assessing the stewardship of the plan's administrators; an appropriate supplemental objective is to provide information about plan benefits and the trends *over time* in the accumulation of resources and benefits.

They believe the total effect of the following factors creates a powerful presumption that the information regarding the actuarial present value of accumulated plan benefits, changes in such actuarial values, and related disclosures (paragraphs 6(c), 6(d), 7, 8, and 16-26) should not be designated as part of the financial statements of the plan:

1. The essence of the information presented is based on estimates of probabilities, conditions, and events that may happen far into the future, vulnerable to all kinds of uncertainties and less reliable than financial statement measurements in general. Although actuarial estimates and judgments are often used in accounting measurements, they are only a part of an accounting presentation and not, as here, the totality of the information content.
2. Accumulated benefits have not been identified as liabilities or other elements of financial statements of pension plans. Trustees and plan administrators are responsible for stewardship of the funds entrusted to them and payment of benefits in compliance with the plan, but only to the extent of those funds.
3. Independent auditors are not trained to perform a substantive audit (that is, make an expert challenge) of the actuarial findings.
4. Congress, in adopting ERISA, identified the financial statements of a plan (Statements of Assets and Liabilities and Changes in Net Assets Available for Plan Benefits) to be covered by the opinion of an independent accountant as separate and distinct from actuarial statements to be covered by the opinion of an enrolled actuary.

They conclude that this presumption has not been overcome and disagree with the Board's determination that what are effectively actuarial statements are to be included within the financial statements. This is not just a theoretical distinction. It has potentially significant cost/benefit implications if the financial statements are audited. If the actuarial data are considered to be within financial statements, there is a presumption that they will be covered by the report of the independent auditor. In their view, the benefits of an auditor's opinion on these actuarial statements are doubtful, but the costs of the audit are real. They believe that a plan's financial report should consist of financial statements accompanied by the report of the independent auditor and actuarial information accompanied by the report of the actuary, if expert opinions are desired.

Messrs. March, Morgan, and Walters believe that the active cooperation between the Board and the actuarial profession in this project is a significant milestone toward more consistent reporting of actuarial data. They believe, however, that the Board has dealt in this Statement with choices of details and refinements in actuarial determinations (paragraphs 17-21) that should be left to the actuarial profession as long as their guidelines produce information relevant to the objectives of financial reporting.

They also are not convinced that plan participants need the detailed disclosures prescribed by this Statement, particularly as to actuarial methods, changes, and assumptions (paragraph 27) and as to the matters in paragraph 28. Users wishing such details for large private plans can obtain them from the annual reports filed with the Department of Labor which are available to participants on request. It should be sufficient to provide summarized benefit information as of the most recent actuarial valuation for plans with fewer than 100 participants, rather than to require an update for each annual report. They understand that less statistical reliability can be expected from actuarial data for these small plans.

Members of the Financial Accounting Standards Board:

Donald J. Kirk, *Chairman*
Frank E. Block
John W. March
Robert A. Morgan
David Mosso
Robert T. Sprouse
Ralph E. Walters

Appendix A

BACKGROUND INFORMATION

31. Financial reporting by defined benefit pension plans in the private sector was generally quite limited before 1976. A few companies included a report of their pension plans in their annual reports to stockholders. Those financial statements that were distributed to participants were frequently limited to summary statements of assets and often did not purport to conform with generally accepted accounting principles.

32. The Employee Retirement Income Security Act of 1974 established minimum standards for participation, vesting, and funding for employee benefit plans of private enterprises. It also requires annual reporting of certain information to particular governmental agencies and summarized information to plan participants. For many plans, the reporting requirements include financial statements prepared in conformity with generally accepted accounting principles.

33. The House Pension Task Force Report indicates that many public employee retirement systems do not report important financial and actuarial information to participants, public officials, and taxpayers.[18] Although ERISA does not apply to those plans, interest in financial information about them has increased since enactment of ERISA, and proposed legislation[19] to establish reporting requirements for them was introduced during the 1978 and 1980 congressional sessions.

34. Prior to this Statement, no authoritative accounting pronouncement issued by the FASB or its predecessor bodies addressed financial accounting and reporting standards specifically for defined benefit pension plans.

35. In recognition of the broadened financial reporting requirements for most employee benefit plans, the significance of both the assets held by pension plans and the benefits accumulated by participants in those plans, and the diversity of existing accounting and reporting practices of employee benefit plans, the FASB placed on its technical agenda in November 1974 a project on accounting and reporting for employee benefit plans.

36. A 10-member task force, composed of individuals from academe, the financial community, government, industry, organized labor, and the public accounting and actuarial professions, was appointed in February 1975 to counsel the Board in preparing a Discussion Memorandum analyzing issues related to the project.

37. In preparing the Discussion Memorandum, the FASB primarily relied on the published research studies and articles that are cited in that document. The additional research undertaken in connection with this project included (a) a review of relevant literature, (b) an examination of selected published annual reports of employee benefit plans and trust funds, and annual reports to stockholders of corporations that included information about pension plans, (c) interviews with actuaries and employee benefit consultants, and (d) analysis of the provisions of ERISA and its related regulations.

38. The Board issued the Discussion Memorandum on October 6, 1975 and held a public hearing on February 4 and 5, 1976. The Board received 104 position papers, letters of comment, and outlines of

[18]U.S. Government Printing Office, *House of Representatives Committee on Education and Labor Pension Task Force Report on Public Employee Retirement Systems* (Washington, D.C., 1978), p. 3.

[19]H.R. 14138, *Public Employee Retirement Income Security Act of 1978*, September 20, 1978, and H.R. 6525, *Public Employee's Retirement Income Security Act of 1980*, February 13, 1980.

oral presentations in response to the Discussion Memorandum, and 23 presentations were made at the public hearing.

39. In its deliberations following the public hearing, the Board concluded for the reason expressed in paragraph 71 that the scope of the initial Statement of Financial Accounting Standards resulting from the project should be limited to financial accounting and reporting by defined benefit pension plans.

40. On April 14, 1977, an FASB Exposure Draft, *Accounting and Reporting by Defined Benefit Pension Plans*, was issued that, if adopted, would have been effective for plan years beginning on or after December 15, 1977. Approximately 700 letters of comment were received in response to that Exposure Draft. The Board announced on September 30, 1977 that because of the need to analyze the large number of responses and the complexity of the issues involved it would be unable to issue a final Statement in 1977.

41. Throughout the project, the FASB worked with the United States Department of Labor, the actuarial profession, and others in an attempt to avoid conflicts, duplication, and confusion in providing meaningful financial reporting. In conjunction with that cooperative effort, the Board decided in the first quarter of 1979 to expose to task force members and certain other interested parties a staff draft of standards that incorporated previously announced tentative conclusions. The Board considered the comments received on that draft. It then concluded that a revised Exposure Draft should be issued for public comment because of the significant changes that had been made to the proposed standards in the April 14, 1977 Exposure Draft.

42. A revised Exposure Draft, *Accounting and Reporting by Defined Benefit Pension Plans*, was issued on July 9, 1979. The Board received approximately 300 letters of comment in response to that Exposure Draft.

Appendix B

BASIS FOR CONCLUSIONS

CONTENTS

Appendix B

BASIS FOR CONCLUSIONS

43. This appendix discusses factors deemed significant by members of the Board in reaching the conclusions in this Statement, including various alternatives considered and reasons for accepting some and rejecting others. Individual Board members gave greater weight to some factors than to others.

REPORTING ENTITY

44. Deciding whether the plan or **pension fund** is the reporting entity is related to the objectives of the financial statements, and many respondents[20] who addressed the issue of the reporting entity did so in that context. Thus, the views expressed in paragraphs 45-47 should be considered together with those expressed in paragraphs 48-69.

45. Arguments presented by proponents of the plan as the reporting entity include the view that a plan has many attributes of a legal entity. It gives rise to participants' rights, plan resources, and employer obligations. That view is reinforced for plans subject to ERISA (**ERISA plans**) by certain sections of the Act.[21] Further, and more importantly, to report only pension fund activities omits reporting the significant information about participants' benefits.

46. Supporting the pension fund as the reporting entity is the view that the pension plan consists only of a set of documents used by various entities, such as the sponsor, trust funds, and insurance companies, to assist in carrying out the terms of the agreement between the employer(s) and the employees. The fact that the plan may possess certain attributes of a legal entity is not viewed as sufficient reason for characterizing it as a reporting entity. Many respondents who supported the pension fund as the reporting entity linked that choice with the impropriety, in their view, of presenting quantitative information about plan benefits in the financial statements.

47. After considering the alternatives, the Board concluded that the needs of financial statement users and the related primary objective of the financial statements (as set forth in following paragraphs) necessitate establishing the plan, rather than the fund, as the reporting entity. The Board believes that financial information about both the promise to provide benefits and any assets committed to fulfill that promise are essential to present financial statements that are most meaningful to users (paragraphs 48-53).

---

[20]This appendix identifies the specific document on which respondents commented only if such comments are limited in their application to that document. Otherwise, the term *respondents* refers to those who responded to one or more documents preceding this Statement, that is, the Discussion Memorandum and the initial and revised Exposure Drafts.

[21]For example, Section 502(d)(1) includes the following statement: "An employee benefit plan may sue or be sued under this title as an entity." Any claims for pension benefits are enforceable against the pension plan as an entity, as provided for in Section 502(d)(2) of the Act: "Any money judgment under this title against an employee benefit plan shall be enforceable only against a plan as an entity and shall not be enforceable against any other person unless liability against such person is established in his individual capacity under this title." The view that the pension plan should be accounted for as if it were a separate accounting entity is also viewed as being compatible with reporting provisions of the Act. For example, Section 103(a)(3)(A) states, in part: ". . . the administrator of an employee benefit plan shall engage, on behalf of all plan participants, an independent qualified public accountant, who shall conduct such an examination of any financial statements of the plan, and of other books and records of the plan, as the accountant may deem necessary to enable the accountant to form an opinion as to whether the financial statements and schedules required to be included in the annual report by subsection (b) of this section are presented fairly in conformity with generally accepted accounting principles applied on a basis consistent with that of the preceding year."

PRIMARY OBJECTIVE OF PLAN FINANCIAL STATEMENTS

Users of Financial Statements

48. Potential users of plan financial statements include those who have an existing or potential relationship with either the plan or the employer(s). The initial Exposure Draft identified plan participants as the primary users of plan financial statements. Many respondents to that Exposure Draft expressed the view that the "typical" plan participant would be uninterested in or unable to properly assimilate the information presented in plan financial statements and thus would be confused and possibly misled.[22] Other respondents thought that Exposure Draft gave insufficient attention to the needs of other users, for example, employers, their investors and creditors, plan administrators, and governmental authorities responsible for regulating pension plans.

49. In response to such comments, the primary objective of plan financial statements as it appeared in that Exposure Draft was revised. Those revisions are intended only as clarifications and shifts in emphasis. For example, the phrase "useful in assessing the plan's present and future ability to pay benefits when due" now appears in place of "useful to plan participants in assessing the security with respect to receipt of their accumulated benefits." Although this Statement does not identify any one group as the primary users, the Board believes that the content of plan financial statements should focus on the needs of plan participants because pension plans exist primarily for their benefit. The Act provides additional support for that view. For example, Section 103(a)(3)(A), quoted in footnote 21, refers to an examination of plan financial statements by an independent accountant engaged on behalf of all plan participants. The Board recognizes, however, that plan financial statements should also be useful to others who either advise or represent participants, are present or potential investors or creditors of the employer(s), are responsible for funding the plan (for example, state legislators), or for other reasons have a derived or indirect interest in the financial status of the plan.

50. The Board recognizes that participants who have not had previous exposure to financial statements may need to be educated regarding the information presented in plan financial statements. However, the Board does not believe that a possible need to educate some users justifies disregarding the financial information needs of other users who have a reasonable understanding of financial reporting and economic activities and are willing to study the information with reasonable diligence. Financial statements should not exclude relevant information merely because it may be difficult for some to understand or because some members of the expected audience choose not to use it. To enhance their usefulness, **plan administrators** may wish to supplement the statements with a brief explanation that highlights those matters expected to be of most interest to participants. Including summary financial information for a period of years in such supplementary information, and thereby disclosing trends, may also be helpful.

51. Some respondents to the initial Exposure Draft who expressed concern regarding the usefulness of plan financial statements to participants presumed that it required that plan financial statements be distributed to all participants. Others interpreted that document as requiring plan financial statements to be audited. This Statement does not require the preparation, distribution, or attestation of any financial statements, but only establishes standards of accounting and reporting to be followed in the preparation of plan financial statements that purport to be in accordance with generally accepted accounting principles.

52. The accounting and reporting standards established by this Statement are intended to result in general purpose external financial statements. To include in financial statements designed to serve many the specialized information needed by a few who can otherwise obtain that information may be uneconomical. For example, the plan administrator may need many kinds of specialized and detailed information to decide day-to-day matters and establish policies. But the plan administrator controls the plan's accounting system, and much of the accounting effort may be managerial accounting designed to help the plan administrator manage and control operations. Similarly, the information needed by the sponsor of a single-employer plan to evaluate potential plan amendments or to determine current minimum funding requirements under the Act is specialized information. But sponsors usually have the ability to acquire the specific information they

[22]Most respondents commented from the perspective of an employer rather than an employee. Thus, those comments may not reflect the views of the "typical" plan participant. A recent nationwide study of attitudes toward pensions and retirement commissioned by Johnson & Higgins and conducted by Louis Harris and Associates surveyed the views of both employers and employees. It found that ". . . business leaders widely misjudge the importance employees place on certain types of information about their pension plans. Among employees who read their most recent pension report, substantial majorities believe it is 'very important' that they receive information about the current financial status of their plan (83%). . . . However, among business leaders whose employees receive annual reports, just 38% feel it is 'very important' that the report contain [that] information. . . ." (Johnson & Higgins, *1979 Study of American Attitudes Toward Pensions and Retirement*, pp. vii and viii.)

need. To the extent that governmental authorities responsible for regulating plans wish to indicate their needs for financial information by requiring submitted financial statements to be prepared in accordance with generally accepted accounting principles, it seems appropriate to consider the needs of those authorities in establishing generally accepted accounting principles for plans (provided those needs do not conflict with the needs of participants and do not entail an adverse cost/benefit relationship). To the extent that governmental authorities need specialized information, they can probably obtain it.

53. Information consistent with the primary objective of plan financial statements (set forth in subsequent paragraphs) is likely to be useful to participants and others who are interested in essentially the same financial aspects of the plan, including those who have an existing or potential relationship with the employer(s). Although information presented in plan financial statements may fulfill certain needs of those who have a relationship with the employer(s), the Board believes that an in-depth consideration of their needs is more appropriately a part of another Board project.[23]

Objectives

54. The Board considered those user needs that could be reasonably satisfied within the constraints of the characteristics and limitations of financial accounting.

55. Because employees generally render service long before they receive the benefits to which they are entitled as a result of that service, they are concerned with the security[24] for their future benefits. Thus, the primary objective of plan financial statements stated in the initial Exposure Draft was to provide information that is useful to plan participants in assessing the security with respect to receipt of their accumulated benefits.

56. A number of respondents thought that primary objective was too narrow. Although the initial Exposure Draft was based on an assumption of an ongoing plan, certain aspects (primarily those relating to measuring the actuarial present value of accumulated plan benefits) were seen as emphasizing the security of participants' benefits in the event of plan termination. Many respondents thought participants and other users should be interested not only in immediate security but in whether adequate progress is being made toward achieving security for the benefits participants expect to receive upon retirement or other termination of service. The Board agreed. Therefore, to emphasize the assumption of an ongoing plan, the phrase "plan's present and future ability to pay benefits when due" was substituted for "security with respect to receipt of [participants'] accumulated benefits."

57. Some respondents to the initial Exposure Draft also expressed the view that providing information useful in assessing the performance of pension plan administrators and other fiduciaries in managing the assets they control should be a part of the primary objective of plan financial statements. The Board believes that providing information useful in an assessment of stewardship is inherent in providing information useful in assessing **benefit security**. However, because of the importance of stewardship to a plan's ability to pay benefits, the Board concluded that that interrelationship should be explicitly indicated. (Paragraph 67 further discusses the use of financial statements in assessing stewardship.)

Other Information Needed in Assessing Benefit Security

58. Some respondents to the Exposure Drafts expressed the view that (a) the continued viability of the employer as an entity willing and able to meet the funding requirements of the plan and (b) (for ERISA plans) the guaranty of the PBGC were more important to long-range benefit security than the assets held by the plan at any given date. In their view, the Exposure Drafts either ignored or dealt inadequately with those factors, and thus the objective of providing information useful in assessing benefit security would not be achieved.

59. As indicated in the Exposure Drafts, the Board recognizes that information beyond that presented in plan financial statements is needed to assess benefit security. Whether participants receive their benefits when due depends not only on the existing relationship between plan resources and accumulated plan benefits but also on (a) the commitment and financial ability of the employer(s) to make future contributions to the plan and (b) (for an ERISA plan) the extent to which payment of benefits is insured by the PBGC. Although the commitment and financial ability of the employer(s) to make future contributions to the plan are primary factors in assessing benefit security, that kind of

[23]Another project on the Board's technical agenda, accounting by employers for pensions, encompasses a reconsideration of present generally accepted accounting principles regarding employer accounting for pension plans.

[24]That view of participants' informational needs appears to be supported by the results of the Harris survey. That survey found that 93 percent of the employees who read the last report thought it was very important that they know how certain it is that they will be paid their pension. (Johnson & Higgins, *1979 Study of American Attitudes Toward Pensions and Retirement*, p. 53.)

information is not within the limits of financial accounting for the plan itself.

60. However, a primary purpose of funding a pension plan is to enhance the plan's present and future ability to pay benefits when due. If a funding program is in effect, participants can look to funds that are irrevocably committed to the payment of benefits. Other factors being equal, the higher the ratio of those funds to the actuarial present value of accumulated plan benefits, the greater is the assurance that present accumulated plan benefits will be paid. With the information presented in plan financial statements, users can assess the extent to which the plan itself is able to pay participants' benefits and the extent to which payment of benefits is dependent on other factors, namely, the commitment and financial ability of the employer(s), and, for ERISA plans, the security provided by the PBGC.

61. The existence of the PBGC guaranty as an element of benefit security was not, as some respondents contended, ignored in the Exposure Drafts. Both drafts required, as does this Statement, that financial statements of ERISA plans include a brief, general description of the PBGC guaranty. However, the initial Exposure Draft's requirement was expanded to require an explanation of the application of the PBGC guaranty to any recent plan amendments (paragraph 265).

62. There is also the view that the primary objective is unattainable because a comparison of the net asset and benefit information as presented in a plan's annual financial statements is not sufficient for an assessment of the plan's future ability to pay benefits when due. The Board recognizes that information regarding the trend of the relationship over time between plan resources and accumulated plan benefits, on both an absolute and a relative basis, can be more useful than information about that relationship at any given date. Information over time is, however, an aggregation of information as of a series of dates. Without annual information, trend information over a period of years cannot be ascertained. Therefore, the Board believes it is appropriate for the primary objective to indicate that the information provided by plan financial statements should be *useful in assessing* (as contrasted with *portraying*) the plan's future as well as present ability to pay benefits when due. Paragraph 50 acknowledges that the usefulness of annual financial statements may be enhanced by supplementing them with summary financial information for a period of years.

63. To summarize, the Board does not believe that the need for information beyond that provided by annual plan financial statements implies that the stated objective of providing information useful in assessing the plan's present and future ability to pay benefits when due is either unattainable or inappropriate. An analogous situation exists with regard to financial reporting by business enterprises. The objectives stated in FASB Concepts Statement No. 1, *Objectives of Financial Reporting by Business Enterprises,* focus on providing "information that is useful to present and potential investors and creditors and other users in making rational investment, credit, and similar decisions."[25] That document recognizes, however, that financial reporting is but one source of economic information about business enterprises. The financial information provided by financial reporting for business enterprises should be used in combination with pertinent information from other sources, for example, information about general economic conditions or expectations, political events and political climate, or industry outlook.[26] Similarly, financial information presented in plan financial statements should be used in combination with other pertinent information, including information about the financial condition of the employer(s) and, for ERISA plans, the guaranty of the PBGC. Concepts Statement 1 also implicitly recognizes that financial reporting by a business enterprise for any one period may be insufficient to fulfill users' needs. For example, paragraph 48 indicates that ". . . procedures such as averaging or normalizing reported earnings for several periods . . . are commonly used in estimating 'earning power'." Users of plan financial statements may likewise need financial information for several years in assessing benefit security.

Alternatives Considered

64. Alternatives suggested by respondents primarily focused on the objectives presented in the Discussion Memorandum, namely:

a. To provide information useful for assessing the aggregate future benefits payable to participants and the resources available to meet those payments
b. To provide information useful to individual pension plan participants for assessing the degree of risk that may be associated with the future receipt of their pension benefits
c. To provide information useful for assessing, in terms of amount, timing, and related uncertainty, the aggregate future benefits payable to participants should the pension plan be terminated
d. To provide information useful for assessing the

[25]Concepts Statement 1, par. 34.

[26]Ibid., par. 22.

performance of pension plan administrators and other fiduciaries in discharging their various responsibilities
e. To provide information useful for assessing the performance of pension plan administrators and other fiduciaries solely with regard to managing the assets that they control
f. To provide information useful for assessing the need for future contributions to the pension plan in terms of amount and timing
g. To provide information useful for assessing future earnings of the pension plan in terms of amount and timing.

65. As was indicated in the Discussion Memorandum and the Exposure Drafts, selection of a particular objective does not necessarily mean exclusion of an alternative; rather, selection of objectives determines the matters to be emphasized.

66. The Board views objectives (a)-(c) as falling within the broad objective of providing financial information that is useful in assessing the plan's present and future ability to pay benefits when due. However, each of those objectives and the views of respondents supporting them suggest an alternative manner of either measuring or displaying particular elements of the financial information. Accordingly, those alternatives are addressed in subsequent paragraphs that deal with the determination and presentation of benefit information.

67. Objectives (d) and (e) are concerned with whether the financial statements should be primarily oriented toward reporting what the plan administrator and other fiduciaries have done to carry out their duties. As indicated in paragraph 57, objective (e) is, to a significant degree, considered inherent in the broad objective adopted by the Board. In accomplishing that objective, plan financial statements will provide information regarding the management of plan assets together with information pertaining to participants' accumulated plan benefits as well as the results of transactions and events that affect those assets and benefits. Although that information should be useful in assessing performance, factors that are beyond the control of plan management, such as the financial condition of the employer(s), participants' longevity, and general economic conditions, may contribute to plan performance. Plan financial statements provide information about a plan when it was under the direction of a particular management but cannot separate the effect of management performance from the effects of other factors. Users therefore need to form their own assessment of the effect of management performance on plan performance. Further, to focus solely on objectives relating to performance might, based on certain respondents' views, result in the exclusion of benefit information. The Board does not believe such exclusion would result in meaningful financial statements. Therefore, the Board does not believe that an objective relating to performance should, by itself, constitute the primary objective of plan financial statements.

68. Objectives (f) and (g) were rejected as primary objectives for reasons somewhat similar to those expressed in paragraph 67. To the extent that users' expectations about future plan performance are based on past plan performance, information about existing plan assets and the income from those assets together with information about present accumulated plan benefits may be useful in assessing the need for future contributions to the plan and future earnings of the plan. However, plan financial statements cannot provide information about assets or benefits that do not currently exist. Users need to assess the possible impact of factors that may cause change and form their own expectations about the future and its relation to the past.

69. Some respondents suggested another objective, namely that the financial statements for ERISA plans provide only the information required by ERISA and its related regulations. In their view, Congress established that pension plan financial statements serve plan participants and prescribed the information that it deemed appropriate for that purpose. The Board noted, however, that Section 103(a)(3)(A) (quoted in footnote 21) refers to financial statements "presented fairly in conformity with generally accepted accounting principles." The Board sees no indication in the Act that those principles of accounting are intended to be found in the Act's requirements or in regulations to be issued thereunder. It is the purpose of, and the Board believes Congress recognized the need for, financial accounting standards to determine the content of plan financial statements.

SCOPE OF THIS STATEMENT

70. This Statement establishes standards of financial accounting and reporting for defined benefit pension plans. In contrast, the Discussion Memorandum comprehended various types of employee benefit plans. However, most respondents to the Discussion Memorandum directed their attention to accounting and reporting for defined benefit pension plans—presumably the area of most concern to them. Some respondents to the Exposure Drafts suggested that the scope of this Statement should be expanded to include other types of employee benefit plans. Although requested to do so by paragraph 43 of the initial Exposure Draft, very few respondents to that document identified specific aspects of the accounting and reporting by other types of employee benefit plans that they believed the Board should focus on.

71. Because of respondents' overriding interest in reporting by defined benefit pension plans, the Board concluded that this Statement should focus on those plans. That focus is not intended to imply that the Board has concluded that the standards of financial accounting and reporting for other types of employee benefit plans should be the same as or different from those described in this Statement.

72. Some respondents to the initial Exposure Draft suggested that the scope of this Statement include interim as well as annual financial statements. Because few, if any, plans publish complete interim financial statements and because the consideration of related issues would delay issuance of this Statement, the Board did not consider interim financial statements.

73. Defined benefit pension plans of state and local governmental units are included in the scope of this Statement. Certain respondents suggested that because of the unique characteristics of governmental units, such as their taxing power and perpetual life, their plans are inherently different from private plans and therefore should be excluded. Others contended that governmental plans should be excluded because they may differ from private plans with respect to funding requirements, vesting and benefit provisions, or both.

74. Some respondents to the Exposure Drafts expressed the view that plans of state and local governmental units should be excluded because the stated primary objective of plan financial statements was not appropriate for such plans. In their view, because public plans are less likely to terminate than private plans, providing information useful in assessing benefit security is not relevant. The view was also expressed that the initial Exposure Draft's identification of participants as the primary users of plan financial statements was not appropriate for governmental plans. Those respondents thought the financial statements of such plans should be directed specifically to users other than plan participants (for example, public officials, state legislators, taxpayer groups, bond underwriters, potential investors, etc.) and that those users might have objectives other than assessing benefit security.

75. The Board recognizes that there are distinctions between business enterprises and governmental units. The Board also recognizes that the financial condition of the employer is of extreme importance for benefit security. However, the Board believes that only the characteristics of the plans themselves, not the characteristics of their sponsors, should affect the accounting and reporting by pension plans. The Board also did not find persuasive the argument that plans of state and local governmental units should be excluded because their vesting and benefit provisions may differ from those of private plans. The vesting and benefit provisions of private plans are not all the same. Such differences will be reflected in plan financial statements prepared in accordance with this Statement. (Paragraph 165 discusses how the basic method for determining the benefit information accommodates differences in such factors as plan provisions.)

76. The Board also believes that there is a need, as evidenced by the increasing interest[27] in financial information about public plans and by the House Pension Task Force Report on Public Employee Retirement Systems,[28] to establish standards of financial accounting and reporting for plans of state and local governmental units. That report states: "Serious deficiencies exist among public employee retirement systems at all levels of government regarding the extent to which important information is reported and disclosed to plan participants, public officials, and taxpayers."[29] It also states that participants in such plans "do face the risk of pension benefit reductions or other benefit curtailments due to reasons other than plan termination," and that "the financing of many pension plans covering local government employees lacks stability and predictability due to state imposed taxing restrictions as well as to the indeterminate amount of funds available from federal revenue sharing, state insurance premium taxes, etc."[30] In view of the foregoing, the Board concluded that the primary objective of providing information useful in assessing the plan's ability to pay benefits when due is as appropriate for plans of state and local governmental units as it is for private plans.

77. Views regarding the needs of financial statement users other than participants were previously addressed (paragraph 49). Further, the primary objective adopted by the Board does not necessarily deny other objectives that are associated with those users. However, to the extent that certain users need specialized or detailed information and can otherwise obtain that information, the Board con-

[27]The recent Harris survey (footnote 22) provides evidence of that interest. That survey found that public plan compliance with private plan regulations is favored by 68 percent of current and retired employees (14 percent opposed) and by 93 percent of business leaders. Moreover, such compliance is favored by a sizeable 65 percent majority of employees currently covered by public plans and opposed by only 18 percent. (Johnson & Higgins, *1979 Study of American Attitudes Toward Pensions and Retirement*, p. xi.)

[28]U.S. Government Printing Office, *House of Representatives Committee on Education and Labor Pension Task Force Report on Public Employee Retirement Systems* (Washington, D.C., 1978).

[29]Ibid., p. 3.

[30]Ibid., p. 102.

cluded (paragraph 52) that such information should not be required in general purpose external financial statements.

78. Government-sponsored social security plans (for example, the U.S. Social Security program and similar plans of foreign countries) are not included in the scope of this Statement. The scope of the Discussion Memorandum did not include those plans nor did the Board consider them in its deliberations.

79. This Statement does not differentiate among plans based on plan size. Some respondents to the initial Exposure Draft suggested that the cost of implementing that document would be excessive for small plans, and therefore such plans should be exempted. (Paragraphs 272-279 discuss certain changes made to that Exposure Draft's requirements to reduce the perceived implementation costs.) Other respondents objected because they interpreted the inclusion of small plans as requiring them to issue audited annual financial statements. As indicated in paragraph 2, this Statement does *not* require the preparation, distribution, or attestation of any plan's financial statements. The Board recognizes that ERISA plans with fewer than 100 participants are not required to have their annual financial statements audited and are subject to less detailed requirements regarding their annual reports to governmental agencies.

80. The Board believes that small plans should be included in the scope of this Statement. The financial information needed in assessing a plan's ability to pay benefits is not dependent on its size. Further, any size criterion selected for excluding plans would be arbitrary. To exclude small plans from the scope of this Statement would be justified only if the usefulness of the required information did not justify its cost. However, that cost/benefit relationship is difficult to determine. It is recognized that the incremental cost per participant to implement this Statement will be generally higher for smaller plans. Accordingly, the Board considered how the provisions of the Statement, primarily those relating to benefit information, might be modified to apply to small plans. The Board noted that the American Academy of Actuaries in its Interpretation 2, *Interpretation of Recommendations Concerning the Calculation of the Actuarial Present Value of Accrued Benefits under an Active Plan,* does not differentiate among plans based on plan size. Although their basic method is the same for large and small plans, the Board is aware that certain actuaries use simplified techniques in applying that method to minimize the costs for small plans. As indicated in paragraph 29, this Statement permits the use of averages or other methods of approximation, including those consistent with recommended actuarial practice, provided the results obtained are substantially the same as the results contemplated by this Statement. That paragraph also notes that such approaches may be particularly useful for plans sponsored by small employers.

81. The revised Exposure Draft requested respondents, particularly those associated with small plans that intended to issue financial statements in accordance with generally accepted accounting principles, to express their views regarding whether the provisions of that document should be modified for small plans and, if so, to what extent. Of those relatively few respondents who thought modifications should be made, most suggested exempting small plans from the requirement to present benefit information. For such an exemption to be appropriate, it would be necessary to conclude that the primary objective of financial statements for a small plan is different from that for a large plan. The Board does not support that conclusion (paragraph 80).

82. The Board considered the American Society of Pension Actuaries' response to the revised Exposure Draft regarding specific simplified techniques that, in the Society's view, should be permitted in valuing small plans' ancillary benefits. Paragraph 29 of this Statement permits the use of such simplified techniques. Further, one reason for the delayed effective date of this Statement is so that small plans that intend to adopt this Statement will have additional time to develop the necessary procedures, which may include appropriate simplified techniques.

83. For plans maintained outside the United States that are similar to plans maintained in the United States, this Statement applies only when financial statements of such plans are intended to conform with U.S. generally accepted accounting principles.

84. The scope of this Statement excludes a plan that has been or is expected to be terminated. The event of termination, particularly for an ERISA plan, would make various requirements of this Statement inappropriate because they are based on the assumption of an ongoing plan.

85. This Statement applies to an unfunded plan. Although principally limited to the information required by paragraphs 6(c) and 6(d), the Board nevertheless considers that financial information useful in assessing such a plan's ability to pay benefits when due.

INFORMATION REGARDING NET ASSETS AVAILABLE FOR BENEFITS

86. Because a plan's net assets are the existing means by which it may provide benefits, **net asset information** is necessary in assessing a plan's ability

to pay benefits when due. This Statement requires that information to be presented as of the end of the plan year. If the benefit information date is the beginning of the year, a statement that includes net asset information as of that date is also required. (Paragraphs 244-246 discuss the Board's conclusions regarding the format for presenting that information.)

Basis of Accounting

87. The Discussion Memorandum referred to the following bases of accounting for the net assets of a pension plan: cash basis, accrual basis, and a modified cash or modified accrual basis. Most respondents who addressed the issue indicated a preference for the accrual basis. Some who favored either the cash basis or a modified basis cited the administrative convenience of such an approach and noted that, in many instances, the difference from the accrual basis would not be material. Respondents favoring the accrual basis generally indicated that it is the only basis that provides complete financial information relating to transactions and events occurring during the period. The Board agreed with the latter argument and believes that basis is the only one that is consistent with the primary objective.

88. Some respondents to the Discussion Memorandum objected to the accrual basis because it would require that purchases and sales of securities be recorded on a trade-date basis. They contended that present recordkeeping is geared to a settlement-date basis, that a change in reporting would be an administrative burden, and that the information produced by the two methods would not be significantly different for most plans. The Board concluded that, subject to materiality considerations, the accrual basis should be used. Therefore, if the results are not significantly different from the results on a trade-date basis, accounting for sales and purchases of securities on a settlement-date basis is acceptable (footnote 3).

Receivables from Employer(s) and Others

89. This Statement requires reporting as contributions receivable those amounts that, as of the reporting date, are due the plan from the employer(s), participants, and other sources of funding. Amounts due include those pursuant to formal commitments as well as legal or contractual requirements.

90. The initial Exposure Draft did not address receivables from sources other than the employer(s) and participants. However, certain other sources (for example, state subsidies and federal grants) constitute a significant source of financing for many plans of state and local governmental units.[31] Accordingly, receivables from such sources should be included and separately identified. However, funds from sources such as federal revenue-sharing programs that are used for plan funding purposes at the employer's discretion are, in effect, employer contributions and should be reported as such.

91. The initial Exposure Draft limited employer contributions receivable to amounts legally or contractually due the plan. A number of respondents indicated that some employers (but not employers participating in collectively bargained multiemployer plans) contribute amounts in excess of legal or contractual minimums and, in some cases, those contributions are made after the plan's year-end. Respondents questioned the appropriateness of excluding those "excess" amounts from plan receivables. Some indicated that determining the amounts that are "legally or contractually" due could be burdensome if such amounts are less than actual contributions. The Board agreed and concluded that contributions receivable should include amounts evidenced by a formal commitment. Paragraph 10 indicates certain factors that may provide evidence of a formal commitment. The revised Exposure Draft did not include the employer's recognition as of the reporting date of a contribution payable to the plan as possible evidence of a formal commitment. Certain respondents suggested that that factor be added. The Board agreed that such a factor could provide *additional* support for the existence of a formal commitment. (Paragraph 92 indicates that the existence of accrued pension costs does not, by itself, provide sufficient support.) Receipt of formally committed amounts soon after the plan's year-end provides additional evidence of the existence of a receivable at year-end. In accordance with existing generally accepted accounting principles applicable to receivables, an adequate allowance should be provided for estimated uncollectible amounts.

92. Certain respondents favored treating as receivables all amounts reported as accrued pension costs by the employer(s). That position was generally founded on the belief that there should be symmetry in the financial reporting of the employer(s) and the plan. The Board has on its technical agenda a project on accounting by employers for pensions. The Board intends to consider further the issue of symmetry in that project. While neither accepting nor rejecting the concept of symmetry at this time (paragraph 163), the Board concluded that present practices of employers in accounting for pension costs are not a sufficient basis on which to account for

[31]U.S. Government Printing Office, *House of Representatives Committee on Education and Labor Task Force Report on Public Employee Retirement Systems*, p. 141.

employer contributions receivable. For various reasons, amounts recorded as accrued pension costs by an employer may differ from amounts formally committed to the plan. For example, the method used for measurement of periodic pension costs for the employer's financial statements may differ from the method used for determining the amount and incidence of employer contributions.

93. A few respondents to the initial Exposure Draft questioned whether the entire amount of "unfunded **prior service costs**" is a receivable of the plan. Because at the reporting date that amount is not due from the employer(s), it is not a receivable of the plan. The employer(s) may or may not intend to eventually contribute amounts sufficient to eliminate the "unfunded prior service costs." Until such payments are formally committed to the plan, "unfunded prior service costs" do not constitute a recordable resource of the plan. For similar reasons, any existing excess of the actuarial present value of accumulated plan benefits over the net assets available for benefits (excluding contributions receivable) is not a plan receivable unless at the reporting date that amount is legally, contractually, or pursuant to a formal commitment due the plan.

Alternatives Considered for Measuring Investments (Other Than Contracts with Insurance Companies)

94. Alternatives presented in the Discussion Memorandum encompassed the following approaches to measuring plan investments: fair value, historical cost, and certain hybrid methods. Opinion was divided among respondents as to whether a single method should be used for all investments.

Single Method

95. Most respondents to the Discussion Memorandum who favored a single method advocated fair value. In their view, the fair value of plan investments is the most relevant information that can be provided for assessing (a) the security within the plan for participants' benefits and (b) the plan's investment performance. Further, for ERISA plans, a number of respondents noted that there would be no additional administrative burden caused by requiring its use because fair value is presently required in financial data filed with certain governmental agencies.

96. Some respondents favoring use of only one method advocated historical cost. Generally, they emphasized the high degree of objectivity associated with that method and that its use does not result in the recognition of unrealized gains or losses as do other methods. Certain respondents who advocated that the primary objective of plan financial statements be limited to portraying stewardship responsibility considered historical cost to be the most useful measure for achieving that objective. Many who supported historical cost nevertheless advocated supplemental disclosure of fair value.

97. A number of respondents preferred a method other than fair value or historical cost. Two such methods were the moving-average-market-value method and the long-range-appreciation method. Support for those methods generally was based on the view that the effects of short-term market fluctuations on financial position and investment performance should be avoided. In addition, because investments are normally held for a long time, the current fair value of those investments is not necessarily indicative of the amount to be ultimately realized.

98. Some respondents to the Exposure Drafts favored a method other than fair value based on their perceptions of the possible effects that disclosing fluctuations in fair values might have on a plan's investment policy. In their view, measurement of investments at fair value is undesirable because plan sponsors or administrators might attempt to avoid the financial statement effects of fluctuating fair values by adopting a more conservative investment policy or by avoiding certain types of investments whose fair values may be subject to wide fluctuations. Some who expressed that view favored historical cost for either all or certain types of investments; others favored some type of averaging method.

99. To avoid additional administrative costs and possible confusion of users of plan financial statements, some respondents argued in favor of using whatever method was used in determining the **actuarial asset value.**

Different Methods

100. Some respondents favored use of different methods for different types of investments. The principal investment categories addressed were fixed-income securities, not-readily-marketable investments, and contracts with insurance companies. (Paragraphs 112-126 discuss the last category.) The views supporting particular methods for marketable equity securities were basically the same as those indicated in paragraphs 95-99.

101. Regardless of the method(s) used to measure other types of investments, certain respondents advocated use of (amortized) historical cost for long-term, fixed-income investments that the plan had both the intent and ability to hold to maturity. They argued that measuring those investments at fair value does not reflect the amounts ultimately

expected to be received. Further, any appreciation or depreciation that is recognized using fair value will ultimately be reversed in subsequent periods.

102. Certain respondents focused on investments that are not readily marketable. They advocated use of historical cost for those investments. In their view, if market quotations are not available, determining fair value is highly subjective. Because users of plan financial statements might be misled by subjective measurements, historical cost should be used.

Conclusions on Measuring Investments (Other Than Contracts with Insurance Companies)

103. The Board concluded that plan investments (excluding contracts with insurance companies) should be measured at fair value. The Board believes that basis provides the most relevant information about the resources of a plan consistent with the primary objective of the financial statements. The Board recognizes that there may be practical problems in determining the fair value of certain types of investments. Notwithstanding those difficulties, the Board believes that the relevance of fair value is so great as to override any objections to its use.

104. If available, the Board considers quoted market prices to be the most objective and relevant measure of fair value. Paragraph 11 provides certain guidelines for determining fair value if no active market exists. The use of independent experts who are qualified to estimate fair value may be necessary for certain investments.

105. The Board rejected using historical cost because prices in past exchanges do not provide the most relevant information about the present ability of the plan's assets to provide participants' benefits. Further, the Board does not believe that historical cost is the most appropriate measure for use in assessing how the stewardship responsibility for plan assets has been discharged. Plan administrators or other fiduciaries who manage plan assets are accountable not only for the custody and safekeeping of those assets but also for their efficient and profitable use in producing additional assets for use in paying benefits. Investment performance is an essential element of stewardship responsibility. Measuring changes in fair value provides information necessary for assessing annual investment performance and stewardship responsibility. Historical cost provides that information only when investments are sold.

106. The Board does not consider perceived effects on investment policies to be an appropriate factor on which to base conclusions concerning measurement of investments. The Board has considered and rejected similar arguments regarding perceived effects of accounting standards on management decisions in conjunction with other projects on its agenda. Even if accounting results were to influence some managers' decisions, it does not follow that accounting standards should be designed to encourage or discourage an action by management. Developing accounting standards on that basis would require a judgment by the Board as to which actions are desirable and which are undesirable. The role of financial reporting is to provide neutral, evenhanded, or unbiased information that is useful to those (including management) who make economic decisions. It is not a function of financial reporting to try to influence those decisions. Even if an approach based on an attempt to avoid possible effects on investment decisions were deemed appropriate, an equally valid argument might be made against the use of historical cost. That is, if investments were presented at historical cost, decisions regarding timing of disposition of investments might be influenced by the effect on reported gains or losses.

107. For fixed-income investments held to maturity, the Board recognizes that market fluctuations will reverse before maturity (assuming no defaults). However, at the reporting date, it is the fair value, not the historical cost or the expected value at maturity, that is relevant to an assessment of the plan's ability to pay benefits. Changes in value from period to period are relevant to an assessment of investment performance and discharge of stewardship responsibility. Presenting fixed-income investments at historical cost (whether or not the intent is to hold them to maturity) does not provide essential information about the effect on investment performance of the decision to hold. Further, it may be difficult to determine whether the plan has both the intent and ability to hold a particular fixed-income investment to maturity.

108. At least two additional issues would need to be considered if fixed-income investments were to be presented at historical cost. First, some respondents contended that recognizing a gain or loss (based on historical cost) is inappropriate for a bond swap, that is, when one bond is sold and replaced by a similar investment-grade bond. Those respondents consider such gains and losses to be, in effect, modifications of future interest income. Therefore, to accomplish the desired results, gain/loss deferral and amortization approaches have been used. Those approaches, however, result in a measure of historical cost of fixed-income investments that other respondents believe is inconsistent with the generally accepted notion that historical cost represents exchange price at date of acquisition. The second issue is that the historical cost of a fixed-income

investment reflects the effective interest rate at the date the plan acquired the investment rather than current and prospective interest rates which are considered more relevant for purposes of measuring the actuarial present value of accumulated plan benefits. The use of historical cost would necessitate resolving that inconsistency in order for the net asset and benefit information to be comparably measured. Presenting fixed-income investments at fair value eliminates any need to address those issues.

109. To address the concerns expressed about the subjectivity of fair value determinations for certain investments, this Statement requires that information regarding a plan's investments indicate whether their fair values have been measured by quoted prices in an active market or are fair values otherwise determined. That requirement replaces the initial Exposure Draft's requirement to segment investments into those that are readily marketable and those that are not. Some respondents expressed the view that a criterion of "readily marketable" would be difficult to apply and would not necessarily be interpreted on a consistent basis among plans. The Board agreed and concluded that the intent of that requirement, namely to provide an indication of (a) the relative degree of subjectivity in the valuation of plan investments and (b) the relative liquidity of the investments, could be achieved by substituting the revised requirement.

110. Because the Board believes that quoted market prices, or in their absence other methods (for example, discounted cash flows or appraisals), are more relevant indicators of fair value than are any of the measures produced by hybrid methods, it rejected those methods for measuring investments.

111. For reasons similar to those expressed in paragraphs 165 and 166, the Board concluded that the measure of investments reported in financial statements should not be dependent on actuarial asset valuations. The Board believes that actuarial asset valuation methods are used in conjunction with objectives, principally determining measures of pension costs for purposes of financial reporting by the employer(s) and for determining periodic funding requirements, that differ from the primary objective of plan financial statements.

Alternatives Considered for Measuring Contracts with Insurance Companies

112. A plan may enter into various contractual agreements with an insurance company. Such agreements may be distinguished based on whether related payments to the insurance company are currently used to purchase immediate or deferred annuities for participants (**allocated contracts**) or are accumulated in an unallocated fund (**unallocated contracts**) to be used to meet benefit payments when employees retire, either directly or through the purchase of annuities. Funds in an unallocated contract may also be withdrawn and otherwise invested.

113. Under an allocated contract (for example, a group deferred annuity contract), the insurance company has a legal obligation to make all benefit payments for which it has received the premiums or consideration requested.

114. An example of an unallocated contract is a group deposit administration *(DA)* contract. Under a DA contract, payments to the insurance company that are intended to provide future benefits to present employees are credited to an account. For investment purposes, the monies in the account are commingled with other assets of the insurance company. The account is credited with interest at the rate specified in the contract; it is charged with the purchase price of annuities when employees retire and with any incidental benefits (death, disability, and withdrawal) disbursed directly from the account.

115. The immediate participation guarantee *(IPG)* contract is a variation of the DA contract. In an IPG contract, the account is credited with the contributions received during the contract period plus its share of the insurance company's actual investment income. The IPG contract is written in two forms. Under either form the insurance company is obligated to make lifetime benefit payments to retired employees. One form provides for the actual purchase of annuities as employees retire. There is an annual adjustment to the account to reflect the insurance company's experience under the annuities. In the other form, the IPG contract may accomplish the same objective through a different technique. When an employee retires, pension payments are made directly from the account without the purchase of an annuity. However, the balance of the account must be maintained at the amount required, according to a premium schedule in the contract, to provide for the remaining pension benefits for all current retirees. That portion of the account is referred to as the **retired life fund.** Thus, if necessary, the account could always be used to buy all annuities in force.

116. Allocated contracts may or may not provide for plan participation in the investment performance and experience (for example, mortality experience) of the insurance company. Under those that do (**participating contracts**), the right to receive future dividends is referred to as a **participation right.**

117. The initial Exposure Draft prescribed that contracts whereby an insurance company was required

to pay certain specified benefits were to be excluded from plan assets. If no such obligation existed, the contracts were to be included in plan assets.

118. Certain respondents to that Exposure Draft favored excluding allocated contracts from plan assets and including unallocated contracts. Others favored excluding contracts under which funds were *assigned* to provide benefits that the insurance company is obligated to pay. Presumably, both proposals are based on the view that when an insurance company agrees to provide certain benefits, it incurs (and removes from the plan) the obligation to pay those benefits. To assess the security for those benefits, one should look to the financial statements of the insurance company rather than those of the plan. By paying premiums for the purchase of annuities, the plan has fulfilled its obligation to provide those benefits and ceases to be the focal point for financial information about those particular benefits and the assets that will be used to pay them.

119. Although the preceding proposals are similar, there may be a significant distinction between them regarding the retired life fund of an IPG contract. Although an IPG contract is an unallocated contract, the retired life fund could be viewed as having been effectively and permanently transferred to the insurance company (that is, the funds have been assigned) in return for the insurance company's agreement to provide certain benefits. Because no annuities are purchased while the contract is active, the funds are not physically transferred. However, because the plan is required to maintain the retired life fund at a level sufficient to purchase annuity contracts to provide the retired participants' remaining benefits, it could be argued that the insurance company has control of that fund.

120. Certain respondents favored including in plan assets all contracts with insurance companies. Some expressed the view that all contracts represent plan assets and to exclude certain contracts would be inconsistent with the reporting of assets and liabilities by other types of entities. Others favor such an approach because they believe the value of participation rights under allocated contracts should be included in plan assets. Presumably, those respondents believe that when a plan purchases a participating contract at a cost that is higher than that for a nonparticipating contract, it purchases an asset (the participation right) in exchange for the incremental cost because under either contract the insurance company is obligated to provide the same benefits. Presumably, subsequent values for the participation right can be determined, for example, upon cancellation of the contract. Thus, an asset with a determinable value (the participation right) seems to be created when the contract is purchased. A subsequent valuation of the participation right may be more or less objective depending on when it is made.

121. The initial Exposure Draft required that contracts included in plan assets be measured at fair value. Certain respondents preferred to measure those contracts at amounts determined by the insurance company in accordance with the terms of the contract. For purposes of this Statement, those values are referred to as **contract values.** Those respondents argued that, except for investments held in an insurance company's **separate account,** it is impossible for anyone other than the insurance company to determine a value for those contracts. They also argued that requiring a fair value approach for contracts under which the plan's investment is maintained in an insurance company's **general account** would necessitate extra calculations, whereas the information for determining contract values is readily available. Some respondents requested guidance as to how fair value should be determined for specific types of contracts, for example, IPG contracts and deposit administration contracts.

122. In view of certain respondents' comments, the Board solicited additional information from certain persons, including members of the project's task force and members of the insurance industry, before issuing the revised Exposure Draft. The issues raised were (a) what criteria should be used to determine the elements of contracts with insurance companies that constitute assets to be recognized in plan financial statements and (b) how to measure those elements that do constitute assets. Views regarding whether it was feasible to determine the value of participation rights were specifically requested. Some respondents indicated such valuation could be very difficult. Others indicated that it could be done.

Conclusions on Measuring Contracts with Insurance Companies

123. The initial Exposure Draft's requirements regarding contracts with insurance companies were changed to require that those contracts be presented in the same manner as that contained in the annual report filed by the plan with certain governmental agencies pursuant to ERISA. A plan not subject to ERISA is required to similarly present its contracts, that is, as if it were subject to the reporting requirements of ERISA. For 1979 plan years, the pertinent governmental reporting requirements relate to item 13 of either Form 5500 or Form 5500-C. Essentially, allocated contracts are excluded from, and unallocated contracts are included in, plan assets.

124. The Board believes that certain aspects of contracts with insurance companies might be appro-

priately accounted for in a manner different from the regulatory reporting requirements. For example, the applicable instructions for the 1979 Form 5500 and Form 5500-C appear to result in the inclusion of retired life funds under IPG contracts as plan assets and the exclusion of participation rights from plan assets. As discussed in paragraphs 119 and 120, it *may* be conceptually more appropriate to exclude retired life funds and include participation rights. Further, Form 5500 and Form 5500-C permit unallocated contracts recognized as plan assets to be measured at either fair value or at amounts determined by the insurance company (that is, contract value). The Board recognizes that presenting contracts with insurance companies at contract value is inconsistent with requiring all other plan investments to be presented at fair value. However, as previously discussed, the information required for determining contract value is readily available, whereas a fair value approach would necessitate extra calculations that, according to information the Board received (paragraph 122), might be extremely complex. The Board concluded that it did not have sufficient information at this time to enable it to reach definitive conclusions concerning matters such as the recognition of retired life funds and participation rights as plan assets and the feasibility of determining a contract's fair value. Moreover, obtaining the information considered necessary to properly assess both the conceptual and the cost/benefit considerations involved would unduly delay the issuance of this Statement. During the Board's deliberations, it was noted that the PBGC and the IRS had proposed certain regulations.[32] Before reaching definitive conclusions, it was thought advisable to consider any final regulations relating to contracts with insurance companies. For the present, the Board concluded that it should adopt the practical solution stated in paragraph 123.

125. Certain respondents to the revised Exposure Draft objected to inclusion of a reference to governmental reporting requirements in a Statement of Financial Accounting Standards and suggested that the pertinent instructions to Form 5500 be incorporated into this Statement. Because the Board has not concluded that those instructions contain the conceptually appropriate treatment of contracts with insurance companies, it rejected that suggestion.

126. Some respondents asked whether benefits to be provided by contracts excluded from plan assets should be excluded from the benefit information. Paragraph 18(d) provides an affirmative response to that query. As discussed in paragraph 118, the insurance company rather than the plan may be viewed as the principal obligor of such benefits. Nevertheless, the fact that contracts excluded from plan assets exist is considered useful information. Accordingly, the Board concluded that the plan's policy with regard to the purchase of excluded contracts should be disclosed. The Board believes that information together with the required disclosure of payments to insurance companies to purchase contracts that are excluded from plan assets (paragraph 15(g)) will adequately inform users that certain benefits will be provided by means of excluded contracts. To inform users that a plan has participation rights and that plan assets reflect dividend income but not the source of that income, the Board concluded that disclosure of the year's income that is related to excluded contracts should be required.

Assets Employed in Operations

127. Certain respondents who advocated use of fair value to measure investments also advocated measuring assets employed in operations at fair value. In their view, a consistent measurement basis should be used for all plan assets. They also noted that fair value is presently required in the financial data filed with governmental agencies pursuant to ERISA.

128. Other respondents favored using historical cost (adjusted for any depreciation or amortization). Some argued that measuring operating assets at historical cost and appropriately allocating that cost to each plan year is the appropriate manner for recognizing that portion of the administrative expenses incurred to provide benefits. Expenditures for operating assets are in the nature of advance payments for future administrative services; in that respect they differ from investments which are expected to generate future cash flows that will be used to provide benefits. Others noted that ERISA reporting requirements are not applicable to plans of state and local governmental units and that requiring fair value could increase their administrative costs.

129. The Board considered the foregoing views together with the objective of the financial statements and concluded that operating assets should be measured at historical cost less accumulated depreciation or amortization.

[32]Pension Benefit Guaranty Corporation [29 CFR Parts 2608 and 2611], *Federal Register,* Vol. 42 (April 18, 1977), pp. 20156-20162; Department of the Treasury, Internal Revenue Service [26 CFR Part 1], *Federal Register,* Vol. 43 (August 25, 1978), pp. 38027-38029. Shortly before the issuance of this Statement, the PBGC announced that it had dropped its proposals [*Federal Register,* Vol. 44 (December 20, 1979), pp. 75405 and 75406].

INFORMATION REGARDING ACTUARIAL PRESENT VALUE OF ACCUMULATED PLAN BENEFITS

The Need to Present Benefit Information

130. To be useful in assessing a plan's present and future ability to pay benefits when due, it is essential that the financial statements present information about both the net assets available for benefits and the benefits to be paid.

131. Some respondents opposed disclosure of any benefit information on the basis that it was outside the scope of financial statements. They asserted that the information is appropriately the province of the actuarial report. In their view, to include such information would at least duplicate information available elsewhere (the actuary's report) and might be confusing and misleading if it differed from amounts reported by the actuary.

132. Similarly, some respondents interpreted certain provisions of the Act to mean that any disclosure of benefits for an ERISA plan is an issue that should be resolved independently of the plan's financial statements. Some who expressed that view thought that excluding benefit information from the financial statements is preferable because it alleviates the possibility of conflicts between the responsibilities of auditors and those of actuaries in the certifications required by the Act.

133. The Board considered whether the need to involve members of the actuarial profession in the development of financial information should be a factor that constrains the content of financial statements. From the project's inception, the Board has recognized the essential role of actuaries in developing any required benefit information. It undertook an extensive cooperative effort with the American Academy of Actuaries *(Academy)* to develop a basic method of determining benefit information that would be both meaningful and implementable. The Board appreciates the Academy's willingness to undertake that effort. The substantial agreement reached (discussed further in subsequent paragraphs of this appendix) should enhance the necessary ongoing cooperative effort among those who have a responsibility regarding the development or dissemination of plan financial information.

134. The Board believes that actuaries are best qualified to develop the benefit information required by this Statement because of their unique professional qualifications and their existing relationship with plans on other matters (for example, funding policy and measurement of pension costs). Although it acknowledges the role of the actuarial profession in developing certain financial information, the Board does not accept the notion that if the preparation of information does not fall within the professional qualifications of accountants, it is outside the scope of financial accounting. Certain financial information presently disclosed in financial statements of business enterprises is prepared exclusively by or with the assistance of professionals other than accountants. For example, the aggregate reserves for life, accident, and health policies of stock life insurance companies that appear in those entities' financial statements and measurements of pension costs in employers' financial statements are prepared by actuaries. The use of appraisers is common in establishing the value of nonmonetary assets acquired in a business combination accounted for as a purchase and may be necessary in conjunction with accounting for certain troubled debt restructurings. (With respect to plan reporting, paragraph 104 of this Statement recognizes that appraisers may be needed to determine the fair value of certain plan investments.) Information oriented to engineering and law may also enter into the preparation of financial accounting information. Thus, the Board rejected the view that the need, by itself, to involve actuaries should be a constraint on the content of financial statements.

135. The Board believes that unnecessary differences between the benefit information presented in plan financial statements and related information presented in schedules filed by ERISA plans pursuant to the Act could result in additional costs being incurred by preparers of the information and might also cause some confusion to those who use the information. Therefore, the Board worked closely with the Department of Labor *(Department)* in an attempt to avoid such unnecessary differences. As discussed further in subsequent paragraphs, that cooperative effort was successful in developing a basic method of determining benefit information that will satisfy both financial reporting requirements and Form 5500 reporting requirements.

136. The Board recognizes that there will be available other actuarial information concerning a plan that may differ from the benefit information in plan financial statements. The Board recognizes (and believes that both the Academy and the Department also recognize) that such differences are unavoidable when the information is intended to serve different purposes. For example, information that is useful in assessing the plan's ability to pay benefits may not be the most useful for determining periodic cost measurements or establishing minimum funding requirements pursuant to ERISA. The Board acknowledges that care needs to be exercised in the presentation of financial accounting information to mitigate any confusion that might result from the presence of other information about the plan. If other information that is made available to users of

plan financial statements is accompanied by appropriate disclosure of its nature and purpose, possible confusion on the part of certain users may be avoided.

137. The view expressed in paragraph 132 apparently reflects a concern that inclusion of benefit information will involve auditors in actuarial matters because of their examination of the plan's financial statements in accordance with generally accepted auditing standards. This Statement does not mandate auditor involvement in financial statements; matters relating to the attest function are not within the scope of the Board's authority. The Board recognizes, however, that both the auditing and actuarial professions have responsibilities under the Act and that their respective professional bodies have promulgated standards or recommendations regarding the conduct of their members. It is not within the Board's authority to attempt to resolve any issues relating to the relationship between those professions. The Board is aware of ongoing efforts by the interested parties to resolve certain such issues and is hopeful that those efforts will result in prompt solutions that are acceptable to all involved. The Board does not agree, however, that the proper manner of resolution is to omit from the financial statements information that is essential to users of those statements. Further, the Board does not believe that considerations relating to whether or by whom certain information should be audited are, of themselves, relevant to a determination of whether the information should be presented in financial statements. For example, Section 2520.103-8 of Department of Labor regulations provides that the auditor's examination need not include any statement or information regarding plan assets held by a bank or insurance carrier if the bank or insurance company is regulated, supervised, and subject to periodic examination by a state or federal agency and the bank or insurance company certifies to the correctness of the statement or information. In the absence of such regulations, it would be equally inappropriate to exclude information regarding those assets from plan financial statements to avoid attestation by an auditor.

Alternatives Considered for Determining Benefit Information

138. Having concluded that benefit information should be in the financial statements, the Board considered how that information should be determined. Respondents' recommendations can be broadly categorized as follows:

a. Some focused on benefit information that would represent those benefits to which employees would be entitled if they terminated their employment at the benefit information date. For present employees, the benefit information would include only that portion of the benefits accumulated under the plan's benefit accrual provision that is vested at that date.
b. Some focused on benefit information that would represent those benefits that are at risk at the benefit information date. The benefit information would include the benefits accumulated by present employees under the plan's benefit accrual provision, without adjustment for future withdrawal. This method is independent of the plan's vesting provision.
c. Some focused on benefit information that would represent the benefits attributable to employees' service to the benefit information date. Respondents' recommendations for determining those benefits can be broadly categorized as follows:
    i. Some would include the benefits of present employees determined as in (a) above (vested benefits) plus that portion of present employees' accumulated plan benefits, determined in accordance with the benefit accrual provision, that is expected to become vested. Some proponents of this approach believe that the benefit information should differ from that determined in (b) above only in that future withdrawal should be recognized. Others would include some portion of certain types of benefits (for example, death and disability benefits) for which the plan does not clearly specify the amount attributable to each year of service.
    ii. Others would measure the benefits as some pro rata portion of the expected benefits to be received by present employees who retire or terminate in a vested status after the benefit information date. That pro rata portion would relate in some manner the service rendered to date with total service expected to be rendered.
d. Some focused on the amount that is assigned by the **actuarial cost method** to periods before the benefit information date.

139. Categories (a)-(c) above refer to present employees; there is little, if any, difference of opinion about how to determine the accumulated plan benefits of employees who have retired or terminated before reaching retirement age. Accordingly, paragraphs 140-168 primarily focus on determining the accumulated plan benefits of present employees. Those paragraphs elaborate on the preceding alternatives. They do not focus on other measurement factors, such as various assumptions (other

than withdrawal)[33] used in determining the benefit information. Paragraphs 169-204 address that aspect of the measurement process.

Vested Benefits

140. Some respondents emphasized that only **vested benefit information** should be presented. Nonvested benefits are forfeitable if certain conditions (primarily age and length of service) are not met, whereas vested benefits are not. Thus, some believe that only vested benefit information could be properly presented as a plan liability. Some respondents to the initial Exposure Draft (which required presentation of information about both vested and nonvested benefits) believe that ERISA supports their view. Under ERISA the legal obligation of the plan upon plan termination cannot exceed vested benefits except to the extent that plan assets are available to provide benefits in excess of vested benefits.

141. Certain respondents to the Exposure Drafts expressed the view that participants would be confused and unduly alarmed by the fluctuations in the security for nonvested benefits that, in their view, are a likely result of the combination of the subordinate status of nonvested benefits and the presentation of plan investments at fair value. However, others argued that employees do not expect any security until they have met the plan's vesting requirements. It was also suggested that presenting **nonvested benefit information** might affect management decisions about plan funding. Respondents who expressed the foregoing views believed that presenting only vested benefit information would avoid such perceived effects and is therefore preferable.

Benefits at Risk

142. Some respondents recommended that the benefit information represent potential claims of employees in the event of plan termination. A defined benefit pension plan normally contains a formula or schedule that specifies the rate at which employees accumulate their benefits. That benefit accrual provision is necessary primarily to determine the benefits attributable to service rendered by an employee who separates from service before retirement. In the view of some, that provision best defines the benefits that are at risk at any time. Because nonvested benefits become vested to the extent of available assets upon plan termination, they are considered equally at risk as vested benefits and therefore could be included in the benefit information under this approach. Because future service is not a factor in measuring benefits at risk, those who support this approach would not adjust the benefit information for future withdrawal. Some view this approach as providing benefit information that is most useful to participants because of its comparability with the computational basis used to prepare the individual statements of accrued benefits that participants in an ERISA plan are entitled to receive. In their view, reflecting future withdrawal would decrease the usefulness of the resulting benefit information. Supporters of this approach do not consider it inconsistent with the concept of an ongoing plan. Providing the specified benefit information is not the same as providing a measure of the benefits that would be paid assuming plan termination. Providing the latter measure would be consistent with the assumption that the plan had, in fact, terminated.

Benefits Attributable to Service Already Rendered

143. Some respondents recommended that the benefit information represent the benefits to which employees are entitled as a result of their service to the benefit information date. For purposes of this Statement, the two basic approaches to determining those benefits are referred to as (a) vested benefits and those accumulated plan benefits expected to become vested and (b) pro rata allocation of projected benefits.

Vested benefits and those expected to become vested

144. Some respondents recommended that the benefit information include benefits presently vested plus that portion of employees' accumulated plan benefits at the benefit information date that is expected to become vested. Those holding this view object to presenting only vested benefit information because that information fails to recognize the benefits that may be reasonably expected to be paid for services already rendered. Adjusting the benefit information for future withdrawal is inherent in the notion of benefits expected to become vested. Thus, this approach differs in that respect from a benefits-at-risk approach. Some holding this view would include in the benefit information a portion of certain nonvested benefits for which the plan does not clearly specify the amount attributable to each year of service, for example, death and disability benefits. The benefits-at-risk approach, on the other hand, would include such benefits only to the extent that employees presently have vested rights to them.

[33]All approaches to determining benefit information discussed in this Statement utilize various assumptions to estimate the probability that benefits will be paid. The approaches differ somewhat with respect to which assumptions are recognized. For convenience, the discussion in paragraphs 140-168 refers to certain assumptions only when necessary to distinguish between approaches. Assumptions relating to the probability of payment of benefits are discussed in more detail in paragraphs 180-186.

Pro rata allocation of projected benefits

145. Some respondents recommended that the benefit information be determined on the basis of the relationship between the total benefits expected to be ultimately paid to present employees and the service rendered in exchange for those benefits. Inherent in this view is the projection of future benefits determined in accordance with employees' projected future pay, service, or both. The relationship between projected benefits and service rendered can be determined by various methods. For purposes of this Statement, those methods are referred to as:

a. The benefit-compensation-correlation method
b. The cost-compensation-correlation method
c. The benefit-years of service-correlation method
d. The cost-years of service-correlation method.

Benefit-compensation-correlation method

146. One method of relating benefits to service is to relate the *benefits* (rather than the cost of such benefits) to compensation. Under that method, the percentage of (a) the actuarial present value at retirement date (or date of termination, if earlier) of the total estimated benefits to (b) the total estimated compensation to retirement (or termination, if earlier) is first determined for each employee.[34] That percentage is then applied to the employee's compensation each year to determine the *benefits* attributable to that year's service. The benefits so determined are then discounted to reflect the time value of money. The benefit information would be the aggregate of those discounted benefits attributable to all present employees' years of service to the benefit information date, increased for interest for the period from the year of service to the benefit information date.

Cost-compensation-correlation method

147. Under the method in which the *cost* of providing benefits (rather than the benefits) is correlated with compensation, a determination is made for each employee[35] of the percentage relationship of (a) the actuarial present value at retirement date (or date of termination, if earlier) of the total estimated benefits to (b) the total estimated compensation to retirement (or termination, if earlier) adjusted to reflect an interest factor from the period that service is rendered to that date. The resulting percentage is then applied to each year's compensation to allocate the employer's *cost* of providing benefits attributable, on the basis of compensation, to that year's service. This method results in each year's cost allocation remaining a constant percentage of each year's compensation. (That is not the case under the benefit-compensation-correlation method.) The benefit information would be the aggregate cost of benefits attributable to all present employees' years of service to the benefit information date, increased for interest for the period from the year of service to the benefit information date.

Years of service-correlation methods

148. The years of service-correlation methods are basically the same as the compensation-correlation methods described in paragraphs 146 and 147 except for the basis of allocation. Similar to the benefit-compensation-correlation method, the benefit-years of service-correlation method allocates a constant percentage of total estimated benefits to each year of service and discounts that amount to reflect the time value of money. Likewise, the cost-years of service-correlation method allocates to each year of service a constant dollar cost for providing the estimated total benefits.

Actuarial Cost Methods

149. Actuarial cost methods are primarily used to determine annual pension cost estimates; those cost estimates may be used for determining the amount and incidence of employer contributions, establishing tax deductibility of the amounts funded, determining pension expense for recognition in the employer's financial statements, determining the minimum funding required by the Act, and possibly other purposes. The view discussed here is not whether the use of actuarial cost methods is appropriate for financial reporting by the employer but whether actuarial cost methods, in general, produce measures that are acceptable for determining the benefit information to be presented in plan financial statements.

150. Certain respondents recommended that determination of any benefit information be left to the discretion of the actuary and that all actuarial cost methods acceptable under the Act be acceptable for plan financial statement purposes. In their view, the actuary is best qualified by training to select the appropriate measure. Certain respondents to the Exposure Drafts (which rejected actuarial cost methods for determining the benefit information) objected to the cost of requiring a method for determining benefit information that might differ from the actuarial cost method. In their view, requiring plans to incur such costs for financial reporting purposes alone would be inappropriate. It was also sug-

[34]In practice, the approach probably would be applied to all employees as a group, or to particular groups of employees, rather than on an individual employee basis.

[35]See footnote 34.

gested that the apparent comparability among plans achieved by the initial Exposure Draft's requirement for use of both a uniform basic method and uniform assumptions would be illusory because differences in plan provisions, characteristics of participants, and investment strategies would not be reflected. Other respondents thought use of the actuarial cost method used for funding purposes was appropriate because the resulting benefit information would be determined in the same way as employer contributions.

Conclusions on Determining Benefit Information

151. The Board concluded that the benefit information should include vested benefits plus employees' nonvested benefits expected to become vested as determined by the plan's benefit accrual provision using primarily employees' history of pay and service to the benefit information date. Projected service should be a factor only in determining employees' expected eligibility for particular benefits such as those listed in paragraph 18(b). The actuarial present value of those benefits should then be determined using appropriate actuarial assumptions to reflect the time value of money (through discounts for interest) and the probability of payment (by means of decrements such as for death, disability, withdrawal, or retirement) between the benefit information date and the expected date of payment.

152. The benefit information required by the initial Exposure Draft was based entirely on employees' history of pay and service and other appropriate factors at the benefit information date. Therefore, benefits such as those listed in paragraph 18(b) were not included, except to the extent that employees' eligibility for them at the benefit information date was not dependent on future service. That method of determining benefit information was primarily based on the benefits-at-risk approach. A number of respondents expressed the view that that approach was not as useful in an assessment of benefit security on an ongoing plan basis as would be an approach that included estimated amounts for benefits such as those listed in paragraph 18(b) for all employees expected to receive such benefits, to the extent those benefits related to service already rendered. For reasons discussed in the following paragraphs, the Board agreed.

153. The Board believes that the benefit information should relate to the benefits reasonably expected to be paid in exchange for employees' service to the benefit information date. In the Board's view, vested benefits and nonvested benefits expected to become vested, determined primarily in accordance with the benefit accrual provision and employees' history of pay and service to the benefit information date, best represent the benefits attributable to service already rendered. For example, if a plan provides a benefit of 2 percent of final 5-year average salary per year of service, the accumulated pension benefit for an employee with 10 years of service would be 10 times 2 percent of the employee's average salary for the 5 years immediately preceding the benefit information date.

154. In the Board's view, future service should be considered only in determining employees' expected eligibility for certain benefits. The need to consider projected service for that purpose can be illustrated by assuming an employee[36] becomes eligible for a disability benefit in the 15th year of service pursuant to a plan that provides disability benefits when an active employee with 10 or more years of service becomes totally and permanently disabled. If projected disability in a future year of service is not considered during the first 14 years of service in determining that employee's expected eligibility for the disability benefit, the entire incremental actuarial present value of that benefit (that is, the excess, if any, over the actuarial present value of the normal retirement benefit previously recognized) is recognized in the 15th year of service, as if it were all attributable to that year of service. In the Board's view, the disability benefit should be related to the service rendered during the employee's entire career. A portion of the disability benefit should thus be attributed to each of the employee's 15 years of service. Similar illustrations could be developed for other types of benefits. For example, future service should be considered for determining an employee's expected eligibility for an early retirement benefit in order to appropriately relate that benefit to each year of service rendered; not doing so would result in attributing the entire incremental actuarial present value of the early retirement benefit to years after the employee initially becomes eligible for an early retirement benefit.

155. In the Board's view, the approach discussed in paragraphs 153 and 154 results in a measure of accumulated plan benefits that is most useful in assessing the plan's present and future ability to pay, when due, the benefits to which employees will ultimately be entitled as a result of their service to the benefit information date. Therefore, the approach is consis-

[36]For purposes of illustration, the discussion is in terms of an individual employee. In practice, such benefits would be recognized on an aggregate rather than individual basis because it is usually not possible to predict whether and when an individual employee will become disabled (or elect early retirement, die in active service, etc.). It is, however, possible to estimate the disability (or early retirement, death, etc.) benefits expected to become payable for a group of employees through the application of appropriate probability factors. The basic principle, however, is the same whether the computations are performed on an aggregate or an individual basis.

tent with the primary objective of plan financial statements.

156. For certain types of benefits, the amount attributable to each year of service cannot be directly determined from the plan's provisions. The manner in which such benefits should be considered to accumulate depends on whether the benefit is includable in vested benefits. To illustrate, assume a plan provides a supplemental early retirement benefit of $200 per month upon early retirement at age 55 with at least 25 years of service, payable from the date of early retirement until age 62 (the eligibility age for collecting Social Security benefits). If that benefit becomes a vested benefit after 25 years of service, it should be considered to accumulate in proportion to the ratio of the number of years of service completed to the benefit information date to the projected number of years of service that will have been completed when the benefit first becomes fully vested. Therefore, 1/25 of the $200 benefit (that is, $8) is attributed to each year of service (assuming the employee is expected to render at least 25 years of service).[37] In the case of a benefit that does not become a vested benefit (for example, a $5,000 death benefit that is payable only if death occurs during active service), the benefit should be considered to accumulate in proportion to the ratio of the number of years of service completed at the benefit information date to the number of years of service completed at the estimated time of separation from covered employment. For example, if the foregoing $5,000 death benefit is expected to be paid after the 20th year of service (that is, the employee is expected to die at the end of the 20th year of service), 1/20 of the benefit should be attributed to each year of service. Thus, after 5 years of service, the employee's accumulated death benefit is $1,250.[38]

157. Because the Board considered vested benefit information to be too restrictive of the benefits reasonably expected to be paid as a result of service rendered to the benefit information date, it rejected the views expressed in paragraphs 140 and 141. As further discussed in subsequent paragraphs regarding the location of benefit information, the Board concluded that it need not decide whether any part or all of the benefit information is a plan liability. Therefore, views regarding the liability nature of vested benefit information were not considered relevant.

158. The Board also did not find persuasive the views regarding perceived effects of presenting nonvested benefit information. If participants are properly educated in the use of financial statements (paragraph 50), the Board believes that they should not be confused or unduly alarmed if the portion of nonvested benefits that is covered by plan assets changes between periods. Further, information about such fluctuations, if they occur, is pertinent to an assessment of the plan's ability to pay benefits. (The Board also notes that the view that participants will be alarmed by information about such fluctuations in security for nonvested benefits and the view that participants do not expect security for nonvested benefits appear somewhat contradictory.) Arguments similar to the views regarding perceived effects on funding decisions were discussed in paragraph 106. As stated in that paragraph, the Board does not believe that accounting standards should be designed to encourage or discourage an action by management.

159. The initial Exposure Draft's approach to determining benefit information was primarily a benefits-at-risk approach. For reasons discussed in preceding paragraphs, the Board concluded that the method required by this Statement would result in more useful benefit information for assessing benefit security on an ongoing plan basis. Further, the revised approach is believed to be consistent both with the views of the Department of Labor as reflected in the revised Schedule B, "Actuarial Information," of Form 5500 (footnote 41) and with the views of the American Academy of Actuaries as reflected in its Interpretation 2 (paragraph 80). That Interpretation was developed during the previously mentioned cooperative effort between the Board and the Academy. Paragraphs 17-20 essentially reiterate the recommendations contained in Interpretation 2 and also provide certain additional guidance to ensure that the resulting benefit information is relevant for financial reporting purposes.

160. The Board also rejected the pro rata allocation methods discussed in paragraphs 145-148. In the Board's view, benefit information intended to be useful in assessing the plan's ability to pay benefits attributable to service already rendered should be based primarily on pay already earned and service already rendered. One significant difference between the method adopted by the Board and the pro rata allocation methods relates to whether future salary increases are considered in measuring benefits attributable to service already rendered. Because that difference relates to the assumptions to be considered in determining the benefit information, it is addressed in subsequent paragraphs that

[37]Footnote 36 discusses the estimation of benefits for a group of employees through application of appropriate probability factors. In determining the benefit information, such probability factors are used to estimate whether an employee will render at least 25 years of service, and whether and when that employee will elect early retirement.

[38]See footnotes 36 and 37.

focus on that aspect of the measurement process.

161. The Board recognizes that financial accounting measures are rarely exact and that the uncertainty that surrounds economic activities often requires use of approximations or predictions of various amounts and judgment about their inclusion and disclosure in financial statements. The foregoing is particularly true in determining benefit information. However, because the method it adopted does not necessitate subjective assumptions about future salary increases, the Board believes that method results in benefit information that is more objective and verifiable than the benefit information that results from the pro rata allocation methods.

162. It was also apparent from the responses of certain supporters of the pro rata allocation methods that their views were significantly affected by the view that there should be symmetry in the accounting by the employer(s) and the plan regarding the measure of *earned* benefits.

163. The Board considered and rejected the view that symmetrical reporting should be a necessary factor in selecting the method for determining benefit information for purposes of plan reporting. The information that is useful in assessing the plan's ability to pay benefits may differ from the information that would best serve the objectives of accounting by employers for pensions. The Board will consider those objectives in another project.[39] Further, those who support symmetrical reporting are presumably influenced by the view that if benefit information is presented as a liability in the financial statements of both the employer(s) and the plan, the liability should be determined in the same manner by both parties. Because the Board concluded that the benefit information need not be presented as a plan liability (paragraph 231), the issue of symmetry may not be pertinent even though some amount may appear as a liability in financial statements of the employer(s).

164. The Board rejected the two cost-correlation methods for an additional reason. Those methods focus solely on the principle of income statement cost-allocation rather than on attributing *benefits* to service rendered. Therefore, the Board does not believe that the measures that are by-products of those methods provide information useful in achieving the primary objective of plan financial statements.

165. For similar reasons, the Board rejected use of actuarial cost methods. APB Opinion No. 8, *Accounting for the Cost of Pension Plans,* recognizes several actuarial cost methods as acceptable for determining employers' costs. Likewise, a number of actuarial cost methods are recognized by ERISA as acceptable for funding purposes. Each of those methods is designed to allocate the expected ultimate cost of the plan to particular time periods. (The pro rata allocation methods discussed in preceding paragraphs are, in effect, applications of allocation approaches employed under certain actuarial cost methods.) The portion allocated to periods before a valuation date, formerly identified as *prior service costs,* the *accrued liability,* or *prior service liability,* but now described as the **supplemental actuarial value,**[40] will vary widely from method to method. Although that variation may be appropriate for funding purposes, the Board considers it inappropriate for plan financial reporting. The Board has previously considered the question of accounting alternatives and has concluded that using different accounting methods for the same types of facts and circumstances impairs the comparability of financial statements and thus significantly detracts from their usefulness. Use of actuarial cost methods for determining the benefit information could result in two plans with essentially the same benefit provisions, participant populations, etc., reporting widely differing benefit information because different actuarial cost methods were used. Further, the Board does not believe that differences in factors such as benefit provisions, participant populations, and investment policies constitute different facts and circumstances that justify use of a different basic method for determining the benefit information. Differences in such factors are appropriately accommodated by the method adopted by the Board. For example, that method requires that employees' accumulated plan benefits be determined in accordance with the individual plan's benefit provisions. Differences in factors such as rates of disability, withdrawal, or mortality and differences in investment policies are reflected in the selection of assumptions that reflect the best estimate of the plan's expected experience with respect to those factors.

166. The Board also rejected the view that using the actuarial cost method used for determining employer contributions would result in an appropriate comparison of net asset and benefit information. Determination of benefit information in accordance with the actuarial cost method used for funding purposes might produce a measure that would be useful in assessing the progress of the funding program relative to the actuarial cost method. However, because most actuarial cost methods are not designed to attribute benefits to

[39]See footnote 23.

[40]Interprofessional Pension Actuarial Advisory Group, *Pension Terminology Final Report,* January 1978, p. 17.

service rendered, such an approach would not, in most cases, produce benefit information that would be useful in achieving the primary objective of plan financial statements. Further, that view taken to its logical conclusion would mean that no benefit information would be presented by an unfunded plan.

167. The Board's conclusions with respect to the appropriate method of determining the benefit information are based solely on plan accounting considerations. It recognizes that other methods, including actuarial cost methods and specifically the cost-correlation methods discussed above, are widely used by actuaries in establishing pension funding programs; the Board is not concerned with, nor does it question, their appropriateness for that purpose.

168. In rejecting the use of actuarial cost methods, the Board is *not* rejecting the use of actuarial expertise in determining the benefit information. On the contrary, the Board recognizes that it is critical to the measurement process.

Assumptions Used in Determining Benefit Information

169. The following paragraphs discuss the Board's conclusions regarding the more significant assumptions that may be used in determining the actuarial present value of accumulated plan benefits.

Future Salary Increases

170. As previously indicated, some believe that an assumption regarding present employees' future salary increases should be considered in measuring benefits attributable to service already rendered (at least when benefits are stated in terms of future salary as, for example, in a final-pay plan).[41] In rejecting that view, some Board members gave greater weight to some factors than to others.

171. Certain Board members believe that benefits attributable to future salary increases should not be considered "earned" until the related compensation is earned. That view holds that the total increase in an employee's accumulated plan benefit attributable to compensation earned in a given year of service is properly considered to have been earned in that year, not in an earlier year.

172. Certain Board members also believe that future salary increases are not unlike certain other future price changes, the accounting effects of which are recognized in the periods in which the price changes occur. Future salary increases may be related to employees' future productivity levels, as well as to changes in wage levels (either as a result of general price changes or changes in the factors of supply and demand). This view considers it inappropriate to reflect salary increases due to either changing levels of productivity or changes in the exchange prices for constant levels of productivity until the economic conditions giving rise to those changes are also present. However, this view distinguishes those prices to be paid in exchange for future service and future price increases that will affect the exchange prices for past service. Thus, this view does not consider it inconsistent to reflect automatic cost-of-living adjustments (which affect the price paid for past service) and not reflect future salary increases (which are prices paid for future service). (The Board's conclusions regarding automatic cost-of-living adjustments are discussed in paragraphs 176-178.)

173. The American Academy of Actuaries' position in its Interpretation 2 was an additional factor that influenced certain Board members' conclusions. For both conceptual and practical reasons, the Academy opposes considering future salary increases. Because of the actuary's important role in developing the benefit information, those Board members gave particular weight to the Academy's views. As a result of not considering future salary increases, the Board's and the Academy's views on the basic method for determining employees' accumulated plan benefits appear to be substantially the same. Therefore, those Board members believe that not considering future salary increases will not only result in benefit information that is meaningful for an assessment of benefit security but will also enhance the necessary ongoing cooperative relationship among those who have a responsibility regarding the development or dissemination of plan financial information.

174. To a lesser degree, some Board members are concerned about certain implementation problems that might arise were it necessary to consider both past and future salary in determining the benefits attributable to service already rendered. Such potential problems include the availability of historical salary information needed to apply a compensation-allocation basis and the possible need to develop detailed guidelines for applying that allocation basis for various types of benefit formulas and fact situations.

[41] On September 26, 1978, the Department of Labor proposed such an approach for determining the benefit information to be reported by ERISA plans on the revised Schedule B ("Actuarial Information") of Form 5500. The Board testified in support of the method required by this Statement at hearings concerning the Schedule B proposals held by the Department on November 20, 1978; in that testimony the Board expressed its views regarding future salary increases. The Board is pleased that the revised Schedule B subsequently issued by the Department requires a method that is believed to be consistent with that required by this Statement.

175. Certain respondents to the Exposure Drafts linked the propriety of considering future salary increases with funding considerations. For example, the view was expressed that not considering future salary increases for a public plan would be inconsistent with assumptions used for funding purposes and might therefore influence the decisions of those responsible for allocating public funds to the plan. As previously stated, the Board's conclusions are based solely on plan accounting considerations. The benefit information presented in plan financial statements is intended to be useful in assessing benefit security. Other measurement methods may be more useful for determining periodic funding requirements. Further, as previously discussed, the Board does not consider it appropriate to establish accounting and reporting standards based on the perceived effects on management decisions. Regarding future salary increases, certain Board members consider it appropriate to note that the concept of long-term funding requirements should not be confused with the concept of benefits accumulated by employees. The former may require projections based on all relevant future factors, including future salary increases. The latter, however, carries with it a notion of "what has occurred to date" to determine the benefits attributable to service rendered to date.

Automatic Cost-of-Living Adjustments

176. Unlike future salary increases, automatic benefit increases specified by the plan, such as automatic cost-of-living adjustments, may be appropriately considered a part of the benefits exchanged for employee service already rendered. The propriety of that view can be illustrated with an example of a plan that provides that a retiree's monthly benefit will be increased on each January 1 by the percentage increase reflected in the change in the Consumer Price Index from the preceding January 1, up to a maximum increase of three percent in a single year. Recognizing amounts payable to a retiree pursuant to that plan provision only as benefits are increased would result in attributing the effect of the cost-of-living adjustment to periods after the employee's retirement, that is, *after* all service had been rendered. The Board considers that result inappropriate. The effects of automatic cost-of-living adjustments should be attributed in an appropriate manner to each year during which an employee renders service.

177. The initial Exposure Draft proscribed recognizing automatic cost-of-living adjustments in determining the benefit information. Some respondents expressed the view that exclusion of such amounts was inappropriate for purposes of providing information useful in assessing benefit security on an ongoing plan basis. As indicated in the preceding paragraph, the Board agreed.

178. This Statement requires that assumed rates of inflation used in measuring benefits attributable to automatic cost-of-living adjustments be consistent with those inherent in assumed rates of return (that is, interest rates). (Paragraphs 187-197 address the Board's conclusion regarding assumed rates of return.) Interest rates are generally perceived as comprising several factors, including a factor to compensate the lender for expected inflation during the life of the loan. The assumed rates of return required by this Statement relate to the periods for which payment of benefits is deferred and therefore encompass the periods on which automatic cost-of-living adjustments are based. Thus, the inflation assumptions for such periods used to reflect automatic cost-of-living adjustments should be consistent with the inflation assumptions inherent in the assumed rates of return for those periods. If an automatic cost-of-living adjustment is subject to a maximum annual percentage increase (sometimes referred to as a "cap"), the assumed rate of benefit increase may differ from the assumed rate of inflation. For example, in the illustration discussed in paragraph 176, which has a three percent "cap," the assumed annual rate of benefit increase would not exceed three percent regardless of the assumed rate of inflation.

Social Security Payments

179. Certain plans integrate pension benefits with payments provided under the federal Social Security program. That integration may take a variety of forms. Whatever the form, certain provisions of the Social Security law are used in determining the benefit information. Therefore, an issue arises regarding whether the benefit information should reflect (a) the Social Security provisions in effect at the benefit information date, (b) the provisions of the present Social Security law scheduled to be in effect at employees' assumed dates of retirement or other termination, or (c) the provisions of possible amendments to the Social Security law in effect at employees' assumed dates of retirement or other termination. This Statement requires that Social Security provisions in effect at the benefit information date be used ((a) above). Because both levels of Social Security payments and taxable wage bases are related to employees' salary, the Board concluded that use of presently effective provisions of the Social Security law is consistent with use of historical salary information.

Certain Assumptions Relating to the Probability and Timing of Benefit Payments

180. Among the more significant assumptions relating to whether and when benefits will initially become payable and for how long they will be paid are (a) pre- and post-retirement mortality, (b) with-

drawal, (c) disability, and (d) ages at which employees will retire.

Mortality

181. Pension benefits are not paid unless employees live to retirement, and they cease upon death unless there is a co-annuitant, as in the case of a joint and survivor option. Therefore, accumulated plan benefits should be adjusted to reflect participants' longevity. If a plan provides death benefits, those benefits should also be reflected in the benefit information.

182. The initial Exposure Draft required that certain plans use the mortality and interest rates prescribed by the PBGC to value benefits upon plan termination. Because most respondents' comments focused on PBGC interest rates rather than mortality rates, their use is discussed in that context (paragraphs 188 and 189).

Withdrawal

183. For reasons other than death or disability (which are addressed in paragraphs 181 and 185, respectively), employees may cease rendering service. If they do so before their pension benefits become fully vested, some or all of those benefits (depending on the plan's vesting provision) are forfeited. For multiemployer plans, withdrawal includes termination of service resulting from withdrawal of a participating employer from the plan. For reasons discussed in paragraph 142, the initial Exposure Draft proscribed adjusting the benefit information for those benefits that may be so forfeited in the future.

184. Although not necessarily disagreeing on a conceptual basis with the views stated in that Exposure Draft about the relationship between future withdrawal and benefits at risk, certain respondents nevertheless felt that nonrecognition of future withdrawal overstated the benefits reasonably expected to become payable. The Board agreed. It also believes that consideration of future withdrawal is consistent with consideration of future service in determining employees' expected eligibility for increased benefits (paragraph 154).

Disability

185. Certain plans provide disability benefits. Because it primarily focused on a benefits-at-risk approach, the initial Exposure Draft required that the benefit information exclude those benefits expected to become payable if an employee became disabled while in service. Some respondents thought excluding such benefits understated the benefits reasonably expected to become payable as a result of service already rendered. As previously indicated, the Board agreed.

Early retirement

186. Certain plans provide that an employee may retire early, subject to the attainment of a specified age, typically 55. Additional conditions may also be imposed. As previously discussed, the Board concluded that the benefit information should reflect the estimated early retirement benefits to be paid to those employees expected to become eligible for and to elect early retirement. The initial Exposure Draft's requirements and respondents' comments regarding early retirement benefits were similar to those regarding disability benefits. In addition, a few respondents asked whether rates of early retirement should be assumed based on an ongoing or a terminating plan. This Statement requires that all assumptions be consistent with an ongoing plan.

Rates of Return

187. To be of use in assessing benefit security, the net asset and benefit information must be determined on a comparable basis. Therefore, accumulated plan benefits must be discounted to reflect the time value of money in order for the benefit information to be on a basis comparable to the net asset information, which is stated in terms of present dollars. Few, if any, respondents who advocated presenting benefit information in the financial statements disagreed. To increase the comparability of the net asset and benefit information, this Statement requires that assumed rates of return used to discount the accumulated plan benefits reflect the expected rates of return on plan investments applicable to the periods for which payment of benefits is deferred.

188. A principal factor behind the initial Exposure Draft's requirement that certain plans use PBGC interest (and mortality) rates to determine the benefit information was that the initial interest rates used by the PBGC were derived from annuity price data obtained from the private insurance industry. PBGC rates therefore represented currently available interest rates, and their use resulted in benefit information that was comparable with the net asset information. Certain respondents objected to the use of PBGC rates. They viewed those rates as relating to a "guaranty" basis rather than a "best estimate" basis and thus unduly conservative for an ongoing plan. The view was also expressed that requiring the use of the same interest and mortality rates by a wide divergency of plans was inappropriate. Questions also were raised about the feasibility of mandatory use of PBGC rates; those questions primarily related to the timeliness of their availability.

189. Because of (a) inherent differences among plans as to investment policies and participants' longevity and (b) questions about the appropriateness of using PBGC rates (that is, the view that their use implies plan termination), the Board concluded that requiring use of assumptions that reflect the plan's expected experience would result in more appropriate benefit information than would requiring the use of PBGC interest and mortality rates.

190. The determination of assumed rates of return for most plans is, to a significant degree, a matter of judgment. Thus, various factors should be considered in estimating rates of return to be used in determining the actuarial present value of accumulated plan benefits. Among them are (a) rates of return expected from investments currently held or available in the marketplace, (b) rates of return expected from the reinvestment of actual returns from those investments, and (c) the investment policy of the plan, including the diversity of investments currently held and expected to be held in the future.

191. Accordingly, accumulated plan benefits will generally not be discounted solely at rates of return expected on existing investments, and changes in assumed rates of return will probably not equal the change during the reporting period in either short-term or long-term interest rates.[42] However, to the extent that assumed rates of return are affected by the rates of return expected from existing investments, this Statement requires that those expected rates be based on the values presented for those investments in the plan's financial statements. Further, the assumed rates of return at which accumulated plan benefits are discounted should be reconsidered in light of changes in the fair values of investments between one period and another.

192. Some believe that year-to-year changes in reported benefit information as a result of changes in assumed rates of return should be avoided to the maximum extent possible. In their view, some averaging technique should be used to smooth out potential year-to-year changes so that assumed rates of return are changed only when it is apparent that the long-term trend has changed. The Board recognizes that long-term rates of return must be considered in determining appropriate assumed rates of return. However, it rejects the view that apparent material changes in long-term rates should be ignored on an annual basis solely to avoid annually adjusting assumed rates of return. Over a period of years, plan financial statements may display a trend of assumed rates of return. However, the Board believes that an assessment of that trend should be based on information determined in a neutral manner rather than on information that is biased so as to produce a presumed trend.

193. Some who object to potential year-to-year changes in assumed rates of return are apparently influenced by funding considerations. An approach to selecting assumed rates of return designed to avoid changing the size of annual contributions may be appropriate for funding purposes. However, the Board does not believe that such a smoothing approach is appropriate for purposes of determining the benefit information to be presented in plan financial statements. As discussed in paragraph 187, determining the benefit and net asset information on a consistent basis is necessary for an appropriate assessment of benefit security. Therefore, to employ a smoothing approach to determining assumed rates of return would require employing a similar approach (for example, certain actuarial asset valuation methods) to determining the values at which investments are presented in plan financial statements. As discussed in paragraph 111, the Board rejected such asset valuation methods for purposes of plan financial statements.

194. Certain respondents to the revised Exposure Draft expressed the view that if it was inappropriate to recognize future salary increases in determining the accumulated plan benefits under plans whose benefit formulas include employees' compensation (for example, final-pay plans), it was equally inappropriate to discount those benefits at rates of return that inherently reflect anticipated future inflation. Those respondents would prefer to recognize future salary increases (at least the inflation component thereof) in determining employees' accumulated plan benefits. However, as a less preferable alternative, they suggested excluding any inflation component from the rates of return used to discount benefits.

195. As acknowledged by its supporters, excluding the inflation component from the assumed rates of return is essentially an attempt to compensate for the exclusion of future salary increases in determining accumulated plan benefits. For the reasons discussed in paragraphs 170-175, the Board rejected considering future salary increases in determining accumulated plan benefits. The Board rejected the suggested approach because it attempts to nullify that decision.

196. In the Board's view, the appropriate method of determining accumulated plan benefits and the selection of assumed rates of return at which to discount those benefits are separate issues. The pur-

[42]A factor to consider in assessing the extent to which short-term and long-term interest rates should impact assumed rates of return is the degree to which the timing of cash inflows from related existing or potential investments matches the timing of payments of accumulated plan benefits.

pose of the former is to determine the benefits attributable under a plan's benefit formula to the service employees have rendered. The latter, however, is designed to present the net asset and benefit information on comparable bases and is independent of the plan's benefit formula. That is, the purpose of the discounting process is the same regardless of a plan's benefit formula, for example, whether it is a final-pay or flat-benefit plan. Given the purpose of the discounting process, the Board believes the appropriate relationship is between the measurement bases for plan investments and assumed rates of return, not between the method of determining accumulated plan benefits and assumed rates of return. Rates of return on plan investments are economic factors related to the plan's existing investments and investment policy, not to its benefit formula. Further, to be consistent, the suggested approach might make it necessary to attempt to exclude the effects of future inflation from all factors[43] used in determining the actuarial present value of accumulated plan benefits, and perhaps also from the values of plan investments. The Board believes that such potential modifications, if adopted, would result in financial information that is less useful in achieving the primary objective of plan financial statements.

197. The suggested approach of discounting benefits at assumed rates of return that exclude future inflation seems inappropriate for additional reasons. For example, future salary increases are a factor only in determining nonvested benefits. Therefore, to achieve the result desired by its supporters (that is, to compensate for the nonrecognition of future salary increases), it would seem necessary to modify the approach so that it would affect only the determination of the actuarial present value of nonvested benefits. Also, the period for which salary increases due to inflation might be a factor (that is, an employee's service period) is less than the period for which payment of benefits is deferred. Therefore, without certain modifications, the suggested approach would not result in the same total actuarial present value of accumulated plan benefits as that which would result from incorporating future salary increases into the measurement process. Modifications of the suggested approach that might be necessary for it to accomplish its intended purpose could be impractical to implement as well as difficult for users of plan financial statements to understand.

Administrative Expenses

198. Because administrative expenses are incurred when making benefit payments, those expenses should be considered in determining the benefit information. That is commonly done by reducing assumed rates of return by an appropriate factor. The initial Exposure Draft required use of that method. Certain respondents expressed the view that assigning anticipated administrative expenses to future periods and discounting them to the benefit information date should also be acceptable. Because the Board is not aware of any conceptual arguments supporting the preferability of either method and because the resulting benefit information should be the same, the Board concluded that both methods are acceptable. However, in similar circumstances, their use results in the disclosure (pursuant to paragraph 27(b)) of different rates of return. The Board therefore concluded that the adjustment of assumed rates of return should be disclosed if that method is used.

Explicit Approach

199. This Statement requires that each significant assumption used in determining the benefit information reflect the best estimate of the plan's future experience solely with respect to that assumption. That method of selecting assumptions is referred to as an *explicit approach*. An *implicit approach,* on the other hand, means that two or more assumptions do not individually represent the best estimate of the plan's future experience with respect to those assumptions. Rather, the aggregate effect of their combined use is presumed to be approximately the same as that of an explicit approach. The Board believes that an explicit approach results in more useful information regarding (a) components of the benefit information, (b) changes in the benefit information, and (c) the choice of significant assumptions used to determine the benefit information.

200. The following illustrates the preferability of an explicit approach as it relates to measuring components of the benefit information (that is, vested benefits of participants currently receiving payments, other vested benefits, and nonvested benefits). Under an implicit approach, it might be assumed that the net result of assuming no withdrawal before vesting and increasing assumed rates of return by a specified amount would approximate the same actuarial present value of total accumulated plan benefits as that which would result from using assumed rates of return and withdrawal rates determined by an explicit approach. Even if that were true, increasing assumed rates of return to compensate for withdrawal before vesting might sig-

[43]Factors that may be directly or indirectly affected by future inflation are discussed in "Recognition of Inflation in the Calculation of Actuarial Present Values under Pension Plans," American Academy of Actuaries, *Bylaws, Guide to Professional Conduct, Standards of Practice, February 1, 1978* (Chicago: American Academy of Actuaries), pp. 98-103.

nificantly misstate components of the benefit information. Withdrawal before vesting relates only to nonvested benefits. Therefore, discounting vested benefits at rates of return that have been adjusted to implicitly reflect that withdrawal understates that component of the benefit information and correspondingly overstates the nonvested benefit information.

201. The disadvantage of an implicit approach with respect to information regarding changes in the benefit information can be similarly illustrated. Assume that under an implicit approach, assumed rates of return are decreased to implicitly reflect the effects of a plan's provision for an automatic cost-of-living adjustment *(COLA)*. In that situation, the effect of a plan amendment relating to the automatic COLA, for example, an amendment to increase the "cap" on the COLA from three percent to four percent, might be obscured. If significant, the effect of such an amendment should, pursuant to the requirements of this Statement, be disclosed as the effect of a plan amendment. If an implicit approach is used, however, assumed rates of return would be adjusted to reflect the effect of that amendment and accordingly, some part or all of the effect might be presented as the effect of a change in an actuarial assumption rather than as the effect of a plan amendment (particularly if assumed rates of return are also changed for other reasons).

202. In addition to the foregoing possible disadvantages, an implicit approach might result in less meaningful disclosure of the significant assumptions used to determine the benefit information. For example, disclosure of the assumed rates of return resulting from the implicit approaches described in paragraphs 200 and 201 could mislead users of the financial statements regarding the plan's investment return expectations and could result in noncomparable reporting for two plans with the same investment return expectations. Users might also draw erroneous conclusions about the relationship between the plan's actual and assumed rates of return.

Insurance Company Premium Rates

203. Paragraph 21 provides that in selecting certain assumptions, an acceptable alternative to the requirements in paragraph 20 is to use those assumptions that are inherent in the estimated cost at the benefit information date to obtain a contract with an insurance company to provide participants with their accumulated plan benefits. Those other assumptions that are necessary but are not inherent in that estimated cost should be selected pursuant to the requirements in paragraph 20. For plans below a certain size, that alternative may be preferable to selection of certain assumptions (for example, mortality rates) appropriate for the participant group because the validity of actuarial assumptions is dependent on the law of large numbers. It has also been suggested that use of insurance company premium rates might reduce for some plans the cost of implementing this Statement. Because the alternative approach results in benefit information that is useful in assessing benefit security and because it also appears desirable on a practical basis, the Board concluded that it should be allowed.

204. The revised Exposure Draft requested those plans that used or intended to use the alternative approach to comment about the difficulty of obtaining information about the significant assumptions inherent in premium rates. The few respondents who commented expressed differing views regarding the difficulty of obtaining that information. It should be noted that paragraph 21 merely establishes an alternative; it does not require any plan to use that alternative. Because some plans apparently wish to use the alternative and expect to be able to obtain the necessary information, the insurance company premium rate approach has been retained.

Date of Required Benefit Information

205. The initial Exposure Draft required that the benefit information and net asset information be determined as of the same date. Thus, if the plan's annual financial statements were as of the end of the plan year, end-of-year benefit information was required. A number of respondents expressed the view that determination of end-of-year benefit information on a timely basis was not practical and would cause increased actuarial fees. They indicated that most actuarial valuations are performed during the year using data as of the beginning of the year. Changing that practice at this time might create significant timing problems in terms of scheduling the actuaries' workload and, in some cases, obtaining necessary end-of-year data.

206. Schedule B of Form 5500, as revised, requires that both net asset and benefit information be presented as of the beginning of the plan year. As originally proposed, the revised Schedule B would have required end-of-year benefit information. In response to that proposal, the Department received comments similar to those received by the Board in response to the initial Exposure Draft.

207. After considering the letters of comment on the initial Exposure Draft and certain of those received by the Department on the Schedule B proposal, the Board concluded that, at present, the perceived costs of requiring end-of-year benefit information may exceed the potential benefits of such information. Among the costs considered was

the cost to ERISA plans of financial reporting requirements that would differ from Schedule B requirements. Therefore, this Statement provides for the presentation of benefit information as of either the beginning or end of the year. However, the Board continues to believe that presenting both net asset and benefit information as of the same date is necessary for a presentation of the financial status of the plan. Therefore, if the benefit information date is the beginning of the year, only the net asset and benefit information presented as of that date may be considered to present the financial status of the plan. In that situation, the year-end net asset information required by paragraph 6(a) is an incomplete presentation of the plan's financial status.

208. The Board considered allowing the benefit information date to be any date within the year. However, presentation of benefit information as of an interim date would necessitate presentation of net asset information, at least the aggregate amount thereof, as of that interim date if the financial statements were to be useful in assessing the plan's ability to pay benefits. The Board believes that (a) requiring net asset information as of an interim date might cause certain difficulties (for example, determining contributions receivable at that date) and could cause plans to incur additional expense (for example, determining fair values of investments more often than annually) and (b) use of benefit information dates other than the beginning or end of the year is not a common practice. Accordingly, the Board decided not to permit interim benefit information dates.

209. The revised Exposure Draft encouraged respondents that used a benefit information date other than the beginning or end of the year to comment on whether disallowing interim benefit information dates would cause substantial problems. Follow-up discussions with most of those respondents who indicated that such action would cause them substantial problems revealed that the majority had interpreted the revised Exposure Draft as disallowing the roll-back to the beginning of the year of detailed employee data as of a date within the year. Paragraph 29 indicates that that method of approximating beginning-of-year benefit information is acceptable, provided the results obtained are substantially the same as those that would be determined using employee data as of the beginning of the year.

210. Although the Board decided not to require end-of-year benefit information, it considers presentation of such information to be a desirable goal. Plans are encouraged to develop procedures to enable them to use an end-of-year benefit information date. In that regard, paragraph 29 of this Statement provides, as did the Exposure Drafts, that detailed service-related data for individual employees as of a date preceding the end of the year may be projected to that latter date, provided the results obtained are substantially the same as those that would be determined using data as of the end of the year.

211. Because ERISA permits benefit valuations for funding purposes to be performed on a triennial rather than annual basis, certain respondents opposed requiring annual benefit valuations for financial reporting purposes. This Statement permits detailed service-related data for individual employees collected at an earlier date to be projected to the benefit information date. However, based on testimony by certain actuaries at hearings held by the Department of Labor regarding the proposed revision of Schedule B of Form 5500 (footnote 41), projecting beginning-of-year employee data to year-end would be difficult. Therefore, it is expected that only in unusual circumstances will projecting the data collected during a triennial valuation to a benefit information date in a subsequent year satisfy the criterion of providing results that are substantially the same as those that would be obtained using data as of that latter date. An example of such unusual circumstances might be a small plan with a stable participant population.

Minimum Required Display of Benefit Information

212. Unless all participants' benefits represent claims against plan assets of equal status and timing, any assessment of benefit security for an individual participant or group of similarly situated participants would be impaired to the extent it was based solely on the relationship between total net assets available for benefits and the actuarial present value of all accumulated plan benefits. (Paragraph 219 discusses required disclosure regarding the priority order of participants' claims to plan assets.) It seems reasonable to assume, however, that the benefits of participants who are already receiving payments *(benefits in pay status)* will generally be paid sooner than will the benefits of present or terminated employees. In determining their respective actuarial present values, fewer subjective assumptions are required for benefits in pay status than are required for benefits not in pay status. For example, assumptions regarding when benefit payments will begin are required for the latter but not for the former. Thus, the actuarial present value of benefits in pay status is a more objective measurement. Similar relationships exist between other vested benefits and nonvested benefits.

213. Some respondents view vested and nonvested benefits differently. As previously indicated, some believe that only vested benefits are a plan liability.

For an ERISA plan, nonvested benefits do not enter into the determination of an employer's contingent liability to the PBGC upon plan termination. That contingent liability relates to the value of PBGC-guaranteed benefits, and that value will probably differ from the vested benefit information presented in plan financial statements. Nevertheless, in the absence of more accurate information, some consider vested benefit information useful in assessing an employer's potential liability in the event of plan termination.

214. This Statement requires that the benefit information be segmented into at least the following categories:

a. Vested benefits of participants currently receiving payments
b. Other vested benefits
c. Nonvested benefits.

The Board concluded that such minimum segmentation would be useful in assessing a plan's near-term vs. long-range liquidity requirements. It might also provide some indication of the relative degree of objectivity or subjectivity inherent in determining the benefit information and would provide information needed by those who wish to make certain judgments or wish to compute certain financial ratios, for example, net asset information to vested benefit information. (Paragraph 221 discusses another ratio sometimes used.) Certain actuaries with whom the Board consulted indicated that the required segmentation could be provided at minimal cost.

215. The initial Exposure Draft required similar benefit segmentation. However, it also required further segmentation if that would provide information particularly useful in assessing the security for the benefits of a significant number of participants. That additional requirement was consistent with that Exposure Draft's focus on a benefits-at-risk approach and its requirement that certain plans use PBGC rates to determine the benefit information.

216. Only in the event of plan termination is the security for each participant's benefits actually determined. Should that event occur, the degree of risk that particular participants bear depends on their benefits' priority position in the allocation of plan assets. For most **noncontributory plans**, benefits in pay status generally have the highest priority, followed by other vested benefits and then nonvested benefits. (In contributory plans, benefits derived from participants' contributions normally have the highest priority.) Additional priority positions may be specified within those broad classifications. In an ERISA plan, for example, vested benefits that are insured by the PBGC generally have a higher priority than do vested benefits that are not so insured.

217. The initial Exposure Draft recognized that, particularly for ERISA plans, segmenting the benefit information by plan termination priority class could be a complex procedure, and its intent was to require that procedure only in certain limited circumstances. Because termination priorities govern the allocation of plan assets upon plan termination, those priorities are an essential element in assessing benefit security. Further, when an ERISA plan terminates, PBGC rates are used to value participants' benefits for purposes of determining plan sufficiency and allocating the assets of an insufficient plan. Thus, for ERISA plans, that Exposure Draft's requirement for the use of PBGC rates would (when the further segmentation provisions applied) generally have allocated to each applicable termination priority category the same actuarial present value that would have been allocated to it if the plan had been terminated at the benefit information date.

218. Many respondents objected to the benefit segmentation requirements of the initial Exposure Draft. Some objected to the basic segmentation. However, most objections focused on the possible additional segmentation requirement. Reasons for those objections included (a) the complexity and expense of making the termination priority allocations pursuant to Section 4044 of ERISA, (b) the view that termination priorities are irrelevant for an ongoing plan, and (c) concern that employers might become reluctant to improve benefits because of the resulting disclosure of the effect that plan amendments have in reallocating available assets among various categories of benefits in the event of plan termination.

219. Because (a) this Statement places more emphasis than did the initial Exposure Draft on providing information useful in assessing future rather than immediate security and (b) the requirement for use of PBGC rates was deleted, the Board concluded that the further segmentation requirement should not be retained. If the benefit information for an ERISA plan is determined using other than PBGC rates, the amount allocated to a given termination priority category may differ significantly from the amount that would be allocated to that category in the event of plan termination. However, because the primary objective adopted by the Board encompasses both the present and future ability of the plan to pay benefits (that is, both immediate and future security) the Board does not agree that disclosure of termination priorities is irrelevant for an ongoing plan. Therefore, this Statement requires that plan financial statements include a brief, general description of the priority order of participants' claims to the assets of the plan upon plan termination. The

Board concluded that such a description will serve to alert participants that a comparison of total net assets with the total actuarial present value of accumulated plan benefits (or with the three minimum required categories of benefit information) does not necessarily indicate which benefits would be covered by plan assets in the event of plan termination. However, the Board believes that unnecessary duplication of disclosures should be avoided. Therefore, if a description of termination priorities is otherwise published and made available to participants, the required description may be omitted if both a reference to such other source and a statement such as that illustrated in footnote 16 are made.

220. For reasons similar to those in paragraph 106, respondents' views regarding perceived effects on employers' decisions were rejected. Even if they had been accepted, the Board believes that at least as strong a case might be made that disclosure of termination priorities is appropriate because both employers and participants should understand the effect of plan amendments on benefit security.

221. Certain respondents to the initial Exposure Draft indicated that disclosure of present employees' accumulated contributions (including interest, if any) would provide useful information. Terminating employees are generally entitled to return of their accumulated contributions (sometimes with interest). Therefore, regardless of their overall view on the accounting nature of the benefit information, some view present employees' accumulated contributions as a plan liability. Others consider present employees' accumulated contributions to be a contingent liability that should be disclosed. It has been suggested that the relationship between net assets and the sum of accumulated employee contributions (including interest, if any) and the actuarial present value of benefits in pay status provides a useful measure for assessing minimum funding adequacy. That is, some believe that net assets available for benefits should, at a minimum, be adequate to provide all benefits in pay status and to refund present employees' accumulated contributions. The recommended disclosure would also provide some indication of relative amounts of plan assets that originated from employee contributions. Based on the foregoing, the Board concluded that disclosure of present employees' accumulated contributions (including interest, if any) should be required. Because the rate of interest credited on employees' contributions may vary among plans, disclosure of that interest rate is also required. Because plans generally maintain records of employee contributions, the Board believes that the benefits of the required disclosure can be obtained at minimal incremental cost.

222. If some or all employee contributions have been used to purchase contracts with insurance companies that are excluded from plan assets, comparison of the total amount of present employees' accumulated contributions with plan assets might be misleading as an indication of relative amounts of plan assets that originated from employee contributions. Therefore, employee contributions that have been so used should be excluded when making the required disclosure. The revised Exposure Draft asked respondents that have used employee contributions in the manner described to comment on the feasibility of determining the amount to be excluded. Responses generally indicated that that determination would be feasible.

Alternatives Considered for Location of Benefit Information

223. Respondents suggested the following alternative locations for presenting benefit information: as a liability, as an equity interest, as supplemental disclosure, or as a combination of the foregoing.

224. Certain respondents contended that a liability should be recognized to the extent that participants have legally enforceable rights to their benefits. They argued that generally accepted accounting principles require other accounting entities to recognize as liabilities those claims that are legally enforceable against them and that there is no reason to apply a different standard to pension plans. Other respondents advocated a liability presentation because they believed that, regardless of the legal relationship, benefits are an equitable obligation of the plan. In their view, participants earn their benefits as they perform services. Therefore, the financial statements should present as a liability those benefits considered earned by participants.

225. Certain respondents advocated presentation of benefit information as participants' equity in the net assets of the plan. Some did not believe that the benefit information satisfied present criteria for recognizing an accounting liability. Because they considered it necessary to display the measure in a prominent manner so users could focus on the relationship between the plan's resources and the benefits accumulated under the plan, they favored presentation of benefit information as an equity interest. Others considered that presentation appropriate because they view the relationship between the plan and its participants primarily as a fiduciary one. In their view, the plan's resources are held in trust for participants who have a beneficial interest in those resources.

226. Some respondents favored presenting benefit information in the notes to the financial statements. Others preferred a separate financial statement. For some, presenting the benefit information as either a

liability or an equity interest limited the information to less than that considered necessary in assessing the plan's ability to pay benefits. Others did not view benefit information as satisfying the criteria for either a liability or an equity interest. Certain respondents who expressed that view nevertheless felt that the benefit and net asset information should be combined and presented in a single financial statement. Those respondents believed that the relationship between the net assets available for benefits and the actuarial present value of accumulated plan benefits should be made explicit.

227. Certain respondents advocated some combination of the foregoing. Generally, those recommendations were based on what was perceived to be (a) an appropriate measure of a liability for an ongoing plan and (b) information necessary in assessing benefit security. Thus, certain respondents advocated presenting vested benefit information as a liability in the basic financial statements and nonvested benefit information in the accompanying notes.

228. For reasons similar to those discussed in paragraphs 131 and 132, other respondents favored presenting the benefit information as supplemental information, that is, in a financial report but outside of the financial statements.

Conclusions on Location of Benefit Information

229. Certain Board members are not convinced that the benefit information required by this Statement satisfies the criteria for presentation as a liability *of the plan*. Employees render services *to the employer* in exchange for their benefits. Therefore, if any liability exists, it is more likely that of the employer(s) rather than that of the plan.[44] Other Board members believe that the benefit information does represent a liability of the plan. Certain Board members believe that provided the benefit information is located in the financial statements, the primary objective is satisfied; that is, it is not necessary to resolve whether the benefit information constitutes a liability of the plan or the employer(s).

230. Although there is a fiduciary relationship between a plan and its participants, an equity presentation would have the disadvantage of limiting the net equity of participants to the plan's net assets available for benefits.

231. Notwithstanding the divergence of individual Board members' views regarding the accounting nature of the benefit information, the Board concluded that that issue need not be resolved at this time. As part of its ongoing effort to develop a conceptual framework for financial accounting and reporting, another project on the Board's agenda addresses the definitions of elements of financial statements.[45] If in the future it becomes necessary to readdress the accounting nature of the benefit information, that effort should be facilitated by the existence of a Statement of Financial Accounting Concepts that contains definitions of assets, liabilities, and equity interests. Because of its decision not to resolve the issue at this time, the Board concluded that this Statement should not restrict the location of the benefit information within the financial statements. However, because the primary objective of plan financial statements focuses on providing information useful in assessing the plan's ability to pay, when due, the aggregate benefits attributable to service already rendered, the Board concluded that the benefit information (that is, categories (a), (b), and (c) identified in paragraph 22) should be presented together. The Board believes that the usefulness of the financial statements in assessing benefit security might be impaired if the user had to extract portions of the benefit information from various locations. Further, those who favored a combination approach (paragraph 227) generally did so because of their views about the liability nature of certain components of the benefit information. Although it decided not to resolve the issue of whether some part or all of the benefit information is a plan liability, the Board considered it inappropriate to have differing views on that issue serve as a basis for allowing portions of the benefit information to be presented in different locations.

232. The Board decided not to restrict the location of the benefit information within the financial statements, but it did conclude that the benefit information should not be presented as supplemental information outside of the financial statements. To require presentation outside of the financial statements, the Board believes it would be necessary to conclude that no part of the benefit information is an essential element of plan financial statements, that is, that the benefit information, either in part or in total, is neither a liability of nor an equity interest in the plan. The Board did *not* reach that conclusion; rather, it decided that it was not necessary at this time to resolve the nature of the benefit information.

233. The Board has on its agenda a project to develop guidelines for determining where information that meets the objectives of financial reporting should be disclosed—either within or outside of

[44]Board members did not focus on the issue of what is the appropriate measure of the employer's obligation. That issue is presently covered by Opinion 8 and will be reconsidered in another Board project (footnote 23).

[45]An FASB revised Exposure Draft, *Elements of Financial Statements of Business Enterprises,* was issued on December 28, 1979.

financial statements. In the absence of such guidelines, the Board compared the benefit information with the types of information that it has previously decided should be presented outside of financial statements (for example, the current cost and historical cost/constant dollar information required by FASB Statement No. 33, *Financial Reporting and Changing Prices*). It noted that other information permitted to be reported outside of financial statements was supplemental to the primary information about elements presented in an enterprise's financial statements (that is, the enterprise's assets, liabilities, owners' equity, revenues, expenses, etc.). Such supplemental information is not the only information about those elements that appears in the financial report of the enterprise. In the absence of that supplemental information, the information contained in the financial statements would still present the enterprise's financial condition and results of operations. An analogous situation does not exist with regard to the benefit information. The benefit information does not supplement other information about an element in a plan's financial statements. It is the only information required to be presented about the benefits attributable to the service rendered by employees—which information is necessary to present the plan's financial status and to achieve the primary objective of plan financial statements. The Board believes that distinction supports requiring the benefit information to be presented within the financial statements.

234. Some who favored reporting the benefit information outside of the financial statements expressed views similar to those discussed in paragraphs 131 and 132. That is, they thought the benefit information was appropriately the province of actuaries rather than accountants. Some also wished to exclude the benefit information from the scope of an independent accountant's audit. As discussed in paragraph 134, the Board does not accept the notion that if the preparation of financial information is not within the professional qualifications of accountants, it is outside the scope of financial statements. Further, inclusion of the benefit information within plan financial statements does not necessarily require it to be audited by an independent accountant. A plan administrator's assessment of various factors, including the needs of particular users of the plan's financial statements, may determine the extent of auditor involvement. For example, as allowed by ERISA regulations, some plan administrators are presently choosing to exclude certain plan investments from the scope of an audit (paragraph 137). The Board does not believe it is appropriate or necessary to exclude the benefit information from plan financial statements solely for the purpose of avoiding auditor involvement.

CHANGES IN NET ASSET AND BENEFIT INFORMATION

235. The information about a plan's ability to pay benefits when due that is provided by the plan's financial statements is affected whenever transactions and other events affect the net asset or benefit information presented in those statements. Normally, a plan's ability to pay participants' benefits does not remain constant. Therefore, users of the financial statements are concerned with assessing the plan's ability to pay participants' benefits not only as of a point in time but also on a continuing basis. To facilitate that latter assessment, users need to know whether perceived changes in the plan's ability to pay benefits result from changes in investment performance, levels of contributions, improvements of benefits, changes in assumptions, or other factors. Further, as previously indicated, information regarding changes in the value of plan assets is essential in assessing stewardship responsibility. Accordingly, this Statement requires that plan financial statements include (a) a statement that contains information regarding changes during the year in the plan's net assets and (b) disclosure of the effects, if significant, of certain factors affecting the year-to-year change in the benefit information. Presenting information regarding both the changes in the net assets available for benefits and the changes in the actuarial present value of accumulated plan benefits for the same period is necessary to present the changes in the plan's financial status for that period. Therefore, if the benefit information date is the beginning of the year, this Statement requires that information regarding changes in the net asset information for the preceding year also be presented. In that situation, information regarding changes in the net asset information during the current year is an incomplete presentation of the changes in the plan's financial status during that year.

Changes in Net Asset Information

236. Information regarding changes in net assets available for benefits is to be presented in enough detail to identify the significant changes during the year. Paragraph 15 indicates particular items to be separately identified. The Board considered those items to be of such significance that they are required, to the extent applicable, for all plans. Paragraph 15 is not intended to limit the amount of detail or manner of presenting information regarding changes in the net asset information. Subclassifications and additional classifications may be useful. For example, separately reporting refunds of terminated employees' contributions may be useful. Alternatively, such refunds may be netted against

contributions received from participants or included in benefits paid. The Board has not considered issues relating to detailed application of the general guidance provided in paragraph 15. Accordingly, plan administrators should use their best judgment in light of the relevant circumstances.

237. The initial Exposure Draft required separate disclosure of (a) the net change in the fair value of investments sold during the year and (b) the net change in the fair value of investments held at year-end. Some respondents suggested that combining those two amounts would provide a sufficiently informative measure of the change in the fair value of the plan's investments during the year and would avoid substantial detailed calculations. The Board agreed.

238. That Exposure Draft also required disclosure of the net gain or loss realized during the year on sales of investments. Some respondents expressed the view that disclosure of realized gains and losses is not relevant in a fair value reporting environment. The Board is not convinced that disclosing the net gain or loss realized on investments sold during the year would enhance an assessment of the plan's ability to pay benefits when due. The Board believes that the basic rationale for requiring a fair value reporting basis for plan investments (excluding contracts with insurance companies) does not support *requiring* disclosure of realized gains and losses. Such disclosure, however, is not proscribed.

239. To further assist users in understanding the changes in net assets during the year, this Statement requires disclosure of the net change in fair value for each significant class of investment, segregated between investments whose fair values have been measured by quoted prices in an active market and those whose fair values have been otherwise determined. The Board believes that information may be useful in assessing the relative degree of objectivity or subjectivity in measuring the plan's investments and the relationship thereof to investment performance during the year. Disclosure of the change in fair value for each significant class of investments provides useful information because different types of investments may perform differently and those differences may be assessed differently. For example, a decrease in the fair value of bonds during a period of rising interest rates may be assessed differently than a decrease or an increase in the fair value of equity securities during the same period.

Changes in Benefit Information

240. The initial Exposure Draft required that the effects of all significant factors affecting the year-to-year change in the benefit information be presented in a statement format. Although such presentation remains acceptable, that requirement has been modified to permit disclosure of only the significant effects of certain factors such as plan amendments and changes in actuarial assumptions. A number of respondents expressed concern about the perceived complexity and expense of developing the information required by the initial Exposure Draft. However, certain respondents and certain actuaries with whom the Board consulted, including representatives of the American Academy of Actuaries and the American Society of Pension Actuaries, agreed that disclosure of at least certain factors having significant effects is important in understanding the year-to-year change in the benefit information. The Board concluded that the minimum required disclosure specified in paragraph 25 would provide that information. The Board believes that each of those factors is distinct in nature. Therefore, their effects should be separately disclosed. The minimum required disclosure may be presented either in a statement format (with the addition of an unidentified "other" category to reconcile beginning and ending balances) or elsewhere in the financial statements.

241. The Board believes that identification of the significant effects of all factors affecting the year-to-year change in the benefit information provides additional information useful in understanding that change. Therefore, disclosure of the effects of the additional factors identified in paragraph 25 is encouraged. The items specified in paragraph 25 are not intended to be an exhaustive list of all factors that may affect the change in the benefit information during the year. If additional information regarding that change is presented, it need not be limited to nor include all other factors identified in paragraph 25.

242. Certain respondents expressed concern that disclosing the effects of plan amendments might affect union negotiations or result in pitting one group of participants against another, as in the case of a benefit increase for retirees that present employees believe decreases the security for their benefits. Similar arguments regarding perceived effects of accounting and reporting standards on the decisions of those responsible for managing plan assets, plan funding, or deciding whether to amend the plan were addressed in preceding paragraphs (paragraphs 106, 158, and 220). The Board considers the reasons stated in those paragraphs for rejecting such arguments to be equally applicable to this concern.

243. Certain respondents to the Exposure Drafts suggested that the Board prescribe a uniform order for calculating the effects of individual factors on the change in the benefit information. They indicated that the effects of factors such as those enu-

merated in paragraph 25 are not all independent and that the order in which they are calculated will vary among plans. The Board recognizes that the determined effects of factors comprising the net change in the benefit information will vary depending on the order in which the effects are calculated. The Board solicited additional information from certain sources for use in considering the order in which the effects of individual factors should be determined; such information, however, was not forthcoming. Because the Board is not aware of any conceptual basis supporting a particular approach to determining the effects of individual factors, any prescribed order would be somewhat arbitrary. Thus, the Board concluded that at this time it would not prescribe an order.

FORMAT FOR PRESENTING FINANCIAL INFORMATION

244. The Board recognizes that divergent views exist about the appropriate format for presenting the net asset and benefit information (and changes therein) required by this Statement. Certain of those views have been previously discussed. In addition, many respondents to the Discussion Memorandum favored presenting net asset information in the format of a statement of net assets available for benefits because that is the statement that ERISA plans presently file with governmental agencies.

245. In view of the Board's conclusion not to restrict the location of benefit information in the financial statements, this Statement permits certain flexibility in presenting the benefit information and changes therein required by paragraphs 6(c) and 6(d). Net asset and benefit information may be presented with equal prominence but in separate financial statements, or benefit information may be presented in notes to a statement of net assets available for benefits. A statement that combines net asset and benefit information is also acceptable. Similar alternative methods of presenting information regarding changes in benefit information are permitted.

246. All financial information presented in a single financial statement is generally understood to be determined as of the same date or for the same period. For a comparison of two amounts or a deduction of one amount from the other to be valid, both amounts must be determined on a comparable basis. Therefore, this Statement permits a single statement that combines benefit and net asset information only if the benefit information is determined as of the same date as the net asset information. Likewise, a single statement that combines information regarding changes in the benefit and net asset information is permitted only if the respective change information is for the same period.

DISCLOSURES

247. The Board concluded that the financial statements should provide (a) information about the results of transactions and events that affect the net asset and benefit information and (b) other factors necessary for users to understand the information provided. Disclosure of underlying methods, assumptions, and estimates, including an indication of their objective/subjective nature, aids users in evaluating the information provided.

248. The Discussion Memorandum considered 4 broad areas of disclosure and within those areas 23 possible disclosures. A number were of the type required for business enterprises; others were specifically enumerated by ERISA as worthy of consideration for disclosure in financial statements filed pursuant to the Act. Opinion was divided among respondents who addressed the issue as to which specific disclosures should be required. The basis for the Board's conclusions regarding certain disclosures required by paragraphs 28(c) and 28(e) were previously discussed (paragraphs 219 and 126, respectively). The following paragraphs discuss the Board's conclusions with respect to other disclosure requirements. As indicated in paragraph 4, the financial accounting standards dealt with in this Statement are those of particular importance to pension plans or that differ from existing generally accepted accounting principles. Accordingly, this Statement does not address all disclosures required by generally accepted accounting principles for other types of entities that are also applicable to pension plans.

Plan Description

249. The Board concluded that a brief plan description could assist users, particularly nonparticipants, in understanding the financial statements. Of those who addressed the issue, many respondents favored that disclosure. Others were opposed because, for many plans, that information is available from other sources. The view was also expressed that it would be difficult to describe briefly but adequately the possibly numerous and complex provisions of a plan. The Board did not find those arguments persuasive. The Board believes that the usefulness of plan financial statements will be increased with a brief description of the plan and that, although there may be some difficulty in initially preparing that information, there should be little, if any, difficulty in presenting it in subsequent plan financial statements. Additionally, for plans not covered by ERISA, a summary plan description may not be readily available. However, the Board also believes that unnecessary duplication of disclosures should be avoided. Accordingly, the Board concluded that if a plan agreement or a description thereof providing the required information is otherwise published

and made available, the plan description required by this Statement may be omitted provided reference to such other source is made.

Methods and Assumptions Used to Determine Fair Value of Investments and Reported Value of Contracts with Insurance Companies

250. This Statement requires that the plan's accounting policy disclosure include a description of the methods and assumptions used to determine the fair value of investments and the reported value of contracts with insurance companies. Investments are normally the principal resource of a plan. Therefore, their measurement can significantly affect an assessment of the plan's ability to pay benefits when due. Most respondents who addressed the issue urged disclosure of the methods and assumptions used for measuring investments. The Board agreed.

Significant Investments

251. Some respondents to the initial Exposure Draft favored disclosure of significant investments. Presumably, they believe that such information is useful in assessing stewardship and investment performance and the degree of risk related to future changes in the fair value of a plan's investments. Because (a) certain securities' market prices may fluctuate more than others and (b) determination of the fair value of investments by means other than quoted prices in an active market may be subjective, the degree of risk related to changes in the fair value of a plan's investments may depend, to some extent, on the degree of diversification and the nature of a plan's investment portfolio.

252. Presumably, the more information that is disclosed about plan investments, the more useful are the financial statements in assessing the plan's ability to pay benefits when due. However, there is a cost associated with detailed disclosure. Therefore, this Statement requires only identification of significant investments, that is, those that represent five percent or more of the net assets available for benefits. Identification of other investments, however, is not proscribed. Because no more than 20 investments need be identified, the Board believes the incremental cost to provide the information will not be significant.

Cost Basis of Investments Presented at Fair Value

253. The initial Exposure Draft required that the historical cost of investments, at least for each significant category, be disclosed. A number of respondents urged deleting that requirement because, in their view, historical cost information is not relevant in a fair value reporting environment and does not provide information useful in assessing benefit security. Questions were raised regarding how to determine historical cost, including its application to bond swaps (paragraph 108). The Board is not convinced that knowledge of the historical cost of significant classes of plan investments would necessarily enhance a user's assessment of the plan's ability to pay benefits when due. Thus, it concluded that such disclosure should not be required. However, it is not proscribed. Given the Board's conclusion, it was not deemed necessary to resolve issues relating to determination of historical cost.

Transactions with Certain Related Parties

254. A number of respondents advocated disclosure of investments in, or transactions with, related parties—primarily the plan sponsor, the employer(s), and the employee organization(s). An investment in an employer is viewed as increasing the degree to which a plan's ability to pay participants' benefits depends on the financial condition of the employer. Accordingly, disclosure is considered necessary to allow financial statement users to evaluate the relative significance of such investments. Because the sponsor, employer(s), and employee organization(s) may have close relationships with the plan, disclosure of transactions with those parties may provide information useful in assessing stewardship responsibility.

255. Because this Statement requires identification of investments that represent five percent or more of the net assets available for benefits, the Board concluded that it need not specifically require disclosure of investments in the employer(s). However, disclosure of other significant transactions with the employer(s), the sponsor (if not the employer), or the employee organization(s) is required.

Method and Assumptions Used to Determine the Benefit Information

256. The actuarial present value of accumulated plan benefits is an essential factor for assessing a plan's ability to pay benefits when due. Many users will be unaware of this Statement's requirements regarding how that amount is calculated. Therefore, the Board concluded that the usefulness of the financial statements would be enhanced by requiring disclosure of the method and significant assumptions used to determine the benefit information.

257. Numerous assumptions are used in determining the benefit information. A given percentage variation in certain of those assumptions may be expected to result in a greater percentage variation in the actuarial present value of accumulated plan benefits than would the same variation in other assumptions (that is, the benefit information is

more sensitive with respect to certain assumptions than to others). The Board believes that users of financial statements should be aware of the degree to which financial information is affected by estimates and judgment. Accordingly, the Board believes that the usefulness of plan financial statements would be enhanced by disclosure of the estimated effect on the benefit information, or on the difference between the net asset information and the benefit information, of a given variation in the assumptions to which that information is most sensitive. Examples of such assumptions are assumed rates of return and, for plans that provide automatic cost-of-living adjustments, assumed inflation rates. However, the Board does not have sufficient information to assess the cost/benefit implications of *requiring* that disclosure. Therefore, at this time it is only encouraging plans to experiment with such disclosure.

Changes in the Plan, Methods of Measurement, or Assumptions

258. The requirement that plan financial statements include (a) a description of significant plan amendments made during the year ending on the latest benefit information date and (b) a description of significant changes in assumptions stems from the conclusion that the financial statements should include information about other factors necessary for users to understand the information provided. The Board believes that users' understanding of the significant effects of plan amendments and changes in actuarial assumptions will be enhanced if descriptions of those events are provided. In addition, users need to know what plan provisions serve as a basis for the benefit information. Accordingly, the Board concluded that if any significant amendments are adopted between the latest benefit information date and year-end, the financial statements should indicate that the benefit information does not reflect those amendments.

259. Some respondents to the initial Exposure Draft opposed requiring a description of significant plan amendments because such information is included in the ERISA-required summary plan description. The Board recognizes that a supplement to the summary plan description concerning any "material modifications" to the plan must be provided to participants by 210 days after the end of the plan year during which the modification became effective. However, because of the potential significance of plan amendments to the year-to-year change in the actuarial present value of accumulated plan benefits and thus to an assessment of the plan's ability to pay benefits, the Board concluded that providing a brief description of the plan amendment in the notes is preferable to incorporating by reference that supplement to the summary plan description in the financial statements. Further, for plans not subject to ERISA, a description of the plan amendment may not be readily available elsewhere.

260. The Board concluded that disclosure of changes in methods or assumptions used to determine the net asset information should be in accordance with existing generally accepted accounting principles. For example, a change from contract value to fair value for measuring contracts with insurance companies should be viewed as a change in accounting principles pursuant to APB Opinion No. 20, *Accounting Changes.*

Funding Policy

261. Many respondents advocated disclosure of the funding policy. A primary purpose of funding is to enable a plan to pay benefits when due. Assessment of the plan's ability to pay benefits is therefore enhanced if information about the pattern of funding adopted by the employer(s) and, if applicable, participants and other sources is also disclosed. Accordingly, this Statement requires disclosure of the funding policy and any changes therein. Some respondents to the initial Exposure Draft suggested that the disclosure for ERISA plans indicate whether the minimum funding requirements of the Act have been met. The Board agreed that such information could be useful in assessing benefit security. Thus, that disclosure is required.

262. Certain respondents to that Exposure Draft suggested that the requirement for disclosure of the funding policy be more specific about the nature of the required information. For example, it was suggested that the actuarial cost method and the amortization period for the unfunded supplemental actuarial value be disclosed. Other respondents suggested that the funding policy be specifically related to the benefit information, to any existing difference between the net asset and benefit information, or to both. Although the Board believes it unlikely that a funding policy disclosure incorporating the technical name of the actuarial cost method and the amortization period for the unfunded supplemental actuarial value would be meaningful to most users, such disclosure is not proscribed. The Board believes that a brief description, in general terms and in layman's language, of how contributions are determined pursuant to the actuarial cost method would be more understandable and therefore more useful. Thus, the latter disclosure is considered preferable.

263. The Board agreed that information regarding the estimated future impact of the funding policy on an existing difference between the net asset and benefit information would be useful in assessing the plan's future ability to pay benefits. However, at this

time, sufficient information to develop and evaluate specific requirements regarding that type of disclosure has not been received. Therefore, it is not required. However, the Board encourages plans to experiment with such disclosures.

Tax Status of the Plan

264. A principal reason for funding a pension plan through a qualified trust or contract with an insurance company is to avoid having participants or the plan pay current federal income taxes on employer contributions and the plan's investment earnings. Virtually all defined benefit pension plans are designed to qualify for exemption from income taxes. Failure to obtain, or to maintain, an exempt status could have a significant effect on a plan. Because of its significance, some respondents recommended that the tax status of the plan be disclosed in all cases. However, because (a) the vast majority of private defined benefit pension plans receive favorable letters of determination from the IRS as to their tax-exempt status, (b) it is the *lack* or *loss* of an exempt status that could have a significant effect on a plan's ability to pay benefits, and (c) the Board believes that disclosures required annually for all plans should be kept to a minimum, the Board concluded that disclosure of a plan's tax status should be required only if the plan has not received a favorable letter of determination, or if that letter has not been maintained. However, disclosure of the plan's tax status is not proscribed in other circumstances.

Description of Benefits Guaranteed by the PBGC

265. For plans that are subject to Title IV of ERISA, the guaranty of the PBGC provides an additional source of security for certain participants' benefits. Providing information about that guaranty enhances the usefulness of the financial statements in assessing benefit security. Accordingly, the Board concluded that ERISA plans should provide a brief description of the benefits guaranteed by the PBGC. Because coverage by the PBGC of increased benefits resulting from plan amendments is phased-in over a period of years, the Board also concluded that the description should include an indication of the application of the PBGC guaranty to any recent plan amendments. For the same reason as that stated in paragraph 219, if the required disclosure is otherwise published and made available, it may be omitted from the financial statements provided the statements make reference to such other source.

266. Some respondents favored placing more emphasis on the PBGC guaranty, and a few favored disclosure of quantified amounts of PBGC-guaranteed benefits. Others, however, contended that calculation of the benefits guaranteed by the PBGC would be administratively burdensome for an ongoing plan. The Board has not assessed the additional cost of measuring the benefits guaranteed by the PBGC, but has concluded that requiring that disclosure is not necessary to achieve the primary objective of plan financial statements.

Unusual or Infrequent Events

267. The benefit information presented in plan financial statements is intended to provide information as of a specific date, that is, the benefit information date. Measures of that information at subsequent dates will necessarily change as events (for example, service rendered) affect the measurement basis. This Statement does not contemplate disclosure of normal changes after the benefit information date, such as benefits attributable to service rendered after that date. However, the Board recognizes that an unusual or infrequent event or transaction that might significantly affect an assessment of the plan's ability to pay participants' benefits may occur after the latest benefit information date and therefore should be disclosed. For example, a plan amendment that significantly increases benefits for service rendered before the latest benefit information date should be disclosed. If reasonably determinable, the effects of such an event or transaction should be disclosed.

EFFECTIVE DATE AND TRANSITION

268. The effective date in paragraph 30 is one year later than that proposed in the revised Exposure Draft. ERISA plans with at least 100 participants are presently required to prepare benefit information for Form 5500 reporting purposes that is similar to that required by this Statement. The Board believes that many of those plans should be able to comply with this Statement in financial statements prepared for the 1980 plan year, and they are encouraged to do so. However, the Board recognizes that small plans and plans of state and local governmental units are not presently required to prepare the benefit information. Those that choose to issue financial statements in accordance with this Statement may need additional time to develop the necessary procedures. Accordingly, the Board concluded that the effective date specified in paragraph 30 is appropriate.

269. In the Board's view, the usefulness of the financial statements in assessing benefit security and changes therein over time will be enhanced by restating the financial statements of prior years if those prior years' statements are presented together with financial statements for plan years that are subject to this Statement. Accordingly, the Board concluded

that retroactive application of this Statement is appropriate.

270. Certain respondents to the initial Exposure Draft expressed the view that restating the financial statements of prior years could be difficult and expensive and suggested that the requirement be eliminated. The Board believes that some respondents misinterpreted that Exposure Draft as *requiring presentation* of restated prior years' statements, rather than as requiring only that such statements be restated *if they are presented*. This Statement does *not* require presentation of the financial statements of prior years.

271. A few respondents to the Exposure Drafts suggested that information regarding changes in the net asset and benefit information not be required for the initial year of compliance with this Statement. Regarding changes in net asset information, the Board notes that ERISA plans presently file similar information with governmental agencies. For plans not subject to ERISA, it does not appear that initially providing that information should be that difficult. Because of the Board's conclusions that (a) beginning-of-year benefit information is acceptable, (b) a statement of changes in benefit information that identifies the effects of all significant factors is not required, and (c) the Statement is not effective until the 1981 plan year, the Board concluded that there should be sufficient time to develop the required information regarding changes in the benefit information. Accordingly, the Board concluded that an exemption for the initial year of compliance should not be provided.

REDUCTIONS IN PERCEIVED COST OF IMPLEMENTING INITIAL EXPOSURE DRAFT

272. Many respondents to the initial Exposure Draft were concerned that compliance with its requirements would impose a substantial and inappropriate cost burden on plans. Those concerns primarily related to the required benefit information and the changes therein, although some concerns addressed other requirements, including the required net asset information and the changes therein. Certain of those concerns were apparently based at least partially on misinterpretations of the requirements. For example, some respondents apparently interpreted that Exposure Draft as requiring that annual financial statements for a plan, regardless of its size, be prepared, audited, and distributed to all participants. Others thought that restated financial statements for one or more prior years were required. This Statement does not require the preparation, attestation, or distribution of any financial statements. It is applicable only to financial information that purports to be in accordance with generally accepted accounting principles. Whether a plan prepares such information; who, if anyone, attests to that information, either in part or in total; and who receives that information are issues that are not within the scope of this Statement.

273. The Board recognizes that certain other concerns were not based on misinterpretations. The Board agrees that the benefits of providing financial information should be expected to exceed (or at least equal) the cost involved. A number of changes made to the initial Exposure Draft's requirements were directly related to the Board's desire to reduce the perceived implementation costs.

274. Most concerns about implementing the requirements regarding the net asset information and the changes therein related to (a) determination of the fair value of contracts with insurance companies and (b) segregating the net change in fair value of investments during the year into the net change in fair value of investments held at year-end and the net change in fair value of investments sold during the year. Those requirements have been deleted. This Statement permits contracts with an insurance company to be measured at amounts determined by the insurance company. It also provides for disclosing in a single amount the net change during the year in the fair value of investments.

275. Rather extensive changes were made to the initial Exposure Draft's requirements relating to benefit information and the changes therein. In response to concerns that determination of end-of-year benefit information would impose a substantial cost burden for many plans, this Statement permits a benefit information date that is either the beginning or the end of the year. Because of the cooperative effort between the Board and the Department of Labor, it appears that the benefit information determined pursuant to this Statement should serve both financial reporting purposes and, for ERISA plans, Form 5500 reporting purposes. The Board's desire to avoid unnecessary differences between those requirements was a significant factor that influenced its conclusion regarding the benefit information date.

276. Another concern regarding the benefit information was the requirement that certain plans use PBGC interest and mortality rates in determining that information. Some viewed that requirement as creating timing problems and causing plans to incur additional costs. They indicated that issuance of PBGC rates has, in the past, generally been subject to a lag of several months. If those rates were not available when other aspects of the benefit information were determined, plans might incur additional

costs when the determination process was completed at a later date. For that reason and others previously discussed, this Statement does not require use of PBGC rates.

277. Many respondents objected to the complexity and resulting expense relating to the initial Exposure Draft's requirement that the benefit information be segmented beyond certain categories if that would provide information particularly useful to a significant class of participants in their assessment of the security for their benefits. Although some objections were apparently based on a misinterpretation that such further segmentation would be required annually for all plans, that requirement has been deleted upon consideration of respondents' concerns and other reasons indicated in paragraph 219.

278. Many respondents contended that it would be complex and costly to comply with the initial Exposure Draft's requirement for a statement of changes in benefit information that identified the effects of all significant factors. As an alternative, this Statement permits disclosing only the significant effects of certain factors affecting the year-to-year change in the benefit information.

279. The Board believes that the changes discussed in the preceding paragraphs, on an individual and aggregate basis, should significantly reduce the perceived incremental costs that were of concern to respondents. The Board believes that the implementation of this Statement will have a favorable cost/benefit relationship. The Board recognizes that neither all benefits from nor all costs of financial information can be measured objectively; different persons may honestly disagree about whether the benefits of providing certain information justify the related costs.

Appendix C

GLOSSARY

280. This appendix defines certain terms, acronyms, and phrases used for convenience in this Statement.

Accumulated plan benefits
Benefits that are attributable under the provisions of a pension plan to employees' service rendered to the benefit information date.

Act
The Employee Retirement Income Security Act of 1974.

Actuarial asset value
A value assigned by an actuary to the assets of a plan generally for use in conjunction with an actuarial cost method.

Actuarial cost method
A recognized actuarial technique used for establishing the amount and incidence of employer contributions or accounting charges for pension cost under a pension plan.

Actuarial present value of accumulated plan benefits
The amount as of a benefit information date that results from applying actuarial assumptions to the benefit amounts determined pursuant to paragraphs 16-18 of this Statement (that is, the accumulated plan benefits), with the actuarial assumptions being used to adjust those amounts to reflect the time value of money (through discounts for interest) and the probability of payment (by means of decrements such as for death, disability, withdrawal, or retirement) between the benefit information date and the expected date of payment.

Allocated contract
A contract with an insurance company under which related payments to the insurance company are currently used to purchase immediate or deferred annuities for individual participants.

Benefit information
The actuarial present value of accumulated plan benefits.

Benefit information date
The date as of which the actuarial present value of accumulated plan benefits is presented.

Benefit security
The plan's present and future ability to pay benefits when due.

Benefits
Payments to which participants may be entitled under a pension plan, including pension benefits, disability benefits, death benefits, and benefits due on termination of employment.

Contract value
The value of an unallocated contract that is determined by the insurance company in accordance with the terms of the contract.

Contributory plan
A pension plan under which participants bear part of the cost.

Defined benefit pension plan
A pension plan that specifies a determinable pension benefit, usually based on factors such as

age, years of service, and salary. Even though a plan may be funded pursuant to periodic agreements that specify a fixed rate of employer contributions (for example, a collectively bargained multiemployer plan), such a plan may nevertheless be a defined benefit pension plan as that term is used in this Statement. For example, if the plan prescribes a scale of benefits and experience indicates or it is expected that employer contributions are or will be periodically adjusted to enable such stated benefits to be maintained, this Statement considers such a plan to be a defined benefit pension plan. Further, a plan that is subject to ERISA and considered to be a defined benefit pension plan under the Act is a defined benefit pension plan for purposes of applying this Statement.

Employee
A person who has rendered or is presently rendering service.

ERISA
The Employee Retirement Income Security Act of 1974.

ERISA plan
A plan that is subject to ERISA.

Funding agency
An organization or individual, such as a specific corporate or individual trustee or an insurance company, that provides facilities for the accumulation of assets to be used for paying benefits under a pension plan; an organization, such as a specific life insurance company, that provides facilities for the purchase of such benefits.

Funding policy
The program regarding the amounts and timing of contributions by the employer(s), participants, and any other sources (for example, state subsidies or federal grants) to provide the benefits a pension plan specifies.

General account
An undivided fund maintained by an insurance company that commingles plan assets with other assets of the insurance company for investment purposes. That is, funds held by an insurance company that are not maintained in a separate account are in its general account.

Net asset information
Information regarding the net assets available for benefits.

Net assets available for benefits
The difference between a plan's assets and its liabilities. For purposes of this definition, a plan's liabilities do not include participants' accumulated plan benefits.

Noncontributory plan
A pension plan under which participants do not make contributions.

Nonvested benefit information
The actuarial present value of nonvested accumulated plan benefits.

Participant
Any employee or former employee, or any member or former member of a trade or other employee association, or the beneficiaries of those individuals, for whom there are accumulated plan benefits.

Participating contract
An allocated contract that provides for plan participation in the investment performance and experience (for example, mortality experience) of the insurance company.

Participation right
A plan's right under a participating contract to receive future dividends from the insurance company.

PBGC
The Pension Benefit Guaranty Corporation.

Pension benefits
Periodic (usually monthly) payments made to a person who has retired from employment.

Pension fund
The assets of a pension plan held by a funding agency.

Pension plan
See **defined benefit pension plan**.

Plan
See **defined benefit pension plan**.

Plan administrator
The person or group of persons responsible for the content and issuance of a plan's financial statements in much the same way that *management* is responsible for the content and issuance of a business enterprise's financial statements.

Prior service costs
See **supplemental actuarial value**.

Reporting date
The date as of which information regarding the net assets available for benefits is presented.

Retired life fund
That portion of the funds under an immediate participation guarantee contract that is designated as supporting benefit payments to current retirees.

Separate account
A special account established by an insurance company solely for the purpose of investing the assets of one or more plans. Funds in a separate account are not commingled with other assets of the insurance company for investment purposes.

Service
Periods of employment taken into consideration under a pension plan.

Sponsor
In the case of a pension plan established or maintained by a single employer, the employer; in the case of a plan established or maintained by an employee organization, the employee organization; in the case of a plan established or maintained jointly by two or more employers or by one or more employers and one or more employee organizations, the association, committee, joint board of trustees, or other group of representatives of the parties who have established or who maintain the pension plan.

Supplemental actuarial value
The amount assigned under the actuarial cost method in use to years before a given date.

Unallocated contract
A contract with an insurance company under which related payments to the insurance company are accumulated in an unallocated fund to be used to meet benefit payments when employees retire, either directly or through the purchase of annuities. Funds in an unallocated contract may also be withdrawn and otherwise invested.

Vested benefit information
The actuarial present value of vested accumulated plan benefits.

Vested benefits
Benefits that are not contingent on an employee's future service.

Appendix D

ILLUSTRATION OF FINANCIAL STATEMENTS

281. This appendix illustrates certain applications of the requirements of this Statement that are applicable for the 1981 annual financial statements of a hypothetical plan, the C&H Company Pension Plan. It does not illustrate other requirements of this Statement that might be applicable in circumstances other than those assumed for the C&H Company Pension Plan. The formats presented and the wording of accompanying notes are only illustrative and do not necessarily reflect a preference of the Board. Further, the circumstances assumed for the C&H Company Pension Plan are designed to facilitate illustration of many of this Statement's requirements. Therefore, the notes to the illustrative financial statements probably are more extensive than would be expected for a typical plan.

282. Included are illustrations of the following alternatives permitted by paragraphs 6, 8, 25, and 26:

a. An end-of-year vs. beginning-of-year benefit information date
b. Separate vs. combined statements for presenting information regarding (a) the net assets available for benefits and the actuarial present value of accumulated plan benefits and (b) changes in the net assets available for benefits and changes in the actuarial present value of accumulated plan benefits
c. A separate statement that reconciles the year-to-year change in the actuarial present value of accumulated plan benefits vs. presenting the effects of a change in actuarial assumptions on the face of the statement of accumulated plan benefits.

Although not illustrated, paragraph 8 of this Statement permits the information regarding the actuarial present value of accumulated plan benefits and changes therein to be presented as notes to the financial statements.

CONTENTS

I. Illustrations Assuming an End-of-Year Benefit Information Date

Exhibit D-1

C&H COMPANY PENSION PLAN
STATEMENT OF NET ASSETS AVAILABLE FOR BENEFITS

	December 31 1981
Assets	
Investments, at fair value (Notes B(1) and E)	
United States government securities	$ 350,000
Corporate bonds and debentures	3,500,000
Common stock	
C&H Company	690,000
Other	2,250,000
Mortgages	480,000
Real estate	270,000
	7,540,000
Deposit administration contract, at contract value (Notes B(1) and F)	1,000,000
Total investments	8,540,000
Receivables	
Employees' contributions	40,000
Securities sold	310,000
Accrued interest and dividends	77,000
	427,000
Cash	200,000
Total assets	9,167,000
Liabilities	
Accounts payable	70,000
Accrued expenses	85,000
Total liabilities	155,000
Net assets available for benefits	$9,012,000

The accompanying notes are an integral part of the financial statements.

Exhibit D-2

C&H COMPANY PENSION PLAN
STATEMENT OF CHANGES IN NET ASSETS AVAILABLE FOR BENEFITS

	Year Ended December 31 1981
Investment income	
Net appreciation in fair value of investments (Note E)	$ 207,000
Interest	345,000
Dividends	130,000
Rents	55,000
	737,000
Less investment expenses	39,000
	698,000
Contributions (Note C)	
Employer	780,000
Employees	450,000
	1,230,000
Total additions	1,928,000
Benefits paid directly to participants	740,000
Purchases of annuity contracts (Note F)	257,000
	997,000
Administrative expenses	65,000
Total deductions	1,062,000
Net increase	866,000
Net assets available for benefits	
Beginning of year	8,146,000
End of year	$9,012,000

The accompanying notes are an integral part of the financial statements.

Exhibit D-3

C&H COMPANY PENSION PLAN
STATEMENT OF ACCUMULATED PLAN BENEFITS

	December 31 1981
Actuarial present value of accumulated plan benefits (Notes B(2) and C)	
Vested benefits	
Participants currently receiving payments	$ 3,040,000
Other participants	8,120,000
	11,160,000
Nonvested benefits	2,720,000
Total actuarial present value of accumulated plan benefits	$13,880,000

The accompanying notes are an integral part of the financial statements.

Exhibit D-4

C&H COMPANY PENSION PLAN
STATEMENT OF CHANGES IN ACCUMULATED PLAN BENEFITS

	Year Ended December 31 1981
Actuarial present value of accumulated plan benefits at beginning of year	$11,880,000
Increase (decrease) during the year attributable to:	
Plan amendment (Note G)	2,410,000
Change in actuarial assumptions (Note B(2))	(1,050,500)
Benefits accumulated	895,000
Increase for interest due to the decrease in the discount period (Note B(2))	742,500
Benefits paid	(997,000)
Net increase	2,000,000
Actuarial present value of accumulated plan benefits at end of year	$13,880,000

The accompanying notes are an integral part of the financial statements.

Exhibit D-5

C&H COMPANY PENSION PLAN
STATEMENT OF ACCUMULATED PLAN BENEFITS AND NET ASSETS AVAILABLE FOR BENEFITS
[An alternative for Exhibits D-1 and D-3]

	December 31 1981
Accumulated Plan Benefits (Notes B(2) and C)	
Actuarial present value of vested benefits	
Participants currently receiving payments	$ 3,040,000
Other participants	8,120,000
	11,160,000
Actuarial present value of nonvested benefits	2,720,000
Total actuarial present value of accumulated plan benefits	13,880,000
Net Assets Available for Benefits	
Investments, at fair value (Notes B(1) and E)	
United States government securities	350,000
Corporate bonds and debentures	3,500,000
Common stock	
C&H Company	690,000
Other	2,250,000
Mortgages	480,000
Real estate	270,000
	7,540,000
Deposit administration contract, at contract value (Notes B(1) and F)	1,000,000
Total investments	8,540,000
Receivables	
Employees' contributions	40,000
Securities sold	310,000
Accrued interest and dividends	77,000
	427,000
Cash	200,000
Total assets	9,167,000
Accounts payable	70,000
Accrued expenses	85,000
Total liabilities	155,000
Net assets available for benefits	9,012,000
Excess of actuarial present value of accumulated plan benefits over net assets available for benefits	$ 4,868,000

The accompanying notes are an integral part of the financial statements.

Exhibit D-6

C&H COMPANY PENSION PLAN
STATEMENT OF CHANGES IN ACCUMULATED PLAN BENEFITS AND NET ASSETS AVAILABLE FOR BENEFITS
[An alternative for Exhibits D-2 and D-4]

	Year Ended December 31 1981
Net Increase in Actuarial Present Value of Accumulated Plan Benefits	
Increase (decrease) during the year attributable to:	
Plan amendment (Note G)	$ 2,410,000
Change in actuarial assumptions (Note B(2))	(1,050,500)
Benefits accumulated	895,000
Increase for interest due to the decrease in the discount period (Note B(2))	742,500
Benefits paid	(997,000)
Net increase	2,000,000
Net Increase in Net Assets Available for Benefits	
Investment income	
Net appreciation in fair value of investments (Note E)	207,000
Interest	345,000
Dividends	130,000
Rents	55,000
	737,000
Less investment expenses	39,000
	698,000
Contributions (Note C)	
Employer	780,000
Employees	450,000
	1,230,000
Total additions	1,928,000
Benefits paid directly to participants	740,000
Purchases of annuity contracts (Note F)	257,000
	997,000
Administrative expenses	65,000
Total deductions	1,062,000
Net increase	866,000
Increase in excess of actuarial present value of accumulated plan benefits over net assets available for benefits	1,134,000
Excess of actuarial present value of accumulated plan benefits over net assets available for benefits	
Beginning of year	3,734,000
End of year	$ 4,868,000

The accompanying notes are an integral part of the financial statements.

Exhibit D-7

C&H COMPANY PENSION PLAN
STATEMENT OF NET ASSETS AVAILABLE FOR BENEFITS
[If a beginning-of-year benefit information date is selected]

	December 31	
	1981	1980
Assets		
Investments, at fair value (Notes B(1) and E)		
United States government securities	$ 350,000	$ 270,000
Corporate bonds and debentures	3,500,000	3,670,000
Common stock		
C&H Company	690,000	880,000
Other	2,250,000	1,860,000
Mortgages	480,000	460,000
Real estate	270,000	240,000
	7,540,000	7,380,000
Deposit administration contract, at contract value (Notes B(1) and F)	1,000,000	890,000
Total investments	8,540,000	8,270,000
Receivables		
Employees' contributions	40,000	35,000
Securities sold	310,000	175,000
Accrued interest and dividends	77,000	76,000
	427,000	286,000
Cash	200,000	90,000
Total assets	9,167,000	8,646,000
Liabilities		
Accounts payable		
Securities purchased	—	400,000
Other	70,000	60,000
	70,000	460,000
Accrued expenses	85,000	40,000
Total liabilities	155,000	500,000
Net assets available for benefits	$9,012,000	$8,146,000

The accompanying notes are an integral part of the financial statements.

Exhibit D-8

C&H COMPANY PENSION PLAN
STATEMENT OF CHANGES IN NET ASSETS AVAILABLE FOR BENEFITS
[If a beginning-of-year benefit information date is selected]

	Year Ended December 31	
	1981	**1980**
Investment income		
Net appreciation (depreciation) in fair value of investments (Note E)	$ 207,000	$ (72,000)
Interest	345,000	320,000
Dividends	130,000	110,000
Rents	55,000	43,000
	737,000	401,000
Less investment expenses	39,000	35,000
	698,000	366,000
Contributions (Note C)		
Employer	780,000	710,000
Employees	450,000	430,000
	1,230,000	1,140,000
Total additions	1,928,000	1,506,000
Benefits paid directly to participants	740,000	561,000
Purchases of annuity contracts (Note F)	257,000	185,000
	997,000	746,000
Administrative expenses	65,000	58,000
Total deductions	1,062,000	804,000
Net increase	866,000	702,000
Net assets available for benefits		
Beginning of year	8,146,000	7,444,000
End of year	$9,012,000	$8,146,000

The accompanying notes are an integral part of the financial statements.

Exhibit D-9

C&H COMPANY PENSION PLAN
STATEMENT OF ACCUMULATED PLAN BENEFITS
[If a beginning-of-year benefit information date is selected]

	December 31 1980
Actuarial present value of accumulated plan benefits (Notes B(2) and C)	
Vested benefits	
Participants currently receiving payments	$ 2,950,000
Other participants	6,530,000
	9,480,000
Nonvested benefits	2,400,000
Total actuarial present value of accumulated plan benefits	$11,880,000

The accompanying notes are an integral part of the financial statements.

At December 31, 1979, the total actuarial present value of accumulated plan benefits was $10,544,000. During 1980, the actuarial present value of accumulated plan benefits increased $700,000 as a result of a change in actuarial assumptions (Note B(2)). Also see Note G.

C&H COMPANY PENSION PLAN

NOTES TO FINANCIAL STATEMENTS[46]

A. Description of Plan

The following brief description of the C&H Company Pension Plan *(Plan)* is provided for general information purposes only. Participants should refer to the Plan agreement for more complete information.

1. *General*. The Plan is a defined benefit pension plan covering substantially all employees of C&H Company *(Company)*. It is subject to the provisions of the Employee Retirement Income Security Act of 1974 *(ERISA)*.
2. *Pension Benefits*. Employees with 10 or more years of service are entitled to annual pension benefits beginning at normal retirement age (65) equal to 1 1/2% of their final 5-year average annual compensation for each year of service. The Plan permits early retirement at ages 55-64. Employees may elect to receive their pension benefits in the form of a joint and survivor annuity. If employees terminate before rendering 10 years of service, they forfeit the right to receive the portion of their accumulated plan benefits attributable to the Company's contributions. Employees may elect to receive the value of their accumulated plan benefits as a lump-sum distribution upon retirement or termination, or they may elect to receive their benefits as a life annuity payable monthly from retirement. For each employee electing a life annuity, payments will not be less than the greater of (a) the employee's accumulated contributions plus interest or (b) an annuity for five years.
3. *Death and Disability Benefits*. If an active employee dies at age 55 or older, a death benefit equal to the value of the employee's accumulated pension benefits is paid to the employee's beneficiary. Active employees who become totally disabled receive annual disability benefits that are equal to the normal retirement benefits they have accumulated as of the time they become disabled. Disability benefits are paid until normal retirement age at which time disabled participants begin receiving normal retirement benefits computed as though they had been employed to normal retirement age with their annual compensation remaining the same as at the time they became disabled.

B. Summary of Accounting Policies

The following are the significant accounting policies followed by the Plan:

1. *Valuation of Investments*. If available, quoted market prices are used to value investments. The amounts shown in Note E for securities that have no quoted market price represent estimated fair value. Many factors are considered in arriving at that fair value. In general, however, corporate bonds are valued based on yields currently available on comparable securities of issuers with similar credit ratings. Investments in certain restricted common stocks are valued at the quoted market price of the issuer's unrestricted common stock less an appropriate discount. If a quoted market price for unrestricted common stock of the issuer is not available, restricted common stocks are valued at a multiple of current earnings less an appropriate discount. The multiple chosen is consistent with multiples of similar companies based on current market prices.

   Mortgages have been valued on the basis of their future principal and interest payments discounted at prevailing interest rates for similar instruments. The fair value of real estate investments, principally rental property subject to long-term net leases, has been estimated on the basis of future rental receipts and estimated residual values discounted at interest rates commensurate with the risks involved.

   The Plan's deposit administration contract with the National Insurance Company *(National)* (Note F) is valued at contract value. Contract value represents contributions made under the contract, plus interest at the contract rate, less funds used to purchase annuities and pay administration expenses charged by National. Funds under the contract that have been allocated and

[46]The notes are for the accompanying illustrative financial statements that use an end-of-year benefit information date. Modifications necessary to accompany the illustrative financial statements that use a beginning-of-year benefit information date are presented in brackets.

applied to purchase annuities (that is, National is obligated to pay the related pension benefits) are excluded from the Plan's assets.

2. *Actuarial Present Value of Accumulated Plan Benefits*. Accumulated plan benefits are those future periodic payments, including lump-sum distributions, that are attributable under the Plan's provisions to the service employees have rendered. Accumulated plan benefits include benefits expected to be paid to (a) retired or terminated employees or their beneficiaries, (b) beneficiaries of employees who have died, and (c) present employees or their beneficiaries. Benefits under the Plan are based on employees' compensation during their last five years of credited service. The accumulated plan benefits for active employees are based on their average compensation during the five years ending on the date as of which the benefit information is presented (the *valuation date*). Benefits payable under all circumstances—retirement, death, disability, and termination of employment—are included, to the extent they are deemed attributable to employee service rendered to the valuation date. Benefits to be provided via annuity contracts excluded from plan assets are excluded from accumulated plan benefits.

   The actuarial present value of accumulated plan benefits is determined by an actuary from the AAA Company and is that amount that results from applying actuarial assumptions to adjust the accumulated plan benefits to reflect the time value of money (through discounts for interest) and the probability of payment (by means of decrements such as for death, disability, withdrawal, or retirement) between the valuation date and the expected date of payment. The significant actuarial assumptions used in the valuations as of December 31, 1981 [1980] and December 31, 1980 [1979] were (a) life expectancy of participants (the 1971 Group Annuity Mortality Table was used), (b) retirement age assumptions (the assumed average retirement age was 60), and (c) investment return. The 1981 [1980] and 1980 [1979] valuations included assumed average rates of return of 7% [6.25%] and 6.25% [6.75%], respectively, including a reduction of .2% to reflect anticipated administrative expenses associated with providing benefits. The foregoing actuarial assumptions are based on the presumption that the Plan will continue. Were the Plan to terminate, different actuarial assumptions and other factors might be applicable in determining the actuarial present value of accumulated plan benefits.

C. Funding Policy

As a condition of participation, employees are required to contribute 3% of their salary to the Plan. Present employees' accumulated contributions at December 31, 1981 [1980] were $2,575,000 [$2,325,000], including interest credited at an interest rate of 5% compounded annually. The Company's funding policy is to make annual contributions to the Plan in amounts that are estimated to remain a constant percentage of employees' compensation each year (approximately 5% for 1981 [and 1980]), such that, when combined with employees' contributions, all employees' benefits will be fully provided for by the time they retire. Beginning in 1982, the Company's contribution is expected to increase to approximately 6% to provide for the increase in benefits attributable to the Plan amendment effective July 1, 1981 (Note G). The Company's contributions for 1981 [and 1980] exceeded the minimum funding requirements of ERISA.

Although it has not expressed any intention to do so, the Company has the right under the Plan to discontinue its contributions at any time and to terminate the Plan subject to the provisions set forth in ERISA.

D. Plan Termination

In the event the Plan terminates, the net assets of the Plan will be allocated, as prescribed by ERISA and its related regulations, generally to provide the following benefits in the order indicated:

a. Benefits attributable to employee contributions, taking into account those paid out before termination.
b. Annuity benefits former employees or their beneficiaries have been receiving for at least three years, or that employees eligible to retire for that three-year period would have been receiving if they had retired with benefits in the normal form of annuity under the Plan. The priority amount is limited to the lowest benefit that was payable (or would have been payable) during those three years. The amount is further limited to the lowest benefit that would be payable under plan provisions in effect at any time during the five years preceding plan termination.
c. Other vested benefits insured by the Pension Benefit Guaranty Corporation (*PBGC*) (a U.S. governmental agency) up to the applicable limitations (discussed below).
d. All other vested benefits (that is, vested benefits not insured by the PBGC).
e. All nonvested benefits.

Benefits to be provided via contracts under which National (Note F) is obligated to pay the benefits would be excluded for allocation purposes.

Certain benefits under the Plan are insured by the PBGC if the Plan terminates. Generally, the PBGC guarantees most vested normal age retirement benefits, early retirement benefits, and certain disability and survivor's pensions. However, the PBGC does not guarantee all types of benefits under the Plan, and the amount of benefit protection is subject to certain limitations. Vested benefits under the Plan are guaranteed at the level in effect on the date of the Plan's termination. However, there is a statutory ceiling on the amount of an individual's monthly benefit that the PBGC guarantees. For plan terminations occurring during 1981 and 1980, that ceiling which is adjusted periodically was $ X,XXX.XX and $1,159.09 per month, respectively. That ceiling applies to those pensioners who elect to receive their benefits in the form of a single-life annuity and are at least 65 years old at the time of retirement or plan termination (whichever comes later). For younger annuitants or for those who elect to receive their benefits in some form more valuable than a single-life annuity, the corresponding ceilings are actuarially adjusted downward. Benefit improvements attributable to the Plan amendment effective July 1, 1981 (Note G) may not be fully guaranteed even though total benefit entitlements fall below the aforementioned ceilings. For example, none of the improvement would be guaranteed if the plan were to terminate before July 1, 1982. After that date, the PBGC would guarantee 20% of any benefit improvements that resulted in benefits below the ceiling, with an additional 20% guaranteed each year the plan continued beyond July 1, 1982. If the amount of the benefit increase below the ceiling is also less than $100, $20 of the increase (rather than 20%) becomes guaranteed by the PBGC each year following the effective date of the amendment. As a result, only the primary ceiling would be applicable after July 1, 1986.

Whether all participants receive their benefits should the Plan terminate at some future time will depend on the sufficiency, at that time, of the Plan's net assets to provide those benefits and may also depend on the level of benefits guaranteed by the PBGC.

E. Investments Other Than Contract with Insurance Company

Except for its deposit administration contract (Note F), the Plan's investments are held by a bank-administered trust fund. The following table presents the fair values of those investments. Investments that represent 5% or more of the Plan's net assets are separately identified.

	December 31, 1981		December 31, 1980	
	Number of Shares or Principal Amount	Fair Value	Number of Shares or Principal Amount	Fair Value
Investments at Fair Value As Determined by Quoted Market Price				
United States government securities		$ 350,000		$ 270,000
Corporate bonds and debentures				
National Locomotive 6% series C bonds due 1990	$600,000	480,000	$600,000	492,000
General Design Corp. 5 1/2% convertible debentures due 1993	$700,000	520,000	$350,000	250,000
Other		2,260,000		2,618,000
Common stocks				
C&H Company	25,000	690,000	25,000	880,000
Reliable Manufacturing Corp.	12,125	625,000	9,100	390,000
American Automotive, Inc.	5,800	475,000	6,800	510,000
Other		680,000		500,000
		6,080,000		5,910,000
Investments at Estimated Fair Value				
Corporate bonds and debentures		240,000		310,000
Common stocks		470,000		460,000
Mortgages		480,000		460,000
Real estate		270,000		240,000
		1,460,000		1,470,000
		$7,540,000		$7,380,000

During 1981 [and 1980], the Plan's investments (including investments bought, sold, as well as held during the year) appreciated [(depreciated)] in value by $207,000 [and ($72,000), respectively], as follows:

Net Appreciation (Depreciation) in Fair Value

	Year Ended December 31 1981	Year Ended December 31 1980
Investments at Fair Value as Determined by Quoted Market Price		
United States Government securities	$ (10,000)	$ 8,000
Corporate bonds and debentures	(125,000)	50,000
Common stocks	228,000	(104,000)
	93,000	(46,000)
Investments at Estimated Fair Value		
Corporate bonds and debentures	(11,000)	9,000
Common stocks	100,000	(49,000)
Mortages	(5,000)	4,000
Real estate	30,000	10,000
	114,000	(26,000)
	$ 207,000	$ (72,000)

F. Contract with Insurance Company

In 1978, the Company entered into a deposit administration contract with the National Insurance Company under which the Plan deposits a minimum of $100,000 a year. National maintains the contributions in an unallocated fund to which it adds interest at a rate of 8%. The interest rate is guaranteed through 1983 but is subject to change for each succeeding five-year period. When changed, the new rate applies only to funds deposited from the date of change. At the direction of the Plan's administrator, a single premium to buy an annuity for a retiring employee is withdrawn by National from the unallocated fund. Purchased annuities are contracts under which National is obligated to pay benefits to named employees or their beneficiaries. The premium rates for such annuities to be purchased in the future and maximum administration expense charges against the fund are also guaranteed by National on a five-year basis. The annuity contracts provide for periodic dividends at National's discretion on the basis of its experience under the contracts. Such dividends received by the Plan for the year[s] ended December 31, 1981 [and 1980] were $25,000 [and $24,000, respectively]. In reporting changes in net assets, those dividends have been netted against amounts paid to National for the purchase of annuity contracts.

G. Plan Amendment

Effective July 1, 1981, the Plan was amended to increase future annual pension benefits from 1 1/4% to 1 1/2% of final 5-year average annual compensation for each year of service, including service rendered before the effective date. The retroactive effect of the Plan amendment, an increase in the actuarial present value of accumulated plan benefits of $2,410,000, was accounted for in the year ended December 31, 1981. [The actuarial present values of accumulated plan benefits at December 31, 1980 and December 31, 1979 do not reflect the effect of that Plan amendment. The Plan's actuary estimates that the amendment's retroactive effect on the actuarial present value of accumulated plan benefits at December 31, 1980 was an increase of approximately $1,750,000, of which approximately $1,300,000 represents an increase in vested benefits.]

H. Accounting Changes

In 1981, the Plan changed its method of accounting and reporting to comply with the provisions of Statement of Financial Accounting Standards No. 35 issued by the Financial Accounting Standards Board. Previously reported financial information pertaining to 1980 [and 1979] has been restated to present that information on a comparable basis.

Appendix E

ILLUSTRATION OF MEASUREMENT OF ACCUMULATED PLAN BENEFITS[47]

283. It is assumed that the actuary uses a full range of decrements including termination rates and disablement rates at ages below age 65, early retirement rates at ages when eligible below age 65, and normal retirement rates at ages 65 and over.

a. Given:
   i. Benefit rate of $10 per month per year of service.
   ii. Normal retirement at age 65, irrespective of service. Retirement not compulsory.
   iii. Unreduced immediate benefit upon early retirement from active employment at age 62 with 20 years of service.
   iv. Unreduced immediate benefit upon early retirement from active employment before age 62 with 30 years of service. Social Security make-up benefit of $200 per month payable until age 62.
   v. Reduced immediate benefit upon early retirement from active employment after age 55 and before age 62 with 20 years of service. Reduction is 4% for each year by which retirement precedes age 62.
   vi. Unreduced immediate benefit upon total and permanent disability before age 65 with 10 years of service.
   vii. Deferred vested benefit, commencing at age 65, upon termination with 10 years of service. Benefit payments (at full actuarially reduced value) may also be elected to commence as early as age 55 if 20 or more years of service have been completed.
   viii. Spouse's benefit upon death in service after meeting eligibility requirements for early or normal retirement (30 years of service, age 55 and 20 years of service, or age 65) equal to $5 per month per year of service.

b. [Follows on page 1533.]

[47]This appendix illustrates the measurement of accumulated plan benefits pursuant to the provisions of paragraphs 18(a) and 18(b) of this Statement. The example has been reproduced from Interpretation 2: *Interpretation of Recommendations Concerning the Calculation of the Actuarial Present Value of Accrued Benefits under an Active Plan,* as presented in American Academy of Actuaries, *Bylaws, Guides to Professional Conduct, Standards of Practice, February 1, 1979* (Chicago: American Academy of Actuaries), pp. 106-113.

Type of Benefit	Payable upon Separation from Service at Ages	Amount of Benefit	Benefit Starts at	Duration of Benefit
		Age 25 and 5 Years of Service		
(1) Deferred Vested	30-49	$50	Age 65	Life
(2) Unreduced Early	50-64	50	Retirement	Life
(3) Social Security Makeup	50-61	33*	Retirement	To Age 62
(4) Normal	65 and Over	50	Retirement	Life
(5) Spouse	50 and Over	25	Death in Service	Life of Spouse
(6) Disability	30-64	50	Disablement	Life
		Age 40 and 5 Years of Service		
(1) Deferred Vested	45-54	$50	Age 65	Life
(2) Reduced Early	55-61	36 at Age 55 Increasing $2 a Year to Age 61	Retirement	Life
(3) Unreduced Early	62-64	50	Retirement	Life
(4) Normal	65 and Over	50	Retirement	Life
(5) Spouse	55 and Over	25	Death in Service	Life of Spouse
(6) Disability	45-64	50	Disablement	Life
		Age 45 and 10 Years of Service		
(1) Deferred Vested	45-54	$100	Age 65	Life
(2) Reduced Early	55-61	72 at Age 55 Increasing $4 a Year to Age 61	Retirement	Life
(3) Unreduced Early	62-64	100	Retirement	Life
(4) Normal	65 and Over	100	Retirement	Life
(5) Spouse	55 and Over	50	Death in Service	Life of Spouse
(6) Disability	45-64	100	Disablement	Life
		Age 50 and 20 Years of Service		
(1) Deferred Vested	50-54	$200	Age 65	Life
(2) Reduced Early	55-59	144 at Age 55 Increasing $8 a Year to Age 59	Retirement	Life
(3) Unreduced Early	60-64	200	Retirement	Life
(4) Social Security Makeup	60-61	133*	Retirement	To Age 62
(5) Normal	65 and Over	200	Retirement	Life
(6) Spouse	55 and Over	100	Death in Service	Life of Spouse
(7) Disability	50-64	200	Disablement	Life
		Age 50 and 30 Years of Service		
(1) Unreduced Early	50-64	$300	Retirement	Life
(2) Social Security Makeup	50-61	200*	Retirement	To Age 62
(3) Normal	65 and Over	300	Retirement	Life
(4) Spouse	50 and Over	150	Death in Service	Life of Spouse
(5) Disability	50-64	300	Disablement	Life
		Age 60 and 10 Years of Service		
(1) Deferred Vested	60-64	$100	Age 65	Life
(2) Normal	65 and Over	100	Retirement	Life
(3) Spouse	65 and Over	50	Death in Service	Life of Spouse
(4) Disability	60-64	100	Disablement	Life

*Because this benefit type is one which is includible in the computation of the present value of vested benefits, the $200 monthly benefit is assumed to accrue uniformly over the first 30 years of service (see I(b)(ii)). If, on the other hand, there had been specified a benefit which never is includible in the computation of the present value of vested benefits, such as a $200 monthly benefit payable in the event of the employee's death after 30 years of service, the accrued death benefit to be valued in the age 25 and 5 years of service example would have been $33 (5/30 of $200) for death at age 50, $32 (5/31 of $200) for death at age 51, etc.

c. If, in the example, there were a maximum service limit of 30 years applicable at normal or early retirement or disablement, with a pro-rata portion of the expected normal retirement benefit payable on vested termination, the only changes in the amount of benefit would be for the deferred vested benefit:

Age 25 and 5 Years of Service	$ 33 (5/45 of $300)
Age 50 and 20 Years of Service	171 (20/35 of $300)

Statement of Financial Accounting Standards No. 36
Disclosure of Pension Information

an amendment of APB Opinion No. 8

STATUS

Issued: May 1980

Effective Date: For fiscal years beginning after December 15, 1979 and for complete interim statements issued after June 30, 1980 for interim periods within those fiscal years

Affects: Supersedes APB 8, paragraph 46

Affected by: No other pronouncements

SUMMARY

There is a need for comparability in disclosures about the financial status of pension plans made in employers' financial statements. Accordingly, this Statement requires revised disclosures about defined benefit pension plans in employers' financial statements. The revised disclosures include the actuarial present value of accumulated plan benefits and the pension plan assets available for those benefits, both as determined in accordance with FASB Statement No. 35, *Accounting and Reporting by Defined Benefit Pension Plans.* Employers having plans for which accumulated benefit information is not available will (1) continue to make the disclosures with respect to vested benefits called for by APB Opinion No. 8, *Accounting for the Cost of Pension Plans,* and (2) disclose the reasons why the information required by this Statement is not provided.

Statement of Financial Accounting Standards No. 36
Disclosure of Pension Information

an amendment of APB Opinion No. 8

CONTENTS

INTRODUCTION AND BACKGROUND INFORMATION

1. In March 1980, the FASB issued Statement No. 35, *Accounting and Reporting by Defined Benefit Pension Plans,* which focuses on accounting and reporting by pension plans. A Discussion Memorandum for a project on accounting by employers for pensions is presently being prepared. It will address the issues relating to employers' accounting for pension and other retirement benefits.

2. As an interim measure, pending completion of the latter project, the Board has decided that the lack of comparable disclosures in employers' financial statements about the financial status of their pension plans requires an amendment of existing disclosure standards. Many publicly held companies presently disclose in their financial statements the amount of unfunded past service costs, which the Securities and Exchange Commission requires to be disclosed in Form 10-K. The amount of past service costs can vary considerably or be nonexistent depending on the actuarial cost method selected, without any differences in other facts or circumstances. For that reason, the Board believes that disclosure of unfunded past service cost is not as useful as other information for evaluating the impact of pension plans on employers. Also, APB Opinion No. 8, *Accounting for the Cost of Pension Plans,* does not specify the basis that should be used for valuing pension plan assets in determining the amount of unfunded vested benefits that Opinion requires to be disclosed. Various valuation methods exist in practice. The Board believes that pension disclosures in financial statements would be more useful if employers with defined benefit pension plans disclosed the actuarial present value of accumulated plan benefits and net assets available for those benefits, as determined in accordance with Statement 35.

3. As a part of its ongoing effort to develop a conceptual framework for financial accounting and reporting, the Board has on its agenda a project that addresses the definitions of liabilities as well as assets and equity interests. At present, the accounting nature of employees' accumulated plan benefits has not been determined. That issue will be addressed, from the employer's perspective, in the project on accounting by employers for pensions. In the meantime, the Board has concluded that summary information of the financial status of the employer's pension plans should be provided to an employer's existing and potential creditors and investors. The Board has also concluded that the information developed for disclosure by the pension plan was a logical basis for the employer's disclosures because of its relevance and because little or no additional cost would be involved.

4. This Statement does not alter the definitions of a defined benefit pension plan and a defined contribution plan contained in Appendix B of Opinion 8. Also, this Statement does not change the requirements of paragraph 39 of Opinion 8; that paragraph requires some defined contribution plans to comply with the requirements applicable to defined benefit plans when careful analysis indicates that the substance of the plan is to provide defined benefits.

5. An Exposure Draft of a proposed Statement, *Disclosure of Pension and Other Post-Retirement Benefit Information,* was issued on July 12, 1979. The Board received 228 letters of comment in response to the Exposure Draft. Certain of the comments received and the Board's consideration of them are discussed in Appendix B, "Summary of Consideration of Comments on Exposure Draft."

6. The Board has concluded that it can reach an informed decision on the basis of existing data without a public hearing and that the effective date

and transition specified in paragraph 11 are advisable in the circumstances.

STANDARDS OF FINANCIAL ACCOUNTING AND REPORTING

7. The Board believes that pension plans are of sufficient importance to an understanding of financial position and results of operations that the disclosures set forth in this paragraph and paragraph 8 shall be made in financial statements or the notes thereto:

a. A statement that pension plans exist, identifying or describing the employee groups covered,
b. A statement of the company's accounting and funding policies,
c. The provision for pension cost for the period,
d. Nature and effect of significant matters affecting comparability for all periods presented, such as changes in accounting methods (actuarial cost method, amortization of past and prior service cost, treatment of actuarial gains and losses, etc.), changes in circumstances (actuarial assumptions, etc.), or adoption or amendment of a plan.

8. For its defined benefit pension plans, an employer shall disclose for each complete set of financial statements the following data determined in accordance with Statement 35 as of the most recent benefit information date[1] for which the data are available:

a. The actuarial present value of vested accumulated plan benefits,
b. The actuarial present value of nonvested accumulated plan benefits,
c. The plans' net assets available for benefits,[2]
d. The assumed rates of return used in determining the actuarial present values of vested and nonvested accumulated plan benefits,
e. The date as of which the benefit information was determined.

The data may be reported in total for all plans, separately for each plan, or in such subaggregations as are considered most useful.[3] For plans for which the above data are not available,[4] the employer shall continue to comply with the disclosure requirements originally contained in Opinion 8, namely, the excess, if any, of the actuarially computed value of vested benefits over the total of the pension fund and any balance sheet pension accruals, less any pension prepayments or deferred charges. The reasons why the information required by (a) through (e) above is not provided for those plans shall be disclosed.

9. In some cases, the relative position and undertakings of an employer associated with a multiemployer plan that, pursuant to paragraph 39 of Opinion 8, is considered to be a defined benefit plan may not be determinable. If that situation exists and the circumstances are disclosed, the requirements of paragraph 8 are waived with regard to that plan.

Amendment to APB Opinion No. 8

10. This Statement supersedes paragraph 46 of Opinion 8. The example following item 5 of paragraph 46 of Opinion 8 is replaced by the example that appears in Appendix A. The requirements of paragraph 46 of Opinion 8 have been carried forward without change except as to item 4 of that paragraph, which is changed by paragraphs 8 and 9 of this Statement.

Effective Date and Transition

11. This Statement shall be effective for annual financial statements for fiscal years beginning after December 15, 1979 and for a complete set of financial statements for interim periods within those fiscal years issued after June 30, 1980. Earlier application is encouraged. The disclosures required by this Statement need not be included in financial statements for periods beginning before the effective date of this Statement that are being presented for comparative purposes with financial statements for periods after the effective date, but if included, that information shall be presented in conformity with the provisions of this Statement.

[1]The benefit information date is the date as of which the actuarial present value of accumulated plan benefits is determined. In comparative financial statements, data disclosed for earlier periods shall be the data available when the earlier financial statements were originally issued.

[2]For purposes of this Statement, an employer's accrued pension liability, as of the benefit information date, shall be added to the plan's net assets to the extent that it exceeds contributions receivable from the employer included in the plan's net assets available for benefits.

[3]There may be circumstances in which significant unfunded amounts of an individual plan are offset by the aggregation of assets in excess of accumulated benefits in other plans. Separate disclosure of such unfunded amounts may be desirable if a significant number of participants in such an unfunded plan are employed by a subsidiary or division that is unprofitable or experiencing a continuous decline in business.

[4]Plans for which the information may not be available are expected to be only those plans that do not report such information with certain governmental agencies pursuant to the Employee Retirement Income Security Act of 1974 (ERISA).

The provisions of this Statement need not be applied to immaterial items.

This Statement was adopted by the affirmative votes of six members of the Financial Accounting Standards Board. Mr. Morgan dissented.

Mr. Morgan dissents to this Statement because: (a) he does not believe the need is urgent, (b) he sees no conceptual or pragmatic reason to require that sponsors and plans have symmetrical reporting, and (c) he believes that until the Board's project on accounting by employers for pensions is completed, the Board should not attempt to change rules concerning disclosure of pension plan information because such changes may become only temporary changes contributing more to misunderstanding than to improved understanding by the users of such information.

Members of the Financial Accounting Standards Board:

Donald J. Kirk, *Chairman*
Frank E. Block
John W. March
Robert A. Morgan
David Mosso
Robert T. Sprouse
Ralph E. Walters

Appendix A

EXAMPLE OF PENSION PLAN DISCLOSURE

12. The company and its subsidiaries have several pension plans covering substantially all of their employees, including certain employees in foreign countries. The total pension expense for 19X1 and 19X2 was $XXX and $XXX respectively, which includes, as to certain defined benefit plans, amortization of past service cost over XX years. The company makes annual contributions to the plans equal to the amounts accrued for pension expense. A change during 19X2 in the actuarial cost method used in computing pension cost had the effect of reducing net income for the year by approximately $XXX. A comparison of accumulated plan benefits and plan net assets for the company's domestic defined benefit plans is presented below:

	January 1, 19X1	January 1, 19X2
Actuarial present value of accumulated plan benefits:		
Vested	$XXX	$XXX
Nonvested	XXX	XXX
	$XXX	$XXX
Net assets available for benefits	$XXX	$XXX

The weighted average assumed rate of return used in determining the actuarial present value of accumulated plan benefits was X percent for both 19X1 and 19X2. The company's foreign pension plans are not required to report to certain governmental agencies pursuant to ERISA and do not otherwise determine the actuarial value of accumulated benefits or net assets available for benefits as calculated and disclosed above. For those plans, the actuarially computed value of vested benefits as of December 31, 19X1 and December 31, 19X2 exceeded the total of those plans' pension funds and balance sheet accruals less pension prepayments and deferred charges by approximately $XXX and $XXX respectively.

Appendix B

SUMMARY OF CONSIDERATION OF COMMENTS ON EXPOSURE DRAFT

13. Some respondents questioned whether an amendment to Opinion 8 should be issued at this time because the project on accounting by employers for pensions is on the agenda and will include a comprehensive examination of employer accounting for pension and other retirement benefits. Other respondents supported issuance of the Statement because present requirements do not provide comparable and meaningful pension disclosures. The Board agrees with the latter arguments and believes the improved comparability among employers' financial statements about the financial status of their pension plans warrants proceeding with the issuance of this Statement.

14. The Exposure Draft would have required a description of all significant actuarial assumptions used to determine the actuarial present value of accumulated plan benefits. Some respondents stated that the highly technical and complex nature of actuarial assumptions would require extensive disclosures to provide adequate information for the user. Others stated that meaningful disclosure of actuarial assumptions would be further complicated

for companies with multiple pension plans. Some respondents proposed the disclosure of actuarial assumptions be limited to the assumed rate(s) of investment return as that was considered the most significant assumption. Although the Board recognizes there may be additional significant assumptions, it agreed with the latter respondents and limited disclosure of actuarial assumptions to the assumed rate(s) of return.

15. The Exposure Draft would have required disclosing a description of other retirement benefits, a description of accounting policies followed with respect to those benefits, and the cost of those benefits included in determining net income for the period. Some respondents objected to such disclosures because they felt that the costs of other retirement benefits were not material when compared to similar costs for active employees. Some respondents stated that because specific accounting standards for such benefits have not been established, disclosure requirements should be postponed pending development of such standards. Other respondents indicated that the only significant disclosure regarding other retirement benefits would be the difference between the amount charged to expense and the amount that would be required using a generally accepted method of accounting for other retirement benefits. Because there is no authoritative generally accepted method of accounting for other retirement benefits, disclosure of that information would be premature at this time. The Board agreed with the comments of those respondents and, because accounting for other retirement benefits is included within the scope of the project on accounting by employers for pensions, the Board deleted that proposed disclosure requirement.

16. Some respondents indicated that the Exposure Draft's statement that the proposed disclosures would cause little or no additional cost to the employer was not valid in certain cases. For example, because certain plans (e.g., foreign plans) are not required to report information to certain governmental agencies pursuant to ERISA, employers sponsoring those plans would have to determine the information in paragraph 8 solely for purposes of complying with this Statement. Similarly, plans having fewer than 100 participants that report under ERISA are not required to report accumulated benefit information to those agencies unless that information is calculated. The Board was persuaded by the arguments of those respondents and concluded that the appropriate criterion for requiring the new disclosures required by this Statement should be the availability of the information. If that information is not available, then employers are required to continue to comply with the disclosure requirements originally contained in paragraph 46(4) of Opinion 8. The Board believes this approach provides improved disclosure in those circumstances where the information is available and will involve little additional cost. It will also not diminish the present disclosure by those employers with plans for which the information is not available.

17. The Exposure Draft required that employers with more than one defined benefit pension plan group those plans as to (a) those with accumulated plan benefits exceeding assets and (b) those having assets exceeding accumulated plan benefits. A number of respondents objected to that requirement because they felt that separate disclosure of "overfunded" and "underfunded" pension plans would be confusing and direct the reader's attention away from the relevance of the combined amounts to the employer's future pension commitments. Other respondents stated that users do not gain significantly meaningful information from such a division. The Board considered the comments of those respondents and agreed to permit, instead of require, such presentation.

Statement of Financial Accounting Standards No. 37
Balance Sheet Classification of Deferred Income Taxes

an amendment of APB Opinion No. 11

STATUS

Issued: July 1980

Effective Date: For periods ending after December 15, 1980

Affects: Amends APB 11, paragraph 57

Affected by: No other pronouncements

SUMMARY

This Statement specifies the basis for classification of deferred income taxes in a classified balance sheet. Deferred income taxes related to an asset or liability are classified the same as the related asset or liability. Deferred income taxes that are not related to an asset or liability are classified according to the expected reversal date of the timing difference.

Statement of Financial Accounting Standards No. 37
Balance Sheet Classification of Deferred Income Taxes

an amendment of APB Opinion No. 11

CONTENTS

INTRODUCTION

1. The FASB has been asked to clarify the classification of deferred income tax charges and credits related to the tax effects of certain timing differences (hereinafter referred to as "deferred income taxes"). The FASB also has been asked to clarify the balance sheet classification of the tax benefits related to "stock relief" under FASB Statement No. 31, *Accounting for Tax Benefits Related to U.K. Tax Legislation concerning Stock Relief*.

2. Paragraph 57 of APB Opinion No. 11, *Accounting for Income Taxes* (see paragraph 6 of this Statement), requires deferred income taxes to be classified in a balance sheet as current or noncurrent based on the classification of assets or liabilities related to the timing differences. Some timing differences, however, are not related to an asset or liability. Accordingly, the Board has concluded that it should amend paragraph 57 to clarify the classification of deferred income taxes when there is no asset or liability in the balance sheet related to the timing difference.

3. The Board also has concluded that it can reach an informed decision on the basis of existing data without a public hearing and that the effective date and transition specified in paragraph 5 are advisable in the circumstances.

STANDARDS OF FINANCIAL ACCOUNTING AND REPORTING

Amendment to APB Opinion No. 11

4. The last two sentences of paragraph 57 of Opinion 11 are deleted and the following sentences and related footnotes are added to that paragraph:

> A deferred charge or credit is related to an asset or liability if reduction* of the asset or liability causes the timing difference to reverse. A deferred charge or credit that is related to an asset or liability shall be classified as current or noncurrent based on the classification of the related asset or liability. A deferred charge or credit that is not related to an asset or liability because (a) there is no associated asset or liability or (b) reduction of an associated asset or liability will not cause the timing difference to reverse shall be classified based on the expected reversal date of the specific timing difference.† Such classification disregards any additional timing differences that may arise and is based on the criteria used for classifying other assets and liabilities.

*As used here, the term "reduction" includes amortization, sale, or other realization of an asset and amortization, payment, or other satisfaction of a liability.

†Tax benefits related to "stock relief" that have been deferred under FASB Statement No. 31, *Accounting for Tax Benefits Related to U.K. Tax Legislation concerning Stock Relief*, are not timing differences and should be classified the same as other liabilities based on the period of potential recapture.

Effective Date and Transition

5. This Statement shall be effective for financial statements for periods ending after December 15, 1980, with earlier application encouraged. Reclassification in previously issued financial statements is permitted but not required.

The provisions of this Statement need not be applied to immaterial items.

This Statement was adopted by the unanimous vote of the seven members of the Financial Accounting Standards Board.

Donald J. Kirk, *Chairman*
Frank E. Block
John W. March
Robert A. Morgan
David Mosso
Robert T. Sprouse
Ralph E. Walters

Appendix A

BACKGROUND INFORMATION

6. Paragraph 57 of Opinion 11 states:

> Deferred charges and deferred credits relating to timing differences represent the cumulative recognition given to their tax effects and as such do not represent receivables or payables in the usual sense. They should be classified in two categories—one for the net current amount and the other for the net noncurrent amount. This presentation is consistent with the customary distinction between current and noncurrent categories and also recognizes the close relationship among the various deferred tax accounts, all of which bear on the determination of income tax expense. The current portions of such deferred charges and credits should be those amounts which relate to assets and liabilities classified as current. Thus, if installment receivables are a current asset, the deferred credits representing the tax effects of uncollected installment sales should be a current item; if an estimated provision for warranties is a current liability, the deferred charge representing the tax effect of such provision should be a current item.

7. Under Opinion 11, deferred income taxes are classified as current and noncurrent on the basis of how the related assets and liabilities are classified. The Board concluded that it should amend paragraph 57 of Opinion 11 to address the classification of deferred taxes when either (a) the timing difference is not related to an asset or liability because reduction of the asset or liability does not result in reversal of the timing difference or (b) there is no asset or liability related to the deferred income taxes.

8. Paragraph 10 of Statement 31 states that the Board believes U.K. "stock relief" does not have the characteristics of a timing or permanent difference. Therefore, the classification criterion of paragraph 57 of Opinion 11 does not apply. Those tax benefits shall be classified the same as other liabilities based on the period of potential recapture.

9. A proposed Interpretation, *Balance Sheet Classification of Deferred Income Taxes,* was released for comment on June 22, 1979. The proposed Interpretation of Opinion 11 addressed the classification of deferred income taxes related to timing differences associated with long-term construction contracts, undistributed earnings of subsidiaries, and a change in method of accounting for income tax reporting purposes. Fifty-one comment letters were received. The Interpretation proposed to clarify that deferred income taxes classified as current should be reclassified to noncurrent only if the related asset or liability is reclassified to noncurrent. Many respondents to the proposed Interpretation questioned the appropriate balance sheet classification when the timing difference is not related to an asset or liability because realization of the asset or liquidation of the liability does not result in reversal of the timing difference. Others commented that there is no asset or liability related to the deferred income taxes for certain timing differences.The Board concluded that it should amend paragraph 57 of Opinion 11 to address the balance sheet classification of deferred income taxes in those circumstances.

10. An Exposure Draft of a proposed Statement, on *Balance Sheet Classification of Deferred Income Taxes,* an amendment of APB Opinion No. 11, was issued for public comment on March 14, 1980.The Board received 67 letters of comment in response to the Exposure Draft.

11. Some respondents suggested classifying deferred income taxes based on the net effect of (a) reversals of existing timing differences and (b) any additional timing differences that may arise. The Board concluded that balance sheet classification of deferred income taxes is based on the deferred income taxes that exist at the balance sheet date.

12. Other respondents suggested classifying *all* deferred income taxes based on when the timing differences reverse or classifying as current only those deferred income taxes that will actually be paid. The Board concluded, however, that such criteria would involve a more fundamental change in paragraph 57 of Opinion 11 that should not be considered at this time.

13. Several respondents to the Exposure Draft commented about the operating cycle in the illustration of construction contracts. The Board did not intend to address or change how an operating cycle is determined. Accordingly, that illustration has been revised to be consistent with the operating cycle concepts expressed in Chapter 3A, "Current Assets and Current Liabilities," of ARB 43.

14. Several comments were received on the capital lease illustration. Those comments suggested classifying the deferred income taxes like the asset or like the liability. The Board concluded that, based on the facts set forth in the capital lease illustration, the nature of lease timing differences and the classification of the associated deferred income taxes described in paragraph 27 are appropriate.

15. Some respondents of regulated utilities stated that regulatory accounting instructions for their industry required deferred income taxes to be classified with the associated asset or liability. Another respondent stated that their required system of accounts makes no provision for a current classification of deferred income taxes. This Statement clarifies classification of deferred income taxes when there is no asset or liability in the balance sheet related to the timing difference and does not otherwise change the classification criteria of Opinion 11. Also, this Statement does not modify the provision in paragraph 6 of Opinion 11 which states that Opinion 11 "does not apply . . . to regulated industries in those circumstances where the standards described in the Addendum (which remains in effect) to APB Opinion No. 2 are met. . . ."

Appendix B

ILLUSTRATIONS OF BALANCE SHEET CLASSIFICATION OF DEFERRED INCOME TAXES

16. The examples in this appendix illustrate the balance sheet classification of certain types of deferred income taxes but do not encompass all possible circumstances. Accordingly, each situation should be resolved based on an evaluation of the facts, using the examples in this appendix as guides to the extent that they are applicable.

Installment Receivables

17. An enterprise reports profit on installment sales for tax purposes on the installment basis as receivables are collected. For financial reporting purposes, profit on installment sales is reported when the merchandise is delivered. The enterprise uses a one-year time period as the basis for classifying current assets and current liabilities on its balance sheet. Deferred income taxes are computed on the net change method. At December 31, 19X1, the balances of receivables reported on the installment method for tax purposes and of related deferred income taxes are as follows:

Installment Receivables:	
Amounts Due within One Year	$1,491,560
Amounts Due after One Year	3,835,440
Total	$5,327,000
Accumulated Deferred Income Tax Credits Related to Installment Receivables	$1,065,000

18. The deferred income tax credits relate to the installment receivables because collection of the receivables will cause the timing differences to reverse.[1] Accordingly, the enterprise would classify the deferred income tax credits the same as the related trade receivables. The trade receivables due within the next year represent 28 percent of the total trade receivables ($1,491,560/$5,327,000). Therefore, 28 percent of the related deferred income tax credits would be classified as current ($298,200).

Accounting Change for Tax Purposes

19. Deferred income taxes associated with an accounting change for tax purposes would be classified like the associated asset or liability if reduction of that associated asset or liability will cause the timing difference to reverse. If there is no associated asset or liability or if the timing difference will reverse only over a period of time, the deferred income taxes would be classified based on the expected reversal date of the specific timing difference.

20. An enterprise changes its method of handling bad debts for tax purposes from the cash method to the reserve method. Ten percent of the effect of the change at the beginning of calendar year 19X1 will be included as a deduction from taxable income each year for 10 years. The enterprise uses a one-year time period as the basis for classifying current assets and current liabilities on its balance sheet. At

[1]Under the net change method, deferred income taxes are computed as though the timing differences at the end of the period were the same timing differences that existed at the beginning of the period except to the extent that the aggregate amount changes. That approach is not used for balance sheet classification because balance sheet classification is based on the nature of the specific timing differences that exist and that relate to the deferred income taxes at the balance sheet date.

December 31, 19X1, the amount of the effect of the change that is yet to be included as a deduction from taxable income and the balance of the related deferred income taxes are as follows:

Amount of the effect of the change that is yet to be included as a deduction from taxable income (9/10 of total effect of the change)	$5,125,000
Accumulated Deferred Income Tax Debits Related to Accounting Change	$2,357,500

21. The deferred income taxes do not relate to trade receivables or provisions for doubtful accounts because collection or write-off of the receivables will not cause the timing differences to reverse; the timing differences will reverse over time. Accordingly, the enterprise would classify the deferred income tax debits based on the scheduled reversal of the related timing differences. One-ninth of the remaining timing differences are scheduled to reverse in 19X2, so one-ninth of the related deferred income tax debits would be classified as current at December 31, 19X1 ($261,944).

Method of Reporting Construction Contracts

22. An enterprise reports profits on construction contracts on the completed contract method for tax purposes and the percentage-of-completion method for financial reporting purposes. The deferred income tax credits do not relate to an asset or liability that appears on the enterprise's balance sheet; the timing differences will only reverse when the contracts are completed. Receivables that result from progress billings can be collected with no effect on the timing differences; likewise, contract retentions can be collected with no effect on the timing differences, and the timing differences will reverse when the contracts are deemed to be complete even if there is a waiting period before retentions will be received. Accordingly, the enterprise would classify the deferred income tax credits based on the estimated reversal of the related timing differences. Deferred income tax credits related to timing differences that will reverse within the same time period used in classifying other contract-related assets and liabilities as current (for example, an operating cycle) would be classified as current.

Unremitted Foreign Earnings of Subsidiaries

23. An enterprise provides U.S. income taxes on the portion of its unremitted foreign earnings that are not considered to be permanently reinvested in its consolidated foreign subsidiary. The foreign earnings are included in U.S. taxable income in the year in which dividends are paid. The enterprise uses a one-year time period as the basis for classifying current assets and current liabilities on its balance sheet. At December 31, 19X1, the accumulated amount of unremitted earnings on which taxes have been provided and the balance of the related deferred income taxes are as follows:

Accumulated unremitted earnings on which taxes have been provided:	
Expected to be remitted within one year	$ 9,800,000
Not expected to be remitted within one year	2,700,000
Total	$12,500,000
Accumulated Deferred Income Tax Credits Related to Unremitted Earnings	$ 1,250,000

24. The deferred income tax credits do not relate to an asset or liability on the consolidated balance sheet; the timing difference will only reverse when the unremitted earnings are received from the foreign subsidiary by the parent. A payment between consolidated affiliates does not change the consolidated balance sheet, so no item on the consolidated balance sheet would be liquidated. Unremitted earnings expected to be remitted within the next year represent 78 percent of the total unremitted earnings for which tax has been provided ($9,800,000/$12,500,000). Therefore, 78 percent of the related deferred income tax credits would be classified as current on the consolidated balance sheet ($975,000).

25. If the subsidiary were accounted for on the equity method rather than consolidated (e.g., a subsidiary reported on the equity method in separate parent company financial statements), the deferred income taxes would relate to the recorded investment in the subsidiary. The payment of dividends that causes the reversal of the timing difference would be accompanied by a reduction of the recorded investment in the subsidiary. Therefore, the deferred income tax credits would be classified the same as the related investment in the subsidiary.

Capital Lease

26. An enterprise is the lessee under one major lease that is reported as an operating lease for tax purposes and as a capital lease for financial reporting purposes. The enterprise uses a one-year time period as the basis for classifying current assets and current liabilities on its balance sheet. At December 31, 19X1, certain data related to the lease are as follows:

Accumulated Lease Timing Differences[2]		$1,020,900
Accumulated Deferred Income Tax Charges Related to Lease Timing Differences		410,000
Amounts relevant to 19X2:		
Rental expense for tax purposes		$579,000
Book expenses:		
Depreciation	$250,000	
Interest	210,500	460,500
Net Reversing Timing Differences		$ 118,500

27. The lease timing differences result from the difference between rental expense reported for tax purposes and the total of interest expense and depreciation expense for financial reporting. Therefore, the deferred income taxes could be considered to relate to both the capitalized leased asset and the recorded lease obligation and not to any specific asset or liability. Accordingly, the enterprise would classify the deferred income tax charges based on the estimated reversal of the related timing differences. The timing differences that will reverse within the next year amount to $118,500 or 12 percent of the total accumulated lease timing differences ($118,500/$1,020,900). Therefore, 12 percent of the related deferred tax charges would be classified as current ($49,200).

Depreciation

28. An enterprise computes its depreciation expense on accelerated methods for tax purposes. For financial reporting purposes, depreciation expense is computed on the straight-line method. The enterprise uses a one-year time period as the basis for classifying current assets and current liabilities on its balance sheet.

29. The deferred income tax credits relate to the fixed assets because sale of the assets would cause the timing differences to reverse.[3] Accordingly, the enterprise would classify the deferred income taxes the same as the related fixed assets. No portion of those deferred income tax credits would be classified as current.

[2]The accumulated timing differences related to a lease that is reported as a capital lease for financial reporting purposes and as an operating lease for tax purposes could be determined based on amounts in the balance sheet rather than based on the difference in amounts reported as expense for book and tax purposes in prior years. If there is no accrued or prepaid rent for tax purposes, the accumulated timing differences would be the difference between the present value of the lease obligation and the net book value of the leased asset, both as reported in the financial statements.

[3]See footnote 1.

Statement of Financial Accounting Standards No. 38
Accounting for Preacquisition Contingencies of Purchased Enterprises

an amendment of APB Opinion No. 16

STATUS

Issued: September 1980

Effective Date: For business combinations initiated after December 15, 1980

Affects: Amends APB 16, paragraph 88

Affected by: No other pronouncements

SUMMARY

This Statement specifies how an acquiring enterprise should account for contingencies of an acquired enterprise that were in existence at the purchase date and for subsequent adjustments that result from those contingencies. Amounts that can be reasonably estimated for contingencies that are considered probable are recorded as a part of the allocation of the purchase price. Subsequent adjustments are included in net income when the adjustments are determined except in limited circumstances described in this Statement.

Statement of Financial Accounting Standards No. 38 Accounting for Preacquisition Contingencies of Purchased Enterprises

an amendment of APB Opinion No. 16

CONTENTS

INTRODUCTION

1. The FASB has been asked to specify the application of FASB Statements No. 5, *Accounting for Contingencies*, and 16, *Prior Period Adjustments*, and APB Opinion No. 16, *Business Combinations,* to preacquisition contingencies[1] of purchased enterprises and adjustments that result from resolution of those contingencies. For example, an acquired enterprise might have litigation pending at the acquisition date, or an unexpected lawsuit relating to events that occurred before the acquisition might be filed shortly after that date. In such cases, do the criteria of Statement 5 apply to the estimate recorded as a part of the purchase price allocation, or, if not, what criteria do apply? Also, does Statement 16 require that a subsequent adjustment that results from a settlement of that litigation or from an estimate of the cost of a future settlement of that litigation be reported by the acquiring enterprise as an item of profit or loss in the period in which the settlement occurs or can be estimated? Alternatively, does Opinion 16 require the subsequent adjustment to be reported by the acquiring enterprise as an adjustment of the purchase allocation?

2. The Board concluded that it should amend Opinion 16 to specify criteria for recording contingent assets, contingent liabilities, and contingent impairments of assets as a part of the allocation of the cost of an enterprise that is acquired in a business combination accounted for by the purchase method. This Statement requires either the fair value of contingencies or other amounts that can be reasonably estimated for contingencies that are considered probable to be used as the basis of allocation of the purchase price during the "allocation period" as defined in paragraph 4. Subsequent adjustments are included in the determination of net income in the period in which the adjustments are determined. This Statement does not apply to potential income tax benefits of preacquisition net operating loss carryforwards or adjustments that result from realization of those benefits. APB Opinion No. 11, *Accounting for Income Taxes*, and Opinion 16 specify the accounting for those items.

3. Appendix A provides additional background information on preacquisition contingencies. Appendix B explains the basis for the Board's conclusions. The Board has concluded that it can make an informed decision on the basis of existing information without a public hearing and that the effective date and transition specified in paragraphs 8-10 are advisable in the circumstances.

STANDARDS OF FINANCIAL ACCOUNTING AND REPORTING

Definitions

4. For purposes of applying this Statement, certain terms are defined as follows:

a. *Preacquisition contingency*. A contingency of an enterprise that is acquired in a business combination accounted for by the purchase method and that is in existence before the consummation of the combination. A preacquisition contingency can be a contingent asset, a contingent liability, or a contingent impairment of an asset.

[1] Statement 5 defines a contingency as an existing condition, situation, or set of circumstances involving uncertainty as to possible gain or loss to an enterprise that will ultimately be resolved when one or more future events occur or fail to occur.

b. *Allocation period*. The period that is required to identify and quantify the assets acquired and the liabilities assumed. The "allocation period" ends when the acquiring enterprise is no longer waiting for information that it has arranged to obtain and that is known to be available or obtainable. Thus, the existence of a preacquisition contingency for which an asset, a liability, or an impairment of an asset cannot be estimated does not, of itself, extend the "allocation period." Although the time required will vary with circumstances, the "allocation period" should usually not exceed one year from the consummation of a business combination.

Allocation of the Purchase Price

5. A preacquisition contingency other than the potential tax benefit of a loss carryforward[2] shall be included in the purchase allocation based on an amount determined as follows:

a. If the fair value of the preacquisition contingency can be determined during the "allocation period," that preacquisition contingency shall be included in the allocation of the purchase price based on that fair value.[3]
b. If the fair value of the preacquisition contingency cannot be determined during the "allocation period," that preacquisition contingency shall be included in the allocation of the purchase price based on an amount determined in accordance with the following criteria:

 (1) Information available prior to the end of the "allocation period" indicates that it is probable that an asset existed, a liability had been incurred, or an asset had been impaired at the consummation of the business combination. It is implicit in this condition that it must be probable that one or more future events will occur confirming the existence of the asset, liability, or impairment.
 (2) The amount of the asset or liability can be reasonably estimated.

 The criteria of this subparagraph shall be applied using the guidance provided in Statement 5 and the related FASB Interpretation No. 14, *Reasonable Estimation of the Amount of a Loss*, for application of the similar criteria of paragraph 8 of Statement 5.[4]

Subsequent Adjustments

6. After the end of the "allocation period," an adjustment that results from a preacquisition contingency other than a loss carryforward[5] shall be included in the determination of net income in the period in which the adjustment is determined.

Amendment to APB Opinion No. 16

7. The following footnote is added to the end of the last sentence of paragraph 88 of Opinion 16:

> Paragraphs 4 through 6 of FASB Statement No. 38, *Accounting for Preacquisition Contingencies of Purchased Enterprises,* specify how the general guidelines of this paragraph shall be applied to preacquisition contingencies.

Effective Date and Transition

8. The provisions of this Statement shall be effective for preacquisition contingencies assumed in business combinations initiated[6] after December 15, 1980.

9. Application of the provisions of this Statement to preacquisition contingencies assumed in business combinations initiated prior to December 16, 1980 is encouraged but not required. An enterprise electing to apply the provisions of this Statement to such preacquisition contingencies shall apply either the provisions of subparagraph (a) below or the provisions of subparagraphs (a) and (b) below:

a. The provisions of this Statement shall be applied to *all* preacquisition contingencies assumed in business combinations for which the "allocation

---

[2]Paragraph 49 of Opinion 11 and paragraph 88 of Opinion 16 (paragraphs 15 and 16 of this Statement) specify the accounting for the potential tax benefit of a loss carryforward of a purchased subsidiary. Opinion 11 specifies that such tax benefits are to be recognized as assets at the date of the purchase only if realization is assured beyond any reasonable doubt; otherwise, they are recognized only when realized. In the latter case. Opinion 16 specifies that those tax benefits retroactively reduce goodwill when realized.

[3]For example, if it can be demonstrated that the parties to a business combination agreed to adjust the total consideration by an amount as a result of a newly discovered contingency, that amount would be a determined fair value of that contingency

[4]Interpretation 14 specifies the amount to be accrued if the reasonable estimate of the amount is a range. If some amount within the range appears at the time to be a better estimate than any other amount within the range, that amount is accrued. If no amount within the range is a better estimate than any other amount, however, the minimum amount in the range is accrued.

[5]See footnote 2.

[6]The date on which a business combination is "initiated" is defined in paragraph 46(a) of Opinion 16 as "the earlier of (1) the date that the major terms of a plan, including the ratio of exchange of stock, are announced publicly or otherwise formally made known to the stockholders of any one of the combining companies or (2) the date that stockholders of a combining company are notified in writing of an exchange offer."

period" *has not* ended at the date of initial application. If application of this Statement to such preacquisition contingencies requires adjustments of amounts previously recorded, those adjustments shall be reported the same as other adjustments of preliminary amounts recorded during the "allocation period." Also, if the enterprise so elects,

b. The provisions of this Statement shall be applied to *all other* unresolved preacquisition contingencies[7] at the date of initial application. If the application permitted by this subparagraph is elected, adjustments that result from resolution or revised estimates of *all other* unresolved preacquisition contingencies shall be reported in accordance with the provisions of paragraph 6 of this Statement. If the previous reporting of those preacquisition contingencies in the allocation of the purchase price was not in conformity with paragraph 5 of this Statement, the provisions of this Statement may be applied retroactively at the date of initial application to *all other* unresolved preacquisition contingencies.

Except as provided in this paragraph, this Statement shall not be applied retroactively to previously issued annual or interim financial statements.

10. If the provisions of paragraph 6 of this Statement are not applied to all unresolved preacquisition contingencies as permitted by paragraph 9, financial statements for periods ending after December 15, 1980 shall include disclosure of the amount and nature of adjustments determined after December 15, 1980 that result from preacquisition contingencies and that are reported other than as specified in paragraph 6. The disclosure shall include a description of how those adjustments are reported and the effect of the adjustments on current or expected future cash flows of the enterprise.

The provisions of this Statement need not be applied to immaterial items.

This Statement was adopted by the affirmative votes of five members of the Financial Accounting Standards Board. Messrs. March and Morgan dissented.

Messrs. March and Morgan dissent because they believe that the accounting for a business acquisition required by this Statement does not properly reflect the outcome of many preacquisition contingencies. They believe subsequent adjustments arising from such contingencies should be reflected as adjustments in the purchase allocation (the alternative summarized in paragraph 26) and not as an increase or decrease in net income of the period in which the adjustment is determined necessary (the requirement in paragraph 6 of this Statement). In their view, reporting the allocated cost of assets acquired and goodwill (positive or negative) based upon the best information obtainable, including hindsight, provides more reliable information to users. They do not agree that the fine distinction made in paragraphs 19 and 21 between an amount deemed paid for an item that includes an element of risk attributable to an uncertainty and the outcome of that uncertainty is sufficiently substantive to require differences in accounting between the amount estimated for the contingency and its ultimate resolution. They also do not agree with paragraphs 4(b) and 5(b) which for all practical purposes require that the outcome be reasonably estimable within one year to be considered in the purchase allocation. The ability to predict the resolution of litigation and later-asserted claims within one year of an acquisition is often doubtful. Legal processes involve much longer time periods, particularly for more significant cases. Although they would oppose a time limit as a matter of principle, Messrs. March and Morgan believe approximately five years would be more realistic if a period were considered desirable for practical considerations.

Members of the Financial Accounting Standards Board:

Donald J. Kirk, *Chairman*
Frank E. Block
John W. March
Robert A. Morgan
David Mosso
Robert T. Sprouse
Ralph E. Walters

[7]"*All other* unresolved preacquisition contingencies" in this paragraph refers to all unresolved preacquisition contingencies assumed in business combinations for which the "allocation period" has ended at the date of initial application of this Statement.

Appendix A

BACKGROUND INFORMATION

11. The original request referred to in paragraph 1 was for an interpretation of Statement 16. The request indicated that the guidance of paragraphs 10 and 21 of Statement 16 could be considered to be in conflict. Paragraphs 12 and 13 of this appendix cite those provisions of Statement 16, and paragraphs 14-16 of this appendix cite the provisions of other authoritative literature that are referred to in paragraph 21 of Statement 16.

12. Paragraph 10 of Statement 16 requires that, with specified exceptions, ". . . items of profit and loss recognized during a period, . . . including accruals of estimated losses from loss contingencies, shall be included in the determination of net income for that period. . . ." The specified exceptions are described in paragraphs 11, 13, and 14 of Statement 16 and consist of:

a. Correction of an error in the financial statements of a prior period,
b. Adjustments that result from realization of income tax benefits of preacquisition operating loss carryforwards of purchased subsidiaries, and
c. Certain adjustments related to prior interim periods of the current fiscal year.

13. With respect to adjustments that are required by Opinions 9, 11, and 16 to be reported as adjustments to paid-in capital, goodwill, or other assets, paragraph 21 of Statement 16 states that "this Statement is not intended to require those adjustments to be included in the determination of net income of the current period." Paragraphs 14 and 15, below, cite the provisions of Opinions 9 and 11 that require adjustments to be reported as adjustments to paid-in capital, goodwill, or other assets. Paragraph 16, below, describes the provisions of Opinion 16 applicable to the purchase method of accounting for a business combination that require adjustments that result from preacquisition contingencies to be reported as adjustments to paid-in capital, goodwill, or other assets.

14. Paragraph 28 of APB Opinion No. 9, *Reporting the Results of Operations*, states that ". . . the following should be excluded from the determination of net income or the results of operations under all circumstances: (a) adjustments or charges or credits resulting from transactions in the company's own capital stock, . . . (b) transfers to and from accounts properly designated as appropriated retained earnings . . . and (c) adjustments made pursuant to a quasi-reorganization."

15. Paragraph 49 of Opinion 11 addresses reporting the tax effects of loss carryforwards of purchased subsidiaries, if not previously recognized. The paragraph states that those tax effects "should be recognized as assets at the date of purchase only if realization is assured beyond any reasonable doubt. Otherwise they should be recognized only when the tax benefits are actually realized and should be recorded as retroactive adjustments . . . of the purchase transactions. . . ." Paragraph 52 of Opinion 11 requires allocation of taxes to prior periods (or the opening balance of retained earnings) and to other stockholders' equity accounts in certain circumstances, none of which relate to preacquisition contingencies.

16. Paragraph 88 of Opinion 16 provides "general guides for assigning amounts to the individual assets acquired and liabilities assumed, except goodwill." The general guides in paragraph 88 include an acknowledgment that allowances for uncollectibility of receivables may be necessary and also include the statement that "an acquiring corporation should reduce the acquired goodwill retroactively for the realized tax benefits of loss carry-forwards of an acquired company not previously recorded by the acquiring corporation." Opinion 16 does not otherwise directly address preacquisition contingencies.

17. An Exposure Draft of a proposed Statement, *Accounting for Preacquisition Contingencies of Purchased Enterprises*, was issued on December 26, 1979. The Board received 59 letters of comment in response to the Exposure Draft.

Appendix B

BASIS FOR CONCLUSIONS

18. This appendix contains a discussion of the factors deemed significant by members of the Board in reaching the conclusions in this Statement, including various alternatives considered and reasons for accepting some and rejecting others. Individual Board members gave greater weight to some factors than to others.

Overall Approach Adopted by the Board

19. This Statement distinguishes between (a) an amount deemed to have been paid for an item that includes an element of risk and (b) the gain or loss that results from the risk assumed.

20. Paragraph 5 requires that the amount paid for the contingent asset or liability be estimated. If its fair value can be determined, that fair value is used as the basis for recording the asset or liability.

Otherwise, an amount determined on the basis of criteria drawn from Statement 5 is used as the best available estimate of fair value. In accordance with the rationale of Opinion 16 (which requires that all assets and liabilities of the acquired enterprise, whether recorded or unrecorded, be identified and recorded by the acquiring enterprise and that only the residual purchase price that cannot be allocated to specific assets and liabilities be allocated to goodwill), this Statement allows a period of time (the "allocation period") for discovery and quantification of preacquisition contingencies.

21. Paragraph 6 requires that subsequent adjustments of the amounts recorded as a part of the purchase allocation be included in the determination of net income in the period in which the adjustments are determined. In contrast to the amounts deemed paid for the asset or liability, those subsequent adjustments are gains or losses that result from the uncertainties and related risks assumed in the purchase.

Contingent Consideration

22. A number of respondents to the Exposure Draft questioned the difference in the accounting required for preacquisition contingencies by this Statement and the accounting required for contingent consideration by Opinion 16. Opinion 16 requires that contingent consideration be accounted for based on its nature. The following examples illustrate the relationship of the accounting for contingent consideration to the nature of the agreement and contrast the nature of each agreement with the nature of a preacquisition contingency:

a. If the contingent consideration is based on subsequent earnings, the additional consideration, when determinable, increases the purchase price because the increased value that was purchased has been demonstrated. Additional goodwill was proven to exist by the achievement of the specified level of earnings. In contrast, when an enterprise changes its estimate of a preacquisition contingent liability, there is nothing to indicate that additional value has been created. A payment is expected to be required, but the payment does not demonstrate that an asset exists or is more valuable than before the payment was anticipated.
b. If the contingent consideration represents payment of amounts withheld to insure against the existence of contingencies, neither the payment of the contingent consideration nor the payment of a liability that results from the contingency with the funds withheld affects the acquiring enterprise's accounting for the business combination. The escrow is a way of protecting the buyer against risk. The buyer has agreed to pay the amount either to the seller or to a third-party claimant; and thus, the only uncertainty to the buyer is the identity of the payee. The amount of the agreed consideration that is withheld would be recorded as part of the purchase price in the original allocation. In contrast, a change in an estimate of a preacquisition contingency for which the acquiring enterprise assumed responsibility represents a change in the total amount that will be paid out or received by the acquiring enterprise. The buyer assumed the risk and is subject to the results of that risk.

Contingencies That Result from a Purchase

23. A number of respondents to the Exposure Draft questioned whether this Statement should be applied to contingencies that arise from the acquisition and that did not exist prior to the acquisition. Examples provided included litigation over the acquisition and the tax effect of the purchase. The Board concluded that such contingencies are the acquiring enterprise's contingencies, rather than preacquisition contingencies of the acquired enterprise. Accordingly, Statement 16 applies to those contingencies after the initial purchase allocation.

Criteria for Inclusion in Purchase Allocation

24. Some believe that a distinction should be made based on whether contingencies were known to the acquiring enterprise at the date of the purchase. In their opinion, the initial recorded estimate for contingencies that were identified at the date of the purchase should be an adjustment of the purchase price and its allocation regardless of when that estimate becomes determinable. The acquiring enterprise agreed to assume those identified contingencies as a condition of the purchase, and presumably that assessment was considered directly in arriving at the purchase price; accordingly, they should be accounted for as part of the purchase. On the other hand, the discovery of contingent assets or liabilities that were *not* identified at the date of the purchase should not affect the allocation of a purchase price because unknown contingencies could not enter directly in the determination of the purchase price and discovery of unexpected assets or liabilities should not affect cost assigned to the other assets and liabilities acquired.

25. The Board rejected the approach outlined in paragraph 24 for a number of reasons, including the following:

a. An approach that would base the allocation of the purchase price on whether an item was known to the acquiring enterprise at the date of the purchase would conflict with the requirements of Opinion 16 for allocation of the cost of an enterprise accounted for by the purchase method. Paragraph 87 of Opinion 16 requires the acquiring enterprise to assign "a portion of the cost of the acquired company" to "all identifiable assets acquired . . . and liabilities assumed . . . , whether or not shown in the financial statements of the acquired company." The reference to "identifiable" does not indicate an intent to limit the allocation to items that were known at the date of the purchase.

b. A distinction based on whether contingencies were known to the acquiring enterprise at the date of the purchase could be viewed as only partially reflecting the economics of many purchase combinations. Many factors affect the purchase price in a business combination. Known contingencies would be one of those factors. Other factors might include amounts of earnings, demonstrated growth in earnings, and unknown preacquisition contingencies, the potential existence of which would nevertheless enter into an assessment of risk and affect the purchase price.
c. If all preacquisition contingencies that result from a cause that was identified at the date of the purchase were considered part of the purchase consideration, the distinction between an identified contingency and one that was not identified would be vague.
d. A requirement that initial recorded estimates for some contingencies be recorded as adjustments of the purchase allocation could discourage an enterprise from recording timely estimates.

26. Some believe that all adjustments that result from preacquisition contingencies should be excluded from income of the acquiring enterprise because they are not related to the acquiring enterprise's business operations. Some of those who hold this view would accept a time limit because they believe that the connection between the adjustment and any underlying event becomes less evident as the underlying event becomes more remote; however, the time limit would be an extended period of several years.

27. The Board rejected the approach outlined in paragraph 26 for a number of reasons, including the following:

a. The usual practice in the current accounting environment is for irregularly occurring costs that result from risks assumed by the enterprise to be reflected in income when they occur. The Board did not believe that it should differentiate between risks assumed by purchase and other business risks.
b. The distinction between an adjustment related to a preacquisition contingency and an adjustment that results from current events is not always clear. For example, an enterprise may settle litigation because the cost of a successful defense would exceed the cost of the settlement. The opinion of counsel may be that the case can be successfully defended. In that case, whether the cost of the settlement relates to the preacquisition event that is the stated cause of the litigation or to the current litigious environment is not clear.

28. Some believe that all adjustments related to preacquisition contingencies should be included in income of the acquired enterprise in the period in which the adjustments are determined. They note that Statement 16 requires accruals of estimated losses from loss contingencies to be included in income in the period in which they are determined, and they believe that contingencies assumed through purchase should be accounted for the same as other contingencies. Although the Board generally agreed, it concluded that an "allocation period" was needed to permit adequate time to make reasonable estimates for the purchase allocation required by Opinion 16.

29. Several respondents to the Exposure Draft stated that changes in an estimate should be accounted for the same as the original estimate. In examining the nature of a preacquisition contingency, the Board concluded that an estimate that can be made soon after the purchase likely would approximate the amount by which the purchase price reflected that contingency. If the eventual outcome of that contingency is significantly different, it is likely that the acquiring enterprise assumed a risk that turned out differently than expected. As indicated in paragraphs 19-21 above, the Board believes that it is appropriate for the result of a risk assumed by an enterprise to be accounted for differently than the transaction that resulted in the assumption of the risk.

Criteria for Amount to Be Included in Purchase Allocation

30. Paragraph 87 of Opinion 16 describes an acquiring enterprise's allocation of the cost of an acquired company to the assets acquired and liabilities assumed. That paragraph states:

> First, all identifiable assets acquired, either individually or by type, and liabilities assumed in a business combination, whether or not shown in the financial statements of the acquired company, should be assigned a portion of the cost of the acquired company, normally equal to their fair values at date of acquisition.
>
> Second, the excess of the cost of the acquired company over the sum of the amounts assigned to identifiable assets acquired less liabilities assumed should be recorded as goodwill.

If "identifiable assets" includes contingent assets, paragraph 87 could be viewed as inconsistent with the practice described in paragraph 17(a) of Statement 5 that "contingencies that might result in gains usually are not reflected in the accounts since to do so might be to recognize revenue prior to its realization." The Board concluded that this usual practice is not applicable to a purchase allocation because revenue does not result from such an allocation; rather, the question is whether to allocate amounts paid to identifiable assets that have value or to goodwill.

31. In the Exposure Draft, the Board proposed that all contingent assets, liabilities, and impairments of assets existing in an acquired enterprise at the acquisition date be recorded based on criteria similar to the criteria in Statement 5 for recognition of an estimated loss from a loss contingency. A number of respondents to the Exposure Draft stated that the fair value of a preacquisition contingency can sometimes be determined and that fair value might not equal the amount determined in accordance with the criteria based on Statement 5.

32. The Board did not intend to modify the general requirement of paragraph 87 of Opinion 16, cited in paragraph 30 above, that the purchase allocation be based on the fair value of the assets acquired and the liabilities assumed. Rather, the criteria were provided because fair value of a preacquisition contingency usually would not be determinable. Accordingly, the Board added paragraph 5(a) to this Statement, to permit recording a preacquisition contingency based on its fair value if that fair value can be determined. Otherwise, paragraph 5(b) requires that the amount recorded be based on the criteria included in the Exposure Draft.

33. Some respondents to the Exposure Draft inquired whether it would be appropriate to base the amount recorded on the present value of the amount determined in accordance with the criteria in paragraph 5(b) because the nature of the resulting amount would be a monetary asset or liability. The Board concluded that it should not specify such a requirement because the timing of payment or receipt of a contingent item seldom would be sufficiently determinable to permit the use of a present value technique on a reasonable basis. However, this Statement does not prohibit the use of a present value if appropriate.

Allocation Period

34. Opinion 16 provides the general principles of accounting for a business combination by the purchase method. The acquiring enterprise determines the value of the consideration given to the sellers, the present value of the liabilities assumed, and the value of the assets acquired. The total value of the consideration given and the liabilities assumed is then allocated among the identifiable assets acquired based on their value; and the balance, if any, is allocated to "goodwill."

35. The Board recognizes that completion of the allocation process that is required by Opinion 16 may sometimes require an extended period of time. For example, appraisals might be required to determine replacement cost of plant and equipment acquired, a discovery period may be needed to identify and value intangible assets acquired, and an actuarial determination may be required to determine the pension liability to be accrued.

36. If a business combination is consummated toward the end of an acquiring enterprise's fiscal year or the acquired enterprise is very large or unusually complex, the acquiring enterprise may not be able to obtain some of the data required to complete the allocation of the cost of the purchased enterprise for inclusion in its next annual financial report. In that case, a tentative allocation might be made using the values that have been determined and preliminary estimates of the values that have not yet been determined. The portions of the allocation that relate to the data that were not available subsequently are adjusted to reflect the finally determined amounts, usually by adjusting the preliminary amount with a corresponding adjustment of goodwill.

37. The Board considered specifying a time period during which estimates of preacquisition contingencies could be recorded as part of the purchase allocation. The Board concluded that it should relate the recording of preacquisition contingencies in the purchase allocation to the nature and process of the allocation, rather than to an arbitrary time limit. However, to indicate the Board's intent that the defined "allocation period" should not be unreasonably extended, paragraph 4(b) notes that the existence of a preacquisition contingency for which an amount cannot be estimated does not, of itself, extend the "allocation period." For example, the existence of litigation for which no estimate can be made in advance of the disposition by a court does not extend the "allocation period." That paragraph also notes that the "allocation period" should usually not exceed one year from the consummation date.

38. The "allocation period" is intended to differentiate between amounts that are determined as a result of the identification and valuation process required by Opinion 16 for all assets acquired and liabilities assumed and amounts that are determined because information that was not previously obtainable becomes obtainable. Thus, the "allocation

period" would continue while the acquiring enterprise's counsel was making an evaluation of a claim, but it would not continue if the counsel's evaluation were complete and resulted in the conclusion that no estimate could be made pending further negotiations with the claimant.

Preacquisition Net Operating Loss Carryforwards

39. A number of respondents cited the similarity of preacquisition net operating loss carryforwards to the other types of preacquisition contingencies that are addressed by this Statement and suggested that the accounting be conformed. The Board decided that it should not make that change in this Statement.

40. Some of those respondents asked whether the Board intended to completely exempt potential tax benefits of loss carryforwards from the provisions of this Statement or only to exempt them from the provisions that addressed the accounting for and reporting of subsequent changes in estimates. The Board did not intend to change the provisions of Opinions 11 and 16 with respect to preacquisition net operating loss carryforwards. Accordingly, paragraph 5 was modified to indicate the Board's intent.

Effective Date and Transition

41. A number of respondents to the Exposure Draft urged that the Statement be effective for adjustments resulting from purchases initiated after the effective date rather than for adjustments determined after that date. They indicated that, if the accounting required by this Statement had been in effect, the purchase price of some acquisitions would have been different or the acquisitions might not have been consummated. Several of those respondents indicated that they had disclosed the existence of a preacquisition contingency to their shareholders and had indicated that any resulting adjustment would be an adjustment of the purchase allocation.

42. The Board concluded that this Statement should be effective for preacquisition contingencies assumed in business combinations initiated after December 15, 1980. In arriving at that conclusion, the Board was concerned about the lack of comparability that may exist during a somewhat indefinite transition period, but it was influenced by expectations that may have existed at the time acquisitions were made (see preceding paragraph) and by the peculiar nature of the items in question. Disclosure of the nature of the items in question and their effect or potential effect on the enterprise's cash flows should provide adequate information for assessing the significance of those items. To ensure that adjustments of contingencies not reported in accordance with the general provisions of this Statement are disclosed, the Board specified the disclosures that are required by paragraph 10.

43. To enhance comparability, the Board also concluded that it should encourage but not require application to preacquisition contingencies assumed in business combinations initiated prior to December 16, 1980. To enhance comparability, all similar preacquisition contingencies of an enterprise should be reported in a consistent manner. Therefore, an enterprise that elects to apply this Statement to such preacquisition contingencies must apply the Statement to *all* preacquisition contingencies assumed in business combinations for which the "allocation period" *has not* ended at the date of initial application of this Statement. With respect to other unresolved preacquisition contingencies, an enterprise making the above election may also elect to apply the provisions of the Statement that address reporting of adjustments after the end of the "allocation period" to those preacquisition contingencies. That election, if exercised, must also be applied to *all other* unresolved preacquisition contingencies.

44. The Board is aware that some enterprises may not have recorded amounts as a part of a purchase allocation because better estimates, when they became available, were expected to be recorded retroactively as a part of that allocation. Accordingly, the Board concluded that enterprises that elect to apply this Statement to existing unresolved preacquisition contingencies should be permitted to record those contingent items as they would have been recorded if this Statement had been in effect at the acquisition date. That procedure should alleviate any problems that would result from applying this Statement to existing preacquisition contingencies. However, that election must be applied to *all* unresolved preacquisition contingencies if it is exercised.

Other Matters

45. Several respondents to the Exposure Draft requested clarification of the accounting required by this Statement in the event that the "allocation period" extends beyond a fiscal year-end. For example, would a change in the purchase allocation determined in a subsequent fiscal year result in a corresponding retroactive restatement of previously recorded amortization or depreciation? The Board decided that the same question would arise whenever the valuations required by Opinion 16 are not finalized until a subsequent fiscal year. The issue is not created by the "allocation period" used in this Statement, and that larger issue should not be resolved in this limited-scope Statement. The Board also noted that the amounts involved usually are not material because they consist of amortization of long-lived assets for a short time period.

Statement of Financial Accounting Standards No. 39 Financial Reporting and Changing Prices: Specialized Assets—Mining and Oil and Gas

a supplement to FASB Statement No. 33

STATUS

Issued: October 1980

Effective Date: For fiscal years ending on or after December 25, 1980

Affects: Amends FAS 33, paragraphs 30(a) through (c), 35(c)(1) through (4)
Supersedes FAS 33, paragraphs 51(b), 52(b), and 53

Affected by: Paragraph 10 superseded by FAS 69
Paragraph 11 superseded by FAS 69
Paragraph 12 superseded by FAS 40
Paragraph 12 superseded by FAS 41
Paragraph 12 amended by FAS 46
Paragraph 12 superseded by FAS 69

SUMMARY

FASB Statement No. 33, *Financial Reporting and Changing Prices*, requires companies that meet specified size tests to disclose certain supplementary information on both a historical cost/constant dollar basis and a current cost basis. This Statement:

- Applies the provisions of Statement 33 for measuring current costs to the mineral resource assets of mining and oil and gas enterprises
- Requires the disclosure of information about quantities, production, and selling prices of mineral resources other than oil and gas reserves.

The information required by this Statement, like the information required by Statement 33, is experimental. This Statement will be reviewed comprehensively, at the same time as Statement 33, after a period of not more than four years.

In recent years, extensive new disclosure requirements have been imposed on the oil and gas industry. The Board intends to study further the usefulness of those requirements in providing information about the effects of changing prices. It intends to work with the oil and gas industry and the Securities and Exchange Commission to refine the requirements and to develop improved methods of presentation.

Statement of Financial Accounting Standards No. 39
Financial Reporting and Changing Prices: Specialized Assets—Mining and Oil and Gas

a supplement to FASB Statement No. 33

CONTENTS

INTRODUCTION

1. FASB Statement No. 33, *Financial Reporting and Changing Prices*, establishes standards for reporting certain effects of price changes on business enterprises. Statement 33 requires that large public enterprises disclose information on both historical cost/constant dollar and current cost bases. However, that Statement does not contain provisions for measuring income-producing real estate or unprocessed natural resources and related depreciation, depletion, and amortization expense on a current cost basis for fiscal years ended on or after December 25, 1980. The Board decided to undertake further studies of the usefulness of current cost information for those types of assets and expenses. This Statement supplements Statement 33 by requiring measurement of mineral resource assets and related expenses at current cost or lower recoverable amount.

2. The current cost of mineral resource assets is given by current market buying prices or by the current cost of finding and developing mineral reserves. The Board recognizes that no generally accepted approach exists for measuring the current finding cost of mineral reserves. To indicate the effects of changes in current costs, it may be impracticable to do more than adjust historical cost by an index of the changes in specific prices of the inputs concerned. That approach may fail to yield a close approximation of the current cost of finding and developing new reserves. In recognition of this difficulty, the requirements of this Statement are flexible regarding the approach used to measure current cost. The approach may include use of specific price indexes, direct information about market buying prices, and other statistical evidence of the cost of acquisitions; enterprises are required to disclose the types of information that have been used. The Board believes that historical costs adjusted by specific price indexes can be useful for the assessment of certain effects of changing prices on an enterprise. For the purposes of aggregate measurements on a current cost basis, that information is preferable to the alternatives of making no adjustment to historical cost or of using historical cost adjusted for changes in the general price level.

3. Statement 33 refers to the need for experimentation on the usefulness of alternative types of information about the effects of changing prices on business enterprises. It also provides, within certain guidelines, flexibility to encourage the development of new techniques that fit the circumstances of particular enterprises. Those considerations are equally applicable to the provisions of this Statement. The Board intends to review the requirements of this Statement on an ongoing basis and to add, amend, or withdraw requirements whenever that course is justified by the evidence. This Statement will be reviewed comprehensively at the same time as Statement 33.

4. The oil and gas industry is the subject of a large number of disclosure requirements (including

reserve recognition accounting) introduced by the Board and the Securities and Exchange Commission (SEC). The Board has decided not to call for the disclosure of any new information, apart from information on a current cost basis, until it has studied further the usefulness of all requirements for assessing the effects of changing prices. The Board intends to work with the industry and with the SEC during 1981 to attempt to refine disclosure requirements. As part of that process, it will consider the usefulness of additional disclosures supported by commentators on the FASB Exposure Draft, *Financial Reporting and Changing Prices: Specialized Assets*, including separate information about income from oil and gas producing activities and information that is useful for assessing the fair value of mineral resource assets; for example, current prices, planned rates of production, and current lifting costs.

STANDARDS OF FINANCIAL ACCOUNTING AND REPORTING

Definitions and Scope

5. For the purposes of this Statement, certain terms are defined as follows:

a. *Mineral resource assets* are assets that are directly associated with and derive value from all minerals that are extracted from the earth. Such minerals include oil and gas, ores containing ferrous and nonferrous metals, coal, shale, geothermal steam, sulphur, salt, stone, phosphate, sand, and gravel. Mineral resource assets include mineral interests in properties, completed and uncompleted wells, and related equipment and facilities, and other facilities required for purposes of extraction (FASB Statement No. 19, *Financial Accounting and Reporting by Oil and Gas Producing Companies*, paragraph 11). The definition does not cover support equipment because that equipment is included in the property, plant, and equipment for which current cost measurements are required by Statement 33.
b. *Proved mineral reserves in extractive industries other than oil and gas*[1] are the estimated quantities of commercially recoverable reserves that, on the basis of geological, geophysical, and engineering data, can be demonstrated with a reasonably high degree of certainty to be recoverable in the future from known mineral deposits by either primary or improved recovery methods.
c. *Probable mineral reserves in extractive industries other than oil and gas*[2] are the estimated quantities of commercially recoverable reserves that are less well defined than proved reserves and that may be estimated or indicated to exist on the basis of geological, geophysical, and engineering data.
d. *Unprocessed natural resources* encompass mineral resource assets, timberlands, and growing timber.

6. The requirements of this Statement apply to the enterprises identified in paragraphs 23 and 24 of Statement 33 and in the manner specified in paragraphs 26-28 of that Statement. The Board encourages nonpublic enterprises and enterprises that do not meet the size tests in paragraph 23 of Statement 33 to present the information called for by this Statement.

7. An enterprise shall disclose the principal types of information used to measure the current cost of mineral resource assets.

8. The disclosures described in paragraphs 9-14 are required by this Statement. Enterprises are encouraged to provide additional information to help users of financial reports understand the effects of changing prices on the activities of the enterprise. Formats that may be used for the presentation of the supplementary information are illustrated in Appendix A of both Statement 33 and this Statement.

Current Cost Information

9. Statement 33, paragraphs 30(a)-(c) and 35(c)(1)-(4), requires the disclosure of supplementary information on a current cost basis. This Statement applies those provisions to mineral resource assets. Accordingly, an enterprise shall measure the current cost or lower recoverable amount[3] of mineral resource assets and related depreciation, depletion, and amortization expense in computations of:

a. Income from continuing operations on a current cost basis;
b. The current cost amounts of inventory and property, plant, and equipment;[4]
c. Increases or decreases in the current cost amounts of inventory and property, plant, and

[1] FASB Discussion Memorandum, *Financial Accounting and Reporting in the Extractive Industries*, December 1976. The various classes of oil and gas reserves are defined in FASB Statement No. 25, *Suspension of Certain Accounting Requirements for Oil and Gas Producing Companies*, February 1979.

[2] Discussion Memorandum on financial accounting and reporting in the extractive industries.

[3] Statement 33, paragraph 62.

[4] Statement 33, paragraph 23, footnote 1, provides that "for the purposes of this Statement, except where otherwise provided, inventory and property, plant, and equipment shall include land and other natural resources. . . ."

equipment, net of inflation;

d. Current cost information in the five-year summary of selected financial data.

10. Paragraph 51 of Statement 33 deals with the measurement of the current cost amounts of inventory and property, plant, and equipment. Subparagraph 51(b) excludes income-producing real estate and unprocessed natural resources from provisions applicable to property, plant, and equipment. That subparagraph is superseded by the following:

> Property, plant, and equipment at the current cost or lower recoverable amount (paragraphs 57-64) of the assets' remaining service potential at the measurement date. (This provision is qualified by paragraph 53 as amended by FASB Statement No. 39, *Financial Reporting and Changing Prices: Specialized Assets—Mining and Oil and Gas*, in respect of income-producing real estate and unprocessed natural resources.)

11. Paragraph 52 of Statement 33 deals with the measurement of cost of goods sold and depreciation and amortization expense. Line 4 of paragraph 52 shall be amended by the insertion of the word "depletion" after "depreciation." Subparagraph 52(b) excludes income-producing real estate and unprocessed natural resources from provisions applicable to property, plant, and equipment. Subparagraph 52(b) is superseded by the following:

> Depreciation, depletion, and amortization expense of property, plant, and equipment shall be measured on the basis of the average current cost or lower recoverable amount (paragraphs 57-64) of the assets' service potential during the period of use. (This provision is qualified by paragraph 53 in respect of income-producing real estate and unprocessed natural resources.)

12. Paragraph 53 of Statement 33 contains interim provisions for the measurement of income-producing real estate and unprocessed natural resources. It is superseded by the following:

> This Statement does not contain provisions for the measurement, on a current cost basis, of income-producing real estate and unprocessed natural resources and related expenses for fiscal years ended before December 25, 1980 (paragraph 19). If an enterprise presents information on a current cost basis for a fiscal year ended before December 25, 1980, it may measure those assets and related expenses at their historical cost/constant dollar amounts or by reference to an appropriate index of specific price changes. When an enterprise presents information on a current cost basis for fiscal years ended on or after December 25, 1980, it shall measure mineral resource assets and related depreciation, depletion, and amortization expense in accordance with the provisions in this Statement for the measurement of property, plant, and equipment and related expenses.

Quantity and Price Information

13. Enterprises that own mineral reserves other than oil and gas[5] shall disclose the following information for each of their five most recent fiscal years:

a. Estimates of significant quantities of proved, or proved and probable (whichever is used for cost amortization purposes) mineral reserves, other than oil and gas, at the end of the year or at the most recent date during the year for which estimates can be made. If estimates are not made as of the end of the year, the disclosures shall indicate the dates for which they apply.
b. The estimated quantity, expressed in physical units or in percentages of reserves, of each mineral product that is recoverable in significant commercial quantities if the mineral reserves included under section (a) include deposits containing one or more significant mineral products.
c. The quantities of each significant mineral produced during the year. If the mineral reserves included under section (a) are ores that are milled or similarly processed, the quantity of each significant mineral product produced by the milling or similar process shall also be disclosed.
d. The quantity of significant proved, or proved and probable, mineral reserves purchased or sold in place during the year.
e. For each significant mineral product, the average market price, or for mineral products transferred within an enterprise, the equivalent market price prior to use in a manufacturing process.

14. In determining the quantities to be reported in conformity with paragraph 13:

a. If the enterprise issues consolidated financial statements, 100 percent of the quantities attributable to the parent company and 100 percent of the quantities attributable to its consolidated subsidiaries (whether or not wholly owned) shall be included.
b. If the enterprise's financial statements include investments that are proportionately consolidated, the enterprise's quantities shall include its proportionate share of the investee's quantities.
c. If the enterprise's financial statements include investments that are accounted for by the equity

[5]Quantity disclosures for oil and gas reserves are required by Statement 19.

method, the investee's quantities shall not be included in the disclosures of the enterprise's quantities. However, the enterprise's (investor's) share of the investee's quantities of reserves shall be reported separately, if significant.

Effective Date and Transition

15. The provisions of this Statement shall be effective for fiscal years ended on or after December 25, 1980. Disclosure of information incorporating current cost measurements of mineral resource assets and information about quantities and prices for fiscal years ended before December 25, 1980 is encouraged but not required.

16. An enterprise that is first required to apply the provisions of this Statement for fiscal years ended on or after December 25, 1981 is not required to disclose the information for earlier years, although disclosure for earlier years is encouraged.

The provisions of this Statement need not be applied to immaterial items.

This Statement was adopted by the affirmative votes of five members of the Financial Accounting Standards Board. Messrs. Sprouse and Walters dissented.

Messrs. Sprouse and Walters dissent primarily because they believe that requiring enterprises to attempt to estimate the current cost of finding oil and gas reserves is a futile exercise that tends to detract significantly from the usefulness and credibility of disclosures of current cost information about other assets and by other enterprises for which provision of that information is reasonably feasible and meaningful.

This Statement provides some flexibility for determining current cost information, but basically it provides that current cost should reflect the method of acquisition that would currently be appropriate in the circumstances of the enterprise. That approach may be reasonable for assets that can be purchased or manufactured within a reasonable period of time, but estimating the current costs of finding oil and gas reserves by applying specific price indexes to historical costs or by substituting current costs for the amount of labor, materials, and activities used to discover oil and gas reserves in the past is seriously defective. Because that aspect of reliability referred to as representational faithfulness is totally lacking in that approach, the credibility of supplementary information about changing prices generally is likely to be diminished. The defects are accentuated in the case of oil and gas reserves because two significantly different methods of accounting for the historical costs of finding those reserves are presently in use.

Determining the current cost of finding oil and gas reserves in existing quantities is simply not feasible. Indeed, it may not be possible to find existing quantities at any cost and it is impossible to estimate the quantity that might be found at any particular cost. Therefore, attempts to estimate the current cost of finding oil and gas reserves are unlikely to provide relevant and reliable information for users' assessments of future cash flows, maintenance of operating capability, or financial performance. Unfortunately, requiring that such estimates be inextricably intermingled with other current cost information that could be relevant and reasonably reliable detracts seriously from the usefulness of that other information as well.

Messrs. Sprouse and Walters believe that estimates of fair value of mineral reserves would be highly relevant, but they agree that such estimates are not sufficiently reliable at present to serve as a basis for a supplementary calculation of income from continuing operations or to be presented separately as supplementary information. Instead, they would favor requiring presentation of supplementary information about oil and gas reserves that is similar to that required by this Statement for other mineral reserves: estimated reserve quantities by major geographical areas, current unit prices and current unit production (lifting) costs for those areas, and current production and near-term production plans (e.g., two to three years) for those areas. To enhance comparability and retain the usefulness of current cost information about other assets and downstream activities (e.g., the refining and marketing activities of an integrated oil and gas enterprise), current cost information should be limited to those other assets and activities. It also should be disclosed separately from information about oil and gas producing activities, as proposed in the April 21, 1980 Exposure Draft of this Statement.

In their view, that information would (a) provide an acceptably reliable basis for users' assessments of future cash flows, maintenance of operating capability, and financial performance; (b) provide comparable information regardless of the accounting method used by an enterprise; and (c) hopefully, provide an equally relevant and more reliable substitute for the reserve recognition accounting presently required by the SEC. It has been observed that much of the information that Messrs. Sprouse and Walters would favor is presently required in filings with the SEC, but that observation does not relieve the Board of its responsibility to identify and require information that it concludes is sufficient and necessary.

Appendix A

ILLUSTRATIONS OF DISCLOSURES

17. This appendix illustrates a format for presenting quantity and price information relating to an enterprise's mineral reserves other than oil and gas. The format given here is only an illustration and is not intended to constrain enterprises from experimenting with the use of different forms of presentation. Illustrations of formats for presenting information on a current cost basis are given in Statement 33, Appendix A.

ILLUSTRATION OF SUPPLEMENTARY OPERATING STATISTICS FOR A MINING ENTERPRISE FOR THE FIVE YEARS ENDED 19X5

	19X5	19X4	19X3	19X2	19X1
Proven and probable ore reserves at beginning of year (Note)					
Tons (thousands)	21,000	21,500	22,000	23,000	24,000
Copper (percent)	1.10	1.10	1.10	1.10	1.10
Lead (percent)	5.99	5.98	5.98	5.98	5.98
Silver (ounces/tons)	3.79	3.80	3.80	3.75	3.75
Tons of ore milled (thousands)	1,025	1,000	890	900	850
Metal produced (thousands)					
-copper (pounds)	17,250	18,480	16,880	10,980	11,220
-lead (pounds)	92,700	92,400	75,450	53,910	45,750
-silver (ounces)	2,800	2,803	2,270	1,850	1,540
Average market price					
-copper (cents per pound)	85	75	68	72	61
-lead (cents per pound)	44	40	36	36	32
-silver (cents per ounce)	510	400	350	368	325

Proved reserves—The estimated quantities of commercially recoverable reserves that, on the basis of geological, geophysical, and engineering data, can be demonstrated with a reasonably high degree of certainty to be recoverable in the future from known mineral deposits by either primary or improved recovery methods.

Probable reserves—The estimated quantities of commercially recoverable reserves that are less well defined than proved reserves and that may be estimated or indicated to exist on the basis of geological, geophysical, and engineering data.

This form illustrates one method of disclosing information about quantities of minerals owned, marketable products produced, and average market prices for those products. Other formats are acceptable. Information about ore grades and differentiation between the production of ores and of marketable product may not be appropriate for some minerals. The classification and degree of detail should follow normal industry practice. Beginning-of-year reserves are used for illustrative purposes. The requirement is for end-of-year or the most recent date during the year. Ranges of prices during the year may be supplied in addition to average prices.

Appendix B

BACKGROUND

18. Statement 33, issued in September 1979, does not contain provisions for the measurement, on a current cost basis, of income-producing real estate or unprocessed natural resources and related expenses, for periods ending after December 25, 1980 (paragraph 53, Statement 33). The Board concluded in Statement 33 that further studies were required to provide a basis for decisions on the applicability to those assets of the requirement to present information on a current cost basis.

19. Many different categories of assets could have been chosen as suitable subjects for special study, and the identification of categories that merited special treatment involved subjective judgment. The

Board began its studies of the measurement of specialized assets on a current cost basis by selecting six industries in which special types of assets were judged to be particularly important, and by forming task groups to advise it on the applicability to the industries concerned of the proposals in the FASB Exposure Draft, *Financial Reporting and Changing Prices,* issued December 28, 1978. Those task groups dealt with banking, forest products, insurance, mining, oil and gas, and real estate. All six task groups held meetings that were open to the public, issued preliminary and interim reports that were widely distributed, and made presentations at a conference on financial reporting and changing prices. The Board concluded in Statement 33 that the general provisions of that Statement were useful and applicable to banking and insurance.

20. With respect to oil and gas, the Board adopted a form of successful efforts accounting in FASB Statement No. 19, *Financial Accounting and Reporting by Oil and Gas Producing Companies,* issued in December 1977. Before that Statement became effective, the Securities and Exchange Commission issued ASR No. 253, *Adoption of Requirements for Financial Accounting and Reporting Practices for Oil and Gas Producing Activities*. That release (a) adopted the form of successful efforts accounting called for in Statement 19, (b) indicated an intention to adopt a form of full cost accounting (which was subsequently done), (c) permitted the use of either (a) or (b) for SEC reporting purposes, and (d) concluded that both forms of historical cost accounting fail to provide sufficient information on the financial position and operating results of oil and gas producing companies. Therefore, the release indicated that steps should be taken to develop an accounting method based on valuation of proved oil and gas reserves (reserve recognition accounting). In order to avoid conflicting requirements, the Board suspended the effective date of that part of Statement 19 pertaining to the successful efforts method. After forming the Oil and Gas Advisory Committee and following its due process procedures, the SEC issued ASR No. 269, *Oil and Gas Producers—Supplemental Disclosures on the Basis of Reserve Recognition Accounting* (RRA).

21. Although RRA information, as promulgated by the SEC, is based on a discounted cash flow or a present value methodology, it is not intended to result in a fair value basis of presentation where fair value is the price that would be accepted as reasonable in a transaction between a willing buyer and a willing seller. The valuations under RRA do not represent an estimate of fair value because the methodology does not permit full consideration of expected future economic conditions, varying discount rates, or quantities of probable reserves.

22. The Board and its staff have followed closely the development of RRA. Representatives have attended all meetings of the SEC Advisory Committee and its working committee on measurement. All public comment letters to the SEC have been reviewed by the FASB staff and summarized for the Board's information.

23. Since Statement 33 was issued, the Oil and Gas, Mining, Real Estate, and Forest Products Task Groups have each met one or more times with the FASB staff.

24. On April 21, 1980, the Board issued an FASB Exposure Draft, *Financial Reporting and Changing Prices: Specialized Assets*. The Board received 124 letters of comment on the Exposure Draft.

25. In July 1980, the Board conducted a public hearing on the Exposure Draft. Twenty-one organizations and individuals presented their views at the two-day hearing.

26. After issuing the Exposure Draft, the Board held five open meetings at which it considered the issues dealt with in the Exposure Draft.

27. This Statement differs from the Exposure Draft principally in that it deals with only the mining and oil and gas industries and that it contains no provision for the *separate* disclosure of current cost information for mineral resource assets nor any requirement to disclose information about the fair values of oil and gas reserves. The Board will issue separate Statements dealing with financial reporting and changing prices for (a) timberland and growing timber and (b) income-producing real estate.

Appendix C

BASIS FOR CONCLUSIONS

Introduction

28. This appendix reviews considerations that members of the Board deemed significant in reaching the conclusions in this Statement; it includes reasons for accepting certain views and rejecting others. Individual Board members gave greater weight to some factors than to others.

29. Statement 33 calls for the presentation of supplementary information about the effects of changing prices on certain large public enterprises according to a historical cost/constant dollar basis and a current cost basis. It requires the presentation of information on a historical cost/constant dollar basis for all those enterprises. However, it contains

only interim provisions, applicable to years ended before December 25, 1980, for the presentation of supplementary information on a current cost basis for mineral resource assets. The purpose of this Statement is to set forth provisions for the measurement of mineral resource assets and related expenses in information prepared on a current cost basis.

30. The general objectives of reporting the effects of changing prices are discussed in Statement 33 (paragraphs 92-96). That discussion provides a starting point for the conclusions in this Statement. In summary, the objectives call for the provision of information that would help users to:

a. Assess future cash flows,
b. Assess the maintenance of operating capability,
c. Assess financial performance, and
d. Assess the maintenance of general purchasing power.

Those objectives are derived from the objectives of financial reporting set out in FASB Concepts Statement No. 1, *Objectives of Financial Reporting by Business Enterprises*.

The Accounting Alternatives

31. The reasons for the Board's decision that special consideration should be given to the measurement of mineral resource assets are set out in paragraph 156 of Statement 33:

> Special considerations arise in the choice of a system for measuring the effects of changing prices on enterprises that own particular categories of assets. Discussions about which attribute of an asset should be measured involve weighing the relevance and reliability of various alternatives, taking account of the costs of preparing the information. Consideration of those factors may suggest the desirability of measuring different attributes of different assets. The Board has concluded that current cost is a useful measurement for inventory and property, plant, and equipment. However, measurements of the current costs of some assets may have relatively low relevance and reliability while other measures, for example net present value of future cash flows, may have more relevance and an acceptable level of reliability. In such cases, it may be desirable to call for measurement of a different attribute from the one that is required for other assets, provided that information about the measurements can be presented in a format that enables users to understand its significance.

32. The Board considered the following alternatives for the measurement of expenses related to the use and sale of mineral resource assets in the computation of income from continuing operations on a current cost basis:

a. Use measures based on fair values or present values,
b. Use measures based on current cost or lower recoverable amount,
c. Use measures based on historical cost/constant dollar amounts,
d. Use measures based on historical cost/nominal dollar amounts, and
e. Exclude activities that involve the use of mineral resource assets from current cost income measurements.

33. Statement 33 calls for information about the current cost amounts of inventory and property, plant, and equipment and about changes in current cost amounts, net of inflation. The Board considered the following main alternatives relating to the application of those requirements to mineral resource assets:

a. Exclude mineral resource assets from any such requirement;
b. Include mineral resource assets on the same basis as inventory and property, plant, and equipment;
c. Measure mineral resource assets on a current cost basis and disclose the information separately;
d. Measure mineral resource assets on a fair value basis and disclose the information separately; or
e. Measure mineral resource assets on a fair value basis and aggregate those measures with current cost measures for other assets.

34. The Board also considered what sources of information would provide useful bases for alternative measurements of mineral resource assets and related expenses. If those assets and expenses are to be measured at current cost, it is necessary to consider whether an enterprise should be able to use both direct pricing methods and methods depending on specific price indexes (paragraph 60, Statement 33). If assets and expenses are to be measured at fair value, similar kinds of questions arise regarding the admissibility of alternative sources of information.

35. If the current costs of assets and related expenses are to be measured, the procedures used to estimate those costs may become critical. Current cost measures can vary significantly according to which costs are to be capitalized and which are to be treated as expenses when they arise. Particular difficulties arise in determining the cost of mineral resource assets, and the Board consequently considered whether special provisions were required to identify the costs that should be capitalized in the measurements of those assets.

36. The Board also has assessed the usefulness of information about the quantities of resources available to the enterprise and the selling prices of those resources.

Current Cost

37. Paragraph 58 of Statement 33 states that for inventory and property, plant, and equipment ". . . the sources of information used to measure current cost should reflect whatever method of acquisition would currently be appropriate in the circumstances of the enterprise." Application of that provision to the assets covered by this Statement indicates that the current cost of an asset may be measured by (a) the estimated buying price for an asset having the same characteristics as the asset owned or (b) the estimated cost of some other method of acquisition; for example, exploration and development.

38. The provision in paragraph 58 of Statement 33, given in the preceding paragraph, identifies information that may be helpful in assessing whether an enterprise is capable of maintaining its operating capability. The provision is applicable to mineral resource assets as well as other assets. Consider, for example, a case in which the enterprise intends to maintain operating capability by acquiring resources that are similar to those used or sold. Current cost is equal to replacement cost. If depletion, depreciation, and amortization expense, measured at current cost, is deducted from revenues, a basis is provided for assessing the maintenance of operating capability. If revenues exceed expenses, measured at current costs where appropriate, and it has not been necessary to invest the excess in other assets, such as receivables, the enterprise may be expected to be able to finance the replacement of resources without borrowing. However, for that argument to hold, current cost must reflect the actual cash needed to acquire the new resources. The cost of buying the asset may exceed the cost of other methods of acquisition. In that case, assuming that the other methods of acquisition are possible, the purchase price would overstate the measure of cost required to assess the maintenance of operating capability. Another possibility is that the purchase price may be less than the cost of other methods of acquisition. In that case, purchase must be assumed to be the usual method of acquisition, and the purchase price is the appropriate basis for measurement of current cost. It also is possible that the costs of replacement by alternative methods are approximately equal. In that case, all methods may be acceptable as bases for the estimation of current cost, and the choice may depend on the reliability of alternative sources of information.

39. It is important to consider the implications of the timing of new acquisitions. If an enterprise were to attempt to replace its mineral resource assets immediately after their use, without advance planning, it probably would find that the only way to avoid a substantial waiting period would be to purchase assets developed by another enterprise. Such a purchase might be the best course of action because waiting would involve a significant loss of income. A similar situation can arise with inventory and property, plant, and equipment. An asset normally cannot be obtained with negligible lead time. Those considerations do not in themselves establish the case for measuring the current cost of mineral resource assets on the basis of purchase prices. An enterprise normally will plan its acquisition of new resources in sufficient time; measurement of current cost at current purchase price may misstate the basis for assessing the maintenance of operating capability if new supplies of the resources can be obtained by less costly methods.

40. One special feature of mineral resource assets is the possibility that replacement, except by purchase, may be impracticable or uneconomic or may require an indeterminate period of time or be of indeterminate feasibility. Additional supplies may be limited or the risks of failure to obtain new supplies by exploration may be great. In such cases, measures of current cost, based on methods of acquisition other than purchase, may be quite uncertain and possibly higher than purchase price; and application of concepts may suggest that current cost or lower recoverable amount should be measured by reference to the purchase price of a comparable existing asset or value in use (the present value of future cash flows).

41. As noted above, the definition of the current cost of mineral resource assets may call for a measurement of the current cost of acquiring, by means other than purchase, resources that are similar to those owned or used and sold; it also may call for measurement at current buying price. However, the Board recognizes that no generally accepted methods exist for those measurements in the cases of mineral resource assets. Moreover, many people believe that such methods are unlikely to be developed in the foreseeable future. The current cost of depletion of oil and gas reserves, for example, depends on the cost of finding new reserves in currently unknown locations and quantities and on the cost of providing facilities to extract the oil and gas from those locations, which may pose new technological problems. In such circumstances, it may be impracticable to obtain a better estimate of current cost than that found from adjustment of historical cost by an index of specific price changes. Some Board members believe that it may be useful to define operating capability in terms of the ability to repeat today the activities that originally were undertaken to find and develop the nonrenewable natural resources of the enterprise. That belief supports the

use of historical costs, adjusted for specific price changes, in the assessment of the maintenance of operating capability.

42. Estimates of the current cost of finding nonrenewable natural resources must depend partly on computations that are predictions rather than measurements in the normal sense. Uncertainty about the ability to find and, therefore, about the cost of finding nonrenewable natural resources makes it difficult to draw general conclusions about the relationship between their costs of purchase and their costs by other methods of acquisition. It is possible that the costs are similar by alternative methods of acquisition and that buying prices should be regarded as one important source of evidence about current cost of acquisition by discovery. However, the existence of price controls for oil and gas reserves might weaken greatly any relationships between cost of purchase and cost by other methods of acquisition. Experience with current cost measurements may well lead to an improved understanding of the advantages and disadvantages of different measurement methods and to the development of improved measurement methods. In the meantime, the Board concluded that a choice of method should be permitted for the estimation of current cost. The preparers of financial reports can, accordingly, use their judgment in selecting a method that provides the best reflection of current costs in the circumstances of the enterprise. The requirement to disclose the types of information on which measurements are based will help users to interpret the measurements.

43. Information about the current cost or lower recoverable amount of assets at the end of the year and about the increase or decrease in current cost amounts during the year is intended to provide information for the assessment of enterprise performance, taking into account changes in the potential of the enterprise's assets to produce future cash flows. Practical difficulties in the measurement of the current cost of mineral resource assets may limit the usefulness of current cost information for the assessment of enterprise performance. However, the Board believes that the measurements required by this Statement are likely to assist with the assessment of cash flows to some extent; and that this belief should be tested by the inclusion of the assets covered by this Statement in the experiment with information about the effects of changing prices.

44. Commentators on the Exposure Draft had various opinions about the usefulness of current cost measures of mineral resource assets. Most commentators recognized the limitations of those measures for assessments of future cash flows, given that the current cost of finding and developing the reserves held may bear little relationship to the cost of finding and developing reserves in the future. Some of those who argued against a requirement for current cost measures did so because of doubts about the general usefulness of current cost accounting. Other commentators emphasized the possible usefulness of current cost measures as indicators of enterprise performance; they favored the application of the current cost provisions of Statement 33 to mineral resource assets in order to obtain experience in all industries in the experiment with the presentation and use of information about the effects of changing prices. Commentators suggested that the incremental costs of preparing current cost information for mineral resource assets were of minor importance.

45. The Board concluded that information about mineral resource assets on a current cost basis should be required in the same way as information about the current cost of other kinds of property, plant, and equipment. That information may be useful for the assessment of both enterprise performance and the maintenance of operating capability. The Board believes that there is an urgent need to provide information about the effects of specific price changes on enterprises that use mineral resource assets. There is a serious gap in public understanding of income levels that may appear large under historical cost measures and yet be inadequate to provide for the maintenance of operating capability. Current cost measures, even if they are subject to difficulties of estimation, are likely to be a useful supplement to historical cost measures by contributing to the development of public understanding.

46. The primary financial statements of different mining and oil and gas enterprises lack comparability because they have adopted materially different accounting policies for capitalizing expenditures as part of the cost of mineral resource assets. It follows that current cost measures also lack comparability if they are obtained by adjusting historical cost measures by specific price indexes. However, the Board believes it to be beyond the scope of this Statement to attempt to attain uniformity in the supplementary information about changing prices for those industries.

Fair Value

47. One of the purposes of financial reporting is to provide information that is useful for the assessment of future cash flows. Such information could possibly be provided directly by reporting estimates of future cash flows or estimates of the net present value of future cash flows associated with assets. Information about the estimated fair values of assets, defined as the prices that would be accepted as reasonable in transactions between a willing

buyer and a willing seller, is another potential source of useful information. Fair values are likely to have a closer and more stable relationship than historical cost to the net present value of cash flows: The buyer of an asset is likely to regard the net present value of estimated cash flows from using an asset as the maximum acceptable price, and the seller is likely to regard that amount as the minimum acceptable price. In an active and efficient market, the price is likely to be approximately equal to net present value of future cash flows.

48. A measurement that reflects the net present value of the cash flows from an asset, if it has sufficient reliability, may provide a useful basis for the assessment of overall enterprise performance. As noted in paragraph 120 of Statement 33, the measurement of assets at current cost or lower recoverable amount may be regarded as partial recognition of the present values of future cash flows; income from continuing operations on a current cost basis and the increase or decrease in current cost amounts then may be regarded as two factors useful for the assessment of overall performance.

49. The actual relationship between current cost and fair value is uncertain; the two concepts overlap to a considerable extent. Measurements of current cost may be based on information about current market prices (i.e., fair value) or current costs of other methods of acquisition. If the current cost of other methods of acquisition, such as exploration and development, is believed to be lower than fair value, it may be assumed that the enterprise normally will not purchase assets and that "other acquisition cost" will be the appropriate basis for estimating current cost. In other cases, fair value will be an appropriate basis for estimating current cost either because the enterprise normally buys its assets or because fair value is approximately equal to "other acquisition cost." Current buying price is a market price and is, therefore, likely to be indistinguishable from fair value. Consequently, current cost is likely to differ from fair value only when the costs of methods of acquisition, other than purchase, are believed to be lower than purchase price.

50. Some people believe that, if measurement difficulties are ignored, the value to the business of a specialized asset is represented better by fair value than by the cost of other methods of acquisition. Value to the business is defined in paragraph 99 of Statement 33, and it is the concept that leads normally to measurement at current cost or lower recoverable amount. It may be identified by assuming that an enterprise has been deprived of the use of an asset and asking what loss it then would incur. The loss may exceed normal acquisition cost because the normal process of acquisition may be lengthy, and net income would be lost during the waiting period. Fair value may be a better measure of the loss than "other acquisition cost" because it represents the cost of obtaining an asset fairly quickly when lengthy planning of the acquisition is not possible. The excess of fair value over "other acquisition cost" (if any) may then be regarded as partly attributable to the worth of the cash flow that would be lost during the planning period if purchase were not undertaken. Arguments for disclosure of information about the fair value of assets may be relatively strong when doubts exist about the relationships between historical cost and fair value at the date of acquisition. In that case, information about fair value may contribute to the assessment of the reliability of current cost measures.

51. Paragraphs 47-50, above, summarize the reasons for believing that information about fair values may be relevant in helping users with the assessment of future cash flows and with related needs. However, information also must satisfy a test of reliability before its disclosure is required in financial reports. The measurement of the fair value of oil and gas and other mineral reserves depends on estimates of the physical quantities of the reserves, the rate of extraction, future selling prices, future development and extraction costs, and the discount rate. Recent research, described at the Board's July public hearing, has shown that estimates of physical quantities of oil and gas reserves are subject to extensive revisions as time passes; that research also has provided examples of material differences among the estimates of independent assessors.[6] Information provided by the Mining Task Group and respondents to the Exposure Draft indicates that similar findings would be likely to apply to estimates of the quantities of other mineral reserves. Consideration of the other factors involved in estimates of fair value indicates that their overall reliability is likely to be low since they involve forecasts of future events, particularly price changes, of a type that previously have been subject to high variability as a result of economic and political changes. Comments by financial analysts on the Exposure Draft suggested that the users of financial reports prefer to make their own assessments of fair value rather than rely on direct assessments provided by the enterprise.

52. The Board also considered the relationship between the proposals in its Exposure Draft and the SEC's existing requirements for disclosure of information about the net present value of proved oil and gas reserves. Respondents emphasized the cost of providing value information on a basis different from that required by the SEC, and the confusion expected to result from requirements for the disclo-

[6]Stanley P. Porter, *Study of the Subjectivity of Reserve Estimates and Its Relation to Financial Reporting*, 1980.

sure of two different types of value information. The SEC's requirements have avoided some of the uncertainties in the measurement of fair value by specifying that expected future price changes are not to be taken into account and by requiring the use of a specified discount rate. Consequently, the value number required by the SEC has a higher verifiability than fair value but it does not represent fair value; fair value depends partly on expectations of changing prices and changing discount rates. The Board intends to evaluate the usefulness of the SEC's requirement and to study the use actually made of the required information as part of an ongoing review of the accounting and reporting requirements for this industry (paragraph 4).

53. After considering the measurement difficulties discussed in paragraphs 51 and 52, and the information provided by respondents to the Exposure Draft, the Board concluded that the reliability of measurements of fair value of mineral resource assets was inadequate for disclosure to be required at the present time. The evidence on reliability cited above relates to measures of the quantities of reserves as well as other factors. Enterprises are, nonetheless, required by this Statement (mineral reserves other than oil and gas) and by Statement 19 (oil and gas reserves) to provide information about those quantities. The Board believes that information about quantities can be useful and that the main arguments distinguishing the reporting of quantities from the reporting of fair values are (a) the cumulative effect on reliability of all the components of fair value measures (fair values have lower reliability than quantities) and (b) the possibility of giving a misleading impression of reliability in the disclosure of a composite number representing fair value.

Other Issues

54. The Exposure Draft called for separate disclosure of information about income from continuing operations for (a) oil and gas producing activities and (b) other activities of an oil and gas producing enterprise. The main purpose of that requirement was to facilitate comparisons of the results of "other activities" among enterprises that use the full cost method for capitalizing expenditures on the one hand and the successful efforts method on the other hand. If current cost is estimated by adjusting historical cost for specific price changes, similar enterprises would report different numbers for current cost income from continuing operations depending on which costing method was used. Separate reporting of income for oil and gas producing activities would leave income from other activities on a comparable basis. However, that course of action would not resolve the basic problem. Some respondents to the Exposure Draft argued that such requirements amounted to a significant extension of FASB Statement No. 14, *Financial Reporting for Segments of a Business Enterprise*, and that they should not be adopted without consideration of the implications for Statement 14. The Board noted that some financial analysts regarded the separate disclosure of information about income from producing activities as useful. However, the Board concluded that the net benefits from such a requirement had not been demonstrated clearly enough to justify the requirement at the present time. It will reconsider this requirement as part of the additional work described in paragraph 4.

55. As noted above, estimates of the fair value of mineral resource assets can be computed from estimates of the quantities of mineral reserves, the rate of production, future selling prices, future production and development costs, and the future cost of capital. The Board considered the usefulness of requirements to disclose estimates of those items or requirements to disclose past information that would be useful for forming such estimates. Disclosure of information that would enable users of financial reports to estimate fair values might be useful and it would minimize the danger, attributed to direct reporting of fair values, that users might develop an exaggerated impression of the reliability of the numbers. The SEC already requires some disclosures of this type of information. In the case of the mining industry, the Exposure Draft proposed disclosure of information about quantities and selling prices of minerals. Respondents to the Exposure Draft generally supported the proposals and the Board concluded that they should be incorporated in this Statement. In the case of the oil and gas industry, the requirements of the SEC are already extensive. The Board concluded that it should not introduce any additional requirements at the present time. It plans to continue to work with the industry and the SEC to study the interrelationships of existing requirements with the purpose of limiting the disclosure requirements to those most effective in achieving the objectives of financial reporting.

56. The quantities of mineral reserves other than oil and gas, disclosure of which is required by this Statement, need not be the quantities at year-end but may be the quantities at the beginning of the year or some other date during the year. The Board weighed the advantage of mandating more current information provided by year-end disclosure against the cost and the possible delay in issuing annual reports. The Board understands that information about year-end reserves may not always be available in a timely manner and that a requirement for year-end disclosure might cause a delay in the issuance of annual reports. New discoveries are not frequent, but a long period of time is required for the assessment of quantities and grades. Current information about discoveries can be provided by management discus-

sion. The Board concluded that the additional value of mandating more current information about reserve quantities did not justify the probable cost and delay in the issuance of annual reports.

57. Several respondents to the Exposure Draft requested clarification of the disclosures required of reserves held by subsidiaries and other investees. The Board concluded that the reporting of those reserves should follow as closely as possible the methods used to incorporate the results of the investee in the primary financial statements. Those provisions (paragraph 14) are similar to provisions contained in Statement 19 for the reporting of oil and gas reserves.

58. Several respondents to the Exposure Draft asked for clarification of the nature of the assets, described as "proved oil and gas reserves," and by other expressions in the Exposure Draft. The Board decided to adopt the term "mineral resource assets" in this Statement. This term was previously used in the SEC's SAB No. 18, *Amended Interpretation Regarding Disclosure of Replacement Cost Data for Mineral Resource Assets Employed in Mining Operations*. It includes mineral interests in properties, completed and uncompleted wells, and related equipment and facilities and other facilities used for purposes of extraction. It does not include movable equipment and support facilities that are covered by the provisions of Statement 33 relating to property, plant, and equipment.

Statement of Financial Accounting Standards No. 40
Financial Reporting and Changing Prices: Specialized Assets—Timberlands and Growing Timber

a supplement to FASB Statement No. 33

STATUS

Issued: November 1980

Effective Date: For fiscal years ending on or after December 25, 1980

Affects: Supersedes FAS 33, paragraph 53

Affected by: Paragraph 6 superseded by FAS 41
Paragraph 6 amended by FAS 46
Paragraph 6 superseded by FAS 69
Paragraph 12 superseded by FAS 39

SUMMARY

This Statement extends the interim provisions in FASB Statement No. 33, *Financial Reporting and Changing Prices,* for the measurement of timberlands, growing timber, and related expenses, in information on a current cost basis. It requires enterprises that present information on a current cost basis to combine measures of those assets and expenses at either historical cost/constant dollar amounts or current cost amounts with current cost measures of other assets and expenses. Statement 33 provides that an enterprise need not present information on a current cost basis if there would be no material difference between that information and information on a historical cost/constant dollar basis. Therefore, an enterprise needs to present information on a current cost basis only if it has significant holdings of inventory, property, plant, and equipment apart from timberlands and growing timber. This Statement applies to fiscal years ended on or after December 25, 1980.

The Board will continue to work with its advisory task group for the forest products industry to develop, as soon as possible, improved methods of measuring the effects of changing prices on this industry.

Statement of Financial Accounting Standards No. 40 Financial Reporting and Changing Prices: Specialized Assets—Timberlands and Growing Timber

a supplement to FASB Statement No. 33

CONTENTS

INTRODUCTION

1. FASB Statement No. 33, *Financial Reporting and Changing Prices,* establishes standards for reporting certain effects of price changes on business enterprises. Statement 33 requires large public enterprises to disclose information on both a historical cost/constant dollar basis and a current cost basis. Current cost information is required for fiscal years ended on or after December 25, 1979, but first presentation of the information can be postponed for one year.

2. If an enterprise does not postpone its first presentation of current cost information, it is required to follow the provisions of Statement 33 for the preparation of that information. Under those provisions inventory, most kinds of property, plant, and equipment and related expenses are measured at current cost amounts but timberlands, growing timber, timber harvested, and certain other specialized assets may be included at historical cost adjusted by either a specific price index or a general price index.

3. The provisions of Statement 33 for the measurement of timberlands and growing timber, in information on a current cost basis, are interim provisions applicable for fiscal years ended before December 25, 1980. This Statement extends those interim provisions. It requires enterprises that present information on a current cost basis to combine measures of timberlands, growing timber, and related expenses at either historical cost/constant dollar amounts or at current cost amounts with current cost measures of other assets and expenses. This Statement permits use of the same approaches as were permitted under the interim provisions of Statement 33 but it also permits the use of other methods of estimating current costs. This Statement provides greater flexibility in measurement because current cost is a broader measure than historical cost adjusted by a specific price index.

4. Statement 33, paragraph 31, provides that an enterprise need not present information on a current cost basis if there would be no material difference between that information and historical cost/constant dollar information. That provision, together with the provisions in this Statement, means that an enterprise needs to present information on a current cost basis only if it has significant holdings of inventory, property, plant, and equipment apart from timberlands and growing timber.

5. This Statement does not set a time limit on the applicability of these interim provisions. However, the Board will work with its advisory task group for the forest products industry to develop improved methods of measuring the effects of specific price changes on timberlands and growing timber; it will issue a Statement to supersede the interim provisions of this Statement as soon as that action is justified by the available evidence.

STANDARDS OF FINANCIAL ACCOUNTING AND REPORTING

Supplement to FASB Statement No. 33

6. Paragraph 53 of Statement 33, as amended by paragraph 12 of FASB Statement No. 39, *Financial Reporting and Changing Prices: Specialized Assets—Mining and Oil and Gas,* is superseded as follows:

This Statement does not contain provisions for the measurement, on a current cost basis, of income-producing real estate and unprocessed natural resources and related depreciation, depletion, and amortization expense for fiscal years ended before December 25, 1980 (paragraph 19). If an enterprise presents information on a current cost basis for a fiscal year ended before December 25, 1980, it may measure those assets and related expenses, at their historical cost/constant dollar amounts or by reference to an appropriate index of specific price changes.

a. When an enterprise presents information on a current cost basis for fiscal years ended on or after December 25, 1980, it shall measure: *Mineral resource assets* and related depreciation, depletion, and amortization expenses in accordance with the provisions of this Statement for the measurement of property, plant, and equipment and related expenses;
b. When an enterprise presents information on a current cost basis for fiscal years ended on or after December 25, 1980, it shall measure: *Timberlands and growing timber* (including timber held under cutting contracts) and related expenses at either their historical cost/constant dollar amounts or at current cost or lower recoverable amounts.

7. If an enterprise estimates the current cost of growing timber and timber harvested by adjusting historical cost for the changes in specific prices, those historical costs may either (a) be limited to the costs that are capitalized in the primary financial statements or (b) include all costs that are directly related to reforestation and forest management, such as planting, fertilization, fire protection, property taxes, and nursery stock, whether or not those costs are capitalized in the primary financial statements.

Effective Date and Transition

8. The provisions of this Statement shall be effective for fiscal years ended on or after December 25, 1980.

The provisions of this Statement need not be applied to immaterial items.

This Statement was adopted by the affirmative votes of five members of the Financial Accounting Standards Board. Messrs. March and Mosso dissented.

Messrs. March and Mosso dissent because there is not adequate reason to delay adoption of the current cost approach proposed in paragraphs 42-44 of the FASB Exposure Draft, *Financial Reporting and Changing Prices: Specialized Assets.* There was substantial support for that approach, particularly for the measurement of income from continuing operations. The principal focus of criticism was on the issue of capitalizing interest on standing timber. Resolution of that issue could easily have been postponed without indefinitely delaying the adoption of current cost measures for income from continuing operations. There are other problems as well, but they are no more severe than the problems in other industries and they could best be resolved, as in other industries, in the context of on-going supplemental reporting. The urgency of getting on with the development of techniques for measuring the erosive effects of inflation on business capital does not permit the leisurely pace exhibited by this Statement.

Members of the Financial Accounting Standards Board:

Donald J. Kirk, *Chairman*
Frank E. Block
John W. March
Robert A. Morgan
David Mosso
Robert T. Sprouse
Ralph E. Walters

Appendix A

BACKGROUND

9. Statement 33, issued in September 1979, does not contain provisions for the measurement on a current cost basis of certain assets and expenses for periods ended on or after December 25, 1980. The Board concluded in Statement 33 that further studies were required to provide a basis for decisions on the applicability to those assets of the requirement to present information on a current cost basis.

10. On April 21, 1980, the Board issued an FASB Exposure Draft, *Financial Reporting and Changing Prices: Specialized Assets.* The Board received 124 letters of comment on the Exposure Draft.

11. In July 1980, the Board conducted a public hearing on the Exposure Draft. Twenty-one organizations and individuals presented their views at the two-day hearing.

12. After issuing the Exposure Draft the Board held five open meetings at which it considered the matters dealt with in the Exposure Draft. In addition, the staff has held meetings with the Forest Products Task Group.

13. This Statement differs from the Exposure Draft principally in that it deals only with timberlands and growing timber and that it contains no requirement for the *separate* disclosure of current cost information for timberlands and growing timber nor any requirement to disclose information about the fair value of timberlands and growing timber. The Board is issuing separate Statements dealing with financial reporting and changing prices for (a) mineral resource assets and (b) income-producing real estate.

Appendix B

BASIS FOR CONCLUSIONS

Introduction

14. This appendix reviews considerations that members of the Board deemed significant in reaching the conclusions in this Statement; it includes reasons for accepting certain views and rejecting others. Individual Board members gave greater weight to some factors than to others.

15. Statement 33 requires large public enterprises to disclose supplementary information on a current cost basis. However, it contains only interim provisions applicable to years ended before December 25, 1980 for the measurement of income-producing real estate and unprocessed natural resources. This Statement extends those interim provisions for the measurement of timberlands and growing timber for years ended on or after December 25, 1980.

16. During its deliberations on this Statement, the Board considered the following main possibilities:

a. Require measurements on a current cost basis
b. Require information about fair values, defined as the prices that would be accepted as reasonable in transactions between a willing buyer and a willing seller
c. Continue interim provisions similar to those contained in Statement 33; require measurement, in information prepared on a current cost basis, at either historical cost/constant dollar amounts or at current cost amounts at the option of the preparer
d. Exempt activities that use timberlands and growing timber from the requirement to present information on a current cost basis.

Current Cost

17. Timberlands and growing timber have certain special features that raise doubts about the usefulness of the type of current cost measures required for other assets. Those special features are of unusual importance in the case of timber but they are not unique to that asset. They arise because timber grows while it is held and because time elapses between planting and maturity.

18. For most assets, information about current costs may be useful because it has a closer and more stable relationship than historical cost to the present value of future cash flows (Statement 33, paragraphs 116-123). Such a relationship is most likely to exist when current cost is measured by a buying price.

19. Some costs of growing timber are not capitalized in the primary statements at the present time. Adjustment of the carrying value of timberlands and growing timber by a specific price index to produce a current cost measurement would probably do little to improve the basis for assessing future cash flows. The development of new procedures for the capitalization of costs might produce a useful measure of current cost, but more work is required to identify improved procedures. The basis for assessing future cash flows might be improved if forest management and similar costs were to be capitalized more comprehensively than at present. Timber takes a long time to grow. Consequently, interest costs or imputed cost of capital also may need to be included in the asset measurement.

20. Information about current costs also may be useful for assessing the ability of an enterprise to maintain its operating capability. For this purpose, expenses should reflect the current cost of resources used or sold during the year. Two cases need to be considered. First, the enterprise may be operating on a sustained-yield basis, with growth approximately equal to the quantity of timber cut. In that case, decisions on what costs should be capitalized make little difference. A change in capitalization procedures, for example, resulting in the capitalization of additional costs, would not significantly affect the amount of income. Expenses for the current year would be reduced by the amount of forest management costs that were to be capitalized but expenses also would be increased by certain forest management costs, capitalized in previous years, and now included at current cost in depreciation, depletion, and amortization expense: the increase would approximately equal the reduction.

21. The second case arises when growth is not equal to the quantity cut. Capitalization procedures then can make a significant difference to income

measurement. Improvements in capitalization procedures could give an expense measurement that was better related to quantities cut and, hence, might provide an improved basis for assessing the maintenance of operating capability. However, further study is required to develop a basis for decisions on capitalization under this approach.

22. Several respondents to the Exposure Draft emphasized the lack of significance of current cost asset measurements obtained under the procedures set out in the Exposure Draft. They favored measurement of income from continuing operations on a current cost basis but thought that information about the current cost of the asset was unreliable and should not be reported. Their comments raise the issue of whether an expense measure can be reliable when the corresponding asset measure is not. After considering the foregoing arguments, the Board decided not to call for measurement of timberlands and growing timber according to the full current cost requirements of Statement 33. It decided that such a requirement should not be imposed until additional work has been undertaken to resolve the difficulties discussed in the preceding paragraphs and until further evidence is available to indicate that the benefits of the information are likely to exceed the costs.

Fair Value

23. Information about the fair value of timberlands and growing timber would be relevant as a basis for assessment of future cash flows. However, some commentators stated that fair values could not be measured with sufficient reliability to justify a requirement for disclosure at the present time. Fair values could be estimated either: (a) by referring to prices at which sales of similar assets had been made or (b) by estimating the net present value of cash flows to be derived from the asset. Application of the first approach would be limited but not excluded because of the absence of sufficient transactions in directly comparable assets. The second approach would depend on estimates of the discount rate, quantities of timber to be harvested in each future year, the future value of logs at the processing point, and future costs of cutting, transportation, and management. Even if quantities were estimable with acceptable reliability, future prices and costs would be highly uncertain, particularly since the processing facility to be used may not exist at the time the computation is made. Accordingly, the Board was not satisfied that fair value would meet the minimum standards of reliability appropriate to inclusion in financial reporting. In addition, some Board members believe that fair value involves a focus on an exit price and, accordingly, has implications that go beyond reporting the effects of changing prices.

24. Some Board members believe that enterprises should be required to present information that would be useful for assessments by users of fair value. They think that the disclosure of information about the quantity of timber on hand, current market prices, and current operating costs may be useful for users while avoiding the danger, in direct reporting of estimated fair value, of giving a misleading impression of reliability. The Board intends to undertake further study of this possibility.

Other Reporting Alternatives

25. The Board considered the exemption of the activities of growing and cutting timber from the current cost reporting requirement. The Board rejected that alternative as an interim provision because of the difficulties in separating the results of various activities in an integrated enterprise and because the proposal would complicate an analysis of differences between the operations reported on a current cost basis and the operations reported in the primary financial statements.

26. The Board also concluded that it should not permit the measurement of timberlands and growing timber at historical cost/nominal dollars for purposes of disclosures otherwise on a current cost basis. Statement 33 requires current cost measures in constant dollars (which are equal to current dollars). To ensure that all the measures involved in current cost income from continuing operations are in constant dollars, timberlands and growing timber should, at least, be measured in historical cost/constant dollars.

Conclusion

27. The Board concluded that either historical cost/constant dollar amounts or current cost measurements should be permitted as they were in paragraph 53 of Statement 33. Flexibility also would be allowed regarding the method of estimating current costs. In this manner, experimentation may be encouraged without the imposition of the costs of preparing particular computations before sufficient information is available about their usefulness.

Statement of Financial Accounting Standards No. 41 Financial Reporting and Changing Prices: Specialized Assets—Income-Producing Real Estate

a supplement to FASB Statement No. 33

STATUS

Issued: November 1980

Effective Date: For fiscal years ending on or after December 25, 1980

Affects: Supersedes FAS 33, paragraph 53
Supersedes FAS 39, paragraph 12
Supersedes FAS 40, paragraph 6

Affected by: Paragraph 7 amended by FAS 46
Paragraph 7 superseded by FAS 69

SUMMARY

This Statement supplements FASB Statement No. 33, *Financial Reporting and Changing Prices*. It requires enterprises that present information on a current cost basis to combine measures of income-producing real estate and related expenses at either historical cost/constant dollar amounts or at current cost amounts with current cost measures of other assets and expenses. Statement 33 provides that an enterprise need not present information on a current cost basis if there would be no material difference between that information and information on a historical cost/constant dollar basis. Therefore, an enterprise needs to present information on a current cost basis only if it has significant holdings of inventory, property, plant, and equipment apart from income-producing real estate. This Statement applies to fiscal years ended on or after December 25, 1980.

The Board will continue to work with its advisory task group for the real estate industry to develop improved methods of measuring the effects of changing prices on this industry.

Statement of Financial Accounting Standards No. 41
Financial Reporting and Changing Prices: Specialized Assets—Income-Producing Real Estate

a supplement to FASB Statement No. 33

CONTENTS

INTRODUCTION

1. FASB Statement No. 33, *Financial Reporting and Changing Prices,* establishes standards for reporting certain effects of price changes on business enterprises. Statement 33 requires large public enterprises to disclose information on both a historical cost/constant dollar basis and a current cost basis. Current cost information is required for fiscal years ended on or after December 25, 1979, but first presentation of the information can be postponed for one year.

2. If an enterprise does not postpone its first presentation of current cost information, it is required to follow the provisions of Statement 33 for the preparation of that information. Under those provisions, inventory, most kinds of property, plant, and equipment and related expenses are measured at current cost amounts but income-producing real estate and certain other specialized assets may be included at historical cost adjusted by either a specific price index or a general price index.

3. The provisions of Statement 33 for the measurement of income-producing real estate, in information on a current cost basis, are interim provisions applicable for fiscal years ended before December 25, 1980. This Statement extends those interim provisions. It requires enterprises that present information on a current cost basis to combine measures of income-producing real estate and related expenses at either historical cost/constant dollar amounts or at current cost amounts with current cost measures of other assets and expenses. The provisions of this Statement permit use of the same approaches to the measurement of current cost as were permitted under the interim provisions of Statement 33; it also permits the use of other approaches.

4. Statement 33, paragraph 31, provides that an enterprise need not present information on a current cost basis if there would be no material difference between that information and historical cost/constant dollar information. That provision, together with the provisions in this Statement, means that an enterprise needs to present information on a current cost basis only if it has significant holdings of inventory, property, plant, and equipment apart from income-producing real estate and certain other specialized assets.

5. This Statement does not set a time limit on the applicability of its interim provisions. However, the Board will continue to work with its advisory task group for the real estate industry to develop improved methods of measuring income-producing real estate. That work will focus on the relevance, verifiability, and representational faithfulness of various measures, including current cost and fair value, and also on a comparison of the characteristics of various types of assets. In assigning a priority to the work, the Board will take account of the small number of enterprises for which income-producing real estate comprises a major part of their assets. Moreover, several of these enterprises are likely to present information about fair values voluntarily. However, the Board will issue a Statement to

supersede the interim provisions of this Statement as soon as that action is justified by the available evidence.

STANDARDS OF FINANCIAL ACCOUNTING AND REPORTING

Definition

6. For the purposes of this Statement, the term *income-producing real estate* is defined as follows:

Income-producing real estate comprises properties that meet all of the following criteria:

a. Cash flows can be directly associated with a long-term leasing agreement with unaffiliated parties.
b. The property is being operated. (It is not in a construction phase.)
c. Future cash flows from the property are reasonably estimable.
d. Ancillary services are not a significant part of the lease agreement.

Supplement to FASB Statement No. 33

7. Paragraph 53 of Statement 33, as amended by Statements 39 and 40, is superseded by the following:

This Statement does not contain provisions for the measurement on a current cost basis of income-producing real estate and unprocessed natural resources and related depreciation, depletion, and amortization expense for fiscal years ended before December 25, 1980 (paragraph 19). If an enterprise presents information on a current cost basis for a fiscal year ended before December 25, 1980, it may measure those assets and related expenses at their historical cost/constant dollar amounts or by reference to an appropriate index of specific price changes.

a. When an enterprise presents information on a current cost basis for fiscal years ended on or after December 25, 1980, it shall measure: *Mineral resource assets* and related depreciation, depletion, and amortization expense in accordance with the provisions of this Statement for the measurement of property, plant, and equipment and related expenses;
b. When an enterprise presents information on a current cost basis for fiscal years ended on or after December 25, 1980, it shall measure: *Timberlands and growing timber* and related expenses at either their historical cost/constant dollar amounts or at current cost or lower recoverable amounts;
c. When an enterprise presents information on a current cost basis for fiscal years ended on or after December 25, 1980, it shall measure: *Income-producing real estate* and related expenses at either their historical cost/constant dollar amounts or at current cost or lower recoverable amounts.

Effective Date and Transition

8. The provisions of this Statement shall be effective for fiscal years ended on or after December 25, 1980.

The provisions of this Statement need not be applied to immaterial items.

This Statement was adopted by the affirmative votes of four members of the Financial Accounting Standards Board. Messrs. Mosso, Sprouse, and Walters dissented.

Messrs. Mosso, Sprouse, and Walters dissent because this Statement, which is part of a comprehensive standard for measurement of the effects of changing prices, and which concerns a kind of asset that has been dramatically affected by specific price changes, does not deal with that issue in a positive way.

The Board received overwhelming testimony that neither the constant dollar nor the current cost method produces useful information for assessing the impact of specific price changes on real estate investment properties, yet this Statement permits either method to be used in current cost presentations. Of special concern is the relevance of deducting current cost depreciation to measure income from a property that is being maintained to last indefinitely and that is continuing to appreciate in value. Because income-producing real estate is generally held as an investment rather than as an operating capability involving continuous disposals and replacements of components, the effect of changing specific prices on depreciation is not a significant concern. Cash flows and value changes are the critical factors just as they are with other kinds of marketable investments. The relevant accounting analogy is to an investment portfolio not, as implicit in this Statement, to property, plant, and equipment. Estimated fair values and changes in fair values are the most relevant information that can be provided about the effects of changing prices on income-producing real estate; those estimates are sufficiently reliable to be required as supplementary information. The information obtained during the two years' attention given specifically to the effects of changing prices on income-producing real estate strongly suggests that further delay will not produce new information that might lead to a different conclusion.

Members of the Financial Accounting Standards Board:

Donald J. Kirk, *Chairman*	John W. March	Robert T. Sprouse
Frank E. Block	Robert A. Morgan	Ralph E. Walters
	David Mosso	

Appendix A

BACKGROUND

9. Statement 33, issued in September 1979, does not contain provisions for the measurement, on a current cost basis, of certain assets and related expenses for periods ended on or after December 25, 1980. The Board concluded in Statement 33 that further studies were required to provide a basis for decisions on the applicability to those assets of the requirement to present information on a current cost basis.

10. On April 21, 1980, the Board issued an FASB Exposure Draft, *Financial Reporting and Changing Prices: Specialized Assets*. The Board received 124 letters of comment on the Exposure Draft.

11. In July 1980, the Board conducted a public hearing on the Exposure Draft. Twenty-one organizations and individuals presented their views at the two-day hearing.

12. After the issuance of the Exposure Draft, the Board held five open meetings at which it considered the issues dealt with in the Exposure Draft. In addition, the staff has met with the Real Estate Task Group.

13. This Statement differs from the Exposure Draft in that it deals with only income-producing real estate, and it contains no requirement for the separate disclosure of current cost information for income-producing real estate nor any requirement to disclose information about the fair value of income-producing real estate. The Board has issued separate Statements dealing with financial reporting and changing prices for (a) mineral resource assets and (b) timberlands and growing timber.

Appendix B

BASIS FOR CONCLUSIONS

Introduction

14. This appendix reviews considerations that members of the Board deemed significant in reaching the conclusions in this Statement; it includes reasons for accepting certain views and rejecting others. Individual Board members gave greater weight to some factors than to others.

15. Statement 33 requires certain large public enterprises to disclose supplementary information on a current cost basis. However, it contains only interim provisions, applicable to years ended before December 25, 1980, for the measurement of income-producing real estate and unprocessed natural resources in information prepared on a current cost basis. This Statement contains further interim provisions for the measurement of income-producing real estate and related expenses for years ended on or after December 25, 1980.

16. During its deliberations on this Statement, the Board considered the following alternatives:

a. Require measurements on a current cost basis
b. Require information about fair values, defined as the prices that would be accepted as reasonable in transactions between a willing buyer and a willing seller
c. Continue provisions similar to those contained in Statement 33; require measurement in information prepared on a current cost basis at either historical cost/constant dollar amounts or at current cost amounts at the option of the preparer
d. Exempt income-producing real estate from the requirement to present information on a current cost basis.

Current Cost

17. Income-producing real estate has certain special features that raise doubts about the usefulness of the types of current cost measures required for other assets. Those special features affect the relevance of current cost information for the assessment of the maintenance of operating capability, for the assessment of future cash flows, and for the assessment of financial performance.

18. Some Board members and respondents to the Exposure Draft believe that the assessment of the maintenance of operating capability is not important in relation to income-producing real estate.

Investors and creditors do not wish to focus on the ability of an enterprise to maintain its physical capability. Such a focus would not contribute significantly to the overall assessment of cash flows. Rather, income-producing real estate should be regarded as investments, much like marketable securities, and assessments should focus directly on the maintenance of the enterprise's ability to generate future cash flows. This approach raises doubts about one of the main uses of current cost information—provision of a basis of assessing operating capability.

19. Some Board members and respondents to the Exposure Draft also believe that conventional methods of measuring depreciation expense (such as the straight-line method) fail to provide useful information about the way in which use of a building is associated with a reduction in expectations of future cash flows. They believe that conventional depreciation methods assume an expiration of service potential that frequently does not, in fact, take place in a well-maintained building. This point of view raises doubts about the usefulness of information about depreciation on a current cost basis for the assessment of enterprise performance.

20. Other Board members believe that a measure of current cost depreciation is needed for income-producing real estate. They believe that income-producing real estate is more similar to other kinds of property, plant, and equipment than to marketable securities and that current cost measures are useful for assessments of enterprise performance. They believe that a conventional measure of depreciation expense can provide information that is useful for the evaluation of managerial performance in operating and leasing real estate, taking account of the expiration of the service potential of the facilities being leased. They also believe that a conventional measure of depreciation expense is needed to distinguish return on capital from return of capital.

21. The Board concluded that some measure of depreciation expense for income-producing real estate is needed in computations of income from continuing operations on a current cost basis. However, it believes that the arguments in favor of requiring current cost information are less strong for income-producing real estate than for other types of property, plant, and equipment. Accordingly, the Board concluded that it should not require enterprises to incur the cost of undertaking current cost measurements of income-producing real estate without further evidence to indicate that the benefits of the information are likely to exceed the costs. Therefore, it decided to permit the use of either historical cost/constant dollar measures or current cost measures of those properties in information on a current cost basis. Accordingly, an enterprise needs to present information on a current cost basis only if it has significant holdings of inventory, property, plant, and equipment apart from income-producing real estate and certain other specialized assets.

Fair Value

22. Information about the fair value of income-producing real estate would be relevant as a basis for assessment of future cash flows if it could be measured with sufficient reliability. Some Board members and respondents to the Exposure Draft favor disclosure of fair value information. They believe that disclosure of estimated fair value information would be more relevant than disclosure of current cost. In addition, some enterprises that own income-producing real estate are likely to disclose information about fair value even if it is not required. These Board members believe it is preferable to provide authoritative guidance about measurement and disclosure rather than allow diverse practices to develop.

23. Other Board members are opposed to the introduction of a requirement for disclosure of fair value information at the present time. They believe that disclosure of fair value involves a focus on an exit price and, accordingly, has implications that go beyond reporting the effects of changing prices. In addition, they are not satisfied that fair value measurements would meet minimum standards of reliability appropriate to inclusion in financial reports. Some of these Board members believe that disclosure of fair value measurements should not be considered until further progress has been made with the conceptual framework at which time it should be possible to have a better understanding of the broad implications of the uses of such measurements in the real estate industry as well as others. Others believe that low reliability will remain a decisive argument against a requirement to disclose fair values for real estate even after the conceptual framework has been further developed. The Board concluded that no requirements for disclosure of fair value measures should be introduced at the present time.

Definition

24. The Exposure Draft reflected the Board's conclusion that income-producing real estate should include only properties that are leased or are ready for leasing, and real estate for which cash flows are reasonably estimable. Those qualifications were intended to ensure that disclosures of fair value be required only for assets for which the measurements would be reasonably reliable. Comments received on the Exposure Draft indicate that only a small number of companies would have significant amounts of income-producing real estate assets.

Hotels, for example, which have occupancy rates and related cash flows that may fluctuate to a relatively large extent, do not meet the criteria for income-producing real estate. While this Statement does not require disclosure of information about fair value, the Board concluded that the definition remains useful. Properties that are not rented for long periods are often used in conjunction with the provision of other services. For the purposes of Statement 33, those properties are included in property, plant, and equipment and are not covered by the special provisions of income-producing real estate. In those cases, the maintenance of operating capability, and, hence, information about current cost, may have greater relevance.

Conclusion

25. The Board concluded that either historical cost/constant dollar amounts or current cost measurements should be permitted as they are in paragraph 53 of Statement 33. In this manner, experimentation may be encouraged without the imposition of the costs of preparing particular computations before sufficient information is available about their usefulness.

Statement of Financial Accounting Standards No. 42
Determining Materiality for Capitalization of Interest Cost

an amendment of FASB Statement No. 34

STATUS

Issued: November 1980

Effective Date: For fiscal years beginning after December 15, 1979, unless enterprise had already adopted FAS34; if so, effective for fiscal years beginning after October 15, 1980

Affects: Amends FAS 34, paragraphs 8 and 9

Affected by: No other pronouncements

SUMMARY

This Statement amends FASB Statement No. 34, *Capitalization of Interest Cost,* (1) to delete language that some believe allows capitalization of interest to be avoided under certain circumstances and (2) to make clear that Statement 34 does not establish new tests of materiality.

Statement of Financial Accounting Standards No. 42
Determining Materiality for Capitalization of Interest Cost

an amendment of FASB Statement No. 34

CONTENTS

INTRODUCTION

1. Paragraph 8 of FASB Statement No. 34, *Capitalization of Interest Cost,* states that:

> In concept, interest cost is capitalizable for all assets that require a period of time to get them ready for their intended use (an "acquisition period"). However, in many cases, the benefit in terms of information about enterprise resources and earnings may not justify the additional accounting and administrative cost involved in providing the information. The benefit may be less than the cost because the effect of interest capitalization and its subsequent amortization or other disposition, compared with the effect of charging it to expense when incurred, would not be material. In that circumstance, interest capitalization is not *required* by this Statement.

Paragraph 9 of Statement 34 begins as follows:

> Subject to the provisions of paragraph 8, interest shall be capitalized for the following types of assets ("qualifying assets"). . . .

2. The Board has received a number of questions concerning how paragraph 8 should be construed in deciding whether capitalization of interest is required. Some have stated that paragraph 8 appears to establish new tests of materiality that allow an enterprise to measure the effect of interest capitalization on income by a pro forma prospective or retroactive computation without also considering the effect on current year income. The Board has concluded that new tests of materiality should not be established for interest capitalization and has, accordingly, decided to amend paragraph 8 of Statement 34 to delete the language that gave rise to those questions.

3. The Board has concluded that it can reach an informed decision on the basis of existing information without a public hearing and that the effective date and transition specified in paragraph 5 are advisable in the circumstances.

STANDARDS OF FINANCIAL ACCOUNTING AND REPORTING

Amendment to FASB Statement No. 34

4. The last two sentences of paragraph 8 of Statement 34 are superseded and replaced by the following sentence:

> Accordingly, interest shall not be capitalized in the situations described in paragraph 10.

The introduction of paragraph 9 of Statement 34 is amended to read as follows:

> Interest shall be capitalized for the following types of assets ("qualifying assets"):

Effective Date and Transition

5. This Statement shall be effective for fiscal years beginning after December 15, 1979. The provisions of this Statement shall be applied at the same time as the provisions of Statement 34 are first applied. Enterprises that already have adopted the provisions of Statement 34 shall apply the provisions of this Statement in their next fiscal year beginning after October 15, 1980 and may, but are not required to, restate their financial statements for the year of initial adoption to reflect the provisions of this Statement.

Determining Materiality for Capitalization of Interest Cost

The provisions of this Statement need not be applied to immaterial items.

This Statement was adopted by the affirmative votes of five members of the Financial Accounting Standards Board. Messrs. March and Mosso dissented.

Messrs. March and Mosso dissent. They believe Statement 34 wisely introduced some flexibility to minimize the additional cost of implementing a new accounting procedure for many enterprises. They would not change the provisions or intent of paragraphs 8 and 9 of that Statement and would interpret it to permit the use of evaluations like the pro forma approaches described in paragraph 6 of this Statement in assessing materiality from a cost-benefit standpoint. In their view, the incremental gain in informational value from a requirement to capitalize interest on construction programs of a continuing level of activity involving many asset items may be insufficient to offset the accounting costs that would in many instances be involved.

Although this Statement acknowledges the appropriateness of minimum threshold policies, Messrs. March and Mosso would interpret Statement 34 as originally issued to permit a broader application of the same reasoning that supported the exclusion of routinely manufactured inventories as qualifying assets in paragraph 10 of Statement 34. Judgments on such cost-benefit evaluations should be left to those able to examine specific facts and circumstances.

Members of the Financial Accounting Standards Board:

Donald J. Kirk, *Chairman*
Frank E. Block
John W. March
Robert A. Morgan
David Mosso
Robert T. Sprouse
Ralph E. Walters

Appendix A

BACKGROUND AND BASIS FOR CONCLUSIONS

6. The Board received a number of questions concerning how paragraph 8 of Statement 34 should be construed in deciding whether capitalization of interest is required. Some asked whether capitalization is required if a pro forma prospective computation indicates that equilibrium between the amount of interest capitalized and amortized each period would be reached after a few years. If equilibrium would be reached ultimately, those favoring this approach believe the benefits perceived by the Board for interest capitalization would be small compared with the accounting and administrative costs involved in providing the information. Others inquired if paragraph 8 would permit an enterprise to make pro forma computations of (a) the effect that capitalizing interest in prior years and subsequently amortizing it would have on the level of earnings in the current year and on the trend of earnings of preceding, current, and future years and (b) the effect of always expensing interest on the level of earnings in the current year and on the trend of earnings over those years. Under that pro forma retroactive approach, they believe an enterprise would not be required to capitalize interest if a comparison of the computations showed no material difference in the effect on the current year's earnings or in the effect on the trend of earnings.

7. An Exposure Draft of a proposed Statement, *Determining Materiality for Capitalization of Interest Cost,* was issued on April 22, 1980. The Board received 63 letters of comment in response to the Exposure Draft. The Exposure Draft concluded that the pro forma prospective approach should not be adopted in Statement 34 because it focuses on expectations of future activities and developments rather than on measurement and reporting of current earnings from past events and transactions. The Exposure Draft also concluded that the pro forma retroactive approach should not be adopted because, among other reasons, the computations focus on avoiding the requirements of the Statement while at the same time incurring the costs of calculation. The Board, therefore, concluded that the usual materiality tests are sufficient for implementation of Statement 34. Some respondents stated that the views expressed above in paragraph 6 are consistent with the usual materiality tests. However, the Board believes those views are not consistent with the usual materiality tests for the reasons explained below in paragraphs 8 and 9.

8. The usual tests of materiality for accounting changes are set forth in APB Opinion No. 20, *Accounting Changes.* Paragraph 38 of Opinion 20 requires disclosure of an accounting change that has a material effect on income before extraordinary items or net income of the current period. In addition, paragraph 38 requires disclosure of an accounting change that has a material effect on the enterprise's trend of earnings. The views expressed

in paragraph 6 suggest that interest capitalization should not be required if the effect is material in the current year but immaterial to the trend of earnings because of the "roll-over" effect that would occur from amortizing previously capitalized interest. In effect, those views imply that immateriality to the trend of earnings in the future should negate materiality to the current year income statement. Opinion 20, however, requires determining the effect on the trend of earnings to provide disclosure of an accounting change that would otherwise not be disclosed because of its immaterial effect on current period income, not to eliminate disclosure of an accounting change for which disclosure would otherwise be required. In other words, the test of the effect on trend of earnings is an additional test of materiality that increases the probability that an accounting change will be deemed material.

9. Consistent with the approach of Opinion 20, pro forma retroactive or prospective computations might be used as part of the assessment of materiality to income in implementing Statement 34 but not as the overriding test of materiality. If the effect of capitalizing interest on current year income is not material, an enterprise might wish to use a pro forma prospective computation to determine whether the effect is likely to be material in future years. Likewise, if the effect of capitalizing interest on current year income is only marginally material, a pro forma prospective computation indicating that the effect will not be material in future years could aid a determination that the current effect is not material. Pro forma retroactive and prospective computations can confirm whether the effect of capitalizing interest is or is not material, but immateriality on a pro forma retroactive or prospective test does not override a determination that an accounting change is material to current year income, the balance sheet, or other measures.

10. Some respondents expressed concern that paragraphs 5 and 6 of the Exposure Draft indicated that the Board opposes the use of minimum threshold levels in implementing Statement 34. That is not the case. Minimum threshold levels are common in inventory and property, plant, and equipment accounting. Many enterprises do not include the costs of minor items in inventory, and many enterprises do not capitalize individual items of property, plant, and equipment, the costs of which are less than a specified threshold. Such thresholds are designed to minimize the burden of capitalizing large numbers of assets and accounting for those costs as the assets are used. Those thresholds are justified on the grounds that the assets whose costs are charged to expense as purchased are immaterial both individually and in the aggregate. This Statement affirms the usual tests of materiality and does not affect threshold levels established in conformity with usual materiality tests.

11. Some respondents stated that the transition provisions did not address those enterprises that had elected early application of Statement 34 and might believe they were exempt from the provisions of this Statement. The Board intended that this Statement should apply to those enterprises and has clarified paragraph 5 to state that those who elected early application of Statement 34 are subject to the provisions of this Statement in the future. Those enterprises may, but are not required to, restate financial statements to the year of initial adoption of Statement 34.

Statement of Financial Accounting Standards No. 43
Accounting for Compensated Absences

STATUS

Issued: November 1980

Effective Date: For fiscal years beginning after December 15, 1980

Affects: No other pronouncements

Affected by: Paragraph 3 superseded by FAS 71

SUMMARY

This Statement requires an employer to accrue a liability for employees' rights to receive compensation for future absences when certain conditions are met. For example, this Statement requires a liability to be accrued for vacation benefits that employees have earned but have not yet taken; however, it generally does not require a liability to be accrued for future sick pay benefits, holidays, and similar compensated absences until employees are actually absent.

Statement of Financial Accounting Standards No. 43
Accounting for Compensated Absences

CONTENTS

INTRODUCTION AND BACKGROUND INFORMATION

1. The FASB has been asked to consider practices used by employers to account for employee absences, such as vacation, illness, and holidays, for which it is expected that employees will be paid (referred to in this Statement as *compensated absences*). The Board has been advised that the following alternative accounting practices exist with respect to compensated absences: (a) the cost is accrued over some period before payment or (b) the cost is recognized when paid. The Board has considered those alternative accounting practices and concluded that a liability for employees' rights to receive compensation for future absences should be accrued as specified by this Statement.

2. This Statement does not apply to severance or termination pay, postretirement benefits, deferred compensation, stock or stock options issued to employees, or other long-term fringe benefits, such as group insurance or long-term disability pay. This Statement does not address the allocation of costs of compensated absences to interim periods. Furthermore, because the appropriate structure for setting accounting standards for state and local governmental units is currently under discussion, the FASB is proposing no change with respect to the nature of its involvement with pronouncements in the governmental area until that matter is resolved. Consequently, the Board has deferred a decision regarding whether this Statement should apply to state and local governmental units.

3. The Addendum to APB Opinion No. 2, *Accounting for the "Investment Credit,"* states that ". . . differences may arise in the application of generally accepted accounting principles as between regulated and nonregulated businesses, because of the effect in regulated businesses of the rate-making process . . ." and discusses the application of generally accepted accounting principles to regulated industries. Accordingly, the provisions of the Addendum govern the application of this Statement to those operations of an employer that are regulated for rate-making purposes on an individual-company-cost-of-service basis.

4. An Exposure Draft of a proposed Statement, *Accounting for Compensated Absences*, was issued on December 17, 1979. The Board received 217 comment letters in response to the Exposure Draft. Certain of the comments received and the Board's consideration of them are discussed in Appendix A, "Summary of Consideration of Comments on Exposure Draft."

5. The Board has concluded that it can reach an informed decision on the basis of existing data without a public hearing and that the effective date and transition specified in paragraphs 8 and 9 are advisable in the circumstances.

STANDARDS OF FINANCIAL ACCOUNTING AND REPORTING

6. An employer shall accrue a liability for employees' compensation for future absences if *all* of the following conditions are met:

a. The employer's obligation relating to employees' rights to receive compensation for future absences is attributable to employees' services already rendered,
b. The obligation relates to rights that vest[1] or accumulate,[2]
c. Payment of the compensation is probable, and
d. The amount can be reasonably estimated.

If an employer meets conditions (a), (b), and (c) and

[1]In this Statement, *vested* rights are those for which the employer has an obligation to make payment even if an employee terminates; thus, they are not contingent on an employee's future service.

[2]For purposes of this Statement, *accumulate* means that earned but unused rights to compensated absences may be carried forward to one or more periods subsequent to that in which they are earned, even though there may be a limit to the amount that can be carried forward.

does not accrue a liability because condition (d) is not met, that fact shall be disclosed.

7. Notwithstanding the conditions specified in paragraph 6, an employer is not required to accrue a liability for nonvesting accumulating rights to receive sick pay benefits[3] (that is, compensation for an employee's absence due to illness) for the reasons stated in paragraph 15.

Effective Date and Transition

8. This Statement shall be effective for fiscal years beginning after December 15, 1980, with earlier application encouraged. Accounting changes adopted to conform to the provisions of this Statement shall be applied retroactively. In the year that this Statement is first applied, the financial statements shall disclose the nature of any restatement and its effect on income before extraordinary items, net income, and related per share amounts for each year restated.

9. If retroactive restatement of all years presented is not practicable, the financial statements presented shall be restated for as many consecutive years as practicable and the cumulative effect of applying the Statement shall be included in determining net income of the earliest year restated (not necessarily the earliest year presented). If it is not practicable to restate any prior year, the cumulative effect shall be included in net income in the year in which the Statement is first applied. (See paragraph 20 of APB Opinion No. 20, *Accounting Changes*.) The effect on income before extraordinary items, net income, and related per share amounts of applying this Statement in a year in which the cumulative effect is included in determining that year's net income shall be disclosed for that year.

The provisions of this Statement need not be applied to immaterial items.

This Statement was adopted by the affirmative votes of five members of the Financial Accounting Standards Board. Messrs. Kirk and Sprouse dissented.

Messrs. Kirk and Sprouse dissent because they believe the condition relating to "rights that vest or accumulate" (paragraph 6(b)) introduces unnecessary and irrelevant considerations in determining whether a liability for compensated absences has been incurred that should be recognized.

For benefits that have vesting provisions, the employee need not be absent to be compensated; therefore, services already rendered (condition 6(a)) is necessarily the past transaction or event that is referred to in the definition of liabilities as creating the obligation. For benefits that do not have vesting provisions, whether the benefits accumulate or are bestowed by outright grant by the employer is irrelevant and tends to detract from the central issue. The crucial question is whether the employer's liability is the result of employees rendering service (past presences) or being absent (future absences). Messrs. Kirk and Sprouse distinguish among the types of plans covered by this Statement believing, for example, that compensation for absences contingent on a specific event outside the control of the employer and employee, such as illness or jury duty, is attributable to those events. Compensation for absences that is not contingent on such events, for example vacations, is attributable to rendering service. Specifically, they believe the employer has a recordable liability for vacation pay and a contingency, but not a recordable liability for sick pay. Until illness occurs the employer has no liability; the employer does not owe anything until the contingent event, an illness, occurs.

Messrs. Kirk and Sprouse also are concerned that identical situations may continue to be accounted for differently because, under paragraph 7, a liability for nonvesting sick pay is not required but rather is permitted.

Members of the Financial Accounting Standards Board:

Donald J. Kirk, *Chairman*
Frank E. Block
John W. March
Robert A. Morgan
David Mosso
Robert T. Sprouse
Ralph E. Walters

[3]In accounting for compensated absences, the form of an employer's policy for compensated absences should not prevail over actual practices. For example, if employees are customarily paid "sick pay" benefits even though their absences from work are not actually the result of illness or if employees are routinely allowed to take compensated "terminal leave" for accumulated unused sick pay benefits prior to retirement, such benefits shall not be considered sick pay benefits for purposes of applying the provisions of paragraph 7 but rather should be accounted for in accordance with paragraph 6.

Appendix A

SUMMARY OF CONSIDERATION OF COMMENTS ON EXPOSURE DRAFT

10. Some respondents questioned the need for a project on accounting for compensated absences. They indicated that the informational benefits of requiring a liability for compensated absences to be accrued do not justify the costs of doing so. The accrual ordinarily would create a one-time significant adjustment with little financial statement effect among periods thereafter. The Accounting Standards Division of the AICPA asked the FASB to consider the alternative practices used by employers to account for compensated absences because of the potential for significant unrecorded or understated liabilities in certain cases. In view of the existence of significantly different alternative practices, the universality of the transactions, and the potential for understatement of liabilities, the Board concluded that a Statement on the subject should be issued (a) to affirm that generally accepted accounting principles require that compensated absences be accounted for on the accrual basis and (b) to clarify the accounting for those absences.

11. Some respondents requested guidance on how compensated absences should be accounted for in interim periods. Other respondents indicated that providing interim reporting guidance in this Statement would involve significant issues that are currently being addressed in the elements and recognition phases of the Board's conceptual framework project. Those respondents recommended that, in light of the Board's decision to defer further action on its interim reporting project until those conceptual issues are resolved, the Statement should specify that it does not change existing interim reporting practices and that the provisions of APB Opinion No. 28, *Interim Financial Reporting*, are still appropriate. The Board agreed; accordingly, this Statement is concerned with the accrual of a liability for compensated absences rather than with the allocation of the costs of such absences to interim periods.

12. Some respondents indicated that accrual of a liability for compensated absences should be limited to those absences for which the right to receive compensation is vested. The liability would then reflect only amounts that employees would be paid for their rights to compensated absences if their employment terminated. The Board believes that those respondents' comments generally reflect an approach that is more restrictive than called for by the Board's definition of a liability in paragraph 22 of the revised FASB Exposure Draft, *Elements of Financial Statements of Business Enterprises* (elements Exposure Draft), which states:

> Liabilities are probable future sacrifices of economic benefits stemming from present legal, equitable, or constructive obligations of a particular enterprise to transfer assets or provide services to other entities in the future as a result of past transactions or events affecting the enterprise.

The Board believes that a liability for amounts to be paid as a result of employees' rights to compensated absences should be accrued, considering anticipated forfeitures, in the year in which earned. For example, if new employees receive vested rights to two-weeks' paid vacation at the beginning of their second year of employment with no pro rata payment in the event of termination during the first year, the two-weeks' vacation would be considered to be earned by work performed in the first year and an accrual for vacation pay would be required for new employees during their first year of service, allowing for estimated forfeitures due to turnover. Furthermore, the proposed definition of a liability does not limit an employer's liability for compensated absences solely to rights to compensation for those absences that eventually vest. The definition also encompasses a constructive obligation for reasonably estimable compensation for past services that, based on the employer's past practices, probably will be paid and can be reasonably estimated. Individual facts and circumstances must be considered in determining when nonvesting rights to compensated absences are earned by services rendered.

13. The requirement to accrue a liability for nonvesting rights to compensated absences depends on whether the unused rights (a) expire at the end of the year in which earned or (b) accumulate and are carried forward to succeeding years, thereby increasing the benefits that would otherwise be available in those later years. If the rights expire, the Board believes that a liability for future absences should not be accrued at year-end because the benefits to be paid in subsequent years would not be attributable to employee services rendered in prior years. (Jury duty and military leave benefits generally do not accumulate if unused and, unless they accumulate, a liability for those benefits would not be accrued at year-end.) On the other hand, if unused rights do accumulate and increase the benefits otherwise available in subsequent years, the Board believes a liability should be accrued at year-end to the extent that it is probable that employees will be paid in subsequent years for the increased benefits attributable to the accumulated rights and the amount can be reasonably estimated.

14. Board members' views differ regarding whether employees' rights to receive compensation for

unused sick days that accumulate for possible future use but do not vest qualify as a liability in terms of the definition in the elements Exposure Draft. Some Board members believe that the relevant "past transaction or event" that creates an obligation to transfer assets to (that is, compensate) employees is the illness and that only a potential liability (that is, a loss contingency) exists before the illness occurs. However, the Board concluded that the relevant event is the past event of working; permitting accumulated sick days to be carried forward for use in future periods represents part of the employees' compensation for past work performed. The accumulated amount at year-end is an obligation that leaves the employer with little or no discretion to avoid future payment. Therefore, a liability exists to the extent that some or all of the accumulated sick days are likely to be used. That view parallels the reasoning of FASB Statement No. 5, *Accounting for Contingencies*, which requires a loss contingency to be accrued if (a) it is probable that a liability has been incurred and that future events will confirm the fact of loss and (b) the amount of loss can be reasonably estimated.

15. Notwithstanding the Board's conclusion that accrual of a liability for the probable payment of accumulated unused sick days is appropriate under the liability definition in the elements Exposure Draft, the Board was influenced by respondents' comments that the amounts involved generally would not be large enough to justify the cost of computing the probable payments for nonvesting accumulating sick pay benefits. The Board concluded that accrual should not be required for an obligation related to employees' accumulating rights to receive compensation for future absences that are contingent on the absences being caused by an employee's future illness because, in the Board's judgment, the lower degree of reliability of estimates of future sick pay and the cost of making and evaluating those estimates do not justify a requirement for such accrual. Furthermore, the Board believes that the probable payments for accumulating sick pay benefits rarely would be material unless they vest or are otherwise normally paid without an illness-related absence (as discussed in the following paragraph), in which cases the benefits would not be dependent on an employee's future illness and the criteria of paragraph 6 would apply. On the other hand, this Statement does not prohibit an employer from accruing a liability for such nonvesting accumulating sick pay benefits, providing the criteria of paragraph 6 are met.

16. The Board believes that the employer's actual administration of sick pay benefits should determine the appropriate accounting. For example, if employees are customarily paid "sick pay" benefits even though their absences from work are not actually the result of illness or if employees are routinely allowed to take compensated "terminal leave" for nonvesting accumulated unused sick pay benefits prior to retirement, the Board believes such accumulated benefits should not be considered as sick pay benefits for purposes of the exclusion described in paragraph 7 but rather should be accounted for in accordance with paragraph 6.

17. Some respondents said that requiring employers to estimate and accrue a liability for compensated absences could be an undue burden for employers, particularly smaller enterprises with limited staff and resources. The Board believes that the accrual accounting specified in paragraph 6 ordinarily will not cause an additional significant record-keeping burden because it centers on employee rights that accumulate or vest. Records maintained by employers for the administration of employee benefits ordinarily will be adequate to provide information for such an accrual. By excluding nonvesting sick pay benefits from required accruals, the Board sought to minimize the estimating burden.

18. Some respondents questioned whether the Board intended this Statement to apply to a sabbatical leave. The Board believes that the appropriate accounting for a sabbatical leave depends on the purpose of the leave. If a sabbatical leave is granted only to perform research or public service to enhance the reputation of or otherwise benefit the employer, the compensation is not attributable to services already rendered (paragraph 6(a)); a liability should not be accrued in advance of the employee's services during such leave. If the leave is granted to provide compensated unrestricted time off for past service and the other conditions for accrual are met, a liability for sabbatical leave should be accrued.

19. Some respondents questioned whether the absence of a reference in the Exposure Draft to the Addendum to Opinion 2 indicated that the Statement would apply to rate-regulated industries. The Board currently is considering the effect of rate regulation on regulated companies in another project. In the meantime, paragraph 3 was added to acknowledge that the provisions of the Addendum govern the application of this Statement to those operations of a company that are regulated for rate-making purposes on a basis of individual company cost of service.

20. Some respondents requested guidance on how an employer should estimate its liability for compensated absences. The respondents asked (a) whether the liability should be based on current or on future rates of pay, (b) whether it should be discounted, and (c) when the effect of scheduled increases should be accrued. The Board noted that it expects to be studying similar issues in its project on

accounting by employers for pensions as well as in a possible project on discounting[4] and, accordingly, concluded to defer a decision on such issues at this time.

21. Some respondents viewed the transition provisions in the Exposure Draft as inconsistent with present generally accepted accounting principles proscribing direct charges to retained earnings. They also expressed the view that required methods of transition should not differ for material and immaterial adjustments. The Board considered those views and changed the transition provisions consistent with several prior FASB Statements.

[4]The AICPA is currently developing an issues paper on discounting for consideration by the FASB.

Statement of Financial Accounting Standards No. 44 Accounting for Intangible Assets of Motor Carriers

an amendment of Chapter 5 of ARB No. 43 and an interpretation of APB Opinions 17 and 30

STATUS

Issued: December 1980

Effective Date: December 19, 1980 for financial statements for fiscal periods ending after December 15, 1980

Affects: Amends ARB 43, Chapter 5, Paragraphs 8 and 10

Affected by: No other pronouncements

SUMMARY

Enactment of the Motor Carrier Act of 1980, deregulating motor carriers, raises questions regarding whether certain intangible assets of motor carriers should continue to be reported as assets or charged to income. This Statement requires the unamortized costs of motor carrier intangible assets representing interstate rights to transport goods with limited competition to be charged to income and, if material, reported as an extraordinary item. This Statement does not affect the accounting for other intangible assets of motor carriers, such as goodwill.

Statement of Financial Accounting Standards No. 44
Accounting for Intangible Assets of Motors Carriers

an amendment of Chapter 5 of ARB No. 43 and an interpretation of APB Opinions 17 and 30

CONTENTS

INTRODUCTION

1. The FASB has been asked to clarify the accounting for certain intangible assets of motor carriers because enactment of the Motor Carrier Act of 1980[1] (Act) on July 1, 1980 raises questions regarding whether those intangibles should continue to be reported as assets or charged to income. Appendix A provides additional background information and Appendix B provides the basis for the Board's conclusions.

2. The Board has concluded that it can reach an informed decision on the basis of existing data without a public hearing and that the effective date and transition specified in paragraph 8 are advisable in the circumstances.

STANDARDS OF FINANCIAL ACCOUNTING AND REPORTING

3. When acquired, intangible assets of motor carriers may have included costs[2] related to expected benefits from established routes or customers, marketing or operating efficiencies, knowledge of the business, and other elements of goodwill as well as from specifically identifiable intangible assets, such as customer lists, favorable leases, or operating rights.[3] The costs of intangible assets acquired may have been identified previously as operating rights or as goodwill. If not separately allocated in the past, the costs of intangible assets shall now be assigned to (a) interstate operating rights, (b) other identifiable intangible assets (including intrastate operating rights[4]), and (c) goodwill; the cost of identifiable intangible assets (including operating rights) shall not be included in goodwill.

4. For purposes of identifying and assigning costs to interstate operating rights, other identifiable intangible assets, and goodwill, a motor carrier shall apply the criteria in paragraph 88 of APB Opinion No. 16, *Business Combinations*, and paragraphs 24-26 of APB Opinion No. 17, *Intangible Assets*, based on the circumstances existing when the assets were acquired. Costs assigned to intangible assets shall not reflect costs of developing, maintaining, or restoring those intangibles after they were acquired. Costs assigned to identifiable intangibles, including operating rights, shall not be merged with or be replaced by amounts relating to other identifiable intangibles or goodwill. Paragraphs 8 and 10 of Chapter 5, "Intangible Assets," of ARB No. 43 are amended by this paragraph and paragraph 3 of this Statement with regard to the intangible assets addressed by this Statement.

5. If a motor carrier cannot separately identify its interstate operating rights, other identifiable intangible assets, and goodwill and cannot assign costs to them as specified by this Statement or finds that it is impracticable to do so, that motor carrier shall presume that all of those costs relate to interstate operating rights.

6. Unamortized costs of interstate operating rights subject to the provisions of the Act shall be charged

[1]Public Law 96-296, 96th Congress, July 1, 1980.

[2]*Cost*, as used in this Statement, refers to the original cost or the unamortized cost of intangible assets as appropriate in the situation.

[3]An *operating right* (also known as an *operating authority*), as used in this Statement, is a franchise or permit issued by the Interstate Commerce Commission (ICC) or a similar state agency to a motor carrier to transport specified commodities over specified routes with limited competition. Those rights were either granted directly by the ICC or state agency, purchased from other motor carriers, or acquired through business combinations.

[4]See paragraph 7.

to income and, if material, reported as an extraordinary item in accordance with paragraph 11 of APB Opinion No. 30, *Reporting the Results of Operations*. Subsequently, the cost of any other identifiable intangible asset or goodwill that is charged to income for reasons attributable to the Act shall not be reported as an extraordinary item. Tax benefits, if any, relating to the costs of interstate operating rights charged to income shall be reported in accordance with the provisions of APB Opinion No. 11, *Accounting for Income Taxes*, and paragraph 25 of Opinion 30.

7. Other identifiable intangible assets and goodwill relating to motor carrier operations shall be accounted for in accordance with Chapter 5 of ARB 43 or Opinion 17, as appropriate. However, the cost of intrastate operating rights shall be accounted for in accordance with the provisions of this Statement if a state deregulates motor carriers with effects similar to those of the Act.

Effective Date and Transition

8. The provisions of this Statement shall be effective on December 19, 1980 for financial statement for fiscal periods ending after December 15, 1980. Earlier application is encouraged for financial statements for fiscal periods ending before the effective date of this Statement that have not been issued before December 19, 1980. This Statement shall not be applied retroactively to previously issued financial statements.

The provisions of this Statement need not be applied to immaterial items.

This Statement was adopted by the affirmative votes of five members of the Financial Accounting Standards Board. Messrs. March and Walters dissented.

Messrs. March and Walters dissent because they believe that the attempt in this Statement to differentiate between operating rights and other intangible assets is misplaced emphasis on form at the expense of substance. Operating rights represent a franchise to conduct business over a route with the objective of making a profit.

Because of the limited or exclusive nature of those rights in the past, their value often could be supported by reference to a resale market. The Act effectively eliminates this market. The fact that the rights have lost the value that attaches to exchangeability creates a presumption that their value has diminished. However, in the FASB Exposure Draft, *Elements of Financial Statements of Business Enterprises*, the Board said that exchangeability is not a necessary characteristic of an asset. A required characteristic of an asset is the capacity, either singly or in combination with other assets, to contribute to future net cash inflows. In some cases, there may be persuasive evidence that the real asset, the purchased opportunity to conduct business over a specific route with the objective of making a profit, is in fact generating, and is expected to continue to generate, profits. In those cases, an immediate charge to income of the cost of operating rights is not consistent with the economic facts and does not measure properly either the operating resources or the return on investment of the enterprise.

Messrs. March and Walters further believe that the conclusion by the Board that all interstate operating rights have lost their value is a finding that substitutes the Board's judgment for the individual evaluations that should be made by the motor carriers and reviewed by their auditors. They believe that the Board should concern itself with setting standards. Application of standards to specific fact situations is a primary function of management. Existing accounting pronouncements are relatively clear in the requirements to charge to income the cost of intangible assets that no longer have value and to revise the periods of amortization when warranted by changed circumstances. At the very most, all that is needed is an interpretation of those pronouncements to demonstrate how they should apply to motor carriers.

Members of the Financial Accounting Standards Board:

Donald J. Kirk, *Chairman*	John W. March	Robert T. Sprouse
Frank E. Block	Robert A. Morgan	Ralph E. Walters
	David Mosso	

Appendix A

BACKGROUND INFORMATION

9. The Board understands that the Motor Carrier Act of 1980 provides for:

a. Easier entry into the motor carrier industry by new carriers and easier route expansion for existing carriers
b. Removal of most route restrictions and a

broadening of the classification of commodities that carriers are permitted to haul

c. Eventual freedom for motor carriers to change freight rates without the ICC's permission
d. Limitations on the scope of collective rate making exempt from antitrust considerations.

10. The Accounting Standards Division of the AICPA prepared an Issues Paper, *Accounting for Intangibles in the Motor Carrier Industry*, and asked the Board to consider the impact of the Act on accounting for intangible assets of motor carriers. The Board has considered the accounting issues relating to the impact of the Act on intangible assets and reached the conclusions presented in this Statement.

11. The Board understands that intangible assets of motor carriers consist principally of operating rights and goodwill. Most motor carriers have not distinguished among operating rights acquired (a) from the ICC or other licensing agency, (b) from other motor carriers, or (c) through business combinations, nor have they distinguished operating rights from other purchased intangibles, such as goodwill, in their financial statements. Intangible assets of motor carriers generally have been reported in general purpose financial statements at original cost, as permitted by Chapter 5 of ARB 43, or amortized over 40 years, the maximum life permitted by Opinion 17, depending on the date of acquisition of those assets.

12. An Exposure Draft of a proposed Statement, *Accounting for Intangible Assets of Motor Carriers*, was issued on October 24, 1980. The Board received 41 comment letters in response to the Exposure Draft. Certain of the comments received and the Board's consideration of them are discussed in Appendix B, "Basis for Conclusions."

Appendix B

BASIS FOR CONCLUSIONS

13. This appendix discusses the factors that the Board considered significant in reaching the conclusions in this Statement, including various alternatives considered and reasons for accepting some and rejecting others. Individual Board members gave greater weight to some factors than to others.

14. Some respondents questioned the need for a project on accounting for motor carrier intangible assets. They indicated that current accounting pronouncements (Chapter 5 of ARB 43, Opinions 11, 17, and 30, and FASB Statement No. 5, *Accounting for Contingencies*) provide adequate guidance for evaluating those intangibles. They also said that those evaluations should be made on a case-by-case basis and that any uniform standard would fail to reflect the circumstances of individual motor carriers. The Board concluded that, although those existing pronouncements do provide some guidance with respect to the effect of passage of the Act on the costs of intangible assets of motor carriers, the provisions of paragraph 8 of Chapter 5 of ARB 43, which permits substitution or merging of intangible assets, should be modified and the other pronouncements should be clarified as discussed in paragraphs 15, 18, 19, and 21 of this Statement to ensure comparability in accounting for the impact of the Act. In addition, the Board concluded that motor carriers should allocate the costs of their intangible assets to identifiable intangible assets and goodwill. That allocation may not have been made in the past because paragraph 10 of Chapter 5 of ARB 43 does not require specific identification of intangible assets with no limited term of existence.

15. Operating rights generally have represented the right to haul specified commodities between two points with limited competition; that is, the rights included oligopolistic or monopolistic benefits. The past resale and collateral values of the rights support that view. Comments received from the motor carrier industry and other sources have convinced the Board that interstate operating rights have been substantially and permanently impaired as a result of the passage of the Act. The Board believes that this economic loss is evidenced further by the significant loss in resale and collateral values and the current nominal replacement cost of operating rights and that this loss should be reflected in the financial statements of motor carriers. Therefore, the Board has concluded that the unamortized costs of those operating rights should be charged to income immediately.

16. Some respondents stated that operating rights may continue to have value irrespective of the provisions of the Act and, in those cases, should not be charged to income. They indicated that operating rights are still required for motor carrier operations and that those rights principally represent a franchise to conduct business over a route with the objective of making a profit. They acknowledge that the value of operating rights often could be supported by reference to a resale market in the past, but they believe that the loss of exchangeability does not necessarily diminish the value of the asset. They believe that operating rights continue to qualify as assets as long as the rights, either singly or in combination with other assets, contribute to future net cash inflows. They believe that in those cases an immediate charge to income of the cost of operating rights is not consistent with economic facts and does not properly portray either the operating resources or the operating performance of the motor carrier.

The Board concluded, however, that operating rights no longer qualify as an asset because those rights no longer provide motor carriers with the benefit of protection from unlimited competition. Loss of exchange value is a consequence of the loss of that benefit.

17. Some respondents indicated that (a) time will be required to evaluate the impact of the Act on ICC actions and (b) the economic impact of increased competition resulting from the Act will take several years. They said that to date the ICC has not responded clearly to the provisions of the Act. They suggested that the uncertainty in the timing and amount of impairment of operating rights could be reflected best by amortizing the cost of the rights over an arbitrary short period, such as three years. They believe that amortization over a short period is consistent with the development of additional competition expected to result from the Act and with the transition provisions of the Act under which certain changes will be phased in over the next few years. The Board concluded that, in accordance with the provisions of Statement 5, a loss is both probable and reasonably estimable and that an arbitrarily short amortization period would defer recognition of the loss resulting from passage of the Act. Also, the Board believes that any arbitrary amortization period selected would not reflect either the general or specific impact of the Act.

18. Some respondents indicated that operating rights may include valuable benefits in addition to the right to provide transportation services with limited competition, such as the potential to increase a motor carrier's marketing or operating efficiency. They indicated that their purchases of operating rights were in combination with other benefits, such as a customer base, favorable leases on established freight terminals and equipment, and qualified and experienced personnel. The Board agrees that intangible assets acquired by motor carriers may have included benefits in addition to being able to operate with limited competition, for example, the potential to increase a motor carrier's operating efficiency. The Board concluded that an enterprise that has not done so should now assign costs to its identifiable intangible motor carrier assets, whether the assets were acquired before or after October 31, 1970, from the ICC, from other motor carriers, or through business combinations. The Board concluded that the cost assignment should be based on the circumstances existing when the assets were acquired. Some respondents indicated that the majority of motor carrier intangibles relate to operating rights. If identification and assignment cannot be made or if it is impracticable to do, the Board concluded that all unidentifiable intangible assets should be presumed to be interstate operating rights.

19. Other respondents indicated that their operating rights are as valuable today as they ever were because they have developed a customer base, favorable locations for operations, and qualified and experienced personnel. The Board recognizes that many enterprises build successful businesses and generate goodwill based on franchises such as operating rights; however, only purchased goodwill is capitalizable under present generally accepted accounting principles. The Board believes that costs assigned to intangible assets should not reflect costs of developing, maintaining, or restoring operating rights after they were acquired. The Board also believes that costs originally related to operating rights should not be merged with or be replaced by amounts relating to other identifiable intangibles or goodwill as would be permitted by paragraph 8 of Chapter 5 of ARB 43 for intangibles subject to the provisions of that chapter. Opinions 16 and 17 do not permit such combining or merging and the Board believes that paragraph 8 of Chapter 5 of ARB 43 should be amended to make it consistent with those Opinions.

20. The Board believes that, as long as intangible assets other than operating rights provide a motor carrier with continuing benefits, costs relating to those assets should continue to be subject to existing accounting pronouncements rather than be addressed by this Statement. Although other intangible assets may be impaired as a result of the Act, the Board believes that existing accounting pronouncements (Chapter 5 of ARB 43, Opinions 11, 17, and 30, and Statement 5) provide adequate guidance for accounting for those intangible assets.

21. The Board believes that the loss of limited competition resulting from the Act is both unusual and infrequent and that charging the costs of operating rights to income as an extraordinary item is appropriate under Opinion 30. The loss of the benefits of limited competition is unusual because the Act significantly alters the regulatory and operating environment of motor carriers. Also, the loss resulting from the Act is infrequent because it can happen only once. Therefore, the Board concluded that the charge to income of the cost of operating rights, if material, should be reported as an extraordinary item in accordance with Opinion 30.

22. Some respondents said that a requirement to charge operating rights to income could create an undue burden for some motor carriers because such a requirement could needlessly force some motor carriers to violate debt covenants. Those respondents recommended a grace period for those motor carriers. The Board believes that the significant loss in value of operating rights is an economic fact that should not be masked by deferring recognition of the loss.

23. Some respondents expressed concern that the Act would have significant impact on intrastate operating rights and that in many cases the unamortized cost of those rights also should be charged to income. This concern is based on increased competition from interstate carriers operating along intrastate routes. The Board decided to address in this Statement only the direct effects of the Act, that is, the effect on interstate operating rights. Intrastate operating rights may or may not continue to provide motor carriers with benefits. The Board believes that existing accounting pronouncements (Chapter 5 of ARB 43, Opinions 11, 17, and 30, and Statement 5) provide adequate guidance for accounting for those rights. However, if a state deregulates motor carriers with effects similar to those of the Act, the Board concluded that the cost of intrastate operating rights should be accounted for in accordance with the provisions of this Statement.

24. Some respondents said that the guidance in the Exposure Draft regarding any income tax benefits relating to the charge to income of the unamortized cost of operating rights was inadequate. The Board concluded that existing accounting pronouncements (particularly Opinion 11 and paragraph 25 of Opinion 30) provide adequate guidance regardless of how the income tax issue ultimately is resolved. In most cases, those pronouncements would require tax benefits related to the charge to income of operating rights to be considered an adjustment of the extraordinary item. Therefore, the Board believes that in most cases any material recognized tax benefits should be included in motor carriers' financial statements as an extraordinary item whenever reported.

25. Some respondents indicated that the disclosure requirements in the Exposure Draft already exist in other accounting pronouncements. After considering those comments, the Board agreed and concluded that the disclosure requirements in the Exposure Draft were unnecessary.

Statement of Financial Accounting Standards No. 45
Accounting for Franchise Fee Revenue

STATUS

Issued: March 1981

Effective Date: For fiscal years beginning after June 15, 1981

Affects: Amends FAS 32, Appendix A

Affected by: No other pronouncements

SUMMARY

This Statement extracts the specialized accounting principles and practices from the AICPA Industry Accounting Guide, *Accounting for Franchise Fee Revenue*, and establishes accounting and reporting standards for franchisors. It requires that franchise fee revenue from individual and area franchise sales be recognized only when all material services or conditions relating to the sale have been substantially performed or satisfied by the franchisor. This Statement also establishes accounting standards for continuing franchise fees, continuing product sales, agency sales, repossessed franchises, franchising costs, commingled revenue, and relationships between a franchisor and a franchisee.

Statement of Financial Accounting Standards No. 45
Accounting for Franchise Fee Revenue

CONTENTS

INTRODUCTION AND BACKGROUND INFORMATION

1. As discussed in FASB Statement No. 32, *Specialized Accounting and Reporting Principles and Practices in AICPA Statements of Position and Guides on Accounting and Auditing Matters,* the FASB is extracting the specialized[1] accounting and reporting principles and practices from AICPA Statements of Position (SOPs) and Guides on accounting and auditing matters and issuing them in FASB Statements after appropriate due process. This Statement extracts the specialized principles and practices from the AICPA Industry Accounting Guide, *Accounting for Franchise Fee Revenue* (Guide), and establishes accounting and reporting standards for franchise fee revenue that is obtained through a **franchise agreement.**[2]

2. The Board has not undertaken a comprehensive reconsideration of the accounting issues discussed in the Guide and has extracted the specialized accounting and reporting principles without significant change. Accordingly, some of the background material and discussion of accounting alternatives have not been carried forward from the Guide. The Board's conceptual framework project on accounting recognition criteria will address revenue recognition issues similar to those addressed in this Statement. A Statement of Financial Accounting Concepts resulting from that project in due course will serve as a basis for evaluating existing standards and practices. Accordingly, the Board may wish to evaluate the standards in this Statement when its conceptual framework project is completed.

3. The Guide was developed to clarify and standardize accounting by **franchisors,** particularly the timing of recognizing revenue from **initial franchise fees.** Before 1970, franchisors generally recognized revenue from initial franchise fees when franchises were sold. The Guide recommended that revenue from initial franchise fees be recognized when the franchise sale transaction was completed, that is, when all material services or conditions relating to the sale had been substantially performed or satisfied by the franchisor. In addition, the Guide stated a presumption that commencement of operations by the **franchisee** ordinarily would be the earliest point at which substantial performance could occur.

4. The Board has concluded that it can reach an informed decision on the basis of existing information without a public hearing and that the effective date and transition specified in paragraph 25 are advisable in the circumstances.

[1]The term *specialized* is used to refer to those accounting and reporting principles and practices in AICPA Guides and SOPs that are neither superseded by nor contained in Accounting Research Bulletins, APB Opinions, FASB Statements, or FASB Interpretations.

[2]Terms defined in the glossary (Appendix A) are in **boldface type** the first time they appear in this Statement.

STANDARDS OF FINANCIAL ACCOUNTING AND REPORTING

Individual Franchise Sales

5. Franchise fee revenue from an individual franchise sale ordinarily shall be recognized, with an appropriate provision for estimated uncollectible amounts, when all material services or conditions relating to the sale have been substantially performed or satisfied by the franchisor. Substantial performance for the franchisor means that (a) the franchisor has no remaining obligation or intent—by agreement, trade practice, or law—to refund any cash received or forgive any unpaid notes or receivables; (b) substantially all of the **initial services** of the franchisor required by the franchise agreement have been performed; and (c) no other material conditions or obligations related to the determination of substantial performance exist. If the franchise agreement does not require the franchisor to perform initial services but a practice of voluntarily rendering initial services exists or is likely to exist because of business or regulatory circumstances, substantial performance shall not be assumed until either the initial services have been substantially performed or reasonable assurance exists that the services will not be performed. The commencement of operations by the franchisee shall be presumed to be the earliest point at which substantial performance has occurred, unless it can be demonstrated that substantial performance of all obligations, including services rendered voluntarily, has occurred before that time.

6. Installment or cost recovery accounting methods[3] shall be used to account for franchise fee revenue only in those exceptional cases when revenue is collectible over an extended period and no reasonable basis exists for estimating collectibility.

7. Sometimes, large initial franchise fees are required but **continuing franchise fees** are small in relation to future services. If it is probable that the continuing fee will not cover the cost of the continuing services to be provided by the franchisor and a reasonable profit on those continuing services, then a portion of the initial franchise fee shall be deferred and amortized over the life of the franchise. The portion deferred shall be an amount sufficient to cover the estimated cost in excess of continuing franchise fees and provide a reasonable profit on the continuing services.

Area Franchise Sales

8. Initial franchise fees relating to **area franchise** sales shall be accounted for following the same principles described in paragraphs 5-7 for individual franchise sales, that is, revenue ordinarily shall be recognized when all material services or conditions relating to the sale(s) have been substantially performed or satisfied by the franchisor. If the franchisor's substantial obligations under the franchise agreement relate to the area franchise and do not depend significantly on the number of individual franchises to be established, substantial performance shall be determined using the same criteria applicable to individual franchises (paragraph 5). However, if the franchisor's substantial obligations depend on the number of individual franchises established within the area, area franchise fees shall be recognized in proportion to the initial mandatory services provided. Revenue that may have to be refunded because future services are not peformed shall not be recognized by the franchisor until the franchisee has no right to receive a refund.

9. The substance of an area franchise agreement shall determine when material services or conditions relating to a sale have been substantially performed or satisfied. Sometimes, the efforts and total cost relating to initial services are not affected significantly by the number of outlets opened in an area and, therefore, the area franchise sale is similar to an individual franchise sale. Conversely, when the efforts and total cost relating to initial services are affected significantly by the number of outlets opened in an area, it may be necessary to regard the franchise agreement as a divisible contract and to estimate the number of outlets involved so that revenue may be recognized in proportion to the outlets for which the required services have been substantially performed. Estimates shall consider the anticipated number of outlets based on the terms of the franchise agreement (for example, time limitations and any specified minimum or maximum number of outlets). Any change in estimate resulting from a change in circumstance shall result in recognizing remaining fees as revenue in proportion to remaining services to be performed.

Relationships between Franchisor and Franchisee

10. A franchisor may guarantee borrowings of a franchisee, have a creditor interest in the franchisee, or control a franchisee's operations by sales or other agreements to such an extent that the franchisee is, for all practical purposes, an affiliate of the franchisor. Sometimes, two franchisors may agree to pool their risks by selling their respective franchises to each other. In all those circumstances, revenue shall not be recognized if all material services, conditions, or obligations relating to the sale have not been substantially performed or satisfied (paragraph 5).

[3]See footnote 8 of APB Opinion No. 10, *Omnibus Opinion—1966*.

11. A franchise agreement may give the franchisor an option to purchase the franchisee's business. For example, a franchisor may purchase a profitable franchised outlet as a matter of management policy, or purchase a franchised outlet that is in financial difficulty or unable to continue in business to preserve the reputation and goodwill of the franchise system. If such an option exists, the likelihood of the franchisor's acquiring the franchised outlet shall be considered in accounting for the initial franchise fee. If at the time the option is given, an understanding exists that the option will be exercised or it is probable that the franchisor ultimately will acquire the franchised outlet, the initial franchise fee shall not be recognized as revenue but shall be deferred. When the option is exercised, the deferred amount shall reduce the franchisor's investment in the outlet.

Commingled Revenue

12. The franchise agreement ordinarily establishes a single initial franchise fee as consideration for the franchise rights and the initial services to be performed by the franchisor. Sometimes, however, the fee also may cover tangible property, such as signs, equipment, inventory, and land and building. In those circumstances, the portion of the fee applicable to the tangible assets shall be based on the fair value of the assets and may be recognized before or after recognizing the portion applicable to the initial services. For example, when the portion of the fee relating to the sale of specific tangible assets is objectively determinable, it would be appropriate to recognize that portion when their titles pass, even though the balance of the fee relating to services is recognized when the remaining services or conditions in the franchise agreement have been substantially performed or satisfied.

13. Although a franchise agreement may specify portions of the total fee that relate to specific services to be provided by the franchisor, the services usually are interrelated to such an extent that the amount applicable to each service cannot be segregated objectively. The fee shall not be allocated among the different services as a means of recognizing any part of the fee for services as revenue before all the services have been substantially performed unless actual transaction prices are available for individual services; for example, through recent sales of the separate specific services.

Continuing Franchise Fees

14. Continuing franchise fees shall be reported as revenue as the fees are earned and become receivable from the franchisee. Costs relating to continuing franchise fees shall be expensed as incurred. Although a portion of the continuing fee may be designated for a particular purpose, such as an advertising program, it shall not be recognized as revenue until the fee is earned and becomes receivable from the franchisee. An exception to the foregoing exists if the franchise constitutes an agency relationship under which a designated portion of the continuing fee is required to be segregated and used for a specified purpose. In that case, the designated amount shall be recorded as a liability against which the specified costs would be charged.

Continuing Product Sales

15. The franchisee may purchase some or all of the equipment or supplies necessary for its operations from the franchisor. Sometimes, the franchisee is given the right to make **bargain purchases** of equipment or supplies for a specified period or up to a specified amount, when the initial franchise fee is paid. If the bargain price is lower than the selling price of the same product to other customers or if the price does not provide the franchisor a reasonable profit on the equipment or supply sales, then a portion of the initial franchise fee shall be deferred and accounted for as an adjustment of the selling price when the franchisee purchases the equipment or supplies. The portion deferred shall be either (a) the difference between the selling price to other customers and the bargain purchase price or (b) an amount sufficient to cover any cost in excess of the bargain purchase price and provide a reasonable profit on the sale, as appropriate.

Agency Sales

16. Some franchisors engage in transactions in which they are, in substance, an agent for franchisees by placing orders for inventory and equipment and selling to franchisees at no profit. The franchisor shall account for such transactions as receivables and payables in its balance sheet and not as revenue and costs or expenses.

Franchising Costs

17. Direct (incremental) costs relating to franchise sales for which revenue has not been recognized ordinarily shall be deferred until the related revenue is recognized; however, the deferred costs shall not exceed anticipated revenue less estimated additional related costs. Indirect costs of a regular and recurring nature that are incurred irrespective of the level of sales, such as general, selling, and administrative costs, shall be expensed as incurred. Costs yet to be incurred shall be accrued and charged against income no later than the period in which the related revenue is recognized. Because of the concept of substantial performance (paragraph 5), such costs should be relatively minor.

Repossessed Franchises

18. A franchisor may recover franchise rights through repossession if a franchisee decides not to open an outlet. If, for any reason, the franchisor refunds the consideration received, the original sale is canceled, and revenue previously recognized shall be accounted for as a reduction in revenue in the period the franchise is repossessed. If franchise rights are repossessed but no refund is made, (a) the transaction shall not be regarded as a sale cancellation, (b) no adjustment shall be made to any previously recognized revenue, (c) any estimated uncollectible amounts resulting from unpaid receivables shall be provided for, and (d) any consideration retained for which revenue was not previously recognized shall be reported as revenue.

Business Combinations

19. A transaction in which a franchisor acquires the business of an operating franchisee ordinarily shall be accounted for as a business combination in accordance with APB Opinion No. 16, *Business Combinations,* assuming no relationship existed at the time of the franchise sale to preclude revenue recognition (paragraphs 10 and 11). If the transaction is accounted for as a pooling of interests, the financial statements of the two entities are retroactively combined and the original franchise sales transaction as well as any product sales shall be eliminated in the combined financial statements. If the transaction is accounted for as a purchase, the financial statements of the two entities are not retroactively combined and revenue shall not be adjusted. If such a transaction is, in substance, a cancellation of an original franchise sale, the transaction shall be accounted for in accordance with paragraph 18.

Disclosures

20. The nature of all significant commitments and obligations resulting from franchise agreements, including a description of the services that the franchisor has agreed to provide for agreements that have not yet been substantially performed, shall be disclosed.

21. If no basis for estimating the collectibility of specific franchise fees exists, the notes to the financial statements shall disclose whether the installment or cost recovery method is being used to account for the related franchise fee revenue. Furthermore, the sales price of such franchises, the revenue and related costs deferred (both currently and on a cumulative basis), and the periods in which such fees become payable by the franchisee shall be disclosed. Any amounts originally deferred but later recognized because uncertainties regarding the collectibility of franchise fees are resolved also shall be disclosed.

22. Initial franchise fees shall be segregated from other franchise fee revenue if they are significant. If it is probable that initial franchise fee revenue will decline in the future because sales predictably reach a saturation point, disclosure of that fact is desirable. Disclosure of the relative contribution to net income of initial franchise fees also is desirable if not apparent from the relative amounts of revenue.

23. Revenue and costs related to franchisor-owned outlets shall be distinguished from revenue and costs related to franchised outlets when practicable. That may be done by segregating revenue and costs related to franchised outlets. If there are significant changes in franchisor-owned outlets or franchised outlets during the period, the number of (a) franchises sold, (b) franchises purchased during the period, (c) franchised outlets in operation, and (d) franchisor-owned outlets in operation shall be disclosed.

Amendment to Other Pronouncement

24. The reference to the AICPA Industry Accounting Guide, *Accounting for Franchise Fee Revenue,* is deleted from Appendix A of Statement 32. The specialized accounting provisions of that Guide are superseded by this Statement.

Effective Date and Transition

25. This Statement shall be effective for financial statements for fiscal years beginning after June 15, 1981. Earlier application is encouraged. The provisions of this Statement shall be applied retroactively and any accompanying financial statements presented for prior periods shall be restated.

The provisions of this Statement need not be applied to immaterial items.

This Statement was adopted by the unanimous vote of the seven members of the Financial Accounting Standards Board:

Donald J. Kirk, *Chairman*
Frank E. Block
John W. March
Robert A. Morgan
David Mosso
Robert T. Sprouse
Ralph E. Walters

Appendix A

GLOSSARY

26. This appendix defines certain terms that are used in this Statement.

Area franchise

An agreement that transfers franchise rights within a geographical area permitting the opening of a number of franchised outlets. Under those circumstances, decisions regarding the number of outlets, their location, and so forth are more likely made unilaterally by the franchisee than in collaboration with the franchisor. A franchisor may sell an area franchise to a franchisee who operates the franchised outlets or the franchisor may sell an area franchise to an intermediary franchisee who then sells individual franchises to other franchisees who operate the outlets.

Bargain purchase

A transaction in which the franchisee is allowed to purchase equipment or supplies for a price that is significantly lower than the fair value of the equipment or supplies.

Continuing franchise fee

Consideration for the continuing rights granted by the franchise agreement and for general or specific services during its life.

Franchise agreement[4]

A written business agreement that meets the following principal criteria:

a. The relation between the franchisor and franchisee is contractual, and an agreement, confirming the rights and responsibilities of each party, is in force for a specified period.
b. The continuing relation has as its purpose the distribution of a product or service, or an entire business concept, within a particular market area.
c. Both the franchisor and the franchisee contribute resources for establishing and maintaining the franchise. The franchisor's contribution may be a trademark, a company reputation, products, procedures, manpower, equipment, or a process. The franchisee usually contributes operating capital as well as the managerial and operational resources required for opening and continuing the franchised outlet.
d. The franchise agreement outlines and describes the specific marketing practices to be followed, specifies the contribution of each party to the operation of the business, and sets forth certain operating procedures that both parties agree to comply with.
e. The establishment of the franchised outlet creates a business entity that will, in most cases, require and support the full-time business activity of the franchisee. (There are numerous other contractual distribution arrangements in which a local businessperson becomes the "authorized distributor" or "representative" for the sale of a particular good or service, along with many others, but such a sale usually represents only a portion of the person's total business.)
f. Both the franchisee and the franchisor have a common public identity. This identity is achieved most often through the use of common trade names or trademarks and is frequently reinforced through advertising programs designed to promote the recognition and acceptance of the common identity within the franchisee's market area.

The payment of an initial franchise fee or a continuing royalty fee is not a necessary criterion for an agreement to be considered a franchise agreement.

Franchisee

The party who has been granted business rights (the franchise) to operate the franchised business.

Franchisor

The party who grants business rights (the franchise) to the party (the franchisee) who will operate the franchised business.

Initial franchise fee

Consideration for establishing the franchise relationship and providing some initial services. Occasionally, the fee includes consideration for initially required equipment and inventory, but those items usually are the subject of separate consideration.

Initial services

Common provision of a franchise agreement in which the franchisor usually will agree to provide a variety of services and advice to the franchisee, such as the following:

a. Assistance in the selection of a site. The assistance may be based on experience with factors, such as traffic patterns, residential configurations, and competition.
b. Assistance in obtaining facilities, including related financing and architectural and engineering services. The facilities may be pur-

[4]This definition has been developed for purposes of this Statement and may not be appropriate for other uses.

chased or leased by the franchisee, and lease payments may be guaranteed by the franchisor.

c. Assistance in advertising, either for the individual franchisee or as part of a general program.
d. Training of the franchisee's personnel.
e. Preparation and distribution of manuals and similar material concerning operations, administration, and record keeping.
f. Bookkeeping and advisory services, including setting up the franchisee's records and advising the franchisee about income, real estate, and other taxes or about local regulations affecting the franchisee's business.
g. Inspection, testing, and other quality control programs.

Appendix B

SUMMARY OF CONSIDERATION OF COMMENTS ON EXPOSURE DRAFT

27. An Exposure Draft of a proposed Statement, *Accounting for Franchise Fee Revenue*, was issued December 1, 1980. The Board received 25 comment letters in response to the Exposure Draft. Certain of the comments received and the Board's consideration of them are discussed in this appendix.

28. Some respondents indicated that the requirement in the last sentence of paragraph 5 that the commencement of operations by the franchisee shall be presumed to be the earliest point at which substantial performance has occurred was too restrictive. They said that the Guide was less restrictive because it provided for recognition of revenue before the franchisee began operations when substantial performance could be demonstrated. The Board agrees with those respondents and has clarified paragraph 5 to state that the presumption may be overcome if the franchisor can demonstrate that it has substantially performed all of its obligations, including services rendered voluntarily, before the franchisee begins operations.

29. Some respondents requested that the phrase "portion of the initial franchise fee" in paragraphs 7 and 15 be clarified. They indicated that the phrase could be interpreted to mean either an amount necessary to cover net future costs only or an amount sufficient to cover net future costs plus a reasonable profit. The Board agrees with those respondents and has clarified those paragraphs to indicate that the appropriate portion represents cost and reasonable profit in excess of anticipated continuing franchise fees (paragraph 7) or bargain purchase price (paragraph 15).

30. Several individual respondents suggested various substantive changes to the Exposure Draft. Adoption of those suggestions would have required a reconsideration of the provisions of the Guide. Those suggestions were not adopted because such a reconsideration is beyond the scope of extracting the specialized accounting and reporting principles and practices from the Guide and because none of the changes was broadly supported.

Statement of Financial Accounting Standards No. 46
Financial Reporting and Changing Prices: Motion Picture Films

a supplement to FASB Statement No. 33

STATUS

Issued: March 1981

Effective Date: For fiscal years ending on or after March 31, 1981

Affects: Amends FAS 33, paragraph 53
Amends FAS 39, paragraph 12
Amends FAS 40, paragraph 6
Amends FAS 41, paragraph 7

Affected by: Paragraph 8 superseded by FAS 69

SUMMARY

This Statement supplements FASB Statement No. 33, *Financial Reporting and Changing Prices*. It requires enterprises that present information on a current cost basis to combine measures of motion picture films and related expenses at either historical cost/constant dollar amounts or at current cost amounts with current cost measures of other assets and expenses. This Statement is effective for fiscal years ended on or after March 31, 1981 and may be applied in financial reports for periods ending before it is issued that have not yet been published.

The Board will continue to work with the motion picture film industry to develop improved methods of measuring the effects of changing prices on this industry.

Statement of Financial Accounting Standards No. 46
Financial Reporting and Changing Prices: Motion Picture Films
a supplement to FASB Statement No. 33

CONTENTS

INTRODUCTION AND BACKGROUND INFORMATION

1. FASB Statement No. 33, *Financial Reporting and Changing Prices*, establishes standards for reporting certain effects of price changes on business enterprises. Statement 33 requires that large public enterprises disclose information on both a historical cost/constant dollar basis and a current cost basis. Current cost information is required for fiscal years ended on or after December 25, 1979, but first presentation of the information can be postponed for one year.

2. Several representatives of the motion picture film industry have met with the FASB staff and the Board to discuss their concerns about the current cost requirements as they apply to films. Based on discussions with the industry representatives and on reactions to a proposed FASB Technical Bulletin on the subject, the Board has concluded that additional flexibility should be provided for measurements of the effects of specific price changes on motion picture films. The Board believes that the doubts about the feasibility and usefulness of current cost measures for motion picture films, and the need for further study of current cost, net realizable value, and other disclosures, justify the alternatives that this Statement provides.

3. An Exposure Draft of a proposed Statement, *Financial Reporting and Changing Prices: Motion Picture Films*, was issued on February 9, 1981. The Board received 18 comment letters in response to the Exposure Draft. All of the respondents favored issuance of the Statement. Four letters suggested minor clarification of wording. The definition of motion picture films has been broadened in response to these suggestions.

4. This Statement allows enterprises that present information on a current cost basis to combine measures of motion picture films and related expenses at either historical cost/constant dollar amounts or at current cost amounts with current cost measures of other assets and expenses.

5. This Statement does not set a time limit on the applicability of its provisions. However, the Board will continue to work with the motion picture film industry to develop improved methods of reflecting effects of price changes on films. That work will focus on the relevance and reliability of various measures, including current cost and net realizable value. In assigning a priority to the work, the Board will take into account the small number of enterprises for which motion picture films are a major part of their assets. However, the Board will issue a Statement to supersede the provisions of this Statement as soon as that action is justified by the available evidence.

6. The Board has concluded that it can reach an informed decision on the basis of existing data without a public hearing and that the effective date and transition specified in paragraph 9 are advisable in the circumstances.

STANDARDS OF FINANCIAL ACCOUNTING AND REPORTING

Definition

7. For the purposes of this Statement, the term *motion picture films* includes all types of films and videotapes and disks, including features, television specials, series, and cartoons that are (a) exhibited in theaters; (b) licensed for exhibition by individual television stations, groups of stations, networks, cable television systems, or other means; or (c) licensed for commercial reproduction (e.g., for the home viewing market).

Supplement to FASB Statement No. 33

8. The following paragraph is added after paragraph 53 of Statement 33, as amended by Statements 39, 40, and 41:

> When an enterprise presents information on a current cost basis, it shall measure motion picture films and related amortization expense at

either their historical cost/constant dollar amounts or at current cost or lower recoverable amounts.

Effective Date and Transition

9. The provisions of this Statement shall be effective for fiscal years ended on or after March 31, 1981. Earlier application is encouraged for financial reports for fiscal periods ending before March 31, 1981 that have not been issued at that date.

The provisions of this Statement need not be applied to immaterial items.

This Statement was adopted by the unanimous vote of the seven members of the Financial Accounting Standards Board:

Donald J. Kirk,
Chairman
Frank E. Block
John W. March
Robert A. Morgan
David Mosso
Robert T. Sprouse
Ralph E. Walters

Statement of Financial Accounting Standards No. 47
Disclosure of Long-Term Obligations

STATUS

Issued: March 1981

Effective Date: For fiscal years ending after June 15, 1981

Affects: No other pronouncements

Affected by: No other pronouncements

SUMMARY

This Statement requires that an enterprise disclose its commitments under unconditional purchase obligations that are associated with suppliers' financing arrangements. Such obligations often are in the form of take-or-pay contracts and throughput contracts. This Statement also requires disclosure of future payments on long-term borrowings and redeemable stock. For long-term unconditional purchase obligations that are associated with suppliers' financing and are not recognized on purchasers' balance sheets, the disclosures include the nature of the obligation, the amount of the fixed and determinable obligation in the aggregate and for each of the next five years, a description of any portion of the obligation that is variable, and the purchases in each year for which an income statement is presented. For long-term unconditional purchase obligations that are associated with suppliers' financing and are recognized on purchasers' balance sheets, payments for each of the next five years shall be disclosed. For long-term borrowings and redeemable stock, the disclosures include maturities and sinking fund requirements (if any) for each of the next five years and redemption requirements for each of the next five years, respectively.

Statement of Financial Accounting Standards No. 47
Disclosure of Long-Term Obligations

CONTENTS

INTRODUCTION

1. The Board has received requests to consider the subjects of accounting for **project financing arrangements**[1] and accounting for **take-or-pay contracts, throughput contracts,** and other unconditional purchase obligations typically associated with project financing arrangements. Some have stated that certain of those arrangements and contracts result in acquisitions of ownership interests and obligations to make future cash payments that should be recognized as assets and liabilities on participants' balance sheets. Others consider such arrangements and contracts to result in commitments or contingent liabilities that should not be recognized on balance sheets.

2. The Board currently has on its agenda three topics that are part of the conceptual framework for financial accounting and reporting and that pertain to those requests:

a. Accounting recognition criteria for elements, which will address the types of transactions, events, and circumstances that should lead to recognition in financial statements of items that qualify as assets, liabilities, revenues, expenses, etc., under the definitions of elements of financial statements[2]
b. Measurement of the elements of financial statements, which will consider how assets, liabilities, and other elements should be measured
c. Funds flows, liquidity, and financial flexibility, which will determine the kinds of information that should be reported to facilitate assessments of an enterprise's flow of funds, liquidity, and ability to obtain cash to adapt to unexpected difficulties or opportunities

The Board believes that the questions raised in paragraph 1 can be addressed more readily after further work is completed on some or all of those conceptual framework projects.

3. The arrangements and contracts discussed in paragraph 1 and in the remainder of this Statement are sometimes recognized on balance sheets. If they are not recognized on balance sheets, they often are disclosed in the notes to financial statements. If disclosed, the disclosure sometimes quantifies the enterprise's rights and obligations. As an interim measure, pending further work on those conceptual framework projects identified in paragraph 2, the Board has concluded that unconditional purchase obligations associated with financing arrangements should be disclosed and quantified. The Board also has concluded that enterprises should disclose future cash payments in a manner similar to existing disclosures of capital lease obligations for long-term borrowings and capital stock with mandatory redemption requirements. This Statement provides standards of disclosure.

4. Appendix A provides additional background information and the basis for the Board's conclusions. Appendix C illustrates applications of this Statement.

5. The Board has concluded that it can reach an informed decision on the basis of existing data without a public hearing and that the effective date and transition specified in paragraph 11 are advisable in the circumstances.

---

[1]Terms defined in the glossary (Appendix B) are in **boldface type** the first time they appear in this Statement.

[2]The question of when rights and obligations that arise under contracts should be recognized as assets and liabilities in financial statements is addressed in an FASB Research Report, *Recognition of Contractual Rights and Obligations*, prepared by Professor Yuji Ijiri of Carnegie-Mellon University as part of the accounting recognition criteria project. The Research Report discusses several possible recognition points, including initiation of the contract, delivery of the contracted goods or services, and payment for those goods or services.

STANDARDS OF FINANCIAL ACCOUNTING AND REPORTING

Definition and Scope

6. An unconditional purchase obligation is an obligation to transfer funds in the future for fixed or minimum amounts or quantities of goods or services at fixed or minimum prices (for example, as in take-or-pay contracts or throughput contracts). An unconditional purchase obligation that has all of the following characteristics shall be disclosed in accordance with paragraph 7 (if not recorded on the purchaser's balance sheet) or in accordance with paragraph 10(a) (if recorded on the purchaser's balance sheet):

a. Is noncancelable, or cancelable only
   (1) Upon the occurrence of some remote contingency or
   (2) With the permission of the other party or
   (3) If a replacement agreement is signed between the same parties or
   (4) Upon payment of a penalty in an amount such that continuation of the agreement appears reasonably assured
b. Was negotiated as part of arranging financing for the facilities that will provide the contracted goods or services or for costs related to those goods or services (for example, carrying costs for contracted goods)
c. Has a remaining term in excess of one year

Future minimum lease payments under leases that have those characteristics need not be disclosed in accordance with this Statement if they are disclosed in accordance with FASB Statement No. 13, *Accounting for Leases*.

Unrecorded Obligations

7. A purchaser shall disclose unconditional purchase obligations that meet the criteria of paragraph 6 and that have not been recognized on its balance sheet. The disclosures shall include:

a. The nature and term of the obligation(s)
b. The amount of the fixed and determinable portion of the obligation(s) as of the date of the latest balance sheet presented in the aggregate and, if determinable, for each of the five succeeding fiscal years (paragraph 8)
c. The nature of any variable components of the obligation(s)
d. The amounts purchased under the obligation(s) (for example, the take-or-pay or throughput contract) for each period for which an income statement is presented

Disclosures of similar or related unconditional purchase obligations may be combined. These disclosures may be omitted only if the aggregate commitment for all such obligations not disclosed is immaterial.

8. Disclosure of the amount of imputed interest necessary to reduce the unconditional purchase obligation(s) to present value is encouraged but not required. The discount rate shall be the effective initial interest rate of the borrowings that financed the facility (or facilities) that will provide the contracted goods or services, if known by the purchaser. If not, the discount rate shall be the **purchaser's incremental borrowing rate** at the date the obligation is entered into.

Recorded Obligations and Redeemable Stock

9. Certain unconditional purchase obligations are presently recorded as liabilities on purchasers' balance sheets with the related assets also recognized. This Statement does not alter that accounting treatment or the treatment of future unconditional purchase obligations that are substantially the same as those obligations already recorded as liabilities with related assets, nor does it suggest that disclosure is an appropriate substitute for accounting recognition if the substance of an arrangement is the acquisition of an asset and incurrence of a liability.

10. The following information shall be disclosed for each of the five years following the date of the latest balance sheet presented:

a. The aggregate amount of payments for unconditional purchase obligations that meet the criteria of paragraph 6 and that have been recognized on the purchaser's balance sheet
b. The combined aggregate amount of maturities and sinking fund requirements for all long-term borrowings
c. The amount of redemption requirements for all issues of capital stock that are redeemable at fixed or determinable prices on fixed or determinable dates, separately by issue or combined

Effective Date and Transition

11. This Statement shall be effective for financial statements for fiscal years ending after June 15, 1981. Earlier application is encouraged. The disclosures required by paragraph 7(d) need not be included in financial statements for periods beginning before the effective date of this Statement that are being presented for comparative purposes with financial statements for periods after the effective date.

The provisions of this Statement need not be applied to immaterial items.

This Statement was adopted by the affirmative votes of six members of the Financial Accounting Standards Board. Mr. Morgan dissented.

Mr. Morgan dissents to issuance of this Statement because he believes it is not needed. In his opinion, conscientious preparers and auditors will disclose the existence of unconditional purchase obligations associated with financing arrangements if there is a reasonable possibility that a payment will be required without the purchaser receiving an asset of comparable value in return. Such disclosure seems to be required by FASB Statement No. 5, *Accounting for Contingencies*; if Statement 5 is ambiguous in that regard, an Interpretation would be sufficient. Mr. Morgan does not believe that there is a need for specific disclosure requirements for unconditional purchase obligations associated with financing arrangements, particularly if there is only a remote possibility that payment will be required without the purchaser receiving an asset of comparable value in return. Also, Mr. Morgan believes that the disclosure of obligations for each of the next five years may convey a notion of a contractual period longer than is realistic. He believes that such agreements are renegotiated frequently in practice.

Mr. Morgan also disagrees with mandating disclosure of next-five-year repayment requirements on long-term borrowings and redemption requirements on redeemable stock. He does not recall any requests to the Board to consider such disclosures.

Mr. Morgan's preference would be to delay action on this Statement until completion of the Board's conceptual framework project on accounting recognition criteria. That project could provide the Board a basis to conclude that unconditional purchase obligations should be recorded on the balance sheet, disclosed in the notes to financial statements, or both.

The members of the Financial Accounting Standards Board:

Donald J. Kirk, *Chairman*
Frank E. Block
John W. March
Robert A. Morgan
David Mosso
Robert T. Sprouse
Ralph E. Walters

Appendix A

BACKGROUND INFORMATION AND BASIS FOR CONCLUSIONS

12. As noted in the introduction, the FASB was asked to consider accounting for project financing arrangements. The particular requests related to whether the unconditional purchase obligations and indirect guarantees of indebtedness of others typical of project financing arrangements result in participants acquiring ownership interests and obligations to make future cash payments that should be recognized as assets and liabilities on their balance sheets. The Board concluded, as noted in paragraph 2, that those accounting questions could be answered better after further progress is made on the conceptual framework for financial accounting and reporting.

13. Paragraphs 40 and 41 of FASB Concepts Statement No. 1, *Objectives of Financial Reporting by Business Enterprises*, state one objective of financial reporting:

> Financial reporting should provide information about the economic resources of an enterprise, the claims to those resources (obligations of the enterprise to transfer resources to other entities and owners' equity), and the effects of transactions, events, and circumstances that change resources and claims to those resources. . . .
>
> Financial reporting should provide information about an enterprise's economic resources, obligations, and owners' equity. That information helps investors, creditors, and others identify the enterprise's financial strengths and weaknesses and assess its liquidity and solvency. Information about resources, obligations, and owners' equity also provides . . . direct indications . . . of the cash needed to satisfy many, if not most, obligations. . . . Many obligations are direct causes of cash payments by the enterprise, and reasonably reliable measures of . . . future net cash outflows are often possible for those . . . obligations.

Existing accounting for and disclosure of unconditional purchase obligations associated with financing arrangements are inconsistent among enterprises and often fail to satisfy that objective of financial reporting. In addition, as noted in paragraph 1, the unconditional purchase obligations discussed in this

Statement have some of the characteristics of liabilities. Accordingly, as an interim measure pending a decision on whether the obligations should be recognized on purchasers' balance sheets, the Board decided that disclosures of unconditional purchase obligations associated with financing arrangements should be expanded and standardized to satisfy that objective of financial reporting.

14. On March 31, 1980, the FASB released an Exposure Draft, *Disclosure of Guarantees, Project Financing Arrangements, and Other Similar Obligations* (March Exposure Draft). The FASB received 102 letters of comment on the March Exposure Draft. Based on the comments received, the content of the March Exposure Draft was separated into two documents that were exposed concurrently for comment on November 14, 1980: a revised Exposure Draft, *Disclosure of Unconditional Obligations*, and a proposed Interpretation, *Disclosure of Indirect Guarantees of Indebtedness of Others*.

15. The Board received 67 letters of comment on the revised Exposure Draft. Certain of the comments received and the Board's consideration of them are discussed in paragraphs 16-22.

16. Some respondents stated that the revised Exposure Draft did not distinguish clearly between the unconditional obligations that would have been required to be disclosed and the unconditional obligations that would have been excluded. The distinction between long-term purchase commitments and take-or-pay contracts was of particular concern. Other respondents suggested that the Board should limit the disclosures to unconditional obligations with clear financing elements. Based on those comments, the Board reconsidered the scope of this Statement. The Board's accounting recognition criteria project will consider criteria for balance sheet recognition of all contractual rights and obligations, whether or not unconditional and whether or not associated with financing arrangements. With respect to most contractual rights and obligations, the Board believes existing disclosures are adequate until the fundamental accounting concepts are resolved. Unconditional purchase obligations associated with financing arrangements, however, have many similarities to borrowings and to lease obligations, and the Board believes that existing disclosures often fail to adequately inform readers of the significance of those obligations. Accordingly, this Statement establishes standards of disclosure for unconditional purchase obligations associated with financing arrangements.

17. Some expressed concern that this Statement might impose on purchasers a burden of determining whether a supplier has used an unconditional purchase obligation to arrange financing without the purchaser's direct involvement or knowledge. The Board believes that, for most arrangements covered by this Statement, financing considerations are an integral part of negotiating the terms of the unconditional purchase obligation. There is no intent to require a purchaser to investigate whether a supplier used an unconditional purchase obligation to help secure financing, if the purchaser would otherwise be unaware of that fact.

18. Some respondents believe that FASB Statement No. 5, *Accounting for Contingencies*, already provides for adequate disclosure of unconditional purchase obligations associated with financing arrangements. They state that quantification of the obligation should be required only if a loss under the contract is reasonably possible. As stated in paragraph 13, however, the Board believes that existing disclosures of unconditional purchase obligations often fail to provide adequate information about an enterprise's economic resources and claims to those resources. Statement 5 contains requirements pertaining to accounting for and reporting loss contingencies, but does not otherwise address long-term unconditional obligations that are not required to be disclosed as loss contingencies but that nevertheless impose significant future financial commitments for which cash must be available.

19. Some respondents stated that the disclosures required by this Statement might be misleading to readers of financial statements because the obligations are disclosed but the associated benefits are not disclosed. Some respondents described the approach of the revised Exposure Draft as a liquidation perspective rather than a going-concern approach. The Board has not included explicit requirements to disclose associated benefits because the expected benefits may be difficult to quantify and may not be assured of realization. Paragraph 7(a) of this Statement requires a description of the nature of the obligation, and each of the first three illustrations in Appendix C describes the obligation and the associated benefit (access to processing facilities, availability of needed pipeline capacity, and an assured supply of ammonia, respectively). The lack of explicit requirements to disclose associated benefits does not preclude an enterprise from describing those benefits.

20. Several respondents noted that the requirements in Statement 13 to disclose future lease obligations apply to leases with initial or remaining terms in excess of one year and suggested conforming the requirements in this Statement. The Board has adopted that suggestion both to conform with Statement 13 and to reduce the costs of applying this Statement by eliminating the need to review short-term unconditional purchase obligations.

21. The revised Exposure Draft and this Statement require quantification of the fixed and determinable portion of unrecorded purchase obligations and description, but not quantification, of the variable portion of unrecorded obligations. Several respondents noted that the variable portion is similar to contingent rentals on leases. They suggested that the purchases made in each period for which an income statement is presented should be disclosed, similar to the disclosure of contingent rental expense, to help readers of financial statements estimate future payments under the variable portions. The Board adopted that suggestion.

22. Paragraphs 7 and 10(a) of this Statement require purchasers to disclose future payments under long-term unconditional purchase obligations associated with financing arrangements, and Statement 13 requires lessees to disclose future payments under capital and operating leases. The Board believes it would be anomalous to require those disclosures but not to require disclosures of maturities and sinking fund requirements on long-term borrowings and of mandatory redemption requirements on capital stock that are similarly relevant in assessing future cash requirements. This Statement, therefore, includes standards of disclosure pertaining to long-term borrowings and capital stock with mandatory redemption features. Those standards are substantially the same as disclosures currently required by Regulation S-X of the Securities and Exchange Commission for publicly held enterprises.

Appendix B

GLOSSARY

23. For purposes of this Statement, certain terms are defined as follows:

a. *Project financing arrangement*. The financing of a major capital project in which the lender looks principally to the cash flows and earnings of the project as the source of funds for repayment and to the assets of the project as collateral for the loan. The general credit of the project entity is usually not a significant factor, either because the entity is a corporation without other assets or because the financing is without direct recourse to the owner(s) of the entity.
b. *Purchaser's incremental borrowing rate*. The rate that, at the inception of an unconditional purchase obligation, the purchaser would have incurred to borrow over a similar term the funds necessary to discharge the obligation.
c. *Take-or-pay contract*. An agreement between a purchaser and a seller that provides for the purchaser to pay specified amounts periodically in return for products or services. The purchaser must make specified minimum payments even if it does not take delivery of the contracted products or services.
d. *Throughput contract*. An agreement between a shipper (processor) and the owner of a transportation facility (such as an oil or natural gas pipeline or a ship) or a manufacturing facility that provides for the shipper (processor) to pay specified amounts periodically in return for the transportation (processing) of a product. The shipper (processor) is obligated to provide specified minimum quantities to be transported (processed) in each period and is required to make cash payments even if it does not provide the contracted quantities.

Appendix C

ILLUSTRATIONS OF THE APPLICATION OF THIS STATEMENT TO COMMON ARRANGEMENTS

Example 1

24. B Company has entered into a throughput agreement with a manufacturing plant providing that B will submit specified quantities of a chemical (representing a portion of plant capacity) for processing through the plant each period while the debt used to finance the plant remains outstanding. B's processing charges are intended to be sufficient to cover a proportional share of fixed and variable operating expenses and debt service of the plant. If, however, the processing charges do not cover such operating expenses and debt service, B must advance additional funds to cover a specified percentage of operating expenses and debt service. Such additional funds are considered advance payments for future throughput.

25. B's unconditional obligation to pay a specified percentage of the plant's fixed operating expenses and debt service is fixed and determinable, while the amount of variable operating expenses that B is obligated to pay will vary depending on plant operations and economic conditions.

26. B's disclosure might be as follows:

To secure access to facilities to process chemical X, the company has signed a processing agreement with a chemical company allowing B Company to submit 100,000 tons for processing annually for 20 years. Under the terms of the agreement, B Company may be required to advance funds against future processing charges if the chemical company is unable to meet its financial obligations. The aggregate amount of required payments at December 31, 19X1 is as follows (in thousands):

19X2	$ 10,000
19X3	10,000
19X4	9,000
19X5	8,000
19X6	8,000
Later years	100,000
Total	145,000
Less: Amount representing interest	(45,000)
Total at present value	$100,000

In addition, the company is required to pay a proportional share of the variable operating expenses of the plant. The company's total processing charges under the agreement in each of the past 3 years have been $12 million.

Example 2

27. C Company has entered into a throughput agreement with a natural gas pipeline providing that C will provide specified quantities of natural gas (representing a portion of capacity) for transportation through the pipeline each period while the debt used to finance the pipeline remains outstanding. The tariff approved by the Federal Energy Regulatory Commission contains two portions, a demand charge and a commodity charge. The demand charge is computed to cover debt service, depreciation, and certain expected expenses. The commodity charge is intended to cover other expenses and provide a return on the pipeline company's investment. C Company must pay the demand charge based on the contracted quantity regardless of actual quantities shipped, while the commodity charge is applied to actual quantities shipped. Accordingly, the demand charge multiplied by the contracted quantity represents a fixed and determinable payment.

28. C's disclosure might be as follows:

C Company has signed an agreement providing for the availability of needed pipeline transportation capacity through 1990. Under that agreement, the company must make specified minimum payments monthly. The aggregate amount of such required payments at December 31, 19X1 is as follows (in thousands):

19X2	$ 5,000
19X3	5,000
19X4	5,000
19X5	4,000
19X6	4,000
Later years	26,000
Total	49,000
Less: Amount representing interest	(9,000)
Total at present value	$ 40,000

In addition, the company is required to pay additional amounts depending on actual quantities shipped under the agreement. The company's total payments under the agreement were (in thousands) $6,000 in 19W9 and $5,500 both in 19X0 and in 19X1.

Example 3

29. A subsidiary of F Company has entered into a take-or-pay contract with an ammonia plant. F's subsidiary is obligated to purchase 50 percent of the planned capacity production of the plant each period while the debt used to finance the plant remains outstanding. The monthly payment equals the sum of 50 percent of raw material costs, operating expenses, depreciation, interest on the debt used to finance the plant, and a return on the owner's equity investment.

30. F's disclosure might be as follows:

To assure a long-term supply, one of the company's subsidiaries has contracted to purchase half the output of an ammonia plant through the year 2005 and to make minimum annual payments as follows, whether or not it is able to take delivery (in thousands):

19X2 through 19X6 ($6,000 per annum)	$ 30,000
Later years	120,000
Total	150,000
Less: Amount representing interest	(65,000)
Total at present value	$ 85,000

In addition, the subsidiary must reimburse the owner of the plant for a proportional share of raw material costs and operating expenses of the plant. The subsidiary's total purchases under the agreement were (in thousands) $7,000, $7,100, and $7,200 in 19W9, 19X0, and 19X1, respectively.

Example 4

31. D Company has outstanding two long-term borrowings and one issue of preferred stock with mandatory redemption requirements. The first borrowing is a $100 million sinking fund debenture with annual sinking fund payments of $10 million in 19X2, 19X3, and 19X4, $15 million in 19X5 and 19X6, and $20 million in 19X7 and 19X8. The second borrowing is a $50 million note due in 19X5. The $30 million issue of preferred stock requires a 5 percent annual cumulative sinking fund payment of $1.5 million until retired.

32. D's disclosure might be as follows:

Maturities and sinking fund requirements on long-term debt and sinking fund requirements on preferred stock subject to mandatory redemption are as follows (in thousands):

	Long-term debt	Preferred stock
19X2	$10,000	$1,500
19X3	10,000	1,500
19X4	10,000	1,500
19X5	65,000	1,500
19X6	15,000	1,500

Statement of Financial Accounting Standards No. 48
Revenue Recognition When Right of Return Exists

STATUS

Issued: June 1981

Effective Date: For fiscal years beginning after June 15, 1981

Affects: Amends FAS 32, Appendix A

Affected by: No other pronouncements

SUMMARY

This Statement specifies how an enterprise should account for sales of its product in which the buyer has a right to return the product. Revenue from those sales transactions shall be recognized at time of sale only if *all* of the conditions specified by the Statement are met. If those conditions are not met, revenue recognition is postponed; if they are met, sales revenue and cost of sales reported in the income statement shall be reduced to reflect estimated returns and expected costs or losses shall be accrued.

Statement of Financial Accounting Standards No. 48
Revenue Recognition When Right of Return Exists

CONTENTS

INTRODUCTION

1. As discussed in FASB Statement No. 32, *Specialized Accounting and Reporting Principles and Practices in AICPA Statements of Position and Guides on Accounting and Auditing Matters,* the FASB is extracting the specialized[1] accounting and reporting principles and practices from AICPA Statements of Position (SOPs) and Guides on accounting and auditing matters and issuing them in FASB Statements after appropriate due process. This Statement extracts the specialized principles and practices from SOP 75-1, *Revenue Recognition When Right of Return Exists,* and establishes accounting and reporting standards for sales of an enterprise's product in which the buyer has a right to return the product.

2. The Board has concluded that it can reach an informed decision on the basis of existing information without a public hearing and that the effective date and transition specified in paragraphs 10-12 are advisable in the circumstances.

APPLICABILITY AND SCOPE

3. This Statement specifies criteria for recognizing revenue on a sale in which a product may be returned, whether as a matter of contract or as a matter of existing practice, either by the ultimate customer or by a party who resells the product to others. The product may be returned for a refund of the purchase price, for a credit applied to amounts owed or to be owed for other purchases, or in exchange for other products. The purchase price or credit may include amounts related to incidental services, such as installation.

4. This Statement does not apply to: (a) accounting for revenue in service industries if part or all of the service revenue may be returned under cancellation privileges granted to the buyer, (b) transactions involving real estate or leases, or (c) sales transactions in which a customer may return defective goods, such as under warranty provisions.

5. This Statement does not modify any of the provisions of FASB Statement No. 49, *Accounting for Product Financing Arrangements.* A product financing arrangement as defined in that Statement should be accounted for as a borrowing rather than as a sale.

STANDARDS OF FINANCIAL ACCOUNTING AND REPORTING

Criteria for Recognizing Revenue When Right of Return Exists

6. If an enterprise sells its product but gives the buyer the right to return the product, revenue from the sales transaction shall be recognized at time of sale only if *all* of the following conditions are met:

a. The seller's price to the buyer is substantially fixed or determinable at the date of sale.
b. The buyer has paid the seller, or the buyer is obligated to pay the seller and the obligation is not contingent on resale of the product.
c. The buyer's obligation to the seller would not be changed in the event of theft or physical destruction or damage of the product.
d. The buyer acquiring the product for resale has economic substance apart from that provided by the seller.[2]

[1]The term *specialized* is used to refer to those accounting and reporting principles and practices in AICPA Guides and SOPs that are neither superseded by nor contained in Accounting Research Bulletins, APB Opinions, FASB Statements, or FASB Interpretations.

[2]This condition relates primarily to buyers that exist "on paper," that is, buyers that have little or no physical facilities or employees. It prevents enterprises from recognizing sales revenue on transactions with parties that the sellers have established primarily for the purpose of recognizing such sales revenue.

e. The seller does not have significant obligations for future performance to directly bring about resale of the product by the buyer.
f. The amount of future returns[3] can be reasonably estimated (paragraph 8).

Sales revenue and cost of sales that are not recognized at time of sale because the foregoing conditions are not met shall be recognized either when the return privilege has substantially expired or if those conditions subsequently are met, whichever occurs first.

7. If sales revenue is recognized because the conditions of paragraph 6 are met, any costs or losses that may be expected in connection with any returns shall be accrued in accordance with FASB Statement No. 5, *Accounting for Contingencies.* Sales revenue and cost of sales reported in the income statement shall be reduced to reflect estimated returns.

8. The ability to make a reasonable estimate of the amount of future returns depends on many factors and circumstances that will vary from one case to the next. However, the following factors may impair the ability to make a reasonable estimate:

a. The susceptibility of the product to significant external factors, such as technological obsolescence or changes in demand
b. Relatively long periods in which a particular product may be returned
c. Absence of historical experience with similar types of sales of similar products, or inability to apply such experience because of changing circumstances, for example, changes in the selling enterprise's marketing policies or relationships with its customers
d. Absence of a large volume of relatively homogeneous transactions

The existence of one or more of the above factors, in light of the significance of other factors, may not be sufficient to prevent making a reasonable estimate; likewise, other factors may preclude a reasonable estimate.

Amendment to Statement 32

9. The reference to SOP 75-1, *Revenue Recognition When Right of Return Exists,* is deleted from Appendix A of Statement 32. The specialized accounting provisions of that SOP are superseded by this Statement.

Effective Date and Transition

10. This Statement shall be effective for fiscal years beginning after June 15, 1981, with earlier application encouraged. Accounting changes adopted to conform to the provisions of this Statement shall be applied retroactively. In the year that this Statement is first applied, the financial statements shall disclose the nature of any restatement and its effect on sales, income before extraordinary items, net income, and related per-share amounts for each year restated.

11. If retroactive restatement of all years presented is not practicable, the financial statements presented shall be restated for as many consecutive years as practicable and the cumulative effect of applying the Statement shall be included in determining net income of the earliest year restated (not necessarily the earliest year presented). If it is not practicable to restate any prior year, the cumulative effect shall be included in net income in the year in which the Statement is first applied. (Refer to paragraph 20 of APB Opinion No. 20, *Accounting Changes.*) The effect on sales, income before extraordinary items, net income, and related per-share amounts of applying this Statement in a year in which the cumulative effect is included in determining that year's net income shall be disclosed for that year.

12. Retroactive application of the provisions of paragraph 7 may require estimates of returns and costs or losses from returns that the enterprise has not previously made; information that may have become available after the year being restated may be considered in making those estimates.

The provisions of this Statement need not be applied to immaterial items.

This Statement was adopted by the unanimous vote of the seven members of the Financial Accounting Standards Board:

Donald J. Kirk, *Chairman*
Frank E. Block
John W. March
Robert A. Morgan
David Mosso
Robert T. Sprouse
Ralph E. Walters

[3]Exchanges by ultimate customers of one item for another of the same kind, quality, and price (for example, one color or size for another) are not considered returns for purposes of this Statement.

Appendix A

BACKGROUND INFORMATION

13. It is the practice in some industries for customers to be given the right to return a product to the seller under certain circumstances. In the case of sales to the ultimate customer, the most usual circumstance is customer dissatisfaction with the product. For sales to customers engaged in the business of reselling the product, the most usual circumstance is that the customer has not been able to resell the product to another party. (Arrangements in which customers buy products for resale with the right to return products often are referred to as *guaranteed sales.*)

14. Sometimes, the returns occur very soon after a sale is made, as in the newspaper and perishable food industries. In other cases, returns occur over a longer period, such as with book publishing and equipment manufacturing. The rate of returns varies considerably from a low rate usually found in the food industry to a high rate often found in the publishing industry.

15. Situations that pose particular problems occur when sales result in significant overstocking by customers acquiring product for resale. In those situations, the recognition of revenue in one period often is followed by substantial returns in a later period.

16. SOP 75-1 was developed to reduce diversity in the accounting for revenue when the right of return exists. The following alternative accounting practices were being used when the SOP was issued: (a) no sale was recognized until the product was unconditionally accepted, (b) a sale was recognized and an allowance for estimated returns was provided, and (c) a sale was recognized without providing an allowance for returns and, instead, sales returns were recognized when the product was returned. The SOP established criteria that had to be met before sales revenue could be recognized.

17. The Board has not undertaken a comprehensive reconsideration of the accounting issues discussed in SOP 75-1 and has extracted the specialized accounting and reporting principles without significant change. Accordingly, some of the background material and discussion of accounting alternatives have not been carried forward from the SOP. The Board's conceptual framework project on accounting recognition criteria will address revenue recognition issues that may pertain to those addressed in this Statement. A Statement of Financial Accounting Concepts resulting from that project in due course will serve as a basis for evaluating existing standards and practices. Accordingly, the Board may wish to evaluate the standards in this Statement when its conceptual framework project is completed.

Appendix B

SUMMARY OF CONSIDERATION OF COMMENTS ON EXPOSURE DRAFT

18. An Exposure Draft of a proposed Statement, *Revenue Recognition When Right of Return Exists,* was issued February 9, 1981. The Board received 36 comment letters in response to the Exposure Draft. Certain of the comments received and the Board's consideration of them are discussed in this appendix.

19. Some respondents requested that the Statement not apply to enterprises that account for inventory using the retail method of accounting. They recommended that sales returns of retailers be permitted to be recognized when merchandise actually is returned for refund or credit. They said that method is appropriate because accounting for sales returns at time of sale for each product sold is not cost justified, for three reasons. First, they believe that the results of recognizing sales returns when returns are made gives substantially the same results as applying the provisions of the Statement, that is, the Statement would have an insignificant effect on sales, gross margins, and earnings. Second, they state that enterprises using the retail method have not maintained historic data on sales returns. They believe that determining the percentage of sales of one accounting period returned in a later accounting period would be time-consuming and costly, because of the number of transactions to be reviewed. Third, if they were to follow the provisions of the Statement, providing for estimated returns for each product would be complex and costly. Others disagreed with the suggestion of exempting retailers from the Statement.

20. The Board believes that the fundamental issue is materiality. The Board recognizes that the provisions of this Statement may not materially affect the financial position and results of operations of some enterprises that currently account differently than specified by this Statement. Like other FASB Statements, the provisions of this Statement need not be applied to immaterial items. With respect to those enterprises for which this Statement would have a material effect, the Board recognizes that detailed record keeping for returns for each product line might be costly in some cases; this Statement permits reasonable aggregations and approximations of product returns.

21. Some respondents suggested that exchanges by ultimate customers of one item for another of the

same kind, quality, and price (for example, one color or size for another) should not be treated as sales returns for purposes of this Statement. They noted that retailers do not account for those exchanges as sales returns. The Board adopted that suggestion in footnote 3.

22. Several respondents, particularly in the publishing industry, expressed concern that the wording of the condition in paragraph 6(b) (paragraph 11(b) of the Exposure Draft) changed its meaning from the similar condition in SOP 75-1. The Board has refined the wording to clarify that the condition is met if the buyer pays the seller at time of sale or if the buyer does not pay at time of sale but is obligated to pay at a specified date or dates. If, however, the buyer does not pay at time of sale and the buyer's obligation to pay is contractually or implicitly excused until the buyer resells the product, then the condition is not met.

23. The transition provisions in the Exposure Draft proposed that either prospective application with cumulative effect of a change in accounting principles or retroactive restatement be permitted. The Notice for Recipients of the Exposure Draft requested respondents to comment on whether the proposed transition is appropriate or whether the transition provisions should be limited to one of the alternatives. Of those respondents who commented on the transition provisions, a substantial majority recommended that one method be specified, but they disagreed on which method. The Board believes that, for recurring revenue recognition issues, comparability is enhanced if enterprises apply accounting standards retroactively by restating the financial statements of previous periods, and the Board has, therefore, adopted that method in this Statement. This Statement, however, calls for enterprises that are unable to restate previous years' financial statements to include the cumulative effect of those years in the earliest year restated.

24. Several individual respondents suggested various substantive changes to the Exposure Draft. Adoption of those suggestions would have required a reconsideration of the provisions of SOP 75-1. Those suggestions were not adopted because such a reconsideration is beyond the scope of extracting the specialized accounting and reporting principles and practices from the SOP, none of the changes was broadly supported, and the Board believes the suggestions should not be adopted.

25. Several respondents requested guidance regarding specific implementation questions; for example, treatment of partial or limited refunds and balance sheet presentation of accruals for expected returns. SOP 75-1 did not provide specific guidance about those questions and the Board concluded that it should not address those questions at this time.

Statement of Financial Accounting Standards No. 49
Accounting for Product Financing Arrangements

STATUS

Issued: June 1981

Effective Date: For product financing arrangements entered into after June 15, 1981

Affects: Amends FAS 32, Appendix A

Affected by: Paragraph 7 superseded by FAS 71

SUMMARY

This Statement specifies criteria for determining when an arrangement involving the sale of inventory is in substance a financing arrangement. A product financing arrangement is a transaction in which an enterprise sells and agrees to repurchase inventory with the repurchase price equal to the original sale price plus carrying and financing costs, or other similar transactions. This Statement requires that a product financing arrangement be accounted for as a borrowing rather than as a sale.

Statement of Financial Accounting Standards No. 49
Accounting for Product Financing Arrangements

CONTENTS

INTRODUCTION

1. As discussed in FASB Statement No. 32, *Specialized Accounting and Reporting Principles and Practices in AICPA Statements of Position and Guides on Accounting and Auditing Matters,* the FASB is extracting the specialized[1] accounting and reporting principles and practices from AICPA Statements of Position (SOPs) and Guides on accounting and auditing matters and issuing them in FASB Statements after appropriate due process. This Statement extracts the specialized principles and practices from SOP 78-8, *Accounting for Product Financing Arrangements,* and establishes accounting and reporting standards for product financing arrangements.

2. The Board has concluded that it can reach an informed decision on the basis of existing information without a public hearing and that the effective date and transition specified in paragraph 11 are advisable in the circumstances.

APPLICABILITY AND SCOPE

3. Product financing arrangements include agreements in which a sponsor (the enterprise seeking to finance product pending its future use or resale):

a. Sells the product to another entity (the enterprise through which the financing flows), and in a related transaction agrees to repurchase the product (or a substantially identical product);
b. Arranges for another entity to purchase the product on the sponsor's behalf and, in a related transaction, agrees to purchase the product from the other entity; or
c. Controls the disposition of the product that has been purchased by another entity in accordance with the arrangements described in either (a) or (b) above.

In all of the foregoing cases, the sponsor agrees to purchase the product, or processed goods of which the product is a component, from the other entity at specified prices over specified periods or, to the extent that it does not do so, guarantees resale prices to third parties (paragraph 5(a)(1)). Appendix C illustrates each of the types of arrangements described in (a) and (b) above.

4. Other characteristics that commonly exist in product financing arrangements but that are not necessarily present in all such arrangements are:

a. The entity that purchases the product from the sponsor or purchases it directly from a third party on behalf of the sponsor was established expressly for that purpose or is an existing trust, nonbusiness organization, or credit grantor.
b. The product covered by the financing arrangement is to be used or sold by the sponsor, although a portion may be sold by the other entity directly to third parties.
c. The product covered by the financing arrangement is stored on the sponsor's premises.
d. The debt of the entity that purchases the product being financed is guaranteed by the sponsor.

5. This Statement applies to product financing arrangements for products[2] that have been produced by or were originally purchased by the sponsor or purchased by another entity on behalf of the sponsor and have both of the following characteristics:

a. The financing arrangement requires the sponsor

[1]The term *specialized* is used to refer to those accounting and reporting principles and practices in AICPA Guides and SOPs that are neither superseded by nor contained in Accounting Research Bulletins, APB Opinions, FASB Statements, or FASB Interpretations.

[2]Unmined or unharvested natural resources and financial instruments are not considered to be a product for purposes of this Statement.

to purchase the product, a substantially identical product, or processed goods of which the product is a component at specified prices. The specified prices are not subject to change except for fluctuations due to finance and holding costs. This characteristic of predetermined prices also is present if any of the following circumstances exists:

(1) The specified prices in the financing arrangement are in the form of resale price guarantees under which the sponsor agrees to make up any difference between the specified price and the resale price for products sold to third parties.
(2) The sponsor is not required to purchase the product but has an option to purchase the product, the economic effect of which compels the sponsor to purchase the product; for example, an option arrangement that provides for a significant penalty if the sponsor does not exercise the option to purchase.
(3) The sponsor is not required by the agreement to purchase the product but the other entity has an option whereby it can require the sponsor to purchase the product.

b. The payments that the other entity will receive on the transaction are established by the financing arrangement, and the amounts to be paid by the sponsor will be adjusted, as necessary, to cover substantially all fluctuations in costs incurred by the other entity in purchasing and holding the product (including interest).[3]

6. This Statement does not modify any of the provisions of FASB Statement No. 48, *Revenue Recognition When Right of Return Exists,* and does not apply to transactions for which sales revenue is recognized currently in accordance with the provisions of that Statement.

7. The Addendum to APB Opinion No. 2, *Accounting for the "Investment Credit,"* (paragraph 2) states that ". . . differences may arise in the application of generally accepted accounting principles as between regulated and nonregulated businesses, because of the effect in regulated businesses of the rate-making process . . ." and discusses the application of generally accepted accounting principles to regulated industries. Accordingly, the provisions of the Addendum govern the application of this Statement to those operations of an enterprise that are regulated for rate-making purposes on an individual-company-cost-of-service basis.

STANDARDS OF FINANCIAL ACCOUNTING AND REPORTING

8. Product and obligations under product financing arrangements that have both of the characteristics described in paragraph 5 shall be accounted for by the sponsor as follows:

a. If a sponsor sells a product to another entity and, in a related transaction, agrees to repurchase the product (or a substantially identical product) or processed goods of which the product is a component, the sponsor shall record a liability at the time the proceeds are received from the other entity to the extent that the product is covered by the financing arrangement. The sponsor shall not record the transaction as a sale and shall not remove the covered product from its balance sheet.
b. If the sponsor is a party to an arrangement whereby another entity purchases a product on the sponsor's behalf and, in a related transaction, the sponsor agrees to purchase the product or processed goods of which the product is a component from the entity, the sponsor shall record the asset and the related liability when the product is purchased by the other entity.

9. Costs of the product, excluding processing costs, in excess of the sponsor's original production or purchase costs or the other entity's purchase costs represent financing and holding costs. The sponsor shall account for such costs in accordance with the sponsor's accounting policies applicable to financing and holding costs as those costs are incurred by the other entity. For example, if insurance costs ordinarily are accounted for as period costs by the sponsor, similar costs associated with the product covered by financing arrangements shall be expensed by the sponsor as those costs are incurred by the other entity. Interest costs associated with the product covered by financing arrangements shall be identified separately and accounted for by the sponsor in accordance with FASB Statement No. 34, *Capitalization of Interest Cost,* as those costs are incurred by the other entity.

Amendment to Statement 32

10. The reference to SOP 78-8, *Accounting for Product Financing Arrangements,* is deleted from Appendix A of Statement 32. The specialized accounting provisions of that SOP are superseded by this Statement.

[3]The characteristic described in paragraph 5(b) ordinarily is not present in purchase commitments or contractor-subcontractor relationships. (Refer to paragraph 18.)

Effective Date and Transition

11. This Statement shall be applied prospectively to product financing arrangements entered into after June 15, 1981.

The provisions of this Statement need not be applied to immaterial items.

This Statement was adopted by the unanimous vote of the seven members of the Financial Accounting Standards Board:

Donald J. Kirk, *Chairman*
Frank E. Block
John W. March
Robert A. Morgan
David Mosso
Robert T. Sprouse
Ralph E. Walters

Appendix A

BACKGROUND INFORMATION

12. SOP 78-8 was developed to establish standards for product financing arrangements, such as transactions in which an enterprise sells and agrees to repurchase inventory (or substantially identical inventory) with the repurchase price equal to the original sale price plus carrying and financing costs. For example, an enterprise (sponsor) would sell a product and in a related transaction would agree to repurchase the product or processed goods of which the product was a component at a specified price over a specified period. The buyer, using the product and sometimes the financing arrangement as collateral, would borrow against the value of the product from a lending institution or other credit grantor and would remit the proceeds to the sponsor as payment for the product. As the terms of the financing arrangement were fulfilled by the sponsor, the buyer of the product would reduce its borrowing from the financial institution.

13. The following alternative accounting practices were being used when SOP 78-8 was issued: (a) product and obligations under product financing arrangements were reported as assets and liabilities in the sponsor's financial statements and (b) product and obligations under product financing arrangements were not reported as assets and liabilities in the sponsor's financial statements; instead, the obligations were disclosed as commitments. In addition, financing and holding costs incurred by the buyer often were not reported by the sponsor until the product was repurchased from the buyer.

14. The SOP concluded that (a) product financing arrangements, such as the one described in paragraph 12, did not transfer the risks and rewards of ownership of the product; (b) product financing arrangements are financing transactions rather than sales; and (c) a sponsor of an arrangement to finance product should account for the transaction as a borrowing rather than as a sale and, accordingly, should report the asset and related liability resulting from the arrangement on its balance sheet.

15. The Board has not undertaken a comprehensive reconsideration of the accounting issues discussed in SOP 78-8 and has extracted the specialized accounting and reporting principles without significant change. Accordingly, some of the background material and discussion of accounting alternatives have not been carried forward from the SOP. The Board's conceptual framework project on accounting recognition criteria will address criteria for recognizing a transaction as a sale that may pertain to the issues addressed in this Statement. A Statement of Financial Accounting Concepts resulting from that project in due course will serve as a basis for evaluating existing standards and practices. Accordingly, the Board may wish to evaluate the standards in this Statement when its conceptual framework project is completed.

Appendix B

SUMMARY OF CONSIDERATION OF COMMENTS ON EXPOSURE DRAFT

16. An Exposure Draft of a proposed Statement, *Accounting for Product Financing Arrangements,* was issued February 9, 1981. The Board received 34 comment letters in response to the Exposure Draft. Certain of the comments received and the Board's consideration of them are discussed in this appendix.

17. In the Exposure Draft, the Board requested respondents to consider the implication of provisions of the proposed Statement on the accounting for certain contractor-subcontractor relationships, such as a contract in which specifications are provided by a customer for the manufacture of product. Some respondents indicated that the provisions of the proposed Statement were too broad and could result in certain contractor-subcontractor rela-

tionships, as well as purchase commitments, being accounted for inappropriately as product financing arrangements. They believe that the distinguishing characteristic of a product financing arrangement is that the sponsor retains the risks and rewards of ownership of the product while the buyer merely holds the product for the sponsor. They stated that the purpose of a purchase commitment is to assure the supply of product, rather than to provide the financing for an entity's inventory, and should not be considered a product financing arrangement. They believe that a product financing arrangement does not exist if a supplier has the risks and rewards of ownership until the product is transferred to the sponsor. They also noted that in a typical contractor-subcontractor relationship, the purchase of product by a subcontractor on behalf of a contractor ordinarily leaves a significant portion of the subcontractor's obligation unfulfilled. The subcontractor has the risks of ownership of the product until it has met all the terms of a contract. Accordingly, they believe that the typical contractor-subcontractor relationship also should not be considered a product financing arrangement.

18. The Board believes that SOP 78-8 was intended to apply only to arrangements in which the sponsor is in substance the owner of the product and the other entity holds the product to facilitate a financing arrangement. The Board does not believe that SOP 78-8 was intended to apply to (a) ordinary purchase commitments in which the risks and rewards of ownership are retained by the seller (for example, a manufacturer or other supplier) until the product is transferred to a purchaser or (b) typical contractor-subcontractor relationships in which the contractor is not in substance the owner of product held by the subcontractor and the obligation of the contractor is contingent on substantial performance on the part of the subcontractor. Accordingly, the Board has modified paragraph 5(b) to indicate that this Statement applies only to product financing arrangements in which the payments that the other entity will receive are established by the financing arrangement and the amounts to be paid will be adjusted, as necessary, to cover substantially all fluctuations in purchasing and holding costs. Most purchase commitments do not have that characteristic because the supplier's profit could fluctuate if the supplier's costs of fulfilling the commitment, including holding costs, change before the commitment is fulfilled. Most contractor-subcontractor relationships, including those having cost-plus-fixed-fee provisions, are not product financing arrangements as contemplated in this Statement. Paragraph 5(a) states that in product financing arrangements "the specified prices are not subject to change except for fluctuations due to finance and holding costs." Paragraph 5(b) states that the ". . . amounts to be paid by the sponsor will be adjusted, as necessary, to cover substantially all fluctuations in costs incurred by the other entity in purchasing and holding the product. . . ." A cost-plus-fixed-fee contract typically provides for reimbursement of labor and other costs, not just finance and holding costs and, therefore, does not qualify as a product financing arrangement under paragraph 5(a). A fixed price contract typically is not adjusted to cover fluctuations in costs incurred by the subcontractor in purchasing and holding product and, therefore, does not qualify as a product financing arrangement under paragraph 5(b).

19. Some respondents suggested that arrangements involving the sale and repurchase of financial instruments be excluded from this Statement. The Board does not believe that SOP 78-8 was intended to encompass financial instruments as products. That conclusion is based, in part, on the existence of specialized accounting principles for agreements to sell and repurchase financial instruments in AICPA documents other than SOP 78-8. Accordingly, footnote 2 excludes financial instruments from the definition of product. In addition, footnote 2 carries forward from SOP 78-8 without change the exclusion of unmined or unharvested natural resources.

20. Some respondents requested the Board to explain why the accounting for product financing arrangements specified by this Statement differs from the accounting for long-term unconditional purchase obligations (for example, take-or-pay contracts) specified by FASB Statement No. 47, *Disclosure of Long-Term Obligations.* They noted that this Statement requires a sponsor to recognize an asset and a liability for a product financing arrangement; Statement 47 requires disclosure, but not necessarily balance sheet recognition of an asset and a liability for an unconditional purchase obligation by a purchaser.

21. There are similarities between a sponsor's rights and obligations under a product financing arrangement and a purchaser's rights and obligations under an unconditional purchase obligation. Both the sponsor and the purchaser obtain probable future economic benefits from the assured source of product. Both are obligated to make future cash payments to the other party to the agreement. Beyond those similarities, however, there is a substantial difference in the related accounting issues.

22. The accounting issue with respect to an unconditional purchase obligation is whether at the time the contract is entered into the purchaser should report rights to receive future product or services as an asset and obligations to make future payments for product or services as a liability. Under a product financing arrangement, the product already exists and the other entity's purchase cost is known. The

accounting issue addressed in this Statement is whether the sponsor should report the existing product currently held by the other entity as an asset and the obligation to pay the other entity as a liability. This Statement concludes that the sponsor is in substance the owner of the product and that the sponsor should, therefore, report the product as an asset and the related obligation as a liability. At the time a take-or-pay contract is entered into, by contrast, either the product does not yet exist (for example, electricity) or the product exists in a form unsuitable to the purchaser (for example, unmined coal); the purchaser has a right to receive future product but is not the substantive owner of existing product.

23. Some respondents questioned whether the absence of a reference in the Exposure Draft to the Addendum to Opinion 2 indicated that the Statement would apply to rate-regulated enterprises. The Board currently is considering the effect of rate regulation on regulated enterprises in another project. In the meantime, paragraph 7 was added to acknowledge that the provisions of the Addendum govern the application of this Statement to those operations of an enterprise that are regulated for rate-making purposes on a basis of individual company cost of service.

24. Several individual respondents suggested various substantive changes to the Exposure Draft. Adoption of those suggestions would have required a reconsideration of the provisions of SOP 78-8. Those suggestions were not adopted because such a reconsideration is beyond the scope of extracting the specialized accounting and reporting principles and practices from the SOP and because none of the changes was broadly supported.

Appendix C

ILLUSTRATIONS OF THE APPLICATION OF THIS STATEMENT TO COMMON PRODUCT FINANCING ARRANGEMENTS

25. This appendix illustrates how this Statement applies to two common product financing arrangements. The facts assumed in the examples are illustrative only and are not intended to modify or limit in any way the provisions of this Statement. The facts assumed in each case could vary in one or more respects without altering the application of the provisions of this Statement.

Example 1

26. An enterprise (sponsor) sells a portion of its inventory to another entity (the entity through which the financing flows), and in a related transaction agrees to repurchase the inventory (paragraph 3(a)).

Assumptions and Provisions of the Financing Arrangement

27. The sponsor arranges for the other entity to acquire a portion of the sponsor's inventory. The other entity's sole asset is the transferred inventory that is, in turn, used as collateral for bank financing. The proceeds of the bank financing are then remitted to the sponsor. The debt of the other entity is guaranteed by the sponsor. The inventory is stored in a public warehouse during the holding period. The sponsor, in connection with the "sale" (legal title passes to the entity), enters into a financing arrangement under which:

a. The sponsor agrees to pay all costs of the other entity associated with the inventory, including holding and storage costs.
b. The sponsor agrees to pay the other entity interest on the purchase price of the inventory equivalent to the interest and fees incurred in connection with the bank financing.
c. The sponsor agrees to repurchase the inventory from the other entity at a specified future date for the same price originally paid by the entity to purchase the inventory irrespective of changes in market prices during the holding period.
d. The other entity agrees not to assign or otherwise encumber the inventory during its ownership period, except to the extent of providing collateral for the bank financing.

Application of the Provisions of This Statement

28. In the product financing arrangement outlined above, both of the characteristics in paragraph 5 are present; accordingly, the sponsor neither records the transaction as a sale of inventory nor removes the inventory from its balance sheet. The sponsor recognizes a liability when the proceeds are received from the other entity. Financing and holding costs are accrued by the sponsor as incurred by the other entity and accounted for in accordance with the sponsor's accounting policies for such costs. Interest costs are separately identified and accounted for in accordance with Statement 34.

Example 2

29. A sponsor arranges for another entity to buy product on the sponsor's behalf with a related agreement to purchase the product from the other entity (paragraph 3(b)).

Assumptions and Provisions of the Financing Arrangement

30. The sponsor arranges for the other entity to purchase on its behalf an existing supply of fuel. In

a related agreement, the sponsor agrees to purchase the fuel from the other entity over a specified period and at specified prices. The prices established are adequate to cover all financing and holding costs of the other entity. The other entity finances the purchase of fuel using the fuel and the agreement as collateral.

Application of the Provisions of This Statement

31. In the product financing arrangement described above, both of the characteristics in paragraph 5 are present; accordingly, the sponsor reports the asset (fuel) and the related liability on its balance sheet when the fuel is acquired by the other entity. Financing and holding costs are accrued by the sponsor as incurred by the other entity and accounted for in accordance with the sponsor's accounting policies for financing and holding costs. Interest costs are separately identified and accounted for in accordance with Statement 34.

Statement of Financial Accounting Standards No. 50 Financial Reporting in the Record and Music Industry

STATUS

Issued: November 1981

Effective Date: For fiscal years beginning after December 15, 1981

Affects: Amends FAS 32, Appendix A

Affected by: No other pronouncements

SUMMARY

This Statement extracts the specialized accounting principles and practices from AICPA Statement of Position 76-1, *Accounting Practices in the Record and Music Industry,* and establishes standards of financial accounting and reporting for licensors and licensees in the record and music industry. If a license agreement is, in substance, an outright sale and collectibility of the licensing fee is reasonably assured, this Statement requires the licensor to recognize the licensing fee as revenue. This Statement requires a licensee to record minimum guarantees as assets and charge them to expense in accordance with the terms of the license agreement. It also establishes accounting standards for artist compensation cost and cost of record masters.

Statement of Financial Accounting Standards No. 50
Financial Reporting in the Record and Music Industry

CONTENTS

INTRODUCTION AND BACKGROUND INFORMATION

1. As discussed in FASB Statement No. 32, *Specialized Accounting and Reporting Principles and Practices in AICPA Statements of Position and Guides on Accounting and Auditing Matters,* the FASB is extracting the specialized[1] accounting and reporting principles and practices from AICPA Statements of Position (SOPs) and Guides on accounting and auditing matters and issuing them in FASB Statements after appropriate due process. This Statement extracts the specialized principles and practices from SOP 76-1, *Accounting Practices in the Record and Music Industry,* and establishes financial accounting and reporting standards for the industry.

2. The Board has not undertaken a comprehensive reconsideration of the accounting issues discussed in SOP 76-1 and has extracted the specialized accounting and reporting principles without significant change. Accordingly, some of the background material, discussion of accounting alternatives, and general accounting guidance have not been carried forward from the SOP. The Board's conceptual framework project on accounting recognition criteria will address revenue recognition issues that may pertain to those addressed in this Statement. A Statement of Financial Accounting Concepts resulting from that project in due course will serve as a basis for evaluating existing standards and practices. Accordingly, the Board may wish to evaluate the standards in this Statement when its conceptual framework project is completed.

3. SOP 76-1 was developed to clarify and standardize accounting by the record and music industry, particularly when manufacturers and distributors should recognize revenue from sales. Before 1976, manufacturers and distributors usually recorded sales when inventory was shipped in accordance with normal trade terms and, because of the return or exchange privileges that characterize the industry, usually provided for the anticipated return of records from current and prior sales. The SOP notes that manufacturers and distributors in the record and music industry must be able to make a reasonable estimate of returns to account for shipments to customers as sales. The SOP also presents conclusions about the accounting by music publishers and other licensors when music copyrights or **record masters**[2] are licensed, for compensation to recording artists in the form of **royalties,** and for costs of record masters and about the accounting by licensees for various fees.

4. An Exposure Draft of a proposed Statement, *Financial Accounting and Reporting in the Record and Music Industry,* was issued June 12, 1981. The Board received 12 comment letters in response to the Exposure Draft. Several respondents suggested minor clarifications that were adopted. No substantive changes were made.

5. The conclusions in SOP 76-1 regarding recognition of sales revenue when right of return exists are based upon SOP 75-1, *Revenue Recognition When Right of Return Exists.* The FASB has issued FASB Statement No. 48, *Revenue Recognition When Right of Return Exists,* that extracts the specialized principles from SOP 75-1. Because the principles for revenue recognition when right of return exists are not unique to the record and music industry, this Statement does not address that subject.

6. The Board has concluded that it can reach an informed decision on the basis of existing information without a public hearing and that the effective date and transition specified in paragraph 17 are advisable in the circumstances.

---

[1]The term *specialized* is used to refer to those accounting and reporting principles and practices in AICPA Guides and SOPs that are neither superseded by nor contained in Accounting Research Bulletins, APB Opinions, FASB Statements, or FASB Interpretations.

[2]Terms defined in the glossary (appendix) are in **boldface type** the first time they appear in this Statement.

STANDARDS OF FINANCIAL ACCOUNTING AND REPORTING

Licensor Accounting

Revenues

7. Substantial revenues may be realized by the owner of a record master or music copyright by entering into **license agreements.** A license agreement may be, in substance, an outright sale. If the licensor has signed a noncancelable contract, has agreed to a fixed fee, has delivered the rights to the licensee who is free to exercise them, and has no remaining significant obligations to furnish music or records, the earnings process is complete and the licensing fee shall be reported as revenue if collectibility of the full fee is reasonably assured.

8. A **minimum guarantee** may be paid in advance by a licensee. The licensor shall report such a minimum guarantee as a liability initially and recognize the guarantee as revenue as the license fee is earned under the agreement. If the licensor cannot otherwise determine the amount of the license fee earned, the guarantee shall be recognized as revenue equally over the remaining performance period, which is generally the period covered by the license agreement.

9. Other fees (for example, for free records distributed by a record club in excess of a stipulated number) also may be required under the license agreement. Such other fees that are not fixed in amount prior to the expiration date of the agreement shall be recognized as revenue by the licensor only when reasonable estimates of such amounts can be made or the agreement has expired.

Artist Compensation Cost

10. The amount of royalties earned by artists, as adjusted for anticipated returns, shall be charged to expense of the period in which the sale of the record takes place. An **advance royalty** paid to an artist shall be reported as an asset if the past performance and current popularity of the artist to whom the advance is made provide a sound basis for estimating that the amount of the advance will be recoverable from future royalties to be earned by the artist. Advances shall be charged to expense as subsequent royalties are earned by the artist. Any portion of advances that subsequently appear not to be fully recoverable from future royalties to be earned by the artist shall be charged to expense during the period in which the loss becomes evident. Advance royalties shall be classified as current and noncurrent assets, as appropriate.

Cost of Record Masters

11. The portion of the cost of a record master borne by the record company shall be reported as an asset if the past performance and current popularity of the artist provides a sound basis for estimating that the cost will be recovered from future sales. Otherwise, that cost shall be charged to expense. The amount recognized as an asset shall be amortized over the estimated life of the recorded performance using a method that reasonably relates the amount to the net revenue expected to be realized.

12. The portion of the cost of a record master recoverable from the artist's royalties shall be accounted for as an advance royalty, as discussed in paragraph 10.

Disclosure

13. Commitments for artist advances payable in future years and future royalty guarantees shall be disclosed.

14. The portion of the cost of record masters borne by the record company that are recorded as assets shall be disclosed separately.

Licensee Accounting

15. If minimum guarantees are paid in advance by a licensee, such minimum guarantees shall be reported as an asset by the licensee and subsequently charged to expense in accordance with the terms of the license agreement. If all or a portion of the minimum guarantee subsequently appears not to be recoverable through future use of the rights obtained under the license, the nonrecoverable portion shall be charged to expense. Other fees, if any, required by the licensing agreement (for example, for free records distributed by a record club in excess of a stipulated number) that are not fixed in amount prior to the expiration date of the agreement shall be estimated and accrued on a license-by-license basis by the licensee.

Amendment to Statement No. 32

16. The reference to AICPA Statement of Position 76-1, *Accounting Practices in the Record and Music Industry,* is deleted from Appendix A of Statement 32.

Effective Date and Transition

17. This Statement shall be effective for financial statements for fiscal years beginning after December 15, 1981. Earlier application is encouraged. The provisions of this Statement shall be applied retroactively and any accompanying financial statements presented for prior periods shall be restated.

The provisions of this Statement need not be applied to immaterial items.

This Statement was adopted by the unanimous vote of the seven members of the Financial Accounting Standards Board:

Donald J. Kirk, *Chairman*
Frank E. Block
John W. March
Robert A. Morgan
David Mosso
Robert T. Sprouse
Ralph E. Walters

Appendix

GLOSSARY

18. This appendix defines certain terms that are used in this Statement.

Advance Royalty
An amount paid to music publishers, record producers, songwriters, or other artists in advance of their earning royalties from record or music sales. Such an amount is based on contractual terms and is generally nonrefundable.

License Agreements
Contractual arrangements entered into by an owner (licensor) of a record master or music copyright with a licensee granting the licensee the right to sell or distribute records or music for a fixed fee paid to the licensor or for a fee based on sales of records or music. License agreements are modifications of the compulsory provisions of the copyright law.

Minimum Guarantee
An amount paid in advance by a licensee to a licensor for the right to sell or distribute records or music.

Record Master
The master tape resulting from the performance of the artist. It is used to produce molds for commercial record production and other tapes for use in making cartridges, cassettes, and reel tapes. The costs of producing a record master include (a) the cost of the musical talent (musicians, vocal background, and arrangements); (b) the cost of the technical talent for engineering, directing, and mixing; (c) costs for the use of the equipment to record and produce the master; and (d) studio facility charges. Under the standard type of artist contract, the record company bears a portion of the costs and recovers a portion of the cost from the artist out of designated royalties earned. However, either party may bear all or most of the cost.

Royalties
Amounts paid to record producers, songwriters, or other artists for their participation in making records and to music publishers for their copyright interest in music. Amounts for artists are determined by the terms of personal service contracts negotiated between the artists and record companies and usually are determined based upon a percentage of sales activity and license fee income, adjusted for estimated sales returns. Royalties for publishing are based on the copyright or other applicable laws, but the requirements of the law may be modified by licenses issued by the publishers.

Statement of Financial Accounting Standards No. 51
Financial Reporting by Cable Television Companies

STATUS

Issued: November 1981

Effective Date: For fiscal years beginning after December 15, 1981

Affects: Amends FAS 32, Appendix A

Affected by: Paragraph 2 superseded by FAS 71

SUMMARY

This Statement extracts the specialized accounting principles and practices from AICPA Statement of Position 79-2, *Accounting by Cable Television Companies,* and establishes standards of financial accounting and reporting for costs, expenses, and revenues applicable to the construction and operation of a cable television system. During a period while a cable television system is partially under construction and partially in service (the prematurity period), costs incurred that relate to both current and future operations shall be partially capitalized and partially expensed.

Statement of Financial Accounting Standards No. 51
Financial Reporting by Cable Television Companies

CONTENTS

INTRODUCTION

1. As discussed in FASB Statement No. 32, *Specialized Accounting and Reporting Principles and Practices in AICPA Statements of Position and Guides on Accounting and Auditing Matters,* the FASB is extracting the specialized[1] accounting and reporting principles and practices from AICPA Statements of Position (SOPs) and Guides on accounting and auditing matters and issuing them in FASB Statements after appropriate due process. This Statement extracts the specialized principles and practices from SOP 79-2, *Accounting by Cable Television Companies,* and establishes financial accounting and reporting standards for certain costs, expenses, and revenues related to cable television systems.

2. The FASB currently has a project under consideration for the effect of rate regulation on accounting for regulated enterprises. Under current practice, the Addendum to APB Opinion No. 2, *Accounting for the "Investment Credit,"* applies only to businesses that are regulated for rate-making purposes on an individual-company-cost-of-service basis and, therefore, does not apply to the financial statements of cable television companies.

3. The Board has concluded that it can reach an informed decision on the basis of existing information without a public hearing and that the effective date and transition specified in paragraph 16 are advisable in the circumstances.

STANDARDS OF FINANCIAL ACCOUNTING AND REPORTING

Prematurity Period

4. Before revenue is earned from the first subscriber, management shall establish the beginning and end of the **prematurity period,**[2] subject to a presumption that the prematurity period usually will not exceed two years. The prematurity period frequently will be shorter than two years; a longer period may be reasonably justified only in major urban markets. After the prematurity period is established by management, it shall not be changed except as a result of highly unusual circumstances.

5. A portion[3] of a cable television system that is in the prematurity period and can be clearly distinguished from the remainder of the system shall be accounted for separately. Such a portion would have most of the following characteristics:

a. Geographical differences, such as coverage of a noncontiguous or separately awarded franchise area
b. Mechanical differences, such as a separate head-end[4]
c. Timing differences, such as starting construction or marketing at a significantly later date
d. Investment decision differences, such as separate break-even and return-on-investment analyses or separate approval of start of construction

---

[1]The term *specialized* is used to refer to those accounting and reporting principles and practices in AICPA Guides and SOPs that are neither superseded by nor contained in Accounting Research Bulletins, APB Opinions, FASB Statements, or FASB Interpretations.

[2]Terms defined in the glossary (Appendix A) are in **boldface type** the first time they appear in this Statement.

[3]Some cable television companies have used the word *segment* to refer to a portion of a cable television system. In view of the use of *segment* in a different context in FASB Statement No. 14, *Financial Reporting for Segments of a Business Enterprise,* the word *portion* has been used here.

[4]Refer to paragraph 17 for a description of *head-end* in the definition of **cable television plant.**

e. Separate accounting records, separate budgets and forecasts, or other accountability differences

Costs incurred by the remainder of the system shall be charged to the portion in the prematurity period only if they are specifically identified with the operations of that portion. Separate projections for the portion shall be developed and the portion's capitalized costs shall be evaluated separately during the prematurity period for recoverability (paragraph 14).

6. During the prematurity period:

a. Costs of cable television plant, including materials, direct labor, and construction overhead shall continue to be capitalized in full.
b. **Subscriber-related costs** and general and administrative expenses shall be expensed as period costs.
c. Programming costs and other system costs[5] that are incurred in anticipation of servicing a fully operating system and that will not vary significantly regardless of the number of subscribers shall be allocated between current and future operations. The proportion attributable to current operations shall be expensed currently and the remainder shall be capitalized. The amount to be expensed currently shall be determined by multiplying the total of such costs for the month by the fraction described in paragraph 7 determined for that month.

7. The following fraction shall be determined each month of the prematurity period. The denominator of the fraction shall be the total number of subscribers expected at the end of the prematurity period. The numerator of the fraction shall be the greatest of (a) the average number of subscribers expected that month as estimated at the beginning of the prematurity period, (b) the average number of subscribers that would be attained using at least equal (that is, straight-line) monthly progress in adding new subscribers towards the estimate of subscribers at the end of the prematurity period, and (c) the average number of actual subscribers.

8. During the prematurity period, depreciation and amortization expense shall be determined by multiplying (a) the monthly depreciation and amortization of total capitalized costs expected on completion of the prematurity period by (b) the fraction described in paragraph 7, using the depreciation method that will be applied by the company after the prematurity period.

9. The amount of interest cost that is capitalized during the prematurity period shall be determined in accordance with FASB Statement No. 34, *Capitalization of Interest Cost,* by applying an interest capitalization rate determined in accordance with paragraphs 13 and 14 of Statement 34 to the average amount of qualifying assets[6] for the system during the period. Qualifying assets shall be determined in accordance with the guidance in paragraphs 16 and 18 of Statement 34. The amount of interest cost capitalized shall not exceed the total amount of interest cost incurred by the cable television system in that period.

Amortization of Capitalized Costs

10. Costs that have been capitalized in accordance with paragraph 6(c) shall be amortized over the same period used to depreciate the main cable television plant.

Hookup Revenue and Costs

11. Initial hookup revenue shall be recognized as revenue to the extent of **direct selling costs**[7] incurred. The remainder shall be deferred and amortized to income over the estimated average period that subscribers are expected to remain connected to the system.

12. Initial subscriber installation costs, including material, labor, and overhead costs of the drop,[8] shall be capitalized and depreciated over a period no longer than the depreciation period used for cable television plant. The costs of subsequently disconnecting and reconnecting shall be charged to expense.

Franchise Costs

13. Costs of successful franchise applications shall be capitalized and amortized in accordance with the provisions of APB Opinion No. 17, *Intangible Assets.* Costs of unsuccessful franchise applications and abandoned franchises shall be charged to expense.

[5]Those costs include property taxes based on valuation as a fully operating system; pole, underground duct, antenna site, and microwave rental based on rental costs for a fully operating system; and local origination programming to satisfy franchise requirements.

[6]During the prematurity period, a portion of the system is in use in the earnings activity of the enterprise and is not eligible for interest capitalization. The portion of the cost of the system that represents a qualifying asset is the amount of accumulated expenditures in excess of the fraction specified in paragraph 7 of the total estimated cost of the system at the end of the prematurity period.

[7]Such costs are subscriber-related costs that are expensed in accordance with paragraph 6(b).

[8]Refer to paragraph 17 for a description of *drop* in the definition of *cable television plant.*

Recoverability

14. Capitalized plant and intangible assets shall be evaluated periodically to determine whether the costs are recoverable (through operations or sale of the system). If recoverability is doubtful, capitalized costs shall be written down to recoverable values. Capitalization of costs shall not cease when the total cost reaches an amount that is not fully recoverable. Capitalization of costs shall continue, and the provision required to reduce capitalized costs to recoverable value shall be increased.

Amendment to Statement No. 32

15. The reference to AICPA Statement of Position 79-2, *Accounting by Cable Television Companies,* is deleted from Appendix A of Statement 32.

Effective Date and Transition

16. The provisions of this Statement shall be effective for fiscal years beginning after December 15, 1981. Earlier application is permitted but not required. The provisions of this Statement may be, but are not required to be, applied retroactively for previously issued financial statements. If applied retroactively and if the estimates of subscribers needed to make the calculations required by some provisions of this Statement are not readily available, actual historical subscriber data may be used instead.

The provisions of this Statement need not be applied to immaterial items.

This Statement was adopted by the unanimous vote of the seven members of the Financial Accounting Standards Board:

Donald J. Kirk, *Chairman*
Frank E. Block
John W. March
Robert A. Morgan
David Mosso
Robert T. Sprouse
Ralph E. Walters

Appendix A

GLOSSARY

17. This appendix defines certain terms that are used in this Statement.

Cable Television Plant

The cable television plant required to render service to the subscriber includes the following equipment:

a. *Head-end*—This includes the equipment used to receive signals of distant television or radio stations, whether directly from the transmitter or from a microwave relay system. It also includes the studio facilities required for operator-originated programming, if any.

b. *Cable*—This consists of cable and amplifiers (which maintain the quality of the signal) covering the subscriber area, either on utility poles or underground.

c. *Drops*—These consist of the hardware that provides access to the main cable, the short length of cable that brings the signal from the main cable to the subscriber's television set, and other associated hardware, which may include a trap to block particular channels.

d. *Converters and descramblers*—These devices are attached to the subscriber's television sets when more than 12 channels are provided or when special services are provided, such as "pay cable" or 2-way communication.

Direct Selling Costs

Direct selling costs include commissions, the portion of a salesperson's compensation other than commissions for obtaining new subscribers, local advertising targeted for acquisition of new subscribers, and costs of processing documents related to new subscribers acquired. Direct selling costs do not include supervisory and administrative expenses or indirect expenses, such as rent and costs of facilities.

Prematurity Period

During the prematurity period, the cable television system is partially under construction and partially in service. The prematurity period begins with the first earned subscriber revenue. Its end will vary with circumstances of the system but will be determined based on plans for completion of the first major construction period[9] or achievement of a specified predeter-

[9]The construction period of a cable television system varies with the size of the franchise area, density of population, and difficulty of physical construction. The construction period is not completed until the head-end, main cable, and distribution cables are installed, and includes a reasonable time to provide for installation of subscriber drops and related hardware. During the construction period, many system operators complete installation of drops and begin to provide service to some subscribers in some parts of the system while construction continues. Providing the signal for the first time is referred to as "energizing" the system.

mined subscriber level at which no additional investment will be required for other than cable television plant. The length of the prematurity period varies with the franchise development and construction plans. Such plans may consist of:

a. Small franchise that is characterized by the absence of free television signal and a short construction period. The entire system is "energized" at one time near the end of the construction period.
b. Medium-size franchise that is characterized by some direct competition from free television and by a more extensive geographical franchise area lending itself to incremental construction. Some parts of the system are "energized" as construction progresses.
c. Large metropolitan franchise that is characterized by heavy direct competition from free television and fringe area signal inadequacy, high cost, and difficult construction. Many parts of the system are "energized" as construction progresses.

Except in the smallest systems, programming is usually delivered to portions of the system and some revenues are obtained before construction of the entire system is complete. Thus, virtually every cable television system experiences a prematurity period during which it is receiving some revenue while continuing to incur substantial costs related to the establishment of the total system.

Subscriber-Related Costs
These are costs incurred to obtain and retain subscribers to the cable television system and include costs of billing and collection, bad debts, and mailings; repairs and maintenance of taps and connections; franchise fees related to revenues or number of subscribers; general and administrative system costs, such as salary of the system manager and office rent; programming costs for additional channels used in the marketing effort or costs related to revenues from, or number of subscribers to, per channel or per program service; and direct selling costs.

Appendix B

BACKGROUND INFORMATION AND SUMMARY OF CONSIDERATION OF COMMENTS ON EXPOSURE DRAFT

18. This Statement extracts the specialized accounting and reporting principles and practices from SOP 79-2 and codifies them as FASB standards without significant change. Board members have assented to the issuance of this Statement on the basis that it is an appropriate extraction of those existing specialized principles and practices and that a comprehensive reconsideration of those principles and practices was not contemplated in undertaking this FASB project. Some of the background material, discussion of accounting alternatives, and general accounting guidance have not been carried forward from the SOP. The Board's conceptual framework project on accounting recognition criteria will address revenue recognition issues that may pertain to those addressed in this Statement. A Statement of Financial Accounting Concepts resulting from that project in due course will serve as a basis for evaluating existing standards and practices. Accordingly, the Board may wish to evaluate the standards in this Statement when its conceptual framework project is completed.

19. SOP 79-2 was developed to clarify and standardize the diverse accounting practices being followed in the cable television industry, particularly the practices relating to accounting for costs during the prematurity period while the cable television system is partially under construction and partially in service. Before 1979, cable television companies differed as to the types of costs capitalized during the prematurity period and used different criteria to determine the date at which capitalization of some costs ceases and amortization of those costs begins. The SOP specified that all direct construction costs should be capitalized and that costs attributable to current operations and their administration should be charged to expense. For certain costs that relate to the cable television system and that benefit both current and future operations, the SOP specified that a proportion of such costs should be charged to current operations and the remainder should be capitalized.

20. An Exposure Draft of a proposed Statement, *Financial Accounting and Reporting by Cable Television Companies,* was issued June 12, 1981. The Board received 23 comment letters in response to the Exposure Draft. Certain of the comments received and the Board's consideration of them are discussed in this appendix.

21. The transition provisions in the Exposure Draft called for retroactive restatement except for companies that do not expect to have systems in the prematurity period in the future. These companies were permitted to continue their previous method of accounting for already mature systems. Several respondents from the cable television industry suggested that the transition provisions be modified to allow prospective application because retroactive application would require greater accounting effort than the resulting informational benefits. They believe that many cable television companies were

expensing some costs that SOP 79-2 recommended be capitalized. They recommended that prospective application be permitted because of the additional administrative burden that retroactive application would entail. The Board has considered these comments and the fact that major cable television companies have complied with SOP 79-2 and concluded that prospective application should be permitted.

22. Some respondents stated that paragraph 8(a) of the Exposure Draft implied that all interest cost incurred during the prematurity period should be capitalized, even though a portion of the cable television system is in use. The Board believes that paragraph 18 of Statement 34 prohibits capitalization of interest cost on the portion of the cable television system that is substantially complete and ready for its intended use. Accordingly, this Statement clarifies that all interest cost incurred during the prematurity period is not necessarily eligible to be capitalized.

23. Some respondents requested that guidance be included regarding accounting for costs of franchise applications. They indicated that practice varies with respect to the accounting for such costs and that additional guidance would enhance uniformity in practice. The Board has included such guidance to clarify the accounting for costs of franchise applications.

24. Some respondents suggested that the definition of direct selling costs be clarified regarding the circumstances under which advertising may be included. The Board believes that the intent of SOP 79-2 was to limit such costs to those pertaining to direct efforts to obtain new subscribers. Accordingly, the definition has been clarified to indicate that local advertising targeted for acquisition of new subscribers is a direct selling cost.

25. Several respondents suggested various substantive changes to the Exposure Draft (such as eliminating certain of the choices for the numerator of the capitalization fraction, reconsideration of provisions for deferral of hookup revenue and expensing of direct selling costs, changing the amortization period for costs capitalized during the prematurity period, and including certain general and administrative costs with other costs that are deferred during the prematurity period). Adoption of those suggestions would have required a reconsideration of some of the provisions of SOP 79-2. Such a reconsideration is not contemplated in the extraction project unless a proposed change meets one of the three criteria for change included in the "Notice for Recipients of This Exposure Draft" or is broadly supported. None of the proposed changes met the criteria for change and none was broadly supported. Accordingly, the Board did not adopt those suggestions.

Statement of Financial Accounting Standards No. 52
Foreign Currency Translation

STATUS

Issued: December 1981

Effective Date: For fiscal years beginning on or after December 15, 1982

Affects: Amends ARB 43, Chapter 12, paragraph 5
Supersedes ARB 43, Chapter 12, paragraphs 7 and 10 through 22
Supersedes APB 6, paragraph 18
Amends APB 22, paragraph 13
Supersedes FAS 1
Supersedes FAS 8
Supersedes FAS 20
Supersedes FIN 15
Supersedes FIN 17

Affected by: No other pronouncements

SUMMARY

Application of this Statement will affect financial reporting of most companies operating in foreign countries. The differing operating and economic characteristics of varied types of foreign operations will be distinguished in accounting for them. Adjustments for currency exchange rate changes are excluded from net income for those fluctuations that do not impact cash flows and are included for those that do. The requirements reflect these general conclusions:

- The economic effects of an exchange rate change on an operation that is relatively self-contained and integrated within a foreign country relate to the net investment in that operation. Translation adjustments that arise from consolidating that foreign operation do not impact cash flows and are not included in net income.
- The economic effects of an exchange rate change on a foreign operation that is an extension of the parent's domestic operations relate to individual assets and liabilities and impact the parent's cash flows directly. Accordingly, the exchange gains and losses in such an operation are included in net income.
- Contracts, transactions, or balances that are, in fact, effective hedges of foreign exchange risk will be accounted for as hedges without regard to their form.

More specifically, this Statement replaces FASB Statement No. 8, *Accounting for the Translation of Foreign Currency Transactions and Foreign Currency Financial Statements,* and revises the existing accounting and reporting requirements for translation of foreign currency transactions and foreign currency financial statements. It presents standards for foreign currency translation that are designed to (1) provide information that is generally compatible with the expected economic effects of a rate change on an enterprise's cash flows and equity and (2) reflect in consolidated statements the financial results and relationships as measured in the primary currency in which each entity conducts its business (referred to as its "functional currency").

An entity's functional currency is the currency of the primary economic environment in which that entity operates. The functional currency can be the dollar or a foreign currency depending on the facts. Normally, it will be the currency of the economic environment in which cash is generated and expended by the entity. An entity can be any form of operation, including a subsidiary, division, branch, or joint venture. The Statement provides guidance for this key determination in which management's judgment is essential in assessing the facts.

A currency in a highly inflationary environment (3-year inflation rate of approximately 100 percent or more) is not considered stable enough to serve as a functional currency and the more stable currency of the reporting parent is to be used instead.

The functional currency translation approach adopted in this statement encompasses:

a. Identifying the functional currency of the entity's economic environment
b. Measuring all elements of the financial statements in the functional currency
c. Using the current exchange rate for translation from the functional currency to the reporting currency, if they are different
d. Distinguishing the economic impact of changes in exchange rates on a net investment from the impact of such changes on individual assets and liabilities that are receivable or payable in currencies other than the functional currency

Translation adjustments are an inherent result of the process of translating a foreign entity's financial statements from the functional currency to U.S. dollars. Translation adjustments are *not* included in determining net income for the period but are disclosed and accumulated in a separate component of consolidated equity until sale or until complete or substantially complete liquidation of the net investment in the foreign entity takes place.

Transaction gains and losses are a result of the effect of exchange rate changes on transactions denominated in currencies other than the functional currency (for example, a U.S. company may borrow Swiss francs or a French subsidiary may have a receivable denominated in kroner from a Danish customer). Gains and losses on those foreign currency transactions are generally included in determining net income for the period in which exchange rates change unless the transaction hedges a foreign currency commitment or a net investment in a foreign entity. Intercompany transactions of a long-term investment nature are considered part of a parent's net investment and hence do not give rise to gains or losses.

Statement of Financial Accounting Standards No. 52
Foreign Currency Translation

CONTENTS

INTRODUCTION

1. FASB Statement No. 8, *Accounting for the Translation of Foreign Currency Transactions and Foreign Currency Financial Statements,* was issued in October 1975 and was effective for fiscal years that began on or after January 1, 1976. In May 1978, the Board issued an invitation for public comment on Statements 1-12, each of which had been in effect for at least two years. **Foreign currency translation*** was the subject of most of the comments received. In January 1979, the Board added to its agenda a project to reconsider Statement 8. This Statement is the result of that project.

2. This Statement establishes revised standards of financial accounting and reporting for **foreign currency transactions** in financial statements of a **reporting enterprise** (hereinafter, **enterprise**). It also revises the standards for translating foreign currency financial statements (hereinafter, **foreign currency statements**) that are incorporated in the financial statements of an enterprise by consolidation, combination, or the equity method of accounting. **Translation** of financial statements from one currency to another for purposes other than consolidation, combination, or the equity method is beyond the scope of this Statement. For example, this Statement does not cover translation of the financial statements of an enterprise from its **reporting currency** into another currency for the convenience of readers accustomed to that other currency.

3. This Statement supersedes FASB Statement No. 8, *Accounting for the Translation of Foreign Currency Transactions and Foreign Currency Financial Statements,*[1] FASB Statement No. 20, *Accounting for Forward Exchange Contracts,* FASB Interpretation No. 15, *Translation of Unamortized Policy Acquisition Costs by a Stock Life Insurance Company,* and FASB Interpretation No. 17, *Applying the Lower of Cost or Market Rule in Translated Financial Statements.*

*Terms defined in the glossary (Appendix E) are in **boldface type** the first time they appear in this Statement.

[1]The following pronouncements, which were superseded or amended by Statement 8, are also superseded or amended by this Statement: paragraphs 7 and 10-22 of Chapter 12, "Foreign Operations and Foreign Exchange," of ARB No. 43; paragraph 18 of APB Opinion No. 6, *Status of Accounting Research Bulletins;* and FASB Statement No. 1, *Disclosure of Foreign Currency Translation Information.* The last sentence of paragraph 5 of ARB 43, Chapter 12, is amended to delete "and they should be reserved against to the extent that their realization in dollars appears to be doubtful," and paragraph 13 of APB Opinion No. 22, *Disclosure of Accounting Policies,* is amended to delete "translation of foreign currencies" as an example of disclosure "commonly required with respect to accounting policies."

STANDARDS OF FINANCIAL ACCOUNTING AND REPORTING

Objectives of Translation

4. Financial statements are intended to present information in financial terms about the performance, financial position, and cash flows of an enterprise. For this purpose, the financial statements of separate **entities** within an enterprise, which may exist and operate in different economic and currency environments, are consolidated and presented as though they were the financial statements of a single enterprise. Because it is not possible to combine, add, or subtract measurements expressed in different currencies, it is necessary to translate into a single reporting currency[2] those assets, liabilities, revenues, expenses, gains, and losses that are measured or denominated in a **foreign currency.**[3] However, the unity presented by such translation does not alter the underlying significance of the results and relationships of the constituent parts of the enterprise. It is only through the effective operation of its constituent parts that the enterprise as a whole is able to achieve its purpose. Accordingly, the translation of the financial statements of each component entity of an enterprise should accomplish the following objectives:

a. Provide information that is generally compatible with the expected economic effects of a rate change on an enterprise's cash flows and equity
b. Reflect in consolidated statements the financial results and relationships of the individual consolidated entities as measured in their **functional currencies** in conformity with U.S. generally accepted accounting principles

The Functional Currency

5. The assets, liabilities, and operations of a **foreign entity** shall be measured using the functional currency of that entity. An entity's functional currency is the currency of the primary economic environment in which the entity operates; normally, that is the currency of the environment in which an entity primarily generates and expends cash. Appendix A provides guidance for determination of the functional currency. The economic factors cited in Appendix A, and possibly others, should be considered both individually and collectively when determining the functional currency.

6. For an entity with operations that are relatively self-contained and integrated within a particular country, the functional currency generally would be the currency of that country. However, a foreign entity's functional currency might not be the currency of the country in which the entity is located. For example, the parent's currency generally would be the functional currency for foreign operations that are a direct and integral component or extension of the parent company's operations.

7. An entity might have more than one distinct and separable operation, such as a division or branch, in which case each operation may be considered a separate entity. If those operations are conducted in different economic environments, they might have different functional currencies.

8. The functional currency (or currencies) of an entity is basically a matter of fact, but in some instances the observable facts will not clearly identify a single functional currency. For example, if a foreign entity conducts significant amounts of business in two or more currencies, the functional currency might not be clearly identifiable. In those instances, the economic facts and circumstances pertaining to a particular foreign operation shall be assessed in relation to the Board's stated objectives for foreign currency translation (paragraph 4). Management's judgment will be required to determine the functional currency in which financial results and relationships are measured with the greatest degree of relevance and reliability.

9. Once the functional currency for a foreign entity is determined, that determination shall be used consistently unless significant changes in economic facts and circumstances indicate clearly that the functional currency has changed. Previously issued financial statements shall not be restated for any change in the functional currency.

---

[2]For convenience, this Statement assumes that the enterprise uses the U.S. dollar (dollar) as its reporting currency. However, a currency other than the dollar may be the reporting currency in financial statements that are prepared in conformity with U.S. generally accepted accounting principles. For example, a foreign enterprise may report in its **local currency** in conformity with U.S. generally accepted accounting principles. If so, the requirements of this Statement apply.

[3]To measure in foreign currency is to quantify an **attribute** of an item in a unit of currency other than the reporting currency. Assets and liabilities are denominated in a foreign currency if their amounts are fixed in terms of that foreign currency regardless of exchange rate changes. An asset or liability may be both measured and denominated in one currency, or it may be measured in one currency and denominated in another. To illustrate: Two foreign branches of a U.S. company, one Swiss and one German, purchase identical assets on credit from a Swiss vendor at identical prices stated in Swiss francs. The German branch measures the cost (an attribute) of that asset in German marks. Although the corresponding liability is also measured in marks, it remains denominated in Swiss francs since the liability must be settled in a specified number of Swiss francs. The Swiss branch measures the asset and liability in Swiss francs. Its liability is both measured and denominated in Swiss francs. Although assets and liabilities can be measured in various currencies, rights to receive or obligations to pay fixed amounts of a currency are, by definition, denominated in that currency.

10. If an entity's books of record are not maintained in its functional currency, remeasurement into the functional currency is required. That remeasurement is required before translation into the reporting currency. If a foreign entity's functional currency is the reporting currency, remeasurement into the reporting currency obviates translation. The remeasurement process is intended to produce the same result as if the entity's books of record had been maintained in the functional currency. The remeasurement of and subsequent accounting for transactions denominated in a currency other than the functional currency shall be in accordance with the requirements of this Statement (paragraphs 15 and 16). Appendix B provides guidance for remeasurement into the functional currency.

The Functional Currency in Highly Inflationary Economies

11. The financial statements of a foreign entity in a highly inflationary economy shall be remeasured as if the functional currency were the reporting currency. Accordingly, the financial statements of those entities shall be remeasured into the reporting currency according to the requirements of paragraph 10. For the purposes of this requirement, a highly inflationary economy is one that has cumulative inflation of approximately 100 percent or more over a 3-year period.

Translation of Foreign Currency Statements

12. All elements of financial statements shall be translated by using a **current exchange rate.** For assets and liabilities, the exchange rate at the balance sheet date shall be used. For revenues, expenses, gains, and losses, the exchange rate at the dates on which those elements are recognized shall be used. Because translation at the exchange rates at the dates the numerous revenues, expenses, gains, and losses are recognized is generally impractical, an appropriately weighted average exchange rate for the period may be used to translate those elements.

13. If an entity's functional currency is a foreign currency, **translation adjustments** result from the process of translating that entity's financial statements into the reporting currency. Translation adjustments shall not be included in determining net income but shall be reported separately and accumulated in a separate component of equity.

14. Upon sale or upon complete or substantially complete liquidation of an investment in a foreign entity, the amount attributable to that entity and accumulated in the translation adjustment component of equity shall be removed from the separate component of equity and shall be reported as part of the gain or loss on sale or liquidation of the investment for the period during which the sale or liquidation occurs.

Foreign Currency Transactions

15. Foreign currency transactions are transactions denominated in a currency other than the entity's functional currency. Foreign currency transactions may produce receivables or payables that are fixed in terms of the amount of foreign currency that will be received or paid. A change in exchange rates between the functional currency and the currency in which a transaction is denominated increases or decreases the expected amount of functional currency cash flows upon settlement of the transaction. That increase or decrease in expected functional currency cash flows is a foreign currency **transaction gain or loss** that generally shall be included in determining net income for the period in which the exchange rate changes. Likewise, a transaction gain or loss (measured from the **transaction date** or the most recent intervening balance sheet date, whichever is later) realized upon settlement of a foreign currency transaction generally shall be included in determining net income for the period in which the transaction is settled. The exceptions to this requirement for inclusion in net income of transaction gains and losses are set forth in paragraphs 20 and 21 and pertain to certain intercompany transactions and to transactions that are designated as, and effective as, economic hedges of net investments and foreign currency commitments.

16. For other than **forward exchange contracts** (paragraphs 17-19), the following shall apply to all foreign currency transactions of an enterprise and its investees:

a. At the date the transaction is recognized, each asset, liability, revenue, expense, gain, or loss arising from the transaction shall be measured and recorded in the functional currency of the recording entity by use of the exchange rate in effect at that date (paragraphs 26-28).
b. At each balance sheet date, recorded balances that are denominated in a currency other than the functional currency of the recording entity shall be adjusted to reflect the current exchange rate.

Forward Exchange Contracts

17. A forward exchange contract (forward contract) is an agreement to exchange different currencies at a specified future date and at a specified rate (the **forward rate**). A forward contract is a foreign currency transaction. A gain or loss on a forward contract that does not meet the conditions described in paragraph 20 or 21 shall be included in determin-

ing net income in accordance with the requirements for other foreign currency transactions (paragraph 15). Agreements that are, in substance, essentially the same as forward contracts, for example, **currency swaps,** shall be accounted for in a manner similar to the accounting for forward contracts.

18. A gain or loss (whether or not deferred) on a forward contract, except a forward contract of the type discussed in paragraph 19, shall be computed by multiplying the foreign currency amount of the forward contract by the difference between the **spot rate** at the balance sheet date and the spot rate at the date of inception of the forward contract (or the spot rate last used to measure a gain or loss on that contract for an earlier period). The **discount or premium on a forward contract** (that is, the foreign currency amount of the contract multiplied by the difference between the contracted forward rate and the spot rate at the date of inception of the contract) shall be accounted for separately from the gain or loss on the contract and shall be included in determining net income over the life of the forward contract. However, if a gain or loss is deferred under paragraph 21, the forward contract's discount or premium that relates to the commitment period may be included in the measurement of the basis of the related foreign currency transaction when recorded. If a gain or loss is accounted for as a hedge of a net investment under paragraph 20, the forward contract's discount or premium may be included with translation adjustments in the separate component of equity.

19. A gain or loss on a speculative forward contract (that is, a contract that does not hedge an exposure) shall be computed by multiplying the foreign currency amount of the forward contract by the difference between the forward rate available for the remaining maturity of the contract and the contracted forward rate (or the forward rate last used to measure a gain or loss on that contract for an earlier period). No separate accounting recognition is given to the discount or premium on a speculative forward contract.

Transaction Gains and Losses to Be Excluded from Determination of Net Income

20. Gains and losses on the following foreign currency transactions shall not be included in determining net income but shall be reported in the same manner as translation adjustments (paragraph 13):

a. Foreign currency transactions that are designated as, and are effective as, economic hedges of a net investment in a foreign entity, commencing as of the designation date
b. Intercompany foreign currency transactions that are of a long-term-investment nature (that is, settlement is not planned or anticipated in the foreseeable future), when the entities to the transaction are consolidated, combined, or accounted for by the equity method in the reporting enterprise's financial statements

21. A gain or loss on a forward contract or other foreign currency transaction that is intended to hedge an identifiable foreign currency commitment (for example, an agreement to purchase or sell equipment) shall be deferred and included in the measurement of the related foreign currency transaction (for example, the purchase or the sale of the equipment). Losses shall not be deferred, however, if it is estimated that deferral would lead to recognizing losses in later periods. A foreign currency transaction shall be considered a hedge of an identifiable foreign currency commitment provided both of the following conditions are met:

a. The foreign currency transaction is designated as, and is effective as, a hedge of a foreign currency commitment.
b. The foreign currency commitment is firm.

The required accounting shall commence as of the designation date. The portion of a hedging transaction that shall be accounted for pursuant to this paragraph is limited to the amount of the related commitment. If a hedging transaction that meets conditions (a) and (b) above exceeds the amount of the related commitment, the gain or loss pertaining to the portion of the hedging transaction in excess of the commitment shall be deferred to the extent that the transaction is intended to provide a hedge on an after-tax basis. A gain or loss so deferred shall be included as an offset to the related tax effects in the period in which such tax effects are recognized; consequently, it shall not be included in the aggregate transaction gain or loss disclosure required by paragraph 30. A gain or loss pertaining to the portion of a hedging transaction in excess of the amount that provides a hedge on an after-tax basis shall not be deferred. Likewise, a gain or loss pertaining to a period after the transaction date of the related commitment shall not be deferred. If a foreign currency transaction previously considered a hedge of a foreign currency commitment is terminated before the transaction date of the related commitment, any deferred gain or loss shall continue to be deferred and accounted for in accordance with the requirements of this paragraph.

Income Tax Consequences of Rate Changes

22. Interperiod tax allocation is required in accordance with APB Opinion No. 11, *Accounting for Income Taxes,* if taxable exchange gains or tax-deductible exchange losses resulting from an entity's foreign currency transactions are included in net

income in a different period for financial statement purposes from that for tax purposes.

23. Translation adjustments shall be accounted for in the same way as timing differences under the provisions of APB Opinions 11, 23, and 24. APB Opinion No. 23, *Accounting for Income Taxes—Special Areas,* provides that deferred taxes shall not be provided for unremitted earnings of a subsidiary in certain instances; in those instances, deferred taxes shall not be provided on translation adjustments.

24. Opinion 11 requires income tax expense to be allocated among income before extraordinary items, extraordinary items, adjustments of prior periods (or of the opening balance of retained earnings), and direct entries to other equity accounts. Some transaction gains and losses and all translation adjustments are reported in a separate component of equity. Any income taxes related to those transaction gains and losses and translation adjustments shall be allocated to that separate component of equity.

Elimination of Intercompany Profits

25. The elimination of intercompany profits that are attributable to sales or other transfers between entities that are consolidated, combined, or accounted for by the equity method in the enterprise's financial statements shall be based on the exchange rates at the dates of the sales or transfers. The use of reasonable approximations or averages is permitted.

Exchange Rates

26. The exchange rate is the ratio between a unit of one currency and the amount of another currency for which that unit can be exchanged at a particular time. If exchangeability between two currencies is temporarily lacking at the transaction date or balance sheet date, the first subsequent rate at which exchanges could be made shall be used for purposes of this Statement. If the lack of exchangeability is other than temporary, the propriety of consolidating, combining, or accounting for the foreign operation by the equity method in the financial statements of the enterprise shall be carefully considered (ARB 43, Chapter 12, paragraph 8).

27. The exchange rates to be used for translation of foreign currency transactions and foreign currency statements are as follows:

a. *Foreign Currency Transactions*—The applicable rate at which a particular transaction could be settled at the transaction date shall be used to translate and record the transaction. At a subsequent balance sheet date, the current rate is that rate at which the related receivable or payable could be settled at that date.
b. *Foreign Currency Statements*—In the absence of unusual circumstances, the rate applicable to **conversion** of a currency for purposes of dividend remittances shall be used to translate foreign currency statements.[4]

28. If a foreign entity whose balance sheet date differs from that of the enterprise is consolidated or combined with or accounted for by the equity method in the financial statements of the enterprise, the current rate is the rate in effect at the foreign entity's balance sheet date for purposes of applying the requirements of this Statement to that foreign entity.

Use of Averages or Other Methods of Approximation

29. Literal application of the standards in this Statement might require a degree of detail in record keeping and computations that could be burdensome as well as unnecessary to produce reasonable approximations of the results. Accordingly, it is acceptable to use averages or other methods of approximation. For example, the propriety of using average rates to translate revenue and expense amounts is noted in paragraph 12. Likewise, the use of other time- and effort-saving methods to approximate the results of detailed calculations is permitted.

Disclosure

30. The aggregate transaction gain or loss included in determining net income for the period shall be disclosed in the financial statements or notes thereto. For that disclosure, gains and losses on forward contracts determined in conformity with the requirements of paragraphs 18 and 19 shall be considered transaction gains or losses. Certain enterprises, primarily banks, are dealers in foreign exchange. Although certain gains or losses from dealer transactions may fit the definition of transaction gains or losses in this Statement, they may be disclosed as dealer gains or losses rather than as transaction gains or losses.

31. An analysis of the changes during the period in the separate component of equity for cumulative translation adjustments shall be provided in a sepa-

[4]If unsettled intercompany transactions are subject to and translated using preference or penalty rates, translation of foreign currency statements at the rate applicable to dividend remittances may cause a difference between intercompany receivables and payables. Until that difference is eliminated by settlement of the intercompany transaction, the difference shall be treated as a receivable or payable in the enterprise's financial statements.

rate financial statement, in notes to the financial statements, or as part of a statement of changes in equity. At a minimum, the analysis shall disclose:

a. Beginning and ending amount of cumulative translation adjustments
b. The aggregate adjustment for the period resulting from translation adjustments (paragraph 13) and gains and losses from certain hedges and intercompany balances (paragraph 20)
c. The amount of income taxes for the period allocated to translation adjustments (paragraph 24)
d. The amounts transferred from cumulative translation adjustments and included in determining net income for the period as a result of the sale or complete or substantially complete liquidation of an investment in a foreign entity (paragraph 14)

32. An enterprise's financial statements shall not be adjusted for a rate change that occurs after the date of the enterprise's financial statements or after the date of the foreign currency statements of a foreign entity if they are consolidated, combined, or accounted for by the equity method in the financial statements of the enterprise. However, disclosure of the rate change and its effects on unsettled balances pertaining to foreign currency transactions, if significant, may be necessary.

Effective Date and Transition

33. This Statement shall be effective for fiscal years beginning on or after December 15, 1982, although earlier application is encouraged. The initial application of this Statement shall be as of the beginning of an enterprise's fiscal year. Financial statements for fiscal years before the effective date, and financial summaries or other data derived therefrom, may be restated to conform to the provisions of paragraphs 5-29 of this Statement. In the year that this Statement is first applied, the financial statements shall disclose the nature of any restatement and its effect on income before extraordinary items, net income, and related per share amounts for each fiscal year restated. If the prior year is not restated, disclosure of income before extraordinary items and net income for the prior year computed on a pro forma basis is permitted.

34. The effect of translating all of a foreign entity's assets and liabilities from a foreign functional currency into the reporting currency at the current exchange rate as of the beginning of the year for which this Statement is first applied shall be reported as the opening balance of the cumulative translation adjustments component of equity. The effect of remeasuring a foreign entity's deferred income taxes and life insurance policy acquisition costs at the current exchange rate (paragraph 54) as of the beginning of the year for which this Statement is first applied shall be reported as an adjustment of the opening balance of retained earnings.

35. Amounts deferred on forward contracts that (a) under Statement 8 were accounted for as hedges of identifiable foreign currency commitments to receive proceeds from the use or sale of nonmonetary assets translated at historical rates, and (b) are canceled at the time this Statement is first applied, shall be included in the opening balance of the cumulative translation adjustments component of equity up to the amount of the offsetting adjustment attributable to those nonmonetary assets.

36. Financial statements for periods beginning on or after the effective date of this Statement shall include the disclosures specified by paragraphs 30-32. To the extent practicable, those disclosures shall also be included in financial statements for earlier periods that have been restated pursuant to paragraph 33.

37. Financial statements of enterprises that first adopt this standard for fiscal years ending on or before March 31, 1982 shall disclose the effect of adopting the new standard on income before extraordinary items, net income, and related per share amounts for the year of the change. Those disclosures are not required for financial statements of enterprises that first adopt this standard for subsequent fiscal years.

38. The Board expects to issue an Exposure Draft proposing an amendment of FASB Statement No. 33, *Financial Reporting and Changing Prices,* to be consistent with the functional currency approach to foreign currency translation. Prior to issuance of a final amendment of Statement 33, enterprises that adopt this Statement and that are subject to the requirements of Statement 33 shall have either of the following options:

a. They may prepare the supplementary information based on this Statement and on the proposed amendment of Statement 33.
b. They may prepare the supplementary information based on the application of Statement 8 and on the provisions of existing Statement 33. (Under this option, historical cost information based on the application of Statement 8 shall be presented in the supplementary information for comparison with the constant dollar and current cost information.)

Enterprises that would become subject to the requirements of Statement 33 as a result of adopting this Statement are exempt from the requirements of Statement 33 until the effective date of this Statement.

The provisions of this Statement need not be applied to immaterial items.

This Statement was adopted by the affirmative votes of four members of the Financial Accounting Standards Board. Messrs. Block, Kirk, and Morgan dissented.

Messrs. Block, Kirk, and Morgan dissent to the issuance of this Statement. They start from a premise different from that underlying this Statement. They believe that more meaningful consolidated results are attained by measuring costs, cost recovery, and exchange risk from a dollar perspective rather than from multiple functional currency perspectives. Accordingly, the dissenters do not believe that this Statement improves financial reporting. In their opinion, improved financial reporting would have resulted from an approach that:

a. Adopted objectives of translation that retained the concept of a single consolidated entity and a single **unit of measure** (that is, all elements of U.S. consolidated financial statements would be measured in dollars rather than multiple functional currencies)
b. Avoided creating direct entries to equity
c. Essentially retained Statement 8's translation method, with an exception being translation of locally sourced inventory at the current rate
d. Recognized all gains and losses in net income (that is, no separate and different accounting for transaction gains or losses and translation adjustments), but allowed for a separate and distinct presentation of those gains and losses within the income statement
e. Recognized additional contractual arrangements (for example, operating leases and take-or-pay contracts) that effectively hedged an exposed net monetary liability position

The dissenters recognize that such an approach would not satisfy all of the critics of Statement 8, but they believe it would have avoided the more far-reaching implications of the functional currency theory. They acknowledge that translating certain inventories at current rates departs from historical cost in dollars. However, they would accept that departure on pragmatic grounds as part of a solution to an exceedingly difficult problem.

As further discussed in subsequent paragraphs, the dissenting Board members do not support this Statement because in their opinion it:

a. Builds on two incompatible premises and, as a result, produces anomalies and a significant but unwarranted reporting distinction between transaction gains and losses and translation adjustments
b. Adopts objectives and methods that are at variance with fundamental concepts that underlie present financial reporting
c. Incorrectly assumes that an aggregation of the results of foreign operations measured in functional currencies and *expressed* in dollars, rather than consolidated results *measured* in dollars, assists U.S. investors and creditors in assessing future cash flows to them
d. Will not result in similar accounting for similar circumstances

Incompatibility of Underlying Premises

The standards for translating foreign currency financial statements set forth in this Statement stem from two premises that are incompatible with each other. The first premise is that it is a parent company's net investment in a foreign operation that is subject to exchange rate risk rather than the foreign operation's individual assets and liabilities. The second premise is that translation should retain the relationships in foreign currency financial statements as measured by the functional currency. The premise of a parent company's exposed net investment reflects a dollar perspective of exchange rate risk, and that calls for a dollar measure of the effects of exchange rate changes. The premise of retaining the relationships of measurements in functional currency financial statements calls for a functional currency measure of the effects of exchange rate changes.

The dissenting Board members note that although the translation process can retain certain intraperiod relationships reported in functional currency financial statements, it cannot retain interperiod functional currency relationships when exchange rates change. Further, when an exchange rate changes between the dollar and a foreign currency, the value of any holdings of that currency changes and, from a dollar perspective, the resulting gain or loss is either real, or unreal, in its entirety. However, to implement the functional currency perspective, the standards result in a division of that gain or loss into two components. One is considered in measuring consolidated net income and the other is considered a translation adjustment. Thus, the standards require a transaction gain in income on a foreign operation's holdings of a third currency when that currency strengthens in relation to the functional currency, even if the third currency has weakened in terms of dollars. That gain will be reported in consolidated net income despite the fact that it does not exist in dollar terms and can never provide increased dollar cash flows to U.S. investors and creditors. The standards inherently recognize that fact by requiring a compensating debit translation adjustment. (Examples that further illustrate these concerns are contained in paragraphs 111-113 of the August 28, 1980 Exposure Draft, *Foreign Currency Translation.*)

The dissenters believe that the need for a translation adjustment that adjusts consolidated equity to the same amount as would have resulted had all foreign currency transactions of foreign operations been measured in dollars demonstrates the incompatibility of the two underlying premises. They believe that incompatibility is further demonstrated by the differing views of the nature of translation adjustments described in paragraphs 113 and 114. In the dissenters' opinion, translation adjustments are, from a dollar perspective, gains and losses as defined in FASB Concepts Statement No. 3, *Elements of Financial Statements of Business Enterprises,* which should be reported in net income when exchange rates change. The dissenters believe that from a functional currency perspective, translation adjustments fail to meet any definition of an element of financial statements because they do not exist in terms of functional currency cash flows.

Relationship to Preexisting Fundamental Concepts

The dissenters believe the two premises underlying this Statement (discussed above) challenge and reject the dollar perspective that underlies existing theories of historical cost and capital maintenance, inflation accounting, consolidation, and realization. The rejection of the dollar perspective has ramifications far beyond this project and was unnecessary in a translation project.

While not explicitly stated, today's accounting model includes the capital maintenance concept that income of a consolidated U.S. entity exists only after recovery of historical cost measured in dollars. For example, prior to this Statement, the gain on the sale by a foreign operation of an internationally priced inventory item or a marketable security would have been measured by comparing the dollar equivalent sales price with the fixed dollar equivalent historical cost of the item. This Statement changes that. It remeasures the dollar equivalent cost while the item is held (measured by changes in the exchange rate between the foreign currency and the dollar) and treats that remeasurement as a translation adjustment, seldom if ever to be reported in net income. Under this Statement, consolidated net income, although expressed in dollars, does not represent the measure of income after maintaining capital measured in dollars. The dissenters believe that U.S. investors' and creditors' decisions are based on a dollar perspective of capital maintenance. Not only does this Statement change income measurement and capital maintenance concepts in the primary financial statements but it also implies the need to modify the measurement of changes in current costs (sometimes referred to as holding gains or losses) in Statement 33 and, likewise, to change that Statement's requirements for constant dollar accounting to constant functional currency accounting.

This Statement abandons the long-standing principle that consolidated results should be measured from a single perspective rather than multiple perspectives. The dissenters believe (for the reasons set forth in paragraphs 83-95 of Statement 8) that a single perspective is essential for (a) valid addition and subtraction in the measurement of financial position and periodic net income and (b) the understandability and representational faithfulness of consolidated results presented in dollars and described as being prepared on the historical cost basis. The dissenters believe that readers of financial statements are better served by having consolidated financial statements prepared in terms of a common bench mark—a single unit of measure. This means to the dissenters that the translation process is one of remeasurement of the individual items of foreign financial statements (not net investments) into dollars—much in the same way as Statement 33 presently requires a remeasurement of individual items of financial statements (not net investments) from nominal dollar measures into constant dollars.

The Statement introduces a concept of realization (paragraphs 71, 111, 117, and 119) different from any previously applied in consolidated financial statements. It requires the results of foreign operations to be measured in various functional currencies and then translated into dollars and included in consolidated net income. It defers recognizing in net income the effects of exchange rate changes from a dollar perspective on the individual assets and liabilities of those same foreign operations until an indefinite future period that will almost always be beyond the point in time that those individual assets and liabilities have ceased to exist. As a result, the dollar effects of a rate change on current operating revenues are recognized when they occur by reporting in the translated income statement an increased or decreased dollar equivalent for those revenues versus the dollar equivalent of identical revenues generated before the rate change. However, the effects of the same rate change on the uncollected receivables from those previous revenue transactions are not included in net income until liquidation of the foreign operation. By not recognizing in net income the effects of exchange rate changes on existing receivables, this Statement results in sales denominated in a foreign currency being accounted for as if they had been denominated in dollars. That result is a focal point of the criticism made in this Statement (paragraph 75) about Statement 8. However, unlike this Statement, Statement 8 recognized that foreign currency sales are not denominated in dollars and therefore it required that the effects of exchange rate changes on all foreign currency denominated receivables be recognized in net income. To do otherwise places the enterprise in the anomalous position of having recognized the entire effect of the rate change on a current transaction while holding in suspense its effect on a previous transaction until liquidation of the foreign operation.

This Statement accepts the use of the Statement 8 methodology (that is, using the dollar as the functional currency) for some foreign operations (including all operations in highly inflationary economies), but at the same time criticizes that methodology. It asserts that the Statement 8 methodology results in accounting as if all transactions were conducted in the economic environment of the United States and in dollars (paragraphs 74, 75, and 86). The dissenters believe such views were convincingly rebutted in paragraphs 94 and 95 of Statement 8, as follows:

> Some respondents to the Exposure Draft criticized that objective as an attempt to account for local and foreign currency transactions of foreign operations as if they were dollar transactions or, to a few respondents, as if they were dollar transactions in the United States. In the Board's judgment, those criticisms are not valid. Neither the objective nor the procedures to accomplish it change the denomination of a transaction or the environment in which it occurs. The procedures adopted by the Board are consistent with the purpose of consolidated financial statements. The foreign currency transactions of an enterprise and the local and foreign currency transactions of its foreign operations are translated and accounted for as transactions of a single enterprise. The denomination of transactions and the location of assets are not changed; however, the separate corporate identities within the consolidated group are ignored. Translation procedures are merely a means of remeasuring in dollars amounts that are denominated or originally measured in foreign currency. That is, the procedures do *not* attempt to simulate what the cost of a foreign plant would have been had it been located in the United States; instead, they recognize the factors that determined the plant's cost in the foreign location and express that cost in dollars.
>
> If translation procedures were capable of changing the denomination of an asset or liability from foreign currency to dollars, no exchange risk would be present.

Effects on Cash Flow Assessments

The dissenters believe that U.S. investors and creditors should be provided with information about a multinational enterprise's performance measured in dollars because that is the currency in which, ultimately, the enterprise makes cash payments to them. Foreign exchange exposure to a U.S. investor or creditor is the exposure to increased or decreased potential dollar cash flows caused by changes in exchange rates between foreign currencies and the dollar. Changes in exchange rates between two foreign currencies are not relevant, except to the extent that each such foreign currency's exchange rate for the dollar changes.

Supporting the functional currency perspective is the assenters' view (paragraphs 73, 75, 97, and elsewhere) that a translated functional currency income statement better provides U.S. investors and creditors with information necessary in assessing future cash flows than does an income statement whose components have been measured from a dollar perspective. The dissenting view is that a translated functional currency income statement is inappropriate because it can include items that (a) do not exist for the consolidated enterprise (for example, transaction gains on intercompany trade receivables or monetary items denominated in dollars) or (b) are incorrectly measured (for example, a gain on a holding of a third currency that significantly strengthens against the dollar but only moderately strengthens against the functional currency). It can also exclude items that do exist for the consolidated enterprise (for example, a gain on a monetary asset denominated in a foreign operation's functional currency when that currency strengthens against the dollar).

The dissenters see no persuasive reasoning to support the belief that external users want or need to know the amount of transaction gains or losses as measured from the perspective of the manager of the foreign operation (that is, in functional currency), while at the same time wanting a balance sheet that is measured from a dollar perspective—a balance sheet that denies the usefulness of the foreign perspective. (The previously referenced examples in the August 1980 Exposure Draft also further illustrate this concern.)

Similar Accounting for Similar Circumstances

The dissenters believe that the criteria in paragraph 42 for deciding between the Statement 8 translation method and the current rate method are inappropriate (for the reasons set forth in paragraphs 140-151 of Statement 8). They also believe that application of those criteria will not result in similar accounting for similar situations.

Likewise, the absence of effective criteria that would objectively indicate when foreign currency transactions (paragraph 20(a)) and forward exchange contracts (paragraph 21) are hedges creates the possibility that transaction gains or losses that should be reported in net income currently may instead be reported as translation adjustments or deferred as hedges of commitments.

The variety of permissible methods of transition from the existing Statement 8 requirements may also result in similar circumstances being accounted for differently. Mr. Morgan believes the transition paragraphs should have required that the amount necessary to adjust from the Statement 8 basis to the new basis be reported as the opening translation adjustment in equity for the first year in which the new Statement becomes effective. To restate any year prior to the effective date of this Statement may foster an inappropriate conclusion, namely, that those restated results are the results an entity might have experienced had the new Statement been in effect for earlier periods. There is considerable evidence that many enterprises alter their hedging of foreign exchange exposure depending on the accounting standards currently in effect. Thus, restated financial statements for those entities, whether required or done voluntarily, could not accurately reflect what might have happened had this Statement been in effect. Voluntary restatement also diminishes the comparability of financial reporting among companies. In Mr. Morgan's view, the Board should have prohibited restatement as a method of transition to this new Statement.

Members of the Financial Accounting Standards Board:

Donald J. Kirk, *Chairman*
Frank E. Block
John W. March
Robert A. Morgan
David Mosso
Robert T. Sprouse
Ralph E. Walters

Appendix A

DETERMINATION OF THE FUNCTIONAL CURRENCY

39. An entity's functional currency is the currency of the primary economic environment in which the entity operates; normally, that is the currency of the environment in which an entity primarily generates and expends cash. The functional currency of an entity is, in principle, a matter of fact. In some cases, the facts will clearly identify the functional currency; in other cases they will not.

40. It is neither possible nor desirable to provide unequivocal criteria to identify the functional currency of foreign entities under all possible facts and circumstances and still fulfill the objectives of foreign currency translation. Arbitrary rules that might dictate the identification of the functional currency in each case would accomplish a degree of superficial uniformity but, in the process, might diminish the relevance and reliability of the resulting information.

41. The Board has developed, with significant input from its task force and other advisors, the following general guidance on indicators of facts to be considered in identifying the functional currency. In those instances in which the indicators are mixed and the functional currency is not obvious, management's judgment will be required in order to determine the functional currency that most faithfully portrays the economic results of the entity's operations and thereby best achieves the objectives of foreign currency translation set forth in paragraph 4. Management is in the best position to obtain the pertinent facts and weigh their relative importance in determining the functional currency for each operation. It is important to recognize that management's judgment is essential and paramount in this determination, provided only that it is not contradicted by the facts.

42. The salient economic factors set forth below, and possibly others, should be considered both individually and collectively when determining the functional currency.

a. Cash flow indicators
   (1) Foreign Currency—Cash flows related to the foreign entity's individual assets and liabilities are primarily in the foreign currency and do not directly impact the parent company's cash flows.
   (2) Parent's Currency—Cash flows related to the foreign entity's individual assets and liabilities directly impact the parent's cash flows on a current basis and are readily available for remittance to the parent company.
b. Sales price indicators
   (1) Foreign Currency—Sales prices for the foreign entity's products are not primarily responsive on a short-term basis to changes in exchange rates but are determined more by local competition or local government regulation.
   (2) Parent's Currency—Sales prices for the foreign entity's products are primarily responsive on a short-term basis to changes in exchange rates; for example, sales prices are determined more by worldwide competition or by international prices.
c. Sales market indicators
   (1) Foreign Currency—There is an active local sales market for the foreign entity's products, although there also might be significant amounts of exports.
   (2) Parent's Currency—The sales market is mostly in the parent's country or sales contracts are denominated in the parent's currency.

d. Expense indicators
  (1) Foreign Currency—Labor, materials, and other costs for the foreign entity's products or services are primarily local costs, even though there also might be imports from other countries.
  (2) Parent's Currency—Labor, materials, and other costs for the foreign entity's products or services, on a continuing basis, are primarily costs for components obtained from the country in which the parent company is located.

e. Financing indicators
  (1) Foreign Currency—Financing is primarily denominated in foreign currency, and funds generated by the foreign entity's operations are sufficient to service existing and normally expected debt obligations.
  (2) Parent's Currency—Financing is primarily from the parent or other dollar-denominated obligations, or funds generated by the foreign entity's operations are not sufficient to service existing and normally expected debt obligations without the infusion of additional funds from the parent company. Infusion of additional funds from the parent company for expansion is not a factor, provided funds generated by the foreign entity's expanded operations are expected to be sufficient to service that additional financing.

f. Intercompany transactions and arrangements indicators
  (1) Foreign Currency—There is a low volume of intercompany transactions and there is not an extensive interrelationship between the operations of the foreign entity and the parent company. However, the foreign entity's operations may rely on the parent's or affiliates' competitive advantages, such as patents and trademarks.
  (2) Parent's Currency—There is a high volume of intercompany transactions and there is an extensive interrelationship between the operations of the foreign entity and the parent company. Additionally, the parent's currency generally would be the functional currency if the foreign entity is a device or shell corporation for holding investments, obligations, intangible assets, etc., that could readily be carried on the parent's or an affiliate's books.

43. In some instances, a foreign entity might have more than one distinct and separable operation. For example, a foreign entity might have one operation that sells parent-company-produced products and another operation that manufactures and sells foreign-entity-produced products. If those two operations are conducted in different economic environments, those two operations might have different functional currencies. Similarly, a single subsidiary of a financial institution might have relatively self-contained and integrated operations in each of several different countries. In circumstances such as those described above, each operation may be considered to be an entity as that term is used in this Statement; and, based on the facts and circumstances, each operation might have a different functional currency.

44. Foreign investments that are consolidated or accounted for by the equity method are controlled by or subject to significant influence by the parent company. Likewise, the parent's currency is often used for measurements, assessments, evaluations, projections, etc., pertaining to foreign investments as part of the management decision-making process. Such management control, decisions, and resultant actions may reflect, indicate, or create economic facts and circumstances. However, the exercise of significant management control and the use of the parent's currency for decision-making purposes do not determine, per se, that the parent's currency is the functional currency for foreign operations.

45. Once a determination of the functional currency is made, that decision shall be consistently used for each foreign entity unless significant changes in economic facts and circumstances indicate clearly that the functional currency has changed. (APB Opinion No. 20, *Accounting Changes,* paragraph 8, states that "adoption or modification of an accounting principle necessitated by transactions or events that are clearly different in substance from those previously occurring" is not a change in accounting principles.)

46. If the functional currency changes from a foreign currency to the reporting currency, translation adjustments for prior periods should not be removed from equity and the translated amounts for nonmonetary assets at the end of the prior period become the accounting basis for those assets in the period of the change and subsequent periods. If the functional currency changes from the reporting currency to a foreign currency, the adjustment attributable to current-rate translation of nonmonetary assets as of the date of the change should be reported in the cumulative translation adjustments component of equity.

Appendix B

REMEASUREMENT OF THE BOOKS OF RECORD INTO THE FUNCTIONAL CURRENCY*

Introduction

47. Paragraph 12 of this Statement requires that all of a foreign entity's assets and liabilities shall be translated from the entity's functional currency into the reporting currency using the current exchange rate. Paragraph 12 also requires that revenues, expenses, gains, and losses be translated using the rates on the dates on which those elements are recognized during the period. The specified result can be reasonably approximated by using an appropriately weighted average exchange rate for the period. If an entity's books of record are not maintained in its functional currency, this Statement (paragraph 10) requires remeasurement into the functional currency prior to the translation process. If a foreign entity's functional currency is the reporting currency, remeasurement into the reporting currency obviates translation. The remeasurement process should produce the same result as if the entity's books of record had been initially recorded in the functional currency. To accomplish that result, it is necessary to use historical exchange rates between the functional currency and another currency in the remeasurement process for certain accounts (the current rate will be used for all others), and this appendix identifies those accounts. To accomplish that result, it is also necessary to recognize currently in income all exchange gains and losses from remeasurement of monetary assets and liabilities that are not denominated in the functional currency (for example, assets and liabilities that are not denominated in dollars if the dollar is the functional currency).

48. The table below lists common nonmonetary balance sheet items and related revenue, expense, gain, and loss accounts that should be remeasured using historical rates in order to produce the same result in terms of the functional currency that would have occurred if those items had been initially recorded in the functional currency.

Accounts to Be Remeasured Using Historical Exchange Rates

Marketable securities carried at cost
- Equity securities
- Debt securities not intended to be held until maturity

Inventories carried at cost

Prepaid expenses such as insurance, advertising, and rent

Property, plant, and equipment

Accumulated depreciation on property, plant, and equipment

Patents, trademarks, licenses, and formulas

Goodwill

Other intangible assets

Deferred charges and credits, except deferred income taxes and policy acquisition costs for life insurance companies

Deferred income

Common stock

Preferred stock carried at issuance price

Examples of revenues and expenses related to nonmonetary items:
- Cost of goods sold
- Depreciation of property, plant, and equipment
- Amortization of intangible items such as goodwill, patents, licenses, etc.
- Amortization of deferred charges or credits except deferred income taxes and policy acquisition costs for life insurance companies

---

*The guidance in this appendix applies only to those instances in which the books of record are not maintained in the functional currency.

Inventories—Applying the Rule of Cost or Market, Whichever Is Lower, to Remeasure Inventory Not Recorded in the Functional Currency

49. The rule of cost or market, whichever is lower (as described in Statement 6 of Chapter 4, "Inventory Pricing," of ARB 43), requires special application when the books of record are not kept in the functional currency. Inventories carried at cost in the books of record in another currency should be first remeasured to cost in the functional currency using historical exchange rates. Then, historical cost in the functional currency is compared with market as stated in the functional currency. Application of the rule in functional currency may require write-downs to market in the functional currency statements even though no write-down has been made in the books of record maintained in another currency. Likewise, a write-down in the books of record may need to be reversed if market exceeds historical cost as stated in the functional currency. If inventory[5] has been written down to market in the functional currency statements, that functional currency amount shall continue to be the carrying amount in the functional currency financial statements until the inventory is sold or a further write-down is necessary.

50. Literal application of the rule of cost or market, whichever is lower, may require an inventory write-down[6] in functional currency financial statements for locally acquired inventory[7] if the value of the currency in which the books of record are maintained has declined in relation to the functional currency between the date the inventory was acquired and the date of the balance sheet. Such a write-down may not be necessary, however, if the replacement costs or selling prices expressed in the currency in which the books of record are maintained have increased sufficiently so that market exceeds historical cost as measured in functional currency. Paragraphs 51-53 illustrate this situation.

51. Assume the following:

a. When the rate is BR*1 = FC2.40, a foreign subsidiary of a U.S. company purchases a unit of inventory at a cost of BR500 (measured in functional currency, FC1,200).
b. At the foreign subsidiary's balance sheet date, the current rate is BR1 = FC2.00 and the current replacement cost of the unit of inventory is BR560 (measured in functional currency, FC1,120).
c. Net realizable value is BR630 (measured in functional currency, FC1,260).
d. Net realizable value reduced by an allowance for an approximately normal profit margin is BR550 (measured in functional currency, FC1,100).

Because current replacement cost as measured in the functional currency (FC1,120) is less than historical cost as measured in the functional currency (FC1,200), an inventory write-down of FC80 is required in the functional currency financial statements.

52. Continue to assume the same information in the preceding example but substitute a current replacement cost at the foreign subsidiary's balance sheet date of BR620. Because market as measured in the functional currency (BR620 × FC2.00 = FC1,240) exceeds historical cost as measured in the functional currency (BR500 × FC2.40 = FC1,200), an inventory write-down is not required in the financial statements.

53. As another example, assume the information in paragraph 51, except that selling prices in terms of the currency in which the books of record are maintained have increased so that net realizable value is BR720 and net realizable value reduced by an allowance for an approximately normal profit margin is BR640. In that case, because replacement cost measured in functional currency (BR560 × FC2.00 = FC1,120) is less than net realizable value reduced by an allowance for an approximately normal profit margin measured in functional currency (BR640 × FC2.00 = FC1,280), market is FC1,280. Because market as measured in the functional currency (FC1,280) exceeds historical cost as measured in the functional currency (BR500 × FC2.40 = FC1,200),

[5]An asset other than inventory may sometimes be written down from historical cost. Although that write-down is not under the rule of cost or market, whichever is lower, the approach described in this paragraph might be appropriate. That is, a write-down may be required in the functional currency statements even though not required in the books of record, and a write-down in the books of record may need to be reversed before remeasurement to prevent the remeasured amount from exceeding functional currency historical cost.

[6]This paragraph is not intended to preclude recognition of gains in a later interim period to the extent of inventory losses recognized from market declines in earlier interim periods if losses on the same inventory are recovered in the same year, as provided by paragraph 14(c) of APB Opinion No. 28, *Interim Financial Reporting,* which states: "Inventory losses from market declines should not be deferred beyond the interim period in which the decline occurs. Recoveries of such losses on the same inventory in later interim periods of the same fiscal year through market price recoveries should be recognized as gains in the later interim period. Such gains should not exceed previously recognized losses. Some market declines at interim dates, however, can reasonably be expected to be restored in the fiscal year. Such *temporary* market declines need not be recognized at the interim date since no loss is expected to be incurred in the fiscal year."

[7]An inventory write-down also may be required for imported inventory.

*BR = Currency in which the books of record are maintained
FC = Functional currency

an inventory write-down is not required in the functional currency financial statements.

Deferred Taxes and Policy Acquisition Costs

54. Statement 8 required certain deferred taxes that do not relate to assets or liabilities translated at current rates to be translated at historical rates.[8] Interpretation 15 required unamortized policy acquisition costs of a stock life insurance company to be translated at historical rates.[9] In Statement 33, the Board decided that, because of the close relationship of those accounts to related monetary items, a monetary classification should be used for the purposes of constant dollar accounting. For similar reasons, the Board decided to retain the classification required by Statement 33 for the purposes of remeasurement of an entity's books of record into its functional currency.

Appendix C

BASIS FOR CONCLUSIONS

CONTENTS

Appendix C

BASIS FOR CONCLUSIONS

Introduction

55. This appendix reviews considerations that were deemed significant by members of the Board in reaching the conclusions in this Statement. The Board members who assented to this Statement did so on the basis of the overall considerations; individual members gave greater weight to some factors than to others.

Nature of the Problem

56. Operations and transactions of an enterprise are affected by the changing prices of goods and services it buys and sells relative to a unit of currency, which is usually also the measuring unit for financial reporting.

57. If the enterprise operates in more than one currency environment, it is affected by the changing prices of goods and services in more than one economic environment and, additionally, by changes in relative prices among the several units of currency in which it conducts its business.

[8]Statement 8, paragraphs 50-52.

[9]Interpretation 15, paragraph 4.

58. The accounting model, generally referred to as the historical cost model, does not generally recognize the effect of changing prices of goods and services until there has been an exchange transaction, usually a sale or purchase. In general, then, it does not recognize unrealized holding gains resulting from changes in the price of goods and services relative to the unit of currency.

59. For enterprises conducting activities in more than a single currency, the practical necessities of financial reporting in a single currency require that the changing prices between two units of currency be accommodated in some fashion. People generally agree on this practical necessity but disagree on concepts and details of implementation. As a result, there is significant disagreement among informed observers regarding the basic nature, information content, and meaning of results produced by various methods of translating amounts from foreign currencies into the reporting currency. Each method has strong proponents and severe critics.

60. In dealing with this dilemma, the Board was faced with the following basic choices:

a. Changing the accounting model to one that recognizes currently the effects of all changing prices in the primary financial statements
b. Deferring any recognition of changing currency prices until they are realized by an actual exchange of foreign currency into the reporting currency
c. Recognizing currently the effect of changing currency prices on the carrying amounts of designated foreign assets and liabilities
d. Recognizing currently the effect of changing currency prices on the carrying amounts of all foreign assets and liabilities

61. Alternative (a) runs counter to the Board's approach in Statement 33, which fosters experimentation with supplemental reporting to test the feasibility, usefulness, and cost of various techniques for reporting the effects of changing prices. Accordingly, the Board did not consider a change in the primary financial statement model to be a reasonable alternative for this project on foreign currency translation.

62. Alternative (b) has little or no support from the Board or its constituents. All transactions and balances would be translated at historical exchange rates—a formidable clerical task—until conversion to the parent's currency occurred. Postponing recognition would fail to reflect the effects of possibly very significant economic events at the time they occurred, particularly those that affect transactions that must be settled under changed currency prices. Most would consider this a retreat rather than an advance toward more useful financial reporting.

63. Alternative (c) is the approach taken in Statement 8. Although some believe this approach is conceptually consistent with the historical cost model, others do not agree. In any event, this approach has produced results that the Board and many constituents believe do not reflect the underlying economic reality of many foreign operations and thereby produces results that are not relevant. A summary of the more common criticisms of Statement 8 is included in paragraphs 153-156 of Appendix D.

64. Some constituents urged the Board to introduce a selective departure from the rationale of Statement 8 by simply adding selected assets to or deleting selected liabilities from the list of those for which the effect of changing currency prices is currently recognized under Statement 8. The most frequent proposals would translate all or some portion of inventory at current exchange rates. This approach would reduce the reported exchange gains and losses of many enterprises, but it would increase the reported exchange gains and losses of other enterprises. It would do nothing to lessen the impact of temporal method gains and losses on enterprises that have no significant amounts of inventory, such as financial institutions; nor would it resolve problems caused by large amounts of debt-financed property, plant, and equipment. Thus, it is not a general cure for the cited deficiencies and it has little or no conceptual basis.

65. Those who advocate a limited modification to translate inventories at the current rate generally oppose translating property, plant, and equipment and other nonmonetary assets on the same basis. As a result, depreciation allocated to inventory and cost of sales would be translated at the current rate, while depreciation allocated directly to expense would be translated at historical rates. This is inconsistent in concept and result. In the absence of any conceptual distinction among nonmonetary items, the list of modifications would be subject to requests for continuous revisions that could be assessed only on an arbitrary, ad hoc basis. Selective modifications of Statement 8 were rejected by the Board primarily on those grounds.

66. The Board decided that, of the practical alternatives available to it, alternative (d) has the most conceptual merit, particularly for foreign operations that are reasonably self-contained. It will result in reports of financial condition and results of operations that, within the constraints of the historical cost model, will most closely reflect economic effects.

67. The problem is complicated by the fact that foreign operations differ greatly in structure and substance. In some situations, only certain assets and liabilities are exposed to foreign exchange risk, whereas in others the entire foreign operation or net

investment is exposed to foreign exchange risk. These differences can significantly change the economic effect of exchange rate fluctuations.

68. The Board agreed that these variations in economic facts and circumstances should be recognized to the degree it is practical to do so and, accordingly, settled on the functional currency approach to translation as one that accommodates alternative (d) above, but recognizes situational differences. The nature of these differences and guidance for identifying the functional currency appears in paragraphs 41 and 42 of Appendix A.

69. A feature of the functional currency approach is the current rate translation method. The Board recognizes that the current rate method, although common in some other countries, has not been extensively used in the United States. Based on extensive study and due process, however, the Board believes that the functional currency approach best recognizes the substantive differences among foreign operations and best reflects the underlying economic effects of exchange rate changes in the consolidated financial statements. The functional currency approach encompasses:

a. Identifying the functional currency of the entity's economic environment
b. Measuring all elements of the financial statements in the functional currency
c. Using the current exchange rate for translation from the functional currency to the reporting currency, if they are different
d. Distinguishing the economic impact of changes in exchange rates on a net investment from the impact of such changes on individual assets and liabilities that are receivable or payable in currencies other than the functional currency

Objectives of Translation

70. The functional currency approach was adopted after considering the following objectives of foreign currency translation:

a. To provide information that is generally compatible with the expected economic effects of a rate change on an enterprise's cash flows and equity
b. To present the consolidated financial statements of an enterprise in conformity with U.S. generally accepted accounting principles
c. To reflect in consolidated financial statements the financial results and relationships of the individual consolidated entities as measured in their functional currencies
d. To use a "single unit of measure" for financial statements that include translated foreign amounts

71. Objective (a), to provide information that is generally compatible with the expected economic effects of a rate change, was adopted by the Board as the basic objective. This was responsive to the pervasive criticism that translation results under Statement 8 do not reflect the underlying reality of foreign operations. The Board focused on two aspects of accounting results and their compatibility with the economic effects of a rate change—changes in equity and cash flow consequences. Compatibility in terms of effect on equity is achieved, for example, if an exchange rate change that is favorable to an enterprise's exposed position produces an accounting result that increases equity. Compatibility in terms of cash flow consequences is achieved if rate changes that are reasonably expected to impact either functional or reporting currency cash flows are reflected as gains or losses in determining net income for the period, and the effect of rate changes that have only remote and uncertain implications for realization are excluded from determining net income for the period.

72. The Board believes that objective (b), conformity with U.S. generally accepted accounting principles, is implicit in and basic to the purpose of all the Board's activities on every technical project and need not be singled out as a separate objective for foreign currency translation.

73. The primary focus of financial reporting is information about an enterprise's performance provided by measures of income and its components. Those who are concerned with the prospects for net cash flows are especially interested in that information.[10] The prospects for net cash flows of a foreign entity are necessarily derived from its performance in terms of transactions and events that occur in its functional currency; in turn, prospects for net cash flows to the consolidated enterprise from the foreign entity are necessarily derived from reinvestment of those functional currency net cash flows or their conversion and distribution. Accordingly, the Board believes that the performance of a foreign entity is best measured by U.S. generally accepted accounting principles applied in terms of the functional currency in which the entity primarily conducts its business, generates and expends cash, and reinvests or converts and distributes cash to its parent.

74. The purpose of translating the functional currency to the reporting currency, if the two are different, is to restate the functional currency financial

[10]FASB Concepts Statement No. 1, *Objectives of Financial Reporting by Business Enterprises,* paragraph 43.

statements in terms of the reporting currency for inclusion in consolidated financial statements. The process should retain the financial results and relationships that were created in the economic environment of the foreign operations; it should not remeasure individual financial statement elements as if the operations had been conducted in the economic environment of the reporting currency. Only by retaining the functional currency relationships of each operating entity is it possible to portray aggregate performance in different operating environments for purposes of consolidation. Accordingly, in addition to adopting objective (a), the Board also adopted objectives (b) and (c) in combination.

75. Objective (d), to use a "single unit of measure" (for example, the dollar) for financial statements that include translated amounts, is the stated premise of the temporal method set forth in Statement 8. In the Board's view, that premise reflects in consolidated financial statements the transactions of the entire group, including foreign operations, as though all operations were extensions of the parent's domestic activities and all transactions were conducted and measured in the parent's reporting currency. That premise does not recognize that the assets, liabilities, and operations of foreign entities frequently exist, in fact, in other economic and currency environments and produce and consume foreign currency cash flows in those other environments. By requiring all foreign currency transactions to be remeasured as if they all had occurred in dollars, the "single unit of measure" approach obscures the fact that foreign entities acquire assets, incur and settle liabilities, and otherwise conduct their operations in multiple foreign currencies. Foreign operations are frequently conducted exclusively in foreign currencies, and the flow of dollars to the parent enterprise is dependent upon the foreign currency net cash flows generated by the foreign entity and remitted to the parent. Because it does not accord with relevant economic facts, reliance on a "single unit of measure" is not always compatible with the nature of foreign operations that is described and discussed in subsequent sections of this basis for conclusions. Accordingly, objective (d) was not adopted.

76. The Board also believes that, to the extent practicable, the accounting for the translation of foreign currency transactions and financial statements in the United States should harmonize with related accounting practices followed in other countries of the world. The Board maintained close liaison with representatives of the International Accounting Standards Committee and the accounting standards-setting bodies in Canada and the United Kingdom and Ireland as this Statement was developed. Representatives from each of those groups were active participants with the Board's foreign currency task force. The Accounting Standards Committee in the United Kingdom and Ireland has issued a proposed standard for foreign currency translation that is compatible with the standards set forth in this Statement.

The Functional Currency

77. An entity's functional currency is the currency of the primary economic environment in which the entity operates; normally, that is the currency of the environment in which an entity primarily generates and expends cash.

78. The Board believes that the most meaningful measurement unit for the assets, liabilities, and operations of an entity is the currency in which it primarily conducts its business, assuming that currency has reasonable stability.

79. Multinational enterprises may consist of entities operating in a number of economic environments and dealing in a number of foreign currencies. All foreign operations are not alike. In order to fulfill the objectives adopted by the Board, it is necessary to recognize at least two broad classes of foreign operations.

80. In the first class are foreign operations that are relatively self-contained and integrated within a particular country or economic environment. The day-to-day operations are not dependent upon the economic environment of the parent's functional currency; the foreign operation primarily generates and expends foreign currency. The foreign currency net cash flows that it generates may be reinvested or converted and distributed to the parent. For this class, the foreign currency is the functional currency.

81. In the second class are foreign operations that are primarily a direct and integral component or extension of the parent company's operations. Significant assets may be acquired from the parent enterprise or otherwise by expending dollars and, similarly, the sale of assets may generate dollars that are available to the parent. Financing is primarily by the parent or otherwise from dollar sources. In other words, the day-to-day operations are dependent on the economic environment of the parent's currency, and the changes in the foreign entity's individual assets and liabilities impact directly on the cash flows of the parent company in the parent's currency. For this class, the dollar is the functional currency.

82. The Board recognizes that some foreign operations will not fit neatly in either of the two broad classes described in paragraphs 80 and 81. Management's judgment will be required in order to select

the functional currency in those instances. Guidance for management in this process is included in Appendix A.

83. Experience with Statement 8, responses to both Exposure Drafts, and testimony at the public hearing repeatedly evidenced that no translation method can yield reliable or economically credible results if it fails to recognize differences in economic substance among different foreign currency operations. Statement 8 did not recognize those differences. Implicitly, the dollar was designated the functional currency for all foreign operations. For those operations for which the functional currency was, in fact, the foreign currency, the reported results created by exchange rate changes did not conform with the underlying economic facts and were, therefore, not understood or not credible.

84. Some allege that the functional currency approach does not "result in similar accounting for similar situations." The Board believes a significant virtue of that approach is that it provides different accounting for significantly different economic facts. Because the facts will sometimes give mixed signals, and because management's judgment will be required to identify, weigh, and interpret the facts within the objectives and guidance in this Statement, the Board acknowledges the possibility that, occasionally, situations that appear similar may be accounted for in different ways. That is always a risk when standards must be applied with judgment. The Board believes that risk is likely to do less damage to the usefulness of financial reporting than arbitrary rules that overlook economic differences and require different situations to be accounted for as though they were the same.

Consolidation of Foreign Currency Statements

85. Critics of the functional currency approach assert that it is not consistent with consolidation theory and that it violates the single entity and "single unit of measure" concepts that they believe underlie consolidated financial statements. The Board believes that, for an enterprise operating in multiple currency environments, a true "single unit of measure" does not, as a factual matter, exist.

86. As noted elsewhere, multiple units of currency are an economic fact of foreign operations, and a translation method cannot prevent the effects of multiple units from showing up in financial statements. The temporal method obscures the fact of multiple units by requiring all transactions to be measured as if the transactions occurred in dollars. As a result, it produces profit margins and earnings fluctuations that do not synchronize with the economic events that affect an entity's operations. All translation methods, including both the temporal and current rate methods, involve multiple currency units at the foreign entity level and a single currency unit, the dollar, at the consolidated reporting level. They only differ in how they bridge from multiple units to the single unit.

87. Proponents of a "single unit of measure" would require the historical cost of inventories and property, plant, and equipment acquired by a foreign entity in a foreign currency to be measured in terms of the equivalent number of dollars at the date of acquisition; that is, they would translate the foreign currency acquisition cost using the historical exchange rate. Statement 8 is based on that proposition. At the same time, however, many of those same proponents recommend that present standards (that is, Statement 8) be improved by requiring the foreign currency acquisition cost of inventories to be translated using the current exchange rate. Whether that proposal is presented as a departure from their perception of generally accepted accounting principles that require inventories to be measured at historical cost or as a departure from their perception of a "single unit of measure" is not always clear. Whatever the nature of the exception, some of those recommending it would have it apply to all inventories acquired by a foreign entity, others only to inventories for which the last-in, first-out method is not used, others only for inventory acquired locally, and still others to various combinations of those possibilities. No matter how the proposal might be applied, it would be impossible to adopt it and retain both the "single unit of measure" and accounting for inventories at historical cost.

88. Statement 8 is frequently described as a faithful application of the "single unit of measure" and the historical cost principle. Most agree that the faithful application of the "single unit of measure" and the historical cost principle produces results that are not compatible with the expected economic effects of changes in exchange rates. The Board concluded that for many foreign entities, adhering to a "single unit of measure" was artificial and illusory.

89. The Board also considered the assertion made by some that the functional currency approach is inconsistent with the presentation of consolidated financial statements that include the individual financial statement elements (that is, assets, liabilities, revenues, expenses, gains, losses, etc.) of foreign entities. That assertion seems to be based on the notion that, because the functional currency approach generally considers the relevant economic effect of exchange rate changes to be on the net investment in a foreign entity rather than on certain of its individual financial statement elements, including in consolidated financial statements the individual elements that underlie that net investment is inappropriate. The Board believes that assertion is without merit.

90. As stated in paragraph 1 of ARB No. 51, *Consolidated Financial Statements:*

> The purpose of consolidated statements is to present, primarily for the benefit of the shareholders and creditors of the parent company, the results of operations and the financial position of a parent company and its subsidiaries essentially as if the group were a single company with one or more branches or divisions. There is a presumption that consolidated statements are more meaningful than separate statements and that they are usually necessary for a fair presentation when one of the companies in the group directly or indirectly has a controlling financial interest in the other companies.

91. The Board agrees with the presumption in ARB 51 that presenting in consolidated financial statements the individual assets, liabilities, revenues, expenses, and other elements that underlie a net investment in a foreign entity in which there is a controlling financial interest is indeed more meaningful than merely presenting the net investment as a single item, as in the parent company's separate financial statements. Nothing in the functional currency approach suggests that the various entities that are included in consolidated financial statements are not components of a single enterprise. The same individual financial statement elements are aggregated in consolidated financial statements using the functional currency approach as under the temporal method or any of the other methods found in practice prior to Statement 8. Measures of some of the elements presented in consolidated financial statements differ depending on the approach to translation, but the component entities and elements of the consolidated enterprise are the same.

92. Some have also suggested that adoption of the functional currency approach causes reporting currency measures of items presented in consolidated financial statements to depart from the historical cost model found in present practice. The Board has concluded that is not the case. Costs are incurred and exchange transactions take place in the functional currency; the functional currency approach preserves those historical costs and exchange prices. If the functional currency and reporting currency are different, translation of functional currency historical costs and exchange prices into their current dollar equivalent is essential to the process of consolidation, but the exchange rate changes affect the dollar equivalents of those historical costs and exchange prices, not the historical costs and exchange prices actually experienced by the foreign entity. As explained elsewhere, the Board concluded that the most relevant information about the performance and financial position of foreign entities is provided by the functional currency financial statements of those entities. Using the current exchange rate to restate those functional currency financial statements in terms of their current dollar equivalents preserves that most relevant information.

93. Those who believe that the functional currency approach is inconsistent with consolidation principles sometimes put the argument in terms of a U.S. perspective versus a local perspective. They contend that the local perspective incorrectly assumes that U.S. investors and creditors are interested in functional currency cash flows rather than in dollar cash flows. To the contrary, the Board has adopted the functional currency approach because it believes that approach provides the best basis for assessing an enterprise's dollar cash flows. The foreign entity's net cash flows are one source of dollar cash flows. However, it is only after a foreign entity has realized net cash flows in its functional currency that those cash flows can be converted to dollars. For example, the property, plant, and equipment of a foreign entity is used directly to produce functional currency revenues, and it is only indirectly through the entire earnings process of the foreign entity that the net functional currency cash flows become available for conversion into dollar cash flows.

Translation of Foreign Currency Statements

94. Fundamental to the functional currency approach to translation is the view that, generally, a U.S. enterprise is exposed to exchange risk to the extent of its net investment in a foreign operation. This view derives from a broad concept of economic hedging. An asset, such as plant and equipment, that produces revenues in the functional currency of an entity can be an effective hedge of debt that requires payments in that currency. Therefore, functional currency assets and liabilities hedge one another, and only the net assets are exposed to exchange risk.

95. If all of a foreign entity's assets and liabilities are measured in its functional currency and are translated at the current exchange rate, the net accounting effect of a change in the exchange rate is the effect on the net assets of the entity. That accounting result is compatible with the broad concept of economic hedging on which the net investment view is based. No gains or losses arise from hedged assets and liabilities and the dollar equivalent of the unhedged net investment increases or decreases when the functional currency strengthens or weakens.

96. If a foreign entity transacts business in a currency other than its functional currency, it is exposed to exchange risk on assets and liabilities denominated in those currencies. That risk will be reflected through gains and losses in the functional currency.

Those gains and losses affect the foreign entity's functional currency net cash flows that may be reinvested by it or converted and distributed to the parent. That is equally the case for transactions of the foreign entity denominated in the reporting currency.

97. Another aspect of the functional currency approach pertains to the financial results and relationships of a foreign entity. The functional currency approach views the parent company as having an investment in a foreign business whose foreign currency earnings are generated in its local economic, legal, and political environment and accrue to the benefit of the parent company in the amount of the dollar equivalent of those earnings. That concept views the accounts of the foreign business measured in its functional currency in accordance with U.S. generally accepted accounting principles as the best available indicators of its performance and financial condition.

98. A foreign entity's assets, liabilities, and operations exist in the economic environment of its functional currency. Its costs are incurred in its functional currency and its revenues are produced in its functional currency. Use of a current exchange rate retains those historical costs and other measurements but restates them in terms of the reporting currency, thereby preserving the relationships established in the entity's economic environment. Accordingly, use of the current exchange rate reflects in the consolidated financial statements the inherent relationships appearing in the functional currency financial statements. If a foreign entity is producing net income in its functional currency, the dollar equivalent of that net income will be reflected in the consolidated financial statements. If different exchange rates are used for monetary and nonmonetary items, as in Statement 8, the translated dollar results inevitably differ from the entity's functional currency results. At an extreme, if different rates are used for monetary and nonmonetary items, the results of operations for a foreign entity that, in fact, is operating profitably and is generating functional currency net cash flows may be converted to a loss merely as a result of the mechanical translation process. The Board believes that by preserving the actual indicators of performance and financial condition of each component entity, the consolidated financial statements will portray the best information about the enterprise as a whole.

99. Paragraph 12 of this Statement requires that a foreign entity's revenues, expenses, gains, and losses be translated in a manner that produces amounts approximately as if the underlying elements had been translated on the dates they were recognized (sometimes referred to as the weighted average exchange rate). This also applies to accounting allocations (for example, depreciation, cost of sales, and amortization of deferred revenues and expenses) and requires translation at the current exchange rates applicable to the dates those allocations are included in revenues and expenses (that is, not the rates on the dates the related items originated). The objectives of the functional currency approach, particularly as expressed in paragraph 70(c), might be best served by application of a single current rate, such as the rate at the end of the period, to those elements. This would, however, require restating prior interim periods or recording a catch-up adjustment in income if rates change. The Board therefore rejected this alternative on practical grounds.

100. Translation of the statement of changes in financial position was the subject of frequent comment on both Exposure Drafts on foreign currency translation. APB Opinion No. 19, *Reporting Changes in Financial Position,* permits some flexibility and judgment to meet the stated objectives of a statement of changes and the Board does not intend to change that either by prescribing the form and content of the statement of changes or by requiring a separate compilation of complete information for each foreign operation. However, Opinion 19 does require disclosure of all important changes in financial position regardless of whether cash or working capital is directly affected and that requirement is not changed in any way by this Statement.

101. The functional currency approach applies equally to translation of financial statements of foreign investees whether accounted for by the equity method or consolidated. It also applies to translation after a business combination. Therefore, the foreign statements and the foreign currency transactions of an investee that are accounted for by the equity method should be translated in conformity with the requirements of this Statement in applying the equity method. Likewise, after a business combination accounted for by the purchase method, the amount allocated at the date of acquisition to the assets acquired and the liabilities assumed (including *goodwill* or *an excess of acquired net assets over cost* as those terms are used in APB Opinion No. 16, *Business Combinations)* should be translated in conformity with the requirements of this Statement. Accumulated translation adjustments attributable to minority interests should be allocated to and reported as part of the minority interest in the consolidated enterprise.

Translation of Operations in Highly Inflationary Economies

102. Translation of operations in highly inflationary economies is frequently cited as a problem if

all assets and liabilities are translated using current exchange rates. In the historical cost model, a reasonably stable measuring unit is an essential ingredient to useful reporting of financial position and operating results over periods of time. Any degree of inflation affects the usefulness of information measured in nominal currency units. If historical costs are measured in nominal currency units in a highly inflationary environment, those measures of historical cost rapidly lose relevance.

103. Because it is a common condition, users of financial statements have developed tolerance for some inflation and in varying degrees compensate for it in their analyses. As inflation increases or persists, however, nominal currency units of the inflationary environment are not useful measures of performance or investment, and a more stable unit of measure must be found.

104. The point at which a substitute measuring unit is necessary is a subjective one. It depends on a number of factors, including the current and cumulative rates of inflation and the capital intensiveness of the operation. In principle, however, a more stable measuring unit is always preferable to a less stable one.

105. The Board has considered a number of alternative methods for restating to a more stable measuring unit. None of the methods is completely satisfactory at this time, either because they are deemed to be incompatible with the functional currency concept or because they involve some aspect of accounting for the effects of inflation in the basic financial statements. Statement 33 calls for experimentation with reporting the effects of inflation on a supplemental basis, not in the basic financial statements. Accordingly, in the 1980 Exposure Draft, the Board proposed not to specify special translation provisions for reporting on operations in highly inflationary economies, pending resolution of the issues being tested in supplemental reporting on the effects of inflation.

106. Virtually every respondent to the 1980 Exposure Draft who addressed translation of operations in highly inflationary economies pointed out that, unless special provisions are made, the proposed translation method could report misleading results. Accordingly, in the revised Exposure Draft, the Board proposed that the financial statements of a foreign entity with a functional currency of a country that has a highly inflationary economy be restated to reflect changes in the general price level in that country prior to translation. Many respondents objected to the revision, generally on one or more of the following grounds:

a. Information restated to reflect changes in the general price level should not be required in the primary financial statements until and unless the usefulness of that information has been adequately demonstrated in the Statement 33 experiment.
b. The primary financial statements should not mix information presented in constant measuring units that reflect changes in the general price level with information presented in nominal monetary units.
c. The lack of reliable and timely price-level indexes in some highly inflationary economies constitutes a significant obstacle to practical application of the proposal.

107. In view of the difficulties with the proposal, the Board decided that the practical alternative, recommended by many respondents, is to require that the financial statements of foreign entities in those economies that meet the definition of highly inflationary be remeasured as if the functional currency were the reporting currency. This is essentially a pragmatic decision. The Board nonetheless believes that a currency that has largely lost its utility as a store of value cannot be a functional measuring unit. If the reporting currency is more stable, it can be used as the functional currency without introducing a form of inflation accounting.

108. The revised Exposure Draft also allowed latitude for restatement of operations in economies that are less than highly inflationary. Many respondents believed that this flexibility would significantly reduce the consistency and comparability of reporting among companies. The Board agreed and removed the latitude in the final Statement.

109. The definition of a highly inflationary economy as one that has cumulative inflation of *approximately* 100 percent or more over a 3-year period is necessarily an arbitrary decision. In some instances, the trend of inflation might be as important as the absolute rate. It is the Board's intention that the definition of a highly inflationary economy be applied with judgment.

Translation Adjustments

110. Translation adjustments arise from either consolidation or equity method accounting for a net investment in another entity having a different functional currency from that of the investor.

111. Translation adjustments do not exist in terms of functional currency cash flows. Translation adjustments are solely a result of the translation process and have no direct effect on reporting currency cash flows. Exchange rate changes have an indirect effect on the net investment that may be realized upon sale or liquidation, but that effect is related to

the net investment and not to the operations of the investee. Prior to sale or liquidation, that effect is so uncertain and remote as to require that translation adjustments arising currently should not be reported as part of operating results.

112. Assenting Board members hold two views of the nature of translation adjustments. Since both views exclude these adjustments from net income and include them in equity, the Board did not consider it necessary to settle on which view should be accepted.

113. The first view is described in terms of a parent (investor) with the dollar as the reporting and functional currency and an investment position in another entity with a functional currency other than the dollar. A change in the exchange rate between the dollar and the other currency produces a change in the dollar equivalent of the net investment although there is no change in the net assets of the other entity measured in its functional currency. A favorable exchange rate change enhances the dollar equivalent; an unfavorable exchange rate change reduces the dollar equivalent. Accordingly, the translation adjustment reflects an economic effect of exchange rate changes. However, that change in the dollar equivalent of the net investment is an unrealized enhancement or reduction, having no effect on the functional currency net cash flows generated by the foreign entity which may be currently reinvested or distributed to the parent. For that reason, the translation adjustment is reported separately from the determination of net income. That adjustment is accumulated separately as part of equity. Concepts Statement 3 defines *comprehensive income* as the change in equity (net assets) of an entity during a period from transactions from nonowner sources. The first view considers the translation adjustment to be an unrealized component of comprehensive income that, for the reasons given above, should be reported separately from net income.

114. The second view regards the translation adjustment as merely a mechanical by-product of the translation process, a process that is essential to providing aggregated information about a consolidated enterprise. An analogy may be drawn between the cumulative foreign currency translation adjustment and the difference between equity (net assets) measured in constant dollars and the same net assets measured in nominal dollars. Viewed as such, the translation adjustment for a period should be excluded from the determination of net income, reported separately, and included as a separate component of equity. In this respect, it represents a restatement of previously reported equity similar to that developed in constant dollar accounting to restate equity in constant dollars from an earlier date to a current date after a change in the constant dollar unit of measure has occurred. Concepts Statement 3, in paragraph 58, anticipated that such restatements would be made to equity without being included in current-period comprehensive income.

115. Both views of the nature of translation adjustments report the same measure of net income and the same information about equity. The Board believes its requirements for disposition and disclosure of translation adjustments are consistent with both views.

116. The Board considered whether at some time the separately reported component of equity should be included in net income. Under the first view, the adjustments have already been included in comprehensive income and should not be included again. Any elimination of the separate component of equity should be accomplished by combining the different classes of items in equity. Under the second view, the translation adjustments are a direct restatement of equity, a form of capital adjustment. It would be contrary to that view to include them in income at any time.

117. Some respondents suggested that the translation adjustments be amortized to income over the lives or maturities of the individual assets and liabilities of the investee, or some relatively long arbitrary period. The Board did not adopt that approach because, as previously stated, translation adjustments are unrealized and do not have the characteristics of items generally included in determining net income.

118. The 1980 Exposure Draft called for recognition of translation adjustments in determining net income based upon permanent impairment of a net investment. That proposal was reconsidered and rejected. The Board concluded that any required provisions for asset-impairment adjustments should be made prior to translation and consolidation.

119. Pending completion of its project on reporting comprehensive income, however, the Board decided to include the accumulated translation adjustments in net income as part of the net gain or loss from sale or complete or substantially complete liquidation of the related investment. Sale and complete or substantially complete liquidation were selected because those events generally cause a related gain or loss on the net investment to be recognized in net income at that time. That procedure recognizes the"unrealized" translation adjustment as a component of net income when it becomes "realized." Although the information is probably marginal, the Board believes that this disposition is desirable until the concepts of reporting all components of comprehensive income are further developed. This dis-

position also can be considered to be in line with the existing view that nonowner transactions or events that change equity should be recognized in net income at some point.

Transaction Gains and Losses

120. A foreign currency transaction is a transaction that is denominated (requires settlement) in a currency other than the functional currency of an entity. Foreign currency transactions typically result from the import or export of goods, services, or capital. Examples include a sale denominated in Swiss francs, a Swiss franc loan, and the holding of Swiss francs by an entity whose functional currency is the dollar. Likewise, a Swiss franc denominated transaction by a German entity or other entity whose functional currency is not the Swiss franc is a foreign currency transaction. For any entity whose functional currency is *not* the dollar, a dollar-denominated transaction is also a foreign currency transaction.

121. The Board has concluded that gains and losses from foreign currency transactions have a different economic nature and therefore require different accounting treatment from that applied to adjustments arising from translating the financial statements of foreign entities from their functional currencies into the reporting currency for the purposes of consolidation. Accordingly, the accounting requirements for disposing of transaction gains and losses and translation adjustments are different.

122. Transaction gains or losses arise when monetary assets and liabilities (cash, receivables, and payables) are denominated in a currency other than the functional currency and the exchange rate between those currencies changes. They can arise at either or both the parent and the subsidiary entity level.

123. Transaction gains and losses have direct cash flow effects when foreign-denominated monetary assets or liabilities are settled in amounts greater or less than the functional currency equivalent of the original transactions.

124. The Board has concluded that such gains or losses should be reflected in income when the exchange rates change rather than when the transaction is settled or at some other intermediate date or period. This is consistent with accrual accounting; it results in reporting the effect of a rate change that will have cash flow effects when the event causing the effect takes place.

125. Some have proposed that a transaction gain or loss should be deferred if the rate change that caused it might be reversed before the transaction is settled. The argument is that to recognize transaction gains and losses from rate changes in determining net income creates needless fluctuations in reported income if those transaction gains and losses might be canceled by future reversals of rate changes. The Board rejected the proposal on both conceptual and practical grounds. Past rate changes are historical facts, and the Board believes that users of financial statements are best served by accounting for rate changes that affect the functional currency cash flows of a foreign entity as those rate changes occur. The proposal is also impractical; future changes, including reversals, cannot be reliably predicted. As a result, a transaction gain or loss might ultimately have to be recognized during a period in which rate changes are unrelated to the recognized gain or loss.

126. The Board saw no conceptual basis for an alternative proposal for recognition of transaction gains or losses when unsettled balances are classified as current assets and liabilities (or as they became due within one year). Such a requirement would place emphasis on the balance sheet classification or settlement date rather than on the economic effect of the exchange rate movement. It would also add a further accounting complexity without a compensating benefit.

127. Others have proposed that transaction gains and losses, particularly those related to long-term debt, should be deferred and amortized over the life of the related liabilities as part of the costs of borrowing. The Board agrees that transaction gains and losses on amounts borrowed in a different currency might be considered part of the cost of the borrowed funds. However, no rational procedure can be prescribed to accrue the total cost at an average effective rate because until the liability is settled that average rate cannot be objectively determined. Amortization of the effect of past exchange rate changes over the remaining life of the borrowing does not accomplish that result. It changes the pattern of gain or loss recognition in net income, but it may retain much of the volatility that advocates seek to eliminate. Further, amortization allocates the effect of an exchange rate change to periods not related in any way to changes in rates or other economic events affecting the enterprise.

Foreign Currency Transactions That Hedge a Net Investment

128. Paragraph 20(a) of this Statement provides that transaction gains and losses attributable to a foreign currency transaction that is designated as, and is effective as, an economic hedge of a net investment in a foreign entity shall be reported in the same manner as translation adjustments and that such accounting shall commence as of the designation date. If a foreign currency transaction is in fact an economic hedge of a net investment, then the

accounting for the effect of a rate change on the transaction should be the same as the accounting for the effect of the rate change on the net investment, that is, both of those partially or fully offsetting amounts should be included in the separate component of equity.

129. An example of the situation contemplated in paragraph 20(a) would be a U.S. parent company with a net investment in a subsidiary that is located in Switzerland and for which the Swiss franc is the functional currency. The U.S. parent might also borrow Swiss francs and designate the Swiss franc loan as a hedge of the net investment in the Swiss subsidiary. The loan is denominated in Swiss francs which are not the functional currency of the U.S. parent and, therefore, the loan is a foreign currency transaction. The loan is a liability, and the net investment in the Swiss subsidiary is an asset. Subsequent to a change in exchange rates, the adjustment resulting from translation of the Swiss subsidiary's balance sheet would go in the opposite direction from the adjustment resulting from translation of the U.S. parent company's Swiss franc debt. To the extent that the adjustment from translation of the Swiss franc loan (after tax effects, if any) is less than or equal to the adjustment from translation of the Swiss subsidiary's balance sheet, both adjustments should be included in the analysis of changes in the cumulative translation adjustment and reflected in the separate component of equity. However, any portion of the adjustment from translation of the U.S. parent company's Swiss franc debt (after tax effects, if any) that exceeds the adjustment from translation of the Swiss subsidiary's balance sheet is a transaction gain or loss that should be included in the determination of net income.

130. Ordinarily, a transaction that hedges a net investment should be denominated in the same currency as the functional currency of the net investment hedged. In some instances, it may not be practical or feasible to hedge in the same currency and, therefore, a hedging transaction also may be denominated in a currency for which the exchange rate generally moves in tandem with the exchange rate for the functional currency of the net investment hedged.

Transaction Gains and Losses Attributable to Intercompany Transactions

131. Paragraph 20(b) of this Statement addresses transaction gains and losses attributable to intercompany foreign currency transactions that are of a long-term investment nature. Transactions and balances for which settlement is not planned or anticipated in the foreseeable future are considered to be part of the net investment. This might include balances that take the form of an advance or a demand note payable provided that payment is not planned or anticipated in the foreseeable future. Accordingly, related gains or losses are to be reported and accumulated in the same manner as translation adjustments when financial statements for those entities are consolidated, combined, or accounted for by the equity method. Transaction gains and losses attributable to other intercompany transactions and balances, however, affect functional currency cash flows; and increases or decreases in actual and expected functional currency cash flows should be included in determining net income for the period in which exchange rates change.

Foreign Currency Transactions That Hedge Foreign Currency Commitments

132. In response to the Board's invitation for public comment on Statements 1-12, most of the comments received that addressed accounting for forward exchange contracts requested that the Board reconsider the requirement that a forward contract must extend from the foreign currency commitment date to the anticipated transaction date or a later date if the forward contract is to be accounted for as a hedge of a foreign currency commitment. Other commentators have requested that transactions other than forward exchange contracts (for example, a cash balance) also should be accounted for as a hedge of a commitment.

133. The Board believes that if a foreign currency commitment is hedged by a forward contract or by any other type of foreign currency transaction, the accounting for the foreign currency transaction should reflect the economic hedge of the foreign currency commitment. The existence of an economic hedge is a question of fact, not of form. Therefore, the Board did not require any linkage of the date of the hedging transaction with the date of the hedged commitment. However, the foreign currency transaction must be designated as, and effective as, a hedge of a foreign currency commitment. In some instances, it may not be practical or feasible to hedge in the same currency and, therefore, a hedging transaction also may be denominated in a currency for which the exchange rate generally moves in tandem with the exchange rate for the currency in which the hedged commitment is denominated.

Income Tax Consequences of Rate Changes

134. The Board has concluded that interperiod tax allocation is required if transaction gains and losses from foreign currency transactions are included in income in a different period for financial statement purposes than for tax purposes. This is consistent with the requirements of Opinion 11.

135. The Board also has considered the possible need to provide deferred taxes related to translation adjustments resulting from translation of functional currency statements. Translation adjustments are accumulated and reported in a separate component of equity. Reported as such, translation adjustments do not affect pretax accounting income and most such adjustments also do not affect taxable income. Adjustments that do not affect either accounting income or taxable income do not create timing differences as defined by Opinion 11. However, reporting those adjustments as a component of equity does have the effect of increasing or decreasing equity, that is, increasing or decreasing an enterprise's net assets. Potential future tax effects related to those adjustments would partially offset the increase or decrease in net assets. Therefore, the Board decided that timing differences relating to translation adjustments should be accounted for in the same way as timing differences relating to accounting income. The need for and the amount of deferred taxes should be determined according to the other requirements of Opinions 11, 23, and 24. For example, paragraph 23 of this Statement provides that deferred taxes should not be provided for translation adjustments attributable to an investment in a foreign entity for which deferred taxes are not provided on unremitted earnings. Similarly, Opinions 11, 23, and 24 provide guidance as to how to compute the amount of deferred taxes. Deferred taxes on translation adjustments should be computed in the same manner.

Elimination of Intercompany Profits

136. An intercompany sale or transfer of inventory, machinery, etc., frequently produces an intercompany profit for the selling entity and, likewise, the acquiring entity's cost of the inventory, machinery, etc., includes a component of intercompany profit. The Board considered whether computation of the amount of intercompany profit to be eliminated should be based on exchange rates in effect on the date of the intercompany sale or transfer, or whether that computation should be based on exchange rates as of the date the asset (inventory, machinery, etc.) or the related expense (cost of sales, depreciation, etc.) is translated.

137. The Board decided that any intercompany profit occurs on the date of sale or transfer and that exchange rates in effect on that date or reasonable approximations thereof should be used to compute the amount of any intercompany profit to be eliminated. The effect of subsequent changes in exchange rates on the transferred asset or the related expense is viewed as being the result of changes in exchange rates rather than being attributable to intercompany profit.

Exchange Rates

138. The Board has concluded that if multiple rates exist, the rate to be used to translate foreign statements should be, in the absence of unusual circumstances, the rate applicable to dividend remittances. Use of that rate is more meaningful than any other rate because cash flows to the reporting enterprise from the foreign entity can be converted at only that rate, and realization of a net investment in a foreign entity will ultimately be in the form of cash flows from that entity.

139. If a foreign entity's financial statements are as of a date that is different from that of the enterprise and they are combined, consolidated, or accounted for by the equity method in the financial statements of the enterprise, the Board concluded that for purposes of applying the requirements of this Statement, the current rate is the rate in effect at the entity's balance sheet date. The Board believes that use of that rate most faithfully presents the dollar equivalent of the functional currency performance during the entity's fiscal period and position at the end of that period. Paragraph 4 of ARB 51 and paragraph 19(g) of APB Opinion No. 18, *The Equity Method of Accounting for Investments in Common Stock,* address consolidation and application of the equity method when a parent and a subsidiary have different fiscal periods. The Board believes its conclusion is consistent with those pronouncements.

Use of Averages or Other Methods of Approximation

140. Paragraph 12 permits the use of average rates to translate revenues, expenses, gains, and losses. Average rates used should be appropriately weighted by the volume of functional currency transactions occurring during the accounting period. For example, to translate revenue and expense accounts for an annual period, individual revenue and expense accounts for each quarter or month may be translated at that quarter's or that month's average rate. The translated amounts for each quarter or month should then be combined for the annual totals.

Disclosure

141. Paragraph 30 requires disclosure of the aggregate transaction gain or loss included in the determination of net income for the period. A transaction gain or loss does not measure, nor is it necessarily an indicator of, the full economic effect of a rate change on an enterprise. However, the Board believes that disclosing the aggregate transaction gain or loss may provide information about the effects of rate changes that is useful in evaluating and comparing reported results of operations.

142. Paragraph 31 requires an analysis of the separate component of equity in which translation adjustments, certain transaction gains and losses, and related tax effects are accumulated and reported. Generally accepted accounting principles presently require an analysis of changes in all equity accounts. Nevertheless, the Board has decided that it should specifically require an analysis of the separate component of equity disclosing the major changes in each period for which financial statements are presented. The analysis may be presented in a separate financial statement, in the notes to the financial statements, or as part of the statement of changes in equity. This separate component of equity might be titled "Equity Adjustment from Foreign Currency Translation" or given a similar title.

143. The Board considered whether an enterprise's financial statements should be adjusted for a change in rate subsequent to the date of the financial statements. The Board concluded that financial statements should not be adjusted for such rate changes. However, disclosure of the rate change and the estimated effect on unsettled balances pertaining to foreign currency transactions, if significant, may be necessary. If disclosed, the disclosure should include consideration of changes in unsettled transactions from the date of the financial statements to the date the rate changed. The Board recognizes that in some cases it may not be practicable to determine these changes; if so, that fact should be stated.

144. The Board considered a proposal for financial statement disclosure that would describe and possibly quantify the effects of rate changes on reported revenue and earnings. This type of disclosure might have included the mathematical effects of translating revenue and expenses at rates that are different from those used in a preceding period as well as the economic effects of rate changes, such as the effects on selling prices, sales volume, and cost structures. After considering information that it received on this matter, the Board has decided not to require disclosure of this type of information, primarily because of the wide variety of potential effects, the perceived difficulties of developing the information, and the impracticality of providing meaningful guidelines. However, the Board encourages management to supplement the disclosures required by this Statement with an analysis and discussion of the effects of rate changes on the reported results of operations. The purpose is to assist financial report users in understanding the broader economic implications of rate changes and to compare recent results with those of prior periods.

Effective Date and Transition

145. The Board considered and rejected both a completely prospective and a completely retroactive application of the accounting standards required by this Statement.

146. A completely prospective application was rejected because continued translation of previously acquired nonmonetary assets and related expenses at historical rates is inconsistent with the Board's other decisions regarding foreign currency translation. Regarding retroactive application, there are two possible effects resulting from the change to the accounting requirements of this Statement. Those effects are:

a. An increase or decrease in the enterprise's net assets resulting from translating all of a foreign entity's assets and liabilities at the current exchange rate for that entity's functional currency.
b. A reclassification between retained earnings and the new separate component of equity for cumulative translation adjustments so that retained earnings would equal an amount as if, since inception, translation adjustments had not been recognized in income and as if expenses related to nonmonetary items had not been translated at historical rates. (Such a reclassification between retained earnings and cumulative translation adjustments would have no effect on an enterprise's net assets or the total amount of equity.)

The Board has decided that the effect on net assets (first possible effect listed above) should be reported as the opening balance of the separate component of equity for cumulative translation adjustments as of the beginning of the year for which this Statement is first applied. Reclassification of amounts between retained earnings and the separate component of equity (second possible effect listed above) would require recomputation of amounts for all prior years for which an enterprise had foreign investments. The Board has decided that the benefits of such a recomputation, even if possible, would not justify the cost and should not be required.

147. The Board recognizes that Statement 8 accounting exposure has been hedged by the management of some enterprises and that different management actions might have been taken if Statement 8 had not been in effect. Therefore, restatement of financial statements presented for fiscal years prior to the effective date of this Statement is not required. However, restatement is permitted

and, if the prior fiscal year is not restated, disclosure of income before extraordinary items and net income for the prior year computed on a pro forma basis is permitted. If pro forma amounts are disclosed, such pro forma amounts should be computed in accordance with Opinion 20.

148. The Board's decision that this Statement should be effective for fiscal years beginning on or after December 15, 1982 is based on the belief that such an effective date will provide sufficient time for enterprises (a) to make any desired changes in financial policies that might be prompted by this Statement and (b) to prepare internally for the accounting requirements of this Statement. Enterprises that want to adopt the provisions of this Statement at an earlier date, however, are encouraged to do so. If adopted for a fiscal year ending on or before March 31, 1982, disclosure of the effect of adopting the new standard is required to provide comparability between those enterprises that do adopt and those that do not adopt the standard before the effective date. This disclosure is not required for fiscal years ending after March 31, 1982 because many enterprises will have terminated some or all hedges of the previous Statement 8 accounting exposure, thereby rendering any determination of the effect virtually impossible. Furthermore, the cost of requiring two systems of translation beyond early 1982 is not justified.

149. The Board is considering an amendment of Statement 33 to provide information that is compatible with the functional currency approach to foreign currency translation. The Board believes that the transition provisions of this Statement provide appropriate flexibility to accommodate any amendment of Statement 33.

Appendix D

BACKGROUND INFORMATION

150. The extensive currency realignments and the major revisions of the international monetary system in the early 1970s, together with the existence in practice of several significantly different methods of accounting for the translation of foreign currency transactions and financial statements, highlighted the need to address foreign currency translation at that time. Statement 8, which was issued in October 1975 and was effective for fiscal years that began on or after January 1, 1976, established standards of financial accounting and reporting for foreign currency translation and eliminated the use of alternative methods.

151. Responding to a recommendation by the Structure Committee of the Financial Accounting Foundation that it experiment with a more formal postenactment review process, the Board issued in May 1978 an invitation for public comment on FASB Statements 1-12, each of which had been in effect for at least two years. More than 200 letters were received, and Statement 8 was the subject of most of the comments received.

152. Respondents were nearly unanimous in their call for changes to Statement 8 but had conflicting views as to what those changes should be. Changes were suggested both in the method to be used in translating financial statements and in the method of disposition of the resulting translation adjustments and transaction gains and losses from foreign currency transactions. Most respondents who suggested changes in the translation method also suggested changes in the method of recognition of the resulting translation effects.

153. Respondents' concerns with Statement 8 reflect the perception that the results of translation under that Statement frequently do not reflect the underlying economic reality of foreign operations. The perceived failure of accounting results to portray the underlying economic circumstances is underscored heavily in two respects: (a) the volatility of reported earnings and (b) the abnormality of financial results and relationships. The sources of both problems are attributed to the requirements for (a) current recognition of unrealized exchange adjustments and (b) that inventories and fixed assets are translated at historical rates under Statement 8, whereas debt is translated at current rates.

154. Many respondents believe that the exchange risk exposure on foreign currency debt is effectively hedged in many cases by the foreign currency revenue potential of operating assets, but that this hedge is not recognized in the Statement 8 translation process. One result is large and frequent fluctuations in reported earnings, which many believe misrepresent the real performance of a company and obscure operating trends. Another result is said to be erratic operating margins and irregular financial relationships that make operating performance difficult to interpret.

155. Recommendations regarding changes in the method of translation of foreign currency statements were that some or all nonmonetary assets (primarily inventories and, less frequently, fixed assets) should be translated at current exchange rates or that long-term debt should be translated at historical rates.

156. The most frequently made recommendations regarding changes to Statement 8 were for some form of deferral or nonrecognition of the exchange adjustments that result from its application. Some

respondents stated that exchange rates are affected by rumor, politics, speculation, and other factors so that foreign currency exchange rates at any particular moment in time are temporary, and that changes over a relatively short time span are not likely to have a long-term effect on a company's earnings or financial position. Those respondents believe that exchange adjustments resulting from transitory rate changes are subject to misinterpretation because short-term rate fluctuations are poor indicators of long-term trends. Moreover, many of those respondents indicated that exchange adjustments from translation of foreign currency statements have not been realized and often will never be realized in amounts approximating the amounts reported in financial statements as required by Statement 8.

157. In January 1979, after considering the FASB staff's analysis of the comment letters, the Board added to its agenda a project to reconsider Statement 8. In February 1979, a task force was appointed to advise the Board during its deliberations on this project. The task force is composed of 22 members and observers from academe, the financial community, government, industry, and public accounting, as well as representatives from the International Accounting Standards Committee, the Accounting Standards Committee of the United Kingdom and Ireland, and the Canadian Institute of Chartered Accountants.

158. Subsequently, foreign currency translation was addressed at 18 public Board meetings and at 4 public task force meetings. In August 1980, the Board issued an Exposure Draft that set forth new proposals for foreign currency translation.

159. The Exposure Draft had a 3-month comment period, and more than 360 comment letters were received. The Board conducted a public hearing on the Exposure Draft in December 1980, and 47 organizations and individuals presented their views at the 4-day hearing.

160. Between January and June 1981, foreign currency translation was addressed at four additional public Board meetings and one public task force meeting. The Board's consideration of the issues resulted in modifications that the Board believed were significant in the aggregate. Accordingly, a revised Exposure Draft was issued on June 30, 1981.

161. The revised Exposure Draft had a 90-day comment period, and more than 260 comment letters were received. In October and November 1981, foreign currency translation was addressed at two additional public Board meetings and one public task force meeting. Consideration of the written comments resulted in further modifications as reflected in this Statement.

Appendix E

GLOSSARY

162. This appendix defines terms that are essential to clear comprehension of this Statement. They are set in **boldface type** the first time they appear in this Statement.

Attribute
The quantifiable characteristic of an item that is measured for accounting purposes. For example, historical cost and current cost are attributes of an asset.

Conversion
The exchange of one currency for another.

Currency Swaps
An exchange between two enterprises of the currencies of two different countries pursuant to an agreement to reexchange the two currencies at the same rate of exchange at a specified future date.

Current Exchange Rate
The current exchange rate is the rate at which one unit of a currency can be exchanged for (converted into) another currency. For purposes of translation of financial statements referred to in this Statement, the current exchange rate is the rate as of the end of the period covered by the financial statements or as of the dates of recognition in those statements in the case of revenues, expenses, gains, and losses. The requirements for applying the current exchange rate for translating financial statements are set forth in paragraph 12. Further information regarding exchange rates is provided in paragraphs 26-28.

Discount or Premium on a Forward Contract
The foreign currency amount of the contract multiplied by the difference between the contracted forward rate and the spot rate at the date of inception of the contract.

Enterprise
See Reporting Enterprise.

Entity
See Foreign Entity.

Foreign Currency
A currency other than the functional currency of the entity being referred to (for example, the dollar could be a foreign currency for a foreign entity). Composites of currencies, such as the Special Drawing Rights on the International

Monetary Fund (SDRs), used to set prices or denominate amounts of loans, etc., have the characteristics of foreign currency for purposes of applying this Statement.

Foreign Currency Statements
Financial statements that employ as the unit of measure a functional currency that is not the reporting currency of the enterprise.

Foreign Currency Transactions
Transactions whose terms are denominated in a currency other than the entity's functional currency. Foreign currency transactions arise when an enterprise (a) buys or sells on credit goods or services whose prices are denominated in foreign currency, (b) borrows or lends funds and the amounts payable or receivable are denominated in foreign currency, (c) is a party to an unperformed forward exchange contract, or (d) for other reasons, acquires or disposes of assets, or incurs or settles liabilities denominated in foreign currency.

Foreign Currency Translation
The process of expressing in the reporting currency of the enterprise those amounts that are denominated or measured in a different currency.

Foreign Entity
An operation (for example, subsidiary, division, branch, joint venture, etc.) whose financial statements (a) are prepared in a currency other than the reporting currency of the reporting enterprise and (b) are combined or consolidated with or accounted for on the equity basis in the financial statements of the reporting enterprise.

Forward Exchange Contract
An agreement to exchange at a specified future date currencies of different countries at a specified rate (forward rate).

Forward Rate
See Forward Exchange Contract.

Functional Currency
An entity's functional currency is the currency of the primary economic environment in which the entity operates; normally, that is the currency of the environment in which an entity primarily generates and expends cash. (See Appendix A.)

Local Currency
The currency of a particular country being referred to.

Reporting Currency
The currency in which an enterprise prepares its financial statements.

Reporting Enterprise
An entity or group whose financial statements are being referred to. In this Statement, those financial statements reflect (a) the financial statements of one or more foreign operations by combination, consolidation, or equity accounting; (b) foreign currency transactions; or (c) both of the foregoing.

Spot Rate
The exchange rate for immediate delivery of currencies exchanged.

Transaction Date
The date at which a transaction (for example, a sale or purchase of merchandise or services) is recorded in accounting records in conformity with generally accepted accounting principles. A long-term commitment may have more than one transaction date (for example, the due date of each progress payment under a construction contract is an anticipated transaction date).

Transaction Gain or Loss
Transaction gains or losses result from a change in exchange rates between the functional currency and the currency in which a foreign currency transaction is denominated. They represent an increase or decrease in (a) the actual functional currency cash flows realized upon settlement of foreign currency transactions and (b) the expected functional currency cash flows on unsettled foreign currency transactions.

Translation
See Foreign Currency Translation.

Translation Adjustments
Translation adjustments result from the process of translating financial statements from the entity's functional currency into the reporting currency.

Unit of Measure
The currency in which assets, liabilities, revenues, expenses, gains, and losses are measured.

Statement of Financial Accounting Standards No. 53 Financial Reporting by Producers and Distributors of Motion Picture Films

STATUS

Issued: December 1981

Effective Date: For fiscal years beginning after December 15, 1981

Affects: Amends FAS 32, Appendix A

Affected by: No other pronouncements

SUMMARY

This Statement extracts the specialized accounting principles and practices from the AICPA Industry Accounting Guide, *Accounting for Motion Picture Films,* and AICPA Statement of Position 79-4, *Accounting for Motion Picture Films,* and establishes standards of financial accounting and reporting for producers and distributors of motion picture films. Exhibition rights transferred under license agreements for television program material shall be accounted for like sales by the licensor. The sale shall be recognized by the licensor when the license period begins and certain specified conditions have been met. Producers and distributors that license film exhibition rights to movie theaters generally shall recognize revenue when the films are shown. This Statement also describes how producers and distributors shall account for film costs and participation agreements.

Statement of Financial Accounting Standards No. 53
Financial Reporting by Producers and Distributors of Motion Picture Films

CONTENTS

INTRODUCTION

1. As discussed in FASB Statement No. 32, *Specialized Accounting and Reporting Principles and Practices in AICPA Statements of Position and Guides on Accounting and Auditing Matters,* the FASB is extracting the specialized[1] accounting and reporting principles and practices from AICPA Statements of Position (SOPs) and Guides on accounting and auditing matters and issuing them in FASB Statements after appropriate due process. This Statement extracts the specialized principles and practices from the AICPA Industry Accounting Guide, *Accounting for Motion Picture Films* (Guide), and SOP 79-4, *Accounting for Motion Picture Films,* and establishes financial accounting and reporting standards for **producers**[2] and **distributors** of **motion picture films** (films).

2. The Board has concluded that it can reach an informed decision on the basis of existing information without a public hearing and that the effective date and transition specified in paragraph 25 are advisable in the circumstances.

STANDARDS OF FINANCIAL ACCOUNTING AND REPORTING

Revenue

Films Licensed to Movie Theaters

3. Motion picture exhibition rights are generally sold (licensed) to theaters on the basis of a percentage of the box office receipts or for a flat fee in some markets. In certain instances, the licensor may receive a nonrefundable guarantee against a percentage of box office receipts. In some markets, for example in many foreign markets, those guarantees are essentially outright sales because the licensor has no reasonable expectations of receiving additional revenues based on percentages of box office receipts, particularly where there is a lack of control over distribution.

4. A licensor shall recognize revenues on the dates of exhibition for both percentage and flat fee engagements. In most cases, nonrefundable guarantees shall be deferred in the accounts and recognized

---

[1]The term *specialized* is used to refer to those accounting and reporting principles and practices in AICPA Guides and Statements of Position that are neither superseded by nor contained in Accounting Research Bulletins, APB Opinions, FASB Statements, or FASB Interpretations.

[2]Terms defined in the glossary (Appendix A) are in **boldface type** the first time they appear in this Statement.

as revenues on the dates of exhibition. Guarantees that are, in substance, outright sales, shall be recognized as revenue if the conditions specified in paragraph 6 are met.

Films Licensed to Television

5. Motion picture companies and **independent producers** and distributors (licensors) shall consider a **license agreement for television program material** as a sale of a right or a group of rights.

6. A licensor shall recognize revenue from a license agreement for television program material when the license period begins *and* all of the following conditions have been met:

a. The license fee for each film is known.
b. The cost of each film is known or reasonably determinable.
c. Collectibility of the full license fee is reasonably assured.
d. The film has been accepted by the licensee in accordance with the conditions of the license agreement.
e. The film is available for its first showing or telecast. Unless a conflicting license prevents usage by the licensee, restrictions under the same license agreement or another license agreement with the same licensee on the timing of subsequent showings shall not affect this condition.

7. Ordinarily, when the conditions specified in paragraph 6 are met, both the licensee and licensor are contractually obligated under a noncancelable license agreement and are able to perform in compliance with all the significant terms of the license agreement. If significant factors raise doubt about the obligation or ability of either party to perform under the agreement, revenue recognition shall be delayed until such factors no longer exist. Insignificant factors, such as the actual delivery of an existing print of a previously accepted film, are not a sufficient basis for delaying revenue recognition. Amendments to an existing license shall receive appropriate accounting recognition consistent with the accounting described in this Statement.

8. Revenues from the licensing of a film shall be recognized in the same sequence as the **market**-by-market exploitation of the film and at the time the licensee is able to exercise rights under the agreement. That time would be the later of the commencement of the license period (the right then being exercisable by the licensee) or the expiration of a conflicting license (the right then being deliverable by the licensor).

9. The amount of the license fee for each film ordinarily is specified in the contract, and the present value of that amount, computed in accordance with the provisions of APB Opinion No. 21, *Interest on Receivables and Payables,* generally shall be used as the sales price for each film.

Costs and Expenses

Production Costs

10. Costs to produce a film **(production costs)** shall be capitalized as film cost inventory and shall be amortized using the individual-film-forecast-computation method (paragraphs 11 and 12 and Appendix D). The periodic-table-computation method (paragraph 13) may be used if the result would approximate the result achieved using the individual-film-forecast-computation method. Amortization shall reasonably relate the film costs to the gross revenues reported and shall yield a constant rate of gross profit before period expenses. Amortization of film costs shall begin when a film is released and revenues on that film are recognized.

11. The individual-film-forecast-computation method amortizes film costs in the same ratio that current gross revenues bear to anticipated total gross revenues. That method requires the determination of a fraction, the numerator being gross revenues from the film for the period and the denominator being the anticipated total gross revenues from the film during its useful life, including future estimated total gross revenues from exploitation in all markets. Estimated revenues from the sale of long-term, noninterest-bearing television exhibition rights shall be included in the denominator in an amount equal to the total estimated present value of those revenues as of the date they are expected to be recognized, computed in accordance with the provisions of Opinion 21. Accordingly, in the period those revenues are recognized, the numerator shall include only that present value (not gross proceeds). The resulting fraction is applied to production and other capitalized film costs to determine the amortization for each period.

12. Due to the uncertainties in the estimating process, anticipated total gross revenues may vary from actual total gross revenues. Estimates of anticipated total gross revenues shall be reviewed periodically and revised when necessary to reflect more current information. When anticipated total gross revenues are revised, a new denominator shall be determined to include only the anticipated total gross revenues from the beginning of the current year; the numerator (actual gross revenues for the current period) is not affected. The revised fraction is applied to the unrecovered film costs (production and other capitalized film costs) as of the beginning of the current year.

13. The periodic-table-computation method amortizes film costs using tables prepared from the historic revenue patterns of a large group of films. That revenue pattern is assumed to provide a reasonable guide to the experience of succeeding groups of films produced and distributed under similar conditions. The periodic-table-computation method ordinarily is used only to amortize that portion of film costs relating to film rights licensed to movie theaters, and film costs accordingly shall be allocated between those markets for which the table is used and other markets. If that method is used to amortize film costs, the periodic tables shall be reviewed regularly and updated whenever revenue patterns change significantly. Such tables shall not be used for a film whose distribution pattern differs significantly from those used in compiling the table, for example, a film released for reserved seat theater exhibition.

Participations

14. If it is anticipated that compensation will be payable under a **participation** agreement, including residuals, the total expected participation shall be charged to expense in the same manner as amortization of production costs as described in paragraphs 10-13, that is, in the same ratio as current gross revenues bear to anticipated total gross revenues.

Exploitation Costs

15. Costs incurred to exploit a film **(exploitation costs)** that clearly benefit future periods shall be capitalized as film cost inventory and amortized as described in paragraphs 10-13. Examples of those costs are film prints, and prerelease and early release advertising that is expected to benefit the film in future markets. Cooperative or other forms of local advertising that are not clearly expected to benefit the film in future markets, and rent, salaries, and other expenses of distribution shall be charged to expense in the period incurred.

Inventory Valuation

16. Unamortized production and exploitation costs shall be compared with **net realizable value** each reporting period on a film-by-film basis. If estimated future gross revenues from a film are not sufficient to recover the unamortized film costs, other direct distribution expenses, and participations, the unamortized film costs shall be written down to net realizable value. Film costs that are written down to net realizable value during a fiscal year may be written back up during that same fiscal year in an amount not to exceed the current year write-down, if the motion picture company increases its estimate of future gross revenues. The adjustments shall be recorded in the interim period in which the revised estimates are made; previously reported interim amounts shall not be restated. Film costs that are reduced to net realizable value at the end of a fiscal year shall not be written back up in subsequent fiscal years. In unusual cases, such as a change in public acceptance of certain types of films or actual costs substantially in excess of budgeted costs, a write-down to net realizable value may be required before the film is released.

Story Costs and Scenarios

17. The cost of film inventories ordinarily includes expenditures for properties, such as film rights to books, stage plays, original screenplays, etc. The stories and scenarios generally must be adapted to the production techniques for motion picture films. The cost of the adaptation is included in the cost of the particular property. Those properties shall be reviewed periodically and, if it is determined that a property will not be used in the production of a film, the cost shall be charged to production overhead in the current period. There is a presumption that story costs shall be charged to production overhead if the property has been held for three years and has not been set for production. Once charged off, story costs shall not be reinstated if subsequently set for production.

Investments in Films Produced by Independent Producers

18. Cash advances made by motion picture companies to independent producers shall be included in film cost inventory of the motion picture company. Amounts of loans to independent producers that are guaranteed by a motion picture company shall be recorded by the motion picture company as film cost inventory and as a liability when funds are disbursed. Revenues and expenses shall be accounted for and reported following the same principles described in paragraphs 3-17.

Balance Sheet Classification

19. A license agreement for sale of film rights for television exhibition shall not be reported on the balance sheet until the time of revenue recognition. Amounts received on such agreements prior to revenue recognition shall be reported as advance payments and included in current liabilities, if those advance payments relate to film cost inventory classified as current assets.

20. Either a classified or unclassified balance sheet may be presented. If a classified balance sheet is presented, film costs shall be segregated on the balance sheet between current and noncurrent assets. The following film costs shall be classified as current assets: unamortized costs of film inventory released

and allocated to the primary market, completed films not released (reduced by the portion allocated to secondary markets), and television films in production that are under contract of sale. All other capitalized film costs shall be classified as noncurrent assets.

21. The allocated portion of film costs expected to be realized from secondary television or other exploitation shall be reported as a noncurrent asset and amortized as revenues are recorded.

Home Viewing Market

22. Motion picture companies may earn additional revenues by licensing films to the **home viewing market.** Some of those transactions have characteristics similar to the transactions described in paragraph 3 of this Statement and some have characteristics similar to the transactions described in paragraph 5. Accordingly, programs licensed to the home viewing market shall be reported as described in paragraphs 3-21, as appropriate.

Disclosure

23. The components of film inventories (including films released, completed but not released, and in process and story rights and scenarios) shall be disclosed.

Amendment to FASB Statement No. 32

24. The references to the AICPA Industry Accounting Guide, *Accounting for Motion Picture Films,* and AICPA Statement of Position 79-4, *Accounting for Motion Picture Films,* are deleted from Appendix A of Statement 32.

Effective Date and Transition

25. This Statement shall be effective for financial statements for fiscal years beginning after December 15, 1981, with earlier application encouraged. Restatement of previously issued financial statements to conform to the provisions of this Statement is encouraged but not required.

The provisions of this Statement need not be applied to immaterial items.

This Statement was adopted by the unanimous vote of the seven members of the Financial Accounting Standards Board:

Donald J. Kirk, *Chairman*
Frank E. Block
John W. March
Robert A. Morgan
David Mosso
Robert T. Sprouse
Ralph E. Walters

Appendix A

GLOSSARY

26. This appendix defines certain terms that are used in this Statement.

Distributor
A film distributor owns the rights to distribute films, which are sold (licensed) to movie theaters, individual television stations, groups of stations, networks, or others. This definition excludes syndicators or other independent sales organizations that act only as sales agents for producers or owners of films under agreements that do not call for the sharing of profits.

Exploitation Costs
Exploitation costs are costs incurred during the final production phase and during the release periods of films in both primary and secondary markets. Examples of such costs are film prints, advertising, rents, salaries, and other distribution expenses.

Home Viewing Market
The home viewing market includes all means by which films are sold or otherwise made available to residential viewers for a fee. Examples are video cassettes and disks and all forms of pay television, including cable and over-the-air transmission.

Independent Producer
Motion picture companies frequently advance funds or guarantee loans for the production of films by independent producers. Certain legal rights of ownership, including the copyright, may be retained by the independent producer. The motion picture company frequently has a participation in the net revenues from the film and generally has additional attributes of ownership, such as the right to exploit the film and the risk of loss. The financing arrangement usually provides that the production loan by the motion picture company (or the guaranteed loan) is repayable only from the revenues from the particular film. The independent producer does not have general liability with respect to such a loan. Consequently, the motion picture company bears substantially all the risks of ownership.

License Agreement for Television Program Material

A typical license agreement for television program material covers several films (a package) and grants a broadcaster (licensee) the right to telecast either a specified number or an unlimited number of showings over a maximum period of time (license period) for a specified fee. Ordinarily, the fee is paid in installments over a period generally shorter than the license period. The agreement usually contains a separate license for each film in the package. The license expires at the earlier of the last allowed telecast or the end of the license period. The licensee pays the required fee whether or not the rights are exercised. If the licensee does not exercise the contractual rights, the rights revert to the licensor with no refund to the licensee. The license period generally is not intended to provide continued use of the film throughout that period but rather to define a reasonable period of time within which the licensee can exercise the limited rights to use the film.

Market

The first market in which a film is exploited is called the primary market because that is the market for which a film principally is produced. All other exploitation is in the secondary market. Generally, the markets are mutually exclusive; that is, a film cannot be exploited in more than one market at a time, because of the contract terms or sound marketing techniques.

There is only one first-run telecast of a particular film in a given market, and film rights are marketed in a manner to avoid conflict in a given market. For example, conflict may exist in a market between (a) theaters and television stations, (b) premium cable or broadcast subscription television and network television, (c) network television and local stations, and (d) two or more local stations within the market area. To avoid conflict between theaters and television, a producer may impose restrictions on distribution that would prohibit the licensing of the film for television while the film is being shown in movie theaters.

The market in which a film is exhibited is a prime determinant of the value of the film. A film's previous exposure in a market will generally have an effect on the price the exhibitor is willing to pay for exhibition rights. In addition, the size and demographics of a particular market and the audience's acceptance of the film affect the price that a telecaster can charge for advertising time.

Motion Picture Film (Film)

The term *film* refers to all types of films and video cassettes and disks, including features, television specials, series, and cartoons that are (a) exhibited in theaters; (b) licensed for exhibition by individual television stations, groups of stations, networks, cable television systems, or other means; or (c) licensed for the home viewing market.

Net Realizable Value

Net realizable value is the estimated selling price (rental value) in the ordinary course of business less estimated costs to complete and exploit in a manner consistent with realization of that income.

Participation

Frequently, persons involved in the production of a motion picture film are compensated, in part or in full, with a participation in the income from the film. Determination of the amount of compensation payable to the participant is usually based on percentages of revenues or profits from the film from some or all sources. Television residuals are comparable to participations and are generally based on the number of times the film is exhibited on television or as a percentage of revenues from such exhibition.

Producer

A film producer is an individual or a motion picture company that produces films for exhibition in movie theaters, on television, or elsewhere.

Production Costs

Production costs include the cost of a story and scenario to be used for a film and other costs to produce a film, for example, salaries of cast, directors, producers, extras, and miscellaneous staff; cost of set construction and operations, wardrobe, and all accessories; cost of sound synchronization; production overhead, including depreciation and amortization of studio equipment and leasehold improvements used in production; and rental of facilities on location. Production costs ordinarily are accumulated by individual films in four chronological steps: (a) acquisition of the story rights; (b) preproduction, which includes script development, costume design, and set design and construction; (c) principal photography, which includes shooting the film; and (d) postproduction, which includes sound synchronization, and editing, culminating in a completed master negative.

Appendix B

BACKGROUND INFORMATION AND SUMMARY OF CONSIDERATION OF COMMENTS ON EXPOSURE DRAFT

27. This Statement extracts the specialized accounting and reporting principles and practices from the Motion Picture Guide and SOP 79-4 and codifies them as FASB standards without significant change. Board members have assented to the issuance of this Statement on the basis that it is an appropriate extraction of those existing specialized principles and practices and that a comprehensive reconsideration of those principles and practices was not contemplated in the undertaking of this FASB project. Some of the background material and discussion of accounting alternatives have not been carried forward from the Guide and SOP. The Board's conceptual framework project on accounting recognition criteria will address revenue recognition issues that may pertain to those addressed in this Statement. A Statement of Financial Accounting Concepts resulting from that project in due course will serve as a basis for evaluating existing standards and practices. Accordingly, the Board may wish to evaluate the standards in this Statement when its conceptual framework project is completed.

28. The Guide was developed to clarify and standardize accounting by motion picture companies for revenues and costs, particularly the timing of revenue recognition and the treatment of production and exploitation costs. Before 1973, motion picture companies accounted for revenue from films licensed to television under several different methods, each of which resulted in recognizing revenue at a different point in time, ranging from the date the agreement was signed to apportioning the revenue over the license period. In addition, industry practice varied with respect to capitalization, amortization, and balance sheet classification of film costs. The Guide recommended that revenue from films licensed for telecasting be recognized when the license period began, the film became available to the licensee, and certain other specified conditions were met that, in effect, contractually obligated the licensor and licensee. The Guide also recommended the amortization of film costs by the individual-film-forecast-computation method and the write-down of those costs to net realizable value when estimated gross revenues were not sufficient to recover the film's unamortized costs.

29. An Exposure Draft of a proposed Statement, *Financial Accounting and Reporting by Producers and Distributors of Motion Picture Films,* was issued June 12, 1981. The Board received 23 letters of comment on the Exposure Draft. The Board's consideration of certain of the comments received are discussed in the following paragraphs.

30. Some respondents believe that a license agreement for television program material should not be considered as a sale of a right or a group of rights, but rather should be reported like an operating lease even though FASB Statement No. 13, *Accounting for Leases,* does not apply to license agreements. They believe that such an agreement has many characteristics of an operating lease. If a licensor accounted for a license agreement as an operating lease, revenues would be recognized over the license period and film costs would be amortized as revenue is recognized.

31. Other respondents believe that a license agreement differs from an operating lease and should not be reported like an operating lease. They believe that a license agreement is a sale of a right. They noted that the licensor has satisfied substantially all of its obligations at the date the film becomes available to the licensee and, accordingly, there is no basis for deferring recognition of revenue beyond that point. They further noted that each sale of a motion picture exhibition right constitutes the final step in the realization process and, accordingly, should be reported as income when the conditions specified in paragraph 6 (paragraph 8 of the Exposure Draft) have been met. The Board agrees with those respondents.

32. Paragraphs 22 and 23 of the Exposure Draft required the segregation of film costs between current and noncurrent assets. Generally, costs allocated to primary markets would be classified as current assets and costs allocated to secondary markets would be classified as noncurrent assets. Several respondents prefer an unclassified balance sheet because they believe that the distinction between primary and secondary markets has blurred in recent years. The Board agrees that a classified balance sheet should not be required (paragraph 20 of this Statement). However, the Board believes that if a classified balance sheet is presented, segregation between current and noncurrent based on primary and secondary markets continues to represent a more meaningful presentation for this industry than other possible methods.

33. Paragraph 17 of the Exposure Draft required exploitation costs that clearly benefit future periods to be capitalized and amortized using the individual-film-forecast-computation method. Costs to be capitalized would have included prerelease and early release national advertising. Cooperative and all other forms of local advertising and distribution expenses would have been charged to expense in the period incurred. Some respondents stated that, in recent years, cooperative and local advertising have

increased substantially, especially in major urban and local media centers. They believe that certain local advertising expenditures benefit future periods by developing a market for the film, thereby increasing its value in other markets. They believe that requiring those local advertising costs to be charged to expense as incurred may result in depressed operating results in the early release period of a film, even for a film expected to be commercially successful. Accordingly, they believe the reporting provisions in paragraph 17 of the Exposure Draft would have mismatched costs and revenues. The Board agrees with those respondents and has broadened the example of advertising costs that may be capitalized under paragraph 15 of this Statement.

34. Some respondents suggested that this Statement specify the accounting for films licensed to the home viewing market. They noted that recent technology has significantly expanded that market and that its increasing economic importance indicates a need for reporting guidance. They believe that some home viewing market transactions have characteristics similar to the transactions described in paragraph 3 (paragraph 5 of the Exposure Draft) and some have characteristics similar to the transactions described in paragraph 5 (paragraph 7 of the Exposure Draft). The Board agrees with those respondents. Accordingly, paragraph 22 has been added to this Statement to specify that films licensed to the home viewing market shall be reported in accordance with the principles described in paragraphs 3-21 of this Statement, as appropriate. A definition of the home viewing market also has been added to the glossary.

35. Paragraph 6 of the Exposure Draft stated that nonrefundable guarantees that are, in substance, outright sales, would be recognized as revenue on execution of a noncancelable contract. Some respondents noted that film producers may sell off exhibition rights during film production and recognize revenue before the film is completed and available for exploitation. They suggested that such nonrefundable guarantees should not be recognized as revenue until the conditions specified in paragraph 6 (paragraph 8 of the Exposure Draft) have been met. The Board adopted that suggestion in paragraph 4 of this Statement.

36. Several respondents suggested other changes to the Exposure Draft. None of those proposed changes met the criteria for change included in the Notice for Recipients of the Exposure Draft. Accordingly, the Board did not adopt those suggestions.

Appendix C

ILLUSTRATION OF REVENUE RECOGNITION CONCEPT

37. This appendix illustrates when revenue shall be recognized under a license agreement for television program material in accordance with paragraphs 5-9 of this Statement.

38. Assumptions

a. End of Fiscal Year—December 31
b. Contract Execution Date—July 31, 19X1
c. Number of Films and Telecasts Permitted—4 films, 2 telecasts each
d. Payment Schedule—$1,000,000 at contract execution date, $6,000,000 on January 1, 19X2, 19X3, and 19X4
e. Appropriate Interest Rate for Imputation of Interest—12 percent per year
f. Fees, License Periods, and Film Availability Dates:

Film	Total Fee	Stated License Periods From	Stated License Periods To[3]	Film Availability Dates
A	$ 8,000,000	10/1/X1	9/30/X3	9/1/X1
B	5,000,000	10/1/X1	9/30/X3	9/1/X1
C	3,750,000	9/1/X2	8/31/X4	12/1/X1
D	2,250,000	9/1/X3	8/31/X5	12/1/X2
	$19,000,000			

For purposes of determining the present value of the payments in accordance with Opinion 21, it is assumed that the $1,000,000 payment on July 31, 19X1 and the $6,000,000 payments on January 1, 19X2 and 19X3 relate to films A and B and the $6,000,000 payment on January 1, 19X4 relates to films C and D. Other simplifying assumptions or methods of assigning the payments to the films could be made.

[3]The actual license periods expire at the earlier of (a) the second telecast or (b) the end of the stated license period.

	Payment		Discounted Present Value (rounded to 000s)	
Film	Date	Amount	As of Date	Amount
A&B	7/31/X1	$ 1,000,000	10/1/X1	$ 1,000,000
	1/1/X2	6,000,000	10/1/X1	5,825,000
	1/1/X3	6,000,000	10/1/X1	5,201,000
		$13,000,000		$12,026,000
C	1/1/X4	$ 3,750,000	9/1/X2	$ 3,219,000
D	1/1/X4	$ 2,250,000	9/1/X3	$ 2,163,000
		$ 6,000,000		

39. Income Recognition

	License Period		Year of Income Recognition		
Film	From	To	19X1	19X2	19X3
A&B	10/1/X1	9/30/X3	$12,026,000(R)		
			331,000(I)(a)	$ 643,000(I)(b)	
C	9/1/X2	8/31/X4		3,219,000(R)	
				129,000(I)(c)	$ 402,000(I)(d)
D	9/1/X3	8/31/X5			2,163,000(R)
					87,000(I)(e)
			$12,357,000	$3,991,000	$2,652,000

(R) Revenue
(I) Imputed interest income
(a) Interest at 12 percent for 3 months on receivable of $11,026,000
(b) Interest at 12 percent for 1 year on receivable of $5,357,000 ($11,026,000 plus $331,000 less 1/1/X2 payment of $6,000,000)
(c) Interest at 12 percent for 4 months on receivable of $3,219,000
(d) Interest at 12 percent for 1 year on receivable of $3,348,000 ($3,219,000 plus $129,000)
(e) Interest at 12 percent for 4 months on receivable of $2,163,000

Appendix D

ILLUSTRATION OF INDIVIDUAL-FILM-FORECAST-COMPUTATION METHOD OF AMORTIZATION

40. This appendix illustrates the individual-film-forecast-computation method used by a licensor to amortize film costs.

41. Assumptions

• Film cost	$10,000,000
• Actual gross revenues:	
First year	12,000,000
Second year	3,000,000
Third year	1,000,000
• Anticipated total gross revenues:	
At end of first year	24,000,000
At end of second and third years	20,000,000

42. Amortization

				Amount of Amortization
First-year amortization				
$12,000,000 / $24,000,000	×	$10,000,000	=	$5,000,000
Second-year amortization (anticipated total gross revenues reduced from $24,000,000 to $20,000,000) (a)				
$3,000,000 / $8,000,000(d)	×	$5,000,000(c)	=	$1,875,000
Third-year amortization				
$1,000,000 / $8,000,000(d)	×	$5,000,000(d)	=	$ 625,000

(a) If there were no change in anticipated total gross revenues, the second-year amortization would be as follows:

$ 3,000,000 / $24,000,000	×	$10,000,000	=	$1,250,000

(b) $20,000,000 minus $12,000,000 or anticipated total gross revenues from beginning of period

(c) $10,000,000 minus $5,000,000 or cost less accumulated amortization at beginning of period

(d) The $8,000,000 and $5,000,000 need not be reduced by the second-year gross revenue ($3,000,000) and second-year amortization ($1,875,000), respectively, because anticipated gross revenues did not change from the second to the third year (paragraph 12). If such reduction were made, the amount of amortization would be the same as follows:

$1,000,000 / $5,000,000	×	$3,125,000	=	$ 625,000

Statement of Financial Accounting Standards No. 54 Financial Reporting and Changing Prices: Investment Companies

an amendment of FASB Statement No. 33

STATUS

Issued: January 1982

Effective Date: January 27, 1982 retroactive to fiscal years ending on or after December 25, 1979

Affects: Amends FAS 33, paragraph 23

Affected by: No other pronouncements

SUMMARY

This Statement amends FASB Statement No. 33, *Financial Reporting and Changing Prices,* to eliminate the requirement that investment companies disclose supplemental information adjusted for effects of changing prices.

Statement of Financial Accounting Standards No. 54
Financial Reporting and Changing Prices: Investment Companies

an amendment of FASB Statement No. 33

CONTENTS

INTRODUCTION AND BACKGROUND INFORMATION

1. FASB Statement No. 33, *Financial Reporting and Changing Prices,* establishes standards for reporting certain effects of price changes on business enterprises. Statement 33 applies to publicly held business enterprises that have, at the beginning of the fiscal year for which financial statements are being presented, either of the following characteristics:

a. Inventory and property, plant, and equipment amounting in the aggregate to more than $125 million
b. Total assets amounting to more than $1 billion

2. Several representatives of the investment company industry met with the FASB staff and with the Board to discuss their concerns about the Statement 33 requirements as they apply to investment companies. Based on discussions with the industry representatives and others on the subject, the Board concluded that the information required to be disclosed by Statement 33 in part is not relevant for investment companies and in part is already provided in their primary financial statements. The rest of the required information can be determined readily by readers of those financial statements. Accordingly, the Board concluded that investment companies need not provide the supplemental information about effects of changing prices called for by Statement 33.

STANDARDS OF FINANCIAL ACCOUNTING AND REPORTING

Amendment to FASB Statement No. 33

3. The first sentence of paragraph 23 of Statement 33 is amended to read:

> The requirements of this Statement apply to public enterprises, except for investment companies as defined in Section 3 of the Investment Company Act of 1940, as amended, that prepare their primary financial statements . . .

Effective Date and Transition

4. This Statement shall be effective on January 27, 1982, retroactive to fiscal years ending on or after December 25, 1979.

The provisions of this Statement need not be applied to immaterial items.

This Statement was adopted by the affirmative votes of four members of the Financial Accounting Standards Board. Messrs. Mosso, Sprouse, and Walters dissented.

Messrs. Mosso, Sprouse, and Walters dissent to the issuance of this Statement. Statement 33 acknowledges that some of the supplementary disclosures that are applicable to enterprises having inventories and property, plant, and equipment are not applicable to enterprises that do not have such assets and it provides for omission of those inapplicable disclosures. The dissenting Board members agree that those and certain other Statement 33 disclosures are not applicable to investment companies, but they believe that complete exemption from presenting supplementary information about changing prices is not justified. The Statement 33 requirement that a five-year summary of key information be presented in constant dollars is especially useful in assessing the trend of an enterprise's performance relative to general inflation over a period of time. That assessment is just as important for an investment company as for an enterprise in any other industry. It is also essential for comparing the performance of investment companies with that of enterprises in other industries. Because the primary financial statements of investment companies already reflect current prices measured in nominal dollars, the Statement 33 supplementary information for investment companies should focus on a five-year summary of net investment income per share, dividends per share, and underlying net asset value per share, all measured in constant dollars. Statement 33 disclosures of that kind have been presented effectively in the annual reports of a number of investment companies, primarily money market funds.

Members of the Financial Accounting Standards Board:

Donald J. Kirk, *Chairman*
Frank E. Block
John W. March
Robert A. Morgan
David Mosso
Robert T. Sprouse
Ralph E. Walters

Appendix

BASIS FOR CONCLUSIONS

5. This appendix reviews considerations that were deemed significant by members of the Board in reaching the conclusions in this Statement. The Board members who assented to this Statement did so on the basis of the overall considerations. Individual Board members gave greater weight to some factors than to others.

6. An Exposure Draft of a proposed Statement, *Financial Reporting and Changing Prices: Investment Companies,* was issued on November 16, 1981. The Board received 27 comment letters in response to the Exposure Draft.

7. The four principal objectives of disclosures about effects of changing prices are outlined in paragraph 3 of Statement 33 and are developed in paragraphs 94 and 116-155 of that Statement. The four objectives are:

a. *Assessment of future cash flows.* Providing information about changes in prices of assets while they are held rather than waiting until they are sold provides an up-to-date basis for assessing future cash flows from those assets.
b. *Assessment of erosion of operating capability.* Providing information about the current prices of assets enables users of financial reports to assess the enterprise's ability to maintain, through replacement or otherwise, its ability to supply a fixed quantity of goods and services.
c. *Assessment of financial performance.* Information about the sum of changes in the current prices of assets and income from operations may provide an improved basis for comprehensively assessing an enterprise's performance.
d. *Assessment of erosion of general purchasing power.* Information about specific price changes combined with information about changes in the purchasing power of money can provide an improved basis for evaluation of whether an enterprise or a shareholder has maintained the general purchasing power of its capital.

8. The Board believes that the "value" amounts reported by investment companies in their primary financial statements are substantially equivalent to current cost amounts and that those financial statements, therefore, already provide the essential information required by Statement 33 to assess financial performance and future cash flows. Investment companies do not supply goods or services and generally do not own inventory or property, plant, and equipment. The Board believes, therefore, that the objective of providing information about maintenance of operating capability in the context of Statement 33 does not apply to investment companies. No respondent disagreed with that conclusion.

9. The Board also believes that some of the constant dollar disclosures required by Statement 33, such as income from continuing operations, operating revenue, and net assets, are of limited significance to investment companies and that disclosure of those items is not necessary for investment companies. No respondent disagreed with that conclusion.

10. Some respondents believe that investment companies should present a five-year summary of income, dividends, and end-of-year market price per share on a constant dollar basis to facilitate assessing the trend of those items after taking general inflation into account. The Board notes that Statement 33 requires those items to be included in the five-year summary in part because they interact with one another and with net assets to produce restated price/earnings ratios, dividend payout ratios, and book value/market value ratios. Because investment companies present all of those items on a substantially current cost basis in their primary

financial statements, the constant dollar restatements of those items do not change the ratios. Therefore, the Board concludes that disclosure of restated earnings per share, dividends per share, and market price per share is not as useful for investment companies as it is for other enterprises. The Board also notes that the need for disclosure of those items is reduced for investment companies because those restated amounts can be determined by users of the financial reports based on the nominal dollar amounts in the primary financial statements and changes in the Consumer Price Index. For other enterprises, restated earnings per share and the ratios cannot be readily determined from the primary financial statements because detailed information about the age and depreciable lives of those enterprises' inventory and property, plant, and equipment is not available to the public. That information is necessary to restate income from continuing operations and net assets.

11. Some respondents viewed the Exposure Draft as relieving an entire industry from participation in the Statement 33 experiment. They believe that all industries should provide information about the impact of inflation that is most meaningful in the circumstances. The Board notes that relatively few investment companies exceed the size tests established in Statement 33. At December 31, 1980, there were more than 500 publicly traded investment companies, 26 of which exceeded $1 billion in total assets. Furthermore, the Board believes that this Statement merely recognizes that the information required by Statement 33 either is provided in investment companies' primary financial statements, is not relevant for them, or can be determined readily by readers of those financial statements. The Board is not aware of any other industry that meets those unusual circumstances.

12. The Board concluded that it could reach an informed decision on the basis of existing data without a public hearing and that the effective date and transition specified in paragraph 4 are advisable in the circumstances.

13. The Board will reconsider this Statement as part of its comprehensive assessment of disclosures about effects of changing prices called for by Statement 33.

Statement of Financial Accounting Standards No. 55
Determining whether a Convertible Security Is a Common Stock Equivalent

an amendment of APB Opinion No. 15

STATUS

Issued: February 1982

Effective Date: For convertible securities issued after February 28, 1982

Affects: Amends APB 15, paragraph 33 and footnote 10
Amends AIN-APB 15, Interpretation No. 2
Supersedes AIN-APB 15, Interpretation No. 38

Affected by: No other pronouncements

SUMMARY

APB Opinion No. 15, *Earnings per Share,* states that a convertible security is a common stock equivalent if it has a cash yield at the time of issuance of less than 66 2/3 percent of the then current bank prime interest rate. The Board has concluded that the prime rate should be replaced as the benchmark interest rate in the cash yield test. This Statement substitutes the average Aa corporate bond yield as the new benchmark rate.

Statement of Financial Accounting Standards No. 55
Determining whether a Convertible Security Is a Common Stock Equivalent

an amendment of APB Opinion No. 15

CONTENTS

INTRODUCTION AND BACKGROUND INFORMATION

1. APB Opinion No. 15, *Earnings per Share,* requires that earnings per share computations reflect the dilutive effect of convertible securities. That dilutive effect is computed by assuming that a convertible security was converted into common stock as of the beginning of the period (or at time of issuance, if later). Conversion is assumed for purposes of computing primary earnings per share only if the convertible security is a common stock equivalent and the assumed conversion reduces earnings per share.

2. Opinion 15 discusses several possible tests to determine whether a convertible security is a common stock equivalent. The Accounting Principles Board concluded that the best type of test is a cash yield test. Certain other possible tests of common stock equivalence were rejected as "too subjective and not sufficiently practicable." The cash yield test specifies that a convertible security is a common stock equivalent if the cash yield to the holder at the time of issuance is significantly below what would be a comparable rate for a similar security of the issuer without the conversion option.

3. Paragraph 33 of Opinion 15 describes the specific terms of the cash yield test:

> . . . A convertible security should be considered as a common stock equivalent at the time of issuance if, based on its market price . . . it has a cash yield of less than 66 2/3% of the then current bank prime interest rate. . . .

4. The bank prime interest rate was adopted because it was a "practicable, simple, and readily available basis on which to establish the criteria for determining a common stock equivalent" and because at that time there was "a high degree of correlation" between the bank prime interest rate and rates of return on long-term debt and preferred stock.

5. In recent years, the bank prime interest rate has been more volatile than it was in the years preceding the issuance of Opinion 15. In addition, the United States and certain other countries recently have experienced an inverted yield curve, in which short-term interest rates exceed long-term interest rates. During periods of interest rate inversion, the effect of Opinion 15 has been to categorize as common stock equivalents convertible securities with cash yields that are similar to those of comparable securities without a conversion option. The Board does not believe that was the intent of Opinion 15.

6. The Board believes that the disadvantages of using the prime rate to determine whether a convertible security is a common stock equivalent have increased in recent years and more than offset the advantages of practicability, simplicity, and ready availability. Accordingly, the Board has decided to amend the cash yield test of Opinion 15. The Board believes this problem does not warrant a major reexamination of Opinion 15 or of the various methods of determining whether convertible securities are common stock equivalents. Its principal objective in amending the cash yield test is to allow that test to function as the Accounting Principles Board had intended when Opinion 15 was issued. It believes that objective can be satisfactorily achieved if the cash yield test is amended to substitute a new benchmark interest rate.

STANDARDS OF FINANCIAL ACCOUNTING AND REPORTING

Amendments to APB Opinion No. 15

7. The phrase "bank prime interest rate" in para-

graph 33 of Opinion 15 is deleted and replaced by "average Aa corporate bond yield.*"

*The designation Aa refers to the quality of the individual bonds that make up the average yield applied in the cash yield test. In the context of this Statement, the Board intends Aa to refer to bonds of equal quality to those rated Aa by either *Moody's* or *Standard & Poor's*. Those two organizations define Aa bonds as being of high quality and as having a very stong capacity to pay interest and repay principal. Bond yield information is widely and regularly published by a number of financial institutions and investor information services.

For purposes of applying the cash yield test, the *average* bond yield shall be based on bond yields for a brief period of time, for example, one week, including or immediately preceding the date of issuance of the security being tested.

Footnote 10 is deleted and replaced by the following:

If convertible securities are sold or issued outside the United States, the most comparable long-term yield in the foreign country should be used for this test.

Effective Date and Transition

8. The provisions of this Statement shall be applied to determine whether convertible securities issued after February 28, 1982 are common stock equivalents. The provisions of this Statement may, but are not required to be applied to convertible securities issued before March 1, 1982 in fiscal periods for which annual financial statements have not previously been issued.

The provisions of this Statement need not be applied to immaterial items.

This Statement was adopted by the affirmative votes of six members of the Financial Accounting Standards Board. Mr. Walters dissented.

Mr. Walters dissents from the issuance of this Statement because it fine tunes, and thereby perpetuates, a notion that he believes is fundamentally defective.

Information about securities or arrangements that have the potential to significantly dilute share values and cash returns is important to the investor. Accordingly, financial reports must include *factual data* to help the user estimate the probability, timing, and amount of potential dilution. The estimating process is a highly subjective analytical function, not a financial reporting function.

In his opinion, primary earnings per share based on the common stock equivalency notion of APB Opinion 15 does not possess the qualities of relevance and reliability essential to financial information. It is not relevant because it furnishes little or no incremental information about the probability, timing, or amount of potential dilution. It is not reliable, that is, representationally faithful, because it implies imminent or predictable dilution, whereas research suggests that it has been a poor predictor of dilution.

He believes the appropriate Board response is to amend APB Opinion 15 to eliminate the notion of common stock equivalency.

Members of the Financial Accounting Standards Board:

Donald J. Kirk, *Chairman*
Frank E. Block
John W. March
Robert A. Morgan
David Mosso
Robert T. Sprouse
Ralph E. Walters

Appendix A

BASIS FOR CONCLUSIONS

9. An Exposure Draft of a proposed Statement, *Determining whether a Convertible Security Is a Common Stock Equivalent,* was issued November 6, 1981. The Board received 68 comment letters in response to the Exposure Draft. This appendix discusses the factors, including certain comments received on the Exposure Draft, that the Board considered significant in reaching the conclusions in this Statement.

10. The Board believes the rate selected as the new benchmark should meet the following criteria: (a) its ability to function as a test of common stock equivalence should not be impaired by changing market conditions of a recurring nature, (b) it should be economically related to yields of corporate convertible securities, and (c) it should be practical to apply. The Board concluded that the existing prime rate benchmark should be replaced with a new

benchmark of the average Aa corporate bond yield. That rate was selected because the Board believes it satisfies more of the criteria listed above than do other possible interest rates.

11. Unlike the prime rate, the average Aa corporate bond yield is a long-term rate. It represents the composite yield to maturity of a representative sample of currently outstanding bonds of varying lives, generally from 10 to 30 years. Because it is a long-term rate, its usefulness as a benchmark in the cash yield test is relatively unaffected over time by such factors as interest rate inversion and market turbulence. The susceptibility of the prime rate to those market factors was perceived as a principal shortcoming in its performance as the benchmark rate.

12. The Board also notes that Aa corporate bonds are economically related to corporate convertible securities in that most economic developments that affect yields of Aa corporate bonds will similarly affect yields of convertible securities at the time they are issued. That relationship is consistent with the basic function of the cash yield test, which is to approximate the relationship between the yields of convertible and nonconvertible corporate bonds. The Board believes that economic link adds to the relevance of Aa corporate bond yields as the new benchmark rate.

13. Finally, the Board believes Aa corporate bond yields are "practicable, simple, and readily available." Bond yield quotations are frequently and widely published. The Board selected the Aa category from the various categories of published corporate bond yields because the Aa quotation is among the most widely published.

14. The Board also considered substituting a treasury bond yield for the prime rate in the cash yield test. A treasury bond yield benchmark was rejected, however, because it did not meet criterion (b) of paragraph 10 and, because composite treasury yields are not widely quoted, it was judged less practical to apply than a corporate bond yield.

15. The Board also considered whether it should revise the 66 2/3 percent factor that is applied to the benchmark rate in the cash yield test. The Board concluded that no such change was necessary because the existing 66 2/3 percent factor, when applied retroactively to the new benchmark of average Aa corporate bond yields, would have produced consistent results with those of Opinion 15 at its inception. The Board has previously stated that achieving this consistency is a principal objective of amending the cash yield test.

16. Some Board members believe that the common stock equivalent information derived under Opinion 15 is not necessarily a relevant or reliable indicator of the dilutive effect of convertible securities on earnings per share data. Nevertheless, they believe there is an urgent need to adopt a more realistic interest rate benchmark for the cash yield test. The Board has concluded that an undertaking to study the concept of common stock equivalency would involve a major reconsideration of Opinion 15. It therefore believes a more limited project addressing only the cash yield test constitutes a better use of the Board's resources at this time.

17. Some respondents recommended that rates other than the average Aa corporate bond yield be used as the new benchmark rate in the cash yield test. Some believe the new benchmark should be the yield on bonds of the specific credit rating of the issuer. They believe that approach satisfies the criteria specified for the new benchmark in paragraph 10 while recognizing that differences in risk exist among the securities of different issuers. The Board rejected that recommendation because the introduction of a benchmark that varies by issuer would require consideration of issues that were not addressed in Opinion 15 and that are beyond the stated scope of this project. It also believes a variable benchmark is not as simple and practical to apply because average yields for rating categories other than Aa are generally not as widely published as Aa yields.

18. The Board similarly rejected other suggested rates because they were judged less successful than the average Aa corporate bond yield at satisfying the criteria in paragraph 10.

19. The Board was asked to consider whether amending the cash yield test results in the need to also amend the second sentence of paragraph 28 of Opinion 15. That sentence requires "convertible securities outstanding or subsequently issued with the same terms as those of a common stock equivalent [to] be classified as common stock equivalents." The Board concluded that the introduction of the Aa benchmark creates no new problem concerning the application of the second sentence of paragraph 28 and that the language should therefore not be amended.

20. The Board concluded that it can reach an informed decision on the basis of existing data without a public hearing and that the effective date and transition specified in paragraph 8 are advisable in the circumstances.

Statement of Financial Accounting Standards No. 56 Designation of AICPA Guide and Statement of Position (SOP) 81-1 on Contractor Accounting and SOP 81-2 concerning Hospital-Related Organizations as Preferable for Purposes of Applying APB Opinion 20

an amendment of FASB Statement No. 32

STATUS

Issued: February 1982

Effective Date: For fiscal years beginning after December 31, 1981

Affects: Amends FAS 32, Appendixes A and B

Affected by: No other pronouncements

SUMMARY

This Statement specifies that the specialized accounting and reporting principles and practices contained in the AICPA *Audit and Accounting Guide for Construction Contractors* and in AICPA Statements of Position 81-1, *Accounting for Performance of Construction-Type and Certain Production-Type Contracts,* and 81-2, *Reporting Practices concerning Hospital-Related Organizations,* are preferable accounting principles for purposes of justifying a change in accounting principles under APB Opinion No. 20, *Accounting Changes.*

Statement of Financial Accounting Standards No. 56
Designation of AICPA Guide and Statement of Position (SOP) 81-1 on Contractor Accounting and SOP 81-2 concerning Hospital-Related Organizations as Preferable for Purposes of Applying APB Opinion 20

an amendment of FASB Statement No. 32

CONTENTS

INTRODUCTION AND BACKGROUND INFORMATION

1. FASB Statement No. 32, *Specialized Accounting and Reporting Principles and Practices in AICPA Statements of Position and Guides on Accounting and Auditing Matters,* states that the specialized accounting and reporting principles and practices contained in AICPA Statements of Position (SOPs) and Guides on accounting and auditing matters that are listed in Appendix A of that Statement are preferable accounting principles for the purposes of applying APB Opinion No. 20, *Accounting Changes.*

2. Appendix B of Statement 32 contains a list of projects in process that the Accounting Standards Executive Committee (AcSEC) of the AICPA expects will result in the issuance of SOPs or Guides. Statement 32 states that the Board may designate the specialized accounting and reporting principles and practices in future AICPA SOPs and Guides, either related to AcSEC projects listed in Appendix B or undertaken by AcSEC at the Board's request, as preferable for purposes of justifying a change in accounting principles.

3. This Statement designates the specialized accounting and reporting principles and practices contained in the AICPA *Audit and Accounting Guide for Construction Contractors* (Guide), and SOPs 81-1, *Accounting for Performance of Construction-Type and Certain Production-Type Contracts,* and 81-2, *Reporting Practices concerning Hospital-Related Organizations,* as preferable for purposes of applying Opinion 20 and amends Appendix A of Statement 32 by substituting the Guide for the AICPA Industry Audit Guide, *Audits of Construction Contractors,* and by adding SOP 81-1 and SOP 81-2. This Statement also deletes the Guide and those SOPs from the AICPA projects in process listed in Appendix B of Statement 32.

4. An Exposure Draft of a proposed Statement, *Applicability of FASB Statement No. 32 to AICPA Statements of Position and Guides on Accounting and Auditing Matters,* was issued November 6, 1981. The Board received 25 comment letters in response to the Exposure Draft, most of which expressed agreement.

5. A few respondents suggested that the Board not designate as preferable for purposes of applying Opinion 20 the specialized accounting principles in SOP 81-1 and the Contractor Guide because they object to certain provisions in those documents. Their primary concern is that application of SOP 81-1 and the Guide will restrict the use of the completed-contract method to circumstances more limited than from application of ARB No. 45, *Long-Term Construction-Type Contracts.*

6. The percentage-of-completion and completed-contract methods are not intended to be free choice alternatives for the same circumstances under either ARB 45 or SOP 81-1. ARB 45 states that "when estimates of costs to complete and extent of progress toward completion of long-term contracts are reasonably dependable, the percentage-of-completion method is preferable" and "when lack of dependable estimates or inherent hazards cause forecasts to be doubtful, the completed-contract method is preferable." SOP 81-1 states that the two methods "should not be acceptable alternatives for the same circumstances" and specifies criteria for choice of method similar to those in ARB 45. In applying either ARB 45 or SOP 81-1, a contractor should evaluate the facts and circumstances pertaining to contract work performed and decide which of the two methods is appropriate.

7. In designating as preferable for purposes of

applying Opinion 20 the specialized accounting principles in SOP 81-1 and the Contractor Guide, this Statement provides justification for a contractor to make an accounting change from the completed-contract method in a circumstance not specifically provided for in ARB 45. That circumstance occurs when a reasonable estimate of the final profit cannot be made but a loss is not expected. In that case, the contractor may adopt the percentage-of-completion method with a zero estimate of profit. The income reported is the same; but, the percentage-of-completion method reports revenues and costs from construction activity as they occur, whereas the completed-contract method does not report revenues and costs from construction activity until contracts are completed. This Statement also justifies a change from estimating a profit to estimating a zero profit under the percentage-of-completion method when a profit cannot be reasonably estimated, but it does not provide justification for a change of accounting method to the completed-contract method beyond that in ARB 45.

8. The FASB will consider adopting the accounting and reporting principles and practices in SOP 81-1 and the Contractor Guide and issue them in an FASB Statement only after appropriate due process. Such plans have not been completed but do include allowing sufficient time for the documents to be used in practice to provide a basis for determining their usefulness. In the meantime, ARB 45 provides authoritative requirements for accounting for long-term construction-type contracts and the Board is clarifying the status of the specialized accounting principles in SOP 81-1 and the Guide by designating them as preferable for purposes of applying Opinion 20.

9. The Board has concluded that it can reach an informed decision on the basis of existing information without a public hearing and that the effective date specified in paragraph 12 is advisable in the circumstances.

STANDARDS OF FINANCIAL ACCOUNTING AND REPORTING

10. The specialized accounting and reporting principles and practices contained in the following AICPA Guide and AICPA Statements of Position are preferable accounting principles for purposes of applying Opinion 20:

a. *Audit and Accounting Guide for Construction Contractors*
b. SOP 81-1, *Accounting for Performance of Construction-Type and Certain Production-Type Contracts*
c. SOP 81-2, *Reporting Practices concerning Hospital-Related Organizations*

Amendment to FASB Statement No. 32

11. The references to the Guide and SOPs listed in paragraph 10 are deleted from the AICPA projects in process listed in Appendix B of Statement 32 and added to Appendix A of that Statement. The AICPA Industry Audit Guide, *Audits of Construction Contractors,* is deleted from Appendix A of Statement 32.

Effective Date

12. The provisions of this Statement shall be effective for financial statements for fiscal years beginning after December 31, 1981.

The provisions of this Statement need not be applied to immaterial items.

This Statement was adopted by the affirmative votes of five members of the Financial Accounting Standards Board. Messrs. March and Walters dissented.

Messrs. March and Walters dissent from this Statement principally because they believe SOP 81-1 substantively changes the application of the criteria established in paragraph 15 of ARB No. 45 for selecting the preferable accounting method. SOP 81-1 states that it "does not amend" ARB 45. This is literally true because the issuer of the SOP does not have the authority to amend ARBs. Nonetheless, the tone and thrust of the SOP suggest that the completed-contract method is seldom acceptable. This is not done directly but rather by establishing a presumption (paragraph 24) and taking positions that effectively limit the completed-contract method to cases where the choice of method makes no difference or where unusual "inherent hazards" raise serious questions about the outcome of the contract or the ability of the contractor or the customer to perform.

They believe the expression of preferability for the percentage-of-completion method with a zero estimate of profit in the circumstances described in paragraph 7 of this Statement (1) is a direct contradiction of paragraph 15 of ARB 45, and (2) entitles the user to assume that the contractor estimates a break-even, which is not a fact.

The Board has not considered a need to amend ARB 45. Messrs. March and Walters believe it is inconsistent and confusing for the Board to confer preferability on accounting principles that, in their view, substantively modify existing and continuing generally accepted accounting principles. The Board has a process for considering and interpreting or changing existing principles. This is not it.

Members of the Financial Accounting Standards Board:

Donald J. Kirk, *Chairman*
Frank E. Block
John W. March
Robert A. Morgan
David Mosso
Robert T. Sprouse
Ralph E. Walters

Statement of Financial Accounting Standards No. 57
Related Party Disclosures

STATUS

Issued: March 1982

Effective Date: For fiscal years ending after June 15, 1982

Affects: No other pronouncements

Affected by: No other pronouncements

SUMMARY

This Statement establishes requirements for related party disclosures. The requirements of this Statement are generally consistent with those in Statement on Auditing Standards No. 6, *Related Party Transactions,* issued by the Auditing Standards Executive Committee of the American Institute of Certified Public Accountants.

Statement of Financial Accounting Standards No. 57
Related Party Disclosures

CONTENTS

INTRODUCTION

1. The FASB has been asked to provide guidance on disclosures of transactions between **related parties.**[1] Examples of related party transactions include transactions between (a) a parent company and its subsidiaries; (b) subsidiaries of a common parent; (c) an enterprise and trusts for the benefit of employees, such as pension and profit-sharing trusts that are managed by or under the trusteeship of the enterprise's **management;** (d) an enterprise and its **principal owners,** management, or members of their **immediate families;** and (e) **affiliates.** Transactions between related parties commonly occur in the normal course of business. Some examples of common types of transactions with related parties are: sales, purchases, and transfers of realty and personal property; services received or furnished, for example, accounting, management, engineering, and legal services; use of property and equipment by lease or otherwise; borrowings and lendings; guarantees; maintenance of bank balances as compensating balances for the benefit of another; intercompany billings based on allocations of common costs; and filings of consolidated tax returns. Transactions between related parties are considered to be related party transactions even though they may not be given accounting recognition. For example, an enterprise may receive services from a related party without charge and not record receipt of the services.

STANDARDS OF FINANCIAL ACCOUNTING AND REPORTING

Disclosures

2. Financial statements shall include disclosures of material related party transactions, other than compensation arrangements, expense allowances, and other similar items in the ordinary course of business. However, disclosure of transactions that are eliminated in the preparation of consolidated or combined financial statements is not required in those statements.[2] The disclosures shall include:[3]

a. The nature of the relationship(s) involved
b. A description of the transactions, including transactions to which no amounts or nominal amounts were ascribed, for each of the periods for which income statements are presented, and such other information deemed necessary to an understanding of the effects of the transactions on the financial statements
c. The dollar amounts of transactions for each of the periods for which income statements are presented and the effects of any change in the method of establishing the terms from that used in the preceding period
d. Amounts due from or to related parties as of the date of each balance sheet presented and, if not otherwise apparent, the terms and manner of settlement

---

[1] Terms defined in the glossary (Appendix B) are in **boldface type** the first time they appear in this Statement.

[2] The requirements of this Statement are applicable to separate financial statements of each or combined groups of each of the following: a parent company, a subsidiary, a corporate joint venture, or a 50-percent-or-less owned investee. However, it is not necessary to duplicate disclosures in a set of separate financial statements that is presented in the financial report of another enterprise (the primary reporting enterprise) if those separate financial statements also are consolidated or combined in a complete set of financial statements and both sets of financial statements are presented in the same financial report.

[3] In some cases, aggregation of similar transactions by type of related party may be appropriate. Sometimes, the effect of the relationship between the parties may be so pervasive that disclosure of the relationship alone will be sufficient. If necessary to the understanding of the relationship, the name of the related party should be disclosed.

3. Transactions involving related parties cannot be presumed to be carried out on an arm's-length basis, as the requisite conditions of competitive, free-market dealings may not exist. Representations about transactions with related parties, if made, shall not imply that the related party transactions were consummated on terms equivalent to those that prevail in arm's-length transactions unless such representations can be substantiated.

4. If the reporting enterprise and one or more other enterprises are under common ownership or management **control** and the existence of that control could result in operating results or financial position of the reporting enterprise significantly different from those that would have been obtained if the enterprises were autonomous, the nature of the control relationship shall be disclosed even though there are no transactions between the enterprises.

Effective Date and Transition

5. This Statement shall be effective for financial statements for fiscal years ending after June 15, 1982. Earlier application is encouraged but is not required.

The provisions of this Statement need not be applied to immaterial items.

This Statement was adopted by the unanimous vote of the seven members of the Financial Accounting Standards Board:

Donald J. Kirk, *Chairman*
Frank E. Block
John W. March
Robert A. Morgan
David Mosso
Robert T. Sprouse
Ralph E. Walters

Appendix A

BACKGROUND INFORMATION AND BASIS FOR CONCLUSIONS

6. This appendix discusses the factors that the Board considered significant in reaching the conclusions in this Statement. Individual Board members gave greater weight to some factors than to others.

7. AICPA Statement on Auditing Standards No. 6, *Related Party Transactions* (SAS 6), and interpretations of SAS 6 provide guidance on related party financial statement disclosures. However, authoritative auditing pronouncements are intended to direct the activities of auditors, not of reporting enterprises.

8. As part of Accounting Series Release No. 280, *General Revisions of Regulation S-X,* the Securities and Exchange Commission integrated the disclosure requirements of SAS 6 pertaining to related party transactions into Regulation S-X. Regulation S-X, however, applies only to enterprises subject to the filing requirements of the SEC.

9. Because guidance for related party disclosures was not included in the authoritative literature on generally accepted accounting principles, the Accounting Standards Division of the AICPA asked the FASB to consider providing such guidance in a Statement of Financial Accounting Standards.

10. As discussed in paragraphs 12-18, the Board believes that it is appropriate to establish standards that apply to all enterprises for disclosure of information about related party transactions and certain control relationships. The Board has not undertaken a comprehensive reconsideration of the accounting and reporting issues discussed in SAS 6 and related interpretations thereof. The related party disclosure requirements contained in those documents have been extracted without significant change, except that this Statement does not address the issues pertaining to economic dependency. Other FASB projects may address issues related to those in this Statement, and the Board may reconsider the standards in this Statement when those projects are completed.

11. An Exposure Draft of a proposed Statement, *Related Party Disclosures,* was issued on November 6, 1981. The Board received 66 comment letters in response to that Exposure Draft. Certain of the comments received and the Board's consideration of them are discussed in paragraphs 19-22 of this appendix.

Usefulness of Related Party Disclosures

12. FASB Concepts Statement No. 2, *Qualitative Characteristics of Accounting Information,* examines the characteristics of accounting information that make it useful. That Statement concludes that for accounting information to be useful, it should be relevant (meaning that it has predictive or

feedback value) and reliable (meaning that it has representational faithfulness, verifiability, and neutrality). That Statement further concludes that information about an enterprise increases in usefulness if it can be compared with similar information about other enterprises and with similar information about the same enterprise for some other period or point in time.

13. Accounting information is relevant if it is "capable of making a difference in a decision by helping users to form predictions about the outcomes of past, present, and future events or to confirm or correct expectations."[4] Relationships between parties may enable one of the parties to exercise a degree of influence over the other such that the influenced party may be favored or caused to subordinate its independent interests. Related party transactions may be controlled entirely by one of the parties so that those transactions may be affected significantly by considerations other than those in arm's-length transactions with unrelated parties. Some related party transactions may be the result of the related party relationship and without the relationship may not have occurred or may have occurred on different terms. For example, the terms under which a subsidiary leases equipment to another subsidiary of a common parent may be imposed by the common parent and might vary significantly from one lease to another because of circumstances entirely unrelated to market prices for similar leases.

14. Sometimes two or more enterprises are under common ownership or management control but do not transact business with each other. The common control, however, may result in operating results or financial position significantly different from that which would have been obtained if the enterprises were autonomous. For example, two or more enterprises in the same line of business may be controlled by a party that has the ability to increase or decrease the volume of business done by each. Disclosure of information about certain control relationships and transactions with related parties helps users of financial statements form predictions and analyze the extent to which those statements may have been affected by that relationship.

15. Reliability of financial information involves "assurance that accounting measures represent what they purport to represent."[5] Without disclosure to the contrary, there is a general presumption that transactions reflected in financial statements have been consummated on an arm's-length basis between independent parties. However, that presumption is not justified when related party transactions exist because the requisite conditions of competitive, free-market dealings may not exist. Because it is possible for related party transactions to be arranged to obtain certain results desired by the related parties, the resulting accounting measures may not represent what they usually would be expected to represent. Reduced representational faithfulness and verifiability of amounts used to measure transactions with related parties weaken the reliability of those amounts. That weakness cannot always be cured by reference to market measures because in many cases there may be no arm's-length market in the goods or services that are the subject of the related party transactions.

16. The Board believes that an enterprise's financial statements may not be complete without additional explanations of and information about related party transactions and thus may not be reliable. Completeness implies that ". . . nothing material is left out of the information that may be necessary to insure that it validly represents the underlying events and conditions."[6]

17. The Board also believes that relevant information is omitted if disclosures about significant related party transactions required by this Statement are not made. "Completeness of information also affects its relevance. Relevance of information is adversely affected if a relevant piece of information is omitted, even if the omission does not falsify what is shown."[7]

18. Information about transactions with related parties is useful to users of financial statements in attempting to compare an enterprise's results of operations and financial position with those of prior periods and with those of other enterprises. It helps them to detect and explain possible differences. Therefore, information about transactions with related parties that would make a difference in decision making should be disclosed so that users of the financial statements can evaluate their significance.

Consideration of Comments on Exposure Draft

19. Some respondents were troubled by the proposal in the Exposure Draft to require disclosure of only those transactions "that are necessary for users to understand the financial statements." They generally expressed the view that it would be difficult to apply such a criterion and that it was unclear how that criterion interacted with materiality judgments.

---

[4]Concepts Statement 2, paragraph 47.

[5]Ibid., paragraph 81.

[6]Ibid., paragraph 79.

[7]Ibid., paragraph 80.

In addition, some respondents also interpreted that language combined with the Exposure Draft's omission of the specific exclusion provided in SAS 6 for disclosure of compensation arrangements, expense allowances, and other similar items in the ordinary course of business as a requirement that such items be disclosed. The Board does not intend to imply that disclosure of related party transactions and certain control relationships is a separate objective of financial reporting, nor does the Board intend to introduce a new concept of materiality. Rather, disclosure of related party transactions and certain control relationships is required solely for the purpose of enhancing the understanding of the financial statements and the fact that such matters have, or could have, an effect on the financial statements. Disclosure of compensation arrangements, expense allowances, and other similar items in the ordinary course of business is not necessary for a user to understand the financial statements. The standard has been revised accordingly.

20. The Exposure Draft would have prohibited representations to the effect that related party transactions were consummated on an arm's-length basis. While recognizing the difficulty in many situations of determining the terms on which a transaction might have occurred if the parties were unrelated, many respondents pointed out that certain related party transactions occur on terms available to unrelated parties or on terms established by regulatory agencies. They believe that representations as to the terms of a related party transaction should not be prohibited if they can be substantiated. The Board agreed, and the requirement (paragraph 3) has been modified accordingly.

21. SAS 6 and interpretations thereof call for disclosure of the nature of common control relationships if the controlling party has the ability to affect the reporting enterprise in a manner that could lead to significantly different operating results or financial position than if the enterprises were autonomous. The Exposure Draft would have gone beyond those requirements to require disclosure of all control relationships. Some respondents expressed doubt about the usefulness of some of the disclosures that would result. They indicated that the requirement would be burdensome particularly for closely held enterprises that might have numerous relationships with owners and their families, lenders, and possibly others that might be deemed to be "control." The Board agreed that requiring disclosure of all control relationships might be of limited usefulness. Accordingly, the requirement (paragraph 4) was revised to conform more closely to that discussed in SAS 6.

22. Several respondents asked the FASB to provide additional guidance on disclosures about economic dependency but did not provide information to define the issues involved, nor did they provide evidence as to why additional guidance is needed. Therefore, the Board concluded that issuance of this Statement should not be delayed to consider that issue.

23. The Board has concluded that it can reach an informed decision on the basis of existing information without a public hearing and that the effective date and transition specified in paragraph 5 are advisable in the circumstances.

Appendix B

GLOSSARY

24. For purposes of this Statement, certain terms are defined as follows:

a. **Affiliate.** A party that, directly or indirectly through one or more intermediaries, controls, is controlled by, or is under common control with an enterprise.
b. **Control.** The possession, direct or indirect, of the power to direct or cause the direction of the management and policies of an enterprise through ownership, by contract, or otherwise.
c. **Immediate family.** Family members whom a principal owner or a member of management might control or influence or by whom they might be controlled or influenced because of the family relationship.
d. **Management.** Persons who are responsible for achieving the objectives of the enterprise and who have the authority to establish policies and make decisions by which those objectives are to be pursued. Management normally includes members of the board of directors, the chief executive officer, chief operating officer, vice presidents in charge of principal business functions (such as sales, administration, or finance), and other persons who perform similar policy-making functions. Persons without formal titles also may be members of management.
e. **Principal owners.** Owners of record or known beneficial owners of more than 10 percent of the voting interests of the enterprise.
f. **Related parties.** Affiliates of the enterprise; entities for which investments are accounted for by the equity method by the enterprise; trusts for the benefit of employees, such as pension and profit-sharing trusts that are managed by or under the trusteeship of management; principal owners of the enterprise; its management; members of the immediate families of principal owners of the enterprise and its management; and other parties with which the enterprise may deal if one party

controls or can significantly influence the management or operating policies of the other to an extent that one of the transacting parties might be prevented from fully pursuing its own separate interests. Another party also is a related party if it can significantly influence the management or operating policies of the transacting parties or if it has an ownership interest in one of the transacting parties and can significantly influence the other to an extent that one or more of the transacting parties might be prevented from fully pursuing its own separate interests.

Statement of Financial Accounting Standards No. 58 Capitalization of Interest Cost in Financial Statements That Include Investments Accounted for by the Equity Method

an amendment of FASB Statement No. 34

STATUS

Issued: April 1982

Effective Date: For investments made after June 30, 1982 but optional for investments contracted for but not yet made at that date

Affects: Amends ARB 51, paragraph 10
Amends APB 18, paragraph 19(m)
Amends APB 20, paragraph 34
Amends FAS 34, paragraphs 9, 10, and 20

Affected by: No other pronouncements

SUMMARY

This Statement amends FASB Statement No. 34, *Capitalization of Interest Cost,* (1) to limit capitalization of consolidated interest cost to qualifying assets of the parent company and consolidated subsidiaries and (2) to include investments (equity, loans, and advances) accounted for by the equity method as qualifying assets of the investor while the investee has activities in progress necessary to commence its planned principal operations provided that the investee's activities include the use of funds to acquire qualifying assets for its operations. This Statement does not affect the accounting for and reporting of capitalized interest cost in the separate financial statements of investees.

Statement of Financial Accounting Standards No. 58 Capitalization of Interest Cost in Financial Statements That Include Investments Accounted for by the Equity Method

an amendment of FASB Statement No. 34

CONTENTS

INTRODUCTION

1. The FASB has received several inquiries concerning (a) the limitations of FASB Statement No. 34, *Capitalization of Interest Cost,* relating to capitalization of interest cost in situations involving investees accounted for by the equity method and (b) the inconsistent requirements between (i) the limitations of Statement 34 on the capitalization of interest cost in situations involving investees accounted for by the equity method and (ii) the requirement of APB Opinion No. 18, *The Equity Method of Accounting for Investments in Common Stock,* that income and owners' equity amounts should be the same whether a subsidiary is consolidated or accounted for by the equity method.

2. The basic issue is whether Statement 34 distinguishes qualifying assets owned by the parent and consolidated subsidiaries from those owned by unconsolidated subsidiaries, joint ventures, and other investees accounted for by the equity method for purposes of determining the amount of interest cost to be capitalized in the investor's financial statements. Although paragraph 15 of Statement 34 clearly limits the amount of interest available for capitalization in consolidated financial statements to that shown in those statements, neither paragraph 9 nor paragraph 15 of Statement 34 is explicit regarding any similar limitations on qualifying assets.

3. The Board has concluded that qualifying assets as described in Statement 34 are limited to those of the parent company and consolidated subsidiaries. The Board has also concluded that certain investments (equity, loans, and advances) accounted for by the equity method are qualifying assets of the investor (including parent company and consolidated subsidiaries). For the investment to be a qualifying asset, the investee must be undergoing activities in preparation for its planned principal operations provided that the investee's activities include the use of funds to acquire qualifying assets for its operations. The investment ceases to be a qualifying asset when those operations begin. Subsequent accounting for interest capitalized on the investment is specified by paragraph 19(b) of Opinion 18.

4. This Statement does not affect the accounting for and reporting of capitalized interest cost in the separate financial statements of investees.

STANDARDS OF FINANCIAL ACCOUNTING AND REPORTING

Amendments to FASB Statement No. 34

5. The following subparagraph is added to paragraph 9 of Statement 34, which specifies the qualifying assets for which interest is to be capitalized:

c. Investments (equity, loans, and advances) accounted for by the equity method while the investee has activities in progress necessary to commence its planned principal operations provided that the investee's activities include the use of funds to acquire qualifying assets for its operations.

6. The following subparagraphs are added to paragraph 10 of Statement 34, which specifies the types of assets for which interest is not capitalized:

c. Assets that are not included in the consolidated balance sheet of the parent company and consolidated subsidiaries
d. Investments accounted for by the equity method after the planned principal operations of the investee begin
e. Investments in regulated investees that are capitalizing both the cost of debt and equity capital

7. The following sentence is added to paragraph 20 of Statement 34, which specifies the accounting for interest after it is capitalized:

> Interest capitalized on an investment accounted for by the equity method shall be accounted for in accordance with paragraph 19(b) of Opinion 18 which states: "A difference between the cost of an investment and the amount of underlying equity in net assets of an investee should be accounted for as if the investee were a consolidated subsidiary."

Amendments to Other Pronouncements

8. Paragraph 10 of ARB No. 51, *Consolidated Financial Statements,* requires accounting for a subsidiary on a step-by-step basis if control is obtained through purchase of two or more blocks of stock. Paragraph 19(m) of Opinion 18 requires retroactive adjustment for an investee that was previously accounted for on other than the equity method when that investee becomes qualified for use of the equity method. Paragraph 34 of APB Opinion No. 20, *Accounting Changes,* requires restatement of prior financial statements for changes in reporting entities. The following footnote is added to each of those paragraphs:

> *The amount of interest cost capitalized through application of FASB Statement No. 58, *Capitalization of Interest Cost in Financial Statements That Include Investments Accounted for by the Equity Method,* shall not be changed when restating financial statements of prior periods.

Effective Date and Transition

9. This Statement shall be effective for investments made after June 30, 1982 except that investments contracted for but not yet made may be accounted for as specified in the next sentence. Investments existing at the effective date or date of earlier adoption of this Statement (a) may be accounted for according to the provisions of this Statement or (b) may continue to be accounted for by the method of interest capitalization previously used even though not in accordance with the provisions of this Statement. Earlier application is encouraged. This Statement may be applied retroactively for annual financial statements that have not been issued but shall not be applied retroactively for previously issued annual financial statements.

The provisions of this Statement need not be applied to immaterial items.

This Statement was adopted by the affirmative votes of four members of the Financial Accounting Standards Board. Messrs. Block, Kirk, and Morgan dissented.

Messrs. Block, Kirk, and Morgan are not persuaded by the arguments in this Statement that an investor should consider an investment in certain types of investees accounted for by the equity method as a qualifying asset for purposes of applying Statement 34. They see merit in an approach that would permit the inclusion of the qualifying assets of the investee in the qualifying assets of the entity (parent company and consolidated subsidiaries) issuing consolidated financial statements. However, they are convinced that there are serious complications in application of such an approach (paragraph 19). They also acknowledge the validity of the argument (paragraph 11) that there is a fundamental distinction between (a) the individual assets acquired by subsidiaries that are considered to be an integral part of the entity issuing consolidated financial statements and (b) the individual assets acquired by other investees that are excluded from consolidated financial statements. Therefore, they favor an interpretation of Statement 34 that, for future transactions, consolidated interest should not be capitalized on the qualifying assets of investees accounted for by the equity method. They note that the investee is subject to Statement 34 and will capitalize its own interest on qualifying assets.

Members of the Financial Accounting Standards Board:

Donald J. Kirk, *Chairman*
Frank E. Block
John W. March
Robert A. Morgan
David Mosso
Robert T. Sprouse
Ralph E. Walters

Appendix

BACKGROUND INFORMATION AND BASIS FOR CONCLUSIONS

10. As stated in paragraph 1, the Board has received several inquiries concerning (a) the limitations of FASB Statement No. 34, *Capitalization of Interest Cost,* relating to capitalization of interest cost in situations involving investees accounted for by the equity method and (b) the inconsistent requirements between (i) the limitations of Statement 34 on the capitalization of interest cost in situations involving investees accounted for by the equity method and (ii) the requirement of APB Opinion No. 18, *The Equity Method of Accounting for Investments in Common Stock,* that income and owners' equity amounts should be the same whether a subsidiary is consolidated or accounted for by the equity method.

11. Some believe that Statement 34 proscribes capitalization of consolidated interest cost on qualifying assets of investees accounted for by the equity method. They believe that there is a fundamental distinction between (a) the individual costs incurred and assets acquired by subsidiaries that are considered to be an integral part of the entity issuing consolidated financial statements and (b) the individual costs incurred and assets acquired by other investees that are excluded from consolidated financial statements. They believe that the individual assets, liabilities, revenues, and expenses reflected in consolidated financial statements should relate to only the entity defined by those consolidated statements (that is, to only the parent company and consolidated subsidiaries) and should be complete. They believe that the equity method of accounting for investees appropriately reflects only the consolidated entity's net investment in and share of net income of the investee. Otherwise, users cannot use the amounts reported in the consolidated financial statements for their assessments of financial trends and relationships of the consolidated economic entity (for example, sales, gross profit percentages, current ratios, returns on total assets, etc.). Those who would proscribe capitalization of consolidated interest cost on qualifying assets of investees accounted for by the equity method do not believe that Opinion 18 precludes differences in net income and owners' equity, depending on whether an investment in a subsidiary is accounted for under the equity method or the subsidiary is consolidated.

12. Others believe that Statement 34 properly does not distinguish between qualifying assets of the investor (parent company and consolidated subsidiaries) and those of investees accounted for by the equity method. They believe that Opinion 18 generally precludes differences in net income and owners' equity for investees accounted for by the equity method. Accordingly, they believe both qualifying assets and interest cost of all investees accounted for by the equity method should be included in the application of Statement 34. They believe that consistent application of Opinion 18 is necessary because changes in the form of a transaction could otherwise affect the amount of interest capitalized. For example, the amount of interest capitalized could be affected because of either differences in interest rates or amounts eliminated in preparation of the investor's financial statements if the parent were to borrow and lend to the investee instead of the investee's borrowing directly from an independent third party with the parent company's guarantee.

13. Still others believe that investments (equity, loans, and advances) in investees that have not begun their planned principal operations are qualifying assets. They believe those investments meet the intent of paragraph 7 of Statement 34 (which states that the objectives of capitalizing interest are (a) to obtain a measure of acquisition cost that more closely reflects the enterprise's total investment in the asset and (b) to charge a cost that relates to the acquisition of a resource that will benefit future periods against the revenues of the periods benefited) because the investor's funds have been invested in an asset that is not ready for its intended use until the investee commences those principal operations. They believe this is particularly evident in the case of projects organized by a limited number of investors to pool resources in developing production or other facilities. Others believe that investments in investees accounted for by the equity method are never qualifying assets because they believe that such investments do not meet the description of qualifying assets in paragraph 9 of Statement 34.

14. An Exposure Draft of a proposed Statement, *Capitalization of Interest Cost in Financial Statements That Include Investments Accounted for by the Equity Method,* was issued on September 30, 1981. The Board received 72 letters of comment in response to the Exposure Draft. Certain of the comments received and the Board's consideration of them, including various alternatives considered and reasons for accepting some and rejecting others, are discussed in the remaining paragraphs.

15. Several respondents to the Exposure Draft stated that investments in investees accounted for by the equity method should be considered qualifying assets only to the extent that the investments in the investee have been reinvested in qualifying assets as defined in Statement 34. The Board concluded, for the reasons cited in paragraph 11, above, that qual-

ifying assets as described in Statement 34 should be limited to those of the parent company and consolidated subsidiaries. The Board also concluded that an investment accounted for by the equity method that has not begun its planned principal operations should be a qualifying asset of the investor while the investee has activities in progress necessary to commence its planned principal operations provided that the investee's activities include the use of funds to acquire qualifying assets for its operations. An investment in an investee that is not undergoing activities necessary to commence planned principal operations is not intended to be a qualifying asset under this Statement. The Board believes these conclusions are consistent with the objectives included in paragraph 7 of Statement 34. The Board believes that consideration of the individual qualifying assets of investees accounted for by the equity method would contradict the rationale in paragraph 11, above, for exclusion from consolidated financial statements of the individual assets and liabilities of such investees.

16. Some respondents stated that including investments in investees accounted for by the equity method in qualifying assets of the investor is undesirable because it would result in an additional exception to paragraph 19 of Opinion 18 that states that net income and stockholders' equity are the same whether an investment in a subsidiary is accounted for under the equity method or the subsidiary is consolidated. The Board realizes that application of Statement 34 and this Statement may produce results that are an exception to paragraph 19 of Opinion 18; that is, consolidated net income and owners' equity may be affected by whether an investee entity is consolidated or accounted for by the equity method. The Board noted the existing exceptions in (a) paragraph 19(i) of Opinion 18 and (b) footnote 5 of FASB Statement No. 12, *Accounting for Certain Marketable Securities,* as establishing circumstances in which net income and stockholders' equity may differ, depending on whether an investment in a subsidiary is accounted for by the equity method or the subsidiary is consolidated. The Board believes paragraph 19 of Opinion 18 provides important general guidance but was not intended to be inviolable in specific circumstances.

17. Some respondents concluded that consolidated interest cost should not be capitalized on the investment in investees accounted for by the equity method. They believe that such investments do not meet the definition of a qualifying asset in Statement 34 because they are not constructed or produced for the consolidated enterprise's own use. The Board has concluded, for reasons cited in paragraphs 11 and 15, above, that the asset that is relevant for determining the qualifying assets of the consolidated group is the investment in the equity method investee until the investee has begun its planned principal operations.

18. Several respondents suggested that subsequent investments in investees that have begun their planned principal operations should qualify for interest capitalization. They believe that allowing capitalization of interest cost on investments in investees accounted for by the equity method that have not begun their planned principal operations while prohibiting capitalization of interest cost on similar investments of an established investee that is undergoing substantial expansion creates a situation in which similar circumstances may be accounted for differently. If an investee has several distinct projects in process and each becomes operational at different times, these respondents believe that allocation of the investment by the investor should be allowed, with capitalization of interest cost taking place on those projects that have not begun their planned principal operations. The Board concluded that the investor's investment in the investee, not the individual assets or projects of the investee, is the qualifying asset for purposes of interest capitalization.

19. Some respondents suggested that the investor should capitalize interest in consolidation on its proportionate share of the equity method investee's average amount of qualifying assets on which the equity method investee has not capitalized interest. The Board considered and rejected this approach because it concluded that (a) the investment in the investee is the qualifying asset for purposes of interest capitalization, (b) only limited guidance is currently available for application of the method, and (c) it involves complex calculations using arbitrary assumptions. The Board recently added to its agenda a project that will consider issues regarding the proportionate method of consolidation and also believes that it would not be prudent to specify a method of accounting that is currently under consideration in a major agenda project and is not clearly defined in current accounting literature.

20. Some respondents asked for clarification of the term *when planned principal operations begin* to be able to determine when the investment in the investee that is the qualifying asset is "ready for its intended use" and interest capitalization ceases under Statement 34. The Board has used that term in this Statement to have the same meaning as in FASB Statement No. 7, *Accounting and Reporting by Development Stage Enterprises.* Statement 7 considers an enterprise to be in the development stage if planned principal operations have not commenced and if it is devoting substantially all of its efforts to establishing a new business through activities such as financial planning; raising capital; exploring for natural resources; developing natural

resources; research and development; establishing sources of supply; acquiring property, plant, and equipment or other operating assets, such as mineral rights; recruiting and training personnel; developing markets; and starting up production.

21. Some respondents stated that a form of "double counting" may result if the investor capitalizes interest on its investment in an equity method investee and that investment also includes the investor's share of the investee's earnings (losses) that, in turn, may reflect the investee's own capitalization of interest on its qualifying assets. The Board believes, however, that the interest capitalized by the investee is a cost like any other cost of acquiring a qualified asset and is not reflected in the investee's earnings any differently than those other costs (for example, materials and labor) that are included in acquisition cost rather than deducted as expenses in determining earnings. The Board also believes that in situations involving intercompany interest there should be little effect because capitalized intercompany interest should be eliminated in accordance with Opinion 18 and ARB 51.

22. A few respondents requested guidance regarding application of the proposed Statement to an investment by an investor in a regulated investee that is accounted for by the equity method while the investee is constructing qualifying assets. The regulated investee capitalizes both a cost of debt and a cost of equity capital during its construction period rather than the amount of interest that it would capitalize in accordance with Statement 34. That method imputes a cost to the investee's equity capital and recognizes that cost as part of the carrying amount of the asset under construction and as current earnings of the investee. Since the investor, by recognizing its equity in the investee's current earnings, includes its prorated share of that imputed cost in the carrying amount of its investment and in its current earnings, the investor should not capitalize an additional cost.

23. Some respondents requested clarification regarding the meaning of the term *goodwill* in paragraph 12 of the Exposure Draft. They suggested that the capitalized interest should be associated with the related assets of the investee and amortized on the basis of the estimated useful lives of those assets. The situation referred to in paragraph 12 of the Exposure Draft was generally limited to one in which the investee would not have underlying qualifying assets. The intent of this Statement is to require capitalization of interest cost on an investment accounted for by the equity method that has not begun its planned principal operations while the investee has activities in progress necessary to commence its planned principal operations provided that the investee's activities include the use of funds to acquire qualifying assets for its operations. Under those circumstances, capitalized interest cost may be associated with the estimated useful lives of the investee's assets and amortized over the same period as those assets. Interest capitalized on the investments accounted for by the equity method is amortized consistent with paragraph 19(b) of Opinion 18. This Statement therefore does not refer to goodwill.

24. Some respondents requested clarification regarding whether the transition provisions of the Exposure Draft permitted retroactive application in previously issued financial statements and whether a qualifying investment existing on the effective date may be included in qualifying expenditures. The Board has revised the transition provisions to indicate that retroactive application in previously issued annual financial statements is not permitted and to clarify that an investment existing or contracted for on the effective date or date of earlier adoption (a) may be accounted for according to the provisions of this Statement or (b) may continue to be accounted for by the method of interest capitalization previously used for those investments even though not in accordance with the provisions of this Statement. The Board concluded that an investor that made an investment or contracted to do so prior to the effective date of this Statement should not be required to change its method of accounting to conform to the provisions of this Statement.

25. The Board concluded that it can reach an informed decision on the basis of existing information without a public hearing and that the effective date and transition specified in paragraph 9 are advisable in the circumstances.

Statement of Financial Accounting Standards No. 59 Deferral of the Effective Date of Certain Accounting Requirements for Pension Plans of State and Local Governmental Units

an amendment of FASB Statement No. 35

STATUS

Issued: April 1982

Effective Date: April 1982 retroactive to fiscal years beginning after December 15, 1980

Affects: Amends FAS 35, paragraph 30

Affected by: Superseded by FAS 75

SUMMARY

This Statement amends FASB Statement No. 35, *Accounting and Reporting by Defined Benefit Pension Plans.* It defers the effective date of Statement 35 for 18 months for plans that are sponsored by state or local governments.

Statement of Financial Accounting Standards No. 59
Deferral of the Effective Date of Certain Accounting Requirements for Pension Plans of State and Local Governmental Units

an amendment of FASB Statement No. 35

CONTENTS

INTRODUCTION

1. FASB Statement No. 35, *Accounting and Reporting by Defined Benefit Pension Plans,* was issued in March 1980 and defines generally accepted accounting principles for general purpose external financial reports of defined benefit pension plans. It applies both to plans in the private sector and to plans sponsored by state and local governmental units. It is effective for plan years beginning after December 15, 1980.

2. In December 1981, the Board received a request from the National Council on Governmental Accounting (NCGA) to suspend Statement 35 as it applies to pension plans sponsored by state and local governmental units. For the reasons given in the appendix, the Board has concluded that it is appropriate to defer the effective date of Statement 35 for those plans.

STANDARDS OF FINANCIAL ACCOUNTING AND REPORTING

Amendment to FASB Statement 35

3. The first sentence of paragraph 30 of Statement 35 is superseded and replaced by the following sentence:

> This Statement shall be effective for plan years beginning after December 15, 1980, except that it shall be effective for plan years beginning after June 15, 1982 for plans that are sponsored by, and provide benefits for the employees of, one or more state or local governments.

Effective Date and Transition

4. This Statement shall be effective upon issuance retroactive to fiscal years beginning after December 15, 1980.

This Statement was approved by the unanimous vote of the seven members of the Financial Accounting Standards Board:

Donald J. Kirk, *Chairman*
Frank E. Block
John W. March
Robert A. Morgan
David Mosso
Robert T. Sprouse
Ralph E. Walters

Appendix

BACKGROUND AND BASIS FOR CONCLUSIONS

5. This appendix reviews considerations that were deemed significant by members of the Board in reaching the conclusions in this Statement. The Board members who assented to this Statement did so on the basis of the overall considerations. Individual members gave greater weight to some factors than to others.

Inclusion of Plans Sponsored by State and Local Governmental Units in Statement 35

6. The Board's reasons for including plans sponsored by state and local governments within the scope of Statement 35 are detailed in paragraphs 75-77 of that Statement. As noted in those paragraphs, the Board believes that the characteristics of the plans rather than those of their sponsors should affect accounting by the plans. The Board also believes, as stated in paragraph 76, that ". . . the primary objective of providing information useful in assessing the plan's ability to pay benefits when

due is as appropriate for plans of state and local governmental units as it is for private plans." The Board reaffirmed that basic conclusion in FASB Concepts Statement No. 4, *Objectives of Financial Reporting by Nonbusiness Organizations,* issued in December 1980. That Statement notes, "based on its study, the Board believes that the objectives of general purpose external financial reporting for government-sponsored entities . . . engaged in activities that are not unique to government should be similar to those of business enterprises or other nonbusiness organizations engaged in similar activities" (paragraph 5).

NCGA Interpretation 4

7. In December 1981, the NCGA issued Interpretation 4, *Accounting and Financial Reporting for Public Employee Retirement Systems and Pension Trust Funds.* The Interpretation is effective for years ending after December 15, 1981. The Interpretation generally requires disclosure of the information required by Statement 35 but differs from that Statement in certain respects.

8. The most significant difference between FASB Statement 35 and NCGA Interpretation 4 is the basis for valuing plan investments. Statement 35 requires presentation of investments at fair value. The Interpretation requires valuing debt securities at amortized cost and equity securities in accordance with FASB Statement No. 12, *Accounting for Certain Marketable Securities.* The Interpretation also requires footnote disclosure of the market value (that is, fair value as defined in Statement 35) of debt and equity securities. The difference in asset valuation also affects information about changes in net assets available for benefits.

Structure for Setting Accounting Standards for State and Local Governmental Units

9. During the period since Board deliberations on Statement 35, an ad hoc Governmental Accounting Standards Board Organization Committee (GASBOC), which included a representative of the Financial Accounting Foundation (FAF), studied the appropriate organizational structure for establishing accounting standards for state and local governments and related entities. On October 13, 1981, GASBOC issued its final report. In that report, GASBOC recommended that a Government Accounting Standards Board be established under the auspices of the FAF to issue pronouncements on governmental accounting standards following due process procedures that provide for broad public participation at all stages of the standard-setting process. Since the issuance of that report, the FAF has organized a committee to advise it regarding implementation of the recommendations of GASBOC. Among the questions that remain to be resolved in implementing those recommendations is how standards should be set for government-related entities (such as hospitals, municipal utilities, universities, and pension plans) that are similar to entities in the private sector.

10. The Board believes that the current efforts to establish a new structure for setting accounting standards for state and local governmental units bear on the request to amend Statement 35. The Board believes that those efforts would not be facilitated by imposition of new standards at this time or by the existence of differing standards issued by different bodies.

11. The FASB and its staff discussed with NCGA representatives the possibility of deferring the applicability of both FASB Statement 35 and NCGA Interpretation 4 for a specific period by changing the effective dates of both to a future date. The Board has concluded that such a mutual deferral would eliminate the potential conflict between those documents while discussions of the appropriate structure are in progress. In March 1982, the NCGA voted to change the effective date of its Interpretation.

12. The Board has concluded that it can reach an informed decision on the basis of existing information without a public hearing and that the effective date and transition specified in paragraph 4 are advisable in the circumstances.

Statement of Financial Accounting Standards No. 60 Accounting and Reporting by Insurance Enterprises

STATUS

Issued: June 1982

Effective Date: For fiscal years beginning after December 15, 1982

Affects: Amends APB 11, paragraph 6
Supersedes APB 23, paragraphs 26 through 30 and footnote 11
Amends APB 30, footnote 8
Amends FAS 5, paragraphs 41 and 102
Amends FAS 32, Appendix A and B
Amends FIN 15, paragraphs 2 and 4
Amends FIN 22, paragraph 7

Affected by: No other pronouncements

SUMMARY

This Statement extracts the specialized principles and practices from the AICPA insurance industry related Guides and Statements of Position and establishes financial accounting and reporting standards for insurance enterprises other than mutual life insurance enterprises, assessment enterprises, and fraternal benefit societies.

Insurance contracts, for purposes of this Statement, need to be classified as short-duration or long-duration contracts. Long-duration contracts include contracts, such as whole-life, guaranteed renewable term life, endowment, annuity, and title insurance contracts, that are expected to remain in force for an extended period. All other insurance contracts are considered short-duration contracts and include most property and liability insurance contracts.

Premiums from short-duration contracts ordinarily are recognized as revenue over the period of the contract in proportion to the amount of insurance protection provided. Claim costs, including estimates of costs for claims relating to insured events that have occurred but have not been reported to the insurer, are recognized when insured events occur.

Premiums from long-duration contracts are recognized as revenue when due from policyholders. The present value of estimated future policy benefits to be paid to or on behalf of policyholders less the present value of estimated future net premiums to be collected from policyholders are accrued when premium revenue is recognized. Those estimates are based on assumptions, such as estimates of expected investment yields, mortality, morbidity, terminations, and expenses, applicable at the time the insurance contracts are made. Claim costs are recognized when insured events occur.

Costs that vary with and are primarily related to the acquisition of insurance contracts (acquisition costs) are capitalized and charged to expense in proportion to premium revenue recognized.

Investments are reported as follows: common and nonredeemable preferred stocks at market, bonds and redeemable preferred stocks at amortized cost, mortgage loans at outstanding principal or amortized cost, and real estate at depreciated cost. Realized investment gains and losses are reported in the income statement below operating income and net of applicable income taxes. Unrealized investment gains and losses, net of applicable income taxes, are included in stockholders' (policyholders') equity.

Statement of Financial Accounting Standards No. 60
Accounting and Reporting by Insurance Enterprises

CONTENTS

INTRODUCTION

1. The primary purpose of insurance is to provide economic protection from identified risks occurring or discovered within a specified period. Some types of risks insured include death, disability, property damage, injury to others, and business interruption. Insurance transactions may be characterized generally by the following:

a. The purchaser of an insurance contract makes an initial payment or deposit to the insurance enterprise in advance of the possible occurrence or discovery of an insured event.
b. When the insurance contract is made, the insurance enterprise ordinarily does not know if, how much, or when amounts will be paid under the contract.

2. Two methods of premium revenue and contract liability recognition for insurance contracts have developed, which are referred to as short-duration and long-duration contract accounting in this Statement. Generally, the two methods reflect the nature of the insurance enterprise's obligations and policyholder rights under the provisions of the contract.

3. Premiums from short-duration insurance contracts, such as most property and liability insurance contracts, are intended to cover expected **claim**[1] costs resulting from insured events that occur during a fixed period of short duration. The insurance enterprise ordinarily has the ability to cancel the contract or to revise the premium at the beginning of each contract period to cover future insured events. Therefore, premiums from short-duration contracts ordinarily are earned and recognized as revenue evenly as insurance protection is provided.

4. Premiums from long-duration insurance contracts, including many life insurance contracts, generally are level even though the expected policy benefits and services do not occur evenly over the periods of the contracts. Functions and services provided by the insurer include insurance protection, sales, premium collection, claim payment, investment, and other services. Because no single function or service is predominant over the periods of most types of long-duration contracts, premiums are recognized as revenue over the premium-paying periods of the contracts when due from policyholders. Premium revenue from long-duration contracts generally exceeds expected policy benefits in

[1]Terms defined in the glossary (Appendix A) are in **boldface type** the first time they appear in this Statement.

the early years of the contracts and it is necessary to accrue, as premium revenue is recognized, a liability for costs that are expected to be paid in the later years of the contracts. Accordingly, a liability for expected costs relating to most types of long-duration contracts is accrued over the current and expected renewal periods of the contracts.

5. Title insurance contracts provide protection for an extended period and therefore are considered long-duration contracts. Premiums from title insurance contracts ordinarily are recognized as revenue on the effective date of the contract because most of the services associated with the contract have been rendered by that time. Estimated claim costs are recognized when premium revenue is recognized because the insurance provides protection against claims caused by problems with title to real estate arising out of ascertainable insured events that generally exist at that time.

APPLICABILITY AND SCOPE

6. This Statement establishes accounting and reporting standards for the general-purpose financial statements of stock **life insurance enterprises, property and liability insurance enterprises,**[2] and **title insurance enterprises.** Except for the sections on premium revenue and claim cost recognition and **acquisition costs** (paragraphs 9-11, 13-18, and 20-31), this Statement applies to **mortgage guaranty insurance enterprises.** It does not apply to mutual life insurance enterprises, **assessment enterprises,** or **fraternal benefit societies.**

STANDARDS OF FINANCIAL ACCOUNTING AND REPORTING

General Principles

7. Insurance contracts, for purposes of this Statement, shall be classified as short-duration or long-duration contracts depending on whether the contracts are expected to remain in force[3] for an extended period. The factors that shall be considered in determining whether a particular contract can be expected to remain in force for an extended period are:

a. *Short-duration contract.* The contract provides insurance protection for a fixed period of short duration and enables the insurer to cancel the contract or to adjust the provisions of the contract at the end of any contract period, such as adjusting the amount of premiums charged or coverage provided.
b. *Long-duration contract.* The contract generally is not subject to unilateral changes in its provisions, such as a noncancelable or guaranteed renewable contract, and requires the performance of various functions and services (including insurance protection) for an extended period.

8. Examples of short-duration contracts include most property and liability insurance contracts and certain **term life insurance** contracts, such as **credit life insurance.** Examples of long-duration contracts include **whole-life contracts,** guaranteed renewable term life contracts, **endowment contracts, annuity contracts,** and title insurance contracts. Accident and health insurance contracts may be short-duration or long-duration depending on whether the contracts are expected to remain in force for an extended period. For example, individual and **group insurance** contracts that are noncancelable or guaranteed renewable (renewable at the option of the insured), or collectively renewable (individual contracts within a group are not cancelable), ordinarily are long-duration contracts.

9. Premiums from short-duration insurance contracts ordinarily shall be recognized as revenue over the period of the contract in proportion to the amount of insurance protection provided. A **liability for unpaid claims** (including estimates of costs for claims relating to insured events that have occurred but have not been reported to the insurer) and a **liability for claim adjustment expenses** shall be accrued when insured events occur.

10. Premiums from long-duration contracts shall be recognized as revenue when due from policyholders. A liability for expected costs relating to most types of long-duration contracts shall be accrued over the current and expected renewal periods of the contracts. The present value of estimated future policy benefits to be paid to or on behalf of policyholders less the present value of estimated future **net premiums** to be collected from policyholders **(liability for future policy benefits)** shall be accrued when premium revenue is recognized. Those estimates shall be based on assumptions, such as estimates of expected investment yields, **mortality, morbidity, terminations,** and expenses, applicable at the time the insurance contracts are made. In addition, liabilities for unpaid claims and claim adjustment expenses shall be accrued when insured events occur.

[2] Property and liability insurance enterprises, for purposes of this Statement, include stock enterprises, mutual enterprises, and **reciprocal or interinsurance exchanges.**

[3] *In force* refers to the period of coverage, that is, the period during which the occurrence of insured events can result in liabilities of the insurance enterprise.

11. Costs that vary with and are primarily related to the acquisition of insurance contracts (acquisition costs) shall be capitalized and charged to expense in proportion to premium revenue recognized. Other costs incurred during the period, such as those relating to investments, general administration, and policy **maintenance**, shall be charged to expense as incurred.

12. Accounting for investments by insurance enterprises presumes that (a) insurance enterprises have both the ability and the intent to hold long-term investments, such as bonds, mortgage loans, and redeemable preferred stocks, to maturity and (b) there is no decline in the market value of the investments other than a temporary decline. Accordingly, bonds, mortgage loans, and redeemable preferred stocks shall be reported at amortized cost. Common and nonredeemable preferred stocks shall be reported at market, and real estate shall be reported at depreciated cost.

Premium Revenue Recognition

Short-Duration Contracts

13. Premiums from short-duration contracts ordinarily shall be recognized as revenue over the period of the contract in proportion to the amount of insurance protection provided. For those few types of contracts for which the period of risk differs significantly from the contract period, premiums shall be recognized as revenue over the period of risk in proportion to the amount of insurance protection provided. That generally results in premiums being recognized as revenue evenly over the contract period (or the period of risk, if different), except for those few cases in which the amount of insurance protection declines according to a predetermined schedule.

14. If premiums are subject to adjustment (for example, retrospectively rated or other experience-rated insurance contracts for which the premium is determined after the period of the contract based on claim experience or reporting-form contracts for which the premium is adjusted after the period of the contract based on the value of insured property), premium revenue shall be recognized as follows:

a. If, as is usually the case, the ultimate premium is reasonably estimable, the estimated ultimate premium shall be recognized as revenue over the period of the contract. The estimated ultimate premium shall be revised to reflect current experience.

b. If the ultimate premium cannot be reasonably estimated, the **cost recovery method** or the **deposit method** may be used until the ultimate premium becomes reasonably estimable.

Long-Duration Contracts

15. Premiums from long-duration contracts, such as whole-life contracts (including limited-payment and single-premium life contracts), guaranteed renewable term life contracts, endowment contracts, annuity contracts, and title insurance contracts, shall be recognized as revenue when due from policyholders.

16. Premiums from title insurance contracts shall be considered due from policyholders and, accordingly, recognized as revenue on the effective date of the insurance contract. However, the binder date (the date a commitment to issue a policy is given) is appropriate if the insurance enterprise is legally or contractually entitled to the premium on the binder date. If reasonably estimable, premium revenue and costs relating to title insurance contracts issued by agents shall be recognized when the agents are legally or contractually entitled to the premiums, using estimates based on past experience and other sources. If not reasonably estimable, premium revenue and costs shall be recognized when agents report the issuance of title insurance contracts.

Claim Cost Recognition

17. A liability for unpaid claim costs relating to insurance contracts other than title insurance contracts, including estimates of costs relating to **incurred but not reported claims,** shall be accrued when insured events occur. A liability for estimated claim costs relating to title insurance contracts, including estimates of costs relating to incurred but not reported claims, shall be accrued when title insurance premiums are recognized as revenue (paragraphs 15 and 16).

18. The liability for unpaid claims shall be based on the estimated ultimate cost of settling the claims (including the effects of inflation and other societal and economic factors), using past experience adjusted for current trends, and any other factors that would modify past experience.[4] Changes in estimates of claim costs resulting from the continuous review process and differences between estimates and payments for claims shall be recognized in income of the period in which the estimates are changed or payments are made. Estimated recoveries on unsettled claims, such as **salvage, subroga-**

[4]Certain disclosures are required if the time value of money is considered in estimating liabilities for unpaid claims and claim adjustment expenses relating to short-duration contracts (paragraph 60(d)).

tion, or a potential ownership interest in real estate, shall be evaluated in terms of their estimated realizable value and deducted from the liability for unpaid claims. Estimated recoveries on settled claims other than mortgage guaranty and title insurance claims also shall be deducted from the liability for unpaid claims.

19. Real estate acquired in settling mortgage guaranty and title insurance claims shall be reported at fair value, that is, the amount that reasonably could be expected to be received in a current sale between a willing buyer and a willing seller. If no market price is available, the expected cash flows (anticipated sales price less maintenance and selling costs of the real estate) may aid in estimating fair value provided the cash flows are discounted at a rate commensurate with the risk involved. Real estate acquired in settling claims shall be separately reported in the balance sheet and shall not be classified as an investment. Subsequent reductions in the reported amount and realized gains and losses on the sale of real estate acquired in settling claims shall be recognized as an adjustment to claim costs incurred.

20. A liability for all costs expected to be incurred in connection with the settlement of unpaid claims (**claim adjustment expenses**) shall be accrued when the related liability for unpaid claims is accrued. Claim adjustment expenses include costs associated directly with specific claims paid or in the process of settlement, such as legal and adjusters' fees. Claim adjustment expenses also include other costs that cannot be associated with specific claims but are related to claims paid or in the process of settlement, such as internal costs of the claims function.[5]

Liability for Future Policy Benefits

21. A liability for future policy benefits relating to long-duration contracts other than title insurance contracts (paragraph 17) shall be accrued when premium revenue is recognized. The liability, which represents the present value of future benefits to be paid to or on behalf of policyholders and related expenses less the present value of future net premiums (portion of **gross premium** required to provide for all benefits and expenses), shall be estimated using methods that include assumptions, such as estimates of expected investment yields, mortality, morbidity, terminations, and expenses, applicable at the time the insurance contracts are made. The liability also shall consider other assumptions relating to guaranteed contract benefits, such as coupons, annual endowments, and conversion privileges. The assumptions shall include provision for the **risk of adverse deviation.** Original assumptions shall continue to be used in subsequent accounting periods to determine changes in the liability for future policy benefits (often referred to as the "lock-in concept") unless a premium deficiency exists (paragraphs 35-37). Changes in the liability for future policy benefits that result from its periodic estimation for financial reporting purposes shall be recognized in income in the period in which the changes occur.

Investment Yields

22. Interest assumptions used in estimating the liability for future policy benefits shall be based on estimates of investment yields (net of related investment expenses) expected at the time insurance contracts are made. The interest assumption for each block of new insurance contracts (a group of insurance contracts that may be limited to contracts issued under the same plan in a particular year) shall be consistent with circumstances, such as actual yields, trends in yields, portfolio mix and maturities, and the enterprise's general investment experience.

Mortality

23. Mortality assumptions used in estimating the liability for future policy benefits shall be based on estimates of expected mortality.

Morbidity

24. Morbidity assumptions used in estimating the liability for future policy benefits shall be based on estimates of expected incidences of disability and claim costs. Expected incidences of disability and claim costs for various types of insurance (for example, noncancelable and guaranteed renewable accident and health insurance contracts) and other factors, such as occupational class, waiting period, sex, age, and benefit period, shall be considered in making morbidity assumptions. The risk of antiselection (the tendency for lower terminations of poor risks) also shall be considered in making morbidity assumptions.

Terminations

25. Termination assumptions used in estimating the liability for future policy benefits shall be based on anticipated terminations and **nonforfeiture benefits,** using anticipated **termination rates** and contractual nonforfeiture benefits. Termination rates may vary by plan of insurance, age at issue, year of issue, frequency of premium payment, and other factors. If composite rates are used, the rates shall be repre-

[5]Title insurance internal claim adjustment expenses, which generally consist of fixed costs associated with a permanent staff handling a variety of functions including claim adjustment, ordinarily are expensed as period costs because the costs are insignificant.

sentative of the enterprise's actual mix of business. Termination assumptions shall be made for long-duration insurance contracts without termination benefits because of the effects of terminations on anticipated premiums and claim costs.

Expenses

26. Expense assumptions used in estimating the liability for future policy benefits shall be based on estimates of expected nonlevel costs, such as termination or settlement costs, and costs after the premium-paying period. Renewal expense assumptions shall consider the possible effect of inflation on those expenses.

Costs Other Than Those Relating to Claims and Policy Benefits

27. Costs incurred during the period, such as those relating to investments, general administration, and policy maintenance, that do not vary with and are not primarily related to the acquisition of new and renewal insurance contracts shall be charged to expense as incurred.

Acquisition Costs

28. Acquisition costs are those costs that vary with and are primarily related to the acquisition of new and renewal insurance contracts. Commissions and other costs (for example, salaries of certain employees involved in the underwriting and policy issue functions, and medical and inspection fees) that are primarily related to insurance contracts issued or renewed during the period in which the costs are incurred shall be considered acquisition costs.

29. Acquisition costs shall be capitalized and charged to expense in proportion to premium revenue recognized. To associate acquisition costs with related premium revenue, acquisition costs shall be allocated by groupings of insurance contracts consistent with the enterprise's manner of acquiring, servicing, and measuring the profitability of its insurance contracts. Unamortized acquisition costs shall be classified as an asset.

30. If acquisition costs for short-duration contracts are determined based on a percentage relationship of costs incurred to premiums from contracts issued or renewed for a specified period, the percentage relationship and the period used, once determined, shall be applied to applicable unearned premiums throughout the period of the contracts.

31. Actual acquisition costs for long-duration contracts shall be used in determining acquisition costs to be capitalized as long as gross premiums are sufficient to cover actual costs. However, estimated acquisition costs may be used if the difference is not significant. Capitalized acquisition costs shall be charged to expense using methods that include the same assumptions used in estimating the liability for future policy benefits.

Premium Deficiency

32. A probable loss on insurance contracts exists if there is a premium deficiency relating to short-duration or long-duration contracts. Insurance contracts shall be grouped consistent with the enterprise's manner of acquiring, servicing, and measuring the profitability of its insurance contracts to determine if a premium deficiency exists.

Short-Duration Contracts

33. A premium deficiency shall be recognized if the sum of expected claim costs and claim adjustment expenses, expected **dividends to policyholders,** unamortized acquisition costs, and maintenance costs exceeds related unearned premiums.[6]

34. A premium deficiency shall first be recognized by charging any unamortized acquisition costs to expense to the extent required to eliminate the deficiency. If the premium deficiency is greater than unamortized acquisition costs, a liability shall be accrued for the excess deficiency.

Long-Duration Contracts

35. Original policy benefit assumptions for long-duration contracts ordinarily continue to be used during the periods in which the liability for future policy benefits is accrued (paragraph 21). However, actual experience with respect to investment yields, mortality, morbidity, terminations, or expenses may indicate that existing contract liabilities, together with the present value of future gross premiums, will not be sufficient (a) to cover the present value of future benefits to be paid to or on behalf of policyholders and settlement and maintenance costs relating to a block of long-duration contracts and (b) to recover unamortized acquisition costs. In those circumstances, a premium deficiency shall be determined as follows:

[6]Disclosure is required regarding whether the insurance enterprise considers anticipated investment income in determining if a premium deficiency relating to short-duration contracts exists (paragraph 60(e)).

Present value of future payments for benefits and related settlement and maintenance costs, determined using revised assumptions based on actual and anticipated experience	$XX
Less the present value of future gross premiums, determined using revised assumptions based on actual and anticipated experience	XX
Liability for future policy benefits using revised assumptions	XX
Less the liability for future policy benefits at the valuation date, reduced by unamortized acquisition costs	XX
Premium deficiency	$XX

36. A premium deficiency shall be recognized by a charge to income and (a) a reduction of unamortized acquisition costs or (b) an increase in the liability for future policy benefits. If a premium deficiency does occur, future changes in the liability shall be based on the revised assumptions. No loss shall be reported currently if it results in creating future income. The liability for future policy benefits using revised assumptions based on actual and anticipated experience shall be estimated periodically for comparison with the liability for future policy benefits (reduced by unamortized acquisition costs) at the valuation date.

37. A premium deficiency, at a minimum, shall be recognized if the aggregate liability on an entire line of business is deficient. In some instances, the liability on a particular line of business may not be deficient in the aggregate, but circumstances may be such that profits would be recognized in early years and losses in later years. In those situations, the liability shall be increased by an amount necessary to offset losses that would be recognized in later years.

Reinsurance

38. Amounts that are recoverable from reinsurers and that relate to paid claims and claim adjustment expenses shall be classified as assets, with an allowance for estimated uncollectible amounts. Estimated amounts recoverable from reinsurers that relate to the liabilities for unpaid claims and claim adjustment expenses shall be deducted from those liabilities. Ceded unearned premiums shall be netted with related unearned premiums. Receivables and payables from the same reinsurer, including amounts withheld, also shall be netted. **Reinsurance** premiums ceded and reinsurance recoveries on claims may be netted against related earned premiums and incurred claim costs in the income statement.

39. Proceeds from reinsurance transactions that represent recovery of acquisition costs shall reduce applicable unamortized acquisition costs in such a manner that net acquisition costs are capitalized and charged to expense in proportion to net revenue recognized (paragraph 29). If the ceding enterprise has agreed to service all of the related insurance contracts without reasonable compensation, a liability shall be accrued for estimated excess future servicing costs under the reinsurance contract. The net cost to the assuming enterprise shall be accounted for as an acquisition cost.

40. To the extent that a reinsurance contract does not, despite its form, provide for indemnification of the ceding enterprise by the reinsurer against loss or liability, the premium paid less the premium to be retained by the reinsurer shall be accounted for as a deposit by the ceding enterprise. Those contracts may be structured in various ways, but if, regardless of form, their substance is that all or part of the premium paid by the ceding enterprise is a deposit, the amount paid shall be accounted for as such. A net credit resulting from the contract shall be reported as a liability by the ceding enterprise. A net charge resulting from the contract shall be reported as an asset by the reinsurer.

Policyholder Dividends

41. Policyholder dividends shall be accrued using an estimate of the amount to be paid.

42. If limitations exist on the amount of net income from **participating insurance** contracts of life insurance enterprises that may be distributed to stockholders, the policyholders' share of net income on those contracts that cannot be distributed to stockholders shall be excluded from stockholders' equity by a charge to operations and a credit to a liability relating to participating policyholders' funds in a manner similar to the accounting for net income applicable to minority interests. Dividends declared or paid to participating policyholders shall reduce that liability; dividends declared or paid in excess of the liability shall be charged to operations. Income-based dividend provisions shall be based on net income that includes adjustments between general-purpose and statutory financial statements that will reverse and enter into future calculations of the dividend provision.

43. For life insurance enterprises for which there are no net income restrictions and that use life insurance dividend scales unrelated to actual net income, policyholder dividends (based on dividends anticipated or intended in determining gross premiums or

as shown in published dividend illustrations at the date insurance contracts are made) shall be accrued over the premium-paying periods of the contracts.

Retrospective and Contingent Commission Arrangements

44. If retrospective commission or experience refund arrangements exist under experience-rated insurance contracts, a separate liability shall be accrued for those amounts, based on experience and the provisions of the contract. Income in any period shall not include any amounts that are expected to be paid to agents or others in the form of experience refunds or additional commissions. Contingent commissions receivable or payable shall be accrued over the period in which related income is recognized.

Investments

45. Bonds shall be reported at amortized cost if the insurance enterprise has both the ability and the intent to hold the bonds until maturity and there is no decline in the market value of the bonds other than a temporary decline. If an insurance enterprise is a trader in bonds and does not intend to hold the bonds until maturity, bonds shall be reported at market and temporary changes in the market value of the bonds shall be recognized as unrealized gains or losses (paragraph 50).

46. Common and nonredeemable preferred stocks shall be reported at market and temporary changes in the market value of those securities shall be recognized as unrealized gains or losses (paragraph 50). Preferred stocks that by their provisions must be redeemed by the issuer shall be reported at amortized cost if the insurance enterprise has both the ability and the intent to hold the stocks until redemption and there is no decline in the market value of the stocks other than a temporary decline.

47. Mortgage loans shall be reported at outstanding principal balances if acquired at par value, or at amortized cost if purchased at a discount or premium, with an allowance for estimated uncollectible amounts, if any. Amortization and other related charges or credits shall be charged or credited to investment income. Changes in the allowance for estimated uncollectible amounts relating to mortgage loans shall be included in realized gains and losses.

48. Real estate investments shall be reported at cost less accumulated depreciation and an allowance for any impairment in value. Depreciation and other related charges or credits shall be charged or credited to investment income. Changes in the allowance for any impairment in value relating to real estate investments shall be included in realized gains and losses.

49. Normal commitment fees received in connection with the placement of mortgage loans (less direct costs) shall be capitalized and recognized as revenue over the commitment period. Commitment fees that exceed current (normal) fees for mortgage loan commitments shall be considered an adjustment of the effective interest yield on the loan. Those excess fees shall be capitalized until the loan is made and then recognized as revenue over the period of the mortgage loan. If the mortgage loan is not ultimately made, the unamortized commitment fee shall be recognized as revenue at the end of the commitment period.

50. Realized gains and losses on all investments (including, but not limited to, stocks, bonds, mortgage loans, real estate, and joint ventures) shall be reported in the income statement below operating income and net of applicable income taxes. Realized gains and losses on the sale of assets other than investments, such as real estate used in the business, shall be reported in accordance with APB Opinion No. 30, *Reporting the Results of Operations.* Unrealized investment gains and losses, net of applicable income taxes, shall be reported as a separate component of stockholders' (policyholders') equity. Except as discussed in paragraph 51, unrealized gains or losses on common stocks, preferred stocks, or publicly traded bonds shall not be recognized in income until the sale, maturity, or other disposition of the investment.[7]

51. If a decline in the value of a common stock, preferred stock, or publicly traded bond below its cost or amortized cost is considered to be other than temporary, the investment shall be reduced to its net realizable value, which becomes the new cost basis. The amount of the reduction shall be reported as a realized loss. A recovery from the new cost basis shall be recognized as a realized gain only at the sale, maturity, or other disposition of the investment.

Real Estate Used in the Business

52. Real estate shall be classified either as an investment or as real estate used in the enterprise's operations, depending on its predominant use. Depreciation and other real estate operating costs shall be classified as investment expenses or operating expenses consistent with the balance sheet classification of the related asset. Imputed investment

[7]This paragraph is not intended to preclude the accrual of losses on private-placement bonds when both conditions in paragraph 8 of FASB Statement No. 5, *Accounting for Contingencies,* are met.

income and rental expense shall not be recognized for real estate used in the business.

Separate Accounts

53. Separate accounts represent assets and liabilities that are maintained by an insurance enterprise for purposes of funding fixed-benefit or **variable annuity contracts,** pension plans, and similar activities. The contract holder generally assumes the investment risk, and the insurance enterprise receives a fee for investment management, certain administrative expenses, and mortality and expense risks assumed.

54. Investments in separate accounts shall be reported at market except for separate account contracts with guaranteed investment returns. For those separate accounts, the related assets shall be reported in accordance with paragraphs 45-51. Separate account assets and liabilities ordinarily shall be reported as summary totals in the financial statements of the insurance enterprise.

Income Taxes of Life Insurance Enterprises

Deferred Income Taxes

55. Because of the provisions of the Life Insurance Company Income Tax Act of 1959 (Act),[8] timing differences (paragraph 13(e) of APB Opinion No. 11, *Accounting for Income Taxes*) of life insurance enterprises arising in the current period may not affect the determination of income taxes in future periods when those timing differences reverse. Amounts determined in the with-and-without calculation (paragraph 36 of Opinion 11) need to be considered further to determine whether the difference will reverse in the future. Deferred taxes need not be provided for the current tax effect of timing differences if circumstances indicate that the current tax effect will not reverse in the future. Similarly, a change in category of taxation (the basis on which the enterprise determines its income tax liability) resulting from the with-and-without calculation need not be recognized unless circumstances indicate that a change in category will result when the timing difference reverses. If the reversal of tax effects cannot be reasonably determined, deferred income taxes shall be provided based on the differential determined using the with-and-without calculation as if the enterprise's tax return was filed on the basis on which financial statements are prepared, including any resulting change in category of taxation.

56. Although (a) special deductions (allowable only for income tax purposes) never enter into the determination of pretax accounting income in any period and (b) the amount of policyholder dividend deductions and special deductions may be limited on the tax return (the unused deductions cannot be carried forward to subsequent periods), the amount of policyholder dividend deductions and available special deductions and limitations on those deductions may properly be determined based on pretax accounting income. For example, unused policyholder dividend deductions and special deductions may be used to offset timing differences that affect taxable income to the extent that the limitations on those deductions change when based on pretax accounting income, unless known or anticipated circumstances indicate that future taxable income resulting from the reversal of timing differences will not be offset by like deductions. In the case of provisions for policyholder dividends (including policyholder dividends deducted as part of the change in the liability for future policy benefits), which may be timing differences themselves, statutory limitations shall not be applied to eliminate their current tax effect unless circumstances indicate that the dividends will be limited when the timing differences reverse. Special deductions that are directly affected by timing differences need to be redetermined in the with-and-without calculation unless circumstances indicate that future special deductions will not be directly affected by the timing differences when the timing differences reverse. If the reversal of tax effects cannot be reasonably determined, special deductions that are not affected by timing differences and, therefore, do not reverse shall be limited to amounts available in the tax return.

57. A life insurance enterprise's liability for future policy benefits and capitalization and amortization of acquisition costs indirectly affect the amount of taxable investment income used in determining the income tax provision for financial reporting purposes. Differences in taxable investment income caused by differences between the liability for future policy benefits and capitalization and amortization of acquisition costs for income tax and financial

[8]The Act contemplated taxation of total income of life insurance enterprises, but the determination of tax is complex because of the manner in which total taxable income is classified as investment income, gain from operations (including investment income and less special deductions for certain accident and health, group life, and nonparticipating insurance contracts), policyholders' surplus (gain from operations previously excluded from tax and the special deductions), and the interrelationship of those elements. Taxable income consists of (a) taxable investment income, (b) 50 percent of the amount by which gain from operations exceeds taxable investment income, and (c) any reductions in policyholders' surplus. If gain from operations is less than taxable investment income, the lesser amount, plus any reductions in policyholders' surplus, is taxable income. If a loss from operations occurs, there is no taxable income except to the extent that there are reductions in policyholders' surplus. Deductions from gain from operations for policyholder dividends and the special deductions are limited and unused deductions cannot be carried forward to subsequent periods.

reporting purposes shall be considered permanent differences (paragraph 13(f) of Opinion 11).

58. If deferred income taxes have not been provided on timing differences on the presumption that the timing differences will not have tax effects when they reverse and circumstances change so that it becomes apparent that tax effects will result, deferred income taxes attributable to those timing differences shall be accrued and reported as income tax expense in that period; those income taxes shall not be reported as an extraordinary item. If deferred income taxes have been provided on timing differences and circumstances change so that it becomes apparent that the tax effects will differ from those originally expected, income taxes previously deferred shall be included in income only as the related timing differences reverse, regardless of whether the life insurance enterprise uses the gross change or net change method (paragraph 37 of Opinion 11).

Policyholders' Surplus

59. A difference between taxable income and pretax accounting income attributable to amounts designated as policyholders' surplus of a life insurance enterprise may not reverse until indefinite future periods or may never reverse. The insurance enterprise controls the events that create the tax consequences, and the enterprise generally is required to take specific action before the initial difference reverses. Therefore, a life insurance enterprise shall not accrue income taxes on the difference between taxable income and pretax accounting income attributable to amounts designated as policyholders' surplus. However, if circumstances indicate that the insurance enterprise is likely to pay income taxes, either currently or in later years, because of a known or expected reduction in policyholders' surplus, income taxes attributable to that reduction shall be accrued as a tax expense of the current period; the accrual of those income taxes shall not be accounted for as an extraordinary item.

Disclosures

60. Insurance enterprises shall disclose the following in their financial statements:

a. The basis for estimating the liabilities for unpaid claims and claim adjustment expenses
b. The methods and assumptions used in estimating the liability for future policy benefits with disclosure of the average rate of assumed investment yields in effect for the current year encouraged
c. The nature of acquisition costs capitalized, the method of amortizing those costs, and the amount of those costs amortized for the period
d. The carrying amount of liabilities for unpaid claims and claim adjustment expenses relating to short-duration contracts that are presented at present value in the financial statements and the range of interest rates used to discount those liabilities
e. Whether the insurance enterprise considers anticipated investment income in determining if a premium deficiency relating to short-duration contracts exists
f. The nature and significance of reinsurance transactions to the insurance enterprise's operations, including reinsurance premiums assumed and ceded, and estimated amounts that are recoverable from reinsurers and that reduce the liabilities for unpaid claims and claim adjustment expenses
g. The relative percentage of participating insurance, the method of accounting for policyholder dividends, the amount of dividends, and the amount of any additional income allocated to participating policyholders
h. The following information relating to stockholders' equity, statutory capital and surplus, and the effects of **statutory accounting practices** on the enterprise's ability to pay dividends to stockholders:
   (1) The amount of statutory capital and surplus
   (2) The amount of statutory capital and surplus necessary to satisfy regulatory requirements (based on the enterprise's current operations) if significant in relation to the enterprise's statutory capital and surplus
   (3) The nature of statutory restrictions on the payment of dividends and the amount of retained earnings that is not available for the payment of dividends to stockholders
i. For life insurance enterprises or a parent of a life insurance enterprise that is either consolidated or accounted for by the equity method:
   (1) The treatment of policyholders' surplus under the U.S. Internal Revenue Code and that income taxes may be payable if the enterprise takes certain specified actions, which shall be appropriately described
   (2) The accumulated amount of policyholders' surplus for which income taxes have not been accrued
j. For life insurance enterprises, any retained earnings in excess of policyholders' surplus on which no current or deferred federal income tax provisions have been made and the reasons for not providing the deferred taxes

Amendments to Other Pronouncements

61. The following footnote is added to the end of paragraph 6 of Opinion 11:

> For life insurance enterprises, also refer to paragraphs 55-59 and subparagraphs 60(i) and 60(j)

of FASB Statement No. 60, *Accounting and Reporting by Insurance Enterprises.*

62. The provisions of APB Opinion No. 23, *Accounting for Income Taxes—Special Areas,* that discuss policyholders' surplus of life insurance enterprises have been included in this Statement without reconsideration, and paragraphs 26-30 and footnote 11 of Opinion 23 are superseded by this Statement.

63. The references to AICPA insurance industry related Guides in footnote 8 of Opinion 30, paragraphs 41 and 102 of FASB Statement No. 5, *Accounting for Contingencies,* paragraph 4 of FASB Interpretation No. 15, *Translation of Unamortized Policy Acquisition Costs by a Stock Life Insurance Company,* and paragraph 7 of FASB Interpretation No. 22, *Applicability of Indefinite Reversal Criteria to Timing Differences,* are replaced by a reference to FASB Statement No. 60, *Accounting and Reporting by Insurance Enterprises.* The references to AICPA Statements of Position (SOPs) 78-6, *Accounting for Property and Liability Insurance Companies,* and 79-3, *Accounting for Investments of Stock Life Insurance Companies,* and to the AICPA Industry Audit Guides, *Audits of Fire and Casualty Insurance Companies* and *Audits of Stock Life Insurance Companies,* are deleted from Appendix A of FASB Statement No. 32, *Specialized Accounting and Reporting Principles and Practices in AICPA Statements of Position and Guides on Accounting and Auditing Matters.* The reference to the AICPA project on accounting by title insurance companies, which resulted in the issuance of SOP 80-1, *Accounting for Title Insurance Companies,* is deleted from Appendix B of Statement 32.

Effective Date and Transition

64. This Statement shall be effective for fiscal years beginning after December 15, 1982, with earlier application encouraged. Accounting changes adopted to conform to the provisions of this Statement shall be applied retroactively. In the year that this Statement is first applied, the financial statements shall disclose the nature of any restatement and its effect on income before extraordinary items, net income, and related per share amounts for each year presented. The individual effects of changing to conform to the provisions of this Statement shall be disclosed in the financial statements.

65. If retroactive restatement of all years presented is not practicable, the financial statements presented shall be restated for as many consecutive years as practicable and the cumulative effect of applying this Statement shall be included in determining net income of the earliest year restated (not necessarily the earliest year presented). If it is not practicable to restate any prior year, the cumulative effect shall be included in net income in the year in which this Statement is first applied. (Refer to paragraph 20 of APB Opinion No. 20, *Accounting Changes.*)

The provisions of this Statement need not be applied to immaterial items.

This Statement was approved by the unanimous vote of the seven members of the Financial Accounting Standards Board:

Donald J. Kirk, *Chairman*
Frank E. Block
John W. March
Robert A. Morgan
David Mosso
Robert T. Sprouse
Ralph E. Walters

Appendix A

GLOSSARY

66. This appendix defines certain terms that are used in this Statement.

Acquisition costs
Costs incurred in the acquisition of new and renewal insurance contracts. Acquisition costs include those costs that vary with and are primarily related to the acquisition of insurance contracts (for example, agent and broker commissions, certain underwriting and policy issue costs, and medical and inspection fees).

Annuity contract
A contract that provides fixed or variable periodic payments made from a stated or contingent date and continuing for a specified period, such as for a number of years or for life. Also refer to variable annuity contract.

Assessment enterprise
An insurance enterprise that sells insurance to groups with similar interests, such as church denominations or professional groups. Some assessment enterprises also sell insurance directly to the general public. If funds are not sufficient

to pay claims, then assessments may be made against members.

Claim
A demand for payment of a policy benefit because of the occurrence of an insured event, such as the death or disability of the insured; the maturity of an endowment; the incurrence of hospital or medical bills; the destruction or damage of property and related deaths or injuries; defects in, liens on, or challenges to the title to real estate; or the occurrence of a surety loss.

Claim adjustment expenses
Expenses incurred in the course of investigating and settling claims. Claim adjustment expenses include any legal and adjusters' fees, and the costs of paying claims and all related expenses.

Cost recovery method
Under the cost recovery method, premiums are recognized as revenue in an amount equal to estimated claim costs as insured events occur until the ultimate premium is reasonably estimable, and recognition of income is postponed until that time.

Credit life insurance
Life insurance, generally in the form of decreasing term insurance, that is issued on the lives of borrowers to cover payment of loan balances in case of death.

Deposit method
Under the deposit method, premiums are not recognized as revenue and claim costs are not charged to expense until the ultimate premium is reasonably estimable, and recognition of income is postponed until that time.

Dividends to policyholders
Amounts distributable to policyholders of participating insurance contracts as determined by the insurer. Under various state insurance laws, dividends are apportioned to policyholders on an equitable basis. The dividend allotted to any contract often is based on the amount that the contract, as one of a class of similar contracts, has contributed to the income available for distribution as dividends.

Endowment contract
An insurance contract that provides insurance from inception of the contract to the maturity date (endowment period). The contract specifies that a stated amount, adjusted for items such as policy loans and dividends, if any, will be paid to the beneficiary if the insured dies before the maturity date. If the insured is still living at the maturity date, the policyholder will receive the maturity amount under the contract after adjustments, if any. Endowment contracts generally mature at a specified age of the insured or at the end of a specified period.

Fraternal benefit society
An organization that provides life or health insurance to its members and their beneficiaries. Policyholders normally participate in the earnings of the society, and insurance contracts stipulate that the society has the power to assess its members if the funds available for future policy benefits are not sufficient to provide for benefits and expenses.

Gross premium
The premium charged to a policyholder for an insurance contract. Also refer to net premium.

Group insurance
Insurance protecting a group of persons, usually employees of an entity and their dependents. A single insurance contract is issued to their employer or other representative of the group. Individual certificates often are given to each insured individual or family unit. The insurance usually has an annual renewable contract period, although the insurer may guarantee premium rates for two or three years. Adjustments to premiums relating to the actual experience of the group of insured persons are common.

Incurred but not reported claims
Claims relating to insured events that have occurred but have not yet been reported to the insurer or reinsurer as of the date of the financial statements.

Liability for claim adjustment expenses
The amount needed to provide for the estimated ultimate cost required to investigate and settle claims relating to insured events that have occurred on or before a particular date (ordinarily, the balance sheet date), whether or not reported to the insurer at that date.

Liability for future policy benefits
An accrued obligation to policyholders that relates to insured events, such as death or disability. The liability for future policy benefits can be viewed as either (a) the present value of future benefits to be paid to or on behalf of policyholders and expenses less the present value of future net premiums payable under the insurance contracts or (b) the accumulated amount of net premiums already collected less the accumulated amount of benefits and expenses already paid to or on behalf of policyholders.

Liability for unpaid claims
The amount needed to provide for the estimated ultimate cost of settling claims relating to insured events that have occurred on or before a particular date (ordinarily, the balance sheet date). The estimated liability includes the amount of money that will be required for future payments on both (a) claims that have been reported to the insurer and (b) claims relating to insured events that have occurred but have not been reported to the insurer as of the date the liability is estimated.

Life insurance enterprise
An enterprise that can issue annuity, endowment, and accident and health insurance contracts as well as life insurance contracts. Life insurance enterprises may be either stock or mutual organizations.

Maintenance costs
Costs associated with maintaining records relating to insurance contracts and with the processing of premium collections and commissions.

Morbidity
The relative incidence of disability due to disease or physical impairment.

Mortality
The relative incidence of death in a given time or place.

Mortgage guaranty insurance enterprise
An insurance enterprise that issues insurance contracts that guarantee lenders, such as savings and loan associations, against nonpayment by mortgagors.

Net premium
As used in this Statement for long-duration insurance contracts, the portion of the gross premium required to provide for all benefits and expenses.

Nonforfeiture benefits
Those benefits in a life insurance contract that the policyholder does not forfeit, even for failure to pay premiums. Nonforfeiture benefits usually include cash value, paid-up insurance value, or extended-term insurance value.

Participating insurance
Insurance in which the policyholder is entitled to participate in the earnings or surplus of the insurance enterprise. The participation occurs through the distribution of dividends to policyholders.

Property and liability insurance enterprise
An enterprise that issues insurance contracts providing protection against (a) damage to, or loss of, property caused by various perils, such as fire and theft, or (b) legal liability resulting from injuries to other persons or damage to their property. Property and liability insurance enterprises also can issue accident and health insurance contracts. The term *property and liability insurance enterprise* is the current terminology used to describe a fire and casualty insurance enterprise. Property and liability insurance enterprises may be either stock or mutual organizations.

Reciprocal or interinsurance exchange
A group of persons, firms, or corporations commonly referred to as "subscribers" that exchange insurance contracts through an attorney-in-fact (an attorney authorized by a person to act in that person's behalf).

Reinsurance
A transaction in which a reinsurer (assuming enterprise), for a consideration (premium), assumes all or part of a risk undertaken originally by another insurer (ceding enterprise). However, the legal rights of the insured are not affected by the reinsurance transaction and the insurance enterprise issuing the insurance contract remains liable to the insured for payment of policy benefits.

Risk of adverse deviation
A concept used by life insurance enterprises in estimating the liability for future policy benefits relating to long-duration contracts. The risk of adverse deviation allows for possible unfavorable deviations from assumptions, such as estimates of expected investment yields, mortality, morbidity, terminations, and expenses. The concept is referred to as *risk load* when used by property and liability insurance enterprises.

Salvage
The amount received by an insurer from the sale of property (usually damaged) on which the insurer has paid a total claim to the insured and has obtained title to the property.

Statutory accounting practices
Accounting principles required by statute, regulation, or rule, or permitted by specific approval, that an insurance enterprise is required to follow when submitting its financial statements to state insurance departments.

Subrogation
The right of an insurer to pursue any course of recovery of damages, in its name or in the name of the policyholder, against a third party who is liable for costs relating to an insured event that have been paid by the insurer.

Term life insurance
Insurance that provides a benefit if the insured dies within the period specified in the contract. The insurance is for level or declining amounts for stated periods, such as 1, 5, or 10 years, or to a stated age. Term life insurance generally has no loan or cash value.

Termination
In general, the failure to renew an insurance contract. Involuntary terminations include death, expirations, and maturities of contracts. Voluntary terminations of life insurance contracts include lapses with or without cash surrender value and contract modifications that reduce paid-up whole-life benefits or term-life benefits.

Termination rate
The rate at which insurance contracts fail to renew. Termination rates usually are expressed as a ratio of the number of contracts on which insureds failed to pay premiums during a given period to the total number of contracts at the beginning of the period from which those terminations occurred. The complement of the termination rate is persistency, which is the renewal quality of insurance contracts, that is, the number of insureds that keep their insurance in force during a period. Persistency varies by plan of insurance, age at issue, year of issue, frequency of premium payment, and other factors.

Title insurance enterprise
An enterprise that issues title insurance contracts to real estate owners, purchasers, and mortgage lenders, indemnifying them against loss or damage arising out of defects in, liens on, or challenges to their title to real estate.

Variable annuity contract
An annuity in which the amount of payments to be made are specified in units, rather than in dollars. When payment is due, the amount is determined based on the value of the investments in the annuity fund.

Whole-life contract
Insurance that may be kept in force for a person's entire life by paying one or more premiums. It is paid for in one of three different ways: (a) ordinary life insurance (premiums are payable as long as the insured lives), (b) limited-payment life insurance (premiums are payable over a specified number of years), and (c) single-premium life insurance (a lump-sum amount paid at the inception of the insurance contract). The insurance contract pays a benefit (contractual amount adjusted for items such as policy loans and dividends, if any) at the death of the insured. Whole-life insurance contracts also build up nonforfeiture benefits.

Appendix B

BACKGROUND INFORMATION AND SUMMARY OF CONSIDERATION OF COMMENTS ON EXPOSURE DRAFT

67. As discussed in Statement 32, the FASB is extracting the specialized[9] accounting and reporting principles and practices from AICPA SOPs and Guides on accounting and auditing matters and issuing them as FASB Statements after appropriate due process. This Statement extracts without significant change the specialized principles and practices relating to insurance enterprises from the AICPA Industry Audit Guides, *Audits of Stock Life Insurance Companies* and *Audits of Fire and Casualty Insurance Companies;* AICPA SOPs 78-6, 79-3, and 80-1; and Opinion 23. Accounting and reporting standards that apply to enterprises in general also apply to insurance enterprises, and the standards in this Statement are in addition to those standards.

68. Board members have assented to the issuance of this Statement on the basis that it is an appropriate extraction of existing specialized principles and practices and that a comprehensive reconsideration of those principles and practices was not contemplated in undertaking this FASB project. Most of the background material and discussion of accounting alternatives have not been carried forward from the AICPA insurance industry related Guides and SOPs. The Board's conceptual framework project on accounting recognition criteria will address recognition issues relating to elements of financial statements. A Statement of Financial Accounting Concepts resulting from that project in due course will serve as a basis for evaluating existing standards and practices. Accordingly, the Board may wish to evaluate the standards in this Statement when its conceptual framework project is completed.

69. This Statement does not address issues that currently are being studied by the insurance industry and the accounting and actuarial professions. Some of those issues include:

a. What financial accounting and reporting principles should mutual life insurance enterprises, assessment enterprises, and fraternal benefit societies follow in their general-purpose financial statements?

[9]The term *specialized* is used to refer to those accounting and reporting principles and practices in AICPA Guides and SOPs that are neither superseded by nor contained in Accounting Research Bulletins, APB Opinions, FASB Statements, or FASB Interpretations.

b. How should universal life insurance contracts and similar products that have been developed since the AICPA insurance industry related Guides and SOPs were originally issued be accounted for?
c. For short-duration contracts:
   (1) Should certain claim liabilities be discounted?
   (2) Should anticipated investment income be considered in determining if a premium deficiency exists?
d. What circumstances constitute a transfer of economic risk under a reinsurance contract?

70. An Exposure Draft of a proposed FASB Statement, *Accounting and Reporting by Insurance Enterprises,* was issued on November 18, 1981. The Board received 56 comment letters in response to the Exposure Draft. Certain of the comments received and the Board's consideration of them are discussed in this appendix.

Criteria for Distinguishing between Short-Duration and Long-Duration Contracts

71. Respondents commented on the appropriateness of the proposed criteria for distinguishing between short-duration and long-duration contracts and on whether the criteria could be improved. Some respondents said that the criteria were not well defined and could result in unintended changes in current accounting principles or practices because the criteria focused too narrowly on whether an insurance contract can be expected to remain in force for an extended period. They suggested that the criteria be clarified so that the nature of the insurance enterprise's obligations and policyholder rights under the provisions of the contract is considered.

72. Other respondents recommended that (a) accounting for insurance contracts should depend on the type of insurance enterprise issuing the contract, (b) the criteria for distinguishing between the two types of contracts should be based on the period of the contract, or (c) contracts should be specified by type of insurance protection that should be considered short-duration or long-duration so that the Statement can be specifically applied without exception or ambiguity.

73. In extracting the specialized principles and practices from the AICPA insurance industry related Guides and SOPs, the Board decided to establish a framework for accounting by insurance enterprises based on the nature of insurance contracts rather than type of insurance enterprise. The Board concluded that the criteria for distinguishing between short-duration and long-duration contracts should be clarified so that the nature of the insurance enterprise's obligations and policyholder rights under the provisions of the contract is considered, because that is consistent with (a) a general framework, (b) the principles in the AICPA insurance industry related Guides and SOPs, and (c) current practice.

Impairment in Value of Publicly Traded Securities

74. If an investment in a publicly traded security is reduced to its net realizable value, paragraph 51 requires that a gain not be recognized until the sale, maturity, or other disposition of the investment. Some respondents argued that permanent impairment is too absolute and often cannot be determined until after the event causing the impairment has occurred. In addition, they said that accounting for impaired amounts relating to publicly traded securities should be consistent with accounting for mortgage loans and real estate investments and reflective of an insurance enterprise's estimate of its ability to recover the carrying amount of those securities. They suggested that a standard consistent with Statement 5 be included to require adjustments of the carrying amount as circumstances change.

75. Other respondents agreed with paragraph 51 because it is an accurate extraction of SOPs 78-6, 79-3, and 80-1 and is consistent with principles and practices applicable to enterprises in other industries. Based on that reasoning, the Board concluded that adjustments for increases in value of previously impaired publicly traded securities should continue to be proscribed.

Acquisition Costs: Primarily versus Directly Related

76. Some respondents commented on the definition in paragraph 28 that states that acquisition costs are those costs that vary with and are *primarily* related to the acquisition of new and renewal insurance contracts. They pointed out that, while the term *primarily* currently is used in practice by life insurance enterprises, the term *directly* is used in practice by property and liability insurance enterprises. They said that using the term *primarily* for all insurance enterprises could produce a different result for property and liability insurance enterprises. They recommended that the distinction between *primarily* and *directly* be retained in prescribing accounting principles for acquisition costs.

77. The Board believes that accounting principles and practices should not be applied differently among insurance enterprises without differences in underlying circumstances. Because the term *primarily* encompasses *directly,* the Board acknowledges that use of the term *primarily* might allow property and liability insurance enterprises to adopt broader

guidelines in defining acquisition costs that are capitalizable. However, the Board believes that the use of the term *primarily* should not cause insurance enterprises to change their methods of defining acquisition costs to be capitalized.

Disclosure of the Average Rate of Assumed Investment Yields

78. Respondents commented on the benefits and costs of specifically requiring a disclosure of the average rate of assumed investment yields used in estimating the liability for future policy benefits. Some respondents said that disclosure of the average rate of assumed investment yields should be required because the disclosure would be relevant to users in assessing the reasonableness of estimated rates of return in relation to current investment yields and in comparing insurance enterprises. They also expressed the view that the cost to the reporting enterprise would be minimal and that the benefit to users of insurance enterprise financial statements would outweigh the related cost.

79. Other respondents said it is likely that the development of a single average interest rate would involve a time-consuming and costly process that would not be justified by the benefit. They also argued that the weighted average of interest rate assumptions has little meaning when there are other significant assumptions that also must be considered in estimating the liability for future policy benefits and that the disclosure would likely result in a general perception that the rate possessed more significance and value than deserved.

80. The Board agrees with those respondents that said disclosure of the average rate of assumed investment yields is useful in assessing the reasonableness of estimated rates of return in relation to current investment yields and in comparing insurance enterprises. However, because of uncertainties relating to the cost of providing that disclosure, the Board decided to encourage but not require disclosure of that yield rate.

Disclosure of Discounting Short-Duration Contract Claim Liabilities and Considering Anticipated Investment Income in Determining Premium Deficiencies

81. The Exposure Draft would have required disclosure of (a) the effects (including amounts) of discounting short-duration contract claim liabilities and (b) the effects (including amounts) of an enterprise's considering anticipated investment income in determining if a premium deficiency relating to short-duration contracts exists. Some respondents said that insurance enterprises generally are not disclosing *amounts* in their notes because they believe disclosure of amounts is not required in the AICPA insurance industry related Guides and SOPs, which require disclosure of only the *effects*. Other respondents recommended that the Exposure Draft be revised to require disclosure of the carrying amount of claim liabilities carried at present value in the balance sheet, the range of interest rates used to discount the claim liabilities, and the period of years over which the claims are being paid.

82. The phrase *including amounts* was included in the Exposure Draft to clarify what the Board understands was meant by *effects on the financial statements* in SOP 78-6. The Board believes that quantitative disclosures relating to the discounting of short-duration claim liabilities is necessary and, accordingly, decided to require disclosure of the carrying amount of short-duration contract liabilities that are presented at present value and the range of discount rates. However, the Board agreed that disclosure of amounts relating to an insurance enterprise's consideration of anticipated investment income in determining whether a premium deficiency exists is not necessary, and decided to require disclosure of only whether the insurance enterprise considers anticipated investment income in making that determination.

Disclosure of Statutory Requirements

83. With respect to the proposed disclosure of information relating to statutory capital and surplus requirements, some respondents suggested that disclosure be limited to the amount of statutory capital and surplus, minimum statutory requirements when significant, and statutory limitations on the payment of dividends. Other respondents recommended that the proposed disclosures parallel those in the SEC's recent revision of Article 7 of Regulation S-X. The Board agreed that the disclosure relating to statutory requirements needed clarification and revised the disclosure in accordance with the first sentence of this paragraph.

Reconciliation Disclosure

84. Respondents commented on whether disclosure of a reconciliation between financial reporting and statutory capital and income should be required. Some respondents said the disclosure should be required because the differences between statutory accounting practices and generally accepted accounting principles are an important element in the analysis of an insurance enterprise's general-purpose financial statements. They pointed out that statutory accounting determines the amount of dividends that can be paid as well as the sufficiency of statutory capital and surplus for regulatory purposes and, therefore, is important to users of insurance enterprise financial statements.

85. Other respondents said the reconciliation disclosure should not be required because the original purpose of the reconciliation was intended principally to provide relevant information during the life insurance industry's transition from statutory reporting. They also said that the disclosure may cast doubt on the appropriateness of accounting principles used in the general-purpose financial statements.

86. The Board believes that the disclosure in paragraph 60(h) relating to statutory requirements is sufficient for the general-purpose financial statements of insurance enterprises.

Other Comments

87. Some respondents noted that paragraph 10 of the Exposure Draft would require a liability for claim adjustment expenses to be accrued when insured events occur and that life insurance enterprises currently are not accruing those costs. They said that accruing claim adjustment expenses associated with unpaid claims would require an accounting change for life insurance enterprises and that, although it may be appropriate to require life insurance enterprises to accrue a liability for those costs, those enterprises should be excluded from that requirement since the AICPA stock life insurance guide does not require that accrual. However, they acknowledged that the change is not likely to significantly affect the financial statements of life insurance enterprises. The Board believes that the requirement is appropriate and that it meets a criterion for change—that is, practices among insurance enterprises are different without differences in circumstances. In addition, the Board believes the requirement is consistent with the provisions of Statement 5.

88. Several respondents suggested various substantive changes to the Exposure Draft. Adoption of those suggestions would have required a reconsideration of some of the provisions of the Guides and SOPs. Such a reconsideration is not contemplated in the extraction project unless a proposed change meets one of the three criteria for change included in the "Notice for Recipients" of the Exposure Draft or is broadly supported. The proposed changes did not meet the criteria for change and were not broadly supported. Accordingly, the Board did not adopt those suggestions. However, based on suggestions from respondents to the Exposure Draft, the Board has made several other changes that it believes clarify the Statement.

89. The Board has concluded that it can reach an informed decision on the basis of existing information without a public hearing and that the effective date and transition specified in paragraphs 64 and 65 are advisable in the circumstances.

Statement of Financial Accounting Standards No. 61
Accounting for Title Plant

STATUS

Issued: June 1982

Effective Date: For fiscal years beginning after December 15, 1982

Affects: No other pronouncements

Affected by: No other pronouncements

SUMMARY

This Statement extracts the specialized principles and practices for title plant from AICPA Statement of Position 80-1, *Accounting for Title Insurance Companies,* and applies to enterprises, such as title insurance enterprises, title abstract enterprises, and title agents, that use a title plant in their operations. This Statement requires that costs directly incurred to construct a title plant be capitalized until the enterprise can use the title plant to do title searches. This Statement also requires that capitalized costs of a title plant not be depreciated and that costs of maintaining a title plant and doing title searches be expensed as incurred.

Statement of Financial Accounting Standards No. 61
Accounting for Title Plant

CONTENTS

INTRODUCTION

1. A title plant consists of (a) indexed and catalogued information for a period concerning the ownership of, and encumbrances on, parcels of land in a particular geographic area; (b) information relating to persons having an interest in real estate; (c) maps and plats; (d) copies of prior title insurance contracts and reports; and (e) other documents and records. In summary, a title plant constitutes a historical record of all matters affecting title to parcels of land in a particular geographic area. The number of years covered by a title plant varies, depending on regulatory requirements and the minimum information period considered necessary to issue title insurance policies efficiently. Title plants are updated on a daily or other frequent basis by adding copies of documents on the current status of title to specific parcels of real estate.

APPLICABILITY AND SCOPE

2. This Statement applies to enterprises that use a title plant in their operations. Those enterprises include, but are not limited to, title insurance enterprises (underwriters), title abstract enterprises, and title agents.

STANDARDS OF FINANCIAL ACCOUNTING AND REPORTING

Capitalization of Title Plant

3. Costs incurred to construct a title plant, including the costs incurred to obtain, organize, and summarize historical information in an efficient and useful manner, shall be capitalized until the title plant can be used by the enterprise to do title searches. To qualify for capitalization, costs need to be directly related to, and properly identified with, the activities necessary to construct the title plant.

4. Purchased title plant, including a purchased undivided interest in title plant, shall be recorded at cost at the date of acquisition. For title plant acquired separately, cost shall be measured by the fair value of the consideration given.

5. An enterprise may decide to construct or purchase a title plant that antedates the period covered by its existing title plant (backplant). Costs to construct a backplant need to be identifiable to qualify for capitalization.

6. Capitalized costs of title plant shall not be depreciated or charged to income unless circumstances indicate that the value of the title plant has been impaired. The following circumstances may indicate that the value of title plant has been impaired:

a. Changes in legal requirements or statutory practices
b. Effects of obsolescence, demand, and other economic factors
c. Actions of competitors and others that may affect competitive advantages
d. Failure to maintain the title plant properly on a current basis
e. Abandonment of title plant or other circumstances that indicate obsolescence

If the value of a title plant decreases below its adjusted cost, that impairment shall be recognized in income.

Title Plant Maintenance and Title Searches

7. Costs incurred to maintain a title plant and to do title searches shall be expensed as incurred. Title plant maintenance involves the updating of the title

plant on a daily or other frequent basis by adding (a) reports on the current status of title to specific parcels of real estate and (b) other documents, such as records relating to security or other ownership interests. Title searches involve the process of searching through records for all recorded documents or updating information summarized in the most recently issued title report.

Storage and Retrieval

8. Costs incurred after a title plant is operational (a) to convert the information from one storage and retrieval system to another or (b) to modify or modernize the storage and retrieval system shall not be capitalized as title plant. Those costs, however, may be capitalized separately and charged to expense in a systematic and rational manner.

Sale of Title Plant

9. The sale of a title plant shall be reported separately as follows:

a. If the enterprise sells its title plant and relinquishes all rights to its future use, the reported amount shall be the amount received net of the adjusted cost of the title plant.
b. If the enterprise sells an undivided ownership interest in its title plant (that is, the right to its joint use), the reported amount shall be the amount received net of a pro rata portion of the adjusted cost of the title plant.
c. If the enterprise sells a copy of its title plant or the right to use it, the reported amount shall be the amount received. Ordinarily, no cost shall be allocated to the sale of a copy of or the right to use a title plant unless the value of the title plant decreases below its adjusted cost as a result of the sale (paragraph 6).

Effective Date and Transition

10. This Statement shall be effective for fiscal years beginning after December 15, 1982, with earlier application encouraged. Accounting changes adopted to conform to the provisions of this Statement shall be applied retroactively. In the year that this Statement is first applied, the financial statements shall disclose the nature of any restatement and its effect on income before extraordinary items, net income, and related per share amounts for each year presented.

11. If retroactive restatement of all years presented is not practicable, the financial statements presented shall be restated for as many consecutive years as practicable and the cumulative effect of applying this Statement shall be included in determining net income of the earliest year restated (not necessarily the earliest year presented). If it is not practicable to restate any prior year, the cumulative effect shall be included in net income in the year in which this Statement is first applied. (Refer to paragraph 20 of APB Opinion No. 20, *Accounting Changes*.)

The provisions of this Statement need not be applied to immaterial items.

This Statement was approved by the unanimous vote of the seven members of the Financial Accounting Standards Board:

Donald J. Kirk, *Chairman*
Frank E. Block
John W. March
Robert A. Morgan
David Mosso
Robert T. Sprouse
Ralph E. Walters

Appendix

BACKGROUND INFORMATION AND SUMMARY OF CONSIDERATION OF COMMENTS ON EXPOSURE DRAFT

12. As discussed in FASB Statement No. 32, *Specialized Accounting and Reporting Principles and Practices in AICPA Statements of Position and Guides on Accounting and Auditing Matters,* the FASB is extracting the specialized[1] accounting and reporting principles and practices from AICPA Statements of Position (SOPs) and Guides on accounting and auditing matters and issuing them as FASB Statements after appropriate due process. This Statement extracts the specialized principles and practices for title plant from SOP 80-1,

[1]The term *specialized* is used to refer to those accounting and reporting principles and practices in AICPA Guides and SOPs that are neither superseded by nor contained in Accounting Research Bulletins, APB Opinions, FASB Statements, or FASB Interpretations.

Accounting for Title Insurance Companies,[2] without significant change.

13. Board members have assented to the issuance of this Statement on the basis that it is an appropriate extraction of those existing specialized principles and practices and that a comprehensive reconsideration of those principles and practices was not contemplated in undertaking this FASB project. Some of the background material and discussion of accounting alternatives have not been carried forward from the SOP. The Board's conceptual framework project on accounting recognition criteria will address recognition issues relating to elements of financial statements. A Statement of Financial Accounting Concepts resulting from that project in due course will serve as a basis for evaluating existing standards and practices. Accordingly, the Board may wish to evaluate the standards in this Statement when its conceptual framework project is completed.

14. An Exposure Draft of a proposed FASB Statement, *Accounting for Title Plant,* was issued on November 18, 1981. The Board received 14 comment letters in response to the Exposure Draft, most of which expressed agreement. Certain of the comments received and the Board's consideration of them are discussed in this appendix.

15. Some respondents stated that title plant is unique to the title insurance industry and that all accounting principles for title insurance enterprises, including title plant, should be included in a separate FASB Statement. The Board has concluded that it is more appropriate to include accounting standards relating to all insurance enterprises in one Statement and that separate Statements for each type of insurance enterprise are unnecessary. The Board concluded that a separate Statement on accounting for title plant was necessary because enterprises that are not insurance enterprises, such as title abstract enterprises and title agents, may use a title plant in their operations.

16. The Board has concluded that it can reach an informed decision on the basis of existing information without a public hearing and that the effective date and transition specified in paragraphs 10 and 11 are advisable in the circumstances.

[2]Other specialized principles and practices from SOP 80-1 are included in FASB Statement No. 60, *Accounting and Reporting by Insurance Enterprises.*

Statement of Financial Accounting Standards No. 62 Capitalization of Interest Cost in Situations Involving Certain Tax-Exempt Borrowings and Certain Gifts and Grants

an amendment of FASB Statement No. 34

STATUS

Issued: June 1982

Effective Date: For tax-exempt borrowing arrangements entered into and gifts or grants received after August 31, 1982

Affects: Amends FAS 34, paragraphs 10, 13, and 17
Supersedes FTB 81-5

Affected by: No other pronouncements

SUMMARY

This Statement amends FASB Statement No. 34, *Capitalization of Interest Cost,* (a) to require capitalization of interest cost of restricted tax-exempt borrowings less any interest earned on temporary investment of the proceeds of those borrowings from the date of borrowing until the specified qualifying assets acquired with those borrowings are ready for their intended use and (b) to proscribe capitalization of interest cost on qualifying assets acquired using gifts or grants that are restricted by the donor or grantor to acquisition of those assets.

Statement of Financial Accounting Standards No. 62 Capitalization of Interest Cost in Situations Involving Certain Tax-Exempt Borrowings and Certain Gifts and Grants

an amendment of FASB Statement No. 34

CONTENTS

INTRODUCTION

1. The FASB has received a number of requests to reconsider the issue of offsetting interest income against interest cost in the application of FASB Statement No. 34, *Capitalization of Interest Cost,* for purposes of determining either capitalization rates or limitations on the amount of interest to be capitalized. FASB Technical Bulletin No. 81-5, *Offsetting Interest Cost to Be Capitalized with Interest Income,* states that Statement 34 does not permit such offsetting. Other requests have been received to consider the issue of capitalization of interest cost in situations in which qualifying assets are acquired using gifts and grants restricted to the purchase of the specified assets.

2. The Board has concluded that Statement 34 should be amended to require offsetting of interest income against interest cost in certain circumstances involving tax-exempt borrowings that are externally restricted as specified in paragraph 3. Those situations include many governmental borrowings and most governmentally sponsored borrowings (such as industrial revenue bonds and pollution control bonds). In such situations, interest earned generally is considered in and is significant to the initial decision to acquire the asset, and the capitalization of net interest cost provides a better measure of the entity's net investment in the qualifying assets. The Board believes that in those circumstances the association is direct and the funds flows from borrowing, temporary investment, and construction expenditures are so intertwined and restricted as to require accounting for the total net cost of financing as a cost of the qualifying assets. The Board also concluded that in all other situations offsetting of interest income against interest cost is not appropriate. The Board further concluded that qualifying assets acquired with externally restricted gifts or grants should not be subject to capitalization of interest cost under Statement 34.

STANDARDS OF FINANCIAL ACCOUNTING AND REPORTING

3. Interest earned shall not be offset against interest cost in determining either capitalization rates or limitations on the amount of interest cost to be capitalized except in situations involving acquisition of qualifying assets financed with the proceeds of tax-exempt borrowings if those funds are externally restricted to finance acquisition of specified qualifying assets or to service the related debt.

4. The amount of interest cost capitalized on qualifying assets acquired with proceeds of tax-exempt borrowings that are externally restricted as specified in paragraph 3 shall be all interest cost of the borrowing less any interest earned on related interest-bearing investments acquired with proceeds of the related tax-exempt borrowings[1] from the date of the borrowing until the assets are ready for their intended use. Interest cost of a tax-exempt borrowing shall be eligible for capitalization on other qualifying assets of the entity when the specified qualifying assets are no longer eligible for interest capitalization.

[1]The interest cost and interest earned on any portion of the proceeds of the tax-exempt borrowings that are not designated for the acquisition of specified qualifying assets and servicing the related debt are excluded. The entire interest cost on that portion of the proceeds that is available for other uses (such as refunding of an existing debt issue other than a construction loan related to those assets) is eligible for capitalization on other qualifying assets.

Amendments to FASB Statement No. 34

5. The following subparagraph is added to paragraph 10 of Statement 34, which specifies the types of assets for which interest is not capitalized:

f. Assets acquired with gifts and grants that are restricted by the donor or grantor to acquisition of those assets to the extent that funds are available from such gifts and grants. Interest earned from temporary investment of those funds that is similarly restricted shall be considered an addition to the gift or grant for this purpose.

6. The following footnote is added at the end of the first sentence of paragraph 13 of Statement 34, which deals with determining the amount of interest cost to be capitalized:

*If qualifying assets are financed with the proceeds of tax-exempt borrowings and those funds are externally restricted to the acquisition of specified qualifying assets or to service the related debt, the amount of interest cost capitalized shall be determined in accordance with FASB Statement No. 62, *Capitalization of Interest Cost in Situations Involving Certain Tax-Exempt Borrowings and Certain Gifts and Grants.*

7. The following footnote is added to paragraph 17 of Statement 34, which specifies the period for interest capitalization:

*In situations involving qualifying assets financed with the proceeds of tax-exempt borrowings that are externally restricted as specified in Statement 62, the capitalization period begins at the date of the borrowing.

Rescission of Technical Bulletin

8. FASB Technical Bulletin No. 81-5, *Offsetting Interest Cost to Be Capitalized with Interest Income,* is rescinded upon issuance of this Statement.

Effective Date and Transition

9. This Statement shall be effective for tax-exempt borrowing arrangements entered into and gifts or grants received after August 31, 1982, with earlier application encouraged in financial statements that have not been previously issued. This Statement may be, but is not required to be, applied retroactively to previously issued financial statements for fiscal years beginning after December 15, 1979. If previously issued financial statements are restated, the financial statements shall, in the year that this Statement is first applied, disclose the nature of any restatement and its effects on income before extraordinary items, net income, and related per share amounts for each restated year presented.

The provisions of this Statement need not be applied to immaterial items.

This Statement was adopted by the affirmative votes of four members of the Financial Accounting Standards Board. Messrs. Block, Morgan, and Walters dissented.

Mr. Block does not support this standard because it merges the accounting for three dissimilar business activities into one: the borrowing of funds, the temporary investment of funds, and the acquisition of capital assets. Users of financial statements find it useful to calculate rates of return to providers of capital, such as return on equity, return on long-term capital, and return on total capital, as well as returns on various types of investment assets and operating assets. Under this standard, interest income will not be reported as a return on the investment asset, interest expense will not be reported as a return on borrowed funds, and a net amount of interest expense or income will be amortized over the life of a fixed asset as depreciation rather than recognized currently as interest. This obscures information significant to users, particularly to those who look upon depreciation as a return *of* capital, interest cost as a return *on* capital, and interest income as a return on a financial asset. In addition, this standard calls for an unwarranted extension of the capitalization period to include a period when no acquisition activities are under way, contrary to two of the three requirements of paragraph 17 of Statement 34. The extension of the capitalization period is defended (paragraphs 2 and 14 of this Statement) on grounds that the investment and financing activities are generally considered in the decision to acquire the asset. Mr. Block believes that accounting should reflect the nature and circumstances of transactions and not the unverifiable motivations and expectations that led to them. He doubts that the deferred net interest credit generated during the pre-acquisition period meets the definition of any element other than revenue as set forth in FASB Concepts Statement No. 3, *Elements of Financial*

Statements of Business Enterprises, and is troubled by the possibility that in extreme cases the acquired asset could be carried at a negative cost.

Mr. Morgan and Mr. Walters believe that offsetting related interest income and expense during the acquisition period is appropriate and consistent with the avoidable-interest-cost notion that is embodied in Statement 34. They disagree with this Statement, however, because it restricts offsetting to tax-exempt borrowings. In their opinion, the reasoning for this narrow approach is based on a conclusion that only the tax-exempt situations are so closely intertwined with the asset acquisition as to require association when, in all likelihood, such intertwining may exist regardless of the tax status of the borrowings. In addition, they believe that it is inconsistent to view the borrowings as intertwined with the asset during the capitalization period and as part of the pool of fungible funds from which interest is available for capitalization on other assets after the capitalization period.

Members of the Financial Accounting Standards Board:

Donald J. Kirk, *Chairman*
Frank E. Block
John W. March
Robert A. Morgan
David Mosso
Robert T. Sprouse
Ralph E. Walters

Appendix A

EXAMPLE OF APPLICATION OF THIS STATEMENT

10. The following example illustrates the application of this Statement in the situation described below:

a. The entity is committed to construct Project A at a cost of $10 million. Project A is to be financed from three sources:
   (1) $4 million government grant restricted to use for the specified construction project, payable $1 million per year
   (2) $4 million tax-exempt borrowing at an interest rate of 8 percent ($320,000 per year)
   (3) $2 million from operations
b. The entity has $10 million in other borrowings that are outstanding throughout the construction of Project A. The interest rate on those borrowings is 6 percent. Other qualifying assets of the entity never exceed $5 million during the construction of Project A.
c. The proceeds from the borrowing and the initial phase of the grant are received 1 year in advance of starting construction on Project A and are temporarily invested in interest-bearing investments yielding 12 percent. Interest income earned from temporary investments is not reinvested.
d. Project A will take 4 years after start of construction to complete.
e. The table on the following page sets forth the amount of interest to be capitalized as part of the entity's investment in Project A.
f. Over the course of construction the net cost of financing is $678,000, the sum of the interest capitalized for the 5 years. Accordingly, the entity's total net investment in Project A will be $10,678,000.

	19X1	19X2	19X3	19X4	19X5
	(amounts in thousands)				
(1) Assumed average qualifying assets	$ 0	$2,000	$5,000	$8,000	$9,000
(2) Average funding received					
borrowing	4,000	4,000	4,000	4,000	4,000
grant	1,000	2,000	3,000	4,000	4,000
(3) Average temporary investments ((2) − (1), not less than zero)*					
borrowing	4,000	3,000	1,000	0	0
grant	1,000	1,000	1,000	0	0
(4) Interest earned ((3) × 12 percent)					
(a) borrowing	480	360	120	0	0
(b) grant	120	120	120	0	0
(5) Average qualifying assets in excess of borrowing, grant, and interest earned on grant†	0	0	0	0	640
(6) Interest cost capitalized—other borrowings ((5) × 6 percent)	0	0	0	0	38
(7) Interest cost—tax-exempt borrowings	320	320	320	320	320
(8) Interest capitalized ((6) + (7) − (4)(a))‡	(160)	(40)	200	320	358

*Balances of unexpended borrowings and unexpended grants can vary depending on the source from which the entity elects to disburse funds.

†That is, (1) average qualifying assets minus the sum of ((2) average funding received plus (4)(b) cumulative interest earned on grant), not less than zero.

‡Note that amounts in parentheses are reductions in the cost of the asset.

Appendix B

BASIS FOR CONCLUSIONS

11. An Exposure Draft of a proposed Statement, *Capitalization of Interest Cost in Situations Involving Tax-Exempt Borrowings and Certain Gifts and Grants,* was issued on December 22, 1981. The Board received 94 letters of comment in response to the Exposure Draft. This appendix discusses the factors that the Board considered significant in reaching the conclusions in this Statement. The Board members who assented to this Statement did so on the basis of the overall considerations. Individual Board members gave greater weight to some factors than to others.

Tax-Exempt Borrowings

12. Many respondents recommended that offsetting interest income against interest expense be extended to situations in addition to tax-exempt borrowings. They believe that the tax status of the borrowings should not determine the accounting and that offsetting should be required in situations that involve borrowings that are externally restricted for use on particular projects specified under the terms of the borrowing agreement and that externally restrict the interest on temporary investment of the proceeds to finance construction or service the related debt. They believe that the association of such borrowings with the specified projects is direct and that offsetting is appropriate under those circumstances.

13. Some respondents stated that interest income earned prior to acquisition or construction is related to investment decisions and not to acquisition decisions. They would not offset the interest earned for the period from the date of the borrowing to the beginning of the acquisition period even in situations involving tax-exempt borrowings.

14. Statement 34 requires that interest cost be capitalized only on funds that actually have been expended in the process of acquiring a qualifying asset. Obviously, those expended funds cannot be earning interest income. Identifying a borrowing with a specific acquisition and requiring that interest income be offset against interest cost in determining the amount of interest to be capitalized necessarily involves extending the beginning of the capitalization period from the date actual expenditures are made to the date of the borrowing. The Board does not believe that extending the capitalization period in that way and thereby generally increasing the amount of capitalized interest is appropriate. As stated in paragraph 6 of Statement 34, "the historical cost of acquiring an asset includes the costs necessarily incurred to bring it to the condition and location necessary for its intended use." Borrowing for indeterminate periods in advance of actual expenditures cannot be said generally to be a necessary part of acquiring an asset. The Board is persuaded, however, that an exception should be made in the case of tax-exempt borrowings specified by this Statement. The timing and use of tax-exempt borrowings are generally an integral part of the decision to acquire the related asset, and the net interest cost from the date of borrowing to the time the acquired asset is substantially complete and ready for its intended use is an essential part of the cost of acquiring that asset.

15. Some respondents questioned the appropriateness of a net reduction in the cost of an asset that may occur if the interest earned from the date of borrowing is greater than the interest accrued on the debt during the capitalization period. The Board believes, for the reasons indicated in paragraph 14, that interest earned on the temporary investment of the proceeds of certain tax-exempt borrowings from the date of borrowing until the specified qualifying assets are ready for their intended use is a part of the net cost of financing that is properly included as a cost of the qualifying asset. This may result in a net reduction in the cost of an asset.

16. Some respondents stated that interest cost of a tax-exempt borrowing should not be eligible for capitalization on other qualifying assets of the entity if the specified qualifying asset is no longer eligible for capitalization. They believe that this conflicts with the notion of specific association between the tax-exempt borrowings and the assets acquired and that the initial association of the borrowing with the qualifying asset nullifies subsequent capitalization of interest cost of the borrowing. The Board believes that the avoidable-interest concept explained in paragraph 12 of Statement 34 requires that interest cost of tax-exempt borrowings be eligible for capitalization on other qualifying assets acquired after completion of the specified qualifying assets. For the same reason, the interest cost on funds provided from the tax-exempt borrowings that are not designated for the acquisition of qualifying assets and servicing the related debt during the capitalization period are eligible for capitalization on other qualifying assets.

Gifts and Grants

17. Nearly all of the respondents who commented on the proposed treatment for qualifying assets acquired with a restricted gift or grant and for interest earned on the temporary investment of those funds supported the Exposure Draft. They believe that qualifying assets acquired with restricted gifts and grants should not be subject to capitalization of interest cost under Statement 34 because they believe there is no economic cost of financing associated with a gift or grant. They believe such an exemption is appropriate only if the gift or grant is restricted by the donor or grantor to the acquisition of the specified asset (or otherwise required to be returned to the donor or grantor). Accordingly, they would capitalize no interest cost during the acquisition of the qualifying asset to the extent that funds are available from such gifts and grants. They would also consider restricted interest earned from temporary investment of the gift or grant as an enhancement to and consequently an integral part of the gift or grant. The Board concurred and has adopted those provisions of the Exposure Draft.

Transition

18. Some respondents requested that the transition provisions of the Exposure Draft be modified to permit retroactive application. They believe that permitting retroactive application would enable enterprises to eliminate problems of lack of comparability resulting from applying Statement 34 and Bulletin 81-5 that prohibit offsetting and the provisions of this Statement that require offsetting. The Board concurred and has revised the transition provisions to permit retroactive application to the effective date of Statement 34. Statement 34 was effective prospectively for fiscal years beginning after December 15, 1979.

19. The Board concluded that it can reach an informed decision on the basis of existing information without a public hearing and that the effective date and transition specified in paragraph 9 are advisable in the circumstances.

Statement of Financial Accounting Standards No. 63
Financial Reporting by Broadcasters

STATUS

Issued: June 1982

Effective Date: For fiscal years beginning after December 15, 1982

Affects: Amends FAS 32, Appendix A

Affected by: No other pronouncements

SUMMARY

This Statement extracts and modifies the specialized accounting principles and practices contained in AICPA Statement of Position (SOP) 75-5, *Accounting Practices in the Broadcasting Industry,* and establishes standards of financial accounting and reporting for broadcasters. Exhibition rights acquired under a license agreement for program material shall be accounted for as a purchase of rights by the licensee. The asset and liability for a license agreement shall be reported by the licensee, at either the present value or the gross amount of the liability, when the license period begins and certain specified conditions have been met. This Statement also establishes standards of reporting by broadcasters for barter transactions and network affiliation agreements.

Statement of Financial Accounting Standards No. 63
Financial Reporting by Broadcasters

CONTENTS

INTRODUCTION

1. As discussed in FASB Statement No. 32, *Specialized Accounting and Reporting Principles and Practices in AICPA Statements of Position and Guides on Accounting and Auditing Matters,* the FASB is extracting the specialized[1] accounting and reporting principles and practices from AICPA Statements of Position (SOPs) and Guides on accounting and auditing matters and issuing them in FASB Statements after appropriate due process. This Statement extracts and modifies the specialized principles and practices contained in SOP 75-5, *Accounting Practices in the Broadcasting Industry,* and establishes accounting and reporting standards for **Broadcasters.**[2] Appendix C illustrates applications of this Statement.

STANDARDS OF FINANCIAL ACCOUNTING AND REPORTING

License Agreements for Program Material

Financial Statement Presentation

2. A broadcaster (licensee) shall account for a **license agreement for program material** as a purchase of a right or group of rights.

3. A licensee shall report an asset and a liability for the rights acquired and obligations incurred under a license agreement when the license period begins *and* all of the following conditions have been met:

a. The cost of each program is known or reasonably determinable.
b. The program material has been accepted by the licensee in accordance with the conditions of the license agreement.
c. The program is available for its first showing or telecast. Except when a conflicting license prevents usage by the licensee, restrictions under the same license agreement or another license agreement with the same licensor on the timing of subsequent showings shall not affect this availability condition.

The asset shall be segregated on the balance sheet between current and noncurrent based on estimated time of usage. The liability shall be segregated between current and noncurrent based on the payment terms.

4. A licensee shall report the asset and liability for a broadcast license agreement either (a) at the present value of the liability calculated in accordance with the provisions of APB Opinion No. 21, *Interest on Receivables and Payables,* or (b) at the gross amount of the liability. If the present value approach is used, the difference between the gross and net liability shall be accounted for as interest in accordance with Opinion 21.

Amortization

5. The capitalized costs to be amortized shall be determined under one of the methods specified in

[1]The term *specialized* is used to refer to those accounting and reporting principles and practices in AICPA Guides and Statements of Position that are neither superseded by nor contained in Accounting Research Bulletins, APB Opinions, FASB Statements, or FASB Interpretations.

[2]Terms defined in the glossary (Appendix A) are in **boldface type** the first time they appear in this Statement.

paragraph 4. Those costs shall be allocated to individual programs within a package on the basis of the relative value of each to the broadcaster, which ordinarily would be specified in the contract. The capitalized costs shall be amortized based on the estimated number of future showings, except that licenses providing for unlimited showings of cartoons and programs with similar characteristics may be amortized over the period of the agreement because the estimated number of future showings may not be determinable.

6. Feature programs shall be amortized on a program-by-program basis; however, amortization as a package may be appropriate if it approximates the amortization that would have been provided on a program-by-program basis. Program series and other syndicated products shall be amortized as a series. If the first showing is more valuable to a station than reruns, an accelerated method of amortization shall be used. However, the straight-line amortization method may be used if each showing is expected to generate similar revenues.

Valuation

7. The capitalized costs of rights to program materials shall be reported in the balance sheet at the lower of unamortized cost or estimated net realizable value on a program-by-program, series, package, or **daypart** basis, as appropriate. If management's expectations of the programming usefulness of a program, series, package, or daypart are revised downward, it may be necessary to write down unamortized cost to estimated net realizable value. A write-down from unamortized cost to a lower estimated net realizable value establishes a new cost basis.

Barter Transactions

8. Broadcasters may **barter** unsold advertising time for products or services. All barter transactions except those involving the exchange of advertising time for network programming[3] shall be reported at the estimated fair value of the product or service received, in accordance with the provisions of paragraph 25 of APB Opinion No. 29, *Accounting for Nonmonetary Transactions.* Barter revenue shall be reported when commercials are broadcast, and merchandise or services received shall be reported when received or used. If merchandise or services are received prior to the broadcast of the commercial, a liability shall be reported. Likewise, if the commercial is broadcast first, a receivable shall be reported.

Network Affiliation Agreements

9. Network affiliation agreements and other such items ordinarily are presented in the balance sheet of a broadcaster as intangible assets. If a network affiliation is terminated and not immediately replaced or under agreement to be replaced, the unamortized balance of the amount originally allocated to the network affiliation agreement shall be charged to expense. If a network affiliation is terminated and immediately replaced or under agreement to be replaced, a loss shall be recognized to the extent that the unamortized cost of the terminated affiliation exceeds the fair value of the new affiliation. Gain shall not be recognized if the fair value of the new network affiliation exceeds the unamortized cost of the terminated affiliation.

Disclosure

10. Disclose commitments for license agreements that have been executed but were not reported because they do not meet the conditions of paragraph 3.

Amendment to FASB Statement No. 32

11. The reference to AICPA Statement of Position (SOP) 75-5, *Accounting Practices in the Broadcasting Industry,* is deleted from Appendix A of Statement 32.

Effective Date and Transition

12. This Statement shall be effective for financial statements for fiscal years beginning after December 15, 1982, with earlier application encouraged. If application of this Statement results in a change in accounting, restatement of previously issued annual financial statements to conform to the provisions of this Statement is encouraged but not required. If it is not practicable or if the issuer of financial statements elects not to restate any prior year, the cumulative effect shall be included in net income in the year in which the Statement is first applied. (Refer to paragraph 20 of APB Opinion No. 20, *Accounting Changes.*) The effect on income before extraordinary items, net income, and related per share amounts of applying this Statement in a year in which the cumulative effect is included in determining that year's net income shall be disclosed for that year.

13. If previously issued financial statements are restated, the financial statements shall disclose, in

[3]As the definition of **network affiliation agreement** in the glossary to this Statement describes in further detail, a network affiliate does not incur program cost for network programming it carries; likewise, it does not sell the related advertising time but instead receives compensation from the network.

the year that this Statement is first applied, the nature of any restatement and its effects on income before extraordinary items, net income, and related per share amounts for each restated year presented. If retroactive restatement of all years presented is not practicable, the financial statements presented shall be restated for as many consecutive years as practicable and the cumulative effect of applying the Statement shall be included in determining net income of the earliest year restated (not necessarily the earliest year presented).

The provisions of this Statement need not be applied to immaterial items.

This Statement was adopted by the affirmative votes of six members of the Financial Accounting Standards Board. Mr. Sprouse dissented.

Mr. Sprouse dissents from the issuance of this Statement. In his opinion, this Statement is retrogressive in two important respects: (a) it flies in the face of Opinion 21 by permitting the asset and liability arising from a license agreement to be reported at the gross amount of future cash payments necessary to settle the obligation, and (b) it ignores the need for comparability, an important qualitative characteristic of accounting information, by designating as equally acceptable two different methods of accounting for the asset and liability arising from license agreements under identical facts and circumstances. Mr. Sprouse believes that the principles enunciated in Opinion 21 are fundamental and sound. In FASB Statement No. 53, *Financial Reporting by Producers and Distributors of Motion Picture Films,* those principles were applied in measuring the receivable and revenue of the other party to a license agreement. Requiring the seller's receivable and revenue to be reported at the present value of the future license payments and permitting the purchaser's asset and payable to be reported at either the gross amount or present value of those future cash payments can only serve to detract from the credibility and usefulness of financial reporting.

Members of the Financial Accounting Standards Board:

Donald J. Kirk, *Chairman*
Frank E. Block
John W. March
Robert A. Morgan
David Mosso
Robert T. Sprouse
Ralph E. Walters

Appendix A

GLOSSARY

14. This appendix defines certain terms that are used in this Statement.

Barter
The exchange of unsold advertising time for products or services. The broadcaster benefits (providing the exchange does not interfere with its cash sales) by exchanging otherwise unsold time for such things as programs, fixed assets, merchandise, other media advertising privileges, travel and hotel arrangements, entertainment, and other services or products.

Broadcaster
An entity or an affiliated group of entities that transmits radio or television program material.

Daypart
An aggregation of programs broadcast during a particular time of day (for example, daytime, evening, late night) or programs of a similar type (for example, sports, news, children's shows). Broadcasters generally sell access to viewing audiences to advertisers on a daypart basis.

License agreement for program material
A typical license agreement for program material (for example, features, specials, series, or cartoons) covers several programs (a package) and grants a television station, group of stations, network, pay television, or cable television system (licensee) the right to broadcast either a specified number or an unlimited number of showings over a maximum period of time (license period) for a specified fee. Ordinarily, the fee is paid in installments over a period generally shorter than the license period. The agreement usually contains a separate license for each program in the package. The license expires at the earlier of the last allowed telecast or the end of the license period. The licensee pays the required fee whether or not the rights are exercised. If the licensee does not exercise the con-

tractual rights, the rights revert to the licensor with no refund to the licensee. The license period is not intended to provide continued use of the program material throughout that period but rather to define a reasonable period of time within which the licensee can exercise the limited rights to use the program material.

Network affiliation agreement

A broadcaster may be affiliated with a network under a network affiliation agreement. Under the agreement, the station receives compensation for the network programming that it carries based on a formula designed to compensate the station for advertising sold on a network basis and included in network programming. Program costs, a major expense of television stations, are generally lower for a network affiliate than for an independent station because an affiliate does not incur program costs for network programs.

Appendix B

BACKGROUND INFORMATION AND BASIS FOR CONCLUSIONS

15. SOP 75-5 was developed to narrow the range of acceptable alternative accounting practices among broadcasters, particularly accounting for program rights and related license fees. Before 1975, some broadcasters treated the unpaid fees stipulated in license agreements for program material as commitments and recorded neither the program rights nor the related obligations on their balance sheets. Other broadcasters recorded the program rights and the related obligations as assets and liabilities, respectively, but practice varied with respect to measuring the amount at which the asset and liability were reported and with respect to classification and method of amortizing the assets. SOP 75-5 concluded that assets and liabilities should be reported at the present value of the future license payments determined using an imputed discount rate, that interest should be accrued on the liability, that assets should be classified based on estimated usage, and that accelerated amortization based on estimated future showings generally should be used. The Board has been informed that the variety of practices in existence prior to the issuance of SOP 75-5 has continued to date.

16. The Board has extracted the specialized accounting and reporting principles of SOP 75-5 without significant change except for providing an option in paragraph 4 to report the asset and liability for a license agreement at the gross amount of the liability. Some of the background material, discussion of accounting alternatives, and general accounting guidance have not been carried forward from the SOP. The Board's conceptual framework project on accounting recognition criteria will address issues of recognizing contractual rights and obligations that may pertain to those addressed in this Statement. A Statement of Financial Accounting Concepts resulting from that project in due course will serve as a basis for evaluating existing standards and practices. Accordingly, the Board may wish to evaluate the standards in this Statement when its conceptual framework project is completed.

17. An Exposure Draft of a proposed Statement, *Financial Accounting and Reporting by Broadcasters,* was issued June 12, 1981 for a 90-day comment period. The Board received 45 letters of comment on the Exposure Draft. Two issues were addressed by the majority of respondents: (a) Should a license agreement for television program material be treated by a licensee as a purchase of a right or as an operating lease, and (b) if the license agreement is treated as a purchase of a right, and an asset and a liability are reported, should the liability be reported in accordance with Opinion 21 at its present value determined by discounting future license payments using an imputed rate of interest? This appendix discusses the factors deemed significant by the Board in reaching the conclusions of this Statement. The Board members who assented to this Statement did so on the basis of the overall considerations; individual members gave greater weight to some factors than to others.

Reporting the Asset and Liability

18. Many respondents believe that a license agreement for program material should be accounted for as an operating lease, that no receivable or payable should be reported at the inception of the agreement, and that footnote disclosure of program commitments is adequate. They believe that such an agreement has many characteristics of an operating lease, even though FASB Statement No. 13, *Accounting for Leases,* does not apply to license agreements. They further believe that if license agreements were classified in accordance with the criteria of paragraph 7 of Statement 13, a majority would be considered operating leases rather than capital leases. They note that if a license agreement were accounted for as an operating lease, no asset or liability would be reported by the licensee and Opinion 21 would not be applicable. A few respondents believe broadcast license agreements are similar to executory contracts and that an asset and liability should therefore not be reported.

19. Many other respondents believe that a license agreement for program material should be reported as a purchase of a right to broadcast that material.

Programs available under license agreements are an important source of future advertising revenue to a broadcaster. Those respondents believe that reporting an asset that will produce future revenues and a liability that will require future license payments is necessary for readers of financial statements to assess the resources, obligations, and future cash flows of the enterprise. They rejected accounting for license agreements as operating leases because under that approach the balance sheet of a broadcaster would reflect only a net debit or a net credit representing the difference between cumulative license payments and cumulative amortization of program costs to date.

20. Some respondents stated that reporting program license agreements as a purchase of a right and the incurrence of a liability is consistent with the definitions of an asset and a liability in FASB Concepts Statement No. 3, *Elements of Financial Statements of Business Enterprises.* The right to broadcast program material during the license period is an asset—a probable future economic benefit that is obtained by the broadcaster as a result of a past transaction—signing the license agreement. Similarly, the broadcaster's obligation to make future payments under the license agreement is a liability—a probable future sacrifice of cash that arises from a present obligation of the broadcaster as a result of a past transaction. They also believe that symmetry in accounting is desirable and that both parties to a contract generally should account for it similarly. Statement 53 considers a license agreement to be a sale of a right by a producer or distributor (licensor) of program material.

21. The Board concluded that exhibition rights acquired under a license agreement for program material should be accounted for as a purchase of rights by the licensee. The Board believes that reporting an asset and a liability for such an agreement is consistent with the definitions of an asset and a liability in Concepts Statement 3 and that information concerning the resources and obligations of the enterprise is necessary for readers of financial statements to assess future cash flows. It also believes that a broadcast license agreement differs from an executory contract because the obligation to make license payments is absolute and because the subject of the agreement—program material—is at hand and available for use.

Date of Recording the License Agreement

22. The Exposure Draft stated that a broadcaster should report the asset and liability for a license agreement when the license period begins, the program is available for its first broadcast, and other specified conditions have been met. A few respondents believe the asset and liability should be reported on the date the agreement is signed. They believe that signing the agreement is the event by which the licensee acquires rights to use the program material and that reporting the asset and liability on that date best portrays in the financial statements the broadcaster's rights to future program material and obligations for future cash payments.

23. The Board believes that an asset and a liability for a license agreement should be reported when the conditions specified in paragraph 3 are met. The Board believes that at the date of signing, a substantial degree of uncertainty about cost, acceptability, and availability exists, particularly if a license agreement is signed for program material that does not yet exist. The major uncertainties are eliminated when the conditions specified in paragraph 3 are met, and the asset and liability should be reported then.

Recognition of Imputed Interest

24. Many respondents in the broadcasting industry stated that if an asset and a liability for a license agreement are reported, the asset and liability should be reported at the gross amount of future license payments rather than at the present value of those future payments determined using an imputed discount rate. Some believe that accruing interest on the liability would not properly match revenue and expense. They believe that the gross amount of the license payments should be amortized to expense in the periods in which the program is broadcast and generates advertising revenue. Accruing interest on the liability would result in recognizing interest expense in different periods from those in which advertising revenue is earned. Other respondents believe that accruing interest results in timing of expense recognition similar to that which would exist if the broadcaster paid the cash equivalent amount of the liability at the outset of the arrangement using borrowed funds. They believe that interest expense arises from the way in which the license agreement asset is financed. In their opinion, recognizing interest expense in a different pattern from amortization of the asset is a faithful representation of the different patterns of license payments and utilization of the licensed rights.

25. Several respondents stated that, for many license agreements, accounting separately for interest expense would not have a material impact on the pattern of expense recognition. They believe that imputing interest is burdensome, especially when it must be applied to the large number of contracts a broadcaster may have. They infer from this that an accounting requirement that would call for the asset and liability to be reported initially at their present values is inappropriate. Others similarly observe that many individual contracts would be

excluded from the scope of Opinion 21 because they are short-term or because the timing of payments is based on the uncertain timing of future broadcasts.

26. Some respondents stated that they view the entire program cost as an operating expense. They do not recognize interest as a component of this cost, either during negotiations with licensors or later as payments are made. They believe the reporting of that "noncash" interest expense distorts operating results and segment disclosures and will confuse readers and management. Other respondents believe that a cash payment of interest is included in each cash payment for the license and that the concept of the time value of money, and therefore interest, is implicit to some degree in every license agreement, regardless of whether interest is specifically discussed during negotiations or separately identified as a component of license fee payments.

27. Some respondents believe that Opinion 21 excludes program license agreements from its scope. They believe that a license agreement is by its nature a prepayment because the payments are made over a period generally shorter than the broadcast period. Paragraph 3(b) of Opinion 21 excludes certain advance payments from the scope of that Opinion. Other respondents stated that a license agreement is not an advance payment because the licensor has fulfilled all of its responsibilities at the time the programs are made available to the licensee.

28. A few respondents believe that Opinion 21 does not apply because, even if a complete package or series of programs is made available to the broadcaster at the inception of a license agreement, it cannot use those programs all at once but will instead use them over an extended period of time as marketing and scheduling factors permit. They believe that, in substance, this is equivalent to delivery of the programs over time and that an ongoing flow of product in exchange for an ongoing payment stream does not involve a payment for interest.

29. Some Board members believe the asset and liability for a broadcast license agreement should be reported at the present value of the liability determined using an imputed interest rate, and that interest should be accrued on the liability in accordance with Opinion 21 and consistent with SOP 75-5. They believe that interest arises from the manner in which the acquisition of program materials is financed and that recognizing the difference between the gross and net liability as interest is a faithful representation of that cost.

30. Some Board members agree that the asset and liability for a license agreement should be reported at the present value of the liability. However, they believe that (a) in each period the amortization of discount on the liability should be accounted for as additional program cost rather than as interest cost as would be required under Opinion 21 and (b) program expense should be determined by amortizing undiscounted program cost, that is, the aggregate of all payments under the license. That approach was described in paragraph 31 of the Exposure Draft. The Board members who support the approach believe it should be followed whenever a normal business arrangement calls for later payment for supplies or services that is linked to use of the related specific assets in future operations. Those Board members believe such an approach should not be required in this Statement because in their opinion it would be premature to decide whether accounting for broadcast license agreements should reflect imputed interest on an interest method or on a program cost method like the one described in this paragraph until broader issues concerning recognition of contractual rights and obligations have been examined.

31. In the "Notice for Recipients" of the Exposure Draft, the Board stated that changes may be needed in the accounting principles and reporting practices to be extracted from SOP 75-5 if those principles and practices are not being followed. The Board has been advised by the FASB Task Force on Specialized Principles for the Entertainment Industry, and by many respondents, that for the reasons cited in paragraphs 18 and 24-28, (a) some broadcasters do not report an asset and a liability for rights acquired and obligations incurred under a license agreement and (b) few of those who report an asset and a liability recognize imputed interest. Some Board members support the view in paragraph 29; others support the view in paragraph 30. One Board member supports the view in paragraph 18. In addition, some Board members believe broadcasters should not be required to report the asset and liability for a license agreement at the present value of the liability until the broad subject of discounting has been considered by the Board. The assenting Board members have concluded that a standard is required, however, to reduce the number of reporting practices now used by broadcasters. Therefore, the Board believes tnat the option in this Statement that permits reporting the asset and liability for a license agreement at either the present value or gross amount of the liability will be an improvement in financial reporting by broadcasters.

Other Issues

32. SOP 75-5 concluded that broadcasting intangibles are subject to the amortization provisions of APB Opinion No. 17, *Intangible Assets*. Several respondents stated that this Statement should specifically exempt intangible assets such as network affil-

iation agreements and broadcasting licenses from the provisions of Opinion 17. They believe such intangibles are marketable assets whose values do not diminish over time and, therefore, the intangibles should not be required to be amortized.

33. The Board did not consider the accounting for broadcasting intangible assets because a reconsideration of the provisions of Opinion 17 is beyond the scope of this project.

34. Some respondents requested guidance regarding the treatment of changes in estimates of net realizable value during interim periods. SOP 75-5 did not provide guidance in that area and the Board concluded that it should not address that matter at this time.

35. The Board has concluded that it can reach an informed decision on the basis of existing information without a public hearing and that the effective date and transition specified in paragraphs 12 and 13 are advisable in the circumstances.

Appendix C

ILLUSTRATION OF ACCOUNTING FOR LICENSE AGREEMENTS FOR PROGRAM MATERIAL

36. This appendix illustrates accounting for a license agreement for television program material in accordance with this Statement.

37. Assumptions

a. End of Fiscal Year—December 31
b. Contract Execution Date—July 31, 19X1
c. Number of Films and Telecasts Permitted—4 films, 2 telecasts each
d. Payment Schedule—$1,000,000 at contract execution date, $6,000,000 on January 1, 19X2, 19X3, and 19X4
e. Appropriate Interest Rate for Imputation of Interest—12 percent per year
f. Fees, License Periods, and Film Availability Dates

Film	Total Fee	Stated License Periods From	Stated License Periods To[4]	Film Availability Dates
A	$ 8,000,000	10/1/X1	9/30/X3	9/1/X1
B	5,000,000	10/1/X1	9/30/X3	9/1/X1
C	3,750,000	9/1/X2	8/31/X4	12/1/X1
D	2,250,000	9/1/X3	8/31/X5	12/1/X2
	$19,000,000			

g. Telecast Dates and Revenues

Film	First Telecast Date	First Telecast Percent of Total Revenue	Second Telecast Date	Second Telecast Percent of Total Revenue
A	3/1/X2	60%	6/1/X3	40%
B	5/1/X2	70%	7/1/X3	30%
C	6/1/X3	75%	6/1/X4	25%
D	12/1/X4	65%	8/1/X5	35%

38. For purposes of imputing interest in accordance with Opinion 21, it is assumed that the $1,000,000 payment on July 31, 19X1 and the $6,000,000 payments on January 1, 19X2 and 19X3 relate to films A and B and the $6,000,000 payment on January 1, 19X4 relates to films C and D. Other simplifying assumptions or methods of assigning the payments to the films could be made.

[4]The actual license periods expire at the earlier of (a) the second telecast or (b) the end of the stated license period.

Film	Payment Date	Payment Amount	Discounted Present Value (rounded to 000s) As of Date	Discounted Present Value (rounded to 000s) Amount
A&B	7/31/X1	$ 1,000,000	10/1/X1	$ 1,000,000
	1/1/X2	6,000,000	10/1/X1	5,825,000
	1/1/X3	6,000,000	10/1/X1	5,201,000
		$13,000,000		$12,026,000
C	1/1/X4	$ 3,750,000	9/1/X2	$ 3,219,000
D	1/1/X4	$ 2,250,000	9/1/X3	$ 2,163,000
		$ 6,000,000		

39. Asset and Liability Recognition (Present Value Approach)

Film	License Period From	License Period To	Year of Asset and Liability Recognition 19X1	19X2	19X3
A	10/1/X1	9/30/X3	$7,401,000(a)		
B	10/1/X1	9/30/X3	4,625,000(a)		
C	9/1/X2	8/31/X4		$3,219,000	
D	9/1/X3	8/31/X5			$2,163,000

(a) Discounted present value of $12,026,000 allocated 8/13 to film A and 5/13 to film B based on stated license fees.

40. Expense Recognition (Present Value Approach)

Film	Year of Expense Recognition 19X1	19X2	19X3	19X4	19X5
A	$204,000(I)(a)	$ 396,000(I)(b)			
		4,441,000(A)(c)	$2,960,000(A)(d)		
B	127,000(I)(e)	247,000(I)(f)			
		3,238,000(A)(g)	1,387,000(A)(h)		
C		129,000(I)(i)	402,000(I)(j)		
			2,414,000(A)(k)	$ 805,000(A)(l)	
D			87,000(I)(m)		
				1,406,000(A)(n)	$757,000(A)(o)
	$331,000	$8,451,000	$7,250,000	$2,211,000	$757,000

(I) Accrued interest expense
(A) Amortization of program cost
(a) Interest at 12% for 3 months on liability of $11,026,000 allocated 8/13 to film A
(b) Interest at 12% for 1 year on liability of $5,357,000 ($11,026,000 plus $331,000 less 1/1/X2 payment of $6,000,000) allocated 8/13 to film A
(c) $7,401,000 × 60%
(d) $7,401,000 × 40%
(e) Interest at 12% for 3 months on liability of $11,026,000 allocated 5/13 to film B
(f) Interest at 12% for 1 year on liability of $5,357,000 ($11,026,000 plus $331,000 less 1/1/X2 payment of $6,000,000) allocated 5/13 to film B
(g) $4,625,000 × 70%
(h) $4,625,000 × 30%
(i) Interest at 12% for 4 months on liability of $3,219,000
(j) Interest at 12% for 1 year on liability of $3,348,000 ($3,219,000 plus $129,000)
(k) $3,219,000 × 75%
(l) $3,219,000 × 25%
(m) Interest at 12% for 4 months on liability of $2,163,000
(n) $2,163,000 × 65%
(o) $2,163,000 × 35%

41. Asset and Liability Recognition (Gross Approach)

	License Period		Year of Asset and Liability Recognition		
Film	**From**	**To**	**19X1**	**19X2**	**19X3**
A	10/1/X1	9/30/X3	$8,000,000		
B	10/1/X1	9/30/X3	5,000,000		
C	9/1/X2	8/31/X4		$3,750,000	
D	9/1/X3	8/31/X5			$2,250,000

42. Expense Recognition (Gross Approach)

	Year of Expense Recognition(a)				
Film	**19X1**	**19X2**	**19X3**	**19X4**	**19X5**
A		$4,800,000(b)	$3,200,000(c)		
B		3,500,000(d)	1,500,000(e)		
C			2,813,000(f)	$ 937,000(g)	
D				1,463,000(h)	$787,000(i)
	$ —	$8,300,000	$7,513,000	$2,400,000	$787,000

(a) Under the Gross Approach, all costs under a license agreement are recorded as amortization of program cost.
(b) $8,000,000 × 60%
(c) $8,000,000 × 40%
(d) $5,000,000 × 70%
(e) $5,000,000 × 30%
(f) $3,750,000 × 75%
(g) $3,750,000 × 25%
(h) $2,250,000 × 65%
(i) $2,250,000 × 35%

Statement of Financial Accounting Standards No. 64 Extinguishments of Debt Made to Satisfy Sinking-Fund Requirements

an amendment of FASB Statement No. 4

STATUS

Issued: September 1982

Effective Date: For extinguishments of debt occurring after September 30, 1982

Affects: Amends FAS 4, paragraph 8 and footnote 2

Affected by: No other pronouncements

SUMMARY

This Statement amends FASB Statement No. 4, *Reporting Gains and Losses from Extinguishment of Debt,* so that (a) gains and losses from extinguishments of debt made to satisfy sinking-fund requirements that an enterprise must meet within one year of the date of the extinguishment are not required to be classifed as extraordinary items and (b) the classification of gains and losses from extinguishments of debt made to satisfy sinking-fund requirements are to be determined without regard to the means used to achieve the extinguishment.

Statement of Financial Accounting Standards No. 64
Extinguishments of Debt Made to Satisfy Sinking-Fund Requirements

an amendment of FASB Statement No. 4

CONTENTS

INTRODUCTION

1. The FASB has been requested to reconsider two provisions of FASB Statement No. 4, *Reporting Gains and Losses from Extinguishment of Debt,* regarding the classification of gains and losses from extinguishments of debt made to satisfy current or future sinking-fund requirements. Paragraph 8 of Statement 4 states:

> Gains and losses from extinguishment of debt that are included in the determination of net income shall be aggregated and, if material, . . . classified as an extraordinary item, net of related income tax effect. That conclusion shall apply whether an extinguishment is early or at scheduled maturity date or later. The conclusion does not apply, however, to gains or losses from cash purchases of debt made to satisfy current or future sinking-fund requirements.[2] Those gains and losses shall be aggregated and the amount shall be identified as a separate item.

[2]Some obligations to acquire debt have the essential characteristics of sinking-fund requirements, and resulting gains or losses are not required to be classified as extraordinary items. For example, if an enterprise is required each year to purchase a certain percentage of its outstanding bonds before their scheduled maturity, the gain or loss from such purchase is not required to be classified as an extraordinary item. Debt maturing serially, however, does not have the characteristics of sinking-fund requirements, and gain or loss from extinguishment of serial debt shall be classified as an extraordinary item.

2. With respect to the requirements of paragraph 8, the FASB has been asked:

a. Whether gains and losses from extinguishments of debt made to satisfy future sinking-fund requirements are exempt from the extraordinary-item classification requirement of Statement 4 regardless of when in the future those sinking-fund requirements have to be met

b. Whether the exemption from extraordinary-item classification also should apply to gains and losses resulting from noncash extinguishments of debt made to satisfy sinking-fund requirements

3. The Board has concluded that the exemption from the general extraordinary-item classification requirement of Statement 4 should be limited to gains and losses from extinguishments of debt made to satisfy sinking-fund requirements that an enterprise must meet within one year of the date of the extinguishment. The Board also has decided that the classification of gains and losses from extinguishments of debt made to satisfy sinking-fund requirements should be determined without regard to the means used to achieve the extinguishment. Accordingly, gains and losses resulting from noncash extinguishments of debt made to satisfy sinking-fund requirements shall be classified in the same manner as gains and losses from cash extinguishments.

STANDARDS OF FINANCIAL ACCOUNTING AND REPORTING

Amendment to FASB Statement No. 4

4. The third sentence of paragraph 8 of Statement 4 and the first sentence of footnote 2 to that paragraph are amended to read as follows:

> The conclusion does not apply, however, to gains or losses from extinguishments of debt made to satisfy sinking-fund requirements that an enterprise must meet within one year of the date of the extinguishment.[2]

[2]Some obligations to acquire debt have the essential characteristics of sinking-fund requirements, and resulting gains or losses are not required to be classified as extraordinary items if the obligations must be met within one year of the date of the extinguishment.

Effective Date and Transition

5. This Statement shall be effective for extinguishments of debt occurring after September 30, 1982 with earlier application encouraged in annual financial statements that have not previously been issued. The provisions of this Statement shall not be applied retroactively to previously issued annual financial statements.

The provisions of this Statement need not be applied to immaterial items.

This Statement was adopted by the unanimous vote of the seven members of the Financial Accounting Standards Board:

Donald J. Kirk, *Chairman*	John W. March	Robert T. Sprouse
Frank E. Block	Robert A. Morgan	Ralph E. Walters
	David Mosso	

Appendix

BACKGROUND INFORMATION AND BASIS FOR CONCLUSIONS

6. As stated in paragraph 2, the Board was asked (a) whether gains and losses from extinguishments of debt made to satisfy future sinking-fund requirements are exempt from the extraordinary-item classification requirement of Statement 4 regardless of when in the future those sinking-fund requirements have to be met and (b) whether the exemption from extraordinary-item classification also should apply to gains and losses resulting from noncash extinguishments of debt made to satisfy sinking-fund requirements.

7. The Board has been advised that diverse accounting practices have developed as a result of different interpretations of the phrase *future sinking-fund requirements* in paragraph 8. Some have interpreted that paragraph to exempt all gains and losses from extinguishments of debt subject to future sinking-fund requirements from the extraordinary-item classification requirement regardless of when in the future those requirements have to be met. Others, however, have interpreted that phrase to mean only those future sinking-fund requirements that have to be met in the near future. In the Exposure Draft, the Board proposed that the exemption be limited to gains and losses from extinguishments of debt made to satisfy sinking-fund requirements that an enterprise must meet within the next year.

8. Paragraph 8 of Statement 4 specifically exempts from the extraordinary-item classification requirement those gains or losses resulting from *cash purchases* of debt made to satisfy current or future sinking-fund requirements. Those raising this question believe that the method of achieving the extinguishment should not determine the manner in which the resulting gains and losses are classified in the financial statements. They point out that APB Opinion No. 26, *Early Extinguishment of Debt,* indicates that all extinguishments of debt before scheduled maturities are fundamentally alike and that the accounting for such transactions should be the same regardless of the means used to achieve the extinguishment. They believe that similar reasoning should be adopted in paragraph 8 of Statement 4 and that the classification of gains and losses resulting from extinguishments of debt made to satisfy sinking-fund requirements should not be based on the means used to effect the extinguishments. The Board agrees and deleted the reference to "cash purchases" in the third sentence of paragraph 8 of Statement 4.

9. An Exposure Draft of a proposed Statement, *Extinguishments of Debt Made to Satisfy Sinking-Fund Requirements,* was issued on February 23, 1982. The Board received 90 letters of comment in response to the Exposure Draft. Certain of the comments received and the Board's consideration of them, including various alternatives considered and reasons for accepting some and rejecting others, are discussed in the remaining paragraphs.

10. Many respondents to the Exposure Draft opposed issuance of a final Statement because they believe the extraordinary-item criteria in APB Opinion No. 30, *Reporting the Results of Operations,* are preferable to the provisions of Statement 4 for purposes of classifying gains and losses resulting from the extinguishment of *all* forms of debt. Those respondents recommended that the Board rescind, or consider rescinding, Statement 4 rather than proceeding with the proposal in the Exposure Draft. The Board notes that the general issue of how to report components of comprehensive income is

being considered in the Board's conceptual framework project on reporting income, cash flows, and financial position of business enterprises. The Board has concluded that the general requirement of Statement 4 (extraordinary-item classification of gains and losses from extinguishment of debt) should not be reconsidered until that conceptual framework project is completed.

11. Other respondents opposed the proposed amendment because they view it as a major extension of Statement 4. They viewed Statement 4 as removing all *nonsinking-fund* debt extinguishments from the classification criteria of Opinion 30, and they now view the proposed amendment as removing many *sinking-fund* debt extinguishments from those same criteria. They believe that the criteria of Opinion 30 should continue to be applied to gains and losses resulting from the extinguishment of sinking-fund debt. The Board believes that the exemption from extraordinary-item classification is appropriate in circumstances in which an enterprise extinguishes debt annually to meet its pending sinking-fund requirements. The Board notes, however, that extinguishments of debt made in anticipation of future sinking-fund requirements are not required to be made currently to meet continuing contractual requirements. Instead, the Board believes those extinguishments are similar in nature to extinguishments of debt not subject to sinking-fund requirements for which resulting gains and losses must be classified as extraordinary items. The Board recognizes, however, that, as a practical matter, an enterprise may extinguish debt somewhat in advance of a sinking-fund due date to satisfy the requirement at that date.

12. Many respondents stated that the proposed one-year time frame is too restrictive and could have adverse economic effects and suggested the time frame be extended. They argued that such a one-year limitation may induce enterprises to delay purchases of sinking-fund debt until one year from the due date to avoid extraordinary-item classification of resulting gains and losses. They pointed out that sinking-fund debt often is extinguished several years in advance of its due date to take advantage of temporary changes in interest rates and believe that such a policy is a prudent and normal business practice that should not be discouraged by an accounting standard. Other respondents noted that some sinking-fund debt issues are held primarily by a small number of institutional investors and are not widely traded. Those respondents pointed out that the market price of sinking-fund debt will rise to a level higher than would prevail in a free market situation as the sinking fund due date approaches. They believe enterprises need flexibility to minimize the costs of their sinking-fund repurchase programs and also that the proposed amendment would, in effect, impair that flexibility. Those respondents who opposed the one-year time frame suggested various alternative limitations. Most recommended a three-year limitation.

13. The Board was not persuaded by the arguments summarized in the previous paragraph. The Board believes gains and losses from extinguishments of sinking-fund debt should be exempt from extraordinary-item classification only if those sinking-fund requirements for which the debt was acquired must be met currently. The Board acknowledges that an enterprise may determine that extinguishment of several years' sinking-fund requirements or an entire sinking-fund debt issue is advisable in the circumstances. However, the Board does not believe that fact should affect the classification of the resulting gains or losses. Further, several Board members rejected the arguments in paragraph 12 because they believe the sinking-fund exemption in Statement 4 should be eliminated completely.

14. The Board concluded that it can reach an informed decision on the basis of existing information without a public hearing and that the effective date and transition specified in paragraph 5 are advisable in the circumstances.

Statement of Financial Accounting Standards No. 65 Accounting for Certain Mortgage Banking Activities

STATUS

Issued: September 1982

Effective Date: For transactions entered into after December 31, 1982

Affects: Amends FAS 32, Appendix A

Affected by: No other pronouncements

SUMMARY

This Statement extracts the specialized accounting and reporting principles and practices from AICPA Statements of Position 74-12, *Accounting Practices in the Mortgage Banking Industry,* and 76-2, *Accounting for Origination Costs and Loan and Commitment Fees in the Mortgage Banking Industry,* and establishes accounting and reporting standards for certain mortgage banking activities.

Mortgage loans and mortgage-backed securities held for sale are reported at the lower of cost or market value. Origination costs associated with loan applications received directly from borrowers are expensed as period costs. The premium paid for the right to service loans in a purchase of mortgage loans ordinarily is capitalized as the cost of acquiring that right.

This Statement also establishes accounting and reporting standards for several different types of loan and commitment fees. Loan origination fees, to the extent they represent reimbursement of loan origination costs, are recognized as revenue when the loan is made. Loan commitment fees ordinarily are recognized as revenue or expense when the loans are sold to permanent investors. Fees for services performed by third parties and loan placement fees are recognized as revenue when all significant services have been performed. Land acquisition, development, and construction loan fees and standby and gap commitment fees are recognized as revenue over the combined commitment and loan periods.

Statement of Financial Accounting Standards No. 65
Accounting for Certain Mortgage Banking Activities

CONTENTS

INTRODUCTION

1. Mortgage banking activities primarily consist of two separate but interrelated activities: (a) the origination or acquisition of mortgage loans and the sale of the loans to **permanent investors**[1] and (b) the subsequent long-term **servicing** of the loans. Mortgage loans are acquired for sale to permanent investors from a variety of sources, including applications received directly from borrowers (in-house originations), purchases from realtors and brokers, purchases from investors, and conversions of various forms of interim financing to permanent financing.

2. A **mortgage banking enterprise** usually retains the right to service mortgage loans it sells to permanent investors. A servicing fee, usually based on a percentage of the outstanding principal balance of the mortgage loan, is received for performing loan administration functions. When servicing fees exceed the cost of performing servicing functions, the existing contractual right to service mortgage loans has economic value. Because of their value, rights to service mortgage loans frequently have been purchased and sold.

APPLICABILITY AND SCOPE

3. This Statement establishes accounting and reporting standards for certain activities of a mortgage banking enterprise. Other enterprises, such as commercial banks and thrift institutions, may conduct operations that are substantially similar to the primary operations of a mortgage banking enterprise (for example, through subsidiaries or divisions). In those circumstances, this Statement also applies to those operations. This Statement does not apply, however, to the normal lending activities of those other enterprises.

STANDARDS OF FINANCIAL ACCOUNTING AND REPORTING

Mortgage Loans and Mortgage-Backed Securities

4. Mortgage loans and **mortgage-backed securities** held for sale shall be reported at the lower of cost or market value, determined as of the balance sheet date. The amount by which cost exceeds market value shall be accounted for as a valuation allowance. Changes in the valuation allowances shall be included in the determination of net income of the period in which the change occurs.

5. Purchase discounts on mortgage loans and mortgage-backed securities shall not be amortized as interest revenue during the period the loans or securities are held for sale.

6. A mortgage loan or mortgage-backed security transferred to a long-term-investment classification shall be transferred at the lower of cost or market

[1]Terms defined in the glossary (Appendix A) are in **boldface type** the first time they appear in this Statement.

value on the transfer date. Any difference between the carrying amount of the loan or security and its outstanding principal balance shall be amortized to income over the estimated life of the loan or security using the interest method.[2] A mortgage loan or mortgage-backed security shall not be classified as a long-term investment unless the mortgage banking enterprise has both the ability and the intent to hold the loan or security for the foreseeable future or until maturity.

7. If ultimate recovery of the carrying amount of a mortgage loan or mortgage-backed security held as a long-term investment is doubtful and the impairment is considered to be other than temporary, the carrying amount of the loan or security shall be reduced to its expected collectible amount, which becomes the new cost basis. The amount of the reduction shall be reported as a loss. A recovery from the new cost basis shall be reported as a gain only at the sale, maturity, or other disposition of the loan or security.

8. As a means of financing its mortgage loans or mortgage-backed securities held for sale, a mortgage banking enterprise may transfer mortgage loans or mortgage-backed securities temporarily to banks or other financial institutions under formal repurchase agreements that indicate that control over the future economic benefits relating to those assets and risk of market loss are retained by the mortgage banking enterprise. Under those agreements, those same mortgage loans or mortgage-backed securities generally are reacquired from the banks or other financial institutions when the mortgage banking enterprise sells the loans or securities to permanent investors. Mortgage loans or mortgage-backed securities also may be transferred temporarily without a repurchase agreement but under circumstances that indicate a repurchase agreement exists on an informal basis, for example, when the mortgage banking enterprise (a) makes all of the necessary marketing efforts, (b) retains any positive or negative interest spread on the loans or securities, (c) retains the risk of fluctuations in loan or security market values, (d) reacquires any uncollectible loans, or (e) routinely reacquires all or almost all of the loans or securities from the bank or other financial institution and sells them to permanent investors. Mortgage loans and mortgage-backed securities held for sale that are transferred under formal or informal repurchase agreements of the nature described in this paragraph shall (1) be accounted for as collateralized financing arrangements and (2) continue to be reported by the transferor as being held for sale.

9. The market value of mortgage loans and mortgage-backed securities held for sale shall be determined by type of loan. At a minimum, separate determinations of market value for residential (one- to four-family dwellings) and commercial mortgage loans shall be made. Either the aggregate or individual loan basis may be used in determining the lower of cost or market value for each type of loan. Market value for loans subject to investor purchase commitments (committed loans) and loans held on a speculative basis (uncommitted loans)[3] shall be determined separately as follows:

a. *Committed Loans and Mortgage-Backed Securities.* Market value for mortgage loans and mortgage-backed securities covered by investor commitments shall be based on commitment prices. Any commitment price that provides for servicing fee rates materially different from current servicing fee rates shall be adjusted in accordance with paragraph 11.
b. *Uncommitted Loans.* Market value for uncommitted loans shall be based on the market in which the mortgage banking enterprise normally operates. That determination would include consideration of the following:
   (1) Commitment prices, to the extent the commitments clearly represent market conditions at the balance sheet date
   (2) Market prices and yields sought by the mortgage banking enterprise's normal market outlets
   (3) Quoted **Government National Mortgage Association (GNMA)** security prices or other public market quotations for long-term mortgage loan rates
   (4) **Federal Home Loan Mortgage Corporation (FHLMC)** and **Federal National Mortgage Association (FNMA)** current delivery prices
c. *Uncommitted Mortgage-Backed Securities.* Market value for uncommitted mortgage-backed securities that are collateralized by a mortgage banking enterprise's own loans ordinarily shall be based on the market value of the securities. If the trust holding the loans may be readily terminated and the loans sold directly, market value for the securities shall be based on the market value of the loans or the securities, depending on the mortgage banking enterprise's sales intent. Market value for other uncommitted mortgage-backed securities shall be based on published mortgage-backed securities yields.

10. Capitalized costs of acquiring rights to service mortgage loans, associated with the purchase of existing mortgage loans (paragraphs 16 through 19),

[2]The interest method is discussed in paragraph 15 of APB Opinion No. 21, *Interest on Receivables and Payables,* and paragraphs 16 and 17 of APB Opinion No. 12, *Omnibus Opinion—1967.*

[3]A mortgage loan shall be considered uncommitted for purposes of determining market value if the loan does not meet the specific terms of a commitment or if a reasonable doubt exists about the acceptance of the loan under a commitment.

shall be excluded from the cost of mortgage loans for the purpose of determining the lower of cost or market value.

Servicing Fees

11. If mortgage loans are sold with servicing retained and the stated servicing fee rate differs materially from a **current (normal) servicing fee rate,** the sales price shall be adjusted, for purposes of determining gain or loss on the sale, to provide for the recognition of a normal servicing fee in each subsequent year. The amount of the adjustment shall be the difference between the actual sales price and the estimated sales price that would have been obtained if a normal servicing fee rate had been specified.[4] The adjustment and any gain or loss to be recognized shall be determined as of the date the mortgage loans are sold. In addition, if normal servicing fees are expected to be less than estimated servicing costs over the estimated life of the mortgage loans, the expected loss on servicing the loans shall be accrued at that date.

Transactions with an Affiliated Enterprise[5]

12. The carrying amount of mortgage loans or mortgage-backed securities to be sold to an **affiliated enterprise** shall be adjusted to the lower of cost or market value of the loans or securities as of the date management decides that a sale to an affiliated enterprise will occur. The date shall be determined based on, at a minimum, formal approval by an authorized representative of the purchaser, issuance of a commitment to purchase the loans or securities, and acceptance of the commitment by the selling enterprise. The amount of any adjustment shall be charged to income.

13. If a particular class of mortgage loans or all loans are originated exclusively for an affiliated enterprise, the originator is acting as an agent of the affiliated enterprise, and the loan transfers shall be accounted for at the originator's acquisition cost. Such an agency relationship, however, would not exist in the case of "right of first refusal" contracts or similar types of agreements or commitments if the originator retains all the risks associated with ownership of the loans.

In-House Origination Costs

14. Costs associated with loan applications received directly from borrowers (in-house originations) shall be expensed as period costs. Those costs include (a) direct costs, such as personnel, financing, and marketing costs, and (b) general and administrative costs, such as occupancy and equipment rental costs.

Costs of Issuing Certain GNMA Securities

15. One month's interest cost, which is required to be paid to a trustee by issuers of GNMA securities electing the **internal reserve method,** shall be capitalized and amortized. The aggregate amount capitalized, including amounts capitalized under other provisions of this Statement, shall not exceed the present value of net future servicing income (paragraph 18).

Servicing Rights

16. The right to service mortgage loans for other than an enterprise's own account is an intangible asset that may be acquired separately, in a purchase of mortgage loans, or in a business combination. Subject to the limitations specified in paragraphs 17 and 18, the cost of acquiring that right from others shall be capitalized and amortized in accordance with the requirements of paragraph 19.

17. A mortgage banking enterprise acquiring the right to service loans in a purchase of mortgage loans shall capitalize the portion of the purchase price representing the cost of acquiring that right if a definitive plan for the sale of the mortgage loans exists when the transaction is initiated.[6] A definitive plan exists if (a) the mortgage banking enterprise has obtained, before the purchase date, commitments from permanent investors to purchase the mortgage loans or related mortgage-backed securities, or makes a commitment within a reasonable period (usually not more than 30 days after the purchase date) to sell the mortgage loans or related mortgage-backed securities to a permanent investor or underwriter, and (b) the plan includes estimates of the purchase price and selling price. The amount capitalized shall not exceed (1) the purchase price of

[4]The adjustment ordinarily will approximate the present value, based on an appropriate interest rate, of the difference between normal and stated servicing fees over the estimated life of the mortgage loans.

[5]This section on "Transactions with an Affiliated Enterprise" applies to only the separate financial statements of a mortgage banking enterprise. The provisions of FASB Statement No. 57, *Related Party Disclosures,* also apply to the separate financial statements of a mortgage banking enterprise. The provisions of ARB No. 51, *Consolidated Financial Statements,* and APB Opinion No. 18, *The Equity Method of Accounting for Investments in Common Stock,* apply when a mortgage banking enterprise is either consolidated or accounted for by the equity method.

[6]In the absence of a definitive plan for the sale of the related mortgage loans, the cost of acquiring the right to service mortgage loans generally is included as part of the cost of the loans for purposes of determining the lower of cost or market value.

the loans, including any transfer fees paid, in excess of the market value of the loans without servicing rights at the purchase date or (2) the present value of net future servicing income, determined in accordance with paragraph 18. The amount capitalized shall be reduced by any amount that the final sales price to the permanent investor exceeds the market value of the loans at the purchase date. All other costs, such as salaries and general and administrative expenses, shall be expensed as period costs.

18. The amount capitalized as the right to service mortgage loans shall not exceed the amount by which the present value of estimated future servicing revenue exceeds the present value of expected future servicing costs. Estimates of future servicing revenue shall include expected late charges and other ancillary revenue. Estimates of expected future servicing costs shall include direct costs associated with performing the servicing function and appropriate allocations of other costs. Estimated future servicing costs may be determined on an incremental cost basis. The rate used to determine the present value shall be an appropriate long-term interest rate.

19. The amount capitalized as the right to service mortgage loans and the amount capitalized by certain issuers of GNMA securities (paragraph 15) shall be amortized in proportion to, and over the period of, estimated net servicing income (servicing revenue in excess of servicing costs).

Loan and Commitment Fees

20. Mortgage banking enterprises may receive or pay nonrefundable loan and commitment fees representing compensation for a variety of services. Those fees may include components representing, for example, an adjustment of the interest yield on the loan, a fee for designating funds for the borrower, or an offset of loan origination costs. Loan and commitment fees shall be accounted for as set forth in paragraphs 21 through 27.

Loan Origination Fees

21. Fees representing reimbursement of the mortgage banking enterprise's costs of processing mortgage loan applications, reviewing legal title to real estate, and performing other loan origination procedures (loan origination fees) shall be recognized as revenue when the loan is made. If origination costs are not reasonably estimable, a portion of the fees, not to exceed the amount allowable by the Department of Housing and Urban Development and the Veterans Administration, may be recognized as revenue when the loan is made because fees based on those rates generally do not exceed loan origination costs. Any fees in excess of the amount considered to be a reimbursement of loan origination costs shall be recognized as revenue in accordance with paragraphs 23 through 26.

Fees for Services Rendered

22. Fees representing reimbursement for the costs of specific services performed by third parties with respect to originating a loan, such as appraisal fees, shall be recognized as revenue when the services have been performed.

Fees Relating to Loans Held for Sale

23. Fees received for guaranteeing the funding of mortgage loans to borrowers, builders, or developers and fees paid to permanent investors to ensure the ultimate sale of the loans (residential or commercial loan commitment fees) shall be recognized as revenue or expense when the loans are sold to permanent investors or when it becomes evident the commitment will not be used. Because residential loan commitment fees ordinarily relate to blocks of loans, fees recognized as revenue or expense as the result of individual loan transactions shall be based on the ratio of the individual loan amount to the total commitment amount.

24. Fees for arranging a commitment directly between a permanent investor and a borrower (loan placement fees) shall be recognized as revenue when all significant services have been performed. In addition, if a mortgage banking enterprise obtains a commitment from a permanent investor before or at the time a related commitment is made to a borrower and if the commitment to the borrower will require (a) simultaneous assignment of the commitment to the investor and (b) simultaneous transfer to the borrower of the amount received from the investor, the related fees also shall be accounted for as loan placement fees.

Fees Relating to Loans Not Held for Sale

25. Fees for guaranteeing the funding of a mortgage loan to acquire or develop land or to construct residential or income-producing properties shall be recognized as revenue over the combined commitment and loan periods using the best estimate of that period. The straight-line method shall be used during the commitment period to recognize the fee revenue, and the interest method shall be used during the loan period to recognize the remaining fee revenue. If it is not practicable to apply the

interest method during the loan period,[7] the straight-line method shall be used. If the original estimate of the combined commitment and loan periods is revised significantly, the remaining commitment fee shall be recognized as revenue over the revised period. Additional fees received as a result of changes in the period shall be recognized as revenue over the revised period.

26. **Standby commitment** and **gap commitment** fees for issuing a commitment to fund a standby or gap loan for purposes such as interim or construction financing shall be recognized as revenue over the combined commitment and loan periods. The straight-line method shall be used during the commitment period to recognize the fee revenue, and the interest method shall be used during the loan period to recognize the remaining fee revenue. If it is not practicable to apply the interest method during the loan period, the straight-line method shall be used. Any additional fees received when the loan is made shall be recognized as revenue over the loan period.

Expired Commitments and Prepayments of Loans

27. If a loan commitment expires without the loan being made or if a loan is repaid before the estimated repayment date, any related unrecognized fees shall be recognized as revenue or expense at that time.

Balance Sheet Classification

28. Mortgage banking enterprises using either a classified or unclassified balance sheet shall distinguish between (a) mortgage loans and mortgage-backed securities held for sale and (b) mortgage loans and mortgage-backed securities held for long-term investment.

Disclosures

29. The method used in determining the lower of cost or market value of mortgage loans and mortgage-backed securities (that is, aggregate or individual loan basis) shall be disclosed.

30. The amount capitalized during the period in connection with acquiring the right to service mortgage loans (paragraph 16), the method of amortizing the capitalized amount, and the amount of amortization for the period shall be disclosed.

Amendments to Statement 32

31. The references to AICPA Statements of Position (SOPs) 74-12, *Accounting Practices in the Mortgage Banking Industry,* and 76-2, *Accounting for Origination Costs and Loan and Commitment Fees in the Mortgage Banking Industry,* are deleted from Appendix A of FASB Statement No. 32, *Specialized Accounting and Reporting Principles and Practices in AICPA Statements of Position and Guides on Accounting and Auditing Matters.*

Effective Date and Transition

32. The provisions of this Statement, other than those of paragraphs 4 and 28 through 30, shall be applied prospectively to transactions entered into after December 31, 1982, with earlier application encouraged. The provisions of paragraphs 4 and 28 through 30 shall be effective for financial statements for fiscal years beginning after December 15, 1982, with earlier application encouraged. If application of paragraph 4 of this Statement results in a change in accounting, restatement of previously issued annual financial statements to conform to the provisions of that paragraph is encouraged but not required. If it is not practicable or if the issuer of financial statements elects not to restate any prior year, the cumulative effect shall be included in net income in the year in which this Statement is first applied. (Refer to paragraph 20 of APB Opinion No. 20, *Accounting Changes.*) The effect on income before extraordinary items, net income, and related per share amounts of applying this Statement in a year in which the cumulative effect is included in determining that year's net income shall be disclosed for that year.

33. If previously issued financial statements are restated, the financial statements shall be restated for as many consecutive years as practicable. In the year that this Statement is first applied, the nature of any restatement and its effect on income before extraordinary items, net income, and related per share amounts for each restated year presented shall be disclosed. The cumulative effect of applying this Statement shall be included in determining net income of the earliest year restated (not necessarily the earliest year presented).

The provisions of this Statement need not be applied to immaterial items.

[7]For example, if a construction loan is to be funded over time in proportion to the progress of the construction, the interest method may not be practicable to apply.

This Statement was approved by the unanimous vote of the seven members of the Financial Accounting Standards Board:

Donald J. Kirk, *Chairman*	John W. March	Robert T. Sprouse
Frank E. Block	Robert A. Morgan	Ralph E. Walters
	David Mosso	

Appendix A

GLOSSARY

34. This appendix defines certain terms that are used in this Statement.

Affiliated enterprise
An enterprise that directly or indirectly controls, is controlled by, or is under common control with another enterprise; also, a party with which the enterprise may deal if one party has the ability to exercise significant influence over the other's operating and financial policies as discussed in paragraph 17 of APB Opinion No. 18, *The Equity Method of Accounting for Investments in Common Stock.*

Current (normal) servicing fee rate
A servicing fee rate that is representative of servicing fee rates most commonly used in comparable servicing agreements covering similar types of mortgage loans.

Federal Home Loan Mortgage Corporation (FHLMC)
Often referred to as "Freddie Mac," FHLMC is a private corporation authorized by Congress to assist in the development and maintenance of a secondary market in conventional residential mortgages. FHLMC purchases mortgage loans and sells mortgages principally through mortgage participation certificates (PCs) representing an undivided interest in a group of conventional mortgages. FHLMC guarantees the timely payment of interest and the collection of principal on the PCs.

Federal National Mortgage Association (FNMA)
Often referred to as "Fannie Mae," FNMA is an investor-owned corporation established by Congress to support the secondary mortgage loan market by purchasing mortgage loans when other investor funds are limited and selling mortgage loans when other investor funds are available.

Gap commitment
A commitment to provide interim financing while the borrower is in the process of satisfying provisions of a permanent loan agreement, such as obtaining a designated occupancy level on an apartment project. The interim loan ordinarily finances the difference between the floor loan (the portion of a mortgage loan commitment that is less than the full amount of the commitment) and the maximum permanent loan.

Government National Mortgage Association (GNMA)
Often referred to as "Ginnie Mae," GNMA is a U.S. governmental agency that guarantees certain types of securities (mortgage-backed securities) and provides funds for and administers certain types of low-income housing assistance programs.

Internal reserve method
A method for making payments to investors for collections of principal and interest on mortgage loans by issuers of GNMA securities. An issuer electing the internal reserve method is required to deposit in a custodial account an amount equal to one month's interest on the mortgage loans that collateralize the GNMA security issued.

Mortgage-backed securities
Securities issued by a governmental agency or corporation (for example, GNMA or FHLMC) or by private issuers (for example, FNMA, banks, and mortgage banking enterprises). Mortgage-backed securities generally are referred to as *mortgage participation certificates* or *pass-through certificates* (PCs). A PC represents an undivided interest in a pool of specific mortgage loans. Periodic payments on GNMA PCs are backed by the U.S. government. Periodic payments on FHLMC and FNMA PCs are guaranteed by those corporations, but are not backed by the U.S. government.

Mortgage banking enterprise
An enterprise that is engaged primarily in originating, marketing, and servicing real estate mortgage loans for other than its own account. Mortgage banking enterprises, as local representatives of institutional lenders, act as correspondents between lenders and borrowers.

Permanent investor
An enterprise that invests in mortgage loans for its own account, for example, an insurance enterprise, commercial or mutual savings bank, savings and loan association, pension plan, real estate investment trust, or FNMA.

Servicing

Mortgage loan servicing includes collecting monthly mortgagor payments, forwarding payments and related accounting reports to investors, collecting escrow deposits for the payment of mortgagor property taxes and insurance, and paying taxes and insurance from escrow funds when due.

Standby commitment

A commitment to lend money with the understanding that the loan probably will not be made unless permanent financing cannot be obtained from another source. Standby commitments ordinarily are used to enable the borrower to obtain construction financing on the assumption that permanent financing will be available on more favorable terms when construction is completed. Standby commitments normally provide for an interest rate substantially above the market rate in effect when the commitment is issued.

Appendix B

BACKGROUND INFORMATION AND SUMMARY OF CONSIDERATION OF COMMENTS ON EXPOSURE DRAFT

35. As discussed in Statement 32, the FASB is extracting the specialized[8] accounting and reporting principles and practices (specialized principles) from AICPA SOPs and Guides on accounting and auditing matters and issuing them as FASB Statements after appropriate due process. This Statement extracts the specialized principles from SOPs 74-12 and 76-2. Accounting and reporting standards that apply to enterprises in general also apply to mortgage banking enterprises, and the standards in this Statement are in addition to those standards.

36. The Board has not undertaken a comprehensive reconsideration of the specialized principles in SOPs 74-12 and 76-2. Also, most of the background material and discussion of accounting alternatives have not been carried forward from the SOPs. The Board's conceptual framework project on accounting recognition criteria will address recognition issues relating to elements of financial statements. A Statement of Financial Accounting Concepts resulting from that project in due course will serve as a basis for evaluating existing standards and practices. Accordingly, the Board may wish to evaluate the standards in this Statement when its conceptual framework project is completed.

37. An Exposure Draft of a proposed FASB Statement, *Accounting for Certain Mortgage Banking Activities,* was issued on February 3, 1982. The Board received 42 comment letters in response to the Exposure Draft. Certain of the comments received and the Board's consideration of them are discussed in this appendix.

Applicability and Scope

38. Respondents commented on the appropriateness of this Statement's applying to the mortgage banking operations of other enterprises, such as commercial banks and thrift institutions, when those enterprises conduct operations that are substantially similar to the operations of a mortgage banking enterprise. Some respondents said that it would be difficult to define "substantially similar" operations and that the scope of the Statement could result in unintended changes in current accounting principles or practices followed by other enterprises, such as commercial banks and thrift institutions. Those enterprises may engage in some, but generally not all, of the activities of a mortgage banking enterprise. A mortgage banker primarily is engaged in originating, selling, and servicing mortgage loans for other than its own account. However, it also may originate loans for investment purposes and collect related loan fees. Commercial banks and thrift institutions may primarily be engaged in those latter activities and occasionally may sell mortgage loans to others for liquidity or other reasons. Those respondents questioned whether this Statement was intended to apply broadly to all activities discussed in the Statement regardless of the basic nature of the enterprise involved. Other respondents pointed out that commercial banks and thrift institutions originate many types of loans other than mortgage loans and questioned whether the Statement also would apply to activities relating to those loans. Still other respondents said that the scope of the Statement could be viewed as establishing broadly applicable standards with respect to the basis of carrying mortgage loans and to the accounting for servicing rights and loan and commitment fees. They suggested that the scope of the Statement be limited solely to mortgage banking enterprises.

39. In extracting the specialized principles from SOPs 74-12 and 76-2, the Board decided that those principles should apply to mortgage banking operations whether those operations are conducted by a mortgage banking enterprise or by another enterprise. That notion is consistent with the recommendations in SOP 76-2. However, the Board

[8]The term *specialized* is used to refer to those accounting and reporting principles and practices in AICPA Guides and SOPs that are neither superseded by nor contained in Accounting Research Bulletins, APB Opinions, FASB Statements, or FASB Interpretations.

decided not to establish in this project broadly applicable standards for each type of activity in which a mortgage banking enterprise generally is engaged because this project did not include a comprehensive consideration of whether the circumstances in other industries do or do not justify different reporting for those activities. Accordingly, the Board has clarified the scope to indicate that the Statement does not apply to the normal lending activities of those other enterprises.

Sales of Mortgage Loans to an Affiliated Enterprise

40. The "Notice for Recipients" of the Exposure Draft requested respondents to comment on whether the Statement should specify the amount at which sales of loans to an affiliated enterprise are to be reported in the separate financial statements of a mortgage banking enterprise. Of those respondents who commented, a majority recommended that the Statement specify how those sales should be reported. Some respondents noted that separate financial statements of mortgage banking enterprises are common in the mortgage banking industry and that guidance is necessary to ensure continued consistency of reporting among those enterprises. Those respondents pointed out that mortgage banking enterprises generally are required, by terms of their various selling and servicing contracts, to issue separate financial statements. Those financial statements are used for regulatory, credit, and other purposes and may be used by potential purchasers of loans to evaluate the mortgage banking enterprise's ability to perform required services under the servicing agreements.

41. Other respondents said that transactions with affiliated enterprises are not unique to mortgage banking enterprises and that issues relating to the accounting for transactions with an affiliated enterprise should be addressed in a separate Board project covering all enterprises. They also argued that transactions with an affiliated enterprise should not be addressed in this Statement because they believe that disclosures required by FASB Statement No. 57, *Related Party Disclosures,* provide financial statement users with sufficient information to understand and evaluate the significance of sales of mortgage loans to affiliated enterprises. They suggested that the section on transactions with an affiliated enterprise be deleted.

42. Primarily for the reasons given in paragraph 41, the Board has decided not to specify for mortgage banking enterprises a common basis of measuring transactions with affiliates, except as provided in paragraph 13. However, the Board decided to clarify in paragraph 12 that the carrying amount of mortgage loans or mortgage-backed securities to be sold to an affiliated enterprise must be adjusted to the lower of cost or market value. The Board believes the clarification is consistent with the intent of SOP 74-12. The Board also indicated in a footnote to paragraph 12 that the provisions of Statement 57 apply to the separate financial statements of a mortgage banking enterprise.

Transition

43. The Exposure Draft proposed that accounting changes adopted to conform to the provisions of this Statement be applied retroactively by restating financial statements for as many years as practicable, with the cumulative effect included in income of the earliest year restated. That method of transition was proposed on the premise that it would afford maximum comparability among financial statements. Some respondents disagreed with the proposed transition provisions because they believe the application of certain provisions of the Exposure Draft would be difficult to implement retroactively. In particular, they noted that the Statement specifies different methods of reporting loans and certain fees based on whether an enterprise intends to sell the applicable loans or hold them as investments. Those respondents noted that retroactive restatement may require an enterprise that was not following the provisions of SOPs 74-12 and 76-2 to reconstruct its intent as of the end of several prior reporting periods, a process that would be difficult and time-consuming. They also noted that the provisions of the Statement relating to the acquisition of servicing rights may be difficult to implement retroactively for enterprises that were following the SOPs because, as noted in the "Notice for Recipients" of the Exposure Draft, this Statement changes the reporting of certain acquisitions of servicing rights. They recommended that prospective application be required.

44. The Board considered those views and concluded that prospective application of the transaction-related provisions of this Statement is appropriate. Because the provisions of paragraph 4 relate to the measurement and reporting of mortgage loan and mortgage-backed security portfolios, the Board concluded that those portfolios should be reported by a single method, that is, the lower of cost or market value. The Board also concluded that comparability would be enhanced if enterprises apply the provisions of that paragraph retroactively by restating the financial statements of previous periods. Because the benefits of restatement may not justify the cost of restating in some cases, however, the Board decided to permit rather than require retroactive restatement in applying the provisions of paragraph 4.

Other Comments

45. Some respondents noted that the provisions of the Exposure Draft relating to sales of mortgage loans with servicing retained are not followed universally by enterprises in other industries, although those provisions currently are being followed by most mortgage banking enterprises. Paragraph 11 requires that, when mortgage loans are sold with servicing retained, the sales price should be adjusted, for purposes of determining gain or loss on the sale, if the stated servicing fee rate differs materially from normal servicing fee rates. The adjustment is determined by the difference between the actual sales price and the estimated sales price that would have been obtained if a normal servicing fee rate had been specified. Those respondents said that some financial institutions are recognizing in income the present value of all future servicing income (stated servicing fees in excess of estimated servicing costs) when mortgage loans are sold rather than over the period servicing is performed. The Board believes that the present value of excess servicing fees (the portion that exceeds normal servicing fees) should be recognized as an additional element of the sales price. However, the Board believes that it is inappropriate to recognize, in effect, the present value of all future servicing income as an element of the sales price when loan servicing is a primary revenue-producing activity of an enterprise. Accordingly, this Statement requires that a normal servicing fee be recognized as revenue when the servicing is performed.

46. The Exposure Draft proposed that commitment fees received for issuing floating-rate commitments for certain loans, such as land development and construction loans, should be recognized in income over the commitment period rather than over the combined commitment and loan periods as recommended in SOP 76-2. The provision was included so that the accounting for those fees would more closely parallel the accounting by other financial institutions for similar fees. Some respondents expressed concern about the proposed provision because it was not identical to existing practices of either banks or thrift institutions. Other respondents pointed out that a task force of the AICPA currently is studying issues relating to the accounting for loan origination and commitment fees by all enterprises. They recommended that the current accounting for those fees not be changed until that task force completes its study and the resulting recommendations are sent to the FASB for consideration. Based on those respondents' comments, the Board concluded that the provisions of this Statement relating to fees on loans not held for sale (paragraphs 25 and 26) should be revised to conform more closely to the existing recommendations in SOP 76-2 (that is, commitment fees should be recognized as revenue over the combined commitment and loan periods regardless of whether the commitment is fixed or floating rate).

47. Several respondents suggested that this Statement address the accounting and reporting of certain transactions that are not covered by SOPs 74-12 and 76-2. Those respondents recommended that the Board (a) specify the accounting for interest rate futures contracts and forward commitments to purchase or sell mortgage loans and (b) address the issue of whether the issuance of a mortgage-backed security collateralized by the issuer's own loans should be reported as a sale of the mortage loans or as a borrowing. The Board notes that it currently has other projects in which those and related issues are being considered. For that reason and because the issues are not unique to mortgage banking enterprises, the Board decided not to adopt the suggestions.

48. Several respondents suggested various substantive changes to the Exposure Draft. Adoption of those suggestions would have required reconsideration of some of the provisions of SOPs 74-12 and 76-2. Those suggestions were not adopted because such a reconsideration is beyond the scope of extracting the specialized principles from the SOPs and because none of the changes was broadly supported. However, based on suggestions from respondents to the Exposure Draft, the Board has made several other changes that it believes clarify the Statement.

49. The Board has concluded that it can reach an informed decision on the basis of existing information without a public hearing and that the effective date and transition specified in paragraphs 32 and 33 are advisable in the circumstances.

Statement of Financial Accounting Standards No. 66 Accounting for Sales of Real Estate

STATUS

Issued: October 1982

Effective Date: For real estate sales transactions entered into after December 31, 1982

Affects: Amends FAS 26, paragraph 7
Amends FAS 28, paragraphs 3 and 23 through 25 and footnote *
Amends FAS 32, Appendix A

Affected by: No other pronouncements

SUMMARY

This Statement establishes accounting standards for recognizing profit or loss on sales of real estate. It adopts the specialized profit recognition principles in the AICPA Industry Accounting Guides, *Accounting for Profit Recognition on Sales of Real Estate* and *Accounting for Retail Land Sales;* and AICPA Statements of Position 75-6, *Questions Concerning Profit Recognition on Sales of Real Estate,* and 78-4, *Application of the Deposit, Installment, and Cost Recovery Methods in Accounting for Sales of Real Estate.*

For retail land sales, this Statement requires that the seller's receivables from the land sales be collectible and that the seller have no significant remaining obligations for construction or development before profits are recognized by the full accrual method. Other sales in retail land sales projects are to be reported under either the percentage-of-completion or the installment method, for which the Statement establishes criteria based on the collectibility of the seller's receivables from the land sales and the seller's remaining obligations.

For other sales of real estate, this Statement provides for profit recognition by the full accrual and several other methods, depending on whether a sale has been consummated, the extent of the buyer's investment in the property being sold, whether the seller's receivable is subject to future subordination, and the degree of the seller's continuing involvement with the property after the sale. Paragraphs 3-5 set forth the general requirements for recognition of all the profit at the date of sale. Paragraphs 6-18 elaborate on those general rules. Paragraphs 19-43 provide more detailed guidance for a variety of more complicated circumstances if the criteria for immediate profit recognition are not met.

* * *

Certain provisions of this Statement that relate to accounting for sales of real estate are summarized in decision trees that appear on pages 1793-97.

Statement of Financial Accounting Standards No. 66
Accounting for Sales of Real Estate

CONTENTS

INTRODUCTION

1. This Statement establishes standards for recognition of profit on all real estate sales transactions without regard to the nature of the seller's business. The Statement distinguishes between retail land sales and other sales of real estate because differences in terms of sales and selling procedures lead to different profit recognition criteria and methods. Accounting for real estate sales transactions that are not retail land sales is specified in paragraphs 3-43. Accounting for retail land sales transactions is specified in paragraphs 44-50. This Statement does not cover exchanges of real estate for other real estate, the accounting for which is covered in APB Opinion No. 29, *Accounting for Nonmonetary Transactions.*

2. Although this Statement applies to all sales of real estate, many of the extensive provisions were developed over several years to deal with complex transactions that are frequently encountered in enterprises that specialize in real estate transactions. The decision trees on pages 1793-97 highlight the major provisions of the Statement and will help a user of the Statement identify criteria that determine when and how profit is recognized. Those using this Statement to determine the accounting for relatively simple real estate sales transactions will need to apply only limited portions of the Statement. The general requirements for recognizing all of the profit on a nonretail land sale at the date of sale are set forth in paragraphs 3-5 and are highlighted on the decision tree on page 1793. Paragraphs 6-18 elaborate on those general provisions. Paragraphs 19-43 provide more detailed guidance for a variety of more complex transactions.

STANDARDS OF FINANCIAL ACCOUNTING AND REPORTING

Real Estate Sales Other Than Retail Land Sales

Recognition of Profit by the Full Accrual Method

3. Profit shall be recognized in full when real estate is sold, provided (a) the profit is determinable, that is, the collectibility of the sales price is reasonably assured or the amount that will not be collectible can be estimated, and (b) the earnings process is virtually complete, that is, the seller is not obliged to perform significant activities after the sale to earn the profit. Unless both conditions exist, recognition of all or part of the profit shall be postponed. Recognition of all of the profit at the time of sale or at some later date when both conditions exist is referred to as the *full accrual method* in this Statement.

4. In accounting for sales of real estate, collectibility of the sales price is demonstrated by the buyer's commitment to pay, which in turn is supported by substantial initial and continuing investments that give the buyer a stake in the property sufficient that the risk of loss through default motivates the buyer to honor its obligation to the seller. Collectibility shall also be assessed by considering factors such as the credit standing of the buyer, age and location of the property, and adequacy of cash flow from the property.

5. Profit on real estate sales transactions[1] shall not be recognized by the full accrual method until all of the following criteria are met:

a. A sale is consummated (paragraph 6).
b. The buyer's initial and continuing investments are adequate to demonstrate a commitment to pay for the property (paragraphs 8-16).
c. The seller's receivable is not subject to future subordination (paragraph 17).
d. The seller has transferred to the buyer the usual risks and rewards of ownership in a transaction that is in substance a sale and does not have a substantial continuing involvement with the property (paragraph 18).

Paragraphs 19-43 describe appropriate accounting if the above criteria are not met.

Consummation of a Sale

6. A sale shall not be considered consummated until (a) the parties are bound by the terms of a contract, (b) all consideration has been exchanged, (c) any permanent financing for which the seller is responsible has been arranged, and (d) all conditions[2] precedent to closing have been performed. Usually, those four conditions are met at the time of closing or after closing, not when an agreement to sell is signed or at a preclosing.

Buyer's Initial and Continuing Investment

7. "Sales value" shall be determined by:

a. Adding to the stated sales price the proceeds from the issuance of a real estate option that is exercised and other payments that are in substance additional sales proceeds. These nominally may be management fees, points, or prepaid interest or fees that are required to be maintained in an advance status and applied against the amounts due to the seller at a later date.
b. Subtracting from the sale price a discount to reduce the receivable to its present value and by the net present value of services that the seller commits to perform without compensation or by the net present value of the services in excess of the compensation that will be received. Paragraph 31 specifies appropriate accounting if services are to be provided by the seller without compensation or at less than prevailing rates.

8. Adequacy of a buyer's initial investment shall be measured by (a) its composition (paragraphs 9-10) and (b) its size compared with the sales value of the property (paragraph 11).

9. The buyer's initial investment shall include only: (a) cash paid as a down payment, (b) the buyer's notes supported by irrevocable letters of credit from an independent established lending institution,[3] (c) payments by the buyer to third parties to reduce existing indebtedness on the property, and (d) other amounts paid by the buyer that are part of the sales value. Other consideration received by the seller, including other notes of the buyer, shall be included as part of the buyer's initial investment only when that consideration is sold or otherwise converted to cash without recourse to the seller.

10. The initial investment shall not include:

a. Payments by the buyer to third parties for improvements to the property
b. A permanent loan commitment by an independent third party to replace a loan made by the seller
c. Any funds that have been or will be loaned, refunded, or directly or indirectly provided to the buyer by the seller or loans guaranteed or collateralized by the seller for the buyer[4]

11. The buyer's initial investment shall be adequate to demonstrate the buyer's commitment to pay for the property and shall indicate a reasonable likelihood that the seller will collect the receivable. Lending practices of independent established lending institutions provide a reasonable basis for assessing the collectibility of receivables from buyers of real estate. Therefore, to qualify, the initial investment shall be equal to at least a major part of the difference between usual loan limits and the sales value of the property. Guidance on minimum initial investments in various types of real estate is provided in paragraphs 53 and 54.

12. The buyer's continuing investment in a real estate transaction shall not qualify unless the buyer is contractually required to pay each year on its total debt for the purchase price of the property an amount at least equal to the level annual payment that would be needed to pay that debt and interest on the unpaid balance over no more than (a) 20 years for debt for land and (b) the customary amortization term of a first mortgage loan by an indepen-

---

[1]Profit on a sale of a partial interest in real estate shall be subject to the same criteria for profit recognition as a sale of a whole interest.

[2]Paragraph 20 provides an exception to this requirement if the seller is constructing office buildings, condominiums, shopping centers, or similar structures.

[3]An "independent established lending institution" is an unrelated institution such as a commercial bank unaffiliated with the seller.

[4]As an example, if unimproved land is sold for $100,000, with a down payment of $50,000 in cash, and the seller plans to loan the buyer $35,000 at some future date, the initial investment is $50,000 minus $35,000, or $15,000.

dent established lending institution for other real estate. For this purpose, contractually required payments by the buyer on its debt shall be in the forms specified in paragraph 9 as acceptable for an initial investment. Except as indicated in the following sentence, funds to be provided directly or indirectly by the seller (paragraph 10(c)) shall be subtracted from the buyer's contractually required payments in determining whether the initial and continuing investments are adequate. If a future loan on normal terms from an established lending institution bears a fair market interest rate and the proceeds of the loan are conditional on use for specified development of or construction on the property, the loan need not be subtracted in determining the buyer's investment.

Release Provisions

13. An agreement to sell property (usually land) may provide that part or all of the property may be released from liens securing related debt by payment of a release price or that payments by the buyer may be assigned first to released property. If either of those conditions is present, a buyer's initial investment shall be sufficient both to pay release prices on property released at the date of sale and to constitute an adequate initial investment on property not released or not subject to release at that time in order to meet the criterion of an adequate initial investment for the property as a whole.

14. If the release conditions described in paragraph 13 are present, the buyer's investment shall be sufficient, after the released property is paid for, to constitute an adequate continuing investment on property not released in order to meet the criterion of an adequate continuing investment for the property as a whole (paragraph 12).

15. If the amounts applied to unreleased portions do not meet the initial and continuing-investment criteria as applied to the sales value of those unreleased portions, profit shall be recognized on each released portion when it meets the criteria in paragraph 5 as if each release were a separate sale.

16. Tests of adequacy of a buyer's initial and continuing investments described in paragraphs 8-15 shall be applied cumulatively when the sale is consummated and annually afterward. If the initial investment exceeds the minimum prescribed, the excess shall be applied toward the required annual increases in the buyer's investment.

Future Subordination

17. The seller's receivable shall not be subject to future subordination. This restriction shall not apply if (a) a receivable is subordinate to a first mortgage on the property existing at the time of sale or (b) a future loan, including an existing permanent loan commitment, is provided for by the terms of the sale and the proceeds of the loan will be applied first to the payment of the seller's receivable.

Continuing Involvement without Transfer of Risks and Rewards

18. If a seller is involved with a property after it is sold in any way that results in retention of substantial risks or rewards of ownership, except as indicated in paragraph 43, the absence-of-continuing-involvement criterion has not been met. Forms of involvement that result in retention of substantial risks or rewards by the seller, and accounting therefor, are described in paragraphs 25-42.

Recognition of Profit When the Full Accrual Method Is Not Appropriate

19. If a real estate sales transaction does not satisfy the criteria in paragraphs 3-18 for recognition of profit by the full accrual method, the transaction shall be accounted for as specified in the following paragraphs.

Sale Not Consummated

20. The deposit method of accounting described in paragraphs 65-67 shall be used until a sale has been consummated (paragraph 6). "Consummation" usually requires that all conditions precedent to closing have been performed, including that the building be certified for occupancy. However, because of the length of the construction period of office buildings, apartments, condominiums, shopping centers, and similar structures, such sales and the related income may be recognized during the process of construction, subject to the criteria in paragraphs 41 and 42, even though a certificate of occupancy, which is a condition precedent to closing, has not been obtained.

21. If the net carrying amount of the property exceeds the sum of the deposit received, the fair value of the unrecorded note receivable, and the debt assumed by the buyer, the seller shall recognize the loss at the date the agreement to sell is signed.[5] If a buyer defaults, or if circumstances after the transaction indicate that it is probable the buyer will default and the property will revert to the seller, the seller shall evaluate whether the circumstances indicate a decline in the value of the property for which an allowance for loss should be provided.

[5]Paragraph 24 of FASB Statement No. 67, *Accounting for Costs and Initial Rental Operations of Real Estate Projects,* specifies the accounting for an excess of costs over net realizable value for property that has not yet been sold.

Initial or Continuing Investments Do Not Qualify

22. If the buyer's initial investment does not meet the criteria specified in paragraphs 8-11 for recognition of profit by the full accrual method and if recovery of the cost of the property is reasonably assured if the buyer defaults, the installment method described in paragraphs 56-61 shall be used. If recovery of the cost of the property is not reasonably assured if the buyer defaults or if cost has already been recovered and collection of additional amounts is uncertain, the cost recovery method (described in paragraphs 62-64) or the deposit method (described in paragraphs 65-67) shall be used. The cost recovery method may be used to account for sales of real estate for which the installment method would be appropriate.

23. If the initial investment meets the criteria in paragraphs 8-11 but the continuing investment by the buyer does *not* meet the criteria in paragraphs 12 and 16, the seller shall recognize profit by the reduced profit method described in paragraphs 68 and 69 at the time of sale if payments by the buyer each year will at least cover both of the following:

a. The interest and principal amortization on the maximum first mortgage loan that could be obtained on the property
b. Interest, at an appropriate rate,[6] on the excess of the aggregate actual debt on the property over such a maximum first mortgage loan

If the criteria specified in this paragraph for use of the reduced profit method are not met, the seller may recognize profit by the installment method (paragraphs 56-61) or the cost recovery method (paragraphs 62-64).

Receivable Subject to Future Subordination

24. If the seller's receivable is subject to future subordination as described in paragraph 17, profit shall be recognized by the cost recovery method (paragraphs 62-64).

Continuing Involvement without Transfer of Risks and Rewards

25. If the seller has some continuing involvement with the property and does not transfer substantially all of the risks and rewards of ownership, profit shall be recognized by a method determined by the nature and extent of the seller's continuing involvement. Generally, profit shall be recognized at the time of sale if the amount of the seller's loss of profit because of continued involvement with the property is limited by the terms of the sales contract. The profit recognized shall be reduced by the maximum exposure to loss. Paragraphs 26-43 describe some common forms of continuing involvement and specify appropriate accounting if those forms of involvement are present. If the seller has some other form of continuing involvement with the property, the transaction shall be accounted for according to the nature of the involvement.

26. *The seller has an obligation to repurchase the property, or the terms of the transaction allow the buyer to compel the seller or give an option*[7] *to the seller to repurchase the property.* The transaction shall be accounted for as a financing, leasing, or profit-sharing arrangement rather than as a sale.

27. *The seller is a general partner in a limited partnership that acquires an interest in the property sold (or has an extended, noncancelable management contract requiring similar obligations) and holds a receivable from the buyer for a significant*[8] *part of the sales price.* The transaction shall be accounted for as a financing, leasing, or profit-sharing arrangement.

28. *The seller guarantees*[9] *the return of the buyer's investment or a return on that investment for a limited or extended period.* For example, the seller guarantees cash flows, subsidies, or net tax benefits. If the seller guarantees return of the buyer's investment or if the seller guarantees a return on the investment for an extended period, the transaction shall be accounted for as a financing, leasing, or

---

[6]Paragraphs 13 and 14 of APB Opinion No. 21, *Interest on Receivables and Payables,* provide criteria for selecting an appropriate rate for present-value calculations.

[7]A right of first refusal based on a bona fide offer by a third party ordinarily is not an obligation or an option to repurchase.

[8]For this purpose, a significant receivable is a receivable in excess of 15 percent of the maximum first-lien financing that could be obtained from an independent established lending institution for the property. It would include:

a. A construction loan made or to be made by the seller to the extent that it exceeds the minimum funding commitment for permanent financing from a third party that the seller will not be liable for
b. An all-inclusive or wraparound receivable held by the seller to the extent that it exceeds prior-lien financing for which the seller has no personal liability
c. Other funds provided or to be provided directly or indirectly by the seller to the buyer
d. The present value of a land lease when the seller is the lessor (footnote 15)

[9]Guarantees by the seller may be limited to a specified period of time.

profit-sharing arrangement. If the guarantee of a return on the investment is for a limited period, the deposit method shall be used until operations of the property cover all operating expenses, debt service, and contractual payments. At that time, profit shall be recognized on the basis of performance of the services required, as illustrated in paragraphs 84-88.

29. *The seller is required to initiate or support operations or continue to operate the property at its own risk, or may be presumed to have such a risk, for an extended period, for a specified limited period, or until a specified level of operations has been obtained, for example, until rentals of a property are sufficient to cover operating expenses and debt service.* If support is required or presumed to be required[10] for an *extended* period of time, the transaction shall be accounted for as a financing, leasing, or profit-sharing arrangement. If support is required or presumed to be required for a *limited* time, profit on the sale shall be recognized on the basis of performance of the services required. Performance of those services shall be measured by the costs incurred and to be incurred over the period during which the services are performed. Profit shall begin to be recognized when there is reasonable assurance that future rent receipts will cover operating expenses and debt service including payments due the seller under the terms of the transaction. Reasonable assurance that rentals will be adequate would be indicated by objective information regarding occupancy levels and rental rates in the immediate area. In assessing whether rentals will be adequate to justify recognition of profit, total estimated future rent receipts of the property shall be reduced by one-third as a reasonable safety factor unless the amount so computed is less than the rents to be received from signed leases. In this event, the rents from signed leases shall be substituted for the computed amount. Application of this method is illustrated in paragraphs 84-89.

30. If the sales contract does not stipulate the period during which the seller is obligated to support operations of the property, support shall be presumed for at least two years from the time of initial rental unless actual rental operations cover operating expenses, debt service, and other contractual commitments before that time. If the seller is contractually obligated for a longer time, profit recognition shall continue on the basis of performance until the obligation expires. Calculation of profits on the basis of performance of services is illustrated in paragraphs 84-89.

31. If the sales contract requires the seller to provide management services relating to the property after the sale without compensation or at compensation less than prevailing rates for the service required (paragraph 7) or on terms not usual for the services to be rendered (footnote 10(d)), compensation shall be imputed when the sale is recognized and shall be recognized in income as the services are performed over the term of the management contract.

32. *The transaction is merely an option to purchase the property.* For example, undeveloped land may be "sold" under terms that call for a very small initial investment by the buyer (substantially less than the percentages specified in paragraph 54) and postponement of additional payments until the buyer obtains zoning changes or building permits or other contingencies specified in the sales agreement are satisfactorily resolved. Proceeds from the issuance of the option by a property owner shall be accounted for as a deposit (paragraphs 65-67). Profit shall not be recognized until the option either expires or is exercised. When an option to purchase real estate is sold by an option holder,[11] the seller of the option shall recognize income by the cost recovery method (paragraphs 62-64) to the extent nonrefundable cash proceeds exceed the seller's cost of the option if the buyer's initial and continuing investments are not adequate for profit recognition by the full accrual method (paragraphs 7-16).

33. *The seller has made a partial sale.* A sale is a partial sale if the seller retains an equity interest in the property or has an equity interest in the buyer. Profit (the difference between the sales value and the proportionate cost of the partial interest sold) shall be recognized at the date of sale if:

a. The buyer is independent of the seller.
b. Collection of the sales price is reasonably assured (paragraph 4).
c. The seller will not be required to support the operations of the property or its related obligations to an extent greater than its proportionate interest.

---

[10]Support shall be presumed to be required if: (a) a seller obtains an interest as a general partner in a limited partnership that acquires an interest in the property sold; (b) a seller retains an equity interest in the property, such as an undivided interest or an equity interest in a joint venture that holds an interest in the property; (c) a seller holds a receivable from a buyer for a significant part of the sales price and collection of the receivable depends on the operation of the property; or (d) a seller agrees to manage the property for the buyer on terms not usual for the services to be rendered, and the agreement is not terminable by either the seller or the buyer.

[11]When an option to purchase real estate is sold by an option holder, the sales value includes the exercise price of the option and the sales price of the option. For example, if the option is sold for $150,000 ($50,000 cash and a $100,000 note) and the exercise price is $500,000, the sales value is $650,000.

34. If the buyer is not independent of the seller, for example, if the seller holds or acquires an equity interest in the buyer, the seller shall recognize the part of the profit proportionate to the outside interests in the buyer at the date of sale. If the seller controls the buyer, no profit on the sale shall be recognized until it is realized from transactions with outside parties through sale or operations of the property.

35. If collection of the sales price is not reasonably assured, the cost recovery or installment method of recognizing profit shall be used.

36. If the seller is required to support the operations of the property after the sale, the accounting shall be based on the nature of the support obligation. For example, the seller may retain an interest in the property sold and the buyer may receive preferences as to profits, cash flows, return on investment, and so forth. If the transaction is in substance a sale, the seller shall recognize profit to the extent that proceeds from the sale, including receivables from the buyer, exceed all of the seller's costs related to the entire property. Other examples of support obligations are described in paragraphs 29-31.

37. If individual units in condominium projects[12] or time-sharing interests are being sold separately and all the following criteria are met, profit shall be recognized by the percentage-of-completion method on the sale of individual units or interests:

a. Construction is beyond a preliminary stage.[13]
b. The buyer is committed to the extent of being unable to require a refund except for nondelivery of the unit or interest.[14]
c. Sufficient units have already been sold to assure that the entire property will not revert to rental property. In determining whether this condition has been met, the seller shall consider the requirements of state laws, the condominium or time-sharing contract, and the terms of the financing agreements.
d. Sales prices are collectible (paragraph 4).
e. Aggregate sales proceeds and costs can be reasonably estimated. Consideration shall be given to sales volume, trends of unit prices, demand for the units including seasonal factors, developer's experience, geographical location, and environmental factors.

If any of the above criteria is not met, proceeds shall be accounted for as deposits until the criteria are met.

38. *The seller sells property improvements and leases the underlying land to the buyer of the improvements.* In these circumstances, the transactions are interdependent and it is impracticable to distinguish between profits on the sale of the improvements and profits under the related lease. The transaction shall be accounted for as a lease of both the land and improvements if the term of the land lease to the buyer from the seller of the improvements either (a) does not cover substantially all of the economic life of the property improvements, thus strongly implying that the transaction is in substance a lease of both land and improvements, or (b) is not for a substantial period, for example, 20 years.

39. If the land lease described in paragraph 38 covers substantially all of the economic life of the improvements and extends for at least 20 years, the profit to be recognized on the sale of the improvements at the time of sale shall be (a) the present value of the rental payments[15] not in excess of the

[12]A condominium project may be a building, a group of buildings, or a complete project.

[13]Construction is not beyond a preliminary stage if engineering and design work, execution of construction contracts, site clearance and preparation, excavation, and completion of the building foundation are incomplete.

[14]The buyer may be able to require a refund, for example, if a minimum status of completion of the project is required by state law and that status has not been attained; if state law requires that a "Declaration of Condominium" be filed and it has not been filed, except that in some states the filing of the declaration is a routine matter and the lack of such filing may not make the sales contract voidable; if the sales contract provides that permanent financing at an acceptable cost must be available to the buyer at the time of closing and it is not available; or if the condominium units must be registered with either the Office of Interstate Land Sales Registration of the Department of Housing and Urban Development or the Securities and Exchange Commission, and they are not so registered.

[15]The present value of the specified rental payments is the present value of the lease payments specified in the lease over the term of the primary indebtedness, if any, on the improvements, or over the customary amortization term of primary debt instruments on the type of improvements involved. The present value is computed at an interest rate appropriate for (a) primary debt if the lease is not subordinated or (b) secondary debt if the lease is subordinated to loans with prior liens.

seller's cost of the land plus (b) the sales value of the improvements minus (c) the carrying value of the improvements and the land. Profit on (1) the buyer's rental payments on the land in excess of the seller's cost of the land and (2) the rent to be received on the land after the maturity of the primary indebtedness on the improvements or other customary amortization term shall be recognized when the land is sold or the rents in excess of the seller's cost of the land are accrued under the lease. Calculations of profit in those circumstances are illustrated in paragraphs 82 and 83.

40. *The sale of the property is accompanied by a leaseback to the seller of all or any part of the property for all or part of its remaining economic life.* Real estate sale and leaseback transactions shall be accounted for in accordance with the provisions of this Statement and FASB Statements No. 13, *Accounting for Leases,* and 28, *Accounting for Sales with Leasebacks.* Statement 13 as amended by Statement 28 provides criteria for determining if a leaseback is a capital lease or an operating lease. If the leaseback is a capital lease, the seller-lessee shall record an asset and an obligation as prescribed by Statement 13. Regardless of whether the leaseback is a capital lease or an operating lease, a sale shall be recorded, and the property sold and any related debt assumed by the buyer shall be removed from the seller-lessee's balance sheet. The criteria in this Statement then shall be used to determine the amount of profit that would be recognized at the date of sale, absent the leaseback provisions. The profit so determined shall be accounted for in accordance with the provisions of Statements 13 and 28 (usually deferred and amortized over the term of the lease) unless other provisions of this Statement require postponement of profit recognition until a later event.

41. *The sales contract or an accompanying agreement requires the seller to develop the property in the future, to construct facilities on the land, or to provide off-site improvements or amenities.* The seller is involved with future development or construction work if the buyer is unable to pay amounts due for that work or has the right under the terms of the arrangement to defer payment until the work is done. If future costs of development can be reasonably estimated at the time of sale, profit allocable to (a) performance before the sale of the land and (b) the sale of the land shall be recognized when the sale of the land meets the criteria in paragraph 5. Profit allocable to performance after the sale shall be recognized by the percentage-of-completion method as development and construction proceed, provided that cost and profit can be reasonably estimated from the seller's previous experience.

42. The profit shall be allocated to the sale of the land and the later development or construction work on the basis of estimated costs of each activity; the same rate of profit shall be attributed to each activity. No profit shall be recognized at the time of sale if future costs of development cannot be reasonably estimated at that time.

43. *The seller will participate in future profit from the property without risk of loss (such as participation in operating profits or residual values without further obligation).* If the transaction otherwise qualifies for recognition of profit by the full accrual method, the transfer of risks and rewards of ownership and absence of continuing involvement criterion shall be considered met. The contingent future profits shall be recognized when they are realized.[16] All the costs of the sale shall be recognized at the time of sale; none shall be deferred to periods when the contingent profits are recognized.

Retail Land Sales

44. A single method of recognizing profit shall be applied to all sales transactions within a project[17] that have been consummated.[18] That method of recognizing profit shall be changed when certain conditions are met for the entire project (paragraph 49).

Recognition of Profit

45. The full accrual method of accounting described in paragraphs 70-72 shall be applied to a sale if *all* of the following conditions are met:

a. *Expiration of refund period.* The buyer has made the down payment and each required subsequent payment until the period of cancellation with refund has expired. That period shall be the longest period of those required by local law, established by the seller's policy, or specified in the contract.
b. *Sufficient cumulative payments.* The cumulative payments of principal and interest equal or exceed 10 percent of the contract sales price.
c. *Collectibility of receivables.* Collection experience for the project in which the sale is made or for the seller's prior projects indicates that at least 90 percent of the contracts in the project in which the sale is made that are in force 6 months after the criteria in paragraph 46 are met will be

[16]Paragraph 17 of FASB Statement No. 5, *Accounting for Contingencies,* addresses accounting for gain contingencies.

[17]A retail land sales "project" is a homogeneous, reasonably contiguous area of land that may, for development and marketing, be subdivided in accordance with a master plan.

[18]Retail land sales shall be considered consummated when all of the criteria in paragraph 47 are met.

collected in full.[19] The collection experience with the seller's prior projects may be applied to a new project if the prior projects:

(1) Had predominantly the same characteristics (type of land, environment, clientele, contract terms, sales methods)[20] as the new project.

(2) Had a sufficiently long collection period to indicate the percentage of current sales of the new project that will be collected to maturity.

A down payment of at least 20 percent shall be an acceptable indication of collectibility.

d. *Nonsubordination of receivables.* The receivable from the sale is not subject to subordination to new loans on the property except that subordination by an individual lot buyer for home construction purposes is permissible if the collection experience on those contracts is the same as on contracts not subordinated.

e. *Completion of development.* The seller is not obligated to complete improvements of lots sold or to construct amenities or other facilities applicable to lots sold. In addition, there shall be no indication of significant delaying factors, such as the inability to obtain permits, contractors, personnel, or equipment, and estimates of costs to complete and extent of progress toward completion shall be reasonably dependable.

f. *Development is practical.* There is a reasonable expectation that the land can be developed for the purposes represented and the properties will be useful for those purposes at the end of the normal payment period. For example, it should be expected that legal restrictions, including environmental restrictions, will not seriously hamper development and that improvements such as access roads, water supply, and sewage treatment or removal are feasible within a reasonable time.

Paragraphs 46-49 specify accounting methods that shall be used if the above criteria are not met.

46. The percentage-of-completion method of accounting[21] described in paragraphs 73-75 shall be applied to a sale that meets all of the following criteria:

a. *The period of cancellation with refund has expired* (paragraph 45(a)).
b. *Cumulative payments equal or exceed 10 percent* (paragraph 45(b)).
c. *Receivables are collectible* (paragraph 45(c)).
d. *Receivables are not subject to subordination* (paragraph 45(d)).
e. *There has been progress on improvements.* The project's improvements have progressed beyond preliminary stages, and there are indications that the work will be completed according to plan. Some indications of progress are:
   (1) The expenditure of funds on the proposed improvements.
   (2) Initiation of work on the improvements.
   (3) Existence of engineering plans and work commitments relating to lots sold.
   (4) Completion of access roads and amenities such as golf courses, clubs, and swimming pools.

Paragraphs 47 and 48 specify accounting methods that shall be used if the above criteria are not met.

47. The installment method of accounting described in paragraphs 56-61 shall be applied to a sale that meets all of the following criteria:

a. *The period of cancellation with refund has expired* (paragraph 45(a)).
b. *Cumulative payments equal or exceed 10 percent* (paragraph 45(b)).
c. *The seller is financially capable.* The seller is clearly capable of providing both land improvements and off-site facilities promised in the contract and of meeting all other representations it has made. It is financially capable of funding or bonding the planned improvements in the project when required. That capability may be indicated by the seller's equity capitalization, its borrowing capacity, or its positive cash flow from operations.

48. If a retail land sale transaction does not meet the criteria for accounting by the methods described in paragraphs 45-47, that transaction shall be accounted for as a deposit as described in paragraphs 65-67.

Change from Installment to Percentage-of-Completion Method

49. When all of the conditions in paragraph 46 are satisfied on a retail land sales project originally reported by the installment method, the percentage-

[19]The six-month period is solely a test of eligibility for the accrual method and is not intended to restrict the recognition of profit before the six-month period expires.

[20]Examples of sales methods include telephone sales, broker sales, and site-visitation sales.

[21]In the AICPA Guide, *Accounting for Retail Land Sales,* this was called the "accrual method."

of-completion method of accounting may be adopted for the entire project (current and prior sales) and the effect accounted for as a change in accounting estimate.[22]

Financial Statement Presentation and Disclosures

50. In addition to disclosures otherwise required by generally accepted accounting principles, the financial statements of enterprises with retail land sales operations shall disclose:

a. Maturities of accounts receivable for each of the five years following the date of the financial statements
b. Delinquent accounts receivable and the method(s) for determining delinquency
c. The weighted average and range of stated interest rates of receivables
d. Estimated total costs and estimated dates of expenditures for improvements for major areas from which sales are being made over each of the five years following the date of the financial statements
e. Recorded obligations for improvements

Financial statement presentations of retail land sales transactions are illustrated in paragraphs 95-97.

Amendments to Other Pronouncements

51. The references to the AICPA Industry Accounting Guides, *Accounting for Profit Recognition on Sales of Real Estate* and *Accounting for Retail Land Sales,* and the AICPA Statements of Position (SOPs) 75-6, *Questions Concerning Profit Recognition on Sales of Real Estate* and 78-4, *Application of the Deposit, Installment, and Cost Recovery Methods in Accounting for Sales of Real Estate,* are deleted from Appendix A of FASB Statement No. 32, *Specialized Accounting and Reporting Principles and Practices in AICPA Statements of Position and Guides on Accounting and Auditing Matters.* The references to the profit recognition Guide in paragraph 7 of FASB Statement No. 26, *Profit Recognition on Sales-Type Leases of Real Estate,* and in footnote "*" and paragraphs 23-25 of Statement 28 are amended to refer to Statement No. 66, *Accounting for Sales of Real Estate.*

Effective Date and Transition

52. This Statement shall be applied to real estate sales transactions entered into after December 31, 1982 and to changes in methods of accounting for real estate sales transactions made after that date. Earlier application is encouraged but not required. The disclosures required by paragraph 50 shall be provided in financial statements for periods ending after December 15, 1982.

The provisions of this Statement need not be applied to immaterial items.

This Statement was adopted by the affirmative votes of five members of the Financial Accounting Standards Board. Messrs. Morgan and Walters dissented.

Mr. Morgan dissents to the issuance of this Statement. Although he recognizes the Board's commitment to extract specialized principles and practices from SOPs and Guides and to issue them as FASB Statements, as stated in paragraph 2 of Statement 32, and the fact that issuance of this Statement is considered by a majority of Board members to be a fulfillment of part of that commitment, Mr. Morgan believes this Statement should be deferred until certain other projects are completed.

Incorporation of these detailed guidelines into accounting standards is inappropriate at this time in view of three projects in process that should bear on the nature and effect of accounting standards in this area:

a. The Board's conceptual framework project on accounting recognition, which should establish a basic framework for all revenue recognition
b. The Board's project on financial reporting by private and small public companies
c. The August 1982 report of the Financial Accounting Foundation's Structure Committee, which acknowledges the comments of many respondents that the Board should deal primarily with broad accounting standards issues and charges the Board to develop a plan, for consideration by the Trustees, to provide timely *guidance* for implementation questions and emerging issues

Mr. Morgan believes that no urgent need for an FASB Statement on this subject has been demonstrated. Accordingly, he believes it more prudent to complete the broader, more general projects before further considering whether this Statement is needed.

[22]The credit to income resulting from the change is the profit not yet recognized less (a) a discount, if required, to reduce the receivable balances to their present values at the date of change to the percentage-of-completion method (using the appropriate interest rates, as specified in paragraphs 13 and 14 of Opinion 21, in effect at the time of the original sales) and (b) the liability (also discounted) for remaining future performance. The computation is illustrated in paragraph 97.

Mr. Walters dissents to the issuance of this Statement primarily because he objects to incorporating these complex, rigid, and detailed rules into accounting standards. Entirely aside from the conceptual merit of these rules, which is at least debatable, he believes the Board should focus at about the level expressed in paragraphs 3 and 4 of this Statement. Beyond that, he believes the accounting profession can serve its members by offering more specific *guidance* for applying the standards in particular specialized areas, but such detailed and arbitrary guidelines should not be dignified as accounting standards. To do so debases accounting standards and inevitably will diminish the stature and effectiveness of the accounting profession, whose strength and purpose arise from applying broad accounting and reporting objectives and standards to specific circumstances with professional judgment and objectivity. That judgment is the hallmark of a true profession.

Secondarily, he believes that incorporation of these detailed guidelines into accounting standards is particularly inappropriate at this time for the reasons cited by Mr. Morgan.

Members of the Financial Accounting Standards Board:

Donald J. Kirk, *Chairman*	John W. March	Robert T. Sprouse
Frank E. Block	Robert A. Morgan	Ralph E. Walters
	David Mosso	

Appendix A

MINIMUM INITIAL INVESTMENTS

53. Minimum initial investment requirements for sales, other than retail land sales, that are to be accounted for by the full accrual method are specified in paragraph 11. The table of minimum initial investments in paragraph 54 is based on usual loan limits for various types of properties. However, lenders' appraisals of specific properties may differ. Therefore, if a recently placed permanent loan or firm permanent loan commitment for maximum financing of the property exists with an independent established lending institution, the minimum initial investment should be whichever of the following is greater:

a. The minimum percentage of the sales value (paragraph 7) of the property specified in paragraph 54
b. The lesser of:
   (1) The amount of the sales value of the property in excess of 115 percent of the amount of a newly placed permanent loan or firm permanent loan commitment from a primary lender that is an independent established lending institution
   (2) Twenty-five percent of the sales value

54. This table does not cover every type of real estate property. To evaluate initial investments on other types of property, enterprises may make analogies to the types of properties specified, or the risks of a particular property can be related to the risks of the properties specified. Use of this table is illustrated in paragraphs 77-83.

	Minimum Initial Investment Expressed as a Percentage of Sales Value
Land	
Held for commercial, industrial, or residential development to commence within two years after sale	20
Held for commercial, industrial, or residential development to commence after two years	25
Commercial and Industrial Property	
Office and industrial buildings, shopping centers, and so forth:	
Properties subject to lease on a long-term lease basis to parties with satisfactory credit rating; cash flow currently sufficient to service all indebtedness	10
Single-tenancy properties sold to a buyer with a satisfactory credit rating	15
All other	20
Other income-producing properties (hotels, motels, marinas, mobile home parks, and so forth):	
Cash flow currently sufficient to service all indebtedness	15
Start-up situations or current deficiencies in cash flow	25
Multifamily Residential Property	
Primary residence:	
Cash flow currently sufficient to service all indebtedness	10
Start-up situations or current deficiencies in cash flow	15
Secondary or recreational residence:	
Cash flow currently sufficient to service all indebtedness	15
Start-up situations or current deficiencies in cash flow	25
Single-Family Residential Property (including condominium or cooperative housing)	
Primary residence of the buyer	5[a]
Secondary or recreational residence	10[a]

[a]If collectibility of the remaining portion of the sales price cannot be supported by reliable evidence of collection experience, the minimum initial investment shall be at least 60 percent of the difference between the sales value and the financing available from loans guaranteed by regulatory bodies such as the Federal Housing Authority (FHA) or the Veterans Administration (VA), or from independent, established lending institutions. This 60-percent test applies when independent first-mortgage financing is not utilized and the seller takes a receivable from the buyer for the difference between the sales value and the initial investment. If independent first mortgage financing is utilized, the adequacy of the initial investment on sales of single-family residential property should be determined in accordance with paragraph 53.

Appendix B

DESCRIPTION OF CERTAIN METHODS OF ACCOUNTING FOR REAL ESTATE SALES TRANSACTIONS

55. This appendix describes several of the methods of profit recognition that are provided for by this Statement.

Installment Method

56. The installment method apportions each cash receipt and principal payment by the buyer on debt assumed between cost recovered and profit. The apportionment is in the same ratio as total cost and total profit bear to the sales value. The calculation is illustrated in paragraph 90.

57. If the stated interest rate is equal to or less than an appropriate interest rate, it is acceptable not to reduce the receivable to its present value. This ordinarily results in reducing profit recognized in the earlier years.

58. Under the installment method, the receivable less profits not recognized does not exceed what the property value would have been if the property had not been sold.

59. The income statement, or related footnotes, for the period including the date of sale presents the sales value, the gross profit that has not yet been recognized, and the total cost of the sale. Revenue and cost of sales (or gross profit) are presented as separate items on the income statement or are disclosed in the footnotes when profit is recognized as earned. This presentation is illustrated in paragraph 96.

60. Paragraph 75 describes accounting for obligations for future improvement costs under the percentage-of-completion method. That description applies as well to accounting for those obligations under the installment method.

61. If after adoption of the installment method the transaction meets the requirements for the full accrual method (specified in paragraphs 3-18) of recognizing profit for real estate sales other than retail land sales, the seller may then change to the full accrual method. The remaining profit that was not recognized is recognized in income at that time.

Cost Recovery Method

62. Under the cost recovery method, no profit is recognized until cash payments by the buyer, including principal and interest on debt due to the seller and on existing debt assumed by the buyer, exceed the seller's cost of the property sold.[23] The receivable less profits not recognized, if any, does not exceed what the depreciated property value would have been if the property had not been sold.

63. The income statement for the period including the date of sale presents the sales value, the gross profit that has not yet been recognized, and the total cost of the sale. Gross profit not yet recognized is offset against the related receivable on the balance sheet. Principal collections reduce the related receivable, and interest collections on such receivables increase the unrecognized gross profit on the balance sheet. Gross profit is presented as a separate item of revenue on the income statement when it is recognized as earned.

64. If, after the adoption of the cost recovery method, the transaction meets the requirements for the full accrual method (specified in paragraphs 3-18), the seller may then change to the full accrual method. The remaining profit that was not recognized is recognized in income at that time.

Deposit Method

65. Under the deposit method, the seller does not recognize any profit, does not record notes receivable, continues to report in its financial statements the property and the related existing debt even if it has been assumed by the buyer, and discloses that those items are subject to a sales contract. The seller continues to charge depreciation to expense as a period cost for the property for which deposits have been received. Cash received from the buyer, including the initial investment and subsequent collections of principal and interest, is reported as a deposit on the contract except that, for sales that are not retail land sales, portions of cash received that are designated by the contract as interest and are not subject to refund offset carrying charges (property taxes and interest on existing debt) on the property. Interest collected that is subject to refund and is included in the deposit account before a sale is consummated is accounted for as part of the buyer's initial investment (paragraph 7) at the time the sale is consummated.

66. When a contract is canceled without a refund, deposits forfeited are recognized as income. When deposits on retail land sales are ultimately recognized as sales, the interest portion is recognized as interest income.

67. The seller's balance sheet presents nonrecourse debt assumed by the buyer among the liabilities; the debt assumed is not offset against the related property. The seller reports the buyer's principal payments on mortgage debt assumed as additional deposits with corresponding reductions of the carrying amount of the mortgage debt.

Reduced-Profit Method

68. A reduced profit is determined by discounting the receivable from the buyer to the present value of the lowest level of annual payments required by the sales contract over the maximum period specified in paragraph 12 and excluding requirements to pay lump sums. The present value is calculated using an appropriate interest rate,[24] but not less than the rate stated in the sales contract. This method permits profit to be recognized from level payments on the buyer's debt over the maximum term established in paragraph 12 and postpones recognition of other profits until lump sum or other payments are made.

69. To illustrate, assume a sale of land that cost the seller $800,000 and is being sold for $1,000,000 with the following financing:

Buyer's initial investment	$ 250,000
First mortgage note payable to an independent lending institution (Terms—15 percent interest payable annually over 20 years: $79,881 per year including principal and interest)	500,000
Second mortgage note payable to seller (Terms—12 percent interest payable annually over 25 years: $31,875 per year including principal and interest)	250,000
Total selling price	$1,000,000

The amortization term of the second mortgage (25 years) exceeds the term permitted by paragraph 12 (20 years for sales of land). It is assumed that the payments by the buyer each year will meet the requirement in paragraph 23, that the reduced-profit method is to be applied, and that the market interest rate is 16 percent.

[23]For an all-inclusive or "wrap-around" receivable held by the seller, interest collected is recognized as income to the extent of, and as an appropriate offset to, interest expense on prior-lien financing for which the seller remains responsible.

[24]Paragraphs 13 and 14 of Opinion 21 provide criteria for selecting an appropriate rate for present-value calculations.

The present value of $31,875 per year for 20 years at a market rate of 16 percent is $31,875 × 5.92884 = $188,982.

The profit to be recognized at the time of sale is reduced by the difference between the face amount of the seller's receivable ($250,000) and the reduced amount ($188,982), or $61,018. The profit recognized at the time of sale is $1,000,000 (sales price) minus $800,000 (cost) minus $61,018, or $138,982. Additional profit of $61,018 is recognized as the second mortgage payments are received in years 21 through 25.

Full Accrual Method—Retail Land Sales

70. Revenues and costs are accounted for under the accrual method as follows:

a. The net receivable is discounted to the present value of the payments required. The present value is determined using an appropriate interest rate,[25] not less than the rate stated in the sales contract. The objective is to value the net receivable at the amount at which it could be sold without recourse to the seller at the date of the sales contract.
b. An allowance is provided for receivables that are not expected to be collected because of cancellation in subsequent periods. Receivable balances applicable to canceled contracts are charged in their entirety to the allowance for contract cancellations when those contracts are canceled.
c. Costs of sales (land and improvement costs incurred, carrying costs, and so forth) are based on sales net of those sales expected to be canceled in future periods.

71. Historical data is evaluated to predict the collection of receivables from current sales. The historical data is selected from a representative sample of receivables that reflect the latest available collection data and cover an adequate period of time. The receivables in the sample are considered uncollectible and the allowance for contract cancellations provided for previously recognized sales (paragraph 70(b)) is appropriately adjusted if payments due are unpaid at the end of the sample period selected for the following delinquency periods:

Percent of Contract Price Paid	Delinquency Period
Less than 25 percent	90 days
25 percent but less than 50 percent	120 days
50 percent and over	150 days

The specified delinquency periods may be extended if the seller's recent experience has been better or if the buyer has accepted, or is willing to accept, personal liability on its debt, provided that the buyer's ability to complete payment on the contract can be determined.

72. Many sellers have programs to accelerate collections of receivables or contract provisions that encourage prepayment with a reduction of the principal as the major incentive for prepayment. If a seller expects to institute those or similar programs in the future, the amount of profit recognized at the date of sale is reduced through charges to income for anticipated discounts not otherwise recognized. Reductions that are given sporadically are charged to income in the period they occur.

Percentage-of-Completion Method—Retail Land Sales

73. The earnings process is not complete if a seller is obliged to complete improvements of lots sold or to construct amenities and other facilities applicable to lots sold, if those obligations are significant in relation to total costs, and if they remain unperformed at the time the sale is recognized. Therefore, the amount of revenue recognized (the discounted contract price) at the time a sale is recognized is measured by the relationship of costs already incurred to total estimated costs to be incurred, including costs of the marketing effort. If performance[26] is incomplete, the portion of revenue related to costs not yet incurred is recognized as the costs are incurred.

74. The costs already incurred and total costs to be incurred include land cost, costs previously charged to expense, such as interest and project carrying costs incurred prior to sale, and selling costs[27] directly associated with a project. The accounting

[25]Paragraphs 13 and 14 of Opinion 21 provide criteria for selecting an appropriate rate for present-value calculations.

[26]*Performance* means completion of the improvements required under the sales contract by either the seller or contractors retained by the seller. However, payments made to municipalities or other governmental organizations not under the direct or joint control of the seller constitute performance by the seller if those organizations are not financed solely by liens on property in the project and they undertake to complete the improvements without further risk or obligation of the seller.

[27]Accounting for selling costs is addressed in FASB Statement No. 67, *Accounting for Costs and Initial Rental Operations of Real Estate Projects.*

described in this paragraph and paragraph 73 is illustrated in paragraphs 91-95.

75. If there is an obligation for future improvement costs that is recognized under the percentage-of-completion method:

a. Estimates are based on costs generally expected in the construction industry locally.
b. Unrecoverable costs of off-site improvements, utilities, and amenities are provided for. In determining the amount of unrecoverable costs, estimates of amounts to be recovered from future sale of the improvements, utilities, and amenities are discounted to present value as of the date the net unrecoverable costs are recognized.

76. Estimates of future improvement costs are reviewed at least annually. Changes in those estimates do not lead to adjustment of revenue applicable to future improvements that has been previously recorded unless the adjusted total estimated cost exceeds the applicable revenue. When cost estimates are revised, the relationship of the two elements included in the revenue not yet recognized—costs and profit—is recalculated on a cumulative basis to determine future income recognition as performance takes place. If the adjusted total estimated cost exceeds the applicable revenue previously recognized, the total anticipated loss is charged to income when it meets the criteria in paragraph 8 of Statement 5. When anticipated losses on lots sold are recognized, the enterprise also considers recognizing a loss on land and improvements not yet sold.

Appendix C

ILLUSTRATIONS OF CALCULATIONS FOR RECOGNITION OF PROFIT ON SALES OF REAL ESTATE OTHER THAN RETAIL LAND SALES[28]

Exhibits

Exhibit I—Illustration of Effect of Land Lease—New Multifamily Residential Property

77. Land improvements may be sold and concurrently the land under the improvements may be leased to the buyer of the improvements.

78. This exhibit illustrates the effect of loans issued in connection with long-term land leases on evaluations of the adequacy of a buyer's initial investment if improvements on the land are sold separately. In addition, it demonstrates the limit that a lease places on profit recognition if the leased land is owned by the seller of the improvements, making the lease of land and sale of improvements interdependent transactions.

79. The calculations are illustrated for four different circumstances: two examples with a primary land lease and two with a subordinated land lease.

[28]The financing and interest rate assumptions in this appendix are based on conditions at the time the profit recognition Guide was issued. They should not be considered as indicative of financing and interest rate assumptions that would be appropriate under different circumstances and at different times.

80. Primary Land Lease: Land Owned by Third Party Lessor—Nonqualifying

Assumptions:

Sales price of improvements	$875,000

Represented by proceeds of:

Cash down payment	$125,000
Loan by insurance company—lien on leasehold improvements, 28-year term, 8 1/2%, payable in equal monthly installments of principal and interest	657,000
Note received by seller from buyer: 12-year term, 9 1/2%, payable in equal monthly installments of principal and interest	93,000
	$875,000

Land lease for 99 years @ $19,000/year, net, payable monthly in advance
Cost of constructing improvements—$750,000
No continuing involvement by seller

Computations:

Present value of 336 monthly payments on land lease of $1,583.33 discounted at 8 1/2% (interest rate on loan from insurance company): $1,583.33 + ($1,583.33 × 127.9071)	$ 204,000
Loan from insurance company	657,000
Equivalent primary debt	861,000
Note receivable from buyer	93,000
Total debt or equivalent	954,000
Down payment	125,000
Sales value	$1,079,000

Because 15% of the sales value of the improvements is $161,850, the initial investment of $125,000 (about 12% of adjusted sales value) is inadequate to recognize profit on the sale of improvements. The second test is therefore irrelevant.

81. Primary Land Lease: Land Owned by Third Party Lessor—Qualifying

Assumptions:

Sales price of improvements	$875,000

Represented by proceeds of:

Cash down payment	$165,000
Loan by insurance company: lien on leasehold improvements, 28-year term, 8 1/2%, payable in equal monthly installments of principal and interest	657,000
Note received by seller from buyer: 12-year term, 9 1/2%, payable in equal monthly installments of principal and interest	53,000
	$875,000

Land lease for 99 years @ $17,880/year, net, payable monthly in advance
Cost of constructing improvements—$750,000
No continuing involvement by seller

Computations:

Present value of 336 monthly payments on land lease of $1,490 discounted at 8 1/2% (interest rate on loan from insurance company): $1,490 + ($1,490 × 127.9071)	$ 192,000
Loan from insurance company	657,000
Equivalent primary debt	849,000
Note receivable from buyer	53,000
Total debt or equivalent	902,000
Down payment	165,000
Sales value	$1,067,000

Because 15% of the sales value of the improvements is $160,050, the initial investment of $165,000 (15% of the sales value) is adequate to recognize profit on the sale of improvements. However, the second test must also be applied.

The initial investment required by the second test is:

Sales value	$1,067,000
115% of $849,000 (loan from primary lender)	976,350
	$ 90,650

The initial investment of $165,000 exceeds the amount required, so recognition of profit on sale of improvements is appropriate. The second test may alternatively be applied as the ratio of total debt or equivalent to the equivalent primary debt: $902,000/$849,000 = 106%. Because 106% is less than 115%, the initial investment exceeds the difference between the sales value of the property and 115% of the equivalent primary debt.

Profit recognition:

Sales price of improvements	$875,000
Less: Cost of improvements	750,000
Profit recognized at time of sale	$125,000

82. Subordinated Land Lease: Land Owned by Seller—Qualifying

Assumptions:

Sales price of improvements	$914,000

Represented by proceeds of:

Cash down payment	$154,000
Loan by insurance company: first lien on the fee or on subordinated leasehold, 28-year term, 8 1/4%, payable in equal monthly installments of principal and interest	760,000
	$914,000

Land lease for 99 years @ $11,580/year, net, payable monthly in advance, and 5% of gross rents
Cost of land—$200,000
Cost of constructing improvements—$750,000
No continuing involvement by seller

Computations:

Present value of 336 monthly payments on land lease at $965 discounted at 12% (imputed interest for a second lien receivable): $965 + ($965 × 96.432696)		$ 94,000
Loan from insurance company (primary debt)		760,000
Total debt or equivalent		854,000
Down payment		154,000
Sales value		$1,008,000

The initial investment ($154,000) is more than 15% of the sales value. (15% × $1,008,000 = $151,200).

The initial investment is also larger than the excess of the sales value over 115% of the primary debt.

Sales value	$1,008,000
115% of $760,000	874,000
Excess of sales value over 115% of debt	$ 134,000

Therefore, the initial investment of $154,000 is adequate, and recognizing profit on the sale of the improvements is appropriate.

Profit recognition:

Sales value		$1,008,000
Less: Cost of improvements	$750,000	
Cost of land	200,000	950,000
Profit recognized at time of sale		$ 58,000

The effect of including the present value of the lease is to reduce profit recognized by $106,000: $94,000 (present value of the land lease) – $200,000 (cost of land).

83. Subordinated Land Lease: Land Owned by Seller—Nonqualifying

Assumptions:

Sales price of improvements	$875,000

Represented by proceeds of:

Cash down payment	$132,000
Loan by insurance company: first lien on the fee or on subordinated leasehold, 28-year term, 8 1/4%, payable in equal monthly installments of principal and interest	743,000
	$875,000

Land lease for 99 years @ $19,332/year, net, payable monthly in advance
Cost of land—$200,000
Cost of improvements—$750,000
No continuing involvement by seller

Computations:

Present value of 336 monthly payments on land lease of $1,611 discounted at 12% (imputed interest for a second lien receivable): $1,611 + ($1,611 × 96.432696)	$ 157,000
Loan from insurance company (primary debt)	743,000
Total debt or equivalent	900,000
Down payment	132,000
Sales value	$1,032,000

The initial investment ($132,000) is less than 15% of the sales value (15% × $1,032,000 = $154,800), and therefore is inadequate to recognize profit on sale of improvements. Profit recognized at time of sale should not exceed that recognizable under the installment method as if the subordinated lease were an installment receivable.

Profit recognition on installment method:

Sales value		$1,032,000
Less: Cost of improvements	$750,000	
Cost of land	200,000	950,000
Anticipated profit on sale of improvements		$ 82,000

Cash received or to be received by the seller, other than the proceeds of the primary loan, is:

Down payment	$132,000
Present value of land lease payments	157,000
	$289,000

The percentage of profit in each collection is therefore:

$$\frac{\$\ 82,000}{\$289,000} = 28.37\%$$

Profit recognizable in the period of sale is 28.37% of the down payment of $132,000, or $37,450. The remaining profit of $44,550 will be recognized at the rate of 28.37% of the portion of each lease payment that is equivalent to a reduction of principal on a loan of $157,000 for 28 years at 12%.

The effect of including the present value of the lease in the sales value of the improvements is to reduce the profit recognized on the improvements by $43,000: $157,000 (present value of the land lease) − $200,000 (cost of the land).

Exhibit II—Illustration of Profit Recognition—Sale of Property with Construction and Support Obligations by Seller

84. This exhibit illustrates the method of accounting required for a sale of property in which the seller is obligated to construct multifamily units and in which cash flow deficits are anticipated. The example applies to obligations of the seller specified in paragraphs 28-30.

85. Assumptions:

a. Company X develops and sells multifamily residential projects. The Company performs directly all developmental activities, including initial planning, site acquisition, obtaining of financing, and physical construction of the project.
b. During the year ended December 31, 19X1 the Company began a project of 100 units. The project was planned and substantial activity had been performed in 19X1 but physical construction had not started as of December 31, 19X1. However, all contracts had been let, and the Company had obtained construction financing.
c. On December 31, 19X1, the Company sold the project to a limited partnership syndication (fully formed) in which it is the sole general partner:

Sales value	$1,100,000
Represented by proceeds of:	
Cash down payment	$ 165,000
Permanent financing assumed by the buyer, consisting of a 28-year 8 1/2% fully amortizing first mortgage loan by a conventional lender, payable in equal monthly payments of principal and interest to maturity	825,000
Second mortgage note received by the Company payable in equal monthly installments including interest at 9 1/2% over 12 years	110,000
	$1,100,000

d. The closing occurred on December 31, 19X1 and included delivery or performance of the following:
   (1) The Company delivered to the buyer a legal title to the land and all existing improvements.
   (2) The Company delivered to the buyer a firm commitment from an outside lender for permanent financing, and the buyer assumed permanent financing formerly in the name of the Company.
   (3) The Company received from the buyer $165,000 cash and a second mortgage note for $110,000.
   (4) The Company signed a contract to deliver the completed project for a single price of $1,100,000.
e. Costs incurred by the Company and total costs estimated to complete the project, as of December 31, 19X1, were:

	Costs to Date	Estimated Costs to Complete	Total Estimated Costs
Land	$117,000		$117,000
Feasibility, zoning, architectural	35,000		35,000
Finance and other	85,000	$ 10,000	95,000
Site improvements		20,000	20,000
Building construction		571,000	571,000
Total	$237,000	$601,000	$838,000

f. The Company has completed an extensive market research and feasibility study analyzing its cost estimates, the rent-up incubation period, and subsequent rent levels. The initial rent-up will commence in 19X2. Accordingly, a support period of two years is presumed for 19X3 and 19X4.

g. Based on its market analysis, the projected results are as follows:

	19X2	19X3	19X4
Rental expense	$ 37,000	$ 58,000	$ 58,000
Debt service	93,000	93,000	93,000
Total	130,000	151,000	151,000
Rental revenue	(75,000)	(150,000)	(180,000)*
Anticipated net deficit (surplus) in cash flow	55,000	1,000	(29,000)
Safety factor of 1/3 of rental revenue	25,000	50,000	60,000
Adjusted anticipated net deficit in cash flow	$ 80,000	$ 51,000	$ 31,000

*$180,000 equals 95% of gross scheduled rents.

h. Initial cost estimates by the Company on previous projects have never varied from final costs by more than one-half of one % of total costs.

86. Calculations of Profit to Be Recognized:

Schedules A and B (paragraphs 87 and 88) illustrate calculations of profit to be recognized in the period of sale, in the period of construction, and in each period in which the seller will support operations (19X2-19X4). The following features should be noted:

a. The percentage of estimated total profit to be recognized each period is determined by the ratio of gross costs incurred to the end of the period to total estimated gross costs of the project, including gross costs during the period of support of operations. (Construction costs should be included even if construction is performed by parties other than the seller.)

b. The estimated total profit that is the basis of the calculation in each period (that is, the profit to which the percentage in (a) is applied) is determined by adding the sales value and two-thirds of the projected revenue during the period of support of operations and deducting the estimated total costs of the project, including costs of operating the property and debt service.

(1) Actual amounts of revenue and costs are substituted for estimated amounts in the calculation as the actual amounts are known. However, in this illustration, remaining estimates of future revenue and expense are not changed because of actual results even though experience might indicate that projections of future amounts should be revised.

(2) Projected and actual revenues in the calculation should exclude amounts that accrue to the buyer, for example, revenue in excess of the sum of operating expenses and debt service.

(3) One-third of projected revenue should be excluded from the estimate of profit to provide a margin of safety (paragraph 85(g)). Actual results incorporated in the calculation need not be reduced by a safety factor.

(4) The calculation illustrated should be applied only if objective information is available regarding occupancy levels and rental rates for similar property in the immediate area. This will provide reasonable assurance that rent revenue from the project will be sufficient to cover operating expenses and debt service, including payments due to the seller under the terms of the transaction. Unless that evidence is available, no profit should be recognized on the transaction until rent revenue actually reaches levels that assure coverage of those costs.

c. Schedule A shows calculation of profit to be recognized each period on the assumption that actual revenue and costs are the same as those projected in paragraph 85(g) *adjusted* for the safety margin of one-third of revenue.

d. Schedule B shows calculation of profit to be recognized each period on the assumption that actual revenue and costs are the same as those projected in paragraph 85(g) *before* adjustment for safety margin.

e. Schedule C illustrates the calculation of estimated future rent receipts by adjustment for a safety margin.

87. **Schedule A**

Example of Profit Calculation
(assuming actual rental revenue equals *adjusted* projection)

REVENUES	
Sales value	$1,100,000
Adjusted—projected rental revenue[29]	
19X2	50,000
19X3	100,000
19X4	120,000
	1,370,000
COSTS	
Total estimated costs of project (paragraph 85(e))	838,000
Estimated rental expenses and debt service	
19X2	130,000
19X3	151,000
19X4	151,000
	1,270,000
TOTAL PROJECTED PROFIT	$ 100,000

Profit to be recognized:

$$\frac{\text{Cost to date} \times \text{projected profit}}{\text{Total costs}}$$

Profit recognized in period of sale:

$$\frac{\$237,000 \times \$100,000}{1,270,000} = \$18,661$$

Total profit to date	$ 18,661
Less profit previously reported	0
Current profit recognition	$ 18,661

Profit recognized in period of construction:

$$\frac{\$838,000 \times \$100,000}{1,270,000} = \$65,984$$

Total profit to date	$ 65,984
Less profit previously recognized	18,661
Current profit recognition	$ 47,323

Profit recognized during support period (19X2):

$$\frac{\$968,000 \times \$100,000}{1,270,000} = \$76,221$$

Total profit to date	$ 76,221
Less profit previously recognized	65,984
Current profit recognition	$ 10,237

Profit recognized during support period (19X3):

$$\frac{\$1,119,000 \times \$100,000}{1,270,000} = \$88,110$$

Total profit to date	$ 88,110
Less profit previously recognized	76,221
Current profit recognition	$ 11,889

Profit recognized during support period (19X4):

$$\frac{\$1,270,000 \times \$100,000}{1,270,000} = \$100,000$$

Total profit to date	$ 100,000
Less profit previously recognized	88,110
Current profit recognition	$ 11,890

[29]Two-thirds of projected revenue during periods of support of operations; this can also be calculated as projected rental expenses plus projected debt service less projected deficit cash flow.

88. **Schedule B**

Example of Profit Calculation
(assuming actual rental revenue equals *unadjusted* projection)
(in thousands)

	Profit Recognized in Period of Sale	Profit Recognized in Period of Construction	Profit Recognized during Support Period 19X2	19X3	19X4
REVENUES					
Sales value	$1,100	$1,100	$1,100	$1,100	$1,100
Adjusted—projected rental revenue*					
19X2	50	50	75†	75†	75†
19X3	100	100	100	150†	150†
19X4	120	120	120	150§	151‡
	1,370	1,370	1,395	1,475	1,476
COSTS					
Same as Schedule A	1,270	1,270	1,270	1,270	1,270
TOTAL PROJECTED PROFIT	$ 100	$ 100	$ 125	$ 205	$ 206

Profit to be recognized:

$$\frac{\text{Cost to date}}{\text{Total costs}} \times \text{projected profit}$$

Profit recognized in period of sale:

$$\frac{\$237{,}000}{1{,}270{,}000} \times \$100{,}000 = \$18{,}661$$

Total profit to date	$ 18,661
Less profit previously reported	0
Current profit recognition	$ 18,661

Profit recognized in period of construction

$$\frac{\$838{,}000}{1{,}270{,}000} \times \$100{,}000 = \$65{,}984$$

Total profit to date	$ 65,984
Less profit previously reported	18,661
Current profit recognition	$ 47,323

Profit recognized during support period (19X2):

$$\frac{\$968{,}000}{1{,}270{,}000} \times \$125{,}000 = \$95{,}276$$

Total profit to date	$ 95,276
Less profit previously reported	65,984
Current profit recognition	$ 29,292

*Two-thirds of projected revenue during periods of support of operation; this can also be calculated as projected rental expenses plus projected debt service less projected deficit cash flow.

†Actual rental revenue.

‡Because the property has attained a level of occupancy in excess of the original adjusted projection, and there is no reason to believe that such occupancy level cannot be sustained, the projected 19X4 rental revenue should be adjusted to 19X3 actual rental revenue.

§Actual rental revenue excluding amounts not needed to meet cash flow requirements of the property.

Profit recognized during support period (19X3):

$$\frac{\$1,119,000 \times \$205,000}{1,270,000} = \$180,626$$

Total profit to date	$180,626
Less profit previously reported	95,276
Current profit recognition	$ 85,350

Profit recognized during support period (19X4):

$$\frac{\$1,270,000 \times \$206,000}{1,270,000} = \$206,000$$

Total profit to date	$206,000
Less profit previously reported	180,626
Current profit recognition	$ 25,374

89. **Schedule C**

Calculation of Adjusted Projected Rental Revenue

Assume an office building under development is sold together with an agreement to support operations of the property for three years. The projected annual rent roll is $1,000,000 of which $350,000 is supported by signed lease agreements. The projected rental revenue for the first year of operation is $600,000; the second year $750,000; and the third year $1,000,000. At the time of sale, the amounts to be included in the calculation would be as follows:

Year	Projected Rental Revenue	Safety Factor (33-1/3%)	Adjusted Projected Rental Revenue
1	$ 600,000	$200,000	$400,000
2	750,000	250,000	500,000
3	1,000,000	333,333	666,667

If at the time of sale there were signed lease agreements for $450,000, then the $450,000 would be used in year 1 because it is greater than the adjusted projected rental revenue. The adjusted projected rental revenue for years 2 and 3 would remain $500,000 and $666,667, respectively.

Exhibit III—Illustration of Profit Recognition—Installment Method, with Debt Assumed by Buyer

90. Assumptions:

Cash down payment	$ 150,000
Second mortgage payable by buyer to seller (10-year amortization of principal plus interest)	350,000
Total cash to be received by seller	500,000
First mortgage assumed by buyer (20-year amortization of principal plus interest)	500,000
Total sales price and sales value	1,000,000
Cost	600,000
Total profit	$ 400,000

The initial investment is assumed to be inadequate for full profit recognition, and the installment method of accounting is assumed to be appropriate. It is also assumed that, after the down payment, the buyer pays $25,000 of principal on the first mortgage and $35,000 of principal on the second mortgage.

Profit recognition: Under the installment method, profit recognition attributable to the down payment is $60,000, representing 40% ($400,000/$1,000,000) of $150,000.

Profit recognition attributable to the principal payments by the buyer on the first and second mortgages is $24,000, representing 40% of $60,000 ($25,000 + $35,000).

Appendix D

ILLUSTRATIONS OF CALCULATIONS FOR RECOGNITION OF PROFIT ON RETAIL LAND SALES[30]

Exhibits

Exhibit I—Initial Measure of Consideration
(Percentage-of-Completion Method)
(amounts in thousands)

91. Assumptions:

Gross sales contracts recorded in year 1 (stated interest of 6%)	$1,000
Estimated uncollectible principal amount (sales contracts of $200* less estimated down payments to be forfeited of $20)	(180)
Net sales contracts receivable	820
Down payments and collections in year 1 relative to above sales contracts ($80 + $20)	100
Collections projected (principal amounts) for years 2 through 10	$ 720
Land cost (applicable to sales contracts of $800)	$ 60
Selling expenses in year 1	300
Future improvement costs (applicable to sales contracts of $800)	120
Minimum annual yield required on contracts receivable	12%

Discount Required:

Sales contracts receivable in year 1 (see above)	$ 720
Present value of 108 level monthly payments of $8.65 on sales contracts receivable (discounted at 12%) (Schedule A)	570
Discount required	$ 150

Computation of Revenue Applicable to Future Improvements:

$$\frac{\$120}{\$60 + \$300 + \$120} = 25\%$$

$$25\% \times \$650\ (\$1000 - \$200 - \$150) = \$163$$

[30]The financing and interest rate assumptions in this appendix are based on conditions at the time the retail land sales Guide was issued. They should not be considered as indicative of financing and interest rate assumptions that would be appropriate under different circumstances and at different times.

*It is assumed that experience shows that 90% of contracts in force 6 months after sales are recognized will ultimately be collected in full (paragraph 45).

Profit Recognition in Year 1:	
Revenue recognized:	
Cash received in year 1	$100
Present value of balance of sales contracts receivable	570
(Net sales $820, less discount $150)	670
Less: Revenue applicable to future improvements	163
Net revenue	507
Less: Costs and expenses ($60 + $300)	360
Pretax income	$147

92. **Schedule A**

Present Value of Sales Contracts Receivable
(amounts in thousands)

Year	Receivable Collections: Principal	Receivable Collections: Interest*	Annual Collections	Present Value @ 12%
2	$ 62	$ 42	$104	$ 97
3	66	38	104	87
4	70	34	104	77
5	75	29	104	68
6	79	25	104	60
7	84	20	104	53
8	89	15	104	47
9	95	9	104	43
10	100	4	104	38
	$720	$216	$936	$570

*Assumes no interest for year 1.

93. **Schedule B**

Computation of Interest Income for Financial Reporting Purposes
(amounts in thousands)

Year	Debit: Cash	Debit: Unamortized Valuation Discount	Credit: Contracts Receivable	Credit: Interest Income*
2	$104	$ 24	($ 62)	($ 66)
3	104	24	(66)	(62)
4	104	22	(70)	(56)
5	104	21	(75)	(50)
6	104	19	(79)	(44)
7	104	16	(84)	(36)
8	104	12	(89)	(27)
9	104	8	(95)	(17)
10	104	4	(100)	(8)
	$936	$150	($720)	($366)

*Total interest income equals $216 stated interest plus $150 discount, or $366.

94. **Schedule C**

Determination of Income Tax Payable
(amounts in thousands)

Year	Principal Receipts	Profit from Installment Sale	Interest Income from Receivable	Selling Expense	Taxable Income (Loss)	Tax	Tax Effect of Loss Carry-forward from Year 1	Net Tax
1	$100	$ 82*		($300)	($218)			
2	62	48	$ 42		90	($ 43)	$ 43	
3	66	51	38		89	(43)	43	
4	70	54	34		88	(42)	19	($ 23)
5	75	58	29		87	(42)		(42)
6	79	61	25		86	(41)		(41)
7	84	65	20		85	(41)		(41)
8	89	69	15		84	(40)		(40)
9	95	74	9		83	(40)		(40)
10	100	78	4		82	(40)		(40)
	$820	$640	$216	($300)	$556	($372)	$105†	($267)

Assumption: The installment method is used for income tax purposes.

---

*Profit on land sale computed on installment method as follows:

Gross profit = \$800 - \$180 = \$620

Principal payment × profit margin: \$80 × $\frac{\$620}{\$800}$ = \$62

Forfeited down payments 20

\$82

†Carryforward amount is 48% of \$218 = \$105.

95. **Schedule D**

Percentage-of-Completion Method—Illustration of Financial Statement Presentation of Transactions Assumed in Paragraph 91
(amounts in thousands)

Balance Sheets	**Beginning of Year 1**	End of Year **1**	**2**	**3**	**4**	**5**	**6**	**7**	**8**	**9**	**10**
Assets:											
Cash	$300	$100	$204	$308	$389	$451	$514	$547	$581	$615	$649
Contracts receivable		720	658	592	522	447	368	284	195	100	
Less: Allowance for contract cancellations*		—									
Unamortized valuation discount		(150)	(126)	(102)	(80)	(59)	(40)	(24)	(12)	(4)	
		570	532	490	442	388	328	260	183	96	
Land	75	15	15	15	15	15	15	15	15	15	15
	$375	$685	$751	$813	$846	$854	$857	$822	$779	$726	$664
Liabilities and equity:											
Deferred income taxes		$ 71	$103	$133	$137	$119	$100	$ 81	$ 59	$ 32	
Revenue applicable to future improvements†		163	163	163	163	163	163	122	81	40	
Capital stock	$375	375	375	375	375	375	375	375	375	375	375
Retained earnings		76	110	142	171	197	219	244	264	279	289
	$375	$685	$751	$813	$846	$854	$857	$822	$779	$726	$664

Schedule D (Cont.)

Income Statements	Year 1	2	3	4	5	6	7	8	9	10	Total
Revenues:											
Gross Sales	$1,000										$1,000
Less:											
Estimated uncollectible sales	(180)										(180)
Revenue applicable to future improvements	(163)										(163)
Valuation discount	(150)										(150)
Net sales	507										507
Improvement revenue—prior sales							$ 41	$ 41	$ 41	$ 40	163
Interest income (Schedule B)		$ 66	$ 62	$ 56	$ 50	$ 44	36	27	17	8	366
	507	66	62	56	50	44	77	68	58	48	1,036
Costs and expenses:											
Cost of sales	60										60
Improvement costs—prior sales							30	30	30	30	120
Selling expenses	300										300
	360	—	—	—	—	—	30	30	30	30	480
Income before provision for income taxes	147	66	62	56	50	44	47	38	28	18	556
Provision for income taxes:											
Current				23	42	41	41	40	40	40	267
Deferred	71	32	30	4	(18)	(19)	(19)	(22)	(27)	(32)	
	71	32	30	27	24	22	22	18	13	8	267
Net Income	$ 76	$ 34	$ 32	$ 29	$ 26	$ 22	$ 25	$ 20	$ 15	$ 10	$ 289

*Assumes that all cancellations occurred in year 1 without refunds of down payments.

†Assumes that future performance occurred equally in years 7, 8, 9, and 10.

Note: The illustrative statements are not intended to represent retail land sales company financial statements because they include only items necessary to illustrate timing of revenue and income recognition.

Exhibit II—Installment Method

96. Schedule A

Illustration of Financial Statement Presentation
Based on Assumptions in Paragraph 91
(amounts in thousands)

Balance Sheets	Beginning of Year 1	End of Year 1	2	3	4	5	6	7	8	9	10
Assets:											
Cash	$300	$100	$204	$308	$389	$451	$514	$547	$581	$615	$649
Contracts receivable		720	658	592	522	447	368	284	195	100	
Less: Profit applicable to future improvements		(342)	(313)	(282)	(249)	(213)	(175)	(135)	(93)	(48)	
		378	345	310	273	234	193	149	102	52	
Land	75	15	15	15	15	15	15	15	15	15	15
	$375	$493	$564	$633	$677	$700	$722	$711	$698	$682	$664
Liabilities and equity:											
Deferred income taxes			$ 33	$ 66	$ 75	$ 64	$ 54	$ 42	$ 29	$ 15	
Liability for future improvements		$120	120	120	120	120	120	90	60	30	
Capital stock	$375	375	375	375	375	375	375	375	375	375	$375
Retained earnings (deficit)		(2)	36	72	107	141	173	204	234	262	289
	$375	$493	$564	$633	$677	$700	$722	$711	$698	$682	$664

Schedule A (Cont.)

Income Statements	**Point of Sale in Year 1**	**Year 1**	**2**	**3**	**4**	**5**	**6**	**7**	**8**	**9**	**10**	**Total**
Revenues:												
Sales	$1,000	$1,000										$1,000
Interest income			$ 42	$ 38	$ 34	$ 29	$ 25	$ 20	$ 15	$ 9	$ 4	216
Profit deferred*	(427)	(427)										(427)
Profit recognized†			29	31	33	36	38	40	42	45	48	342
	573	573	71	69	67	65	63	60	57	54	52	1,131
Costs and expenses:												
Cost of Sales‡	225	225										225
Selling expenses	300	300										300
Loss on cancellations§		50										50
	525	575	—	—	—	—	—	—	—	—	—	575
Income (loss) before provision for income taxes	48	(2)	71	69	67	65	63	60	57	54	52	556
Provision for income taxes:												
Current					23	42	41	41	40	40	40	267
Deferred	23		33	33	9	(11)	(10)	(12)	(13)	(14)	(15)	
	23		33	33	32	31	31	29	27	26	25	267
Net income (loss)	$ 25	($ 2)	$ 38	$ 36	$ 35	$ 34	$ 32	$ 31	$ 30	$ 28	$ 27	$ 289

See Notes to Exhibit II, Schedule A, on next page.

Notes to Exhibit II, Schedule A:

		(amounts in thousands)
*Computation of profit deferred:		
Sales		$1,000
Cost of sales (see Note ‡)		(225)
Selling expense		(300)
Profit		$ 475
Percentage		47.5%.
Uncollected receivables		$ 900
Profit percentage		47.5%
Profit deferred		$ 427

†Profit recognized is 47.5% of principal collections.

‡Costs applicable to *gross* sales contracts:		
Land		$ 75
Future development		150
		$ 225
§Loss on cancellations:		
Contracts cancelled in Year 1		$ 200
Unpaid balance		$ 180
Costs recovered (credited to cost of sales):		
Land at cost	$15	
Future development	30	(45)
Profit at 47.5% of $180		(85)
Unrecovered selling cost		$ 50

97. **Schedule B**

Installment Method Changed to Percentage-of-Completion Method at Beginning of Year 4
(amounts in thousands)

Balance Sheets	End of Year 1	2	3	4	5	6	7	8	9	10
Assets:										
Cash	$100	$204	$308	$389	$451	$514	$547	$581	$615	$649
Contracts receivable	720	658	592	522	447	368	284	195	100	
Less:										
Profit applicable to future improvements	(342)	(313)	(282)							
Unamortized valuation discount				(80)	(59)	(40)	(24)	(12)	(4)	
	378	345	310	442	388	328	260	183	96	
Land	15	15	15	15	15	15	15	15	15	15
	$493	$564	$633	$846	$854	$857	$822	$779	$726	$664
Liabilities and equity:										
Deferred income taxes		$33	$66	$137	$119	$100	$81	$59	$32	
Liability for future improvements (revenue applicable to future improvements after Year 3)	$120	120	120	163	163	163	122	81	40	
Capital stock	375	375	375	375	375	375	375	375	375	$375
Retained earnings (deficit)	(2)	36	72	171	197	219	244	264	279	289
	$493	$564	$633	$846	$854	$857	$822	$779	$726	$664

Schedule B (Cont.)

Income Statements	Year 1	2	3	4	5	6	7	8	9	10	Total
Revenues:											
Gross sales contracts recorded	$1,000										$1000
Improvement revenue—prior sales							$41	$41	$41	$40	163
Profit deferred	(427)										(427)
Profit recognized		$29	$31								60
Interest income*		42	38	$56	$50	$44	36	27	17	8	318
Income resulting from change from installment to percentage-of-completion method† (described fully in notes to financial statements)				137							137
	573	71	69	193	50	44	77	68	58	48	1,251
Costs and expenses:											
Cost of sales	225										225
Improvement costs—prior sales							30	30	30	30	120
Selling expenses	300										300
Loss on cancellations	50										50
	575	—	—	—	—	—	30	30	30	30	695
Income (loss) before provision for income taxes	(2)	71	69	193	50	44	47	38	28	18	556
Provision for income taxes:											
Current				23	42	41	41	40	40	40	267
Deferred		33	33	71	(18)	(19)	(19)	(22)	(27)	(32)	—
		33	33	94	24	22	22	18	13	8	267
Net income (loss)	($ 2)	$38	$36	$99	$26	$22	$25	$20	$15	$10	$289

See Notes to Exhibit II, Schedule B, on next page.

Schedule B (Cont.)

Notes to Exhibit II, Schedule B:

*Interest at stated rate for Years 2 and 3; 12% after change from installment to percentage-of-completion method.

†Computation of effect of change from installment to percentage-of-completion method:

	(Amounts in thousands)	
Profit not yet recognized under installment method:		
Original	$427	
Recognized in prior years	(60)	
Applicable to canceled contracts	(85)	$282
Less, valuation discount required:		
Receivables at beginning of Year 4	592	
Present value of payments due (principal and interest) at 12%	(490)	102
		180
Less:		
Revenue to be recognized in future as performance takes place	163	
Costs to be recognized in future	(120)	43
Net amount credited to income (before taxes)		$137

Appendix E

BACKGROUND INFORMATION AND SUMMARY OF CONSIDERATION OF COMMENTS ON EXPOSURE DRAFT

98. As discussed in FASB Statement No. 32, *Specialized Accounting and Reporting Principles and Practices in AICPA Statements of Position and Guides on Accounting and Auditing Matters,* the FASB is extracting the specialized[31] accounting and reporting principles and practices from AICPA Statements of Position (SOPs) and Guides on accounting and auditing matters and issuing them as FASB Statements after appropriate due process. This Statement extracts the specialized sale and profit recognition principles and practices from the AICPA Industry Accounting Guides, *Accounting for Profit Recognition on Sales of Real Estate* and *Accounting for Retail Land Sales,* and SOPs 75-6, *Questions Concerning Profit Recognition on Sales of Real Estate,* and 78-4, *Application of the Deposit, Installment, and Cost Recovery Methods in Accounting for Sales of Real Estate.* The provisions of the retail land sales Guide that address costs have been included in FASB Statement No. 67, *Accounting for Costs and Initial Rental Operations of Real Estate Projects.*

99. Board members have assented to the issuance of this Statement on the basis that it is an appropriate extraction of existing specialized principles and practices and that a comprehensive reconsideration of those principles and practices was not contemplated in undertaking this FASB project. Most of the background material and discussion of accounting alternatives has not been carried forward from the Guides and SOPs. The Board's conceptual framework project on accounting recognition criteria will address recognition issues relating to elements of financial statements. A Statement of Financial Accounting Concepts resulting from that project in due course will serve as a basis for evaluating existing standards and practices. Accordingly, the Board may wish to evaluate the standards in this Statement when its conceptual framework project is completed. However, the Board concluded that this Statement should not be postponed indefinitely to await completion of a Statement of concepts on recognition issues.

100. Retail land sales are sales, on a volume basis, of lots that are subdivisions of large tracts of land. They are characterized by down payments so small that local banks and savings and loan institutions would not loan money on the property at market rates or purchase the buyer's note for the remaining purchase price without a substantial discount. The seller is unable to enforce the sales contract or the buyer's note against the buyer's general credit. If the buyer cancels the contract within an established cancellation period, its money is refunded. Defaults by the buyer after the cancellation period result in recovery of the land by the seller and forfeiture of at least some principal payments made by the buyer.[32]

[31]The term *specialized* is used to refer to those accounting and reporting principles and practices in AICPA Guides and Statements of Position that are neither superseded by nor contained in Accounting Research Bulletins, APB Opinions, FASB Statements, or FASB Interpretations.

[32]Federal and state laws may affect the amount that can be retained by the seller.

101. Examples of real estate sales transactions that are not retail land sales include sales of lots to builders; sales of homes, buildings, and parcels of land to builders and others; sales of corporate stock of enterprises with substantial real estate, sales of partnership interests,[33] and sales of time-sharing interests[34] if the sales are in substance sales of real estate; and sales of options to purchase real estate.

102. The retail land sales Guide was developed to clarify and standardize accounting for retail land sales, particularly the timing and methods of revenue and profit recognition. The Guide recommended conditions to be met by both the buyer and the seller before the seller reported a sale. It also recommended criteria for the use of the full accrual, percentage-of-completion, and installment methods for recognizing profit.

103. The profit recognition Guide addressed real estate sales transactions other than retail land sales. It was developed to standardize accounting for transactions that had become increasingly diverse and complex. The Guide addressed the timing of profit recognition and recommended criteria for determining appropriate methods for profit recognition. SOPs 75-6 and 78-4 clarified and elaborated on the recommendations of the Guide.

104. A draft of this Statement was reviewed by the FASB Task Force on Specialized Principles for the Real Estate Industry to ensure that the specialized principles in the Guides and SOPs had been extracted correctly. Based on the task force's comments, the Board believes that the specialized profit recognition principles in the Guides and SOPs have been correctly identified and included in this Statement.

105. An Exposure Draft of a proposed FASB Statement, *Accounting for Sales of Real Estate,* was issued on December 15, 1981. The Board received 47 comment letters in response to the Exposure Draft. Certain of the comments received and the Board's consideration of them are discussed in this appendix.

Accounting for Sales of Time-Sharing Interests

106. The Exposure Draft proposed that sales of time-sharing interests in real estate that represent either fee simple ownership or are sales-type leases under Statement 13 should be accounted for as sales of real estate other than retail land sales under the provisions of this Statement. Sales of time-sharing interests were not addressed in the Guides and SOPs whose principles are extracted in this Statement.

107. The majority of respondents commenting on this issue agreed that accounting for sales of time-sharing interests should be covered in this Statement and that the accounting proposed in the Exposure Draft is appropriate. Some respondents felt that accounting for sales of time-sharing interests in real estate should not be dealt with as part of this Statement because the Guides and SOPs being extracted did not deal with that subject. Other respondents believe that this Statement should provide additional guidance on accounting for revenue and costs of time-sharing interests.

108. The Board concurred with those respondents who believe that it is appropriate to require that sales of real estate time-sharing interests be accounted for in accordance with the provisions of this Statement but that additional guidance should not be provided as part of this extraction project.

Discount Rate for Valuation of Retail Land Sales Receivables

109. Paragraph 79(a) of the Exposure Draft proposed that a net retail land sales receivable be valued at an amount at which it could be sold on a volume basis without recourse to the seller at the time of the initial transaction. It referred to APB Opinion No. 21, *Interest on Receivables and Payables,* for guidance on selection of an appropriate interest rate. The retail land sales Guide had provided a more specific recommendation—that those receivables be discounted at a rate not less than the rate charged locally for financing installment purchases of soft goods and appliances.

110. Many respondents agreed that the guidance proposed in the Exposure Draft was appropriate. Others suggested that additional guidance be provided as to selection of a discount rate, such as the seller's incremental borrowing rate, the yield rate established by recent sales of Government National Mortgage Association (GNMA) securities, or an average rate charged by local savings and loan associations. Other respondents objected to the principle of valuing receivables at an amount at which they could be sold on a volume basis without recourse. They believe that there is not a market for this type of paper or an opportunity for nonrecourse discounting with lending institutions.

[33]An example of a sale of a partnership interest that is in substance a sale of real estate would be an enterprise forming a partnership, arranging for the partnership to acquire the property directly from third parties, and selling an interest in the partnership to investors who then become limited partners.

[34]For purposes of this Statement, a time-sharing interest that is in substance a sale of real estate is the exclusive right to occupy a specified dwelling unit for a designated period each year and represents (a) fee simple ownership of real estate or (b) a right-to-use time-sharing interest that is a sales-type lease as defined in Statement 13, as amended and interpreted.

111. The Board believes that determination of an appropriate interest rate should be governed by the principles of Opinion 21 and that designation of specific rates would be arbitrary. Therefore, the Board believes that the general guidance proposed in the Exposure Draft should be retained. However, the idea of valuation at the amount at which receivables could be sold without recourse has been expressed as an objective rather than as a prescribed methodology.

Condensed Disclosure Requirements

112. The Exposure Draft proposed that certain detailed disclosures that were recommended by the retail land sales Guide not be required by this Statement because they are already required by other authoritative literature. Most of the comment letters agreed with that proposal. A few respondents suggested adding specific disclosures or eliminating one or more specific items, but those suggestions were not generally supported. The Board considered those suggestions and determined that no significant changes should be made to the Exposure Draft.

Loans to Buyers by Sellers of Real Estate

113. The Exposure Draft noted that financing institutions occasionally sell land and make development or construction loans to the buyers. It proposed that the buyer's initial investment not include such funds and that anticipated future loans from the seller be subtracted from the initial and continuing investments.

114. Several respondents agreed with that provision. Others disagreed and suggested that it is not appropriate to subtract future loans from sellers that are established lending institutions if those loans will be used to add value to the property, especially if the future loan is on normal lending terms. They agreed, however, that the future loans should not be included as part of the buyer's initial investment.

115. The Board has considered those comments and concluded that future loans from an established lending institution need not be subtracted if (a) they are on normal terms, (b) they bear fair-market interest rates, and (c) the proceeds of the loans are conditional on use for specified development of or construction on the property. Those requirements are designed to preclude an effective reduction in the buyer's investment in the property to less than the minimum requirement by a subsequent loan from the seller.

Sale and Leaseback of Real Estate

116. Several respondents recommended that paragraph 8 of the Exposure Draft clarify the relative applicability of this Statement and FASB Statements 13 and 28. Paragraph 40 of this Statement has been added to indicate that (a) recognition of a sale in a sale-leaseback shall be governed by Statements 13 and 28, (b) the amount of the profit on sale-leaseback transactions is to be determined by the provisions of this Statement, and (c) the profit so determined is to be accounted for in accordance with the provisions of Statements 13 and 28 unless other provisions of this Statement require postponement of profit recognition until a later event.

Due Process

117. Several respondents questioned the appropriateness of extracting specialized accounting principles from AICPA documents that had not been subjected to the FASB's extensive due process procedures. They noted the Guides and SOPs were promulgated through a process that did not include input from industry, academe, or the general public and that those documents were not exposed for comments before they were issued.

118. The extraction process is described in paragraph 98 of this Statement, paragraphs 1-9 of Statement 32, and the FASB's *Request for Written Comments on an FASB Proposal for Dealing with Industry Accounting Matters and Accounting Questions of Limited Application*. Input from the public has been received and carefully considered:

a. At a meeting of the Financial Accounting Standards Advisory Council in July 1978 at which the extraction process was discussed
b. In the form of 157 letters of comment on the request for written comments described above
c. In the form of 53 letters of comment in response to the Exposure Draft, *Specialized Accounting and Reporting Principles and Practices in AICPA Industry Accounting Guides, Industry Audit Guides, and Statements of Position*
d. At two meetings of the FASB Task Force on Specialized Principles for the Real Estate Industry held in 1981
e. In extensive oral and written comments from task force members on several drafts of the Exposure Draft, *Accounting for Sales of Real Estate,* and of this Statement
f. In the form of 47 letters of comment on the Exposure Draft

The Board believes it has followed its required due process procedures and that it is appropriate to issue this Statement.

Other

119. Several respondents suggested various sub-

stantive changes to the Exposure Draft. Adoption of those suggestions would have required a reconsideration of some of the provisions of the Guides and SOPs. Such a reconsideration is not contemplated in the extraction project unless a proposed change meets one of the three criteria for change included in the "Notice for Recipients" section of the Exposure Draft or is broadly supported. The proposed changes did not meet the criteria for change and were not broadly supported. Accordingly, the Board did not adopt those suggestions. However, based on suggestions from respondents to the Exposure Draft, the Board has made several other changes, including an internal reorganization of this Statement, that it believes clarify the Statement.

120. It was suggested that compliance with this Statement would be burdensome to small practitioners and enterprises that sell real estate infrequently. In response to that suggestion, the Board considered limiting the scope and applicability of this Statement, for example, to publicly held enterprises and privately owned real estate enterprises. However, the Board believes further consideration is necessary before income measurement standards such as those in this Statement are applied differently based on the size or form of ownership of an enterprise. The Board notes that its project on financial reporting by private and small public companies will consider characteristics of those enterprises and how their financial reporting needs differ from those of other business enterprises. The Board may reconsider the need for applying some or all of the provisions of this Statement to certain private and small public enterprises when that project is completed.

121. In its August 1982 report, the Structure Committee of the Financial Accounting Foundation recommended that the Board develop a plan to provide timely guidance for implementation questions (pages 18 and 19 of the report). The committee also said it believes the program to extract specialized accounting standards from AICPA pronouncements and issue them as FASB Statements is consistent with the Board's mission (page 18 of the report).

122. The Board has concluded that it can reach an informed decision on the basis of existing information without a public hearing and that the effective date and transition specified in paragraph 52 are advisable in the circumstances.

Appendix F

DECISION TREES

123. The following decision trees are intended to provide an overview of the major provisions in this Statement that relate to the accounting for sales of real estate. They should not be used without further reference to the Statement. Two decision trees are provided—one for retail land sales and a second for all other sales of real estate. The highlighted boxes on this page describe the general requirements for recognizing all of the profit on a sale of real estate other than a retail land sale at the date of sale.

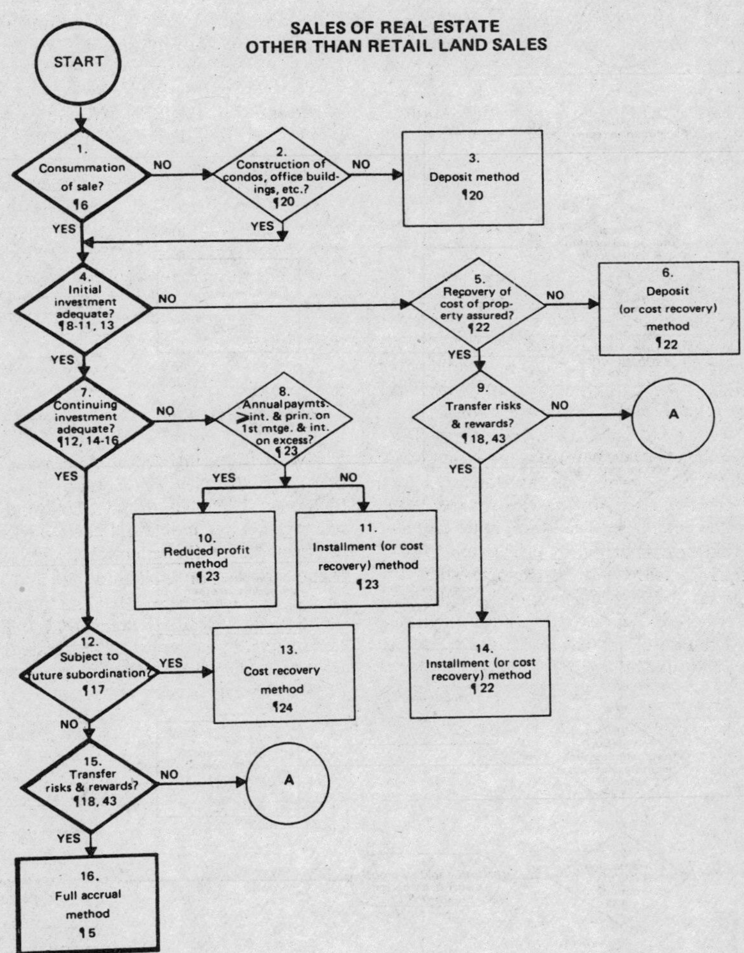
SALES OF REAL ESTATE
OTHER THAN RETAIL LAND SALES
START
1. Consummation of sale? ¶6
NO
YES
2. Construction of condos, office buildings, etc.? ¶20
NO
YES
3. Deposit method ¶20
4. Initial investment adequate? ¶8-11, 13
NO
YES
5. Recovery of cost of property assured? ¶22
NO
YES
6. Deposit (or cost recovery) method ¶22
7. Continuing investment adequate? ¶12, 14-16
NO
YES
8. Annual paymts. > int. & prin. on 1st mtge. & int. on excess? ¶23
YES
NO
9. Transfer risks & rewards? ¶18, 43
NO
YES
A
10. Reduced profit method ¶23
11. Installment (or cost recovery) method ¶23
12. Subject to future subordination? ¶17
YES
NO
13. Cost recovery method ¶24
14. Installment (or cost recovery) method ¶22
15. Transfer risks & rewards? ¶18, 43
NO
YES
A
16. Full accrual method ¶5

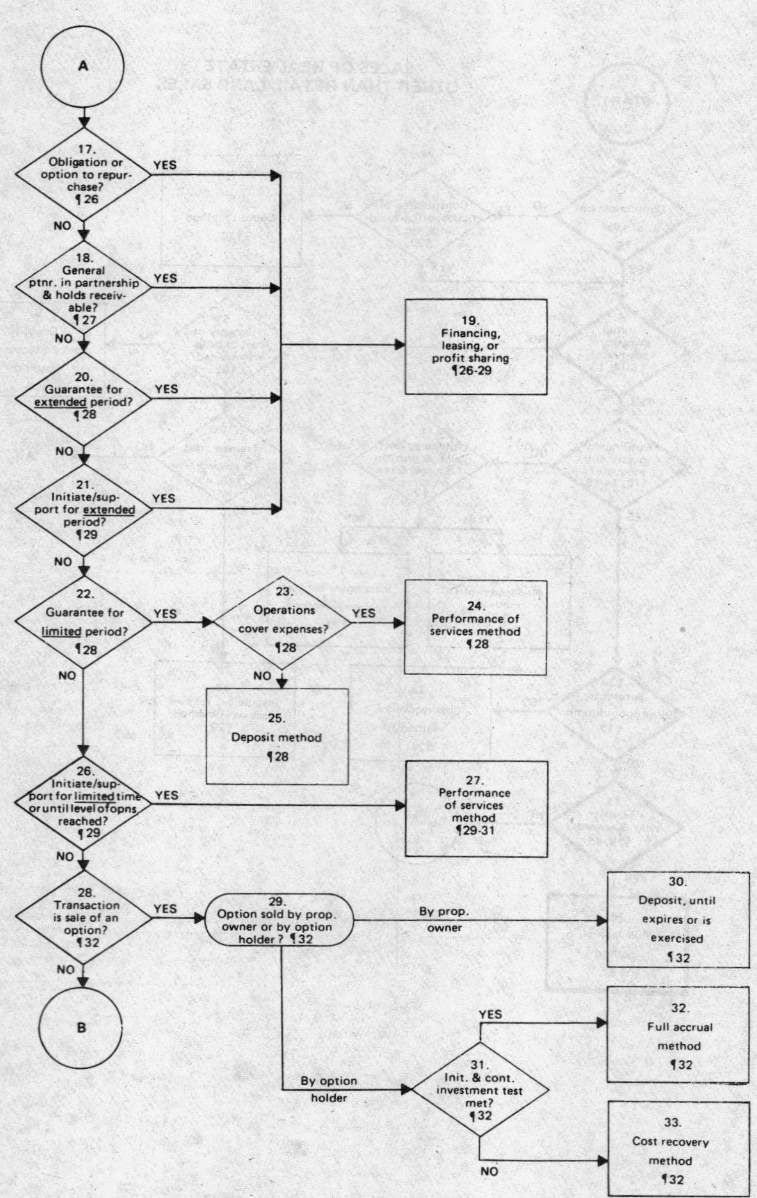
A
17. Obligation or option to repurchase? ¶26
YES
NO
18. General ptnr. in partnership & holds receivable? ¶27
YES
NO
19. Financing, leasing, or profit sharing ¶26-29
20. Guarantee for extended period? ¶28
YES
NO
21. Initiate/support for extended period? ¶29
YES
NO
22. Guarantee for limited period? ¶28
YES
NO
23. Operations cover expenses? ¶28
YES
NO
24. Performance of services method ¶28
25. Deposit method ¶28
26. Initiate/support for limited time or until level of opns reached? ¶29
YES
NO
27. Performance of services method ¶29-31
28. Transaction is sale of an option? ¶32
YES
NO
29. Option sold by prop. owner or by option holder? ¶32
By prop. owner
30. Deposit, until expires or is exercised ¶32
B
By option holder
31. Init. & cont. investment test met? ¶32
YES
NO
32. Full accrual method ¶32
33. Cost recovery method ¶32

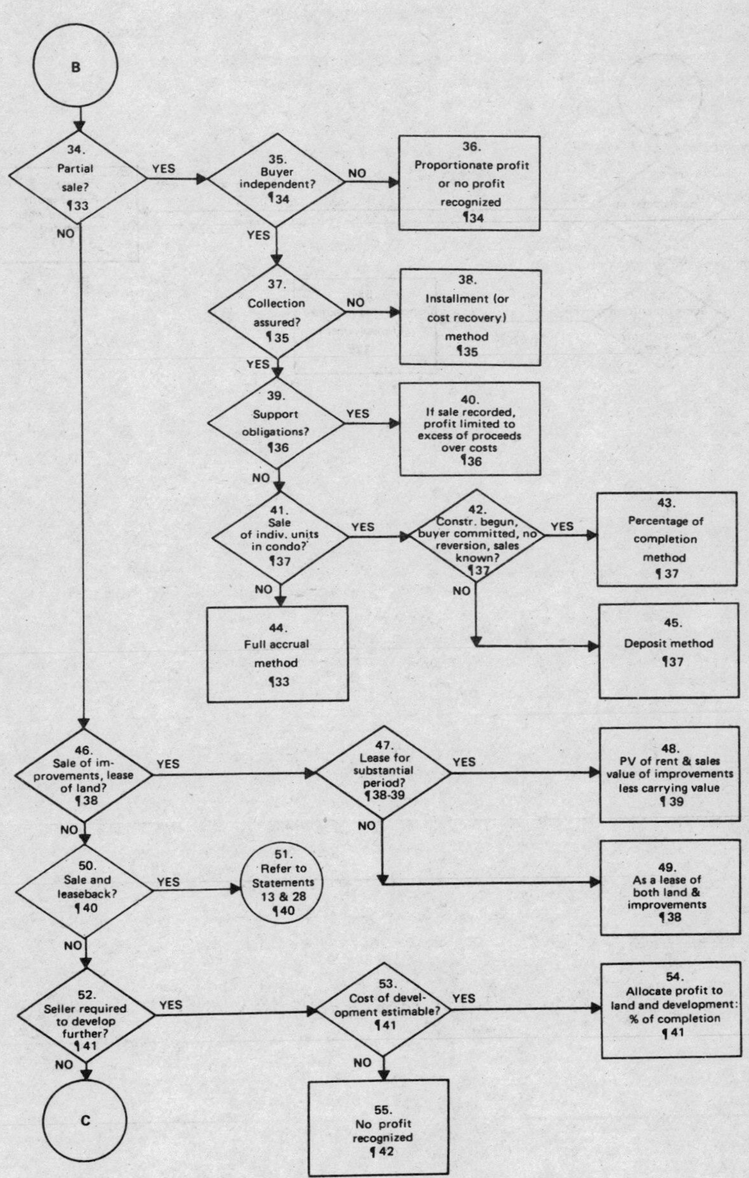
B
34. Partial sale? ¶33
YES
NO
35. Buyer independent? ¶34
NO
YES
36. Proportionate profit or no profit recognized ¶34
37. Collection assured? ¶35
NO
YES
38. Installment (or cost recovery) method ¶35
39. Support obligations? ¶36
YES
NO
40. If sale recorded, profit limited to excess of proceeds over costs ¶36
41. Sale of indiv. units in condo? ¶37
YES
NO
42. Constr. begun, buyer committed, no reversion, sales known? ¶37
YES
NO
43. Percentage of completion method ¶37
44. Full accrual method ¶33
45. Deposit method ¶37
46. Sale of improvements, lease of land? ¶38
YES
NO
47. Lease for substantial period? ¶38-39
YES
NO
48. PV of rent & sales value of improvements less carrying value ¶39
49. As a lease of both land & improvements ¶38
50. Sale and leaseback? ¶40
YES
NO
51. Refer to Statements 13 & 28 ¶40
52. Seller required to develop further? ¶41
YES
NO
53. Cost of development estimable? ¶41
YES
NO
54. Allocate profit to land and development: % of completion ¶41
55. No profit recognized ¶42
C

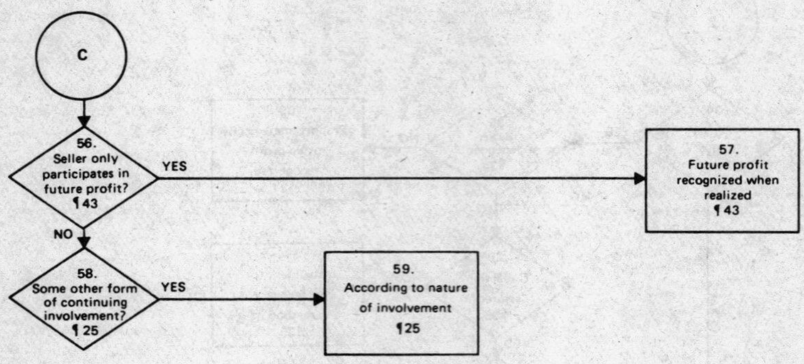
C
56.
Seller only
participates in
future profit?
¶43
YES
57.
Future profit
recognized when
realized
¶43
NO
58.
Some other form
of continuing
involvement?
¶25
YES
59.
According to nature
of involvement
¶25

RETAIL LAND SALES

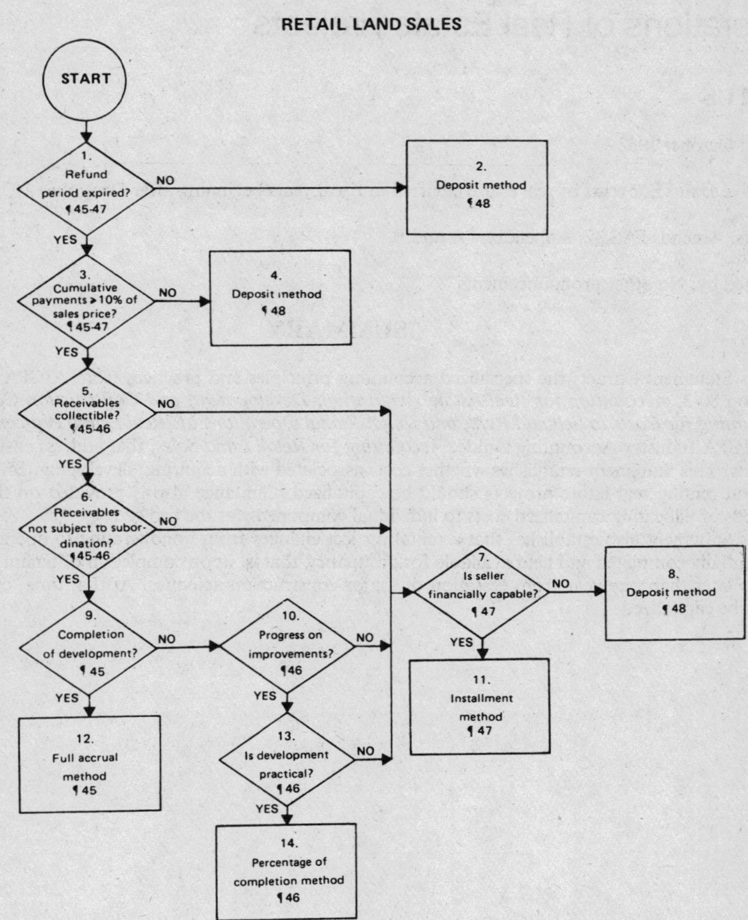

Statement of Financial Accounting Standards No. 67 Accounting for Costs and Initial Rental Operations of Real Estate Projects

STATUS

Issued: October 1982

Effective Date: For costs of real estate incurred in fiscal years beginning after December 31, 1982

Affects: Amends FAS 32, Appendixes A and B

Affected by: No other pronouncements

SUMMARY

This Statement extracts the specialized accounting principles and practices from AICPA Statements of Position 80-3, *Accounting for Real Estate Acquisition, Development, and Construction Costs,* and 78-3, *Accounting for Costs to Sell and Rent, and Initial Rental Operations of, Real Estate Projects,* and those in the AICPA Industry Accounting Guide, *Accounting for Retail Land Sales,* that address costs of real estate projects. This Statement establishes whether costs associated with acquiring, developing, constructing, selling, and renting real estate projects should be capitalized. Guidance also is provided on the appropriate methods of allocating capitalized costs to individual components of the project.

This Statement also establishes that a rental project changes from nonoperating to operating when it is substantially completed and held available for occupancy, that is, upon completion of tenant improvements but no later than one year from cessation of major construction activities. At that time, costs should no longer be capitalized.

Statement of Financial Accounting Standards No. 67
Accounting for Costs and Initial Rental Operations of Real Estate Projects

CONTENTS

INTRODUCTION

1. This Statement establishes accounting and reporting standards for acquisition, development, construction, selling, and rental costs associated with real estate projects. It also provides guidance for the accounting for initial rental operations and criteria for determining when the status of a rental project changes from nonoperating to operating.

SCOPE AND APPLICABILITY

2. This Statement does not apply to:

a. Real estate developed by an enterprise for use in its own operations,[1] other than for sale or rental.
b. "Initial direct costs" of sales-type, operating, and other types of leases, which are defined in FASB Statement No. 17, *Accounting for Leases—Initial Direct Costs.* The accounting for initial direct costs is prescribed in FASB Statement No. 13, *Accounting for Leases.*
c. Costs directly related to manufacturing, merchandising, or service activities as distinguished from real estate activities.

Paragraphs 20-23 of this Statement do not apply to real estate rental activity in which the predominant rental period is less than one month.

STANDARDS OF FINANCIAL ACCOUNTING AND REPORTING

General

3. Paragraphs 4-25 specify the accounting for the following as they relate to real estate projects: (a) **preacquisition costs,**[2] (b) taxes and insurance, (c) **project costs,** (d) **amenities,** (e) **incidental operations,** (f) allocation of capitalized costs to components of a real estate project, (g) revisions of estimates, (h) abandonments and changes in use, (i) selling costs, (j) rental costs, and (k) costs in excess of estimated **net realizable value.**

Acquisition, Development, and Construction Costs

Preacquisition Costs

4. Payments to obtain an option to acquire real property shall be capitalized as incurred. All other costs related to a property that are incurred before the enterprise acquires the property, or before the enterprise obtains an option to acquire it, shall be capitalized if all of the following conditions are met and otherwise shall be charged to expense as incurred:

a. The costs are directly identifiable with the specific property.

[1]In this context, "real estate developed by an enterprise for use in its own operations" includes real estate developed by a member of a consolidated group for use in the operations of another member of the group (for example, a manufacturing facility developed by a subsidiary for use in its parent's operations) when the property is reported in the group's consolidated financial statements. However, such property is not "real estate developed for use in the enterprise's operations" when reported in the separate financial statements of the entity that developed it.

[2]Terms defined in the glossary (Appendix A) are in **boldface type** the first time they appear in this Statement.

b. The costs would be capitalized if the property were already acquired.
c. Acquisition of the property or of an option to acquire the property is probable.[3] This condition requires that the prospective purchaser is actively seeking to acquire the property and has the ability to finance or obtain financing for the acquisition and that there is no indication that the property is not available for sale.

5. Capitalized preacquisition costs (a) shall be included as project costs upon the acquisition of the property or (b) to the extent not recoverable by the sale of the options, plans, etc., shall be charged to expense when it is probable that the property will not be acquired.

Taxes and Insurance

6. Costs incurred on real estate for property taxes and insurance shall be capitalized as property cost only during periods in which activities necessary to get the property ready for its intended use are in progress.[4] Costs incurred for such items after the property is substantially complete and ready for its intended use[5] shall be charged to expense as incurred.

Project Costs

7. Project costs clearly associated with the acquisition, development, and construction of a real estate project shall be capitalized as a cost of that project. **Indirect project costs** that relate to several projects shall be capitalized and allocated to the projects to which the costs relate. Indirect costs that do not clearly relate to projects under development or construction, including general and administrative expenses, shall be charged to expense as incurred.

Amenities

8. Accounting for costs of amenities shall be based on management's plans for the amenities in accordance with the following:

a. If an amenity is to be sold or transferred in connection with the sale of individual units, costs in excess of anticipated proceeds shall be allocated as **common costs** because the amenity is clearly associated with the development and sale of the project. The common costs include expected future operating costs to be borne by the developer until they are assumed by buyers of units in a project.
b. If an amenity is to be sold separately or retained by the developer, capitalizable costs of the amenity in excess of its estimated **fair value** as of the expected date of its substantial physical completion shall be allocated as common costs. For the purpose of determining the amount to be capitalized as common costs, the amount of cost previously allocated to the amenity shall not be revised after the amenity is substantially completed and available for use. A later sale of the amenity at more or less than its estimated fair value as of the date of substantial physical completion, less any accumulated depreciation, results in a gain or loss that shall be included in net income in the period in which the sale occurs.

Costs of amenities shall be allocated among land parcels[6] benefited and for which development is probable.

9. Before an amenity is substantially completed and available for use, operating income (or loss) of the amenity shall be included as a reduction of (or an addition to) common costs. When an amenity to be sold separately or retained by the developer is substantially completed and available for use, current operating income and expenses of the amenity shall be included in current operating results.

Incidental Operations

10. **Incremental revenue from incidental operations** in excess of **incremental costs of incidental operations** shall be accounted for as a reduction of capitalized project costs. Incremental costs in excess of incremental revenue shall be charged to expense as incurred, because the incidental operations did not achieve the objective of reducing the costs of developing the property for its intended use.

Allocation of Capitalized Costs to the Components of a Real Estate Project

11. The capitalized costs of real estate projects shall be assigned to individual components of the project based on specific identification. If specific identification is not practicable, capitalized costs shall be allocated as follows:

---

[3]*Probable* is defined in FASB Statement No. 5, *Accounting for Contingencies,* as "likely to occur" and is used in the same sense in this Statement.

[4]The phrase *activities necessary to get the property ready for its intended use are in progress* is used here with the same meaning as it has for interest capitalization in paragraph 17 of FASB Statement No. 34, *Capitalization of Interest Cost.*

[5]The phrase *substantially complete and ready for its intended use* is used here with the same meaning as it has for interest capitalization in paragraph 18 of Statement 34.

[6]A land parcel may be considered to be an individual lot or unit, an amenity, or a **phase**.

a. Land cost and all other common costs[7] (prior to construction) shall be allocated to each land parcel benefited. Allocation shall be based on the **relative fair value before construction.**
b. Construction costs shall be allocated to individual units in the phase on the basis of relative sales value of each unit.

If allocation based on relative value also is impracticable, capitalized costs shall be allocated based on area methods (for example, square footage) or other value methods as appropriate under the circumstances.

Revisions of Estimates

12. Estimates and cost allocations shall be reviewed at the end of each financial reporting period until a project is substantially completed and available for sale. Costs shall be revised and reallocated as necessary for material changes on the basis of current estimates.[8] Changes in estimates shall be reported in accordance with paragraph 31 of APB Opinion No. 20, *Accounting Changes.*

Abandonments and Changes in Use

13. If real estate, including rights to real estate, is abandoned (for example, by allowing a mortgage to be foreclosed or a purchase option to lapse), capitalized costs of that real estate shall be expensed. Such costs shall not be allocated to other components of the project or to other projects even if other components or other projects are capable of absorbing the losses.

14. Real estate donated to municipalities or other governmental agencies for uses that will benefit the project are not abandonments. The cost of the real estate donated shall be allocated as a common cost of the project.

15. Changes in the use of real estate comprising a project or a portion of a project may arise after significant development and construction costs have been incurred. If the change in use is made pursuant to a formal plan for a project that is expected to produce a higher economic yield (as compared to its yield based on use before change), the development and construction costs to be charged to expense shall be limited to the amount by which the capitalized costs incurred and to be incurred exceed the estimated value of the revised project when it is substantially complete and ready for its intended use.

16. In the absence of a formal plan for a project that is expected to produce a higher economic yield, the project costs to be charged to expense shall be limited to the amount by which total project costs exceed the estimated net realizable value of the property determined on the assumption it will be sold in its present state.

Costs Incurred to Sell and Rent Real Estate Projects, Including Initial Rental Operations

Costs Incurred to Sell Real Estate Projects

17. **Costs incurred to sell real estate projects** shall be capitalized if they (a) are reasonably expected to be recovered from the sale of the project or from incidental operations and (b) are incurred for (1) tangible assets that are used directly throughout the selling period to aid in the sale of the project or (2) services that have been performed to obtain regulatory approval of sales. Examples of costs incurred to sell real estate projects that ordinarily meet the criteria for capitalization are costs of model units and their furnishings, sales facilities, legal fees for preparation of prospectuses, and semipermanent signs.

18. Other costs incurred to sell real estate projects shall be capitalized as prepaid costs if they are directly associated with and their recovery is reasonably expected from sales that are being accounted for under a method of accounting other than full accrual.[9] Costs that do not meet the criteria for capitalization shall be expensed as incurred.

19. Capitalized selling costs shall be charged to expense in the period in which the related revenue is recognized as earned. When a sales contract is canceled (with or without refund) or the related receivable is written off as uncollectible, the related unrecoverable capitalized selling costs shall be charged to expense or an allowance previously established for that purpose.

Costs Incurred to Rent Real Estate Projects

20. If **costs incurred to rent real estate projects,** other than initial direct costs,[10] under operating leases are related to and their recovery is reasonably expected from future rental operations, they shall be capitalized. Examples of such costs are costs of model units and their furnishings, rental facilities, semipermanent signs, "grand openings," and unused rental brochures. Costs that do not meet the

[7]Including the costs of amenities to be allocated as common costs (paragraphs 8 and 9).

[8]Paragraph 76 of Statement No. 66, *Accounting for Sales of Real Estate,* discusses revisions of estimates relating to retail land sales accounted for by the percentage-of-completion method.

[9]FASB Statement 66 discusses the circumstances under which the appropriate accounting methods are to be applied, including the full accrual method.

[10]Initial direct costs are defined in Statement 17. The accounting for initial direct costs is prescribed in Statement 13.

criteria for capitalization shall be expensed as incurred, for example, rental overhead.

21. Capitalized rental costs directly related to revenue from a specific operating lease shall be amortized over the lease term. Capitalized rental costs not directly related to revenue from a specific operating lease shall be amortized over the period of expected benefit. The amortization period shall begin when the project is substantially completed and held available for occupancy.[11] Estimated unrecoverable amounts of unamortized capitalized rental costs associated with a lease or group of leases shall be charged to expense when it becomes probable that the lease(s) will be terminated.

Initial Rental Operations

22. When a real estate project is substantially completed and held available for occupancy, rental revenues and operating costs shall be recognized in income and expense as they accrue, all carrying costs (such as real estate taxes) shall be charged to expense when incurred, depreciation on the cost of the project shall be provided, and costs to rent the project shall be amortized in accordance with paragraph 21 of this Statement. A real estate project shall be considered substantially completed and held available for occupancy upon completion of tenant improvements by the developer but no later than one year from cessation of major construction activity (as distinguished from activities such as routine maintenance and cleanup).

23. If portions of a rental project are substantially completed and occupied by tenants or held available for occupancy and other portions have not yet reached that stage, the substantially completed portions shall be accounted for as a separate project. Costs incurred shall be allocated between the portions under construction and the portions substantially completed and held available for occupancy.

Recoverability

24. The carrying amount of a real estate project, or parts thereof, held for sale or development and sale shall not exceed net realizable value. If costs exceed net realizable value, capitalization of costs associated with development and construction of a property shall not cease, but rather an allowance shall be provided to reduce the carrying amount to estimated net realizable value, determined on the basis of an evaluation of individual projects. An individual project, for this purpose, consists of components that are relatively homogeneous, integral parts of a whole (for example, individual houses in a residential tract, individual units in a condominium complex, and individual lots in a subdivision and amenities). Therefore, a multiphase development consisting of a tract of single-family houses, a condominium complex, and a lot subdivision generally would be evaluated as three separate projects.

25. Evidence of insufficient rental demand for a rental project currently under construction may indicate an impairment of the carrying value. If it is probable that the insufficient rental demand is other than temporary, an allowance for losses shall be provided, whether or not construction is actually suspended.

Amendments to Other Pronouncement

26. The references to AICPA Statements of Position 78-3, *Accounting for Costs to Sell and Rent, and Initial Rental Operations of, Real Estate Projects,* and 80-3, *Accounting for Real Estate Acquisition, Development, and Construction Costs,* are deleted from Appendixes A and B of FASB Statement No. 32, *Specialized Accounting and Reporting Principles and Practices in AICPA Statements of Position and Guides on Accounting and Auditing Matters,* respectively.

Effective Date and Transition

27. This Statement shall be applied to costs of real estate projects incurred in fiscal years beginning after December 31, 1982. Earlier application is encouraged but not required.

The provisions of this Statement need not be applied to immaterial items.

This Statement was adopted by the affirmative votes of six members of the Financial Accounting Standards Board. Mr. Morgan dissented.

Mr. Morgan dissents to the issuance of this Statement. Although he recognizes the Board's commitment, as stated in paragraph 2 of Statement 32, to extract specialized principles and practices from SOPs and Guides and to issue them as FASB Statements and the fact that issuance of this Statement is considered by a majority of Board members as a fulfillment of part of that commitment, Mr. Morgan believes this Statement should be deferred until certain other projects are completed.

[11]Refer to paragraph 22 for the definition of *substantially completed and held available for occupancy.*

Incorporation of these detailed guidelines into accounting standards is inappropriate at this time in view of two projects in process that should bear on the nature and effect of accounting standards in this area.

a. The Board's project on financial reporting by private and small public companies
b. The August 1982 report of the Financial Accounting Foundation Structure Committee, which acknowledges the comments of many respondents that the Board should deal primarily with broad accounting standards issues and charges the Board to develop a plan, for consideration by the Trustees, to provide timely *guidance* for implementation questions and emerging issues

Mr. Morgan believes that no urgent need for an FASB Statement on this subject has been demonstrated. Accordingly, he believes it more prudent to complete the broader, more general projects before further considering whether this Statement is needed.

Members of the Financial Accounting Standards Board:

Donald J. Kirk, *Chairman*
Frank E. Block
John W. March
Robert A. Morgan
David Mosso
Robert T. Sprouse
Ralph E. Walters

Appendix A

GLOSSARY

28. This glossary defines certain terms as they are used in this Statement.

Amenities
Examples of amenities include golf courses, utility plants, clubhouses, swimming pools, tennis courts, indoor recreational facilities, and parking facilities.

Common Costs
Costs that relate to two or more units within a real estate project.

Costs Incurred to Rent Real Estate Projects
Examples of such costs include costs of model units and their furnishings, rental facilities, semipermanent signs, rental brochures, advertising, "grand openings," and rental overhead including rental salaries.

Costs Incurred to Sell Real Estate Projects
Examples of such costs include costs of model units and their furnishings, sales facilities, sales brochures, legal fees for preparation of prospectuses, semipermanent signs, advertising, "grand openings," and sales overhead including sales salaries.

Fair Value
The amount in cash or cash equivalent value of other consideration that a real estate parcel would yield in a current sale between a willing buyer and a willing seller (i.e., selling price), that is, other than in a forced or liquidation sale. The fair value of a parcel is affected by its physical characteristics, its probable ultimate use, and the time required for the buyer to make such use of the property considering access, development plans, zoning restrictions, and market absorption factors.

Incidental Operations
Revenue-producing activities engaged in during the holding or development period to reduce the cost of developing the property for its intended use, as distinguished from activities designed to generate a profit or a return from the use of the property.

Incremental Costs of Incidental Operations
Costs that would not be incurred except in relation to the conduct of incidental operations. Interest, taxes, insurance, security, and similar costs that would be incurred during the development of a real estate project regardless of whether incidental operations were conducted are not incremental costs.

Incremental Revenues from Incidental Operations
Revenues that would not be produced except in relation to the conduct of incidental operations.

Indirect Project Costs
Costs incurred after the acquisition of the property, such as construction administration (for example, the costs associated with a field office at a project site and the administrative personnel that staff the office), legal fees, and various office costs, that clearly relate to projects under development or construction. Examples of office costs that may be considered indirect project costs are cost accounting, design, and other departments providing services that are clearly related to real estate projects.

Net Realizable Value
The estimated selling price in the ordinary

course of business less estimated costs of completion (to the stage of completion assumed in determining the selling price), holding, and disposal.

Phase
A parcel on which units are to be constructed concurrently.

Preacquisition Costs
Costs related to a property that are incurred for the express purpose of, but prior to, obtaining that property. Examples of preacquisition costs may be costs of surveying, zoning or traffic studies, or payments to obtain an option on the property.

Project Costs
Costs clearly associated with the acquisition, development, and construction of a real estate project.

Relative Fair Value before Construction
The fair value of each land parcel in a real estate project in relation to the fair value of the other parcels in the project, exclusive of value added by on-site development and construction activities.

Appendix B

BACKGROUND INFORMATION AND SUMMARY OF CONSIDERATION OF COMMENTS ON EXPOSURE DRAFT

29. As discussed in Statement 32, the FASB is extracting the specialized[12] accounting and reporting principles and practices from AICPA SOPs and Guides on accounting and auditing matters and issuing them in FASB Statements after appropriate due process. This Statement extracts without significant changes the specialized principles and practices from AICPA SOPs 80-3, *Accounting for Real Estate Acquisition, Development, and Construction Costs,* and 78-3, *Accounting for Costs to Sell and Rent, and Initial Rental Operations of, Real Estate Projects,* and those from the AICPA Industry Accounting Guide (Guide), *Accounting for Retail Land Sales,* that address costs of real estate projects. Accounting and reporting standards that apply to costs in general also apply to real estate costs, and the standards in this Statement are in addition to those standards.

30. SOP 80-3 was developed to provide guidance in accounting for costs associated with real estate acquisition, development, and construction. Trends in real estate development activities at the time SOP 80-3 was developed had dramatically increased the size of enterprises engaged in real estate development, the cost of individual projects, and the time required to complete the development of individual projects. Those trends focused attention on the need for guidance. SOP 80-3 specifies when costs related to a real estate project should be capitalized and how those costs should be allocated to the components of a real estate project.

31. SOP 78-3 was developed to eliminate the wide diversity in practice in accounting for costs to sell and rent real estate projects and the costs and revenues during the initial operating period of a rental project before occupancy stabilizes (sometimes referred to as the "rent-up" period).

32. The Guide was developed to clarify and standardize the accounting for retail land sales. The Guide discusses both the timing of revenue and income recognition and costs to be capitalized. This Statement incorporates only the principles addressing the accounting for costs. The specialized principles dealing with revenue and income recognition have been extracted into Statement 66.

33. Board members have assented to the issuance of this Statement on the basis that it is an appropriate extraction of existing specialized principles and practices and that a comprehensive reconsideration of those principles and practices was not contemplated in undertaking this FASB project. Most of the background material and discussion of accounting alternatives have not been carried forward from the AICPA real estate related SOPs and Guide. The Board's conceptual framework project on accounting recognition criteria will address recognition issues relating to elements of financial statements. A Statement of Financial Accounting Concepts resulting from that project in due course will serve as a basis for evaluating existing standards and practices. Accordingly, the Board may wish to evaluate the standards in this Statement when its conceptual framework project is completed.

34. An Exposure Draft of a proposed FASB Statement, *Accounting for Costs and Initial Rental Operations of Real Estate Projects,* was issued on December 15, 1981. The Board received 37 comment letters in response to the Exposure Draft. Certain of the comments received and the Board's consideration of them are discussed in this appendix.

---

[12]The term *specialized* is used to refer to those accounting and reporting principles and practices in AICPA Guides and SOPs that are neither superseded by nor contained in Accounting Research Bulletins, APB Opinions, FASB Statements, or FASB Interpretations.

Due Process

35. Several respondents questioned the appropriateness of extracting specialized accounting principles from AICPA documents that had not been subjected to the FASB's extensive due process procedures. They noted the Guides and SOPs were promulgated through a process that did not include input from industry, academe, or the general public and that those documents were not exposed for comments before they were issued.

36. The extraction process is described in paragraph 29 of this Statement, paragraphs 1-9 of FASB Statement 32, and the FASB's *Request for Written Comments on an FASB Proposal for Dealing with Industry Accounting Matters and Accounting Questions of Limited Application.* Input from the public has been received and carefully considered:

a. At a meeting of the Financial Accounting Standards Advisory Council in July 1978 at which the extraction process was discussed
b. In the form of 157 letters of comment on the request for written comments described above
c. In the form of 53 letters of comment in response to the Exposure Draft, *Specialized Accounting and Reporting Principles and Practices in AICPA Industry Accounting Guides, Industry Audit Guides, and Statements of Position*
d. At two meetings of the FASB Task Force on Specialized Principles for the Real Estate Industry in 1981
e. In extensive oral and written comments from task force members on several drafts of the Exposure Draft, *Accounting for Costs and Initial Rental Operations of Real Estate Projects,* and of this Statement
f. In the form of 37 letters of comment on the Exposure Draft

The Board believes it has followed its required due process procedures and that it is appropriate to issue this Statement. In addition, in its August 1982 report, the Structure Committee of the Financial Accounting Foundation said it believes the program to extract specialized accounting standards from AICPA pronouncements and issue them as FASB Statements is consistent with the Board's mission (page 18 of the report).

Initial Rental Operations

37. Respondents commented on the appropriateness of the proposed provision that a rental project changes from nonoperating to operating status when it is substantially completed and held available for occupancy. Some respondents said that the proposed provision was acceptable although they suggested that further clarification of the phrase *substantially completed and held available for occupancy* was necessary, specifically, how tenant improvements should be treated. Some respondents suggested that a limit of one year be placed on the length of time a project that is substantially completed (other than tenant improvements) and held available for occupancy can remain in a nonoperating status.

38. Other respondents recommended that the "percentage-of-occupancy" method, or some variation thereof, be used to phase in depreciation and other operating costs. The Board considered the percentage-of-occupancy method but concurred with a majority of respondents that the method proposed in the Exposure Draft, modified by a one-year maximum period, was more appropriate. The Board has therefore modified the provisions of the Exposure Draft to state that a project shall be considered to be substantially completed and held available for occupancy upon completion of tenant improvements by the developer but no later than one year from cessation of major construction activity.

Amenities

39. With respect to the proposed accounting for amenities, some respondents indicated that the Exposure Draft appropriately extracted the relevant provisions of SOP 80-3. A few of those respondents also indicated that paragraph 13(b) of the Exposure Draft should be modified to indicate that downward revision of costs allocated to an amenity would be appropriate in the event of an impairment.

40. A few respondents believe that the provisions of the retail land sales Guide should have been extracted instead of the provisions of SOP 80-3. They believe those provisions would not have required any adjustment for fair value at the date of substantial physical completion.

41. Although the Board agrees that the provisions of the retail land sales Guide would not have required a fair value adjustment, it concluded that any excess of capitalizable costs over fair value should be allocated as common costs and no changes have been made to the provisions of the Exposure Draft.

Revisions of Estimates

42. Some respondents commented that the seller's performance of development and construction work is very similar to the long-term construction contracts discussed in SOP 81-1, *Accounting for Performance of Construction-Type and Certain Production-Type Contracts.* SOP 81-1 requires that revisions of estimates be accounted for by the cumu-

lative catch-up method and those respondents believed that the accounting for real estate should be consistent.

43. The provisions in the Exposure Draft extracted from SOP 80-3 are consistent with paragraph 31 of Opinion 20, which requires that a change in estimate should be accounted for in (a) the period of change if the change affects that period only or (b) the period of change and future periods if the change affects both. The Board has concluded that this Statement should rely on the general provisions of Opinion 20. The provisions of SOP 81-1 will be considered when the specialized accounting principles and practices from that AICPA document are extracted.

Interest as a Holding Cost

44. Some of the respondents indicated that the definition of net realizable value needed clarification, particularly whether interest not capitalized under Statement 34 should be considered as a holding cost in determining net realizable value.

45. The Board considered the need to address the issue of interest as a holding cost in this document. The Board concluded that it was not appropriate to address this issue within the real estate extraction project because the issue is not limited to real estate transactions.

Allocation of Capitalized Costs to the Components of Real Estate Projects

46. A number of respondents commented that the guidance in the Exposure Draft on allocation of capitalized costs to the components of real estate projects precluded the use of "area" and "other value" methods as provided in the retail land sales Guide. Those respondents indicated that this omission would have a significant impact on the real estate industry.

47. The Board has agreed with those respondents. The paragraph has been revised to allow for area or other value methods to be used if specific identification or relative fair and sales value methods, as originally proposed, are impracticable.

Other Comments

48. Several respondents suggested various substantive changes to the Exposure Draft. Adoption of those suggestions would have required a reconsideration of some of the provisions of the Guide and SOPs. Such a reconsideration is not contemplated in the extraction project unless a proposed change meets one of the three criteria for change included in the "Notice for Recipients" of the Exposure Draft or is broadly supported. The proposed changes did not meet the criteria for change and were not broadly supported. Accordingly, the Board did not adopt those suggestions. However, based on suggestions from respondents to the Exposure Draft, the Board has made several other changes that it believes clarify the Statement.

49. The Board has concluded that it can reach an informed decision on the basis of existing information without a public hearing and that the effective date and transition specified in paragraph 27 are advisable in the circumstances.

Statement of Financial Accounting Standards No. 68
Research and Development Arrangements

STATUS

Issued: October 1982

Effective Date: For research and development arrangements entered into after December 31, 1982

Affects: No other pronouncements

Affected by: No other pronouncements

SUMMARY

This Statement specifies how an enterprise should account for its obligation under an arrangement for the funding of its research and development by others. The enterprise must determine whether it is obligated only to perform contractual research and development for others, or is otherwise obligated. To the extent that the enterprise is obligated to repay the other parties, it records a liability and charges research and development costs to expense as incurred.

Statement of Financial Accounting Standards No. 68
Research and Development Arrangements

CONTENTS

INTRODUCTION

1. The FASB has been asked how an enterprise should account for an arrangement through which research and development is funded by other parties. Some consider a research and development arrangement to be simply a contract to do research for others. Others believe that such arrangements are, in essence, borrowings by the enterprise. They believe the research and development expenditures should be reflected in the enterprise's financial statements as current expenses in accordance with FASB Statement No. 2, *Accounting for Research and Development Costs.* As a result of those different views, the reporting of similar arrangements has been inconsistent.

2. The legal structure of a research and development arrangement may take a variety of forms and often is influenced by federal and state income tax and securities regulations. An enterprise might have an equity interest in the arrangement, or its legal involvement might be only contractual (for example, a contract to provide services and an option to acquire the results of the research and development).

SCOPE

3. This Statement establishes standards of financial accounting and reporting for an enterprise that is a party to a research and development arrangement through which it can obtain the results of research and development funded partially or entirely by others. It applies whether the research and development is performed by the enterprise, the funding parties, or a third party. Although the limited-partnership form of arrangement is used for illustrative purposes in this Statement, the standards also apply for other forms. This Statement does not address reporting of government-sponsored research and development.

STANDARDS OF FINANCIAL ACCOUNTING AND REPORTING

4. An enterprise shall determine the nature of the obligation it incurs when it enters into an arrangement with other parties who fund its research and development. The factors discussed in paragraphs 5-11 and other factors that may be present and relevant to a particular arrangement shall be considered when determining the nature of the enterprise's obligation.

Obligation Is a Liability to Repay the Other Parties

5. If the enterprise is obligated to repay any of the funds provided by the other parties regardless of the outcome of the research and development, the enterprise shall estimate and recognize that liability. This requirement applies whether the enterprise may settle the liability by paying cash, by issuing securities, or by some other means.

6. To conclude that a liability does not exist, the transfer of the financial risk involved with research and development from the enterprise to the other parties must be substantive and genuine. To the extent that the enterprise is committed to repay any of the funds provided by the other parties regardless of the outcome of the research and development, all or part of the risk has not been transferred. The following are some examples in which the enterprise is committed to repay:

a. The enterprise guarantees, or has a contractual commitment that assures, repayment of the funds provided by the other parties regardless of the outcome of the research and development.

b. The other parties can require the enterprise to purchase their interest in the research and development regardless of the outcome.

c. The other parties automatically will receive debt or equity securities of the enterprise upon termination or completion of the research and development regardless of the outcome.

7. Even though the written agreements or contracts under the arrangement do not require the enterprise to repay any of the funds provided by the other parties, surrounding conditions might indicate that the enterprise is likely to bear the risk of failure of the research and development. If those conditions suggest that it is probable[1] that the enterprise will repay any of the funds regardless of the outcome of the research and development, there is a presumption that the enterprise has an obligation to repay the other parties. That presumption can be overcome only by substantial evidence to the contrary.

8. Examples of conditions leading to the presumption that the enterprise will repay the other parties include the following:

a. The enterprise has indicated an intent to repay all or a portion of the funds provided regardless of the outcome of the research and development.

b. The enterprise would suffer a severe economic penalty if it failed to repay any of the funds provided to it regardless of the outcome of the research and development. An economic penalty is considered "severe" if in the normal course of business an enterprise would probably choose to pay the other parties rather than incur the penalty. For example, an enterprise might purchase the partnership's interest in the research and development if the enterprise had provided the partnership with proprietary basic technology necessary for the enterprise's ongoing operations without retaining a way to recover that technology, or prevent it from being transferred to another party, except by purchasing the partnership's interest.

c. A significant related party[2] relationship between the enterprise and the parties funding the research and development exists at the time the enterprise enters into the arrangement.

d. The enterprise has essentially completed the project before entering into the arrangement.

9. An enterprise that incurs a liability to repay the other parties shall charge the research and development costs to expense as incurred. The amount of funds provided by the other parties might exceed the enterprise's liability. That might be the case, for example, if license agreements or partial buy-out provisions permit the enterprise to use the results of the research and development or to reacquire certain basic technology or other assets for an amount that is less than the funds provided. Those agreements or provisions might limit the extent to which the enterprise is economically compelled to buy out the other parties regardless of the outcome. In those situations, the liability to repay the other parties might be limited to a specified price for licensing the results or for purchasing a partial interest in the results. If the enterprise's liability is less than the funds provided, the enterprise shall charge its portion of the research and development costs to expense in the same manner as the liability is incurred. For example, the liability might arise as the initial funds are expended, or the liability might arise on a pro rata basis.

Obligation Is to Perform Contractual Services

10. To the extent that the financial risk associated with the research and development has been transferred because repayment of any of the funds provided by the other parties depends *solely* on the results of the research and development having future economic benefit, the enterprise shall account for its obligation as a contract to perform research and development for others.

11. If the enterprise's obligation is to perform research and development for others and the enterprise subsequently decides to exercise an option to purchase the other parties' interests in the research and development arrangement or to obtain the exclusive rights to the results of the research and development, the nature of those results and their future use shall determine the accounting for the purchase transaction.[3]

Loan or Advance to the Other Parties

12. If repayment to the enterprise of any loan or advance by the enterprise to the other parties depends solely on the results of the research and development having future economic benefit, the

[1] *Probable* is used here consistent with its use in FASB Statement No. 5, *Accounting for Contingencies,* to mean that repayment is likely.

[2] *Related parties* are defined in FASB Statement No. 57, *Related Party Disclosures.*

[3] Paragraph 5 of FASB Interpretation No. 4, *Applicability of FASB Statement No. 2 to Business Combinations Accounted for by the Purchase Method,* states: ". . . the accounting for the cost of an item to be used in research and development activities is the same under paragraphs 11 and 12 of Statement 2 whether the item is purchased singly, or as part of a group of assets, or as part of an entire enterprise in a business combination accounted for by the purchase method." The accounting for other identifiable intangible assets acquired by the enterprise is specified in APB Opinion No. 17, *Intangible Assets.*

loan or advance shall be accounted for as costs incurred by the enterprise. The costs shall be charged to research and development expense unless the loan or advance to the other parties can be identified as relating to some other activity, for example, marketing or advertising, in which case the costs shall be accounted for according to their nature.

Issuance of Warrants or Similar Instruments

13. If warrants or similar instruments are issued in connection with the arrangement, the enterprise shall report a portion of the proceeds to be provided by the other parties as paid-in capital. The amount so reported shall be the fair value of the instruments at the date of the arrangement.

Disclosures

14. An enterprise that under the provisions of this Statement accounts for its obligation under a research and development arrangement as a contract to perform research and development for others shall disclose[4] the following:[5]

a. The terms of significant agreements under the research and development arrangement (including royalty arrangements, purchase provisions, license agreements, and commitments to provide additional funding) as of the date of each balance sheet presented
b. The amount of compensation earned and costs incurred under such contracts for each period for which an income statement is presented

Effective Date and Transition

15. The provisions of this Statement shall be effective for research and development arrangements covered by this Statement that are entered into after December 31, 1982 with earlier application encouraged in financial statements that have not been previously issued. This Statement may be, but is not required to be, applied retroactively to previously issued financial statements. If previously issued financial statements are restated, the financial statements shall, in the year that this Statement is first applied, disclose the nature of any restatement and its effects on income before extraordinary items, net income, and related per share amounts for each restated year presented.

The provisions of this Statement need not be applied to immaterial items.

This Statement was adopted by the unanimous vote of the seven members of the Financial Accounting Standards Board:

Donald J. Kirk, *Chairman*
Frank E. Block
John W. March
Robert A. Morgan
David Mosso
Robert T. Sprouse
Ralph E. Walters

Appendix A

BACKGROUND INFORMATION

16. Research and development arrangements have been used to finance the research and development of a variety of new products, such as information processing systems, medical technology, experimental drugs, electronic devices, and aerospace equipment. Enterprises may enter into arrangements for different reasons. The objectives of entering into an arrangement may be to:

a. Transfer all or part of the uncertainty and risk involved with the research and development to others
b. Obtain the benefit of funds that are made available because of tax incentives for investors
c. Attract qualified research and development personnel who otherwise might be concerned that funding might not be assured
d. Avoid expanding the ownership of the enterprise and the impact on earnings per share that would result from issuing equity securities
e. Avoid debt service expenditures and the impact on the enterprise's debt-to-equity ratio that would result from issuing debt securities
f. Avoid the impact on the enterprise's near-term earnings that would result if it incurred the related research and development expenses

17. Many arrangements have been formed as limited partnerships. In some, the enterprise or a related party is the general partner who manages the research and development activities. Sometimes, the limited partners are related to the enterprise. In some arrangements, the enterprise has the basic

[4]Statement 57 specifies additional disclosure requirements for related party transactions and certain control relationships.

[5]An enterprise that is a party to more than one research and development arrangement need not separately disclose each arrangement unless separate disclosure is necessary to understand the effects on the financial statements. Aggregation of similar arrangements by type may be appropriate.

technology needed for the research and development and has performed preliminary research and development work to determine the attractiveness of further work. The enterprise might contribute the preliminary research and development work and basic technology to the partnership for a minor equity interest or might license or give the rights to the preliminary work and basic technology to the partnership.

18. The terms of the arrangement usually contemplate, but do not guarantee, that the funds provided by the limited partners will be sufficient to complete the intended research and development. However, some agreements permit or require the general partner to sell additional limited-partnership interests or to use its own funds if the funds provided are insufficient to complete the research and development effort. The enterprise sometimes provides additional funds through loans or advances to the partnership. Repayment of the loans or advances sometimes is guaranteed by the partnership although repayment sometimes is contingent on realization of future economic benefits of the research and development; for example, repayment might be made through offsets against the purchase price for the results of the project or against royalty payments.

19. The enterprise or a related party of the enterprise usually performs the research and development work under a contract with the partnership. The compensation under the research and development contract usually is either a fixed fee or reimbursement of direct costs plus a fixed fee or fixed percentage of those costs. The work is performed on a best-efforts basis with no guarantee of either technological or commercial success. The partnership retains legal ownership of the results of the research and development and sometimes retains legal rights to the basic technology provided by the enterprise.

20. Either as part of the partnership agreement or through contracts with the partnership, the enterprise usually has an option either to purchase the partnership's interest in or to obtain the exclusive rights to the entire results of the research and development in return for a lump sum payment or royalty payments to the partnership. Some arrangements contain a provision that permits the enterprise to acquire complete ownership of the results for a specified amount of the enterprise's stock or cash at some future time. In some of those purchase agreements, the partnership has the option to receive either the enterprise's stock or cash; in others, the enterprise makes the decision. Sometimes, warrants or similar instruments to purchase the enterprise's stock are issued in connection with the arrangement.

21. An enterprise that is a party to an arrangement through which research and development is funded by other parties usually incurs an obligation when it enters into the arrangement. The nature and extent of the enterprise's obligation are sometimes difficult to determine and can range from an obligation to perform contract research and development work to an obligation to repay the other parties, with a return, for the funds provided.

22. If the results of the research and development are determined to have sufficient future economic benefit, the enterprise probably will exercise its option either to purchase the partnership's interests in or to obtain the exclusive rights to the entire results. If the results do not have future economic benefit, the enterprise usually is not legally required to exercise its option; however, there may be valid business reasons for the enterprise to acquire the results even though the original objectives of the research and development are not met. For example, the enterprise may want to obtain ownership of results that have value to the enterprise even though they do not meet the original objectives. Other reasons may be to maintain the ability to enter into another arrangement with the same parties or similar arrangements with other parties; to recover the ownership of or rights to the enterprise's basic technology or to prevent the partnership from providing that technology to others; to avoid any potential future claim against the use of the results; or to fulfill a moral obligation (for example, the enterprise is the general partner and due to a conflict of interest feels compelled to exercise its option).

23. Although the enterprise's legal liabilities will be specified in the various contracts and agreements under the arrangement, accounting representations should not necessarily be limited to legal requirements. Depending on the facts and circumstances involved in a particular research and development arrangement, future payments by the enterprise to the other parties ostensibly for royalties or to purchase the partnership's interests in or to obtain the exclusive rights to the research and development results might actually be any of the following: (a) the settlement of a borrowing, (b) the purchase price of an asset, or (c) royalties for the use of an asset. The financial reporting of an enterprise that is a party to a research and development arrangement should represent faithfully what it purports to represent and should not subordinate substance to form.

Appendix B

BASIS FOR CONCLUSIONS

24. An Exposure Draft of a proposed Statement, *Research and Development Arrangements,* was

issued on April 27, 1982. The Board received 37 letters of comment in response to that Exposure Draft. This appendix discusses the factors that the Board considered significant in reaching the conclusions in this Statement. Individual Board members gave greater weight to some factors than to others.

25. Several respondents to the Exposure Draft questioned the need for a project to specify how an enterprise that is a party to a research and development arrangement should account for its obligation under the arrangement. Although they generally agreed with the principles proposed in the Exposure Draft, they expressed the view that a careful reading of other Statements, such as FASB Statements No. 2, *Accounting for Research and Development Costs,* No. 5, *Accounting for Contingencies,* and No. 57, *Related Party Disclosures,* would lead to the correct answers. However, because information received by the Board showed significant diversity in the accounting practices of enterprises involved in similar research and development arrangements, the Board concluded that those Statements do not provide adequate guidance. Some enterprises accounted for the proceeds received from the other parties as contract revenues from performing research and development for others while other enterprises accounted for the proceeds from similar arrangements as borrowings. Various regulatory agencies raised questions about the diversity in accounting for similar arrangements, and industry and the accounting profession asked the FASB to provide guidance.

26. Some people believe that most, if not all, research and development arrangements are borrowing transactions. Those with that view believe that in most, if not all, cases the enterprise controls the right to the future economic benefits of the research and development and has in one form or another an obligation to repay principal and pay interest on the borrowed funds, even though those amounts may be paid in the form of royalties.

27. Others argue for contract accounting because they believe that in most, if not all, research and development arrangements the financial risk is transferred to others, the results of the research and development belong to the partnership, and the enterprise is not obligated to acquire the results or to acquire the partnership's interest therein. They believe that the enterprise has a liability only if it decides to exercise its option.

28. The Board believes that each of the above positions is appropriate in certain situations and that neither position is universally applicable to all research and development arrangements. The Board's conclusions in this Statement are derived from FASB Concepts Statement No. 3, *Elements of Financial Statements of Business Enterprises,* which defines liabilities as:

> . . . Probable . . . future sacrifices of economic benefits arising from present obligations . . . of a particular entity to transfer assets or provide services to other entities in the future as a result of past transactions or events. [paragraph 28]

Concepts Statement 3 uses the term *obligation* to include duties imposed legally or socially; that is, what an enterprise is bound to do by contract, promise, or moral responsibility. Therefore, an enterprise may have a liability that is recognized for financial reporting even though it is not a legal liability.

29. Some respondents believed that the Board should have based its conclusions on the definition of a loss contingency in Statement 5 rather than on the definition of a liability in Concepts Statement 3. The Board concluded that Statement 5 does not address the primary issue involved in determining whether an enterprise involved in a research and development arrangement has a liability. Statement 5 deals with contingencies; that is, an existing condition, situation, or set of circumstances involving *uncertainty as to possible gain or loss* that will ultimately be resolved when one or more future events occur or fail to occur. This Statement deals with a transaction in which the issue is whether at the time an enterprise enters into a research and development arrangement (a) it is *committed* to repay any of the funds provided by the other parties regardless of the outcome of the research and development, (b) existing conditions indicate that it is likely that the enterprise will repay the other parties regardless of the outcome, or (c) the enterprise is obligated only to perform research and development work for others.

30. Some people consider the likelihood of success of the research and development as the key issue in who bears the risk of failure of those activities. However, even though future benefits from a particular project may be foreseen, the amount generally cannot be measured with a reasonable degree of certainty. The key question in determining who bears the risk of failure is whether the enterprise is obligated to repay any of the funds provided by the other parties regardless of the outcome of the research and development. Concepts Statement 3 states that "an enterprise is not obligated to sacrifice assets in the future if it can avoid the future sacrifice at its discretion without significant penalty."[6] A deter-

[6]Concepts Statement 3, paragraph 135.

mination must be made of the penalty, if any, that the enterprise will incur if it does not repay any of the funds provided.

31. If an enterprise is contractually committed to repay any of the funds provided or has guaranteed or assured the other parties of repayment of the funds provided, regardless of the outcome of the research and development, the enterprise clearly has a liability to repay the other parties. However, because of tax considerations, the agreements and contracts under the arrangement normally state that the enterprise is obligated only to perform services and generally do not require the enterprise to repay any of the funds provided if the research and development does not have future economic benefit. Nonetheless, the Board believes that substantive and genuine transfer of risk is essential for the enterprise's obligation to be limited to performing contractual services and that certain conditions create a presumption that the transfer of risk to the other parties may not be substantive or genuine. An enterprise involved in a research and development arrangement might incur equitable or constructive obligations through actions that bind the enterprise or by circumstances that change the nature of the enterprise's obligation from one to perform services for a fee to one to repay amounts provided by the other parties. For example, an enterprise might provide the partnership with basic technology necessary for the enterprise's ongoing operations without retaining a way to recover that technology, or to prevent it from being transferred to another party, except by purchasing the partnership's interest in the research and development. Another example might be that there is a conflict of interest and the limited partners could reasonably be expected to litigate successfully if the enterprise does not buy out the partnership.

32. Some respondents questioned whether the mere presence in a research and development arrangement of parties related to the enterprise should lead to a presumption that a liability has been incurred. In particular, they questioned the relevance of the enterprise's role as general partner. Although transactions between related parties commonly occur in the normal course of business, the conditions of competitive free-market dealings between independent parties may not exist. Accordingly, the enterprise might be influenced by considerations other than those that would exist in arm's-length transactions with unrelated parties. This is particularly true if the related parties can directly or indirectly influence the enterprise's decision whether or not to acquire the results of the research and development. The Board concluded that the combined attractiveness of "off-balance-sheet" financing for the enterprise and tax incentives for related party investors may cause the substance of such an arrangement to differ from its form. However, the Board does not believe that the enterprise's obligation should be accounted for as a liability just because the enterprise is the general partner. The example in paragraph 8(c) has been revised accordingly.

33. The Board believes that the enterprise should account for the amount of any loan or advance to the partnership, the collection of which is contingent on the results of the research and development having future economic benefit, as costs incurred by the enterprise because of the uncertainty of recovery of those loans and advances. As discussed in the "Basis for Conclusions" of Statement 2, "estimates of the rate of success of research and development projects vary markedly—depending in part on how narrowly one defines a 'project' and how one defines 'success'—but all such estimates indicate a high failure rate."[7] Statement 2 further states that "even after a project has passed beyond the research and development stage, and a new or improved product or process is being marketed or used, the failure rate is high."[8] Statement 2 requires any research and development costs to be charged to expense as those costs are incurred. If the costs relate to some other activity, for example, marketing or advertising, the costs should be accounted for according to their nature.

34. If the enterprise exercises an option to purchase the partnership's interest in or to obtain the exclusive rights to the results of the research and development, a question arises as to whether the amount paid should be an expense or the purchase price of an intangible asset. If an intangible asset is developed, the Board believes that there is a distinction between an amount paid for the results of a known successful project and the costs incurred in ongoing research and development whose ultimate success or failure is unknown. An enterprise exercising a purchase option on a successful project has made a decision about the results of past research and development costs. The uncertainty usually has diminished to the point that an evaluation, comparable to an evaluation made when an intangible asset is acquired from an independent party, can be made about the future economic benefits of the results. If a purchase price is reported as the cost of an intangible asset, the provisions of FASB Interpretation No. 4, *Applicability of FASB Statement No. 2 to Business Combinations Accounted for by the Purchase Method,* or of APB Opinion No. 17, *Intangible Assets,* apply.

[7]Statement 2, paragraph 39.

[8]Ibid., paragraph 40.

35. If the enterprise's liability is less than the amount of funds provided by the other parties, the Exposure Draft would have required an enterprise to charge its portion of the research and development costs relating to the research and development to expense on a pro rata basis. Several respondents argued that a pro rata approach is appropriate only if the enterprise must repay on a pro rata basis. In some instances, the enterprise's liability might arise as the initial funds are spent. The Board agreed that a pro rata approach might not be appropriate in all circumstances. Paragraph 9 has been revised to require that the enterprise charge its portion of the research and development costs to expense in the same manner as the enterprise's liability is incurred.

36. Several respondents suggested that the final Statement provide detailed guidance for the various aspects of research and development arrangements. Most of the guidance sought deals with accounting in general or is addressed by other existing generally accepted accounting principles; for example, guidance for discounting a liability is contained in APB Opinion No. 21, *Interest on Receivables and Payables,* and guidance for recognition of losses on cost overruns is contained in Statement 5. Accordingly, the Board concluded that it is unnecessary to specify such detailed guidance in this Statement. Some respondents also requested that the final Statement specify the accounting and reporting for contract revenues and costs under a research and development arrangement. Those issues relate to accounting and reporting for contracts in general, which is beyond the scope of this Statement.

37. The Exposure Draft included a notice to recipients specifically requesting comments on the proposed disclosures. Several respondents said that the proposed disclosure requirements were excessive for an enterprise's obligation accounted for as a liability because adequate disclosures are required by other existing generally accepted accounting principles. The Board agreed with those respondents and, accordingly, the disclosure requirements for an obligation accounted for as a liability have not been carried forward from the Exposure Draft. Some respondents also disagreed with requiring the disclosures as of each balance sheet presented and about requiring that the disclosures be presented in the footnotes. The Board concluded that the disclosures required by this Statement should be provided for each balance sheet presented because the research and development activities often are long-term in nature and the disclosures are useful for comparison. The Board agreed that it is acceptable to present the disclosures either in the primary financial statements or in the footnotes and revised the disclosure requirements accordingly.

38. Some respondents requested that the transition provisions of the Exposure Draft be modified to permit retroactive restatement of previously issued financial statements. They believe that permitting retroactive restatement would enable enterprises that have used various accounting alternatives to report old and new arrangements consistently and thereby improve overall comparability. The Board agreed and revised the transition to permit retroactive restatement for previously issued financial statements.

39. The Board concluded that it can reach an informed decision on the basis of existing information without a public hearing and that the effective date and transition specified in paragraph 15 are advisable in the circumstances.

Statement of Financial Accounting Standards No. 69
Disclosures about Oil and Gas Producing Activities

an amendment of FASB Statements 19, 25, 33, and 39

STATUS

Issued: November 1982

Effective Date: For fiscal years beginning on or after December 15, 1982

Affects: Supersedes FAS 19, paragraphs 48 through 59
Supersedes FAS 25, paragraphs 6 and 8
Supersedes FAS 33, paragraphs 51(b), 52(b), and 53(a)
Supersedes FAS 39, paragraphs 10, 11, and 12
Supersedes FAS 40, paragraph 6
Supersedes FAS 41, paragraph 7
Supersedes FAS 46, paragraph 8

Affected by: No other pronouncements

SUMMARY

This Statement establishes a comprehensive set of disclosures for oil and gas producing activities and replaces requirements of several earlier Statements. The requirement to disclose the method of accounting for costs incurred in oil and gas producing activities and the manner of disposing of related capitalized costs is continued for both publicly traded and other enterprises. None of the other requirements in this Statement is extended to enterprises that are not publicly traded, thereby eliminating existing requirements for them to disclose information about proved oil and gas reserve quantities, capitalized costs, and costs incurred.

Publicly traded enterprises with significant oil and gas activities, when presenting a complete set of annual financial statements, are to disclose the following as supplementary information, but not as a part of the financial statements:

a. Proved oil and gas reserve quantities
b. Capitalized costs relating to oil and gas producing activities
c. Costs incurred in oil and gas property acquisition, exploration, and development activities
d. Results of operations for oil and gas producing activities
e. A standardized measure of discounted future net cash flows relating to proved oil and gas reserve quantities

This Statement eliminates a previous requirement to disclose capitalized costs in complete sets of interim financial statements.

In addition, this Statement permits historical cost/constant dollar measures to be used for oil and gas mineral interests when presenting current cost information under the provisions of FASB Statement No. 39, *Financial Reporting and Changing Prices: Specialized Assets—Mining and Oil and Gas.*

NOTE

Paragraph 5 of FAS 69 originally stated:

> "(Amendments to Statements 19 and 33 contained in this Statement are indicated by shading.)"

This comment, and the shading described in the comment, have been deleted in the ensuing reprint because shading in this volume indicates paragraphs superseded or amended by subsequent pronouncements. No other changes have been made to FAS 69.

Statement of Financial Accounting Standards No. 69
Disclosures about Oil and Gas Producing Activities

an amendment of FASB Statements 19, 25, 33, and 39

CONTENTS

INTRODUCTION

1. This Statement amends FASB Statement No. 19, *Financial Accounting and Reporting by Oil and Gas Producing Companies,* by establishing disclosures about oil and gas producing activities[1] to be made for publicly traded enterprises[2] when presenting a complete set of annual financial statements.[3] Those disclosures include the information required by Statement 19 and FASB Statement No. 25, *Suspension of Certain Accounting Requirements for Oil and Gas Producing Companies,* concerning proved oil and gas reserve quantities, capitalized costs, costs incurred, and the method of accounting for costs incurred for an enterprise's oil and gas producing activities. Information about the results of operations for oil and gas producing activities, a standardized measure of discounted future net cash flows relating to proved oil and gas reserve quantities, and summary information about oil and gas producing activities associated with equity investments and minority interests also is required to be disclosed. The accounting method shall be disclosed within the financial statements; the other disclosures are considered to be supplementary information.

2. This Statement also amends Statement 19 to eliminate, for enterprises that are not publicly traded, the requirement to disclose information concerning capitalized costs, costs incurred, and proved oil and gas reserve quantities. However, this Statement maintains the requirement of Statement 25 for all enterprises to disclose the method of accounting for costs incurred in oil and gas producing activities and the manner of disposing of capitalized costs relating to those activities.

3. In addition, this Statement permits historical

[1]Statement 19 defines oil and gas producing activities as "those activities [that] involve the acquisition of mineral interests in properties, exploration (including prospecting), development, and production of crude oil, including condensate and natural gas liquids, and natural gas . . ." (par. 1).

[2]For purposes of this Statement, a publicly traded enterprise is a business enterprise (a) whose securities are traded in a public market on a domestic stock exchange or in the domestic over-the-counter market (including securities quoted only locally or regionally) or (b) whose financial statements are filed with a regulatory agency in preparation for the sale of any class of securities in a domestic market.

[3]FASB Statement No. 24, *Reporting Segment Information in Financial Statements That Are Presented in Another Enterprise's Financial Report,* refers to a complete set of financial statements as "a set of financial statements (including necessary footnotes) that present financial position, results of operations, and changes in financial position in conformity with generally accepted accounting principles" (footnote 2).

cost/constant dollar measures to be used when presenting current cost information about oil and gas mineral interests under the provisions of FASB Statement No. 39, *Financial Reporting and Changing Prices: Specialized Assets—Mining and Oil and Gas.*

4. Appendix A contains summaries and illustrations of certain disclosures about oil and gas producing activities set forth in this Statement. Background information highlighting the pertinent events that preceded the issuance of this Statement is set forth in Appendix B. The basis for the Board's conclusions, including alternative approaches considered in developing the disclosures for oil and gas producing activities, is discussed in Appendix C.

STANDARDS OF FINANCIAL ACCOUNTING AND REPORTING

Amendments to Statements 19, 25, 33, and 39

5. Paragraphs 48-59 of Statement 19, as amended by Statement 25, are superseded by paragraphs 6-34 of this Statement. Paragraphs 51-53 of FASB Statement No. 33, *Financial Reporting and Changing Prices,* as amended by Statement 39, are amended by paragraphs 35-38 of this Statement.

Applicability and Scope

6. All enterprises engaged in oil and gas producing activities shall disclose in their financial statements the method of accounting for costs incurred in those activities and the manner of disposing of capitalized costs relating to those activities.

7. In addition, publicly traded enterprises that have significant oil and gas producing activities shall disclose with complete sets of annual financial statements the information required by paragraphs 10-34 of this Statement. Those disclosures relate to the following and are considered to be supplementary information:

a. Proved oil and gas reserve quantities
b. Capitalized costs relating to oil and gas producing activities
c. Costs incurred for property acquisition, exploration, and development activities
d. Results of operations for oil and gas producing activities
e. A standardized measure of discounted future net cash flows relating to proved oil and gas reserve quantities

8. For purposes of this Statement, an enterprise is regarded as having significant oil and gas producing activities if it satisfies one or more of the following tests. The tests shall be applied separately for each year for which a complete set of annual financial statements is presented.

a. Revenues from oil and gas producing activities, as defined in paragraph 25 (including both sales to unaffiliated customers and sales or transfers to the enterprise's other operations), are 10 percent or more of the combined revenues (sales to unaffiliated customers and sales or transfers to the enterprise's other operations) of all of the enterprise's industry segments.[4]
b. Results of operations for oil and gas producing activities, excluding the effect of income taxes, are 10 percent or more of the greater of:
   (1) The combined operating profit of all industry segments that did not incur an operating loss
   (2) The combined operating loss of all industry segments that did incur an operating loss
c. The identifiable assets, defined in a similar manner as in paragraph 10 of FASB Statement No. 14, *Financial Reporting for Segments of a Business Enterprise,* relating to oil and gas producing activities are 10 percent or more of the combined identifiable assets of all industry segments.

9. The disclosures set forth in this Statement are not required in interim financial reports. However, interim financial reports shall include information about a major discovery or other favorable or adverse event that causes a significant change from the information presented in the most recent annual financial report concerning oil and gas reserve quantities.

Disclosure of Proved Oil and Gas Reserve Quantities

10. Net quantities of an enterprise's interests in proved reserves and proved developed reserves of (a) crude oil (including condensate and natural gas liquids)[5] and (b) natural gas shall be disclosed as of the beginning and the end of the year. "Net" quantities of reserves include those relating to the enterprise's operating and nonoperating interests in properties as defined in paragraph 11(a) of Statement 19. Quantities of reserves relating to royalty

[4]FASB Statement No. 14, *Financial Reporting for Segments of a Business Enterprise,* defines an industry segment as "a component of an enterprise engaged in providing a product or service or a group of related products and services primarily to unaffiliated customers (i.e., customers outside the enterprise) for a profit" (par. 10).

[5]If significant, the reserve quantity information shall be disclosed separately for natural gas liquids.

interests owned shall be included in "net" quantities if the necessary information is available to the enterprise; if reserves relating to royalty interests owned are not included because the information is unavailable, that fact and the enterprise's share of oil and gas produced for those royalty interests shall be disclosed for the year. "Net" quantities shall not include reserves relating to interests of others in properties owned by the enterprise.

11. Changes in the net quantities of an enterprise's proved reserves of oil and of gas during the year shall be disclosed. Changes resulting from each of the following shall be shown separately with appropriate explanation of significant changes:

a. *Revisions of previous estimates.* Revisions represent changes in previous estimates of proved reserves, either upward or downward, resulting from new information (except for an increase in proved acreage) normally obtained from development drilling and production history or resulting from a change in economic factors.
b. *Improved recovery.* Changes in reserve estimates resulting from application of improved recovery techniques shall be shown separately, if significant. If not significant, such changes shall be included in revisions of previous estimates.
c. *Purchases of minerals in place.*
d. *Extensions and discoveries.* Additions to proved reserves that result from (1) extension of the proved acreage of previously discovered (old) reservoirs through additional drilling in periods subsequent to discovery and (2) discovery of new fields with proved reserves or of new reservoirs of proved reserves in old fields.
e. *Production.*
f. *Sales of minerals in place.*

12. If an enterprise's proved reserves of oil and of gas are located entirely within its home country, that fact shall be disclosed. If some or all of its reserves are located in foreign countries, the disclosures of net quantities of reserves of oil and of gas and changes in them required by paragraphs 10 and 11 shall be separately disclosed for (a) the enterprise's home country (if significant reserves are located there) and (b) each foreign geographic area in which significant reserves are located. Foreign geographic areas are individual countries or groups of countries as appropriate for meaningful disclosure in the circumstances.

13. Net quantities disclosed in conformity with paragraphs 10-12 shall not include oil or gas subject to purchase under long-term supply, purchase, or similar agreements and contracts, including such agreements with ~~foreign~~ governments or authorities. However, quantities of oil or gas subject to such agreements with ~~foreign~~ governments or authorities as of the end of the year, and the net quantity of oil or gas received under the agreements during the year, shall be separately disclosed if the enterprise participates in the operation of the properties in which the oil or gas is located or otherwise serves as the "producer" of those reserves, as opposed, for example, to being an independent purchaser, broker, dealer, or importer.

14. In determining the reserve quantities to be disclosed in conformity with paragraphs 10-13:

a. If the enterprise issues consolidated financial statements, 100 percent of the net reserve quantities attributable to the parent company and 100 percent of the net reserve quantities attributable to its consolidated subsidiaries (whether or not wholly owned) shall be included. If a significant portion of those reserve quantities at the end of the year is attributable to a consolidated subsidiary(ies) in which there is a significant minority interest, that fact and the approximate portion shall be disclosed.
b. If the enterprise's financial statements include investments that are proportionately consolidated, the enterprise's reserve quantities shall include its proportionate share of the investees' net oil and gas reserves.
c. If the enterprise's financial statements include investments that are accounted for by the equity method, the investees' net oil and gas reserve quantities shall *not* be included in the disclosures of the enterprise's reserve quantities. However, the enterprise's (investor's) share of the investees' net oil and gas reserve quantities shall be separately disclosed as of the end of the year.

15. In reporting reserve quantities and changes in them, oil reserves and natural gas liquids reserves shall be stated in barrels, and gas reserves in cubic feet.

16. If important economic factors or significant uncertainties affect particular components of an enterprise's proved reserves, explanation shall be provided. Examples include unusually high expected development or lifting costs, the necessity to build a major pipeline or other major facilities before production of the reserves can begin, and contractual obligations to produce and sell a significant portion of reserves at prices that are substantially below those at which the oil or gas could otherwise be sold in the absence of the contractual obligation.

17. If a government restricts the disclosure of estimated reserves for properties under its authority, or of amounts under long-term supply, purchase, or similar agreements or contracts, or if the government requires the disclosure of reserves other than

proved, the enterprise shall indicate that the disclosed reserve estimates or amounts do not include figures for the named country or that reserve estimates include reserves other than proved.

Disclosure of Capitalized Costs Relating to Oil and Gas Producing Activities

18. The aggregate capitalized costs relating to an enterprise's oil and gas producing activities (paragraph 11 of Statement 19) and the aggregate related accumulated depreciation, depletion, amortization, and valuation allowances shall be disclosed as of the end of the year. Paragraph 5 of APB Opinion No. 12, *Omnibus Opinion—1967,* requires disclosure of "balances of major classes of depreciable assets, by nature or function." Thus, separate disclosure of capitalized costs for asset categories (a) through (d) in paragraph 11 of Statement 19 or for a combination of those categories often may be appropriate.

19. If significant, capitalized costs of unproved properties shall be separately disclosed. Capitalized costs of support equipment and facilities may be disclosed separately or included, as appropriate, with capitalized costs of proved and unproved properties.

20. If the enterprise's financial statements include investments that are accounted for by the equity method, the enterprise's share of the investees' net capitalized costs relating to oil and gas producing activities as of the end of the year shall be separately disclosed.

Disclosure of Costs Incurred in Oil and Gas Property Acquisition, Exploration, and Development Activities

21. Each of the following types of costs for the year shall be disclosed (whether those costs are capitalized or charged to expense at the time they are incurred under the provisions of paragraphs 15-22 of Statement 19):[6]

a. Property acquisition costs
b. Exploration costs
c. Development costs
~~d. Production (lifting) costs~~

22. If some or all of those costs are incurred in foreign countries, the amounts shall be disclosed separately for each of the geographic areas for which reserve quantities are disclosed (paragraph 12). If significant costs have been incurred to acquire mineral interests that have proved reserves, those costs shall be disclosed separately from the costs of acquiring unproved properties.

23. If the enterprise's financial statements include investments that are accounted for by the equity method, the enterprise's share of the investees' property acquisition, exploration, and development costs incurred in oil and gas producing activities shall be separately disclosed for the year, in the aggregate and for each geographic area for which reserve quantities are disclosed (paragraph 12).

Disclosure of the Results of Operations for Oil and Gas Producing Activities

24. The results of operations for oil and gas producing activities shall be disclosed for the year. That information shall be disclosed in the aggregate and for each geographic area for which reserve quantities are disclosed (paragraph 12). The following information relating to those activities shall be presented:[7]

a. Revenues
b. Production (lifting) costs
c. Exploration expenses[8]
d. Depreciation, depletion, and amortization, and valuation provisions
e. Income tax expenses
f. Results of operations for oil and gas producing activities (excluding corporate overhead and interest costs)

25. Revenues shall include sales to unaffiliated enterprises and sales or transfers to the enterprise's other operations (for example, refineries or chemical plants). Sales to unaffiliated enterprises and sales or transfers to the enterprise's other operations shall be disclosed separately. Revenues shall include sales to unaffiliated enterprises attributable to net working interests, royalty interests, oil payment interests, and net profits interests of the reporting enterprise. Sales or transfers to the enterprise's other operations

[6]As defined in the paragraphs cited, exploration and development costs include depreciation of support equipment and facilities used in those activities and do not include the expenditures to acquire support equipment and facilities.

[7]If oil and gas producing activities represent substantially all of the business activities of the reporting enterprise and those oil and gas activities are located substantially in a single geographic area, the information required by paragraphs 24-29 of this Statement need not be disclosed if that information is provided elsewhere in the financial statements. If oil and gas producing activities constitute a business segment, as defined by Statement 14, paragraph 10(a), and the business segment activities are located substantially in a single geographic area, the results of operations information required by paragraphs 24-29 of this Statement may be included with segment information disclosed elsewhere in the financial report.

[8]Generally, only enterprises utilizing the successful efforts accounting method will have exploration expenses to disclose, since enterprises utilizing the full cost accounting method generally capitalize all exploration costs when incurred and subsequently reflect those costs in the determination of earnings through depreciation, depletion, and amortization, and valuation provisions.

shall be based on market prices determined at the point of delivery from the producing unit. Those market prices shall represent prices equivalent to those that could be obtained in an arm's-length transaction. Production or severance taxes shall not be deducted in determining gross revenues, but rather shall be included as part of production costs. Royalty payments and net profits disbursements shall be excluded from gross revenues.

26. Income taxes shall be computed using the statutory tax rate for the period, applied to revenues less production (lifting) costs, exploration expenses, depreciation, depletion, and amortization, and valuation provisions. Calculation of income tax expenses shall reflect permanent differences and tax credits and allowances relating to the oil and gas producing activities that are reflected in the enterprise's consolidated income tax expense for the period.

27. Results of operations for oil and gas producing activities are defined as revenues less production (lifting) costs, exploration expenses, depreciation, depletion, and amortization, valuation provisions, and income tax expenses. General corporate overhead and interest costs[9] shall not be deducted in computing the results of operations for an enterprise's oil and gas producing activities. However, some expenses incurred at an enterprise's central administrative office may not be general corporate expenses, but rather may be operating expenses of oil and gas producing activities, and therefore should be reported as such. The nature of an expense rather than the location of its incurrence shall determine whether it is an operating expense. Only those expenses identified by their nature as operating expenses shall be allocated as operating expenses in computing the results of operations for oil and gas producing activities.

28. The amounts disclosed in conformity with paragraphs 24-27 shall include an enterprise's interests in proved oil and gas reserves (paragraph 10) and in oil and gas subject to purchase under long-term supply, purchase, or similar agreements and contracts in which the enterprise participates in the operation of the properties on which the oil or gas is located or otherwise serves as the producer of those reserves (paragraph 13).

29. If the enterprise's financial statements include investments that are accounted for by the equity method, the investees' results of operations for oil and gas producing activities shall not be included in the enterprise's results of operations for oil and gas producing activities. However, the enterprise's share of the investees' results of operations for oil and gas producing activities shall be separately disclosed for the year, in the aggregate and by each geographic area for which reserve quantities are disclosed (paragraph 12).

Disclosure of a Standardized Measure of Discounted Future Net Cash Flows Relating to Proved Oil and Gas Reserve Quantities

30. A standardized measure of discounted future net cash flows relating to an enterprise's interests in (a) proved oil and gas reserves (paragraph 10) and (b) oil and gas subject to purchase under long-term supply, purchase, or similar agreements and contracts in which the enterprise participates in the operation of the properties on which the oil or gas is located or otherwise serves as the producer of those reserves (paragraph 13) shall be disclosed as of the end of the year. The standardized measure of discounted future net cash flows relating to those two types of interests in reserves may be combined for reporting purposes. The following information shall be disclosed in the aggregate and for each geographic area for which reserve quantities are disclosed in accordance with paragraph 12:

a. *Future cash inflows.* These shall be computed by applying year-end prices of oil and gas relating to the enterprise's proved reserves to the year-end quantities of those reserves. Future price changes shall be considered only to the extent provided by contractual arrangements in existence at year-end.
b. *Future development and production costs.* These costs shall be computed by estimating the expenditures to be incurred in developing and producing the proved oil and gas reserves at the end of the year, based on year-end costs and assuming continuation of existing economic conditions. If estimated development expenditures are significant, they shall be presented separately from estimated production costs.
c. *Future income tax expenses.* These expenses shall be computed by applying the appropriate year-end statutory tax rates, with consideration of future tax rates already legislated, to the future pretax net cash flows relating to the enterprise's proved oil and gas reserves, less the tax basis of the properties involved. The future income tax expenses shall give effect to permanent differences and tax credits and allowances relating to the enterprise's proved oil and gas reserves.
d. *Future net cash flows.* These amounts are the result of subtracting future development and production costs and future income tax expenses from future cash inflows.

[9]The disposition of interest costs that have been capitalized as part of the cost of acquiring qualifying assets used in oil and gas producing activities shall be the same as that of other components of those assets' costs.

e. *Discount.* This amount shall be derived from using a discount rate of 10 percent a year to reflect the timing of the future net cash flows relating to proved oil and gas reserves.
f. *Standardized measure of discounted future net cash flows.* This amount is the future net cash flows less the computed discount.

31. If a significant portion of the economic interest in the consolidated standardized measure of discounted future net cash flows reported is attributable to a consolidated subsidiary(ies) in which there is a significant minority interest, that fact and the approximate portion shall be disclosed.

32. If the financial statements include investments that are accounted for by the equity method, the investees' standardized measure of discounted future net cash flows relating to proved oil and gas reserves shall not be included in the disclosure of the enterprise's standardized measure. However, the enterprise's share of the investees' standardized measure of discounted future net cash flows shall be separately disclosed for the year, in the aggregate and by each geographic area for which quantities are disclosed (paragraph 12).

33. The aggregate change in the standardized measure of discounted future net cash flows shall be disclosed for the year. If individually significant, the following sources of change shall be presented separately:

a. Net change in sales and transfer prices and in production (lifting) costs related to future production
b. Changes in estimated future development costs
c. Sales and transfers of oil and gas produced during the period
d. Net change due to extensions, discoveries, and improved recovery
e. Net change due to purchases and sales of minerals in place
f. Net change due to revisions in quantity estimates
g. Previously estimated development costs incurred during the period
h. Accretion of discount
i. Other—unspecified
j. Net change in income taxes

In computing the amounts under each of the above categories, the effects of changes in prices and costs shall be computed before the effects of changes in quantities. As a result, changes in quantities shall be stated at year-end prices and costs. The change in computed income taxes shall reflect the effect of income taxes incurred during the period as well as the change in future income tax expenses. Therefore, all changes except income taxes shall be reported pretax.

34. Additional information necessary to prevent the disclosure of the standardized measure of discounted future net cash flows and changes therein from being misleading also shall be provided.

Disclosure of Current Cost Information

35. In applying the provisions of Statement 39 for presenting supplementary information on a current cost basis, this Statement permits enterprises to use historical cost/constant dollar measures of oil and gas mineral resource assets and related expense. As a result of this provision, together with the provision of paragraph 31 of Statement 33, an enterprise needs to present supplementary information on a current cost basis only if it has significant holdings of inventory and property, plant, and equipment apart from oil and gas producing activities or certain other specialized assets.

36. Paragraph 53(a) of Statement 33, as amended by Statements 39, 40, 41, and 46,[10] is superseded by the following:

a. When an enterprise presents information on a current cost basis for fiscal years ended on or after December 15, 1982, it shall measure:
   (1) Oil and gas mineral resource assets and related expenses at either their historical cost/constant dollar amounts or current cost or lower recoverable amounts
   (2) Mining mineral resource assets and related expenses at their current cost or lower recoverable amounts

37. Paragraph 51(b) of Statement 33, as amended by Statements 39, 40, 41, and 46, is superseded by the following:

b. Property, plant, and equipment at the current cost or lower recoverable amount (paragraphs 57-64) of the assets' remaining service potential at the measurement date. (This provision is qualified by paragraph 53 with respect to timberlands and growing timber, income-producing real estate, motion picture films, and oil and gas mineral resource assets.)

[10]FASB Statements No. 40, *Financial Reporting and Changing Prices: Specialized Assets—Timberlands and Growing Timber,* No. 41, *Financial Reporting and Changing Prices: Specialized Assets—Income-Producing Real Estate,* and No. 46, *Financial Reporting and Changing Prices: Motion Picture Films.*

38. Paragraph 52(b) of Statement 33, as amended by Statements 39, 40, 41, and 46, is superseded by the following:

b. Depreciation, depletion, and amortization expense of property, plant, and equipment shall be measured on the basis of the average current cost or lower recoverable amount (paragraphs 57-64) of the assets' service potential during the period of use. (This provision is qualified by paragraph 53 with respect to timberlands and growing timber, income-producing real estate, motion picture films, and oil and gas mineral resource assets.)

Effective Date and Transition

39. This Statement shall be effective for fiscal years beginning on or after December 15, 1982. Earlier application is encouraged but is not required.

The provisions of this Statement need not be applied to immaterial items.

This Statement was adopted by the affirmative votes of four members of the Financial Accounting Standards Board. Messrs. March, Morgan, and Sprouse dissented.

Messrs. March, Morgan, and Sprouse dissent to this Statement because they are opposed to requiring the disclosure of the computation and analysis of a standardized measure of discounted future net cash flows relating to proved oil and gas reserves (paragraphs 30-34). They believe that a requirement to disclose supplementary historical information about proved reserve quantities (paragraphs 10-17), capitalized and incurred costs (paragraphs 18-23), and results of producing activities (paragraphs 24-29) by significant geographic area is adequate to achieve the objectives of this Statement. Those disclosures are important for understanding oil and gas producing activities due to (a) the significance of oil and gas reserves as an economic resource; (b) the relatively long cycle from resource exploration to production, product sale, and ultimate cash flow; and (c) the risks related to geographic location. They help to fill a void caused by the absence of reliable measurements of the cost of finding and developing oil and gas reserves and the lack of a relationship between those costs and the revenues and cash inflows resulting from their disposition in the normal course of business.

Elsewhere, the Board has stated that relevance and reliability are the two primary qualities that make accounting useful for decision making and has adopted the position that if either of those qualities is completely missing, the information will not be useful (FASB Concepts Statement No. 2, *Qualitative Characteristics of Accounting Information*). The dissenting Board members believe that the proposed standardized measure of discounted future net cash flows is completely lacking in reliability. The reliability of a measure rests on the faithfulness with which it represents what it purports to represent (representational faithfulness), coupled with an assurance for the user that it has that representational quality (verifiability). Representational faithfulness is correspondence or agreement between a measure or description of an economic resource and the phenomenon that the measure or description purports to represent. The phenomenon being measured or described must be something that actually exists; the arithmetical results of a prescribed calculation that does not even purport to represent current cost, historical cost, fair market value, or any other real-world phenomenon cannot have representational faithfulness. Indeed, one of the concerns is that many users would not understand that the result of the standardized calculation itself is not intended to measure fair market value, the present value of future net cash flows, value to the business, or any other economic attribute (paragraphs 77 and 83) and might assume erroneously that it is some kind of an estimate of fair value.

Although it would be possible to provide assurance to users that the arithmetic involved in computing the standardized measure has been properly performed, it is impossible to verify the future. The standardized calculation depends largely upon management's forecasts of future production quantities, not only for the immediate future but for the entire period required to exhaust the existing estimated quantity of proved reserves. It is true that the discounting process automatically gives less weight to those forecasts the further into the future they extend, but the proposed disclosures do not provide adequate information for users, other than perhaps the most sophisticated, to assess the underlying production forecast itself.

Although the Board has not taken a position on reporting management forecasts generally, in Concepts Statement No. 1, *Objectives of Financial Reporting of Business Enterprises,* it characterizes financial statements and financial reporting as largely reflecting the financial effects of transactions and events that have already happened. Those who use the information provided by financial reporting may try to predict the future, but that is the essence of investment decision making, not the objective of financial reporting. The dissenting Board members are unconvinced that the case for a standardized measure of discounted future net cash flows that depends on management production forecasts is greater for enterprises engaged in oil and gas producing activities than for enterprises engaged in any other activity.

The dissenting Board members also are not convinced of the purported usefulness of the standardized measure as a benchmark to permit comparison of enterprises on a relative scale. The subjectivity of the estimates of quantities and production rates is too great. Each management's different expectations about what the future holds (for example, the future demand for energy, future use of alternative sources of energy, and future political stability among oil and gas producing nations) will be reflected in its critical production forecasts. Only if a user reflects his or her own set of expectations in predicting the future activities and results of various enterprises is comparability possible.

Disclosures of historical information about revenues, costs, and production permit users to determine average unit prices received and average unit costs incurred in each significant geographic area and to make their own predictions about future production, prices, costs, net cash flows, and risks. Predicting the future is the users' responsibility; it is not an appropriate objective of financial reporting. The cost of calculating a standardized measure in which comprehensive management production forecasts are inextricably intermingled with current costs and prices and weighted with a prescribed 10-percent discount rate is likely to exceed the limited benefits of that disclosure.

Members of the Financial Accounting Standards Board:

Donald J. Kirk, *Chairman*	John W. March	Robert T. Sprouse
Frank E. Block	Robert A. Morgan	Ralph E. Walters
	David Mosso	

Appendix A

SUMMARIES AND ILLUSTRATIONS OF CERTAIN DISCLOSURES ABOUT OIL AND GAS PRODUCING ACTIVITIES

40. Following are summaries and illustrations of certain of the disclosure requirements for oil and gas producing activities required by this Statement.

	Disclosure Illustration
Accounting Method	
Method of accounting for costs incurred and the manner of disposing of capitalized costs relating to oil and gas producing activities	—
Capitalized Costs	
Aggregate amount of capitalized costs and related accumulated depreciation, depletion, and amortization, and valuation allowances (If significant, capitalized costs of unproved properties shall be separately disclosed.)	1
Enterprise's share of equity method investees' capitalized costs in the aggregate at the end of the year	1
Costs Incurred in Oil and Gas Property Acquisition, Exploration, and Development	
Cost incurred in oil and gas producing activities in the aggregate, by type, and by geographic area during the year (If significant, costs of acquiring existing mineral interests that have proved reserves shall be disclosed separately from the costs of acquiring unproved properties.)	2
Enterprise's share of equity method investees' costs incurred in the aggregate and by geographic area during the year	2

Results of Operations

	Paragraph
Results of operations for the year from oil and gas producing activities and the major components of those activities in the aggregate and by geographic area	3
Enterprise's share of equity method investees' results of operations for the year from oil and gas producing activities in the aggregate and by geographic area	3

Reserve Quantity Information

Net quantities of proved reserves and proved developed reserves at the beginning and end of the year and changes in proved reserves in the aggregate, by type, and by geographic area	4
Reserves subject to purchase under supply agreements with governments or authorities in which the enterprise acts as producer, and reserves received under those agreements during the year in the aggregate and by geographic area	4
Enterprise's share of equity method investees' proved reserves at the end of the year in the aggregate and by geographic area	4
Approximate portion of reserves quantities at the end of the year attributable to a consolidated subsidiary(ies) in which there is a significant minority interest	4
Important economic factors and significant uncertainties affecting an enterprise's proved reserves	—
Governmental restrictions on reporting reserve information	—

Standardized Measure of Discounted Future Net Cash Flows

Standardized measure of discounted future net cash flows and major components of that calculation relating to proved reserve quantities (including those relating to long-term supply agreements for which the enterprise acts as producer) at the end of the year in the aggregate and by geographic area, based on year-end prices, costs, and statutory tax rates (adjusted for permanent differences) and a 10-percent annual discount rate	5
Enterprise's share of equity method investees' standardized measure of discounted future net cash flows in the aggregate and by geographic area	5
Approximate portion of economic interests in the consolidated standardized measure of discounted future net cash flows at the end of the year attributable to a consolidated subsidiary(ies) in which there is a significant minority interest	5
Summary of changes in the standardized measure of discounted future net cash flows during the year in the aggregate	5
Additional information concerning the standardized measure of discounted future net cash flows required to prevent the information from being misleading	—

41. The following illustrations present formats that may be used to disclose certain information required by this Statement when a complete set of annual financial statements is presented for one year.

Illustration 1

CAPITALIZED COSTS RELATING TO OIL AND GAS PRODUCING ACTIVITIES AT DECEMBER 31, 19XX

	Total
Unproved oil and gas properties	$X
Proved oil and gas properties	X
	X
Accumulated depreciation, depletion, and amortization, and valuation allowances	X
Net capitalized costs	$X
Enterprise's share of equity method investees' net capitalized costs	$X

Illustration 2

COSTS INCURRED IN OIL AND GAS PROPERTY ACQUISITION, EXPLORATION, AND DEVELOPMENT ACTIVITIES FOR THE YEAR ENDED DECEMBER 31, 19XX

	Total	**United States**	**Foreign Geographic Area A**	**Foreign Geographic Area B**	**Other Foreign Geographic Areas**
Acquisition of properties					
—Proved	$X	$X	$X	$X	$X
—Unproved	X	X	X	X	X
Exploration costs	X	X	X	X	X
Development costs	X	X	X	X	X
Enterprise's share of equity method investees' costs of property acquisition, exploration, and development	X	X	X	X	X

Illustration 3

RESULTS OF OPERATIONS FOR PRODUCING ACTIVITIES FOR THE YEAR ENDED DECEMBER 31, 19XX

	Total	United States	Foreign Geographic Area A	Foreign Geographic Area B	Other Foreign Geographic Areas
Revenues					
Sales	$ X	$ X	$ X	$ X	$ X
Transfers	X	X	X	X	X
Total	X	X	X	X	X
Production costs	(X)	(X)	(X)	(X)	(X)
Exploration expenses	(X)	(X)	(X)	(X)	(X)
Depreciation, depletion, and amortization, and valuation provisions	(X)	(X)	(X)	(X)	(X)
	X	X	X	X	X
Income tax expenses	(X)	(X)	(X)	(X)	(X)
Results of operations from producing activities (excluding corporate overhead and interest costs)	$ X	$ X	$ X	$ X	$ X
Enterprise's share of equity method investees' results of operations for producing activities	$ X	$ X	$ X	$ X	$ X

Illustration 4

RESERVE QUANTITY INFORMATION*
FOR THE YEAR ENDED DECEMBER 31, 19XX

	Total		United States		Foreign Geographic Area A		Foreign Geographic Area B		Other Foreign Geographic Areas	
	Oil	Gas	Oil	Gas	Oil	Gas	Oil	Gas	Oil	Gas
Proved developed and undeveloped reserves:										
Beginning of year	X	X	X	X	X	X	X	X	X	X
Revisions of previous estimates	X	X	X	X	X	X	X	X	X	X
Improved recovery	X	X	X	X	X	X	X	X	X	X
Purchases of minerals in place	X	X	X	X	X	X	X	X	X	X
Extensions and discoveries	X	X	X	X	X	X	X	X	X	X
Production	(X)	(X)	(X)	(X)	(X)	(X)	(X)	(X)	(X)	(X)
Sales of minerals in place	(X)	(X)	(X)	(X)	(X)	(X)	(X)	(X)	(X)	(X)
End of year	X†	X	X	X	X	X	X	X	X	X
Proved developed reserves:										
Beginning of year	X	X	X	X	X	X	X	X	X	X
End of year	X	X	X	X	X	X	X	X	X	X

Illustration 4 (continued)

	Total		United States		Foreign Geographic Area A		Foreign Geographic Area B		Other Foreign Geographic Areas	
	Oil	Gas	Oil	Gas	Oil	Gas	Oil	Gas	Oil	Gas
Oil and gas applicable to long-term supply agreements with governments or authorities in which the enterprise acts as producer:										
Proved reserves—end of year	X	X			X	X				
Received during the year	X	X			X	X				
Enterprise's proportional interest in reserves of investees accounted for by the equity method—end of year	X	X	X	X	X	X	X	X	X	X

*Oil reserves stated in barrels; gas reserves stated in cubic feet.

†Includes reserves of X barrels attributable to a consolidated subsidiary in which there is an X-percent minority interest.

Illustration 5

STANDARDIZED MEASURE OF DISCOUNTED FUTURE NET CASH FLOWS AND CHANGES THEREIN RELATING TO PROVED OIL AND GAS RESERVES AT DECEMBER 31, 19XX

	Total	United States	Foreign Geographic Area A	Foreign Geographic Area B	Other Foreign Geographic Areas
Future cash inflows*	$ X	$ X	$ X	$ X	$ X
Future production and development costs*	(X)	(X)	(X)	(X)	(X)
Future income tax expenses*	(X)	(X)	(X)	(X)	(X)
Future net cash flows	X	X	X	X	X
10% annual discount for estimated timing of cash flows	(X)	(X)	(X)	(X)	(X)
Standardized measure of discounted future net cash flows	$ X †	$ X	$ X	$ X	$ X
Enterprise's share of equity method investees' standardized measure of discounted future net cash flows	$ X	$ X	$ X	$ X	$ X

Illustration 5 (continued)

	Total	United States	Foreign Geographic Area A	Foreign Geographic Area B	Other Foreign Geographic Areas
The following are the principal sources of change in the standardized measure of discounted future net cash flows during 19XX:					
Sales and transfers of oil and gas produced, net of production costs	$(X)				
Net changes in prices and production costs	X				
Extensions, discoveries, and improved recovery, less related costs	X				
Development costs incurred during the period	(X)				
Revisions of previous quantity estimates	X				
Accretion of discount	X				
Net change in income taxes	X				
Other	X				

*Future net cash flows were computed using year-end prices and costs, and year-end statutory tax rates (adjusted for permanent differences) that relate to existing proved oil and gas reserves in which the enterprise has mineral interests, including those mineral interests related to long-term supply agreements with governments for which the enterprise serves as the producer of the reserves.

†Includes $X attributable to a consolidated subsidiary in which there is an X-percent minority interest.

Appendix B

BACKGROUND INFORMATION

42. In December 1977, Statement 19 was issued by the Board. That Statement adopted a form of successful efforts accounting and required disclosure of proved oil and gas reserve quantities, capitalized costs, and costs incurred in oil and gas producing activities.

43. Before Statement 19 became effective, the Securities and Exchange Commission (SEC) issued, in August 1978, ASR No. 253, *Adoption of Requirements for Financial Accounting and Reporting Practices for Oil and Gas Producing Activities.*[11] That release (a) adopted the form of successful efforts accounting prescribed by Statement 19, (b) indicated an intention to adopt the disclosures prescribed by Statement 19 (which was subsequently done), (c) indicated an intention to adopt a form of the full cost accounting method (which was subsequently done), (d) permitted the use of either (a) or (c) for SEC reporting purposes, and (e) adopted rules requiring disclosure of certain financial and operating information beyond that required in Statement 19. The SEC took those actions because it believed that neither the full cost nor the successful efforts method provided sufficient information on the financial position and operating results of oil and gas producing enterprises. Accordingly, the SEC concluded that a new method of accounting that is based on valuations of proved oil and gas reserves and that would replace both the successful efforts and full cost accounting methods should be developed for the primary financial statements. The SEC initiated the development of that new accounting method (which it referred to as reserve recognition accounting [RRA]) by requiring supplemental disclosures on that basis. The SEC also indicated (and subsequently carried out) its intention to require the disclosure of a supplemental earnings summary to reflect estimated additions to proved reserves and changes in valuation of estimated proved reserves, based on current prices and a 10-percent discount rate. All costs associated with finding and developing such additions and all costs determined to be nonproductive during the period are deducted in determining that supplemental measure of earnings.

44. In February 1979—because Statement 19 requirements would be imposed only on enterprises not subject to SEC reporting requirements and therefore would not achieve comparability—the Board issued Statement 25, which suspended the effective date of Statement 19 as to the accounting method to be used in financial statements but not as to the disclosure requirements.

45. Further supplemental information is presently required to be disclosed by Statements 33 and 39. Those Statements require large publicly held oil and gas enterprises to report the effects of changes in general prices and changes in specific prices of certain types of assets.

46. During the development of Statement 39, the Board recognized that the accumulation of both the Board's and the SEC's disclosure requirements placed a significant burden on oil and gas producing enterprises. It recognized that the disclosures made in response to those requirements may have become unnecessarily voluminous and complex without a corresponding increase in their usefulness to the users of financial statements. Furthermore, other information, frequently suggested by some financial analysts as useful, was not presented. Accordingly, the Board indicated that it would study the usefulness of the existing and proposed disclosures and would work with the oil and gas industry, the SEC, and users to develop a single, coherent set of disclosure requirements for oil and gas producing enterprises.

47. On February 26, 1981, the SEC issued ASR No. 289, *Financial Reporting by Oil and Gas Producers,* which states that the SEC no longer considers RRA to be a potential method of accounting in the primary financial statements of oil and gas producers. That release also announced the Commission's "support of an undertaking by the Financial Accounting Standards Board to develop a comprehensive package of disclosures for those engaged in oil and gas producing activities." The Commission indicated in that release that it expected to amend its rules to be consistent with the disclosure standards for oil and gas producers to be developed by the FASB for oil and gas producers.

48. The Board added a project on disclosures about oil and gas producing activities to its agenda on March 4, 1981.

49. A task force comprising 20 people from the oil and gas industry, petroleum engineering and geological consulting firms, the financial community, the public accounting profession, and academe was formed at the outset of the project to advise the staff on technical matters encompassed in the scope of the project.

50. On May 13, 1981, the Board published the

[11]In April 1982, the SEC codified the relevant ASRs concerning accounting and auditing matters in Financial Reporting Release No. 1, *Codification of Financial Reporting Policies.*

FASB Invitation to Comment, *Disclosures about Oil and Gas Producing Activities.* The Board received 120 letters in response to that Invitation to Comment.

51. In August 1981, the Board conducted a public hearing on the Invitation to Comment. Twenty-eight organizations and individuals presented their views at the two-day hearing.

52. On April 15, 1982, the Board issued an FASB Exposure Draft, *Disclosures about Oil and Gas Producing Activities.* The Board received 113 letters of comment on that Exposure Draft.

53. Since the project was added to the Board's agenda, the Board held 10 open meetings at which the project's issues were discussed. The Task Force on Disclosures about Oil and Gas Producing Activities met three times with the FASB staff, and individuals serving on the task force participated in open educational Board meetings held on the project's issues. Task force members provided the Board and its staff with comments on those issues.

Appendix C

BASIS FOR CONCLUSIONS

CONTENTS

Appendix C

BASIS FOR CONCLUSIONS

Introduction

54. This appendix reviews considerations that were deemed significant by members of the Board in reaching the conclusions in this Statement. It includes reasons for accepting certain views and rejecting others. Individual Board members gave greater weight to some factors than to others.

55. The underlying causes of the problem leading to this Statement relate to some significant and unusual economic characteristics of oil and gas producing activities:

a. The principal assets are oil and gas reserves.
b. There is no necessary correlation between the costs and the values of oil and gas reserves.
c. The costs of finding specific reserves are unique.

The costs of existing reserves, therefore, are not relevant indicators of either (a) cash inflows from production and sale of those reserves or (b) cash outflows necessary to replace those reserves.

56. An important quality of information that is useful in making rational investment, credit, and similar decisions is its predictive value—specifically, its usefulness in assessing the amounts, timing, and uncertainty of prospective net cash inflows to the enterprise. Historical cost based financial statements for oil and gas producing enterprises have limited predictive value. Their usefulness is further reduced because a uniform accounting method is not required to be used for costs incurred in oil and gas producing activities.

57. The inherent limitations involved in using historical cost based information relative to mineral interests in properties have long been recognized. Various attempts have been made to standardize the industry's method of accounting for costs incurred in oil and gas producing activities. Those attempts have not been successful.

58. Other attempts have been made by the FASB and the SEC (current cost accounting and RRA) to develop disclosures to assist the user to:

a. Assess future net cash flows
b. Estimate the values or replacement costs of mineral reserves
c. Compare financial positions and operating results of enterprises in the industry

59. Those attempts have resulted in a great volume

of additional disclosures, particularly for publicly owned oil and gas producing enterprises. The Board's project is an attempt, by agreement with the SEC, to analyze the problem, to sort out the reasonable needs of users, and to determine what information will help to meet those needs at a reasonable cost.

60. In summary, the primary objectives of this Statement are:

a. To develop disclosure requirements that are useful and in particular would compensate, in some measure, for recognized deficiencies in the comparability and predictive value of financial statement information of oil and gas enterprises
b. To consider cost-benefit relationships of alternative disclosures and to reduce the quantity and cost of existing disclosures

Alternatives Considered

61. The Board considered four basic approaches to developing comprehensive oil and gas disclosures:

A — Historical cost based information and reserve quantity information *only*

B — Historical cost based information and reserve quantity information *plus* future estimated costs and reserve production information

C — Historical cost based information and reserve quantity information *plus* information about estimated future net cash flows relating to oil and gas reserves

D — Historical cost based information and reserve quantity information plus information about estimated future net cash flows relating to oil and gas reserves *and* an alternative measure of income based on changes in those future net cash flows

62. Most respondents to the Invitation to Comment and the Exposure Draft support the Board's conclusion in Statement 19 that for users to understand and interpret an enterprise's financial statements, information about its oil and gas producing activities must be supplemented by information about its mineral interests. The discovery of proved oil and gas reserves is a critical event in the oil and gas producing cycle, and information about those reserves and changes in them are key indicators of the success of an enterprise. That information is considered so useful in decision making that the lack of precision associated with the estimate of proved oil and gas reserve quantities is more than compensated for by the added relevance to users.

63. All four alternatives considered by the Board provide historical cost based and reserve quantity information. However, they differ on the extent to which that information is considered sufficient to meet the objectives of financial reporting for oil and gas producing activities.

Historical Cost Based Information and Reserve Quantity Information

64. Some respondents to the Invitation to Comment and the Exposure Draft support disclosure of only historical cost based information and proved oil and gas reserve quantity information (Alternative A). They believe that users can apply current costs and prices or their own estimates of future costs and prices to an extrapolation of historical production trends to estimate future net cash flows related to the enterprise's proved oil and gas reserves. Supporters of this alternative generally believe that disclosure of fair market value, discounted future net cash flows, or projections of future events or conditions relating to an enterprise's proved oil and gas reserves should not be part of financial reporting.

65. In the Board's view, historical cost based financial information and proved oil and gas reserve quantity information are crude tools for any predictive analytical process for many reasons, the most notable of which are:

a. Mineral interests in proved oil and gas reserves may have significantly different economic values because of such features as location, qualitative properties, development status, and tax status. Reserve quantity information does not give a comparable base for comparison over time or among companies.
b. Historical production trends, even if determinable, may differ significantly from management's future production plans.

66. Alternative A, then, is subject (as are all alternatives considered) to the challenge of the reliability of the proved oil and gas reserve estimates and, in addition, does not add materially to users' ability to make comparisons and to assess the future net cash flows of oil and gas producing enterprises.

Estimated Future Costs and Reserve Production Information

67. A few respondents to the Invitation to Comment and the Exposure Draft support, in addition to historical cost based information and proved oil and gas reserve quantity information, disclosure of additional information about oil and gas producing activities that would provide forecasts of (a) estimated future costs of production (lifting) and development of existing proved oil and gas reserves and (b) estimated timing of future production of those reserves (Alternative B). Supporters of this alternative generally suggest limiting the disclosure requirements for that information to a period encompass-

ing the following three to five years. This alternative is intended to allow users of the financial reports of oil and gas producing enterprises to compute estimated near-term future cash flows using their own assumptions concerning future prices and risks.

68. The lack of broad support for Alternative B seems to reflect primarily three views:

a. An objection to presenting explicit forecasts of production and costs in financial reports
b. A concern that, for data to be useful, they would have to be presented separately for each significant field
c. A belief that the data would tend to be used by only the most sophisticated industry analysts

69. The Board was dissuaded from this alternative primarily by the combination of the large volume of data to be presented and the limited number of probable users.

Information about Future Net Cash Flows

70. Some respondents to the Invitation to Comment and to the Exposure Draft supported disclosure of summary information regarding the future net cash flows associated with an enterprise's existing proved oil and gas reserves (Alternative C). This Statement reflects an Alternative C approach to developing disclosure requirements for oil and gas producing activities.

71. The Board considered various means of providing relevant summary information:

a. Fair market value
b. Estimate of discounted net cash flows based on future prices and costs and an enterprise-specific discount rate
c. Standardized measure of discounted future net cash flows with major factors separately reported

Fair Market Value

72. *Fair market value* is usually defined as the exchange price that reasonably could be expected in an arm's-length transaction between a willing buyer and a willing seller. If ascertainable, fair market value would be better than historical cost for indicating future net cash flows relating to oil and gas properties. It also would have been better than the standardized discounted future net cash flows approach required by this Statement because, among other factors, the fair market value of mineral interests in properties includes the "value" of all the various categories of reserves (proved, possible, and probable) as well as undeveloped acreage.

73. Nevertheless, the Board concluded that a requirement to disclose fair market value would be impracticable because:

a. Relatively few exchanges of oil and gas mineral interests take place.
b. Mineral interests that are exchanged tend to be interests in smaller properties that principally involve undeveloped acreage.
c. The geological characteristics of each oil and gas property are unique to that individual mineral interest.
d. The amount of information concerning sales price and stratigraphic data available to parties not directly involved in the exchange is limited because that information usually is considered confidential.

Discounted Future Net Cash Flows

74. The Board considered the use of discounted future net cash flows based on estimated future prices and costs, production timing, and an enterprise-specific discount rate as a surrogate for fair market value. The Board rejected that approach, however, for a number of reasons.

75. As a practical matter, the estimate would have to be limited to proved reserves because information about probable and possible reserves and undeveloped acreage can be little more than conjectural. Limiting the estimate to proved reserves, however, would seriously detract from the estimate as a representation of fair market value.

76. Estimates of future costs and prices are highly subjective, depending on political events (for example, price controls, tax policy, embargoes, and political upheavals) in addition to supply and demand factors. Estimates of future production are also subject to a wide range of error, and selection of a discount rate is subjectively variable due to individual assessments of political, operating, and general business risks. This combination of subjective estimating variables could not result in information with the necessary degree of verifiability and comparability required for financial reporting.

Standardized Measure of Discounted Net Cash Flows

77. The Board finally settled on a standardized measure of discounted net cash flows to achieve some of the characteristics of a fair market value measure without the extreme subjectivity inherent in either direct estimation of market value or entity-specific discounted net cash flows. Although it cannot be considered an estimate of fair market value, the standardized measure of discounted net cash flows should be responsive to some of the key variables that affect fair market value, namely, changes

in reserve quantities, selling prices, production costs, and tax rates.

78. Some respondents to the Invitation to Comment and the Exposure Draft, including financial analysts who specialize in oil and gas securities and petroleum engineers, believe that the disclosure of a standardized measure of discounted future net cash flows associated with an enterprise's proved oil and gas reserves is useful.[12] In ASR 253, the SEC required a measure based on year-end prices and costs specific to the enterprise's proved oil and gas reserves, a standard discount rate of 10 percent, and an estimate of the production timing of those reserves. The Board has adopted that approach to requiring information about future net cash flows.

79. One criticism of a standardized measure of discounted net cash flows has been that it is limited to proved reserves, omitting probable and possible reserves. The Board believes, however, that limiting the estimate to proved reserves is appropriate because:

a. Only proved reserves have been defined in a manner that has gained general acceptance by the petroleum engineering profession.
b. Information on proved reserves is already used within the industry to describe and compare oil and gas mineral interests.

Further, proved reserves ordinarily will be produced sooner than other categories of reserves and are weighted more heavily than other types of reserves in calculating discounted net cash flows. Additionally, more risk is associated with other types of reserves, and consequently the cash flows relating to those reserves probably would be discounted at a higher rate than proved reserves. Those two factors would tend to mitigate the effects of limiting the estimated discounted future net cash flows disclosed to proved reserves.

80. Disclosure of the principal components of the standardized measure of discounted future net cash flows provides users with information concerning the factors involved in making the calculation. Users then have standardized data they can adjust as necessary for their own individual estimates of future changes and risks in order to prepare their own assessments of future cash flows. In addition, disclosing both undiscounted and discounted net cash flows provides a means of comparing proved oil and gas reserves both with and without the subjectivity introduced by management's estimate of production timing, although management generally is in a better position than a user to forecast both the production timing and the recovery method of the enterprise's proved oil and gas reserves.

81. Government participation in oil and gas producing activities takes various forms, ranging from participation in production (royalties, either in cash or in kind) to income taxes. As governments devise different methods of participating, problems of classification arise. For example, excise taxes are based on production or revenue and are generally classified as a part of production costs. Other taxes are based on revenues less certain costs and are generally classified as income taxes. Because of those differences in classification, a standardized measure of discounted future net cash flows relating to proved reserves must reflect income taxes to reflect all forms of taxation (those considered as costs of production and those considered as income taxes). The Board also noted that several enterprises already disclose in their annual reports the effects of income taxes on a standardized measure of estimated net cash flows relating to proved reserves.

82. The Board decided not to require disclosure of the periods in which the calculated net cash flows are expected to be realized. That type of detailed information would add some predictive value to the disclosure, but the Board did not consider the added benefits to be sufficient to justify the additional volume of information that would be included in financial reports if that requirement were adopted. Based on respondents' comments to the Exposure Draft, the Board also decided not to require disclosure by geographic area of changes in the standardized measure that occurred during the period. The Board believes that the small reduction in the feedback value of the disclosure caused by the elimination of geographic area information for the types of changes is acceptable considering the resulting large reduction in volume of information from that initially proposed in the Exposure Draft.

83. The Board was persuaded by respondents' comments that the standardized information can be useful and is, in fact, being used. The Board is concerned, at the same time, that users of financial statements understand that it is neither fair market value nor the present value of future cash flows. It is a rough surrogate for such measures, a tool to allow for a reasonable comparison of mineral reserves and changes through the use of a standardized method

[12]A survey of 190 oil and gas financial analysts (conducted by Edward B. Deakin and James W. Deitrick of the University of Texas at Austin) shows that 90 percent supported disclosure of reserve values. Approximately 80 percent of those supporters indicated that the disclosures should be based on specified, uniform pricing and discounting assumptions. A survey of members of the Society of Petroleum Evaluation Engineers (conducted by B. P. Huddleston & Co., Inc.) indicated that over 70 percent of the 102 respondents believe that the "present value" of proved oil and gas reserves should be reported by publicly traded companies, based on current price information. Approximately 58 percent of those who responded support the use of a standard 10-percent discount rate in that calculation.

that recognizes qualitative, quantitative, geographic, and temporal characteristics. Absent such a tool, there is no reasonable basis for comparing these most important assets and activities; values are not determinable and quantities are not comparable. In addition, the standardized measure provides users with a common base upon which they can prepare their own estimates of future cash flows.

84. Largely because of the limitations of the standardized measure, the Board rejected the presentation of an alternative measure of income based on changes in the standardized cash flows (Alternative D).

Historical Cost Based Information and Reserve Quantity Information

85. This Statement sets forth disclosure requirements for historical cost based information and reserve quantity information about oil and gas producing activities of the type presently required by the FASB and the SEC. Some of those existing disclosure requirements have been continued in this Statement, while other requirements have either been reorganized or omitted from the Board's disclosure requirements. The Board's considerations of the principal disclosures of historical cost based information and reserve quantity information are discussed below.

Accounting Method

86. Because of past SEC action and the related FASB suspension of the effective date for the accounting requirements of Statement 19, all oil and gas producing enterprises do not use a single method of accounting for costs incurred in oil and gas producing activities. Therefore, the Board has continued the requirement in Statement 25 to disclose in the financial statements the method of accounting and the manner of disposition of capitalized costs.

Capitalized Costs

87. Separately disclosing capitalized costs related to proved and unproved properties will assist users in assessing the degree of risk associated with those two different types of assets. Unproved properties have a much higher degree of risk associated with them since many of them may never result in additions to an enterprise's proved oil and gas reserves. Disclosure of the costs associated with unproved properties also helps users of an oil and gas enterprise's financial statements to assess the enterprise's efforts to maintain an inventory of properties in which it seeks to find additional oil and gas reserves and thereby to maintain or increase its existing oil and gas production level. The Board and most respondents therefore believe that it is appropriate to continue the requirement in Statement 19 to disclose the aggregate amount of capitalized costs and to expand it to require separate disclosure of capitalized costs related to unproved properties.

88. Some respondents suggested that capitalized costs information be required to be disclosed by geographic area to allow an evaluation of an enterprise's risks by geographic area. The Board disagrees with that suggestion because information concerning the enterprise's risks by geographic area is provided to the users of the enterprise's financial reports by the reserve quantity and standardized measure information required to be disclosed.

Costs Incurred

89. The Board and most respondents believe that it is necessary to continue the requirement in Statement 19 to disclose information about costs incurred during the period because that information indicates management's efforts to replace its existing proved reserves. Disclosure of costs by type also allows users of the financial statements to assess the emphasis of the enterprise's oil and gas producing activities because the disclosure provides information about the enterprise's efforts to find new reserves, to develop existing proved reserves, or both. The accomplishments of those efforts over time are indicated by the reserve quantity disclosures and the analysis of changes in a standardized measure of discounted future net cash flows.

90. Several respondents to the Exposure Draft suggested that costs incurred to acquire proved reserves should be disclosed separately, if significant. They believe it is useful to report the costs of acquiring mineral interests in proved reserves separately from the costs of acquiring unproved mineral leases because of the implications and risks associated with each of those types of expenditures. The Board agreed and believes the data is readily obtainable.

91. Several respondents noted that the Exposure Draft proposed that production costs information should be disclosed in both the costs incurred and results of operations information. Those respondents believe that there is no need for this duplicative disclosure of production costs and suggested that the disclosure of production costs be eliminated from the schedule of costs incurred. The Board agreed and eliminated the requirement of Statement 19 to report production costs as part of costs incurred information.

Results of Operations

92. Disclosing the results of operations for oil and gas producing activities by geographic area is useful in evaluating historical results of operations, cash

flows, and risks associated with an important portion of a vertically integrated oil and gas enterprise's activities. It is also useful in comparing the historical performance of independent exploration and production enterprises with the producing activities of integrated enterprises and in comparing the performance of one integrated enterprise with that of another.

93. The November 1981 FASB Exposure Draft, *Reporting Income, Cash Flows, and Financial Position of Business Enterprises,* stresses the relevance of separately disclosing information about different activities within complex enterprises. Analysis aimed at predicting the amount, timing, and uncertainty of future cash flows is facilitated by segregating financial information into homogeneous groups. Oil and gas producing activities of an integrated oil and gas enterprise are subject to significantly different degrees of risk than are its other activities (for example, refining and marketing). Therefore, separately reporting the results of oil and gas producing activities is likely to enhance the predictive value of the information presented by vertically integrated oil and gas producing enterprises.

94. Disclosing the results of operations for oil and gas producing activities also complements the disclosure of the standardized measure of discounted future net cash flows and changes therein. The results of operations provide historical information that may help users to confirm or correct prior expectations about the factors involved in assessing the near-term cash flow potential of the proved reserves from the trends of the historical results of operations.

95. The reasons for requiring the results of operations for oil and gas producing activities to be reported on an after-tax basis are the same as those provided for the standardized measure of discounted future net cash flows (paragraph 81). That is, there are significant differences in the total governmental participation in oil and gas producing activities and differences in the methods by which that participation is achieved (for example, different mixes of royalties, excise taxes, income taxes, and so forth). The Board believes that to provide comparable information all forms of taxation must be reflected in the disclosure.

96. This Statement requires that general corporate expenses and interest expenses not be added to or deducted from the results of operations for an enterprise's oil and gas producing activities because the allocation of those expenses would be subjective and would tend to decrease the comparability of the disclosure.

97. Some Board members and respondents expressed concern about the reliability of using a transfer price between oil and gas producing activities and other internal operations (for example, refining) for vertically integrated enterprises. However, a reliable transfer price appears to be obtainable since local regulatory and taxation authorities ordinarily require separate information about an enterprise's oil and gas producing activities. The price used to prepare that information reflects the effective price after separation of the oil and gas found in the reserves. The requirement to use established prices will increase the comparability of the information in making comparisons of the revenues and results of operations of enterprises' oil and gas producing activities.

98. Another possible transfer-pricing method considered by the Board is the wellhead price, which is the market price established at the well location where the reserves are produced (lifted). The wellhead price ordinarily is comparable to the point-of-delivery price from the producing unit, except for reserves in remote locations for which the initial processing to separate gas from oil is delayed. The Board considers the wellhead price to be less satisfactory because wellhead prices generally do not exist for reserves in remote locations.

99. The Board agreed, however, with those respondents to the Exposure Draft who suggested separate disclosure of revenues from sales and transfers to other operations of the enterprise, and revenues from sales to unaffiliated customers. That disclosure would indicate the interrelationship between the oil and gas producing activities and the enterprise's other activities. The disclosure of that information makes the disclosure of revenues from oil and gas producing activities consistent with the Statement 14 requirements for business segments.

Reserve Quantity Information

100. As previously indicated, most respondents to the Invitation to Comment and to the Exposure Draft agreed with the Board's conclusions in Statement 19 that information about quantities of oil and gas reserves is useful to understanding and interpreting the financial statements of an oil and gas producing enterprise. The discovery of reserves is a critical event in the oil and gas producing cycle, and reserves and changes in them are key indicators of the success of an enterprise.

101. Respondents also agreed with the Board's conclusions in Statement 19 that reserve quantities and changes in them should be reported separately for each geographic area in which significant reserves are located since such reporting assists in assessing the risks associated with those reserves.

102. Some governments have nationalized or otherwise taken over, in whole or in part, certain properties in which oil and gas producing enterprises previously had mineral interests. Some of those interests have been converted into long-term supply, purchase, or similar agreements with a government or a governmental authority. In some countries, oil and gas producing enterprises can obtain access to oil and gas reserves only through such agreements and not through direct acquisition of mineral interests. If an oil and gas producing enterprise participates in the operation of a property subject to such an agreement or otherwise serves as "producer" of the reserves from the property, disclosure of the reserve quantities identified with, and quantities of oil or gas received under, that type of agreement with those governments or authorities provides useful information. The fact that the reserves are available to an enterprise requires their inclusion to give a complete presentation of the enterprise's reserve position. However, because of the different nature of those agreements (that is, they do not represent direct ownership interests in reserves), those reserve quantities are to be reported separately from the enterprise's own proved reserves.

103. The requirement of Statement 19 to disclose important economic factors and significant uncertainties affecting an enterprise's proved reserves is continued because it provides information that assists users in assessing the economic resources of an oil and gas producing enterprise. Examples of this type of disclosure include expectation of unusually high development or lifting costs, the necessity to build a major pipeline or other major facility before production of the reserves can begin, or contractual obligations to produce and sell a significant portion of reserves at prices that are substantially below those at which the oil and gas could otherwise be sold.

104. Certain governments restrict the disclosure of reserves located within their jurisdiction. Disclosure of restrictions informs users about the completeness and uniformity of the reserve information presented. Therefore, the Board decided to require disclosure of the existence of any governmental restrictions that affect the completeness of reporting the reserve information.

Equity Method Investees and Minority Interests

105. An enterprise may carry out significant operations through investees to share the high risks of exploration and the high costs of development in some areas. Respondents' comments indicate that such sharing of risks and costs is increasing and that they generally favor disclosing supplemental information about equity investees' oil and gas producing activities. It is most commonly achieved by joint participation agreements without formation of a separate entity. However, if a separate entity is formed and accounted for by the equity method, information needs to be provided about the enterprise's share of the equity investees' capitalized costs, costs incurred, results of operation, proved oil and gas reserve quantities, and standardized measure of discounted future net cash flows. That information should be disclosed for the same reasons that the Board requires disclosure of similar information about an enterprise's consolidated operations—so users can obtain a meaningful understanding of all the oil and gas operations of the enterprise.

106. Several respondents to the Exposure Draft also noted that an enterprise's consolidated financial statements may include subsidiaries with significant minority interests related to oil and gas producing activities. The Board believes that unless significant minority interests in reported oil and gas producing activities are disclosed, users may overestimate the portion of future cash flows that may accrue to an enterprise's shareholders. As indicated earlier, it is important to include disclosures about equity method investees; it is equally important to include disclosures about significant minority interests in consolidated subsidiaries.

107. The Board acknowledges that disclosures about equity investees and minority interests may have implications for other industries that operate through equity investees and that have significant minority interests. Therefore, the Board may reassess the requirements to report information about equity investments and minority interests contained in this Statement upon completion of a project on consolidated financial statements, the equity method, and other procedures for accounting for investments in or other relations with affiliated entities.

Reasons for Omitting Other Disclosures

108. Other disclosures of historical cost based information suggested by respondents or required by the SEC were rejected either because they do not assist in meeting the objectives of financial reporting in a cost-beneficial manner or because their usefulness would overlap that of the disclosures required by this Statement.

109. In the Exposure Draft, the Board specifically requested comment on the usefulness of requiring operational disclosures concerning acreage. Some respondents to the Invitation to Comment and the Exposure Draft expressed the view that disclosure of the quantity of undeveloped acreage would provide some indication of the enterprise's future explora-

tion and production efforts. However, most respondents to the Exposure Draft stated that disclosure of information about undeveloped acreage should not be required by this Statement principally because: (a) the quality of the acreage and its precise location are more important than its quantity, (b) that type of detailed information would be unduly voluminous and would be considered proprietary, and (c) information that describes general physical facilities is readily available outside of financial reports. Therefore, the Board did not require the disclosure of this type of operational information.

Interim Reporting

110. The Board and the majority of respondents to the Invitation to Comment and to the Exposure Draft believe that the disclosure requirements for oil and gas producing activities should apply to only complete sets of annual financial statements. Statement 19 specifically omits from its requirements for interim statements disclosure of information about reserve quantities and costs incurred. That Statement indicates that "the Board reached that conclusion principally because problems in gathering data of that type on a timely basis become especially acute at interim reporting dates and, for some companies, the costs of that effort may be unduly burdensome" (paragraph 234). The Board believes that those reasons for not requiring information about reserve quantities and costs incurred to be disclosed in interim reports are still valid. For the same reasons, information about the results of operations and discounted future net cash flows also should not be required in interim reports.

111. The Board rescinded the requirement in Statement 19 to report information about capitalized costs for oil and gas producing activities in interim financial statements or reports because that information is not essential for an understanding of the performance and financial position of the enterprise. That rescission is consistent with the provisions of FASB Statement No. 18, *Financial Reporting for Segments of a Business Enterprise—Interim Financial Statements.*

112. However, if interim financial statements or reports are presented, this Statement requires disclosure of information about a major discovery or other event that causes a significant change from the information reported in the most recent financial statements. That approach is consistent with Statement 19, paragraph 49, and APB Opinion No. 28, *Interim Financial Reporting,* paragraph 32, both of which seek commentary relating to the effects of significant events in interim financial statements or reports.

Applicability

113. If information about an enterprise's oil and gas producing activities meets the objectives of financial reporting and possesses the necessary degree of relevance and reliability, the Board believes that the only justification for excluding a particular enterprise (or group of enterprises) from the disclosure requirements would be that the costs of providing that information exceed the benefits. Respondents to the Invitation to Comment and to the Exposure Draft raised that argument concerning the application of this Statement's requirements to enterprises that are not publicly traded and to publicly traded enterprises that do not have significant oil and gas producing activities. Furthermore, responses to the Invitation to Comment and to the Exposure Draft and testimony received at the public hearing specified the following reasons for omitting enterprises that are not publicly traded from specialized disclosure requirements:

a. The users of financial statements of enterprises that are not publicly traded are generally its owners and creditors. Those users usually are knowledgeable about the individual enterprise and its industry and frequently are directly involved in the management of the enterprise or have the ability to demand and obtain the information they need (for example, creditors).
b. In assessing the creditworthiness of enterprises that are not publicly traded, lending institutions generally require that their own staffs prepare estimates of reserve quantities and information about estimated future net cash flows from the petroleum engineer's report. Therefore, to require enterprises that are not publicly traded to report that information cannot be cost justified since those lending institutions would not be expected to use the information.

114. As previously indicated, the informational needs of the users of financial reports are the same for enterprises that are publicly traded and enterprises that are not publicly traded. However, creditors of and investors in enterprises that are not publicly traded, if they do not already have the information they require, usually are able to obtain it. Therefore, a Board requirement to report specialized information about oil and gas producing activities would provide little additional benefit to the users of those financial reports. The Board acknowledges that there are instances in which certain investors in closely held businesses may not have the ability to get the information necessary for decision making. However, comments received in the course of this project do not indicate that this is a widespread problem. The Board may need to reassess a possible requirement for enterprises that are not publicly traded to provide the information after completion of the Board's project on financial reporting by private and small public companies.

Location of Information within Financial Reports

115. The requirement to report specialized information about oil and gas producing activities and the issue of where that information should be reported were considered by the Board in 1979 as part of its consideration of Statement 25 requirements. Since that time, the Board has issued an Exposure Draft on reporting income, which offers some guidance on the placement of information within financial reports.

116. That Exposure Draft indicates that information with a different perspective from that reported in the body of the financial statements (for example, other than historical cost based information) can be reported as supplementary information. Presenting information about proved reserve quantities and estimated discounted future net cash flows as supplementary disclosures would be consistent with that suggestion. In addition, cost-benefit considerations (as well as reliability considerations) indicate that information about the reserve quantities, estimated discounted future net cash flows, and results of operations should be supplementary because the placement of information outside the financial statements may result in lower auditing costs.

117. Also, that Exposure Draft indicates that detailed information or information useful for specialized analysis of financial reports can appropriately be considered supplementary. That supports the inclusion of the whole disclosure package for oil and gas producing activities—except for the disclosure of the enterprise's accounting method—as supplementary information. Reporting specialized information on oil and gas producing activities in a single location within a financial report is a desired objective of this Statement so as to make the relationship among the different types of information easier to analyze.

118. Since the industry does not use a uniform accounting method for costs incurred in oil and gas producing activities, this Statement retains the requirements of Statement 25 to disclose the accounting method within the financial statements.

Current Cost Information

119. Most comments received in response to the Exposure Draft's specific question concerning current cost for oil and gas producing activities addressed the decision usefulness of that information. The principal reason given by respondents who do not consider current cost information useful for oil and gas mineral interests is that it is not representationally faithful. That is, the amount does not represent the cost of replacing the enterprise's mineral interests. Respondents who supported disclosure of current cost information for oil and gas producing activities generally view it as a mechanical necessity to report current cost information in their consolidated operations. In addition, some supporters of current cost information for oil and gas producing activities believe that the information is useful since it provides information about part of the change in current cost—the part attributed to price changes—even though the uncertainty concerning future exploration and development defies measurement.

120. Respondents to the Invitation to Comment and to the Exposure Draft indicated that current cost measurements of oil and gas interests presented in annual reports for 1980 and 1981 usually reflected an indexed cost, in many cases the result of applying a general price index to past costs incurred to find oil and gas reserves, not a current finding cost of the same quantity and quality of mineral interests. Therefore, the Board has modified the requirements of Statement 39 to permit enterprises to use historical cost/constant dollar measures for oil and gas mineral resource assets in presenting supplementary information on a current cost basis.

121. The effect of the modification is to require enterprises to present information on a current cost basis only if the enterprise has significant holdings of inventory and property, plant, and equipment apart from its oil and gas mineral resource assets or certain other specialized assets. However, the modifications allow enterprises to continue experimenting with developing current cost information for oil and gas mineral interests, and also allow the use of the present value of future cash flows associated with those mineral interests for enterprises that would expect to replace their oil and gas mineral interests by purchase.

Statement of Financial Accounting Standards No. 70 Financial Reporting and Changing Prices: Foreign Currency Translation

an amendment of FASB Statement No. 33

STATUS

Issued: December 1982

Effective Date: For fiscal years ending after December 15, 1982 for which an enterprise has applied FAS 52

Affects: Supersedes FAS 33, paragraph 22(c)
Amends FAS 33, paragraphs 22, 29(a), 30, 31, 34, 35, 35(c), 36, 39, 41, 50, 53, 56, 59, and 66

Affected by: No other pronouncements

SUMMARY

This Statement amends FASB Statement No. 33, *Financial Reporting and Changing Prices,* to implement revisions to the supplementary information about the effects of changing prices necessitated by changes in the method of translating foreign currency financial statements set out in FASB Statement No. 52, *Foreign Currency Translation.* However, this Statement has no effect on the reporting of supplementary information about changing prices by enterprises for which the U.S. dollar is the functional currency for all significant operations. The provisions of Statement 33 continue to apply to those enterprises.

An enterprise that measures a significant part of its operations in functional currencies other than the U.S. dollar is exempted from Statement 33's requirements to present historical cost information measured in units of constant purchasing power. Enterprises without significant amounts of inventory and property, plant, and equipment that have used historical cost information measured in units of constant purchasing power to satisfy Statement 33's current cost requirements may continue to do so.

Operations that use functional currencies other than the U.S. dollar should measure current cost amounts and increases or decreases therein in the functional currency. Adjustments to current cost information to reflect the effects of general inflation may be based on either the U.S. CPI(U) or functional currency general price level indexes.

Statement of Financial Accounting Standards No. 70
Financial Reporting and Changing Prices: Foreign Currency Translation

an amendment of FASB Statement No. 33

CONTENTS

INTRODUCTION

1. FASB Statement No. 33, *Financial Reporting and Changing Prices,* requires presentation of supplementary information about selected financial data using alternative accounting measurement systems. The provisions of Statement 33 concerning foreign currency translation were based on FASB Statement No. 8, *Accounting for the Translation of Foreign Currency Transactions and Foreign Currency Financial Statements.* FASB Statement No. 52, *Foreign Currency Translation,* supersedes Statement 8 and revises the requirements for translating foreign currency financial statements for purposes of preparing the primary financial statements of an enterprise. This Statement implements amendments to Statement 33 necessitated by those revisions.

2. This Statement applies to an enterprise that (a) presents supplementary information about the effects of changing prices in conformity with Statement 33 (as supplemented by Statements 39, 40, 41, 46, and 69)[1] and (b) measures the results of a significant part of its operations in one or more functional currencies other than the U.S. dollar. This Statement does not affect the reporting of supplementary information about changing prices by enterprises for which the U.S. dollar is the functional currency for all significant operations. The provisions of Statement 33 continue to apply to those enterprises.

STANDARDS OF FINANCIAL ACCOUNTING AND REPORTING

3. An enterprise that measures a significant part of its operations in one or more functional currencies[2] other than the U.S. dollar is not required to disclose historical cost information measured in units of constant purchasing power for either the current or prior years, provided that current cost information is disclosed for those years. Enterprises that do not have significant amounts of inventory and property, plant, and equipment may continue to disclose historical cost information measured in units of constant purchasing power as a substitute for current cost information.

4. Current cost amounts and increases or decreases therein shall be first measured in the functional currency[3] and then translated into U.S. dollar equivalents in accordance with paragraph 12 of Statement 52. The effects of general inflation on the current cost information shall be measured either (a) after translation and based on the U.S. CPI(U) (the *translate-restate method*) or (b) before translation and based on the functional currency general price level index (the *restate-translate method*). The same method shall be used for all operations measured in functional currencies other than the U.S. dollar and for all periods presented. Regardless of which method is used, end-of-year net assets and the

[1]FASB Statements No. 39, *Financial Reporting and Changing Prices: Specialized Assets—Mining and Oil and Gas,* No. 40, *Financial Reporting and Changing Prices: Specialized Assets—Timberlands and Growing Timber,* No. 41, *Financial Reporting and Changing Prices: Specialized Assets—Income-Producing Real Estate,* No. 46, *Financial Reporting and Changing Prices: Motion Picture Films,* and No. 69, *Disclosures about Oil and Gas Producing Activities.*

[2]*Functional currency* is defined in paragraph 5 of Statement 52 as the currency of the primary economic environment in which an entity operates.

[3]Paragraph 59 of Statement 33, as amended by this Statement, provides guidance concerning remeasurement of current cost amounts initially measured in a currency other than the functional currency. This Statement does not change the provisions of paragraphs 57, 58, or 60 or the discussion in paragraph 181 of Statement 33 concerning initial measurement of current cost amounts.

change in net assets during the year shall be measured in either average-for-the-year or end-of-year U.S. dollars. The translate-restate method is essentially the same as the original requirements of Statement 33 concerning disclosure of current cost/constant dollar information, except that translation adjustments are to be disclosed as a separate line item rather than included in measuring income from continuing operations and increases or decreases in current cost amounts. The method used shall be disclosed.

5. Paragraphs 6-19 set forth the technical amendments to Statement 33 needed to implement the standards in paragraphs 3 and 4 of this Statement. In addition, paragraphs 31-37 of Appendix A illustrate the preparation of current cost information based on the translate-restate method; paragraphs 38-45 of that appendix illustrate the preparation of current cost information based on the restate-translate method.

Amendments to FASB Statement No. 33

Definitions

6. Subparagraph 22(c) of Statement 33, which defines current cost/constant dollar accounting, is superseded by the following definition:

> *Current cost/constant purchasing power accounting.* A method of accounting based on measures of current cost or lower recoverable amount in units of currency that each have the same general purchasing power. For operations for which the U.S. dollar is the functional currency, the general purchasing power of the dollar is used. For operations for which the functional currency is other than the U.S. dollar, the general purchasing power of either (a) the dollar or (b) the functional currency is used.

The references in Statement 33, paragraphs 36, 56, 66, and 137 to *current cost/constant dollar* are hereby amended to read *current cost/constant purchasing power.* In addition, the following definition is added as subparagraph 22(i) of Statement 33:

> *Current cost/nominal functional currency accounting.* A method of accounting based on measures of current cost or lower recoverable amount in units of the functional currency that do not each have the same general purchasing power.

Deletion of Historical Cost/Constant Dollar Requirements

7. Subparagraph 29(a) of Statement 33 is amended to read as follows:

> Information on income from continuing operations for the current fiscal year on a historical cost/constant dollar basis (paragraphs 39-46); however, this requirement does not apply to an enterprise that measures a significant part of its operations in one or more functional currencies other than the U.S. dollar, except as provided in paragraph 31.*

*An enterprise with significant operations measured in functional currencies other than the U.S. dollar that voluntarily wishes to present historical cost information measured in units of constant purchasing power should prepare historical cost/constant functional currency information using a functional currency general price index to *restate* the functional currency amounts and then *translate* those amounts into U.S. dollar equivalents. In that situation, the restate-translate method shall be used to prepare current cost/constant purchasing power information.

8. The first sentence of paragraph 35 of Statement 33, which specifies the information to be disclosed in the five-year summary of selected financial data, is revised to read as follows:

> An enterprise is required to disclose the following information for each of its five most recent fiscal years (paragraphs 65 and 66); however, the historical cost/constant dollar disclosures specified by items b(1), b(2), and b(3) do not apply to an enterprise that measures a significant part of its operations in one or more functional currencies other than the U.S. dollar:

9. The following provision is added at the end of paragraph 31 of Statement 33:

> An enterprise that measures a significant part of its operations in one or more functional currencies other than the U.S. dollar and that does not have significant amounts of inventory and property, plant, and equipment may substitute other information for the current cost information required by subparagraphs 30(a), 30(b), and 30(d) or 30(e). The substituted information shall be historical cost information measured either (a) in units of constant U.S. general purchasing power or (b) in units of constant functional currency purchasing power translated into dollar equivalents in accordance with paragraph 12 of FASB Statement No. 52, *Foreign Currency Translation.*

10. The following provision is added at the end of paragraph 53 of Statement 33, as amended by Statements 39, 40, 41, 46, and 69:

> Operations measured in a functional currency other than the U.S. dollar may adjust the func-

tional currency historical cost (and related expenses) of timberlands and growing timber, income-producing real estate, motion picture films, and oil and gas mineral resource assets by a functional currency general price level index and then translate those restated amounts to dollar equivalents in accordance with paragraph 12 of Statement 52 as a substitute for the current cost or lower recoverable amount of those assets.

Remeasurement of Current Cost Amounts

11. Paragraph 59 of Statement 33 is amended to read as follows:

> If current cost is measured in a foreign currency, other than the functional currency, the amount shall be remeasured into the functional currency at the current exchange rate, that is, the rate at the date of use, sale, or commitment to a specific contract (in the cases of depreciation expense and cost of goods sold) or the rate at the balance sheet date (in the cases of inventory and property, plant, and equipment).

The Translate-Restate Method

12. The following disclosure requirement is added to paragraph 30 of Statement 33, which specifies the current cost information to be disclosed for the current fiscal year:

> d. If inflation-adjusted current cost information for operations measured in a functional currency other than the U.S. dollar is based on the translate-restate method, the aggregate foreign currency translation adjustment for the period, on the current cost basis, less any income taxes for the period allocated to the aggregate translation adjustment in the primary financial statements (Statement 52, subparagraphs 31(b) and 31(c)).

13. The following disclosure requirement is added to subparagraph 35(c) of Statement 33, which specifies the current cost information to be disclosed in the five-year summary of selected financial data:

> (5) If inflation-adjusted current cost information for operations measured in functional currencies other than the U.S. dollar is based on the translate-restate method, the aggregate foreign currency translation adjustment, on the current cost basis, less any income taxes allocated to the aggregate translation adjustment in the primary financial statements (Statement 52, subparagraphs 31(b) and 31(c)).

The Restate-Translate Method

14. The following disclosure requirement is added to paragraph 30 of Statement 33, which specifies the current cost information to be disclosed for the current fiscal year:

> e. If inflation-adjusted current cost information for operations measured in functional currencies other than the U.S. dollar is based on the restate-translate method, the aggregate foreign currency translation adjustment for the period, on the current cost basis, net of both any income taxes for the period allocated to the aggregate translation adjustment in the primary financial statements (Statement 52, subparagraphs 31(b) and 31(c)) and the aggregate parity adjustment (FASB Statement No. 70, *Financial Reporting and Changing Prices: Foreign Currency Translation,* paragraphs 74 and 75). The parity adjustment shall be the amount needed to measure end-of-year net assets and the change in net assets during the year in (1) average-for-the-year dollars, if income from continuing operations is measured in average-for-the-year functional currency units, or (2) end-of-year dollars, if income from continuing operations is measured in end-of-year functional currency units.

15. The following disclosure requirement is added to subparagraph 35(c) of Statement 33, which specifies the current cost information to be disclosed in the five-year summary of selected financial data:

> (6) If current cost information for operations measured in functional currencies other than the U.S. dollar is based on the restate-translate method, the aggregate foreign currency translation adjustment, on the current cost basis, net of both any income taxes allocated to the aggregate translation adjustment in the primary financial statements (Statement 52, subparagraphs 31(b) and 31(c)) and the aggregate parity adjustment (Statement 70, paragraphs 74 and 75). The parity adjustment shall be the amount needed to measure end-of-year net assets and the change in net assets during the year in (a) average-for-the-year dollars, if income from continuing operations is measured in average-for-the-year functional currency units, or (b) end-of-year dollars, if income from continuing operations is measured in end-of-year functional currency units.

16. The following provisions are added at the end of paragraph 39 of Statement 33 concerning the general price level index to be used:

The index used to compute information in units of constant functional currency purchasing power shall be a broad-based measure of the change in the general purchasing power of that functional currency. If no reliable index is available for a particular functional currency, management shall estimate the change in the general purchasing power of that currency (Statement 70, paragraphs 81 and 82).

17. Paragraph 41 of Statement 33 is amended to insert a provision concerning a foreign index, so that the paragraph reads as follows:

If the level of the Consumer Price Index or a foreign functional currency general price level index at the end of the year and the data required to compute the average level of the index over the year have not been published in time for preparation of the annual report, they may be estimated by referring to published forecasts based on economic statistics or by extrapolation based on recently reported changes in the index.

18. The following sentences are added after the first sentence of paragraph 50 of Statement 33 concerning computation of the purchasing power gain or loss:

If inflation-adjusted current cost information for operations measured in functional currencies other than the U.S. dollar is based on the restate-translate method, the purchasing power gain or loss on net monetary items shall be equal to the net gain or loss determined by restating the opening and closing balances of, and transactions in, monetary assets and liabilities in units of constant functional currency purchasing power. The purchasing power gain or loss computed in that manner shall be translated into its dollar equivalent at the average exchange rate for the period.

Disclosure of Method

19. The following disclosure requirement is added at the end of paragraph 34 of Statement 33, which specifies disclosures to be made in notes to the supplementary information:

An enterprise that measures a significant part of its operations in one or more functional currencies other than the U.S. dollar shall disclose whether adjustments to the current cost information to reflect the effects of general inflation are based on the U.S. CPI(U) or on functional currency general price level indexes.

Effective Date and Transition

20. The provisions of this Statement shall be effective for fiscal years ending after December 15, 1982 for which an enterprise has applied Statement 52. Restatement of supplementary information for prior periods in the five-year summary of selected financial data to conform to the provisions of this Statement is required only if the primary financial statements for those prior periods have been restated to conform to the provisions of Statement 52.

21. The method (either translate-restate or restate-translate) used in any restatement pursuant to paragraph 20 shall be the same as the method chosen for fiscal years for which this Statement is effective. If the restate-translate method is chosen, information prepared in accordance with the provisions of the Exposure Draft, *Financial Reporting and Changing Prices: Foreign Currency Translation,* issued December 22, 1981, need not be restated.

The provisions of this Statement need not be applied to immaterial items.

This Statement was adopted by the affirmative votes of six members of the Financial Accounting Standards Board. Mr. Morgan dissented.

Mr. Morgan disagrees with the conclusions expressed in this Statement because he believes that continuing to require enterprises that use foreign functional currencies for a significant part of their operations to disclose current cost information imposes a cost greater than the potential benefit. As acknowledged in paragraph 86, application of the provisions of this Statement will affect the comparability of the supplementary current cost information prepared before and after its adoption. Mr. Morgan believes that the discontinuity of information thus created will impair the usefulness of the information for discerning trends in data items and thus will probably render conclusions of researchers attempting to use the data invalid or subject to many unquantifiable reservations.

Not all accounting changes cause discontinuity of data as significant as that which resulted from the introduction of the functional currency concept in Statement 52. Most accounting changes merely result in a different measurement or presentation of identical or similar economic facts, and the effect of the change generally can be measured with reasonable reliability. In the instance of foreign currency translation, there is evidence that enterprises altered their ways of doing business to minimize reportable exchange losses under Statement 8. It seems logical to assume that further changes in business practices will result when enterprises adopt Statement 52 and the effect of such changes cannot be measured with reasonable reliability. Accordingly, the discontinuity created by Statement 52 is different from the discontinuity arising from other accounting changes.

In Mr. Morgan's opinion, it also is not cost beneficial to consider that the experiment with alternative measurement systems for enterprises that use foreign functional currencies for a significant part of their operations constitutes two experiments—one before adoption of Statement 52 and the other after adoption of Statement 52. Because the data for each of those experiments would be for such a short time period (between two and three years), researchers would have difficulty analyzing whether meaningful trends or random events were responsible for the observable changes.

Members of the Financial Accounting Standards Board:

Donald J. Kirk, *Chairman*	John W. March	Robert T. Sprouse
Frank E. Block	Robert A. Morgan	Ralph E. Walters
	David Mosso	

Appendix A

ILLUSTRATIVE CALCULATIONS TO COMPUTE CURRENT COST/CONSTANT PURCHASING POWER INFORMATION

Introduction

22. This appendix presents an example of the methodology that might be used to calculate supplementary current cost information for a foreign subsidiary that uses the local currency as its functional currency. To simplify the calculations, the company is assumed to have a fixed asset but no inventory. The mechanics of restating inventory and cost of goods sold on a current cost basis are similar to those illustrated for property, plant, and equipment and depreciation.

23. The methodology used in this example is essentially the same as that illustrated in Appendix E of Statement 33. The major adaptation needed to accommodate the functional currency concept is first to measure not only current cost amounts but also increases or decreases therein for the foreign subsidiary in its local currency and then to translate those amounts into U.S. dollar equivalents in accordance with Statement 52. The effect of general inflation may be measured either (a) after translation and based on the U.S. CPI(U) or (b) before translation and based on the local price index. To prepare consolidated supplementary information, dollar equivalent amounts determined in accordance with either (a) or (b) would be aggregated with dollar equivalent amounts computed in a similar fashion for other subsidiaries with foreign functional currencies and dollar amounts for operations for which the U.S. dollar is the functional currency. Statement 33 (paragraph 27) encourages presentation of information by segments of business enterprises, and it may be helpful to present foreign operations separately.

24. Throughout this illustration, CFC indicates constant functional currency amounts, and CFC$ indicates the translated dollar equivalents of CFC amounts. Nominal functional currency is indicated by FC, and C$E indicates dollar equivalents of FC amounts restated by the U.S. index.

Assumptions

25. The functional currency financial statements of Sub Company appear [on page 1847]:

Sub Company
Historical Cost FC Balance Sheets

	December 31	
	1982	**1981**
Cash	FC2,550	FC1,250
Equipment	2,500	2,500
Accumulated depreciation	750	500
Net equipment	1,750	2,000
Total assets	FC4,300	FC3,250
Current liabilities	FC 600	FC 500
Long-term debt	2,000	1,500
Total liabilities	2,600	2,000
Capital stock	500	500
Retained earnings	1,200	750
Total equity	1,700	1,250
Total liabilities and equity	FC4,300	FC3,250

Sub Company
Historical Cost FC Statement of Income and Retained Earnings
Year Ending December 31, 1982

Revenue	FC5,000
Salaries	2,500
General and administrative expenses	1,000
Depreciation	250
Interest	350
	4,100
Income before taxes	900
Income taxes	450
Net income	450
Retained earnings—beginning of year	750
Retained earnings—end of year	FC1,200

26. The fixed asset was acquired on December 31, 1979. It is depreciated on a straight-line basis over 10 years and is expected to have no salvage value. There were no acquisitions or disposals of assets during the year.

27. Exchange rates between the functional currency and the dollar are:

December 31, 1981	FC1 = $1.20
Average 1982	FC1 = $1.10
December 31, 1982	FC1 = $1.00

28. Management has measured the current cost of equipment at December 31, 1981 and 1982 as follows:

	1982	**1981**
Current cost	FC5,500	FC4,000
Accumulated depreciation	(1,650)	(800)
Net current cost	FC3,850	FC3,200

The "net recoverable amount" has been determined to be in excess of net current cost at both dates.

29. Current cost equity in nominal FC at the beginning and end of the year may be computed by adding net monetary items and net property, plant, and equipment at current cost. To determine current cost equity in nominal dollars, those FC amounts are translated at the appropriate exchange rate:

	December 31					
	1982			1981		
	FC	Exchange Rate	$	FC	Exchange Rate	$
Monetary items (par. 25):						
Cash	FC2,550	$1	$2,550	FC1,250	$1.20	$1,500
Current liabilities	(600)	$1	(600)	(500)	$1.20	(600)
Long-term debt	(2,000)	$1	(2,000)	(1,500)	$1.20	(1,800)
Net monetary liabilities	FC (50)		$ (50)	FC (750)		$ (900)
Equipment—net (par. 28)	FC3,850	$1	$3,850	FC3,200	$1.20	$3,840
Equity at current cost	FC3,800		$3,800	FC2,450		$2,940

30. The U.S. and local general price level indexes are:

	Local	U.S.
December 1981	144	281.5
Average 1982	158	292.5*
December 1982	173	303.5*

*Assumed for illustrative purposes.

The Translate-Restate Method

31. To apply the translate-restate method, amounts measured in nominal FC are first translated into their dollar equivalents. Changes in those dollar equivalent amounts are then restated to reflect the effects of U.S. inflation.

Current Cost Depreciation and Income from Continuing Operations

32. The first step is to determine current cost depreciation for the year as follows:

Current cost—beginning of year	FC4,000
Current cost—end of year	5,500
	9,500
	÷ 2
Average current cost, gross	FC4,750

Current cost depreciation expense for the year measured in average 1982 CFC is CFC475 (FC4,750 × 10%). Computation of current cost depreciation and income from continuing operations does not involve use of a general price level index if measurements are made in average-for-the-year currency units. Accordingly, reported current cost depreciation under the translate-restate method is $523 (FC475 × $1.10).

33. Income from continuing operations on a current cost basis measured in average 1982 CFC is computed by simply replacing historical cost depreciation in income from continuing operations in the primary financial statements with the current cost amount. Accordingly, current cost income from continuing operations measured in average 1982 CFC is:

Net income + historical cost depreciation − current cost depreciation = income from continuing operations

FC450 (par. 25) + FC250 (par. 25) − FC475 (par. 32) = CFC225

Reported current cost income from continuing operations under the translate-restate method is C$E248 (CFC225 × $1.10).

Excess of Increase in Specific Prices over Increase in General Price Level

34. The second step is to compute the change in the current cost of equipment and the effect of the increase in the general price level. To measure the increase in current cost of equipment in nominal FC dollar equivalents, the effect of the exchange rate change must be excluded (paragraphs 60-62). One way to accomplish that is to translate the 12/31/81 and 12/31/82 FC current cost amounts to dollar equivalents at the average exchange rate and then restate those dollar amounts to average 1982 constant dollar equivalents:

	Current Cost/FC	Exchange Rate	Current Cost/$	Conversion Factor	Current Cost/C$E
Current cost, net—12/31/81 (par. 28)	FC3,200	$1.10	$3,520	292.5(Avg.1982) / 281.5(Dec.1981)	C$E3,658
Depreciation	(475)	$1.10	(523)	*	(523)
Current cost, net—12/31/82 (par. 28)	3,850	$1.10	4,235	292.5(Avg.1982) / 303.5(Dec.1982)	4,081
Increase in current cost	FC1,125		$1,238		C$E 946

*Assumed to be in average 1982 C$E.

The inflation component of the increase in current cost amount is the difference between the nominal dollar and the constant dollar equivalent amounts:

Increase in current cost ($)	$1,238
Increase in current cost (C$E)	C$E 946
Inflation component	292

Purchasing Power Gain or Loss on Net Monetary Items

35. The third step is to compute the purchasing power gain or loss on net monetary items. Under the translate-restate method, the translated beginning and ending net monetary liabilities are restated to average 1982 dollars. The U.S. purchasing power gain is then the balancing amount:

	FC	Exchange Rate	$
Net monetary liabilities—12/31/81 (par. 29)	FC750	$1.20	$900
Net monetary liabilities—12/31/82 (par. 29)	50	$1.00	50
Decrease during the year	FC700		$850

	$	Conversion Factor	C$E
Net monetary liabilities 12/31/81	$900	292.5(Avg. 1982) / 281.5(Dec. 1981)	C$E935
Decrease during the year	(850)	*	(850)
Net monetary liabilities 12/31/82	$ 50	292.5(Avg. 1982) / 303.5(Dec. 1982)	48
Purchasing power gain			C$E 37

*Assumed to be in average 1982 C$E.

The above computation is the same as that used to compute the purchasing power gain or loss on net monetary items under the original translate-restate provisions of Statement 33. In some circumstances, that procedure will include a part of the effect of exchange rate changes on net monetary items in the purchasing power gain or loss. A more theoretically correct computation that would completely exclude the effect of exchange rate changes would be to compute a separate purchasing power gain or loss for each functional currency operation in a manner similar to that illustrated in paragraph 34 for the increase in specific prices. For the example, that alternative method produces a purchasing power gain of $34:

	FC	Average Exchange Rate	$	Conversion Factor	C$E
Net monetary liabilities—12/31/81 (par. 29)	FC750	$1.10	$825	292.5 (Avg. 1982) / 281.5 (Dec. 1981)	C$E857
Decrease during the year	(700)	$1.10	770	*	(770)
Net monetary liabilities—12/31/82 (par. 29)	FC50	$1.10	$ 55	292.5 (Avg. 1982) / 303.5 (Dec. 1982)	53
Purchasing power gain					C$E34

*Assumed to be in average 1982 C$E.

However, the first procedure illustrated is less costly because it can be applied on a consolidated basis, and it generally provides a reasonable approximation. Accordingly, that method is acceptable.

Reconciliation of Equity

36. Although neither Statement 33 nor this Statement requires disclosure of a reconciliation of equity, such a reconciliation serves as a check of the calculations and is a convenient way to compute the translation adjustment:

Equity at 12/31/81 in average 1982 C$ $2,940 (par. 29) x 292.5/281.5		C$3,055
Income from continuing operations (par. 33)	C$E248	
Purchasing power gain (par. 35)	37	
Excess of increase in specific prices over increase in general price level (par. 34)	946	
Translation adjustment (par. 37)	(624)	
Increase in equity in terms of U.S. purchasing power		607
		C$3,662
Equity at 12/31/82 in average 1982 C$ $3,800 (par. 29) × 292.5/303.5		C$3,662

Translation adjustment

37. The translation adjustment is the amount needed to balance the reconciliation of equity. The translation adjustment determined under the translate-restate method may be checked by translating the beginning- and end-of-year equity on a C$ basis into FC amounts and using those FC amounts in a calculation similar to that illustrated in paragraph 61 of Appendix B:

	C$	Exchange Rate	FC
Equity at 12/31/81 in average 1982 C$ (par. 36)	C$3,055	$0.833*	FC2,545
Equity at 12/31/82 in average 1982 C$ (par. 36)	3,662	$1.00	3,662
Increase in equity	C$ 607		FC1,117

Restated opening equity	FC2,545
Exchange rate change during 1982 ($1.20 − $1.00)	× (.20)
	$ (509)
Plus increase in equity	FC1,117
Difference between ending exchange rate and average rate for 1982 ($1.10 − $1.00)	× (.10)
	$ (112)
Translation adjustment	$ (621)

*1FC ÷ $1.20 = $0.833.

The difference of $3 ($624 − $621) between the translation adjustment computed above and the translation adjustment that appears in paragraph 36 reflects the $3 difference ($37 − $34) between the short-cut and theoretically correct procedures illustrated in paragraph 35.

The Restate-Translate Method

38. To apply the restate-translate method, the steps illustrated in paragraphs 31-35 are followed except that all restatements to reflect the effects of general inflation are made before translation to dollar

equivalents and using the local general price level index.

Current Cost Depreciation and Income from Continuing Operations

39. Current cost depreciation and income from continuing operations are CFC475 and CFC225, respectively, as determined in paragraphs 32 and 33.

Purchasing Power Gain or Loss on Net Monetary Items

40. To apply the restate-translate method, the FC amount of net monetary items at the beginning of the year, changes in the net monetary items, and the amount at the end of the year are restated into average 1982 CFC. The purchasing power gain or loss on net monetary items is then the balancing item:

	FC	Conversion Factor	CFC
Net monetary liabilities 12/31/81 (par. 29)	FC750	158 (Avg.1982) / 144 (Dec.1981)	CFC823
Decrease during the year	(700)	*	(700)
Net monetary liabilities 12/31/82 (par. 29)	FC 50	158 (Avg.1982) / 173 (Dec.1982)	46
Purchasing power gain			CFC 77

*Assumed to be in average 1982 CFC.

Excess of Increase in Specific Prices over Increase in General Price Level

41. Under the restate-translate method, the local index is used to restate the beginning and ending current cost/FC amounts into average 1982 CFC:

	Current Cost/FC	Conversion Factor	Current Cost/CFC
Current cost, net—12/31/81	FC3,200	158 (Avg.1982) / 144 (Dec.1981)	CFC3,511
Depreciation	(475)	*	(475)
Current cost, net—12/31/82	(3,850)	158 (Avg.1982) / 173 (Dec.1982)	(3,516)
Increase in current cost	FC1,125		CFC 480

*Assumed to be in average 1982 CFC.

The inflation component of the increase in current cost amount is the difference between the nominal functional currency and constant functional currency amounts:

Increase in current cost (FC)	FC1,125
Increase in current cost (CFC)	CFC 480
Inflation component	645

Reconciliation of Equity

42. As with the translate-restate method, a reconciliation of equity acts as a check of the calculations. A reconciliation of equity also is a convenient point at which to translate the functional currency amounts determined in the preceding paragraphs into dollar equivalents and is a convenient way to compute the translation and parity adjustments.

43. If opening and closing equity are restated to average 1982 CFC using the local index, the reconciliation of equity under the restate-translate method would be:

	CFC	Exchange Rate	CFC$
Equity at 12/31/81 in average 1982 CFC FC2,450 (par. 29) × 158/144	CFC2,688	1.20	CFC$3,225
Income from continuing operations (par. 39)	225	1.10	248
Purchasing power gain (par. 40)	77	1.10	85
Excess of increase in specific prices over increase in general price level (par. 41)	480	1.10	528
Translation adjustment (par. 44)			(616)
	CFC3,470		CFC$3,470
Equity at 12/31/82 in average 1982 CFC FC3,800 (par. 29) × 158/173	CFC3,470	1.00	CFC$3,470

Translation adjustment

44. The translation adjustment is the amount needed to balance the CFC$ reconciliation of equity. The adjustment may be computed as (a) the change in exchange rates during the period multiplied by the restated amount of net assets at the beginning of the period plus (b) the difference between the average exchange rate for the period and the end-of-period exchange rate multiplied by the increase or decrease in restated net assets for the period. Accordingly, the translation adjustment under the restate-translate method is:

Restated opening equity (par. 43)	CFC2,688
Exchange rate change during 1982 ($1.20 – $1.00)	× (.20)
	$ (538)
Plus (equity at 12/31/82 minus equity at 12/31/82 = 3,470 – 2,688)	CFC 782
Difference between ending exchange rate and average rate for 1982 ($1.10 – $1.00)	× (.10)
	(78)
Translation adjustment	$ (616)

Parity adjustment

45. The reconciliation of equity in paragraph 43, in which beginning-of-year and end-of-year equity are stated in average 1982 CFC, is needed to calculate the translation adjustment in CFC$. However, beginning-of-year and end-of-year equity and the increase in equity must be stated in average 1982 constant dollars in the supplementary current cost information. Beginning-of-year and end-of-year equity in average 1982 constant dollars are C$3,055 and C$3,662, respectively, as computed in paragraph 36. The overall increase in U.S. purchasing power for the year thus is C$3,662 – C$3,055 = C$607. The difference between that amount and the increase of CFC$245 (CFC$3,470 – CFC$3,225) that appears in the reconciliation of equity in paragraph 43 is the parity adjustment needed to adjust the ending net investment and the increase in the net investment to measures in average 1982 constant dollars (paragraph 74). Accordingly, the parity adjustment is C$607 – CFC$245 = $362. That amount represents (a) the effect of the difference between local and U.S. inflation from 12/31/81 to average for 1982 on the restatement of opening equity to average units plus (b) the effect of the difference between local and U.S. inflation from average for 1982 to 12/31/82 on the restatement of ending nominal dollar equity to average units:

Equity at 12/31/81 (par. 29)	$ 2,940
Difference between local and U.S. inflation from 12/31/81 to average 1982 (158/144 − 292.5/281.5)	× 0.0581
	$ 171
Plus equity at 12/31/82 (par. 29)	$ 3,800
Difference between U.S. and local inflation from average 1982 to 12/31/82 (292.5/303.5 − 158/173)	× 0.0504
	$ 191
Parity adjustment	$ 362

For display purposes, the parity adjustment is combined with the $(616) translation adjustment (paragraph 43). Accordingly, the net translation adjustment disclosed in the supplementary current cost information prepared using the restate-translate method would be $(616) + $362 = $(254). The components of current cost information based on the restate-translate method thus would be:

Beginning-of-year equity		C$3,055
Income from continuing operations	CFC$248	
Purchasing power gain	85	
Excess of increase in specific prices over increase in general price level	528	
Translation and parity adjustments	(254)	
Increase in equity in terms of U.S. purchasing power		607
End-of-year equity		C$3,662

Appendix B

BACKGROUND INFORMATION AND BASIS FOR CONCLUSIONS

CONTENTS

Appendix B

BACKGROUND INFORMATION AND BASIS FOR CONCLUSIONS

Introduction

46. This appendix reviews considerations deemed significant by members of the Board in reaching the conclusions in this Statement. The Board members who assented to this Statement did so on the basis of the overall considerations. Individual members gave greater weight to some factors than to others.

Change in Objectives of Foreign Currency Translation

47. An objective of foreign currency translation stated in Statement 8 was to remeasure in U.S. dollars assets, liabilities, revenues, and expenses originally measured or denominated in a foreign currency. The original provisions of Statement 33 concerning foreign currency translation were based on the Statement 8 approach. Amounts that were originally measured in a foreign currency were first remeasured into U.S. dollars and then restated into constant dollars.

48. In contrast, Statement 52 requires that the financial statements of an enterprise reflect the financial results and relationships as measured in the functional currencies in which it conducts its business. Paragraph 74 of Statement 52 indicates that the translation process should retain the functional currency relationships created in the economic environment of the foreign operations; it should not remeasure individual financial statement elements as if the operations had been conducted in the economic environment of the reporting currency.

49. The possible need for a change in the method of calculating the supplementary information for foreign operations following completion of the Board's review of Statement 8 was anticipated in paragraph 192 of Statement 33. Accordingly, in recognition of the change in objectives of foreign currency translation, the Board in October 1981 added to its agenda a project to amend Statement 33 to maintain consistency between the data reported in the primary financial statements under Statement 52 and the supplementary information about the effects of changing prices. On December 22, 1981, the Board issued for a 120-day comment period an Exposure Draft that set forth proposals designed to achieve that consistency.

50. Sixty-nine comment letters were received in response to that initial Exposure Draft. Many respondents expressed the view that the costs of implementing the proposed requirements would exceed the related benefits. In June 1982, after considering the comment letters received, the Board decided that the Exposure Draft should be revised and reissued for public comment. On August 19, 1982, a revised Exposure Draft was issued for a 60-day comment period. Seventy-one comment letters were received.

Historical Cost/Constant Functional Currency Information

51. For operations measured in a foreign functional currency, the initial Exposure Draft proposed replacing the existing historical cost/constant dollar measurements with historical cost/constant functional currency measurements. That change would have required that the functional currency historical cost of inventory and property, plant, and equipment first be restated into units of constant functional currency purchasing power using an index of general price level changes in the local environment and then translated into dollar equivalents in accordance with the requirements of Statement 52.

52. Although respondents to the initial Exposure Draft generally agreed that instituting a *restate-translate* procedure to determine constant functional currency information would be consistent with the functional currency approach of Statement 52, many objected to the proposed requirements. Those respondents generally expressed the view that the restate-translate approach would be significantly more complex and difficult to understand, and more expensive to prepare, than the procedures used to prepare constant dollar information. In particular, the start-up costs would be substantial, and the ongoing costs for an enterprise with many subsidiaries that use functional currencies other than the U.S. dollar also could be significant. Many respondents expressed the view that requiring such a costly change to the historical cost/constant dollar requirements would be inappropriate, particularly considering the limited time remaining before the Board is scheduled to begin its evaluation of the results of the Statement 33 experiment.

53. Many respondents to the initial Exposure Draft also expressed the view that the historical cost/constant dollar aspect of the Statement 33 experiment appeared to be generating less interest on the part of users than current cost information. Accordingly, they objected to requirements that would significantly increase the costs associated with an accounting system of uncertain value. Many of those respondents recommended that the historical cost/constant dollar requirements be terminated.

54. Because the restate-translate methodology does not affect those enterprises subject to Statement 33

that either do not have foreign operations or that use the U.S. dollar as the functional currency for all significant foreign operations, the Board decided that the historical cost/constant dollar requirements should not be immediately discontinued for all companies. However, the Board concluded that the additional costs associated with requiring historical cost/constant functional currency information could not be justified at this time. Accordingly, in the revised Exposure Draft, the Board proposed exempting enterprises that use functional currencies other than the U.S. dollar for a significant part of their operations from the historical cost/constant purchasing power requirements of Statement 33 until the usefulness of that information has been evaluated.

55. Some respondents to the revised Exposure Draft expressed the view that continuing to require enterprises for which the U.S. dollar is the functional currency for all significant operations to disclose historical cost/constant dollar information was not justified. They generally believed that exempting a large number of the enterprises subject to Statement 33 from those requirements would effectively end and perhaps prejudge the results of the constant dollar aspect of the Statement 33 experiment. The Board disagrees with that view. A substantial number of enterprises included in the Statement 33 sample—probably more than half of the total—are not significantly affected by the adoption of Statement 52. The Board believes that those enterprises will constitute a continuing sample of sufficient size to provide useful experience with historical cost/constant dollar data. Moreover, exempting those enterprises for which continued experimentation at this time would not be cost effective is not intended to prejudge the usefulness of historical cost/constant purchasing power information generally. If the evaluation of Statement 33 indicates that historical cost information measured in units of constant purchasing power is useful, at least for certain types of enterprises or assets, whether to require historical cost/constant functional currency information can be reconsidered.

56. Some respondents to the revised Exposure Draft suggested that the Board define *significant* for purposes of the exemption from historical cost/constant dollar requirements. The Board considered specifying a percentage size test but rejected that approach because it believes the assessment of significance should take into account the facts and circumstances of a particular enterprise. The Board believes management is in the best position to make that assessment. If foreign functional currency operations are not deemed to be significant, historical cost/constant dollar information prepared under the translate-restate method should be presented.

57. The exemption discussed in paragraphs 54 and 55 relates only to disclosure of historical cost information measured in units of constant purchasing power as one of two alternative measurement systems. Statement 33 permits historical cost/constant dollar measures to be substituted for current cost measures of timberlands and growing timber, income-producing real estate, motion picture films, and oil and gas mineral resources. In addition, enterprises that do not have material amounts of inventory and property, plant, and equipment are not required to disclose both historical cost/constant dollar and current cost information because the two sets of information would be essentially the same. The Board concluded that enterprises that have disclosed historical cost information measured in units of constant purchasing power as a substitute for current cost information should continue to do so. Although that substitution will require use of a functional currency general price level index to adjust the functional currency historical cost of certain specialized assets, the Board does not believe that will impose an undue burden on preparers. In that situation, the functional currency general price level index merely serves as a substitute for a specific price index.

Current Cost Information

Nominal Current Cost Measures

58. Paragraph 59 of Statement 33 requires current cost amounts that are originally measured in a foreign currency to be translated into U.S. dollars at the exchange rate in effect at the date of that foreign currency measure. The increase or decrease in current cost amounts for the period is then computed by comparing the dollar current cost measures of assets at their "entry dates" for the year with dollar current cost measures of the assets at their "exit dates" for the year (paragraph 55 of Statement 33). Under the original requirements of Statement 33, the increase or decrease in the dollar current cost amount of an asset originally measured in a foreign currency includes two components:

a. The change in the foreign currency current cost of the asset
b. The effect of any change in exchange rates during the holding period for the asset

Statement 33 does not require those components to be separately disclosed.

59. Statement 52 requires a foreign entity's assets and liabilities to be measured in its functional currency and places importance on reporting in the income statement the effects of transactions and events as measured in the functional currency environment. Accordingly, the Board concluded

that the concepts underlying Statement 52 require that the increase or decrease in current cost amounts initially be measured in the functional currency and then translated into dollar equivalents at the average exchange rate for the holding period. As a result, the effect of exchange rate changes is reflected in a separate line item, "translation adjustment."

60. The distinction between (a) measures of current cost amounts and increases or decreases therein in U.S. dollars as described in paragraph 58 and (b) measures in the functional currency as described in paragraph 59 can be illustrated with a simple example in which a foreign entity's only asset is inventory with a current cost of FC200 and FC400 at the beginning and end of the year, respectively. The exchange rates between the functional currency and the dollar are:

Beginning of year	FC1 = $1.00
Average for year	FC1 = $0.90
End of year	FC1 = $0.80

Measuring the increase or decrease in current cost in dollars under the original requirements of Statement 33 produces the following results:

End-of-year current cost	FC400 × $0.80 =	$320
Beginning-of-year current cost	FC200 × $1.00 =	200
Increase in current cost		$120

If there are no other activities during the period, the increase in the parent's net investment on a current cost basis is $120.

61. In contrast, measuring the increase in current cost in the functional currency and then translating that amount into its dollar equivalent using the average exchange rate produces the following results:

End-of-year current cost	FC400	
Beginning-of-year current cost	200	
Increase in current cost	FC200	× $0.90 = $180

The effect of exchange rate changes during the holding period of the inventory is reflected separately. It consists of (a) the product of the beginning functional currency current cost amount and the total exchange rate change plus (b) the product of the change in current cost and the difference between the average and ending exchange rates:

Beginning-of-year current cost		FC200
Exchange rate change during the year ($1.00 − $0.80)	×	(.20)
		$(40)
Plus increase in current cost		FC200
Difference between average and ending exchange rates ($0.90 − $0.80)	×	(.10)
		$(20)
Translation adjustment		$(60)

Accordingly, the nominal dollar increase in the parent's net investment on a current cost basis under the approach required by this Statement consists of two components:

Increase in current cost	$180
Translation adjustment	(60)
	$120

62. It is important to note that both approaches produce the same dollar amounts of ending net investment and increase for the year in the net investment. The difference between the approaches is the combined or separate disclosure of the effects of two kinds of price changes—changes in the functional currency specific prices of assets and changes in exchange rates. The method required by this Statement separates the effects of those two distinct kinds of price changes, each of which may have different significance in assessments of future cash flows.

Inflation-Adjusted Current Cost Measures

63. Application of the functional currency theory to current cost information measures the parent's net investment in foreign entities, and the change in that net investment, in nominal U.S. dollars. Accordingly, the Board concluded that current cost information measured in units of constant purchasing power should reflect the change in the net investment during the year in terms of U.S. purchasing power. The Board believes that either of two approaches to accomplishing that result has conceptual merit. Current cost amounts in nominal units of the functional currency might be (a) translated into dollar equivalents and changes in those amounts restated to reflect the effect of U.S. inflation *(translate-restate)* or (b) first adjusted to reflect the effect of local inflation and those restated amounts then translated to dollar equivalents *(restate-translate)*. Under the latter approach, a parity

adjustment that reflects the difference between U.S. and local inflation is needed to adjust the total change in the parent's net investment to a U.S. perspective because the individual line items reflect a local perspective. Those two approaches are discussed in paragraphs 64-75.

64. Some believe that extension of the functional currency theory to current cost information measured in units of constant purchasing power should reflect (a) the effect of local inflation on the foreign entity's individual financial statement elements and (b) the effect of U.S. inflation on the total change for the year in the net investment (net assets of the foreign entity). They believe that approach would provide information useful for assessing both the performance of the foreign entity in maintaining its purchasing power in the functional currency environment and the performance of the enterprise as a whole in maintaining the purchasing power of its equity (net assets) in relation to the U.S. dollar.

65. Others believe that reporting individual components of the current cost information (that is, income from continuing operations and the increase or decrease in current cost amount) measured in nominal functional currency units and reflecting the effect of U.S. inflation on the dollar equivalent amounts, perhaps through a one-line capital maintenance adjustment, would best achieve the objectives of (a) maintaining the financial results and relationships created in the functional currency environment and (b) reporting the total performance of the enterprise from a U.S. perspective. They are not convinced that achieving the objective of the functional currency theory requires use of a restate-translate methodology to reflect the effects of local inflation on individual components of the current cost information if combined current cost information for the entire enterprise is to be reported to those concerned with changes in U.S. dollar equity.

66. The relationship between the two approaches described above can be illustrated by extending the example introduced in paragraph 60 to assume that the foreign entity also holds FC100 cash during the year. Accordingly, the foreign entity's net assets at the beginning of the year are FC300. Local inflation for the year is assumed to be 20 percent, and U.S. inflation is 10 percent. Paragraphs 67-71 illustrate the approach described in paragraph 65; paragraphs 72-75 illustrate the approach described in paragraph 64.

The translate-restate approach

67. The view described in paragraph 65 would report current cost information measured in nominal functional currency units translated into dollar equivalents and then adjusted to reflect the effect of U.S. inflation. That might be accomplished by means of a one-line capital maintenance adjustment, computed as the U.S. inflation component of the nominal increase or decrease in the net investment during the year. In the example introduced in paragraph 66, the capital maintenance adjustment in end-of-year dollars would be the product of the beginning-of-year nominal dollar net investment ($300) and the U.S. inflation rate for the year (10 percent), or $30.

68. Under the capital maintenance adjustment approach, individual line items of the current cost information would be measured in nominal functional currency dollar equivalents. Presentation of individual financial statement elements in constant purchasing power terms would be limited to the five-year summary, in which prior years' data would be restated by the U.S. CPI(U) to provide a statistical display of interperiod relationships on a constant basis. Accordingly, current cost information[4] for the current year in the example would be:

Beginning-of-year net investment in end-of-year dollars $300 × 110/100	$330
Increase in specific prices	180
Translation adjustment	(80)
Capital maintenance adjustment	(30)
End-of-year net investment	$400

The translation adjustment of $(80) is stated in nominal U.S. dollars; it is (a) the $(60) computed in paragraph 61 plus (b) a $20 loss on the FC100 cash held during the year. Although omitted from the example for simplicity, income from continuing operations on a current cost basis also would be measured in nominal functional currency dollar equivalents.

69. That capital maintenance adjustment of $30 may be split into 2 components: (a) a U.S. purchasing power loss on net monetary items of $10 ($100 × 10%) plus (b) the amount needed to maintain the U.S. purchasing power represented by the beginning dollar equivalent current cost of inventory, or $20

[4]Throughout the illustrations in this Statement, current cost information is displayed in a reconciliation-of-equity format. Neither Statement 33 nor this Statement requires use of that format for reporting purposes, although some respondents expressed the view that disclosure of a reconciliation of equity would help users to understand the relationships among the various pieces of information disclosed. Under the usual Statement 33 display, beginning-of-year net assets measured in current-year dollars would appear only in the five-year summary. The purpose of the format used in the illustrations is to demonstrate the similarities and differences of the various methods.

($200 × 10%). Some Board members believe that reporting those components separately may be useful; in particular, they believe that the purchasing power gain or loss on net monetary items may be significant when compared with interest expense in evaluating an enterprise's use of borrowed funds. That point is explained more fully in paragraphs 150-155 of Statement 33. Other Board members believe that the one-line capital maintenance adjustment approach may be the eventual solution to reporting inflation-adjusted current cost information but that such a change would have implications for the reporting of current cost information by all enterprises—not only those that measure a significant part of their operations in functional currencies other than the U.S. dollar. The one-line capital maintenance adjustment approach therefore would be difficult to introduce into the Statement 33 experiment at this time. Accordingly, those Board members also would separate the capital maintenance adjustment into its two components for display purposes, at least until the Board has evaluated the results of the Statement 33 experiment.

70. The revised Exposure Draft specifically requested respondents to comment on the capital maintenance adjustment approach. Most respondents who did so agreed that an alternate display of adjustments to current cost information to reflect the effects of changes in the general price level should not be introduced at this time. Many expressed the opinion, however, that the capital maintenance adjustment approach should be explored further as part of the comprehensive evaluation of Statement 33. Accordingly, the Board decided not to require or permit the capital maintenance adjustment display at this time.

71. In the example introduced in paragraph 66, the elements of the current cost information disclosed under the translate-restate approach required by this Statement would be (a) a purchasing power loss of $10 and (b) an inflation-adjusted increase in current cost of inventory computed as the dollar equivalent of the nominal functional currency increase ($180) less the U.S. inflation component ($20), or $160.

The restate-translate approach

72. In contrast, the restate-translate approach described in paragraph 64 would measure the purchasing power gain or loss on net monetary items and the inflation component of the increase in the current cost of inventory and property, plant, and equipment in terms of local inflation in the functional currency environment. For the example discussed in paragraphs 67-71, measuring in end-of-year constant functional currency units (CFC) would result in (a) a purchasing power loss of CFC20 (FC100 × 20%) and (b) an inflation-adjusted increase in current cost amount of CFC160—computed as the nominal functional currency increase of FC200 (paragraph 61) minus the amount needed to maintain the local purchasing power represented by the beginning current cost amount, or FC40 (FC200 × 20%).

73. If beginning-of-year net assets also are restated to end-of-year constant functional currency under a restate-translate approach, a reconciliation of equity would appear as follows:

	CFC	Exchange Rate	CFC$
Beginning-of-year equity in end-of-year CFC FC300 × 120/100	CFC360	$1.00	CFC$360
Purchasing power loss	(20)	.90	(18)
Excess of increase in specific prices over increase in general price level	160	.90	144
Translation adjustment			(86)
	CFC500		CFC$400
End-of-year equity in end-of-year CFC	CFC500	.80	CFC$400

The translation adjustment of $(86) also can be computed directly:

Beginning-of-year equity		CFC360
Exchange rate change during the year ($1.00 – $0.80)	×	(.20)
		$(72)
Plus increase in equity (CFC500 – CFC360)		CFC140
Difference between average and ending exchange rates ($0.90 – $0.80)	×	(.10)
		$(14)
Translation adjustment		$(86)

74. The above reconciliation reflects only the effect of local inflation and indicates an increase in the dollar equivalent of the net investment of $40 (CFC$400 – CFC$360). However, the view described in paragraph 64 requires that supplementary current cost information reflect the change in the net investment during the year in terms of U.S. purchasing power. Determining the increase in the U.S. purchasing power represented by the net investment requires comparing end-of-year equity with beginning-of-year equity restated by the U.S. general price level index and thus is $70 ($400 – [$300 × 110/100] = $400 – $330). Adjusting the reported change in the net investment to a U.S. perspective therefore requires a parity adjustment of $30 ($70 – $40), which represents the product of the difference between local and U.S. inflation for the year (10 percent) and the beginning-of-year net investment (equity) measured in nominal dollars ($300).[5]

75. The translation adjustment and the parity adjustment do not affect assessments of functional currency cash flows. Both of those adjustments are required to adjust the end-of-year net investment and the change in the net investment to U.S. dollar measures, however, and this Statement requires them to be combined for display purposes. If the differential rates of U.S. and local inflation were reflected in the exchange rates (parity), the parity adjustment and the translation adjustment on beginning-of-year net assets would net to zero. The combined amount therefore represents the effect of exchange rate changes in excess of (or less than) that needed to maintain purchasing power parity between the functional currency and the U.S. dollar. In the example introduced in paragraph 66, the end-of-year exchange rate under conditions of parity would be 1FC = $1 × 110/120 = $0.9167. Therefore, a translation adjustment of $(30) (CFC360 × [$1 – 0.9167]) would arise on the restated beginning-of-year equity and would be exactly offset by the parity adjustment of $30. Combining the translation adjustment of $(86) (paragraph 73) and the parity adjustment of $30 yields a dollar loss of $56 that results from the failure of purchasing power parity to hold.

Comparison of approaches

76. The two approaches to preparing inflation-adjusted current cost information permitted by this Statement produce the following results for the example discussed in paragraphs 67-75:

[5]If measures are made in end-of-year constant functional currency, it might be considered appropriate to translate the components of change in net assets during the year at the end-of-year exchange rate rather than the average rate as this Statement requires. However, the Board decided not to require use of end-of-year rates because it would necessitate retranslating revenues and expenses at rates different from those used in the primary financial statements and thus would be more costly. Moreover, use of end-of-year rates would include a part of the effect of exchange rate changes during the year in individual line items rather than with the translation adjustment.

	Translate-Restate		Restate-Translate	
Beginning-of-year net investment in end-of-year dollars $300 × 110/100		$330		$330
Purchasing power loss		(10)		(18)
Increase in specific prices	$180		$180	
Effect of increase in general price level	(20)		(36)	
Excess of increase in specific prices over increase in general price level		160		144
Translation adjustment		(80)		(56)
Increase in net investment in terms of U.S. purchasing power		$ 70		$ 70
End-of-year net investment		$400		$400

Both approaches provide the same information in total. Moreover, both produce the same nominal increase in specific prices. (Income from continuing operations in nominal units also would be the same.) The difference between them is whether the inflation adjustments to individual components of the current cost information reflect U.S. or local inflation.

Conclusions concerning inflation-adjusted current cost information

77. Although some Board members believe the restate-translate approach is preferable because it provides information about both local and U.S. inflation, they are concerned about the implementation costs of an approach that would require the use of multiple functional currency general price level indexes. Accordingly, those Board members believe that for cost-benefit reasons enterprises should be permitted to use the translate-restate approach that involves use of only the U.S. inflation index. The revised Exposure Draft therefore proposed that enterprises be permitted to use either method and specifically asked for comments on the merits of such an option.

78. The majority of the respondents who expressed a view considered it appropriate in an experimental standard to provide enterprises the flexibility to consider cost-benefit implications and to choose between the translate-restate and restate-translate methods. Although many respondents believed that most enterprises would choose the translate-restate method because of its lower implementation cost, some expressed concerns about the potential loss of comparability among enterprises. The Board concluded that the benefits of permitting experimentation with two methods outweigh any potential loss of comparability. The Board believes that conclusion is consistent with other alternatives permitted in Statement 33, such as the option to choose either partial or comprehensive restatement. Therefore, this Statement permits enterprises to use either the translate-restate or restate-translate method. Because a choice is permitted, the method used is required to be disclosed.

Disclosure of Translation and Parity Adjustments

79. Some respondents to the revised Exposure Draft disagreed with the required disclosure of the translation adjustment (if the translate-restate method is used) or the combined translation and parity adjustments (if the restate-translate method is used). They expressed the view that computing those amounts would unduly increase the implementation costs and that the potential usefulness of translation adjustments and parity adjustments had not been demonstrated.

80. The Board believes the discussion and illustrations in paragraphs 67-76 indicate the need to disclose the translation adjustment on a current cost basis. Although translation adjustments do not affect functional currency cash flows, they result from an important type of price change (exchange rate changes) and eventually can have a significant impact on U.S. dollar cash flows. Moreover, the translation adjustment and, under the restate-translate approach, the parity adjustment are required to portray the total change in equity during the year in terms of U.S. purchasing power. The Board recognizes that computation of the translation adjustment will increase the costs of preparing current cost information for enterprises with many

functional currencies. However, Statement 33 emphasizes the appropriateness of reasonable approximations and short-cut methods. Moreover, the exemption from historical cost/constant dollar requirements granted enterprises that measure a significant part of their operations in functional currencies other than the U.S. dollar should at least partly offset the increased costs of preparing current cost information. Accordingly, the Board does not believe required disclosure of translation adjustments will constitute an undue burden.

Functional Currency General Price Level Index

81. The Board concluded that the index to be used in determining constant functional currency amounts should be one that measures the change in the general level of prices in the functional currency environment in a reasonably reliable manner. Some respondents suggested that the Board specify the index to be used for each functional currency. However, the Board believes flexibility is necessary in choosing an appropriate functional currency general price level index. The choice should take into account the availability, reliability, and timeliness of a general price level index and the frequency with which it is adjusted. In providing that flexibility, the Board is aware that comparability among enterprises may be impaired if different enterprises select different indexes for a particular functional currency (other than the U.S. dollar). However, disclosure of the effects of changing prices requires management's judgment in many areas, and the Board believes that allowing flexibility in this area is consistent with the experimental nature of Statement 33.

82. The Board anticipates that an appropriate index of the change in the general price level will be available for most functional currencies. Indexes are published in most countries, and some indexes are periodically published by organizations such as the International Monetary Fund, the Organization for Economic Co-Operation and Development, and the United Nations. However, in some cases indexes may not be available on a timely basis or may not be sufficiently reliable. In those circumstances, management should estimate the change in the general price level.

Five-Year Summary of Selected Financial Data

83. Paragraph 65 of Statement 33 requires that amounts in the five-year summary of selected data be expressed in a unit of constant purchasing power. The initial Exposure Draft indicated that the Board had considered whether prior years' data for foreign functional currency entities in the five-year summary should be restated into (a) units of constant functional currency using the functional currency general price level indexes or (b) constant dollar equivalent units using the Consumer Price Index for All Urban Consumers (CPI(U)). That Exposure Draft required use of the CPI(U) for several reasons, including the fact that use of multiple functional currency indexes might impose significant costs on preparers.

84. Some respondents to both the initial and revised Exposure Drafts favored use of the functional currency general price level index to restate amounts in the five-year summary. They expressed the view that that approach would be more consistent with the functional currency theory. Although some Board members tend to agree with that view, the Board concluded that use of the CPI(U) should be required. That approach was deemed to be more consistent with the requirement of this Statement that the supplementary current cost information should present the increase or decrease for the year in the net investment in terms of U.S. purchasing power, regardless of whether inflation adjustments to current cost information are based on the translate-restate or the restate-translate approach.

Alternative Approaches Considered

85. The Board considered the possibility of requiring enterprises to continue to present constant dollar information based on the Statement 8 translation procedure and the original provisions of Statement 33. The Board rejected that approach because it not only could be costly but also would retain a measure of income from continuing operations that would be inconsistent with information in the primary financial statements prepared by applying Statement 52.

86. The Board also considered exempting enterprises that use foreign functional currencies for a significant part of their operations from the current cost requirements. The Board recognizes that application of the provisions of this Statement will affect the comparability of the supplementary current cost information prepared before and after its adoption. That discontinuity may impair the usefulness of the supplementary information for discerning trends in the data items, but all accounting changes have that effect. The Board considered whether the discontinuity and possible difficulties for users in reorienting their evaluations to accommodate the new information might cause the costs of the supplementary information to exceed the prospective benefits. However, it decided not to terminate the current cost requirements. Statement 33 is an experiment with alternative measurement systems. Information about the usefulness of supplementary current cost information prepared under the new rules for foreign currency translation is needed to assist the Board in making decisions

about the usefulness of that alternative measurement system.

Transition and Effective Date

87. If the experiment with supplementary information about the effects of changing prices is to serve its intended purpose of providing a basis on which to evaluate alternative measurement systems, the Board believes the supplementary current cost information must be prepared on a basis generally consistent with that used in the primary financial statements. Accordingly, this Statement requires restatement of prior years' supplementary information if Statement 52 is applied by restating the primary financial statements for those years.

88. The Board concluded that it can reach an informed decision on the basis of existing information without a public hearing and that the effective date specified in paragraph 20 is advisable in the circumstances.

Statement of Financial Accounting Standards No. 71
Accounting for the Effects of Certain Types of Regulation

STATUS

Issued: December 1982

Effective Date: For fiscal years beginning after December 15, 1983

Affects: Supersedes ARB 44 (Rev.), paragraphs 8 and 9
Amends ARB 51, paragraph 6
Supersedes APB 1, paragraph 7
Supersedes APB 2, paragraph 17 and Addendum
Supersedes APB 6, paragraph 20
Amends APB 11, paragraph 6
Supersedes APB 16, paragraph 6
Supersedes APB 17, paragraph 7
Amends APB 20, paragraph 3
Supersedes APB 23, paragraph 4
Supersedes APB 24, paragraph 3
Amends APB 26, paragraph 2
Amends APB 29, paragraph 4 and footnote 4
Supersedes AIN-APB 8, Interpretation No. 22
Amends AIN-APB 11, Interpretation No. 4
Supersedes FAS 2, paragraph 14
Supersedes FAS 4, paragraph 7
Supersedes FAS 5, paragraph 13
Amends FAS 7, paragraph 5
Supersedes FAS 13, paragraph 3
Supersedes FAS 15, paragraph 9
Supersedes FAS 16, paragraph 9
Supersedes FAS 19, paragraph 9
Supersedes FAS 22, paragraph 11
Supersedes FAS 34, paragraph 5
Supersedes FAS 43, paragraph 3
Supersedes FAS 49, paragraph 7
Supersedes FAS 51, paragraph 2
Supersedes FIN 18, paragraph 4
Supersedes FIN 22, paragraph 8
Supersedes FIN 25, paragraph 9

Affected by: No other pronouncements

SUMMARY

This Statement provides guidance in preparing general purpose financial statements for most public utilities. Certain other companies with regulated operations that meet specified criteria are also covered.

In general, the type of regulation covered by this Statement permits rates (prices) to be set at levels intended to recover the estimated costs of providing regulated services or products, including the cost of capital (interest costs and a provision for earnings on shareholders' investments).

For a number of reasons, revenues intended to cover some costs are provided either before or after the costs are incurred. If regulation provides assurance that incurred costs will be recovered in the future, this Statement requires companies to capitalize those costs. If current recovery is provided for costs that are expected to be incurred in the future, this Statement requires companies to recognize those current receipts as liabilities.

This Statement also requires recognition, as costs of assets and increases in net income, of two types of allowable costs that include amounts not usually accepted as costs in the present accounting framework for nonregulated enterprises, as follows:

- If rates are based on allowable costs that include an allowance for the cost of funds used during construction (consisting of an equity component and a debt component), the company should capitalize and increase net income by the amount used for rate-making purposes—instead of capitalizing interest in accordance with FASB Statement No. 34, *Capitalization of Interest Cost.*
- If rates are based on allowable costs that include reasonable intercompany profits, the company should not eliminate those intercompany profits in its financial statements.

Pending completion of the Board's current project on accounting for income taxes, this Statement continues current practices of most utilities with respect to accounting for deferred income taxes. Accordingly, if the current income tax benefits (or costs) of timing differences are passed through to customers in current prices and it is probable that any resulting income taxes payable in future years will be recovered through future rates, the company should not record deferred income taxes resulting from those timing differences. However, the company should disclose the cumulative net amounts of timing differences for which deferred taxes have not been recorded.

This Statement may require that a cost be accounted for in a different manner from that required by another authoritative pronouncement. In that case, this Statement is to be followed because it reflects the economic effects of the rate-making process—effects not considered in other authoritative pronouncements. All other provisions of that other authoritative pronouncement apply to the regulated enterprise.

This Statement clarifies the application of certain other authoritative pronouncements, which is expected to result in at least two changes in general-purpose financial statements of certain public utilities. First, expected refunds of revenue collected in prior years will be charged to income in the period in which those refunds are first recognized. Second, leases will be classified (as capital or operating leases) in accordance with FASB Statement No. 13, *Accounting for Leases,* as amended. Because Statement 13 has not been applied by some utilities in the past, this Statement provides a four-year transition period before retroactive application of lease capitalization is required. Statement 13 provided a similar transition period for unregulated enterprises.

Statement of Financial Accounting Standards No. 71
Accounting for the Effects of Certain Types of Regulation

CONTENTS

INTRODUCTION

1. Regulation of an enterprise's prices (hereinafter referred to as *rates*) is sometimes based on the enterprise's costs. Regulators use a variety of mechanisms to estimate a regulated enterprise's allowable costs,[1] and they allow the enterprise to charge rates that are intended to produce revenue approximately equal to those allowable costs. Specific costs that are allowable for rate-making purposes result in revenue approximately equal to the costs.

2. In most cases, allowable costs are used as a means of estimating costs of the period during which the rates will be in effect, and there is no intent to permit recovery of specific prior costs. The process is a way of setting prices—the results of the process are reported in general-purpose financial statements in accordance with the same accounting principles that are used by unregulated enterprises.

3. Regulators sometimes include costs in allowable costs in a period other than the period in which the costs would be charged to expense by an unregulated enterprise. That procedure can create assets (future cash inflows that will result from the rate-making process), reduce assets (reductions of future cash inflows that will result from the rate-making process), or create liabilities (future cash outflows that will result from the rate-making process) for the regulated enterprise. For general-purpose financial reporting, an incurred cost for which a regulator permits recovery in a future period is accounted for like an incurred cost that is reimbursable under a cost-reimbursement-type contract.

4. Accounting requirements that are not directly related to the economic effects of rate actions may be imposed on regulated businesses by orders of regulatory authorities and occasionally by court decisions or statutes. This does not necessarily mean that those accounting requirements conform with generally accepted accounting principles. For example, a regulatory authority may order an enterprise to capitalize[2] and amortize a cost that would be charged to income currently by an unregulated enterprise. Unless capitalization of that cost is appropriate under this Statement, generally accepted accounting principles require the regulated enterprise to charge the cost to income currently.

STANDARDS OF FINANCIAL ACCOUNTING AND REPORTING

Scope

5. This Statement applies to general-purpose

[1]The term *allowable costs* is used throughout this Statement to refer to all costs for which revenue is intended to provide recovery. Those costs can be actual or estimated. In that context, allowable costs include interest cost and amounts provided for earnings on shareholders' investments.

[2]*Capitalize* is used in this Statement to indicate that the cost would be recorded as the cost of an asset. That procedure is often referred to as "deferring a cost," and the resulting asset is sometimes described as a "deferred cost."

external financial statements of an enterprise that has regulated operations that meet all of the following criteria:

a. The enterprise's rates for regulated services or products provided to its customers are established by or are subject to approval by an independent, third-party regulator or by its own governing board empowered by statute or contract to establish rates that bind customers.[3]
b. The regulated rates are designed to recover the specific enterprise's costs of providing the regulated services or products.
c. In view of the demand for the regulated services or products and the level of competition, direct and indirect, it is reasonable to assume that rates set at levels that will recover the enterprise's costs can be charged to and collected from customers. This criterion requires consideration of anticipated changes in levels of demand or competition during the recovery period for any capitalized costs.

6. If some of an enterprise's operations are regulated and meet the criteria of paragraph 5, this Statement shall be applied to only that portion of the enterprise's operations.

7. Authoritative accounting pronouncements that apply to enterprises in general also apply to regulated enterprises. However, enterprises subject to this Statement shall apply it instead of any conflicting provisions of standards in other authoritative pronouncements.[4]

8. This Statement does not apply to accounting for price controls that are imposed by governmental action in times of emergency, high inflation, or other unusual conditions. Nor does it cover accounting for contracts in general. However, if the terms of a contract between an enterprise and its customer are subject to regulation and the criteria of paragraph 5 are met with respect to that contract, this Statement shall apply.

General Standards of Accounting for the Effects of Regulation

9. Rate actions of a regulator can provide reasonable assurance of the existence of an asset. An enterprise shall capitalize all or part of an incurred cost[5] that would otherwise be charged to expense if both of the following criteria are met:

a. It is probable[6] that future revenue in an amount at least equal to the capitalized cost will result from inclusion of that cost in allowable costs for rate-making purposes.
b. Based on available evidence, the future revenue will be provided to permit recovery of the previously incurred cost rather than to provide for expected levels of similar future costs. If the revenue will be provided through an automatic rate-adjustment clause, this criterion requires that the regulator's intent clearly be to permit recovery of the previously incurred cost.

10. Rate actions of a regulator can reduce or eliminate the value of an asset. If a regulator excludes all or part of a cost from allowable costs and it is not probable that the cost will be included as an allowable cost in a future period, the cost cannot be expected to result in future revenue through the rate-making process. Accordingly, the carrying amount of any related asset shall be reduced to the extent that the asset has been impaired. Whether the asset has been impaired shall be judged the same as for enterprises in general.

11. Rate actions of a regulator can impose a liability on a regulated enterprise. Such liabilities are usually obligations to the enterprise's customers. The following are the usual ways in which liabilities can be imposed and the resulting accounting:

a. A regulator may require refunds to customers.[7] Refunds that meet the criteria of paragraph 8 (accrual of loss contingencies) of FASB State-

[3]The appropriate structure for setting accounting standards for state and local governmental units is currently under discussion. The FASB is proposing no change with respect to the applicability or use of its pronouncements in the governmental area until that matter is resolved.

[4]For example, a regulator might authorize a regulated enterprise to incur a major research and development cost because the cost is expected to benefit future customers. The regulator might also direct that cost to be capitalized and amortized as an allowable cost over the period of expected benefit. If the criteria of paragraph 9 of this Statement were met, the enterprise would capitalize that cost even though FASB Statement No. 2, *Accounting for Research and Development Costs,* requires such costs to be charged to income currently. Statement 2 would still apply to accounting for other research and development costs of the regulated enterprise, as would the disclosure requirements of Statement 2.

[5]An *incurred cost* is "a cost arising from cash paid out or obligation to pay for an acquired asset or service, a loss from any cause that has been sustained and has been or must be paid for" (Eric L. Kohler, *A Dictionary for Accountants,* 5th ed. [Englewood Cliffs, N.J.: Prentice-Hall, Inc., 1975], p. 253).

[6]The term *probable* is used in this Statement with its usual general meaning, rather than in a specific technical sense, and refers to that which can reasonably be expected or believed on the basis of available evidence or logic but is neither certain nor proved (*Webster's New World Dictionary of the American Language,* 2d college ed. [New York and Cleveland: World Publishing Company, 1972], p. 1132). That is the meaning referred to by FASB Concepts Statement No. 3, *Elements of Financial Statements of Business Enterprises.*

[7]Refunds can be paid to the customers who paid the amounts being refunded; however, they are usually provided to current customers by reducing current charges.

ment No. 5, *Accounting for Contingencies,* shall be recorded as liabilities and as reductions of revenue or as expenses of the regulated enterprise.

b. A regulator can provide current rates intended to recover costs that are expected to be incurred in the future with the understanding that if those costs are not incurred future rates will be reduced by corresponding amounts. If current rates are intended to recover such costs and the regulator requires the enterprise to remain accountable for any amounts charged pursuant to such rates and not yet expended for the intended purpose,[8] the enterprise shall not recognize as revenues amounts charged pursuant to such rates. Those amounts shall be recognized as liabilities and taken to income only when the associated costs are incurred.

c. A regulator can require that a gain or other reduction of net allowable costs be given to customers over future periods. That would be accomplished, for rate-making purposes, by amortizing the gain or other reduction of net allowable costs over those future periods and reducing rates to reduce revenues in approximately the amount of the amortization. If a gain or other reduction of net allowable costs is to be amortized over future periods for rate-making purposes, the regulated enterprise shall not recognize that gain or other reduction of net allowable costs in income of the current period. Instead, it shall record it as a liability for future reductions of charges to customers that are expected to result.

12. Actions of a regulator can eliminate a liability only if the liability was imposed by actions of the regulator.

13. Appendix B illustrates the application of the general standards of accounting for the effects of regulation.

Specific Standards Derived from the General Standards

14. The following specific standards are derived from the general standards in paragraphs 9-12. The specific standards shall not be used as guidance for other applications of those general standards.

Allowance for Funds Used during Construction

15. In some cases, a regulator requires an enterprise subject to its authority to capitalize, as part of the cost of plant and equipment, the cost of financing construction as financed partially by borrowings and partially by equity. A computed interest cost and a designated cost of equity funds are capitalized, and net income for the current period is increased by a corresponding amount. After the construction is completed, the resulting capitalized cost is the basis for depreciation and unrecovered investment for rate-making purposes. In such cases, the amounts capitalized for rate-making purposes as part of the cost of acquiring the assets shall be capitalized for financial reporting purposes instead of the amount of interest that would be capitalized in accordance with FASB Statement No. 34, *Capitalization of Interest Cost.*[9] The income statement shall include an item of other income, a reduction of interest expense, or both, in a manner that indicates the basis for the amount capitalized.

Intercompany Profit[10]

16. Profit on sales to regulated affiliates shall not be eliminated in general-purpose financial statements[11] if both of the following criteria are met:

a. The sales price is reasonable.
b. It is probable that, through the rate-making process, future revenue approximately equal to the sales price will result from the regulated affiliate's use of the products.

17. The sales price usually shall be considered reasonable if the price is accepted or not challenged by the regulator that governs the regulated affiliate. Otherwise, reasonableness shall be considered in light of the circumstances. For example, reasonableness might be judged by the return on investment earned by the manufacturing or construction operations or by a comparison of the transfer prices with prices available from other sources.

Other Specific Standards

Accounting for Income Taxes

18. Items of revenue and expense are sometimes

---

[8]The usual mechanism used by regulators for this purpose is to require the regulated enterprise to record the anticipated cost as a liability in its regulatory accounting records.

[9]Statement 34 requires capitalization of interest cost on certain qualifying assets. The amount capitalized is the portion of the interest cost incurred during the period that theoretically could have been avoided if the expenditures had not been made.

[10]The term *intercompany profit* is used in this Statement to include both profits on sales from one company to another within a consolidated or affiliated group and profits on sales from one operation of a company to another operation of the same company.

[11]ARB No. 51, *Consolidated Financial Statements,* requires that profit on sales of assets remaining in the consolidated group be eliminated in consolidated financial statements. APB Opinion No. 18, *The Equity Method of Accounting for Investments in Common Stock,* effectively extends that requirement to affiliated entities reported on the equity method.

taxable or deductible in periods other than the periods in which those items are recognized for financial reporting purposes. In some cases, a regulator does not include the income tax effect of certain transactions in allowable costs in the period in which the transactions are reported but includes income taxes related to those transactions in allowable costs in the period in which the taxes become payable. In such cases, if it is probable that income taxes payable in future years because of net reversal of timing differences will be recovered through rates based on taxes payable at that time, the enterprise shall record neither the deferred income taxes[12] that result from those timing differences nor the related asset (the probable future benefits that will result from payment of the taxes). However, the enterprise shall disclose the cumulative net amount of income tax timing differences for which deferred income taxes have not been provided. That disclosure supplements the requirements of paragraph 63 of Opinion 11 for disclosure of operating loss carryforwards, significant amounts of other unused deductions or credits, and reasons for significant variations in the customary relationships between income tax expense and pretax accounting income. Except as provided in this paragraph, regulated enterprises shall apply the requirements of Opinion 11.

Other Disclosure

19. For refunds that are recognized in a period other than the period in which the related revenue was recognized and that have a material effect on net income, the enterprise shall disclose the effect on net income and indicate the years in which the related revenue was recognized. Such effect may be disclosed by including it, net of related income taxes, as a line item in the income statement. However, that item shall not be presented as an extraordinary item.

20. In some cases, a regulator may permit an enterprise to include a cost that would be charged to expense by an unregulated enterprise as an allowable cost over a period of time by amortizing that cost for rate-making purposes, but the regulator does not include the unrecovered amount in the rate base. That procedure does not provide a return on investment during the recovery period. If recovery of such major costs is provided without a return on investment during the recovery period, the enterprise shall disclose the remaining amounts of such assets and the remaining recovery period applicable to them.

Amendments to Existing Pronouncements

21. Appendix A lists the amendments to existing pronouncements that result from this Statement.

Effective Date and Transition

22. This Statement shall be effective for fiscal years beginning after December 15, 1983. Earlier application is encouraged. Accounting changes adopted to conform to the provisions of this Statement shall be applied retroactively, except that:

a. Previously issued financial statements shall not be restated for changes in accounting for refunds.
b. Leases for which the inception[13] is after December 31, 1982 shall be classified in accordance with FASB Statement No. 13, *Accounting for Leases,* in financial statements commencing with initial application of this Statement. Leases for which the inception of the lease is before January 1, 1983 may be classified as they would have been classified before this Statement was issued until fiscal years beginning after December 15, 1986. Commencing no later than the first fiscal year beginning after December 15, 1986, those leases shall be retroactively classified in accordance with Statement 13 as amended.

23. If leases are not retroactively classified in accordance with Statement 13 in financial statements for fiscal years beginning after December 15, 1983 and before December 15, 1986 as permitted by paragraph 22(b), lessees shall disclose the amounts of additional capitalized leased assets and lease obligations that would be included in each balance sheet presented if Statement 13 had been applied retroactively.

24. In the year that this Statement is first applied, the financial statements shall disclose the nature of any restatement and its effect on income before extraordinary items, net income, and related per-share amounts[14] for each year restated. If retroactive restatement of all years presented is not practicable, the financial statements shall be restated for as many consecutive years as is practicable, and the cumulative effect of applying this Statement shall be included in determining net income of the earliest year restated (not necessarily the earliest year presented). If it is not practicable to restate any prior year, the cumulative effect shall be included in net income in the year in which this Statement is first applied. (See paragraph 20 of APB Opinion No. 20,

[12]APB Opinion No. 11, *Accounting for Income Taxes,* requires comprehensive interperiod allocation of the income tax effect of timing differences, that is, differences between the timing of income or expense recognition in financial statements and in income tax returns.

[13]The inception of a lease is defined in FASB Statement No. 23, *Inception of the Lease.*

[14]The effect on related per-share amounts need not be disclosed if the enterprise does not disclose earnings per share.

Accounting Changes.) The effect on income before extraordinary items, net income, and related per-share amounts[15] of applying this Statement in a year in which the cumulative effect is included in determining that year's net income shall be disclosed for that year.

The provisions of this Statement need not be applied to immaterial items.

This Statement was adopted by the affirmative votes of four members of the Financial Accounting Standards Board. Messrs. Block, Kirk, and Sprouse dissented.

Mr. Block dissents to the issuance of this Statement. He believes that the regulatory environment as it exists today does not provide the necessary assurance of realization of future revenues to justify the standards in this Statement.

In his opinion, the creation of an asset by a regulator requires, at a minimum, an exclusive franchise to deliver goods and services for which demand is insensitive to price. This means that the goods and services must be necessities and that no alternative goods and services exist as competition. Further, the creation of long-lived assets requires assurance that the regulatory environment will remain unchanged for long periods. The nature of assets created by a regulator (future amounts receivable from customers) would appear to require assurance that the customers will exist, the goods and services will be delivered to customers, and the customers will pay the decreed rates. Mr. Block does not believe that rate regulators can provide such assurances in the industries to which this Statement is likely to be applied. Because of those beliefs, Mr. Block concludes that the rate-making process should have no bearing on principles for cost capitalization and loss recognition. Those principles should be the same for rate-regulated enterprises as they are for unregulated enterprises.

Mr. Block further believes that the assets created by regulation under this Statement are merely future accounts receivable for future sales. While he is opposed to recognizing such receivables, he notes that APB Opinion No. 21, *Interest on Receivables and Payables,* requires discounting of long-term receivables on which there is no stated interest rate or the stated rate is unreasonable. Thus, in his view, if such receivables are to be recognized, discounting at market rates of return should be required.

Mr. Kirk dissents to the issuance of this Statement because he believes the immediate increases in income resulting from the capitalization of costs imputed for equity funds used during construction (paragraph 15) and intercompany profit (paragraphs 16 and 17) are not valid reflections of the economics of rate regulation or in accordance with other generally accepted accounting principles. Unlike other allowable costs, imputed costs have not been incurred. In Mr. Kirk's opinion, even if capitalization is deemed appropriate for financial reporting purposes, income should not be recognized. The income related to allowable but imputed costs should be recognized when the rates covering the costs are charged to customers, not before.

Mr. Sprouse dissents primarily because he does not agree with the thrust of paragraph 11 related to liabilities. He agrees that a regulator can impose a liability on a regulated enterprise by requiring the enterprise to make refunds to its customers (paragraph 11(a)). In his opinion, however, "refunds" involve reductions in existing assets—either cash settlements or lump-sum deductions from the amounts due from customers. Reductions in future rates do not "refund" anything and, therefore, do not create a liability. Indeed, reductions in future rates do not obligate a regulated enterprise to transfer assets or use them in any way that would not be required in the absence of those reductions. Of course, a sufficiently severe reduction in future rates might trigger the need to recognize impairment of assets.

In Mr. Sprouse's view, paragraph 11(b) tends to confuse the use of a formula that a regulator might properly use to set reasonably stable rates with real, often sporadic, economic events, the effects of which should be recognized in financial statements if and when they have actually occurred. In setting rates, a regulator may include a "provision for noninsurance" among the allowable costs, but that does not create a present obligation to repair unusual storm damage that has not yet occurred (paragraphs 11(b), 38, and 39). If over a period of time the amounts of uninsured losses are sufficiently less than the "provisions for noninsurance" included in allowable costs, the regulator may reduce or eliminate future allowed provisions and reduce rates accordingly. As explained in the previous paragraph, however, possible future rate reductions do not create a liability. The possibility that sometime in the future the regulator might require cash refunds to customers to reduce or eliminate the cumulative "provision for noninsurance" is too remote to be recognized as a liability.

Similarly, in a formula designed to maintain reasonably stable rates, a regulatory agency may wish

[15]See footnote 14.

to spread a gain on early extinguishment of debt over some arbitrary period, but that does not create a present obligation for the regulated enterprise to transfer assets or to use them in any way that would not be required in the absence of such a gain (paragraphs 11(c) and 35-37).

Mr. Sprouse does agree that, to the extent that there is adequate evidence that the rates set by a regulator will cause a specific cost or other amount to be recovered through future incremental revenues, the regulated enterprise has an asset or asset enhancement (a quasi-receivable) that is properly measured by that incurred cost or other amount. Accordingly, he agrees that those circumstances may call for capitalizing (a) unusual storm losses, property abandonments, plant conversions, and similar costs that have occurred (paragraph 9); (b) an imputed cost of equity funds (paragraph 15); and (c) intercompany profits included in transfer prices to affiliates (paragraphs 16 and 17).

Messrs. Kirk and Sprouse also dissent because they believe the amendment to APB Opinion 30 in paragraph 19 of this Statement that suggests that refunds be reported in income net of taxes but not as extraordinary items is unrelated to the economics of rate regulation and therefore inappropriate. They see no reason why a potentially recurring charge to income should be singled out from all other recurring or even unusual items for this special treatment.

Members of the Financial Accounting Standards Board:

Donald J. Kirk, *Chairman*
Frank E. Block
John W. March
Robert A. Morgan
David Mosso
Robert T. Sprouse
Ralph E. Walters

Appendix A

AMENDMENTS TO EXISTING PRONOUNCEMENTS

25. This Statement supersedes the Addendum, *Accounting Principles for Regulated Industries,* to APB Opinion 2.

26. Paragraph 7 provides for this Statement to be applied by enterprises that are subject to it instead of conflicting provisions of other authoritative pronouncements. The Board sees no need for references to this Statement in either existing pronouncements or future authoritative pronouncements. That conclusion requires the following amendments to existing pronouncements:

a. ARB No. 44 (Revised), *Declining-Balance Depreciation,* as amended by APB Opinion No. 6, *Status of Accounting Research Bulletins.* Delete paragraphs 8 and 9.
b. ARB 51. Delete the last sentence of paragraph 6.
c. APB Opinion No. 1, *New Depreciation Guidelines and Rules.* Delete paragraph 7.
d. APB Opinion No. 2, *Accounting for the "Investment Credit."* Delete paragraph 17.
e. APB Opinion 11. In the second sentence of paragraph 6, delete the words "(a) to regulated industries in those circumstances where the standards described in the Addendum (which remains in effect) to APB Opinion No. 2 are met and (b)."
f. APB Opinion No. 16, *Business Combinations.* Delete paragraph 6.
g. APB Opinion No. 17, *Intangible Assets.* Delete paragraph 7.
h. APB Opinion 20. Delete the last two sentences of paragraph 3.
i. APB Opinion No. 23, *Accounting for Income Taxes—Special Areas.* Delete paragraph 4.
j. APB Opinion No. 24, *Accounting for Income Taxes.* Delete paragraph 3.
k. APB Opinion No. 26, *Early Extinguishment of Debt.* Delete the last sentence of paragraph 2.
l. APB Opinion No. 29, *Accounting for Nonmonetary Transactions.* In the first sentence following subparagraph 4(d), delete the words "applies to regulated companies in accordance with the Addendum to APB Opinion No. 2, *Accounting for the Investment Credit,* 1962 and it."
m. FASB Statement No. 2, *Accounting for Research and Development Costs.* Delete paragraph 14.
n. FASB Statement No. 4, *Reporting Gains and Losses from Extinguishment of Debt.* Delete paragraph 7.
o. FASB Statement 5. Delete paragraph 13.
p. FASB Statement No. 7, *Accounting and Reporting by Development Stage Enterprises.* Delete the second sentence of paragraph 5.
q. FASB Statement 13. Delete paragraph 3.
r. FASB Statement No. 15, *Accounting by Debtors and Creditors for Troubled Debt Restructurings.* Delete paragraph 9.
s. FASB Statement No. 16, *Prior Period Adjustments.* Delete paragraph 9.
t. FASB Statement No. 19, *Financial Accounting and Reporting by Oil and Gas Producing Companies.* Delete paragraph 9.
u. FASB Statement No. 22, *Changes in the Provisions of Lease Agreements Resulting from Refundings of Tax-Exempt Debt.* Delete paragraph 11.
v. FASB Statement 34. Delete paragraph 5.

w. FASB Statement No. 43, *Accounting for Compensated Absences*. Delete paragraph 3.
x. FASB Statement No. 49, *Accounting for Product Financing Arrangements*. Delete paragraph 7.
y. FASB Statement No. 51, *Financial Reporting by Cable Television Companies*. Delete paragraph 2.
z. FASB Interpretation No. 18, *Accounting for Income Taxes in Interim Periods*. Delete paragraph 4.
aa. FASB Interpretation No. 22, *Applicability of Indefinite Reversal Criteria to Timing Differences*. Delete paragraph 8.
bb. FASB Interpretation No. 25, *Accounting for an Unused Investment Tax Credit*. Delete paragraph 9.

Appendix B

APPLICATION OF GENERAL STANDARDS TO SPECIFIC SITUATIONS

27. This appendix provides guidance for application of this Statement to some specific situations. The guidance does not address all possible applications of this Statement. All of the examples assume that the enterprise meets the criteria in paragraph 5 of this Statement; thus, recovery of any cost is probable if that cost is designated for future recovery by the regulator. The examples also assume that the items addressed are material. The provisions of this Statement need not be applied to immaterial items.

28. Specific situations discussed in this appendix are:

	Paragraph Numbers
Intangible assets	29—30
Accounting changes	31—32
Recovery of costs without return on investment	33—34
Early extinguishment of debt	35—37
Accounting for contingencies	38—39
Accounting for leases	40—43
Revenue collected subject to refund	44—45
Refunds to customers	46—47
Accounting for compensated absences	48—49

Intangible Assets

29. Opinion 17 requires that the cost of an intangible asset acquired after October 30, 1970 be amortized over the shorter of its estimated useful life or 40 years. That Opinion also requires that a company continually evaluate the period of amortization to determine whether later events and circumstances warrant a revised estimate of the useful life and whether the unamortized cost should be reduced significantly by a charge to income. For rate-making purposes, a regulator may permit an enterprise to amortize purchased goodwill over a specified period. In other cases, a regulator may direct an enterprise not to amortize goodwill acquired in a business combination after October 30, 1970 or to write off that goodwill.

30. If the regulator permits the goodwill to be amortized over a specific time period as an allowable cost for rate-making purposes, the regulator's action provides reasonable assurance of the existence of an asset (paragraph 9). The goodwill would then be amortized for financial reporting purposes over the period during which it will be allowed for rate-making purposes. If the regulator excludes amortization of goodwill from allowable costs for rate-making purposes, either by not permitting amortization or by directing the enterprise to write off the goodwill, the value of the goodwill may be reduced or eliminated (paragraph 10). If there is no indication that the amortization will be allowed in a subsequent period, the goodwill would be amortized for financial reporting purposes and continually evaluated to determine whether the unamortized cost should be reduced significantly by a charge to income in accordance with Opinion 17.

Accounting Changes

31. Opinion 20 defines various types of accounting changes and establishes guidelines for reporting each type. Other authoritative pronouncements specify the manner of reporting initial application of those pronouncements.

32. If a regulated enterprise changes accounting methods and the change does not affect costs that are allowable for rate-making purposes, the regulated enterprise would apply the change in the same manner as would an unregulated enterprise. Capitalization of leases with no income statement effect (paragraphs 40-43) is an example of that type of change. If a regulated enterprise changes accounting methods and the change affects allowable costs for rate-making purposes, the change generally would be implemented in the way that it is implemented for regulatory purposes. A change in the method of accounting for research and development costs, either from a policy of capitalization and amortization to one of charging those costs to expense as incurred or vice versa, is an example of that type of change.

Recovery of Costs without Return on Investment

33. In some cases, a regulator may approve rates that are intended to recover an incurred cost over an extended period without a return on the unrecovered cost during the recovery period.

34. The regulator's action provides reasonable assurance of the existence of an asset (paragraph 9). Accordingly, the regulated enterprise would capitalize the cost and amortize it over the period during which it will be allowed for rate-making purposes. That cost would not be recorded at discounted present value. If the amounts are material, the disclosures specified in paragraph 20 of this Statement would be furnished.

Early Extinguishment of Debt

35. Opinion 26 requires recognition in income of a gain or loss on an early extinguishment of debt in the period in which the debt is extinguished. For rate-making purposes, the difference between the enterprise's net carrying amount of the extinguished debt and the reacquisition price may be amortized as an adjustment of interest expense over some future period.

36. If the debt is reacquired for an amount in excess of the enterprise's net carrying amount, the regulator's decision to increase future rates by amortizing the difference for rate-making purposes provides reasonable assurance of the existence of an asset (paragraph 9). Accordingly, the regulated enterprise would capitalize the excess cost and amortize it over the period during which it will be allowed for rate-making purposes.

37. If the debt is reacquired for an amount that is less than the enterprise's net carrying amount, the regulator's decision to reduce future rates by amortizing the difference for rate-making purposes imposes a liability on the regulated enterprise (paragraph 11(c)). Accordingly, the enterprise would record the difference as a liability and amortize it over the period during which permitted rates will be reduced.

Accounting for Contingencies

38. Statement 5 specifies criteria for recording estimated losses from loss contingencies. A regulator may direct a regulated enterprise to include an amount for a contingency in allowable costs for rate-making purposes even though the amount does not meet the criteria of Statement 5 for recording. For example, a regulator may direct a regulated enterprise to include an amount for repairs of expected future uninsured storm damage.

39. If the regulator requires the enterprise to remain accountable for any amounts charged pursuant to such rates and not yet expended for the intended purpose, the resulting increased charges to customers create a liability (paragraph 11(b)). If a cost to repair storm damage is not subsequently incurred, the increased charges will have to be refunded to customers through future rate reductions. Accordingly, the regulated enterprise would recognize the amounts charged pursuant to such rates as liabilities rather than as revenues. If a cost to repair storm damage is subsequently incurred, the enterprise would charge that cost to expense and reduce the liabilities at that time by recognizing income in amounts equal to the cost.

Accounting for Leases

40. Statement 13, as amended, specifies criteria for classification of leases and the method of accounting for each type of lease. For rate-making purposes, a lease may be treated as an operating lease even though the lease would be classified as a capital lease under the criteria of Statement 13. In effect, the amount of the lease payment is included in allowable costs as rental expense in the period it covers.

41. For financial reporting purposes, the classification of the lease is not affected by the regulator's actions. The regulator cannot eliminate an obligation that was not imposed by the regulator (paragraph 12). Also, by including the lease payments as allowable costs, the regulator sets rates that will provide revenue approximately equal to the combined amount of the capitalized leased asset and interest on the lease obligation over the term of the lease and, thus, provides reasonable assurance of the existence of an asset (paragraph 9). Accordingly, regulated enterprises would classify leases in accordance with Statement 13 as amended.

42. The nature of the expense elements related to a capitalized lease (amortization of the leased asset and interest on the lease obligation) is not changed by the regulator's action; however, the timing of expense recognition related to the lease would be modified to conform to the rate treatment. Thus, amortization of the leased asset would be modified so that the total of interest on the lease obligation and amortization of the leased asset would equal the rental expense that was allowed for rate-making purposes.

43. The Board notes that generally accepted accounting principles do not require interest expense or amortization of leased assets to be classified as separate items in an income statement. For example, the amounts of amortization of capitalized leased nuclear fuel and interest on the related lease obliga-

tion could be combined with other costs and displayed as "fuel cost." However, the disclosure of total interest cost incurred, required by Statement 34, would include the interest on that lease obligation; and the disclosure of the total amortization charge, required by Statement 13, would include amortization of that leased asset.

Revenue Collected Subject to Refund

44. In some cases, a regulated enterprise is permitted to bill requested rate increases before the regulator has ruled on the request.

45. When the revenue is originally recorded, the criteria in paragraph 8 of Statement 5 would determine whether a provision for estimated refunds should be accrued as a loss contingency. That provision would be adjusted subsequently if the estimate of the refund changes (paragraph 11(a)).[16]

Refunds to Customers

46. Statement 16 limits prior period adjustments (other than those that result from reporting accounting changes) to corrections of errors, adjustments that result from realization of income tax benefits of preacquisition operating loss carryforwards of purchased subsidiaries, and adjustments related to prior interim periods of the current fiscal year.

47. In accordance with Statement 16, estimated refunds that were not previously accrued would be charged to income in the first period in which they meet the criteria for accrual (paragraph 8 of Statement 5). If the amounts are material, the disclosures specified in paragraph 19 of this Statement would be furnished.

Accounting for Compensated Absences

48. Statement 43 specifies criteria for accrual of a liability for employees' compensation for future absences. For rate-making purposes, compensation for employees' absences may be included in allowable costs when the compensation is paid.

49. The liability, if any, would be accrued in accordance with Statement 43 because rate actions of the regulator cannot eliminate obligations that were not imposed by the regulator (paragraph 12). By including the accrued compensation in future allowable costs on an as-paid basis, the regulator provides reasonable assurance of the existence of an asset. The asset is the probable future benefit (increased revenue) that will result from the regulatory treatment of the subsequent payment of the liability (paragraph 9). Accordingly, the enterprise also would record the asset that results from the regulator's actions.

[16]Revenue collected subject to refund is similar to sales with warranty obligations. Paragraph 25 of Statement 5 states that "inability to make a reasonable estimate of the amount of a warranty obligation at the time of sale because of significant uncertainty about possible claims . . . precludes accrual and, if the range of possible loss is wide, may raise a question about whether a sale should be recorded. . . ." Similarly, if the range of possible refund is wide and the amount of the refund cannot be reasonably estimated, there may be a question about whether it would be misleading to recognize the provisional revenue increase as income.

Appendix C

BASIS FOR CONCLUSIONS

CONTENTS

Appendix C

BASIS FOR CONCLUSIONS

Introduction

50. This appendix discusses factors deemed significant by members of the Board in reaching the conclusions in this Statement. It includes descriptions of the various alternatives considered and the Board's reasons for accepting some and rejecting others. Individual Board members gave greater weight to some factors than to others.

Relationship of Regulatory-Prescribed Accounting to Generally Accepted Accounting Principles

51. The FASB Discussion Memorandum, *Effect of Rate Regulation on Accounting for Regulated Enterprises,* presented a threshold issue: "Should accounting prescribed by regulatory authorities be considered in and of itself generally accepted for purposes of financial reporting by rate-regulated enterprises?"

52. Virtually all respondents to the Discussion Memorandum indicated that accounting prescribed by regulatory authorities should not be considered in and of itself generally accepted for purposes of financial reporting by rate-regulated enterprises. Respondents noted that the function of accounting is to report economic conditions and events. Unless an accounting order indicates the way a cost will be handled for rate-making purposes, it causes no economic effects that would justify deviation from the generally accepted accounting principles applicable to business enterprises in general. The mere issuance of an accounting order not tied to rate treatment does not change an enterprise's economic resources or obligations. In other words, the economic effect of regulatory decisions—not the mere existence of regulation—is the pervasive factor that determines the application of generally accepted accounting principles.

53. Respondents also noted that regulatory-prescribed accounting has not been considered generally accepted per se in the past.

54. The Board concluded that regulatory-prescribed accounting should not be considered generally accepted per se, but rather that the Board should specify how generally accepted accounting principles apply in the regulatory environment.

55. Some respondents to the FASB Exposure Draft, *Accounting for the Effects of Regulation of an Enterprise's Prices Based on Its Costs,* suggested that the Board clarify the relationship of this State-

ment to an enterprise's regulatory accounting and to regulators' actions. This Statement does not address an enterprise's regulatory accounting. Regulators may require regulated enterprises to maintain their accounts in a form that permits the regulator to obtain the information needed for regulatory purposes. This Statement neither limits a regulator's actions nor endorses them. Regulators' actions are based on many considerations. Accounting addresses the effects of those actions. This Statement merely specifies how the effects of different types of rate actions are reported in general-purpose financial statements.

Economic Effects of Regulation

56. The second threshold issue in the Discussion Memorandum was: "Does rate regulation introduce an economic dimension in some circumstances that should affect the application of generally accepted accounting principles to rate-regulated enterprises?"

57. Most respondents to the Discussion Memorandum indicated that rate regulation does introduce such an economic dimension in some circumstances. Respondents cited the cause-and-effect relationship of costs and revenues as the principal economic effect of regulation that affects accounting for regulated enterprises. They noted that cost might be one factor used by unregulated enterprises to establish prices, but it would often not be the most important factor. Usually, prices are limited by the market. An unregulated enterprise might desire to price its goods or services at a level that would recover all costs and a reasonable profit; however, the market might not permit that price. Alternatively, an unregulated enterprise might be able to increase its prices and its profit if competition does not limit its prices. In either case, cost often is not the principal determinant of prices. In contrast, for an enterprise with prices regulated on the basis of its costs, allowable costs are the principal factor that influences its prices.

58. The economic effect cited by most respondents is the ability of a regulatory action to create a future economic benefit—the essence of an asset. For example, consider a regulated enterprise that incurs costs to repair damage caused by a major storm. If the regulator approves recovery of the costs through rates over some future period or is expected to do so, the rate action of the regulator creates a new asset that offsets the reduction in the damaged asset. The enterprise has probable future economic benefits—the additional revenue that will result from including the cost in allowable costs for rate-making purposes. The future benefits are obtained or controlled by the enterprise as a result of a past event—incurring the cost that results in the rate order. Thus, the criteria of Concepts Statement 3 for an asset are met.

59. Most respondents that opposed special accounting for the effects of regulation cited the need for comparability between regulated and unregulated enterprises. Paragraph 119 of FASB Concepts Statement No. 2, *Qualitative Characteristics of Accounting Information,* indicates that ". . . the purpose of comparison is to detect and explain similarities and differences." The Board concluded that comparability would not be enhanced by accounting as though regulation had no effect. Regulation creates different circumstances that require different accounting.

Scope

60. The Discussion Memorandum discussed regulation of various industries, and it asked whether a Board pronouncement should identify specific industries that are affected. Most respondents indicated that applicability of an FASB Statement on rate regulation should be specified by clearly describing the nature of the regulated operations to which it applies rather than by attempting to delineate specific industries. Some noted that changes in the political environment can cause changes in the nature of regulation. Accordingly, whether an industry meets the criteria for applicability might change over time. The Board agreed with those respondents and, accordingly, specified criteria that focus on the nature of regulation rather than on specific industries.

61. This Statement specifies the economic effects that result from the cause-and-effect relationship of costs and revenues in the rate-regulated environment and how those effects are to be accounted for. The nature of those effects led to the criteria for applicability of this Statement (paragraph 5).

62. The first criterion is the existence of third-party regulation. That criterion is intended to exclude contractual arrangements in which the government, or another party that could be viewed as a "regulator," is a party to a contract and is the enterprise's principal customer. For example, the normal Medicare and Medicaid arrangements are excluded from the scope of this Statement because they are contractual-type arrangements between the provider and the governmental agency that is responsible for payment for services provided.

63. Some respondents to the Exposure Draft indicated that cooperative utilities should be included in the scope of this Statement. They observed that some cooperative utilities' rates are subject to third-party regulation, but others' rates are set by their own governing board. The governing board is elected by the members of the cooperative, and it has the same authority as an independent, third-party regulator. In their view, the difference between

cooperative utilities that are subject to third-party regulation and those that are not does not justify different accounting. The Board agreed with those respondents, and modified the first criterion to include enterprises with rates established by their own governing board providing that board is empowered by statute or by contract to establish rates that bind customers.

64. A number of governmental utility respondents to the Exposure Draft asked that governmental utilities be included within the scope of this Statement. They noted that many governmental utilities have been guided by the same accounting practices and standards as investor-owned utilities in their general-purpose financial statements, and they expressed the view that users' emphasis on comparability supports continuation of that practice. In their view, the Board's decision not to address governmental utilities in this Statement should not preclude them from applying it. The Board agreed with those respondents and modified paragraph 5(a) so as not to preclude application by governmental utilities with rates set by their own governing board.

65. The second criterion is that the regulated rates are designed to recover the specific enterprise's costs of providing the regulated services or products. If rates are based on industry costs or some other measure that is not directly related to the specific enterprise's costs, there is no cause-and-effect relationship between the enterprise's costs and its revenues. In that case, costs would not be expected to result in revenues approximately equal to the costs; thus, the basis for the accounting specified in this Statement is not present under that type of regulation. That criterion is intended to be applied to the substance of the regulation, rather than its form. If an enterprise's regulated rates are based on the costs of a group of companies and the enterprise is so large in relation to the group of companies that its costs are, in essence, the group's costs, the regulation would meet the second criterion for that enterprise.

66. The last criterion requires that it be reasonable to assume that rates set at levels that will recover the enterprise's costs can be charged to and collected from customers. Regardless of the actions of the regulator, if the market for the enterprise's regulated services or products will not support a price based on cost, the enterprise's rates are at least partially controlled by the market. In that case, the cause-and-effect relationship of costs and revenues that is the basis for the accounting required by this Statement cannot be assumed to exist, and this Statement would not apply.

67. The Board does not intend the last criterion as a requirement that the enterprise earn a fair return on shareholders' investment under all conditions; an enterprise can earn less than a fair return for many reasons unrelated to the ability to bill and collect rates that will recover allowable costs.[17] For example, mild weather might reduce demand for energy utility services. In that case, rates that were expected to recover an enterprise's allowable costs might not do so. The resulting decreased earnings do not demonstrate an inability to charge and collect rates that would recover the enterprise's costs; rather, they demonstrate the uncertainty inherent in estimating weather conditions.

68. The last criterion also requires reasonable assurance that the regulated environment and its economic effects will continue. That requirement must be evaluated in light of the circumstances. For example, if the enterprise has an exclusive franchise to provide regulated services or products in an area and competition from other services or products is minimal, there is usually a reasonable expectation that it will continue to meet the other criteria. Exclusive franchises can be revoked, but they seldom are. If the enterprise has no exclusive franchise but has made the very large capital investment required to provide either the regulated services or products or an acceptable substitute, future competition also may be unlikely.

69. Some respondents to the Discussion Memorandum questioned whether, in light of recent events, it would ever be reasonable to assume that rates set at levels that will recover the enterprise's costs can be charged to and collected from customers. They cited recent developments—such as the use of solar devices as alternatives to certain energy utility services, increasing competition in the telecommunications industry, and deregulation of various transportation industries—as evidence that the environment of a regulated enterprise can change rapidly. The Board concluded that users of financial statements should be aware of the possibility of rapid, unanticipated changes in an industry, but accounting should not be based on such possibilities unless their occurrence is considered probable. However, changes of a long-term nature could modify the demand for an enterprise's regulated services sufficiently to affect its qualifying under the criterion of subparagraph 5(c).

70. The first scope limitation of paragraph 8—excluding accounting for price controls imposed by governmental action in times of emergency, high inflation, or other unusual conditions—was included in the Discussion Memorandum. Price

[17]As indicated in footnote 1, the term *allowable costs* is used here to include earnings permitted on shareholders' investment.

controls imposed in periods of unusual conditions are not expected to be applied consistently over an extended period. Indeed, their duration usually is limited by statute. In that environment, assurance of future benefits cannot be provided by probable future actions of the price control regulator because that regulator may not exist at a given future date.

71. Accounting for contracts in general was also excluded from the scope of the Discussion Memorandum. The economic effects of cost reimbursement contracts are in some respects similar to the economic effects of the type of regulation addressed by this Statement. However, most contracts tend to be relatively short-term, whereas regulation of enterprises covered by this Statement is expected to continue beyond the foreseeable future. The Board noted that other authoritative literature addresses contract accounting and concluded that it should exclude the general issue of contract accounting from the scope of this Statement.

72. The Discussion Memorandum described rate-making processes in several industries and asked whether each process justified the application of this Statement. As noted in paragraph 60, the Board concluded that applicability of this Statement should be specified by describing the nature of the regulated operations and the type of rate making to which it applies rather than by attempting to delineate specific industries.

73. In view of the nature of comments received, the Board concluded that the possible application of this Statement to the health care industry should be discussed. The Board does not intend to preclude application of the provisions of this Statement to the health care industry or to any other industry. Rather, application of this Statement is limited to regulated operations that meet the specified criteria for application.

74. In general, rates for services in the health care industry are not regulated based on the provider's costs. The federal Medicare and Medicaid programs usually are applied through a contractual-type arrangement (paragraph 62). Some states are applying comprehensive, prospective rate making to health care providers. In some cases, the rates set by state regulatory agencies are accepted for Medicare and Medicaid reimbursement purposes. There is some disagreement about the extent to which such rates are based on a provider's costs. If regulatory agencies in those states base rates on the provider's costs and adopt a permanent system of regulation, health care providers in those jurisdictions could be subject to the provisions of this Statement. However, the criterion in subparagraph 5(c) also would have to be considered to determine whether the Statement applies to the enterprise.

General Standards of Accounting for the Effects of Regulation

75. The Board concluded that, for general-purpose financial reporting, the principal economic effect of the regulatory process is to provide assurance of the existence of an asset or evidence of the diminution or elimination of the recoverability of an asset. The regulator's rate actions affect the regulated enterprise's probable future benefits or lack thereof. Thus, an enterprise should capitalize a cost if it is probable that future revenue approximately equal to the cost will result through the rate-making process.

76. A number of respondents to the Exposure Draft asked for clarification of the types of costs addressed by paragraph 9. Those respondents expressed the view that tangible assets should be capitalized based on the criteria used by unregulated companies; paragraph 9 should be limited to other assets. Paragraph 9 was intended to address only accounting for costs that would be charged to expense by an unregulated enterprise, and the Board modified the paragraph to so indicate.

77. The regulatory process, as usually practiced, has two aspects. First, either historical or projected test period costs are used to compute the revenues necessary to provide for similar costs during the period in which the rates will be in force. Second, test period costs are adjusted to provide for recovery or to prevent recovery of costs that are considered unusual or unpredictable. If unusual or unpredictable costs are not provided for in advance, they may be recovered after their incurrence through increased rates provided for that purpose. In some cases, rate orders do not specify whether costs are (a) included as normal test period costs, used to compute rates that are intended to provide for similar future costs, or (b) incurred costs designated for specific recovery. The Board concluded that costs should be capitalized only if the future revenue is expected to be provided to permit recovery of the previously incurred cost rather than merely to provide for recovery of higher levels of similar future costs.

78. If rates are designed to be adjusted automatically for changes in operating expenses (e.g., costs of purchased fuel), the regulator's intent could be either to permit recovery of the incurred cost or merely to provide for recovery of similar future costs. Normal operating expenses such as fuel costs usually are provided for in current rates. In that case, the presumption is that the rate increase is intended to permit recovery of similar future costs. That presumption, which would preclude capitalizing the incurred cost, can be overcome only if it is clear that the regulator's intent is to provide recovery of the incurred cost.

79. Rate actions of a regulator can also impose a liability on a regulated enterprise in the following ways:

a. A regulator can order a regulated enterprise to refund previously collected revenues.
b. A regulator can provide rates intended to recover costs that are expected to be incurred in the future. Paragraphs 38 and 39 illustrate that possibility. The resulting increased charges to customers are liabilities and not revenues for the enterprise—the enterprise undertakes to provide the services for which the increased charges were collected, and it is obligated to return those increased charges if the future cost does not occur. The obligation will be fulfilled either by refunding the increased charges through future rate reductions or by paying the future costs with no corresponding effect on future rates. The resulting increases in charges to customers are unearned revenues until they are earned by their use for the intended purpose.
c. For rate-making purposes, a regulator can recognize a gain or other reduction of overall allowable costs over a period of time. Paragraphs 35-37 illustrate that possibility. By that action, the regulator obligates the enterprise to give the gain or other reduction of overall allowable costs to customers by reducing future rates. Accordingly, the amount of the gain or cost reduction is the appropriate measure of the obligation.

80. A number of respondents to the Exposure Draft asked the Board to clarify whether paragraph 11(b), discussed in paragraph 79(b) above, was intended to apply to costs such as nuclear plant decommissioning costs. Decommissioning costs are incurred costs in the current accounting framework. Those costs and the related liabilities are imposed by regulation or statute, similar to the liability to restore the land after strip mining, discussed in paragraph 142 of Concepts Statement 3. Accordingly, paragraph 11(b) does not address those costs.

Specific Standards Derived from the General Standards

81. The specific standards derived from the general standards deal with recognition, as assets and increases in net income, of allowable costs that are not usually accepted as incurred costs in the present accounting framework. For the reasons explained below, the Board concluded that recognition is appropriate for those allowable costs. However, the Board does not intend them to be used as guidance for other applications of the general standards in paragraphs 9-12.

Allowance for Funds Used during Construction

82. Most respondents to the Discussion Memorandum supported the present practices of public utilities in accounting for the allowance for funds used during construction. They noted that the current income statement display reflects the regulatory process used in determining the amount to be capitalized and, thus, aids the user in understanding the regulatory environment. They cited the regulator's determination of the "cost" of equity capital as a basis for accepting that amount as a cost, and they noted that unregulated enterprises do not have a similar basis. They also noted that most utilities have an obligation to construct the facilities necessary to provide regulated services. Thus, there is no option of not obtaining the required funds or using accumulated funds to retire debt instead of investing in construction, and there is no available "avoidable cost" to use as the measure of the cost of the funds used.

83. Respondents who opposed present practices of accounting for the allowance for funds used during construction indicated that the cost of equity funds should be excluded from that allowance. Those respondents cited paragraph 49 of Statement 34, which states that ". . . recognition of the cost of equity capital does not conform to the present accounting framework." However, the arguments presented by those respondents supported capitalization of interest in accordance with Statement 34. Capitalization of interest in accordance with Statement 34 would be based on actual interest rates on outstanding debt and limited to the total amount of interest cost incurred during the period. In most cases, the effect on net income would be similar to capitalizing an allowance that included a cost of equity funds.

84. Some Board members believe that the allowances for funds used during construction, computed under current utility practices, are appropriate measures of the costs of financing construction and that the regulators' actions provide reasonable assurance of the existence of assets that should be measured by the amount on which rates will be based. Other Board members believe that those amounts are acceptable substitutes for the amount of interest that would be capitalized in accordance with Statement 34 and that, absent a change in regulatory practices, the cost of a change in those accounting practices would exceed any perceived benefits. The Board concluded that the amounts capitalized for rate-making purposes also should be capitalized for financial reporting purposes.

Intercompany Profit

85. Most respondents to the Discussion Memorandum indicated that enterprises should not eliminate intercompany profits on sales to regulated affiliates if it is probable that, through the rate-making pro-

cess, future revenues in amounts approximately equal to the intercompany transfer price will be provided. That revenue would result from inclusion of the intercompany profits in the amount used by the regulator as allowable cost for purposes of depreciation and return on investment. They noted that an enterprise does not recognize profits on sales to unregulated affiliates because the profits are not validated by transactions with outside parties. According to those respondents, however, an enterprise should recognize profits on sales to a regulated affiliate to the extent that the profits are included in allowable costs in the rate-making process because the profits are validated by the rate actions of the regulator. The regulator's acceptance of the transfer price provides evidence of recoverability. For rate-making purposes, the intercompany profits will be included in the depreciation used as an allowable cost, and the undepreciated amount will be included in the investment on which a return is provided as an allowable cost. Those respondents noted that ARB 51 did not require elimination of intercompany profits on sales to regulated affiliates.

86. The Board concluded that intercompany profits on sales of assets to regulated affiliates should not be eliminated in consolidated financial statements if the transfer price is reasonable and it is probable that, through the rate-making process, future revenue approximately equal to the transfer price will result from the regulated affiliate's use of those assets. In view of existing regulatory practices, the Board further concluded that the transfer price usually should be considered reasonable if the price is accepted or not challenged by the regulator that governs the regulated affiliate. Otherwise, reasonableness should be considered in light of the circumstances. For example, reasonableness might be judged by the return on investment earned by the manufacturing or construction operations or by a comparison of the transfer prices with prices available from other sources.

Other Specific Standards

Accounting for Income Taxes

87. In the past, enterprises generally have not provided for deferred income taxes if regulated rates to customers were based on taxes currently payable. Most respondents to the Discussion Memorandum supported that practice based on the rationale of Opinion 11. Opinion 11 indicates that deferred taxes are the result of comprehensive interperiod allocation of income taxes to achieve a proper "matching" of revenues and expenses. Those respondents indicated that a provision for deferred income taxes does not achieve a proper "matching" if rates to customers are based on taxes currently payable. In that situation, the income tax expense should be recorded in the future periods in which the taxes become payable and the regulator grants a resulting rate increase. Those respondents also noted that Concepts Statement 3 concluded that deferred taxes computed under the deferred method that is prescribed by Opinion 11 do not meet the definition of a liability. They expressed the view that the Board should not require utilities to commence to apply Opinion 11 when the Board may reconsider that Opinion in the near future.

88. Other respondents indicated that deferred income taxes should be recorded in all cases. However, if rates charged to customers are based on taxes currently payable, the recorded deferred taxes should also result in an asset—the future benefit that will result from treatment of the taxes as allowable costs for regulatory purposes in the period in which those taxes become payable.

89. Some Board members believe that the general standards (paragraphs 9-12) would require a regulated enterprise to record deferred income taxes. If it is probable that income taxes payable in future years because of net reversal of timing differences will be recovered through rates based on taxes payable at that time, the enterprise also would record an asset in an amount equal to the deferred income taxes. Offsetting those deferred income taxes against the related asset normally would not be appropriate because the asset will be realized through collections from customers and the deferred income taxes will not be paid to the customers. However, the Board concluded that any possible benefits of commencing to record deferred income taxes and an offsetting asset at this time probably would not exceed the cost. Accordingly, if rates are based on income taxes currently payable and it is probable that income taxes payable in future years because of net reversal of timing differences will be recovered through rates based on income taxes payable at that time, this Statement does not permit deferred income taxes to be computed or recorded in accordance with Opinion 11. However, it does require disclosure of the cumulative amount of timing differences for which deferred income taxes have not been provided. Approximate amounts of cumulative timing differences can be estimated without the complex calculations required by Opinion 11. That information, together with the disclosures required by Opinion 11, should help users in estimating the possible future income tax and rate effects of those timing differences. The Board will reconsider its conclusions on this matter in the course of its project on accounting for income taxes, which was added to the agenda in January 1982.

90. A number of respondents to the Exposure Draft indicated that the disclosures required by this Statement would be misunderstood by users. In

their view, users might attempt to estimate unrecorded deferred taxes as a charge to current income. The Board believes that users will understand the required disclosures if affected companies explain that deferred taxes are not provided because the method of rate making assures future recovery of future taxes. The Board believes that it is important to disclose those costs which have to be recovered from future customers through future rates.

Other Specific Accounting Matters

Recovery of Cost without Return on Investment

91. The Discussion Memorandum asked whether the recoverability criterion for capitalization of costs should be based on recovery of cost (which excludes a return on equity capital) or on recovery of cost of service (which includes a return on equity capital). In some cases, a regulator may provide rates intended to recover an incurred cost over an extended period without a return on the unrecovered cost during the recovery period. That issue was intended to elicit comments on whether the capitalized costs should be carried at the present value of the amount to be recovered in those cases. Most respondents interpreted that issue as asking whether any capitalization of costs was justified if the enterprise would recover its cost but would not realize a return on the unrecovered cost during the recovery period. Thus, many of the responses did not address the valuation of the resulting asset.

92. The Board concluded that capitalized costs not related to a tangible asset provide a measure of an intangible asset. Generally accepted accounting principles do not necessarily require the carrying amount of an intangible asset to be its discounted present value, nor do they necessarily require an enterprise to consider a return on investment when evaluating possible impairment of an intangible or depreciable asset. Accordingly, the Board concluded that it should not impose such a requirement on regulated enterprises.

93. Some respondents to the Exposure Draft indicated that disclosure should be required for capitalized costs that are recovered over an extended period without a return on investment during the recovery period. Those respondents indicated that regulated enterprises should provide the same types of disclosure for a given item as unregulated enterprises do.

94. The situations in question usually result from a problem encountered by a regulated enterprise—an abandoned plant, major storm damage, or a similar event. For troubled debt restructurings, which are similar to the events in question, Statement 15 requires creditors that agree to forego interest on outstanding loans to disclose the amounts of nonearning assets included in the balance sheet. The Board agreed that regulated enterprises with capitalized costs that are recovered over an extended period without a return on investment during the recovery period should provide similar disclosure and, thus, added the requirements of paragraph 20.

Accounting for Leases

95. Statement 13, as amended, specifies criteria for classification of leases and the method of accounting for each type of lease. For rate-making purposes, a regulator may include lease payments in allowable costs as rental expense even though the lease would be classified as a capital lease under the criteria of Statement 13. The Discussion Memorandum asked for views on the economic effects of that regulatory treatment and how to account for those effects.

96. A number of respondents indicated that the classification of a lease is not affected by the regulator's actions. In their view, rate actions of the regulator cannot eliminate obligations to third parties unless the obligations were created by the regulator. Also, they observed that, over the term of a capital lease, the aggregate lease payments are equal to aggregate amortization of the leased asset and aggregate interest on the lease obligation. Thus, the regulator, by including the lease payments in allowable costs, establishes the existence of probable future benefits approximately equal to the combined amount of the capitalized leased asset and interest on the lease obligation over the term of the lease. In their view, regulated enterprises should classify leases in accordance with Statement 13 as amended. The Board agrees with that view.

97. Other respondents indicated that the regulator's action establishes that there is no asset related to the lease. They indicated that an income statement display consisting of amortization and interest would mislead users if the regulatory process based rates on rental expense. In their view, regulated enterprises should classify leases in accordance with their classification for rate-making purposes. The Board concluded that such a view focuses on the mechanics of the rate-making process rather than on the economic effects of the process. This Statement requires that regulated enterprises account for the economic effects of the rate-making process; it does not attempt to portray the mechanics of that process in financial statements.

98. The Board concluded that the nature of the expense elements for a capitalized lease (amortization and interest) are not changed by the regulator's action; however, the timing of expense recognition related to the lease should be modified to conform with the rate treatment. Thus, amortization of the

leased asset would be modified so that the total interest and amortization recognized during a period would equal the rental expense included in allowable cost for rate-making purposes during that period. Although this Statement requires the expense elements of a capitalized lease to consist of amortization and interest regardless of the regulatory treatment, the Board notes that generally accepted accounting principles do not require interest expense or amortization expense to be shown as such in an income statement.

Revenue Collected Subject to Refund

99. In some jurisdictions, regulated enterprises are permitted to bill and collect requested rate increases before the regulator has ruled on the request.

100. Some respondents opposed reducing net income by the amount expected to be disallowed prior to the final rate action. In their view, if the enterprise requests the increase, the increase must be supported by the evidence. In that case, management could not take the position that some portion of the request is likely to be disallowed without providing the regulator a possible basis for disallowance. Other respondents supported application of the loss contingency provisions of Statement 5 to those rate increases. They indicated that utilities usually can predict the outcome of a rate hearing by considering recent actions of the regulator. They also indicated that it is misleading to include in net income revenue that is expected to be refunded.

101. The Board concluded that regulation does not have a unique economic effect that requires special accounting for anticipated refunds of revenue. Rather, regulation results in a contingency that should be accounted for in accordance with Statement 5, the same as other contingencies.

Refunds to Customers

102. The Discussion Memorandum asked whether the effects of rate-making transactions applicable to prior periods should be charged to income in the year in which they become estimable, as required by Statement 16 for other adjustments applicable to prior periods, or accounted for as prior period adjustments.

103. Some respondents opposed applying Statement 16 to utility refunds. Most of those respondents indicated that Statement 16 is not presently applied to significant refunds that could not be estimated in advance. They indicated that including refunds in a year other than that in which the amount refunded was included in income misstates both years, because the financial statements would not accurately reflect permitted rates of return, trends, etc. They also noted that current earnings could be reduced to a level at which existing covenants or state regulations governing investments by certain institutional investors could preclude necessary financing.

104. Respondents who favored applying Statement 16 to refunds indicated that the regulatory process does not introduce unique economic effects that warrant different accounting. In their view, the arguments supporting prior period adjustments for regulated enterprises are the same arguments that were made by unregulated enterprises before Statement 16 was issued.

105. The Board concluded that regulation does not have a unique economic effect that requires special accounting for refunds. Rather, regulation results in resolution of a previous contingency that should be accounted for the same as resolution of contingencies by unregulated enterprises. Reconsideration of Statement 16 was not within the scope of this Statement.

106. The Exposure Draft would have required disclosure of the pro forma effect of refunds on net income of each period presented, computed as though the refunds were retroactively recorded in the prior periods in which the revenue was recognized. A number of respondents objected to that requirement on the basis that the proposed disclosure indicates a need for restatement.

107. The Board believes that users are interested in two aspects of refunds. They are concerned about the impact of the refund in the year of the refund, and they also are concerned about the effect of the refund on trends of permitted earnings. Neither prior period adjustment nor current income charge provides all of the needed information. The Board concluded that users' needs could be satisfied by disclosure of (a) the effect of the refund on net income of the current year and (b) the years in which the refunded revenue was recognized.

108. In making its determination, the Board considered whether the amount disclosed should be net of related taxes. APB Opinion No. 30, *Reporting the Results of Operations,* prohibits net-of-tax disclosure of unusual or infrequently occurring items that are not extraordinary items. The Board concluded that users would not be confused by a net-of-tax disclosure of the effect of refunds. Users understand that refunds occur from time to time in public utilities—and they are concerned with the net effect rather than the gross amounts refunded. Accordingly, the Board concluded that refunds should be disclosed net of their related tax effects. Based on comments received and its deliberations, the Board decided that a narrow amendment of

Opinion 30 for utility refunds was justified. However, the Board's action is limited to utility refunds, and it is not intended to otherwise modify or question the requirements of Opinion 30.

Rate Making Based on a Fair Value Rate Base

109. Some state regulatory commissions use a "fair value rate base" for determining allowable return *on* invested capital. Normally, those commissions do not permit recovery *of* the fair value of the enterprise's assets by including depreciation of the fair value in allowable cost; rather, depreciation is based on historical cost. The Discussion Memorandum asked whether that procedure provides a basis for accounting for utility plant at its "fair value" in financial statements prepared in accordance with generally accepted accounting principles.

110. Virtually all respondents opposed the use of fair value in financial statements. Respondents indicated that fair value would present the enterprise's assets at an amount in excess of the recoverable amount of those assets. The use of depreciation based on historical cost for rate-making purposes limits recovery to that historical cost. Respondents also noted that the realized rate of return based on historical cost is not proportionately greater in jurisdictions that base rates on a fair value rate base than in other jurisdictions; thus, they question whether there is substance to that special treatment.

111. The Board concluded that if the return on investment permitted in a jurisdiction is based on fair value but recovery of cost is based on historical cost, the fair value of the assets should not be recognized in general-purpose financial statements. The Board did not need to address the accounting implications if a commission were to use fair value to determine both recovery of cost and return on capital invested because that practice currently is not used by regulators.

Acquisition Adjustments

112. A number of respondents to the Exposure Draft asked the Board to address accounting for *acquisition adjustments.* Those adjustments are the differences between the amounts paid for an acquired utility and the acquired utility's book value of its assets and liabilities. Those respondents indicated that utilities do not have goodwill because a utility cannot realize excess profits. Thus, they considered the example of goodwill in Appendix B unnecessary.

113. Opinion 16 describes how the amount paid in a business combination is allocated to the assets obtained and the liabilities assumed. Acquisition adjustments are values in excess of book value of identifiable assets obtained, valuation adjustments applicable to liabilities assumed, or goodwill or a combination of those items. Opinion 16 does not allow another possibility. The example of accounting for intangibles in Appendix B of this Statement indicates the appropriate accounting for goodwill. Additional guidance should not be needed about accounting for any portions of acquisition adjustments that represent amounts allocable to identifiable assets or liabilities such as property and equipment or intangibles amortizable over specific benefit periods.

Evidence

114. Several issues in the Discussion Memorandum identified types of evidence that might be available before a rate order is received and asked whether each would provide sufficient assurance to warrant capitalizing costs. A number of respondents indicated that judgment is needed to determine the adequacy of available evidence. In their view, all of the available evidence has to be evaluated, and the resulting decision cannot be standardized. Other respondents indicated that specific items did or did not provide adequate evidence; however, their responses appeared to differ based on the regulator involved and on their assumptions about other related circumstances.

115. The Board concluded that it should not attempt to categorize types of evidence and the reliance that should be based on each. Rather, this Statement indicates the degree of assurance required, and judgment must be exercised to evaluate whether that degree of assurance is present in various circumstances. In general, the Board concluded that costs should be capitalized only if (a) it is probable that future revenue in an amount at least equal to the cost will result from inclusion of that cost in allowable costs for rate-making purposes and (b) the future revenue will be provided to permit recovery of the previously incurred cost rather than to provide for expected levels of similar future costs.

Effective Date and Transition

116. This Statement prescribes the circumstances in which regulation has an economic effect that affects the application of generally accepted accounting principles, and it outlines the accounting that should result. Accounting changes that result from initial application of this Statement will involve accounting for the effects of regulation that have not been accounted for in the past and revising previous accounting that was not in accordance with the provisions of this Statement. Those changes are not expected to cause changes in the methods or in the results of regulation.

117. The Exposure Draft proposed that the Statement be effective for fiscal years beginning after December 15, 1982. A number of respondents suggested that the effective date be delayed to provide time for companies to determine how the Statement would affect them. The Board agreed that the proposed effective date could cause some hardship. Accordingly, this Statement is effective for fiscal years beginning after December 15, 1983.

118. Implementation of this Statement is not expected to have major effects on the accounting of most regulated enterprises. This Statement is considerably more specific than the Addendum; however, its thrust is similar. Accordingly, the Board concluded that comparability would be best achieved if this Statement were applied retroactively to the extent practicable. The Board did not extend that general approach to application of Statement 16, because Statement 16 does not permit retroactive application.

119. A number of respondents to the Exposure Draft urged the Board to permit affected companies to defer retroactive application of Statement 13. They noted that Statement 13 did not require retroactive application until the fourth year after its effective date, and they urged the Board to afford regulated enterprises the same consideration.

120. Retroactive application of Statement 13 was delayed to permit affected enterprises time to work out any resulting problems, such as indenture covenant restrictions. The Board agreed that regulated enterprises might have the same problems; thus, retroactive application of Statement 13 is not required until the first fiscal year beginning after December 15, 1986. The Board also decided that, pending retroactive application of Statement 13, regulated enterprises should furnish the same disclosure as was required of unregulated enterprises under Statement 13. Retroactive application of Statement 13 should not affect a regulated enterprise's net income or shareholders' equity. Thus, only the effect of retroactive application on the balance sheet is required by this Statement.

Appendix D

BACKGROUND INFORMATION

121. The Addendum to APB Opinion 2, issued in December 1962, outlined the general approach that has been used for accounting by regulated enterprises. On November 18, 1977, in response to requests from the Acting Chief Accountant of the Securities and Exchange Commission and from the AICPA's Accounting Standards Division, the FASB initiated a project to consider the effects of rate regulation on accounting for regulated enterprises.

122. An FASB Discussion Memorandum on rate regulation was issued on December 31, 1979. The Board received 197 letters of comment in response to the Discussion Memorandum. In May 1980, the Board conducted a public hearing on the issues in the Discussion Memorandum. Twenty-four individuals and organizations presented their views at the two-day hearing.

123. An Exposure Draft of a proposed Statement was issued on March 4, 1982. The Board received 172 letters of comment in response to that Exposure Draft.

124. An FASB task force provided counsel in preparing the Discussion Memorandum and in preparing material for Board consideration during the course of Board deliberations concerning this Statement. The task force included persons from the investment community, industry, public accounting, academe, and regulatory authorities.

Statement of Financial Accounting Standards No. 72 Accounting for Certain Acquisitions of Banking or Thrift Institutions

an amendment of APB Opinion No. 17, an interpretation of APB Opinions 16 and 17, and an amendment of FASB Interpretation No. 9

STATUS

Issued: February 1983

Effective Date: For business combinations initiated after September 30, 1982

Affects: Amends APB 17, paragraphs 29 through 31
Amends FIN 9, paragraphs 8 and 9

Affected by: No other pronouncements

SUMMARY

This Statement amends APB Opinion No. 17, *Intangible Assets,* with regard to the amortization of the unidentifiable intangible asset (commonly referred to as goodwill) recognized in certain business combinations accounted for by the purchase method. If, and to the extent that, the fair value of liabilities assumed exceeds the fair value of identifiable assets acquired in the acquisition of a banking or thrift institution, the unidentifiable intangible asset recognized generally shall be amortized to expense by the interest method over a period no longer than the discount on the long-term interest-bearing assets acquired is to be recognized as interest income. This Statement also specifies that financial assistance granted to an enterprise by a regulatory authority in connection with a business combination shall be accounted for as part of the combination if receipt of the assistance is probable and the amount is reasonably estimable.

Statement of Financial Accounting Standards No. 72

Accounting for Certain Acquisitions of Banking or Thrift Institutions

an amendment of APB Opinion No. 17, an interpretation of APB Opinions 16 and 17, and an amendment of FASB Interpretation No. 9

CONTENTS

INTRODUCTION

1. The FASB has been asked to address the accounting for certain acquisitions of banking or thrift institutions. Those making the requests indicate that APB Opinions No. 16, *Business Combinations,* and No. 17, *Intangible Assets,* do not adequately address the conditions that have been present in some recent business combinations involving those institutions and that the use of the purchase method of accounting accompanied by the use of long amortization periods for purchased goodwill has produced postcombination operating results that are not reliable. Such combinations have recently become more frequent as a result of the economic climate, the move toward deregulation of certain financial institutions, and the involvement of financial institution regulators.

SCOPE AND APPLICABILITY

2. This Statement applies to the acquisition of a commercial bank, a savings and loan association, a mutual savings bank, a credit union, other depository institutions having assets and liabilities of the same types as those institutions, and branches of such enterprises. Paragraphs 5 and 6 of this Statement apply to only those acquisitions in which the fair value of liabilities assumed by the acquiring enterprise exceeds the fair value of tangible and identifiable intangible assets acquired, and those provisions specify an amortization method for the portion of any unidentifiable intangible asset up to the amount of that excess. Opinion 17 and FASB Interpretation No. 9, *Applying APB Opinions No. 16 and 17 When a Savings and Loan Association or a Similar Institution Is Acquired in a Business Combination Accounted for by the Purchase Method,* also provide guidance as to the amortization of any additional unidentifiable intangible asset recognized in the acquisition. The provisions of paragraphs 4 and 7 apply to all acquisitions of banking and thrift institutions.

3. The provisions of paragraphs 8 through 11, which relate to the reporting of regulatory financial assistance, apply to all acquisitions of banking or thrift institutions. The Board understands that regulatory financial assistance agreements are not standardized and that the conditions under which assistance will be granted vary widely. As a result, this Statement does not specifically address all forms of regulatory financial assistance, but its provisions should serve as a general guide.

STANDARDS OF FINANCIAL ACCOUNTING AND REPORTING

Identified Intangible Assets

4. In a business combination accounted for by the purchase method involving the acquisition of a banking or thrift institution, intangible assets

acquired that can be separately identified shall be assigned a portion of the total cost of the acquired enterprise if the fair values of those assets can be reliably[1] determined. The fair values of such assets that relate to depositor or borrower relationships[2] shall be based on the estimated benefits attributable to the relationships that *exist* at the date of acquisition without regard to new depositors or borrowers that may replace them. Those identified intangible assets shall be amortized over the estimated lives of those existing relationships.

Unidentifiable Intangible Asset

5. If, in such a combination, the fair value of liabilities assumed exceeds the fair value of tangible and identified intangible assets acquired, that excess constitutes an unidentifiable intangible asset. That asset shall be amortized to expense over a period no greater than the estimated remaining life of the long-term interest-bearing assets[3] acquired. Amortization shall be at a constant rate when applied to the carrying amount[4] of those interest-bearing assets that, based on their terms, are expected to be outstanding at the beginning of each subsequent period. The prepayment assumptions, if any, used to determine the fair value of the long-term interest-bearing assets acquired also shall be used in determining the amount of those assets expected to be outstanding. However, if the assets acquired in such a combination do not include a significant amount of long-term interest-bearing assets, the unidentifiable intangible asset shall be amortized over a period not exceeding the estimated average remaining life of the existing customer (deposit) base acquired. The periodic amounts of amortization shall be determined as of the acquisition date and shall not be subsequently adjusted except as provided by paragraphs 6 and 7 of this Statement. Notwithstanding the other provisions of this paragraph, the period of amortization shall not exceed 40 years.

6. Paragraph 31 of Opinion 17 specifies, among other things, that an enterprise should evaluate the periods of amortization of intangible assets continually to determine whether later events and circumstances warrant revised estimates of useful lives. In no event, however, shall the useful life of the unidentifiable intangible asset described in paragraph 5 of this Statement be revised upward.

7. For purposes of applying paragraph 32 of Opinion 17,[5] if a large segment or separable group of the operating assets of an acquired banking or thrift institution, such as branches, is sold or liquidated, the portion of the unidentifiable intangible asset attributable to that segment or separable group shall be included in the cost of the assets sold. If a large segment or separable group of the interest-bearing assets of an acquired institution is sold or liquidated and if the benefits attributable to the unidentifiable intangible asset have been significantly reduced,[6] that reduction shall be recognized as a charge to income.

Regulatory-Assisted Combinations

8. In connection with a business combination, a regulatory authority may agree to pay amounts by which future interest received or receivable on the interest-bearing assets acquired is less than the interest cost of carrying those assets for a period by a stated margin. In such a case, the projected assistance, computed as of the date of acquisition based on the interest-rate margin existing at that date, shall be considered as additional interest on the interest-bearing assets acquired in determining their fair values for purposes of applying the purchase method (paragraphs 87 and 88 of Opinion 16). The carrying amount of those interest-bearing assets shall not be adjusted for subsequent changes in the estimated amount of assistance to be received. Actual assistance shall be reported in income of the period in which it accrues. Notwithstanding the above provisions, if an enterprise intends to sell all or a portion of the interest-bearing assets acquired, those assets shall not be stated at amounts in excess of their current market values.

9. Other forms of financial assistance may be granted to a combining enterprise or the combined enterprise by a regulatory authority in connection with a business combination accounted for by the purchase method. If receipt of the assistance is

[1]Reliability embodies the characteristics of representational faithfulness and verifiability, as discussed in FASB Concepts Statement No. 2, *Qualitative Characteristics of Accounting Information*.

[2]Examples of intangible assets related to depositor or borrower relationships are described in paragraphs 8(a) and 8(b) of Interpretation 9.

[3]For purposes of this Statement, long-term interest-bearing assets are interest-bearing assets with a remaining term to maturity of more than one year.

[4]*Carrying amount* is the face amount of the interest-bearing asset plus (or minus) the unamortized premium (or discount).

[5]Paragraph 32 of Opinion 17 states: "a large segment or separable group of assets of an acquired company or the entire acquired company may be sold or otherwise liquidated, and all or a portion of the unamortized cost of the goodwill recognized in the acquisition should be included in the cost of the assets sold."

[6]For example, if a sale of a large group of interest-bearing assets is accompanied by the loss of a significant and valuable customer base, a reduction in goodwill likely would be appropriate. On the other hand, if the proceeds of sale are reinvested in other forms of interest-bearing or other assets, no such reduction may be necessary.

probable and the amount is reasonably estimable, that portion of the cost of the acquired enterprise shall be assigned to such assistance. Assets and liabilities that have been or will be transferred to or assumed by a regulatory authority shall not be recognized in the acquisition. If receipt of the assistance is not probable or the amount is not reasonably estimable, any assistance subsequently recognized in the financial statements shall be reported as a reduction of the unidentifiable intangible asset, described in paragraph 5, that was recognized in the acquisition. Subsequent amortization shall be adjusted proportionally. Assistance recognized in excess of that intangible asset shall be reported in income.

10. Under certain forms of assistance granted in connection with a business combination, the combined enterprise may agree to repay all or a portion of the assistance if certain criteria related to the level of future revenues, expenses, or profits are met. Such a repayment obligation shall be recognized as a liability and as a charge to income at the time the conditions in paragraph 8 of FASB Statement No. 5, *Accounting for Contingencies,* are met. This paragraph does not address repayments of assistance granted in exchange for debt or equity instruments.

Disclosures

11. The nature and amounts of any regulatory financial assistance granted to or recognized by an enterprise during a period in connection with the acquisition of a banking or thrift institution shall be disclosed.

Amendments to Other Pronouncements

12. The following footnote is added to the end of (a) paragraph 29 of Opinion 17, (b) the first sentence of paragraph 30 of Opinion 17, (c) the second sentence of paragraph 31 of Opinion 17, and (d) paragraph 9 of Interpretation 9:

> *Paragraphs 5 and 6 of FASB Statement No. 72, *Accounting for Certain Acquisitions of Banking or Thrift Institutions,* specify an exception to the provisions of this [Opinion/Interpretation] with respect to the amortization of goodwill recognized in certain acquisitions of banking or thrift institutions.

13. The second sentence of paragraph 8 of Interpretation 9 is amended to insert the word *reliably* and the related footnote as follows:

> If the amount paid for any such factor can be reliably* determined, that amount shall not be included in goodwill.
>
> *Reliability embodies the characteristics of representational faithfulness and verifiability, as discussed in FASB Concepts Statement No. 2, *Qualitative Characteristics of Accounting Information.*

14. The following sentence is added to the end of paragraph 8 of Interpretation 9:

> The fair values of identified intangible assets that relate to depositor or borrower relationships (refer to paragraphs 8(a) and 8(b)) shall be based on the estimated benefits attributable to the relationships that *exist* at the date of acquisition without regard to new depositors or borrowers that may replace them. Those identified intangible assets shall be amortized over the estimated lives of those existing relationships.

Effective Date and Transition

15. This Statement shall be applied prospectively to business combinations initiated[7] after September 30, 1982 with earlier application encouraged. Retroactive application to a business combination initiated prior to October 1, 1982 is permitted but not required. If, prior to March 1, 1983, an enterprise has issued financial statements in which the provisions of this Statement have not been applied to a business combination initiated and consummated after September 30, 1982, those financial statements shall be restated when they are first presented with financial statements for subsequent periods, or the opening balance of retained earnings for that subsequent period shall be appropriately adjusted if they are omitted. In addition, the financial statements shall, in the year the standards are first applied, disclose the nature of any restatement and its effect on income before extraordinary items, net income, and related per share amounts for each restated year presented.

[7]Refer to Opinion 16, paragraph 46(a) and footnote 14 to paragraph 97. Planned combinations involving a banking or thrift institution may be subject to approval by a regulatory authority and to a final determination concerning the amount of regulatory financial assistance to be granted. Under those circumstances, a combination shall be considered initiated if an announcement or notification as required by paragraph 46(a) of Opinion 16 has been made. A plan of combination involving only mutual banking or thrift institutions often is communicated by an enterprise to the board of directors of an institution rather than to the owners of the institution. In those circumstances, notification to a board of directors constitutes notification to shareholders for purposes of determining the date a business combination is initiated.

Accounting for Certain Acquisitions of Banking or Thrift Institutions

The provisions of this Statement need not be applied to immaterial items.

This Statement was adopted by the unanimous vote of the seven members of the Financial Accounting Standards Board:

Donald J. Kirk, *Chairman*
Frank E. Block
Victor H. Brown
John W. March
David Mosso
Robert T. Sprouse
Ralph E. Walters

Appendix A

BACKGROUND INFORMATION

16. Business combinations involving banking or thrift institutions have become frequent. Such combinations have increased, in part, as a result of the relaxed restrictions on interstate banking, the involvement of financial institution regulators, and the current trend toward deregulation of those industries. Various accounting and reporting questions have been raised as a result of those combinations.

17. Banking and thrift institutions, whose primary assets and liabilities are interest-bearing instruments, generally are regulated under laws of the various states or the federal government, or both. The qualified deposits of most banking and thrift institutions are insured by regulatory agencies, and as a result, those institutions are subject to the rules and regulations of those agencies. Because of its position as an insurer, a regulatory agency may provide financial assistance to an institution to minimize the agency's risk of loss.

18. Current economic and competitive conditions have adversely affected the financial position and operations of many financial institutions, particularly savings and loan associations and mutual savings banks. In particular, continued high interest rates have eroded interest margins, and competitive pressures in some cases have resulted in depositors' transferring funds to other kinds of enterprises. Many savings and loan associations and mutual savings banks have reported net losses during recent periods and some have failed to meet the minimum net worth requirements established by regulatory agencies. Failure to meet those requirements may result in a regulator's arranging or encouraging a merger with another enterprise. In some cases, a regulatory authority such as the Federal Deposit Insurance Corporation, the Federal Savings and Loan Insurance Corporation, the National Credit Union Share Insurance Fund, or a state insurance fund may grant financial assistance to an enterprise as an inducement for that enterprise to assume the assets, liabilities, and operations of a banking or thrift institution that has failed, or is about to fail, those minimum regulatory net worth requirements.

19. A majority of the recent business combinations referred to above were mergers of mutual thrift institutions. Most thrifts are mutual institutions, that is, they are owned by their depositors, rather than by stockholders. The combination of two mutual thrifts generally is effected without any payment of cash or other assets by either institution to the previously separate ownership interests. Instead, one institution absorbs the operations of the other institution, thereby obtaining the assets and assuming the liabilities of that institution. Prior to 1981, substantially all mergers of mutual thrifts were accounted for using the pooling-of-interests method described in Opinion 16. Recently, however, the majority of such mergers have been accounted for using the purchase method of accounting.

20. Opinion 16 and Interpretation 9 specify how an acquiring enterprise should allocate the cost of an acquired enterprise to the assets acquired and the liabilities assumed in applying the purchase method. Paragraph 88 of Opinion 16 indicates that, as a general guide, a portion of the cost should be assigned to intangible assets that can be identified and named based on appraised values. Paragraph 87 of that Opinion indicates that the cost of the acquired enterprise in excess of the sum of the amounts assigned to identifiable assets acquired less liabilities assumed should be reported as goodwill, which is an unidentifiable intangible asset. Opinion 17 and Interpretation 9 also apply to intangible assets acquired in business combinations accounted for by the purchase method.

21. Opinion 17 specifies that any intangible asset should be amortized by systematic charges to income over the period to be benefited, but that period may not exceed 40 years. That Opinion sets forth factors that should be considered in estimating the useful lives of intangible assets. Paragraph 27(c) of that Opinion specifies that the "effects of obsolescence, demand, competition, and other economic factors may reduce a useful life."

22. When banking or thrift institutions are acquired in periods of high interest rates, application of the purchase method and subsequent amortization of acquired intangibles over an extended period of time may produce a significant effect on the subsequent reported results of operations of the combined enterprise. In such periods, if low-rate interest-bearing assets are discounted to their fair values using current interest rates, the fair value of liabilities assumed may exceed by a substantial amount the fair value of tangible and identifiable intangible assets acquired. That excess often has been reported as goodwill in applying the purchase method under Opinion 16. The discount on the interest-bearing assets is amortized to income over the remaining lives of those assets using the interest method. If the goodwill is amortized straight-line over a period that exceeds the period the discount is amortized to income, the subsequent reported earnings for the combined enterprise may show a dramatic increase compared with the sum of the separate results of those enterprises absent the combination.

23. Some believe that the goodwill recognized in such circumstances generally does not represent a negotiated premium paid for intangible factors that are expected to enhance future profit levels. They contend that the amount recognized is often merely a function of current interest rates. Others believe that the current economic and competitive conditions facing the banking and thrift industries do not support the selection of a 40-year estimated useful life, especially in view of the anomalous effect on postcombination earnings that the use of such an extended life can produce. Still others believe that goodwill recognized in the acquisition of such institutions is not different in nature from goodwill recognized in other acquisitions and that the existing provisions of Opinion 17 provide adequate guidance in determining the estimated life.

24. In July 1982, the Accounting Standards Executive Committee of the AICPA requested the FASB to address the accounting for business combinations of mutual thrift institutions. The committee requested the Board to issue guidance that would produce meaningful results in accounting for these combinations and reduce the diversity in practice. On August 11, 1982, the Board added to its agenda a project to address the amortization of the unidentifiable intangible asset recognized in certain acquisitions of banking or thrift institutions. On October 7, 1982, the Board issued an FASB Exposure Draft, *Accounting for Certain Acquisitions of Banking or Thrift Institutions.* The Board received 80 letters of comment on that Exposure Draft. On December 13, 1982, the Board conducted a public hearing on the Exposure Draft. Thirteen organizations and individuals presented their views at the hearing.

Appendix B

BASIS FOR CONCLUSIONS

25. This appendix discusses the significant comments received on the Exposure Draft and the factors deemed significant by the Board in reaching the conclusions in this Statement, including alternatives considered and reasons for accepting some and rejecting others. Individual Board members gave greater weight to some factors than to others.

Scope

26. Many respondents to the Exposure Draft pointed out that the issues of purchase accounting and the recognition and amortization of intangible assets are not unique to acquisitions of banking and thrift institutions. They suggested that if the Board perceives a problem with respect to those issues, it should undertake a comprehensive project to readdress the accounting for business combinations by all types of enterprises. They stated that the Exposure Draft discriminated against thrift institutions in particular and that such an approach ran counter to the Board's general practice of promulgating standards that are evenhanded and applicable to all enterprises.

27. Board members agree that questions concerning purchase accounting and the recognition and amortization of intangible assets are not unique to acquisitions of banking and thrift institutions but believe that a comprehensive reconsideration of Opinions 16 and 17 should not be undertaken at this time. Accounting for business combinations and intangible assets are subjects with a long history of diverse views and controversy among standard setters and among others interested in financial reporting—preparers, users, auditors, academics, and the financial press. As one would expect, individual Board members have different views on those subjects, and it is neither feasible nor appropriate to reconsider the pervasive issues of business combinations and intangible assets in the context of this narrow, but significant and urgent, practice problem. Accordingly, the Board decided to restrict the scope of this Statement to certain combinations involving the acquisition of a banking or thrift institution in order to address that problem in a timely manner. However, most Board members believe that if goodwill is recognized in the acquisition of any enterprise having liabilities in excess of its assets it generally would be short-lived.

Unidentifiable Intangible Asset

28. Many respondents stated that the Board's proposal to equate the amortization period for an

unidentifiable intangible asset with the average life of the interest-bearing assets acquired is arbitrary and conceptually unsound, and they urged the Board to abandon the project. They stated that enterprises that acquire banking and thrift institutions pay a premium to gain entry into new markets, to acquire established branches with existing customer relationships, to acquire an existing deposit base, and for other factors. They also indicated that goodwill recognized in a banking or thrift acquisition relates to the expectation of enhanced future earnings just as it does in acquisitions of other types of enterprises. They pointed out that the proposed amortization method implies that an acquiring enterprise has paid a premium to acquire an institution's interest-bearing assets, when in fact that aspect of the acquisition is of least importance. Most of those respondents stated that the existing guidance in Opinion 17 is sufficient to allow enterprises and auditors to reach reasonable conclusions about the useful life of the unidentifiable intangible.

29. All Board members recognize that acquisitions of banking and thrift institutions seldom, if ever, are consummated for the purpose of acquiring a portfolio of interest-bearing assets. In both Interpretation 9 and this Statement, the Board has emphasized that intangible factors of the nature referred to in the preceding paragraph should be identified and recognized if their fair values can be reliably measured. The Board understands that identified intangibles have not always been separately recognized in the past.

30. The Board believes that the use of a 40-year maximum amortization period in the face of existing economic and competitive uncertainties confronting the banking and thrift industries is inappropriate. That accounting for such combinations produces results that lack economic substance, that destroy both consistency of reporting by the enterprise and comparability among similar enterprises, and that have the capacity to mislead users and damage the credibility of financial reporting. Accordingly, the Board concluded that more explicit guidance was needed to improve the relevance and reliability of financial reporting.

31. For a variety of reasons discussed below, the Board believes that if the fair value of the liabilities assumed in an acquisition exceeds the fair value of tangible and identified intangible assets acquired, the remaining life of the long-term interest-bearing assets acquired is an appropriate maximum period for amortizing the unidentifiable intangible asset attributable to that excess. It is important to observe that Board members support this industry-specific standard primarily because they agree that a rapid and pragmatic resolution of the problem is essential.

32. Most Board members believe that Opinion 16 requires that the amount by which the fair value of liabilities assumed exceeds the fair value of identifiable assets acquired be recognized as an unidentifiable intangible asset. They also believe that this excess should be amortized over a relatively short period because of the uncertainty about the nature and extent of the estimated future benefits related to that asset. Ordinarily, the form of consideration given in a business combination (for example, cash, assumption of debt, or issuance of stock) does not affect the reporting of the transaction. However, the Board believes that a deficiency of identifiable assets (determined using fair values) is indicative of uncertainty as to the recoverability of any unidentifiable intangible and augments the uncertainty inherent in the economic and competitive environment of banking and thrift institutions. In many cases, the acquired banking or thrift institution has incurred recent operating losses, and its prospects for returning (or contributing) to profitable operations in the future depend in large part on the level of future interest rates. The nature and extent of future benefits related to the intangible asset also may be impacted by the possible deregulation of the banking and thrift industries.

33. Most Board members also support the amortization method specified in paragraph 5 as a practical solution for eliminating what they believe is an unwarranted positive effect on earnings when a troubled financial institution is acquired and an unidentifiable intangible asset is recognized and amortized over an extended period. They agree that an increase in earnings may occur after a business combination as a result of acquiring a profitable enterprise or because of economic advantages that the combination has produced, but they believe that reporting a substantial increase in earnings without any substantive change in the economic condition of the combined enterprise is not representationally faithful and that the frequency of such reporting has harmed the credibility of financial reporting in general. Some Board members also support an amortization method based on the lives of the interest-bearing assets acquired because they believe that that period more closely approximates the useful life of a customer list or deposit base than does a 40-year period.

34. Some Board members also believe that the purchase method of accounting may be inappropriate for most combinations of *mutual* banking and thrift institutions and note that a majority of thrift institutions are organized under that form of ownership. Combinations of those institutions generally do not involve the transfer of cash, other assets, or equity interests to the previous owners of the acquired institution. Those Board members further support the amortization method specified in paragraph 5

because it often results in reporting approximately the same amount of postcombination net income that would have been reported if the combination had been accounted for by combining the previous carrying amounts of the two enterprises.

Nature of Problem

35. Several respondents said the Board should reexamine the applicability of Opinion 16 to a combination of mutual banking or thrift institutions instead of pursuing the tentative conclusions in the Exposure Draft. They stated that Opinion 16's criteria for using the pooling-of-interests method are difficult to apply in a combination of mutuals and indicated that those criteria were not designed with mutual institutions in mind. Some of those respondents recommended that the Board explain how the pooling-of-interests criteria should be applied in a combination of mutuals. Others stated that the Board should mandate the use of the pooling-of-interests method in such combinations. Still others indicated that purchase accounting should be used.

36. Board members considered addressing the question of whether the methods of accounting for a business combination specified in Opinion 16 (that is, the purchase method and the pooling-of-interests method) are appropriate for business combinations of mutual banking and thrift institutions. Most Board members believe that (a) the Accounting Principles Board in Opinion 16 did not specifically consider such combinations and (b) application of the criteria in paragraphs 46-48 of Opinion 16 to combinations of mutual institutions is not clear. Most Board members believe such a reconsideration would be time-consuming and would delay resolution of the pressing accounting question at hand. The Board also notes that the reporting problem being addressed is not limited to combinations of mutuals. Stockholder-owned banking and thrift institutions are also involved in business combinations. The Board concluded that a broad consideration of accounting for business combinations of mutuals should be included as part of any future project to readdress accounting for business combinations in general.

37. Some respondents stated that the reporting problems addressed in this project have resulted from the failure of enterprises and auditors to properly apply the existing guidance in Opinion 17. Some of those respondents said that a 40-year life for goodwill may not be appropriate in many circumstances but suggested that the Board view the current problem as an auditing or enforcement matter and not take on the role of a mediator. They believe that the existing principles of Opinion 17 are sound and should not be changed to address such a limited problem. Some of those respondents provided the Board with data indicating the problem was not as widespread as some others had asserted. However, research by the FASB staff indicated that the use of a 40-year life for goodwill has become common. The Board assessed both the severity of the problem and the adequacy of existing guidance and concluded that, on balance, more explicit guidance was needed to minimize diversity in practice and to improve the relevance and reliability of financial reporting.

Perceived Economic Consequences

38. Some respondents recommended that the Board withdraw the proposal because its adoption would have adverse economic consequences. Those respondents stated that the adoption of the provisions of the Exposure Draft in a final Statement would (a) prevent economically sound mergers from occurring, (b) put a strain on the resources of regulatory insurance agencies because potential acquiring enterprises would demand an increased amount of financial assistance, (c) frustrate the thrift industry's survival plans, or (d) impair an enterprise's ability to restructure and meet changing economic conditions. The Board was not persuaded by those arguments. The Board believes that this Statement will not affect an enterprise's ability to survive or restructure. Those abilities are a function of future cash flows, management action, and legal and regulatory restrictions rather than a function of accounting standards. In addition, the Board believes that the amortization provisions of this Statement will produce accounting information that is more relevant, reliable, and neutral for purposes of decision making. A primary focus of financial reporting is information about an enterprise's performance provided by measures of earnings and its components. The need for relevant and reliable measures of earnings following the acquisition of a banking or thrift institution was a major factor contributing to the Board's decision.

Subsequent Dispositions of Interest-Bearing Assets

39. Many respondents asked whether the proposed amortization method and the provision of paragraph 11(b) of the Exposure Draft were intended to require an enterprise to reduce goodwill proportionally when all or a portion of the acquired interest-bearing assets are sold subsequent to the acquisition date. Some of those respondents stated that such reporting may be appropriate, but only if the acquiring enterprise sells or liquidates a large segment or separable group of those assets (paragraph 32 of Opinion 17). They requested the Board to clarify the meaning of *large segment or separable group of assets* in the context of the banking and thrift industries. Other respondents also asked for clarification and stated that paragraph 32 of Opin-

ion 17 should not apply in *any* subsequent sale of acquired interest-bearing assets, such as mortgage loans and investment securities. They pointed out that some banking and thrift institutions sell and reinvest in interest-bearing assets every day and that the benefits attributable to goodwill are unaffected by the presence or absence of such fungible assets. The Board generally agreed with that latter view, and this Statement specifies that the sale of all or a portion of acquired interest-bearing assets does not automatically require a reduction in goodwill. A determination of whether a reduction in goodwill is appropriate should be based on the individual facts and circumstances. For example, if a sale of a large group of interest-bearing assets is accompanied by the loss of a significant and valuable customer base, a reduction in goodwill likely would be appropriate. On the other hand, if the proceeds of sale are reinvested in other forms of interest-bearing or other assets, no such reduction is necessary if there has been no reduction in the benefits attributable to goodwill.

Identified Intangibles

40. Several respondents stated that the adoption of a shorter useful life for goodwill recognized in certain acquisitions of banking or thrift institutions would induce affected enterprises to assign a greater portion (or all) of the excess purchase price to identified intangibles rather than to goodwill. Some of those respondents said that amounts often have not been assigned in the past to identified intangibles because (a) appraised values were not readily determinable, (b) those intangible factors often have indefinite lives, and (c) factors such as core deposits, branch networks, and territorial advantages represent the essence of goodwill. They questioned whether the benefits of separate identification would justify the costs. Other respondents said the Board should clarify Opinion 16 and Interpretation 9 to indicate that the measurements of such identified intangibles must be representationally faithful and verifiable. They stated that, without such guidance, unreliable amounts may be assigned to identified intangibles, thus circumventing this Statement's intent.

41. The Board reaffirms the principles in Opinion 16 and Interpretation 9 that require identified intangibles to be recognized apart from goodwill and amortized over their estimated useful lives. The Board does not view as undesirable any increased effort to identify and measure specific intangible assets acquired in a business combination. However, the Board agrees with those respondents who stated that such intangible assets should be recognized only when they can be separately identified and their fair values can be reliably measured. Accordingly, this Statement specifies that the measurements of identified intangible assets must be verifiable and representationally faithful. The Board disagrees with those respondents who stated that intangible assets attributed to deposit accounts and customer relationships generally have indefinite lives. Those respondents viewed such relationships as being constantly renewed and growing and, therefore, indicated that a 40-year useful life may often be appropriate. The Board notes that Interpretation 9 refers to intangible factors representing the capacity of *existing* accounts to generate future income or new business. The Board recognizes that many enterprises purchase a banking or thrift institution with the expectation of maintaining and even expanding the existing customer base and, thereby, the value of the related intangible asset; however, only purchased intangible assets are capitalizable under present generally accepted accounting principles. The Board believes that the cost and useful life of acquired intangible assets should not reflect the costs and expectations of developing, maintaining, or restoring such intangibles after they are acquired.

Other Matters

42. A few respondents requested the Board to explain how the provisions of the Exposure Draft should be applied when a combination does not involve the acquisition of a significant amount of interest-bearing assets, such as in the acquisition of a branch location. The Board understands that such acquisitions often involve the assumption of deposit liabilities by the acquiring enterprise in exchange for a cash payment in an amount less than the fair value of the deposit liabilities assumed. In such circumstances, the Board believes identifiable intangible assets should be recognized as provided in Opinion 16, Interpretation 9, and paragraph 4 of this Statement. If a portion of the purchase price is allocated to an unidentifiable intangible, the Board believes that amount should be amortized over a relatively short period of time, not to exceed the estimated average remaining life of the existing customer base acquired. The value of a customer base was cited most often by respondents as the primary factor acquired in such transactions.

43. Some respondents questioned portions of the Exposure Draft that dealt with reporting regulatory financial assistance granted to an enterprise as an inducement for that enterprise to acquire a banking or thrift institution. Some stated that subsequent repayments of regulatory assistance should not be charged to income automatically because such reporting may not be consistent with the initial reporting of the assistance. The Board understands that repayment requirements generally are related to future profitability levels or other criteria based on future revenues or expenses. In those cases, the Board believes the nature of the repayment is similar

to a profit-sharing arrangement and that the repayments should be charged to expense, regardless of the manner in which the assistance was initially reported.

44. A few respondents stated that estimates of regulatory reimbursements for any future operating losses should not be recognized at the time of combination because the amount of assistance cannot be reliably measured. The Board is in general agreement with those respondents. However, the Board believes that certain forms of regulatory assistance expected to be effective in indemnifying an enterprise from all or a portion of any losses that may result from holding certain low-rate interest-bearing assets acquired in a combination accounted for using the purchase method should be taken into consideration in determining the fair value of the assets acquired. Those forms of assistance represent probable future economic benefits that will result in future cash flows as a result of either (a) payment by a regulatory authority (if interest rates increase or remain constant) or (b) reduced cost of funds (if interest rates decline). The Board believes that reporting the effect of this benefit as part of the carrying amount of the interest-bearing assets acquired is a reasonable approach.

45. A few respondents suggested that this Statement should be effective for business combinations initiated after the issuance of the Statement rather than for combinations initiated after September 30, 1982. They argued that it is inappropriate to establish a retroactive effective date in a Statement that changes existing standards, especially when those standards have previously been acceptable. Although the Board hopes that the conditions that led to the reporting problems addressed by this Statement are temporary, the accounting for intangible assets may affect financial reporting for an extended period. The Board considered when this Statement should become effective and the transition method that should be applied by enterprises in adopting it in that light, weighing considerations of consistent, comparable, and credible reporting with fairness to preparers who have adopted or may yet adopt practices this Statement would change, fairness to those who did not, and fairness to users of financial reports. Those are subjective considerations and individual Board members attached differing weights. Accordingly, the effective date of September 30, 1982 and the prospective application reflect a compromise among Board members, some of whom would prefer an earlier effective date or retroactive application or both, and others who would prefer that the Statement become effective upon issuance.

Statement of Financial Accounting Standards No. 73
Reporting a Change in Accounting for Railroad Track Structures

an amendment of APB Opinion No. 20

STATUS

Issued: August 1983

Effective date: For changes from retirement-replacement-betterment accounting to depreciation accounting made after June 30, 1983

Affects: Amends APB 20, paragraph 27

Affected by: No other pronouncements

SUMMARY

This Statement amends APB Opinion No. 20, *Accounting Changes,* to specify that a change to depreciation accounting for railroad track structures shall be reported by restating financial statements of all prior periods presented. The Statement is effective for changes made after June 30, 1983; however, earlier application is encouraged but not required. Prior to 1983, railroads generally followed betterment accounting for track structures in their general purpose financial statements. In 1983, the Interstate Commerce Commission (ICC) adopted changes requiring depreciation accounting in ICC filings. As a result, railroads and their accountants requested a determination of how best to report a voluntary change from betterment to depreciation accounting for general purpose financial reporting. This Statement is a response to that request.

Statement of Financial Accounting Standards No. 73
Reporting a Change in Accounting for Railroad Track Structures

an amendment of APB Opinion No. 20

CONTENTS

INTRODUCTION

1. This Statement amends APB Opinion No. 20, *Accounting Changes,* to specify that a change to depreciation accounting for railroad track structures should be reported by restating financial statements of all prior periods presented.

STANDARDS OF FINANCIAL ACCOUNTING AND REPORTING

Amendment to APB Opinion No. 20

2. A change from retirement-replacement-betterment accounting (RRB) to depreciation accounting is added to the last sentence of paragraph 27 of Opinion 20, which will read as follows:

The changes that should be accorded this treatment are: (a) a change from the LIFO method of inventory pricing to another method, (b) a change in the method of accounting for long-term construction-type contracts, (c) a change to or from the "full cost" method of accounting which is used in the extractive industries, and (d) a change from retirement-replacement-betterment accounting to depreciation accounting.

Effective Date and Transition

3. This Statement shall be effective for changes in accounting from RRB to depreciation accounting made after June 30, 1983. Earlier application is encouraged but is not required.

The provisions of this Statement need not be applied to immaterial items

This Statement was adopted by the unanimous vote of the seven members of the Financial Accounting Standards Board:

Donald J. Kirk, *Chairman*
Frank E. Block
Victor H. Brown
John W. March
David Mosso
Robert T. Sprouse
Ralph E. Walters

Appendix

BACKGROUND INFORMATION AND BASIS FOR CONCLUSIONS

4. Railroads and their accountants requested a determination by the Board of how best to report a voluntary change from betterment to depreciation accounting for general purpose reporting.

5. On February 17, 1983, the Interstate Commerce Commission (ICC) ruled that railroads must use depreciation accounting for railroad track structures in reports to the ICC. The ruling is effective for 1983 annual filings, 1984 quarterly filings, and all filings thereafter with the ICC. The ICC previously had required RRB for railroad track structures in reports to the ICC.

6. Under RRB, the initial costs of installing track

are capitalized, not depreciated, and remain capitalized until the track is retired. The costs of replacing track are expensed unless a betterment (for example, replacing a 110-lb. rail with a 132-lb. rail) occurs. In that case, the amount by which the cost of the new part exceeds the current cost of the part replaced is considered a betterment and is capitalized but not depreciated, and the current cost of the part replaced is expensed. Railroads generally have used RRB for financial reporting.

7. The ICC ruling does not apply to financial reporting by railroads, but the Board has been informed that many railroads plan to adopt depreciation accounting for financial reporting. A change from RRB to depreciation accounting would be a change in accounting principle under Opinion 20.

8. Opinion 20 specifies that most changes in accounting principle should be reported by including the cumulative effect of the change in net income of the period of change. The Opinion provides for certain exceptions that should be reported by restating financial statements of all prior periods presented. Those exceptions are: (a) a change from the LIFO method of inventory pricing to another method, (b) a change in the method of accounting for long-term construction-type contracts, and (c) a change to or from the "full cost" method of accounting which is used in the extractive industries.

9. The Board believes that a change from RRB to depreciation accounting should be included among the exceptions noted in paragraph 8 because that change is another specific instance in which the advantages of comparability of financial statements resulting from restating financial statements outweigh the disadvantages. Therefore, the Board decided to amend Opinion 20 to specify that a change from RRB to depreciation accounting should be reported by restating financial statements of all prior periods presented.

10. An Exposure Draft of a proposed Statement, *Reporting a Change in Accounting for Railroad Track Structures,* was issued on April 12, 1983. The Board received 28 comment letters in response to the Exposure Draft, most of which expressed agreement. Certain of the comments received and the Board's consideration of them are discussed in the remaining paragraphs.

11. Some respondents stated that the Board should reconsider all of the provisions of Opinion 20. Those respondents suggested that a reconsideration of Opinion 20 would eliminate the need to amend that Opinion for exceptions as they arise. The Board concluded that a separate Statement on reporting a change in accounting for railroad track structures is appropriate because a need for timely guidance was demonstrated and there is no evidence that Opinion 20 needs to be reconsidered in its entirety. Also, voluntary accounting changes are infrequent, and the Board sees little benefit in attempting to devise a new implementation method applicable to all such changes.

12. Some respondents indicated that a Statement should not be issued on reporting a change in accounting for railroad track structures because it is a narrow issue. The Board considered other means of addressing this issue, such as through a Technical Bulletin, but concluded that at this time a response to the issue should be effected through a Statement.

13. The Board concluded that it could reach an informed decision on the basis of existing information without a public hearing and that the effective date and transition specified in paragraph 3 are advisable in the circumstances.

Statement of Financial Accounting Standards No. 74 Accounting for Special Termination Benefits Paid to Employees

STATUS

Issued: August 1983

Effective Date: For special termination benefits offered after June 30, 1983

Affects: Amends APB 8, paragraph 31

Affected by: No other pronouncements

SUMMARY

This Statement applies when an employer offers for a short period of time special termination benefits to its employees. The employer is to recognize special termination benefits as a liability and an expense when the employees accept the offer and the amount can be reasonably estimated. The amount to be recognized includes any lump-sum payments and the present value of any expected future payments. If reliably measurable, certain changes in the estimated costs of other employee benefits are also to be included in measuring the expense.

This Statement applies for special termination benefits offered after June 30, 1983, with earlier application encouraged. Restatement of previously issued financial statements is permitted.

Statement of Financial Accounting Standards No. 74
Accounting for Special Termination Benefits Paid to Employees

CONTENTS

INTRODUCTION

1. An employer may offer for a short period of time special benefits to its employees in connection with their termination of employment (special termination benefits). The employees to whom the benefits are offered may vary but often include employees who have reached the early retirement age specified in the employer's pension plan. The special termination benefits can take different forms, such as a lump-sum payment or periodic future payments or both. They may be paid directly from an employer's assets, an existing pension plan, a new employee benefit plan, or a combination of those means. Some believe that the cost of special termination benefits should be recognized as an expense of future periods. Others believe that the cost of those benefits should be immediately expensed. The AICPA Accounting Standards Executive Committee requested that the FASB provide guidance on this issue because of the diversity of views. That diversity was confirmed by the comments received in response to the FASB Exposure Draft, *Accounting for Special Termination Benefits Paid to Employees* (December 28, 1982).

STANDARDS OF FINANCIAL ACCOUNTING AND REPORTING

2. An employer that offers for a short period of time special termination benefits to employees shall recognize a liability and an expense when the employees accept the offer and the amount can be reasonably estimated. The amount recognized shall include any lump-sum payments and the present value of any expected future payments.

3. The termination of employees under a special termination benefit arrangement may affect the estimated costs of other employee benefits, such as pension benefits, because of differences between past assumptions and actual experience. If reliably measurable, the effects of any such changes on an employer's previously accrued expenses for those benefits that result directly from the termination of employees shall be included in measuring the termination expense.[1]

Amendment to APB Opinion No. 8

4. The following footnote is added to the end of the last sentence of paragraph 31 of APB Opinion No. 8, *Accounting for the Cost of Pension Plans,* to elaborate on the examples cited in that paragraph:

> *Paragraph 3 of FASB Statement No. 74, *Accounting for Special Termination Benefits Paid to Employees,* identifies another situation for which an actuarial gain or loss is immediately recognized.

Effective Date and Transition

5. This Statement shall be applied for special termination benefits offered after June 30, 1983. Earlier application is encouraged. Restatement of previously issued financial statements is permitted but is not required.

The provisions of this Statement need not be applied to immaterial items.

[1]Additional guidance for applying this provision is provided in paragraphs 14 through 17.

This Statement was adopted by the affirmative votes of six members of the Financial Accounting Standards Board. Mr. March dissented.

Mr. March dissents because he believes that the requirement in paragraph 2 making employee acceptance of the employer's offer of termination benefits a condition precedent to recognizing a liability is an undesirable bar to recognition that could cause failure to report a loss known to have occurred. The definition of a liability, cited in paragraph 11 of this Statement, does not require acceptance by the obligee when the effect of probable acceptance is known or reasonably estimable and when, as the Board finds in paragraph 12, such acceptance does not give rise to the future acquisition of an asset (future economic benefit). He believes that users' reasonable expectations are that known losses have been reflected in financial statements. That objective should take priority over the emphasis on legal obligation that is implicit in requiring prior acceptance. He also believes that the Board's decision to require acceptance is inconsistent with the guidance for accruing severance pay and additional pension costs in paragraph 17 of APB Opinion No. 30, *Reporting the Results of Operations,* for discontinuance of a business segment, cited in paragraph 12 of this Statement as being a similar situation. The provisions of paragraphs 2 and 3 of the Statement (as explained in paragraph 17) specifying that the effect of employees' acceptances must be "reasonably estimated" or "reliably measurable" are adequate assurance against accruals for offers of uncertain outcome.

Members of the Financial Accounting Standards Board:

Donald J. Kirk, *Chairman*
Frank E. Block
Victor H. Brown
John W. March
David Mosso
Robert T. Sprouse
Ralph E. Walters

Appendix

BASIS FOR CONCLUSIONS

6. An Exposure Draft of a proposed Statement, *Accounting for Special Termination Benefits Paid to Employees,* was issued on December 28, 1982. The Board received 160 letters of comment in response to the Exposure Draft. The Board concluded that it could reach an informed decision on the basis of existing information without a public hearing. This appendix discusses the significant comments received on the Exposure Draft and the factors deemed significant by the Board in reaching the conclusions in this Statement. Individual Board members gave greater weight to some factors than to others.

Need for Statement

7. Many respondents suggested that the Board combine the project on special termination benefits with its project on employers' accounting for pensions and other postemployment benefits. Other respondents questioned the need for a Statement that specifies how an employer should account for special termination benefits. Although they generally agreed with the proposed standards, they expressed the view that a careful reading of Opinion 8 and FASB Statement No. 5, *Accounting for Contingencies,* leads to the same result.

8. The Board concluded that it should address this issue now because of the significance of recent termination offers and the differences of opinion on the proper accounting for special termination benefits as evidenced by respondents' comments.

Recognition and Measurement

9. Some respondents expressed the view that Opinion 8 applies if special termination benefits are offered through an amendment to an existing pension plan. They concluded that special termination benefits offered through a plan amendment represent prior service costs which are recognized as an expense of future periods under Opinion 8.

10. The Board recognizes that special termination benefits may be paid from a pension plan, but it believes that the source of payment should not determine the accounting. The Board believes that an assumption underlying Opinion 8 is an employer's ongoing commitment to provide pension benefits in exchange for employees' services. Because special termination benefits are offered only for a short period of time and in exchange for employees' termination of service, the Board concluded that the accounting for those benefits is excluded from the scope of Opinion 8.

11. Paragraph 28 of FASB Concepts Statement No. 3, *Elements of Financial Statements of Business Enterprises,* states:

> Liabilities are probable future sacrifices of economic benefits arising from present obligations of a particular entity to transfer assets or provide services to other entities in the future as

a result of past transactions or events. [Footnote references omitted.]

The Board believes that an employer's obligation for special termination benefits meets that definition of a liability when the employees accept the offer (paragraph 18).

12. Some respondents believe that an employer's incurring a liability for special termination benefits results in its acquiring future economic benefits that should be recognized as an asset. Most of those respondents stated that the future economic benefits are the salaries and other employee costs that will be avoided because of the employees' termination. The Board believes that the avoidance of future employee costs does not result in the acquisition of an asset under the facts and circumstances dealt with in this Statement. Special termination benefits are generally offered to eliminate or mitigate an existing unfavorable situation. Termination of employees' services is similar to discontinuance of a business segment in that as a result of either of those actions future results of operations provided by the remaining assets or work force may improve when compared with the past performance of the enterprise. Other respondents indicated that the future economic benefits could also include improved productivity and reduced employee turnover, thereby enhancing the value of continuing employees' future services. The Board believes that there is sufficient uncertainty about whether and to what extent the employer will obtain those benefits to preclude recognition of an asset.

13. Some respondents suggested that special termination benefits are similar to improvements in retirees' benefits and pointed to Preliminary Views of the FASB, *Employers' Accounting for Pensions and Other Postemployment Benefits,* which indicates that such improvements give rise to probable future economic benefits that qualify as an intangible asset. All Board members agree that incurring an obligation for special termination benefits does not result in the acquisition of an asset. The Board notes that it will not reach a conclusion on the issue concerning improvements in retirees' benefits until after the Board has considered comments on the Preliminary Views and further deliberated all of the issues concerning employers' accounting for pensions. However, the Board believes that conclusion would not affect the decision relating to special termination benefits.

14. The Exposure Draft specified that any "accounting actuarial gain (loss)" related to an existing employee benefit plan that results from the employee terminations should be immediately recognized. Some respondents indicated that the term *accounting actuarial gain (loss)* was confusing and requested that the Board further clarify the nature of that gain (loss). Other respondents indicated that it is difficult, if not impossible, to reliably measure those gains (losses) in many circumstances, and therefore, immediate recognition should not be required.

15. The Board agreed that the term *accounting actuarial gain (loss)* was not clear. Accordingly, the Board decided to clarify the matter and not use that term. The termination of employees under a special termination benefit arrangement may affect the cost of other employee benefits, such as pension benefits, because of differences between past assumptions and actual experience. For example, there may be an additional pension cost if the pension plan does not require any actuarial reduction of benefits for early retirement and previously estimated pension costs for the terminating employees have been based on the assumption of a later retirement age. As another example, pension costs for the terminating employees may be reduced if they have been based on expected salary levels and service to normal retirement age. The Board believes that the effects of any such changes on an employer's previously accrued expenses for other employee benefits that result *directly* from the termination of employees should be included in measuring the termination expense. The Board believes that this result is consistent with the intent of paragraph 31 of Opinion 8.

16. Terminating employees may have other benefits whose costs have not been fully accrued. The Board concluded that previously existing unaccrued costs should not be considered in measuring the termination expense. Any increases in those unaccrued costs that result directly from the termination of employees would be included in measuring the termination expense. However, any decreases in those unaccrued costs would not be included in measuring the expense. For example, the actuarial liability under the actuarial cost method used by the employer for its pension plan may be reduced as a result of the termination of employees. Termination expense would be reduced only to the extent that the actuarial liability being reduced represents pension expense previously accrued in the employer's financial statements. The Board also concluded that past investment performance more or less favorable than that assumed in measuring previously accrued pension expense should not be included in measuring the termination expense.

17. The Board agrees with those respondents who indicated that it may not be possible in many situations to reliably measure the effects of the employees' termination on the costs of other benefits that should be immediately recognized. Situations cited include (a) an implicit (versus explicit) approach to

actuarial assumptions has been followed, (b) changes in actuarial assumptions have preceded the offer of termination benefits, and (c) previously accrued expenses cannot be allocated between terminated employees and other plan participants. Accordingly, this Statement requires that such effects be immediately recognized only if reliably measurable.

18. Some respondents asked the Board to clarify whether the termination liability and expense should be recognized when the employer offers termination benefits or when employees accept the offer. As noted in paragraphs 2 and 11, the Board concluded that the employer incurs a liability when employees accept the offer and that the termination expense should be recognized at that time. The Board believes that a liability and an expense for special termination benefits result from an exchange transaction and that neither a liability nor an expense is incurred until that exchange takes place. That accounting is consistent with accounting for other exchange transactions. Although there are similarities between termination of employees through an offer of special termination benefits and discontinuance of a business segment (paragraph 12), the Board believes the differences between them call for recognizing their effects at different dates. APB Opinion No. 30, *Reporting the Results of Operations,* requires severance pay and additional pension costs expected in connection with the discontinuance of a business segment to be accrued when management adopts a formal plan for such discontinuance. That Opinion is concerned with recognizing the impairment of assets intended to be disposed of and any related expenses. In that situation, employees' termination is a unilateral decision of the employer, not an exchange transaction.

19. Some respondents expressed the view that, if adopted, the provisions of the Exposure Draft would deter employers from offering special termination benefits. The Board was not persuaded by that view. The Board believes that financial reporting must reflect economic activity as faithfully as possible without coloring the image it communicates for the purpose of influencing behavior in any particular direction.

Effective Date and Transition

20. The Exposure Draft proposed that this Statement be effective for special termination benefits offered in fiscal years ending after April 15, 1983. The Board concluded, however, that the effective date and transition specified in paragraph 5 are advisable primarily because of the additional clarification concerning the "accounting actuarial gain (loss)."

Statement of Financial Accounting Standards No. 75 Deferral of the Effective Date of Certain Accounting Requirements for Pension Plans of State and Local Governmental Units

an amendment of FASB Statement No. 35

STATUS

Issued: November 1983

Effective Date: November 1983 retroactive for fiscal years beginning after December 15, 1980

Affects: Amends FAS 35, paragraph 30
Supersedes FAS 59

Affected by: No other pronouncements

SUMMARY

This Statement amends FASB Statement No. 35, *Accounting and Reporting by Defined Benefit Pension Plans,* to defer indefinitely its applicability to pension plans of state and local governmental units pending further action by the Board.

Statement of Financial Accounting Standards No. 75

Deferral of the Effective Date of Certain Accounting Requirements for Pension Plans of State and Local Governmental Units

an amendment of FASB Statement No. 35

CONTENTS

INTRODUCTION

1. In February 1983, the Board received a request from the AICPA Accounting Standards Executive Committee urging the Board to extend the effective date of FASB Statement No. 35, *Accounting and Reporting by Defined Benefit Pension Plans,* for pension plans of state and local governmental units. For the reasons given in the appendix, the Board has concluded that it is appropriate to further defer the effective date of Statement 35 for those plans.

STANDARDS OF FINANCIAL ACCOUNTING AND REPORTING

Amendment to FASB Statement No. 35

2. The first sentence of paragraph 30 of Statement 35 is superseded and replaced by the following two sentences:

This Statement shall be effective for plan years beginning after December 15, 1980, except for plans that are sponsored by and provide benefits for the employees of one or more state or local governmental units. For those plans, the effective date of this Statement is deferred indefinitely pending further action by the Board.

Supersession of FASB Statement No. 59

3. This Statement supersedes FASB Statement No. 59, *Deferral of the Effective Date of Certain Accounting Requirements for Pension Plans of State and Local Governmental Units.*

Effective Date

4. This Statement shall be effective upon issuance retroactive to fiscal years beginning after December 15, 1980.

This Statement was adopted by the unanimous vote of the seven members of the Financial Accounting Standards Board:

Donald J. Kirk, *Chairman*
Frank E. Block
Victor H. Brown
John W. March
David Mosso
Robert T. Sprouse
Ralph E. Walters

Appendix

BACKGROUND INFORMATION AND BASIS FOR CONCLUSIONS

5. Statement 35 was issued in March 1980 and defines generally accepted accounting principles for general purpose external financial reports of defined benefit pension plans. It was intended to apply both to plans in the private sector and to plans sponsored by state and local governmental units. As originally issued, Statement 35 was to be effective for plan years beginning after December 15, 1980.

6. In April 1982, the Board issued Statement 59. That Statement amended Statement 35 by deferring its applicability until plan years beginning after June 15, 1982 for plans that are sponsored by and provide benefits for the employees of one or more state or local governmental units.

7. In November 1982, the Financial Accounting Foundation (FAF) reached agreement with the Municipal Finance Officers Association, the National Association of State Auditors, Comptrollers and Treasurers, and the American Institute of Certified Public Accountants regarding the establishment of a Governmental Accounting Standards Board (GASB). The Foundation's trustees have approved the formation of an FAF committee to oversee all aspects of implementation of the agreement. Among the questions that remain to be resolved is how standards should be set for government-related entities (such as hospitals, municipal utilities, universities, and pension plans) that are similar to entities in the private sector.

8. As indicated in paragraph 1, the Board has been requested to further extend the effective date of Statement 35 for pension plans of state and local governmental units. The Board believes that the current efforts to establish a new structure for setting accounting standards for state and local governmental units bear on the consideration to amend Statement 35. The Board believes that those efforts might be impaired by imposition of new standards at this time or by the existence of differing standards issued by different bodies.

9. On June 7, 1983, the FASB issued an Exposure Draft proposing deferral of the effective date for application of Statement 35 to pension plans of state and local governmental units until plan years beginning after June 15, 1985. The Exposure Draft was issued after the Board was informed by representatives of the National Council on Governmental Accounting (NCGA) that the NCGA would consider at its June 1983 meeting taking similar action regarding its recently issued Statement 6, *Pension Accounting and Financial Reporting: Public Employee Retirement Systems and State and Local Government Employers*. NCGA Statement 6 differs significantly from Statement 35 in the measurement of participants' benefits and the basis for valuing plan investments. The Board received 10 letters of comment in response to the Exposure Draft, all of which generally supported extending the period of mutual deferral of both Statement 35 and NCGA Statement 6. Subsequent to issuance of the Exposure Draft, the NCGA has taken various actions regarding the effective date of Statement 6. The Board understands that the NCGA will soon issue its Interpretation 8 which will extend indefinitely the effective date of Statement 6.

10. The Board believes that a mutual deferral of both Statement 35 and NCGA Statement 6 is appropriate while discussions relating to the formation and operation of the GASB are in progress. Accordingly, the Board decided to defer indefinitely the applicability of Statement 35 to pension plans of state and local governmental units pending further action by the Board.

11. The Board has concluded that it can reach an informed decision on the basis of existing information without a public hearing and that the effective date specified in paragraph 4 is advisable in the circumstances.

Statement of Financial Accounting Standards No. 76
Extinguishment of Debt

an amendment of APB Opinion No. 26

STATUS

Issued: November 1983

Effective Date: For transaction entered into after December 31, 1983

Affects: Supersedes APB 26, paragraph 2
Supersedes APB 26, paragraph 3(a)
Amends APB 26, paragraph 3(c)
Amends APB 26, paragraph 19
Amends APB 26, paragraph 21
Amends APB 26, footnote 1
Amends AIN-APB 26, Interpretation No. 1
Supersedes FAS 22, footnote 1
Amends FAS 32, Appendix A, SOP 78-5

Affected by: No other pronouncements

SUMMARY

This Statement provides guidance to debtors as to when debt should be considered to be extinguished for financial reporting purposes. This project was undertaken in response to requests to clarify the circumstances that constitute extinguishment and because the Board learned of growing diversity in practice.

This Statement specifies that debt is to be considered extinguished if the debtor is relieved of primary liability for the debt by the creditor and it is probable that the debtor will not be required to make future payments as guarantor of the debt. This Statement also specifies that, even though the creditor does not relieve the debtor of its primary obligation, debt is to be considered extinguished if (a) the debtor irrevocably places cash or other essentially risk-free monetary assets in a trust solely for satisfying that debt and (b) the possibility that the debtor will be required to make further payments is remote. This Statement amends APB Opinion No. 26, *Early Extinguishment of Debt,* to make it apply to all extinguishments of debt, whether early or not, other than those currently exempted from its scope, such as debt conversions and troubled debt restructurings.

This Statement is applicable to transactions occurring after December 31, 1983, with earlier application encouraged in annual financial statements that have not been previously issued. This Statement also permits the restatement of previously issued financial statements to apply this Statement retroactively.

Statement of Financial Accounting Standards No. 76
Extinguishment of Debt

an amendment of APB Opinion No. 26

CONTENTS

INTRODUCTION AND SCOPE

1. This Statement addresses what shall be considered to be an extinguishment of debt, which in turn affects when the debtor recognizes a gain or loss on extinguishment. This Statement does not address the accounting for redeemable preferred stock. The circumstances for an extinguishment of debt described in paragraphs 3(b) and 3(c) do not apply to debt that is convertible into the debtor's equity securities. Furthermore, the circumstances for an extinguishment of debt described in paragraph 3(c) apply only to debt with specified maturities and fixed payment schedules; consequently, those circumstances do not apply to debt with variable terms that do not permit advance determination of debt service requirements, such as debt with a floating interest rate.

2. Because extinguishment of debt currently is addressed by APB Opinion No. 26, *Early Extinguishment of Debt,* that Opinion is amended to refer to the standards in this Statement for guidance about what shall be considered to be an extinguishment of debt. This Statement also amends that Opinion to make it apply to all extinguishments of debt, whether early or not, other than those currently exempted from its scope, such as debt conversions as described in that Opinion and troubled debt restructurings as described in FASB Statement No. 15, *Accounting by Debtors and Creditors for Troubled Debt Restructurings.*

STANDARDS OF FINANCIAL ACCOUNTING AND REPORTING

Circumstances for an Extinguishment of Debt

3. A debtor shall consider debt to be extinguished for financial reporting purposes in the following circumstances:

a. The debtor pays the creditor and is relieved of all its obligations with respect to the debt. This includes the debtor's reacquisition of its outstanding debt securities in the public securities markets, regardless of whether the securities are cancelled or held as so-called treasury bonds.
b. The debtor is legally released[1] from being the primary obligor under the debt either judicially or by the creditor and it is probable[2] that the debtor will not be required to make future payments with respect to that debt under any guarantees.
c. The debtor irrevocably places cash or other assets in a trust to be used solely for satisfying scheduled payments of both interest and principal of a specific obligation and the possibility that the debtor will be required to make future payments with respect to that debt is remote. In this circumstance, debt is extinguished even though the debtor is not legally released from being the primary obligor under the debt obligation.

---

[1]If nonrecourse debt (such as certain mortgages) is assumed by a third party in conjunction with the sale of an asset that serves as the sole collateral for that debt, the sale and related assumption effectively accomplish a legal release of the seller/debtor for purposes of applying this Statement.

[2]*Probable* is used here, consistent with its use in FASB Statement No. 5, *Accounting for Contingencies,* to mean that it is likely that no payments will be required.

Restrictions on the Nature of Assets in Trust

4. The following requirements regarding the nature of the assets held by the trust shall be met to effect an extinguishment of debt under paragraph 3(c):

a. The trust shall be restricted to owning only monetary assets[3] that are *essentially risk free* as to the amount, timing, and collection of interest and principal. The monetary assets shall be denominated in the currency in which the debt is payable. For debt denominated in U.S. dollars, essentially risk-free monetary assets shall be limited to:
   (1) Direct obligations of the U.S. government
   (2) Obligations guaranteed by the U.S. government
   (3) Securities that are backed by U.S. government obligations as collateral under an arrangement by which the interest and principal payments on the collateral generally flow immediately through to the holder of the security.

   However, some securities described in the previous sentence can be paid prior to scheduled maturity and so are not essentially risk free as to the *timing* of the collection of interest and principal; thus, they do not qualify for ownership by the trust.
b. The monetary assets held by the trust shall provide cash flows (from interest and maturity of those assets) that approximately coincide, as to timing and amount, with the scheduled interest and principal payments on the debt that is being extinguished.

Costs Related to Placing Assets in Trust

5. If, in conjunction with placing assets in trust to effect an extinguishment of debt, it is expected that trust assets will be used to pay related costs, such as trustee fees, as well as to satisfy scheduled interest and principal payments of a specific debt, those costs shall be considered in determining the amount of funds required by the trust. On the other hand, if the debtor incurs an obligation to pay any related costs, the debtor shall accrue a liability for those probable future payments in the period that the debt is recognized as extinguished.

Disclosures

6. If debt is considered to be extinguished under the provisions of paragraph 3(c), a general description of the transaction and the amount of debt that is considered extinguished at the end of the period shall be disclosed so long as that debt remains outstanding.

Amendments to Other Pronouncements

7. Paragraph 2 of Opinion 26, which addresses the applicability of that Opinion, is superseded and replaced by the following:

> *Applicability.* This Opinion applies to all extinguishments of debt, whether early or not, except debt that is extinguished through a troubled debt restructuring and debt that is converted to equity securities of the debtor pursuant to conversion privileges provided in terms of the debt at issuance. It supersedes Chapter 15 of ARB No. 43 and paragraph 19 of APB Opinion No. 6. However, it does not alter the accounting for convertible debt securities described in APB Opinion No. 14.

8. Paragraph 3(a) of Opinion 26, which defines *early extinguishment,* is superseded and replaced by the following:

> a. *Extinguishment of debt.* FASB Statement No. 76, *Extinguishment of Debt,* defines transactions that the debtor shall recognize as an extinguishment of debt.

9. The following terms and phrases are deleted from Opinion 26 as indicated:

a. In paragraph 3(c), the term *early*
b. In paragraph 19, the phrase *before scheduled maturities*
c. In paragraph 21, the phrase *before maturity.*

10. The last sentence of footnote 1 of FASB Statement No. 22, *Changes in the Provisions of Lease Agreements Resulting from Refundings of Tax-Exempt Debt,* which refers to AICPA Statement of Position (SOP) 78-5, *Accounting for Advance Refundings of Tax-Exempt Debt,* is superseded and replaced by the following:

> FASB Statement No. 76, *Extinguishment of Debt,* provides criteria for determining whether the advance refunding should be recognized as an extinguishment of the existing debt at the date of the advance refunding.

11. The reference to SOP 78-5, *Accounting for Advance Refundings of Tax-Exempt Debt,* is deleted from Appendix A of FASB Statement No. 32, *Specialized Accounting and Reporting Principles and Practices in AICPA Statements of Position and Guides on Accounting and Auditing Matters.*

Effective Date and Transition

12. This Statement shall be effective for transactions entered into after December 31, 1983. Earlier

[3]A monetary asset is money or a claim to receive a sum of money that is fixed or determinable without reference to future prices of specific goods or services.

application of this Statement is encouraged for transactions in fiscal years for which annual financial statements have not previously been issued. Furthermore, retroactive application of this Statement to transactions occurring during fiscal years for which annual financial statements have previously been issued is permitted, in which case the effects on restated per share amounts of prior years shall be disclosed.

The provisions of this Statement need not be applied to immaterial items.

This Statement was adopted by the affirmative votes of four members of the Financial Accounting Standards Board. Messrs. Kirk, March, and Mosso dissented.

Messrs. Kirk, March, and Mosso dissent from this Statement because they do not believe that extinguishment of debt accounting and resultant gain or loss recognition should be extended to situations wherein the "debtor is not legally released from being the primary obligor under the debt obligation." (Refer to paragraph 3(c).) They believe such accounting should be limited to situations described in paragraphs 3(a) and 3(b), which are more consistent with both present practice and the concept in paragraph 143 of FASB Concepts Statement No. 3, *Elements of Financial Statements of Business Enterprises,* that "a liability once incurred by an enterprise remains a liability until it is satisfied in another transaction or other event or circumstance affecting the enterprise." In their opinion, the setting aside of assets in trust does not, in and of itself, constitute either the disposition of assets with potential gain or loss recognition or the satisfaction of a liability with potential gain or loss recognition. Though dedicated to a single purpose, assets in the trust continue to be assets (that is, probable future economic benefits) of the debtor until applied to payment of the debt. Likewise, the liability continues to be a liability of the original debtor until satisfied by payment or by agreement of the creditor that the debtor is no longer the primary obligor. Dedicating the assets might ensure that the debt is serviced in timely fashion, but that event alone just matches up cash flows; it does not satisfy, eliminate, or extinguish the obligation. For a debt to be satisfied, the creditor must be satisfied.

Members of the Financial Accounting Standards Board:

Donald J. Kirk, *Chairman*
Frank E. Block
Victor H. Brown
John W. March
David Mosso
Robert T. Sprouse
Ralph E. Walters

Appendix A

BACKGROUND INFORMATION

Introduction

13. This project was undertaken because the FASB was asked to clarify the circumstances that should cause debt to be considered to be extinguished. Specific inquiries focused on a type of transaction discussed in SOP 78-5. That SOP is one of the AICPA documents from which the FASB is extracting specialized accounting and reporting principles and practices[4] and is issuing them in FASB Statements after appropriate due process, as discussed in Statement 32.

14. SOP 78-5 stipulates that, in an advance refunding,[5] a debtor has extinguished its tax-exempt debt if a legal defeasance[6] of that debt has occurred. The SOP also establishes criteria for determining when a debtor would account for a transaction as an extinguishment of its tax-exempt debt even though legal defeasance of the debt has not occurred. Those transactions, which are described in SOP 78-5 and are referred to as "in-substance defeasance," involve placing assets in trust and irrevocably restricting their use solely to satisfy specific debt. The FASB was specifically asked whether the criteria for "in-substance defeasance" of tax-exempt debt could be used in determining if debt other than tax-exempt debt has been extinguished.

[4]The term *specialized* is used to refer to those accounting and reporting principles and practices in AICPA Guides and SOPs that are neither superseded by nor contained in Accounting Research Bulletins, APB Opinions, FASB Statements, or FASB Interpretations.

[5]SOP 78-5 defines an *advance refunding* as a transaction in which refunding debt is issued to replace refunded debt at a specified future date, with the proceeds placed in trust or otherwise restricted to replacing the refunded debt.

[6]*Defeasance* connotes the debtor's release from legal liability.

Issuance of Exposure Drafts

15. An Exposure Draft of a proposed Statement, *Extinguishment of Debt and the Offsetting of Restricted Assets against Related Debt,* was issued on October 13, 1982 with a 60-day comment period. The Exposure Draft proposed a new exception to the general principle in paragraph 7 of APB Opinion No. 10, *Omnibus Opinion—1966,* that assets and liabilities should not be offset unless right of setoff exists. The Exposure Draft also proposed that debt be considered to be extinguished only when the debtor's obligation to the creditor has been satisfied, thereby not permitting "in-substance defeasance" transactions to be accounted for as extinguishments. In addition, the Exposure Draft proposed that debt not be considered to be extinguished if there is any continuing or contingent recourse to the debtor with respect to the debt. The Board received 62 letters of comment in response to the Exposure Draft. Respondents indicated concerns about portions of that Exposure Draft.

16. After considering the comments received, the Board concluded that the Exposure Draft should be revised and reissued for public comment. On July 14, 1983, the Board issued a revised Exposure Draft, *Extinguishment of Debt,* with the following principal changes from the October 1982 Exposure Draft:

a. Debt would be considered extinguished if the debtor is relieved by the creditor from being primarily liable for the debt and is virtually assured that it will not be required to make future payments as guarantor of the debt. Furthermore, even though the creditor does not relieve the debtor of its primary obligation, debt would be considered extinguished if the debtor irrevocably places cash or other assets in a trust to be used solely for satisfying specific debt service requirements of that debt obligation and the debtor is virtually assured that it will not be required to make further payments with respect to the debt that is being recognized as extinguished.
b. No change was proposed to the general principle in Opinion 10 that assets and liabilities should not be offset unless right of setoff exists.

The Board received 75 comment letters on the revised Exposure Draft.

Appendix B

BASIS FOR CONCLUSIONS

17. This appendix discusses the significant comments received on the revised Exposure Draft and the factors deemed significant by members of the Board in reaching the conclusions in this Statement, including alternatives considered and reasons for accepting some and rejecting others. The Board concluded that it could reach an informed decision on the basis of existing information without a public hearing. Individual Board members gave greater weight to some factors than to others.

Assumption of Debt by Third Party

18. The Board believes there is a substantive difference between being primarily liable for an obligation and being only secondarily liable for that obligation. Thus, the Board believes that the assumption by a third party of a debtor's obligation to pay a debt and the concurrent agreement by the creditor to look primarily to that third party and only secondarily to the original debtor is an event that affects the original debtor's accounting for that debt. FASB Concepts Statement No. 3, *Elements of Financial Statements of Business Enterprises,* states in paragraph 143 that "a liability once incurred by an enterprise remains a liability until it is satisfied in another transaction or other event or circumstance affecting the enterprise." The Board believes that being legally released from being the primary obligor for a debt is "another transaction or other event or circumstance affecting the enterprise" that satisfies a debtor's obligation if it is probable that the debtor will not be required to make future payments with respect to the debt. Concepts Statement 3 also recognizes the substantive difference between being primarily and secondarily liable in paragraphs 136 and 137, which state:

> . . . Most liabilities bind a single enterprise or other entity, and those that bind two or more enterprises or other entities are commonly ranked rather than shared. For example, a primary debtor and guarantor may both be obligated for a debt, but they do not have the same obligation—the guarantor must pay only if the primary debtor defaults and thus has a contingent or secondary obligation, which ranks lower than that of the primary debtor.
>
> . . . The probability that a secondary or lower ranked obligation will actually have to be paid must be assessed to apply the definition [of a liability].

Accordingly, the Board stated in paragraph 3(b) of the revised Exposure Draft that a debtor shall consider debt to be extinguished for financial reporting purposes, even though the creditor has not been paid in full, if the debtor is legally released from being the primary obligor under the debt either judicially or by the creditor and is virtually assured that it will not be required to make future payments with respect to that debt under any guarantees. Although the respondents supported the Board's distinction between being primarily liable for an obligation and being only secondarily liable for that obligation, many felt that paragraph 3(b) posed implementation problems in two respects: (a) use of the term *virtually assured* and (b) requirement for a legal release from the creditor.

Use of the Term **Virtually Assured**

19. Many respondents stated that the revised Exposure Draft's requirement that the debtor be *virtually assured* that it will not be required to make future payments with respect to the debt imposes too high a level of confidence when applied to debt assumptions, particularly real estate transactions. Because the debtor legally has only a contingent liability, the accounting for which is addressed by FASB Statement No. 5, *Accounting for Contingencies*, respondents generally suggested that the term *virtually assured* be replaced by the term *probable* as used in Statement 5. The Board concurs with those respondents and has changed paragraph 3(b) accordingly.

Requirement for a Legal Release from the Creditor

20. Some respondents thought the requirement in paragraph 3(b) for a legal release from the creditor was too strict and would change current practice for some real estate transactions. They suggested that debt be considered extinguished whenever a "debt assumption" gives the debtor assurance that it will not be required to make future payments, even though the debtor is not legally released from being the primary obligor under the debt obligation. The Board decided to retain the requirement for a legal release in paragraph 3(b) because that subparagraph focuses on the important distinction between being primarily liable for an obligation and being only secondarily liable for that obligation. The Board specifies in paragraphs 3(c) and 4 the conditions for an extinguishment when the debtor continues to be legally liable as the primary obligor. The Board believes third party debt "assumptions" without a legal release from the primary obligation effectively create for the debtor a receivable from the third party for the payments expected to be made by that party on the debtor's behalf.

21. Some respondents asked whether a legal release by the creditor is necessary for the extinguishment of nonrecourse debt that is assumed in conjunction with the sale of assets that serve as sole collateral for that debt. The Board believes that such a sale and related assumption effectively accomplish a "legal release" for the seller/debtor and has added a footnote to paragraph 3(b) to clarify that point.

In-Substance Defeasance and Extinguishment of Debt

22. The Board believes that, in general, recognizing the effect of in-substance defeasance transactions as extinguishing debt is reasonable because settlement in cash is not always feasible and the effect of an in-substance defeasance is essentially the same. Accordingly, the Board believes that, in certain circumstances, debt should be considered extinguished for financial reporting purposes even though the debtor is not legally released from being the primary obligor under the debt obligation. In the July 1983 revised Exposure Draft, the Board proposed in paragraph 3(c) that debt be considered extinguished if the debtor irrevocably places cash or other assets in a trust to be used solely for satisfying specific debt service requirements of a debt obligation and the debtor is virtually assured that it would not be required to make future payments with respect to that debt, even though the debtor was not legally released from being the primary obligor under the debt obligation. The revised Exposure Draft also would have imposed certain restrictions in paragraph 4 regarding the nature of the assets held by the trust to reinforce the high threshold imposed by the Board for recognizing an extinguishment of debt when the debtor remains the primary obligor.

23. Most respondents supported the concept that an in-substance defeasance is an extinguishment of debt for financial reporting purposes, although some respondents suggested changes to the revised Exposure Draft. Many respondents commented about (a) the requirement in paragraph 3(c) that the debtor be *virtually assured* and (b) the requirement in paragraph 4 that the trust assets be *essentially risk free*.

Use of the Term **Virtually Assured**

24. The respondents' most frequent concern was about the use of the term *virtually assured*. Some perceived the term as requiring a level of confidence so near absolute certainty as to be unworkable—a level that goes beyond the intent of the conceptual framework. Others objected to use of the term because it was undefined and no substantive guidance was provided to apply it. Still other respondents were concerned because they saw no need for a new term. Many respondents recommended that the Board use terms that are used in other accounting standards, such as *probable* and *remote* as defined in Statement 5.

25. The Board agreed that use of a new term is unnecessary and changed paragraph 3(c) to use the term *remote*. In doing so, the Board does not intend to lower the high threshold of this Statement for in-substance defeasance transactions; the term *remote* establishes a high test and the trust assets are still required by paragraph 4 to be essentially risk free.

26. As discussed above, paragraph 3(c) of this Statement now requires that the possibility be remote that the debtor will be required to make

future payments with respect to the debt. That requires an assessment of the circumstances at the date of the in-substance defeasance transaction regarding the likelihood of the debtor's being required to make such future payments. A requirement for such future payments by the debtor could arise due to an inadequacy of trust assets attributable not only to a failure to realize scheduled cash flows from trust assets but also to an acceleration of the debt's maturity due to a violation of a covenant of the debt issue being extinguished or, if cross-default provisions exist, of a covenant of another debt issue.

27. The Board believes that a debtor's placing assets irrevocably in a trust to be used solely to pay the debtor's obligation is "another transaction or other event or circumstance affecting the enterprise" (refer to paragraph 18 of this Statement) that effectively satisfies a debtor's obligation if the possibility is remote that the debtor will be required to make further payments with respect to the debt that is being recognized as extinguished. The Board believes that such an arrangement ensures that the debtor has no "probable future sacrifices of economic benefits arising from present obligations of a particular entity to transfer assets or provide services to other entities in the future as a result of past transactions or events," the definition of a liability in paragraph 28 of Concepts Statement 3 (footnote references omitted). Thus, the Board believes that the debtor should remove the liability for the debt from its balance sheet.

Requirement That Assets Be Essentially Risk Free

28. The revised Exposure Draft stipulated two requirements that the assets placed in trust in an in-substance defeasance had to meet:

a. They are monetary assets that are *essentially risk free* as to collection of interest and principal.
b. Their maturities do not extend beyond the maturity of the debt that is being extinguished.

Those requirements were intended to eliminate nearly all risk that the trust would not have funds available to meet the scheduled interest and principal repayments on the defeased debt.

29. Most respondents requested further guidance about what assets should be considered essentially risk free. Some respondents considered investments in direct obligations of the U.S. government as the only monetary assets that could be considered essentially risk free because they alone were cited as an example. Some respondents disputed the Board's view that an investment in highly rated corporate securities should not be considered to be essentially risk free as to collection of interest and principal. A few respondents asked whether trust assets also had to be risk free with respect to the timing of the collection of principal and interest.

30. The Board believes the concept of in-substance defeasance requires trust assets to be risk free not only with respect to the collection of principal and interest but also with respect to the timing of those collections. Paragraph 4(a) clarifies that point.

31. Although it would prefer to provide only broad guidance as to what monetary assets are to be considered essentially risk free under paragraph 4, the Board decided that specific guidance is needed to preserve the high threshold it considers necessary for in-substance defeasance transactions. Accordingly, the Board stipulated that, for debt denominated in U.S. dollars, essentially risk-free assets shall be limited to direct obligations of the U.S. government, obligations guaranteed by the U.S. government, and securities collateralized by U.S. government obligations, provided such monetary assets are essentially risk free as to both the collection of interest and principal and the timing of such collections. The Board believes that securities that are backed by U.S. government obligations as collateral should be considered essentially risk free as to the timing of the collection of interest and principal only if an arrangement exists in which the interest and principal payments on the collateral generally flow immediately through to the holder of the security, for example, as in a closed trust.

32. Several respondents asked the Board to provide guidance regarding the in-substance defeasance of debt denominated in foreign currencies and whether the trust can use forward contracts to protect against exchange rate changes if only U.S. government obligations qualify for trust assets. The Board concluded that neither U.S. government obligations nor such forward contracts would be essentially risk-free monetary assets to defease debt denominated in foreign currencies. Consequently, paragraph 4(a) requires that the trust invest only in monetary assets that are denominated in the currency in which the debt is payable. The level of assurance with respect to the collection of interest and principal, and the timing of such collections, from monetary assets denominated in foreign currencies should be equivalent to that required for the in-substance defeasance of debt denominated in U.S. dollars.

33. Some respondents questioned the accounting for reacquiring in the marketplace debt that has previously been extinguished due to an in-substance defeasance, specifically whether further gain or loss could be recognized. The Board believes that, if a debtor purchases its own debt securities that have

previously been recognized as extinguished in an in-substance defeasance, the debtor is making an investment in the future cash flows from the trust and should report its investment as an asset in its balance sheet. The debtor should not be considered to be reextinguishing its debt. Thus, no gain or loss should be recognized from such purchase of those debt securities.

The Need for Matching Maturities and the Effect of Reinvestment Earnings

34. Inherent in the concept of in-substance defeasance is the matching of the trust's cash inflows from its investments with its cash outflows for paying periodic interest payments and principal repayment. The Board believes that matching of assured inflows with scheduled outflows is important so that the trust is not exposed to any risk on reinvesting premature inflows. SOP 78-5 recognized the importance of matching cash flows and required that "the funds used to consummate the advance refunding [be] invested in qualifying securities with maturities that approximate the debt service requirements of the trust." As a surrogate for requiring the matching of trust inflows and outflows, the revised Exposure Draft (a) required that the monetary assets held by the trust have maturities not extending beyond the maturity of the debt being extinguished and (b) excluded from the defeasance computation any earnings from the reinvestment of the scheduled net inflows from maturity of the trust's initial investments. That exclusion was intended to preclude significant mismatching of cash flows. Some respondents incorrectly interpreted the exclusion of reinvestment earnings as a prohibition against compounding interest.

35. The Board has decided to address more directly the need for matching the trust's cash flows. Consequently, paragraph 4(b) requires that the monetary assets held by the trust provide cash flows (from interest and maturity) that approximately coincide, as to timing and amount, with the scheduled interest and principal payments on the debt that is being extinguished. That requirement will serve to minimize significant reinvestment earnings.

Partial Defeasances

36. Some respondents asked whether the in-substance defeasance of only a portion of the obligations under a debt issue was permitted by the revised Exposure Draft. Although in-substance defeasance transactions have typically, as the Board understands, comprehended an entire debt issue, the Board believes that conceptually there is no impediment to a partial in-substance defeasance. In a partial in-substance defeasance, the debt considered extinguished will be either (a) a pro rata portion of all remaining interest and principal repayment obligations of the debt issue or (b) the principal and interest payments for a specific debt instrument (such as a serial bond with a specific scheduled maturity). Thus, the debtor cannot recognize a partial defeasance of the obligation for only the interest payments or for only the principal repayment.

Applicability

37. Several respondents asked whether the revised Exposure Draft permits the in-substance defeasance of convertible debentures, debt with floating interest rates, and capitalized lease obligations. Respondents also asked whether the document was intended to apply to preferred stock with mandatory redemptions provisions. The Board has concluded that the provisions for an extinguishment in paragraphs 3(b) and 3(c) do not apply to convertible debentures due to the inseparability of the debt and the conversion option and to the fact that there will be no obligation to pay if the debentures are converted. The Board decided that the circumstances for an extinguishment of debt described in paragraph 3(c) apply only to debt with specified maturities and fixed payment schedules; consequently, the provisions for in-substance defeasance in paragraph 3(c) do not apply to debt with floating interest rates because of the uncertainty of the future debt service requirements. However, the provisions for in-substance defeasance generally apply to capitalized lease obligations if the lease obligation has a specified maturity and a fixed payment schedule. The Statement does not apply to preferred stock with mandatory redemption provisions because the Board has not addressed whether such preferred stock should be accounted for as debt.

38. Consistent with Opinion 26, this Statement does not address extinguishment through conversion of debt by exchange for equity securities of the debtor pursuant to conversion privileges provided in the terms of the debt at issuance. In addition, this Statement amends Opinion 26 to apply to an extinguishment of debt whether or not the extinguishment was early, consistent with FASB Statement No. 4, *Reporting Gains and Losses from Extinguishment of Debt,* which also applies to all debt extinguishments. The Board understands that extinguishments at scheduled maturity would seldom involve gain or loss under Opinion 26.

Disclosure Requirements

39. Some respondents opposed the requirement in the revised Exposure Draft to continue disclosing in the financial statements of subsequent periods information about debt that had been extinguished in a defeasance transaction until that specific debt issue no longer remained outstanding. Those

respondents considered the continuing disclosures to be unnecessary, particularly since Statement 5 addresses disclosures for contingencies. Those respondents also considered the continuing disclosures to contradict the substance of the transaction and to raise doubt about the propriety of recognizing an extinguishment. The Board believes that, because an outstanding defeased debt issue is not reported in the balance sheet, continuing disclosures are needed in the notes to provide useful information to the creditors and investors about that debt issue. Accordingly, the requirement was retained.

Offsetting Assets against Liabilities

40. Several respondents to the revised Exposure Draft commented about offsetting assets against liabilities, though it was apparent that some respondents had confused *offsetting* with *extinguishment*. In the Board's view, *offsetting* is a display issue—how recognized assets and recognized liabilities should be presented in a balance sheet (or how other recognized elements should be displayed in a basic financial statement). In contrast, *extinguishment* is a recognition issue—whether an asset or a liability exists and whether continued recognition is warranted in the basic financial statements. This Statement addresses when debt ceases to be a liability that warrants continued recognition in the balance sheet.

41. The Board has concluded that there is no need to create an additional exception to the general principle in Opinion 10 that the offsetting of assets and liabilities in the balance sheet is improper except if a right of setoff exists.

AICPA Statement of Position 78-5 and Extinguishment of Tax-Exempt Debt

42. The Board considered whether SOP 78-5 contains specialized accounting and reporting principles and practices that warrant extraction and issuance in an FASB Statement, as discussed in paragraph 13. "In-substance defeasance" transactions that have been accounted for as extinguishments under SOP 78-5 generally will continue to be accounted for as extinguishments under this Statement; thus, the related provisions of the SOP are no longer "specialized." Other provisions of the SOP relate to accounting by state and local governmental units and are not being extracted pending resolution of the FASB's involvement with standard setting for those entities. (Refer to paragraph 8 of Statement 32.) The Board believes the remainder of SOP 78-5 consists of descriptions and examples of refunding transactions that are not specialized accounting and reporting principles; thus, extraction is not warranted. Accordingly, this Statement deletes the reference to SOP 78-5 from Appendix A of Statement 32.

Amendment to Statement 22

43. Statement 22 addresses changes to lease agreements resulting from refundings of tax-exempt debt and specifies different accounting depending on whether the refunding is accounted for as an extinguishment. Footnote 1 of that Statement refers to SOP 78-5 for "descriptions of advance refundings that are and are not accounted for as early extinguishments of debt." This Statement amends Statement 22 to replace the footnote reference to SOP 78-5 with a reference to this Statement.

Effective Date and Transition

44. Several respondents suggested that the final Statement should permit, but not require, retroactive implementation and restatement of previously issued financial statements for transactions occurring in years previously reported so that similar transactions can be reported similarly. The Board concurs in that recommendation and has modified the Statement accordingly.

Statement of Financial Accounting Standards No. 77 Reporting by Transferors for Transfers of Receivables with Recourse

STATUS

Issued: December 1983

Effective Date: For transfers of receivables with recourse entered into after December 31, 1983

Affects: Amends FAS 13, paragraph 20
Amends FAS 32, Appendix A

Affected by: No other pronouncements

SUMMARY

This Statement specifies that a transferor ordinarily should report a sale of receivables with recourse transaction as a sale if (a) the transferor surrenders its control of the future economic benefits relating to the receivables, (b) the transferor can reasonably estimate its obligation under the recourse provisions, and (c) the transferee cannot return the receivables to the transferor except pursuant to the recourse provisions. If those conditions do not exist, the amount of proceeds from the transfer should be reported as a liability.

This Statement is effective for transfers made after December 31, 1983, including those made pursuant to earlier agreements. It amends a minor provision of FASB Statement No. 13, *Accounting for Leases.*

This project was undertaken in response to an Issues Paper prepared by the AICPA and in considering an AICPA Statement of Position, both of which addressed transfers of receivables with recourse. The conclusions of this Statement differ from those reached by the AICPA. It is not expected to change predominant practice generally except that gain or loss on a transfer will be recognized when a transfer is made rather than over the period the receivables remain outstanding.

Statement of Financial Accounting Standards No. 77
Reporting by Transferors for Transfers of Receivables with Recourse

CONTENTS

INTRODUCTION

1. An enterprise may borrow money and pledge receivables as collateral for a loan or may sell receivables with **recourse.**[1] Whether the enterprise pledges or sells the receivables, either the borrower-seller or the lender-purchaser may thereafter bill and collect the receivables, or they may share the servicing of the receivables. Sales of receivables with recourse may have many of the same characteristics as loans collateralized by receivables, and, therefore, the FASB has been asked to clarify the circumstances under which a transfer of receivables with recourse should be recognized by the transferor as a loan or, alternatively, as a sale.

2. In Statement of Position (SOP) 74-6, *Recognition of Profit on Sales of Receivables with Recourse,* the AICPA addressed profit or loss recognition on receivables sold with recourse (paragraph 16). This Statement reaches a conclusion different from that in SOP 74-6.

SCOPE

3. This Statement establishes standards of financial accounting and reporting by transferors for transfers of receivables with recourse that purport to be sales of receivables. It also applies to participation agreements (that is, transfers of specified interests in a particular receivable or pool of receivables) that provide for recourse, factoring agreements that provide for recourse, and sales or assignments with recourse of leases or property subject to leases that were accounted for as sales-type or direct financing leases.[2]

4. This Statement does not address accounting and reporting by transferees, nor does it address accounting and reporting of loans collateralized by receivables, for which the receivables and the loan are reported on the borrower's balance sheet. It also does not address the accounting and reporting for exchanges of substantially identical receivables or exchanges of other assets.

STANDARDS OF FINANCIAL ACCOUNTING AND REPORTING

Transfer Recognized as a Sale

5. A transfer of receivables with recourse shall be recognized as a sale if all of the following conditions are met:

a. *The transferor surrenders control of the future economic benefits embodied in the receivables.* Control has not been surrendered if the transferor has an option[3] to repurchase the receivables at a later date.
b. *The transferor's obligation under the recourse provisions can be reasonably estimated.* Lack of experience with receivables with characteristics similar to those being transferred or other factors

[1]Terms defined in the glossary (Appendix A) are in **boldface type** the first time they appear in this Statement.

[2]Refer to FASB Statement No. 13, *Accounting for Leases,* paragraph 6(b), and also paragraph 20, which is amended by this Statement.

[3]A right of first refusal based on a bona fide offer by an unrelated third party ordinarily is not an option to repurchase.

that affect a determination at the transfer date of the collectibility of the receivables may impair the ability to make a reasonable estimate of the probable bad debt losses and related costs of collections and repossessions. A transfer of receivables shall not be recognized as a sale if collectibility of the receivables and related costs of collection and repossession are not subject to reasonable estimation.

c. *The transferee cannot require the transferor to repurchase the receivables except pursuant to the recourse provisions.*[4]

6. If a transfer qualifies to be recognized as a sale, all **probable adjustments** in connection with the recourse obligations to the transferor shall be accrued in accordance with FASB Statement No. 5, *Accounting for Contingencies.* The difference between (a) the sales price (adjusted for the accrual for probable adjustments) and (b) the **net receivables** shall be recognized as a gain or loss on the sale of receivables. If receivables are sold with servicing retained and the stated servicing fee rate differs materially from a **current (normal) servicing fee rate** or no servicing fee is specified, the sales price shall be adjusted to provide for a normal servicing fee in each subsequent servicing period, which shall not be less than the estimated servicing costs.

7. If a transfer qualifies to be recognized as a sale and the sales price is subject to change during the term of the receivables because of a floating interest rate provision, the sales price shall be estimated using an appropriate market interest rate[5] at the transfer date. Subsequent changes in interest rates from the rate used at the transfer date shall be considered changes in the estimate of the sales price and not as interest cost or interest income. The effect shall be reported in income in the period the interest rate changes in accordance with paragraph 31 of APB Opinion No. 20, *Accounting Changes.*

Transfer Recognized as a Liability

8. If any of the conditions in paragraph 5 is not met, the amount of the proceeds from the transfer of receivables shall be reported as a liability.

Disclosures

9. For transfers of receivables with recourse reported as sales, the transferor's financial statements shall disclose[6] (a) the proceeds to the transferor during each period for which an income statement is presented and (b), if the information is available, the balance of the receivables transferred that remain uncollected at the date of each balance sheet presented.[7]

Amendments to Other Pronouncements

10. The reference to SOP 74-6, *Recognition of Profit on Sales of Receivables with Recourse,* is deleted from Appendix A of FASB Statement No. 32, *Specialized Accounting and Reporting Principles and Practices in AICPA Statements of Position and Guides on Accounting and Auditing Matters.* The last sentence of paragraph 20 of FASB Statement No. 13, *Accounting for Leases,* is amended to read as follows:

> Any profit or loss on the sale or assignment shall be recognized at the time of the transaction except that (a) if the sale or assignment is between related parties, the provisions of paragraphs 29 and 30 shall be applied or (b) if the sale or assignment is with recourse, it shall be accounted for in accordance with FASB Statement No. 77, *Reporting by Transferors for Transfers of Receivables with Recourse.*

Effective Date and Transition

11. This Statement shall be effective for transfers of receivables with recourse after December 31, 1983, including transfers after that date that are made pursuant to the terms of earlier agreements. Earlier application of this Statement is encouraged in annual or interim financial statements that have not been previously issued.

The provisions of this Statement need not be applied to immaterial items.

[4]Some transfer agreements require or permit the transferor to repurchase transferred receivables when the amount of outstanding receivables is minor to keep the cost of servicing those receivables from becoming unreasonable. If those reversionary interests are not significant to the transferor, their existence alone does not preclude a transfer from being recognized as a sale.

[5]Paragraph 14 of APB Opinion No. 21, *Interest on Receivables and Payables,* discusses the considerations that may affect the selection of a rate.

[6]As discussed in paragraph 39 of this Statement, other pronouncements also require disclosures about transfers of receivables with recourse. This Statement does not alter those already existing disclosure requirements.

[7]Aggregation of similar transfers may be appropriate for these disclosures.

This Statement was adopted by the affirmative votes of five members of the Financial Accounting Standards Board. Messrs. March and Sprouse dissented.

Mr. March and Mr. Sprouse dissent because they believe that a transfer of receivables with recourse, hypothecated receivables, and a loan collateralized by receivables are merely different forms of financing transactions having substantially similar substance. They believe that the proceeds from those transactions, including transfer of receivables with recourse, should be reported initially as liabilities and that the particular form of the transaction should not produce significantly different accounting results. That conclusion is in general agreement with the recommendations of the AICPA in the March 1980 Issues Paper, "Accounting for Transfers of Receivables with Recourse."

Whether an asset of the transferor (the receivables) has or has not been eliminated by a transfer with recourse should depend on whether the "probable future economic benefits" embodied in the asset have in fact been transferred or whether those benefits continue to reside with the transferor. To have an asset, a business enterprise must control its probable future economic benefits to the extent that the enterprise is in a position to receive those benefits to the general exclusion of others. Probable future benefits and related inherent risks cannot be dissociated; bearing related risks is necessarily implicit in controlling future benefits. When a holdback, dealer's reserve, or other arrangement provides adequate protection against loss to the transferee, the economic benefits and inherent risks related to receivables transferred with recourse are controlled by the transferor—that is, the benefits and risks accrue to the transferor to the general exclusion of others. The financial well-being of the transferor is improved by collection; the well-being of the transferee is unchanged. Either the receivables are collected or the transferor makes them good; presumably, the transferee is indifferent as to who pays.

Those circumstances are critically different from the sale of a nonmonetary asset (for example, a manufactured product) with an implied or express warranty. The "probable future economic benefit" embodied in a nonmonetary asset is its service potential—the ability of a truck to provide transportation, a building to provide shelter, a machine to perform a particular function, a product to be resold, and so forth. The purchaser controls the future benefit of a nonmonetary asset to the general exclusion of others to the extent that it alone is in a position of utilizing or failing to utilize that service potential effectively in its attempt to generate future cash flows. The purchaser's future cash flows associated with a nonmonetary asset generally are neither contractually limited nor guaranteed by the seller. Accordingly, it is the financial well-being of the purchaser, not that of the seller, that is primarily affected by the future cash flows associated with nonmonetary assets. If that is not the case, the transfer of a nonmonetary asset also should not be recognized as a sale. For example, FASB Statement No. 48, *Revenue Recognition When Right of Return Exists,* precludes recognition of a "sale" of a product if the purchaser's obligation is contingent on resale, or if the seller has significant obligations for future performance to bring about resale, or if the buyer's obligation to the seller is changed in the event of theft or damage of the product. In those circumstances the financial well-being of the seller is still at stake and a "sale" of its product is not recognized for accounting purposes.

The sheer ability to estimate the amount of product that will not be resold in the future or the amount of transferred receivables that will not be collected in the future is not a sufficient condition to recognize a "sale." The critical question is whose financial well-being—that is, whose future benefits and related inherent risks—is at stake. In the case of transfers of receivables with recourse, the analogy with hypothecated receivables and a loan collateralized by receivables is clear; a sale of product with an implied or express product warranty is readily distinguishable.

That the transferor controls the probable future economic benefits—that is, that the transferor is the primary beneficiary of future benefits and is the bearer of related future risks—seems especially clear if the agreement stipulates that the "sales price" is subject to adjustment due to prepayments by debtors or to a floating interest rate provision. The transferor's retention of credit risk through the recourse provisions and retention of interest rate risk through the floating interest rate provision leave the transferor in a position whose economic substance is indistinguishable from that of a borrower with a floating interest rate loan.

Having concluded that the transfer of receivables with recourse does not trigger the elimination of the transferor's asset, it follows that the receipt of proceeds from the transferee creates a liability on the part of the transferor. As a result of the transaction, the transferor incurs a present obligation for future cash payments to the transferee. The substance of the obligation is the same whether the cash payments are collected primarily from the receivables (if the transferee services the receivables) or entirely from the transferor (if the transferor services the receivables).

Appendix A

GLOSSARY

12. For purposes of this Statement, certain terms are defined as follows:

Current (normal) servicing fee rate
A servicing fee rate that is representative of servicing fee rates most commonly used in comparable servicing agreements covering similar types of receivables.

Net receivables
The gross amount of the receivables, including finance and service charges and fees owed by the debtor included in the recorded receivables, less related unearned finance and service charges and fees.

Probable adjustments
Adjustments for (a) failure of the debtors to pay when due, for example, estimated bad debt losses and related costs of collections and repossessions accounted for in accordance with Statement 5, (b) estimated effects of prepayments, and (c) defects in the eligibility of the transferred receivables, for example, defects in the legal title of the transferred receivables.

Recourse
The right of a transferee of receivables to receive payment from the transferor of those receivables for (a) failure of the debtors to pay when due, (b) the effects of prepayments, or (c) adjustments resulting from defects in the eligibility of the transferred receivables.

Appendix B

BACKGROUND INFORMATION

13. Recourse provisions vary. Examples of various forms of recourse provisions include the following:

a. Under some recourse provisions, the transferor must reimburse the transferee in full (by repurchasing the receivable or otherwise) in the event of default by the debtor regardless of whether property that is collateral for the receivable is recovered from the debtor.
b. Under other recourse provisions, the transferee is obligated to repossess property that is collateral for the receivable from the debtor and return it to the transferor before the transferor is compelled to perform under the recourse provisions. Sometimes a recourse provision is effective only if the property is reacquired within a stated period of time, such as 90 days. The recourse provision may require that the transferee sell the repossessed property, apply the proceeds against the balance of the receivable, and charge the transferor for any remaining receivable balance.
c. Under some recourse provisions, the right of the transferee to demand payment from the transferor is limited to a stipulated maximum dollar amount or percentage of transferred receivables. Depending on the type of receivables transferred and the value of collateral securing the receivables, transfers that appear to be with limited recourse actually might be with full recourse. For example, in the absence of unusual economic conditions or of a material unexpected loss, a recourse provision for an amount in excess of the anticipated loss might assure that the transferee will recover its investment and will suffer no loss from defaults on the receivables.
d. Sometimes the transferee may retain a portion of the transfer price of the receivables until the receivables are collected to ensure performance by the transferor under the recourse provisions. The retained amounts are generally referred to as dealers' reserves or holdbacks, and the terms governing them usually are specified in the transfer agreement. The amount of a dealer's reserve may be determined by the transferee based on previous experience in transactions with the transferor or others. Amounts retained in a dealer's reserve account are sometimes remitted to the transferor as the reserve account exceeds stipulated percentages of the uncollected receivables. Agreements may provide that the dealer's reserve be charged for credit losses if a debtor defaults. Some agreements may limit the transferee's recourse to the transferor to the amount set aside in the dealer's reserve. The holdback is the mechanism by which the recourse provisions in the agreement are effected; they are part of the transfer price and are a receivable of the transferor from the transferee if the transfer qualifies to be recognized as a sale.

14. Sometimes the transferor guarantees the transferee a minimum specified return or profit on the transfer. For example, the transferor guarantees that the transferee will earn 10 percent after deducting all expenses and credit losses. Those arrangements may require the transferor to provide the required yield in addition to repurchasing a defaulted receivable. Prepayments by debtors also might reduce the transferee's yield and require the transferor to pay the difference.

15. The transfer agreement normally stipulates which party is to perform the administration and routine collection functions (usually referred to as "servicing") for the receivables that are transferred. If the transferor retains the servicing function when receivables are sold, the agreement may require the transferee to pay a servicing fee. Even though the agreement does not specifically provide for compensation to the party performing the servicing, com-

pensation for the future servicing will nevertheless be reflected in the transfer price of the receivables.

16. In the early 1970s, the AICPA became concerned about diverse practices in recognizing income on transfers of receivables with recourse. SOP 74-6 was developed to eliminate the use of two different accounting methods by which transferors recognized gains and losses on transfers of receivables with recourse. Some transferors were treating transfers of receivables with recourse as completed transactions and recognizing gains or losses at the time of transfer. Other transferors were deferring gains and recognizing them in income in a systematic manner over the terms of the transferred receivables. Transferors who deferred gains generally recognized losses immediately at the time of transfer, although some deferred both gains and losses. SOP 74-6 concluded that both gains and losses should be deferred and recognized in income in a systematic manner over the terms of the transferred receivables. SOP 74-6 did not address the presentation of transfers of receivables with recourse in the transferor's balance sheet, which was addressed in an Issues Paper, "Accounting for Transfers of Receivables with Recourse," prepared by the Accounting Standards Division of the AICPA in March 1980. That Issues Paper addressed the types of transfers that should be accounted for as loans and those that should be accounted for as sales. Even though SOP 74-6 was issued in 1974 and the Issues Paper in 1980, the Board was advised that practice continued to be diverse.

17. The Board issued an Exposure Draft of a proposed Statement, *Accounting and Reporting by Transferors for Transfers of Receivables with Recourse,* on November 18, 1981 and received 120 comment letters. Respondents indicated concerns about portions of that Exposure Draft. After considering the comments received, the Board concluded that the Exposure Draft should be revised and reissued for public comment. On August 31, 1982, the Board issued a revised Exposure Draft, *Reporting by Transferors for Transfers of Receivables with Recourse,* with the following principal changes from the November 1981 Exposure Draft:

a. A transfer of receivables with recourse could qualify to be recognized as a sale even though the transfer price is subject to adjustment because of a floating interest rate provision.
b. The "economic substance" criterion contained in paragraph 7(d) of the November 1981 Exposure Draft was not carried forward. That criterion was intended to have the same meaning as that of a similar criterion in FASB Statement No. 48, *Revenue Recognition When Right of Return Exists,* relating primarily to enterprises that exist "on paper," that is, buyers that have little or no physical facilities or employees. It prevents an enterprise from recognizing sales revenue on transactions with parties that the sellers have established primarily for the purpose of recognizing such sales revenue. However, many respondents interpreted the "economic substance" criterion in the November 1981 Exposure Draft as requiring all transfers to a wholly owned unconsolidated finance subsidiary to be reported as loans. Those respondents argued that such reporting effectively would produce results similar to consolidation of the finance subsidiary. The issue of consolidation of finance subsidiaries is beyond the scope of this Statement and will be considered in another project on the Board's agenda addressing consolidation and the equity method of accounting.

The Board received 72 comment letters on the revised Exposure Draft.

Appendix C

BASIS FOR CONCLUSIONS

Appendix C

BASIS FOR CONCLUSIONS

Introduction

18. This appendix discusses the significant comments received on the revised Exposure Draft and the factors deemed significant by members of the Board in reaching the conclusions in this Statement, including alternatives considered and reasons for accepting some and rejecting others. The Board concluded that it could reach an informed decision on the basis of existing information without a public hearing. Individual Board members gave greater weight to some factors than to others.

Board's Conclusions versus SOP 74-6

19. The conclusions in SOP 74-6 were based on two reasons: (a) transfers of receivables with recourse have many of the same characteristics that collateralized loans have and (b) the transferor's retention of risk through the recourse provision precludes immediate recognition of gain or loss. Those reasons also were used to support the conclusions in the AICPA's March 1980 Issues Paper on transfers of receivables with recourse. Although transfers of receivables with recourse may have many of the same characteristics that collateralized loans have, the Board concluded that a substantive distinction can and should be made between transactions accounted for as sales of receivables with recourse and loans collateralized by receivables. Further, the Board believes that the retention of risk should not automatically disqualify a transaction for recognition as a sale if the retained risk can be reasonably estimated.

Scope

20. Some respondents expressed concern that the concepts of this Statement would be extended in practice to types of transactions not addressed by it, including types of transactions already addressed by other pronouncements. The scope of this Statement is specified by paragraphs 3 and 4. Except as discussed in paragraph 10, this Statement does not modify any of the provisions of any Accounting Research Bulletin, APB Opinion, or FASB Statement and does not apply to transactions for which the accounting or reporting is specified by those pronouncements. In addition, the provisions of other pronouncements apply to transfers of receivables with recourse as appropriate. For example, the requirements for elimination of intercompany gain or loss of ARB No. 51, *Consolidated Financial Statements,* and APB Opinion No. 18, *The Equity Method of Accounting for Investments in Common Stock,* apply to a transfer of receivables to a finance subsidiary.

Analysis of Transaction

21. In ascertaining whether a transfer of receivables with recourse should be recognized as a loan or a sale, determinations must be made as to (a) the party that controls the future economic benefits embodied in the receivables and (b) each party's rights and obligations resulting from the transfer. To have an asset, a business enterprise must control the future economic benefits embodied in that asset and generally must be able to deny or regulate access to those benefits by others. "The enterprise having an asset is the one that can exchange it, use it to produce goods or services, exact a price for others' use of it, use it to settle liabilities, hold it, or perhaps distribute it to owners."[8] A seller of receivables with recourse surrenders its control of the related future economic benefits embodied in the receivables, receives cash in exchange for the receivables, and incurs a contractual obligation under the recourse provisions. Sometimes the transferor also acquires a contractual right to receive additional cash or incurs a contractual obligation to pay cash pursuant to the terms of the transfer agreement if the interest rate used to discount the receivables fluctuates subsequent to the transfer date. A borrower retains both the future economic benefits and the risks embodied in the pledged receivables and has an obligation to repay the loan.

Retention of Risk

22. Several respondents stated that the transferor's retention of risk through the recourse provisions should preclude recognizing a transfer of receivables with recourse as a sale. As justification, some of them referred to Statement 48, which specifies how an enterprise should account for sales of its product in which the buyer has a right to return the product. The provisions of Statement 48 were extracted from SOP 75-1, *Revenue Recognition When Right of Return Exists,* without substantive change. Both Statement 48 and SOP 75-1 state six conditions that must be met to recognize revenue at the time of a sale. Neither precludes recognition of a sale merely because some risks are retained, such as credit risk and guarantees of quality. The Board believes that some risk retention by itself is not sufficient to prohibit recognizing a sale. The Board also believes that the basic conclusion of Statement 48 is consistent with the provisions of this Statement. Statement 48 provides that when a right of return exists a seller shall recognize a transaction as a sale only if the amount of future returns can be reasonably estimated. Consistent with that, this Statement requires that the transferor of receivables with recourse must

[8]FASB Concepts Statement No. 3, *Elements of Financial Statements of Business Enterprises,* par. 116.

be able to reasonably estimate its obligations under the recourse provisions before the transfer can qualify to be reported as a sale.

23. The Board believes that the uncertainty relating to the transferor's probable future sacrifice under the recourse provisions is similar to the uncertainty relating to a bad debt allowance or to a warranty obligation. Paragraph 23 of Statement 5 states that "inability to make a reasonable estimate of the amount of loss from uncollectible receivables . . . precludes accrual [of the loss] and may, if there is significant uncertainty as to collection, suggest that the installment method, the cost recovery method, or some other method of revenue recognition be used. . . ." Similarly, paragraph 25 of Statement 5 states that "inability to make a reasonable estimate of the amount of a warranty obligation at the time of sale because of significant uncertainty about possible claims . . . precludes accrual [of the warranty obligation] and, if the range of possible loss is wide, may raise a question about whether a sale should be recorded prior to expiration of the warranty period. . . ." Accordingly, the transfer should not be recognized as a sale if the collectibility of the receivables and related costs of collection and repossession are not subject to reasonable estimation.

24. The Board believes that application of a criterion that retention of risks of ownership automatically precludes reporting a sale would require transferors to report liabilities that do not exist in many instances. Risks retained by the seller should be recognized either by accruing the costs to be incurred or, if those costs are not subject to reasonable estimation, by postponing recognition of the sale. In most transactions, the benefits of ownership can be transferred even though some of the risks of ownership are retained. The Board believes, therefore, that the benefits and risks of ownership are separable. Although recognition of a sale may be postponed because the amount of risk retained cannot be reasonably estimated, that postponement is not because risk is retained per se. Rather, postponing recognition of the sale is prudent reporting in the circumstances because of the significance of the uncertainty of the amount of the obligation for the risk retained. Reporting the sale in one period and the costs of the risk retained in a later period when those costs become reasonably estimable would not provide reliable information about enterprise performance in either period because costs would not be charged against revenues of the period benefited.

Control of Future Economic Benefits

25. Another basic question is whether the probable future economic benefits embodied in the receivables have been disposed of by the transferor. An asset is disposed of if a transaction results in either a loss of its future economic benefits or relinquishing control over the future economic benefits. In a transfer of receivables with recourse, the transferor has received the future economic benefits (cash) relating to the receivables. Accordingly, the significant question is whether the transferor has relinquished control.

26. In considering whether control has been relinquished, paragraph 115 of FASB Concepts Statement No. 3, *Elements of Financial Statements of Business Enterprises,* is pertinent. It states in part:

> Every asset is an asset of some entity; moreover, no asset can simultaneously be an asset of more than one entity. . . . To have an asset, a business enterprise must control future economic benefit to the extent that it can benefit from the asset and generally can deny or regulate access to that benefit by others. . . .

To apply that concept to a transfer of receivables with recourse, determining what constitutes control over a receivable is necessary. Although the legal document relating to a transfer of receivables may specify which party has legal title to the related future economic benefits, paragraph 119 of Concepts Statement 3 states that ". . . legal enforceability of a right is not an indispensible prerequisite for an enterprise to have an asset if the enterprise otherwise will probably obtain the future economic benefit involved."

27. One process that might be used to determine who has control is to consider what could happen if interest rates declined subsequent to the date of transfer. The enterprise that controls the receivables could transfer the receivables at a higher price or lower interest rate. Thus, if the transferor has an option to reacquire the receivables at a later date, the transferor would retain an essential characteristic of control of the asset and incur an obligation (a loan).

28. Some respondents suggested that an option to reacquire the receivables at fair value should not preclude sale treatment for a transfer that meets the other criteria in paragraph 5 of this Statement. However, the Board believes that the transferor retains control if it has the right to repurchase the receivables at a later date or to negotiate new favorable changes in the terms of the transfer. Accordingly, the Board believes that such a transfer should not be recognized as a sale.

29. A view has been expressed that the transferor (seller) of receivables remains the primary beneficiary of the future benefits (cash inflows) embodied in the receivables; thus, they remain the transferor's assets. The Board believes that view is not generally observed in accounting. In general business practice, assets are sold subject to implied or express warranty of fitness to perform an intended function—food is fit for human consumption; an automobile

is capable of transporting passengers. Receivables are expected to generate cash, which is their only function. A seller benefits when an asset sold performs as intended, for there will be no sacrifice under the warranty. In practice, however, the buyer-owner is considered the primary beneficiary of the future benefits embodied in the asset, including future cash inflows. The Board believes that a logical extension of the concept that the seller is the primary beneficiary of the future benefits would defer recognition of the sale of an asset until it has performed its intended function. It might also suggest that the guarantor of a debt should record a liability and an asset of equal amount until the debtor settles the debt under a theory that the guarantor is the primary beneficiary.

Transferor's Liability to the Transferee

30. In considering whether the transferor is obligated to repay the transfer proceeds, paragraph 28 of Concepts Statement 3 is relevant. That paragraph states:

> Liabilities are probable future sacrifices of economic benefits arising from present obligations of a particular entity to transfer assets or provide services to other entities in the future as a result of past transactions or events. [Footnote references omitted.]

Further, Concepts Statement 3 discusses the substantive difference between being primarily obligated and being secondarily obligated for a liability:

> . . . Most liabilities bind a single enterprise or other entity, and those that bind two or more enterprises or other entities are commonly ranked rather than shared. For example, a primary debtor and a guarantor may both be obligated for a debt, but they do not have the same obligation—the guarantor must pay only if the primary debtor defaults and thus has a contingent or secondary obligation, which ranks lower than that of the primary debtor. [paragraph 136]
>
> . . . The probability that a secondary or lower ranked obligation will actually have to be paid must be assessed to apply the definition. [paragraph 137]

In a transfer of receivables that qualifies as a sale, the transferor is a guarantor to the extent of the recourse provision and therefore is secondarily obligated. The debtors on the receivables transferred are the primary debtors; the transferor must pay only if the primary debtors do not and only to the extent of the recourse provisions—not the entire amount of proceeds received on receivables transferred.

31. The Board believes that the transferor's probable future sacrifice is limited to the estimated payments under the recourse provisions. The transferor does not have a present obligation to return the transfer proceeds (that is, to repay a loan); rather, the transferor has an obligation to perform under the recourse provisions. To the extent specified by the recourse provisions, the transferor has a contingent liability and, in effect, is a guarantor that the underlying debtors will pay the amounts when due. In that respect, the transferor's obligation is similar to a seller's obligation when there is a right of return (paragraph 22) or to a warranty obligation (paragraph 23).

Transferee's Put Option

32. If the transferee can require the transferor to repurchase the receivables other than through the recourse provisions because of a "put" option, the Board believes that the possibility of the transferee's exercising its option and thereby reversing the transfer creates significant uncertainty about disposition of the receivables by the transferor. A transferee's put option, in the Board's view, therefore requires postponement of recognizing the transfer as a sale.

33. Some respondents disagreed with the Board and indicated that reporting a transfer as a loan if the transferee has a put option is inconsistent because the transferor in fact surrenders control of the asset. They suggested that the transferor should recognize the transfer as a sale and allocate the transfer price between the sale of the receivable and the writing of a put option, with the put option accounted for on a mark-to-market or higher-of-cost-or-market approach. The Board believes that implementing the suggestion to allocate the transfer price between the sale of the receivables and the writing of a put option would depend on the ability to make a reasonable estimate of the value of the put option. Although a put option may have some characteristics similar to a standby commitment or an interest rate futures contract, factors such as the varying terms and quality of receivables sold, terms of recourse provisions, and a floating interest rate provision in many cases preclude an objective measurement of the value of the put option, and it has no market. Therefore, the Board believes the suggestion is incapable of being implemented and rejected it.

34. Some respondents further suggested that if a transferor desires to avoid reporting a transfer as a sale (for example, to avoid loss recognition), the transferor could include a put option (or a call option) in the transfer agreement solely for that reason with terms to ensure that the option would never be exercised. Paragraph 160 of FASB Concepts Statement No. 2, *Qualitative Characteristics of Accounting Information,* states that "the quality of reliability and, in particular, of representational faithfulness leaves no room for accounting representations that subordinate substance to form." If

respondents were suggesting options without economic substance, the Board believes that professional judgment can eliminate abuses.

Interest Rate Changes

35. Some respondents suggested that a provision for adjustments to the sales price pursuant to a floating interest rate provision creates an unresolved sales price that is subject to the swings of the economy and, therefore, the transfer of receivables should not be recognized as a sale. The Board believes that the issue of the ability to estimate the ultimate sales price is separate from the question of whether a sale took place (asset derecognition). If the transfer qualifies to be recognized as a sale, the Board concluded that the adjustments from changes in interest rates are changes in the estimate of the sales price and should be reported in income in the period the interest rate changes in accordance with paragraph 31 of Opinion 20.[9]

36. A provision for adjustments to the sales price pursuant to a floating interest rate provision is a pricing consideration related to the time value of money. The Board believes that such adjustments do not automatically change the nature of the transaction from a sale to a borrowing but rather that those adjustments arise from a contractual right or contractual obligation created when the transferor and transferee enter into the transfer agreement. Further, the right acquired and the obligation incurred by the transferor are conditional because they require the occurrence of an event (change in interest rate) before the transferor will receive additional cash from the transferee or will pay additional cash to the transferee. Accordingly, the Board concluded that the nature of the transfer does not hinge on whether there is a floating interest rate provision.

Cost-Benefit Considerations

37. In addition to the conceptual reasons for reporting transfers of receivables with recourse as sales, the Board believes that cost-benefit considerations also favor that approach. Established accounting practice for some time has been to report many transfers of receivables with recourse as sales. There is little evidence that financial statements would be more useful if transfers of receivables were reported as collateralized loans rather than sales. On the other hand, the Board has received a number of indications that modifying current practice to require loan treatment would have significant attendant costs. It has been argued that, at a minimum, many existing transfer agreements (including those with captive finance companies) would have to be revised and that financings might be adversely impacted by requiring loan treatment. While those types of arguments, per se, are not persuasive, they add support to retaining what the Board believes is a conceptually sound accounting method.

Disclosures

38. The Board believes that an enterprise should disclose information about sales of receivables with recourse in its financial statements. A sale of receivables with recourse has the effect of accelerating cash receipts that, in the normal course of collections, would extend over a period of time. In that respect, a sale of receivables with recourse has much the same effect on cash flows as a loan collateralized by receivables. Accordingly, disclosure of the proceeds from transfers of receivables with recourse reported as sales and the balance outstanding would help users of financial statements in assessing the enterprise's ability to generate favorable cash flows, in evaluating its financing activities, and in assessing its liquidity or solvency. The Board chose not to specify the format of the disclosure.

39. Some respondents suggested that the Board should expand the disclosure requirements of this Statement for sales of receivables with recourse to include other disclosures, such as the amount of any contingent liability, significant terms of the transfer agreement and recourse provisions, related party transactions, and so forth. The Board believes that most of those disclosures, if material, are already required by other authoritative pronouncements. The following are examples:

a. Paragraph 12 of Statement 5 requires disclosure of the nature and amount of certain contingencies even though the possibility of loss may be remote. Examples of such contingencies include guarantees to repurchase receivables under recourse provisions (or, in some cases, to repurchase the repossessed property underlying the receivables) and guarantees of a specified return or yield on the transferred receivables, including a floating interest rate provision. Paragraph 17 of Statement 5 also requires disclosure of contingencies that might result in gains.
b. Paragraph 26 of APB Opinion No. 30, *Reporting the Results of Operations—Reporting the Effects of Disposal of a Segment of a Business, and Extraordinary, Unusual and Infrequently Occurring Events and Transactions,* requires that the nature and financial effects of a material transaction that occurs infrequently be disclosed

[9]That conclusion is consistent with the Board's conclusion in paragraph 17(b) of Statement 13 as amended by FASB Statement No. 29, *Determining Contingent Rentals,* that a lease having contingent rentals based on the prime interest rate may qualify as a sales-type lease. In such a case, the lease is reported as a sales-type lease with contingent rentals based on the prime rate in effect at the inception of the lease included in minimum lease payments, the present value of which is reported as the sales price. Amounts related to subsequent changes in the prime rate are included in income as they are accruable.

as a separate component of income from continuing operations on the face of the income statement or in the notes thereto. A material gain or loss on a sale of receivables with recourse might qualify.

c. Paragraph 33 of Opinion 20 requires disclosure of the effect on income before extraordinary items, net income, and related per share amounts of the current period for a change in estimate that affects several future periods, such as a change in interest rates if the sales price of a sale of receivables with recourse is subject to a floating interest rate provision.
d. Paragraph 2 of FASB Statement No. 57, *Related Party Disclosures,* requires disclosure of material related party transactions, such as a sale of receivables with recourse by a parent company or an affiliate to an unconsolidated finance subsidiary.

This Statement does not alter already existing disclosure requirements. Accordingly, the Board believes that it is unnecessary to duplicate those requirements in this Statement.

Statement of Financial Accounting Standards No. 78
Classification of Obligations That Are Callable by the Creditor

an amendment of ARB No. 43, Chapter 3A

STATUS

Issued: December 1983

Effective Date: For financial statements for fiscal years beginning after December 15, 1983 and for interim accounting periods within those fiscal years

Affects: Amends ARB 43, Chapter 3A, paragraph 7

Affected by: No other pronouncements

SUMMARY

This Statement amends ARB No. 43, Chapter 3A, "Current Assets and Current Liabilities," to specify the balance sheet classification of obligations that, by their terms, are or will be due on demand within one year (or operating cycle, if longer) from the balance sheet date. It also specifies the classification of long-term obligations that are or will be callable by the creditor either because the debtor's violation of a provision of the debt agreement at the balance sheet date makes the obligation callable or because the violation, if not cured within a specified grace period, will make the obligation callable. Such callable obligations are to be classified as current liabilities unless one of the following conditions is met:

a. The creditor has waived or subsequently lost the right to demand repayment for more than one year (or operating cycle, if longer) from the balance sheet date.
b. For long-term obligations containing a grace period within which the debtor may cure the violation, it is probable that the violation will be cured within that period, thus preventing the obligation from becoming callable.

Short-term obligations expected to be refinanced on a long-term basis, including those callable obligations discussed herein, continue to be classified in accordance with FASB Statement No. 6, *Classification of Short-Term Obligations Expected to Be Refinanced.* This Statement is effective for financial statements for fiscal years beginning after December 15, 1983 and for interim periods within those fiscal years.

Statement of Financial Accounting Standards No. 78
Classification of Obligations That Are Callable by the Creditor

an amendment of ARB No. 43, Chapter 3A

CONTENTS

INTRODUCTION

1. The FASB has been requested to clarify how obligations that are callable[1] by the creditor should be presented by the debtor in a balance sheet in which liabilities are classified as current or noncurrent. Specifically, the issue is whether an obligation should be classified as a current liability if the debtor is in violation of a provision[2] of a long-term debt agreement at the balance sheet date and (a) the violation makes the obligation callable by the creditor within one year from the balance sheet date or (b) the violation, if not cured within a specified grace period, will make the obligation callable within one year from the balance sheet date (or operating cycle in both cases, if longer). In considering that issue, the Board also decided to clarify whether an obligation should be classified as a current liability if the obligation, by its terms, is or will be due on demand within that period.

2. Some obligations, by their terms, are due on demand; that is, they are callable by the creditor. Other obligations have scheduled future maturities but nevertheless are callable if the debtor is in violation of certain provisions of the related debt agreement or if the creditor has the right to accelerate those maturities for other reasons. Some obligations with scheduled future maturities will become callable if an existing violation of a provision of the debt agreement is not cured within a specified grace period.

3. Paragraph 7 of ARB No. 43, Chapter 3A, "Current Assets and Current Liabilities," discusses obligations that should be considered current liabilities and states:

> The term *current liabilities* is used principally to designate obligations whose liquidation is reasonably expected to require the use of existing resources properly classifiable as current assets, or the creation of other current liabilities. . . .

FASB Statement No. 6, *Classification of Short-Term Obligations Expected to Be Refinanced,* amends ARB 43, Chapter 3A to require short-term obligations arising from transactions in the normal course of business that are due in customary terms (such as trade payables, advance collections, and accrued expenses) to be classified as current liabilities in all instances. Other short-term obligations are excluded from current liabilities under that Statement only if the enterprise intends to refinance the obligation on a long-term basis and such intent is supported by an ability to consummate the refinancing, demonstrated by either a financing agreement or the post-balance-sheet-date issuance of a long-term obligation or equity securities. Neither ARB 43, Chapter 3A nor Statement 6, however, discusses how obligations that are callable by the creditor should be presented in a classified balance sheet. As a result of differing views on such presentation, the same types of obligations have been classified differently by various entities in similar circumstances.

[1]An obligation is *callable* at a given date if the creditor has the right at that date to demand, or to give notice of its intention to demand, repayment of the obligation owed to it by the debtor.

[2]A *violation of a provision* is the failure to meet a condition in a debt agreement or a breach of a provision in the agreement for which compliance is objectively determinable, whether or not a grace period is allowed or the creditor is required to give notice of its intention to demand repayment.

APPLICABILITY AND SCOPE

4. This Statement applies to obligations reported in classified balance sheets and to disclosures made about maturities of obligations reported in both classified and unclassified balance sheets. It does not modify Statement 6 or FASB Statement No. 47, *Disclosure of Long-Term Obligations.*

STANDARDS OF FINANCIAL ACCOUNTING AND REPORTING

Amendment to ARB No. 43, Chapter 3A

5. The following sentences and footnotes are added to the end of paragraph 7 of ARB 43, Chapter 3A:

> The current liability classification is also intended to include obligations that, by their terms, are due on demand or will be due on demand within one year (or operating cycle, if longer) from the balance sheet date, even though liquidation may not be expected within that period. It is also intended to include long-term obligations that are or will be callable by the creditor either because the debtor's violation of a provision of the debt agreement at the balance sheet date makes the obligation callable or because the violation, if not cured within a specified grace period, will make the obligation callable. Accordingly, such callable obligations shall be classified as current liabilities unless one of the following conditions is met:
>
> a. The creditor has waived* or subsequently lost† the right to demand repayment for more than one year (or operating cycle, if longer) from the balance sheet date.
> b. For long-term obligations containing a grace period within which the debtor may cure the violation, it is probable‡ that the violation will be cured within that period, thus preventing the obligation from becoming callable.
>
> If an obligation under (b) above is classified as a long-term liability (or, in the case of an unclassified balance sheet, is included as a long-term liability in the disclosure of debt maturities), the circumstances shall be disclosed. Short-term obligations that are expected to be refinanced on a long-term basis, including those callable obligations discussed herein, shall be classified in accordance with FASB Statement No. 6, *Classification of Short-Term Obligations Expected to Be Refinanced.*
>
> *If the obligation is callable because of violations of certain provisions of the debt agreement, the creditor needs to waive its right with regard only to those violations.
>
> †For example, the debtor has cured the violation after the balance sheet date and the obligation is not callable at the time the financial statements are issued.
>
> ‡*Probable* is defined in FASB Statement No. 5, *Accounting for Contingencies,* as "likely to occur" and is used in the same sense in this paragraph.

Effective Date and Transition

6. This Statement shall be effective for financial statements for fiscal years beginning after December 15, 1983 and for interim accounting periods within those fiscal years. Earlier application is encouraged in financial statements that have not previously been issued. This Statement may be, but is not required to be, applied retroactively to previously issued financial statements.

The provisions of this Statement need not be applied to immaterial items.

This Statement was adopted by the affirmative votes of four members of the Financial Accounting Standards Board. Messrs. Block, Brown, and Walters dissented.

Messrs. Block, Brown, and Walters dissent from this Statement because they see no demonstrated need for it and because it is a further step to supplant judgment in financial reporting with arbitrary rules.

The concept of current liabilities, which was adopted over 35 years ago, comprises obligations whose liquidation is *reasonably expected* to consume existing current assets within a certain time span—usually one year. The reasonable-expectation notion implies that judgment should be applied to known facts and circumstances to assess the probable timing of liquidation. Statement 6 pointed out that reasonable expectations in the cases it considered must be supported by intent and evidence of an ability to refinance; but the Board then specifically rejected a strict maturity date (or worst-case) approach "because . . . [it] is not necessarily indicative of the point in time at which that obligation will require the use of the enterprise's funds" and because "that approach would also result in a major change in the concept of current liabilities described in . . . *ARB No. 43* . . ." (Statement 6, paragraph

23). The Board should not now change that concept of current liabilities unless it is able to demonstrate clearly how information that will result from the new concept is expected to be more useful.

This standard is a major change in the concept of current liabilities. It is based on a notion that obligations should be classified as current when they are legally callable within one year, whether or not they are likely to be called. This is a worst-case notion, not a reasonable-expectation notion. While the two notions may often give the same answer, they will not in all cases. It is asserted that this amendment will improve comparability. It will, in fact, cause situations to appear the same even when underlying facts and circumstances are sufficiently different to justify different reasonable expectations. This is not comparability; it is substituting an arbitrary rule for judgment.

Not only will the amendment classify essentially different situations similarly but it will also cause essentially similar situations to be classified differently. For example, the dissenters do not perceive any substantive difference between a demand loan and a loan with a subjective acceleration clause. In each case there must be cause for repayment to be demanded and the lender must not be unreasonable in demanding repayment. Thus, essentially similar liabilities could be classified as current under this Statement and as noncurrent under FASB Technical Bulletin No. 79-3, *Subjective Acceleration Clauses in Long-Term Debt Agreements.*

Members of the Financial Accounting Standards Board:

Donald J. Kirk, *Chairman*
Frank E. Block
Victor H. Brown
John W. March
David Mosso
Robert T. Sprouse
Ralph E. Walters

Appendix

BACKGROUND INFORMATION AND BASIS FOR CONCLUSIONS

Introduction

7. An Exposure Draft of a proposed Statement, *Classification of Obligations That Are Callable by the Creditor,* was issued on July 30, 1982. The Board received 85 comment letters in response to the Exposure Draft. This appendix discusses the significant comments received during the exposure period and the factors deemed significant by the Board in reaching the conclusions in this Statement, including alternatives considered and reasons for accepting some and rejecting others. Individual Board members gave greater weight to some factors than to others. The Board concluded that it could reach an informed decision on the basis of existing information without a public hearing and that the effective date and transition specified in paragraph 6 are advisable in the circumstances.

8. Some have questioned the value of the current asset and current liability classifications which they believe are, at best, crude and superficial indicators of liquidity. Some Board members share those concerns; nonetheless, they recognize that those classifications and the resulting terms and ratios are widely used by creditors and are often incorporated in financing agreements. In addition, they believe that any reconsideration of the broad issue of balance sheet classification should be addressed in the Board's major agenda project on the reporting of income, cash flows, and financial position. Accordingly, until other measures of liquidity or funds flow are determined to be preferable, those Board members agreed to clarify the classification of obligations under the present system by proceeding with this project.

9. Several respondents to the Exposure Draft questioned the need for a Statement to specify how an enterprise should classify an obligation that is callable by the creditor. They stated that the issues covered by the Exposure Draft are narrow, that adequate accounting guidance already exists, and that the exercise of judgment in the context of existing standards, such as ARB 43, Chapter 3A and Statement 6, provides satisfactory results. Other respondents said that the issues covered by the Exposure Draft are important practice problems that need an objective standard for resolution. Comments received on the Exposure Draft and other information received by the Board showed that, under similar facts and circumstances, significant diversity in reporting practices of enterprises exists with respect to the classification of obligations that are callable by the creditor. Accordingly, the Board concluded that this Statement should be issued.

Subjective Acceleration Clauses

10. The Exposure Draft disclosed the Board's intent not to address the effects of a subjective acceleration

clause[3] in classifying a debtor's obligation. However, some respondents recommended that the Statement be expanded to include that issue since they believe it is similar to those currently being addressed and should be resolved in a consistent manner. Other respondents disagreed with the assertion in paragraph 13 of the Exposure Draft that, in principle, a long-term obligation that contains a subjective acceleration clause is callable by the creditor. They indicated that although compliance with the conditions of a subjective acceleration clause may not, by definition, be objectively determinable, such clauses do require the occurrence of some event of noncompliance, regardless of how subjective the determination of that occurrence may be, before the obligation can be called. Furthermore, they stated that the creditor must be "reasonable" in making any subjective determination to sustain a demand for repayment.

11. In determining the effect of a subjective acceleration clause on classification, FASB Technical Bulletin No. 79-3, *Subjective Acceleration Clauses in Long-Term Debt Agreements,* indicates that a debtor should assess the likelihood that the creditor will accelerate the debt's maturity under that clause, whereas this Statement does not permit a debtor to use such an assessment in determining the classification of obligations with objectively determinable provisions. The Board understands, however, that long-term debt agreements containing subjective acceleration clauses also typically include objectively determinable provisions, such as working capital or net worth requirements. The Board believes that creditors and debtors perceive a substantive difference between the rights that a creditor has under such a subjective acceleration clause and the rights that a creditor has under either (a) an obligation that is due on demand or (b) an obligation that is callable because of a violation of an objectively determinable provision. Accordingly, the Board has concluded that this Statement should not modify Bulletin 79-3.

Classification of Various Callable Obligations

12. Most respondents generally favored the proposals in the Exposure Draft and stated that requiring all callable obligations to be classified as current liabilities will promote more comparable financial reporting among various entities. Some respondents, however, disagreed with the classifications that would be required for specific types of callable obligations and implied that classifying those obligations in a similar manner would create an unwarranted uniformity of presentation. Many of the latter respondents expressed the view that a callable obligation should be classified as a noncurrent liability if the creditor has not demanded repayment and there is no indication that the creditor intends to do so within the next year, a situation sometimes referred to as "continued forbearance." They maintained that classifying an obligation based on the discussion of current liabilities in ARB 43, Chapter 3A (particularly the phrase *reasonably expected to require the use of existing resources* in paragraph 7) would provide users of financial statements with the most useful information.

13. The Board believes that, for purposes of balance sheet classification, all obligations that are callable at the creditor's discretion are fundamentally alike and that the merits of setting an objective standard for determining classification outweigh the disadvantages. The Board further believes that assessments of liquidity and financial flexibility and comparisons of current liability positions may be obscured if the balance sheet classification of such callable obligations is based on the debtor's subjective expectations of the creditor's intent. Accordingly, the Board has concluded that, as a general principle, classification of debt in a debtor's balance sheet should be based on facts existing at the balance sheet date rather than on expectations. If the creditor has at that date, or will have within one year (or operating cycle, if longer) from that date, the unilateral right to demand immediate repayment of the debt under any provision of the debt agreement, the Board concluded that the obligation should be classified as a current liability unless (a) one of the conditions in paragraph 5 is met or (b) the obligation is expected to be refinanced on a long-term basis and the provisions of Statement 6 are met.

14. Some respondents disagreed with the provision of the Exposure Draft with respect to an obligation that is not currently callable but will become so within one year (or operating cycle, if longer) from the balance sheet date if an existing violation is not cured within a specified grace period. They stated that the obligation should be classified as a noncurrent liability because the creditor does not have the right to demand repayment at the balance sheet date and will not have that right within one year from the balance sheet date if the violation is cured or if the grace period will not expire within the next year (or operating cycle in both cases, if longer). They argued that requiring an obligation to be classified as a current liability in those circumstances negates the purpose of a grace period, which is to permit the debtor time to cure a violation without being subjected to its consequences. Other respondents agreed with the tentative conclusion of the Exposure Draft that would have required current classifica-

[3]A *subjective acceleration clause* is a provision in a debt agreement that states that the creditor may accelerate the scheduled maturities of the obligation under conditions that are not objectively determinable (for example, "if the debtor fails to maintain satisfactory operations" or "if a material adverse change occurs").

tion in all such circumstances. They stated that classification of such an obligation should not be based on an assessment of the likelihood of future changes in circumstances, that is, on the debtor's assessment of the likelihood that the violation will be cured before the grace period expires.

15. Because the violation will make the obligation callable if conditions existing at the balance sheet date do not change within the grace period, the Board considers such liabilities to be presumptively current. However, because the creditor does not have the right to call the obligation at the balance sheet date, the Board believes that the presumption for current classification can be overcome if it is also probable that the creditor will not obtain such a right under that provision of the debt agreement during the next year (or operating cycle, if longer). Accordingly, the Board concluded that such obligations should be classified as current liabilities unless it is probable that the violation will be cured within the grace period, thus preventing the obligation from becoming callable. This approach calls for an assessment of the probability that the debtor's own actions will prevent the creditor from *obtaining* the unilateral right to demand repayment within the next year; it differs from the approach favored by some respondents to assess the probability that another party (the creditor) will exercise an *existing* right. (Refer to paragraph 12.) Therefore, the Board believes that evaluating the probability that the violation will be cured within the grace period is not in conflict with the general principle described in paragraph 13 or with the classification required for the other types of callable obligations addressed by this Statement.

Other Matters

16. Some respondents suggested that the final Statement should distinguish between the consequences of significant violations of critical conditions and technical violations that are considered not to be of substance. They stated that implementation of the provisions of the Exposure Draft could result in serious and unintended consequences even in situations involving minor and easily correctible violations of debt agreement provisions. Other respondents said that the Exposure Draft substantially removes any auditor judgment in evaluating how an obligation should be classified when a violation exists. The Board believes that drawing a distinction between significant violations of critical conditions and technical violations is not practicable. A violation that a debtor considers to be technical may be considered critical by the creditor. Furthermore, a creditor may choose to use a technical violation as a means to withdraw from its lending relationship with the debtor. The Board believes that if the violation is considered insignificant by the creditor, then the debtor should be able to obtain a waiver as discussed in paragraph 5.

17. Some respondents recommended that the Statement be expanded to address the effect of a violation of a debt agreement that occurs between the balance sheet date and the date the financial statements are issued. Because accounting for events occurring after the balance sheet date is a pervasive issue that is beyond the scope of this project, the Board decided that consideration of that topic should not delay issuance of a final Statement.

18. Some respondents suggested that the Statement require specific disclosures when a debtor is in violation of a debt agreement provision. The Board concluded that existing disclosure practices for obligations classified as current liabilities are adequate. However, the Board decided to require disclosure of the circumstances for situations in which a debtor is in violation of a provision of the loan agreement but classifies the related debt as a long-term liability because it is probable that the violation will be cured within a specified grace period that extends beyond the date that the financial statements are to be issued.

19. Some respondents requested that additional time be provided for enterprises to implement this Statement to enable them to cure existing debt agreement violations or to renegotiate loan provisions that are likely to cause what they consider to be technical violations. The Board extended the effective date to include financial statements for fiscal years beginning after December 15, 1983 to be responsive to those concerns.

Statement of Financial Accounting Standards No. 79
Elimination of Certain Disclosures for Business Combinations by Nonpublic Enterprises

an amendment of APB Opinion No. 16

STATUS

Issued: February 1984

Effective Date: For financial statements for fiscal years beginning after December 15, 1983

Affects: Amends APB 16, paragraph 96

Affected by: No other pronouncements

SUMMARY

This Statement amends APB Opinion No. 16, *Business Combinations,* to eliminate the requirement for nonpublic enterprises to disclose pro forma results of operations for business combinations accounted for by the purchase method. Disclosure requirements for public enterprises are not changed by this Statement.

This Statement is a product of FASB research on financial reporting by private and small public companies. A number of participants in those research efforts cited accounting and disclosure requirements that they believe should not apply to nonpublic enterprises, including the pro forma disclosures prescribed by Opinion 16. The Board has concluded that the costs of providing the pro forma disclosures prescribed by Opinion 16 generally exceed the benefits for the users of nonpublic company financial statements.

This Statement is effective for financial statements for fiscal years beginning after December 15, 1983, with earlier application permitted in financial statements that have not previously been issued.

Statement of Financial Accounting Standards No. 79

Elimination of Certain Disclosures for Business Combinations by Nonpublic Enterprises

an amendment of APB Opinion No. 16

CONTENTS

INTRODUCTION

1. The FASB has undertaken research on financial reporting by private and small public companies to obtain information about the practices and views of managers, financial statement users, and public accountants involved with those companies.[1] A number of participants in those research efforts stated that the requirement to disclose pro forma results of operations for business combinations accounted for by the purchase method was unnecessary and too costly for private companies.

2. Paragraph 96 of APB Opinion No. 16, *Business Combinations,* requires an acquiring enterprise to disclose the following information in financial statements of the period in which a business combination accounted for by the purchase method occurs:

a. Results of operations for the current period as though the enterprises had combined at the beginning of the period, unless the acquisition was at or near the beginning of the period
b. Results of operations for the immediately preceding period as though the enterprises had combined at the beginning of that period if comparative financial statements are presented.

3. The Board has concluded that the disclosures prescribed by paragraph 96 of Opinion 16 should not be required in the financial statements of nonpublic enterprises. The basis for the Board's conclusions is presented in the appendix to this Statement.

STANDARDS OF FINANCIAL ACCOUNTING AND REPORTING

4. Disclosures of pro forma results of operations prescribed in paragraph 96 of Opinion 16 for business combinations accounted for by the purchase method are not required for nonpublic enterprises.

5. For purposes of this Statement, a nonpublic enterprise is an enterprise other than one (a) whose debt or equity securities are traded in a public market, including those traded on a stock exchange or in the over-the-counter market (including securities quoted only locally or regionally), or (b) whose financial statements are filed with a regulatory agency in preparation for the sale of any class of securities.

Amendment to APB Opinion No. 16

6. The following footnote is added to the end of paragraph 96 of Opinion 16:

> *The disclosures prescribed by paragraph 96 are not required in the financial statements of nonpublic enterprises as defined by FASB Statement No. 79, *Elimination of Certain Disclosures for Business Combinations by Nonpublic Enterprises.*

[1]Refer to (a) FASB Invitation to Comment, *Financial Reporting by Private and Small Public Companies,* 1981; (b) FASB Special Report, *Financial Reporting by Privately Owned Companies: Summary of Responses to FASB Invitation to Comment,* 1983; and (c) FASB Research Report, *Financial Reporting by Private Companies: Analysis and Diagnosis,* prepared by A. Rashad Abdel-khalik, 1983.

Effective Date

7. This Statement shall be effective for financial statements for fiscal years beginning after December 15, 1983. Earlier application is permitted in financial statements that have not previously been issued.

This Statement was adopted by the unanimous vote of the seven members of the Financial Accounting Standards Board:

Donald J. Kirk, *Chairman*	Victor H. Brown	David Mosso
Frank E. Block	Raymond C. Lauver	Robert T. Sprouse
	John W. March	

Appendix

BACKGROUND INFORMATION AND BASIS FOR CONCLUSIONS

8. An Exposure Draft of a proposed Statement, *Elimination of Certain Disclosures for Business Combinations by Nonpublic Enterprises,* was issued on October 4, 1983. In response to the Exposure Draft the Board received 46 comment letters, most of which expressed agreement. This appendix discusses factors deemed significant by the Board in reaching the conclusions in this Statement. Individual Board members gave greater weight to some factors than to others. The Board concluded that it could reach an informed decision on the basis of existing information without a public hearing and that the effective date specified in paragraph 7 is advisable in the circumstances.

Responses to Invitation to Comment

9. Many public accountants who responded to the FASB Invitation to Comment, *Financial Reporting by Private and Small Public Companies,* criticized the requirement in Opinion 16 to disclose pro forma information as unnecessary and too costly for nonpublic companies. They stated that those companies are frequently unable to make the pro forma calculations themselves and that the public accountants frequently have to develop the information, which increases the costs of compliance. They also stated that they believe many users of nonpublic company financial statements do not use the information.

10. Responses to the Invitation to Comment indicate that bankers are the primary external users of the financial statements of most nonpublic companies. Bankers responding to the Invitation to Comment did not identify as unnecessary the requirement to disclose pro forma information. However, in follow-up discussions with the FASB's small business advisory group and others, bankers indicated that they do not believe the pro forma disclosures are always necessary.

Costs and Benefits of Providing Pro Forma Information

11. FASB Concepts Statements No. 1, *Objectives of Financial Reporting by Business Enterprises,* and No. 2, *Qualitative Characteristics of Accounting Information,* both recognize the constraint of costs in relation to benefits in considering the information required to be disclosed in financial statements. Paragraph 23 of Concepts Statement 1 states:

> The information provided by financial reporting involves a cost to provide and use, and generally the benefits of information provided should be expected to at least equal the cost involved.

12. The preparation of pro forma disclosures is usually costly because necessary information is not always readily available and the compilation of the disclosures is complex. Most nonpublic companies are relatively small and often do not have extensive accounting expertise. They usually obtain outside assistance to prepare financial reporting disclosures that are required only infrequently. Consequently, the Board believes that the disclosures of pro forma results of operations that are required in the event of business combinations are relatively costly for nonpublic enterprises.

13. The primary users of financial statements of nonpublic enterprises believe that the pro forma disclosures required by Opinion 16 are not always needed, and when the financial statement users want information about a significant business acquisition they frequently desire and obtain different information.

14. The Board's decision to eliminate the pro forma disclosure requirements in Opinion 16 for nonpublic enterprises is based on the assessment that the costs of requiring all nonpublic enterprises to provide those disclosures generally exceed the benefits to the users of nonpublic company financial statements. The disclosure requirements in paragraph 95 of Opinion 16 continue unchanged, including the

requirement to disclose the period for which results of operations of the acquired company are included in the income statement of the acquiring enterprise.

Mutual and Cooperative Organizations

15. Some Board members believe that the definition of nonpublic enterprises in paragraph 5 of this Statement inappropriately includes mutual and cooperative organizations whose financial statements are broadly distributed. Many of those organizations have large numbers of depositors, policyholders, patrons, and other interested parties whose primary source of financial information about the organization may be the financial statements. They believe that those organizations are public companies in a practical sense. They also note that those organizations are frequently involved in business combinations.

16. A few respondents to the Exposure Draft agreed with the Board members' views described in paragraph 15 and stated that the definition of a nonpublic enterprise in paragraph 5 should be changed to exclude mutual and cooperative organizations whose financial statements are broadly distributed. The Board decided not to address mutual and cooperative organizations separately in this Statement because it would raise additional issues (including those referred to in paragraph 17) that might impede its efforts to provide timely relief from pro forma disclosure requirements for nonpublic enterprises.

Applicability to Public Enterprises

17. A few respondents to the Exposure Draft stated that the pro forma disclosures required by Opinion 16 are not cost effective for public enterprises, and should be eliminated for those enterprises also. The Board did not address the cost effectiveness of the pro forma disclosures required by Opinion 16 for public enterprises. Such an undertaking would necessarily involve broader issues, including a review of other disclosures required for business combinations by public companies. The Board believes that such a review would unnecessarily delay providing relief from pro forma disclosure requirements for nonpublic enterprises.

(The next page is 3021.)

Interpretations

TABLE OF CONTENTS

Table of Contents

Table of Contents

(The next page is 3031.)

FASB Interpretation No. 1
Accounting Changes Related to the Cost of Inventory

an interpretation of APB Opinion No. 20

STATUS

Issued: June 1974

Effective Date: July 1, 1974

Affects: No other pronouncements

Affected by: No other pronouncements

FASB Interpretation No. 1
Accounting Changes Related to the Cost of Inventory

an interpretation of APB Opinion No. 20

INTRODUCTION

1. *Accounting Principles Board (APB) Opinion No. 20* specifies how changes in accounting principles should be reported in financial statements and what is required to justify such changes. Under that Opinion, the term *accounting principle* includes "not only accounting principles and practices but also the methods of applying them."

2. Paragraph 5 of Chapter 4 of *Accounting Research Bulletin No. 43* states "there is a presumption that inventories should be stated at cost," which is "understood to mean acquisition and production cost." It further states that "the exclusion of all overheads from inventory costs does not constitute an accepted accounting procedure."

3. Internal Revenue Service (IRS) Regulation 1.471—11, adopted in September 1973, specifies how certain costs should be treated in determining inventory costs for income tax reporting. Under IRS Reg. 1.471—11, some costs must be included in inventory or excluded from inventory for income tax reporting *regardless* of their treatment for financial reporting. Other costs must be included in inventory or excluded from inventory for income tax reporting *depending upon* their treatment for financial reporting, "but only if such treatment is not inconsistent with generally accepted accounting principles." Among the costs listed in IRS Reg. 1.471—11 in this last category are taxes other than income taxes, depreciation, cost depletion, factory administrative expenses, and certain insurance costs.

4. Taxable income and accounting income are based on common information about transactions of an enterprise. However, the objectives of income determination for Federal income taxation and the objectives of income determination for financial statements of business enterprises are not always the same.

INTERPRETATION

5. A change in composition of the elements of cost included in inventory is an accounting change. A company which makes such a change for financial reporting shall conform to the requirements of *APB Opinion No. 20*, including justifying the change on the basis of preferability as specified by paragraph 16 of *APB Opinion No. 20*. In applying *APB Opinion No. 20*, preferability among accounting principles shall be determined on the basis of whether the new principle constitutes an improvement in financial reporting and not on the basis of the income tax effect alone.

EFFECTIVE DATE

6. This Interpretation shall be effective on July 1, 1974.

This Interpretation was adopted by the unanimous vote of the seven members of the Financial Accounting Standards Board following submission to the members of the Financial Accounting Standards Advisory Council.

Marshall S. Armstrong, *Chairman*
Donald J. Kirk
Arthur L. Litke
Robert E. Mays
John W. Queenan
Walter Schuetze
Robert T. Sprouse

FASB Interpretation No. 2
Imputing Interest on Debt Arrangements Made under the Federal Bankruptcy Act

an interpretation of APB Opinion No. 21

STATUS

Issued: June 1974

Effective Date: For transactions after June 30, 1974

Affects: No other pronouncements

Affected by: Superseded by FAS 15

FASB Interpretation No. 2
Imputing Interest on Debt Arrangements Made under the Federal Bankruptcy Act

an interpretation of APB Opinion No. 21

INTRODUCTION

1. The Financial Accounting Standards Board has been asked to clarify the application of *Accounting Principles Board (APB) Opinion No. 21* with respect to debt issued in connection with arrangements made under the Federal Bankruptcy Act and Federal statutes related thereto (Federal Bankruptcy Act). *APB Opinion No. 21* does not specifically address bankruptcy accounting and this Interpretation is limited in scope to clarification of the application of that Opinion in such circumstances.

2. Paragraph 12 of *APB Opinion No. 21* generally requires that interest be imputed by recording either discount or premium on a note* exchanged for property, goods, or service if (1) interest is not stated, or (2) the stated interest rate is unreasonable, or (3) the stated face amount of the note is materially different from the current cash sales price for the same or similar items or from the market value of the note at the date of the transaction. Likewise, when a note is received or issued for cash and there is at the same time an exchange of rights or privileges, paragraph 11 of *APB Opinion No. 21* requires that accounting recognition be given to the value of the rights or privileges exchanged by establishing a note discount or premium account.

3. Under a reorganization, arrangement, or other provisions of the Federal Bankruptcy Act, modification, alteration, or other changes of notes may be made in satisfaction of creditors' claims. For example, this may be accomplished through a provision for a debtor to issue equity securities and/or notes having a different interest rate and/or principal amount in exchange for existing notes. Likewise, a modification, alteration, or other change may involve an agreement whereby a creditor forgives part of the existing debt or extends the payment period with interest at a rate different from the market rate for the debtor.

INTERPRETATION

4. *APB Opinion No. 21* applies to notes issued by a debtor in a reorganization, arrangement, or under other provisions of the Federal Bankruptcy Act. A note issued under such circumstances in exchange (in whole or in part) for an existing note or notes shall be considered a "note exchanged for property" for purposes of applying *APB Opinion No. 21*. In addition, an existing note shall be considered as originating in a reorganization, arrangement, or under other provisions of the Federal Bankruptcy Act and therefore as being a new note if its original terms are modified, altered, or otherwise changed as a part of the agreement with creditors. Accordingly, interest shall be imputed by applying *APB Opinion No. 21* if the new note does not specify interest or specifies an interest rate which is unreasonable in the particular circumstances.

EFFECTIVE DATE

5. This Interpretation shall be effective for notes issued, modified, altered, or otherwise changed after June 30, 1974 in reorganizations, arrangements, or under other provisions of the Federal Bankruptcy Act.

This Interpretation was adopted by the unanimous vote of the seven members of the Financial Accounting Standards Board following submission to the members of the Financial Accounting Standards Advisory Council.

Marsh[illegible] A[illegible]ong,	Arthur L. Litke	Walter Schuetze
	Robert E. Mays	Robert T. Sprouse
	John W. Queenan	

[illegible]inition of the term "note."

FASB Interpretation No. 3
Accounting for the Cost of Pension Plans Subject to the Employee Retirement Income Security Act of 1974

an interpretation of APB Opinion No. 8

STATUS

Issued: December 1974

Effective Date: December 31, 1974

Affects: No other pronouncements

Affected by: No other pronouncements

FASB Interpretation No. 3
Accounting for the Cost of Pension Plans Subject to the Employee Retirement Income Security Act of 1974

an interpretation of APB Opinion No. 8

INTRODUCTION

1. The Employee Retirement Income Security Act of 1974 (commonly referred to as the Pension Reform Act) became law on September 2, 1974. It is principally concerned with the funding of pension plans, the conditions for employee participation and for vesting of benefits, and the safeguarding of employees' pension rights. Pension plans adopted after January 1, 1974 are subject to the participation, vesting, and funding requirements of the Act for plan years beginning after September 2, 1974. Pension plans in existence on January 1, 1974 are not subject to those requirements until plan years beginning after December 31, 1975, unless earlier compliance is elected.

2. The Financial Accounting Standards Board has analyzed the Act to determine whether there is a need to reconsider *APB Opinion No. 8*, "Accounting for the Cost of Pension Plans." As a result of that analysis, the Board has placed the overall subject of pension accounting, including accounting and reporting by pension trusts, on its technical agenda. Pending completion of that project, the Board is issuing this Interpretation to clarify the accounting for the cost of pension plans covered by the Act.

INTERPRETATION

3. A fundamental concept of *APB Opinion No. 8* is that the annual pension cost to be charged to expense for financial accounting purposes is not necessarily determined by the funding of a pension plan. Therefore, no change in the minimum and maximum limits for the annual provision for pension cost set forth in paragraph 17 of *APB Opinion No. 8* is required as a result of the Act. Compliance with the Act's participation, vesting, or funding requirements may result, however, in a change in the amount of pension cost to be charged to expense periodically for financial accounting purposes even though no change in accounting methods is made. Paragraph 17 of *APB Opinion No. 8* requires that "the entire cost of benefit payments ultimately to be made should be charged against income subsequent to the adoption or amendment of a plan." Consistent with that requirement and within the minimum and maximum limits of paragraph 17 of *APB Opinion No. 8*, any change in pension cost resulting from compliance with the Act shall enter into the determination of periodic provisions for pension expense *subsequent* to the date a plan becomes subject to the Act's participation, vesting, and funding requirements. That date will be determined either by the effective dates prescribed by the Act or by an election of earlier compliance with the requirements of the Act.

4. If, *prior* to the date a plan becomes subject to the Act's participation, vesting, and funding requirements, it appears likely that compliance will have a significant effect in the future on the amount of an enterprise's (a) periodic provision for pension expense, (b) periodic funding of pension costs, or (c) unfunded vested benefits, this fact and an estimate of the effect shall be disclosed in the notes to the financial statements.[1]

5. Based on an analysis of information presently available, the Board does not believe that the Act creates a legal obligation for unfunded pension costs that warrants accounting recognition as a liability pursuant to paragraph 18 of *APB Opinion No. 8* except in the following two respects. First, an enterprise with a plan subject to the Act must fund a minimum amount annually unless a waiver is obtained from the Secretary of the Treasury. If a waiver is not obtained, the amount currently required to be funded shall be recognized as a liability by a charge to pension expense for the period, by a deferred charge, or by a combination of both, whatever is appropriate under *APB Opinion No. 8*. Second, in the event of the termination of a pension plan, the Act imposes a liability on an enterprise. When there is convincing evidence that a pension plan will be terminated, evidenced perhaps by a formal commitment by management to terminate the plan, and the liability on termination will exceed fund assets and related prior accruals, the excess liability shall be accrued. If the amount of the excess liability cannot be reasonably determined, disclosure of the circumstances shall be made in the notes to the financial statements, including an estimate of the possible range of the liability.

EFFECTIVE DATE

6. This Interpretation shall be effective on December 31, 1974.

[1] The Board recognizes that actuarial computations or other information may not be available in time to permit disclosure of an estimate of the effect in notes to financial statements for fiscal periods ending in 1974 or early in 1975. If an estimate cannot be furnished, an explanation shall be provided.

Accounting for the Cost of Pension Plans Subject to the Employee Retirement Income Security Act of 1974

This Interpretation was adopted by the unanimous vote of the seven members of the Financial Accounting Standards Board following submission to the members of the Financial Accounting Standards Advisory Council.

FASB Interpretation No. 4
Applicability of FASB Statement No. 2 to Business Combinations Accounted for by the Purchase Method

an interpretation of FASB Statement No. 2

STATUS

Issued: February 1975

Effective Date: For business combinations initiated after March 31, 1975

Affects: No other pronouncements

Affected by: No other pronouncements

FASB Interpretation No. 4
Applicability of FASB Statement No. 2 to Business Combinations Accounted for by the Purchase Method

an interpretation of FASB Statement No. 2

INTRODUCTION

1. The FASB has been asked to explain the applicability of *FASB Statement No. 2,* "Accounting for Research and Development Costs," to the cost of tangible and intangible assets to be used in research and development activities of an enterprise when those assets are acquired in a business combination accounted for by the purchase method.

2. Broad guidelines about the activities to be classified as research and development and the elements of costs to be identified with those activities are set forth in paragraphs 8-11 of *Statement No. 2.* Paragraph 12 of that Statement provides that research and development costs shall be charged to expense when incurred. However, some costs associated with research and development activities shall be capitalized if the item has alternative future uses in research and development or otherwise (see paragraphs 11(a) and 11(c) of *Statement No. 2*). The cost of materials consumed, the depreciation of equipment and facilities used, and the amortization of intangibles used in research and development activities are research and development costs.

3. *Statement No. 2* amends *APB Opinion No. 17,* "Intangible Assets," to exclude from the scope of that Opinion those research and development costs encompassed by the Statement but does not amend *APB Opinion No. 16,* "Business Combinations." Paragraph 34 of the Statement indicates that paragraph 11(c) is not intended to alter the conclusions in paragraphs 87-88 of *APB Opinion No. 16* regarding allocation of cost to assets acquired in a business combination accounted for by the purchase method.

INTERPRETATION

4. The intent of paragraph 34 of *Statement No. 2* is that the allocation of cost to the identifiable assets of an acquired enterprise shall be made in accordance with the provisions of *APB Opinion No. 16.* Therefore, costs shall be assigned to all identifiable tangible and intangible assets, including any *resulting from* research and development activities of the acquired enterprise or *to be used in* research and development activities of the combined enterprise. Identifiable assets *resulting from* research and development activities of the acquired enterprise might include, for example, patents received or applied for, blueprints, formulas, and specifications or designs for new products or processes. Identifiable assets *to be used in* research and development activities of the combined enterprise might include, for example, materials and supplies, equipment and facilities, and perhaps even a specific research project in process. In either case, the costs to be assigned under *APB Opinion No. 16* are determined from the amount paid by the acquiring enterprise and *not* from the original cost to the acquired enterprise.

5. The subsequent accounting by the combined enterprise for the costs allocated to assets[1] *to be used in* research and development activities shall be determined by reference to *Statement No. 2.* Paragraph 12 of *Statement No. 2* requires that costs identified with research and development activities shall be charged to expense when incurred unless the test of alternative future use in paragraph 11(a) or 11(c) is met. That requirement also applies in a business combination accounted for by the purchase method. Accordingly, costs assigned to assets to be used in a particular research and development project and that have no alternative future use shall be charged to expense at the date of consummation of the combination. Therefore, the accounting for the cost of an item to be used in research and development activities is the same under paragraphs 11 and 12 of *Statement No. 2,* whether the item is purchased singly, or as part of a group of assets, or as part of an entire enterprise in a business combination accounted for by the purchase method.

EFFECTIVE DATE AND TRANSITION

6. Because there have been varying interpretations of *Statement No. 2* with respect to the accounting for the cost of tangible and intangible assets covered by this Interpretation, the Board has concluded that it shall be effective as follows:

a. Application of this Interpretation to business combinations accounted for by the purchase method that are initiated[2] after March 31, 1975 is required.

[1] In this regard, paragraph 69 of *APB Opinion No. 16* states in part that: "The nature of an asset and not the manner of its acquisition determines an acquirer's subsequent accounting for the cost of that asset."

[2] See paragraph 46(a) of *APB Opinion No. 16* for the definition of "initiated."

b. Application of this Interpretation to business combinations accounted for by the purchase method that are initiated prior to April 1, 1975 and consummated after March 31, 1975 is encouraged but is not required. It may be applied selectively to those combinations.
c. Application of this Interpretation to business combinations accounted for by the purchase method that were initiated and consummated prior to April 1, 1975 is encouraged but is not required. If an enterprise chooses to apply this Interpretation to those combinations, it shall be applied retroactively as described in paragraphs 15 and 16 of *Statement No. 2* to *all* business combinations accounted for by the purchase method that were consummated prior to April 1, 1975.

7. This Interpretation shall not be applied prior to the initial application of *Statement No. 2*.

This Interpretation was adopted by the unanimous vote of the seven members of the Financial Accounting Standards Board following submission to the members of the Financial Accounting Standards Advisory Council.

Marshall S. Armstrong, *Chairman*
Oscar S. Gellein
Donald J. Kirk
Arthur L. Litke
Robert E. Mays
Walter Schuetze
Robert T. Sprouse

FASB Interpretation No. 5
Applicability of FASB Statement No. 2 to Development Stage Enterprises

an interpretation of FASB Statement No. 2

STATUS

Issued: February 1975

Effective Date: March 31, 1975 for fiscal periods beginning on or after January 1, 1975

Affects: No other pronouncements

Affected by: Superseded by FAS 7

FASB Interpretation No. 5
Applicability of FASB Statement No. 2 to Development Stage Enterprises

an interpretation of FASB Statement No. 2

INTRODUCTION

1. The FASB has been asked to explain the applicability of *FASB Statement No. 2,* "Accounting for Research and Development Costs," to development stage enterprises.

2. In July 1974 the FASB issued an exposure draft of a proposed Statement titled "Accounting and Reporting by Development Stage Companies, Subsidiaries, Divisions and Other Components." A final Statement on this subject has not yet been issued.

3. Broad guidelines about the activities to be classified as research and development and the elements of costs to be identified with those activities are set forth in paragraphs 8-11 of *Statement No. 2.* Paragraph 12 of that Statement provides that research and development costs shall be charged to expense when incurred. However, some costs associated with research and development activities shall be capitalized if the item has alternative future uses in research and development or otherwise (see paragraphs 11(a) and 11(c) of *Statement No. 2*). The costs of materials consumed, the depreciation of equipment and facilities used, and the amortization of intangibles used in research and development activities are research and development costs.

4. Some development stage enterprises have adopted special accounting practices or forms of financial statement presentation and types of disclosure that are different from those used by established operating enterprises. Special accounting practices include deferral of preoperating costs (sometimes including general and administrative costs and interest costs), non-assignment of dollar amounts to shares of stock issued for consideration other than cash, and offset of revenue against deferred costs. Special financial reporting formats may consist of presentation of statements of (a) assets and unrecovered preoperating costs, (b) liabilities, (c) capital shares, and (d) cash receipts and disbursements; or other formats.

5. Other development stage enterprises prepare financial statements like those of established operating enterprises that present financial position, changes in financial position, or results of operations in conformity with generally accepted accounting principles.

INTERPRETATION

6. *Statement No. 2* applies to the accounting for research and development costs of development stage enterprises whose financial statements present financial position, changes in financial position, or results of operations in conformity with generally accepted accounting principles. *Statement No. 2* also applies to the accounting for research and development costs of a development stage enterprise when the financial statements of that enterprise are included, either by consolidation or by the equity method, in financial statements of others that present financial position, changes in financial position, or results of operations in conformity with generally accepted accounting principles.

7. Pending the issuance of a Statement on the subject (see paragraph 2), a development stage enterprise that issues financial statements that do not purport to present financial position, changes in financial position, or results of operations in conformity with generally accepted accounting principles need not apply *Statement No. 2* in accounting for its research and development costs. However, at such time as a development stage enterprise commences issuing financial statements that present financial position, changes in financial position, or results of operations in conformity with generally accepted accounting principles, *Statement No. 2* shall apply. At that time, the requirement of paragraph 12 of *Statement No. 2* that research and development costs be charged to expense when incurred shall be applied retroactively by prior period adjustment (described in paragraphs 18 and 26 of *APB Opinion No. 9,* "Reporting the Results of Operations"). If financial statements that present financial position, changes in financial position, or results of operations in conformity with generally accepted accounting principles are not also presented for prior periods, the disclosures specified by paragraphs 15 and 16 of *Statement No. 2* and by paragraph 26 of *APB Opinion No. 9* shall be limited to the effects of the prior period adjustment on retained earnings at the beginning of the period.

EFFECTIVE DATE

8. This Interpretation shall be effective on March 31, 1975 for fiscal years beginning on or after January 1, 1975. Earlier application is encouraged,

except that this Interpretation shall not be applied prior to initial application of *Statement No. 2.* When initially applied, this Interpretation shall be applied retroactively as described in paragraphs 15 and 16 of *Statement No. 2.*

This Interpretation was adopted by the unanimous vote of the seven members of the Financial Accounting Standards Board following submission to the members of the Financial Accounting Standards Advisory Council.

Marshall S. Armstrong, *Chairman*
Oscar S. Gellein
Donald J. Kirk
Arthur L. Litke
Robert E. Mays
Walter Schuetze
Robert T. Sprouse

FASB Interpretation No. 6
Applicability of FASB Statement No. 2 to Computer Software

an interpretation of FASB Statement No. 2

STATUS

Issued: February 1975

Effective Date: For fiscal years beginning on or after April 1, 1975

Affects: No other pronouncements

Affected by: No other pronouncements

FASB Interpretation No. 6 Applicability of FASB Statement No. 2 to Computer Software

an interpretation of FASB Statement No. 2

INTRODUCTION

1. The FASB has been asked to explain the applicability of *FASB Statement No. 2,* "Accounting for Research and Development Costs," to costs incurred to obtain or develop computer software.

2. Broad guidelines about the activities to be classified as research and development and the elements of costs to be identified with those activities are set forth in paragraphs 8-11 of *Statement No. 2.* Paragraph 12 of that Statement provides that research and development costs shall be charged to expense when incurred. However, some costs associated with research and development activities shall be capitalized if the item has alternative future uses in research and development or otherwise (see paragraphs 11(a) and 11(c) of *Statement No. 2*). The costs of materials consumed, the depreciation of equipment and facilities used, and the amortization of intangibles used in research and development activities are research and development costs.

3. Paragraph 31 of *Statement No. 2* states the following about the activities for which computer software is developed:

> Computer software is developed for many and diverse uses. Accordingly, in each case the nature of the activity for which the software is being developed should be considered in relation to the guidelines in paragraphs 8-10 to determine whether software costs should be included or excluded [in research and development]. For example, efforts to develop a new or higher level of computer software capability intended for sale (but not under a contractual arrangement) would be a research and development activity encompassed by this Statement.

INTERPRETATION

4. Paragraph 8 of *Statement No. 2* defines research and development to include those activities aimed at developing or significantly improving a product or service (hereinafter "product") or a process or technique (hereinafter "process") whether the product or process is intended for sale or use. A process may be a system whose output is to be sold, leased, or otherwise marketed to others. A process also may be used internally as a part of a manufacturing activity or a service activity where the service itself is marketed. A process may be intended to achieve cost reductions as opposed to revenue generation. Paragraph 8(b) of *Statement No. 2,* however, specifically excludes from research and development activities "market research or market testing activities." Those activities were excluded because they relate to the selling function of an enterprise. Thus, while in the broadest sense of the word, a process may be used in all of an enterprise's activities, the Board's intent in *Statement No. 2* was that the acquisition, development, or improvement of a process by an enterprise for use in its selling or administrative activities be excluded from the definition of research and development activities.[1] To the extent, therefore, that the acquisition, development, or improvement of a process by an enterprise for use in its selling or administrative activities includes costs for computer software, those costs are not research and development costs. Examples of the excluded costs of software are those incurred for development by an airline of a computerized reservation system or for development of a general management information system.

Purchase or Lease of Software

5. Costs incurred to purchase or lease computer software developed by others are not research and development costs under *Statement No. 2* unless the software is for use in research and development activities. When software for use in research and development activities is purchased or leased, its cost shall be accounted for as specified by paragraphs 11(c) and 12 of *Statement No. 2.* That is, the cost shall be charged to expense as incurred unless the software has alternative future uses (in research and development or otherwise).

Internal Development of Software

6. An enterprise may undertake development of computer software internally for its own use or as a product or process to be sold, leased, or otherwise marketed to others for their use. If development is undertaken for the enterprise's own use, the software may be intended, for example, to be used in the research and development activities of the enterprise or as a part of a newly developed or significantly improved product or process.

---

[1] General and administrative costs are discussed in paragraphs 11(e) and 35 of *Statement No. 2.*

7. *Development of software as a product or process to be sold, leased, or otherwise marketed.* Accounting for the cost of developing software for others under a contractual arrangement is beyond the scope of *Statement No. 2,* because paragraph 2 of the Statement indicates that this is part of accounting for contracts in general. On the other hand, if the development of software is undertaken to create a new or significantly improved product or process without any contractual arrangement, costs incurred for *conceptual formulation or the translation of knowledge into a design* would be research and development costs (see paragraph 8 of *Statement No. 2*). Other costs, including those incurred for programming and testing software, are research and development costs when incurred in the search for or the evaluation of product or process alternatives or in the design of a pre-production model. On the other hand, costs for programming and testing are *not* research and development costs when incurred, for example, in routine or other on-going efforts to improve an existing product or adapt a product to a particular requirement or customer's need. Because the term *product* also encompasses services that are sold, leased, or otherwise marketed to others, this paragraph applies, for example, to costs incurred in developing software to be used by a data processing service bureau or a computer time-sharing company.

8. *Development of software to be used in research and development activities.* Developing or significantly improving a product or process that is intended to be sold, leased, or otherwise marketed to others is a research and development activity (see paragraph 8 of *Statement No. 2*). Similarly, developing or significantly improving a process whose output is a product that is intended to be sold, leased, or otherwise marketed to others is a research and development activity. Costs incurred by an enterprise in developing computer software internally for use in its research and development activities are research and development costs and, therefore, shall be charged to expense when incurred.[2] This includes costs incurred during all phases of software development because all of those costs are incurred in a research and development activity.

9. *Development of software to be used as a part of a product or process.* An enterprise may undertake internal development of software as a part of a newly developed or significantly improved product or process that will be sold, leased, or otherwise marketed to others, or as a part of a process whose output is a product that will be sold, leased, or otherwise marketed to others. For example, a manufacturer of computerized typesetting machinery may undertake to develop and use software as a part of that machinery, or a medical laboratory may undertake to develop software for use in a newly developed analytical process. In those cases, costs incurred for *conceptual formulation or the translation of knowledge into a design* would be research and development costs (see paragraph 8 of *Statement No. 2*). Other costs, including those incurred for programming and testing software, are research and development costs when incurred in the search for or the evaluation of product or process alternatives or in the design of a pre-production model. On the other hand, costs for programming and testing are *not* research and development costs when incurred, for example, in routine or other on-going efforts to improve an existing product or process or adapt a product or process to a particular requirement or customer's need.

EFFECTIVE DATE AND TRANSITION

10. Because there have been varying interpretations of *Statement No. 2* with respect to costs of computer software, this Interpretation shall be effective for fiscal years beginning on or after April 1, 1975. Earlier application is encouraged, except that this Interpretation shall not be applied prior to initial application of *Statement No. 2.* Retroactive application of this Interpretation, as described in paragraphs 15 and 16 of *Statement No. 2,* to costs incurred in prior fiscal years is also encouraged but is not required.

This Interpretation was adopted by the unanimous vote of the seven members of the Financial Accounting Standards Board following submission to the members of the Financial Accounting Standards Advisory Council.

Marshall S. Armstrong, *Chairman*	Donald J. Kirk	Walter Schuetze
Oscar S. Gellein	Arthur L. Litke	Robert T. Sprouse
	Robert E. Mays	

[2]The alternative future use test does not apply to the internal development of computer software; paragraph 11(c) of *Statement No. 2* applies only to intangibles *purchased from others.*

FASB Interpretation No. 7
Applying FASB Statement No. 7 in Financial Statements of Established Operating Enterprises

an interpretation of FASB Statement No. 7

STATUS

Issued: October 1975

Effective Date: For fiscal periods beginning on or after January 1, 1976

Affects: No other pronouncements

Affected by: No other pronouncements

FASB Interpretation No. 7
Applying FASB Statement No. 7 in Financial Statements of Established Operating Enterprises

an interpretation of FASB Statement No. 7

INTRODUCTION

1. The FASB has been asked to explain the applicability of *FASB Statement No. 7,* "Accounting and Reporting by Development Stage Enterprises," to an established operating enterprise's financial statements that include the financial statements of a development stage subsidiary or other investee either by consolidation or by the equity method,[1] in terms of the following questions:

a. Must the effect of a change in accounting principle adopted in the separate financial statements of a development stage subsidiary to conform to the provisions of *Statement No. 7* be reflected in the consolidated financial statements of an established operating enterprise that include the financial statements of that subsidiary?
b. If it is appropriate that the established operating enterprise's consolidated financial statements reflect the effect of its development stage subsidiary's change to a new principle of accounting adopted to conform to the provisions of *Statement No. 7,* how should the effect of the change be reported in the established operating enterprise's financial statements?

2. Paragraph 10 of *Statement No. 7* states:

> Financial statements issued by a development stage enterprise shall present financial position, changes in financial position, and results of operations in conformity with the generally accepted accounting principles that apply to established operating enterprises. . . . Generally accepted accounting principles that apply to established operating enterprises shall govern the recognition of revenue by a development stage enterprise and shall determine whether a cost incurred by a development stage enterprise is to be charged to expense when incurred or is to be capitalized or deferred. Accordingly, capitalization or deferral of costs shall be subject to the same assessment of recoverability that would be applicable in an established operating enterprise. For a development stage subsidiary or other investee, the recoverability of costs shall be assessed within the entity for which separate financial statements are being presented.

3. Paragraph 14 of *Statement No. 7* provides for initial application of the Statement as follows:

> This Statement shall be effective for fiscal periods beginning on or after January 1, 1976, although earlier application is encouraged. Thereafter, when financial statements, or financial summaries or other data derived therefrom, are presented for periods prior to the effective date of this Statement, they shall be restated, where necessary, to conform to the provisions of this Statement. Accordingly, any items that would have been accounted for differently by a development stage enterprise if the provisions of paragraph 10 had then been applicable shall be accounted for by prior period adjustment (described in paragraphs 18 and 26 of *APB Opinion No. 9,* "Reporting the Results of Operations").

Further, paragraph 1 of *Statement No. 7* states, in part, that "the transition requirements of this Statement are also applicable to certain established operating enterprises" and makes specific reference to paragraphs 14-16 of *Statement No. 7* by footnote.

INTERPRETATION

4. *Statement No. 7* does not address and does not alter generally accepted accounting principles for the preparation of consolidated financial statements. Therefore, *Statement No. 7* does not address the question of whether the effect of a change in accounting principle adopted in the separate financial statements of a development stage subsidiary to conform to the provisions of that Statement must be reflected in an established operating enterprise's consolidated financial statements that include the financial statements of the subsidiary. However, paragraph 10 of the Statement specifies that "capitalization or deferral of costs shall be subject to the same assessment of recoverability that would be applicable in an established operating enterprise" and further specifies that "for a development stage subsidiary or other investee, the recoverability of costs shall be assessed within the entity for which separate financial statements are being presented." In specifying that the same assessment of recovera-

[1]Hereinafter, in this Interpretation, the term *subsidiary* comprehends all *investees* that are accounted for by the equity method as described in *APB Opinion No. 18,* "The Equity Method of Accounting for Investments in Common Stock." Likewise, the term *consolidated financial statements* hereinafter comprehends the *equity method of accounting.*

bility be made, the Statement does not require that the results of that assessment must necessarily be the same. Further, the Statement does not affect any accepted practice in consolidation of financial statements where the results of an assessment of recoverability of a cost may be different (a) in the broader context of a consolidated enterprise and (b) in the context of a development stage subsidiary standing alone. Under any such accepted practice, a cost incurred by a development stage subsidiary could be assessed as recoverable within the consolidated enterprise and be capitalized or deferred in consolidated financial statements even though that cost is assessed as not being recoverable within a development stage subsidiary and, therefore, charged to expense in the separate financial statements of the development stage subsidiary.

5. Except in the circumstances described in the preceding paragraph, the effect of a development stage subsidiary's change in accounting principle to conform its accounting to the requirements of *Statement No. 7* generally would be reflected in an established operating enterprise's consolidated financial statements that include that subsidiary. When a development stage subsidiary adopts a new accounting principle to conform its accounting to the requirements of *Statement No. 7* and the effect of that subsidiary's accounting change is also reflected in an established operating enterprise's consolidated financial statements that include that subsidiary, the provisions of paragraph 14 of *Statement No. 7* apply. In that situation, the established operating enterprise's consolidated financial statements for periods prior to the period in which the subsidiary's accounting change is made and financial summaries and other data derived therefrom shall be restated by prior period adjustment. It should be noted that *Statement No. 7* does not address the question of how an established operating enterprise should report accounting changes adopted with respect to the revenue and costs related to activities of the parent company or any subsidiaries that are not in the development stage; that question is covered by *APB Opinion No. 20,* "Accounting Changes."

EFFECTIVE DATE

6. This Interpretation shall be effective for fiscal periods beginning on or after January 1, 1976, although earlier application is encouraged, except that it shall not be applied prior to initial application of *Statement No. 7*.

This Interpretation was adopted by the affirmative votes of five members of the Financial Accounting Standards Board following submission to the members of the Financial Accounting Standards Advisory Council. Mr. Mays and Mr. Schuetze dissented.

Mr. Mays and Mr. Schuetze dissent because, in their view, the response to the first of the two questions addressed is ambiguous and serves to create additional uncertainty as to the substance of paragraph 10 of *FASB Statement No. 7*.

If different conclusions as to recoverability can be justified on the basis that the two entities are making their assessments within different "contexts," as paragraph 4 attempts to rationalize, would not a development stage enterprise and an established operating enterprise always have different contexts for such assessments? How, then, they ask, is the development stage enterprise subject to "the same assessment of recoverability that would be applicable in an established operating enterprise" as required by paragraph 10 of the Statement? They find equivocal the explanation that although the assessments must be the same the conclusions may be different.

In their opinion, the only appropriate response to the question in paragraph 1(a) is to require that the effect of the change in principle and the assessment of recoverability in the development stage subsidiary be preserved and reflected in the consolidated financial statements in the same manner as in the subsidiary's financial statements.

Members of the Financial Accounting Standards Board:

Marshall S. Armstrong, *Chairman*
Oscar S. Gellein
Donald J. Kirk
Arthur L. Litke
Robert E. Mays
Walter Schuetze
Robert T. Sprouse

FASB Interpretation No. 8
Classification of a Short-Term Obligation Repaid Prior to Being Replaced by a Long-Term Security

an interpretation of FASB Statement No. 6

STATUS

Issued: January 1976

Effective Date: For balance sheets and statements of changes in financial position dated on or after February 29, 1976

Affects: No other pronouncements

Affected by: No other pronouncements

FASB Interpretation No. 8
Classification of a Short-Term Obligation Repaid Prior to Being Replaced by a Long-Term Security

an interpretation of FASB Statement No. 6

INTRODUCTION

1. *FASB Statement No. 6,* "Classification of Short-Term Obligations Expected to Be Refinanced," specifies that a short-term obligation shall be excluded from current liabilities only if the enterprise intends to refinance the obligation on a long-term basis and before the balance sheet is issued has either (a) completed the refinancing by issuing a long-term obligation or by issuing equity securities or (b) has entered into a financing agreement that permits refinancing on a long-term basis. (See paragraphs 9-11 of the Statement.)

2. The FASB has been asked to clarify whether a short-term obligation should be included in or excluded from current liabilities if it is repaid after the balance sheet date and subsequently replaced by long-term debt before the balance sheet is issued. For example, assume that an enterprise has issued $3,000,000 of short-term commercial paper during the year to finance construction of a plant. At June 30, 1976, the enterprise's fiscal year end, the enterprise intends to refinance the commercial paper by issuing long-term debt. However, because the enterprise temporarily has excess cash, in July 1976 it liquidates $1,000,000 of the commercial paper as the paper matures. In August 1976, the enterprise completes a $6,000,000 long-term debt offering. Later during the month of August, it issues its June 30, 1976 financial statements. The proceeds of the long-term debt offering are to be used to replenish $1,000,000 in working capital, to pay $2,000,000 of commercial paper as it matures in September 1976, and to pay $3,000,000 of construction costs expected to be incurred later that year to complete the plant.

INTERPRETATION

3. The concept that a short-term obligation will not require the use of current assets during the ensuing fiscal year if it is to be excluded from current liabilities underlies *FASB Statement No. 6* (see paragraphs 1, 2, and 20 of the Statement). That concept is also fundamental to Chapter 3A, "Current Assets and Current Liabilities," of *ARB No. 43,* which was not changed by *FASB Statement No. 6* (except as specified in paragraph 16 of the Statement). Repayment of a short-term obligation *before* funds are obtained through a long-term refinancing requires the use of current assets. Therefore, if a short-term obligation is repaid after the balance sheet date and subsequently a long-term obligation or equity securities are issued whose proceeds are used to replenish current assets before the balance sheet is issued, the short-term obligation shall not be excluded from current liabilities at the balance sheet date.

4. In the example described in paragraph 2 above, the $1,000,000 of commercial paper liquidated in July would be classified as a current liability in the enterprise's balance sheet at June 30, 1976. The $2,000,000 of commercial paper liquidated in September 1976 but refinanced by the long-term debt offering in August 1976 would be excluded from current liabilities in balance sheets at the end of June 1976, July 1976, and August 1976.[1] It should be noted that the existence of a financing agreement at the date of issuance of the financial statements rather than a completed financing at that date would not change these classifications.

EFFECTIVE DATE

5. This Interpretation shall be effective February 29, 1976 and shall apply to balance sheets dated on or after that date and to related statements of changes in financial position. Reclassification in financial statements for periods ending prior to February 29, 1976 is permitted but not required.

This Interpretation was adopted by the unanimous vote of the seven members of the Financial Accounting Standards Board following submission to the members of the Financial Accounting Standards Advisory Council.

Marshall S. Armstrong, *Chairman*
Oscar S. Gellein
Donald J. Kirk
Arthur L. Litke
Robert E. Mays
Walter Schuetze
Robert T. Sprouse

[1] At the end of August 1976, $2,000,000 of cash would be excluded from current assets or if included in current assets, a like amount of debt would be classified as a current liability. (See footnote 1 and paragraph 40 of *FASB Statement No. 6.*)

FASB Interpretation No. 9
Applying APB Opinions No. 16 and 17 When a Savings and Loan Association or a Similar Institution Is Acquired in a Business Combination Accounted for by the Purchase Method

an interpretation of APB Opinions No. 16 and 17

STATUS

Issued: February 1976

Effective Date: For business combinations initiated on or after March 1, 1976

Affects: No other pronouncements

Affected by: Paragraphs 8 and 9 amended by FAS 72

FASB Interpretation No. 9
Applying APB Opinions No. 16 and 17 When a Savings and Loan Association or a Similar Institution Is Acquired in a Business Combination Accounted for by the Purchase Method

an interpretation of APB Opinions No. 16 and 17

INTRODUCTION

1. The FASB has been asked to explain how the provisions of *APB Opinions No. 16,* "Business Combinations," and *No. 17,* "Intangible Assets," should be applied to account for the acquisition of a savings and loan association[1] in a business combination accounted for by the purchase method. In this regard, the FASB has been asked (1) whether the *net-spread* method or the *separate-valuation* method is appropriate for determining the amounts assigned to the assets and liabilities of the acquired savings and loan association and (2) whether any cost not assigned to the identifiable assets acquired less liabilities assumed may be amortized using an accelerated method of amortization rather than the straight-line method of amortization.

2. Under the net-spread method, the acquisition of a savings and loan association is viewed as the acquisition of a leveraged whole rather than the acquisition of the separate assets and liabilities of the association. Therefore, if the spread between the rates of interest received on mortgage loans and the rates of interest (often called *dividends* in the industry) paid on savings accounts is normal for the particular market area, the acquired savings and loan association's principal assets and liabilities, i.e., its mortgage loan portfolio and savings accounts, are brought forward at the carrying amounts shown in the financial statements of the acquired association.

3. Under the separate-valuation method, each of the identifiable assets and liabilities of the acquired savings and loan association is accounted for in the consolidated financial statements at an amount based on fair value at the date of acquisition, either individually or by types of assets and types of liabilities.

INTERPRETATION

4. Paragraph 87 of *APB Opinion No. 16* states the general principle that "all identifiable assets acquired, either individually or by type, and liabilities assumed in a business combination . . . should be assigned a portion of the cost of the acquired company, normally equal to their fair values at date of acquisition." Because the net-spread method ignores fair value of individual assets and liabilities or types of assets and liabilities, that method is inappropriate under *APB Opinion No. 16.*

5. Paragraph 88 of *APB Opinion No. 16* provides "general guides for assigning amounts to the individual assets acquired and liabilities assumed, except goodwill." In paragraph 88(b), the general guide for receivables is "present values of amounts to be received determined at appropriate current interest rates, less allowances for uncollectibility and collection costs, if necessary." Ascertaining appropriate current interest rates (and the periods over which the receivables are to be discounted) requires an analysis of the many factors that determine the fair value of the portfolio of loans acquired.

6. In paragraph 88(e), the general guide for "intangible assets which can be identified and named, including contracts, patents, franchises, customer and supplier lists, and favorable leases" is "appraised values." A footnote to that paragraph states that "fair values should be ascribed to specific assets; identifiable assets should not be included in goodwill."

7. In paragraph 88(g), the general guide for "accounts and notes payable, long-term debt, and other claims payable" is "present values of amounts to be paid determined at appropriate current interest rates." That present value for savings deposits due on demand is their face amount plus interest accrued or accruable as of the date of acquisition. That present value for other liabilities assumed, e.g., time savings deposits, borrowings from a Federal Home Loan Bank, or other borrowings, shall be determined by using prevailing interest rates for similar liabilities at the acquisition date.

8. The purchase price paid for a savings and loan association may include an amount for one or more factors, such as the following:

a. Capacity of existing savings accounts and loan

[1] This Interpretation applies not only in the case of the acquisition of a savings and loan association but also in the case of the acquisition of a savings and loan association holding company, a savings and loan branch, or other financial institution having similar types of assets and liabilities.

accounts to generate future income,

b. Capacity of existing savings accounts and loan accounts to generate additional business or new business, and
c. Nature of territory served.

If the amount paid for any such factor can be determined, that amount shall not be included in goodwill. Rather, the amount paid for that separately identified intangible shall be recorded as the cost of the intangible and amortized over its estimated life as specified by *APB Opinion No. 17.* Any portion of the purchase price that cannot be assigned to specifically identifiable tangible and intangible assets acquired (see paragraph 6 above) less liabilities assumed shall be assigned to goodwill.

9. Paragraph 30 of *APB Opinion No. 17* requires that goodwill be amortized using the straight-line method "unless a company demonstrates that another systematic method is more appropriate." An accelerated method would be appropriate and may be used to amortize goodwill when a company demonstrates that (a) the amount assigned to goodwill represents an amount paid for factors such as those listed in paragraph 8 but there is not a satisfactory basis for determining appraised values for the individual factors, and (b) the benefits expected to be received from the factors decline over the expected life of those factors. Unless both (a) and (b) are demonstrated, straight-line amortization shall be used.

EFFECTIVE DATE AND TRANSITION

10. This Interpretation shall be effective for business combinations initiated on or after March 1, 1976. Application to business combinations initiated before March 1, 1976 but consummated on or after that date is encouraged but not required. Application to a business combination consummated prior to March 1, 1976 is permitted if the annual financial statements for the fiscal year in which the business combination was consummated have not yet been issued; if applied to such a combination, financial statements for interim periods of that fiscal year shall be restated if subsequently presented. Previously issued annual financial statements shall not be restated.

This Interpretation was adopted by the unanimous vote of the seven members of the Financial Accounting Standards Board following submission to the members of the Financial Accounting Standards Advisory Council.

Marshall S. Armstrong, *Chairman*
Oscar S. Gellein
Donald J. Kirk
Arthur L. Litke
Robert E. Mays
Walter Schuetze
Robert T. Sprouse

FASB Interpretation No. 10
Application of FASB Statement No. 12 to Personal Financial Statements

an interpretation of FASB Statement No. 12

STATUS

Issued: September 1976

Effective Date: For annual and interim periods ending after October 15, 1976

Affects: No other pronouncements

Affected by: No other pronouncements

FASB Interpretation No. 10
Application of FASB Statement No. 12 to Personal Financial Statements

an interpretation of FASB Statement No. 12

INTRODUCTION

1. Paragraph 5 of *FASB Statement No. 12,* "Accounting for Certain Marketable Securities," enumerates the entities excluded from the scope of the Statement but does not mention individuals. The AICPA Industry Audit Guide, "Audits of Personal Financial Statements," states that ". . . financial statements for individuals should be prepared on a cost basis, in conformity with generally accepted accounting principles" and that ". . . financial information on an estimated value basis is useful . . . as additional financial information" (pages 2 and 3). Further, the Industry Audit Guide recommends a two-column presentation of personal financial statements: "The first column should present financial data on the cost basis, paralleled by a second column presenting estimated values" (page 3). The FASB has been asked to clarify whether in personal financial statements prepared in conformity with generally accepted accounting principles the presentation of marketable equity securities on an estimated value basis in the second column supplants the requirement of paragraph 8 of *FASB Statement No. 12* to carry marketable equity securities at the lower of aggregate cost or aggregate market value in the first column.

INTERPRETATION

2. Personal financial statements prepared in conformity with generally accepted accounting principles are included in the scope of *FASB Statement No. 12.* The presentation of marketable equity securities on an estimated value basis as additional financial information in the second column does not supplant the requirement of paragraph 8 of *FASB Statement No. 12* to carry marketable equity securities at the lower of aggregate cost or aggregate market value in the first column.

EFFECTIVE DATE AND TRANSITION

3. The provisions of this Interpretation shall be effective for financial statements for annual and interim periods ending after October 15, 1976. Earlier application is encouraged in financial statements for annual and interim periods ending before October 16, 1976 that have not been previously issued. This Interpretation shall not be applied retroactively for previously issued annual or interim financial statements.

This Interpretation was adopted by the unanimous vote of the six members of the Financial Accounting Standards Board following submission to the members of the Financial Accounting Standards Advisory Council.

Marshall S. Armstrong, *Chairman*
Oscar S. Gellein
Donald J. Kirk
Arthur L. Litke
Robert E. Mays
Robert T. Sprouse

FASB Interpretation No. 11
Changes in Market Value after the Balance Sheet Date

an interpretation of FASB Statement No. 12

STATUS

Issued: September 1976

Effective Date: For annual and interim periods ending after October 15, 1976

Affects: No other pronouncements

Affected by: No other pronouncements

FASB Interpretation No. 11
Changes in Market Value after the Balance Sheet Date

an interpretation of FASB Statement No. 12

INTRODUCTION

1. Paragraphs 13 and 17[1] of *FASB Statement No. 12,* "Accounting for Certain Marketable Securities," specify in part that "an enterprise's financial statements shall not be adjusted for realized gains or losses or for changes in market prices with respect to marketable equity securities when such gains or losses or changes occur after the date of the financial statements but prior to their issuance, except for situations covered by paragraph 21." The Board has been requested to clarify the meaning of the qualification, *except for situations covered by paragraph 21.*

2. Paragraph 21 of *FASB Statement No. 12* states:

> For those marketable securities for which the effect of a change in carrying amount is included in stockholders' equity rather than in net income (including marketable securities in unclassified balance sheets), a determination must be made as to whether a decline in market value below cost as of the balance sheet date of an individual security is other than temporary. . . . If the decline is judged to be other than temporary, the cost basis of the individual security shall be written down to a new cost basis and the amount of the write-down shall be accounted for as a realized loss. The new cost basis shall not be changed for subsequent recoveries in market value.

The Board also has been asked to elaborate on the amount of the write-down that shall be accounted for as a realized loss when the "decline in market value below cost *as of the balance sheet date* of an individual security is other than temporary." (Emphasis added.)

INTERPRETATION

3. In the case of those marketable securities for which the effect of a change in carrying amount is included in stockholders' equity rather than in net income, the phrase "except for situations covered by paragraph 21" in paragraphs 13 and 17 refers to the provisions in paragraph 21 requiring a decline in market value below cost as of the balance sheet date of an individual security that is determined to be other than temporary to be accounted for as a realized loss. In judging whether a decline in market value below cost at the balance sheet date is other than temporary, a gain or loss realized on subsequent disposition or changes in market price occurring after the date of the financial statements but prior to their issuance shall be taken into consideration along with other factors.

4. The amount of decline in market value below cost of an individual marketable equity security that is accounted for as a realized loss as of the balance sheet date because the decline is other than temporary shall not exceed the difference between market value at the balance sheet date and cost of the marketable equity security. Further declines in market value after the balance sheet date might indicate that the decline in market value below cost at the balance sheet date was other than temporary. However, those declines result from information, events, or changes in expectations occurring after the balance sheet date. Accordingly, if a decline in market value below cost as of the balance sheet date of an individual security is judged to be other than temporary, further declines in market value occurring after the date of the balance sheet shall not be included in the amount that is accounted for as a realized loss as of the balance sheet date. Recoveries in market value after the balance sheet date also result from information, events, or changes in expectations occurring after the balance sheet date, but they tend to indicate that a portion or all of the decline at the balance sheet date was in fact temporary. Accordingly, such recoveries shall be considered when estimating the amount of decline as of the balance sheet date that is judged to be other than temporary.

EFFECTIVE DATE AND TRANSITION

5. The provisions of this Interpretation shall be effective for financial statements for annual and interim periods ending after October 15, 1976. Earlier application is encouraged in financial statements for annual and interim periods ending before October 16, 1976 that have not been previously issued. This Interpretation shall not be applied retroactively for previously issued annual or interim financial statements.

---

[1]Paragraph 13 applies to enterprises in industries not having specialized accounting practices with respect to marketable securities, and paragraph 17 applies to enterprises in industries having specialized accounting practices with respect to marketable securities.

This Interpretation was adopted by the unanimous vote of the six members of the Financial Accounting Standards Board following submission to the members of the Financial Accounting Standards Advisory Council.

Marshall S. Armstrong, *Chairman*
Oscar S. Gellein
Donald J. Kirk
Arthur L. Litke
Robert E. Mays
Robert T. Sprouse

FASB Interpretation No. 12
Accounting for Previously Established Allowance Accounts

an interpretation of FASB Statement No. 12

STATUS

Issued: September 1976

Effective Date: For annual and interim periods ending after October 15, 1976

Affects: No other pronouncements

Affected by: No other pronouncements

FASB Interpretation No. 12
Accounting for Previously Established Allowance Accounts

an interpretation of FASB Statement No. 12

INTRODUCTION

1. Paragraph 8 of *FASB Statement No. 12,* "Accounting for Certain Marketable Securities," specifies that the "carrying amount of a marketable equity securities portfolio shall be the lower of its aggregate cost or market value, determined at the balance sheet date." Paragraph 7(e) of *FASB Statement No. 12* defines "cost" of a marketable equity security as "original cost . . . unless a new cost basis has been assigned based on recognition of an impairment of value that was deemed other than temporary. . . . In such cases, the new cost basis shall be the cost. . . ."

2. Prior to the issuance of *FASB Statement No. 12,* some enterprises that carried marketable equity securities at cost had reduced the carrying amount of individual marketable equity securities to market value through an allowance account with a corresponding amount included in the determination of net income. In some of those cases, a new cost basis was not established for individual securities and the allowance account was expected to increase or decrease depending on fluctuations in the market price of the marketable equity security because the decline in market value below cost was assessed to be temporary. The Board has been asked to clarify whether, in those cases, the original cost of the individual securities or the original cost reduced by an existing allowance account should be used in applying paragraphs 7(e) and 8 of *FASB Statement No. 12.*

INTERPRETATION

3. The original cost of individual marketable equity securities shall be used in applying paragraphs 7(e) and 8 of *FASB Statement No. 12* by an enterprise that carried marketable equity securities at cost and that (a) had reduced the carrying amount of individual marketable equity securities through an allowance account with a corresponding amount included in the determination of net income prior to the effective date of the Statement and (b) expected the allowance account to increase or decrease in the future based on fluctuations in the market price of the security because the decline in market value below cost was assessed to be temporary. Any balance remaining in such an existing allowance account shall be eliminated and credited to income in the period in which this Interpretation is initially applied. The valuation allowance would then be determined in accordance with paragraph 8 of *FASB Statement No. 12.*

4. If, prior to the effective date of *FASB Statement No. 12,* a new cost basis had been assigned to a marketable equity security based on recognition of an impairment of value that was deemed other than temporary, the new cost basis shall be used in applying the provisions of *FASB Statement No. 12.*

EFFECTIVE DATE AND TRANSITION

5. The provisions of this Interpretation shall be effective for financial statements for annual and interim periods ending after October 15, 1976. Earlier application is encouraged in financial statements for annual and interim periods ending before October 16, 1976 that have not been previously issued. This Interpretation shall not be applied retroactively for previously issued annual or interim financial statements.

This Interpretation was adopted by the unanimous vote of the six members of the Financial Accounting Standards Board following submission to the members of the Financial Accounting Standards Advisory Council.

Marshall S. Armstrong, *Chairman*
Oscar S. Gellein
Donald J. Kirk
Arthur L. Litke
Robert E. Mays
Robert T. Sprouse

FASB Interpretation No. 13
Consolidation of a Parent and Its Subsidiaries Having Different Balance Sheet Dates

an interpretation of FASB Statement No. 12

STATUS

Issued: September 1976

Effective Date: For annual and interim periods ending after October 15, 1976

Affects: No other pronouncements

Affected by: No other pronouncements

FASB Interpretation No. 13
Consolidation of a Parent and Its Subsidiaries Having Different Balance Sheet Dates

an interpretation of FASB Statement No. 12

INTRODUCTION

1. Paragraphs 8, 9, and 15 of *FASB Statement No. 12,* "Accounting for Certain Marketable Securities," set forth the requirements of the portfolio basis for comparing cost and market value. The portfolio basis requires that marketable equity securities owned by enterprises that are consolidated and that do not follow specialized accounting practices with respect to marketable equity securities, or that are consolidated and follow the same specialized accounting practices with respect to marketable equity securities, shall be aggregated into separate portfolios according to the current or noncurrent classifications of the securities. The aggregate cost and aggregate market value of the portfolios are compared to determine carrying amount.

2. Paragraph 13 of *FASB Statement No. 12,* which applies to enterprises in industries not having specialized accounting practices with respect to marketable securities, states:

> An enterprise's financial statements shall not be adjusted for realized gains or losses or for changes in market prices with respect to marketable equity securities when such gains or losses or changes occur after *the date of the financial statements* but prior to their issuance, except for situations covered by paragraph 21. However, significant net realized and net unrealized gains and losses arising after *the date of the financial statements,* but prior to their issuance, applicable to marketable equity securities owned at the date of the most recent balance sheet shall be disclosed. (Emphasis added.)

Paragraph 17 of *FASB Statement No. 12,* which applies to enterprises in industries having specialized accounting practices with respect to marketable securities, is in substance identical to paragraph 13 of the Statement.

3. The financial statements of a subsidiary sometimes are consolidated with the financial statements of its parent even though the financial statements of the subsidiary are as of a date different from the financial statements of the parent. The use of different dates is permitted by paragraph 4 of *ARB No. 51,* "Consolidated Financial Statements," which states:

> A difference in fiscal periods of a parent and a subsidiary does not of itself justify the exclusion of the subsidiary from consolidation. It ordinarily is feasible for the subsidiary to prepare, for consolidation purposes, statements for a period which corresponds with or closely approaches the fiscal period of the parent. However, where the difference is not more than about three months, it usually is acceptable to use, for consolidation purposes, the subsidiary's statements for its fiscal period; when this is done, recognition should be given by disclosure or otherwise to the effect of intervening events which materially affect the financial position or results of operations.

4. The Board has been requested to clarify application of the portfolio basis specified in *FASB Statement No. 12* when the financial statements of a subsidiary are as of a date different from that of its parent and are consolidated with the financial statements of its parent. Further, the Board has been asked to explain the meaning of "the date of the financial statements" in paragraphs 13 and 17 of *FASB Statement No. 12* when the financial statements of a subsidiary or investee are as of a date different from that of its parent or investor and are consolidated with or accounted for by the equity method in the financial statements of its parent or investor.

INTERPRETATION

5. To compute the amount of any valuation allowance(s) required by *FASB Statement No. 12* in the consolidated financial statements, aggregate cost and aggregate market value of the portfolio(s) shall be determined for each subsidiary that is consolidated as of the date of each subsidiary's balance sheet, and those aggregates shall be combined with aggregate cost and aggregate market value of the parent's portfolio(s) determined as of the parent's balance sheet date. For example, assume that consolidated financial statements dated December 31, 1976 and issued on March 1, 1977 include the financial statements of the parent as of December 31, 1976 and of the subsidiary as of October 31, 1976. The cost of the marketable equity securities owned by the subsidiary at October 31, 1976 is added to the cost of the marketable equity securities owned by the parent at December 31, 1976. The market values

at October 31, 1976 of the securities owned by the subsidiary and the market values at December 31, 1976 of the securities owned by the parent are aggregated in the same manner. The aggregate cost and aggregate market value of the portfolios are compared to determine the carrying amount in the consolidated financial statements.

6. For purposes of applying paragraphs 13 and 17 of *FASB Statement No. 12,* "the date of the financial statements" shall be for each subsidiary or investee the date of the financial statements that are consolidated with or accounted for by the equity method in the financial statements of its parent or investor. The last sentence in each of those paragraphs requires disclosure of significant net realized gains or losses and of significant net unrealized gains or losses arising after the date of the financial statements. Using the assumptions in the example in paragraph 5 above, aggregate amounts are computed as follows for possible disclosure: the net *realized* gains or losses arising after October 31, 1976 and prior to March 1, 1977 applicable to the marketable equity securities in the portfolio of the subsidiary at October 31, 1976 are aggregated with the net *realized* gains or losses arising after December 31, 1976 and prior to March 1, 1977 applicable to the marketable equity securities in the portfolio of the parent at December 31, 1976. Likewise, net *unrealized* gains or losses arising in the portfolio of the subsidiary after October 31, 1976 and prior to March 1, 1977 applicable to the marketable equity securities in the portfolio of the subsidiary at October 31, 1976 are aggregated with the net *unrealized* gains or losses arising after December 31, 1976 and prior to March 1, 1977 applicable to the marketable equity securities in the portfolio of the parent at December 31, 1976. If significant, each of the aggregate amounts shall be disclosed.

7. If the financial statements of a subsidiary are consolidated with the financial statements of its parent and the financial statements of the subsidiary are as of a date different from the financial statements of the parent, paragraph 4 of *ARB No. 51* requires that "recognition should be given by disclosure or otherwise to the effect of intervening events which materially affect the financial position or results of operations." In the case of the subsidiary in the example in paragraph 5 above, that requirement pertains to the period from October 31, 1976 to December 31, 1976. Accordingly, in addition to the disclosure required by paragraph 6 above, the net realized gains or losses and the net unrealized gains or losses arising after October 31, 1976 and prior to December 31, 1976 applicable to the marketable equity securities of the subsidiary shall be disclosed if they "materially affect the financial position or results of operations." Further, as required by paragraphs 13 and 17 of *FASB Statement No. 12,*[1] the subsidiary's financial statements shall not be adjusted for realized gains or losses or for changes in market prices with respect to its marketable equity securities occurring after October 31, 1976 and prior to December 31, 1976, unless the decline in market value below cost of an individual marketable equity security is determined to be other than temporary and, accordingly, shall be accounted for as a realized loss.

EFFECTIVE DATE AND TRANSITION

8. The provisions of this Interpretation shall be effective for financial statements for annual and interim periods ending after October 15, 1976. Earlier application is encouraged in financial statements for annual and interim periods ending before October 16, 1976 that have not been previously issued. This Interpretation shall not be applied retroactively for previously issued annual or interim financial statements.

This Interpretation was adopted by the unanimous vote of the six members of the Financial Accounting Standards Board following submission to the members of the Financial Accounting Standards Advisory Council.

Marshall S. Armstrong, *Chairman*
Oscar S. Gellein
Donald J. Kirk
Arthur L. Litke
Robert E. Mays
Robert T. Sprouse

[1]See also *FASB Interpretation No. 11,* "Changes in Market Value after the Balance Sheet Date: an interpretation of FASB Statement No. 12."

FASB Interpretation No. 14
Reasonable Estimation of the Amount of a Loss

an interpretation of FASB Statement No. 5

STATUS

Issued: September 1976

Effective Date: For annual and interim periods ending after October 15, 1976

Affects: No other pronouncements

Affected by: No other pronouncements

FASB Interpretation No. 14
Reasonable Estimation of the Amount of a Loss

an interpretation of FASB Statement No. 5

INTRODUCTION

1. The two conditions for accrual of an estimated loss from a loss contingency set forth in paragraph 8 of *FASB Statement No. 5,* "Accounting for Contingencies," are that "(a) information available prior to issuance of the financial statements indicates that it is probable that an asset had been impaired or a liability had been incurred at the date of the financial statements . . ." and "(b) the amount of loss can be reasonably estimated." In some situations in which condition (a) in paragraph 8 is met, a range of loss can be reasonably estimated but no single amount within the range appears at the time to be a better estimate than any other amount within the range. The Board has been asked to clarify whether, in those situations, condition (b) in paragraph 8 also is met and, if so, to explain what amount of loss should be accrued.

INTERPRETATION

2. As indicated in paragraph 59 of *FASB Statement No. 5,* the purpose of the two conditions in paragraph 8 of the Statement is "to require accrual of losses when they are reasonably estimable and relate to the current or a prior period." Condition (b) in paragraph 8, that "the amount of loss can be reasonably estimated," does not delay accrual of a loss until only a single amount can be reasonably estimated. To the contrary, when condition (a) in paragraph 8 is met, i.e., "it is probable that an asset had been impaired or a liability had been incurred," and information available indicates that the estimated amount of loss is within a range of amounts, it follows that some amount of loss has occurred and can be reasonably estimated.

3. When condition (a) in paragraph 8 is met with respect to a particular loss contingency and the reasonable estimate of the loss is a range, condition (b) in paragraph 8 is met and an amount shall be accrued for the loss. When some amount within the range appears at the time to be a better estimate than any other amount within the range, that amount shall be accrued. When no amount within the range is a better estimate than any other amount, however, the minimum amount in the range shall be accrued.[1] In addition, paragraph 9 of the Statement may require disclosure of the nature and, in some circumstances, the amount accrued, and paragraph 10 requires disclosure of the nature of the contingency and the additional exposure to loss if there is at least a reasonable possibility of loss in excess of the amount accrued.

4. As an example, assume that an enterprise is involved in litigation at the close of its fiscal year ending December 31, 1976 and information available indicates that an unfavorable outcome is probable. Subsequently, after a trial on the issues, a verdict unfavorable to the enterprise is handed down, but the amount of damages remains unresolved at the time the financial statements are issued. Although the enterprise is unable to estimate the exact amount of loss, its reasonable estimate at the time is that the judgment will be for not less than $3 million or more than $9 million. No amount in that range appears at the time to be a better estimate than any other amount. *FASB Statement No. 5* requires accrual of the $3 million at December 31, 1976, disclosure of the nature of the contingency and the exposure to an additional amount of loss of up to $6 million, and possibly disclosure of the amount of the accrual.

5. The same answer would result under the example in paragraph 4 above if it is probable that a verdict will be unfavorable even though the trial has not been completed before the financial statements are issued. In that situation, condition (a) in paragraph 8 would be met because information available to the enterprise indicates that an unfavorable verdict is probable. An assessment that the range of loss is between $3 million and $9 million would meet condition (b) in paragraph 8. If no single amount in that range is a better estimate than any other amount, *FASB Statement No. 5* requires an accrual of $3 million at December 31, 1976, disclosure of the nature of the contingency and the exposure to an additional amount of loss of up to $6 million, and possibly disclosure of the amount of the accrual. Note, however, that if the enterprise had assessed the verdict differently (e.g., that an unfavorable verdict was *not* probable but was only reasonably possible), condition (a) in paragraph 8 would not have been met and no amount of loss would be accrued but the nature of the contingency and any amount of loss that is reasonably possible would be disclosed.

[1]Even though the minimum amount in the range is not necessarily the amount of loss that will be ultimately determined, it is not likely that the ultimate loss will be less than the minimum amount.

6. Assume that in the examples given in paragraphs 4 and 5 above condition (a) in paragraph 8 has been met and a reasonable estimate of loss is a range between $3 million and $9 million but a loss of $4 million is a better estimate than any other amount in that range. In that situation, *FASB Statement No. 5* requires accrual of $4 million, disclosure of the nature of the contingency and the exposure to an additional amount of loss of up to $5 million, and possibly disclosure of the amount of the accrual.

7. As a further example, assume that at December 31, 1976 an enterprise has an investment of $1,000,000 in the securities of another enterprise that has declared bankruptcy, and there is no quoted market price for the securities. Condition (a) in paragraph 8 has been met because information available indicates that the value of the investment has been impaired, and a reasonable estimate of loss is a range between $300,000 and $600,000. No amount of loss in that range appears at the time to be a better estimate of loss than any other amount. *FASB Statement No. 5* requires accrual of the $300,000 loss at December 31, 1976, disclosure of the nature of the contingency and the exposure to an additional amount of loss of up to $300,000, and possibly disclosure of the amount of the accrual.

EFFECTIVE DATE AND TRANSITION

8. The provisions of this Interpretation shall be effective for financial statements for annual and interim periods beginning after October 15, 1976. Earlier application is encouraged in financial statements for annual and interim periods beginning before October 15, 1976 that have not been previously issued. An accrual for a loss contingency or an adjustment of an established accrual for a loss contingency resulting from application of this Interpretation shall be accounted for as a change in estimate in accordance with the requirements of paragraph 31 of *APB Opinion No. 20,* "Accounting Changes." This Interpretation shall not be applied retroactively for previously issued annual and interim financial statements.

This Interpretation was adopted by the unanimous vote of the six members of the Financial Accounting Standards Board following submission to the members of the Financial Accounting Standards Advisory Council.

Marshall S. Armstrong, *Chairman*
Oscar S. Gellein
Donald J. Kirk
Arthur L. Litke
Robert E. Mays
Robert T. Sprouse

FASB Interpretation No. 15
Translation of Unamortized Policy Acquisition Costs by a Stock Life Insurance Company

an interpretation of FASB Statement No. 8

STATUS

Issued: September 1976

Effective Date: For annual and interim periods ending after December 15, 1976

Affects: No other pronouncements

Affected by: Superseded by FAS 52
Paragraphs 2 and 4 amended by FAS 60

FASB Interpretation No. 15
Translation of Unamortized Policy Acquisition Costs by a Stock Life Insurance Company

an interpretation of FASB Statement No. 8

INTRODUCTION

1. The FASB has been requested to clarify the application of *FASB Statement No. 8,* "Accounting for the Translation of Foreign Currency Transactions and Foreign Currency Financial Statements," to the translation of the unamortized policy acquisition costs of a foreign stock life insurance company whose foreign currency financial statements are incorporated in the financial statements of an enterprise by consolidation, combination, or the equity method of accounting. Policy acquisition costs include commissions paid to agents for selling policies and other costs that vary with and are primarily related to the production of new business. The following three approaches have been suggested to the Board:

a. Unamortized policy acquisition costs are deferred charges and should be translated at historical rates. They represent expenses that have been incurred in past transactions that are deferred and amortized in proportion to the related anticipated premium revenue.
b. Unamortized policy acquisition costs are in the nature of long-term receivables and should be translated at the current rate. They represent past services paid for to receive future premium revenue and are recoverable from those future revenues.
c. Unamortized policy acquisition costs and the liability for future policy benefits are so interconnected that they both should be translated at the current rate. Unamortized policy acquisition costs are classified on the balance sheet among assets as an accounting convention for separate disclosure but this method of disclosure does not change their fundamental nature of being an integral part of the liability for future policy benefits.

In addition, if unamortized policy acquisition costs are translated at historical rates, the Board has been asked if Statement No. 8 requires that a "reserve deficiency computation" be made in dollars.

2. The FASB has not considered the specialized accounting practices for life insurance companies. Those practices are specified for stock life insurance companies by the AICPA Industry Audit Guide, "Audits of Stock Life Insurance Companies." That Audit Guide requires that, because of their nature, unamortized policy acquisition costs should be classified as a deferred charge (page 74). The Guide also requires that unamortized policy acquisition costs be included in the computation of a deficiency, if any, in the reserve[1] applicable to a block of insurance policies; any deficiency is corrected "by a charge to earnings to increase reserves and/or reduce deferred acquisition expense" (page 87).

3. *FASB Statement No. 8* requires that asset and liability balances representing cash and amounts receivable or payable that are denominated in a foreign currency shall be translated into dollars at the current rate. All other asset and liability accounts measured in a foreign currency shall generally be translated in a manner that retains their measurement bases; that is, accounts carried at prices in past exchanges shall be translated at historical rates and accounts carried at prices in current or future exchanges shall be translated at the current rate. The Statement also requires that existing U.S. generally accepted accounting principles be followed and specifies that translation should change only the unit of measure without changing the accounting principles.

INTERPRETATION

4. According to the AICPA Industry Audit Guide, "Audits of Stock Life Insurance Companies," unamortized policy acquisition costs of a stock life insurance company are deferred charges under present generally accepted accounting principles. Because *FASB Statement No. 8* relies on generally accepted accounting principles, which for stock life insurance companies are set forth in the Audit Guide, those costs shall be translated at historical rates.

5. Present generally accepted accounting principles require that a stock life insurance company recognize a loss represented by a reserve deficiency as a charge to current earnings (see paragraph 2 above). *FASB Statement No. 8* requires that the dollar financial statements be in conformity with generally accepted accounting principles. Accordingly, com-

[1]The Audit Guide uses the term "reserve" to describe the actuarially determined liability for future benefits on insurance policies in force. Because that term has a special meaning in the insurance industry, it is also used in this Interpretation in referring to that *liability.*

putation of a reserve deficiency shall be made *in dollars* after translation of the unamortized policy acquisition costs at historical rates and the liability for future policy benefits at the current rate. Computation of a reserve deficiency *in dollars* may require a charge (or an increased charge) to current earnings in the dollar statements for a reserve deficiency even though no such charge is required in the foreign statements. It may also require a charge to current earnings in the foreign statements to be reversed in whole or in part in preparing the dollar statements if the translated charge to current earnings exceeds the reserve deficiency computed in dollars. (See paragraph 14 of Statement No. 8.)

EFFECTIVE DATE AND TRANSITION

6. This Interpretation shall be effective for all unamortized policy acquisition costs reported in financial statements for annual and interim periods ending after December 15, 1976, except that it shall not be applied prior to initial application of *FASB Statement No. 8*. Earlier application is encouraged in financial statements for annual and interim periods ending before December 16, 1976 that have not been previously issued. If initially applied concurrently with the initial application of *FASB Statement No. 8,* this Interpretation shall be applied in the same manner as the initial application of that Statement. Enterprises that have adopted Statement No. 8 prior to the effective date of this Interpretation and that have reported unamortized policy acquisition costs differently from the requirements of this Interpretation are encouraged to apply this Interpretation in the same manner as they initially applied Statement No. 8 (see paragraphs 35 and 36 of the Statement), but if they choose not to do so, those enterprises shall report the cumulative effect of applying this Interpretation in the year that it is adopted in the manner required by *APB Opinion No. 20,* "Accounting Changes," and *FASB Statement No. 3,* "Reporting Accounting Changes in Interim Financial Statements."

This Interpretation was adopted by the unanimous vote of the six members of the Financial Accounting Standards Board following submission to the members of the Financial Accounting Standards Advisory Council.

Marshall S. Armstrong, *Chairman*
Oscar S. Gellein
Donald J. Kirk
Arthur L. Litke
Robert E. Mays
Robert T. Sprouse

FASB Interpretation No. 16
Clarification of Definitions and Accounting for Marketable Equity Securities That Become Nonmarketable

an interpretation of FASB Statement No. 12

STATUS

Issued: February 1977

Effective Date: For annual and interim periods ending after March 15, 1977

Affects: No other pronouncements

Affected by: No other pronouncements

FASB Interpretation No. 16
Clarification of Definitions and Accounting for Marketable Equity Securities That Become Nonmarketable

an interpretation of FASB Statement No. 12

INTRODUCTION

1. The FASB has been asked to clarify the definitions of the terms "marketable" and "restricted stock" as used in *FASB Statement No. 12,* "Accounting for Certain Marketable Securities," and to clarify whether paragraph 10 of *FASB Statement No. 12* requires a new cost basis to be assigned when a marketable equity security becomes nonmarketable if its market value is less than its cost at that time.

2. For purposes of applying paragraphs 8-13, 15, 17, and 19 of *FASB Statement No. 12,* the term "marketable" is defined in paragraph 7(b) of the Statement as follows:

> *Marketable,* as applied to an equity security, means an equity security as to which sales prices or bid and ask prices are currently available on a national securities exchange (i.e., those registered with the Securities and Exchange Commission) or in the over-the-counter market. In the over-the-counter market, an equity security shall be considered marketable when a quotation is publicly reported by the National Association of Securities Dealers Automatic Quotations System or by the National Quotations Bureau Inc. (provided, in the latter case, that quotations are available from at least three dealers). Equity securities traded in foreign markets shall be considered marketable when such markets are of a breadth and scope comparable to those referred to above. Restricted stock[3] does not meet this definition.

Footnote 3 to that paragraph defines restricted stock as follows:

> Restricted stock for purposes of this Statement shall mean securities for which sale is restricted by a governmental or contractual requirement except where such requirement terminates within one year or where the holder has the power by contract or otherwise to cause the requirement to be met within one year. Any portion of the stock which can reasonably be expected to qualify for sale within one year, such as may be the case under Rule 144 or similar rules of the Securities and Exchange Commission, is not considered restricted [under *FASB Statement No. 12*].

3. Paragraph 10 of *FASB Statement No. 12* states:

> If there is a change in the classification of a marketable equity security between current and noncurrent, the security shall be transferred between the corresponding portfolios at the lower of its cost or market value at date of transfer. If market value is less than cost, the market value shall become the new cost basis, and the difference shall be accounted for as if it were a realized loss and included in the determination of net income.

INTERPRETATION

Definitions

4. For purposes of applying paragraphs 8-13, 15, 17, and 19 of *FASB Statement No. 12,* an equity security is not considered marketable if market price quotations specified by the Statement (see paragraph 2 above) are not available or if it is "restricted stock" as defined in the Statement (see paragraph 2 above) even though market price quotations are available for securities of the same class that are not restricted.

5. The determination of whether an equity security is marketable is made as of the balance sheet date,[1] but a temporary lack of trades or price quotations for an equity security at the balance sheet date does not make it nonmarketable for purposes of applying *FASB Statement No. 12* if the required market prices are available on days closely preceding and following the balance sheet date. In that situation, the market price of a security traded on a national securities exchange shall be determined from the sales or bid and ask prices on the first day following the balance sheet date that the information is available. If the lack of a publicly reported quotation by the National Association of Securities Dealers Automatic Quotations System or the lack of three quotations by the National Quotations Bureau Inc. is a mere temporary condition as described above for a security traded in the over-the-counter market, its market price shall be determined from:

[1] If the balance sheet date falls on a date that securities are not normally traded (e.g., Saturday or Sunday), the availability of market price quotations shall be determined as of the most recent business day preceding the balance sheet date.

a. The quotation publicly reported by the National Association of Securities Dealers Automatic Quotations System on the first day following the balance sheet date that a quotation is publicly reported, or
b. The quotation(s) reported by the National Quotations Bureau Inc. as of the balance sheet date if at least one quotation is available as of that date or on the first day following the balance sheet date that quotations are reported if no quotations are available on the balance sheet date.

6. If it can be reasonably expected that a security "for which sale is restricted by a governmental or contractual requirement" can qualify for sale within one year of the balance sheet date and market price quotations for unrestricted securities of the same class are available as of the balance sheet date, the security is considered marketable at the balance sheet date for purposes of applying *FASB Statement No. 12* (see paragraph 2 above). In this situation, market price quotations for unrestricted shares of the same class at the balance sheet date provide a surrogate market price for the restricted shares and shall be considered as the market price for the security. If the restricted security cannot qualify for sale within one year or market price quotations are not available for unrestricted shares of the same class, the security is considered nonmarketable for purposes of applying the Statement.

7. As an example of the application of paragraph 6 above, assume that an enterprise pledges a marketable equity security as collateral for a loan due in three years. Normally, debt agreements permit substitution for the collateral or sale of the collateral if the proceeds are used to repay the loan. However, if the debt agreement prohibits sale of or substitution for the collateral for the term of the loan, the pledged security becomes "restricted stock" and nonmarketable for purposes of applying *FASB Statement No. 12* at the time it is pledged and shall be excluded from the enterprise's portfolio of marketable equity securities from that date until one year before expiration of the long-term debt agreement.

8. As a further example, assume that an enterprise owns common stock that cannot be sold to the public, except pursuant to Rule 144 of the Securities and Exchange Commission (see explanation below), until a registration statement has been filed with the SEC and has become effective. Also assume that the stock is marketable at one balance sheet date pursuant to an effective registration statement. At the next balance sheet date, the registration statement is no longer effective and the enterprise does not have the power to cause another one to be filed within one year. Then, only the portion of the stock that "can reasonably be expected to qualify for sale within one year . . . under Rule 144 . . . is not considered restricted" under *FASB Statement No. 12.* Rule 144 specifies that if certain conditions are met a security may be sold to the public without an effective registration statement on file with the SEC, subject to a limitation on the number of shares that may be sold during a given time period. The number of shares eligible for sale is based on the total number of shares of the security outstanding or the average weekly trading volume of the security for a stated past period. Changes in the number of shares outstanding or in trading volume change the number of shares that qualify for sale under Rule 144. The number of shares considered marketable for purposes of applying the Statement are those that "can reasonably be expected to qualify for sale within one year"; the determination of such number is a matter of judgment based on past trading volumes, the presently outstanding shares and plans for changes therein, and other relevant factors. The number of shares considered nonmarketable are those that cannot qualify for sale within one year under the preceding sentence.

Accounting

9. Paragraph 10 of *FASB Statement No. 12* applies to all transfers between current and noncurrent classifications of equity securities that are marketable, as that term is defined in the Statement (see paragraph 2 above). If the change in the classification of an equity security is coincident with a change in its status from marketable to nonmarketable or from nonmarketable to marketable, paragraph 10 of the Statement shall apply to the transfer between current and noncurrent classifications. Paragraph 10 of the Statement requires that if the market value of the security is less than its cost when it is transferred between current and noncurrent classifications, "the market value shall become the new cost basis, and the difference shall be accounted for as if it were a realized loss and included in the determination of net income." In that situation, market value shall be the security's last available market price if the transfer between classifications is coincident with a change in status from marketable to nonmarketable and the first available market price if the transfer between classifications is coincident with a change in status from nonmarketable to marketable.

10. The accounting for a nonmarketable security is outside of the scope of *FASB Statement No. 12.* When a marketable equity security becomes nonmarketable, the cost of that security shall be excluded from the portfolio of marketable equity securities of which it was a part for purposes of applying the Statement. When a nonmarketable

equity security becomes marketable, that security shall be included in the portfolio of marketable equity securities at cost. The term *cost* is defined in paragraph 7(e) of the Statement as "the original cost . . . unless a new cost basis has been assigned based on recognition of an impairment of value that was deemed other than temporary or as the result of a transfer between current and noncurrent classifications as described in paragraph 10 [of the Statement]. In such cases, the new cost basis shall be the cost for the purposes of this Statement."

EFFECTIVE DATE AND TRANSITION

11. The provisions of this Interpretation shall be effective for financial statements for annual and interim periods ending after March 15, 1977. Earlier application is encouraged in financial statements for annual and interim periods ending before March 16, 1977 that have not been previously issued. This Interpretation shall not be applied retroactively for previously issued annual or interim financial statements.

This Interpretation was adopted by the unanimous vote of the six members of the Financial Accounting Standards Board following submission to the members of the Financial Accounting Standards Advisory Council.

Marshall S. Armstrong, *Chairman*
Oscar S. Gellein
Donald J. Kirk
Arthur L. Litke
Robert E. Mays
Robert T. Sprouse

FASB Interpretation No. 17
Applying the Lower of Cost or Market Rule in Translated Financial Statements

an interpretation of FASB Statement No. 8

STATUS

Issued: February 1977

Effective Date: For annual and interim periods ending after March 15, 1977

Affects: No other pronouncements

Affected by: Superseded by FAS 52

FASB Interpretation No. 17
Applying the Lower of Cost or Market Rule in Translated Financial Statements

an interpretation of FASB Statement No. 8

INTRODUCTION

1. The FASB has been asked to clarify the determination of *market* when applying the rule of *cost or market, whichever is lower,* in translated financial statements. The FASB also has been requested to clarify the manner of reporting a write-down of inventory resulting from application of that rule in the translated financial statements.

2. *FASB Statement No. 8,* "Accounting for the Translation of Foreign Currency Transactions and Foreign Currency Financial Statements," relies on existing U.S. generally accepted accounting principles which for purposes of pricing inventories are set forth in Chapter 4, "Inventory Pricing," of *ARB No. 43.* Chapter 4 specifies that inventory should be stated at *cost or market, whichever is lower.* To ensure that inventory in the translated statements conforms to that rule, paragraph 14 of Statement No. 8 requires that the rule of *cost or market, whichever is lower,* be applied *in dollars.*[1]

3. Appendix A of *FASB Statement No. 8* explains and illustrates how to apply the rule of *cost or market, whichever is lower,* in translated financial statements. Paragraph 46 of Statement No. 8 states that "to apply the rule of *cost or market, whichever is lower* (as described in Statement 6 of Chapter 4, 'Inventory Pricing,' of *ARB No. 43*), *translated historical cost* shall be compared with *translated market.*"

4. Statement 6 of Chapter 4 of *ARB No. 43* is as follows:

> As used in the phrase *lower of cost or market* . . . the term *market* means current replacement cost (by purchase or by reproduction, as the case may be) except that:
>
> (1) Market should not exceed the net realizable value (i.e., estimated selling price in the ordinary course of business less reasonably predictable costs of completion and disposal); and
>
> (2) Market should not be less than net realizable value reduced by an allowance for an approximately normal profit margin.

Although the above is referred to as the rule of *cost or market, whichever is lower,* the discussion of Statement 6 in Chapter 4 of *ARB No. 43* states that "because of the many variations of circumstances encountered in inventory pricing, Statement 6 is intended as a guide rather than a literal rule."

INTERPRETATION

5. Because *FASB Statement No. 8* relies on U.S. generally accepted accounting principles, *translated market* for inventory shall be determined in accordance with the provisions of Chapter 4 of *ARB No. 43.* When applying the literal rule of *cost or market, whichever is lower,* in translated financial statements, *translated market* shall be current foreign currency replacement cost translated at the current rate,[2] except that:

a. *Translated market* shall not exceed foreign currency net realizable value translated at the current rate;[3] and

b. *Translated market* shall not be less than foreign currency net realizable value reduced by an allowance for an approximately normal profit margin translated at the current rate.[4]

6. Literal application of the rule of *cost or market, whichever is lower,* will require an inventory write-

---

[1]For convenience, both *FASB Statement No. 8* and this Interpretation assume that the translated financial statements are prepared using the U.S. dollar (dollar) as the unit of measure. See footnote 1 to *FASB Statement No. 8.*

[2]In the case of replacement by *reproduction,* certain elements of replacement cost (e.g., depreciation included in inventory) may need to be translated at historical rates to determine *translated market.*

[3]See footnote 2 above.

[4]In the case of replacement by *purchase,* if *normal profit margin* is viewed as being other than *gross profit margin,* translation entirely at the current rate may not be appropriate. In the case of replacement by *reproduction,* if *normal profit margin* is viewed as other than *gross profit margin,* certain elements, in addition to those referred to in footnote 2, may need to be translated at historical rates.

down[5] in dollar financial statements for locally acquired inventory[6] if the value of the foreign currency has declined in relation to the dollar between the date the foreign operation acquired its inventory and the date of the foreign operation's balance sheet unless foreign currency replacement costs or selling prices have increased sufficiently so that translated market measured in dollars exceeds translated historical cost. Paragraphs 7-9 illustrate literal application of the rule *in dollars.*

7. Assume the following:

a. When the rate is FC 1 = \$2.40, a foreign subsidiary of a U.S. company purchases a unit of inventory at a cost of FC 500 (measured in dollars, \$1,200),
b. At the foreign subsidiary's balance sheet date, the current rate is FC 1 = \$2.00 and the current replacement cost of the unit of inventory is FC 560 (measured in dollars, \$1,120),
c. Net realizable value is FC 630 (measured in dollars, \$1,260),
d. Net realizable value reduced by an allowance for an approximately normal profit margin is FC 550 (measured in dollars, \$1,100).

Because current replacement cost measured in dollars (\$1,120) is less than translated historical cost (\$1,200), an inventory write-down of \$80 is required in the dollar financial statements.

8. Assume the same information as given in the preceding example except that current replacement cost at the foreign subsidiary's balance sheet date is FC 620. Because market measured in dollars (FC 620 × \$2.00 = \$1,240) exceeds translated historical cost (FC 500 × \$2.40 = \$1,200), an inventory write-down is not required in the dollar financial statements.

9. As a further example, assume the same information given in paragraph 7 except that foreign currency selling prices have increased so that net realizable value is FC 720, and net realizable value reduced by an allowance for an approximately normal profit margin is FC 640. In this case, because replacement cost measured in dollars (FC 560 × \$2.00 = \$1,120) is less than net realizable value reduced by an allowance for an approximately normal profit margin measured in dollars (FC 640 × \$2.00 = \$1,280), translated market is \$1,280. Because translated market (\$1,280) exceeds translated historical cost (FC 500 × \$2.40 = \$1,200), an inventory write-down is not required in the dollar financial statements.

10. Disclosure of inventory write-downs that result from applying the rule of *cost or market, whichever is lower,* is specified by *ARB No. 43,* Chapter 4, paragraph 14, as follows:

> When substantial and unusual losses result from the application of this rule it will frequently be desirable to disclose the amount of the loss in the income statement as a charge separately identified from the consumed inventory costs described as *cost of goods sold.*

Paragraph 16 of Statement No. 8 specifies that "exchange gains or losses are a consequence of translation . . ."; that is, "they result from the procedures specified in paragraphs 7(b) and 11-13. . . ." Inventory write-downs are a consequence of applying the rule of *cost or market, whichever is lower,* in translated financial statements as required by paragraph 14 of Statement No. 8 and, accordingly, are not exchange losses. Therefore, such inventory write-downs in translated financial statements shall *not* be included in the aggregate exchange gain or loss required to be disclosed pursuant to paragraph 32 of Statement No. 8, but shall be reported in accordance with paragraph 14 of Chapter 4 of *ARB No. 43* and, in addition, included in the disclosures made pursuant to paragraph 33 of Statement No. 8.

EFFECTIVE DATE AND TRANSITION

11. The provisions of this Interpretation shall be effective for financial statements for annual and interim periods ending after March 15, 1977. Earlier application is encouraged in financial statements for annual and interim periods ending before March 16, 1977 that have not been previously issued. This Interpretation shall not be applied retroactively for previously issued annual or interim financial statements unless it is being applied concurrently with initial application of *FASB Statement No. 8,* in which case previously issued financial statements shall be restated in accordance with either paragraph 35 or 36 of Statement No. 8.

---

[5]As to interim periods, paragraph 14(c) of *APB Opinion No. 28,* "Interim Financial Reporting," states:

> Inventory losses from market declines should not be deferred beyond the interim period in which the decline occurs. Recoveries of such losses on the same inventory in later interim periods of the same fiscal year through market price recoveries should be recognized as gains in the later interim period. Such gains should not exceed previously recognized losses. Some market declines at interim dates, however, can reasonably be expected to be restored in the fiscal year. Such *temporary* market declines need not be recognized at the interim date since no loss is expected to be incurred in the fiscal year.

[6]An inventory write-down may also be required for imported inventory.

This Interpretation was adopted by the unanimous vote of the six members of the Financial Accounting Standards Board following submission to the members of the Financial Accounting Standards Advisory Council.

Marshall S. Armstrong, *Chairman*
Oscar S. Gellein
Donald J. Kirk
Arthur L. Litke
Robert E. Mays
Robert T. Sprouse

FASB Interpretation No. 18
Accounting for Income Taxes in Interim Periods

an interpretation of APB Opinion No. 28

STATUS

Issued: March 1977

Effective Date: For financial statements issued after March 31, 1977 for interim periods beginning after December 15, 1976

Affects: No other pronouncements

Affected by: Paragraph 4 superseded by FAS 71

CONTENTS

FASB Interpretation No. 18
Accounting for Income Taxes in Interim Periods

an interpretation of APB Opinion No. 28

INTRODUCTION AND BACKGROUND INFORMATION

1. The FASB has been asked to clarify the application of *APB Opinion No. 28,* "Interim Financial Reporting," with respect to accounting for income taxes in interim periods. In general, that Opinion requires that an estimated annual effective tax rate be used to determine interim period income tax provisions. Application of the general guideline to specific situations has resulted in differences in accounting for similar situations by different enterprises.

2. This Interpretation describes (a) the general computation of interim period income taxes (paragraphs 8 and 9), (b) the application of the general computation to specific situations (paragraphs 10-15), (c) the computation of interim period income taxes applicable to significant unusual or infrequently occurring items, discontinued operations, extraordinary items, and cumulative effects of changes in accounting principles (paragraphs 16-21), (d) special computations applicable to operations taxable in multiple jurisdictions (paragraph 22), (e) guidelines for reflecting the effects of new tax legislation in interim period income tax provisions (paragraphs 23 and 24), and (f) disclosure requirements (paragraph 25). Appendix A, "Excerpts from APB Opinions," quotes from *APB Opinion No. 28* on accounting for income taxes in interim financial reports and from the paragraphs of *APB Opinion No. 11,* "Accounting for Income Taxes," that prescribe the annual accounting for income taxes in certain situations. The computations described in paragraphs 10-24 are illustrated in Appendix C, "Examples of Computations of Interim Period Income Taxes."

3. An Exposure Draft of a proposed Interpretation on "Accounting for Income Taxes in Interim Periods" was issued October 7, 1976. The Board received 99 letters of comment in response to the Exposure Draft. This Interpretation incorporates a number of changes suggested by those respondents. Appendix E, "Summary of Consideration of Comments on Exposure Draft," describes certain of the comments and the FASB's consideration of them.

4. The Addendum to *APB Opinion No. 2,* "Accounting for the 'Investment Credit'," states that "differences may arise in the application of generally accepted accounting principles as between regulated and nonregulated businesses, because of the effect . . . of the rate-making process," and discusses the application of generally accepted accounting principles to regulated industries. FASB Statements and Interpretations should therefore be applied to regulated companies that are subject to the rate-making process in accordance with the provisions of the Addendum.

INTERPRETATION

Definition of Terms

5. As a matter of convenience of expression, certain terms are defined in this Interpretation as follows:

a. *"Ordinary" income (or loss)* refers to "income (or loss) from continuing operations before income taxes (or benefits)" excluding significant "unusual or infrequently occurring items." Extraordinary items, discontinued operations, and cumulative effects of changes in accounting principles are also excluded from this term.[1] The term is *not* used in the income tax context of ordinary income v. capital gain.
b. *Tax (or benefit)* is the total income tax expense (or benefit), including the provision (or benefit) for income taxes both currently payable and deferred.

Concept of APB Opinion No. 28

6. *APB Opinion No. 28* specifies that the tax (or benefit) for an interim period shall be determined under the provisions of *APB Opinion No. 11, APB Opinion No. 23,* "Accounting for Income Taxes-Special Areas," and *APB Opinion No. 24,* "Accounting for Income Taxes-Invesments in Common Stock Accounted for by the Equity Method (Other than Subsidiaries and Corporate Joint Ventures)."[2] The tax (or benefit) related to "ordinary" income (or loss) shall be computed at an estimated

[1]The terms used in this definition are described in *APB Opinion No. 20,* "Accounting Changes," and in *APB Opinion No. 30,* "Reporting the Results of Operations." See paragraph 8 of *APB Opinion No. 30* for *income (or loss) from continuing operations before income taxes (or benefits)* and *discontinued operations,* paragraph 10 for *extraordinary items,* and paragraph 26 for *unusual items* and *infrequently occurring items.* See paragraph 20 of *APB Opinion No. 20* for *cumulative effects of changes in accounting principles.*

[2]*APB Opinions No. 23* and *24* are not specifically described herein because no questions were raised regarding application of those Opinions for interim periods.

annual effective tax rate and the tax (or benefit) related to all other items shall be individually computed and recognized when the items occur. Application of this general guidance to specific situations is described in the following paragraphs and illustrated in Appendix C.

Tax (or Benefit) Applicable to "Ordinary" Income (or Loss)

7. Paragraphs 8 and 9 describe the computation of interim period tax (or benefit) related to "ordinary" income (or loss). Paragraphs 10-15 describe the application of paragraphs 8 and 9 to specific situations. Paragraphs 14 and 15 describe special limitations that apply to the computations in paragraphs 8 and 9 if an enterprise has a year-to-date "ordinary" loss or anticipates an "ordinary" loss for the fiscal year.

8. *Estimated annual effective tax rate.*[3] Paragraph 19 of *APB Opinion No. 28*[4] requires than an enterprise determine an estimated annual effective tax rate.[5] That rate "should reflect anticipated investment tax credits, foreign tax rates, percentage depletion, capital gains rates, and other available tax planning alternatives."[6] The rate is revised, if necessary, as of the end of each successive interim period during the fiscal year to the enterprise's best *current* estimate of its annual effective tax rate. In some cases, the rate will be the statutory rate modified as may be appropriate in particular circumstances. In other cases, the rate will be the enterprise's estimate of the tax (or benefit) that will be provided for the fiscal year, stated as a percentage of its estimated "ordinary" income (or loss) for the fiscal year (see paragraphs 14 and 15 if an "ordinary" loss is anticipated for the fiscal year).[7]

9. *Computation of interim period tax (or benefit).* The estimated annual effective tax rate, described in paragraph 8 above, shall be applied to the year-to-date "ordinary" income (or loss) at the end of each interim period to compute the year-to-date tax (or benefit) applicable to "ordinary" income (or loss).[8] The interim period tax (or benefit) related to "ordinary" income (or loss) shall be the difference between the amount so computed and the amounts reported for previous interim periods of the fiscal year.

"Ordinary" income anticipated for fiscal year

10. *Year-to-date "ordinary" income.* If an enterprise has "ordinary" income for the year-to-date at the end of an interim period and anticipates "ordinary" income for the fiscal year, the interim period tax shall be computed as described in paragraph 9 above.

11. *Year-to-date "ordinary" loss.* If an enterprise has an "ordinary" loss for the year-to-date at the end of an interim period and anticipates "ordinary" income for the fiscal year, the interim period tax benefit shall be computed as described in paragraph 9 above, except that the year-to-date tax benefit recognized shall be limited to the amount determined in accordance with paragraphs 14 and 15 below.

---

[3]See also paragraph 22 below when the enterprise has operations taxable in multiple jurisdictions.

[4]See Appendix A, paragraph 28.

[5]Enterprises in some industries report certain items of "ordinary" income net of their related tax effect. For example, the AICPA Industry Audit Guide, "Audits of Stock Life Insurance Companies," illustrates a caption "Realized investment gains and losses, net of related income taxes of $. . ." in its suggested format of a stock life insurance company's statement of income. If an enterprise follows such an accepted industry practice, the item that will be reported net of tax and its related tax (or benefit) shall be excluded from the computation of the estimated annual effective tax rate and interim period tax (or benefit). A separate estimated annual effective tax rate shall be computed for the item, and applied to that item in accordance with paragraphs 9-15 below.

[6]Certain investment tax credits may be excluded from the estimated annual effective tax rate. If an enterprise includes allowable investment tax credits as part of its provision for income taxes over the productive life of acquired property and not entirely in the year the property is placed in service, amortization of deferred investment tax credits need not be taken into account in estimating the annual effective tax rate; however, if the investment tax credits are taken into account in the estimated annual effective tax rate, the amount taken into account shall be the amount of amortization that is anticipated to be included in income in the current year (see paragraphs 13 and 15 of *APB Opinion No. 2).* Further, paragraphs 43 and 44 of *FASB Statement No. 13*, "Accounting for Leases," specify that investment tax credits related to leases that are accounted for as leveraged leases shall be deferred and accounted for as return on the net investment in the leveraged leases in the years in which the net investment is positive. Footnote 25 of Statement No. 13 explains that the use of the term "years" is not intended to preclude application of the accounting described to shorter periods. If an enterprise accounts for investment tax credits related to leveraged leases in accordance with paragraphs 43 and 44 of Statement No. 13 for interim periods, those investment tax credits shall not be taken into account in estimating the annual effective tax rate.

[7]Estimates of the annual effective tax rate at the end of interim periods are, of necessity, based on evaluations of possible future events and transactions and may be subject to subsequent refinement or revision. If a reliable estimate cannot be made, the actual effective tax rate for the year-to-date may be the best estimate of the annual effective tax rate. If an enterprise is unable to estimate a part of its "ordinary" income (or loss) or the related tax (or benefit) but is otherwise able to make a reliable estimate, the tax (or benefit) applicable to the item that cannot be estimated shall be reported in the interim period in which the item is reported.

[8]One result of the year-to-date computation is that, if the tax benefit of an "ordinary" loss that occurs in the early portions of the fiscal year is not recognized because realization of the tax benefit is not assured, tax is not provided for subsequent "ordinary" income until the unrecognized tax benefit of the earlier "ordinary" loss is offset (see Appendix A, paragraph 32).

"Ordinary" loss anticipated for fiscal year

12. *Year-to-date "ordinary" income.* If an enterprise has "ordinary" income for the year-to-date at the end of an interim period and anticipates an "ordinary" loss for the fiscal year, the interim period tax shall be computed as described in paragraph 9 above. The estimated tax benefit for the fiscal year, used to determine the estimated annual effective tax rate described in paragraph 8 above, shall not exceed the tax benefit determined in accordance with paragraphs 14 and 15 below.

13. *Year-to-date "ordinary" loss.* If an enterprise has an "ordinary" loss for the year-to-date at the end of an interim period and anticipates an "ordinary" loss for the fiscal year, the interim period tax benefit shall be computed as described in paragraph 9 above. The estimated tax benefit for the fiscal year, used to determine the estimated annual effective tax rate described in paragraph 8 above, shall not exceed the tax benefit determined in accordance with paragraphs 14 and 15 below. In addition to that limitation in the effective rate computation, if the year-to-date "ordinary" loss exceeds the anticipated "ordinary" loss for the fiscal year, the tax benefit recognized for the year-to-date shall not exceed the tax benefit determined, based on the year-to-date "ordinary" loss, in accordance with paragraphs 14 and 15 below.

Limitations applicable to losses

14. *Recognition of the tax benefit of a loss.* Paragraphs 44 and 45 of *APB Opinion No. 11*[9] require that the tax benefit of a loss shall not be recognized until it is realized, unless future realization is assured beyond any reasonable doubt at the time the loss occurs. Therefore, the estimated tax benefit of an "ordinary" loss for the fiscal year, used to determine the estimated annual effective tax rate described in paragraph 8 above, and the year-to-date tax benefit of a loss recognized at an interim date shall be limited to the tax benefit realized or assured of future realization beyond any reasonable doubt. Paragraph 47 of *APB Opinion No. 11*[10] describes circumstances that may assure future realization of the tax benefit of a loss for a fiscal year beyond any reasonable doubt. Assurance beyond any reasonable doubt of future realization of the tax benefit of a loss at an interim date may also result from established seasonal patterns, as described in paragraph 20 of *APB Opinion No. 28.*[11] (See also paragraph 15 below.)

15. *Reversal of net deferred tax credits.* If an enterprise anticipates an "ordinary" loss for the fiscal year or has a year-to-date "ordinary" loss in excess of the anticipated "ordinary" loss for the fiscal year and all or a part of the tax benefit of the loss will not be realized or its realization is not assured beyond any reasonable doubt, existing deferred tax credits arising from timing differences shall be adjusted as required by paragraph 48 of *APB Opinion No. 11.*[12] The amount of the adjustment shall not exceed the lower of (a) the otherwise unrecognized tax benefit of the loss or (b) the amount of the net deferred tax credits that would otherwise be amortized during the carryforward period attributable to the loss. If the adjustment relates to an estimated "ordinary" loss for the fiscal year, the amount of the adjustment shall be considered additional current year tax benefit in the determination of the estimated annual effective tax rate described in paragraph 8 above.[13] If the adjustment relates to a year-to-date "ordinary" loss, the amount of the adjustment shall be considered additional tax benefit in computing the maximum tax benefit that shall be recognized for the year-to-date.[14]

Tax (or Benefit) Applicable to Significant Unusual or Infrequently Occurring Items, Discontinued Operations, or Extraordinary Items

16. *Basis of tax provision.* Paragraph 19 of *APB Opinion No. 28*[15] excludes taxes related to "significant unusual or extraordinary items that will be separately reported or reported net of their related tax effect"[16] from the estimated annual effective tax rate calculation. Paragraph 21 of *APB Opinion No. 28*[17] requires that those items be recognized in the interim period in which they occur. Paragraph 52 of *APB Opinion No. 11*[18] describes the method of applying tax allocation within a period. Under para-

[9]See Appendix A, paragraphs 29 and 30.

[10]See Appendix A, paragraph 31.

[11]See Appendix A, paragraph 32.

[12]See Appendix A, paragraph 33.

[13]See Appendix A, paragraph 34.

[14]Paragraph 48 of *APB Opinion No. 11* describes the reinstatement of previously eliminated deferred tax credits when the tax benefit of the loss is subsequently realized.

[15]See Appendix A, paragraph 28.

[16]In the context of paragraph 21 of *APB Opinion No. 28* (see Appendix A, paragraph 35), which is consistent with *APB Opinion No. 30,* this description includes unusual items, infrequently occurring items, discontinued operations, and extraordinary items.

[17]See Appendix A, paragraph 35.

[18]See Appendix A, paragraph 36.

graph 52 of Opinion No. 11, the difference between the tax computed on income including an item described in footnote 16 below and the tax computed on income excluding that item is the tax related to the item. This computation shall be made using the estimated fiscal year "ordinary" income and the items described in footnote 16 below for the year-to-date.

17. *Financial statement presentation.* Extraordinary items and discontinued operations that will be presented net of related tax effects in the financial statements for the fiscal year shall be presented net of related tax effects in interim financial statements. Unusual or infrequently occurring items that will be separately disclosed in the financial statements for the fiscal year shall be separately disclosed as a component of pretax income from continuing operations, and the tax (or benefit) related to such items shall be included in the tax (or benefit) related to continuing operations. Paragraphs 18 and 19 describe the application of the above to specific situations.

18. *Recognition of the tax benefit of a loss.* If an enterprise has a significant unusual, infrequently occurring, or extraordinary loss or a loss from discontinued operations, the tax benefit of that loss shall not be recognized until it is realized or realization is assured beyond any reasonable doubt. Realization is assured beyond any reasonable doubt (a) by offsetting year-to-date "ordinary" income, (b) by offsetting taxable income from an unusual, infrequently occurring, or extraordinary item, or from discontinued operations, or items credited directly to stockholders' equity accounts, or (c) if the loss can be carried back (after any anticipated fiscal year "ordinary" loss is carried back). Realization beyond any reasonable doubt would also appear to be assured by future taxable income that is virtually certain to occur soon enough to provide realization during the carryforward period, including anticipated "ordinary" income for the current year expected to result from an established seasonal pattern of loss in early interim periods offset by income in later interim periods.[19] If previously recorded net deferred tax credits that would be amortized during the carryforward period of the loss are present and all or a portion of the tax benefit of the loss is not realized and future realization is not assured beyond any reasonable doubt, see paragraph 15 above. If all or a part of the tax benefit is not realized and future realization is not assured beyond any reasonable doubt in the interim period of occurrence but becomes assured beyond any reasonable doubt in a subsequent interim period of the same fiscal year, the previously unrecognized tax benefit shall be reported in that subsequent interim period in the same manner that it would have been reported if realization had been assured beyond any reasonable doubt in the interim period of occurrence, i.e., as a tax benefit relating to continuing operations, discontinued operations, or an extraordinary item.

19. *Discontinued operations.* The computations described in paragraphs 16-18 shall be the basis for the tax (or benefit) related to both (a) the income (or loss) from operations of the discontinued segment[20] prior to the measurement date and (b) the gain (or loss) on disposal of discontinued operations (including any provision for operating loss subsequent to the measurement date). Income (or loss) from operations of the discontinued segment prior to the interim period in which the measurement date occurs will have been included in "ordinary" income (or loss) of prior periods and thus will have been included in the estimated annual effective tax rate and tax (or benefit) calculations described in paragraphs 8-15 above. The *total* tax (or benefit) provided in the prior interim periods shall not be recomputed but shall be divided into two components, applicable to the remaining "ordinary" income (or loss) and to the income (or loss) from operations of the discontinued segment as follows. A revised estimated annual effective tax rate and resulting tax (or benefit) shall be computed, in accordance with paragraphs 8-15 above, for the remaining "ordinary" income (or loss), based on the estimates applicable to such operations used in the original calculations for each prior interim period. The tax (or benefit) related to the operations of the discontinued segment shall be the total of (a) the difference between the tax (or benefit) originally computed for "ordinary" income (or loss) and the recomputed amount for the remaining "ordinary" income (or loss) and (b) the tax computed in accordance with paragraphs 16-18 above for any unusual or infrequently occurring items of the discontinued segment.

Using a Prior Year Operating Loss Carryforward

20. Paragraph 61 of *APB Opinion No. 11*[21] requires that the tax benefit of an operating loss carryforward recognized in a subsequent year be reported as an extraordinary item. Paragraph 19 of *APB Opinion No. 28*[22] excludes extraordinary items from the effective tax rate computation, and para-

[19]See paragraph 47 of *APB Opinion No. 11* (see Appendix A, paragraph 31) and paragraph 20 of *APB Opinion No. 28* (see Appendix A, paragraph 32).

[20]The term "discontinued segment" refers to a discontinued segment of the business as described in paragraph 13 of *APB Opinion No. 30.*

[21]See Appendix A, paragraph 38.

[22]See Appendix A, paragraph 28.

graph 21 of *APB Opinion No. 28*[23] specifies that extraordinary items should not be prorated over the balance of the year. Accordingly, the tax benefit of a prior year operating loss carryforward shall be recognized as an extraordinary item in each interim period to the extent that income in the period and for the year-to-date is available to offset the operating loss carryforward.

Cumulative Effects of Changes in Accounting Principles

21. *FASB Statement No. 3,* "Reporting Accounting Changes in Interim Financial Statements," specifies that the cumulative effect of a change in accounting principle on retained earnings at the beginning of the year shall be reported in the first interim period of the fiscal year. *APB Opinion No. 20,* "Accounting Changes," specifies that the related income tax effect of a cumulative effect type accounting change shall be computed as though the new accounting principle had been applied retroactively for all prior periods that would have been affected.

Operations Taxable in Multiple Jurisdictions

22. If an enterprise that is subject to tax in multiple jurisdictions pays taxes based on identified income in one or more individual jurisdictions, interim period tax (or benefit) related to consolidated "ordinary" income (or loss) for the year-to-date shall be computed in accordance with paragraphs 8-15 above using one overall estimated annual effective tax rate except that:

a. If in a separate jurisdiction an enterprise anticipates an "ordinary" loss for the fiscal year or has an "ordinary" loss for the year-to-date for which, in accordance with paragraphs 14 and 15 above, no tax benefit can be recognized, the enterprise shall exclude "ordinary" income (or loss) in that jurisdiction and the related tax (or benefit) from the overall computations of the estimated annual effective tax rate and interim period tax (or benefit). A separate estimated annual effective tax rate shall be computed for that jurisdiction and applied to "ordinary" income (or loss) in that jurisdiction in accordance with paragraphs 9-15 above.
b. If an enterprise is unable to estimate an annual effective tax rate in a foreign jurisdiction in dollars or is otherwise unable to make a reliable estimate of its "ordinary" income (or loss) or of the related tax (or benefit) for the fiscal year in a jurisdiction, the enterprise shall exclude "ordinary" income (or loss) in that jurisdiction and the related tax (or benefit) from the overall computations of the estimated annual effective tax rate and interim period tax (or benefit). The tax (or benefit) related to "ordinary" income (or loss) in that jurisdiction[24] shall be recognized in the interim period in which the "ordinary" income (or loss) is reported.

Effect of New Tax Legislation

23. Paragraph 20 of *APB Opinion No. 28*[25] states that changes resulting from new tax legislation shall be "reflected after the effective dates prescribed in the statutes." If new tax legislation prescribes changes that become effective during an enterprise's fiscal year, the tax effect of those changes shall be reflected in the computation of the estimated annual effective tax rate beginning with the first interim period that ends after the new legislation becomes effective. Paragraph 24 describes the determination of when new legislation becomes effective.

24. *Effective date.* Legislation generally becomes effective on the date prescribed in the statutes. However, tax legislation may prescribe changes that become effective during an enterprise's fiscal year that are administratively implemented by applying a portion of the change to the full fiscal year. For example, if the statutory tax rate applicable to calendar-year corporations were increased from 48 percent to 52 percent, effective January 1, the increased statutory rate might be administratively applied to a corporation with a fiscal year ending at June 30 in the year of the change by applying a 50 percent rate to its taxable income for the fiscal year, rather than 48 percent for the first six months and 52 percent for the last six months. In that case the legislation becomes effective for that enterprise at the beginning of the enterprise's fiscal year.

Disclosure

25. Application of the provisions of *APB Opinion No. 28* that are described in this Interpretation may result in a significant variation in the customary relationship between income tax expense and pretax accounting income. The reasons for significant variations in the customary relationship between income tax expense and pretax accounting income shall be disclosed if they are not otherwise apparent

[23]See Appendix A, paragraph 35.

[24]The tax (or benefit) related to "ordinary" income (or loss) in a jurisdiction may not be limited to tax (or benefit) in that jurisdiction. It might also include tax (or benefit) in another jurisdiction that results from providing taxes on unremitted earnings, foreign tax credits, etc.

[25]See Appendix A, paragraph 39.

from the financial statements or from the nature of the enterprise's business.[26]

Effective Date and Transition

26. The provisions of this Interpretation shall be effective for financial statements issued after March 31, 1977 for interim periods in fiscal years beginning after December 15, 1976. Earlier application is encouraged for any interim financial statements that have not been previously issued. This Interpretation shall not be applied retroactively for previously issued interim financial statements.

This Interpretation was adopted by the unanimous vote of the six members of the Financial Accounting Standards Board:

Marshall S. Armstrong, *Chairman*
Oscar S. Gellein
Donald J. Kirk
Arthur L. Litke
Robert E. Mays
Robert T. Sprouse

Appendix A

EXCERPTS FROM APB OPINIONS

27. This Appendix contains relevant excerpts from APB Opinions that relate to this Interpretation. It repeats the general guidance of *APB Opinion No. 28* on accounting for income taxes in interim financial reports and the specific paragraphs of *APB Opinion No. 11* that prescribe the annual accounting for income taxes in certain situations.

General Guidelines

28. Paragraph 19 of *APB Opinion No. 28* contains the following general guidelines for the computation of income tax provisions for interim periods:

> In reporting interim financial information, income tax provisions should be determined under the procedures set forth in APB Opinion Nos. 11, 23, and 24. At the end of each interim period the company should make its best estimate of the effective tax rate expected to be applicable for the full fiscal year. The rate so determined should be used in providing for income taxes on a current year-to-date basis. The effective tax rate should reflect anticipated investment tax credits, foreign tax rates, percentage depletion, capital gains rates, and other available tax planning alternatives.

The paragraph continues with the following regarding the tax effects of unusual or extraordinary items:

> However, in arriving at this effective tax rate no effect should be included for the tax related to significant unusual or extraordinary items that will be separately reported or reported net of their related tax effect in reports for the interim period or for the fiscal year. . . .

Recognition of the Tax Benefit of a Loss

29. Paragraph 44 of *APB Opinion No. 11* states the following with respect to tax benefits of loss carrybacks:

> The tax effects of any realizable loss carry*backs* should be recognized in the determination of net income (loss) of the loss periods. The tax loss gives rise to a refund (or claim for refund) of past taxes, which is both measurable and currently realizable; therefore the tax effect of the loss is properly recognizable in the determination of net income (loss) for the loss period. (Emphasis in original.)

30. Paragraph 45 of *APB Opinion No. 11* states the following with respect to tax benefits of loss carryforwards:

> The tax effects of loss carry*forwards* also relate to the determination of net income (loss) of the loss periods. However, a significant question generally exists as to realization of the tax effects of the carry*forwards,* since realization is dependent upon future taxable income. Accordingly, the Board [APB] has concluded that the tax benefits of loss carry*forwards* should not be recognized until they are actually realized, except in unusual circumstances when realization is *assured beyond any reasonable doubt* at the time the loss carry*forwards* arise. (Emphasis in original.)

31. Paragraph 47 of *APB Opinion No. 11* describes the circumstances that may assure future realization of the tax benefit of a loss carryforward beyond any reasonable doubt as follows:

> Realization of the tax benefit of a loss carry*forward* would appear to be assured beyond any reasonable doubt when both of the following conditions exist: (a) the loss results from an iden-

[26]See Appendix A, paragraph 37.

> tifiable, isolated and nonrecurring cause and the company either has been continuously profitable over a long period or has suffered occasional losses which were more than offset by taxable income in subsequent years, and (b) future taxable income is virtually certain to be large enough to offset the loss carry*forward* and will occur soon enough to provide realization during the carry*forward* period. (Emphasis in original.)

32. Paragraph 20 of *APB Opinion No. 28* states the following with respect to losses that arise in the early portion of a fiscal year:

> The tax effects of losses that arise in the early portion of a fiscal year (in the event carryback of such losses is not possible) should be recognized only when realization is assured beyond any reasonable doubt (paragraph 45 of APB Opinion No. 11). An established seasonal pattern of loss in early interim periods offset by income in later interim periods should constitute evidence that realization is assured beyond reasonable doubt, unless other evidence indicates the established seasonal pattern will not prevail. The tax effects of losses incurred in early interim periods may be recognized in a later interim period of a fiscal year if their realization, although initially uncertain, later becomes assured beyond reasonable doubt. When the tax effects of losses that arise in the early portions of a fiscal year are not recognized in that interim period, no tax provision should be made for income that arises in later interim periods until the tax effects of the previous interim losses are utilized. . . .

Reversal of Net Deferred Tax Credits

33. Paragraph 48 of *APB Opinion No. 11* states the following with respect to reversal in a loss year of existing net deferred tax credits arising from timing differences:

> Net deferred tax credits arising from timing differences may exist at the time loss carry*forwards* arise. In the usual case when the tax effect of a loss carry*forward* is not recognized in the loss period, adjustments of the existing net deferred tax credits may be necessary in that period or in subsequent periods. In this situation net deferred tax credits should be eliminated to the extent of the lower of (a) the tax effect of the loss carry*forward,* or (b) the amortization of the net deferred tax credits that would otherwise have occurred during the carry*forward* period. (Emphasis in original.)

34. Paragraph 46 of *APB Opinion No. 11* suggests that existing net deferred tax credits arising from timing differences that will be amortized during the carryforward period of a current year operating loss carryforward should be accounted for the same as if there were assurance of realization of the tax benefits of the loss carryforward beyond any reasonable doubt when it states:

> In those rare cases in which realization of the tax benefits of loss carry*forwards* is assured beyond any reasonable doubt, the potential benefits should be associated with the periods of loss and should be recognized in the determination of results of operations for those periods. Realization is considered to be assured beyond any reasonable doubt when conditions such as those set forth in paragraph 47 are present. (Also see paragraph 48.) (Emphasis in original.)

Tax (or Benefit) Applicable to Significant Unusual or Infrequently Occurring Items, Discontinued Operations, or Extraordinary Items

35. Paragraph 21 of *APB Opinion No. 28* states the following with respect to significant unusual or infrequently occurring items, discontinued operations, or extraordinary items:

> Extraordinary items should be disclosed separately and included in the determination of net income for the interim period in which they occur. In determining materiality, extraordinary items should be related to the estimated income for the full fiscal year. Effects of disposals of a segment of a business and unusual and infrequently occurring transactions and events that are material with respect to the operating results of the interim period but that are not designated as extraordinary items in the interim statements should be reported separately. . . . Extraordinary items, gains or losses from disposal of a segment of a business, and unusual or infrequently occurring items should not be prorated over the balance of the fiscal year.

Tax Allocation within a Period

36. Paragraph 52 of *APB Opinion No. 11* states the following concerning tax allocation within a period:

> The Board [APB] has concluded that tax allocation within a period should be applied to obtain an appropriate relationship between income tax expense and (a) income before extraordinary items, (b) extraordinary items, (c) adjustments of prior periods (or of the opening balance of retained earnings) and (d) direct entries to other stockholders' equity accounts. The income tax expense attributable to income before extraordinary items is computed by

determining the income tax expense related to revenue and expense transactions entering into the determination of such income, without giving effect to the tax consequences of the items excluded from the determination of income before extraordinary items. The income tax expense attributable to other items is determined by the tax consequences of transactions involving these items. If an operating loss exists before extraordinary items, the tax consequences of such loss should be associated with the loss.

Disclosure

37. Footnote 2 to paragraph 19 of *APB Opinion No. 28* states the following concerning the annual effective tax rate:

> Disclosure should be made of the reasons for significant variations in the customary relationship between income tax expense and pretax accounting income, if they are not otherwise apparent from the financial statements or from the nature of the entity's business (see APB Opinion No. 11, paragraph 63).

Paragraph 63 of *APB Opinion No. 11* requires disclosure of:

> Reasons for significant variations in the customary relationships between income tax expense and pretax accounting income, if they are not otherwise apparent from the financial statements or from the nature of the entity's business.

Using a Prior Year Operating Loss Carryforward

38. Paragraph 61 of *APB Opinion No. 11* specifies:

> When the tax benefit of an operating loss carry*forward* is realized in full or in part in a subsequent period, and has not been previously recognized in the loss period, the tax benefit should be reported as an extraordinary item . . . in the results of operations of the period in which realized. (Emphasis in original.)

Effect of New Tax Legislation

39. Paragraph 20 of *APB Opinion No. 28* also contains the following guidance with respect to the effect of new tax legislation:

> Changes resulting from new tax legislation should be reflected after the effective dates prescribed in the statutes.

Appendix B

CROSS REFERENCE TABLE

40. This Appendix provides a cross reference from the paragraphs of this Intepretation to the paragraphs in Appendixes C and D that illustrate the application of those paragraphs.

Interpretation Paragraph Numbers		Example at Paragraph Numbers
8	Estimated annual effective tax rate	43, 49, 53, 54
	Changes in estimates	48
9	Computation of interim period tax (or benefit) applicable to "ordinary" income (or loss):	
	"Ordinary" income anticipated for fiscal year:	
10	Year-to-date "ordinary" income	44, 45
11	Year-to-date "ordinary" loss	46, 47
	"Ordinary" loss anticipated for fiscal year:	
12	Year-to-date "ordinary" income	51, 54
13	Year-to-date "ordinary" loss	50, 52, 53
14	Recognition of the tax benefit of a loss	50, 52, 53, 54
	Year-to-date loss-special computation	46, 47, 51
15	Reversal of net deferred tax credits	55
16	Tax (or benefit) applicable to significant unusual, infrequently occurring, or extraordinary items	57, 58
17	Financial statement presentation	71
18	Recognition of the tax benefit of a loss	57, 58
19	Tax (or benefit) applicable to discontinued operations	62
20	Using a prior year operating loss carryforward	59, 60, 61
21	Cumulative effects of changes in accounting principles	63, 64
22	Operations taxable in multiple jurisdictions	65
22a	"Ordinary" loss, realization not assured	66
22b	Unable to estimate in a jurisdiction	67
	Effect of new tax legislation:	
23	Effective in a future interim period	69
23	Effective in a past interim period	70

Appendix C

EXAMPLES OF COMPUTATIONS OF INTERIM PERIOD INCOME TAXES

41. This Appendix provides examples of application of this Interpretation for some specific situations. In general, the examples illustrate matters unique to accounting for income taxes at interim dates. The examples do not include consideration of the nature of tax credits and permanent differences or illustrate all possible combinations of circumstances.

42. Specific situations illustrated in this Appendix are:

Accounting for Income Taxes Applicable to "Ordinary" Income (or Loss) at an Interim Date If "Ordinary" Income Is Anticipated for the Fiscal Year

43. The following assumed facts are applicable to the examples of application of this Interpretation in paragraphs 44-47.

For the full fiscal year, an enterprise anticipates "ordinary" income of $100,000. All income is taxable in one jurisdiction at a 50 percent rate.

Anticipated tax credits for the fiscal year total $10,000. No permanent differences are anticipated. No changes in estimated "ordinary" income, tax rates, or tax credits occur during the year.

Computation of the estimated annual effective tax rate applicable to "ordinary" income is as follows:

Tax at statutory rate ($100,000 at 50%)	$ 50,000
Less anticipated tax credits	(10,000)
Net tax to be provided	$ 40,000
Estimated annual effective tax rate ($40,000 ÷ $100,000)	40%

Tax credits are generally subject to limitations, usually based on the amount of tax payable before the credits. In computing the estimated annual effective tax rate, anticipated tax credits are limited to the amounts that are expected to be realized or are expected to be assured of future realization beyond any reasonable doubt at year-end. An exception to this general rule occurs in the computation of deferred taxes resulting from timing differences. If tax credits are not realized but the credits would have been realized if timing differences were not present, the credits are accounted for as a tax benefit and included in the estimated annual effective tax rate. If an enterprise is unable to estimate the amount of its tax credits for the year, see footnote 7 to paragraph 8.

44. Assume the facts stated in paragraph 43. The enterprise has "ordinary" income in all interim periods. Quarterly tax computations are:

	"Ordinary" income		Estimated annual	Tax		
Reporting Period	Reporting period	Year-to-date	effective tax rate	Year-to-date	Less previously provided	Reporting period
First quarter	$ 20,000	$ 20,000	40%	$ 8,000	$ —	$ 8,000
Second quarter	20,000	40,000	40%	16,000	8,000	8,000
Third quarter	20,000	60,000	40%	24,000	16,000	8,000
Fourth quarter	40,000	100,000	40%	40,000	24,000	16,000
Fiscal year	$100,000					$40,000

45. Assume the facts stated in paragraph 43. The enterprise has "ordinary" income and losses in interim periods; there is not an "ordinary" loss for the fiscal year-to-date at the end of any interim period. Quarterly tax computations are:

	"Ordinary" income (loss)		Estimated annual	Tax (or benefit)		
Reporting Period	Reporting period	Year-to-date	effective tax rate	Year-to-date	Less previously provided	Reporting period
First quarter	$ 40,000	$ 40,000	40%	$16,000	$ —	$16,000
Second quarter	40,000	80,000	40%	32,000	16,000	16,000
Third quarter	(20,000)	60,000	40%	24,000	32,000	(8,000)
Fourth quarter	40,000	100,000	40%	40,000	24,000	16,000
Fiscal year	$100,000					$40,000

46. Assume the facts stated in paragraph 43. The enterprise has "ordinary" income and losses in interim periods, and there is an "ordinary" loss for the year-to-date at the end of an interim period. Established seasonal patterns assure the realization of the tax benefit of the year-to-date loss and realization of anticipated tax credits beyond any reasonable doubt. Quarterly tax computations are:

	"Ordinary" income (loss)		Estimated annual	Tax (or benefit)		
Reporting Period	Reporting period	Year-to-date	effective tax rate	Year-to-date	Less previously provided	Reporting period
First quarter	$ (20,000)	$ (20,000)	40%	$ (8,000)	$ —	$ (8,000)
Second quarter	10,000	(10,000)	40%	(4,000)	(8,000)	4,000
Third quarter	15,000	5,000	40%	2,000	(4,000)	6,000
Fourth quarter	95,000	100,000	40%	40,000	2,000	38,000
Fiscal year	$100,000					$40,000

47. Assume the facts stated in paragraph 43. The enterprise has "ordinary" income and losses in interim periods, and there is a year-to-date "ordinary" loss during the year. There is no established seasonal pattern, and realization of the tax benefit of the year-to-date loss and realization of the anticipated tax credits are not otherwise assured beyond any reasonable doubt. Quarterly tax computations are:

	"Ordinary" income (loss)		Estimated annual	Tax		
Reporting Period	Reporting period	Year-to-date	effective tax rate	Year-to-date	Less previously provided	Reporting period
First quarter	$ (20,000)	$ (20,000)	—*	$ —	$ —	$ —
Second quarter	10,000	(10,000)	—*	—	—	—
Third quarter	15,000	5,000	40%	2,000	—	2,000
Fourth quarter	95,000	100,000	40%	40,000	2,000	38,000
Fiscal year	$100,000					$40,000

*No benefit is recognized because realization of the tax benefit of the year-to-date loss is not assured beyond any reasonable doubt.

48. During the fiscal year, all of an enterprise's operations are taxable in one jurisdiction at a 50 percent rate. No permanent differences are anticipated. Estimates of "ordinary" income for the year and of anticipated credits at the end of each interim period are as shown below. Changes in the estimated annual effective tax rate result from changes in the ratio of anticipated tax credits to tax computed at the statutory rate. Changes consist of an unanticipated strike that reduced income in the second quarter, an increase in the capital budget resulting in an increase in anticipated investment tax credit in the third quarter, and better than anticipated sales and income in the fourth quarter. The enterprise has "ordinary" income in all interim periods. Computations of the estimated annual effective tax rate based on the estimate made at the end of each quarter are:

	Estimated, end of			Actual fiscal
	First quarter	Second quarter	Third quarter	year
Estimated "ordinary" income for the fiscal year	$100,000	$80,000	$80,000	$100,000
Tax at 50% statutory rate	$ 50,000	$40,000	$40,000	$ 50,000
Less anticipated credits	(5,000)	(5,000)	(10,000)	(10,000)
Net tax to be provided	$ 45,000	$35,000	$30,000	$ 40,000
Estimated annual effective tax rate	45%	43.75%	37.5%	40%

Quarterly tax computations are:

	"Ordinary" income		Estimated annual effective tax rate	Tax		
Reporting Period	Reporting period	Year-to-date		Year-to-date	Less previously provided	Reporting period
First quarter	$ 25,000	$ 25,000	45%	$11,250	$ —	$11,250
Second quarter	5,000	30,000	43.75%	13,125	11,250	1,875
Third quarter	25,000	55,000	37.5%	20,625	13,125	7,500
Fourth quarter	45,000	100,000	40%	40,000	20,625	19,375
Fiscal year	$100,000					$40,000

Accounting for Income Taxes Applicable to "Ordinary" Income (or Loss) at an Interim Date If an "Ordinary" Loss Is Anticipated for the Fiscal Year

49. The following assumed facts are applicable to the examples of application of this Interpretation in paragraphs 50-54.

For the full fiscal year, an enterprise anticipates an "ordinary" loss of $100,000. The enterprise operates entirely in one jurisdiction where the tax rate is 50 percent. Anticipated tax credits for the fiscal year total $10,000. No permanent differences are anticipated.

If realization of the tax benefit of the loss and realization of tax credits were assured beyond any reasonable doubt, computation of the estimated annual effective tax rate applicable to the "ordinary" loss would be as follows:

Tax benefit at statutory rate ($100,000 at 50%)	$(50,000)
Tax credits	(10,000)
Net tax benefit	$(60,000)
Estimated annual effective tax rate ($60,000 ÷ $100,000)	60%

The examples in paragraphs 50-54 state varying assumptions with respect to assurance of realization of the components of the net tax benefit. When the realization of a component of the benefit is not assured beyond any reasonable doubt, that component is not included in the computation of the estimated annual effective tax rate.

50. Assume the facts stated in paragraph 49. The enterprise has "ordinary" losses in all interim periods. Realization of the full tax benefit of the anticipated "ordinary" loss and realization of anticipated tax credits are assured beyond any reasonable doubt because they will be carried back. Quarterly tax computations are:

	"Ordinary" loss		Estimated annual effective tax rate	Tax benefit		
Reporting Period	Reporting period	Year-to-date		Year-to-date	Less previously provided	Reporting period
First quarter	$ (20,000)	$ (20,000)	60%	$(12,000)	$ —	$(12,000)
Second quarter	(20,000)	(40,000)	60%	(24,000)	(12,000)	(12,000)
Third quarter	(20,000)	(60,000)	60%	(36,000)	(24,000)	(12,000)
Fourth quarter	(40,000)	(100,000)	60%	(60,000)	(36,000)	(24,000)
Fiscal year	$(100,000)					$(60,000)

51. Assume the facts stated in paragraph 49. The enterprise has "ordinary" income and losses in interim periods and for the year-to-date. Realization of the full tax benefit of the anticipated "ordinary" loss and realization of the anticipated tax credits are assured beyond any reasonable doubt because they will be carried back. Realization of the full tax benefit of the maximum year-to-date "ordinary" loss is also assured beyond any reasonable doubt. Quarterly tax computations are:

	"Ordinary" income (loss)		Estimated annual	Tax (or benefit)			
				Year-to-date		Less	
Reporting period	Reporting period	Year-to-date	effective tax rate	Computed	Limited to	previously provided	Reporting period
First quarter	$ 20,000	$ 20,000	60%	$ 12,000		$ —	$ 12,000
Second quarter	(80,000)	(60,000)	60%	(36,000)		12,000	(48,000)
Third quarter	(80,000)	(140,000)	60%	(84,000)	$(80,000)*	(36,000)	(44,000)
Fourth quarter	40,000	(100,000)	60%	(60,000)		(80,000)	20,000
Fiscal year	$(100,000)						$(60,000)

*Because the year-to-date "ordinary" loss exceeds the anticipated "ordinary" loss for the fiscal year, the tax benefit recognized for the year-to-date is limited to the amount that would be recognized if the year-to-date "ordinary" loss were the anticipated "ordinary" loss for the fiscal year. The limitation is computed as follows:

Year-to-date "ordinary" loss times the statutory rate ($140,000 at 50%)	$(70,000)
Estimated tax credits for the year	(10,000)
Year-to-date benefit limited to	$(80,000)

52. In the examples in paragraphs 50 and 51, if neither realization of the tax benefit of the anticipated loss for the fiscal year nor realization of anticipated tax credits were assured beyond any reasonable doubt, the estimated annual effective tax rate for the year would be zero and no tax (or benefit) would be recognized in any quarter. That conclusion is not affected by changes in the mix of income and loss in interim periods during a fiscal year. However, see footnote 7 to paragraph 8 above.

53. Assume the facts stated in paragraph 49. The enterprise has an "ordinary" loss in all interim periods. Realization of the tax benefit of the loss is assured beyond any reasonable doubt only to the extent of $40,000 of prior income available to be offset by carryback ($20,000 of tax at the 50 percent statutory rate). Therefore the estimated annual effective tax rate is 20 percent ($20,000 benefit assured divided by $100,000 estimated fiscal year "ordinary" loss). Quarterly tax computations are:

	"Ordinary" loss		Estimated annual	Tax benefit		
Reporting Period	Reporting period	Year-to-date	effective tax rate	Year-to-date	Less previously provided	Reporting period
First quarter	$ (20,000)	$ (20,000)	20%	$ (4,000)	$ —	$ (4,000)
Second quarter	(20,000)	(40,000)	20%	(8,000)	(4,000)	(4,000)
Third quarter	(20,000)	(60,000)	20%	(12,000)	(8,000)	(4,000)
Fourth quarter	(40,000)	(100,000)	20%	(20,000)	(12,000)	(8,000)
Fiscal year	$(100,000)					$(20,000)

54. Assume the facts stated in paragraph 49. The enterprise has "ordinary" income and losses in interim periods and for the year-to-date. Realization of the tax benefit of the anticipated "ordinary" loss is assured beyond any reasonable doubt only to the extent of $40,000 of prior income available to be offset by carryback ($20,000 of tax at the 50 percent statutory rate). Therefore the estimated annual effective tax rate is 20 percent ($20,000 benefit assured divided by $100,000 estimated fiscal year "ordinary" loss), and the benefit that can be recognized for the year-to-date is limited to $20,000 (the benefit that is assured of realization). Quarterly tax computations are:

	"Ordinary" income (loss)		Estimated annual	Tax (or benefit)			
				Year-to-date		Less	
Reporting period	Reporting period	Year-to-date	effective tax rate	Computed	Limited to	previously provided	Reporting period
First quarter	$ 20,000	$ 20,000	20%	$ 4,000		$ —	$ 4,000
Second quarter	(80,000)	(60,000)	20%	(12,000)		4,000	(16,000)
Third quarter	(80,000)	(140,000)	20%	(28,000)	$(20,000)	(12,000)	(8,000)
Fourth quarter	40,000	(100,000)	20%	(20,000)		(20,000)	—
Fiscal year	$(100,000)						$(20,000)

55. The enterprise anticipates a fiscal year "ordinary" loss. The loss cannot be carried back, and future profits are not assured beyond any reasonable doubt. Net deferred tax credits arising from timing differences are present. A portion of the timing differences relating to those credits will reverse within the loss carryforward period. Computation of the estimated annual effective tax rate to be used is as follows:

Estimated fiscal year "ordinary" loss		$(100,000)
The tax benefit to be recognized is the lesser of:		
Tax effect of the loss carryforward ($100,000 at 50% statutory rate)	$50,000	
Amount of the net deferred tax credits that would otherwise have been amortized during the carryforward period	$24,000	
Estimated annual effective tax rate ($24,000 ÷ $100,000)		24%

Quarterly tax computations are:

	"Ordinary" loss		Estimated annual	Tax benefit		
Reporting Period	Reporting period	Year-to-date	effective tax rate	Year-to-date	Less previously provided	Reporting period
First quarter	$ (20,000)	$ (20,000)	24%	$ (4,800)	$ —	$ (4,800)
Second quarter	(20,000)	(40,000)	24%	(9,600)	(4,800)	(4,800)
Third quarter	(20,000)	(60,000)	24%	(14,400)	(9,600)	(4,800)
Fourth quarter	(40,000)	(100,000)	24%	(24,000)	(14,400)	(9,600)
Fiscal year	$(100,000)					$(24,000)

Note: Changes in the timing of the loss by quarter would not change the above computation.

Accounting for Income Taxes Applicable to Unusual, Infrequently Occurring, or Extraordinary Items

56. The examples of computations in paragraphs 57 and 58 illustrate the computation of the tax (or benefit) applicable to unusual, infrequently occurring, or extraordinary items when "ordinary" income is anticipated for the fiscal year. These examples are based on the facts and computations given in paragraphs 43-47 plus additional information supplied in paragraphs 57 and 58. The computation of the tax (or benefit) applicable to the "ordinary" income is not affected by the occurrence of an unusual, infrequently occurring, or extraordinary item; therefore, each example refers to one or more of the examples of that computation in paragraphs 44-47 and does not reproduce the computation and the facts assumed. The income statement display for tax (or benefit) applicable to unusual, infrequently occurring, or extraordinary items is illustrated in Appendix D.

57. As explained in paragraph 56, this example is based on the computations of tax applicable to "ordinary" income that are illustrated in paragraph 44 above. In addition, the enterprise experiences a tax-deductible unusual, infrequently occurring, or extraordinary loss of $50,000 (tax benefit $25,000) in the second quarter. Because the loss can be carried back, the benefit of the loss is assured beyond any reasonable doubt at the time of occurrence. Quarterly tax provisions are:

			Tax (or benefit) applicable to	
Reporting period	"Ordinary" income	Unusual, infrequently occurring, or extraordinary loss	"Ordinary" income	Unusual, infrequently occurring, or extraordinary loss
First quarter	$ 20,000		$ 8,000	
Second quarter	20,000	$(50,000)	8,000	$(25,000)
Third quarter	20,000		8,000	
Fourth quarter	40,000		16,000	
Fiscal year	$100,000	$(50,000)	$40,000	$(25,000)

Note: Changes in assumptions would not change the timing of the recognition of the tax benefit applicable to the unusual, infrequently occurring, or extraordinary item as long as realization is assured beyond any reasonable doubt.

58. As explained in paragraph 56, this example is based on the computations of tax applicable to "ordinary" income that are illustrated in paragraphs 44 and 45 above. In addition, the enterprise experiences a tax-deductible unusual, infrequently occurring, or extraordinary loss of $50,000 (potential benefit $25,000) in the second quarter. The loss cannot be carried back, and the current projection of "ordinary" income is not considered sufficiently reliable to assure realization of the tax benefit of the year-to-date loss beyond any reasonable doubt. As a result, realization of the tax benefit of the unusual, infrequently occurring, or extraordinary loss is not assured beyond any reasonable doubt except to the extent of offsetting "ordinary" income for the year-to-date. Quarterly tax provisions under two different assumptions for the occurrence of "ordinary" income are:

			Tax (or benefit) applicable to				
			"Ordinary" income (loss)		Unusual, infrequently occurring, or extraordinary loss		
Assumptions and reporting period	"Ordinary" income (loss)	Unusual, infrequently occurring, or extraordinary loss	Reporting period	Year-to-date	Year-to-date	Less previously provided	Reporting period
Income in all quarters:							
First quarter	$ 20,000		$ 8,000	$ 8,000			
Second quarter	20,000	$(50,000)	8,000	16,000	$(16,000)	$ —	$(16,000)
Third quarter	20,000		8,000	24,000	(24,000)	(16,000)	(8,000)
Fourth quarter	40,000		16,000	40,000	(25,000)	(24,000)	(1,000)
Fiscal year	$100,000	$(50,000)	$40,000				$(25,000)
Income and loss quarters:							
First quarter	$ 40,000		$16,000	$16,000			
Second quarter	40,000	$(50,000)	16,000	32,000	$ (25,000)	$ —	$ (25,000)
Third quarter	(20,000)		(8,000)	24,000	(24,000)	(25,000)	1,000
Fourth quarter	40,000		16,000	40,000	(25,000)	(24,000)	(1,000)
Fiscal year	$100,000	$(50,000)	$40,000				$ (25,000)

Using a Prior Year Operating Loss Carryforward

59. The examples of computations in paragraphs 60 and 61 illustrate the computation of the tax benefit that results from using a prior year operating loss carryforward. The examples are based on the following assumed facts.

For the full fiscal year, an enterprise anticipates "ordinary" income of $100,000. All income is taxable in one jurisdiction at a 50 percent rate. No tax credits or permanent differences are anticipated. If an operating loss carryforward is available, the estimated tax (or benefit) applicable to "ordinary" income (or loss) for the year is divided by the estimated "ordinary" income (or loss) for the year to arrive at an estimated annual effective tax rate. That rate is 50 percent in these examples. The estimated annual effective tax rate is applied to "ordinary" income (or loss) for the year-to-date to determine the year-to-date tax (or benefit) applicable to "ordinary" income (or loss), similar to the computations that are illustrated in paragraphs 44-47.

60. Assume the facts stated in paragraph 59. In addition, an operating loss carryforward is available that exceeds the estimated "ordinary" income for the year. Because *APB Opinion No. 28* required that an extraordinary item be recognized in the interim period of its occurrence and not spread over the year, the extraordinary credit recognized for the year-to-date at the end of each interim period is the amount that is realized by offsetting year-to-date taxable income. Quarterly tax provisions under various assumptions for the occurrence of "ordinary" income are:

Assumptions and reporting period	"Ordinary" income (loss)	Tax (or benefit) Reporting period	Year-to-date	Extraordinary charge (or credit)* Year-to-date	Less previously provided	Reporting period
Income in all quarters:						
First quarter	$ 20,000	$10,000	$10,000	$(10,000)	$ —	$(10,000)
Second quarter	20,000	10,000	20,000	(20,000)	(10,000)	(10,000)
Third quarter	20,000	10,000	30,000	(30,000)	(20,000)	(10,000)
Fourth quarter	40,000	20,000	50,000	(50,000)	(30,000)	(20,000)
Fiscal year	$100,000	$50,000				$(50,000)
Income and loss quarters; no year-to-date losses:						
First quarter	$ 40,000	$20,000	$20,000	$(20,000)	$ —	$(20,000)
Second quarter	40,000	20,000	40,000	(40,000)	(20,000)	(20,000)
Third quarter	(20,000)	(10,000)	30,000	(30,000)	(40,000)	10,000
Fourth quarter	40,000	20,000	50,000	(50,000)	(30,000)	(20,000)
Fiscal year	$100,000	$50,000				$(50,000)
Income and loss quarters and including year-to-date loss (realization of the tax benefit of the year-to-date "ordinary" loss and realization of anticipated tax credits are assured beyond any reasonable doubt by seasonal patterns):						
First quarter	$ (20,000)	$(10,000)	$(10,000)	$ —	$ —	$ —
Second quarter	10,000	5,000	(5,000)	—	—	—
Third quarter	15,000	7,500	2,500	(2,500)	—	(2,500)
Fourth quarter	95,000	47,500	50,000	(50,000)	(2,500)	(47,500)
Fiscal year	$100,000	$50,000				$(50,000)
Income and loss quarters, including year-to-date loss (realization of the tax benefit of the year-to-date "ordinary" loss and realization of anticipated tax credits are not assured beyond any reasonable doubt):						
First quarter	$ (20,000)	$ —	$ —	$ —	$ —	$ —
Second quarter	10,000	—	—	—	—	—
Third quarter	15,000	2,500	2,500	(2,500)	—	(2,500)
Fourth quarter	95,000	47,500	50,000	(50,000)	(2,500)	(47,500)
Fiscal year	$100,000	$50,000				$(50,000)

*Tax benefit resulting from using the operating loss carryforward.

61. Assume the facts stated in paragraph 59. In addition, an operating loss carryforward of $30,000 (tax benefit $15,000 at the 50 percent statutory rate) is available. Because *APB Opinion No. 28* requires that an extraordinary item be recognized in the interim period of its occurrence and not spread over the year, the extraordinary credit recognized for the year-to-date at the end of each interim period is the amount that is realized by offsetting year-to-date taxable income. Quarterly tax provisions are:

		Tax provision		Extraordinary credit		
Reporting period	"Ordinary" income	Reporting period	Year-to-date	Year-to-date	Less previously provided	Reporting period
First quarter	$ 20,000	$10,000	$10,000	$(10,000)	$ —	$(10,000)
Second quarter	20,000	10,000	20,000	(15,000)	(10,000)	(5,000)
Third quarter	20,000	10,000	30,000	(15,000)	(15,000)	—
Fourth quarter	40,000	20,000	50,000	(15,000)	(15,000)	—
Fiscal year	$100,000	$50,000				$(15,000)

Note: Differing patterns of occurrence of "ordinary" income and loss would result in computations similar to those in paragraph 60.

Accounting for Income Taxes Applicable to Income (or Loss) from Discontinued Operations at an Interim Date

62. An enterprise anticipates "ordinary" income for the year of $100,000 and tax credits of $10,000. The enterprise has "ordinary" income in all interim periods. The estimated annual effective tax rate is 40 percent, computed as follows:

Estimated pretax income	$ 100,000
Tax at 50% statutory rate	$ 50,000
Less anticipated credits	(10,000)
Net tax to be provided	$ 40,000
Estimated annual effective tax rate	40%

Quarterly tax computations for the first two quarters are:

	"Ordinary" income			Tax		
Reporting Period	Reporting period	Year-to-date	Estimated annual effective tax rate	Year-to-date	Less previously provided	Reporting period
First quarter	$20,000	$20,000	40%	$ 8,000	$ —	$ 8,000
Second quarter	25,000	45,000	40%	18,000	8,000	10,000

In the third quarter a decision is made to discontinue the operations of Division X, a segment of the business that has recently operated at a loss (before income taxes). The pretax income (and losses) of the continuing operations of the enterprise and of Division X through the third quarter and the estimated fourth quarter results are as follows:

		Division X	
Reporting period	Revised "ordinary" income from continuing operations	Loss from operations	Provision for loss on disposal
First quarter	$ 25,000	$ (5,000)	
Second quarter	35,000	(10,000)	
Third quarter	50,000	(10,000)	$(55,000)
Fourth quarter	50,000*	—	—
Fiscal year	$160,000	$(25,000)	$(55,000)

*Estimated.

No changes have occurred in continuing operations that would affect the estimated annual effective tax rate. Anticipated annual tax credits of $10,000 included $2,000 of credits related to the operations of Division X. The revised estimated annual effective tax rate applicable to "ordinary" income from continuing operations is 45 percent, computed as follows:

Estimated "ordinary" income from continuing operations	$160,000
Tax at 50% statutory rate	$ 80,000
Less anticipated tax credits applicable to continuing operations	(8,000)
Net tax to be provided	$ 72,000
Estimated annual effective tax rate	45%

Quarterly computations of tax applicable to "ordinary" income from continuing operations are as follows:

	"Ordinary" income		Estimated annual effective tax rate	Tax		
Reporting Period	Reporting period	Year-to-date		Year-to-date	Less previously provided	Reporting period
First quarter	$ 25,000	$ 25,000	45%	$11,250	$ —	$11,250
Second quarter	35,000	60,000	45%	27,000	11,250	15,750
Third quarter	50,000	110,000	45%	49,500	27,000	22,500
Fourth quarter	50,000	160,000	45%	72,000	49,500	22,500
Fiscal year	$160,000					$72,000

Tax benefit applicable to Division X for the first two quarters is computed as follows:

	Tax applicable to "ordinary" income		
Reporting period	Previously reported (A)	Recomputed (above) (B)	Tax benefit applicable to Division X (A – B)
First quarter	$ 8,000	$11,250	$(3,250)
Second quarter	10,000	15,750	(5,750)
			$(9,000)

The third quarter tax benefits applicable to both the loss from operations and the provision for loss on disposal of Division X are computed based on estimated annual income with and without the effects of the Division X losses. Current year tax credits related to the operations of Division X have not been recognized. It is assumed that the tax benefit of those credits will not be realized because of the discontinuance of Division X operations. Any reduction in tax benefits resulting from recapture of previously recognized tax credits resulting from discontinuance or current year tax credits applicable to the discontinued operations would be reflected in the tax benefit recognized for the loss on disposal or loss from operations as appropriate. If, because of capital gains and losses, etc., the individually computed tax effects of the items do not equal the aggregate tax effects of the items, the aggregate tax effects are allocated to the indiviaul items in the same manner that they will be allocated in the annual financial statements. The computations are as follows:

	Loss from operations Division X	Provision for loss on disposal
Estimated annual income from continuing operations	$160,000	$160,000
Loss from Division X operations	(25,000)	
Provision for loss on disposal of Division X		(55,000)
Total	$135,000	$105,000
Tax at 50% statutory rate	$ 67,500	$ 52,500
Anticipated credits from continuing operations	(8,000)	(8,000)
Tax credits of Division X and recapture of previously recognized tax credits resulting from discontinuance	—	—
Taxes on income after effect of Division X losses	59,500	44,500
Taxes on income before effect of Division X losses—see computation above	72,000	72,000
Tax benefit applicable to the losses of Division X	(12,500)	(27,500)
Amounts previously recognized—see computation above	(9,000)	—
Tax benefit recognized in third quarter	$ (3,500)	$ (27,500)

The resulting revised quarterly tax provisions are summarized as follows:

	Pretax income (loss)			Tax (or benefit) applicable to		
Reporting period	Continuing operations	Operations of Division X	Provision for loss on disposal	Continuing operations	Operations of Division X	Provision for loss on disposal
First quarter	$ 25,000	$ (5,000)		$11,250	$ (3,250)	
Second quarter	35,000	(10,000)		15,750	(5,750)	
Third quarter	50,000	(10,000)	$(55,000)	22,500	(3,500)	$(27,500)
Fourth quarter	50,000			22,500		
Fiscal year	$160,000	$(25,000)	$(55,000)	$72,000	$(12,500)	$(27,500)

Accounting for Income Taxes Applicable to the Cumulative Effect of a Change in Accounting Principle

63. The tax (or benefit) applicable to the cumulative effect of the change on retained earnings at the beginning of the fiscal year shall be computed the same as for the annual financial statements.

64. When an enterprise makes a cumulative effect type accounting change in other than the first interim period of the enterprise's fiscal year, paragraph 10 of *FASB Statement No. 3,* "Reporting Accounting Changes in Interim Financial Statements," requires that financial information for the pre-change interim periods of the fiscal year shall be restated by applying the newly adopted accounting principle to those pre-change interim periods. The tax (or benefit) applicable to those pre-change interim periods shall be recomputed. The restated tax (or benefit) shall reflect the year-to-date amounts and annual estimates originally used for the pre-change interim periods, modified only for the effect of the change in accounting principle on those year-to-date and estimated annual amounts.

Accounting for Income Taxes Applicable to "Ordinary" Income If an Enterprise Is Subject to Tax in Multiple Jurisdictions

65. An enterprise operates through separate corporate entities in two countries. Applicable tax rates are 50 percent in the United States and 20 percent in Country A. The enterprise has no unusual or extraordinary items during the fiscal year and anticipates no tax credits or permanent differences. (The effect of foreign tax credits and the necessity of providing tax on undistributed earnings are ignored

because of the wide range of tax planning alternatives available.) For the full fiscal year the enterprise anticipates "ordinary" income of $60,000 in the United States and $40,000 in Country A. The enterprise is able to make a reliable estimate of its Country A "ordinary" income and tax for the fiscal year in dollars. Computation of the overall estimated annual effective tax rate is as follows:

Anticipated "ordinary" income for the fiscal year:	
In the U.S.	$ 60,000
In Country A	40,000
Total	$100,000
Anticipated tax for the fiscal year:	
In the U.S. ($60,000 at 50% statutory rate)	$ 30,000
In Country A ($40,000 at 20% statutory rate)	8,000
Total	$ 38,000
Overall estimated annual effective tax rate ($38,000 ÷ $100,000)	38%

Quarterly tax computations are as follows:

Reporting Period	"Ordinary" income U.S.	Country A	Total	Year-to-date	Overall estimated annual effective tax rate	Tax Year-to-date	Less previously reported	Reporting period
First quarter	$ 5,000	$15,000	$ 20,000	$ 20,000	38%	$ 7,600	$ —	$ 7,600
Second quarter	10,000	10,000	20,000	40,000	38%	15,200	7,600	7,600
Third quarter	10,000	10,000	20,000	60,000	38%	22,800	15,200	7,600
Fourth quarter	35,000	5,000	40,000	100,000	38%	38,000	22,800	15,200
Fiscal year	$60,000	$40,000	$100,000					$38,000

66. Assume the facts stated in paragraph 65. In addition the enterprise operates through a separate corporate entity in Country B. Applicable tax rates in Country B are 40 percent. Operations in Country B have resulted in losses in recent years and an "ordinary" loss is anticipated for the current fiscal year in Country B. Realization of the tax benefit of those losses is not assured beyond any reasonable doubt; accordingly, no tax benefit is recognized for losses in Country B, and interim period tax (or benefit) is separately computed for the "ordinary" loss in Country B and for the overall "ordinary" income in the United States and Country A. The tax applicable to the overall "ordinary" income in the United States and Country A is computed as in paragraph 65. Quarterly tax provisions are as follows:

Reporting Period	"Ordinary" income (or loss) U.S.	Country A	Combined excluding Country B	Country B	Total	Tax (or benefit) Overall excluding Country B	Country B	Total
First quarter	$ 5,000	$15,000	$ 20,000	$ (5,000)	$15,000	$ 7,600	$ —	$ 7,600
Second quarter	10,000	10,000	20,000	(25,000)	(5,000)	7,600	—	7,600
Third quarter	10,000	10,000	20,000	(5,000)	15,000	7,600	—	7,600
Fourth quarter	35,000	5,000	40,000	(5,000)	35,000	15,200	—	15,200
Fiscal year	$60,000	$40,000	$100,000	$(40,000)	$60,000	$38,000	$ —	$38,000

67. Assume the facts stated in paragraph 65. In addition the enterprise operates through a separate corporate entity in Country C. Applicable tax rates in Country C are 40 percent in foreign currency. Depreciation in that country is large and exchange rates have changed in prior years. The enterprise is unable to make a reasonable estimate of its "ordinary" income for the year in Country C and

thus is unable to reasonably estimate its annual effective tax rate in Country C in dollars. Accordingly, tax (or benefit) in Country C is separately computed as "ordinary" income (or loss) occurs in Country C. The tax applicable to the overall "ordinary" income in the United States and Country A is computed as in paragraph 65. Quarterly computations of tax applicable to Country C are as follows:

	Foreign currency amounts		Translated amounts in dollars	
Reporting period	"Ordinary" income in reporting period	Tax (at 40% rate)	"Ordinary" income in reporting period	Tax
First quarter	FC 10,000	FC 4,000	$12,500	$ 3,000
Second quarter	5,000	2,000	8,750	1,500
Third quarter	30,000	12,000	27,500	9,000
Fourth quarter	15,000	6,000	16,250	4,500
Fiscal year	FC 60,000	FC 24,000	$65,000	$18,000

Quarterly tax provisions are as follows:

	"Ordinary" income					Tax		
Reporting Period	U.S.	Country A	Combined excluding Country C	Country C	Total	Overall excluding Country C	Country C	Total
First quarter	$ 5,000	$15,000	$ 20,000	$12,500	$ 32,500	$ 7,600	$ 3,000	$10,600
Second quarter	10,000	10,000	20,000	8,750	28,750	7,600	1,500	9,100
Third quarter	10,000	10,000	20,000	27,500	47,500	7,600	9,000	16,600
Fourth quarter	35,000	5,000	40,000	16,250	56,250	15,200	4,500	19,700
Fiscal year	$ 60,000	$40,000	$100,000	$65,000	$165,000	$38,000	$18,000	$56,000

Effect of New Tax Legislation

68. The following assumed facts are applicable to the examples of application of this Interpretation in paragraphs 69 and 70.

For the full fiscal year, an enterprise anticipates "ordinary" income of $100,000. All income is taxable in one jurisdiction at a 50 percent rate. Anticipated tax credits for the fiscal year total $10,000. No permanent differences are anticipated.

Computation of the estimated annual effective tax rate applicable to "ordinary" income is as follows:

Tax at statutory rate ($100,000 at 50%)	$ 50,000
Less anticipated tax credits	(10,000)
Net tax to be provided	$ 40,000
Estimated annual effective tax rate ($40,000 ÷ $100,000)	40%

69. Assume the facts stated in paragraph 68. In addition, assume that new legislation creating additional tax credits is enacted during the second quarter of the enterprise's fiscal year. The new legislation is effective on the first day of the third quarter. As a result of the estimated effect of the new legislation, the enterprise revises its estimate of its annual effective tax rate to the following:

Tax at statutory rate ($100,000 at 50%)	$ 50,000
Less anticipated tax credits	(12,000)
Net tax to be provided	$ 38,000
Estimated annual effective tax rate ($38,000 ÷ $100,000)	38%

The effect of the new legislation shall not be reflected until it is effective or administratively effective. Accordingly, quarterly tax computations are:

	"Ordinary" income		Estimated	Tax		
Reporting Period	Reporting period	Year-to-date	annual effective tax rate	Year-to-date	Less previously provided	Reporting period
First quarter	$ 20,000	$ 20,000	40%	$ 8,000	$ —	$ 8,000
Second quarter	20,000	40,000	40%	16,000	8,000	8,000
Third quarter	20,000	60,000	38%	22,800	16,000	6,800
Fourth quarter	40,000	100,000	38%	38,000	22,800	15,200
Fiscal year	$100,000					$38,000

70. Assume the facts stated in paragraph 68. In addition, assume that new legislation creating additional tax credits is enacted after the end of the third quarter of the enterprise's fiscal year but before the enterprise has reported the results of its operations for the third quarter. The new legislation is effective retroactive to the first day of the third quarter. The new legislation results in the following revised estimated annual effective tax rate:

Tax at statutory rate ($100,000 at 50%)	$ 50,000
Less anticipated tax credits	(12,000)
Net tax to be provided	$ 38,000
Estimated annual effective tax rate ($38,000 ÷ $100,000)	38%

Quarterly tax computations are:

	"Ordinary" income		Estimated	Tax		
Reporting Period	Reporting period	Year-to-date	annual effective tax rate	Year-to-date	Less previously provided	Reporting period
First quarter	$ 20,000	$ 20,000	40%	$ 8,000	$ —	$ 8,000
Second quarter	20,000	40,000	40%	16,000	8,000	8,000
Third quarter	20,000	60,000	38%	22,800	16,000	6,800
Fourth quarter	40,000	100,000	38%	38,000	22,800	15,200
Fiscal year	$100,000					$38,000

Appendix D

ILLUSTRATION OF INCOME TAXES IN INCOME STATEMENT DISPLAY

71. The following illustrates the location in an income statement display of the various tax amounts computed under this Interpretation:

*Net sales		$XXXX
*Other income		XXX
		XXXX
Costs and expenses:		
*Cost of sales	$XXXX	
*Selling, general, and administrative expenses	XXXX	
*Interest expense	XXX	
*Other deductions	XX	
Unusual items	XXX	
Infrequently occurring items	XXX	XXXX
Income (loss) from continuing operations before income taxes and other items listed below		XXXX
†Provision for income taxes (benefit)		XXXX
Income (loss) from continuing operations before other items listed below		XXXX
Discontinued operations:		
Income (loss) from operations of discontinued Division X (less applicable income taxes of $XXXX)	XXXX	
Income (loss) on disposal of Division X, including provision of $XXXX for operating losses during phase-out period (less applicable income taxes of $XXXX)	XXXX	XXXX
Income (loss) before extraordinary items and cumulative effect of a change in accounting principle		XXXX
Extraordinary items (less applicable income taxes of $XXXX)		XXXX
‡Cumulative effect on prior years of a change in accounting principle (less applicable income taxes of $XXXX)		XXXX
Net income (loss)		$XXXX

*Components of "ordinary" income (loss).

†Consists of the total of income taxes (or benefit) applicable to (a) "ordinary" income, (b) unusual items, and (c) infrequently occurring items.

‡This amount is net of applicable income taxes. The amount of the applicable income taxes is usually separately disclosed but that is not required.

Appendix E

SUMMARY OF CONSIDERATION OF COMMENTS ON EXPOSURE DRAFT

72. The "Notice of Exposure and Request for Comments" accompanying the Exposure Draft issued October 7, 1976 for this Interpretation stated:

> The Interpretation set forth in this EXPOSURE DRAFT explains, clarifies, and elaborates on the requirements of *APB Opinion No. 28,* "Interim Financial Reporting," which relies in part on *APB Opinion No. 11,* "Accounting for Income Taxes," and on other APB Opinions with respect to accounting for income taxes in interim periods.
>
> The FASB currenlty has on its technical agenda a project entitled Interim Financial Reporting. As part of that project, the Board will examine possible methods of accounting for income taxes in interim periods. At the completion of that project, the Board expects to issue a comprehensive Statement specifying the financial accounting and reporting standards to be applied in interim financial reporting. The Board recognizes that some might prefer methods of accounting for income taxes in interim periods other than those required by the concepts of *APB Opinion No. 28.* However, the Board is of the view that any other methods should be considered as part of the FASB's technical agenda project on Interim Financial Reporting.
>
> The FASB Rules of Procedure permit the

issuance of a final Interpretation without exposure for public comment but allow public exposure prior to final issuance when the Board deems such procedure to be advisable. The Board has reached that conclusion here and has also concluded that a public comment period extending to November 15, 1976 is appropriate.

73. In response to the request for comments on the Exposure Draft, the FASB received and considered 99 letters of comment. Certain of the comments and the FASB's consideration of them are summarized in paragraphs 74-85.

Issuance of the Interpretation

74. Many respondents recommended that the FASB not issue a final Interpretation on "Accounting for Income Taxes in Interim Periods" at this time. Some of those respondents recommended that the project be deferred until the FASB issues its comprehensive Statement on Interim Financial Reporting. Others questioned if the number of existing differences in accounting for similar situations was great enough to require an Interpretation at this time.

75. It is not likely that a final Statement for the Board's current agenda project on Interim Financial Reporting will be issued and effective before 1979. Comments received in respect of the Exposure Draft indicate that there is, currently, diversity of practice. The Board concluded that the provisions of *APB Opinion No. 28* are sufficiently clear to provide a basis for an Interpretation and that a final Interpretation should be issued.

Applicability to Annual Financial Statements

76. Some respondents stated that the proposed Interpretation and the examples in Appendix B implicitly included a number of interpretations of the application of *APB Opinion No. 11* to annual financial statements. They recommended that, if the Board intends to interpret Opinion No. 11, the intent should be stated. The Board does not intend to modify annual accounting practices in this Interpretation. Accordingly, specific guidance on those matters that appeared to imply interpretations of the application of *APB Opinion No. 11* to annual financial statements was deleted.

77. Some respondents asked if the example in paragraph 49 of Appendix C of this Interpretation was intended to change the annual accounting for investment tax credits. Paragraph 49 includes "tax credits" in the computed tax benefit of an "ordinary" loss, but does not identify those "tax credits" as "investment tax credits." Various tax credits other than investment tax credits may be available to an enterprise. This Interpretation is not intended to change annual accounting for unrealized investment tax credits.

Applicability to Regulated Industries

78. A number of respondents stated that the proposed Interpretation should not apply to regulated industries. Some respondents noted that the Addendum to *APB Opinion No. 2* may provide an exemption from the Interpretation for certain enterprises in regulated industries. The Board is aware that differing applications of the Addendum exist in practice and has not addressed that issue.

Amortization of Deferred Investment Tax Credits

79. Several respondents recommended that the amortization of deferred investment tax credits be excluded from the estimated annual effective tax rate. Some stated that the rationale of *APB Opinion No. 2* requires those items to be allocated among interim periods on the same basis as depreciation expense for the property giving rise to the credit. Paragraph 13 of Opinion No. 2 states that "the . . . investment credit should be reflected in net income over the productive life of acquired property and not in the year in which it is placed in service."[27] Footnote 6 to paragraph 8 of this Interpretation was revised to indicate that amortization of deferred investment tax credits need not be taken into account in estimating the annual effective tax rate. However, if an enterprise elects to consider investment tax credits in estimating the annual effective tax rate, the amount to be taken into account shall be the estimated amount of the current year's amortization and not the amount that reduces income tax payable on the enterprise's tax return.

Tax Exempt Interest

80. A number of respondents recommended that tax-exempt interest income be excluded from "ordinary" income in estimating the annual effective tax rate and in computing the year-to-date tax (or benefit). A number of them stated that the tax effect of tax-exempt interest income must be reported on a discrete period basis to reflect the economic effects of tax-exempt investments. A few respondents noted that the practice of excluding tax-exempt interest income from "ordinary" income in estimating the annual effective tax rate and in computing interim period tax (or benefit) is followed by virtually all financial institutions. The Board noted

[27]That conclusion was amended by *APB Opinion No. 4*, "Accounting for the 'Investment Credit'." Paragraph 10 of Opinion No. 4 permits "the alternative method of treating the credit as a reduction of Federal income taxes of the year in which the credit arises. . . ."

that the accounting practice described above for tax-exempt interest income in interim periods appears to be uniform and concluded that it should not address the issue in this Interpretation.

Exchange Gains and Losses

81. Several respondents requested that the Board provide guidance on accounting for the tax effects of exchange gains and losses in interim periods. Paragraphs 166 and 192 of *FASB Statement No. 8,* "Accounting for the Translation of Foreign Currency Transactions and Foreign Currency Financial Statements," indicate that it would be rare that the timing, direction, and magnitude of future exchange rate changes and the enterprise's financial position at the time of an expected future exchange rate change could each be reasonably estimated. Footnote 7 to paragraph 8 has been expanded to explain that the tax (or benefit) applicable to an item that cannot be estimated shall be reported in the interim period in which the item is reported.

Estimated Annual Effective Tax Rate

82. Several respondents recommended that an estimated annual effective tax rate not be applied in various specific circumstances. Circumstances mentioned included (a) if the rate is extremely high or low, (b) if an "ordinary" loss is expected for the year, and (c) if an enterprise has a year-to-date "ordinary" income and anticipates an "ordinary" loss for the year. An example cited was an enterprise that experienced "ordinary" income in an early part of the year and anticipated offsetting "ordinary" losses in the balance of the year, resulting in zero estimated "ordinary" income and no tax (or benefit). Such unusual circumstances may result in significant variations in the customary relationship between income tax expense and pretax accounting income in interim periods and footnote 2 to paragraph 19 of Opinion No. 28 requires disclosure of the reasons for those variations. Footnote 7 to paragraph 8 of this Interpretation states that if a reliable estimate cannot be made the actual effective tax rate for the year-to-date may be the best estimate of the annual effective tax rate. What is and what is not a "reliable estimate" is a matter of judgment. In the break-even situation cited above, a small change in the enterprise's estimated "ordinary" income could produce a large change in the estimated annual effective tax rate. In those circumstances, a break-even estimate would not be reliable if a small change in the estimated "ordinary" income were considered likely to occur.

Operations Taxable in Multiple Jurisdictions

83. Many respondents stated that the intent of Opinion No. 28 was to apply one overall estimated annual effective tax rate to "ordinary" income for the consolidated reporting entity. Several respondents stated that interrelationships between jurisdictions would make the use of separate rates impractical. Paragraph 22 was modified to indicate that one overall estimated annual effective tax rate shall be used with the two exceptions described in that paragraph and discussed further in paragraphs 84 and 85 below.

84. If an enterprise that operates in multiple jurisdictions has losses in one or more of the jurisdictions and realization of the tax benefit of the losses is not assured beyond any reasonable doubt, use of one overall estimated annual effective tax rate can result in the recognition of tax benefits for the year-to-date for those losses. Paragraph 20 of Opinion No. 28 states that "the tax effects of losses that arise in the early portion of a fiscal year (in the event carryback of such losses is not possible) should be recognized only when realization is assured beyond any reasonable doubt. . . ." Accordingly, a separate computation is necessary for the tax (or benefit) applicable to "ordinary" income (or loss) in those jurisdictions.

85. The effect of translating foreign currency financial statements may make it difficult to estimate an annual effective foreign currency tax rate in dollars. For example, depreciation is translated at historical exchange rates, whereas many transactions included in income are translated at current period average exchange rates. If depreciation is large in relation to earnings, a change in the estimated "ordinary" income that does not change the effective foreign currency tax rate can change the effective tax rate in the dollar financial statements. This result can occur with no change in exchange rates during the current year if there have been exchange rate changes in past years. If the enterprise is unable to estimate its annual effective tax rate in dollars or is otherwise unable to make a reliable estimate of its "ordinary" income (or loss) or of the related tax (or benefit) for the fiscal year in a jurisdiction, the tax (or benefit) applicable to "ordinary" income (or loss) in that jurisdiction shall be recognized in the interim period in which the "ordinary" income (or loss) is reported, as described in footnote 7 to paragraph 8.

FASB Interpretation No. 19
Lessee Guarantee of the Residual Value of Leased Property

an interpretation of FASB Statement No. 13

STATUS

Issued: October 1977

Effective Date: For leasing transactions and revisions entered into on or after January 1, 1978

Affects: No other pronouncements

Affected by: No other pronouncements

FASB Interpretation No. 19
Lessee Guarantee of the Residual Value of Leased Property

an interpretation of FASB Statement No. 13

INTRODUCTION

1. The FASB has been asked to clarify whether a particular kind of lease provision constitutes a guarantee by the lessee of the residual value of leased property at the expiration of the lease term to be included in *minimum lease payments* in accordance with paragraph 5(j)(i)(b) of *FASB Statement No. 13,* "Accounting for Leases," and to clarify whether certain provisions in lease agreements and certain other circumstances limit the amount of a lessee guarantee to be included in minimum lease payments to an amount less than a stipulated residual value of the leased property at the end of the lease term. Paragraph 5(j)(i)(b) of the Statement states that minimum lease payments from the standpoint of the lessee shall include a "guarantee by the lessee . . . of the residual value at the expiration of the lease term, whether or not payment of the guarantee constitutes a purchase of the leased property. . . . When the lessee agrees to make up any deficiency below a stated amount in the lessor's realization of the residual value, the guarantee to be included in the minimum lease payments shall be the stated amount, rather than an estimate of the deficiency to be made up."

2. Specifically, the Board has been asked the following three questions:

a. Does a lease provision requiring the lessee to make up a residual value deficiency that is attributable to damage, extraordinary wear and tear, or excessive usage (e.g., excessive mileage on a leased vehicle) constitute a lessee guarantee of the residual value such that the estimated residual value of the leased property at the end of the lease term should be included in minimum lease payments under paragraph 5(j)(i)(b) of *FASB Statement No. 13*?
b. Some lease agreements limit the amount of a residual value deficiency that a lessee can be required to make up to an amount that is (1) less than the stipulated residual value of the leased property at the end of the lease term but (2) clearly in excess of any reasonable estimate of a deficiency that might be expected to arise in normal circumstances. In those cases, is the amount of the lessee's guarantee to be included in minimum lease payments under paragraph 5(j)(i)(b) of *FASB Statement No. 13* limited to the specified maximum deficiency that the lessee can be required to make up, or is it the stipulated residual value of the leased property at the end of the lease term?
c. If a lessee who is obligated to make up a deficiency in the lessor's realization of the residual value obtains a guarantee of the residual value from an unrelated third party, may the lessee reduce the amount of his minimum lease payments under paragraph 5(j)(i)(b) of *FASB Statement No. 13* by the amount of the third-party guarantee?

INTERPRETATION

3. A lease provision requiring the lessee to make up a residual value deficiency that is attributable to damage, extraordinary wear and tear, or excessive usage is similar to contingent rentals in that the amount is not determinable at the inception of the lease.[1] Such a provision does not constitute a lessee guarantee of the residual value for purposes of paragraph 5(j)(i)(b) of *FASB Statement No. 13.*

4. If a lease limits the amount of the lessee's obligation to make up a residual value deficiency to an amount less than the stipulated residual value of the leased property at the end of the lease term, the amount of the lessee's guarantee to be included in minimum lease payments under paragraph 5(j)(i)(b) of *FASB Statement No. 13* shall be limited to the specified maximum deficiency the lessee can be required to make up. In other words, the "stated amount" referred to in the last sentence of paragraph 5(j)(i)(b) is the specified maximum deficiency that the lessee is obligated to make up. If that maximum deficiency clearly exceeds any reasonable estimate of a deficiency that might be expected to arise in normal circumstances, the lessor's risk associated with the portion of the residual in excess of the maximum may appear to be negligible. However, the fact remains that the lessor must look to the resale market or elsewhere rather than to the lessee to recover the unguaranteed portion of the stipulated residual value of the leased property. The lessee has not guaranteed full recovery of the residual value,

[1]Contingent rentals are not included in *minimum lease payments* as defined in paragraph 5(j) of *FASB Statement No. 13.* Contingent rentals are to be recognized as period costs when incurred (or revenue when receivable). (See paragraphs 12, 17(b), and 18(b) of Statement No. 13.)

and the parties should not base their accounting on the assumption that the lessee has guaranteed it. The 90 percent test specified in criterion (d) of paragraph 7 of Statement No. 13 is stated as a lower limit rather than as a guideline.

5. A guarantee of the residual value obtained by the lessee from an unrelated third party for the benefit of the lessor shall not be used to reduce the amount of the lessee's minimum lease payments under paragraph 5(j)(i)(b) of *FASB Statement No. 13* except to the extent that the lessor explicitly releases the lessee from obligation, including secondary obligation if the guarantor defaults, to make up a residual value deficiency. Amounts paid in consideration for a guarantee by an unrelated third party are executory costs and are not included in the lessee's minimum lease payments.

EFFECTIVE DATE AND TRANSITION

6. The provisions of this Interpretation shall be effective for leasing transactions and lease agreement revisions (see paragraph 9 of *FASB Statement No. 13*) entered into on or after January 1, 1978. Earlier application is encouraged. In addition, the provisions of this Interpretation shall be applied retroactively at the same time and in the same manner as the provisions of *FASB Statement No. 13* are applied retroactively (see paragraphs 49 and 51 of the Statement). Enterprises that have already applied the provisions of Statement No. 13 retroactively and have published financial statements based on the retroactively adjusted accounts before the effective date of this Interpretation may, but are not required to, apply the provisions of this Interpretation retroactively.

This Interpretation was adopted by the unanimous vote of the seven members of the Financial Accounting Standards Board:

Marshall S. Armstrong, *Chairman*
Oscar S. Gellein
Donald J. Kirk
Arthur L. Litke
Robert E. Mays
Robert T. Sprouse
Ralph E. Walters

FASB Interpretation No. 20 Reporting Accounting Changes under AICPA Statements of Position

an interpretation of APB Opinion No. 20

STATUS

Issued: November 1977

Effective Date: December 1, 1977

Affects: No other pronouncements

Affected by: No other pronouncements

FASB Interpretation No. 20
Reporting Accounting Changes under AICPA Statements of Position

an interpretation of APB Opinion No. 20

CONTENTS

INTRODUCTION AND BACKGROUND INFORMATION

1. The Accounting Standards Division of the AICPA has asked the FASB to either reconsider certain provisions of *APB Opinion No. 20,* "Accounting Changes," or to clarify whether statements of position issued by the AICPA may specify how to report a change to adopt its recommendations for purposes of applying that Opinion.

2. Paragraph 4 of *APB Opinion No. 20* indicates that each APB Opinion specifies how to report a change to conform with the conclusions of the Opinion and further states:

> An industry audit guide prepared by a committee of the American Institute of Certified Public Accountants may also prescribe the manner of reporting a change in accounting principle. Accordingly, the provisions of this Opinion do not apply to changes made in conformity with such pronouncements issued in the past or in the future.

3. At the time *APB Opinion No. 20* was issued in July 1971, the Accounting Principles Board issued Opinions on financial accounting and reporting and various AICPA industry committees issued industry audit guides that dealt with both the specialized auditing procedures and the specialized accounting practices applicable to enterprises in those industries. Subsequently, specialized industry accounting practices were dealt with in a new series of industry accounting guides issued by the AICPA, each of which specified how to report a change in accounting to conform with the conclusions of the guide. In July 1973, the FASB replaced the APB; the AICPA discontinued the industry accounting guides and its Accounting Standards Division began issuing statements of position[1] covering specialized industry accounting practices.

4. The FASB believes that in due course *APB Opinion No. 20* should be reconsidered. The FASB believes further, however, that pending that reconsideration, issuance of this Interpretation will result in improvements in financial accounting and reporting.

INTERPRETATION

5. For purposes of applying *APB Opinion No. 20,* an enterprise making a change in accounting principle to conform with the recommendations of an AICPA statement of position shall report the change as specified in the statement. If an AICPA statement of position does not specify the manner of reporting a change in accounting principle to conform with its recommendations, an enterprise making a change in accounting principle to conform with the recommendations of the statement shall report the change as specified by Opinion No. 20.

EFFECTIVE DATE

6. This Interpretation shall be effective December 1, 1977.

---

[1]In the introduction to previously issued statements of position, the AICPA indicates that "Statements of Position of the Accounting Standards Division are issued for the general information of those interested in the subject. They present the conclusions of at least a majority of the Accounting Standards Executive Committee, which is the senior technical body of the [AICPA] authorized to speak for the [AICPA] in the areas of financial accounting and reporting and cost accounting.

"The objective of Statements of Position is to influence the development of accounting and reporting standards in directions the Division believes are in the public interest. It is intended that they should be considered, as deemed appropriate, by bodies having authority to issue pronouncements on the subject. However, Statements of Position do not establish standards enforceable under the [AICPA's] Code of Professional Ethics."

Reporting Accounting Changes under AICPA Statements of Position

This Interpretation was adopted by the affirmative votes of four members of the Financial Accounting Standards Board following submission to the members of the Financial Accounting Standards Advisory Council. Messrs. Armstrong, Kirk, and Mays dissented.

Messrs. Armstrong, Kirk, and Mays dissent from this Interpretation because they believe that the FASB should reconsider currently *APB Opinion No. 20* on its merit instead of permitting the AICPA to grant selective dispensations from the requirements of that Opinion.

Further, Mr. Mays dissents because he believes that this Interpretation, in effect, constitutes an unwarranted delegation of authority to the AICPA to establish standards of financial accounting and reporting.

Members of the Financial Accounting Standards Board:

Marshall S. Armstrong, *Chairman*
Oscar S. Gellein
Donald J. Kirk
Arthur L. Litke
Robert E. Mays
Robert T. Sprouse
Ralph E. Walters

FASB Interpretation No. 21
Accounting for Leases in a Business Combination

an interpretation of FASB Statement No. 13

STATUS

Issued: April 1978

Effective Date: For business combinations initiated on or after May 1, 1978

Affects: No other pronouncements

Affected by: No other pronouncements

FASB Interpretation No. 21
Accounting for Leases in a Business Combination

an interpretation of FASB Statement No. 13

Contents

INTRODUCTION AND BACKGROUND INFORMATION

1. The FASB has been asked to clarify the application of *FASB Statement No. 13*, "Accounting for Leases," in business combinations. Specifically, this involves the following questions:

a. Does the consummation of a business combination require the combined enterprise to treat leases of the combining companies as new leases to be classified according to the criteria set forth in Statement No. 13, based on conditions as of the date of the combination?
b. If the consummation of a business combination does not require enterprises to treat leases of the combining companies as new leases as of the date of the combination, how should Statement No. 13 be applied[1] to the leases of the combined enterprise?
c. How do the requirements of *APB Opinion No. 16,* "Business Combinations," for assigning amounts to the assets acquired and liabilities assumed in a business combination that is accounted for by the purchase method affect the application of Statement No. 13 by the combined enterprise to leases of the acquired company?

2. Paragraph 40 of *FASB Statement No. 13* requires the new lessee under a sublease or similar transaction to classify the lease in accordance with the criteria in Statement No. 13 and to account for it as a new lease. Subparagraphs (b) and (c) of paragraph 35 of Statement No. 13 describe the transactions similar to subleases that are subject to the requirements of paragraph 40 of the Statement as follows:

b. A new lessee is substituted under the original lease agreement. The new lessee becomes the primary obligor under the agreement, and the original lessee may or may not be secondarily liable.
c. A new lessee is substituted through a new agreement, with cancellation of the original lease agreement.

The question has been raised as to whether the provisions of paragraphs 35 and 40 ever require that leases in a business combination be treated as new leases by the combined enterprise.

3. In connection with a business combination, changes may be made in the provisions of existing leases of a combining enterprise. Paragraph 9 of *FASB Statement No. 13* discusses changes in the provisions of leases as follows:

> If at any time the lessee and lessor agree to change the provisions of the lease, other than by renewing the lease or extending its term, in a manner that would have resulted in a different classification of the lease under the criteria in paragraphs 7 and 8 had the changed terms been in effect at the inception of the lease, the revised agreement shall be considered as a new agreement over its term, and the criteria in paragraphs 7 and 8 shall be applied for purposes of classifying the new lease. Likewise, except when a guarantee or penalty is rendered inoperative as described in paragraphs 12 and 17(e), any action that extends the lease beyond the expiration of the existing lease term (see paragraph 5(f)), such as the exercise of a lease renewal option other than those already included in the lease term, shall be considered as a new agreement, which

[1]See paragraphs 49 and 51 of *FASB Statement No. 13* regarding retroactive application of Statement No. 13.

shall be classified according to the provisions of paragraphs 6-8. Changes in estimates (for example, changes in estimates of the economic life or of the residual value of the leased property) or changes in circumstances (for example, default by the lessee), however, shall not give rise to a new classification of a lease for accounting purposes.

4. Paragraph 88 of *APB Opinion No. 16* provides "general guides for assigning amounts to the individual assets acquired and liabilities assumed, except goodwill . . ." in a business combination that is accounted for by the purchase method. The guides in subparagraphs of paragraph 88 indicate the method of valuation to be used for various types of assets and liabilities. The concepts underlying *FASB Statement No. 13* that govern classification of leases differ in some respects from the concepts of prior APB Opinions on accounting for leases. Thus, the subparagraphs of paragraph 88 of Opinion No. 16 that were applied prior to Statement No. 13 may not be the appropriate subparagraphs to be applied under Statement No. 13. In addition, some provisions of Statement No. 13 (e.g., interest rates used) may suggest that certain of the general guidelines in paragraph 88 should be applied differently from the way they may have been applied in the past.

5. An Exposure Draft of a proposed Interpretation on "Accounting for Leases in a Business Combination" was issued on December 19, 1977. The Board received 27 letters of comment in response to the Exposure Draft. Certain of those comments and the Board's consideration of them are discussed in paragraphs 6-10 below.

6. One respondent requested that the Interpretation provide for circumstances in which determinations at the inception of the lease are not possible. The Board is aware that in some cases it is difficult to obtain accurate data relating to the remote past of an acquired enterprise but believes that reasonable estimates can be derived based on the information that is available.

7. Some respondents expressed the belief that the concept of purchase accounting in *APB Opinion No. 16* requires the acquiring enterprise to classify the acquired enterprise's leases as new leases at the date of a business combination that is accounted for by the purchase method and stated that the acquiring enterprise should apply the criteria of *FASB Statement No. 13* for classifying the acquired leases at the date of the acquisition. The Board does not believe that Opinion No. 16 requires reconsideration of the classification of existing leases that are already classified in conformity with Statement No. 13; rather, the Board views Opinion No. 16 as requiring valuation of the existing assets and obligations of the acquired company, including assets and obligations pertaining to leases, and allocation of cost to those assets and obligations. Also, the Board views the procedure suggested as contrary to Statement No. 13. Paragraph 8 below describes the basis for classification of a lease under Statement No. 13.

8. Paragraph 7 of *FASB Statement No. 13* states that "the criteria for classifying leases set forth in this paragraph and in paragraph 8 derive from the concept set forth in paragraph 60." Paragraph 60 of Statement No. 13 describes the underlying concept as follows:

> The provisions of this Statement derive from the view that a *lease that transfers* substantially all of the benefits and risks incident to the ownership of property should be accounted for as the acquisition of an asset and the incurrence of an obligation by the lessee and as a sale or financing by the lessor. All other leases should be accounted for as operating leases. . . . [Emphasis added.]

Statement No. 13 requires that the classification of a lease (an agreement between a lessee and a lessor) be determined at the inception of *the lease*. Once that determination is made, the classification of the lease is not reexamined unless either (a) both parties to the lease agree to a revision that would have resulted in a different classification of the lease had the changed terms been in effect at the inception of the lease or (b) the lease is extended or renewed. Paragraphs 36-40 of Statement No. 13 apply similar procedures with respect to classification to the parties affected by a sublease, as follows:

a. *The original lessor* retains the classification of the original lease unless it is replaced by a new agreement.
b. *The original lessee* retains the original classification of the original lease unless the original lessee is relieved of the primary obligation. (If the lessee is relieved of the primary obligation, the original lessor will have agreed to a revision.)
c. *The new lessee* has agreed to the terms of a lease, either with the original lessee (in effect, a sublease) or with the original lessor (a new lease). Accordingly, the new lessee is required to classify the new lease at the date of the new agreement.

Statement No. 13 applies the same rationale to an enterprise that purchases the lessor's interest in an existing lease from the original lessor. The Statement does not permit an enterprise that purchases property from a lessor while the property is leased to a third party lessee to classify the acquired lease as a new lease at the acquisition date. The lessee is not a party to the transaction and the original lessor ceases to be a party to the lease; thus, there has been no new agreement between a lessee and a lessor and the purchase date is not the inception of a new lease requiring classification at that date. The Board views the substance of a business combination that is accounted for under the purchase method to be the purchase of the lessor's or lessee's interest in an existing lease. The original lessor or lessee does not become a party to a new agreement; accordingly, there is no new agreement to be classified, and Statement No. 13 does not permit reclassification of the existing lease unless the provisions of the lease are modified. The Board is aware that the identity of a party to a lease may change in a business combination and that the lease may be modified to reflect that change. If the provisions of the lease are not changed (see paragraph 3 above), the modification does not represent a new agreement between the lessee and lessor in substance, and the lease should not be reclassified.

9. Some respondents suggested that the Board expand the scope of this Interpretation to address asset acquisitions that are not business combinations. As explained in paragraph 8 above, the Board believes that *FASB Statement No. 13* provides adequate guidance for those transactions.

10. Some enterprises have already applied the provisions of *FASB Statement No. 13* retroactively and have published financial statements based on the retroactively adjusted accounts. The Exposure Draft proposed that those enterprises would be permitted, but not required, to apply the provisions of this Interpretation retroactively. Some respondents' comments indicated that they interpreted the reference to "published financial statements" in the Exposure Draft to include financial summaries of interim results. The Board had intended the reference to "published financial statements" to exclude those summaries. Upon further consideration, the Board modified the wording of paragraph 18 to "published *annual* financial statements."

11. This Interpretation applies to the accounting for leases by combined enterprises at the date of and subsequent to a business combination.

INTERPRETATION

Summary

12. The classification of a lease in accordance with the criteria of *FASB Statement No. 13* shall not be changed as a result of a business combination unless the provisions of the lease are modified. (See paragraph 13.)

Changes in the Provisions of the Lease

13. If in connection with a business combination, whether accounted for by the purchase method or by the pooling of interests method, the provisions of a lease are modified in a way that would require the revised agreement to be considered a new agreement under paragraph 9 of *FASB Statement No. 13,* the new lease shall be classified by the combined enterprise according to the criteria set forth in Statement No. 13, based on conditions as of the date of the modification of the lease.

Application of FASB Statement No. 13 in a Pooling of Interests

14. In a business combination that is accounted for by the pooling of interests method, each lease shall retain its previous classification under *FASB Statement No. 13* unless the provisions of the lease are modified as indicated in paragraph 13 above and shall be accounted for by the combined enterprise in the same manner that it would have been classified and accounted for by the combining enterprise.

Application of FASB Statement No. 13 in a Purchase Combination

15. In a business combination that is accounted for by the purchase method, the acquiring enterprise shall retain the previous classification in accordance with *FASB Statement No. 13* for the leases of an acquired enterprise unless the provisions of the lease are modified as indicated in paragraph 13 above.[2] The amounts assigned to individual assets acquired and liabilities assumed at the date of the combination shall be determined in accordance with the general guides for that type of asset or liability in paragraph 88 of *APB Opinion No. 16*. Subsequent to the recording of the amounts called for by Opinion No. 16, the leases shall thereafter be accounted for in accordance with Statement No. 13.[3] Paragraph 16 below explains the application of this paragraph to a leveraged lease by an enterprise that acquires a lessor.

16. In a business combination that is accounted for by the purchase method, the acquiring enterprise shall apply the following procedures to the acquired enterprise's investment as a lessor in a leveraged lease. The acquiring enterprise shall retain the classification of a leveraged lease at the date of the com-

[2]If the acquired enterprise has not applied *FASB Statement No. 13* retroactively at the date of the business combination, the acquiring enterprise shall classify the leases of the acquired enterprise as they would have been classified if the acquired enterprise had applied Statement No. 13 retroactively at that date.

[3]*FASB Statement No. 13* does not address the subsequent accounting for amounts recorded for favorable or unfavorable operating leases. Accordingly, present practice is not changed with respect to the amortization of those amounts.

bination. The acquiring enterprise shall assign an amount to the acquired net investment in the leveraged lease in accordance with the general guides in paragraph 88 of *APB Opinion No. 16*, based on the remaining future cash flows and giving appropriate recognition to the estimated future tax effects of those cash flows. Once determined, that net investment shall be broken down into its component parts, namely, net rentals receivable, estimated residual value, and unearned income including discount to adjust other components to present value. The acquiring enterprise thereafter shall account for that investment in a leveraged lease in accordance with the provisions of *FASB Statement No. 13*. Appendix A illustrates the application of this paragraph.

17. When an enterprise that has acquired another enterprise in a business combination accounted for by the purchase method prior to the effective date of this Interpretation applies the provisions of *FASB Statement No. 13* retroactively, leases acquired in the business combination shall be classified as they would have been classified if the acquired enterprise had applied Statement No. 13 retroactively at the date of the business combination. The amounts retroactively recorded for those leases shall be the amounts that would have been allocated under *APB Opinion No. 16* by the acquiring enterprise at the purchase date if the leases had been classified in accordance with the provisions of Statement No. 13 at that date. The following examples illustrate the application of this paragraph:

a. In the case of a lease for which the lessee's classification is changed by the retroactive application of Statement No. 13 from an operating lease to a capital lease, the favorable or unfavorable amount recorded under Opinion No. 16 at the date of the combination shall be restated to record an asset and a liability, each to be assigned an amount in accordance with Opinion No. 16. The net of the restated asset and liability may equal the amount previously recorded for a favorable or unfavorable operating lease. However, if the net of the restated asset and liability differs from the amount that was originally recorded under Opinion No. 16 for that lease, the difference is a retroactive adjustment of the allocation of the cost of the acquired enterprise with an offsetting retroactive adjustment, usually to goodwill.
b. In the case of a lease for which the lessor's classification is changed by the retroactive application of Statement No. 13 from an operating lease to a direct financing lease, the carrying amount of the leased asset and any favorable or unfavorable amount recorded under Opinion No. 16 at the date of the combination shall be restated to record a net investment in the direct financing lease determined in accordance with Opinion No. 16 and consisting of the gross receivable, residual value, and unearned income. If the restated amount allocated to the net investment in the direct financing lease differs from the net amount that was originally recorded for that lease, the difference is a retroactive adjustment of the allocation of the cost of the acquired enterprise with an offsetting retroactive adjustment, usually to goodwill.

Effective Date and Transition

18. The provisions of this Interpretation shall be effective for business combinations that are initiated[4] on or after May 1, 1978. Earlier application is encouraged. In addition, the provisions of this Interpretation shall be applied retroactively at the same time and in the same manner as the provisions of *FASB Statement No. 13* are applied retroactively (see paragraphs 49 and 51 of Statement No. 13). Enterprises that have already applied the provisions of Statement No. 13 retroactively and have published annual financial statements based on the retroactively adjusted accounts before the effective date of this Interpretation may, but are not required to, apply the provisions of this Interpretation retroactively.

This Interpretation was adopted by the unanimous vote of the seven members of the Financial Accounting Standards Board:

Donald J. Kirk, *Chairman*
Oscar S. Gellein
John W. March
Robert A. Morgan
David Mosso
Robert T. Sprouse
Ralph E. Walters

Appendix A

ILLUSTRATION OF THE ACCOUNTING FOR A LEVERAGED LEASE IN A PURCHASE COMBINATION

19. This Appendix illustrates one way that a lessor's investment in a leveraged lease might be valued by the acquiring enterprise in a business combination accounted for by the purchase method and the subsequent accounting for the investment in accordance with *FASB Statement No. 13*. The elements of accounting and reporting illustrated for this example are as follows:

1. Leveraged lease example—terms and assumptions, Schedule 1

[4]See paragraph 46(a) of *APB Opinion No. 16* for the definition of "initiated."

2. Acquiring enterprise's cash flow analysis by years, Schedule 2
3. Acquiring enterprise's valuation of investment in the leveraged lease, Schedule 3
4. Acquiring enterprise's allocation of annual cash flow to investment and income, Schedule 4
5. Journal entry for recording allocation of purchase price to net investment in the leveraged lease, Schedule 5
6. Journal entries for the year ending December 31, 1984 (year 10 of the lease), Schedule 6

SCHEDULE 1

Leveraged Lease Example Term and Assumptions

Cost of leased asset (equipment)	$1,000,000
Lease term	15 years, dating from January 1, 1975
Lease rental payments	$90,000 per year (payable last day of each year)
Residual value	$200,000 estimated to be realized one year after lease termination
Financing:	
Equity investment by lessor	$400,000
Long-term nonrecourse debt	$600,000, bearing interest at 9% and repayable in annual installments (on last day of each year) of $74,435.30
Depreciation allowable to lessor for income tax purposes	Seven-year ADR life using double-declining-balance method for the first two years (with the half-year convention election applied in the first year) and sum-of-years digits method for remaining life, depreciated to $100,000 salvage value
Lessor's income tax rate (federal and state)	50.4% (assumed to continue in existence throughout the term of the lease)
Investment tax credit	10% of equipment cost or $100,000 (realized by the lessor on last day of first year of lease)
Initial direct costs	For simplicity, initial direct costs have not been included in the illustration
Date of business combination	January 1, 1982
Tax status of business combination	Non-taxable transaction
Appropriate interest rate for valuing net-of-tax return on investment	4 1/2%

SCHEDULE 2

Acquiring Enterprise's Cash Flow Analysis by Years

	1	2	3	4	5	6	7
Year	Gross lease rentals and residual value	Depreciation (for income tax purposes)	Loan interest payments	Taxable income (col. 1-2-3)	Income tax (charges) (col. 4 × 50.4%)	Loan principal payments	Annual cash flow (col. 1 − 3 + 5 − 6)
8	$ 90,000	—	$ 37,079	$ 52,921	$ (26,672)	$ 37,357	$(11,108)
9	90,000	—	33,717	56,283	(28,367)	40,719	(12,803)
10	90,000	—	30,052	59,948	(30,214)	44,383	(14,649)
11	90,000	—	26,058	63,942	(32,227)	48,378	(16,663)
12	90,000	—	21,704	68,296	(34,421)	52,732	(18,857)
13	90,000	—	16,957	73,043	(36,813)	57,478	(21,248)
14	90,000	—	11,785	78,215	(39,420)	62,651	(23,856)
15	90,000	—	6,145	83,855	(42,263)	68,290	(26,698)
16	200,000	$100,000	—	100,000	(50,400)	—	149,600
Totals	$920,000	$100,000	$183,497	$636,503	$(320,797)	$411,988	$ 3,718

SCHEDULE 3

Acquiring Enterprise's Valuation of Investment in the Leveraged Lease

Cash flow	Present value at 4 1/2% net-of-tax rate
1. Rentals receivable (net of principal and interest on the nonrecourse debt) ($15,564.70 at the end of each year for 8 years)	$ 102,663
2. Estimated residual value ($200,000 realizable at the end of 9 years)	134,581
3. Future tax payments (various amounts payable over 9 years—see Schedule 2)	(253,489)
Net present value	$ (16,245)

SCHEDULE 4

Acquiring Enterprise's
Allocation of Annual Cash Flow to Investment and Income

	1	2	3	4	5	6
		Annual Cash Flow			Components of Income[2]	
Year	Net investment at beginning of year	Total from Schedule 2, col. 7	Allocated to investment	Allocated to income[1]	Pretax income	Tax effect of pretax income
8	$ (16,245)	$ (11,108)	$ (11,108)	—	—	—
9	(5,137)	(12,803)	(12,803)	—	—	—
10	7,666	(14,649	(14,973	$ 324	$ 5,530	$ (5,206)
11	22,639	(16,663)	(17,621)	958	16,353	(15,395)
12	40,260	(18,857)	(20,561)	1,704	29,087	(27,383)
13	60,821	(21,248)	(23,822)	2,574	43,937	(41,363)
14	84,643	(23,856)	(27,439)	3,583	61,160	(57,577)
15	112,082	(26,698)	(31,443)	4,745	80,995	(76,250)
16	143,525	149,600	143,525	6,075	103,698	(97,623)
Totals		$ 3,718	$ (16,245)	$19,963	$340,760	$(320,797)

[1]Lease income is recognized as 4.233% of the unrecovered investment at the beginning of each year in which the net investment is positive. The rate is that rate which when applied to the net investment in the years in which the net investment is positive will distribute the net income (net cash flow) to those years. The rate for allocation used in this Schedule is calculated by a trial and error process. The allocation is calculated based upon an initial estimate of the rate as a starting point. If the total thus allocated to income (column 4) differs under the estimated rate from the net cash flow (column 2 less column 3) the estimated rate is increased or decreased, as appropriate, to derive a revised allocation. This process is repeated until a rate is selected which develops a total amount allocated to income that is precisely equal to the net cash flow. As a practical matter, a computer program is used to calculate Schedule 4 under successive iterations until the correct rate is determined.

[2]Each component is allocated among the years of positive net investment in proportion to the allocation of net income in column 4. Journal Entry 2 in Schedule 6 of this Appendix includes an example of this computation.

SCHEDULE 5

Illustrative Journal Entry for Recording Allocation of Purchase Price to Net Investment in the Leveraged Lease

	Debit	Credit
Rentals receivable (Schedule 2, total of column 1 less residual value, less totals of columns 3 and 6)	$124,515	
Estimated residual value (Schedule 1)	200,000	
Purchase price allocation clearing account (Schedule 3, present value)	16,245	
Unearned and deferred income (Schedule 3, present value, less total of rentals receivable and estimated residual value)		$340,760

SCHEDULE 6

Illustrative Journal Entries for Year Ending December 31, 1984

Third Year of Operation after the Business Combination (Year 10 of the Lease)

Journal Entry 1

	Debit	Credit
Cash	$15,565	
Rentals receivable (Schedule 2, column 1 less columns 3 and 6)		$15,565
Collection of year's net rental		

Journal Entry 2

	Debit	Credit
Unearned and Deferred Income	$ 5,530	
Income from Leveraged Leases (Schedule 4, column 5)		$ 5,530

Recognition of pretax income for the year allocated in the same proportion as the allocation of total income

$$\left(\frac{\$\ \ 324}{\$19{,}963} \times \$340{,}760 = \$5{,}530\right)$$

Journal Entry 3

	Debit	Credit
Deferred taxes (Schedule 2, column 5, less Schedule 4, column 6)	$25,008	
Income tax expense (Schedule 4, column 6)	5,206	
Cash (Schedule 2, column 5)		$30,214

To record payment of tax for the year

FASB Interpretation No. 22
Applicability of Indefinite Reversal Criteria to Timing Differences

an interpretation of APB Opinions No. 11 and 23

STATUS

Issued: April 1978

Effective Date: For timing differences occurring in fiscal years beginning after June 15, 1978

Affects: No other pronouncements

Affected by: Paragraph 7 amended by FAS 60
Paragraph 8 superseded by FAS 71

FASB Interpretation No. 22
Applicability of Indefinite Reversal Criteria to Timing Differences

an interpretation of APB Opinions No. 11 and 23

CONTENTS

INTRODUCTION AND BACKGROUND INFORMATION

1. The FASB has been asked to clarify whether the indefinite reversal criteria described in *APB Opinion No. 23,* "Accounting for Income Taxes—Special Areas," are applicable beyond the four special areas addressed by that Opinion, for example, in connection with the costs of railroad gradings and tunnel bores that are reported differently for financial statement purposes and income tax purposes.

2. Paragraph 13 of *APB Opinion No. 11,* "Accounting for Income Taxes," defines differences between taxable income and pretax accounting income as either timing differences or permanent differences and provides criteria for distinguishing between the differences. Timing differences are "differences between the periods in which transactions affect taxable income and the periods in which they enter into the determination of pretax accounting income. Timing differences originate in one period and reverse or 'turn around' in one or more subsequent periods." Permanent differences are "differences between taxable income and pretax accounting income arising from transactions that, under applicable tax laws and regulations, will not be offset by corresponding differences or 'turn around' in other periods." Opinion No. 11 recognizes five special areas with unique aspects in which reversal of the tax consequences of some timing differences may be indefinite and defers any conclusion as to whether interperiod tax allocation should be required in those areas. The five special areas are:

a. Undistributed earnings of subsidiaries.
b. Intangible development costs in the oil and gas industry.
c. "General reserves" of stock savings and loan associations.
d. Amounts designated as "policyholders' surplus" by stock life insurance companies.
e. Deposits in statutory reserve funds by United States steamship companies.

Except for those special areas, Opinion No. 11 requires interperiod income tax allocation under the comprehensive allocation view adopted in the Opinion for timing differences.

3. *APB Opinion No. 23* addresses three of the special areas identified in *APB Opinion No. 11:* undistributed earnings of subsidiaries,[1] "general reserves" of stock savings and loan associations, and amounts designated as "policyholders' surplus" by stock life insurance companies and also addresses undistributed earnings of corporate joint ventures. Opinion No. 23 concludes that because of special provisions of the United States Internal Revenue Code that are unique to the four special areas addressed, an enterprise might postpone indefinitely the payment of income taxes on certain differences between pretax accounting income and taxable income that would otherwise require tax allocation for financial reporting purposes. The Opinion further indicates that an enterprise must take specific action for income tax purposes before taxes on those timing differences become payable and the taxes may never become payable unless the enterprise takes those actions. However, if circumstances indicate that the enterprise is likely to pay taxes on those differences, either currently or in later years because of known or expected actions, income taxes should be accrued as tax expense of the current period. Further, the Opinion indicates that there is a presumption that interperiod income tax allocation applies to timing differences in the four special areas addressed even though the presumption may be overcome in each case.

4. Paragraphs 5 and 6 of *APB Opinion No. 23* dis-

[1]Footnote 2 of Opinion No. 23 states that the conclusions on undistributed earnings of a subsidiary also apply to the portion of the earnings of a Domestic International Sales Corporation (DISC) that is eligible for tax deferral.

cuss permanent and timing differences. Paragraph 6 states:

> A timing difference arises when the initial difference between taxable income and pretax accounting income originates in one period and predictably reverses or turns around in one or more subsequent periods. The reversal of a timing difference at some future date is definite and the period of reversal is generally predictable within reasonable limits. Sometimes, however, reversals of a difference cannot be predicted because the events that create the tax consequences are controlled by the taxpayer and frequently require that the taxpayer take specific action before the initial difference reverses.

Some have suggested that the discussion of timing differences in Opinion No. 23 amends the definition of timing differences in *APB Opinion No. 11* (see paragraph 2 above).

5. *APB Opinion No. 24,* "Accounting for Income Taxes—Investments in Common Stock Accounted for by the Equity Method (Other than Subsidiaries and Corporate Joint Ventures)," which was issued concurrently with *APB Opinion No. 23,* requires tax allocation for an investor's equity in the undistributed earnings of an investee other than a subsidiary or corporate joint venture, both of which are addressed by Opinion No. 23.

6. *FASB Statement No. 19,* "Financial Accounting and Reporting by Oil and Gas Producing Companies," which supersedes *FASB Statement No. 9,* "Accounting for Income Taxes—Oil and Gas Producing Companies," addresses income tax allocation for intangible development costs in the oil and gas industry. Statement No. 19 requires comprehensive interperiod income tax allocation by oil and gas producing companies and prohibits "interaction" of book/tax timing differences (see paragraphs 60-62 and 260-264 of that Statement).

7. This Interpretation does not modify *APB Opinion No. 17,* "Intangible Assets," or the AICPA Industry Audit Guide, "Audits of Stock Life Insurance Companies." This Interpretation does not apply to deposits in capital construction funds or statutory reserve funds by United States steamship companies, for which *APB Opinions No. 11* and *23* did not reach a conclusion as to whether interperiod tax allocation should be required.

8. The Addendum to *APB Opinion No. 2,* "Accounting for the 'Investment Credit'," states that "differences may arise in the application of generally accepted accounting principles as between regulated and nonregulated businesses, because of the effect in regulated businesses of the rate-making process" and discusses the application of generally accepted accounting principles to regulated industries. Accordingly, the provisions of the Addendum shall govern the application of this Interpretation to those operations of a company that are regulated for rate-making purposes on an individual-company-cost-of-service basis.

9. Although *APB Opinion No. 23* discusses criteria for identifying a special category of timing differences involving indefinite reversal, it carefully limited the application of those criteria to specified transactions and only under certain circumstances. The Board believes that Opinion No. 23 was not intended to establish general criteria applicable beyond the specified areas. The Board recognizes that the income tax benefits resulting from amortization and depreciation of railroad gradings and tunnel bores, and possibly other transactions, have characteristics that might be considered similar in some respects to the four special areas addressed in Opinion No. 23. However, the Board is engaged in other studies which may lead to a comprehensive reexamination of tax allocation concepts and believes that it should not reopen the matter of tax allocation at this time or extend the range of exceptions to *APB Opinion No. 11.* Accordingly, the Board reaffirms the applicability of Opinion No. 11, which requires comprehensive interperiod tax allocation for timing differences unless specifically exempted by other APB Opinions or FASB Statements.

INTERPRETATION

10. *APB Opinion No. 23* acknowledges that reversal of some timing differences cannot be predicted because of special provisions in the tax law that allow a taxpayer to control the events that control the tax consequences in certain areas. Opinion No. 23 does not require interperiod tax allocation for timing differences in the four special areas addressed in that Opinion except in specified circumstances, and the indefinite reversal criteria of that Opinion apply only to the four special areas addressed. *APB Opinion No. 11* as amended to date requires interperiod tax allocation under the comprehensive allocation view adopted in that Opinion except for the four special areas addressed in Opinion No. 23 and for the areas described in paragraph 7 of this Interpretation.

11. The income tax benefits resulting from amortization and depreciation of railroad gradings and tunnel bores for income tax reporting purposes are timing differences for which comprehensive interperiod income tax allocation is required. The provisions of *APB Opinion No. 23* do not apply to those timing differences.

EFFECTIVE DATE AND TRANSITION

12. The provisions of this Interpretation shall be applied prospectively for timing differences occurring in fiscal years beginning after June 15, 1978. Timing differences that result from depreciation or amortization reported in fiscal years beginning after June 15, 1978, shall be subject to the provisions of this Interpretation. Earlier application is encouraged in financial statements for fiscal years beginning before June 16, 1978, that have not been previously issued.

13. If early application is adopted in financial reports for interim periods of a fiscal year beginning before June 16, 1978, previously issued financial information for any interim periods of that fiscal year that precede the period of adoption shall be restated to give effect to the provisions of this Interpretation and any subsequent presentation of that information shall be on the restated basis.

This Interpretation was adopted by the affirmative votes of five members of the Financial Accounting Standards Board following submission to the members of the Financial Accounting Standards Advisory Council. Messrs. Sprouse and Walters dissented.

Messrs. Sprouse and Walters dissent because they believe this Interpretation is inconsistent with the reasoning applied to the issues resolved in *APB Opinions No. 23* and *24.* In their view, if the accounting issue related to railroad gradings and tunnel bores that arose as a result of the Tax Reform Act of 1976 had existed and been resolved in 1972 when Opinion No. 23 was adopted, one must assume that issue would have been resolved consistently with the indefinite reversal criteria that served as the basis for that Opinion. They consider it relevant to note that the APB itself did not restrict its application of those criteria to the "special areas" cited in paragraph 38 of *APB Opinion No. 11;* in Opinion No. 23, those criteria were explicitly applied to an additional "special area" that arose subsequent to the adoption of Opinion No. 11.

Messrs. Sprouse and Walters agree that "a reexamination of tax allocation concepts" is appropriate in due course but, meanwhile, they believe that in interpreting the application of existing standards the Board should strive to account for similar situations in a similar way.

Members of the Financial Accounting Standards Board:

Donald J. Kirk,
Chairman
Oscar S. Gellein
John W. March
Robert A. Morgan
David Mosso
Robert T. Sprouse
Ralph E. Walters

FASB Interpretation No. 23
Leases of Certain Property Owned by a Governmental Unit or Authority

an interpretation of FASB Statement No. 13

STATUS

Issued: August 1978

Effective Date: For leasing transactions and revisions recorded as of December 1, 1978

Affects: No other pronouncements

Affected by: No other pronouncements

SUMMARY

This Interpretation clarifies that portion of paragraph 28 of *FASB Statement No. 13*, "Accounting for Leases," stating that leases of certain property owned by a governmental unit or authority shall be classified as operating leases.

The Interpretation describes six conditions that must be met for a lease of government owned property to be automatically classified as an operating lease. If all of the six conditions are not met, the criteria for classifying leases under Statement No. 13 that are applicable to leases generally are also applicable to leases involving government owned property.

FASB Interpretation No. 23
Leases of Certain Property Owned by a Governmental Unit or Authority

an interpretation of FASB Statement No. 13

CONTENTS

INTRODUCTION AND BACKGROUND INFORMATION

1. The FASB has been asked to clarify that portion of paragraph 28 of *FASB Statement No. 13*, "Accounting for Leases," stating that leases of certain property owned by a governmental unit or authority shall be classified as operating leases. That portion of paragraph 28 is as follows:

> Because of special provisions normally present in leases involving terminal space and other airport facilities owned by a governmental unit or authority, the economic life of such facilities for purposes of classifying the lease is essentially indeterminate. Likewise, the concept of fair value is not applicable to such leases. Since such leases also do not provide for a transfer of ownership or a bargain purchase option, they shall be classified as operating leases. Leases of other facilities owned by a governmental unit or authority wherein the rights of the parties are essentially the same as in a lease of airport facilities described above shall also be classified as operating leases. Examples of such leases may be those involving facilities at ports and bus terminals.

2. That provision of paragraph 28 was further explained in paragraph 106 of *FASB Statement No. 13* as follows:

> A number of respondents pointed out that leases of facilities such as airport and bus terminals and port facilities from governmental units or authorities contain features that render the criteria of paragraph 7 inappropriate for classifying such leases. Leases of such facilities do not transfer ownership or contain bargain purchase options. By virtue of its power to abandon a facility during the term of a lease, the governmental body can effectively control the lessee's continued use of the property for its intended purpose, thus making its economic life essentially indeterminate. Finally, since neither the leased property nor equivalent property is available for sale, a meaningful fair value cannot be determined, thereby invalidating the 90 percent recovery criterion. For those reasons, the Board concluded that such leases shall be classified as operating leases by both the lessee and lessor.

3. The Board has been asked to clarify the conditions that shall cause leases of certain property owned by a governmental unit or authority to be classified as operating leases.

4. A draft of a proposed Interpretation on "Leases of Certain Property Owned by a Governmental Unit or Authority" was issued on April 7, 1978. The Board received 43 letters of comment in response to the proposed Interpretation. Some respondents disagreed with the proposed Interpretation because they believe that a lessee's classification of leases of government owned property should be determined by the same criteria as those applied to leases generally. A few respondents expressed neither overall agreement nor disagreement but offered comments or suggestions about specific matters. The remainder of the respondents expressed general agreement with the proposed Interpretation.

5. The Board also considered the possibility of amending *FASB Statement No. 13* to delete that portion of paragraph 28 that applies to leases of certain property owned by a governmental unit or authority. As stated in the proposed Interpretation that was released for comment, some Board members believe that a lessee's classification of leases of government owned property should be determined by the same criteria as those applied to leases generally. However, in the interest of a timely resolution of the matter, the Board concluded that further consideration of amending the applicable portion of paragraph 28 of Statement No. 13 should not delay the issuance of this Interpretation.

6. A number of respondents recommended that the Board clarify subparagraph 8(d) with respect to the

lessor's right to terminate the lease during the lease term. Some of those respondents stated that the existence of the termination right was the significant issue and that such a right can exist even though explicit reference to the right is not contained in the lease agreement. The Board did not intend that leases of government-owned property would be classified as operating leases merely because sovereign rights, such as the right of eminent domain, exist. Accordingly, the Board has modified subparagraph 8(d) to clarify its intent.

7. Some respondents suggested that the Board define the term "equivalent property in the same service area" as that term is used in subparagraph 8(f), and a footnote has been added to that subparagraph to provide additional guidance.

INTERPRETATION

8. The provisions of paragraph 28 of *FASB Statement No. 13* stating that certain leases shall be classified as operating leases are intended to apply to leases only if all of the following conditions are met:

a. The leased property is owned by a governmental unit or authority.
b. The leased property is part of a larger facility, such as an airport, operated by or on behalf of the lessor.
c. The leased property is a permanent structure or a part of a permanent structure, such as a building, that normally could not be moved to a new location.
d. The lessor, or in some cases a higher governmental authority, has the explicit right under the lease agreement or existing statutes or regulations applicable to the leased property to terminate the lease at any time during the lease term, such as by closing the facility containing the leased property or by taking possession of the facility.
e. The lease neither transfers ownership of the leased property to the lessee nor allows the lessee to purchase or otherwise acquire ownership of the leased property.
f. The leased property or equivalent property in the same service area[1] cannot be purchased nor can such property be leased from a nongovernmental unit or authority.

9. Leases of property not meeting all of the conditions of paragraph 8 of this Interpretation are subject to the same criteria for classifying leases under *FASB Statement No. 13* that are applicable to leases not involving government owned property.

EFFECTIVE DATE AND TRANSITION

10. The provisions of this Interpretation shall be effective for leasing transactions recorded and lease agreement revisions (see paragraph 9 of *FASB Statement No. 13*) recorded as of December 1, 1978 or thereafter. Earlier application is encouraged. In addition, except as provided in the next sentence, the provisions of this Interpretation shall be applied retroactively at the same time and in the same manner as the provisions of Statement No. 13 are applied retroactively (see paragraphs 49 and 51 of Statement No. 13). Enterprises that have already applied the provisions of Statement No. 13 retroactively and have published annual financial statements based on the retroactively adjusted accounts before the effective date of this Interpretation may, but are not required to, apply the provisions of this Interpretation retroactively.

This Interpretation was adopted by the affirmative votes of six members of the Financial Accounting Standards Board following submission to the members of the Financial Accounting Standards Advisory Council and the Screening Committee on Emerging Problems. Mr. Walters dissented.

Mr. Walters cannot support further efforts to apply different capitalization criteria for leases of government owned property, and he believes that this Interpretation shows the futility of attempting to rationalize that position. Among the conditions cited in paragraph 8 of this Interpretation, the only one that is relatively unique to leases of government property is the unilateral right to terminate the lease. Special consideration of this condition if termination is a remote contingency, in his view, denies the definition of "lease term" in paragraph 5(f) of *FASB Statement No. 13*.

Members of the Financial Accounting Standards Board:

Donald J. Kirk, *Chairman*
Oscar S. Gellein
John W. March
Robert A. Morgan
David Mosso
Robert T. Sprouse
Ralph E. Walters

[1]As used in this Interpretation, equivalent property in the same service area is property that would allow continuation of essentially the same service or activity as afforded by the leased property without any appreciable difference is economic results to the lessee.

FASB Interpretation No. 24
Leases Involving Only Part of a Building

an interpretation of FASB Statement No. 13

STATUS

Issued: September 1978

Effective Date: For leasing transactions and revisions recorded as of December 1, 1978

Affects: No other pronouncements

Affected by: No other pronouncements

SUMMARY

This Interpretation concerns that portion of *FASB Statement No. 13*, "Accounting for Leases," stating that "when the leased property is part of a larger whole, its cost (or carrying amount) and fair value may not be objectively determinable, as for example, when an office or a floor of a building is leased."

This Interpretation recognizes that reasonable estimates of the leased property's fair value might be objectively determinable from other information if sales of property similar to the leased property do not exist.

FASB Interpretation No. 24
Leases Involving Only Part of a Building

an interpretation of FASB Statement No. 13

CONTENTS

INTRODUCTION AND BACKGROUND INFORMATION

1. Paragraph 28 of *FASB Statement No. 13*, "Accounting for Leases," states that "when the leased property is part of a larger whole, its cost (or carrying amount) and fair value may not be objectively determinable, as for example, when an office or floor of a building is leased. If the cost and fair value of the leased property are objectively determinable, both the lessee and the lessor shall classify and account for the lease according to the provisions of paragraph 26." Paragraph 28 goes on to state that "if the fair value of the leased property is not objectively determinable, the lessee shall classify the lease according to the criterion of paragraph 7(c) only. . . ." Paragraph 5(c) of Statement No. 13 defines the fair value of leased property as "the price for which the property could be sold in an arm's-length transaction between unrelated parties."

2. The FASB has been asked if a fair value can be objectively determined for a lease involving only part of a building if there are no sales of property similar to the leased property to use as a basis for estimating the leased property's fair value for purposes of applying *FASB Statement No. 13*.

3. A draft of a proposed Interpretation on "Leases Involving Only Part of a Building" was issued on April 20, 1978. The Board received 29 letters of comment on the proposed Interpretation. The Board's consideration of certain of the respondents' comments is discussed in paragraphs 4 and 5 below.

4. A number of respondents questioned whether the proposed Interpretation would provide meaningful guidance. Some respondents noted that, in many cases, information providing a basis for a reasonable estimate of the leased property's fair value would not be available. Other respondents agreed that information providing a basis for a reasonable estimate of fair value might be obtained through an appraisal or other similar valuation. The Board does not intend to impose a requirement to obtain an appraisal or similar valuation as a general matter but does believe that kind of information should be obtained whenever possible if (a) classification as a capital lease seems likely and (b) the effects of capital lease classification would be significant to the financial statements of a lessee. Other respondents stated that the applicability of the Interpretation should be limited to lessees of a significant portion of a facility. Although that view was not adopted, the Board recognizes that a lessee's ability to make a reasonable estimate of the leased property's fair value will vary depending on the size of the leased property in relation to the entire facility. For example, obtaining a meaningful appraisal of an office or a floor of a multi-story building may not be possible whereas similar information may be readily obtainable if the leased property is a major part of that facility.

5. Some respondents stated that replacement cost measures costs of physical attributes but does not necessarily measure fair value. Two of those respondents stated that replacement cost would not reflect the value attributable to factors such as location of the leased property or traffic patterns of a larger complex. One respondent stated that a determination of replacement cost for only part of a building would require arbitrary cost allocations and subjective considerations. Paragraph 5(c)(ii) of *FASB Statement No. 13* states, in part, "when the lessor is not a manufacturer or dealer, the fair value of the property at the inception of the lease will ordinarily be its cost. . . ." That paragraph further provides that if there is a significant lapse of time between construction or acquisition of the property and inception of the lease, the determination of fair value shall be made in light of the market conditions at inception. The Board recognizes that replacement cost will not reflect the fair value of the leased property in all cases. However, if the leased facility has been recently constructed or acquired, cost estimates may provide a reasonable basis for estimating the property's fair value for purposes of applying the recovery criterion of paragraph 7(d) of Statement No. 13.

INTERPRETATION

6. For purposes of applying paragraph 28 of *FASB Statement No. 13* to leases involving only part of a building, other evidence may provide a basis for an objective determination of fair value even if there are no sales of property similar to the leased property. For example, reasonable estimates of the leased property's fair value might be objectively determined by referring to an independent appraisal of the leased property or to estimated replacement cost information.

EFFECTIVE DATE AND TRANSITION

7. The provisions of this Interpretation shall be effective for leasing transactions recorded and lease agreement revisions (see paragraph 9 of *FASB Statement No. 13*) recorded as of December 1, 1978 or thereafter. Earlier application is encouraged. In addition, except as provided in the next sentence, the provisions of this Interpretation shall be applied retroactively at the same time and in the same manner as the provisions of Statement No. 13 are applied retroactively (see paragraphs 49 and 51 of Statement No. 13). Enterprises that have already applied the provisions of Statement No. 13 retroactively and have published annual financial statements based on the retroactively adjusted accounts before the effective date of this Interpretation may, but are not required to, apply the provisions of this Interpretation retroactively.

This Interpretation was adopted by the affirmative votes of six members of the Financial Accounting Standards Board following submission to the members of the Financial Accounting Standards Advisory Council and the Screening Committee on Emerging Problems. Mr. Walters dissented.

Mr. Walters believes this is not a valid interpretation of *FASB Statement No. 13*. That Statement defines fair value as "the price for which the property could be sold in an arm's-length transaction between unrelated parties." Except for condominium or cooperative arrangements, fair value as defined does not exist for part of a building. Since it does not exist, it cannot be determined, objectively or otherwise. He believes this Interpretation contradicts the stated definition of fair value, and in effect selectively amends that definition as it relates to part of a building.

Members of the Financial Accounting Standards Board:

Donald J. Kirk,
Chairman
Oscar S. Gellein

John W. March
Robert A. Morgan
David Mosso

Robert T. Sprouse
Ralph E. Walters

FASB Interpretation No. 25
Accounting for an Unused Investment Tax Credit

an interpretation of APB Opinions No. 2, 4, 11, and 16

STATUS

Issued: September 1978

Effective Date: Prospectively for fiscal years beginning after December 15, 1978

Affects: No other pronouncements

Affected by: Paragraph 9 superseded by FAS 71
Footnote 5 superseded by FIN 32

SUMMARY

This Interpretation concerns recognition of investment tax credits in computing financial statement provisions for income tax expense. An investment tax credit should be recognized to the extent that the credit would have been realized on the tax return if taxes payable had been based on pretax accounting income. Any remaining available investment tax credit should be recognized to the extent that existing net deferred tax credits would reverse during the investment tax credit carryforward period, subject to limitations. The credit should not be recognized simply because the enterprise believes that future realization of the benefit is assured beyond a reasonable doubt.

The Interpretation also addresses the accounting for investment tax credits existing in an acquired company at the time of a business combination accounted for by the purchase method. If those investment tax credits are subsequently realized on the tax return, goodwill should be reduced by an equivalent amount until it is reduced to zero. Any additional amounts realized should be applied to reduce specified noncurrent assets until they are reduced to zero. Any remaining amount realized should be recorded as a deferred credit and amortized to income over a period not to exceed 40 years.

FASB Interpretation No. 25
Accounting for an Unused Investment Tax Credit

an interpretation of APB Opinions No. 2, 4, 11, and 16

CONTENTS

INTRODUCTION AND BACKGROUND INFORMATION

1. The FASB has been asked to clarify the circumstances, if any, under which an enterprise may recognize the benefit of an investment tax credit prior to its realization as an offset against federal income tax liability.

2. Paragraph 16 of *APB Opinion No. 2,* "Accounting for the 'Investment Credit'," states:

> An investment credit should be reflected in the financial statements only to the extent that it has been used as an offset against income tax liability. . . . A carryforward of unused investment credit should ordinarily be reflected only in the year in which the amount becomes "allowable," in which case the unused amount would not appear as an asset. Material amounts of unused investment credits should be disclosed.

Paragraph 10 of *APB Opinion No. 4 (Amending No. 2),* "Accounting for the 'Investment Credit'," amended paragraph 13 of *APB Opinion No. 2*[1] and states that "treating the credit as a reduction of federal income taxes of the year in which the credit *arises* is also acceptable" [emphasis added].

3. With respect to accounting for investment tax credits, paragraph 4 of *APB Opinion No. 11,* "Accounting for Income Taxes," states:

> *Investment Credits.* The [Accounting Principles] Board is continuing its study on accounting for "Investment Credits" and intends to issue a new Opinion on the subject as soon as possible. In the meantime APB Opinion No. 2, *Accounting for the "Investment Credit,"* and APB Opinion No. 4 (Amending No. 2), *Accounting for the "Investment Credit,"* remain in effect.

4. For tax years beginning before January 1, 1976, federal income tax law required that an investment tax credit arising in a particular tax year was to be offset against federal income tax liability before any investment tax credit carryovers to that year. Because the carryforward period was limited to seven years, an investment tax credit could expire unused. The Tax Reform Act of 1976 establishes a first-in, first-out treatment of investment tax credits for tax years beginning after December 31, 1975. Investment tax credit carryovers are to be used to reduce federal income taxes otherwise payable *before* investment tax credits arising from additions to assets in the current tax year. If unused investment tax credits from more than one tax year are carried over to a subsequent year, the credit from the earliest year is used first. As a result of that change in the federal income tax law and other features of the Tax Reform Act of 1976, some enterprises have concluded that an investment tax credit may be recognized in advance of realization because they believe its future realization is assured. Although the Tax Reform Act of 1976 has changed the *order* in which unused investment tax credits are used, an investment tax credit carryover can still expire unused.

5. A draft of a proposed Interpretation, "Accounting for an Unused Investment Tax Credit," was issued on December 16, 1977. The Board received 32 letters of comment in response to the proposed Interpretation. A few respondents disagreed with the proposed Interpretation and others expressed neither overall agreement nor disagreement but

[1]As to accounting for the investment tax credit, paragraph 13 of Opinion No. 2 states that "the allowable investment credit should be reflected in net income over the productive life of acquired property and not in the year in which it is placed in service."

offered comments or suggestions about specific matters. The remainder expressed general agreement.

6. Some respondents urged the Board to conform the accounting for unused investment tax credit to that specified by *APB Opinion No. 11* for net operating losses. Others recommended that investment tax credit should be recognized as an asset if future realization is assured beyond any reasonable doubt. The Board considered those recommendations and concluded that adoption of either might require an amendment. The Board believes that other aspects of accounting for the investment credit would require further consideration if an amendment were contemplated. The Board believes issuance of this Interpretation should not be delayed pending that further consideration.

7. Other respondents recommended that the investment tax credit should be recognized only when realized as an offset against federal income tax liability. Under comprehensive interperiod tax allocation by the deferred method required by *APB Opinion No. 11* and as interpreted by AICPA Accounting Interpretation No. 18 of Opinion No. 11, the investment tax credit is recognized before it is realized as an offset against federal income tax liability under the "with and without" method described in paragraph 36 of that Opinion. The Board has concluded that this practice should not be changed without a reconsideration of accounting for income taxes.

8. A number of respondents recommended that the Board clarify the computational guidelines in the proposed Interpretation for recognizing the investment tax credit, including the limitations on recognition of unused investment tax credit. Several respondents also suggested that examples of the application of the requirements of the proposed Interpretation should be provided. The computational guidelines have been clarified and Appendix A, Examples of Computations of Investment Tax Credit Recognized, has been added to the Interpretation setting forth some examples. The examples do not attempt to illustrate all of the various possible combinations of circumstances that may affect the amount of investment tax credit recognized.

9. The Addendum to *APB Opinion No. 2* states that "differences may arise in the application of generally accepted accounting principles as between regulated and nonregulated businesses, because of the effect in regulated businesses of the rate-making process," and discusses the application of generally accepted accounting principles to regulated industries. Accordingly, the provisions of the Addendum shall govern the application of this Interpretation to those operations of a company that are regulated for rate-making purposes on an individual-company-cost-of-service basis.

INTERPRETATION

Interperiod Tax Allocation

10. The tax benefit of investment tax credits becoming available in the current period (excluding investment tax credits carried back to previous years[2]) or carried forward from a prior period shall be recognized in measuring income tax expense for the current period[3] by the deferred method to the extent that the benefit would have been realized if taxes payable had been based on pretax accounting income adjusted for permanent differences. In addition, any remaining unused investment tax credit shall be offset against existing net deferred tax credits[4] to the extent that those net deferred tax credits would reverse during the investment tax credit carryforward period, disregarding any timing differences that may originate in that carryforward period. The statutory limitation on offsets of the investment tax credit against federal income taxes payable[5] shall be applied to each determination of amounts of investment tax credit to be recognized in accordance with the provisions of this Interpretation.

[2]The tax benefit of investment tax credits carried back to previous tax years and realized as a refund of federal income taxes previously paid is added to the amount of investment tax credits recognized in measuring income tax expense for the current period in accordance with paragraph 10 above.

[3]Some enterprises recognize the tax benefit of investment tax credits only to the extent realized as an offset to federal income tax liability and defer and amortize such credits over the productive life of acquired property. This Interpretation does not modify that practice.

[4]As used in this Interpretation, the term "net deferred tax credits" represents the net of aggregate deferred tax credits and aggregate deferred tax debits.

[5]Currently, the federal statutory limitation is generally 100 percent of the first $25,000 and 50 percent of the remaining federal income taxes payable for most enterprises.

11. The guidelines set forth in paragraphs 45-47 of *APB Opinion No. 11*[6] that permit the recognition of the tax benefit of an *operating loss* carryforward when future realization is assured beyond any reasonable doubt *do not apply* to recognition of an unused investment tax credit.

12. When the tax benefit of an unused investment tax credit that was recognized through offset of net deferred tax credits (see paragraph 10 above) is subsequently realized as a reduction of federal income taxes payable, an equivalent amount of deferred tax credits shall be reinstated. The reinstated deferred tax credits shall be amortized in the periods in which the related timing differences reverse.

Unused Investment Tax Credit Acquired in a Business Combination Accounted for by the Purchase Method

13. Paragraphs 66-96 of *APB Opinion No. 16,* "Business Combinations," specify the accounting for a business combination by the purchase method. Paragraph 87 of that Opinion requires that all identifiable assets acquired and liabilities assumed, whether or not shown in the financial statements of the acquired enterprise, shall be assigned a portion of the cost of the acquired enterprise and that the excess of the cost of the acquired enterprise over the sum of the amounts assigned to the identifiable assets acquired less liabilities assumed shall be recorded as goodwill. Paragraphs 87, 91 and 92 of the Opinion also specify the accounting for the cost of an acquired enterprise if the market or appraisal values of identifiable assets acquired less liabilities assumed exceeds the cost of the acquired enterprise.

14. *APB Opinion No. 2* does not permit an unused investment tax credit to be recognized as an asset.

15. An acquiring enterprise shall reduce the goodwill recognized in a business combination by the amount of tax benefits realized from an unused investment tax credit of an acquired enterprise in the period in which that credit offsets federal income tax liability. Goodwill shall not be reduced (or "negative goodwill"[7] shall not be increased) retroactively to the date of the business combination and the results of operations of previous periods shall not be retroactively restated for revised amortization of goodwill. Rather, the adjusted goodwill (or "negative goodwill") shall be amortized over the remainder of the amortization period. Paragraph 16 of this Interpretation specifies the accounting for the realized tax benefits from an acquired enterprise's unused investment tax credit that exceed the remaining unamortized goodwill recognized in the business combination.

16. If there is no remaining unamortized goodwill from the business combination, the realized tax benefits from an acquired enterprise's unused investment tax credit shall be applied to reduce any remaining unamortized balances of amounts assigned to noncurrent assets acquired in the combination as specified in paragraphs 87, 91 and 92 of *APB Opinion No. 16.* Those amounts shall not be reduced retroactively to the date of the business combination and the results of operations for previous periods shall not be retroactively restated for revised depreciation, depletion, or amortization expense. If the unused investment tax credit realized reduces the unamortized balance of noncurrent assets acquired in the combination to zero, any further tax benefits realized from unused investment tax credit acquired in the combination shall be recorded as a deferred credit and shall be amortized systematically to income over the estimated period to be benefited, not to exceed forty years.

EFFECTIVE DATE AND TRANSITION

17. The provisions set forth in paragraphs 10-12 of this Interpretation shall be applied prospectively in fiscal years beginning after December 15, 1978. Investment tax credits related to acquisitions in fiscal years beginning after December 15, 1978 shall be accounted for in accordance with this Interpretation. Unused investment tax credits related to acquisitions in fiscal years beginning before December 16, 1978 shall be accounted for in accordance with the enterprise's present method of accounting for unused investment tax credits. Earlier application is encouraged in financial statements for fiscal years beginning before December 16, 1978 that have not been previously issued.

---

[6]Paragraph 45 of *APB Opinion No. 11* states that "the tax benefits of loss carryforwards should not be recognized until they are actually realized, except in unusual circumstances when realization is assured beyond any reasonable doubt at the time the loss carryforwards arise." Paragraph 47 of that Opinion states:

> Realization of the tax benefit of the loss carryforward would appear to be assured beyond any reasonable doubt when both of the following conditions exist: (a) the loss results from an identifiable, isolated and nonrecurring cause and the company either has been continuously profitable over a long period or has suffered occasional losses which were more than offset by taxable income in subsequent years, and (b) future taxable income is virtually certain to be large enough to offset the loss carryforward and will occur soon enough to provide realization during the carryforward period.

[7]See paragraph 87 of *APB Opinion No. 16.*

18. The provisions set forth in paragraphs 13-16 of this Interpretation shall be applied prospectively in annual financial statements for fiscal years beginning after December 15, 1978 and for financial reports for interim periods within those fiscal years, regardless of the date of the business combination. Earlier application is encouraged in financial statements for fiscal years beginning before December 16, 1978 that have not been previously issued.

19. If early application is adopted in financial reports for interim periods of a fiscal year beginning before December 16, 1978, previously issued financial information for any interim periods of that fiscal year that precede the period of adoption shall be restated to give effect to the provisions of this Interpretation and any subsequent presentation of that information shall be on the restated basis. This Interpretation shall not be applied retroactively for previously issued annual financial statements.

This Interpretation was adopted by the affirmative votes of six members of the Financial Accounting Standards Board following submission to members of the Financial Accounting Standards Advisory Council and Screening Committee on Emerging Problems. Mr. Sprouse dissented.

Mr. Sprouse dissents because he believes this Interpretation is inherently contradictory in two respects:

1. Paragraph 16 of *APB Opinion No. 2* is cited as stating that "an investment credit should be reflected in the financial statements only to the extent that it has been used as an offset against income tax liability." For that reason, the Board rejected recognition of an unrealized investment tax credit even though future realization is assured beyond any reasonable doubt (paragraph 11). At the same time, the Interpretation requires recognition of an unrealized investment credit "in measuring income tax expense for the current period by the deferred method to the extent that the benefit would have been realized if taxes payable had been based on pretax accounting income adjusted for permanent differences" (paragraph 10).
2. The Interpretation states that under the "with and without" method described in paragraph 36 of *APB Opinion No. 11* the investment credit *is* recognized before it is realized and that the Board concluded that this practice should not be changed (paragraph 7). At the same time, the Interpretation states that, if the "with and without" method is used by an enterprise that defers and amortizes realized investment credits over the productive life of acquired property, the "with and without" method need not recognize an unused investment credit before it is realized (footnote 3).

Mr. Sprouse believes that paragraph 16 of *APB Opinion No. 2,* taken as a whole (that is, including the portion omitted in the quotation in paragraph 2 of this Interpretation), could reasonably be interpreted either (i) to provide that an investment credit be recognized only to the extent it has been realized (see paragraph 7 of this Interpretation) or (ii) to provide that an unused investment credit be accounted for "consistent with the provisions" (of *APB Opinion No. 11*) for accounting for an operating loss carryforward (see paragraph 6 of this Interpretation), but not partly (i) and partly (ii). In his opinion the latter interpretation is preferable.

Members of the Financial Accounting Standards Board:

Donald J. Kirk, *Chairman*
Oscar S. Gellein
John W. March
Robert A. Morgan
David Mosso
Robert T. Sprouse
Ralph E. Walters

Appendix A

EXAMPLES OF COMPUTATIONS OF INVESTMENT TAX CREDIT RECOGNIZED

20. This Appendix illustrates the application of the provisions of paragraphs 10-12 of this Interpretation in computing the amount of investment tax credit recognized. The examples do not comprehend all possible combinations of circumstances.

General Assumptions

21. The general assumptions on which the following examples are based are:

1. The statutory tax rate is 48 percent.
2. Investment tax credit that may be offset against federal income taxes payable is limited to 50 percent of taxes payable.
3. There are no permanent differences.
4. There are no investment tax credit carrybacks.
5. The "net change" method of computing deferred taxes is used (paragraph 37, *APB Opinion No. 11*).

EXAMPLE 1

22. This example illustrates the computation of investment tax credit to be recognized had taxes payable been based on pretax accounting income. In addition, investment tax credit is also recognized as

an offset against existing net deferred tax credits that would reverse in the investment tax credit carryforward period.

Additional assumptions:

Pretax accounting income	$1,000,000
Net timing differences	(300,000)
Taxable income	$ 700,000
Available investment tax credit (for both financial reporting and tax purposes)	$ 925,000
Existing net deferred tax credits	$2,000,000
Existing net deferred tax credits to be amortized in the investment tax credit carryforward period	$1,200,000

The maximum amount of investment tax credit recognizable is computed as follows:

Investment tax credit recognized based upon tax on pretax accounting income ($1,000,000 × 48% × 50% limitation)	$ 240,000
Investment tax credit recognized as an offset against existing net deferred tax credits to be amortized in the investment tax credit carryforward period ($1,200,000 × 50% limitation)	600,000
Maximum investment tax credit recognizable (limited to $925,000 available)	$ 840,000

Computation of the provision for income taxes:

Tax on pretax accounting income ($1,000,000 × 48%)	$480,000	
Less investment tax credit ($480,000 × 50% limitation)	(240,000)	$ 240,000
Tax on taxable income ($700,000 × 48%)	$336,000	
Less investment tax credit ($336,000 × 50% limitation)	(168,000)	(168,000)
Deferred tax expense (differential equivalent to tax effects of timing differences to be added to deferred tax credits)		72,000
Investment tax credit offset against net deferred tax credits		(600,000)
Provision for deferred taxes (credit)		(528,000)
Taxes currently payable—above		168,000
Provision for income taxes (credit)		$ (360,000)

Investment tax credit recognized:

As a reduction of taxes on pretax accounting income	$ 240,000
As an offset against net deferred tax credits	600,000
Total	$840,000

Changes in net deferred tax credits:

Balance, beginning of period	$2,000,000
Deferred tax on net timing differences ($480,000 – 336,000)	144,000
Investment tax credit offset against deferred tax credits ($240,000 – 168,000 + 600,000)	(672,000)
Balance, end of period	$1,472,000

EXAMPLE 2

23. This example illustrates the reinstatement of deferred tax credits that have been offset by investment tax credit to the extent that the tax benefit of the investment tax credit is subsequently realized (a continuation of Example 1).

Additional assumptions:

Pretax accounting income	$2,000,000
Net timing differences	(125,000)
Taxable income	$1,875,000
Available investment tax credit (all amounts carried forward from prior year):	
Financial reporting ($925,000 – 840,000)	$ 85,000
Tax return ($925,000 – 168,000)	$ 757,000
Existing net deferred tax credits	$1,472,000

Investment tax credit recognizable:

Investment tax credit recognized based upon tax on pretax accounting income ($2,000,000 × 48% × 50% limitation = $480,000; limited to available investment tax credit)	$ 85,000

Computation of the provision for income taxes:

Tax on pretax accounting income ($2,000,000 × 48%)	$960,000	
Less investment tax credit (limited to available investment tax credit)	(85,000)	$ 875,000
Tax on taxable income ($1,875,000 × 48%)	$900,000	
Less investment tax credit ($900,000 × 50% limitation)	(450,000)	(450,000)
Deferred tax expense (differential equivalent to tax effects of timing differences and reinstatement of deferred tax credits for investment tax credit realized that was recognized in a previous period)		425,000*
Taxes currently payable—above		450,000
Provision for income taxes		$ 875,000

*Deferred tax expense is comprised of the following:

Investment tax credit realized as an offset to taxes currently payable	$ 450,000
Less investment tax credit recognized in the computation of taxes on pretax accounting income for the current period and included in $450,000 above	(85,000)
Deferred taxes reinstated for investment tax credit realized that was recognized in a previous period	365,000
Tax effects of net timing differences ($125,000 × 48%)	60,000
Total	$ 425,000

Changes in net deferred tax credits:

Balance, beginning of period	$1,472,000
Deferred tax on net timing differences	60,000
Deferred tax credits reinstated	365,000
Balance, end of period	$1,897,000

FASB Interpretation No. 26
Accounting for Purchase of a Leased Asset by the Lessee during the Term of the Lease

an interpretation of FASB Statement No. 13

STATUS

Issued: September 1978

Effective Date: For purchases of leased property recorded as of December 1, 1978

Affects: No other pronouncements

Affected by: No other pronouncements

SUMMARY

This Interpretation clarifies the application of paragraph 14 of *FASB Statement No. 13,* "Accounting for Leases," to a termination of a capital lease that results from the purchase of a leased asset by the lessee.

The purchase by the lessee of property under a capital lease and the related lease termination are accounted for as a single transaction. The difference, if any, between the purchase price and the carrying amount of the lease obligation is recorded as an adjustment of the carrying amount of the asset. The Board also noted that Statement No. 13 does not prohibit recognition of a loss if a loss has been incurred.

FASB Interpretation No. 26
Accounting for Purchase of a Leased Asset by the Lessee during the Term of the Lease

an interpretation of FASB Statement No. 13

CONTENTS

INTRODUCTION AND BACKGROUND INFORMATION

1. The FASB has been asked to clarify whether a termination of a capital lease that results from the purchase of a leased asset by the lessee is the type of transaction contemplated by paragraph 14(c) of *FASB Statement No. 13,* "Accounting for Leases." That paragraph states that "a termination of a capital lease shall be accounted for by removing the asset and obligation, with gain or loss recognized for the difference."

2. A draft of a proposed Interpretation on "Accounting for Purchase of a Leased Asset by the Lessee during the Term of the Lease" was issued on April 28, 1978. The Board received 27 letters of comment in response to the proposed Interpretation. Certain of the comments received and the Board's consideration of them are discussed in paragraphs 3 and 4 below.

3. A number of respondents stated that the purchase of a leased asset by the lessee during the term of a capital lease gives rise to an early extinguishment of debt for which the accounting is prescribed in *APB Opinion No. 26,* "Early Extinguishment of Debt." The Board concluded that it should look to *FASB Statement No. 13* to clarify the accounting for the termination of a lease instead of Opinion No. 26. Statement No. 13 specifies different accounting for the termination of a capital lease for which the leased asset ceases to be carried on the enterprise's balance sheet and for a renewal or extension for which the leased asset continues to be carried on the enterprise's balance sheet. The Board views the purchase of the leased asset by the lessee during the term of the lease as a transaction for which similar rights for the same asset continue to be carried on the enterprise's balance sheet. The Board is aware that some extensions of capital leases and purchases of leased assets could be viewed as similar to early extinguishments of debt. Other extensions of capital leases and purchases of leased assets could be viewed as nonmonetary transactions with an amount of monetary consideration of the type (exchanges of rights to productive assets not held for sale in the ordinary course of business) for which *APB Opinion No. 29,* "Accounting for Nonmonetary Transactions," does not permit recognition of gain. The Board considered the possible applicability of both Opinion No. 26 and Opinion No. 29 during its deliberations on the provisions of Statement No. 13 that address accounting for extensions and other terminations of capital leases. The subjectivity of an allocation of the purchase price between retirement of the lease obligation and acquisition of additional property rights was also a consideration in the determination that recognition of gain or loss should not be required if the asset continued to be carried on the enterprise's balance sheet.

4. Some respondents stated that this Interpretation should require recognition of a loss if a loss is indicated by the terms of the transaction. The Board noted that *FASB Statement No. 13* does not include a requirement for loss recognition on an extension of a capital lease. Therefore, an Interpretation of Statement No. 13 could not include such a requirement. However, the Board also noted that Statement No. 13 does not prohibit recognition of a loss if a loss has been incurred.

INTERPRETATION

5. The termination of a capital lease that results from the purchase of a leased asset by the lessee is not the type of transaction contemplated by paragraph 14(c) of *FASB Statement No. 13* but rather is an integral part of the purchase of the leased asset. The purchase by the lessee of property under a capital lease shall be accounted for like a renewal or extension of a capital lease that, in turn, is classified

as a capital lease,[1] that is, any difference between the purchase price and the carrying amount of the lease obligation shall be recorded as an adjustment of the carrying amount of the asset.

EFFECTIVE DATE AND TRANSITION

6. The provisions of this Interpretation shall be effective for purchases of leased property recorded as of December 1, 1978 or thereafter. Earlier application is encouraged. In addition, except as provided in the next sentence, the provisions of this Interpretation shall be applied retroactively at the same time and in the same manner as the provisions of *FASB Statement No. 13* are applied retroactively (see paragraphs 49 and 51 of Statement No. 13). Enterprises that have already applied the provisions of Statement No. 13 retroactively and have published annual financial statements based on the retroactively adjusted accounts before the effective date of this Interpretation may, but are not required to, apply the provisions of this Interpretation retroactively.

This Interpretation was adopted by the unanimous vote of the seven members of the Financial Accounting Standards Board following submission to the Financial Accounting Standards Advisory Council and the Screening Committee on Emerging Problems.

Members of the Financial Accounting Standards Board:

Donald J. Kirk, *Chairman*
Oscar S. Gellein
John W. March
Robert A. Morgan
David Mosso
Robert T. Sprouse
Ralph E. Walters

[1]Paragraph 14(b)(i) of *FASB Statement No. 13* refers to paragraph 14(a) of the Statement for the accounting for a renewal or an extension of a capital lease that is also classified as a capital lease.

FASB Interpretation No. 27
Accounting for a Loss on a Sublease

an interpretation of FASB Statement No. 13 and APB Opinion No. 30

STATUS

Issued: November 1978

Effective Date: For transactions with measurement dates on or after March 1, 1979

Affects: No other pronouncements

Affected by: No other pronouncements

SUMMARY

This Interpretation clarifies that recognition of a loss by an original lessee who disposes of leased property or mitigates the cost of an existing lease commitment by subleasing the property is not prohibited by *FASB Statement No. 13,* "Accounting for Leases."

This Interpretation also clarifies the treatment of a sublease that is part of a disposal of a segment. The determination of a gain or loss on disposal of the segment, under the provisions of *APB Opinion No. 30,* "Reporting the Results of Operations," comprehends amounts related to an original lease and a sublease entered into as part of the decision to dispose of the segment. Any gain or loss on the sublease becomes an indistinguishable part of the gain or loss on the disposal.

FASB Interpretation No. 27
Accounting for a Loss on a Sublease

an interpretation of FASB Statement No. 13 and APB Opinion No. 30

CONTENTS

INTRODUCTION

1. The FASB has been asked to clarify whether paragraph 39 of *FASB Statement No. 13,* "Accounting for Leases," prohibits the recognition of a loss by an original lessee[1] who disposes of property that was used in a discontinued operation or mitigates the cost of a lease commitment related to a discontinued operation by subleasing the property. In those circumstances, paragraphs 15-17 of *APB Opinion No. 30* may require recognition of a loss. Appendix A provides additional background information about this matter.

INTERPRETATION

2. Paragraph 39 of *FASB Statement No. 13* does not prohibit the recognition of a loss by an original lessee[2] who disposes of leased property or mitigates the cost of an existing lease commitment by subleasing the property.

3. If a sublease is entered into as part of a disposal of a segment of a business[3] as defined in paragraph 13 of *APB Opinion No. 30,* the anticipated future cash flows that will result from the original lease and the sublease, as well as the carrying amount of any related recorded assets or obligations, shall be taken into account in determining the overall gain or loss on the disposal.

EFFECTIVE DATE AND TRANSITION

4. The provisions of this Interpretation shall be effective for estimates of losses on a disposal of a segment of a business recorded as of a measurement date[4] occurring on or after March 1, 1979 and for subleases recorded as of March 1, 1979 or thereafter. Earlier application is encouraged. In addition, except as provided in the next sentence, the provisions of this Interpretation shall be applied retroactively at the same time and in the same manner as the provisions of *FASB Statement No. 13* are applied retroactively (see paragraphs 49 and 51 of Statement No. 13). Enterprises that have already applied the provisions of Statement No. 13 retroactively and have published annual financial statements based on the retroactively adjusted accounts before the effective date of this Interpretation may, but are not required to, apply the provisions of this Interpretation retroactively.

This Interpretation was adopted by the unanimous vote of the seven members of the Financial Accounting Standards Board following submission to the Financial Accounting Standards Advisory Council and the Screening Committee on Emerging Problems.

Members of the Financial Accounting Standards Board:

Donald J. Kirk, *Chairman*
Oscar S. Gellein
John W. March
Robert A. Morgan
David Mosso
Robert T. Sprouse
Ralph E. Walters

[1]An "original lessee" is used in this Interpretation and in *FASB Statement No. 13* to include any lessee who acts as sublessor on a sublease.

[2]See Footnote 1.

[3]An AICPA Accounting Interpretation of APB Opinion No. 30, "Illustrations of the Application of APB Opinion No. 30," issued in November 1973, states that "the gain or loss on a sale of a portion of a line of business which is not a segment of a business . . . should be calculated using the same measurement principles as if it were a segment of a business (paragraphs 15-17 of the Opinion)."

[4]See paragraph 14 of *APB Opinion No. 30* for the definition of "measurement date."

Appendix A

BACKGROUND INFORMATION

5. Paragraph 39 of *FASB Statement No. 13* specifies the accounting by an original lessee for both an original lease and a sublease or similar transaction if the original lessee is not relieved of the primary obligation under the original lease. Under that paragraph, the original lessee accounts for a sublease as a sales-type, direct financing, or operating lease, based partly on the classification of the original lease and partly on the criteria of Statement No. 13 for those classifications. If the sublease is classified as an operating lease, the original lessee continues to account for the original lease as before. If the sublease is classified as a direct financing or sales-type lease, the unamortized balance of the asset under the original lease is treated as the cost of the subleased property, and the original lessee continues to account for the obligation related to the original lease as before. Paragraph 39 does not specifically address recognition of a loss on a sublease except when the sublease meets the criteria for classification as a sales-type lease.

6. Paragraphs 15-17 of *APB Opinion No. 30* describe how an enterprise determines a gain or loss on disposal of a segment of a business. Paragraph 17 of Opinion No. 30 states that "costs and expenses *directly* associated with the decision to dispose include items such as . . . future rentals on long-term leases to the extent they are not offset by sublease rentals." The provision for a loss on a sublease would be based on the net expected future cash disbursements if both the original lease and the sublease were classified as operating leases.

7. If an original lease was classified as a capital lease, a comparison of future rentals on the original lease with sublease rentals would not necessarily be indicative of the future loss on the sublease transaction. A loss, if any, would generally have to be measured based on other provisions of *APB Opinion No. 30*. Paragraph 15 of Opinion No. 30 states that "if it is expected that net losses from operations will be incurred between the measurement date and the expected disposal date, the computation of the gain or loss on disposal should also include an estimate of such amounts." Paragraph 16 of Opinion No. 30 states that "adjustments, costs, and expenses which (a) are clearly a *direct* result of the decision to dispose of the segment and (b) are clearly not the adjustments of carrying amounts or costs, or expenses that should have been recognized on a going-concern basis prior to the measurement date should be included in determining the gain or loss on disposal."

8. A draft of a proposed Interpretation on "Accounting for a Loss on a Sublease" was issued on April 28, 1978. The Board received 20 letters of comment in response to the proposed Interpretation. Certain of the comments received and the Board's consideration of them are discussed in paragraphs 9-11 below.

9. The proposed Interpretation was limited to subleases for which *APB Opinion No. 30* requires recognition of a loss. A number of respondents suggested that the proposed Interpretation be expanded to encompass all subleases. Paragraph 2 of this Interpretation is intended to clarify the Board's view that paragraph 39 of *FASB Statement No. 13* does not prohibit recognition of a loss on a sublease whether or not the sublease is part of a disposal of a segment. Paragraph 3 of this Interpretation is intended to indicate that determination of a gain or loss on disposal of a segment will comprehend amounts relating to an original lease and a sublease entered into as part of a decision to dispose of the segment. Any gain or loss on the lease or sublease becomes an indistinguishable part of the gain or loss on disposal. If a sublease is not entered into as part of a decision to dispose of the segment, Statement No. 13 does not specifically require recognition of an indicated loss except for a sales-type loss on a sales-type sublease. The Board has a possible amendment of Statement No. 13 under consideration that would specify the computation of an indicated loss to be recognized on a sublease that is not entered into as part of a disposal of a segment. However, the Board concluded that it should not delay issuance of this Interpretation pending a final decision on whether to proceed with that amendment.

10. A number of respondents stated that *FASB Statement No. 5,* "Accounting for Contingencies," requires recognition of a loss on a sublease. The Board views most subleases as outside the scope of Statement No. 5 by reason of the exclusion from the coverage of that Statement of write-downs of operating assets (paragraph 31 of Statement No. 5). In addition, if a sublease covered all of the remaining term of the original lease and no contingent rentals were involved, the only uncertainty would be the collectibility of the sublease rentals, and thus Statement No. 5 would not apply to the determination of any loss that would occur if all sublease rentals were collected.

11. A number of respondents suggested that the proposed Interpretation be expanded to address the application of *APB Opinion No. 30* to other specific matters. The essence of this Interpretation is that the application of Opinion No. 30 was not affected by the issuance of *FASB Statement No. 13*. Accordingly, the Board concluded that it should not expand the scope of this Interpretation to describe the application of Opinion No. 30.

FASB Interpretation No. 28
Accounting for Stock Appreciation Rights and Other Variable Stock Option or Award Plans

an interpretation of APB Opinions No. 15 and 25

STATUS

Issued: December 1978

Effective Date: For awards granted in fiscal years beginning after December 15, 1978

Affects: No other pronouncements

Affected by: Paragraph 6 amended by FIN 31

SUMMARY

This Interpretation clarifies aspects of accounting for compensation related to stock appreciation rights and other variable stock option or award plans. The Interpretation specifies that compensation should be measured at the end of each period as the amount by which the quoted market value of the shares of the enterprise's stock covered by a grant exceeds the option price or value specified under the plan and should be accrued as a charge to expense over the periods the employee performs the related services. Changes in the quoted market value should be reflected as an adjustment of accrued compensation and compensation expense in the periods in which the changes occur until the date the number of shares and purchase price, if any, are both known.

FASB Interpretation No. 28
Accounting for Stock Appreciation Rights and Other Variable Stock Option or Award Plans

an interpretation of APB Opinions No. 15 and 25

CONTENTS

INTRODUCTION

1. The FASB has been asked to clarify whether the provisions of *APB Opinion No. 25,* "Accounting for Stock Issued to Employees," apply to stock appreciation rights and, if so, how the Opinion should be applied. Similar questions have been raised about awards under other stock compensation plans with variable terms, that is, plans for which the number of shares of stock the employee may receive, the price per share the employee must pay, or both the number of shares and the price are unknown at the date of grant or award. Appendix A provides additional background information about these matters. Appendix B illustrates applications of this Interpretation.

INTERPRETATION

2. *APB Opinion No. 25* applies to plans for which the employer's stock is issued as compensation or the amount of cash paid as compensation is determined by reference to the market price of the stock or to changes in its market price. Plans involving stock appreciation rights and other variable plan awards[1] are included in those plans dealt with by Opinion No. 25. When stock appreciation rights or other variable plan awards are granted, an enterprise shall measure compensation as the amount by which the quoted market value of the shares of the enterprise's stock covered by the grant exceeds the option price or value specified, by reference to a market price or otherwise, subject to any appreciation limitations under the plan. Changes, either increases or decreases, in the quoted market value of those shares between the date of grant and the measurement date[2] result in a change in the measure of compensation for the right or award.

3. Compensation determined in accordance with paragraph 2 shall be accrued as a charge to expense over the period or periods the employee performs the related services (hereinafter referred to as the "service period"). If the stock appreciation rights or other variable plan awards are granted for past services, compensation shall be accrued as a charge to expense of the period in which the rights or awards are granted. If the service period is not defined in the plan or some other agreement, such as an employment agreement, as a shorter or previous period, the service period shall be presumed to be the vesting period.[3]

4. Compensation accrued during the service period in accordance with paragraph 3 shall be adjusted in subsequent periods up to the measurement date[4] for

---

[1]Plans for which the number of shares of stock that may be acquired by or awarded to an employee or the price or both are not specified or determinable until after the date of grant or award are referred to in this Interpretation as "variable plan awards." However, plans described in paragraph 11(c) of Opinion No. 25 (see paragraph 12 in Appendix A of this Interpretation) and book value stock option, purchase, or award plans are not covered by this Interpretation. Plans under which an employee may receive cash in lieu of stock or additional cash upon the exercise of a stock option are variable plans for purposes of this Interpretation if the amount is contingent on the occurrence of future events.

[2]Paragraph 10 of Opinion No. 25 defines the measurement date as "the first date on which are known both (1) the number of shares that an individual employee is entitled to receive and (2) the option or purchase price, if any." Generally, the number of shares of stock that may be acquired or awarded under stock appreciation rights and many other variable plan awards are not known until the date that they are exercised.

[3]For purposes of this Interpretation, stock appreciation rights and other variable plan awards become vested when the employee's right to receive or retain shares or cash under the rights or awards is not contingent upon the performance of additional services. Frequently, the vesting period is the period from the date of grant to the date the rights or awards become exercisable.

[4]See footnote 2.

changes, either increases or decreases, in the quoted market value of the shares of the enterprise's stock covered by the grant but shall not be adjusted below zero. The offsetting adjustment shall be made to compensation expense of the period in which changes in the market value occur. Except as provided in paragraph 5, the accrued compensation for a right that is forfeited or cancelled shall be adjusted by decreasing compensation expense in the period of forfeiture, in accordance with paragraph 15 of *APB Opinion No. 25.*

5. For purposes of applying paragraph 11(h)[5] of *APB Opinion No. 25,* compensation expense for a combination plan[6] involving stock appreciation rights or other variable plan awards (including those that are granted after the date of grant of related stock options) shall be measured according to the terms the employee is most likely to elect based on the facts available each period. An enterprise shall presume that the employee will elect to exercise the stock appreciation rights or other variable plan awards, but the presumption may be overcome if past experience or the terms of a combination plan that limit the market appreciation available to the employee in the stock appreciation rights or other variable plan awards provide evidence that the employee will elect to exercise the related stock option. If an enterprise has been accruing compensation for a stock appreciation right or other variable plan award and a change in circumstances provides evidence that the employee will likely elect to exercise the related stock option, accrued compensation recorded for the right or award shall *not* be adjusted.[7] If the employee elects to exercise the stock option, the accrued compensation recorded for the right or award shall be recognized as a consideration for the stock issued. If all parts of the grant or award (e.g., both the option and the right or award) are forfeited or cancelled, accrued compensation shall be adjusted by decreasing compensation expense in that period.

6. Stock appreciation rights and other variable plan awards are common stock equivalents to the extent payable in stock for purposes of applying the provisions of *APB Opinion No. 15,* "Earnings per Share." Accrued compensation for those rights or awards shall be considered additional "proceeds" for purposes of applying the treasury stock method described in paragraph 36 of Opinion No. 15 for determining the dilutive effect of options in earnings per share computations. Stock appreciation rights and other variable plan awards payable only in cash are not common stock equivalents for the computation of earnings per share under that Opinion.

EFFECTIVE DATE AND TRANSITION

7. The provisions of this Interpretation shall be applied prospectively for stock appreciation rights and other variable plan awards granted in fiscal years beginning after December 15, 1978. Early application is encouraged for stock appreciation rights and other variable plan awards granted in fiscal years beginning before December 16, 1978 for which financial statements have not been previously issued. In addition, this Interpretation may be, but is not required to be, adopted for stock appreciation rights and other variable plan awards granted in fiscal years beginning before December 16, 1978 for which financial statements have been previously issued; if so adopted, an accrual of compensation expense or an adjustment of accrued compensation resulting from the application of this Interpretation for stock appreciation rights and other variable plan awards granted in fiscal years beginning before December 16, 1978 shall be accounted for as a change in estimate in the period of change (see paragraphs 31-33 of *APB Opinion No. 20*). This Interpretation shall not be applied retroactively for previously issued annual financial statements.

8. If early application is adopted in financial reports for interim periods of a fiscal year beginning before December 16, 1978, previously issued financial information for any interim periods of that fiscal year that precede the period of adoption shall be restated to give effect to the provisions of this Interpretation. Any subsequent presentation of that information shall be on the restated basis.

This Interpretation was adopted by the unanimous vote of the seven members of the Financial Accounting Standards Board following submission to the Financial Accounting Standards Advisory Council and the Screening Committee on Emerging Problems.

[5]See paragraph 13 in Appendix A of this Interpretation.

[6]See paragraph 10 in Appendix A of this Interpretation.

[7]A change in the circumstances may be indicated by market appreciation in excess of any appreciation limitations under the plan or the cancellation or forfeiture of the stock appreciation right or other variable plan award without a concurrent cancellation or forfeiture of the related stock option. A subsequent decrease in market value that reduces the appreciation to a level below the limitations under the plan would require adjustment of accrued compensation in accordance with paragraph 4 of this Interpretation if evidence then indicates that the employee will elect to exercise the stock appreciation right or other variable plan award.

Appendix A

BACKGROUND INFORMATION

9. Stock appreciation rights are awards entitling employees to receive cash, stock, or a combination of cash and stock in an amount equivalent to any excess of the market value of a stated number of shares of the employer company's stock over a stated price. The form of payment may be specified when the rights are granted or may be determined when they are exercised; in some plans the employee may choose the form of payment.

10. Stock appreciation rights are usually granted in combination with compensatory stock options but also may be granted separately. Combination plans usually provide that the rights are exercisable for the same period as the companion stock options and that the exercise of either cancels the other. In some combination plans, the enterprise may grant stock appreciation rights either when the options are granted or at a later date. In some cases the holder of stock options may apply to receive share appreciation in cash or stock with the approval of the enterprise, in lieu of exercising the options.

11. Paragraph 10 of *APB Opinion No. 25* specifies that "compensation for services that a corporation receives as consideration for stock issued through employee stock option, purchase, and award plans should be measured by the quoted market price of the stock at the measurement date less the amount, if any, that the employee is required to pay." Paragraphs 12-15 of Opinion No. 25 refer to accrual of compensation in periods for which service is rendered before issuance of stock. Paragraph 13 states that "the employer corporation should accrue compensation expense in each period in which the services are performed" and "if the measurement date is later than the date of grant or award, an employer corporation should record the compensation expense each period from date of grant or award to date of measurement based on the quoted market price of the stock at the end of each period." Paragraph 15 of Opinion No. 25 states that the effect of the change in estimated compensation expense should be accounted for in the period of change in accordance with paragraphs 31-33 of *APB Opinion No. 20,* "Accounting Changes."

12. Paragraph 11(c) of *APB Opinion No. 25* states that "the measurement date of an award of stock for current service may be the end of the fiscal period, which is normally the effective date of the award, instead of the date that the award to an employee is determined if (1) the award is provided for by the terms of an established formal plan, (2) the plan designates the factors that determine the total dollar amount of awards to employees for the period (for example, a percent of income), although the total amount or the individual awards may not be known at the end of the period, and (3) the award pertains to current service of the employee for the period.

13. Paragraph 11(h) of *APB Opinion No. 25* states that "compensation cost for a combination plan permitting an employee to elect one part should be measured according to the terms that an employee is most likely to elect based on the facts available each period." Although Opinion No. 25 principally addresses the measurement of compensation when stock is issued to an employee, the Opinion also addresses situations in which cash or stock is paid to an employee for appreciation in the market price of an enterprise's stock. Paragraph 32 of the Opinion states that "the terms of some plans, often called *phantom stock* or *shadow stock* plans, base the obligations for compensation on increases in market price of or dividends distributed on a specified or variable number of shares of stock of the employer corporation but provide for settlement of the obligation to the employee in cash, in stock of the employer corporation, or a combination of cash and stock."

14. A draft of a proposed Interpretation, "Accounting for Stock Appreciation Rights and Other Compensation Plans with Variable Terms Related to the Price of a Company's Stock," was released for comment August 17, 1978. The Board received 62 letters of comment in response to the proposed Interpretation. Certain of the comments received and the Board's consideration of them are discussed in paragraphs 15-18 below.

15. The proposed Interpretation required that compensation expense for stock appreciation rights and other variable plan awards be accrued to the extent that the quoted market value of the shares of the enterprise's stock covered by the grant exceeds the value specified. A majority of the respondents disagreed with that provision as a required allocation method and recommended that other methods be permitted for allocating compensation cost as an expense in the periods in which the related services

are performed. In adopting that recommendation, the Board concluded that the recommendation is consistent with the recognition principles underlying *APB Opinion No. 25.*

16. The proposed Interpretation specified that compensation expense for stock appreciation rights and other variable plan awards should be measured by the extent that the quoted market value of the shares of the enterprise's stock covered by the grant exceeds the value specified, by reference to a market price or otherwise. Several respondents recommended that the compensation expense be measured by using the average market price of the stock, the value of the right or award at the date of grant, or some other value. The Board considered those recommendations and concluded that the method of measuring compensation for stock appreciation rights and other variable plan awards should not be changed without a comprehensive reexamination of the measurement principles underlying *APB Opinion No. 25*. The Board plans such a reexamination in the future but has concluded that issuance of this Interpretation should not be delayed in the meantime.

17. Some respondents requested guidance on whether stock appreciation rights and other variable plan awards are common stock equivalents for purposes of computing earnings per share. Guidance in this regard is provided in paragraph 6 of this Interpretation.

18. The transition called for by the proposed Interpretation required that an accrual of compensation expense or an adjustment of accrued compensation resulting from initial application of the Interpretation should be accounted for as a change in estimate in the period of change. The proposed effective date was for annual periods *ending* after December 15, 1978. Several respondents recommended either prospective or retroactive application because, in their view, the application of the Interpretation would result in a change in accounting method for some enterprises. The Board concluded that the effective date and transition should be changed to prospective application for stock appreciation rights and other variable plan awards granted in fiscal years *beginning* after December 15, 1978. The Interpretation also provides an election that it may be applied to grants made in fiscal years beginning before December 16, 1978 as a change in estimate in the period of the change.

Appendix B

ILLUSTRATION OF THE ACCOUNTING FOR STOCK APPRECIATION RIGHTS AND OTHER VARIABLE STOCK OPTION OR AWARD PLANS

19. This Appendix illustrates applications of this Interpretation in accounting for stock appreciation rights and other variable stock option or award plans when the service period is presumed to be the vesting period. The examples do not comprehend all possible combinations of circumstances nor do the examples illustrate the computation of deferred income taxes.

20. Provisions of the agreements:

Stock appreciation rights are granted in tandem with stock options for market value appreciation in excess of the option price. Exercise of the rights cancels the option for an equal number of shares and vice versa. Share appreciation is payable in stock, cash, or a combination of stock and cash at the enterprise's election.

Date of grant	January 1, 1979
Expiration date	December 31, 1988
Vesting	100% at the end of 1982
Number of shares under option	1,000
Option price	$10 per share
Quoted market price at date of grant	$10 per share

21. Market price assumptions:

Quoted market price per share at December 31 of subsequent years:

1979—$11
1980— 12
1981— 15
1982— 14
1983— 15
1984— 18

EXAMPLE 1

22. The following example illustrates the annual computation of compensation expense for the above described stock appreciation right plan.

		Compensation					Accrual of Expense by Year (3)					
Date	Market Price	Per Share	Aggregate (1)	Percentage Accrued (2)	Compensation Accrued to Date	1979	1980	1981	1982	1983	1984
12/31/79	$11	$1	$1,000	25%	$ 250	$250					
					750		$750				
12/31/80	12	2	2,000	50	1,000						
					2,750			$2,750			
12/31/81	15	5	5,000	75	3,750						
					250				$250		
12/31/82	14	4	4,000	100	4,000						
					1,000					$1,000	
12/31/83	15	5	5,000	100	5,000						
					3,000						$3,000
12/31/84	18	8	8,000	100	$8,000						

Notes

(1) Aggregate compensation for unexercised shares to be allocated to periods service performed.

(2) The percentage accrued is based upon the four-year vesting period.

(3) A similar computation would be made for interim reporting periods.

EXAMPLE 2

23. If the stock appreciation rights vested 25 percent per year commencing in 1979, the computation of compensation expense in the preceding example would change as illustrated in the following examples.

24. Because 25 percent of the rights vest each year commencing in 1979, the service period over which compensation is accrued as a charge to expense is determined separately for each 25 percent portion. For example, the services for the 25 percent portion of the rights vesting in 1980 are performed in both 1979 and 1980 and the related compensation is accrued proportionately as a charge to expense in each year. Similarly, compensation for rights vesting in 1981 is proportionately accrued as a charge to expense in 1979, 1980, and 1981. In this way, compensation related to the portion of the rights vesting in 1979 is recognized in 1979, compensation related to the portion of the rights vesting in 1980 is recognized in 1979 and 1980, and so forth. The following schedule indicates the service period for each 25 percent portion of the rights and the computation of the *aggregate* percentage of compensation accrued by the end of each year of service (the vesting period). A similar computation would be made for interim reporting periods.

		Aggregate Percentage of Compensation Accrued by the End of Each Year of Service			
For Rights Vesting in	Service Period	1979	1980	1981	1982
1979	1 year	25%	25%	25%	25%
1980	2 years	12.5	25	25	25
1981	3 years	8.33	16.67	25	25
1982	4 years	6.25	12.5	18.75	25
Aggregate percentage accrued at the end of each year		52.08%	79.17%	93.75%	100%
Rounded for purposes of Examples 2 and 3		52%	79%	94%	100%

For periods ending after 1982, 100 percent of the aggregate compensation should be accrued.

25. Additional Assumptions:

On December 31, 1981, the employee exercises the right to receive share appreciation on 300 shares.

On March 15, 1982, the employee exercises the right to receive share appreciation on 100 shares; quoted market price $15 per share.

On June 15, 1983, the employee exercises the right to receive share appreciation on 100 shares; quoted market price $16 per share.

On December 31, 1983, the employee exercises the right to receive share appreciation on 300 shares.

On December 31, 1984, the employee exercises the right to receive share appreciation on 200 shares.

Date	Trans-action	Number of Shares	Market Price	Compensation Per Share	Compensation Aggregate (1)	Compensation Percentage Accrued (2)	Compensation Accrued to Date	Accrual of Expense by Year (3) 1979	1980	1981	1982	1983	1984
12/31/79	A		$11	$1	$1,000	52%	$ 520	$520					
	A						1,060		$1,060				
12/31/80			12	2	2,000	79	1,580						
	A						3,120			$3,120			
12/31/81			15	5	5,000	94	4,700						
12/31/81	E	300	15	5	(1,500)	—	(1,500)						
							3,200						
3/15/82	E	100	15	5	(500)	—	(500)						
							2,700						
	A						(300)				$(300)		
12/31/82			14	4	2,400	100	2,400						
6/15/83	E	100	16	6	(600)	—	(400)					$200	
							2,000						
	A						500					500	
12/31/83			15	5	2,500	100	2,500						
12/31/83	E	300	15	5	(1,500)	—	(1,500)						
							1,000						
	A						600						$600
12/31/84			18	8	1,600	100	1,600						
12/31/84	E	200	18	8	(1,600)	—	(1,600)						
							$ —						

Transaction Codes

A - Adjustment for changes in the market price of the stock.
E - Exercise of a stock appreciation right.

Notes

(1) Aggregate compensation for unexercised shares to be allocated to periods service performed.

(2) See the schedule in paragraph 24 of this Interpretation.

(3) A similar computation would be made for interim reporting periods.

EXAMPLE 3

26. If the plan limits the amount of share appreciation that the employee can receive to $5, the computation of compensation expense in Example 2 would change as illustrated in the following example.

27. When the quoted market price exceeds the appreciation limitation, the employee is more likely to exercise the related stock option rather than the stock appreciation right. Therefore, accrued compensation is *not* adjusted for changes in the quoted market price of the stock. The assumptions stated in paragraph 25 of this Interpretation are changed to the extent that on June 15, 1983 and December 31, 1984 the employee exercises the related stock option instead of the stock appreciation right. Accordingly, accrued compensation for the equivalent number of rights is recognized as part or all of the consideration for the stock issued in accordance with paragraph 5 of this Interpretation.

Date	Transaction	Number of Shares	Market Price	Per Share	Compensation: Aggregate (1)	Compensation: Percentage Accrued (2)	Compensation Accrued to Date	Accrual of Expense by Year (3): 1979	1980	1981	1982	1983	1984
12/31/79	A		$11	$1	$1,000	52%	$ 520	$520					
	A						1,060		$1,060				
12/31/80			12	2	2,000	79	1,580						
	A						3,120			$3,120			
12/31/81			15	5	5,000	94	4,700						
12/31/81	E	300	15	5	(1,500)	—	(1,500)						
							3,200						
3/15/82	E	100	15	5	(500)	—	(500)						
							2,700						
	A						(300)				$(300)		
12/31/82			14	4	2,400	100	2,400						
6/15/83	O	100	16	5	(500)	—	(400)					$100	
							2,000						
	A						500					500	
12/31/83			15	5	2,500	100	2,500						
12/31/83	E	300	15	5	(1,500)	—	(1,500)						
							1,000						
	NA						—						$ —
12/31/84			18	5	1,000	100	1,000						
12/31/84	O	200	18	5	(1,000)	—	(1,000)						
							$ —						

Transaction Codes

A - Adjustment for changes in the market price of the stock.
NA - No adjustment required because the market price exceeds the appreciation limitation.
E - Exercise of a stock appreciation right.
O - Exercise of the related stock option.

Notes

(1) Aggregate compensation for unexercised shares to be allocated to periods service performed.

(2) See the schedule in paragraph 24 of this Interpretation.

(3) A similar computation would be made for interim reporting periods.

FASB Interpretation No. 29
Reporting Tax Benefits Realized on Disposition of Investments in Certain Subsidiaries and Other Investees

an interpretation of APB Opinions No. 23 and 24

STATUS

Issued: February 1979

Effective Date: For dispositions of investments occurring after March 31, 1979

Affects: No other pronouncements

Affected by: No other pronouncements

SUMMARY

Because of divergent practices in reporting tax benefits realized on dispositions of certain investments, the FASB was asked to clarify the reporting of those benefits. This Interpretation requires tax benefits realized on disposition of investments in certain subsidiaries and other investees relating to a difference between the accounting and tax basis of the investment to be classified the same as the classification accorded the gain or loss on disposition of the investment (for example, as results of continuing operations, as extraordinary, or as disposal of a segment of a business).

FASB Interpretation No. 29
Reporting Tax Benefits Realized on Disposition of Investments in Certain Subsidiaries and Other Investees

an interpretation of APB Opinions No. 23 and 24

CONTENTS

INTRODUCTION

1. The FASB has been asked to clarify the reporting of income tax benefits realized by an investor from the disposition of an investment in certain subsidiaries and other investees.[1] Losses of a subsidiary or other investee that have been included in the investor's financial statements may have created a difference[2] between the accounting basis and the tax basis of the investment in the subsidiary or other investee because the investor could not deduct those losses for income tax purposes. No recognition is given to the tax effect relating to the difference between the accounting basis and the tax basis in the years prior to disposition of the investment if realization of the tax benefit is not assured beyond any reasonable doubt. Upon disposition of the investment, a question arises as to whether tax benefits realized on disposition of the investment relating to a difference between the accounting basis and the tax basis of the investment in the subsidiary or other investee should be reported in the investor's financial statements as an extraordinary credit or as a reduction of income taxes on continuing operations. Appendix A provides additional background information about this matter.

INTERPRETATION

2. The accounting for the effect of a difference between taxable income and pretax accounting income as stated in paragraphs 11 and 17 of *APB Opinion No. 23,* "Accounting for Income Taxes—Special Areas," and paragraph 9 of *APB Opinion No. 24,* "Accounting for Income Taxes—Investments in Common Stock Accounted for by the Equity Method (Other than Subsidiaries and Corporate Joint Ventures)," applies to an investor's accounting for the operating losses and the related tax benefits of operating loss carrybacks or carryforwards that may be realized by a subsidiary, a corporate joint venture, or other investee under applicable tax laws and regulations and does not apply to tax benefits that may be realized by the investor from disposition of the related investment. An investor shall classify tax benefits realized[3] on disposition of an investment relating to a difference[4] between the accounting basis and the tax basis of the investment in the subsidiary or other investee in the same manner as the classification accorded the gain or loss on disposition of the investment.

3. If reporting tax benefits in accordance with paragraph 2 of this Interpretation creates a significant variation in the customary relationship between income tax expense and pretax accounting income, that fact shall be disclosed in accordance with paragraph 63(c) of *APB Opinion No. 11,* "Accounting for Income Taxes."

EFFECTIVE DATE AND TRANSITION

4. The provisions of this Interpretation shall be effective for dispositions of investments in certain

[1]The term "subsidiary or other investee," as used in this Interpretation, refers to a subsidiary that files separate income tax returns (whether consolidated or accounted for by the equity method for financial reporting) or to a corporate joint venture or other nonsubsidiary investee accounted for by the equity method.

[2]A "difference between the accounting basis and the tax basis of the investment in the subsidiary or other investee," as used in this Interpretation, refers to a difference attributable to prior year losses of a subsidiary or other investee that have been included in the investor's financial statements and could not be deducted by the investor for income tax purposes.

[3]The term "tax benefits realized" as used in this Interpretation refers to either realization by inclusion in an income tax return or the determination that realization is assured beyond any reasonable doubt.

[4]See footnote 2.

subsidiaries and other investees occurring after March 31, 1979. Earlier application is encouraged. Reclassification in previously issued financial statements is permitted but not required.

This Interpretation was adopted by the affirmative votes of five members of the Financial Accounting Standards Board following submission to members of the Financial Accounting Standards Advisory Council and the Screening Committee on Emerging Problems. Mr. Walters dissented.

Mr. Walters dissents because he believes that, in combination, paragraphs 11 and 17 of *APB Opinion No. 23,* paragraph 9 of *APB Opinion No. 24,* and paragraphs 45 and 61 of *APB Opinion No. 11* specify that a realized tax benefit attributable to prior years' losses of a subsidiary or investee shall be reported as an extraordinary credit. The APB left this specification intact when it overtly excluded *APB Opinion No. 11* from the modifications made by *APB Opinion No. 30.* He therefore believes the assertion in paragraph 2 of this Interpretation that this treatment "does not apply to tax benefits that may be realized by the investor from disposition of the related investment" is an amendment of *APB Opinions No. 23* and *24.* Aside from the validity of the Interpretation, he believes that a tax benefit arising from prior years' losses in a liquidated investment has no place in results of continuing operations. In his view this Interpretation detracts from the usefulness of financial reporting.

Members of the Financial Accounting Standards Board:

Donald J. Kirk, *Chairman*
John W. March
Robert A. Morgan
David Mosso
Robert T. Sprouse
Ralph E. Walters

Appendix A

BACKGROUND INFORMATION

5. Paragraph 11 of *APB Opinion No. 23* states:

> The tax effect of a difference between taxable income and pretax accounting income attributable to losses of a subsidiary should be accounted for in accordance with the Board's conclusions on operating losses in paragraphs 44 through 50 of *APB Opinion No. 11.*

Paragraph 17 of Opinion No. 23 applies the same provision to an investment in a corporate joint venture that is accounted for by the equity method. Paragraph 9 of *APB Opinion No. 24* has an identical provision for losses of an investee other than a subsidiary or corporate joint venture.

6. Paragraphs 44 through 50 of *APB Opinion No. 11* address the accounting for operating loss carrybacks and carryforwards. Paragraph 45 states: "When the tax benefits of loss carry*forwards* are not recognized until realized in full or in part in subsequent periods, the tax benefits should be reported in the results of operations of those periods as extraordinary items."

7. *APB Opinion No. 30,* "Reporting the Results of Operations—Reporting the Effects of Disposal of a Segment of a Business, and Extraordinary, Unusual and Infrequently Occurring Events and Transactions," requires income taxes applicable to a disposal of a segment of a business and to an extraordinary item to be associated with the gain or loss on disposal of the segment or the extraordinary item reported in an income statement.

8. The following three approaches have been suggested to the Board for classification of tax benefits realized on disposition of an investment relating to a difference between the accounting basis and the tax basis of an investment in the subsidiary or other investee:

a. Report the tax benefits as a reduction of income taxes from continuing operations for the current period, because the benefits are attributable to a decision made and an action taken (i.e., disposition of an investment) in the current period.
b. Classify the tax benefits in the investor's financial statements the same as the classification accorded the gain or loss on disposition of the related investment (for example, as a reduction of income taxes on continuing operations, as extraordinary, or as disposal of a segment of a business).
c. Report the tax benefits as an extraordinary credit in accordance with paragraph 45 of *APB Opinion No. 11* because the difference in bases "is attributable to losses of an investee," as referred to in paragraphs 11 and 17 of *APB Opinion No. 23* and paragraph 9 of *APB Opinion No. 24.*

9. A draft of a proposed Interpretation on "Reporting Tax Benefits Realized on Disposition of Investments in Certain Subsidiaries and Other Investees" was issued on September 22, 1978. The Board received 22 letters of comment in response to the proposed Interpretation. Virtually all respondents expressed agreement with the proposed Interpretation. However, a few respondents ques-

tioned whether the proposed Interpretation amounted to an amendment of *APB Opinions No. 23* and *24,* and the Board concluded that it does not. The Board believes that Opinions No. 23 and 24 address the reporting of operating losses and related tax benefits of operating loss carrybacks or carryforwards available to a subsidiary or other investee but does not address the reporting of tax benefits realized by an investor from disposition of the related investment. The Board believes that the differences between tax benefits arising from the utilization by an investee of its tax loss carryforwards and the tax consequences to an investor upon disposition of its investment justify differences in reporting.

FASB Interpretation No. 30 Accounting for Involuntary Conversions of Nonmonetary Assets to Monetary Assets

an interpretation of APB Opinion No. 29

STATUS

Issued: September 1979

Effective Date: For fiscal years beginning after November 15, 1979

Affects: No other pronouncements

Affected by: No other pronouncements

SUMMARY

This Interpretation clarifies the accounting for involuntary conversions of nonmonetary assets (such as property or equipment) to monetary assets (such as insurance proceeds). Examples of such conversions are total or partial destruction or theft of insured nonmonetary assets and the condemnation of property in eminent domain proceedings. A diversity in practice exists in accounting for the difference between the cost of a nonmonetary asset that is involuntarily converted and the amount of monetary assets received. Generally, that difference has been recognized in income as a gain or loss. In other cases, that difference has been accounted for as an adjustment to the cost of subsequently acquired replacement property. This Interpretation requires that gain or loss be recognized when a nonmonetary asset is involuntarily converted to monetary assets even though an enterprise reinvests or is obligated to reinvest the monetary assets in replacement nonmonetary assets.

FASB Interpretation No. 30
Accounting for Involuntary Conversions of Nonmonetary Assets to Monetary Assets

an interpretation of APB Opinion No. 29

CONTENTS

INTRODUCTION

1. The FASB has been asked whether gain or loss results from an involuntary conversion of a nonmonetary asset to monetary assets if the monetary assets are subsequently reinvested in a similar nonmonetary asset.[1] Generally, if a nonmonetary asset is involuntarily converted, gain or loss for the difference between the cost[2] of the nonmonetary asset and the amount of monetary assets received has been recognized in income in the period of the involuntary conversion. In other cases, that difference has been accounted for as an adjustment to the cost basis of a nonmonetary asset that is subsequently acquired as replacement property.

INTERPRETATION

2. Involuntary conversions of nonmonetary assets to monetary assets are monetary transactions for which gain or loss shall be recognized even though an enterprise reinvests or is obligated to reinvest the monetary assets in replacement nonmonetary assets. As discussed in paragraph 11 of this Interpretation, however, the requirement to recognize gain does not apply to certain involuntary conversions of LIFO inventories.[3]

3. In some cases, a nonmonetary asset may be destroyed or damaged in one accounting period, and the amount of monetary assets to be received is not determinable until a subsequent accounting period. In those cases, gain or loss shall be recognized in accordance with FASB Statement No. 5, *Accounting for Contingencies.*

4. Gain or loss resulting from an involuntary conversion of a nonmonetary asset to monetary assets shall be classified in accordance with the provisions of APB Opinion No. 30, *Reporting the Results of Operations—Reporting the Effects of Disposal of a Segment of a Business, and Extraordinary, Unusual and Infrequently Occurring Events and Transactions.*

5. Gain or loss resulting from an involuntary conversion of a nonmonetary asset to monetary assets that is not recognized for income tax reporting purposes in the same period in which the gain or loss is recognized for financial reporting purposes is a timing difference for which comprehensive interperiod tax allocation, as described in APB Opinion No. 11, *Accounting for Income Taxes,* is required.

EFFECTIVE DATE AND TRANSITION

6. The provisions of this Interpretation shall be applied prospectively for involuntary conversions of nonmonetary assets to monetary assets occurring in fiscal years beginning after November 15, 1979. Earlier application is encouraged in financial statements for fiscal years beginning before November 16, 1979 that have not been previously issued.

Appendix A

BACKGROUND INFORMATION

7. APB Opinion No. 29, *Accounting for Nonmonetary Transactions,* concludes that the account-

[1]The terms "nonmonetary" and "monetary" as used in this Interpretation have the same meaning as those terms have in APB Opinion No. 29, *Accounting for Nonmonetary Transactions.*

[2]As used in this Interpretation, the term cost refers to the cost of a nonmonetary asset or to its carrying amount, if different.

[3]Paragraph 14(b) of APB Opinion No. 28, *Interim Financial Reporting,* provides an exception for the liquidation of a LIFO inventory at an interim date if replacement is expected by year-end. Accordingly, that exception applies to an involuntary conversion of a LIFO inventory if replacement is expected by year-end.

ing for nonmonetary transactions should generally be the same as for monetary transactions and that the basic principle of recognizing a gain or loss based on the fair values of the assets (or services) involved should be applied for nonmonetary transactions as for monetary transactions. However, in some cases, modifications of that basic principle are required. For example, paragraph 21 of Opinion 29 provides that an exchange of a nonmonetary asset for a similar nonmonetary asset that is not essentially the culmination of an earnings process should be accounted for based on the recorded amount of the nonmonetary asset relinquished.

8. Paragraph 4 of Opinion 29 states, in part:

> For purposes of applying this Opinion, events and transactions in which nonmonetary assets are involuntarily converted (for example, as a result of total or partial destruction, theft, seizure, or condemnation) to monetary assets that are then reinvested in other nonmonetary assets are monetary transactions *since the recipient is not obligated to reinvest the monetary consideration in other nonmonetary assets.* (Emphasis added.)

Paragraph 22 of Opinion 29 addresses exchanges of nonmonetary assets that involve some monetary consideration. That paragraph requires the recipient of monetary consideration to recognize a gain on the exchange to the extent that the amount of monetary receipt exceeds a proportionate share of the recorded amount of the asset surrendered.

9. A draft of a proposed Interpretation on *Accounting for Involuntary Conversions of Nonmonetary Assets to Monetary Assets* was released for comment on April 11, 1979. The Board received 31 letters of comment on the proposed Interpretation.

10. Some respondents disagreed with the proposed Interpretation, suggesting that the difference between the cost of a nonmonetary asset that is involuntarily converted and the amount of monetary assets received should be accounted for as an adjustment to the cost of subsequently acquired replacement property. For the most part, those respondents expressed the view that an involuntary conversion of a nonmonetary asset to monetary assets that are reinvested in replacement property is, in essence, an exchange transaction, as described in paragraph 21 of Opinion 29. Some of those respondents also noted that an involuntary conversion should be accounted for as an exchange transaction rather than as a monetary transaction if the recipient of monetary assets is obligated to reinvest the monetary assets in a nonmonetary asset similar to that which was destroyed. They contended that that position was consistent with paragraph 4 of Opinion 29, which states, in part, ". . . events and transactions in which nonmonetary assets are involuntarily converted . . . to monetary assets . . . are monetary transactions *since the recipient is not obligated to reinvest the monetary consideration in other nonmonetary assets.*" (Emphasis added.) However, the Board does not believe that an involuntary conversion of a nonmonetary asset to monetary assets and the subsequent reinvestment of the monetary assets is equivalent to an exchange transaction between an enterprise and another entity. In the Board's view, the conversion of a nonmonetary asset to monetary assets is a monetary transaction, whether the conversion is voluntary or involuntary, and such a conversion differs from exchange transactions that involve only nonmonetary assets. To the extent the cost of a nonmonetary asset differs from the amount of monetary assets received, the transaction results in the realization of a gain or loss that should be recognized. Furthermore, the cost of subsequently acquired nonmonetary assets should be measured by the consideration paid and not be affected by a previous transaction.

11. A question was raised as to the application of this Interpretation to an involuntary conversion of a LIFO inventory if the monetary assets are expected to be reinvested in replacement inventory. APB Opinion No. 28, *Interim Financial Reporting,* addresses that situation if the LIFO inventory replacement is expected before year-end, and footnote 3 has been added to provide an exception to conform with Opinion 28. If the LIFO inventory replacement is not made by year-end and a taxpayer does not recognize a gain for income tax reporting purposes, it has been asserted that application of this Interpretation might invalidate a taxpayer's LIFO election. The Board concluded that issuance of this Interpretation should not be delayed to resolve that matter and has exempted it from the provisions of this Interpretation. Accordingly, the requirement of this Interpretation with respect to gain recognition does not apply to an involuntary conversion of a LIFO inventory for which replacement is intended but not made by year-end and the taxpayer does not recognize gain for income tax reporting purposes.

This Interpretation was adopted by the affirmative votes of six members of the Financial Accounting Standards Board following submission to the members of the Financial Accounting Standards Advisory Council and the Screening Committee on Emerging Problems. Mr. Morgan dissented.

Mr. Morgan dissents because he believes that this Interpretation emphasizes form over substance. He disagrees with the statement in paragraph 10 that the conversion of a nonmonetary asset to monetary assets is a monetary transaction that differs from exchange transactions that involve only nonmonetary assets and that a gain should be recognized. He believes that the earnings process is not culminated simply because monetary assets are received if there is an economic incentive to reinvest the proceeds of an involuntary conversion of a productive asset. He also believes that financial statements reporting improved earnings as a result of the destruction or incapacitation of significant productive assets are misleading and therefore fail to comply with the objectives of financial reporting as described in paragraph 32 *et seq* of FASB Concepts Statement No. 1, *Objectives of Financial Reporting by Business Enterprises.*

Members of the Financial Accounting Standards Board:

Donald J. Kirk, *Chairman*	John W. March	Robert T. Sprouse
Frank E. Block	Robert A. Morgan	Ralph E. Walters
	David Mosso	

FASB Interpretation No. 31 Treatment of Stock Compensation Plans in EPS Computations

an interpretation of APB Opinion No. 15 and a modification of FASB Interpretation No. 28

STATUS

Issued: February 1980

Effective Date: For fiscal years beginning after December 15, 1979

Affects: Amends FIN 28, paragraph 6
Modifies AIN-APB 15, Interpretation No. 82

Affected by: No other pronouncements

SUMMARY

Earnings per share data reflect the dilutive effect of outstanding stock options, including stock appreciation rights and other variable plan awards, computed by application of the treasury stock method under APB Opinion No. 15, *Earnings per Share*. Under that method, earnings per share data are computed as if the options were exercised at the beginning of the period (or at date of grant, if later) and as if the funds obtained thereby were used to purchase common stock. This Interpretation specifies that the funds used in applying the treasury stock method are the sum of the cash to be received on exercise, the compensation related to the options to be charged to expense in the future, and any tax benefit to be credited to capital. The Interpretation also provides guidance for how to include the effect of variable plans, combination plans, or plans payable in cash or in stock in earnings per share computations.

FASB Interpretation No. 31
Treatment of Stock Compensation Plans in EPS Computations

an interpretation of APB Opinion No. 15 and a modification of FASB Interpretation No. 28

CONTENTS

INTRODUCTION

1. The FASB received several requests to clarify the provisions of FASB Interpretation No. 28, *Accounting for Stock Appreciation Rights and Other Variable Stock Option or Award Plans,* that discuss the dilutive effect of stock appreciation rights and other variable plan awards in EPS computations. Some believed that FASB Interpretation 28 conflicted with earlier pronouncements with respect to the composition of funds obtained from the assumed exercise of stock options, including stock appreciation rights and other variable plan awards. Such funds are hereinafter referred to as "exercise proceeds."

2. This Interpretation modifies AICPA Interpretation No. 82 of APB Opinion No. 15, *Earnings per Share,* and supersedes the second sentence of paragraph 6 of FASB Interpretation 28. This Interpretation is not intended to alter the treatment of shares issuable contingent upon certain conditions being met, as discussed in paragraphs 61-64 of Opinion 15. Appendix A provides additional background information about this Interpretation. Appendix B illustrates applications of this Interpretation.

INTERPRETATION

3. In applying the treasury stock method of paragraph 36 of Opinion 15 to stock options, including stock appreciation rights and other variable plan awards, the exercise proceeds of the options are the sum of the amount the employee must pay, the amount of measurable compensation ascribed to future services and not yet charged to expense (whether or not accrued), and the amount of any "windfall" tax benefit[1] to be credited[2] to capital. Exercise proceeds shall not include compensation ascribed to past services.

4. The dilutive effect of stock appreciation rights and other variable plan awards on primary earnings per share shall be computed using the average aggregate compensation and average market price for the period. The market price of an enterprise's stock and the resulting aggregate compensation used to compute the dilutive effect of stock appreciation rights and other variable plan awards in fully diluted earnings per share computations shall be the more dilutive of the market price and aggregate compensation at the close of the period being reported upon or the average market price and average aggregate compensation for that period.[3]

5. If an enterprise has a combination plan allowing the enterprise or the employee to make an election involving stock appreciation rights or other variable plan awards, earnings per share for a period shall be computed based on the terms used in the computation of compensation expense for that period.

[1]The "windfall" tax benefit is the tax credit resulting from a tax deduction for compensation in excess of compensation expense recognized for financial reporting purposes. Such credit arises from an increase in the market price of the stock under option between the measurement date (as defined in APB Opinion No. 25, *Accounting for Stock Issued to Employees*) and the date at which the compensation deduction for income tax purposes is determinable. The amount of the "windfall" tax benefit shall be determined by a "with-and-without" computation as described in paragraph 36 of APB Opinion No. 11, *Accounting for Income Taxes.*

[2]Paragraph 17 of Opinion 25 states that there may be instances when the tax deduction for compensation is less than the compensation expense recognized for financial reporting purposes. If the resulting difference in income tax will be deducted from capital in accordance with that paragraph, such taxes to be deducted from capital shall be treated as a reduction of exercise proceeds.

[3]If the rights or awards were granted during the period, the shares issuable must be weighted to reflect the portion of the period during which the rights or awards were outstanding.

6. If stock appreciation rights or other variable plan awards are payable in stock or in cash at the election of the enterprise or the employee, the decision of whether such rights or awards are common stock equivalents shall be made according to the terms most likely to be elected based on the facts available each period. It shall be presumed that such rights or awards will be paid in stock, but that presumption may be overcome if past experience or a stated policy provides a reasonable basis to believe that the rights or awards will be paid partially or wholly in cash.

EFFECTIVE DATE AND TRANSITION

7. The provisions of this Interpretation shall be effective for financial statements for fiscal years beginning after December 15, 1979. Earlier application is encouraged in financial statements for fiscal years beginning before December 16, 1979 that have not been previously issued. This Interpretation may be, but is not required to be, applied retroactively to previously issued financial statements.

This Interpretation was adopted by the unanimous vote of the seven members of the Financial Accounting Standards Board following submission to the Financial Accounting Standards Advisory Council and the Screening Committee on Emerging Problems.

Members of the Financial Accounting Standards Board:

Donald J. Kirk, *Chairman*
Frank E. Block
John W. March
Robert A. Morgan
David Mosso
Robert T. Sprouse
Ralph E. Walters

Appendix A

BACKGROUND INFORMATION

8. Paragraph 35 of Opinion 15 states that stock options "should be regarded as common stock equivalents at all times" and that ". . . earnings per share should reflect the dilution that would result from exercise . . . of these securities and use of the funds, if any, obtained." Paragraph 6 of FASB Interpretation 28 states that "stock appreciation rights and other variable plan awards are common stock equivalents to the extent payable in stock. . . ." Paragraph 36 of Opinion 15 discusses the treatment of stock options in earnings per share computations and provides that:

> . . . the amount of dilution to be reflected in earnings per share data should be computed by application of the "treasury stock" method. Under this method, earnings per share data are computed as if the options . . . were exercised at the beginning of the period (or at time of issuance, if later) and as if the funds obtained thereby were used to purchase common stock. . . .

The dilutive effect that would result from assumed exercise of stock options is reflected in the earnings per share computation by an increase in shares assumed to be outstanding equal to the number of shares issuable upon exercise of the stock options less the number of shares assumed to be purchased with the funds obtained from such exercise.

9. AICPA Interpretation 82 defines exercise proceeds as the sum of the amount the employee must pay, the unamortized deferred compensation, and the "windfall" tax benefit credited to capital surplus. That definition results in treating shares "earned" by past services as outstanding for earnings per share computations. The Board believes that definition is an appropriate interpretation of Opinion 15 and has accordingly adopted a similar definition of exercise proceeds in this Interpretation.

10. Stock appreciation rights are often granted in combination with stock options. Such combination plans usually provide that the rights are exercisable for the same period as the companion stock options and that the exercise of either cancels the other. Compensation expense and earnings per share for a period could differ depending on which terms (options or rights) were used in the computations. Paragraph 5 of FASB Interpretation 28 states that compensation expense for a combination plan "shall be measured according to the terms the employee is most likely to elect based on the facts available each period." The Board has concluded that earnings per share for a period should be computed according to the same terms used in the computation of compensation expense for that period.

11. A draft of a proposed Interpretation, *Treatment of Stock Compensation Plans in EPS Computations,* was released for comment October 1, 1979. The Board received 35 letters of comment in response to the proposed Interpretation. Certain of the comments received and the Board's consideration of them are discussed in paragraphs 12 and 13.

12. To simplify the EPS computation, the proposed Interpretation stated that "windfall" tax benefits

credited to capital are not part of exercise proceeds. Some respondents contended that "windfall" tax benefits should be included in the definition of exercise proceeds because they represent a potential future cash flow to the enterprise. The definition of exercise proceeds in paragraph 3 has been modified to include "windfall" tax benefits.

13. Some respondents requested clarification or guidance on how to treat stock appreciation rights that are payable in cash or in stock at the option of the enterprise or the employee in EPS computations. As noted in paragraph 8, stock appreciation rights and other variable plan awards are common stock equivalents to the extent payable in stock. The Board has decided that to provide a conservative estimate of potential dilution, such rights and awards should be presumed to be payable in stock unless there is a reasonable basis to believe that they will be paid in cash. That guidance is provided in paragraph 6 of this Interpretation.

Appendix B

ILLUSTRATION OF THE APPLICATION OF THE TREASURY STOCK METHOD FOR STOCK APPRECIATION RIGHTS AND OTHER VARIABLE STOCK OPTION AWARD PLANS

14. This appendix illustrates applications of this Interpretation in computing the dilutive effect on earnings per share of stock appreciation rights and other variable stock option or award plans when the service period is presumed to be the vesting period. The examples do not comprehend all possible combinations of circumstances. Amounts and quantities have been rounded down to whole units for simplicity.

15. Provisions of the agreements:

Stock appreciation rights are granted in tandem with stock options for market value appreciation in excess of the option price. Exercise of the rights cancels the options for an equal number of shares and vice versa. Share appreciation is payable in stock, cash, or a combination of stock and cash at the enterprise's election.

Date of grant	January 1, 1979
Expiration date	December 31, 1988
Vesting	100% at the end of 1982
Number of shares under option	1,000
Option price	$10 per share
Quoted market price at date of grant	$10 per share

16. Assumptions:

There are no circumstances in these three examples that would overcome the presumption that the rights are payable in stock.

The tax deduction for compensation will equal the compensation recognized for financial reporting purposes.

Quoted market price per share at December 31 of subsequent years:

1979 — $11
1980 — 12
1981 — 15
1982 — 14
1983 — 15
1984 — 18

EXAMPLE 1

17. The following example illustrates the annual computation of incremental shares for the above described stock appreciation right plan. A single annual computation is shown for simplicity in this and the following examples. Normally, a computation would be done monthly or quarterly.

		COMPENSATION							FOR PRIMARY EARNINGS PER SHARE			FOR FULLY DILUTED EARNINGS PER SHARE		
Date	Market Price	Per Share	Aggregate (1)	Percentage Accrued (2)	Compensation-Accrued to Date	Measurable Compensation Ascribed to Future Periods (3)	Amount to Be Paid by Employee	Exercise Proceeds	Shares Issuable (4)	Treasury Shares Assumed Repurchased (5)	Incremental Shares	Shares Issuable (6)	Treasury Shares Assumed Repurchased (7)	Incremental Shares
12/31/79	$11	$1	$1,000	25%	$ 250	$ 750	—	$ 750	47	35	12	90	68	22
12/31/80	12	2	2,000	50	1,000	1,000	—	1,000	130	76	54	166	83	83
12/31/81	15	5	5,000	75	3,750	1,250	—	1,250	259	83	176	333	83	250
12/31/82	14	4	4,000	100	4,000	—	—	—	310	43	267	285	—	285
12/31/83	15	5	5,000	100	5,000	—	—	—	310	—	310	333	—	333
12/31/84	18	8	8,000	100	8,000	—	—	—	393	—	393	444	—	444

Notes
(1) Aggregate compensation for unexercised shares to be allocated to periods service performed.
(2) The percentage accrued is based upon the four-year vesting period.
(3) Unaccrued compensation in this example.
(4) Average aggregate compensation divided by average market price.*
(5) Average exercise proceeds divided by average market price.*
(6) End-of-year aggregate compensation divided by market price as of year-end.
(7) End-of-year exercise proceeds divided by market price as of year-end.

Illustration of computation for one year (1982)

Date	Market Price	Aggregate Compensation	Exercise Proceeds	Shares Issuable	Treasury Shares Assumed Repurchased	Incremental Shares
12/31/81 (beginning of year)	$15	$5000	$1250	N/A	N/A	N/A
12/31/82 (end of year)	14	4000	—	285	—	285
Average	14.50	4500	625	310	43	267

If average incremental shares were higher than end-of-year incremental shares, average incremental shares would be used for both primary and fully diluted earnings per share computations.

*These computations could also be done using other methods of averaging.

EXAMPLE 2

18. If the stock appreciation rights vested 25 percent per year commencing in 1979, the annual computation of incremental shares for primary earnings per share in the preceding example would change as illustrated in the following example. Similar computations would be made for fully diluted earnings per share. The computation of compensation expense is explained in FASB Interpretation 28, Appendix B, Example 2.

19. Additional Assumptions:

On December 31, 1981, the employee exercises the right to receive share appreciation on 300 shares.

On March 15, 1982, the employee exercises the right to receive share appreciation on 100 shares; quoted market price $15 per share.

On June 15, 1983, the employee exercises the right to receive share appreciation on 100 shares; quoted market price $16 per share.

On December 31, 1983, the employee exercises the right to receive share appreciation on 300 shares.

On December 31, 1984, the employee exercises the right to receive share appreciation on 200 shares.

					COMPENSATION						ADDITIONAL SHARES FOR PRIMARY EARNINGS PER SHARE				
Date	Transaction	Number of Shares	Market Price	Per Share	Aggregate (1)	Percentage Accrued (2)	Compensation Accrued to Date	Measurable Compensation Ascribed to Future Periods (3)	Amount to Be Paid by Employee	Exercise Proceeds	Shares Issuable (4)	Treasury Shares Assumed Repurchased (5)	Incremental Shares	Weighted Average Shares Outstanding (6)	Total Shares
12/31/79			$11	$1	$1,000	52%	$ 520	$480	—	$480	47	22	25	—	25
12/31/80			12	2	2,000	79	1,580	420	—	420	130	39	91	—	91
12/31/81			15	5	5,000	94	4,700	300	—	300	259	26	233	—	233
12/31/81	E	300	15	5	(1,500)	—									
3/15/82	E	100	15	5	(500)	—									
12/31/82			14	4	2,400	100	2,400	—	—	—	193	10	183	126	309
6/15/83	E	100	16	6	(600)	—									
12/31/83			15	5	2,500	100	2,500	—	—	—	170	—	170	153	323
12/31/83	E	300	15	5	(1,500)	—									
12/31/84			18	8	1,600	100	1,600	—	—	—	78	—	78	270	348
12/31/84	E	200	18	8	(1,600)	—									

Transaction Code
E—Exercise of a stock appreciation right.

Notes
(1) Aggregate compensation for unexercised shares to be allocated to periods service performed.
(2) See the schedule in paragraph 24 of FASB Interpretation 28.
(3) Unaccrued compensation in this example.
(4) Average aggregate compensation divided by average market price, weighted for proportion of period during which rights were unexercised.
(5) Average exercise proceeds divided by average market price.
(6) Shares issued upon exercise of stock appreciation rights. These would be included in the enterprise's total weighted average shares outstanding.

Illustration of computation for one year (1982)

	Number of Shares	Average Market Price	Average Aggregate Compensation	Aggregate Shares Issuable	Weighing Factor	Shares Issuable
Rights outstanding entire year	600	$14.50	$2700	186	12/12	186
Rights outstanding 1/1-3/15	100	15.00	500	33	2.5/12	7
						193

EXAMPLE 3

20. If the plan limits the amount of share appreciation that the employee can receive to $5, the computation of additional shares in Example 2 would change as illustrated in the following example.

21. When the quoted market price exceeds the appreciation limitations, the employee is more likely to exercise the related stock option rather than the stock appreciation right. Therefore, accrued compensation is not adjusted for changes in the quoted market price of the stock. The assumptions stated in paragraph 19 of this Interpretation are changed to the extent that on June 15, 1983 and December 31, 1984 the employee exercises the related stock option instead of the stock appreciation right. In addition, it is assumed that the market price does not exceed $15 for substantially all of a three-month period until 1984. Therefore, for earnings per share purposes the incremental shares are computed based on assumed exercise of the stock appreciation rights prior to 1984 and on assumed exercise of the stock options in 1984.

				COMPENSATION							ADDITIONAL SHARES FOR PRIMARY EARNINGS PER SHARE (6)				
Date	Transaction	Number of Shares	Market Price	Per Share	Aggregate (1)	Percentage Accrued (2)	Compensation Accrued to Date	Measurable Compensation Ascribed to Future Periods (3)	Amount to Be Paid by Employee	Exercise Proceeds	Shares Issuable (4)	Treasury Shares Assumed Repurchased (5)	Incremental Shares	Weighted Average Shares Outstanding (7)	Total Shares
12/31/79			$11	$1	$1,000	52%	$ 520	$480	—	$480	47	22	25	—	25
12/31/80			12	2	2,000	79	1,580	420	—	420	130	39	91	—	91
12/31/81			15	5	5,000	94	4,700	300	—	300	259	26	233	—	233
12/31/81	E	300	15	5	(1,500)	—									
3/15/82	E	100	15	5	(500)	—									
12/31/82			14	4	2,400	100	2,400	—	—	—	193	10	183	126	309
6/15/83	O	100	16	5	(500)	—									
12/31/83			15	5	2,500	100	2,500	—	—	—	170	—	170	187	357
12/31/83	E	300	15	5	(1,500)	—									
12/31/84			18	5	1,000	100	1,000	—	$2,000	2,000	200	121	79	333	412
12/31/84	O	200	18	5	(1,000)	—									

Transaction Codes

E—Exercise of a stock appreciation right.

O—Exercise of the related stock option.

Notes

(1) Aggregate compensation for unexercised shares to be allocated to periods service performed.
(2) See the schedule in paragraph 24 of FASB Interpretation 28.
(3) Unaccrued compensation in this example.
(4) Average aggregate compensation divided by average market price, weighted for proportion of period during which options or rights were unexercised.
(5) Average exercise proceeds divided by average market price.
(6) Similar computations would be made for fully diluted earnings per share.
(7) Shares issued upon exercise of stock appreciation rights and stock options. These would be included in the enterprise's total weighted average shares outstanding.

FASB Interpretation No. 32
Application of Percentage Limitations in Recognizing Investment Tax Credit

an interpretation of APB Opinions No. 2, 4, and 11

STATUS

Issued: March 1980

Effective Date: For fiscal years beginning after December 15, 1979

Affects: Supersedes FIN 25, footnote 5

Affected by: No other pronouncements

SUMMARY

The Revenue Act of 1978 changed the statutory percentage limitations that determine the extent to which federal income tax otherwise payable is offset by investment tax credit. This Interpretation clarifies the percentage limitations to be used in recognizing investment tax credit in the computation of income tax expense for financial reporting purposes.

FASB Interpretation No. 32
Application of Percentage Limitations in Recognizing Investment Tax Credit

an interpretation of APB Opinions No. 2, 4, and 11

CONTENTS

INTRODUCTION

1. The FASB has been asked to clarify the application of paragraph 10 of FASB Interpretation No. 25, *Accounting for an Unused Investment Tax Credit*, with respect to the statutory limitation to be used in recognizing unused investment tax credit. Appendix A contains background information about that request.

INTERPRETATION

2. The percentage limitation on the amount of federal income tax payable that can be offset by investment tax credit in the "with-and-without" computation[1] shall be the statutory percentage limitations in effect for the year for which the computation is being made.

3. The limitations to be used in recognizing investment tax credit in addition to that recognized in the "with-and-without" computation shall be the statutory percentage limitations applicable to the years in which previously recorded deferred tax credits are expected to reverse. Only net deferred tax credits that have not been previously offset and that will reverse during the investment tax credit carryforward period, disregarding any timing differences that may originate in that carryforward period, shall be offset by investment tax credit.

4. Net deferred tax credits offset in prior years shall not be adjusted to reflect changes in the statutory percentage limitations.

EFFECTIVE DATE AND TRANSITION

5. The provisions of this Interpretation shall be applied prospectively for recognition of investment tax credit[2] in fiscal years beginning after December 15, 1979. Earlier application is encouraged in financial statements for fiscal years beginning before December 16, 1979 that have not been previously issued.

6. If early application is adopted in financial statements for a fiscal year beginning before December 16, 1979, previously issued financial information for any interim periods of that fiscal year that precede the period of adoption shall be restated to give effect to the provisions of this Interpretation. Any subsequent presentation of that information shall be on a restated basis. This Interpretation shall not be applied retroactively for previously issued annual financial statements.

This Interpretation was adopted by the affirmative votes of six members of the Financial Accounting Standards Board. Mr. Walters dissented.

Mr. Walters dissents from this Interpretation because it is unnecessarily complex to apply and the result has no meaning in either the conceptual or the real world. In his view, the objective of this exercise should be to accrue the benefit that is assured from unused investment tax credits. In the worst case, that is the deferred taxes that will not be paid because of the availability of those investment tax credits. This should be determined by applying the statutory percentage limitations that will be in effect when the timing differences are expected to reverse (within the investment tax credit carryforward period).

[1]See paragraph 9.

[2]Paragraph 17 of Interpretation 25 specifies that unused investment tax credit related to property acquired in fiscal years beginning before December 16, 1978 shall be accounted for in accordance with the enterprise's method of accounting for unused investment tax credit in those years.

Appendix A

BACKGROUND INFORMATION

7. Paragraph 10 of Interpretation 25 states:

> The tax benefit of investment tax credits becoming available in the current period (excluding investment tax credits carried back to previous years . . .) or carried forward from a prior period shall be recognized in measuring income tax expense for the current period . . . by the deferred method to the extent that the benefit would have been realized if taxes payable had been based on pretax accounting income adjusted for permanent differences. In addition, any remaining unused investment tax credit shall be offset against existing net deferred tax credits . . . to the extent that those net deferred tax credits would reverse during the investment tax credit carryforward period, disregarding any timing differences that may originate in that carryforward period. *The statutory limitation on offsets of the investment tax credit against federal income taxes payable . . . shall be applied to each determination of amounts of investment tax credit to be recognized in accordance with the provisions of this Interpretation.* [Emphasis added.]

8. The Revenue Act of 1978 changed the statutory percentage limitations that determine the extent to which federal income tax otherwise payable may be offset by investment tax credit.[3] The FASB has been asked whether an enterprise should use the limitation currently in effect or the limitation that is scheduled to be in effect in the year that the timing difference is expected to reverse in determining the amount of investment tax credit to be recognized in applying Interpretation 25.

9. Paragraph 36 of APB Opinion No. 11, *Accounting for Income Taxes*, and paragraph 10 of Interpretation 25 require that the tax effect of timing differences be computed by the "with-and-without" method. Under that method, the tax effect of a timing difference is the difference between income taxes on income "with" the timing difference included and "without" it and results in deferred income tax debits or credits. The deferred taxes are based on tax rates in effect when the timing differences originate.

10. A proposed Interpretation, *Application of Percentage Limitations in Recognizing Investment Tax Credits under FASB Interpretation No. 25*, was issued November 14, 1979. The Board received 28 letters of comment on the proposed Interpretation.

11. Under Interpretation 25, the amount of investment tax credit recognized in the computation of income tax expense for the current period includes investment tax credit recognized (a) in the "with-and-without" computation and (b) as an offset against existing net deferred tax credits. Some respondents questioned the rationale for limiting investment tax credit recognized in the "with-and-without" computation to the limitation in effect for the year for which the computation is being made but using future limitations in offsetting investment tax credit against existing net deferred tax credits. Other respondents suggested that the additional investment tax credit to be recognized as an offset of existing net deferred tax credits should not be limited to deferred tax credits that have not been previously offset.

[3]Prior to the Revenue Act of 1978, the statutory limitation was 100 percent of the first $25,000 of federal income taxes payable plus a percentage of the remaining federal income taxes payable. That Act changed the percentage limitation applicable to the remaining federal income taxes payable as follows:

	Percentage Limitation for Taxes over $25,000			
	Most Enterprises		Airlines and Railroads	
Fiscal Year Ending in	Prior Law	Revenue Act of 1978	Prior Law	Revenue Act or 1978
1978	50%		100%	
1979	50	60%	90	90%
1980	50	70	80	80
1981	50	80	70	80
1982	50	90	60	90
1983 and thereafter	50	90	50	90

12. The first sentence of paragraph 10 of Interpretation 25 provides for the recognition of investment tax credit in the "with-and-without" computation under comprehensive interperiod income tax allocation by the deferred method. The deferred method of interperiod tax allocation uses the tax rates currently in effect, does not consider future tax rates, and does not adjust for subsequent changes in rates (paragraph 19 of Opinion 11). Therefore, the amount of investment tax credit recognized in the "with-and-without" computation is determined by applying the limitation in effect for the year for which the computation is being made (paragraph 36 of Opinion 11). Deferred tax credits offset in the "with-and-without" computation are considered fully offset.

13. In determining the amount of investment tax credit to be recognized as an offset against existing net deferred tax credits, prospective percentage limitations are applied to existing net deferred tax credits from prior years that have not been previously offset. Prospective limitations are applied only to existing net deferred tax credits not previously offset because application of prospective limitations to existing net deferred tax credits that have been previously offset would result in subsequently adjusting the limitation applied in the "with-and-without" computation. This concept under Interpretation 25 is similar to recognizing currently the tax benefit of an operating loss carryforward as an offset against existing net deferred tax credits (paragraph 48 of Opinion 11).

14. A footnote in the proposed Interpretation stated that the most current statutory percentage limitations in effect should be used if the limitations change after the end of the reporting period but before the financial statements are issued. Several respondents disagreed with that approach as not being consistent with Opinion 11. That footnote was deleted and the statutory percentage limitations to be used in applying paragraph 3 are those that have been enacted by the end of the reporting period as being applicable to the years in which the deferred tax credits are expected to reverse.

Appendix B

EXAMPLE OF COMPUTATIONS FOR RECOGNIZING INVESTMENT TAX CREDIT

15. This example illustrates one method of computing the amount of investment tax credit to be recognized in financial statement provisions for income tax expense in the "with-and-without" computation and as an offset against existing net deferred tax credits under this Interpretation. Note that paragraph 4 specifies that net deferred tax credits previously offset shall not be adjusted to reflect changes in the statutory limitations. The example does not comprehend all possible combinations of circumstances.

General Assumptions

16. The general assumptions on which the following example is based are:

a. There are no permanent differences.
b. There are no investment tax credit carrybacks.
c. The "net change" method of computing deferred taxes is used (paragraph 37 of Opinion 11).
d. As of January 1, 1979, the deferred tax account consists of the following:

Deferred tax credits resulting from timing differences aggregating $260,000	$119,600
Less investment tax credit recognized but not realized	35,000
Net deferred tax credits	$ 84,600

e. The federal income tax rate before recognition of any tax credits is 46 percent.
f. The statutory percentage limitations in effect are those specified in footnote 3 to paragraph 8 of this Interpretation.
g. Reinstatement of deferred tax credits only arises when investment tax credit realized on the tax return exceeds the amount recognized for financial reporting purposes in the current period.

Timing Differences

17. Timing differences are summarized as follows:

a. Scheduled Reversal of Timing Differences by Year of Origin

Year of Reversal	Total Reversal	Timing Differences Originating In 1976	1977	1978	1979	1980	1981
1979	$ 12,000	$ 12,000					
1980	20,000	12,000	$ 8,000				
1981	230,000	12,000	8,000	$ 6,000	$204,000		
1982		12,000	8,000	6,000	204,000		
1983		12,000	8,000	6,000	204,000		
1984		12,000	8,000	6,000	—		
1985		12,000	8,000	6,000	—		
1986		12,000	8,000	6,000	—		
1987		12,000	8,000	6,000	—	$210,000	
1988		12,000	8,000	6,000	—	210,000	
1989		—	8,000	6,000	—	—	$365,000
1990		—	—	6,000	—	—	365,000
Total		$120,000	$80,000	$60,000	$612,000	$420,000	$730,000

b. Summary of Cumulative Net Timing Differences

End of Year	Total	Timing Differences 1976	1977	1978	1979	1980	1981
1979	$ 860,000	$108,000	$80,000	$60,000	$612,000		
1980	1,260,000	96,000	72,000	60,000	612,000	$420,000	
1981	1,760,000	84,000	64,000	54,000	408,000	420,000	$730,000

c. Summary of Timing Differences Originating Prior to the Beginning of the Period That Are Still in Existence at the End of the Period

End of Year	Total	Timing Differences 1976	1977	1978	1979	1980
1979	$ 248,000	$108,000	$80,000	$60,000		
1980	840,000	96,000	72,000	60,000	$612,000	
1981	1,030,000	84,000	64,000	54,000	408,000	$420,000

Additional Assumptions

18. Additional assumptions on which the following example is based are:

		1979	1980	1981
Pretax accounting income		$1,500,000	$1,000,000	$1,600,000
Timing differences:				
Originating		(612,000)	(420,000)	(730,000)
Reversing		12,000	20,000	230,000
Net		(600,000)	(400,000)	(500,000)
Taxable income		$ 900,000	$ 600,000	$1,100,000
Originating investment tax credit		$ 325,000	$ 370,000	$ 675,000
Federal income tax based on pretax accounting income at 46%	(1)	$ 690,000	$ 460,000	$ 736,000
Federal income tax based on taxable income at 46%	(2)	$ 414,000	$ 276,000	$ 506,000
Difference [(1) − (2)]		$ 276,000	$ 184,000	$ 230,000

"With-and-without" Computation

19. Investment tax credit recognized under the "with-and-without" method is computed as follows:

		1979	1980	1981
Investment tax credit based on the federal income tax on pretax accounting income:				
First $25,000 × 100%		$ 25,000	$ 25,000	$ 25,000
Remainder of federal income tax:				
($690,000 − $25,000) × 60%		399,000		
($460,000 − $25,000) × 70%			304,500	
($736,000 − $25,000) × 80%				568,800
Total		$424,000	$329,500	$593,800
Amount recognized (lesser of amount computed above or amount available)	(1)	$325,000	$329,500	$593,800
Investment tax credit realized on taxable income (cannot exceed amount available for tax purposes):				
First $25,000 of federal income tax × 100%		$ 25,000	$ 25,000	$ 25,000
Remainder of federal income tax:				
($414,000 − $25,000) × 60%		233,400		
($276,000 − $25,000) × 70%			175,700	
($506,000 − $25,000) × 80%				384,800
Total	(2)	$258,400	$200,700	$409,800
Investment tax credit recognized in the "with-and-without" computation in excess of that realized on taxable income [(1) − (2)]		$ 66,600	$128,800	$184,000

Offset of Unrecognized Investment Tax Credit against Existing Net Deferred Tax Credits

20. Remaining unused investment tax credit, after the "with-and-without" computation, is recognized as an offset against existing net deferred tax credits that would reverse in the investment tax credit carryforward period. Investment tax credit offset against existing net deferred tax credits is summarized as follows:

		1979	1980	1981
Unrecognized investment tax credit after "with-and-without" computation (available for offset against existing net deferred tax credits):				
Unrecognized investment tax credit carried forward from prior years		$ —	$ —	$ —
Originating in current year		325,000	370,000	675,000
		325,000	370,000	675,000
Recognized in "with-and-without" computation		325,000	329,500	593,800
Unrecognized investment tax credit available for offset against existing net deferred tax credits	(1)	$ —	$ 40,500	$ 81,200
Existing net deferred tax credits at the beginning of the year, available for offset at the end of the year:				
Paragraph 21			$205,400	
Paragraph 22				$ 61,831
Multiplied by limitation rate in years of expected reversal[4]			80% & 90%[5]	90%
Offset limitation based on existing net deferred tax credits available for offset	(2)	N/A	$183,088	$ 55,648
Investment tax credit recognized by offset [lesser of (1) or (2)]	(3)	N/A	$ 40,500	$ 55,648
Investment tax credit carried forward [(1) − (3)]		$ —	$ —	$ 25,552

[4]The first $25,000 of federal income tax payable may be completely offset by investment tax credit, but the complications involved and additional record keeping that would be necessary would generally cause the cost to exceed the benefit from the greater precision.

[5]In 1980, the existing net deferred tax credits at the beginning of the year available for offset at the end of the year relate to the 1979 originating timing difference in the amount of $612,000. The offset limitation based on existing net deferred tax credits available for offset is determined as follows:

A		B	C	D	E	F
Reversal of Timing Difference (paragraph 17 (a))		Deferred Tax Credits (paragraph 21)	Deferred Tax Credit Considered to Have Been Previously Offset (paragraph 21)	Difference (B − C)	Limitation Rate in Year of Expected Reversal	Offset Limitation (E × D)
Year	Amount					
1981	$204,000	$ 93,840	$76,120	$ 17,720	80%	$ 14,176
1982	204,000	93,840	—	93,840	90	84,456
1983	204,000	93,840	—	93,840	90	84,456
	$612,000	$281,520	$76,120	$205,400		$183,088

Because the investment tax credit recognized by offset is limited to $40,500, the deferred tax credits considered offset by the $40,500 is determined as follows:

Investment Tax Credit Recognized	Deferred Tax Credits Offset
$14,176 ÷ 80%	$17,720
26,324 ÷ 90%	29,249
$40,500	$46,969

Offset Computation

21. The computation of deferred tax credits available for offset in 1980 is as follows:

			Timing Differences Originating In			
		Total	1976	1977	1978	1979
Timing differences (paragraph 17(c))[6]		$840,000	$ 96,000	$ 72,000	$ 60,000	$612,000
Deferred tax credits at average rate[7]	(1)	$386,400	$44,160	$ 33,120	$ 27,600	$281,520
Deferred tax credits considered to have been previously offset:[8]						
Investment Tax Credit Recognized						
Pre-1979 $35,000 ÷ 50%		70,000	44,160	25,840	—	—
1979 66,600 ÷ 60%		111,000	—	7,280	27,600	76,120
Total deferred tax credits offset	(2)	181,000	44,160	33,120	27,600	76,120
Difference [(1)-(2)]	(3)	205,400	$ —	$ —	$ —	205,400
Deferred tax credits that will reverse beyond the carryforward period for 1980 investment tax credits[9]	(4)	—				—
Existing net deferred tax credits available for offset under paragraph 3 [(3)-(4)]		$205,400				$205,400

Paragraph 3 specifies that only net deferred tax credits that have *not* been previously offset and that will reverse during the investment tax credit carryforward period shall be offset by investment tax credit. The above computation disregards any timing differences that may originate in that carryforward period. Hence, identification of specific timing differences is necessary.

[6]Represents the amount of timing differences originating prior to the beginning of the period that are still in existence at the end of the period. Originating timing differences (current period) are offset in the "with-and-without" computation and are not eligible for additional offset.

[7]The average rate that is applied to the timing differences is calculated as the balance in the deferred tax account plus the total recognized but unrealized investment tax credit divided by the cumulative net timing differences; all at the beginning of the period. The 1980 computation consists of:

$$\frac{\$294{,}000 \text{ (paragraph 23(b))} + \$101{,}600 \text{ (paragraph 23(a))}}{\$860{,}000 \text{ (paragraph 17(b))}} = 46\%$$

[8]The investment tax credit previously recognized is divided by the percentage limitation that was used in determining the amount of investment tax credit recognized. The resultant amount equals the deferred tax credits that have been offset. The total amount of deferred tax credits considered offset is then allocated to deferred taxes on originating timing differences starting with the earliest year, irrespective of when the investment tax credit was recognized. This allocation procedure is necessary because the net change method does not result in the investment tax credit being directly associated with specific originating timing differences.

[9]In 1980, the only deferred tax credits that have not been fully offset relate to timing differences originating in 1979; all reverse within the carryforward period for 1980 investment tax credits.

22. The computation of deferred tax credits available for offset in 1981 is as follows:

			Timing Differences Originating In				
		Total	**1976**	**1977**	**1978**	**1979**	**1980**
Timing differences (paragraph 17 (c))[10]		$1,030,000	$84,000	$64,000	$54,000	$408,000	$420,000
Deferred tax credits at average rate[11]	(1)	$ 473,800	$38,640	$29,440	$24,840	$187,680	$193,200
Deferred tax credits considered to have been previously offset:[12]							
Investment Tax Credit Recognized							
Pre-1979 $ 35,000 ÷ 50%		70,000	38,640	29,440	1,920	—	—
1979 66,600 ÷ 60%		111,000	—	—	22,920	88,080	—
1980 128,800 ÷ 70%		184,000	—	—	—	99,600	84,400
1980 40,500 ÷ 80% & 90%		46,969	—	—	—	—	46,969
Total deferred tax credits offset	(2)	411,969	38,640	29,440	24,840	187,680	131,369
Difference [(1)-(2)]	(3)	61,831	$ —	$ —	$ —	$ —	61,831
Deferred tax credits that will reverse beyond the carryforward period for 1981 investment tax credits[13]	(4)	—					—
Existing net deferred tax credits available for offset under paragraph 3 [(3) − (4)]		$ 61,831					$ 61,831

[10]See footnote 6.

[11]See footnote 7. The 1981 computation consists of:

$$\frac{\$308{,}700 \text{ (paragraph 23(b))} + \$270{,}900 \text{ (paragraph 23(a))}}{\$1{,}260{,}000 \text{ (paragraph 17(b))}} = 46\%$$

[12]See footnote 8.

[13]In 1981, the only deferred tax credits that have not been fully offset relate to timing differences originating in 1980; all reverse within the carryforward period for 1981 investment tax credits.

Summary of Investment Tax Credit Recognized But Not Realized and Deferred Tax Account Activity

23. The computations in paragraphs 18-22 are summarized as follows:

a. Investment Tax Credit Recognized But Not Realized

	Investment Tax Credit	Percentage Limitation	Deferred Tax Credits Offset
As of 1978	$ 35,000	50%	$ 70,000
1979			
"With-and-without"	66,600	60	111,000
Offset	—		—
Cumulative subtotal	101,600		181,000
1980			
"With-and-without"	128,800	70	184,000
Offset	40,500	80 & 90	46,969
Cumulative subtotal	270,900		411,969
1981			
"With-and-without"	184,000	80	230,000
Offset	55,648	90	61,831
Cumulative Total	$510,548		$ 703,800

b. Deferred Tax Account Activity

	DR	CR	Balance
1978 assumed (paragraph 16(d))	$ 35,000	$119,600	$ 84,600
1979			
"With-and-without"	66,600	276,000	
Offset	—	—	294,000
1980			
"With-and-without"	128,800	184,000	
Offset	40,500	—	308,700
1981			
"With-and-without"	184,000	230,000	
Offset	55,648	—	$ 299,052

FASB Interpretation No. 33
Applying FASB Statement No. 34 to Oil and Gas Producing Operations Accounted for by the Full Cost Method

an interpretation of FASB Statement No. 34

STATUS

Issued: August 1980

Effective Date: For fiscal years beginning after December 15, 1979 and for interim periods within those years

Affects: No other pronouncements

Affected by: No other pronouncements

SUMMARY

FASB Statement No. 34, *Capitalization of Interest Cost*, establishes standards for capitalizing interest cost as part of the historical cost of acquiring certain assets. This Interpretation clarifies that the assets of an oil and gas producing operation accounted for by the full cost method that qualify for capitalization of interest are:

a. Those unusually significant investments in unproved properties and major development projects that are not being depreciated, depleted, or amortized currently and
b. Significant properties and projects in cost centers with no production,

provided that exploration or development activities on such assets are in progress.

FASB Interpretation No. 33
Applying FASB Statement No. 34 to Oil and Gas Producing Operations Accounted for by the Full Cost Method

an interpretation of FASB Statement No. 34

CONTENTS

INTRODUCTION

1. The FASB received several inquiries from oil and gas producing enterprises that use the full cost method of accounting asking how they should apply FASB Statement No. 34, *Capitalization of Interest Cost*, to their operations. Appendix A contains background information about those inquiries.

INTERPRETATION

2. For purposes of applying Statement 34 to oil and gas producing operations accounted for by the full cost method, assets whose costs are being currently depreciated, depleted, or amortized are assets in use in the earning activities of the enterprise and are not assets qualifying for capitalization of interest cost as defined in paragraph 9 of Statement 34. Unusually significant investments in unproved properties and major development projects that are not being currently depreciated, depleted, or amortized and on which exploration or development activities are in progress are assets qualifying for capitalization of interest cost. Similarly, in a cost center with no production, significant properties and projects on which exploration or development activities are in progress are assets qualifying for capitalization of interest cost.

EFFECTIVE DATE AND TRANSITION

3. The provisions of this Interpretation shall be effective for annual financial statements for fiscal years beginning after December 15, 1979 and for interim periods within those fiscal years, with earlier application encouraged. Enterprises that have applied Statement 34 in a manner contrary to this Interpretation in previously issued annual financial statements are encouraged, but are not required, to restate those financial statements and financial information for interim periods within those fiscal years to give effect to the provisions of this Interpretation. If those annual financial statements are not restated, the effect that the provisions of this Interpretation would have had in those financial statements shall be disclosed in the annual financial statements in which this Interpretation is first applied. Likewise, the effect that this Interpretation would have had on the financial information for interim periods within those years shall be disclosed whenever financial information for those interim periods is presented.

4. If the change to conform to the provisions of this Interpretation is made in *other than* the first interim period of an enterprise's fiscal year, financial information for the prechange interim periods of that fiscal year shall be restated by applying the newly adopted method of applying Statement 34 to those prechange interim periods. Whenever financial information that includes those prechange interim periods is presented, it shall be presented on the restated basis. In addition, the following disclosures shall be made for the interim period in which the provisions of this Interpretation are adopted:

a. The nature of the change in method of applying Statement 34;
b. The effect of the change on income from continuing operations. net income, and related per share amounts for each prechange interim period of that fiscal year; and
c. Income from continuing operations, net income, and related per share amounts for each prechange interim period restated in accordance with this Interpretation.

Appendix A

BACKGROUND INFORMATION

5. Paragraph 9 of Statement 34 states that interest shall be capitalized on "assets that are constructed

or otherwise produced for an enterprise's own use (including assets constructed or produced for the enterprise by others for which deposits or progress payments have been made)." Such assets are referred to as "qualifying assets." Paragraph 10 of Statement 34, however, states that interest shall not be capitalized on:

a. Assets that are in use or ready for their intended use in the earning activities of the enterprise
b. Assets that are not being used in the earning activities of the enterprise and that are not undergoing the activities necessary to get them ready for use.

6. Appendix B of FASB Statement No. 19, *Financial Accounting and Reporting by Oil and Gas Producing Companies*, discusses the full cost method. Paragraph 104 states that:

> Under the full cost concept, all costs incurred in acquiring, exploring, and developing properties within a relatively large geopolitical (as opposed to geological) cost center (such as a country) are capitalized when incurred and are amortized as mineral reserves in the cost center are produced, subject to a limitation that the capitalized costs not exceed the value of those reserves.

Paragraph 107 further states that:

> . . . acquisition, exploration, and development costs are sometimes included in the pool of capitalized costs associated with a cost center when incurred, so that if the cost center is producing, those costs are subject to amortization at once. In some cases, however, certain significant costs, such as those associated with offshore U.S. operations, are deferred separately without amortization until the specific property to which they relate is found to be either productive or nonproductive, at which time those deferred costs and any reserves attributable to the property are included in the computation of amortization in the cost center.

Proponents of the full cost method have traditionally argued that all exploratory and development costs should be capitalized because such costs represent the historical cost of an enterprise's proved oil and gas reserves. As stated in paragraph 102 of Statement 19:

> . . . all costs incurred in oil and gas producing activities are regarded as integral to the acquisition, discovery, and development of whatever reserves ultimately result from the efforts as a whole, and are thus associated with the company's reserves.

7. Securities and Exchange Commission (SEC) ASR No. 258, *Oil and Gas Producers—Full Cost Accounting Practices*, established "uniform requirements for financial accounting and reporting practices of oil and gas producers following the full cost method of accounting" and subject to SEC Rules. ASR 258 requires that costs to be amortized include "all capitalized costs, less accumulated amortization, other than the cost . . . of unusually significant investments in unproved properties and major development projects," plus certain other costs.

8. A proposed Interpretation, *Applying FASB Statement No. 34 to Oil and Gas Producing Operations Accounted for by the Full Cost Method*, was released for comment on January 28, 1980. The Board received 28 letters of comment to the proposed Interpretation. Certain of the comments received and the Board's consideration of them are discussed in paragraphs 9-15.

9. Two views have been expressed regarding what constitute the qualifying assets of an oil and gas producing operation accounted for by the full cost method. The first view is that major exploration or development projects constitute qualifying assets as long as exploration or development activities are in progress. Interest capitalization ends when those activities cease or when the property begins producing oil or gas, whichever comes first. Under this view, the qualifying assets of an oil and gas producing enterprise for purposes of capitalizing interest are the same regardless of whether the enterprise uses the successful efforts method or the full cost method.

10. Others argue that the first view fails to reflect the conceptual basis of the full cost method. Proponents of the full cost method have traditionally argued that the assets of an oil and gas producing company are not its individual properties, platforms, wells, and equipment, but are, rather, its underground oil and gas reserves. The historical acquisition cost of those reserves is the cumulative exploration and development expenditures of the enterprise and, accordingly, all exploration and development costs are capitalized. As reserves are produced, the costs of those reserves (the capitalized costs in the cost center) are amortized on a units-of-production basis. The cumulative capitalized costs in the cost center, therefore, represent the cost of one asset—proved oil and gas reserves—not an aggregation of the costs of separately identifiable assets each of which may or may not be ready for use. Once production begins, that asset is in use "in the earning activities of the enterprise" and is, therefore, not a qualifying asset for purposes of capitalizing interest. ASR 258 permits the costs of major nonproducing properties to be accounted for as separate assets excluded from the full cost pool and not

amortized because the reserves related to those costs are not yet known. Nonproducing properties whose costs are excluded from the full cost pool and are not being currently amortized are not in use "in the earning activities of the enterprise."

11. The Board believes that the view expressed in paragraph 10 is consistent with the conceptual basis of the full cost method. By contrast, the view expressed in paragraph 9, that the assets of an oil or gas producer that qualify for capitalization of interest should be the same regardless of the accounting method used, creates conceptual implementation problems. Assume that an oil and gas producer drills three exploratory wells on a property, that the first two wells are dry holes, and that the third well locates proved reserves. If the enterprise uses the successful efforts method, it will charge the costs of the first two wells to expense when they are determined to be dry holes and cease to capitalize interest on them. Under the view expressed in paragraph 9, an enterprise that uses the full cost method would capitalize interest as a cost of the wells and would stop capitalization of interest on the first two wells when they are determined to be dry holes. The full cost method, however, does not differentiate an exploratory dry hole from a successful exploratory well. All exploration costs are considered costs of locating proved reserves and the full cost method treats all exploration costs the same. Therefore, the arguments advanced in paragraph 9 would create a distinction between dry holes and successful wells that is incompatible with the full cost method.

12. Some respondents requested that the Board provide guidance to determine what constitute "unusually significant" investments and "major" projects. Those terms are taken from ASR 258, and enterprises subject to SEC rules have experience in applying those terms to their amortization policies. For enterprises not subject to SEC rules, the Board believes that judgments as to what constitute "unusually significant" investments and "major" projects should be determined by an enterprise and its auditors based upon the enterprise's facts and circumstances.

13. Some respondents suggested that the proposed Interpretation contradicted paragraph 18 of Statement 34, which states:

> The capitalization period shall end when the asset is substantially complete and ready for its intended use. Some assets are completed in parts, and each part is capable of being used independently while work is continuing on other parts. An example is a condominium. For such assets, interest capitalization shall stop on each part when it is substantially complete and ready for use. . . . Some assets cannot be used effectively until a separate facility has been completed. Examples are the oil wells drilled in Alaska before completion of the pipeline. For such assets, interest capitalization shall continue until the separate facility is substantially complete and ready for use.

Those respondents maintain that paragraph 18 of Statement 34 supports the view expressed in paragraph 9 of this appendix. Paragraph 18 of Statement 34, however, deals with the end of the capitalization period; it does not address what assets are qualifying assets. If an asset is not a qualifying asset for purposes of interest capitalization, then the duration of the capitalization period is not relevant.

14. The concept of assets completed in parts with each part capable of being used independently is compatible with this Interpretation. Interest may be capitalized as a part of the cost of unusually significant investments in unproved properties and major development projects that are not being currently depreciated, depleted, or amortized and on which exploration or development activities are in progress. Properties and projects whose costs are included in producing cost centers lose their separate identity, however, and are treated as part of a single, indivisible asset.

15. Some respondents found the effective date and transition provisions of the proposed Interpretation unclear. Other respondents objected to the requirement for enterprises that elected early implementation of Statement 34 in a manner not compatible with the proposed Interpretation to restate their previously issued financial statements or financial information. The effective date and transition section has been revised to encourage, but not require, restatement.

This Interpretation was adopted by the affirmative votes of six members of the Financial Accounting Standards Board following submission to the members of the Financial Accounting Standards Advisory Council and the Screening Committee on Emerging Problems. Mr. Mosso dissented.

Mr. Mosso dissents because he believes this Interpretation misapplies (1) the basic premise stated in paragraph 6 of Statement 34 that the cost of acquiring an asset includes interest as part of "the costs necessarily incurred to bring it to the *condition and location* necessary for its intended use" and (2) that part of paragraph 18 which reads "Some assets are completed in parts. . . . interest capitalization shall stop *on each part* when it is substantially complete and ready for use" (emphasis added).

The Interpretation hinges on rejection of the applicability of paragraph 18 of Statement 34 which deals with the end of the capitalization period for assets that are partly ready for use and partly not. Rejection of paragraph 18 requires a determination that a producing cost center for oil and gas reserves represents a single, indivisible asset, wholly ready for use when it satisfies an accounting test, current amortization. That determination, however, ignores the fact that readiness for use is defined in paragraph 6 of Statement 34 essentially in terms of satisfying physical tests, condition and location, and the further fact that similar physical tests are implicit in the SEC rule for full cost accounting.

The SEC rule for amortizing a full cost pool reads in part: "Costs to be amortized shall include . . . the estimated future expenditures . . . to be incurred in developing proved reserves. . . ." The fact that estimated future development costs are required to be included in the current amortization charge is clear recognition that some portions of proved reserves may not be physically ready for current production even though other portions are currently producing. It is recognition that a proved but undeveloped oil and gas field constitutes an incomplete part of a larger asset complex, the full cost pool. Interest in that context is as much a future development cost as any other kind of capitalizable cost.

Members of the Financial Accounting Standards Board:

FASB Interpretation No. 34
Disclosure of Indirect Guarantees of Indebtedness of Others

an interpretation of FASB Statement No. 5

STATUS

Issued: March 1981

Effective Date: For fiscal years ending after June 15, 1981

Affects: No other pronouncements

Affected by: No other pronouncements

SUMMARY

This Interpretation clarifies that the disclosures that FASB Statement No. 5, *Accounting for Contingencies*, requires of guarantees of indebtedness of others also are required of indirect guarantees.

FASB Interpretation No. 34
Disclosure of Indirect Guarantees of Indebtedness of Others

an interpretation of FASB Statement No. 5

CONTENTS

INTRODUCTION

1. The Board has been asked to clarify the disclosures that are required of indirect guarantees of indebtedness of others. Paragraph 12 of FASB Statement No. 5, *Accounting for Contingencies*, requires disclosure of guarantees of indebtedness of others:

> Certain loss contingencies are presently being disclosed in financial statements even though the possibility of loss may be remote. The common characteristic of those contingencies is a guarantee, normally with a right to proceed against an outside party in the event that the guarantor is called upon to satisfy the guarantee. Examples include (a) guarantees of indebtedness of others. . . . The Board concludes that disclosure of those loss contingencies, and others that in substance have the same characteristic, shall be continued. The disclosure shall include the nature and amount of the guarantee. Consideration should be given to disclosing, if estimable, the value of any recovery that could be expected to result, such as from the guarantor's right to proceed against an outside party.

INTERPRETATION

2. An indirect guarantee of the indebtedness of another arises under an agreement that obligates one entity to transfer funds to a second entity upon the occurrence of specified events, under conditions whereby (a) the funds are legally available to creditors of the second entity and (b) those creditors may enforce the second entity's claims against the first entity under the agreement. Examples of indirect guarantees include agreements to advance funds if a second entity's income, coverage of fixed charges, or working capital falls below a specified minimum.[1]

3. The term *guarantees of indebtedness of others* in paragraph 12 of Statement 5 includes indirect guarantees of indebtedness of others as described in paragraph 2 of this Interpretation.

EFFECTIVE DATE AND TRANSITION

4. This Interpretation shall be effective for financial statements for fiscal years ending after June 15, 1981. Earlier application is encouraged.

This Interpretation was adopted by the affirmative votes of six members of the Financial Accounting Standards Board following submission to the members of the Financial Accounting Standards Advisory Council. Mr. Morgan dissented.

Mr. Morgan dissents to issuance of this Interpretation because he believes that it is not needed. In his opinion, paragraph 12 of Statement 5 already requires disclosure of indirect guarantees of indebtedness of others.

One of the examples that paragraph describes is "guarantees of indebtedness of others" without explicitly referring to "indirect" guarantees. However, the paragraph's main point is that contingencies based on guarantees shall be disclosed, and it states that ". . . disclosure of those loss contingencies, and *others that in substance have the same characteristic*, shall be continued" (emphasis added).

Mr. Morgan believes new financial accounting pronouncements should be issued only when GAAP is to be charged or expanded and should be avoided when earlier pronouncements seem clear to *most* concerned parties but lack the specificity that *some* parties desire. A trend toward more and more specificity in financial accounting pronouncements would seem to be a trend toward substituting the

[1]Disclosure of an indirect guarantee is not required by this Interpretation if it is otherwise disclosed in an entity's financial statements.

Board's judgment in place of the judgment of preparers and attestors who are most familiar with the pertinent facts and circumstances.

The members of the Financial Accounting Standards Board:

Appendix A

BACKGROUND INFORMATION

5. The FASB released an Exposure Draft of a proposed Statement on March 31, 1980 titled *Disclosure of Guarantees, Project Financing Arrangements, and Other Similar Obligations* (March Exposure Draft), that would have amended Statement 5 to explicitly include in paragraph 12 both unconditional obligations and indirect guarantees of indebtedness of others. The FASB received 102 letters of comment on the March Exposure Draft. Based on the comments received, the content of the March Exposure Draft was separated into two documents that were exposed concurrently for comment on November 14, 1980: a proposed Interpretation, *Disclosure of Indirect Guarantees of Indebtedness of Others*, and a revised Exposure Draft, *Disclosure of Unconditional Obligations*.

6. The Board received 51 letters of comment on the proposed Interpretation. Certain of the comments received and the Board's consideration of them are discussed in paragraphs 7-10.

7. Some respondents stated that disclosure of indirect guarantees should not be required unless loss is probable. The approach suggested by those respondents would require an amendment of Statement 5, which requires disclosure of guarantees even though the possibility of loss may be remote. The Board does not believe those respondents have presented evidence sufficient to warrant an amendment.

8. Some respondents suggested that enterprises regulated on an individual-company-cost-of-service basis should be exempted from the requirements of this Interpretation. They state that payments required under indirect guarantees usually would be recovered through the rate-making process, and no loss would result. Statement 5 requires disclosure of guarantees, however, even though the possibility of loss may be remote. The fact that the possibility of loss is remote for those regulated enterprises does not distinguish them or provide a basis for exemption.

9. Some respondents requested clarification of the definition of an indirect guarantee and the difference between direct and indirect guarantees of indebtedness of others. Both direct and indirect guarantees of indebtedness involve three parties: a debtor, a creditor, and a guarantor. In a direct guarantee, the guarantor states that if the debtor fails to make payment to the creditor when due, the guarantor will pay the creditor. If the debtor defaults, the creditor has a direct claim on the guarantor. Under an indirect guarantee, there is an agreement between the debtor and the guarantor requiring the guarantor to transfer funds to the debtor upon the occurrence of specified events. The creditor has only an indirect claim on the guarantor by enforcing the debtor's claim against the guarantor. After funds are transferred from the guarantor to the debtor, the funds become available to the creditor through its claim against the debtor.

10. The proposed Interpretation stated that a general partner's responsibility for the indebtedness of a partnership is an indirect guarantee. Several respondents suggested deleting that sentence for various reasons. A creditor has a direct claim against the general partners of a debtor partnership and, accordingly, a general partner's responsibility for the indebtedness of a partnership is not an indirect guarantee as discussed in paragraph 9. The Board, therefore, deleted the sentence.

FASB Interpretation No. 35
Criteria for Applying the Equity Method of Accounting for Investments in Common Stock

an interpretation of APB Opinion No. 18

STATUS

Issued: May 1981

Effective Date: For fiscal years beginning after June 15, 1981

Affects: No other pronouncements

Affected by: No other pronouncements

SUMMARY

This Interpretation clarifies the criteria for applying the equity method of accounting for investments of 50 percent or less of the voting stock of an investee enterprise (other than a corporate joint venture). APB Opinion No. 18, *The Equity Method of Accounting for Investments in Common Stock*, states that use of the equity method of accounting for the investment is required if the investor has the ability to exercise significant influence over operating and financial policies of the investee. Opinion 18 includes presumptions, based on the investor's percentage ownership, as to whether the investor has that ability, but those presumptions can be overcome by evidence to the contrary and do not override the need for judgment. If there is an indication that an investor owning 20 percent or more of an investee's voting stock is unable to exercise significant influence over the investee's operating and financial policies, all the facts and circumstances related to the investment shall be evaluated to determine whether the presumption of ability to exercise significant influence over the investee is overcome.

FASB Interpretation No. 35 Criteria for Applying the Equity Method of Accounting for Investments in Common Stock

an interpretation of APB Opinion No. 18

CONTENTS

INTRODUCTION

1. The Board has been asked to clarify the provisions of APB Opinion No. 18, *The Equity Method of Accounting for Investments in Common Stock*, regarding application of that method to investments of 50 percent or less of the voting stock of an investee enterprise (other than a corporate joint venture).

INTERPRETATION

2. Opinion 18 requires that the equity method of accounting be followed by an investor whose investment in voting stock gives it the ability to exercise significant influence over operating and financial policies of an investee. The presumptions in paragraph 17 of Opinion 18 are intended to provide a reasonable degree of uniformity in applying the equity method. The presumptions can be overcome by predominant evidence to the contrary.

3. Evidence that an investor owning 20 percent or more of the voting stock of an investee may be unable to exercise significant influence over the investee's operating and financial policies requires an evaluation of all the facts and circumstances relating to the investment. The presumption that the investor has the ability to exercise significant influence over the investee's operating and financial policies stands until overcome by predominant evidence to the contrary.[1]

4. Examples of indications that an investor may be unable to exercise significant influence over the operating and financial policies of an investee include:

a. Opposition by the investee, such as litigation or complaints to governmental regulatory authorities, challenges the investor's ability to exercise significant influence.
b. The investor and investee sign an agreement under which the investor surrenders significant rights as a shareholder.[2]
c. Majority ownership of the investee is concentrated among a small group of shareholders who operate the investee without regard to the views of the investor.
d. The investor needs or wants more financial information to apply the equity method than is available to the investee's other shareholders (for example, the investor wants quarterly financial information from an investee that publicly reports only annually), tries to obtain that information, and fails.[3]
e. The investor tries and fails to obtain representation on the investee's board of directors.

This list is illustrative and is not all-inclusive. None of the individual circumstances is necessarily conclusive that the investor is unable to exercise significant influence over the investee's operating and financial policies. However, if any of these or similar circumstances exists, an investor with ownership of 20 percent or more shall evaluate all facts and circumstances relating to the investment to reach a judgment about whether the presumption that the investor has the ability to exercise significant influence over the investee's operating and financial policies is overcome. It may be necessary to evaluate the facts and circumstances for a period of time before reaching a judgment.

[1]Subject to the limitations on the use of the equity method identified in footnote 4 of Opinion 18. That footnote states that conditions that represent limitations on consolidation shall be applied as limitations to the use of the equity method.

[2]See paragraph 9 of this Interpretation for a discussion of such agreements.

[3]The subject of inability to obtain financial information also is addressed in the American Institute of Certified Public Accountants' *Codification of Statements on Auditing Standards*, AU Section 332, "Evidential Matter for Long-Term Investments," paragraph 9.

EFFECTIVE DATE AND TRANSITION

5. The provisions of this Interpretation shall be effective for fiscal years beginning after June 15, 1981, with earlier application encouraged. Changes in the method of accounting for investments required by this Interpretation shall be recorded in accordance with paragraphs 19(l) and (m) of Opinion 18, which provide that:

a. If the investor discontinues application of the equity method, the earnings and losses of the investee that were previously accrued shall remain as part of the carrying amount of the investment. The carrying amount of the investment shall not be adjusted retroactively.
b. If the investor begins applying the equity method, the investment, results of operations (current and prior periods presented), and retained earnings of the investor shall be adjusted retroactively.

This Interpretation was adopted by the unanimous vote of the seven members of the Financial Accounting Standards Board following submission to the Financial Accounting Standards Advisory Council.

Members of the Financial Accounting Standards Board:

Donald J. Kirk, *Chairman*
Frank E. Block
John W. March
Robert A. Morgan
David Mosso
Robert T. Sprouse
Ralph E. Walters

Appendix A

BACKGROUND INFORMATION AND BASIS FOR CONCLUSIONS

6. Paragraph 17 of Opinion 18 establishes standards for use of the equity method to account for investments in common stock other than subsidiaries and corporate joint ventures. It states that:

> The [Accounting Principles] Board concludes that the equity method of accounting for an investment in common stock should also be followed by an investor whose investment in voting stock gives it the ability to exercise significant influence over operating and financial policies of an investee even though the investor holds 50% or less of the voting stock. Ability to exercise that influence may be indicated in several ways, such as representation on the board of directors, participation in policy making processes, material intercompany transactions, interchange of managerial personnel, or technological dependency. Another important consideration is the extent of ownership by an investor in relation to the concentration of other shareholdings, but substantial or majority ownership of the voting stock of an investee by another investor does not necessarily preclude the ability to exercise significant influence by the investor. The [Accounting Principles] Board recognizes that determining the ability of an investor to exercise such influence is not always clear and applying judgment is necessary to assess the status of each investment. In order to achieve a reasonable degree of uniformity in application, the [Accounting Principles] Board concludes that an investment (direct or indirect) of 20% or more of the voting stock of an investee should lead to a presumption that in the absence of evidence to the contrary an investor has the ability to exercise significant influence over an investee. Conversely, an investment of less than 20% of the voting stock of an investee should lead to a presumption that an investor does not have the ability to exercise significant influence unless such ability can be demonstrated. When the equity method is appropriate, it should be applied in consolidated financial statements and in parent-company financial statements prepared for issuance to stockholders as the financial statements of the primary reporting entity.

7. The basic question raised is how to decide when use of the equity method is appropriate; in particular, how much weight should be given to the statement that ". . . applying judgment is necessary to assess the status of each investment" and how much weight to the presumptions based on percentage ownership? The Board has been advised that some investors view the presumptions as rigid rules and believe that achievement of 20 percent ownership requires use of the equity method to account for the investment regardless of circumstances. This Interpretation clarifies that the presumptions are to be applied using judgment and may be overcome by predominant evidence to the contrary.

8. A related question involves how an investor owning 20 percent or more of the voting stock of an investee should account for the investment if the investee opposes the investor. That opposition might be in the form of the investee's filing a lawsuit against the investor or the investee's making allegations to appropriate governmental regulatory authorities. This Interpretation clarifies that opposition by the investee requires an assessment by the investor of all the facts and circumstances of the investment to determine whether they are sufficient to overcome the presumption.

9. A third question relates to the appropriateness of using the equity method if an investor and an investee have signed an agreement under which the investor agrees to limit its shareholding in the investee. (Because the investor usually agrees not to increase its current holdings, such agreements often are called "stand-still agreements.") Those agreements are commonly used to compromise disputes when an investee is fighting against a takeover attempt or an increase in an investor's percentage ownership. Depending on their provisions, the agreements may modify an investor's rights or may increase certain rights and restrict others compared with the situation of an investor without such an agreement. If the investor surrenders significant rights as a shareholder under the provisions of such an agreement, this Interpretation clarifies that the investor shall assess all the facts and circumstances of the investment to determine whether they are sufficient to overcome the presumption.

10. A proposed Interpretation, *Criteria for Applying the Equity Method of Accounting for Investments in Common Stock*, was released for comment on December 19, 1980. The Board received 45 letters of comment on the proposed Interpretation. Certain of the comments received and the Board's consideration of them are discussed in paragraphs 11-14.

11. Some respondents believed that the Board should not finalize the proposed Interpretation because the document did not provide guidance beyond that contained in Opinion 18. The Board believes that this Interpretation provides additional guidance in two respects:

a. It provides examples of indications that an investor may be unable to exercise significant influence over operating and financial policies of an investee.
b. It affirms that the presumptions in Opinion 18 may be overcome by contrary evidence.

12. Some respondents suggested that the Interpretation would strengthen investees relative to investors in takeover disputes by making it more difficult for the investor to use the equity method to account for its investment. The Board disagrees with that suggestion for two reasons. First, the Board believes this Interpretation is a faithful interpretation of Opinion 18. The Board has not attempted to favor either investors or investees and does not believe that its role is to do so. The Board's role on this project is to faithfully interpret Opinion 18. Second, the Board notes that the actual cash returns on an investment and the income taxes that would be paid are unaffected by the method of accounting for the investment. Therefore, a decision not to proceed with an otherwise attractive investment simply because the equity method of accounting cannot be used would seem to be unlikely for the vast majority of companies. Conversely, an investment that is not otherwise attractive does not become so simply because the equity method will be used to account for that investment in the investor's financial statements.

13. Some respondents requested that the Interpretation explicitly provide guidance on accounting for investments of less than 20 percent. Paragraph 2 of this Interpretation states that the presumptions in paragraph 17 of Opinion 18 can be overcome. The Board believes that that statement plus the examples in Opinion 18 of ways an investor might indicate ability to exercise significant influence provide adequate guidance on accounting for investments of less than 20 percent.

14. Some respondents requested that the Interpretation provide more specific guidance, perhaps by providing some examples. The subject of "stand-still agreements" (paragraphs 4(b) and 9) was suggested as one for which guidance is particularly needed. The Board believes, as one respondent stated, that "every investor-investee relationship is unique. . . ." Even if the Board were to provide examples, they would not necessarily be applicable to unique facts and circumstances. Professional judgment would be required in any case. Accordingly, the Board has concluded that adding examples to this Interpretation would not reduce the degree of professional judgment required.

FASB Interpretation No. 36
Accounting for Exploratory Wells in Progress at the End of a Period

an interpretation of FASB Statement No. 19

STATUS

Issued: October 1981

Effective Date: For fiscal years beginning after December 15, 1981 and for interim periods within those years

Affects: No other pronouncements

Affected by: No other pronouncements

SUMMARY

FASB Statement No. 19, *Financial Accounting and Reporting by Oil and Gas Producing Companies,* requires that the costs of exploratory wells that do not locate proved oil and gas reserves (exploratory dry holes) be charged to expense. Questions have been raised about when to charge to expense the costs of an exploratory well in progress at the end of a period that is determined to be a dry hole before the financial statements for that period are issued. This Interpretation clarifies that the costs incurred through the end of the period shall be charged to expense for that period.

FASB Interpretation No. 36
Accounting for Exploratory Wells in Progress at the End of a Period

an interpretation of FASB Statement No. 19

CONTENTS

INTRODUCTION

1. The FASB has been asked to clarify certain provisions of FASB Statement No. 19, *Financial Accounting and Reporting by Oil and Gas Producing Companies,* relating to accounting for the costs of exploratory wells and exploratory-type stratigraphic test wells (both referred to generally as exploratory wells in this Interpretation) that are in progress at the end of a period and that are determined not to have found proved oil and gas reserves before issuance of the financial statements for the period. The Board has been advised that oil and gas producing enterprises are following differing accounting practices for those wells. Those practices are described in Appendix A.

INTERPRETATION

2. If an exploratory well or exploratory-type stratigraphic test well is in progress at the end of a period and the well is determined not to have found proved reserves before the financial statements for that period are issued, the costs incurred through the end of the period, net of any salvage value, shall be charged to expense for that period. Previously issued financial statements shall not be retroactively restated.

EFFECTIVE DATE AND TRANSITION

3. This Interpretation shall be effective for financial statements for fiscal years beginning after December 15, 1981 and for interim accounting periods within those fiscal years. Earlier application is encouraged but is not required.

This Interpretation was adopted by the affirmative votes of six members of the Financial Accounting Standards Board. Mr. Kirk dissented.

Mr. Kirk dissents to issuance of this Interpretation because, in his opinion, the positions stated in paragraphs 5(c) and 7 of this Interpretation, though rejected in this Interpretation, are consistent with the intention of Statement 19. Paragraph 11(d) of Statement 19 expressly defines costs incurred to "drill and equip wells that are not yet completed" as assets.

Mr. Kirk believes that while drilling is still in process, an exploratory well has value; industry experts indicate interests in uncompleted wells can be sold. As of the balance sheet date, therefore, it is entirely appropriate to recognize the costs of an uncompleted well as an asset, though, if significant, disclosure of the subsequent determination that the well was unsuccessful may be required. Moreover, Mr. Kirk believes that Statement 19's intent was to avoid suggesting the need for an impairment of value assessment for the capitalized costs of exploratory wells in process, similar to the assessment explicitly required in Statement 19 (paragraph 28) for unproved properties.

Appendix A

BACKGROUND INFORMATION

4. Paragraphs 19, 27, 31, 33, and 39 of Statement 19 are relevant to this matter. The substance of the relevant portions of paragraphs 19, 27, 31, and 33 is as follows:

a. The costs of drilling exploratory wells shall be capitalized as part of the enterprise's uncompleted wells, equipment, and facilities pending determination of whether the well has found proved reserves. That determination is usually made on or shortly after completion of drilling the well.

b. If the well has found proved reserves, the capitalized costs of drilling the well shall be reclassified as part of the enterprise's wells and related equipment and facilities.

c. If the well has not found proved reserves, the capitalized costs of drilling the well, net of any salvage value, shall be charged to expense.

Paragraph 39 states that:

> Information that becomes available after the end of the period covered by the financial statements but before those financial statements are issued shall be taken into account in evaluating conditions that existed at the balance sheet date, for example, in assessing unproved properties (paragraph 28) and in determining whether an exploratory well or exploratory-type stratigraphic test well had found proved reserves (paragraphs 31-34).

5. The Board has been advised that three different accounting practices are now being followed for exploratory wells that are in progress at the end of a period and that are determined not to have found proved reserves before financial statements are issued.

a. Some enterprises believe the costs incurred on the well through the end of the period should be charged to expense. They believe that the determination, after the end of the period, that the exploratory well has not found proved reserves (is a "dry hole") confirms a condition that existed all the time. That condition is not affected by whether the well was completed at the end of the period. They believe, therefore, that paragraph 39 of Statement 19 requires charging the costs incurred through the end of the period to expense.

b. Other enterprises agree with the view in subparagraph (a) and in addition believe that the costs to complete the well should be accrued and charged to expense as of the end of the period. The subsequent determination that the well has not found proved reserves means that the total cost of the well represents a loss. They believe that the total loss, both already incurred and yet to be incurred, should be recognized at the end of the period. Those who hold the view stated in subparagraph (a) disagree because they feel continued drilling in the next period should not affect the results of the previous period. They believe that the costs of unsuccessful exploratory wells under Statement 19 are not comparable to costs of contractual commitments requiring recognition of losses.

c. A third group of enterprises capitalizes the costs incurred through the end of the period as uncompleted wells, equipment, and facilities. They believe that paragraphs 19, 27, 31, and 33 of Statement 19 require capitalization of the costs of an exploratory well until a determination is made of whether the well has found proved reserves. Because the determination cannot be made until the well is completed, the costs should not be charged to expense before the date of completion. They believe that paragraph 39 of Statement 19 is only applicable to exploratory wells that have been completed but not yet evaluated at the end of a period. Determination before issuance of financial statements that a completed well had not found proved reserves would result in charging the costs of the well to expense in the period of completion.

6. A draft of a proposed Interpretation, *Accounting for Exploratory Wells in Progress at the End of a Period,* was released for comment November 26, 1980. The Board received 48 letters of comment in response to the proposed Interpretation. Certain of the comments received and the Board's consideration of them are discussed in paragraphs 7-10.

7. Most of the respondents who disagreed with the proposed Interpretation believe that the proper method of accounting for an exploratory well in progress at the end of a period is that described in paragraph 5(c) of this Interpretation (i.e., that such costs should remain capitalized until the well is completed and determined to be dry). Those respondents relied heavily on the language in paragraph 19 of Statement 19, which provides that the cost of drilling an exploratory well shall be capitalized pending determination of whether the well has found proved reserves, and on paragraph 31, which addresses accounting when drilling of an exploratory well *is completed.* They believe that Statement 19 requires capitalization of the costs of an exploratory well until the well is completed, at which time an assessment is made and the cost of an unsuccessful well is charged to expense. They believe that paragraph 39 of Statement 19 does not apply to an exploratory well in progress at the end of a period.

8. Paragraph 198 of Statement 19 refers to capitalizing "the costs of drilling all exploratory wells *pending* determination of success or failure, that is, *pending* determination of whether proved reserves are found" (emphasis added). Paragraph 205 further explains that "the existence of future benefits is not known until the well is drilled. Future benefits depend on whether reserves are found." Also, that "an exploratory well must be assessed on its own, and the direct discovery of oil and gas reserves can be the sole determinant of whether future benefits exist and, therefore, whether an asset

should be recognized." The Board believes that the existence of future benefits is an essential characteristic of an asset. An exploratory well that is determined to be dry is not an asset. The timing of that determination has no bearing on the obligation to account for the nonexistence of the asset at the end of the period in yet-to-be issued financial statements for the period. A determination that is made after the end of the period but before financial statements for that period are issued is not an event that eliminates previously existing future benefits; the determination merely provides information as to whether future benefits did or did not exist at the end of the period and, therefore, whether an asset did or did not exist at that time.

9. Many respondents expressed concern that to finalize the proposed Interpretation would impair the comparability of financial statements of (a) different enterprises that issue their financial statements at different dates and (b) individual enterprises that issue financial statements at different times after the end of interim and annual accounting periods. They also believe that gathering data relating to exploratory wells in progress at the end of a period would be costly and might delay the release of financial statements. The Board believes these problems are not unique to this issue and exist for all contingencies that exist at the date of the financial statements.

10. A number of respondents requested that the Board define the term "before the issuance of financial statements" as it appears in this Interpretation. The Board did not do so because such a definition is beyond the scope of this Interpretation and is not unique to accounting for exploratory wells.

FASB Interpretation No. 37
Accounting for Translation Adjustments upon Sale of Part of an Investment in a Foreign Entity

an interpretation of FASB Statement No. 52

STATUS

Issued: July 1983

Effective Date: For partial sales investments after June 30, 1983

Affects: No other pronouncements

Affected by: No other pronouncements

SUMMARY

Upon sale or complete or substantially complete liquidation of an investment in a foreign entity, FASB Statement No. 52, *Foreign Currency Translation,* requires that the accumulated translation adjustment component of equity related to that investment be included in measuring the resulting gain or loss. Members of the Board's advisory group on implementation of Statement 52 and others have asked the Board to clarify the application of that requirement to a sale of part of an investment. This Interpretation indicates that the prescribed accounting applies to an enterprise's partial, as well as complete, disposal of its ownership interest.

This Interpretation is effective for transactions entered into after June 30, 1983.

FASB Interpretation No. 37
Accounting for Translation Adjustments upon Sale of Part of an Investment in a Foreign Entity

an interpretation of FASB Statement No. 52

CONTENTS

INTRODUCTION

1. The Board has been asked to clarify the application of paragraph 14 of FASB Statement No. 52, *Foreign Currency Translation,* to the sale of part of an investment in a foreign entity. That paragraph states:

> Upon sale or upon complete or substantially complete liquidation of an investment in a foreign entity, the amount attributable to that entity and accumulated in the translation adjustment component of equity shall be removed from the separate component of equity and shall be reported as part of the gain or loss on sale or liquidation of the investment for the period during which the sale or liquidation occurs.

INTERPRETATION

2. If an enterprise sells part of its ownership interest in a foreign entity, a pro rata portion of the accumulated translation adjustment component of equity attributable to that investment shall be recognized in measuring the gain or loss on the sale.[1]

EFFECTIVE DATE AND TRANSITION

3. This Interpretation shall be applied to the sale of part of an investment after June 30, 1983. Earlier application is encouraged. Restatement of previously issued financial statements is permitted but is not required.

This Interpretation was adopted by the unanimous vote of the seven members of the Financial Accounting Standards Board.

Members of the Financial Accounting Standards Board:

Donald J. Kirk, *Chairman*
Frank E. Block
Victor H. Brown
John W. March
David Mosso
Robert T. Sprouse
Ralph E. Walters

Appendix

BACKGROUND INFORMATION

4. Paragraph 111 of Statement 52 explains the rationale for excluding translation adjustments from current operating results:

> Translation adjustments do not exist in terms of functional currency cash flows. Translation adjustments are solely a result of the translation process and have no direct effect on reporting currency cash flows. Exchange rate changes have an indirect effect on the net investment that may be realized upon sale or liquidation, but that effect is related to the net investment and not to the operations of the investee. Prior to sale or liquidation, that effect is so uncertain and remote as to require that translation adjustments arising currently should not be reported as part of operating results.

Upon sale or upon complete or substantially complete liquidation of an investment in a foreign entity, paragraph 14 of Statement 52 requires that the accumulated translation adjustment attributable to that investment be removed from equity and included in determining the gain or loss on sale or liquidation. Paragraph 119 of Statement 52 indicates that:

[1]Under APB Opinion No. 30, *Reporting the Results of Operations,* a gain or loss on disposal of part or all of a net investment may be recognized in a period other than that in which actual sale or liquidation occurs. Paragraph 14 of Statement 52 does not alter the period in which a gain or loss on sale or liquidation is recognized under existing generally accepted accounting principles.

> . . . Sale and complete or substantially complete liquidation were selected because those events generally cause a related gain or loss on the net investment to be recognized in net income at that time. That procedure recognizes the "unrealized" translation adjustment as a component of net income when it becomes "realized."

5. Some members of the Board's advisory group on implementation of Statement 52 and others have questioned whether an enterprise's sale of part of its ownership interest in a foreign entity requires that a pro rata part of the accumulated translation adjustment attributable to that investment be recognized in measuring the gain or loss on the sale.

6. A proposed Interpretation, *Accounting for Translation Adjustments upon Sale of Part of an Investment in a Foreign Entity,* was released for public comment on February 16, 1983. The Board received 45 letters of comment on the proposed Interpretation. Certain of the comments received and the Board's consideration of them are discussed in paragraphs 7 and 8.

7. Respondents unanimously agreed with the Board's conclusion that the rationale stated in paragraph 119 of Statement 52 for recognition of translation adjustments in income when realized through sale of an investment requires proportionate recognition when an enterprise sells part of its ownership interest. However, some respondents believe that events other than a sale of some or all of an investor's ownership interest and complete or substantially complete liquidation of an investment should require recognition of translation adjustments in net income. Views concerning which additional events should require such recognition included a subsidiary's sale of additional stock, liquidations of assets and liabilities by a subsidiary, and any reduction in an investor's net investment, including dividends and the payment of long-term intercompany accounts.

8. As discussed in paragraphs 110-119 of Statement 52, whether events other than an investor's sale of an ownership interest and complete or substantially complete liquidation should cause recognition of translation adjustments in net income was thoroughly considered by the Board before the issuance of that Statement. Information and developments that have come to the Board's attention since that time have not caused the Board to reconsider its conclusions with respect to that issue. For example, the Board is aware that a partial liquidation by a subsidiary may be considered to be similar to a sale of part of an ownership interest if the liquidation proceeds are distributed to the parent. However, extending pro rata recognition to such partial liquidations would require that their substance be distinguished from ordinary dividends. The Board is unconvinced that such a distinction is either possible or desirable. Further, paragraph 119 of Statement 52 states the Board's view that the information provided by recognizing "realized" translation adjustments in net income is probably marginal and gives the reasons for restricting recognition to sale and complete or substantially complete liquidation. Accordingly, this Interpretation is restricted to clarifying that a sale includes an investor's partial, as well as complete, disposal of its ownership interest.

(The next page is 4017.)

Statements of
Financial Accounting Concepts

TABLE OF CONTENTS

Statement of Financial Accounting Concepts No. 1
Objectives of Financial Reporting by Business Enterprises

STATUS

Issued: November 1978

HIGHLIGHTS

[Best understood in context of full Statement]

- Financial reporting is not an end in itself but is intended to provide information that is useful in making business and economic decisions.
- The objectives of financial reporting are not immutable—they are affected by the economic, legal, political, and social environment in which financial reporting takes place.
- The objectives are also affected by the characteristics and limitations of the kind of information that financial reporting can provide.

  —The information pertains to business enterprises rather than to industries or the economy as a whole.

  —The information often results from approximate, rather than exact, measures.

  —The information largely reflects the financial effects of transactions and events that have already happened.

  —The information is but one source of information needed by those who make decisions about business enterprises.

  —The information is provided and used at a cost.

- The objectives in this Statement are those of general purpose external financial reporting by business enterprises.

  —The objectives stem primarily from the needs of external users who lack the authority to prescribe the information they want and must rely on information management communicates to them.

  —The objectives are directed toward the common interests of many users in the ability of an enterprise to generate favorable cash flows but are phrased using investment and credit decisions as a reference to give them a focus. The objectives are intended to be broad rather than narrow.

  —The objectives pertain to financial reporting and are not restricted to financial statements.

- The objectives state that:

  —Financial reporting should provide information that is useful to present and potential investors and creditors and other users in making rational investment, credit, and similar decisions. The information should be comprehensible to those who have a reasonable understanding of business and economic activities and are willing to study the information with reasonable diligence.

—Financial reporting should provide information to help present and potential investors and creditors and other users in assessing the amounts, timing, and uncertainty of prospective cash receipts from dividends or interest and the proceeds from the sale, redemption, or maturity of securities or loans. Since investors' and creditors' cash flows are related to enterprise cash flows, financial reporting should provide information to help investors, creditors, and others assess the amounts, timing, and uncertainty of prospective net cash inflows to the related enterprise.

—Financial reporting should provide information about the economic resources of an enterprise, the claims to those resources (obligations of the enterprise to transfer resources to other entities and owners' equity), and the effects of transactions, events, and circumstances that change its resources and claims to those resources.

- "Investors" and "creditors" are used broadly and include not only those who have or contemplate having a claim to enterprise resources but also those who advise or represent them.

- Although investment and credit decisions reflect investors' and creditors' expectations about future enterprise performance, those expectations are commonly based at least partly on evaluations of past enterprise performance.

- The primary focus of financial reporting is information about earnings and its components.

- Information about enterprise earnings based on accrual accounting generally provides a better indication of an enterprise's present and continuing ability to generate favorable cash flows than information limited to the financial effects of cash receipts and payments.

- Financial reporting is expected to provide information about an enterprise's financial performance during a period and about how management of an enterprise has discharged its stewardship responsibility to owners.

- Financial accounting is not designed to measure directly the value of a business enterprise, but the information it provides may be helpful to those who wish to estimate its value.

- Investors, creditors, and others may use reported earnings and information about the elements of financial statements in various ways to assess the prospects for cash flows. They may wish, for example, to evaluate management's performance, estimate "earning power," predict future earnings, assess risk, or to confirm, change, or reject earlier predictions or assessments. Although financial reporting should provide basic information to aid them, they do their own evaluating, estimating, predicting, assessing, confirming, changing, or rejecting.

- Management knows more about the enterprise and its affairs than investors, creditors, or other "outsiders" and accordingly can often increase the usefulness of financial information by identifying certain events and circumstances and explaining their financial effects on the enterprise.

* * * * *

Statement of Financial Accounting Concepts No. 1
Objectives of Financial Reporting by Business Enterprises

STATEMENTS OF FINANCIAL ACCOUNTING CONCEPTS

This is the first in a series of Statements of Financial Accounting Concepts. The purpose of the series is to set forth fundamentals on which financial accounting and reporting standards will be based. More specifically, Statements of Financial Accounting Concepts are intended to establish the objectives and concepts that the Financial Accounting Standards Board will use in developing standards of financial accounting and reporting.

The Board itself is likely to be the major user and thus the most direct beneficiary of the guidance provided by the new series. However, knowledge of the objectives and concepts the Board uses should enable all who are affected by or interested in financial accounting standards to better understand the content and limitations of information provided by financial accounting and reporting, thereby furthering their ability to use that information effectively and enhancing confidence in financial accounting and reporting. That knowledge, if used with care, may also provide guidance in resolving new or emerging problems of financial accounting and reporting in the absence of applicable authoritative pronouncements.

Unlike a Statement of Financial Accounting Standards, a Statement of Financial Accounting Concepts does not establish generally accepted accounting principles and therefore is not intended to invoke the application of Rule 203 of the Rules of Conduct of the Code of Professional Ethics of the American Institute of Certified Public Accountants (or successor rule or arrangement of similar scope and intent).* Like other pronouncements of the Board, a Statement of Financial Accounting Concepts may be amended, superseded, or withdrawn by appropriate action under the Board's *Rules of Procedure.*

The Board recognizes that in certain respects current generally accepted accounting principles may be inconsistent with those that may derive from the objectives and concepts set forth in this Statement and others in the series. In due course, the Board expects to reexamine its pronouncements, pronouncements of predecessor standard-setting bodies, and existing financial reporting practice in the light of newly enunciated objectives and concepts. In the meantime, a Statement of Financial Accounting Concepts does not (a) require a change in existing generally accepted accounting principles, (b) amend, modify, or interpret Statements of Financial Accounting Standards, Interpretations of the FASB, effective Opinions of the Accounting Principles Board, or effective Bulletins of the Committee on Accounting Procedure, or (c) justify either changing existing generally accepted accounting and reporting practices or interpreting the pronouncements listed in (b) based on personal interpretations of the objectives and concepts in the Statements of Financial Accounting Concepts.

To establish objectives and concepts will not, by itself, directly solve financial accounting and reporting problems. Rather, objectives and concepts are tools for solving problems. Moreover, although individual Statements of Financial Accounting Concepts may be issued serially, they will form a cohesive set of interrelated concepts and will often need to be used jointly.

The new series of Statements of Financial Accounting Concepts is intended and expected to serve the public interest within the context of the role of financial accounting and reporting in the economy—to provide evenhanded financial and other information that, together with information from other sources, facilitates efficient functioning of capital and other markets and otherwise assists in promoting efficient allocation of scarce resources in the economy.

*Rule 203 prohibits a member of the American Institute of Certified Public Accountants from expressing an opinion that financial statements conform with generally accepted accounting principles if those statements contain a material departure from an accounting principle promulgated by the Financial Accounting Standards Board, unless the member can demonstrate that because of unusual circumstances the financial statements otherwise would have been misleading.

Contents

This Statement contains no conclusions about matters expected to be covered in other Statements resulting from the Board's conceptual framework project, such as objectives of financial reporting by organizations other than business enterprises; elements of financial statements and their recognition, measurement, and display; capital maintenance; unit of measure; criteria for distinguishing information to be included in financial statements from that which should be provided by other means of financial reporting; and criteria for evaluating and selecting accounting information (qualitative characteristics).

INTRODUCTION AND BACKGROUND

1. This Statement establishes the objectives of general purpose external financial reporting by business enterprises. Its concentration on business enterprises is not intended to imply that the Board has concluded that the uses and objectives of financial reporting by other kinds of entities are, or should be, the same as or different from those of business enterprises. Those and related matters, including whether and, if so, how business enterprises and other organizations should be distinguished for the purpose of establishing objectives of and basic concepts underlying financial reporting, are issues in another phase of the Board's conceptual framework project.[1]

2. This Statement is the first of a planned series of publications in the Board's conceptual framework project. Later Statements are expected to cover the elements of financial statements and their recognition, measurement, and display as well as related matters such as capital maintenance, unit of measure, criteria for distinguishing information to be included in financial statements from that which should be provided by other means of financial reporting, and criteria for evaluating and selecting accounting information (qualitative characteristics). Accordingly, this Statement contains no conclusions about matters such as the identity, number, or form of financial statements or about the attributes to be measured[2] or the unit of measure to be used. Thus, although designation in the objectives of certain information as relevant has implications for communicating the information, the Statement should not be interpreted as implying a particular set of financial statements. Nor should the Statement be interpreted as suggesting that the relative merits of various attributes, such as historical cost/historical proceeds or current cost/current proceeds, have been resolved. Similarly, references in it to measures in units of money should not be interpreted as precluding the possibility of measures in constant dollars (units of money having constant purchasing power).

3. This Statement also does not specify financial accounting standards prescribing accounting procedures or disclosure practices for particular items or events; rather it describes concepts and relations that will underlie future financial accounting standards and practices and in due course serve as a basis for evaluating existing standards and practices. Its effect on financial reporting will be reflected primarily in Statements of Financial Accounting Standards (please see "Statements of Financial Accounting Concepts" on page 4023). Until the FASB reexamines its pronouncements, pronouncements of predecessor standard-setting bodies, and existing financial reporting practices, pronounce-

[1] In August 1977, the Board announced its sponsorship of a research study on the objectives and basic concepts underlying financial reporting by organizations other than business enterprises. The Board published the research report, *Financial Accounting in Nonbusiness Organizations: An Exploratory Study of Conceptual Issues,* by Robert N. Anthony, in May 1978. It issued a *Discussion Memorandum,* "Objectives of Financial Reporting by Nonbusiness Organizations," in June 1978 and held public hearings in October and November 1978.

[2] "Attributes to be measured" refers to the traits or aspects of an element to be quantified or measured, such as historical cost/historical proceeds, current cost/current proceeds, etc. Attribute is a narrower concept than measurement, which includes not only identifying the attribute to be measured but also selecting a scale of measurement (for example, units of money or units of constant purchasing power). "Property" is commonly used in the sciences to describe the trait or aspect of an object being measured, such as the length of a table or the weight of a stone. But "property" may be confused with land and buildings in financial reporting contexts, and "attribute" has become common in accounting literature and is used in this Statement.

ments such as *APB Statement No. 4,* "Basic Concepts and Accounting Principles Underlying Financial Statements of Business Enterprises," or the *Accounting Terminology Bulletins* will continue to serve their intended purpose—to describe objectives and concepts underlying standards and practices existing before the issuance of this Statement.

4. This Statement includes a brief exposition of the reasons for the Board's conclusions.[3] It therefore includes no separate Appendix containing a basis for conclusions. Appendix A to this Statement contains background information for the Statement.

Financial Statements and Financial Reporting

5. The objectives in this Statement pertain to financial reporting and are not restricted to information communicated by financial statements. Although financial reporting and financial statements have essentially the same objectives, some useful information is better provided by financial statements and some is better provided, or can only be provided, by means of financial reporting other than financial statements. The following paragraphs briefly describe some major characteristics of financial reporting and financial statements and give some examples, but they draw no clear distinction between financial reporting and financial statements and leave extremely broad the scope of financial reporting. The Board will draw boundaries, as needed, in other parts of the conceptual framework project or in financial accounting standards.

6. Financial statements are a central feature of financial reporting. They are a principal means of communicating accounting information to those outside an enterprise. Although financial statements may also contain information from sources other than accounting records, accounting systems are generally organized on the basis of the elements of financial statements (assets, liabilities, revenues, expenses, etc.) and provide the bulk of the information for financial statements. The financial statements now most frequently provided are (a) balance sheet or statement of financial position, (b) income or earnings statement, (c) statement of retained earnings, (d) statement of other changes in owners' or stockholders' equity, and (e) statement of changes in financial position (statement of sources and applications of funds). To list those examples from existing practice implies no conclusions about the identity, number, or form of financial statements because those matters are yet to be considered in the conceptual framework project (paragraph 2).

7. Financial reporting includes not only financial statements but also other means of communicating information that relates, directly or indirectly, to the information provided by the accounting system—that is, information about an enterprise's resources, obligations, earnings, etc. Management may communicate information to those outside an enterprise by means of financial reporting other than formal financial statements either because the information is required to be disclosed by authoritative pronouncement, regulatory rule, or custom or because management considers it useful to those outside the enterprise and discloses it voluntarily. Information communicated by means of financial reporting other than financial statements may take various forms and relate to various matters. Corporate annual reports, prospectuses, and annual reports filed with the Securities and Exchange Commission are common examples of reports that include financial statements, other financial information, and nonfinancial information. News releases, management's forecasts or other descriptions of its plans or expectations, and descriptions of an enterprise's social or environmental impact are examples of reports giving financial information other than financial statements or giving only nonfinancial information.

8. Financial statements are often audited by independent accountants for the purpose of enhancing confidence in their reliability. Some financial reporting by management outside the financial statements is audited, or is reviewed but not audited, by independent accountants or other experts, and some is provided by management without audit or review by persons outside the enterprise.

Environmental Context of Objectives

9. Financial reporting is not an end in itself but is intended to provide information that is useful in making business and economic decisions—for making reasoned choices among alternative uses of scarce resources in the conduct of business and economic activities. Thus, the objectives set forth stem largely from the needs of those for whom the information is intended, which in turn depend significantly on the nature of the economic activities and decisions with which the users are involved. Accordingly, the objectives in this Statement are affected by the economic, legal, political, and social environment in the United States. The objectives are also affected by characteristics and limitations of the information that financial reporting can provide (paragraphs 17-23).

[3]The Board has previously provided a more detailed discussion of the environment of financial reporting and the basis underlying the Board's conclusions on objectives of financial reporting by business enterprises in Chapters 1-3 of *Tentative Conclusions on Objectives of Financial Statements of Business Enterprises* (Stamford, CT: Financial Accounting Standards Board, December 2, 1976). The Board may reissue pertinent parts of that discussion, and perhaps other related material, in a more permanent publication.

10. The United States has a highly developed exchange economy. Most goods and services are exchanged for money or claims to money instead of being consumed by their producers. Most goods and services have money prices, and cash (ready money, including currency, coins, and money on deposit) is prized because of what it can buy. Members of the society carry out their consumption, saving, and investment decisions by allocating their present and expected cash resources.

11. Production and marketing of goods and services often involve long, continuous, or intricate processes that require large amounts of capital, which in turn require substantial saving in the economy. Savings are often invested through a complex set of intermediaries which offer savers diverse types of ownership and creditor claims, many of which can be freely traded or otherwise converted to cash.

12. Most productive activity in the United States is carried on through investor-owned business enterprises, including many large corporations that buy, sell, and obtain financing in national or multinational markets. Since investor-owners are commonly more interested in returns from dividends and market price appreciation of their securities than in active participation in directing corporate affairs, directors and professional managers commonly control enterprise resources and decide how those resources are allocated in enterprise operations. Management is accountable to owner-investors, both directly and through an elected board of directors, for planning and controlling enterprise operations in their interests, including gaining or maintaining competitive advantage or parity in the markets in which the enterprise buys, sells, and obtains financing and considering and balancing various other, often competing interests, such as those of employees, customers, lenders, suppliers, and government.

13. Business enterprises raise capital for production and marketing activities not only from financial institutions and small groups of individuals but also from the public through issuing equity and debt securities that are widely traded in highly developed securities markets. Numerous, perhaps most, transactions in those markets are transfers from one investor or creditor to another with no part of the exchange price going to the issuing enterprise. But those transactions set the market prices for particular securities and thereby affect an enterprise's ability to attract investment funds and its cost of raising capital. Those having funds to invest normally assess the expected costs, expected returns, and expected risks of alternative investment opportunities. They attempt to balance expected risks and returns and generally invest in high risk ventures only if they expect commensurately high returns and will accept low expected returns only if expected risk is commensurately low. A business enterprise is unlikely to be able to compete successfully in the markets for lendable or investment funds unless lenders and investors expect the enterprise to be able to sell its output at prices sufficiently in excess of its costs to enable them to expect a return from interest or dividends and market price appreciation commensurate with the risks they perceive. Thus, well-developed securities markets tend to allocate scarce resources to enterprises that use them efficiently and away from inefficient enterprises.

14. In the United States, productive resources are generally privately owned rather than government owned. Markets—which vary from those that are highly competitive, including many commodities and securities markets, to those that involve regulated monopolies, including markets for telephone service or electricity—are significant factors in resource allocation in the economy. However, government intervenes in the allocation process in many ways and for various purposes. For example, it intervenes directly by collecting taxes, borrowing, and spending for its purchases of goods and services for government operations and programs; by regulating business activities; or by paying subsidies. It intervenes less directly through broad tax, monetary, and fiscal policies. Government also has a broad interest in the impact of business enterprises on the community at large and may intervene to alter that impact. Many government interventions are expressly designed to work through market forces, but even government actions that are not so designed may significantly affect the balance of market forces.

15. Moreover, government is a major supplier of economic statistics and other economic information that are widely used by management, investors, and others interested in individual business enterprises and are commonly included in news reports and other statistics and analyses in ways that may broadly affect perceptions about business and economic matters. Although government statistics are primarily "macro" in nature (pertaining to the economy as a whole or to large segments of it) and do not generally disclose much about individual business enterprises, they are based to a considerable extent on information of the kind provided by financial reporting by individual business enterprises.

16. The effectiveness of individuals, enterprises, markets, and government in allocating scarce resources among competing uses is enhanced if

those who make economic decisions have information that reflects the relative standing and performance of business enterprises to assist them in evaluating alternative courses of action and the expected returns, costs, and risks of each. The function of financial reporting is to provide information that is useful to those who make economic decisions about business enterprises and about investments in or loans to business enterprises. Independent auditors commonly examine or review financial statements and perhaps other information, and both those who provide and those who use that information often view an independent auditor's opinion as enhancing the reliability or credibility of the information.

Characteristics and Limitations of Information Provided

17. The objectives of financial reporting are affected not only by the environment in which financial reporting takes place but also by the characteristics and limitations of the kind of information that financial reporting, and particularly financial statements, can provide. The information is to a significant extent financial information based on approximate measures of the financial effects on individual business enterprises of transactions and events that have already happened; it cannot be provided or used without incurring a cost.

18. The information provided by financial reporting is primarily financial in nature—it is generally quantified and expressed in units of money. Information that is to be formally incorporated in financial statements must be quantifiable in units of money. Other information can be disclosed in financial statements (including notes) or by other means, but financial statements involve adding, subtracting, multiplying, and dividing numbers depicting economic things and events and require a common denominator. The numbers are usually exchange prices or amounts derived from exchange prices. Quantified nonfinancial information (such as number of employees or units of product produced or sold) and nonquantified information (such as descriptions of operations or explanations of policies) that are reported normally relate to or underlie the financial information. Financial information is often limited by the need to measure in units of money or by constraints inherent in procedures, such as verification, that are commonly used to enhance the reliability or objectivity of the information.

19. The information provided by financial reporting pertains to individual business enterprises, which may comprise two or more affiliated entities, rather than to industries or an economy as a whole or to members of society as consumers. Financial reporting may provide information about industries and economies in which an enterprise operates but usually only to the extent the information is relevant to understanding the enterprise. It does not attempt to measure the degree to which the consumption of wealth satisfies consumers' wants. Since business enterprises are producers and distributors of scarce resources, financial reporting bears on the allocation of economic resources to producing and distributing activities and focuses on the creation of, use of, and rights to wealth and the sharing of risks associated with wealth.

20. The information provided by financial reporting often results from approximate, rather than exact, measures. The measures commonly involve numerous estimates, classifications, summarizations, judgments, and allocations. The outcome of economic activity in a dynamic economy is uncertain and results from combinations of many factors. Thus, despite the aura of precision that may seem to surround financial reporting in general and financial statements in particular, with few exceptions the measures are approximations, which may be based on rules and conventions, rather than exact amounts.

21. The information provided by financial reporting largely reflects the financial effects of transactions and events that have already happened. Management may communicate information about its plans or projections, but financial statements and most other financial reporting are historical. For example, the acquisition price of land, the current market price of a marketable equity security, and the current replacement price of an inventory are all historical data—no future prices are involved. Estimates resting on expectations of the future are often needed in financial reporting, but their major use, especially of those formally incorporated in financial statements, is to measure financial effects of past transactions or events or the present status of an asset or liability. For example, if depreciable assets are accounted for at cost, estimates of useful lives are needed to determine current depreciation and the current undepreciated cost of the asset. Even the discounted amount of future cash payments required by a long-term debt contract is, as the name implies, a "present value" of the liability. The information is largely historical, but those who use it may try to predict the future or may use the information to confirm or reject their previous predictions. To provide information about the past as an aid in assessing the future is not to imply that the future can be predicted merely by extrapolating past trends or relationships. Users of the information need to assess the possible or probable impact of factors that may cause change and form their own expectations about the future and its relation to the past.

22. Financial reporting is but one source of information needed by those who make economic decisions about business enterprises. Business enterprises and those who have economic interests in them are affected by numerous factors that interact with each other in complex ways. Those who use financial information for business and economic decisions need to combine information provided by financial reporting with pertinent information from other sources, for example, information about general economic conditions or expectations, political events and political climate, or industry outlook.

23. The information provided by financial reporting involves a cost to provide and use, and generally the benefits of information provided should be expected to at least equal the cost involved. The cost includes not only the resources directly expended to provide the information but may also include adverse effects on an enterprise or its stockholders from disclosing it. For example, comments about a pending lawsuit may jeopardize a successful defense, or comments about future plans may jeopardize a competitive advantage. The collective time needed to understand and use information is also a cost. Sometimes a disparity between costs and benefits is obvious. However, the benefits from financial information are usually difficult or impossible to measure objectively, and the costs often are; different persons will honestly disagree about whether the benefits of the information justify its costs.

Potential Users and Their Interests

24. Many people base economic decisions on their relationships to and knowledge about business enterprises and thus are potentially interested in the information provided by financial reporting. Among the potential users are owners, lenders, suppliers, potential investors and creditors, employees, management, directors, customers, financial analysts and advisors, brokers, underwriters, stock exchanges, lawyers, economists, taxing authorities, regulatory authorities, legislators, financial press and reporting agencies, labor unions, trade associations, business researchers, teachers and students, and the public. Members and potential members of some groups—such as owners, creditors, and employees—have or contemplate having direct economic interests in particular business enterprises. Managers and directors, who are charged with managing the enterprise in the interest of owners (paragraph 12), also have a direct interest. Members of other groups—such as financial analysts and advisors, regulatory authorities, and labor unions—have derived or indirect interests because they advise or represent those who have or contemplate having direct interests.

25. Potential users of financial information most directly concerned with a particular business enterprise are generally interested in its ability to generate favorable cash flows because their decisions relate to amounts, timing, and uncertainties of expected cash flows. To investors, lenders, suppliers, and employees, a business enterprise is a source of cash in the form of dividends or interest and perhaps appreciated market prices, repayment of borrowing, payment for goods or services, or salaries or wages.They invest cash, goods, or services in an enterprise and expect to obtain sufficient cash in return to make the investment worthwhile. They are directly concerned with the ability of the enterprise to generate favorable cash flows and may also be concerned with how the market's perception of that ability affects the relative prices of its securities. To customers, a business enterprise is a source of goods or services, but only by obtaining sufficient cash to pay for the resources it uses and to meet its other obligations can the enterprise provide those goods or services. To managers, the cash flows of a business enterprise are a significant part of their management responsibilities, including their accountability to directors and owners. Many, if not most, of their decisions have cash flow consequences for the enterprise. Thus, investors, creditors, employees, customers, and managers significantly share a common interest in an enterprise's ability to generate favorable cash flows. Other potential users of financial information share the same interest, derived from investors, creditors, employees, customers, or managers whom they advise or represent or derived from an interest in how those groups (and especially stockholders) are faring.

26. Some of the potential users listed in paragraph 24 may have specialized needs but also have the power to obtain information needed. For example, both the information needed to enforce tax laws and regulations and the information needed to set rates for public utilities are specialized needs. However, although both taxing authorities and rate-making bodies often use the information in financial statements for their purposes, both also have statutory authority to require the specific information they need to fulfill their functions and do not need to rely on information provided to other groups. Some investors and creditors or potential investors and creditors may also be able to require a business enterprise to provide specified information to meet a particular need—for example, a bank or insurance company negotiating with an enterprise for a large loan or private placement of securities can often obtain desired information by making the information a condition for completing the transaction.

27. Except for management, and to some extent directors, the potential users listed in paragraph 24 are commonly described as "external users," and accounting and reporting are sometimes divided conventionally into internal and external parts. That broad distinction more nearly suits the purposes of this Statement than does another common conventional distinction—that between managerial or management accounting (which is designed to assist management decision making, planning, and control at the various administrative levels of an enterprise) and financial accounting (which is concerned with accounting for an enterprise's assets, liabilities, revenues, expenses, earnings, etc.)[4] because management uses information provided by both management accounting and financial accounting. Management needs, in addition to financial accounting information, a great deal of management accounting information to carry out its responsibilities in planning and controlling operations. Much of that information relates to particular decisions or to particular cost or profit centers and is often provided in more detail than is considered necessary or appropriate for external financial reporting, even though the same accounting system normally accumulates, processes, and provides the information whether it is called managerial or financial or internal or external. Directors usually have access to at least some information available to management that is normally not provided outside an enterprise. Since management accounting is internal to an enterprise, it can usually be tailored to meet management's informational needs and is beyond the scope of this Statement.

General Purpose External Financial Reporting

28. The objectives in this Statement are those of general purpose external financial reporting by business enterprises. The objectives stem primarily from the informational needs of external users who lack the authority to prescribe the financial information they want from an enterprise and therefore must use the information that management communicates to them. Those potential users include most of the groups listed in paragraph 24.

29. Financial reporting has both an internal and an external aspect, and this Statement focuses on the external aspect. Management is as interested in information about assets, liabilities, earnings, and related elements as external users and, among its other requirements, generally needs the same kinds of information about those elements as external users (paragraph 25). Thus, management is a major user of the same information that is provided by external financial reporting. However, management's primary role in external financial reporting is that of communicating information for use by others. For that reason, it has a direct interest in the cost, adequacy, and understandability of external financial reporting.

30. General purpose external financial reporting is directed toward the common interest of various potential users in the ability of an enterprise to generate favorable cash flows (paragraph 25). Thus, the objectives in this Statement are focused on information for investment and credit decisions for reasons that are largely pragmatic, not to narrow their scope. The objectives need a focus to avoid being vague or highly abstract. Investors and creditors and their advisors are the most obvious prominent external groups who use the information provided by financial reporting and who generally lack the authority to prescribe the information they want. Their decisions and their uses of information have been studied and described to a much greater extent than those of other external groups, and their decisions significantly affect the allocation of resources in the economy. In addition, information provided to meet investors' and creditors' needs is likely to be generally useful to members of other groups who are interested in essentially the same financial aspects of business enterprises as investors and creditors.

31. For convenience, *financial reporting* is used in place of *general purpose external financial reporting by business enterprises* in the remainder of this Statement.

OBJECTIVES OF FINANCIAL REPORTING

32. The following objectives of financial reporting flow from the preceding paragraphs and proceed from the more general to the more specific. The objectives begin with a broad focus on information that is useful in investment and credit decisions; then narrow that focus to investors' and creditors' primary interest in the prospects of receiving cash from their investments in or loans to business enterprises and the relation of those prospects to the enterprise's prospects; and finally focus on information about an enterprise's economic resources, the claims to those resources, and changes in them, including measures of the enterprise's performance, that is useful in assessing the enterprise's cash flow prospects. The reasons for focusing the objectives of financial reporting primarily on investment, credit,

[4]That distinction between managerial and financial accounting is made, for example, by Eric L. Kohler, *A Dictionary for Accountants,* 5th ed. (Englewood Cliffs, NJ: Prentice-Hall, Inc., 1975), pp. 208 and 303, and by Sidney Davidson, James S. Schindler, Clyde P. Stickney, and Roman L. Weil, *Accounting: The Language of Business,* 3rd ed. (Glen Ridge, NJ: Thomas Horton and Daughters, Inc., 1977), pp. 24 and 34.

and similar decisions are given in paragraph 30. That focus and wording do not mean that the objectives apply only to investors and creditors and exclude everyone else. To the contrary, information that satisfies the objectives should be useful to all who are interested in an enterprise's future capacity to pay or in how investors or creditors are faring.

33. The objectives are those of financial reporting rather than goals for investors, creditors, or others who use the information or goals for the economy or society as a whole. The role of financial reporting in the economy is to provide information that is useful in making business and economic decisions, not to determine what those decisions should be. For example, saving and investing in productive resources (capital formation) are generally considered to be prerequisite to increasing the standard of living in an economy. To the extent that financial reporting provides information that helps identify relatively efficient and inefficient users of resources, aids in assessing relative returns and risks of investment opportunities, or otherwise assists in promoting efficient functioning of capital and other markets, it helps to create a favorable environment for capital formation decisions. However, investors, creditors, and others make those decisions, and it is not a function of financial reporting to try to determine or influence the outcomes of those decisions. The role of financial reporting requires it to provide evenhanded, neutral, or unbiased information. Thus, for example, information that indicates that a relatively inefficient user of resources is efficient or that investing in a particular enterprise involves less risk than it does and information that is directed toward a particular goal, such as encouraging the reallocation of resources in favor of a particular segment of the economy, are likely to fail to serve the broader objectives that financial reporting is intended to serve.

Information Useful in Investment and Credit Decisions

34. Financial reporting should provide information that is useful to present and potential investors and creditors and other users in making rational investment, credit, and similar decisions. The information should be comprehensible to those who have a reasonable understanding of business and economic activities and are willing to study the information with reasonable diligence.

35. This Statement uses the terms investors and creditors broadly. The terms include both those who deal directly with an enterprise and those who deal through intermediaries, both those who buy securities from other investors or creditors and those who buy newly issued securities from the enterprise or an underwriter, both those who commit funds for long periods and those who trade frequently, both those who desire safety of investment and those who are willing to accept risk to obtain high rates of return, both individuals and specialized institutions. The major groups of investors are equity securityholders and debt securityholders. The major groups of creditors are suppliers of goods and services who extend credit, customers and employees with claims, lending institutions, individual lenders, and debt securityholders.[5] The terms also may comprehend security analysts and advisors, brokers, lawyers, regulatory agencies, and others who advise or represent the interests of investors and creditors or who otherwise are interested in how investors and creditors are faring.

36. Individual investors, creditors, or other potential users of financial information understand to varying degrees the business and economic environment, business activities, securities markets, and related matters. Their understanding of financial information and the way and extent to which they use and rely on it also may vary greatly. Financial information is a tool and, like most tools, cannot be of much direct help to those who are unable or unwilling to use it or who misuse it. Its use can be learned, however, and financial reporting should provide information that can be used by all—nonprofessionals as well as professionals—who are willing to learn to use it properly. Efforts may be needed to increase the understandability of financial information. Cost-benefit considerations may indicate that information understood or used by only a few should not be provided. Conversely, financial reporting should not exclude relevant information merely because it is difficult for some to understand or because some investors or creditors choose not to use it.

Information Useful in Assessing Cash Flow Prospects

37. Financial reporting should provide information to help present and potential investors and creditors and other users in assessing the amounts, timing, and uncertainty of prospective cash receipts from dividends or interest and the proceeds from the sale, redemption, or maturity of securities or loans. The prospects for those cash receipts are affected by an enterprise's ability to generate enough cash to meet its obligations when due and its other cash operating needs, to reinvest in operations, and to pay cash

[5]Debt securityholders are included in both groups because they are investors as that term is commonly used as well as creditors by contract and usual legal definition. Moreover, it is often convenient to refer to them as investors without making a precise distinction between "investors in debt securities" and "investors in equity securities." That distinction is made if it is significant.

dividends and may also be affected by perceptions of investors and creditors generally about that ability, which affect market prices of the enterprise's securities. Thus, financial reporting should provide information to help investors, creditors, and others assess the amounts, timing, and uncertainty of prospective net cash inflows to the related enterprise.[6]

38. People engage in investing, lending, and similar activities primarily to increase their cash resources. The ultimate test of success (or failure) of those activities is the extent to which they return more (or less) cash than they cost.[7] A successful investor or creditor receives not only a return *of* investment but also a return *on* that investment (cash, goods, or services) commensurate with the risk involved. Moreover, investment, credit, and similar decisions normally involve choices between present cash and future cash—for example, the choice between the price of a security that can be bought or sold or the amount of a loan and rights to expected future cash receipts from dividends or interest and proceeds from resale or repayment. Investors, creditors, and others need information to help them form rational expectations about those prospective cash receipts and assess the risk that the amounts or timing of the receipts may differ from expectations, including information that helps them assess prospective cash flows to the enterprise in which they have invested or to which they have loaned funds.

39. Business enterprises, like investors and creditors, invest cash in noncash resources to earn more cash. The test of success (or failure) of the operations of an enterprise is the extent to which the cash returned exceeds (or is less than) the cash spent (invested) over the long run (footnote 7).[8] A successful enterprise receives not only a return *of* its investment but also a satisfactory return *on* that investment. The market's assessment of an enterprise's expected success in generating favorable cash flows affects the relative market prices of its securities, although the level of market prices of securities is affected by numerous factors—such as general economic conditions, interest rates, market psychology, and the like—that are not related to particular enterprises. Thus, since an enterprise's ability to generate favorable cash flows affects both its ability to pay dividends and interest and the market prices of its securities, expected cash flows to investors and creditors are related to expected cash flows to the enterprise in which they have invested or to which they have loaned funds.

Information about Enterprise Resources, Claims to Those Resources, and Changes in Them

40. Financial reporting should provide information about the economic resources of an enterprise, the claims to those resources (obligations of the enterprise to transfer resources to other entities and owners' equity), and the effects of transactions, events, and circumstances that change resources and claims to those resources.[9]

Economic Resources, Obligations, and Owners' Equity

41. Financial reporting should provide information about an enterprise's economic resources, obligations, and owners' equity. That information helps investors, creditors, and others identify the enterprise's financial strengths and weaknesses and assess its liquidity and solvency. Information about resources, obligations, and owners' equity also provides a basis for investors, creditors, and others to

[6]Several respondents to the Exposure Draft, "Objectives of Financial Reporting and Elements of Financial Statements of Business Enterprises," interpreted this objective as requiring "cash flow information," "current value information," or "management forecast information." However, the objective focuses on the purpose for which information provided should be useful—emphasizing the importance of cash to people and the activities they use to increase cash inflows that also help increase the productive resources and outputs of goods and services in an economy—rather than the kinds of information that may be useful for that purpose. The objective neither requires nor prohibits "cash flow information," "current value information," "management forecast information," or any other specific information. Conclusions about "current value information" and "management forecast information" are beyond the scope of this Statement. Paragraphs 42-44 note that information about cash receipts and disbursements is not usually considered to be the most useful information for the purposes described in this objective.

[7]Questions of measurement scale and unit of measure are beyond the scope of this Statement (paragraph 2). Therefore, the description in paragraphs 38, 39, and others ignore, for example, that a dollar of cash received as dividends, interest, or proceeds from resale or repayment is not necessarily equal in purchasing power to a dollar invested or loaned earlier, a dollar of cash collected from customers is not necessarily equal in purchasing power to a dollar spent earlier, and a dollar of cash paid to a creditor is not necessarily equal in purchasing power to a dollar received earlier.

[8]Descriptions of operations of business enterprises commonly describe a cycle that begins with cash outlays and ends with cash receipts. That description is not only straightforward and convenient but also generally fits manufacturing, merchandising, financial, and service enterprises whose operations comprise primarily activities such as acquiring goods and services, increasing their value by adding time, place, or form utility, selling them, and collecting the selling price. Cash receipts may precede cash payments, however, and commonly do in the operations of some service and financial enterprises. The order of cash flows does not affect the basic nature of operations but may complicate descriptions and analyses.

[9]Economic resources, claims to those resources, changes in resources and claims, and the elements that represent them in financial statements are the subject of the next phase in the Board's conceptual framework project on elements of financial statements of business enterprises.

evaluate information about the enterprise's performance during a period (paragraphs 42-48). Moreover, it provides direct indications of the cash flow potentials of some resources and of the cash needed to satisfy many, if not most, obligations. That is, some of an enterprise's resources are direct sources of cash to the enterprise, many obligations are direct causes of cash payments by the enterprise, and reasonably reliable measures of future net cash inflows or future net cash outflows are often possible for those resources and obligations. Many cash flows cannot be identified with individual resources (or some obligations), however, because they are the joint result of combining various resources in the enterprise's operations. Indirect measures of cash flow potential are widely considered necessary or desirable, both for particular resources and for enterprises as a whole. That information may help those who desire to estimate the value of a business enterprise, but financial accounting is not designed to measure directly the value of an enterprise.

Enterprise Performance and Earnings

42. Financial reporting should provide information about an enterprise's financial performance during a period. Investors and creditors often use information about the past to help in assessing the prospects of an enterprise. Thus, although investment and credit decisions reflect investors' and creditors' expectations about future enterprise performance, those expectations are commonly based at least partly on evaluations of past enterprise performance.[10]

43. The primary focus of financial reporting is information about an enterprise's performance provided by measures of earnings and its components. Investors, creditors, and others who are concerned with assessing the prospects for enterprise net cash inflows are especially interested in that information. Their interest in an enterprise's future cash flows and its ability to generate favorable cash flows leads primarily to an interest in information about its earnings rather than information directly about its cash flows. Financial statements that show only cash receipts and payments during a short period, such as a year, cannot adequately indicate whether or not an enterprise's performance is successful.

44. Information about enterprise earnings and its components measured by accrual accounting generally provides a better indication of enterprise performance than information about current cash receipts and payments. Accrual accounting attempts to record the financial effects on an enterprise of transactions and other events and circumstances that have cash consequences for an enterprise in the periods in which those transactions, events, and circumstances occur rather than only in the periods in which cash is received or paid by the enterprise. Accrual accounting is concerned with the process by which cash expended on resources and activities is returned as more (or perhaps less) cash to the enterprise, not just with the beginning and end of that process. It recognizes that the buying, producing, selling, and other operations of an enterprise during a period, as well as other events that affect enterprise performance, often do not coincide with the cash receipts and payments of the period.

45. Periodic earnings measurement involves relating to periods the benefits from and the costs[11] of operations and other transactions, events, and circumstances that affect an enterprise. Although business enterprises invest cash to obtain a return *on* investment as well as a return *of* investment, the investment of cash and its return often do not occur in the same period. Modern business activities are largely conducted on credit and often involve long and complex financial arrangements or production or marketing processes. An enterprise's receivables and payables, inventory, investments, property, plant, equipment, and other noncash resources and obligations are the links between its operations and other transactions, events, and circumstances that affect it and its cash receipts and outlays. For example, labor is often used by an enterprise before it is paid for, requiring that salaries and wages payable be accrued to recognize the obligation and measure the effects on earnings in the period the labor is used rather than when the payroll checks are issued. Conversely, resources such as raw materials and equipment may be paid for by an enterprise in a period that does not coincide with their use, requiring that the resources on hand be recognized and that the effect on earnings be deferred until the periods the resources are used. Similarly, receivables and the related effects on earnings must often be accrued before the related cash is received, or obligations must be recognized when cash is received and the effects on earnings must be identified with the

[10]Investors and creditors ordinarily invest in or lend to enterprises that they expect to continue in operation—an expectation that is familiar to accountants as "the going concern" assumption. Information about the past is usually less useful in assessing prospects for an enterprise's future if the enterprise is in liquidation or is expected to enter liquidation. Then, emphasis shifts from performance to liquidation of the enterprise's resources and obligations. The objectives of financial reporting do not necessarily change if an enterprise shifts from expected operation to expected liquidation, but the information that is relevant to those objectives, including measures of elements of financial statements may change.

[11]"Cost" is the sacrifice incurred in economic activities—that which is given up or foregone to consume, to save, to exchange, to produce, etc. For example, the value of cash or other resources given up (or the present value of an obligation incurred) in exchange for a resource is the cost of the resource acquired. Similarly, the expiration of future benefits caused by using a resource in production is the cost of using it.

periods in which goods or services are provided. The goal of accrual and deferral of benefits and sacrifices is to relate the accomplishments and the efforts so that reported earnings measures an enterprise's performance during a period instead of merely listing its cash receipts and outlays.[12]

46. Earnings and its components relate to an individual enterprise during a particular period. Over the life of an enterprise (or other very long period), total reported earnings equals the net cash receipts excluding those from capital changes (ignoring changes in value of money noted in footnote 7), but that relationship between earnings and cash flows rarely, if ever, holds for periods as short as a year. The major difference between periodic earnings measured by accrual accounting and statements of cash receipts and outlays is timing of recognition of the components of earnings.

47. Investors, creditors, and others often use reported earnings and information about the components of earnings in various ways and for various purposes in assessing their prospects for cash flows from investments in or loans to an enterprise. For example, they may use earnings information to help them (a) evaluate management's performance, (b) estimate "earning power" or other amounts they perceive as "representative" of long-term earning ability of an enterprise, (c) predict future earnings, or (d) assess the risk of investing in or lending to an enterprise. They may use the information to confirm, reassure themselves about, or reject or change their own or others' earlier predictions or assessments. Measures of earnings and information about earnings disclosed by financial reporting should, to the extent possible, be useful for those and similar uses and purposes.

48. However, accrual accounting provides measures of earnings rather than evaluations of management's performance, estimates of "earning power," predictions of earnings, assessments of risk, or confirmations or rejections of predictions or assessments. Investors, creditors, and other users of the information do their own evaluating, estimating, predicting, assessing, confirming, or rejecting. For example, procedures such as averaging or normalizing reported earnings for several periods and ignoring or averaging out the financial effects of "nonrepresentative" transactions and events are commonly used in estimating "earning power." However, both the concept of "earning power" and the techniques for estimating it are part of financial analysis and are beyond the scope of financial reporting.

Liquidity, Solvency, and Funds Flows

49. Financial reporting should provide information about how an enterprise obtains and spends cash, about its borrowing and repayment of borrowing, about its capital transactions, including cash dividends and other distributions of enterprise resources to owners, and about other factors that may affect an enterprise's liquidity or solvency. For example, although reports of an enterprise's cash receipts and cash outlays during a period are generally less useful than earnings information for measuring enterprise performance during a period and for assessing an enterprise's ability to generate favorable cash flows (paragraphs 42-46), information about cash flows or other funds flows may be useful in understanding the operations of an enterprise, evaluating its financing activities, assessing its liquidity or solvency, or interpreting earnings information provided. Information about earnings and economic resources, obligations, and owners' equity may also be useful in assessing an enterprise's liquidity or solvency.

Management Stewardship and Performance

50. Financial reporting should provide information about how management of an enterprise has discharged its stewardship responsibility to owners (stockholders) for the use of enterprise resources entrusted to it. Management of an enterprise is periodically accountable to the owners not only for the custody and safekeeping of enterprise resources but also for their efficient and profitable use and for protecting them to the extent possible from unfavorable economic impacts of factors in the economy such as inflation or deflation and technological and social changes. To the extent that management offers securities of the enterprise to the public, it voluntarily accepts wider responsibilities for accountability to prospective investors and to the public in general. Society may also impose broad or specific responsibilities on enterprises and their managements.

51. Earnings information is commonly the focus for assessing management's stewardship or accountability. Management, owners, and others emphasize enterprise performance or profitability in describing how management has discharged its stewardship accountability. A central question for owners, managers, potential investors, the public, and government is how an enterprise and its owners are faring. Since earnings and its components for a single period are often an insufficient basis for assessing management's stewardship, owners and others may

[12]The process described in this paragraph is commonly called the "matching of costs and revenues," and "matching" is a significant part of it, though not the whole. "Matching" is one of the subjects of the next phase in the conceptual framework project on elements of financial statements.

estimate "earning power" or other average they consider "representative" of long-term performance. As noted in paragraph 48, however, accrual accounting measures earnings for a period rather than "earning power" or other financial analysis concepts.

52. Financial reporting should provide information that is useful to managers and directors in making decisions in the interests of owners. Although this Statement is concerned primarily with providing information to external users, managers and directors are responsible to owners (and other investors) for enterprise performance as reflected by financial reporting and they are judged at least to some extent on the enterprise performance reported. Thus, how owners have fared during a period is of equal concern to managers and owners, and information provided should be useful to both in meeting their common goal.

53. Financial reporting, and especially financial statements, usually cannot and does not separate management performance from enterprise performance. Business enterprises are highly complex institutions, and their production and marketing processes are often long and intricate. Enterprise successes and failures are the result of the interaction of numerous factors. Management ability and performance are contributing factors, but so are events and circumstances that are often beyond the control of management, such as general economic conditions, supply and demand characteristics of enterprise inputs and outputs, price changes, and fortuitous events and circumstances. What happens to a business enterprise is usually so much a joint result of a complex interaction of many factors that neither accounting nor other statistical analysis can discern with reasonable accuracy the degree to which management, or any other factor, affected the joint result. Actions of past managements affect current periods' earnings, and actions of current management affect future periods' earnings. Financial reporting provides information about an enterprise during a period when it was under the direction of a particular management but does not directly provide information about that management's performance. The information is therefore limited for purposes of assessing management performance apart from enterprise performance.

Management Explanations and Interpretations

54. Financial reporting should include explanations and interpretations to help users understand financial information provided. For example, the usefulness of financial information as an aid to investors, creditors, and others in forming expectations about a business enterprise may be enhanced by management's explanations of the information. Management knows more about the enterprise and its affairs than investors, creditors, or other "outsiders" and can often increase the usefulness of financial information by identifying certain transactions, other events, and circumstances that affect the enterprise and explaining their financial impact on it. In addition, dividing continuous operations into accounting periods is a convention and may have arbitrary effects. Management can aid investors, creditors, and others in using financial information by identifying arbitrary results caused by separating periods, explaining why the effect is arbitrary, and describing its effect on reported information. Moreover, financial reporting often provides information that depends on, or is affected by, management's estimates and judgment. Investors, creditors, and others are aided in evaluating estimates and judgmental information by explanations of underlying assumptions or methods used, including disclosure of significant uncertainties about principal underlying assumptions or estimates. Financial reporting may, of course, provide information in addition to that specified by financial accounting standards, regulatory rules, or custom.

THE CONCEPTUAL FRAMEWORK: A PERSPECTIVE

55. Paragraphs 40-54 focus the objectives of financial reporting by business enterprises on information about the economic resources of an enterprise, the claims to those resources, and the effects of transactions, events, and circumstances that change resources and claims to them. The paragraphs emphasize information about an enterprise's performance provided by measures of earnings and its components and also broadly describe other kinds of information that financial reporting should provide. The objectives lead to, but leave unanswered, questions such as the identity, number, and form of financial statements; elements of financial statements and their recognition, measurement, and display; information that should be provided by other means of financial reporting; and meanings and balancing or trading-off of relevance, reliability, and other criteria for evaluating and selecting accounting information (qualitative characteristics). Those matters are, as noted in paragraph 2, topics of other Statements that are expected to follow this Statement on objectives.

56. Financial statements are the basic means of communicating the information described in paragraphs 40-54 to those who use it. The elements of financial statements provide "... information about the economic resources of an enterprise, the claims to those resources (obligations of the enterprise to transfer resources to other entities and owners' equity), and the effects of transactions, events, and

circumstances that change resources and claims to those resources" (paragraph 40), including "... information about an enterprise's performance provided by measures of earnings and its components" (paragraph 43). Thus, the next phase of the conceptual framework project pertains to the elements of financial statements.

This Statement was adopted by the unanimous vote of the seven members of the Financial Accounting Standards Board:

Donald J. Kirk, *Chairman*
Oscar S. Gellein
John W. March
Robert A. Morgan
David Mosso
Robert T. Sprouse
Ralph E. Walters

Appendix A

BACKGROUND INFORMATION

57. The need for a conceptual framework for financial accounting and reporting, beginning with consideration of the objectives of financial reporting, is generally recognized. The Accounting Principles Board issued *APB Statement No. 4,* "Basic Concepts and Accounting Principles Underlying Financial Statements of Business Enterprises," in 1970. When the Financial Accounting Standards Board came into existence, the Study Group on the Objectives of Financial Statements was at work, and its report, "Objectives of Financial Statements," was published in October 1973 by the American Institute of Certified Public Accountants.

58. The Financial Accounting Standards Board issued a Discussion Memorandum, "Conceptual Framework for Accounting and Reporting: Consideration of the Report of the Study Group on the Objectives of Financial Statements," dated June 6, 1974 and held a public hearing on September 23 and 24, 1974 on the objectives of financial statements. The Discussion Memorandum and the hearing were based primarily on the *Report of the Study Group on the Objectives of Financial Statements.* The Board received 95 written communications responding to the Discussion Memorandum, and 20 parties presented their views orally and answered Board Members' questions at the hearing.

59. On December 2, 1976, the Board issued three documents:

Tentative Conclusions on Objectives of Financial Statements of Business Enterprises,

FASB Discussion Memorandum, "Conceptual Framework for Financial Accounting and Reporting: Elements of Financial Statements and Their Measurement," and

Scope and Implications of the Conceptual Framework Project.

The same task force, with only one membership change, provided counsel in preparing both Discussion Memoranda. Eleven persons from academe, the financial community, industry, and public accounting served on the task force while the Discussion Memoranda were written.

60. The Board considered the 12 objectives of financial statements in the Study Group Report but has not attempted to reach conclusions on some of them—for example, reporting current value and changes in current value, providing a statement of financial activities, providing financial forecasts, determining the objectives of financial statements for governmental and not-for-profit organizations, and reporting enterprise activities affecting society. Some issues about reporting current values and changes in current values were discussed in the Discussion Memorandum, "Elements of Financial Statements and Their Measurement," and the Board has a project on supplementary disclosures of the effects of changing prices on business enterprises (paragraph 61). The Board also has a project on objectives of financial reporting by organizations other than business enterprises (footnote 1). The other matters may be dealt with in later phases of the conceptual framework project.

61. The Board held public hearings (a) August 1 and 2, 1977 on the *Tentative Conclusions on Objectives of Financial Statements* and Chapters 1-5 of the Discussion Memorandum concerning definitions of the elements of financial statements and (b) January 16-18, 1978 on the remaining chapters of the Discussion Memorandum concerning capital maintenance or cost recovery, qualities of useful financial information ("qualitative characteristics"), and measurement of the elements of financial statements.

62. The Board received 283 written communications on the subject of the August 1977 hearing, of which 214 commented on the objectives and 221 commented on the elements, and 27 parties presented their views orally and answered Board Members' questions at the hearing. The Board issued an Exposure Draft of a proposed Statement of Finan-

cial Accounting Concepts on "Objectives of Financial Reporting and Elements of Financial Statements of Business Enterprises," dated December 29, 1977 and received 135 letters of comment.

63. The major difference between this Statement and the Exposure Draft is the scope of the subject matter. "Elements of financial statements of business enterprises" and the brief comments on "qualitative characteristics" (paragraphs 41-66 and 69-75, respectively, of the Exposure Draft) have been omitted to be the subjects of separate exposure drafts. Other significant changes are (a) the "Highlights" preceding the text, (b) the subheadings in the third objective (paragraphs 40-54), and (c) reorganization of the "Introduction and Background" paragraphs, including the position of "characteristics and limitations of information provided" in the forepart of the Statement.

Statement of Financial Accounting Concepts No. 2
Qualitative Characteristics of Accounting Information

STATUS

Issued: May 1980

SUMMARY OF PRINCIPAL CONCLUSIONS

The purpose of this Statement is to examine the characteristics that make accounting information useful. Those who prepare, audit, and use financial reports, as well as the Financial Accounting Standards Board, must often select or evaluate accounting alternatives. The characteristics or qualities of information discussed in this Statement are the ingredients that make information useful and are the qualities to be sought when accounting choices are made.

All financial reporting is concerned in varying degrees with decision making (though decision makers also use information obtained from other sources). The need for information on which to base investment, credit, and similar decisions underlies the objectives of financial reporting. The usefulness of information must be evaluated in relation to the purposes to be served, and the objectives of financial reporting are focused on the use of accounting information in decision making.

The central role assigned to decision making leads straight to the overriding criterion by which all accounting choices must be judged. The better choice is the one that, subject to considerations of cost, produces from among the available alternatives information that is most useful for decision making.

Even objectives that are oriented more towards stewardship are concerned with decisions. Stewardship deals with the efficiency, effectiveness, and integrity of the steward. To say that stewardship reporting is an aspect of accounting's decision making role is simply to say that its purpose is to guide actions that may need to be taken in relation to the steward or in relation to the activity that is being monitored.

A Hierarchy of Accounting Qualities

The characteristics of information that make it a desirable commodity can be viewed as a hierarchy of qualities, with usefulness for decision making of most importance. Without usefulness, there would be no benefits from information to set against its costs.

User-Specific Factors

In the last analysis, each decision maker judges what accounting information is useful, and that judgment is influenced by factors such as the decisions to be made, the methods of decision making to be used, the information already possessed or obtainable from other sources, and the decision maker's capacity (alone or with professional help) to process the information. The optimal information for one user will not be optimal for another. Consequently, the Board, which must try to cater to many different users while considering the burdens placed on those who have to provide information, constantly treads a fine line between requiring disclosure of too much or too little information.

The hierarchy separates user-specific qualities, for example, understandability, from qualities inherent in information. Information cannot be useful to decision makers who cannot understand it, even though it may otherwise be relevant to a decision and be reliable. However, understandability of information is related to the characteristics of the decision maker as well as the characteristics of the information itself and, therefore, understandability cannot be evaluated in overall terms but must be judged in relation to a specific class of decision makers.

Primary Decision-Specific Qualities

Relevance and *reliability* are the two primary qualities that make accounting information useful for decision making. Subject to constraints imposed by cost and materiality, increased relevance and increased reliability are the characteristics that make information a more desirable commodity—that is, one useful in making decisions. If either of those qualities is completely missing, the information will not be useful. Though, ideally, the choice of an accounting alternative should produce information that is both more reliable and more relevant, it may be necessary to sacrifice some of one quality for a gain in another.

To be relevant, information must be timely and it must have predictive value *or* feedback value or both. To be reliable, information must have representational faithfulness and it must be verifiable and neutral. Comparability, which includes consistency, is a secondary quality that interacts with relevance and reliability to contribute to the usefulness of information. Two constraints are included in the hierarchy, both primarily quantitative in character. Information can be useful and yet be too costly to justify providing it. To be useful *and* worth providing, the benefits of information should exceed its cost. All of the qualities of information shown are subject to a materiality threshold, and that is also shown as a constraint.

Relevance

- Relevant accounting information is capable of making a difference in a decision by helping users to form predictions about the outcomes of past, present, and future events or to confirm or correct prior expectations. Information can make a difference to decisions by improving decision makers' capacities to predict or by providing feedback on earlier expectations. Usually, information does both at once, because knowledge about the outcomes of actions already taken will generally improve decision makers' abilities to predict the results of similar future actions. Without a knowledge of the past, the basis for a prediction will usually be lacking. Without an interest in the future, knowledge of the past is sterile.
- Timeliness, that is, having information available to decision makers before it loses its capacity to influence decisions, is an ancillary aspect of relevance. If information is not available when it is needed or becomes available so long after the reported events that it has no value for future action, it lacks relevance and is of little or no use. Timeliness alone cannot make information relevant, but a lack of timeliness can rob information of relevance it might otherwise have had.

Reliability

- The reliability of a measure rests on the faithfulness with which it represents what it purports to represent, coupled with an assurance for the user that it has that representational quality. To be useful, information must be reliable as well as relevant. Degrees of reliability must be recognized. It is hardly ever a question of black or white, but rather of more reliability or less. Reliability rests upon the extent to which the accounting description or measurement is verifiable and representationally faithful. Neutrality of information also interacts with those two components of reliability to affect the usefulness of the information.
- Verifiability is a quality that may be demonstrated by securing a high degree of consensus among independent measurers using the same measurement methods. Representational faithfulness, on the other hand, refers to the correspondence or agreement between the accounting numbers and the resources or events those numbers purport to represent. A high degree of correspondence, however, does not guarantee that an accounting measurement will be relevant to the user's needs if the resources or events represented by the measurement are inappropriate to the purpose at hand.
- Neutrality means that, in formulating or implementing standards, the primary concern should be the relevance and reliability of the information that results, not the effect that the new rule may have on a particular interest. A neutral choice between accounting alternatives is free from bias towards a predetermined result. The objectives of financial reporting serve many different information users who have diverse interests, and no one predetermined result is likely to suit all interests.

Comparability and Consistency

- Information about a particular enterprise gains greatly in usefulness if it can be compared with similar information about other enterprises and with similar information about the same enterprise for some other period or some other point in time. Comparability between enterprises and consistency in the application of methods over time increases the informational value of comparisons of relative economic opportunities or performance. The significance of information, especially quantitative information, depends to a great extent on the user's ability to relate it to some benchmark.

Materiality

- Materiality is a pervasive concept that relates to the qualitative characteristics, especially relevance and reliability. Materiality and relevance are both defined in terms of what influences or makes a difference to a decision maker, but the two terms can be distinguished. A decision not to disclose certain information may be made, say, because investors have no need for that kind of information (it is not relevant) or because the amounts involved are too small to make a difference (they are not material). Magnitude by itself, without regard to the nature of the item and the circumstances in which the judgment has to be made, will not generally be a sufficient basis for a materiality judgment. The Board's present position is that no general standards of materiality can be formulated to take into account all the considerations that enter into an experienced human judgment. Quantitative materiality criteria may be given by the Board in specific standards in the future, as in the past, as appropriate.

Costs and Benefits

- Each user of accounting information will uniquely perceive the relative value to be attached to each quality of that information. Ultimately, a standard-setting body has to do its best to meet the needs of society as a whole when it promulgates a standard that sacrifices one of those qualities for another; and it must also be aware constantly of the calculus of costs and benefits. In order to justify requiring a particular disclosure, the perceived benefits to be derived from that disclosure must exceed the perceived costs associated with it. However, to say anything precise about their incidence is difficult. There are costs of using information as well as of providing it; and the benefits from providing financial information accrue to preparers as well as users of that information.
- Though it is unlikely that significantly improved means of measuring benefits will become available in the foreseeable future, it seems possible that better ways of quantifying the incremental costs of regulations of all kinds may gradually be developed, and the Board will watch any such developments carefully to see whether they can be applied to financial accounting standards. The Board cannot cease to be concerned about the cost-effectiveness of its standards. To do so would be a dereliction of its duty and a disservice to its constituents.

Statement of Financial Accounting Concepts No. 2
Qualitative Characteristics of Accounting Information

STATEMENTS OF FINANCIAL ACCOUNTING CONCEPTS

This Statement of Financial Accounting Concepts is one of a series of publications in the Board's conceptual framework for financial accounting and reporting. Statements in the series are intended to set forth objectives and fundamentals that will be the basis for development of financial accounting and reporting standards. The objectives identify the goals and purposes of financial reporting. The fundamentals are the underlying concepts of financial accounting—concepts that guide the selection of transactions, events, and circumstances to be accounted for, their recognition and measurement, and the means of summarizing and communicating them to interested parties. Concepts of that type are fundamental in the sense that other concepts flow from them and repeated reference to them will be necessary in establishing, interpreting, and applying accounting and reporting standards.

The conceptual framework is a coherent system of interrelated objectives and fundamentals that is expected to lead to consistent standards and that prescribes the nature, function, and limits of financial accounting and reporting. It is expected to serve the public interest by providing structure and direction to financial accounting and reporting to facilitate the provision of evenhanded financial and related information that is useful in assisting capital and other markets to function efficiently in allocating scarce resources in the economy.

Establishment of objectives and identification of fundamental concepts will not directly solve financial accounting and reporting problems. Rather, objectives give direction, and concepts are tools for solving problems.

The Board itself is likely to be the most direct beneficiary of the guidance provided by the Statements in this series. They will guide the Board in developing accounting and reporting standards by providing the Board with a common foundation and basic reasoning on which to consider merits of alternatives.

However, knowledge of the objectives and concepts the Board will use in developing standards should also enable those who are affected by or interested in financial accounting standards to understand better the purposes, content, and characteristics of information provided by financial accounting and reporting. That knowledge is expected to enhance the usefulness of, and confidence in, financial accounting and reporting. Careful use of the concepts may also provide guidance in resolving new or emerging problems of financial accounting and reporting in the absence of applicable authoritative pronouncements.

Statements of Financial Accounting Concepts do not establish standards prescribing accounting procedures or disclosure practices for particular items or events, which are issued by the Board as Statements of Financial Accounting Standards. Rather, Statements in this series describe concepts and relations that will underlie future financial accounting standards and practices and in due course serve as a basis for evaluating existing standards and practices.*

The Board recognizes that in certain respects current generally accepted accounting principles may be inconsistent with those that may derive from the objectives and concepts set forth in Statements in this series. However, a Statement of Financial Accounting Concepts does not (a) require a change in existing generally accepted accounting principles, (b) amend, modify, or interpret Statements of Financial Accounting Standards, Interpretations of the FASB, Opinions of the Accounting Principles Board, or Bulletins of the Committee on Accounting Procedure that are in effect, or (c) justify either changing existing generally accepted accounting and reporting practices or interpreting the pronouncements listed in item (b) based on personal interpretations of the objectives and concepts in the Statements of Financial Accounting Concepts.

Since a Statement of Financial Accounting Concepts does not establish generally accepted accounting principles or standards for the disclosure of financial information outside of financial statements in published financial reports, it is not intended to invoke application of Rule 203 or 204 of the Rules of Conduct of the Code of Professional Ethics of the American Institute of Certified Public Accountants (or successor rules or arrangements of similar scope and intent). †

Like other pronouncements of the Board, a Statement of Financial Accounting Concepts may be

---

*Pronouncements such as APB Statement No. 4, *Basic Concepts and Accounting Principles Underlying Financial Statements of Business Enterprises,* and the Accounting Terminology Bulletins will continue to serve their intended purpose—they describe objectives and concepts underlying standards and practices existing at the time of their issuance.

† Rule 203 prohibits a member of the American Institute of Certified Public Accountants from expressing an opinion that financial statements conform with generally accepted accounting principles if those statements contain a material departure from an accounting principle promulgated by the Financial Accounting Standards Board, unless the member can demonstrate that because of unusual circumstances the financial statements otherwise would have been misleading. Rule 204 requires members of the Institute to justify departures from standards promulgated by the Financial Accounting Standards Board for the disclosure of information outside of financial statements in published financial reports.

amended, superseded, or withdrawn by appropriate action under the Board's *Rules of Procedure.*

FASB PUBLICATIONS ON CONCEPTUAL FRAMEWORK

Statements of Financial Accounting Concepts

No. 1, *Objectives of Financial Reporting by Business Enterprises* (November 1978)

Exposure Drafts Being (or Yet to Be) Considered by the Board

Elements of Financial Statements of Business Enterprises (December 28, 1979)

Objectives of Financial Reporting by Nonbusiness Organizations (March 14, 1980)

Discussion Memorandums and Invitations to Comment Having Issues Being Considered by the Board

Reporting Earnings (July 31, 1979)

Financial Statements and Other Means of Financial Reporting (May 12, 1980)

Other Projects in Process

Accounting Recognition Criteria
Funds Flows and Liquidity

CONTENTS

GLOSSARY OF TERMS

Bias

Bias in measurement is the tendency of a measure to fall more often on one side than the other of what it represents instead of being equally likely to fall on either side. Bias in accounting measures means a tendency to be consistently too high or too low.

Comparability
The quality of information that enables users to identify similarities in and differences between two sets of economic phenomena.

Completeness
The inclusion in reported information of everything material that is necessary for faithful representation of the relevant phenomena.

Conservatism
A prudent reaction to uncertainty to try to ensure that uncertainty and risks inherent in business situations are adequately considered.

Consistency
Conformity from period to period with unchanging policies and procedures.

Feedback Value
The quality of information that enables users to confirm or correct prior expectations.

Materiality
The magnitude of an omission or misstatement of accounting information that, in the light of surrounding circumstances, makes it probable that the judgment of a reasonable person relying on the information would have been changed or influenced by the omission or misstatement.

Neutrality
Absence in reported information of bias intended to attain a predetermined result or to induce a particular mode of behavior.

Predictive Value
The quality of information that helps users to increase the likelihood of correctly forecasting the outcome of past or present events.

Relevance
The capacity of information to make a difference in a decision by helping users to form predictions about the outcomes of past, present, and future events or to confirm or correct prior expectations.

Reliability
The quality of information that assures that information is reasonably free from error and bias and faithfully represents what it purports to represent.

Representational Faithfulness
Correspondence or agreement between a measure or description and the phenomenon that it purports to represent (sometimes called validity).

Timeliness
Having information available to a decision maker before it loses its capacity to influence decisions.

Understandability
The quality of information that enables users to perceive its significance.

Verifiability
The ability through consensus among measurers to ensure that information represents what it purports to represent or that the chosen method of measurement has been used without error or bias.

INTRODUCTION

1. The purpose of this Statement is to examine the characteristics of accounting information[1] that make that information useful. This Statement is one of a planned series of publications in the Board's conceptual framework project. It should be seen as a bridge between FASB Concepts Statement No. 1, *Objectives of Financial Reporting By Business Enterprises,* and other Statements to be issued covering the elements of financial statements and their recognition, measurement, and display. The Statement on objectives was concerned with the *purposes* of financial reporting. Later Statements will be concerned with questions about *how* those purposes are to be attained; and the standards that the Board has issued and will issue from time to time are also intended to attain those purposes. The Board believes that, in between the "why" of objectives and the "how" of other Statements and standards, it is helpful to share with its constituents its thinking about the characteristics that the information called for in its standards should have. It is those characteristics that distinguish more useful accounting information from less useful information.

2. Although those characteristics are expected to be stable, they are not immutable. They are affected by the economic, legal, political, and social environment in which financial reporting takes place and they may also change as new insights and new research results are obtained. Indeed, they ought to change if new knowledge shows present judgments to be outdated. If and when that happens, revised concepts Statements will need to be issued.

3. Although conventionally referred to as qualitative characteristics, some of the more important of the characteristics of accounting information that make it useful, or whose absence limit its usefulness, turn out on closer inspection to be quantitative in nature (for example, costliness) or to be partly quali-

[1] "Accounting information," "information provided by financial reporting," and variations on those descriptions are used interchangeably in this Statement.

tative and partly quantitative (for example, reliability and timeliness). While it will sometimes be important to keep those distinctions in mind, it will usually be convenient, and not misleading, to refer to all of the characteristics of information discussed in this Statement as "qualities" of information.

4. Although the discussion of the qualities of information and the related examples in this Statement refer primarily to business enterprises, the Board has tentatively concluded that similar qualities also apply to financial information reported by nonbusiness organizations. The Board intends to solicit views regarding its tentative conclusion.[2]

5. To maximize the usefulness of accounting information, subject to considerations of the cost of providing it, entails choices between alternative accounting methods. Those choices will be made more wisely if the ingredients that contribute to "usefulness" are better understood. The characteristics or qualities of information discussed in this Statement are, indeed, the ingredients that make information useful. They are, therefore, the qualities to be sought when accounting choices are made. They are as near as one can come to a set of criteria for making those choices.

The Nature of Accounting Choices

6. Accounting choices are made at two levels at least. At one level they are made by the Board or other agencies that have the power to require business enterprises to report in some particular way or, if exercised negatively, to prohibit a method that those agencies consider undesirable. An example of such a choice, made many years ago but still accepted as authoritative, is the pronouncement by the Committee on Accounting Procedure of the American Institute of Certified Public Accountants that ". . . the exclusion of all overheads from inventory costs does not constitute an accepted accounting procedure"[3] for general purpose external financial reporting.

7. Accounting choices are also made at the level of the individual enterprise. As more accounting standards are issued, the scope for individual choice inevitably becomes circumscribed. But there are now and will always be many accounting decisions to be made by reporting enterprises involving a choice between alternatives for which no standard has been promulgated or a choice between ways of implementing a standard.

8. Those who are unfamiliar with the nature of accounting are often surprised at the large number of choices that accountants are required to make. Yet choices arise at every turn. Decisions must first be made about the nature and definition of assets and liabilities, revenues and expenses, and the criteria by which they are to be recognized. Then a choice must be made of the attribute of assets to be measured—historical cost, current cost, current exit value, net realizable value, or present value of expected cash flows. If costs have to be allocated, either among time periods (for example, to compute depreciation) or among service beneficiaries (for example, industry segments), methods of allocation must be chosen. Further, choices must be made concerning the level of aggregation or disaggregation of the information to be disclosed in financial reports. Should a particular subsidiary company be consolidated or should its financial statements be presented separately? How many reportable segments should a company recognize? Choices involving aggregation arise at every point. Still other choices concern the selection of the terminal date of an enterprise's financial year, the form of descriptive captions to be used in its financial statements, the selection of matters to be commented on in notes or in supplementary information, and the wording to be used.

9. That list of choices, which is by no means comprehensive, illustrates some of the more important choices that arise in financial reporting. References throughout this Statement to alternative accounting policies, methods, or choices refer to the kinds of alternatives illustrated above.

10. If alternative accounting methods could be given points for each ingredient of usefulness in a particular situation, it would be an easy matter to add up each method's points and select the one (subject to its cost) that scored highest—so long, of course, as there were general agreement on the scoring system and how points were to be awarded. There are some who seem to harbor the hope that somewhere waiting to be discovered there is a comprehensive scoring system that can provide the universal criterion for making accounting choices. Unfortunately, neither the Board nor anyone else has such a system at the present time, and there is little probability that one will be forthcoming in the foreseeable future. Consequently, those who must choose among alternatives are forced to fall back on human judgment to evaluate the relative merits of

[2]The Board's consideration of aspects of the conceptual framework that pertain to nonbusiness organizations began later than its consideration of aspects that pertain to business enterprises. To date, the Board has sponsored and published a research study on the objectives and basic concepts underlying financial reporting by organizations other than business enterprises: FASB Research Report, *Financial Accounting in Nonbusiness Organizations,* by Robert N. Anthony; issued a Discussion Memorandum, *Conceptual Framework for Financial Accounting and Reporting: Objectives of Financial Reporting by Nonbusiness Organizations;* held public hearings on the Discussion Memorandum; and issued an Exposure Draft, *Objectives of Financial Reporting by Nonbusiness Organizations.* At its May 7, 1980 meeting, the Board authorized the staff to proceed with the consideration of concepts and standards issues relating to nonbusiness organizations that are beyond the scope of the existing nonbusiness objectives project.

[3]Accounting Research Bulletin No. 43, *Restatement and Revision of Accounting Research Bulletins,* Chapter 4, par. 5.

competing methods. If it were not so, there would be no need for a standard-setting authority; for by means of the comprehensive scoring system, agreement on the "best" methods would easily be secured.

11. That does not mean that nothing can be done to aid human judgment. By identifying and defining the qualities that make accounting information useful, this Statement develops a number of generalizations or guidelines for making accounting choices that are intended to be useful to the Board, to its staff, to preparers of financial statements, and to all others interested in financial reporting. For the Board and its staff, the qualities of useful accounting information should provide guidance in developing accounting standards that will be consistent with the objectives of financial reporting. This Statement also provides a terminology that should promote consistency in standard setting. For preparers of financial information, the qualities of useful accounting information should provide guidance in choosing between alternative ways of representing economic events, especially in dealing with situations not yet clearly covered by standards. This Statement also should be useful to those who use information provided by financial reporting. For them, its main value will be in increasing their understanding of both the usefulness and the limitations of the financial information that is provided by business enterprises and other organizations, either directly by financial reporting or indirectly through the commentaries of financial analysts and others. That increased understanding should be conducive to better-informed decisions.

12. The need for improved communication, especially between the Board and its constituents, provides much of the rationale for the whole conceptual framework project and particularly for this Statement. Indeed, improved communication may be the principal benefit to be gained from it. It is important that the concepts used by the Board in reaching its conclusions be understood by those who must apply its standards and those who use the results, for without understanding, standards become mere arbitrary edicts. Communication will also be facilitated if there is widespread use of a common terminology and a common set of definitions. The terminology used in this Statement is already widely, though not universally, used and its general adoption could help to eliminate many misunderstandings. The definitions of the principal terms used have been brought together in the glossary on pages 4041 and 4042.

13. It should perhaps be emphasized here that this Statement is not a standard. Its purpose is not to make rules but to provide part of the conceptual base on which rule making can stand. Unless that distinction is understood, this Statement may be invested with more authority than a discussion of concepts has a right to carry.

14. Whether at the level of the Board or the individual preparer, the primary criterion of choice between two alternative accounting methods involves asking which method produces the better—that is, the more useful—information. If that question can be answered with reasonable assurance, it is then necessary to ask whether the value of the better information sufficiently exceeds that of the inferior information to justify its extra cost, if any. If a satisfactory answer can again be given, the choice between the alternative methods is clear.

15. The qualities that distinguish "better" (more useful) information from "inferior" (less useful) information are primarily the qualities of relevance and reliability, with some other characteristics that those qualities imply. Subject to considerations of cost, the objective of accounting policy decisions is to produce accounting information that is relevant to the purposes to be served and is reliable. The meaning of those terms, the recognition that there are gradations of relevance and reliability, and the problems that arise if trade-offs between them are necessary all are matters discussed in later paragraphs of this Statement.

16. Accounting choices made by the Board and those made by individual statement preparers have this in common: they both aim to produce information that satisfies those criteria. Yet, though the objectives of the Board and of individual preparers are alike in that respect, the Board does not expect all its policy decisions to accord exactly with the preferences of every one of its constituents. Indeed, they clearly cannot do so, for the preferences of its constituents do not accord with each other. Left to themselves, business enterprises, even in the same industry, would probably choose to adopt different reporting methods for similar circumstances. But in return for the sacrifice of some of that freedom, there is a gain from the greater comparability and consistency that adherence to externally imposed standards brings with it. There also is a gain in credibility. The public is naturally skeptical about the reliability of financial reporting if two enterprises account differently for the same economic phenomena.

17. Throughout this Statement, readers should keep in mind the objectives of the Board in issuing accounting standards of widespread applicability and those of individual preparers who are concerned with the informational needs of a particular enterprise. Though the criteria by which information should be judged are the same whether the judgment is made by the Board or by a preparer, they cannot be expected always to produce agreement on a preferred choice of accounting method. The best accounting policies will provide information that best achieves the objectives of financial

reporting. But whatever information is provided, it cannot be expected to be equally useful to all preparers and users, for the simple reason that individual needs and objectives vary. The Board strives to serve the needs of all, knowing that in doing so some individual preferences are sacrificed. Like motorists who observe traffic laws in the interest of their own and general traffic safety, so long as others do the same, in general, those who have to subordinate their individual preferences to observe common accounting standards will, in the long run, gain more than they lose.

18. The analogy between accounting standards and traffic laws merits closer examination. Traffic laws impose certain minima or maxima in regulating behavior but still permit considerable flexibility in driving habits. A speed limit leaves slow drivers to choose their speed below the maximum and does not prohibit passing by other drivers. Even a requirement to drive on the right allows a driver to choose and to change lanes on all but very narrow roads. The point is that in most respects the traffic laws allow for considerable variations within a framework of rules. In setting accounting standards, the Board also strives to leave as much room as possible for individual choices and preferences while securing the degree of conformity necessary to attain its objectives.

19. This Statement must be seen as part of the larger conceptual framework, an important part of the foundations of which were laid with the publication of Concepts Statement 1. This Statement, with the proposed Statement on the elements of financial statements of business enterprises, is part of the second stage of the structure. With successive stages, the level of abstraction will give way to increasing specificity. The qualitative characteristics discussed in this document are formulated in rather general terms. As they are brought to bear on particular situations in subsequent pronouncements, however, those generalizations will give way to specific applications.

20. While this Statement concentrates on guidelines for making accounting choices, either by the Board or by those who provide financial information, its function is not to make those choices. Insofar as those choices lie within the Board's responsibility, some of them (for example, those relating to the attributes of assets and liabilities that should be measured and presented in financial statements) will be made in other parts of the conceptual framework project. Other choices will be made in the standards to be issued by the Board from time to time. The qualitative characteristics put forward in this Statement are intended to facilitate those choices and to aid in making them consistent with one another.

The Objectives of Financial Reporting

21. The objectives of financial reporting underlie judgments about the qualities of financial information, for only when those objectives have been established can a start be made on defining the characteristics of the information needed to attain them. In Concepts Statement 1, the Board set out the objectives of financial reporting for business enterprises that will guide it. The information covered by that Statement was not limited to the contents of financial statements. "Financial reporting," the Statement said, "includes not only financial statements but also other means of communicating information that relates, directly or indirectly, to the information provided by the accounting system—that is, information about an enterprise's resources, obligations, earnings, etc. [paragraph 7]."

22. The objectives of financial reporting are summarized in the following excerpts from the Statement:

> Financial reporting should provide information that is useful to present and potential investors and creditors and other users in making rational investment, credit, and similar decisions. The information should be comprehensible to those who have a reasonable understanding of business and economic activities and are willing to study the information with reasonable diligence [paragraph 34].
>
> Financial reporting should provide information to help present and potential investors and creditors and other users in assessing the amounts, timing, and uncertainty of prospective cash receipts from dividends or interest and the proceeds from the sale, redemption, or maturity of securities or loans. The prospects for those cash receipts are affected by an enterprise's ability to generate enough cash to meet its obligations when due and its other cash operating needs, to reinvest in operations, and to pay cash dividends and may also be affected by perceptions of investors and creditors generally about that ability, which affect market prices of the enterprise's securities. Thus, financial reporting should provide information to help investors, creditors, and others assess the amounts, timing, and uncertainty of prospective net cash inflows to the related enterprise [paragraph 37].
>
> Financial reporting should provide information about the economic resources of an enterprise, the claims to those resources (obligations of the enterprise to transfer resources to other entities and owners' equity), and the effects of transactions, events, and circum-

stances that change resources and claims to those resources [paragraph 40].

Financial reporting should provide information about an enterprise's financial performance during a period. Investors and creditors often use information about the past to help in assessing the prospects of an enterprise. Thus, although investment and credit decisions reflect investors' and creditors' expectations about future enterprise performance, those expectations are commonly based at least partly on evaluations of past enterprise performance [paragraph 42].

The primary focus of financial reporting is information about an enterprise's performance provided by measures of earnings and its components [paragraph 43].

Financial reporting should provide information about how an enterprise obtains and spends cash, about its borrowing and repayment of borrowing, about its capital transactions, including cash dividends and other distributions of enterprise resources to owners, and about other factors that may affect an enterprise's liquidity or solvency [paragraph 49].

Financial reporting should provide information about how management of an enterprise has discharged its stewardship responsibility to owners (stockholders) for the use of enterprise resources entrusted to it [paragraph 50].

Financial reporting should provide information that is useful to managers and directors in making decisions in the interests of owners [paragraph 52].

23. The Statement on objectives makes clear (paragraph 31) that *financial reporting* means *general purpose external financial reporting by business enterprises.* General purpose financial reporting attempts to meet "the informational needs of external users who lack the authority to prescribe the financial information they want from an enterprise and therefore must use the information that management communicates to them" (paragraph 28). General purpose statements are not all purpose statements, and never can be.

24. An analogy with cartography has been used to convey some of the characteristics of financial reporting, and it may be useful here. A map represents the geographical features of the mapped area by using symbols bearing no resemblance to the actual countryside, yet they communicate a great deal of information about it. The captions and numbers in financial statements present a "picture" of a business enterprise and many of its external and internal relationships more rigorously—more informatively, in fact—than a simple description of it. There are, admittedly, important differences between geography and economic activity and, therefore, between maps and financial statements. But the similarities may, nevertheless, be illuminating.

25. A "general purpose" map that tried to be "all purpose" would be unintelligible, once information about political boundaries, communications, physical features, geological structure, climate, economic activity, ethnic groupings, and all the other things that mapmakers can map were put on it. Even on a so-called general purpose map, therefore, the cartographer has to select the data to be presented. The cartographer, in fact, has to decide to serve some purposes and neglect others. The fact is that all maps are really special purpose maps, but some are more specialized than others. And so are financial statements. Some of the criticisms of financial statements derive from a failure to understand that even a general purpose statement can be relevant to and can, therefore, serve only a limited number of its users' needs.

26. The objectives focus financial reporting on a particular kind of economic decision—committing (or continuing to commit) cash or other resources to a business enterprise with expectation of future compensation or return, usually in cash but sometimes in other goods or services. Suppliers, lenders, employees, owners, and, to a lesser extent, customers commonly make decisions of that kind, and managers continually make them about an enterprise's resources. Concepts Statement 1 uses investment and credit decisions as prototypes of the kind of decisions on which financial reporting focuses. Nevertheless, as just noted, the Board, in developing the qualities in this Statement, must be concerned with groups of users of financial information who have generally similar needs. Those qualities do not necessarily fit all users' needs equally well.

THE CENTRAL ROLE OF DECISION MAKING

27. All financial reporting is concerned in varying degrees with decision making (though decision makers also use information obtained from other sources). The need for information on which to base investment, credit, and similar decisions underlies the objectives of financial reporting cited earlier.

28. Even objectives that are oriented more towards stewardship are concerned with decisions. The broader stewardship use of accounting, which is concerned with the efficiency, effectiveness, and integrity of the steward, helps stockholders or other financially interested parties (for example, bondholders) to evaluate the management of an enterprise. But that would be a pointless activity if

there were no possibility of taking action based on the results. Management is accountable to stockholders through an elected board of directors, but stockholders are often passive and do not insist on major management changes as long as an enterprise is reasonably successful. Their appraisals of management's stewardship help them to assess prospects for their investments, and stockholders who are dissatisfied with management's stewardship of those investments commonly sell their stock in the enterprise. Bondholders are concerned with management's compliance with bond indentures and may take legal action if covenants are broken. Thus, decision making and stewardship are interrelated accounting objectives. Indeed, the stewardship role of accounting may be viewed as subordinate to and a part of the decision making role, which is virtually all encompassing.

29. That view of the stewardship use of accounting in no way diminishes its importance, nor does it elevate the predictive value of accounting information above its confirmatory value. In its stewardship use, accounting compiles records of past transactions and events and uses those records to measure performance. The measurement confirms expectations or shows how far actual achievements diverged from them. The confirmation or divergence becomes the basis for a decision—which will often be a decision to leave things alone. To say that stewardship reporting is an aspect of accounting's decision making role is simply to say that its purpose is to guide actions that *may* need to be taken in relation to the steward or in relation to the activity that is being monitored.

30. The central role assigned here to decision making leads straight to the overriding criterion by which all accounting choices must be judged. The better choice is the one that, subject to considerations of cost, produces from among the available alternatives information that is most useful for decision making.[4]

31. So broad a generalization looks self-evident. Indeed, it says no more than the Board said in Concepts Statement 1 (paragraph 9): "Financial reporting is not an end in itself but is intended to provide information that is useful in making business and economic decisions. . . ." The challenge is to define in more detail what makes accounting information useful for decision making. If there is a serious difference of opinion, it is not over the general nature of characteristics such as relevance and reliability, which clearly occupy important places in the hierarchy of qualities that make information useful. There may indeed be some disagreement about their relative importance. But more serious disagreement arises over the choice between two accounting methods (for example, methods of allocating costs or recognizing revenues) if the choice involves a judgment about which method will produce more relevant or more reliable results or a judgment about whether the superior relevance of the results of one method outweighs the superior reliability of the results of the other.

A HIERARCHY OF ACCOUNTING QUALITIES

32. The characteristics of information that make it a desirable commodity guide the selection of preferred accounting policies from among available alternatives. They can be viewed as a hierachy of qualities, with usefulness for decision making of most importance. Without usefulness, there would be no benefits from information to set against its costs. The hierarchy is represented in Figure 1.

Features and Limitations of the Chart

33. Before discussing the informational characteristics shown on the chart, some words of explanation are offered about what the chart attempts to convey. It is a limited device—limited, for example, by being in two dimensions only—for showing certain relationships among the qualities that make accounting information useful. The primary qualities are that accounting information shall be relevant and reliable. If either of those qualities is completely missing, the information will not be useful. Relevance and reliability can be further analyzed into a number of components. To be relevant, information must be timely and it must have predictive value *or* feedback value or both. To be reliable, information must have representational faithfulness and it must be verifiable and neutral (the meaning of these terms, like all the other terms used in the chart, will be discussed later). Comparability, including consistency, is a secondary quality that interacts with relevance and reliability to contribute to the usefulness of information. Finally, two constraints are shown on the chart, both primarily quantitative rather than qualitative in character. Information can be useful and yet be too costly to justify providing it. To be useful and worth providing, the benefits of information should exceed its cost. All of the qualities shown are subject to a materiality threshold, and that is also shown as a constraint. The requirement that information be reliable can still be met even though it may contain immaterial errors, for errors that are not material will not perceptibly diminish its usefulness. Similar considerations apply to the other characteristics of information shown on the chart.

[4]The divergence among individual needs was noted in paragraph 17. It needs to be considered here and throughout this Statement.

FIGURE 1

A HIERARCHY OF ACCOUNTING QUALITIES

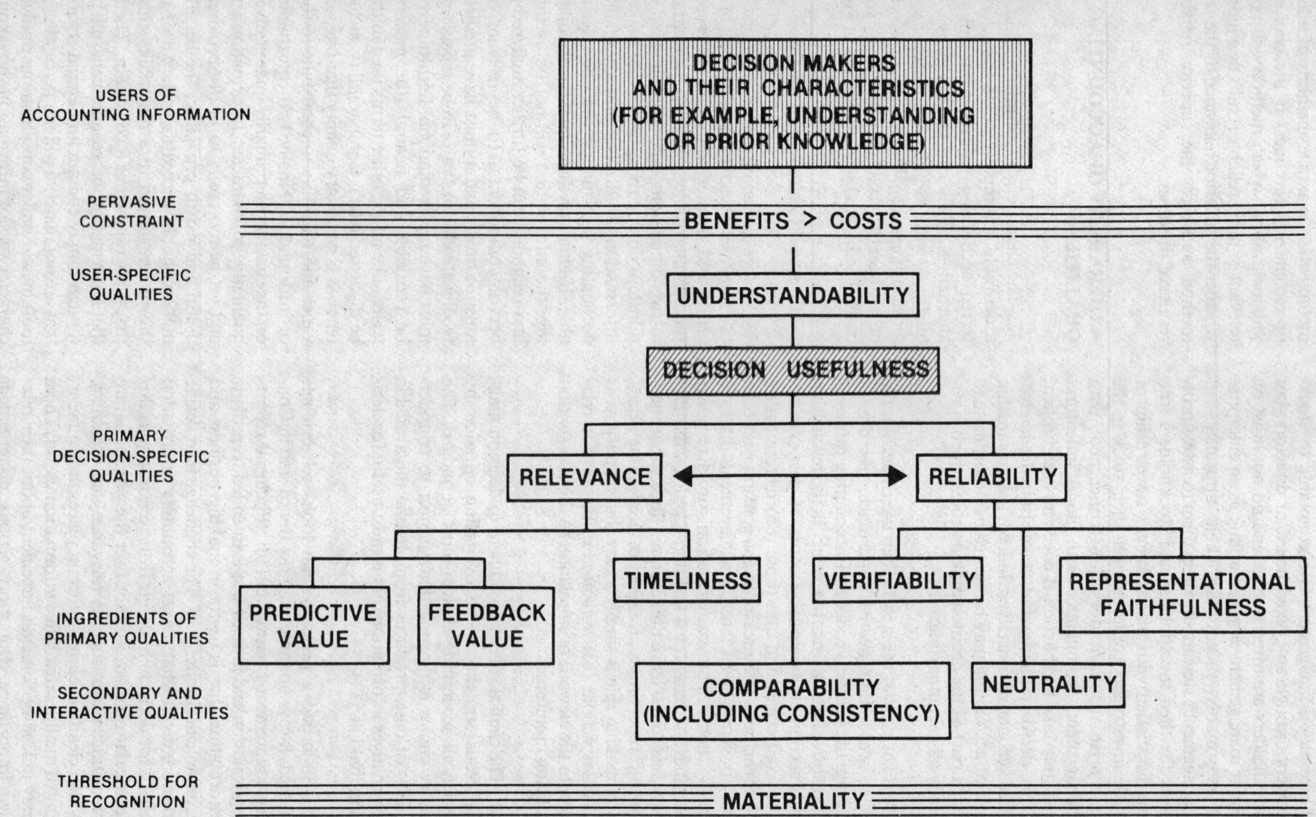

34. An important limitation of the hierarchy is that while it does distinguish between primary and other qualities, it does not assign priorities among qualities. That limitation is a salutary one, however, for the relative weight to be given to different qualities must vary according to circumstances. The hierarchy should be seen as no more than an explanatory device, the purpose of which is to clarify certain relationships rather than to assign relative weights. To be useful, financial information must have each of the qualities shown to a minimum degree. Beyond that, the rate at which one quality can be sacrificed in return for a gain in another quality without making the information less useful overall will be different in different situations.

35. Several characteristics that some would wish to see included in the hierarchy are not shown there. Rather than confuse a discussion of its positive features by explaining at this point why certain items have been excluded, discussion of that matter has been placed in Appendix B with other responses to comment letters that have been received by the Board.

Decision Makers and Their Characteristics

36. In the last analysis, each decision maker judges what accounting information is useful, and that judgment is influenced by factors such as the decisions to be made, the methods of decision making to be used, the information already possessed or obtainable from other sources, and the decision maker's capacity (alone or with professional help) to process the information. The optimal information for one user will not be optimal for another. Consequently, the Board, which must try to cater to many different users while considering the burdens placed on those who have to provide information, constantly treads a fine line between requiring disclosure of too much information and requiring too little.

37. The better informed decision makers are, the less likely it is that any new information can add materially to what they already know. That may make the new information less useful, but it does not make it less relevant to the situation. If an item of information reaches a user and then, a little later, the user receives the same item from another source, it is not less relevant the second time, though it will have less value. For that reason, relevance has been defined in this Statement (paragraphs 46 and 47) in terms of the capacity of information to make a difference (to someone who does not already have it) rather than in terms of the difference it actually does make. The difference it actually does make may be more a function of how much is already known (a condition specific to a particular user) than of the content of the new messages themselves (decision-specific qualities of information).

38. Thus, management in general and owners of small or closely held enterprises may find at least some information provided by external financial reporting to be less useful to them than it is to stockholders of large or publicly held enterprises. The latter must rely on financial reporting for information that the former has access to as a result of their intimate relationship to their enterprise.

39. Similarly, information cannot be useful to a person who cannot understand it. However, information may be relevant to a situation even though it cannot be understood by the person who confronts the situation. Its relevance will depend on its capacity to reduce uncertainty about the situation, even though it may call for more understanding to interpret it than its prospective user can command. For example, a hungry vegetarian traveling in a foreign country may experience difficulty in obtaining acceptable food when ordering from a menu printed in an unfamiliar language. The listing of items on the menu is relevant to the decision to be made but the traveler cannot use that information unless it is translated into another (understandable) language. Thus, the information may not be useful to a particular user even though it is relevant to the situation that the user faces. Information that cannot be understood, like information that is not available, may be relevant, but its relevance will be wasted because its capacity to make a difference cannot be utilized.

Understandability and Other User-Specific Qualities

40. The Board said in Concepts Statement 1 (paragraph 34) that information provided by financial reporting should be comprehensible to those who have a reasonable understanding of business and economic activities and are willing to study the information with reasonable diligence. The Board elaborated as follows:

> Financial information is a tool and, like most tools, cannot be of much direct help to those who are unable or unwilling to use it or who misuse it. Its use can be learned, however, and financial reporting should provide information that can be used by all—nonprofessionals as well as professionals—who are willing to learn to use it properly. Efforts may be needed to increase the understandability of financial information. Cost-benefit considerations may indicate that information understood or used by only a few should not be provided. Conversely, financial reporting should not exclude relevant information merely because it is difficult for some to understand or because some investors or creditors choose not to use it [paragraph 36].

The benefits of information may be increased by

making it more understandable and, hence, useful to a wider circle of users. Understandability of information is governed by a combination of user characteristics and characteristics inherent in the information, which is why understandability and other user-specific characteristics occupy a position in the hierarchy of qualities as a link between the characteristics of users (decision makers) and decision-specific qualities of information. Other parts of the conceptual framework project that will deal with displays of financial information will have a contribution to make to this matter.

41. Understandability and similar qualities of information, for example, newness, are closely related to the characteristics of *particular* decision makers as well as *classes* of decision makers. However, the Board is concerned with qualities of information that relate to broad classes of decision makers rather than to particular decision makers. Understandability can be classified as relating to particular decision makers (does the decision maker speak that language?) or relating to classes of decision makers (is the disclosure intelligible to the audience for which it is intended?). Newness of information can be classified similarly to understandability. The Board can influence the newness of information to broad classes of decision makers, for example, by requiring the disclosure of relevant information that was not previously available. However, the newness to a particular decision maker of generally available information depends largely on the timing of the receipt of that information by the decision maker, and that timing is subject to the effects of many variables extraneous to accounting and financial reporting. The Board establishes concepts and standards for general purpose external financial reporting by considering the needs of broad classes of decision makers and cannot base its decisions on the specific circumstances of individual decision makers.

Relative Importance and Trade-Offs

42. Although financial information must be both relevant and reliable to be useful, information may possess both characteristics to varying degrees. It may be possible to trade relevance for reliability or vice versa, though not to the point of dispensing with one of them altogether. Information may also have other characteristics shown on the chart to varying degrees, and other trade-offs between characteristics may be necessary or beneficial.

43. The question has been raised whether the relative importance to be attached to relevance and reliability should be different in financial statements and in other means of financial reporting. The issuance in September 1979 of FASB Statement No. 33, *Financial Reporting and Changing Prices*, calling for reporting by certain enterprises of supplementary information on both constant dollar and current cost bases outside of the primary financial statements, has brought into prominence the question of whether information reported outside financial statements should be allowed to be less reliable than what is reported in them.

44. Although there seems to be considerable support for the view that reliability should be the dominant quality in the information conveyed in financial statements, even at the expense of relevance, while the opposite is true of information conveyed outside the financial statements, that view has in it the seeds of danger. Like most potentially harmful generalizations, it does contain a germ of truth: almost everyone agrees that criteria for formally recognizing elements in financial statements call for a minimum level or threshold of reliability of measurement that should be higher than is usually considered necessary for disclosing information outside financial statements. But the remainder of the proposition does not follow. If it were carried to its logical conclusion and resulted in a downgrading of relevance of information in financial statements, the end would be that most really useful information provided by financial reporting would be conveyed outside the financial statements, while the audited financial statements would increasingly convey highly reliable but largely irrelevant, and thus useless, information. Those matters are germane to another part of the conceptual framework, the project on financial statements and other means of financial reporting.

45. This Statement discusses trade-offs between characteristics at several points. Those discussions apply generally to kinds of decisions and to groups of users of accounting information but do not necessarily apply to individual users. In a particular situation, the importance attached to relevance in relation to the importance of other decision specific qualities of accounting information (for example, reliability) will be different for different information users, and their willingness to trade one quality for another will also differ. The same thing is true of other considerations such as timeliness. That fact has an important bearing on the question of preferability, for it probably puts unanimity about preferences among accounting alternatives out of reach. Even though considerable agreement exists about the qualitative characteristics that "good" accounting information should have, no consensus can be expected about their relative importance in a specific situation because different users have or perceive themselves to have different needs and, therefore, have different preferences.

RELEVANCE

46. In discussions of accounting criteria, relevance has usually been defined in the dictionary sense, as pertaining to or having a bearing on the matter in question. That broad definition is satisfactory as far as it goes—information must, of course, be logically related to a decision in order to be relevant to it. Mistaken attempts to base decisions on logically unrelated information cannot convert irrelevant information into relevant information[5] any more than ignoring relevant information makes it irrelevant. However, the meaning of relevance for financial reporting needs to be made more explicit. Specifically, it is information's capacity to "make a difference" that identifies it as relevant to a decision.

47. To be relevant to investors, creditors, and others for investment, credit, and similar decisions, accounting information must be capable of making a difference in a decision by helping users to form predictions about the outcomes of past, present, and future events or to confirm or correct expectations. "Event" is a happening of consequence to an enterprise (Exposure Draft on elements, paragraph 67), and in this context can mean, for example, the receipt of a sales order or a price change in something the enterprise buys or sells. "Outcome" is the effect or result of an event or series of events and in this context can mean, for example, that last year's profit was $X or the expectation that this year's profit will be $Y. The event in question may be a past event the outcome of which is not already known, or it may be a future event the outcome of which can only be predicted.

48. Information need not itself be a prediction of future events or outcomes to be useful in forming, confirming, or changing expectations about future events or outcomes. Information about the present status of economic resources or obligations or about an enterprise's past performance is commonly a basis for expectations (Concepts Statement 1, paragraph 42).

49. Information may confirm expectations or it may change them. If it confirms them, it increases the probability that the results will be as previously expected. If it changes them, it changes the perceived probabilities of the previous possible outcomes. Either way, it makes a difference to one who does not already have that information. Decisions already made need not be changed, nor need a course of action already embarked on be altered by the information. A decision to hold rather than to sell an investment is a decision, and information that supports holding can be as relevant as information that leads to a sale. Information is relevant if the degree of uncertainty about the result of a decision that has already been made is confirmed or altered by the new information; it need not alter the decision.

50. One of the more fundamental questions raised by the search for relevance in accounting concerns the choice of attribute to be measured for financial reporting purposes. Will financial statements be more relevant if they are based on historical costs, current costs, or some other attribute? The question must be left for consideration in other parts of the conceptual framework project; but because of lack of experience with information providing measures of several of those attributes and differences of opinion about their relevance and reliability, it is not surprising that agreement on the question is so difficult to obtain.

Feedback[6] Value and Predictive Value as Components of Relevance

51. Information can make a difference to decisions by improving decision makers' capacities to predict or by confirming or correcting their earlier expectations. Usually, information does both at once, because knowledge about the outcome of actions already taken will generally improve decision makers' abilities to predict the results of similar future actions. Without a knowledge of the past, the basis for a prediction will usually be lacking. Without an interest in the future, knowledge of the past is sterile.

52. The same point can be made by saying that information is relevant to a situation if it can reduce uncertainty about the situation. Information that was not known previously about a past activity clearly reduces uncertainty about its outcome, and information about past activities is usually an indispensable point of departure for attempts to foresee the consequences of related future activities. Disclosure requirements almost always have the dual purpose of helping to predict and confirming or correcting earlier predictions. The reporting of business results by segments is a good example of accounting reports whose relevance is believed to lie both in the information they convey about the past performance of segments and in their contribution to an investor's ability to predict the trend of earnings of a diversified company. Another example is to be found in interim earnings reports, which provide both feedback on past performance and a basis for

[5]Information theorists assert that "relevant" as an adjective qualifying "information" is redundant, for irrelevant information is mere data. This Statement does not follow that usage.

[6]This inelegant term is used because no other single word has been found to comprehend both confirmation or corroboration and their opposites.

prediction for anyone wishing to forecast annual earnings before the year-end.

53. To say that accounting information has *predictive value* is not to say that it is itself a *prediction*. It may be useful here to draw an analogy between the financial information that analysts and others use in predicting earnings or financial position and the information that meteorologists use in forecasting weather. Meteorologists gather and chart information about actual conditions—temperatures, barometric pressures, wind velocities at various altitudes, and so on—and draw their conclusions from the relationships and patterns that they detect. Success in forecasting the weather has increased as new methods of gathering information have been developed. New kinds of information have become available, and with greater speed than was previously possible. To the simple sources of information available to our ancestors have been added satellite photographs, radar, and radiosondes to give information about the upper atmosphere. New information makes possible more sophisticated predictive models. When a meteorologist selects from among the alternative sources of information and methods of gathering information—about existing conditions, since future conditions cannot be known—those sources and methods that have the greatest predictive value can be expected to be favored. So it is with information about the existing financial state of a company and observed changes in that state from which predictions of success, failure, growth, or stagnation may be inferred. Users can be expected to favor those sources of information and analytical methods that have the greatest predictive value in achieving their specific objectives. Predictive value here means value as an *input* into a predictive process, not value directly as a prediction.

54. An important similarity and an important difference between predicting the weather and predicting financial performance may be noted. The similarity is that the meteorologist's information and the information derived from financial reporting both have to be fed into a predictive model[7] before they can throw light on the future. Financial predictions, like weather forecasts, are the joint product of a model and the data that go into it. A choice between alternative accounting methods on the basis of their predictive value can be made only if the characteristics of the model to be used are generally known. For example, the econometric models now used for economic forecasting are designed to use as data financial aggregates (among other things) as those aggregates are compiled at present. They might work less well if price-level adjusted data were used. However, it might be possible to revise the model for use with that kind of data so that even better predictions could be made. The point is that the predictive value of information cannot be assessed in the abstract. It has to be transformed into a prediction, and the nature of the transformation as well as the data used determine the outcome.

55. The important difference between meteorological and financial predictions is that only exceptionally can meteorological predictions have an effect on the weather, but business or economic decision makers' predictions often affect their subjects. For example, the use of financial models to predict business failures looks quite successful judged in the light of hindsight by looking at the financial history of failed firms during their last declining years. But a prediction of failure can be self-fulfilling by restricting a company's access to credit. The prediction could also bring about a recovery by initiating action by managers or bankers to avert failure. Because information affects human behavior and because different people react differently to it, financial information cannot be evaluated by means of a simple tally of the correct predictions that are based on it. Nevertheless, predictive value is an important consideration in distinguishing relevant from irrelevant accounting information.

Timeliness

56. Timeliness is an ancillary aspect of relevance. If information is not available when it is needed or becomes available only so long after the reported events that it has no value for future action, it lacks relevance and is of little or no use. Timeliness in the present context means having information available to decision makers before it loses its capacity to influence decisions. Timeliness alone cannot make information relevant, but a lack of timeliness can rob information of relevance it might otherwise have had.

57. Clearly, there are degrees of timeliness. In some situations, the capacity of information to influence decisions may evaporate quickly, as, for example, in a fast-moving situation such as a take-over bid or a strike, so that timeliness may have to be measured in days or perhaps hours. In other contexts, such as routine reports by an enterprise of its annual results, it may take a longer delay to diminish materially the relevance and, therefore, the usefulness of the information. But a gain in relevance that comes with increased timeliness may entail sacrifices of other desirable characteristics of information, and as a result there may be an overall gain or loss in usefulness. It may sometimes be desirable, for example, to

[7]A model is no more than a simplified, scaled-down representation of a situation that is to be analyzed. Typically, sophisticated models are expressed in terms of mathematical equations.

sacrifice precision for timeliness, for an approximation produced quickly is often more useful than precise information that takes longer to get out. Of course, if, in the interest of timeliness, the reliability of the information is sacrificed to a material degree, the result may be to rob the information of much of its usefulness. What constitutes a material loss of reliability is discussed in later paragraphs. Yet, while every loss of reliability diminishes the usefulness of information, it will often be possible to approximate an accounting number to make it available more quickly without making it materially unreliable. As a result, its overall usefulness may be enhanced.

RELIABILITY

58. That information should be reliable as well as relevant is a notion that is central to accounting. It is, therefore, important to be clear about the nature of the claim that is being made for an accounting number that is described as reliable.

59. The reliability of a measure rests on the faithfulness with which it represents what it purports to represent, coupled with an assurance for the user, which comes through verification, that it has that representational quality. Of course, degrees of reliability must be recognized. It is hardly ever a question of black or white, but rather of more reliability or less.

60. Two different meanings of reliability can be distinguished and illustrated by considering what might be meant by describing a drug as reliable. It could mean that the drug can be relied on to cure or alleviate the condition for which it was prescribed, or it could mean that a dose of the drug can be relied on to conform to the formula shown on the label. The first meaning implies that the drug is effective at doing what it is expected to do. The second meaning implies nothing about effectiveness but does imply a correspondence between what is represented on the label and what is contained in the bottle.[8]

61. Effectiveness is indeed a quality that is necessary in information, but in an accounting context it goes by another name—relevance. It is not always easy to maintain a clear distinction between relevance and reliability, as in the drug illustration, yet it is important to try to keep the two concepts apart. Given at least a minimum acceptable level of reliability, the choice of a drug will depend on its effectiveness in treating the condition for which it is prescribed.

62. Use of the term reliability in this Statement implies nothing about effectiveness. Accounting information is reliable to the extent that users can depend on it to represent the economic conditions or events that it purports to represent. As indicated in paragraph 59, reliability of accounting information stems from two characteristics that it is desirable to keep separate, representational faithfulness and verifiability. Neutrality of information also interacts with those two characteristics to affect its usefulness.

Representational Faithfulness

63. Representational faithfulness is correspondence or agreement between a measure or description and the phenomenon it purports to represent. In accounting, the phenomena to be represented are economic resources and obligations and the transactions and events that change those resources and obligations.[9]

64. Clearly, much depends on the meaning of the words "purports to represent" in the preceding paragraphs. Sometimes, but rarely, information is unreliable because of simple misrepresentation. Receivables, for example, may misrepresent large sums as collectible that, in fact, are uncollectible. Unreliability of that kind may not be easy to detect, but once detected its nature is not open to argument. More subtle is the information conveyed by an item such as "goodwill." Does a balance sheet that shows goodwill as an asset purport to represent the company as having no goodwill except what is shown? An uninformed reader may well think so, while one who is familiar with present generally accepted accounting principles will know that nonpurchased goodwill is not included. The discussion of reliability in this Statement assumes a reasonably informed user (paragraphs 36-41), for example, one who understands that the information provided by financial reporting often results from approximate, rather than exact, measures involving numerous estimates, classifications, summarizations, judgments, and allocations. The following paragraphs elaborate on and illustrate the concept of representational faithfulness used in this Statement, including the considerations noted in this and the preceding paragraphs.

Degrees of Representational Faithfulness

65. The cost of acquiring assets is more often than not capable of being determined unambiguously,

[8]Perhaps, more accurately, there is also a third meaning—that the drug does not have hidden undesirable side effects. The alleged undesirable economic impact of certain FASB standards is perhaps an accounting analogue to side effects of drugs, which are, in essence, costs to be considered in a cost-benefit analysis.

[9]Representational faithfulness is closely related to what behavioral scientists call "validity," as in the statement that intelligence quotients are (or are not) a valid measure of intelligence. Validity is a more convenient term than representational faithfulness, but out of its scientific context it has too broad a connotation for it to be an appropriate substitute.

but that is by no means always the case. Thus, if a collection of assets is bought for a specified amount, the cost attributable to each individual item may be impossible to ascertain. The acquisition cost may also be difficult to determine if assets are acquired in exchange for assets other than cash, by issuing stock, or in transactions with related parties. If assets are converted into other assets within an enterprise, as when raw materials are converted into finished products, or buildings or equipment are constructed by an enterprise for its own use, the multiplicity of costing conventions that can be used, all within the boundaries of present generally accepted accounting principles, make it impossible to attach a unique cost to the finished asset. Thus, it may not be certain that the cost for the asset in the enterprise's records does faithfully represent its cost.

66. The problem of determining cost becomes more difficult if assets are fungible. If there have been several purchases at different prices and a number of disposals at different dates, only by the adoption of some convention (such as first-in, first-out) can a cost be attributed to the assets on hand at a particular date. Since what is shown as the assets' cost is only one of several alternatives, it is difficult to substantiate that the chosen amount does represent the economic phenomena in question.

67. In the absence of market prices for the assets in question, representational faithfulness of amounts purporting to be current costs or fair values of assets also involves the same kinds of difficulties as those already described. For example, unless there are markets for used equipment or partially processed products, the current costs or fair values of those assets can be determined only by means such as deducting estimated depreciation from current costs or fair values of similar new assets, applying price indexes to past acquisition costs, or combining the current costs of the materials, labor, and overhead used. The allocations required by those procedures inevitably cast at least some doubt on the representational faithfulness of the results.

68. As accounting concepts become more complex, assessing the faithfulness of accounting representations of economic phenomena becomes increasingly difficult, and separating relevance or effectiveness from reliability becomes much more difficult than in the drug example used earlier (paragraphs 60 and 61). Social scientists have much discussed the concept of representational faithfulness (which they call validity) in connection with educational testing, and though that field may seem remote from accounting, the difficulties that beset it in some respects bear a close resemblance to some of those encountered in accounting. If two students score 640 and 580, respectively, in a scholastic aptitude test of verbal skills, it is inferred that the first student has more verbal aptitude than the second. But does the test really measure verbal aptitude? Is it, in other words, a valid test of verbal aptitude? That is a very difficult question to answer, for what is verbal aptitude? Without a definition of the quality to be measured, the validity of the test cannot be assessed. The problem of defining intelligence and of judging whether intelligence tests validly measure it may be even more difficult because of the many different manifestations of intelligence, the problems of separating innate and acquired abilities, standardizing for differences in social conditions, and many other things.

69. The nature of the problem just described can be clarified by means of an example. A spelling test is administered orally to a group of students. The words are read aloud by the tester, and the students are required to write down the test words. Some students, though they can usually spell well, fail the test. The reason, it turns out, is that they have hearing problems. The test score purports to measure ability to spell, whereas it, in fact, is partly measuring aural acuity. The test score lacks true representational faithfulness.

70. Another example, perhaps more closely related to accounting, may serve to further highlight some possible ways in which a representation may not be faithful to the economic phenomena that it purports to represent. The Consumer Price Index for All Urban Consumers (CPI-U) is an index of price level changes affecting consumers generally and is often used to measure changes in the general purchasing power of the monetary unit itself. However, if it were used as a measure of the price change of a specific asset, a purchase of a specific consumer, or an acquisition of a specific enterprise, it would not likely provide a faithful representation. The CPI-U is a "market basket" index, based on the average price a typical consumer would pay for a selection of consumer goods. Specific price changes experienced by specific consumers will differ from the index to the extent their consumption patterns are different from the selection of goods in the index market basket if the price changes on the goods they purchase are not perfectly correlated to the changes in the index. General price indexes, such as the CPI-U, cannot acknowledge individual differences, but they may provide a reasonable measure of the loss in the general purchasing power of the monetary unit. The index must be interpreted in the context of what it was designed to do and in view of the limitations of any averaging process.

71. The discussion in the preceding paragraph illustrates some of the problems that may arise when representations of economic phenomena are used in different contexts than those for which they were designed. Accounting information, for example, purports to reflect the activities of a particular

enterprise. However, aggregating the amounts reported by all businesses may not result in a faithful representation of total activity in the business sector, for that is not the purpose for which the accounting information was intended. Information that is representationally faithful in the context for which it was designed, therefore, may not be reliable when used in other contexts.

Precision and Uncertainty

72. Reliability does not imply certainty or precision. Indeed, any pretension to those qualities if they do not exist is a negation of reliability. Sometimes, a range within which an estimate may fall will convey information more reliably than can a single (point) estimate. In other cases, an indication of the probabilities attaching to different values of an attribute may be the best way of giving information reliably about the measure of the attribute and the uncertainty that surrounds it. Reporting accounting numbers as certain and precise if they are not is a negation of reliable reporting.

73. Different uses of information may require different degrees of reliability and, consequently, what constitutes a material loss or gain in reliability may vary according to use. An error in timekeeping of a few seconds a day will usually be acceptable to the owner of an ordinary wristwatch, whereas the same error would normally cause a chronometer to be judged unreliable. The difference is linked to use—a wristwatch is used for purposes for which accuracy within a few seconds (or perhaps a few minutes) is satisfactory; a chronometer is used for navigation, scientific work, and the like, uses for which a high degree of accuracy is required because an error of a few seconds or a fraction of a second may have large consequences. In everyday language, both the wristwatch and the chronometer are said to be reliable. By the standard of the chronometer, the wristwatch, in fact, is unreliable. Yet the watch's owner does not perceive it to be unreliable, for it is not expected to have the accuracy of a chronometer.

74. Fortunately, that is well understood by accountants. They recognize that a difference between an estimate and an accurate measurement may be material in one context and not material in another. The relationship between the concepts of reliability and materiality, including what constitutes *material* unreliability, will be discussed later in this Statement.

75. Reliability as a quality of a predictor has a somewhat different meaning from reliability as a quality of a measure. The reliability of a barometer should be judged in terms of the accuracy with which it measures air pressure and changes in air pressure. That is all that a barometer is constructed to do. Yet questions about its reliability are more likely to be couched in terms of its accuracy as a predictor of the weather, even though weather conditions in any location are the result of many factors besides air pressure in that location. Though much of the relevance of accounting information may derive from its value as input to a prediction model, the probability that it will lead to correct predictions does not determine its reliability as a set of measurements. The correctness of predictions depends as much on the predictive model used as on the data that go into the model. Thus, the result of a predictive process cannot be used to assess the reliability of the inputs into it any more than a run of successes by a barometer in forecasting the weather can tell us much about the accuracy with which it measures the pressure of the atmosphere.

76. The financial statements of a business enterprise can be thought of as a representation of the resources and obligations of an enterprise and the financial flows into, out of, and within the enterprise—as a model of the enterprise.[10] Like all models, it must abstract from much that goes on in a real enterprise. No model, however sophisticated, can be expected to reflect all the functions and relationships that are found within a complex organization. To do so, the model would have to be virtually a reproduction of the original. In real life, it is necessary to accept a much smaller degree of correspondence between the model and the original than that. One can be satisfied if none of the important functions and relationships are lost. Before an accounting model—either the one now used or an alternative—can be judged to represent an enterprise reliably, it must be determined that none of the important financial functions of the enterprise or its relationships have been lost or distorted. The mere fact that model works—that when it receives inputs it produces outputs—gives no assurance that it faithfully represents the original. Just as a distorting mirror reflects a warped image of the person standing in front of it or just as an inexpensive loudspeaker fails to reproduce faithfully the sounds that went into the microphone or onto the phonograph records, so a bad model gives a distorted representation of the system that it models. The question that accountants must face continually is how much distortion is acceptable. The cost of a perfect sound reproduction system puts it out of reach of most people, and perfect reliability of accounting information is equally unattainable.

[10]Nothing is implied here about the possible predictive uses of the model. While it is true that models are generally used to make predictions, they need not be so used. A model is no more than a representation of certain aspects of the real world.

Effects of Bias

77. Bias in measurement is the tendency of a measure to fall more often on one side than the other of what it represents instead of being equally likely to fall on either side. Bias in accounting measures means a tendency to be consistently too high or too low.

78. Accounting information may not represent faithfully what it purports to represent because it has one or both of two kinds of bias. The measurement method may be biased, so that the resulting measurement fails to represent what it purports to represent. Alternatively, or additionally, the measurer, through lack of skill or lack of integrity, or both, may misapply the measurement method chosen. In other words, there may be bias, not necessarily intended, on the part of the measurer. Those two kinds of bias are further discussed in the following paragraphs and in the next section on "verifiability." Intentional bias introduced to attain a predetermined result or induce a particular mode of behavior is discussed under "neutrality" (paragraphs 98-110).

Completeness

79. Freedom from bias, both in the measurer and the measurement method, implies that nothing material is left out of the information that may be necessary to insure that it validly represents the underlying events and conditions. Reliability implies completeness of information, at least within the bounds of what is material and feasible, considering the cost. A map that is 99 percent reliable but fails to show a bridge across a river where one exists can do much harm. Completeness, however, must always be relative, for neither maps nor financial reports can show everything.

80. Completeness of information also affects its relevance. Relevance of information is adversely affected if a relevant piece of information is omitted, even if the omission does not falsify what is shown. For example, in a diversified enterprise a failure to disclose that one segment was consistently unprofitable would not, before the issuance of FASB Statement No. 14, *Accounting for Segments of a Business Enterprise,* have caused the financial reporting to be judged unreliable, but that financial reporting would have been (as it would now be) deficient in relevance. Thus, completeness, within the bounds of feasibility, is necessary to both of the primary qualities that make information useful.

Verifiability

81. The quality of verifiability contributes to the usefulness of accounting information because the purpose of verification is to provide a significant degree of assurance that accounting measures represent what they purport to represent. Verification is more successful in minimizing measurer bias than measurement bias, and thus contributes in varying degrees toward assuring that particular measures represent faithfully the economic things or events that they purport to represent. Verification contributes little or nothing toward insuring that measures used are relevant to the decisions for which the information is intended to be useful.

82. Measurer bias is a less complex concept than measurement bias. In its simplest form, it arises from intentional misrepresentation. But even honest measurers may get different results from applying the same measurement method, especially if it involves a prediction of the outcome of a future event, such as the realization of an asset. Measurer bias can be detected and eliminated by having the measurement repeated with the same result. It is, therefore, a desirable quality of an accounting measure that it should be capable of replication. The Accounting Principles Board (APB) called this characteristic verifiability, and defined it in APB Statement No. 4, *Basic Concepts and Accounting Principles Underlying Financial Statements of Business Enterprises:* "Verifiable financial accounting information provides results that would be substantially duplicated by independent measurers using the same measurement methods" (paragraph 90).

83. The last five words of the APB's definition are significant for they imply that alternative methods may be available. Verification does not guarantee the appropriateness of the method used, much less the correctness of the resulting measure. It does carry some assurance that the measurement rule used, whatever it was, was applied carefully and without personal bias on the part of the measurer.

84. Verification implies consensus. Verifiability can be measured by looking at the dispersion of a number of independent measurements of some particular phenomenon. The more closely the measurements are likely to be clustered together, the greater the verifiability of the number used as a measure of the phenomenon.

85. Some accounting measurements are more easily verified than others. Alternative measures of cash will be closely clustered together, with a consequently high level of verifiability. There will be less unanimity about receivables (especially their net value), still less about inventories, and least about depreciable assets, for there will be disagreements about depreciation methods to be used, predictions of asset lives, and (if book values are based on historical cost) even which expenditures should be included in the investment base. More than one

empirical investigation has concluded that accountants may agree more about estimates of the market values of certain depreciable assets than about their carrying values. Hence, to the extent that verification depends on consensus, it may not always be those measurement methods widely regarded as "objective" that are most verifiable.

86. The elimination of measurer bias alone from information does not insure that the information will be reliable. Even though several independent measurers may agree on a single measurement method and apply it honestly and skillfully, the result will not be reliable if the method used is such that the measure does not represent what it purports to represent. Representational faithfulness of reported measurements lies in the closeness of their correspondence with the economic transactions, events, or circumstances that they represent.

87. Two further points about verifiability and representational faithfulness need to be emphasized. First, when accountants speak of verification they may mean either that an accounting measure itself has been verified or only that the procedures used to obtain the measure have been verified. For example, the price paid to acquire a block of marketable securities or a piece of land is normally directly verifiable, while the amount of depreciation for a period is normally only indirectly verifiable by verifying the depreciation method, calculations used, and consistency of application (paragraphs 65-67). Direct verification of accounting measures tends to minimize both personal bias introduced by a measurer (measurer bias) and bias inherent in measurement methods (measurement bias). Verification of only measurement methods tends to minimize measurer bias but usually preserves any bias there may be in the selection of measurement or allocation methods.

88. Second, measurement or allocation methods are often verifiable even if the measures they produce result in a very low degree of representational faithfulness. For example, before FASB Statement No. 5, *Accounting for Contingencies,* some enterprises that were "self-insured" recorded as an expense a portion of expected future losses from fire, flood, or other casualties. If an enterprise had a large number of "self-insured" assets, expectations of future losses could be actuarially computed, and the methods of allocating expected losses to periods could be readily verified. However, since uninsured losses occurred only when a casualty damaged or destroyed a particular asset or particular assets, the representational faithfulness of the resulting allocated measures was very low. In years in which no casualties were suffered by an enterprise, the allocated expenses or losses represented nonexistent transactions or events; while in years in which assets were actually damaged or destroyed, the allocated expenses or losses may have fallen far short of representing the losses.

89. In summary, verifiability means no more than that several measurers are likely to obtain the same measure. It is primarily a means of attempting to cope with measurement problems stemming from the uncertainty that surrounds accounting measures and is more successful in coping with some measurement problems than others. Verification of accounting information does not guarantee that the information has a high degree of representational faithfulness, and a measure with a high degree of verifiability is not necessarily relevant to the decision for which it is intended to be useful.

Reliability and Relevance

90. Reliability and relevance often impinge on each other. Reliability may suffer when an accounting method is changed to gain relevance, and vice versa. Sometimes it may not be clear whether there has been a loss or gain either of relevance or of reliability. The introduction of current cost accounting will illustrate the point. Proponents of current cost accounting believe that current cost income from continuing operations is a more relevant measure of operating performance than is operating profit computed on the basis of historical costs. They also believe that if holding gains and losses that may have accrued in past periods are separately displayed, current cost income from continuing operations better portrays operating performance. The uncertainties surrounding the determination of current costs, however, are considerable, and variations among estimates of their magnitude can be expected. Because of those variations, verifiability or representational faithfulness, components of reliability, might diminish. Whether there is a net gain to users of the information obviously depends on the relative weights attached to relevance and reliability (assuming, of course, that the claims made for current cost accounting are accepted).

Conservatism

91. Nothing has yet been said about conservatism, a convention that many accountants believe to be appropriate in making accounting decisions. To quote APB Statement 4:

> Frequently, assets and liabilities are measured in a context of significant uncertainties. Historically, managers, investors, and accountants have generally preferred that possible errors in measurement be in the direction of understatement rather than overstatement of net income and net assets. This has led to the convention of conservatism . . . [paragraph 171].

92. There is a place for a convention such as conservatism—meaning prudence—in financial accounting and reporting, because business and economic activities are surrounded by uncertainty, but it needs to be applied with care. Since a preference "that possible errors in measurement be in the direction of understatement rather than overstatement of net income and net assets" introduces a bias into financial reporting, conservatism tends to conflict with significant qualitative characteristics, such as representational faithfulness, neutrality, and comparability (including consistency). To be clear about what conservatism does not mean may often be as important as to be clear about what it means.

93. Conservatism in financial reporting should no longer connote deliberate, consistent understatement of net assets and profits. The Board emphasizes that point because conservatism has long been identified with the idea that deliberate understatement is a virtue. That notion became deeply ingrained and is still in evidence despite efforts over the past 40 years to change it. The convention of conservatism, which was once commonly expressed in the admonition to "anticipate no profits but anticipate all losses," developed during a time when balance sheets were considered the primary (and often only) financial statement, and details of profits or other operating results were rarely provided outside business enterprises. To the bankers or other lenders who were the principal external users of financial statements, understatement for its own sake became widely considered to be desirable, since the greater the understatement of assets the greater the margin of safety the assets provided as security for loans or other debts.

94. Once the practice of providing information about periodic income as well as balance sheets became common, however, it also became evident that understated assets frequently led to overstated income in later periods. Perceptive accountants saw that consistent understatement was difficult to maintain over a lengthy period, and the Committee on Accounting Procedure began to say so, for example, in ARB No. 3, *Quasi-Reorganization or Corporate Readjustment—Amplification of Institute Rule No. 2 of 1934:* "Understatement as at the effective date of the readjustment of assets which are likely to be realized thereafter, though it may result in conservatism in the balance-sheet, may also result in overstatement of earnings or of earned surplus when the assets are subsequently realized. Therefore, in general, assets should be carried forward as of the date of readjustment at a fair and not unduly conservative value." The Committee also formulated the "cost or market rule" in ARB No. 29, *Inventory Pricing,* in such a way that decreases in replacement costs do not result in writing down inventory unless (a) the expected selling price also decreases or (b) costs to complete and sell inventory increase; unless those conditions are met, recognition of a loss by writing down inventory merely increases income in one or more later periods. (ARB 3 and 29 became, respectively, chapters 7A and 4 of ARB No. 43, *Restatement and Revision of Accounting Research Bulletins.*) Among the most recent admonitions on the point is that of the International Accounting Standards Committee (IASC) in International Accounting Standard No. 1, *Disclosure of Accounting Policies:* "Uncertainties inevitably surround many transactions. This should be recognized by exercising prudence in preparing financial statements. Prudence does not, however, justify the creation of secret or hidden reserves."

95. Conservatism is a prudent reaction to uncertainty to try to ensure that uncertainties and risks inherent in business situations are adequately considered. Thus, if two estimates of amounts to be received or paid in the future are about equally likely, conservatism dictates using the less optimistic estimate; however, if two amounts are not equally likely, conservatism does not necessarily dictate using the more pessimistic amount rather than the more likely one. Conservatism no longer requires deferring recognition of income beyond the time that adequate evidence of its existence becomes available or justifies recognizing losses before there is adequate evidence that they have been incurred.

96. The Board emphasizes that any attempt to understate results consistently is likely to raise questions about the reliability and the integrity of information about those results and will probably be self-defeating in the long run. That kind of reporting, however well-intentioned, is not consistent with the desirable characteristics described in this Statement. On the other hand, the Board also emphasizes that imprudent reporting, such as may be reflected, for example, in overly optimistic estimates of realization, is certainly no less inconsistent with those characteristics. Bias in estimating components of earnings, whether overly conservative or unconservative, usually influences the timing of earnings or losses rather than their aggregate amount. As a result, unjustified excesses in either direction may mislead one group of investors to the possible benefit or detriment of others.

97. The best way to avoid the injury to investors that imprudent reporting creates is to try to ensure that what is reported represents what it purports to represent. It has been pointed out in this Statement that the reliability of financial reporting may be enhanced by disclosing the nature and extent of the uncertainty surrounding events and transactions reported to stockholders and others. In assessing the prospect that as yet uncompleted transactions will be concluded successfully, a degree of skepticism is

often warranted. The aim must be to put the users of financial information in the best possible position to form their own opinion of the probable outcome of the events reported. Prudent reporting based on a healthy skepticism builds confidence in the results and, in the long run, best serves all of the divergent interests that are represented by the Board's constituents.

NEUTRALITY

98. Neutrality in accounting has a greater significance for those who set accounting standards than for those who have to apply those standards in preparing financial reports, but the concept has substantially the same meaning for the two groups, and both will maintain neutrality in the same way. Neutrality means that either in formulating or implementing standards, the primary concern should be the relevance and reliability of the information that results, not the effect that the new rule may have on a particular interest.

99. To say that information should be free from bias towards a predetermined result is not to say that standard setters or providers of information should not have a *purpose* in mind for financial reporting. Of course, information must be purposeful. But a predetermined purpose should not imply a predetermined result. For one thing, the purpose may be to serve many different information users who have diverse interests, and no one predetermined result is likely to suit them all.

100. Neutrality does not mean "without purpose," nor does it mean that accounting should be without influence on human behavior. Accounting information cannot avoid affecting behavior, nor should it. If it were otherwise, the information would be valueless—by definition, irrelevant—and the effort to produce it would be futile. It is, above all, the predetermination of a desired result, and the consequential selection of information to induce that result, that is the negation of neutrality in accounting. To be neutral, accounting information must report economic activity as faithfully as possible, without coloring the image it communicates for the purpose of influencing behavior in *some particular direction*.

101. Behavior will be influenced by financial information just as it is influenced and changed by the results of elections, college examinations, and sweepstakes. Elections, examinations, and sweepstakes are not unfair—nonneutral—merely because some people win and others lose. So it is with neutrality in accounting. The effect of "capitalization" of leases on enterprises in the leasing industry is a case in point. Recording of certain leases as assets and liabilities has been opposed by many of those enterprises on the grounds that, by making "off balance sheet" financing more difficult, it would make leasing less attractive to lessees, and that would have a detrimental effect on the business of lessors. Although it is at least debatable whether that kind of effect actually would result from lease capitalization, standard setters have not been indifferent to those fears. After carefully weighing the matter, various standard setters (including the Board) have generally concluded that those fears could not be allowed to stand in the way of what the Board and others considered to be a gain in the relevance and reliability of financial statements.

102. Some reject the notion of accounting neutrality because they think it is impossible to attain because of the "feedback effect." Information that reports on human activity itself influences that activity, so that an accountant is reporting not on some static phenomenon but on a dynamic situation that changes because of what is reported about it. But that is not an argument against neutrality in measurement. Many measurements relating to human beings—what they see when they step on a scale, what the speedometer registers when they drive a car, their performance in an athletic contest, or their academic performance, for example—have an impact on their behavior, for better or worse. No one argues that those measurements should be biased in order to influence behavior. Indeed, most people are repelled by the notion that some "big brother," whether government or private, would tamper with scales or speedometers surreptitiously to induce people to lose weight or obey speed limits or would slant the scoring of athletic events or examinations to enhance or decrease someone's chances of winning or graduating. There is no more reason to abandon neutrality in accounting measurement.

103. Another argument against the acceptance of neutrality as a necessary characteristic of accounting information is that it would inhibit the Board from working for the achievement of national goals. That view raises several issues. First, there would have to be agreement on national goals. For example, should the United States work to make energy cheap and plentiful or should it conserve natural resources for the benefit of posterity? Furthermore, governments come and go, and administrations change their political color and their policies. The Board concludes that it is not feasible to change financial accounting standards that accountants use every time governmental policy changes direction, even if it were desirable to do so. Moreover, only if accounting information is neutral can it safely be used to help guide those policies as well as to measure their results.

104. But more importantly, it is not desirable for the Board to tack with every change in the political wind, for politically motivated standards would quickly lose their credibility, and even standards that were defensible if judged against the criteria discussed in this Statement would come under suspicion because they would be tainted with guilt by association. The chairman of the SEC made the point in his statement on oil and gas accounting on August 29, 1978:

> If it becomes accepted or expected that accounting principles are determined or modified in order to secure purposes other than economic measurement—even such virtuous purposes as energy production—we assume a grave risk that confidence in the credibility of our financial information system will be undermined.[11]

105. For a standard to be neutral, it is not necessary that it treat everyone alike in all respects. A standard could require less disclosure from a small enterprise than it does from a large one without having its neutrality impugned, if the Board were satisfied that a requirement that was cost-effective if imposed on a large enterprise would be more burdensome than it was worth if imposed on a small one. Nevertheless, in general, standards that apply differentially need to be looked at carefully to ensure that the criterion of neutrality is not being transgressed.

106. While rejecting the view that financial accounting standards should be slanted for political reasons or to favor one economic interest or another, the Board recognizes that a standard-setting authority must be alert to the economic impact of the standards that it promulgates. The consequences of those standards will usually not be easy to isolate from the effects of other economic happenings, and they will be even harder to predict with confidence when a new standard is under consideration but before it has gone into effect. Nevertheless, the Board will consider the probable economic impact of its standards as best it can and will monitor that impact as best it can after a standard goes into effect. For one thing, a markedly unexpected effect on business behavior may point to an unforeseen deficiency in a standard in the sense that it does not result in the faithful representation of economic phenomena that was intended. It would then be necessary for the standard to be revised.

107. Neutrality in accounting is an important criterion by which to judge accounting policies, for information that is not neutral loses credibility. If information can be verified and can be relied on faithfully to represent what it purports to represent—*and if there is no bias in the selection of what is reported*—it cannot be slanted to favor one set of interests over another. It may in fact favor certain interests, but only because the information points that way, much as a good examination grade favors a good student who has honestly earned it.

108. The italicized words deserve comment. It was noted earlier in this Statement that reliability implies completeness of information, at least within the bounds of what is material and feasible, considering the cost. An omission can rob information of its claim to neutrality if the omission is material and is intended to induce or inhibit some particular mode of behavior.

109. Though reliability and the absence of bias in what is to be reported bring neutrality as a by-product, the converse is not true. Information may be unreliable even though it is provided without any intention on the part of the provider to influence behavior in a particular direction. Good intentions alone do not guarantee representational faithfulness.

110. Can information that is undeniably reliable produce undesirable consequences? The answer must be another question—consequences for whom? The consequences may indeed be bad for some interests. But the dissemination of unreliable and potentially misleading information is, in the long run, bad for all interests. It may be the responsibility of other agencies to intervene to take care of special interests that they think might be injured by an accounting standard. The Board's responsibility is to the integrity of the financial reporting system, which it regards as its paramount concern.

COMPARABILITY

111. Information about an enterprise gains greatly in usefulness if it can be compared with similar information about other enterprises and with similar information about the same enterprise for some other period or some other point in time. The significance of information, especially quantitative information, depends to a great extent on the user's ability to relate it to some benchmark. The comparative use of information is often intuitive, as when told that an enterprise has sales revenue of $1,000,000 a year, one forms a judgment of its size by ranking it with other enterprises that one knows. Investing and lending decisions essentially involve evaluations of alternative opportunities, and they

[11]Harold M. Williams, Chairman, Securities and Exchange Commission, "Accounting Practices for Oil and Gas Producers" (Washington, D.C., 1978), p. 12.

cannot be made rationally if comparative information is not available.

112. The difficulty in making financial comparisons among enterprises because of the use of different accounting methods has been accepted for many years as the principal reason for the development of accounting standards. Indeed, the only other possible reason for wanting accounting standards would be a belief that there was one right method among the available alternatives, and few people, if any, hold any such belief.

113. The purpose of comparison is to detect and explain similarities and differences. But, in comparing complex entities, such as human beings or business enterprises, it is useless to try to consider all similarities and differences at once, for to assess the significance of any one of them will then be impossible. Valid comparison, therefore, usually requires attention to be focused on one or two characteristics at a time. Other characteristics that are in no way correlated with those under inquiry can be ignored. Characteristics that are correlated with those under inquiry must be standardized to avoid affecting the comparison. For example, to find whether a man is overweight, one compares his weight with that of other men—not women—of the same height. That is, valid comparisons involve standardizing for gender and height because those characteristics are correlated with weight. It is not necessary to standardize for intelligence, for example, by comparing a man's weight with that of other males of similar height and intelligence because weight is not correlated with intelligence. Intelligence as a characteristic can be ignored.

114. Simple comparisons can often be made without the use of measurements expressed in units, but as the number of items to be compared increases, or if comparisons over an interval of time are desired, a unit of measure becomes indispensable. If valid comparisons are to be made over time, the unit of measurement used must be invariant. Units of money used in money measurement are not in one significant sense—their command over goods and services—invariant over time.

115. Defined in the broadest terms, comparability is the quality or state of having certain characteristics in common, and comparison is normally a quantitative assessment of the common characteristic. Clearly, valid comparison is possible only if the measurements used—the quantities or ratios—reliably represent the characteristic that is the subject of comparison. To cite a nonaccounting example, it may be desired to compare the fertility of land in Florida and Oregon. If that were done by comparing crop yields per acre, it should be obvious that crop yield is not a reliable representation of fertility. Many other factors, such as climate and human efficiency, help to determine yields, and to use too broad a gauge to measure the characteristic of fertility invalidates the comparison.

116. While a particular datum, in some appropriate context, can be said to be relevant or reliable, it cannot be said to be comparable. Comparability is not a quality of information in the same sense as relevance and reliability are, but is rather a quality of the relationship between two or more pieces of information. Improving comparability may destroy or weaken relevance or reliability if, to secure comparability between two measures, one of them has to be obtained by a method yielding less relevant or less reliable information. Historically, extreme examples of this have been provided in some European countries in which the use of standardized charts of accounts has been made mandatory in the interest of interfirm comparability but at the expense of relevance and often reliability as well. That kind of uniformity may even adversely affect comparability of information if it conceals real differences between enterprises.

117. Generally, noncomparability is thought to arise because business enterprises do not use similar inputs, do not apply similar procedures, or do not use the same systems of classification of costs and revenues or assets and liabilities, and it is usually assumed that removal of those inconsistencies will make the results comparable. Certainly, comparability cannot be achieved without consistency of inputs and classification. For example, comparing liquidity between two enterprises by comparing their current ratios would usually not be valid if one enterprise valued its inventory on a last-in, first-out basis while the other valued inventory on first-in, first-out. The difference in practice would affect the comparison adversely to the first company, but its appearance of inferior liquidity would result from an invalid comparison, for the current value of its inventory may not have been less than that of the other company.

118. That kind of noncomparability imposes costs on users of financial statements and is best avoided, but it is relatively easy to diagnose and, with sufficient disclosure, can be rectified by a user of the information. A more difficult kind of noncomparability to deal with is the kind that results when ill-chosen or incomplete data inputs are used to generate information that fails one test of reliability—it does not truly represent what it purports to represent. If data inputs are ill-chosen or incomplete, the measures that result will not be truly comparable no matter how consistent the procedures are that are applied to them. For example, suppose it is desired to compare the performance of two investment managers. Each starts with the same

portfolio, but their portfolios at the end of the year are different as a result of trades during the year. Realized gains of the two managers are equal. The ending portfolio of one shows substantial unrealized gains, the other does not. To compare their performance by comparing only realized gains implies a definition of performance that many people would regard as incomplete and, therefore, as an unreliable representation.

119. To repeat what was said earlier, the purpose of comparison is to detect and explain similarities and differences. Comparability should not be confused with identity, and sometimes more can be learned from differences than from similarities if the differences can be explained. The ability to explain phenomena often depends on the diagnosis of the underlying causes of differences or the discovery that apparent differences are without significance. Much insight into the functioning of the capital market, for example, has been obtained from observing how market forces affect different stocks differently. Something has been learned, too, from observing that the market generally ignores apparent (cosmetic) differences among stocks that were formerly thought to be significant. Greater comparability of accounting information, which most people agree is a worthwhile aim, is not to be attained by making unlike things look alike any more than by making like things look different. The moral is that in seeking comparability accountants must not disguise real differences nor create false differences.

Consistency

120. Consistency in applying accounting methods over a span of time has always been regarded as an important quality that makes accounting numbers more useful. The standard form of an auditor's report states that the financial statements have been prepared "in conformity with generally accepted accounting principles consistently applied." The Accounting Principles Board stated in APB Opinion No. 20, *Accounting Changes,* that ". . . in the preparation of financial statements there is a presumption that an accounting principle once adopted should not be changed in accounting for events and transactions of a similar type. Consistent use of accounting principles from one accounting period to another enhances the utility of financial statements to users by facilitating analysis and understanding of comparative accounting data [paragraph 15]."

121. The same considerations apply whether comparisons involve time series data, with which discussions of consistency are mostly concerned, or cross-sectional data, which raise more general issues of comparability. Like comparability, consistency is a quality of the relationship between two accounting numbers rather than a quality of the numbers themselves in the sense that relevance and reliability are. The consistent use of accounting methods, whether from one period to another within a single firm, or within a single period across firms, is a necessary but not a sufficient condition of comparability. Consistency without genuine comparability is illustrated by time series data using units of money during periods of inflation. A 10-year summary of sales revenues covering a period when the purchasing power of the monetary unit has been declining may convey an exaggerated picture of growth unless the user of the information is accustomed to making purchasing power corrections. As before, it is the representational faithfulness of the measurements used, rather than simply the unchanging nature of the measurement rules or the classification rules, that results in true comparability over time.

122. Consistent use of accounting principles from one accounting period to another, if pushed too far, can inhibit accounting progress. No change to a preferred accounting method can be made without sacrificing consistency, yet there is no way that accounting can develop without change. Fortunately, it is possible to make the transition from a less preferred to a more preferred method of accounting and still retain the capacity to compare the periods before and after the change if the effects of the change of method are disclosed. If a change will bring only a small improvement, the trade-off between the improvement and the loss of consistency may make it hard to judge where the advantage lies. As in all trade-offs, it is a question of costs and benefits; and the costs include the psychological cost of adopting the change. If the cost of the added disclosure that will enable the user of accounting information to compare the prechange and postchange results is less than the expected benefits from making the change, the change should be made.

MATERIALITY

123. Those who make accounting decisions and those who make judgments as auditors continually confront the need to make judgments about materiality. Materiality judgments are primarily quantitative in nature. They pose the question: Is this item large enough for users of the information to be influenced by it? However, the answer to that question will usually be affected by the nature of the item; items too small to be thought material if they result from routine transactions may be considered material if they arise in abnormal circumstances.

124. Throughout this Statement, emphasis has been placed on relevance and reliability as the primary qualitative characteristics that accounting information must have if it is to be useful. Material-

ity is not a primary characteristic of the same kind. In fact, the pervasive nature of materiality makes it difficult to consider the concept except as it relates to the other qualitative characteristics, especially relevance and reliability.

125. Relevance and materiality have much in common—both are defined in terms of what influences or makes a difference to an investor or other decision maker. Yet the two concepts can be distinguished. A decision not to disclose certain information may be made, say, because investors have no interest in that kind of information (it is not relevant) or because the amounts involved are too small to make a difference (they are not material). But as was noted above, magnitude by itself, without regard to the nature of the item and the circumstances in which the judgment has to be made, will not generally be a sufficient basis for a materiality judgment.

126. Materiality judgments are concerned with screens or thresholds. Is an item, an error, or an omission large enough, considering its nature and the attendant circumstances, to pass over the threshold that separates material from immaterial items? An example of an applicant for employment who is negotiating with an employment agency will illustrate the relationship of the materiality concept to relevance and reliability. The agency has full information about a certain job for which the applicant is suited and will furnish any item of information about it. The applicant will certainly want information about the nature of the duties, the location of the job, the pay, the hours of work, and the fringe benefits. Information about vacations and job security may or may not be important enough to affect a decision concerning accepting the job. Further, the applicant may not be concerned at all with whether the office floor is carpeted or about the quality of the food in the cafeteria. All of those items are, in the broadest sense, relevant to an evaluation of the job. But some of them make no difference in a decision to accept it or not. The values placed on them by the applicant are too small for them to be material. They are not important enough to matter.

127. The employment agency example can also help to explain what is meant by a materiality threshold for reliability. Salary information accurate only to the nearest thousand dollars might not be acceptable to an applicant for an $8,000 a year job, but will almost certainly be acceptable if the job pays $100,000 a year. An error of a percentage point in the employee's rate of pension contribution would rarely make information about fringe benefits unacceptable. An error of a year in the retirement date of someone who would block the applicant's advancement might be quite material. An error of a year in the applicant's mandatory retirement date will probably be immaterial to a person 20 years old, but quite material to a 63-year-old person.

128. The more important a judgment item[12] is, the finer the screen should be that will be used to determine whether it is material. For example:

a. An accounting change in circumstances that puts an enterprise in danger of being in breach of covenant regarding its financial condition may justify a lower materiality threshold than if its position were stronger.
b. A failure to disclose separately a nonrecurrent item of revenue may be material at a lower threshold than would otherwise be the case if the revenue turns a loss into a profit or reverses the trend of earnings from a downward to an upward trend.
c. A misclassification of assets that would not be material in amount if it affected two categories of plant or equipment might be material if it changed the classification between a noncurrent and a current asset category.
d. Amounts too small to warrant disclosure or correction in normal circumstances may be considered material if they arise from abnormal or unusual transactions or events.

129. Almost always, the relative rather than the absolute size of a judgment item determines whether it should be considered material in a given situation. Losses from bad debts or pilferage that could be shrugged off as routine by a large business may threaten the continued existence of a small one. An error in inventory valuation may be material in a small enterprise for which it cut earnings in half but immaterial in an enterprise for which it might make a barely perceptible ripple in the earnings. Some of the empirical investigations referred to in Appendix C throw light on the considerations that enter into materiality judgments.

130. Another factor in materiality judgments is the degree of precision that is attainable in estimating the judgment item. The amount of deviation that is considered immaterial may increase as the attainable degree of precision decreases. For example, accounts payable usually can be estimated more accurately than can contingent liabilities arising from litigation or threats of it, and a deviation considered to be material in the first case may be quite trivial in the second.

[12]A judgment item is whatever has to be determined to be material or immaterial. It may be an asset or liability item, a transaction, an error, or any of a number of things.

131. Some hold the view that the Board should promulgate a set of quantitative materiality guides or criteria covering a wide variety of situations that preparers could look to for authoritative support. That appears to be a minority view, however, on the basis of representations made to the Board in response to the Discussion Memorandum, *Criteria for Determining Materiality.* The predominant view is that materiality judgments can properly be made only by those who have all the facts. The Board's present position is that no general standards of materiality could be formulated to take into account all the considerations that enter into an experienced human judgment. However, that position is not intended to imply either that the Board may not in the future review that conclusion or that quantitative guidance on materiality of specific items may not appropriately be written into the Board's standards from time to time. That has been done on occasion already (for example, in the Statement on financial reporting by segments of a business enterprise), and the Board recognizes that quantitative materiality guidance is sometimes needed. Appendix C lists a number of examples of quantitative guidelines that have been applied both in the law and in the practice of accounting. However, whenever the Board or any other authoritative body imposes materiality rules, it is substituting generalized collective judgments for specific individual judgments, and there is no reason to suppose that the collective judgments are always superior. In any case, it must be borne in mind that if, to take one example, some minimum size is stipulated for recognition of a material item (for example, a segment having revenue equal to or exceeding 10 percent of combined revenues shall be recognized as a reportable segment), the rule does not prohibit the recognition of a smaller segment. Quantitative materiality guidelines generally specify minima only. They, therefore, leave room for individual judgment in at least one direction.

132. Individual judgments are required to assess materiality in the absence of authoritative criteria or to decide that minimum quantitative criteria are not appropriate in particular situations. The essence of the materiality concept is clear. The omission or misstatement of an item in a financial report is material if, in the light of surrounding circumstances, the magnitude of the item is such that it is probable that the judgment of a reasonable person relying upon the report would have been changed or influenced by the inclusion or correction of the item.

COSTS AND BENEFITS[13]

133. Accounting information must attain some minimum level of relevance and also some minimum level of reliability if it is to be useful. Beyond those minimum levels, sometimes users may gain by sacrificing relevance for added reliability or by sacrificing reliability for added relevance; and some accounting policy changes will bring gains in both. Each user will uniquely perceive the relative value to be attached to each quality. Ultimately, a standard-setting body has to do its best to meet the needs of society as a whole when it promulgates a standard that sacrifices one of those qualities for the other; and it must also be aware constantly of the calculus of costs and benefits.

134. Unless the benefits to be derived from a commodity or service exceed the costs associated with it, it will not be sought after. When a decision to acquire a commodity is being considered, the prospective buyer will compare the costs of acquisition and maintenance with the benefits of owning the commodity. Once the purchase has been made, the owner must decide—continually, from day to day—whether the opportunity cost of ownership, the sacrifice of the sale price that cannot be realized so long as ownership continues, is less than the benefits of continued ownership. Thus, both before and after acquisition, costs and benefits must be compared, though the comparison takes a somewhat different form according to whether the acquisition has or has not been consummated.

135. Financial information is unlike other commodities in certain important respects. While, in general, it will not be desired unless its benefits exceed its costs, what makes it different from other commodities, or at least from those that are traded in the marketplace, is that whereas those other commodities are private goods, to be enjoyed only by the buyer and those with whom the buyer chooses to share them, the benefits of information cannot always be confined to those who pay for it. If the whole government and private system by which the flow of financial information is regulated could now be dismantled, if information could be traded between buyers and sellers like other commodities and could be kept from those who did not pay for it, and if consumers of information were willing to rely on their own inquiries, the balance of costs and benefits could be left to the market. But in the real world the market for information is less complete than most other markets, and a standard-setting authority must concern itself with the perceived costs and benefits of the standards it sets—costs and benefits to both users and preparers of such information, to others, like auditors, who are also concerned with it, and to anyone else in society who may be affected.

[13]This section expands on the considerations mentioned in paragraph 23 of Concepts Statement 1.

136. Most of the costs of providing financial information fall initially on the preparers, while the benefits are reaped by both preparers and users. Ultimately, the costs and benefits are diffused quite widely. The costs are mostly passed on to the users of information and to the consumers of goods and services. The benefits also are presumably passed on to consumers by assuring a steady supply of goods and services and more efficient functioning of the marketplace. But, even if the costs and benefits are not traced beyond the preparers and users of information, to say anything precise about their incidence is difficult. There are costs of using information as well as of preparing it; and much published information would be compiled for the preparer's own use even if providing it to stockholders and others were not required. The preparer enjoys other benefits also, such as improved access to capital markets, favorable impact on the enterprise's public relations, and so on.

137. The costs of providing information are of several kinds, including costs of collecting and processing the information, costs of audit if it is subject to audit, costs of disseminating it to those who must receive it, costs associated with the dangers of litigation, and in some instances costs of disclosure in the form of a loss of competitive advantages vis-a-vis trade competitors, labor unions (with a consequent effect on wage demands), or foreign enterprises. The costs to the users of information, over and above those costs that preparers pass on to them, are mainly the costs of analysis and interpretation and may include costs of rejecting information that is redundant, for the diagnosis of redundancy is not without its cost.

138. Society needs information to help allocate resources efficiently, but the benefit to any individual or company from that source is not measurable. Nor is the spur to efficiency that comes from making managers account to stockholders capable of evaluation, either at the level of the enterprise or the economy. It is impossible to imagine a highly developed economy without most of the financial information that it now generates and, for the most part, consumes; yet it is also impossible to place a value on that information.

139. From the point of view of society, the loss of competitive advantage that is said to result from some disclosure requirements is clearly in a different category from the other costs involved. Although the loss to one business enterprise may be a gain to another, the Board is aware of and concerned about the economic effects of the possible discouragement of initiative, innovation, and willingness to take risks if a reward to risk taking is denied. That is another cost that is impossible to begin to quantify.

140. The burden of the costs and the incidence of benefits fall quite unevenly throughout the economy, and it has been rightly observed that ". . . the matter of establishing disclosure requirements becomes not only a matter of judgment but also a complex balancing of many factors so that all costs and benefits receive the consideration they merit. For example, a simple rule that any information useful in making investment decisions should be disclosed fails as completely as a rule that says disclosure should not be required if competitive disadvantage results."[14] The problem is to know how to accomplish that "complex balancing."

141. The Board has watched with sympathetic interest the efforts of the Cost Accounting Standards Board (CASB) to come to grips with the task of comparing the costs and benefits of its standards. The Report of the special group of consultants who were asked by the CASB to examine this matter was submitted on November 13, 1978. The conclusions were quite negative.

> Our conclusion is that no objective cost benefit calculation in aggregate quantitative terms is possible for CASB standards as a whole or for any of them individually. Reasonable people, with some experience in such matters, acting responsibly in a spirit of compromise, using such reliable information as can be gathered together, will make a "calculation," as they must if anything is to be done. But the calculation will be in ordinal rather than cardinal terms; it will be rough rather than precise; it will always be subject to revision, rather than fixed in stone. The situation is not different from that concerning the merits of many other laws, rules, regulations, and administrative decisions. Nor is our conclusion different from the conclusion reached by those concerned with the cost-benefit problem confronting the Paperwork Commission, for example.[15]

142. As the CASB's consultants point out, the reasons for that negative conclusion can be simply stated. The costs and benefits of a standard are both direct and indirect, immediate and deferred. They may be affected by a change in circumstances not foreseen when the standard was promulgated. There are wide variations in the estimates that different people make about the dollar values involved and the rate of discount to be used in reducing them to a

[14]R. K. Mautz and William G. May, *Financial Disclosure in a Competitive Economy* (New York: Financial Executives Research Foundation, 1978), p. 6.

[15]Robert N. Anthony et al., "Report to the Cost Accounting Standards Board by a Special Group of Consultants to Consider Issues Relating to Comparing Costs with Benefits" (1978), p. 1.

present value. "For these reasons," the consultants conclude, "the merits of any Standard, or of the Standards as a whole, can be decided finally only by judgments that are largely subjective. They cannot be decided by scientific test."

143. Despite the difficulties, the Board does not conclude that it should turn its back on the matter, for there are some things that it can do to safeguard the cost-effectiveness of its standards. Before a decision is made to develop a standard, the Board needs to satisfy itself that the matter to be ruled on represents a significant problem and that a standard that is promulgated will not impose costs on the many for the benefit of a few. If the proposal passes that first test, a second test may subsequently be useful. There are usually alternative ways of handling an issue. Is one of them less costly and only slightly less effective? Even if absolute magnitudes cannot be attached to costs and benefits, a comparison between alternatives may yet be possible and useful.

144. Though it is unlikely that significantly improved means of measuring benefits will become available in the foreseeable future, it seems possible that better ways of quantifying the incremental costs of regulations of all kinds may gradually be developed, and the Board will watch any such developments carefully to see whether they can be applied to financial accounting standards. Even if that hope proves to be a vain one, however, the Board cannot cease to be concerned about the cost-effectiveness of its standards. To do so would be a dereliction of its duty and a disservice to its constituents.

This Statement was adopted by the unanimous vote of the seven members of the Financial Accounting Standards Board:

Donald J. Kirk, *Chairman*
Frank E. Block
John W. March
Robert A. Morgan
David Mosso
Robert T. Sprouse
Ralph E. Walters

Appendix A

BACKGROUND INFORMATION

145. The need for a conceptual framework for financial accounting and reporting, beginning with consideration of the objectives of financial reporting, is generally recognized. The Accounting Principles Board issued APB Statement No. 4 on basic concepts and accounting principles in 1970. When the Financial Accounting Standards Board came into existence, the Study Group on the Objectives of Financial Statements was at work, and its Report, *Objectives of Financial Statements,* was published in October 1973 by the American Institute of Certified Public Accountants. A chapter of that report briefly described "certain characteristics . . . [information should possess] to satisfy users' needs"—relevance and materiality, form and substance, reliability, freedom from bias, comparability, consistency, and understandability—which the Study Group called "qualitative characteristics of reporting."

146. The Financial Accounting Standards Board issued FASB Discussion Memorandum, *Conceptual Framework for Accounting and Reporting: Consideration of the Report of the Study Group on the Objectives of Financial Statements,* dated June 6, 1974, and held a public hearing on September 23 and 24, 1974 on the objectives of financial statements. The Discussion Memorandum and the hearing were based primarily on the Report of the Study Group on the Objectives of Financial Statements. The Discussion Memorandum asked respondents to comment on the acceptability of the seven qualitative characteristics in the Report and to suggest needed modifications. The Board received 95 written communications responding to the Discussion Memorandum, and 20 parties presented their views orally and answered Board members' questions at the hearing.

147. On December 2, 1976, the Board issued three documents:

Tentative Conclusions on Objectives of Financial Statements of Business Enterprises,

FASB Discussion Memorandum, *Conceptual Framework for Financial Accounting and Reporting: Elements of Financial Statements and Their Measurement,* and

Scope and Implications of the Conceptual Framework Project.

One chapter of the Discussion Memorandum was entitled, "Qualities of Useful Financial Information." Although it raised no specific issues, it asked respondents to explain what they meant by relevance, reliability, comparability, and other "qualitative characteristics" and to illustrate those meanings in responding to the issues about elements of financial statements and their measurement and by completing a set of matrixes designed to show trade-offs between various qualities or characteristics. The same task force, with one membership change, provided counsel in preparing both Discussion Memorandums. Eleven persons from academe, the financial community, industry, and public accounting served on the task force while the Discussion Memorandums were written.

148. The Board held public hearings (a) August 1 and 2, 1977 on the *Tentative Conclusions on Objectives of Financial Statements of Business Enterprises* and Chapters 1-5 of the Discussion Memorandum (December 1976) concerning definitions of the elements of financial statements and (b) January 16-18, 1978 on the remaining chapters of that Discussion Memorandum concerning capital maintenance or cost recovery, qualities of useful financial information ("qualitative characteristics"), and measurement of the elements of financial statements. The Board received 332 written communications on the Discussion Memorandum, of which 143 commented on the "qualitative characteristics." Twenty-seven parties presented their views orally and answered Board members' questions at the January 1978 hearing.

149. The Board issued an Exposure Draft of a proposed Statement of Financial Accounting Concepts, *Objectives of Financial Reporting and Elements of Financial Statements of Business Enterprises,* dated December 29, 1977, which included a very brief discussion of some "characteristics or qualities that make financial information useful," noting that those characteristics were to be the subject of another phase of the conceptual framework project. The Board received 135 letters of comment, of which 36 commented on the paragraphs discussing "qualitative characteristics." That discussion was not included in Concepts Statement 1.

150. The Board also issued FASB Discussion Memorandum, *Criteria for Determining Materiality,* on March 21, 1975 and held public hearings on it May 20 and 21, 1976. The Board received 96 written communications on the Discussion Memorandum, and 16 parties presented their views orally and answered Board members' questions at the hearing. The Board explored incorporating the conceptual aspects of the materiality project into the qualitative characteristics project during 1977 and 1978 and formally did so in October 1978.

151. Professor David Solomons, the Arthur Young Professor of Accounting at the Wharton School of the University of Pennsylvania, served as consultant to the Board and staff on the qualitative characteristics project.

Appendix B

PRINCIPAL RESPECTS IN WHICH THIS STATEMENT DIFFERS FROM THE EXPOSURE DRAFT AND OTHER RESPONSES TO LETTERS OF COMMENT ON THE EXPOSURE DRAFT

152. Of the changes made to the Exposure Draft that was issued on August 9, 1979, many were in response to suggestions that were made in the 89 comment letters received during the exposure period. One suggestion was that the definitions that were scattered throughout the Exposure Draft should be brought together in a glossary. That has now been done.

153. The chart that appears on page 4048 now distinguishes between primary qualities, ingredients of primary qualities, and secondary qualities that make information useful. The chart also now explicitly introduces decision makers and their characteristics as factors that help to determine what information will be useful in particular situations. Those characteristics include how much knowledge decision makers already have and how well they understand the significance of new information that comes to them. That makes it possible to view relevance as a quality that information has in relation to a situation or a decision rather than as a quality that depends on the personal characteristics of the decision maker. Thus, if information that is relevant to a decision were conveyed in a language that some decision makers did not understand, it would not be useful to them because of their lack of understanding. However, understandability of information is a prerequisite to the information being useful to particular decision makers.

154. The discussion of relevance has been further clarified by recognizing more explicitly the value of information about past activities as distinct from its value for predictive purposes. Thus, predictive value and feedback value are shown as coequal ingredients of relevance. To be relevant, information must have one of them or both, and it must be timely.

155. A clearer distinction is now drawn between the degree of reliability that can be achieved in a particular situation and the perceived need for more reliability or less. In terms of the chronometer-wristwatch analogy in paragraph 73, the wristwatch is not as reliable a timekeeper as the chronometer. It does not need to be. It is the perceived *need* for

reliability that is different because of the different uses to which the two instruments are put. That difference does not affect the *nature* of reliability but only the degree of reliability that may be needed for particular uses.

156. The discussion of materiality has been considerably recast, with much of the detail moved into Appendix C. Though the definition of materiality is not substantially changed, its quantitative character is now given a more central position, enabling the distinction between materiality and relevance to be stated more clearly. Though both qualities are present in information only if it "can make a difference" to a decision, relevance stems from the *nature* of the information while materiality depends on the *size* of the judgment item in particular circumstances.

157. Several of those who commented on the Exposure Draft doubted that the qualitative characteristics discussed in it were "operational" in the sense that they provided clear criteria for the selection of a preferred accounting method if two or more alternatives were available. Only in a few cases were other methods of selection proposed that were claimed to be more operational, and after careful review by the Board's staff, those claims had to be rejected as being unrealistic. The Board believes that the approach to preferability choices put forward in this Statement achieves as much operationality as is feasible in the present state of knowledge.The true test will be in the contributions that the criteria discussed here can make to the formulation of future standards. Unanimous acclaim for the Board's decisions is not to be expected; but the basis for those decisions should be better understood if they can be seen to be aimed at obtaining an optimal mix (as judged by the Board) of certain clearly defined informational characteristics.

158. A number of respondents urged the Board to include additional qualitative characteristics in its "hierarchy." All of the proposed additions had already been considered and excluded because they seemed to add little value to other characteristics that were already included. The more items are added, the more the impact of each is diluted. To earn a place, therefore, something really important must be added. None of the new candidates passed that test. For example, objectivity was mentioned by several respondents. Yet, verifiability better expresses the quality that those respondents were concerned with preserving. "Objective" means having an existence independent of the observer. That does not fit accounting measurements at all well, especially measurements such as profit, depreciation and other cost allocations, earnings per share, and others of like kind. Accounting terminology will be improved if verifiability, which reflects what accountants do, replaces objectivity in the accountant's lexicon.

159. Feasibility was another candidate for inclusion in the hierarchy. That has been excluded because it adds nothing to the cost-benefit constraint. In accounting as in other fields, many things are feasible *at a cost*. But an accounting method that, though feasible, yields information that is worth less than it costs is not a good one to choose. For that reason, feasibility has not been included in the hierarchy.

160. Substance over form is an idea that also has its proponents, but it is not included because it would be redundant. The quality of reliability and, in particular, of representational faithfulness leaves no room for accounting representations that subordinate substance to form. Substance over form is, in any case, a rather vague idea that defies precise definition.

Appendix C

QUANTITATIVE MATERIALITY CONSIDERATIONS

161. Each Statement of Financial Accounting Standards issued by the Board has concluded by stating that: "The provisions of this Statement need not be applied to immaterial items." Rule 3-02 of the Securities and Exchange Commission's (SEC) Regulation S-X, "Form and Content of Financial Statements," states that if an "amount which would otherwise be required to be shown with respect to any item is not material, it need not be separately set forth."

162. Those who turn to SEC Regulation S-X for help in understanding the concept of materiality learn that a material matter is one "about which an average prudent investor ought reasonably to be informed" (Rule 1-02) and that material information is "such . . . information as is necessary to make the required statements, in the light of the circumstances under which they are made not misleading" (Rule 3-06). But those statements are not really definitions of materiality in that they provide only general guidance in distinguishing material from immaterial information.

163. The courts have stepped in to fill the gap. It is the impact of information on an investor's judgment that is at the heart of the distinction. To quote the Tenth Circuit Court of Appeals, information is material if ". . . the trading judgment of reasonable investors would not have been left untouched upon

receipt of such information."[16] That is very close to the definition of materiality adopted in the *BarChris* decision, in which the judge said that a material fact was one "which if it had been correctly stated or disclosed would have deterred or tended to deter the average prudent investor from purchasing the securities in question."[17] Both statements refer to one particular kind of user of information—a prudent investor—but, of course, the essential idea that they convey is applicable to other users also.

164. Statements by the Supreme Court have given added authority to that view of materiality. In the important case of *TSC Industries Inc.* v. *Northway Inc.*,[18] a case which concerned the omission of certain facts from a proxy statement, the Court held that:

> An omitted fact is material if there is a substantial likelihood that a reasonable shareholder would consider it important in deciding how to vote. This standard is fully consistent with the . . . general description of materiality as a requirement that "the defect have a significant *propensity* to affect the voting process." It does not require proof of a substantial likelihood that disclosure of the omitted fact would have caused the reasonable investor to change his vote. What the standard does contemplate is a showing of a substantial likelihood that, under all the circumstances, the omitted fact would have assumed actual significance in the deliberations of the reasonable shareholder. Put another way, there must be a substantial likelihood that the disclosure of the omitted fact would have been viewed by the reasonable investor as having significantly altered the "total mix" of information made available.

165. Until such time as the Supreme Court returns to this question, the *Northway* case provides the most authoritative judicial definition of what constitutes a material omitted fact. Examples, taken from earlier cases, of facts that have been held to be "material" are:[19]

1. Failure to disclose a greatly enhanced inventory value (carried on the corporation's financial statements at historical cost) and an intention to realize on it by liquidation. *Speed* v. *Transamerica Corp.*, 99 F. Supp. 808 (D. Del. 1951), *modified and aff'd.*, 235 F.2d 369 (3d Cir. 1956).
2. Failure to disclose pending negotiations to sell all of the assets of the corporation at a price per share substantially larger than that being paid to a selling shareholder. *Kardon* v. *National Gypsum Co.*, 69 F. Supp. 512 (E.D. Pa. 1946), *on the merits,* 73 F. Supp. 798 (E.D. Pa. 1947).
3. Failure to disclose the imminence of a highly profitable transaction by the corporation. *Northern Trust Co.* v. *Essaness Theatres Corp.*, 103 F. Supp. 954 (N.D. Ill. 1952).
4. Failure to disclose a readjustment of reported earnings from 85¢ per share for the first five months of the fiscal year to 12¢ per share for the first six months. *Financial Industrial Fund, Inc.* v. *McDonnell Douglas Corp.*, CCH Fed. Sec. L. Rep. ¶93,004 (D. Col. 1971).
5. Failure to disclose that investigations were pending by the SEC. *Hill York Corp.* v. *American International Franchises, Inc.*, 448 F.2d 680 (5th Cir. 1971).
6. Failure to disclose firm offers, in contrast to appraisals, greatly higher than the book value for the physical facilities of the acquired company which the acquiring company intended to liquidate as soon as possible. *Gerstle* v. *Gamble-Skogmo, Inc.*, 478 F2d 1281, 1295 (2d Cir. 1973).
7. Failure to disclose active negotiations by tender offeror to sell significant assets substantially below book value. *Chris Craft Industries, Inc.* v. *Piper Aircraft Corp.*, 480 F.2d 341, 367 (2d Cir. 1973).

166. The Discussion Memorandum on materiality cited some of the quantitative guides to materiality in authoritative statements issued by the SEC and other regulatory agencies and standard-setting bodies. It may be helpful to be reminded how certain specific situations have been dealt with in practice. Some of these examples of materiality are brought together again in the accompanying table.

---

[16] *Mitchell* v. *Texas Gulf Sulphur Co.*, 446 F.2D 90, at 99-100 (10th Circuit, 1971).

[17] *Escott et al.* v. *BarChris Construction Corporation et al.*, 283 Fed. Supp. (District Ct. S.D. New York, 1968), p. 681.

[18] CCH *Federal Securities Law Reports* ¶95,615 (US Sup Ct. June 14, 1976).

[19] The following list is taken from James O. Hewitt, "Developing Concepts of Materiality and Disclosure," *The Business Lawyer,* Vol. 32 (April 1977), pp. 910 and 911. A word of caution may be in order. The extreme brevity of the citations given here inevitably causes many important aspects of these cases to be omitted.

Table 1

EXAMPLES OF QUANTITATIVE MATERIALITY GUIDELINES

Subject	Authority	Materiality Guidelines
Dilution of earnings per share (EPS)	APB Opinion No. 15	Reduction of EPS of less than 3% in the aggregate not material.
Separate disclosure of balance sheet items	SEC Accounting Series Release No. 41	If 10% or more of their immediate category or more than 5% of total assets.
Receivables from officers and stockholders	SEC Regulation S-X, Rule 5-04	Disclose details of receivables from any officer or principal stockholder if it equals or exceeds $20,000 or 1% of total assets.
Segmental reporting: recognition of reportable segment	Statement of Financial Accounting Standards No. 14	Revenue equals or exceeds 10% of combined revenues, etc.
Gross rental expense under leases	SEC Accounting Series Release No. 147	Disclose total rental expense, etc., if gross rents exceed 1% of consolidated revenue.
Information on present value of lease commitments under noncapitalized financing leases	SEC Accounting Series Release No. 147	Disclose if present value is 5% or more of total of long-term debt, stockholders' equity, and present value of commitments, or if impact of capitalization on income is 3% or more of average net income for most recent 3 years.
Proved oil and gas reserves	SEC Accounting Series Release No. 258	Disclose quantities of proved oil and gas reserves and historical financial data unless, for each of the two most recent years, revenues and income from oil and gas producing activities and certain oil and gas capital values do not exceed 10% of the related company totals.

167. One approach in seeking guidance about what constitutes a material item or a material error is to examine current practice empirically. One study[20] investigated the factors that entered into judgments about the materiality of an error and found that the primary factor was the ratio of the error to current income before tax. The error took on special significance if it changed the trend in income. Another study[21] examined a sample of audit reports to try to determine the factors that caused auditors to render

[20]Sam M. Woolsey, "Materiality Survey," *The Journal of Accountancy* (September 1973), pp. 91 and 92.

[21]Paul Frishkoff, "An Empirical Investigation of the Concept of Materiality in Accounting," *Empirical Research in Accounting: Selected Studies* (1970), pp. 116-129.

qualified opinions when there was an accounting change. The effect on net income (as a percentage) was found to be the only significant variable, but there was little uniformity among auditors about when an accounting change was material. A much more extensive study, conducted for the Financial Executives Research Foundation[22] examined several kinds of materiality judgments. Perhaps its principal conclusion was that a "rule of thumb" of 5-10 percent of net income is widely used as a general materiality criterion.

168. A different approach looks to security prices to determine materiality norms. According to that view, "an observed association between extant security prices and reported accounting data (or changes therein) provides prima facie evidence as to the informational content of accounting numbers."[23] That means that the materiality of information released to the market can be tested by observing its impact on security prices. Of course, that can only be done after the event, whereas preparers and auditors have to make materiality judgments before information is released to the market. Presumably they are to act in the light of market behavior observed in similar circumstances.

169. Without doubt, observations of market behavior can improve understanding of what constitutes material information. But the market's anticipation of accounting information months before it is released and the dilution of accounting influences on prices by other factors acting concurrently make price fluctuations, in the present state of knowledge, too blunt an instrument to be depended on to set materiality guidelines.

170. It is already possible to simulate some aspects of the decision making processes of auditors by constructing a model that will bring into play many of the decision variables that enter into materiality judgments.[24] Those variables would normally include the nature and size of the judgment item in question (for example, an accounting change or a contingent liability), the size of the enterprise, its financial condition and recent changes in condition, present and recent profitability, and as many as possible of the other significant factors that affect materiality judgments. Further development of such models is perhaps the most promising line of research that needs to be pursued before accountants can hope to be relieved of the onerous duty of making materiality decisions. But, until further progress has been made, that duty must continue to be discharged by the exercise of judgment taking into account as many relevant considerations as possible.

[22]James W. Pattillo, *The Concept of Materiality in Financial Reporting* (New York: Financial Executives Research Foundation, 1976).

[23]Melvin C. O'Connor and Daniel W. Collins, "Toward Establishing User-Oriented Materiality Standards," *The Journal of Accountancy* (December 1974), p. 70.

[24]For an example, see "Policy-Capturing on Selected Materiality Judgments," by James R. Boatsman and Jack C. Robertson (*Accounting Review,* April 1974, pp. 342-352).

Statement of Financial Accounting Concepts No. 3
Elements of Financial Statements of Business Enterprises

STATUS

Issued: December 1980

HIGHLIGHTS

[*Best understood in context of full Statement*]

- Elements of financial statements are the building blocks with which financial statements are constructed—the classes of items that financial statements comprise. The items in financial statements represent in words and numbers certain enterprise resources, claims to those resources, and the effects of transactions and other events and circumstances that result in changes in those resources and claims.

- This Statement defines 10 interrelated elements that are directly related to measuring performance and status of an enterprise. (Other possible elements of financial statements are not addressed.)

  —Assets are probable future economic benefits obtained or controlled by a particular entity as a result of past transactions or events.

  —Liabilities are probable future sacrifices of economic benefits arising from present obligations of a particular entity to transfer assets or provide services to other entities in the future as a result of past transactions or events.

  —Equity is the residual interest in the assets of an entity that remains after deducting its liabilities. In a business enterprise, the equity is the ownership interest.

  —Investments by owners are increases in net assets of a particular enterprise resulting from transfers to it from other entities of something of value to obtain or increase ownership interests (or equity) in it. Assets are most commonly received as investments by owners, but that which is received may also include services or satisfaction or conversion of liabilities of the enterprise.

  —Distributions to owners are decreases in net assets of a particular enterprise resulting from transferring assets, rendering services, or incurring liabilities by the enterprise to owners. Distributions to owners decrease ownership interests (or equity) in an enterprise.

  —Comprehensive income is the change in equity (net assets) of an entity during a period from transactions and other events and circumstances from nonowner sources. It includes all changes in equity during a period except those resulting from investments by owners and distributions to owners.

  —Revenues are inflows or other enhancements of assets of an entity or settlements of its liabilities (or a combination of both) during a period from delivering or producing goods, rendering services, or other activities that constitute the entity's ongoing major or central operations.

  —Expenses are outflows or other using up of assets or incurrences of liabilities (or a combination of both) during a period from delivering or producing goods, rendering services, or carrying out other activities that constitute the entity's ongoing major or central operations.

—Gains are increases in equity (net assets) from peripheral or incidental transactions of an entity and from all other transactions and other events and circumstances affecting the entity during a period except those that result from revenues or investments by owners.

—Losses are decreases in equity (net assets) from peripheral or incidental transactions of an entity and from all other transactions and other events and circumstances affecting the entity during a period except those that result from expenses or distributions to owners.

- The Statement also defines or describes certain other concepts that underlie or are otherwise closely related to the 10 elements defined in the Statement.

- The Statement does not define the term *earnings,* which is reserved for possible use to designate a significant intermediate measure or component that is part of comprehensive income.

- The Board expects most assets and liabilities in present practice to continue to qualify as assets or liabilities under the definitions in this Statement. The Board emphasizes that the definitions neither require nor presage upheavals in present practice, although they may in due time lead to some evolutionary changes in practice or at least in the ways certain items are viewed. They should be especially helpful in understanding the content of financial statements and in analyzing and resolving new financial accounting issues as they arise.

- The appendixes are not part of the definitions but are intended for readers who may find them useful. They describe the background of the Statement and elaborate on the descriptions of the essential characteristics of the elements, including some discussions and illustrations of how to apply the definitions and what they mean.

Statement of Financial Accounting Concepts No. 3
Elements of Financial Statements of Business Enterprises

Statements of Financial Accounting Concepts

This Statement of Financial Accounting Concepts is one of a series of publications in the Board's conceptual framework for financial accounting and reporting. Statements in the series are intended to set forth objectives and fundamentals that will be the basis for development of financial accounting and reporting standards. The objectives identify the goals and purposes of financial reporting. The fundamentals are the underlying concepts of financial accounting—concepts that guide the selection of transactions, events, and circumstances to be accounted for; their recognition and measurement; and the means of summarizing and communicating them to interested parties. Concepts of that type are fundamental in the sense that other concepts flow from them and repeated reference to them will be necessary in establishing, interpreting, and applying accounting and reporting standards.

The conceptual framework is a coherent system of interrelated objectives and fundamentals that is expected to lead to consistent standards and that prescribes the nature, function, and limits of financial accounting and reporting. It is expected to serve the public interest by providing structure and direction to financial accounting and reporting to facilitate the provision of evenhanded financial and related information that helps promote the efficient allocation of scarce resources in the economy and society, including assisting capital and other markets to function efficiently.

Establishment of objectives and identification of fundamental concepts will not directly solve financial accounting and reporting problems. Rather, objectives give direction and concepts are tools for solving problems.

The Board itself is likely to be the most direct beneficiary of the guidance provided by the Statements in this series. They will guide the Board in developing accounting and reporting standards by providing the Board with a common foundation and basic reasoning on which to consider merits of alternatives.

However, knowledge of the objectives and concepts the Board will use in developing standards also should enable those who are affected by or interested in financial accounting standards to understand better the purposes, content, and characteristics of information provided by financial accounting and reporting. That knowledge is expected to enhance the usefulness of, and confidence in, financial accounting and reporting. The concepts also may provide some guidance in analyzing new or emerging problems of financial accounting and reporting in the absence of applicable authoritative pronouncements.

Statements of Financial Accounting Concepts do not establish standards prescribing accounting procedures or disclosure practices for particular items or events, which are issued by the Board as Statements of Financial Accounting Standards. Rather, Statements in this series describe concepts and relations that will underlie future financial accounting standards and practices and in due course serve as a basis for evaluating existing standards and practices.*

The Board recognizes that in certain respects current generally accepted accounting principles may be inconsistent with those that may derive from the objectives and concepts set forth in Statements in this series. However, a Statement of Financial Accounting Concepts does not (a) require a change in existing generally accepted accounting principles; (b) amend, modify, or interpret Statements of Financial Accounting Standards, Interpretations of the FASB, Opinions of the Accounting Principles Board, or Bulletins of the Committee on Accounting Procedure that are in effect; or (c) justify either changing existing generally accepted accounting and reporting practices or interpreting the pronouncements listed in item (b) based on personal interpretations of the objectives and concepts in the Statements of Financial Accounting Concepts.

Since a Statement of Financial Accounting Concepts does not establish generally accepted accounting principles or standards for the disclosure of financial information outside of financial statements in published financial reports, it is not intended to invoke application of Rule 203 or 204 of the Rules of Conduct of the Code of Professional Ethics of the American Institute of Certified Public Accountants (or successor rules or arrangements of similar scope and intent).†

Like other pronouncements of the Board, a Statement of Financial Accounting Concepts may be amended, superseded, or withdrawn by appropriate action under the Board's *Rules of Procedure.*

*Pronouncements such as APB Statement No. 4, *Basic Concepts and Accounting Principles Underlying Financial Statements of Business Enterprises,* and the Accounting Terminology Bulletins will continue to serve their intended purpose — they describe objectives and concepts underlying standards and practices existing at the time of their issuance.

†Rule 203 prohibits a member of the American Institute of Certified Public Accountants from expressing an opinion that financial statements conform with generally accepted accounting principles if those statements contain a material departure from an accounting principle promulgated by the Financial Accounting Standards Board, unless the member can demonstrate that because of unusual circumstances the financial statements otherwise would have been misleading. Rule 204 requires members of the Institute to justify departures from standards promulgated by the Financial Accounting Standards Board for the disclosure of financial information outside of financial statements in published financial reports.

Elements of Financial Statements of Business Enterprises

FASB PUBLICATIONS ON CONCEPTUAL FRAMEWORK

Statements of Financial Accounting Concepts

No. 1, *Objectives of Financial Reporting by Business Enterprises* (November 1978)

No. 2, *Qualitative Characteristics of Accounting Information* (May 1980)

No. 4, *Objectives of Financial Reporting by Nonbusiness Organizations* (December 1980)

Discussion Memorandums and Invitations to Comment Having Issues Being (or Yet to Be) Considered by the Board

Elements of Financial Statements and Their Measurement (December 2, 1976)

Reporting Earnings (July 31, 1979)

Financial Statements and Other Means of Financial Reporting (May 12, 1980)

Reporting Funds Flows, Liquidity, and Financial Flexibility (December 15, 1980)

Other Projects in Process

Accounting Recognition Criteria

CONTENTS

INTRODUCTION

Scope and Content of Statement

1. This Statement defines 10 elements of financial statements of business enterprises: assets, liabilities, equity, investments by owners, distributions to owners, comprehensive income,[1] revenues, expenses, gains, and losses. The Statement also defines or describes certain other concepts that underlie or are otherwise related to the 10 elements listed (Summary Index, page 79). It contains no conclusions about matters that are intended to be decided in other phases of the Board's conceptual framework project (paragraphs 16 and 17).

2. Although this Statement is entitled *Elements of Financial Statements of Business Enterprises,* the Board has tried to word several of the definitions so that they could also apply to organizations other than business enterprises. Assets and liabilities are common to all organizations, and the Board sees no reason to define them differently for business and nonbusiness organizations. The Board also expects

[1]*Comprehensive income* is the name used in this Statement for the concept that was called *earnings* in the FASB Exposure Draft, *Objectives of Financial Reporting and Elements of Financial Statements of Business Enterprises* (December 1977), FASB Concepts Statement No. 1, *Objectives of Financial Reporting by Business Enterprises,* and other conceptual framework documents previously issued (*Tentative Conclusions on Objectives of Financial Statements of Business Enterprises* [December 1976]; FASB Discussion Memorandum, *Elements of Financial Statements and Their Measurement* [December 1976]; and FASB Discussion Memorandum, *Reporting Earnings* [July 1979]). *Earnings* is not defined in this Statement. The Board has decided to reserve the term for possible use to designate a component part, as yet undetermined, of comprehensive income (par. 58).

the definitions of equity, revenues, expenses, gains, and losses to fit both business and nonbusiness organizations. In contrast, nonbusiness organizations have no need for elements such as investments by owners, distributions to owners, and comprehensive income but may need other elements not needed by business enterprises. In the near future, the Board expects to consider and to solicit views about which, if any, of the definitions are inappropriate or may require modification for nonbusiness organizations and whether other elements are needed for financial statements of nonbusiness organizations.

Other Possible Elements of Financial Statements of Business Enterprises

3. Although the elements defined in this Statement include basic elements and are probably those most commonly identified as elements of financial statements of business enterprises, they are not the only elements of financial statements. The elements defined in this Statement are a related group with a particular focus—on assets, liabilities, equity, and other elements directly related to measuring performance and status of an enterprise. Information about an enterprise's performance and status provided by accrual accounting is the primary focus of financial reporting (FASB Concepts Statement No. 1, *Objectives of Financial Reporting by Business Enterprises,* paragraphs 40-48). Other focuses may require other elements.[2]

4. Variations of possible statements showing the effects on assets and liabilities of transactions or other events and circumstances during a period are almost limitless, and all of them have classes of items that may be called elements of financial statements. For example, a statement showing funds flows or cash flows during a period may include categories for funds or cash provided by (a) operations, (b) borrowings, (c) issuing equity securities, (d) sale of assets, and so forth. Other phases of the conceptual framework project may define additional elements of financial statements as needed.

Elements and Financial Representations

5. Elements of financial statements are the building blocks with which financial statements are constructed—the classes of items that financial statements comprise. *Elements* refers to broad classes, such as assets, liabilities, revenues, and expenses. Particular economic things and events, such as cash on hand or selling merchandise, that may meet the definitions of elements are not elements as the term is used in this Statement. Rather, they are called *items* or other descriptive names. This Statement focuses on the broad classes and their characteristics instead of defining particular assets, liabilities, or other items. Although notes to financial statements are described in some authoritative pronouncements as an integral part of financial statements, they are not elements. They serve different functions, including amplifying or complementing information about items in financial statements.

6. The items that are formally incorporated in financial statements are financial representations (depictions in words and numbers) of certain resources of an entity, claims to those resources, and the effects of transactions and other events and circumstances that result in changes in those resources and claims. That is, symbols (words and numbers) in financial statements stand for cash in a bank, buildings, wages due, sales, use of labor, earthquake damage to property, and a host of other economic things and events pertaining to an entity existing and operating in what is sometimes called the "real world."

7. This Statement follows the common practice of calling by the same names both the financial representations in financial statements and the resources, claims, transactions, events, or circumstances that they represent. For example, *inventory* or *asset* may refer either to merchandise on the floor of a retail enterprise or to the words and numbers that represent that merchandise in the enterprise's financial statements; and *sale* or *revenue* may refer either to the transaction by which some of that merchandise is transferred to a customer or to the words and numbers that represent the transaction in the enterprise's financial statements.[3]

Other Scope and Content Matters

8. Appendix A to this Statement contains background information for the Statement. Appendix B contains explanations and examples pertaining to

[2]Some respondents to the Exposure Draft interpreted the discussion of other possible elements to mean that financial statements now called balance sheets and income statements might have elements other than those defined. However, the other elements referred to pertain to other possible financial statements. Although this Statement contains no conclusions about the identity, number, or form of financial statements, it defines all elements for balance sheets and income statements in their present forms except perhaps *earnings* (par. 1, footnote 1).

[3]The FASB Exposure Draft, *Objectives of Financial Reporting and Elements of Financial Statements of Business Enterprises* (December 29, 1977), attempted to distinguish the representations from what they represent by giving them different names. For example, *assets* referred only to the financial representations in financial statements, and *economic resources* referred to the real-world things that assets represented in financial statements. That aspect of the Exposure Draft caused considerable confusion and was criticized by respondents. The revised Exposure Draft, *Elements of Financial Statements of Business Enterprises,* reverted to the more common practice of using the same names for both, and this Statement adopts the same usage.

the characteristics of assets, liabilities, equity, and comprehensive income and its components.

Objectives, Qualitative Characteristics, and Elements

9. Decision usefulness in investment, credit, and similar decisions is the focus of both of the concepts Statements that precede this one: FASB Concepts Statement No. 1, *Objectives of Financial Reporting by Business Enterprises,* and FASB Concepts Statement No. 2, *Qualitative Characteristics of Accounting Information.* Usefulness of financial reporting information for those decisions rests on the cornerstones of relevance and reliability.

10. The definitions in this Statement are of economic things and events that are relevant to investment, credit, and similar decisions and thus are relevant to financial reporting.[4] Those decisions involve committing (or continuing to commit) resources to a business enterprise. The elements defined are an enterprise's resources, the claims to or interests in those resources, and the changes therein from transactions and other events and circumstances involved in its use of resources to earn a profit. Relevance of information about those elements stems from the significance of resources and profitability in the activities of business enterprises.

11. Economic resources or assets and changes in them are central to the existence and operations of an individual business enterprise. Business enterprises are in essence resource or asset processors, and a resource's capacity to be exchanged for cash or other resources or to be combined with other resources to produce exchangeable goods or services gives it utility and value (future economic benefit) to an enterprise. Since resources or assets confer their benefits on an enterprise by being exchanged, used, or otherwise invested, changes in resources or assets are the purpose, the means, and the result of an enterprise's operations, and a business enterprise exists primarily to acquire, use, produce, and distribute resources. Through those activities it both provides goods or services to society and obtains cash and other assets with which it compensates those who provide it with resources, including its owners.

12. Although the relation between profit of an enterprise[5] and compensation received by owners is complex and often indirect, profit is the basic source of compensation to owners for providing equity or risk capital to an enterprise. Profitable operations generate resources that can be distributed to owners or reinvested in the enterprise, and investors' expectations about both distributions to owners and reinvested profit may affect market prices of the enterprise's equity securities. Expectations that owners will be adequately compensated—that they will receive returns *on* their investments commensurate with their risks—are as necessary to attract equity capital to an enterprise as are expectations of wages and salaries to attract employees' services, expectations of repayments of borrowing with interest to attract borrowed funds, or expectations of payments on account to attract raw materials or merchandise.

13. Repayment or compensation of lenders, employees, suppliers, and other nonowners for resources provided is also related to profit or loss in the sense that profitable enterprises (and those that break even) generally are able to repay borrowing with interest, pay adequate wages and salaries, and pay for other goods and services received, while unprofitable enterprises often become less and less able to pay and thus find it increasingly difficult to obtain the resources they need to continue operations. Thus, information about profit and its components is of interest to suppliers, employees, lenders, and other providers of resources as well as to owners.

Interrelation of Elements—Articulation

14. Elements of financial statements are of two different kinds or classes, which are sometimes explained as being analogous to photographs and motion pictures. The elements defined in this Statement include three of one class and seven of the other. Assets, liabilities, and equity describe levels or amounts of resources or claims to resources at a moment of time. All other elements describe effects of transactions and other events and circumstances that affect an enterprise during intervals of time (periods). They include comprehensive income and its components—revenues, expenses, gains, and

[4]Decision usefulness of information provided about those relevant economic things and events depends not only on their relevance but also on the reliability (especially representational faithfulness) of the financial representations called assets, liabilities, revenues, expenses, etc., in financial statements. Representational faithfulness depends not only on the way the definitions are applied but also on recognition and measurement decisions that are beyond the scope of this Statement (pars. 16 and 17).

[5]*Profit* is used in this and the following paragraphs in a broad descriptive sense to refer to an enterprise's successful performance during a period. It is not intended to have a technical accounting meaning or to imply resolution of classification and display matters that are beyond the scope of this Statement, and no specific relation between *profit* and either *comprehensive income* or *earnings* (par. 1, footnote 1) is implied. *Loss* as in *profit or loss* (in contrast to *gain or loss*) is also used in a broad descriptive sense to refer to negative profit or unsuccessful performance and is not intended to have a technical accounting meaning.

losses—as well as investments by owners and distributions to owners.[6]

15. The two classes of elements are related in such a way that (a) assets, liabilities, and equity are changed by elements of the other class and at any time are their cumulative result and (b) an increase (decrease) in an asset cannot occur without a corresponding decrease (increase) in another asset or a corresponding increase (decrease) in a liability or equity. Those relations are sometimes collectively referred to as "articulation." They result in financial statements that are fundamentally interrelated so that statements that show elements of the second class depend on statements that show elements of the first class and vice versa.[7]

Definition, Recognition, Measurement, and Display

16. All matters of recognition, measurement, and display have purposely been separated from the definitions of the elements of financial statements in the Board's conceptual framework project. The definitions in this Statement are concerned with the essential characteristics of elements of financial statements. Other phases of the conceptual framework project are concerned with questions such as which financial statements should be provided; which items that qualify under the definitions should be included in those statements; when particular items that qualify as assets, liabilities, revenues, expenses, and so forth should be formally recognized in the financial statements; which attributes of those items should be measured; which unit of measure should be used; and how the information included should be classified and otherwise displayed.

17. Definitions of elements of financial statements are a significant first screen in determining the content of financial statements. An item's having the essential characteristics of one of the elements is a necessary but not a sufficient condition for formally recognizing the item in the entity's financial statements. To be included in a particular set of financial statements, an item must not only qualify under the definition of an element but also must meet criteria for recognition and have a relevant attribute (or surrogate for it) that is capable of reasonably reliable measurement or estimate.[8] Thus, some items that meet the definitions may have to be excluded from formal incorporation in financial statements because of recognition or measurement considerations (paragraphs 37-42).

DEFINITIONS OF ELEMENTS

18. All elements are defined in relation to a particular entity, which may be a business enterprise, an educational or charitable organization, a governmental unit, a natural person, or the like (paragraph 2). Items that qualify under the definitions are a particular entity's asset, liability, revenue, expense, etc. An entity may comprise two or more affiliated entities and does not necessarily correspond to what is often described as a "legal entity." The definitions may also refer to "other entity," "other entities," or "entities other than the enterprise," which may include individuals, other business enterprises, nonbusiness organizations, and the like. For example, employees, suppliers, customers, lenders, stockholders, and governments are all "other entities" to a particular business enterprise. A subsidiary company that is part of the same entity as its parent company in consolidated financial statements is an "other entity" in the separate financial statements of its parent.

---

[6]The two classes can also be distinguished as financial position and changes in financial position, without meaning to imply or describe particular financial statements. Used broadly, financial position refers to state or status of assets or claims to assets at moments in time, and changes in financial position refers to flows or changes in assets or claims to assets over time. In that sense, for example, both income statements and statements of sources and applications of funds (now commonly called statements of changes in financial position) show changes in financial position in present practice. Other statements, such as statements of retained earnings or analyses of property, plant, and equipment, may show aspects of both financial position at the beginning and end of a period and changes in financial position during a period. For business enterprises, at least, the other possible elements of financial statements referred to in paragraphs 3 and 4 also fall into this second class. That is, they are changes in financial position, describing effects of transactions and other events and circumstances that affect assets, liabilities, or equity during a period, for example, acquisitions and dispositions of assets, borrowings, and repayments of borrowings.

[7]The two relations described in this paragraph are commonly expressed as (a) balance at beginning of period ± changes during period = balance at end of period and (b) assets = liabilities + equity. "Double entry," the mechanism by which accrual accounting formally includes particular items that qualify under the elements definitions in articulated financial statements, incorporates those relations.

[8]Decisions about recognizing, measuring, and displaying elements of financial statements depend significantly on evaluations such as what information is most relevant for investment, credit, and similar decisions and whether the information is reliable enough to be trusted. Other significant evaluations of the information involve its comparability with information about other periods or other enterprises, its materiality, and whether the benefits from providing it exceed the costs of providing it. Those matters are discussed in Concepts Statement 2.

Assets

19. Assets are probable[9] future economic benefits obtained or controlled by a particular entity as a result of past transactions or events.

Characteristics of Assets of Business Enterprises

20. An asset has three essential characteristics: (a) it embodies a probable future benefit that involves a capacity, singly or in combination with other assets, to contribute directly or indirectly to future net cash inflows, (b) a particular enterprise can obtain the benefit and control others' access to it, and (c) the transaction or other event giving rise to the enterprise's right to or control of the benefit has already occurred. Assets commonly have other features that help identify them—for example, assets may be acquired at a cost[10] and they may be tangible, exchangeable, or legally enforceable. However, those features are not essential characteristics of assets. Their absence, by itself, is not sufficient to preclude an item's qualifying as an asset. That is, assets may be acquired without cost, they may be intangible, and although not exchangeable they may be usable by the enterprise in producing or distributing other goods or services. Similarly, although the ability of an enterprise to obtain benefit from an asset and to control others' access to it generally rests on a foundation of legal rights, legal enforceability of a claim to the benefit is not a prerequisite for a benefit to qualify as an asset if its receipt by the enterprise is otherwise probable.

21. The kinds of items that qualify as assets under the definition in paragraph 19 are also commonly called economic resources. They are the scarce means that are useful for carrying out economic activities, such as consumption, production, and exchange.

22. The common characteristic possessed by all assets and economic resources is "service potential" or "future economic benefit," the capacity to provide services or benefits to the entities that use them. In a business enterprise, that service potential or future economic benefit eventually results in net cash inflows to the enterprise. That characteristic is the primary basis of the definition of assets in this Statement.

23. Money (cash, including deposits in banks) is valuable because of what it can buy. It can be exchanged for virtually any good or service that is available or it can be saved and exchanged for them in the future. Money's "command over resources"—its purchasing power—is the basis of its value and future economic benefits.[11]

24. Assets other than cash benefit a business enterprise by being exchanged for cash or other goods or services, by being used to produce or otherwise increase the value of other assets, or by being used to settle liabilities. Services provided by other entities, including personal services, cannot be stored and are received and used simultaneously. They can be assets of a business enterprise only momentarily—as the enterprise receives and uses them—although their use may create or add value to other assets of the enterprise. Rights to receive services of other entities for specified or determinable future periods can be assets of particular business enterprises.

Transactions and Events That Change Assets

25. Assets of a business enterprise are changed both by its transactions and activities and by events that happen to it. A business enterprise obtains assets from other entities and adds value through operations to assets it already has. It transfers assets to other entities and uses assets in its operations. Some transactions or other events decrease one asset and increase another. An enterprise's assets or their values are also commonly increased or decreased by other events and circumstances that may be partly or entirely beyond the control of the enterprise and its management, for example, price changes, interest rate changes, technological changes, impositions of taxes and regulations, discovery, growth or accretion, shrinkage, vandalism, thefts, expropriations, wars, fires, and natural disasters.

26. Once acquired, an asset continues as an asset of

[9] *Probable* is used with its usual general meaning, rather than in a specific technical sense (such as that in FASB Statement No. 5, *Accounting for Contingencies,* par. 3), and refers to that which can reasonably be expected or believed on the basis of available evidence or logic but is neither certain nor proved (*Webster's New World Dictionary of the American Language,* 2d college ed. [New York and Cleveland: World Publishing Company, 1972], p. 1132). Its inclusion in the definition is intended to acknowledge that business and economic activities occur in an environment characterized by uncertainty in which few outcomes are certain (pars. 37-40), not to describe a criterion for recognizing assets in financial statements, which is beyond the scope of this Statement.

[10] *Cost* is the sacrifice incurred in economic activities—that which is given up or forgone to consume, to save, to exchange, to produce, etc. For example, the value of cash or other resources given up (or the present value of an obligation incurred) in exchange for a resource measures the cost of the resource acquired. Similarly, the expiration of future benefits caused by using a resource in production is the cost of using it.

[11] Money's command over resources, or purchasing power, declines during periods of inflation and increases during periods of deflation (increases and decreases, respectively, in the level of prices in general). Since matters of measurement and unit of measure are beyond the scope of this Statement, it recognizes but does not emphasize that characteristic of money.

the enterprise until the enterprise collects it, transfers it to another entity, or uses it, or some other event or circumstance destroys the future benefit or removes the enterprise's ability to obtain it.

Valuation Accounts

27. A separate item that reduces or increases the carrying amount of an asset is sometimes found in financial statements. For example, an estimate of uncollectible amounts reduces receivables to the amount expected to be collected, or a premium on a bond receivable increases the receivable to its cost or present value. Those "valuation accounts" are part of the related assets and are neither assets in their own right nor liabilities.[12]

Liabilities

28. Liabilities are probable[13] future sacrifices of economic benefits arising from present obligations[14] of a particular entity to transfer assets or provide services to other entities in the future as a result of past transactions or events.

Characteristics of Liabilities of Business Enterprises

29. A liability has three essential characteristics: (a) it embodies a present duty or responsibility to one or more other entities that entails settlement by probable future transfer or use of assets at a specified or determinable date, on occurrence of a specified event, or on demand, (b) the duty or responsibility obligates a particular enterprise, leaving it little or no discretion to avoid the future sacrifice, and (c) the transaction or other event obligating the enterprise has already happened. Liabilities commonly have other features that help identify them—for example, most liabilities require the obligated enterprise to pay cash to one or more identified other entities and are legally enforceable. However, those features are not essential characteristics of liabilities. Their absence, by itself, is not sufficient to preclude an item's qualifying as a liability. That is, liabilities may not require an enterprise to pay cash but to convey other assets, to provide or stand ready to provide services, or to use assets. And as long as payment or other transfer of assets to settle an existing obligation is probable, the identity of the recipient need not be known to the obligated enterprise before the time of settlement. Similarly, although most liabilities rest generally on a foundation of legal rights and duties, existence of a legally enforceable claim is not a prerequisite for an obligation to qualify as a liability if the future payment of cash or other transfer of assets to settle the obligation is otherwise probable.

30. Most liabilities stem from human inventions—such as financial instruments, contracts, and laws—that facilitate the functioning of a highly developed economy and are commonly embodied in legal obligations and rights (or the equivalent) with no existence apart from them. Liabilities facilitate the functioning of a highly developed economy primarily by permitting delay—delay in payment, delay in delivery, and so on.[15]

31. Enterprises routinely incur most liabilities to acquire the funds, goods, and services they need to operate and just as routinely settle the liabilities they incur. For example, borrowing cash obligates an enterprise to repay the amount borrowed, usually with interest; acquiring assets on credit obligates an enterprise to pay for them, perhaps with interest to compensate for the delay in payment; using employees' knowledge, skills, time, and efforts obligates an enterprise to pay for their use, often including fringe benefits; selling products with a warranty or guarantee obligates an enterprise to pay cash or to repair or replace those that prove defective; and accepting a cash deposit or prepayment obligates an enterprise to provide goods or services or to refund the cash. In short, most liabilities are incurred in exchange transactions to obtain needed resources or their use, and most liabilities incurred in exchange transactions are contractual in nature—based on written or oral agreements to pay cash or to provide goods or services to specified or determinable entities on demand, at specified or determinable dates, or on occurrence of specified events.

32. Although most liabilities result from agreements between entities, some obligations are imposed on business enterprises by government or courts or are accepted to avoid imposition by government or courts (or costly efforts related thereto), and some relate to other nonreciprocal transfers

[12]Although this kind of distinction must be clearly drawn in concept because it is often essential to clear thinking, to maintain it in practice may not always be possible because of practical considerations relating to recognition and measurement stemming ultimately from the effects of uncertainty (pars. 16, 17, 41, 42, and 107-108).

[13]*Probable* is used with its usual general meaning, rather than in a specific accounting or technical sense (such as that in Statement 5, par. 3), and refers to that which can reasonably be expected or believed on the basis of available evidence or logic but is neither certain nor proved (*Webster's New World Dictionary,* 2d college ed., p. 1132). Its inclusion in the definition is intended to acknowledge that business and economic activities occur in an environment characterized by uncertainty in which few outcomes are certain (pars. 37-40), not to describe a criterion for recognizing liabilities in financial statements, which is beyond the scope of this Statement.

[14]*Obligations* in the definition is broader than *legal obligations.* It is used with its usual general meaning to refer to duties imposed legally or socially; to that which one is bound to do by contract, promise, moral responsibility, etc. (*Webster's New World Dictionary,* 2d college ed., p. 981). It includes equitable and constructive obligations as well as legal obligations (pars. 30-33).

[15]A common feature of liabilities is interest—the time value of money or the price of delay.

from a business enterprise to owners or to one or more other entities. Thus, taxes, laws, regulations, and other governmental actions commonly require business enterprises to pay cash, convey other assets, or provide services either directly to specified governmental units or to others for purposes or in ways specified by government. An enterprise may also incur liabilities for cash dividends declared but not paid or for donations pledged to educational or charitable organizations.

33. Similarly, although most liabilities stem from legally enforceable obligations, some liabilities rest on equitable or constructive obligations, including some that arise in exchange transactions. Liabilities stemming from equitable or constructive obligations are commonly paid in the same way as legally binding contracts, but they lack the legal sanction that characterizes most liabilities and may be binding primarily because of social or moral sanctions or custom. An equitable obligation stems from ethical or moral constraints rather than rules of common or statute law, that is, from a duty to another entity to do that which an ordinary conscience and sense of justice would deem fair, just, and right—to do what one ought to do rather than what one is legally required to do. For example, an enterprise may have an equitable obligation to complete and deliver a product to a customer that has no other source of supply even though its failure to deliver would legally require only return of the customer's deposit. A constructive obligation is created, inferred, or construed from the facts in a particular situation rather than contracted by agreement with another entity or imposed by government. For example, an enterprise may create a constructive obligation to employees for vacation pay or year-end bonuses by paying them every year even though it is not contractually bound to do so and has not announced a policy to do so. The line between equitable or constructive obligations and obligations that are enforceable in courts of law is not always clear, and the line between equitable or constructive obligations and no obligations may often be even more troublesome because to determine whether an enterprise is actually bound by an obligation to a third party in the absence of legal enforceability is often extremely difficult. Thus, the concepts of equitable and constructive obligations must be applied with great care. To interpret equitable and constructive obligations too narrowly will tend to exclude significant actual obligations of an enterprise, while to interpret them too broadly will effectively nullify the definition by including items that lack an essential characteristic of liabilities.

Transactions and Events That Change Liabilities

34. Liabilities of a business enterprise are changed both by its transactions and activities and by events that happen to it. The preceding paragraphs note most major sources of changes in liabilities. An enterprise's liabilities are also sometimes affected by price changes, interest rate changes, or other events and circumstances that may be partly or wholly beyond the control of an enterprise and its management.

35. Once incurred, a liability continues as a liability of the enterprise until the enterprise settles it, or another event or circumstance discharges it or removes the enterprise's responsibility to settle it.

Valuation Accounts

36. A separate item that reduces or increases the carrying amount of a liability is sometimes found in financial statements. For example, a bond premium or discount increases or decreases the face value of a bond payable to its proceeds or present value. Those "valuation accounts" are part of the related liability and are neither liabilities in their own right nor assets.

Effects of Uncertainty

37. Uncertainty about economic and business activities and results is pervasive, and it often clouds whether a particular item qualifies as an asset or a liability of a particular enterprise at the time the definitions are applied. The presence or absence of future economic benefit that can be obtained and controlled by the enterprise or of the enterprise's legal, equitable, or constructive obligation to sacrifice assets in the future can often be discerned reliably only with hindsight. As a result, some items that with hindsight actually qualified as assets or liabilities of the enterprise under the definitions may, as a practical matter, have been recognized as expenses, losses, revenues, or gains or remained unrecognized in its financial statements because of uncertainty about whether they qualified as assets or liabilities of the enterprise or because of recognition and measurement considerations stemming from uncertainty at the time of assessment. Conversely, some items that with hindsight did not qualify under the definitions may have been included as assets or liabilities because of judgments made in the face of uncertainty at the time of assessment.

38. An effect of uncertainty is to increase the costs of financial reporting in general and the costs of recognition and measurement in particular. Some items that qualify as assets or liabilities under the definitions may therefore be recognized as expenses, losses, revenues, or gains or remain unrecognized as a result of cost and benefit analyses indicating that their formal incorporation in financial statements is not useful enough to justify the time and effort needed to do it. It may be possible, for example, to make the information more reliable in the face of uncertainty by exerting greater effort or by spending more money, but it also may not be worth the added cost.

39. A highly significant practical consequence of

the features described in the preceding two paragraphs is that the existence or amount (or both) of most assets and many liabilities can be probable but not certain.[16] The definitions in this Statement are not intended to require that the existence and amounts of items be certain for them to qualify as assets, liabilities, revenues, expenses, etc., and estimates and approximations will often be required unless financial statements are to be restricted to reporting only cash transactions.

40. To apply the definitions of assets and liabilities (and other elements of financial statements) thus commonly requires assessments of probabilities, but degrees of probability are not part of the definitions. That is, the degree of probability of a future economic benefit (or of a future cash outlay or other sacrifice of future economic benefits) and the degree to which its amount can be estimated with reasonable reliability that are required to recognize an item as an asset (or a liability) are matters of recognition and measurement that are beyond the scope of this Statement. The distinction needs to be maintained between the definitions themselves and steps that may be needed to apply them. Matters involving measurement problems, effects of uncertainty, reliability, and numerous other factors may be significant in applying a definition, but they are not part of the definition. Particular items that qualify as assets or liabilities under the definitions may need to be excluded from formal incorporation in financial statements for reasons relating to measurement, uncertainty, or unreliability, but they are not excluded by the definitions. Similarly, the attitude commonly known as conservatism may be appropriate in applying the definitions under uncertain conditions, but conservatism is not part of the definitions. Definition, recognition, measurement, and display are separate in the Board's conceptual framework (paragraphs 16 and 17).[17]

Note on Uncertainty and Certain Recognition Matters

41. All practical financial accounting and reporting models have limitations. The preceding paragraphs describe one limit that may affect various models—how recognition or measurement considerations stemming from uncertainty may result in not recognizing as assets or liabilities some items that qualify as such under the definitions or may result in postponing recognition of some assets or liabilities until their existence becomes more probable or their measures become more reliable.

42. That propensity to defer recognition of or to not recognize assets and liabilities, particularly assets, may create problems in recognizing losses of future economic benefits. The situation may arise if the events or circumstances causing the losses have occurred, and the related future sacrifice of assets has become virtually inevitable, but (a) affected assets either are not recognized or separately identified in the financial statements or are recorded at amounts significantly less than the cash or other outlays needed to restore the lost future benefits and (b) the amounts to be spent in the future to restore the lost benefits are not yet owed to anyone. To recognize those kinds of losses, an enterprise may need to recognize, and display among either its assets or its liabilities, a "valuation account" (paragraph 27) that either relates to unrecorded assets or reduces recorded assets to negative amounts.[18]

Equity[19]

43. Equity is the residual interest in the assets of an entity that remains after deducting its liabilities. In a business enterprise, the equity is the ownership interest.

Characteristics of Equity of Business Enterprises

44. Equity in a business enterprise stems from ownership rights (or the equivalent).[20] It involves a relation between an enterprise and its owners *as owners* rather than as employees, suppliers, cus-

[16]The meaning of *probable* in these paragraphs is described in par. 19, footnote 9, and par. 28, footnote 13.

[17]The Board's projects on accounting recognition criteria (par. 63, footnote 30) and qualitative characteristics (par. 17, footnote 8) bear directly on the matter discussed in pars. 37-42.

[18]Since the description in paragraphs 41 and 42 involves recognition matters that are beyond the scope of this Statement, it is not intended to imply that the kinds of items described should necessarily be recognized. It notes an existing practical problem stemming from uncertainty, however, and is intended to make clear that the possibility of recognition is not precluded. Appendix B includes a brief discussion of the matter, including examples (pars. 174-178).

[19]This Statement defines equity only as a whole, although the discussion of equity of business enterprises in this Statement notes that different owners of an enterprise may have different kinds of ownership rights and that equity has various sources. In financial statements of business enterprises, various distinctions *within* equity, such as those between common stockholders' equity and preferred stockholders' equity, between contributed capital and earned capital, or between stated or legal capital and other equity, are primarily matters of display that are beyond the scope of this Statement.

[20]Other entities with proprietary or ownership interests in a business enterprise are commonly known by specialized names, such as stockholders, partners, and proprietors, and by more general names, such as investors, but all are also covered by the descriptive term *owners*. Equity of business enterprises is thus commonly known by several names, such as owners' equity, stockholders' equity, ownership, equity capital, partners' capital, and proprietorship. Some enterprises (for example, mutual organizations) do not have stockholders, partners, or proprietors in the usual sense of those terms but do have participants whose interests are essentially ownership interests, residual interests, or both.

tomers, lenders, or in some other nonowner role.[21] Since it ranks after liabilities as a claim to or interest in the assets of the enterprise, it is a residual interest: (a) equity is the same as net assets, the difference between the enterprise's assets and its liabilities, and (b) equity is enhanced or burdened by increases and decreases in net assets from sources other than investments by owners and distributions to owners.

45. Equity represents the source of distributions by an enterprise to its owners, whether in the form of cash dividends or other distributions of assets. Owners' and others' expectations about distributions to owners may affect the market prices of an enterprise's equity securities, thereby indirectly affecting owners' compensation for providing equity or risk capital to the enterprise (paragraph 12). Thus, the essential characteristics of equity center on the conditions for transferring enterprise assets to owners. Equity—an excess of assets over liabilities—is a necessary but not sufficient condition; distributions to owners are at the discretion and volition of the owners or their representatives after satisfying restrictions imposed by law, regulation, or agreements with other entities. Generally, an enterprise is not obligated to transfer assets to owners except in the event of the enterprise's liquidation unless the enterprise formally acts to distribute assets to owners, for example, by declaring a dividend.[22] Owners may sell their interests in an enterprise to others and thus may be able to obtain a return *of* part or all of their investments and perhaps a return *on* investments through a securities market, but those transactions do not normally affect the equity of an enterprise or its assets or liabilities.

46. An enterprise may have several classes of equity (for example, one or more classes each of common stock or preferred stock) with different degrees of risk stemming from different rights to participate in distributions of enterprise assets or different priorities of claims on enterprise assets in the event of liquidation. That is, some classes of owners may bear relatively more of the risks of an enterprise's unprofitability or may benefit relatively more from its profitability (or both) than other classes of owners. However, all classes depend at least to some extent on enterprise profitability for distributions of enterprise assets, and no class of equity carries an unconditional right to receive future transfers of assets from the enterprise except in liquidation, and then only after liabilities have been satisfied.

47. Equity is originally created by owners' investments in an enterprise and may from time to time be augmented by additional investments by owners. Equity is reduced by distributions by the enterprise to owners. However, the distinguishing characteristic of equity is that it inevitably is affected by the enterprise's operations and other events and circumstances affecting the enterprise (which together constitute comprehensive income—paragraph 56).

Equity and Liabilities

48. An enterprise's assets, liabilities, and equity all pertain to the same set of probable future economic benefits. Assets are probable future economic benefits owned or controlled by the enterprise. Its liabilities and equity are mutually exclusive claims to or interests in the enterprise's assets by entities other than the enterprise. In a business enterprise, equity or the ownership interest is a residual interest, remaining after liabilities are deducted from assets and depending significantly on the profitability of the enterprise. Distributions to owners are discretionary, depending on the volition of owners or their representatives after considering the needs of the enterprise and restrictions imposed by law, regulations, or agreement. An enterprise is generally not obligated to transfer assets to owners except in the event of the enterprise's liquidation. In contrast, liabilities, once incurred, involve nondiscretionary future sacrifices of assets that must be satisfied on demand, at a specified or determinable date, or on occurrence of a specified event, and they take precedence over ownership interests.

49. Although the line between equity and liabilities is clear in concept, it may be obscured in practice. Applying the definitions to particular situations may involve practical problems because several kinds of securities issued by business enterprises seem to have characteristics of both liabilities and equity in varying degrees or because the names given some securities may not accurately describe their essential characteristics. For example, convertible

[21]Distinctions between liabilities and equity generally depend on the nature of the claim rather than on the identity of the claimant. The same entities may simultaneously be both owners and employees, owners and creditors, owners and customers, creditors and customers, or some other combination. For example, an investor may hold both debt and equity securities of the same enterprise, or an owner of an enterprise may become also its creditor by lending to it or by receiving rights to unpaid cash dividends that it declares. Wages due, products or services due, accounts payable due, and other amounts due to owners in their roles as employees, customers, suppliers, and the like are liabilities, not part of equity. Exceptions involve situations in which doubts exist that the transactions are "at arm's length." In some circumstances, for example, a loan to an enterprise by a controlling stockholder may be considered to be in substance an investment by owners and thus may not qualify as a liability.

[22]A controlling interest or an interest that confers an ability to exercise significant influence over the operations of an enterprise may have more potential than other ownership interests to control or affect assets of the enterprise or distributions of assets to owners. Procedures such as consolidated financial statements and the equity method of accounting for intercorporate investments have been developed to account for the rights and relations involved.

debt instruments have both liability and residual interest characteristics, which may create problems in accounting for them. (APB Opinion No. 14, *Accounting for Convertible Debt and Debt Issued with Stock Purchase Warrants,* and APB Opinion No. 15, *Earnings per Share,* both discuss problems of that kind.) Preferred stock also often has both debt and equity characteristics, and some preferred stocks may effectively have maturity amounts and dates at which they must be redeemed for cash. To determine whether specific securities of the kinds illustrated are liabilities or equity presents practical problems of applying definitions rather than problems of determining the essential characteristics of those definitions. Adequate definitions are the starting point. They provide a basis for assessing, for example, the extent to which a particular application meets the qualitative characteristic of representational faithfulness, which includes the notion of reporting economic substance rather than legal form (Concepts Statement 2, paragraphs 63-80 and 160).

Transactions and Events That Change Equity

50. The diagram on the next page shows the sources of changes in equity (class B) and distinguishes them from each other and from other transactions, events, and circumstances affecting an enterprise during a period (classes A and C). Specifically, the diagram shows that (a) class B (changes in equity) comprises two mutually exclusive classes of transactions and other events and circumstances, B1 and B2, each of which also comprises two (or perhaps more) significant subclasses, and (b) classes B1, B2, and A are the sources of all increases and decreases in assets and liabilities of an enterprise; class C includes no changes in assets or liabilities. Shaded bands rather than clear boundary lines separate classes B1(a) and B1(b) and fall within class B1(b) in the diagram because of display considerations that are beyond the scope of this Statement. First, paragraphs 63-73 of this Statement define and discuss revenues, expenses, gains, and losses as elements of financial statements but do not precisely distinguish between revenues and gains on the one hand or between expenses and losses on the other. Second, the definitions of gains and losses include the possibility of other descriptions for some items in that class (paragraphs 57 and 58). Fine distinctions between revenues and gains and between expenses and losses as well as other distinctions *within* comprehensive income are more appropriately considered as part of display or reporting.

51. The full width of the diagram, represented by the two-pointed arrow labeled "All transactions and other events and circumstances that affect an enterprise during a period," encompasses all potentially recordable events and circumstances affecting an enterprise. Moving from top to bottom of the diagram, each level divides the preceding level into classes that are significant for the definitions and related concepts in this Statement. (Size of classes does not indicate their relative volume or significance.)

A. All changes in assets and liabilities not accompanied by changes in equity. This class comprises four kinds of exchange transactions that are common in most business enterprises (exchanges that affect equity belong in class B rather than class A).[23]

1. Exchanges of assets for assets, for example, purchases of assets for cash or barter exchanges
2. Exchanges of liabilities for liabilities, for example, issues of notes payable to settle accounts payable or refundings of bonds payable by issuing new bonds to holders that surrender outstanding bonds
3. Acquisitions of assets by incurring liabilities, for example, purchases of assets on account, borrowings, or receipts of cash advances for goods or services to be provided in the future
4. Settlements of liabilities by transferring assets, for example, repayments of borrowings, payments to suppliers on account, payments of accrued wages or salaries, or repairs (or payments for repairs) required by warranties.

B. All changes in assets or liabilities accompanied by changes in equity. This class is the subject of this section and comprises:

1. Comprehensive income (defined in paragraph 56) whose components are:
   a. Revenues and expenses (broadly defined and discussed in paragraphs 63-66)
   b. Gains and losses (broadly defined and discussed in paragraphs 67-73)
2. All changes in equity from transfers between the enterprise and its owners (defined in paragraphs 52 and 53)
   a. Investments by owners in the enterprise
   b. Distributions by the enterprise to owners

[23]The diagram reflects the concept that value added by productive activities increases assets as production takes place, which is the basis for the common observation that revenues are *earned* by the entire process of acquiring goods and services, using them to produce other goods or services, selling the output, and collecting the sales price or fee. However, that value added is commonly *recognized* after production is complete, usually when product is delivered or sold but sometimes when cash is received or product is completed. Under those bases of recognition, certain internal transfers are viewed as falling into class A rather than class B. For example, using a sale basis of revenue recognition, internal transfers such as from raw materials on hand to product in process of production or from product in process to completed product fall into class A1 rather than class B1. The diagram does not, of course, settle recognition issues.

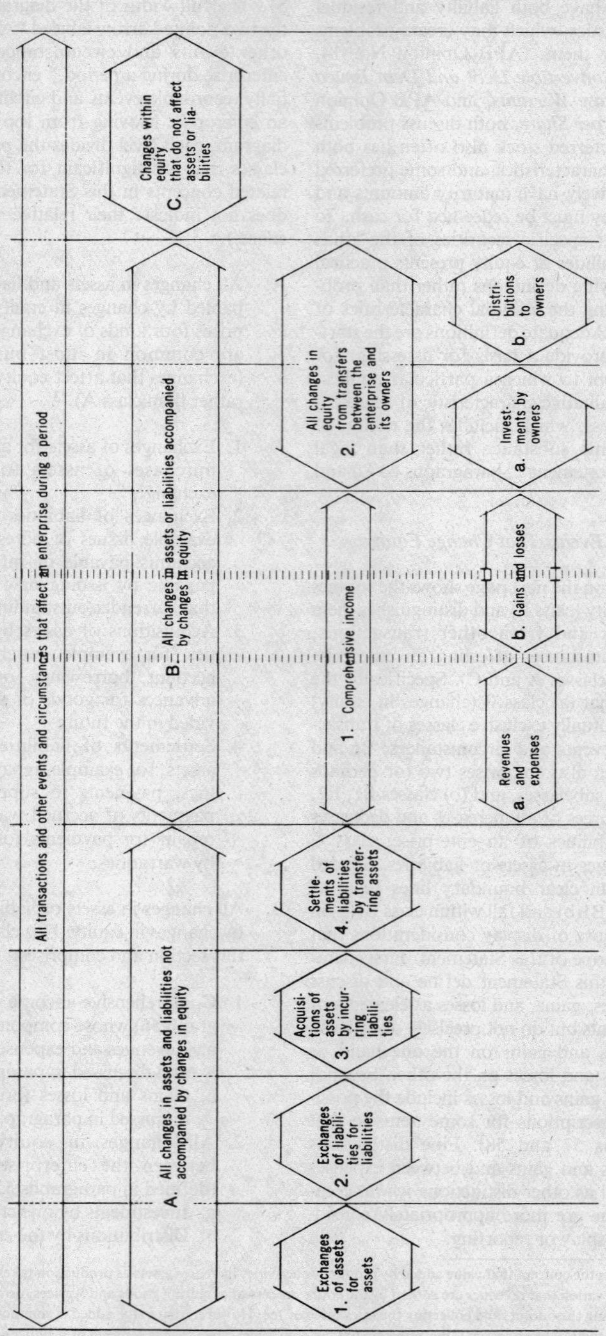
All transactions and other events and circumstances that affect an enterprise during a period
A. All changes in assets and liabilities not accompanied by changes in equity
B. All changes in assets or liabilities accompanied by changes in equity
C. Changes within equity that do not affect assets or liabilities
1. Exchanges of assets for assets
2. Exchanges of liabilities for liabilities
3. Acquisitions of assets by incurring liabilities
4. Settlements of liabilities by transferring assets
1. Comprehensive income
2. All changes in equity from transfers between the enterprise and its owners
a. Revenues and expenses
b. Gains and losses
a. Investments by owners
b. Distributions to owners

C. Changes within equity that do not affect assets or liabilities (for example, stock dividends, conversions of preferred stock into common stock, and some stock recapitalizations). This class contains only changes *within* equity and does not affect the definition of equity or its amount.

The definitions in paragraphs 56, 63, 65, 67, and 68 are those in class B1 and its subclasses (a) and (b): comprehensive income, revenues, expenses, gains, and losses.

Investments by and Distributions to Owners[24]

52. Investments by owners are increases in net assets of a particular enterprise resulting from transfers to it from other entities of something valuable to obtain or increase ownership interests (or equity) in it. Assets are most commonly received as investments by owners, but that which is received may also include services or satisfaction or conversion of liabilities of the enterprise.

53. Distributions to owners are decreases in net assets of a particular enterprise resulting from transferring assets, rendering services, or incurring liabilities by the enterprise to owners. Distributions to owners decrease ownership interest (or equity) in an enterprise.

Characteristics of Investments by and Distributions to Owners

54. Investments by owners and distributions to owners are transactions between an enterprise and its owners *as owners*. Through investments by owners, an enterprise obtains resources it needs to begin or expand operations, to retire debt securities or other liabilities, or for other business purposes; as a result of investing resources in the enterprise, other entities obtain ownership interests in the enterprise or increase ownership interests they already had. Not all investments in the equity securities of an enterprise by other entities are investments by owners as that concept is defined in this Statement. In an investment by owners, the enterprise that issues the securities acquired by an owner always receives the proceeds or their benefits; its net assets increase. If the purchaser of equity securities becomes an owner or increases its ownership interest in an enterprise by purchasing those securities from another owner that is decreasing or terminating its ownership interest, the transfer does not affect the net assets of the enterprise.

55. Distributions by an enterprise to its owners decrease its net assets and decrease or terminate ownership interests of those that receive them. Reacquisition by an entity of its own equity securities by transferring assets or incurring liabilities to owners is a distribution to owners as that concept is defined in this Statement. Since owners become creditors for a dividend declared until it is paid, an enterprise's incurrence of a liability to transfer assets to owners in the future converts a part of the equity or ownership interest of the enterprise into a creditors' claim; settlement of the liability by transfer of the assets is a transaction in class A4 in the diagram in paragraph 50 rather than in class B2(b). That is, equity is reduced by the incurrence of the liability to owners, not by its settlement.

Comprehensive Income

56. Comprehensive income is the change in equity (net assets) of an entity during a period from transactions and other events and circumstances from nonowner sources. It includes all changes in equity during a period except those resulting from investments by owners and distributions to owners.

Concepts of Capital Maintenance

57. A concept of maintenance of capital or recovery of cost is a prerequisite for separating return *on* capital from return *of* capital because only inflows in excess of the amount needed to maintain capital are a return *on* equity. Two major concepts of capital maintenance exist, both of which can be measured in units of either money or constant purchasing power: the financial capital concept and the physical capital concept (which is often expressed in terms of maintaining operating capability, that is, maintaining the capacity of an enterprise to provide a constant supply of goods or services). The major difference between them involves the effects of price changes on assets held and liabilities owed during a period. Under the financial capital concept, if the effects of those price changes are recognized, they are called *holding gains and losses* and are included in return on capital. Under the physical capital concept, those changes are recognized but are called *capital maintenance adjustments* and are included directly in equity and are *not* included in return on capital. Under that concept, capital maintenance adjustments are a separate element rather than being gains and losses.

58. The financial capital concept is the traditional view and is generally the capital maintenance concept in present primary financial statements. Comprehensive income as defined in paragraph 56 is a return *on* financial capital. However, the reason for using *comprehensive income* rather than *earnings* in this Statement is that the Board has decided to

[24]Investments by owners are sometimes called capital contributions. Distributions to owners are sometimes called capital distributions; distributions of earnings, profits, or income; or dividends.

reserve *earnings* for possible use to designate a different concept that is a component part of—that is, is narrower than or less than—comprehensive income,[25] and *earnings,* when defined, may be a return *on* physical capital or may be a return *on* financial capital. The Board emphasizes that capital maintenance concepts are the subject of another project and that the Board has not chosen between the financial and physical capital maintenance concepts for deciding the meaning and appropriate display of *earnings* and thus has not decided whether *capital maintenance adjustments* should be considered to be a separate element of financial statements.[26] For that reason, gains and losses in the diagram in paragraph 50 (class B1(b)) and in the discussions in the remainder of this Statement explicitly or implicitly include the possibility that some items included in that class may more appropriately be described by other terms, including perhaps *capital maintenance adjustments.*

Characteristics, Sources, and Components of Comprehensive Income of Business Enterprises

59. Over the life of a business enterprise, its comprehensive income equals the net of its cash receipts and cash outlays, excluding cash investments by owners and cash distributions to owners (Concepts Statement 1, paragraph 46). That characteristic holds whether the amounts of cash and comprehensive income are measured in nominal dollars or constant dollars. Although the amounts in constant dollars may differ from those in nominal dollars, the basic relationship is not changed because both nominal and constant dollars express the same thing using different measuring units. Matters such as recognition criteria and choice of attributes to be measured[27] also do not affect the amounts of comprehensive income and net cash receipts over the life of an enterprise but do affect the time and way parts of the total are identified with the periods that constitute the entire life. Timing of recognition of revenues, expenses, gains, and losses is also a major difference between accounting based on cash receipts and outlays and accrual accounting. Accrual accounting may encompass various timing possibilities—for example, when goods or services are provided, when cash is received, or when prices change—that are being considered in the project on accounting recognition criteria.

60. Comprehensive income results from (a) exchange transactions and other transfers between the enterprise and other entities that are not its owners, (b) the enterprise's productive efforts,[28] and (c) price changes, casualties, and other effects of interactions between the enterprise and the economic, legal, social, political, and physical environment of which it is part. An enterprise's productive efforts and most of its exchange transactions with other entities are ongoing major activities that constitute the enterprise's central operations by which it attempts to fulfill its basic function in the economy of producing and distributing goods or services at prices that are sufficient to enable it to pay for the goods and services it uses and to provide a satisfactory return to its owners. Although those ongoing major or central operations are generally intended to be the primary source of comprehensive income, they are not the only source. Most enterprises occasionally engage in activities that are peripheral or incidental to their central activities. Moreover, all enterprises are affected by the economic, legal, social, political, and physical environment of which they are part, and comprehensive income of each enterprise is affected by events and circumstances that may be partly or

---

[25]Examples of the kinds of items that *might* be included in *comprehensive income* but not in *earnings,* when it is defined, include prior period adjustments and cumulative effects of changes in accounting principles. (The latter and many of the former are included in *net income* in present practice.)

[26]FASB Statement No. 33, *Financial Reporting and Changing Prices* (September 1979), par. 104. Capital maintenance concepts are the subject of Chapter 6 of the FASB Discussion Memorandum, *Elements of Financial Statements and Their Measurement* (December 2, 1976).

[27]" 'Attributes to be measured' refers to the traits or aspects of an element to be quantified or measured, such as historical cost/historical proceeds, current cost/current proceeds, etc. Attribute is a narrower concept than measurement, which includes not only identifying the attribute to be measured but also selecting a scale of measurement (for example, units of money or units of constant purchasing power). 'Property' is commonly used in sciences to describe the trait or aspect of an object being measured, such as the length of a table or the weight of a stone. But 'property' may be confused with land and buildings in financial reporting contexts, and 'attribute' has become common in accounting literature and is used in this Statement" (Concepts Statement 1, par. 2, footnote 2).

[28]An enterprise increases the values of goods or services it holds or acquires by adding time, place, or form utility. Thus, *productive efforts* and *producing and distributing activities* include not only manufacturing and other conversion processes but also other productive activities such as storing, transporting, lending, insuring, and providing professional services that might be overlooked if *producing* were narrowly equated with *manufacturing.*

wholly beyond the control of individual enterprises and their managements.[29]

61. Although cash resulting from various sources of comprehensive income is the same, receipts from various sources may vary in stability, risk, and predictability. That is, characteristics of various sources of comprehensive income may differ significantly from one another, indicating a need for information about various components of comprehensive income. That need underlies the distinctions between revenues and gains, between expenses and losses, between various kinds of gains and losses, and between measures found in present practice such as income from continuing operations and income after extraordinary items and cumulative effect of change in accounting principle.

62. Comprehensive income comprises two related but distinguishable types of components. Comprehensive income consists of not only its basic components—revenues, expenses, gains, and losses—but also various intermediate components or measures that result from combining the basic components. Revenues, expenses, gains, and losses can be combined in various ways to obtain several measures of enterprise performance with varying degrees of inclusiveness. Examples of intermediate components or measures are gross margin, contribution margin, income from continuing operations before taxes, income from continuing operations, and operating income. Those intermediate components or measures are, in effect, subtotals of comprehensive income and often of one another in the sense that they can be combined with each other or with the basic components to obtain other intermediate measures of comprehensive income.

Revenues

63. Revenues are inflows or other enhancements of assets of an entity or settlements of its liabilities (or a combination of both) during a period from delivering or producing goods, rendering services, or other activities that constitute the entity's ongoing major or central operations.[30]

Characteristics of Revenues of Business Enterprises

64. Revenues represent actual or expected cash inflows (or the equivalent) that have occurred or will eventuate as a result of the enterprise's ongoing major or central operations during the period. The assets increased by revenues[31] may be of various kinds—for example, cash, claims against customers or clients, other goods or services received, or increased value of a product resulting from production. Similarly, the transactions and events from which revenues arise and the revenues themselves are in many forms and are called by various names—for example, output, deliveries, sales, fees, interest, dividends, royalties, and rent—depending on the kinds of operations involved and the way revenues are recognized.

Expenses

65. Expenses are outflows or other using up of assets or incurrences of liabilities (or a combination

---

[29]Comprehensive income is a broad concept, broad enough to include changes in net assets from price changes, casualties, and other sources in the environment as well as changes from sales of product or amortization of costs. Being broad, (a) it is neutral regarding measurement matters not yet considered in the Board's conceptual framework and (b) it includes those kinds of changes in present practice (accounting for construction contracts by a percentage-of-completion method, accounting for marketable securities at market values, accounting for inventories and marketable securities at the lower of cost and market, accounting for other impairments of assets, and accounting for flood and fire losses, for example). This Statement contains no conclusions about which attributes (for example, historical costs or "current values") of elements of financial statements should be measured or which unit of measure should be used and is intended to imply none.

[30]Timing of recognition of revenues—including existing recognition procedures, which usually recognize revenues when goods are delivered or services are performed but may sometimes recognize them when cash is received, when production is completed, or as production progresses—is major subject matter for the Board's conceptual framework project on accounting recognition criteria. This Statement contains no conclusions about recognition of revenues or of any other elements.

[31]In concept, revenues increase assets rather than decrease liabilities, but a convenient shortcut is often to record directly reduction of liabilities. Production is essentially an asset conversion process to create future economic benefit (par. 60, footnote 28, and par. 51, footnote 23). It adds utility and value to assets and is the primary source of revenue, which may be recognized (as noted in the preceding footnote) when product is delivered, when cash is received, or when production is completed rather than as production takes place. Production does not directly incur or settle liabilities but is often closely related to exchange transactions in which liabilities are incurred or settled. Business enterprises acquire assets (economic benefits), not expenses or losses, to carry out their production operations, and most expenses are at least momentarily assets. Since many goods and services acquired are used either simultaneously with acquisition or soon thereafter, it is common practice to record them as expenses at acquisition. However, to record an expense as resulting from incurring a liability is a useful shortcut that combines two conceptually separate events: (a) an exchange transaction in which an asset was acquired and (b) an internal event (production) in which an asset was used up. The assets produced by operations may be used to settle liabilities (for example, by delivering product that has been paid for in advance). However, again, to record a liability as being directly reduced by recording revenue is a useful shortcut that combines two conceptually separate events: (a) an internal event (production) that resulted in an asset and revenue and (b) an exchange transaction in which the asset was transferred to another entity to satisfy a liability. In the diagram in par. 50, the exchange transactions are in class A, while the internal events (production) that result in revenues or expenses are in class B1.

of both) during a period from delivering or producing goods,[32] rendering services, or carrying out other activities that constitute the entity's ongoing major or central operations.

Characteristics of Expenses of Business Enterprises

66. Expenses represent actual or expected cash outflows (or the equivalent) that have occurred or will eventuate as a result of the enterprise's ongoing major or central operations during the period. The assets that flow out or are used or the liabilities that are incurred[33] may be of various kinds—for example, units of product delivered or produced, kilowatt hours of electricity used to light an office building, or taxes on current income. Similarly, the transactions and events from which expenses arise and the expenses themselves are in many forms and are called by various names—for example, cost of goods sold, cost of services provided, depreciation, interest, rent, and salaries and wages—depending on the kinds of operations involved and the way expenses are recognized.[34]

Gains and Losses[35]

67. Gains are increases in equity (net assets) from peripheral or incidental transactions of an entity and from all other transactions and other events and circumstances affecting the entity during a period except those that result from revenues or investments by owners.

68. Losses are decreases in equity (net assets) from peripheral or incidental transactions of an entity and from all other transactions and other events and circumstances affecting the entity during a period except those that result from expenses or distributions to owners.

Characteristics of Gains and Losses of Business Enterprises

69. Gains and losses result from enterprises' peripheral or incidental transactions and from other events and circumstances stemming from the environment that may be largely beyond the control of individual enterprises and their managements. Thus, gains and losses are not all alike. There are several kinds, even in a single enterprise, and they may be described or classified in a variety of ways that are not necessarily mutually exclusive.

70. Gains and losses may be described or classified according to sources. Some gains or losses are net results of comparing the proceeds and sacrifices (costs) in peripheral or incidental transactions with other entities—for example, from sales of investments in marketable securities, from dispositions of used equipment, or from settlements of liabilities at other than their carrying amounts. Other gains or losses result from nonreciprocal transfers between an enterprise and other entities that are not its owners—for example, from gifts or donations, from winning a lawsuit, from thefts, and from assessments of fines or damages by courts. Still other gains or losses result from holding assets or liabilities while their values change—for example, from price changes that cause inventory items to be written down from cost to market, from changes in market prices of investments in marketable equity securities accounted for at market values or at the lower of cost and market, and from changes in foreign exchange rates. And still other gains or losses result from other environmental factors, such as natural catastrophes—for example, damage to or destruction of property by earthquake or flood.

71. Gains and losses may also be described or classified as "operating" or "nonoperating," depending on their relation to an enterprise's major ongoing or central operations. For example, losses on writing down inventory from cost to market are usually considered to be operating losses, while major casualty losses are usually considered nonoperating losses.

Revenues, Expenses, Gains, and Losses

72. Revenues and gains are similar, and expenses

[32]If manufactured products are accounted for at accumulated costs until sold, as is common in present practice, production costs are recognized as expenses in the periods in which product is sold rather than in periods in which assets are used to produce output. For example, use of raw materials and depreciation of factory machinery are included in the cost of product and are recognized as expenses as part of the cost of goods sold. In contrast, if products are accounted for at net realizable value using a percentage-of-completion method, as output under construction contracts often is, production costs such as raw materials used and depreciation of construction equipment are recognized as expenses in the periods in which the assets are used to produce output.

[33]In concept, most expenses decrease assets rather than increase liabilities. They involve using (sacrificing) goods or services, not acquiring them. However, acquisition and use of many goods or services may occur simultaneously or during the same period, and a convenient shortcut is often to record directly increases of liabilities (par. 64, footnote 31). Taxes and other expenses resulting from nonreciprocal transfers, as several comment letters noted, commonly do result directly from incurring liabilities.

[34]Some have held that an imputed cost of (imputed interest on) equity capital should be accounted for the same as interest on borrowed funds. Thus, it might be included in the cost of certain assets and would be deducted, either directly as interest expense or indirectly as perhaps depreciation or cost of goods sold, in measuring operating income or income from continuing operations. The matter involves the so-called entity theory vs. proprietary theory, specifically whether an intermediate component of comprehensive income (which is a return on equity) should be designated as *income (or earnings) of the enterprise,* a question that the Board has not considered. The measurement and display issues raised by that kind of proposal are, of course, beyond the scope of this Statement, and this Statement contains no conclusions on the procedure suggested, but the definitions in this Statement are not intended to foreclose it.

[35]The terms *gains and losses* and *gains or losses* in this Statement include the possibility of *other appropriately descriptive terms* for reasons given in par. 58.

and losses are similar, but some differences are significant in conveying information about an enterprise's performance. Revenues and expenses result from an enterprise's ongoing major or central operations and activities—that is, from activities such as producing or delivering goods, rendering services, lending, insuring, investing, and financing. In contrast, gains and losses result from incidental or peripheral transactions of an enterprise with other entities and from other events and circumstances affecting it. Some gains and losses may be considered "operating" gains and losses and may be closely related to revenues and expenses. Revenues and expenses are commonly displayed as gross inflows or outflows of net assets, while gains and losses are usually displayed as net inflows or outflows.

73. The definitions and discussion of revenues, expenses, gains, and losses in this Statement give broad guidance but do not distinguish precisely between revenues and gains or between expenses and losses. Distinctions between revenues and gains and between expenses and losses in a particular enterprise depend to a significant extent on the nature of the enterprise, its operations, and its other activities. Items that are revenues for one kind of enterprise are gains for another, and items that are expenses for one kind of enterprise are losses for another. For example, investments in securities that may be sources of revenues and expenses for insurance or investment companies may be sources of gains and losses in manufacturing or merchandising companies. Technological changes may be sources of gains or losses to most kinds of enterprises but may be characteristic of the operations of high-technology or research-oriented enterprises. Events such as commodity price changes and foreign exchange rate changes that occur while assets are being used or produced or liabilities are owed may directly or indirectly affect the *amounts* of revenues or expenses for most enterprises, but they are *sources* of revenues or expenses only for enterprises for which trading in foreign exchange or commodities is a major or central activity. Since a primary purpose of distinguishing gains and losses from revenues and expenses is to make displays of information about an enterprise's sources of comprehensive income as useful as possible, fine distinctions between revenues and gains and between expenses and losses are principally matters of display or reporting (paragraphs 50, 151, and 152).

Accrual Accounting and Related Concepts

74. Items that qualify under the definitions of elements of financial statements and that meet criteria for recognition and measurement (paragraph 17) are accounted for and included in financial statements by the use of accrual accounting procedures. Accrual accounting and related concepts are therefore significant not only for defining elements of financial statements but also for understanding and considering other aspects of the conceptual framework for financial accounting and reporting. Paragraphs 75-89 define or describe several significant financial accounting and reporting concepts that are used in this Statement or will be needed in related projects.

Transactions, Events, and Circumstances

75. This Statement commonly uses "transactions and other events and circumstances affecting an entity" to describe the sources or causes of the components of comprehensive income and other changes in assets, liabilities, and equity. An event is a happening of consequence to an entity. It may be an internal event that occurs within an entity, such as using raw materials or equipment in production, or it may be an external event that involves interaction between an entity and its environment, such as a transaction with another entity, a change in price of a good or service that an entity buys or sells, a flood or earthquake, or an improvement in technology by a competitor.[36] Many events are combinations. For example, acquiring services of employees or others involves exchange transactions, which are external events; using those services, often simultaneously with their acquisition, is part of production, which involves a series of internal events (paragraph 64, footnote 31). An event may be initiated by an entity, such as a purchase of merchandise or use of a building, or it may be partly or wholly beyond the control of an entity and its management, such as an interest rate change, an act of vandalism or theft, or the imposition of taxes.

76. Circumstances are a condition or set of conditions that develop from an event or a series of events, which may occur almost imperceptibly and may converge in random or unexpected ways to create situations that might otherwise not have occurred and might not have been anticipated. To see the circumstance may be fairly easy, but to discern specifically when the event or events that caused it occurred may be difficult or impossible. For example, a debtor's going bankrupt or a thief's stealing gasoline may be an event, but a creditor's facing the situation that its debtor is bankrupt or a warehouse's facing the fact that its tank is empty may be a circumstance.

77. A transaction is a particular kind of external event, namely, an external event involving transfer of something of value (future economic benefit)

[36]In contrast, APB Statement 4, *Basic Concepts and Accounting Principles Underlying Financial Statements of Business Enterprises* (October 1970), par. 62, distinguishes external and internal events as follows: external events are "events that affect the enterprise in which other entities participate," while internal events are "events in which only the enterprise participates." In that classification, so-called acts of God, such as floods and earthquakes, which are external events in this Statement, are internal events.

between two (or more) entities. The transaction may be an exchange in which each participant both receives and sacrifices value, such as purchases or sales of goods or services; or the transaction may be a nonreciprocal transfer in which an entity incurs a liability or transfers an asset to another entity (or receives an asset or cancellation of a liability) without directly receiving (or giving) value in exchange. Nonreciprocal transfers contrast with exchanges, which are reciprocal transfers, and include, for example, investments by owners, distributions to owners, impositions of taxes, gifts, charitable contributions, and thefts.[37]

78. This Statement does not use the term *internal transaction* (which is essentially contradictory). Transferring materials to production processes, using plant and equipment whose wear and tear is represented by depreciation, and other events that happen within an entity are internal events, not internal transactions.

Accrual Accounting

79. "Accrual accounting attempts to record the financial effects on an enterprise of transactions and other events and circumstances that have cash consequences for the enterprise in the periods in which those transactions, events, and circumstances occur rather than only in the periods in which cash is received or paid by the enterprise. Accrual accounting is concerned with the process by which cash expended on resources and activities is returned as more (or perhaps less) cash to the enterprise, not just with the beginning and end of that process. It recognizes that the buying, producing, selling, and other operations of an enterprise during a period, as well as other events that affect enterprise performance, often do not coincide with the cash receipts and payments of the period" (FASB Concepts Statement No. 1, *Objectives of Financial Reporting by Business Enterprises,* paragraph 44).

80. Thus, accrual accounting is based not only on cash transactions but also on credit transactions, barter exchanges, changes in prices, changes in form of assets or liabilities, and other transactions, events, and circumstances that have cash consequences for an enterprise but involve no concurrent cash movement. By accounting for noncash assets, liabilities, revenues, expenses, gains, and losses, accrual accounting links an enterprise's operations and other transactions, events, and circumstances that affect it with its cash receipts and outlays whose assessment looms large in the objectives of financial reporting by business enterprises (Concepts Statement 1, paragraphs 37 and 45).

Accrual and Deferral (Including Allocation and Amortization)

81. Accrual accounting attempts to recognize noncash events and circumstances as they occur and involves not only accruals but also deferrals, including allocations and amortizations. Accrual is concerned with expected future cash receipts and payments: it is the accounting process of recognizing assets, liabilities, or components of comprehensive income for amounts expected to be received or paid, usually in cash, in the future. Deferral is concerned with past cash receipts and payments—with prepayments received (often described as collected in advance) or paid: it is the accounting process of recognizing a liability resulting from a current cash receipt or an asset resulting from a current cash payment with deferred recognition of components of comprehensive income. Common examples of accruals include purchases and sales of goods or services on account, interest, rent (not yet paid), wages and salaries, taxes, and decreases and increases in marketable securities accounted for at lower of cost and market. Common examples of deferrals include prepaid insurance and unearned subscriptions.[38]

82. Allocation is the accounting process of assigning or distributing an amount according to a plan or a formula. It is broader than and includes amortization, which is the accounting process of reducing an amount by periodic payments or write-downs. Specifically, amortization is the process of reducing a liability recorded as a result of a cash receipt by recognizing revenues or reducing an asset recorded as a result of a cash payment by recognizing expenses or costs of production. That is, amortization is an allocation process for accounting for prepayments and deferrals. Common examples of allocations include assigning manufacturing costs to production departments or cost centers and thence to units of product to determine "product cost," apportioning the cost of a "basket purchase" to the individual assets acquired on the basis of their relative market values, and spreading the cost of an insurance policy or a building to two or more accounting periods. Common examples of amortizations include recognizing expenses for depreciation, depletion, and insurance and recognizing earned subscription revenues.

[37]APB Statement 4, par. 62, and APB Opinion No. 29, *Accounting for Nonmonetary Transactions,* beginning with par. 5.

[38]The expressions *accrued depreciation* or *to accrue depreciation* are sometimes used, but depreciation in present practice is technically the result of allocation or amortization, which are deferral, not accrual, techniques. Conversely, the expressions *unamortized debt discount or premium* and *to amortize debt discount or premium* are sometimes used, but accounting for debt securities issued (or acquired as an investment) at a discount or premium by the "interest" method is technically the result of accrual, not deferral or amortization, techniques (pars. 159-162 of this Statement). The "interest" method is described in APB Opinion No. 12, *Omnibus Opinion—1967,* pars. 16 and 17, and APB Opinion No. 21, *Interest on Receivables and Payables,* pars. 15 and 16.

Realization and Recognition

83. Realization in the most precise sense means the process of converting noncash resources and rights into money and is most precisely used in accounting and financial reporting to refer to sales of assets for cash or claims to cash. The related terms *realized* and *unrealized* therefore identify revenues or gains or losses on assets sold and unsold, respectively. Those are the meanings of realization and related terms in the Board's conceptual framework. Recognition is the process of formally recording or incorporating an item in the financial statements of an entity. Thus, an asset, liability, revenue, expense, gain, or loss may be recognized (recorded) or unrecognized (unrecorded). *Realization* and *recognition* are not used as synonyms, as they sometimes are in accounting and financial literature.

Recognition, Matching, and Allocation for Business Enterprises

84. A major difference between accrual accounting and accounting based on cash receipts and outlays is timing of recognition of revenues, expenses, gains, and losses. Investments by an enterprise in goods and services for its operations or other activities commonly do not all occur in the same period as revenues or other proceeds from selling the resulting products or providing the resulting services. Several periods may elapse between the time cash is invested in raw materials or plant, for example, and the time cash is returned by collecting the sales price of products from customers. A report showing cash receipts and cash outlays of an enterprise for a short period cannot indicate how much of the cash received is return *of* investment and how much is return *on* investment and thus cannot indicate whether or to what extent an enterprise is successful or unsuccessful. Cash receipts in a particular period may largely reflect the effects of activities of the enterprise in earlier periods, while many of the cash outlays may relate to activities and efforts expected in future periods.

85. Accrual accounting uses accrual, deferral, and allocation procedures whose goal is to relate revenues, expenses, gains, and losses to periods to reflect an enterprise's performance during a period instead of merely listing its cash receipts and outlays. Thus, recognition of revenues, expenses, gains, and losses and the related increments or decrements in assets and liabilities—including matching of costs and revenues, allocation, and amortization—is the essence of using accrual accounting to measure performance of business enterprises. The goal of accrual accounting for a business enterprise is to account in the periods in which they occur for the effects of transactions and other events and circumstances, to the extent that those financial effects are recognizable and measurable.

86. Matching of costs and revenues is combined or simultaneous recognition of the revenues and expenses that result directly and jointly from the same transactions or other events. In most business enterprises, some transactions or events result simultaneously in both a revenue and one or more expenses. The revenue and expense(s) are directly related to each other and require recognition at the same time. In present practice, for example, a sale of product or merchandise involves both revenue (sales revenue) for receipt of cash or a receivable and expense (cost of goods sold) for sacrifice of the product or merchandise sold to customers. Other examples of expenses that may result from the same transaction and be directly related to sales revenues are transportation to customers, sales commissions, and perhaps certain other selling costs.

87. Many expenses, however, are not related directly to particular revenues but can be related to a period on the basis of transactions or events occurring in that period or by allocation. Recognition of those expenses is largely independent of recognition of particular revenues, but they are deducted from particular revenues by being recognized in the same period.[39]

88. Some costs that cannot be directly related to particular revenues are incurred to obtain benefits that are exhausted in the period in which the costs are incurred. For example, salesmen's monthly salaries and electricity used to light an office building usually fit that description and are usually recognized as expenses in the period in which they are incurred. Other costs are also recognized as expenses in the period in which they are incurred because the period to which they otherwise relate is indeterminable or not worth the effort to determine.

89. However, many assets yield their benefits to an enterprise over several periods, for example, prepaid insurance, buildings, and various kinds of equipment. Expenses resulting from their use are normally allocated to the periods of their estimated useful lives (the periods over which they are expected to provide benefits) by a "systematic and rational" allocation procedure, for example, by recognizing depreciation or other amortization. Although the purpose of expense allocation is the same as that of other expense recognition—to

[39]APB Statement 4 (pars. 154-161) describes "three pervasive expense recognition principles": associating cause and effect, systematic and rational allocation, and immediate recognition. Paragraphs 86-89 of this Statement describe generally the same three bases for recognizing expenses but not in the same order.

reflect the using up of assets as a result of transactions or other events or circumstances affecting an enterprise—allocation is applied if causal relations are generally, but not specifically, identified. For example, wear and tear from use is known to be a major cause of the expense called depreciation, but the amount of depreciation caused by wear and tear in a period normally cannot be measured. Those expenses are not related directly to either specific revenues or particular periods. Usually no traceable relationship exists, and they are recognized by allocating costs to periods in which assets are expected to be used and are related only indirectly to the revenues that are recognized in the same period.

This Statement was adopted by the unanimous vote of the seven members of the Financial Accounting Standards Board:

Donald J. Kirk, *Chairman*
Frank E. Block
John W. March
Robert A. Morgan
David Mosso
Robert T. Sprouse
Ralph E. Walters

Appendix A

BACKGROUND INFORMATION

90. The need for a conceptual framework for financial accounting and reporting, beginning with consideration of the objectives of financial reporting, is generally recognized. The Accounting Principles Board issued APB Statement No. 4, *Basic Concepts and Accounting Principles Underlying Financial Statements of Business Enterprises,* in 1970. When the Financial Accounting Standards Board came into existence, the Study Group on the Objectives of Financial Statements was at work, and its report, *Objectives of Financial Statements,* was published in October 1973 by the American Institute of Certified Public Accountants.

91. The Financial Accounting Standards Board issued a Discussion Memorandum, *Conceptual Framework for Accounting and Reporting: Consideration of the Report of the Study Group on the Objectives of Financial Statements,* dated June 6, 1974, and held a public hearing on September 23 and 24, 1974 on the objectives of financial statements. On December 2, 1976, the Board issued three documents:

Tentative Conclusions on Objectives of Financial Statements of Business Enterprises,

FASB Discussion Memorandum, *Conceptual Framework for Financial Accounting and Reporting: Elements of Financial Statements and Their Measurement,* and

Scope and Implications of the Conceptual Framework Project.

The same task force, with only one membership change, provided counsel in preparing both Discussion Memorandums. Eleven persons from academe, the financial community, industry, and public accounting served on the task force while the Discussion Memorandums were written.

92. The Board held public hearings (a) August 1 and 2, 1977 on the *Tentative Conclusions on Objectives of Financial Statements* and on Chapters 1-5 of the Discussion Memorandum concerning definitions of the elements of financial statements and (b) January 16-18, 1978 on the remaining chapters of the Discussion Memorandum concerning capital maintenance or cost recovery, qualities of useful financial information (qualitative characteristics), and measurement of the elements of financial statements.

93. The Board received 283 written communications on the subject of the August 1977 hearing, of which 221 commented on the elements, and 27 parties presented their views orally and answered Board members' questions at the hearing. The Board issued an Exposure Draft of a proposed Statement of Financial Accounting Concepts, *Objectives of Financial Reporting and Elements of Financial Statements of Business Enterprises,* dated December 29, 1977 and received 135 letters of comment.

94. During 1978, the Board divided the subject matter of the Exposure Draft. One part became FASB Concepts Statement No. 1, *Objectives of Financial Reporting by Business Enterprises,* which was issued in November 1978. Another part became the basis for the revised Exposure Draft, *Elements of Financial Statements of Business Enterprises,* issued December 28, 1979, on which the Board received 92 letters of comment.

95. Although some changes in wording and organization have been made, the Board believes that the substance of this Statement is essentially the same as that of the revised Exposure Draft.

Appendix B

CHARACTERISTICS OF ASSETS, LIABILITIES, EQUITY, AND COMPREHENSIVE INCOME AND ITS COMPONENTS

Purpose and Summary of Appendix

96. This appendix elaborates on the descriptions of the essential characteristics that items must have to qualify under the definitions of elements of financial statements in this Statement. It includes some discussion and illustrations of how to assess the characteristics of items that are potential candidates for formal inclusion in financial statements and in general how to apply the definitions.

97. The remainder of this introductory section briefly illustrates the relationship of the definitions to recognition, measurement, and display issues and the function and some consequences of the definitions. It is followed by a discussion of the characteristics of assets, liabilities, equity, and comprehensive income and its components. The appendix concludes with a series of examples that are intended to illustrate the meanings of the definitions and the essential characteristics that form them.

98. This Statement emphasizes that the definitions of elements are not intended to answer recognition, measurement, or display questions, which are issues in other phases of the conceptual framework project. The definitions are, however, a significant first step in determining the content of financial statements. They screen out items that lack one or more characteristics of assets, liabilities, revenues, expenses, or other elements of financial statements (paragraphs 16 and 17).

99. Thus, unless an item qualifies as an asset of an enterprise under the definition in paragraph 19, for example, questions do not arise about whether to recognize it as an asset of the enterprise, which of its attributes to measure, or how to display it as an asset in the financial statements of the enterprise. Although items that fail to qualify under the definitions of elements during a period do not raise recognition issues, they may nevertheless raise issues about whether and, if so, how and at what amounts they should be disclosed. For example, contingencies that have not yet, and may never, become assets or liabilities may need to be estimated and disclosed. Thus, the first question about each potential candidate for formal inclusion in financial statements is whether it qualifies under one of the definitions of elements; recognition, measurement, and display questions follow.

100. An item does not qualify as an asset or liability of an enterprise if it lacks one or more essential characteristics. Thus, for example, an item does not qualify as an asset of an enterprise under the definition in paragraph 19 if (a) the item involves no future economic benefit, (b) the item involves future economic benefit, but the enterprise cannot obtain it, or (c) the item involves future economic benefit that the enterprise may in the future obtain, but the events or circumstances that give the enterprise access to and control of the benefit have not yet occurred (or the enterprise in the past had the ability to obtain or control the future benefit, but events or circumstances have occurred to remove that ability). Similarly, an item does not qualify as a liability of an enterprise under the definition in paragraph 28 if (a) the item entails no future sacrifice of assets, (b) the item entails future sacrifice of assets, but the enterprise is not obligated to make the sacrifice, or (c) the item involves a future sacrifice of assets that the enterprise will be obligated to make, but the events or circumstances that obligate the enterprise have not yet occurred (or the enterprise in the past was obligated to make the future sacrifice, but events or circumstances have occurred to remove that obligation).

101. This appendix contains numerous examples of items that commonly qualify as assets or liabilities of an enterprise under the definitions in this Statement. It also includes several illustrations showing that items that may not qualify as assets may readily qualify as reductions (valuation accounts) of liabilities and that items that may not qualify as liabilities may readily qualify as reductions (valuation accounts) of assets. The following examples illustrate items that do not qualify as assets or liabilities of an enterprise under the definitions: (a) "dry holes" drilled by an exploration enterprise that has not yet discovered hydrocarbon, mineral, or other reserves are not assets (except to the extent of salvageable materials or equipment) because they provide no access to probable future economic benefit;[40] (b) estimated possible casualty losses from future floods or fires are not liabilities or impairments of assets because an event incurring a liability or impairing an asset has not occurred; (c) inventories or depreciable assets required (but not yet ordered) to replace similar items that are being or have been used up are not assets because no future economic benefits have been acquired, and the requirement to sacrifice assets to obtain them is not a liability because the enterprise is not yet obligated to sacrifice assets in the future; (d) deferrals relating to assets no longer held or liabilities no longer owed—such as a deferred loss on selling an asset for cash or a deferred gain on settling a liability for cash—are not assets or liabilities because they

[40] Paragraph 170 notes an aspect of the cost of some "dry holes" in different circumstances.

involve no future economic benefit or no required future sacrifice of assets; (e) receipts of grants of cash or other assets with no strings attached do not create liabilities because the enterprise is not required to sacrifice assets in the future; (f) other receipts of cash in return for which an enterprise is in no way obligated to pay cash, transfer other assets, or provide services do not create liabilities because the enterprise is not required to sacrifice assets in the future; (g) "know-how" of NASA or other governmental agencies placed in the public domain is not an asset of an enterprise unless the enterprise spends funds or otherwise acts to secure benefits not freely available to everyone; (h) estimated losses for two years from a decision to start up a new product line next year are not liabilities because the enterprise is not legally, equitably, or constructively obligated to sacrifice assets in the future; and (i) "stock dividends payable" are not liabilities because they do not involve an obligation to make future sacrifices of assets.

102. The Board expects most assets and liabilities in present practice to continue to qualify as assets or liabilities under the definitions in this Statement. That expectation is supported by the examples in the preceding paragraph as well as by those throughout this appendix. The Board emphasizes that the definitions in this Statement neither require nor presage upheavals in present practice, although they may in due time lead to some evolutionary changes in practice or at least in the ways certain items are viewed. They should be especially helpful, however, in understanding the content of financial statements and in analyzing and resolving new financial accounting issues as they arise.

Characteristics of Assets of Business Enterprises

103. Paragraph 19 defines assets as "probable future economic benefits obtained or controlled by a particular entity as a result of past transactions or events." The following discussion amplifies that definition and illustrates its meaning under three headings that correspond to the three essential characteristics of assets described in paragraph 20: future economic benefits, control by a particular enterprise, and occurrence of a past transaction or event.

Future Economic Benefits

104. Future economic benefit is the essence of an asset (paragraphs 21-24). An asset has the capacity to serve the enterprise by being exchanged for something else of value to the enterprise, by being used to produce something of value to the enterprise, or by being used to settle its liabilities.

105. The most obvious evidence of future economic benefit is a market price. Anything that is commonly bought and sold has future economic benefit, including the individual items that a buyer obtains and is willing to pay for in a "basket purchase" of several items or in a business combination. Similarly, anything that creditors or others commonly accept in settlement of liabilities has future economic benefit, and anything that is commonly used to produce goods or services, whether tangible or intangible and whether or not it has a market price or is otherwise exchangeable, also has future economic benefit.[41] Incurrence of costs may be significant evidence of acquisition or enhancement of future economic benefits (paragraphs 110-112).

106. To assess whether a particular item constitutes an asset of a particular enterprise at a particular time requires at least two considerations in addition to the general kinds of evidence just described: (a) whether the item obtained by the enterprise actually embodied future economic benefit in the first place and (b) whether all or any of the future economic benefit to the enterprise remains at the time of assessment.

107. Uncertainty about business and economic outcomes often clouds whether or not particular items that might be assets have the capacity to provide future economic benefits to the enterprise (paragraphs 37-40), sometimes precluding their recognition as assets. The kinds of items that may be recognized as expenses or losses rather than as assets because of uncertainty are some in which management's intent in taking certain steps or initiating certain transactions is clearly to acquire or enhance future economic benefits available to the enterprise. Thus, enterprises engage in research and development activities, advertise, develop markets, open new branches or divisions, and the like, and spend significant funds to do so. The uncertainty is not about the intent to increase future economic benefits but about whether and, if so, to what extent they succeeded in doing so. Certain expenditures for research and development, advertising, training, start-up and preoperating activities, development stage enterprises, relocation or rearrangement, and goodwill are examples of the kinds of items for which assessments of future economic benefits may be especially uncertain.

108. Since many of the activities described in the preceding paragraph involve incurring costs, the distinction between the items just listed and assets, such as prepaid insurance and prepaid rent, that are described in paragraph 113 is often difficult to draw because the two groups tend to shade into each other. Indeed, the distinction is not based on the def-

[41]Absence of a market price or exchangeability of an asset may create measurement and recognition problems but it in no way negates future economic benefit that can be obtained by use as well as by exchange.

inition of assets in paragraph 19 but rather on the practical considerations of coping with the effects of uncertainty. If research or development activities or advertising result in an enterprise's acquiring or increasing future economic benefit, that future economic benefit qualifies as an asset as much as do the future benefits from prepaid insurance or prepaid rent. The practical problem is whether future economic benefit is actually present and, if so, how much—an assessment that is greatly complicated by the feature that the benefits may be realized far in the future, if at all.

109. Most assets presently included in financial statements qualify as assets under the definition in paragraph 19 because they have future economic benefits. Cash, accounts and notes receivable, interest and dividends receivable, investments in securities of other entities, and similar items so obviously qualify as assets that they need no further comment except to note that uncollectible receivables do not qualify as assets. Inventories of raw materials, supplies, partially completed product, finished goods, and merchandise likewise obviously fit the definition as do productive resources, such as property, plant, equipment, tools, furnishings, leasehold improvements, natural resource deposits, and patents. They are mentioned separately from cash, receivables, and investments only because they have commonly been described in accounting literature as "deferred costs" or occasionally as "deferred charges" to revenues. The point requires noting because comments received on the Discussion Memorandum and Exposure Drafts have manifested some misunderstanding: some respondents apparently concluded that all or most deferrals of costs were precluded by the definition of assets.

Assets and costs

110. A business enterprise commonly incurs costs to obtain future economic benefits, either to acquire assets from other entities in exchange transactions or to add value through operations to assets it already has (paragraph 25). An enterprise acquires assets in exchanges with other entities by sacrificing other assets or by incurring liabilities to transfer assets to the other entity later. An enterprise also incurs a cost when it uses an asset in production—future economic benefits are partially or wholly used up to produce or acquire other assets, for example, product in process, completed product, or receivables from customers.

111. Although an enterprise normally incurs costs to acquire or use assets, costs incurred are not themselves assets. The essence of an asset is its future economic benefit rather than whether or not it was acquired at a cost. However, costs may be significant to applying the definition of assets in at least two ways: as evidence of acquisition of an asset or as a measure of an attribute of an asset.

112. First, since an enterprise commonly obtains assets by incurring costs, incurrence of a cost may be evidence that an enterprise has acquired one or more assets, but it is not conclusive evidence. Costs may be incurred without receiving services or enhanced future economic benefits. Or, enterprises may obtain assets without incurring costs—for example, from investment in kind by owners. The ultimate evidence of the existence of assets is the future economic benefit, not the costs incurred.

113. Second, cost may measure an attribute of future economic benefit. Costs of assets such as inventories, plant, equipment, and patents are examples of costs or unamortized costs of future benefits from present practice, as are prepayments such as prepaid insurance and prepaid rent, which are unamortized costs of rights to receive a service or use a resource.

114. Losses have no future economic benefits and cannot qualify as assets under the definition in paragraph 19. Stated conversely, items that have future economic benefits are not in concept losses, although practical considerations may sometimes make it impossible to distinguish them from expenses or losses.

Control by a Particular Enterprise

115. Paragraph 19 defines assets in relation to specific entities. Every asset is an asset of some entity; moreover, no asset can simultaneously be an asset of more than one entity, although a particular physical thing or other agent that provides future economic benefit may provide separate benefits to two or more entities at the same time (paragraph 117). To have an asset, a business enterprise must control future economic benefit to the extent that it can benefit from the asset and generally can deny or regulate access to that benefit by others, for example, by permitting access only at a price.

116. Thus, an asset of a business enterprise is future economic benefit that the enterprise can control and thus can, within limits set by the nature of the benefit or the enterprise's right to it, use as it pleases. The enterprise having an asset is the one that can exchange it, use it to produce goods or services, exact a price for others' use of it, use it to settle liabilities, hold it, or perhaps distribute it to owners.

117. The definition of assets focuses primarily on the future economic benefit to which an enterprise has access and only secondarily on the physical things and other agents that provide future economic benefits. Many physical things and other

agents are in effect bundles of future economic benefits that can be unbundled in various ways, and two or more entities may have different future economic benefits from the same agent at the same time or the same continuing future economic benefit at different times. For example, two or more entities may have undivided interests in a parcel of land. Each has a right to future economic benefit that may qualify as an asset under the definition in paragraph 19, even though the right of each is subject at least to some extent to the rights of the other(s). Or, one entity may have the right to the interest from an investment, while another has the right to the principal. Leases are common examples of agreements that unbundle the future economic benefits of a single property to give a lessee a right to possess and use the property and give a lessor a right to receive rents and a right to the residual value. Moreover, a mortgagee may also have a right to receive periodic payments that is secured by the leased property.

Control and legal rights

118. As some of the preceding discussion indicates, an entity's ability to obtain the future economic benefit of an asset commonly stems from legal rights. Those rights share the common feature of conferring ability to obtain future economic benefits, but they vary in other ways. For example, ownership, a contract to use, and a contract to receive cash confer different rights.

119. Although the ability of an enterprise to obtain the future economic benefit of an asset and to deny or control access to it by others rests generally on a foundation of legal rights, legal enforceability of a right is not an indispensible prerequisite for an enterprise to have an asset if the enterprise otherwise will probably obtain the future economic benefit involved. For example, exclusive access to future economic benefit may be maintained by keeping secret a formula or process.

Noncontrolled benefits

120. Some future economic benefits cannot meet the test of control. For example, public highways and stations and equipment of municipal fire and police departments may qualify as assets of governmental units but they cannot qualify as assets of individual business enterprises under the definition in paragraph 19. Similarly, general access to things such as clean air or water resulting from environmental laws or requirements cannot qualify as assets of individual business enterprises, even if the enterprises have incurred costs to help clean up the environment.

121. Those examples should be distinguished from similar future economic benefits that an individual enterprise can control and thus are its assets. For example, an enterprise can control benefits from a private road on its own property, clean air it provides in a laboratory or water it provides in a storage tank, or a private fire department or a private security force, and the related equipment probably qualifies as an asset even if it has no other use to the enterprise and cannot be sold except as scrap. Equipment used to help provide clean air or water in the general environment may provide future economic benefit to the user, even if it has no other use and cannot be sold except as scrap. Moreover, a specific right to use a public highway from which the licensee might otherwise be excluded—for example, a license to operate a truck on the highways within a state—may have future economic benefit to the licensee even though it does not keep everyone else off the highway. Similarly, riparian rights and airspace rights may confer future economic benefits on their holders even though they do not keep others' boats off the river or prevent airplanes from flying overhead.

Occurrence of a Past Transaction or Event

122. The definition of assets in paragraph 19 distinguishes between the future economic benefits of present and future assets of an enterprise. Only present abilities to obtain future economic benefits are assets under the definition, and they become assets of particular enterprises as a result of transactions or other events or circumstances affecting the enterprise. For example, the future economic benefits of a particular building can be an asset of a particular entity only after a transaction or other event—such as a purchase or a lease agreement—has occurred that gives it access to and control of those benefits. Similarly, although an oil deposit may have existed in a certain place for millions of years, it can be an asset of a particular enterprise only after the enterprise either has discovered it in circumstances that permit the enterprise to exploit it or has acquired the rights to exploit it from whoever had them.

123. Since the transaction or event giving rise to the enterprise's right to the future economic benefit must already have occurred, the definition excludes from assets items that may in the future become an enterprise's assets but have not yet become its assets. An enterprise has no asset for a particular future economic benefit if the transactions or events that give it access to and control of the benefit are yet in the future. The corollary is that an enterprise still has an asset if the transactions or events that use up or destroy a particular future economic benefit or remove the enterprise's access to and control of it are yet in the future. For example, an enterprise does not acquire an asset merely by budgeting the purchase of a machine and does not lose an asset from

fire until a fire destroys or damages some asset.

Characteristics of Liabilities of Business Enterprises

124. Paragraph 28 defines liabilities as "probable future sacrifices of economic benefits arising from present obligations of a particular entity to transfer assets or provide services to other entities in the future as a result of past transactions or events." The following discussion amplifies that definition and illustrates its meaning under three headings that correspond to the three essential characteristics of liabilities described in paragraph 29: required future sacrifice of assets, obligation of a particular enterprise, and occurrence of a past transaction or event.

Required Future Sacrifice of Assets

125. The essence of a liability is a duty or requirement to sacrifice assets in the future. A liability requires an enterprise to transfer assets, provide services, or otherwise expend assets to satisfy a responsibility to one or more other entities that it has incurred or that has been imposed on it.

126. The most obvious evidence of liabilities are contracts or other agreements resulting from exchange transactions and laws or governmental regulations that require expending assets to comply. Although receipt of proceeds is not conclusive evidence that a liability has been incurred (paragraph 130), receipt of cash, other assets, or services without an accompanying cash payment is often evidence that a liability has been incurred. Evidence of liabilities may also be found in declarations of dividends, lawsuits filed or in process, infractions that may bring fines or penalties, and the like. Reductions in prices paid or offered to acquire an enterprise or a significant part of it to allow for items that a buyer must assume that require future transfers of assets or providing of services also may indicate the kinds of items that qualify as liabilities. Moreover, liabilities that are not payable on demand normally have specified or determinable maturity dates or specified events whose occurrence requires that they must be settled, and absence of a specified maturity date or event may cast doubt that a liability exists.

127. To assess whether a particular item constitutes a liability of a particular enterprise at a particular time requires at least two considerations in addition to the general kinds of evidence just described: (a) whether the enterprise actually incurred a responsibility to sacrifice assets in the future and (b) whether all or any of the responsibility remains unsatisfied at the time of assessment.

128. Most liabilities presently included in financial statements qualify as liabilities under the definition in paragraph 28 because they require an enterprise to sacrifice assets in the future. Thus, accounts and notes payable, wages and salaries payable, long-term debt, interest and dividends payable, and similar requirements to pay cash so obviously qualify as liabilities that they need no further comment. Responsibilities such as those to pay pensions, deferred compensation, and taxes and to honor warranties and guarantees also create liabilities under the definition. That they may be satisfied by providing goods or services instead of cash, that their amounts or times of settlement must be estimated, or that the identity of the specific entities to whom an enterprise is obligated is as yet unknown does not disqualify them under the definition, although some may not be recognized because of uncertainty or measurement problems (paragraphs 37-40).

129. Deposits and prepayments received for goods or services to be provided—"unearned revenues," such as subscriptions or rent collected in advance—likewise qualify as liabilities under the definition because an enterprise is required to provide goods or services to those who have paid in advance. They are mentioned separately from other liabilities only because they have commonly been described in the accounting literature and financial statements as "deferred credits" or "reserves." Comments on the Discussion Memorandum and Exposure Drafts have manifested some misunderstanding: some respondents apparently concluded that all or most "deferred credits" and "reserves" were precluded by the definition of liabilities.

Liabilities and Proceeds

130. An enterprise commonly receives cash, goods, or services by incurring liabilities (paragraph 31), and that which is received is often called proceeds, especially if cash is received. Receipt of proceeds may be evidence that an enterprise has incurred one or more liabilities, but it is not conclusive evidence. Proceeds may be received from cash sales or by issuing ownership shares—that is, from revenues or other sales of assets or from investments by owners—and enterprises may incur liabilities without receiving proceeds—for example, by imposition of taxes. The essence of a liability is a legal, equitable, or constructive obligation to sacrifice economic benefits in the future rather than whether proceeds were received by incurring it. Proceeds themselves are not liabilities.

Obligation of a Particular Enterprise

131. Paragraph 28 defines liabilities in relation to specific entities. A required future sacrifice of assets

is a liability of the particular entity that must make the sacrifice.

132. To have a liability, a business enterprise must be obligated to sacrifice its assets in the future—that is, it must be bound by a legal, equitable, or constructive duty or responsibility to transfer assets or provide services to one or more other entities. Not all probable future sacrifices of economic benefits (assets) are liabilities of an enterprise. For example, an enterprise's need to replace merchandise sold or raw materials or equipment used up, no matter how pressing, does not by itself constitute a liability of the enterprise because no obligation to another entity is present.

133. Most obligations that underlie liabilities stem from contracts and other agreements that are enforceable by courts or from governmental actions that have the force of law,[42] and the fact of an enterprise's obligation is so evident that it is often taken for granted. To carry out its operations, an enterprise routinely makes contracts and agreements that obligate it to repay borrowing, to pay suppliers and employees for goods and services they provide, to provide goods or services to customers or clients, or to repair or replace defective products sold with warranties or guarantees. Governmental units also routinely assess tax obligations against business enterprises, and courts may impose obligations for damages or fines on business enterprises.

134. Equitable or constructive obligations may underlie liabilities as well as those that are legally enforceable. Legal obligations are much more common, and their existence may be more readily substantiated, but other kinds of obligations are sometimes liabilities. For example, the question, which has resulted in differences of opinion, of the extent to which future payments under a lease agreement are legally enforceable against lessees is not necessarily significant in determining whether the obligations under lease agreements qualify as liabilities.

135. An enterprise may incur equitable or constructive obligations by actions to bind itself or by finding itself bound by circumstances, rather than by making contracts or participating in exchange transactions. An enterprise is not obligated to sacrifice assets in the future if it can avoid the future sacrifice at its discretion without significant penalty. The example of an enterprise that binds itself to pay employees vacation pay or year-end bonuses by paying them every year even though it is not contractually bound to do so and has not announced a policy to do so has already been noted (paragraph 33). It could refuse to pay only by risking substantial employee relations problems.

136. Most liabilities are obligations of only one enterprise at a time. Some liabilities are shared—for example, two or more entities may be "jointly and severally liable" for a debt or for the unsatisfied liabilities of a partnership. But most liabilities bind a single enterprise or other entity, and those that bind two or more enterprises or other entities are commonly ranked rather than shared. For example, a primary debtor and a guarantor may both be obligated for a debt, but they do not have the same obligation—the guarantor must pay only if the primary debtor defaults and thus has a contingent or secondary obligation, which ranks lower than that of the primary debtor.

137. Secondary, and perhaps even lower ranked, obligations may qualify as liabilities under the definition in paragraph 28, but recognition criteria are highly significant in deciding whether they should formally be included in financial statements because of the effects of uncertainty (paragraphs 37-40). For example, the probability that a secondary or lower ranked obligation will actually have to be paid must be assessed to apply the definition.

Occurrence of a Past Transaction or Event

138. The definition of liabilities in paragraph 28 distinguishes between present and future obligations of an enterprise. Only present obligations are liabilities under the definition, and they are liabilities of a particular enterprise as a result of the occurrence of transactions or other events or circumstances affecting the enterprise.

139. Most liabilities result from exchange transactions in which an enterprise borrows funds or acquires goods or services and agrees to repay borrowing, usually with interest, or to pay for goods or services received. For example, using employees' services obligates an enterprise to pay wages or salaries and usually fringe benefits.

140. In contrast, the acts of budgeting the purchase of a machine and budgeting the payments required to obtain it result neither in acquiring an asset nor in incurring a liability. No transaction or event has occurred that gives the enterprise access to or con-

[42]Contracts and agreements and enforceability of agreements and statutes are necessary parts of the environment in which business and economic activities and financial reporting take place. Business and economic activities in the United States depend on flows of money and credit, and the fact that the participants largely keep their promises to pay money or provide goods or services is a necessary stabilizing factor. But, the definitions in this Statement are not legal definitions and do not necessarily agree with legal definitions of the same or related terms (which have a propensity to have diverse meanings, often depending on the context or the branch of law that is involved). Nor is existence of a legally enforceable obligation inevitably required for an enterprise to have a liability (pars. 30-33).

trol of future economic benefit or obligates it to transfer assets or provide services to another entity.

141. Many agreements specify or imply how a resulting obligation is incurred. For example, borrowing agreements specify interest rates, periods involved, and timing of payments; rental agreements specify rentals and periods to which they apply; and royalty agreements may specify payments relating to periods or payments relating to production or sales. The occurrence of the specified event or events results in a liability. For example, interest accrues with the passage of time (that is, providing loaned funds for another hour, day, week, month, or year), while royalties may accrue either with the passage of time or as units are produced or sold, depending on the agreement.

142. Transactions or events that result in liabilities imposed by law or governmental units also are often specified or inherent in the nature of the statute or regulation involved. For example, taxes are commonly assessed for calendar or fiscal years, fines and penalties stem from infractions of the law or failure to comply with provisions of laws or regulations, damages result from selling defective products, and restoring the land after strip-mining the mineral deposit is a consequence of removing the ground cover or overburden and ore. For those imposed obligations, as for obligations resulting from exchange transactions, no liability is incurred until the occurrence of an event or circumstance that obligates an enterprise to pay cash, transfer other assets, or provide services to other entities in the future.

143. A liability once incurred by an enterprise remains a liability until it is satisfied in another transaction or other event or circumstance affecting the enterprise. Most liabilities are satisfied by cash payments. Others are satisfied by the enterprise's transferring assets or providing services to other entities, and some of those—for example, liabilities to provide magazines under a prepaid subscription agreement—involve performance to earn revenues. Liabilities are also sometimes eliminated by forgiveness, compromise, incurring another liability, or changed circumstances.

Characteristics of Equity of Business Enterprises

144. Paragraph 43 defines equity as the "the residual interest in the assets of an entity that remains after deducting its liabilities." It adds that "in a business enterprise, the equity is the ownership interest." Characteristics of equity of business enterprises are briefly discussed under the headings: residual or ownership interest and invested and earned equity. Although *capital* is not a precise term in referring to ownership interests because it is also applied to assets and liabilities in various ways, it is used in this discussion because *capital* is part of so many terms commonly used to describe aspects of ownership interests; for example, investments by owners are commonly called capital contributions, distributions to owners are commonly called capital distributions, and discussions of comprehensive income and its components often refer to capital maintenance.

Residual or Ownership Interest

145. Equity is the cumulative result of investments by owners, comprehensive income, and distributions to owners. That characteristic, coupled with the characteristic that liabilities have priority over ownership interest as claims against enterprise assets, makes equity not determinable independently of assets and liabilities. Although equity can be described in various ways, and different recognition criteria and measurement procedures can affect its amount, equity always equals net assets (assets − liabilities). That is why it is a residual interest.

Invested and Earned Equity

146. Equity is defined only in total in this Statement. Although equity of business enterprises is commonly displayed in two or more classes, usually based on actual or presumed legal distinctions, those classes may not correspond to the two sources of equity: investments by owners and comprehensive income. For example, a traditional classification for corporate equity is capital stock, other contributed capital, and retained or undistributed profit, with the first two categories described as invested or contributed capital and the third described as earned capital or capital from operations. That distinction holds reasonably well in the absence of distributions to owners or stock dividends; and cash dividends or dividends in kind that are "from profit" may not cause significant classification problems. However, transactions and events such as stock dividends (proportional distributions of an enterprise's own stock accompanied by a transfer of retained or undistributed profit to capital stock and other contributed capital) and reacquisitions and reissues of ownership interests (commonly called treasury stock transactions in corporations) mix the sources and make tracing of sources impossible except by using essentially arbitrary allocations. Thus, categories labeled invested or contributed capital or earned capital may or may not accurately reflect the sources of equity of an enterprise. However, those problems are problems of measurement and display, not problems of definition.

Characteristics of Comprehensive Income and Its Components

147. Paragraph 56 defines comprehensive income as "the change in equity (net assets) of an entity during a period from transactions and other events and circumstances from nonowner sources." It adds that "it includes all changes in equity during a period except those resulting from investments by owners and distributions to owners." Comprehensive income comprises four basic components—revenues, expenses, gains and losses—that are defined in paragraphs 63, 65, 67, and 68.

148. Comprehensive income and investments by and distributions to owners account for all changes in equity (net assets) of a business enterprise during a period, but not for all changes in its assets and liabilities. The diagram in paragraph 50 shows those relations. That makes the sources of comprehensive income significant to those attempting to use financial statements to help them with investment, credit, and similar decisions, especially since various sources may differ from each other in stability, risk, and predictability. That underlies the distinctions between revenues, expenses, gains, and losses as well as other components of comprehensive income that result from combining revenues, expenses, gains, and losses in various ways (paragraphs 59-62).

149. The principal distinction between revenues and expenses on the one hand and gains and losses on the other is that between an enterprise's ongoing major or central operations and its peripheral and incidental transactions and activities. Revenues and expenses result from an enterprise's productive efforts and most of its exchange transactions with other entities that constitute the enterprise's ongoing major or central operations. The details vary with the type of enterprise and activities involved. For example, a manufacturing or construction enterprise buys or contracts to use labor, raw materials, land, plant, equipment, and other goods and services it needs. Its manufacturing or construction operations convert those resources into a product—output of goods—that is intended to have a greater utility, and therefore a higher price, than the combined inputs. Sale of the product should therefore bring in more cash or other assets than were spent to produce and sell it. Other kinds of enterprises earn more cash or other assets than they spend in producing and distributing goods or services through other kinds of operations—for example, by buying and selling goods without changing their form (such as retailers or wholesalers), by providing one or more of a wide variety of services (such as garages, professional firms, insurance companies, and banks), or by investing in securities of other enterprises (such as mutual funds, insurance companies, and banks). Some enterprises simultaneously engage in many different ongoing major or central activities.

150. Most enterprises also occasionally engage in activities that are peripheral or incidental to their ongoing major or central operations. For example, many enterprises invest in securities of other enterprises to earn a return on otherwise idle assets (rather than to control or influence the other enterprise's operations). Moreover, all enterprises are affected by price changes, interest rate changes, technological changes, thefts, fires, natural disasters, and similar events and circumstances that may be wholly or partly beyond the control of individual enterprises and their managements. The kinds of events and circumstances noted in this paragraph are commonly sources of gains and losses for business enterprises. Of course, the distinction between revenues and gains and between expenses and losses depends significantly on the nature of an enterprise and its activities (paragraphs 72 and 73).

Interest in Information about Sources of Comprehensive Income

151. Information about various components of comprehensive income is usually more useful than merely its aggregate amount to investors, creditors, managers, and others who are interested in knowing not only that an enterprise's net assets have increased (or decreased) but also *how* and *why*. The amount of comprehensive income for a period can, after all, be measured merely by comparing the ending and beginning equity and eliminating the effects of investments by owners and distributions to owners, but that procedure has never provided adequate information about an enterprise's performance. Investors, creditors, managers, and others need information about the causes of changes in assets and liabilities.

152. As the preceding paragraphs imply, financial accounting and reporting information that is intended to be useful in assessing an enterprise's performance or profitability focuses on certain components of comprehensive income. Ways of providing information about various sources of comprehensive income are the subject of conceptual framework projects on display, particularly the project on reporting earnings.[43] Pertinent issues involve questions such as: Should all components of comprehensive income be displayed in a single financial statement or in two or more statements and, if the latter, which statements should be provided? What level of aggregation or disaggregation is needed for

[43]An FASB Discussion Memorandum, *Reporting Earnings,* was issued July 31, 1979. *Earnings* in the title of the Discussion Memorandum has the same meaning as *comprehensive income* in this Statement (par. 1, footnote 1).

revenues, expenses, gains, and losses? Which intermediate components or measures resulting from combining those elements should be emphasized and which, if any, should be emphasized to the extent of being the "bottom line" of a financial statement? Which, if any, intermediate component or components should be designated as *earnings*? May or should some components of comprehensive income be displayed as direct increases or decreases of equity?

Examples to Illustrate Concepts

153. The following paragraphs illustrate some possible applications of the definitions and related concepts. Two cautions apply. First, although the points involved are conceptually significant, they may be practically trivial—that is, the results may appear to make little difference in practice. However, since this Statement is part of the Board's conceptual framework project, it is intended to emphasize concepts and sound analysis and to foster careful terminology, classification, and disclosure. The illustrations are meant to focus on substance rather than form. They illustrate, among other things, (a) that the presence or absence of future economic benefit rather than whether or not an enterprise incurred a cost ultimately determines whether it has a particular kind of asset, (b) that the presence or absence of a legal, equitable, or constructive obligation entailing future sacrifice of economic benefit (assets) rather than whether or not an enterprise received proceeds ultimately determines whether it has a particular kind of liability, and (c) that debit balances are not necessarily assets and credit balances are not necessarily liabilities.

154. Second, the examples used are intended to illustrate concepts and are not intended to imply that the accounting illustrated or the display described should necessarily be adopted in practice. Statements of Financial Accounting Standards, not Statements of Financial Accounting Concepts, establish generally accepted accounting principles. Decisions about what should be adopted in practice involve not only concepts but also practical considerations, including the relative benefits and costs of procedures and the reliability of measures. For example, some of the kinds of items illustrated are significantly affected by the uncertainty that surrounds the activities of business enterprises (paragraphs 37-40), and those effects should be considered in applying the definitions in this Statement.

155. A particular item to which the definitions may be applied may belong to either of two groups of elements:

First Group

an asset,
a reduction of a liability
(liability valuation),
an expense, or
a loss.

Second Group

a liability,
a reduction of an asset
(asset valuation),
a revenue, or
a gain.

(None of the examples involves investments by owners or distributions to owners, and only the last one involves equity; those elements are therefore omitted from the two groups.) The nature of the elements and the relations between them dictate that the same item can be, for example, either an asset or an expense or either a liability or a gain, but the same item cannot be, for example, either an asset or a liability or either an expense or a gain. (Those who are familiar with the mechanics of accounting will recognize that the first group includes "debits" and the second group includes "credits.") Thus, to apply the definitions involves determining the group to which an item belongs and the element within the group whose definition it fits.

Deferred Gross Profit on Installment Sales

156. Deferred gross profit on installment sales falls into the second group. It is neither a revenue nor a gain; the recognition basis that results in deferred gross profit (in substance a cash receipts basis) permits no revenue or gain to be recognized at the time of sale, except to the extent of gross profit in a down payment. Designating the amount as "deferred gross profit" also indicates that it is not now a revenue or gain, although it may be in the future.

157. Nor is the deferred gross profit a liability. The selling enterprise is not obligated to pay cash or to provide goods or services to the customer, except perhaps to honor a warranty or guarantee on the item sold, but that is a separate liability rather than part of the deferred gross profit. The deferred gross profit resulted because of doubt about the collectibility of the sales price (installment receivable), not because of cash payments or other asset transfers that the seller must make.

158. The essence of the installment sale transaction (using the recognition basis involved) is that the sale resulted in an increase in installment receivables and

a decrease in inventory of equal amounts—the receivable reflects the unrecovered cost of the inventory sold. Gross profit (revenue less the related cost of goods sold) is recognized as cash is collected on the installment receivable, and the receivable continues to reflect the unrecovered cost—as it should using a cash receipts basis of recognition—if the deferred gross profit is deducted from it. Thus, no matter how it is displayed in financial statements, deferred gross profit on installment sales is conceptually an asset valuation—that is, a reduction of an asset.

Debt Discount, Premium, and Issue Cost

159. Unamortized or deferred debt discount belongs to the first group (paragraph 155) and was long commonly reported as an asset and amortized to interest expense by straight-line methods. APB Opinion No. 21, *Interest on Receivables and Payables,* changed that practice by requiring debt discount to be (a) deducted directly from the liability (as a "valuation account") and (b) "amortized" by the "interest" method using the effective interest or discount rate implicit in the borrowing transaction. That accounting reports the liability at the present value of the future cash payments for interest and maturity amount, discounted at the effective rate (which is higher than the nominal rate specified in the debt agreement), and reports interest expense at an amount determined by applying the effective rate to the amount of the liability at the beginning of the period.

160. The definitions in this Statement support the accounting required by Opinion 21. The debt discount is not an asset because it provides no future economic benefit. The enterprise has the use of the borrowed funds but it pays a price for that use—interest. A bond discount means that the enterprise borrowed less than the face or maturity amount of the debt instrument and therefore pays a higher actual (effective) interest rate than the rate (nominal rate) specified in the debt agreement. Conceptually, debt discount is a liability valuation—that is, a reduction of the face or maturity amount of the related liability.

161. Debt issue cost also falls into the first group of elements and is either an expense or a reduction of the related debt liability. Debt issue cost is not an asset for the same reason that debt discount is not—it provides no future economic benefit. Debt issue cost in effect reduces the proceeds of borrowing and increases the effective interest rate and thus may be accounted for the same as debt discount. However, debt issue cost may also be considered to be an expense of the period of borrowing.

162. Unamortized or deferred debt premium is the exact counterpart of unamortized or deferred debt discount, and Opinion 21 requires counterpart accounting. Unamortized debt premium is not itself a liability—it has no existence apart from the related debt—and is accounted for under the Opinion by being (a) added directly to the related liability and (b) "amortized" by the "interest" method using the effective interest or discount rate implicit in the borrowing transaction. The lower interest rate and lower interest cost result because the proceeds of borrowing exceeded the face or maturity amount of the debt. Conceptually, debt premium is a liability valuation, that is, an addition to the face or maturity amount of the related liability.

Deferred Income Tax Credits

163. One view of deferred income tax credits—the liability method—is that they are taxes payable in future periods, that is, they are obligations of an enterprise that entail future cash payments. Another view—the net-of-tax method—is that they are valuations related to the effects of taxability and tax deductibility on individual assets. Deferred tax credits belong in the second group (paragraph 155), and the two views just noted exhaust the possibilities—deferred tax credits cannot be revenues or gains.[44] Both the liability method and the net-of-tax method are compatible with the definitions in this Statement.

164. Only the deferred method that is prescribed by APB Opinion No. 11, *Accounting for Income Taxes,* does not fit the definitions. Deferred income tax credits are neither liabilities nor reductions of assets in Opinion 11. That Opinion rejects the liability method and specifically denies that deferred tax credits are "payables in the usual sense" (paragraph 57). The Opinion also proscribes the net-of-tax method. It requires accounting for deferred tax credits as "tax effects of current timing differences [that] are deferred currently and allocated to income tax expense of future periods when the timing differences reverse" (paragraph 19) rather than either as accrued taxes to be paid in future periods when the timing differences reverse or as reductions in related assets.[45]

---

[44]Deferred tax charges are not discussed separately in this Statement. However, they are assets—prepaid taxes—in the liability method and reductions of related liabilities in the net-of-tax method.

[45]Some proponents of the deferred method hold that it is actually a variation of the net-of-tax method despite rejection of that method in Opinion 11. They view the deferred tax charges and credits as the separate display of the effects of interperiod tax allocation instead of as reductions of the related assets, liabilities, revenues, expenses, gains, and losses. They argue that separate display is necessary or desirable, but it is a matter of "geography" in financial statements rather than a matter of the nature of deferred income tax credits.

165. The compatibility of two of the three most widely suggested methods of accounting for tax effects of timing differences with the definitions in this Statement (and a possible compatible rationale for the results of the third method) is noted because several comments on the Discussion Memorandum and 1977 Exposure Draft had concluded, some with dismay and some with satisfaction, that the definitions ruled out deferred tax accounting or interperiod income tax allocation. However, the definitions are neutral on that recognition question: they affect only the method of allocation and neither require tax allocation nor rule it out.

Deferred Investment Tax Credits

166. Deferred investment tax credits were created by APB Opinion No. 2, *Accounting for the "Investment Credit,"* and the concept of deferred investment tax credits in that opinion is the basis of this example. Those deferred credits fall into the second group (paragraph 155) and are neither revenues nor gains. Deferred investment tax credits differ from deferred income tax credits in lacking a characteristic of liabilities that deferred income tax credits may have: deferred investment tax credits do not involve an obligation to pay taxes or otherwise sacrifice assets in the future. Conceptually, if investment tax credits are to be deferred and amortized over the life of the related assets, they are reductions of the acquisition costs of assets, not liabilities.

167. The Accounting Principles Board concluded in Opinion 2 that an investment tax credit was in substance a reduction of the cost of the related asset acquired and thereby a reduction of depreciation expense over the life of the asset rather than a reduction of income tax expense for the period of acquisition. The APB therefore concluded that "reflection of the allowable credit as a reduction in the net amount at which the acquired property is stated (either directly or by inclusion in an offsetting account)" was "preferable in many cases," and it permitted accounting for the credit as "deferred income" (a deferred credit) only if it were amortized over the productive life of the property (Opinion 2, paragraph 14). In other words, a deferred investment tax credit could be displayed as if it were a liability, and its amortization could be displayed as a reduction of income tax expense, but it must be accounted for as a reduction of an asset.[46]

168. The issue of whether the tax credit is a liability (deferred credit) or a reduction of the assets acquired is a significant conceptual question with a much less significant practical effect. Indeed, some consider the matter trivial because it does not affect reported profit. The issue of whether the investment tax credit is an asset valuation or a liability focuses, however, directly on the heart of the definition of liabilities. The essence of a liability is a legal, equitable, or constructive obligation to sacrifice economic benefits (assets) in the future, and a deferred investment tax credit based on the analysis in Opinion 2 wholly lacks that characteristic. If, therefore, liabilities were defined in a way that those deferred investment tax credits could qualify as liabilities, the concept would have virtually no meaning—almost any credit balance would qualify as a liability. A definition must set limits to be useful, and a definition broad enough to include deferred investment tax credits would be of little or no help in determining whether any other particular item were a liability of a particular enterprise.

Deferred Costs of Assets

169. Accountants, and others, are accustomed to describing costs incurred as assets, but costs incurred are at best evidence of the existence of assets (paragraphs 110-112). They result in assets only if an enterprise acquires or increases future economic benefits available to it in exchange transactions or through production. Once that conceptual point is made, however, it is obvious that cost incurred (acquisition cost or sometimes "historical cost") is commonly the attribute that is measured in financial reporting for many assets. Thus, inventories, plant, equipment, land, and a host of other future economic benefits are now represented in financial statements by some variation of costs incurred to acquire or make them.

170. Other "deferred costs" that are not themselves assets may be costs of the kinds of assets of an enterprise described in the preceding paragraph. For example, a procedure so long established that it rarely rates a second thought is to account for the costs (less salvage value, if any) of units normally spoiled in producing a product as additional costs of the salable units produced. Similarly, although a "dry hole" cannot by itself qualify as an asset, except perhaps for some salvageable materials or equipment, the costs of drilling a dry hole may be part of the cost of developing the future economic benefits of a mineral deposit that has been discov-

[46]The definitions in this Statement do not bear on the question of whether an investment tax credit should be accounted for by the "deferral and amortization" method (which is described in this paragraph) or the "flow-through" method (which the Board also accepted in Opinion 4 [amending Opinion 2]). That issue involves whether the tax credit reduces the cost of the asset and depreciation over its life or reduces income tax expense in the period of acquisition, which is a recognition or measurement question. The existence of an asset from whose cost the credit may be deducted is not in doubt.

ered.[47] Or, the legal and other costs of successfully defending a patent from infringement are "deferred legal costs" only in the sense that they are part of the cost of retaining and obtaining the future economic benefit of the patent.

171. The examples in the preceding paragraph illustrate costs that are accounted for in current practice as costs of other assets rather than as assets by themselves. The examples in this and the next two paragraphs illustrate costs that are of the same general nature but have sometimes been accounted for, and are commonly described, as if they were themselves assets. For example, enterprises that incur relocation, repair, training, advertising, or similar costs usually receive services (that is, something of value) in exchange for cash paid or obligations incurred. The question that needs to be answered to apply the definition of assets is whether the economic benefit received by incurring those costs was used up at the time the costs were incurred or shortly thereafter or future economic benefit remains at the time the definition is applied. Costs such as those of relocation, repair, training, or advertising services do not *by themselves* qualify as assets under the definition in paragraph 19 any more than do spoiled units, dry holes, or legal costs. The reason for considering the possibility that they might be accounted for as if they were assets stems from their possible relationship to future economic benefits.

172. Costs incurred for services such as research and development, relocation, repair, training, or advertising relate to future economic benefits in one of two ways. First, costs may represent rights to unperformed services yet to be received from other entities. For example, advertising cost incurred may be for a series of advertisements to appear in national news magazines over the next three months. Those kinds of costs incurred are similar to prepaid insurance or prepaid rent. They are payments in advance for services to be rendered to the enterprise by other entities in the future. Second, they may represent future economic benefit that is expected to be obtained within the enterprise by using assets or in future exchange transactions with other entities. For example, prerelease advertising of a motion picture may increase the future economic benefits of the product, or repairs may increase the future economic benefits of a piece of equipment. Those kinds of costs may be accounted for as assets either by being added to other assets or by being disclosed separately. If costs are to be included in assets because they enhance future economic benefits of two or more assets, the only practical alternative to arbitrarily allocating them to those other assets may be to show them as separate assets.

173. The examples do not, of course, preclude accounting for the kinds of costs involved as expenses of the period in which they are incurred. Many, perhaps most, will not be shown as assets at all for practical reasons stemming from considerations of uncertainty or measurement (paragraphs 37-40 and 107-108).

Estimated Loss on Purchase Commitments

174. Estimated loss on purchase commitments belongs in the second group of elements (paragraph 155). It is not a revenue or gain because it results from a loss. It is at best part of a liability and is not *by itself* an obligation to pay cash or otherwise sacrifice assets in the future. There is no asset from which it may be a deduction in present practice. Thus, it seems not to fit in the second group, after all. That predicament results, however, because estimated loss on purchase commitments is the recorded part of a series of transactions and events that are mostly unrecorded.

175. A purchase commitment involves both an item that might be recorded as an asset and an item that might be recorded as a liability. That is, it involves both a right to receive assets and an obligation to pay for them.[48] A decrease in the price that leaves the committed buyer in the position of now being able to buy the assets cheaper were it not committed to buy them at the former, higher price does not by itself create an obligation that was not already present. If both the right to receive assets and the obligation to pay for them were recorded at the time of the purchase commitment, the nature of the loss and the valuation account that records it when the price falls would be clearly seen. The obligation to pay has been unaffected by the price decrease—the full amount must be paid if the assets are delivered. However, the future economic benefit and value of the right to receive the assets has decreased because the market value of the assets to be received has declined, and the estimated loss on purchase commitment is in concept a reduction of that asset.

176. As long as the commitment transaction remains unrecorded, however, the only way to recognize the loss on the commitment is to do as is

[47]"The cost of a development well [in contrast to that of an exploratory well] is a part of the cost of a bigger asset—a producing system of wells and related equipment and facilities intended to extract, treat, gather, and store known reserves" (FASB Statement No. 19, *Financial Accounting and Reporting by Oil and Gas Producing Companies,* par. 205). The "full-costing" method incorporates the same notion—costs of dry holes are not themselves assets but are costs of mineral deposits.

[48]Whether those rights and obligations might be accounted for as assets and liabilities is a subject for the Board's project on accounting recognition criteria. Although the definitions in this Statement do not exclude the possibility of recording assets and liabilities for purchase commitments, the Statement contains no conclusion or implications about whether they should be recorded.

done in current practice—to recognize the valuation account for estimated loss on purchase commitments and include it among the assets or liabilities. Although it can be deducted from assets in some way, even though the asset to which it applies is not recorded, it is sometimes shown among the liabilities. Paragraph 42, footnote 18, specifically notes that the Board does not intend to foreclose that latter possibility by issuing this Statement.

Other Losses Incurred

177. The Board also does not wish to foreclose similar accounting for certain other items. Some events and circumstances that are largely beyond the control of an enterprise or its management may reduce or make unavailable to the enterprise future economic benefits of its existing assets in ways that virtually force the enterprise to pay cash or otherwise transfer or use assets in the future to restore the future economic benefit that has been diminished or lost. For example, a storm may destroy a bridge that provides the only access to a plant but is owned by another entity that has granted an easement and has no incentive to rebuild the bridge; grain stored in an elevator may spoil leaving the elevator unusable until it is cleaned out; a flood may deposit mud or other debris on the floor of a warehouse; a tornado may leave the customers' parking lot covered with rubble, wrecked automobiles, and trees; a snowfall may bury railroad tracks, access roads, or parking lots. Each of those examples involves a situation in which an asset that is essentially undamaged itself cannot provide services to the owning enterprise until the enterprise spends cash or uses other assets to rebuild the bridge, clean out the warehouse or elevator, or clean off the tracks, access roads, or parking lots. The cost of restoring the future economic benefits lost or diminished may sometimes exceed the carrying amount of the affected asset.

178. It is always conceptually sound accounting to reduce the assets affected for the losses that have been incurred from events and circumstances such as those described in the preceding paragraph. However, if an event or circumstance has occurred causing a loss of the kinds described, and a future sacrifice of assets to restore future economic benefit lost is probable, it may be necessary as a practical matter to recognize the loss by recognizing an amount akin to the estimated loss on purchase commitments described earlier. The amount recognized might be the expected cash outlays or other future sacrifice needed to restore the diminished or lost economic benefits.

Minority Interests and Stock Purchase Warrants

179. Minority interests in net assets of consolidated subsidiaries do not represent present obligations of the enterprise to pay cash or distribute other assets to minority stockholders. Rather, those stockholders have ownership or residual interests in components of a consolidated enterprise. The definitions in this Statement do not, of course, preclude showing minority interests separately from majority interests or preclude emphasizing the interests of majority stockholders for whom consolidated statements are primarily provided. Stock purchase warrants are also sometimes called liabilities but entirely lack the characteristics of liabilities. They also are part of equity.

Examples Do Not Govern Practice

180. The Board reiterates that the examples in paragraphs 156-179 are intended to illustrate the definitions and related concepts, not to establish standards for accounting practice (paragraph 154). The examples are intended to help readers understand the essential characteristics of the definitions and related concepts and thereby to help them understand the definitions in this Statement.

Summary Index of Concepts Defined or Discussed

In addition to defining ten elements of financial statements, this Statement defines or discusses other concepts, terms, or phrases that are used in the definitions or explanations or are otherwise related to the elements defined. This index identifies the paragraphs in which the ten elements and certain other significant concepts, terms, or phrases are defined or discussed.

Statement of Financial Accounting Concepts No. 4
Objectives of Financial Reporting by Nonbusiness Organizations

STATUS

Issued: December 1980

HIGHLIGHTS

[*Best understood in context of full Statement*]

- This Statement establishes the objectives of general purpose external financial reporting by nonbusiness organizations.

  —Based on its review of those objectives and the objectives set forth in FASB Concepts Statement No. 1, *Objectives of Financial Reporting by Business Enterprises,* the Board has concluded that it is not necessary to develop an independent conceptual framework for any particular category of entities.

  —The two sets of objectives will serve as the foundation of an integrated conceptual framework for financial accounting and reporting that, when completed, will have relevance to all entities while providing appropriate consideration of any different reporting objectives and concepts that may apply to only certain types of entities.

  —Pending resolution of the appropriate structure for setting financial accounting and reporting standards for state and local governmental units, the Board has deferred a final decision on whether the objectives in this Statement should apply to general purpose external financial reporting of those units. On the basis of its study to date, the Board is aware of no persuasive evidence that the objectives in this Statement are inappropriate for that type of financial reporting by state and local governmental units.

  —Based on its study, the Board believes that the objectives of general purpose external financial reporting for government-sponsored entities (for example, hospitals, universities, or utilities) engaged in activities that are not unique to government should be similar to those of business enterprises or other nonbusiness organizations engaged in similar activities.

- This Statement focuses on organizations that have predominantly nonbusiness characteristics that heavily influence the operations of the organization.

  —The major distinguishing characteristics of nonbusiness organizations include: (a) receipts of significant amounts of resources from resource providers who do not expect to receive either repayment or economic benefits proportionate to resources provided, (b) operating purposes that are primarily other than to provide goods or services at a profit or profit equivalent, and (c) absence of defined ownership interests that can be sold, transferred, or redeemed, or that convey entitlement to a share of a residual distribution of resources in the event of liquidation of the organization.

  —These characteristics result in certain types of transactions that are infrequent in business enterprises, such as contributions and grants, and in the absence of transactions with owners.

  —The line between nonbusiness organizations and business enterprises is not always sharp since the incidence and relative importance of those characteristics in any organization are different. This suggests that, for purposes of developing financial reporting objectives, a spectrum of organizations exists ranging from those with clearly dominant nonbusiness characteristics to those with wholly business characteristics.

—Examples of organizations that clearly fall outside the focus of this Statement include all investor-owned enterprises and other types of organizations, such as mutual insurance companies and other mutual cooperative entities that provide dividends, lower costs, or other economic benefits directly and proportionately to their owners, members, or participants.

—Examples of organizations that clearly fall within the focus of this Statement include most human service organizations, churches, foundations, and some other organizations, such as those private nonprofit hospitals and nonprofit schools that receive a significant portion of their financial resources from sources other than the sale of goods and services.

—Borderline cases may exist where organizations possess some of the distinguishing characteristics but not others. Examples are those private nonprofit hospitals and nonprofit schools that may receive relatively small amounts of contributions and grants but finance their capital needs largely from the proceeds of debt issues and their operating needs largely from service charges. As a result, the objectives of Concepts Statement 1 may be more appropriate for those organizations.

- The objectives in this Statement stem from the common interests of those who provide resources to nonbusiness organizations in the services those organizations provide and their continuing ability to provide services.

- Nonbusiness organizations generally have no single indicator of performance comparable to a business enterprise's profit. Thus, other indicators of performance usually are needed.

- The performance of nonbusiness organizations generally is not subject to the test of direct competition in markets to the extent that business enterprises are.

—Other kinds of controls introduced to compensate for the lesser influence of markets are a major characteristic of their operations and affect the objectives of their financial reporting. Controls, such as formal budgets and donor restrictions on the use of resources, give managers a special responsibility to ensure compliance. Information about departures from those mandates is important in assessing how well managers have discharged their stewardship responsibilities.

- The objectives in this Statement apply to general purpose external financial reporting by nonbusiness organizations.

—The objectives stem primarily from the needs of external users who generally cannot prescribe the information they want from an organization.

—In addition to information provided by general purpose external financial reporting, managers and, to some extent, governing bodies need a great deal of internal accounting information to carry out their responsibilities in planning and controlling activities. That information and information directed at meeting the specialized needs of users having the power to obtain the information they need are beyond the scope of this Statement.

- The objectives of financial reporting are affected by the economic, legal, political, and social environment in which financial reporting takes place.

—The operating environments of nonbusiness organizations and business enterprises are similar in many ways. Both nonbusiness organizations and business enterprises produce and distribute goods and services and use scarce resources in doing so.

—Differences between nonbusiness organizations and business enterprises arise in the ways they obtain resources. Noneconomic reasons are commonly factors in decisions to provide resources to particular nonbusiness organizations.

- The objectives also are affected by the characteristics and limitations of the kind of information that financial reporting can provide.

  —The information provided by financial reporting is primarily financial in nature: It is generally quantified and expressed in units of money. However, quantified information expressed in terms other than units of money and nonquantified information may be needed to understand the significance of information expressed in units of money or to help in assessing the performance of a nonbusiness organization.

  —The information provided by financial reporting pertains to individual reporting entities, often results from approximate rather than exact measures, largely reflects the effects of transactions and events that have already happened, is but one source of information needed by those who make decisions about nonbusiness organizations, and is provided and used at a cost.

- The objectives state that:

  —Financial reporting by nonbusiness organizations should provide information that is useful to present and potential resource providers and other users in making rational decisions about the allocation of resources to those organizations.

  —Financial reporting should provide information to help present and potential resource providers and other users in assessing the services that a nonbusiness organization provides and its ability to continue to provide those services.

  —Financial reporting should provide information that is useful to present and potential resource providers and other users in assessing how managers of a nonbusiness organization have discharged their stewardship responsibilities and about other aspects of their performance.

  —Financial reporting should provide information about the economic resources, obligations, and net resources of an organization, and the effects of transactions, events, and circumstances that change resources and interests in those resources.

  —Financial reporting should provide information about the performance of an organization during a period. Periodic measurement of the changes in the amount and nature of the net resources of a nonbusiness organization and information about the service efforts and accomplishments of an organization together represent the information most useful in assessing its performance.

  —Financial reporting should provide information about how an organization obtains and spends cash or other liquid resources, about its borrowing and repayment of borrowing, and about other factors that may affect an organization's liquidity.

  —Financial reporting should include explanations and interpretations to help users understand financial information provided.

- Background information relating to the development of this Statement is included in paragraphs 57-66. Paragraph 67 contains a comparison of the objectives in this Statement to those in Concepts Statement 1.

Statement of Financial Accounting Concepts No. 4
Objectives of Financial Reporting by Nonbusiness Organizations

Statements of Financial Accounting Concepts

This Statement of Financial Accounting Concepts is one of a series of publications in the Board's conceptual framework for financial accounting and reporting. Statements in the series are intended to set forth objectives and fundamentals that will be the basis for development of financial accounting and reporting standards. The objectives identify the goals and purposes of financial reporting. The fundamentals are the underlying concepts of financial accounting—concepts that guide the selection of transactions, events, and circumstances to be accounted for; their recognition and measurement; and the means of summarizing and communicating them to interested parties. Concepts of that type are fundamental in the sense that other concepts flow from them and repeated reference to them will be necessary in establishing, interpreting, and applying accounting and reporting standards.

The conceptual framework is a coherent system of interrelated objectives and fundamentals that is expected to lead to consistent standards and that prescribes the nature, function, and limits of financial accounting and reporting. It is expected to serve the public interest by providing structure and direction to financial accounting and reporting to facilitate the provision of evenhanded financial and related information that helps promote the efficient allocation of scarce resources in the economy and society, including assisting capital and other markets to function efficiently.

Establishment of objectives and identification of fundamental concepts will not directly solve financial accounting and reporting problems. Rather, objectives give direction and concepts are tools for solving problems.

The Board itself is likely to be the most direct beneficiary of the guidance provided by the Statements in this series. They will guide the Board in developing accounting and reporting standards by providing the Board with a common foundation and basic reasoning on which to consider merits of alternatives.

However, knowledge of the objectives and concepts the Board will use in developing standards also should enable those who are affected by or interested in financial accounting standards to understand better the purposes, content, and characteristics of information provided by financial accounting and reporting. That knowledge is expected to enhance the usefulness of, and confidence in, financial accounting and reporting. The concepts also may provide some guidance in analyzing new or emerging problems of financial accounting and reporting in the absence of applicable authoritative pronouncements.

Statements of Financial Accounting Concepts do not establish standards prescribing accounting procedures or disclosure practices for particular items or events, which are issued by the Board as Statements of Financial Accounting Standards. Rather, Statements in this series describe concepts and relations that will underlie future financial accounting standards and practices and in due course serve as a basis for evaluating existing standards and practices.*

The Board recognizes that in certain respects current generally accepted accounting principles may be inconsistent with those that may derive from the objectives and concepts set forth in Statements in this series. However, a Statement of Financial Accounting Concepts does not (a) require a change in existing generally accepted accounting principles; (b) amend, modify, or interpret Statements of Financial Accounting Standards, Interpretations of the FASB, Opinions of the Accounting Principles Board, or Bulletins of the Committee on Accounting Procedure that are in effect; or (c) justify either changing existing generally accepted accounting and reporting practices or interpreting the pronouncements listed in item (b) based on personal interpretations of the objectives and concepts in the Statements of Financial Accounting Concepts.

Since a Statement of Financial Accounting Concepts does not establish generally accepted accounting principles or standards for the disclosure of financial information outside of financial state-

*Generally accepted accounting principles for nonbusiness organizations are primarily set forth in publications of the American Institute of Certified Public Accountants (AICPA) and other bodies, such as the National Council on Governmental Accounting (NCGA). The Board has agreed to exercise responsibility, except as noted below, for all the specialized accounting and reporting principles and practices in AICPA Statements of Position and Guides that are neither superseded by nor contained in Accounting Research Bulletins, Accounting Principles Board Opinions, FASB Statements, and FASB Interpretations. The Board deferred similar action with regard to those specialized accounting and reporting principles and practices contained in the AICPA Industry Audit Guide, *Audits of State and Local Governmental Units,* and the three Statements of Position (75-3, *Accruals of Revenues and Expenditures by State and Local Governmental Units;* 77-2, *Accounting for Interfund Transfers of State and Local Governmental Units;* and 80-2, *Accounting and Financial Reporting by Governmental Units*) that supplement that Guide. In so doing, the Board noted that at the present time the accounting and reporting by such governmental units is addressed by the AICPA and the NCGA. The Board also noted that discussions are continuing among interested parties, including the AICPA, the Financial Accounting Foundation (FAF), and NCGA, as to what the appropriate structure for accounting standard setting for such governmental units should be. Until the matter is resolved, the FASB proposes no changes with respect to its involvement with pronouncements in that area (paragraphs 3-5).

ments in published financial reports, it is not intended to invoke application of Rule 203 or 204 of the Rules of Conduct of the Code of Professional Ethics of the American Institute of Certified Public Accountants (or successor rules or arrangements of similar scope and intent).*

Like other pronouncements of the Board, a Statement of Financial Accounting Concepts may be amended, superseded, or withdrawn by appropriate action under the Board's *Rules of Procedure*.

FASB PUBLICATIONS ON CONCEPTUAL FRAMEWORK

Statements of Financial Accounting Concepts

No. 1, *Objectives of Financial Reporting by Business Enterprises* (November 1978)

No. 2, *Qualitative Characteristics of Accounting Information* (May 1980)

No. 3, *Elements of Financial Statements of Business Enterprises* (December 1980)

Discussion Memorandums and Invitations to Comment Having Issues Being (or Yet to Be) Considered by the Board

Elements of Financial Statements and Their Measurement (December 2, 1976)

Reporting Earnings (July 31, 1979)

Financial Statements and Other Means of Financial Reporting (May 12, 1980)

Reporting Funds Flows, Liquidity, and Financial Flexibility (December 15, 1980)

Other Projects in Process

Accounting Recognition Criteria

CONTENTS

*Rule 203 prohibits a member of the American Institute of Certified Public Accountants from expressing an opinion that financial statements conform with generally accepted accounting principles if those statements contain a material departure from an accounting principle promulgated by the Financial Accounting Standards Board, unless the member can demonstrate that because of unusual circumstances the financial statements otherwise would have been misleading. Rule 204 requires members of the Institute to justify departures from standards promulgated by the Financial Accounting Standards Board for the disclosure of information outside of financial statements in published financial reports.

INTRODUCTION AND BACKGROUND

Scope

General

1. This Statement establishes the objectives of general purpose external financial reporting by nonbusiness organizations. Those objectives, together with the objectives set forth in FASB Concepts Statement No. 1, *Objectives of Financial Reporting by Business Enterprises,* will serve as the foundation of the conceptual framework the Board is developing for financial accounting and reporting. Based on its review of the similarities and differences between those two sets of objectives, the Board has concluded that it is not necessary to develop an independent conceptual framework for any particular category of entities (e.g., nonbusiness organizations or business enterprises). Rather, its goal is to develop an integrated conceptual framework that has relevance to all entities and that provides appropriate consideration of any different reporting objectives and concepts that may apply to only certain types of entities. Consideration of the differences between the objectives of financial reporting set forth in this Statement and those in Concepts Statement 1 will be most useful in helping to identify those areas that may require unique treatment. Appendix A to this Statement provides background information. Appendix B compares the objectives of this Statement and Concepts Statement 1, noting the many areas of similarity and the few, but important, areas of difference (paragraph 9).

2. This Statement uses terminology that has been chosen carefully to avoid prejudging issues that may be subjects of other conceptual framework projects. For example, it uses the terms *resource inflows* and *outflows* rather than *revenues, expenses,* and *expenditures.* The reasons for the Board's conclusions are included in the text rather than in a separate appendix.

State and Local Governmental Units

3. From its outset, the project leading to this Statement has included governmental units in its scope, and the Exposure Draft included governmental examples. On the basis of its study to date, the Board is aware of no persuasive evidence that the objectives in this Statement are inappropriate for general purpose external financial reports of governmental units. Nonetheless, the appropriate structure for setting financial accounting and reporting standards for state and local governmental units continues to be discussed.[1] Pending resolution of that issue, the Board has deferred a final decision on whether the objectives set forth in this Statement should apply to general purpose external financial reporting by state and local governmental units.

4. If the responsibility for standard setting was ultimately given to the Financial Accounting Standards Board, the Board would expect to consider the findings of research in process by the National Council on Governmental Accounting (NCGA), the Council of State Governments (CSG) (paragraphs 65 and 66), and other intervening research. Before reaching a decision, it would also solicit additional views regarding the applicability of the conclusions in this Statement to general purpose external financial reporting of state and local governmental units.

5. Based on its study, the Board believes that the objectives of general purpose external financial reporting for government-sponsored entities (for example, hospitals, universities, or utilities) engaged in activities that are not unique to government should be similar to those of business enterprises or other nonbusiness organizations engaged in similar activities. Accordingly, examples of such government-sponsored organizations and activities are included in the sections of this Statement that discuss the environment in which nonbusiness organizations operate and the users of their financial reports.

Distinguishing Characteristics of Nonbusiness Organizations

6. The major distinguishing characteristics of nonbusiness organizations include:

a. Receipts of significant amounts of resources from resource providers who do not expect to receive either repayment or economic benefits proportionate to resources provided
b. Operating purposes that are other than to provide goods or services at a profit or profit equivalent

[1]The Board recognizes that standard setting for the federal government is not in question. Although the Board sees no conceptual reasons why the objectives in this Statement could not be applied to general purpose external financial reporting by the federal government, the Board acknowledges that determination is the responsibility of others.

c. Absence of defined ownership interests that can be sold, transferred, or redeemed, or that convey entitlement to a share of a residual distribution of resources in the event of liquidation of the organization.

These characteristics result in certain types of transactions that are largely, although not entirely, absent in business enterprises, such as contributions and grants,[2] and to the absence of transactions with owners, such as issuing and redeeming stock and paying dividends. Because the authoritative accounting literature has largely focused on problems commonly encountered in business enterprises, it has not dealt comprehensively with these unique areas in nonbusiness organizations.

7. This Statement focuses on organizations that have predominantly nonbusiness characteristics that heavily influence the operations of the organization. The line between nonbusiness organizations and business enterprises is not always sharp since the incidence and relative importance of those characteristics in any organization are different. This suggests that, for purposes of developing financial reporting objectives, a spectrum of organizations exists ranging from those with clearly dominant nonbusiness characteristics to those with wholly business characteristics. Examples of organizations that clearly fall outside the focus of this Statement include all investor-owned enterprises and other types of organizations, such as mutual insurance companies and other mutual cooperative entities that provide dividends, lower costs, or other economic benefits directly and proportionately to their owners, members, or participants. The objectives of financial reporting set forth in Concepts Statement 1 are appropriate for those types of organizations. Examples of organizations that clearly fall within the focus of this Statement include most human service organizations, churches, foundations, and some other organizations, such as those private nonprofit hospitals and nonprofit schools that receive a significant portion of their financial resources from sources other than the sale of goods and services.[3] As happens with any distinction, there will be borderline cases. This will be true especially for organizations that possess some of the distinguishing characteristics of nonbusiness organizations but not others.

8. Some organizations have no ownership interests but are essentially self-sustaining from fees they charge for goods and services. Examples are those private nonprofit hospitals and nonprofit schools that may receive relatively small amounts of contributions and grants but finance their capital needs largely from the proceeds of debt issues and their operating needs largely from service charges rather than from private philanthropy or governmental grants. As a result, assessment of amounts, timing, and uncertainty of cash flows becomes the dominant interest of their creditors and other resource providers and profitability becomes an important indicator of performance. Consequently, the objectives of Concepts Statement 1 may be more appropriate for those organizations.[4]

9. The objectives in this Statement stem from the common interests of those who provide resources to nonbusiness organizations in the services those organizations provide and their continuing ability to provide services. In contrast, the objectives of financial reporting of Concepts Statement 1 stem from the interests of resource providers in the prospects of receiving cash as a return of and return on their investment.[5] Despite different interests, resource providers of all entities look to information about economic resources, obligations, net resources, and changes in them for information that is useful in assessing their interests. All such resource providers focus on indicators of organization performance and information about management stewardship. Nonbusiness organizations generally have no single indicator of performance comparable to a business enterprise's profit. Thus, other indicators of perfor-

[2]These types of transactions are classified in APB Statement No. 4, *Basic Concepts and Accounting Principles Underlying Financial Statements of Business Enterprises,* as nonreciprocal transfers. Nonreciprocal transfers are therein defined as "transfers in one direction of resources or obligations, either from the enterprise to other entities or from other entities to the enterprise" (paragraphs 62 and 182). Two types of such transfers noted are: (a) transfers between the enterprise and its owners and (b) transfers between the enterprise and entities other than owners. Transactions of the second type frequently are found in nonbusiness organizations.

[3]The FASB Research Report, *Financial Accounting in Nonbusiness Organizations,* distinguishes two types of nonprofit organizations based "on a difference in the source of the financial resources" (page 161). A Type A nonprofit organization is therein defined as "a nonprofit organization whose financial resources are obtained, entirely, or almost entirely, from revenues from the sale of goods and services" (page 162). A Type B nonprofit organization, in contrast, is defined as "a nonprofit organization that obtains a significant amount of financial resources from sources other than the sale of goods and services" (page 162). The Type B category corresponds to the type of organizations that clearly falls within the focus of this Statement.

[4]The organizations described in this paragraph correspond to the Type A category described in the preceding footnote. To the extent, however, that Type A organizations have the unique transactions described in paragraph 6, they naturally will be impacted by standards promulgated by the Board in those areas.

[5]Creditors of nonbusiness organizations are also interested in receiving cash. Because of the differences in environment (principally the motivations of other resource providers) and different indicators of the performance of a nonbusiness organization, creditors also look to information useful in assessing the services that type of organization provides and its ability to continue to provide services to satisfy their basic interest in the prospect for cash flows.

mance are usually needed. This Statement sets forth two performance indicators for nonbusiness organizations: information about the nature of and relation between inflows and outflows of resources and information about service efforts and accomplishments. Moreover, the performance of nonbusiness organizations generally is not subject to the test of direct competition in markets to the extent that business enterprises are. Other kinds of controls introduced to compensate for the lesser influence of markets are a major characteristic of their operations and affect the objectives of their financial reporting. Controls, such as formal budgets and donor restrictions on the use of resources, give managers a special responsibility to ensure compliance. Information about departures from those mandates that may impinge upon an organization's financial performance or its ability to provide a satisfactory level of services is important in assessing how well managers have discharged their stewardship responsibilities. Paragraphs 13-22 compare the environments of nonbusiness organizations and business enterprises and provide a basis for the similarities and differences noted in this section and elsewhere in this Statement.

General Purpose External Financial Reporting

10. The objectives in this Statement apply to general purpose external financial reporting by nonbusiness organizations. The aim of that type of financial reporting is limited. It does not attempt to meet all informational needs of those interested in nonbusiness organizations nor to furnish all the types of information that financial reporting can provide. For example, although managers and governing bodies of nonbusiness organizations are interested in the information provided by general purpose external financial reporting, they also need additional information to help them carry out their planning, controlling, and other stewardship responsibilities (paragraph 32). Nor is general purpose external financial reporting intended to meet specialized needs of regulatory bodies, some donors or grantors, or others having the authority to obtain the information they need (paragraph 31). Rather, general purpose external financial reporting focuses on providing information to meet the common interests of external users who generally cannot prescribe the information they want from an organization. Those users must use the information that is communicated to them by the organization. The most obvious and important users fitting that description in the nonbusiness environment are resource providers, such as members, taxpayers, contributors, and creditors (paragraph 36).

11. The objectives in this Statement are not restricted to information communicated by financial statements. Financial reporting includes not only financial statements but also other means of communicating information that relates, directly or indirectly, to the information provided by the accounting system, that is, information about an organization's resources and obligations.[6]

12. For convenience, *financial reporting* is used in place of *general purpose external financial reporting by nonbusiness organizations* in the remainder of this Statement.

Environmental Context of Objectives

13. Financial reporting is not an end in itself but is intended to provide information that is useful in making economic decisions—for making reasoned choices among alternative uses of scarce resources.[7] Thus, the objectives in this Statement stem largely from the needs of those for whom the information is intended. Those needs depend significantly on the activities of nonbusiness organizations and the decisions that users of the information make about them. Accordingly, the objectives in this Statement are affected by the economic, legal, political, and social environment within which those organizations function in the United States. The objectives are also affected by the characteristics and limitations of the information that financial reporting can provide (paragraphs 23-28).

14. The operating environments of nonbusiness organizations and business enterprises are similar in many ways. Both nonbusiness organizations and business enterprises produce and distribute goods or services and use scarce resources in doing so. They sometimes provide essentially the same goods or services. For example, both municipal transportation systems significantly subsidized by general tax revenues and private bus lines may carry passengers within a large city, and both private nonprofit organizations supported by significant philanthropy and investor-owned enterprises may operate theatri-

[6]Distinctions between financial reporting and financial statements are discussed at more length in Concepts Statement 1 (paragraphs 5-8), and are the subject of another phase of the Board's conceptual framework project.

[7]Economic decisions about nonbusiness organizations may take different forms depending on the factors that are evident in the resource allocation process affecting an organization. For example, if an element of compulsion is present as it is with members paying dues or taxpayers paying taxes, this Statement describes processes, such as approval of budgets, elections, referendums, and involvement in legislative processes, through which resource providers decide or influence decisions about matters that affect the amount and use of resources allocated to organizations. A member may discontinue membership or a taxpayer may choose to locate in one governmental jurisdiction rather than another as a result of assessment of their respective policies. That kind of action also represents, in part, the result of an economic decision.

cal, dance, and musical organizations.[8] Both nonbusiness organizations and business enterprises obtain resources from external sources and are accountable to those who provide resources or their representatives. Both are integral parts of the national economy and interrelate directly or indirectly with other organizations. Both own or control supplies of resources, some of which are used in current operations and some of which are held for use in future periods. Both incur obligations. Some nonbusiness organizations, as well as business enterprises, incur and pay taxes, and both are subject to governmental laws and regulations. Both must be financially viable: To achieve their operating objectives, they must, *in the long run,* receive at least as many resources as they need to provide goods and services at levels satisfactory to resource providers and other constituents.[9] Both generally obtain resources from the same pool of resource providers, and the resources available for use by all organizations are limited.

15. Differences between nonbusiness organizations and business enterprises arise principally in the ways they obtain resources. The following descriptions begin with areas of greatest similarity between nonbusiness organizations and business enterprises and end with the areas of greatest difference.

16. Both nonbusiness organizations and business enterprises obtain resources in exchange transactions in markets. Both obtain labor, materials, and facilities or their use by paying for them or agreeing to pay for them in the future.[10] Both may borrow funds through bank loans, mortgages, or other direct loans or through issuing debt securities to creditors who commonly may evaluate and compare the risks and returns of securities of both nonbusiness organizations and business enterprises.

17. Both nonbusiness organizations and business enterprises may obtain resources by charging a price or fee for goods or services they provide, but the purpose of sales of goods or services is different. Some nonbusiness organizations may sell goods or services at prices that equal or exceed costs, but many nonbusiness organizations commonly provide goods or services at prices less than costs. Nonbusiness organizations also commonly provide goods or services free of charge. Moreover, those that charge prices sufficient to cover costs often use resources from those sales to subsidize other activities within the organization. For example, the football or basketball program at a college or university may finance both intercollegiate and intramural athletic programs. Although sales of goods or services may be important sources of financing for some nonbusiness organizations, nonbusiness organizations generally are not expected to and do not need to cover all costs, and perhaps earn profits, by sales because they rely significantly on other continuing sources of financing (paragraph 18). For example, some nonbusiness organizations have the power to assess dues, taxes, or other compulsory contributions, and others depend significantly on voluntary contributions. In contrast, business enterprises attempt to sell goods or services at prices that enable them to repay or compensate all resource providers, including owners and others who expect a monetary return for providing resources. Profit is the basis for compensating owners and others for providing resources, and expectations of profit are necessary to attract resources. Moreover, unprofitable business enterprises find it increasingly difficult to borrow or otherwise obtain resources. Sales of goods or services are not only significant sources of resources for business enterprises but also underlie their ability to obtain resources from other sources.

18. Members, contributors, taxpayers, and others who provide resources to nonbusiness organizations do so for reasons different from those of owners of business enterprises. All nonbusiness organizations obtain significant resources from resource providers who either expect no economic benefits or expect benefits received not to be proportionate to the resources provided. Those resources are often provided for charitable, humanitarian, religious, or other noneconomic reasons.[11] As a result, those who provide resources to a nonbusiness organization and those who benefit from the goods or services it provides may be different individuals or groups. Owners of business enterprises, in contrast, generally expect returns through dividends or price appreciation of their securities commensurate with the perceived risk.

19. As the preceding paragraphs indicate, non-

[8]Other nonprofit organizations (paragraph 8) lacking all the distinguishing characteristics of nonbusiness organizations also may provide the services described in this sentence.

[9]Some nonbusiness organizations are established for short-term purposes and are not intended to survive after completing their operating objectives, such as an organization established to erect a memorial.

[10]Nonbusiness organizations also may receive significant donations of labor, materials, and facilities or their use from resource providers.

[11]Contributors to nonbusiness organizations often provide resources, such as property, materials, and uncompensated volunteer labor, in addition to financial resources. In many nonbusiness organizations, such as charities and youth groups, these donated materials and services are significant factors in the organization's operations. In other nonbusiness organizations, especially those operated by religious bodies, services contributed by personnel at far less than their market value are equally significant. Such donated or contributed services and materials are rarely found in business enterprises.

economic reasons are commonly factors in decisions to provide resources to particular nonbusiness organizations. For example, contributors[12] to philanthropic organizations, such as charities, and to some membership organizations, such as churches, generally seek no direct economic benefits. Rather, their reasons for voluntarily providing resources relate to their interests in furthering the purpose and goals of the organization. The goals may involve a wide range of endeavors including those of a charitable, cultural, educational, economic, religious, scientific, social, or political nature. Some kinds of membership organizations, such as professional and trade associations, assess membership dues. Persons joining these organizations often seek noneconomic benefits, such as recognition or prestige, in addition to direct service benefits.

20. Nonbusiness organizations and business enterprises have different degrees of involvement with markets. Most transactions of business enterprises with other entities involve exchange prices in active markets; that market mechanism provides a measure of the utility and satisfaction of goods and services businesses buy and sell and of the overall performance of those enterprises. Nonbusiness organizations also borrow money and buy goods and services in markets and may or may not sell goods or services in markets. However, market transactions play a more limited role in the resource allocation process of nonbusiness organizations because those organizations do not finance their operations through equity markets and they commonly receive resources and provide goods or services in other than market transactions. Since market controls exist to a lesser degree for nonbusiness organizations than for business enterprises, other kinds of controls are introduced to compensate for their absence.

21. Resource providers or governing bodies may restrict or mandate the ways a nonbusiness organization may spend the resources provided. Spending mandates generally take one of two forms: specific budgetary appropriations or direct restrictions by donors or grantors. For example, a budgetary appropriation may limit the amount that a church may spend for its educational program or that a governmental unit may spend to subsidize its public transportation system, a donor or grantor may specify that a gift to a museum must be used to construct a new wing, or an agency of the federal government may specify that its grant to a university must be used for medical research. Those mandates give managers of nonbusiness organizations a special responsibility to ensure compliance. Although spending mandates also may exist in business enterprises, they are less common. Their effects on the conduct and control of the activities of business enterprises are less pervasive than in nonbusiness organizations.

22. Budgets are particularly significant in the nonbusiness environment. Both business and nonbusiness organizations use budgets to allocate and control uses of resources. However, in nonbusiness organizations for which providing resources is compulsory (for example, many membership organizations and governmental units), budgets are significant factors not only in allocating resources within an organization but also in obtaining resources. For example, budgets in membership organizations and governmental units are often pivotal in establishing the level of dues, taxes, or fees to be imposed; the level of services to be provided; and the desired relation between the two. Members and taxpayers may have the opportunity, either by direct vote or through elected representatives, to participate in developing and approving budgets. Elections and referendums also offer opportunities to change policies and the amounts and uses of resources provided. In other kinds of nonbusiness organizations, budgets may be important to voluntary donors in deciding whether to provide resources to nonbusiness organizations and in establishing the level of their giving.

Characteristics and Limitations of Information Provided by Financial Reporting

23. The objectives of financial reporting by nonbusiness organizations are affected not only by the environment in which financial reporting takes place but also by the characteristics and limitations of the kind of information that financial reporting, and particularly financial statements, can provide. The information provided by financial reporting is primarily financial in nature: It is generally quantified and expressed in terms of units of money. Information that is to be incorporated formally in financial statements must be quantifiable in terms of units of money. Other information can be disclosed in financial statements (including notes) or by other means, but financial statements involve adding, subtracting, multiplying, and dividing numbers that depict economic things and events and require a common denominator. Quantified information expressed in terms other than units of money (such as number of employees or units of services or products provided) and nonquantified information (such as descriptions of operations or explanations of policies) that are reported normally relate to or underlie the financial information. Information that is not expressed in terms of units of money may be needed

[12]Contributors include donors and prospective donors, grantors and prospective grantors, and federated fund-raising organizations that solicit contributions and then redistribute those contributions to nonbusiness organizations after deducting fund-raising and other costs.

to understand the significance of information expressed in terms of units of money or to help in assessing the performance of a nonbusiness organization (paragraphs 47-53). Financial reporting by nonbusiness organizations, however, is limited in its ability to provide direct measures of the quality of goods and services provided in the absence of market-determined exchange prices or the degree to which they satisfy the needs of service beneficiaries and other consumers.

24. The information provided by financial reporting pertains to individual nonbusiness reporting entities. This Statement, however, does not include criteria for determining the appropriate reporting entity for purposes of financial reporting by nonbusiness organizations. That matter will need to be addressed by other projects.[13]

25. The information provided by financial reporting often results from approximate, rather than exact, measures. The measures commonly involve numerous estimates, classifications, summarizations, judgments, and allocations. Thus, despite the aura of precision that may seem to surround financial reporting in general and financial statements in particular, with few exceptions the measures are approximations which may be based on rules and conventions rather than exact amounts.

26. The information provided by financial reporting largely reflects the effects of transactions and events that have already happened. Governing bodies and managers may use budgets to communicate information about plans or projections, but most of the information provided by financial reporting is historical, including comparisons of actual results with previously approved budgets. The acquisition price of land and the current market price of a marketable equity security are other examples of historical data included in financial reports. No future amounts or events are involved. Estimates resting on expectations of the future are often needed in financial reporting, but their major use, especially of those formally incorporated in financial statements, is to measure financial effects of past transactions or events or the present status of an asset or liability.

27. Financial reporting is but one source of information needed by those who make economic decisions about nonbusiness organizations. They need to combine information provided by financial reporting with relevant social, economic, and political information from other sources.

28. The information provided by financial reporting involves a cost to provide and use. The cost includes not only the resources directly expended to provide the information but also may include adverse effects on an organization from disclosing it. For example, comments about a pending lawsuit may jeopardize a successful defense. The collective time needed to understand and use information is also a cost. Generally, the benefits of information provided should be expected to at least equal the cost involved.[14] However, the benefits and costs usually are difficult to measure. Different persons will honestly disagree about whether the benefits of the information justify its cost.

Types of Users and Their Interests

29. Many people base economic decisions on their relationships to and knowledge about nonbusiness organizations and, thus, are interested in the information provided by financial reporting. Among present and potential users are members, taxpayers, contributors, grantors, lenders, suppliers, creditors, employees, managers, directors and trustees, service beneficiaries, financial analysts and advisors, brokers, underwriters, lawyers, economists, taxing authorities, regulatory authorities, legislators, the financial press and reporting agencies, labor unions, trade associations, researchers, teachers, and students. The following groups are especially interested in information provided by the financial reporting of a nonbusiness organization:

a. *Resource providers.* Resource providers include those who are directly compensated for providing resources—lenders, suppliers, and employees (paragraph 16)—and those who are not directly and proportionately compensated—members, contributors, and taxpayers (paragraph 18).[15]
b. *Constituents.* Constituents are those who use and benefit from the services rendered by the organization. In some nonbusiness organizations, constituents include resource providers (for example, members who pay dues or taxpayers), and distinguishing constituents from

[13]A discussion of the reporting entity issue can be found in the FASB Research Report on financial accounting in nonbusiness organizations, pages 18-21.

[14]Paragraphs 133-144 of FASB Concepts Statement No. 2, *Qualitative Characteristics of Accounting Information,* expand on the cost/benefit considerations discussed in this paragraph. The Board intends to solicit views regarding its tentative conclusion that the qualities of information set forth in Concepts Statement 2 also apply to accounting information of nonbusiness organizations.

[15]Taxpayers provide resources to nonbusiness organizations both directly and indirectly. They pay taxes to all levels of government. Governments (especially federal and state), in turn, provide funding to other levels of government, government-sponsored entities, and private nonbusiness organizations.

resource providers may serve no function. However, resource providers and service beneficiaries are largely different groups or individuals in some organizations. The degree to which service beneficiaries are a distinctive part of a constituency depends largely on the extent of separation between those providing the resources and those using and receiving the service benefits.

c. *Governing and oversight bodies.* Governing and oversight bodies are those responsible for setting policies and for overseeing and appraising managers of nonbusiness organizations. Governing bodies include boards of trustees, boards of overseers or regents, legislatures, councils, and other bodies with similar responsibilities. Oversight bodies also are responsible for reviewing the organization's conformance with various laws, restrictions, guidelines, or other items of a similar nature. Oversight bodies include national headquarters of organizations with local chapters, accrediting agencies, agencies acting on behalf of contributors and constituents, oversight committees of legislatures, and governmental regulatory agencies. In some nonbusiness organizations, governing bodies commonly are elected representatives of a constituency that is largely comprised of resource providers. In other nonbusiness organizations, governing bodies may be self-perpetuating through election of their successors.

d. *Managers.* Managers of an organization are responsible for carrying out the policy mandates of governing bodies and managing the day-to-day operations of an organization. Managers include certain elected officials; managing executives appointed by elected governing bodies, such as school superintendents, agency heads, and executive directors; and staff, such as fund-raising and program directors.

30. Present and potential users of the information provided by financial reporting by a particular nonbusiness organization share a common interest in information about the services provided by the nonbusiness organization, its efficiency and effectiveness in providing those services, and its ability to continue to provide those services. Resource providers, such as members and contributors, may be interested in that information as a basis for assessing how well the organization has met its objectives and whether to continue support. Taxpayers may need similar information to help them assess whether governmental units and government-sponsored entities have achieved their operating objectives. In addition, they may want to know how the services provided by the governmental unit or government-sponsored entity are likely to affect the amount of taxes and fees they will be required to pay. Resource providers, such as lenders, suppliers, and employees, view a nonbusiness organization as a source of payment for the cash, goods, or services they supply. Their interest stems from concern about the organization's ability to generate cash flows for timely payment of the organization's obligations to them. Governing and oversight bodies also use information about services rendered to help them evaluate whether managers have carried out their policy mandates and to change or formulate new policies for the organization. That information also is important to managers in evaluating the accomplishment of the responsibilities for which they are accountable to governing bodies, resource providers, and other constituents. Constituents, including recipients and beneficiaries of services who as a group are distinct from resource providers, share a direct interest in similar information.

31. Some users have specialized needs but also have the power to obtain the information they need. For example, donors and grantors who restrict the use of resources they provide often stipulate that they be apprised periodically of the organization's compliance with the terms and conditions of the gift or grant. Creditors also may be able to stipulate that certain specialized types of information be provided. Special-purpose reports directed at those kinds of needs are beyond the scope of this Statement.

32. Managers and, to some extent, governing bodies commonly are described as "internal users." In addition to the information provided by financial reporting, they need a great deal of internal accounting information to carry out their responsibilities in planning and controlling activities. Much of that information relates to particular decisions or to managers' exercise of their stewardship responsibility to ensure that resources are used for their intended purposes. For example, governing bodies and managers need information to evaluate properly the competing requests for funding of capital projects. They also need information to assist them in complying or overseeing compliance with spending mandates established by budgetary appropriations or donor or grantor restrictions. They need to know how much of a budgetary appropriation or restricted grant is unspent or uncommitted. They need to know that restricted resources were expended or committed in compliance with related mandates. Generally, both the number of spending mandates and the detail about them required to meet the informational needs of managers are so great that the usefulness of general purpose external financial reports would be reduced significantly if they reported the status of compliance with each mandate (paragraph 41). Since the type of reporting described in this paragraph needs to be tailored to

meet the specialized needs of managers and governing bodies of particular organizations, it is beyond the scope of this Statement.

OBJECTIVES OF FINANCIAL REPORTING

33. The following objectives of financial reporting flow from the preceding paragraphs and proceed from the general to the specific. The objectives begin with a broad focus on information that is useful to resource providers and other users in making rational decisions about allocating resources to nonbusiness organizations. The focus is then narrowed to the needs of resource providers and other users for information about the services an organization provides and its ability to continue to provide those services. That directs their attention to information about the organization's performance and how its managers have discharged their stewardship responsibility. Finally, the objectives focus on the types of information financial reporting can provide to meet those needs. The reasons for focusing the objectives of financial reporting on decisions generally made by resource providers are given in paragraph 36. That focus and wording do not mean that the objectives apply to only resource providers. On the contrary, information that satisfies the objectives should be useful to all who are interested in a nonbusiness organization's present and future capacity to render service and achieve its operating goals.

34. The objectives are those of financial reporting rather than goals for resource providers or others who use the information or for the economy or society as a whole. The role of financial reporting in the economy and society is to provide information that is useful in making decisions about allocating scarce resources, not to determine what those decisions should be. For example, information that tries to indicate that a relatively inefficient user of resources is efficient or information that is directed toward a particular goal, such as encouraging the reallocation of resources in favor of certain programs or activities of nonbusiness organizations, is likely to fail to serve the broader objectives that financial reporting is intended to serve. The role of financial reporting requires it to provide neutral information.

Information Useful in Making Resource Allocation Decisions

35. Financial reporting by nonbusiness organizations should provide information that is useful to present and potential resource providers and other users in making rational decisions about the allocation of resources to those organizations. The information should be comprehensible to those who have a reasonable understanding of an organization's activities and are willing to study the information with reasonable diligence.

36. Resource providers are important users of information provided by financial reporting who generally cannot prescribe the information they want. Their decisions significantly affect both nonbusiness organizations and the allocation of resources in society generally. In addition, information provided to meet the needs of present and potential resource providers is likely to be useful to others who are interested in essentially the same aspects of nonbusiness organizations as resource providers.

37. The potential users listed in paragraph 29 understand, to varying degrees, the environment within which a nonbusiness organization operates, the nature of its activities, and related matters. Their understanding of information provided by financial reporting and the extent to which they use and rely on it also varies greatly. Financial reporting information is a tool and, like most tools, cannot be of much direct help to those who are unable or unwilling to use it or who misuse it. Its use can be learned, however, and financial reporting should provide information that can be used by all who are willing to learn to use it properly. Efforts may be needed to increase the understandability of information provided by financial reporting. Cost/benefit considerations may indicate that information understood or used by only a few should not be provided.[16] Conversely, financial reporting should not exclude relevant information merely because it is difficult for some to understand or because some choose not to use it.

Information Useful in Assessing Services and Ability to Provide Services

38. Financial reporting should provide information to help present and potential resource providers and other users in assessing the services[17] that a nonbusiness organization provides and its ability to continue to provide those services.[18] They are interested in that information because the services are the end for which the resources are provided. The relation of the services provided to the resources used to provide them helps resource providers and others assess the extent to which the organization is successful in

[16]See footnote 14.

[17]The term *services* in this context encompasses the goods as well as the services a nonbusiness organization may provide.

[18]An organization's ability to continue to provide services ultimately depends on its ability to obtain resources from resource providers. The ability to obtain sufficient resources normally is not discussed in general purpose external financial reports unless that ability is in doubt. Paragraphs 43-55 discuss the type of information financial reporting can provide to meet the objective in paragraph 38.

carrying out its service objectives.

39. Resources are the lifeblood of an organization in the sense that it uses resources to provide services. A nonbusiness organization cannot, in the long run, continue to achieve its operating objectives unless the resources made available to it at least equal the resources needed to provide services at levels satisfactory to resource providers and other constituents. Although decisions of potential and present resource providers to provide or continue to provide resources involve expectations about future services of an organization, those expectations commonly are based at least partly on evaluations of past performance. Thus, resource providers tend to direct their interest to information about the organization's resources and how it acquires and uses resources. The focus of that interest is information about the organization's performance and how its managers have discharged their stewardship responsibility during a period.

Information Useful in Assessing Management Stewardship and Performance

40. Financial reporting should provide information that is useful to present and potential resource providers and other users in assessing how managers of a nonbusiness organization have discharged their stewardship responsibilities and about other aspects of their performance. Managers of an organization are accountable to resource providers and others, not only for the custody and safekeeping of organization resources, but also for their efficient and effective use. Those who provide resources to nonbusiness organizations do not have a profit indicator to guide their resource allocation decisions and may not have an immediate choice about the amounts of their contributions. They must look to managers to represent their interests and to make operating cost/benefit judgments that achieve the objectives of the organizations with minimum use of resources. Managers also are accountable for compliance with statutory, contractual, or other limitations.

41. Information about an organization's performance (paragraphs 47-53) should be the focus for assessing the stewardship or accountability of managers of a nonbusiness organization. Users also need assurance that managers have exercised their special responsibilities to ensure that an organization uses resources in the manner specifically designated by resource providers. General purpose external financial reporting can best meet that need by disclosing failures to comply with spending mandates that may impinge on an organization's financial performance or on its ability to continue to provide a satisfactory level of services.

42. Financial reporting is limited in its ability to distinguish the performance of managers from that of the organization itself. Nonbusiness organizations are often highly complex institutions, and the processes by which they acquire resources and render services often are long and intricate. Organizational successes and failures are the result of numerous factors. The ability and performance of managers are contributing factors, as are events and circumstances that often are beyond the control of managers. It is usually not possible to determine the degree to which managers, or any other specific factors, have affected the result. Actions of past managers affect current periods' performance, and actions of present managers affect future periods' performance.

Information about Economic Resources, Obligations, Net Resources, and Changes in Them

43. Financial reporting should provide information about the economic resources, obligations, and net resources of an organization and the effects of transactions, events, and circumstances that change resources and interests in those resources.[19] That type of information is useful in achieving each of the above objectives.

Economic Resources, Obligations, and Net Resources

44. Financial reporting should provide information about an organization's economic resources, obligations, and net resources. That information helps resource providers and others identify the organization's financial strengths and weaknesses, evaluate information about the organization's performance during a period (paragraphs 47-53), and assess its ability to continue to render services.

45. Information about an organization's economic resources, obligations, and net resources also provides direct indications of the cash flow potential of some resources and of the cash needed to satisfy many, if not most, obligations. The assessment of cash flow potential is important because it relates directly to the organization's ability to provide the goods and services for which it exists.

46. Resources provided to nonbusiness organizations often are restricted by providers as to time and for particular purposes (paragraph 21). Accord-

[19]In FASB Concepts Statement No. 3, *Elements of Financial Statements of Business Enterprises,* the Board has attempted to define many elements (for example, assets and liabilities) in a way that they could apply to all types of entities. In the near future, the Board expects to consider and solicit views about which, if any, of the definitions are inappropriate or may require modification for nonbusiness organizations and whether other elements are needed for financial statements of nonbusiness organizations.

ingly, information about restrictions on the use of resources is important for assessing the types and levels of services an organization is able to provide. That information is also important to creditors in assessing their prospects for receiving cash.[20]

Organization Performance

47. Financial reporting should provide information about the performance of an organization during a period. Periodic measurement of the changes in the amount and nature of the net resources of a nonbusiness organization and information about the service efforts and accomplishments of an organization together represent the information most useful in assessing its performance.

Nature of and Relation between Inflows and Outflows

48. Financial reporting should provide information about the amounts and kinds of inflows and outflows of resources during a period. It should distinguish resource flows that change net resources, such as inflows of fees or contributions and outflows for wages and salaries, from those that do not change net resources, such as borrowings or purchases of buildings. It also should identify inflows and outflows of restricted resources.

49. Financial reporting should provide information about the relation between inflows and outflows of resources during a period. Those who provide resources to a nonbusiness organization and others want to know how and why net resources changed during a period. To meet that need, financial reporting must distinguish between resource flows that are related to operations and those that are not.[21] In this way, financial reporting may provide information that is useful in assessing whether the activities of a nonbusiness organization during a particular period have drawn upon, or have contributed to, past or future periods. Thus, it should show the relation of resources used in operations of a period to resource inflows available to finance those operations. Similarly, it should provide information about changes in resources that are not related to operations. For example, resource providers to colleges or universities need information about changes in an organization's endowment and plant to understand more fully the changes in its net resources during a period.

50. The information described in paragraphs 47-49 measured by accrual accounting generally provides a better indication of an organization's performance than does information about cash receipts and payments.[22] Accrual accounting attempts to record the financial effects of transactions, events, and circumstances that have cash consequences for an organization in the periods in which those transactions, events, and circumstances occur rather than in only the periods in which cash is received or paid by the organization. Accrual accounting is concerned with the process by which cash is obtained and used, not with just the beginning and end of that process. It recognizes that the acquisition of resources needed to provide services and the rendering of services by an organization during a period often do not coincide with the cash receipts and payments of the period.[23]

Service efforts and accomplishments

51. Information about an organization's service efforts and accomplishments is useful to resource providers and others in assessing the performance of a nonbusiness organization and in making resource allocation decisions, particularly because:

a. The accomplishments of nonbusiness organizations generally cannot be measured in terms of sales, profit, or return on investment.
b. Resource providers often are not in a position to have direct knowledge of the goods or services provided when they also are not users or beneficiaries of those goods and services.

52. Financial reporting should provide information about the service efforts of a nonbusiness organization. Information about service efforts should focus on how the organization's resources (inputs such as money, personnel, and materials) are used in providing different programs or services. Techniques for measuring the costs of significant programs or ser-

---

[20] Issues that affect how, if at all, restricted resources are displayed in financial statements, for example, by using multi-column presentations or disclosure in the notes, are outside the scope of this Statement and may be the subject of future Board projects.

[21] Resource flows that are not related to operations have been described in various ways, for example, as "nonexpendable," "capital," or "restricted" flows. The Board's endorsement of distinguishing these types of flows is not intended to prejudge future determinations of (a) the criteria that should be used in making this distinction and (b) how and in what financial statements different types of flows might be displayed.

[22] In some relatively small organizations, the benefits of the better information obtained from accrual accounting may not justify the costs of obtaining that information (footnote 14).

[23] Accrual accounting is concerned with the timing of recognizing transactions, events, and circumstances that have financial effects on an organization. This paragraph is not intended to prejudge specific recognition and measurement issues involved in applying accrual accounting in the nonbusiness area. For example, whether certain inflows of financial resources, such as taxes, grants, and contributions, should be recognized in the period when a claim arises, when they are received, when they are appropriated for use, when they are used, or when other events occur, is beyond the scope of this Statement.

vices are well developed and this information normally should be included in financial statements.

53. Ideally, financial reporting also should provide information about the service accomplishments of a nonbusiness organization. Information about service accomplishments in terms of goods or services produced (outputs) and of program results[24] may enhance significantly the value of information provided about service efforts. However, the ability to measure service accomplishments, particularly program results, is generally undeveloped. At present, such measures may not satisfy the qualitative characteristics of accounting information identified in Concepts Statement 2. Research should be conducted to determine if measures of service accomplishments with the requisite characteristics of relevance, reliability, comparability, verifiability, and neutrality can be developed. If such measures are developed, they should be included in financial reports. In the absence of measures suitable for financial reporting, information about service accomplishments may be furnished by managers' explanations and sources other than financial reporting.

Liquidity

54. Financial reporting should provide information about how an organization obtains and spends cash or other liquid resources, about its borrowing and repayment of borrowing, and about other factors that may affect its liquidity. Information about those resource flows may be useful in understanding the operations of an enterprise, evaluating its financing activities, assessing its liquidity, or interpreting performance information provided. Information about performance and economic resources, obligations, and net resources also may be useful in assessing an enterprise's liquidity.

Managers' Explanations and Interpretations

55. Financial reporting should include explanations and interpretations to help users understand financial information provided. For example, the usefulness of financial information to resource providers and others may be enhanced by managers' explanations of the information. Since managers usually know more about the organization and its affairs than do resource providers or others outside the organization, they often can increase the usefulness of information provided by financial reporting by identifying certain transactions, events, and circumstances that affect the organization and by explaining their financial impact.[25] In addition, dividing continuous operations into accounting periods is a convention and may have arbitrary effects. Managers can enhance the usefulness of information contained in financial reports by identifying arbitrary results caused by allocations between periods and by describing the effects of those allocations on reported information. Moreover, financial reporting often provides information that depends on, or is affected by, managers' estimates and judgments. Users are aided in evaluating estimates and judgments by explanations of underlying assumptions and methods used, including disclosure of significant uncertainties about principal underlying assumptions or estimates.

THE NONBUSINESS OBJECTIVES PROJECT—A PERSPECTIVE

56. Paragraphs 43-54 focus on information that assists resource providers and other users in assessing an organization's financial viability, its performance, and how the organization's managers have discharged their stewardship responsibilities. Those paragraphs emphasize information about an organization's economic resources, obligations, and net resources and its performance during a period. The objectives lead to, but leave unanswered, questions such as the identity, number, and form of financial statements; elements of financial statements and their recognition, measurement, and display; and criteria for determining the reporting entity. The Board's approach to resolving those questions will be to integrate consideration of nonbusiness organizations into its series of conceptual framework projects. That integration may involve initiating new projects to deal with issues that may be more prevalent in or unique to nonbusiness organizations.

This Statement was adopted by the unanimous vote of the seven members of the Financial Accounting Standards Board:

Donald J. Kirk, *Chairman*
Frank E. Block
John W. March
Robert A. Morgan
David Mosso
Robert T. Sprouse
Ralph E. Walters

[24]Service accomplishments generally may be viewed as the results of service efforts. The FASB Research Report, *Reporting of Service Efforts and Accomplishments,* distinguishes two possible measures of accomplishments, outputs and results. "*Outputs* usually are observable directly as a result of service delivery; they describe goods and services provided by service delivery but do not measure impact upon clients or problems. . . . *Results* . . . represent impact upon clients or problem situations" (page 7). In discussing this latter measure, this Statement uses the term *program results.*

[25]These discussions may include information about service efforts and accomplishments as described in paragraphs 51-53.

Appendix A

BACKGROUND INFORMATION

Brief History of FASB Nonbusiness Objectives Project

57. The Board's project on objectives of financial reporting by nonbusiness organizations is related to and part of its effort to develop a conceptual framework for financial reporting. The Board began its work on a conceptual framework in 1973 and used as a point of departure the Report of the Study Group on the Objectives of Financial Statements, *Objectives of Financial Statements* (Trueblood Report), published by the American Institute of Certified Public Accountants in October 1973. That report included governmental and not-for-profit organizations in its scope.

58. As more fully discussed in paragraphs 57-62 of Concepts Statement 1, the Board initially considered the 12 objectives of financial statements in the Trueblood Report but decided to concentrate its initial efforts on formulating objectives of financial reporting by business enterprises. Initially, therefore, the Board did not attempt to reach conclusions on the objectives of financial reporting for governmental and not-for-profit organizations.

59. The need to consider the objectives of general purpose external financial reporting by nonbusiness organizations generally is recognized. An increasing number of public officials and private citizens are questioning the relevance and reliability of financial accounting and reporting by nonbusiness organizations. That concern has been reflected in legislative initiatives and well-publicized allegations of serious deficiencies in the financial reporting of various types of nonbusiness organizations.

60. In response to those concerns, the Board, in August 1977, engaged Professor Robert N. Anthony of the Harvard Business School to prepare a research report aimed at identifying the objectives of financial reporting by organizations other than business enterprises. A 53-member advisory group was appointed to assist in that effort. When the Board began consideration of objectives of financial reporting by nonbusiness organizations in August 1977, significant progress already had been made on the objectives of financial reporting by business enterprises. Rather than delay progress on that project to include nonbusiness organizations in its scope, and to explore thoroughly the issues in the nonbusiness area, the Board proceeded with two separate objectives projects. The Board issued Concepts Statement 1 in November 1978. Paragraph 1 of Concepts Statement 1 states:

> This Statement establishes the objectives of general purpose external financial reporting by business enterprises. Its concentration on business enterprises is not intended to imply that the Board has concluded that the uses and objectives of financial reporting by other kinds of entities are, or should be, the same as or different from those of business enterprises. Those and related matters, including whether and, if so, how business enterprises and other organizations should be distinguished for the purpose of establishing objectives of and basic concepts underlying financial reporting, are issues in another phase of the Board's conceptual framework project.

61. In May 1978, the Board published the FASB Research Report, *Financial Accounting in Nonbusiness Organizations,* prepared by Professor Anthony. The Board added the nonbusiness objectives project to its technical agenda on May 11, 1978 and directed the staff to prepare a Discussion Memorandum to solicit public comment. The Discussion Memorandum was issued on June 15, 1978. It focused on specific issues discussed in the Research Report and identified those on which the Board sought comments.

62. The Board held public hearings in Washington, D.C. on October 12 and 13, 1978; in San Francisco on October 19 and 20, 1978; and in Chicago on November 3, 1978. The Board received 87 written responses to the Discussion Memorandum, and 48 oral presentations were made at the public hearings.

63. The Board issued an Exposure Draft, *Objectives of Financial Reporting by Nonbusiness Organizations,* on March 14, 1980. In preparing the Exposure Draft, the Board deliberated the issues at meetings which were open to public observation. FASB Board and staff members have met with and maintained close liaison with various groups and individuals in the community of nonbusiness organizations since the outset of this project. In addition, persons from academe, public accounting, and various nonbusiness organizations provided counsel to the Board and its staff in preparing the Exposure Draft. The Board received 77 letters of comment on the Exposure Draft and considered the issues raised by respondents in those comment letters at meetings which were open to public observation.

64. The major differences between this Statement and the Exposure Draft are revisions to the scope of the document. The types of organizations to which the objectives in this document apply have been clarified (paragraph 1 of the Exposure Draft), and a discussion has been added concerning the relationship of this Statement to Concepts Statement 1.

Other significant changes are (a) the addition of examples of various types of nonbusiness organizations in the environment section (paragraphs 13-22); (b) greater emphasis on distinguishing flows that affect operations from those that do not (paragraph 49); (c) greater emphasis on the need for research to determine if measures of service accomplishments with the requisite characteristics of relevance, reliability, comparability, verifiability, and neutrality can be developed; and (d) acknowledgement that, in the absence of that financial reporting capability, information about service accomplishments may be furnished by managers' explanations and sources other than financial reporting.

State and Local Governmental Units

65. Others have been studying the objectives of financial reporting by governmental units during the period that the Board has been deliberating the issues and preparing this concepts Statement. The National Council on Governmental Accounting is sponsoring research in the broad area of a conceptual framework for governmental accounting, which includes the objectives of external financial reporting by state and local governmental units. A state accounting project that was commissioned by the Council of State Governments includes a study of objectives of accounting and financial reporting by state governments. The U.S. General Accounting Office is developing a statement of the objectives of financial reporting by the federal government and its agencies.

66. Since the publication of the Exposure Draft of this concepts Statement, the Board and its staff have monitored developments on the three projects discussed above. This monitoring has consisted of reviewing and analyzing working drafts of certain materials made available to the FASB by the NCGA and other researchers. On the basis of its study to date, the Board is aware of no persuasive evidence that the objectives in this Statement are inappropriate for general purpose external financial reports of governmental units.

Appendix B

COMPARISON OF OBJECTIVES IN THIS STATEMENT TO THOSE IN CONCEPTS STATEMENT 1

67. This Statement follows the *structure* of Concepts Statement 1. Both sets of objectives are based on the fundamental notion that financial accounting and reporting concepts and standards should be based on their decision usefulness. Thus, the objectives in this Statement and in Concepts Statement 1 focus on:

a. Types of users of the information provided by financial reporting and the types of decisions they make
b. The broad interests of the users identified and the information they need to assist them in making decisions
c. The type of information financial reporting can provide to help satisfy their informational needs.

The chart on pages 4127-29 compares the similarities and differences of this Statement and Concepts Statement 1 in each of those areas.

Purpose of Objectives	Nonbusiness Organizations Concepts Statement 4	Business Enterprises Concepts Statement 1	Comparison of Objectives
a. Identifies (1) the types of users that financial reporting should focus on in providing information and (2) the types of decisions those users make.	a. Financial reporting by nonbusiness organizations should provide information that is useful to present and potential resource providers and other users in making rational decisions about the allocation of resources to those organizations (paragraph 35).	a. Financial reporting should provide information that is useful to present and potential investors and creditors and other users in making rational investment, credit, and similar decisions (paragraph 34).	a(1) Investors and creditors are major resource providers to business enterprises. Thus, resource providers, as a type of user, include investors and creditors as well as the other groups identified in Concepts Statement 4. a(2) Both Statements focus on providing information useful in deciding whether to provide resources to an entity. The reasons for providing the resources, in each case, are quite different. Investors and creditors of business enterprises seek monetary repayment of and a return on resources they provide. Nonbusiness organizations, in contrast, obtain significant resources from resource providers who either expect no economic benefits or expect benefits that are not proportionate to the resources provided.
b. Identifies the broad interests of the users identified and the information they need to assist them in making the type of decisions described above.	b(1) Financial reporting should provide information to help present and potential resource providers and other users in assessing the services that a nonbusiness organization provides and its ability to continue to provide those services (paragraph 38). b(2) Financial reporting should provide information that is useful to present and potential resource providers and other users in assessing how managers of a nonbusiness	b(1) Financial reporting should provide information to help present and potential investors and creditors and other users in assessing the amounts, timing, and uncertainty of prospective cash receipts from dividends or interest and the proceeds from the sale, redemption, or maturity of securities or loans (paragraph 37). b(2) Financial reporting should provide information about how management of an enterprise has discharged its stewardship respon-	b(1)These two objectives reflect the different interests of the respective resource providers. Those different interests lead to the other major area of difference in the objectives: the types of information financial reporting should provide about performance. b(2) The substance of these two objectives is similar but their placement within the two Statements is different. In this concepts Statement, the objective is viewed as a

Purpose of Objectives	Nonbusiness Organizations Concepts Statement 4	Business Enterprises Concepts Statement 1	Comparison of Objectives
	organization have discharged their stewardship responsibilities and about other aspects of their performance (paragraph 40).	sibility to owners (stockholders) for the use of enterprise resources entrusted to it (paragraph 50).	basic information need of users. In Concepts Statement 1, it was viewed as information financial reporting could provide to satisfy other basic information needs. That difference in placement arises from the importance of stewardship information in the environment of nonbusiness organizations. It is more important because the organization often is not self-sustaining (not profit oriented) and is dependent upon the continuing support of its resource providers. Consequently, there often is a more direct relationship between resource providers and the entity than for a business enterprise.
c. Identifies the type of information financial reporting can provide to help satisfy users' informational needs.	c. Financial reporting should provide information about the economic resources, obligations, and net resources of an organization and the effects of transactions, events and circumstances that change resources and interests in those resources (paragraph 43).	c. Financial reporting should provide information about the economic resources of an enterprise, the claims to those resources (obligations of the enterprise to transfer resources to other entities and owners' equity), and the effects of transactions, events, and circumstances that change resources and claims to those resources (paragraph 40).	c. The objectives are similar except for differences in terminology that reflect one of the distinguishing characteristics of nonbusiness organizations—the lack of ownership interests entitled to a residual distribution in the event of liquidation.
	(1) Financial reporting should provide information about an organization's economic resources, obligations, and net resources (paragraph 44).	(1) Financial reporting should provide information about an enterprise's economic resources, obligations, and owners' equity (paragraph 41).	(1) Except for differences in terminology, these objectives are the same.

(2) Financial reporting should provide information about the performance of an organization during a period. Periodic measurement of the changes in the amount and nature of the net resources of a nonbusiness organization and information about the service efforts and accomplishments of an organization together represent the information most useful in assessing its performance (paragraph 47).	(2) Financial reporting should provide information about an enterprise's financial performance during a period. The primary focus of financial reporting is information about an enterprise's performance provided by measures of earnings and its components (paragraphs 42 and 43).	(2) The goals of the two objectives are the same but, because of the distinguishing characteristics of nonbusiness organizations, somewhat different information is required to satisfy those goals. Both seek to measure the efforts and accomplishments of the entity but assessment of performance in nonbusiness lacks earnings as a focal measure. This creates the need for information on service efforts and accomplishments.
(3) Financial reporting should provide information about how an organization obtains and spends cash or other liquid resources, about its borrowing and repayment of borrowing, and about other factors that may affect its liquidity (paragraph 54).	(3) Financial reporting should provide information about how an enterprise obtains and spends cash, about its borrowing and repayment of borrowing, about its capital transactions, including cash dividends and other distributions of enterprise resources to owners, and about other factors that may affect an enterprise's liquidity or solvency (paragraph 49).	(3) Except for differences in terminology and circumstances that reflect the lack of ownership interests entitled to receive cash dividends and other distributions of entity resources in nonbusiness organizations, these objectives are the same.
(4) Financial reporting should include explanations and interpretations to help users understand financial information provided (paragraph 55).	(4) Financial reporting should include explanations and interpretations to help users understand financial information provided (paragraph 54).	(4) These objectives are the same.

(The next page is 5000.)

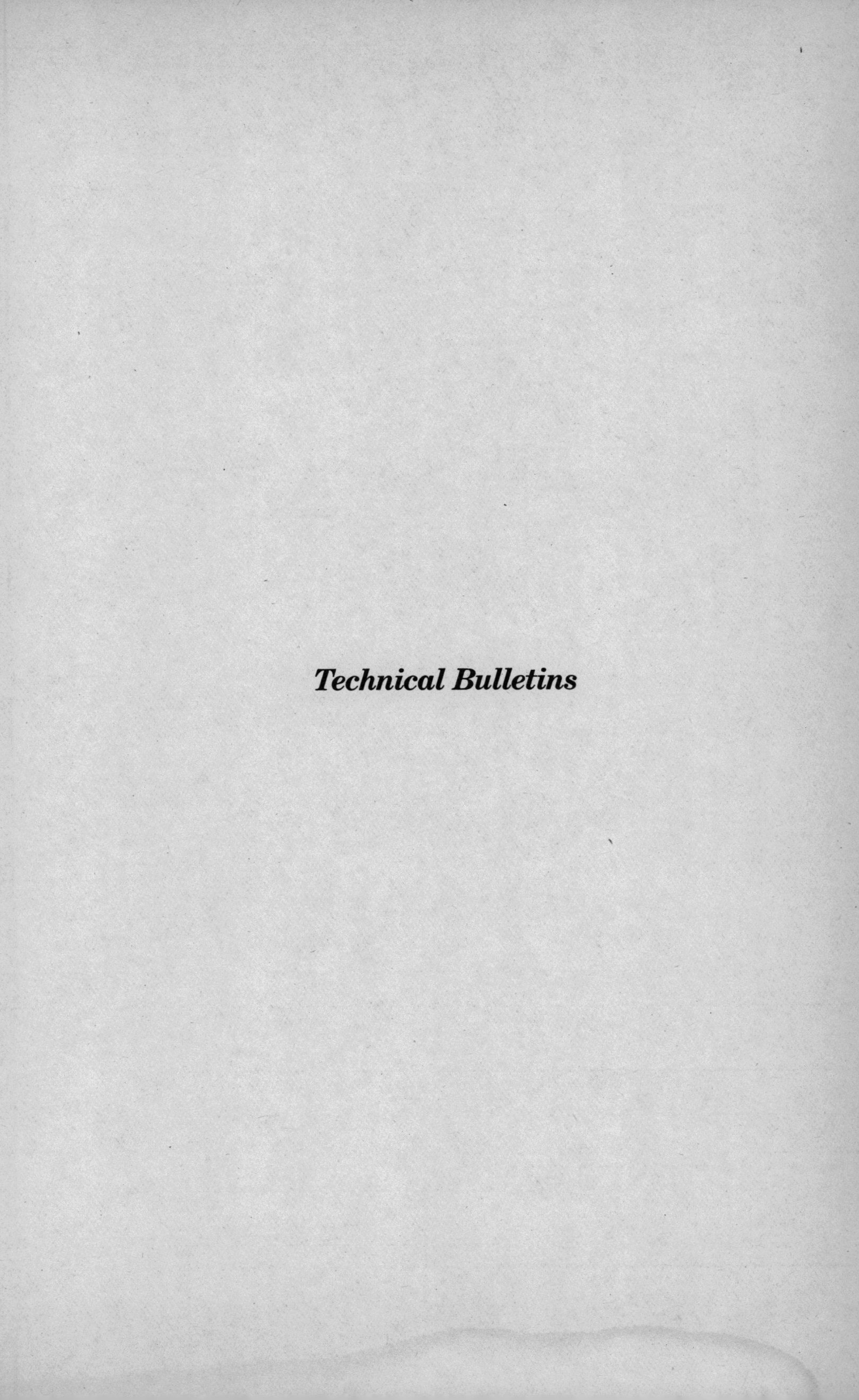

Technical Bulletins

FASB TECHNICAL BULLETINS

TABLE OF CONTENTS

Table of Contents

(The next page is 5011.)

FASB Technical Bulletin No. 79-1
Purpose and Scope of FASB Technical Bulletins and Procedures for Issuance

STATUS

Issued: December 28, 1979

Affected by: No other pronouncements

Note: Technical Bulletins (FTBs) have no effective date; the date indicated is the date issued.

FASB Technical Bulletin No. 79-1
Purpose and Scope of FASB Technical Bulletins and Procedures for Issuance

1. The Financial Accounting Standards Board has authorized its staff to issue FASB Technical Bulletins to provide guidance on certain financial accounting and reporting problems on a timely basis. The first Bulletin describes the purpose and scope of FASB Technical Bulletins, the procedures for issuing them, and related background information. Those procedures have been approved by the Board.

Background

2. The scope of FASB Technical Bulletins and the procedures for issuing them were developed through the solicitation of the public's views in the *Request for Written Comments on an FASB Proposal for Dealing with Industry Accounting Matters and Accounting Questions of Limited Application* issued on November 7, 1978 and *Information about FASB Technical Bulletins* issued August 10, 1979.

- Some respondents suggested that the FASB identify its procedures for issuing FASB Technical Bulletins. That has been done in this Bulletin.
- Some respondents stated that all proposed FASB Technical Bulletins should be exposed to knowledgeable parties for comment. Although most proposed Bulletins will be exposed to knowledgeable parties, such as the FASB's Screening Committee on Emerging Problems, exposure is not mandated because some problems to which the answers are clear may require immediate resolution, which could not be accomplished with formal exposure requirements.
- Some respondents expressed concerns about guidelines for the kinds of problems that could be addressed in FASB Technical Bulletins. This Bulletin outlines guidelines that indicate that issuance of a Bulletin would be appropriate for resolving a specific financial accounting and reporting problem. However, the Board can at any time address a matter discussed in a Bulletin or proposed Bulletin.
- Some respondents also questioned the level of Board involvement in Technical Bulletins. Even though the Board does not approve Bulletins, each Board member receives a copy of proposed Bulletins prior to issuance. Board members are thereby provided an opportunity to express concerns about the answer or to decide that the matter should be addressed in a Board pronouncement.

Purpose and Scope of FASB Technical Bulletins and Procedures for Issuance

3. FASB Technical Bulletins provide guidance concerning the application of FASB Statements or Interpretations, APB Opinions, or Accounting Research Bulletins. FASB Technical Bulletins are not Statements of Financial Accounting Standards or Interpretations as defined[1] in the FASB's *Rules of Procedure* and do not establish new financial accounting and reporting standards or amend existing standards.

4. FASB Technical Bulletins generally address implementation questions and other matters that have heretofore been covered by FASB letter communications, summaries of which have been published in *Status Report*. The FASB plans to issue those previous letters of broad interest as the first series of FASB Technical Bulletins.

5. An accounting or reporting problem that comes to the FASB's attention is analyzed to determine whether the problem might be resolved by issuing an FASB Technical Bulletin. Issuance of an FASB Technical Bulletin is generally viewed as appropriate if the financial accounting and reporting problem can be resolved within the following guidelines:

- The intent of the underlying standard is documented or otherwise known to the staff and the answer to the problem in the Bulletin does no more than clarify, explain, or elaborate upon the underlying standard,
- The answer is not expected to have a significant effect on either financial reporting in general or most organizations affected by the underlying standard, and
- The administrative cost that may be involved in implementing the answer is not expected to be significant to most affected organizations.

If the appropriateness of resolving a problem by issuing an FASB Technical Bulletin is in doubt, that

[1]Rule 203 of the Rules of Conduct of the AICPA Code of Professional Ethics applies to FASB Statements of Financial Accounting Standards and, through the AICPA's Interpretation 203-2 of the Code, Rule 203 applies to FASB Interpretations.

problem is referred to the Board for its consideration.

6. FASB Technical Bulletins are not approved by the Board, but Board members are informed of all matters proposed for Bulletins and are provided with copies of all proposed FASB Technical Bulletins prior to issuance. In some cases, Bulletins may be issued for matters that the Board has considered and concluded not to add to its agenda. In such cases, the Board may provide guidance for the preparation of a Bulletin. However, the issues addressed in Bulletins have not necessarily been deliberated by the Board.

7. In addition to distributing proposed FASB Technical Bulletins to Board members, the Director of Research and Technical Activities may decide to expose proposed Bulletins to the public in general or to selected knowledgeable persons or groups for comment prior to issuance.

8. The Board monitors the issuance of FASB Technical Bulletins and, if deemed advisable, may modify the above procedures from time to time. Any modifications will be announced publicly.

9. FASB Technical Bulletins are generally in question-and-answer format and are published with the following legend:

> The Financial Accounting Standards Board has authorized its staff to issue FASB Technical Bulletins to provide guidance on certain financial accounting and reporting problems on a timely basis. Although Board Members are provided with copies of proposed Bulletins prior to issuance, the Board does not approve them.

FASB Technical Bulletin No. 79-2 Computer Software Costs

STATUS

Issued: December 28, 1979

Affected by: No other pronouncements

Note: Technical Bulletins (FTBs) have no effective date; the date indicated is the date issued.

FASB Technical Bulletin No. 79-2
Computer Software Costs

References:

FASB Statement No. 2, *Accounting for Research and Development Costs,* paragraphs 8-10
FASB Interpretation No. 6, *Applicability of FASB Statement No. 2 to Computer Software*

Question

1. Are *all* costs incurred to produce computer software considered "research and development costs" under Statement 2 and Interpretation 6?

Background

2. Statement 2 requires all research and development costs encompassed by that Statement to be charged to expense as incurred. Interpretation 6 clarifies the applicability of Statement 2 to certain costs incurred to obtain or develop computer software.

Response

3. Statement 2 and Interpretation 6 do not require that all computer software production costs be considered research and development costs as defined in paragraph 8 of Statement 2. Statement 2 specifies certain activities that are to be identified as research and development costs for financial accounting and reporting purposes. The activities described in paragraphs 9 and 10 of Statement 2 give appropriate recognition to the fact that all costs incurred in producing a given software product or process are not necessarily research and development costs. However, a determination that software production costs are not research and development costs does not necessarily mean that they would be inventoriable or deferrable to future operations. Those decisions can only be made in light of all of the facts and circumstances surrounding the particular situation.

The Financial Accounting Standards Board has authorized its staff to issue FASB Technical Bulletins to provide guidance on certain financial accounting and reporting problems on a timely basis. Although Board members are provided with copies of proposed Bulletins prior to issuance, the Board does not approve them.

FASB Technical Bulletin No. 79-3 Subjective Acceleration Clauses in Long-Term Debt Agreements

STATUS

Issued: December 28, 1979

Affected by: No other pronouncements

Note: Technical Bulletins (FTBs) have no effective date; the date indicated is the date issued.

FASB Technical Bulletin No. 79-3
Subjective Acceleration Clauses in Long-Term Debt Agreements

Reference:

FASB Statement No. 6, *Classification of Short-Term Obligations Expected to Be Refinanced*

Question

1. Should long-term debt be classified as a current liability if the long-term debt agreement contains a subjective clause that may accelerate the due date?

Background

2. Statement 6 indicates that a subjective acceleration clause contained in a financing agreement that would otherwise permit a short-term obligation to be refinanced on a long-term basis would preclude that short-term obligation from being classified as long-term. Statement 6 does not address financing agreements other than those related to short-term obligations.

Response

3. In some situations, the circumstances (for example, recurring losses or liquidity problems) would indicate that long-term debt subject to a subjective acceleration clause should be classified as a current liability. Other situations would indicate only disclosure of the existence of such clauses. It would also seem that neither reclassification nor disclosure would be required if the likelihood of the acceleration of the due date were remote, such as when the lender historically has not accelerated due dates of loans containing similar clauses and the financial condition of the borrower is strong and its prospects are bright.

The Financial Accounting Standards Board has authorized its staff to issue FASB Technical Bulletins to provide guidance on certain financial accounting and reporting problems on a timely basis. Although Board members are provided with copies of proposed Bulletins prior to issuance, the Board does not approve them.

FASB Technical Bulletin No. 79-4
Segment Reporting of Puerto Rican Operations

STATUS

Issued: December 28, 1979

Affected by: No other pronouncements

Note: Technical Bulletins (FTBs) have no effective date; the date indicated is the date issued.

FASB Technical Bulletin No. 79-4
Segment Reporting of Puerto Rican Operations

Reference:

FASB Statement No. 14, *Financial Reporting for Segments of a Business Enterprise*, paragraphs 31-38

Question

1. Are Puerto Rican operations and operations relating to other areas under U.S. sovereignty or some type of American jurisdiction, such as the Virgin Islands and American Samoa, to be considered *foreign* operations and thus subject to the disclosure requirements of paragraphs 31-38 of Statement 14?

Background

2. Paragraphs 31-38 of Statement 14 require disclosure of information about an enterprise's foreign operations and export sales. Paragraph 31 states that "for purposes of this Statement, an enterprise's foreign operations include those revenue-producing operations . . . that (a) *are located outside the enterprise's home country (the United States for U.S. enterprises)*. . . ." (Emphasis added.)

Response

3. Statement 14 allows judgment (paragraph 83) to distinguish between domestic and foreign operations based on the features of the operation and the facts and circumstances of the enterprise (paragraph 31). Based on those guidelines the degree of interrelationship between the United States and Puerto Rico (as well as non-self-governing U.S. territories such as the Virgin Islands and American Samoa) is such that Puerto Rican operations of U.S. enterprises should be considered domestic operations. Factors such as proximity, economic affinity, and similarities in business environments also indicate this classification for the Puerto Rican operations of U.S. enterprises. It should be noted that the Statement does not prohibit additional disclosures about Puerto Rican operations that might be useful in analyzing and understanding an enterprise's financial statements.

FASB Technical Bulletin No. 79-5
Meaning of the Term "Customer" as It Applies to Health Care Facilities under FASB Statement No. 14

STATUS

Issued: December 28, 1979

Affected by: No other pronouncements

Note: Technical Bulletins (FTBs) have no effective date; the date indicated is the date issued.

FASB Technical Bulletin No. 79-5
Meaning of the Term "Customer" as It Applies to Health Care Facilities under FASB Statement No. 14

Reference:

FASB Statement No. 14, *Financial Reporting for Segments of a Business Enterprise*, paragraph 39

Question

1. Would an insuring entity (such as Blue Cross) be considered a "customer" of a health care facility as that term is defined in paragraph 39 of Statement 14?

Background

2. Paragraph 39 of Statement 14 requires that if 10 percent or more of an enterprise's revenue is derived from sales to any single customer, that fact and the amount of revenue from each such customer should be disclosed. A group of customers under common control is regarded as a single customer for purposes of that requirement.

Response

3. An insuring entity should not be considered the "customer" of a health care facility as that term is used in Statement 14. The fact that an insuring entity is a paying agent for the patient does not make the insuring entity the customer of the health care facility because the insuring entity does not decide which services to purchase and from which health care facility to purchase the services. The latter two factors are important in determining the customer.

The Financial Accounting Standards Board has authorized its staff to issue FASB Technical Bulletins to provide guidance on certain financial accounting and reporting problems on a timely basis. Although Board members are provided with copies of proposed Bulletins prior to issuance, the Board does not approve them.

FASB Technical Bulletin No. 79-6
Valuation Allowances Following Debt Restructuring

STATUS

Issued: December 28, 1979

Affected by: No other pronouncements

Note: Technical Bulletins (FTBs) have no effective date; the date indicated is the date issued.

FASB Technical Bulletin No. 79-6
Valuation Allowances Following Debt Restructuring

Reference:

FASB Statement No. 15, *Accounting by Debtors and Creditors for Troubled Debt Restructurings,* paragraphs 1 and 29

Question

1. Must the collectibility of a receivable whose terms have been modified and carrying basis adjusted in a troubled debt restructuring under Statement 15 be evaluated to determine the need for subsequent valuation allowances?

Background

2. Statement 15 addresses the accounting appropriate at the time that a restructuring occurs but does not specifically address the accounting for allowances for estimated uncollectible amounts.

Response

3. Statement 15 does not proscribe subsequent provisions for anticipated losses on assets adjusted or acquired in a troubled debt restructuring. Paragraphs 1, 29, 60, 90, and 91 and footnotes 18 and 34 of that Statement are relevant in this respect. Furthermore, FASB Statement No. 5, *Accounting for Contingencies,* requires recognition of anticipated losses whenever they are probable and reasonably estimable. Thus, an assessment of the collectibility of a receivable with modified terms is necessary for a troubled debt restructuring subject to Statement 15.

The Financial Accounting Standards Board has authorized its staff to issue FASB Technical Bulletins to provide guidance on certain financial accounting and reporting problems on a timely basis. Although Board members are provided with copies of proposed Bulletins prior to issuance, the Board does not approve them.

FASB Technical Bulletin No. 79-7
Recoveries of a Previous Writedown under a Troubled Debt Restructuring Involving a Modification of Terms

STATUS

Issued: December 28, 1979

Affected by: No other pronouncements

Note: Technical Bulletins (FTBs) have no effective date; the date indicated is the date issued.

FASB Technical Bulletin No. 79-7
Recoveries of a Previous Writedown under a Troubled Debt Restructuring Involving a Modification of Terms

Reference:

FASB Statement No. 15, *Accounting by Debtors and Creditors for Troubled Debt Restructurings,* paragraph 30 and footnote 17

Question

1. May a creditor reverse a previous direct writedown of a receivable when, under a restructuring of a troubled loan through a modification of terms, the future cash receipts exceed the recorded investment in the receivable?

Background

2. Paragraph 30 of Statement 15 discusses the accounting by a creditor for a restructuring involving only a modification of terms and states that the recorded investment in the receivable is not changed unless that amount exceeds the total future cash receipts specified by the new terms, in which case the investment is reduced to an amount equal to the total future cash receipts and a loss recognized. If the total future cash receipts exceed the recorded investment in the receivable, the excess is recognized as interest over the remaining term of the loan. Footnote 17 states that the recorded investment in the receivable is the face amount decreased by the amount of any previous direct writedown.

Response

3. The future cash receipts in excess of the recorded investment in the receivable shall be accounted for as interest income even if a previous direct writedown results in an unusually high effective interest rate on the recorded investment. The amount of the direct writedown should not be reversed.

4. Paragraph 40(a) of Statement 15 does not require disclosures related to a receivable whose terms have been modified if its effective interest rate is equal to or greater than the rate that the creditor was willing to accept for a new receivable with comparable risk; however, disclosure of the amount and source of interest income on such receivables is permitted.

FASB Technical Bulletin No. 79-8 Applicability of FASB Statements 21 and 33 to Certain Brokers and Dealers in Securities

STATUS

Issued: December 28, 1979

Affected by: No other pronouncements

Note: Technical Bulletins (FTBs) have no effective date; the date indicated is the date issued.

FASB Technical Bulletin No. 79-8
Applicability of FASB Statements 21 and 33 to Certain Brokers and Dealers in Securities

References:

FASB Statement No. 21, *Suspension of the Reporting of Earnings per Share and Segment Information by Nonpublic Enterprises,* paragraph 13
FASB Statement No. 33, *Financial Reporting and Changing Prices,* paragraph 22(h)

Question

1. Should closely held brokers or dealers in securities that file financial statements with the Securities and Exchange Commission (SEC) be considered nonpublic enterprises for purposes of applying Statements 21 and 33?

Background

2. Statement 21 suspends the requirements of FASB Statement No. 14, *Financial Reporting for Segments of a Business Enterprise,* and APB Opinion No. 15, *Earnings Per Share,* for nonpublic enterprises.

3. Statement 33 establishes standards for reporting effects of price changes by certain large, public enterprises.

4. To be considered a nonpublic enterprise under Statement 21, an enterprise must meet two specific conditions, one of which is that the enterprise is not required to file financial statements with the SEC. Reciprocally, Statement 33 states that an enterprise that is required to file financial statements with the SEC is a public enterprise.

5. All security brokers and dealers registered with the SEC must file complete sets of financial statements with the SEC for use by the SEC's Division of Market Regulation for regulatory purposes, whether they are closely held or publicly held. Although the statement of financial condition filed by a broker-dealer must be available for public inspection, the income statement and statement of changes in financial position may be treated as "confidential" if so requested by the broker-dealer. A publicly held broker-dealer that is subject to sections 12 and 13 of the Securities Exchange Act of 1934 must, in addition, file a complete set of financial statements and various forms with the SEC in the same manner as is required of other publicly held enterprises subject to those sections of the 1934 Act.

Response

6. The fact that financial statements are required to be filed for broker-dealer regulatory purposes with the SEC does not make an otherwise "nonpublic" enterprise public for purposes of Statements 21 and 33. Thus, the Statement 21 suspension applies to, and the Statement 33 definition of a public enterprise excludes, closely held broker-dealers that are required to file financial statements with the SEC only for use by its Division of Market Regulation, principally because the broker-dealer can cause a significant portion of those financial statements (that is, the income statement and statement of changes in financial position) to be unavailable for public inspection by requesting confidential treatment.

FASB Technical Bulletin No. 79-9 Accounting in Interim Periods for Changes in Income Tax Rates

STATUS

Issued: December 28, 1979

Affected by: No other pronouncements

Note: Technical Bulletins (FTBs) have no effective date; the date indicated is the date issued.

FASB Technical Bulletin No. 79-9
Accounting in Interim Periods for Changes in Income Tax Rates

Reference:

FASB Interpretation No. 18, *Accounting for Income Taxes in Interim Periods,* paragraph 24

Question

1. How should a company with a fiscal year other than a calendar year account during interim periods for the reduction in the corporate tax rate resulting from the Revenue Act of 1978?

Background

2. The Revenue Act of 1978, among other things, reduced the corporate income tax rate from 48 percent to 46 percent.

Response

3. Paragraph 24 of Interpretation 18 requires that the effect of a change in tax rates be reflected in a revised annual effective tax rate calculation in the same way that the change will be applied to the company's taxable income for the year. The revised annual effective tax rate would then be applied to pretax income for the year-to-date at the end of the current interim period. Paragraph 13 of FASB Statement No. 16, *Prior Period Adjustments,* indicates that previous interim periods of the company's current fiscal year would be restated by prior period adjustment if the effect is material.

The Financial Accounting Standards Board has authorized its staff to issue FASB Technical Bulletins to provide guidance on certain financial accounting and reporting problems on a timely basis. Although Board members are provided with copies of proposed Bulletins prior to issuance, the Board does not approve them.

FASB Technical Bulletin No. 79-10
Fiscal Funding Clauses in Lease Agreements

STATUS

Issued: December 28, 1979

Affected by: No other pronouncements

Note: Technical Bulletins (FTBs) have no effective date; the date indicated is the date issued.

FASB Technical Bulletin No. 79-10
Fiscal Funding Clauses in Lease Agreements

Reference:

FASB Statement No. 13, *Accounting for Leases,* paragraph 5(f)

Question

1. What effect, if any, should the existence of a fiscal funding clause in a lease agreement have on the classification of the lease under Statement 13?

Background

2. A fiscal funding clause is commonly found in a lease agreement in which the lessee is a governmental unit. A fiscal funding clause generally provides that the lease is cancelable if the legislature or other funding authority does not appropriate the funds necessary for the governmental unit to fulfill its obligations under the lease agreement.

Response

3. Paragraph 5(f) of Statement 13 requires that a cancelable lease, such as a lease containing a fiscal funding clause, be evaluated to determine whether the uncertainty of possible lease cancellation is a remote contingency. That paragraph states that "a lease which is cancelable (i) only upon occurrence of some *remote* contingency . . . shall be considered 'noncancelable' for purposes of this definition" of lease term. (Emphasis added.)

4. In discussing the likelihood of the occurrence of a future event or events to confirm a loss contingency, paragraph 3 of FASB Statement No. 5, *Accounting for Contingencies,* defines *remote* as relating to conditions when "the chance of the future event or events occurring is slight." The evaluation of the uncertainty of possible lease cancellation should be consistent with that definition.

5. The existence of a fiscal funding clause in a lease agreement would necessitate an assessment of the likelihood of lease cancellation through exercise of the fiscal funding clause. If the likelihood of exercise of the fiscal funding clause is assessed as being remote, a lease agreement containing such a clause would be considered a noncancelable lease; otherwise, the lease would be considered cancelable and thus classified as an operating lease.

The Financial Accounting Standards Board has authorized its staff to issue FASB Technical Bulletins to provide guidance on certain financial accounting and reporting problems on a timely basis. Although Board members are provided with copies of proposed Bulletins prior to issuance, the Board does not approve them.

FASB Technical Bulletin No. 79-11
Effect of a Penalty on the Term of a Lease

STATUS

Issued: December 28, 1979

Affected by: No other pronouncements

Note: Technical Bulletins (FTBs) have no effective date; the date indicated is the date issued.

FASB Technical Bulletin No. 79-11
Effect of a Penalty on the Term of a Lease

Reference:

FASB Statement No. 13, *Accounting for Leases,* paragraph 5(f)

Question

1. In determining the lease term under the provisions of Statement 13, does the existence of a penalty that would reasonably assure renewal of a lease need to be stated in the lease agreement?

Background

2. Paragraph 5(f) of Statement 13 states that the lease term includes "all periods, if any, for which failure to renew the lease imposes a penalty on the lessee in an amount such that renewal appears, at the inception of the lease, to be reasonably assured."

Response

3. The "penalty" referred to in paragraph 5(f) of Statement 13 is not limited to a penalty imposed by the lease agreement. Accordingly, the lease term would also include any periods for which failure to renew the lease would result in an economic penalty as a result of factors external to the lease so long as (a) the existence of the penalty were known at the inception of the lease and (b) the nature and estimated amount of the penalty at the inception of the lease were such that renewal would appear to be reasonably assured.

FASB Technical Bulletin No. 79-12
Interest Rate Used in Calculating the Present Value of Minimum Lease Payments

STATUS

Issued: December 28, 1979

Affected by: No other pronouncements

Note: Technical Bulletins (FTBs) have no effective date; the date indicated is the date issued.

FASB Technical Bulletin No. 79-12
Interest Rate Used in Calculating the Present Value of Minimum Lease Payments

Reference:

FASB Statement No. 13, *Accounting for Leases,* paragraphs 5(l) and 7(d)

Question

1. May a lessee use its secured borrowing rate in calculating the present value of minimum lease payments in applying the provisions of Statement 13?

Background

2. Paragraph 7(d) of Statement 13 requires the lessee to use its incremental borrowing rate (or the lessor's implicit interest rate in certain circumstances) to calculate the present value of minimum lease payments. The incremental borrowing rate is defined in paragraph 5(l) as "the rate that . . . the lessee would have incurred to borrow over a similar term the funds necessary to purchase the leased asset."

Response

3. Paragraph 5(l) of Statement 13 does not proscribe the lessee's use of a secured borrowing rate as its incremental borrowing rate if that rate is determinable, reasonable, and consistent with the financing that would have been used in the particular circumstances.

The Financial Accounting Standards Board has authorized its staff to issue FASB Technical Bulletins to provide guidance on certain financial accounting and reporting problems on a timely basis. Although Board members are provided with copies of proposed Bulletins prior to issuance, the Board does not approve them.

FASB Technical Bulletin No. 79-13
Applicability of FASB Statement No. 13 to Current Value Financial Statements

STATUS

Issued: December 28, 1979

Affected by: No other pronouncements

Note: Technical Bulletins (FTBs) have no effective date; the date indicated is the date issued.

FASB Technical Bulletin No. 79-13
Applicability of FASB Statement No. 13 to Current Value Financial Statements

Reference:

FASB Statement No. 13, *Accounting for Leases,* paragraphs 7 and 8

Question

1. Are financial statements prepared on a current value basis exempt from the provisions of Statement 13?

Response

2. Statement 13 would not be inapplicable merely because financial statements are prepared on a current value basis. For example, if at its inception a lease involving property meets one or more of the four criteria of paragraph 7 and both of the criteria of paragraph 8 of Statement 13, the lessor would classify the lease as a sales-type or direct financing lease, whichever is appropriate. Subsequently, the carrying amount of the recorded investment in the lease payments receivable would be adjusted in accordance with the valuation techniques employed in preparing the financial statements on a current value basis.

The Financial Accounting Standards Board has authorized its staff to issue FASB Technical Bulletins to provide guidance on certain financial accounting and reporting problems on a timely basis. Although Board members are provided with copies of proposed Bulletins prior to issuance, the Board does not approve them.

FASB Technical Bulletin No. 79-14
Upward Adjustment of Guaranteed Residual Values

STATUS

Issued: December 28, 1979

Affected by: No other pronouncements

Note: Technical Bulletins (FTBs) have no effective date; the date indicated is the date issued.

FASB Technical Bulletin No. 79-14
Upward Adjustment of Guaranteed Residual Values

Reference:

FASB Statement No. 13, *Accounting for Leases,* paragraphs 17(d), 18(d), and 46

Question

1. Does the prohibition against upward adjustments of estimated residual values in Statement 13 also apply to upward adjustments that result from renegotiations of the guaranteed portions of residual values?

Background

2. Paragraphs 17(d), 18(d), and 46 of Statement 13 require the lessor to review annually the estimated residual value of sales-type leases, direct financing leases, and leveraged leases, respectively. Those paragraphs also contain a provision that prohibits any upward adjustment of the estimated residual value.

Response

3. The prohibitions of paragraphs 17(d), 18(d), and 46 of Statement 13 against upward adjustments to the leased property's estimated residual value are equally applicable to the guaranteed portion. If a lease initially transferred substantially all of the benefits and risks incident to the ownership of the leased property, it would not seem appropriate that the lessor could subsequently increase the benefits that were accounted for as having been retained initially.

4. Recording upward adjustments to the leased property's residual value would, in essence, result in recognizing a sale of the residual value interest. In this respect, the prohibition of an upward adjustment in the leased property's residual value is similar to the prohibition in paragraph 17 of FASB Statement No. 5, *Accounting for Contingencies,* of recognizing gain contingencies because to do so might be recognizing revenue before realization. Realization of the residual value interest might also be contingent on factors, such as the physical condition of the leased property or the requirements and related costs, if any, relating to remarketing agreements at the end of the lease term.

The Financial Accounting Standards Board has authorized its staff to issue FASB Technical Bulletins to provide guidance on certain financial accounting and reporting problems on a timely basis. Although Board members are provided with copies of proposed Bulletins prior to issuance, the Board does not approve them.

FASB Technical Bulletin No. 79-15 Accounting for Loss on a Sublease Not Involving the Disposal of a Segment

STATUS

Issued: December 28, 1979

Affected by: No other pronouncements

Note: Technical Bulletins (FTBs) have no effective date; the date indicated is the date issued.

FASB Technical Bulletin No. 79-15
Accounting for Loss on a Sublease Not Involving the Disposal of a Segment

References:

FASB Statement No. 13, *Accounting for Leases,* paragraphs 35-39
FASB Interpretation No. 27, *Accounting for a Loss on a Sublease*

Question

1. Should a loss on a sublease not involving the disposal of a segment be recognized and how is it determined?

Response

2. The general principle of recognizing losses on transactions and the applicability of that general principle to contracts that are expected to result in a loss are well established. Accordingly, if costs expected to be incurred under an operating sublease (that is, executory costs and either amortization of the leased asset or rental payments on an operating lease, whichever is applicable) exceed anticipated revenue on the operating sublease, a loss should be recognized by the sublessor. Similarly, a loss should be recognized on a direct financing sublease if the carrying amount of the investment in the sublease exceeds the total of rentals expected to be received and estimated residual value unless the sublessor's tax benefits from the transaction are sufficient to justify that result.

3. The absence of explicit reference to accounting for these transactions in Statement 13 does not affect the necessity to follow general principles of loss recognition.

The Financial Accounting Standards Board has authorized its staff to issue FASB Technical Bulletins to provide guidance on certain financial accounting and reporting problems on a timely basis. Although Board members are provided with copies of proposed Bulletins prior to issuance, the Board does not approve them.

FASB Technical Bulletin No. 79-16 (Revised) Effect of a Change in Income Tax Rate on the Accounting for Leveraged Leases

STATUS

Issued: February 29, 1980

Affected by: No other pronouncements

Note: Technical Bulletins (FTBs) have no effective date; the date indicated is the date issued.

FASB Technical Bulletin No. 79-16 (Revised) Effect of a Change in Income Tax Rate on the Accounting for Leveraged Leases

Reference:

FASB Statement No. 13, *Accounting for Leases,* paragraph 46

Question

1. What effect, if any, does a change[1] in the income tax rate have on the accounting for leveraged leases under Statement 13?

Background

2. Paragraph 46 of Statement 13 provides that, when an important assumption changes, the rate of return and the allocation of income shall be recalculated from the inception of the lease, and the change in the recalculated balances of net investment shall be recognized as a gain or loss in the year in which the assumption is changed.

Response

3. The lessor's income tax rate is an important assumption in accounting for a leveraged lease. Accordingly, the income effect of a change in the income tax rate should be recognized in the first accounting period ending on or after the date on which the legislation effecting a rate change becomes law.[2]

4. If accounting for the effect on leveraged leases of the change in tax rates results in a significant variation from the customary relationship between income tax expense and pretax accounting income and the reason for that variation is not otherwise apparent, paragraph 63 of APB Opinion No. 11, *Accounting for Income Taxes,* requires that the reason for that variation should be disclosed.

[1]FASB Technical Bulletin No. 79-16 addressed the effect of a reduction in the corporate income tax rate from 48 percent to 46 percent. Because the response is applicable to increases as well as decreases in the tax rate, this revised Bulletin has been generalized to address the effect of all income tax changes on the accounting for leveraged leases.

[2]Bulletin 79-16 stated "ending on or after the *effective date of the rate change*." (Emphasis added.) This revised Bulletin clarifies the ambiguity of that phrase.

FASB Technical Bulletin No. 79-17
Reporting Cumulative Effect Adjustment from Retroactive Application of FASB Statement No. 13

STATUS

Issued: December 28, 1979

Affected by: No other pronouncements

Note: Technical Bulletins (FTBs) have no effective date; the date indicated is the date issued.

FASB Technical Bulletin No. 79-17
Reporting Cumulative Effect Adjustment from Retroactive Application of FASB Statement No. 13

Reference:

FASB Statement No. 13, *Accounting for Leases,* paragraph 51

Question

1. If a company presents in its annual report five annual income statements that were retroactively restated to apply the provisions of paragraphs 1-47 of Statement 13, must the cumulative effect of applying those provisions be included in determining net income of any period presented?

Background

2. Paragraph 49 of Statement 13 requires retroactive application of the provisions of that Statement in financial statements for fiscal years beginning after December 31, 1980. Financial statements presented for prior periods are to be restated. Paragraph 51 of that Statement requires that the cumulative effect on the retained earnings at the beginning of the earliest period restated shall be included in determining the net income of that period.

Response

3. The cumulative effect of applying the provisions of paragraphs 1-47 of Statement 13 would *not* be included in net income of any period presented unless the year prior to the earliest year presented could not be restated. Paragraph 51 does not refer to the earliest period *presented* but rather refers to the earliest period *restated.* Thus, if income statements for five years are presented and the next prior year cannot be restated, the cumulative effect would be included in the determination of net income of the first year presented. In that same situation, if a company presented income statements only for the current year and the immediately preceding year, neither income statement would include a cumulative effect adjustment.

The Financial Accounting Standards Board has authorized its staff to issue FASB Technical Bulletins to provide guidance on certain financial accounting and reporting problems on a timely basis. Although Board members are provided with copies of proposed Bulletins prior to issuance, the Board does not approve them.

FASB Technical Bulletin No. 79-18
Transition Requirement of Certain FASB Amendments and Interpretations of FASB Statement No. 13

STATUS

Issued: December 28, 1979

Affected by: No other pronouncements

Note: Technical Bulletins (FTBs) have no effective date; the date indicated is the date issued.

FASB Technical Bulletin No. 79-18
Transition Requirement of Certain FASB Amendments and Interpretations of FASB Statement No. 13

References:

FASB Statements 17, 22, 23, 26, 27, 28, and 29
FASB Interpretations 19, 21, 23, 24, 26, and 27
[All related to FASB Statement No. 13, *Accounting for Leases*]

Question

1. In applying the transition requirement of the amendments and interpretations of Statement 13, what is meant by the phrase "have published annual financial statements" and what disclosure is required to indicate that Statement 13 had been applied retroactively without restatement of the prior years' financial statements due to immateriality?

Background

2. The relevant portion of the transition requirement in FASB amendments and interpretations of Statement 13 states:

> In addition, except as provided in the next sentence, the provisions of this [Interpretation/Statement] shall be applied retroactively at the same time and in the same manner as the provisions of FASB Statement No. 13 are applied retroactively (see paragraphs 49 and 51 of Statement No. 13). Enterprises that *have already applied the provisions of Statement No. 13 retroactively and have published annual financial statements* based on the retroactively adjusted accounts before the effective date of this [Interpretation/Statement] may, but are not required to, apply the provisions of this [Interpretation/Statement] retroactively. [Emphasis added.]

Response

3. The phrase "have published annual financial statements" generally refers to those financial statements that a company normally includes in its annual report to shareholders for its established 12-month reporting period (that is, its fiscal year). Inclusion of the word "published" in the transition requirement emphasizes that the annual financial statements should be those that are distributed to all shareholders. For a publicly held company, those financial statements would normally be accompanied by an independent auditor's opinion.

4. Although the phrase "have published annual financial statements" generally refers to the financial statements included in a company's annual reports to shareholders, other circumstances, such as in a filing under the requirements of the Federal Securities Act, may necessitate the issuance to all shareholders of complete financial statements for a company's established 12-month reporting period. For example, if a calendar-year company files a registration statement with the Securities and Exchange Commission in October 1978 and subsequently delivers a proxy statement containing complete financial statements for its year ended December 31, 1977 to all shareholders, the 1977 financial statements (which would include all footnotes contained in the annual report to shareholders) that are included in the proxy statement could constitute published annual financial statements as contemplated by the transition requirement of the amendments and interpretations of Statement 13.

5. On the other hand, the "have published annual financial statements" provision would not be met if the calendar-year company referred to in the above example included its 1977 financial statements, restated to adopt the requirements of Statement 13 retroactively, in the 1978 third quarter interim report to shareholders unless inclusion of its normal fiscal year financial statements is consistent with that company's previously established reporting practices. In addition, the issuance of complete financial statements for a 12-month period that is not the company's established fiscal year would not constitute published annual financial statements for purposes of satisfying the transition requirement in question.

6. Amendments and interpretations of Statement 13 should be applied retroactively as they become effective unless Statement 13 had been applied retroactively in published annual financial statements to shareholders at an earlier date. The retroactive application of Statement 13 would not necessarily require the recording of an adjustment in a company's accounting records when the effects of applying Statement 13 on a retroactive basis call for adjustments that are clearly immaterial. However, in those instances, it could be expected that the notes to the published annual financial statements would have included appropriate disclosure to indicate that the company had adopted Statement 13 retroactively and that prior years' financial statements were not restated because the effects of retroactive application were immaterial. The absence of such disclosures would indicate that Statement 13 had not yet been adopted retroactively. Similarly, if the notes to financial statements in an annual report to shareholders include the "as if" disclosures required by paragraph 50 of Statement 13, it would also be apparent that a company had not adopted the provisions of Statement 13 on a retroactive basis in those earlier financial statements.

FASB Technical Bulletin No. 79-19
Investor's Accounting for Unrealized Losses on Marketable Securities Owned by an Equity Method Investee

STATUS

Issued: December 28, 1979

Affected by: No other pronouncements

Note: Technical Bulletins (FTBs) have no effective date; the date indicated is the date issued.

FASB Technical Bulletin No. 79-19
Investor's Accounting for Unrealized Losses on Marketable Securities Owned by an Equity Method Investee

References:

FASB Statement No. 12, *Accounting for Certain Marketable Securities,* paragraph 9 and footnote 5
APB Opinion No. 18, *The Equity Method of Accounting for Investments in Common Stock,* paragraph 19

Question

1. How should a parent or investor account for its share of the accumulated changes in the valuation allowance for marketable equity securities included in stockholders' equity of an investee accounted for under the equity method?

Background

2. Paragraph 9 of Statement 12 specifies in part that "the portfolios of marketable equity securities owned by an entity (subsidiary or investee) that is accounted for by the equity method shall not be combined with the portfolios of marketable equity securities owned by any other entity included in the financial statements. However, such an entity is, itself, subject to the requirements of this Statement." (Footnote reference omitted.)

3. Under Statement 12, if the aggregate cost of a portfolio of marketable equity securities exceeds the aggregate market value of the portfolio, the difference is accounted for as a valuation allowance and the securities are thereby carried at market value. For a portfolio of marketable equity securities classified as a noncurrent asset or included in an unclassified balance sheet, an amount equal to the accumulated changes in the valuation allowance is included in the equity section of the investee's balance sheet and shown separately. On the other hand, for a portfolio of marketable equity securities classified as a current asset, an amount equal to the changes in the valuation allowance is included in the determination of net income by the investee and the parent or investor includes its proportionate share of the investee's earnings or losses in income.

4. Opinion 18 states in paragraph 19:

> *Applying the equity method.* The difference between consolidation and the equity method lies in the details reported in the financial statements. Thus, an investor's net income for the period and its stockholders' equity at the end of the period are the same whether an investment in a subsidiary is accounted for under the equity method or the subsidiary is consolidated. . . . A transaction of an investee of a capital nature that affects the investor's share of stockholders' equity of the investee should be accounted for as if the investee were a consolidated subsidiary.

5. Footnote 5 of Statement 12 recognizes that exclusion of the securities owned by a subsidiary that is accounted for by the equity method from the parent company's portfolio of marketable equity securities may result in income different from that which would have resulted if that subsidiary had been consolidated rather than accounted for by the equity method because portfolios of consolidated subsidiaries are combined while portfolios of entities accounted for by the equity method are not combined. However, that footnote does not describe, as an exception to paragraph 19 of Opinion 18, any difference in stockholders' equity from applying the portfolio approach required by Statement 12.

Response

6. If a subsidiary or other investee that is accounted for by the equity method is required to include accumulated changes in a valuation allowance for a portfolio of marketable equity securities in the stockholders' equity section of its balance sheet pursuant to the provisions of Statement 12, the parent or investor shall reduce its investment in that investee by its proportionate share of the accumulated changes in the valuation allowance and a like amount shall be included in the stockholders' equity section of its balance sheet.

FASB Technical Bulletin No. 80-1
Early Extinguishment of Debt through Exchange for Common or Preferred Stock

STATUS

Issued: December 19, 1980

Affected by: Amended by FAS 76

Note: Technical Bulletins (FTBs) have no effective date; the date indicated is the date issued.

FASB Technical Bulletin No. 80-1 Early Extinguishment of Debt through Exchange for Common or Preferred Stock

References:

APB Opinion No. 26, *Early Extinguishment of Debt*
FASB Statement No. 4, *Reporting Gains and Losses from Extinguishment of Debt*
FASB Statement No. 15, *Accounting by Debtors and Creditors for Troubled Debt Restructurings*

Question

1. Does Opinion 26 apply to early extinguishments of debt effected by issuance of common or preferred stock, including redeemable and fixed-maturity preferred stock?

Background

2. Under Opinion 26, the conversion of debt to common or preferred stock is not an early extinguishment if the conversion represents the exercise of a conversion right contained in the terms of the debt issue. Other exchanges of common or preferred stock for debt before the scheduled maturity of the debt would constitute early extinguishment.

Response

3. All early extinguishments of debt must be accounted for in accordance with either Statement 15 or Opinion 26. Statement 15 applies to extinguishments effected in a troubled debt restructuring; Opinion 26 applies to all other early extinguishments of debt.

4. Thus, Opinion 26 applies to all early extinguishments of debt effected by issuance of common or preferred stock, including redeemable and fixed-maturity preferred stock, unless the extinguishment is a troubled debt restructuring or a conversion by the holder pursuant to conversion privileges contained in the original debt issue. Paragraph 20 of Opinion 26 requires the difference between the net carrying amount of the extinguished debt and the reacquisition price of the extinguished debt to be recognized currently in income of the period of extinguishment. Paragraph 8 of Statement 4 requires any such difference, if material, to be classified as an extraordinary item, net of related income tax effect. The reacquisition price of the extinguished debt is to be determined by the value of the common or preferred stock issued or the value of the debt—whichever is more clearly evident.

The Financial Accounting Standards Board has authorized its staff to issue FASB Technical Bulletins to provide guidance on certain financial accounting and reporting problems on a timely basis. Although Board members are provided with copies of proposed Bulletins prior to issuance, the Board does not approve them.

FASB Technical Bulletin No. 80-2 Classification of Debt Restructurings by Debtors and Creditors

STATUS

Issued: December 19, 1980

Affected by: No other pronouncements

Note: Technical Bulletins (FTBs) have no effective date; the date indicated is the date issued.

FASB Technical Bulletin No. 80-2 Classification of Debt Restructurings by Debtors and Creditors

Reference:

FASB Statement No. 15, *Accounting by Debtors and Creditors for Troubled Debt Restructurings*

Question

1. In applying Statement 15, can a debt restructuring be a troubled debt restructuring for a debtor but not for the creditor?

Background

2. Paragraph 2 of Statement 15 states that "a restructuring of a debt constitutes a *troubled debt restructuring* for purposes of this Statement if the creditor for economic or legal reasons related to the debtor's financial difficulties grants a concession to the debtor that it would not otherwise consider." Paragraph 7 points out that a debt restructuring is not necessarily a troubled debt restructuring simply because the debtor is experiencing some financial difficulties. That paragraph states in part:

> For example, a troubled debt restructuring is not involved if (a) the fair value[2] of cash, other assets, or an equity interest accepted *by a creditor* from a debtor in full satisfaction of its receivable at least equals *the creditor's* recorded investment in the receivable;[3] (b) the fair value of cash, other assets, or an equity interest transferred *by a debtor* to a creditor in full settlement of its payable at least equals the *debtor's* carrying amount of the payable; (c) the creditor reduces the effective interest rate on the debt primarily to reflect a decrease in market interest rates in general or a decrease in the risk so as to maintain a relationship with a debtor that can readily obtain funds from other sources at the current market interest rate; or (d) the debtor issues in exchange for its debt new marketable debt having an effective interest rate based on its market price that is at or near the current market interest rates of debt with similar maturity dates and stated interest rates issued by nontroubled debtors. [Emphasis added.]

[2]Defined in paragraph 13 [of Statement 15].

[3]Defined in footnote 17 [of Statement 15].

Response

3. Yes, a debtor may have a troubled debt restructuring under Statement 15 even though the related creditor does not have a troubled debt restructuring. The debtor and creditor must individually apply Statement 15 to the specific facts and circumstances to determine whether a troubled debt restructuring has occurred. Example (a) in paragraph 7 of Statement 15 identifies a type of debt restructuring that is *not* a troubled debt restructuring for purposes of the creditor's application of Statement 15; similarly, example (b) in paragraph 7 identifies a type of debt

restructuring that is *not* a troubled debt restructuring for purposes of the debtor's application of Statement 15. Thus, Statement 15 establishes tests for applicability that are not symmetrical as between the debtor and the creditor when the debtor's carrying amount and the creditor's recorded investment differ.

Illustration

4. Creditor A makes a $10,000 interest-bearing loan to Debtor X and, when Debtor X later encounters financial difficulties, sells its receivable from Debtor X to Creditor B for $4,000 on a nonrecourse basis. Following the sale, the carrying amount of the loan payable by Debtor X would still be $10,000 and the recorded investment of the loan by Creditor B would be $4,000. If Debtor X subsequently transfers to Creditor B assets with a fair value of $5,500 in full settlement of the loan, that transaction would be a troubled debt restructuring for Debtor X because the fair value of the assets is less than the carrying amount of the loan, whereas Creditor B would not have a troubled debt restructuring because the fair value of the assets received exceeds its recorded investment in the loan.

The Financial Accounting Standards Board has authorized its staff to issue FASB Technical Bulletins to provide guidance on certain financial accounting and reporting problems on a timely basis. Although Board members are provided with copies of proposed Bulletins prior to issuance, the Board does not approve them.

FASB Technical Bulletin No. 81-1 Disclosure of Interest Rate Futures Contracts and Forward and Standby Contracts

STATUS

Issued: February 6, 1981

Affected by: No other pronouncements

Note: Technical Bulletins (FTBs) have no effective date; the date indicated is the date issued.

FASB Technical Bulletin No. 81-1 Disclosure of Interest Rate Futures Contracts and Forward and Standby Contracts

Reference:

APB Opinion No. 22, *Disclosure of Accounting Policies*

Question

1. Do the disclosure requirements of Opinion 22 apply to interest rate futures contracts, forward contracts, and standby contracts?

Background

2. In October 1980, the SEC identified a need for disclosure standards for interest rate futures contracts, forward contracts, and standby contracts until the accounting issues related to those transactions are addressed. The FASB issued an Exposure Draft of a proposed Statement, *Disclosure of Interest Rate Futures Contracts and Forward and Standby Contracts*, for public comment on November 14, 1980. The Board received 51 letters of comment in response to the Exposure Draft, many of which pointed out significant implementation problems for some of the disclosures proposed. In addition, in late December 1980, the FASB received an AICPA Issues Paper titled "Accounting for Forward Placement and Standby Commitments and Interest Rate Futures Contracts." At the January 7, 1981 Board meeting, the Board decided not to issue a final FASB Statement on disclosure of those contracts because of the implementation problems identified.

3. Interest rate futures contracts are standardized contracts or agreements to make or take delivery of a standardized amount of a financial instrument of deliverable grade at a specified price during a specific month under conditions established by the commodity exchange on which the contracts are traded. Those contracts are traded on a commodity futures exchange that is regulated by the Commodity Futures Trading Commission, an independent agency of the federal government.

4. Forward contracts are similar to futures. However, forwards are not traded in regulated contract markets; rather, they are transactions between two parties. The buyer agrees to purchase and the seller agrees to deliver a financial instrument at a future time under such conditions as the two agree. In contrast with futures, the terms of forward contracts are *not* standardized and generally can be terminated only with the consent of both parties. *Forwards*, as used in this Bulletin, do not include commitments to lend funds in the future at some specified rate (i.e., loan commitments).

5. Standby contracts are optional delivery forward contracts. The buyer of a standby (put option) pays a fee for the right or option to sell (deliver) to the issuer at a specified future date a financial instrument either at a fixed price or specified yield. The seller of a standby (the issuer) receives the fee and must stand ready to buy the financial instrument at the other party's option. *Standbys*, as used in this Bulletin, do not include commitments to lend funds in the future at some specified rate (i.e., loan commitments).

6. The term *financial instrument*, as used in this Bulletin, refers to debt instruments of the U.S. government (Treasury bills, notes, and bonds), obligations of the Federal National Mortgage Association, obligations of U.S. governmental agencies (e.g., Federal Home Loan Mortgage Corporation and Government National Mortgage Association), general obligations of states and political subdivi-

sions, and money market instruments including bankers acceptances, certificates of deposit, and commercial paper.

Response

7. Opinion 22 requires disclosure of all significant accounting policies where alternative accounting principles or practices exist, including the methods of applying those accounting principles that materially affect the determination of financial position, changes in financial position, and results of operations. Because alternative accounting practices exist for interest rate futures contracts, forward contracts, and standby contracts, the accounting policies or practices followed for those contracts should be disclosed in accordance with that Opinion. Such disclosure should include the method(s) of accounting for contracts and related commitment fees and the method(s) of recognizing gains and losses on the contracts. Disclosures in addition to those required by Opinion 22 also may be appropriate in specific circumstances.

8. This Bulletin does not address the accounting for interest rate futures contracts, forward contracts, and standby contracts.

FASB Technical Bulletin No. 81-2 Accounting for Unused Investment Tax Credits Acquired in a Business Combination Accounted for by the Purchase Method

STATUS

Issued: February 6, 1981

Affected by: No other pronouncements

Note: Technical Bulletins (FTBs) have no effective date; the date indicated is the date issued.

FASB Technical Bulletin No. 81-2 Accounting for Unused Investment Tax Credits Acquired in a Business Combination Accounted for by the Purchase Method

References:

FASB Statement No. 38, *Accounting for Preacquisition Contingencies of Purchased Enterprises*
FASB Interpretation No. 25, *Accounting for an Unused Investment Tax Credit*

Question

1. Does Statement 38 supersede Interpretation 25? Specifically, if an enterprise acquires another enterprise that has unused investment tax credits, does Statement 38 require that (a) an estimate of the tax benefits of those unused investment tax credits be included in the initial purchase allocation and (b) subsequent changes in estimate be included in income in the period in which they occur?

Background

2. Paragraphs 13-16 of Interpretation 25 specify the accounting for unused investment tax credits acquired in a business combination accounted for by the purchase method. Paragraph 14 states that "*APB Opinion No. 2* does not permit an unused investment tax credit to be recognized as an asset." Paragraph 15 states that "an acquiring enterprise shall reduce the goodwill recognized in a business combination by the amount of tax benefits realized from an unused investment tax credit of an acquired enterprise in the period in which that credit offsets federal income tax liability." The paragraph further provides that "goodwill shall not be reduced (or 'negative goodwill' . . . shall not be increased) retroactively to the date of the business combination and the results of operations of previous periods shall not be retroactively restated for revised amortization of goodwill."

3. Statement 38 addresses accounting for "a preacquisition contingency other than the potential tax benefit of a loss carryforward." Footnote 2 of Statement 38 indicates that "paragraph 49 of Opinion 11 and paragraph 88 of Opinion 16 . . . specify the accounting for the potential tax benefit of a loss carryforward of a purchased subsidiary." Statement 38 does not indicate that it modifies or supersedes Interpretation 25.

Response

4. Statement 38 does not modify or supersede Interpretation 25. An unused investment tax credit of an acquired enterprise should be accounted for in accordance with Interpretation 25, which does not permit an estimate of the eventual tax benefit to be included in the initial allocation of the purchase price. Rather, under Interpretation 25, tax benefits subsequently realized are accounted for as adjustments of goodwill in the period in which they are realized, and the adjusted balance of goodwill is amortized over its remaining useful life.

The Financial Accounting Standards Board has authorized its staff to issue FASB Technical Bulletins to provide guidance on certain financial accounting and reporting problems on a timely basis. Although Board members are provided with copies of proposed Bulletins prior to issuance, the Board does not approve them.

FASB Technical Bulletin No. 81-3
Multiemployer Pension Plan Amendments Act of 1980

STATUS

Issued: February 6, 1981

Affected by: No other pronouncements

Note: Technical Bulletins (FTBs) have no effective date; the date indicated is the date issued.

FASB Technical Bulletin No. 81-3
Multiemployer Pension Plan Amendments Act of 1980

References:

APB Opinion No. 8, *Accounting for the Cost of Pension Plans*, paragraphs 18 and 39
FASB Interpretation No. 3, *Accounting for the Cost of Pension Plans Subject to the Employee Retirement Income Security Act of 1974*, paragraph 5
FASB Statement No. 36, *Disclosure of Pension Information*

Question

1. What are the accounting implications for employers of the Multiemployer Pension Plan Amendments Act of 1980 (Act)?

Background

2. The recent Act establishes new funding requirements and obligations for employers that participate in multiemployer pension plans. One effect of the new Act is to obligate a participating employer who withdraws from a multiemployer plan for a part of the plan's unfunded vested benefits. The resulting withdrawal obligation is similar to that created by the Employee Retirement Income Security Act of 1974 (ERISA) for the sponsor of a single employer plan that is terminated. The Act also imposes obligations on participating employers when a plan terminates.

3. The FASB has on its agenda a project to reconsider accounting by employers for pensions. That project will consider the effects of the Act. In the interim, this Bulletin responds to questions concerning the accounting implications of the Act under existing authoritative pronouncements.

Response

4. Statement 36 addresses disclosures of pension information and continues to be applicable to employers participating in plans covered by the Act. The Act establishes new funding requirements and obligations for employers that participate in multiemployer pension plans subject to the Act. Paragraph 7(d) of Statement 36 requires disclosure of the nature and effect of such changes in circumstances.

5. For defined benefit plans, paragraph 18 of Opinion 8 provides that if a company has a legal obligation for pension cost in excess of amounts paid or accrued, the excess should be shown in the balance sheet as both a liability and a deferred charge. Interpretation 3 was issued by the FASB in response to ERISA. Paragraph 5 of that Interpretation indicates that the Board concluded that ERISA did not create a legal obligation for unfunded pension costs that warrants accounting recognition as a liability pursuant to paragraph 18 of Opinion 8, except in two specified situations. The Act is an amendment of ERISA. Therefore, employers participating in multiemployer plans deemed to be defined benefit plans subject to the Act should look to Interpretation 3 for guidance.

6. Paragraph 39 of Opinion 8 indicates that plans that have both defined contributions and defined benefits require careful analysis. When the substance of the plan is to provide defined benefits, the annual pension cost should be determined in accordance with the conclusions of Opinion 8 applicable to defined benefit plans. Employers should consider the impact of the Act on the analysis specified in that paragraph.

The Financial Accounting Standards Board has authorized its staff to issue FASB Technical Bulletins to provide guidance on certain financial accounting and reporting problems on a timely basis. Although Board members are provided with copies of proposed Bulletins prior to issuance, the Board does not approve them.

FASB Technical Bulletin No. 81-4
Classification as Monetary or Nonmonetary Items

STATUS

Issued: February 6, 1981

Affected by: No other pronouncements

Note: Technical Bulletins (FTBs) have no effective date; the date indicated is the date issued.

FASB Technical Bulletin No. 81-4
Classification as Monetary or Nonmonetary Items

Reference:

FASB Statement No. 33, *Financial Reporting and Changing Prices*, paragraphs 47 and 48 and Appendix D

Question

1. For purposes of determining a purchasing power gain or loss on net monetary items, should the following items that are not listed in Appendix D of Statement 33 be classified as monetary or nonmonetary?

- Trading account investments in fixed income securities owned by banks, investment brokers, and others
- The unguaranteed residual value of property owned by a lessor and leased under direct financing, sales-type, and leveraged leases
- Commodity inventories whose values are hedged by futures contracts whose contract amounts have not been recorded in the financial statements
- Portion of the carrying amount of lessors' assets leased under noncancellable operating leases that represent claims to fixed sums of money
- Vested pension benefits in excess of fund assets or other accrued pension obligations, recorded in a business combination accounted for by the purchase method
- Investment tax credits that are deferred by a lessor as part of the unearned income of a leveraged lease
- Minority interests in consolidated subsidiaries
- Capital stock of the enterprise or of its consolidated subsidiaries subject to mandatory redemption at fixed amounts

Background

2. Paragraphs 47 and 48 of Statement 33 state:

47. A monetary asset is money or a claim to receive a sum of money the amount of which is fixed or determinable without reference to future prices of specific goods or services. A monetary liability is an obligation to pay a sum of money the amount of which is fixed or determinable without reference to future prices of specific goods or services. The economic significance of monetary assets and liabilities (monetary items) depends heavily on the general purchasing power of money, although other factors, such as the credit worthiness of debtors, may affect their significance.

48. All assets and liabilities that are not monetary are nonmonetary. The economic significance of nonmonetary items depends heavily on the value of specific goods and services. Nonmonetary assets include (a) goods held primarily for resale or assets held primarily for direct use in providing services for the business of the enterprise, (b) claims to cash in amounts dependent on future prices of specific goods or services, and (c) residual rights such as goodwill or equity interests. Nonmonetary liabilities include (a) obligations to furnish goods or services in quantities that are fixed or determinable without reference to changes in prices or (b) obligations to pay cash in amounts dependent on future prices of specific goods or services.

3. Paragraph 208 in Appendix D of Statement 33 states, in part:

208. This appendix provides guidance . . . for the classification of certain asset and liability items as monetary or nonmonetary. The . . . table is not intended to provide answers that should be followed regardless of the circumstances of the case. Rather, the intent is to illustrate the application of the definitions to common cases under typical circumstances. In other circumstances the classification should be resolved by reference to the definitions.

Response

4. The following table summarizes the response in paragraphs 5-19.

	Monetary	Nonmonetary
Trading account investments in fixed-income securities owned by banks, investment brokers, and others		X
The unguaranteed residual value of property owned by a lessor and leased under direct financing, sales-type, and leveraged leases	See discussion	
Commodity inventories whose values are hedged by futures contracts whose contract amounts have not been recorded in the financial statements	See discussion	
Portion of the carrying amount of lessors' assets leased under noncancellable operating leases that represent claims to fixed sums of money		X
Vested pension benefits in excess of fund assets or other accrued pension obligations, recorded in a business combination accounted for by the purchase method		X
Investment tax credits that are deferred by a lessor as part of the unearned income of a leveraged lease	See discussion	
Minority interests in consolidated subsidiaries		X
Capital stock of the enterprise or of its consolidated subsidiaries subject to mandatory redemption at fixed amounts	X	

5. *Trading account investments in fixed-income securities owned by banks, investment brokers, and others*. Trading account securities are "securities of all types carried . . . in a dealer trading account (or accounts) that are held principally for resale to customers."[1] The predominant practice by banks is to carry these securities at the lower of cost or market, although a substantial minority carry them at market value. Trading account investments include both fixed-income securities (e.g., nonconvertible preferred stock, convertible bonds, and other bonds) and other securities (e.g., common stock). Usually, trading account securities are held for extremely short periods of time—sometimes for only a few hours. Frequently, the enterprise buys and sells the securities expecting to make a profit on the difference between dealer and retail, or bid and asked prices, rather than on price changes during the period securities are held. However, the prices of the securities change with market forces.

6. Trading account investments in fixed-income securities are not "claim[s] to receive a sum of money . . . which is fixed or determinable" (paragraph 47 of Statement 33). The market prices of the securities might and frequently do change while the securities are held. Appendix D of Statement 33 indicates that, generally, nonconvertible and nonparticipating preferred stock, convertible bonds that the market values primarily as bonds rather than as stocks, and nonconvertible bonds should be classified as monetary items. However, those classifications were based, in part, on the assumption that those securities would be held for long periods, if not to maturity. Trading account investments, on the other hand, are held for shorter periods and so their value depends much less heavily on the general purchasing power of money and depends more on the specific values of the securities. Therefore, trading account investments in fixed-income securities should be classified as nonmonetary.

7. *The unguaranteed residual value of property owned by a lessor and leased under direct financing, sales-type, and leveraged leases*. The unguaranteed residual value is included with the minimum lease payments, at present value, in the net investment in the lease.

[1] Office of the Federal Register, *Code of Federal Regulations*, Vol. 12 (Washington, D.C.: U.S. Government Printing Office, 1980), p. 217.

8. The minimum lease payments are monetary items because they are claims to fixed sums of money. The residual value is not a claim to a fixed sum of money, so it is a nonmonetary item. Some assets and liabilities, of which the net investment in the lease is a good example, are combinations of claims to (or obligations of) fixed amounts and claims to (or obligations of) variable amounts. Ideally, those claims should be separated for purposes of classifying them as monetary and nonmonetary. However, if the information necessary to make the separation is not available or is impracticable to obtain, such items need not be divided into monetary and nonmonetary components and would be classified according to their dominant element. If the net investment in leases is principally claims to fixed amounts, it would be classified as monetary; it would be classified as nonmonetary if it is principally claims to residuals.

9. *Commodity inventories whose values are hedged by futures contracts whose contract amounts have not been recorded in the financial statements*. Many enterprises hedge commodity inventories (such as grain or metals). "Selling hedges" are designed to provide a degree of assurance that a decline in the price of the commodity would be offset by an increase in the value of the hedge contract. Selling hedges thus help protect the value of the inventory that is hedged.

10. There are certain similarities between inventories that are hedged and inventories that are used on or committed to a contract. In each case, the risk of gain or loss due to price changes before the inventory is sold is largely or entirely eliminated. Statement 33 states that "inventories may need to be reclassified as monetary assets at the date of the use on or commitment to a contract . . ." (paragraph 42). To the extent that hedges fix the value of an inventory in dollars, the inventory effectively becomes a monetary item. However, in some cases, hedging positions may not be identifiable with specific inventory positions. In those cases, the inventory should be classified as nonmonetary.

11. Some inventory may be hedged and other inventory not hedged. As discussed in paragraph 8 above, in those cases the ideal solution would be to separately classify the hedged and non-hedged portions. However, if the information is not available or is impracticable to obtain, the enterprise would classify the entire inventory according to its dominant element as either monetary or nonmonetary.

12. *Portion of the carrying amount of lessors' assets leased under noncancellable operating leases that represent claims to fixed sums of money*. These assets are carried at depreciated historical cost under generally accepted accounting principles and are classified with or near property, plant, and equipment. Appendix D of Statement 33 indicates that property, plant, and equipment are nonmonetary.

13. The classification of a lease as an operating lease under FASB Statement No. 13, *Accounting for Leases*, indicates that the lease has not transferred substantially all of the benefits and risks incident to ownership to the lessee. Thus the economic significance of the asset continues to depend heavily on the value of the future lease rentals, residual values, and associated costs.Therefore, an asset subject to an operating lease should be classified as nonmonetary.

14. *Vested pension benefits in excess of fund assets or other accrued pension obligations, recorded in a business combination accounted for by the purchase method*. Appendix D of Statement 33 indicates that fixed amounts of accrued pension obligations that are payable to a fund are monetary; all other accrued pension obligations are nonmonetary. Other liabilities mentioned in Appendix D are monetary, except those to be satisfied by providing goods and services (e.g., obligations under warranties) and accrued vacation pay if it is to be paid at wage rates as of the vacation dates and if those rates may vary from rates in effect at the balance sheet date.

15. Under APB Opinion No. 16, *Business Combinations*, vested pension benefits in excess of fund assets sometimes are recorded as liabilities on the occurrence of business combinations treated as purchases. The amounts may be similar to accrued vacation pay that is to be paid at rates in effect as of the vacation dates—the pension benefits to be paid also may depend on future salary and wage rates, dates of retirement, and future changes in pension plan benefits. Therefore, vested pension benefits in excess of fund assets should be classified as nonmonetary items.

16. *Investment tax credits that are deferred by a lessor as part of the unearned income of a leveraged lease*. Under Statement 13, the deferred investment tax credit related to the leased asset is subtracted from rentals receivable and estimated residual value as part of the calculation of the lessor's investment in the leveraged lease. The investment, including the deferred investment tax credit related to the leveraged lease, is presented as one amount in the balance sheet. As indicated in paragraph 8 above, the investment in a leveraged lease would be classified as monetary or nonmonetary according to its dominant element.

17. As indicated in Appendix D of Statement 33, a deferred investment tax credit should be classified as nonmonetary but, if it is part of an investment in a leveraged lease and if the information necessary to

separate its elements is not available or is impracticable to obtain, the investment would be classified according to its dominant element.

18. *Minority interests in consolidated subsidiaries.* The interests of minority shareholders in the earnings and equity of subsidiaries are, from the consolidated entity's point of view, claims that are not fixed. Rather, they are residuals that will vary based on the subsidiary's earnings, dividends, and other transactions affecting its equity and so are nonmonetary. (See paragraph 19 below as to classification of capital stock of the enterprise or of its consolidated subsidiaries subject to mandatory redemption at fixed amounts.)

19. *Capital stock of the enterprise or of its consolidated subsidiaries subject to mandatory redemption at fixed amounts.* Such securities are claims of the stockholders to a fixed number of dollars and therefore are monetary. Classification as a monetary item called for in this Bulletin is only for purposes of determining a purchasing power gain or loss. This Bulletin does not address how such securities should be classified in balance sheets or the accounting for dividends on those securities.

The Financial Accounting Standards Board has authorized its staff to issue FASB Technical Bulletins to provide guidance on certain financial accounting and reporting problems on a timely basis. Although Board members are provided with copies of proposed Bulletins prior to issuance, the Board does not approve them.

FASB Technical Bulletin No. 81-5
Offsetting Interest Cost to Be Capitalized with Interest Income

STATUS

Issued: February 6, 1981

Affected by: Superseded by FAS 62

Note: Technical Bulletins (FTBs) have no effective date; the date indicated is the date issued.

FASB Technical Bulletin No. 81-5 Offsetting Interest Cost to Be Capitalized with Interest Income

Reference:

FASB Statement No. 34, *Capitalization of Interest Cost*, paragraphs 1, 7, 12, 13, and 14

Question

1. In determining the amount of interest cost to be capitalized as part of the cost of acquiring qualifying assets, under what circumstances, if any, should interest income earned from investments be offset or netted against interest cost incurred?

Background

2. In certain circumstances, proceeds from borrowings may be temporarily invested in designated interest-bearing securities prior to funding construction projects.Those proceeds are typically restricted as to use and may be held in escrow or in the custody of a trustee. Interest income earned may exceed the amount of interest cost on the borrowing for a period of time prior to or during the early stages of construction.

3. Paragraph 1 of Statement 34 states:

> . . . *Interest cost* includes interest recognized on obligations having explicit interest rates, . . . interest imputed on certain types of payables, . . . and interest related to a capital lease. . . .

4. Paragraph 7 of Statement 34 states:

> The objectives of capitalizing interest are (a) to obtain a measure of acquisition cost that more closely reflects the enterprise's total investment in the asset and (b) to charge a cost that relates to the acquisition of a resource that will benefit future periods against the revenues of the periods benefited.

5. Paragraph 12 of Statement 34 states:

> The amount of interest cost to be capitalized for qualifying assets is intended to be that portion of the interest cost incurred during the assets' acquisition periods that theoretically could have been avoided (for example, by avoiding additional borrowings or by using the funds expended for the assets to repay existing borrowings) if expenditures for the assets had not been made.

6. Paragraph 13 of Statement 34 states:

> The capitalization rates used in an accounting period shall be based on the rates applicable to borrowings outstanding during the period.

7. Paragraph 14 of Statement 34 states:

> However, the use of judgment in determining capitalization rates shall not circumvent the requirement that a capitalization rate be applied to all capitalized expenditures for a qualifying asset to the extent that interest cost has been incurred during an accounting period.

Response

8. The method to be used in determining the rate at which interest is capitalized and the limitations on the amount of interest to be capitalized are specified in Statement 34. The provisions for determining the amount of interest cost to be capitalized deal solely with the interest cost incurred and the rates applicable to borrowings outstanding. Temporary or short-term investment decisions are not related to the determination of the acquisition cost of the asset or to the allocation of that cost against revenues of the periods benefited by the asset. Accordingly, netting or offsetting of interest income against interest cost is not permitted by Statement 34.

9. The following example illustrates the computation of the avoidable interest cost as set forth in Statement 34 using the following assumptions:

a. Borrowing proceeds of $10,000,000 are received in advance of beginning construction, placed in escrow, and temporarily invested until used for the restricted purpose of constructing a plant. Interest is paid on the borrowings at a rate of 8 percent or $800,000 per year. The enterprise has no other debt. Therefore, the limit on the amount of capitalizable interest for the year is $800,000.
b. The average accumulated qualifying expenditures for the year are $5,500,000. The $10,000,000 construction project is completed at the end of the year. The enterprise has no other qualifying expenditures during the year.
c. Temporary investments average $4,500,000 ($10,000,000 proceeds minus average accumulated qualifying expenditures of $5,500,000) during the year and yield a 14 percent annual rate. Interest income earned during the year is $630,000 ($4,500,000 × .14).

The amount of interest cost to be capitalized in accordance with the avoidable interest concept in paragraph 12 of Statement 34 is $440,000 ($5,500,000 × .08). The amounts expended for qualifying assets are amounts that could have been used to repay the outstanding borrowing thereby avoiding the related interest cost. The amounts held in temporary investments and the related interest income of $630,000 do not affect the computation of avoidable interest cost.

10. The Addendum to APB Opinion No. 2, *Accounting for the "Investment Credit,"* (paragraph 2) states that ". . . differences may arise in the application of generally accepted accounting principles as between regulated and nonregulated businesses, because of the effect in regulated businesses of the rate-making process, . . ." and discusses the application of generally accepted accounting principles to regulated industries. Accordingly, the provisions of the Addendum shall govern the application of this Bulletin to those operations of an enterprise that are regulated for rate-making purposes on an individual-company-cost-of-service basis.

The Financial Accounting Standards Board has authorized its staff to issue FASB Technical Bulletins to provide guidance on certain financial accounting and reporting problems on a timely basis. Although Board members are provided with copies of proposed Bulletins prior to issuance, the Board does not approve them.

FASB Technical Bulletin No. 81-6 Applicability of Statement 15 to Debtors in Bankruptcy Situations

STATUS

Issued: November 30, 1981

Affected by: No other pronouncements

Note: Technical Bulletins (FTBs) have no effective date; the date indicated is the date issued.

FASB Technical Bulletin No. 81-6 Applicability of Statement 15 to Debtors in Bankruptcy Situations

Reference:

FASB Statement No. 15, *Accounting by Debtors and Creditors for Troubled Debt Restructurings,* paragraph 10

Question

1. Does Statement 15 apply to troubled debt restructurings of debtors involved in bankruptcy proceedings?

Background

2. Some confusion has arisen about the interaction of paragraph 10 and footnote 4 of Statement 15. Paragraph 10 indicates that the Statement applies to troubled debt restructurings consummated under reorganization, arrangement, or other provisions of the Federal Bankruptcy Act or other federal statutes related thereto. However, footnote 4 to that paragraph states that the Statement does not apply ". . . if, under provisions of those Federal statutes or in a quasi-reorganization or corporate readjustment (*ARB No. 43,* Chapter 7, Section A, 'Quasi-Reorganization or Corporate Readjustment . . .') with which a troubled debt restructuring coincides, the debtor restates its liabilities generally."

Response

3. Statement 15 does not apply to debtors who, in connection with bankruptcy proceedings, enter into troubled debt restructurings that result in a general restatement of the debtor's liabilities, that is, when such restructurings or modifications accomplished under purview of the bankruptcy court encompass most of the amount of the debtor's liabilities.

4. For example, companies involved with Chapter XI bankruptcy proceedings frequently reduce all or most of their indebtedness with the approval of their creditors and the court in order to provide an opportunity for the company to have a fresh start. Such reductions are usually by a stated percentage so that, for example, the debtor owes only 60 cents on the dollar. Because the debtor would be restating its liabilities generally, Statement 15 would not apply to the debtor's accounting for such reduction of liabilities.

5. On the other hand, Statement 15 would apply to an isolated troubled debt restructuring by a debtor involved in bankruptcy proceedings if such restructuring did not result in a general restatement of the debtor's liabilities.

The Financial Accounting Standards Board has authorized its staff to issue FASB Technical Bulletins to provide guidance on certain financial accounting and reporting problems on a timely basis. Although Board members are provided with copies of proposed Bulletins prior to issuance, the Board does not approve them.

FASB Technical Bulletin No. 82-1
Disclosure of the Sale or Purchase of Tax Benefits through Tax Leases

STATUS

Issued: January 27, 1982

Affected by: No other pronouncements

Note: Technical Bulletins (FTBs) have no effective date; the date indicated is the date issued.

FASB Technical Bulletin No. 82-1 Disclosure of the Sale or Purchase of Tax Benefits through Tax Leases

References:

ARB No. 43, *Restatement and Revision of Accounting Research Bulletins,* Chapter 2A, paragraph 2
APB Opinion No. 11, *Accounting for Income Taxes,* paragraph 63
APB Opinion No. 22, *Disclosure of Accounting Policies*
APB Opinion No. 30, *Reporting the Results of Operations,* paragraph 26
FASB Statement No. 5, *Accounting for Contingencies*

Question

1. What disclosures are required for the sale or purchase of tax benefits through tax leases?

Background

2. The term *tax leases,* as used in this Bulletin, refers to leases that are entered into to transfer certain tax benefits as allowed by the leasing provisions of the Economic Recovery Tax Act of 1981. The tax benefits that can be transferred are deductions under the Accelerated Cost Recovery System and credits such as the investment tax credit and energy credit. Temporary Treasury regulations were issued on October 20, 1981, November 10, 1981, and December 28, 1981 that prescribe the conditions that must be met for a transaction to be characterized as a "safe harbor" lease for federal income tax purposes, thus enabling the parties to the transaction to transfer certain tax benefits between them.

3. The FASB issued an Exposure Draft of a proposed Statement, *Accounting for the Sale or Purchase of Tax Benefits through Tax Leases,* for public comment on October 29, 1981, and received over 160 letters of comment. At the December 16, 1981 Board meeting, the Board concluded that the provisions of that Exposure Draft should be revised and that it should be reexposed for public comment. In late December 1981, a need was identified for disclosure of transactions involving solely the sale or purchase of tax benefits through tax leases until the accounting issues related to those transactions are resolved.

Response

4. Opinion 22 requires disclosure of all significant accounting policies where alternative accounting principles or practices exist, including the methods of applying those accounting principles that materially affect the determination of financial position, changes in financial position, and results of operations. Because alternative accounting practices may exist until the FASB issues a final Statement addressing the sale or purchase of tax benefits through tax leases, the accounting policies or practices followed for those transactions should be disclosed in accordance with that Opinion. The disclosure should include the method of accounting for those transactions and the methods of recognizing revenue and allocating income tax benefits and asset costs to current and future periods.

5. Paragraph 63 of Opinion 11 requires disclosure of the reasons for significant variations in the customary relationships between income tax expense and pretax accounting income if they are not otherwise apparent from the financial statements or from the nature of the enterprise's business. Accordingly, any significant variation in the customary relationship between income tax expense and pretax accounting income resulting from transactions involving the sale or purchase of tax benefits through tax leases should be disclosed in accordance with Opinion 11.

6. Paragraph 26 of Opinion 30 requires disclosure of material events or transactions that are unusual in nature or occur infrequently as a separate component of income from continuing operations. If material and unusual or infrequent to the enterprise, the nature and financial effects of transactions involving the sale or purchase of tax benefits through tax leases should be disclosed on the face of the income statement or, alternatively, in notes to the financial statements in accordance with Opinion 30.

7. Disclosures in addition to those required by Opinions 11, 22, and 30 as discussed above also may be appropriate depending on the circumstances involved. For example, if significant contingencies exist with respect to the sale or purchase of tax benefits, disclosures in accordance with Statement 5 may be warranted. Also, as referred to in paragraph 2 of Chapter 2A of ARB 43, if comparative financial statements are presented, disclosure should be made of any change in practice that significantly affects comparability.

8. This Bulletin does not address the accounting for the sale or purchase of tax benefits through tax leases.

The Financial Accounting Standards Board has authorized its staff to issue FASB Technical Bulletins to provide guidance on certain financial accounting and reporting problems on a timely basis. Although Board members are provided with copies of proposed Bulletins prior to issuance, the Board does not approve them.

Technical Bulletin No. 82-2 Accounting for the Conversion of Stock Options into Incentive Stock Options as a Result of the Economic Recovery Tax Act of 1981

STATUS

Issued: March 31, 1982

Affected by: No other pronouncements

Note: Technical Bulletins (FTBs) have no effective date; the date indicated is the date issued.

Technical Bulletin No. 82-2
Accounting for the Conversion of Stock Options into Incentive Stock Options as a Result of the Economic Recovery Tax Act of 1981

References:

ARB No. 43, *Restatement and Revision of Accounting Research Bulletins,* Chapter 13B, "Compensation Involved in Stock Option and Stock Purchase Plans"
APB Opinion No. 25, *Accounting for Stock Issued to Employees*
FASB Interpretation No. 28, *Accounting for Stock Appreciation Rights and Other Variable Stock Option or Award Plans*

Question

1. What are the accounting implications for enterprises that convert previously issued stock options into incentive stock options (ISOs) as a result of the Economic Recovery Tax Act of 1981 (Act)?

Background

2. The Act includes provisions that grant favorable tax treatment to individuals who own incentive stock options. Enterprises can provide individuals with ISOs in two ways, by issuing new ISOs and by converting previously issued options into ISOs through changes to conform those options to the requirements of the Act. Accounting issues arise for enterprises with respect to plan modifications that are undertaken to convert existing options into ISOs.

3. One ISO requirement is that the option price must either equal or exceed the fair market value of the stock either at the date of grant or, if the option has been modified or renewed, at the date of the most recent amendment providing benefits to the option holder. This is commonly referred to as the "repricing" requirement of the Act. Enterprises electing to convert existing options into ISOs may be forced to raise option prices to meet the repricing requirement.

4. The Act allows enterprises to limit or eliminate the need to raise option prices by canceling certain prior plan amendments. For example, assume the option price and stock price at date of grant are $8 and $10, respectively, for a nonqualified plan and that a plan amendment is later introduced when the stock price is $17. By canceling the amendment, the option can be repriced at $10, resulting in $2 of additional cost to the employee; if the amendment is not canceled, the repricing is at $17 and the employee's additional cost is $9. In recent years, several stock option plans have been amended to add a tandem stock appreciation right (SAR). Therefore, if they are converting the underlying stock option into an ISO, some enterprises may elect to cancel SARs that were previously added through plan amendments.

5. ARB 43, Chapter 13B, states in paragraph 10 that ". . . in most cases . . . valuation should be made of the option as of the date of grant." Opinion 25 did not change that underlying principle for plans that do not have variable terms. Paragraph 29 of Opinion 25 defines plans with variable terms:

> . . . The characteristic that identifies plans in this group is that the terms prevent determining at the date of grant or award either the number of shares of stock that may be acquired by or awarded to an employee or the price to be paid by the employee, or both.

Regarding the determination of the measurement date, paragraph 10(b) of Opinion 25 states that:

> *The measurement date* for determining compensation cost in stock option, purchase, and award plans is the first date on which are known both (1) the number of shares that an individual employee is entitled to receive and (2) the option or purchase price, if any. . . . The measurement date may be later than the date of grant or award in plans with variable terms that depend on events after date of grant or award.

6. Paragraph 5 of Interpretation 28 addresses tandem plans and states that:

> . . . If an enterprise has been accruing compensation for a stock appreciation right or other variable plan award and a change in circumstances provides evidence that the employee will likely elect to exercise the related stock option, accrued compensation recorded for the right or award shall *not* be adjusted.[7] If the employee elects to exercise the stock option, the accrued compensation recorded for the right or award shall be recognized as a consideration for the stock issued. If all parts of the grant or award (e.g., both the option and the right or award) are

forfeited or cancelled, accrued compensation shall be adjusted by decreasing compensation expense in that period.

[7]A change in the circumstances may be indicated by . . . cancellation or forfeiture of the stock appreciation right or other variable plan award without a concurrent cancellation or forfeiture of the related stock option.

7. Paragraph 17 of Opinion 25 describes accounting for income tax benefits under stock option plans:

> An employer corporation should reduce income tax expense for a period by no more of a tax reduction under a stock option, purchase, or award plan than the proportion of the tax reduction that is related to the compensation expense for the period. . . . The remainder of the tax reduction, if any, is related to an amount that is deductible for income tax purposes but does not affect net income. The remainder of the tax reduction should not be included in income but should be added to capital in addition to par or stated value of capital stock in the period of the tax reduction. Conversely, a tax reduction may be less than if recorded compensation expenses were deductible for income tax purposes. If so, the corporation may deduct the difference from additional capital in the period of the tax reduction to the extent that tax reductions under the same or similar compensatory stock option, purchase, or award plans have been included in additional capital.

Response

Repricing

8. Opinion 25 requires that an enterprise record compensation for services it receives for stock issued to employees through a stock option plan. That compensation is equal to the quoted market price of the stock on the measurement date less the amount the employee is required to pay. The compensation cost is charged to expense over the periods in which the employee performs the related services. Increasing the option price to meet the repricing requirement described in paragraph 3 of this Bulletin results in the enterprise's recapturing the compensation cost that arose when the option was granted. In recognition of that recapture, enterprises should reverse, in the period in which the option price is increased, the portion of total compensation cost that arose when the option was granted and has been charged to expense in subsequent periods.

9. A variable plan is a plan that has variable terms at its inception, as described in paragraph 5 of this Bulletin. A variable plan therefore differs from a plan with terms that are fixed at inception, modified once to increase the option price to conform to the Act, and remain fixed thereafter. A stock option plan that has fixed terms does not become a variable plan simply because the option price is raised to meet the repricing requirements of the Act. Accordingly, the increase in the option price to 100 percent of the fair market value at the date of grant to qualify an option under the Act does not result in a new measurement date.

Tandem Plans

10. *Presumption as to Exercise.* Interpretation 28 clarifies how compensation expense shall be recorded in connection with a combination or tandem stock option and SAR plan. Paragraph 5 of that Interpretation states that ". . . compensation expense . . . shall be measured according to the terms an employee is most likely to elect based on the facts available each period. An enterprise shall presume that the employee will elect to exercise the stock appreciation rights or other variable plan awards, but the presumption may be overcome. . . ." The fact that the Act grants more favorable tax treatment to holders of stock options does not invalidate the presumption of Interpretation 28 that the SAR will be exercised. However, it may be an important factor in evaluating what the employee is most likely to elect.

11. *Cancellation of SAR Only.* Interpretation 28 also discusses accounting for the cancellation of the SAR in a tandem SAR and stock option plan. Paragraph 5 and footnote 7 of that Interpretation (refer to paragraph 6 of this Bulletin) state that accrued compensation recorded for an SAR shall not be adjusted if cancellation or forfeiture of the SAR occurs without a concurrent cancellation or forfeiture of the related stock option. Enterprises that cancel SARs under the circumstances described in paragraph 4 of this Bulletin should look to paragraph 5 and footnote 7 of Interpretation 28 for guidance. Those sections of Interpretation 28 also include guidance concerning the ultimate disposition of the accrued compensation amount if the option is exercised, canceled, or forfeited.

Combination of Circumstances

12. A combination of certain of the circumstances described in the preceding paragraphs may exist. For example, the cancellation of a tandem SAR may be combined with the repricing of the underlying option. If that happens, the portion of total accrued compensation that relates to the repricing should be reversed as described in paragraph 8 of this Bulletin; the balance of accrued compensation relates to the cancellation of the SAR and should be accounted for under the provisions of paragraph 11 of this Bulletin. As an illustration, assume the following: (a) a

nonqualified option for $110 was granted when the market value of the stock was $130, (b) a tandem SAR was subsequently introduced through a plan amendment, (c) all compensation costs for the option and SAR relate to prior periods and have been charged to expense, and (d) the enterprise decides to cancel the SAR and reprice the stock option to a $130 option price when the market value of the stock is $180. The accounting result is that $20 of accrued compensation (computed $130 − $110) is reversed in the current period and the remaining $50 (computed $180 − $130) is retained as accrued compensation.

Taxes

13. Certain of the guidance in this Bulletin involves adjustments to compensation expense. For accounting purposes, the tax effects of those adjustments should be determined in accordance with the general guidance concerning accounting for income tax benefits under stock option plans found in paragraph 17 of Opinion 25 (refer to paragraph 7 of this Bulletin). For example, a reversal of compensation expense in connection with a repricing as described in paragraph 8 of this Bulletin results in a corresponding reversal of the related deferred tax benefits. Likewise, if a tandem SAR is canceled as described in paragraph 11, the tax benefit is not adjusted, but is retained along with the accrued compensation that gave rise to it. Ultimately, depending on the employee's actions, the compensation and tax benefit are disposed of in the same manner—together, they are either reversed or applied to additional paid-in capital.

The Financial Accounting Standards Board has authorized its staff to issue FASB Technical Bulletins to provide guidance on certain financial accounting and reporting problems on a timely basis. Although Board members are provided with copies of proposed Bulletins prior to issuance, the Board does not approve them.

FASB Technical Bulletin No. 83-1 Accounting for the Reduction in the Tax Basis of an Asset Caused by the Investment Tax Credit

STATUS

Issued: July 26, 1983

Affected by: No other pronouncements

Note: Technical Bulletins (FTBs) have no effective date; the date indicated is the date issued.

FASB Technical Bulletin No. 83-1
Accounting for the Reduction in the Tax Basis of an Asset Caused by the Investment Tax Credit

References:

APB Opinion No. 11, *Accounting for Income Taxes*
AICPA Accounting Interpretation 8, *Permanent Differences,* of Opinion 11

Question

1. Section 205 of the Tax Equity and Fiscal Responsibility Act of 1982 (Act) provides a taxpayer with the choice of either (a) taking the full amount of Accelerated Cost Recovery System (ACRS) deductions and a reduced investment tax credit[1] or (b) taking the full investment tax credit and a reduced amount of ACRS deductions. The deferral and flow-through methods of accounting for investment tax credits are well established as acceptable alternatives; however, how should enterprises that recognize investment tax credits by the flow-through method[2] account for the reduction in the tax basis of an asset caused by the investment tax credit?

Response

2. Some believe that the reduction in the tax basis of an asset caused by the investment tax credit represents solely a reduction of ACRS benefits and would account for it as a permanent difference. However, the reduction in the tax basis of an asset results from taking the full amount of investment tax credit; that basis reduction would not exist independently of the investment tax credit. As further evidence that the reduction in the tax basis of an asset is directly related to the investment tax credit, the basis reduction is restored if the investment tax credit is recaptured and an additional deduction is allowed if the investment tax credit expires.

3. Others believe AICPA Accounting Interpretation 8 of Opinion 11 (paragraph 13 of this Technical Bulletin) applies to a reduction in the tax basis of an asset caused by the investment tax credit. AICPA Interpretation 8 indicates that a permanent difference results if different bases of carrying property produce different amounts of depreciation for income tax and financial reporting. However, AICPA Interpretation 8 does not apply to the reduction in the tax basis of an asset caused by the investment tax credit. The reduction in the tax basis of an asset caused by the investment tax credit is unlike the different bases of carrying property cited in AICPA Interpretation 8. The tax effects of the different bases of carrying property addressed in AICPA Interpretation 8 do not reverse in other periods. In contrast, as a result of the reduction in the tax basis occurring under the Act, an amount equivalent to a portion of the investment tax credit reverses in other periods because of the related lower ACRS deductions.

4. The portion of the investment tax credit that reduces the tax basis of an asset is, in substance, a timing difference (paragraph 14) rather than a permanent difference (paragraph 12) because it will be offset by corresponding differences (reduced ACRS deductions) or "turn around" in other periods. The combination of the investment tax credit and the accompanying reduction in ACRS deductions reduces income taxes payable in one period and increases income taxes payable in subsequent periods. Accordingly, the effect of the basis reduction should be reported as a timing difference under Opinion 11. Deferred taxes should be provided for a reduction in the tax basis of an asset in the year that the related investment tax credit is recognized as a credit to income tax expense. Those deferred taxes should be amortized to income tax expense as taxable income exceeds financial reporting income as a result of the basis reduction. Likewise, deferred taxes should be recognized by a lessee claiming an investment tax credit passed through by a lessor if the lessee is required to adjust taxable income over the ACRS recovery period for the asset because of the credit.

5. This Technical Bulletin does not address accounting for the reduction in the tax basis of an asset by enterprises that recognize investment tax credits by the deferral method. Application of its provisions by those enterprises would not affect net income and might cause only minor changes in balance sheet classifications. The benefits of the application of this Technical Bulletin by such enterprises probably would not justify the costs they would incur to implement it.

[1]For purposes of this Technical Bulletin, regular investment tax credit, energy investment tax credit, and credit for qualified rehabilitation expenditures are all referred to as "investment tax credit."

[2]The reasons for not addressing enterprises that use the deferral method of accounting for investment tax credits are explained in paragraph 5.

Appendix A

EXAMPLE OF ACCOUNTING FOR THE REDUCTION IN THE TAX BASIS OF AN ASSET CAUSED BY THE INVESTMENT TAX CREDIT

6. This example illustrates the accounting for the reduction in the tax basis of an asset caused by the investment tax credit. The example includes the effects on deferred taxes of (a) differences resulting from the reduction in the tax basis of an asset caused by the investment tax credit and (b) differences between financial reporting depreciation and ACRS deductions. Differences between financial reporting depreciation and ACRS deductions are included in the example because, in practice, such differences will often be accounted for in combination with differences resulting from the reduction in the tax basis of an asset. The example does not include all possible combinations of circumstances.

7. The assumptions on which the following illustration is based are:

a. The enterprise recognizes investment tax credits by the flow-through method.
b. The enterprise purchased manufacturing equipment at a cost of $1,000,000. A 10-percent regular investment tax credit is claimed and the tax basis of the asset is reduced $50,000.
c. The asset is depreciated on the straight-line method over 10 years for financial reporting purposes. ACRS guidelines are followed for tax purposes (5 years at 15 percent in year 1, 22 percent in year 2, and 21 percent in years 3, 4, and 5).
d. As a simplifying assumption for purposes of this illustration, the enterprise has no differences between pretax accounting income and taxable income other than differences related to depreciation and the reduction in the tax basis of the equipment.

8. Recognition of deferred taxes in income tax expense for financial reporting purposes is illustrated below. For purposes of this illustration, it is assumed that the "with and without" computation of deferred taxes under Opinion 11 would result in an amount equal to 46 percent of the depreciation differences for each year.

	Income Tax Basis	Financial Reporting Basis	Difference*	Deferred Tax Charge (Credit) to Income Tax Expense
Deferred taxes related to:				
Effect of full investment tax credit flow-through	$ (50,000)	$(100,000)	$ 50,000	$ 23,000
Depreciation:				
Year 1	142,500	100,000	42,500	19,550
2	209,000	100,000	109,000	50,140
3	199,500	100,000	99,500	45,770
4	199,500	100,000	99,500	45,770
5	199,500	100,000	99,500	45,770
6	—	100,000	(100,000)	(46,000)
7	—	100,000	(100,000)	(46,000)
8	—	100,000	(100,000)	(46,000)
9	—	100,000	(100,000)	(46,000)
10	—	100,000	(100,000)	(46,000)
	$900,000	$ 900,000	$ —	$ —

*ACRS deductions in excess of financial reporting depreciation in years 1 through 5 are originating timing differences that are net of the following amounts resulting from the basis reduction: $7,500 (15% of $50,000) in year 1, $11,000 (22% of $50,000) in year 2, and $10,500 (21% of $50,000) in years 3, 4, and 5. Differences after year 5 are reversing timing differences that relate solely to differences between ACRS guidelines and the financial reporting depreciation method.

Appendix B

BACKGROUND INFORMATION

9. Taxpayers electing the full investment tax credit are required under Section 205 of the Act to reduce the tax basis of depreciable assets by one-half of the regular and energy investment tax credits and one-half of the 25-percent investment credit for qualified rehabilitation expenditures for certified historic structures. Taxpayers continue to be required to reduce the tax basis of other rehabilitation expenditures by the full amount of a 15-percent or 20-

percent credit as provided by the Economic Recovery Tax Act of 1981. The reduced basis is used to compute ACRS deductions. If an investment tax credit is recaptured on disposal of the asset, there is an increase in the basis of the asset for determining taxable gain or loss. If the investment tax credit expires, an additional deduction is allowed in the amount of one-half of the unused credit. The Act also requires a lessee claiming an investment tax credit passed through to it by a lessor to include an amount equal to one-half of the credit in taxable income ratably over the ACRS recovery period for the asset.

10. The Board issued an Exposure Draft of a proposed Statement, *Accounting for the Reduction in the Tax Basis of an Asset Caused by the Investment Tax Credit,* on October 26, 1982. That Exposure Draft concluded that (a) the basis reduction functions like a timing difference and, therefore, should be accounted for as a timing difference and (b) enterprises recognizing investment tax credits by the deferral method need not apply the provisions of the proposed Statement for the reasons expressed in paragraph 5 of this Technical Bulletin.

11. Several respondents to the Exposure Draft indicated that an FASB Statement was not needed to address this issue because AICPA Interpretation 8 provides guidance, and others indicated that a Statement should not be issued on accounting for the basis reduction because it is a narrow issue. The Board decided not to issue a Statement on the narrow question of how to account for the basis reduction. However, the Board understood that some of those respondents desired guidance in a form other than a Statement; therefore, the Board encouraged the staff to provide guidance through a Technical Bulletin. This Technical Bulletin is responsive to those comments and will provide adequate guidance by clarifying that AICPA Interpretation 8 does not apply to the reduction in the tax basis of an asset caused by the investment tax credit.

12. Paragraph 13(f) of Opinion 11 defines permanent differences as:

> Differences between taxable income and pretax accounting income arising from transactions that, under applicable tax laws and regulations, will not be offset by corresponding differences or "turn around" in other periods. . . .

13. AICPA Accounting Interpretation 8 of Opinion 11 states:

> A permanent difference also results if different bases of carrying property for accounting purposes and for tax purposes produce amounts for depreciation or amortization different for tax purposes than for accounting purposes. Also, gains or losses for tax purposes upon dispositions of such property may differ from those recognized for accounting purposes. Different bases for property frequently result from write-downs of assets in a reorganization. Different bases may also occur from business combinations accounted for as purchases and treated as tax-free exchanges or from business combinations accounted for as poolings of interests and treated as taxable exchanges. Similarly, in the case of a donation of property, accounting expense could be recorded on the basis of the net carrying amount of the property whereas the tax deduction would be for the fair value on the date of gift.

14. Paragraph 13(e) of Opinion 11 defines timing differences as:

> Differences between the periods in which transactions affect taxable income and the periods in which they enter into the determination of pretax accounting income. Timing differences originate in one period and reverse or "turn around" in one or more subsequent periods. Some timing differences reduce income taxes that would otherwise be payable currently; others increase income taxes that would otherwise be payable currently.

15. Several respondents stated that the reduction in the tax basis of an asset caused by the investment tax credit does not meet the literal definition of either a permanent difference or a timing difference as specified by Opinion 11. However, the effect of the tax requirements causes the reduction to function in substance as a timing difference rather than as a permanent difference because receiving the benefit of the full investment tax credit will result in higher

income taxes through reduced ACRS deductions in years subsequent to acquisition of the asset. For example, assuming (a) a full investment tax credit of $100, (b) a basis reduction of $50, and (c) a 46-percent incremental tax rate, $23 of the investment tax credit received when the asset is acquired effectively will result in higher income taxes in subsequent years.

FASB Technical Bulletin No. 84-1
Accounting for Stock Issued to Acquire the Results of a Research and Development Arrangement

STATUS

Issued: March 15, 1984

Affected by: No other pronouncements

Note: Technical Bulletins (FTBs) have no effective date; the date indicated is the date issued.

FASB Technical Bulletin No. 84-1
Accounting for Stock Issued to Acquire the Results of a Research and Development Arrangement

References:

FASB Statement No. 68, *Research and Development Arrangements,* paragraphs 11, 13, and 20
APB Opinion No. 16, *Business Combinations,* paragraph 67

Question

1. How should an enterprise account for stock issued to acquire the results of a research and development arrangement?

Background

2. Paragraph 20 of Appendix A of Statement 68 describes the usual contractual right of an enterprise to acquire the results of a research and development arrangement (that paragraph describes an arrangement between the enterprise and a partnership):

> Either as part of the partnership agreement or through contracts with the partnership, the enterprise usually has an option either to purchase the partnership's interest in or to obtain the exclusive rights to the entire results of the research and development in return for a lump sum payment or royalty payments to the partnership. Some arrangements contain a provision that permits the enterprise to acquire complete ownership of the results for a specified amount of the enterprise's stock or cash at some future time. In some of those purchase agreements, the partnership has the option to receive either the enterprise's stock or cash; in others, the enterprise makes the decision. Sometimes, warrants or similar instruments to purchase the enterprise's stock are issued in connection with the arrangement.

3. Paragraph 11 of Statement 68 describes the accounting for a purchase of the results of a research and development arrangement:

> If the enterprise's obligation is to perform research and development for others and the enterprise subsequently decides to exercise an option to purchase the other parties' interests in the research and development arrangement or to obtain the exclusive rights to the results of the research and development, the nature of those results and their future use shall determine the accounting for the purchase transaction. [Footnote reference omitted.]

4. Paragraph 67 of Opinion 16 describes the general principles of historical cost accounting that are applied in determining the cost of an asset acquired by issuing shares of stock:

> c. An asset acquired by issuing shares of stock of the acquiring corporation is recorded at the fair value of the asset—that is, shares of stock issued are recorded at the fair value of the consideration received for the stock.
>
> The general principles must be supplemented to apply them in certain transactions. For example, the fair value of an asset received for stock issued may not be reliably determinable, or the fair value of an asset acquired in an exchange may be more reliably determinable than the fair value of a noncash asset given up. Restraints on measurement have led to the practical rule that assets acquired for other than cash, including shares of stock issued, should be stated at "cost" when they are acquired and "cost may be determined either by the fair value of the consideration given or by the fair value of the property acquired, whichever is more clearly evident." . . . [Footnote references omitted.]

5. Paragraph 13 of Statement 68 describes the accounting for the issuance of warrants or similar instruments in connection with a research and development arrangement:

> If warrants or similar instruments are issued in connection with the arrangement, the enterprise shall report a portion of the proceeds to be provided by the other parties as paid-in capital. The amount so reported shall be the fair value of the instruments at the date of the arrangement.

Statement 68 does not address the accounting for a subsequent issuance of stock pursuant to the exercise of warrants or similar instruments issued in connection with a research and development arrangement.

Response

6. When an enterprise that is or was a party to a research and development arrangement acquires the

results of the research and development arrangement in exchange for cash, common stock of the enterprise, or other consideration, the transaction is a purchase of tangible or intangible assets resulting from the activities of the research and development arrangement. Although such a transaction is not a business combination, paragraph 67 of Opinion 16 describes the general principles that apply in recording the purchase of such an asset.

7. Accordingly, when an enterprise that is or was a party to a research and development arrangement exchanges stock for the results of the research and development arrangement, whether pursuant to the exercise of warrants or similar instruments issued in connection with the arrangement or otherwise, the enterprise should record the stock issued at its fair value, or at the fair value of consideration received, whichever is more clearly evident. The transaction should be accounted for in this manner whether the enterprise exchanges stock for the results of the research and development arrangement, for rights to use the results, or for ownership interests in the arrangement or a successor to the arrangement. The fair value should be determined as of the date the enterprise exercises its option to acquire the result of the research and development arrangement.

(The next page is 6001.)

Appendix A

APPENDIX A

AICPA Audit Guides, Accounting Guides, and Statements of Position

This appendix lists the AICPA Audit and Accounting Guides and Statements of Position (some of which have been superseded by FASB Statements). These documents, some of which are referred to in the text, discuss accounting principles applicable to specialized situations.

Audit and Accounting Guides

Accounting for Motion Picture Films, Committee on the Entertainment Industries, 1973; Statement of Position, *Accounting for Motion Picture Films,* Accounting Standards Division, March 1979.

Accounting for Retail Land Sales, Committee on Land Development Companies, 1973.

Accounting for Profit Recognition on Sales of Real Estate, Committee on Accounting for Real Estate Transactions, 1973; Statement of Position, *Questions Concerning Profit Recognition on Sales of Real Estate,* Accounting Standards Division, December 1975; Statement of Position, *Application of the Deposit, Installment, and Cost Recovery Methods in Accounting for Sales of Real Estate,* June 1978.

Audit Sampling, Statistical Sampling Subcommittee, 1983.

The Auditor's Study and Evaluation of Internal Control in EDP Systems, Computer Services Executive Committee, 1977.

Audits of Airlines, Civil Aeronautics Subcommittee, 1981.

Audits of Banks, Committee on Banking, 1983.

Audits of Brokers and Dealers in Securities, Committee on Stockbrokerage Auditing, 1973; Statement of Position, *Audits of Brokers and Dealers in Securities,* Accounting Standards Division, December 1976.

Audits of Certain Nonprofit Organizations, Subcommittee on Nonprofit Organizations, 1981; Statement of Position, *Accounting Principles and Reporting Practices for Certain Nonprofit Organizations,* Accounting Standards Division, December 1978.

Audits of Colleges and Universities, Committee on College and University Accounting and Auditing, 1973; Statement of Position, *Financial Accounting and Reporting by Colleges and Universities,* Accounting Standards Division, August 1974.

Audits of Employee Benefit Plans, Employee Benefit Plans and ERISA Special Committee, 1983.

Audits of Finance Companies, Committee on Finance Companies, 1973.

Audits of Fire and Casualty Insurance Companies, Committee on Insurance Accounting and Auditing, 1966; Statement of Position, *Revision of Form of Auditor's Report,* Auditing Standards Division, July 1974;

Statement of Position, *Accounting for Property and Liability Insurance Companies,* Accounting Standards Division, July 1978; Statement of Position, *Auditing Property and Liability Reinsurance,* Auditing Standards Division, October 1982.

Audits of Government Contractors, Task Force on Defense Contract Agencies, 1975; Statement of Position, *Accounting for Performance of Construction-Type and Certain Production-Type Contracts,* Accounting Standards Division, July 1981.

Audits of Investment Companies, Committee on Investment Companies, 1973; Statement of Position, *Financial Accounting and Reporting by Face-Amount Certificate Companies,* Accounting Standards Division, December 1974; Statement of Position, *Financial Accounting and Reporting by Investment Companies,* Accounting Standards Division, April 1977; Statement of Position, *Accounting for Municipal Bond Funds,* Accounting Standards Division, January 1979.

Audits of Service-Center-Produced Records, Committee on Computer Auditing, 1974.

Audits of State and Local Governmental Units, Committee on Governmental Accounting and Auditing, 1974; Statement of Position, *Accrual of Revenues and Expenditures by State and Local Governmental Units,* Accounting Standards Division, August 1975; Statement of Position, *Accounting for Interfund Transfers of State and Local Governmental Units,* Accounting Standards Division, September 1977; Statement of Position, *Financial Accounting and Reporting by Hospitals Operated by a Governmental Unit,* Accounting Standards Division, July 1978; Statement of Position, *Accounting and Financial Reporting by Governmental Units,* Accounting Standards Division, June 1980.

Audits of Stock Life Insurance Companies, Committee on Insurance Accounting and Auditing, 1972; Statement of Position, *Confirmation of Insurance Policies in Force,* Auditing Standards Division, August 1978; Statement of Position, *Accounting for Investments of Stock Life Insurance Companies,* Accounting Standards Division, March 1979.

Audits of Voluntary Health and Welfare Organizations, Committee on Voluntary Health and Welfare Organizations, 1974.

Computer-Assisted Audit Techniques, Computer Services Executive Committee, 1979.

Construction Contractors, Construction Contractor Guide Committee, 1981; Statement of Position, *Accounting for Performance of Construction-Type and Certain Production-Type Contracts,* Accounting Standards Division, July 1981.

Guide for a Review of a Financial Forecast, Financial Forecasts and Projections Task Force, 1980; Statement of Position, *Presentation and Disclosure of Financial Forecasts,* Accounting Standards Division, August 1975; Statement of Position, *Report on a Financial Feasibility Study,* Auditing Standards Division, October 1982.

Hospital Audit Guide, Committee on Health Care Institutions, 1972; Statement of Position, *Clarification of Accounting, Auditing, and Reporting Practices Relating to Hospital Malpractice Loss Contingencies,* Auditing Standards Division, March 1978; Statement of Position, *Accounting by Hospitals for Certain Marketable Equity Securities,* Accounting Standards Division, May 1978; Statement of Position, *Reporting Practices Concerning Hospital-Related Organizations,* Accounting Standards Division. August 1981.

Personal Financial Statements Guide, Personal Financial Statements Task Force, 1983; Statement of Position, *Accounting and Reporting for Personal Financial Statements,* Accounting Standards Division, October 1982.

Savings and Loan Associations, Committee on Savings and Loan Associations, Revised Edition, 1979.

Statements of Position of the Auditing Standards Division

Revision of Form of Auditor's Report, Audits of Fire and Casualty Insurance Companies	7/74
Audits of Brokers and Dealers in Securities	12/76
Clarification of Accounting, Auditing, and Reporting Practices Relating to Hospital Malpractice Loss Contingencies, Hospital Audit Guide	3/78
Confirmation of Insurance Policies in Force, Audits of Stock Life Insurance Companies	8/78
Report on a Financial Feasibility Study	10/82
Auditing Property and Liability Reinsurance	10/82

Statements of Position of the Accounting Standards Division

Recognition of Profit on Sales of Receivables with Recourse	6/74
Financial Accounting and Reporting by Colleges and Universities	8/74
Financial Accounting and Reporting by Face-Amount Certificate Companies	12/74
Accounting Practices in the Mortgage Banking Industry	12/74
Accounting Practices of Real Estate Investment Trusts	6/75
Accrual of Revenues and Expenditures by State and Local Governmental Units	7/75
Presentation and Disclosure of Financial Forecasts	8/75
Accounting Practices in the Broadcasting Industry	12/75
Questions Concerning Profit Recognition on Sales of Real Estate	12/75
Accounting Practices in the Record and Music Industry	8/76
Accounting for Origination Costs and Commitment Fees in the Mortgage Banking Industry	8/76

Accounting Practices for Certain Employee Stock Ownership Plans	12/76
Financial Accounting and Reporting by Investment Companies	4/77
Accounting for Interfund Transfers of State and Local Governmental Units	9/77
Accounting by Hospitals for Certain Marketable Equity Securities	5/78
Accounting Practices of Real Estate Investment Trusts	5/78
Accounting for Costs to Sell and Rent, and Initial Rental Operations of, Real Estate Projects	6/78
Application of the Deposit, Installment, and Cost Recovery Methods in Accounting for Sales of Real Estate	6/78
Accounting for Advance Refundings of Tax-Exempt Debt	6/78
Accounting for Property and Liability Insurance Companies	7/78
Financial Accounting and Reporting by Hospitals Operated by a Governmental Unit	7/78
Accounting for Investments in Real Estate Ventures	12/78
Accounting Principles and Reporting Practices for Certain Nonprofit Organizations	12/78
Accounting for Municipal Bond Funds	1/79
Accounting by Cable Television Companies	3/79
Accounting for Investments of Stock Life Insurance Companies	3/79
Accounting for Motion Picture Films	3/79
Accounting for Title Insurance Companies	1/80
Accounting and Financial Reporting by Governmental Units	6/80
Accounting for Real Estate Acquisition, Development, and Construction Costs	12/80
Accounting for Performance of Construction-Type and Certain Production-Type Contracts	7/81
Reporting Practices Concerning Hospital-Related Organizations	8/81
Accounting and Financial Reporting for Personal Financial Statements	10/82
Reporting by Banks of Investment Securities Gains or Losses	12/83

(The next page is 6051.)

Appendix B

APPENDIX B

Schedule of Amended and Superseded Accounting Pronouncements

The following schedule lists changes in Accounting Research Bulletins (ARB), APB Opinions (APB), APB Statements (APS), AICPA Accounting Interpretations (AIN-ARB or AIN-APB), FASB Statements of Financial Accounting Standards (FAS), FASB Interpretations (FIN), and FASB Technical Bulletins (FTB) that are readily determinable as the result of subsequent pronouncements. It does not address changes that may have been made implicitly by subsequent pronouncements and cannot be directly related to paragraphs in specific prior pronouncements including those made to APB Statements by FASB Statements of Concepts (CON). Changes that have been explicitly made to APB Statements have been included. Refer to Appendix C for the effective dates of all pronouncements.

Changes in Accounting Pronouncements

ARB	Chap.	Par.	
43	1B		Amended by APB 6
43	2A	3	Amended by APB 20
43	2B		Superseded by APB 9
43	3A	6(a)	Amended by FAS 6
43	3A	6(g)	Amended by APB 21
43	3A	7	*Amended by FAS 78
43	3A	8	Amended by FAS 6
43	3A	10	*Amended by APB 6
43	3A	fn1	Amended by FAS 6
43	3A	fn4	Amended by FAS 6
43	3B		Superseded by APB 10
43	5	5,6	Amended by APB 9
43	5	7	Amended by APB 6
43	5	8	Amended by APB 9
43	5	8	Amended by FAS 44
43	5	9	Amended by APB 9
43	5	10	Superseded prospectively by APB 16
43	5	10	Amended by FAS 44
43	5	fn1	Superseded by APB 9
43	5	1-9	Superseded prospectively by APB 17
43	6		Superseded by FAS 5
43	7B	6	Amended by APB 6
43	7C		Superseded by ARB 48
43	8		Superseded by APB 9
43	8	fn1-5	Superseded by APB 9
43	9B		Superseded by APB 6
43	9C		Amended by APB 6
43	9C	11-13	Amended by APB 11

ARB	Chap.	Par.	
43	10A	19	Amended by APB 9
43	10A	19	Amended by FAS 16
43	10B		Amended by APB 6
43	10B	15,17	Amended by APB 9
43	10B		Superseded by APB 11
43	11B	8	Amended by APB 11
43	11B	9	Amended by APB 9
43	11B	9	Amended by FAS 16
43	11B	fn3	Amended by APB 9
43	11B	fn4	Amended by FAS 16
43	12	5	Amended by FAS 8
43	12	5	Amended by FAS 52
43	12	7	Superseded by FAS 8
43	12	7	Superseded by FAS 52
43	12	12,18	Amended by APB 6
43	12	21	Amended by APB 9
43	12	10-22	Superseded by FAS 8
43	12	10-22	Superseded by FAS 52
43	13A		Superseded by APB 8
43	13B		Amended by APB 25
43	14		Superseded by APB 5
43	15	7	Amended by APB 9
43	15	11	Amended by APB 11
43	15	12	Amended by APB 6
43	15	17	Amended by APB 9
43	15	fn1,fn2	Superseded by APB 26
43	15		Superseded by APB 26
44			Superseded by ARB 44 (Rev.)
44 (Rev.)		3	Amended by APB 20
44 (Rev.)		4,5,7	Amended by APB 11
44 (Rev.)		8	Superseded by FAS 71
44 (Rev.)		9	Amended by APB 6
44 (Rev.)		9	Superseded by FAS 71
44 (Rev.)		10	Amended by APB 11
Letter, Dated April 15,1959			Superseded by APB 11
47			Superseded by APB 8
48		5,6	Amended by APB 6
48		12	Amended by APB 10
48			Superseded by APB 16
49			Superseded by APB 9
50			Superseded by FAS 5
51		6	Amended by FAS 71
51		7,8	Superseded by APB 16
51		10	*Amended by FAS 58
51		16	Superseded by APB 23
51		17	Amended by APB 11
51		19	Amended by APB 6
51		19,20	Amended by APB 10
51		19-21	Amended by APB 18
51		fn1	Superseded by APB 16

Appendix B

APB Opinion	Par.	
1	1,5,6	Amended by APB 11
1	7	Superseded by FAS 71
1	fn1	Amended by APB 11
2		Amended by APB 4
2	17	Superseded by FAS 71
2	Addendum	Superseded by FAS 71
3		Superseded by APB 19
5	14	Amended by APB 31
5	16-18	Superseded by APB 31
5	20	Amended by APB 31
5	21	Amended by APB 11
5	23	Amended by APB 31
5		Superseded by FAS 13
6	12(c)	Superseded by APB 16
6	15	Superseded by APB 17
6	18	Superseded by FAS 8
6	18	Superseded by FAS 52
6	19	Superseded by APB 26
6	20	Superseded by FAS 71
6	21	Superseded by APB 11
6	22	Superseded by APB 16
6	23	Superseded by APB 11
6	fn7,fn8	Superseded by APB 11
7	8	Amended by APB 27
7	12	Superseded by APB 27
7		Superseded by FAS 13
8	31	*Amended by FAS 74
8	46	Superseded by FAS 36
9	3	Amended by APB 30
9	3	Amended by FAS 16
9	6	Amended by APB 13
9	8,17	Amended by APB 30
9	18	Amended by APB 20
9	18	Amended by FAS 16
9	20	Amended by APB 20
9	20-22	Superseded by APB 30
9	23,24	Superseded by FAS 16
9	25	Superseded by APB 20
9	29,Exh. A-D	Superseded by APB 30
9	30-51,Exh. E	Superseded by APB 15
9	fn2	Superseded by APB 30
9	fn6-9	Superseded by APB 15
10	2-4	Superseded by APB 18
10	5	Superseded by APB 16
10	8,9	Amended by APB 12
10	8,9	Superseded by APB 14
10	11(b)	Amended by APB 15

Appendix B

APB Opinion	Par.	
10	fn1-5	Superseded by APB 18
10	fn6	Superseded by APB 16
11	6	Amended by APB 28
11	6	*Amended by FAS 60
11	6	Amended by FAS 71
11	38,39	Superseded by APB 23
11	40	Superseded by FAS 9
11	41	Superseded by APB 23
11	49	Amended by APB 16
11	57	Amended by FAS 37
11	fn14	Amended by FAS 16
12	11-15	Superseded by APB 14
12	fn2	Superseded by APB 14
15	5	Amended by FAS 21
15	13	Amended by APB 20
15	13	Amended by APB 30
15	33	Amended by FAS 55
15	45	Amended by FAS 21
15	fn8	Amended by APB 30
15	fn10	Amended by FAS 55
16	6	Superseded by FAS 71
16	88	Amended by FAS 38
16	96	*Amended by FAS 79
16	99	Amended by FAS 10
17	6	Amended by FAS 2
17	7	Superseded by FAS 71
17	29,30	*Amended by FAS 72
17	31	Amended by APB 30
17	31	*Amended by FAS 72
18	15	Superseded by FAS 13
18	19(d)	Amended by APB 30
18	19(j)	Superseded by APB 23
18	19(m)	*Amended by FAS 58
18	fn5	Superseded by FAS 13
18	fn11	Superseded by APB 23
19	10	Amended by APB 30
20	3	Amended by FAS 71
20	5	Amended by APB 30
20	27	*Amended by FAS 73
20	34	*Amended by FAS 58
20	fn5	Amended by FAS 32
20	fn9	Superseded by FAS 16
21	15,16	Amended by FAS 34
22	13	Amended by FAS 2
22	13	Amended by FAS 8
22	13	Amended by FAS 52
23	2	Amended by FAS 9
23	4	Superseded by FAS 71
23	26-30	Superseded by FAS 60

APB Opinion	Par.	
23	fn11	Superseded by FAS 60
24	3	Superseded by FAS 71
26	2	Amended by FAS 15
26	2	Amended by FAS 71
26	2	Superseded by FAS 76
26	3(a)	*Amended by FAS 15
26	3(a)	Superseded by FAS 76
26	3(c)	Amended by FAS 76
26	19	Amended by FAS 76
26	20	Amended by APB 30
26	20	Amended by FAS 4
26	21	Amended by FAS 76
27		Superseded by FAS 13
28	27	Superseded by FAS 3
28	31	Amended by FAS 3
28	fn5	Superseded by FAS 3
29	4	Amended by FAS 71
29	fn4	Amended by FAS 71
30	20	Amended by FAS 4
30	25	Amended by FAS 16
30	fn8	Amended by FAS 60
31		Superseded by FAS 13

APB Statement	Par.	
4	196	Amended by APB 18
4	14,15,35, 46,80,191	Amended by APB 19
4	199	Amended by APB 20
4	181	Amended by APB 21
4	81,199	Amended by APB 22
4	182	Amended by APB 29
4	198	Amended by APB 30
4	fn51	Amended by APB 29
4	fn53,fn54	Amended by APB 30

AICPA Interpretation of	No.	
ARB 51	1	Superseded by APB 23
APB 4	5	Superseded by FAS 16
APB 7	1	Superseded by FAS 13
APB 8	22	Superseded by FAS 71
APB 9	1	Amended by APB 30
APB 9	2	Superseded by APB 20
APB 11	4	Amended by FAS 71

Appendix B

AICPA Interpretation of	No.	
APB 15	2	Amended by FAS 55
APB 15	38	Superseded by FAS 55
APB 15	82	Modified by FIN 31
APB 16	15-17, 24,26	Amended by FAS 10
APB 22	1	Superseded by FAS 13
APB 26	1	Amended by FAS 76

FASB Statement	Par.	
1		Superseded by FAS 8
1		Superseded by FAS 52
2	14	Superseded by FAS 71
4	7	Superseded by FAS 71
4	8	Amended by FAS 64
4	fn2	Amended by FAS 64
5	13	Superseded by FAS 71
5	20	Amended by FAS 11
5	41,102	Amended by FAS 60
5	fn3	Superseded by FAS 16
7	5	Amended by FAS 71
8	27	Amended by FAS 20
8	35	*Amended by FAS 20
8		Superseded by FAS 52
9		Superseded by FAS 19
13	3	Superseded by FAS 71
13	5(b)	Superseded by FAS 23
13	5(m)	Superseded by FAS 17
13	5(j)(i),(n)	*Amended by FAS 29
13	6(b)(i),(ii)	Superseded by FAS 27
13	8	*Amended by FAS 26
13	8(b),10	*Amended by FAS 23
13	12	Amended by FAS 29
13	12	Amended by FAS 34
13	14	Amended by FAS 22
13	16(a)(iv)	Amended by FAS 29
13	17(a)	*Amended by FAS 23
13	17(b)	Amended by FAS 29
13	17(f)	Amended by FAS 22
13	17(f)(ii)	*Amended by FAS 27
13	18(a)	*Amended by FAS 23
13	18(b)	Amended by FAS 29
13	20	*Amended by FAS 77
13	26(a)(i)	*Amended by FAS 23
13	32,33	Superseded by FAS 28
13	43(c)	*Amended by FAS 23

FASB Statement	Par.	
13	fn13	Superseded by FAS 29
14	4	Superseded by FAS 18
14	7	*Amended by FAS 24
14	39	Superseded by FAS 30
14	41	Amended by FAS 18
14	41	*Amended by FAS 21
14	73	Superseded by FAS 18
14	fn15	Superseded by FAS 18
15	9	Superseded by FAS 71
16	9	Superseded by FAS 71
19	9	Superseded by FAS 71
19	48†	Amended by FAS 25
19	48-59	Superseded by FAS 69
19	63	Amended by FAS 25
19	271	Superseded by FAS 25
19	fn11, fn12	Superseded by FAS 25
20		Superseded by FAS 52
22	11	Superseded by FAS 71
22	fn1	Superseded by FAS 76
25	6,8	Superseded by FAS 69
26	7	Amended by FAS 66
28	3,23-25	Amended by FAS 66
28	fn*	Amended by FAS 66
32	App.A SOP74-6	Amended by FAS 77
32	App.A SOP74-12	Amended by FAS 65
32	App.A SOP75-1	Amended by FAS 48
32	App.A SOP75-5	Amended by FAS 63
32	App.A SOP75-6	Amended by FAS 66
32	App.A SOP76-1	Amended by FAS 50
32	App.A SOP76-2	Amended by FAS 65
32	App.A SOP78-3	Amended by FAS 67
32	App.A SOP78-4	Amended by FAS 66
32	App.A SOP78-5	Amended by FAS 76
32	App.A SOP78-6	Amended by FAS 60
32	App.A SOP78-8	Amended by FAS 49
32	App.A SOP79-2	Amended by FAS 51

FASB Statement	Par.	
32	App.A SOP79-3	Amended by FAS 60
32	App.A SOP79-4	Amended by FAS 53
32	App.A Construction Contractors‡	Amended by FAS 56
32	App.A Franchise Fee Revenue§	Amended by FAS 45
32	App.A Insurance‡	Amended by FAS 60
32	App.A Motion Picture Films§	Amended by FAS 53
32	App.A Real Estate§	Amended by FAS 66
32	App.B SOP80-1	Amended by FAS 60
32	App.B SOP80-3	Amended by FAS 67
32	App.B SOP81-1	*Amended by FAS 56
32	App.B SOP81-2	*Amended by FAS 56
33	22(c)	Superseded by FAS 70
33	22	*Amended by FAS 70
33	23	Amended by FAS 54
33	29(a)	Amended by FAS 70
33	30(a-c)	*Amended by FAS 39
33	30,31,34	*Amended by FAS 70
33	35	Amended by FAS 70
33	35(c)(1-4)	*Amended by FAS 39
33	35(c)	*Amended by FAS 70
33	36	Amended by FAS 70
33	39	*Amended by FAS 70
33	41	Amended by FAS 70
33	50	*Amended by FAS 70
33	51(b)	Amended by FAS 39
33	51(b)	Superseded by FAS 69
33	52	Amended by FAS 39
33	52(b)	Superseded by FAS 39
33	52(b)	Superseded by FAS 69
33	53	Superseded by FAS 39
33	53	Superseded by FAS 40
33	53	Superseded by FAS 41
33	53	*Amended by FAS 46
33	53	*Amended by FAS 70
33	53(a)	Superseded by FAS 69
33	56,59,66	Amended by FAS 70
34	5	Superseded by FAS 71

Appendix B

FASB Statement	Par.	
34	8,9	Amended by FAS 42
34	9,10	*Amended by FAS 58
34	10,13,17	*Amended by FAS 62
34	20	*Amended by FAS 58
35	30	*Amended by FAS 59
35	30	*Amended by FAS 75
39	10,11,12	Superseded by FAS 69
39	12	Superseded by FAS 40
39	12	Superseded by FAS 41
39	12	*Amended by FAS 46
40	6	Superseded by FAS 41
40	6	*Amended by FAS 46
40	6	Superseded by FAS 69
41	7	*Amended by FAS 46
41	7	Superseded by FAS 69
43	3	Superseded by FAS 71
46	8	Superseded by FAS 69
49	7	Superseded by FAS 71
51	2	Superseded by FAS 71
59		Superseded by FAS 75

FASB Interpretation	Par.	
2		Superseded by FAS 15
5		Superseded by FAS 7
9	8,9	*Amended by FAS 72
15		Superseded by FAS 52
15	2,4	Amended by FAS 60
17		Superseded by FAS 52
18	4	Superseded by FAS 71
22	7	Amended by FAS 60
22	8	Superseded by FAS 71
25	9	Superseded by FAS 71
25	fn5	Superseded by FIN 32
28	6	Amended by FIN 31

FASB Technical Bulletin	
80-1	Amended by FAS 76
81-5	Superseded by FAS 62

(The next page is 6151.)

*Denotes an addition to the text; all others are deletions or changes.

†The effective date of certain paragraphs of FASB Statement 19 is suspended by FASB Statement 25 insofar as they pertain to a required form of successful efforts accounting.

‡Refers to Industry Audit Guides, *Audits of Fire and Casualty Insurance Companies* (1966), *Audits of Stock Life Insurance Companies* (1972), and *Audits of Construction Contractors* (1965).

§Refers to Industry Accounting Guides, *Accounting for Profit Recognition on Sales of Real Estate* (1973), *Accounting for Retail Land Sales* (1973), *Accounting for Franchise Fee Revenue* (1973), and *Accounting for Motion Picture Films* (1973).

Appendix C

APPENDIX C

Effective Dates of Pronouncements

This appendix lists effective dates of FASB Statements of Financial Accounting Standards (FAS), FASB Interpretations (FIN), APB Opinions (APB), and Accounting Research Bulletins (ARB), and the issue dates of AICPA Accounting Interpretations (AIN) and FASB Technical Bulletins (FTB).

Only the *principal* effective date is listed below. In many cases the provisions relating to the effective date are complex. Most pronouncements could be applied earlier than the date listed because application earlier than the effective date is usually encouraged. Any questions regarding effective dates should be resolved by referring to the effective date and transition provisions of the original pronouncement. For the convenience of the reader, the appendix presents the transition paragraphs of more recent pronouncements whose effective dates and transition provisions are such that they might be initially applied in annual financial statements issued on or after June 1, 1984.

Pronouncement	**Effective Date**
ARB	
43	June 1953 (replaced ARBs issued September 1939-January 1953)
44	October 1954
44R	July 1958
45	October 1955
46	February 1956
47	September 1956
48	January 1957
49	April 1958
50	October 1958
51	August 1959
APB	
1	November 1962
2	December 1962

Pronouncement	Effective Date
APB	
3	October 1963
4	March 1964
5	September 1964
6	For fiscal periods beginning after December 31, 1965
7	For fiscal periods beginning after December 31, 1966
8	For fiscal periods beginning after December 31, 1966
9	For fiscal periods beginning after December 31, 1966
10	For fiscal periods beginning after December 31, 1966
11	For fiscal periods beginning after December 31, 1967
12	For fiscal periods beginning after December 31, 1967
13	For fiscal periods beginning after December 31, 1968
14	For fiscal periods beginning after December 31, 1966
15	For fiscal periods beginning after December 31, 1968
16	For business combinations initiated after October 31, 1970
17	For intangible assets acquired after October 31, 1970
18	For fiscal periods beginning after December 31, 1971
19	For fiscal periods ending after September 30, 1971
20	For fiscal years beginning after July 31, 1971
21	For transactions on or after October 1, 1971
22	For fiscal years beginning after December 31, 1971
23	For fiscal periods beginning after December 31, 1971
24	For fiscal periods beginning after December 31, 1971
25	For awards granted after December 31, 1972
26	For transactions on or after January 1, 1973
27	For transactions after December 31, 1972
28	For interim periods relating to fiscal years beginning after December 31, 1973
29	For transactions after September 30, 1973
30	For events and transactions after September 30, 1973
31	For fiscal periods ending on or after December 31, 1973

Pronouncement	Effective Date
FAS	
1	For fiscal periods ending after November 30, 1973
2	For fiscal years beginning on or after January 1, 1975
3	For interim periods ending on or after December 31, 1974
4	For extinguishments after March 31, 1975
5	For fiscal years beginning on or after July 1, 1975
6	For fiscal periods ending on or after December 31, 1975
7	For fiscal periods beginning on or after January 1, 1976
8	For fiscal years beginning on or after January 1, 1976
9	For financial statements issued on or after December 1, 1975
10	November 1, 1975
11	For fiscal years beginning on or after July 1, 1975
12	For fiscal periods ending on or after December 31, 1975
13	For leasing transactions and revisions entered into on or after January 1, 1977
14	For fiscal years beginning after December 15, 1976 and interim periods within those years (but amended by FAS18, FAS21, and FAS24)
15	For troubled debt restructurings consummated after December 31, 1977
16	For fiscal years beginning after October 15, 1977
17	For leasing transactions and revisions entered into on or after January 1, 1978
18	December 1, 1977 retroactive to effective date of FAS14
19	For fiscal years beginning after December 15, 1978 and interim periods within those years (but amended by FAS25)
20	January 1, 1978
21	April 30, 1978 retroactive to fiscal years beginning after December 15, 1976
22	For lease agreement revisions entered into on or after July 1, 1978
23	For leasing transactions and revisions recorded as of December 1, 1978

Appendix C

Pronouncement	Effective Date
FAS	
24	January 1, 1979 retroactive to fiscal years beginning after December 15, 1976
25	For fiscal years beginning after December 15, 1978
26	For leasing transactions and revisions recorded as of August 1, 1979
27	For lease agreement renewals and extensions recorded as of September 1, 1979
28	For leasing transactions and revisions recorded as of September 1, 1979
29	For leasing transactions and revisions recorded as of October 1, 1979
30	For fiscal years beginning after December 15, 1979
31	For annual or interim financial statements issued after September 30, 1979 for periods ending on or after July 26, 1979
32	October 31, 1979
33	For fiscal years ending on or after December 25, 1979
34	For fiscal years beginning after December 15, 1979
35	For plan years beginning after December 15, 1980 (but deferred indefinitely by FAS75 for plans sponsored by state or local governments)
36	For fiscal years beginning after December 15, 1979 and for complete interim statements issued after June 30, 1980 for interim periods within those fiscal years
37	For periods ending after December 15, 1980
38	For business combinations initiated after December 15, 1980
39	For fiscal years ending on or after December 25, 1980
40	For fiscal years ending on or after December 25, 1980
41	For fiscal years ending on or after December 25, 1980
42	For fiscal years beginning after December 15, 1979, unless enterprise had already adopted FAS34; if so, effective for fiscal years beginning after October 15, 1980

Pronouncement	Effective Date
FAS	
43	For fiscal years beginning after December 15, 1980
44	December 19, 1980 for financial statements for fiscal periods ending after December 15, 1980
45	For fiscal years beginning after June 15, 1981
46	For fiscal years ending on or after March 31, 1981
47	For fiscal years ending after June 15, 1981
48	For fiscal years beginning after June 15, 1981
49	For product financing arrangements entered into after June 15, 1981
50	For fiscal years beginning after December 15, 1981
51	For fiscal years beginning after December 15, 1981
52	For fiscal years beginning on or after December 15, 1982
53	For fiscal years beginning after December 15, 1981
54	January 27, 1982 retroactive to fiscal years ending on or after December 25, 1979
55	For convertible securities issued after February 28, 1982
56	For fiscal years beginning after December 31, 1981
57	For fiscal years ending after June 15, 1982
58	For investments made after June 30, 1982 but optional for investments contracted for but not yet made at that date
59	April 1982 retroactive to fiscal years beginning after December 15, 1980
60	For fiscal years beginning after December 15, 1982
61	For fiscal years beginning after December 15, 1982
62	For tax-exempt borrowing arrangements entered into and gifts or grants received after August 31, 1982
63	For fiscal years beginning after December 15, 1982
64	For extinguishments of debt occurring after September 30, 1982
65	For transactions entered into after December 31, 1982
66	For real estate sales transactions entered into after December 31, 1982

Pronouncement	Effective Date
FAS	
67	For costs of real estate incurred in fiscal years beginning after December 31, 1982
68	For research and development arrangements entered into after December 31, 1982
69	For fiscal years beginning on or after December 15, 1982
70	For fiscal years ending after December 15, 1982 for which an enterprise has applied FAS52
71	For fiscal years beginning after December 15, 1983
72	For business combinations initiated after September 30, 1982
73	For changes from retirement-replacement-betterment accounting to depreciation accounting made after June 30, 1983
74	For special termination benefits offered after June 30, 1983
75	November 1983 retroactive for fiscal years beginning after December 15, 1980
76	For transactions entered into after December 31, 1983
77	For transfers of receivables with recourse after December 31, 1983
78	For financial statements for fiscal years beginning after December 15, 1983 and for interim accounting periods within those fiscal years
79	For financial statements for fiscal years beginning after December 15, 1983
FIN	
1	July 1, 1974
2	For transactions after June 30, 1974
3	December 31, 1974
4	For business combinations initiated after March 31, 1975
5	March 31, 1975 for fiscal periods beginning on or after January 1, 1975
6	For fiscal years beginning on or after April 1, 1975

Pronouncement	Effective Date
FIN	
7	For fiscal periods beginning on or after January 1, 1976
8	For balance sheets and statements of changes in financial position dated on or after February 29, 1976
9	For business combinations initiated on or after March 1, 1976
10	For annual and interim periods ending after October 15, 1976
11	For annual and interim periods ending after October 15, 1976
12	For annual and interim periods ending after October 15, 1976
13	For annual and interim periods ending after October 15, 1976
14	For annual and interim periods beginning after October 15, 1976
15	For annual and interim periods ending after December 15, 1976
16	For annual and interim periods ending after March 15, 1977
17	For annual and interim periods ending after March 15, 1977
18	For financial statements issued after March 31, 1977 for interim periods beginning after December 15, 1976
19	For leasing transactions and revisions entered into on or after January 1, 1978
20	December 1, 1977
21	For business combinations initiated on or after May 1, 1978
22	For timing differences occurring in fiscal years beginning after June 15, 1978
23	For leasing transactions and revisions recorded as of December 1, 1978
24	For leasing transactions and revisions recorded as of December 1, 1978
25	Prospectively for fiscal years beginning after December 15, 1978
26	For purchases of leased property recorded as of December 1, 1978
27	For transactions with measurement dates on or after March 1, 1979
28	For awards granted in fiscal years beginning after December 15, 1978
29	For dispositions of investments occurring after March 31, 1979

Appendix C

Pronouncement	Effective Date
FIN	
30	For fiscal years beginning after November 15, 1979
31	For fiscal years beginning after December 15, 1979
32	For fiscal years beginning after December 15, 1979
33	For fiscal years beginning after December 15, 1979 and for interim periods within those years
34	For fiscal years ending after June 15, 1981
35	For fiscal years beginning after June 15, 1981
36	For fiscal years beginning after December 15, 1981 and for interim periods within those years
37	For sale of part of an investment after June 30, 1983
FTB*	
79-1 through 79-19	December 28, 1979
79-16 Rev.	February 29, 1980
80-1 and 80-2	December 19, 1980
81-1 through 81-5	February 6, 1981
81-6	November 30, 1981
82-1	January 27, 1982
82-2	March 31, 1982
83-1	July 26, 1983
84-1	March 15, 1984

*Note: Technical Bulletins (FTB) have no effective date; the date indicated is the date issued.

Pronouncement		Effective Date
AIN-ARB		
AIN (Key-Man Life Insurance)		November 1970
43	AIN #1	March 1971
51	AIN #1	February 1972
AIN-APB		
4	AIN #1	February 1972
	AIN #2 through 6	March 1972
7	AIN #1	November 1971
8	AIN (all)	1968
9	AIN #1	February 1971
	AIN #2	April 1971
11	AIN #1	July 1970
	AIN #2 through 23	1969
	AIN #24 and 25	March 1972
15	AIN #1 through 101	July 1970
	AIN #102	September 1971
16	AIN #1 through 7	December 1970
	AIN #8 through 17	April 1971
	AIN #18 through 23	September 1971
	AIN #24 and 25	November 1971
	AIN #26 through 33	December 1971
	AIN #34 and 35	January 1972
	AIN #36	Effective for combinations consummated after May 31, 1972
	AIN #37	November 1972
	AIN #38 and 39	March 1973
17	AIN #1	April 1971
	AIN #2	March 1973
18	AIN #1 and 2	November 1971
	AIN #3	February 1972

Pronouncement		Effective Date
AIN-APB		
19	AIN #1 and 2	February 1972
	AIN #3	June 1972
20	AIN #1 and 2	March 1973
21	AIN #1	June 1972
22	AIN #1	November 1973
23	AIN #1	March 1973
25	AIN #1	June 1973
26	AIN #1	March 1973
30	AIN #1	November 1973

Effective Dates and Transition Provisions of Pronouncements That Might Initially Be Applied in Annual Financial Statements Issued on or after June 1, 1984

FAS60: Accounting and Reporting by Insurance Enterprises

This Statement shall be effective for fiscal years beginning after December 15, 1982, with earlier application encouraged. Accounting changes adopted to conform to the provisions of this Statement shall be applied retroactively. In the year that this Statement is first applied, the financial statements shall disclose the nature of any restatement and its effect on income before extraordinary items, net income, and related per share amounts for each year presented. The individual effects of changing to conform to the provisions of this Statement shall be disclosed in the financial statements. [FAS60, ¶64]

If retroactive restatement of all years presented is not practicable, the financial statements presented shall be restated for as many consecutive years as practicable and the cumulative effect of applying this Statement shall be included in determining net income of the earliest year restated (not necessarily the earliest year presented). If it is not practicable to restate any prior year, the cumulative effect shall be included in net income in the year in which this Statement is first applied. (Refer to paragraph 20 of APB Opinion No. 20, *Accounting Changes* [Section A06, "Accounting Changes," paragraph .116].) [FAS60, ¶65]

FAS61: Accounting for Title Plant

This Statement shall be effective for fiscal years beginning after December 15, 1982, with earlier application encouraged. Accounting changes adopted to conform to the provisions of this Statement shall be applied retroactively. In the year that this Statement is first applied, the financial statements shall disclose the nature of any restatement and its effect on income before extraordinary items, net income, and related per share amounts for each year presented. [FAS61, ¶10]

If retroactive restatement of all years presented is not practicable, the financial statements presented shall be restated for as many consecutive years as practicable and the cumulative effect of applying this Statement shall be included in determining net income of the earliest year restated (not necessarily the earliest year presented). If it is not practicable to restate any prior year, the cumulative effect shall be included in net income in the year in which this Statement is first applied. (Refer to paragraph 20 of APB Opinion No. 20, *Accounting Changes* [Section A06, "Accounting Changes," paragraph .116].) [FAS61, ¶11]

FAS63: Financial Reporting by Broadcasters

This Statement shall be effective for financial statements for fiscal years beginning after December 15, 1982, with earlier application encouraged. If application of this Statement results in a change in accounting, restatement of previously issued annual financial statements to conform to the provisions of this Statement is encouraged but not required. If it is not practicable or if the issuer of financial statements elects not to restate any prior year, the cumulative effect shall be included in net income in the year in which the Statement is first applied. (Refer to paragraph 20 of APB Opinion No. 20, *Accounting Changes* [Section A06, "Accounting Changes," paragraph .116].) The effect on income before extraordinary items, net income, and related per share amounts of applying this Statement in a year in which the cumulative effect is included in determining that year's net income shall be disclosed for that year. [FAS63, ¶12]

If previously issued financial statements are restated, the financial statements shall disclose, in the year that this Statement is first applied, the nature of any restatement and its effects on income before extraordinary items, net income, and related per share amounts for each restated year presented. If retroactive restatement of all years presented is not practicable, the financial statements presented shall be restated for as many consecutive years as practicable and the cumulative effect of applying the Statement shall be included in determining net income of the earliest year restated (not necessarily the earliest year presented). [FAS63, ¶13]

FAS65: Accounting for Certain Mortgage Banking Activities

The provisions of this Statement, other than those of paragraphs 4 and 28 through 30, shall be applied prospectively to transactions entered into after December 31, 1982, with earlier application encouraged. The provisions of [FAS65] paragraphs 4 and 28 through 30 [Section Mo4, "Mortgage Banking Activities," paragraphs .105 and .129 through .131] shall be effective for financial statements for fiscal years beginning after December 15, 1982, with earlier application encouraged. If application of paragraph 4 of this Statement [Section Mo4, paragraph .105] results in a change in accounting, restatement of previously issued annual financial statements to conform to the provisions of that paragraph is encouraged but not required. If it is not practicable or if the issuer of financial statements elects not to restate any prior year, the cumulative effect shall be included in net income in the year in which this Statement is first applied. (Refer to paragraph 20 of APB Opinion No. 20, *Accounting Changes* [Section A06, "Accounting Changes," paragraph .116].) The effect on income before extraordinary items, net income, and related per share amounts of applying this Statement in a year in which the cumulative effect is included in determining that year's net income shall be disclosed for that year. [FAS65, ¶32]

If previously issued financial statements are restated, the financial statements shall be restated for as many consecutive years as practicable. In the year that this Statement is first applied, the nature of any restatement and its effect on income before extraordinary items, net income, and related per share amounts for each restated year presented shall be disclosed. The cumulative effect of applying this Statement shall be included in determining net income of the earliest year restated (not necessarily the earliest year presented). [FAS65, ¶33]

FAS71: Accounting for the Effects of Certain Types of Regulation

This Statement shall be effective for fiscal years beginning after December 15, 1983. Earlier application is encouraged. Accounting changes adopted to conform to the provisions of this Statement shall be applied retroactively, except that:

a. Previously issued financial statements shall not be restated for changes in accounting for refunds.
b. Leases for which the inception is after December 31, 1982 shall be classified in accordance with FASB Statement No. 13, *Accounting for Leases* [Section L10, "Leases"], in financial statements commencing with initial application of this Statement. Leases for which the inception of the lease is before January 1, 1983 may be classified as they would have been classified before this Statement was issued until fiscal years beginning after December 15, 1986. Commencing no later than the first fiscal year beginning after December 15, 1986, those leases shall be retroactively classified in accordance with Statement 13 [Section L10, "Leases"] as amended. [FAS71, ¶22]

If leases are not retroactively classified in accordance with Statement 13 [Section L10, "Leases"] in financial statements for fiscal years beginning after December 15, 1983 and before December 15, 1986 as permitted by [FAS71] paragraph 22(b), lessees shall disclose the amounts of additional capitalized leased assets and lease obligations that would be included in each balance sheet presented if Statement 13 [Section L10, "Leases"] had been applied retroactively. [FAS71, ¶23]

In the year that this Statement is first applied, the financial statements shall disclose the nature of any restatement and its effect on income before extraordinary items, net income, and related per share amounts for each year restated.[14] If retroactive restatement of all years presented is not practicable, the financial statements

[14]The effect on related per share amounts need not be disclosed if the enterprise does not disclose earnings per share.

shall be restated for as many consecutive years as is practicable, and the cumulative effect of applying this Statement shall be included in determining net income of the earliest year restated (not necessarily the earliest year presented). If it is not practicable to restate any prior year, the cumulative effect shall be included in net income in the year in which this Statement is first applied. (See paragraph 20 of APB Opinion No. 20, *Accounting Changes* [Section A06, "Accounting Changes," paragraph .116].) The effect on income before extraordinary items, net income, and related per share amounts[15] of applying this Statement in a year in which the cumulative effect is included in determining that year's net income shall be disclosed for that year. [FAS71, ¶24]

[15]See footnote 14.

FAS73: Reporting a Change in Accounting for Railroad Track Structures

This Statement shall be effective for changes in accounting from RRB to depreciation accounting made after June 30, 1983. Earlier application is encouraged but is not required. [FAS73, ¶3]

FAS74: Accounting for Special Termination Benefits Paid to Employees

This Statement shall be applied for special termination benefits offered after June 30, 1983. Earlier application is encouraged. Restatement of previously issued financial statements is permitted but is not required. [FAS74, ¶5]

FAS75: Deferral of the Effective Date of Certain Accounting Requirements for Pension Plans of State and Local Governmental Units

This Statement shall be effective upon issuance retroactive to fiscal years beginning after December 15, 1980. [FAS75, ¶4]

FAS76: Extinguishment of Debt

This Statement shall be effective for transactions entered into after December 31, 1983. Earlier application of this Statement is encouraged for transactions in fiscal years for which annual financial statements have not previously been issued. Furthermore, retroactive application of this Statement to transactions occurring during fiscal years for which annual financial statements have previously been issued is permitted, in which case the effects on restated per share amounts of prior years shall be disclosed. [FAS76, ¶12]

FAS77: Reporting by Transferors for Transfers of Receivables with Recourse

This Statement shall be effective for transfers of receivables with recourse after December 31, 1983, including transfers after that date that are made pursuant to the terms of earlier agreements. Earlier application of this Statement is encouraged in annual or interim financial statements that have not been previously issued. [FAS77, ¶11]

FAS78: Classification of Obligations That Are Callable by the Creditor

This Statement shall be effective for financial statements for fiscal years beginning after December 15, 1983 and for interim accounting periods within those fiscal years. Earlier application is encouraged in financial statements that have not previously been issued. This Statement may be, but is not required to be, applied retroactively to previously issued financial statements. [FAS78, ¶6]

FAS79: Elimination of Certain Disclosures for Business Combinations by Nonpublic Enterprises

This Statement shall be effective for financial statements for fiscal years beginning after December 15, 1983. Earlier application is permitted in financial statements that have not previously been issued. [FAS79, ¶6]

FIN37: Accounting for Translation Adjustments upon Sale of Part of an Investment in a Foreign Entity

This Interpretation shall be applied to the sale of part of an investment after June 30, 1983. Earlier application is encouraged. Restatement of previously issued financial statements is permitted but is not required. [FIN37, ¶3]

(The next page is 7001.)

Topical Index

TOPICAL INDEX

The index generally excludes references to introductory paragraphs and those paragraphs that provide background information or bases for conclusions. However, if such paragraphs facilitate an understanding of an accounting standard, those paragraphs are referenced. Superseded paragraphs and pronouncements are not indexed.

This volume includes the Schedule of Amended and Superseded Accounting Pronouncements, which lists changes to the original pronouncements as a result of subsequent pronouncements. The effective date and transition paragraphs are not indexed, but the principal effective dates are listed in the schedule of Effective Dates of Pronouncements, which is also included in this volume.

See "Terminology" for references to definitions of terms not separately presented in the index.

See "Terminology" for references to definitions of terms not separately presented in the index.

See "Terminology" for references to definitions of terms not separately presented in the index.

See "Terminology" for references to definitions of terms not separately presented in the index.

CHANGING PRICES:REPORTING THEIR EFFECTS IN FINANCIAL REPORTS—continued

CHANGING PRICES:REPORTING THEIR EFFECTS IN FINANCIAL REPORTS—continued

See "Terminology" for references to definitions of terms not separately presented in the index.

See "Terminology" for references to definitions of terms not separately presented in the index.

See "Terminology" for references to definitions of terms not separately presented in the index.

FAS-FASB Statements FIN-FASB Interpretations FTB-FASB Technical Bulletins
APB-APB Opinions AIN-AICPA Interpretations ARB-Accounting Research Bulletins
CON-FASB Concepts fn-footnote ch-chapter APS-APB Statements

See "Terminology" for references to definitions of terms not separately presented in the index.

See "Terminology" for references to definitions of terms not separately presented in the index.

See "Terminology" for references to definitions of terms not separately presented in the index.

See "Terminology" for references to definitions of terms not separately presented in the index.

See "Terminology" for references to definitions of terms not separately presented in the index.

See "Terminology" for references to definitions of terms not separately presented in the index.

See "Terminology" for references to definitions of terms not separately presented in the index.

See "Terminology" for references to definitions of terms not separately presented in the index.

FAS-FASB Statements | FIN-FASB Interpretations | FTB-FASB Technical Bulletins
APB-APB Opinions | AIN-AICPA Interpretations | ARB-Accounting Research Bulletins
CON-FASB Concepts | fn-footnote | ch-chapter | APS-APB Statements

INCOME TAXES: DEFERRED TAXES AND TAX ALLOCATION—continued

INCOME TAXES: DEFERRED TAXES AND TAX ALLOCATION—continued

INCOME TAXES:FINANCIAL REPORTING

See "Terminology" for references to definitions of terms not separately presented in the index.

See "Terminology" for references to definitions of terms not separately presented in the index.

See "Terminology" for references to definitions of terms not separately presented in the index.

See "Terminology" for references to definitions of terms not separately presented in the index.

See "Terminology" for references to definitions of terms not separately presented in the index.

See "Terminology" for references to definitions of terms not separately presented in the index.

See "Terminology" for references to definitions of terms not separately presented in the index.

M

See "Terminology" for references to definitions of terms not separately presented in the index.

See "Terminology" for references to definitions of terms not separately presented in the index.

See "Terminology" for references to definitions of terms not separately presented in the index.

See "Terminology" for references to definitions of terms not separately presented in the index.

See "Terminology" for references to definitions of terms not separately presented in the index.

See "Terminology" for references to definitions of terms not separately presented in the index.

See "Terminology" for references to definitions of terms not separately presented in the index.

See "Terminology" for references to definitions of terms not separately presented in the index.

See "Terminology" for references to definitions of terms not separately presented in the index.

See "Terminology" for references to definitions of terms not separately presented in the index.

See "Terminology" for references to definitions of terms not separately presented in the index.

See "Terminology" for references to definitions of terms not separately presented in the index.

See "Terminology" for references to definitions of terms not separately presented in the index.